VISUAL BASIC® 2008
HOW TO PROGRAM

Deitel® Ser

How to Program Series

Internet & World Wide Web How to Program, 4/E

Java How to Program, 7/E

C++ How to Program, 6/E

C How to Program, 5/E

Visual Basic® 2008 How to Program

Visual C#® 2008 How to Program, 2/E

Small Java™ How to Program, 6/E

Small C++ How to Program, 5/E

Visual C++® 2008 How to Program, 2/E

Simply Series

Simply C++: An Application-Driven Tutorial Approach

Simply Java™ Programming: An Application-Driven Tutorial Approach

Simply C#: An Application-Driven Tutorial Approach

Simply Visual Basic® 2008, 3/E: An Application-Driven Tutorial Approach

SafariX Web Books

www.deitel.com/books/SafariX.html

C++ How to Program, 5/E & 6/E

Java How to Program, 6/E & 7/E

Simply C++: An Application-Driven Tutorial Approach

Simply Visual Basic 2008: An Application-Driven Tutorial Approach, 3/E

Small C++ How to Program, 5/E

Small Java How to Program, 6/E

Visual Basic 2008 How to Program

Visual C# 2008 How to Program, 3/E

ies Page

LiveLessons Video Learning Products

`www.deitel.com/books/LiveLessons/`

Java Fundamentals Parts 1 and 2
C# Fundamentals Parts 1 and 2

To follow the Deitel publishing program, please register for the free *Deitel® Buzz Online* e-mail newsletter at:

`www.deitel.com/newsletter/subscribe.html`

To communicate with the authors, send e-mail to:

`deitel@deitel.com`

For information on government and corporate on-site seminars offered by Deitel & Associates, Inc. worldwide, visit:

`www.deitel.com/training/`

or write to

`deitel@deitel.com`

For continuing updates on Prentice Hall/Deitel publications visit:

`www.deitel.com`
`www.prenhall.com/deitel`

Check out our Resource Centers for valuable web resources that will help you master C++, other important programming languages, software and Internet- and web-related topics:

`www.deitel.com/ResourceCenters.html`

Library of Congress Cataloging-in-Publication Data
On file

Vice President and Editorial Director, ECS: ***Marcia J. Horton***
Associate Editor: ***Carole Snyder, Lisa Bailey***
Supervisor/Editorial Assistant: ***Dolores Mars***
Director of Team-Based Project Management: ***Vince O'Brien***
Senior Managing Editor: ***Scott Disanno***
Managing Editor: ***Robert Engelhardt***
Production Editor: ***Marta Samsel***
A/V Production Editor: ***Greg Dulles***
Art Director: ***Kristine Carney***
Cover Design: ***Abbey S. Deitel, Harvey M. Deitel, Francesco Santalucia, Kristine Carney***
Interior Design: ***Harvey M. Deitel, Kristine Carney***
Manufacturing Manager: ***Alexis Heydt-Long***
Manufacturing Buyer: ***Lisa McDowell***
Director of Marketing: ***Margaret Waples***
Marketing Manager: ***Chris Kelly***

Upper Saddle River, New Jersey 07458

Printed in the United States of America

10 9 8 7 6 5 4 3 2 1

ISBN 0-13-605305-X

Pearson Education Ltd., *London*
Pearson Education Australia Pty. Ltd., *Sydney*
Pearson Education Singapore, Pte. Ltd.
Pearson Education North Asia Ltd., *Hong Kong*
Pearson Education Canada, Inc., *Toronto*
Pearson Educación de Mexico, S.A. de C.V.
Pearson Education–Japan, *Tokyo*
Pearson Education Malaysia, Pte. Ltd.
Pearson Education, Inc., *Upper Saddle River, New Jersey*

VISUAL BASIC® 2008
HOW TO PROGRAM

P. J. Deitel
Deitel & Associates, Inc.

H. M. Deitel
Deitel & Associates, Inc.

Upper Saddle River, New Jersey 07458

Trademarks

DEITEL, the double-thumbs-up bug and DIVE INTO are registered trademarks of Deitel and Associates, Inc.

Microsoft, Windows, Silverlight, SQL Server, Visual Studio, Visual Basic and Visual Web Developer are either registered trademarks or trademarks of Microsoft Corporation in the United States and/or other countries.

To Abbey S. Deitel
President, Deitel & Associates, Inc.:

For a dozen years of extraordinary leadership and for your unswerving commitment to excellence.

Paul and Harvey

Deitel Resource Centers

Our Resource Centers focus on the vast amounts of free content available online. Find resources, downloads, tutorials, documentation, books, e-books, journals, articles, blogs, RSS feeds and more on many of today's hottest programming and technology topics. For the most up-to-date list of our Resource Centers, visit:

`www.deitel.com/ResourceCenters.html`

Let us know what other Resource Centers you'd like to see! Also, please register for the free *Deitel® Buzz Online* e-mail newsletter at:

`www.deitel.com/newsletter/subscribe.html`

Computer Science
Regular Expressions

Programming
ADO.NET
Adobe Flex
Ajax
Amazon Web Services
Apex
ASP.NET
ASP.NET 3.5
ASP.NET AJAX
C
C++
C++ Boost Libraries
C++ Game Programming
C#
Cloud Computing
Code Search Engines and Code Sites
Computer Game Programming
CSS 2.1
Dojo
Facebook Developer Platform
Flash 9
Google Web Toolkit (GWT)
Java
Java Certification and Assessment Testing
Java Design Patterns
Java EE 5
Java SE 6
Java SE 7 (Dolphin) Resource Center
JavaFX
JavaScript
JSON
Microsoft LINQ
Microsoft Popfly
MySpace Developer Platform
.NET
.NET 3.0
.NET 3.5
OpenGL
Open Social
Perl
PHP
Programming Projects
Python
Refactoring
Regular Expressions
REST Web Services
Ruby
Ruby on Rails
Service-Oriented Architecture (SOA)
Silverlight
Silverlight 2
Visual Basic
Visual Basic 2008
Visual C++
Visual C# 2008 and C# 3.0
Visual Studio Team System
Web 3D Technologies
Web Services
Windows Communication Foundation
Windows Presentation Foundation
XHTML
XAML
XML

Games and Game Programming
Computer Game Programming
Computer Games
Mobile Gaming
Sudoku

Internet Business
Affiliate Programs
Competitive Analysis
Facebook Social Ads
Google AdSense
Google Analytics
Google Services
Government Business
Internet Advertising
Internet Business Initiative
Internet Public Relations
Link Building
Location-Based Services
Online Lead Generation
Podcasting
Search Engine Optimization
Selling Digital Content
Sitemaps
Web Analytics
Website Monetization
YouTube and AdSense

Java
Java
Java Certification and Assessment Testing
Java Design Patterns
Java EE 5
Java SE 6
Java SE 7 (Dolphin) Resource Center
JavaFX

Microsoft
ASP.NET
ASP.NET 3.5
ASP.NET AJAX
C#
DotNetNuke (DNN)
Internet Explorer 7 (IE7)
Microsoft LINQ
Microsoft Popfly
.NET
.NET 3.0
.NET 3.5
SharePoint
Silverlight
Silverlight 2
SQL Server 2008
Visual Basic
Visual Basic 2008
Visual C++
Visual C# 2008 and C# 3.0
Visual Studio Team System
Windows Communication Foundation
Windows Presentation Foundation
Windows Vista
XAML

Open Source & LAMP Stack
Apache
DotNetNuke (DNN)
Eclipse
Firefox
Linux
MySQL
Open Source
Perl
PHP
Python
Ruby

Software
Apache
DotNetNuke (DNN)
Eclipse
Firefox
Firefox 3
Internet Explorer 7 (IE7)
Linux
MySQL
Open Source
Search Engines
SharePoint
Skype
SQL Server 2008
Web Servers
Wikis
Windows Vista

Web 2.0
Alert Services
Avatars
Attention Economy
Blogging
Building Web Communities
Community Generated Content
Facebook Developer Platform
Facebook Social Ads
Google Base
Google Video
Google Web Toolkit (GWT)
Internet Video
Joost
KNOL
Location-Based Services
Mashups
Microformats
Recommender Systems
RSS
Social Graph
Social Media
Social Networking
Software as a Service (SaaS)
Virtual Worlds
Web 2.0
Web 3.0
Widgets

Dive Into Web 2.0 eBook
Web 2 eBook

Database
MySQL
SQL Server 2008

Other Topics
Computer Games
Computing Jobs
Gadgets and Gizmos
Ring Tones
Sudoku

Contents

Chapter 1 thru 8 = VB101 Intro to Visual Basic for Non-Programmers: PART I

Chptrs 9 thru 14 = VB102 Intro to Visual Basic for Non-Programmers: PART II

Chapter 15 thru 24 = Advanced

Preface

"Live in fragments no longer, only connect."
—Edgar Morgan Foster

Welcome to the Visual Basic® 2008 programming language and the world of Microsoft® Windows® and Internet and web programming with Microsoft's .NET 3.5 platform! This book presents leading-edge computing technologies for students, instructors, software developers and IT professionals.

We use the Deitel signature "live-code approach," presenting most concepts in the context of complete working Visual Basic 2008 programs, rather than using code snippets. Each code example is immediately followed by one or more sample executions. All the source code is available at `www.deitel.com/books/vb2008htp/`.

At Deitel & Associates, we write programming-language textbooks and professional books for Prentice Hall, deliver corporate training courses worldwide and develop Web 2.0 Internet businesses. We have updated the previous edition of this book based on Visual Studio 2008 and .NET 3.5.

New and Updated Features

Here are the updates we've made for *Visual Basic 2008 How to Program*:

- ***LINQ.*** Many Microsoft technical evangelists say that LINQ (Language Integrated Query) is the single most important new feature in Visual Basic 2008 and Visual C# 2008. LINQ provides a uniform syntax for querying data and for performing insert, update and delete operations. Strong typing enables Visual Studio to provide *IntelliSense* support for LINQ operations and results. LINQ can be used on different types of data sources, including collections and files (LINQ to Objects, Chapters 9 and 18, respectively), databases (LINQ to SQL, Chapters 20–22) and XML (LINQ to XML, Chapters 19 and 23).
- ***Early Introduction to LINQ and Generic Collections.*** We introduce LINQ early in the book so that you can begin using it as soon as you've been introduced to data structures—our LINQ coverage begins immediately after Chapter 8 on arrays. To enable you to work with more flexible data structures throughout the book, we also now introduce the `List` generic collection—a dynamic data structure—in close proximity to arrays. This enables us to demonstrate the power of LINQ and how it can be applied to most data structures. In addition, the `List` class is a generic collection, which provides strong compile-time type safety—ensuring that all elements of the collection are of the appropriate type.
- ***Databases.*** We use the free Microsoft SQL Server Express Edition and real-world applications to teach the fundamentals of database programming. Chapters 20–22

discuss database and LINQ to SQL fundamentals, presented in the context of an address-book desktop application, a web-based bookstore application and a web-based airline reservation system, respectively. Chapter 20 also demonstrates using the Visual Studio tools to build a GUI application that accesses a database using LINQ to SQL.

- *Windows Presentation Foundation (WPF) GUI and Graphics.* Graphical user interfaces (GUIs) and graphics make applications fun to create and easier to use. We begin our GUI discussion with the traditional Windows `Forms` controls in Chapter 14. We extend our coverage of GUI and graphics in Chapters 15 and 16, respectively, with an introduction to Windows Presentation Foundation (WPF)—Microsoft's new framework that integrates GUI, graphics and multimedia capabilities. To demonstrate WPF GUI and graphics capabilities we present many examples, including a painting application, a text editor, a color chooser, a book-cover viewer, a television video player, a 3-D rotating pyramid and various animations.
- *Windows Communication Foundation (WCF) Web Services.* Microsoft's .NET strategy embraces the Internet and web as integral to software development and deployment. Web services technology enables information sharing, e-commerce and other interactions using standard Internet protocols and technologies, such as Hypertext Transfer Protocol (HTTP), Extensible Markup Language (XML) and Simple Object Access Protocol (SOAP). Web services enable programmers to package application functionality in a manner that turns the web into a library of reusable software components. We replaced our treatment of ASP.NET web services from the previous edition with a discussion of Windows Communication Foundation (WCF) services in Chapter 22. WCF is a set of technologies for building distributed systems in which system components communicate with one another over networks. In earlier versions of .NET, the various types of communication used different technologies and programming models. WCF uses a common framework for all communication between systems, so you need to learn only one programming model. Chapter 22 focuses on WCF web services that use either the SOAP protocol or REST (Representational State Transfer) architecture. The REST examples transmit both XML (eXtensible Markup Language) and JSON (JavaScript Object Notation).
- *ASP.NET 3.5 and ASP.NET AJAX.* The .NET platform enables developers to create robust, scalable web-based applications. Microsoft's .NET server-side technology, ASP.NET 3.5, allows programmers to build web documents that respond to client requests. To enable interactive web pages, server-side programs process information that users input into HTML forms. ASP.NET provides enhanced visual programming capabilities, similar to those used in building Windows `Forms` for desktop programs. Programmers can create web pages visually, by dragging and dropping web controls onto web forms. Chapter 21 introduces these powerful technologies. We present a sequence of examples in which the student builds several web applications, including a web-based bookstore application. The chapter culminates with an example that demonstrates the power of AJAX. Chapter 21 also discusses the ASP.NET Development Server (which en-

ables you to test your web applications on your local computer), multitier architecture and web transactions. The chapter uses ASP.NET 3.5 and LINQ to build a guestbook application that retrieves information from a database and displays it in a web page. We use the new `LinqDataSource` from a web application to manipulate a database. We use ASP.NET AJAX controls to add AJAX functionality to web applications to improve their responsiveness—in particular, we use the `UpdatePanel` control to perform partial-page updates.

- *Silverlight.* In Chapter 23, we introduce Silverlight, Microsoft's technology for building Rich Internet Applications (RIA). Silverlight, a competitor to JavaFX and Adobe's Flash and Flex technologies, allows programmers to create visually stunning, multimedia-intensive user interfaces for web applications using .NET languages such as Visual Basic. Silverlight is a subset of WPF that runs in a web browser using a plug-in. One of Silverlight's most compelling features is its ability to stream high-definition video. The chapter presents powerful multimedia applications, including a weather viewer, Flickr photo viewer, deep zoom book-cover collage and video viewer.

- *New Visual Basic XML Capabilities.* Use of the Extensible Markup Language (XML) is exploding in the software-development industry and in e-business and is pervasive throughout the .NET platform. Because XML is a platform-independent technology for describing data and creating markup languages, its data portability integrates well with Visual Basic-based portable applications and services. Visual Basic 2008 has many new features that integrate XML with the language. In Chapter 19, we use XML axis properties to manipulate elements of an XML document by their element names. We also demonstrate Visual Basic's new support for XML literals—this enables you to embed XML documents and elements directly in your Visual Basic code. In addition, we introduce LINQ to XML for manipulating XML data. As you'll see, the same types of operations performed in our earlier coverage of LINQ can also be applied to XML.

- *New Language Features to Support LINQ.* Many of the new Visual Basic language features we cover in Chapter 10 were introduced to support LINQ. We show how to use extension methods to add functionality to a class without modifying the class's source code. We enhanced our discussion of delegates (objects that hold method references) to support our discussion of Visual Basic's new lambda expressions, which define simple, anonymous functions. Lambda expressions can be used wherever delegates are needed—typically as arguments to method calls or to help create more powerful LINQ queries. You'll learn how to use anonymous types to create simple classes that store data without writing a class definition—a feature used frequently in LINQ.

- *Local Type Inference.* When you initialize a local variable in its declaration, you can now omit the variable's type—the compiler infers it from the variable's initializer value (introduced in Chapter 6). This is another feature used frequently in LINQ.

- *Conditional `If` Expressions.* Visual Basic provides a new conditional `If` expression (introduced in Chapter 5), which consists of a condition, a true expression and a false expression. It tests its condition, then evaluates to either its true expression or its false expression, based on whether the condition is true or false. This can be used as shorthand notation for some `If...Then...Else` statements.

- ***Optional Parameters.*** You can specify method parameters with default values—if a corresponding method argument is not provided in the method call, the compiler inserts the optional parameter's default value in the call (introduced in Chapter 7).
- ***Object Initializers.*** When creating a new object, you can use the new object initializer syntax to assign values to the new object's properties (introduced in Chapter 10).
- ***"Quick Fix" Window.*** The IDE now provides an **Error Correction Options** window that enables you to quickly fix certain common programming errors (introduced in Appendix H).

We updated the entire text to reflect Microsoft's latest release of Visual Basic 2008. New items include:

- Screenshots updated to the Visual Studio 2008 IDE.
- Updated keywords table (Chapter 3) to include the new contextual keywords—words that are considered keywords only in certain contexts. Outside those contexts, such keywords can still be used as valid identifiers. This minimizes the chance that older Visual Basic code will break when upgrading to Visual Basic 2008. Many of these contextual keywords are used with LINQ.
- Pointing out additional ways in which the IDE's *IntelliSense* helps you write code.
- Using local type inference to determine the types of the control variables in `For...Next` and `For Each...Next` statements.
- Using *DataTips* and visualizers to view object contents in the code window during debugging.
- Using LINQ to Objects to manipulate the data in two file-processing examples.
- Using LINQ to SQL in all database-driven examples.

All of this has been carefully reviewed by distinguished academics and industry developers who worked with us on *Visual Basic 2008 How to Program.*

We believe that this book and its support materials will give students and professionals an informative, interesting, challenging and entertaining Visual Basic educational experience. We provide a suite of ancillary materials that help instructors maximize their students' learning experience.

As you read the book, if you have questions, send an e-mail to `deitel@deitel.com`; we'll respond promptly. For updates on this book and the status of all supporting Visual Basic software, and for the latest news on all Deitel publications and services, visit `www.deitel.com`. Sign up at `www.deitel.com/newsletter/subscribe.html` for the free *Deitel® Buzz Online* e-mail newsletter and check out our growing list of Visual Basic and related Resource Centers at `www.deitel.com/ResourceCenters.html`. Each week we announce our latest Resource Centers in the newsletter.

Features

Early Classes and Objects Approach

We introduce basic object-technology concepts and terminology in Chapter 1. Chapter 4 provides a carefully crafted, friendly introduction to classes and objects that gets students working with object orientation comfortably from the start. This chapter was developed with the guidance of a distinguished team of academic and industry reviewers. Chapters 5–8 have been carefully written with a friendly "early classes and objects approach."

Carefully Tuned Treatment of Object-Oriented Programming in Chapters 10–12

We performed a high-precision upgrade for *Visual Basic 2008 How to Program*. This edition is clearer and more accessible—especially if you are new to object-oriented programming.

Case Studies

We include many case studies, some spanning multiple sections and chapters:

- `GradeBook` class in Chapters 4–8.
- Optional OOD/UML ATM system in the Software Engineering sections of Chapters 1, 3–8, 10 and 12. The complete code for the ATM is included in Appendix D.
- `Time` class in several sections of Chapter 10.
- `Employee` payroll application in Chapters 11–12.
- WPF painter application in Chapter 15.
- WPF text editor application in Chapter 15.
- WPF color chooser application in Chapter 15.
- WPF Deitel book cover viewer application in Chapter 15.
- WPF television application in Chapter 16.
- Address book application in Chapter 20.
- Guestbook ASP.NET application in Chapter 21.
- Secure books database ASP.NET application in Chapter 21.
- Airline reservation web service in Chapter 22.
- Blackjack web service in Chapter 22.
- Equation generator web service and math tutor application in Chapter 22.
- Silverlight weather viewer application in Chapter 23.
- Silverlight Flickr™ photo viewer application in Chapter 23.
- Silverlight deep zoom book-cover collage application in Chapter 23.
- Silverlight video viewer application in Chapter 23.

Integrated **GradeBook** *Case Study*

To reinforce our early classes presentation, we present an integrated case study using classes and objects in Chapters 4–8. We incrementally build a `GradeBook` class that represents an instructor's grade book and performs various calculations based on a set of student grades—finding the average, finding the maximum and minimum, and printing a bar chart. Our goal is to familiarize you with the important concepts of objects and classes through a real-world example of a substantial class. We develop this class from the ground up, constructing methods from control statements and carefully developed algorithms, and adding instance variables and arrays as needed to enhance the functionality of the class.

The Unified Modeling Language (UML)—Using the UML 2.0 to Develop an Object-Oriented Design of an ATM

The Unified Modeling Language™ (UML™) has become the preferred graphical modeling language for designing object-oriented systems. All the UML diagrams in the book comply with the UML 2.0 specification. We use UML class diagrams to visually represent classes and their inheritance relationships, and we use UML activity diagrams to demonstrate the flow of control in each of Visual Basic's control statements.

This edition continues to include an optional (and highly recommended) case study on object-oriented design using the UML. The case study was reviewed by a distinguished team of OOD/UML academic and industry professionals, including leaders in the field from Rational (the creators of the UML and now a division of IBM) and the Object Management Group (responsible for maintaining and evolving the UML). In the case study, we design and fully implement the software for a simple automated teller machine (ATM).

The Software Engineering Case Study sections at the ends of Chapters 1, 3–8, 10 and 12 present a carefully paced introduction to object-oriented design using the UML. We introduce a concise, simplified subset of the UML 2.0, then guide the reader through a first design experience intended for the novice object-oriented designer/programmer. The case study is not an exercise; rather, it is an end-to-end learning experience that concludes with a detailed walkthrough of the complete Visual Basic code.

The Software Engineering Case Study sections help readers develop an object-oriented design to complement the object-oriented programming concepts they begin learning in Chapter 1 and implementing in Chapter 4. In the first of these sections at the end of Chapter 1, we introduce basic OOD concepts and terminology. In the optional Software Engineering Case Study sections at the ends of Chapters 3–8, we consider more substantial issues, as we undertake a challenging problem with the techniques of OOD. We analyze a typical requirements document that specifies the system to be built; we determine the classes needed to implement that system, determine the attributes the classes need to have, determine the behaviors the classes need to exhibit and specify how the classes must interact with one another to meet the system requirements. In Appendix D, we include a complete Visual Basic implementation of the object-oriented system that we design in the earlier chapters. We employ a carefully developed, incremental object-oriented design process to produce a UML model for our ATM system. From this design, we produce a substantial working Visual Basic implementation using key programming notions, including classes, objects, encapsulation, visibility, composition, inheritance and polymorphism.

Object-Oriented Programming

Object-oriented programming is today's most widely employed technique for developing robust, reusable software. This text offers a rich treatment of Visual Basic's object-oriented programming features. Chapter 4 introduces how to create classes and objects. These concepts are extended in Chapter 10. Chapter 11 discusses how to create powerful new classes quickly by using inheritance to "absorb" the capabilities of existing classes. Chapter 12 familiarizes the reader with the crucial concepts of polymorphism, abstract classes, concrete classes and interfaces, all of which facilitate powerful manipulations among objects belonging to an inheritance hierarchy.

Visual Studio 2008 Debugger
In Appendix H, we explain how to use key debugger features, such as setting "breakpoints" and "watches," and stepping into and out of methods. Most of the material in this appendix can be covered after Chapter 4. One example uses the `AndAlso` keyword, which is explained in Chapter 6.

Dependency Chart

Figure 1 (on the next page) illustrates the dependencies among chapters in the book. An arrow pointing into a chapter indicates that it depends on the content of the chapter from which the arrow points. Though other approaches may work for you, we recommend that you study all of a given chapter's dependencies before studying that chapter. Some of the dependencies apply only to sections of chapters, so we advise readers to browse the material before designing a course of study. We've commented on some additional dependencies in the diagram's footnotes.

Teaching Approach

Visual Basic 2008 How to Program contains a rich collection of examples. The book concentrates on the principles of good software engineering and stresses program clarity. We teach by example. We are educators who teach leading-edge topics in industry classrooms worldwide. Dr. Harvey M. Deitel has 20 years of experience in college teaching and 19 years in industry teaching. Paul Deitel has taught 17 years in industry. The Deitels have taught courses at all levels to government, industry, military and academic clients of Deitel & Associates.

Live-Code Approach. *Visual Basic 2008 How to Program* is loaded with "live-code" examples. By this we mean that each new concept is presented in the context of a complete working Visual Basic program, followed immediately by one or more actual executions showing the program's inputs and outputs. This style exemplifies the way we teach and write about programming; we call it the "live-code approach."

Syntax Coloring. We syntax color all the Visual Basic code, similar to the way most Visual Basic integrated-development environments and code editors syntax color code. This greatly improves code readability—an especially important goal, given that this book contains approximately 20,000 lines of code. Our syntax-coloring conventions are as follows:

```
comments appear in green
keywords appear in dark blue
errors and ASP.NET delimiters appear in red
constants and literal values appear in light blue
all other code appears in plain black
```

Code Highlighting. We place gray rectangles around the key code segments in each program.

Programming Tips. We include programming tips to help you focus on important aspects of program development. These tips and practices represent the best we have gleaned from

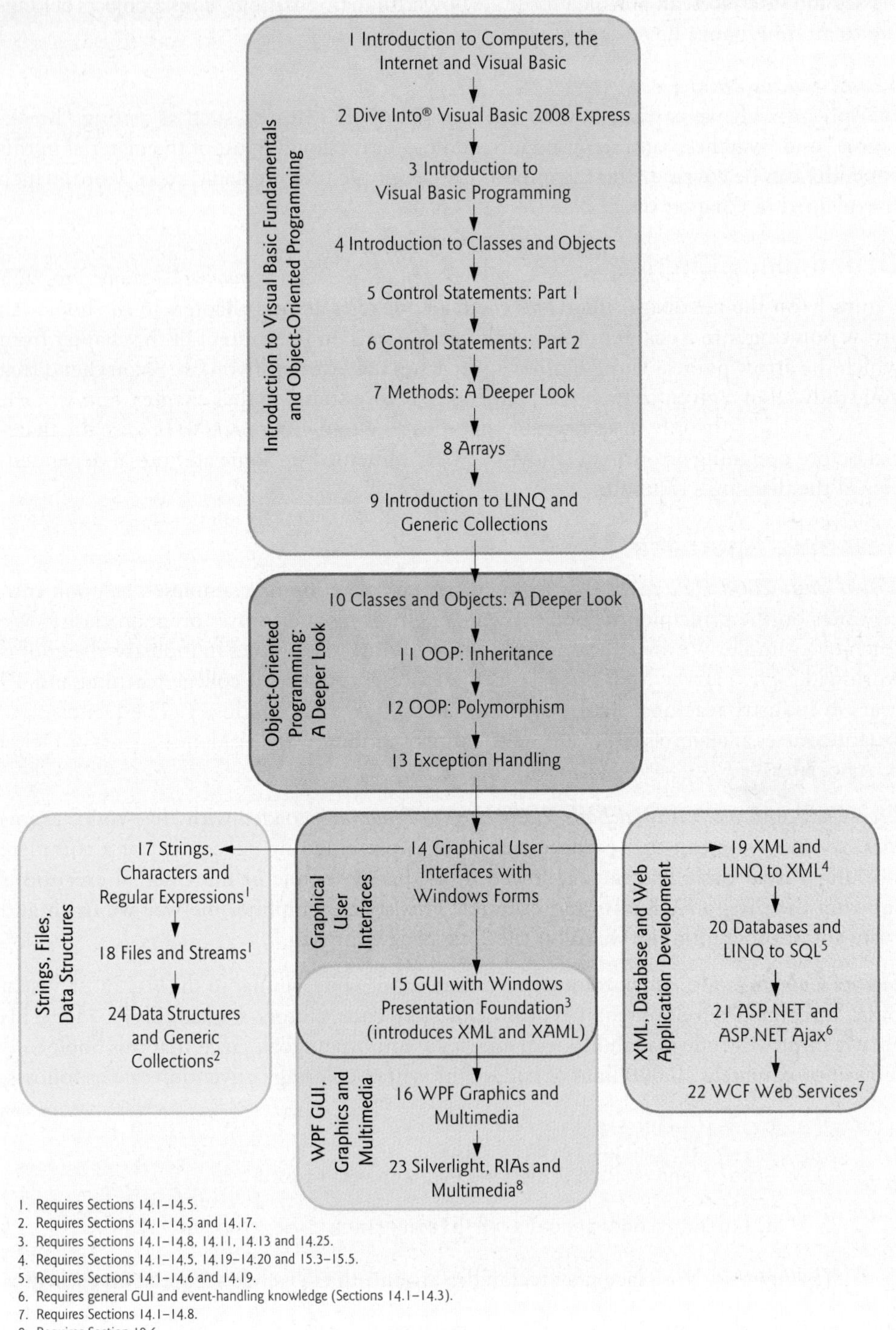

Fig. 1 | *Visual Basic 2008 How to Program* chapter dependency chart.

a combined six decades of programming and teaching experience. One of our students—a mathematics major—likens this approach to the highlighting of axioms, theorems and corollaries in mathematics books; it provides a basis on which to build good software.

Good Programming Practices

Good Programming Practices *will help you produce programs that are clearer, more understandable and more maintainable.*

Common Programming Errors

Students tend to make certain kinds of errors frequently. Pointing out these Common Programming Errors *reduces the likelihood that you'll make the same mistakes.*

Error-Prevention Tips

These tips contain suggestions for exposing bugs and removing them from your programs; many describe aspects of Visual Basic that prevent bugs from getting into programs in the first place.

Performance Tips

Students like to "turbocharge" their programs. These tips highlight opportunities for making your programs run faster or minimizing the amount of memory that they occupy.

Portability Tips

We include Portability Tips *to help you write code that will run on a variety of platforms and to explain how Visual Basic achieves its high degree of portability.*

Software Engineering Observations

The Software Engineering Observations *highlight architectural and design issues that affect the construction of software systems, especially large-scale systems.*

Look-and-Feel Observations

We provide Look-and-Feel Observations *to highlight graphical-user-interface conventions. These observations help you design attractive, user-friendly graphical user interfaces that conform to industry norms.*

Using Fonts and Colors for Emphasis. We place the key terms and the index's page reference for each defining occurrence in **bold blue** text for easier reference. We emphasize on-screen components in the **bold Helvetica** font (e.g., the **File** menu) and Visual Basic program text in the `Lucida` font (e.g., `int x = 5`).

Web Access. All of the source-code examples for *Visual Basic 2008 How to Program* are available for download from:

```
www.deitel.com/books/vb2008htp/
```

Site registration is quick and easy. Download all the examples, then run each program as you read the corresponding text discussions. Making changes to the examples and seeing the effects of those changes is a great way to enhance your Visual Basic learning experience.

Objectives. Each chapter begins with a statement of objectives. This lets you know what to expect and gives you an opportunity, after reading the chapter, to determine if you have met the objectives.

Quotations. The learning objectives are accompanied by quotations. Some are humorous; some are philosophical; others offer interesting insights. We hope that you enjoy relating the quotations to the chapter material.

Outline. The chapter outline helps you approach the material in a top-down fashion, so you can anticipate what is to come and set an effective learning pace.

Illustrations/Figures. Abundant charts, tables, line drawings, programs and program output are included. We model the flow of control in control statements with UML activity diagrams. UML class diagrams model the fields, constructors and methods of classes. We make extensive use of six major UML diagram types in the optional OOD/UML 2 ATM case study.

Wrap-Up Section. Each chapter ends with a brief "wrap-up" section that recaps the chapter content and transitions to the next chapter.

Summary Bullets. Each chapter ends with additional pedagogical features. We present a thorough, bullet-list-style summary of the chapter, section by section.

Terminology. We include an alphabetized list of the important terms defined in each chapter. Each term also appears in the index, with its defining occurrence highlighted with a **bold blue** page number.

Self-Review Exercises and Answers. Extensive self-review exercises and answers are included for self-study.

Exercises. Each chapter concludes with a set of exercises, including simple recall of important terminology and concepts; identifying the errors in code samples; writing individual Visual Basic statements; writing small portions of functions and classes; writing complete Visual Basic functions, classes and programs; and writing major term projects. The large number of exercises enables instructors to tailor their courses to the unique needs of their students and to vary course assignments each semester. Instructors can use these exercises to form homework assignments, short quizzes, major examinations and term projects. See our Programming Projects Resource Center (`www.deitel.com/ProgrammingProjects/`) for additional exercise and project possibilities.

[*NOTE:* **Please do not write to us requesting access to the Prentice Hall Instructor's Resource Center, which contains the exercise solutions and the book's ancillaries. Access is limited strictly to college instructors teaching from the book. Instructors may obtain access only through their Prentice Hall representatives.**]

Thousands of Index Entries. We have included a comprehensive index, which is especially useful when you use the book as a reference.

"Double Indexing" of Visual Basic Live-Code Examples. For every source-code program in the book, we index the figure caption both alphabetically and as a subindex item under "Examples." This makes it easier to find examples using particular features.

A Tour of the Optional Case Study on Object-Oriented Design with the UML

In this section we tour the book's optional case study on object-oriented design with the UML. This tour previews the contents of the Software Engineering Case Study sections (in Chapters 1, 3–8, 10, 12 and Appendix D). After completing this case study, you will be thoroughly familiar with an object-oriented design and implementation for a significant Visual Basic application.

The design presented in the ATM case study was developed at Deitel & Associates, Inc., and scrutinized by a distinguished developmental review team of industry professionals and academics. We crafted this design to meet the requirements of introductory course sequences. Real ATM systems used by banks and their customers worldwide are based on more sophisticated designs that take into consideration many more issues than we have addressed here. Our primary goal throughout the design process was to create a simple design that would be clear to OOD and UML novices, while still demonstrating key OOD concepts and the related UML modeling techniques. We worked hard to keep the design and the code relatively small so that they would work well in the introductory course sequence.

Section 1.19—(Required) Software Engineering Case Study: Introduction to Object Technology and the UML—introduces the object-oriented design case study with the UML. The section presents basic concepts and terminology of object technology, including classes, objects, encapsulation and inheritance. We discuss the history of the UML. This is the only required section of the case study.

Section 3.10—(Optional) Software Engineering Case Study: Examining the ATM Requirements Document—discusses a *requirements document* specifying the requirements for a system that design and implement—the software for a simple automated teller machine (ATM). We investigate the structure and behavior of object-oriented systems in general. We discuss how the UML will facilitate the design process in subsequent Software Engineering Case Study sections by providing several additional types of diagrams to model our system. We include a list of URLs and book references on object-oriented design with the UML. We discuss the interaction between the ATM system and its user. Specifically, we investigate the scenarios that may occur between the user and the system itself—these are called *use cases*. We model these interactions, using UML *use case diagrams*.

Section 4.9—(Optional) Software Engineering Case Study: Identifying the Classes in the ATM Requirements Documents—begins to design the ATM system. We identify its classes by extracting the nouns and noun phrases from the requirements document. We arrange these classes into a UML class diagram that describes the class structure of our simulation. The diagram also describes relationships, known as *associations*, among the classes.

Section 5.16—(Optional) Software Engineering Case Study: Identifying Class Attributes in the ATM System—focuses on the attributes of the classes discussed in Section 3.10. A class contains both *attributes* (data) and *operations* (behaviors). As we see in later sections, changes in an object's attributes often affect its behavior. To determine the attributes for the classes in our case study, we extract the adjectives describing the nouns and noun phrases (which defined our classes) from the requirements document, then place the attributes in the class diagram we created in Section 4.9.

Section 6.11—(Optional) Software Engineering Case Study: Identifying Objects' States and Activities in the ATM System—discusses how an object, at any given time, occupies a specific condition called a *state*. A *state transition* occurs when the object receives a message to change state. The UML provides the *state machine diagram*, which identifies the set of possible states that an object may occupy and models that object's state transitions. An object also has an *activity*—the work it performs in its lifetime. The UML provides the *activity diagram*—a flowchart that models an object's activity. This section uses both diagram types to model behavioral aspects of our ATM system, such as how it carries out a withdrawal transaction and how it responds when the user is authenticated.

Section 7.20—(Optional) Software Engineering Case Study: Identifying Class Operations in the ATM System—identifies the operations, or services, of our classes. We extract from the requirements document the verbs and verb phrases that specify the operations for each class. We then modify the class diagram of Section 4.9 to include each operation with its associated class. At this point in the case study, we will have gathered all information possible from the requirements document. As future chapters introduce such topics as inheritance, we'll modify our classes and diagrams.

Section 8.17—(Optional) Software Engineering Case Study: Collaboration Among Objects in the ATM System—provides a "rough sketch" of the model for our ATM system. In this section, we see how it works. We investigate the behavior of the simulation by discussing *collaborations*—messages that objects send to each other to communicate. The class operations that we identified in Section 7.20 turn out to be the collaborations among the objects in our system. We determine the collaborations, then collect them into a *communication diagram*—the UML diagram for modeling collaborations. This diagram reveals which objects collaborate and when. We present a communication diagram of the collaborations among objects to perform an ATM balance inquiry. We then present the UML *sequence diagram* for modeling interactions in a system. This diagram emphasizes the chronological ordering of messages. A sequence diagram models how objects in the system interact to carry out withdrawal and deposit transactions.

Section 10.19—(Optional) Software Engineering Case Study: Starting to Program the Classes of the ATM System—takes a break from designing the behavior of our system. We begin the implementation process to emphasize the material discussed in Chapter 8. Using the UML class diagram of Section 4.9 and the attributes and operations discussed in Section 5.16 and Section 7.20, we show how to implement a class in Visual Basic from a design. We do not implement all classes—because we have not completed the design process. Working from our UML diagrams, we create code for the `Withdrawal` class.

Section 12.8—(Optional) Software Engineering Case Study: Incorporating Inheritance and Polymorphism into the ATM System—continues our discussion of object-oriented programming. We consider inheritance: classes sharing common characteristics may inherit attributes and operations from a "base" class. In this section, we investigate how our ATM system can benefit from using inheritance. We document our discoveries in a class diagram that models inheritance relationships—the UML refers to these relationships as *generalizations*. We modify the class diagram of Section 4.9 by using inheritance to group classes with similar characteristics. This section concludes the design of the model portion of our simulation.

Appendix D—ATM Case Study Code—The majority of the case study involves designing the model (i.e., the data and logic) of the ATM system. In this appendix, we fully implement that model in Visual Basic, using all the UML diagrams we created. We apply the concepts of object-oriented design with the UML and object-oriented programming in Visual Basic that you learned in the chapters. By the end of this appendix, you'll have completed the design and implementation of a real-world system and should feel confident tackling larger systems, such as those that professional software engineers build.

Appendix E—UML 2: Additional Diagram Types—overviews the UML 2 diagram types not discussed in the OOD/UML Case Study.

Microsoft Developer Network Academic Alliance (MSDNAA) and Microsoft DreamSpark

Microsoft Developer Network Academic Alliance (MSDNAA)—Free Microsoft Software for Academic and Research Purposes
The MSDNAA provides free software for academic and research purposes. For software direct to faculty, visit `www.microsoft.com/faculty`. For software for your department, visit `www.msdnaa.com`.

Microsoft DreamSpark—Professional Developer and Designer Tools for Students
Microsoft provides many of its developer tools to students for free via a program called DreamSpark (`downloads.channel8.msdn.com/`). At the time of this writing, the DreamSpark website states that students in the United States, the United Kingdom, Canada, China, Germany, France, Finland, Spain, Sweden, Switzerland and Belgium can obtain this software after their student status has been verified.

Software for the Book

We use Microsoft Visual Studio 2008 development tools, including the free Visual Basic® 2008 Express Edition and the free Visual Web Developer™ 2008 Express Edition. Per Microsoft's website, Microsoft Express Editions are "lightweight, easy-to-use and easy-to-learn tools for the hobbyist, novice and student developer." The Express Editions provide rich functionality and can be used to build robust .NET applications. They are appropriate for academic courses and for professionals who do not have access to a complete version of Visual Studio 2008.

You may use the Express Editions to compile and execute all the example programs and solve all the exercises in the book (with the exception of Chapter 23, whose software requirements are presented below in the Other Software Requirements section). You may also use the full Visual Studio product to build and run the examples and exercises. All of the features supported by the Express Editions are also available in the complete Visual Studio 2008 editions.

This book includes the Microsoft® Visual Studio® 2008 Express Editions All-in-One DVD, which contains the Visual Basic 2008 Express Edition, the Visual Web Developer 2008 Express Edition and the SQL Server 2005 Express Edition. You can also download the latest versions of these tools from:

```
www.microsoft.com/express/
```

When you install the software (discussed in the Before You Begin section that follows this Preface), you also should install the help documentation and SQL Server 2005 Express. Microsoft provides a dedicated forum for help using the Express Editions at:

```
forums.microsoft.com/msdn/ShowForum.aspx?siteid=1&ForumID=24
```

When the SQL Server 2008 Express Edition becomes available, we'll announce it in our newsletter (`www.deitel.com/newsletter/subscribe.html`) and add information on using it with this book at `www.deitel.com/books/vb2008htp/`.

Windows Vista vs. Windows XP

Readers of this book can use either Windows Vista or Windows XP. We used Windows Vista while developing the book. We use the Windows Vista Segoe UI font in the graphical user interfaces. This font is accessible to Windows XP users—we tell you how to get it in the Before You Begin section. Several of our full-book reviewers tested all the programs on Windows XP and reported no problems. If any Windows XP-specific issues arise after the book is published, we'll post them at `www.deitel.com/books/vb2008htp/` with appropriate instructions. Write to us at `deitel@deitel.com` if you encounter any problems and we'll respond promptly.

Other Software Requirements

For Chapters 20–22, you'll need the SQL Server 2005 Express Edition. Chapters 21 and 22 require Visual Web Developer 2008 Express (or a full Visual Studio 2008 edition).

We present Microsoft Silverlight in Chapter 23. At the time of this writing Silverlight 2 was in beta, and the tools for developing Silverlight applications were available only for Visual Studio 2008 (not Express Editions); tools for developing Silverlight applications with the Express Editions will be available soon. When the final tools become available, we'll post updates at `www.deitel.com/books/vb2008htp/`.

For updates on the software used in this book, subscribe to our free e-mail newsletter at `www.deitel.com/newsletter/subscribe.html` and visit the book's website at `www.deitel.com/books/vb2008htp/`. Also, be sure to visit our Visual Basic 2008 Resource Center (`www.deitel.com/VisualBasic2008/`) frequently for new Visual Basic 2008 resources. We've created Resource Centers for all of the major technologies discussed in this book (`www.deitel.com/resourcecenters.html`)—each week we announce our latest Resource Centers in the newsletter.

Instructor Resources for *Visual Basic 2008 How to Program*

Visual Basic 2008 How to Program has extensive instructor resources. The Prentice Hall *Instructor's Resource Center* contains the *Solutions Manual* with solutions to the vast majority of the end-of-chapter exercises, a *Test Item File* of multiple-choice questions (approximately two per book section) and PowerPoint® slides containing the code and figures in the text, plus bulleted summaries of the key points in the text. Instructors can customize the slides. If you are not already a registered faculty member, contact your Prentice Hall representative or visit `vig.prenhall.com/replocator/`.

[*NOTE:* Please do not write to us requesting access to the Prentice Hall Instructor's Resource Center, which contains the exercise solutions and the book's ancillaries. Access is limited strictly to college instructors teaching from the book. Instructors may obtain access only through their Prentice Hall representatives.]

Deitel® Buzz Online Free E-mail Newsletter

Each week, the *Deitel® Buzz Online* newsletter announces our latest Resource Center(s) and includes commentary on industry trends and developments, links to free articles and resources from our published books and upcoming publications, product-release schedules, errata, challenges, anecdotes, information on our corporate instructor-led training courses and more. It's also a good way for you to keep posted about issues related to *Visual Basic 2008 How to Program*. To subscribe, visit

```
www.deitel.com/newsletter/subscribe.html
```

The Deitel Online Resource Centers

Our website `www.deitel.com` provides more than 100 Resource Centers on various topics including programming languages, software development, Web 2.0, Internet business and open-source projects—see the complete list of Resource Centers in the first few pages of this book or visit `www.deitel.com/ResourceCenters.html`. The Resource Centers evolved out of the research we've done to support our books and business endeavors. We've found many exceptional resources online, including tutorials, documentation, software downloads, articles, blogs, podcasts, videos, code samples, books, e-books and more—most of them are free. Each week we announce our latest Resource Centers in our newsletter, the *Deitel® Buzz Online* (`www.deitel.com/newsletter/subscribe.html`). The following Resource Centers may be of interest to you as you study *Visual Basic 2008 How to Program*:

- Visual Basic 2008
- Visual Basic
- ASP.NET
- ASP.NET 3.5
- ASP.NET AJAX
- Visual Studio Team System
- Code Search Engines and Code Sites
- Computer Game Programming
- Computing Jobs
- LINQ
- Popfly
- Open Source
- Programming Projects
- .NET
- .NET 3.0
- .NET 3.5
- Silverlight
- Silverlight 2.0
- SQL Server 2008
- Web Services
- Windows Communication Foundation
- Windows Presentation Foundation
- Windows Vista

Acknowledgments

It's a pleasure to acknowledge the efforts of people whose names do not appear on the cover, but whose hard work, cooperation, friendship and understanding were crucial to the book's production. Many people at Deitel & Associates, Inc., devoted long hours to this project—thanks especially to Abbey Deitel and Barbara Deitel.

We would also like to thank the participants of our Honors Internship and Co-op programs who contributed to this publication—Greg Ayer, a Computer Science major at Northeastern University; Nicholas Doiron, an Electrical and Computer Engineering major at Carnegie Mellon University; Joseph Itkis, a Mathematics major (Computer Science track) at Yeshiva University; David Keyworth, an Information Technology major at Rochester Institute of Technology; Jehhal Liu, an Electrical and Computer Engineering major at Cornell University; Matthew Pearson, a Computer Science major at Cornell University; Bruce Tu, an Information Science major at Cornell University; and H. Shawn Xu, a Biomedical Engineering and Economics double major at Johns Hopkins University.

We are fortunate to have worked on this project with the talented and dedicated team of publishing professionals at Prentice Hall. We appreciate the extraordinary efforts of Marcia Horton, Editorial Director of Prentice Hall's Engineering and Computer Science Division. Carole Snyder, Lisa Bailey and Dolores Mars did an extraordinary job recruiting the book's review team and managing the review process. Francesco Santalucia (an independent artist) and Kristine Carney of Prentice Hall did a wonderful job designing the book's cover—we provided the concept, and they made it happen. Scott Disanno, Robert Engelhardt and Marta Samsel did a marvelous job managing the book's production. Our marketing manager Chris Kelly and his boss Margaret Waples did a great job marketing the book through academic and professional channels.

We wish to acknowledge the efforts of our reviewers. Adhering to a tight time schedule, they scrutinized the text and the programs, providing countless suggestions for improving the accuracy and completeness of the presentation:

Visual Basic 2008 How to Program *Reviewers*

Academic Reviewers: Douglas B. Bock (MCSD.NET, Southern Illinois University Edwardsville), Amit K. Ghosh (University of Texas at El Paso), James Edward Keysor (Florida Institute of Technology) and Jesús Ubaldo Quevedo-Torrero (University of Wisconsin–Parkside, Department of Computer Science). **Microsoft Reviewers:** Dan Crevier, Marcelo Guerra Hahn, Kim Hamilton (Software Design Engineer and co-author of *Learning UML 2.0*), Huanhui Hu, Vitek Karas, Helena Kotas, Chris Lovett (Software Architect), Timothy Ng, Akira Onishi, Joe Stagner (Senior Program Manager, Developer Tools & Platforms) and Erick Thompson. **Industry Reviewers:** Bashar Lulu (INETA Country Leader, Arabian Gulf), John McIlhinney (Spatial Intelligence; Microsoft MVP 2008 Visual Developer, Visual Basic), Ged Mead (Microsoft Visual Basic MVP, DevCity.net), Anand Mukundan (Architect, Polaris Software Lab Ltd.) and José Antonio González Seco (Parliament of Andalusia).

Visual Basic 2005 How to Program, 3/e *[Previous Edition] Reviewers*

Academic Reviewers: Karen Arlien (Bismarck State College), Robert Benavides (Collin County Community College), Rekha Bhowmik (Winston-Salem State University), Chadi Boudiab (Georgia Perimeter College), Brian Larson (Modesto Junior College), Gavin Osborne (Saskatchewan Institute of Applied Science and Technology) and Warren Wiltsie (Fairleigh Dickinson University). **Microsoft Reviewers:** Corneliu Barsan, Dharmesh Chauhan, John Chen, Eric Gruber, Manish Jayaswal, Cameron McColl, Alexandre Moura, Baiju Nair, Cat Rambo, Thom Robbins, Chris Smith (Compiler UI Team) and Craig Vick. **Industry Reviewers:** Harlan Brewer (SES Consulting), Kunal Cheda (Computer Enterprises, Inc., U.S.), James Huddleston (Independent Consultant), Terrell Hull (Independent Consultant), Amit Kalani (TechContent Corporation), Tysen Leckie (Edge Technologies) and John Mueller (DataCon Services). **UML Case Study Reviewers:** Scott Ambler (Ambysoft, Inc.), Rekha Bhowmik (Winston-Salem State University), Chadi Boudiab (Georgia Perimeter College), Brian Cook (Zurich North America), Sergio Davalos (University of Washington–Tacoma), Sujay Ghuge (Verizon IT), Manu Gupta (Patni Computer Systems), Terrell Hull (Independent Consultant), James Huddleston (Independent Consultant), Jeff Jones (Route Match Software), John Mueller (DataCon Services), Davyd Norris (Rational/IBM) and Gavin Osborne (Saskatchewan Institute).

Well, there you have it! Visual Basic 2008 is a powerful programming language that will help you write programs quickly and effectively. It scales nicely into the realm of enterprise-systems development to help organizations build their business-critical and mission-critical information systems. As you read the book, we would sincerely appreciate your comments, criticisms, corrections and suggestions for improvement. Please address all correspondence to:

```
deitel@deitel.com
```

We'll respond promptly, and we'll post corrections and clarifications on the book's website:

```
www.deitel.com/books/vb2008htp/
```

We hope you enjoy reading *Visual Basic 2008 How to Program* as much as we enjoyed writing it!

Paul J. Deitel
Dr. Harvey M. Deitel

About the Authors

Paul J. Deitel, CEO and Chief Technical Officer of Deitel & Associates, Inc., has 21 years of experience in the computer field. Paul is a graduate of MIT's Sloan School of Management, where he studied Information Technology. Through Deitel & Associates, Inc., he has delivered Visual Basic, C#, C++, C and Java courses to industry clients, including Cisco, IBM, Sun Microsystems, Dell, Lucent Technologies, Fidelity, NASA at the Kennedy Space Center, White Sands Missile Range, the National Severe Storm Laboratory, Rogue Wave Software, Boeing, Stratus, Hyperion Software, Adra Systems, Entergy, CableData Systems, Nortel Networks, Puma, iRobot, Invensys and many more. He holds the Sun Certified Java Programmer and Java Developer certifications and has been designated by Sun Microsystems as a Java Champion. He has lectured on Java and C++ for the Boston Chapter of the Association for Computing Machinery. He and his father, Dr. Harvey M. Deitel, are the world's best-selling programming-language textbook authors.

Dr. Harvey M. Deitel, Chairman and Chief Strategy Officer of Deitel & Associates, Inc., has 47 years of experience in the computer field. Dr. Deitel earned B.S. and M.S. degrees from MIT and a Ph.D. from Boston University. He has extensive college teaching experience, including earning tenure and serving as the Chairman of the Computer Science Department at Boston College before founding Deitel & Associates, Inc., with his son, Paul J. Deitel. Harvey and Paul are the co-authors of dozens of books and multimedia packages and they are writing many more. The Deitels' texts have earned international recognition with translations published in Japanese, German, Russian, Spanish, Traditional Chinese, Simplified Chinese, Korean, French, Polish, Italian, Portuguese, Greek, Urdu and Turkish. Dr. Deitel has delivered hundreds of professional seminars to major corporations, academic institutions, government organizations and the military.

About Deitel & Associates, Inc.

Deitel & Associates, Inc., is an internationally recognized corporate training and content-creation organization specializing in computer programming languages, Internet and web software technology, object-technology education and Internet business development through its Web 2.0 Internet Business Initiative. The company provides instructor-led courses on major programming languages and platforms, such as Visual Basic, C#, Visual C++, C++, Java, C, XML, object technology, Internet and web programming, and a growing list of additional programming and software-development related courses. The founders of Deitel & Associates, Inc., are Paul J. Deitel and Dr. Harvey M. Deitel. The company's clients include many of the world's largest companies, government agencies, branches of the military, and academic institutions. Through its 32-year publishing partnership with Prentice Hall, Deitel & Associates, Inc., publishes leading-edge programming textbooks, professional books, interactive multimedia *Cyber Classrooms*, *LiveLessons* DVD-based and web-based video courses, and e-content for popular course-management systems. Deitel & Associates, Inc., and the authors can be reached via e-mail at:

`deitel@deitel.com`

To learn more about Deitel & Associates, Inc., its publications and its worldwide *Dive Into®* Series Corporate Training curriculum, see the last few pages of this book or visit:

`www.deitel.com`

and subscribe to the free *Deitel® Buzz Online* e-mail newsletter at:

`www.deitel.com/newsletter/subscribe.html`

Individuals wishing to purchase Deitel books, *LiveLessons* DVD and web-based training courses can do so through:

`www.deitel.com`

Bulk orders by corporations, the government, the military and academic institutions should be placed directly with Prentice Hall. For more information, visit

`www.prenhall.com/mischtm/support.html#order`

Before You Begin

This section contains information you should review before using this book and instructions to ensure that your computer is set up properly for use with this book. We'll post updates to this Before You Begin section (if any) on the book's website:

```
www.deitel.com/books/vb2008htp/
```

Font and Naming Conventions

We use fonts to distinguish between features, such as menu names, menu items, and other elements that appear in the program-development environment. Our convention is to emphasize IDE features in a sans-serif bold **Helvetica** font (for example, **Properties** window) and to emphasize program text in a sans-serif `Lucida` font (for example, `Private x As Boolean = True`).

A Note Regarding Software for the Book

This textbook includes a DVD which contains the Microsoft® Visual Studio® 2008 Express Edition integrated development environments for Visual Basic 2008, Visual C# 2008, Visual C++ 2008, Visual Web Developer 2008 and SQL Server 2005. These are also downloadable from `www.microsoft.com/express`. The Express Editions are fully functional, and there is no time limit for using the software. We discuss the setup of this software shortly. You do not need Visual C# or Visual C++ for use with this book.

Hardware and Software Requirements for the Visual Studio 2008 Express Editions

To install and run the Visual Studio 2008 Express Editions, Microsoft recommends these minimum requirements:

- **Operating System:** Windows XP Service Pack 2 (or above), Windows Server 2003 Service Pack 1 (or above), Windows Server 2003 R2 (or above), Windows Vista or Windows Server 2008.
- **Processor:** Computer with a 1.6 GHz or faster processor (2.2 GHz or higher recommended—2.4 GHz on Vista).
- **RAM minimum:** 192 MB; Microsoft recommends 384 MB (768 MB on Vista).
- **Hard Drive:** 1.3 GB for complete install.
- **Display:** 1024 by 768 (1280 by 1024 recommended).
- To test and build the examples in Chapter 20 and some of the examples in Chapters 21–22, **you must install Microsoft's SQL Server 2005 Express**, which is an option during the installation of each Express Edition.
- To test and build the examples in Chapters 21–22, **you must install Microsoft's Visual Web Developer 2008 Express.**

Desktop Theme Settings for Windows Vista Users
If you are using Windows Vista, we assume that your theme is set to **Windows Vista**. Follow these steps to set **Windows Vista** as your desktop theme:

1. Right click the desktop, then click **Personalize**.
2. Click the **Theme** item. Select **Windows Vista** from the **Theme:** drop-down list.
3. Click **Apply** to save the settings.

Desktop Theme Settings for Windows XP Users
If you are using Windows XP, the windows you see on the screen will look slightly different from the screen captures in the book. We assume that your theme is set to **Windows XP**. Follow these steps to set **Windows XP** as your desktop theme:

1. Right click the desktop, then click **Properties**.
2. Click the **Themes** tab. Select **Windows XP** from the **Theme:** drop-down list.
3. Click **OK** to save the settings.

Viewing File Extensions
Several screenshots in *Visual Basic 2008 How to Program* display file names with file-name extensions (e.g., `.txt`, `.vb` or `.png`). Your system's settings may need to be adjusted to display file-name extensions. Follow these steps to configure your computer:

1. In the **Start** menu, select **All Programs**, then **Accessories**, then **Windows Explorer**.
2. In Windows Vista, press *Alt* to display the menu bar, then select **Folder Options...** from **Windows Explorer**'s **Tools** menu. In Windows XP, simply select **Folder Options...** from **Windows Explorer**'s **Tools** menu.
3. In the dialog that appears, select the **View** tab.
4. In the **Advanced settings:** pane, uncheck the box to the left of the text **Hide extensions for known file types**. [*Note*: If this item is already unchecked, no action needs to be taken.]

Notes to Windows XP Users Regarding the Segoe UI Font Used in Many Applications
As part of Windows Vista, Microsoft has released a new font called Segoe UI to make graphical user interfaces (GUIs) more readable. Many of our GUI examples use this font, which is not available by default on Windows XP. You can get it by installing Windows Live Mail—a free download from `get.live.com/wlmail/overview`.

You must also enable ClearType on your system; otherwise, the font will not display correctly. ClearType is a technology for smoothing the edges of fonts displayed on the screen. To enable ClearType, perform the following steps:

1. Right click your desktop and select **Properties...** from the popup menu to view the **Display Properties** dialog.
2. In the dialog, click the **Appearance** tab, then click the **Effects...** button to display the **Effects** dialog.
3. In the **Effects** dialog, ensure that the **Use the following method to smooth edges of screen fonts** checkbox is checked, then select **ClearType** from the combobox below the checkbox.
4. Click **OK** to close the **Effects** dialog. Click **OK** to close the **Display Properties** dialog.

Obtaining the Code Examples

The examples for *Visual Basic 2008 How to Program* are available for download at

```
www.deitel.com/books/vb2008htp/
```

If you are not already registered at our website, go to `www.deitel.com` and click the **Register** link below our logo in the upper-left corner of the page. Fill in your information. There is no charge to register, and we do not share your information with anyone. We send you only account-management e-mails unless you register separately for our free e-mail newsletter at `www.deitel.com/newsletter/subscribe.html`. After registering, you'll receive a confirmation e-mail with your verification code. You need this code to sign in at `www.deitel.com` for the first time.

Next, go to `www.deitel.com` and sign in using the **Login** link below our logo in the upper-left corner of the page. Go to `www.deitel.com/books/vb2008htp/`. Click the **Examples** link to download the `Examples.zip` file to your computer. Write down the location where you choose to save the file on your computer.

We assume the examples are located at `C:\Examples` on your computer. Extract the contents of `Examples.zip` using a tool such as WinZip (`www.winzip.com`) or the built-in capabilities of Windows XP and Windows Vista.

Installing the Software

Before you can run the applications in *Visual Basic 2008 How to Program* or build your own applications, you must install a development environment. We used Microsoft's free Visual Basic 2008 Express Edition in the examples for most chapters and Visual Web Developer 2008 Express Edition for Chapters 21–22. Chapters 20–22 also require SQL Server 2005 Express Edition. (SQL Server 2008 Express Edition was not available at the time of this writing. Once it becomes available, we'll post information about using it with this book at `www.deitel.com/books/vb2008htp/`.) Chapters 23, Silverlight, Rich Internet Applications and Multimedia, currently requires a full Visual Studio 2008 edition. We'll post information on the book's website when Silverlight support for the Express Editions becomes available. All of the Visual Studio Express Editions are included on a DVD bundled with this book and can be downloaded from:

```
www.microsoft.com/express/
```

To install the Visual Basic 2008 and Visual Web Developer 2008 Express Editions:

1. Insert the DVD that accompanies this book into your computer's DVD drive to launch the software installer. If the **Visual Studio 2008 Express Editions Setup** window does not appear, use Windows Explorer to view the contents of the DVD drive and double click `Setup.hta` to launch the installer
2. In the **Visual Studio 2008 Express Editions Setup** window, click **Visual Basic 2008 Express Edition** to display the **Visual Basic 2008 Express Edition Setup** window, then click **Next >**.
3. Carefully read the license agreement. Click the **I have read and accept the license terms** radio button to agree to the terms, then click **Next >**. [*Note:* If you do not accept the license agreement, the software will not install and you will not be able to create or execute Visual Basic applications.]

4. Select the **MSDN Express Library for Visual Studio 2008**, **Microsoft SQL Server 2005 Express Edition (x86)** and **Microsoft Silverlight Runtime** options to install. Click **Next >**. [*Note:* Installing the MSDN documentation is not required but is highly recommended.]
5. Click **Next >**, then click **Finish >** to continue with the installation. The installer will now begin copying the files required by Visual Basic 2008 Express Edition and SQL Server 2005 Express Edition. Wait for the installation to complete before proceeding—the installation process can be quite lengthy. When the installation completes, click **Exit.**.
6. In the **Visual Studio 2008 Express Editions Setup** window, click **Visual Web Developer 2008 Express Edition** to display the **Visual Web Developer 2008 Express Edition Setup** window, then click **Next >**.
7. Carefully read the license agreement. Click the **I have read and accept the license terms** radio button to agree to the terms, then click **Next >**. [*Note:* If you do not accept the license agreement, the software will not install and you will not be able to create or execute web applications with Visual Web Developer.]
8. Click **Install >** to continue with the installation. The installer will now begin copying the files required by Visual Web Developer 2008 Express Edition. This portion of the install process should be much faster, since you've already installed most of the supporting software and files required by Visual Web Developer. When the installation completes, click **Exit**.

Miscellaneous Notes

- Some people like to change the workspace layout in the development tools. You can return the tools to their default layouts by selecting **Window > Reset Window Layout**.
- There are differences between the full Visual Studio 2008 products and the Express Edition products we use in this book, such as additional menu items. One key difference is that the **Database Explorer** we refer to in Chapters 20–22 is called the **Server Explorer** in the full Visual Studio 2008 products.
- Many of the menu items we use in the book have corresponding icons shown with each menu item in the menus. Many of the icons also appear on one of the toolbars at the top of the development environment. As you become familiar with these icons, you can use the toolbars to help speed up your development time. Similarly, many of the menu items have keyboard shortcuts (also shown with each menu item in the menus) for accessing commands quickly.

You are now ready to begin your Visual Basic studies with *Visual Basic 2008 How to Program*. We hope you enjoy the book!

Obtaining the Code Examples

The examples for *Visual Basic 2008 How to Program* are available for download at

```
www.deitel.com/books/vb2008htp/
```

If you are not already registered at our website, go to `www.deitel.com` and click the **Register** link below our logo in the upper-left corner of the page. Fill in your information. There is no charge to register, and we do not share your information with anyone. We send you only account-management e-mails unless you register separately for our free e-mail newsletter at `www.deitel.com/newsletter/subscribe.html`. After registering, you'll receive a confirmation e-mail with your verification code. You need this code to sign in at `www.deitel.com` for the first time.

Next, go to `www.deitel.com` and sign in using the **Login** link below our logo in the upper-left corner of the page. Go to `www.deitel.com/books/vb2008htp/`. Click the **Examples** link to download the `Examples.zip` file to your computer. Write down the location where you choose to save the file on your computer.

We assume the examples are located at `C:\Examples` on your computer. Extract the contents of `Examples.zip` using a tool such as WinZip (`www.winzip.com`) or the built-in capabilities of Windows XP and Windows Vista.

Installing the Software

Before you can run the applications in *Visual Basic 2008 How to Program* or build your own applications, you must install a development environment. We used Microsoft's free Visual Basic 2008 Express Edition in the examples for most chapters and Visual Web Developer 2008 Express Edition for Chapters 21–22. Chapters 20–22 also require SQL Server 2005 Express Edition. (SQL Server 2008 Express Edition was not available at the time of this writing. Once it becomes available, we'll post information about using it with this book at `www.deitel.com/books/vb2008htp/`.) Chapters 23, Silverlight, Rich Internet Applications and Multimedia, currently requires a full Visual Studio 2008 edition. We'll post information on the book's website when Silverlight support for the Express Editions becomes available. All of the Visual Studio Express Editions are included on a DVD bundled with this book and can be downloaded from:

```
www.microsoft.com/express/
```

To install the Visual Basic 2008 and Visual Web Developer 2008 Express Editions:

1. Insert the DVD that accompanies this book into your computer's DVD drive to launch the software installer. If the **Visual Studio 2008 Express Editions Setup** window does not appear, use Windows Explorer to view the contents of the DVD drive and double click `Setup.hta` to launch the installer
2. In the **Visual Studio 2008 Express Editions Setup** window, click **Visual Basic 2008 Express Edition** to display the **Visual Basic 2008 Express Edition Setup** window, then click **Next >**.
3. Carefully read the license agreement. Click the **I have read and accept the license terms** radio button to agree to the terms, then click **Next >**. [*Note:* If you do not accept the license agreement, the software will not install and you will not be able to create or execute Visual Basic applications.]

4. Select the **MSDN Express Library for Visual Studio 2008**, **Microsoft SQL Server 2005 Express Edition (x86)** and **Microsoft Silverlight Runtime** options to install. Click **Next >**. [*Note:* Installing the MSDN documentation is not required but is highly recommended.]
5. Click **Next >**, then click **Finish >** to continue with the installation. The installer will now begin copying the files required by Visual Basic 2008 Express Edition and SQL Server 2005 Express Edition. Wait for the installation to complete before proceeding—the installation process can be quite lengthy. When the installation completes, click **Exit**..
6. In the **Visual Studio 2008 Express Editions Setup** window, click **Visual Web Developer 2008 Express Edition** to display the **Visual Web Developer 2008 Express Edition Setup** window, then click **Next >**.
7. Carefully read the license agreement. Click the **I have read and accept the license terms** radio button to agree to the terms, then click **Next >**. [*Note:* If you do not accept the license agreement, the software will not install and you will not be able to create or execute web applications with Visual Web Developer.]
8. Click **Install >** to continue with the installation. The installer will now begin copying the files required by Visual Web Developer 2008 Express Edition. This portion of the install process should be much faster, since you've already installed most of the supporting software and files required by Visual Web Developer. When the installation completes, click **Exit**.

Miscellaneous Notes

- Some people like to change the workspace layout in the development tools. You can return the tools to their default layouts by selecting **Window > Reset Window Layout**.
- There are differences between the full Visual Studio 2008 products and the Express Edition products we use in this book, such as additional menu items. One key difference is that the **Database Explorer** we refer to in Chapters 20–22 is called the **Server Explorer** in the full Visual Studio 2008 products.
- Many of the menu items we use in the book have corresponding icons shown with each menu item in the menus. Many of the icons also appear on one of the toolbars at the top of the development environment. As you become familiar with these icons, you can use the toolbars to help speed up your development time. Similarly, many of the menu items have keyboard shortcuts (also shown with each menu item in the menus) for accessing commands quickly.

You are now ready to begin your Visual Basic studies with *Visual Basic 2008 How to Program*. We hope you enjoy the book!

Introduction to Computers, the Internet and Visual Basic

The chief merit of language is clearness.
—Galen

High thoughts must have high language.
—Aristophanes

Our life is frittered away with detail. . . . Simplify, simplify.
—Henry David Thoreau

My object all sublime I shall achieve in time.
—W. S. Gilbert

Man is still the most extraordinary computer of all.
—John F. Kennedy

OBJECTIVES

In this chapter you'll learn:

- Basic hardware and software concepts.
- The different types of programming languages.
- Which programming languages are most widely used.
- The history of the Visual Basic programming language.
- Some basics of object technology.
- The history of the UML—the industry-standard object-oriented system modeling language.
- The history of the Internet and the World Wide Web.
- The motivation behind and an overview of Microsoft's .NET initiative, which involves the Internet in developing and using software systems.
- To test-drive a Visual Basic 2008 application that enables you to draw on the screen.

Outline

1.1 Introduction

Welcome to Visual Basic 2008! We've worked hard to provide you with accurate and complete information regarding this powerful computer programming language which, from this point forward, we'll refer to simply as Visual Basic. Visual Basic is appropriate for technically oriented people with little or no programming experience, and for experienced programmers to use in building substantial information systems. *Visual Basic 2008 How to Program* is an effective learning tool for both audiences. We hope that working with this text will be an informative, challenging and entertaining learning experience for you.

How can one book appeal to both novices and skilled programmers? The core of this book emphasizes achieving program clarity through the proven techniques of object-oriented programming (OOP) and event-driven programming. Nonprogrammers learn skills that underlie good programming; experienced developers receive a rigorous explanation of the language and may improve their programming styles. Perhaps most important, the book presents hundreds of complete, working Visual Basic programs and depicts their inputs and outputs. We call this the **live-code approach.** All of the book's examples may be downloaded from `www.deitel.com/books/vb2008htp/`.

Computer use is increasing in almost every field of endeavor. Computing costs have been decreasing dramatically due to rapid developments in both hardware and software technologies. Computers that might have filled large rooms and cost millions of dollars a few decades ago can now be inscribed on silicon chips smaller than a fingernail, costing a few dollars each. Fortunately, silicon is one of the most abundant materials on earth—it's an ingredient in common sand. Silicon chip technology has made computing so economical that about a billion general-purpose computers are in use worldwide, helping people in business, industry and government, and in their personal lives.

We hope that you'll enjoy learning with *Visual Basic 2008 How to Program*. You are embarking on a challenging and rewarding path. As you proceed, if you have any questions, please send e-mail to

```
deitel@deitel.com
```

To keep current with Visual Basic developments at Deitel & Associates and to receive updates to this textbook, please register for our free e-mail newsletter, the *Deitel® Buzz Online,* at

```
www.deitel.com/newsletter/subscribe.html
```

Check out our growing list of Visual Basic and related Resource Centers at

```
www.deitel.com/ResourceCenters.html
```

1.2 What Is a Computer?

A **computer** is a device that can perform calculations and make logical decisions millions, billions and even trillions of times faster than humans can. For example, many of today's personal computers can perform billions of additions per second. A person operating a desk calculator might require a lifetime to complete the same number of calculations that a powerful personal computer can perform in one second. Today's fastest **supercomputers** are already performing trillions of additions per second!

Computers process **data**, using sets of instructions called **computer programs**. These programs guide computers through orderly sets of actions that are specified by people known as **computer programmers**.

A computer consists of various devices referred to as **hardware** (e.g., the keyboard, screen, mouse, hard drive, memory, DVDs and processing units). The programs that run on a computer are referred to as **software** (e.g., word processing programs, e-mail, games, etc.). Hardware costs have been declining dramatically in recent years, to the point that personal computers have become a commodity. Historically, however, software development costs have risen steadily as programmers develop ever more powerful and complex applications without being able to significantly improve the software development process. Object-oriented programming (which models real-world objects with software counterparts), available in Visual Basic and other programming languages, is a significant breakthrough that can greatly enhance your productivity.

1.3 Computer Organization

Computers can be thought of as being divided into six units:

1. **Input unit**. This "receiving" section of the computer obtains information (data and computer programs) from various **input devices**, such as the keyboard and

the mouse. Other input devices include microphones (for recording speech to the computer), scanners (for scanning images) and digital cameras (for taking photographs and making videos).

2. Output unit. This "shipping" section of the computer takes information that the computer has processed and places it on various output devices, making the information available for use outside the computer. Output can be displayed on screens, printed on paper, played on audio/video devices, transmitted over the Internet, etc. Output also can be used to control other devices, such as robots used in manufacturing.
3. Memory unit. This rapid-access, relatively low-capacity "warehouse" section of the computer stores data temporarily while an application is running. The memory unit retains information that has been entered through input devices, so that information is immediately available for processing. To be executed, computer programs must be in memory. The memory unit also retains processed information until it can be sent to output devices on which it is made available to users. Often, the memory unit is called either memory or primary memory. Random-access memory (RAM) is an example of primary memory. Primary memory is usually volatile, which means that it is erased when the machine is powered off.
4. Central processing unit (CPU). The CPU serves as the "administrative" section of the computer, supervising the operation of the other sections. The CPU alerts the input unit when information should be read into the memory unit, instructs the ALU when to use information from the memory unit in calculations and tells the output unit when to send information from the memory unit to certain output devices. Many of today's more powerful desktop computers have several CPUs.
5. Arithmetic and logic unit (ALU). The ALU (a part of the CPU) is the "manufacturing" section of the computer. It performs calculations such as addition, subtraction, multiplication and division. It also makes decisions, allowing the computer to perform such tasks as determining whether two items stored in memory are equal.
6. Secondary storage unit. This unit is the long-term, high-capacity "warehousing" section of the computer. Secondary storage devices, such as hard drives, CD-ROM drives, DVD drives, and USB memory sticks, normally hold programs or data that other units are not actively using. The computer can retrieve this information when it is needed—immediately or possibly hours, days, months or even years later. Information in secondary storage takes much longer to access than information in primary memory. However, secondary storage is much less expensive than primary memory. Secondary storage is nonvolatile, retaining information even when the computer is powered off.

1.4 Early Operating Systems

Computers of the 1950s could perform only one job or task at a time. This is often called single-user batch processing. The computer runs one program at a time while processing data in groups or batches. In these early systems, users generally submitted their jobs to a computer center on decks of punched cards and often had to wait hours or even days before printouts were returned to their desks. Computers were very large (often filling entire rooms) and expensive (often costing millions of dollars). Personal computers did not exist; people did not have computers in their offices and homes.

Software systems called operating systems were developed to make using computers more convenient. Early operating systems smoothed and speeded up the transition between jobs, increasing the amount of work, or throughput, computers could process.

As computers became more powerful, it became evident that single-user batch processing was inefficient, because so much time was spent waiting for slow input/output devices to complete their tasks. It was thought that many jobs or tasks could share the resources of the computer to achieve better utilization. This is achieved by multiprogramming—the simultaneous operation of many jobs that are competing to share the computer's resources. With early multiprogramming operating systems, users still submitted jobs on decks of punched cards and waited hours or days for results.

In the 1960s, several groups in industry and the universities pioneered timesharing operating systems. Timesharing is a special case of multiprogramming in which users access the computer through terminals, typically devices with keyboards and screens. Dozens or even hundreds of users share the computer at once. The computer actually does not run the users' jobs simultaneously. Rather, it runs a small portion of one user's job, then moves on to service the next user, perhaps providing service to each user several times per second. Thus, the users' programs *appear* to be running simultaneously. An advantage of timesharing is that user requests receive almost immediate responses.

1.5 Personal Computing, Distributed Computing and Client/Server Computing

In the early years of computing, computer systems were too large and expensive for individuals to own. In the 1970s, silicon chip technology appeared, making it possible for computers to be much smaller and so economical that individuals and small organizations could own these machines. In 1977, Apple Computer—creator of today's popular Mac personal computers and iPod digital music players—popularized personal computing. In 1981, IBM, the world's largest computer vendor, introduced the IBM Personal Computer, legitimizing personal computing in business, industry and government organizations.

These computers were "stand-alone" units—people transported disks back and forth between computers to share information (creating what was often called "sneakernet"). Although early personal computers were not powerful enough to timeshare several users, these machines could be linked together in computer networks, sometimes over telephone lines and sometimes in local area networks (LANs) within an organization. This led to the phenomenon of distributed computing, in which an organization's computing, instead of being performed only at some central computer installation, is distributed over networks to the geographically dispersed sites where the organization's work is performed. Personal computers were powerful enough to handle the computing requirements of individual users as well as the basic communications tasks of passing information between computers electronically.

Today's personal computers are as powerful as the million-dollar machines of just a few decades ago; complete personal computer systems often sell for as little as $500–1000.

The most powerful desktop machines provide individual users with enormous capabilities. Information is shared easily across computer networks, where computers called servers offer a common data store that may be used by client computers distributed throughout the network, hence the term client/server computing. In Chapters 21–23 you'll learn how to build Internet- and web-based applications; we'll talk about web servers (computers that distribute content over the web) and web clients (computers that request and receive the content offered up by web servers).

1.6 Hardware Trends

Every year, people generally expect to pay at least a little more for most products and services. The opposite has been the case in the computer and communications fields, especially with regard to the costs of hardware supporting these technologies. For many decades, hardware costs have fallen rapidly, if not precipitously. Every year or two, the capacities of computers have approximately doubled without any increase in price. This often is called Moore's Law, named after the person who first identified and explained the trend, Gordon Moore, co-founder of Intel—the company that manufactures the vast majority of the processors in today's personal computers. Moore's Law is especially true in relation to the amount of memory that computers have for programs, the amount of secondary storage (such as disk storage) they have to hold programs and data over longer periods of time, and their processor speeds—the speeds at which computers execute their programs (i.e., do their work). Similar growth has occurred in the communications field, in which costs have plummeted as enormous demand for communications bandwidth has attracted intense competition. We know of no other fields in which technology improves so quickly and costs fall so rapidly. Such phenomenal improvement in the computing and communications fields is truly fostering the so-called Information Revolution.

When computer use exploded in the 1960s and 1970s, many people discussed the dramatic improvements in human productivity that computing and communications would cause, but these improvements did not materialize. Organizations were spending vast sums of money on these technologies, but without realizing the expected productivity gains. The invention of microprocessor chip technology and its wide deployment in the late 1970s and 1980s laid the groundwork for the productivity improvements that individuals and businesses have achieved in recent years.

1.7 Microsoft's Windows® Operating System

Microsoft Corporation became the dominant software company in the 1980s and 1990s. In 1981, Microsoft released the first version of its DOS operating system for the IBM Personal Computer (DOS is an acronym for "Disk Operating System"). In the mid-1980s, Microsoft developed the Windows operating system, a graphical user interface built on top of DOS. Microsoft released Windows 3.0 in 1990; this new version featured a user-friendly interface and rich functionality. The Windows operating system became incredibly popular after the 1993 release of Windows 3.1, whose successors, Windows 95 and Windows 98, virtually cornered the desktop operating systems market by the late 1990s. These operating systems, which borrowed from many concepts (such as icons, menus and windows) popularized by early Apple Macintosh operating systems, enabled users to navigate multiple applications simultaneously. Microsoft entered the corporate operating systems market with the 1993 release of Windows NT. Windows XP, which is based on the Windows NT operating system, was released in 2001 and combines Microsoft's corporate and consumer operating system lines. Windows Vista, released in 2007, is Microsoft's latest operating system offering. This book is intended for Windows XP and Windows Vista users. Windows is by far the world's most widely used operating system.

The biggest competitor to the Windows operating system is Linux. The name Linux derives from Linus, after Linus Torvalds, who developed Linux, and UNIX—the operating system on which Linux is based; UNIX was developed at Bell Laboratories and was written in the C programming language. Linux is a free, open-source operating system, unlike Windows, which is proprietary (owned and controlled by Microsoft). The source code for Linux is freely available to users, and they can modify it to fit their needs.

1.8 Machine Languages, Assembly Languages and High-Level Languages

Programmers write instructions in various programming languages. Some of these are directly understandable by computers, and others require intermediate translation steps. Although hundreds of computer languages are in use today, they can be divided into three general types:

1. Machine languages
2. Assembly languages
3. High-level languages

A computer can directly understand only its own machine language. As the "natural language" of a particular computer, machine language is defined by the computer's hardware design. Machine languages generally consist of streams of numbers (ultimately reduced to 1s and 0s) that instruct computers how to perform their most elementary operations. You normally work in the decimal number system with digits in the range 0–9. The number system with only 1s and 0s is called the binary number system. Machine-language programs are sometimes called "binaries" for that reason. Machine languages are machine dependent, which means that a particular machine language can be used on only one type of computer. The following section of an early machine-language program, which adds *overtime pay* to *base pay* and stores the result in *gross pay*, demonstrates the incomprehensibility of machine language to humans:

```
+1300042774
+1400593419
+1200274027
```

As the popularity of computers increased, machine-language programming proved to be slow and error prone. Instead of using the strings of numbers that computers could directly understand, programmers began using English-like abbreviations to represent the computer's basic operations. These abbreviations formed the basis of assembly languages. Translator programs called assemblers convert assembly-language programs to machine language at computer speeds. The following section of an assembly-language program also adds *overtime pay* to *base pay* and stores the result in *gross pay*, but the steps are somewhat clearer to human readers than in the machine-language example:

```
LOAD   BASEPAY
ADD    OVERPAY
STORE  GROSSPAY
```

Although it is clearer to humans, computers cannot understand assembly-language code until it is translated into machine language by an assembler program.

The speed at which programmers could write programs increased rapidly with the creation of assembly languages, but these languages still require many instructions to accomplish even the simplest tasks. To speed up the programming process, **high-level languages** (in which single program statements accomplish more substantial tasks) were developed. Translator programs called **compilers** convert high-level-language programs into machine language. High-level languages enable programmers to write instructions that look almost like everyday English and contain common mathematical notations. For example, a payroll application written in a high-level language might contain a statement such as

```
grossPay = basePay + overTimePay
```

From these examples, it is clear why programmers prefer high-level languages to either machine languages or assembly languages. Figure 1.1 compares machine, assembly and high-level languages. Visual Basic is one of the world's most popular high-level programming languages. In the next section, you learn about Microsoft's latest version of this language, called Visual Basic 2008.

	Sample code	Translator	From the programmer's perspective	From the computer's perspective

Machine language	`+1300042774`
	`+1400593419`
	`+1200274027`
		None	Slow, tedious, error prone	Natural lanugage of a computer; the only language the computer can understand directly

Assembly language	`LOAD BASEPAY`
	`ADD OVERPAY`
	`STORE GROSSPAY`
		Assembler	English-like abbreviations, easier to understand	Assemblers convert assembly language into machine language so the computer can understand

High-level language	`grossPay = basePay + overTimePay`	Compiler	Instructions resemble everyday English; single statements accomplish substantial tasks	Compilers convert high-level languages into machine language so the computer can understand

Fig. 1.1 | Comparing machine, assembly and high-level languages.

1.9 Visual Basic

Visual Basic evolved from BASIC (Beginner's All-purpose Symbolic Instruction Code), developed in the mid-1960s by Professors John Kemeny and Thomas Kurtz of Dartmouth College as a language for writing simple programs quickly and easily. BASIC's primary purpose was to teach novices fundamental programming techniques.

When Bill Gates founded Microsoft Corporation in the 1970s, he implemented BASIC on several early personal computers. In the late 1980s and the early 1990s, Microsoft developed the Microsoft Windows graphical user interface (GUI)—the visual part of the operating system with which users interact. With the creation of the Windows GUI, the natural evolution of BASIC was to Visual Basic, introduced by Microsoft in 1991 to make programming Windows applications easier.

Until Visual Basic appeared, developing Microsoft Windows-based applications was a difficult process. Visual Basic is now an object-oriented, event-driven visual programming language in which programs are created with the use of a software tool called an Integrated Development Environment (IDE). With Microsoft's Visual Studio IDE, you can write, run, test and debug Visual Basic programs quickly and conveniently.

The latest versions of Visual Basic are fully object oriented—you'll learn some basics of object technology shortly and will study a rich treatment in the remainder of the book. Visual Basic is event driven—you'll write programs that respond to user-initiated events such as mouse clicks, keystrokes and timer expirations. It is a visual programming language—in addition to writing program statements to build portions of your applications, you'll also use Visual Studio's graphical user interface to conveniently drag and drop predefined objects like buttons and textboxes into place on your screen, and label and resize them. Visual Studio will write much of the GUI code for you.

Microsoft introduced its .NET (pronounced "dot-net") strategy in 2000. The .NET platform—the set of software components that enables .NET programs to run—allows applications to be distributed to a variety of devices (such as cell phones) as well as to desktop computers. The .NET platform offers a programming model that allows software components created in different programming languages (such as Visual Basic and C#) to communicate with one another. We discuss .NET in more detail in Section 1.16.

1.10 C, C++, Java and Visual C#

C

The C programming language was implemented by Dennis Ritchie at Bell Laboratories in 1973. C first gained widespread recognition as the development language of the UNIX operating system. C is a hardware-independent language, and, with careful design, it is possible to write C programs that are portable to most computers.

C++

C++ was developed by Bjarne Stroustrup in the early 1980s at Bell Laboratories. C++ provides a number of features that "spruce up" the C language, but, more important, it provides capabilities for object-oriented programming (OOP). Many of today's major operating systems are written in C or C++. At a time when the demand for new and more powerful software is soaring, the ability to build software quickly, correctly and economically remains an elusive goal. This problem can be addressed in part through the use of objects, or reusable software components that model items in the real world (we'll discuss object technology in Section 1.19). A modular, object-oriented approach to design and implementation can make software development groups much more productive than is possible using earlier programming techniques. Furthermore, object-oriented programs are often easier to understand, correct and modify.

Java

Microprocessors are having a profound impact in intelligent consumer electronic devices. Recognizing this, Sun Microsystems in 1991 funded an internal corporate research project that resulted in the development of a C++-based language. When a group of Sun people visited a local coffee shop, the name Java was suggested and it stuck. As the World Wide Web exploded in popularity in 1993, Sun saw the possibility of using Java to add dynamic content (e.g., interactivity, animations and the like) to web pages. Sun formally announced the language in 1995. This generated immediate interest in the business community because of the commercial potential of the web. Java is now used to develop large-scale enterprise applications, to enhance the functionality of web servers (the computers that provide the content we see in our web browsers), to provide applications for consumer devices (such as cell phones, pagers and personal digital assistants) and for many other purposes. Visual Basic is similar in capability to Java.

C#

In 2000, Microsoft announced the C# (pronounced "C-Sharp") programming language—created specifically for the .NET platform (which is discussed in Section 1.16). C# has roots in C, C++ and Java, adapting the best features of each. Like Visual Basic, C# is object oriented and has access to a powerful class library of prebuilt components, enabling programmers to develop applications quickly—Visual Basic and C# share the .NET Framework Class Library, discussed in Section 1.17. Both languages have similar capabilities to Java and are appropriate for demanding application development tasks, especially for building today's popular web-based applications.

1.11 Other High-Level Languages

Although hundreds of high-level languages have been developed, only a few have achieved broad acceptance. IBM Corporation developed Fortran (Formula Translator) in the mid-1950s to create scientific and engineering applications that require complex mathematical computations. Fortran is still widely used.

COBOL was developed in the late 1950s by a group of computer manufacturers in conjunction with government and industrial computer users. COBOL is used primarily for business applications that require the manipulation of large amounts of data. A considerable portion of today's business software is still programmed in COBOL.

1.12 Structured Programming

During the 1960s, software-development efforts often ran behind schedule, costs greatly exceeded budgets and the finished products were unreliable. People began to realize that software development was a far more complex activity than they had imagined. Research activity intended to address these issues resulted in the evolution of structured programming—a disciplined approach to creating clear, correct and easy to modify programs.

One result of this research was the development of the Pascal programming language in 1971. Pascal, named after the 17th-century mathematician and philosopher Blaise Pascal, was designed for teaching structured programming and rapidly became the preferred introductory programming language in most colleges. Unfortunately, the language lacked many features needed to make it useful in commercial, industrial and government applications. By contrast, C, which also arose from research on structured programming, did not have the limitations of Pascal, and professional programmers quickly adopted it.

The Ada programming language, based on Pascal, was developed under the sponsorship of the U.S. Department of Defense (DOD) during the 1970s and early 1980s. The language was named after Ada Byron, Lady Lovelace, daughter of the poet Lord Byron. Lady Lovelace is generally acknowledged as the world's first computer programmer, having written an application in the early 1800s for Charles Babbage's Analytical Engine mechanical computing device.

1.13 Key Software Trend: Object Technology

As the benefits of structured programming were realized in the 1970s, improved software technology began to appear. Not until object-oriented programming became widely used in the 1980s and 1990s, however, did software developers feel they had the tools to dramatically improve the software development process.

What are objects, and why are they special? Object technology is a packaging scheme for creating meaningful software units. There are date objects, time objects, paycheck objects, invoice objects, automobile objects, people objects, audio objects, video objects, file objects, record objects and so on. In fact, almost any noun can be reasonably represented as a software object. Objects have properties (also called attributes), such as color, size and weight; and perform actions (also called behaviors or methods), such as moving, sleeping or drawing. Classes are types of related objects. For example, all cars belong to the "car" class, even though individual cars vary in make, model, color and options packages. A class specifies the general format of its objects, and the properties and actions available to an object depend on its class. An object is related to its class in much the same way as a building is related to its blueprint from which the building is constructed. Contractors can build many buildings from the same blueprint; programmers can instantiate (create) many objects from the same class.

Before object-oriented languages appeared, procedural programming languages (such as Fortran, Pascal, BASIC and C) focused on actions (verbs) rather than things or objects (nouns). This made programming a bit awkward. However, using today's popular object-oriented languages, such as Visual Basic, C++, Java and C#, you can program in an object-oriented manner that more naturally reflects the way in which you perceive the world. This has resulted in significant productivity gains.

With object technology, properly designed classes can be reused on future projects. Using libraries of classes can greatly reduce the amount of effort required to implement new systems. Some organizations report that the key benefit they get from object-oriented programming is not, in fact, software reusability. Rather, it is the production of software that is more understandable because it is better organized and has fewer maintenance requirements.

Object orientation allows you to focus on the "big picture." Instead of worrying about the minute details of how reusable objects are implemented, you can focus on the behaviors and interactions of objects. A road map that showed every tree, house and driveway would be difficult, if not impossible, to read. When such details are removed and only the essential information (roads) remains, the map becomes easier to understand. In the same way, an application that is divided into objects is easy to understand, modify and update because it hides much of the detail.

It is clear that object-oriented programming will be the key programming methodology for the next several decades. Visual Basic is one of the world's most widely used object-oriented languages.

1.14 The Internet and the World Wide Web

In the late 1960s, ARPA—the Advanced Research Projects Agency of the Department of Defense—rolled out plans to network the main computer systems of approximately a dozen ARPA-funded universities and research institutions. The computers were to be connected with communications lines operating at a then-stunning 56 Kbps (1 Kbps is equal to 1,024 bits per second), at a time when most people (of the few who even had networking access) were connecting over telephone lines to computers at a rate of 110 bits per second. Academic research was about to take a giant leap forward. ARPA proceeded to implement what quickly became known as the ARPAnet, the grandparent of today's Internet.

Things worked out differently from the original plan. Although the ARPAnet enabled researchers to network their computers, its main benefit proved to be the capability for quick and easy communication via what came to be known as electronic mail (e-mail). This is true even on today's Internet, with e-mail, instant messaging and file transfer allowing more than a billion people worldwide to communicate with each other.

The protocol (in other words, the set of rules) for communicating over the ARPAnet became known as the Transmission Control Protocol (TCP). TCP ensured that messages, consisting of pieces called "packets," were properly routed from sender to receiver, arrived intact and were assembled in the correct order.

In parallel with the early evolution of the Internet, organizations worldwide were implementing their own networks for both intraorganization (that is, within an organization) and interorganization (that is, between organizations) communication. A huge variety of networking hardware and software appeared. One challenge was to enable these different networks to communicate with each other. ARPA accomplished this by developing the Internet Protocol (IP), which created a true "network of networks," the current architecture of the Internet. The combined set of protocols is now called TCP/IP.

Businesses rapidly realized that by using the Internet, they could improve their operations and offer new and better services to their clients. Companies started spending large amounts of money to develop and enhance their Internet presence. This generated fierce competition among communications carriers and hardware and software suppliers to meet the increased infrastructure demand. As a result, bandwidth—the information-carrying capacity of communications lines—on the Internet has increased tremendously, while hardware costs have plummeted.

The World Wide Web is a collection of hardware and software associated with the Internet that allows computer users to locate and view multimedia-based documents (documents with various combinations of text, graphics, animations, audios and videos) on almost any subject. Even though the Internet was developed more than three decades ago, the introduction of the World Wide Web (WWW) was a relatively recent event. In 1989, Tim Berners-Lee of CERN (the European Organization for Nuclear Research) began to develop a technology for sharing information via "hyperlinked" text documents. Berners-Lee called his invention the HyperText Markup Language (HTML). He also wrote communication protocols such as HyperText Transfer Protocol (HTTP) to form the backbone of his new hypertext information system, which he referred to as the World Wide Web.

In October 1994, Berners-Lee founded an organization, called the World Wide Web Consortium (W3C, `www.w3.org`), devoted to developing technologies for the World Wide Web. One of the W3C's primary goals is to make the web universally accessible to everyone regardless of disabilities, language or culture.

The Internet and the web will surely be listed among the most important creations of humankind. In the past, most computer applications ran on "stand-alone" computers (computers that were not connected to one another). Today's applications can be written with the aim of communicating among the world's computers. In fact, as you'll see, this is the focus of Microsoft's .NET strategy. The Internet and the web make information instantly and conveniently accessible to large numbers of people, enabling even individuals and small businesses to achieve worldwide exposure. They are profoundly changing the way we do business and conduct our personal lives.

1.15 Extensible Markup Language (XML)

As the popularity of the web exploded, HTML's limitations became apparent. HTML's lack of extensibility (the ability to change or add features) frustrated developers, and its ambiguous definition allowed erroneous HTML to proliferate. The need for a standardized, fully extensible and structurally strict language was apparent. As a result, XML was developed by the W3C.

Data independence, the separation of content from its presentation, is the essential characteristic of XML. Because XML documents describe data, any application conceivably can process them. Software developers are integrating XML into their applications to improve web functionality and interoperability.

XML is not limited to web applications. For example, it is increasingly being employed in databases—the structure of an XML document enables it to be integrated easily with database applications. As applications become more web enabled, it is likely that XML will become the universal technology for data representation. All applications employing XML would be able to communicate with one another, provided that they could understand their respective XML markup schemes, or vocabularies.

The Simple Object Access Protocol (SOAP) is a technology for the transmission of objects (marked up as XML) over the Internet. Microsoft's .NET technologies (discussed in the next two sections) use XML and SOAP to mark up and transfer data over the Internet. XML and SOAP are at the core of .NET—they allow software components to interoperate (i.e., communicate easily with one another). Since SOAP's foundations are in XML and HTTP (Hypertext Transfer Protocol—the key communication protocol of the web), it is supported on most types of computer systems. We discuss XML in Chapter 19, XML and LINQ to XML and SOAP in Chapter 22, Windows Communication Foundation (WCF) Web Services.

1.16 Introduction to Microsoft .NET

In June 2000, Microsoft announced its .NET initiative (www.microsoft.com/net), a broad new vision for using the Internet and the web in the development, engineering, distribution and use of software. Rather than forcing developers to use a single programming language, the .NET initiative permits developers to create .NET applications in any .NET-compatible language (such as Visual Basic, Visual C++, C# and others). Part of the initiative includes Microsoft's ASP.NET technology, which allows you to create web applications. You will use ASP.NET 3.5 (the current version) to build the web-based secure books database application later in the book.

The .NET strategy extends the idea of software reuse to the Internet by allowing programmers to concentrate on their specialties without having to implement every component of every application. Visual programming (which you'll learn throughout this book) has become popular because it enables programmers to create Windows and web applications easily, using such prepackaged controls as buttons, textboxes and scrollbars.

The Microsoft .NET Framework is at the heart of the .NET strategy. This framework executes applications and web services, contains a class library (called the .NET Framework Class Library) and provides many other programming capabilities that you'll use to build Visual Basic applications. Steve Ballmer, Microsoft's CEO, has stated that Microsoft is "betting the company" on .NET. Such a dramatic commitment surely indicates a bright future for Visual Basic 2008 programmers.

1.17 The .NET Framework and the Common Language Runtime

The details of the .NET Framework are found in the Common Language Infrastructure (CLI), which contains information about the storage of data types (i.e., data that has predefined characteristics such as a date, percentage or currency amount), objects and so on. The CLI has been standardized by Ecma International, making it easier to create the .NET Framework for other platforms. This is like publishing the blueprints of the framework—anyone can build it by following the specifications. The specification is available from www.ecma-international.org/publications/standards/Ecma-335.htm.

The Common Language Runtime (CLR) is another central part of the .NET Framework—it executes .NET programs. Programs are compiled into machine-specific instructions in two steps. First, the program is compiled into Microsoft Intermediate Language (MSIL), which defines instructions for the CLR. Code converted into MSIL from other languages and sources can be woven together by the CLR. The MSIL for an application's components is placed into the application's executable file. When the application executes, another compiler (known as the just-in-time compiler or JIT compiler) in the CLR translates the MSIL in the executable file into machine-language code (for a particular platform), then the machine-language code executes on that platform.

If the .NET Framework exists (and is installed) for a platform, that platform can run any .NET program. The ability of a program to run (without modification) across multiple platforms is known as platform independence. Code written once can be used on another type of computer without modification, saving time and money. In addition, software can target a wider audience—previously, companies had to decide whether converting their programs to different platforms (sometimes called porting) was worth the cost. With .NET, porting programs is no longer an issue (at least once .NET itself has been made available on the platforms).

The .NET Framework also provides a high level of language interoperability. Programs written in different languages (e.g., Visual Basic and C#) are all compiled into MSIL—the different parts can be combined to create a single unified program. MSIL allows the .NET Framework to be language independent, because .NET programs are not tied to a particular programming language. Any language that can be compiled into MSIL is called a .NET-compliant language.

The .NET Framework Class Library can be used by any .NET language. The library contains a variety of reusable components, saving programmers the trouble of creating new components. This book explains how to develop .NET software with Visual Basic.

1.18 Test-Driving the Visual Basic Advanced Painter Application

In this section, you'll "test-drive" a Visual Basic application that enables you to draw on the screen using the mouse. You'll run and interact with the working application. You'll build a similar application in Chapter 15, GUI with Windows Presentation Foundation.

The **Advanced Painter** application allows you to draw with different brush sizes and colors. The elements and functionality you see in this application are typical of what you'll learn to program in this text. We use fonts to distinguish between IDE features (such as menu names and menu items) and other elements that appear in the IDE. Our convention is to emphasize IDE features (such as the **File** menu) in a bold **sans-serif Helvetica** font and to emphasize other elements, such as file names (e.g., `Form1.vb`), in a `sans-serif Lucida` font. The following steps show you how to test-drive the application.

1. ***Checking your setup.*** Confirm that you have set up your computer properly by reading the Before You Begin section located after the Preface.

2. ***Locating the application directory.*** Open a Windows Explorer window and navigate to the `C:\Examples\ch01` directory (Fig. 1.2).

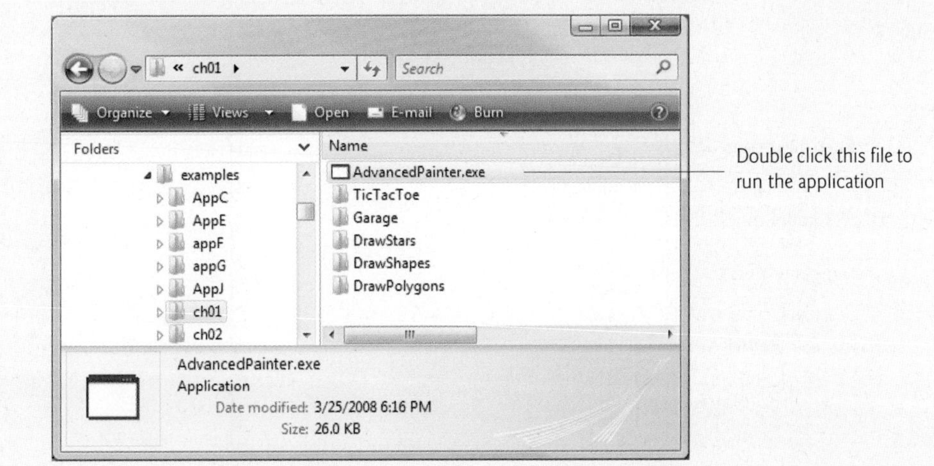

Fig. 1.2 | Contents of `C:\Examples\ch01`.

3. ***Running the* Advanced Painter *application.*** Now that you are in the proper directory, double click the file name `AdvancedPainter.exe` (Fig. 1.2) to run the application (Fig. 1.3).

   In Fig. 1.3, several graphical elements—called controls—are labeled. The controls include `GroupBoxes`, `RadioButtons`, a `Panel` and `Buttons` (these controls are discussed in depth later in the text). The application allows you to draw with a red, blue, green or black brush of small, medium or large size. You'll explore these options in this test-drive. You can also undo your previous operation or clear the drawing to start from scratch.

   By using existing controls—which are objects—you can create powerful applications in Visual Basic much faster than if you had to write all the code yourself. In this text, you'll learn how to use many preexisting controls, as well as how to write your own program code to customize your applications.

   The brush's properties, selected in the `RadioButtons` labeled **Black** and **Medium**, are default settings—the initial settings you see when you first run the application. You include default settings to provide visual cues for users to choose their own settings. Now you'll choose your own settings.

4. ***Changing the brush color.*** Click the `RadioButton` labeled **Red** to change the color of the brush and **Small** to change the size of the brush. Position the mouse over the white `Panel`, then press and hold down the left mouse button to draw with the brush. Draw flower petals, as shown in Fig. 1.4. Then click the `RadioButton` labeled **Green** to change the color of the brush again.

5. ***Changing the brush size.*** Click the `RadioButton` labeled **Large** to change the size of the brush. Draw grass and a flower stem, as shown in Fig. 1.5.

6. ***Finishing the drawing.*** Click the **Blue** and **Medium** `RadioButtons`. Draw raindrops, as shown in Fig. 1.6, to complete the drawing.

7. ***Closing the application.*** Close your running application by clicking its close box, X (Fig. 1.6).

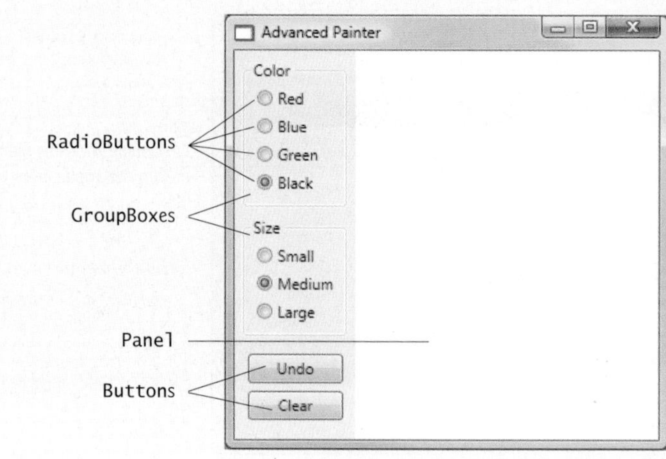

Fig. 1.3 | Visual Basic **Advanced Painter** application.

Fig. 1.4 | Drawing with a new brush color.

Fig. 1.5 | Drawing with a new brush size.

Fig. 1.6 | Finishing the drawing.

Additional Applications in Visual Basic 2008 How to Program

Figure 1.7 lists a few of the hundreds of applications in the examples and exercises in this text. We encourage you to practice running some of them. The examples folder for Chapter 1 contains the files required to run each application listed in Fig. 1.7. Simply double click the file names for any application you would like to run. [*Note:* The `Garage.exe` application assumes that the user inputs a value from 0 to 24.]

Application name	File to execute
Parking Fees	`Garage.exe`
Tic Tac Toe	`TicTacToe.exe`
Drawing Stars	`DrawStars.exe`
Drawing Shapes	`DrawShapes.exe`
Drawing Polygons	`DrawPolygons.exe`

Fig. 1.7 | Examples of Visual Basic applications found in this book.

1.19 (Only Required Section of the Case Study) Software Engineering Case Study: Introduction to Object Technology and the UML

Now we begin our early introduction to object orientation, a natural way of thinking about the world and writing computer programs. Chapters 1, 3–8, 10 and 12 each end with a brief Software Engineering Case Study section in which we present a carefully paced introduction to object orientation. Our goal here is to help you develop an object-oriented way of thinking and to introduce you to the Unified Modeling Language™ (UML™)—a graphical language that allows people who design object-oriented software systems to use an industry-standard notation to represent them.

In this, the only required section of the case study (because it contains foundational information for all readers), we introduce basic object-oriented concepts and terminology. The optional case study sections in Chapters 3–8, 10 and 12, and in Appendix D present an object-oriented design and implementation of the software for a simple automated teller machine (ATM) system. The Software Engineering Case Study sections at the ends of Chapters 3–8

- analyze a typical requirements document that describes a software system (the ATM) to be built
- determine the objects required to implement that system
- determine the attributes the objects will have
- determine the behaviors these objects will exhibit
- specify how the objects will interact with one another to meet the system requirements

The Software Engineering Case Study sections at the ends of Chapters 8, 10 and 12 modify and enhance the design presented in Chapters 3–7. Appendix D contains a complete, working Visual Basic implementation of the object-oriented ATM system.

Although our case study is a scaled-down version of an industry-level problem, we nevertheless cover many common industry practices. You'll experience a solid introduction to object-oriented design with the UML. Also, you'll sharpen your code-reading skills by touring a complete, straightforward and well-documented Visual Basic implementation of the ATM.

Basic Object-Technology Concepts

We begin our introduction to object orientation with some key terminology. Everywhere you look in the real world you see objects—people, animals, plants, cars, planes, buildings, computers and so on. Humans think in terms of objects. Telephones, houses, traffic lights, microwave ovens and water coolers are just a few more objects we see around us every day.

We sometimes divide objects into two categories: animate and inanimate. Animate objects are "alive" in some sense—they move around and do things. Inanimate objects do not move on their own. Objects of both types, however, have some things in common. They all have attributes (e.g., size, shape, color and weight), and they all exhibit behaviors (e.g., a ball rolls, bounces, inflates and deflates; a baby cries, sleeps, crawls, walks and blinks; a car accelerates, brakes and turns; a towel absorbs water). We'll study the kinds of attributes and behaviors that software objects have.

Humans learn about objects by studying their attributes and observing their behaviors. Different objects can have similar attributes and can exhibit similar behaviors. Comparisons can be made, for example, between babies and adults and between humans and chimpanzees.

Object-oriented design (OOD) models software in terms similar to those that people use to describe real-world objects. It takes advantage of class relationships, where objects of a certain class, such as a class of vehicles, have the same characteristics—cars, trucks, little red wagons and roller skates have much in common. OOD takes advantage of inheritance relationships, where new classes of objects are derived by absorbing characteristics of existing classes and adding unique characteristics of their own. An object of class "convertible" certainly has the characteristics of the more general class "automobile," but more specifically, the roof goes up and down.

Object-oriented design provides a natural and intuitive way to view the software design process—namely, modeling objects by their attributes, behaviors and interrelationships, just as we describe real-world objects. OOD also models communication between objects. Just as people send messages to one another (e.g., a sergeant commands a soldier to stand at attention), objects also communicate via messages. A bank-account object may receive a message to decrease its balance by a certain amount because the customer has withdrawn that amount of money.

OOD encapsulates (i.e., wraps) attributes and operations (behaviors) into objects—an object's attributes and operations are intimately tied together. Objects have the property of information hiding. This means that objects may know how to communicate with one another across well-defined interfaces, but normally they are not allowed to know how other objects are implemented—implementation details are hidden within the objects themselves. You can drive a car effectively, for instance, without knowing the details of how engines, transmissions, brakes and exhaust systems work internally—as long as you know how to use the accelerator pedal, the brake pedal, the steering wheel and so on. Information hiding, as you'll see, is crucial to good software engineering.

Languages like Visual Basic are object oriented. Programming in such a language is called object-oriented programming (OOP), and it allows computer programmers to conveniently implement an object-oriented design as a working software system. Languages like C, on the other hand, are procedural, so programming tends to be action oriented. In C, the unit of programming is the function. In Visual Basic, the unit of programming is the class from which objects are eventually instantiated (an OOP term for "created"). Visual Basic classes contain methods (Visual Basic's equivalent of C's functions) that implement operations, and data that implements attributes.

Classes, Fields and Methods

Visual Basic programmers concentrate on creating their own user-defined types called classes. Each class contains data as well as the set of methods that manipulate that data and provide services to clients (i.e., other classes that use the class). The data components of a class are called attributes or fields. For example, a bank-account class might include an account number and a balance. The operation components of a class are called methods. For example, a bank-account class might include methods to make a deposit (increase the balance), make a withdrawal (decrease the balance) and inquire what the current balance is. Programmers use built-in types and user-defined types as the "building blocks" for constructing new user-defined types (classes). The nouns in a system specification help the Visual Basic programmer determine the set of classes from which objects are created that work together to implement the system.

Classes are to objects as blueprints are to houses—a class is a "plan" for building objects of the class. Just as we can build many houses from one blueprint, we can instantiate (create) many objects from one class. You cannot cook meals in the kitchen of a blueprint, but you can cook meals in the kitchen of a house. You cannot sleep in the bedroom of a blueprint, but you can sleep in the bedroom of a house.

Classes can have relationships with other classes. For example, in an object-oriented design of a bank, the "bank teller" class needs to relate to other classes, such as the "customer" class, the "cash drawer" class, the "safe" class, and so on. These relationships are called associations.

Packaging software as classes makes it possible for future software systems to reuse the classes. Groups of related classes often are packaged as reusable components. Just as realtors often say that the three most important factors affecting the price of real estate are "location, location and location," people in the software development community often say that the three most important factors affecting the future of software development are "reuse, reuse and reuse."

Software Engineering Observation 1.1

Reuse of existing classes when building new classes and programs saves time, money and effort. Reuse also helps programmers build more reliable and effective systems, because existing classes and components often have gone through extensive testing, debugging and performance tuning.

Indeed, with object technology, you can build much of the new software you'll need by combining existing classes, just as automobile manufacturers combine interchangeable parts. Each new class you create will have the potential to become a valuable software asset that you and other programmers can reuse to speed and enhance the quality of future software development efforts.

Introduction to Object-Oriented Analysis and Design (OOAD)

Soon you'll be writing programs in Visual Basic. How will you create the code for your programs? Perhaps, like many beginning programmers, you'll simply turn on your computer and start typing. This approach may work for small programs (like the ones we present in the early chapters of the book), but what if you were asked to create a software system to control thousands of automated teller machines for a major bank? Or what if you were asked to work on a team of 1,000 software developers building the next generation of the U.S. air traffic control system? For projects so large and complex, you could not simply sit down and start writing programs.

To create the best solutions, you should follow a detailed process for analyzing your project's requirements (i.e., determining *what* your system is supposed to do) and developing a design that satisfies them (i.e., deciding *how* your system should do it). Ideally, you would go through this process and carefully review the design (and have your design reviewed by other software professionals) before writing any code. If this process involves analyzing and designing your system from an object-oriented point of view, it is called object-oriented analysis and design (OOAD). Experienced programmers know that proper analysis and design can save many hours by helping avoid an ill-planned system development approach that has to be abandoned partway through its implementation, possibly wasting considerable time, money and effort.

OOAD is the generic term for analyzing a problem and developing an approach for solving it. Small problems, such as the ones discussed in the first few chapters of this book, do not require an exhaustive OOAD process. It may be sufficient, before you begin writing Visual Basic code, to write pseudocode—an informal text-based means of expressing program logic. Pseudocode is not actually a programming language, but we can use it as a kind of outline to guide us as we write our code. We introduce pseudocode in Chapter 5.

As problems and the groups of people solving them increase in size, OOAD quickly becomes more appropriate than pseudocode. Ideally, a group should agree on a strictly defined process for solving its problem and a uniform way of communicating the results of that process to one another. Although many different OOAD processes exist, a single graphical language for communicating the results of *any* OOAD process has come into wide use. This language, known as the Unified Modeling Language (UML), was developed in the mid-1990s under the initial direction of three software methodologists: Grady Booch, James Rumbaugh and Ivar Jacobson.

History of the UML

In the 1980s, increasing numbers of organizations began using OOP to build their applications, and a need developed for a standard object-oriented analysis and design (OOAD) process. Many methodologists—including Grady Booch, James Rumbaugh and Ivar Jacobson—individually produced and promoted separate processes to satisfy this need. Each process had its own notation, or "language" (in the form of graphical diagrams), to convey the results of analysis (i.e., determining *what* a proposed system is supposed to do) and design (i.e., determining *how* a proposed system should be implemented to do what it is supposed to do).

By the early 1990s, different organizations were using their own unique processes and notations. At the same time, these organizations also wanted to use software tools that would support their particular processes. Software vendors found it difficult to provide tools for so many processes. A standard notation and standard process were needed.

In 1994, James Rumbaugh joined Grady Booch at Rational Software Corporation (now a division of IBM), and the two began working to unify their popular processes. They soon were joined by Ivar Jacobson. In 1996, the group released early versions of the UML to the software engineering community and requested feedback. Around the same time, an organization known as the Object Management Group™ (OMG™) invited submissions for a common modeling language. The OMG (`www.omg.org`) is a nonprofit organization that promotes the standardization of object-oriented technologies by issuing guidelines and specifications, such as the UML. Several corporations—among them HP, IBM, Microsoft, Oracle and Rational Software—had already recognized the need for a common modeling language. In response to the OMG's request for proposals, these companies formed the UML Partners—the consortium that developed the UML version 1.1 and submitted it to the OMG. The OMG accepted the proposal and, in 1997, assumed responsibility for the continuing maintenance and revision of the UML. We present the recently adopted UML 2 terminology and notation throughout this book.

What is the UML?

The Unified Modeling Language (UML) is the most widely used graphical representation scheme for modeling object-oriented systems. It has indeed unified the various popular notational schemes. Those who design systems use the language (in the form of diagrams, many of which we discuss throughout our ATM case study and other portions of the book) to model their systems.

An attractive feature of the UML is its flexibility. The UML is extensible (i.e., capable of being enhanced with new features) and is independent of any particular OOAD process. UML modelers are free to use various processes in designing systems, but all developers can now express their designs with one standard set of graphical notations.

The UML is a feature-rich graphical language. In our subsequent (and optional) Software Engineering Case Study sections on developing the software for an automated teller machine (ATM), we present a simple, concise subset of these features. We then use this subset to guide you through a first design experience with the UML. We sincerely hope you enjoy working through it.

Deitel UML Resource Center

For additional information about the UML, refer to our UML Resource Center at `www.deitel.com/UML/`. Here you will find downloads, tutorials, documentation, books, e-books, journals, articles, blogs and more that will help you learn more about the UML.

Section 1.19 Self-Review Exercises

1.1 List three examples of real-world objects that we did not mention. For each object, list several attributes and behaviors.

1.2 Pseudocode is __________.

a) another term for OOAD
b) a programming language used to display UML diagrams
c) an informal means of expressing program logic
d) a graphical representation scheme for modeling object-oriented systems

1.3 The UML is used primarily to __________.
a) test object-oriented systems
b) design object-oriented systems
c) implement object-oriented systems
d) Both a and b

Answers to Section 1.19 Self-Review Exercises

1.1 [*Note:* Answers may vary.] a) A television's attributes include the size of the screen, the number of colors it can display, and its current channel and volume. A television turns on and off, changes channels, displays video and plays sounds. b) A coffee maker's attributes include the maximum volume of water it can hold, the time required to brew a pot of coffee and the temperature of the heating plate under the coffee pot. A coffee maker turns on and off, brews coffee and heats coffee. c) A turtle's attributes include its age, the size of its shell and its weight. A turtle crawls, retreats into its shell, emerges from its shell and eats vegetation.

1.2 c.

1.3 b.

1.20 Wrap-Up

This chapter introduced basic hardware and software concepts and basic object-technology concepts, including classes, objects, attributes and behaviors. We discussed the different types of programming languages and which languages are most widely used. We presented a brief history of operating systems, including Microsoft's Windows. We discussed the history of the Internet and the web. We presented the history of Visual Basic programming and Microsoft's .NET initiative, which allows you to program Internet and web-based applications using Visual Basic (and other languages). You learned the steps for executing a Visual Basic application. You test-drove a sample Visual Basic application similar to the types of applications you'll learn to program in this book. You learned about the history and purpose of the UML—the industry-standard graphical language for modeling software systems. We launched our early objects and classes presentation with the first of our Software Engineering Case Study sections (and the only one which is required). The remaining (all optional) sections of the case study use object-oriented design and the UML to design the software for our simplified automated teller machine system. We present the complete Visual Basic code implementation of the ATM system in Appendix D.

In the next chapter, you'll use the Visual Studio IDE (Integrated Development Environment) to create your first Visual Basic application, using the techniques of visual programming. You'll also learn about Visual Studio's help features.

1.21 Web Resources

The Internet and the web are extraordinary resources. This section includes links to interesting and informative websites. Reference sections like this one are included throughout the book where appropriate.

`www.deitel.com/books/vb2008htp/`
Our Visual Basic Resource Center focuses on the enormous amount of Visual Basic content available online. Search for resources, downloads, tutorials, documentation, books, e-books, journals, articles, blogs and more that will help you develop Visual Basic applications.

`www.deitel.com/ResourceCenters.html`
Deitel.com has a growing list of Visual Basic and related Resource Centers, including ASP.NET, ASP.NET 3.5, ASP.NET Ajax, Microsoft LINQ, Microsoft Popfly, .NET 3.0, .NET 3.5, Silverlight 2, SQL Server 2008, Visual Basic 2008, Visual C++, Visual C# 2008 and C# 3.0 Resource Center, Windows Communication Foundation, Windows Presentation Foundation, Windows Vista, XAML and many more.

`www.deitel.com`
Visit this site for code downloads, updates, corrections and additional resources for Deitel & Associates publications, including *Visual Basic 2008 How To Program* errata, Frequently Asked Questions (FAQs), hot links and code downloads.

`www.prenhall.com/deitel`
The Deitel & Associates page on the Prentice Hall website contains information about our publications and code downloads for this book.

Summary

Section 1.1 Introduction

- Visual Basic is appropriate for technically oriented people with little or no programming experience, and for experienced programmers to use in building substantial information systems.
- Computer use is increasing in almost every field of endeavor.
- Computing costs have been decreasing dramatically due to rapid developments in both hardware and software technologies.
- Silicon chip technology has made computing so economical that about a billion general-purpose computers are in use worldwide, helping people in business, industry and government, and in their personal lives.

Section 1.2 What Is a Computer?

- A computer is a device that can perform calculations and make logical decisions millions, billions and even trillions of times faster than humans can.
- Today's fastest supercomputers are already performing trillions of additions per second!
- Computer programs guide computers through orderly sets of actions that are specified by computer programmers. An application is a program that does something particularly useful.
- A computer is composed of various devices (such as the keyboard, screen, mouse, hard drives, memory, DVD drives, printer and processing units) known as hardware.
- The programs that run on a computer are referred to as software.
- Object-oriented programming, available in Visual Basic and other programming languages, is a significant breakthrough that can greatly enhance your productivity.

Section 1.3 Computer Organization

- The input unit obtains information (data and computer programs) from various input devices, such as the keyboard and the mouse.

- The output unit takes information that the computer has processed and places it on various output devices, making the information available for use outside the computer.
- The memory unit stores information temporarily that has been entered through input devices, so the information is immediately available for processing. The memory unit also retains processed information until it can be sent to output devices.
- The central processing unit (CPU) serves as the "administrative" section of the computer, supervising the operation of the other sections.
- The arithmetic and logic unit (ALU) is the "manufacturing" section of the computer—it performs calculations and makes decisions.
- The secondary storage unit is the long-term, high-capacity "warehousing" section of the computer. Secondary storage devices normally hold programs or data that other units are not actively using. Secondary storage is nonvolatile, retaining information even when the computer is powered off.

Section 1.4 Early Operating Systems

- Early computers were very large (often filling entire rooms) and expensive (often costing millions of dollars) and could perform only one job or task at a time—called single-user batch processing.
- Early operating systems smoothed and speeded up the transition between jobs, increasing the amount of work, or throughput, computers could process.
- Multiprogramming is the simultaneous operation of many jobs that are competing to share the computer's resources.
- Timesharing operating systems allowed dozens or even hundreds of users share the computer at once, accessing the computer through keyboards and screens. The computer runs a small portion of one user's job, then services the next user, perhaps providing service to each user several times per second. An advantage of timesharing is that user requests receive almost immediate responses.

Section 1.5 Personal Computing, Distributed Computing and Client/Server Computing

- Silicon chip technology made it possible for computers to be much smaller and more economical—individuals and small organizations could own these machines.
- In 1977, Apple Computer—creator of today's popular Macintosh personal computers and iPod digital music players—popularized personal computing.
- In 1981, IBM, the world's largest computer vendor, introduced the IBM Personal Computer, legitimizing personal computing in business, industry and government organizations.
- Personal computers could be linked together in computer networks, sometimes over telephone lines and sometimes in local area networks (LANs) within an organization. This led to the phenomenon of distributed computing, in which an organization's computing is distributed over networks to the geographically dispersed sites where the organization's work is performed.
- Personal computers were powerful enough to handle the computing requirements of individuals and the basic communications tasks of passing information between computers electronically.
- Information can be shared easily across computer networks, where computers called file servers offer a common data store that may be used by client computers distributed throughout the network, hence the term client/server computing.

Section 1.6 Hardware Trends

- Moore's Law states that the capacities of computers approximately double every year or two, without any increase in price. Similar growth has occurred in the communications field, in which costs have plummeted as enormous demand for communications bandwidth has attracted intense competition.

- The invention of microprocessor chip technology and its wide deployment in the late 1970s and 1980s laid the groundwork for the productivity improvements that individuals and businesses have achieved in recent years.

Section 1.7 Microsoft's Windows Operating System
- In 1981, Microsoft released the first version of its DOS operating system for the IBM Personal Computer (DOS is an acronym for "Disk Operating System").
- In the mid-1980s, Microsoft developed the Windows operating system, a graphical user interface built on top of DOS.
- Microsoft released Windows 3.0 in 1990; this new version featured a user-friendly interface and rich functionality.
- The Windows operating system became incredibly popular after the 1993 release of Windows 3.1, whose successors, Windows 95 and Windows 98, virtually cornered the desktop operating systems market by the late 1990s.
- Windows XP was released in 2001 and combines Microsoft's corporate and consumer operating system lines.
- Windows Vista, released in 2007, is Microsoft's latest operating system offering.
- The biggest competitor to the Windows operating system is Linux.

Section 1.8 Machine Languages, Assembly Languages and High-Level Languages
- The hundreds of computer languages in use today can be divided into three general types—machine languages, assembly languages, high-level languages.
- As the "natural language" of a particular computer, machine language is defined by the computer's hardware design. Machine languages generally consist of streams of numbers (ultimately reduced to 1s and 0s) that instruct computers how to perform their most elementary operations.
- The number system with only 1s and 0s is called the binary number system. Machine-language programs are sometimes called "binaries" for that reason.
- A particular machine language can be used on only one type of computer.
- Programmers began using English-like abbreviations to represent the computer's basic operations. These abbreviations formed the basis of assembly languages.
- Translator programs called assemblers convert assembly-language programs to machine language at computer speeds.
- High-level languages enable programmers to write instructions that look almost like everyday English and contain common mathematical notations. Translator programs called compilers convert high-level-language programs into machine language.

Section 1.9 Visual Basic
- Visual Basic evolved from BASIC (Beginner's All-purpose Symbolic Instruction Code), developed by Professors John Kemeny and Thomas Kurtz of Dartmouth College. BASIC's primary purpose was to teach novices fundamental programming techniques.
- With the creation of the Windows GUI, the natural evolution of BASIC was to Visual Basic, which made programming Windows applications easier.
- With Microsoft's Visual Studio Integrated Development Environment (IDE), you can write, run, test and debug Visual Basic programs quickly and conveniently.

- Visual Basic is an object-oriented, event-driven language.
- You'll use Visual Studio's graphical user interface to conveniently drag and drop predefined objects like buttons and textboxes into place on your screen, and label and resize them.
- The .NET platform, introduced in 2000, is a set of software components that allow applications to be distributed to a variety of devices (such as cell phones) as well as to desktop computers.

Section 1.10 C, C++, Java and Visual C#

- The C programming language, implemented by Dennis Ritchie at Bell Laboratories in 1973, gained widespread recognition as the development language of the UNIX operating system.
- C is a hardware-independent language, and, with careful design, it is possible to write C programs that are portable to most computers.
- C++ provides a number of features that "spruce up" the C language and provides capabilities for object-oriented programming (OOP).
- A modular, object-oriented approach to design and implementation can make software development groups much more productive. Object-oriented programs are often easier to understand, correct and modify.
- Sun Microsystems developed Java, a C++-based language, which is used to develop large-scale enterprise applications, to enhance the functionality of web servers, to provide applications for consumer devices and for many other purposes.
- C#, created by Microsoft in 2000 specifically for the .NET platform, has roots in C, C++ and Java. C# is object oriented and has access to powerful prebuilt components, enabling programmers to develop applications quickly.

Section 1.11 Other High-Level Languages

- IBM Corporation developed Fortran (Formula Translator) in the mid-1950s to create scientific and engineering applications that require complex mathematical computations.
- COBOL was developed in the late 1950s for business applications that require the manipulation of large amounts of data.

Section 1.12 Structured Programming

- Structured programming is a disciplined approach to creating programs that are clear, correct and easy to modify.
- The Pascal programming language was designed for teaching structured programming and rapidly became the preferred introductory programming language in most colleges.
- The Ada programming language, based on Pascal, was developed under the sponsorship of the U.S. Department of Defense (DOD).

Section 1.13 Key Software Trend: Object Technology

- Object technology is a packaging scheme for creating meaningful software units.
- Objects have properties (also called attributes), such as color, size and weight, and they perform actions (also called behaviors or methods), such as moving, sleeping or drawing.
- Classes are types of related objects. A class specifies the general format of its objects, and the properties and actions available to an object depend on its class.
- Using class libraries can greatly reduce the amount of effort required to implement new systems.
- Object orientation allows you to focus on the "big picture"—the behaviors and interactions of objects. An application that is divided into objects is easy to understand, modify and update because it hides much of the detail.

Section 1.14 The Internet and the World Wide Web

- In the late 1960s, ARPA—the Advanced Research Projects Agency of the Department of Defense—rolled out plans to network the main computer systems of approximately a dozen ARPA-funded universities and research institutions. This became known as the ARPAnet, the grandparent of today's Internet.
- ARPAnet's main benefit proved to be the capability for quick and easy communication via what came to be known as electronic mail (e-mail).
- Transmission Control Protocol (TCP) ensured that messages, consisting of pieces called "packets," were properly routed from sender to receiver, arrived intact and were assembled in the correct order.
- The Internet Protocol (IP) created a true "network of networks," allowing different networks to communicate with each other.
- TCP/IP makes up the current architecture of the Internet.
- Bandwidth—the information-carrying capacity of communications lines—on the Internet has increased tremendously, while hardware costs have plummeted.
- The World Wide Web is a collection of hardware and software associated with the Internet that allows computer users to locate and view multimedia-based documents (documents with various combinations of text, graphics, animations, audios and videos) on almost any subject.
- HyperText Markup Language (HTML) is a technology for sharing information via "hyperlinked" text documents. HyperText Transfer Protocol (HTTP) forms the backbone of the hypertext information system, which is referred to as the World Wide Web.
- The World Wide Web Consortium (W3C, `www.w3.org`) is devoted to developing technologies for the World Wide Web.
- In the past, most computer applications ran on "stand-alone" computers (computers that were not connected to one another).
- The Internet and the web make information instantly and conveniently accessible to large numbers of people, enabling even individuals and small businesses to achieve worldwide exposure.

Section 1.15 Extensible Markup Language (XML)

- Data independence, the separation of content from its presentation, is the essential characteristic of XML.
- As applications become more web enabled, it is likely that XML will become the universal technology for data representation.
- The Simple Object Access Protocol (SOAP) is a technology for the transmission of objects (marked up as XML) over the Internet.
- XML and SOAP are at the core of .NET—they allow software components to interoperate (i.e., communicate easily with one another).

Section 1.16 Introduction to Microsoft .NET

- Microsoft's .NET initiative (`www.microsoft.com/net`) is a broad new vision for using the Internet and the web in the development, engineering, distribution and use of software.
- The .NET initiative permits developers to create .NET applications in any .NET-compatible language (such as Visual Basic, Visual C++, Visual C# and others).
- Part of the .NET initiative includes Microsoft's ASP.NET technology, which allows you to create web applications.

- The .NET strategy extends the idea of software reuse to the Internet—allowing you to concentrate on you specialty without having to implement every component of every application.
- Visual programming has become popular because it enables programmers to create Windows and web applications easily, using such prepackaged graphical components as buttons, textboxes and scrollbars.
- The Microsoft .NET Framework is at the heart of the .NET strategy. This framework executes applications and web services, contains a class library (called the Framework Class Library) and provides many other programming capabilities that you'll use to build Visual Basic applications.

Section 1.17 The .NET Framework and the Common Language Runtime

- The Common Language Runtime (CLR) executes .NET programs. Programs are compiled into machine-specific instructions in two steps. First, the program is compiled into Microsoft Intermediate Language (MSIL), which defines instructions for the CLR. Code converted into MSIL from other languages and sources can be woven together by the CLR.
- The MSIL for an application's components is placed into the application's executable file. When the application executes, another compiler (known as the just-in-time compiler or JIT compiler) in the CLR translates the MSIL in the executable file into machine-language code (for a particular platform), then the machine-language code executes on that platform.
- If the .NET Framework exists (and is installed) for a platform, that platform can run any .NET program. The ability of a program to run (without modification) across multiple platforms is known as platform independence.
- The .NET Framework also provides a high level of language interoperability. Programs written in different languages are all compiled into MSIL—the different parts can be combined to create a single unified program. MSIL allows the .NET Framework to be language independent, because .NET programs are not tied to a particular programming language.
- The .NET Framework Class Library can be used by any .NET language.

Section 1.18 Test-Driving the Visual Basic Advanced Painter *Application*

- You can use existing controls—which are objects—to get powerful applications running in Visual Basic much faster than if you had to write all of the code yourself.
- The default settings for controls are the initial settings you see when you first run the application. Programmers include default settings to provide reasonable choices that the application will use if the user chooses not to change the settings.

Section 1.19 (Only Required Section of the Case Study) Software Engineering Case Study: Introduction to Object Technology and the UML

- The Unified Modeling Language (UML) is a graphical language that allows people who build systems to represent their object-oriented designs in a common notation.
- Object-oriented design (OOD) models software components in terms of real-world objects. It takes advantage of class relationships, where objects of a certain class have the same characteristics. It also takes advantage of inheritance relationships, where newly created classes of objects are derived by absorbing characteristics of existing classes and adding unique characteristics of their own. OOD encapsulates data (attributes) and functions (behavior) into objects—the data and functions of an object are intimately tied together.
- Objects have the property of information hiding—objects of one class are normally not allowed to know how objects of other classes are implemented.
- Object-oriented programming (OOP) allows programmers to implement object-oriented designs as working systems.

- Visual Basic programmers concentrate on creating their own user-defined types called classes. Each class contains data as well as the set of methods that manipulate that data and provide services to clients (i.e., other classes or methods that use the class).
- The data components of a class are called attributes or fields. The operation components of a class are called methods.
- Classes can have relationships with other classes. These relationships are called associations.
- Packaging software as classes makes it possible for future software systems to reuse the classes. Groups of related classes are often packaged as reusable components.
- An instance of a class is called an object.
- With object technology, programmers can build much of the software they will need by combining standardized, interchangeable parts called classes.
- The process of analyzing and designing a system from an object-oriented point of view is called object-oriented analysis and design (OOAD).

Terminology

action
action oriented
Ada programming language
"administrative" section of the computer
arithmetic and logic unit (ALU)
ARPAnet
ASP.NET
assembler
assembly language
association
attribute of a class
bandwitdth
BASIC (Beginner's All-purpose Symbolic Instruction Code)
batch processing
behavior of an object
C programming language
C# programming language
C++ programming language
central processing unit (CPU)
class
class library
client of a class
client/server computing
COBOL programming language
Common Language Infrastructure (CLI)
Common Language Runtime (CLR)
compiler
component
computer
computer program
computer programmer
control
data
data independence
debugging
design
distributed computing
dynamic content
e-mail (electronic mail)
encapsulate
event-driven program
extensible
field of a class
Fortran programming language
function
graphical user interface (GUI)
hardware
hardware platform
high-level language
HTML (HyperText Markup Language)
HTTP (Hypertext Transfer Protocol)
information hiding
inheritance
input device
input unit
instantiate an object of a class
Integrated Development Environment (IDE)
interface
Internet
Java programming language
job
just-in-time (JIT) compiler
language independence
language interoperability in .NET
live-code approach

local area network (LAN)
logical unit
machine dependent
machine language
"manufacturing" section of the computer
member function
memory
memory unit
method
microprocessor
Microsoft .NET
Microsoft Intermediate Language (MSIL)
Moore's Law
multiprocessor
multiprogramming
.NET-compliant language
.NET Framework
.NET Framework Class Library
.NET initiative
.NET platform
nouns in a system specification
object
object oriented
object-oriented analysis and design (OOAD)
object-oriented design (OOD)
object-oriented programming (OOP)
object technology
operating system
operation of a class
output device
output unit
Pascal programming language
personal computer
personal computing
platform independence
portability
primary memory
procedural programming
properties
random-access memory (RAM)
"receiving" section of the computer
requirements
reusable software component
secondary storage unit
server
"shipping" section of the computer
SOAP (Simple Object Access Protocol)
software
software reuse
structured programming
supercomputer
task
throughput
timesharing
translation
translator program
Transmission Control Protocol/Internet Protocol (TCP/IP)
UML (Unified Modeling Language)
user-defined type
Visual Basic programming language
visual programming
Visual Studio
volatile memory
W3C (World Wide Web Consortium)
web service
Windows operating system
World Wide Web (WWW)
XML (Extensible Markup Language)
XML vocabulary

Self-Review Exercises

1.1 Fill in the blanks in each of the following statements:

a) Computers can directly understand only their native _________ language, which is composed only of 1s and 0s.
b) Computers process data under the control of sets of instructions called computer _________.
c) The three types of languages discussed in the chapter are machine languages, _________ and _________.
d) Programs that translate high-level-language programs into machine language are called _________.
e) Visual Studio is a(n) _________ in which Visual Basic programs are developed.
f) C is widely known as the development language of the _________ operating system.
g) The Department of Defense developed the Ada language with a capability called _________, which allows programmers to specify activities that can proceed in parallel.

h) Web services use __________ and __________ to mark up and send information over the Internet, respectively.

1.2 State whether each of the following is *true* or *false*. If *false*, explain why.
a) The UML is used primarily to implement object-oriented systems.
b) Visual Basic is an object-oriented language.
c) Visual Basic is the only language available for programming .NET applications.
d) Procedural programming models the world more naturally than object-oriented programming.
e) Computers can directly understand high-level languages.
f) MSIL is the common intermediate format to which all .NET programs compile, regardless of their original .NET language.
g) The .NET Framework is portable to non-Windows platforms.
h) Multiprogramming involves the simultaneous operation of many jobs that are competing to share the computer's resources.

Answers to Self-Review Exercises

1.1 a) machine. b) programs. c) secondary storage unit. d) assembly languages, high-level languages. e) compilers. f) Integrated Development Environment (IDE). g) UNIX. h) XML, SOAP.

1.2 a) False. The UML is used primarily to design object-oriented systems. b) True. c) False. Visual Basic is one of many .NET languages (others are Visual C# and Visual C++). d) False. Object-oriented programming (because it focuses on *things*) is a more natural way to model the world than procedural programming. e) False. Computers can directly understand only their own machine languages. f) True. g) True.h) True.

Exercises

1.3 Categorize each of the following items as either hardware or software:
a) CPU.
b) Compiler.
c) Input unit.
d) A word-processor program.
e) A Visual Basic program.

1.4 Translator programs, such as assemblers and compilers, convert programs from one language (referred to as the source language) to another language (referred to as the target language). Determine which of the following statements are *true* and which are *false*:
a) A compiler translates high-level language programs into target-language programs.
b) An assembler translates source-language programs into machine-language programs.
c) A compiler converts source-language programs into target-language programs.
d) High-level languages are generally machine dependent.
e) A machine-language program requires translation before it can be run on a computer.
f) The Visual Basic compiler translates high-level-language programs into SMIL.

1.5 What are the basic requirements of a .NET language? What is needed to run a .NET program on a new type of computer (machine)?

1.6 Expand each of the following acronyms:
a) W3C.
b) XML.
c) SOAP.
d) OOP.

e) CLR.
f) CLI.
g) MSIL.
h) UML.
i) OMG.
j) IDE.

1.7 What are the key benefits of the .NET Framework and the CLR? What are the drawbacks?

1.8 What are the advantages to using object-oriented techniques?

1.9 You are probably wearing on your wrist one of the world's most common types of objects—a watch. Discuss how each of the following terms and concepts applies to the notion of a watch: object, attributes and behaviors.

1.10 What was the key reason that Visual Basic was developed as a special version of the BASIC programming language?

1.11 What is the key accomplishment of the UML?

1.12 What did the chief benefit of the early Internet prove to be?

1.13 What is the key capability of the web?

1.14 What is the key vision of Microsoft's .NET initiative?

1.15 How does the .NET Framework Class Library facilitate the development of .NET applications?

1.16 What is the key advantage of standardizing .NET's CLI (Common Language Infrastructure) with Ecma?

1.17 Why is programming in an object-oriented language such as Visual Basic more "natural" than programming in a procedural programming language such as C?

1.18 Despite the obvious benefits of reuse made possible by OOP, what do many organizations report as the key benefit of OOP?

1.19 Why is Visual Basic said to be an event-driven language?

1.20 Why is XML so crucial to the development of future software systems?

2

Dive Into® Visual Basic 2008 Express

Seeing is believing.
—Proverb

Form ever follows function.
—Louis Henri Sullivan

Intelligence … is the faculty of making artificial objects, especially tools to make tools.
—Henri-Louis Bergson

OBJECTIVES

In this chapter you'll learn:

- The basics of the Visual Studio Integrated Development Environment (IDE) that assists you in writing, running and debugging your Visual Basic programs.
- Visual Studio's help features.
- Key commands contained in the IDE's menus and toolbars.
- The purpose of the various kinds of windows in the Visual Studio 2008 IDE.
- What visual programming is and how it simplifies and speeds program development.
- To create, compile and execute a simple Visual Basic program that displays text and an image using the Visual Studio IDE and the technique of visual programming.

Outline

2.1 Introduction

Visual Studio 2008 is Microsoft's Integrated Development Environment (IDE) for creating, running and debugging programs (also called applications) written in various .NET programming languages. This chapter provides an overview of the Visual Studio 2008 IDE and shows how to create a simple Visual Basic program by dragging and dropping predefined building blocks into place—a technique called visual programming.

2.2 Overview of the Visual Studio 2008 IDE

There are many versions of Visual Studio available. This book's examples are based on the *Microsoft Visual Basic 2008 Express Edition*, which supports only the Visual Basic programming language. See the Before You Begin section that follows the Preface for information on installing the software. Microsoft also offers a full version of Visual Studio 2008, which includes support for other languages in addition to Visual Basic, such as Visual C# and Visual C++. Our screen captures and discussions focus on the IDE of the Visual Basic 2008 Express Edition. We assume that you have some familiarity with Windows.

We use fonts to distinguish between IDE features (such as menu names and menu items) and other elements that appear in the IDE. We emphasize IDE features in a sans-serif bold **Helvetica** font (e.g., **File** menu) and emphasize other elements, such as file names (e.g., `Form1.vb`) and program code in a sans-serif `Lucida` font.

Introduction to Microsoft Visual Basic 2008 Express Edition

To start Microsoft Visual Basic 2008 Express Edition, select **Start > All Programs > Microsoft Visual Basic 2008 Express Edition**. Once the Express Edition begins execution, the **Start Page** displays (Fig. 2.1) Depending on your version of Visual Studio, your **Start Page** may look different. The **Start Page** contains a list of links to Visual Studio 2008 IDE resources and web-based resources. From this point forward, we'll refer to the Visual Studio 2008 IDE simply as "Visual Studio" or "the IDE." For experienced developers, this page provides links to the latest Visual Basic developments (such as updates and bug fixes) and to information on advanced programming topics. [*Note:* An internet connection is re-

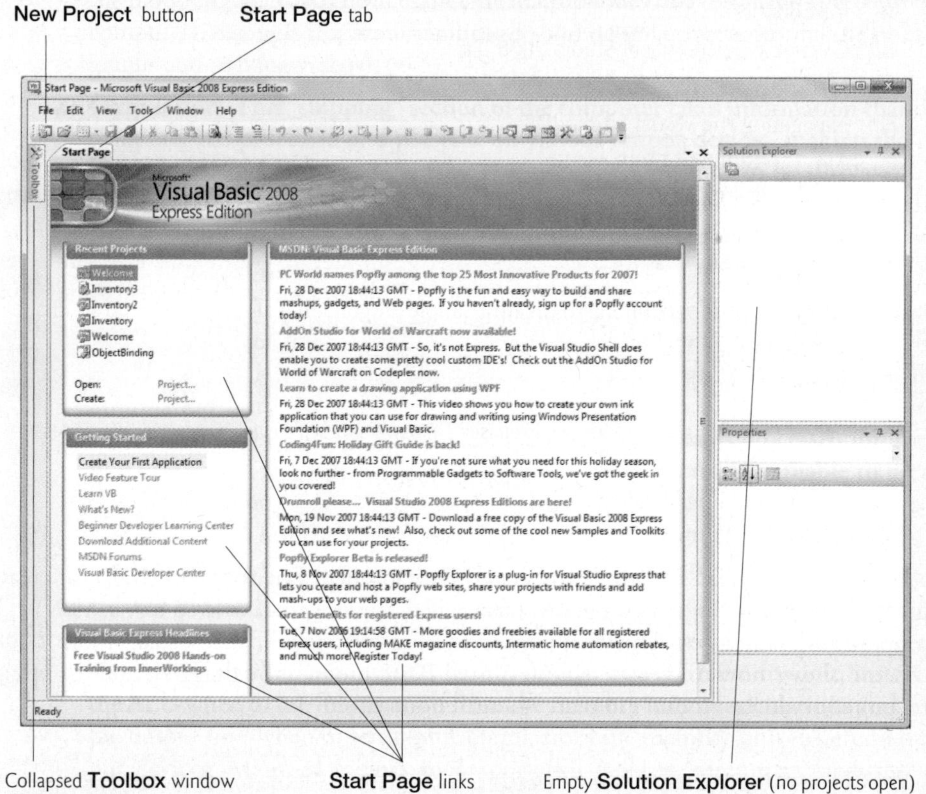

Fig. 2.1 | **Start Page** in Visual Basic 2008 Express Edition.

quired for the IDE to download this information.] At any time, you can return to the **Start Page** by selecting **View > Other Windows > Start Page**. We use the > character to indicate the selection of a menu item from a menu. For example, we use the notation **File > Open File** to indicate that you should select the **Open File** menu item from the **File** menu.

Links on the Start Page

The **Start Page** links are organized into sections—**Recent Projects**, **Getting Started**, **Visual Basic Express Headlines** and **MSDN: Visual Basic Express Edition**—that contain links to helpful programming resources. Clicking any link on the **Start Page** displays relevant information associated with the specific link. We refer to **single clicking** with the left mouse button as **selecting** or **clicking**; we refer to double clicking with the left mouse button simply as **double clicking**.

The **Recent Projects** section contains information on projects you have recently created or modified. You can also open existing projects or create new ones by clicking the links in the section. The **Getting Started** section focuses on using the IDE for creating programs, learning Visual Basic, connecting to the Visual Basic developer community (i.e., other software developers with whom you can communicate through newsgroups and web sites) and providing various development tools.

If you are connected to the Internet, the **Visual Basic Express Headlines** and **MSDN: Visual Basic Express Edition** sections provide links to information about programming in Visual Basic, including online courses and the latest Visual Basic news. To access more extensive information on Visual Studio, you can browse the MSDN (Microsoft Developer Network) online library at `msdn2.microsoft.com/library`. The MSDN site contains articles, downloads and tutorials on technologies of interest to Visual Studio developers. You can also browse the web from the IDE using Internet Explorer (also called the internal web browser in the IDE). To request a web page, type its URL into the location bar (Fig. 2.2) and press the *Enter* key—your computer, of course, must be connected to the Internet. (If the location bar is not already displayed, select **View > Other Windows > Web Browser** or type *<Ctrl> <Alt> R*.) The web page that you wish to view appears as another tab, which you can select, inside the Visual Studio IDE (Fig. 2.2).

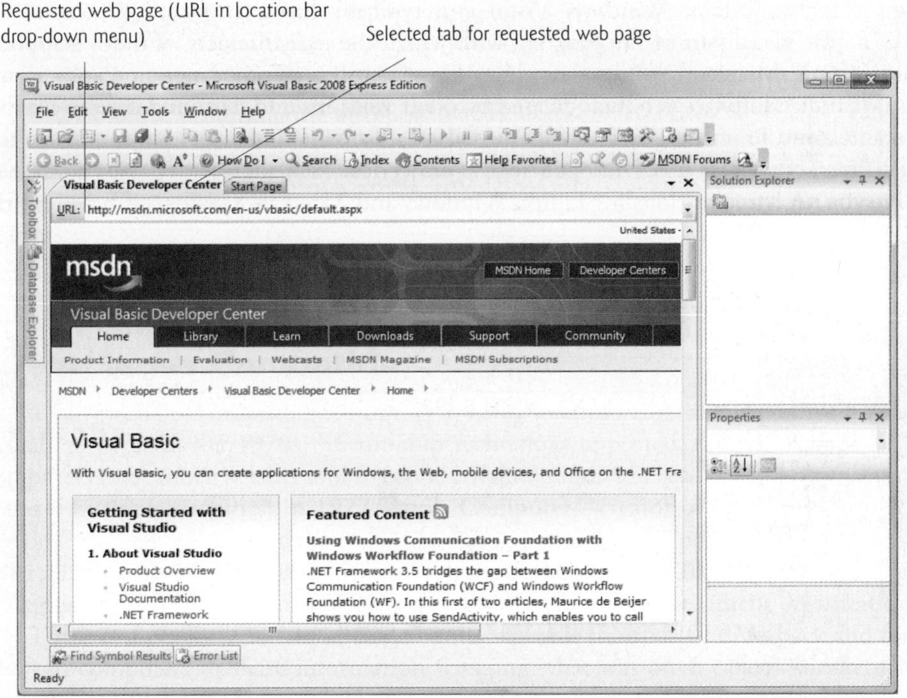

Fig. 2.2 | Displaying a web page in Visual Studio.

Customizing the IDE and Creating a New Project

To begin programming in Visual Basic, you must create a new project or open an existing one. To do so, select either **File > New Project...** to create a new project or **File > Open Project...** to open an existing project. From the **Start Page**, under the **Recent Projects** section, you can also click the links **Create: Project...** or **Open: Project....** A project is a group of related files, such as the Visual Basic code and any images that might make up a program. Visual Studio 2008 organizes programs into projects and solutions, which contain one or more projects. Multiple-project solutions are used to create large-scale programs. Each program we create in this book consists of a single project.

When you select **File > New Project...** or click the **Create: Project...** link on the **Start Page**, the **New Project** dialog (Fig. 2.3) displays. Dialogs are windows that facilitate user–computer communication. We discuss the detailed process of creating new projects momentarily.

Visual Studio provides several templates (Fig. 2.3). Templates are the project types users can create in Visual Basic—Windows Forms applications, console applications, WPF applications and others (in this textbook you'll primarily use Windows Forms applications and console applications). Users can also create their own custom application templates. In this chapter, we build a **Windows Forms Application**. We discuss the **Console Application** template in Chapter 3, Introduction to Visual Basic Programming. We use a WPF application in Chapter 15, GUI with Windows Presentation Foundation. A Windows Forms application is a program that executes within a Windows operating system (e.g., Windows XP or Windows Vista) and typically has a graphical user interface (GUI)—the visual part of the program with which the user interacts. Windows applications include Microsoft software products like Microsoft Word, Internet Explorer and Visual Studio; software products created by other vendors; and customized software that you and other programmers create. You will create many Windows applications in this text. [*Note:* Novell sponsors an open-source project called Mono that enables developers to create .NET applications for Linux, Windows and Mac OS X. Mono is based on the

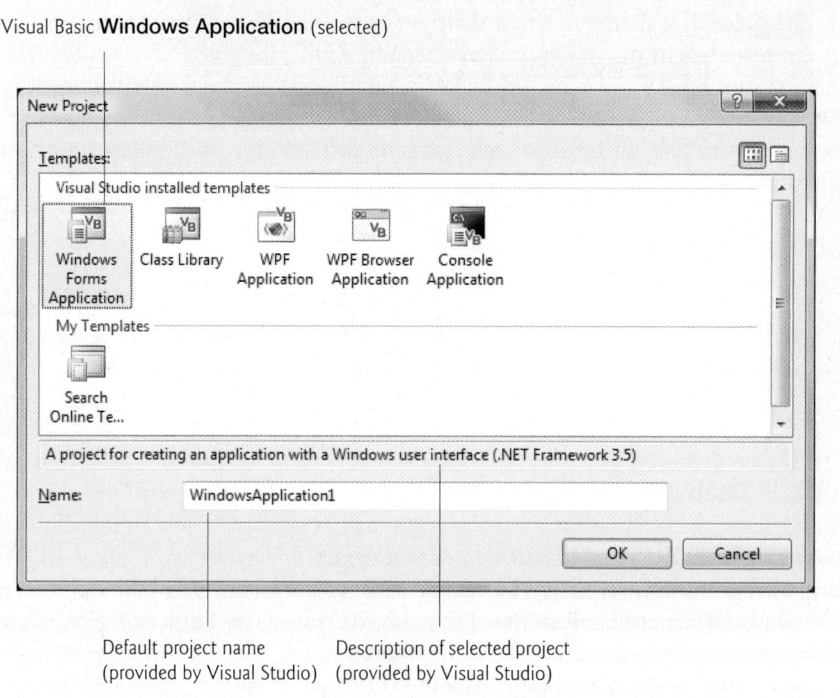

Fig. 2.3 | **New Project** dialog.

Ecma standards for the Common Language Infrastructure (CLI). For more information on Mono, visit `www.mono-project.com`.]

By default, Visual Studio assigns the name **WindowsApplication1** to a new Windows `Forms` Application project and solution (Fig. 2.3). In the **Templates** section of the dialog, select **Windows Forms Application.** Click **OK** to display the IDE in Design view (Fig. 2.4), which contains the features that enable you to create programs. The IDE's **Design** view is also known as the Windows Forms Designer.

The rectangle in the **Design** area titled **Form1** (called a `Form`) represents the main window of the Windows `Forms` application that you are creating. Visual Basic applications can have multiple `Forms` (windows)—however, most applications you'll create in this text use only one `Form`. You'll learn how to customize the `Form` by adding GUI controls—in this example, you'll add a `Label` and a `PictureBox` (Fig. 2.26). A `Label` typically contains descriptive text (e.g., `"Welcome to Visual Basic!"`), and a `PictureBox` displays an image, such as the Deitel bug mascot. Visual Basic Express has 66 preexisting controls and other components you can use to build and customize your programs. Many of these controls are discussed and used throughout the book. Other controls are available from third parties.

In this chapter, you'll work with preexisting controls from the .NET Framework Class Library. As you place controls on the `Form`, you'll be able to modify their properties (discussed in Section 2.4). For example, Fig. 2.5 shows where the `Form`'s title can be modified and Fig. 2.6 shows a dialog in which a control's font properties can be modified.

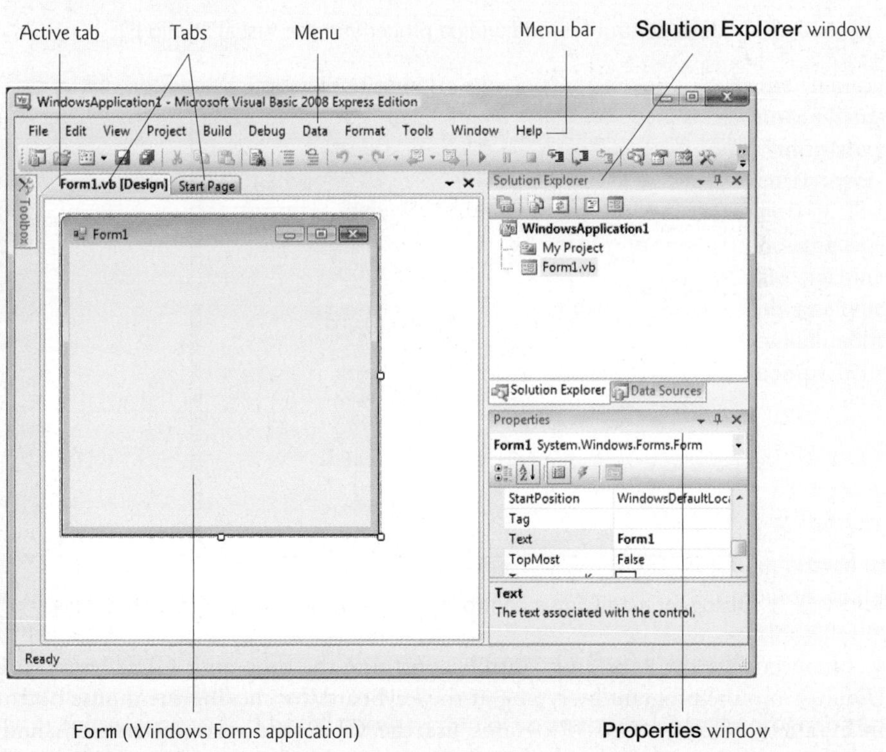

Fig. 2.4 | **Design** view of the IDE.

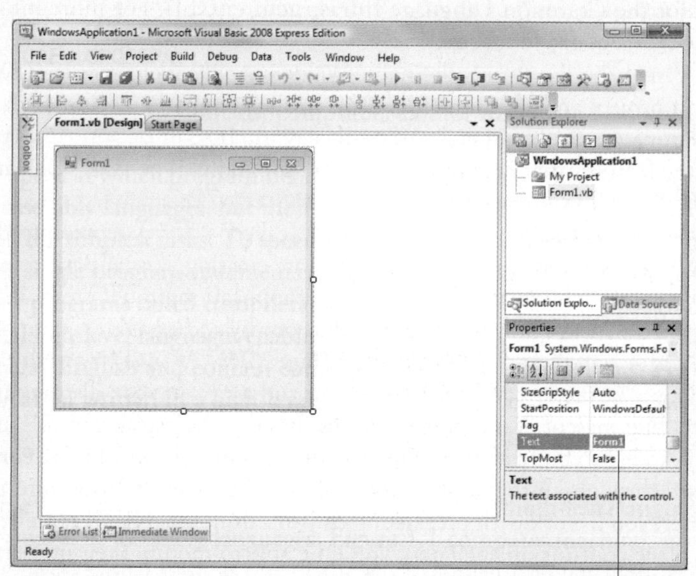

Textbox (displaying the text `Form1`)
which can be modified

Fig. 2.5 | Textbox control for modifying a property in the Visual Studio IDE.

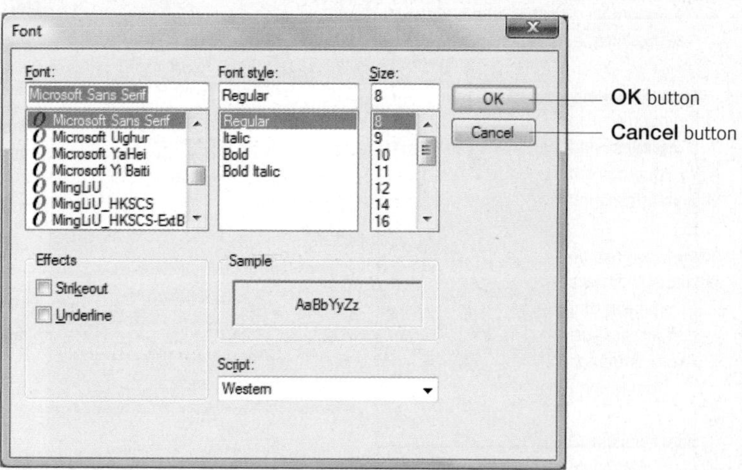

Fig. 2.6 | Dialog for modifying a control's font properties in the Visual Studio IDE.

Collectively, the `Form` and controls constitute the program's GUI. Users enter data (**inputs**) into the program by typing at the keyboard, by clicking the mouse buttons and in a variety of other ways. Programs use the GUI to display instructions and other information (**outputs**) for users to view. For example, the **New Project** dialog in Fig. 2.3 presents a GUI where the user clicks the mouse button to select a template type, then inputs a project name from the keyboard (note that the figure is still showing the default project name **WindowsApplication1** supplied by Visual Studio).

Each open document's name is listed on a tab—in Fig. 2.4, the open documents are **Form1.vb [Design]** and the **Start Page**. To view a document, click its tab. Tabs facilitate easy access to multiple open documents. The active tab (the tab of the document currently displayed in the IDE) is displayed in bold text (e.g., **Form1.vb [Design]** in Fig. 2.4) and is positioned in front of all the other tabs.

2.3 Menu Bar and Toolbar

Commands for managing the IDE and for developing, maintaining and executing programs are contained in menus, which are located on the menu bar of the IDE (Fig. 2.7). The set of menus displayed depends on what you are currently doing in the IDE.

Menus contain groups of related commands (also called menu items) that, when selected, cause the IDE to perform specific actions (e.g., open a window, save a file, print a file and execute a program). For example, new projects are created by selecting **File > New Project....** The menus depicted in Fig. 2.7 are summarized in Fig. 2.8. In Chapter 14, Graphical User Interfaces with Windows Forms, we discuss how to create and add your own menus and menu items to your programs.

File Edit View Project Build Debug Data Format Tools Window Help

Fig. 2.7 | Visual Studio menu bar.

Menu	Description
File	Contains commands for opening, closing, adding and saving projects, as well as printing project data and exiting Visual Studio.
Edit	Contains commands for editing programs, such as cut, copy, paste, undo, redo, delete, find and select.
View	Contains commands for displaying IDE windows (e.g., **Solution Explorer**, **Toolbox**, **Properties** window) and for adding toolbars to the IDE.
Project	Contains commands for managing projects and their files.
Build	Contains commands for compiling Visual Basic programs.
Debug	Contains commands for debugging (i.e., identifying and correcting problems in programs) and running programs.
Data	Contains commands for interacting with databases (i.e., organized collections of data stored on computers), which we discuss in Chapter 20, Databases and LINQ to SQL.

Fig. 2.8 | Summary of Visual Studio 2008 IDE menus. (Part 1 of 2.)

Menu	Description
Format	Contains commands for arranging and modifying a Form's controls. Note that the Format menu appears only when a GUI component is selected in Design view.
Tools	Contains commands for accessing additional IDE tools and options that enable customization of the IDE.
Window	Contains commands for hiding, opening, closing and displaying IDE windows.
Help	Contains commands for accessing the IDE's help features.

Fig. 2.8 | Summary of Visual Studio 2008 IDE menus. (Part 2 of 2.)

Rather than navigating the menus from the menu bar, you can access many of the more common commands from the **toolbar** (Fig. 2.9), which contains graphics, called **icons**, that graphically represent commands. By default, the standard toolbar is displayed when you run Visual Studio for the first time—it contains icons for the most commonly used commands, such as opening a file, adding an item to a project, saving files and running applications (Fig. 2.9). The icons that appear on the standard toolbar may vary, depending on the version of Visual Studio you are using. Some commands are initially disabled (or unavailable to use). These commands are enabled by Visual Studio only when they are necessary. For example, Visual Studio enables the command for saving a file once you begin editing a file.

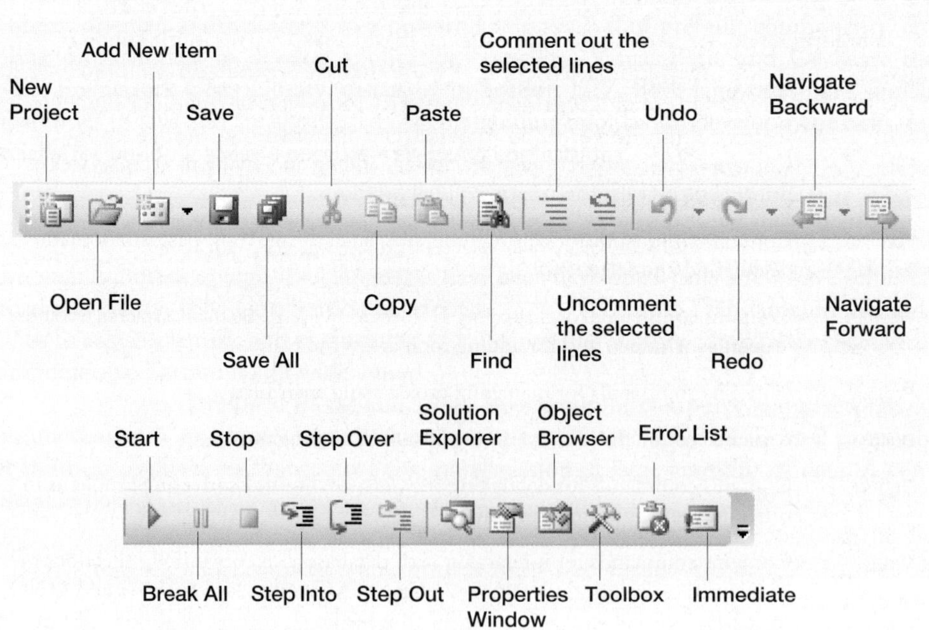

Fig. 2.9 | Standard Visual Studio toolbar.

You can customize the IDE by adding more toolbars. Select **View > Toolbars** (Fig. 2.10). Each toolbar you select is displayed with the other toolbars at the top of the Visual Studio window. To execute a command via the toolbar, click its icon. Some icons contain a down arrow that you can click to display related commands, as shown in Fig. 2.11.

It's difficult to remember what each toolbar icon represents. Positioning the mouse pointer over an icon highlights it and, after a brief pause, displays a description of the icon called a tool tip (Fig. 2.12). Tool tips help novice programmers become familiar with the IDE's features and serve as useful reminders for each toolbar icon's functionality.

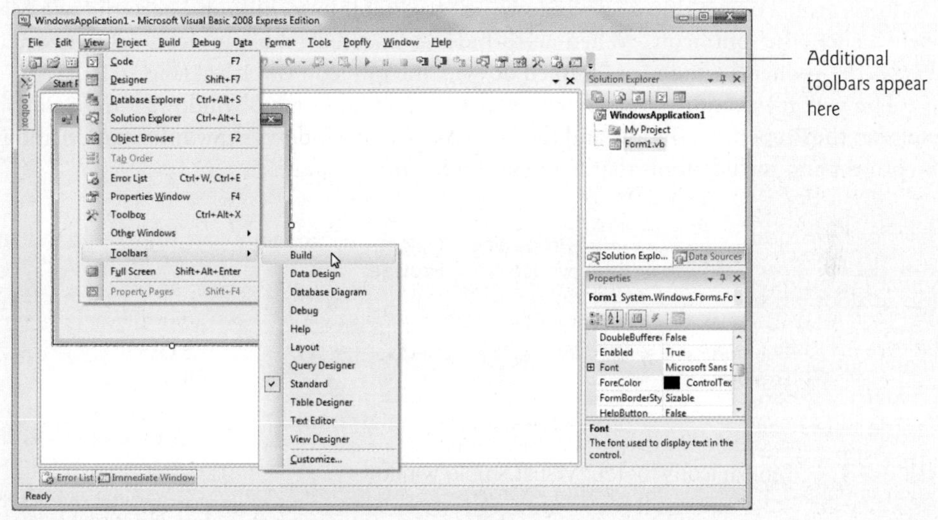

Fig. 2.10 | Adding the **Build** toolbar to the IDE.

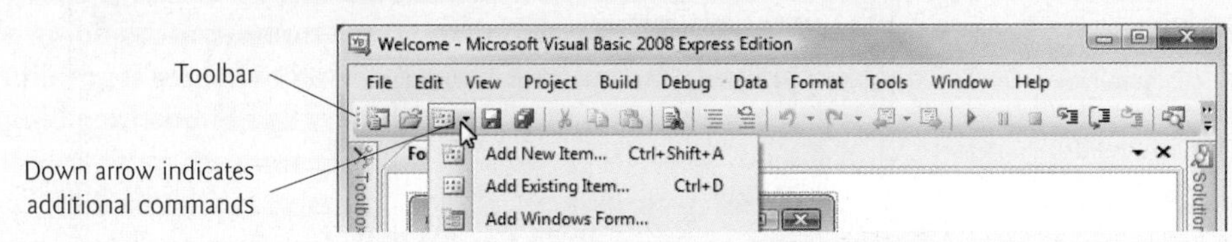

Fig. 2.11 | IDE toolbar icon showing additional commands.

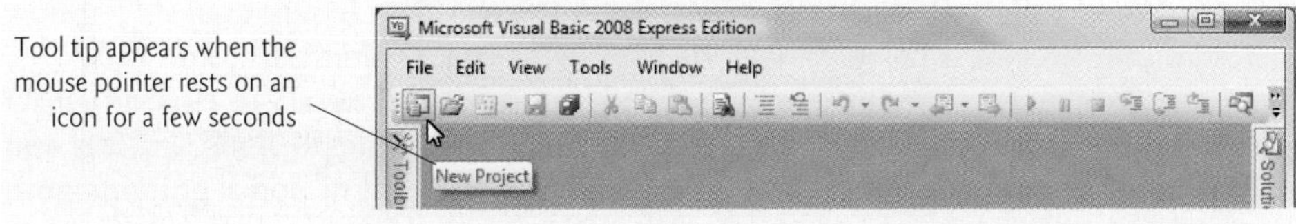

Fig. 2.12 | Tool tip demonstration.

2.4 Navigating the Visual Studio IDE

The IDE provides windows for accessing project files and customizing controls. This section introduces several windows that you'll use frequently when developing Visual Basic programs. These windows can be accessed via the toolbar icons (Fig. 2.13) or by selecting the desired window's name in the **View** menu.

Visual Studio provides a space-saving feature called auto-hide. When auto-hide is enabled, a tab appears along either the left, right or bottom edge of the IDE window (Fig. 2.14). This tab contains one or more icons, each of which identifies a hidden window. Placing the mouse pointer over one of these icons displays that window (Fig. 2.15). The window is hidden again when the mouse pointer is moved outside the window's area. To "pin down" a window (i.e., to disable auto-hide and keep the window open), click the pin icon. When auto-hide is enabled, the pin icon is horizontal (Fig. 2.15)—when a window is "pinned down," the pin icon is vertical (Fig. 2.16).

The next few sections overview three of Visual Studio's main windows—the **Solution Explorer**, the **Properties** window and the **Toolbox**. These windows show information about the project and include tools that help you build your programs.

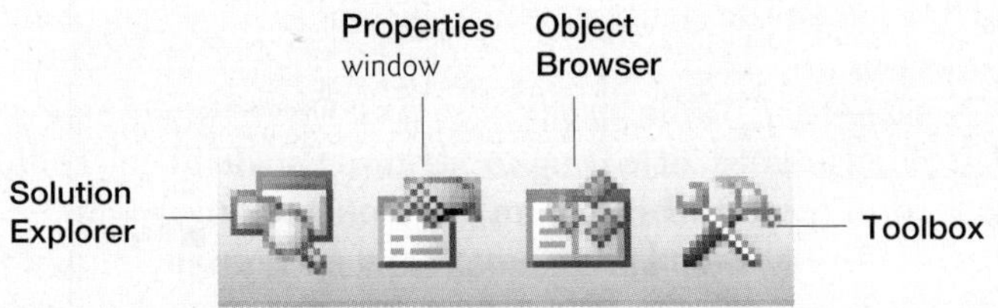

Fig. 2.13 | Toolbar icons for four Visual Studio windows.

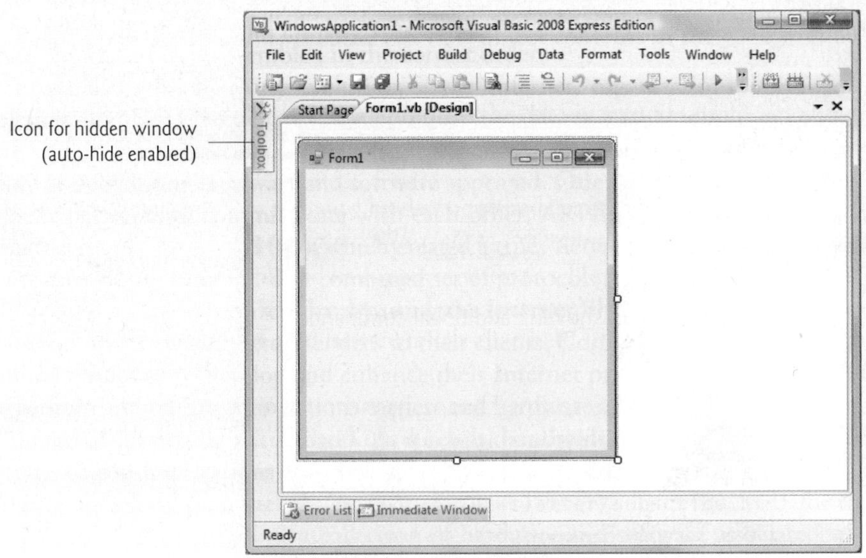

Fig. 2.14 | Auto-hide feature demonstration.

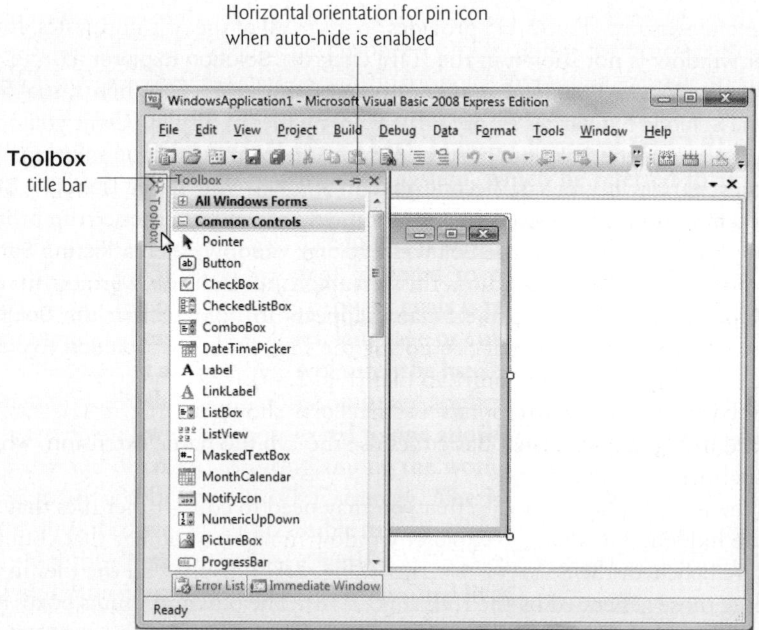

Fig. 2.15 | Displaying a hidden window when auto-hide is enabled.

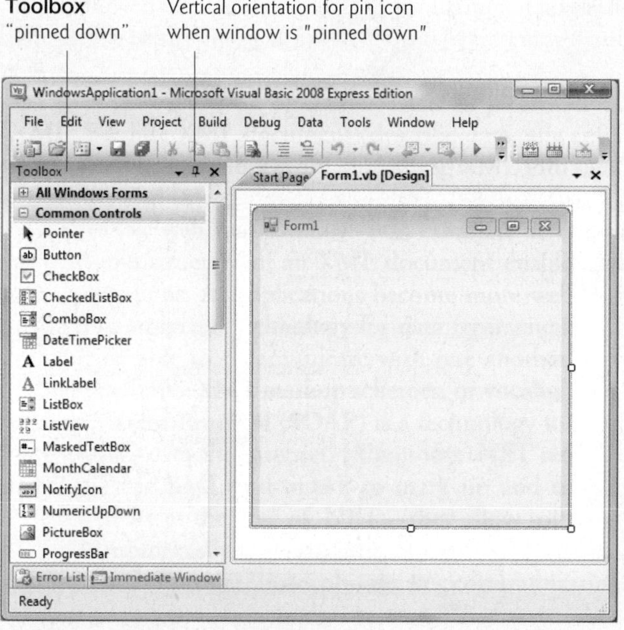

Fig. 2.16 | Disabling auto-hide ("pinning down" a window).

2.4.1 Solution Explorer

The Solution Explorer window (Fig. 2.17) provides access to all of the solution's files. If the **Solution Explorer** window is not shown in the IDE, click the **Solution Explorer** icon in the IDE (Fig. 2.13), select **View > Solution Explorer** or type *<Ctrl> <Alt> L*. When Visual Studio is first run, the **Solution Explorer** is empty—there are no files to display. Once you open a new or existing solution, the **Solution Explorer** displays the contents of the solution.

The solution's startup project is the one that runs when you select **Debug > Start Debugging**. If you have multiple projects in a solution, you can specify the startup project by right-clicking the project name in the **Solution Explorer** window, then selecting **Set as StartUp Project**. For a single-project solution, the startup project is the only project (in this case, **WindowsApplication1**) and the project name appears in bold text in the **Solution Explorer** window. When you use Visual Studio for the first time, the **Solution Explorer** window lists only the **My Project** and **Form1.vb** files (Fig. 2.17).

The Visual Basic file that corresponds to the `Form` shown in Fig. 2.4 is named `Form1.vb` (selected in Fig. 2.17). Visual Basic files use the `.vb` file-name extension, which is short for "Visual Basic."

By default, the IDE displays only files that you may need to edit—other files that the IDE generates are hidden. The **Solution Explorer** window includes a toolbar that contains several icons. When clicked, the Show All Files icon (Fig. 2.17) displays all the files in the solution, including those generated by the IDE (Fig. 2.18). The plus and minus boxes that

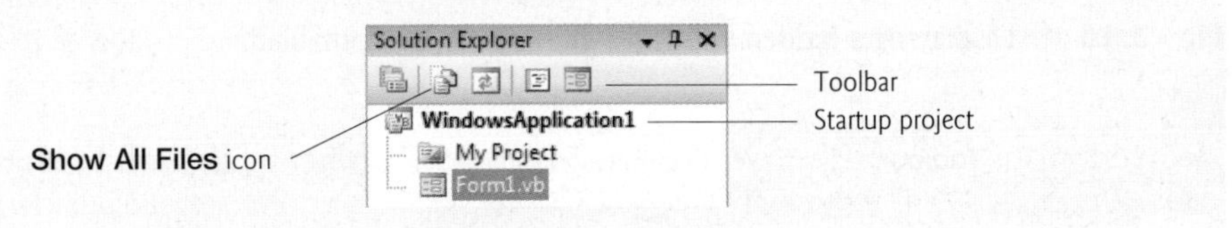

Fig. 2.17 | **Solution Explorer** with an open project.

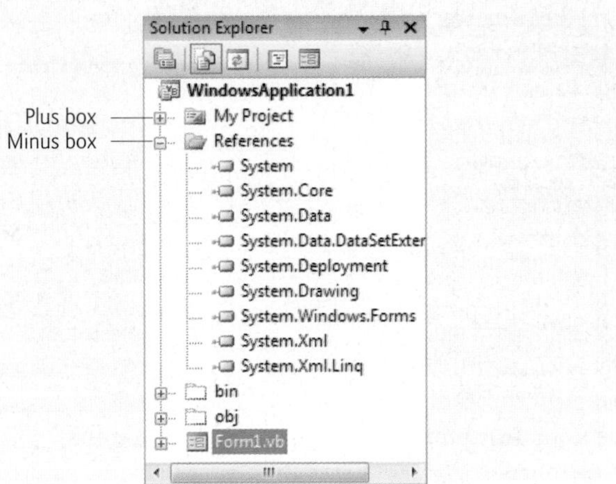

Fig. 2.18 | **Solution Explorer** showing plus boxes and minus boxes for expanding and collapsing the tree to reveal or hide project files.

appear can be clicked to expand and collapse the project tree, respectively. Click the plus box to the left of **My Project** to display items grouped under the heading to the right of the plus box (Fig. 2.19)—click the minus box to collapse the tree from its expanded state (Fig. 2.20). Other Visual Studio windows also use this plus-box/minus-box convention.

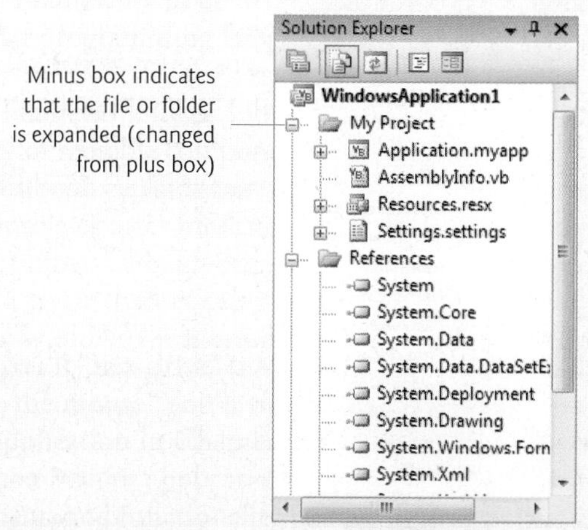

Fig. 2.19 | **Solution Explorer** expanding the **My Project** file after you click its plus box.

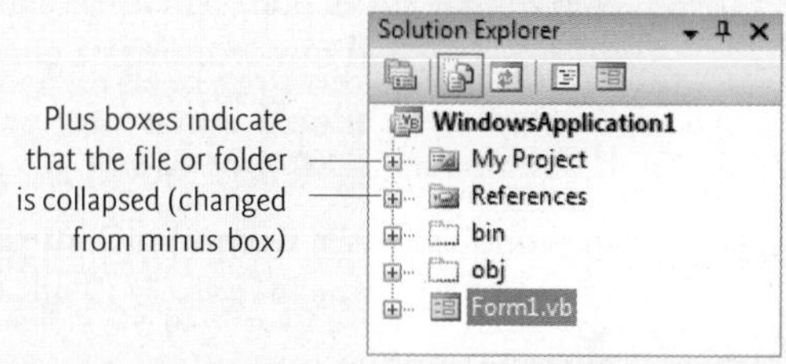

Fig. 2.20 | **Solution Explorer** showing collapsed nodes after all minus boxes are clicked.

2.4.2 Toolbox

The **Toolbox** (**View > Toolbox**) contains icons representing controls used to customize `Forms` (Fig. 2.21). With visual programming, you can "drag and drop" controls onto the `Form` and the IDE will write the code that creates the controls for you, which is faster and simpler than writing this code yourself. Just as you do not need to know how to build an engine to drive a car, you do not need to know how to build controls to use them. Reusing preexisting controls saves time and money when you develop programs. You'll use the **Toolbox** when you create your first program later in the chapter.

The **Toolbox** groups the prebuilt controls into categories—**All Windows Forms**, **Common Controls**, **Containers**, **Menus & Toolbars**, **Data**, **Components**, **Printing**, **Dialogs**, **WPF Interoperability**, **Visual Basic PowerPacks** and **General** are listed in Fig. 2.21. Again, note the use of plus and minus boxes, which can expand or collapse a group of controls. We discuss many of the **Toolbox**'s controls and their functionality throughout the book.

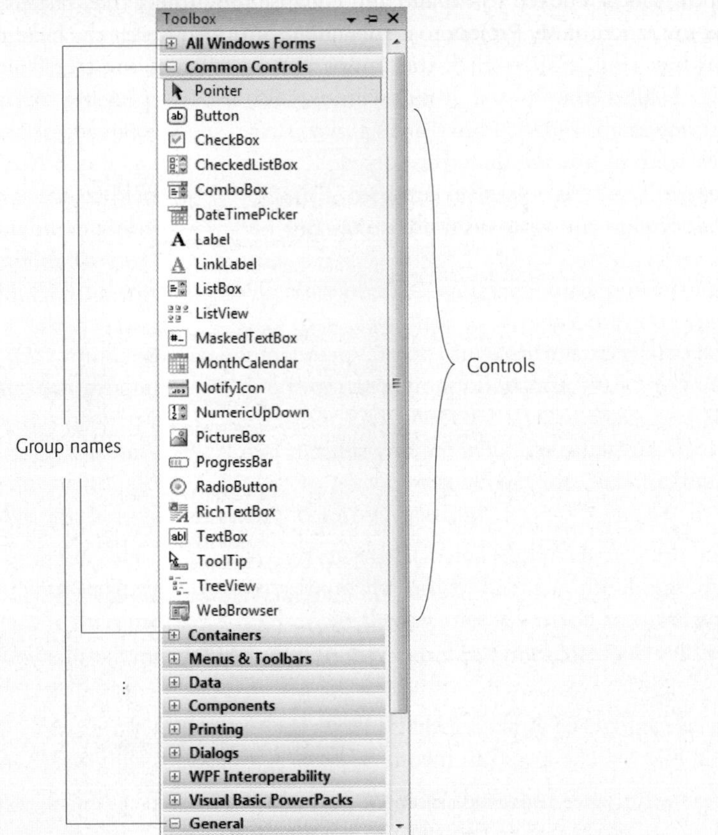

Fig. 2.21 | **Toolbox** window displaying controls for the **Common Controls** group.

2.4.3 Properties Window

To display the **Properties** window, select **View > Properties Window**, click the **Properties** window icon shown in Fig. 2.13, or press the *F4* key. The **Properties window** displays the properties for the currently selected `Form` (Fig. 2.22), control or file in **Design** view. **Properties** specify information about the `Form` or control, such as its size, color and position. Each `Form` or control has its own set of properties—a property's description is displayed at the bottom of the **Properties** window whenever that property is selected.

Figure 2.22 shows `Form1`'s **Properties** window. The left column lists the `Form`'s properties—the right column displays the current value of each property. You can sort the properties either alphabetically (by clicking the **Alphabetical icon**) or categorically (by clicking the **Categorized icon**). The properties can be sorted alphabetically from A–Z or Z–A—sorting by category groups the properties according to their use (i.e., **Appearance**, **Behavior**, **Design**, etc.). Depending on the size of the **Properties** window, some of the properties may be hidden from view on the screen. Users can scroll through the list of properties by **dragging** the **scrollbox** up or down inside the **scrollbar**, or by clicking the arrows at the top and bottom of the scrollbar. We show how to set individual properties later in this chapter.

The **Properties** window is crucial to visual programming—it allows you to modify a control's properties visually, without writing code. You can see which properties are available for modification and, in many cases, can learn the range of acceptable values for a given property. The **Properties** window displays a brief description of the selected property, helping you understand its purpose. A property can be set quickly using this window, and no code needs to be written.

At the top of the **Properties** window is the component selection drop-down list, which allows you to select the Form or control whose properties you wish to display in the **Properties** window (Fig. 2.22). Using the component selection drop-down list is an alternative way to display a Form's or control's properties without clicking the actual Form or control in the GUI.

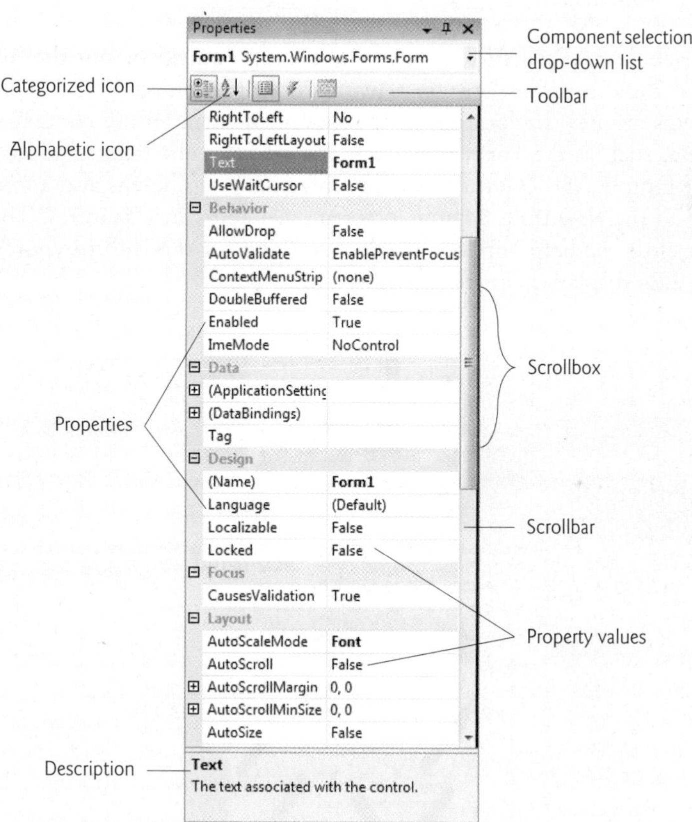

Fig. 2.22 | **Properties** window.

2.5 Using Help

Visual Studio provides extensive help features. Some **Help** menu commands are summarized in Fig. 2.23.

Command	Description
How Do I?	Contains links to relevant topics, including how to upgrade programs and learn more about web services, architecture and design, files and I/O, data, debugging and more.
Search	Finds help articles based on search keywords.
Index	Displays an alphabetized list of topics you can browse.
Contents	Displays a categorized table of contents in which help articles are organized by topic.

Fig. 2.23 | **Help** menu commands.

Using **Help** is an excellent way to get information quickly about the IDE and its features. Visual Basic provides context-sensitive help pertaining to the "current content" (i.e., the items around the location of the mouse cursor). To use context-sensitive help, click an item, such as the `Form`, then press the *F1* key. The help window provides help topics, code samples and "Getting Started" information. There is also a toolbar that provides access to the **How Do I**, **Search**, **Index** and **Contents** help features. To return to the IDE, either close the help window or select the icon for the IDE in your Windows task bar. Figure 2.24 displays help articles related to a `Form`.

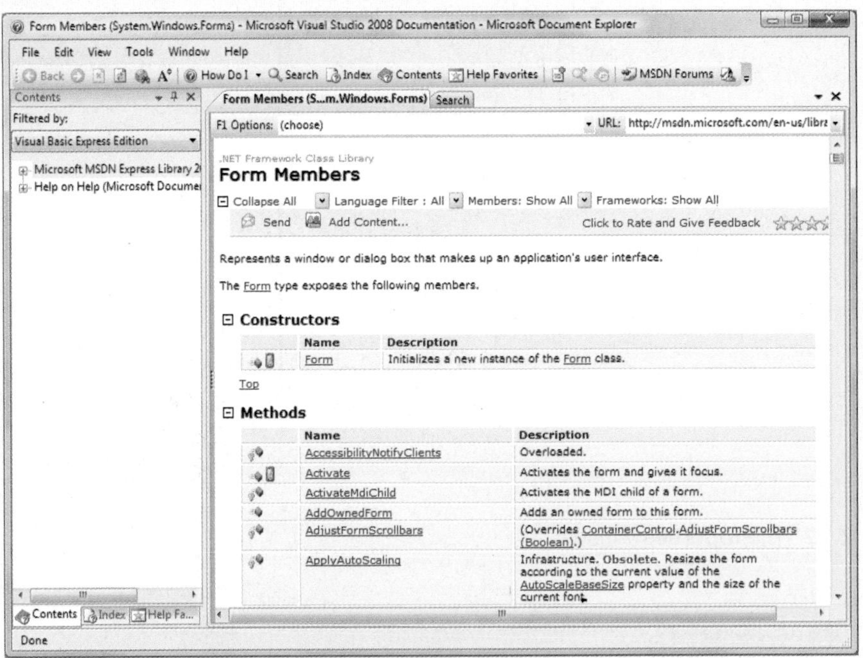

Fig. 2.24 | Using context-sensitive help.

The **Help** options can be set in the **Options** dialog (accessed by selecting **Tools > Options...**). To display all the settings that you can modify (including the settings for the **Help** options), make sure that the **Show all settings** checkbox in the lower-left corner of the dialog is checked (Fig. 2.25). To change whether the **Help** is displayed in the IDE window or in a separate window, select **Help** on the left, then locate the **Show Help using:** drop-down list on the right. Depending on your preference, selecting **External Help Viewer** displays a relevant help article in a separate window outside the IDE (some programmers like to view web pages separately from the project on which they are working in the IDE)—selecting **Integrated Help Viewer** displays a help article as a tabbed window inside the IDE.

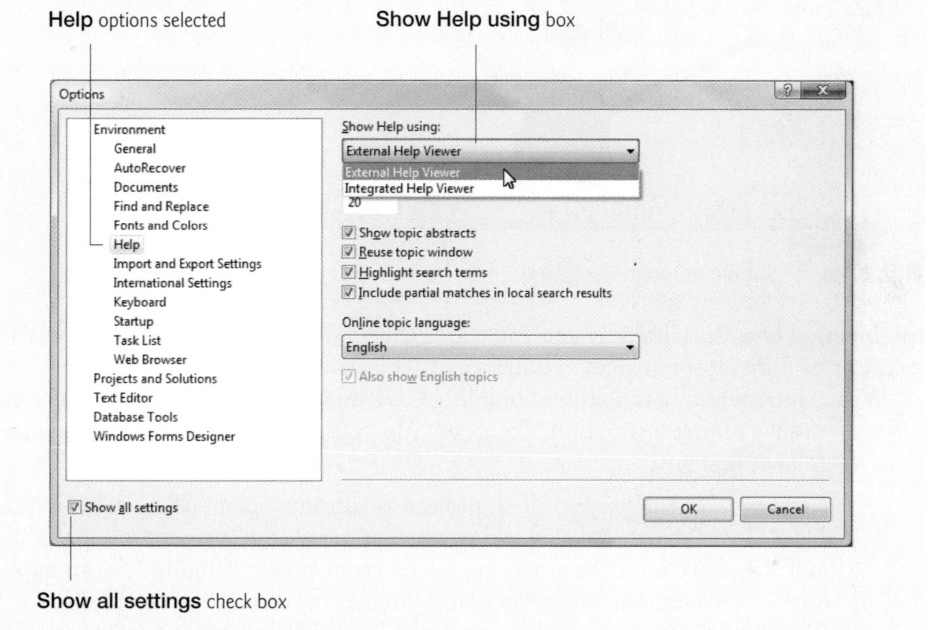

Fig. 2.25 | **Options** dialog displaying **Help** settings.

2.6 Using Visual Programming to Create a Simple Program that Displays Text and an Image

Next, we create a program that displays the text "`Welcome to Visual Basic!`" and an image of the Deitel & Associates bug mascot. The program consists of a single `Form` that uses a `Label` and a `PictureBox`. Figure 2.26 shows the result of the program as it executes. The program and the bug image are available with this chapter's examples. You can download the examples from `www.deitel.com/books/vb2008htp/`. Please read the Before You Begin section to ensure that you install the examples correctly on your computer.

To create the program whose output is shown in Fig. 2.26, you won't write a single line of program code. Instead, you'll use the visual programming techniques. Visual Studio processes your actions (such as mouse clicking, dragging and dropping) to generate program code. Chapter 3 begins our discussion of writing program code. Throughout the book, you produce increasingly substantial and powerful programs that usually include a

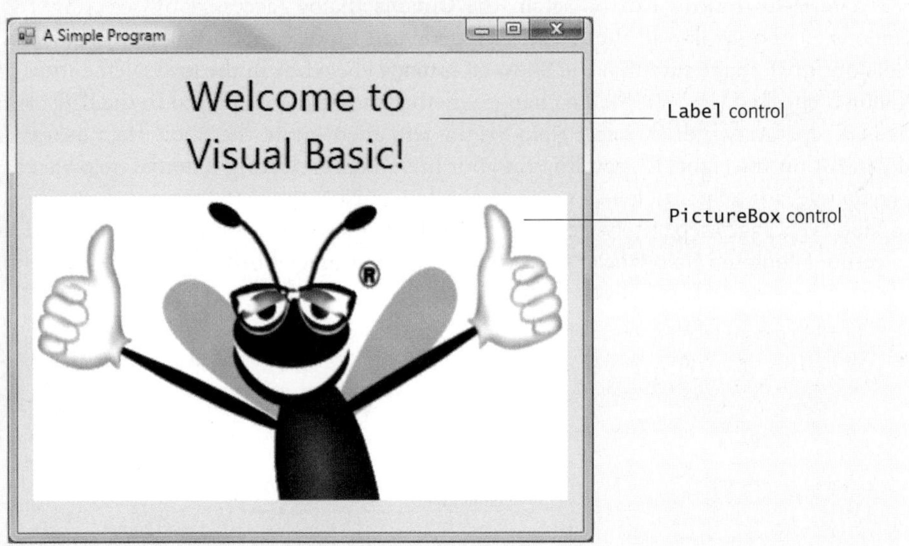

Fig. 2.26 | Simple program executing.

combination of code written by you and code generated by Visual Studio. The generated code can be difficult for novices to understand—but you'll rarely need to look at it.

Visual programming is useful for building GUI-intensive programs that require a significant amount of user interaction. To create, run and terminate this first program, perform the following steps:

1. *Creating the new project.* If a project is already open, close it by selecting **File > Close Project**. A dialog asking whether to save the current project might appear. Click **Save** to save any changes. To create a new Windows Forms application for the program, select **File > New Project...** to display the **New Project** dialog (Fig. 2.27). From the template options, select **Windows Forms Application**. Name the project **ASimpleProgram** and click **OK**. [*Note:* File names must conform to certain rules. For example, file names cannot contain symbols (e.g., ?, :, *, <, >, # and %) or Unicode® control characters (Unicode is a special character set described in Appendix G). Also, file names cannot be system-reserved names, such as "CON", "PRN", "AUX" and "COM1" or "." and "..", and cannot be longer than 256 characters in length.] We mentioned earlier in this chapter that you must set the directory in which the project is saved. To specify the directory in Visual Basic 2008 Express, select **File > Save All** to display the **Save Project dialog** (Fig. 2.28). To set the project location, click the **Browse...** button, which opens the **Project Location dialog** (Fig. 2.29). Navigate through the directories, select one in which to place the project (in our example, we use a directory named **MyProjects**) and click **Select Folder** (**OK** in Windows XP) to close the dialog. Click **Save** in the **Save Project** dialog (Fig. 2.28) to save the project and close the dialog. [*Note:* If you wish to specify the project's directory when you first create the project, select **Tools > Options...**. Then, in the dialog that appears, select **Projects and Solutions** in the list on the left and check the **Save new projects when created** option.]

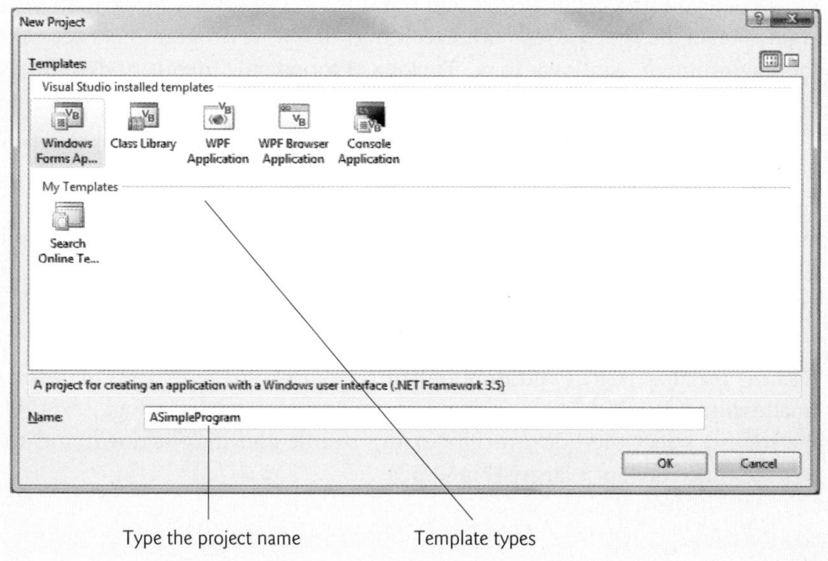

Fig. 2.27 | **New Project** dialog.

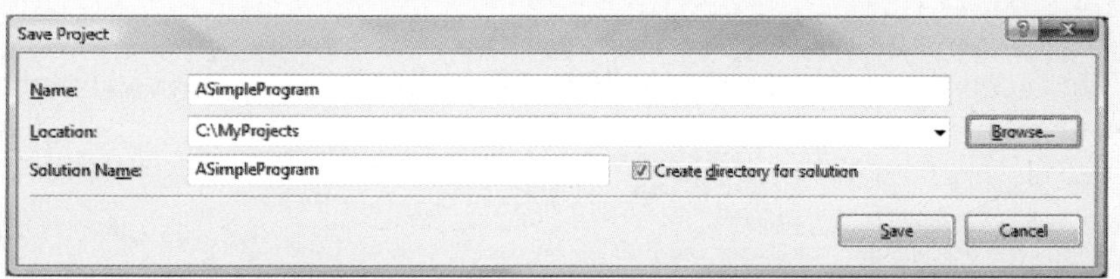

Fig. 2.28 | **Save Project** dialog.

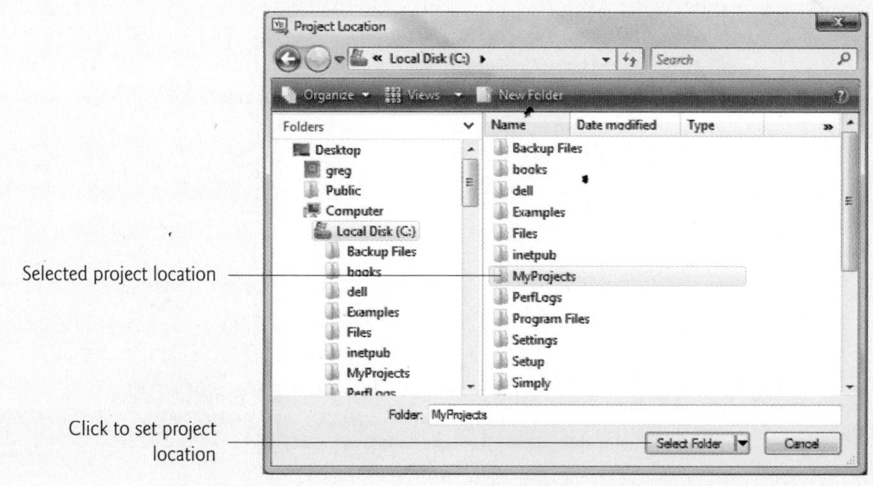

Fig. 2.29 | Setting the project location in the **Project Location** dialog.

When you first begin working in the IDE, it is in design mode (i.e., the program is being designed and is not executing). It allows programmers access to all the environment windows (e.g., **Toolbox**, **Properties**), menus and toolbars, as you'll see shortly.

2. *Seting the text in the* `Form`*'s title bar.* The text in the `Form`'s title bar is determined by the `Form`'s `Text` property (Fig. 2.30). If the **Properties** window is not open, click the properties icon in the toolbar or select **View > Properties Window**. Click anywhere in the `Form` to display the `Form`'s properties in the **Properties** window. Click in the textbox to the right of the `Text` property box and type "`A Simple Program`," as in Fig. 2.30. Press the *Enter* key (*Return* key) when finished—the `Form`'s title bar is updated immediately (Fig. 2.31).
3. *Resizing the* `Form`*.* Click and drag one of the `Form`'s enabled sizing handles (the small white squares that appear around the `Form`, as shown in Fig. 2.31). Using the mouse, select the bottom-right sizing handle and drag it down and to the right to make the `Form` larger (Fig. 2.32).

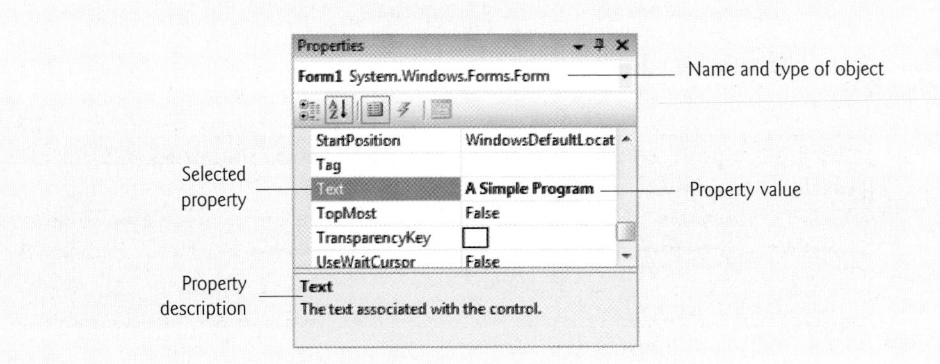

Fig. 2.30 | Setting the `Form`'s `Text` property in the **Properties** window.

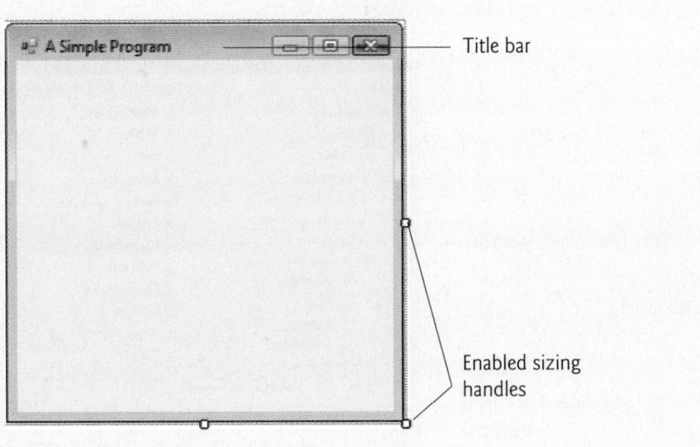

Fig. 2.31 | `Form` with enabled sizing handles.

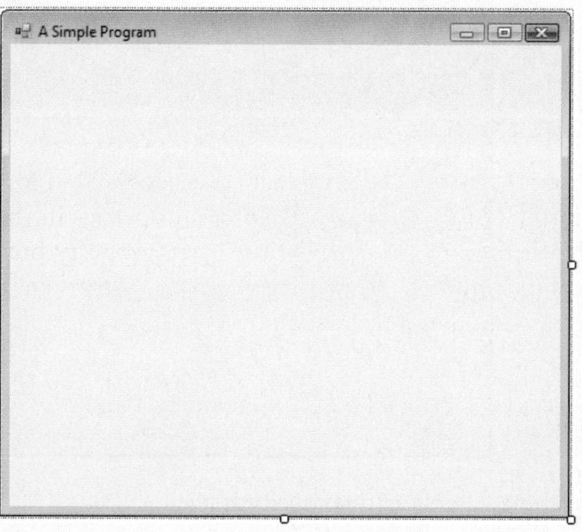

Fig. 2.32 | Resized Form.

4. *Changing the Form's background color.* The BackColor property specifies a Form's or control's background color. Clicking BackColor in the **Properties** window causes a down-arrow button to appear next to the value of the property (Fig. 2.33). When clicked, the down-arrow button displays a set of other options, which vary depending on the property. In this case, the arrow displays tabs for **Custom**, **Web** and **System** (the default). Click the **Custom** tab to display the palette (a grid of colors). Select the box that represents light blue. Once you select the color, the palette closes and the Form's background color changes to light blue (Fig. 2.34).

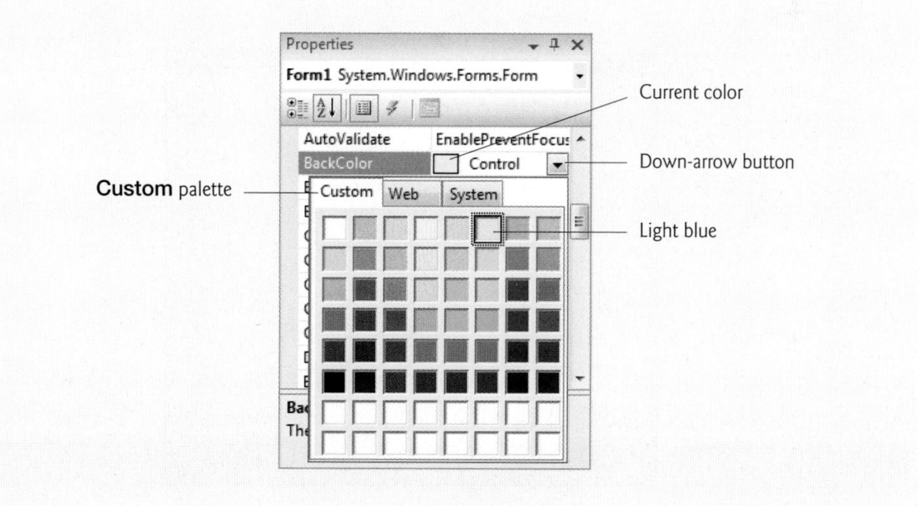

Fig. 2.33 | Changing the Form's BackColor property.

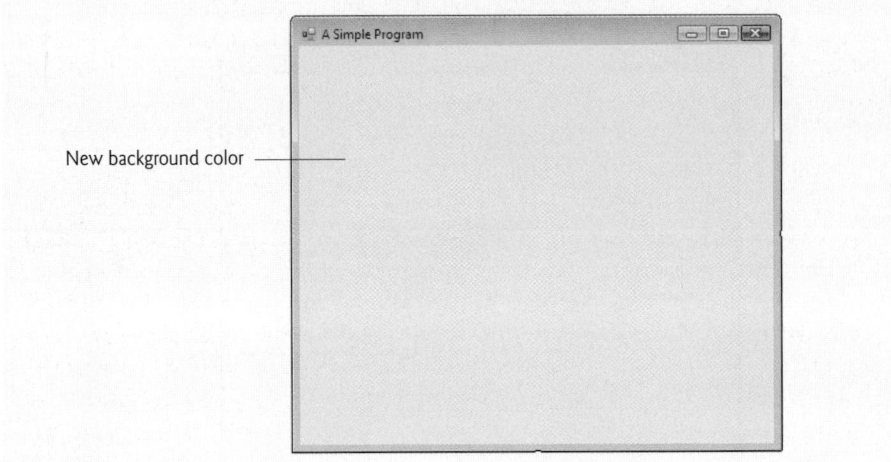

Fig. 2.34 | `Form` with new `BackColor` property applied.

5. *Adding a `Label` control to the `Form`.* If the **Toolbox** is not already open, select **View > Toolbox** to display the set of controls you'll use for creating your programs. For the type of program we are creating in this chapter, the typical controls we use are located in either the **All Windows Forms** category of the **Toolbox** or the **Common Controls** group. If either group name is collapsed, expand it by clicking the plus sign (the **All Windows Forms** and **Common Controls** groups are shown in Fig. 2.21). Next, double click the `Label` control in the **Toolbox**. This action causes a `Label` to appear in the upper-left corner of the `Form` (Fig. 2.35). [*Note:* If the `Form` is behind the **Toolbox**, you may need to hide the **Toolbox** to see the `Label`.] Although double clicking any **Toolbox** control places the control on the `Form`, you also can "drag" controls from the **Toolbox** to the `Form` (you may prefer dragging the control because you can position it wherever you want). Our `Label`

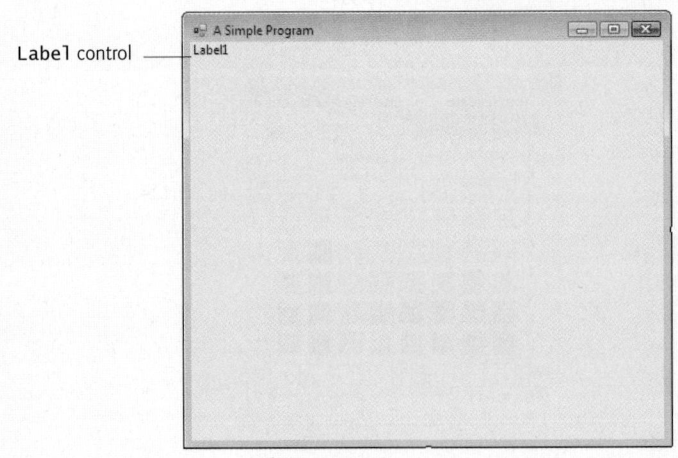

Fig. 2.35 | Adding a `Label` to the `Form`.

displays the text **Label1** by default. Note that our `Label`'s background color is the same as the `Form`'s background color. When a control is added to the `Form`, its `BackColor` property is set to the `Form`'s `BackColor`. You can change the `Label`'s background color by changing its `BackColor` property.

6. *Customizing the `Label`'s appearance.* Select the `Label` by clicking it. Its properties now appear in the **Properties** window. The `Label`'s `Text` property determines the text (if any) that the `Label` displays. The `Form` and `Label` each have their own `Text` property—`Forms` and controls can have the same types of properties (such as `BackColor`, `Text`, etc.) without conflict. Set the `Label`'s `Text` property to **Welcome to Visual Basic!**. Note that the `Label` resizes to fit all the typed text on one line. By default, the `AutoSize` property of the `Label` is set to `True`, which allows the `Label` to update its size to fit all of the text if necessary. Set the `AutoSize` property to `False` (Fig. 2.36) so that you can resize the `Label` on your own. Resize the `Label` (using the sizing handles) so that the text fits. Move the `Label` to the top center of the `Form` by dragging it or by using the keyboard's left and right arrow keys to adjust its position (Fig. 2.37). Alternatively, when the `Label` is selected, you can center the `Label` control horizontally by selecting **Format > Center In Form > Horizontally.**
7. *Setting the `Label`'s font size.* To change the font type and appearance of the `Label`'s text, select the value of the `Font` property, which causes an ellipsis button to appear next to the value (Fig. 2.38). When the ellipsis button is clicked, a dialog that provides additional values—in this case, the **Font** dialog (Fig. 2.39)—is displayed. You can select the font name (e.g., **Microsoft Sans Serif, MingLiU, Mistral, Modern No. 20**—the font options may be different, depending on your system), font style (**Regular, Italic, Bold**, etc.) and font size (**16, 18, 20**, etc.) in this dialog. The text in the **Sample** area provides sample text with the selected font settings. Under **Font**, select **Segoe UI**, Microsoft's recommended font for user interfaces. Under **Size**, select **24** points and click **OK**. If the `Label`'s text does not fit on a single line, it wraps to the next line. Resize the `Label` vertically if it's not large enough to hold the text. You may need to center the `Label` horizontally again after resizing.
8. *Aligning the `Label`'s text.* Select the `Label`'s `TextAlign` property, which determines how the text is aligned within the `Label`. A three-by-three grid of buttons representing alignment choices is displayed (Fig. 2.40). The position of each button

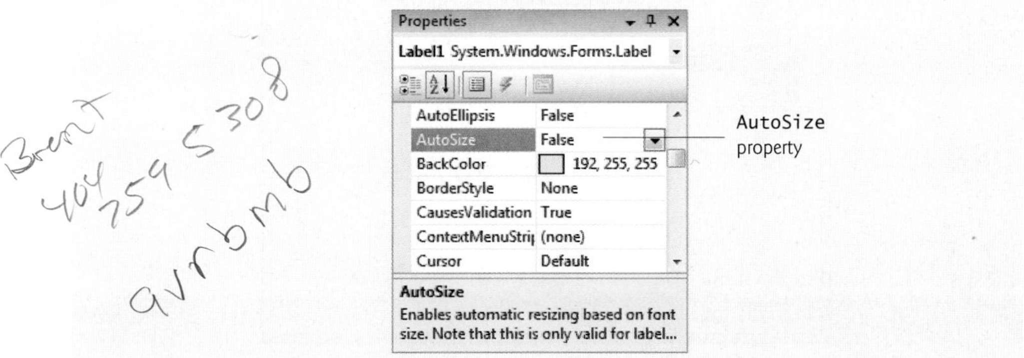

Fig. 2.36 | Changing the `Label`'s `AutoSize` property to `False`.

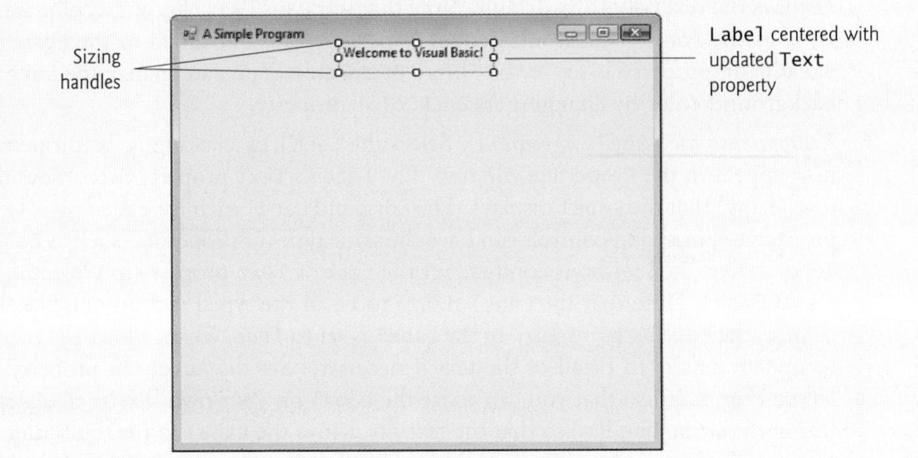

Fig. 2.37 | GUI after the `Form` and `Label` have been customized.

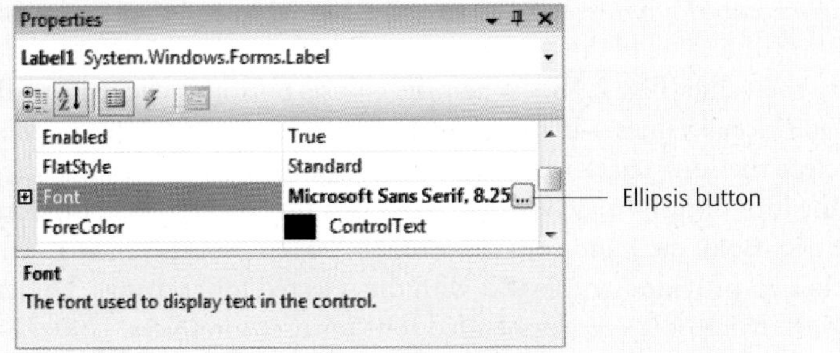

Fig. 2.38 | **Properties** window displaying the `Label`'s properties.

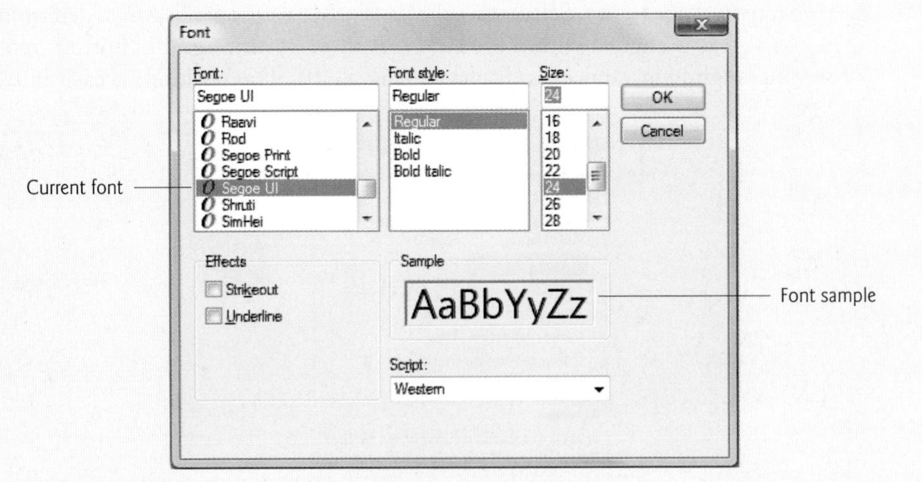

Fig. 2.39 | **Font** dialog for selecting fonts, styles and sizes.

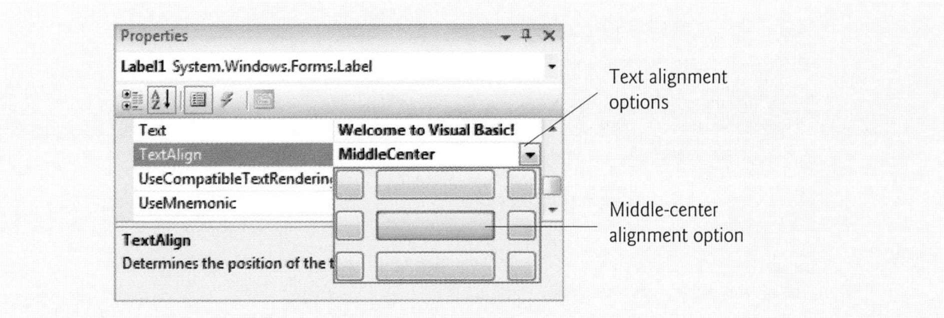

Fig. 2.40 | Centering the `Label`'s text.

corresponds to where the text appears in the `Label`. For this program, set the `TextAlign` property to `MiddleCenter` in the three-by-three grid—this selection causes the text to appear centered in the middle of the `Label`, with equal spacing from the text to all sides of the `Label`. The other `TextAlign` values, such as `TopLeft`, `TopRight`, and `BottomCenter`, can be used to position the text anywhere within a `Label`. Certain alignment values may require that you resize the `Label` larger or smaller to better fit the text.

9. *Adding a `PictureBox` to the `Form`.* The `PictureBox` control displays images. The process involved in this step is similar to that of *Step 5*, in which we added a `Label` to the `Form`. Locate the `PictureBox` in the **Toolbox** (Fig. 2.21) and double click it to add it to the `Form`. When the `PictureBox` appears, move it underneath the `Label`, either by dragging it or by using the arrow keys (Fig. 2.41).
10. *Inserting an image.* Click the `PictureBox` to display its properties in the **Properties** window (Fig. 2.42). Locate the **`Image` property**, which displays a preview of the image, if one exists. No picture has been assigned, so the value of the `Image` property displays **(none)**. Click the ellipsis button to display the **Select Resource**

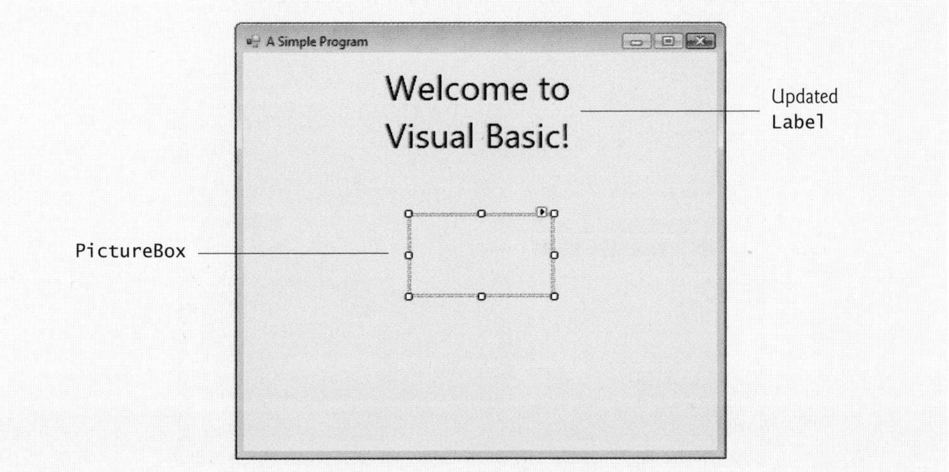

Fig. 2.41 | Inserting and aligning a `PictureBox`.

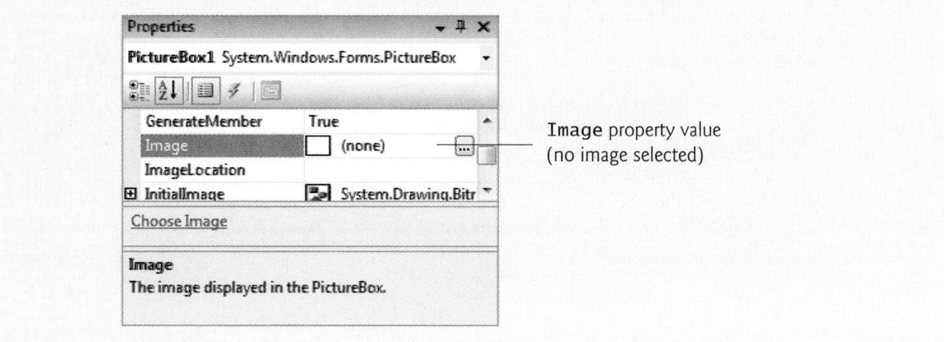

Fig. 2.42 | `Image` property of the `PictureBox`.

dialog (Fig. 2.43). This dialog is used to import files, such as images, to a program. Click the **Import...** button to browse for an image to insert. In our case, the picture is `bug.png` (located in this chapter's examples folder). In the dialog that appears, locate the image file, select it and click **OK**. The image is previewed in the **Select Resource** dialog (Fig. 2.44). Click **OK** to place the image in your program. Supported image formats include PNG (Portable Network Graphics), GIF (Graphic Interchange Format), JPEG (Joint Photographic Experts Group) and BMP (Windows bitmap). Creating a new image requires image-editing software, such as Corel® Paint Shop Pro® Photo X2 (`www.corel.com`), Adobe® Photoshop™ Elements (`www.adobe.com`) or Microsoft Paint (provided with Windows). To size the image to the `PictureBox`, change the `SizeMode` property to `StretchImage` (Fig. 2.45), which scales the image to the size of the `PictureBox`. Resize the `PictureBox`, making it larger (Fig. 2.46).

11. *Saving the project.* Select **File > Save All** to save the entire solution. The solution file (which has the file name extension `.sln`) contains the name and location of its project, and the project file (which has the file name extension `.vbproj`) contains the names and locations of all the files in the project.

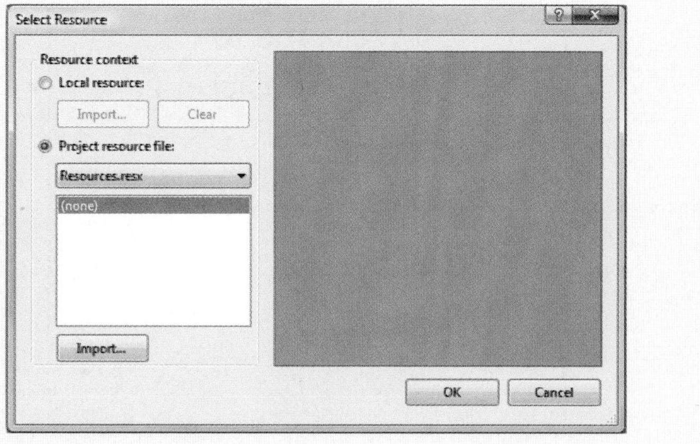

Fig. 2.43 | **Select Resource** dialog to select an image for the `PictureBox`.

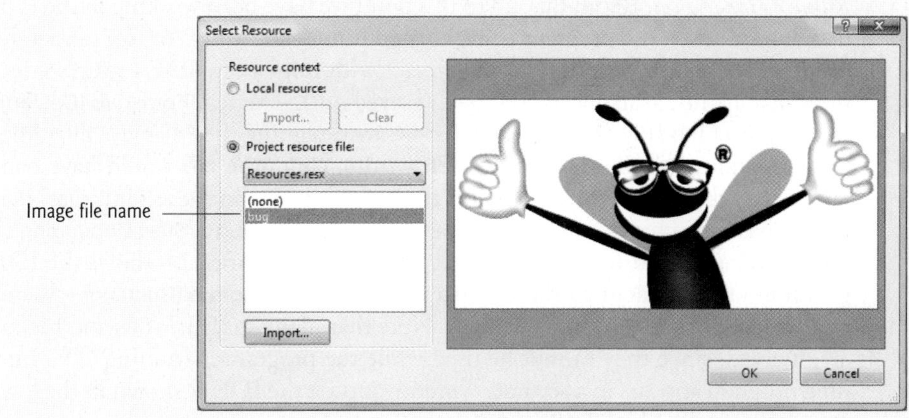

Fig. 2.44 | **Select Resource** dialog displaying a preview of selected image.

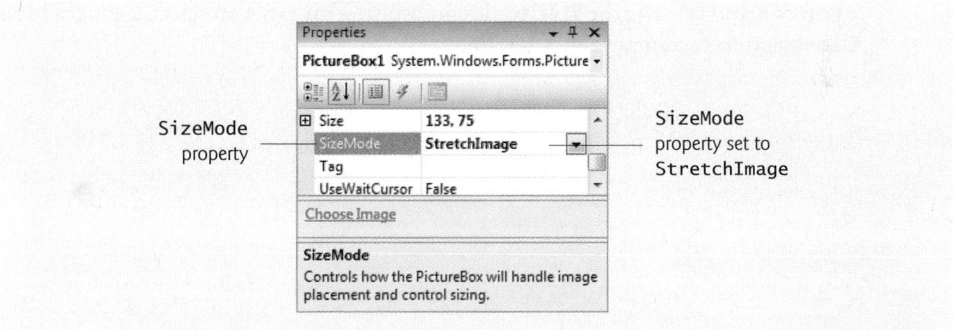

Fig. 2.45 | Scaling an image to the size of the `PictureBox`.

Fig. 2.46 | `PictureBox` displaying an image.

12. *Running the project.* Recall that up to this point we have been working in the IDE design mode (i.e., the program being created is not executing). In run mode, the program is executing, and you can interact with only a few IDE features—features that are not available are disabled (grayed out). The text **Form1.vb [Design]*** in the project tab (Fig. 2.47) means that we are designing the `Form` visually rather than programmatically. If we had been writing code, the tab would have contained only the text **Form1.vb**. The * at the end of the text in the tab indicates that the file has been changed and should be saved. Select **Debug > Start Debugging** to execute the program (or you can select the *F5* key). Figure 2.48 shows the IDE in run mode (indicated by the title-bar text **A Simple Program (Running) – Microsoft Visual Basic 2008 Express Edition**). Note that many toolbar icons and menus are disabled, since they cannot be used while the program is running. The running program appears in a separate window outside the IDE as shown in the lower-right portion of Fig. 2.48.
13. *Terminating execution.* Click the running program's close box (the **X** in the top-right corner of the running program's window). This action stops the program's execution and returns the IDE to design mode. You can also select **Debug > Stop Debugging** to terminate the program.

Fig. 2.47 | Debugging a solution.

IDE - INTEGRATED DEVELOPMENT ENVIRONMENT

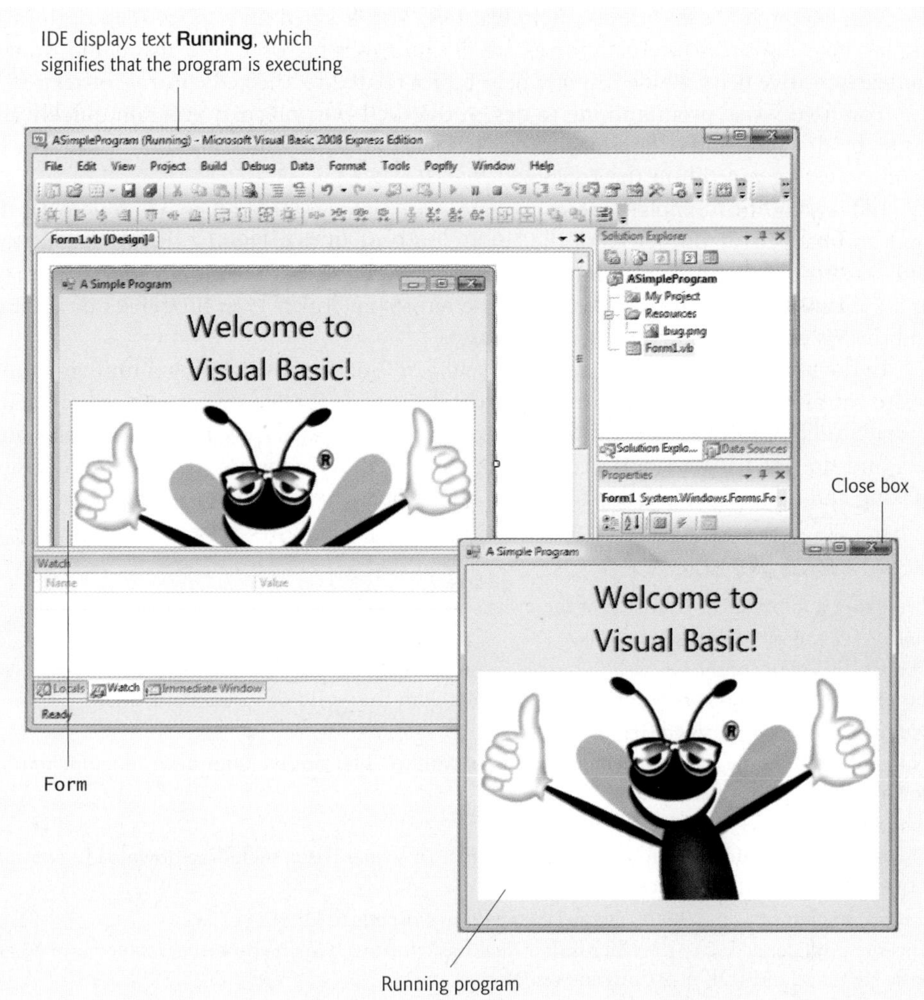

Fig. 2.48 | IDE in run mode, with the running program in the foreground.

2.7 Wrap-Up

In this chapter, we introduced key features of the Visual Studio Integrated Development Environment (IDE). You used the technique of visual programming to create a working Visual Basic program without writing a single line of code. Visual Basic programming is a mixture of the two styles—visual programming allows you to develop GUIs easily and avoid tedious GUI programming; conventional programming (which we introduce in Chapter 3) allows you to specify the behavior of your programs.

You created a Visual Basic Windows Forms application with one `Form`. You worked with the **Solution Explorer**, **Toolbox** and **Properties** windows, which are essential to developing Visual Basic programs. The **Solution Explorer** window allows you to manage your solution's files visually. The **Toolbox** window contains a rich collection of controls for creating GUIs. The **Properties** window allows you to set the attributes of a `Form` and controls.

You explored Visual Studio's help features. You learned how to set **Help** options to display help resources internally or externally in a web browser. We also demonstrated context-sensitive help, which displays help topics related to selected controls or text.

You used visual programming to design the GUI portions of a program quickly and easily, by dragging and dropping controls (a `Label` and a `PictureBox`) onto a `Form` or by double clicking controls in the **Toolbox**.

In creating the **ASimpleProgram** program, you used the **Properties** window to set the `Text` and `BackColor` properties of the `Form`. You learned that `Label` controls display text and that `PictureBox`es display images. You displayed text in a `Label` and added an image to a `PictureBox`. You also worked with the `AutoSize`, `TextAlign` properties of a `Label` and the `SizeMode` property of a `PictureBox`.

In the next chapter, we discuss "nonvisual," or "conventional," programming—you'll create your first programs that contain Visual Basic code that you write, instead of having Visual Studio write the code. You'll study console applications (programs that display only text and do not have a GUI). You'll also learn memory concepts, arithmetic, decision making and how to use a dialog to display a message.

2.8 Web Resources

Please take a moment to visit each of these sites briefly.

`www.deitel.com/VisualBasic2008/`
This site lists many of the key web resources we used as we were preparing to write this book. There's lots of great stuff here to help you become familiar with the world of Visual Basic 2008.

`msdn.microsoft.com/vstudio`
This site is the home page for Microsoft Visual Studio. The site includes news, documentation, downloads and other resources.

`msdn.microsoft.com/vbasic/default.aspx`
This site provides information on the newest release of Visual Basic, including downloads, community information and resources.

`forums.microsoft.com/MSDN/default.aspx?ForumGroupID=10&SiteID=1`
This site provides access to the Microsoft Visual Basic forums, which you can use to get your Visual Basic language and IDE questions answered.

`msdn.microsoft.com/msdnmag/`
This is the Microsoft Developer Network Magazine site. This site provides articles and code on many Visual Basic and .NET programming topics. There is also an archive of past issues.

`www.vbi.org`
This site has Visual Basic articles, reviews of books and software, documentation, downloads, links and more.

`www.vbcity.com`
This site provides Visual Basic articles, tutorials, FAQs and more. Submit your Visual Basic code to be reviewed and rated by other developers. Includes polls on Visual Basic topics.

Summary

Section 2.1 Introduction

- Visual Studio is Microsoft's Integrated Development Environment (IDE) for creating, running and debugging programs written in a variety of .NET programming languages.

- Creating simple programs by dragging and dropping predefined building blocks into place is called visual programming.

Section 2.2 Overview of the Visual Studio 2008 IDE

- The **Start Page** contains a list of links to resources either within the Visual Studio 2008 IDE or on the Internet.
- A project is a group of related files, such as the Visual Basic code and any images that might make up a program.
- The Visual Studio 2008 IDE organizes programs into projects and solutions—a solution may contain one or more projects.
- Dialogs are windows that facilitate user–computer communication.
- Visual Studio provides templates for the project types available for users to create, including Windows Forms applications and console applications.
- The `Form` represents the main window of the Windows Forms application that you are creating.
- Collectively, the `Form` and controls constitute the program's graphical user interface (GUI), which is the visual part of the program with which the user interacts.

Section 2.3 Menu Bar and Toolbar

- Commands for managing the IDE and for developing, maintaining and executing programs are contained in the menus, which are located on the menu bar.
- Menus contain groups of commands (menu items) that, when selected, cause the IDE to perform actions (e.g., open a window, save a file, print a file and execute a program).
- Tool tips help you become familiar with the IDE's features.

Section 2.4 Navigating the Visual Studio IDE

- The **Solution Explorer** window lists all the files in the solution.
- The **Toolbox** contains controls for customizing `Forms`.
- By using visual programming, you can place predefined controls onto the `Form` instead of writing the code yourself.
- Moving the mouse pointer over a hidden window's icon opens that window. When the mouse pointer leaves the area of the window, the window is hidden. This feature is known as auto-hide. To "pin down" a window (i.e., to disable auto-hide), click the pin icon.
- The **Properties** window displays the properties for a `Form`, control or file (in **Design** view). Properties are information about a `Form` or control, such as size, color and position. The **Properties** window allows you to modify controls visually, without writing code.
- Each control has its own set of properties. The left column of the **Properties** window shows the properties of the control—the right column displays property values. This window's toolbar contains options for organizing properties either alphabetically when the **Alphabetic** icon is clicked or categorically (e.g., **Appearance**, **Behavior**, **Design**) when the **Categorized** icon is clicked.

Section 2.5 Using Help

- The **Help** menu contains a variety of options: The **How Do I?** menu provides specific resources to help users accomplish a given task, such as participating in community discussions. The **Contents** menu displays a categorized table of contents; the **Index** menu displays an alphabetical index that the you can browse; the **Search** menu allows you to find particular help articles, by entering search keywords.
- Context-sensitive help brings up a list of relevant help articles. To use context-sensitive help, click an item and press the *F1* key.

Section 2.6 Using Visual Programming to Create a Simple Program that Displays Text and an Image

- Visual Basic programming usually involves a combination of writing a portion of the program code and having the Visual Studio generate the remaining code.
- The text that appears at the top of the `Form` (the title bar) is specified in the `Form`'s `Text` property.
- To resize the `Form`, click and drag one of the `Form`'s enabled sizing handles (the small squares around the `Form`). Enabled sizing handles appear as white boxes.
- The `BackColor` property specifies the background color of a `Form`. The `Form`'s background color is the default background color for any controls added to the `Form`.
- Double clicking any **Toolbox** control icon places a control of that type on the `Form`. Alternatively, you can drag and drop controls from the **Toolbox** to the `Form`.
- The `Label`'s `Text` property determines the text (if any) that the `Label` displays. The `Form` and `Label` each have their own `Text` property.
- A property's ellipsis button, when clicked, displays a dialog containing additional options.
- In the **Font** dialog, you can select the font for a `Form`'s or `Label`'s text.
- The `TextAlign` property determines how the text is aligned within a `Label`'s boundaries.
- The `PictureBox` control displays images. The `Image` property specifies the image to displayed.
- Select **File > Save All** to save the entire solution, including all of its files.
- A program that is in design mode is not executing.
- In run mode, the program is executing—you can interact with only a few IDE features.
- When designing a program visually, the name of the Visual Basic file appears in the project tab, followed by **[Design]**.
- Terminate execution by clicking the close box.

Terminology

active tab
Alphabetical icon
application
auto-hide
`AutoSize` property of `TextBox`
`BackColor` property of `Form`
background color
BMP (Windows bitmap)
Categorized icon
clicking with the mouse
close a project
collapse a tree
component selection
context-sensitive help
customize a `Form`
Data menu
debug a program
Debug menu
design mode
dialog
double clicking
down arrow
dragging
dynamic help
Edit menu
ellipsis button
expand a tree
external help
F1 help key
File menu
`Font` property of `Label`
font size
font style
Font window
`Form`
Format menu
`Form`'s background color
`Form`'s title bar
GIF (Graphics Interchange Format)
graphical user interface (GUI)
Graphics Interchange Format (GIF)
GUI (graphical user interface)

Help menu
icon
IDE (Integrated Development Environment)
Integrated Development Environment (IDE)
Image property of PictureBox
input
internal help
Joint Photographic Experts Group (JPEG)
JPEG (Joint Photographic Experts Group)
Label
menu
menu bar in Visual Studio
menu item
Microsoft Developers Network (MSDN)
Microsoft Visual Basic 2008 Express Edition
mouse pointer
MSDN (Microsoft Developers Network)
New Project dialog
opening a project
output
palette
PictureBox
pin a window
PNG (Portable Network Graphics)
Portable Network Graphics (PNG)
project
Project Location dialog
Project menu
Properties window
property of a Form or control
run mode
Save Project dialog
Select Resource dialog
Show All Files icon
selecting an item with the mouse
SizeMode property of PictureBox
sizing handle
solution
Solution Explorer in Visual Studio
Start Page
startup project
StretchImage value
tabbed window
Text property
TextAlign property of Label
title bar
tool tip
toolbar
toolbar icon
Toolbox
Tools menu
.vb file extension
View menu
visual programming
Visual Basic 2008 Express Edition
Visual Studio
Windows Forms application
Windows menu

Self-Review Exercises

2.1 Fill in the blanks in each of the following statements:

a) The technique of __________ allows you to create GUIs without writing any code.
b) A(n) __________ is a group of one or more projects that collectively form a Visual Basic program.
c) The __________ feature hides a window when the mouse pointer is moved outside the window's area.
d) A(n) __________ appears when the mouse pointer hovers over an icon.
e) The __________ window allows you to browse solution files.
f) A plus box indicates that the tree in the Solution Explorer can __________.
g) The properties in the Properties window can be sorted __________ or __________.
h) A Form's __________ property specifies the text displayed in the Form's title bar.
i) The __________ allows you to add controls to the Form in a visual manner.
j) Using __________ displays relevant help articles, based on the current context.
k) The __________ property specifies how text is aligned within a Label's boundaries.

2.2 State whether each of the following is *true* or *false*. If *false*, explain why.

a) The title bar of the IDE displays the IDE's mode.
b) The X box toggles auto-hide.
c) The toolbar icons represent various menu commands.
d) The toolbar contains icons that represent controls you can drag onto a Form.

e) Both `Forms` and `Labels` have a title bar.
f) Control properties can be modified only by writing code.
g) `PictureBoxes` typically display images.
h) Visual Basic files use the file extension `.bas`.
i) A `Form`'s background color is set using the `BackColor` property.

Answers to Self-Review Exercises

2.1 a) visual programming. b) solution. c) auto-hide. d) tool tip. e) **Solution Explorer**. f) expand. g) alphabetically, categorically. h) `Text`. i) **Toolbox**. j) context-sensitive help. k) `TextAlign`.

2.2 a) True. b) False. The pin icon toggles auto-hide. The **X** box closes a window. c) True. d) False. The **Toolbox** contains icons that represent such controls. e) False. `Forms` have a title bar but `Labels` do not (although they do have `Label` text). f) False. Control properties can be modified using the **Properties** window. g) True. h) False. Visual Basic files use the file extension `.vb`. i) True.

Exercises

2.3 Fill in the blanks in each of the following statements:
a) When an ellipsis button is clicked, a(n) ________ is displayed.
b) To save every file in a solution, select ________.
c) Using ________ help immediately displays a relevant help article. It can be accessed using the ________ key.
d) "GUI" is an acronym for ________.

2.4 State whether each of the following is *true* or *false*. If *false*, explain why.
a) You can add a control to a `Form` by double clicking its control icon in the **Toolbox**.
b) The `Form`, `Label` and `PictureBox` have identical properties.
c) If your machine is connected to the Internet, you can browse the Internet from the Visual Studio IDE.
d) Visual Basic programmers usually create complex programs without writing any code.
e) Sizing handles are visible during execution.

2.5 Some features that appear throughout Visual Studio perform similar actions in different contexts. Explain and give examples of how the plus and minus boxes, ellipsis buttons, down-arrow buttons and tool tips act in this manner. Why do you think the Visual Studio IDE was designed this way?

2.6 Fill in the blanks in each of the following statements:
a) The ________ property specifies which image a `PictureBox` displays.
b) The ________ menu contains commands for arranging and displaying windows.

2.7 Briefly describe each of the following terms:
a) toolbar
b) menu bar
c) **Toolbox**
d) control
e) `Form`
f) solution

[*Note:* In the following exercises, you are asked to create GUIs using controls that we have not yet discussed in this book. The exercises give you practice with visual programming only—the programs do not perform any actions. You place controls from the **Toolbox** on a `Form` to familiarize yourself with what each control looks like. We have provided step-by-step instructions for you. If you follow these, you should be able to replicate the screen images we provide.]

2.8 *(Notepad GUI)* Create the GUI for the notepad as shown in Fig. 2.49.

a) *Manipulating the* `Form`*'s properties.* Change the `Text` property of the `Form` to `My Notepad`. Change the `Font` property to 9pt `Segoe UI`.

b) *Adding a* `MenuStrip` *control to the* `Form`*.* After inserting the `MenuStrip`, add items by clicking the **Type Here** section, typing a menu name (e.g., **File**, **Edit**, **View** and **About**) and then pressing *Enter*.

c) *Adding a* `RichTextBox` *to the* `Form`*.* Drag this control onto the `Form`. Change the `Size` property to `267, 220` or use the sizing handles. This property specifies the width and height of the control within the window. Change the `Text` property to "`Enter Text Here`." Finally, set the `Location` property to `14, 36`. This property specifies the location of the top-left corner of the control relative to the top-left corner of the `Form`.

2.9 *(Calendar and Appointments GUI)* Create the GUI for the calendar as shown in Fig. 2.50.

a) *Manipulating the* `Form`*'s properties.* Change the `Text` property of the `Form` to `My Scheduler`. Change the `Font` property to 9pt `Segoe UI`. Set the `Form`'s `Size` property to `332, 470`.

b) *Adding* `Label`*s to the* `Form`*.* Add two `Label`s to the `Form`. Both should be of equal size (`231, 23`) and should be centered in the `Form` horizontally, as shown. Set the `Label`'s `Text` properties to match the figure as shown, using 12-point font size. Also set the `BackColor` property to `Yellow`.

c) *Adding a* `MonthCalendar` *control to the* `Form`*.* Add this control to the `Form` and center it horizontally in the appropriate place between the two `Label`s.

d) *Adding a* `RichTextBox` *control to the* `Form`*.* Add a `RichTextBox` control to the `Form` and center it below the second `Label`. Resize the `RichTextBox` accordingly.

2.10 *(Calculator GUI)* Create the GUI for the calculator as shown in Fig. 2.51.

a) *Manipulating the* `Form`*'s properties.* Change the `Text` property of the `Form` to `Calculator`. Change the `Font` property to 9pt `Segoe UI`. Change the `Size` property of the `Form` to `272, 204`.

b) *Adding a* `TextBox` *to the* `Form`*.* Set the `TextBox`'s `Text` property in the **Properties** window to `0`. Change the `Size` property to `240, 23`. Set the `TextAlign` property to `Right`—this right aligns text displayed in the `TextBox`. Finally, set the `TextBox`'s `Location` property to `8, 16`.

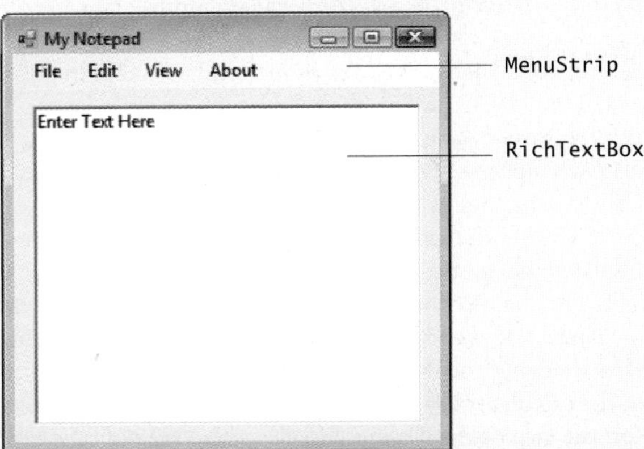

Fig. 2.49 | Notepad GUI.

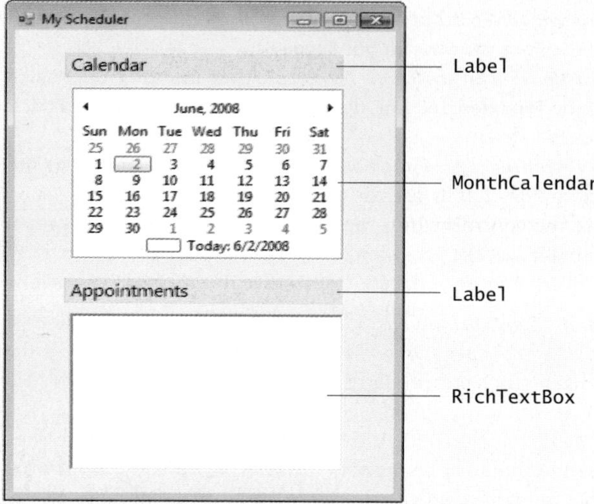

Fig. 2.50 | Calendar and appointments GUI.

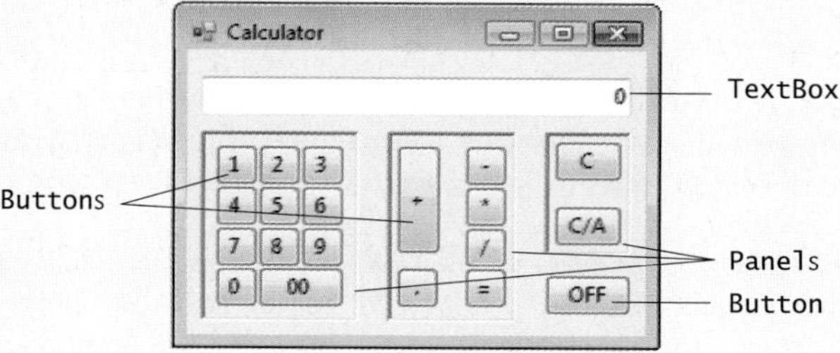

Fig. 2.51 | Calculator GUI.

c) *Adding the first* `Panel` *to the* `Form`*.* `Panel` controls are used to group other controls. Change the `Panel`'s `BorderStyle` property to `Fixed3D` to make the inside of the `Panel` appear recessed. Change the `Size` property to `88, 112`. Finally, set the `Location` property to `8, 48`. This `Panel` contains the calculator's numeric keys.

d) *Adding the second* `Panel` *to the* `Form`*.* Change the `Panel`'s `BorderStyle` property to `Fixed3D`. Change the `Size` property to `72, 112`. Finally, set the `Location` property to `112, 48`. This `Panel` contains the calculator's operator keys.

e) *Adding the third (and last)* `Panel` *to the* `Form`*.* Change the `Panel`'s `BorderStyle` property to `Fixed3D`. Change the `Size` property to `48, 72`. Finally, set the `Location` property to `200, 48`. This `Panel` contains the calculator's **C** (clear) and **C/A** (clear all) keys.

f) *Adding* `Buttons` *to the* `Form`*.* There are 20 `Buttons` on the calculator. Add a `Button` to the `Panel` by dragging and dropping it on the `Panel`. Change the `Text` property of each `Button` to the calculator key it represents. The value you enter in the `Text` property will appear on the face of the `Button`. Finally, resize the `Buttons`, using their `Size` properties. Each `Button` labeled `0`–`9`, `*`, `/`, `-`, `=` and `.` should have a size of `24, 24`. The **00** and **OFF** `Buttons` have size `48, 24`. The **+** `Button` is sized `25, 64`. The **C** (clear) and **C/A** (clear all) `Buttons` are sized `38, 24`.

2.11 *(Alarm Clock GUI)* Create the GUI for the alarm clock as shown in Fig. 2.52.

a) *Manipulating the Form's properties.* Change the Text property of the Form to Alarm Clock. Change the Font property to 9pt Segoe UI. Change the Size property of the Form to 281, 176.

b) *Adding Buttons to the Form.* Add six Buttons to the Form. Change the Text property of each Button to the appropriate text. Change the Size properties of the **Hour** and **Minute** Buttons to 60, 23. Set the Size of the **Second** Button to 65, 23. The **ON** and **OFF** Buttons get size 40, 23. The **Timer** Button gets size 48, 32. Align the Buttons as shown.

c) *Adding a Label to the Form.* Add a Label to the Form. Change the Text property to SNOOZE. Set its Size to 254, 23. Set the Label's TextAlign property to MiddleCenter. Finally, to draw a border around the edge of the **Snooze** Label, change the BorderStyle property of the **Snooze** Label to FixedSingle.

d) *Adding a GroupBox to the Form.* GroupBoxes are like Panels, except that GroupBoxes display a title. Change the Text property to AM/PM, and set the Size property to 72, 72. To place the GroupBox in the correct location on the Form, set the Location property to 104, 29.

e) *Adding* **AM/PM** *RadioButtons to the GroupBox.* Change the Text property of one RadioButton to AM and the other to PM. Then place the RadioButtons as shown by setting the Location of the **AM** RadioButton to 16, 16 and that of the **PM** RadioButton to 16, 40. These coordinates are with respect to the top-left corner of the GroupBox that contains the RadioButtons. Set their Size properties to 48, 24.

f) *Adding the time Label to the Form.* Add a Label to the Form and change its Text property to 00:00:00. Change the BorderStyle property to Fixed3D and the BackColor to Black. Set the Size property to 64, 23. Use the Font property to make the time bold. Change the ForeColor to Silver (located in the **Web** tab) to make the time stand out against the black background. Set TextAlign to MiddleCenter to center the text in the Label. Position the Label as shown.

2.12 *(Radio GUI)* Create the GUI for the radio as shown in Fig. 2.53. [*Note:* All colors used in this exercise are from the **Web** palette, and the image can be found in the examples folder for Chapter 2.]

a) *Manipulating the Form's properties.* Change the Font property to 9pt Segoe UI. Change the Form's Text property to Radio and the Size to 576, 240. Set BackColor to PeachPuff.

b) *Adding the* **Pre-set Stations** *GroupBox and Buttons.* Set the GroupBox's Size to 232, 64, its Text to Pre-set Stations, its ForeColor to Black and its BackColor to RosyBrown. Change its Font to Bold. Finally, set its Location to 24, 16. Add six Buttons to the GroupBox. Set each BackColor to PeachPuff and each Size to 24, 24. Change the Buttons' Text properties to 1, 2, 3, 4, 5, 6, respectively.

c) *Adding the* **Speakers** *GroupBox and CheckBoxes.* Set the GroupBox's Size to 160, 64, its Text to Speakers and its ForeColor to Black. Set its Location to 280, 16. Add two CheckBoxes to the GroupBox. Set each CheckBox's Size to 56, 24. Set the Text properties for the CheckBoxes to Rear and Front.

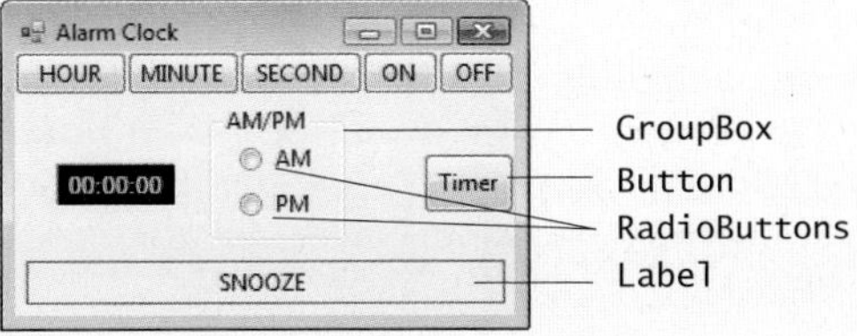

Fig. 2.52 | Alarm clock GUI.

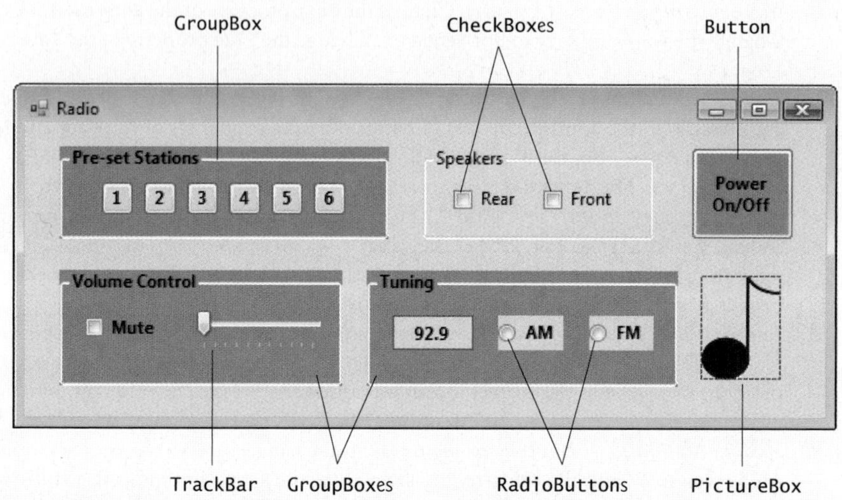

Fig. 2.53 | Radio GUI.

d) *Adding the* **Power On/Off** *Button.* Add a Button to the Form. Set its Text to Power On/Off, its BackColor to RosyBrown, its ForeColor to Black and its Size to 72, 64. Change its Font style to Bold.

e) *Adding the* **Volume Control** *GroupBox, the* **Mute** *CheckBox and the* **Volume** *TrackBar.* Add a GroupBox to the Form. Set its Text to Volume Control, its BackColor to RosyBrown, its ForeColor to Black and its Size to 200, 80. Set its Font style to Bold. Add a CheckBox to the GroupBox. Set its Text to Mute and its Size to 56, 19. Add a TrackBar to the GroupBox.

f) *Adding the* **Tuning** *GroupBox, the radio station Label and the* **AM/FM** *RadioButtons.* Add a GroupBox to the Form. Set its Text to Tuning, its ForeColor to Black and its BackColor to RosyBrown. Set its Font style to Bold and its Size to 216, 80. Add a Label to the Form. Set its BackColor to PeachPuff, its ForeColor to Black, its BorderStyle to FixedSingle, its TextAlign to MiddleCenter and its Size to 56, 24. Set its Text to 92.9. Place the Label as shown in the figure. Add two RadioButtons to the GroupBox. Change the BackColor to PeachPuff and change the Size to 45,24. Set the Text of one to AM and of the other to FM.

g) *Adding the image.* Add a PictureBox to the Form. Set its BackColor to PeachPuff, its SizeMode to StretchImage and its Size to 56, 72. Set the Image property to MusicNote.gif (located in the examples folder for Chapter 2).

3

Comment is free, but facts are sacred.
—C. P. Scott

The creditor hath a better memory than the debtor.
—James Howell

When faced with a decision, I always ask, "What would be the most fun?"
—Peggy Walker

Equality, in a social sense, may be divided into that of condition and that of rights.
—James Fenimore Cooper

Introduction to Visual Basic Programming

OBJECTIVES

In this chapter you'll learn:

- To write simple Visual Basic programs using code rather than visual programming.
- To write statements that input data from the keyboard and output data to the screen.
- To declare and use data of various types.
- To store and retrieve data from memory.
- To use arithmetic operators to perform calculations.
- To use the precedence of arithmetic operators to determine the order in which operators are applied.
- To write decision-making statements.
- To use equality and relational operators to compare operands.
- To use message dialogs to display messages.

Outline

3.1 Introduction

In this chapter, we introduce Visual Basic programming with program code and present examples to demonstrate how your programs can display messages and obtain information from the user at the keyboard for processing. The first two programs simply display text on the screen. The next obtains two numbers from the user, calculates their sum and displays the result. The accompanying discussion shows you how to perform various arithmetic calculations and save their results for later use. The fourth example demonstrates decision-making fundamentals by showing you how to compare two numbers in various ways, then display messages based on the comparison results. The final example demonstrates how to display text in a special window known as a message dialog.

We introduce console applications—that is, applications that do not have a graphical user interface. There are several types of Visual Basic projects (you have already seen Windows applications in Chapter 2); the console application is one of the simplest types. When a console application is executed in Visual Basic 2008 Express, its text output appears in the Console window. A console application can also be executed outside the IDE in a Windows Command Prompt. Programs can input and output information in a variety of ways. For example, in Chapter 2, we created a simple graphical user interface (GUI) for a Windows application, using visual programming techniques. We'll briefly return to Windows applications in Chapter 5, Control Statements: Part 1, and Chapter 6, Control Statements: Part 2, respectively. These chapters provide a more detailed introduction to program development in Visual Basic. We discuss Windows applications in detail in Chapter 14, Graphical User Interfaces with Windows Forms.

3.2 Displaying a Line of Text

We begin by considering a simple program (Fig. 3.1) that displays a line of text. When this program runs, its output appears in a **Command Prompt** window. We show such output in a blue box following the program listing. You'll see exactly what a **Command Prompt** win-

```
1  ' Fig. 3.1: Welcome1.vb
2  ' Simple Visual Basic program.
3
4  Module Welcome1
5
6     Sub Main()
7
8        Console.WriteLine("Welcome to Visual Basic!")
9
10    End Sub ' Main
11
12 End Module ' Welcome1
```

```
Welcome to Visual Basic!
```

Fig. 3.1 | Simple Visual Basic program.

dow looks like later in this section, when we guide you step-by-step through the process of creating a console application.

Analyzing the Program

This program illustrates several important Visual Basic features. For your convenience, all program listings in this text include line numbers—these are not part of the Visual Basic language. The line numbers help us refer to specific parts of a program. You'll soon learn how to display line numbers in program files. Each program is followed by one or more outputs showing the program's execution output.

Line 1 of Fig. 3.1 begins with a **single-quote character** (`'`) which indicates that the remainder of the line is a **comment**. You insert comments in programs to improve the readability of the code—you can write anything you want in a comment. Comments can be placed either on their own lines (we call these "**full-line comments**"; as in lines 1–2) or at the end of a line of Visual Basic code (we call these "**end-of-line comments**"; as in lines 10 and 12).[1] The compiler ignores comments—they do not cause the computer to perform any actions when a program runs. The comment in line 1 simply indicates the figure number (Fig. 3.1) and the file name (`Welcome1.vb`) in which we stored this program. The comment in line 2 provides a brief description of the program. By convention, we begin every program in this manner (you can, of course, say anything you want in a comment).

Visual Basic console applications consist of pieces called **modules**, which are logical groupings of methods that simplify program organization. Lines 4–12 define our first module. These lines collectively are called a **module declaration**. We discuss the method in lines 6–10 momentarily—**methods** perform tasks and can return information when the tasks are completed. Every console application in Visual Basic consists of at least one module and one method in that module. In Chapter 7, Methods: A Deeper Look, we discuss methods in detail.

---

1. Visual Basic also provides documentation comments that begin with `'''` and contain Extensible Markup Language (XML) elements that you can use to describe your code. The IDE can generate documentation for your code based on these comments and can use them with its *IntelliSense* feature (Section 3.3) to provide help while you write code. We discuss documentation comments in Chapter 19, XML and LINQ to XML.

The word `Module` (line 4) is an example of a **keyword**. Keywords are words reserved for use by Visual Basic. A complete list of Visual Basic keywords is presented in Fig. 3.2. We discuss many of Visual Basic's keywords throughout this book. Visual Basic has a larger set of keywords than most other programming languages.

Visual Basic keywords and contextual keywords				
AddHandler	AddressOf	Alias	And	AndAlso
As	Boolean	ByRef	Byte	ByVal
Call	Case	Catch	CBool	CByte
CChar	CDate	CDbl	CDec	Char
CInt	Class	CLng	CObj	Const
Continue	CSByte	CShort	CSng	CStr
CType	CUInt	CULng	CUShort	Date
Decimal	Declare	Default	Delegate	Dim
DirectCast	Do	Double	Each	Else
ElseIf	End	Enum	Erase	Error
Event	Exit	False	Finally	For
Friend	Function	Get	GetType	GetXmlNamespace
Global	GoTo	Handles	If	Implements
Imports	In	Inherits	Integer	Interface
Is	IsNot	Lib	Like	Long
Loop	Me	Mod	Module	MustInherit
MustOverride	MyBase	MyClass	Namespace	Narrowing
New	Next	Not	Nothing	NotInheritable
NotOverridable	Object	Of	On	Operator
Option	Optional	Or	OrElse	Overloads
Overridable	Overrides	ParamArray	Partial	Private
Property	Protected	Public	RaiseEvent	ReadOnly
ReDim	REM	RemoveHandler	Resume	Return
SByte	Select	Set	Shadows	Shared
Short	Single	Static	Step	Stop
String	Structure	Sub	SyncLock	Then
Throw	To	True	Try	TryCast
TypeOf	UInteger	ULong	UShort	Using
When	While	Widening	With	WithEvents
WriteOnly	Xor			
Contextual keywords				
Aggregate	Ansi	Assembly	Auto	Binary
Compare	Custom	Distinct	Equals	Explicit
From	Group By	Group Join	Into	IsFalse
IsTrue	Join	Key	Let	Mid
Off	Order By	Preserve	Skip	Skip While
Strict	Take	Take While	Text	Unicode
Until	Where			
The following are retained as keywords, although they are no longer supported in Visual Basic 2008				
EndIf	GoSub	Variant	Wend	

Fig. 3.2 | Keywords and contextual keywords in Visual Basic.

The name of the `Module`—`Welcome1` in line 4—is known as an identifier, which is a series of characters consisting of letters, digits and underscores (`_`). Identifiers cannot begin with a digit and cannot contain spaces. Examples of valid identifiers are `value1`, `Welcome1`, `xy_coordinate`, `_total` and `grossPay`. The name `7Welcome` is not a valid identifier because it begins with a digit, and the name `input field` is not a valid identifier because it contains a space.

Common Programming Error 3.1

You cannot use a keyword as an identifier, so it is an error, for example, to choose any of the words in Fig. 3.2 as a `Module` name. The Visual Basic compiler helps you locate such errors in your programs. Though keywords cannot be used as identifiers, they can be used in strings and comments. The contextual keywords in Fig. 3.2 can be used as identifiers outside the contexts in which they are keywords, but for clarity this is not recommended.

Visual Basic keywords and identifiers are not case sensitive. Uppercase and lowercase letters are considered to be identical, which causes `welcome1` and `Welcome1` to be interpreted as the same identifier. Although keywords appear to be case sensitive, they are not. Visual Basic Express applies its "preferred" case (i.e., the casing used in Fig. 3.2) to each letter of a keyword, so when you type `module` and press the *Enter* key, Visual Basic changes the lowercase `m` to uppercase, as in `Module`, even though `module` would be correct.

Lines 3, 5, 7, 9 and 11 (Fig. 3.1) are blank lines. Blank lines, space characters and tab characters are used throughout a program to make it easier to read. Collectively, these are called whitespace characters. We use lots of blank lines in our early programs. We'll use fewer later in the book as you become more comfortable reading Visual Basic programs.

Good Programming Practice 3.1

Use whitespace to enhance program readability.

Line 6 is present in all Visual Basic console applications. These begin executing at `Main`, which is known as the entry point of the program. The keyword `Sub` that appears before `Main` indicates that `Main` is a method.

Note that lines 6–10 are indented three spaces relative to lines 4 and 12. Indentation improves program readability—in this case making it clear that `Main` is part of the module `Welcome1`. We refer to spacing conventions that enhance program clarity as *Good Programming Practices*. We show how to set the indent size in Visual Basic Express shortly.

The keyword **`Sub`** (line 6) begins the body of the method declaration (the code that will be executed as part of our program). The keywords **`End Sub`** (line 10) close the method declaration's body. The keyword `Sub` is short for "subroutine"—an early term for method. Note that the line of code (line 8) in the method body is indented three additional spaces to the right relative to lines 6 and 10. This emphasizes that line 8 is part of the `Main` method's body. We do this throughout the text to enhance readability. Again, the indentation is whitespace and is ignored by the compiler. The end-of-line comments in lines 10 and 12 improve readability by indicating which method or module ends at those lines.

Good Programming Practice 3.2

Indent the entire body of each method declaration one additional "level" of indentation. This emphasizes the structure of the method, improving its readability. In this text, one level of indentation is set to three spaces—this keeps the code readable yet concise.

Using `Console.WriteLine` *to Display Text*

Line 8 in Fig. 3.1 does the "real work" of the program, displaying the phrase `Welcome to Visual Basic!` on the screen. Line 8 instructs the computer to perform an action—namely, to print (i.e., display on the screen) the series of characters contained between the double quotation marks. Characters and the surrounding double quotes are called strings, which also are called character strings or string literals.

The entire line, including `Console.WriteLine` and its string in the parentheses, is called a statement. When this statement executes, it displays (or prints) the message `Welcome to Visual Basic!` in the **Console** window (Fig. 3.1).

Note that `Console.WriteLine` contains two identifiers (i.e., `Console` and `WriteLine`) separated by the dot separator (`.`). The identifier to the right of the dot separator is the method name, and the identifier to the left of the dot separator is the class name to which the method belongs. Classes organize groups of related methods and data; methods perform tasks and can return information when the tasks are completed. For instance, the `Console` class contains methods, such as `WriteLine`, that communicate with users via the **Console** window. The statement in line 8 is known as a method call because it "calls" a method (i.e., method `WriteLine` of class `Console`) to ask the method to perform its task. Sometimes a method receives values, known as arguments, from its caller—it uses these arguments while performing its task. In Fig. 3.1, the string in parentheses in line 8 is the argument to method `WriteLine`. We discuss methods and classes in detail in Chapter 10.

When method `WriteLine` completes its task, it positions the output cursor (the location where the next output character will be displayed) at the beginning of the next line in the **Console** window. This behavior is similar to what happens when you press the *Enter* key when typing in a text editor window—the cursor is repositioned at the beginning of the next line. Program execution terminates when the program encounters the keywords `End Sub` in line 10. The `Module` is a package that contains the program's methods; the methods contain the statements that perform the actions of the program.

3.3 Creating Your First Program in Visual Basic Express

Now that we have presented our first console application (Fig. 3.1), we provide a step-by-step explanation of how to create and run it using Visual Basic 2008 Express.

Creating the Console Application

Select **File > New Project...** to display the **New Project** dialog (Fig. 3.3). Click **Console Application** to ensure that it is selected in the section labeled **Visual Studio installed templates.** In the dialog's **Name** field, type `Welcome1`. Click **OK** to create the project. The IDE now contains the open console application, as shown in Fig. 3.4. Note that the editor window contains four lines of Visual Basic code provided by the IDE. The code coloring scheme used by the IDE is called syntax-color highlighting and helps you visually differentiate program elements. Keywords appear in blue and other text is black. When present, comments are colored green. In this book, we color our code similarly—blue for keywords, green for comments, cyan for literals and constants and black for other text. One example of a literal is the string passed to `Console.WriteLine` in line 8 of Fig. 3.1. You can customize the colors shown in the code editor by selecting **Tools > Options...** to display the **Options** dialog. Then select **Fonts and Colors** to display the options for changing the fonts and colors of various code elements.

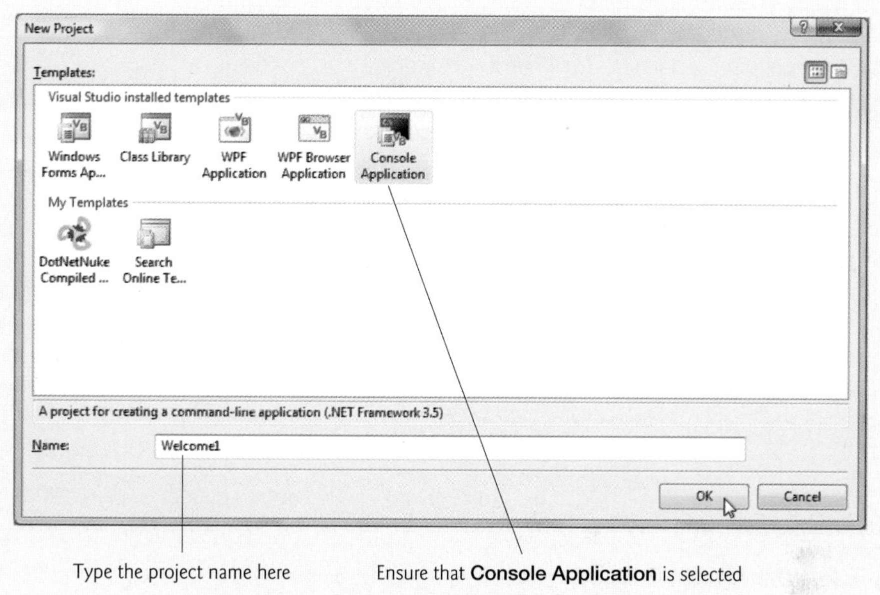

Fig. 3.3 | Creating a **Console Application** with the **New Project** dialog.

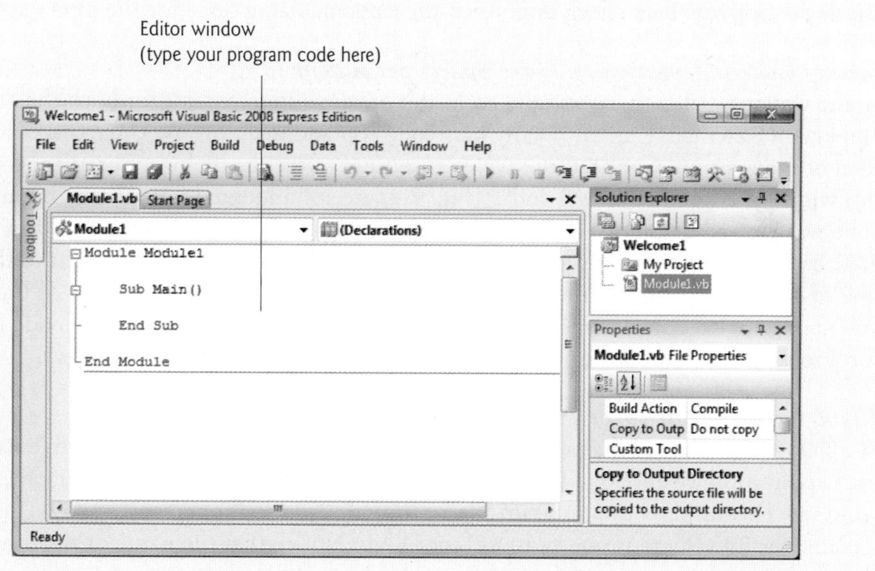

Fig. 3.4 | IDE with an open console application.

Modifying the Editor Settings to Display Line Numbers

Visual Basic 2008 Express provides many ways to personalize your coding experience. You'll now learn how to change the settings so that your code matches ours. To have the IDE display line numbers, select **Tools > Options...**. In the dialog that appears (Fig. 3.5),

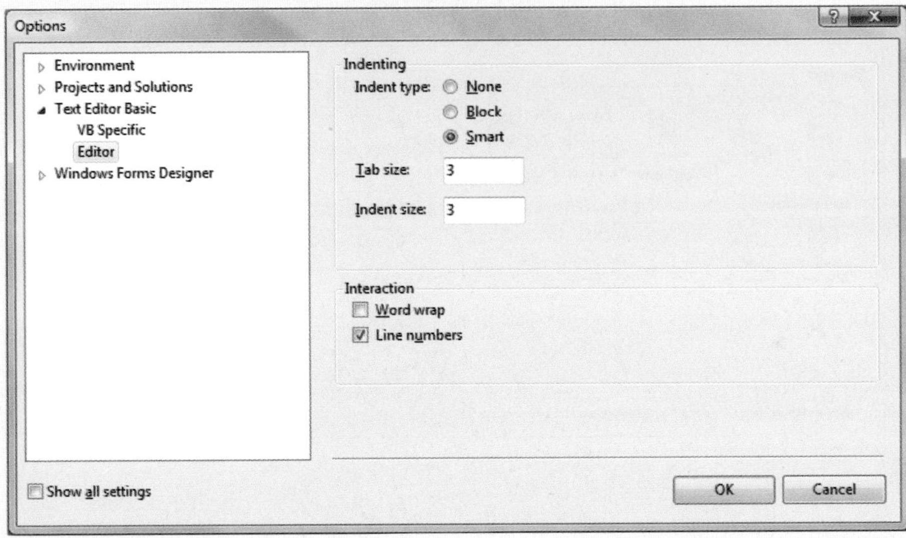

Fig. 3.5 | Modifying the IDE settings.

ensure that the **Show all settings** check box in the dialog's lower-left corner is unchecked. Expand the **Text Editor Basic** category in the left pane, and select **Editor**. Under **Interaction**, check the **Line Numbers** check box. Keep the **Options** dialog open for the next step.

Setting Code Indentation to Three Spaces per Indent

In the **Options** dialog that you opened in the previous step, enter **3** for both the **Tab Size** and **Indent Size** fields (Fig. 3.5). Any new code you add will now use three spaces for each level of indentation. Click **OK** to save your settings, close the dialog and return to the editor window. Note that lines 3 and 5 (Fig. 3.4) are still indented four spaces, because this code was created before we changed the indentation settings. Go to line 3 and move the code back one space to conform to our new convention, then move the cursor to the next line of code. After you do this, line 5 updates its indentation to match that of line 3. As you create applications in this book, Visual Basic Express will often update code to conform to various Visaul Basic code conventions and your current IDE settings.

Changing the Name of the Program File

We change the name of the program file (i.e., `Module1.vb`) to a more descriptive name for each application we develop. To rename the file, click `Module1.vb` in the **Solution Explorer** window. This displays the program file's properties in the **Properties** window (Fig. 3.6). Change the **File Name** property to `Welcome1.vb`. Notice that the name of the module in the source code changes to `Welcome1` (line 1) to match the file name.

Setting the Startup Object

Each Visual Basic project has a startup object that specifies where the application begins executing. If you modify the name of the module where `Main` resides directly in the source code, you must update the application's startup object as well. To do so, double click the **My Project** item in the **Solution Explorer** window (near the top of Fig. 3.6). A page appears

(Fig. 3.7) where you can set several properties of your application. Select **Welcome1** (our new module name) from the **Startup object** drop-down list.

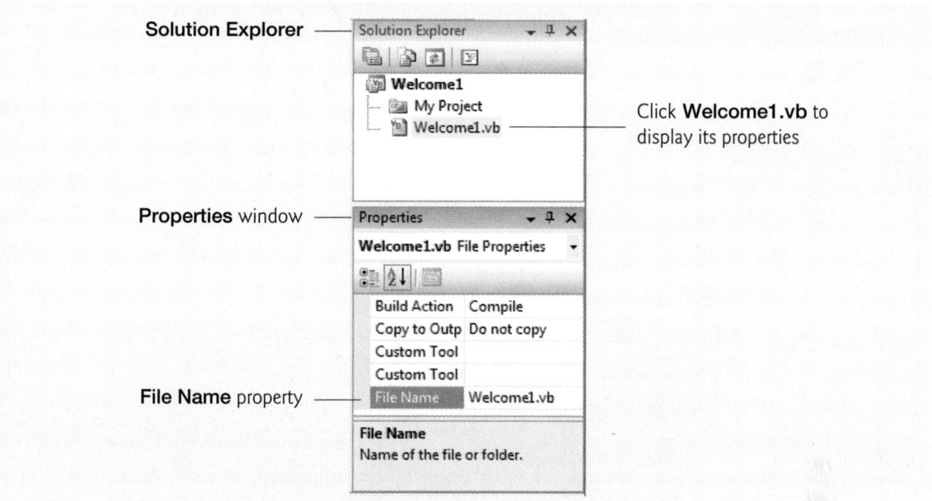

Fig. 3.6 | Renaming the program file in the **Properties** window.

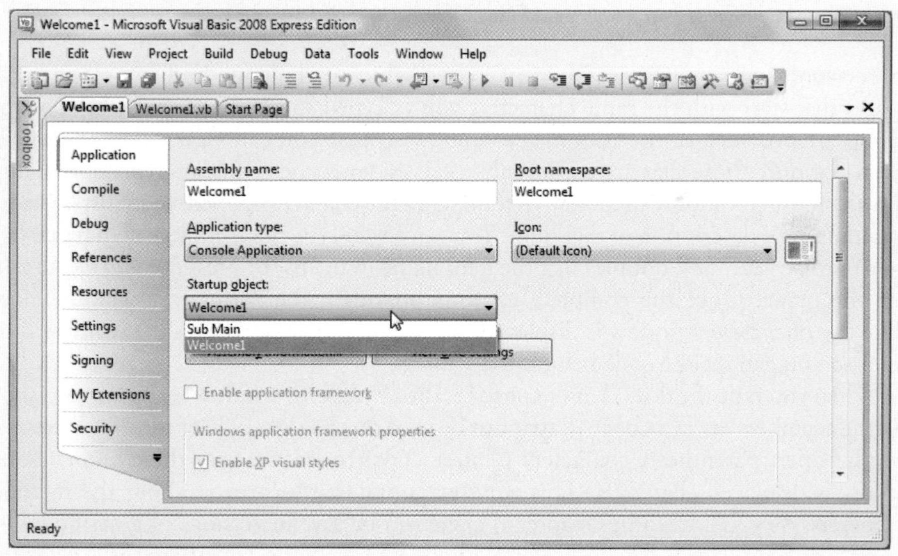

Fig. 3.7 | Setting the startup object.

Writing Code and Using IntelliSense

Click the **Welcome1.vb** tab in the IDE to view the editor window. In the editor window (Fig. 3.4), add the comments from lines 1 and 2 of Fig. 3.1. Then type the code contained in line 8 of Fig. 3.1 between the lines `Sub Main()` and `End Sub`. As you begin typing, a small window containing a scrollbar appears (Fig. 3.8). This IDE feature, called *IntelliSense*,

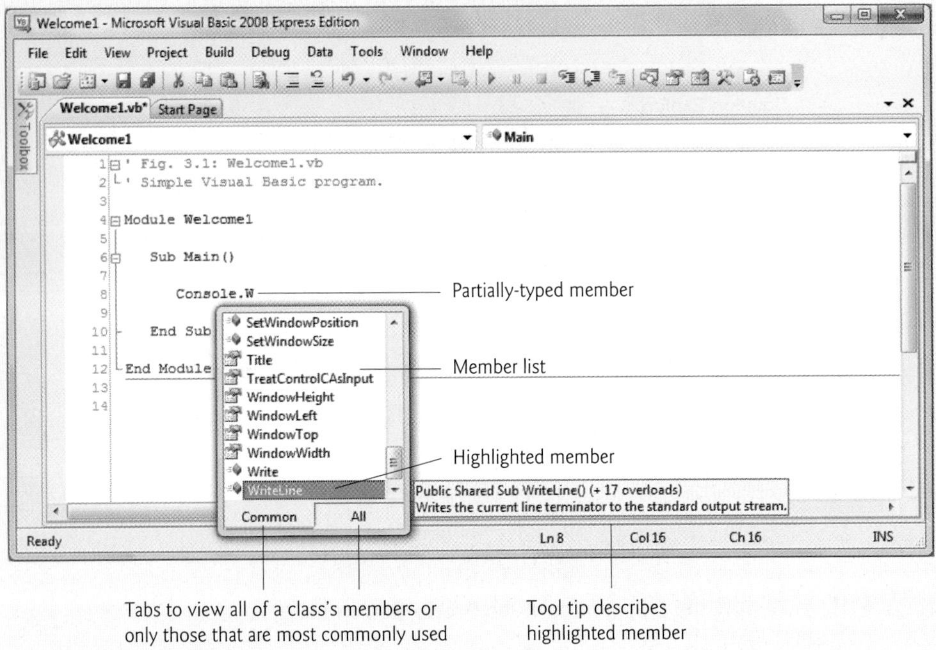

Fig. 3.8 | *IntelliSense* feature of Visual Basic Express.

lists keywords, class names, members of a class (which include method names) and other features that start with the same characters you've typed so far. Note that tabs (**Common** and **All**) are provided in the *IntelliSense* window so that you can view either all available matches or only those that are commonly used. As you type characters, *IntelliSense* highlights the most commonly used item that matches the characters typed, then displays a tool tip containing a description of that item. You can either type the complete item name (e.g., `Console` or `WriteLine`), double click the item name in the list or press the *Tab* key to complete the name. Once the complete name is provided, the *IntelliSense* window closes. While the *IntelliSense* window is displayed, pressing the *Ctrl* key makes the window transparent so you can see the code behind the window.

When you type the dot (`.`) after `Console`, the *IntelliSense* window reappears and shows only the members of class `Console` that can be used on the right side of the dot. When you type the open parenthesis character, `(`, after `Console.WriteLine`, the *Parameter Info* window is displayed (Fig. 3.9). This window contains information about the method's parameters. As you'll learn in Chapter 7, there can be several versions of a method. That is, a class or module can define several methods that have the same name as long as they have different numbers and/or types of parameters—a concept known as overloaded methods. These methods all perform similar tasks. The *Parameter Info* window indicates how many versions of the selected method are available and provides up and down arrows for scrolling through the different versions. For example, there are 18 versions of the `WriteLine` method—we use one of these 18 versions in our program. The *Parameter Info* window is one of the many features provided by the IDE that help you develop programs. In the next several chapters, you'll learn more about the information displayed in these

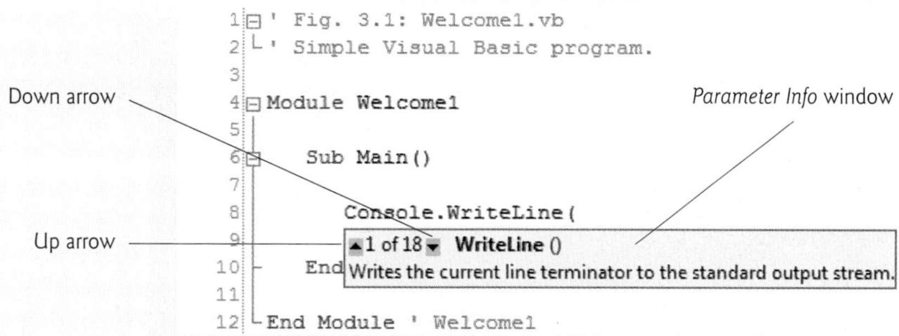

Fig. 3.9 | *Parameter Info* window.

windows. The *Parameter Info* window is especially helpful when you want to see the different ways in which a method can be used. From the code in Fig. 3.1, we already know that we intend to display a string with `WriteLine`, so you can simply close the *Parameter Info* window by pressing the *Esc* key. Finish entering line 8, as well as the comments in lines 10 and 12 of Fig. 3.1.

Saving the Program

Select **File > Save All** to display the **Save Project** dialog (Fig. 3.10). In the **Location** text box, specify the directory where you want to save this project. We choose to save the project in the `MyProjects` directory on the `C:` drive. Select the **Create directory for solution** check box, and click **Save**.

Fig. 3.10 | **Save Project** dialog.

Compiling and Running the Program

You are now ready to compile and execute your program. When you run a program, the IDE first compiles the program. This creates a new file (named `Welcome1.exe`, in the project's directory structure) that contains the Microsoft Intermediate Language (MSIL) code for the program. The **.exe file extension** indicates that the file is **executable**.

To execute this console application (i.e., `Welcome1.exe`), select **Debug > Start Debugging** (or press *F5*), which invokes the `Main` method. The statement in line 8 of `Main` displays `Welcome to Visual Basic!` however, the window appears, then disappears immediately. Figure 3.11 shows the results of the program's execution. To enable the window to remain on the screen so you can view the results, you can use the **Debug** menu's **Start Without Debugging** option (or type *Ctrl + F5*). This option is not in the menu by default, so you must add it. To do so, close any open projects, then select **Tools > Customize...**. In the **Commands** tab of the dialog that appears, select **Debug** from the **Catego-**

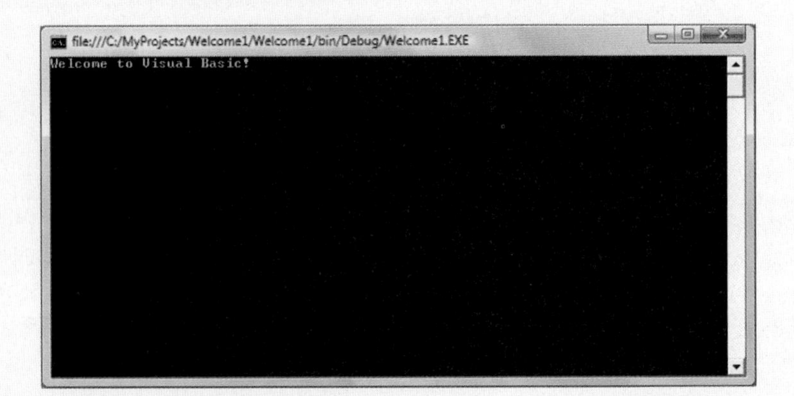

Fig. 3.11 | Executing the program shown in Fig. 3.1.

ries pane, then locate **Start Without Debugging** in the **Commands** pane. Drag the **Start Without Debugging** option over the **Debug** menu in the IDE (which will open the menu), then position the mouse just below the **Start / Continue** option and release the mouse button. Click **Close** to dismiss the **Customize** dialog. You can now execute the program using the select **Debug > Start Without Debugging** option. The window showing the results will remain on the screen until you press a key or click the window's close box. Leave the project open in the IDE, as you'll go back to it later in this section.

Running the Program from the **Command Prompt**

As we mentioned at the beginning of this chapter, you can execute applications outside the IDE in a **Command Prompt**. This is useful when you simply want to run an application rather than open it for modification. To open the **Command Prompt**, click the Windows **Start** button (), then select **All Programs > Accessories > Command Prompt**. The window (Fig. 3.12) displays Microsoft's copyright information followed by a prompt that indicates the current directory. By default, the prompt specifies the current user's directory on the local machine (in our case, `C:\Users\paul`; this would be `C:\Documents and Settings\paul` on Windows XP). On your machine, the folder name `paul` will be replaced with your username. A flashing cursor appears at the end of the prompt to indicate that

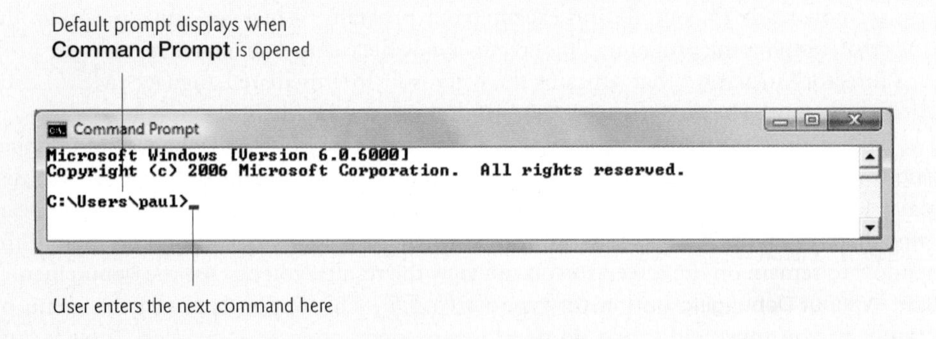

Fig. 3.12 | **Command Prompt** window.

the **Command Prompt** window is waiting for you to type a command. Enter the command `cd` (which stands for "change directory") followed by the directory where the application's `.exe` file is located (i.e., your application's `bin\Debug` or `bin\Release` directory). For example, the command `cd C:\MyProjects\Welcome1\Welcome1\bin\Debug` (Fig. 3.13) changes the current directory to the `Welcome1` application's `bin\Debug` directory. The next prompt displays the new directory followed by the flashing cursor. Now, you can run the compiled application by entering the name of the `.exe` file (i.e., `Welcome1.exe`) with or without the `.exe` extension. The application will run to completion, then the prompt will display again, awaiting your next command. To close the **Command Prompt**, type `exit` and press *Enter* or click the window's close box. [*Note:* **Command Prompt** windows normally have black backgrounds and white text. We adjusted these settings in our environment to make our screen captures more readable.]

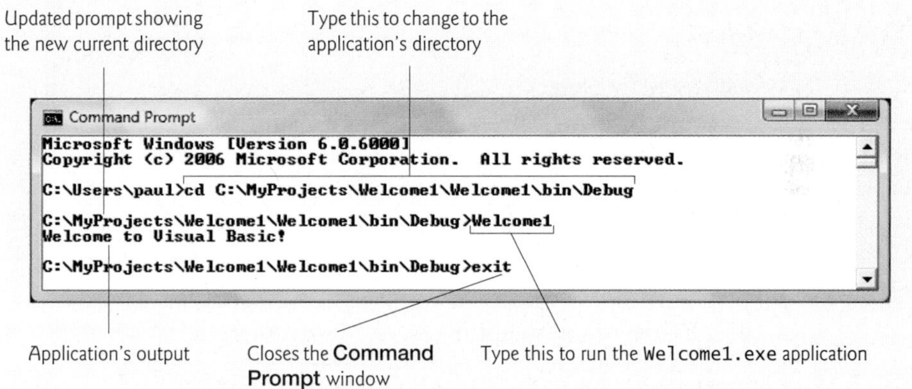

Fig. 3.13 | Executing the program shown in Fig. 3.1 from a **Command Prompt**.

Syntax Errors, Error Messages and the Error List *Window*

Go back to the application in Visual Basic Express. When you type a line of code and press the *Enter* key, the IDE responds either by applying syntax-color highlighting or by generating a syntax error, which indicates a violation of Visual Basic's rules for creating correct programs (i.e., one or more statements are not written correctly). Syntax errors occur for various reasons, such as missing parentheses and misspelled keywords. When a syntax error occurs, the IDE underlines the error in blue and provides a description of the error in the **Error List** window. If the **Error List** window is not visible in the IDE, select **View > Error List** to display it. In Fig. 3.14, we intentionally omitted the first parenthesis in line 8. The first error contains the text "**Method arguments must be enclosed in parentheses.**" and specifies that the error is in column 25 of line 8. This informs you that one or more parentheses are missing in line 8. The second error—"**End of statement expected.**"—specifies that this error is in column 51 of line 8. This error message appears when the compiler thinks that the line contains a complete statement, followed by the beginning of another statement. Visual Basic allows only one statement per line. Although we are attempting to include only one statement in line 8, the missing parenthesis causes the compiler to incorrectly assume that there is more than one statement on that line. You can double click an error message in the **Error List** to jump to the line of code that caused the error.

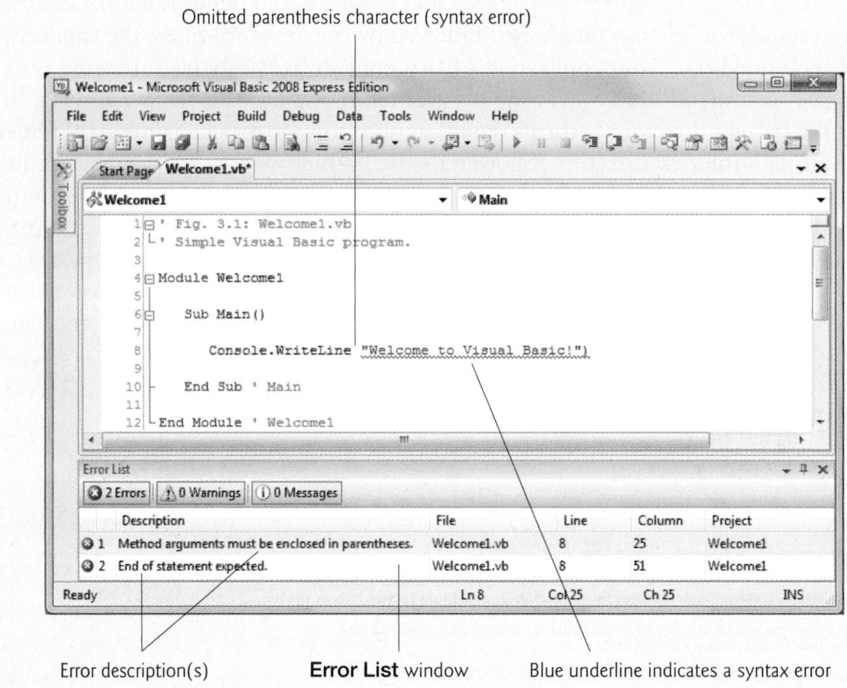

Fig. 3.14 | Syntax error indicated by the IDE.

Error-Prevention Tip 3.1

One syntax error can lead to multiple entries in the **Error List** *window. Each error that you address could eliminate several subsequent error messages. So, when you see a particular error you know how to fix, correct it—this may make the other errors disappear.*

3.4 Displaying a Single Line of Text with Multiple Statements

The message `Welcome to Visual Basic!` can be displayed using multiple statements. Figure 3.15 uses two method calls to produce the same output as the program in Fig. 3.1. Follow the steps in Section 3.3 to create a new console application. You can close the preceding application by selecting **File > Close Project**.

Lines 8–9 of Fig. 3.15 display only one line of text in the **Console** window. The first statement calls `Console` method `Write` to display a string. Unlike `WriteLine`, `Write` does not position the output cursor at the beginning of the next line in the **Console** window after displaying its string. Instead, the next character displayed in the **Console** window appears immediately to the right of the last character displayed with `Write`. Thus, when line 9 executes, the first character displayed ("V") appears immediately after the last character displayed with `Write` (i.e., the space character after the word `"to"` in line 8). Each `Write` or `WriteLine` outputs its characters at the exact location where the previous `Write`'s or `WriteLine`'s output ended.

```
' Fig. 3.15: Welcome2.vb
' Displaying a line of text with multiple statements.

Module Welcome2

   Sub Main()

      Console.Write("Welcome to ")
      Console.WriteLine("Visual Basic!")

   End Sub ' Main

End Module ' Welcome2
```

```
Welcome to Visual Basic!
```

Fig. 3.15 | Displaying a line of text with multiple statements.

3.5 Adding Integers

Our next program (Fig. 3.16) inputs two integers (whole numbers) entered at the keyboard by a user, computes the sum of these integers and displays the result. As the user enters each integer and presses the *Enter* key, the integer is read into the program and added to the total. Follow the steps in Section 3.3 to create a new console application. You can close the preceding application by selecting **File > Close Project**.

Lines 9–11 are declarations, which begin with keyword `Dim` (a contraction of "dimension"). The words `number1`, `number2` and `total` are identifiers for variables—locations in the computer's memory where values can be stored for use by a program. All variables must be declared before they can be used in a program. The declarations in lines 9–11 specify that the variables `number1`, `number2` and `total` are data of type `Integer`; that is, these variables store integer values (i.e., whole numbers such as 919, –11, 0 and 138624). Types already defined in Visual Basic, such as `Integer`, are known as primitive types. Primitive type names are keywords. The 15 primitive types are listed in Fig. 3.17 and discussed further in Chapter 7.

```
1  ' Fig. 3.16: Addition.vb
2  ' Addition program.
3
4  Module Addition
5
6     Sub Main()
7
8        ' variables used in the addition calculation
9        Dim number1 As Integer
10       Dim number2 As Integer
11       Dim total As Integer
12
```

Fig. 3.16 | Addition program that adds two integers entered by the user. (Part 1 of 2.)

```
        ' prompt for and read the first number from the user
        Console.Write("Please enter the first integer: ")
        number1 = Console.ReadLine()

        ' prompt for and read the second number from the user
        Console.Write("Please enter the second integer: ")
        number2 = Console.ReadLine()

        total = number1 + number2 ' add the numbers

        Console.WriteLine("The sum is " & total) ' display the sum

    End Sub ' Main

End Module ' Addition
```

```
Please enter the first integer: 45
Please enter the second integer: 72
The sum is 117
```

Fig. 3.16 | Addition program that adds two integers entered by the user. (Part 2 of 2.)

Primitive types				
`Boolean`	`Byte`	`Char`	`Date`	`Decimal`
`Double`	`Integer`	`Long`	`SByte`	`Short`
`Single`	`String`	`UInteger`	`ULong`	`UShort`

Fig. 3.17 | Primitive types in Visual Basic.

A variable name can be any valid identifier. Variables of the same type can be declared in separate statements or they can be declared in one statement with each variable in the declaration separated by a comma. The latter format uses a comma-separated list of variable names.

Good Programming Practice 3.3

Choosing meaningful variable names helps a program to be "self-documenting"—the program can be understood by others without the use of documentation manuals or excessive comments.

Good Programming Practice 3.4

A common convention (and the one used in this book) is to have the first word in a variable-name identifier begin with a lowercase letter. Every word in the name after the first word should begin with an uppercase letter—this is known as camel case. For example, identifier `firstNumber` *has a capital* `N` *beginning its second word,* `Number`*. We use a similar convention for module names, except that the first letter of the first word is also capitalized—this is known as Pascal case. Although identifiers are not case sensitive, using these conventions helps make your programs more readable. In this book, we use widely adopted Visual Basic naming conventions.*

Good Programming Practice 3.5

Declaring each variable on a separate line allows for easy insertion of an end-of-line comment next to each declaration. We follow this convention.

Line 14 prompts the user to enter the first of two integers that will be summed. Line 15 obtains the value entered by the user and assigns it to variable `number1`. The statement in line 14 is called a **prompt**, because it directs the user to take a specific action. The method **`ReadLine`** (line 15) causes the program to pause and wait for user input. After entering the integer via the keyboard, the user presses the *Enter* key to send the integer to the program.

Once the user has entered a number and pressed *Enter*, the number is assigned to variable `number1` (line 15) by an **assignment**, **`=`**. The statement is read as, "`number1` *gets* the value returned by method `ReadLine` of the `Console` class." We call the entire statement an **assignment statement** because it assigns a value to a variable. Lines 18–19 prompt the user to enter a second integer and assign the entered value to `number2`.

Technically, the user can send any character to the program as input. For this program, if the user types a noninteger value, such as `"hello,"` a **runtime error** (an error that has its effect at execution time) occurs. The message displayed in Fig. 3.18 appears if you ran the application using **Debug > Start Debugging** (or pressed *F5*). Otherwise, Windows will display an error-message dialog indicating that the program stopped working. In this case, you can stop debugging by selecting **Debug > Stop Debugging** or typing *Ctrl* + *Alt* + *Break*. Chapter 13, Exception Handling, discusses how to handle such errors to make programs more robust—that is, able to handle runtime errors and continue executing.

The assignment statement in line 21 (Fig. 3.16) calculates the sum of the `Integer` variables `number1` and `number2` and assigns the result to variable `total`. The statement is read as, "`total` *gets* the value of `number1 + number2`." Most calculations are performed in assignment statements.

Line 23 displays the total of the two values. The argument to method `WriteLine`

```
"The sum is " & total
```

uses the **string concatenation operator**, **`&`**, to combine the string literal `"The sum is "` and the value of the variable `total` (the `Integer` variable containing the sum calculated in line

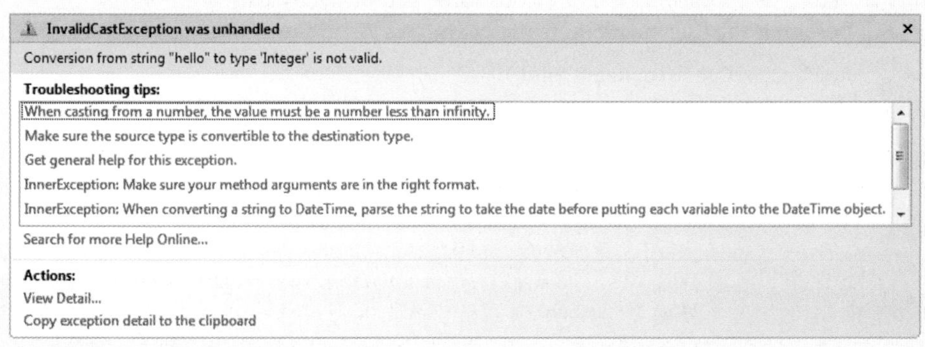

Fig. 3.18 | Dialog displaying a runtime error.

21). The string concatenation operator is called a binary operator, because it has two operands—"The sum is" and total. The string concatenation operator is used to combine two strings (i.e., to join them together). This operation results in a new, longer string. If an operand given to the string concatenation operator is a number (e.g., an integer), the program automatically creates a string representation of the number.

Good Programming Practice 3.6

The Visual Basic IDE places a space on either side of a binary operator, such as the addition operator, to make the operator stand out and improve the readability of the statement. You should also follow this convention when programming in other languages.

When reading or writing a program, you may find it difficult to match End Sub statements with their method declarations. For this reason, you may want to include an end-of-line comment after End Sub (indicating which method is ending), as we do in line 25. This practice is especially helpful when modules contain multiple methods. Although, for now, our modules contain only one method, we place the comment after End Sub as a *Good Programming Practice*.

Good Programming Practice 3.7

Follow a method's End Sub *with an end-of-line comment containing the name of the method that the* End Sub *terminates.*

3.6 Memory Concepts

Variable names, such as number1, number2 and total, correspond to locations in the computer's memory. Every variable has a name, type, size and value. In the addition program of Fig. 3.16, when the statement (line 15)

```
number1 = Console.ReadLine()
```

executes, the data input by the user in the **Console** window is placed into a memory location to which the name number1 has been assigned by the compiler. Suppose the user enters the characters 45 and presses *Enter*. This input is returned by ReadLine and assigned to number1. The program places the Integer value 45 into location number1, as shown in Fig. 3.19.

Whenever a value is placed in a memory location, this value replaces the value previously stored in that location. The previous value is destroyed (lost).

Suppose that the user then enters the characters 72 and presses *Enter*. Line 19

```
number2 = Console.ReadLine()
```

places the Integer value 72 into location number2, and memory appears, as shown in Fig. 3.20.

Once the program has obtained values for number1 and number2, it adds these values and places their total into variable total. The statement (line 21)

number1	45

Fig. 3.19 | Memory location showing name the and value of variable number1.

number1	45
number2	72

Fig. 3.20 | Memory locations after values for variables `number1` and `number2` have been input.

```
total = number1 + number2
```

performs the addition and replaces (i.e., destroys) `total`'s previous value. After `total` is calculated, memory appears, as shown in Fig. 3.21. Note that the values of `number1` and `number2` appear exactly as they did before they were used in the calculation of `total`. Although these values were used when the computer performed the calculation, they were not destroyed. As this illustrates, when a value is read from a memory location, the process is nondestructive.

number1	45
number2	72
total	117

Fig. 3.21 | Memory locations after an addition operation.

3.7 Arithmetic

Most programs perform arithmetic calculations. The arithmetic operators are summarized in Fig. 3.22. Note the use of various special symbols not used in algebra. For example, the asterisk (*) indicates multiplication, and the keyword `Mod` represents the `Mod` operator (also known as the modulus or modulo operator), which will be discussed shortly. Most of the arithmetic operators in Fig. 3.22 are binary operators, because each operates on two operands. For example, the expression `sum + value` contains the binary operator + and the two operands `sum` and `value`. Visual Basic also provides unary operators that take only one operand. For example, unary versions of plus (+) and minus (-) are provided, so that you can write expressions such as `+9` and `-19`.

Division Operators

Visual Basic has separate operators for integer division (the backslash, \) and floating-point division (the forward slash, /). Integer division takes two `Integer` operands and yields an `Integer` result; for example, the expression `7 \ 4` evaluates to `1`, and the expression `17 \ 5` evaluates to `3`. Any fractional part in an `Integer` division result simply is truncated (i.e., discarded)—no rounding occurs. When floating-point numbers (i.e., numbers that contain a decimal point, such as 2.3456 and –845.7840) are used with the integer division operator, the numbers are first rounded to the nearest whole number, then

Visual Basic operation	Arithmetic operator	Algebraic expression	Visual Basic expression
Addition	+	$f + 7$	`f + 7`
Subtraction	–	$p - c$	`p - c`
Multiplication	*	bm	`b * m`
Division (floating point)	/	x / y or $\frac{x}{y}$ or $x \div y$	`x / y`
Division (integer)	\	none	`v \ u`
Modulus	`Mod`	$r \bmod s$	`r Mod s`
Exponentiation	^	q^p	`q ^ p`
Unary minus	-	$-e$	`-e`
Unary plus	+	$+g$	`+g`

Fig. 3.22 | Arithmetic operators.

divided. This means that, although `7.1 \ 4` evaluates to `1` as expected, the statement `7.7 \ 4` evaluates to `2`, because `7.7` is rounded to `8` before the division occurs. To divide floating-point numbers without rounding the operands (which is normally what you want to do), use the floating-point division operator.

Common Programming Error 3.2

Using the integer division operator (\) when the floating-point division operator (/) is expected (i.e., when one or both of the operands is a floating-point value) can lead to incorrect results.

Error-Prevention Tip 3.2

Ensure that each integer division operator has only integer operands.

`Mod` *Operator*

The `Mod` operator yields the remainder after division. The expression `x Mod y` yields the remainder after `x` is divided by `y`. Thus, `7 Mod 4` yields `3`, and `17 Mod 5` yields `2`. You use this operator mostly with `Integer` operands, but it also can be used with other types. In later chapters, we consider interesting applications of the `Mod` operator, such as determining whether one number is a multiple of another.

Arithmetic Expressions in Straight-Line Form

Arithmetic expressions in Visual Basic must be entered into the computer in straight-line form. Thus, expressions such as "a divided by b" must be written as `a / b`, so that all constants, variables and operators appear in a straight line. The algebraic notation

$$\frac{a}{b}$$

is generally not acceptable to compilers, although some special-purpose software packages do exist that support more natural notation for complex mathematical expressions.

Parentheses for Grouping Subexpressions

Parentheses are used in Visual Basic expressions in the same manner as in algebraic expressions. For example, to multiply a times the quantity `b + c`, we write `a * ( b + c )`.

Rules of Operator Precedence

Visual Basic applies the operators in arithmetic expressions in a precise sequence determined by the rules of operator precedence (Fig. 3.23), which are similar to those in algebra. Operators in the same row of the table are said to have the same level of precedence. When we say operators are evaluated from left to right, we are referring to the operators' associativity. All binary operators in Visual Basic associate from left to right. If there are multiple operators, each with the same precedence, the order in which the operators are applied is determined by the operators' associativity. We'll expand Fig. 3.23 as we introduce additional operators in subsequent chapters.

Operators in expressions contained within a pair of parentheses are evaluated before those that are outside a pair of parentheses. Parentheses can be used to group expressions and change the order of evaluation to occur *in any sequence you desire*. With nested parentheses, the operators contained in the innermost pair of parentheses are applied first.

Not all expressions with several pairs of parentheses contain nested parentheses. For example, although the expression

```
a * ( b + c ) + c * ( d + e )
```

contains multiple sets of parentheses, none are nested. Rather, these sets are said to be "on the same level." Appendix A contains a complete operator-precedence chart.

Operator(s)	Operation	Order of evaluation (precedence)
^	Exponentiation	Evaluated first. If there are several such operators, they are evaluated from left to right.
+, -	Sign operations	Evaluated second. If there are several such operators, they are evaluated from left to right.
*, /	Multiplication and Division	Evaluated third. If there are several such operators, they are evaluated from left to right.
\	Integer division	Evaluated fourth. If there are several such operators, they are evaluated from left to right.
Mod	Modulus	Evaluated fifth. If there are several such operators, they are evaluated from left to right.
+, -	Addition and Subtraction	Evaluated sixth. If there are several such operators, they are evaluated from left to right.

Fig. 3.23 | Precedence of arithmetic operators.

Sample Algebraic and Visual Basic Expressions

Now consider several expressions in light of the rules of operator precedence. Each example lists an algebraic expression and its Visual Basic equivalent. The following is an example of an arithmetic mean (average) of five terms:

Algebra: $m = \frac{a + b + c + d + e}{5}$

Visual Basic: `m = ( a + b + c + d + e ) / 5`

The parentheses are required, because floating-point division has higher precedence than addition. The entire quantity `( a + b + c + d + e )` is to be divided by `5`. If the parentheses are erroneously omitted, we obtain `a + b + c + d + e / 5`, which evaluates as

$$a + b + c + d + \frac{e}{5}$$

The following is the equation of a straight line:

Algebra: $y = mx + b$

Visual Basic: `y = m * x + b`

No parentheses are required. The multiplication is applied first, because multiplication has a higher precedence than addition.

The following example contains modulus (`Mod`), multiplication, division, addition and subtraction operations (we use the text "mod" to represent modulus in algebra):

Algebra: $z = pr \bmod q + w/x - y$

Visual Basic:

```
z = p * r Mod q + w / x - y
      1   3     4   2   5
```

The circled numbers under the statement indicate the order in which Visual Basic applies the operators. The multiplication and division operators are evaluated first in left-to-right order (i.e., they associate from left to right). The `Mod` operator is evaluated next. The addition and subtraction operators are applied next, from left to right.

Evaluation of a Second-Degree Polynomial

To develop a better understanding of the rules of operator precedence, consider how the second-degree polynomial $y = ax^2 + bx + c$ is evaluated:

```
y = a * x ^ 2 + b * x + c
      2   1   4   3   5
```

The circled numbers under the statement indicate the order in which Visual Basic applies the operators. In Visual Basic, x^2 is represented as `x ^ 2`.

Now, suppose that `a`, `b`, `c` and `x` in the preceding expression are initialized as follows: `a = 2`, `b = 3`, `c = 7` and `x = 5`. Figure 3.24 illustrates the order in which the operators are applied.

As in algebra, it is acceptable to place unnecessary parentheses in an expression to make the expression clearer—these are called redundant parentheses. For example, many people might parenthesize the preceding assignment statement for clarity as

```
y = ( a * x ^ 2 ) + ( b * x ) + c
```

```
Step 1.   y = 2 * 5 ^ 2 + 3 * 5 + 7      (Exponentiation first)
                  5 ^ 2 is 25

Step 2.   y = 2 * 25 + 3 * 5 + 7         (Leftmost multiplication)
              2 * 25 is 50

Step 3.   y = 50 + 3 * 5 + 7             (Multiplication before addition)
                   3 * 5 is 15

Step 4.   y = 50 + 15 + 7                (Leftmost addition)
              50 + 15 is 65

Step 5.   y = 65 + 7                     (Last addition)
              65 + 7 is 72

Step 6.   y = 72                         (Last operation—place 72 in y)
```

Fig. 3.24 | Order in which a second-degree polynomial is evaluated.

Good Programming Practice 3.8

Redundant parentheses can make complex expressions easier to read.

Error-Prevention Tip 3.3

When you are uncertain about the order of evaluation in a complex expression, use parentheses to force the order, as you would in an algebraic expression. Doing so can help avoid subtle bugs.

3.8 Decision Making: Equality and Relational Operators

This section introduces Visual Basic's `If...Then` statement, which allows a program to make a decision based on the truth or falsity of some expression. The expression in an `If...Then` statement is called a **condition**. If the condition is met (i.e., the condition is true), the statement in the `If...Then` statement's body executes. If the condition is not met (i.e., the condition is false), the body statement is not executed. Conditions in `If...Then` statements can be formed by using the **equality operators** and **relational operators** (also called **comparison operators**), which are summarized in Fig. 3.25. The relational and equality operators all have the same level of precedence and associate from left to right.

Common Programming Error 3.3

It is a syntax error to reverse the symbols in the operators <>, >= and <= (as in ><, =>, =<). The Visual Basic IDE fixes these errors as you type.

The next example uses six `If...Then` statements to compare two numbers entered into a program by the user. If the condition in any of these statements is true, the output state-

Standard algebraic equality operator or relational operator	Visual Basic equality or relational operator	Example of Visual Basic condition	Meaning of Visual Basic condition
Equality operators			
=	=	`x = y`	x is equal to y
≠	<>	`x <> y`	x is not equal to y
Relational operators			
>	>	`x > y`	x is greater than y
<	<	`x < y`	x is less than y
≥	>=	`x >= y`	x is greater than or equal to y
≤	<=	`x <= y`	x is less than or equal to y

Fig. 3.25 | Equality and relational operators.

ment associated with that `If...Then` executes. The user enters these values, which are stored in variables `number1` and `number2`, respectively. The comparisons are performed, and the results of the comparison are displayed in the **Console** window. The program and outputs are shown in Fig. 3.26.

```
' Fig. 3.26: Comparison.vb
' Using equality and relational operators.

Module Comparison

   Sub Main()

      ' declare Integer variables for user input
      Dim number1 As Integer
      Dim number2 As Integer

      ' read first number from user
      Console.Write("Please enter first integer: ")
      number1 = Console.ReadLine()

      ' read second number from user
      Console.Write("Please enter second integer: ")
      number2 = Console.ReadLine()

      If number1 = number2 Then ' number1 is equal to number2
         Console.WriteLine(number1 & " = " & number2)
      End If

      If number1 <> number2 Then ' number1 is not equal to number2
         Console.WriteLine(number1 & " <> " & number2)
      End If
```

Fig. 3.26 | Performing comparisons with equality and relational operators. (Part 1 of 2.)

```
27
28          If number1 < number2 Then ' number1 is less than number2
29             Console.WriteLine(number1 & " < " & number2)
30          End If
31
32          If number1 > number2 Then ' number1 is greater than number2
33             Console.WriteLine(number1 & " > " & number2)
34          End If
35
36          ' number1 is less than or equal to number2
37          If number1 <= number2 Then
38             Console.WriteLine(number1 & " <= " & number2)
39          End If
40
41          ' number1 is greater than or equal to number2
42          If number1 >= number2 Then
43             Console.WriteLine(number1 & " >= " & number2)
44          End If
45
46       End Sub ' Main
47
48    End Module ' Comparison
```

```
Please enter first integer: 1000
Please enter second integer: 2000
1000 <> 2000
1000 < 2000
1000 <= 2000
```

```
Please enter first integer: 515
Please enter second integer: 49
515 <> 49
515 > 49
515 >= 49
```

```
Please enter first integer: 333
Please enter second integer: 333
333 = 333
333 <= 333
333 >= 333
```

Fig. 3.26 | Performing comparisons with equality and relational operators. (Part 2 of 2.)

Lines 9–10 declare the variables that are used in method `Main`. The comment that precedes the declarations indicates the purpose of the variables in the program. Lines 14 and 18 retrieve inputs from the user and assign the values to `Integer` variables `number1` and `number2`, respectively.

The `If...Then` statement in lines 20–22 compares the values of the variables `number1` and `number2` for equality. If the values are equal, the statement in line 21 outputs a string indicating that the two numbers are equal. Note that assignment and the equality operator both use the = symbol. When a condition is expected (such as after the `If` keyword in an `If...Else` statement), the = is used as an equality operator.

If `number1` contains the value `333` and `number2` contains the value `333`, the expression in line 21 evaluates as follows: `number1` is converted to a string and concatenated with the string `" = "`, then `number2` is converted to a string and concatenated with the resulting string from the first concatenation. At this point, the string `"333 = 333"` is displayed by `WriteLine`. As the program proceeds through the remaining `If...Then` statements (lines 24–44), additional strings are output by the `WriteLine` statements. For example, when given the value `333` for `number1` and `number2`, the conditions in lines 37 and 42 also are true. Thus, the output displayed (in the third output of Fig. 3.26) is:

```
333 = 333
333 <= 333
333 >= 333
```

Notice the indentation of the body statements within the `If...Then` statements throughout the program. Such indentation enhances program readability.

Good Programming Practice 3.9

Visual Basic indents the statements in the body of an `If...Then` *statement to emphasize the body statements and enhance program readability. You should also follow this convention when programming in other languages.*

Figure 3.27 shows the precedence of the operators introduced in this chapter. The operators are displayed from top to bottom in decreasing order of precedence.

Operators	Type
`^`	exponentiation
`+ -`	sign operations (unary)
`* /`	multiplication and floating-point division
`\`	`Integer` division
`Mod`	modulus
`+ -`	addition and subtraction (binary)
`= <> < <= > >=`	equality and relational

Fig. 3.27 | Precedence of the operators introduced in this chapter.

3.9 Using a Message Dialog to Display a Message

The programs discussed thus far display output in the **Console** window. Visual Basic programs often use message dialogs to display output. Message dialogs are windows that display messages to the user. Visual Basic provides class `MessageBox` for creating message dialogs. We use a message dialog in Fig. 3.28 to display the square root of 2. For this program to compile and execute, you must perform several steps discussed later in this section. Be sure to read the entire section as you create this example.

```
1  ' Fig. 3.28: SquareRoot.vb
2  ' Displaying the square root of 2 in a dialog.
3
4  Imports System.Windows.Forms ' Namespace containing class MessageBox
5
6  Module SquareRoot
7
8     Sub Main()
9
10       Dim root As Double = Math.Sqrt(2) ' calculate the square root of 2
11
12       ' display the results in a message dialog
13       MessageBox.Show("The square root of 2 is " & root, _
14          "The Square Root of 2")
15
16    End Sub ' Main
17
18 End Module ' SquareRoot
```

Fig. 3.28 | Displaying text in a message dialog.

Note that in the output for Fig. 3.28, the square root of 2 is displayed with many digits to the right of the decimal point. In many applications, you won't need such precise output. In the next chapter, we demonstrate how to display only a few digits to the right of the decimal point.

Displaying a `MessageBox`

Figure 3.28 presents a program that creates a simple GUI (i.e., the message dialog). The .NET Framework Class Library contains a rich collection of classes that can be used to construct GUIs. Framework Class Library classes are grouped by functionality into namespaces, which make it easier for you to find the classes needed to perform particular tasks. Line 4 is an `Imports` statement indicating that we are using the features provided by the namespace `System.Windows.Forms`, which contains windows-related classes (i.e., forms and dialogs). We discuss this namespace in more detail after we discuss the code in this example.

Line 10 calls the `Sqrt` method of the `Math` class to compute the square root of 2. The value returned is a floating-point number, so we declare the variable `root` as type `Double`. Variables of type `Double` can store floating-point numbers. We declare and initialize `root` in a single statement.

Note the use of spacing in lines 13–14 of Fig. 3.28. To improve readability, long statements may be split over several lines using the line-continuation character, _ . Line 13 uses the line-continuation character to indicate that line 14 is a continuation of the preceding line. A single statement can contain as many line-continuation characters as necessary. At least one whitespace character must precede each line-continuation character.

Common Programming Error 3.4

Splitting a statement over several lines without including the line-continuation character is usually a syntax error.

Common Programming Error 3.5

Failure to precede the line-continuation character (_) with at least one whitespace character is a syntax error.

Common Programming Error 3.6

Placing anything, including comments, on the same line after a line-continuation character is a syntax error.

Common Programming Error 3.7

Splitting a statement in the middle of an identifier or string is a syntax error.

Good Programming Practice 3.10

If a single statement must be split across lines, choose breaking points that make sense, such as after a comma in a comma-separated list or after an operator in a lengthy expression. If a statement is split across two or more lines, indent all subsequent lines with one level of indentation.

Lines 13–14 (Fig. 3.28) call method **Show** of class `MessageBox`. This method takes a comma-separated argument list. The first argument is the string that is displayed in the message dialog. The second argument is the string that is displayed in the message dialog's title bar.

Good Programming Practice 3.11

Visual Basic places a space after each comma in a method's argument list to make method calls more readable. You should also follow this convention when programming in other languages.

Analyzing the `MessageBox`

When executed, lines 13–14 (Fig. 3.28) display the message dialog shown in Fig. 3.29. The message dialog includes an **OK** button that allows the user to **dismiss** (i.e., **close**) the message dialog by clicking the button. The program waits for the dialog to be closed before executing the next line of code. This type of dialog is known as a modal dialog. After you

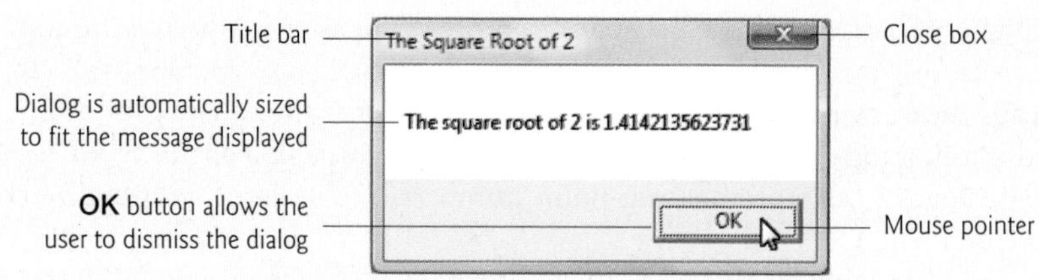

Fig. 3.29 | Message dialog displayed by calling `MessageBox.Show`.

dismiss the message dialog, the program reaches the end of `Main` and terminates. You can also dismiss the message dialog by clicking the dialog's close box—the button with an **X** in the dialog's upper-right corner. You'll see various dialogs throughout this book, some with more buttons than the **OK** button and the close box. In Chapter 14, Graphical User Interfaces with Windows Forms, you'll learn how to determine which button was pressed and have your application respond accordingly. For instance, you can have one action occur when the user clicks the **OK** button and a different action occur when the user clicks the close box. By default, these buttons simply dismiss the dialog.

If you create this example and enter the code in Fig. 3.28, you'll notice that line 13 gives you the error **Name 'MessageBox' is not declared.** Some classes provided by Visual Basic (such as `MessageBox`) must be added to the project before they can be used in a program. These compiled classes are located in a file, called an assembly, that has a `.dll` (dynamic link library) file extension. Information about the assembly our program must reference so that it can use class `MessageBox` can be found in the Visual Basic Express documentation—also called the MSDN (Microsoft Developer Network) Documentation. To locate this information, select **Help > Index**. This displays the Visual Basic Express documentation in a separate window that contains an **Index** (Fig. 3.30).

Type the class name `MessageBox` in the **Look for:** box, and select the appropriate filter, which narrows the search to a subset of the documentation—we selected **.NET Framework** in Fig. 3.30 so that we can see all the classes in the framework. Next, click the **about MessageBox class** link (Fig. 3.30) to display documentation for the `MessageBox` class (Fig. 3.31). The documentation lists the assembly that contains the class. Class `MessageBox` is located in assembly `System.Windows.Forms.dll`.

Adding a Reference to an Assembly

We must add a reference to this assembly if we wish to use class `MessageBox` in our program. Visual Basic 2008 Express provides a simple process for adding a reference. To see which assemblies are currently referenced in a project, you need to view the project's **References** folder. To do this, click the **Show All Files** button of the **Solution Explorer** (Fig. 3.32), which displays any of the project's files that are normally hidden by the IDE. If you expand the **References** folder (i.e., click the **+** to the left of the folder name), you'll see that **System.Windows.Forms** is not listed. It *is* listed in Fig. 3.33(c), which we'll discuss shortly.

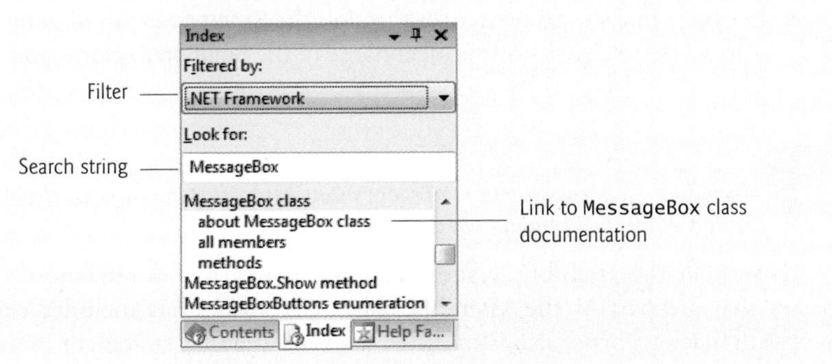

Fig. 3.30 | Obtaining documentation for a class by using the **Index** dialog.

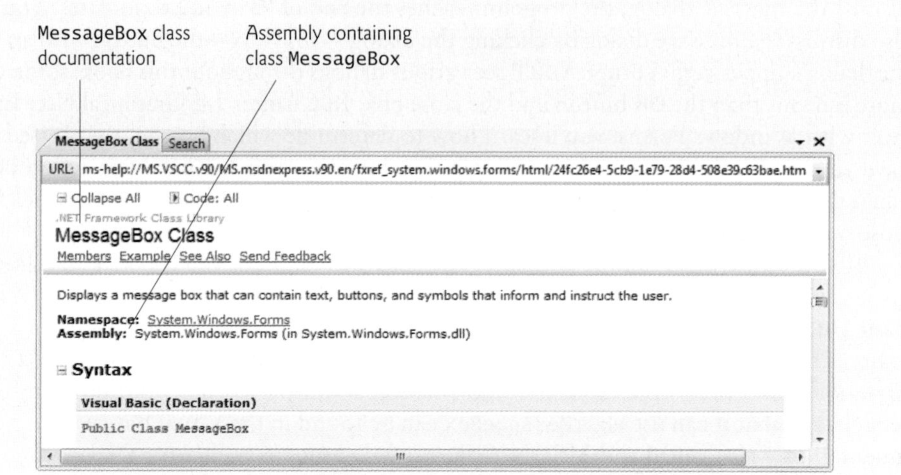

Fig. 3.31 | Documentation for the `MessageBox` class.

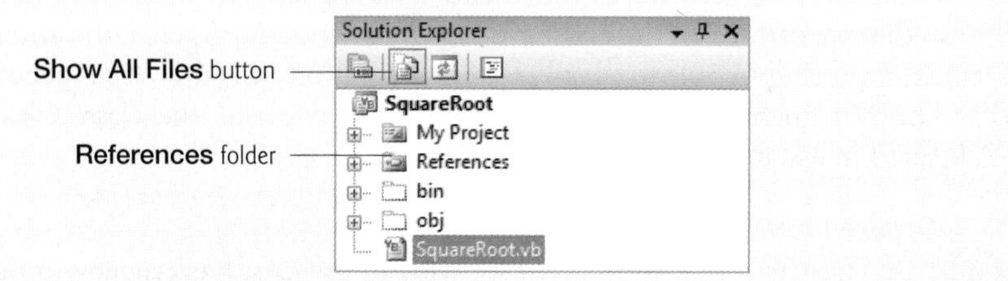

Fig. 3.32 | Viewing a project's references.

To add a reference to an existing project, select **Project > Add Reference...** or right click the **References** folder and select **Add Reference...** to display the **Add Reference dialog** (Fig. 3.33(a)). Scroll through the list of DLLs in the **.NET** tab and click `System.Windows.Forms.dll` to add it to the **References** folder, then click **OK**. Note that **System.Windows.Forms** was not originally listed in the **References** folder (Fig. 3.33(b)), but after we add the reference using the **Add Reference** dialog, it *is* listed (Fig. 3.33(c)). Note that you can also add references through the **References** tab of your projects properties. To do so, double click your project name in the **Solution Explorer** go to the **References** tab.

Common Programming Error 3.8

Including a namespace with the `Imports` statement without adding a reference to the proper assembly results in a compilation error.

Now that the assembly `System.Windows.Forms.dll` is referenced, we can use the classes that are part of the assembly. The namespace that includes class `MessageBox`, `System.Windows.Forms`, also is specified with the `Imports` statement in line 4 of our code (Fig. 3.28). The `Imports` statement is not added to the program by Visual Basic 2008 Express; you must add this line to your code.

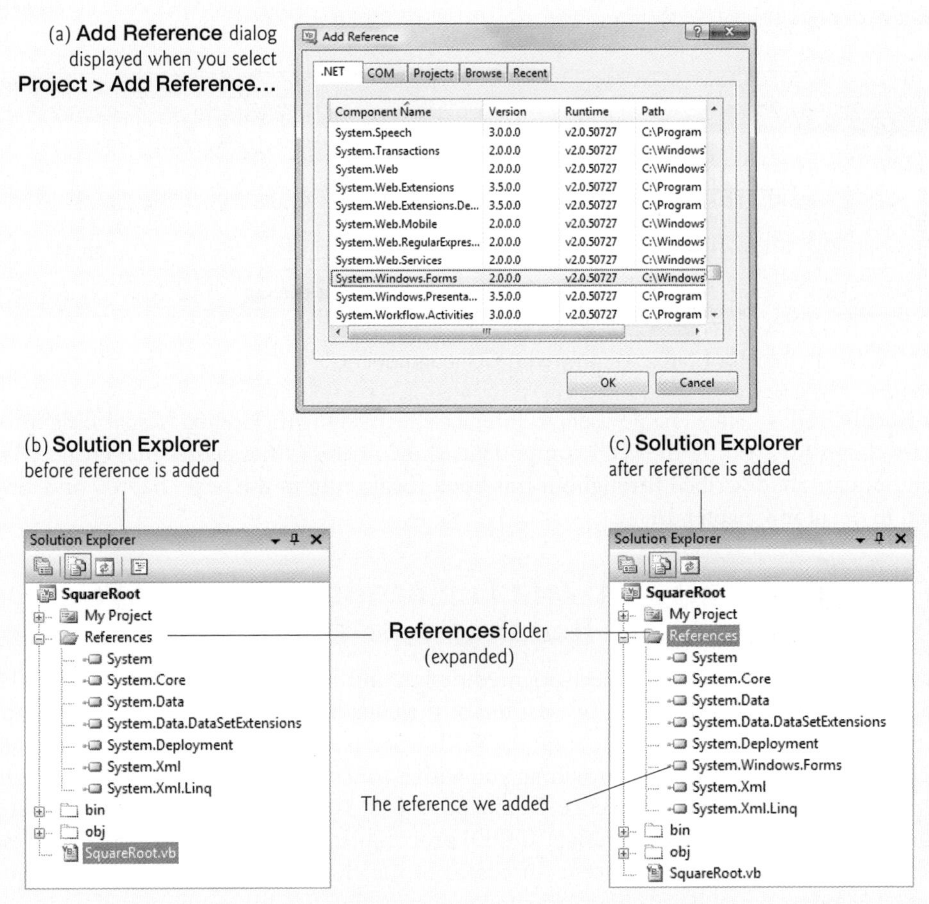

Fig. 3.33 | Adding an assembly reference to a project in the Visual Basic 2008 Express IDE.

We did not have to add references to any of our previous programs, because Visual Basic 2008 Express adds references to some assemblies when the project is created. The references added depend on the project type that you select in the **New Project** dialog. In addition, some assemblies do not need to be referenced. For example, class `Console` is located in the assembly `mscorlib.dll`, but we did not need to reference this assembly explicitly to use it—the IDE does this for us.

GUI Components and the `System.Windows.Forms` *Namespace*

The `System.Windows.Forms` namespace contains many classes that help you define graphical user interfaces (GUIs) for your applications. GUI components (such as `Buttons`) facilitate both data entry by the user and presentation of data outputs to the user. For example, Fig. 3.34 is a Mozilla Firefox browser window with a menu bar containing various menus, such as **File**, **Edit** and **View**. Below the menu bar is a toolbar that consists of buttons. Each button, when clicked, executes a task. In the toolbar is a combo box in which the user can type the location of a website to visit. The menus, buttons, toolbar and combo box are part

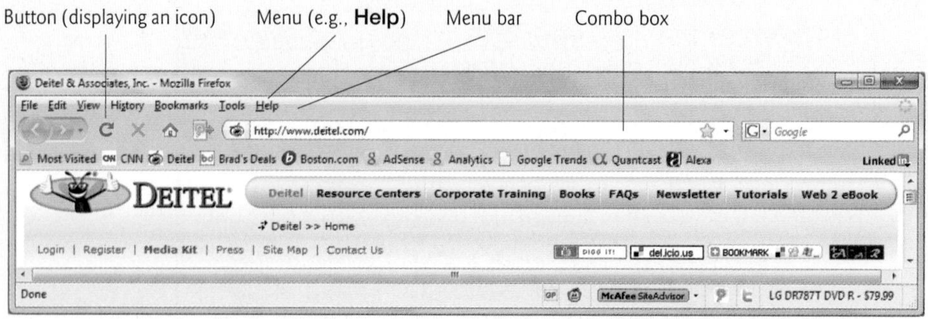

Fig. 3.34 | lMozilla Firefox window with GUI components.

of Firefox's GUI. They enable users to interact effectively with Firefox. Visual Basic provides classes for creating the GUI components shown here. Other classes that create GUI components are described throughout this book (beginning in the next chapter) and covered in detail in Chapter 14.

3.10 (Optional) Software Engineering Case Study: Examining the ATM Requirements Document

Now we begin our optional object-oriented design and implementation case study. The "Software Engineering Case Study" sections at the ends of this and the next several chapters will ease you into object orientation. We'll develop software for a simple automated teller machine (ATM) system, providing you with a concise, carefully paced, complete design and implementation experience. In Chapters 4–8, 10 and 12, we'll perform the various steps of an object-oriented design (OOD) process using the UML, while relating these steps to the object-oriented concepts discussed in the chapters. Appendix D implements the ATM using Visual Basic object-oriented programming (OOP) techniques. We present the complete case-study solution. This is not an exercise; rather, it is an end-to-end learning experience that concludes with a detailed walkthrough of the complete Visual Basic code that implements our design. It will begin to acquaint you with the kinds of substantial problems encountered in industry, and their potential solutions.

We begin our design process by presenting a requirements document that specifies the ATM system's purpose and *what* it must do. Throughout the case study, we refer to the requirements document to determine precisely what functionality the system must provide.

Requirements Document

A small local bank intends to install a new automated teller machine (ATM) to allow users (i.e., bank customers) to perform basic financial transactions (Fig. 3.35). For simplicity, each user can have only one account at the bank. ATM users should be able to view their account balance, withdraw cash (i.e., take money out of an account) and deposit funds (i.e., place money into an account).

The user interface of the automated teller machine contains the following hardware components:

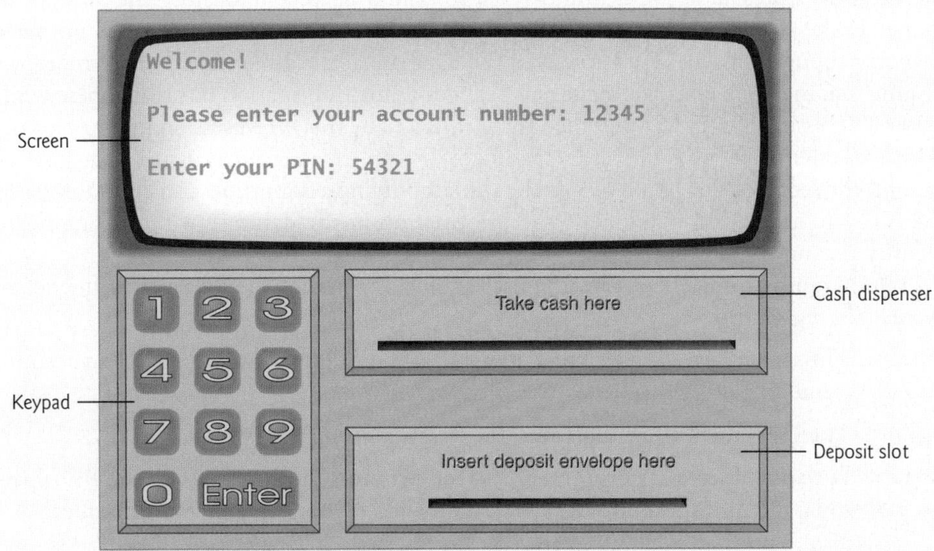

Fig. 3.35 | Automated teller machine user interface.

- a screen that displays messages to the user;
- a keypad that receives numeric input from the user;
- a cash dispenser that dispenses cash to the user; and
- a deposit slot that receives deposit envelopes from the user.

The cash dispenser begins each day loaded with 500 $20 bills. [*Note:* Certain elements of the ATM described here simplify various aspects of a real ATM. For example, commercial ATMs typically contain a device that reads a user's account number from an ATM card, whereas our ATM asks the user to type an account number on the keypad (which you'll simulate with your personal computer's keypad). Also, commercial ATMs usually print a paper receipt at the end of a session, but all output from this ATM appears on the screen.]

The bank wants you to develop software to perform the financial transactions initiated by bank customers through the ATM. The bank will integrate the software with the ATM's hardware at a later time. The software should simulate the functionality of the hardware devices (e.g., cash dispenser, deposit slot) in software components, but it need not concern itself with how these devices perform their duties. The ATM hardware has not been developed yet, so instead of writing your software to run on the ATM, you should develop a first version of the software to run on a personal computer. This version should use the computer's monitor to simulate the ATM's screen, and the computer's keyboard to simulate the ATM's keypad.

An ATM session consists of authenticating a user (i.e., proving the user's identity) based on an account number and personal identification number (PIN), followed by creating and executing financial transactions. To authenticate a user and perform transactions, the ATM must interact with the bank's account information database. [*Note:* A database is an organized collection of data stored on a computer.] For each bank account, the database stores an account number, a PIN and a balance indicating the amount of money in the account. [*Note:* The bank plans to build only one ATM, so we do not need to worry about multiple ATMs accessing the database at the same time. Furthermore, we assume that the bank does not make any changes to the information in the database while a user is accessing the ATM other than those initiated by this ATM session itself. Also, any business system like an ATM faces reasonably complicated security issues that go well beyond the scope of this book—we make the simplifying assumption that the bank trusts the ATM to access and manipulate the information in the database without significant security measures.]

Upon approaching the ATM, the user should experience the following sequence of events (see Fig. 3.35):

1. The screen displays a welcome message and prompts the user to enter an account number.
2. The user enters a five-digit account number, using the keypad.
3. For authentication purposes, the screen prompts the user to enter the PIN (personal identification number) associated with the specified account number.
4. The user enters a five-digit PIN, using the keypad.
5. If the user enters a valid account number and the correct PIN for that account, the screen displays the main menu (Fig. 3.36). If the user enters an invalid account number or an incorrect PIN, the screen displays an appropriate message, then the ATM returns to *Step 1* to restart the authentication process.

After the ATM authenticates the user, the main menu (Fig. 3.36) displays a numbered option for each of the three types of transactions—balance inquiry (option 1), withdrawal (option 2) and deposit (option 3). The main menu also displays an option that

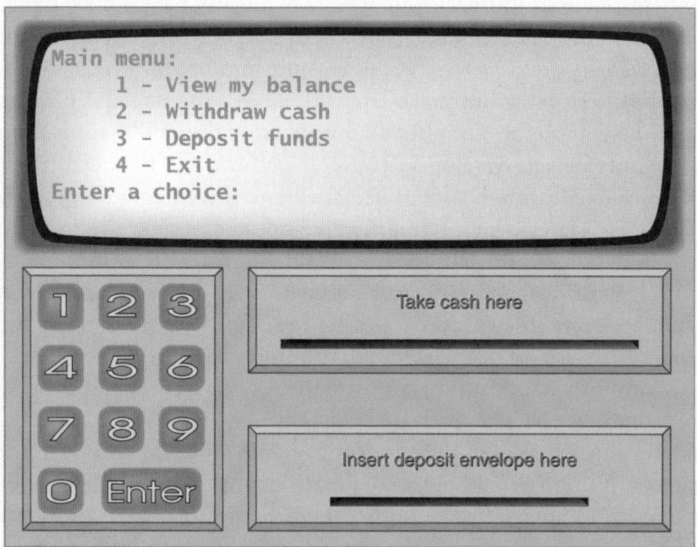

Fig. 3.36 | ATM main menu.

allows the user to exit the system (option 4). The user then chooses either to perform a transaction (by entering 1, 2 or 3) or to exit the system (by entering 4). If the user enters an invalid option, the screen displays an error message, then redisplays the main menu.

If the user enters 1 to make a balance inquiry, the screen displays the user's account balance. To do so, the ATM must retrieve the balance from the bank's database.

The following actions occur when the user enters 2 to make a withdrawal:

1. The screen displays a menu (shown in Fig. 3.37) containing standard withdrawal amounts: $20 (option 1), $40 (option 2), $60 (option 3), $100 (option 4) and $200 (option 5). Option 6 allows the user to cancel the transaction.
2. The user enters a menu selection (1–6) using the keypad.
3. If the withdrawal amount chosen is greater than the user's account balance, the screen displays a message stating this and telling the user to choose a smaller amount. The ATM then returns to *Step 1*. If the withdrawal amount chosen is less than or equal to the user's account balance (i.e., an acceptable withdrawal amount), the ATM proceeds to *Step 4*. If the user cancels the transaction (option 6), the ATM displays the main menu (Fig. 3.36) and waits for user input.
4. If the cash dispenser contains enough cash to satisfy the request, the ATM proceeds to *Step 5*. Otherwise, the screen displays a message indicating the problem and telling the user to choose a smaller withdrawal amount. The ATM then returns to *Step 1*.
5. The ATM debits (reduces) the user's account balance in the bank's database by the withdrawal amount.
6. The cash dispenser dispenses the desired amount of money to the user.
7. The screen displays a message reminding the user to take the money.

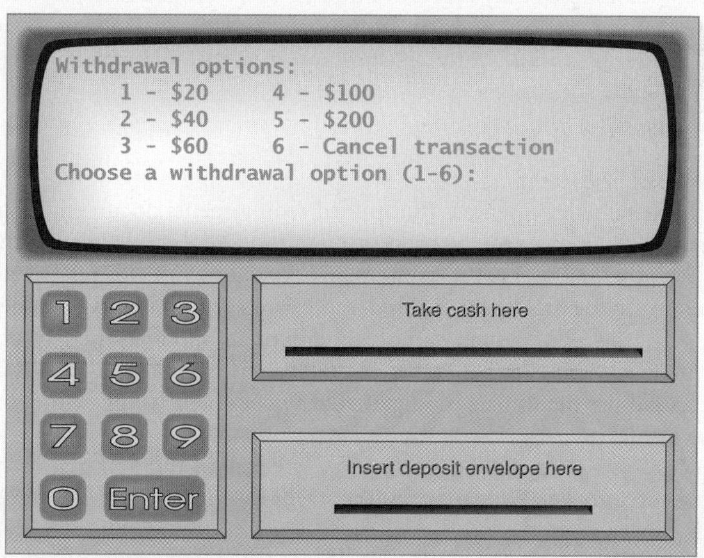

Fig. 3.37 | ATM withdrawal menu.

The following actions occur when the user enters 3 (from the main menu) to make a deposit:

1. The screen prompts the user to enter a deposit amount or to type 0 (zero) to cancel the transaction.
2. The user enters a deposit amount or 0, using the keypad. [*Note:* The keypad does not contain a decimal point or a dollar sign, so the user cannot type a dollar amount (e.g., $147.25). Instead, the user must enter a deposit amount as a number of cents (e.g., 14725). The ATM then divides this number by 100 to obtain a number representing a dollar amount (e.g., 14725 ÷ 100 = 147.25).]
3. If the user specifies a deposit amount, the ATM proceeds to *Step 4.* If the user cancels the transaction (by entering 0), the ATM displays the main menu (Fig. 3.36) and waits for user input.
4. The screen displays a message telling the user to insert a deposit envelope into the deposit slot.
5. If the deposit slot receives a deposit envelope within two minutes, the ATM credits (i.e., increases) the user's account balance in the bank's database by the deposit amount. [*Note:* This money is not immediately available for withdrawal. The bank first must verify the amount of cash in the deposit envelope, and any checks in the envelope must clear (i.e., money must be transferred from the check writer's account to the check recipient's account). When either of these events occurs, the bank appropriately updates the user's balance stored in the database. This occurs independently of the ATM system.] If the deposit slot does not receive a deposit envelope within two minutes, the screen displays a message that the system has canceled the transaction due to inactivity. The ATM then displays the main menu and waits for user input.

After the system successfully executes a transaction, it should redisplay the main menu (Fig. 3.36) so that the user can perform additional transactions. If the user chooses to exit the system (by entering option 4), the screen should display a thank you message, then display the welcome message for the next user.

Analyzing the ATM System

The preceding statement presented a simplified requirements document. Typically, such a document is the result of a detailed process of requirements gathering that might include interviews with potential users of the system and specialists in fields related to the system. For example, a systems analyst who is hired to prepare a requirements document for banking software (e.g., the ATM system described here) might interview people who have used ATMs and financial experts to gain a better understanding of *what* the software must do. The analyst would use the information gathered to compile a list of system requirements to guide systems designers.

The process of requirements gathering is a key task of the first stage of the software life cycle. The software life cycle specifies the stages through which software evolves from the time it is conceived to the time at which it is retired from use. These stages typically include analysis, design, implementation, testing, debugging, deployment, maintenance and retirement. Several software life-cycle models exist, each with its own preferences and specifications for when and how often software engineers should perform the various stages. Waterfall models perform each stage once in succession, whereas iterative models may repeat one or more stages several times throughout a product's life cycle.

The analysis stage of the software life cycle focuses on precisely defining the problem to be solved. When designing any system, one must certainly *solve the problem right*, but of equal importance, one must *solve the right problem*. Systems analysts collect the requirements that indicate the specific problem to solve. Our requirements document describes our simple ATM system in sufficient detail that you do not need to go through an extensive analysis stage—it has been done for you.

To capture what a system should do, developers often employ a technique known as use case modeling. This process identifies the use cases of the system, each representing a different capability that the system provides to its clients. For example, ATMs typically have several use cases, such as "View Account Balance," "Withdraw Cash," "Deposit Funds," "Transfer Funds Between Accounts" and "Buy Postage Stamps." The simplified ATM system we build in this case study requires only the first three use cases.

Each use case describes a typical scenario in which the user uses the system. You have already read descriptions of the ATM system's use cases in the requirements document. The lists of steps required to perform each type of transaction (i.e., balance inquiry, withdrawal and deposit) actually described the three use cases of our ATM—"View Account Balance," "Withdraw Cash" and "Deposit Funds."

Use Case Diagrams

We create a use case diagram to model the interactions between a system's clients (in this case study, bank customers) and the system. The goal is to show the kinds of interactions users have with a system without providing the details—these are shown in other UML diagrams (which we present throughout the case study). Use case diagrams are often accompanied by informal text that describes the use cases in more detail—like the text that appears in the requirements document. Use case diagrams are produced during the analysis stage of the software life cycle. In larger systems, use case diagrams are simple but indispensable tools that help system designers focus on satisfying the users' needs.

Figure 3.38 shows the use case diagram for our ATM system. The stick figure represents an actor, which defines the roles that an external entity—such as a person or another system—plays when interacting with the system. For our automated teller machine, the actor is a User who can view an account balance, withdraw cash and deposit funds using the ATM. The User is not an actual person, but instead comprises the roles that a real person—when playing the part of a User—can play while interacting with the ATM. Note that a use case diagram can include multiple actors. For example, the use case diagram for a real bank's ATM system might also include an actor named Administrator who refills the cash dispenser each day.

We identify the actor in our system by examining the requirements document, which states, "ATM users should be able to view their account balance, withdraw cash and deposit funds." The actor in each of the three use cases is simply the User who interacts with the ATM. An external entity—a real person—plays the part of the User to perform financial transactions. Figure 3.38 shows one actor, whose name, User, appears below the actor in the diagram. The UML models each use case as an oval connected to an actor with a solid line.

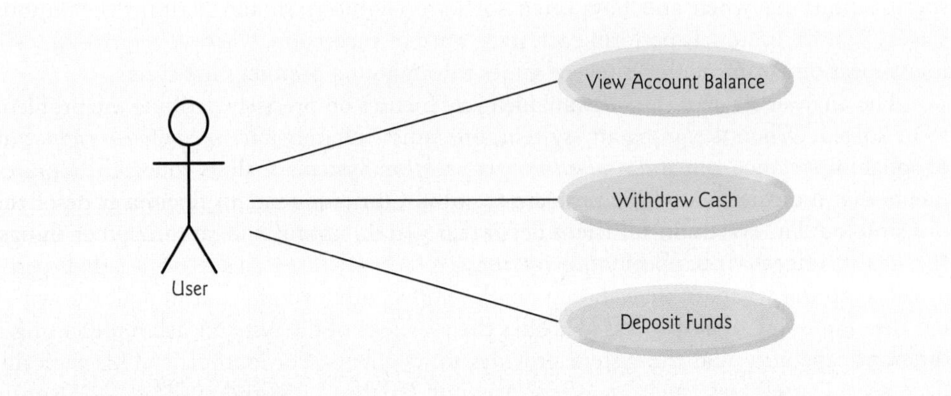

Fig. 3.38 | Use case diagram for the ATM system from the user's perspective.

Systems designers must analyze the requirements document or a set of use cases, and design the system before programmers implement it in a particular programming language. During the analysis stage, systems designers focus on understanding the requirements document to produce a high-level specification that describes *what* the system is supposed to do. The output of the design stage—a design specification—should specify *how* the system should be constructed to satisfy these requirements. In the next several Software Engineering Case Study sections, we perform the steps of a simple object-oriented design (OOD) process on the ATM system to produce a design specification containing a collection of UML diagrams and supporting text. Recall that the UML can be used with any OOD process. Many such processes exist, the best known being the Rational Unified Process™ (RUP) developed by Rational Software Corporation (now a division of IBM). RUP is a rich process for designing "industrial-strength" applications. For this case study, we employ a simplified design process.

Designing the ATM System

We now begin the design stage of our ATM system. A system is a set of components that interact to solve a problem. For example, to perform the ATM system's designated tasks, our ATM system has a user interface (Fig. 3.35), contains software that executes financial transactions and interacts with a database of bank-account information. System structure describes the system's objects and their interrelationships. System behavior describes how the system changes as its objects interact with one another. Every system has structure and behavior—designers must specify both. There are several distinct types of system structures and behaviors. For example, the interactions among objects in the system differ from those between the user and the system, yet both constitute a portion of the system behavior.

The UML 2 specifies 13 diagram types for documenting system models. Each diagram type models a distinct characteristic of a system's structure or behavior—six diagram types relate to system structure; the remaining seven relate to system behavior. We list here only the six types of diagrams used in our case study—one of these (class diagrams) models system structure, and the remaining five model system behavior. We overview the remaining seven UML diagram types in Appendix E, UML 2: Additional Diagram Types:

1. Use case diagrams, such as the one in Fig. 3.38, model the interactions between a system and its external entities (actors) in terms of use cases (system capabilities, such as "View Account Balance," "Withdraw Cash" and "Deposit Funds").
2. Class diagrams, which you'll study in Section 4.9, model the classes, or "building blocks," used in a system. Each noun or "thing" described in the requirements document is a candidate to be a class in the system (e.g., "account," "keypad"). Class diagrams help us specify the structural relationships between parts of the system. For example, the ATM system class diagram will, among other things, specify that the ATM is physically composed of a screen, a keypad, a cash dispenser and a deposit slot.
3. State machine diagrams, which you'll study in Section 6.11, model the ways in which an object changes state. An object's state is indicated by the values of all the object's attributes at a given time. When an object changes state, that object may subsequently behave differently in the system. For example, after validating a user's PIN, the ATM transitions from the "user not authenticated" state to the "user authenticated" state, at which point the ATM allows the user to perform financial transactions (i.e., view account balance, withdraw cash, deposit funds).
4. Activity diagrams, which you'll also study in Section 6.11, model an object's activity—the object's workflow (sequence of events) during program execution. An activity diagram models the actions the object performs and specifies the order in which it performs these actions. For example, an activity diagram shows that the ATM must obtain the balance of the user's account (from the bank's account information database) before the screen can display the balance to the user.
5. Communication diagrams (called collaboration diagrams in earlier versions of the UML) model the interactions among objects in a system, with an emphasis on *what* interactions occur. You'll learn in Section 8.17 that these diagrams show which objects must interact to perform an ATM transaction. For example, the ATM must communicate with the bank's account-information database to retrieve an account balance.
6. Sequence diagrams also model the interactions among the objects in a system, but unlike communication diagrams, they emphasize *when* interactions occur. You'll learn in Section 8.17 that these diagrams help show the order in which interactions occur in executing a financial transaction. For example, the screen prompts the user to enter a withdrawal amount before cash is dispensed.

In Section 4.9, we continue designing our ATM system by identifying the classes from the requirements document. We accomplish this by extracting key nouns and noun phrases from the requirements document. Using these classes, we develop our first draft of the class diagram that models the structure of our ATM system.

Software Engineering Case Study Self-Review Exercises

3.1 Suppose we enabled a user of our ATM system to transfer money between two bank accounts. Modify the use case diagram of Fig. 3.38 to reflect this change.

3.2 __________ model the interactions among objects in a system with an emphasis on *when* these interactions occur.

a) Class diagrams
b) Sequence diagrams
c) Communication diagrams
d) Activity diagrams

3.3 Which of the following choices lists stages of a typical software life cycle in sequential order?
a) design, analysis, implementation, testing
b) design, analysis, testing, implementation
c) analysis, design, testing, implementation
d) analysis, design, implementation, testing

Answers to Software Engineering Case Study Self-Review Exercises

3.1 Figure 3.39 contains a use case diagram for a modified version of our ATM system that also allows users to transfer money between accounts.

3.2 b.

3.3 d.

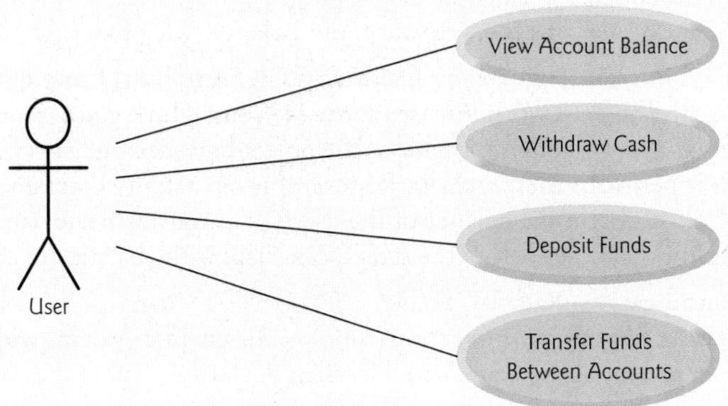

Fig. 3.39 | Use case diagram for a modified version of our ATM system that also allows users to transfer money between accounts.

Internet and Web Resources

The following URLs provide information on object-oriented design with the UML.

`www-306.ibm.com/software/rational/offerings/design.html`
Provides information about IBM Rational software available for designing systems. Provides downloads of 30-day trial versions of several products, such as IBM Rational Application Developer.

`www.borland.com/us/products/together/index.html`
Provides a free 30-day license to download a trial version of Borland® Together® ControlCenter™—a software-development tool that supports the UML.

`www.ilogix.com/sublevel.aspx?id=53`
Provides a free 30-day license to download a trial version of I-Logix Rhapsody®—a UML 2 based model-driven development environment.

`argouml.tigris.org`
Contains information and downloads for ArgoUML, a free open source UML tool written in Java.

`www.objectsbydesign.com/books/booklist.html`
Lists books on the UML and object-oriented design.

`www.objectsbydesign.com/tools/umltools_byCompany.html`
Lists software tools that use the UML, such as IBM Rational Rose, Embarcadero Describe, Sparx Systems Enterprise Architect, I-Logix Rhapsody and Gentleware Poseidon for UML.

`www.ootips.org/ood-principles.html`
Provides answers to the question, "What Makes a Good Object-Oriented Design?"

`parlezuml.com/tutorials/umlforjava.htm`
Provides a UML tutorial for Java developers that presents UML diagrams side by side with the Java code that implements them.

`www.cetus-links.org/oo_uml.html`
Introduces the UML and provides links to numerous UML resources.

`www.agilemodeling.com/essays/umlDiagrams.htm`
Provides in-depth descriptions and tutorials on each of the 13 UML 2 diagram types.

Recommended Readings

The following books provide information on object-oriented design with the UML.

Booch, G. *Object-Oriented Analysis and Design with Applications.* 3rd ed. Boston: Addison-Wesley, 2004.

Eriksson, H., et al. *UML 2 Toolkit.* New York: John Wiley & Sons, 2003.

Fowler, M. *UML Distilled.* 3rd ed. Boston: Addison-Wesley Professional, 2004.

Kruchten, P. *The Rational Unified Process: An Introduction.* Boston: Addison-Wesley, 2004.

Larman, C. *Applying UML and Patterns: An Introduction to Object-Oriented Analysis and Design.* 2nd ed. Upper Saddle River, NJ: Prentice Hall, 2002.

Roques, P. *UML in Practice: The Art of Modeling Software Systems Demonstrated Through Worked Examples and Solutions.* Hoboken, NJ: John Wiley & Sons, 2004.

Rosenberg, D., and K. Scott. *Applying Use Case Driven Object Modeling with UML: An Annotated e-Commerce Example.* Reading, MA: Addison-Wesley, 2001.

Rumbaugh, J., I. Jacobson and G. Booch. *The Complete UML Training Course.* Upper Saddle River, NJ: Prentice Hall, 2000.

Rumbaugh, J., I. Jacobson and G. Booch. *The Unified Modeling Language Reference Manual.* Reading, MA: Addison-Wesley, 1999.

Rumbaugh, J., I. Jacobson and G. Booch. *The Unified Software Development Process.* Reading, MA: Addison-Wesley, 1999.

Schneider, G. and J. Winters. *Applying Use Cases: A Practical Guide.* 2nd ed. Boston: Addison-Wesley Professional, 2002.

3.11 Wrap-Up

You learned many features of Visual Basic in this chapter, including displaying data on the screen, inputting data from the keyboard and declaring variables of primitive types `Integer` and `Double`. You used the `WriteLine`, `Write` and `ReadLine` methods of class `Console` to build simple interactive programs that input and output text. We explained how variables are stored in, and retrieved from, memory. You learned how to use arithmetic operators to perform calculations, and the order in which Visual Basic applies these operators (i.e., the rules of operator precedence). We demonstrated how Visual Basic's `If...Then` statement allows a program to perform actions based on a condition. You learned how to create conditions using the equality and relational operators. You learned how to display `MessageBox` dialogs. We demonstrated several features of Visual Basic 2008 Express, including creating console applications, modifying the IDE's settings and adding references to assemblies.

In the next chapter, we re-introduce Visual Basic Windows applications that provide graphical user interfaces. The chapter begins our discussion of structured programming. We demonstrate creating applications using pseudocode, an informal language that helps you develop programs. We study how to specify and vary the order in which statements are executed—this is called flow of control. You'll learn how to use control statements to select between alternative actions based on the truth or falsity of a condition, or to perform actions repeatedly based on a condition. You'll see several case studies that demonstrate the types of repetition that can occur in Visual Basic programs.

3.12 Web Resources

`www.deitel.com/VisualBasic2008/`

The Deitel Visual Basic 2008 Resource Center contains links to some of the best Visual Basic information on the web. There you'll find categorized links to tutorials, references, code examples, demos, videos, and more. Check out the demos section for more advanced examples of layouts, menus, and other web page components.

Summary

Section 3.1 Introduction

- A console application is an application that does not have a graphical user interface.

Section 3.2 Displaying a Line of Text

- The single-quote character (`'`), when placed outside a string, indicates that the remainder of the line of code is a comment.
- Inserting comments in your programs improves the readability of your code. Comments are ignored by the Visual Basic compiler; they do not cause the computer to perform any actions when the program is run.
- Visual Basic console applications consist of pieces called modules, which are logical groupings of methods that simplify program organization.
- Methods perform tasks and can return information when the tasks are completed. Every console application in Visual Basic consists of at least one module declaration and one method.
- Keywords are words that are reserved for use by Visual Basic; you should use other names as identifiers.
- The name of a module is an identifier. An identifier is a series of characters, consisting of letters, digits and underscores (`_`), that does not begin with a digit and does not contain spaces.
- Visual Basic keywords and identifiers are not case sensitive—uppercase and lowercase letters are considered to be identical. Thus, `welcome1` and `Welcome1` are the same identifier.
- Blank lines, tabs and space characters are often used to make programs easier to read. Collectively, blank lines, tabs and space characters are known as whitespace.
- Console applications begin executing at method `Main`, which is known as the entry point of the program.

- Keyword `Sub` begins the body of a method declaration. Keywords `End Sub` close the method declaration's body.
- Characters delimited by double quotes are called strings, character strings or string literals.
- Methods perform tasks and can return data when the tasks are completed. Groups of related methods are organized into classes or modules.
- The dot separator (`.`) selects a member of a particular class.
- The `Console` class contains methods, such as `WriteLine`, that communicate with users via the **Console** window.
- `Console` method `WriteLine` displays text followed by a newline in the **Console** window.

Section 3.3 Creating Your First Program in Visual Basic Express

- Syntax-color highlighting helps you visually differentiate program elements. In Visual Basic 2008 Express, keywords are blue, text is black and comments are green. You can customize the colors shown in the code editor.
- As you begin typing code, the *IntelliSense* window appears and lists keywords, class names, class members and other features that start with the same characters you've typed so far.
- When you type the opening left parenthesis after a method's name, the *Parameter Info* window displays information about a method's arguments. This window is one of the many features provided by the IDE to aid program development.
- The `.exe` file extension denotes that a file is executable.

Section 3.4 Displaying a Single Line of Text with Multiple Statements

- Unlike `WriteLine`, `Write` does not position the output cursor to the beginning of the next line in the **Console** window after displaying its string.

Section 3.5 Adding Integers

- The `ReadLine` method causes the program to pause and wait for user input. Once the user presses the *Enter* key, the input is returned to the program and execution resumes.
- A syntax error indicates a violation of Visual Basic's rules for creating correct programs (i.e., one or more statements are not written correctly).
- Variables are locations in the computer's memory where values can be stored for use by a program. Every variable has a name, type, size and value.
- All variables must be declared before they can be used in a program.
- Declarations begin with keyword `Dim` and allow you to specify the name and type of a variable.
- Types already defined in Visual Basic, such as `Integer`, are known as primitive types.
- Primitive type names are keywords.
- Variables of type `Integer` store integer values (i.e., whole numbers such as 919, –11 and 0).
- A runtime error is an error that affects the program during execution (unlike a syntax error, which affects the program when it is compiled).
- The symbol = is used to assign a value to a variable.

Section 3.6 Memory Concepts

- Whenever a value is placed in a memory location, it replaces the value previously stored in that location. The previous value is destroyed.
- When a value is read from a memory location, the process is nondestructive, meaning that the value in memory is not changed.

Section 3.7 Arithmetic

- Binary operators operate on two operands; unary operators operate on one operand.
- Visual Basic has separate operators for `Integer` division (the backslash, \) and floating-point division (the forward slash, /). `Integer` division yields an `Integer` result. Any fractional part in `Integer` division is truncated (i.e., discarded).
- The `Mod` operator yields the remainder after division.
- Arithmetic expressions in Visual Basic must be written in straight-line form to enter programs into a computer.
- Parentheses are used in Visual Basic expressions in the same manner as in algebraic expressions.
- Visual Basic applies the operators in arithmetic expressions in a precise sequence, which is determined by the rules of operator precedence.
- If an expression contains multiple operators with the same precedence, the order in which the operators are applied is determined by their associativity. In Visual Basic, all binary operators associate from left to right.
- As in algebra, you can place redundant parentheses in an expression to make it easier to read.

Section 3.8 Decision Making: Equality and Relational Operators

- Visual Basic's `If...Then` statement allows a program to make a decision based on the truth or falsity of a condition. If the condition is true, the statement in the body of the `If...Then` statement executes. If the condition is false, the body statement does not execute.
- Conditions in `If...Then` statements can be formed by using the equality operators and relational operators. Equality operators and relational operators are also called comparison operators.
- Relational and equality operators have the same level of precedence and associate from left to right.

Section 3.9 Using a Message Dialog to Display a Message

- Message dialogs are windows that display messages to the user. Visual Basic provides the class `MessageBox` for creating message dialogs.
- The .NET Framework Class Library organizes groups of related classes into namespaces.
- The `System.Windows.Forms` namespace contains windows-related classes (i.e., forms and dialogs) that help you define graphical user interfaces (GUIs) for their applications.
- GUI components facilitate data entry by the user and the formatting and presenting of data outputs to the user.
- An `Imports` statement indicates that a program uses the features provided by a specific namespace, such as `System.Windows.Forms`.
- To improve readability, long statements may be split over several lines with the line-continuation character (_). Although a single statement can contain as many line-continuation characters as necessary, at least one whitespace character must precede each line-continuation character.
- Assemblies that contain compiled classes for reuse in applications are located in files with a `.dll` (dynamic link library) extension.

Terminology

action
Add Reference dialog
addition operator (+)
argument to a method
arithmetic operator
assembly
assignment (=)
assignment statement
associativity of operators
binary operator

body of a method
case sensitive
character string
class
class name
close a dialog
Command Prompt
comment
comparison operator
condition
console application
`Console` class
Console window
declaration
dialog
`Dim` keyword
dismiss (hide) a dialog
`.dll` file extension
dot separator (`.`)
`Double` primitive type
double quotes (`""`) to delineate a string
dynamic link library (`.dll`)
`End Module` keywords
end-of-line comment
`End Sub` keywords
entry point of a program
equality operator (=)
Error List window
`.exe` file extension
executable file (`.exe`)
exponentiation operator (^)
false condition
File Name property of a file in the **Solution Explorer**
filter
floating-point division operator (/)
floating-point number
flow of control
full-line comment
greater than operator (>)
greater than or equal to operator (>=)
GUI component
identifier
`If...Then` selection statement
implicit conversion
`Imports` statement
inequality operator (<>)
integer division operator (\)
`Integer` primitive type
integer value
IntelliSense
keyword
less than operator (<)
less than or equal to operator (<=)
line-continuation character (_)
location in the computer's memory
`Main` method
`Math` class
member of a class
`MessageBox` class
method
method call
method name
`Mod` (modulus, modulo) operator
module
`Module` keyword
MSDN Documentation
multiplication operator (*)
namespace
nested parentheses
operand
operator precedence
output cursor
Parameter Info window
precedence
primitive type
prompt
`ReadLine` method of class `Console`
redundant parentheses
relational operators (<, >, <=, >=)
rules of operator precedence
runtime error
`Show` method of class `MessageBox`
sign operations (+ and -)
single-line comment
single-quote character (`'`)
`Sqrt` method of class `Math`
startup object
statement
straight-line form
string concatenation operator (&)
string literal
structured programming
`Sub` keyword
subtraction operator (-)
syntax error
syntax-color highlighting
`System.Windows.Forms` namespace
true condition
unary minus operator (-)

unary operator
unary plus operator (+)
variable
variable name
variable size
variable type
variable value
whitespace character
`Write` method of class `Console`
`WriteLine` method of class `Console`

Self-Review Exercises

3.1 Fill in the blanks in each of the following statements:

a) Keyword ________ begins the body of a module, and keywords ________ end the body of a module.
b) The ________ symbol begins a comment.
c) ________, ________ and ________ collectively are known as whitespace.
d) Class ________ contains methods for displaying dialogs.
e) ________ are words reserved for use by Visual Basic.
f) Visual Basic console applications begin execution at method ________.
g) Methods ________ and ________ of class `Console` display information in the **Console** window.
h) A Visual Basic program uses a(n) ________ statement to indicate that a namespace is being used.
i) When a value is placed in a memory location, this value ________ the previous value in that location.
j) The indication that operators are applied from left to right refers to the ________ of the operators.
k) Visual Basic's `If...Then` statement allows a program to make a decision based on whether a condition is ________ or ________.
l) Types such as `Integer` and `Boolean` are often called ________ types.
m) A variable is a location in the computer's ________ where a value can be stored for use by a program.
n) The expression to the ________ of an assignment (=) is always evaluated first before the assignment occurs.
o) Expressions in Visual Basic must be written in ________ form to facilitate entering programs into the computer.

3.2 State whether each of the following is *true* or *false*. If *false*, explain why.

a) Comments cause the computer to print the text after the `'` on the screen when the program executes.
b) All variables must be declared before they can be used in a Visual Basic program.
c) Visual Basic considers the variable names `number` and `NuMbEr` to be different.
d) The arithmetic operators `*`, `/`, `+` and `-` all have the same level of precedence.
e) A string of characters contained between double quotation marks is called a phrase or phrase literal.
f) Method `Display` of class `MessageBox` displays a message dialog.
g) Integer division yields an `Integer` result.

Answers to Self-Review Exercises

3.1 a) `Module`, `End Module`. b) single quotation mark, `'`. c) Blank lines, space characters, tab characters. d) `MessageBox`. e) Keywords. f) `Main`. g) `Write`, `WriteLine`. h) `Imports`. i) replaces. j) associativity. k) true, false. l) primitive. m) memory. n) right. o) straight-line.

3.2 a) False. Comments do not cause any action to be performed when the program executes. They are used to document programs and improve their readability. b) True. c) False. Visual Basic identifiers are not case sensitive, so these variable names are identical. d) False. The operators * and / are on the same level of precedence, and the operators + and - are on a lower level of precedence. e) False. A string of characters is called a string or string literal. f) False. Method `Show` of class `MessageBox` displays a message dialog. g) True.

Exercises

[*Note:* Assume that the exercise outputs are displayed in a **Command Prompt** window unless otherwise directed. For instance, you may be asked to display your output in a message dialog.]

3.3 Write Visual Basic statements that accomplish each of the following tasks:

a) Display the message `"Hello"` with the title bar string `"Message"` using class `MessageBox`.
b) Assign the product of variables `number` and `userData` to variable `result`.
c) State that a program performs a sample payroll calculation (i.e., use text that helps to document a program).

3.4 What displays in the message dialog when each of the following statements is performed? Assume that the value of `x` is `2` and the value of `y` is `3`.

a) `MessageBox.Show(x, "x")`
b) `MessageBox.Show((x + x), "(x + x)")`

3.5 Given $z = 8e^5 - n$, which of the following are correct statements for this equation?

a) `z = 8 * e ^ 5 - n`
b) `z = ( 8 * e ) ^ 5 - n`
c) `z = 8 * ( e ^ 5 ) - n`
d) `z = 8 * e ^ ( 5 - n )`

3.6 Indicate the order of evaluation of the operators in each of the following Visual Basic statements, and show the value of `x` after each statement is performed.

a) `x = 7 + 3 * 3 \ 2 - 1`
b) `x = 2 Mod 2 + 2 * 2 - 2 / 2`
c) `x = ( 3 * 9 * ( 3 + ( 9 * 3 / ( 3 ) ) ) )`

3.7 Write a program that displays the numbers `1` to `4` on the same line, with each pair of adjacent numbers separated by one space. Write the program using the following:

a) Use one `Write` statement.
b) Use four `Write` statements.

3.8 Write a program that prompts the user for two integers, obtains them from the user and prints their sum, product, difference and integer quotient.

3.9 Write a program that inputs from the user the radius of a circle and displays the circle's diameter, circumference and area. Use the following formulas (r is the radius): $diameter = 2r$, $circumference = 2\pi r$, $area = \pi r^2$. Use the constant `Math.PI` from class `Math` for π.

3.10 Write a program that displays a box, an oval, an arrow and a diamond using asterisks (*) as follows:

```
*********     ***       *        *
*       *   *     *    ***      * *
*       *  *       *  *****    *   *
*       *  *       *    *     *     *
*       *  *       *    *    *       *
*       *  *       *    *     *     *
*       *  *       *    *      *   *
*       *   *     *     *       * *
*********     ***       *        *
```

3.11 What does the following group of statements print?

```
Console.Write("*     *")
Console.WriteLine(" *****")
Console.WriteLine("*     *  *    *")
Console.Write(" *   *   **")
Console.WriteLine("***")
Console.WriteLine("  * *    *    *")
Console.Write("   ")
Console.WriteLine("*     *****")
```

3.12 Write a program that reads two integers and determines and prints whether the first is a multiple of the second. For example, if the user inputs `15` and `3`, the first number is a multiple of the second. If the user inputs `2` and `4`, the first number is not a multiple of the second. [*Hint:* Use the `Mod` operator.]

3.13 Write a program that inputs one number consisting of five digits from the user, separates the number into its individual digits and prints the digits separated from one another by three spaces each. For example, if the user types in the number `42339`, the program should display:

```
4   2   3   3   9
```

[*Hint:* This exercise is possible with the techniques discussed in this chapter. You'll need to use both the integer division and modulus operations to "pick off" each digit.]

3.14 Using only the programming techniques discussed in this chapter, write a program that calculates the squares and cubes of the numbers from `0` to `5` and displays the resulting values in table format as follows:

```
number  square  cube
0       0       0
1       1       1
2       4       8
3       9       27
4       16      64
5       25      125
```

3.15 Write an application that reads five integers and determines and prints the largest and the smallest integers in the group. Use only the programming techniques you learned in this chapter.

3.16 Write a program that reads a first name and a last name from the user as two separate inputs and concatenates the first name and last name, separating them by a space. Display the concatenated name in a message dialog. To do this exercise, you'll need to store user input in variables of type `String`, a primitive type used to represent string data. You can create variables of type `String` just as you created variables of types `Integer` and `Double`, except using the keyword `String`:

```
Dim firstName As String
Dim lastName As String
```

Variables `firstName` and `lastName` can now be used to store user input, display text in a message dialog, and perform other tasks. You'll learn more about type `String` in the next chapter.

3.17 Write a program that inputs five numbers and determines and prints the number of negative numbers input, the number of positive numbers input and the number of zeros input. Do not count zero as either a positive or negative number. Display your output in a message dialog.

4

Introduction to Classes and Objects

You will see something new. Two things. And I call them Thing One and Thing Two.

—Dr. Theodor Seuss Geisel

Nothing can have value without being an object of utility.

—Karl Marx

Your public servants serve you right.

—Adlai E. Stevenson

Knowing how to answer one who speaks,
To reply to one who sends a message.

—Amenemope

OBJECTIVES

In this chapter you'll learn:

- What classes, objects, methods, instance variables and properties are.
- How to declare a class and use it to create an object.
- How to implement a class's behaviors as methods.
- How to implement a class's attributes as instance variables and properties.
- How to call an object's methods to make them perform their tasks.
- The differences between instance variables of a class and local variables of a method.
- How to use a constructor to ensure that an object's attributes are initialized when the object is created.
- The differences between value types and reference types.
- How to use properties to ensure that only valid data is placed in attributes.

Outline

4.1 Introduction

We introduced the basic terminology and concepts of object-oriented programming in Section 1.19. In Chapter 3, you began to use those concepts to create simple applications that displayed messages to the user, obtained information from the user, performed calculations and made decisions. One common feature of every application in Chapter 3 was that all the statements that performed tasks were located in method `Main`, in a module. Many of the applications you develop in this book will consist of one or more classes, each containing one or more methods. These classes will then be used in the module that contains `Main`. If you become part of a development team in industry, you may work on applications that contain hundreds, or even thousands, of classes. In this chapter, we present a simple framework for organizing object-oriented applications in Visual Basic.

First, we motivate the notion of classes with a real-world example. Then we present five complete working applications to demonstrate creating and using your own classes. These examples begin our integrated case study on developing a grade-book class that instructors can use to maintain student test scores. This case study is enhanced over the next several chapters, culminating with the version presented in Chapter 8, Arrays.

4.2 Classes, Objects, Methods and Instance Variables

We begin with a simple analogy to help you understand classes and their contents. Suppose you want to drive a car and make it go faster by pressing down on its accelerator pedal. What must happen before you can do this? Well, before you can drive a car, someone has to design the car. A car typically begins as engineering drawings, similar to the blueprints used to design a house. These engineering drawings include the design for an accelerator pedal to make the car go faster. The pedal "hides" the complex mechanisms that actually make the car go faster, just as the brake pedal "hides" the mechanisms that slow the car and the steering wheel "hides" the mechanisms that turn the car. This enables people with little or no knowledge of how automotive hardware works to easily drive a car.

Unfortunately, you cannot drive a car's engineering drawings. Before you can drive a car, the car must be built from the engineering drawings that describe it. A completed car has an actual accelerator pedal to make it go faster, but even that is not enough—the car will not accelerate on its own, so the driver must press the accelerator pedal.

Now let's use our car example to introduce the key programming concepts of this section. Performing a task in a program requires a method. The method describes the mechanisms that actually perform its tasks. The method hides these mechanisms from its user, just as the accelerator pedal of a car hides from the driver the complex mechanisms that make the car go faster. In Visual Basic, we begin by creating a program unit called a class to house a method, just as a car's engineering drawings house the design of an accelerator pedal. In a class, you provide one or more methods that are designed to perform the class's tasks. For example, a class that represents a bank account might contain many methods, including one to deposit money in the account, another to withdraw money from the account and a third to inquire what the current balance is.

Just as you cannot drive an engineering drawing of a car, you cannot "drive" a class. Just as someone has to build a car from its engineering drawings before you can actually drive it, you must build an object of a class before you can get a program to perform the tasks the class describes how to do. That is one reason Visual Basic is known as an object-oriented programming language.

When you drive a car, pressing its gas pedal sends a message to the car to perform a task—that is, to go faster. Similarly, you send **messages** to an object—each message is known as a **method call** and tells one of an object's methods to perform its task.

Thus far, we have used the car analogy to introduce classes, objects and methods. In addition to the capabilities a car provides, it also has many attributes, such as its color, the number of doors, the amount of gas in its tank, its current speed and its odometer reading (i.e., its total miles driven since it was built). Like the car's capabilities, its attributes are represented as part of a car's design in its engineering diagrams. As you drive a car, these attributes are always associated with the car. For example, each car knows how much gas is in its own gas tank, but not how much is in the tanks of other cars. Similarly, an object has attributes that are carried with it as it is used in a program. These attributes are specified in the object's class. For example, a bank-account object has a balance attribute that represents the amount of money in the account. Each bank-account object knows the balance in the account it represents, but not the balances of the other accounts in the bank. Attributes are specified by the class's **instance variables**.

This chapter presents five simple examples that demonstrate the concepts introduced in the context of the car analogy. The examples incrementally build a `GradeBook` class:

1. The first example presents a `GradeBook` class with one method that simply displays a welcome message when it is called. We show how to create an object of the class and call the method so that it displays the welcome message.

2. The second example modifies the first by allowing the method to receive a course name as an argument and display the name as part of the welcome message.

3. The third example shows how to store the course name in a `GradeBook` object. We show how to use the convenient notation of "properties" to set the course name in the object and obtain the course name from the object.

4. The fourth example demonstrates how the data in a `GradeBook` object can be initialized when the object is created—the initialization is performed by the class's constructor (a special initialization method with the name `New`).

5. The last example enhances class GradeBook by introducing data validation, which ensures that data in an object adheres to a particular format or is in a proper value range. For example, a Date object should accept month values only in the range 1–12. In our GradeBook example, the property that sets the course name for a GradeBook object ensures that the course name is 25 or fewer characters. If not, the property uses only the first 25 characters of the course name and displays a warning message. Restrictions like this are common in information systems that have to display data in fixed-size boxes in a form on the screen.

The GradeBook examples in this chapter do not process or store grades. We begin processing grades with the version of class GradeBook in Chapter 5, Control Statements: Part 1, and we store grades in the version of GradeBook in Chapter 8, Arrays.

4.3 Declaring a Class with a Method and Instantiating an Object of a Class

We begin with an example that consists of class GradeBook (Fig. 4.1) and module GradeBookTest (Fig. 4.2). Class GradeBook (declared in file GradeBook.vb) displays a message on the screen (Fig. 4.2) welcoming the instructor to the grade-book application. Module GradeBookTest (declared in file GradeBookTest.vb) contains the Main method that instantiates (creates) and uses an object of class GradeBook. The class and module are placed in separate files for clarity, but it is possible to place them in the same file.

Adding a Class to a Visual Basic Project

For each example in this chapter, you'll add a class to your console application. To do this, right click the project name in the **Solution Explorer** and select **Add > Class...** from the menu that appears. In the **Add New Item** dialog that appears, enter the name of your new file, in this case GradeBook.vb. A new file will be added to your project with an empty GradeBook class. Add the code from Fig. 4.1 to this file—we discuss this code shortly.

Class **GradeBook**

The GradeBook class declaration (Fig. 4.1) contains a DisplayMessage method (lines 5–7) that displays a message on the screen. Recall that a class is like a blueprint—we need to make an object of class GradeBook and call its method to get line 6 to execute and display its message. We do this in the Main method in Fig. 4.2.

The class declaration begins at line 3. The keyword Public is an access modifier. Access modifiers determine the accessibility of an object's properties and methods to other methods in an application. For now, we simply declare every class Public. Every class dec-

```
1  ' Fig. 4.1: GradeBook.vb
2  ' Class declaration with one method.
3  Public Class GradeBook
4     ' display a welcome message to the GradeBook user
5     Public Sub DisplayMessage()
6        Console.WriteLine("Welcome to the Grade Book!")
7     End Sub ' DisplayMessage
8  End Class ' GradeBook
```

Fig. 4.1 | Class declaration with one method.

laration contains keyword Class followed immediately by the class's name. Every class's body ends with the keywords End Class, as in line 8 of class GradeBook.

Method DisplayMessage

Class GradeBook has one method—DisplayMessage (lines 5–7). The method declaration begins with keyword Public to indicate that the method is "available to the public"—that is, it can be called from outside the class declaration's body by methods of other classes or modules (these other classes and modules are called clients of the class). Keyword Sub indicates that this method will perform a task but will not return (i.e., give back) any information to its calling method when it completes its task. You have already used methods that return information—for example, in Chapter 3 you used Console method ReadLine to input an integer typed by the user at the keyboard. When ReadLine inputs a value, it returns that value for use in the program.

The name of the method, DisplayMessage, follows keyword Sub. By convention, method names begin with an uppercase letter and all subsequent words in the name begin with a capital letter (recall that Visual Basic is not case sensitive). The parentheses after the method name are used to indicate any parameters—additional information that is required by the method to perform its task (we discuss parameters in more detail in Section 4.4). An empty set of parentheses, as in line 5, indicates that this method does not require any additional information and does not need any parameters. We refer to the part of the method in line 5 as the method header. Like Main, method DisplayMessage ends with keywords End Sub.

The body of a method contains statements that perform the method's task. In this case, the method contains one statement (line 6) that displays the message "Welcome to the Grade Book!" in the **Console** window. After this statement executes, the method has completed its task.

Note that the DisplayMessage method declaration is similar to the declaration of Main. We discuss methods in depth in Chapter 7, Methods: A Deeper Look.

In Chapter 3, each module we declared had one method named Main. Class GradeBook, likewise, has one method. Recall that Main is a special method that is required to begin the execution of every application. Main is called automatically by the runtime when you execute an application. Most methods do not get called automatically. As you'll soon see, you must call method DisplayMessage to tell it to perform its task.

Using Class GradeBook

You'll now use class GradeBook in an application. A Visual Basic project that contains only class GradeBook is not an application that can be executed, because GradeBook does not contain Main. If you try to compile such a project, you'll get an error message like:

```
'Sub Main' was not found in 'GradeBook.GradeBookTest'.
```

This was not a problem in Chapter 3, because every application you created contained a Main method. To fix this problem for the GradeBook, either we must declare a separate class or module that contains Main, or we must place Main in class GradeBook. We use a separate module (GradeBookTest in this example) containing Main to test each new class we create in this chapter.

Module GradeBookTest

The GradeBookTest module declaration (Fig. 4.2; lines 3–12) contains the Main method (lines 5–11) that controls our application's execution. The module contains only a Main method, which is typical of many modules that begin an application's execution.

Lines 5–11 declare method Main. In this application, we would like to call class GradeBook's DisplayMessage method to display the welcome message in the **Console** window. Typically, you cannot call a method that belongs to another class until you create an object of that class. We begin by declaring variable gradeBook (line 7). Note that the variable's type is GradeBook—the class we declared in Fig. 4.1. Each new class you create becomes a new type in Visual Basic that can be used to declare variables and create objects. You can declare new class types as needed; this is one reason why Visual Basic is known as an extensible language.

Variable gradeBook is initialized with the result of the object-creation expression New GradeBook() (Fig. 4.2; line 7). New creates a new object of the class specified to the right of the New keyword (i.e., GradeBook). The class name is followed by a set of parentheses. As you'll learn in Section 4.7, those parentheses in combination with a class name represent a call to a constructor, a special type of method that is used only when an object is created to initialize the object's data. In that section you'll see that arguments can be placed in the parentheses to specify initial values for the object's data. In this example, we simply leave the parentheses empty. When there are no arguments to be placed in the parentheses, Visual Basic allows for the parentheses to be omitted, as in the next example. Although Visual Basic is not case sensitive, it does allow us to create objects (e.g., gradeBook) with the "same" name as their class (e.g. GradeBook)—we do this throughout the book.

We can now use object gradeBook to call method DisplayMessage. Line 10 calls DisplayMessage (declared in lines 5–7 of Fig. 4.1) using variable gradeBook followed by a dot separator (.), the method name DisplayMessage and an empty set of parentheses. This call causes the DisplayMessage method to perform its task. This method call differs from the method calls in Chapter 3 that displayed information in the **Console** window—each of those method calls provided arguments that specified the data to display. At the beginning of line 10, "gradeBook." indicates that Main should use the object of class

```
1  ' Fig. 4.2: GradeBookTest.vb
2  ' Create a GradeBook object and call its DisplayMessage method.
3  Module GradeBookTest
4     ' Main begins program execution
5     Sub Main()
6        ' initialize gradeBook to refer to a new GradeBook object
7        Dim gradeBook As New GradeBook()
8
9        ' call gradeBook's DisplayMessage method
10       gradeBook.DisplayMessage()
11    End Sub ' Main
12 End Module ' GradeBookTest
```

```
Welcome to the Grade Book!
```

Fig. 4.2 | Creating an object of class GradeBook and calling its DisplayMessage method.

GradeBook that was created in line 7. The empty parentheses in line 5 of Fig. 4.1 indicate that method DisplayMessage has no parameters—that is, DisplayMessage does not require additional information to perform its task. For this reason, the method call (line 10 of Fig. 4.2) specifies an empty set of parentheses after the method name to indicate that no arguments are being passed to method DisplayMessage. When method DisplayMessage completes its task, Main continues executing at line 11, which is the end of method Main, so the program terminates. When you type "gradeBook." (line 10) in the IDE, notice that *IntelliSense* displays the list of items that can be placed after the dot, such as the method DisplayMessage.

UML Class Diagram for Class **GradeBook**

Figure 4.3 presents a UML class diagram for class GradeBook of Fig. 4.1. Recall from Section 1.19 that the UML is a graphical language used to represent object-oriented systems in a standardized manner. In the UML, each class is modeled in a class diagram as a rectangle with three compartments. The top compartment contains the name of the class centered horizontally in boldface type. The middle compartment contains the class's attributes, which correspond to instance variables in Visual Basic. In Fig. 4.3, the middle compartment is empty because the version of class GradeBook in Fig. 4.1 does not have any attributes. The bottom compartment contains the class's operations, which correspond to methods in Visual Basic. The UML models an operation by listing its name followed by a set of parentheses. Class GradeBook has one method, DisplayMessage, so the bottom compartment of Fig. 4.3 lists the operation with this name. Method DisplayMessage does not require additional information to perform its tasks, so the parentheses following DisplayMessage in the class diagram are empty, just as they were in the method's declaration in line 5 of Fig. 4.1. The plus sign (+) in front of the operation name indicates that DisplayMessage is a public operation in the UML (because it is a Public method in Visual Basic). We often use UML class diagrams to summarize a class's attributes and operations.

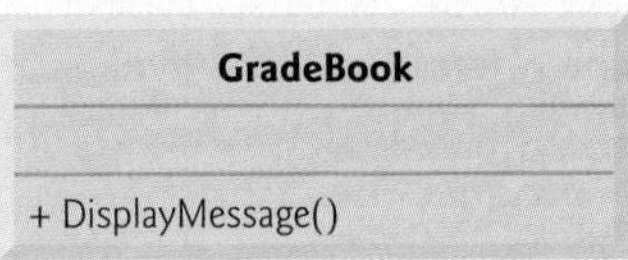

Fig. 4.3 | UML class diagram indicating that class GradeBook has a public DisplayMessage operation.

4.4 Declaring a Method with a Parameter

In our car analogy in Section 4.2, we discussed the fact that pressing a car's gas pedal sends a message to the car to perform a task—make the car go faster. But how fast should the car accelerate? The farther down you press the pedal, the faster the car accelerates. So the message to the car actually includes both the task to perform and additional information that helps the car perform the task. This additional information is known as a parameter (mentioned briefly in Section 4.3)—the value of the parameter helps the car determine how fast to accelerate. Similarly, a method can require one or more parameters that represent additional information it needs to perform its task. A method call supplies values—called arguments—for each method's parameters. For example, the call to `Console.WriteLine` requires an argument that specifies the data to output in a Command Prompt window. Similarly, to deposit funds into a bank account, a `Deposit` method specifies a parameter that represents the deposit amount. When the `Deposit` method is called, the argument value representing the deposit amount is assigned to the method's parameter. The method then makes a deposit of that amount, increasing the balance in the bank account.

Our next example declares class `GradeBook` (Fig. 4.4) with a `DisplayMessage` method that displays the course name as part of the welcome message. (See the sample execution in Fig. 4.5.) The new `DisplayMessage` method requires a parameter that represents the course name to output (line 5).

Note that line 7 contains the identifier, `vbNewLine`, which is not declared explicitly in the program. Identifier `vbNewLine` is one of several predefined constants provided by Visual Basic. Constants contain values that you cannot modify. The constant `vbNewLine` represents a combination of the carriage return and linefeed characters. Outputting this constant's value causes subsequent text to display at the beginning of the next line. The effect of this constant is similar to calling `Console.WriteLine()`.

Although not demonstrated in this example, Visual Basic also provides the `vbTab` constant, which represents a *Tab* character. Both the `vbNewLine` and `vbTab` constants are defined in a module named `Constants`. These constants are available in all Visual Basic programs. To view the complete list of constants, select **Help > Index** and type **Constants module** in the **Look for** field. Then select **Constants module** from the index list to view Visual Basic's predefined constants.

Before discussing the new features of class `GradeBook`, let us see how the new class is used from the `Main` method of module `GradeBookTest` (Fig. 4.5). Line 7 initializes variable `gradeBook` to reference a new `GradeBook` object. Note that empty parentheses are used in the object-creation expression (`New GradeBook()`), because no arguments need to be passed to create a `GradeBook` object. Line 10 prompts the user to enter a course name. Line 13 reads the name from the user and assigns it to the `nameOfCourse` variable, using method `ReadLine` to perform the input. The user types the course name and presses *Enter* to submit the course name to the program. Variable `nameOfCourse` is declared as a `String` (line 13). `String` is the type used for strings of characters in Visual Basic, such as names, addresses, cities, states and product descriptions. `Strings` can consist of up to 2,147,483,648 (2^{31}) characters.

Line 19 calls `gradeBook`'s `DisplayMessage` method. The argument `nameOfCourse` in parentheses is passed to method `DisplayMessage` so that it can perform its task. The value

```
1  ' Fig. 4.4: GradeBook.vb
2  ' Class declaration with a method that has a parameter.
3  Public Class GradeBook
4     ' display a welcome message to the GradeBook user
5     Public Sub DisplayMessage(ByVal courseName As String)
6        Console.WriteLine( _
7           "Welcome to the grade book for " & vbNewLine & courseName & "!")
8     End Sub ' DisplayMessage
9  End Class ' GradeBook
```

Fig. 4.4 | Class declaration with one method that has a parameter.

```
1  ' Fig. 4.5: GradeBookTest.vb
2  ' Create a GradeBook object and call its DisplayMessage method.
3  Module GradeBookTest
4     ' Main begins program execution
5     Sub Main()
6        ' initialize gradeBook to reference a new gradeBook object
7        Dim gradeBook As New GradeBook()
8
9        ' prompt for the course name
10       Console.WriteLine("Please enter the course name:")
11
12       ' read the course name
13       Dim nameOfCourse As String = Console.ReadLine()
14
15       Console.WriteLine() ' output a blank line
16
17       ' call gradeBook's DisplayMessage method
18       ' and pass nameOfCourse as an argument
19       gradeBook.DisplayMessage(nameOfCourse)
20    End Sub ' Main
21 End Module ' GradeBookTest
```

```
Please enter the course name:
CS101 Introduction to Visual Basic Programming

Welcome to the grade book for
CS101 Introduction to Visual Basic Programming!
```

Fig. 4.5 | Creating a `GradeBook` object and passing a `String` to its `DisplayMessage` method.

of variable `nameOfCourse` in `Main` (i.e., whatever course name the user types) becomes the value of method `DisplayMessage`'s parameter `courseName` in line 5 of Fig. 4.4. When you execute this application, you'll see that method `DisplayMessage` outputs a welcome message with the course name you type (Fig. 4.5).

More on Arguments and Parameters

When you declare a method, you must specify in the method's declaration whether the method requires data to perform its task. To do so, you place additional information in the method's parameter list, which is located in the parentheses that follow the method name. The parameter list may contain any number of parameters, including none at all. In Fig. 4.4, `DisplayMessage`'s parameter list (line 5) declares that the method requires one parameter. Each parameter must specify a type and an identifier. In this case, the type `String` and the identifier `courseName` indicate that method `DisplayMessage` requires a `String` parameter named `courseName` to perform its task. At the time the method is called, the argument value in the call (in this case, the value of `nameOfCourse` in line 19 of Fig. 4.5) is assigned to the corresponding parameter in the method header (in this case, `courseName` in line 5 of Fig. 4.4). Then the method body uses the parameter `courseName` to access the value. Lines 6–7 of Fig. 4.4 display parameter `courseName`'s value. The parameter variable's name (Fig. 4.4, line 5) can be the same as or different from the argument variable's name (Fig. 4.5, line 19)—there is no conflict if the names are identical, because as you'll see in Chapter 7, Methods: A Deeper Look, these names appear in different "scopes."

Note that the parameter declaration in the parameter list looks similar to a variable declaration, but uses keyword `ByVal` instead of `Dim`. `ByVal` specifies that the calling program should pass a copy of the value of the argument in the method call to the parameter, which can be used in the method body. Section 7.13 discusses argument-passing options in detail.

A method can specify multiple parameters by separating each from the next with a comma. The number of arguments in a method call must match the number of parameters in the called method's parameter list. Also, the argument types in the method call must be "consistent" with the types of the corresponding parameters in the method's declaration. (As you'll learn in subsequent chapters, an argument's type and its corresponding parameter's type are not always required to be identical.) In our example, the method call (line 19 of Fig. 4.5) passes one argument of type `String` (`nameOfCourse` is declared as a `String` in line 13 of Fig. 4.5) and the method declaration specifies one parameter of type `String` (line 5 in Fig. 4.4), so the type of the argument in the method call is identical to the type of the parameter in the method header.

Updated UML Class Diagram for Class **GradeBook**

The UML class diagram in Fig. 4.6 models class `GradeBook` of Fig. 4.4. Like Fig. 4.1, this `GradeBook` class contains public operation `DisplayMessage`. However, this version of `DisplayMessage` has a parameter. The UML models a parameter a bit differently from Visual Basic, by listing the parameter name in the parentheses following the operation name, followed by a colon and the parameter type. The UML has several data types that are similar to the Visual Basic types. For example, UML types `String` and `Integer` correspond to Visual Basic types `String` and `Integer`, respectively. Unfortunately, the UML does not provide types that correspond to every Visual Basic type. For this reason, and to avoid confusion between UML types and Visual Basic types, we use only Visual Basic types in our UML diagrams. Class `GradeBook`'s method `DisplayMessage` (Fig. 4.4) has a `String` parameter named `courseName`, so Fig. 4.6 lists `courseName : String` between the parentheses following `DisplayMessage`.

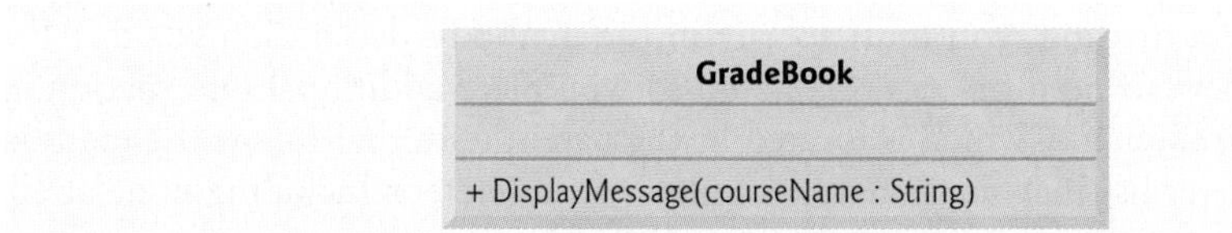

Fig. 4.6 | UML class diagram indicating that class `GradeBook` has a `DisplayMessage` operation with a `courseName` parameter of type `String`.

4.5 Instance Variables and Properties

In Chapter 3, we declared all of an application's variables in the `Main` method. Variables declared in the body of a particular method are known as local variables and can be used only in that method. When a method terminates, the values of its local variables are lost. In contrast, an object's attributes are carried with the object as it is used in a program. Such attributes exist before a method is called on the object, while the method is executing, and after the method completes execution.

Attributes are represented as variables in a class declaration. Such variables are called instance variables and are declared inside a class declaration but outside the bodies of the class's other members, such as methods (and properties, which are discussed later in this section). Each object of a class maintains its own copy of an instance variable—that is, each object (instance) of the class has a separate instance of the variable in memory. [*Note:* In Chapter 10, Classes and Objects: A Deeper Look, we discuss another type of variable called a `Shared` variable, where all objects of a class share one copy of the variable.] The following example demonstrates a `GradeBook` class that contains a `courseNameValue` instance variable to represent a particular `GradeBook` object's course name.

`GradeBook` Class with an Instance Variable and a Property

The next version of class `GradeBook` (Fig. 4.7) maintains the course name as instance variable `courseNameValue` (line 5) so that the course name can be used or modified at any time during an application's execution. The class also contains one method—`DisplayMessage` (lines 19–24)—and one property—`CourseName` (line 8–16). Recall from Chapter 2 that properties are used to manipulate an object's attributes. For example, in that chapter, we used a `Label`'s `Text` property to specify the text to display on the `Label`. In this example, we use a property in code rather than in the **Properties** window of the IDE. To do this, we first declare a property as a member of the `GradeBook` class. As you'll soon see, the `GradeBook`'s `CourseName` property can be used to store a course name in a `GradeBook` (in instance variable `courseNameValue`) or retrieve the `GradeBook`'s course name (from instance variable `courseNameValue`). Method `DisplayMessage`—which now specifies no parameters—still displays a welcome message that includes the course name. However, the method now uses the `CourseName` property to obtain the course name from instance variable `courseNameValue`.

```
1  ' Fig. 4.7: GradeBook.vb
2  ' GradeBook class that contains instance variable courseNameValue
3  ' and a property to get and set its value.
4  Public Class GradeBook
5     Private courseNameValue As String ' course name for this GradeBook
6
7     ' property CourseName
8     Public Property CourseName() As String
9        Get ' retrieve courseNameValue
10          Return courseNameValue
11       End Get
12
13       Set(ByVal value As String) ' set courseNameValue
14          courseNameValue = value ' store the course name in the object
15       End Set
16    End Property ' CourseName
17
```

Fig. 4.7 | `GradeBook` class that contains a `courseNameValue` instance variable and a `CourseName` property. (Part 1 of 2.)

```
18      ' display a welcome message to the GradeBook user
19      Public Sub DisplayMessage()
20         ' use property CourseName to display the
21         ' name of the course this GradeBook represents
22         Console.WriteLine("Welcome to the grade book for " _
23            & vbNewLine & CourseName & "!")
24      End Sub ' DisplayMessage
25   End Class ' GradeBook
```

Fig. 4.7 | `GradeBook` class that contains a `courseNameValue` instance variable and a `CourseName` property. (Part 2 of 2.)

A typical instructor teaches more than one course, each with its own course name. Line 5 declares instance variable `courseNameValue` as a `String`. Line 5 is a declaration for an instance variable because it is in the body of the class (lines 4–25) but outside the bodies of the class's method (lines 19–24) and property (lines 8–16). Every `GradeBook` object requires its own copy of instance variable `courseNameValue` because each object represents a `GradeBook` for a different course. All the methods and properties of class `GradeBook` can directly manipulate its instance variable `courseNameValue`, but it is considered good practice for methods to use properties to manipulate instance variables (as we do in line 23 of method `DisplayMessage`)—you'll see why in Section 4.8.

Access Modifiers `Public` *and* `Private`

Most instance-variable declarations are preceded with the access modifier `Private` (as in line 5 of Fig. 4.7). Variables, methods and properties that are declared `Private` are accessible only to methods and properties of the class in which they are declared. Note that the keyword `Dim` is replaced by `Private` in an instance-variable declaration.

Declaring instance variables with access modifier `Private` is known as information hiding. When a program creates (instantiates) an object of class `GradeBook`, variable `courseNameValue` is encapsulated (hidden) in the object and can be accessed only by methods and properties of the object's class.

Software Engineering Observation 4.1

Precede every instance-variable declaration, method declaration and property declaration with an access modifier. In most cases, instance variables should be declared `Private`*, and methods and properties should be declared* `Public`*. If these modifiers are omitted, instance variables are* `Private` *by default, and methods and properties are* `Public` *by default. (You'll see in Section 10.2 that it is appropriate to declare certain methods and properties* `Private` *if they should be accessed only by other methods and properties of the class.)*

Software Engineering Observation 4.2

Declaring the instance variables of a class as `Private` *and the methods of the class as* `Public` *facilitates debugging, because problems with data manipulations are localized to the class's methods and properties since the* `Private` *instance variables are accessible only to these methods and properties.*

Setting and Getting the Values of `Private` *Instance Variables*

How can we allow a program to manipulate a class's `Private` instance variables but ensure that they remain in a valid state? We need to provide controlled ways for programmers to "get" (i.e., retrieve) the value in an instance variable and "set" (i.e., modify) the value in an instance variable. For these purposes, programmers using languages other than Visual Basic normally use methods known as *get* and *set* methods. These methods typically are made `Public`, and provide ways for the client to access or modify `Private` data. Historically, these methods begin with the words "get" and "set"—in our class `GradeBook`, for example, if we were to use such methods, they might be called `GetCourseNameValue` and `SetCourseNameValue`, respectively. Although it is possible to define methods with these names, Visual Basic properties provide a more elegant solution.

`GradeBook` *Class with a Property*

The `GradeBook` class's `CourseName` property declaration is located in lines 8–16 of Fig. 4.7. The property begins in line 8 with an access modifier (in this case, `Public`), followed by the keyword `Property`, the property's name—`CourseName`—and an empty set of parentheses. The keywords `As String` indicate that property `CourseName` represents a `String` (which in this example is the instance variable `courseNameValue`). The property ends with the keywords `End Property`.

Properties contain accessors that handle the details of returning and modifying data. A property declaration can contain a `Get` accessor, a `Set` accessor or both. The `Get` accessor (lines 9–11) enables a client to read the value of `Private` instance variable `courseNameValue`; the `Set` accessor (lines 13–15) enables a client to modify `courseNameValue`.

Visual Basic has feature called code snippets that allows you to insert predefined code templates into your code. To use the `Property` code snippet, type "`Property`" in the code window and hit the *tab* key. This inserts code for creating a `Private` instance variable and `Public` accessors to get and set that variable. Certain pieces of the code are highlighted for you to easily change the name and type of the property. You can hit *tab* to quickly go from one highlighted piece of text to another. You need to specify the instance variable's name and type, and the property's name. By default, the new `Property`'s type is `String`. The rest of the template is automatically updated for you by the IDE. To get a list of all available code snippets, type "?" and hit tab to display menu of template categories.

After defining a property, you can use it like a variable in your code. For example, you can assign a value to a property using an assignment statement. This executes the code in the property's `Set` accessor to set the value of the corresponding instance variable. Similarly, referencing the property to use its value (for example, to display it on the screen) executes the code in the property's `Get` accessor to obtain the corresponding instance variable's value. We demonstrate how to use properties in a program shortly. When we use properties in our examples, our convention is to append "`Value`" to instance-variable names (e.g., `courseNameValue`). We do this because Visual Basic is not case sensitive, so we cannot have both an instance variable named `courseName` and a property named `CourseName` in the same class.

`Get` *and* `Set` *Accessors*

Let us look more closely at property `CourseName`'s `Get` and `Set` accessors (Fig. 4.7). The `Get` accessor (lines 9–11) begins with the keyword `Get` and ends with the keywords `End`

Get. The accessor's body contains a Return statement, which consists of the keyword Return followed by an expression. The expression's value is returned to the client code that references the property. In this example, the value of courseNameValue is returned when the property CourseName is referenced. For example, the following statement

```
Dim theCourseName As String = gradeBook.CourseName
```

executes property CourseName's Get accessor, which returns the value of instance variable courseNameValue. That value is then stored in variable theCourseName. Note that property CourseName can be used as simply as if it were an instance variable. The property notation allows the client to think of the property as the underlying data. Again, the client cannot directly manipulate instance variable courseNameValue because it is Private.

The Set accessor (lines 13–15) begins with the keyword Set and ends with the keywords End Set. Following the keyword Set in line 13 is a pair of parentheses enclosing the Set accessor's parameter. When the property CourseName appears in an assignment statement, as in

```
gradeBook.CourseName = "CS100 Introduction to Computers"
```

the text "CS100 Introduction to Computers" is automatically passed to the parameter named value in line 13, and the Set accessor executes. Line 14 then stores value in instance variable courseNameValue. Set accessors do not return any data when they complete their tasks.

When you type the first line of a property declaration in the IDE and press *Enter*, the IDE creates empty Get and Set accessors for you. The parameter for the Set accessor is named value by default, so we use this parameter name in our examples. You can choose a different name if you like.

The statements inside the property's accessors at lines 10 and 14 (Fig. 4.7) each access courseNameValue, even though it was declared (as Private) outside the accessors. We can use variable courseNameValue in the methods and properties of class GradeBook because courseNameValue is an instance variable of the class. The order in which methods and properties are declared in a class does not determine when they are called at execution time, so you can declare method DisplayMessage (which uses property CourseName) before you declare property CourseName. Within the property itself, the Get and Set accessors can appear in any order, and either accessor can be omitted. In Chapter 10, we discuss how to omit either a Set or Get accessor to create a "read-only" or "write-only" property, respectively.

Using Property **CourseName** *in Method* **DisplayMessage**

Method DisplayMessage (lines 19–24 of Fig. 4.7) does not receive any parameters. Lines 22–23 output a welcome message that includes the value of instance variable courseNameValue. We do not reference courseNameValue directly. Instead, we access property CourseName (line 23), which automatically executes the property's Get accessor, returning the value of courseNameValue.

GradeBookTest *Module That Demonstrates Class* **GradeBook**

Module GradeBookTest (Fig. 4.8) creates a GradeBook object and demonstrates property CourseName. Line 8 creates a GradeBook object that is referenced by variable gradeBook of

```
1  ' Fig. 4.8: GradeBookTest.vb
2  ' Create and manipulate a GradeBook object.
3  Module GradeBookTest
4     ' Main begins program execution
5     Sub Main()
6        ' line 8 creates a GradeBook object that is referenced by
7        ' variable gradeBook of type GradeBook
8        Dim gradeBook As New GradeBook
9
10       ' display initial value of property CourseName (invokes Get)
11       Console.WriteLine( _
12          "Initial course name is: " & gradeBook.CourseName & vbNewLine)
13
14       ' prompt for course name
15       Console.WriteLine("Please enter the course name:")
16
17       ' read course name
18       Dim theName As String = Console.ReadLine()
19
20       gradeBook.CourseName = theName ' set the CourseName (invokes Set)
21       Console.WriteLine() ' output a blank line
22
23       ' display welcome message including the course name (invokes Get)
24       gradeBook.DisplayMessage()
25    End Sub ' Main
26 End Module ' GradeBookTest
```

```
Initial course name is:

Please enter the course name:
CS101 Introduction to Visual Basic Programming

Welcome to the grade book for
CS101 Introduction to Visual Basic Programming!
```

Fig. 4.8 | Creating and manipulating a `GradeBook` object (invoking properties).

type `GradeBook`. Lines 11–12 display the initial course name by referencing the object's `CourseName` property—this executes the property's `Get` accessor, which returns the value of `courseNameValue`. Note that the first line of the output does not contain a course name. Variables have a **default initial value**—a value provided by Visual Basic when you do not specify the variable's initial value. The default value for numeric types like `Integer` is zero. As you'll see in the next section, `String` is a reference type; the default value for reference types is **`Nothing`**—a keyword which indicates that a variable does not yet refer to an object. When you display a `String` variable that contains the value `Nothing`, no text is displayed on the screen.

Line 15 prompts the user to enter a course name. Local `String` variable `theName` (declared in line 18) is initialized with the course name entered by the user, which is returned by the call to `Console.ReadLine()`. Line 20 assigns `theName` to the `gradeBook` object's `CourseName` property. When a value is assigned to `CourseName`, the value specified (in this case, `theName`) is assigned to parameter `value` (line 13 of Fig. 4.7) of `CourseName`'s

Set accessor (lines 13–15, Fig. 4.7). Then parameter value is assigned by the Set accessor to instance variable courseNameValue (line 14 of Fig. 4.7). Line 21 (Fig. 4.8) displays a blank line, then line 24 calls gradeBook's DisplayMessage method to display the welcome message containing the course name.

GradeBook's UML Class Diagram with a Property

Figure 4.9 contains an updated UML class diagram for the version of class GradeBook in Fig. 4.7. We model properties in the UML as attributes—the property (in this case, CourseName) is listed as a public attribute—as indicated by the plus (+) sign—preceded by the word "Property" in guillemets (« and »). Using descriptive words in guillemets (called stereotypes in the UML) helps distinguish properties from other attributes and operations. The UML indicates the type of the property by placing a colon and a type after the property name. The Get and Set accessors of the property are implied (otherwise, the property would be inaccessible), so they are not listed in the UML diagram. In some cases, a property may require only a Get accessor to allow client code to retrieve the property's value. This is known as a "read-only" property. You can indicate this in a class diagram by placing the annotation {ReadOnly} after the property's type.

The diagram shows that class GradeBook also contains one Public method DisplayMessage, which the class diagram lists in the third compartment. Recall that the plus (+) sign before an operation name indicates that the operation is Public.

A class diagram helps you design a class, so it is not required to show every implementation detail of the class. Since an instance variable that is manipulated by a property is really an implementation detail of that property, our class diagram does not show the courseNameValue instance variable. A programmer implementing the GradeBook class based on this class diagram would create the instance variable courseNameValue as part of the implementation process (as we did in Fig. 4.7).

In some cases, you may find it necessary to model the Private instance variables of a class, because they are not implementation details of properties. Like properties, instance variables are attributes of a class and are modeled in the middle compartment of a class diagram. The UML represents instance variables as attributes by listing the attribute name, followed by a colon and the attribute type. To indicate that an attribute is Private, a class diagram would list a minus sign (-) before the attribute's name. For example, the instance variable courseNameValue in Fig. 4.7 would be modeled as "– courseNameValue : String".

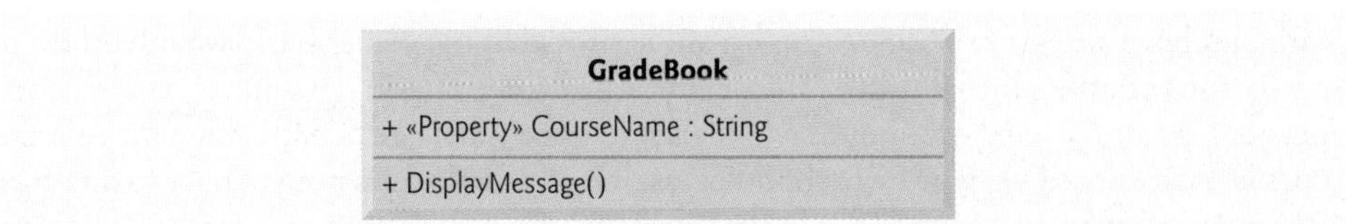

Fig. 4.9 | UML class diagram indicating that class GradeBook has one property and one method.

Software Engineering with Properties and Set and Get Accessors

Using properties as described earlier in this section would seem to violate the notion of Private data. Although providing a property with Get and Set accessors may appear to be the same as making its corresponding instance variable `Public`, this is not the case. A `Public` instance variable can be read or written by any method in the program. If an instance variable is `Private`, the client code can access the instance variable only indirectly through the class's non-`Private` methods or properties. This allows the class to control the manner in which the data is set or returned. For example, `Get` and `Set` accessors can translate between the format of the data used by the client and the format stored in the `Private` instance variable.

Consider a `Clock` class that represents the time of day as a `Private Integer` instance variable `timeValue` containing the number of seconds since midnight. Suppose the class provides a `Time` property of type `String` to manipulate this instance variable. Although `Get` accessors typically return data exactly as it is stored in an object, they need not expose the data in this "raw" format. When a client refers to a `Clock` object's `Time` property, the property's `Get` accessor could use instance variable `timeValue` to determine the number of hours, minutes and seconds since midnight, then return the time as a `String` of the form `"HH:MM:SS"`. Similarly, suppose a `Clock` object's `Time` property is assigned a `String` of the form `"HH:MM:SS"`. Using the `String` capabilities presented in Section 4.8 and the method `Convert.ToInt32` presented in Section 7.10, the `Time` property's `Set` accessor could convert this `String` to an `Integer` number of seconds and store the result in the `Clock` object's `Private` instance variable `timeValue`. The `Time` property's `Set` accessor can also provide **data-validation** capabilities that scrutinize attempts to modify the instance variable's value to ensure that the value it receives represents a valid time (e.g., `"12:30:45"` is valid but `"42:85:70"` is not). We demonstrate data validation in Section 4.8. So, although a property's accessors enable clients to manipulate `Private` data, they carefully control those manipulations, and the object's `Private` data remains safely encapsulated (i.e., hidden) in the object. This is not possible with `Public` instance variables, which can easily be set by clients to invalid values.

Properties of a class should also be used by the class's own methods to manipulate the class's `Private` instance variables, even though the methods can directly access the `Private` instance variables. Accessing an instance variable via a property's accessors—as in the body of method `DisplayMessage` (Fig. 4.7, line 23)—creates a better, more robust class that is easier to maintain and less likely to malfunction. If we decide to change the representation of instance variable `courseNameValue` in some way, the declaration of method `DisplayMessage` will not require modification—only the bodies of property `CourseName`'s `Get` and `Set` accessors that directly manipulate the instance variable will need to change. For example, suppose that we want to represent the course name as two separate instance variables—`courseNumber` (e.g., `"CS101"`) and `courseTitle` (e.g., `"Introduction to Visual Basic Programming"`). The `DisplayMessage` method can still use property `CourseName`'s `Get` accessor to obtain the full course name to display as part of the welcome message. In this case, the `Get` accessor would need to build and return a `String` containing the `courseNumber` followed by the `courseTitle`. Method `DisplayMessage` would continue to display the complete course title "`CS101 Introduction to Visual Basic Programming`," because it is unaffected by the change to the class's instance variables.

Software Engineering Observation 4.3

Accessing `Private` data through `Set` and `Get` accessors not only protects the instance variables from receiving invalid values, but also hides the internal representation of the instance variables from that class's clients. Thus, if representation of the data changes (often, to reduce the amount *of required storage or to improve performance), only the properties' implementations need to change—the clients' implementations need not change as long as the services provided by the properties are preserved.*

4.6 Value Types and Reference Types

Data types in Visual Basic are divided into two categories—value types and reference types. A variable of a value type (such as `Integer`) simply contains a value of that type. For example, Fig. 4.10 shows an `Integer` variable named `count` that contains the value `7`.

By contrast, a variable of a reference type (sometimes called a reference) contains the memory address where the data referred to by that variable is stored. Such a variable is said to refer to an object in the program. Line 8 of Fig. 4.8 creates a `GradeBook` object, places it in memory and stores the object's memory address in reference variable `gradeBook` of type `GradeBook` as shown in Fig. 4.11. Note that the `GradeBook` object is shown with its `courseNameValue` instance variable.

Reference type instance variables (such as `gradeBook` in Fig. 4.11) are initialized by default to the value `Nothing`. Except for type `String`, Visual Basic's primitive types are value types—`String` is a reference type. For this reason, the `String` variable `courseNameValue` is shown in Fig. 4.11 with an empty box representing the variable in memory. Once you assign a value to the `String` variable, the box will not contain the object itself, but rather an arrow referencing that String object.

A client of an object must use a reference to the object to invoke (i.e., call) the object's methods and access the object's properties. In Fig. 4.8, the statements in `Main` use variable `gradeBook`, which contains the `GradeBook` object's reference, to send messages to the `GradeBook` object. These messages are calls to methods (like `DisplayMessage`) or references to properties (like `CourseName`) that enable the program to interact with `GradeBook` objects. For example, the statement (in line 20)

```
gradeBook.CourseName = theName ' set the CourseName (invokes Set)
```

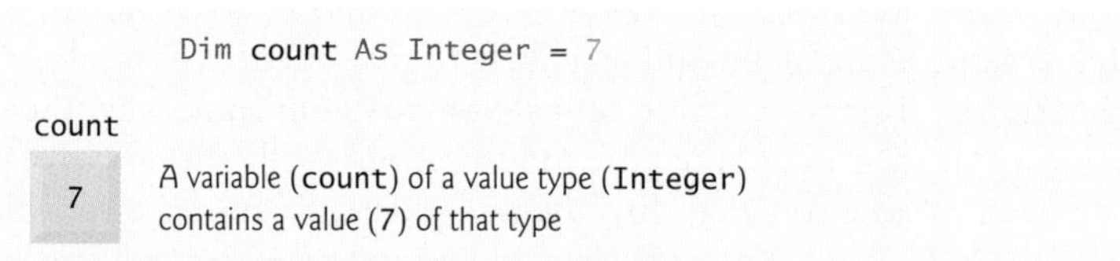
Dim count As Integer = 7
count
7
A variable (count) of a value type (Integer) contains a value (7) of that type

Fig. 4.10 | Value type variable.

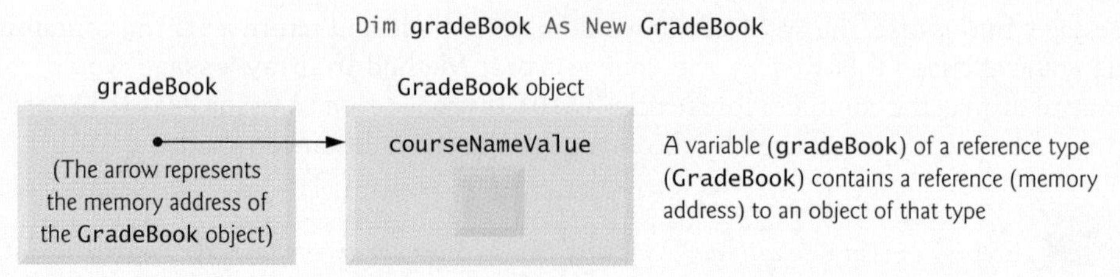
Dim gradeBook As New GradeBook
gradeBook
GradeBook object
courseNameValue
(The arrow represents the memory address of the GradeBook object)
A variable (gradeBook) of a reference type (GradeBook) contains a reference (memory address) to an object of that type

Fig. 4.11 | Reference type variable.

uses gradeBook to set the course name by assigning a value to property CourseName. This sends a message to the GradeBook object to invoke the CourseName property's Set accessor. The message includes as an argument the value (i.e., the value of theName, namely CS101 Introduction to Visual Basic Programming) that CourseName's Set accessor requires to perform its task. The Set accessor uses this information to set the courseNameValue instance variable. In Section 7.11, we discuss value types and reference types in detail.

4.7 Initializing Objects with Constructors

As mentioned in Section 4.5, when an object of class GradeBook (Fig. 4.7) is created, its instance variable courseNameValue is initialized to Nothing by default. What if you want to provide a course name when you create a GradeBook object? Each class you declare can provide a constructor that can be used to initialize an object of the class when the object is created. In fact, Visual Basic requires a constructor call for every object that is created. The New keyword calls the class's constructor to perform the initialization. The constructor call is indicated by the class name followed by parentheses. For example, line 8 of Fig. 4.8 first uses New to create a GradeBook object. The lack of parentheses after "New GradeBook" indicates a call to the class's constructor that takes no arguments and is equivalent to using "New GradeBook()." By default, the compiler provides a **default constructor** with no parameters in any class that does not explicitly include a constructor.

When you declare a class, you can provide your own constructor to specify custom initialization for objects of your class. For example, you might want to specify a course name for a GradeBook object when the object is created, as in

```
Dim gradeBook As New GradeBook( _
   "CS101 Introduction to Visual Basic Programming")
```

This passes the argument "CS101 Introduction to Visual Basic Programming" to the GradeBook object's constructor, which uses the argument value to initialize instance variable courseNameValue. The preceding statement requires that the class provide a constructor with a String parameter. Figure 4.12 contains a modified GradeBook class with such a constructor.

```
' Fig. 4.12: GradeBook.vb
' GradeBook class with a constructor to initialize the course name.
Public Class GradeBook
   Private courseNameValue As String ' course name for this GradeBook

   ' constructor initializes course name with String supplied as argument
   Public Sub New(ByVal name As String)
      CourseName = name ' initialize courseNameValue via property
   End Sub ' New

   ' property CourseName
   Public Property CourseName() As String
      Get ' retrieve courseNameValue
         Return courseNameValue
      End Get
```

Fig. 4.12 | GradeBook class with a constructor that receives a course name. (Part 1 of 2.)

```
16
17          Set(ByVal value As String) ' set courseNameValue
18             courseNameValue = value ' store the course name in the object
19          End Set
20       End Property ' CourseName
21
22       ' display a welcome message to the GradeBook user
23       Public Sub DisplayMessage()
24          ' use property CourseName to display the
25          ' name of the course this GradeBook represents
26          Console.WriteLine("Welcome to the grade book for " _
27             & vbNewLine & CourseName & "!")
28       End Sub ' DisplayMessage
29    End Class ' GradeBook
```

Fig. 4.12 | GradeBook class with a constructor that receives a course name. (Part 2 of 2.)

Lines 7–9 declare the constructor for class GradeBook—a constructor must have the name New. As with the other methods we have declared, a constructor specifies in its parameter list the data it requires to perform its task. When you create a new object, this data is placed in the parentheses that follow the class name (as in lines 8–11 of Fig. 4.13). Line 7 (Fig. 4.12) indicates that class GradeBook's constructor has a parameter called name of type String.

Line 8 of the constructor's body assigns name to property CourseName. This causes the Set accessor of property CourseName to execute, which (in line 18) assigns parameter value to instance variable courseNameValue. You might be wondering why we bother using property CourseName—the constructor certainly could perform the assignment courseNameValue = name. In Section 4.8, we modify the Set accessor of property CourseName to perform validation (in this case, to ensure that the courseNameValue is 25 or fewer characters in length). At that point the benefits of using property CourseName from the constructor will become clear.

Figure 4.13 demonstrates initializing GradeBook objects using this constructor. Lines 8–9 create and initialize a GradeBook object. The constructor of class GradeBook is called with the argument "CS101 Introduction to Visual Basic Programming" to initialize the course name. The object-creation expression in lines 8–9 returns a reference to the new object, which is assigned to variable gradeBook1. Lines 10–11 repeat this process for another GradeBook object, this time passing the argument "CS102 Data Structures in Visual Basic" to initialize the course name for gradeBook2. Lines 14–17 use each object's CourseName property to display the course names and show that they were initialized properly when the objects were created. The output confirms that each GradeBook maintains its own copy of instance variable courseNameValue.

```
1  ' Fig. 4.13: GradeBookTest.vb
2  ' GradeBook constructor used to specify the course name at the
3  ' time each GradeBook object is created.
4  Module GradeBookTest
```

Fig. 4.13 | Constructor used to initialize GradeBook objects. (Part 1 of 2.)

```
    ' Main begins program execution
    Sub Main()
       ' create GradeBook object
       Dim gradeBook1 As New GradeBook( _
          "CS101 Introduction to Visual Basic Programming")
       Dim gradeBook2 As New GradeBook( _
          "CS102 Data Structures in Visual Basic")

       ' display initial value of CourseName for each GradeBook
       Console.WriteLine( _
          "gradeBook1 course name is: " & gradeBook1.CourseName)
       Console.WriteLine( _
          "gradeBook2 course name is: " & gradeBook2.CourseName)
    End Sub ' Main
 End Module ' GradeBookTest
```

```
gradeBook1 course name is: CS101 Introduction to Visual Basic Programming
gradeBook2 course name is: CS102 Data Structures in Visual Basic
```

Fig. 4.13 | Constructor used to initialize `GradeBook` objects. (Part 2 of 2.)

Like other methods, constructors also can take arguments. However, an important difference between constructors and methods is that constructor declarations cannot return values (even though, as you know, each constructor does return a reference—to an object of its class type). Normally, constructors are declared `Public`. If a class does not include a constructor, the class's instance variables are initialized to their default values.

Error-Prevention Tip 4.1

Unless default initialization of your class's instance variables is acceptable, provide a constructor to ensure that these variables are properly initialized with meaningful values when each new object of your class is created.

Adding the Constructor to Class `GradeBook`*'s UML Class Diagram*

The UML class diagram of Fig. 4.14 models the class `GradeBook` of Fig. 4.12, which has a constructor that has a `name` parameter of type `String`. Like operations, the UML models constructors in the third compartment of a class in a class diagram. To distinguish a constructor from a class's operations, the UML places the word "constructor" between guillemets (« and ») before the constructor's name (`New`). It is customary to list constructors before other operations in the third compartment.

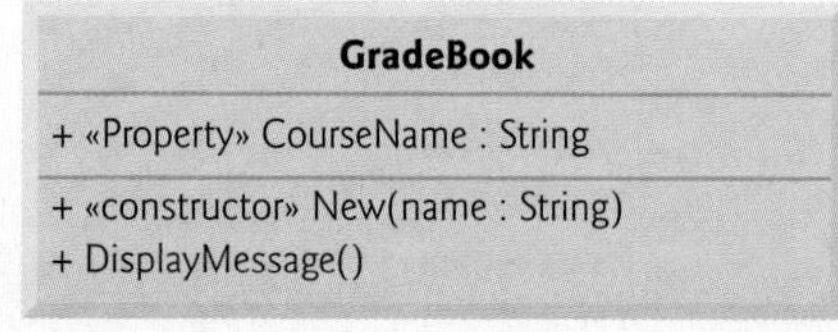

Fig. 4.14 | UML class diagram indicating that class `GradeBook` has a constructor that has a `name` parameter of type `String`.

4.8 Validating Data with Set Accessors in Properties

In Section 4.5, we introduced properties whose `Set` accessors allow clients of a class to modify the value of a `Private` instance variable. In Fig. 4.7, class `GradeBook` defines property `CourseName`'s `Set` accessor to assign the value received in its parameter `value` to instance variable `courseNameValue` (line 14). This `CourseName` property does not ensure that `courseNameValue` contains valid data. In this section, we enhance our property to include data validation in its `Set` accessor. Property `CourseName` (Fig. 4.12) does not ensure that the course name adheres to any particular format or follows any other rules regarding what a "valid" course name is. Suppose that a university can display student transcripts in an online form that can hold course names of only 25 or fewer characters. If the university uses a system containing `GradeBook` objects to generate the transcripts, we might want class `GradeBook` to ensure that its `courseNameValue` never contains more than 25 characters. The program of Figs. 4.15–4.16 enhances class `GradeBook`'s property `CourseName` to perform this validation (also known as validity checking).

`GradeBook` Class Definition

`GradeBook`'s class definition in Fig. 4.15 contains all the same members as Fig. 4.12. Since the name and type of the property remain unchanged, clients of this class need not be changed when the definition of property `CourseName` is modified. This enables clients to take advantage of the improved `GradeBook` class without having to modify their own code.

```
' Fig. 4.15: GradeBook.vb
' GradeBook class with a property that performs validation.
Public Class GradeBook
   Private courseNameValue As String ' course name for this GradeBook

   ' constructor initializes CourseName with String supplied as argument
   Public Sub New(ByVal name As String)
      CourseName = name ' validate and store course name
   End Sub ' New

   ' property that gets and sets the course name; the Set accessor
   ' ensures that the course name has at most 25 characters
   Public Property CourseName() As String
      Get ' retrieve courseNameValue
         Return courseNameValue
      End Get

      Set(ByVal value As String) ' set courseNameValue
         If value.Length <= 25 Then ' if value has 25 or fewer characters
            courseNameValue = value ' store the course name in the object
         End If

         If value.Length > 25 Then ' if value has more than 25 characters
            ' set courseNameValue to first 25 characters of value
            ' start at 0, length of 25
            courseNameValue = value.Substring(0, 25)
```

Fig. 4.15 | Method declarations for class `GradeBook` with a `CourseName` property that validates the length of instance variable `courseNameValue`. (Part 1 of 2.)

```
27
28                Console.WriteLine( _
29                   "Name """ & value & """ exceeds maximum length (25).")
30                Console.WriteLine( _
31                   "Limiting course name to first 25 characters." & vbNewLine)
32             End If
33          End Set
34       End Property ' CourseName
35
36       ' display a welcome message to the GradeBook user
37       Public Sub DisplayMessage()
38          ' this statement uses property CourseName to get the
39          ' name of the course this GradeBook represents
40          Console.WriteLine("Welcome to the grade book for " _
41             & vbNewLine & CourseName & "!")
42       End Sub ' DisplayMessage
43    End Class ' GradeBook
```

Fig. 4.15 | Method declarations for class `GradeBook` with a `CourseName` property that validates the length of instance variable `courseNameValue`. (Part 2 of 2.)

Validating the Course Name with `GradeBook` *Property* `CourseName`

The enhancement to class `GradeBook` is in the definition of `CourseName`'s `Set` accessor (Fig. 4.15, lines 18–33). The `If...Then` statement in lines 19–21 determines whether parameter `value` contains a valid course name (i.e., a `String` of 25 or fewer characters). If the course name is valid, line 20 stores it in instance variable `courseNameValue`. Note the expression `value.Length` in line 19. **`Length`** is a property of class `String` that returns the number of characters in the `String`. Parameter `value` is a `String` object, so the expression `value.Length` returns the number of characters in `value`. If `value.Length` is less than or equal to `25`, `value` is valid and line 20 executes.

The `If...Then` statement in lines 23–32 handles the case in which `CourseName` receives an invalid course name (i.e., a name longer than 25 characters). Even if the `String` in parameter `value` is too long, we still want to leave the `GradeBook` object in a **consistent state**—that is, a state in which the object's instance variable `courseNameValue` contains a `String` of 25 or fewer characters. We choose to truncate (i.e., shorten) the specified course name and assign the first 25 characters of `value` to the `courseNameValue` instance variable (unfortunately, this could truncate the course name awkwardly). Class `String` provides the method **`Substring`** that returns a new `String` object created by copying part of an existing `String` object. The call in line 26 (i.e., `value.Substring(0, 25)`) passes two integers (`0` and `25`) to `value`'s method `Substring`. These arguments indicate the portion of the string `value` that `Substring` should return. The first argument specifies the starting position in the original `String` from which characters are to be copied—the first character in every string is considered to be at position 0. The second argument specifies the number of characters to copy. Therefore, the call in line 26 returns a 25-character substring of `value` starting at position 0 (i.e., the first 25 characters in `value`). For example, if `value` holds `"CS101 Introduction to Visual Basic Programming"`, `Substring` returns `"CS101 Introduction to Vis"`. After the call to `Substring`, line 26 assigns the substring returned by `Substring` to `courseNameValue`. In this way, property `CourseName` ensures that `courseNameValue` is always assigned a string containing 25 or fewer characters. If the property has to truncate the course name to make it valid, lines 28–31 display a warning message. Note that line 29 displays a string of text that includes double quotes ("). Double quotes are normally used to delimit string literals, so to display double quotes in a string, you use two double quotes in a row.

Testing Class **GradeBook**

Figure 4.16 demonstrates the modified version of class `GradeBook` featuring validation. Lines 8–9 create a `GradeBook` object named `gradeBook1`. Note that the `GradeBook` constructor (lines 7–9 of Fig. 4.15) references property `CourseName` to initialize `courseNameValue`. In previous versions of the class, the benefit of referencing the property `CourseName` in the constructor was not evident. Now, however, the constructor takes advantage of the validation provided by the `Set` accessor of the `CourseName` property. The constructor simply assigns a value to `CourseName` rather than duplicate the `Set` accessor's validation code. When line 9 of Fig. 4.16 passes an initial course name of `"CS101 Introduction to Visual Basic Programming"` to the `GradeBook` constructor, the constructor passes this value to the `Set` accessor of `CourseName`, where the actual initialization occurs. This course name contains more than 25 characters, so the body of the second `If...Then` statement (lines 23–32 of Fig. 4.15) executes, causing `courseNameValue` to be initialized to the truncated 25-character course name `"CS101 Introduction to Vis"` (the truncated part of the `String` is

```
1   ' Fig. 4.16: GradeBookTest.vb
2   ' Create and manipulate a GradeBook object; illustrate validation.
3   Module GradeBookTest
4      ' Main begins program execution
5      Sub Main()
6         ' create two GradeBook objects;
7         ' initial course name of gradeBook1 is too long
8         Dim gradeBook1 As New GradeBook( _
9            "CS101 Introduction to Visual Basic Programming")
10        Dim gradeBook2 As New GradeBook("CS102 VB Data Structures")
11
12        ' display each GradeBook's course name (by invoking Get)
13        Console.WriteLine("gradeBook1's initial course name is: " & _
14           gradeBook1.CourseName)
15        Console.WriteLine("gradeBook2's initial course name is: " & _
16           gradeBook2.CourseName)
17        Console.WriteLine() ' display blank line
18
19        ' place in gradeBook1's course name a valid-length String
20        gradeBook1.CourseName = "CS101 VB Programming"
21
22        ' display each GradeBook's course name (by invoking Get)
23        Console.WriteLine( _
24           "gradeBook1's course name is: " & gradeBook1.CourseName)
25        Console.WriteLine( _
26           "gradeBook2's course name is: " & gradeBook2.CourseName)
27     End Sub ' Main
28  End Module ' GradeBookTest
```

Fig. 4.16 | Creating and manipulating a `GradeBook` object in which the course name is limited to 25 characters in length. (Part 1 of 2.)

```
Name "CS101 Introduction to Visual Basic Programming" exceeds maximum length
(25).
Limiting course name to first 25 characters.

gradeBook1's initial course name is: CS101 Introduction to Vis
gradeBook2's initial course name is: CS102 VB Data Structures

gradeBook1's course name is: CS101 VB Programming
gradeBook2's course name is: CS102 VB Data Structures
```

Fig. 4.16 | Creating and manipulating a `GradeBook` object in which the course name is limited to 25 characters in length. (Part 2 of 2.)

highlighted in red in line 9 of Fig. 4.16). The output in Fig. 4.16 contains the warning message output by lines 28–31 of Fig. 4.15. Line 10 of Fig. 4.16 creates another `GradeBook` object called `gradeBook2`—the valid course name passed to the constructor contains fewer than 25 characters (it contains 24 characters, to be exact).

Lines 13–16 of Fig. 4.16 display the truncated course name for `gradeBook1` (we highlight this in red in the program output) and the course name for `gradeBook2`. Line 20 assigns a new value to `gradeBook1`'s `CourseName` property, to change the course name in the `GradeBook` object to a shorter name that does not need to be truncated. Then lines 23–26 output the course names for the `GradeBook` objects again.

A class's `Set` accessors cannot return values that indicate a failed attempt to assign invalid data to objects of the class. Such return values could be useful to a class's clients for handling errors—clients could then take appropriate actions. Chapter 13 presents exception handling—a mechanism that can be used (among other things) to notify a class's clients of attempts to set objects of that class to inconsistent states. To keep the program of Figs. 4.15–4.16 simple at this early point in the book, the `CourseName` property's `Set` accessor in Fig. 4.15 prints an appropriate message on the screen and sets `courseNameValue` to the first 25 characters of the specified course name.

`Set` and `Get` Accessors with Different Access Modifiers

By default, the `Get` and `Set` accessors of a property have the same access as the property—in other words, for a `Public` property, the accessors also are `Public`. In Visual Basic, it is possible to declare the `Get` and `Set` accessors with different access modifiers. In this case, one of the accessors must have the same access as the property and the other must be more restrictive than the property. For example, in a `Public` property, the `Get` accessor might be `Public` and the `Set` accessor might be `Private`. To make a `Set` accessor `Private`, simply type the keyword `Private` before the word `Set` in the accessor's declaration.

Error-Prevention Tip 4.2

The benefits of data integrity are not automatic simply because instance variables are made `Private`—you must provide appropriate validity checking and report the errors.

Error-Prevention Tip 4.3

`Set` accessors that set the values of `Private` data should verify that the intended new values are proper; if they are not, the `Set` accessors should place the `Private` instance variables into an appropriately consistent state.

4.9 (Optional) Software Engineering Case Study: Identifying the Classes in the ATM Requirements Document

Now we begin designing the ATM system that we introduced in Chapter 3. In this section, we identify the classes that are needed to build the ATM system by analyzing the nouns and noun phrases that appear in the requirements document. We introduce UML class diagrams to model the relationships among these classes. This is an important first step in defining the structure of our system.

Identifying the Classes in a System

We begin our OOD process by identifying the classes required to build the ATM system. We eventually describe these classes using UML class diagrams and implement these classes in Visual Basic. First, we review the requirements document of Section 3.10 and find key nouns and noun phrases to help us identify classes that comprise the ATM system. We may decide that some of the nouns and noun phrases are attributes of other classes in the system. We may also conclude that some of the nouns and noun phrases do not correspond to parts of the system and thus should not be modeled at all. Additional classes may become apparent as we proceed through the design process.

Figure 4.17 lists the nouns and noun phrases in the requirements document. We list them from left to right in the order in which they appear in the requirements document.

We create classes only for the nouns and noun phrases that have significance in the ATM system. We do not need to model "bank" as a class, because the bank is not a part of the ATM system—the bank simply wants us to build the ATM. "User" and "customer" also represent entities outside of the system—they are important because they interact with our ATM system, but we do not need to model them as classes in the ATM system itself. Recall that we modeled an ATM user (i.e., a bank customer) as the actor in the use case diagram of Fig. 3.38.

We do not model "$20 bill" or "deposit envelope" as classes. These are physical objects in the real world, but they are not part of what is being automated. We can adequately represent the presence of $20 bills in the system using an attribute of the class that models the cash dispenser. (We assign attributes to classes in Section 5.16.) For example,

Nouns and noun phrases in the requirements document		
bank	money / funds	account number
ATM	screen	PIN
user	keypad	bank database
customer	cash dispenser	balance inquiry
transaction	$20 bill / cash	withdrawal
account	deposit slot	deposit
balance	deposit envelope	

Fig. 4.17 | Nouns and noun phrases in the requirements document.

the cash dispenser maintains a count of the number of bills it contains. The requirements document does not say anything about what the system should do with deposit envelopes after it receives them. We can assume that simply acknowledging the receipt of an envelope—an operation performed by the class that models the deposit slot—is sufficient to represent the presence of an envelope in the system. (We assign operations to classes in Section 7.20.)

In our simplified ATM system, representing various amounts of "money," including the "balance" of an account, as attributes of other classes seems most appropriate. Likewise, the nouns "account number" and "PIN" represent significant pieces of information in the ATM system. They are important attributes of a bank account. They do not, however, exhibit behaviors. Thus, we can most appropriately model them as attributes of an account class.

Though the requirements document frequently describes a "transaction" in a general sense, we do not model the broad notion of a financial transaction at this time. Instead, we model the three types of transactions (i.e., "balance inquiry," "withdrawal" and "deposit") as individual classes. These classes possess specific attributes needed for executing the transactions they represent. For example, a withdrawal needs to know the amount of money the user wants to withdraw. A balance inquiry, however, does not require any additional data if the user is authenticated. Furthermore, the three transaction classes exhibit unique behaviors. A withdrawal includes dispensing cash to the user, whereas a deposit involves receiving a deposit envelope from the user. [*Note:* In Section 12.8, we "factor out" common features of all transactions into a general "transaction" class using the object-oriented concepts of abstract classes and inheritance.]

We determine the classes for our system based on the remaining nouns and noun phrases from Fig. 4.17. Each of these refers to one or more of the following:

- ATM
- screen
- keypad
- cash dispenser
- deposit slot
- account
- bank database
- balance inquiry
- withdrawal
- deposit

The elements of this list are likely to be classes we need to implement our system, although it's too early in our process to claim that this list is complete.

We can now begin modeling the classes in our system based on the list we have created. We capitalize class names in the design process—a UML convention—as we'll do when we write the actual Visual Basic code that implements our design. If the name of a class contains more than one word, we run the words together and capitalize each word (e.g., `MultipleWordName`). Using these conventions, we create classes `ATM`, `Screen`, `Keypad`, `CashDispenser`, `DepositSlot`, `Account`, `BankDatabase`, `BalanceInquiry`, `Withdrawal` and Deposit. We construct our system using all of these classes as building blocks. Before we begin building the system, however, we must gain a better understanding of how the classes relate to one another.

Modeling Classes

The UML enables us to model, via class diagrams, the classes in the ATM system and their interrelationships. Figure 4.18 represents class ATM. In the UML, each class is modeled as a rectangle with three compartments. The top compartment contains the name of the class, centered horizontally and appearing in boldface. The middle compartment contains the class's attributes (which we discuss in Section 5.16 and Section 6.11.) The bottom compartment contains the class's operations (which we discuss in Section 7.20). In Fig. 4.18 the middle and bottom compartments are empty, because we have not yet determined the ATM class's attributes and operations.

Class diagrams also show the relationships between the classes of the system. Figure 4.19 shows how classes ATM and Withdrawal relate to one another. For the moment, we choose to model only this subset of the ATM classes for simplicity. We present a more complete class diagram later in this section. Notice that the rectangles representing classes in this diagram are not subdivided into compartments. The UML allows the suppression of class attributes and operations in this manner, when appropriate, to create more readable diagrams. Such a diagram is said to be an elided diagram—one in which some information, such as the contents of the second and third compartments, is not modeled. We place information in these compartments in Section 5.16 and Section 7.20.

In Fig. 4.19, the solid line that connects the two classes represents an association—a relationship between classes. The numbers near each end of the line are multiplicity values, which indicate how many objects of each class participate in the association. In this case, following the line from the ATM to the Withdrawal reveals that, at any given moment, one ATM object participates in an association with either zero or one Withdrawal objects—zero if the current user is not performing a transaction or has requested a different type of transaction, and one if the user has requested a withdrawal. The UML can model many types of multiplicity (Fig. 4.20).

An association can be named. For example, the word Executes above the line connecting classes ATM and Withdrawal in Fig. 4.19 indicates the name of that association.

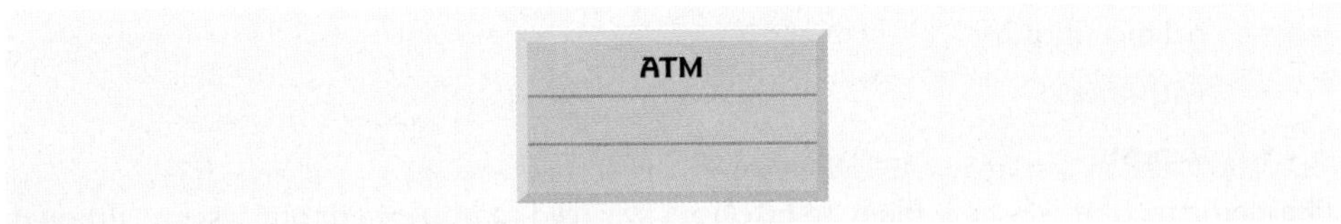

Fig. 4.18 | Representing a class in the UML using a class diagram.

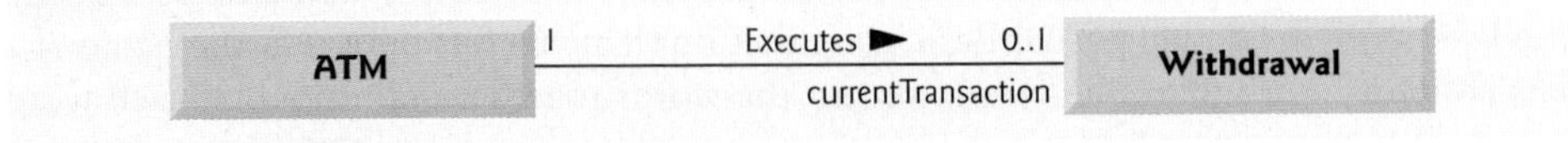

Fig. 4.19 | Class diagram showing an association among classes.

Symbol	Meaning
0	None
1	One
m	An integer value
0..1	Zero or one
m, *n*	*m* or *n*
m..n	At least *m*, but not more than *n*
*	Any nonnegative integer (zero or more)
0..*	Zero or more (identical to *)
1..*	One or more

Fig. 4.20 | Multiplicity types.

This part of the diagram reads "one object of class `ATM` executes zero or one objects of class `Withdrawal`." Note that association names are directional, as indicated by the filled arrowhead—so it would be improper, for example, to read the preceding association from right to left as "zero or one objects of class `Withdrawal` execute one object of class `ATM`."

The word `currentTransaction` at the `Withdrawal` end of the association line in Fig. 4.19 is a role name, which identifies the role the `Withdrawal` object plays in its relationship with the `ATM` object. A role name adds meaning to an association between classes by identifying the role a class plays in the context of an association. A class can play several roles in the same system. For example, in a college personnel system, a person may play the role of "professor" when relating to students. The same person may take on the role of "colleague" when participating in a relationship with another professor, and "coach" when coaching student athletes. In Fig. 4.19, the role name `currentTransaction` indicates that the `Withdrawal` object participating in the `Executes` association with an object of class `ATM` represents the transaction currently being processed by the ATM. In other contexts, a `Withdrawal` object may take on other roles (e.g., the previous transaction). Notice that we do not specify a role name for the `ATM` end of the `Executes` association. Role names in class diagrams are often omitted when the meaning of an association is clear without them.

In addition to indicating simple relationships, associations can specify more complex relationships, such as objects of one class being composed of objects of other classes. Consider a real-world automated teller machine. What "pieces" does a manufacturer put together to build a working ATM? Our requirements document tells us that the ATM is composed of a screen, a keypad, a cash dispenser and a deposit slot.

In Fig. 4.21, the solid diamonds attached to the association lines of class `ATM` indicate that class `ATM` has a composition relationship with classes `Screen`, `Keypad`, `CashDispenser` and `DepositSlot`. Composition implies a whole/part relationship. The class that has the composition symbol (the solid diamond) on its end of the association line is the whole (in this case, `ATM`), and the classes on the other end of the association lines are the parts—in this case, classes `Screen`, `Keypad`, `CashDispenser` and `DepositSlot`. The compositions in

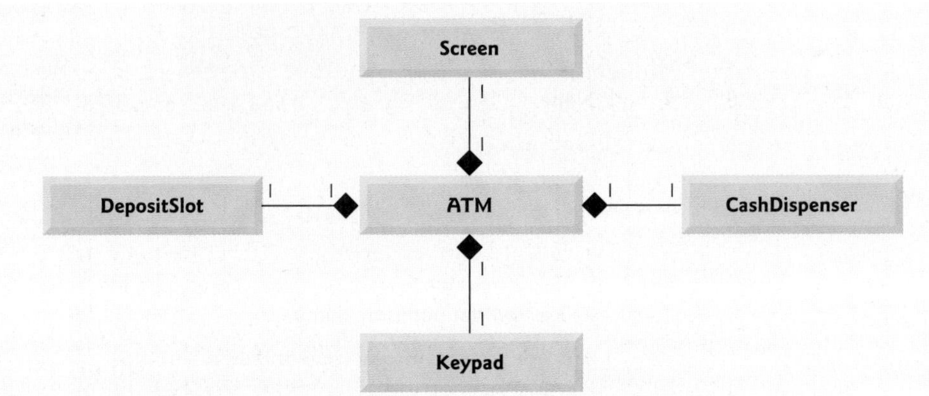

Fig. 4.21 | Class diagram showing composition relationships.

Fig. 4.21 indicate that an object of class `ATM` is formed from one object of class `Screen`, one object of class `CashDispenser`, one object of class `Keypad` and one object of class `DepositSlot`—the ATM *has a* screen, a keypad, a cash dispenser and a deposit slot. The *has-a* relationship defines composition. (You'll see in Section 12.8 that the *is-a* relationship defines inheritance.)

According to the UML specification, composition relationships have the following properties:

1. Only one class in the relationship can represent the whole (i.e., the diamond can be placed on only one end of the association line). For example, either the screen is part of the ATM or the ATM is part of the screen, but the screen and the ATM cannot both represent the whole in the relationship.
2. The parts in the composition relationship exist only as long as the whole, and the whole is responsible for creating and destroying its parts. For example, the act of constructing an ATM includes manufacturing its parts. Furthermore, if the ATM is destroyed, its screen, keypad, cash dispenser and deposit slot are also destroyed.
3. A part may belong to only one whole at a time, although the part may be removed and attached to another whole, which then assumes responsibility for the part.

The solid diamonds in our class diagrams indicate composition relationships that fulfill these three properties. If a *has-a* relationship does not satisfy one or more of these criteria, the UML specifies that hollow diamonds be attached to the ends of association lines to indicate aggregation—a weaker form of composition. For example, a personal computer and a computer monitor participate in an aggregation relationship—the computer *has a* monitor, but the two parts can exist independently, and the same monitor can be attached to multiple computers at once, thus violating the second and third properties of composition.

Figure 4.22 shows a class diagram for the ATM system. This diagram models most of the classes that we identified earlier in this section, as well as the associations between them that we can infer from the requirements document. [*Note:* Classes `BalanceInquiry` and `Deposit` participate in associations similar to those of class `Withdrawal`, so we have chosen

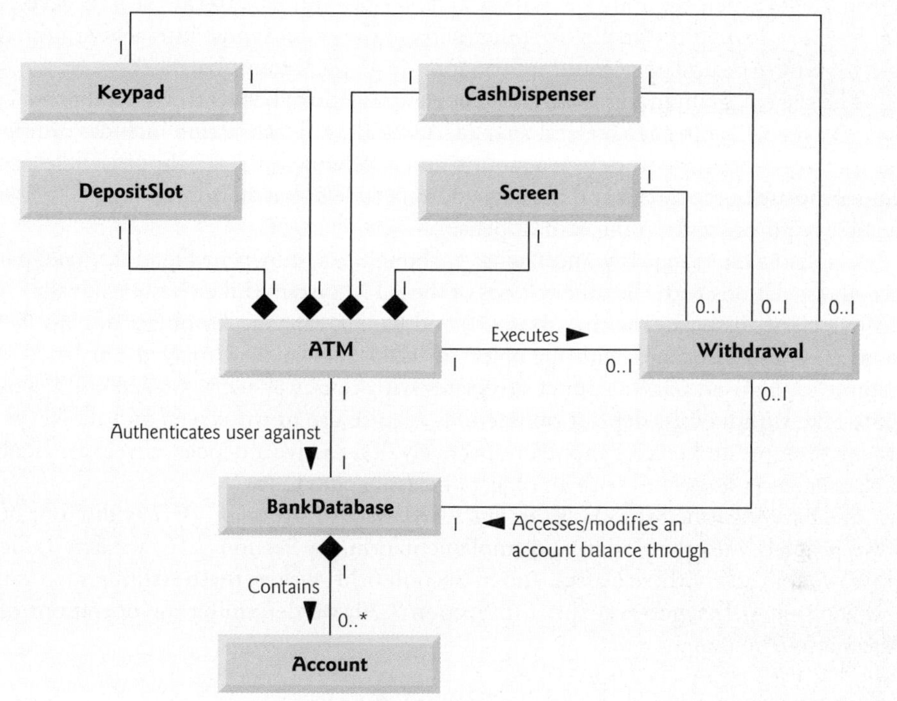

Fig. 4.22 | Class diagram for the ATM system model.

to omit them from this diagram for simplicity. In Chapter 12, we expand our class diagram to include all the classes in the ATM system.]

Figure 4.22 presents a graphical model of the structure of the ATM system. This class diagram includes classes `BankDatabase` and `Account`, and several associations that were not present in either Fig. 4.19 or Fig. 4.21. The class diagram shows that class `ATM` has a **one-to-one relationship** with class `BankDatabase`—one `ATM` object authenticates users against one `BankDatabase` object. In Fig. 4.22, we also model the fact that the bank's database contains information about many accounts—one object of class `BankDatabase` participates in a composition relationship with zero or more `Account` objects. Recall from Fig. 4.20 that the multiplicity value 0..* at the `Account` end of the association between class `BankDatabase` and class `Account` indicates that zero or more objects of class `Account` take part in the association. Class `BankDatabase` has a **one-to-many relationship** with class `Account`—the `BankDatabase` can contain many `Account`s. Similarly, class `Account` has a **many-to-one relationship** with class `BankDatabase`—there can be many `Account`s in the `BankDatabase`. Recall from Fig. 4.20 that the multiplicity value * is identical to 0..*.

Figure 4.22 also indicates that if the user is performing a withdrawal, "one object of class `Withdrawal` accesses/modifies an account balance through one object of class `BankDatabase`." We could have created an association directly between class `Withdrawal` and class `Account`. The requirements document, however, states that the "ATM must interact with the bank's account-information database" to perform transactions. A bank account contains sensitive information, and systems engineers must always consider the security of personal data when designing a system. Thus, only the BankDatabase can access and manipulate an account directly. All other parts of the system must interact with the database to retrieve or update account information (e.g., an account balance).

The class diagram in Fig. 4.22 also models associations between class Withdrawal and classes Screen, CashDispenser and Keypad. A withdrawal transaction includes prompting the user to choose a withdrawal amount and receiving numeric input. These actions require the use of the screen and the keypad, respectively. Furthermore, dispensing cash to the user requires access to the cash dispenser.

Classes BalanceInquiry and Deposit, though not shown in Fig. 4.22, take part in several associations with the other classes of the ATM system. Like class Withdrawal, each of these classes associates with classes ATM and BankDatabase. An object of class BalanceInquiry also associates with an object of class Screen to display the balance of an account to the user. Class Deposit associates with classes Screen, Keypad and DepositSlot. Like withdrawals, deposit transactions require use of the screen and the keypad to display prompts and receive inputs, respectively. To receive a deposit envelope, an object of class Deposit associates with an object of class DepositSlot.

We have identified the classes in our ATM system, although we may discover others as we proceed with the design and implementation. In Section 5.16, we determine the attributes for each of these classes, and in Section 6.11, we use these attributes to examine how the system changes over time. In Section 7.20, we determine the operations of the classes in our system.

Software Engineering Case Study Self-Review Exercises

4.1 Suppose we have a class Car that represents a car. Think of some of the different pieces that a manufacturer would put together to produce a whole car. Create a class diagram (similar to Fig. 4.21) that models some of the composition relationships of class Car.

4.2 Suppose we have a class File that represents an electronic document in a stand-alone, non-networked computer represented by class Computer. What sort of association exists between class Computer and class File?

a) Class Computer has a one-to-one relationship with class File.
b) Class Computer has a many-to-one relationship with class File.
c) Class Computer has a one-to-many relationship with class File.
d) Class Computer has a many-to-many relationship with class File.

4.3 State whether the following statement is *true* or *false*, and if *false*, explain why: A UML class diagram in which a class's second and third compartments are not modeled is said to be an elided diagram.

4.4 Modify the class diagram of Fig. 4.22 to include class Deposit instead of class Withdrawal.

Answers to Software Engineering Case Study Self-Review Exercises

4.1 Figure 4.23 presents a class diagram that shows some of the composition relationships of a class Car.

4.2 c. In a computer network, this relationship could be many-to-many.

4.3 True.

4.4 Figure 4.24 presents a class diagram for the ATM including class Deposit instead of class Withdrawal (as in Fig. 4.22). Note that class Deposit does not associate with class CashDispenser but does associate with class DepositSlot.

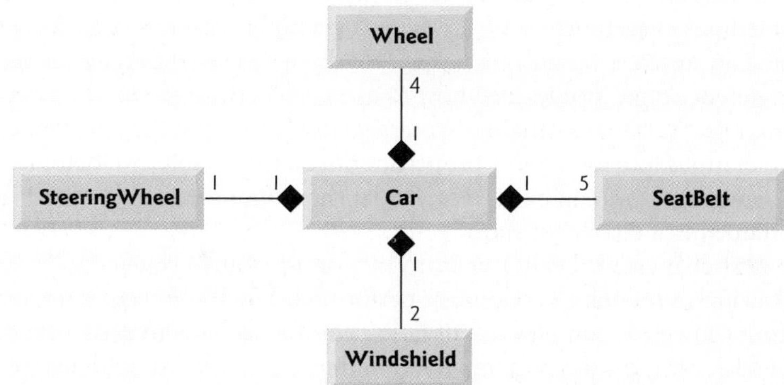

Fig. 4.23 | Class diagram showing some composition relationships of a class `Car`.

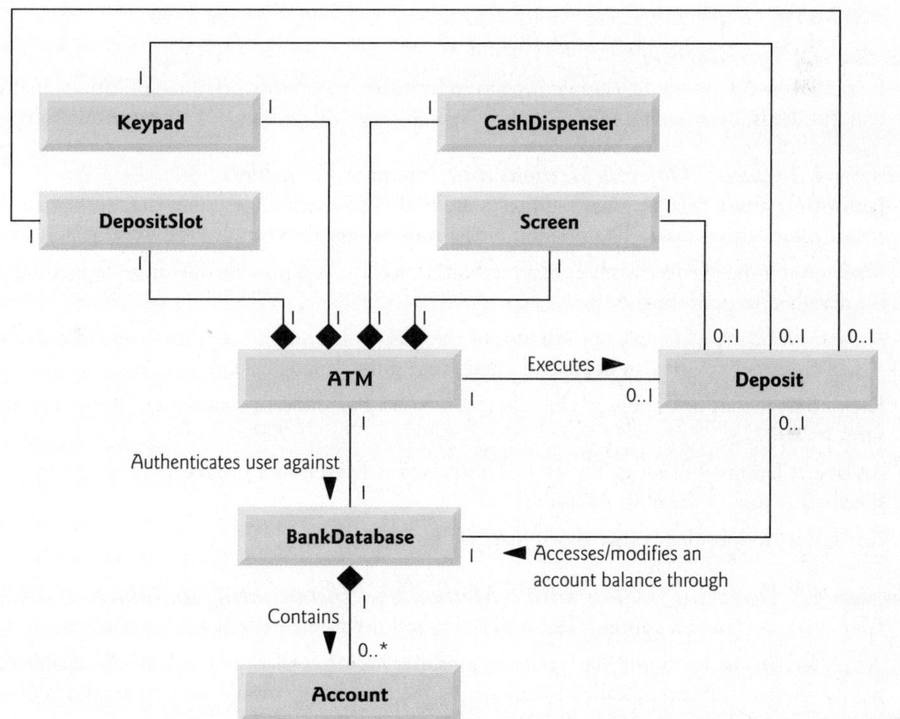

Fig. 4.24 | Class diagram for the ATM system model including class `Deposit`.

4.10 Wrap-Up

In this chapter, you learned the basic concepts of classes, objects, methods, instance variables and properties. You learned how to declare instance variables of a class to maintain separate data for each object of the class, and how to declare methods that operate on that data. You learned how to call a method to tell it to perform its task and how to pass information to methods as arguments. We explained the difference between a local variable of a method and an instance variable of a class. We discussed the difference between a value type and a reference type. You learned how to use a class's constructor to specify the initial values for an object's instance variables. You saw how UML class diagrams model the constructors, operations, attributes and properties of classes. Finally, we demonstrated how `Set` accessors in properties can be used to validate an object's data and ensure that the object is maintained in a consistent state.

In the next chapter we begin our introduction to control statements, which specify the order in which a program's actions are performed. You'll use these statements in your programs to specify more complex sets of tasks. You'll learn how to execute code based on the truth or falsity of a condition, and how to indicate that code should be repeated based on a condition.

Summary

Section 4.1 Introduction

- If you become part of a development team in industry, you may work on applications that contain hundreds, or even thousands, of classes. Each class will contain one or more methods.

Section 4.2 Classes, Objects, Methods and Instance Variables

- Performing a task in a program requires a method. The method describes the mechanisms that actually perform its tasks. The method hides from its user the complex tasks that it performs.
- A program unit called a class houses a method. In a class, you provide one or more methods that are designed to perform the class's tasks.
- A class can be used to create an instance of the class called an object. This is one of the reasons Visual Basic is known as an object-oriented programming language.
- Each message sent to an object is known as a method call and tells a method of the object to perform its task.
- An object has attributes that are carried with it as it is used in a program. These attributes are specified as part of the object's class.
- Attributes are specified by the class's instance variables.

Section 4.3 Declaring a Class with a Method and Instantiating an Object of a Class

- Every class declaration contains keyword `Class` followed immediately by the class's name.
- A method declared with the `Public` access modifier indicates that the method is "available to the public"—that is, it can be called from outside the class declaration's body by methods of other classes or modules.
- Keyword `Sub` indicates that a method will perform a task but will not return (i.e., give back) any information to its calling method when it completes its task.
- By convention, method names begin with an uppercase first letter, and all subsequent words in the name begin with a capital letter (recall that Visual Basic is not case sensitive).
- Empty parentheses after a method name indicate that the method does not require any additional information to perform its task.
- The first line of a method is commonly referred to as the method header.

- The body of a method contains a statement or statements that perform the method's task.
- `Main` is a special method that is always called automatically by the runtime when you execute an application. Most methods do not get called automatically.
- Typically, you cannot call a method that belongs to another class until you create an object of that class.
- Each new class you create becomes a new type in Visual Basic that can be used to declare variables and create objects. You can declare new class types as needed; this is one reason why Visual Basic is known as an extensible language.
- Object-creation expressions beginning with the `New` keyword create new objects.
- To call a method of an object, follow the variable name with a dot separator (`.`), the method name and a set of parentheses containing the method's arguments.
- In the UML, each class is modeled in a class diagram as a rectangle with three compartments. The top compartment contains the name of the class centered horizontally in boldface type. The middle compartment contains the class's attributes, which correspond to instance variables in Visual Basic. The bottom compartment contains the class's operations, which correspond to methods in Visual Basic.
- The UML models operations by listing the operation name followed by a set of parentheses.

Section 4.4 Declaring a Method with a Parameter

- A method can require one or more parameters that represent additional information it needs to perform its task.
- A method call supplies values—called arguments—for each of the method's parameters.
- `String` is a type used for strings of characters in Visual Basic, such as names, addresses, cities, states and product descriptions.
- When you declare a method, you must specify in the method's declaration whether the method requires data to perform its task.
- A parameter list may contain any number of parameters, including none at all. Empty parentheses following the method name indicate that a method does not require any parameters.
- Each parameter must specify a type and an identifier.
- At the time a method is called, the argument value in the call is assigned to the corresponding parameter in the method header. Then the method body uses the parameter to access the value.
- Parameter declarations in the parameter list use keyword `ByVal` to specify that the calling program should pass a copy of the value of the argument in the method call to the parameter.
- The number of arguments in a method call must match the number of parameters in the parameter list of the called method's declaration.
- The argument types in the method call must be consistent with the types of the corresponding parameters in the method's declaration.
- The UML models a parameter a bit differently from Visual Basic by listing the parameter name, followed by a colon and the parameter type in the parentheses following the operation name.

Section 4.5 Instance Variables and Properties

- Variables declared in the body of a particular method are known as local variables and can be used only in that method.
- An object has attributes that are carried with it as it is used in a program. Such attributes exist before a method is called on the object and after the method completes execution.

- Attributes are represented as instance variables and are declared inside a class declaration but outside the bodies of the class's other members.
- Each object of a class maintains its own copy of an instance variable—that is, each object of the class has a separate instance of the variable in memory.
- Variables or methods declared with access modifier `Private` are accessible only to methods and properties of the class in which they are declared.
- Declaring instance variables with access modifier `Private` is known as information hiding.
- In Visual Basic, properties provide a controlled way for you to "get" (i.e., retrieve) the value in an instance variable and "set" (i.e., modify) the value in an instance variable.
- Properties can scrutinize attempts to modify an instance variable's value (known as data validation), thus ensuring that the new value for that instance variable is valid.
- Properties contain accessors that handle the details of modifying and returning data.
- A property declaration can contain a `Get` accessor, a `Set` accessor or both. The `Get` accessor enables a client to read the value of a `Private` instance variable. The `Set` accessor enables a client to modify that instance variable's value.
- After defining a property, you can use it the same way as you use a variable.
- A `Set` accessor can provide data-validation capabilities to ensure that the value is set properly; `Get` and `Set` accessors can translate between the format of the data used by the client and the format used in the `Private` instance variable.
- The UML represents instance variables as attributes by listing the attribute name, followed by a colon and the attribute type.
- Public class members are preceded by a plus (+) sign in UML class diagrams.
- Private class members are preceded by a minus (-) sign in UML class diagrams.
- We model properties in the UML as attributes—a property is listed as an attribute with the word "Property" in guillemets (« and »). Using guillemets helps distinguish properties from other attributes and operations. The UML indicates the type of the property by placing a colon and type after the property name.

Section 4.6 Value Types and Reference Types

- Data types in Visual Basic are divided into two categories—value types and reference types.
- A variable of a value type contains data of that type.
- A variable of a reference type (sometimes called a reference) contains the address of a location in memory where an object is stored.
- Reference type instance variables are initialized by default to the value `Nothing`.
- A client of an object must use a reference to the object to invoke (i.e., call) the object's methods and access the object's properties.

Section 4.7 Initializing Objects with Constructors

- Each class you declare can provide a constructor that can be used to initialize an object of the class when the object is created.
- Keyword `New` calls the class's constructor to perform the initialization.
- By default, the compiler provides a default constructor with no parameters in any class that does not explicitly include a constructor.
- When you declare a class, you can provide your own constructor to specify custom initialization for objects of your class.

- A constructor must have the name New.
- Constructor declarations cannot return values.
- A class's instance variables are initialized to their default values if no constructor is provided.
- Like operations, the UML models constructors in the third compartment of a class in a class diagram. To distinguish a constructor from a class's operations, the UML places the word "constructor" between guillemets (« and ») before the constructor's name.

Section 4.8 Validating Data with Set *Accessors in Properties*

- Properties can be used to keep an object in a consistent state—that is, a state in which the object's instance variables contain valid data.
- A class's Set accessors cannot return values indicating a failed attempt to assign invalid data to objects of the class. Such return values could be useful to a class's clients for handling errors—clients could then take appropriate actions. Chapter 13 presents exception handling—a mechanism that can be used (among other things) to notify a class's clients of attempts to set objects of that class to inconsistent states.
- In Visual Basic, it is possible to declare the Get and Set accessors of a property with different access modifiers. In this case, one of the accessors must have the same access as the property and the other must be more restrictive than the property. Private is more restrictive than Public.

Terminology

access modifier
accessor
attribute in the UML
ByVal keyword
calling method (caller)
carriage return
class diagram in the UML
Class keyword
client of a class
consistent state of an object
constant
constructor
create an object of a class
data validation
declare a method of a class
default constructor
default value of an instance variable
End Class keywords
End Get keywords
End Set keywords
extensible language
Get accessor of a property
information hiding
instance variable
instantiate an object of a class
invoke a method
Length property of class String
line feed
local variable
message (send to an object)
method call
method header
New keyword
Nothing keyword
object-creation expression
operation in the UML
operation parameter in the UML
parameter
parameter list
Private access modifier
property declaration
Property keyword
Public access modifier
refer to an object
reference
reference type
Return statement
Set accessor of a property
String primitive type
Substring method of class String
validation
validity checking
value type
vbNewLine
vbTab

Self-Review Exercises

4.1 Fill in the blanks in each of the following:

a) A house is to a blueprint as a(n) ________ is to a class.
b) Every class declaration contains keyword ________ followed immediately by the class's name.
c) ________ creates an object of the class specified to the right of it.
d) Each parameter must specify both a(n) ________ and a(n) ________.
e) The number of characters in a `String` can be determined using class `String`'s ________ property.
f) When each object of a class maintains its own copy of an attribute, the attribute is represented as a(n) ________.
g) Declaring instance variables with access modifier `Private` is known as ________.
h) Keyword `Public` is a(n) ________.
i) Keyword ________ indicates that a method will perform a task but will not return any information when it completes its task.
j) The keyword ________ represents a "reference to nothing."
k) `String` method ________ returns a new `String` object created by copying part of an existing `String` object.
l) ________ is a primitive type used for strings in Visual Basic, such as names, addresses, cities, states and product descriptions.
m) In a method header, the parentheses after the method name are used to indicate any ________—additional information that is required by the method to perform its task.
n) Methods of a class are depicted as ________ in UML class diagrams.
o) Properties contain ________ and ________ that handle the details of returning and modifying data, respectively.
p) Types in Visual Basic are divided into two categories—________ types and ________ types.

4.2 State whether each of the following is *true* or *false*. If *false*, explain why.

a) By convention, method names begin with a lowercase letter and all subsequent words in the name begin with an uppercase letter.
b) A property's `Get` accessor enables a client to modify the value of the instance variable associated with the property.
c) Empty parentheses following a method name in a method declaration indicate that the method does not require any parameters to perform its task.
d) Variables or methods declared with access modifier `Private` are accessible only to other members of the class in which they are declared.
e) After defining a property, you can use it the same way you use a method, but with empty parentheses because no arguments are passed to a property.
f) Variables declared in the body of a particular method are known as instance variables and can be used in all methods of the class.
g) A client of an object must use a reference to the object to invoke (i.e., call) the object's methods and access the object's properties.
h) A property declaration must contain both a `Get` accessor and a `Set` accessor.
i) Reference type instance variables are initialized by default to `Nothing`.
j) Any class that contains `Main` can be used to execute an application.
k) The number of arguments in a method call must match the number of parameters in the method declaration's parameter list.
l) A class's `Set` accessors can return values indicating failed attempts to assign invalid data to objects of the class.

4.3 What is the difference between a local variable and an instance variable?

4.4 Explain the purpose of a method parameter. What is the difference between a parameter and an argument?

Answers to Self-Review Exercises

4.1 a) object. b) `Class`. c) `New`. d) type, name. e) `Length`. f) instance variable. g) information hiding. h) access modifier. i) `Sub`. j) `Nothing`. k) `Substring`. l) `String`. m) parameters. n) operations. o) `Get` accessors and `Set` accessors. p) value, reference.

4.2 a) False. By convention, method names begin with an uppercase letter, and all subsequent words in the name begin with an uppercase letter. b) False. A property's `Get` accessor enables a client to retrieve the value of the instance variable associated with the property. A property's `Set` accessor enables a client to modify the value of the instance variable associated with the property. c) True. d) True. e) False. After defining a property, you can use it the same way you use a variable. f) False. Such variables are called local variables and can be used only in the method in which they are declared. g) True. h) False. A property declaration can contain a `Get` accessor, a `Set` accessor or both. i) True. j) True. k) True. (You'll learn in Chapter 7 that there is an exception to this with so-called optional arguments.) l) False. A class's `Set` accessors cannot return values indicating failed attempts to assign invalid data to objects of the class. Chapter 13 presents exception handling—a mechanism that can be used (among other things) to notify a class's clients of attempts to set objects of that class to inconsistent states.

4.3 A local variable is declared in the body of a method and can be used only in that method declaration. An instance variable is declared in a class, but not in the body of any of the class's methods or properties. Every object (instance) of a class has a separate copy of the class's instance variables. Also, instance variables are accessible to all methods and properties of the class. (You'll see an exception to this in Chapter 10, Classes and Objects: A Deeper Look; instance variables are not accessible to `Shared` methods of a class.)

4.4 A parameter represents additional information that a method requires to perform its task. Each parameter required by a method is specified in the method's declaration. An argument is the actual value for a method parameter. When a method is called, the argument values are passed to the method so that it can perform its task.

Exercises

4.5 What is the purpose of the `New` keyword? Explain what happens when this keyword is used in an application.

4.6 What is a default constructor? How are an object's instance variables initialized if a class has only a default constructor?

4.7 Explain the purpose of an instance variable.

4.8 Explain why a class might provide a property for an instance variable.

4.9 *(Modifying Class `GradeBook`)* Modify class `GradeBook` (Fig. 4.15) as follows:

a) Include a second `String` instance variable that represents the name of the course's instructor.
b) Provide a property to access and modify the instructor's name. This property does not need to provide any validation.
c) Modify the constructor to specify two parameters—one for the course name and one for the instructor's name.

d) Modify method `DisplayMessage` such that it first outputs the welcome message and course name, then outputs `"This course is presented by: "` followed by the instructor's name.

Use your modified class in a test module that demonstrates the class's new capabilities.

4.10 *(`Account` Class and Introduction to Debugging)* This exercise not only tests concepts in this chapter, but introduces you to debugging. You should first attempt the solution, then read Appendix H, Using the Visual Studio 2008 Debugger, and perform the debugging steps in the appendix. Create a class called `Account` that a bank might use to represent customers' bank accounts. Your class should include one instance variable of type `Integer` to represent the account balance (in whole dollars). [*Note:* In subsequent chapters, you'll use type `Decimal` values to represent dollar amounts with cents.] Your class should provide a constructor that receives an initial balance and uses it to initialize the instance variable. The constructor should validate the initial balance to ensure that it is greater than or equal to 0. The class should provide two methods and a property. Method `Credit` should add an amount to the current balance. Method `Debit` should withdraw money from the `Account` and should ensure that the debit amount does not exceed the `Account`'s balance. If it does, the balance should be left unchanged and the method should print a message indicating `"Debit amount exceeded account balance."` Property `Balance` should provide access to the current balance, but no validation is necessary. Create a module that creates two `Account` objects and tests the methods and property of class `Account`.

4.11 *(`Invoice` Class)* Create a class called `Invoice` that a hardware store might use to represent an invoice for an item sold at the store. An `Invoice` should include four pieces of information as instance variables—a part number (type `String`), a part description (type `String`), a quantity of the item being purchased (type `Integer`) and a price per item (type `Integer`). Your class should have a constructor that initializes the four instance variables. Provide a property for each instance variable. If the quantity is not positive, it should be set to `0`. If the price per item is not positive, it should be set to `0`. Use validation in the properties for these instance variables to ensure that they remain positive. In addition, provide a method named `DisplayInvoiceAmount` that calculates and displays the invoice amount (i.e., multiplies the quantity by the price per item). Write a test module named `InvoiceTest` that demonstrates class `Invoice`'s capabilities. Figure 4.25 shows a sample output of the program.

4.12 *(`Employee` Class)* Create a class called `Employee` that includes three pieces of information as instance variables—a first name (type `String`), a last name (type `String`) and a monthly salary (type `Integer`). Your class should have a constructor that initializes the three instance variables. Provide a property for each instance variable. The property for the monthly salary should ensure that its value remains positive—if an attempt is made to assign a negative value, leave the original value. Write a test module named `EmployeeTest` that demonstrates class `Employee`'s capabilities. Create two `Employee` objects and display each object's *yearly* salary. Then give each `Employee` a 10% raise and display each `Employee`'s yearly salary again.

4.13 *(`DateInformation` Class)* Create a class called `DateInformation` that includes three pieces of information as instance variables—a month (type `Integer`), a day (type `Integer`) and a year (type `Integer`). Your class should provide properties that enable a client of the class to `Get` and `Set` the month, day and year values. The `Set` accessors for the month and day should provide simple validation to ensure that the month value is in the range 1–12 and the day value is in the range 1–31. There is no need to validate the year in this example. [*Note:* In Chapter 10, Classes and Objects: A Deeper Look, we develop a version of this class with more extensive validation that checks for leap years and day ranges specific to each month (e.g., January—31 days, June—30 days, and February—28 days unless it is a leap year).] If the month value is less than 1 or greater than 12, the `Set` accessor for the month should set the month to 1. Similarly, if the day value is less than 1 or greater than 31, the `Set` accessor for the day should set the day to 1. Your class should have a constructor

```
Original invoice information
Part number: 1234
Description: Hammer
Quantity: 2
Price Per Item: 14
Invoice amount: 28

Updated invoice information
Part number: 001234
Description: Yellow Hammer
Quantity: 3
Price Per Item: 19
Invoice amount: 57

Original invoice information
Part number: 5678
Description: Paint Brush
Quantity: 0
Price Per Item: 0
Invoice amount: 0

Updated invoice information
Part number: 5678
Description: Paint Brush
Quantity: 3
Price Per Item: 9
Invoice amount: 27
```

Fig. 4.25 | Sample output for Exercise 4.11.

that initializes the three instance variables and uses the class's properties to set each instance variable's value. This ensures that the month and day are validated. Provide a method `DisplayDate` that displays the month, day and year separated by forward slashes (/). Write a test module named `DateInformationTest` that demonstrates class `DateInformation`'s capabilities.

5

Control Statements: Part 1

Let's all move one place on.
—Lewis Carroll

The wheel is come full circle.
—William Shakespeare

How many apples fell on Newton's head before he took the hint?
—Robert Frost

All the evolution we know of proceeds from the vague to the definite.
—Charles Sanders Peirce

OBJECTIVES

In this chapter you'll learn:

- Basic problem-solving techniques.
- To develop algorithms through the process of top-down, stepwise refinement.
- To use the `If`...`Then` and `If`...`Then`...`Else` selection statements to choose among alternative actions.
- To use the `While`, `Do While`...`Loop` and `Do Until`...`Loop` repetition statements to execute statements in a program repeatedly.
- To use the compound assignment operators to abbreviate assignment operations.
- To use counter-controlled repetition and sentinel-controlled repetition.
- To use nested control statements.
- To add Visual Basic code to a Windows `Forms` application.

Outline

5.1 Introduction

Before writing a program to solve a problem, it is essential to have a thorough understanding of the problem and a carefully planned approach. When writing a program, it is equally important to recognize the types of building blocks that are available and to employ proven program-construction principles. In this chapter and the next, we present the theory and principles of structured programming with control statements. Control statements are important in building and manipulating objects.

In this chapter, we introduce Visual Basic's `If...Then`, `If...Then...Else`, `While`, `Do While...Loop` and `Do Until...Loop` statements, five of the building blocks that allow programmers to specify the logic required for methods to perform their tasks. We devote a portion of this chapter (and Chapters 6–8) to further developing the `GradeBook` class introduced in Chapter 4. In particular, we add a method to the `GradeBook` class that uses control statements to calculate the average of a set of student grades. Another example demonstrates how to combine control statements by "stacking" and "nesting" to solve a particular problem. You'll notice that some examples use classes and a test module to demonstrate a concept, while others use only a module. When it does not make sense to create a reusable class to demonstrate a simple concept, we write the code in the `Main` method of a module.

Throughout most of this chapter we use console applications to demonstrate new programming techniques. We devote one section to enhancing the Windows application you created in Chapter 2 to include your own Visual Basic code.

5.2 Algorithms

Any computing problem can be solved by executing a series of actions in a specific order. A procedure for solving a problem, in terms of

1. the actions to be executed and
2. the order in which these actions are to be executed

is called an algorithm. The following example demonstrates the importance of correctly specifying the order in which the actions are to be executed.

Consider the "rise-and-shine algorithm" followed by one junior executive for getting out of bed and going to work: (1) get out of bed, (2) take off pajamas, (3) take a shower, (4) get dressed, (5) eat breakfast and (6) carpool to work. This routine prepares the executive for a productive day at the office.

However, suppose that the same steps are performed in a slightly different order: (1) get out of bed, (2) take off pajamas, (3) get dressed, (4) take a shower, (5) eat breakfast, (6) carpool to work. In this case, our junior executive shows up for work soaking wet.

Specifying the order in which statements (actions) execute in a program is called program control. This chapter investigates program control using Visual Basic's control statements.

5.3 Pseudocode

Pseudocode is an informal language that helps programmers develop algorithms. It is similar to everyday English; it is convenient and user friendly, but it is not an actual computer programming language. The pseudocode we present is particularly useful for developing algorithms that will be converted to structured portions of Visual Basic programs.

Pseudocode programs are not executed on computers. Rather, they help you "think out" a program before attempting to write it in a programming language, such as Visual Basic. In this chapter, we provide several pseudocode programs.

Software Engineering Observation 5.1

Pseudocode helps you conceptualize a program during the program-design process. The pseudocode program can be converted to Visual Basic at a later point.

The style of pseudocode that we present consists solely of characters, so that programmers can create, share and modify pseudocode programs using text editor programs. You can easily convert a carefully prepared pseudocode program to a corresponding Visual Basic program. Much of this conversion is as simple as replacing pseudocode statements with their Visual Basic equivalents.

Pseudocode normally describes only statements representing the actions that occur after a programmer converts a program from pseudocode to Visual Basic and the program is run on a computer. Such actions might include input, output or calculations. We typically do not include variable declarations such as

```
Dim number As Integer
```

in our pseudocode. However, some programmers choose to list variables and mention their purposes at the beginning of pseudocode algorithms. We show several pseudocode algorithms and explain how you can develop your own.

5.4 Control Structures

Normally, statements in a program are executed one after another in the order in which they are written. This is called sequential execution. However, various Visual Basic statements enable you to specify the next statement to be executed as one that is not the next in sequence. A transfer of control occurs when an executed statement does not directly follow the previously executed statement in the program.

During the 1960s, it became clear that the indiscriminate use of transfers of control was causing difficulty for software development groups. A key problem was the `GoTo` statement, which allows you to specify a transfer of control to one of a wide range of possible destinations in a program. The excessive use of `GoTo` statements caused programs to become quite unstructured and hard to follow—such disorganized programs were referred to as "spaghetti code." Since then, the notion of structured programming has become almost synonymous with "`GoTo` elimination."

The research of Bohm and Jacopini demonstrated that all programs containing `GoTo` statements could be written without them.[1] A challenge of the era was for programmers to shift their styles to "`GoTo`-less programming." It was not until the 1970s that most programmers started taking structured programming seriously. The results were impressive, with software development groups reporting reduced development times, more frequent on-time delivery of systems and more frequent within-budget completion of software projects. The key to these successes is that structured programs are clearer, easier to debug and modify and more likely to be bug free in the first place.

Bohm and Jacopini's work demonstrated that all programs could be written in terms of only three control structures—the sequence structure, the selection structure and the repetition structure. The term "control structures" comes from the field of computer science. When we introduce Visual Basic's implementation of control structures, we will refer to them as "control statements."

Sequence Structure in Visual Basic

The sequence structure is built into Visual Basic. Unless directed to act otherwise, the computer executes Visual Basic statements sequentially. The UML activity diagram in Fig. 5.1 illustrates a sequence structure in which two calculations are performed in order.

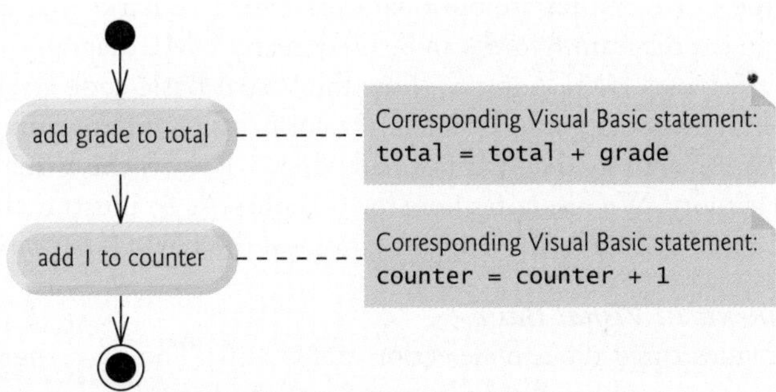

Fig. 5.1 | Sequence-structure activity diagram.

1. C. Bohm and G. Jacopini, "Flow Diagrams, Turing Machines, and Languages with Only Two Formation Rules," *Communications of the ACM*, Vol. 9, No. 5, May 1966, pp. 366–371.

Visual Basic lets us have as many actions as we want in a sequence structure. As we will soon see, anywhere a single action may be placed, we may place several actions in sequence.

The two statements in Fig. 5.1 involve adding a grade to a `total` variable and adding the value 1 to a `counter` variable. Such statements might appear in a program that takes the average of several student grades. To calculate an average, the total of the grades being averaged is divided by the number of grades. A counter variable would be used to keep track of the number of values being averaged. You'll see similar statements in the program in Section 5.11.

UML Activity Diagrams

Activity diagrams are part of the UML. An activity diagram models the workflow (also called the activity) of a portion of a software system. A workflow may include a portion of an algorithm, such as the sequence structure in Fig. 5.1. Activity diagrams are composed of special-purpose symbols, such as the action state symbol (a rectangle with its left and right sides replaced with arcs curving outward; there are two of these in Fig. 5.1), the diamond symbol (there are none in this figure) and the small circle symbol; these symbols are connected by transition arrows, which represent the flow of the activity.

Like pseudocode, activity diagrams help programmers develop and represent algorithms. Activity diagrams clearly show how control structures operate.

Consider the sequence-structure activity diagram in Fig. 5.1. It contains two action states that represent actions to perform. Each action state contains an action expression—"add grade to total" or "add 1 to counter"—that specifies a particular action to perform. Other actions might include calculations or input/output operations. The transition arrows represent transitions that indicate the order in which the actions represented by the action states occur—the program that implements the activities illustrated by the activity diagram in Fig. 5.1 first adds `grade` to `total`, then adds `1` to `counter`.

The solid circle symbol located at the top of the activity diagram represents the activity's initial state—the beginning of the workflow before the corresponding program performs the modeled activities. The solid circle surrounded by a hollow circle that appears at the bottom of the activity diagram represents the final state—the end of the workflow after the corresponding program performs its activities.

Figure 5.1 also includes rectangles with the upper-right corners folded over. These are called notes in the UML. Notes are optional explanatory remarks that describe the purpose of symbols in the diagram. Notes can be used in any UML diagram—not just activity diagrams. Figure 5.1 uses UML notes to show the Visual Basic code associated with each action state in the activity diagram. A dotted line connects each note with the element that the note describes. An activity diagram normally does not show the Visual Basic code that implements the activity. We use notes here for this purpose to illustrate how the diagram relates to Visual Basic code. For more information on the UML, visit `www.uml.org`.

Selection Statements in Visual Basic

Visual Basic provides three types of selection statements. The `If...Then` selection statement (which we introduced briefly in Chapter 3 and study in detail in Section 5.5) either performs (selects) an action (or sequence of actions) if a condition is true, or skips the action (or sequence of actions) if the condition is false. The `If...Then...Else` selection statement, which we introduce in Section 5.6, performs an action (or sequence of actions) if a condition is true, and performs a different action (or sequence of actions) if the condition is false. The `Select...Case` statement, which we introduce in Chapter 6, performs one of many different actions (or sequences of actions), depending on the value of an expression.

The `If...Then` statement is called a single-selection statement because it selects or ignores a single action (or a sequence of actions). The `If...Then...Else` statement is called a double-selection statement because it selects between two different actions (or sequences of actions). The `Select...Case` statement is called a multiple-selection statement because it selects among many different actions or sequences of actions.

Repetition Statements in Visual Basic

Visual Basic provides seven types of repetition statements (also called looping statements or loops) that enable programs to perform statements repeatedly based on the value of a condition. The repetition statements are the `While`, `Do While...Loop`, `Do...Loop While`, `Do Until...Loop`, `Do...Loop Until`, `For...Next` and the `For Each...Next` statements. (The repetition statements `While`, `Do While...Loop` and `Do Until...Loop` are covered in this chapter; the `Do...Loop While`, `Do...Loop Until`, and `For...Next` statements are covered in Chapter 6; and the `For Each...Next` statement is covered in Chapter 8, Arrays.) The words `If`, `Then`, `Else`, `End`, `Select`, `Case`, `While`, `Do`, `Until`, `Loop`, `For`, `Next` and `Each` are all Visual Basic keywords (Fig. 3.2).

Summary of Control Statements in Visual Basic

Visual Basic has only three kinds of control structures, which from this point forward we refer to as control statements: the sequence structure, selection statements (three types—`If...Then`, `If...Then...Else` and `Select...Case`) and repetition statements (seven types—`While`, `Do While...Loop`, `Do...Loop While`, `Do Until...Loop`, `Do...Loop Until`, `For...Next` and `For Each...Next`)—for a total of 11 types of control statements. We combine as many of each type of statement as necessary to make the program flow and work as required. We can model each control statement as an activity diagram. Each diagram contains one initial state and one final state, which represent the control statement's entry point and exit point, respectively. These single-entry/single-exit control statements make it easy to build programs—the control statements are "attached" to one another by "connecting" the exit point of one control statement to the entry point of the next (which we accomplish simply by following one control statement immediately by another). This is similar to stacking building blocks, so we call it control-statement stacking. Section 5.12 shows an example of control-statement stacking. There is only one other way to connect control statements, and that is through control-statement nesting, where one control statement is placed inside another. We discuss control-statement nesting in Sections 5.13 and 5.14.

Software Engineering Observation 5.2

Any Visual Basic program can be constructed from only 11 different types of control statements (sequence, three types of selection statements and seven types of repetition statements) combined in only two ways (control-statement stacking and control-statement nesting).

5.5 If...Then Selection Statement

In a program, a selection statement chooses among alternative courses of action. For example, suppose that the passing grade on an examination is 60 (out of 100). Then the pseudocode statement

If student's grade is greater than or equal to 60 then
Print "Passed"

determines whether the condition "student's grade is greater than or equal to 60" is true or false. If the condition is true, then "Passed" is printed, and the next pseudocode statement in order is "performed" (remember that pseudocode is not a real programming language). If the condition is false, the print statement is ignored, and the next pseudocode statement in order is "performed."

The preceding pseudocode *If* statement may be written in Visual Basic as

```
If studentGrade >= 60 Then
   Console.WriteLine("Passed")
End If
```

Note that the Visual Basic code corresponds closely to the pseudocode, demonstrating the usefulness of pseudocode as a program-development tool. The statement in the body of the `If...Then` statement outputs the string `"Passed"`. Note also that the output statement in this selection statement is indented. Such indentation is optional, but it is recommended because it emphasizes the organization of structured programs.

The Visual Basic compiler ignores whitespace characters, such as spaces, tabs and blank lines used for indentation and vertical spacing, unless the whitespace characters are contained in strings. Some whitespace characters are required, however, such as the space between variable names and keywords. Programmers insert extra whitespace characters to enhance program readability.

The preceding `If...Then` selection statement also could be written on a single line as

```
If studentGrade >= 60 Then Console.WriteLine("Passed")
```

In the multiple-line format, all statements (there can be many) in the `If...Then`'s body execute if the condition is true. In the single-line format, only the statement immediately after the `Then` keyword executes if the condition is true. Although writing the `If...Then` selection statement in the latter format saves space, some programmers feel that the organization of the statement is clearer when the multiple-line format is used.

Whereas syntax errors are caught by the compiler, logic errors, such as the error caused when the wrong relational operator is used in the condition of a selection statement, affect the program only at execution time. A fatal logic error causes a program to fail and terminate prematurely. A nonfatal logic error does not terminate a program's execution but causes the program to produce incorrect results.

Figure 5.2 is an activity diagram that illustrates the single-selection `If...Then` statement. It contains what is perhaps the most important symbol in an activity diagram—the diamond, or decision symbol, which indicates that a decision is to be made. A decision symbol indicates that the workflow will continue along a path determined by the symbol's associated guard conditions, which can be true or false. Each transition arrow emerging from a decision symbol has a guard condition (specified in square brackets above or next to the transition arrow). If a particular guard condition is true, the workflow enters the action state to which that transition arrow points. Exactly one of the guard conditions associated with a decision symbol must be true when a decision is made. In Fig. 5.2, if the grade is greater than or equal to 60, the program prints "Passed" to the screen, then tran-

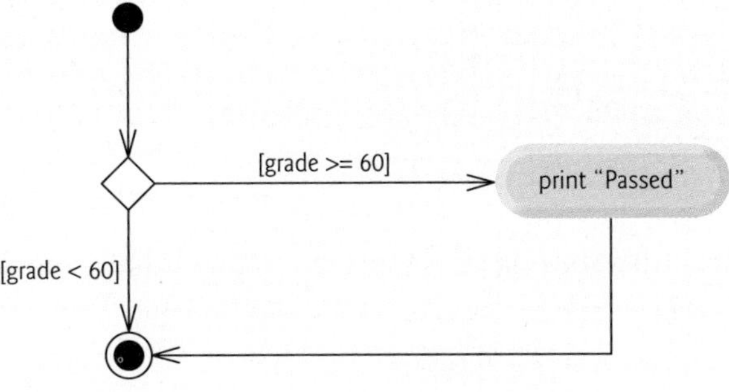

Fig. 5.2 | `If...Then` single-selection statement activity diagram.

sitions to the final state of this activity. If the grade is less than 60, the program immediately transitions to the final state without displaying a message.

Note that the `If...Then` statement is a single-entry/single-exit statement (as are all Visual Basic control statements). The activity diagrams for the remaining control statements also contain initial states, transition arrows, action states that indicate actions to perform, decision symbols (with associated guard conditions) that indicate decisions to be made, and final states.

To understand the process of structured programming better, we can envision 11 bins, each containing single-entry/single-exit UML activity diagrams of a different type of the 11 possible control statements. The activity diagrams in each bin are empty—nothing is written in the action states and no guard conditions are written alongside the transition arrows emerging from the decision symbols. Your task is to assemble a program using as many of these UML activity diagrams as the algorithm demands, combining them in only two possible ways (stacking or nesting) and filling in the actions and decisions and guard conditions in a manner appropriate to the algorithm.

5.6 If...Then...Else Selection Statement

As we have explained, the `If...Then` selection statement performs an indicated action (or sequence of actions) only when the condition evaluates to true; otherwise, the action (or sequence of actions) is skipped. The `If...Then...Else` selection statement allows you to specify that a different action (or sequence of actions) is to be performed when the condition is true than when the condition is false. For example, the pseudocode statement

If student's grade is greater than or equal to 60 then
    Print "Passed"
Else
    Print "Failed"

prints "Passed" if the student's grade is greater than or equal to 60, and prints "Failed" if the student's grade is less than 60. In either case, after printing occurs, the next pseudocode statement in sequence is "performed."

The preceding pseudocode *If...Else* statement may be written in Visual Basic as

```
If studentGrade >= 60 Then
   Console.WriteLine("Passed")
Else
   Console.WriteLine("Failed")
End If
```

Note that the body of the `Else` clause is indented so that it lines up with the body of the `If` clause.

Good Programming Practice 5.1

Visual Basic indents both body statements of an `If...Then...Else` statmement to improve readability.

Good Programming Practice 5.2

A standard indentation convention should be applied consistently throughout your programs. It is difficult to read programs that do not use uniform spacing conventions. Visual Basic automatically applies uniform indentation conventions.

The preceding `If...Then...Else` statement can also be written using a **conditional `If` expression**, as in

```
Console.WriteLine(If(studentGrade >= 60, "Passed", "Failed"))
```

A conditional `If` expression starts with the keyword `If` and is followed by three expressions in parentheses—a condition, the value of the conditional expression if the condition is true and the value if the condition is false. Notice that the call to method `Console.WriteLine` appears outside the conditional `If` expression. The second and third expressions in a conditional `If` expression must evaluate to a value. If a method is used as either the second or third expression, the method must return a value. Method `Console.WriteLine` does not return a value, so it cannot be used in the conditional `If` expression.

Figure 5.3 illustrates the flow of control in the `If...Then...Else` statement. Once again, note that (besides the initial state, transition arrows and final state) the only other symbols in this activity diagram represent action states and decisions.

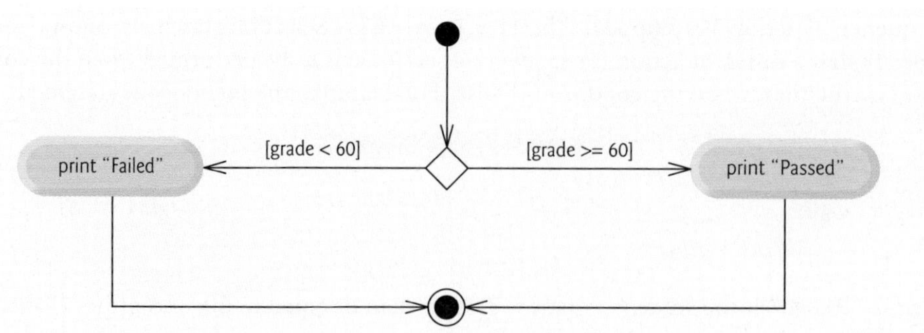

Fig. 5.3 | `If...Then...Else` double-selection statement activity diagram.

Nested `If...Then...Else` Statements

Nested `If...Then...Else` statements test for multiple conditions by placing `If...Then...Else` statements inside other `If...Then...Else` statements. For example, the following pseudocode statement will print "A" for exam grades greater than or equal to 90, "B" for grades in the range 80–89, "C" for grades in the range 70–79, "D" for grades in the range 60–69 and "F" for all other grades.

```
If student's grade is greater than or equal to 90 then
    Print "A"
Else
    If student's grade is greater than or equal to 80 then
        Print "B"
    Else
        If student's grade is greater than or equal to 70 then
            Print "C"
        Else
            If student's grade is greater than or equal to 60 then
                Print "D"
            Else
                Print "F"
```

The preceding pseudocode may be written in Visual Basic as

```
If studentGrade >= 90 Then
   Console.WriteLine("A")
Else
   If studentGrade >= 80 Then
      Console.WriteLine("B")
   Else
      If studentGrade >= 70 Then
         Console.WriteLine("C")
      Else
         If studentGrade >= 60 Then
            Console.WriteLine("D")
         Else
            Console.WriteLine("F")
         End If
      End If
   End If
End If
```

If `studentGrade` is greater than or equal to 90, the first four conditions are true, but only the `Console.WriteLine` statement in the body of the first test is executed. After that particular `Console.WriteLine` executes, the `Else` part of the "outer" `If...Then...Else` statement is skipped, and the program proceeds with the next statement after the last `End If`.

Good Programming Practice 5.3

If there are several levels of indentation, each level should be indented additionally by the same amount of space; this gives programs a neatly structured appearance.

Most Visual Basic programmers prefer to write the preceding `If...Then...Else` statement using the `ElseIf` keyword as

```
If grade >= 90 Then
   Console.WriteLine("A")
ElseIf grade >= 80 Then
   Console.WriteLine("B")
ElseIf grade >= 70 Then
   Console.WriteLine("C")
ElseIf grade >= 60 Then
   Console.WriteLine("D")
Else
   Console.WriteLine("F")
End If
```

Both forms are equivalent, but the latter is popular because it avoids the deep indentation of the code. Such deep indentation often leaves little room on a line, forcing lines to be split and decreasing program readability.

5.7 While Repetition Statement

A repetition statement (also called a looping statement or a loop) allows you to specify that an action should be repeated, depending on the value of a condition (called the loop-continuation condition). The pseudocode statements

While there are more items on my shopping list
Put next item in cart
Cross it off my list

describe the repetitive actions that occur during a shopping trip. The condition "there are more items on my shopping list" can be true or false. If it is true, then the actions "Purchase next item" and "Cross it off my list" are performed in sequence. These actions execute repeatedly while the condition remains true. The statement(s) contained in the *While* repetition statement constitute the body of the *While.* Eventually, the condition becomes false (when the last item on the shopping list has been purchased and crossed off the list). At this point, the repetition terminates, and the first statement after the repetition statement executes.

As an example of a `While` statement (sometimes more formally referred to as the `While...End While` statement), consider a program designed to find the first power of 3 larger than 100 (Fig. 5.4). In line 5, we take advantage of a Visual Basic feature that allows variable initialization to be incorporated into a declaration. When the `While` statement is entered (line 9), `product` is `3`. Variable `product` is repeatedly multiplied by `3` (line 11), taking on the values `3`, `9`, `27`, `81` and `243`, successively. When `product` becomes `243`, the condition `product <= 100` in the `While` statement becomes false. This terminates the repetition with `243` as `product`'s final value. Execution continues with the next statement after the keywords `End While` in line 12. [*Note:* If a `While` statement's condition is initially false, the body statement(s) are not performed.]

The UML activity diagram of Fig. 5.5 illustrates the flow of control that corresponds to the `While` statement shown in Fig. 5.4 (we have omitted the display of `product` each time through the loop at line 10). Once again, the symbols in the diagram (besides the initial state, transition arrows, a final state and three notes) represent an action state and a decision. This diagram also introduces the UML's merge symbol, which joins two flows of activity into one flow of activity. The UML represents both the merge symbol and the

```
' Fig. 5.4: PowersOfThree.vb
' Demonstration of While statement.
Module PowersOfThree
   Sub Main()
      Dim product As Integer = 3

      ' statement multiplies and displays product
      ' while product is less than or equal to 100
      While product <= 100
         Console.Write(product & "  ")
         product = product * 3 ' compute next power of 3
      End While

      Console.WriteLine() ' write blank line

      ' print result
      Console.WriteLine("First power of 3 " & _
         "larger than 100 is " & product)
   End Sub ' Main
End Module ' PowersOfThree
```

```
3  9  27  81
First power of 3 larger than 100 is 243
```

Fig. 5.4 | While repetition statement used to print powers of 3.

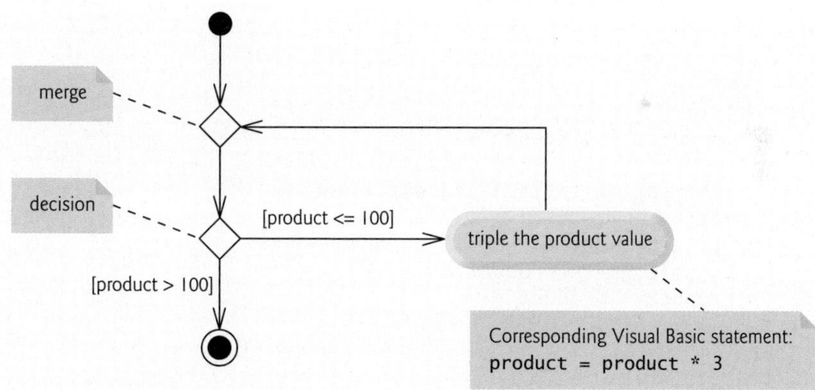

Fig. 5.5 | While repetition statement activity diagram.

decision symbol as diamonds (this can be confusing). In this diagram, the merge symbol joins the transitions from the initial state and the action state, so they both flow into the decision that determines whether the loop should begin (or continue) executing. The decision and merge symbols can be distinguished by the number of “incoming” and “outgoing” transition arrows. A decision symbol has one transition arrow pointing to the diamond and two or more transition arrows pointing out from the diamond to indicate possible transitions from that point. In addition, each transition arrow pointing out of a decision symbol has a guard condition next to it (exactly one of which must be true when a decision is made). A merge symbol has two or more transition arrows pointing to the diamond and only one transition arrow pointing from the diamond, to indicate multiple activity flows merging to continue the activity. Note that, unlike the decision symbol, the merge symbol does not have a counterpart in Visual Basic code. None of the transition arrows associated with a merge symbol have guard conditions.

The activity diagram of Fig. 5.5 clearly shows the repetition of the `While` statement discussed earlier in this section. The transition arrow emerging from the action state connects back to the merge, which transitions back to the decision that is tested each time through the loop until the guard condition `product > 100` becomes true. Then the `While` statement exits (reaches its final state) and control passes to the next statement in sequence in the program.

Common Programming Error 5.1

Failure to provide the body of a `While` statement with an action that eventually causes the loop-continuation condition to become false is a logic error. Normally, such a repetition statement never terminates, resulting in a logic error called an "infinite loop."

5.8 Do While...Loop Repetition Statement

The `Do While...Loop` repetition statement behaves like the `While` repetition statement. As an example of a `Do While...Loop` statement, consider another version of the program designed to find the first power of 3 larger than 100 (Fig. 5.6).

```
' Fig. 5.6: DoWhile.vb
' Demonstration of the Do While...Loop statement.
Module DoWhile
   Sub Main()
      Dim product As Integer = 3 ' initialize product

      ' statement multiplies and displays the
      ' product while it is less than or equal to 100
      Do While product <= 100
         Console.Write(product & "  ")
         product = product * 3
      Loop

      Console.WriteLine() ' write blank line

      ' print result
      Console.WriteLine("First power of 3 " & _
         "larger than 100 is " & product)
   End Sub ' Main
End Module ' DoWhile
```

```
3  9  27  81
First power of 3 larger than 100 is 243
```

Fig. 5.6 | `Do While...Loop` repetition statement demonstration.

When the Do While...Loop statement is entered (line 9), the value of product is 3. The variable product is repeatedly multiplied by 3, taking on the values 3, 9, 27, 81 and 243, successively. When product becomes 243, the condition in the Do While...Loop statement, product <= 100, becomes false. This terminates the repetition, with the final value of product being 243. Program execution continues with the next statement after the Do While...Loop statement. Because the While and Do While...Loop statements behave in the same way, the activity diagram in Fig. 5.5 also illustrates the flow of control of the Do While...Loop repetition statement.

Common Programming Error 5.2

Failure to provide the body of a Do While...Loop *statement with an action that eventually causes the loop-continuation condition in the* Do While...Loop *to become false creates an infinite loop.*

5.9 Do Until...Loop Repetition Statement

Unlike the While and Do While...Loop repetition statements, the **Do Until...Loop** repetition statement tests a condition for falsity for repetition to continue. Statements in the body of a Do Until...Loop are executed repeatedly as long as the condition (known as the **loop-termination condition**) evaluates to false. The program of Fig. 5.7 finds the first power of 3 larger than 100 by using a Do Until...Loop repetition statement.

Once again, the activity diagram of Fig. 5.5 illustrates the flow of control in the Do Until...Loop repetition statement shown in Fig. 5.7. This time, however, we focus on the leftmost guard condition—product > 100—the loop-termination condition for our control statement. Because we are using a Do Until...Loop statement, the statement's actions

```
' Fig. 5.7: DoUntil.vb
' Demonstration of the Do Until...Loop statement.
Module DoUntil
   Sub Main()
      Dim product As Integer = 3

      ' find first power of 3 larger than 100
      Do Until product > 100
         Console.Write(product & "  ")
         product = product * 3
      Loop

      Console.WriteLine() ' write blank line

      ' print result
      Console.WriteLine("First power of 3 " & _
         "larger than 100 is " & product)
   End Sub ' Main
End Module ' DoUntil
```

```
3  9  27  81
First power of 3 larger than 100 is 243
```

Fig. 5.7 | Do Until...Loop repetition statement demonstration.

(lines 9–10) are performed when the statement's loop-termination condition is false (i.e., `product` is less than or equal to `100`). When the loop-termination condition (`product > 100`, the leftmost guard condition) is true, the statement exits.

Common Programming Error 5.3

Failure to provide the body of a `Do Until...Loop` statement with an action that eventually causes the loop-termination condition in the `Do Until...Loop` to become true creates an infinite loop.

5.10 Compound Assignment Operators

Visual Basic provides several compound assignment operators for abbreviating assignment statements. For example, the statement

```
value = value + 3
```

can be abbreviated with the addition assignment operator, += as

```
value += 3
```

The += operator adds the value of the right operand to the value of the left operand and stores the result in the left operand's variable. Any statement of the form

variable = *variable operator expression*

can be written in the form

variable operator = *expression*

where *operator* is one of the binary operators +, -, *, ^, &, / or \, and *variable* is an *lvalue* ("left value"). An *lvalue* is a variable or property that can appear on the left side of an assignment statement. We will learn how to declare constants in Section 7.16—constants cannot be *lvalues*. Figure 5.8 includes the compound assignment operators, sample expressions using these operators, and explanations.

The =, +=, -=, *=, /=, \=, ^= and &= operators are always applied last in an expression. When an assignment (=) is evaluated, the expression to the right of the operator is always

Compound assignment operator	Sample expression	Explanation	Assigns
Assume: `c = 4, d = "He"`			
+=	`c += 7`	`c = c + 7`	`11` to `c`
-=	`c -= 3`	`c = c - 3`	`1` to `c`
*=	`c *= 4`	`c = c * 4`	`16` to `c`
/=	`c /= 2`	`c = c / 2`	`2` to `c`
\=	`c \= 3`	`c = c \ 3`	`1` to `c`
^=	`c ^= 2`	`c = c ^ 2`	`16` to `c`
&=	`d &= "llo"`	`d = d & "llo"`	`"Hello"` to `d`

Fig. 5.8 | Compound assignment operators.

evaluated first, then the value is assigned to the *lvalue* on the left. When a compound assignment is evaluated, the appropriate operator is applied to the *lvalue*'s original value and the value to the operator's right, then the value is assigned to the *lvalue* on the left. Figure 5.9 calculates a power of two using the exponentiation assignment operator. Lines 12 and 16 have the same effect on the variable `result`. Both statements raise `result` to the value of variable `exponent`. Note that the results of these two calculations are identical.

```
1  ' Fig. 5.9: Assignment.vb
2  ' Using a compound assignment operator to calculate a power of 2.
3  Module Assignment
4     Sub Main()
5        Dim exponent As Integer ' power input by user
6        Dim result As Integer = 2 ' number to raise to a power
7
8        ' prompt user for exponent
9        Console.Write("Enter an integer exponent: ")
10       exponent = Console.ReadLine() ' input exponent
11
12       result ^= exponent ' same as result = result ^ exponent
13       Console.WriteLine("result ^= exponent: " & result)
14
15       result = 2 ' reset result to 2
16       result = result ^ exponent ' same as result ^= exponent
17       Console.WriteLine("result = result ^ exponent: " & result)
18    End Sub ' Main
19 End Module ' Assignment
```

```
Enter an integer exponent: 8
result ^= exponent: 256
result = result ^ exponent: 256
```

Fig. 5.9 | Exponentiation using a compound assignment operator.

5.11 Formulating Algorithms: Counter-Controlled Repetition

To illustrate how algorithms are developed, we modify the `GradeBook` class of Chapter 4 to solve two variations of a problem that averages student grades. Consider the following problem statement:

> *A class of 10 students took a quiz. The grades (integers in the range 0 to 100) for this quiz are available to you. Determine the class average on the quiz.*

The class average is equal to the sum of the grades divided by the number of students (10). The algorithm for solving this problem on a computer must input each grade, keep track of the total of all grades input, perform the averaging calculation and print the result.

Pseudocode Algorithm with Counter-Controlled Repetition

Let us use pseudocode to list the actions to execute and specify the order of execution. We use counter-controlled repetition to input and process the grades one at a time. This technique uses a variable called a counter (or control variable) to specify the number of times that a set of statements will execute. Counter-controlled repetition also is called definite repetition because the number of repetitions is known before the loop begins executing. In this example, repetition terminates when the counter exceeds 10. This section presents a fully developed pseudocode algorithm (Fig. 5.10) and a version of class `GradeBook` (Fig. 5.11) that implements the algorithm in a method. The section then presents an application (Fig. 5.12) that demonstrates the algorithm in action. In Sections 5.12—5.14, we demonstrate how to use pseudocode to develop algorithms from scratch.

Note the references in the pseudocode algorithm (Fig. 5.10) to a total and a counter. A total is a variable used to accumulate the sum of several values. A counter is a variable used to count—in this case, the grade counter records the number of grades input by the user. It is important that variables used as totals and counters have appropriate initial values before they are used. Counters usually are initialized to 1 (but we will see examples where it is appropriate to initialize counters to other values, most commonly zero). Totals generally are initialized to zero. In Visual Basic, numeric variables are initialized to 0 when they are declared, unless another value is assigned to the variable in its declaration.

Good Programming Practice 5.4

Although Visual Basic initializes numeric variables to 0, it is a good practice to initialize certain variables explicitly to avoid confusion and improve program readability.

```
Set total to zero
Set grade counter to one

While grade counter is less than or equal to ten
    Prompt the user to enter the next grade
    Input the next grade
    Add the grade into the total
    Add one to the grade counter

Set the class average to the total divided by ten
Print the class average
```

Fig. 5.10 | Pseudocode algorithm that uses counter-controlled repetition to solve the class-average problem.

```
' Fig. 5.11: GradeBook.vb
' GradeBook class that solves class-average problem using
' counter-controlled repetition.
Public Class GradeBook
   Private courseNameValue As String ' course name for this GradeBook

   ' constructor initializes CourseName with String supplied as argument
   Public Sub New(ByVal name As String)
      CourseName = name ' validate and store course name
   End Sub ' New
```

Fig. 5.11 | Counter-controlled repetition: Class-average problem. (Part 1 of 3.)

```

   ' property that gets and sets the course name; the Set accessor
   ' ensures that the course name has at most 25 characters
   Public Property CourseName() As String
      Get ' retrieve courseNameValue
         Return courseNameValue
      End Get

      Set(ByVal value As String) ' set courseNameValue
         If value.Length <= 25 Then ' if value has 25 or fewer characters
            courseNameValue = value ' store the course name in the object
         Else ' if name has more than 25 characters
            ' set courseNameValue to first 25 characters of parameter name
            ' start at 0, length of 25
            courseNameValue = value.Substring(0, 25)

            Console.WriteLine( _
               "Course name (" & value & ") exceeds maximum length (25).")
            Console.WriteLine( _
               "Limiting course name to first 25 characters." & vbCrLf)
         End If
      End Set
   End Property ' CourseName

   ' display a welcome message to the GradeBook user
   Public Sub DisplayMessage()
      ' this statement uses property CourseName to get the
      ' name of the course this GradeBook represents
      Console.WriteLine("Welcome to the grade book for " _
         & vbCrLf & CourseName & "!" & vbCrLf)
   End Sub ' DisplayMessage

   ' determine class average based on 10 grades entered by user
   Public Sub DetermineClassAverage()
      Dim total As Integer ' sum of grades entered by user
      Dim gradeCounter As Integer ' number of grades input
      Dim grade As Integer ' grade input by user
      Dim average As Integer ' average of grades

      ' initialization phase
      total = 0 ' set total to zero
      gradeCounter = 1 ' prepare to loop

      ' processing phase
      While gradeCounter <= 10 ' loop 10 times
         ' prompt for and input grade from user
         Console.Write("Enter grade: ") ' prompt for grade
         grade = Console.ReadLine() ' input the next grade
         total += grade ' add grade to total
         gradeCounter += 1 ' add 1 to gradeCounter
      End While

```

Fig. 5.11 | Counter-controlled repetition: Class-average problem. (Part 2 of 3.)

```
63          ' termination phase
64          average = total \ 10 ' integer division yields integer result
65
66          ' display total and average of grades
67          Console.WriteLine(vbCrLf & "Total of all 10 grades is " & total)
68          Console.WriteLine("Class average is " & average)
69       End Sub ' DetermineClassAverage
70    End Class ' GradeBook
```

Fig. 5.11 | Counter-controlled repetition: Class-average problem. (Part 3 of 3.)

Implementing Counter-Controlled Repetition in Class `GradeBook`

Class `GradeBook` (Fig. 5.11) contains a constructor (lines 8–10) that assigns a value to the class's property `CourseName`. Lines 14–33 and 36–41 declare property `CourseName` and method `DisplayMessage`, respectively. Lines 44–69 declare method `DetermineClassAverage`, which implements the class-averaging algorithm described by the pseudocode in Fig. 5.10.

Lines 45–48 declare local variables `total`, `gradeCounter`, `grade` and `average` to be of type `Integer`. In this example, variable `total` accumulates the sum of the grades entered and `gradeCounter` counts the number of grades entered. Variable `grade` stores the most recent grade value entered (line 58). Variable `average` stores the average grade.

Note that the declarations (in lines 45–48) appear in the body of method `DetermineClassAverage`. Recall that variables declared in a method body are local variables and can be used only from their declaration until the end of the method declaration. A local variable's declaration must appear before the variable is used in that method. A local variable cannot be accessed outside the method in which it is declared.

In the versions of class `GradeBook` in this chapter, we simply read and process a set of grades. The averaging calculation is performed in method `DetermineClassAverage` using local variables—we do not preserve any information about student grades in instance variables of the class. In versions of the class in Chapter 8, we maintain the grades in memory using an instance variable that refers to a data structure known as an array. This allows a `GradeBook` object to perform various calculations on the same set of grades without requiring the user to enter the grades multiple times.

Good Programming Practice 5.5

Separating declarations from other statements with a blank line improves readability.

The assignments (in lines 51–52) initialize `total` to `0` and `gradeCounter` to `1`. Line 55 indicates that the `While` statement should continue looping (also called iterating) as long as the value of `gradeCounter` is less than or equal to 10. While this condition remains true, the `While` statement repeatedly executes the statements in its body (lines 57–60).

Line 57 displays the prompt `"Enter grade: "`. Line 58 reads the grade entered by the user and assigns it to the variable `grade`. Then line 59 adds the new `grade` entered by the user into the variable `total` using the += compound assignment operator.

Line 60 adds `1` to `gradeCounter` to indicate that the program has processed another grade and is ready to input the next grade from the user. Incrementing `gradeCounter` eventually causes it to exceed 10. At that point the `While` loop terminates because its condition (line 55) becomes false.

When the loop terminates, line 64 performs the averaging calculation and assigns its result to the variable `average`. Line 67 displays the text `"Total of all 10 grades is "` followed by variable `total`'s value. Line 68 then displays the text `"Class average is "` followed by variable `average`'s value. Method `DetermineClassAverage` returns control to the calling method (i.e., `Main` in `GradeBookTest` of Fig. 5.12) after reaching line 69.

Software Engineering Observation 5.3

Experience has shown that the most difficult part of solving a problem on a computer is developing the algorithm for the solution. Once a correct algorithm has been specified, the process of producing a working Visual Basic program from the algorithm is normally straightforward.

Module `GradeBookTest`

Module `GradeBookTest` (Fig. 5.12) creates an object of class `GradeBook` (Fig. 5.11) and demonstrates its capabilities. Line 7 of Fig. 5.12 creates a new `GradeBook` object and assigns it to variable `gradeBook`. The string in line 7 is passed to the `GradeBook` constructor (lines 8–10 of Fig. 5.11). Line 9 calls `gradeBook`'s `DisplayMessage` method to display a

```
1  ' Fig. 5.12: GradeBookTest.vb
2  ' Create GradeBook object and invoke its DetermineClassAverage method.
3  Module GradeBookTest
4     Sub Main()
5        ' create GradeBook object gradeBook and
6        ' pass course name to constructor
7        Dim gradeBook As New GradeBook("CS101 Introduction to VB")
8
9        gradeBook.DisplayMessage() ' display welcome message
10       gradeBook.DetermineClassAverage() ' find average of 10 grades
11    End Sub ' Main
12 End Module ' GradeBookTest
```

```
Welcome to the grade book for
CS101 Introduction to VB!

Enter grade: 65
Enter grade: 78
Enter grade: 89
Enter grade: 67
Enter grade: 87
Enter grade: 98
Enter grade: 93
Enter grade: 85
Enter grade: 82
Enter grade: 100

Total of all 10 grades is 844
Class average is 84
```

Fig. 5.12 | Module `GradeBookTest` creates an object of class `GradeBook` (Fig. 5.11) and invokes its `DetermineClassAverage` method.

welcome message to the user. Line 10 then calls `gradeBook`'s `DetermineClassAverage` method to allow the user to enter 10 grades, for which the method then calculates and prints the average, performing the algorithm shown in Fig. 5.10.

Notes on Integer Division

The averaging calculation performed by method `DetermineClassAverage` in response to the method call at line 10 in Fig. 5.12 produces an integer result. The program's output indicates that the sum of the grade values in the sample execution is 844, which, when divided by 10, should yield the floating-point number 84.4. However, the result of the calculation `total \ 10` (line 64 of Fig. 5.11) is the integer 84, because the integer division operator is used. Recall that the integer division operator takes two integer operands and returns an integer result. We use the floating-point division operator in the next section to determine a floating-point average.

Common Programming Error 5.4

Assuming that integer division rounds (rather than truncates) can lead to incorrect results. For example, 7 divided by 4, which yields 1.75 in conventional arithmetic, truncates to 1 in integer arithmetic, rather than rounding to 2.

5.12 Formulating Algorithms: Sentinel-Controlled Repetition

Let us generalize Section 5.11's class-average problem. Consider the following problem:

> *Develop a class-average program that processes grades for an arbitrary number of students each time it is run.*

In the previous class-average example, the problem statement specified the number of students, so the number of grades (10) was known in advance. In this example, no indication is given of how many grades are to be input. The program must process an arbitrary number of grades. How can it determine when to stop the input of grades? How will it know when to calculate and print the class average?

One way to solve this problem is to use a special value called a sentinel value (also called a signal value, a dummy value or a flag value) to indicate "end of data entry." The user enters grades until all legitimate grades have been entered. The user then types the sentinel value to indicate that no more grades will be entered. Sentinel-controlled repetition is called indefinite repetition because the number of repetitions is not known before the loop begins its execution.

It is crucial to employ a sentinel value that cannot be confused with an acceptable input value. Grades on a quiz are nonnegative integers, so –1 is an acceptable sentinel value for this problem. A run of the class-average program might process a stream of inputs such as 95, 96, 75, 74, 89 and –1. The program would then compute and print the class average for the grades 95, 96, 75, 74 and 89. The sentinel value, –1, should not enter into the averaging calculation.

Common Programming Error 5.5

Choosing a sentinel value that is also a legitimate data value could result in a logic error that would cause a program to produce incorrect results.

Developing the Pseudocode Algorithm with Top-Down, Stepwise Refinement: The Top and the First Refinement

When solving more complex problems, such as the one in this example, the pseudocode representation might not be obvious. For this reason we approach the class-average program with top-down, stepwise refinement, a technique for developing well-structured algorithms. We begin with a pseudocode representation of the top—a single statement that conveys the overall function of the program:

Determine the class average for the quiz

The top is, in effect, a *complete* representation of a program. Unfortunately, the top rarely conveys sufficient detail from which to write a Visual Basic program. Therefore, we conduct the refinement process. This involves dividing the top into a series of smaller tasks that are listed in the order in which they must be performed, resulting in the following first refinement:

Initialize variables
Input, sum and count the quiz grades
Calculate and print the class average

Software Engineering Observation 5.4

Each refinement, including the top, is a complete specification of the algorithm; only the level of detail in each refinement varies.

Software Engineering Observation 5.5

Many algorithms can be divided logically into three phases—an initialization phase that initializes the program variables, a processing phase that inputs data values and adjusts program variables accordingly, and a termination phase that calculates and prints the results.

Proceeding to the Second Refinement

The preceding *Software Engineering Observation* is often all you need for the first refinement in the top-down process. To proceed to the second refinement, we commit to specific variables. In this example, we need a running total of the numbers, a count of how many numbers have been processed, a variable to receive the value of each grade as it is input by the user and a variable to hold the calculated average. The pseudocode statement

Initialize variables

can be refined as follows:

Initialize total to zero
Initialize grade counter to zero

Note that only the variables *total* and *counter* need to be initialized before they are used. The variables *average* and *grade* (the program in Fig. 5.14 uses these variables for the calculated average and the user input, respectively) need not be initialized (although, as you know, Visual Basic nevertheless initializes them to the default value zero) because the assignment of their values does not depend on their previous values, as is the case for *total* and *counter*.

The pseudocode statement

Input, sum and count the quiz grades

requires a repetition statement (i.e., a loop) that inputs and processes each grade. We do not know in advance how many grades are to be processed, so we use sentinel-controlled repetition. The user enters legitimate grades one at a time. After the last legitimate grade is typed, the user enters the sentinel value. The program tests for the sentinel value after each grade is input and terminates the loop when the user enters the sentinel value. The second refinement of the preceding pseudocode statement is then

```
Prompt the user to enter the first grade
Input the first grade (possibly the sentinel)

While the user has not yet entered the sentinel
    Add this grade into the running total
    Add one to the grade counter
    Prompt the user to enter the next grade
    Input the next grade (possibly the sentinel)
```

The pseudocode statement

```
Calculate and print the class average
```

can be refined as follows:

```
If the grade counter is not equal to zero then
    Set the average to the total divided by the counter
    Print the class average
Else
    Print "No grades were entered"
```

The counter will be zero if the user enters the sentinel value first. We test for the possibility of division by zero—a logic error that, if undetected, would cause the program to fail or produce invalid output. The complete second refinement of the pseudocode algorithm for the class-average problem is shown in Fig. 5.13.

```
Initialize total to zero
Initialize grade counter to zero

Prompt the user to enter the first grade
Input the first grade (possibly the sentinel)

While the user has not yet entered the sentinel
    Add this grade into the running total
    Add one to the grade counter
    Prompt the user to enter the next grade
    Input the next grade (possibly the sentinel)

If the grade counter is not equal to zero then
    Set the average to the total divided by the counter
    Print the class average
Else
    Print "No grades were entered"
```

Fig. 5.13 | Class-average problem pseudocode algorithm with sentinel-controlled repetition.

Error-Prevention Tip 5.1

When performing division by an expression whose value could be zero, explicitly test for this case and handle it appropriately in your program. Such handling could be as simple as printing an error message. Sometimes more sophisticated processing is required, such as using the techniques of Chapter 13, Exception Handling.

Good Programming Practice 5.6

Include blank lines in pseudocode algorithms to improve readability. The blank lines separate pseudocode control statements and the algorithms' phases.

The pseudocode algorithm in Fig. 5.13 solves the more general class-averaging problem presented at the beginning of this section. This algorithm was developed after only two levels of refinement—sometimes more levels of refinement are necessary.

Software Engineering Observation 5.6

You terminate the top-down, stepwise refinement process when the pseudocode algorithm is specified in sufficient detail for the pseudocode to be converted to a Visual Basic program.

Implementing Sentinel-Controlled Repetition in Class GradeBook

Figure 5.14 shows the Visual Basic class `GradeBook` containing the method `DetermineClassAverage` that implements the pseudocode algorithm of Fig. 5.13. Although each grade is an integer, the averaging calculation is likely to produce a number with a decimal point—a real number or floating-point number. The type `Integer` cannot represent such a number, so method `DetermineClassAverage` uses type `Double` to do so.

```
' Fig. 5.14: GradeBook.vb
' GradeBook class that solves class-average problem using
' sentinel-controlled repetition.
Public Class GradeBook
   Private courseNameValue As String ' course name for this GradeBook

   ' constructor initializes CourseName with String supplied as argument
   Public Sub New(ByVal name As String)
      CourseName = name ' validate and store course name
   End Sub ' New

   ' property that gets and sets the course name; the Set accessor
   ' ensures that the course name has at most 25 characters
   Public Property CourseName() As String
      Get ' retrieve courseNameValue
         Return courseNameValue
      End Get

      Set(ByVal value As String) ' set courseNameValue
         If value.Length <= 25 Then ' if value has 25 or fewer characters
            courseNameValue = value ' store the course name in the object
         Else ' if name has more than 25 characters
            ' set courseNameValue to first 25 characters of parameter name
            ' start at 0, length of 25
```

Fig. 5.14 | Sentinel-controlled repetition: Class-average problem. (Part 1 of 3.)

```
            courseNameValue = value.Substring(0, 25)

            Console.WriteLine( _
               "Course name (" & value & ") exceeds maximum length (25).")
            Console.WriteLine( _
               "Limiting course name to first 25 characters." & vbCrLf)
         End If
      End Set
   End Property ' CourseName

   ' display a welcome message to the GradeBook user
   Public Sub DisplayMessage()
      ' this statement uses property CourseName to get the
      ' name of the course this GradeBook represents
      Console.WriteLine("Welcome to the grade book for " _
          & vbCrLf & CourseName & "!" & vbCrLf)
   End Sub ' DisplayMessage

   ' determine class average based on 10 grades entered by user
   Public Sub DetermineClassAverage()
      Dim total As Integer ' sum of grades entered by user
      Dim gradeCounter As Integer ' number of grades input
      Dim grade As Integer ' grade input by user
      Dim average As Double ' average of all grades

      ' initialization phase
      total = 0 ' clear total
      gradeCounter = 0 ' prepare to loop

      ' processing phase
      ' prompt for input and read grade from user
      Console.Write("Enter grade or -1 to quit: ")
      grade = Console.ReadLine()

      ' sentinel-controlled loop where -1 is the sentinel value
      While grade <> -1
         total += grade ' add grade to total
         gradeCounter += 1 ' add 1 to gradeCounter

         ' prompt for and input next grade from user
         Console.Write("Enter grade or -1 to quit: ") ' prompt
         grade = Console.ReadLine() ' input next grade
      End While

      ' termination phase
      If gradeCounter <> 0 Then ' if user entered at least one grade
         ' calculate average of all grades entered
         average = total / gradeCounter

         ' display total and average (with two digits of precision)
         Console.WriteLine(vbCrLf & "Total of the " & gradeCounter & _
            " grades entered is " & total)
```

Fig. 5.14 | Sentinel-controlled repetition: Class-average problem. (Part 2 of 3.)

```
77             Console.WriteLine("Class average is {0:F}", average)
78          Else ' no grades were entered, so output appropriate message
79             Console.WriteLine("No grades were entered")
80          End If
81       End Sub ' DetermineClassAverage
82    End Class ' GradeBook
```

Fig. 5.14 | Sentinel-controlled repetition: Class-average problem. (Part 3 of 3.)

In this example, we see that control statements may be stacked on top of one another (i.e., placed in sequence) just as a child stacks building blocks. The `While` statement (lines 60–67) is followed in sequence by an `If...Then...Else` statement (lines 70–80). Much of the code in this program is identical to the code in Fig. 5.11, so we concentrate on the new features and issues.

Line 48 declares `Double` variable `average`. This variable allows us to store the calculated class average as a floating-point number. We discuss floating-point numbers in more detail shortly. Line 52 initializes `gradeCounter` to `0`, because no grades have been entered yet. Remember that this program uses sentinel-controlled repetition to input the grades from the user. To keep an accurate record of the number of grades entered, the program increments `gradeCounter` only when the user inputs a valid grade value. Recall that `Integer` variables are initialized to zero by default, so lines 51–52 can be omitted.

Program Logic for Sentinel-Controlled Repetition vs. Counter-Controlled Repetition

Compare the program logic for sentinel-controlled repetition in this application with that for counter-controlled repetition in Fig. 5.11. In counter-controlled repetition, each iteration (repetition) of the `While` statement (e.g., lines 55–61 of Fig. 5.11) reads a value from the user for the specified number of iterations. In sentinel-controlled repetition, the program reads the first value (lines 56–57 of Fig. 5.14) before reaching the `While`. This value determines whether the program's flow of control should enter the body of the `While`. If the condition of the `While` is false, the user entered the sentinel value, so the body of the `While` does not execute (i.e., no grades were entered). If, on the other hand, the condition is true, the body begins execution, and the loop adds the `grade` value to the `total` (line 61). Lines 65–66 in the loop's body input the next value from the user. Next, program control reaches the end of the `While` statement, so execution continues with the test of the `While`'s condition (line 60). The condition uses the most recent `grade` input by the user to determine whether the loop's body should execute again. Note that the value of variable `grade` is always input from the user immediately before the program tests the `While` condition. This allows the program to determine whether the value just input is the sentinel value *before* processing that value (i.e., adding it to the `total`). If the sentinel value is input, the loop terminates, and the program does not add `–1` to the `total`.

Good Programming Practice 5.7

In a sentinel-controlled loop, the prompts requesting data entry should explicitly remind the user of the sentinel value.

After the loop terminates, the `If...Then...Else` statement at lines 70–80 executes. The condition at line 70 determines whether any grades were input. If none were input, the `Else` part (lines 78–79) of the `If...Then...Else` statement executes and displays the message `"No grades were entered"` and the method returns control to the calling method.

Floating-Point Numbers and Type `Double`

Although each grade is an integer, the averaging calculation is likely to produce a number with a decimal point (i.e., a floating-point number). Type `Integer` cannot represent floating-point numbers, so this program uses data type `Double` to store floating-point numbers. Visual Basic provides two primitive types for storing floating-point numbers in memory—`Single` and `Double`. The primary difference between them is that `Double` variables can store numbers of larger magnitude and finer detail (i.e., more digits to the right of the decimal point—also known as the number's precision) than `Single` variables.

Floating-Point-Number Precision and Memory Requirements

Variables of type `Single` represent single-precision floating-point numbers and have seven significant digits. Variables of type `Double` represent double-precision floating-point numbers. These require twice as much memory as `Single` variables and provide 15 significant digits—approximately double the precision of `Single` variables. For the range of values required by most programs, variables of type `Single` should suffice, but you can use `Double` to play it safe. In some applications, even variables of type `Double` will be inadequate—such applications are beyond the scope of this book. Most programmers represent floating-point numbers with type `Double`. In fact, Visual Basic treats all the floating-point numbers you type in a program's source code (such as 7.33 and 0.0975) as `Double` values by default. Such values in the source code are known as floating-point literals. See Section 7.11 for the ranges of values for `Single`s and `Double`s.

Floating-Point Numbers are Approximations

Although floating-point numbers are not always 100% precise, they have numerous applications. For example, when we speak of a "normal" body temperature of 98.6, we do not need to be precise to a large number of digits. When we read the temperature on a thermometer as 98.6, it may actually be 98.5999473210643. Calling this number simply 98.6 is fine for most applications involving body temperatures. Due to the imprecise nature of floating-point numbers, type `Double` is preferred over type `Single` because `Double` variables can represent floating-point numbers more accurately. For this reason, we use type `Double` throughout the book.

Floating-point numbers also arise as a result of division. In conventional arithmetic, when we divide 10 by 3, the result is 3.3333333..., with the sequence of 3s repeating infinitely. The computer allocates only a fixed amount of space to hold such a value, so clearly the stored floating-point value can be only an approximation.

Common Programming Error 5.6

Using floating-point numbers in a manner that assumes they are represented precisely can lead to logic errors.

Implicitly Converting Between Primitive Types

If at least one grade was entered, line 72 of Fig. 5.14 calculates the average of the grades. Recall from Fig. 5.11 that we used the integer division operator to yield an integer result. Since we are now calculating a floating-point value, we use the floating-point division operator. But the operands of the division in line 72 are of type `Integer`. To perform a floating-point calculation with integer values, we must temporarily treat these values as floating-point numbers for use in the calculation.

The floating-point division operator is defined to operate on values of three types—`Single`, `Double` and `Decimal` (you'll learn about type `Decimal` in Chapter 6). To ensure that the operator's operands are one of these three types, Visual Basic performs an operation called implicit conversion on selected operands. For example, in an expression using the floating-point division operator, if both operands are of type `Integer`, the operands will be promoted to `Double` values for use in the expression. In this example, the values of `total` and `gradeCounter` are promoted to type `Double`, then the floating-point division is performed and the result of the calculation is assigned to `average`. You'll learn more about the implicit conversion rules in Section 7.9.

Formatting for Floating-Point Numbers

Line 77 outputs the class average. In this example, we decided to display the class average rounded to the nearest hundredth and to output the average with exactly two digits to the right of the decimal point. Note that the call to method `WriteLine` in line 77 uses the string "`{0:F}`" to indicate that the value of `average` should be displayed in the command prompt as a fixed-point number, (i.e., a number with a specified number of places after the decimal point). This is an example of formatted output, where a value's data is formatted for display purposes. The numeric value that appears before the colon (in this case, `0`) indicates which of `WriteLine`'s arguments will be formatted—`0` specifies the first argument *after* the format string passed to `WriteLine`, namely `average`. Additional values can be inserted into the string to specify other arguments. If we had passed `total` as a third argument to method `WriteLine` and used the string "`{1:F}`", the value to be formatted would be `total`. The value after the colon (in this case, `F`) is known as a format specifier, which indicates how a value is to be formatted. The format specifier `F` indicates that a fixed-point number should (by default) be displayed with two decimal places. The entire placeholder (`{0:F}`) is replaced with the formatted value of variable `average`. This can be changed by placing an integer value after the format specifier—e.g., the string "`{0:F3}`" would display a fixed-point value with three decimal places. Some of the more common format specifiers are summarized in Fig. 5.15. The format specifiers are case insensitive. Also, the format specifiers `D` and `X` can be used only with integer values.

Format code	Description
`C`	Currency. Formats the currency based on the computer's locale setting. For U.S. currency, precedes the value with `$`, uses commas as thousands separators, uses a dot (`.`) as the decimal separator and sets the number of decimal places to two.
`E`	Scientific notation. Displays one digit to the left of the decimal and six digits to the right of the decimal, followed by the character `E` and a three-digit integer representing the exponent of a power of 10. For example, `956.2` is formatted as `9.562000E+002`.
`F`	Fixed point. Sets the number of decimal places to two.

Fig. 5.15 | Formatting codes for `Strings`. (Part 1 of 2.)

Format code	Description
G	General. Visual Basic chooses either E or F for you, depending on which representation generates a shorter string.
D	Decimal integer. Displays an integer as a whole number in standard base-10 format.
N	Number. Separates every three digits with a comma and sets the number of decimal places to two. (Varies by locale.)
X	Hexadecimal integer. Displays the integer in hexadecimal (base-16) notation. We discuss hexadecimal notation in Appendix C.

Fig. 5.15 | Formatting codes for `Strings`. (Part 2 of 2.)

Good Programming Practice 5.8

When formatting with two positions to the right of the decimal point, some programmers prefer to use the format specifier `F2` *for clarity.*

The three grades entered during the sample execution of module `GradeBookTest` (Fig. 5.16) total 257, which yields the average 85.666666…. The format specifier causes the output to be rounded to the specified number of digits. In this program, the average is rounded to the hundredths position and is displayed as `85.67`.

```
' Fig. 5.16: GradeBookTest.vb
' Create GradeBook object and invoke its DetermineClassAverage method.
Module GradeBookTest
   Sub Main()
      ' create GradeBook object gradeBook and
      ' pass course name to constructor
      Dim gradeBook As New GradeBook("CS101 Introduction to VB")

      gradeBook.DisplayMessage() ' display welcome message
      gradeBook.DetermineClassAverage() ' find average of grades
   End Sub ' Main
End Module ' GradeBookTest
```

```
Welcome to the grade book for
CS101 Introduction to VB!

Enter grade or -1 to quit: 97
Enter grade or -1 to quit: 88
Enter grade or -1 to quit: 72
Enter grade or -1 to quit: -1

Total of the 3 grades entered is 257
Class average is 85.67
```

Fig. 5.16 | `GradeBookTest` module creates an object of class `GradeBook` (Fig. 5.14) and invokes its `DetermineClassAverage` method.

5.13 Formulating Algorithms: Nested Control Statements

For the next example, we once again formulate an algorithm by using pseudocode and top-down, stepwise refinement, and write a corresponding Visual Basic program. We have seen that control statements can be stacked on top of one another (in sequence) just as a child stacks building blocks. In this case study, we examine the only other structured way control statements can be combined, namely, through the nesting of one control statement within another.

Consider the following problem statement:

> *A college offers a course that prepares students for the state licensing exam for real-estate brokers. Last year, 10 of the students who completed this course took the licensing exam. The college wants to know how well its students did on the exam. You have been asked to write a program to summarize the results. You have been given a list of the 10 students. Next to each name is written a "P" if the student passed the exam and an "F" if the student failed the exam.*
>
> *Your program should analyze the results of the exam as follows:*
>
> 1. *Input each exam result (i.e., a "P" or an "F"). Display the message "Enter result" on the screen each time the program requests another exam result.*
> 2. *Count the number of passes and failures.*
> 3. *Display a summary of the exam results, indicating the number of students who passed and the number who failed.*
> 4. *If more than eight students passed the exam, print the message "Raise tuition."*

After reading the problem statement carefully, we make the following observations:

1. The program must process exam results for 10 students. A counter-controlled loop can be used because the number of test results is known in advance.
2. Each exam result is a string—either a "P" or an "F". Each time the program reads an exam result, it must determine whether the input is a "P" or an "F". We test for a "P" in our algorithm. If the input is not a "P," we assume it is an "F". An exercise at the end of the chapter considers the consequences of this assumption. For instance, consider what happens in this program when the user enters a lowercase "p."
3. Two counters store the exam results—one counts the number of students who passed the exam and the other counts the number of students who failed the exam.
4. After the program has processed all the exam results, it must determine whether more than eight students passed the exam.

Let us proceed with top-down, stepwise refinement. We begin with a pseudocode representation of the top:

> *Analyze exam results and decide if tuition should be raised*

Once again, the top is a *complete* representation of the program, but several refinements are likely to be needed before the pseudocode can evolve naturally into a Visual Basic program.

Our first refinement is

Initialize variables
Input the 10 exam grades, and count passes and failures
Print a summary of the exam results and decide if tuition should be raised

Here, too, even though we have a complete representation of the entire program, further refinement is necessary. We must commit to specific variables. Counters are needed to record the passes and failures. A counter controls the looping process and a variable stores the user input. The pseudocode statement

Initialize variables

can be refined as follows:

Initialize passes to zero
Initialize failures to zero
Initialize student to one

Only the counters for the number of passes, number of failures and number of students need to be initialized.

The pseudocode statement

Input the 10 exam results, and count passes and failures

requires a loop that successively inputs the result of each exam. We know in advance that there are precisely 10 exam results, so counter-controlled looping is appropriate. Inside the loop (i.e., *nested* within the loop), a double-selection statement will determine whether each exam result is a pass or a failure and will increment the appropriate counter. The refinement of the preceding pseudocode statement is then

```
While student is less than or equal to 10
    Prompt the user to enter the next exam result
    Input the next exam result

    If the student passed then
        Add one to passes
    Else
        Add one to failures

    Add one to student
```

Note the use of blank lines to set off the *If...Else* control statement to improve readability.

The pseudocode statement

Print a summary of the exam results and decide if tuition should be raised

may be refined as follows:

```
Print the number of passes
Print the number of failures

If more than eight students passed then
    Print "Raise tuition"
```

Complete Second Refinement of Pseudocode and Conversion to Class `Analysis`

The complete second refinement of the pseudocode appears in Fig. 5.17. Note that blank lines are also used to set off the *While* statement for readability. This pseudocode is now sufficiently refined for conversion to Visual Basic. The class that implements the pseudocode algorithm is shown in Fig. 5.18, and two sample executions appear in Fig. 5.19.

Lines 7–10 of Fig. 5.18 declare the variables that method `ProcessExamResults` of class `Analysis` uses to process the examination results. Several of these declarations use Visual Basic's ability to incorporate variable initialization into declarations (`passes` is initialized to `0`, `failures` is initialized to `0` and `student` is initialized to `1`).

The `While` statement (lines 13–25) loops 10 times. During each iteration, the loop inputs and processes one exam result. Note that the `If...Then...Else` statement (lines 18–22) for processing each result is nested in the `While` statement. If the `result` is `"P"`, the

```
Initialize passes to zero
Initialize failures to zero
Initialize student to one

While student is less than or equal to 10
    Prompt the user to enter the next exam result
    Input the next exam result

    If the student passed then
        Add one to passes
    Else
        Add one to failures

    Add one to student

Print the number of passes
Print the number of failures

If more than eight students passed then
    Print "Raise tuition"
```

Fig. 5.17 | Pseudocode for examination-results problem.

```
1  ' Fig. 5.18: Analysis.vb
2  ' Analysis of examination results.
3  Public Class Analysis
4     ' input and analyze exam results
5     Public Sub ProcessExamResults()
6        ' initializing variables in declarations
7        Dim passes As Integer = 0 ' number of passes
8        Dim failures As Integer = 0 ' number of failures
9        Dim student As Integer = 1 ' student counter
10       Dim result As String ' one exam result (obtains value from user)
```

Fig. 5.18 | Nested control statements: Examination-results problem. (Part 1 of 2.)

```
11
12         ' process 10 students using counter-controlled loop
13         While student <= 10
14            Console.Write("Enter result (P = pass, F = fail): ")
15            result = Console.ReadLine()
16
17            ' nested control statement
18            If result = "P" Then
19               passes += 1 ' increment number of passes
20            Else
21               failures += 1 ' increment number of failures
22            End If
23
24            student += 1 ' increment student counter
25         End While
26
27         ' display exam results
28         Console.WriteLine( _
29            "Passed: " & passes & vbCrLf & "Failed: " & failures)
30
31         ' raise tuition if more than 8 students passed
32         If passes > 8 Then
33            Console.WriteLine("Raise tuition")
34         End If
35      End Sub ' ProcessExamResults
36   End Class ' Analysis
```

Fig. 5.18 | Nested control statements: Examination-results problem. (Part 2 of 2.)

`If...Then...Else` statement increments `passes`; otherwise, it assumes the `result` is `"F"` and increments `failures`. [*Note:* `Strings` are case sensitive by default—uppercase and lowercase letters are different. Only `"P"` represents a passing grade. In the exercises, we ask you to enhance the program by processing lowercase inputs such as `"p"` and `"f"`.] Line 24 increments `student` before the loop condition is tested again at line 13. After 10 values have been input, the loop terminates and lines 28–29 display the number of `passes` and `failures`. The `If...Then` statement at lines 32–34 determines whether more than eight students passed the exam and, if so, outputs the message `"Raise tuition"`.

`AnalysisTest` Module That Demonstrates Class `Analysis`

Module `AnalysisTest` (Fig. 5.19) creates an `Analysis` object (line 5) and invokes the object's `ProcessExamResults` method (line 6) to process a set of exam results entered by the user. Figure 5.19 shows the input and output from two sample executions of the program. During the first sample execution, the condition at line 32 of method `ProcessExamResults` in Fig. 5.18 is true—more than eight students passed the exam, so the program outputs a message indicating that the tuition should be raised.

```
1   ' Fig. 5.19: AnalysisTest.vb
2   ' Test program for class Analysis.
3   Module AnalysisTest
```

Fig. 5.19 | Test program for class `Analysis` (Fig. 5.18). (Part 1 of 2.)

```
   Sub Main()
      Dim application As New Analysis() ' create Analysis object
      application.ProcessExamResults() ' call method to process results
   End Sub ' Main
End Module ' AnalysisTest
```

```
Enter result (P = pass, F = fail): P
Enter result (P = pass, F = fail): F
Enter result (P = pass, F = fail): P
Enter result (P = pass, F = fail): P
Enter result (P = pass, F = fail): P
Enter result (P = pass, F = fail): P
Enter result (P = pass, F = fail): P
Enter result (P = pass, F = fail): P
Enter result (P = pass, F = fail): P
Enter result (P = pass, F = fail): P
Passed: 9
Failed: 1
Raise tuition
```

```
Enter result (P = pass, F = fail): P
Enter result (P = pass, F = fail): P
Enter result (P = pass, F = fail): P
Enter result (P = pass, F = fail): F
Enter result (P = pass, F = fail): F
Enter result (P = pass, F = fail): P
Enter result (P = pass, F = fail): P
Enter result (P = pass, F = fail): P
Enter result (P = pass, F = fail): P
Enter result (P = pass, F = fail): P
Passed: 8
Failed: 2
```

Fig. 5.19 | Test program for class `Analysis` (Fig. 5.18). (Part 2 of 2.)

5.14 Formulating Algorithms: Nested Repetition Statements

Let us present another complete example. Once again, we formulate the algorithm using pseudocode and top-down, stepwise refinement, then write the corresponding program. We use nested repetition statements to solve the problem.

Consider the following problem statement:

> *Write a program that draws in the command prompt a filled square consisting solely of one type of character, such as the asterisk (*). The side of the square and the character to be used to fill the square should be entered by the user. The length of the side should not exceed 20 characters. If the user enters a value over 20, the message "Side is too large" should be printed.*

Your program should draw the square as follows:

1. Input the side of the square.
2. Validate that the side is less than or equal to 20. [*Note:* It's possible for the user to enter a value less than 1. We explore in the chapter exercises how this can be detected.]
3. Use repetition to draw the square by printing only one fill character at a time.

After reading the problem statement, we make the following observations:

1. The program must draw *side* rows, each containing *side* fill characters, where *side* is the value entered by the user. Counter-controlled repetition should be used.
2. A test must be employed to ensure that the value of *side* is less than or equal to 20. If it is not, the message "Side is too large" should be printed.
3. Four variables should be used—one that represents the length of the side of the square, one that represents (as a `String`) the fill character to be used, one that represents the row in which the next symbol should appear and one that represents the column in which the next symbol should appear.

Evolving the Pseudocode

Let us proceed with top-down, stepwise refinement. We begin with a pseudocode representation of the top:

Draw a square of fill characters

Once again, it is important to emphasize that the top is a complete representation of the program, but several refinements are likely to be needed before the pseudocode can be easily evolved into a program.

Our first refinement is

Prompt for the fill character
Input the fill character

Prompt for the side of the square
Input the side of the square

Draw the square if its side is less than or equal to 20; otherwise print an error message

Here, too, even though we have a complete representation of the entire program, further refinement is necessary.

The pseudocode statement

Draw the square if its side is less than or equal to 20; otherwise print an error message

can be refined as

```
If the side of the square is less than or equal to 20 then
    Draw the square
Else
    Print "Side is too large"
```

which explicitly tests whether *side is less than or equal to 20*. If the condition (i.e., "*side is less than or equal to 20*") is true, the square is drawn. If the condition is false, a message is displayed to the user.

Drawing the Square

The pseudocode statement

Draw the square

can be implemented by using one loop nested inside another. In this example, it is known in advance that there are *side* rows of *side* fill characters each, so counter-controlled repetition is appropriate. One loop controls the row in which each fill character is to be printed. A nested loop prints each fill character (one at a time) for that row. The refinement of the preceding pseudocode statement is

```
Set row to one

While row is less than or equal to side
    Set column to one

    While column is less than or equal to side
        Print the fill character
        Increment column by one

    Print a line feed/carriage return
    Increment row by one
```

The value of *row* is set to one to prepare to display the square's first row. The outer *While* statement loops while *row* is less than or equal to *side*—that is, for each row of the square. Within this *While* statement, *column* is set to one, as we prepare to display the first fill character of the current row. After *column* is set to one, the inner loop executes to completion (i.e., until *column* exceeds *side*). Each iteration of the inner loop prints one fill character (which in line 46 of the class of Fig. 5.21 we follow by a space, to make the output look more like a square). After each row of symbols, a line feed/carriage return is printed to move the cursor to the beginning of the next line, to prepare to print the next row of the square. Variable *row* is incremented by 1. If the outer loop condition allows the body of the loop to be executed again (because *row* is less than or equal to *side*), *column* is reset to 1, and the inner loop executes again, printing another row of fill characters. Variable *row* is incremented by 1. This process is repeated until the value of *row* exceeds *side*, at which point the square of fill characters has been printed.

The complete second refinement appears in Fig. 5.20. Note that blank lines are used to separate the nested control statements for readability.

```
Prompt for the fill character
Input the fill character

Prompt for the side of the square
Input the side of the square

If the side of the square is less than or equal to 20 then
    Set row to one

```

Fig. 5.20 | Second refinement of the pseudocode. (Part 1 of 2.)

```
    While row is less than or equal to side
        Set column to one

        While column is less than or equal to side
            Print the fill character
            Increment column by one

        Print a line feed/carriage return
        Increment row by one
Else
    Print "Side is too large"
```

Fig. 5.20 | Second refinement of the pseudocode. (Part 2 of 2.)

The pseudocode now is refined sufficiently for conversion to Visual Basic. The Visual Basic class and test program are shown in Fig. 5.21 and Fig. 5.22, respectively.

Software Engineering Observation 5.7

Many experienced programmers write programs without ever using program-development tools like pseudocode. They feel that their ultimate goal is to solve the problem on a computer and that writing pseudocode merely delays producing final outputs. Although this might work for simple and familiar problems, it can lead to serious errors and delays in large, complex projects.

```
' Fig. 5.21: Box.vb
' Class can be used to draw a square of a specified length, using
' a specified fill character.
Public Class Box
   Private sideValue As Integer ' length of side of square
   Private fillCharacterValue As String ' character used to draw square

   ' property provides access to side length of box
   Public Property Side() As Integer
      Get
         Return sideValue ' return side length
      End Get

      Set(ByVal value As Integer)
         sideValue = value ' modify side length
      End Set
   End Property ' Side

   ' property provides access to fill character for drawing box
   Public Property FillCharacter() As String
      Get
         Return fillCharacterValue ' return fill character
      End Get

```

Fig. 5.21 | Nested repetition statements used to print a square of symbols. (Part 1 of 2.)

```
      Set(ByVal value As String)
         fillCharacterValue = value ' modify fill character
      End Set
   End Property ' FillCharacter

   ' display box
   Public Sub Display()
      Dim row As Integer ' current row
      Dim column As Integer ' current column

      If Side <= 20 Then ' if true, then print the box
         row = 1

         ' this While is nested inside the If in lines 35-55
         While row <= Side ' controls row being printed
            column = 1 ' prepare to print first character in the row

            ' this loop prints one row of the square
            ' and is nested inside the While in lines 39-52
            While column <= Side
               ' print fill character and a space
               Console.Write(FillCharacter & " ")
               column += 1 ' increment column
            End While

            Console.WriteLine() ' position cursor to next line
            row += 1 ' increment row
         End While
      Else ' Side > 20
         Console.WriteLine("Side too large")
      End If
   End Sub ' Display
End Class ' Box
```

Fig. 5.21 | Nested repetition statements used to print a square of symbols. (Part 2 of 2.)

```
' Fig. 5.22: BoxTest.vb
' Program draws square by creating an object of class Box.
Module BoxTest
   ' Main begins program execution
   Sub Main()
      Dim box As New Box()

      ' obtain fill character and side length from user
      Console.Write("Enter fill character: ")
      box.FillCharacter = Console.ReadLine()
      Console.Write("Enter side length (must be 20 or less): ")
      box.Side = Console.ReadLine()

      box.Display() ' display box
   End Sub ' Main
End Module ' BoxTest
```

Fig. 5.22 | Using class `Box` to draw a square. (Part 1 of 2.)

```
Enter fill character: #
Enter side length (must be 20 or less): 8
# # # # # # # #
# # # # # # # #
# # # # # # # #
# # # # # # # #
# # # # # # # #
# # # # # # # #
# # # # # # # #
# # # # # # # #
```

```
Enter fill character: *
Enter side length (must be 20 or less): 5
* * * * *
* * * * *
* * * * *
* * * * *
* * * * *
```

```
Enter fill character: $
Enter side length (must be 20 or less): 37
Side too large
```

Fig. 5.22 | Using class Box to draw a square. (Part 2 of 2.)

5.15 Visual Basic Programming in a Windows Forms Application

In Chapter 2, we showed how to create a simple GUI application using visual programming—that is, defining the appearance of an application by dragging and dropping GUI controls onto a Form and setting properties in design mode without writing any program code. The application you created in Chapter 2 (Fig. 2.26) displayed text and an image but did not perform any other actions. In Chapters 3, 4 and this chapter we've focused on console applications, which do not provide a GUI but perform various actions, such as finding the average of several grades and displaying the results as text in the command prompt. Most Visual Basic programmers use a combination of visual programming and conventional programming techniques. In this section, you'll see that when you build a GUI, Visual Basic code (which makes use of the Framework Class Library) is generated by the IDE to define that GUI. You'll modify a GUI control's property programmatically, causing the text displayed on the Form to change at runtime. You'll also learn how to add code to a GUI application to perform an action when the Form is loaded.

Before proceeding, load the project ASimpleProgram from your Chapter 5 examples folder into the IDE. This is the same program as the one you created in Chapter 2. Change the name of the file from Form1.vb to ASimpleProgramForm.vb to enhance clarity. Then double click this file in the **Solution Explorer** to open the file in design mode. Select the Form by clicking it. Notice in the **Properties** window that Visual Basic changed the Form's name to ASimpleProgramForm when you changed the name of the file from Form1.vb to ASimpleProgramForm.vb.

Next, let's change the name of the `Form`'s controls for clarity. To do this, simply select the control and modify the `Name` property (listed in the **Properties** window as **(Name)**), entering the new identifier you want to represent the control. Use this technique to change the name of the `Label` to `welcomeLabel` and the name of the `PictureBox` to `bugPictureBox`. This enables us to easily identify the `Form`'s controls in the program code.

Viewing Windows-Generated Code

Let's view the code for our Windows `Forms` application. When you use visual programming to create a program's GUI, the IDE generates the Visual Basic code that defines how the GUI appears. The code that defines the GUI application is stored in two files—one to define the initial appearance of the GUI (e.g., the background color of the `Form` or the size of a `Label`), and one to define the behavior of the GUI (i.e., what happens when a `Button` is clicked or text is entered in a `TextBox`). Unlike a console application's code, a Windows `Forms` application's program code is not displayed initially in the editor window. Once you open the file `ASimpleProgramForm.vb` in design mode, you can view the code by selecting **View > Code** or by pressing *F7*. Figure 5.23 shows the code editor displaying the program code. This is the file that defines your GUI's behavior.

Note that `ASimpleProgramForm.vb` does not contain a `Module`. Instead Windows `Forms` applications use classes. You've used .NET classes, such as `Console` and `MessageBox`, and you've created your own classes in Chapters 4 and this chapter.

The class declared in Fig. 5.23 is called `ASimpleProgramForm` and is currently empty, as we have not yet defined the application's behavior. Recall that the application's initial GUI appearance is defined in another file. To view that file, go into the **Solution Explorer** and click the **Show All Files** button ( ). Then click the plus sign to the left of **ASimpleProgramForm.vb** to expand its node, and double click **ASimpleProgramForm.Designer.vb**. The file is shown in Fig. 5.24.

Though this code appears complex (especially at this early stage in the book), the IDE creates it for you and normally you won't edit it. It is important for novices to be aware of the IDE-generated code, even though much of it is not explained until Chapters 10–14. This type of code is present in every Windows `Forms` application. If the IDE did not provide the code, you would have to write it, which would require a considerable amount of time and would be an error-prone process.

ASimpleProgramForm.vb | ASimpleProgramForm.vb [Design]

```
Public Class ASimpleProgramForm

End Class
```

Fig. 5.23 | IDE showing program code for `ASimpleProgram.vb`.

Inheriting Predefined Functionality

Keyword **`Inherits`** (line 3 of Fig. 5.24) indicates that the class `ASimpleProgramForm` inherits existing pieces from another class. The class from which `ASimpleProgramForm` inherits—`System.Windows.Forms.Form`—appears to the right of the `Inherits` keyword. This is the class `Form` preceded by its namespace and a dot separator. The namespace and class name together form the class's **fully qualified name**. In this inheritance relationship,

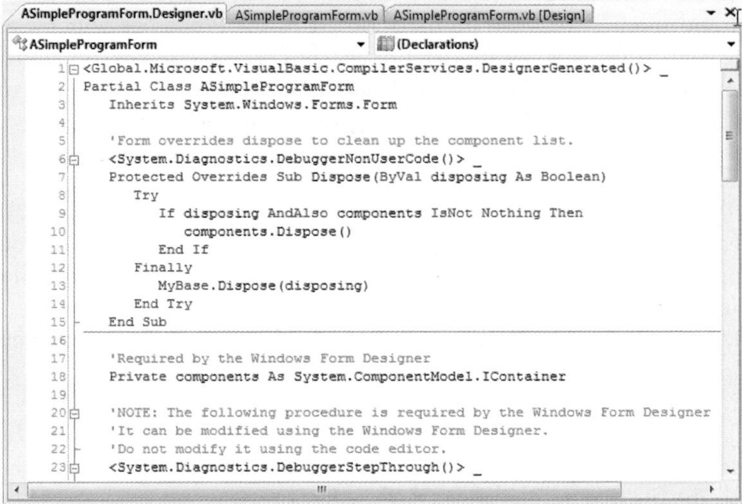

Fig. 5.24 | Windows Form Designer generated code.

`Form` is called the base class, and `ASimpleProgramForm` is called the derived class. This inheritance results in an `ASimpleProgramForm` class definition that has the attributes (data) and behaviors (methods) of class `Form`.

Every Windows `Forms` application consists of at least one class that inherits from class `Form`. A key benefit of inheriting from class `Form` is that someone else has previously defined everything about "what it means to be a `Form`." The Windows operating system expects every window, including `Form`, to have certain capabilities (attributes and behaviors). Because class `Form` already provides these capabilities, you don't need to "reinvent the wheel" by defining all those capabilities yourself. In fact, class `Form` has over 200 methods! Using `Inherits` to absorb class `Form`'s capabilities enables you to create `Forms` quickly and easily.

When you created this application in Chapter 2, you used the **Properties** window to set properties for the `Form`, `Label` and `PictureBox`. Once a property was set, the `Form` or control was updated immediately. `Forms` and controls contain a set of default values for their properties, which are displayed initially in the **Properties** window when a `Form` or control is selected. These default values provide the initial characteristics of a `Form` or control. When a control (such as a `Label`) is first placed on the `Form`, the IDE adds code to the class's designer file (e.g., `ASimpleProgramForm.Designer.vb`) that creates the control and sets some of the control's property values, such as the name of the control and its location on the `Form`. Figure 5.25 shows the portion of `ASimpleProgram.Designer.vb` that sets the `welcomeLabel`'s `Font`, `Location`, `Name`, `Size`, `TabIndex`, `Text` and `TextAlign` properties. These lines specify property values that are set when the `Label` is first placed on the `Form`, or edited by you in the **Properties** window (your line numbers may differ if you have made your own changes to the original application). The control contains many more properties—those not set in the code contain their default values. Recall from Chapter 2 that you explicitly set values for the `Label`'s `Text` and `TextAlign` properties. The values set in the **Properties** window are reflected in this code. Note that the code sets properties of control `welcomeLabel`. Had we not updated the name of this control, every instance of the identifier `welcomeLabel` would be replaced with its default name, in this case `Label1`.

Property initializations for `welcomeLabel`

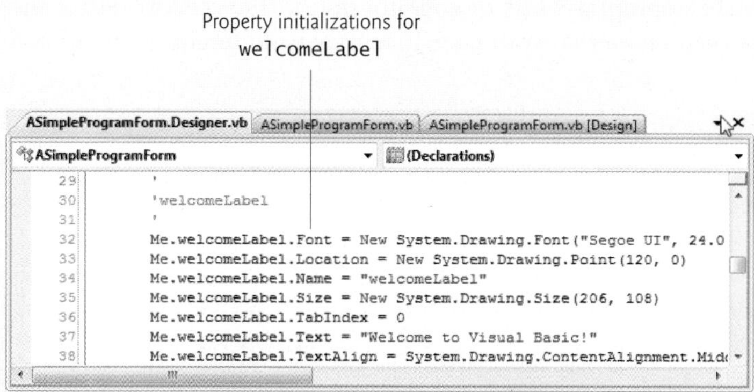

Fig. 5.25 | Property initializations generated by the Windows Form Designer for `welcomeLabel`.

Modifying Properties in Design View

The values assigned to the properties are based on the values in the **Properties** window. We now demonstrate how the IDE updates the generated code when a control's property is modified. While performing the steps in this section, you must switch between code view and design view. To switch views, select the corresponding tabs—**ASimpleProgramForm.vb** or **ASimpleProgramForm.Designer.vb** for code view (we will specify which file as necessary) and **ASimpleProgramForm.vb [Design]** for design view. Alternatively, with the file `ASimpleProgramForm.vb` selected, you can choose **View > Code** (for **ASimpleProgramForm.vb**) or **View > Designer** (for **ASimpleProgramForm.vb [Design]**). Now you'll modify the application's code:

1. *Modifying the* `Label` *control's* `Text` *property using the* **Properties** *window.* If you have not already done so, switch to design view. Recall that properties can be changed in design view by clicking a `Form` or control, then modifying the appropriate property it in the **Properties** window. Select the `Label` (`welcomeLabel`) control and change its `Text` property to "`Deitel and Associates`" (Fig. 5.26).

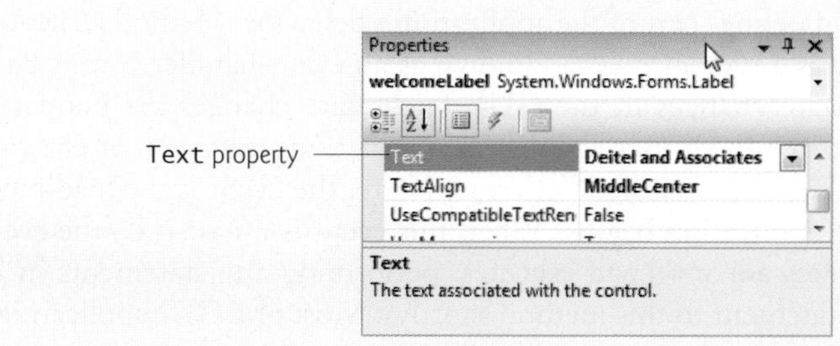

Fig. 5.26 | **Properties** window used to set a property value.

2. *Examining the change in code view.* Switch to code view (`ASimpleProgram.Designer.vb`) and examine the code (Fig. 5.27). Note that the `Label`'s `Text` property is now assigned the text that you entered in the **Properties** window (line 37). When a property is changed in design mode, the Windows Form Designer updates the appropriate line of code for you in the class to reflect the new value. Once again, note that your code lines may be different.

Fig. 5.27 | Windows Form Designer generated code reflecting new property value.

Modifying Properties Programmatically

Now that you have seen how properties are updated in code in response to changes in the **Properties** window, we show how you can write code to modify a property. You'll also see how to specify code that executes when a GUI application loads.

1. *Adding an event handler to your application.* In the preceding steps, we set properties at design time. Often, however, it is necessary to modify a property while a program is running. For example, to display the result of a calculation, a `Label`'s text can be assigned a `String` containing the result. In the applications we have created so far, such code is located in `Main`. In Windows `Forms` applications, you can create a method that executes when the `Form` loads into memory during program execution. Like `Main`, this method is invoked when the program is run. Double clicking the `Form` in design view adds an event handling method named `ASimpleProgramForm_Load` to the class (Fig. 5.28). Be sure to double click the background of the `Form`—that is, the portion of the `Form` that is not covered with another control. Note that `ASimpleProgramForm_Load` is not part of the Windows Form Designer generated code found in `ASimpleProgramForm.Designer.vb`; rather it is added by the IDE to the `ASimpleProgramForm.vb` file. This is because this method defines part of the application's behavior. Method `ASimpleProgramForm_Load` is a type of method known as an event handler. Event handlers respond to state changes in the GUI. Such state changes are known as events. Most events represent user actions, such as clicking a `Button` or entering text in a `TextBox`. For the event handler created here, the event is the loading of the `Form` when the application begins. When this event is raised (i.e., the event occurs), `ASimpleProgramForm_Load` executes, performing any statements in its body (we'll add a statement to this method shortly). Most of a GUI application's functionality executes based on events. You'll see many examples of events and event handling throughout this book.

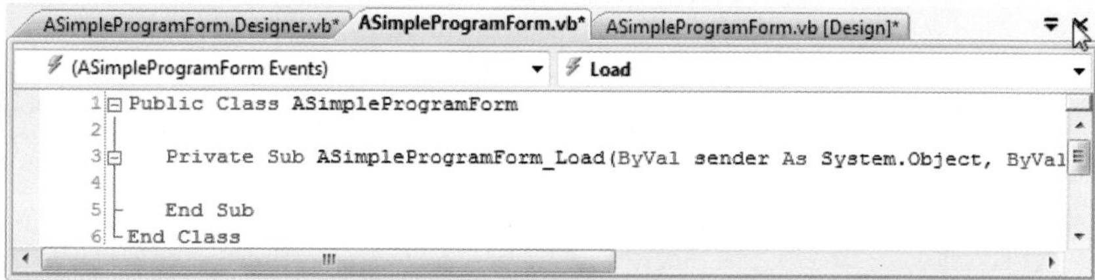

Fig. 5.28 | Method `ASimpleProgramForm_Load` created when `Form` is double clicked.

2. *Changing the `Label`'s `Text` property at runtime.* Add the statement `welcomeLabel.Text = "Visual Basic!"` to the body of the method declaration (Fig. 5.29). Note that we use the dot separator to access a property of `welcomeLabel`. This is because GUI controls are actually objects, just like the objects you created and used in Chapter 4 and this chapter.

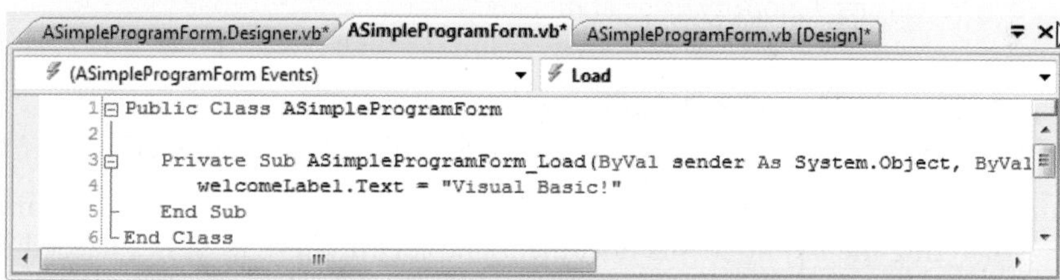

Fig. 5.29 | Method `ASimpleProgramForm_Load` containing program code.

3. *Examining the results of the `ASimpleProgramForm_Load` method.* Switch back to design view. Note that the text in the `Label` is still "`Deitel and Associates`" and that the **Properties** window still displays the value "`Deitel and Associates`" as the `Label`'s `Text` property value. The code generated by the IDE has not changed, either. Instead, the property value is changed in the `ASimpleProgramForm_Load` method, causing the property value to be updated at runtime. Select **Debug > Start Debugging** (or press *F5*) to run the program. When the `Form` displays, the text in the `Label` reflects the property assignment executed in `ASimpleProgramForm_Load` (Fig. 5.30).

4. *Terminating program execution.* Click the close button to the program. Again, notice in the IDE that the `Label` and its `Text` property contain the text "`Deitel and Associates`". Remember that the event handler `ASimpleProgramForm_Load` changes the text to **Visual Basic!** only when the application runs.

This example combined conventional programming and visual programming. We provided a brief overview of the code that the IDE generates for a Windows `Forms` application, and showed how to add code that performs actions when the application's `Form` loads. The topics covered in this section provide a basis for the more complex GUI applications that you'll create throughout this book. Our next Windows `Forms` program appears in Chapter 7.

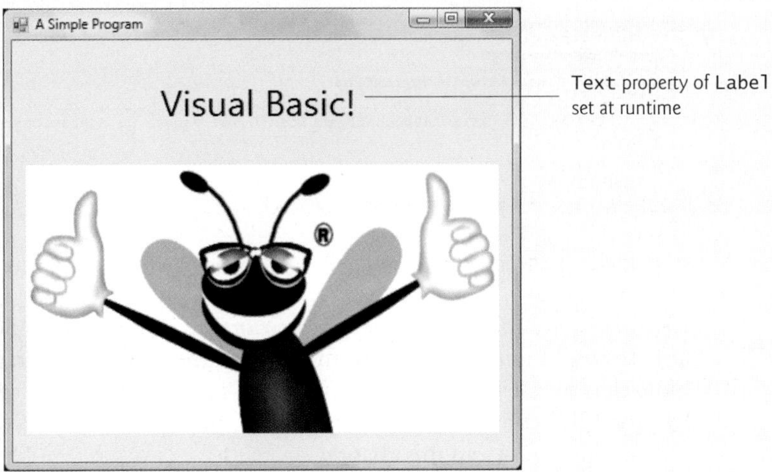

Fig. 5.30 | Changing a property value at runtime.

5.16 (Optional) Software Engineering Case Study: Identifying Class Attributes in the ATM System

In Section 4.9, we began the first stage of an object-oriented design (OOD) for our ATM system—analyzing the requirements document and identifying the classes needed to implement the system. We listed the nouns and noun phrases in the requirements document and identified a separate class for each one that plays a significant role in the ATM system. We then modeled the classes and their relationships in a UML class diagram (Fig. 4.22). Classes have attributes (data) and operations (behaviors). Class attributes are implemented in Visual Basic programs as properties and instance variables (and `Shared` variables, as we will see in Section 10.11), and class operations are implemented as methods and properties. In this section, we determine many of the attributes needed in the ATM system. In Section 6.11, we examine how these attributes represent an object's state. In Section 7.20, we determine the operations for our classes.

Identifying Attributes

Consider the attributes of some real-world objects: A person's attributes include height, weight and whether the person is left-handed, right-handed or ambidextrous. A radio's attributes include its station setting, its volume setting and its AM or FM setting. A car's attributes include its speedometer and odometer readings, the amount of gas in its tank and what gear it is in. A personal computer's attributes include its manufacturer (e.g., Dell, Gateway, Sun, Apple or HP), type of screen (e.g., LCD or CRT), main memory size and hard disk size.

We can identify many attributes of the classes in our system by looking for descriptive words and phrases in the requirements document. For each one we find that plays a significant role in the ATM system, we create an attribute and assign it to one or more of the classes identified in Section 4.9. We also create attributes to represent any additional data that a class may need, as such needs become clear throughout the design process.

Figure 5.31 lists the words or phrases from the requirements document that describe each class. For example, the requirements document describes the steps taken to obtain a "withdrawal amount," so we list "amount" next to class `Withdrawal`.

Figure 5.31 leads us to create one attribute of class `ATM`. Class `ATM` maintains information about the state of the ATM. The phrase "user is authenticated" describes a state of the ATM (we discuss states in detail in Section 6.11), so we include `userAuthenticated` as a `Boolean` attribute (i.e., an attribute that has a value of either `True` or `False`). This attribute indicates whether the ATM has successfully authenticated the current user—`userAuthenticated` must be `True` for the system to allow the user to perform transactions and access account information. This attribute helps ensure the security of the data in the system.

Classes `BalanceInquiry`, `Withdrawal` and `Deposit` share one attribute. Each transaction involves an "account number" that corresponds to the account of the user making the transaction. We assign an integer attribute `accountNumber` to each transaction class to identify the account to which an object of the class applies.

Descriptive words and phrases in the requirements document also suggest some differences in the attributes required by each transaction class. The requirements document indicates that to withdraw cash or deposit funds, users must enter a specific "amount" of money to be withdrawn or deposited, respectively. Thus, we assign to classes `Withdrawal` and `Deposit` an attribute `amount` to store the value supplied by the user. The amounts of money related to a withdrawal and a deposit are defining characteristics of these transactions that the system requires for them to take place. In Visual Basic, monetary amounts

Class	Descriptive words and phrases
`ATM`	user is authenticated
`BalanceInquiry`	account number
`Withdrawal`	account number amount
`Deposit`	account number amount
`BankDatabase`	[no descriptive words or phrases]
`Account`	account number PIN balance
`Screen`	[no descriptive words or phrases]
`Keypad`	[no descriptive words or phrases]
`CashDispenser`	begins each day loaded with 500 $20 bills
`DepositSlot`	[no descriptive words or phrases]

Fig. 5.31 | Descriptive words and phrases from the ATM requirements document.

are represented with type `Decimal` (which you'll learn more about in Chapter 6). Note that class `BalanceInquiry` does not need additional data to perform its task—it requires only an account number to indicate the account whose balance should be retrieved.

Class `Account` has several attributes. The requirements document states that each bank account has an "account number" and a "PIN," which the system uses for identifying accounts and authenticating users. We assign to class `Account` two `Integer` attributes: `accountNumber` and `pin`. The requirements document also specifies that an account maintains a "balance" of the amount of money in the account, and that the money the user deposits does not become available for a withdrawal until the bank verifies the amount of cash in the deposit envelope and any checks in the envelope clear. An account must still record the amount of money that a user deposits, however. Therefore, we decide that an account should represent a balance using two attributes of type `Decimal`—`availableBalance` and `totalBalance`. Attribute `availableBalance` tracks the amount of money that a user can withdraw from the account. Attribute `totalBalance` refers to the total amount of money that the user has "on deposit" (i.e., the amount of money available, plus the amount of cash deposits waiting to be verified or checks waiting to clear). For example, suppose an ATM user deposits $50.00 in cash into an empty account. The `totalBalance` attribute would increase to $50.00 to record the deposit, but the `availableBalance` would remain at $0 until a bank employee counts the amount of cash in the envelope and confirms that it is correct. [*Note:* We assume that the bank updates the `availableBalance` attribute of the `Account` soon after the ATM transaction occurs, in response to confirming that $50 in cash was found in the deposit envelope. We assume that this update occurs through a transaction that a bank employee performs using a bank system other than the ATM. Thus, we do not discuss this "external" transaction in our case study.]

Class `CashDispenser` has one attribute. The requirements document states that the cash dispenser "begins each day loaded with 500 $20 bills." The cash dispenser must keep track of the number of bills it contains to determine whether enough cash is on hand to satisfy withdrawal requests. We assign to class `CashDispenser` an integer attribute `billCount`, which is initially set to `500`.

For real problems in industry, there is no guarantee that requirements documents will be rich enough and precise enough for the object-oriented systems designer to determine all the attributes or even all the classes. The need for additional classes, attributes and behaviors may become clear as the design process proceeds. As we progress through this case study, we too will continue to add, modify and delete information about the classes in our system.

Modeling Attributes

The class diagram in Fig. 5.32 lists some of the attributes for the classes in our system—the descriptive words and phrases in Fig. 5.31 helped us identify these attributes. For simplicity, Fig. 5.32 does not show the associations among classes—we showed these in Fig. 4.22. Systems designers commonly do this. Recall that in the UML, a class's attributes are placed in the middle compartment of the class's rectangle. We list each attribute's name and type separated by a colon (`:`), followed in some cases by an equal sign (`=`) and an initial value.

Consider the `userAuthenticated` attribute of class `ATM`:

```
userAuthenticated : Boolean = False
```

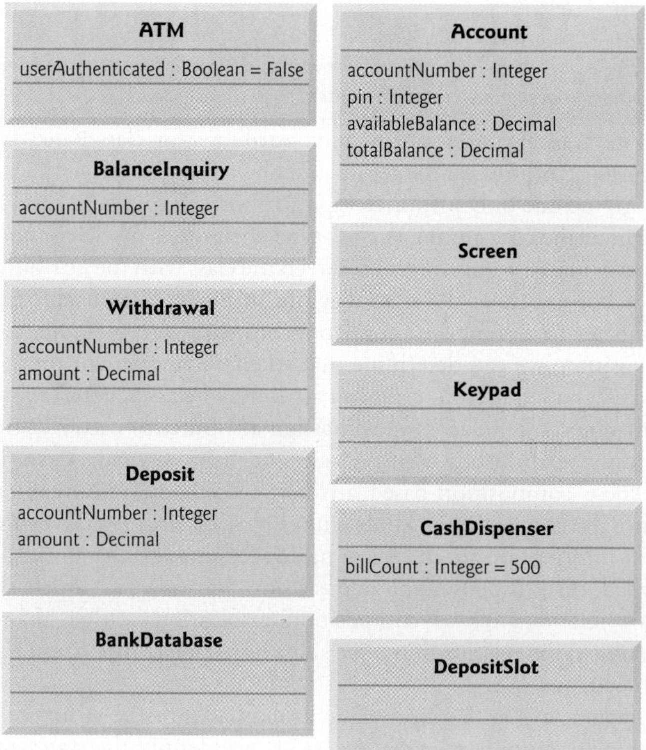

Fig. 5.32 | Classes with attributes.

This attribute declaration contains three pieces of information about the attribute. The attribute name is `userAuthenticated`. The attribute type is `Boolean`. In Visual Basic, an attribute can be represented by a primitive type, such as `Boolean`, `Integer`, `Double` or `Decimal`, or a class type—as discussed in Chapter 4. We have chosen to model only primitive-type attributes in Fig. 5.32—we discuss the reasoning behind this decision shortly. For simplicity, we use Visual Basic primitive type names in our UML diagrams. These type names sometimes differ from those defined in the UML specification.

We can also indicate an initial value for an attribute. Attribute `userAuthenticated` in class `ATM` has an initial value of `False`. This indicates that the system initially does not consider the user to be authenticated. If an attribute has no initial value specified, only its name and type (separated by a colon) are shown. For example, the `accountNumber` attribute of class `BalanceInquiry` is an `Integer`. Here we show no initial value, because the value of this attribute is a number that we do not yet know. This number will be determined at execution time based on the account number entered by the current ATM user. Recall that Visual Basic initializes all instance variables to their default values, so the `accountNumber` will be `0` initially as we have not specified its value.

Figure 5.32 does not contain attributes for classes `Screen`, `Keypad` and `DepositSlot`. These are important components of our system, for which our design process simply has not yet revealed any attributes.

Software Engineering Observation 5.8

Early in the design process classes often lack attributes (and operations). Such classes should not necessarily be eliminated, however, because attributes (and operations) may become evident in the later phases of design and implementation.

Note that Fig. 5.32 also does not include attributes for class `BankDatabase`. Recall that in Visual Basic, attributes can be represented by either primitive types or class types. We have chosen to include only primitive-type attributes in Fig. 5.32 (and in similar class diagrams throughout the case study). A class-type attribute is modeled more clearly as an association (in particular, a composition) between the class with the attribute and the attribute's own class. For example, the class diagram in Fig. 4.22 indicates that class `BankDatabase` participates in a composition relationship with zero or more `Account` objects. From this composition, we can determine that when we implement the ATM system in Visual Basic, we will be required to create an attribute of class `BankDatabase` to hold zero or more `Account` objects. Similarly, we will assign attributes to class `ATM` that correspond to its composition relationships with classes `Screen`, `Keypad`, `CashDispenser` and `DepositSlot`. These composition-based attributes would be redundant if modeled in Fig. 5.32, because the compositions modeled in Fig. 4.22 already convey the fact that the database contains information about zero or more accounts and that an ATM is composed of a screen, keypad, cash dispenser and deposit slot. Software developers typically model these whole/part relationships as composition associations rather than as attributes required to implement the relationships. We show how such composition relationships are implemented in Section 10.8.

The class diagram in Fig. 5.32 provides a solid basis for the structure of our model, but the diagram is not complete. In Section 6.11, we identify the states and activities of the objects in the model, and in Section 7.20 we identify the operations that the objects perform. As we present more of the UML and object-oriented design, we will continue to strengthen the structure of our model.

Software Engineering Case Study Self-Review Exercises

5.1 We typically identify the attributes of the classes in our system by analyzing the __________ in the requirements document.
  a) nouns and noun phrases
  b) descriptive words and phrases
  c) verbs and verb phrases
  d) All of the above

5.2 Which of the following is not an attribute of an airplane?
  a) length
  b) wingspan
  c) fly
  d) number of seats

5.3 Describe the meaning of the following attribute declaration of class `CashDispenser` in the class diagram in Fig. 5.32:

```
billCount : Integer = 500
```

Answers to Software Engineering Case Study Self-Review Exercises

5.1 b.

5.2 c. Fly is an operation or behavior of an airplane, not an attribute.

5.3 This declaration indicates that attribute `billCount` is an `Integer` with an initial value of `500`; `billCount` keeps track of the number of $20 bills available in the `CashDispenser` at any given time.

5.17 Wrap-Up

This chapter presented basic problem-solving techniques that you use to build programs. We demonstrated how to develop an algorithm (i.e., an approach to solving a problem) in pseudocode, evolving it through several refinements until it is ready to be translated to Visual Basic code that can be executed. This process is called top-down, stepwise refinement.

You learned that only three types of control structures—sequence, selection and repetition—are needed to develop an algorithm. We demonstrated the `If...Then` single-selection statement and the `If...Then...Else` double-selection statement. The `If...Then` statement is used to execute a set of one or more statements based on a condition—if the condition is true, the statements execute; if it is false, the statements are skipped. The `If...Then...Else` double-selection statement is used to execute one set of statements if a condition is true, and another set if the condition is false.

We discussed the `While` and `Do While...Loop` repetition statements, where a set of statements is executed repeatedly as long as a loop-continuation condition remains true. We discussed the `Do Until...Loop` repetition statement, where a set of statements is executed repeatedly as long as a loop-termination condition remains false. You learned the UML Activity Diagrams that represent each control statement presented in the chapter.

We used control-statement stacking to compute the average of a set of student grades with counter-controlled repetition and then with sentinel-controlled repetition, and we used control-statement nesting to analyze and make decisions based on a set of exam results, and also to display a square of fill characters. We introduced compound assignment operators, which can be used for abbreviating assignment statements.

The chapter concluded with an introduction to adding event handlers to a GUI application. Here, you learned how to modify a GUI application programmatically. In Chapter 6, Control Statements: Part 2, we present additional selection and repetition statements. In the next few chapters, we build Windows `Forms` applications that interact more with the user.

Summary

Section 5.2 Algorithms

- Computing problems are solved by executing actions in a specific order.
- An algorithm is a procedure for solving a problem in terms of the actions to be executed and the order in which these actions are to be executed.
- Program control refers to the task of ordering a program's statements correctly.

Section 5.3 Pseudocode

- Pseudocode is an informal language that helps programmers develop algorithms and "think out" a program before attempting to write it in a programming language.
- A carefully prepared pseudocode program can be converted easily to a corresponding Visual Basic program.

Section 5.4 Control Structures

- Normally, statements in a program are executed one after another in the order in which they are written. This is called sequential execution.
- Various Visual Basic statements enable you to specify that the next statement to be executed might not be the next one in sequence. This is called a transfer of control.
- Bohm and Jacopini's work demonstrated that all programs could be written in terms of the sequence, selection and repetition structures.
- The sequence structure is built into Visual Basic. Unless directed otherwise, the computer executes Visual Basic statements one after the other in the order in which they are written.
- A UML activity diagram models the workflow (also called the activity) of a software system.
- Activity diagrams are composed of special-purpose symbols, such as action state symbols, diamonds and small circles. These symbols are connected by transition arrows that represent the flow of activity.
- Like pseudocode, activity diagrams help programmers develop and represent algorithms.
- An action state is represented as a rectangle with its left and right sides replaced by arcs curving outward. An action expression appears inside the action state.
- The arrows in an activity diagram represent transitions that indicate the order in which the actions represented by action states occur.
- The solid circle located at the top of an activity diagram represents the initial state—the beginning of the workflow before the program performs the modeled actions.
- The solid circle surrounded by a hollow circle that appears at the bottom of the activity diagram represents the final state—the end of the workflow after the program performs its actions.
- Rectangles with the upper-right corners folded over are called notes in the UML. Notes are optional explanatory remarks that describe the purpose of symbols in the diagram. A dotted line connects each note with the element that it describes.
- The `If...Then` single-selection statement selects or ignores a single action (or a single group of actions) based on the truth or falsity of a condition.
- The `If...Then...Else` double-selection statement selects between two different actions (or groups of actions) based on the truth or falsity of a condition.
- A multiple-selection statement selects among many different actions or groups of actions.
- Visual Basic provides seven types of repetition statements (also called looping statements or loops) that enable programs to perform statements repeatedly based on the value of a condition.
- Programs are formed by combining as many of each type of Visual Basic's 11 control statements as is appropriate for the algorithm the program implements.
- Single-entry/single-exit control statements make it easy to build programs.
- In control-statement stacking, the control statements are attached to one another by connecting the exit point of one control statement to the entry point of the next.
- In control-statement nesting, one control statement is placed inside another.
- Algorithms in Visual Basic programs are constructed from 11 different types of control statements combined in only two ways (control-statement stacking and control-statement nesting).

Section 5.5 `If...Then` Selection Statement

- Syntax errors are caught by the compiler. Logic errors affect the program only at execution time. Fatal logic errors cause a program to fail and terminate prematurely. Nonfatal logic errors do not terminate a program's execution but cause the program to produce incorrect results.

- The diamond or decision symbol in an activity diagram indicates that a decision is to be made. A decision symbol indicates that the workflow will continue along a path determined by the symbol's associated guard conditions, which can be true or false.
- Each transition arrow emerging from a decision symbol has a guard condition (specified in square brackets above or next to the transition arrow). If a particular guard condition is true, the workflow enters the action state to which that transition arrow points.

Section 5.6 `If...Then...Else` *Selection Statement*

- The `If...Then...Else` selection statement allows you to specify that a different action (or sequence of actions) is to be performed when the condition is true than when the condition is false.
- Nested `If...Then...Else` statements test for multiple conditions by placing `If...Then...Else` statements inside other `If...Then...Else` statements.
- Keyword `ElseIf` can be used in nested `If...Then...Else` statements to make them more readable.

Section 5.7 `While` *Repetition Statement*

- The UML's merge symbol joins two flows of activity into one flow of activity. The UML represents both the merge symbol and the decision symbol as diamonds.
- The `While` repetition statement allows you to specify that an action is to be repeated while a specific condition remains true.
- Eventually, the loop-continuation condition in a `While` statement becomes false. At this point, the repetition terminates, and the first statement after the repetition statement executes.
- Failure to provide the body of a `While` statement with an action that eventually causes the loop-continuation condition to become false is a logic error. Normally, such a repetition statement never terminates, resulting in an error called an "infinite loop."

Section 5.8 `Do While...Loop` *Repetition Statement*

- The `Do While...Loop` repetition statement allows you to specify that an action is to be repeated while a specific condition remains true.
- Eventually, the loop-continuation condition in a `Do While...Loop` statement becomes false, the repetition terminates and the first statement after the repetition statement executes.
- Failure to provide in the body of a `Do While...Loop` statement an action that eventually causes the loop-continuation condition to become false is a logic error. Normally, such a repetition statement never terminates, resulting in an infinite loop.

Section 5.9 `Do Until...Loop` *Repetition Statement*

- Statements in the body of a `Do Until...Loop` are executed repeatedly as long as the loop-termination condition evaluates to false.
- Failure to provide the body of a `Do Until...Loop` statement with an action that eventually causes the loop-termination condition in the `Do Until...Loop` to become true creates an infinite loop.

Section 5.10 Compound Assignment Operators

- Visual Basic provides the compound assignment operators `+=`, `-=`, `*=`, `/=`, `\=`, `^=` and `&=` for abbreviating assignment statements.

Section 5.11 Formulating Algorithms: Counter-Controlled Repetition

- In counter-controlled repetition, a counter is used to repeat a set of statements a certain number of times. Counter-controlled repetition is also called definite repetition, because the number of repetitions is known before the loop begins executing.
- A total is a variable used to calculate the sum of a series of values.

Section 5.12 Formulating Algorithms: Sentinel-Controlled Repetition

- In sentinel-controlled repetition, the number of repetitions is not known before the loop begins executing. Sentinel-controlled repetition uses a sentinel value (also called a signal value, dummy value or flag value) to terminate repetition.
- We approach programming problems with top-down, stepwise refinement, a technique essential to the development of well-structured algorithms.
- The top is a single statement that conveys the overall function of the program. As such, the top is a complete representation of a program.
- Through the process of refinement, we divide the top into a series of smaller tasks, listed in the order in which they must be performed. Each refinement, including the top, is a complete specification of the algorithm; only the level of detail in each refinement varies.
- Many algorithms can be divided logically into an initialization phase that initializes the program variables, a processing phase that inputs data values and adjusts program variables such as counts and totals accordingly, and a termination phase that calculates and prints the results.
- You terminate the top-down, stepwise refinement process when the pseudocode algorithm is specified in sufficient detail for the pseudocode to be converted to a Visual Basic program. The implementation of the Visual Basic program is then straightforward.
- Data type `Double` stores double-precision floating-point numbers. Visual Basic also provides data type `Single` for storing single-precision floating-point numbers. Data type `Double` requires more memory to store a floating-point value, but is more accurate than type `Single`. Most programmers use `Double` to represent floating-point numbers.
- A format specifier can be used to indicate how a value is to be formatted for output.

Section 5.13 Formulating Algorithms: Nested Control Statements

- Besides being stacked on top of one another (in sequence), control statements can be combined through the nesting of one control statement within another.

Section 5.14 Formulating Algorithms: Nested Repetition Statements

- Repetition statements can be nested within each other, as well as stacked on top of one another.

Section 5.15 Visual Basic Programming in a Windows **Forms** *Application*

- With visual programming, the IDE generates program code that creates the GUI. This code contains instructions for creating the `Form` and every control on it.
- Using keyword `Inherits` to extend from class `Form` enables programmers to create `Forms` quickly, without reinventing the wheel. Every Windows `Forms` application consists of at least one class that `Inherits` from class `Form` in the `System.Windows.Forms` namespace.
- Forms and controls contain a set of default values for their properties, which are displayed initially in the **Properties** window when a `Form` or control is selected. These default values provide the initial characteristics a `Form` or control has when it is created.
- When a change, such as changing a property value, is made in design mode, the Windows Form Designer creates code that implements the change.
- Often it is necessary to modify a property while a program is running. In Windows `Forms` applications, such code is placed in a method that executes when the `Form` is loaded. This method can be created by double clicking the `Form` in design view.
- Event handlers respond to (i.e., perform actions when) a state change occurs in the GUI. This state change is known as an event. Most events represent user actions, such as clicking a `Button` or altering a value.

Terminology

&= string concatenation assignment operator
*= multiplication assignment operator
+= addition assignment operator
/= division assignment operator
-= subtraction assignment operator
\= integer division assignment operator
^= exponentiation assignment operator
action
action expression in the UML
action state in the UML
action state symbol in the UML
activity diagram in the UML
activity of a portion of a software system
algorithm
arrow in the UML
attribute of a class
carriage return
compound assignment operator
constant
control statement
control-statement nesting
control-statement stacking
control structure
counter
counter-controlled loop
counter-controlled repetition
decision symbol in the UML
definite repetition
diamond symbol in the UML
division by zero
`Do Until...Loop` repetition statement
`Do While...Loop` repetition statement
dotted line in the UML
double-precision floating-point number
double-selection statement
dummy value
event
event handler
`F` format specifier
fatal logic error
final state in the UML
first refinement in pseudocode
fixed-point number
flag value
floating-point literal
flow of control
format specifier
formatted output
fully qualified name
`GoTo` statement
guard condition in the UML
`If...Then...Else` double-selection statement
implicit conversion
indefinite repetition
initial state in the UML
initialization phase
iteration
level of refinement
levels of nesting
logic error
loop
loop-continuation condition
loop-termination condition
looping statement
lvalue ("left value")
merge symbol in the UML
multiple-selection statement
`Name` property of a control
nested control statements
nonfatal logic error
note in the UML
order of actions in an algorithm
precision
procedure for solving a problem
processing phase
program control
program-development tool
promote
pseudocode
pseudocode algorithm
pseudocode statement
raise an event
repetition statement
repetition structure
second refinement in pseudocode
selection statement
selection structure
sentinel-controlled repetition
sentinel value
sequence statement
sequence structure
sequential execution
signal value
single-entry/single-exit control statement
single-precision floating-point number
`Single` primitive type
single-selection statement
small circle symbol in the UML

solid circle symbol in the UML
stacked control statements
stepwise refinement
`String` primitive type
structured programming
top in pseudocode
top-down, stepwise refinement
total
transfer of control
transition arrow in the UML
transition in the UML
visual programming
`While` repetition statement

Self-Review Exercises

5.1 Answer each of the following questions.

a) All programs can be written in terms of three types of control structures: ________, ________ and ________.
b) The ________ statement executes one action (or sequence of actions) when a condition is true and another action (or sequence of actions) when a condition is false.
c) Repetition of a set of instructions a specific number of times is called ________ repetition.
d) When it is not known in advance how many times a set of statements will be repeated, a(n) ________, ________, ________ or ________ value can be used to terminate the repetition.
e) Specifying the order in which statements are to be executed in a computer program is called program ________.
f) ________ is an artificial and informal language that helps programmers develop algorithms.
g) ________ are words reserved by Visual Basic to implement various features, such as the language's control statements.
h) The ________ selection statement is called a multiple-selection statement because it selects among many different actions (or sequences of actions).

5.2 State whether each of the following is *true* or *false*. If *false*, explain why.

a) It is difficult to convert pseudocode into a Visual Basic program.
b) Sequential execution refers to statements in a program that execute one after another.
c) The `If...Then` statement is called a single-selection statement.
d) The sequence structure is not built into Visual Basic.
e) Pseudocode closely resembles actual Visual Basic code.
f) The `While` statement is terminated with the keywords `End While`.

5.3 Write two different Visual Basic statements that each add `1` to `Integer` variable `number`.

5.4 Write a statement or a set of statements to accomplish each of the following:

a) Sum the odd integers between `1` and `99` using a `While` statement. Assume that variables `sum` and `count` have been declared as `Integers`.
b) Sum the squares of the even integers between `1` and `15` using a `Do While...Loop` repetition statement. Assume that the `Integer` variables `sum` and `count` have been declared and initialized to `0` and `2`, respectively.
c) Print the numbers from `20` to `1` to the command prompt using a `Do Until...Loop` and `Integer` counter variable `counterIndex`. Assume that the variable `counterIndex` is initialized to `20`.
d) Repeat Exercise 5.4 (c) using a `Do While...Loop` statement.

5.5 Write a Visual Basic statement to accomplish each of the following tasks:

a) Declare variables `sum` and `number` to be of type `Integer`.
b) Assign `1` to variable `number`.

c) Assign `0` to variable `sum`.
d) Total variables `number` and `sum`, and assign the result to variable `sum`.
e) Print `"The sum is: "` followed by the value of variable `sum` to the command prompt.

5.6 Combine the statements that you wrote in Exercise 5.5 into a program that calculates and prints the sum of the `Integers` from `1` to `10`. Use a `While` statement to loop through the calculation and increment statements. The loop should terminate when the value of control variable `number` becomes `11`.

5.7 Identify and correct the error(s) in each of the following (you may need to add code):

a) Assume that `value` has been initialized to `50`. The values from `0` to `50` should be summed.

```
While value >= 0
   sum += value
End While
```

b) This segment should read an unspecified number of positive values from the user and sum them. Assume that `number` and `total` are declared as `Integers`.

```
   total = 0

   Do Until number = -1
      Console.Write("Enter a positive value; -1 to terminate: ")
      number = Console.ReadLine()
      total += number
   Loop

Console.WriteLine(total)
```

c) The following code should print the squares of `1` to `10`.

```
Dim number As Integer = 1

Do While number < 10
   Console.WriteLine(number ^ 2)
While End
```

d) This segment should print the values from `888` to `1000`. Assume `value` is declared as an `Integer`.

```
value = 888

While value <= 1000
   value -= 1
End While
```

5.8 State whether each of the following is *true* or *false*. If the answer is *false*, explain why.

a) Pseudocode is a structured programming language.
b) The body of a `Do While...Loop` is executed only if the loop-continuation test is false.
c) The body of a `While` is executed only if the loop-continuation test is false.
d) The body of a `Do Until...Loop` is executed only if the loop-termination condition is false.

Answers to Self-Review Exercises

5.1 a) sequence, selection, repetition. b) `If...Then...Else`. c) counter-controlled or definite. d) sentinel, signal, flag or dummy. e) control. f) pseudocode. g) Keywords. h) `Select...Case`.

5.2 a) False. Pseudocode normally converts easily into Visual Basic code. b) True. c) True. d) False. The sequence structure is built into Visual Basic—statements execute in the order in which they are written, unless explicitly directed to do otherwise. e) True. f) True.

5.3

```
number = number + 1
number += 1
```

5.4 a)

```
count = 1
sum = 0

While count <= 99
   sum += count
   count += 2
End While
```

b)

```
Do While count <= 15
   sum += count ^ 2
   count += 2
Loop
```

c)

```
Do Until counterIndex < 1
   Console.Write(counterIndex & " ")
   counterIndex -= 1
Loop
```

d)

```
Do While counterIndex >= 1
   Console.Write(counterIndex & " ")
   counterIndex -= 1
Loop
```

5.5 a) `Dim sum, number As Integer`
b) `number = 1`
c) `sum = 0`
d) `sum += number` or `sum = sum + number`
e) `Console.WriteLine("The sum is: " & sum)`

5.6 See the code below:

```
' Ex. 5.6: Calculate.vb
' Calculates the sum of the integers from 1 to 10.
Module Calculate
   Sub Main()
      Dim sum, number As Integer

      sum = 0
      number = 1

      While number <= 10
         sum += number
         number += 1
      End While

      Console.WriteLine("The sum is: " & sum)
   End Sub ' Main
End Module ' Calculate
```

```
The sum is: 55
```

5.7 a) Error: Repetition condition may never become false, resulting in an infinite loop.

```
While value >= 0
   sum += value
   value -= 1
End While
```

b) Error: The sentinel value (-1) is added to `total`, producing an incorrect sum.

```
total = 0
Console.Write("Enter a positive value; -1 to terminate: ")
number = Console.ReadLine()

Do Until number = -1
   total += number
   Console.Write("Enter a positive value; -1 to terminate: ")
   number = Console.ReadLine()
Loop

Console.WriteLine(total)
```

c) Errors: The counter is never incremented, resulting in an infinite loop. The repetition condition uses the wrong relational operator. Keywords `While End` are used instead of keyword `Loop`.

```
Dim number As Integer = 1

Do While number <= 10
   Console.WriteLine(number ^ 2)
   number += 1
Loop
```

d) Error: The values are never printed and are decremented instead of incremented.

```
value = 888

While value <= 1000
   Console.WriteLine(value)
   value += 1
End While
```

5.8 a) False. Pseudocode is not a programming language.
b) False. The loop condition must evaluate to true for the body to be executed.
c) False. The loop condition must evaluate to true for the body to be executed.
d) True.

Exercises

5.9 Drivers are concerned with the mileage obtained by their automobiles. One driver has kept track of several tankfuls of gasoline by recording the miles driven and the gallons used for each tankful. Develop a program that inputs the miles driven and gallons used (both as `Double`s) for each tankful. The program should calculate and display the miles per gallon obtained for each tankful and print the combined miles per gallon obtained for all tankfuls. All average calculations should produce floating-point results. Use a sentinel value of `-1.0` for the miles driven to terminate repetition. Avoid division by zero—if the user enters zero for the number of gallons, inform the user that the input value for gallons must be greater than zero. Be sure to check the total number of gallons for zero as well (when calculating the combined miles per gallon), in case someone enters `-1.0` before entering a value for gallons greater than zero. [*Note:* Be careful—the miles per gallon for all tankfuls is not the average of the miles-per-gallon figures for each tankful.]

5.10 Develop a program that determines whether a department store customer has exceeded the credit limit on a charge account. For each customer, the following facts are available:

a) Account number
b) Balance at the beginning of the month
c) Total of all items charged by this customer this month
d) Total of all credits applied to this customer's account this month
e) Allowed credit limit

The program should input the account number as an `Integer`, but use `Double`s for the other variables. The program should calculate the new balance (= *beginning balance + charges – credits*), display the new balance and determine whether it exceeds the customer's credit limit. For customers whose credit limit is exceeded, the program should display the message, "Credit limit exceeded." Use a sentinel value of `-1` for the account number to terminate repetition.

5.11 A palindrome is a number or a text phrase that reads the same backward and forward. For example, all of the following five-digit `Integers` are palindromes: 12321, 55555, 45554 and 11611; the five-digit `Integers` 43235, 64445 and 12322 are not palindromes. Write an application that reads in a five-digit `Integer` and determines whether it is a palindrome. [*Hint:* Break the number into its separate digits first. Then check whether the first digit equals the fifth digit, and the second digit equals the fourth digit.]

5.12 A company wants to transmit data over the telephone but is concerned that its phones may be tapped. All the data is transmitted as four-digit `Integers`. The company has asked you to write a program that encrypts its data so that it may be transmitted more securely. Your program should read a four-digit `Integer` entered by the user and encrypt it as follows: Replace each digit by *(the sum of that digit and 7) modulo 10*. Then swap the first digit with the third, and swap the second digit with the fourth. Print the encrypted `Integer`. Write a separate program that inputs an encrypted four-digit `Integer` and decrypts it to form the original number.

5.13 The factorial of a nonnegative `Integer` n (0, 1, 2, …) is written $n!$ (pronounced "*n* factorial") and is defined as follows:

$$n! = n \cdot (n - 1) \cdot (n - 2) \cdot \ldots \cdot 1 \quad \text{(for values of } n \text{ greater than or equal to 1)}$$

and

$$n! = 1 \quad (\text{for } n = 0).$$

For example, $5! = 5 \cdot 4 \cdot 3 \cdot 2 \cdot 1$, which is 120.

a) Write a program that reads a nonnegative `Integer` from the user and computes and prints its factorial. To calculate the factorials of large values of n, data type `Long` (a 64-bit integer value) must be used. Type `Long` is designed to store integer values in a range much larger than that of type `Integer`. We discuss primitive type `Long` in more detail in Chapter 6.

b) Write a program that estimates the value of the mathematical constant e by using the first 15 terms of the series:

$$e = 1 + \frac{1}{1!} + \frac{1}{2!} + \frac{1}{3!} + \ldots$$

c) Write an application that computes the value of e^x by using the first 15 terms of the series:

$$e^x = 1 + \frac{x}{1!} + \frac{x^2}{2!} + \frac{x^3}{3!} + \ldots$$

5.14 Modify the class of Fig. 5.18 to process the four `String`s: `"P"`, `"p"`, `"F"` and `"f"`. If any other `String` input is encountered, a message should be displayed informing the user of invalid input. Increment the loop's counter only if one of the four previously mentioned `Strings` is input. Use the program of Fig. 5.19 to test your new program.

5.15 Modify the class of Fig. 5.21 to test whether the value input for the side is less than `1` and, if it is, issue an appropriate error message. [*Hint:* This requires that another `If...Then` statement be added to the code. In the next chapter we will show you how to solve this problem more elegantly using logical operators.] Use Fig. 5.22 to test your new program.

5.16 Write a program that uses counter-controlled repetition with a `While` statement to print the following table of values: [*Hint:* Use `vbTab` to separate the columns of output.]

```
N       10*N    100*N   1000*N

1       10      100     1000
2       20      200     2000
3       30      300     3000
4       40      400     4000
5       50      500     5000
```

5.17 The process of finding the largest value (i.e., the maximum of a group of values) is used frequently in computer applications. For example, a program that determines the winner of a sales contest would input the number of units sold by each salesperson. The salesperson who sells the most units would win the contest. Write a Visual Basic application that inputs a series of 10 integers and determines and displays the largest. Your program should use at least the following three variables:

a) `counter`: A counter to count to 10 (i.e., to keep track of how many numbers have been input and to determine when all 10 numbers have been processed)
b) `number`: The current integer input to the program
c) `largest`: The largest number found so far

5.18 Write an application that inputs an integer containing only 0s and 1s (i.e., a "binary" integer) and displays its decimal equivalent. [*Hint:* Use the modulus and division operators to pick off the "binary number's" digits one at a time, from right to left. In the decimal number system, the rightmost digit has a positional value of 1 and the next digit to the left has a positional value of 10, then 100, then 1000, and so on. The decimal number 234 can be interpreted as 4 * 1 + 3 * 10 + 2 * 100. In the binary number system, the rightmost digit has a positional value of 1, the next digit to the left has a positional value of 2, then 4, then 8, and so on. The decimal equivalent of binary 1101 is 1 * 1 + 0 * 2 + 1 * 4 + 1 * 8, or 1 + 0 + 4 + 8, or 13.]

6

Control Statements: Part 2

Who can control his fate?
—William Shakespeare

The used key is always bright.
—Benjamin Franklin

Not everything that can be counted counts, and not every thing that counts can be counted.
—Albert Einstein

Every advantage in the past is judged in the light of the final issue.
—Demosthenes

OBJECTIVES

In this chapter you'll learn:

- The essentials of counter-controlled repetition.
- To use the `For`...`Next`, `Do`...`Loop While` and `Do`...`Loop Until` repetition statements to execute statements in a program repeatedly.
- To perform multiple selection using the `Select`...`Case` selection statement.
- To use the `Exit` statement to break out of a repetition statement.
- To use the `Continue` statement to break out of the current iteration of a repetition statement.
- To use logical operators to form more complex conditions.

Outline

6.1 Introduction

Chapter 5 began our introduction to the types of building blocks that are available for problem solving. We used those building blocks to employ proven program-construction techniques. In this chapter, we continue our study of Visual Basic's control statements. The control statements we study here and in Chapter 5 help us build and manipulate objects. We continue our early emphasis on object-oriented programming, presenting the next version of our `GradeBook` class.

We demonstrate the `For...Next`, `Select...Case`, `Do...Loop While` and `Do...Loop Until` control statements. Through a series of short examples using `While...End While` and `For...Next`, we explore the essentials of counter-controlled repetition. We create a `GradeBook` class that uses a `Select...Case` multiple-selection statement to count the number of A, B, C, D and F grades in a set of letter grades entered by the user. We introduce the `Exit` and `Continue` program control statements. Finally, we discuss the logical operators, which enable you to use more powerful conditional expressions in control statements.

6.2 Essentials of Counter-Controlled Repetition

This section uses the `While` repetition statement introduced in Chapter 5 to highlight the elements required to perform counter-controlled repetition. Counter-controlled repetition requires

1. the **name** of a control variable (or loop counter) that is used to determine whether the loop continues to iterate
2. the **initial value** of the control variable
3. the **increment** (or **decrement**) by which the control variable is modified each time through the loop
4. the condition that tests for the **final value** of the control variable (i.e., whether looping should continue)

The example in Fig. 6.1 uses the four elements of counter-controlled repetition to display the even integers in the range 2–10. The declaration in line 5 *names* the control variable (`counter`), indicates that it is of type `Integer`, reserves space for it in memory and sets it to an *initial value* of `2`.

Consider the `While` statement (lines 7–10). Line 8 displays the current value of `counter`, and line 9 *increments* the control variable by `2` to prepare for the next iteration (repetition) of the loop. The loop-continuation condition in the `While` statement (line 7) tests whether the value of the control variable is less than or equal to `10`—the *final value* for which the condition is true. The body of the `While` is performed even when the control variable is `10`. The loop terminates when the control variable exceeds `10` (i.e., when `counter` becomes `12`, because the loop is incrementing by `2` each time).

```
1  ' Fig. 6.1: WhileCounter.vb
2  ' Using the While statement to demonstrate counter-controlled repetition.
3  Module WhileCounter
4     Sub Main()
5        Dim counter As Integer = 2 ' name and initialize loop counter
6
7        While counter <= 10 ' test final value of loop counter
8           Console.Write("{0} ", counter)
9           counter += 2 ' increment counter
10       End While
11
12       Console.WriteLine()
13    End Sub ' Main
14 End Module ' WhileCounter
```

```
2 4 6 8 10
```

Fig. 6.1 | Counter-controlled repetition with the `While...End While` statement.

6.3 For...Next Repetition Statement

Section 6.2 presented the essentials of counter-controlled repetition with the `While` statement. Visual Basic also provides the `For...Next` repetition statement, which specifies the counter-controlled repetition details in a single line of code. In general, it conter-controlled repetition should be implemented with `For...Next`. To illustrate the power of `For...Next`, we rewrite the program of Fig. 6.1 using the `For...Next` statement in Fig. 6.2.

The `Main` method of the program operates as follows: When the `For...Next` statement (lines 7–9) begins its execution, the control variable `counter` is declared as an `Integer` and initialized to `2`, thus addressing the first two elements of counter-controlled repetition—control variable *name* and *initial value*. Next, the implied loop-continuation condition `counter <= 10` is tested. The **`To` keyword** is required in the `For...Next` statement. The optional **`Step` keyword** specifies the increment (i.e., the amount that is added to `counter` each time the `For...Next` body is executed). If `Step` and the value following it are omitted, the increment defaults to `1` (`-1` if the final value is less than the initial value). You typically omit the `Step` portion for increments of `1`. The increment of a `For...Next` statement could be negative, in which case it is a decrement, and the loop actually counts downward.

```
1  ' Fig. 6.2: ForCounter.vb
2  ' Using the For...Next statement for counter-controlled repetition.
3  Module ForCounter
4     Sub Main()
5        ' initialization, repetition condition and
6        ' incrementing are all included in For...Next statement
7        For counter As Integer = 2 To 10 Step 2
8           Console.Write("{0} ", counter)
9        Next
10
11       Console.WriteLine()
12    End Sub ' Main
13 End Module ' ForCounter
```

```
2 4 6 8 10
```

Fig. 6.2 | Counter-controlled repetition with the `For...Next` statement.

In this example, the initial value of `counter` is `2`, so the implied condition is satisfied (i.e., true), and the `counter`'s value `2` is output in line 8. The required **`Next` keyword** marks the end of the `For...Next` repetition statement. When the `Next` keyword is reached, variable `counter` is incremented by the specified value of `2`, and the loop begins again with the loop-continuation test. Some programmers place the control variable name after `Next` as in `Next counter`. This is particularly useful in nested `For...Next` statements to identify the statement to which the `Next` belongs.

Now, the control variable is equal to `4`. This value does not exceed the final value, so the program performs the body statement again. This process continues until the `counter` value of `10` has been printed and the control variable `counter` is incremented to `12`, causing the (implied) loop-continuation test to fail and repetition to terminate. The program continues by performing the first statement after the `For...Next` statement (line 11.)

Good Programming Practice 6.1

Place a blank line before and after each control statement to make it stand out in the program.

Good Programming Practice 6.2

Vertical spacing above and below control statements, as well as indentation of the bodies of control statements, gives programs a two-dimensional appearance that enhances readability.

Error-Prevention Tip 6.1

Use a `For...Next` loop for counter-controlled repetition. Off-by-one errors (which occur when a loop is executed for one more or one less iteration than is necessary) tend to disappear, because the terminating value is clear.

`For...Next` Statement Header Components

Figure 6.3 takes a closer look at the `For...Next` statement from Fig. 6.2. The first line of the `For...Next` statement sometimes is called the **`For...Next` header**. Note that the `For...Next` header specifies each of the items needed for counter-controlled repetition with a control variable.

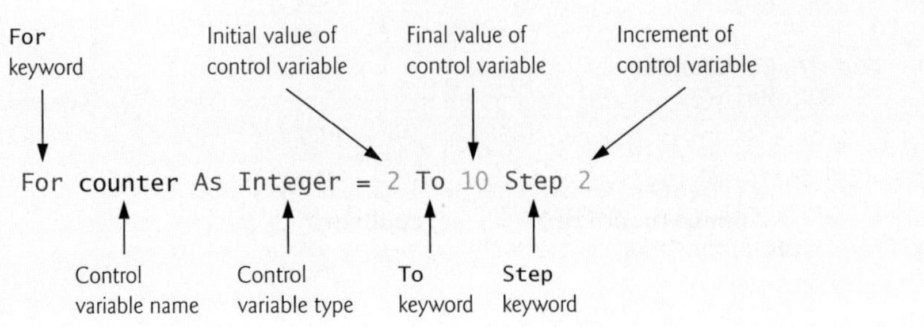

Fig. 6.3 | For...Next header components.

The general form of the For...Next statement is

```
For initialization To finalValue Step increment
   statement
Next
```

where the *initialization* expression initializes the loop's control variable, *finalValue* determines whether the loop should continue executing (if the control variable is less than or equal to *finalValue*) and *increment* specifies the amount the control variable should be incremented each time through the loop. In most cases, the For...Next statement can be represented by an equivalent While statement, as follows:

```
initialization

While variable <= finalValue
   statement
   increment
End While
```

There is an exception to this rule, which we will discuss in Section 6.9.

Note in Fig. 6.3 that the counter variable is both initialized and declared in the For...Next header. The counter variable may be declared before the For...Next statement. For example, the code in Fig. 6.2 could have been written as

```
Dim counter As Integer

For counter = 2 To 10 Step 2
   Console.Write("{0} ", counter)
Next
```

Although both forms are correct, declaring the control variable in the For...Next header is more clear and concise. The difference between the two forms is that if the *initialization* expression in the For...Next statement header declares the control variable (as we have done in Fig. 6.2), the control variable can be used only in the body of the For...Next statement—it will be unknown outside the For...Next statement. This restricted use of the control-variable name is known as the variable's **scope**. The scope of a variable specifies where it can be used in a program. Scope is discussed in detail in Chapter 7, Methods: A

Deeper Look. If the control variable is declared before the `For...Next` statement, it can be used from the point of declaration, inside the control statement's body and after the control statement as well.

The starting value, ending value and increment portions of a `For...Next` statement can contain arithmetic expressions. The expressions are evaluated once (when the `For...Next` statement begins executing) and used as the starting value, ending value and increment of the `For...Next` statement's header. For example, assume that `value1 = 2` and `value2 = 10`. The header

```
For j As Integer = value1 To 4 * value1 * value2 Step value2 \ value1
```

is equivalent to the header

```
For j As Integer = 2 To 80 Step 5
```

If the loop-continuation condition is initially false (e.g., if the starting value is greater than the ending value and the increment is positive), the `For...Next`'s body is not performed. Instead, execution proceeds with the first statement after the `For...Next` statement.

The control variable frequently is printed or used in calculations in the `For...Next` body, but it does not have to be. It is common to use the control variable exclusively to control repetition and never mention it in the `For...Next` body.

Common Programming Error 6.1

Counter-controlled loops should not be controlled with `Float` or `Double` variables. Values of these types are represented only approximately in the computer's memory; this can lead to imprecise counter values and inaccurate tests for termination.

Error-Prevention Tip 6.2

Although the value of the control variable can be changed in the body of a `For...Next` loop, avoid doing so, because this practice can lead to subtle errors.

Common Programming Error 6.2

In nested `For...Next` loops, the use of the same control-variable name in more than one loop is a compilation error.

`For...Next` Statement UML Activity Diagram

The activity diagram for the `For...Next` statement is similar to that of the `While` statement (Fig. 5.5). For example, the activity diagram of the `For...Next` statement

```
For counter As Integer = 1 To 10
   Console.WriteLine("{0} ", counter)
Next
```

is shown in Fig. 6.4. This activity diagram makes it clear that the initialization occurs only once and that incrementing occurs *after* each execution of the body statement. Note that (besides an initial state, transition arrows, a merge, a final state and several notes) the diagram contains only action states and a decision.

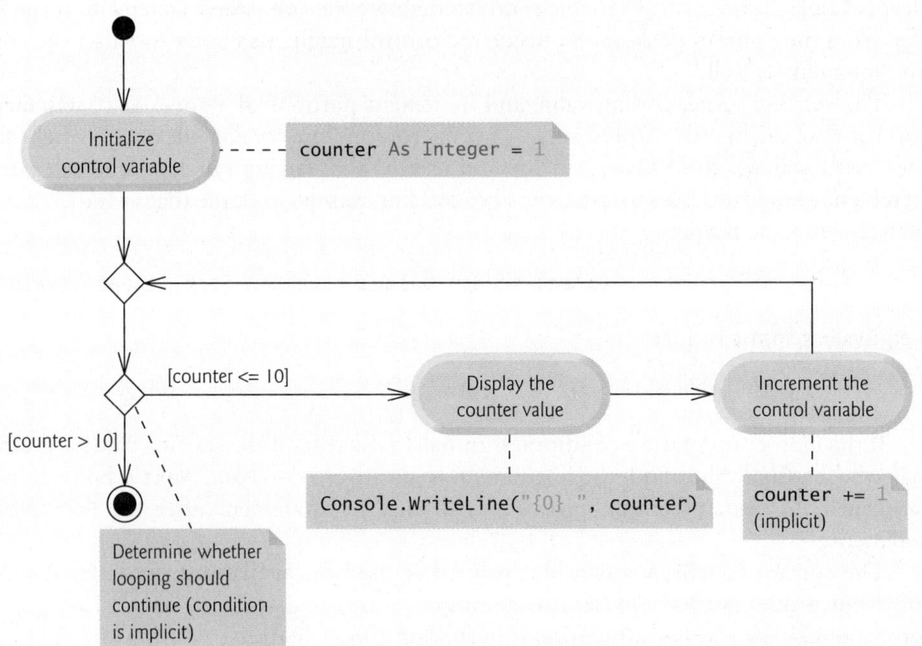

Fig. 6.4 | For...Next repetition statement activity diagram.

Local Type Inference

In each `For...Next` statement presented so far, we declared the control variable's type in the `For...Next` statement's header. The Visual Basic 2008 compiler provides a new feature—called local type inference—that enables it to infer a local variable's type based on the context in which the variable is initialized. Recall that a local variable is any variable declared in the body of a method. For example, in the declaration

```
Dim x = 7
```

the compiler infers that the variable `x` should be of type `Integer`, because the compiler assumes that whole-number values, like `7`, are of type `Integer`. Similarly, in the declaration

```
Dim y = -123.45
```

the compiler infers that the variable `y` should be of type `Double`, because the compiler assumes that floating-point number values, like `-123.45`, are of type `Double`.

You can also use local type inference with control variables in the header of a `For...Next` statement. For example, the `For...Next` header

```
For counter As Integer = 1 To 10
```

can be written as

```
For counter = 1 To 10
```

In this case, `counter` is of type `Integer` because it is initialized with a whole number (`1`).

Local type inference can be used on any variable that is initialized in its declaration. For clarity, we prefer to use it only in `For...Next` statement headers. We'll also use local type inference when we present Language Integrated Query (LINQ) examples starting in Chapter 9. Local type inference is one of several new Visual Basic 2008 features that support LINQ.

6.4 Examples Using the For...Next Statement

The following examples demonstrate different ways of varying the control variable in a `For...Next` statement. In each case, we write the appropriate `For...Next` header.

a) Vary the control variable from `1` to `100` in increments of `1`.

`For i = 1 To 100` or `For i = 1 To 100 Step 1`

b) Vary the control variable from `100` to `1` in increments of `-1` (decrements of `1`).

```
For i = 100 To 1 Step -1
```

c) Vary the control variable from `7` to `77` in increments of `7`.

```
For i = 7 To 77 Step 7
```

d) Vary the control variable from `20` to `2` in increments of `-2` (decrements of `2`).

```
For i = 20 To 2 Step -2
```

e) Vary the control variable over the sequence of the following values: `2`, `5`, `8`, `11`, `14`, `17`, `20`.

```
For i = 2 To 20 Step 3
```

f) Vary the control variable over the sequence of the following values: `99`, `88`, `77`, `66`, `55`, `44`, `33`, `22`, `11`, `0`.

```
For i = 99 To 0 Step -11
```

Application: Summing the Even Integers from 2 to 100

The next two examples demonstrate simple applications of the `For...Next` repetition statement. The program in Fig. 6.5 uses the `For...Next` statement to sum the even integers from `2` to `100`. Remember that to use the `MessageBox` class you must add a reference to `System.Windows.Forms.dll`, as explained in Section 3.9.

```
' Fig. 6.5: Sum.vb
' Using For...Next statement to demonstrate summation.
Imports System.Windows.Forms

Module Sum
   Sub Main()
      Dim sum As Integer = 0
```

Fig. 6.5 | `For...Next` statement used for summation. (Part 1 of 2.)

```
8
9         ' add even numbers from 2 to 100
10        For number = 2 To 100 Step 2
11           sum += number
12        Next
13
14        MessageBox.Show("The sum is " & sum, _
15           "Sum even integers from 2 to 100", _
16           MessageBoxButtons.OK, MessageBoxIcon.Information)
17     End Sub ' Main
18  End Module ' Sum
```

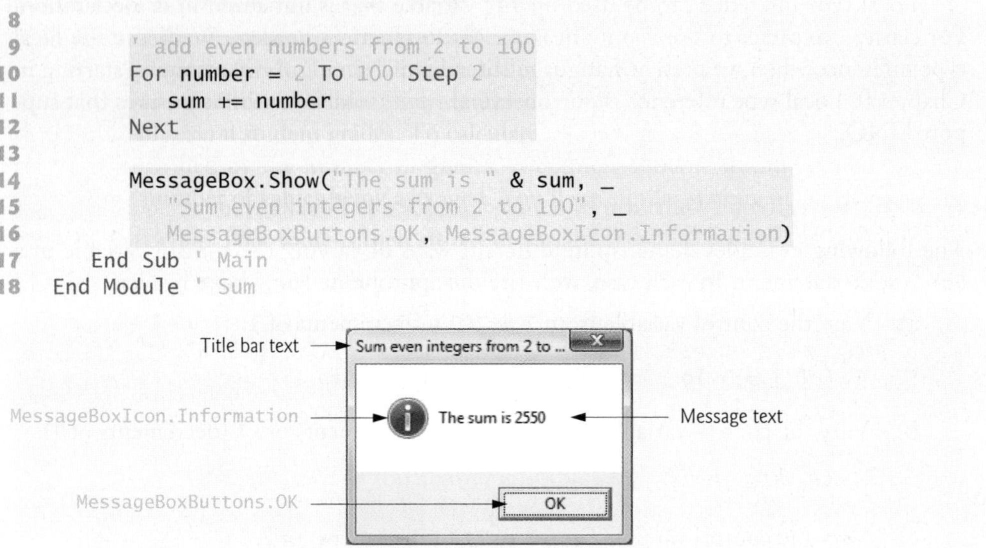

Fig. 6.5 | `For`...`Next` statement used for summation. (Part 2 of 2.)

Message Dialog Buttons and Icons

The version of method `MessageBox.Show` called in Fig. 6.5 (lines 14–16) is different from the version discussed in earlier examples in that it takes four arguments instead of two. The dialog in Fig. 6.5 is labeled to emphasize the effects of the four arguments. The first two arguments are `Strings` displayed in the dialog and the dialog's title bar, respectively. The third argument indicates which button(s) to display, and the fourth argument indicates an icon that appears to the left of the message. The documentation provided with the IDE includes the complete listing of **`MessageBoxButtons`** and **`MessageBoxIcon`** constants. Some message dialog icon options are described in Fig. 6.6; the message dialog button options are described in Fig. 6.7, including how to display multiple buttons. Note that there are multiple icon constants that display the same icon. Sometimes using a different constant name improves program readability. For instance, it may make more sense to use the constant `MessageBoxIcon.Warning` to indicate that a warning is being displayed, while the constant `MessageBoxIcon.Exclamation` would be used to indicate that an unexpected result occurred. Both constants display the same icon, but the names used in the code are clearer based on context.

`MessageBoxIcon` constants	Icon	Description
`MessageBoxIcon.Warning` or `MessageBoxIcon.Exclamation`	⚠	Icon containing an exclamation point. Used to caution the user against potential problems.
`MessageBoxIcon.Information`	ⓘ	Icon containing the letter "i." Used to display information about the state of the application.

Fig. 6.6 | Message dialog icon constants. (Part 1 of 2.)

MessageBoxIcon constants	Icon	Description
MessageBoxIcon.None		No icon is displayed.
MessageBoxIcon.Error	⊗	Icon containing an **X** in a red circle. Used to alert the user to errors or critical situations.

Fig. 6.6 | Message dialog icon constants. (Part 2 of 2.)

MessageBoxButton constants	Description
MessageBoxButtons.OK	**OK** button. Allows the user to acknowledge a message. Included by default.
MessageBoxButtons.OKCancel	**OK** and **Cancel** buttons. Allow the user to either continue or cancel an operation.
MessageBoxButtons.YesNo	**Yes** and **No** buttons. Allow the user to respond to a question.
MessageBoxButtons.YesNoCancel	**Yes**, **No** and **Cancel** buttons. Allow the user to respond to a question or cancel an operation.
MessageBoxButtons.RetryCancel	**Retry** and **Cancel** buttons. Allow the user to retry or cancel an operation that has failed.
MessageBoxButtons.AbortRetryIgnore	**Abort**, **Retry** and **Ignore** buttons. When one of a series of operations has failed, these buttons allow the user to abort the entire sequence, retry the failed operation or ignore the failed operation and continue.

Fig. 6.7 | Message dialog button constants.

Application: Compound-Interest Calculations

The next example computes compound interest using the `For...Next` statement. Consider the following problem statement:

> *A person invests $1000.00 in a savings account that yields 5% interest. Assuming that all the interest is left on deposit, calculate and print the amount of money in the account at the end of each year over a period of 10 years. To determine these amounts, use the following formula:*
>
> $$a = p\,(1 + r)^{n}$$
>
> *where*
>
> p is the original amount invested (i.e., the principal)
> r is the annual interest rate (e.g., .05 stands for 5%)
> n is the number of years
> a is the amount on deposit at the end of the nth year.

This problem involves a loop that performs the indicated calculation for each of the 10 years that the money remains on deposit. The solution is shown in Fig. 6.8.

Lines 7–8 declare two `Decimal` variables. Type **`Decimal`** is used for monetary calculations. Line 9 declares `rate` as type `Double`. Variable `principal` is initialized to `1000.00` and `rate` is initialized to `0.05` (i.e., 5%). Variable `output` (line 12) will be used to store the output that we will eventually display in a message dialog.

```
1  ' Fig. 6.8: Interest.vb
2  ' Calculating compound interest.
3  Imports System.Windows.Forms
4
5  Module Interest
6     Sub Main()
7        Dim amount As Decimal ' dollar amounts on deposit
8        Dim principal As Decimal = 1000.00 ' amount invested
9        Dim rate As Double = 0.05 ' interest rate
10
11       ' amount after each year
12       Dim output As String = _
13          "Year" & vbTab & "Amount on deposit" & vbNewLine
14
15       ' calculate amount after each year
16       For yearValue = 1 To 10
17          amount = principal * (1 + rate) ^ yearValue
18          output &= yearValue & vbTab & String.Format("{0:C}", amount) _
19             & vbNewLine
20       Next
21
22       ' display output
23       MessageBox.Show(output, "Compound Interest", _
24          MessageBoxButtons.OK, MessageBoxIcon.Information)
25    End Sub ' Main
26 End Module ' Interest
```

Compound Interest
Year Amount on deposit
1 $1,050.00
2 $1,102.50
3 $1,157.63
4 $1,215.51
5 $1,276.28
6 $1,340.10
7 $1,407.10
8 $1,477.46
9 $1,551.33
10 $1,628.89
OK

Fig. 6.8 | `For...Next` statement used to calculate compound interest.

The `For...Next` statement (lines 16–20) iterates 10 times, varying control variable `yearValue` from `1` to `10` in increments of `1`. Line 17 performs the calculation from the problem statement

$$a = p\,(1 + r)^{\,n}$$

where a is the `amount`, p is the `principal`, r is the `rate` and n is the `yearValue`.

Formatting Currency Output

Lines 18–19 append text to the end of the `String output`. The text includes the current `yearValue` value, a tab character (`vbTab`) to position to the second column, the result of the method call `String.Format("{0:C}", amount)` and, finally, a `vbNewLine` to start the next output on the next line. Method **`Format`** of class `String` takes a formatted string and the values to be formatted as arguments, and returns the resulting text with the formatting applied. The first argument passed to `Format` is the format string. In Chapter 5, we used the format string `"{0:F}"` to print a floating-point number with two digits after the decimal. Line 18 uses the format string `"{0:C}"`. The **`C`** (for "currency") format specifier indicates that its corresponding value (`amount`) should be displayed in monetary format—with a dollar sign to the left and commas in the proper locations (this will differ based on your locale). For example, the value `1334.50`, when formatted using the `C` format specifier, will appear as "`$1,334.50`."

Type `Decimal` *vs. Type* `Double`

Variables `amount` and `principal` are declared as type `Decimal`. We do this because we are dealing with fractional monetary amounts and need a type that allows precise monetary calculations—`Single` and `Double`, because they only approximate values, do not. Using floating-point types, such as `Single` or `Double`, to represent dollar amounts (assuming that dollar amounts are displayed with two digits to the right of the decimal point) can cause errors. For example, two `Double` dollar amounts stored in the machine could be 14.234 (normally rounded to 14.23) and 18.673 (normally rounded to 18.67). When these amounts are added together, they produce the internal sum 32.907, which normally rounds to 32.91. Thus, the output could appear as

```
  14.23
+ 18.67
-------
  32.91
```

but a person adding the individual numbers as displayed would expect the sum to be 32.90. Therefore, it is inappropriate to use `Single` or `Double` for dollar amounts. You have been warned!

Error-Prevention Tip 6.3

Do not use variables of type `Single` or `Double` to perform precise monetary calculations. The imprecision of floating-point numbers can cause errors that result in incorrect monetary values. Use the type `Decimal` for monetary calculations.

Variable `rate`, of type `Double`, is used in the calculation `1 + rate`, which appears as the left operand of the exponentiation operator. In fact, this calculation produces the same result each time through the loop, so performing the calculation in the body of the `For...Next` loop is wasteful.

Performance Tip 6.1

Avoid placing inside a loop the calculation of an expression whose value does not change each time through the loop. Such an expression should be evaluated only once and prior to the loop.

6.5 GradeBook Case Study: Select...Case Multiple-Selection Statement

Chapter 5 presented the `If...Then` single-selection statement and the `If...Then...Else` double-selection statement. Occasionally, an algorithm contains a series of decisions that test a variable or expression separately for each value that the variable or expression might assume. The algorithm then takes different actions based on those values. Visual Basic provides the `Select...Case` multiple-selection statement to handle such decision making.

***GradeBook* Class with `Select...Case` Statement to Count A, B, C, D and F Grades.** Figure 6.9 contains an enhanced version of the `GradeBook` class introduced in Chapter 4 and further developed in Chapter 5. The new version not only calculates the average of a set of numeric grades entered by the user, but uses a `Select...Case` statement to determine whether each grade is the equivalent of an A, B, C, D or F and to increment the appropriate grade counter. The class also displays a summary of the number of students who received each grade. An extra counter is used to display the number of students who received a perfect score of 100 on the exam. Figure 6.10 shows a sample execution of the `GradeBookTest` module that uses an object of class `GradeBook` to process a set of grades.

Like earlier versions of the class, class `GradeBook` (Fig. 6.9) declares instance variable `courseNameValue` (line 4) and contains property `CourseName` (lines 22–41) and method `DisplayMessage` (lines 44–47), which access the course name and display a welcome message to the user, respectively. The class also contains a constructor (lines 16–18) that initializes the course name.

```
1   ' Fig. 6.9: GradeBook.vb
2   ' GradeBook class uses Select...Case statement to count letter grades.
3   Public Class GradeBook
4      Private courseNameValue As String ' name of course
5      Private total As Integer ' sum of grades
6      Private gradeCounter As Integer ' number of grades entered
7      Private aCount As Integer ' count of A grades
8      Private bCount As Integer ' count of B grades
9      Private cCount As Integer ' count of C grades
10     Private dCount As Integer ' count of D grades
11     Private fCount As Integer ' count of F grades
12     Private perfectScoreCount As Integer ' count of perfect scores
13
14     ' constructor initializes course name;
15     ' Integer instance variables are initialized to 0 by default
16     Public Sub New(ByVal name As String)
17        CourseName = name ' initializes CourseName
18     End Sub ' New
```

Fig. 6.9 | `GradeBook` class uses `Select...Case` statement to count A, B, C, D and F grades. (Part 1 of 3.)

```

   ' property that gets and sets the course name; the Set accessor
   ' ensures that the course name has at most 25 characters
   Public Property CourseName() As String
      Get ' retrieve courseNameValue
         Return courseNameValue
      End Get

      Set(ByVal value As String) ' set courseNameValue
         If value.Length <= 25 Then ' if value has 25 or fewer characters
            courseNameValue = value ' store the course name in the object
         Else ' if name has more than 25 characters
            ' set courseNameValue to first 25 characters of parameter name
            ' start at 0, length of 25
            courseNameValue = value.Substring(0, 25)

            Console.WriteLine( _
               "Course name (" & value & ") exceeds maximum length (25).")
            Console.WriteLine( _
               "Limiting course name to first 25 characters." & vbNewLine)
         End If
      End Set
   End Property ' CourseName

   ' display a welcome message to the GradeBook user
   Public Sub DisplayMessage()
      Console.WriteLine("Welcome to the grade book for " _
         & vbNewLine & CourseName & "!" & vbNewLine)
   End Sub ' DisplayMessage

   ' input arbitrary number of grades from user
   Public Sub InputGrades()
      Console.Write( _
         "Enter the grades in the range 0-100, negative value to quit: ")
      Dim grade As Integer = Console.ReadLine() ' input first grade

      ' loop until user enters a sentinel value
      While grade >= 0
         total += grade ' add grade to total
         gradeCounter += 1 ' increment number of grades

         ' call method to increment appropriate counter
         IncrementLetterGradeCounter(grade)

         ' input next grade
         Console.Write("Enter the grades in the range 0-100, " & _
            "negative value to quit: ")
         grade = Console.ReadLine()
      End While
   End Sub ' InputGrades

```

Fig. 6.9 | GradeBook class uses Select...Case statement to count A, B, C, D and F grades. (Part 2 of 3.)

```
70      ' add 1 to appropriate counter for specified grade
71      Private Sub IncrementLetterGradeCounter(ByVal grade As Integer)
72         Select Case grade ' determine which grade was entered
73            Case 100 ' perfect score
74               perfectScoreCount += 1 ' increment perfectScoreCount
75               aCount += 1 ' increment aCount
76            Case 90 To 99 ' grade was between 90 and 99
77               aCount += 1 ' increment aCount
78            Case 80 To 89 ' grade was between 80 and 89
79               bCount += 1 ' increment bCount
80            Case 70 To 79 ' grade was between 70 and 79
81               cCount += 1 ' increment cCount
82            Case 60 To 69 ' grade was between 60 and 69
83               dCount += 1 ' increment dCount
84            Case Else ' grade was less than 60
85               fCount += 1 ' increment fCount
86         End Select
87      End Sub ' IncrementLetterGradeCounter
88
89      ' display a report based on the grades entered by user
90      Public Sub DisplayGradeReport()
91         Console.WriteLine(vbNewLine & "Grade Report:")
92
93         ' if user entered at least one grade
94         If (gradeCounter > 0) Then
95            ' calculate average of all grades entered
96            Dim average As Double = total / gradeCounter
97
98            ' output summary of results
99            Console.WriteLine("Total of the {0} grades entered is {1}", _
100              gradeCounter, total)
101           Console.WriteLine("Class average is {0:F2}", average)
102           Console.WriteLine("Number of students who received each grade:")
103           Console.WriteLine("A: " & aCount) ' display number of A grades
104           Console.WriteLine("B: " & bCount) ' display number of B grades
105           Console.WriteLine("C: " & cCount) ' display number of C grades
106           Console.WriteLine("D: " & dCount) ' display number of D grades
107           Console.WriteLine("F: " & fCount) ' display number of F grades
108           Console.WriteLine(vbNewLine & "Number of students who " & _
109              "received perfect scores: " & perfectScoreCount)
110        Else ' no grades were entered, so output appropriate message
111           Console.WriteLine("No grades were entered")
112        End If
113     End Sub ' DisplayGradeReport
114  End Class ' GradeBook
```

Fig. 6.9 | GradeBook class uses Select...Case statement to count A, B, C, D and F grades. (Part 3 of 3.)

This version of the GradeBook class declares instance variables total (line 5) and gradeCounter (line 6), which keep track of the sum of the grades entered by the user and the number of grades entered, respectively. Lines 7–11 declare counter variables for each grade category. Line 12 declares perfectScoreCount, a counter for the number of students who received a perfect score of 100 on the exam. The class maintains `total`, `gradeCounter` and the six counters as instance variables so that they can be used or modified in any of the class's methods. Note that the class's constructor (lines 16–18) sets only the course name; the remaining instance variables are `Integer`s and are initialized to `0` by default.

This version of class `GradeBook` contains three additional methods—`InputGrades`, `IncrementLetterGradeCounter` and `DisplayGradeReport`. Method `InputGrades` (lines 50–68) reads an arbitrary number of integer grades from the user using sentinel-controlled repetition and updates instance variables `total` and `gradeCounter`. The method calls method `IncrementLetterGradeCounter` (lines 71–87) to update the appropriate letter-grade counter for each grade entered. Note that method `IncrementLetterGradeCounter` is declared `Private`—we will discuss why later in the section. Method `DisplayGradeReport` (lines 90–113) outputs a report containing the total of all the grades entered, the average of the grades, the number of students who received each letter grade and the number of students who received a perfect score.

Let's examine these methods in more detail. Lines 51–53 in method `InputGrades` prompt the user to enter a grade, which is assigned to variable `grade`. In this example, we are using any negative number as a sentinel. The `While` statement (lines 56–67) executes if there is more data to input (i.e., if the `grade` is not a sentinel value).

Line 57 adds `grade` to `total`. Line 58 increments `gradeCounter`. The `DisplayGradeReport` method uses these variables to compute the average. Line 61 calls method `IncrementLetterGradeCounter` to increment the appropriate letter-grade counter based on the numeric grade entered. Lines 64–66 prompt the user and input the next grade.

Method `IncrementLetterGradeCounter` uses a `Select...Case` statement (lines 72–86) to determine which counter to increment. In this example, we assume that the user enters a valid grade in the range 0–100. A grade in the range 90–100 represents an A, 80–89 represents a B, 70–79 represents a C, 60–69 represents a D and 0–59 represents an F. Line 72

```
Select Case grade
```

begins the `Select...Case` statement. The expression following the keywords `Select Case` (in this case, `grade`) is called the **controlling expression**. The controlling expression is compared sequentially with each `Case`. If a matching `Case` is found, the code in the `Case` executes, then program control proceeds to the first statement after the `Select...Case` statement (line 87).

Common Programming Error 6.3

Duplicate `Case` statements are logic errors. At run time, the first matching `Case` is executed.

The first `Case` statement (line 73) determines whether the value of `grade` is equal to `100`. If this is true, the statements in lines 74–75 execute, incrementing both `aCount` (because a grade of 100 is an A) and `perfectScoreCount`. Note that a `Case` statement can specify multiple actions—in this case, incrementing both `aCount` and `perfectScoreCount`. The next `Case` statement (line 76) determines whether `grade` is between `90` and `99`, inclusive. In this case, only `aCount` is incremented (line 77). Keyword `To` specifies the range; lines 78–83 use this keyword to present a series of similar Cases. Each case increments the appropriate counter.

Common Programming Error 6.4

If the value on the left side of the `To` keyword in a `Case` statement is larger than the value on the right side, the `Case` is ignored during program execution; this is probably a logic error.

If no match occurs between the controlling expression's value and a `Case` label, the optional **`Case Else`** (lines 84–85) executes. We use the `Case Else` in this example to process all controlling-expression values that are less than `60`—that is, all failing grades. If no match occurs and the `Select...Case` does not contain a `Case Else`, program control simply continues with the first statement after the `Select...Case`. `Case Else` commonly is used to deal with invalid input. When employed, the `Case Else` must be the last `Case`.

The required **`End Select`** keywords terminate the `Select...Case` statement. Note that the body parts of the `Select...Case` statement are indented to emphasize structure and improve program readability.

Error-Prevention Tip 6.4

Provide a `Case Else` in `Select...Case` statements. `Case`s not handled in a `Select...Case` statement are ignored unless a `Case Else` is provided. The inclusion of a `Case Else` statement can facilitate the processing of exceptional conditions.

Types of `Case` *Statements*

`Case` statements also can use relational operators to determine whether the controlling expression satisfies a condition. For example

```
Case Is < 0
```

uses keyword **`Is`** along with the relational operator, <, to test for values less than 0.

Multiple values can be tested in a `Case` statement where the values are separated by commas, as in

```
Case 0, 5 To 9
```

which tests for the value 0 or values in the range 5–9. Also, `Case`s can be used to test `String` values.

`GradeBookTest` *Module That Demonstrates Class* `GradeBook`

Module `GradeBookTest` (Fig. 6.10) creates a `GradeBook` object (line 7). Line 9 invokes the object's `DisplayMessage` method to output a welcome message to the user. Line 10 invokes the object's `InputGrades` method to read grades from the user and keep track of the sum of all the grades entered and the number of grades. Recall that method `InputGrades` also calls method `IncrementLetterGradeCounter` to keep track of the number of students who received each letter grade. Line 11 invokes method `DisplayGradeReport` of class `GradeBook`, which outputs a report based on the grades entered (as in the sample execution in Fig. 6.10). Line 94 of class `GradeBook` (Fig. 6.9) determines whether the user entered at least one grade—this helps us avoid dividing by zero. If so, line 96 calculates the average of the grades. Lines 99–109 then output the totals of all the grades, the class average, the number of students who received each letter grade and the number of students who received a perfect score. If no grades were entered, line 111 outputs an appropriate message.

```
1  ' Fig. 6.10: GradeBookTest.vb
2  ' Create GradeBook object, input grades and display grade report.
3  Module GradeBookTest
4     Sub Main()
5        ' create GradeBook object gradeBook1 and
6        ' pass course name to constructor
7        Dim gradeBook1 As New GradeBook("CS101 Introduction to VB")
8
9        gradeBook1.DisplayMessage() ' display welcome message
10       gradeBook1.InputGrades() ' read grades from user
11       gradeBook1.DisplayGradeReport() ' display report based on grades
12    End Sub ' Main
13 End Module ' GradeBookTest
```

```
Welcome to the grade book for
CS101 Introduction to VB!

Enter a grade in the range 0-100, negative value to quit: 99
Enter a grade in the range 0-100, negative value to quit: 92
Enter a grade in the range 0-100, negative value to quit: 45
Enter a grade in the range 0-100, negative value to quit: 57
Enter a grade in the range 0-100, negative value to quit: 63
Enter a grade in the range 0-100, negative value to quit: 71
Enter a grade in the range 0-100, negative value to quit: 76
Enter a grade in the range 0-100, negative value to quit: 85
Enter a grade in the range 0-100, negative value to quit: 90
Enter a grade in the range 0-100, negative value to quit: 100
Enter a grade in the range 0-100, negative value to quit: -1

Grade Report:
Total of the 10 grades entered is 778
Class average is 77.80
Number of students who received each grade:
A: 4
B: 1
C: 2
D: 1
F: 2

Number of students who received a perfect score: 1
```

Fig. 6.10 | GradeBookTest creates a GradeBook object and invokes its methods.

Note that module GradeBookTest (Fig. 6.10) does not directly call GradeBook method IncrementLetterGradeCounter (lines 71–87 of Fig. 6.9). This method is used exclusively by method InputGrades of class GradeBook to update the appropriate letter-grade counter as each new grade is entered by the user. Method IncrementLetterGradeCounter exists solely to support the operation of class GradeBook's other methods and thus is declared Private. Methods declared Private can be called only by other members of the class in which the Private methods are declared. Such Private methods are commonly referred to as utility methods or helper methods.

Using the **With** *Statement*

The With statement allows you to make multiple references to the same object in a concise manner. For example, we can replace lines 9–11 of Fig. 6.10 (which all reference the same object, gradeBook1) with

```
With gradeBook1
   .DisplayMessage() ' display welcome message
   .InputGrades() ' read grades from user
   .DisplayGradeReport() ' display report based on grades
End With
```

These lines of code are collectively known as a **`With` statement block**. At the beginning of the block, we specify the object (`gradeBook1`) that we will be using in the block. The `With` statement allows you to access an object's members in the block without having to specify the name of the object before the dot separator—e.g., `.DisplayMessage()` instead of `gradeBook1.DisplayMessage()`.

`Select...Case` Statement UML Activity Diagram

Figure 6.11 shows the UML activity diagram for the general `Select...Case` statement. Again, note that (besides an initial state, transition arrows, merges, a final state and several notes) the diagram contains only action states and decisions.

In Chapter 12, Object-Oriented Programming: Polymorphism, we present a more elegant method of implementing multiple-selection logic. We use a technique called polymorphism to create programs that are often clearer, more manageable, and easier to extend than programs that use `Select...Case` logic.

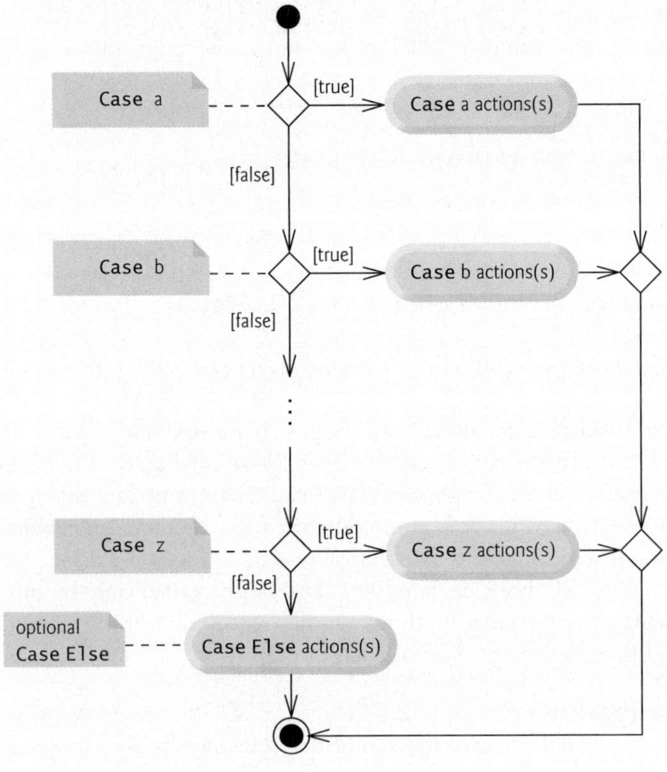

Fig. 6.11 | `Select...Case` multiple-selection statement UML activity diagram.

6.6 Do...Loop While Repetition Statement

The Do...Loop While repetition statement is similar to the While statement and Do While...Loop statement. In the While and Do While...Loop statements, the loop-continuation condition is tested at the *beginning* of the loop, before the body of the loop is performed. The Do...Loop While statement tests the loop-continuation condition *after* the loop body is performed; therefore, in a Do...Loop While statement, the loop body is always executed at least once. When a Do...Loop While statement terminates, execution continues with the statement after the Loop While clause. The program in Fig. 6.12 uses a Do...Loop While statement to output the values 1–5.

Error-Prevention Tip 6.5

Infinite loops occur when the loop-continuation condition in a While, Do While...Loop or Do...Loop While statement never becomes false.

Lines 8–11 demonstrate the Do...Loop While statement. The first time the statement is encountered, lines 9–10 are executed, displaying the value of counter (at this point, 1), then incrementing counter by 1. Then the condition in line 11 is evaluated. Variable counter is 2, which is less than or equal to 5; because the loop-continuation condition is met, the Do...Loop While statement executes again. In the fifth iteration of the statement, line 9 outputs the value 5, and line 10 increments counter to 6. At this point, the loop-continuation condition in line 11 evaluates to false, and the program exits the Do...Loop While statement.

```
1  ' Fig. 6.12: DoLoopWhile.vb
2  ' Demonstrating the Do...Loop While repetition statement.
3  Module DoLoopWhile
4     Sub Main()
5        Dim counter As Integer = 1
6
7        ' print values 1 to 5
8        Do
9           Console.Write("{0} ", counter)
10          counter += 1
11       Loop While counter <= 5
12
13       Console.WriteLine()
14    End Sub ' Main
15 End Module ' DoLoopWhile
```

```
1 2 3 4 5
```

Fig. 6.12 | Do...Loop While repetition statement.

Do...Loop While Statement UML Activity Diagram

The Do...Loop While UML activity diagram (Fig. 6.13) illustrates the fact that the loop-continuation condition is not evaluated until after the statement body is executed at least once. Compare this activity diagram with that of the While statement (Fig. 5.5). Again, note that (besides an initial state, transition arrows, a merge, a final state and several notes) the diagram contains only action states and a decision.

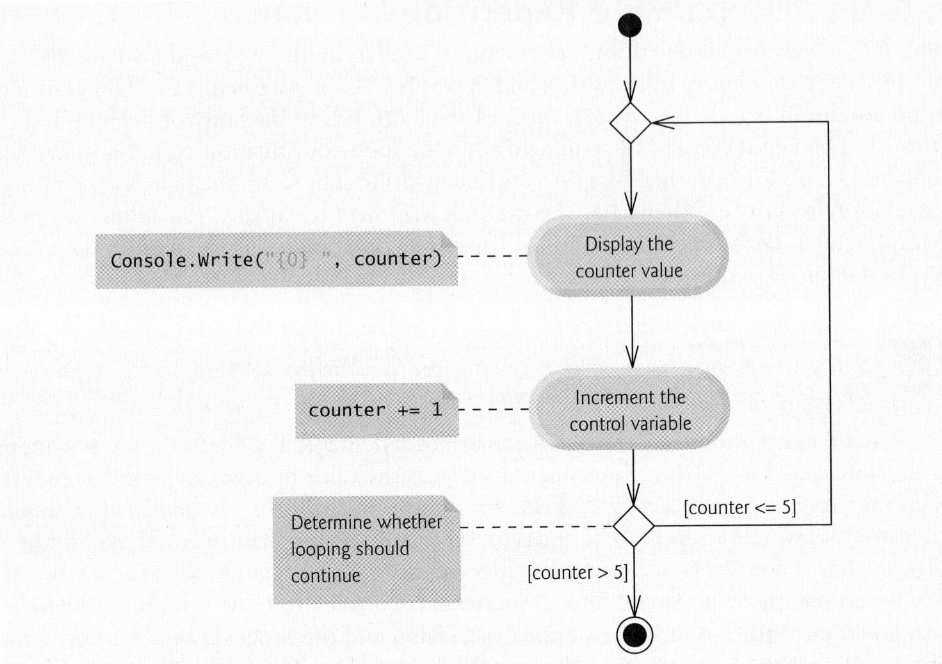

Fig. 6.13 | `Do...Loop While` repetition statement activity diagram.

6.7 Do...Loop Until Repetition Statement

The `Do...Loop Until` repetition statement is similar to the `Do Until...Loop` statement, except that the loop-termination condition is tested after the loop body is performed; therefore, the loop body executes at least once. When a `Do...Loop Until` terminates, execution continues with the statement after the `Loop Until` clause. Figure 6.14 uses a `Do...Loop Until` statement to print the numbers from 1 to 5.

The `Do...Loop Until` statement activity diagram is the same as the one in Fig. 6.13. Note that the loop-termination condition (`counter > 5`) is not evaluated until after the body is executed at least once. If this condition is true, the statement exits. If the condition is false (i.e., the condition `counter <= 5` is true), the loop continues executing.

Common Programming Error 6.5

Including an incorrect relational operator or an incorrect final value for a loop counter in the condition of any repetition statement can cause off-by-one errors.

Error-Prevention Tip 6.6

Infinite loops occur when the loop-termination condition in a `Do Until...Loop` or `Do...Loop Until` statement never becomes true.

Error-Prevention Tip 6.7

In a counter-controlled loop, ensure that the control variable is incremented (or decremented) appropriately in the body of the loop to avoid an infinite loop.

```
' Fig. 6.14: DoLoopUntil.vb
' Using Do...Loop Until repetition statement.
Module DoLoopUntil
   Sub Main()
      Dim counter As Integer = 1

      ' print values 1 to 5
      Do
         Console.Write("{0} ", counter)
         counter += 1
      Loop Until counter > 5

      Console.WriteLine()
   End Sub ' Main
End Module ' DoLoopUntil
```

```
1 2 3 4 5
```

Fig. 6.14 | Do...Loop Until repetition statement.

6.8 Using Exit in Repetition Statements

The **Exit statement** can be used to alter a program's flow of control. There are many forms of the Exit statement, designed to exit different types of code blocks. In this section, we focus on using the Exit statement in repetition statements. The **Exit Do statement** can be executed in a Do While...Loop, Do...Loop While, Do Until...Loop or Do...Loop Until statement, to cause the program to exit immediately from that repetition statement. Similarly, the **Exit For statement** and the **Exit While statement** cause immediate exit from For...Next and While...End While loops, respectively. Execution continues with the first statement after the repetition statement. Figure 6.15 demonstrates the Exit For, Exit Do and Exit While statements in their respective repetition statements.

```
' Fig. 6.15: ExitTest.vb
' Using the Exit statement in repetition statements.
Module ExitTest
   Sub Main()
      Dim counter As Integer ' loop counter

      ' exit For...Next statement
      For counter = 1 To 10
         ' skip remaining code in loop only if counter = 5
         If counter = 5 Then
            Exit For ' break out of loop
         End If

         Console.Write("{0} ", counter) ' output counter
      Next

```

Fig. 6.15 | Exit statement in repetition statements. (Part 1 of 2.)

```
17          Console.WriteLine(vbNewLine & _
18             "Broke out of For...Next at counter = " & counter & vbNewLine)
19          counter = 1 ' reset counter
20
21          ' exit Do Until...Loop statement
22          Do Until counter > 10
23             ' skip remaining code in loop only if counter = 5
24             If counter = 5 Then
25                Exit Do ' break out of loop
26             End If
27
28             Console.Write("{0} ", counter) ' output counter
29             counter += 1 ' increment counter
30          Loop
31
32          Console.WriteLine(vbNewLine & "Broke out of Do Until...Loop " & _
33             " at counter = " & counter & vbNewLine)
34          counter = 1 ' reset counter
35
36          ' exit While statement
37          While counter <= 10
38             ' skip remaining code in loop only if counter = 5
39             If counter = 5 Then
40                Exit While ' break out of loop
41             End If
42
43             Console.Write("{0} ", counter) ' output counter
44             counter += 1 ' increment counter
45          End While
46
47          Console.WriteLine( _
48             vbNewLine & "Broke out of While at counter = " & counter)
49       End Sub ' Main
50    End Module ' ExitTest
```

```
1 2 3 4
Broke out of For...Next at counter = 5

1 2 3 4
Broke out of Do Until...Loop at counter = 5

1 2 3 4
Broke out of While at counter = 5
```

Fig. 6.15 | Exit statement in repetition statements. (Part 2 of 2.)

The header of the `For...Next` statement (line 8) indicates that the body of the loop is to execute 10 times. During each execution, the `If...Then` statement (lines 10–12) determines whether the control variable, `counter`, is equal to `5`. For the first four iterations of the loop (`counter` values `1–4`), this condition is false, so program control proceeds to line 14, which displays the current value of `counter`. Once the value of `counter` reaches 5, the condition in line 10 evaluates to true, so the `Exit For` statement (line 11) executes, terminating the execution of the loop. Program control then proceeds to the output statement in lines 17–18, which displays the value of `counter` after the loop has been exited.

Line 19 resets the value of counter for the next repetition statement. The header of the Do Until...Loop statement (line 22) indicates that the loop should continue executing until counter is greater than 10. When counter has values in the range 1–4, the body of the If...Then statement (lines 24–26) is skipped, the current value of counter is displayed (line 28) and counter is incremented (line 29). However, when counter is 5, the Exit Do statement (line 25) executes, terminating the loop. Lines 32–33 display the value of counter after the loop has been exited. Note that the program does not increment counter (line 29) after the Exit Do statement executes.

Line 34 once again resets the value of counter for the next repetition statement. The header of the While statement (line 37) indicates that the loop should continue executing while counter is less than or equal to 10. When counter is 5, the Exit While statement (line 40) executes, terminating execution of the While statement. Lines 47–48 display the value of counter after the loop has been exited.

The **Exit Select statement** can be used to exit a Select...Case statement. The **Exit Property statement** can be used to exit from a property. We encounter different forms of the Exit statement throughout the book.

6.9 Using Continue in Repetition Statements

The **Continue statement** skips the remaining statements in the loop body of a repetition statement and causes control to proceed to the next iteration of the loop. Like the Exit statement, Continue comes in many forms. The **Continue Do statement** can be executed in a Do While...Loop, Do...Loop While, Do Until...Loop or Do...Loop Until statement to cause the program to skip the remainder of the current iteration of that repetition statement. Similarly, the **Continue For statement** and **Continue While statement** cause the program to skip the remainder of the current iteration of For...Next and While loops, respectively. Unlike the Exit statement, the Continue statement is used to alter program control only in repetition statements.

When Continue For is encountered in a For...Next statement, execution continues with the statement's increment expression, then the program evaluates the loop-continuation test. When Continue is used in another type of repetition statement, the program evaluates the loop-continuation (or loop-termination) test immediately after the Continue statement executes. If a control variable's increment occurs in the loop after the Continue statement, the increment is skipped.

Figure 6.16 demonstrates the Continue For, Continue Do and Continue While statements in their respective repetition statements. Each repetition statement displays the values 1–4 and 6–10; the value 5 is skipped in each case, using an appropriate form of the Continue statement.

```
' Fig. 6.16: ContinueTest.vb
' Using the Continue statement in repetition statements.
Module ContinueTest
   Sub Main()
      Dim counter As Integer ' loop counter

```

Fig. 6.16 | Continue statement in repetition statements. (Part 1 of 2.)

```
      ' skipping an iteration of a For...Next statement
      For counter = 1 To 10
         If counter = 5 Then
            Continue For ' skip to next iteration of loop if counter = 5
         End If

         Console.Write("{0} ", counter) ' output counter
      Next

      Console.WriteLine(vbNewLine & _
         "Skipped printing in For...Next at counter = 5" & vbNewLine)
      counter = 0 ' reset counter

      ' skipping an iteration of a Do Until...Loop statement
      Do Until counter >= 10
         counter += 1 ' increment counter

         If counter = 5 Then
            Continue Do ' skip to next iteration of loop if counter = 5
         End If

         Console.Write("{0} ", counter) ' output counter
      Loop

      Console.WriteLine(vbNewLine & _
         "Skipped printing in Do Until...Loop at counter = 5" & vbNewLine)
      counter = 0 ' reset counter

      ' skipping an iteration of a While statement
      While counter < 10
         counter += 1 ' increment counter

         If counter = 5 Then
            Continue While ' skip to next iteration of loop if counter = 5
         End If

         Console.Write("{0} ", counter) ' output counter
      End While

      Console.WriteLine( _
         vbNewLine & "Skipped printing in While at counter = 5")
   End Sub ' Main
End Module ' ContinueTest
```

```
1 2 3 4 6 7 8 9 10
Skipped printing in For...Next at counter = 5

1 2 3 4 6 7 8 9 10
Skipped printing in Do Until...Loop at counter = 5

1 2 3 4 6 7 8 9 10
Skipped printing in While at counter = 5
```

Fig. 6.16 | `Continue` statement in repetition statements. (Part 2 of 2.)

The header of the For...Next statement (line 8) indicates that the body of the loop is to execute 10 times. During each execution, the If...Then statement (lines 9–11) determines whether the control variable, counter, is equal to 5. If it is not, line 13 displays the current value of counter, and the repetition statement continues to iterate. When the value of counter reaches 5, the Continue For statement (line 10) executes, which terminates the current iteration of the loop, causing the display of the current value of counter to be skipped. The control variable is incremented, then the program evaluates the loop-continuation test. The value of counter is now 6, so the For...Next statement continues to loop, eventually printing the values 1–4 and 6–10.

Line 18 sets counter to 0, so that we can loop through the values 1–10 again, this time using a Do Until...Loop statement. Line 21 indicates that the loop is to continue executing until counter is greater than or equal to 10. Line 22 increments counter. The If...Then statement in lines 24–26 tests whether counter is 5. If it is, the Continue Do statement (line 25) executes, causing the display of the variable counter to be skipped. The program then immediately evaluates the loop-termination test (line 21). The value of counter is still 5, which is not greater than or equal to 10, so the loop continues. During the next iteration, the value of counter is incremented to 6, so the loop executes to completion, eventually displaying the values 1–4 and 6–10. We placed the increment at the beginning of the loop (line 22) so that it would not be skipped during the iteration when the Continue statement executes. If we had placed the increment after the If...Then statement, the value of counter would reach 5 and never be incremented in subsequent iterations. The If...Then condition would repeatedly evaluate to true, causing an infinite loop.

Line 33 once again sets counter to 0. The While statement in lines 36–44 executes while counter is less than 10. Once again, the increment appears at the beginning of the loop. When the value of counter is 5, the If...Then statement's condition (line 39) evaluates to true, and the Continue While statement (line 40) executes, terminating the current iteration of the While statement. Note that the While statement also displays only the values 1–4 and 6–10.

Exit and Continue can be used in nested control statements. For instance, Exit For or Continue For can be used in a While statement, as long as the While statement is itself located in a For...Next statement. In such an example, the Exit or Continue statement would be applied to the proper control statement based on the keywords used in the Exit or Continue statement—in this example, the For keyword is used, so the For...Next statement is the control statement whose flow of control will be altered. If there are nested loops of the same type (e.g., a For...Next statement within a For...Next statement), the statement that immediately surrounds the Exit or Continue statement is the one affected.

In Section 6.3, we stated that While could be used in most cases in place of For...Next. The one exception occurs when the increment expression in the While follows a Continue statement. In this case, the increment does not execute before the program evaluates the repetition-continuation condition, so the While does not execute in the same manner as the For...Next.

6.10 Logical Operators

So far, we have studied only simple conditions, such as count <= 10, total > 1000 and number <> sentinelValue. Each selection and repetition statement evaluated only one condition with one of the operators >, <, >=, <=, = and <>. To make a decision that relied on the evaluation of multiple conditions, we performed these tests in separate statements or in nested `If...Then` or `If...Then...Else` statements.

To handle multiple conditions more efficiently, Visual Basic provides logical operators that can be used to form complex conditions by combining simple ones. The logical operators are `And`, `Or`, `AndAlso`, `OrElse`, `Xor` and `Not`. We consider examples that use each of these operators.

Logical And *Operator*

Suppose we wish to ensure that two conditions are *both* true in a program before a certain path of execution is chosen. In such a case, we can use the logical `And` operator as follows:

```
If gender = "F" And age >= 65 Then
   seniorFemales += 1
End If
```

This `If...Then` statement contains two simple conditions. The condition `gender = "F"` determines whether a person is female and the condition `age >= 65` determines whether a person is a senior citizen. The two simple conditions are evaluated first, because the precedences of = and >= are both higher than the precedence of `And`. The `If...Then` statement then considers the combined condition

```
gender = "F" And age >= 65
```

This condition evaluates to true if and only if *both* simple conditions are true. When this combined condition is true, the `seniorFemales` count is incremented by `1`. However, if either or both simple conditions are false, the program skips the increment and proceeds to the statement following the `If...Then` statement. The readability of the preceding combined condition can be improved by adding redundant (i.e., unnecessary) parentheses:

```
(gender = "F") And (age >= 65)
```

Figure 6.17 illustrates the effect of using the `And` operator with two expressions. The table lists all four possible combinations of true and false values for *expression1* and *expression2*. Such tables often are called truth tables. Visual Basic evaluates to true or false expressions that include relational operators, equality operators and logical operators.

expression1	expression2	expression1 And expression2
False	False	False
False	True	False
True	False	False
True	True	True

Fig. 6.17 | Truth table for the logical `And` operator.

Logical `Or` *Operator*

Now let us consider the `Or` operator. Suppose we wish to ensure that either *or* both of two conditions are true before we choose a certain path of execution. We use the `Or` operator as in the following program segment:

```
If (semesterAverage >= 90 Or finalExam >= 90) Then
   Console.WriteLine("Student grade is A")
End If
```

This statement also contains two simple conditions. The condition `semesterAverage >= 90` is evaluated to determine whether the student deserves an "A" in the course because of an outstanding performance throughout the semester. The condition `finalExam >= 90` is evaluated to determine whether the student deserves an "A" in the course because of an outstanding performance on the final exam. The `If...Then` statement then considers the combined condition

```
(semesterAverage >= 90 Or finalExam >= 90)
```

and awards the student an "A" if either or both of the conditions are true. Note that the text `"Student grade is A"` is *always* printed, unless both of the conditions are false. Figure 6.18 provides a truth table for the `Or` operator. The `And` operator has a higher precedence than the `Or` operator.

expression1	expression2	expression1 Or expression2
False	False	False
False	True	True
True	False	True
True	True	True

Fig. 6.18 | Truth table for the logical `Or` operator.

Logical `AndAlso` *and* `OrElse` *Operators*

The logical AND operator with short-circuit evaluation (`AndAlso`) and the logical inclusive OR operator with short-circuit evaluation (`OrElse`) are similar to the `And` and `Or` operators, respectively, with one exception—an expression containing `AndAlso` or `OrElse` operators is evaluated only until its truth or falsity is known. For example, evaluation of the expression

```
(gender = "F" AndAlso age >= 65)
```

stops immediately if `gender` is not equal to `"F"` (i.e., the entire expression is false); the evaluation of the second expression is irrelevant because the first condition is false. Evaluation of the second condition occurs if and only if `gender` is equal to `"F"` (i.e., the entire expression could still be true if the condition `age >= 65` is true). This performance feature for the evaluation of `AndAlso` and `OrElse` expressions is called short-circuit evaluation.

Performance Tip 6.2

In expressions using operator `AndAlso`, if the separate conditions are independent of one another, place the condition most likely to be false as the leftmost condition. In expressions using operator `OrElse`, make the condition most likely to be true the leftmost condition. Each of these suggestions can reduce a program's execution time.

Normally, the `AndAlso` and `OrElse` operators can be used in place of `And` and `Or`. An exception to this rule occurs when the right operand of a condition produces a side effect such as a modification of a variable's value or a required method call, as in the following program segment:

```
Console.WriteLine("How old are you?")

If (gender = "F" And Console.ReadLine() >= 65) Then
   Console.WriteLine("You are a female senior citizen.")
End If
```

Here, the `And` operator guarantees that the condition `Console.ReadLine() >= 65` is evaluated, so `ReadLine` is called regardless of whether the overall expression is true or false. If operator `AndAlso` had been used, the call to `Console.ReadLine` might not be evaluated. It is better to write this code as two separate statements—a first that stores the result of `Console.ReadLine()` in a variable, and a second that uses the variable with either the operator `AndAlso` or the operator `And` in the condition.

Error-Prevention Tip 6.8

Avoid expressions with side effects in conditions, because side effects often cause subtle errors.

Logical `Xor` *Operator*

A condition containing the logical exclusive OR (`Xor`) operator is true if and only if one of its operands results in a true value and the other results in a false value. If both operands are true or both are false, the entire condition is false. Figure 6.19 presents a truth table for the logical exclusive OR operator (`Xor`). This operator always evaluates both of its operands (i.e., there is no short-circuit evaluation).

expression1	expression2	expression1 Xor expression2
False	False	False
False	True	True
True	False	True
True	True	False

Fig. 6.19 | Truth table for the logical exclusive OR (`Xor`) operator.

Logical `Not` *Operator*

The `Not` (logical negation) operator enables you to "reverse" the meaning of a condition. Unlike the logical operators `And`, `AndAlso`, `Or`, `OrElse` and `Xor`, which each combine two conditions (i.e., these are all binary operators), the logical negation operator is a unary operator, requiring only one operand. The logical negation operator is placed before a condition to choose a path of execution if the original condition (without the logical negation operator) is false. The logical negation operator is demonstrated by the following program segment:

```
If Not (grade = sentinelValue) Then
   Console.WriteLine("The next grade is " & grade)
End If
```

The parentheses around the condition `grade = sentinelValue` are necessary because the logical negation operator (`Not`) has a higher precedence than the equality operator. Figure 6.20 provides a truth table for the logical negation operator.

In most cases, you can avoid using logical negation by expressing the condition differently with relational or equality operators. For example, the preceding statement can be written as follows:

```
If grade <> sentinelValue Then
   Console.WriteLine("The next grade is " & grade)
End If
```

This flexibility helps you express conditions more naturally.

expression	Not expression
`False`	`True`
`True`	`False`

Fig. 6.20 | Truth table for operator `Not` (logical negation).

Logical Operators Example

Figure 6.21 demonstrates the logical operators by displaying their truth tables. Lines 6–10 demonstrate operator `And`; lines 13–17 demonstrate operator `Or`. The remainder of method `Main` demonstrates the `AndAlso`, `OrElse`, `Xor` and `Not` operators. We use keywords **`True`** and **`False`** in the program to specify values of the `Boolean` type. Note that when a `Boolean` value is concatenated to a `String`, Visual Basic concatenates the string `"False"` or `"True"` based on the `Boolean`'s value.

```
1  ' Fig. 6.21: LogicalOperators.vb
2  ' Using logical operators.
3  Module LogicalOperators
4     Sub Main()
5        ' display truth table for And
6        Console.WriteLine("And" & vbNewLine & _
7           "False And False: " & (False And False) & vbNewLine & _
8           "False And True: " & (False And True) & vbNewLine & _
9           "True And False: " & (True And False) & vbNewLine & _
10          "True And True: " & (True And True) & vbNewLine)
```

Fig. 6.21 | Logical operator truth tables. (Part 1 of 3.)

```

      ' display truth table for Or
      Console.WriteLine("Or" & vbNewLine & _
         "False Or False: " & (False Or False) & vbNewLine & _
         "False Or True: " & (False Or True) & vbNewLine & _
         "True Or False: " & (True Or False) & vbNewLine & _
         "True Or True: " & (True Or True) & vbNewLine)

      ' display truth table for AndAlso
      Console.WriteLine("AndAlso" & vbNewLine & _
         "False AndAlso False: " & (False AndAlso False) & vbNewLine & _
         "False AndAlso True: " & (False AndAlso True) & vbNewLine & _
         "True AndAlso False: " & (True AndAlso False) & vbNewLine & _
         "True AndAlso True: " & (True AndAlso True) & vbNewLine)

      ' display truth table for OrElse
      Console.WriteLine("OrElse" & vbNewLine & _
         "False OrElse False: " & (False OrElse False) & vbNewLine & _
         "False OrElse True: " & (False OrElse True) & vbNewLine & _
         "True OrElse False: " & (True OrElse False) & vbNewLine & _
         "True OrElse True: " & (True OrElse True) & vbNewLine)

      ' display truth table for Xor
      Console.WriteLine("Xor" & vbNewLine & _
         "False Xor False: " & (False Xor False) & vbNewLine & _
         "False Xor True: " & (False Xor True) & vbNewLine & _
         "True Xor False: " & (True Xor False) & vbNewLine & _
         "True Xor True: " & (True Xor True) & vbNewLine)

      ' display truth table for Not
      Console.WriteLine("Not" & vbNewLine & "Not False: " & _
         (Not False) & vbNewLine & "Not True: " & (Not True) & vbNewLine)
   End Sub ' Main
End Module ' LogicalOperators
```

```
And
False And False: False
False And True: False
True And False: False
True And True: True

Or
False Or False: False
False Or True: True
True Or False: True
True Or True: True

AndAlso
False AndAlso False: False
False AndAlso True: False
True AndAlso False: False
True AndAlso True: True
```

Fig. 6.21 | Logical operator truth tables. (Part 2 of 3.)

```
OrElse
False OrElse False: False
False OrElse True: True
True OrElse False: True
True OrElse True: True

Xor
False Xor False: False
False Xor True: True
True Xor False: True
True Xor True: False

Not
Not False: True
Not True: False
```

Fig. 6.21 | Logical operator truth tables. (Part 3 of 3.)

Summary of Operator Precedence

Figure 6.22 displays the precedence of the operators introduced so far. The operators are shown from top to bottom in decreasing order of precedence.

Operators	Type
`^`	exponentiation
`+ -`	unary plus and minus
`* /`	multiplicative operators
`\`	integer division
`Mod`	modulus
`+ -`	additive operators
`&`	concatenation
`< <= > >= = <>`	relational and equality
`Not`	logical NOT
`And AndAlso`	logical AND
`Or OrElse`	logical inclusive OR
`Xor`	logical exclusive OR
`= += -= *= /= \= ^= &=`	assignment

Fig. 6.22 | Precedence of the operators discussed so far.

6.11 (Optional) Software Engineering Case Study: Identifying Objects' States and Activities in the ATM System

In Section 5.16, we identified many of the class attributes needed to implement the ATM system and added them to a class diagram (Fig. 5.32). In this section, we show how these attributes represent an object's state. We identify some key states that our objects may occupy and discuss how objects change state in response to various events occurring in the system. We also discuss the workflow, or activities, that objects perform in the ATM system. We present the activities of the `BalanceInquiry` and `Withdrawal` transaction objects.

State Machine Diagrams

Each object in a system goes through a series of discrete states. An object's current state is indicated by the values of the object's attributes at that time. State machine diagrams model key states of an object and show under what circumstances the object changes state. Unlike the class diagrams presented in earlier case study sections, which focused primarily on the system's structure, state machine diagrams model some of the system's behavior.

Figure 6.23 is a simple state machine diagram that models some of the states of an `ATM` object. The UML represents each state in a state machine diagram as a rounded rectangle with the name of the state placed inside it. A solid circle with an attached stick arrowhead designates the initial state. Recall that we modeled this state information as the `Boolean` attribute `userAuthenticated` in the class diagram of Fig. 5.32. This attribute is initialized to `False`, or the "User not authenticated" state, according to the state machine diagram.

The arrows with stick arrowheads indicate transitions between states. An object can transition from one state to another in response to various events that occur in the system. The name or description of the event that causes a transition is written near the line that corresponds to the transition. For example, the `ATM` object changes from the "User not authenticated" state to the "User authenticated" state after the bank database authenticates the user. Recall from the requirements document that the database authenticates a user by comparing the account number and PIN entered by the user with those of the corresponding account in the database. If the database indicates that the user has entered a valid account number and the correct PIN, the `ATM` object transitions to the "User authenticated" state and changes its `userAuthenticated` attribute to a value of `True`. When the user exits the system by choosing the **Exit** option from the main menu, the `ATM` object returns to the "User not authenticated" state in preparation for the next ATM user.

Software Engineering Observation 6.1

Software designers do not generally create state machine diagrams showing every possible state and state transition for all attributes—there are simply too many of them. State machine diagrams typically show only the most important or complex states and state transitions.

Fig. 6.23 | State machine diagram for some of the states of the `ATM` object.

Activity Diagrams

Like a state machine diagram, an activity diagram models aspects of system behavior. Unlike a state machine diagram, an activity diagram models an object's workflow (sequence of tasks) during program execution. An activity diagram models the actions the object will perform and in what order. Recall that we used UML activity diagrams to illustrate the flow of control for the control statements presented in Chapters 5 and this chapter.

The activity diagram in Fig. 6.24 models the actions involved in executing a `BalanceInquiry` transaction. We assume that a `BalanceInquiry` object has already been initialized and assigned a valid account number (that of the current user), so the object knows which balance to retrieve. The diagram includes the actions that occur after the user selects a balance inquiry from the main menu and before the ATM returns the user to the main menu—a `BalanceInquiry` object does not perform or initiate these actions, so we do not model them here. The diagram begins with retrieving the available balance of the user's account from the database. Next, the `BalanceInquiry` retrieves the total balance of the account. Finally, the transaction displays the balances on the screen.

The UML represents an action in an activity diagram as an action state modeled by a rectangle with its left and right sides replaced by arcs curving outward. Each action state contains an action expression—for example, "get available balance of user's account from database"—that specifies an action to be performed. An arrow with a stick arrowhead connects two action states, indicating the order in which the actions represented by the action states occur. The solid circle (at the top of Fig. 6.24) represents the activity's initial state—the beginning of the workflow before the object performs the modeled actions. In this case, the transaction first executes the "get available balance of user's account from database" action expression. Second, the transaction retrieves the total balance. Finally, the transaction displays both balances on the screen. The solid circle enclosed in an open circle (at the bottom of Fig. 6.24) represents the final state—the end of the workflow after the object performs the modeled actions.

Figure 6.25 shows a more complex activity diagram for a `Withdrawal` transaction. We assume that a `Withdrawal` object has been assigned a valid account number. We do not model the user selecting a withdrawal from the main menu or the ATM returning the user to the main menu, because these are not actions performed by a `Withdrawal` object. The transaction first displays a menu of standard withdrawal amounts (Fig. 3.37) and an option to cancel the transaction. The transaction then inputs a menu selection from the user. The activity flow now arrives at a decision symbol to determine the next action based

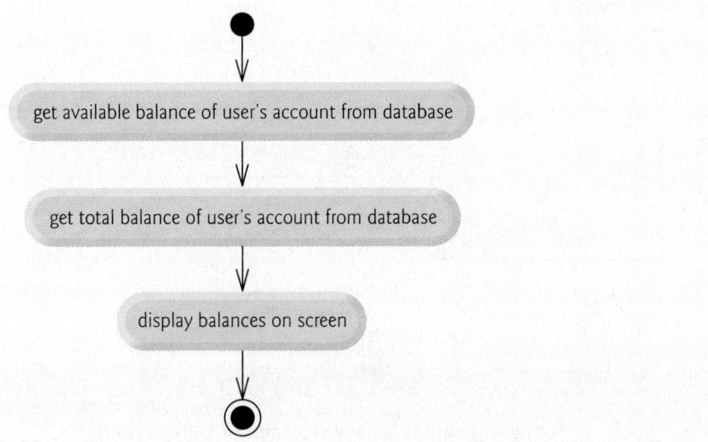

Fig. 6.24 | Activity diagram for a `BalanceInquiry` transaction.

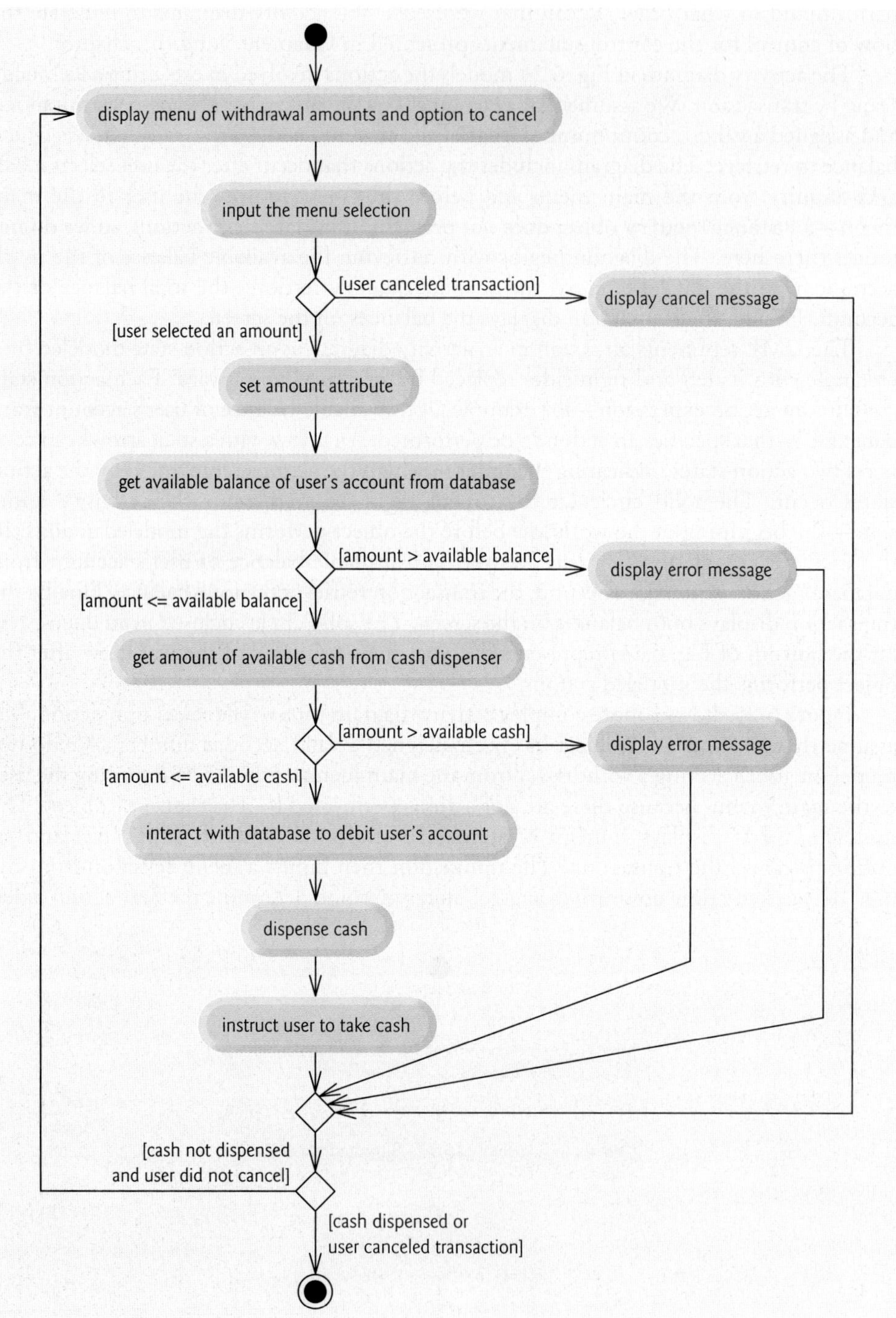

Fig. 6.25 | Activity diagram for a `Withdrawal` transaction.

on the associated guard conditions. If the user cancels the transaction, the system displays an appropriate message and the cancellation flow reaches a merge symbol (at the bottom of the activity diagram), where this activity flow joins the transaction's other possible activity flows (which we discuss shortly). Note that a merge can have any number of incoming transition arrows, but only one outgoing transition arrow. The decision at the bottom of the diagram determines whether the transaction should repeat from the beginning. When the user has canceled the transaction, the guard condition "cash dispensed or user canceled transaction" is true, so control transitions to the activity's final state.

If the user selects a withdrawal amount from the menu, `amount` (an attribute of class `Withdrawal` originally modeled in Fig. 5.32) is set to the value chosen by the user. The transaction next gets the available balance of the user's account (i.e., the `availableBalance` attribute of the user's `Account` object) from the database. The activity flow then arrives at another decision. If the requested withdrawal amount exceeds the user's available balance, the system displays an error message informing the user of the problem. Control then merges with the other activity flows before reaching the decision at the bottom of the diagram. The guard decision "cash not dispensed and user did not cancel" is true, so the activity flow returns to the top of the diagram, and the transaction prompts the user to input a new amount.

If the requested withdrawal amount is less than or equal to the user's available balance, the transaction tests whether the cash dispenser has enough cash to satisfy the request. If it does not, the transaction displays an appropriate error message and passes through the merge before reaching the final decision. Cash was not dispensed, so the activity flow returns to the beginning of the activity diagram, and the transaction prompts the user to choose a new amount. If sufficient cash is available, the transaction interacts with the database to debit the user's account by the withdrawal amount (i.e., subtract the amount from both the `availableBalance` and `totalBalance` attributes of the user's `Account` object). The transaction then dispenses the desired amount of cash and instructs the user to take the cash. The main flow of activity next merges with the two error flows and the cancellation flow. In this case, cash was dispensed, so the activity flow reaches the final state.

We have taken the first steps in modeling the behavior of the ATM system and have shown how an object's attributes affect the object's activities. In Section 7.20, we investigate the operations of our classes to create a more complete model of the system's behavior.

Software Engineering Case Study Self-Review Exercises

6.1 State whether the following statement is *true* or *false*, and if *false*, explain why: State machine diagrams model structural aspects of a system.

6.2 An activity diagram models the __________ that an object performs and the order in which it performs them.

a) actions
b) attributes
c) states
d) state transitions

6.3 Based on the requirements document, create an activity diagram for a deposit transaction.

Answers to Software Engineering Case Study Self-Review Exercises

6.1 False. State machine diagrams model some of the behavior of a system.

6.2 a.

6.3 Figure 6.26 presents an activity diagram for a `Deposit` transaction. The diagram models the actions that occur after the user chooses the deposit option from the main menu and before the ATM returns the user to the main menu. Recall that part of receiving a deposit amount from the user involves converting an integer number of cents to a dollar amount. Also recall that crediting an account by the deposit amount involves increasing only the `totalBalance` attribute of the user's `Account` object. The bank updates the `availableBalance` attribute of the user's `Account` object only after confirming the amount of cash in the deposit envelope and after the enclosed checks clear—this occurs independently of the ATM system.

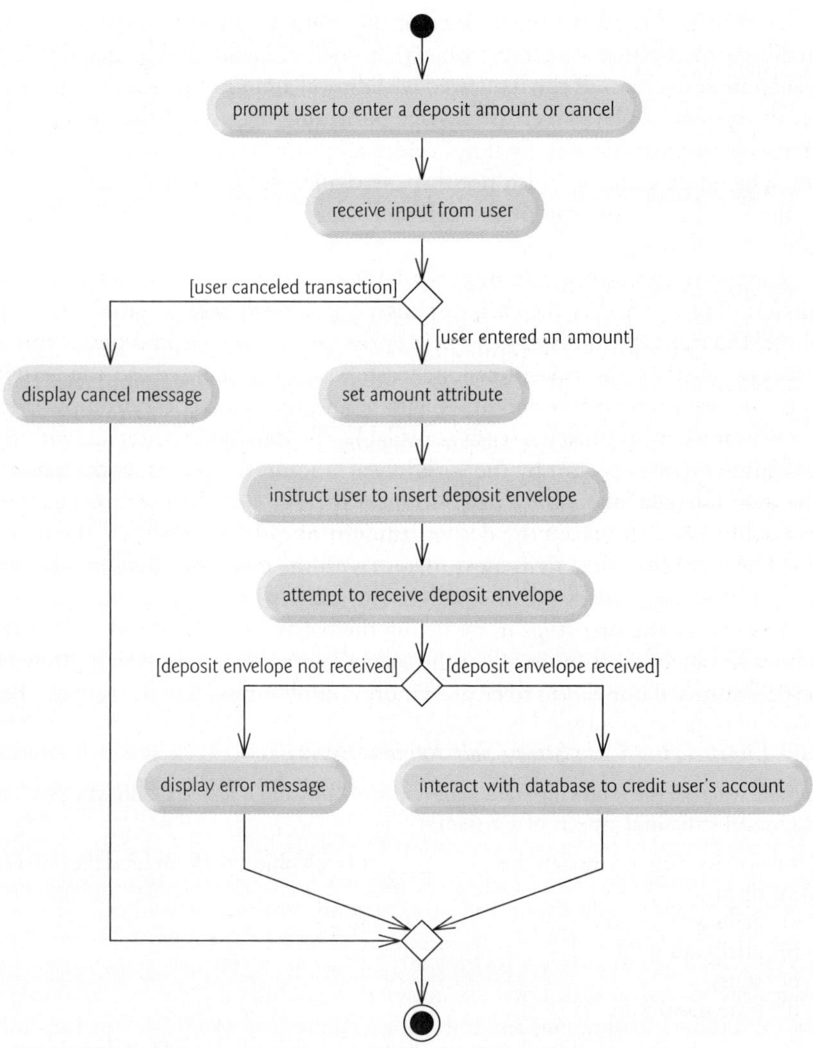

Fig. 6.26 | Activity diagram for a `Deposit` transaction.

6.12 Wrap-Up

In this chapter, we completed our introduction to the control statements that enable you to control the flow of execution. Chapter 5 discussed the `If...Then`, `If...Then...Else`, `While...End While`, `Do While...Loop` and `Do Until...Loop` statements. This chapter demonstrated the `For...Next`, `Select...Case`, `Do...Loop While` and `Do...Loop Until` statements. We have shown that any algorithm can be developed using combinations of the sequence structure (i.e., statements listed in the order in which they are to execute), the three types of selection statements—`If...Then`, `If...Then...Else` and `Select...Case`—and the seven types of repetition statements—`While...End While`, `Do While...Loop`, `Do Until...Loop`, `Do...Loop While`, `Do...Loop Until`, `For...Next` and `For Each...Next` (which we discuss in Chapter 8). In Chapters 5 and 6, we discussed how you can combine these building blocks to utilize proven program-construction and problem-solving techniques. We demonstrated how to alter the flow of program control using the various `Exit` and `Continue` statements. We introduced the logical operators, which enable you to use more complex conditional expressions in control statements. In Chapter 7, we examine methods in greater depth. So far you have learned how to create methods in classes, and a `Main` method in a module. Chapter 7 introduces the different types of methods, including how and when to use each of them. You will learn how to use methods to organize a complex object-oriented program into small, manageable pieces.

Summary

Section 6.2 Essentials of Counter-Controlled Repetition

- Counter-controlled repetition requires the name of a control variable, the initial value of the control variable, the increment (or decrement) by which the control variable is modified each time through the loop and the condition that tests for the final value of the control variable.

Section 6.3 `For...Next` Repetition Statement

- The `For...Next` repetition statement specifies the counter-controlled repetition details in a single line of code.
- The `To` keyword is required in the `For...Next` statement and is followed by the final value of the control variable.
- The optional `Step` keyword specifies the increment (or decrement). If `Step` and the value following it are omitted, the increment defaults to `1` (`-1` if the final value is less than the initial value).
- The required `Next` keyword marks the end of the `For...Next` repetition statement.
- The first line of the `For...Next` statement sometimes is called the `For...Next` header, which specifies each of the items needed for counter-controlled repetition with a control variable.
- The general form of the `For...Next` statement is

```
For initialization To finalValue Step increment
    statement
Next
```

  where the *initialization* expression initializes the loop's control variable, *finalValue* determines whether the loop should continue executing (if the control variable is less than or equal to *finalValue*) and *increment* specifies the amount the control variable should be incremented each time through the loop.

- If the *initialization* expression in the `For...Next` statement header declares the control variable, the control variable can be used only in the body of the `For...Next` statement—the control variable will be unknown outside the statement.
- If the control variable is declared before the `For...Next` statement, it can be used outside the statement.
- The starting value, ending value and increment portions of a `For...Next` statement can contain arithmetic expressions.
- The Visual Basic 2008 compiler provides a new feature—called local type inference—that enables it to infer a local variable's type based on the context in which the variable is initialized.
- You can use local type inference with control variables in the header of a For...Next statement.

Section 6.4 Examples Using the `For...Next` Statement

- Method `MessageBox.Show` can be used to specify a message to be displayed in a message dialog, as well as the icon and button(s) displayed in the dialog.
- The buttons in a message dialog are specified using the `MessageBoxButtons` constants.
- The icon to be displayed in a message dialog is specified using the `MessageBoxIcon` constants.
- Type `Decimal` is used for monetary calculations.
- Using floating-point types, such as `Single` or `Double`, to represent dollar amounts (assuming that dollar amounts are displayed with two digits to the right of the decimal point) can cause errors.
- Method `Format` of class `String` takes a formatted string and the values to be formatted as arguments and returns the resulting text with the formatting applied.
- The `C` (for "currency") format specifier indicates that its corresponding value should be displayed in monetary format.

Section 6.5 `GradeBook` Case Study: `Select...Case` Multiple-Selection Statement

- Occasionally, an algorithm contains a series of decisions in which the algorithm tests a variable or expression separately for each value that the variable or expression might assume. The algorithm then takes different actions based on those values. The `Select...Case` multiple-selection statement handles such decision making.
- The expression following the keywords `Select Case` is called the controlling expression. The controlling expression is compared sequentially with each `Case`. If a matching `Case` is found, the code in the `Case` executes, then program control proceeds to the first statement after the `Select...Case` statement.
- A `Case` statement can use the `To` keyword to specify a range of values to be compared.
- If no match occurs between the controlling expression's value and a `Case` label, the optional `Case Else` executes. `Case Else` commonly is used to deal with invalid input. When employed, the `Case Else` must be the last `Case`.
- The required `End Select` keywords terminate the `Select...Case` statement.
- `Case` statements also can use relational operators to determine whether the controlling expression satisfies a condition. For example

```
Case Is < 0
```

  uses keyword `Is` along with the relational operator, <, to test for values less than 0.
- Methods declared `Private` can be called only by other members of the same class. Such `Private` methods are commonly referred to as utility methods or helper methods, because they are used to support the operation of those members.

- The `With` statement allows you to access an object's members in a block of code without specifying the name of the object before the dot separator. You often employ the `With` statement when there are many references to an object's members in a relatively small region of code.

Section 6.6 `Do...Loop While` *Repetition Statement*

- The `Do...Loop While` statement is similar to the `Do While...Loop` statement, ecvept that the loop-continuation condition is tested *after* the loop body is performed; therefore, in a `Do...Loop While` statement, the loop body is always executed at least once.

Section 6.7 `Do...Loop Until` *Repetition Statement*

- The `Do...Loop Until` repetition statement is similar to the `Do Until...Loop` statement, except that the loop-termination condition is tested after the loop body is performed; therefore, the loop body executes at least once.

Section 6.8 Using `Exit` *in Repetition Statements*

- The `Exit Do` statement can be executed in a `Do While...Loop`, `Do...Loop While`, `Do Until...Loop` or `Do...Loop Until` statement, to cause the program to exit immediately from that repetition statement.
- The `Exit For` and `Exit While` statements cause immediate exit from `For...Next` and `While...End While` loops, respectively.

Section 6.9 Using `Continue` *in Repetition Statements*

- The `Continue` statement skips the remaining statements in the loop body of a repetition statement and causes control to proceed to the next iteration of the loop.
- The `Continue Do` statement can be executed in a `Do While...Loop`, `Do...Loop While`, `Do Until...Loop` or `Do...Loop Until` statement, to cause the program to skip the remainder of the current iteration of that repetition statement.
- The `Continue For` and `Continue While` statements cause the program to skip the remainder of the current iteration of `For...Next` and `While...End While` loops, respectively.
- Unlike the `Exit` statement, the `Continue` statement is used to alter program control only in repetition statements.
- When `Continue For` is encountered in a `For...Next` statement, execution continues with the statement's increment expression, then the program evaluates the loop-continuation test. When `Continue` is used in other repetition statements, the program evaluates the loop-continuation (or loop-termination) test immediately after the `Continue` statement executes. If a control variable's increment occurs in the loop after the `Continue` statement, the increment is skipped.
- The `Exit` and `Continue` statements can be used in nested control statements. For instance, `Exit For` or `Continue For` can be used in a `While` statement, as long as the `While` statement is itself located in a `For...Next` statement.

Section 6.10 Logical Operators

- To handle multiple conditions, Visual Basic provides logical operators that can be used to form complex conditions by combining simple ones.
- The logical `And` operator can be used to ensure that two conditions are *both* true in a program before a certain path of execution is chosen. The complex condition evaluates to true *if and only if* both of the simple conditions are true.
- The logical `Or` operator can be used to ensure that either *or* both of two conditions are true before we choose a certain path of execution. The complex condition evaluates to true except when both of the conditions are false.

- The And operator has a higher precedence than the Or operator.
- The operators AndAlso and OrElse are similar to the And and Or operators, with one exception—an expression containing AndAlso or OrElse operators is evaluated only until its truth or falsity is known. Evaluation of the second condition occurs only as necessary to determine the final result of the expression—this performance feature is called short-circuit evaluation.
- Normally, the AndAlso and OrElse operators can be used in place of And and Or. An exception to this rule occurs when the right operand of a condition produces a side effect (such as a modification of a variable's value or a required method call).
- A condition containing the logical exclusive OR (Xor) operator is true if and only if one of its operands results in a true value and the other results in a false value. If both operands are true or both are false, the entire condition is false.
- The Not operator enables you to "reverse" the meaning of a condition.

Terminology

And operator
AndAlso operator
C format specifier
Case Else statement
Case statement
Continue Do statement
Continue For statement
Continue statement
Continue While statement
control variable name
controlling expression of a Select...Case
Decimal primitive type
decrement of a control variable
Do...Loop Until repetition statement
Do...Loop While repetition statement
Exit Do statement
Exit For statement
Exit Property statement
Exit Select statement
Exit statement
Exit While statement
False keyword
final state
final value of a control variable
For...Next header
For...Next repetition statement
Format method of class String
helper method
increment of a control variable
initial value of a control variable
Is keyword
local type inference
logical operator
MessageBoxButtons constants
MessageBoxIcon constants
name of a control variable
Not operator
Or operator
OrElse operator
scope
Select...Case multiple-selection statement
short-circuit evaluation
side effect
simple condition
Step keyword
To keyword
True keyword
truth table
utility method
With statement
With statement block
Xor (exclusive OR) operator

Self-Review Exercises

6.1 State whether each of the following is *true* or *false*. If *false*, explain why.
a) The Case Else is required in the Select...Case selection statement.
b) The expression x > y And a < b is true if either x > y is true or a < b is true.
c) An expression containing the Or operator is true if either or both of its operands are true.
d) The expression x <= y AndAlso y > 4 is true if x is less than or equal to y and y is greater than 4.

e) Logical operator `Or` performs short-circuit evaluation.
f) A `While...End While` statement with the header

```
While (x > 10 And x < 100)
```

iterates while `10 < x < 100`.
g) The `Exit Do`, `Exit For` and `Exit While` statements, when executed in a repetition statement, cause immediate exit from only the current iteration of the repetition statement.
h) The `Do...Loop While` statement tests the loop-continuation condition before the loop body is performed.
i) The `Or` operator has a higher precedence than the `And` operator.

6.2 Fill in the blanks in each of the following statements:
a) Keyword ________ is optional in a `For...Next` header when the control variable's increment is one.
b) Monetary values should be stored in variables of type ________.
c) A `Case` that handles all values greater than a specified value must precede the > operator with the ________ keyword.
d) In a `For...Next` statement, incrementing occurs ________ the body of the statement is performed.
e) Placing expressions whose values do not change inside ________ statements can lead to poor performance.
f) In a `Do...Loop While` repetition statement, the body of the loop is executed ________.
g) The expression following the keywords `Select Case` is called the ________.

6.3 Write a statement or a set of statements to accomplish each of the following:
a) Sum the odd integers between `1` and `99` using a `For...Next` statement. Assume that the `Integer` variables `sum` and `count` have been declared.
b) Write a statement that exits a `While` loop.
c) Print the integers from `1` to `20`, using a `Do...Loop While` loop and the counter variable `x`. Assume that the variable `x` has been declared but not initialized. Print only five integers per line. [*Hint:* Use the calculation `x Mod 5`. When the value of this is `0`, print a carriage return; otherwise, print a tab character. Call `Console.WriteLine` to output the carriage return and call `Console.Write(vbTab)` to output the tab character.]
d) Repeat part c, using a `For...Next` statement.

Answers to Self-Review Exercises

6.1 a) False. The `Case Else` is optional. b) False. Both of the simple conditions must be true for the entire expression to be true. c) True. d) True. e) False. Logical operator `Or` always evaluates both of its operands. f) True. g) False. The `Exit Do`, `Exit For` and `Exit While` statements, when executed in a repetition statement, cause immediate exit from the repetition statement. The `Continue Do`, `Continue For` and `Continue While` statements, when executed in a repetition statement, cause immediate exit from the current iteration of the repetition statement. h) False. The `Do...Loop While` statement tests the loop-continuation condition after the loop body is performed. i) False. The `And` operator has higher precedence than the `Or` operator.

6.2 a) `Step`. b) `Decimal`. c) `Is`. d) after. e) repetition. f) at least once. g) controlling expression.

6.3 a)

```
sum = 0
For count = 1 To 99 Step 2
   sum += count
Next
```

b)

```
Exit While
```

c)
```
x = 1
Do
   Console.Write(x)
   If x Mod 5 = 0 Then
      Console.WriteLine()
   Else
      Console.Write(vbTab)
   End If
   x += 1
Loop While x <= 20
```

or

```
x = 1
Do
   If x Mod 5 = 0 Then
      Console.WriteLine(x)
   Else
      Console.Write(x & vbTab)
   End If
   x += 1
Loop While x <= 20
```

d)
```
For x = 1 To 20
   Console.Write(x)

   If x Mod 5 = 0 Then
      Console.WriteLine()
   Else
      Console.Write(vbTab)
   End If
Next
```

or

```
For x = 1 To 20
   If x Mod 5 = 0 Then
      Console.WriteLine(x)
   Else
      Console.Write(x & vbTab)
   End If
Next
```

Exercises

6.4 A mail-order house sells five products whose retail prices are as follows: Product 1, $2.98; product 2, $4.50; product 3, $9.98; product 4, $4.49 and product 5, $6.87. Write an application that reads a series of pairs of numbers as follows:

a) product number;
b) quantity sold.

Your program should use a `Select...Case` statement to determine the retail price for each product. It should calculate and display the total retail value of all products sold. Use a sentinel-controlled loop to determine when the program should stop looping and display the final results.

6.5 Modify the compound-interest application of Fig. 6.8 to repeat its steps for interest rates of 5, 6, 7, 8, 9 and 10%. Use a `For...Next` loop to vary the interest rate. Display a `MessageBox` for each interest-rate value.

6.6 Modify the application in Fig. 6.8 to use only integers to calculate the compound interest. [*Hint:* Treat all monetary amounts as integral numbers of pennies. Then "break" the result into its dollars portion and cents portion by using the division and modulus operators, respectively. Insert a period between the dollars and cents portions.]

6.7 The *factorial* method is used frequently in probability problems. The factorial of a positive integer *n* (written *n*! and pronounced "n factorial") is equal to the product of the positive integers from 1 to *n*. Even for relatively small values of *n*, the factorial method yields extremely large numbers. For instance, when *n* is 13, *n*! is 6227020800—a number too large to be represented with type `Integer` (a 32-bit integer value). To calculate the factorials of large values of *n*, type `Long` (a 64-bit integer value) must be used. Write a program that evaluates the factorials of the integers from 1 to 20 using type `Long`—larger factorial values cannot be represented with `Long`. Display the results in a two-column output table. [*Hint:* Create a Windows `Forms` application, use `Labels` as the columns and the `vbNewLine` constant to line up the rows. Create an event handler as you did in Section 5.15 to append text to the `Label`'s `Text` properties. To make the output clearer, set each `Label`'s `BorderStyle` property to `Fixed3D`. Place the code that generates the output in the `Form`'s `Load` event handler, which you can create by double clicking the `Form` in **Design** view.] The first column should display the *n* values (1–20). The second column should display *n*!.

6.8 Write a program that prints a table of the binary, octal, and hexadecimal equivalents of the decimal numbers in the range 1–255. If you are not familiar with these number systems, read Appendix C, Number Systems, first.

6.9 (*Pythagorean Triples*) Some right triangles have sides that are all integers. A set of three integer values for the sides of a right triangle is called a Pythagorean triple. These three sides must satisfy the relationship that the sum of the squares of the two sides is equal to the square of the hypotenuse. Write a program to find all Pythagorean triples for `side1`, `side2` and `hypotenuse`, none larger than 30. Use a triple-nested `For...Next` loop that tries all possibilities. This is an example of "brute force" computing.

6.10 Write a program that displays the following patterns separately, one below the other. Use `For...Next` loops to generate the patterns. All asterisks (*) should be printed by a single statement of the form `Console.Write("*")` (this causes the asterisks to print side by side). A statement of the form `Console.WriteLine()` can be used to position to the next line, and a statement of the form `Console.WriteLine(" ")` can be used to display spaces for the last two patterns. There should be no other output statements in the program. [*Hint:* The last two patterns require that each line begin with an appropriate number of blanks.] Maximize your use of repetition (with nested `For...Next` statements) and minimize the number of output statements.

```
(a)           (b)           (c)           (d)
*             **********    **********             *
**            *********      *********            **
***           ********        ********           ***
****          *******          *******          ****
*****         ******            ******         *****
******        *****              *****        ******
*******       ****                ****       *******
********      ***                  ***      ********
*********     **                    **     *********
**********    *                      *    **********
```

6.11 Modify Exercise 6.10 to combine your code from the four separate triangles of asterisks into a single program that prints all four patterns side by side, making clever use of nested `For...Next` loops.

6.12 Write a program that prints the following diamond shape. You may use output statements that print a single asterisk (*), a single space or a single carriage return. Maximize your use of repetition (with nested `For...Next` statements) and minimize the number of output statements.

```
    *
   ***
  *****
 *******
*********
 *******
  *****
   ***
    *
```

6.13 Modify the program you wrote in Exercise 6.12 to read an odd number in the range from 1 to 19 to specify the number of rows in the diamond. Your program should then display a diamond of the appropriate size. Use a `Do...Loop Until` statement to validate user input.

7

Methods: A Deeper Look

The greatest invention of the nineteenth century was the invention of the method of invention.
—Alfred North Whitehead

Form ever follows function.
—Louis Henri Sullivan

Call me Ishmael.
—Herman Melville

When you call me that, smile!
—Owen Wister

O! call back yesterday, bid time return.
—William Shakespeare

Answer me in one word.
—William Shakespeare

There is a point at which methods devour themselves.
—Frantz Fanon

OBJECTIVES

In this chapter you'll learn:

- To construct programs modularly from methods.
- That `Shared` methods are associated with a class rather than a specific instance of the class.
- To use common `Math` methods from the Framework Class Library.
- To create new methods.
- The mechanisms used to pass information between methods.
- Simulation techniques that employ random-number generation.
- How the visibility of identifiers is limited to specific regions of programs.
- To write and use recursive methods (methods that call themselves).

Outline

7.1 Introduction

Most computer programs that solve real-world problems are much larger than the programs presented in this book's first few chapters. Experience has shown that the best way to develop and maintain a large program is to construct it from small, simple pieces—a technique called divide and conquer. In Chapter 3 we introduced methods. In this chapter we study methods in greater depth. We emphasize how to declare and use methods to facilitate the design, implementation, operation and maintenance of large programs.

You will see that certain methods, called `Shared` methods, can be called without the need for an object of the class to exist. You will learn how to declare a method with more than one parameter. You will also learn how Visual Basic keeps track of which method is currently executing, how local variables of methods are maintained in memory and how a method knows where to return after it finishes executing.

We will take a brief diversion into simulation techniques with random-number generation and develop a version of the casino dice game called craps that will use most of the programming techniques you have learned to this point in the book. In addition, we will introduce two techniques for declaring constants in your programs.

You will learn that applications can have more than one method of the same name. This technique, called overloading, is used for convenience and clarity when implementing methods that perform similar tasks using different types or numbers of arguments. In certain situations, you can replace a series of overloaded method declarations with a single "generic" method—we study this powerful code-reuse capability in Chapter 9, Introduction to LINQ and Generic Collections and Chapter 24, Data Structures and Generic Collections.

7.2 Modules, Classes and Methods

Programs consist of many pieces, including modules and classes. These modules and classes are composed of smaller pieces called methods, instance variables and properties. You combine new modules and classes with "prepackaged" classes available in the .NET Framework Class Library and in various other class libraries. Related classes are typically grouped into namespaces (and compiled into library files) so that they can be imported into programs and reused. You will learn how to package your own classes into class libraries in Section 10.14. The .NET Framework Class Library provides a rich collection of classes and methods for performing common mathematical calculations (Chapter 3), error checking (Chapter 13), building sophisticated GUI applications (Chapters 14–15), graphics (Chapter 16), string and character manipulations (Chapter 17), input/output operations (Chapter 18), XML processing (Chapter 19), database manipulations (Chapter 20), creating applications for the web (Chapters 21–22) and many other useful operations. This framework makes your job easier, because the methods provide many of the capabilities you need. In earlier chapters, we introduced classes such as `Console`, which provides methods for inputting and outputting data and `MessageBox`, used to display message dialogs.

Software Engineering Observation 7.1

When possible, use .NET Framework classes and methods instead of writing new classes and methods. This reduces program-development time and can prevent the introduction of errors.

Performance Tip 7.1

.NET Framework Class Library methods are written to perform efficiently.

You can create your own classes and methods to meet the unique requirements of a particular application. Two types of methods exist: **subroutines** and **functions**. We discuss the differences between them shortly. Throughout this book, unless otherwise noted, the term "method" refers to both subroutines and functions.

You write methods to define specific tasks that a program may use one or more times during its execution. Although the same method can be executed from multiple points in a program, the actual statements that define the method are written only once.

Let's briefly review method basics. A method is invoked (i.e., made to perform its designated task) by a method call. The method call specifies the method name and provides information (as arguments) that the **callee** (i.e, the method being called) requires to do its job. When the method completes its task, it returns control to the caller (i.e., the calling method). In some cases, the method also returns a result to the caller. The code that calls a method is also sometimes known as the client code—as it is a client of the method. A common analogy for calling methods and returning results is the hierarchical form of management. A boss (the caller) asks a worker (the callee) to perform a task and return (i.e., report) the results when the task is done. The boss does not need to know how the worker performs the designated task. The worker might call other workers—the boss would be unaware of this. This **hiding of implementation details** promotes good software engineering. Figure 7.1 depicts a `Boss` method communicating with worker methods `Worker1`, `Worker2` and `Worker3` in a hierarchical manner. Note that in this example `Worker1` also acts as a "boss" method to `Worker4` and `Worker5`.

There are several motivations for dividing code into methods. First, the divide-and-conquer approach makes program development more manageable. Another motivation is software reusability—the ability to use existing methods as building blocks for new programs. When proper naming and definition conventions are applied, programs can be created from standardized pieces that accomplish specific tasks, to minimize the need for customized code. A third motivation is to avoid repeating code in a program—when code is packaged as a method, the code can be executed from various points in a program simply by calling the method.

Software Engineering Observation 7.2

To promote reusability, the capabilities of each method should be limited to the performance of a single, well-defined task, and the name of the method should express that task effectively.

Software Engineering Observation 7.3

If you cannot choose a concise method name that expresses the task performed by a method, the method could be attempting to perform too many diverse tasks. Consider dividing such a method into several smaller methods.

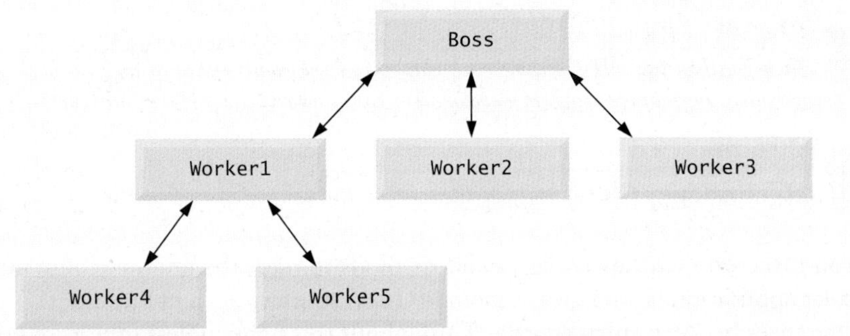

Fig. 7.1 | Hierarchical boss-method/worker-method relationship.

7.3 Subroutines: Methods That Do Not Return a Value

The programs presented earlier in the book each contain at least one method declaration that calls .NET Framework Class Library methods (such as `Console.WriteLine`) to accomplish the program's tasks. All of the methods that you have defined so far, such as `DisplayMessage` in class `GradeBook`, are known as subroutines—methods that perform tasks but do not return a value. Functions are methods that do return a value to the calling method. An example of a function that you have seen is `Console.ReadLine`, which returns to the caller the data entered by the user at the keyboard. We show how to declare functions in Section 7.4.

Consider the console application in Fig. 7.2, which uses a subroutine (invoked from the application's `Main` method) to print a worker's payment information.

The program contains two method declarations. Lines 4–10 define method `Main`, the subroutine that executes when the console application is loaded. Lines 13–16 define method `PrintPay`, a subroutine that executes when it is called from method `Main`.

`Main` makes four calls (lines 6–9) to subroutine `PrintPay`, causing `PrintPay` to execute four times. Although the method arguments in this example are constants, recall that arguments can also be variables or expressions. For example, the statement

```
PrintPay(employeeExtraHours, employeeWage * 1.5)
```

could be used to display payment information for an employee who is being paid time-and-a-half for working overtime—this statement calculates only the overtime portion of the person's pay.

When `Main` calls `PrintPay`, the program makes a copy of the value of each argument (e.g., `40` and `10.5` in line 6), and program control transfers to the first line of method `PrintPay`. Method `PrintPay` receives the copied values and stores them in the parameters `hours` and `wage`. Then `PrintPay` calculates `hours * wage` and displays the result, using the currency format (line 15). When the `End Sub` statement (line 16) is encountered, control is returned to the next statement in the calling method, `Main`.

The first line of method `PrintPay` (line 13) shows that `PrintPay` declares a `Double` parameter `hours` and a `Decimal` parameter `wage`. These parameters hold the values passed to `PrintPay` so that they can be accessed within this method. Note that the entire declaration of method `PrintPay` appears within the body of module `Payment`.

```
1  ' Fig. 7.2: Payment.vb
2  ' Subroutine that prints payment information.
3  Module Payment
4     Sub Main()
5        ' call subroutine PrintPay 4 times
6        PrintPay(40, 10.5)
7        PrintPay(38, 21.75)
8        PrintPay(20, 13)
9        PrintPay(30, 14)
10    End Sub ' Main
11
12    ' print dollar amount earned in console window
13    Sub PrintPay(ByVal hours As Double, ByVal wage As Decimal)
14       ' pay = hours * wage
15       Console.WriteLine("The payment is {0:C}", hours * wage)
16    End Sub ' PrintPay
17 End Module ' Payment
```

```
The payment is $420.00
The payment is $826.50
The payment is $260.00
The payment is $420.00
```

Fig. 7.2 | Subroutine for printing payment information.

Subroutine Declarations

The format of a subroutine declaration is

```
Sub method-name(parameter-list)
    declarations and statements
End Sub
```

Subroutines in previous versions of Visual Basic were referred to as **Sub procedures** because of the use of keyword `Sub`. The *parameter-list* is a comma-separated list in which the subroutine declares each parameter variable's type and name. There must be one argument in the method call for each parameter in the method header (we will see an exception to this when we study `Optional` parameters in Section 7.18). The type of each argument must be consistent with its corresponding parameter's type; i.e., Visual Basic must be able to implicitly convert the value of the argument to a value of the parameter's type. For example, a parameter of type `Double` could receive a value of 7.35, 22 or –0.03546, but not `"hello"`, because a `Double` variable cannot contain a `String`. In Section 7.9 we discuss this issue in detail. If a method does not receive any values, the parameter list is empty (i.e., the method name is followed by an empty set of parentheses).

Common Programming Error 7.1

Declaring a variable in the method's body with the same name as a parameter variable in the method header is a compilation error.

Error-Prevention Tip 7.1

Although it is allowable, an argument passed to a method should not have the same name as the corresponding parameter name in the method declaration. This prevents ambiguity that could lead to logic errors.

The declarations and statements in the method declaration form the method body. The method body contains code that performs actions, generally by manipulating or processing the method's parameters. The body of a method declared with `Sub` must be terminated with keywords `End Sub`. The method body is also referred to as a **block**. A block is a group of declarations and executable statements.

Control returns to the next statement in the caller when execution reaches the `End Sub` statement in the called method.

Software Engineering Observation 7.4

Method names tend to be verbs because methods typically perform actions. By convention, method names begin with an uppercase first letter. For example, a method that sends an e-mail message might be named `SendMail`.

Error-Prevention Tip 7.2

Small methods are easier to test, debug and understand than large methods.

Good Programming Practice 7.1

When a parameter is declared without a type, its type is assumed to be `Object`. *As you'll learn in Chapter 11, Object-Oriented Programming: Inheritance, all values in Visual Basic can be represented as type* `Object`. *Explicitly declaring a parameter's type improves program clarity.*

7.4 Functions: Methods That Return a Value

Functions (known as **Function procedures** in earlier versions of Visual Basic) are methods that **return a value** to the caller (whereas subroutines do not). The console application in Fig. 7.3 uses the function `Square` to calculate the squares of the integers from 1–10.

The `For...Next` statement (lines 8–10) displays the results of squaring the integers from 1–10. Each iteration of the loop calculates and displays the square of control variable `counter` (line 9).

Function `Square` is invoked (line 9) with the expression `Square(counter)`. When program control reaches this expression, the program calls `Square` (lines 14–16). At this point, the program makes a copy of the value of `counter` (the argument), and program control transfers to the first line of `Square`. `Square` receives the copy of `counter`'s value and stores it in the parameter `y`. Line 15 is a **`Return` statement**, which terminates execution of the method and returns the result of `y ^ 2` to the calling program. The result is returned to the point in line 9 where `Square` was invoked. Line 9 displays in the command prompt the value of `counter` and the value returned by `Square`. This process is repeated 10 times. Note that returning a value from a function is similar to returning a value from the `Get` accessor of a property.

```
1  ' Fig. 7.3: SquareInteger.vb
2  ' Function that squares a number.
3  Module SquareInteger
4     Sub Main()
5        Console.WriteLine("Number" & vbTab & "Square")
6
7        ' square integers from 1 to 10
8        For counter = 1 To 10
9           Console.WriteLine(counter & vbTab & Square(counter))
10       Next
11    End Sub ' Main
12
13    ' function Square is executed when it is explicitly called
14    Function Square(ByVal y As Integer) As Integer
15       Return y ^ 2 ' return square of parameter value
16    End Function ' Square
17 End Module ' SquareInteger
```

```
Number  Square
1       1
2       4
3       9
4       16
5       25
6       36
7       49
8       64
9       81
10      100
```

Fig. 7.3 | Function for squaring an integer.

Function Declarations
The format of a function declaration is

```
Function method-name(parameter-list) As return-type
    declarations and statements
End Function
```

The *method-name*, *parameter-list*, and *declarations and statements* in a function declaration behave like the corresponding elements in a subroutine declaration. In the function header, the *return-type* indicates the type of the result returned from the function to its caller. The statement

```
Return expression
```

can occur anywhere in a function body and returns the value of *expression* to the caller. If necessary, Visual Basic attempts to convert the *expression* to the function's return-type. Functions `Return` exactly one value. When a `Return` statement is executed, control returns immediately to the point at which that function was invoked.

Common Programming Error 7.2

If the expression in a `Return` *statement cannot be converted to the function's return-type, a runtime error is generated.*

Common Programming Error 7.3

Failure to return a value from a function (e.g., by forgetting to provide a `Return` *statement) causes the function to return the default value for the return-type, possibly producing incorrect output.*

7.5 Shared Methods and Class `Math`

As you know, every class provides methods that perform common tasks on objects of the class. For example, to display the grade information in a `GradeBook` object, we defined and called method `DisplayGradeReport` (Section 6.5). Recall that when we call `GradeBook` methods such as `DisplayGradeReport`, we first need to create a `GradeBook` object.

Although most methods of a class execute in response to method calls on specific objects, this is not always the case. Sometimes a method performs a task that does not depend on the contents of an object. Such a method applies to the class in which it is declared and is known as a `Shared` method or a class method. It is not uncommon for a class to contain a group of convenient `Shared` methods to perform common tasks. For example, recall that we use method `WriteLine` of class `Console` throughout this book; method `WriteLine` is a `Shared` method.

Methods that are declared in modules are `Shared` by default. To declare a `Shared` method in a class, place the `Shared` modifier before the keyword `Sub` or `Function` in the method's header. To call a `Shared` method, specify the name of the class or module in which the method is declared, followed by the dot (`.`) separator and the method name, as in

```
ClassName.MethodName(arguments)
```

We use various `Math` class `Shared` methods here. Class `Math` provides a collection of methods that enable you to perform common mathematical calculations. For example, you can calculate the square root of `900.0` with the `Shared` method call

```
Math.Sqrt(900.0)
```

which evaluates to and returns `30.0`. Method `Sqrt` takes an argument of type `Double` and returns a result of type `Double`. To output the value of the preceding method call in the command prompt, you could write

```
Console.WriteLine(Math.Sqrt(900.0))
```

In this statement, the value that `Sqrt` returns becomes the argument to method `WriteLine`. Note that we did not create a `Math` object before calling method `Sqrt`, nor did we create an object of class `Console` before calling method `WriteLine`. Most `Math` class methods are `Shared` and are therefore called by preceding the name of the method with the class name `Math` and a dot (`.`) separator.

Software Engineering Observation 7.5

It is not necessary to add an assembly reference to use the `Math` class methods in a program, because class `Math` is located in the assembly `mscorlib.dll`, which is referenced by every .NET application. Also it is not necessary to import class `Math`'s namespace (`System`), because it is implicitly imported in all .NET applications.

Method arguments may be constants, variables or expressions. If `c = 13.0`, `d = 3.0` and `f = 4.0`, then the statement

```
Console.WriteLine(Math.Sqrt(c + d * f))
```

calculates and prints the square root of `13.0 + 3.0 * 4.0 = 25.0`—namely, `5.0`. Figure 7.4 summarizes several `Math` class methods. In the figure, *x* and *y* are of type `Double`. Methods Min and Max have overloaded versions for several types. We discuss method overloading in Section 7.17.

Method	Description	Example

`Abs(x)`	returns the absolute value of *x*	`Abs(23.7)` is `23.7`
		`Abs(0)` is `0`
		`Abs(-23.7)` is `23.7`

`Ceiling(x)`	rounds *x* to the smallest integer not less than *x*	`Ceiling(9.2)` is `10.0` `Ceiling(-9.8)` is `-9.0`
`Cos(x)`	returns the trigonometric cosine of *x* (*x* in radians)	`Cos(0.0)` is `1.0`
`Exp(x)`	returns the exponential e^x	`Exp(1.0)` is approximately `2.71828182845905` `Exp(2.0)` is approximately `7.38905609893065`

Fig. 7.4 | `Math` class methods. (Part 1 of 2.)

Method	Description	Example
`Floor(x)`	rounds x to the largest integer not greater than x	`Floor(9.2)` is `9.0` `Floor(-9.8)` is `-10.0`
`Log(x)`	returns the natural logarithm of x (base e)	`Log(2.7182818284590451)` is approximately `1.0` `Log(7.3890560989306504)` is approximately `2.0`
`Max(x, y)`	returns the larger value of x and y (also has versions for `Single`, `Integer` and `Long` values)	`Max(2.3, 12.7)` is `12.7` `Max(-2.3, -12.7)` is `-2.3`
`Min(x, y)`	returns the smaller value of x and y (also has versions for `Single`, `Integer` and `Long` values)	`Min(2.3, 12.7)` is `2.3` `Min(-2.3, -12.7)` is `-12.7`
`Pow(x, y)`	calculates x raised to the power y (x^y)	`Pow(2.0, 7.0)` is `128.0` `Pow(9.0, .5)` is `3.0`
`Sin(x)`	returns the trigonometric sine of x (x in radians)	`Sin(0.0)` is `0.0`
`Sqrt(x)`	returns the square root of x	`Sqrt(9.0)` is `3.0` `Sqrt(2.0)` is `1.4142135623731`
`Tan(x)`	returns the trigonometric tangent of x (x in radians)	`Tan(0.0)` is `0.0`

Fig. 7.4 | `Math` class methods. (Part 2 of 2.)

`Math` Class Constants `PI` and `E`

Class `Math` also declares two commonly used mathematical constants: `Math.PI` and `Math.E`. The constant `Math.PI` (3.14159265358979323846) is the ratio of a circle's circumference to its diameter. The constant `Math.E` (2.7182818284590452354) is the base value for natural logarithms (calculated with `Shared Math` method `Log`). These values are declared in class `Math` with the modifiers `Public` and `Const`. Making them `Public` allows you to use the values in your own classes. Keyword `Const` declares a constant—a value that cannot be changed after the variable is initialized. Both `PI` and `E` are declared `Const` because their values never change. Constants are implicitly `Shared`, so they can be accessed via the class name `Math` and a dot (`.`) separator, just like class `Math`'s methods. Recall from Section 4.5 that when each object of a class maintains its own copy of an attribute, the variable that represents the attribute is also known as an instance variable—each object (instance) of the class has a separate instance of the variable in memory. There are also variables for which each object of a class does not have a separate instance of the variable. That is the case with `Shared` variables. When objects of a class containing `Shared` variables are created, all the objects of that class share one copy of the class's `Shared` variables. Together the Shared variables and instance variables represent the so-called fields of a class. You'll learn more about Shared members in Section 10.11.

7.6 GradeBook Case Study: Declaring Methods with Multiple Parameters

Chapters 3–6 presented classes containing simple methods that had at most one parameter. Methods often need to receive more than one piece of information to perform their tasks. We now consider how to write methods with multiple parameters.

Declaring Method Maximum

The application in Figs. 7.5–7.6 uses a user-declared method called Maximum to determine and return the largest of three Integer values entered by the user. When the application begins execution, class GradeBookTest's Main method (lines 4–11 of Fig. 7.6) creates one object of class GradeBook (line 6) and uses this object to call method InputGrades (line 9). This method is declared in lines 43–57 of class GradeBook (Fig. 7.5). Lines 48–53 prompt the user to enter three Integer values and read them from the user. Line 56 calls method Maximum (declared in lines 60–76) to determine the largest of the three Integer arguments. When method Maximum returns the result to line 56, the program assigns Maximum's return value to instance variable maximumGrade. Then line 10 of Fig. 7.6 calls method DisplayGradeReport, which outputs the maximum value.

```
1   ' Fig. 7.5: GradeBook.vb
2   ' Definition of class GradeBook that finds the maximum of three grades.
3   Public Class GradeBook
4      Private courseNameValue As String ' name of course
5      Private maximumGrade As Integer ' maximum of three grades
6
7      ' constructor initializes course name
8      Public Sub New(ByVal name As String)
9         CourseName = name ' initializes CourseName
10        maximumGrade = 0 ' this value will be replaced by maximum grade
11     End Sub ' New
12
13     ' property that gets and sets the course name; the Set accessor
14     ' ensures that the course name has at most 25 characters
15     Public Property CourseName() As String
16        Get ' retrieve courseNameValue
17           Return courseNameValue
18        End Get
19
20        Set(ByVal value As String) ' set courseNameValue
21           If value.Length <= 25 Then ' if value has 25 or fewer characters
22              courseNameValue = value ' store the course name in the object
23           Else ' if name has more than 25 characters
24              ' set courseNameValue to first 25 characters of parameter name
25              ' start at 0, length of 25
26              courseNameValue = value.Substring(0, 25)
```

Fig. 7.5 | User-declared method Maximum that has three Integer parameters. (Part 1 of 3.)

```
            Console.WriteLine( _
               "Course name (" & value & ") exceeds maximum length (25).")
            Console.WriteLine( _
               "Limiting course name to first 25 characters." & vbNewLine)
         End If
      End Set
   End Property ' CourseName

   ' display a welcome message to the GradeBook user
   Public Sub DisplayMessage()
      Console.WriteLine("Welcome to the grade book for " _
         & vbNewLine & CourseName & "!" & vbNewLine)
   End Sub ' DisplayMessage

   ' input three grades from user
   Public Sub InputGrades()
      Dim grade1 As Integer ' first grade entered by user
      Dim grade2 As Integer ' second grade entered by user
      Dim grade3 As Integer ' third grade entered by user

      Console.Write("Enter the first grade: ")
      grade1 = Console.ReadLine()
      Console.Write("Enter the second grade: ")
      grade2 = Console.ReadLine()
      Console.Write("Enter the third grade: ")
      grade3 = Console.ReadLine()

      ' store the maximum in maximumGrade
      maximumGrade = Maximum(grade1, grade2, grade3)
   End Sub ' InputGrades

   ' returns the maximum of its three integer parameters
   Function Maximum(ByVal x As Integer, ByVal y As Integer, _
      ByVal z As Integer) As Integer

      Dim maximumValue As Integer = x ' assume x is the largest to start

      ' determine whether y is greater than maximumValue
      If (y > maximumValue) Then
         maximumValue = y ' make y the new maximumValue
      End If

      ' determine whether z is greater than maximumValue
      If (z > maximumValue) Then
         maximumValue = z ' make z the new maximumValue
      End If

      Return maximumValue
   End Function ' Maximum

```

Fig. 7.5 | User-declared method `Maximum` that has three `Integer` parameters. (Part 2 of 3.)

```
   ' display a report based on the grades entered by user
   Public Sub DisplayGradeReport()
      ' output maximum of grades entered
      Console.WriteLine("Maximum of grades entered: " & maximumGrade)
   End Sub ' DisplayGradeReport
End Class ' GradeBook
```

Fig. 7.5 | User-declared method `Maximum` that has three `Integer` parameters. (Part 3 of 3.)

```
' Fig. 7.6: GradeBookTest.vb
' Create a GradeBook object, input grades and display grade report.
Module GradeBookTest
   Sub Main()
      ' create GradeBook object
      Dim gradeBook1 As New GradeBook("CS101 Introduction to VB")

      gradeBook1.DisplayMessage() ' display welcome message
      gradeBook1.InputGrades() ' read grades from user
      gradeBook1.DisplayGradeReport() ' display report based on grades
   End Sub ' Main
End Module ' GradeBookTest
```

```
Welcome to the grade book for
CS101 Introduction to VB!

Enter the first grade: 65
Enter the second grade: 87
Enter the third grade: 45
Maximum of grades entered: 87
```

```
Welcome to the grade book for
CS101 Introduction to VB!

Enter the first grade: 45
Enter the second grade: 65
Enter the third grade: 87
Maximum of grades entered: 87
```

```
Welcome to the grade book for
CS101 Introduction to VB!

Enter the first grade: 87
Enter the second grade: 45
Enter the third grade: 65
Maximum of grades entered: 87
```

Fig. 7.6 | Application to test class `GradeBook`'s `Maximum` method.

Consider method Maximum (lines 60–76). Lines 60–61 indicate that it returns an Integer value, the method's name is Maximum and the method requires three Integer parameters (x, y and z) to accomplish its task. When a method has more than one parameter, the parameters are specified as a comma-separated list. When Maximum is called in line 56, the parameter x is initialized with the value of the argument grade1, the parameter y with the value of the argument grade2 and the parameter z with the value of the argument grade3. There must be one argument in the method call for each parameter (sometimes called a formal parameter) in the method declaration. Also, the type of each argument must be consistent with the type of the corresponding parameter.

To determine the maximum value, we begin with the assumption that parameter x contains the largest value, so line 63 declares local variable maximumValue and initializes it with the value of parameter x. Of course, parameter y or z may contain the actual largest value, so we must compare each of these values with maximumValue. The If...Then statement in lines 66–68 determines whether y is greater than maximumValue, and if so, line 67 assigns y to maximumValue. The If...Then statement in lines 71–73 determines whether z is greater than maximumValue, and if so, line 72 assigns z to maximumValue. At this point the largest of the three values resides in maximumValue, so line 75 returns that value to line 56. When program control returns to the point in the program where Maximum was called, Maximum's parameters x, y and z are no longer accessible to the program—we will see why in Section 7.8. Note that methods can return at most one value, but the returned value could be a reference to an object that contains many values.

Note that maximumGrade is an instance variable in class GradeBook. Variables should be declared as instance variables of a class only if they are required for use in more than one method of the class or if the program should save their values between calls to the class's methods.

Implementing Method **Maximum** *by Reusing Method* **Math.Max**

Recall from Fig. 7.4 that class Math has a Max method that can determine the larger of two values. The entire body of our maximum method could also be implemented with two calls to Math.Max, as follows:

```
Return Math.Max(x, Math.Max(y, z))
```

The outer call to Math.Max specifies arguments x and Math.Max(y, z). Before any method is called, all its arguments are evaluated to determine their values. If an argument is a method call, the method call is performed to determine its return value. So, in the preceding statement, Math.Max(y, z) is evaluated first to determine the maximum of y and z. Then the result is passed as the second argument to the other call to Math.Max, which returns the larger of its two arguments. Using Math.Max in this manner is a good example of software reuse—we find the largest of three values by reusing Math.Max, which finds the largest of two values. Note how concise this code is compared to lines 63–75 of Fig. 7.5.

7.7 Notes on Declaring and Using Methods

There are three ways to call a method:

1. Using a method name by itself to call another method of the same class or module—such as Maximum(number1, number2, number3) in line 56 of Fig. 7.5.

2. Using a variable that contains a reference to an object, followed by a dot (`.`) and the method name to call a method of the referenced object—such as the method call in line 10 of Fig. 7.6, `gradeBook1.DisplayGradeReport()`, which calls a method of class `GradeBook` from the `Main` method of module `GradeBookTest`.
3. Using the class or module name and a dot (`.`) to call a `Shared` method of a class or module (all methods of a module are implicitly `Shared`). One example of this is `Math.Sqrt(900.0)` in Section 7.5.

Note that a `Shared` method can call only other `Shared` methods of the same class directly (i.e., using the method name by itself) and can manipulate only `Shared` members in the same class directly. To access the class's non-`Shared` members, a `Shared` method must use a reference to an object of the class. Recall that `Shared` methods relate to the class, whereas non-`Shared` methods are associated with a specific instance (object) of the class and may manipulate the instance variables of that object. Many objects of a class, each with its own copies of the instance variables, may exist at the same time. Suppose a `Shared` method were to invoke a non-`Shared` method directly. How would the method know which object's instance variables to manipulate? What would happen if no objects of the class existed at the time the non-`Shared` method was invoked? Thus, a `Shared` method cannot access non-`Shared` members of the same class directly.

Control can be returned to the statement that calls a method by using the `Return` statement or by reaching the end of the method (`End Sub` or `End Function`). If the method does not return a result but uses a `Return` statement to return control to the calling method, the `Return` statement cannot include an expression. If the method does return a result, the statement

`Return` *expression*

evaluates the *expression*, then returns the result to the caller.

Common Programming Error 7.4

Declaring a method outside the body of a class or module declaration or inside the body of another method is a syntax error.

Common Programming Error 7.5

Omitting the return-value-type *in a method declaration, if that method is a* `Function`, *is a syntax error.*

Common Programming Error 7.6

Redeclaring a method parameter as a local variable in the method's body is a compilation error.

Common Programming Error 7.7

Returning a value from a method that is a subroutine is a compilation error.

7.8 Method Call Stack and Activation Records

To understand how Visual Basic performs method calls, we first need to consider a data structure (i.e., collection of related data items) known as a stack. You can think of a stack as analogous to a pile of dishes. When a dish is placed on the pile, it is normally placed at the top (referred to as pushing the dish onto the stack). Similarly, when a dish is removed from the pile, it is normally removed from the top (referred to as popping the dish off the stack). Stacks are known as last-in, first-out (LIFO) data structures—the last item pushed (inserted) onto the stack is the first item popped (removed) from the stack.

When a program calls a method, the called method must know how to return to the correct location in its caller, so the return address in the calling method is pushed onto the method call stack. If a series of nested method calls occurs (e.g., method `A` calls method `B`, and method `B` calls method `C`), the successive return addresses are pushed onto the stack in last-in, first-out order so that each method can return to its caller.

The method call stack also contains the memory for the local variables used in each method invocation during a program's execution. A method's local variables also include its parameters. This data, stored as a portion of the method call stack, is known as the activation record or stack frame of the method call. When a method call is made, the activation record for that call is pushed onto the method call stack. When the method returns to its caller, the activation record for the returning method call is popped off the stack, and those local variables are no longer known to the program. If a local variable holding a reference to an object is the only variable in the program with a reference to that object, when the activation record containing that local variable is popped off the stack, the object can no longer be accessed by the program and it will eventually be deleted from memory by the CLR during garbage collection. We discuss garbage collection in Section 10.10.

Of course, the amount of memory in a computer is finite, so only a certain amount of memory can be used to store activation records on the method call stack. If more method calls occur than can have their activation records stored on the method call stack, an error known as a stack overflow occurs.

7.9 Implicit Argument Conversions

An important feature of argument passing is implicit argument conversion—converting an argument's value to a type that the method expects to receive in its corresponding parameter. Visual Basic supports both widening and narrowing conversions. A widening conversion occurs when an argument is converted to a parameter of another type that can hold more data, whereas a narrowing conversion occurs when there is potential for data loss during the conversion (i.e., a conversion to a parameter of a type that holds a smaller amount of data). Figure 7.7 lists the widening conversions supported by Visual Basic that occur between primitive types. In addition to the conversions in Fig. 7.7, all primitive type variables can be converted to type `Object` without losing data.

Type	Conversion types
`Boolean`	No possible widening conversions to other primitive types
`Byte`	`UShort`, `Short`, `UInteger`, `Integer`, `ULong`, `Long`, `Decimal`, `Single` or `Double`

Fig. 7.7 | Widening conversions between primitive types. (Part 1 of 2.)

Type	Conversion types
`Char`	`String`
`Date`	No possible widening conversions to other primitive types
`Decimal`	`Single` or `Double`
`Double`	No possible widening conversions to other primitive types
`Integer`	`Long`, `Decimal`, `Single` or `Double`
`Long`	`Decimal`, `Single` or `Double`
`SByte`	`Short`, `Integer`, `Long`, `Decimal`, `Single` or `Double`
`Short`	`Integer`, `Long`, `Decimal`, `Single` or `Double`
`Single`	`Double`
`String`	No possible widening conversions to other primitive types
`UInteger`	`ULong`, `Long`, `Decimal`, `Single` or `Double`
`ULong`	`Decimal`, `Single` or `Double`
`UShort`	`UInteger`, `Integer`, `ULong`, `Long`, `Decimal`, `Single` or `Double`

Fig. 7.7 | Widening conversions between primitive types. (Part 2 of 2.)

For example, the `Math` class method `Sqrt` can be called with an `Integer` argument, even though the method is defined in class `Math` with a `Double` parameter. The statement

```
Console.Write(Math.Sqrt(4))
```

correctly evaluates `Math.Sqrt(4)` and prints the value `2`. Visual Basic implicitly converts the `Integer` argument `4` to the `Double` value `4.0` before the argument is passed to `Math.Sqrt`. In this case, the argument does not precisely correspond to the parameter type in the method declaration, so an implicit widening conversion changes the value to the proper type before the method is called. Visual Basic also performs narrowing conversions on arguments passed to methods. For example, if a `Double` variable containing the value `4.0` were passed to a method expecting an `Integer` variable, the value would be converted to `4`. Some implicit narrowing conversions can cause runtime errors. In the next section, we discuss measures you can take to avoid such runtime errors. In Chapter 13, Exception Handling, we discuss how to handle the errors caused by failed narrowing conversions.

Common Programming Error 7.8

Converting a primitive-type value to a value of another primitive type may change the value if the conversion is not a widening conversion. For example, converting a floating-point value to an integral value truncates any fractional part of the floating-point value (e.g., 4.7 becomes 4).

Conversions occur not only for values passed as arguments to methods, but also for expressions containing values of two or more types. In such expressions, the values' original types are maintained, while temporary copies of the values are converted for use in the expression. Each value is converted to the "widest" type in the expression (i.e., widening conversions are made until the values are of the same type as the "widest" type). For example, if `singleNumber` is of type `Single` and `integerNumber` is of type `Integer`, when Visual Basic evaluates the expression

```
singleNumber + integerNumber
```

the value of `integerNumber` is converted to type `Single` (the widest type in the expression), then added to `singleNumber`, producing a `Single` result.

7.10 Option Strict and Data-Type Conversions

Visual Basic provides several options for controlling the way the compiler handles types. These options can help you eliminate such errors as those caused by narrowing conversions. **Option Explicit**—which is set to **On** by default and has been enabled in the programs we created in Chapters 2–6—forces you to explicitly declare all variables before they are used in a program. This eliminates various errors. For example, when **Option Explicit** is set to **Off**, the compiler interprets misspelled variable names as new variables and implicitly declares them to be of type `Object`. (Class `Object` is the base type of all types in Visual Basic. We will discuss class `Object` in more detail in Chapter 11.) This creates subtle errors that can be difficult to debug. It is recommended that you leave this option set to **On**. If you wish to set **Option Explicit** to **Off**, double click **My Project** in **Solution Explorer**. This opens a window that allows you to change the properties of the project. In this window, click the **Compile** tab (Fig. 7.8), then select the value **Off** from the **Option Explicit** drop-down list. Note that all variables have a type regardless of whether **Option Explicit** is **On**, so Visual Basic is known as a strongly typed language.

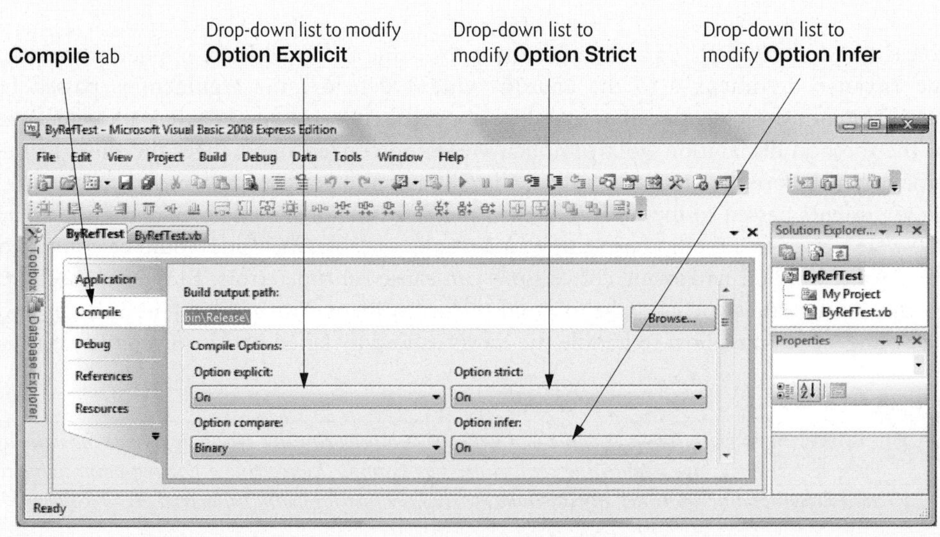

Fig. 7.8 | Modifying `Option Strict` and `Option Explicit`.

A second option, which defaults to **Off**, is **Option Strict**. Visual Basic provides **Option Strict** as a means of increasing program clarity and reducing debugging time. When set to **On**, **Option Strict** causes the compiler to check all conversions and requires you to perform an explicit conversion for all narrowing conversions that could cause data loss (e.g., conversion from `Double` to `Integer`) or program termination (e.g., conversion of a `String`, such as `"hello"`, to type `Integer`). To set **Option Strict** to **On**, select the value **On** in the **Option Strict** drop-down list (Fig. 7.8). An explicit conversion is a conversion that uses a cast operator or a method to force a conversion to occur. In Chapter 12 we discuss using operators known as cast operators to perform explicit conversions. Explicit conversion enables you to "take control" from the compiler. You essentially say, "I know this conversion might cause loss of information, but for my purposes here, that's fine." **Option Infer**, which defaults to `On`, enables the compiler to infer a variable's type based on its intializer value. For example, in the statement

```
Dim x = 7 ' compiler infers that x is an Integer
```

the compiler infers that `x` is an `Integer` because the initializer value is an `Integer` literal. You can set **Option Explicit**, **Option Strict** and **Option Infer** for all future projects as follows. In the IDE, select **Tools > Options...** to display the **Options** dialog. Under **Projects and Solutions**, select **VB Defaults** and choose the appropriate value in each option's `ComboBox`.

Class `Convert`'s methods explicitly convert data from one type to another. The name of each conversion method is the word `To`, followed by the name of the type to which the method converts its argument. For instance, to convert a `String` input by the user to type `Double` (to be stored in variable `number` of type `Double`), we use the statement

```
number = Convert.ToDouble(Console.ReadLine())
```

Likewise, many of the primitive types have a `Parse` method that they can use to convert a `String` to a value of the primitive type. For instance, method `Double.Parse` converts a string representation of a number to a value of type `Double`.

Visual Basic also provides type-conversion functions, such as `CChar` (converts to `Char`), such as `CDec` (converts to `Decimal`), `CInt` (converts to `Integer`) and `CDbl` (converts to `Double`), for converting between built-in types. These conversion functions are defined as part of the Visual Basic language rather than the .NET framework—using them may improve your application's performance. A complete list of the type-conversion functions with descriptions can be found at `msdn.microsoft.com/en-us/library/s2dy91zy.aspx`.

When **Option Strict** is **Off** (as it has been for all the code examples so far in this book), Visual Basic performs such type conversions implicitly, and thus you may not realize that a narrowing conversion is being performed. If the data being converted is incompatible with the new type, a runtime error occurs. `Option Strict` draws your attention to narrowing conversions at compile time so that they can be eliminated or handled properly.

Error-Prevention Tip 7.3

From this point forward, all code examples have **Option Strict** *set to* **On**.

Setting **Option Strict** to **On** applies the change globally, to the entire project. You also can set **Option Strict** within an individual code file by typing `Option Strict On` or `Option Strict Off`—`Option` statements must be placed at the start of the file above any declarations or `Imports` statements.

7.11 Value Types and Reference Types

As we discussed briefly in Chapter 4, all Visual Basic types can be categorized as either value types or reference types. A variable of a value type contains data of that type. Normally, value types are used for a single piece of data, such as an `Integer` or a `Double` value. By contrast, a variable of a reference type contains the address of the location in memory where the data referred to by that variable is stored. The actual object to which the variable refers can contain many individual pieces of data (i.e., its instance variables). Reference types are discussed in more detail in Chapters 10–12.

Both value types and reference types include primitive types and types that you can create. The primitive value types include the integral types (`Byte`, `SByte`, `Short`, `UShort`, `Integer`, `UInteger`, `Long` and `ULong`), the floating-point types (`Single` and `Double`) and types `Boolean`, `Date`, `Decimal` and `Char`. There is only one primitive reference type—`String`. Reference types can be created by declaring classes and modules, as well as delegates and interfaces—constructs that we will discuss in Chapters 10 and 12, respectively. The primitive reference type, `String`, actually represents the `String` class in the .NET framework. Value types can be created by declaring structures and enumerations. Structures, like classes, define types that contain members such as methods and instance variables. Enumerations may only contain sets of integral values. The primitive value types are defined using structures. Most of these structures have the same name as the Visual Basic primitive type (type `Double` is defined by structure `Double`), but others do not (type `Integer` is defined by structure `Int32`). These structures are part of the .NET Framework Class Library, which is used by several languages—as a result, the naming of types in the various .NET languages may not always be identical to their underlying classes and structures in the .NET framework. User-defined types are discussed in greater detail in Chapter 10, Classes and Objects: A Deeper Look and Chapter 17, Strings, Characters and Regular Expressions. Figure 7.9 lists the primitive types, which form the building blocks for more complicated types, such as the `GradeBook` type we have defined in several examples in this book.

Type	Size in bits	Values	Standard	Name of .NET class or structure
`Boolean`		`True` or `False`		`Boolean`
`Byte`	8	0 to 255		`Byte`
`SByte`	8	-128 to 127		`SByte`
`Char`	16	One Unicode character	(Unicode character set)	`Char`
`Date`	64	1 January 0001 to 31 December 9999 12:00:00 AM to 11:59:59 PM		`DateTime`

Fig. 7.9 | Primitive types. (Part 1 of 2.)

Type	Size in bits	Values	Standard	Name of .NET class or structure
`Decimal`	128	`1.0E-28` to `7.9E+28`		`Decimal`
`Double`	64	`±5.0E-324` to `±1.7E+308`	(IEEE 754 floating point)	`Double`
`Integer`	32	`-2,147,483,648` to `2,147,483,647`		`Int32`
`Long`	64	`-9,223,372,036,854,775,808` to `9,223,372,036,854,775,807`		`Int64`
`Short`	16	`-32,768` to `32,767`		`Int16`
`Single`	32	`±1.5E-45` to `±3.4E+38`	(IEEE 754 floating point)	`Single`
`String`		0 to ~2000000000 Unicode characters	(Unicode character set)	`String`
`UInteger`	32	`0` to `4,294,967,295`		`UInt32`
`ULong`	64	`0` to `18,446,744,073,709,551,615`		`UInt64`
`UShort`	16	`0` to `65,535`		`UInt16`

Fig. 7.9 | Primitive types. (Part 2 of 2.)

Each value type in the table is accompanied by its size in bits (there are 8 bits to a byte) and its range of values. To promote portability, Microsoft chose to use internationally recognized standards for character formats (Unicode, `www.unicode.org`) and floating-point numbers (IEEE 754, `grouper.ieee.org/groups/754/`). We discuss the Unicode character formats in Appendix G, Unicode®. In the far right column of the table we display the name of the structure or class that defines the primitive type. Note that these are the names used for the methods of class `Convert` that we discussed in the previous section. For instance, to convert a value to type `Integer`, the name of the proper `Convert` class method would be `Convert.ToInt32`, not `Convert.ToInteger`.

7.12 Framework Class Library Namespaces

As we have seen, the .NET framework contains many predefined classes that are grouped into namespaces. Throughout the text, we have used `Imports` statements to specify the namespaces used in a program. For example, a program includes the declaration

```
Imports System.Windows.Forms
```

to specify that the program uses classes in this namespace, such as class `MessageBox`. This allows you to use the simple class name `MessageBox`, rather than the fully qualified class name `System.Windows.Forms.MessageBox`, in the code. A great strength of Visual Basic is the large number of classes in the .NET framework. Some key namespaces are described in Fig. 7.10, which represents only a small portion of the reusable components in the .NET Framework Class Library.

.NET has over 100 namespaces. In addition to the those summarized in Fig. 7.10, the .NET framework includes namespaces for complex graphics, web services, printing, security and many other capabilities.

You can locate additional information about a predefined .NET class's methods in the Visual Studio 2008 documentation by selecting **Help > Index**. In the window that appears there will be an index to the left. Enter .NET Framework in the **Filtered by** drop-down list, and enter the name of the class in the **Look for** field. You will be provided with links for general information about the class or for a listing of the class's members.

Namespace	Description
`System.Windows.Forms`	Contains the classes required to create and manipulate GUIs. (Various classes in this namespace are discussed in Chapter 14, Graphical User Interfaces with Windows Forms.)
`System.IO`	Contains classes that enable programs to input and output data. (You will learn more about this namespace in Chapter 18, Files and Streams.)
`System.Data`	Contains classes that enable programs to access and manipulate databases (i.e., an organized collection of data).
`System.Web`	Contains classes used for creating and maintaining web applications, which are accessible over the Internet. (You will learn more about this namespace in Chapter 21, ASP.NET and ASP.NET Ajax.)
`System.Xml`	Contains classes for creating and manipulating XML data. Data can be read from or written to XML files. (You will learn more about this namespace in Chapter 19, XML and LINQ to XML.)
`System.Collections.Generics`	Contains classes that define data structures for maintaining collections of data. (You will learn more about this namespace in Chapter 24, Data Structures and Generic Collections.)
`System.Net`	Contains classes that enable programs to communicate via computer networks like the Internet.
`System.Text`	Contains classes and interfaces that enable programs to manipulate characters and strings. (You will learn more about this namespace in Chapter 17, Strings, Characters and Regular Expressions.)
`System.Threading`	Contains classes that enable programs to perform several tasks concurrently, or at the same time.
`System.Drawing`	Contains classes that enable programs to display basic graphics, such as displaying shapes and arcs.

Fig. 7.10 | .NET Framework Class Library namespaces (a subset).

Good Programming Practice 7.2

The Visual Studio 2008 documentation is easy to search and provides many details about each class. As you learn a class in this book, you should read about the class in the online documentation.

7.13 Passing Arguments: Pass-by-Value vs. Pass-by-Reference

Arguments are passed in one of two ways: pass-by-value and pass-by-reference. When an argument is passed by value, the program makes a copy of the argument's value and passes the copy to the called method. With pass-by-value, changes to the called method's copy do not affect the original variable's value in the caller. In contrast, when an argument is passed by reference, the caller gives the called method the ability to access and modify the caller's original data directly. Figure 7.11 demonstrates passing value-type arguments by value and by reference.

```
' Fig. 7.11: ByRefTest.vb
' Demonstrates passing by value and by reference.
Module ByRefTest
   Sub Main()
      Dim number1 As Integer = 2

      Console.WriteLine("Passing a value-type argument by value:")
      Console.WriteLine("Before calling SquareByValue, " & _
         "number1 is {0}", number1)
      SquareByValue(number1) ' passes number1 by value
      Console.WriteLine("After returning from SquareByValue, " & _
         "number1 is {0}" & vbNewLine, number1)

      Dim number2 As Integer = 2

      Console.WriteLine("Passing a value-type argument" & _
         " by reference:")
      Console.WriteLine("Before calling SquareByReference, " & _
         "number2 is {0}", number2)
      SquareByReference(number2) ' passes number2 by reference
      Console.WriteLine("After returning from " & _
         "SquareByReference, number2 is {0}" & vbNewLine, number2)

      Dim number3 As Integer = 2

      Console.WriteLine("Passing a value-type argument" & _
         " by reference, but in parentheses:")
      Console.WriteLine("Before calling SquareByReference " & _
         "using parentheses, number3 is {0}", number3)
      SquareByReference((number3)) ' passes number3 by value
      Console.WriteLine("After returning from " & _
         "SquareByReference, number3 is {0}", number3)
   End Sub ' Main

```

Fig. 7.11 | ByVal and ByRef used to pass value-type arguments. (Part 1 of 2.)

```
35       ' squares number by value (note ByVal keyword)
36       Sub SquareByValue(ByVal number As Integer)
37          Console.WriteLine("After entering SquareByValue, " & _
38             "number is {0}", number)
39          number *= number
40          Console.WriteLine("Before exiting SquareByValue, " & _
41             "number is {0}", number)
42       End Sub ' SquareByValue
43
44       ' squares number by reference (note ByRef keyword)
45       Sub SquareByReference(ByRef number As Integer)
46          Console.WriteLine("After entering SquareByReference" & _
47             ", number is {0}", number)
48          number *= number
49          Console.WriteLine("Before exiting SquareByReference" & _
50             ", number is {0}", number)
51       End Sub ' SquareByReference
52    End Module ' ByRefTest
```

```
Passing a value-type argument by value:
Before calling SquareByValue, number1 is 2
After entering SquareByValue, number is 2
Before exiting SquareByValue, number is 4
After returning from SquareByValue, number1 is 2

Passing a value-type argument by reference:
Before calling SquareByReference, number2 is 2
After entering SquareByReference, number is 2
Before exiting SquareByReference, number is 4
After returning from SquareByReference, number2 is 4

Passing a value-type argument by reference, but in parentheses:
Before calling SquareByReference using parentheses, number3 is 2
After entering SquareByReference, number is 2
Before exiting SquareByReference, number is 4
After returning from SquareByReference, number3 is 2
```

Fig. 7.11 | `ByVal` and `ByRef` used to pass value-type arguments. (Part 2 of 2.)

The program passes three value-type variables, `number1`, `number2` and `number3`, in different ways to methods `SquareByValue` (lines 36–42) and `SquareByReference` (lines 45–51). Keyword `ByVal` in the method header of `SquareByValue` (line 36) indicates that value-type arguments should be passed by value. A parameter declared with keyword `ByVal` is known as a **value parameter**. When `number1` is passed to `SquareByValue` (line 10), a copy of the value stored in `number1` (i.e., 2) is passed to the method. Therefore, the value of `number1` in the calling method, `Main`, is not modified when parameter `number` is squared in method `SquareByValue` (line 39)—only the local copy stored in parameter `number` gets modified. Note that `ByVal` is the default for method parameters and it is not required in the parameter declarations.

Method `SquareByReference` uses **keyword `ByRef`** (line 45) to receive its value-type parameter by reference. A parameter declared with keyword `ByRef` is known as a **reference** parameter. When `Main` calls `SquareByReference` (line 20), a reference to the value stored in `number2` is passed, which gives `SquareByReference` direct access to the value stored in the original variable. Thus, the value stored in `number2` after `SquareByReference` finishes executing is the same as the final value of parameter `number`.

When arguments are enclosed in parentheses, `()`, the expression within the parentheses is evaluated. In line 30, the inner set of parentheses evaluates `number3` to its value (2) and passes this value to the method, even if the method header includes keyword `ByRef`. Thus, the value of `number3` does not change after it is passed to `SquareByReference` (line 30) via parentheses.

Passing value-type arguments with keyword `ByRef` is useful when methods need to alter argument values directly or when methods need to simulate returning multiple values. However, passing by reference can weaken security, because the called method can modify the caller's data. We discuss some of the more complex subtleties of passing arguments by value and by reference in Section 8.16.

When you pass a variable of a reference type to a method that declares the corresponding parameter `ByVal`, a copy of the variable's value is passed. In this case, the value is actually a reference to an object, so the method is able to modify the object in memory. Thus, reference-type variables passed with keyword `ByVal` are effectively passed by reference. Although Visual Basic allows you to use keyword `ByRef` with reference-type parameters, it is usually not necessary to do so except with type `String`. Although they technically are reference types, `String` arguments cannot be modified directly when passed with keyword `ByVal`, due to some subtle details of the `String` type, which we discuss in Chapter 17, Strings, Characters and Regular Expressions. We discuss passing reference types by reference in Section 8.16.

Error-Prevention Tip 7.4

When passing arguments by value, changes to the called method's copy do not affect the original variable's value. This prevents possible side effects that could hinder the development of correct and reliable software systems. Always pass value-type arguments by value unless you explicitly intend the called method to modify the caller's data.

7.14 Scope of Declarations

You have seen declarations of various Visual Basic entities, such as classes, methods, variables and parameters. Declarations introduce names that are used to refer to such entities. A declaration's Scope is the portion of the program that can refer to the declared entity by its name without qualification—i.e., without preceding the entity with a variable name or class name and a dot (`.`) separator. Such an entity is said to be "in scope" for that portion of the program. This section introduces several important scope issues.

The basic scopes are as follows:

1. Block scope—The scope of a variable declared in a block is from the point of the declaration to the end of the block (e.g., a variable declared in a control statement's body is in scope only until the end of that control statement).
2. Method scope—The scope of a method's local-variable declaration or parameter is from the point at which the declaration appears to the end of that method. This is similar to block scope.

3. Module scope—The scope of a class's members or a module's members is the entire body of the class or module. This enables non-`Shared` methods of a class to use all of the class's members. (Note that `Shared` methods of a class can access only the class's `Shared` variables and `Shared` methods.) All module members are implicitly `Shared`, so all methods of a module can access all variables and other methods of the module.
4. Namespace scope—Elements declared in a namespace (i.e., classes, modules, interfaces, delegates, enumerations, structures and other namespaces) are accessible to all other elements in the same namespace. By default, all elements of a project are part of a namespace that uses the project's name. This enables, for example, a module method in the project to create an object of a class that is also part of the project.

Any block may contain variable declarations. If a local variable or parameter in a method has the same name as a field of the class, the field is "hidden" until the block terminates execution—this is called shadowing. In Chapter 10, we discuss how to access shadowed members. Keep in mind that although a variable may not be in scope, it may still exist. A variable's lifetime is the period during which the variable exists in memory. Some variables exist briefly, some are created and destroyed repeatedly, yet others are maintained through the entire execution of a program. Variables normally exist as long as their container exists—for instance, a local variable of a method will exist as long as the method itself exists in memory.

Error-Prevention Tip 7.5

Use different names for fields and local variables to help prevent subtle logic errors that occur when a method is called and a local variable of the method shadows a field of the same name in the class.

The application in Figs. 7.12 and 7.13 demonstrates scoping issues with fields and local variables. When the application begins execution, module `ScopeTest`'s `Main` method (Fig. 7.13, lines 4–7) creates an object of class `Scope` (line 5) and calls the object's `Begin` method (line 6) to produce the program's output (shown in Fig. 7.13).

In class `Scope`, line 5 declares and initializes the instance variable `x` to `1`. This instance variable is shadowed (hidden) in any block (or method) that declares a local variable named `x`. Method `Begin` (lines 9–21) declares a local variable `x` (line 11) and initializes it to `5`. This local variable's value is output to show that the instance variable `x` (whose value is `1`) is shadowed in method `Begin`. The program declares two other methods—`UseLocalVariable` (lines 24–32) and `UseInstanceVariable` (lines 35–41)—each taking no arguments and returning no results. Method `Begin` calls each method twice (lines 15–18). Method `UseLocalVariable` declares local variable `x` (line 25). When method `UseLocalVariable` is first called (line 15), it creates local variable `x` and initializes it to `25` (line 25), outputs the value of `x` (lines 27–28), increments `x` (line 29) and outputs the value of `x` again (lines 30–31). When `UseLocalVariable` is called a second time (line 17), it recreates local variable `x` and reinitializes it to `25`, so the output of each `UseLocalVariable` call is identical.

Method `UseInstanceVariable` does not declare any local variables. Therefore, when it refers to `x`, instance variable `x` (line 5) of the class is used. When method `UseInstance-`

Variable is first called (line 16), it outputs the value (1) of instance variable x (lines 36–37), multiplies the instance variable x by 10 (line 38) and outputs the value (10) of instance variable x again (lines 39–40) before returning. The next time method UseInstanceVariable is called (line 18), the instance variable has its modified value, 10, so the method outputs 10, then 100. Finally, in method Begin, the program outputs the value of local variable x again (line 20) to show that none of the method calls modified Begin's local variable x, because the methods all referred to variables named x in other scopes.

```
1  ' Fig. 7.12: Scope.vb
2  ' Scope class demonstrates instance and local variable scopes.
3  Public Class Scope
4     ' instance variable that is accessible to all methods of this class
5     Private x As Integer = 1
6
7     ' method Begin creates and initializes local variable x and
8     ' calls methods UseLocalVariable and UseInstanceVariable
9     Public Sub Begin()
10       ' method's local variable x shadows instance variable x
11       Dim x As Integer = 5
12
13       Console.WriteLine("local x in method Begin is " & x)
14
15       UseLocalVariable() ' UseLocalVariable has local x
16       UseInstanceVariable() ' uses class Scope's instance variable x
17       UseLocalVariable() ' UseLocalVariable reinitializes local x
18       UseInstanceVariable() ' Scope's instance variable x retains value
19
20       Console.WriteLine(vbNewLine & "local x in method Begin is " & x)
21    End Sub ' Begin
22
23    ' create and initialize local variable x during each call
24    Sub UseLocalVariable()
25       Dim x As Integer = 25 ' initialized in each call
26
27       Console.WriteLine(vbNewLine & _
28          "local x on entering method UseLocalVariable is " & x)
29       x += 1 ' modifies this method's local variable x
30       Console.WriteLine("local variable x before exiting method " & _
31          "UseLocalVariable is " & x)
32    End Sub ' UseLocalVariable
33
34    ' modify class Scope's instance variable x during each call
35    Sub UseInstanceVariable()
36       Console.WriteLine(vbNewLine & "instance variable" & _
37          " x on entering method UseInstanceVariable is " & x)
38       x *= 10 ' modifies class Scope's instance variable x
39       Console.WriteLine("instance variable " & _
40          "x before exiting method UseInstanceVariable is " & x)
41    End Sub ' UseInstanceVariable
42 End Class ' Scope
```

Fig. 7.12 | Scoping rules in a class.

```
' Fig. 7.13: ScopeTest.vb
' Testing class Scope.
Module ScopeTest
   Sub Main()
      Dim testScope As New Scope()
      testScope.Begin()
   End Sub ' Main
End Module ' ScopeTest
```

```
local x in method Begin is 5

local x on entering method UseLocalVariable is 25
local variable x before exiting method UseLocalVariable is 26

instance variable x on entering method UseInstanceVariable is 1
instance variable x before exiting method UseInstanceVariable is 10

local x on entering method UseLocalVariable is 25
local variable x before exiting method UseLocalVariable is 26

instance variable x on entering method UseInstanceVariable is 10
instance variable x before exiting method UseInstanceVariable is 100

local x in method Begin is 5
```

Fig. 7.13 | Module to test class `Scope`.

7.15 Case Study: Random-Number Generation

We now take a brief and hopefully entertaining diversion into a popular programming application—simulation and game playing. In this and the next section, we develop a game-playing program with multiple methods. The program employs many of the control statements presented thus far in the book and introduces several new concepts.

There is something in the air of a gambling casino that invigorates people—from the high rollers at the plush mahogany-and-felt craps tables to the quarter poppers at the one-armed bandits. It is the element of chance, the possibility that luck will convert a pocketful of money into a mountain of wealth. Unfortunately, that rarely happens because the odds, of course, favor the casinos. The element of chance can be introduced through class **Random** (located in namespace `System`).

Class **Random** *and Method* **Next**

Consider the following statements:

```
Dim randomObject As New Random()
Dim randomNumber As Integer = randomObject.Next()
```

The first statement declares `randomObject` as a reference to an object of type `Random` and creates a new `Random` object.

The second statement declares `Integer` variable `randomNumber` and assigns to it the value returned by calling `Random` method **Next**. Method `Next` generates a positive `Integer` value greater than or equal to zero and less than the constant **Int32.MaxValue**

(2,147,483,647). If Next truly produces values at random, every value in this range has an equal chance (or probability) of being chosen when Next is called. The values returned by Next are actually pseudorandom numbers, or a sequence of values produced by a complex mathematical calculation. This calculation requires a seed value. If the seed value is different each time the program is run, the series of values will be different as well (so that the generated numbers are indeed random). When we create a Random object, the seed is based on the current time. Alternatively, we can pass a seed value as an argument in the parentheses after New Random. Passing in the same seed twice results in the same series of random numbers. Using the current time of day as the seed value is effective because the time is likely to change for each Random object we create.

The range of values produced by Next is often different from what is needed in a particular application. For example, a program that simulates coin tossing might require only 0 for "heads" and 1 for "tails." A program that simulates the rolling of a six-sided die would require random integers in the range 1–6. Similarly, a program that randomly predicts the next type of spaceship (out of four possibilities) that flies across the horizon in a video game might require random integers from 1 to 4.

Scaling and Shifting of Random Numbers

By passing an argument to method Next as follows

```
value = 1 + randomObject.Next(6)
```

we can produce integers in the range 1–6. When a single argument is passed to Next, the values returned by Next will be in the range from 0 to (but not including) the value of that argument. This is called scaling. The number 6 is the scaling factor. We shift the range of numbers produced by adding 1 to our previous result, so that the return values are between 1 and 6 rather than 0 and 5.

Visual Basic simplifies the process of specifying a range of random numbers by allowing you to pass two arguments to Next. For example, the preceding statement also could be written as

```
value = randomObject.Next(1, 7)
```

Note that we must use 7 as the second argument to produce integers in the range from 1–6. The first argument indicates the minimum value in our desired range, whereas the second is equal to 1 + the maximum value desired. Figure 7.14 demonstrates the use of class Random and method Next by simulating 20 rolls of a six-sided die and showing the value of each roll. Note that all the values are in the range from 1 to 6, inclusive.

```
' Fig. 7.14: RandomInteger.vb
' Random integers from 1 to 6 created by calling Random method Next
Module RandomInteger
   Sub Main()
      Dim randomObject As New Random() ' create Random object
      Dim randomNumber As Integer

```

Fig. 7.14 | Random integers from 1 to 6 created by calling Random method Next. (Part 1 of 2.)

```
      ' generate 20 random numbers between 1 and 6
      For i = 1 To 20
         randomNumber = randomObject.Next(1, 7)
         Console.Write(randomNumber & " ")

         If i Mod 5 = 0 Then ' is i a multiple of 5?
            Console.WriteLine()
         End If
      Next
   End Sub ' Main
End Module ' RandomInteger
```

```
1 1 3 1 1
2 1 1 3 6
6 3 4 6 6
2 2 3 6 5
```

Fig. 7.14 | Random integers from 1 to 6 created by calling `Random` method `Next`. (Part 2 of 2.)

The program in Fig. 7.15 uses class `Random` to simulate rolling four six-sided dice. We then use some of the functionality from this program in another example (Fig. 7.17) to demonstrate that the numbers generated by `Next` occur with approximately equal likelihood.

```
' Fig. 7.15: RollDice.vb
' Rolling four dice.
Public Class RollDice
   Dim randomObject As New Random() ' create Random object

   ' display results of four rolls
   Private Sub rollButton_Click(ByVal sender As System.Object, _
      ByVal e As System.EventArgs) Handles rollButton.Click
      ' method randomly assigns a face to each die
      DisplayDie(die1PictureBox)
      DisplayDie(die2PictureBox)
      DisplayDie(die3PictureBox)
      DisplayDie(die4PictureBox)
   End Sub ' rollButton_Click

   ' get a random die image
   Sub DisplayDie(ByVal diePictureBox As PictureBox)
      ' generate random integer in range 1 to 6
      Dim face As Integer = randomObject.Next(1, 7)

      ' retrieve specific die image from resources
      Dim pictureResource = My.Resources.ResourceManager.GetObject( _
         String.Format("die{0}", face))

      ' convert pictureResource to type Image and display in PictureBox
      diePictureBox.Image = CType(pictureResource, Image)
   End Sub ' DisplayDie
End Class ' RollDice
```

Fig. 7.15 | Demonstrating four die rolls with graphical output. (Part 1 of 2.)

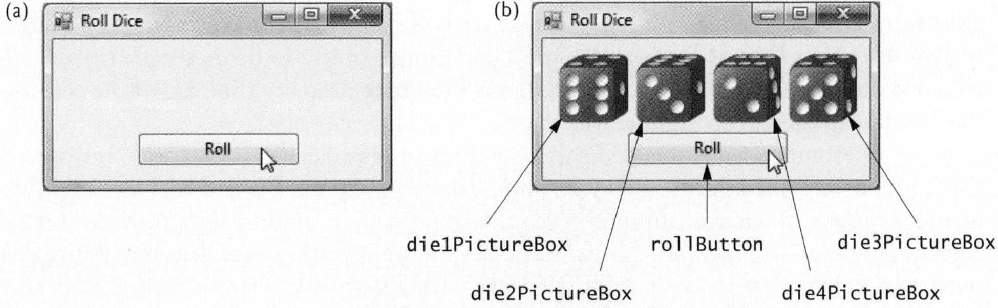

Fig. 7.15 | Demonstrating four die rolls with graphical output. (Part 2 of 2.)

Using `Buttons` *on a GUI*

Before we discuss the use of `Random` in this application, let's analyze the GUI controls we use and the flow of control in this example. The names of the GUI controls are indicated in the output of Fig. 7.15. In this example, we use four `PictureBoxes`. You used `PictureBoxes` in Chapters 2 and 5. In these examples, you used the `PictureBox`'s `Image` property to display an image. We will do the same, but set the control's `Image` property programmatically, so that different die images can be displayed based on the random numbers generated.

In this example, we also use our first `Button` control. Like the other controls we have used, the `Button` control can be simply dragged and dropped onto the `Form` from the **Toolbox**, and its sizing handles can be used to increase or decrease the `Button`'s size. The `Button`'s `Text` property has been set to **Roll**. Name the control `rollButton`.

Creating a `Click` *Event Handler*

Random die images are displayed whenever the user clicks the **Roll** `Button`. To enable such functionality, we need to add an event handler for our `Button`'s `Click` event. Double click the `Button` in design view to create the empty event handler in your code. In Chapter 5 we created an event handler for the `Form`'s `Load` event, which executes when the `Form` loads. An event handler for a `Button`'s `Click` event executes whenever the `Button` is clicked. The event handler with code added to its body is defined in lines 7–14. The name of the event handler is `rollButton_Click`. Note that the event handler method is declared as a `Sub` procedure—the event handler performs actions in response to an event, but does not return a value. The event handler's first argument represents the object with which the user interacted; the second argument is an object that contains information about the event. Event-handler names created by the IDE normally begin with the object's name, followed by an underscore and the event's name. From here on, if you see a method in an example named using this convention, you can assume that it is an event handler. Event handlers are discussed in more detail in Chapter 14.

Displaying Random Images in a `PictureBox`

The body of our event handler calls method `DisplayDie` four times, once for each `PictureBox` on the `Form`. Calling `DisplayDie` (lines 10–13) causes four dice to appear as if they were being rolled each time **Roll** is clicked. When this program runs, the dice images do not appear until the user clicks **Roll** the first time.

Method `DisplayDie` (lines 17–27) specifies the correct image for the face value calculated by method `Next` (line 19). Note that we declare `randomObject` as an instance variable of class `RollDice` (line 4). This allows the same `Random` object to be used each time `DisplayDie` executes. The code in lines 22–26 sets the `Image` property (line 25) of the current `PictureBox` (passed as an argument).

In this example, we embedded the images into the project as resources. This causes the compiler to embed the images in the application's executable file and enables the application to access the images through Visual Basic's `My` namespace, which provides many capabilities that make common Visual Basic programming tasks easier. By embedding the images in the application, you don't need to worry about wrapping the images with the application when you move it to another location or computer. The images used in this example are located with the chapter's examples in the `Images` folder. You can download the examples from `www.deitel.com/books/vb2008htp/`.

If you are creating a new project, use the following steps to add images to the project as resources:

1. After creating your project, double click **My Project** in the **Solution Explorer** to display the project's properties.
2. Click the **Resources** tab.
3. At the top of the **Resources** tab click the down arrow next to the **Add Resource** button (Fig. 7.16) and select **Add Existing File...** to display the **Add** existing file to resources dialog.
4. Locate the image files you wish to add as resources and click the **Open** button.
5. Save your project.

The files now appear in a folder named **Resources** in the **Solution Explorer.** We'll use this technique in most examples that use images going forward. For more details on the `My` namespace visit `msdn.microsoft.com/en-us/vbasic/ms789188.aspx`.

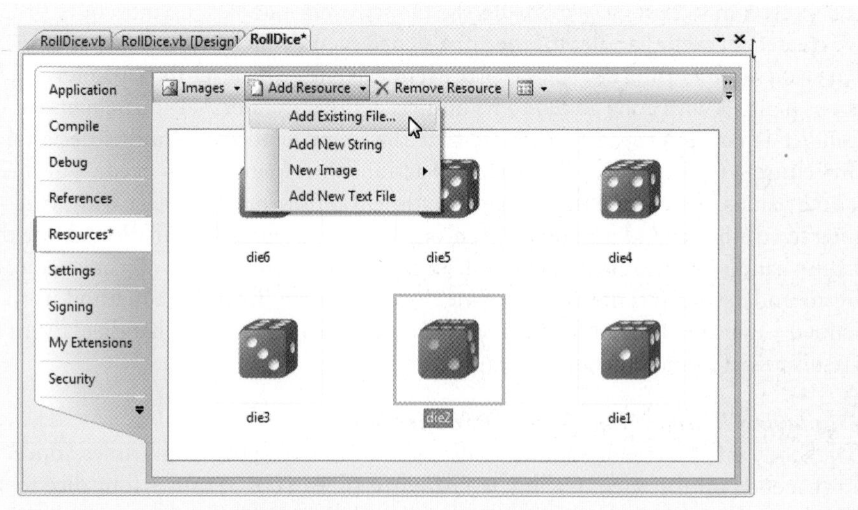

Fig. 7.16 | Images added as resources.

To access an image (or any other resource) in the project's resources, you use the method `My.Resources.ResourceManager.GetObject`, which takes as an argument the resource name as it appears in the **Resources** tab (e.g., `"die1"`) and returns the resource as an `Object`. Lines 22–23 invoke `GetObject` with the result of the expression

```
String.Format("die{0}", face)
```

which builds the name of the resource by placing the random number `face` at the end of the word `"die"`. You must convert this `Object` to type `Image` to assign it to the `PictureBox`'s `Image` property. Line 26 uses Visual Basic's `CType` function to perform the conversion. `CType` converts its first argument to the type specified in its second argument. A conversion performed with the `CType` function is also known as a cast operation.

The `My` namespace also provides direct access to the resources you define with expressions of the form `My.Resources.`*resourceName*, where *resourceName* is the name you provided to the resource when you created it. When using such an expression, the resource returned already has the appropriate type. For example, `My.Resources.die1` is an `Image` object representing the `die1.png` image.

Rolling Dice Repeatedly and Displaying Statistics

The Windows `Forms` application in Fig. 7.17 enables the reader to repeatedly roll 12 dice to show that the numbers generated by class `Random` occur with approximately equal frequencies. The program displays the cumulative frequencies of each face in a `TextBox` control, and the die faces are displayed using 12 `PictureBoxes`.

```
' Fig. 7.17: RollTwelveDice.vb
' Rolling 12 dice with frequency chart.
Public Class RollTwelveDice
   Dim randomObject As New Random() ' generate random number
   Dim ones As Integer ' count of die face 1
   Dim twos As Integer ' count of die face 2
   Dim threes As Integer ' count of die face 3
   Dim fours As Integer ' count of die face 4
   Dim fives As Integer ' count of die face 5
   Dim sixes As Integer ' count of die face 6

   ' display result of twelve rolls
   Private Sub rollButton_Click(ByVal sender As System.Object, _
      ByVal e As System.EventArgs) Handles rollButton.Click

      ' assign random faces to 12 dice using DisplayDie
      DisplayDie(die1PictureBox)
      DisplayDie(die2PictureBox)
      DisplayDie(die3PictureBox)
      DisplayDie(die4PictureBox)
      DisplayDie(die5PictureBox)
      DisplayDie(die6PictureBox)
      DisplayDie(die7PictureBox)
      DisplayDie(die8PictureBox)
      DisplayDie(die9PictureBox)
```

Fig. 7.17 | `Random` class used to simulate rolling 12 six-sided dice. (Part 1 of 3.)

```
      DisplayDie(die10PictureBox)
      DisplayDie(die11PictureBox)
      DisplayDie(die12PictureBox)

      Dim total As Integer = ones + twos + threes + fours + fives + sixes
      Dim output As String

      ' display frequencies of faces
      output = ("Face" & vbTab & "Frequency" & vbTab & "Percent")
      output &= (vbNewLine & "1" & vbTab & ones & _
         vbTab & vbTab & String.Format("{0:P2}", ones / total))
      output &= (vbNewLine & "2" & vbTab & twos & vbTab & _
         vbTab & String.Format("{0:P2}", twos / total))
      output &= (vbNewLine & "3" & vbTab & threes & vbTab & _
         vbTab & String.Format("{0:P2}", threes / total))
      output &= (vbNewLine & "4" & vbTab & fours & vbTab & _
         vbTab & String.Format("{0:P2}", fours / total))
      output &= (vbNewLine & "5" & vbTab & fives & vbTab & _
         vbTab & String.Format("{0:P2}", fives / total))
      output &= (vbNewLine & "6" & vbTab & sixes & vbTab & _
         vbTab & String.Format("{0:P2}", sixes / total) & vbNewLine)
      displayTextBox.Text = output
   End Sub ' rollButton_Click

   ' display a single die image
   Sub DisplayDie(ByVal diePictureBox As PictureBox)
      Dim face As Integer = randomObject.Next(1, 7)

      ' retrieve specific die image from resources
      Dim pictureResource = My.Resources.ResourceManager.GetObject( _
         String.Format("die{0}", face))

      ' convert pictureResource to image type and load into PictureBox
      diePictureBox.Image = CType(pictureResource, Image)

      ' maintain count of die faces
      Select Case face
         Case 1 ' die face 1
            ones += 1
         Case 2 ' die face 2
            twos += 1
         Case 3 ' die face 3
            threes += 1
         Case 4 ' die face 4
            fours += 1
         Case 5 ' die face 5
            fives += 1
         Case 6 ' die face 6
            sixes += 1
      End Select
   End Sub ' DisplayDie
End Class ' RollTwelveDice
```

Fig. 7.17 | Random class used to simulate rolling 12 six-sided dice. (Part 2 of 3.)

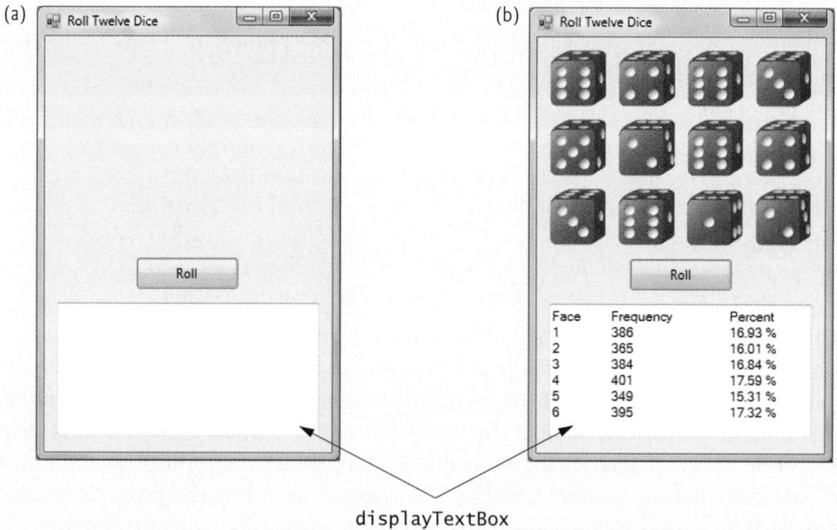

Fig. 7.17 | `Random` class used to simulate rolling 12 six-sided dice. (Part 3 of 3.)

The `TextBox` control is located toward the bottom of the GUI. This control can be used both for displaying data to the user and for inputting data from the user. The data in the `TextBox` can be accessed and modified via the control's `Text` property. This `TextBox`'s name is `displayTextBox` and the font size has been set to 9. Finally, the `TextBox`'s `Multiline` property has been set to `True`, so that multiple lines of text can be displayed.

Figure 7.17 contains two screenshots. The one on the left shows the program when it initially executes, and the one on the right shows the program after the user has clicked **Roll** over 200 times. If the values produced by method `Next` are indeed random, the frequencies of the face values (1–6) should be approximately the same (as Figure 7.17(b) illustrates).

To show that the die rolls occur with approximately equal likelihood, the program in Fig. 7.17 has been modified to keep some simple statistics. We declare counters for each of the possible rolls in lines 5–10. Note that the counters are instance variables. Lines 35–47 display the frequency of each roll as percentages using the `P` format specifier. `P2` indicates that the percentages should be displayed with 2 digits to the right of the decimal point.

As the program output demonstrates, method `Next` can be used to effectively simulate the rolling of a six-sided die. Over the course of many die rolls, each of the possible faces from 1–6 appears with equal likelihood, or approximately one-sixth of the time. Note that *no* `Case Else` is provided in the `Select...Case` statement (lines 62–75), because we know that the values generated are in the range 1–6. In Chapter 8, Arrays, we show the power of arrays by explaining how to replace the entire `Select...Case` statement in this program with a single-line statement.

Run the program several times and observe the results. Note that a different sequence of random numbers is obtained each time the program is executed, causing the resulting frequencies to vary.

7.16 Case Study: A Game of Chance

One of the most popular games of chance is a dice game known as "craps." The rules of the game are straightforward:

> *A player rolls two dice. Each die has six faces. Each face contains 1, 2, 3, 4, 5 or 6 spots. After the dice have come to rest, the sum of the spots on the two upward faces is calculated. If the sum is 7 or 11 on the first throw, the player wins. If the sum is 2, 3 or 12 on the first throw (called "craps"), the player loses (i.e., the "house" wins). If the sum is 4, 5, 6, 8, 9 or 10 on the first throw, that sum becomes the player's "point." To win, players must continue rolling the dice until they "make their point" (i.e., roll their point value). The player loses by rolling a 7 before making the point.*

The application in Fig. 7.18 simulates the game of craps.

The player must roll two dice on the first and all subsequent rolls. When executing the application, click the **Play** `Button` to play the game. The form displays the results of each roll. The screen captures depict the execution of two games. Figure 7.18(a) displays the `Form` before the game has begun, while Fig. 7.18(b) shows the application after the **Play** `Button` has been clicked. In this example, a 9 is rolled, which is the point to make. We click **Roll** again and a 9 is rolled, causing us to win the game (Fig. 7.18(c)). Figure 7.18(d) shows another example game, where the user loses by rolling a 3 on the first roll.

```
' Fig 7.18: CrapsGame.vb
' Craps game using class Random.
Public Class CrapsGame
   ' die-roll constants
   Enum DiceNames
      SNAKE_EYES = 2
      TREY = 3
      LUCKY_SEVEN = 7
      CRAPS = 7
      YO_LEVEN = 11
      BOX_CARS = 12
   End Enum

   Dim myPoint As Integer ' total point
   Dim myDie1 As Integer ' die1 face
   Dim myDie2 As Integer ' die2 face
   Dim randomObject As New Random() ' generate random number

   ' begins new game and determines point
   Private Sub playButton_Click(ByVal sender As System.Object, _
      ByVal e As System.EventArgs) Handles playButton.Click

      ' initialize variables for new game
      myPoint = 0
      pointGroupBox.Text = "Point"
      statusLabel.Text = String.Empty

      ' remove point-die images
      pointDie1PictureBox.Image = Nothing
```

Fig. 7.18 | Craps game using class `Random`. (Part 1 of 3.)

```
      pointDie2PictureBox.Image = Nothing

      Dim sum As Integer = RollDice() ' roll dice and calculate sum

      ' check die roll
      Select Case sum
         Case DiceNames.LUCKY_SEVEN, DiceNames.YO_LEVEN
            rollButton.Enabled = False ' disable Roll button
            statusLabel.Text = "You Win!!!"
         Case DiceNames.SNAKE_EYES, DiceNames.TREY, DiceNames.BOX_CARS
            rollButton.Enabled = False ' disable Roll button
            statusLabel.Text = "Sorry. You Lose."
         Case Else
            myPoint = sum
            pointGroupBox.Text = "Point is " & sum
            statusLabel.Text = "Roll Again!"
            DisplayDie(pointDie1PictureBox, myDie1)
            DisplayDie(pointDie2PictureBox, myDie2)
            playButton.Enabled = False ' disable Play button
            rollButton.Enabled = True ' enable Roll button
      End Select
   End Sub ' playButton_Click

   ' determines outcome of next roll
   Private Sub rollButton_Click(ByVal sender As System.Object, _
      ByVal e As System.EventArgs) Handles rollButton.Click

      Dim sum As Integer = RollDice() ' roll dice and calculate sum

      ' check outcome of roll
      If sum = myPoint Then ' win
         statusLabel.Text = "You Win!!!"
         rollButton.Enabled = False ' disable Roll button
         playButton.Enabled = True ' enable Play button
      ElseIf sum = DiceNames.CRAPS Then ' lose
         statusLabel.Text = "Sorry. You Lose."
         rollButton.Enabled = False ' disable Roll button
         playButton.Enabled = True ' enable Play button
      End If
   End Sub ' rollButton_Click

   ' display die image
   Sub DisplayDie(ByVal diePictureBox As PictureBox, _
      ByVal face As Integer)

      ' retrieve specific die image from resources
      Dim pictureResource = My.Resources.ResourceManager.GetObject( _
         String.Format("die{0}", face))

      ' convert pictureResource to image type and load into PictureBox
      diePictureBox.Image = CType(pictureResource, Image)
   End Sub ' DisplayDie
```

Fig. 7.18 | Craps game using class `Random`. (Part 2 of 3.)

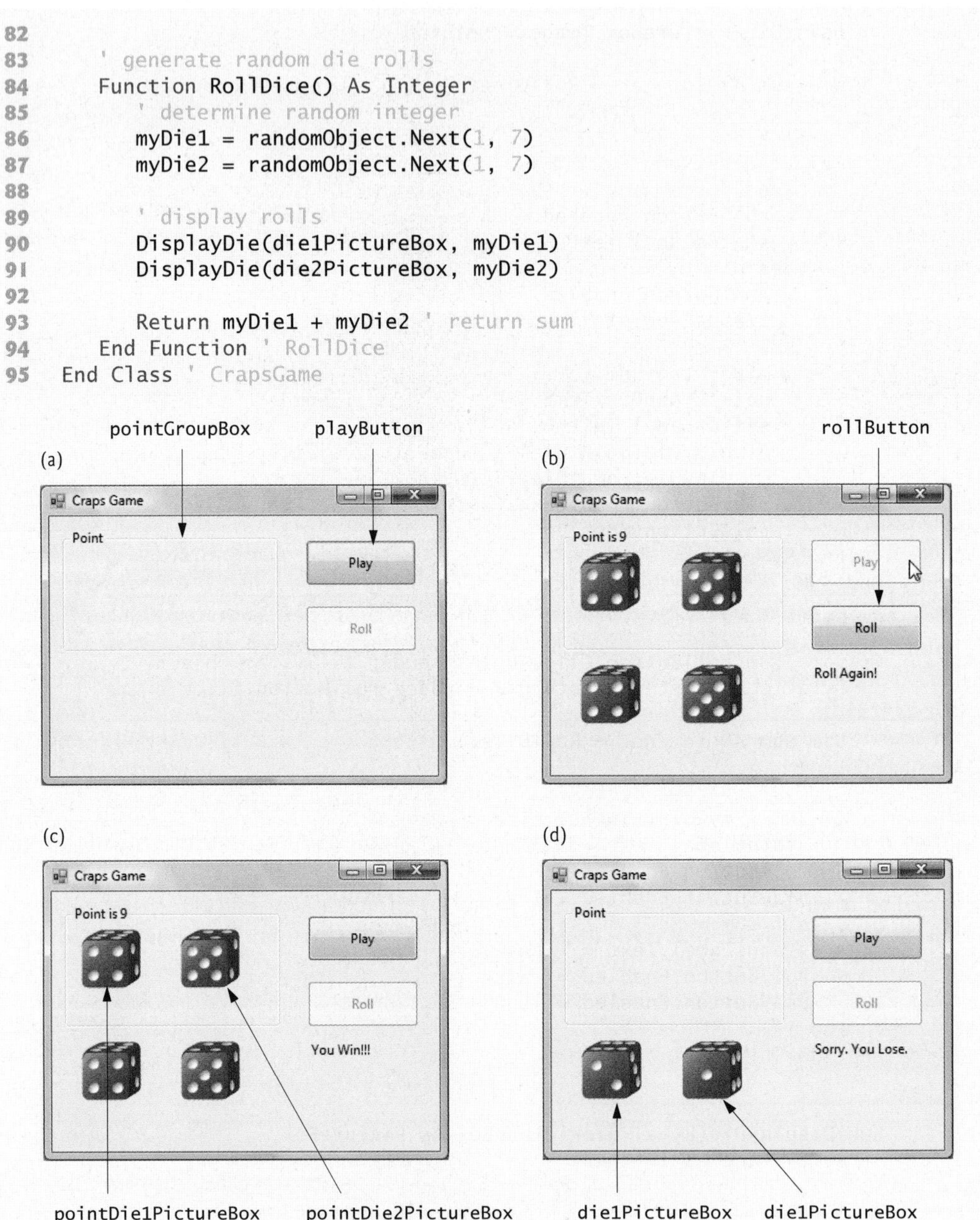

```
      ' generate random die rolls
      Function RollDice() As Integer
         ' determine random integer
         myDie1 = randomObject.Next(1, 7)
         myDie2 = randomObject.Next(1, 7)

         ' display rolls
         DisplayDie(die1PictureBox, myDie1)
         DisplayDie(die2PictureBox, myDie2)

         Return myDie1 + myDie2 ' return sum
      End Function ' RollDice
   End Class ' CrapsGame
```


Fig. 7.18 | Craps game using class `Random`. (Part 3 of 3.)

This program introduces the **`GroupBox`** control, used to display the user's point. A `GroupBox` is a container used to group related controls. Within the `GroupBox` `pointDice-Group`, we add two `PictureBoxes`, which are controls that display images. You can drag and drop a `GroupBox` onto the `Form` the same way you would any other control. When adding other controls to a `GroupBox` (such as the two `PictureBoxes` in this example), drag and drop the controls within the bounds of the GroupBox on the Form. We set the GroupBox's Text property to **Point**. This is the text that displays in the upper-left corner of the GroupBox. Note in the output of Fig. 7.18 that we'll be modifying this text to display the user's point value. If you leave the Text property blank, the GroupBox displays as a simple border without any text.

Enumerations and Constants

Before introducing any method declarations, the program includes several declarations, including our first enumeration. Enumerations enhance program readability by providing descriptive identifiers for constant numbers or Strings. Enumerations help you ensure that values are consistent throughout a program. Enumerations are used to define groups of related constants. (Recall that keyword Const creates a single constant identifier and that such an identifier must be initialized in its declaration.) In this case, we create an Enumeration of descriptive names for the various dice combinations in craps (i.e., SNAKE_EYES, TREY, LUCKY_SEVEN, CRAPS, YO_LEVEN and BOX_CARS). Note that multiple enumeration members can have the same value—in this example, LUCKY_SEVEN and CRAPS both have the value 7. We use two identifiers for program clarity; on the first roll, a seven causes the player to win (LUCKY_SEVEN), and on subsequent rolls, a seven causes the player to lose (CRAPS).

After the declarations for several instance variables (lines 14–17), lines 20–51 declare method playButton_Click to handle playButton's Click event. When the user clicks the **Play** button, method playButton_Click sets up a new game by initializing several values (lines 24–26). Note that line 26 sets our status Label's Text property to String.Empty. This constant from class String represents the so-called empty string (i.e., a string that does not contain any characters), which can also be represented as empty double-quotation characters (""). Nothing appears on the screen when an empty string is displayed. Recall from Chapter 4 that the default value of a String is Nothing, called the null string, which also does not display anything on the screen. The null string and empty string are quite different. The null string represents a String reference that does not yet refer to a String object. The empty string represents a String containing no characters. You can invoke methods on the empty string, but not on the null string.

Setting the Image property of pointDie1PictureBox and pointDie2PictureBox to Nothing (lines 29–30) causes the PictureBoxes to appear blank. Method playButton_Click executes the game's opening roll by calling RollDice (line 38). Internally, RollDice (lines 84–94) generates two random numbers and calls method DisplayDie (lines 72–81), which displays an appropriate die image in its PictureBox argument.

The Select...Case statement (lines 35–50) analyzes the roll returned by RollDice to determine how play should continue (i.e., by terminating the game with a win or loss, or by enabling subsequent rolls). If the user does not win or lose on the first roll, the GroupBox's text is set to display the point value (line 44) and the property images are displayed in the GroupBox's PictureBoxes (lines 46–47). Depending on the value of the roll, Buttons **Roll** and **Play** become either enabled or disabled (lines 37, 40 and 48–49). Disabling a Button means that no action will be performed when the Button is clicked. Buttons can be enabled and disabled by setting the Button's Enabled property to True or False, respectively.

If button **Roll** is enabled, clicking it invokes method `rollButton_Click` (lines 54–69), which executes an additional roll of the dice. Method `rollButton_Click` then analyzes the roll, letting users know whether they have won or lost.

7.17 Method Overloading

Visual Basic provides several ways of allowing methods to have variable sets of parameters. Method overloading allows you to create multiple methods with the same name but different signatures—that is, different numbers and types of parameters—or with different orderings of the parameters (by type). When an overloaded method is called, the compiler selects the proper method by examining the number, types and order (by type) of the arguments. Often, method overloading is used to create several methods with the same name that perform similar tasks on different types of data.

Good Programming Practice 7.3

Overloading methods that perform closely related tasks can make programs clearer.

Figure 7.19 uses overloaded method `Square` to calculate the square of both an `Integer` and a `Double`. If the compiler looked only at method names during compilation, the code in Fig. 7.19 would be ambiguous—the compiler would not know how to differentiate between the two `Square` methods. The compiler uses a process known as overload resolution to determine which method to call. This process first searches for all methods that *could* be used on the basis of the number and type of arguments that are present. Although it might seem that only one method would match, it is important to remember that Visual Basic converts variables as necessary when they are passed as arguments. Once all matching methods are found, the compiler then selects the closest match.

```
' Fig. 7.19: Overload.vb
' Using overloaded methods.
Module Overload
   Sub Main() ' call Square methods with Integer, then with Double
      Console.WriteLine("The square of Integer 7 is " & Square(7) & _
         vbNewLine & "The square of Double 7.5 is " & Square(7.5))
   End Sub ' Main

   ' method Square takes an Integer and returns an Integer
   Function Square(ByVal value As Integer) As Integer
      Return Convert.ToInt32(value ^ 2)
   End Function ' Square

   ' method Square takes a Double and returns a Double
   Function Square(ByVal value As Double) As Double
      Return value ^ 2
   End Function ' Square
End Module ' Overload
```

```
The square of Integer 7 is 49
The square of Double 7.5 is 56.25
```

Fig. 7.19 | Using overloaded methods.

Note that at line 11 we use method `Convert.ToInt32`, which converts its argument to a value of type `Integer`. This explicit conversion is needed because the exponent (`^`) operator expects operands of type `Double` and implicitly converts its operands to that type. This version of method `Square` returns an `Integer` value, so `Convert.ToInt32` performs this conversion. Recall that because we are now using **Option Strict**, such conversion is required to compile the application.

In Fig. 7.19, the compiler might use the logical name "`Square` of `Integer`" for the `Square` method that specifies an `Integer` parameter (line 10) and "`Square` of `Double`" for the `Square` method that specifies a `Double` parameter (line 15). If a method `ExampleSub`'s declaration begins as

```
Function ExampleSub(ByVal a As Integer, ByVal b As Double) _
   As Integer
```

the compiler might use the logical name "`ExampleSub` of `Integer` and `Double`." Similarly, if the parameters are specified as

```
Function ExampleSub(ByVal a As Double, ByVal b As Integer) _
   As Integer
```

the compiler might use the logical name "`ExampleSub` of `Double` and `Integer`." The order of the parameters (by type) is important to the compiler; it considers the preceding two `ExampleSub` methods to be distinct.

So far, the logical method names used by the compiler have not mentioned the methods' return types. This is because method calls cannot be distinguished by return type. The program in Fig. 7.20 illustrates the syntax error that is generated when two methods have the same signature and different return types. Overloaded methods with different parameter lists can have different return types. Overloaded methods need not have the same number of parameters.

Common Programming Error 7.9

Creating overloaded methods with identical parameter lists and different return types is a compilation error.

```
' Fig. 7.20: Overload2.vb
' Using overloaded methods with identical signatures and
' different return types.
Module Overload2
   Sub Main() ' call Square methods with Integer and Double
      Console.WriteLine("The square of Integer 7 is " & Square(7) & _
         vbNewLine & "The square of Double 7.5 is " & Square(7.5))
   End Sub ' Main

   ' method takes a Double and returns an Integer
   Function Square(ByVal value As Double) As Integer
      Return Convert.ToInt32(value ^ 2)
   End Function ' Square

```

Fig. 7.20 | Syntax error generated from overloaded methods with identical parameter lists and different return types. (Part 1 of 2.)

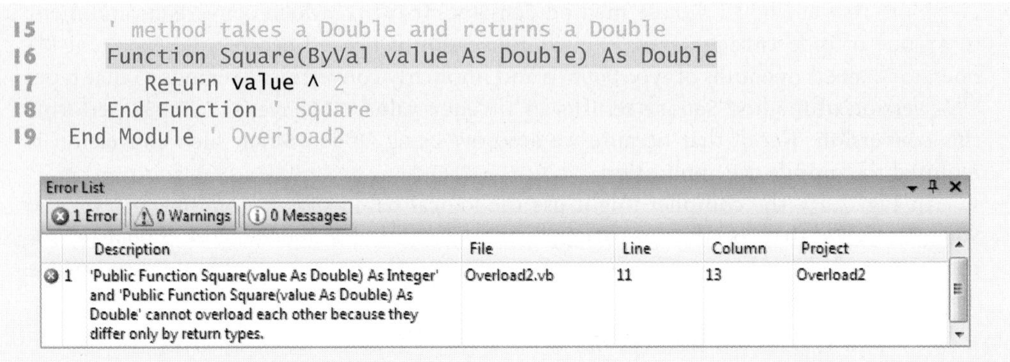

```
    ' method takes a Double and returns a Double
    Function Square(ByVal value As Double) As Double
       Return value ^ 2
    End Function ' Square
End Module ' Overload2
```

Error List

1 Error | 0 Warnings | 0 Messages

	Description	File	Line	Column	Project
1	'Public Function Square(value As Double) As Integer' and 'Public Function Square(value As Double) As Double' cannot overload each other because they differ only by return types.	Overload2.vb	11	13	Overload2

Fig. 7.20 | Syntax error generated from overloaded methods with identical parameter lists and different return types. (Part 2 of 2.)

7.18 Optional Parameters

Methods can have optional parameters. Declaring a parameter as optional allows the calling method to vary the number of arguments to pass. Optional parameters specify a default value that is assigned to the parameter if the optional argument is not passed. Overloaded methods are generally more flexible than methods with optional parameters. For instance, you can specify different return types for overloaded methods.

You can create methods with one or more optional parameters. All optional parameters, however, must be placed to the right of the method's nonoptional parameters—i.e., at the end of the parameter list.

Common Programming Error 7.10

Declaring a non-`Optional` parameter to the right of an `Optional` parameter is a syntax error.

When a parameter is declared as optional, the caller has the *option* of passing that particular argument. Optional parameters are specified in the method header with keyword `Optional`. For example, the method header

```
Sub ExampleMethod(ByVal value1 As Boolean, _
   Optional ByVal value2 As Integer = 0)
```

specifies the last parameter as `Optional`. Any call to `ExampleMethod` must pass at least one argument (the `Boolean`), or else a syntax error is generated. If the caller chooses, a second argument (the `Integer`) can be passed to `ExampleMethod`. Consider the following calls to `ExampleMethod`:

```
ExampleMethod()
ExampleMethod(True)
ExampleMethod(False, 10)
```

The first call to `ExampleMethod` generates a syntax error because a minimum of one argument is required for this method. The second call to `ExampleMethod` is valid because one argument (the `Boolean`) is being passed—the `Optional` argument, corresponding to parameter `value2`, is not specified in the method call. The last call to `ExampleMethod` also is valid: `False` is passed as the one required argument, and `10` is passed as the `Optional` argument.

In the call that passes only one argument (`True`) to `ExampleMethod`, parameter `value2` defaults to `0`, which is the value specified in the method header. `Optional` parameters must specify a default value, using the equals sign followed by the value. For example, the header for `ExampleMethod` sets `0` as the default value for `value2`. Default values can be used only with parameters declared as `Optional`.

Common Programming Error 7.11

Not specifying a default value for an `Optional` *parameter is a syntax error.*

The example in Fig. 7.21 demonstrates the use of optional parameters. The program calculates the result of raising a base to an exponent, both of which are specified by the user. Method `Power` (lines 23–33) specifies that its second parameter is `Optional`. If the user does not specify an exponent, the `Optional` argument is omitted, and the default parameter value, `2`, is used.

```
1  ' Fig 7.21: Power.vb
2  ' Optional argument demonstration with method Power.
3  Public Class Power
4     ' reads input and displays result
5     Private Sub calculateButton_Click(ByVal sender As System.Object, _
6        ByVal e As System.EventArgs) Handles calculateButton.Click
7
8        Dim value As Integer
9
10       ' call version of Power depending on power input
11       If Not String.IsNullOrEmpty(powerTextBox.Text) Then
12          value = Power(Convert.ToInt32(baseTextBox.Text), _
13             Convert.ToInt32(powerTextBox.Text))
14       Else
15          value = Power(Convert.ToInt32(baseTextBox.Text))
16          powerTextBox.Text = Convert.ToString(2)
17       End If
18
19       outputLabel.Text = Convert.ToString(value)
20    End Sub ' calculateButton_Click
21
22    ' use iteration to calculate power
23    Function Power(ByVal base As Integer, _
24       Optional ByVal exponent As Integer = 2) As Integer
25
26       Dim total As Integer = 1 ' initialize total
27
28       For i = 1 To exponent ' calculate power
29          total *= base
30       Next
31
```

Fig. 7.21 | `Optional` argument demonstration with method `Power`. (Part 1 of 2.)

```
32         Return total ' return result
33      End Function ' Power
34   End Class ' Power
```

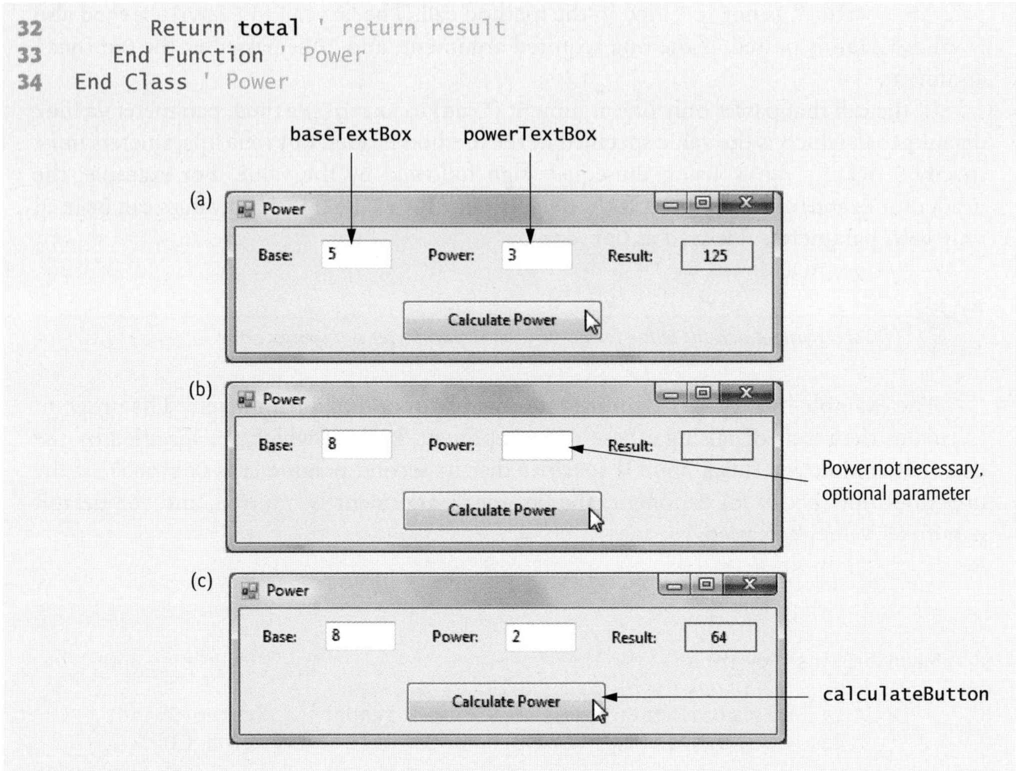

Fig. 7.21 | `Optional` argument demonstration with method `Power`. (Part 2 of 2.)

In this example, we use `TextBoxes` to input data from the user. When the **Calculate Power** `Button` is clicked, line 11 determines whether `powerTextBox` contains a value by passing the value of its `Text` property to `String` method `IsNullOrEmpty`, which returns true if its argument is the value `Nothing` or the empty string. If the condition is true (as in Fig. 7.21(a)), the values in the `TextBoxes` are converted to `Integers` and passed to `Power`. Otherwise, `txtBase`'s value is converted to an `Integer` and passed as the first of two arguments to `Power` in line 15. An example of this is shown in Fig. 7.21(b), where we clicked the **Calculate Power** `Button` without entering an exponent value. The second argument, `2`, is provided by the compiler (using the default value of the `Optional` argument) and is not visible to you in the call. Line 16 displays the value `2` in `txtPower`, for clarity (Fig. 7.21(c)).

7.19 Recursion

It is sometimes useful for methods to call themselves—a recursive method is a method that calls itself either directly or indirectly (i.e., through another method). In this section, we present a simple example of recursion.

Let's first consider recursion conceptually. Recursive problem-solving approaches have a number of elements in common. A recursive method is called to solve a problem. The method actually knows how to solve only the simplest case(s)—the base case(s). If the method is called with a base case, it returns a result. If the method is called with a more complex problem, it divides the problem into two conceptual pieces—a piece that the method knows how to perform (i.e., base case), and a piece that it does not know how to perform. To make recursion feasible, the latter piece must resemble the original problem but be a slightly simpler or smaller version of it. The method invokes (calls) a fresh copy of itself to work on the smaller problem—this is referred to as a recursive call, or recursion step. The recursion step also normally includes the keyword `Return`, because its result will be combined with the portion of the problem that the method knew how to solve. Such a combination will form a result that will be passed back to the original caller.

The recursion step executes while the original call to the method is still "open" (i.e., has not finished executing). The recursion step can result in many more recursive calls, as the method divides each new subproblem into two conceptual pieces. As the method continues to call itself with slightly simpler versions of the original problem, the sequence of smaller and smaller problems must converge on a base case, so that the recursion can eventually terminate. At that point, the method recognizes the base case and returns a result to the previous copy of the method. A sequence of returns ensues up the line until the original method call returns the final result to the caller. As an example of these concepts, let's write a recursive program that performs a popular mathematical calculation.

Determining a Factorial Value Recursively

The factorial of a nonnegative integer *n,* written *n*! (and read "*n* factorial"), is the product

$$n \cdot (n - 1) \cdot (n - 2) \cdot \ldots \cdot 1$$

with 1! equal to 1, and 0! defined as 1. For example, 5! is the product $5 \cdot 4 \cdot 3 \cdot 2 \cdot 1$, which is equal to 120.

The factorial of an integer `number` greater than or equal to 0 can be calculated iteratively (nonrecursively) using a `For...Next` statement, as follows:

```
Dim counter, factorial As Integer = 1

For counter = number To 1 Step -1
   factorial *= counter
Next
```

We arrive at a recursive definition of the factorial method by observing the following relationship:

$$n! = n \cdot (n - 1)!$$

For example, 5! is clearly equal to $5 \cdot 4!$, as is shown by the following:

$$5! = 5 \cdot 4 \cdot 3 \cdot 2 \cdot 1$$
$$5! = 5 \cdot (4 \cdot 3 \cdot 2 \cdot 1)$$
$$5! = 5 \cdot (4!)$$

A recursive evaluation of 5! would proceed as in Fig. 7.22. Figure 7.22(a) shows how the succession of recursive calls proceeds until 1! is evaluated to be 1, which terminates the recursion. Figure 7.22(b) depicts the values that are returned from each recursive call to its caller until the final value is calculated and returned.

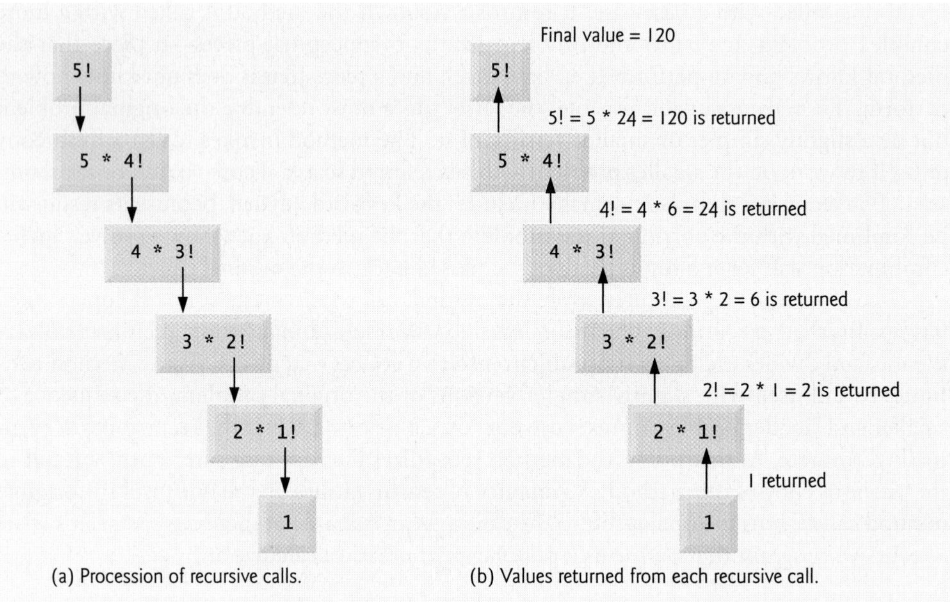

Fig. 7.22 | Recursive evaluation of 5!.

Figure 7.23 recursively calculates and prints factorials. The recursive method `Factorial` (lines 19–25) first tests (line 20) to determine whether its terminating condition is true (i.e., `number` is less than or equal to 1). This determines whether the parameter is one of the base cases (0 or 1). If `number` is less than or equal to 1, `Factorial` returns `1`, no further recursion is necessary and the method returns. If `number` is greater than `1`, line 23 expresses the problem as the product of `number` and a recursive call to `Factorial`, evaluating the factorial of `number - 1`. Note that calculating `Factorial(number - 1)` is slightly simpler than the original calculation, `Factorial(number)`.

```
1  ' Fig. 7.23: FactorialCalculator.vb
2  ' Calculating factorials using recursion.
3  Public Class FactorialCalculator
4     ' calculate factorial
5     Private Sub calculateButton_Click(ByVal sender As System.Object, _
6        ByVal e As System.EventArgs) Handles calculateButton.Click
7
8        ' convert text in TextBox to Integer
9        Dim value As Integer = Convert.ToInt32(inputTextBox.Text)
10       displayTextBox.Clear() ' reset TextBox
11
12       ' call Factorial to perform calculation
13       For i = 0 To value
14          displayTextBox.Text &= i & "! = " & Factorial(i) & vbNewLine
15       Next
16    End Sub ' calculateButton_Click
```

Fig. 7.23 | Recursive factorial program. (Part 1 of 2.)

```
17
18         ' recursively generates factorial of number
19         Function Factorial(ByVal number As Long) As Long
20            If number <= 1 Then ' base case
21               Return 1
22            Else
23               Return number * Factorial(number - 1)
24            End If
25         End Function ' Factorial
26      End Class ' FactorialCalculator
```

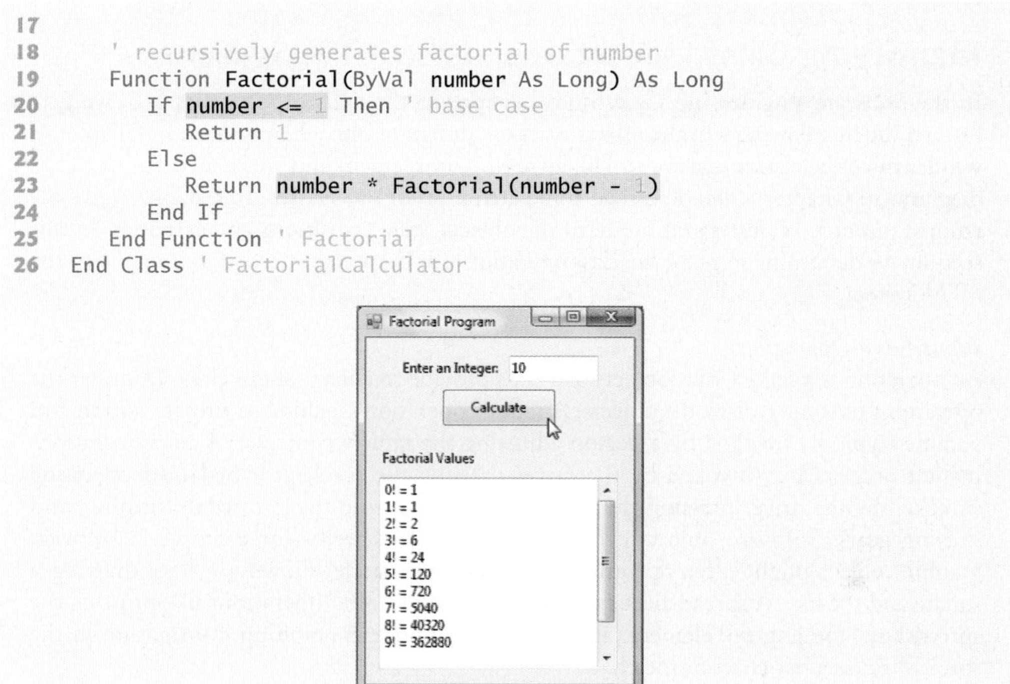

Fig. 7.23 | Recursive factorial program. (Part 2 of 2.)

We have set the output `TextBox`'s `ScrollBars` property to `Vertical`, to display a vertical scrollbar. This allows us to display more outputs than will fit in the space allocated for the `TextBox`. Method `Factorial` (line 19) receives a parameter of type `Long` and returns a result of type `Long`. Type `Long` is designed to store integer values in a range much larger than that of type `Integer`. As is seen in the output window of Fig. 7.23, factorial values grow quickly. We choose type `Long` to enable the program to calculate factorials greater than 12!. Unfortunately, the values produced by the `Factorial` method increase at such a rate that the range of even the `Long` type is quickly exceeded. This points to a weakness in most programming languages—they are not easily extended to handle the unique requirements of various applications, such as the evaluation of large factorials. Recall that Visual Basic is an extensible language—if you have unique requirements, you can extend the language by defining new classes. You could create a `HugeInteger` class that would enable a program to calculate the factorials of arbitrarily large numbers. Note that line 10 introduces the `TextBox`'s `Clear` method, which clears the text in the `TextBox`.

Common Programming Error 7.12

Forgetting to return a value from a recursive method can result in logic errors.

Common Programming Error 7.13

Omitting the base case or writing the recursion step so that it does not converge on the base case will cause infinite recursion, eventually exhausting memory. This is analogous to the problem of an infinite loop in an iterative (nonrecursive) solution.

7.20 (Optional) Software Engineering Case Study: Identifying Class Operations in the ATM System

In the Software Engineering Case Study sections at the ends of Chapters 4–6, we performed the first few steps in the object-oriented design of our ATM system. In Chapter 4, we identified the classes that we will likely need to implement and we created our first class diagram. In Chapter 5, we described some attributes of our classes. In Chapter 6, we examined our objects' states and modeled the objects' state transitions and activities. In this section, we determine some of the class operations (or behaviors) needed to implement the ATM system.

Identifying Operations

An operation is a service that objects of a class provide to clients of the class. Consider the operations of some real-world objects. A radio's operations include setting its station and volume (typically invoked by a person adjusting the radio's controls). A car's operations include accelerating (invoked by the driver pressing the accelerator pedal), decelerating (invoked by the driver pressing the brake pedal or releasing the gas pedal), turning, and shifting gears. Software objects can offer operations as well—for example, a software graphics object might offer operations for drawing a circle, drawing a line, drawing a square and the like. A spreadsheet software object might offer operations like printing the spreadsheet, totaling the elements in a row or column and graphing information in the spreadsheet as a bar chart or pie chart.

We can derive many of the operations of the classes in our ATM system by examining the verbs and verb phrases in the requirements document. We then relate each of these to particular classes in our system (Fig. 7.24). The verb phrases in Fig. 7.24 help us determine the operations of our classes.

Class	Verbs and verb phrases
`ATM`	executes financial transactions
`BalanceInquiry`	[none in the requirements document]
`Withdrawal`	[none in the requirements document]
`Deposit`	[none in the requirements document]
`BankDatabase`	authenticates a user, retrieves an account balance, credits an account by a deposit amount, debits an account by a withdrawal amount
`Account`	retrieves an account balance, credits an account by a deposit amount, debits an account by a withdrawal amount
`Screen`	displays a message to the user
`Keypad`	receives numeric input from the user
`CashDispenser`	dispenses cash, indicates whether it contains enough cash to satisfy a withdrawal request
`DepositSlot`	receives a deposit envelope

Fig. 7.24 | Verbs and verb phrases for each class in the ATM system.

Modeling Operations

To identify operations, we examine the verb phrases listed for each class in Fig. 7.24. The "executes financial transactions" phrase associated with class `ATM` implies that class `ATM` instructs transactions to execute. Therefore, classes `BalanceInquiry`, `Withdrawal` and `Deposit` each need an operation to provide this service to the ATM. We place this operation (which we have named `Execute`) in the third compartment of the three transaction classes in the updated class diagram of Fig. 7.25. During an ATM session, the `ATM` object will invoke the `Execute` operation of each transaction object to tell it to execute.

The UML represents operations (which are implemented as methods in Visual Basic) by listing the operation name, followed by a comma-separated list of parameters in parentheses, a colon and the return type:

operationName(*parameter1*, *parameter2*, ..., *parameterN*) : *returnType*

Each parameter in the comma-separated parameter list consists of a parameter name, followed by a colon and the parameter type:

parameterName : *parameterType*

For the moment, we do not list the parameters of our operations—we will identify and model the parameters of some of the operations shortly. For some of the operations, we do not yet know the return types, so we also omit them from the diagram. These omissions are perfectly normal at this point. As our design and implementation proceed, we will add the remaining return types.

Operations of Class `BankDatabase` *and Class* `Account`

Figure 7.24 lists the phrase "authenticates a user" next to class `BankDatabase`—the database is the object that contains the account information necessary to determine whether the account number and PIN entered by a user match those of an account held at the bank. Therefore, class `BankDatabase` needs an operation that provides an authentication service to the ATM. We place the operation `AuthenticateUser` in the third compartment of class `BankDatabase` (Fig. 7.25). However, an object of class `Account`, not class `BankDatabase`, stores the account number and PIN that must be accessed to authenticate a user, so class `Account` must provide a service to validate a PIN obtained through user input against a PIN stored in an `Account` object. Therefore, we add a `ValidatePIN` operation to class `Account`. Note that we specify a return type of `Boolean` for the `AuthenticateUser` and `ValidatePIN` operations. Each operation returns a value indicating either that the operation was successful in performing its task (i.e., a return value of `True`) or that it was not successful (i.e., a return value of `False`).

Figure 7.24 lists several additional verb phrases for class `BankDatabase`: "retrieves an account balance," "credits an account by a deposit amount" and "debits an account by a withdrawal amount." Like "authenticates a user," these phrases refer to services that the database must provide to the ATM, because the database holds all the account data used to authenticate a user and perform ATM transactions. However, `Account` objects actually perform the operations to which these phrases refer. Thus, class `BankDatabase` and class `Account` both need operations that correspond to each of these phrases. Recall from Section 4.9 that, because a bank account contains sensitive information, we do not allow the ATM to access accounts directly. The database acts as an intermediary between the

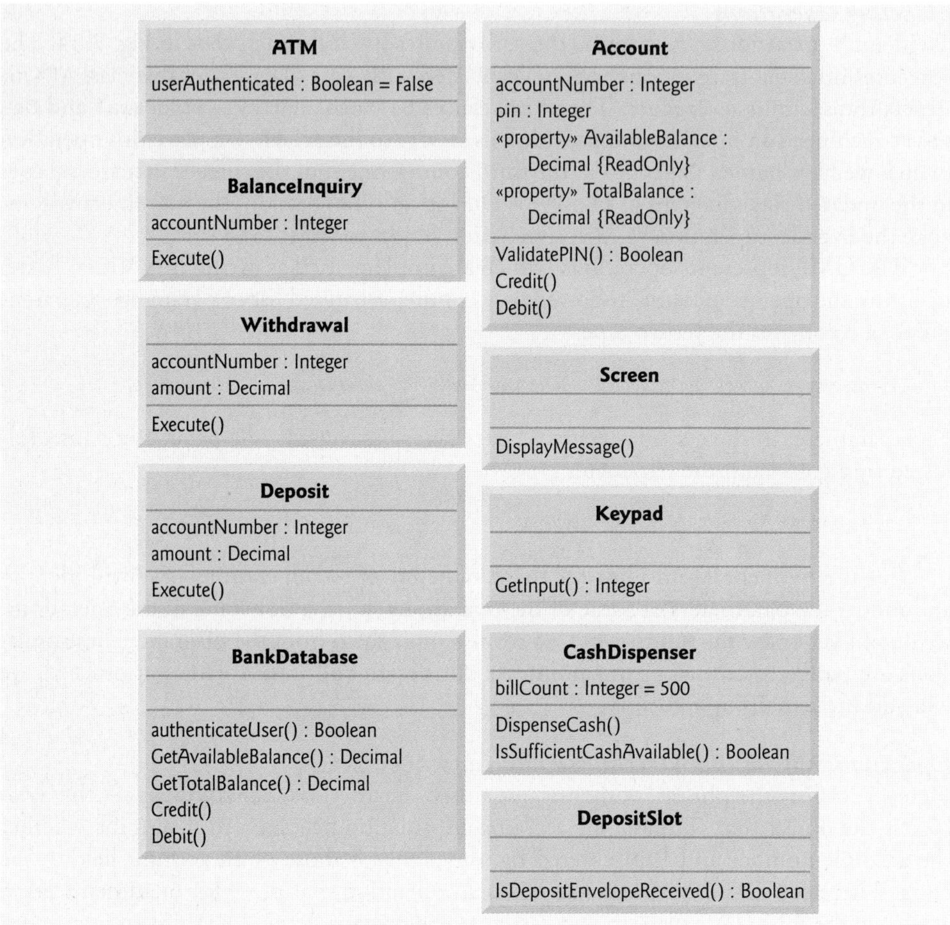

Fig. 7.25 | Classes in the ATM system with attributes and operations.

ATM and the account data, preventing unauthorized access. As we will see in Section 8.17, class `ATM` invokes the operations of class `BankDatabase`, each of which in turn invokes operations (which are the `Get` accessors of `ReadOnly` properties) in class `Account`.

The phrase "retrieves an account balance" suggests that classes `BankDatabase` and `Account` each need an operation that gets the balance. However, recall that Fig. 5.32 specified two attributes in class `Account` to represent a balance—`availableBalance` and `totalBalance`. A balance inquiry requires access to both balance attributes so that it can display them to the user, but a withdrawal needs to check only the value of `availableBalance`. To allow objects in the system to obtain these balance attributes individually from a specific `Account` object in the `BankDatabase`, we add operations `GetAvailableBalance` and `GetTotalBalance` to the third compartment of class `BankDatabase` (Fig. 7.25). We specify a return type of `Decimal` for each of these operations, because the balances which they retrieve are of type `Decimal`.

Once the BankDatabase knows which Account to access, it must be able to obtain each balance attribute individually from that Account. For this purpose, we could add operations GetAvailableBalance and GetTotalBalance to the third compartment of class Account (Fig. 7.25). However, in Visual Basic, simple operations such as getting the value of an attribute are typically performed by a property's Get accessor (at least when that particular class "owns" the underlying attribute). This design is for a Visual Basic application, so rather than modeling operations GetAvailableBalance and GetTotalBalance, we model Decimal properties AvailableBalance and TotalBalance in class Account. Properties are placed in the second compartment of a class diagram. These properties replace the availableBalance and totalBalance attributes that we modeled for class Account in Fig. 5.32. Recall from Chapter 4 that a property's accessors are implied, thus they are not modeled in a class diagram. Figure 7.24 does not mention the need to set the balances, so Fig. 7.25 shows properties AvailableBalance and TotalBalance as ReadOnly properties (i.e., they have only Get accessors). To indicate a ReadOnly property, we follow the property's type with "{ReadOnly}."

You may be wondering why we modeled AvailableBalance and TotalBalance *properties* in class Account, but modeled GetAvailableBalance and GetTotalBalance *operations* in class BankDatabase. Since there can be many Account objects in the BankDatabase, the ATM must specify which Account to access when invoking BankDatabase operations GetAvailableBalance and GetTotalBalance. The ATM does this by passing an account-number argument to each BankDatabase operation. The Get accessors of the properties you have seen in Visual Basic code cannot receive arguments. Thus, we modeled GetAvailableBalance and GetTotalBalance as operations in class BankDatabase so that we could specify parameters to which the ATM can pass arguments. Also, the underlying balance attributes are not owned by the BankDatabase, so Get accessors are not appropriate here. We discuss the parameters for the BankDatabase operations shortly.

The phrases "credits an account by a deposit amount" and "debits an account by a withdrawal amount" indicate that classes BankDatabase and Account must perform operations to update an account during a deposit and withdrawal, respectively. We therefore assign Credit and Debit operations to classes BankDatabase and Account. You may recall that crediting an account (as in a deposit) adds an amount only to the Account's total balance. Debiting an account (as in a withdrawal), on the other hand, subtracts the amount from both the total and available balances. We hide these implementation details inside class Account. This is a good example of encapsulation and information hiding.

If this were a real ATM system, classes BankDatabase and Account would also provide a set of operations to allow another banking system to update a user's account balance after either confirming or rejecting all or part of a deposit. Operation ConfirmDepositAmount, for example, would add an amount to the Account's available balance, thus making deposited funds available for withdrawal. Operation RejectDepositAmount would subtract an amount from the Account's total balance to indicate that a specified amount, which had recently been deposited through the ATM and added to the Account's total balance, was invalidated (or checks may have "bounced"). The bank would invoke operation RejectDepositAmount after determining either that the user failed to include the correct amount of cash or that any checks did not clear (i.e., they "bounced"). While adding these operations would make our system more complete, we do not include them in our class diagrams or implementation because they are beyond the scope of the case study.

Operations of Class **Screen**

Class Screen "displays a message to the user" at various times in an ATM session. All visual output occurs through the screen of the ATM. The requirements document describes many types of messages (e.g., a welcome message, an error message, a thank-you message) that the screen displays to the user. The requirements document also indicates that the screen displays prompts and menus to the user. However, a prompt is really just a message describing what the user should input next, and a menu is essentially a type of prompt consisting of a series of messages (i.e., menu options) displayed consecutively. Therefore, rather than assign class Screen an individual operation to display each type of message, prompt and menu, we simply create one operation that can display any message specified by a parameter. We place this operation (DisplayMessage) in the third compartment of class Screen in our class diagram (Fig. 7.25). Note that we do not worry about the parameter of this operation at this time—we model the parameter momentarily.

Operations of Class **Keypad**

From the phrase "receives numeric input from the user" listed by class Keypad in Fig. 7.24, we conclude that class Keypad should perform a GetInput operation. Because the ATM's keypad, unlike a computer keyboard, contains only the numbers 0–9, we specify that this operation returns an integer value. Recall from the requirements document that in different situations the user may be required to enter a different type of number (e.g., an account number, a PIN, the number of a menu option, a deposit amount as a number of cents). Class Keypad simply obtains a numeric value for a client of the class—it does not determine whether the value meets any specific criteria. Any class that uses this operation must verify that the user enters appropriate numbers, and if not, display error messages via class Screen). [*Note:* When we implement the system, we simulate the ATM's keypad with a computer keyboard, and for simplicity we assume that the user does not enter nonnumeric input using keys on the computer keyboard that do not appear on the ATM's keypad. In Chapter 17, Strings, Characters and Regular Expressions, you will learn how to examine inputs to determine if they are of particular types.]

Operations of Class **CashDispenser** *and Class* **DepositSlot**

Figure 7.24 lists "dispenses cash" for class CashDispenser. Therefore, we create operation DispenseCash and list it under class CashDispenser in Fig. 7.25. Class CashDispenser also "indicates whether it contains enough cash to satisfy a withdrawal request." Thus, we include IsSufficientCashAvailable, an operation that returns a value of type Boolean, in class CashDispenser. Figure 7.24 also lists "receives a deposit envelope" for class DepositSlot. The deposit slot must indicate whether it received an envelope, so we place the operation IsDepositEnvelopeReceived, which returns a Boolean value, in the third compartment of class DepositSlot. [*Note:* A real hardware deposit slot would most likely send the ATM a signal to indicate that an envelope was received. We simulate this behavior, however, with an operation in class DepositSlot that class ATM can invoke to find out whether the deposit slot received an envelope.]

Operations of Class **ATM**

We do not list any operations for class ATM at this time. We are not yet aware of any services that class ATM provides to other classes in the system. When we implement the system in

Visual Basic (Appendix D), however, operations of this class, and additional operations of the other classes in the system, may become apparent.

Identifying and Modeling Operation Parameters

So far, we have not been concerned with the parameters of our operations—we have attempted to gain only a basic understanding of the operations of each class. Let's now take a closer look at some operation parameters. We identify an operation's parameters by examining what data the operation requires to perform its assigned task.

Consider class `BankDatabase`'s `AuthenticateUser` operation. To authenticate a user, this operation must know the account number and PIN supplied by the user. Thus we specify that operation `AuthenticateUser` takes integer parameters `userAccountNumber` and `userPIN`, which the operation must compare to the account number and PIN of an `Account` object in the database. We prefix these parameter names with "user" to avoid confusion between the operation's parameter names and the attribute names that belong to class `Account`. We list these parameters in the class diagram in Fig. 7.26 that models only class `BankDatabase`. [*Note:* It is perfectly normal to model only one class in a class diagram. In this case, we are most concerned with examining the parameters of this one class in particular, so we omit the other classes. In class diagrams later in the case study, in which parameters are no longer the focus of our attention, we omit the parameters to save space. Remember, however, that the operations listed in these diagrams still have parameters.]

Recall that the UML models each parameter in an operation's comma-separated parameter list by listing the parameter name, followed by a colon and the parameter type. Figure 7.26 thus specifies, for example, that operation `AuthenticateUser` takes two parameters—`userAccountNumber` and `userPIN`, both of type `Integer`.

Class `BankDatabase` operations `GetAvailableBalance`, `GetTotalBalance`, `Credit` and `Debit` also each require a `userAccountNumber` parameter to identify the account to which the database must apply the operations, so we include these parameters in the class diagram. In addition, operations `Credit` and `Debit` each require a `Decimal` parameter `amount` to specify the amount of money to be credited or debited, respectively.

The class diagram in Fig. 7.27 models the parameters of class `Account`'s operations. Operation `ValidatePIN` requires only a `userPIN` parameter, which contains the user-specified PIN to be compared with the PIN associated with the account. Like their counterparts in class `BankDatabase`, operations `Credit` and `Debit` in class `Account` each require a `Decimal` parameter `amount` that indicates the amount of money involved in the operation. Note that class `Account`'s operations do not require an account-number parameter—each

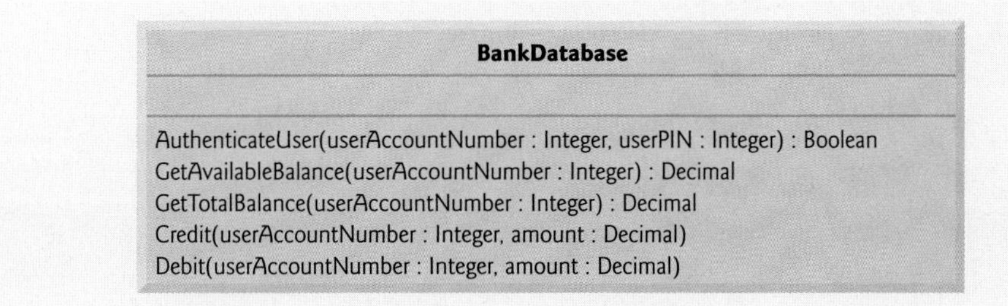

Fig. 7.26 | Class `BankDatabase` with operation parameters.

Account

accountNumber : Integer
pin : Integer
«property» AvailableBalance : Decimal {ReadOnly}
«property» TotalBalance : Decimal {ReadOnly}

ValidatePIN(userPIN: Integer) : Boolean
Credit(amount : Decimal)
Debit(amount : Decimal)

Fig. 7.27 | Class `Account` with operation parameters.

of these operations can be invoked only on the `Account` object in which it is executing, so including a parameter to specify an `Account` is unnecessary.

Figure 7.28 models class `Screen` with a parameter specified for operation `DisplayMessage`. This operation requires only a `String` parameter `message` that indicates the text to be displayed.

The class diagram in Fig. 7.29 specifies that operation `DispenseCash` of class `CashDispenser` takes a `Decimal` parameter `amount` to indicate the amount of cash (in dollars) to be dispensed. Operation `IsSufficientCashAvailable` also takes a `Decimal` parameter `amount` to indicate the amount of cash in question.

Note that we do not discuss parameters for operation `Execute` of classes `BalanceInquiry`, `Withdrawal` and `Deposit`, operation `GetInput` of class `Keypad` and operation `IsDepositEnvelopeReceived` of class `DepositSlot`. At this point in our design process, we cannot determine whether these operations require additional data to perform their tasks, so we leave their parameter lists empty. As we progress through the case study, we may decide to add parameters to these operations.

In this section, we have determined many of the operations performed by the classes in the ATM system. We have identified the parameters and return types of some of the operations. As we continue our design process, the number of operations belonging to each class may vary—we might find that new operations are needed or that some current

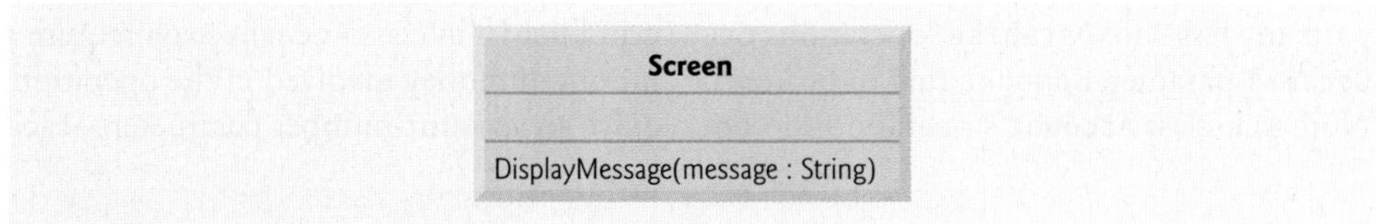

Fig. 7.28 | Class `Screen` with an operation parameter.

CashDispenser

billCount : Integer = 500

DispenseCash(amount : Decimal)
IsSufficientCashAvailable(amount : Decimal) : Boolean

Fig. 7.29 | Class `CashDispenser` with operation parameters.

ones are unnecessary—and we might determine that some of our class operations need additional parameters and different return types. Again, all of this is perfectly normal.

Software Engineering Case Study Self-Review Exercises

7.1 Which of the following is not a behavior?
a) reading data from a file
b) printing output
c) text output
d) obtaining input from the user

7.2 If you were to add to the ATM system an operation that returns the `amount` attribute of class `Withdrawal`, how and where would you specify this operation in the class diagram of Fig. 7.25?

7.3 Describe the meaning of the following operation listing that might appear in a class diagram for an object-oriented design of a calculator:

```
Add( x : Integer, y : Integer ) : Integer
```

Answers to Software Engineering Case Study Self-Review Exercises

7.1 c.

7.2 An operation that retrieves the `amount` attribute of class `Withdrawal` would typically be implemented as a `Get` accessor of a property of class `Withdrawal`. The following would replace attribute `amount` in the attribute (i.e., second) compartment of class `Withdrawal`:

```
«property» Amount : Decimal
```

7.3 This is an operation named `Add` that takes `Integer` parameters `x` and `y` and returns an `Integer` value. This operation would most likely sum its parameters `x` and `y` and return the result.

7.21 Wrap-Up

In this chapter, you studied methods in greater depth. You learned the difference between subroutines and functions, and when to use each type of method. You also learned the difference between non-`Shared` and `Shared` methods and how to call `Shared` methods by preceding the method name with the name of the class in which it appears and a dot (`.`). You learned how to declare named constants using both enumerations and constant variables. You learned about how arguments can be implicitly converted to the type of their corresponding parameters. We demonstrated using **Option Strict**, which causes the compiler to check all conversions and requires you to perform an explicit conversion for all narrowing conversions that could cause data loss or program termination. We discussed how Visual Basic performs method calls using a stack data structure. You saw how to use class `Random` to generate random numbers that can be used for simulations and game playing. You also learned about the scope of instance variables and local variables in classes and methods, respectively. You enhanced your GUI skills, using `PictureBoxes`, `GroupBoxes`, `Buttons` and `TextBoxes`, and created event handlers for `Buttons`. Finally, you learned that multiple methods in one class can be overloaded by providing methods with the same name and different signatures. Such methods can be used to perform the same or similar tasks using different types or different numbers of parameters.

In Chapter 8, you will learn how to maintain lists and tables of data in arrays. You will see a more elegant implementation of the application that rolls a die several times and two enhanced versions of the `GradeBook` case study that you studied in Chapters 4–7.

Summary

Section 7.1 Introduction

- Experience has shown that the best way to develop and maintain a large program is to construct it from small, simple pieces. This technique is called divide and conquer.

Section 7.2 Modules, Classes and Methods

- Although the same method can be executed from multiple points in a program, the actual statements that define the method are written only once.
- A method is invoked by a method call. The method call specifies the method name and provides information, called arguments, that the callee requires to do its job.
- When the method completes its task, it returns control to the caller (i.e., the calling method). In some cases, the method also returns a result to the caller.

Section 7.3 Subroutines: Methods That Do Not Return a Value

- Subroutines are methods that perform tasks but don't return a value.
- The format of a subroutine declaration is

```
Sub method-name(parameter-list)
    declarations and statements
End Sub
```

- Control returns to the caller when execution reaches the `End Sub` statement.

Section 7.4 Functions: Methods That Return a Value

- Functions are methods that perform tasks and return a value.
- The `Return` statement terminates execution of a method and can optionally return a result.
- The format of a function declaration is

```
Function method-name(parameter-list) As return-type
    declarations and statements
End Function
```

- A function's return type indicates the type of the result returned from the function to its caller.
- Functions return exactly one value. When a `Return` statement is executed, control returns immediately to the point at which that function was invoked.

Section 7.5 `Shared` Methods and Class `Math`

- `Shared` methods are associated with the class, but not with any specific object of the class; they perform tasks that do not depend on the contents of any object.
- You call a `Shared` method by specifying the name of the class or module in which the method is declared, followed by the dot (`.`) separator and the method name.
- Any variable declared with keyword `Const` is constant—its value cannot be changed after the variable is initialized. Constants are implicitly `Shared`.
- There are variables for which each object of a class does not have a separate instance of the member. That is the case with `Shared` members. When objects of a class containing `Shared` variables are created, all the objects of that class share one copy of the class's `Shared` variables. Together, the instance variables and `Shared` variables of a class are known as the class's fields.

Section 7.6 `GradeBook` Case Study: Declaring Methods with Multiple Parameters

- In a method with more than one parameter, the parameters are specified as a comma-separated list.

- There must be one argument in the method call for each parameter in the method declaration (except in the case of `Optional` parameters). The type of each argument must be consistent with the type of the corresponding parameter.
- Methods can return at most one value, but the returned value could be a reference to an object that contains many values.

Section 7.7 Notes on Declaring and Using Methods

- There are three ways to call a method: using a method name by itself to call another method of the same class or module, using a variable that contains a reference to an object followed by a dot (`.`) and the method name to call a method of the referenced object, and using the class or module name and a dot (`.`) to call a `Shared` method of a class or module (all methods of a module are implicitly `Shared`).
- Control can be returned to the statement that calls a method by using the `Return` statement or by reaching the end of the method (`End Sub` or `End Function`). If the method does not return a result but uses a `Return` statement to return control to the calling method, the `Return` statement cannot include an expression. If the method does return a result, the statement

  `Return` *expression*

  evaluates the *expression*, then returns the result to the caller.

Section 7.8 Method Call Stack and Activation Records

- Stacks are known as last-in, first-out (LIFO) data structures—the last item pushed (inserted) on the stack is the first item popped (removed) from the stack.
- When a program calls a method, the called method must know how to return to its caller, so the return address of the calling method is pushed onto the method call stack. If a series of nested method calls occurs, the successive return addresses are pushed onto the stack in last-in, first-out order so that each method can return to its caller.
- The method call stack also contains the memory for the local variables used in each invocation of a method during a program's execution. This data is known as the activation record or stack frame of the method call. When a method call is made, the activation record for that method call is pushed onto the method call stack. When the method returns to its caller, the activation record for this method call is popped off the stack, and those local variables are no longer known to the program.

Section 7.9 Implicit Argument Conversions

- An important feature of argument passing is implicit argument conversion—converting an argument's value to the type that a method expects to receive in its corresponding parameter.
- In a widening conversion, data of one type is converted to data of another type without losing data. In a narrowing conversion, there is potential for data loss during the conversion.
- Conversions occur not only for values passed as arguments to methods, but also for expressions containing values of two or more types. In such expressions, each value is converted to the "widest" type in the expression.

Section 7.10 Option Strict and Data-Type Conversions

- **Option Explicit** forces you to explicitly declare all variables before they are used in a program.
- **Option Strict** causes the compiler to check all conversions and requires you to perform an explicit conversion for all narrowing conversions that could cause data loss or program termination.
- The methods in class `Convert` convert data between types explicitly.

Section 7.11 Value Types and Reference Types

- Both value types and reference types include primitive types and types that you can create. The primitive value types include the integral types (`Byte`, `SByte`, `Short`, `UShort`, `Integer`, `UInteger`, `Long` and `ULong`), the floating-point types (`Single` and `Double`) and types `Boolean`, `Date`, `Decimal` and `Char`. There is only one primitive reference type—`String`.
- Reference types can be created by defining classes, modules, interfaces and delegates. Value types can be created by defining structures and enumerations.

Section 7.12 Framework Class Library Namespaces

- A great strength of Visual Basic is the large number of classes in the .NET framework. The set of namespaces available in the .NET Framework Class Library is quite large. This framework includes namespaces for graphics, input/output, database processing, GUI development, web services and many other capabilities.

Section 7.13 Passing Arguments: Pass-by-Value vs. Pass-by-Reference

- When an argument is passed by value, the program makes a copy of the argument's value and passes that copy to the called method. With pass-by-value, changes to the called method's copy do not affect the original variable's value.
- When an argument is passed by reference, the caller gives the called method the ability to access and modify the caller's original data directly.

Section 7.14 Scope of Declarations

- The scope of a declaration is the portion of the program that can refer to the declared entity by its name, without qualification.
- If a local variable or parameter in a method has the same name as a field, the member is "hidden" until the block terminates execution—this is called shadowing.

Section 7.15 Case Study: Random-Number Generation

- The element of chance can be introduced through class `Random` (located in namespace `System`).
- Class `Random`'s `Next` method generates pseudorandom numbers based on a complex mathematical calculation that requires a seed value. If the seed value is different each time the program is run, the series of values will be different as well.
- A `Button`'s `Click` event handler executes whenever the `Button` is clicked.
- The data in a `TextBox` can be accessed and modified via the control's `Text` property.
- You can embed images into a project as resources. This causes the compiler to embed the images in the application's executable file and enables the application to access the images through Visual Basic's `My` namespace, which provides many capabilities that make common Visual Basic programming tasks easier.
- Embedded image files appear in a folder named **Resources** in the **Solution Explorer**.
- To access an image (or any other resource) in the project's resources, you use the method `My.Resources.ResourceManager.GetObject`, which takes as an argument the resource name as it appears in the **Resources** tab and returns the resource as an `Object`.
- The `My` namespace also provides direct access to the resources you define with expressions of the form `My.Resources.`*resourceName*, where resourceName is the name you provided to the resource when you created it. When using such an expression, the resource returned already has the appropriate type.
- Visual Basic's `CType` function converts its first argument to the type specified in its second argument. A conversion performed with the `CType` function is also known as a cast operation.

Section 7.16 Case Study: A Game of Chance

- A GroupBox is a container used to group related controls.
- Constant identifiers and Enumerations enhance program readability by providing descriptive identifiers for constant numbers or Strings.
- Enumerations are used to define groups of related constants.
- Disabling a Button causes no action to be performed when the Button is clicked. Buttons can be enabled and disabled by setting the Button's Enabled property to True or False, respectively.
- The constant String.Empty represents the so-called empty string (i.e., a string that does not contain any characters), which can also be represented as empty double-quotation characters ("").

Section 7.17 Method Overloading

- Method overloading allows you to create multiple methods with the same name but differing numbers and types of parameters, or with different orders of the parameters (by type).
- Overloaded methods are distinguished by their signatures, which are a combination of the method's name and parameter types, and the order of the parameters (by type).

*Section 7.18 **Optional** Parameters*

- Methods can have optional parameters. Declaring a parameter as Optional allows the calling method to vary the number of arguments to pass.
- Optional parameters specify a default value that is assigned to the parameter if the optional argument is not passed.
- For an Optional parameter, the caller has the *option* of passing that particular argument.
- You can create methods with one or more optional parameters. All optional parameters, however, must be placed to the right of the method's nonoptional parameters.
- Default values can be used only with parameters declared as Optional.
- String method IsNullOrEmpty returns True if its argument is the value Nothing or the empty string; otherwise, it returns False.

Section 7.19 Recursion

- A recursive method calls itself either directly or indirectly (i.e., through another method).
- A recursive method knows how to solve only the simplest case(s)—the base case(s). If the method is called with a base case, it returns a result. If the method is called with a more complex problem, it divides the problem into a base case and a recursion step that resembles the original problem but is a slightly simpler or smaller version of it. The recursion step executes while the original call to the method is still "open." The recursion step can result in many more recursive calls as the method divides each new subproblem into two conceptual pieces. Since the method continues to call itself with simpler versions of the original problem, the sequence of smaller and smaller problems must converge on a base case, so that the recursion can eventually terminate. At that point, the method recognizes the base case and returns a result to the previous copy of the method. A sequence of returns ensues until the original method call returns the final result to the caller.

Terminology

activation record
argument conversion
base case(s) in recursion
block
block scope
ByRef keyword
class method
Clear method of a TextBox

`Click` event of a `Button`
`Const` keyword
`Convert` class
`Convert.ToInt32` method
copy of an argument
default value for `Optional` parameter
divide-and-conquer approach
`Double` structure
`Double.Parse` method
empty string
`Enabled` property of class `Button`
`Enum` keyword
enumeration
`Exit Function` statement
`Exit Sub` statement
explicit conversion
field of a class
floating-point type
formal parameter
`FromFile` method of class `Image`
function
`GetCurrentDirectory` method of class `Directory`
`GroupBox` control
implicit argument conversion
infinite recursion
`Int32` structure
`Int32.MaxValue` constant
integral type
`IsNullOrEmpty` method of class `String`
iteratively (nonrecursively) solve a problem
last-in, first-out (LIFO)
lifetime of a variable
`Long` primitive type
method call stack
method overloading
method scope
module scope
`My.Resources.ResourceManager.GetObject`
namespace scope
narrowing conversion
`Next` method of class `Random`
`Object` class
Option Explicit
Option Infer
Option Strict
`Optional` keyword
optional parameter
overload resolution
overloaded methods
`P` format specifier for displaying percentages
pass-by-reference
pass-by-value
pop off a stack
pseudorandom numbers
push onto a stack
recursion
recursion step
recursive call
recursive method
reference parameter
return a value from a method
`Return` statement
return type of a method
scaling factor
scope of a declaration
seed value to generate pseudorandom numbers
shadowing an instance variable
`Shared` method
shifted random integers
signature of a method
stack data structure
stack frame
stack overflow
`String.Empty`
strong typing
subroutine
value parameter
widening conversion

Self-Review Exercises

7.1 Fill in the blanks in each of the following statements:

a) Methods can be declared in __________ and __________.
b) A method is invoked with a(n) __________.
c) A variable known only within the method in which it is declared is called a(n) __________.
d) The __________ statement in a called function can be used to pass the value of an expression back to the calling method.

e) A method declared with keyword __________ does not return a value.
f) The __________ of a variable is the portion of the program in which the variable can be referenced without qualification.
g) Control can be returned from a called subroutine to a caller with the __________ or __________ statements.
h) The __________ method in class `Random` produces random numbers.
i) A method that calls itself either directly or indirectly is a(n) __________ method.
j) A recursive method typically has two components—one that provides a means for the recursion to terminate by testing for a(n) __________ case, and one that expresses the problem as a recursive call for a problem slightly simpler or smaller than the original call.
k) It is possible to have several methods with the same name that operate on different types or numbers of arguments. This is called method __________.
l) A method that performs a task that does not depend on the contents of an object is normally declared as a(n) __________ method.
m) When a program calls a method, the called method must know how to return to its caller, so the return address of the calling method is pushed onto the __________.
n) Recursion terminates when a(n) __________ is reached.
o) The __________ is a comma-separated list containing the declarations of the parameters received by the called method.
p) The __________ is the type of the result returned from a called function.
q) A `Button`'s __________ event occurs when a `Button` is clicked.

7.2 State whether each of the following is *true* or *false*. If *false*, explain why.

a) `Math` method `Abs` rounds its parameter to the smallest integer not less than its parameter.
b) `Math` method `Exp` is the exponential method that calculates e^x.
c) A recursive method is one that calls itself.
d) Conversion of a data item from type `Single` to type `Double` is an example of a widening conversion.
e) Variables of type `Char` cannot be converted to type `Integer`.
f) When a method recursively calls itself, it is known as the base case.
g) Forgetting to return a value from a recursive method when one is needed results in a logic error.
h) **Option Explicit** causes the compiler to check all conversions and requires you to perform an explicit conversion for all narrowing conversions that could cause data loss or program termination.
i) Visual Basic supports `Optional` parameters.
j) When an argument is passed by value, the program makes a copy of the argument's value and passes the copy to the called method.

7.3 Write an application that tests whether the examples of the `Math` class method calls shown in Fig. 7.4 actually produce the indicated results.

7.4 Give the method header for each of the following:

a) Method `Hypotenuse`, which takes two double-precision, floating-point arguments, `side1` and `side2`, and returns a double-precision, floating-point result.
b) Method `Smallest`, which takes three integers, `x`, `y` and `z`, and returns an integer.
c) Method `Instructions`, which does not take any arguments and does not return a value.
d) Method `IntegerToSingle`, which takes an integer argument, `number`, and returns a floating-point result.

7.5 Find the error in each of the following program segments and explain how the error can be corrected:

a)
```
Sub General1()
   Console.WriteLine("Inside method General1")

   Sub General2()
      Console.WriteLine("Inside method General2")
   End Sub ' General2
End Sub ' General1
```
b)
```
Function Sum(ByVal x As Integer, ByVal y As Integer) As Integer
   Dim result As Integer
   result = x + y
End Function ' Sum
```
c)
```
Sub Printer1(ByVal value As Single)
   Dim value As Single
   Console.WriteLine(value)
End Sub ' Printer1
```
d)
```
Sub Product()
   Dim a As Integer = 6
   Dim b As Integer = 5
   Dim result As Integer = a * b
   Console.WriteLine("Result is " & result)
    Return result
End Sub ' Product
```
e)
```
Function Sum(ByVal value As Integer) As Integer
   If value = 0 Then
      Return 0
   Else
      value += Sum(value - 1)
   End If
End Function ' Sum
```

Answers to Self-Review Exercises

7.1 a) classes, modules. b) method call. c) local variable. d) `Return`. e) `Sub`. f) scope. g) `Return`, `End Sub`. h) `Next`. i) recursive. j) base. k) overloading. l) `Shared`. m) method call stack. n) base case. o) parameter list. p) return-value type. q) `Click`.

7.2 a) False. `Math` method `Abs` returns the absolute value of a number. b) True. c) True. d) True. e) False. Type `Char` variables can be converted to type `Integer` with a narrowing conversion. f) False. A method recursively calling itself is known as a recursive call or recursion step. g) True. h) False. **Option Strict** causes the compiler to check all conversions and requires you to perform an explicit conversion for all narrowing conversions that could cause data loss or program termination. **Option Explicit** forces you to explicitly declare all variables before they are used in a program. i) True. j) True.

7.3 The following code demonstrates the use of some `Math` library method calls:

```
' Exercise 7.3 Solution: MathTest.vb
' Testing the Math class methods
Module MathTest
   Sub Main()
      Console.WriteLine("Math.Abs(23.7) = {0}", Math.Abs(23.7))
      Console.WriteLine("Math.Abs(0.0) = {0}", Math.Abs(0.0))
```

```
        Console.WriteLine("Math.Abs(-23.7) = {0}", Math.Abs(-23.7))
        Console.WriteLine("Math.Ceiling(9.2) = {0}", Math.Ceiling(9.2))
        Console.WriteLine("Math.Ceiling(-9.8) = {0}", Math.Ceiling(-9.8))
        Console.WriteLine("Math.Cos(0.0) = {0}", Math.Cos(0.0))
        Console.WriteLine("Math.Exp(1.0) = {0}", Math.Exp(1.0))
        Console.WriteLine("Math.Exp(2.0) = {0}", Math.Exp(2.0))
        Console.WriteLine("Math.Floor(9.2) = {0}", Math.Floor(9.2))
        Console.WriteLine("Math.Floor(-9.8) = {0}", Math.Floor(-9.8))
        Console.WriteLine("Math.Log(2.7182818284590451) = {0}", _
           Math.Log(2.7182818284590451))
        Console.WriteLine("Math.Log(7.3890560989306504) = {0}", _
           Math.Log(7.38905609893065))
        Console.WriteLine("Math.Max(2.3, 12.7) = {0}", Math.Max(2.3, 12.7))
        Console.WriteLine("Math.Max(-2.3, -12.7) = {0}", _
           Math.Max(-2.3, -12.7))
        Console.WriteLine("Math.Min(2.3, 12.7) = {0}", Math.Min(2.3, 12.7))
        Console.WriteLine("Math.Min(-2.3, -12.7) = {0}", _
           Math.Min(-2.3, -12.7))
        Console.WriteLine("Math.Pow(2, 7) = {0}", Math.Pow(2, 7))
        Console.WriteLine("Math.Pow(9, .5) = {0}", Math.Pow(9, 0.5))
        Console.WriteLine("Math.Sin(0.0) = {0}", Math.Sin(0.0))
        Console.WriteLine("Math.Sqrt(9.0) = {0}", Math.Sqrt(9.0))
        Console.WriteLine("Math.Sqrt(2.0) = {0}", Math.Sqrt(2.0))
        Console.WriteLine("Math.Tan(0.0) = {0}", Math.Tan(0.0))
     End Sub ' Main
  End Module ' MathTest
```

```
Math.Abs(23.7) = 23.7
Math.Abs(0.0) = 0
Math.Abs(-23.7) = 23.7
Math.Ceiling(9.2) = 10
Math.Ceiling(-9.8) = -9
Math.Cos(0.0) = 1
Math.Exp(1.0) = 2.71828182845905
Math.Exp(2.0) = 7.38905609893065
Math.Floor(9.2) = 9
Math.Floor(-9.8) = -10
Math.Log(2.7182818284590451) = 1
Math.Log(7.3890560989306504) = 2
Math.Max(2.3, 12.7) = 12.7
Math.Max(-2.3, -12.7) = -2.3
Math.Min(2.3, 12.7) = 2.3
Math.Min(-2.3, -12.7) = -12.7
Math.Pow(2, 7) = 128
Math.Pow(9, .5) = 3
Math.Sin(0.0) = 0
Math.Sqrt(9.0) = 3
Math.Sqrt(2.0) = 1.4142135623731
Math.Tan(0.0) = 0
```

7.4

a)
```
Function Hypotenuse(ByVal side1 As Double, _
   ByVal side2 As Double) As Double
```
b)
```
Function Smallest(ByVal x As Integer, _
   ByVal y As Integer, ByVal z As Integer) As Integer
```
c) `Sub Instructions()`

d) `Function IntegerToSingle(ByVal number As Integer) As Single`

7.5

a) Error: Method `General2` is declared in method `General1`.
Correction: Move the declaration of `General2` out of the declaration of `General1`.

b) Error: The method is supposed to return an `Integer`, but does not.
Correction: Replace the statement `result = x + y` with

```
Return x + y
```

or add the following statement at the end of the method body:

```
Return result
```

c) Error: Parameter `value` is redefined in the method declaration.
Correction: Delete the declaration `Dim value As Single`.

d) Error: The method returns a value, but is declared as a subroutine.
Correction: Change the method to a function with return type `Integer`.

e) Error: The result of `value += Sum(value - 1)` is not returned by this recursive method, resulting in a logic error.
Correction: Rewrite the statement in the `Else` clause as

```
Return value + Sum(value - 1)
```

Exercises

7.6 A gas pump calculates the cost of gas at a local gas station. The station charges `$4.09` per gallon for regular grade gas, `$4.16` per gallon for special grade gas and `$4.26` per gallon for super grade gas. Create an application that simulates the functionality of the gas pump. The user enters the number of gallons to purchase and clicks the desired grade (each grade is represented by a `Button` whose `Text` properties are set to **Regular**, **Special** and **Super+**). The `Click` event handler for each `Button` calls a method to compute the total cost from the number of gallons entered and the selected grade. [*Note:* You can use the `Text` property of each `Button` to pass the selected grade to your method.]

7.7 A lottery commission offers four different lottery games to play: Three-number, Four-number, Five-number and Five-number + 1 lotteries. Each game has independent numbers. Develop an application that randomly picks numbers for all four games and displays the generated numbers in a GUI. Declare a method that generates a random number based on a range given, and returns the random number as a `String`. The games are played as follows:

a) Three-number lotteries require players to choose three numbers in the range 0–9.
b) Four-number lotteries require players to choose four numbers in the range 0–9.
c) Five-number lotteries require players to choose five numbers in the range 1–39.
d) Five-number + 1 lotteries require players to choose five numbers in the range 1–49 and an additional number in the range 1–42.

7.8 Develop an application that calculates a salesperson's commission from the number of items sold. Assume that all items have a fixed price of $10 per unit. Use a `Select...Case` statement to implement the following sales-commission schedule:

a) Up to 50 items sold = 6% commission
b) Between 51 and 100 items sold = 7% commission
c) Between 101 and 150 items sold = 8% commission
d) More than 150 items sold = 9% commission

Create an application that inputs the number of items sold and contains a **Calculate** `Button`. When this `Button` is clicked, three methods should be called—one to calculate gross sales, one to calculate the commission percentage based on the commission schedule above and one to calculate the salesperson's earnings. Earnings are defined as gross sales multiplied by commission percentage, divided by 100 (because we are working with a percentage value). The data returned by these three methods should be displayed in the GUI.

7.9 What is the value of `x` after each of the following statements is performed?

a) `x = Math.Abs(7.5)`
a) `x = Math.Floor(7.5)`
b) `x = Math.Abs(0.0)`

c) `x = Math.Ceiling(0.0)`
d) `x = Math.Abs(-6.4)`
e) `x = Math.Ceiling(-6.4)`
f) `x = Math.Ceiling(-Math.Abs(-8 + Math.Floor(-5.5)))`

7.10 A parking garage charges a $2.00 minimum fee to park for up to three hours. The garage charges an additional $0.50 per hour for each hour *or part thereof* in excess of three hours. The maximum charge for any given 24-hour period is $10.00. Assume that no car parks for longer than 24 hours at a time. Write a program that calculates and displays the parking charges for each customer who parked a car in this garage yesterday. You should enter in a `TextBox` the hours parked for each customer. The program should display the charge for the current customer. The program should use the method `CalculateCharges` to determine the charge for each customer. Use the techniques described in the chapter to read the `Double` value from a `TextBox`. [*Note:* You may need to use methods `Convert.ToDouble` and `Convert.ToDecimal` when doing calculations with the number of hours and charges, respectively.]

7.11 Write a method `IntegerPower(base, exponent)` that returns the value of

$base^{exponent}$

For example, `IntegerPower(3, 4) = 3 * 3 * 3 * 3`. Assume that `exponent` is a positive integer and `base` is an integer. Method `IntegerPower` should use a `For...Next` statement to control the calculation. Do not use any `Math` library methods or the exponentiation operator, `^`. Incorporate this method into a Windows `Forms` application that reads integer values from `TextBoxes` for `base` and `exponent` from the user and performs the calculation by calling method `IntegerPower`. [*Note:* You may need to use method `Convert.ToString` to display numeric output in a `Label`.]

7.12 Declare a method `Hypotenuse` that calculates the length of the hypotenuse of a right triangle when the other two sides are given. The method should take two arguments of type `Double` and return the hypotenuse as a `Double`. Incorporate this method into a Windows `Forms` application that reads integer values for `side1` and `side2` from `TextBoxes` and performs the calculation with the `Hypotenuse` method. Determine the length of the hypotenuse for each of the following triangles:

Triangle	Side 1	Side 2
1	3.0	4.0
2	5.0	12.0
3	8.0	15.0

7.13 Write a method `SquareOfAsterisks` that displays a solid square of asterisks whose side is specified in integer parameter `side`. For example, if `side` is `4`, `SquareOfAsterisks` displays

```
* * * *
* * * *
* * * *
* * * *
```

Incorporate this method into a Windows `Forms` application that reads an integer value for `side` from the user and performs the drawing with `SquareOfAsterisks`. This method should obtain the side of the square from a `TextBox` and should print to a `Label`. Display a space after each asterisk to make the shape appear more like a square on the screen.

7.14 Modify the method created in Exercise 7.13 to form the square out of whatever character is contained in parameter `fillCharacter`. Thus, if `side` is `5` and `fillCharacter` is `"#"`, this method should print

```
# # # # #
# # # # #
# # # # #
# # # # #
# # # # #
```

Display a space after each fill character to make the shape appear more like a square on the screen.

7.15 Write a Windows `Forms` application that simulates coin tossing. Let the program toss the coin each time the user presses the **Toss** button. Count the number of times each side of the coin appears. Display the results. The program should call a separate method `Flip`, which takes no arguments and returns `False` for tails and `True` for heads. Use the head and tail images provided in the `images` folder with this chapter's examples. [*Note:* If the program simulates the coin tossing realistically, each side of the coin should appear approximately half the time.]

7.16 Computers are playing an increasing role in education. Write a program that will help an elementary-school student learn multiplication. Use the `Next` method from an object of type `Random` to produce two positive one-digit integers. It should display a question, such as

```
How much is 6 times 7?
```

The student should then type the answer into a `TextBox`. Your program should check the student's answer. If it is correct, display `"Very good!"` in a `Label`, then ask another multiplication question. If the answer is incorrect, display `"No. Please try again."` in the same `Label`, then let the student try the same question again until the student finally gets it right. A separate method should be used to generate each new question. This method should be called once wWindows `Forms` applicationhen the program begins execution and then each time the user answers a question correctly.

7.17 *(Towers of Hanoi)* Legend has it that in a temple in the Far East, priests are attempting to move a stack of disks from one peg to another. The initial stack had 64 disks threaded onto one peg and arranged from bottom to top by decreasing size. The priests are attempting to move the stack from this peg to a second peg, under the constraints that exactly one disk is moved at a time and that at no time may a larger disk be placed above a smaller disk. A third peg is available for temporarily holding disks. Figure 7.30 shows the Towers of Hanoi with four disks. Supposedly, the world will end when the priests complete their task, so there is little incentive for us to facilitate their efforts.

Let's assume that the priests are attempting to move the disks from peg 1 to peg 3. We wish to develop an algorithm that prints the precise sequence of peg-to-peg disk transfers.

If we were to approach this problem with conventional techniques, we would find ourselves hopelessly knotted up in managing the disks. However, if we approach the problem with recursion in mind, it becomes simpler. Moving n disks can be viewed in terms of moving only $n - 1$ disks (and hence the recursion) as follows:

a) Move $n - 1$ disks from peg 1 to peg 2, using peg 3 as a temporary holding area.
b) Move the last disk (the largest) from peg 1 to peg 3.
c) Move the $n - 1$ disks from peg 2 to peg 3, using peg 1 as a temporary holding area.

The process ends when the last task involves moving $n = 1$ disk (i.e., the base case). This is accomplished by moving the disk without the need for a temporary holding area.

Write a program to solve the Towers of Hanoi problem. Allow the user to enter the number of disks in a `TextBox`. Use a recursive `Tower` method with four parameters:

a) The number of disks to be moved
b) The peg on which the disks are threaded initially

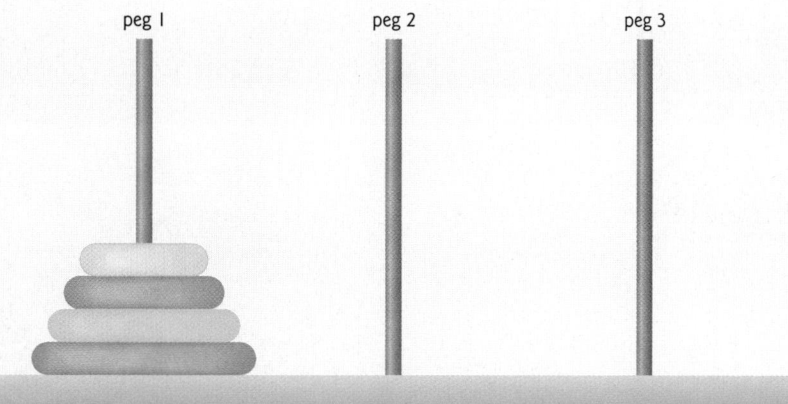

Fig. 7.30 | Towers of Hanoi for the case with four disks.

c) The peg to which this stack of disks is to be moved
d) The peg to be used as a temporary holding area

Your program should display in a `TextBox` with scrolling functionality the precise instructions for moving the disks from the starting peg to the destination peg. For example, to move a stack of three disks from peg 1 to peg 3, your program should print the following series of moves:

1 → 3 (This means move one disk from peg 1 to peg 3.)
1 → 2
3 → 2
1 → 3
2 → 1
2 → 3
1 → 3

8

Arrays

Now go, write it before them in a table, and note it in a book.

—Isaiah 30:8

With sobs and tears he sorted out
Those of the largest size …

—Lewis Carroll

Attempt the end, and never stand to doubt;
Nothing's so hard, but search will find it out.

—Robert Herrick

Begin at the beginning, … and go on till you come to the end: then stop.

—Lewis Carroll

To go beyond is as wrong as to fall short

—Confucius

OBJECTIVES

In this chapter you'll learn:

- To use the array data structure; arrays are objects.
- How arrays are used to store, sort and search lists and tables of values.
- To declare, initialize and refer to individual elements of arrays.
- To pass arrays to methods using `ByVal` and `ByRef`.
- To declare and manipulate multidimensional arrays, especially rectangular arrays and jagged arrays.
- To create variable-length parameter lists.
- To use the `For Each`...`Next` statement to iterate through the elements of arrays without using a loop counter.

Outline

8.1 Introduction

This chapter introduces basic concepts of data structures. Arrays are simple data structures consisting only of data items of the same type. Arrays normally are "static" entities, in that they typically remain the same size once they are created, although you can use the `ReDim` statement or the `Array` class's `Resize` method to resize an array at execution time. We begin by creating and accessing arrays; we then perform more complex manipulations of arrays, including searching and sorting. We discuss arrays with one dimension and with multiple dimensions. Chapter 24, Data Structures and Generic Collections, introduces dynamic data structures, such as lists, queues, stacks and trees, which typically grow and shrink as programs execute. Chapter 24 also presents some of the .NET Framework Class Library's predefined data structures.

8.2 Arrays

An array is a group of variables (called **elements**) containing values that all have the same type. Array names follow the same conventions that apply to other variable names. To refer to a particular element in an array, we specify the name of the array and the **position number** of the element to which we refer. Position numbers are values that indicate specific locations within arrays.

Figure 8.1 shows a logical representation of an integer array called `c`. This array contains 12 elements, any one of which can be referred to by giving the name of the array followed by the position number of the element in parentheses `()`. The first element in every array is the **zeroth element**. Thus, the elements of array `c` are `c(0)`, `c(1)`, `c(2)` and so on. The highest position number in array `c` is 11, which is 1 less than 12—the number of elements in the array.

The position number in parentheses more formally is called an **index** (or a **subscript**). An index must be a nonnegative integer or integer expression. If a program uses an expression as an index, the expression is evaluated first to determine the index. For example, if variable `value1` is equal to `5`, and variable `value2` is equal to `6`, then the statement

```
c(value1 + value2) += 2
```

adds `2` to array element `c(11)`. Note that an **indexed array name** (i.e., the array name followed by an index enclosed in parentheses) is an *lvalue*—it can be used on the left side of an assignment statement to place a new value into an array element.

Let's examine array `c` (Fig. 8.1) more closely. The array's name is `c`. Its 12 elements are referred to as `c(0)` through `c(11)`—pronounced as "c sub zero" through "c sub 11," where "sub" derives from "subscript." The value of `c(0)` is `-45`, the value of `c(1)` is `6`, the value of `c(7)` is `62` and the value of `c(11)` is `78`. Values stored in arrays can be employed in calculations. For example, to determine the total of the values contained in the first three elements of array `c` and then store the result in variable `sum`, we would write

```
sum = c(0) + c(1) + c(2)
```

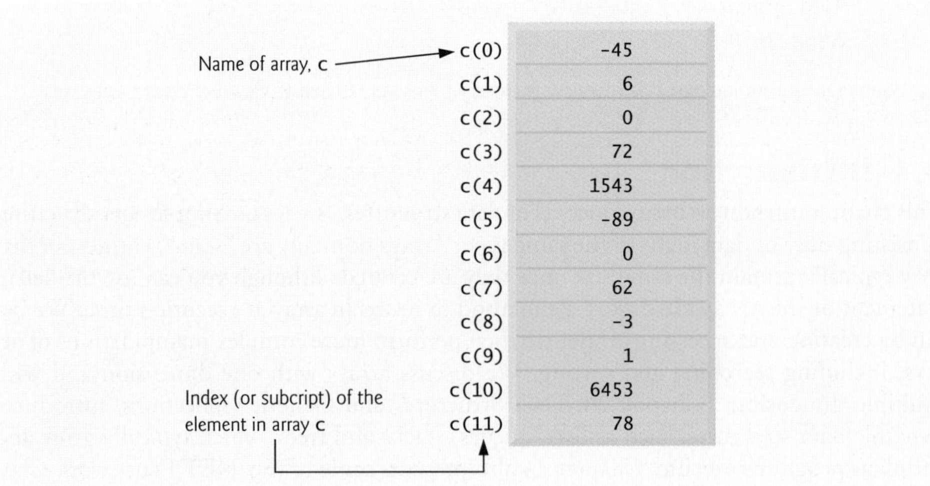

Fig. 8.1 | Array consisting of 12 elements.

To divide the value of `c(6)` by 2 and assign the result to the variable `result`, we'd write

```
result = c(6) \ 2
```

Common Programming Error 8.1

It is important to note the difference between the "seventh element of the array" and "array element seven." Array indices begin at 0, which means that the "seventh element of the array" has the index 6, whereas "array element seven" has the index 7 and is actually the eighth element of the array. This confusion is a common source of "off-by-one" errors. We will avoid such terminology; instead, we refer to all array elements simply by their indexed names—such as `c(0)` *rather than "the first element of* `c`*."*

Every array in Visual Basic "knows" its own length. The length of array `c` (i.e., `12`) is determined by the following expression:

```
c.Length
```

All arrays have access to the methods and properties of class `System.Array`, including the `Length` property. For instance, method `GetUpperBound` returns the index of the last element in the array. Method `GetUpperBound` takes one argument indicating a dimension of the array (e.g., 0 for the first dimension, 1 for the second dimension, and so on). We discuss arrays with multiple dimensions in Section 8.11. For one-dimensional arrays, such as `c`, the argument passed to `GetUpperBound` is `0`. For example, the expression

```
c.GetUpperBound(0)
```

returns `11`. Note that the value returned by method `GetUpperBound` is one less than the value of the array's `Length` property.

8.3 Declaring and Allocating Arrays

Arrays occupy space in memory. The amount of memory an array requires depends on its length and the size of the type of its elements. To declare an array, provide the array's name and type. Either of the following statements can be used to declare the array in Fig. 8.1:

```
Dim c As Integer()
Dim c() As Integer
```

The parentheses that follow the type or the variable name indicate that `c` is an array. Arrays can be declared to contain elements of any type; every element of the array is of that type. For example, every element of an `Integer` array contains an `Integer` value.

Before an array can be used, you must specify its size and allocate memory for it. Recall from Chapter 4 that keyword `New` creates an object. Arrays are objects in Visual Basic, so they too can be allocated using keyword `New`. The value stored in the array variable is actually a reference to the location in the computer's memory where the array object is stored. The statement

```
c = New Integer(11) {}
```

allocates memory for the array `c`. In our example, the number `11` defines the array's upper bound. Array bounds determine what indices can be used to access an element in the array. Here the array bounds are `0` (which is implicit in the preceding statement and is always the lower bound of every array) and `11`—an index outside these bounds cannot be used to access elements in the array c. Note that the actual size of the array is one larger (12) than the specified upper bound. We also can explicitly specify the array bounds, as in

```
c = New Integer(0 To 11) {}
```

The explicit array bounds specified in the preceding statement indicate that the lower bound of the array is 0 and the upper bound is 11. Note that the size of the array is still 12.

Common Programming Error 8.2

Explicitly setting the lower bound of an array to a value other than 0 is a compilation error.

The braces ({ and }) following the array bounds are called an initializer list and specify the initial values of the array's elements. When the initializer list is empty, the elements in the array are initialized to the default value for the array's type. Again, the default value is 0 for numeric primitive data-type variables, False for Boolean variables and Nothing for references. The initializer list also can contain a comma-separated list specifying the initial values of the elements in the array. For instance,

```
Dim numbers As Integer()
numbers = New Integer() {1, 2, 3, 6}
```

declares and allocates an array containing four Integer values. Visual Basic can determine the array bounds from the number of elements in the initializer list—it is not necessary to specify the upper bound of the array when a nonempty initializer list is present. When you explicitly state the upper bound and a nonempty initializer list, ensure that the upper bound of the array is one less than the number of elements in the initializer list; otherwise, a compilation error occurs.

The two preceding statements can be combined into a single statement, as in

```
Dim numbers As Integer() = New Integer() {1, 2, 3, 6}
```

The array declaration and initialization can be further condensed to

```
Dim numbers As Integer() = {1, 2, 3, 6}
```

In this case, the compiler determines the array bounds from the number of elements in the initializer list and implicitly uses the New keyword.

You may be tempted to shorten this statement even further using local type inference to infer the type of numbers (Integer()) from the initializer list, as in

```
Dim numbers = {1, 2, 3, 6}
```

However, in this case, the compiler does not have enough information to determine the type of variable numbers, so the type defaults to Object. This causes a compilation error, because a variable of type Object cannot be initialized with an initializer list. The statement must be written as

```
Dim numbers = New Integer() {1, 2, 3, 6}
```

for the compiler to infer the type of variable numbers correctly.

Although arrays are objects in Visual Basic, they can be created using a syntax that does not use the New keyword. For example, the statement

```
Dim numbers(5) As Integer
```

allocates the six-element array of `Integer`s. Some programmers prefer to use the shorter syntax used above. Throughout the book, we'll use the `New` keyword to emphasize the fact that arrays are objects. This syntax is also consistent with other popular programming languages such as C# or Java, which create arrays with the `New` keyword.

8.4 Examples Using Arrays

This section presents several examples that demonstrate the declaration, allocation and initialization of arrays, as well as various common manipulations of array elements. The examples in this section use arrays that contain elements of type `Integer`.

8.4.1 Allocating an Array

The program in Fig. 8.2 uses the `New` operator to allocate an array of 10 `Integer` elements, which are initially zero (the default value for `Integer` variables). The program displays the array elements in tabular format in a console window.

```
' Fig. 8.2: CreateArray.vb
' Declaring and allocating an array.
Module CreateArray
   Sub Main()
      Dim array As Integer() ' declare array variable

      ' allocate memory for 10-element array using explicit array bounds
      array = New Integer(0 To 9) {}

      Console.WriteLine("Index " & vbTab & "Value")

      ' display values in array
      For i = 0 To array.GetUpperBound(0)
         Console.WriteLine(i & vbTab & array(i))
      Next

      Console.WriteLine(vbNewLine & "The array contains " & _
         array.Length & " elements.")
   End Sub ' Main
End Module ' CreateArray
```

```
Index   Value
0       0
1       0
2       0
3       0
4       0
5       0
6       0
7       0
8       0
9       0

The array contains 10 elements.
```

Fig. 8.2 | Creating an array.

Line 5 declares array—a variable capable of storing a reference to an array of Integers. Line 8 allocates an array of 10 elements (with explicit array bounds 0 to 9) using New and assigns it to array. Line 10 displays the headings for the columns. The columns represent the index for each array element and the value of each array element, respectively.

Lines 13–15 use a For statement to display the index number (i) and the value of each array element (array(i)). We use zero-based counting (recall that array indices start at 0), so that the loop accesses every array element. Also note, in the header of the For statement, the expression array.GetUpperBound(0), used to retrieve the upper bound of the array (in this case, 9). The Length property (line 18) returns the number of elements in the array.

8.4.2 Initializing the Values in an Array

Figure 8.3 creates two 10-element integer arrays and sets their element values, using an initializer list and a For statement, respectively. The arrays are displayed in tabular format.

Lines 7–8 combine the declaration and allocation of array1 into one statement. The compiler implicitly uses New to allocate the array based on the number of values in the initializer list. Line 11 declares and allocates array2, whose size is determined by the expression array1.GetUpperBound(0), meaning that array1 and array2, in this particular program, have the same upper bound (9) and the same size (10).

The For statement in lines 14–16 initializes the elements in array2 to the even integers 2, 4, 6, ..., 20. These numbers are generated by multiplying each successive value of

```
1  ' Fig. 8.3: InitArray.vb
2  ' Initializing arrays.
3  Module InitArray
4     Sub Main()
5        ' initializer list specifies the number of elements
6        ' and the value of each element
7        Dim array1 As Integer() = _
8           {32, 27, 64, 18, 95, 14, 90, 70, 60, 37}
9
10       ' allocate array2 based on length of array1
11       Dim array2 As Integer() = New Integer(array1.GetUpperBound(0)) {}
12
13       ' set values in array2 by a calculation
14       For i = 0 To array2.GetUpperBound(0)
15          array2(i) = 2 + 2 * i ' generate 2, 4, 6, ..., 20
16       Next
17
18       Console.WriteLine("Index " & vbTab & "Array1" & vbTab & "Array2")
19
20       ' display values for both arrays side by side
21       For i = 0 To array1.GetUpperBound(0)
22          Console.WriteLine(i & vbTab & array1(i) & vbTab & array2(i))
23       Next
24    End Sub ' Main
25 End Module ' InitArray
```

Fig. 8.3 | Initializing array elements with an array initializer and a For statement. (Part 1 of 2.)

```
Index   Array1  Array2
0       32      2
1       27      4
2       64      6
3       18      8
4       95      10
5       14      12
6       90      14
7       70      16
8       60      18
9       37      20
```

Fig. 8.3 | Initializing array elements with an array initializer and a For statement. (Part 2 of 2.)

the loop counter by 2 and adding 2 to the product. The For statement in lines 21–23 displays the values in the arrays.

8.4.3 Summing the Elements of an Array

Often, the elements of an array represent a series of values that are employed in a calculation. For example, if the elements of an array represent a group of students' exam grades, the instructor might wish to total the elements of the array, then calculate the class average for the exam. Figure 8.4 sums the values contained in a 10-element integer array.

Line 5 declares, allocates and initializes the 10-element array array. Line 10, in the body of the For statement, performs the addition. Alternatively, the values supplied as initializers for array could have been read into the program. For example, the user could enter the values through a TextBox, or the values could be read from a file on disk. Information about reading values into a program from a file can be found in Chapter 18, Files and Streams.

```
1  ' Fig. 8.4: SumArray.vb
2  ' Computing the sum of the elements in an array.
3  Module SumArray
4     Sub Main()
5        Dim array As Integer() = {1, 2, 3, 4, 5, 6, 7, 8, 9, 10}
6        Dim total As Integer = 0
7
8        ' sum the array element values
9        For i = 0 To array.GetUpperBound(0)
10          total += array(i)
11       Next
12
13       Console.WriteLine("Total of array elements: {0}", total)
14    End Sub ' Main
15 End Module ' SumArray
```

```
Total of array elements: 55
```

Fig. 8.4 | Computing the sum of the elements in an array .

8.4.4 Using Arrays to Analyze Survey Results

Our next example uses arrays to summarize data collected in a survey. Consider the following problem statement:

> *Forty students were asked to rate on a scale of 1 to 10 the quality of the food in the student cafeteria, with 1 being "awful" and 10 being "excellent." Place the 40 responses in an integer array and determine the frequency of each rating.*

This is a typical array-processing application (Fig. 8.5). We wish to summarize the number of responses of each type (i.e., 1–10). Array `responses` (lines 6–8) is a 40-element integer array containing the students' survey responses. We use 11-element array `frequency` to count the number of occurrences of each response. We ignore `frequency(0)` because it is more natural to have the survey response `1` increment `frequency(1)` rather

```
1  ' Fig. 8.5: StudentPoll.vb
2  ' Using arrays to display poll results.
3  Module StudentPoll
4     Sub Main()
5        ' student response array (more typically, input at run time)
6        Dim responses As Integer() = _
7           {1, 2, 6, 4, 8, 5, 9, 7, 8, 10, 1, 6, 3, 8, 6, 10, 3, 8, 2, _
8           7, 6, 5, 7, 6, 8, 6, 7, 5, 6, 6, 5, 6, 7, 5, 6, 4, 8, 6, 8, 10}
9
10       ' response frequency array (indices 0 through 10)
11       Dim frequency As Integer() = New Integer(10) {}
12
13       ' count frequencies
14       For answer = 0 To responses.GetUpperBound(0)
15          frequency(responses(answer)) += 1
16       Next
17
18       Console.WriteLine("Rating " & vbTab & "Frequency ")
19
20       ' display output, ignore element 0 of frequency
21       For rating = 1 To frequency.GetUpperBound(0)
22          Console.WriteLine(rating & vbTab & frequency(rating))
23       Next
24    End Sub ' Main
25 End Module ' StudentPoll
```

```
Rating  Frequency
1       2
2       2
3       2
4       2
5       5
6       11
7       5
8       7
9       1
10      3
```

Fig. 8.5 | Simple student-poll analysis program.

than `frequency(0)`. We can use each response directly as an index on the `frequency` array. Each element of the array is used as a counter for one of the possible types of survey responses—`frequency(1)` counts the number of students who rated the food as 1, `frequency(2)` counts the number of students who rated the food as 2, and so on.

The `For` statement (lines 14–16) reads the responses from the array `responses` one at a time and increments one of the 10 counters in the `frequency` array (`frequency(1)` to `frequency(10)`; we ignore `frequency(0)` because the survey responses are limited to the range 1–10). The key statement in the loop appears in line 15. This statement increments the appropriate `frequency` counter as determined by the value of `responses(answer)`.

Consider several iterations of the `For` statement. When the counter `answer` is `0`, `responses(answer)` is the value of `responses(0)` (i.e., `1`—see line 7). So, `frequency( responses(answer))` is interpreted as `frequency(1)`, and the counter `frequency(1)` increments by one. In evaluating the expression `frequency(responses(answer))`, Visual Basic starts with the value in the innermost set of parentheses (`answer`, currently `0`). The value of `answer` is plugged into the expression, and Visual Basic evaluates the next set of parentheses (`responses(answer)`). That value is used as the index for the `frequency` array to determine which counter to increment (in this case, the `1` counter).

When `answer` is `1`, `responses(answer)` is the value of `responses(1)` (i.e., `2`—see line 7). As a result, `frequency(responses(answer))` is interpreted as `frequency(2)`, causing array element `2` to be incremented.

When `answer` is `2`, `responses(answer)` is the value of `responses(2)` (i.e., `6`—see line 7), so `frequency(responses(answer))` is interpreted as `frequency(6)`, causing array element `6` to be incremented, and so on. Note that, regardless of the number of responses processed in the survey, only an 11-element array (in which we ignore element zero) is required to summarize the results, because all the response values are between 1 and 10, and the index values for an 11-element array are 0–10. Note that, in the output in Fig. 8.5, the numbers in the frequency column correctly total 40 (the elements of the `frequency` array were initialized to zero when the array was allocated with `New`).

If the data contained the out-of-range value 13, the program would attempt to add `1` to `frequency(13)`. This is outside the bounds of the array. In languages like C and C++, such a dangerous out-of-bounds reference would be allowed. The program would "walk" past the end of the array to where it thought element number 13 was located and would add 1 to whatever happened to be stored at that memory location. This could modify another variable in the program, possibly causing incorrect results or even premature program termination. Visual Basic provides mechanisms that prevent accessing elements outside the bounds of arrays.

Common Programming Error 8.3

When a program is executed, array element indices are checked for validity (i.e., all indices must be greater than or equal to 0 and less than the length of the array). If an attempt is made to use an invalid index to access an element, Visual Basic generates an `IndexOutOfRangeException` *exception. Exceptions are discussed in detail in Chapter 13, Exception Handling.*

Error-Prevention Tip 8.1

When looping through an array, the array index should remain between 0 and the upper bound of the array (i.e., the value returned by method `GetUpperBound`*). The initial and final values used in the repetition statement should prevent accessing elements outside this range.*

8.4.5 Using Bar Charts to Display Array Data Graphically

Many programs present data to users in a visual or graphical format. For example, numeric values are often displayed as bars in a bar chart. In such a chart, longer bars represent proportionally larger numeric values. Figure 8.6 displays numeric data graphically by creating a bar chart that shows each numeric value as a bar of asterisks (*).

The program reads numbers from an array and graphs the information as a bar chart. Each number is printed, and a bar consisting of the corresponding number of asterisks is displayed beside the number. The nested `For` loops (lines 11–19) display the bars. Note the end value (`array1(i)`) of the inner `For` statement at line 14. Each time the inner `For` statement is reached (line 14), it counts from `1` to `array1(i)`, using a value in `array1` to determine the final value of the control variable `j`—the number of asterisks to display.

```
1  ' Fig. 8.6: BarChart.vb
2  ' Using data to create bar chart.
3  Module BarChart
4     Sub Main()
5        ' create data array
6        Dim array1 As Integer() = {19, 3, 15, 7, 11, 9, 13, 5, 17, 1}
7
8        Console.WriteLIne("Element " & "Value " & vbTab & "Bar Chart")
9
10       ' display a bar of the bar chart for each element in the array
11       For i = 0 To array1.GetUpperBound(0)
12          Console.Write(i & vbTab & array1(i) & vbTab)
13
14          For j = 1 To array1(i)
15             Console.Write("*") ' display one asterisk
16          Next j
17
18          Console.WriteLine()
19       Next i
20    End Sub ' Main
21 End Module ' BarChart
```

```
Element Value   Bar Chart
0       19      *******************
1       3       ***
2       15      ***************
3       7       *******
4       11      ***********
5       9       *********
6       13      *************
7       5       *****
8       17      *****************
9       1       *
```

Fig. 8.6 | Bar chart printing program.

8.4.6 Using the Elements of an Array as Counters

Sometimes programs use a series of counter variables to summarize data, such as the results of a survey. In Chapter 7, we used a series of counters in our die-rolling program to track the number of occurrences of each face on a six-sided die as the program rolled the die 12 times. We indicated that we can do what we did in Fig. 7.17 in a more elegant way to write the dice-rolling program. An array version of this application is shown in Fig. 8.7. The images of the dice are included in this example's directory.

```
' Fig. 8.7: RollDie.vb
' Rolling 12 dice with frequency chart.
Public Class RollDie
   Dim randomNumber As Random = New Random()
   Dim frequency As Integer() = New Integer(6) {}

   ' event handler for rollButton's Click event
   Private Sub rollButton_Click(ByVal sender As System.Object, _
      ByVal e As System.EventArgs) Handles rollButton.Click

      ' pass PictureBox to a method that assigns a face to each die
      DisplayDie(die1PictureBox)
      DisplayDie(die2PictureBox)
      DisplayDie(die3PictureBox)
      DisplayDie(die4PictureBox)
      DisplayDie(die5PictureBox)
      DisplayDie(die6PictureBox)
      DisplayDie(die7PictureBox)
      DisplayDie(die8PictureBox)
      DisplayDie(die9PictureBox)
      DisplayDie(die10PictureBox)
      DisplayDie(die11PictureBox)
      DisplayDie(die12PictureBox)

      Dim total As Double = 0

      ' total the die faces (used in percentage calculations)
      For i = 1 To frequency.GetUpperBound(0)
         total += frequency(i)
      Next

      displayTextBox.Text = "Face" & vbTab & "Frequency" & _
         vbTab & "Percent" & vbNewLine

      ' output frequency values
      For i = 1 To frequency.GetUpperBound(0)
         displayTextBox.Text &= i & vbTab & frequency(i) & _
            vbTab & vbTab & String.Format("{0:P2}", _
            frequency(i) / total) & "%" & vbNewLine
      Next
   End Sub ' rollButton_Click

   ' simulate roll, display proper image and increment frequency
   Sub DisplayDie(ByVal diePictureBox As PictureBox)
      Dim face As Integer = 1 + randomNumber.Next(6)

```

Fig. 8.7 | Using arrays to eliminate a `Select Case` statement. (Part 1 of 2.)

```
47         ' retrieve specific die image from resources
48         Dim pictureResource = My.Resources.ResourceManager.GetObject( _
49            String.Format("die{0}", face))
50
51         ' convert pictureResource to image type and load into PictureBox
52         diePictureBox.Image = CType(pictureResource, Image)
53
54         frequency(face) += 1 ' increment appropriate frequency counter
55      End Sub ' DisplayDie
56   End Class ' RollDie
```

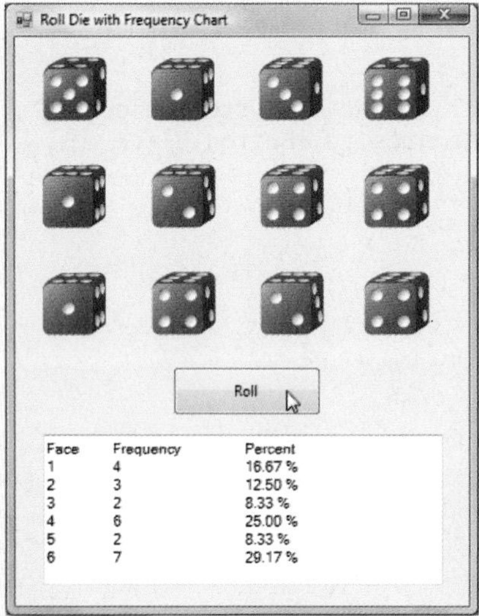

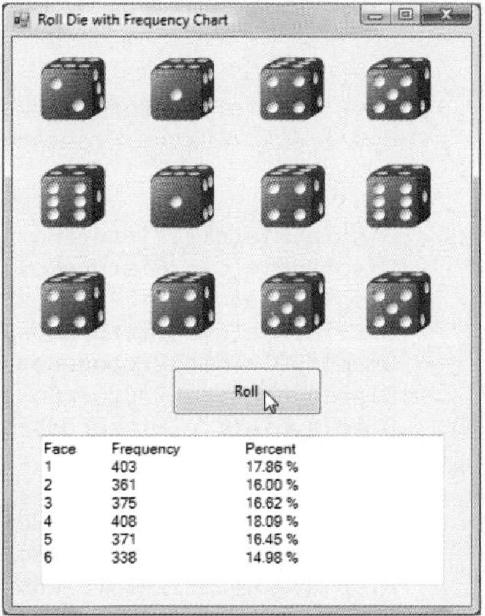

Fig. 8.7 | Using arrays to eliminate a `Select Case` statement. (Part 2 of 2.)

Lines 62–75 of Fig. 7.17 are replaced by line 54 of Fig. 8.7, which uses `face`'s value as the index for array `frequency` to determine which element should be incremented during each iteration of the loop. The random number calculation at line 45 produces numbers from 1 to 6 (the values for a six-sided die); thus, the `frequency` array must have seven elements to allow the index values 1–6. We ignore element 0 of array `frequency`. Lines 36–40 replace lines 35–47 from Fig. 7.17. We can loop through array `frequency`; therefore, we do not have to enumerate each line of text to display in the `PictureBox`, as we did in Fig. 7.17.

8.5 Case Study: Card Shuffling and Dealing Simulation

The examples in the chapter thus far have used arrays containing elements of primitive types. The elements of an array can be of either value types or reference types. This section uses random number generation and an array of reference-type elements, namely references to objects representing playing cards, to develop a class that simulates card shuffling and dealing. You can then use this class to implement applications that play specific card games.

First, we develop class Card (Fig. 8.8), which represents a playing card that has a face (e.g., "Ace", "Deuce", "Three", ..., "Jack", "Queen", "King") and a suit (e.g., "Hearts", "Diamonds", "Clubs", "Spades"). Next, we develop the DeckOfCards class (Fig. 8.9), which creates a deck of 52 playing cards in which each element is a Card object. We then build a test application DeckOfCardsTest (Fig. 8.10) that demonstrates class DeckOfCards's card shuffling and dealing capabilities.

Class **Card**

Class Card (Fig. 8.8) contains two String instance variables—face and suit—that are used to store references to the face name and suit name for a specific Card. The constructor for the class (lines 8–11) receives two Strings that it uses to initialize face and suit. Method ToString (lines 14–16) creates a String consisting of the face of the card, the String " of " and the suit of the card. Card's ToString method can be invoked explicitly to obtain a string representation of a Card object (e.g., "Ace of Spades"). The ToString method of an object is called implicitly when an object is output as a String. For this behavior to occur, ToString must be declared with the header shown in line 14 of Fig. 8.8. We discuss the special method ToString in Chapter 10, Classes and Objects: A Deeper Look.

```
1  ' Fig. 8.8: Card.vb
2  ' Card class represents a playing card.
3  Public Class Card
4     Private face As String ' face of card ("Ace", "Deuce", ...)
5     Private suit As String ' suit of card ("Hearts", "Diamonds", ...)
6
7     ' two-argument constructor initializes card's face and suit
8     Public Sub New(ByVal cardFace As String, ByVal cardSuit As String)
9        face = cardFace ' initialize face of card
10       suit = cardSuit ' initialize suit of card
11    End Sub ' New
12
13    ' return String representation of Card, Overrides defined in Ch 10
14    Public Overrides Function ToString() As String
15       Return face & " of " & suit
16    End Function ' ToString
17 End Class ' Card
```

Fig. 8.8 | Card class represents a playing card.

Class **DeckOfCards**

Class DeckOfCards (Fig. 8.9) declares an instance variable array named deck, which consists of Card objects (line 4). Like primitive-type array declarations, the declaration of an array of objects includes the name of the array variable, followed by the keyword As, the type of the elements in the array and parentheses (e.g., deck As Card()). Class DeckOfCards also declares an integer instance variable currentCard (line 5) representing the next Card to be dealt from the deck array and a named constant NUMBER_OF_CARDS (line 6) indicating the number of Cards in the deck (52).

The class's constructor instantiates the `deck` array (line 15) with upper bound `NUMBER_OF_CARDS - 1`. When first created, the elements of the `deck` array are `Nothing` by default, so the constructor uses a `For` statement (lines 20–22) to fill the `deck` array with `Cards`. This statement initializes control variable `count` to `0` and loops while `count` is less than or equal to `deck.GetUpperBound(0)`, causing `count` to take on each integer value from 0 to 51 (the indices of the `deck` array). Each `Card` is instantiated and initialized with two `Strings`—one from the `faces` array (which contains the `Strings` `"Ace"` through `"King"`) and one from the `suits` array (which contains the `Strings` `"Hearts"`, `"Diamonds"`, `"Clubs"` and `"Spades"`). The calculation `count Mod 13` always results in a value from 0 to 12 (the 13 indices of the `faces` array in lines 11–12), and the calculation `count \ 13` always results in a value from 0 to 3 (the four indices of the `suits` array in line 13). When the `deck` array is initialized, it contains the `Cards` with faces `"Ace"` through `"King"` in order for each suit.

```
1  ' Fig. 8.9: DeckOfCards.vb
2  ' DeckOfCards class represents a deck of playing cards.
3  Public Class DeckOfCards
4     Private deck As Card() ' array of Card objects
5     Private currentCard As Integer ' index of next Card to be dealt
6     Private Const NUMBER_OF_CARDS As Integer = 52 ' number of cards
7     Private randomNumbers As Random ' random number generator
8
9     ' constructor fills deck of Cards
10    Public Sub New()
11       Dim faces As String() = {"Ace", "Deuce", "Three", "Four", "Five", _
12          "Six", "Seven", "Eight", "Nine", "Ten", "Jack", "Queen", "King"}
13       Dim suits As String() = {"Hearts", "Diamonds", "Clubs", "Spades"}
14
15       deck = New Card(NUMBER_OF_CARDS - 1) {} ' create array of Cards
16       currentCard = 0 ' set currentCard so first Card dealt is deck(0)
17       randomNumbers = New Random() ' create random number generator
18
19       ' populate deck with Card objects
20       For count = 0 To deck.GetUpperBound(0)
21          deck(count) = New Card(faces(count Mod 13), suits(count \ 13))
22       Next
23    End Sub ' New
24
25    ' shuffle deck of Cards with simple one-pass algorithm
26    Public Sub Shuffle()
27       ' after shuffling, dealing should start at deck(0) again
28       currentCard = 0 ' reinitialize currentCard
29
30       ' for each Card, pick another random Card and swap them
31       For first = 0 To deck.GetUpperBound(0)
32          ' select a random number between 0 and 51
33          Dim second As Integer = randomNumbers.Next(NUMBER_OF_CARDS)
34
```

Fig. 8.9 | `DeckOfCards` class represents a deck of playing cards that can be shuffled and dealt one at a time. (Part 1 of 2.)

```
35             ' swap current Card with randomly selected Card
36             Dim temp As Card = deck(first)
37             deck(first) = deck(second)
38             deck(second) = temp
39          Next
40       End Sub ' Shuffle
41
42       ' deal one Card
43       Public Function DealCard() As Card
44          ' determine whether Cards remain to be dealt
45          If currentCard <= deck.GetUpperBound(0) Then
46             Dim lastCard = currentCard ' store current card number
47             currentCard += 1 ' increment current card number
48             Return deck(lastCard)
49          Else
50             Return Nothing
51          End If
52       End Function ' DealCard
53    End Class ' DeckOfCards
```

Fig. 8.9 | `DeckOfCards` class represents a deck of playing cards that can be shuffled and dealt one at a time. (Part 2 of 2.)

Method `Shuffle` (lines 26–40) shuffles the `Card`s in the deck. The method loops through all 52 `Card`s (array indices 0 to 51). For each `Card`, a number between 0 and 51 is picked randomly to select another `Card` (line 33). Next, the current `Card` object and the randomly selected `Card` object are swapped in the array (lines 36–38). The extra variable `temp` temporarily stores one of the two `Card` objects being swapped. The swap cannot be performed with only the two statements

```
deck(first) = deck(second)
deck(second) = deck(first)
```

If `deck(first)` is the `"Ace"` of `"Spades"` and `deck(second)` is the `"Queen"` of `"Hearts"`, after the first assignment, both array elements contain the `"Queen"` of `"Hearts"` and the `"Ace"` of `"Spades"` is lost—hence, the extra variable `temp` is needed. After the `For` loop terminates, the `Card` objects are randomly ordered. Only 52 swaps are made in a single pass of the entire array, and the array of `Card` objects is shuffled!

Method `DealCard` (lines 43–52) deals one `Card` in the array. Recall that `currentCard` indicates the index of the next `Card` to be dealt (i.e., the `Card` at the top of the deck). Thus, line 45 compares `currentCard` to the upper bound (51) of the `deck` array. If the `deck` is not empty (i.e., `currentCard` is less than or equal to 51), line 46 assigns `currentCard` (the index of the card that will be returned) to temporary variable `lastCard`, line 47 increments `currentCard` to prepare for the next call to `DealCard` and line 48 returns `deck(lastCard)`, which represents the top card of the deck for this call to `DealCard`. Otherwise, `DealCard` returns `Nothing` to indicate that the deck is empty.

Shuffling and Dealing Cards

Figure 8.10 demonstrates the card dealing and shuffling capabilities of class `DeckOfCards` (Fig. 8.9). Line 5 creates a `DeckOfCards` object named `cards`. Recall that the `DeckOfCards` constructor creates the deck with the 52 `Card` objects in order by suit and face. Line 6 invokes cards's Shuffle method to randomly rearrange the Card objects. The For statement in lines 9–13 deals all 52 Cards in the deck and prints them in four columns of 13 Cards each. Lines 10–12 deal and print four Card objects (on one line), each obtained by invoking cards's DealCard method. When Console.WriteLine outputs a Card with the format specifier {0, -18}, the Card's ToString method (declared in lines 14–16 of Fig. 8.8) is implicitly invoked, and the result is output left justified (because of the minus sign in -18) in a field of width 18, as indicated by the value -18 to the right of the comma. The **field width** specifies the number of character positions in which a value should appear. Positive field widths are right justified. Again, we explain ToString in detail in Chapter 10.

```
1  ' Fig. 8.10: DeckOfCardsTest.vb
2  ' Card shuffling and dealing application.
3  Module DeckOfCardsTest
4     Sub Main()
5        Dim cards As New DeckOfCards()
6        cards.Shuffle() ' place Cards in random order
7
8        ' print all 52 Cards in the order in which they are dealt
9        For i = 0 To 12
10          Console.WriteLine("{0, -18} {1, -18} {2, -18} {3, -18}", _
11             cards.DealCard(), cards.DealCard(), cards.DealCard(), _
12             cards.DealCard())
13       Next
14    End Sub ' Main
15 End Module ' DeckOfCardsTest
```

```
Five of Spades     Nine of Spades     Seven of Hearts    Eight of Clubs
Jack of Spades     Seven of Clubs     Queen of Spades    Ace of Diamonds
Ace of Clubs       Five of Hearts     Ten of Diamonds    Queen of Diamonds
Nine of Diamonds   Four of Hearts     Six of Spades      Six of Diamonds
Ace of Hearts      King of Spades     Jack of Diamonds   Seven of Spades
Four of Spades     Seven of Diamonds  Ten of Spades      Eight of Spades
Deuce of Spades    King of Diamonds   Deuce of Hearts    Nine of Hearts
Three of Clubs     King of Hearts     Six of Hearts      Queen of Hearts
Eight of Hearts    Ten of Hearts      Five of Clubs      King of Clubs
Five of Diamonds   Jack of Clubs      Jack of Hearts     Eight of Diamonds
Six of Clubs       Deuce of Clubs     Ace of Spades      Three of Hearts
Four of Diamonds   Ten of Clubs       Nine of Clubs      Three of Spades
Queen of Clubs     Deuce of Diamonds  Three of Diamonds  Four of Clubs
```

Fig. 8.10 | Card shuffling and dealing (all 52 cards are dealt).

8.6 Passing an Array to a Method

To pass an array argument to a method, specify the name of the array without using parentheses. For example, if array hourlyTemperatures has been declared as

```
Dim hourlyTemperatures As Integer() = New Integer(24) {}
```

the method call

```
DisplayDayData(hourlyTemperatures)
```

passes array hourlyTemperatures to method DisplayDayData.

Every array object "knows" its own upper bound (i.e., the value returned by the method `GetUpperBound`), so when you pass an array object to a method, you do not need to pass the upper bound of the array as a separate argument.

For a method to receive an array through a method call, the method's parameter list must specify that an array will be received. For example, the method header for `DisplayDayData` might be written as

```
Sub DisplayDayData(ByVal temperatureData As Integer())
```

indicating that `DisplayDayData` expects to receive an `Integer` array in parameter `temperatureData`. In Visual Basic, arrays always are passed by reference, yet it is normally inappropriate to use keyword `ByRef` in the method definition header. We discuss this subtle (and somewhat complex) issue in more detail in Section 8.16.

Although entire arrays are always passed by reference, individual array elements can be passed in the same manner as simple variables of that type. For instance, array element values of primitive types, such as `Integer`, can be passed either by value or by reference, depending on the method definition. To pass an array element to a method, use the indexed name of the array element as an argument in the method call. Figure 8.11 demonstrates the difference between passing an entire array and passing an array element.

```
' Fig. 8.11: PassArray.vb
' Passing arrays and individual array elements to methods.
Module PassArray
   Sub Main()
      Dim array1 As Integer() = New Integer() {1, 2, 3, 4, 5}

      Console.WriteLine("EFFECTS OF PASSING AN ENTIRE ARRAY " & _
         "BY REFERENCE:" & vbNewLine & vbNewLine & _
         "The values of the original array are:")

      ' display original elements of array1
      For i = 0 To array1.GetUpperBound(0)
         Console.Write("   " & array1(i))
      Next

      ModifyArray(array1) ' array is passed by reference
      Console.WriteLine(vbNewLine & _
         "The values of the modified array are:")

      ' display modified elements of array1
      For i = 0 To array1.GetUpperBound(0)
         Console.Write("   " & array1(i))
      Next

      Console.WriteLine(vbNewLine & vbNewLine & _
         "EFFECTS OF PASSING AN ARRAY ELEMENT BY VALUE:" & vbNewLine & _
         vbNewLine & "array1(3) before ModifyElementByVal: " & _
         array1(3))

```

Fig. 8.11 | Passing arrays and individual array elements to methods. (Part 1 of 3.)

```
      ModifyElementByVal(array1(3)) ' array element passed by value
      Console.WriteLine("array1(3) after ModifyElementByVal: " & _
         array1(3))
      Console.WriteLine(vbNewLine & "EFFECTS OF PASSING AN " & _
         "ARRAY ELEMENT BY REFERENCE: " & vbNewLine & vbNewLine & _
         "array1(3) before ModifyElementByRef: " & array1(3))

      ModifyElementByRef(array1(3)) ' array element passed by reference
      Console.WriteLine("array1(3) after ModifyElementByRef: " & _
         array1(3))
   End Sub ' Main

   ' method modifies array it receives (note ByVal)
   Sub ModifyArray(ByVal arrayParameter As Integer())
      For j = 0 To arrayParameter.GetUpperBound(0)
         arrayParameter(j) *= 2 ' double the array element
      Next
   End Sub ' ModifyArray

   ' method modifies integer passed to it
   ' original is not modified (note ByVal)
   Sub ModifyElementByVal(ByVal element As Integer)
      Console.WriteLine("Value received in ModifyElementByVal: " & _
         element)
      element *= 2 ' double the array element
      Console.WriteLine("Value calculated in ModifyElementByVal: " & _
         element)
   End Sub ' ModifyElementByVal

   ' method modifies integer passed to it
   ' original is modified (note ByRef)
   Sub ModifyElementByRef(ByRef element As Integer)
      Console.WriteLine("Value received in ModifyElementByRef: " & _
         element)
      element *= 2 ' double the array element
      Console.WriteLine("Value calculated in ModifyElementByRef: " & _
         element)
   End Sub ' ModifyElementByRef
End Module ' PassArray
```

```
EFFECTS OF PASSING AN ENTIRE ARRAY BY REFERENCE:

The values of the original array are:
  1  2  3  4  5
The values of the modified array are:
  2  4  6  8  10

EFFECTS OF PASSING AN ARRAY ELEMENT BY VALUE:

array1(3) before ModifyElementByVal: 8
Value received in ModifyElementByVal: 8
Value calculated in ModifyElementByVal: 16
array1(3) after ModifyElementByVal: 8
```

Fig. 8.11 | Passing arrays and individual array elements to methods. (Part 2 of 3.)

```
EFFECTS OF PASSING AN ARRAY ELEMENT BY REFERENCE:

array1(3) before ModifyElementByRef: 8
Value received in ModifyElementByRef: 8
Value calculated in ModifyElementByRef: 16
array1(3) after ModifyElementByRef: 16
```

Fig. 8.11 | Passing arrays and individual array elements to methods. (Part 3 of 3.)

The `For...Next` statement in lines 12–14 displays the five elements of integer array `array1` (line 5). Line 16 passes `array1` to method `ModifyArray` (lines 43–47), which then multiplies each element by `2` (line 45). To illustrate that `array1`'s elements were modified in the called method (i.e., as enabled by passing by reference), the `For...Next` statement in lines 21–23 displays the five elements of `array1`. As the output indicates, the elements of `array1` are indeed modified by `ModifyArray`.

To show the value of `array1(3)` before the call to `ModifyElementByVal`, lines 25–28 display the value of `array1(3)`. Line 30 invokes method `ModifyElementByVal` (lines 51–57) and passes `array1(3)`. When `array1(3)` is passed by value, the `Integer` value in position 3 of array `array1` (now an `8`) is copied and is passed to method `ModifyElementByVal`, where it becomes the value of parameter `element`. Method `ModifyElementByVal` then multiplies `element` by `2` (line 54). The parameter `element` of `ModifyElementByVal` is a local variable that is destroyed when the method terminates. Thus, when control is returned to `Main`, the unmodified value of `array1(3)` is displayed.

Lines 33–39 demonstrate the effects of method `ModifyElementByRef` (lines 61–67). This method performs the same calculation as `ModifyElementByVal`, multiplying `element` by `2`. In this case, `array1(3)` is passed by reference, meaning that the value of `array1(3)` displayed (lines 38–39) is the same as the value calculated in the method (i.e., the original value in the caller is modified by the called method).

Common Programming Error 8.4

When passing an array to a method, including an empty pair of parentheses after the array name is a syntax error.

8.7 For Each...Next Repetition Statement

Visual Basic provides the **`For Each...Next`** repetition statement for iterating through the values in a data structure, such as an array, without using a loop counter. When used with one-dimensional arrays, `For Each...Next` behaves like a `For...Next` statement that iterates through the range of indices from `0` to the value returned by `GetUpperBound(0)`. Instead of a counter, `For Each...Next` uses a variable to represent the value of each element. The program in Fig. 8.12 uses the `For Each...Next` statement to determine the minimum value in a one-dimensional array of grades.

The header of the `For Each` repetition statement (line 10) specifies an `Integer` variable (`grade`) and an array (`gradeArray`). The type of variable grade is inferred from the elements of `gradeArray`. The `For Each` statement iterates through all the elements in `gradeArray`, sequentially assigning each value to variable `grade`. The values are compared to variable `lowGrade` (line 11), which stores the lowest grade in the array.

```
1  ' Fig. 8.12: ForEach.vb
2  ' Program uses For Each…Next to find the minimum grade.
3  Module ForEach
4     Sub Main()
5        Dim gradeArray As Integer() = _
6           {77, 68, 86, 73, 98, 87, 89, 81, 70, 90, 86, 81}
7        Dim lowGrade As Integer = 100
8
9        ' use For Each…Next to find the minimum grade
10       For Each grade In gradeArray
11          If grade < lowGrade Then
12             lowGrade = grade
13          End If
14       Next
15
16       Console.WriteLine("The minimum grade is: {0}", lowGrade)
17    End Sub ' Main
18 End Module ' ForEach
```

```
The minimum grade is: 68
```

Fig. 8.12 | Using `For Each...Next` with an array.

For one-dimensional arrays, the repetition of the `For Each...Next` statement begins with the element whose index is zero, then iterates through all the indices. In this case, `grade` takes on the successive values as they are ordered in the initializer list in line 6. When all the grades have been processed, `lowGrade` is displayed. Although many array calculations are handled best with a counter, `For Each` is useful when the indices of the elements are not important.

8.8 GradeBook Case Study: Using an Array to Store Grades

This section further evolves class `GradeBook`, introduced in Chapter 4 and expanded in Chapters 5–7. Recall that this class represents a grade book used by a professor to store and analyze a set of student grades. Previous versions of the class process a set of grades entered by the user, but do not maintain the individual grade values in instance variables of the class. Thus, repeat calculations require the user to reenter the same grades. One way to solve this problem would be to store each grade entered in an instance of the class. For example, we could create instance variables `grade1`, `grade2`, …, `grade10` in class `GradeBook` to store 10 student grades. However, the code to total the grades and determine the class average would be cumbersome, and the class would not be able to process any more than 10 grades at a time. In this section, we solve the problem by storing the grades in an array.

Storing Student Grades in an Array in Class **GradeBook**

The version of class `GradeBook` (Fig. 8.13) presented here uses an array of `Integers` to store the grades of several students on a single exam. This eliminates the need to repeatedly input the same set of grades. Array `grades` is declared as an instance variable in line 5—therefore, each `GradeBook` object maintains its own set of grades. The class's constructor (lines 8–11) has two parameters—the name of the course and an array of grades. When an application (e.g., class `GradeBookTest` in Fig. 8.14) creates a `GradeBook` object, the application passes an existing `Integer` array to the constructor, which assigns the array's reference to instance variable `grades` (line 10). The size of the array `grades` is determined by the class that passes the array to the constructor. Thus, a `GradeBook` object can process a variable number of grades. The grade values in the passed array could have been input from a user or read from a file on disk (as discussed in Chapter 18). In our test application, we simply initialize an array with a set of grade values (Fig. 8.14, lines 6–7). Once the grades are stored in instance variable `grades` of class `GradeBook`, all the class's methods can access the elements of `grades` as needed to perform various calculations.

```
1  ' Fig. 8.13: GradeBook.vb
2  ' GradeBook class uses an array to store test grades.
3  Public Class GradeBook
4     Private courseNameValue As String ' name of course
5     Private grades As Integer() ' array of student grades
6
7     ' two-argument constructor initializes courseNameValue and grades
8     Public Sub New(ByVal name As String, ByVal gradesArray As Integer())
9        CourseName = name ' initializes courseNameValue via property
10       grades = gradesArray ' store reference to gradesArray
11    End Sub ' New
12
13    ' property CourseName
14    Public Property CourseName() As String
15       Get
16          Return courseNameValue
17       End Get
18
19       Set(ByVal name As String)
20          courseNameValue = name
21       End Set
22    End Property ' CourseName
23
24    ' display a welcome message to the GradeBook user
25    Public Sub DisplayMessage()
26       Console.WriteLine("Welcome to the grade book for " & vbNewLine & _
27          CourseName & vbNewLine)
28    End Sub ' DisplayMessage
29
30    ' perform various operations on the data
31    Public Sub ProcessGrades()
32       OutputGrades() ' output grades array
33
34       ' call method GetAverage to calculate the average grade
35       Console.WriteLine("Class average is {0:F2}", GetAverage())
36
37       ' call methods GetMinimum and GetMaximum
38       Console.WriteLine("Lowest grade is {0}", GetMinimum())
39       Console.WriteLine("Highest grade is {0}", GetMaximum())
40
```

Fig. 8.13 | GradeBook class using an array to store test grades. (Part 1 of 3.)

```
      ' call OutputBarChart to print grade distribution chart
      OutputBarChart()
   End Sub ' ProcessGrades

   ' find minimum grade
   Public Function GetMinimum() As Integer
      Dim lowGrade As Integer = grades(0) ' assume grades(0) is smallest

      ' loop through grades array
      For Each grade In grades
         ' if grade lower than lowGrade, assign it to lowGrade
         If grade < lowGrade Then
            lowGrade = grade ' new lowest grade
         End If
      Next

      Return lowGrade ' return lowest grade
   End Function ' GetMinimum

   ' find maximum grade
   Public Function GetMaximum() As Integer
      Dim highGrade As Integer = grades(0) ' assume grades(0) is largest

      ' loop through grades array
      For Each grade In grades
         ' if grade greater than highGrade, assign it to highGrade
         If grade > highGrade Then
            highGrade = grade ' new highest grade
         End If
      Next

      Return highGrade ' return highest grade
   End Function ' GetMaximum

   ' determine average grade for test
   Public Function GetAverage() As Double
      Dim total As Integer = 0 ' initialize total

      ' sum grades
      For Each grade In grades
         total += grade
      Next

      ' return average of grades
      Return (total / grades.Length)
   End Function ' GetAverage

   ' output bar chart displaying grade distribution
   Public Sub OutputBarChart()
      Console.WriteLine(vbNewLine & "Grade distribution:")

      ' stores frequency of grades in each range of 10 grades
      Dim frequency As Integer() = New Integer(10) {}
```

Fig. 8.13 | GradeBook class using an array to store test grades. (Part 2 of 3.)

```
94
95          ' for each grade, increment the appropriate frequency
96          For Each grade In grades
97             frequency(grade \ 10) += 1
98          Next
99
100         ' for each grade frequency, print bar in chart
101         For count = 0 To frequency.GetUpperBound(0)
102            ' output bar label ( "00-09: ", ..., "90-99: ", "100: " )
103            If count = 10 Then
104               Console.Write("{0, 5:D}: ", 100)
105            Else
106               Console.Write("{0, 2:D2}-{1, 2:D2}: ", _
107                  count * 10, count * 10 + 9)
108            End If
109
110            ' print bar of asterisks
111            For stars As Integer = 0 To frequency(count) - 1
112               Console.Write("*")
113            Next stars
114
115            Console.WriteLine() ' start a new line of output
116         Next count
117      End Sub ' OutputBarChart
118
119      ' output the contents of the grades array
120      Public Sub OutputGrades()
121         Console.WriteLine("The grades are:" & vbNewLine)
122
123         ' output each student's grade
124         For student = 0 To grades.GetUpperBound(0)
125            Console.WriteLine("Student {0, 2:D}: {1, 3:D}", _
126               student + 1, grades(student))
127         Next
128
129         Console.WriteLine()
130      End Sub ' OutputGrades
131   End Class ' GradeBook
```

Fig. 8.13 | GradeBook class using an array to store test grades. (Part 3 of 3.)

Method `ProcessGrades` (lines 31–43) contains a series of method calls that result in the output of a report summarizing the grades. Line 32 calls method `OutputGrades` to print the contents of the array `grades`. Lines 124–127 in method `OutputGrades` use a `For` statement to output each student's grade. Lines 125–126 use counter variable `student`'s value to output each grade next to a particular student number (see the output in Fig. 8.14). Although array indices start at 0, a professor would typically number students starting at 1. Thus, lines 125–126 output `student + 1` as the student number to produce grade labels `"Student 1: "`, `"Student 2: "`, and so on.

Method `ProcessGrades` next calls method `GetAverage` (line 35) to obtain the average of the grades in the array. Method `GetAverage` (lines 76–86) uses a `For Each` statement to total the values in array `grades` before calculating the average. The loop-control variable declaration in the `For Each`'s header (line 80) indicates that for each iteration, the `Integer` variable `grade` takes on the next successive value in the array `grades`. The averaging calculation in line 85 uses `grades.Length` to determine the number of grades being averaged.

Lines 38–39 in method `ProcessGrades` call methods `GetMinimum` and `GetMaximum` to determine the lowest and highest grades of any student on the exam, respectively. Each of these methods uses a `For Each` statement to loop through array `grades`. Lines 50–55 in method `GetMinimum` loop through the array, and lines 52–54 compare each grade to `lowGrade`. If a grade is less than `lowGrade`, `lowGrade` is set to that grade. When line 57 executes, `lowGrade` contains the lowest grade in the array. Method `GetMaximum` (lines 61–73) works similarly to method `GetMinimum`.

Finally, line 42 in method `ProcessGrades` calls method `OutputBarChart` to print a distribution chart of the grade data using a technique similar to that in Fig. 8.6. Lines 96–98 calculate the frequency of grades in each category. Line 106 passes to the method `Console.Write` the format string `"{0, 2:D2}-{1, 2:D2}"`, which indicates that arguments 0 and 1 (the first two arguments after the format string) should take the format `D2` (base-10 decimal number format using two digits) for display purposes—thus, 8 would be converted to 08 and 10 would remain as 10. Recall that the number `2` before the colon indicates that the result should be output right justified in a field of width 2. The dash that separates the curly braces } and { is printed to display the range of the grades (see the output of Fig. 8.14).

Line 93 declares and creates array `frequency` of 11 `Integers` to store the frequency of grades in each grade category. For each `grade` in array `grades`, lines 96–98 increment the appropriate element of the `frequency` array. To determine which element to increment, line 97 divides the current `grade` by 10 using integer division. For example, if `grade` is `85`, line 97 increments `frequency[ 8 ]` to update the count of grades in the range 80–89. Lines 101–116 next print the bar chart (see the output of Fig. 8.14) based on the values in the `frequency` array. Like lines 14–16 of Fig. 8.6, lines 111–113 of Fig. 8.13 use a value in array `frequency` to determine the number of asterisks to display in each bar.

Class **GradeBookTest** *That Demonstrates Class* **GradeBook**

The application in Fig. 8.14 creates an object of class `GradeBook` (Fig. 8.13) using the `Integer` array `gradesArray` (declared and initialized in lines 6–7). Lines 8–9 pass a course name and `gradesArray` to the `GradeBook` constructor. Line 10 displays a welcome message, and line 11 invokes the `GradeBook` object's `ProcessGrades` method. The output presents an analysis of the 10 grades in `gradeBooks`.

```
1  ' Fig. 8.14: GradeBookTest.vb
2  ' Create GradeBook object using any array of grades.
3  Module GradeBookTest
4     Sub Main()
5        ' array of student grades
6        Dim gradesArray As Integer() = _
7           {87, 68, 94, 100, 83, 78, 85, 91, 76, 87}
```

Fig. 8.14 | `GradeBookTest` creates a `GradeBook` object using an array of grades, then invokes method `ProcessGrades` to analyze them. (Part 1 of 2.)

```
        Dim gradeBooks As New GradeBook( _
            "CS101 Introduction to Visual Basic Programming", gradesArray)
        gradeBooks.DisplayMessage()
        gradeBooks.ProcessGrades()
    End Sub ' Main
End Module ' GradeBookTest
```

```
Welcome to the grade book for
CS101 Introduction to Visual Basic Programming

The grades are:

Student  1:  87
Student  2:  68
Student  3:  94
Student  4: 100
Student  5:  83
Student  6:  78
Student  7:  85
Student  8:  91
Student  9:  76
Student 10:  87

Class average is 84.90
Lowest grade is 68
Highest grade is 100

Grade distribution:
00-09:
10-19:
20-29:
30-39:
40-49:
50-59:
60-69: *
70-79: **
80-89: ****
90-99: **
  100: *
```

Fig. 8.14 | GradeBookTest creates a GradeBook object using an array of grades, then invokes method ProcessGrades to analyze them. (Part 2 of 2.)

Software Engineering Observation 8.1

A test harness (or test application) is responsible for creating an object of the class being tested and providing it with data. This data could come from any of several sources. Test data can be placed directly into an array with an array initializer, entered by the user at the keyboard or read from a file (as you will see in Chapter 18), or the data can arrive over a network. After passing this data to the object (e.g., through the class's constructor or another method), the test harness should call the object's methods to verify that they work properly.

8.9 Sorting an Array with Method Sort of Class Array

Sorting data (i.e., arranging the data in ascending or descending order) is one of the most popular computing applications. For example, a bank sorts all checks by account number, so that it can prepare individual bank statements at the end of each month. Telephone companies sort their lists of accounts by last name and, within last-name listings, by first name, to make it easy to find phone numbers. Virtually every organization must sort some data and, often, massive amounts of it.

Recall that all arrays have access to the methods and properties of class `Array` (in namespace `System`). Class `Array` provides methods for creating, modifying, sorting and searching arrays. By default, `Shared` method **`Sort`** of class `Array` sorts an array's elements into ascending order. The Windows `Forms` application in Fig. 8.15 demonstrates method `Sort` by sorting an array of 10 randomly generated elements (which may contain duplicates).

```
' Fig. 8.15: SortTest.vb
' Program creates random numbers and sorts them.
Public Class SortArray
   Dim integerArray As Integer() = New Integer(9) {}

   ' creates randomly generated numbers
   Private Sub createButton_Click(ByVal sender As System.Object, _
      ByVal e As System.EventArgs) Handles createButton.Click

      Dim output As String = String.Empty
      Dim randomNumber As Random = New Random()

      sortedTextBox.Clear() ' clear sortedTextBox

      ' create 10 random numbers and append to output
      For i = 0 To integerArray.GetUpperBound(0)
         integerArray(i) = randomNumber.Next(100)
         output &= (integerArray(i) & vbNewLine)
      Next

      originalTextBox.Text = output ' display numbers
      sortButton.Enabled = True ' enable Sort button
   End Sub ' createButton_Click

   ' sorts randomly generated numbers
   Private Sub sortButton_Click(ByVal sender As System.Object, _
      ByVal e As System.EventArgs) Handles sortButton.Click

      Dim output As String = String.Empty

      Array.Sort(integerArray) ' sort array integerArray

      ' creates string with sorted numbers
      For i = 0 To integerArray.GetUpperBound(0)
         output &= (integerArray(i) & vbNewLine)
      Next

      sortedTextBox.Text = output ' display numbers
      sortButton.Enabled = False ' disable Sort button
```

Fig. 8.15 | Sorting an array with method `Array.Sort`. (Part 1 of 2.)

```
40      End Sub ' sortButton_Click
41  End Class ' SortTest
```

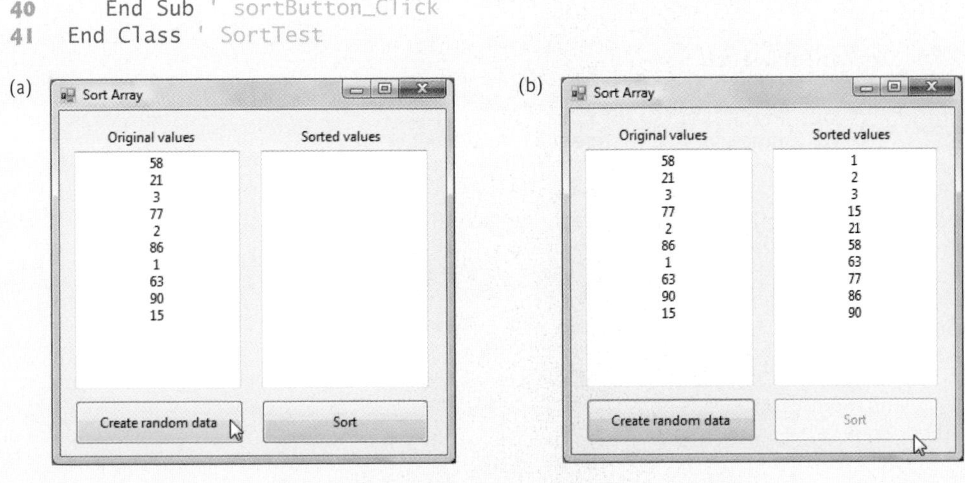

Fig. 8.15 | Sorting an array with method `Array.Sort`. (Part 2 of 2.)

Method `createButton_Click` (lines 7–23) assigns 10 random values to the elements of `integerArray` and displays the contents of the array in the `originalTextBox`. Method `sortButton_Click` (lines 26–41) sorts `array` by calling `Shared` method `Sort` of class `Array`, which takes an array as its argument and sorts the elements in the array in ascending order. To sort an array in descending order, first call method `Sort` to sort the array, then call `Shared` method `Reverse` of class `Array` to reverse the order of the elements in the array. Like method `Sort`, method `Reverse` takes an array as its argument. Exercise 8.6 asks you to modify this program to display an array's values in both ascending and descending order.

8.10 Searching Arrays

Often it is necessary to determine whether an array contains a value that matches a certain key value. The process of locating a particular element value in an array is called searching. In this section, we use two searching techniques—the simple linear search and the more efficient (but more complex) binary search.

8.10.1 Searching an Array with Linear Search

Module `LinearSearch` in Fig. 8.16 contains a function for performing a linear search. Function `Search` simply compares each element of an array with a search key. If the search key is found, the method returns the index value of the matching element. If the search key is not found, the method returns `-1`. The value `-1` is a good choice because it is not a valid index number. If the elements of the array being searched are unordered, it is just as likely that the value will be found in the front half of the array as in the back half, so on average the method will have to compare the search key with half the elements of the array.

Figure 8.17 uses function `Search` in module `LinearSearch` to search a 20-element array filled with random values created when the user clicks the `createButton`. The user types a search key in the `inputTextBox` and clicks the `searchButton` to start the search.

```
' Fig. 8.16: LinearSearch.vb
' Linear search of an array.
Module LinearSearch
   ' iterates through array
   Function Search(ByVal key As Integer, _
      ByVal numbers As Integer()) As Integer

      ' statement iterates linearly through array
      For i = 0 To numbers.GetUpperBound(0)
         If numbers(i) = key Then
            Return i
         End If
      Next

      Return -1 ' indicates the key was not found
   End Function ' Search
End Module ' LinearSearch
```

Fig. 8.16 | Method for performing a linear search.

```
' Fig. 8.17: LinearSearchTest.vb
' Linear search of an array.
Public Class LinearSearchTest
   Dim array1 As Integer() = New Integer(19) {}

   ' create random data
   Private Sub createButton_Click(ByVal sender As System.Object, _
      ByVal e As System.EventArgs) Handles createButton.Click

      Dim randomNumber As Random = New Random()
      Dim output As String = ("Index" & vbTab & "Value" & vbNewLine)

      ' create string containing 20 random numbers
      For i = 0 To array1.GetUpperBound(0)
         array1(i) = randomNumber.Next(1000)
         output &= (i & vbTab & array1(i) & vbNewLine)
      Next

      dataTextBox.Text = output ' display numbers
      inputTextBox.Clear() ' clear search key text box
      searchButton.Enabled = True ' enable search button
   End Sub ' createButton_Click

   ' search array for search key
   Private Sub searchButton_Click(ByVal sender As System.Object, _
      ByVal e As System.EventArgs) Handles searchButton.Click

      ' if search key text box is empty, display
      ' message and exit method
      If String.IsNullOrEmpty(inputTextBox.Text) Then
         MessageBox.Show("You must enter a search key.", "Error", _
            MessageBoxButtons.OK, MessageBoxIcon.Error)
```

Fig. 8.17 | Linear search of an array. (Part 1 of 2.)

```
            Exit Sub
        End If

        Dim searchKey As Integer = Convert.ToInt32(inputTextBox.Text)
        Dim element As Integer = LinearSearch.Search(searchKey, array1)

        If element <> -1 Then
            resultLabel.Text = "Found value in index " & element
        Else
            resultLabel.Text = "Value not found"
        End If
    End Sub ' searchButton_Click
End Class ' LinearSearchTest
```

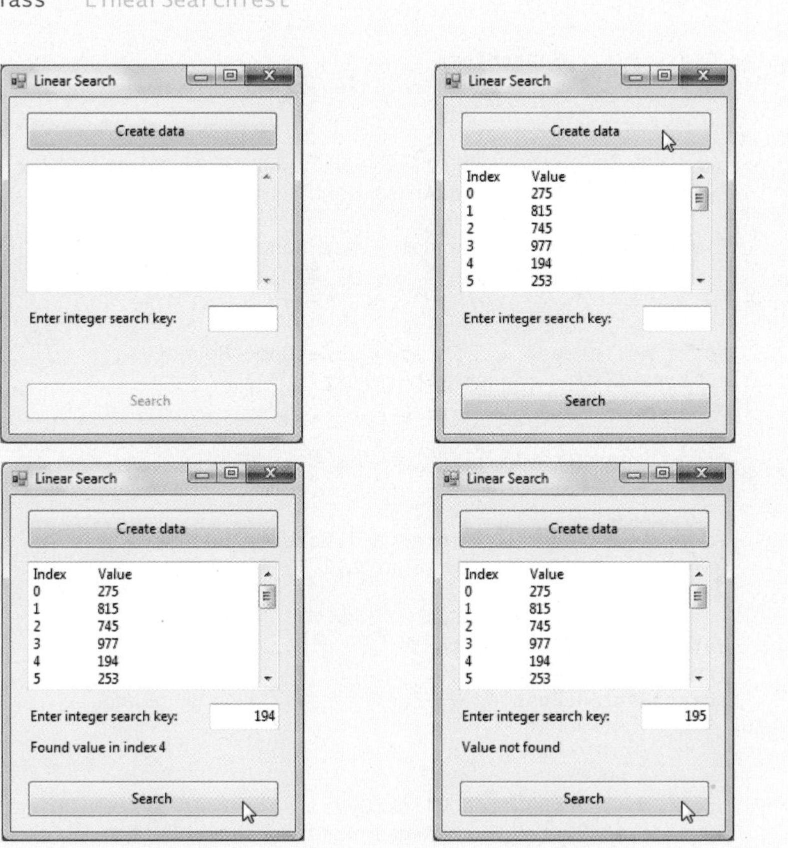

Fig. 8.17 | Linear search of an array. (Part 2 of 2.)

Note that the class `Array` provides a method `IndexOf` that performs the same operation as the `Search` function in Fig. 8.16. Class `Array` also provides methods such as `Find` and `FindAll`, which search the array for element(s) that meet certain criteria. The criteria can be more general than simply searching for an element. For instance, the `FindAll` method allows you to search for all elements in an `Integer` array that have values in a specified range.

8.10.2 Searching a Sorted Array with Array Method BinarySearch

The linear search method works well for small or unsorted arrays. However, for large unsorted arrays, linear searching is inefficient. If the array is sorted, the high-speed binary search technique can be used. Class `Array` provides method `BinarySearch`, which searches a sorted array for a value using binary search.

Figure 8.18 uses method `BinarySearch` of class `Array` to perform a binary search for a key value. The method receives two arguments—integer array `array1` (the array to search) and integer `searchKey` (the search key). If the value is found, method `BinarySearch` returns the index of the search key; otherwise, it returns a negative number.

```
' Fig. 8.18: BinarySearchTest.vb
' Binary search of an array using Array.BinarySearch.
Public Class BinarySearchTest
   Dim array1 As Integer() = New Integer(19) {}

   ' create random data
   Private Sub createButton_Click(ByVal sender As System.Object, _
      ByVal e As System.EventArgs) Handles createButton.Click

      Dim randomNumber As Random = New Random()
      Dim output As String = ("Index" & vbTab & "Value" & vbNewLine)

      ' create random array elements
      For i As Integer = 0 To array1.GetUpperBound(0)
         array1(i) = randomNumber.Next(1000)
      Next

      Array.Sort(array1) ' sort array to enable binary searching

      ' display sorted array elements
      For i As Integer = 0 To array1.GetUpperBound(0)
         output &= (i & vbTab & array1(i) & vbNewLine)
      Next

      dataTextBox.Text = output ' displays numbers
      inputTextBox.Clear() ' clear search key text box
      searchButton.Enabled = True ' enable search button
   End Sub ' createButton_Click

   ' search array for search key
   Private Sub searchButton_Click(ByVal sender As System.Object, _
      ByVal e As System.EventArgs) Handles searchButton.Click

      ' if search key text box is empty, display
      ' message and exit method
      If String.IsNullOrEmpty(inputTextBox.Text) Then
         MessageBox.Show("You must enter a search key.", "Error", _
            MessageBoxButtons.OK, MessageBoxIcon.Error)
         Exit Sub
      End If
```

Fig. 8.18 | Binary search of an array. (Part 1 of 2.)

```
41
42          Dim searchKey As Integer = Convert.ToInt32(inputTextBox.Text)
43          Dim element As Integer = Array.BinarySearch(array1, searchKey)
44
45          If element >= 0 Then
46             resultLabel.Text = "Found Value in index " & element
47          Else
48             resultLabel.Text = "Value Not Found"
49          End If
50       End Sub ' searchButton_Click
51    End Class ' BinarySearchTest
```

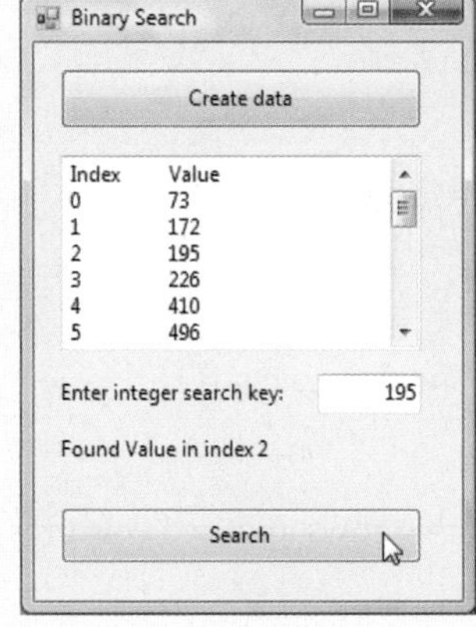

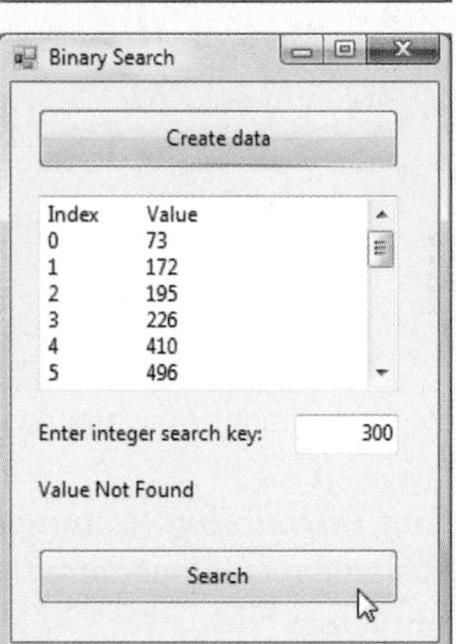

Fig. 8.18 | Binary search of an array. (Part 2 of 2.)

For method `BinarySearch` to perform correctly, the array passed to it must be sorted. Line 18 invokes method `Sort` to sort the randomly generated array elements in ascending order. Line 42 obtains the search key and converts it to an integer. Line 43 then passes the sorted array and the search key to method `BinarySearch`, and assigns the value returned by `BinarySearch` to variable `element`. If the search key is found, the value of variable `element` is greater than or equal to 0; otherwise, the value of variable `element` is less than 0. The `If` statement in lines 45–49 displays the search result.

8.11 Rectangular Arrays

So far, we have studied one-dimensional (or single-subscripted) arrays—arrays that contain one row of values. In this section, we introduce multidimensional (also called multiple-subscripted) arrays, which require two or more indices to identify particular elements. We concentrate on two-dimensional (also called double-subscripted) arrays, or arrays that contain multiple rows of values. There are two types of two-dimensional arrays—rectangular and jagged. We discuss jagged arrays in Section 8.14. Rectangular arrays often represent tables of values consisting of information arranged in rows and columns. Each row is the same size, and each column is the same size (hence the term "rectangular"). To identify a particular table element, we specify two indices—by convention, the first identifies the element's row, the second the element's column. Figure 8.19 illustrates a rectangular array, a, containing three rows and four columns. A rectangular array with m rows and n columns is called an m-by-n array; the array in Fig. 8.19 is referred to as a 3-by-4 array.

Every element in array a is identified in Fig. 8.19 by an element name of the form `a(i, j)`, where a is the name of the array and i and j are the indices that uniquely identify the row and column of each element in array a. Array indices are zero based, so the names of the elements in the first row all have a first index of 0; the names of the elements in the fourth column all have a second index of 3.

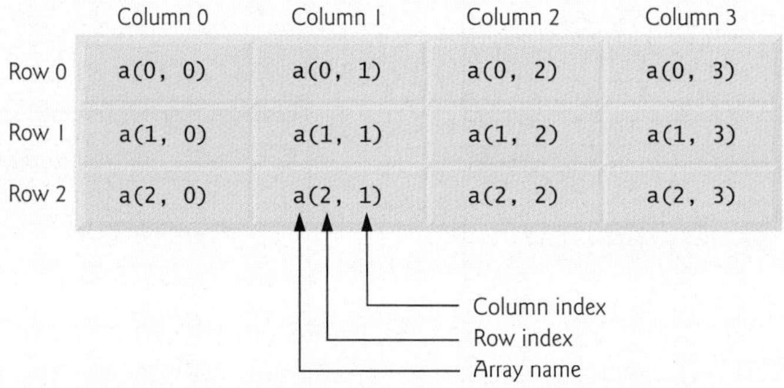

Fig. 8.19 | Two-dimensional array with three rows and four columns.

Declaring and Initializing Rectangular Arrays

A two-dimensional rectangular array numbers with two rows and two columns can be declared and initialized with

```
Dim numbers As Integer(,) = New Integer(1,1) {}

numbers(0, 0) = 1 ' leftmost element in row 0
numbers(0, 1) = 2 ' rightmost element in row 0
numbers(1, 0) = 3 ' leftmost element in row 1
numbers(1, 1) = 4 ' rightmost element in row 1
```

Alternatively, the initialization can be written on one line, as shown below:

```
Dim numbers As Integer(,) = New Integer(,) {{1, 2}, {3, 4}}
```

The values are grouped by row in braces, with 1 and 2 initializing `numbers(0,0)` and `numbers(0,1)`, respectively, and 3 and 4 initializing `numbers(1,0)` and `numbers(1,1)`, respectively. The compiler determines the number of rows by counting the number of subinitializer lists (represented by the sets of data in curly braces) in the main initializer list. Then the compiler determines the number of columns in each row by counting the number of initializer values in the subinitializer list for that row. In rectangular arrays, each row has the same number of values.

The preceding declaration can also be written as

```
Dim numbers As Integer(,) = {{1, 2}, {3, 4}}
```

In this case, the compiler implicitly uses the `New` keyword to create the array object.

The program in Fig. 8.20 demonstrates the initialization of a rectangular array (`array1`) and the use of nested `For...Next` loops to traverse the arrays (i.e., to manipulate every array element).

The program declares a rectangular array in method `Main`. The allocation of rectangular `array1` (line 7) provides six initializers in two sublists. The first sublist initializes row `0` of the array to the values `1`, `2` and `3`; the second sublist initializes row `1` of the array to the values `4`, `5` and `6`.

The nested `For...Next` statements in lines 12–18 display the elements of rectangular array `array1`, traversing the array in two dimensions. The outer `For...Next` statement traverses the rows; the inner `For...Next` statement traverses the columns within a row. Each `For...Next` statement calls method `GetUpperBound` to obtain the upper bound of the dimension it traverses. Note that the dimensions are zero based, meaning that the rows are dimension `0` (line 12) and the columns are dimension `1` (line 13).

```
1  ' Fig. 8.20: RectangularArray.vb
2  ' Initializing a rectangular array.
3  Module RectangularArray
4     Sub Main()
5        ' create rectangular array
6        Dim array1 As Integer(,)
7        array1 = New Integer(,) {{1, 2, 3}, {4, 5, 6}}
8
9        Console.WriteLine("Values in rectangular array1 by row are ")
10
11       ' output array1 elements
12       For i = 0 To array1.GetUpperBound(0)
13          For j = 0 To array1.GetUpperBound(1)
14             Console.Write(array1(i, j) & "  ")
15          Next j
16
17          Console.WriteLine()
18       Next i
19    End Sub ' Main
20 End Module ' RectangularArray
```

```
Values in rectangular array1 by row are
1  2  3
4  5  6
```

Fig. 8.20 | Initializing a rectangular array .

8.12 GradeBook Case Study: Using a Rectangular Array

In Section 8.8, we presented class `GradeBook` (Fig. 8.13), which used a one-dimensional array to store student grades on a single exam. In most semesters, students take several exams. Professors are likely to want to analyze grades across the entire semester, both for a single student and for the class as a whole.

Storing Student Grades in a Rectangular Array in Class **GradeBook**

Figure 8.21 contains a version of class `GradeBook` that uses a rectangular array `grades` to store the grades of several students on multiple exams. Each row of the array represents a single student's grades for the entire course, and each column represents a grade on one of the exams the students took during the course. An application such as `GradeBookTest` (Fig. 8.22) passes the array as an argument to the `GradeBook` constructor. In this example, we use a 10-by-3 array containing ten students' grades on three exams. Five methods perform various array manipulations to process the grades. Each method is similar to its counterpart in the earlier one-dimensional array version of class `GradeBook` (Fig. 8.13). Method `GetMinimum` (lines 45–61) determines the lowest grade of any student for the semester. Method `GetMaximum` (lines 64–80) determines the highest grade of any student for the semester. Method `GetAverage` (lines 83–93) determines a particular student's semester average. Method `OutputBarChart` (lines 96–126) outputs a bar chart of the distribution of all student grades for the semester. Method `OutputGrades` (lines 129–156) outputs the rectangular array in a tabular format, along with each student's semester average.

Methods `GetMinimum`, `GetMaximum`, `OutputBarChart` and `OutputGrades` each loop through array `grades` by using nested `For` statements—for example, the nested `For` statement (lines 50–58) from the declaration of method `GetMinimum`. The outer `For` statement iterates through the rows of two-dimensional array `grades`. To find the lowest overall grade, the inner `For` statement compares the current array element to variable `lowGrade`. For example, on the first iteration of the outer `For`, row 0 of `grades` is used. The inner `For` statement then loops through elements in row 0 and compares each `grade` value with `lowGrade`. If a grade is less than `lowGrade`, `lowGrade` is set to that grade. On the second iteration of the outer `For` statement, row 1 of `grades` is used, and the elements of this row are compared with variable `lowGrade`. This repeats until all the rows of `grades` have been traversed. When execution of the nested statement is complete, `lowGrade` contains the lowest grade in the two-dimensional array. Method `GetMaximum` works similarly to method `GetMinimum`.

```
1  ' Fig. 8.21: GradeBook.vb
2  ' Grade book using a rectangular array to store grades.
3  Public Class GradeBook
4     Private courseNameValue As String ' name of course
5     Private grades As Integer(,) ' rectangular array of student grades
6
7     ' two-argument constructor initializes courseNameValue and Grades
8     Public Sub New(ByVal name As String, ByVal gradesArray As Integer(,))
9        CourseName = name ' initializes courseNameValue via property
10       grades = gradesArray ' store grades
11    End Sub ' New
```

Fig. 8.21 | GradeBook class using a rectangular array to store grades. (Part 1 of 4.)

```

   ' property CourseName
   Public Property CourseName() As String
      Get
         Return courseNameValue
      End Get

      Set(ByVal name As String)
         courseNameValue = name
      End Set
   End Property ' CourseName

   ' display a welcome message to the GradeBook user
   Public Sub DisplayMessage()
      Console.WriteLine("Welcome to the grade book for " & vbNewLine & _
         CourseName & vbNewLine)
   End Sub ' DisplayMessage

   ' perform various operations on the data
   Public Sub ProcessGrades()
      OutputGrades() ' output grades array

      ' call methods GetMinimum and GetMaximum
      Console.WriteLine("Lowest grade in the grade book is {0}", _
         GetMinimum())
      Console.WriteLine("Highest grade in the grade book is {0}", _
         GetMaximum())

      ' call OutputBarChart to print grade distribution chart
      OutputBarChart()
   End Sub ' ProcessGrades

   ' find minimum grade
   Public Function GetMinimum() As Integer
      ' assume first element of grades array is smallest
      Dim lowGrade As Integer = grades(0,0)

      ' loop through grades array
      For i = 0 To grades.GetUpperBound(0)
         ' loop through columns of current row
         For j = 0 To grades.GetUpperBound(1)
            ' if grade lower than lowGrade, assign it to lowGrade
            If grades(i,j) < lowGrade Then
               lowGrade = grades(i,j) ' new lowest grade
            End If
         Next j
      Next i

      Return lowGrade ' return lowest grade
   End Function ' GetMinimum

```

Fig. 8.21 | GradeBook class using a rectangular array to store grades. (Part 2 of 4.)

```
    ' find maximum grade
    Public Function GetMaximum() As Integer
       ' assume first element of grades array is largest
       Dim highGrade As Integer = grades(0,0)

       ' loop through grades array
       For i = 0 To grades.GetUpperBound(0)
          ' loop through columns of current row
          For j = 0 To grades.GetUpperBound(1)
             ' if grade greater than highGrade, assign it to highGrade
             If grades(i,j) > highGrade Then
                highGrade = grades(i,j) ' new highest grade
             End If
          Next j
       Next i

       Return highGrade ' return highest grade
    End Function ' GetMaximum

    ' determine average grade for particular student's grades
    Public Function GetAverage(ByVal row As Integer) As Double
       Dim total As Integer = 0 ' initialize total

       ' sum grades for one student
       For column = 0 To grades.GetUpperBound(1)
          total += grades(row, column)
       Next

       ' return average of grades
       Return (total / (grades.GetUpperBound(1) + 1))
    End Function ' GetAverage

    ' output bar chart displaying grade distribution
    Public Sub OutputBarChart()
       Console.WriteLine(vbNewLine & "Overall grade distribution:")

       ' stores frequency of grades in each range of 10 grades
       Dim frequency As Integer() = New Integer(10) {}

       ' for each grade, increment the appropriate frequency
       For i = 0 To grades.GetUpperBound(0)
          For j = 0 To grades.GetUpperBound(1)
             frequency(grades(i,j) \ 10) += 1
          Next j
       Next i

       ' for each grade frequency, print bar in chart
       For count = 0 To frequency.GetUpperBound(0)
          ' output bar label ( "00-09: ", ..., "90-99: ", "100: " )
          If count = 10 Then
             Console.Write("{0, 5:D}: ", 100)
```

Fig. 8.21 | GradeBook class using a rectangular array to store grades. (Part 3 of 4.)

```
114          Else
115             Console.Write("{0, 2:D2}-{1, 2:D2}: ", _
116                count * 10, count * 10 + 9)
117          End If
118
119          ' print bar of asterisks
120          For stars = 0 To frequency(count) - 1
121             Console.Write("*")
122          Next stars
123
124          Console.WriteLine() ' start a new line of output
125       Next count
126    End Sub ' OutputBarChart
127
128    ' output the contents of the grades array
129    Public Sub OutputGrades()
130       Console.WriteLine("The grades are:" & vbNewLine)
131       Console.Write("            ") ' align column heads
132
133       ' create a column heading for each of the tests
134       For test = 0 To grades.GetUpperBound(1)
135          Console.Write("Test {0:D}  ", test + 1)
136       Next
137
138       Console.WriteLine("Average") ' student average column heading
139
140       ' create rows/columns of text representing array grades
141       For student = 0 To grades.GetUpperBound(0)
142          Console.Write("Student {0, 2:D}", student + 1)
143
144          ' output student's grades
145          For counter = 0 To grades.GetUpperBound(1)
146             Console.Write("{0, 8:D}", grades(student, counter))
147          Next counter
148
149          ' call method GetAverage to calculate student's average grade;
150          ' pass row of grades as the argument to GetAverage
151          Dim average As Double = GetAverage(student)
152          Console.WriteLine("{0, 9:F2}", average)
153       Next student
154
155       Console.WriteLine()
156    End Sub ' OutputGrades
157 End Class ' GradeBook
```

Fig. 8.21 | GradeBook class using a rectangular array to store grades. (Part 4 of 4.)

Method OutputBarChart in Fig. 8.21 is nearly identical to the one in Fig. 8.13. However, to output the overall grade distribution for a whole semester, the method here uses a nested For statement (lines 103–107) to create the one-dimensional array frequency based on all the grades in the rectangular array. The rest of the code in each of the two OutputBarChart methods that displays the chart is identical.

Method `OutputGrades` (lines 129–156) also uses nested `For` statements to output values of the array `grades`, in addition to each student's semester average. The output in Fig. 8.22 shows the result, which resembles the tabular format of a professor's physical grade book. Lines 134–136 (Fig. 8.21) print the column headings for each test. We use a counter-controlled `For` statement here so that we can identify each test with a number. Similarly, the `For` statement in lines 141–153 first outputs a row label using a counter variable to identify each student (line 142). Although array indices start at 0, note that lines 135 and 142 output `test + 1` and `student + 1`, respectively, to produce test and student numbers starting at 1 (see Fig. 8.22). The inner `For` statement in lines 145–147 loops through a specific row of array `grades` and outputs each student's test grades. Finally, line 151 obtains each student's semester average by passing the current row number (i.e., `student`) to method `GetAverage`.

Method `GetAverage` (lines 83–93) takes one argument—an integer which specifies the row number of a particular student. When line 151 calls `GetAverage`, the argument is `student`, which specifies that a particular row number of the rectangular array `grades` should be passed to `GetAverage`. Method `GetAverage` calculates the sum of the array elements, divides the total by the number of test results and returns the floating-point result as a `Double` value (line 92).

Class **GradeBookTest** *That Demonstrates Class* **GradeBook**

The application in Fig. 8.22 creates an object of class `GradeBook` (Fig. 8.21) using the rectangular array of `Integers` named `gradesArray` (declared and initialized in lines 6–9). Lines 11–12 pass a course name and `gradesArray` to the `GradeBook` constructor. Lines 13–14 then invoke `gradeBooks`'s `DisplayMessage` and `ProcessGrades` methods to display a welcome message and obtain a report summarizing the students' grades for the semester, respectively.

```
1  ' Fig. 8.22: GradeBookTest.vb
2  ' Create GradeBook object using a rectangular array of grades.
3  Module GradeBookTest
4     Sub Main()
5        ' array of student grades
6        Dim gradesArray As Integer(,)
7        gradesArray = New Integer(,) {{87, 96, 70}, {68, 87, 90}, _
8           {94, 37, 90}, {100, 81, 82}, {83, 65, 85}, {78, 87, 65}, _
9           {85, 75, 83}, {91, 59, 100}, {76, 72, 84}, {87, 93, 73}}
10
11       Dim gradeBooks As New GradeBook( _
12          "CS101 Introduction to Visual Basic Programming", gradesArray)
13       gradeBooks.DisplayMessage()
14       gradeBooks.ProcessGrades()
15    End Sub ' Main
16 End Module ' GradeBookTest
```

```
Welcome to the grade book for
CS101 Introduction to Visual Basic Programming
```

Fig. 8.22 | Creates `GradeBook` object using a rectangular array of grades, then invokes method `processGrades` to analyze them. (Part 1 of 2.)

```
The grades are:

             Test 1  Test 2  Test 3  Average
Student  1      87      96      70    84.33
Student  2      68      87      90    81.67
Student  3      94      37      90    73.67
Student  4     100      81      82    87.67
Student  5      83      65      85    77.67
Student  6      78      87      65    76.67
Student  7      85      75      83    81.00
Student  8      91      59     100    83.33
Student  9      76      72      84    77.33
Student 10      87      93      73    84.33

Lowest grade in the grade book is 37
Highest grade in the grade book is 100

Overall grade distribution:
00-09:
10-19:
20-29:
30-39: *
40-49:
50-59: *
60-69: ***
70-79: ******
80-89: ***********
90-99: ******
  100: **
```

Fig. 8.22 | Creates GradeBook object using a rectangular array of grades, then invokes method processGrades to analyze them. (Part 2 of 2.)

8.13 Variable-Length Parameter Lists

It's possible to create methods that receive a variable number of arguments, using keyword **ParamArray**. Figure 8.23 calls method AnyNumberOfArguments three times, passing a different number of values each time. The values passed into the method are stored in one-dimensional Integer array array1, which is declared using ParamArray.

```
' Fig. 8.23: ParamArrayTest.vb
' Using ParamArray to create variable-length parameter lists.
Module ParamArrayTest
   Sub Main()
      AnyNumberOfArguments()
      AnyNumberOfArguments(2, 3)
      AnyNumberOfArguments(7, 8, 9, 10, 11, 12)
   End Sub ' Main

   ' receives any number of arguments in array
   Sub AnyNumberOfArguments(ByVal ParamArray array1 As Integer())
      Dim total As Integer = 0
```

Fig. 8.23 | Creating variable-length parameter lists. (Part 1 of 2.)

```
13
14          ' check number of arguments
15          If array1.Length = 0 Then
16             Console.WriteLine("Method AnyNumberOfArguments" & _
17                " received 0 arguments.")
18          Else
19             Console.Write("The total of ")
20
21             ' total array elements
22             For i = 0 To array1.GetUpperBound(0)
23                Console.Write(array1(i) & " ")
24                total += array1(i)
25             Next
26
27             Console.WriteLine("is {0}.", total)
28          End If
29       End Sub ' AnyNumberOfArguments
30    End Module ' ParamArrayTest
```

```
Method AnyNumberOfArguments received 0 arguments.
The total of 2 3 is 5.
The total of 7 8 9 10 11 12 is 57.
```

Fig. 8.23 | Creating variable-length parameter lists. (Part 2 of 2.)

We call method `AnyNumberOfArguments` (lines 5–7), passing a different number of arguments each time. The method (lines 11–29) applies keyword `ParamArray` to `array1` in line 11. The `If` statement in lines 15–28 determines whether the number of arguments passed to the method is zero. If not, lines 19–27 display `array1`'s elements and their sum. All arguments passed to the `ParamArray` array must be of the same type as the array or a type that can be implicitly converted to the type of the array, otherwise a compilation error occurs. Though we used an `Integer` array in this example, any type of array can be used. You can either pass this method several arguments or an array containing those arguments.

In the last chapter, we discussed method overloading. Programmers often prefer to use method overloading rather than write methods with variable-length parameter lists.

Common Programming Error 8.5

Attempting to declare a parameter variable to the right of the `ParamArray` *array variable is a syntax error.*

Common Programming Error 8.6

Using `ByRef` *with* `ParamArray` *is a syntax error.*

8.14 Jagged Arrays

Jagged arrays are maintained as arrays of arrays. Unlike rectangular arrays, rows in jagged arrays can be of different lengths. The program in Fig. 8.24 demonstrates the initialization of a jagged array (`array1`) and the use of nested `For...Next` loops to traverse the array.

The program declares a jagged array in method `Main`. The declaration and allocation of the jagged array `array1` (line 6) create a jagged array of three arrays (specified by the 2

```
1  ' Fig. 8.24: JaggedArray.vb
2  ' Initializing a jagged array.
3  Module JaggedArray
4     Sub Main()
5        ' create jagged array
6        Dim array1 As Integer()() = New Integer(2)() {} ' three rows
7        array1(0) = New Integer() {1, 2} ' row 0 is a single array
8        array1(1) = New Integer() {3} ' row 1 is a single array
9        array1(2) = New Integer() {4, 5, 6} ' row 2 is a single array
10
11       Console.WriteLine("Values in jagged array1 by row are ")
12
13       ' output array1 elements
14       For i = 0 To array1.GetUpperBound(0)
15          For j = 0 To array1(i).GetUpperBound(0)
16             Console.Write(array1(i)(j) & "  ")
17          Next
18
19          Console.WriteLine()
20       Next
21    End Sub ' Main
22 End Module ' JaggedArray
```

```
Values in jagged array1 by row are
1  2
3
4  5  6
```

Fig. 8.24 | Initializing a jagged array .

in the first set of parentheses after keyword `Integer`). Lines 7–9 initialize each subarray so that the first subarray contains the values `1` and `2`, the second contains the value `3` and the last contains the values `4`, `5` and `6`.

The nested `For...Next` statements in lines 14–20 behave similarly to those that manipulate the rectangular array in Fig. 8.20. However, in a jagged array, the second dimension is actually an index into the one-dimensional array that represents the current row. In the example, the inner `For...Next` statement (lines 15–17) uses `GetUpperBound` with the argument `0` to determine the number of columns in each row. In this case, we call `GetUpperBound` on a single row—`array(i)`. Arrays of two or more dimensions can be traversed using a nested `For...Next` statement containing a separate `For...Next` for each dimension.

8.15 Changing the Size of an Array at Execution Time: Using the ReDim Statement

An array's size cannot be changed so a new array must be created if you need to change the size of an existing array. The **`ReDim`** statement and the class `Array`'s **`Resize`** method enable you to dynamically change an array's size. Each of these "resizes" an array by creating a new array and assigning its reference to the specified variable. In this book, we'll use and discuss the `ReDim` statement rather than the `Resize` method. Figure 8.25 demonstrates the `ReDim` statement.

```
1  ' Fig. 8.25: ReDimTest.vb
2  ' Resize an array using the ReDim statement.
3  Module ReDimTest
4     Sub Main()
5        ' create and initialize a 5-element array
6        Dim array As Integer() = {1, 2, 3, 4, 5}
7        Dim arrayCopy As Integer() = array
8
9        ' display array length and the elements in array
10       Console.Write("The original array has {0} elements: ", _
11          array.Length)
12       DisplayArray(array)
13
14       ' change the size of the array without the Preserve keyword
15       ReDim array(6)
16
17       ' display new array length and the elements in array
18       Console.Write("New array (without Preserve) has {0} elements: ", _
19          array.Length)
20       DisplayArray(array)
21
22       ' change the size of the array with the Preserve keyword
23       ReDim Preserve arrayCopy(6)
24       arrayCopy(6) = 7 ' assign 7 to array element 6
25
26       ' display new array length and the elements in array
27       Console.Write("New array (with Preserve) has {0} elements: ", _
28          arrayCopy.Length)
29       DisplayArray(arrayCopy)
30    End Sub ' Main
31
32    ' display array elements
33    Sub DisplayArray(ByVal array As Integer())
34       For Each number In array
35          Console.Write("{0} ", number)
36       Next
37
38       Console.WriteLine()
39    End Sub ' DisplayArray
40 End Module ' ReDimTest
```

```
The original array has 5 elements: 1 2 3 4 5
New array (without Preserve) has 7 elements: 0 0 0 0 0 0 0
New array (with Preserve) has 7 elements: 1 2 3 4 5 0 7
```

Fig. 8.25 | Using ReDim statements to change the array size.

Line 6 creates and initializes a five-element array array. Line 7 creates a second reference to the array named arrayCopy. Lines 10–12 display the size and elements of the original array. Line 15 uses a ReDim statement to change the upper bound of array to 6, so that the array now contains seven elements. The ReDim statement contains keyword ReDim, followed by the name of the array to be resized and the new upper bound in parentheses. Note that after using the ReDim statement, the variables array and arrayCopy no longer reference the same location in memory. The output of Fig. 8.25 shows that after the ReDim statement is executed, the size of the array is changed to 7 and the value of each element is reinitialized to the default value of the type of the array element (i.e., 0 for Integers). To save the original data stored in an array, follow the ReDim keyword with the optional **Preserve** keyword. Line 23 uses Preserve in the ReDim statement to indicate that the existing array elements are to be preserved in the now larger array after the array is resized. If the new array is smaller than the original array, the existing elements that are outside the bounds of the new array are discarded. If the new array is larger than the original array, all the existing elements are preserved in the now larger array, and the extra elements are initialized to the default value of the type of the array element. For example, after line 23 is executed, the value of arrayCopy(5) is 0. Line 24 assigns the value 7 to arrayCopy(6), so that the now larger array arrayCopy contains elements 1, 2, 3, 4, 5, 0 and 7.

In Section 9.3, we introduce class List from the System.Collections.Generic namespace. A List is a dynamically resizable arraylike data structure that mimics the functionality of conventional arrays. Additional List capabilities include inserting elements, searching for elements, removing elements and sorting elements.

8.16 Passing Arrays: ByVal vs. ByRef

A variable that "stores" an object, such as an array, does not actually store the object itself. Instead, the variable stores a reference to the object (i.e., the address of the location in the computer's memory where the object is stored). Recall that in Chapters 4–6, we discussed two types of variables—value types and reference types. The distinction between value-type variables and reference-type variables raises some subtle issues that you must understand to create secure, stable programs.

Effects of **ByVal** *on Value-Type Parameters and Reference-Type Parameters*

Keyword ByVal causes an argument's value to be copied to a parameter—i.e., a local variable—of a method. Changes to the local variable are reflected in the local copy of the variable, but not in the original variable in the caller. If the argument passed is of a reference type, the value being copied is a reference to the original object in memory—any changes you make using that reference will be applied to the original object. So, although the reference itself is passed by value, the object to which the reference refers is passed by reference and can be manipulated directly by the called method.

Performance Tip 8.1

Passing arrays and other objects by reference makes sense for performance reasons. If arrays were passed by value, a copy of each element would be passed. For large, frequently passed arrays, this would waste time and consume considerable storage for the copies of the arrays—both of these problems cause poor performance.

Passing Reference-Type Parameters Using **ByRef**

Visual Basic also allows methods to pass references with keyword ByRef. This is a subtle capability, which, if misused, can lead to problems. For instance, when a reference-type object like an array is passed with ByRef, the called method actually gains control over the original reference in the caller, allowing the called method to replace the reference with one to a different object or even with `Nothing`. Such behavior can lead to unpredictable effects, which can be disastrous in business-critical and mission-critical applications. The program in Fig. 8.26 demonstrates the subtle difference between passing a reference `ByVal` and passing a reference `ByRef`.

```
' Fig. 8.26: ArrayReferenceTest.vb
' Testing the effects of passing array references using ByVal and ByRef.
Module ArrayReferenceTest
   Sub Main()
      ' declare array references
      Dim firstArray As Integer()
      Dim firstArrayCopy As Integer()

      ' allocate firstArray and copy its reference
      firstArray = New Integer() {1, 2, 3}
      firstArrayCopy = firstArray ' reference preceding array

      Console.WriteLine("Passing an array reference using ByVal.")
      Console.Write("Contents of firstArray before calling FirstDouble: ")

      ' print contents of firstArray
      For i = 0 To firstArray.GetUpperBound(0)
         Console.Write(firstArray(i) & " ")
      Next

      FirstDouble(firstArray) ' pass firstArray using ByVal
      Console.Write(vbNewLine & "Contents of firstArray after " & _
         "calling FirstDouble: ")

      ' print contents of firstArray
      For i = 0 To firstArray.GetUpperBound(0)
         Console.Write(firstArray(i) & " ")
      Next

      ' was reference to firstArray changed by FirstDouble?
      If firstArray Is firstArrayCopy Then
         Console.WriteLine(vbNewLine & "The references are equal.")
      Else
         Console.WriteLine(vbNewLine & "The references are not equal.")
      End If

      ' declare array references
      Dim secondArray As Integer()
      Dim secondArrayCopy As Integer()

      ' allocate secondArray and copy its reference
      secondArray = New Integer() {1, 2, 3}
      secondArrayCopy = secondArray

```

Fig. 8.26 | Passing an array reference with `ByVal` and `ByRef`. (Part 1 of 3.)

```
      Console.WriteLine(vbNewLine & "Passing an array " & _
         "reference using ByRef.")
      Console.Write("Contents of secondArray before " & _
         "calling SecondDouble: ")

      ' print contents of secondArray before method call
      For i = 0 To secondArray.GetUpperBound(0)
         Console.Write(secondArray(i) & " ")
      Next

      SecondDouble(secondArray) ' pass secondArray using ByRef
      Console.Write(vbNewLine & "Contents of secondArray " & _
         "after calling SecondDouble: ")

      ' print contents of secondArray after method call
      For i = 0 To secondArray.GetUpperBound(0)
         Console.Write(secondArray(i) & " ")
      Next

      ' was reference secondArray changed by SecondDouble
      If secondArray Is secondArrayCopy Then
         Console.WriteLine(vbNewLine & "The references are equal.")
      Else
         Console.WriteLine(vbNewLine & "The references are not equal.")
      End If
   End Sub ' Main

   ' method modifies elements of array and assigns
   ' new reference (note ByVal)
   Sub FirstDouble(ByVal array As Integer())
      ' double each element value in caller's array
      For i = 0 To array.GetUpperBound(0)
         array(i) *= 2 ' double the ith element
      Next

      ' create a new array and assign its reference to the variable array
      array = New Integer() {11, 12, 13}
   End Sub ' FirstDouble

   ' method modifies elements of array and assigns
   ' new reference (note ByRef)
   Sub SecondDouble(ByRef array As Integer())
      ' double each element value in caller's array
      For i = 0 To array.GetUpperBound(0)
         array(i) *= 2 ' double the ith element
      Next

      ' create a new array and assign its reference to the variable array
      array = New Integer() {11, 12, 13} ' lose the 2, 4, 6 array
   End Sub ' SecondDouble
End Module ' ArrayReferenceTest
```

Fig. 8.26 | Passing an array reference with ByVal and ByRef. (Part 2 of 3.)

```
Passing an array reference using ByVal.
Contents of firstArray before calling FirstDouble: 1 2 3
Contents of firstArray after calling FirstDouble: 2 4 6
The references are equal.

Passing an array reference using ByRef.
Contents of secondArray before calling SecondDouble: 1 2 3
Contents of secondArray after calling SecondDouble: 11 12 13
The references are not equal.
```

Fig. 8.26 | Passing an array reference with `ByVal` and `ByRef`. (Part 3 of 3.)

Lines 6–7 declare two `Integer` array variables, `firstArray` and `firstArrayCopy`. We make `firstArrayCopy` reference the same array as `firstArray` so that we can determine whether the reference `firstArray` gets overwritten by method `FirstDouble`. Line 10 allocates an array containing `Integer` values `1`, `2` and `3` and stores the array reference in variable `firstArray`. The assignment statement at line 11 copies the reference `firstArray` to the reference variable `firstArrayCopy`, causing these variables to reference the same array object. The `For...Next` statement in lines 17–19 prints the contents of `firstArray` before it is passed to method `FirstDouble` at line 21, so we can verify that this array is passed by reference (i.e., the called method indeed changes the array's contents in `Main`).

The `For...Next` statement in method `FirstDouble` (lines 76–78) multiplies the values of all the elements in the array by `2`. Line 81 allocates a new array containing the values `11`, `12` and `13`; the reference for this array then is assigned to parameter `array` (in an attempt to overwrite reference `firstArray` in `Main`—this, of course, does not happen, because the reference `firstArray` was passed `ByVal`). After method `FirstDouble` executes, the `For...Next` statement in lines 26–28 prints the contents of `firstArray`, demonstrating that the values of the elements have been changed by the method `FirstDouble` (and confirming that in Visual Basic arrays are always passed by reference). The `If` statement in lines 31–35 uses the `Is` operator to compare references `firstArray` (which we just attempted to overwrite) and `firstArrayCopy`. Visual Basic provides **operator `Is`** for comparing references to determine whether they are referencing the same object. The expression at line 31 is true if the operands to the binary operator `Is` reference the same object. In this case, the object represented is the array allocated in line 10—not the array allocated in method `FirstDouble` (line 81). Visual Basic also provides **operator `IsNot`** for comparing two references. If two references refer to the same objects, operator `IsNot` returns `False`; otherwise it returns `True`. Line 81 modifies only the parameter `array`, not the variable `firstArray`, because `firstArray` was passed with keyword `ByVal`. We will see in a moment the effect of passing an array with keyword `ByRef`.

Lines 38–69 in method `Main` perform similar tests, using array variables `secondArray` and `secondArrayCopy` and method `SecondDouble` (lines 86–94). Method `SecondDouble` performs the same operations as `FirstDouble`, but receives its array argument with `ByRef`. In this case, the reference stored in `secondArray` after the method call is a reference to the array allocated at line 93 of `SecondDouble`, demonstrating that a reference passed with `ByRef` can be modified by the called method so that the reference actually points to a different object, in this case the array that is allocated in method `SecondDouble`. The `If` statement in lines 65–69 determines that `secondArray` and `secondArrayCopy` no longer represent the same array.

Software Engineering Observation 8.2

Using `ByVal` to receive a reference-type object parameter does not cause the object to pass by value—the object still passes by reference. `ByVal` causes only the object's reference to pass by value. This prevents a called method from overwriting a reference in the caller. In the vast majority of cases, protecting the caller's reference from modification is the desired behavior. If you encounter a situation where you truly want the called method to modify the caller's reference, pass the reference-type object `ByRef`.

8.17 (Optional) Software Engineering Case Study: Collaboration Among Objects in the ATM System

When two objects communicate with each other to accomplish a task, they are said to collaborate. A collaboration consists of an object of one class sending a message to an object of another class. Messages are sent in Visual Basic via method calls. In this section, we concentrate on the collaborations (interactions) among the objects in our ATM system.

In Section 7.20, we determined many of the operations of the classes in our system. In this section, we concentrate on the messages that invoke these operations. To identify the collaborations in the system, we return to the requirements document of Section 3.10. Recall that this document specifies the activities that occur during an ATM session (e.g., authenticating a user, performing transactions). The steps used to describe how the system must perform each of these tasks are our first indication of the collaborations in our system. As we proceed through this and the remaining Software Engineering Case Study sections, we may discover additional collaborations.

Identifying the Collaborations in a System

We begin to identify the collaborations in the system by carefully reading the sections of the requirements document that specify what the ATM should do to authenticate a user and to perform each transaction type. For each action or step described in the requirements document, we decide which objects in our system must interact to achieve the desired result. We identify one object as the sending object (i.e., the object that sends the message) and another as the receiving object (i.e., the object that offers that operation to clients of the class). We then select one of the receiving object's operations (identified in Section 7.20) that must be invoked by the sending object to produce the proper behavior. For example, the ATM displays a welcome message when idle. We know that an object of class `Screen` displays a message to the user via its `DisplayMessage` operation. Thus, we decide that the system can display a welcome message by employing a collaboration between the `ATM` and the `Screen` in which the `ATM` sends a `DisplayMessage` message to the `Screen` by invoking the `DisplayMessage` operation of class `Screen`. [*Note:* To avoid repeating the phrase "an object of class...," we refer to each object simply by using its class name preceded by an article (e.g., "a," "an" or "the")—for example, "the `ATM`" refers to an object of class `ATM`.]

Figure 8.27 lists the collaborations that can be derived from the requirements document. For each sending object, we list the collaborations in the order in which they are discussed in the requirements document. We list each collaboration involving a unique sender, message and recipient only once, even though the collaboration may occur several times during an ATM session. For example, the first row in Fig. 8.27 indicates that the `ATM` collaborates with the `Screen` whenever the `ATM` needs to display a message to the user.

An object of class...	sends the message...	to an object of class...
ATM	DisplayMessage	Screen
	GetInput	Keypad
	AuthenticateUser	BankDatabase
	Execute	BalanceInquiry
	Execute	Withdrawal
	Execute	Deposit
BalanceInquiry	GetAvailableBalance	BankDatabase
	GetTotalBalance	BankDatabase
	DisplayMessage	Screen
Withdrawal	DisplayMessage	Screen
	GetInput	Keypad
	GetAvailableBalance	BankDatabase
	IsSufficientCashAvailable	CashDispenser
	Debit	BankDatabase
	DispenseCash	CashDispenser
Deposit	DisplayMessage	Screen
	GetInput	Keypad
	IsDepositEnvelopeReceived	DepositSlot
	Credit	BankDatabase
BankDatabase	ValidatePIN	Account
	AvailableBalance (Get)	Account
	TotalBalance (Get)	Account
	Debit	Account
	Credit	Account

Fig. 8.27 | Collaborations in the ATM system.

Let's consider the collaborations in Fig. 8.27. Before allowing a user to perform any transactions, the ATM must prompt the user to enter an account number, then to enter a PIN. It accomplishes each of these tasks by sending a DisplayMessage message to the Screen. Both of these actions refer to the same collaboration between the ATM and the Screen, which is already listed in Fig. 8.27. The ATM obtains input in response to a prompt by sending a GetInput message to the Keypad. Next, the ATM must determine whether the user-specified account number and PIN match those of an account in the database. It does so by sending an AuthenticateUser message to the BankDatabase. Recall that the BankDatabase cannot authenticate a user directly—only the user's Account (i.e., the Account that contains the account number specified by the user) can access the user's PIN to authenticate the user. Figure 8.27 therefore lists a collaboration in which the BankDatabase sends a ValidatePIN message to an Account.

After the user is authenticated, the ATM displays the main menu by sending a series of DisplayMessage messages to the Screen and obtains input containing a menu selection by sending a GetInput message to the Keypad. We have already accounted for these collaborations. After the user chooses a type of transaction to perform, the ATM executes the transaction by sending an Execute message to an object of the appropriate transaction class (i.e., a BalanceInquiry, a Withdrawal or a Deposit). For example, if the user chooses to perform a balance inquiry, the ATM sends an Execute message to a BalanceInquiry.

Further examination of the requirements document reveals the collaborations involved in executing each transaction type. A BalanceInquiry retrieves the amount of money available in the user's account by sending a GetAvailableBalance message to the BankDatabase, which sends a Get message to an Account's AvailableBalance property to access the available balance. Similarly, the BalanceInquiry retrieves the amount of money on deposit by sending a GetTotalBalance message to the BankDatabase, which sends a Get message to an Account's TotalBalance property to access the total balance on deposit. To display both measures of the user's balance at the same time, the BalanceInquiry sends DisplayMessage messages to the Screen.

A Withdrawal sends DisplayMessage messages to the Screen to display a menu of standard withdrawal amounts (i.e., $20, $40, $60, $100, $200). The Withdrawal sends a GetInput message to the Keypad to obtain the user's menu selection. Next, the Withdrawal determines whether the requested withdrawal amount is less than or equal to the user's account balance. The Withdrawal can obtain the amount of money available in the user's account by sending a GetAvailableBalance message to the BankDatabase. The Withdrawal then tests whether the cash dispenser contains enough cash by sending an IsSufficientCashAvailable message to the CashDispenser. A Withdrawal sends a Debit message to the BankDatabase to decrease the user's account balance. The BankDatabase in turn sends the same message to the appropriate Account. Recall that debiting an Account decreases both the total balance and the available balance. To dispense the requested amount of cash, the Withdrawal sends a DispenseCash message to the CashDispenser. Finally, the Withdrawal sends a DisplayMessage message to the Screen, instructing the user to take the cash.

A Deposit responds to an Execute message first by sending a DisplayMessage message to the Screen to prompt the user for a deposit amount. The Deposit sends a GetInput message to the Keypad to obtain the user's input. The Deposit then sends a DisplayMessage message to the Screen to tell the user to insert a deposit envelope. To determine whether the deposit slot received an incoming deposit envelope, the Deposit sends an IsDepositEnvelopeReceived message to the DepositSlot. The Deposit updates the user's account by sending a Credit message to the BankDatabase, which subsequently sends a Credit message to the user's Account. Recall that crediting an Account increases the total balance but not the available balance.

Interaction Diagrams

Now that we have identified a set of possible collaborations between the objects in our ATM system, let us graphically model these interactions. The UML provides several types of interaction diagrams that model the behavior of a system by modeling how objects interact with one another. The communication diagram emphasizes *which objects* participate in collaborations. [*Note:* Communication diagrams were called collaboration diagrams in earlier versions of the UML.] Like the communication diagram, the sequence diagram shows collaborations among objects, but it emphasizes *when* messages are sent between objects.

Communication Diagrams

Figure 8.28 shows a communication diagram that models the ATM executing a BalanceInquiry. Objects are modeled in the UML as rectangles containing names in the form objectName : ClassName. In this example, which involves only one object of each type, we disregard the object name and list only a colon followed by the class name. Specifying the name of each object in a communication diagram is recommended when modeling multiple objects of the same type. Communicating objects are connected with solid lines, and messages are passed between objects along these lines in the direction shown by arrows with filled arrowheads. The name of the message, which appears next to the arrow, is the name of an operation (i.e., a method) belonging to the receiving object—think of the name as a service that the receiving object provides to sending objects (its "clients").

The filled arrow in Fig. 8.28 represents a message—or synchronous call—in the UML and a method call in Visual Basic. This arrow indicates that the flow of control is from the sending object (the ATM) to the receiving object (a BalanceInquiry). Since this is a synchronous call, the sending object may not send another message, or do anything at all, until the receiving object processes the message and returns control (and possibly a return value) to the sending object. The sender just waits. For example, in Fig. 8.28, the ATM calls method Execute of a BalanceInquiry and may not send another message until Execute finishes and returns control to the ATM. [*Note:* If this were an asynchronous call, represented by a stick arrowhead, the sending object would not have to wait for the receiving object to return control—it would continue sending additional messages immediately following the asynchronous call. Such calls are beyond the scope of this book.]

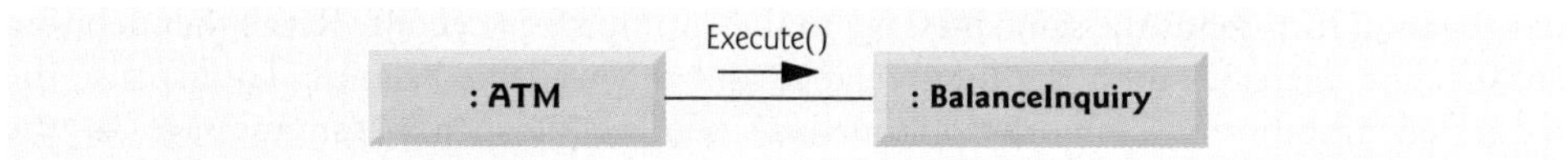

Fig. 8.28 | Communication diagram of the ATM executing a BalanceInquiry.

Sequence of Messages in a Communication Diagram

Figure 8.29 shows a communication diagram that models the interactions among objects in the system when an object of class BalanceInquiry executes. We assume that the object's accountNumber attribute contains the account number of the current user. The collaborations in Fig. 8.29 begin after the ATM sends an Execute message to a BalanceInquiry (i.e., the interaction modeled in Fig. 8.28). The number to the left of a message name indicates the order in which the message is passed. The sequence of messages in a communication diagram progresses in numerical order from least to greatest. In this diagram, the numbering starts with message 1 and ends with message 3. The BalanceInquiry first sends a GetAvailableBalance message to the BankDatabase (message 1), then sends a GetTotalBalance message to the BankDatabase (message 2). Within the parentheses following a message name, we can specify a comma-separated list of the names of the arguments sent with the message (i.e., arguments in a Visual Basic method call)—the BalanceInquiry passes attribute accountNumber with its messages to the BankDatabase to indicate which Account's balance information to retrieve. Recall from Fig. 7.26 that operations GetAvailableBalance and GetTotalBalance of class BankDatabase each

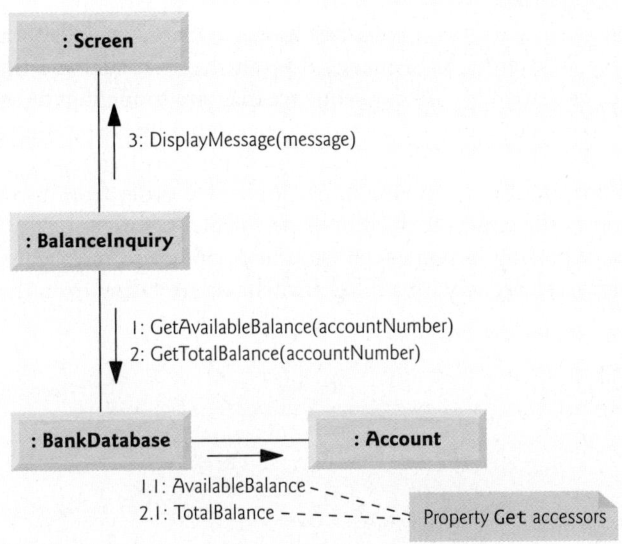

Fig. 8.29 | Communication diagram for executing a `BalanceInquiry`.

require a parameter to identify an account. The `BalanceInquiry` next displays the available balance and the total balance to the user by passing a `DisplayMessage` message to the `Screen` (message 3) that includes a parameter indicating the `message` to be displayed.

Note that Fig. 8.29 models two additional messages passing from the `BankDatabase` to an `Account` (message `1.1` and message `2.1`). To provide the `ATM` with the two balances of the user's `Account` (as requested by messages `1` and `2`), the `BankDatabase` must send `Get` messages to the `Account`'s `AvailableBalance` and `TotalBalance` properties. A message passed within the handling of another message is called a **nested message**. The UML recommends using a decimal numbering scheme to indicate nested messages. For example, message `1.1` is the first message nested in message 1—the `BankDatabase` sends the `Get` message to the `Account`'s `AvailableBalance` property during `BankDatabase`'s processing of a `GetAvailableBalance` message. [*Note:* If the `BankDatabase` needed to pass a second nested message while processing message `1`, the second message would be numbered `1.2`.] A message may be passed only when all the nested messages from the previous message have been passed. For example, the `BalanceInquiry` passes message `3` to the `Screen` only after messages `2` and `2.1` have been passed, in that order.

The nested numbering scheme used in communication diagrams helps clarify precisely when and in what context each message is passed. For example, if we numbered the five messages in Fig. 8.29 using a flat numbering scheme (i.e., `1`, `2`, `3`, `4`, `5`), someone looking at the diagram might not be able to determine that `BankDatabase` passes the `Get` message to an `Account`'s `AvailableBalance` property (message `1.1`) *during* the `BankDatabase`'s processing of message `1`, as opposed to *after* completing the processing of message `1`. The nested decimal numbers make it clear that the `Get` message (message `1.1`) is passed to an `Account`'s `AvailableBalance` property within the handling of the `GetAvailableBalance` message (message `1`) by the `BankDatabase`.

Sequence Diagrams

Communication diagrams emphasize the participants in collaborations but model their timing a bit awkwardly. A sequence diagram helps model the timing of collaborations more clearly. Figure 8.30 shows a sequence diagram modeling the sequence of interactions that occur when a `Withdrawal` executes. The dotted line extending down from an object's rectangle is that object's lifeline, which represents the progression of time. Actions typically occur along an object's lifeline in chronological order from top to bottom—an action near the top of the sequence diagram is performed before one near the bottom.

Message passing in sequence diagrams is similar to message passing in communication diagrams. An arrow with a filled arrowhead extending from the sending object to the

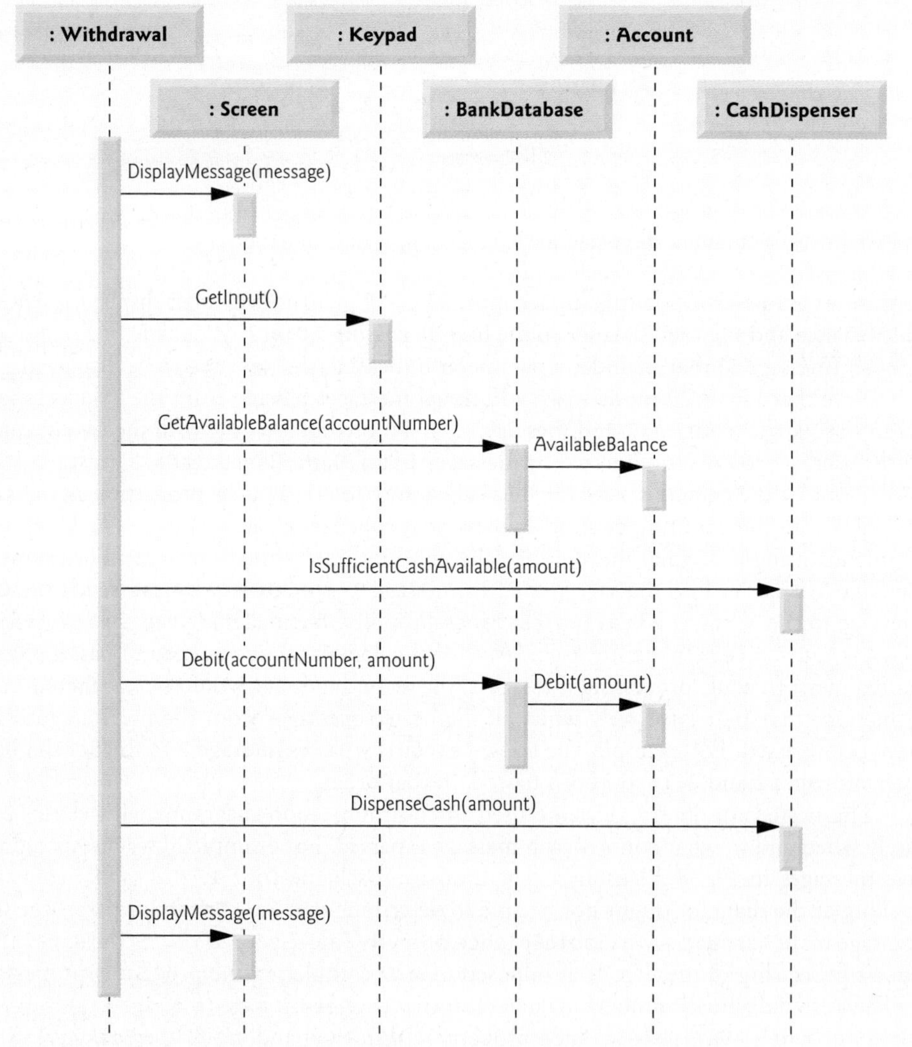

Fig. 8.30 | Sequence diagram that models a `Withdrawal` executing.

receiving object represents a message between two objects. The arrowhead points to an activation on the receiving object's lifeline. An activation, shown as a thin vertical rectangle, indicates that an object is executing. When an object returns control, a return message, represented as a dashed line with a stick arrowhead, extends from the activation of the object returning control to the activation of the object that initially sent the message; to eliminate clutter, we omit the return-message arrows—the UML allows this practice to make diagrams more readable. Like communication diagrams, sequence diagrams can indicate message parameters between the parentheses following a message name.

The sequence of messages in Fig. 8.30 begins when a `Withdrawal` prompts the user to choose a withdrawal amount by sending a `DisplayMessage` message to the `Screen`. The `Withdrawal` then sends a `GetInput` message to the `Keypad`, which obtains input from the user. We have already modeled the control logic involved in a `Withdrawal` in the activity diagram of Fig. 6.25, so we do not show this logic in the sequence diagram of Fig. 8.30. Instead, we model the best-case scenario in which the balance of the user's account is greater than or equal to the chosen withdrawal amount, and the cash dispenser contains a sufficient amount of cash to satisfy the request. For information on how to model control logic in a sequence diagram, please refer to the web resources and recommended readings listed at the end of Section 3.10.

After obtaining a withdrawal amount, the `Withdrawal` sends a `GetAvailableBalance` message to the `BankDatabase`, which in turn sends a `Get` message to the `Account`'s `AvailableBalance` property. Assuming that the user's account has enough money available to permit the transaction, the `Withdrawal` next sends an `IsSufficientCashAvailable` message to the `CashDispenser`. Assuming that there is enough cash available, the `Withdrawal` decreases the balance of the user's account (i.e., both the total balance and the available balance) by sending a `Debit` message to the `BankDatabase`. The `BankDatabase` responds by sending a `Debit` message to the user's `Account`. Finally, the `Withdrawal` sends a `DispenseCash` message to the `CashDispenser` and a `DisplayMessage` message to the `Screen`, telling the user to remove the cash from the machine.

We have identified collaborations among objects in the ATM system and modeled some of these collaborations using UML interaction diagrams—communication diagrams and sequence diagrams. In the next Software Engineering Case Study section (Section 10.19), we enhance the structure of our model to complete a preliminary object-oriented design, then we begin implementing the ATM system in Visual Basic.

Software Engineering Case Study Self-Review Exercises

8.1 A(n) __________ consists of an object of one class sending a message to an object of another class.

a) association
b) aggregation
c) collaboration
d) composition

8.2 Which form of interaction diagram emphasizes *what* collaborations occur? Which form emphasizes *when* collaborations occur?

8.3 Create a sequence diagram that models the interactions among objects in the ATM system that occur when a `Deposit` executes successfully, and explain the sequence of messages modeled by the diagram.

Answers to Software Engineering Case Study Self-Review Exercises

8.1 c.

8.2 Communication diagrams emphasize *what* collaborations occur. Sequence diagrams emphasize *when* collaborations occur.

8.3 Figure 8.31 presents a sequence diagram that models the interactions between objects in the ATM system that occur when a `Deposit` executes successfully. Figure 8.31 indicates that a `Deposit` first sends a `DisplayMessage` message to the `Screen` (to ask the user to enter a deposit amount). Next the `Deposit` sends a `GetInput` message to the `Keypad` to receive the amount of the deposit from the user. The `Deposit` then prompts the user (to enter a deposit envelope) by sending a `DisplayMessage` message to the `Screen`. The `Deposit` next sends an `IsDepositEnvelopeReceived` message to the `DepositSlot` to confirm that the deposit envelope has been received by the ATM. Finally, the `Deposit` increases the total balance (but not the available balance) of the user's `Account` by sending a `Credit` message to the `BankDatabase`. The `BankDatabase` responds by sending the same message to the user's `Account`.

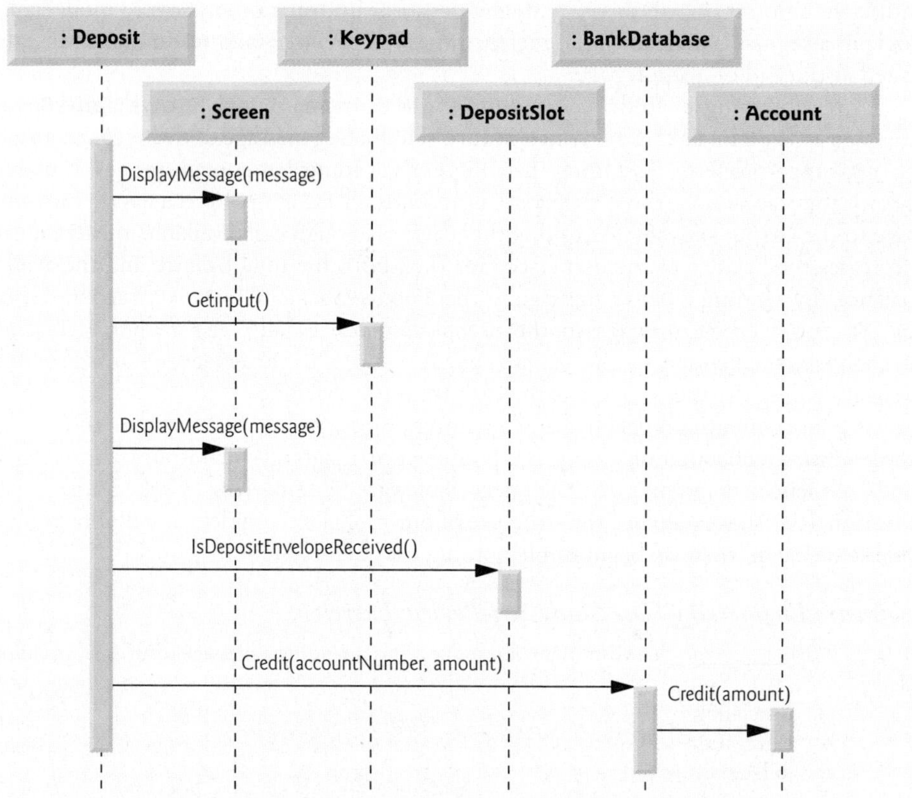

Fig. 8.31 | Sequence diagram that models a `Deposit` executing.

8.18 Wrap-Up

This chapter began our discussion of data structures, exploring the use of arrays to store data in and retrieve data from lists and tables of values. The chapter examples demonstrated how to declare an array, initialize an array and refer to individual elements of an array. We showed how to pass arrays to methods using `ByVal` and `ByRef`. We also showed how to use the `For Each...Next` statement to iterate through the values in an array without using an index. We used method `Sort` of class `Array` to sort an array and method `BinarySearch` of class `Array` to search an array for a specific value. We explained how to declare and manipulate rectangular arrays and jagged arrays. We wrote methods that use variable-length parameter lists. Finally, we demonstrated how to use the `ReDim` statement to dynamically change an array's size.

Chapter 24, Data Structures and Generic Collections, introduces dynamic data structures, such as lists, queues, stacks and trees, that can grow and shrink as programs execute. The chapter also presents generics, which provide the means to create general models of methods and classes that can be declared once but used with many different types, and shows several predefined data structures, which you can use instead of building your own.

In Chapter 9 we introduce the `List` collection which is a type of dynamic data structure. We also introduce one of Visual Basic 2008's key new features—Language Integrated Query (LINQ)—which enables you to write expressions that can retrieve information from a wide variety of data sources, such as arrays and collections. You'll see how to search, sort and filter data using LINQ.

Summary

Section 8.1 Introduction

- Arrays are data structures consisting of data items of the same type.

Section 8.2 Arrays

- An array is a group of variables (called elements) that all have the same type.
- To refer to a particular element in an array, we specify the name of the array and the position number of the element to which we refer.
- Every array begins with a zeroth element (i.e., element 0).
- The position number in parentheses more formally is called an index (or a subscript). An index must be a nonnegative integer or integer expression.
- An indexed array name (i.e., the array name followed by an index enclosed in parentheses) is an *lvalue*—it can be used on the left side of an assignment statement to place a new value into an array element.
- Every array in Visual Basic "knows" its own length. The length of an array named `c` is determined by the expression `c.Length`.
- All arrays have access to the methods and properties of class `System.Array`, including the `Length` property.
- Method `GetUpperBound` returns the index of the last element in the array.

Section 8.3 Declaring and Allocating Arrays

- To declare an array, you provide the array's name and type—for example, `Dim c As Integer()`. The parentheses that follow the type indicate that `c` is an array.
- The declaration of an array creates a variable that can store a reference to any array but does not actually create the array in memory.
- Arrays can be declared to contain any type.

- Before an array can be used, you must specify its size and allocate memory for it.
- Array bounds determine what indices can be used to access an element in the array.
- The initializer list enclosed in braces ({ and }) specifies the initial values of the elements in the array. The initializer list can be a comma-separated list specifying the initial values of the elements in the array.
- When the initializer list is empty, the elements in the array are initialized to the default value for the type of the elements of the array.

Section 8.4 Examples Using Arrays

- All the elements of any array must be of the same type.
- Visual Basic provides mechanisms that prevent accessing elements outside the bounds of arrays.

Section 8.6 Passing an Array to a Method

- To pass an array argument to a method, specify the name of the array without using parentheses.
- Every array object "knows" its own upper bound (i.e., the value returned by the method `GetUpperBound`), so when you pass an array object to a method, you do not need to pass the upper bound of the array as a separate argument.
- For a method to receive an array through a method call, the method's parameter list must specify that an array will be received.
- In Visual Basic, arrays always are passed by reference, yet it is normally inappropriate to use keyword `ByRef` in the method definition header.
- To pass an array element to a method, use the indexed name of the array element as an argument in the method call.

Section 8.7 `For Each...Next` Repetition Statement

- Visual Basic provides the `For Each...Next` repetition statement for iterating through the values in a data structure, such as an array.
- When used with one-dimensional arrays, `For Each...Next` behaves like a `For...Next` statement that iterates through the range of indices from 0 to the value returned by `GetUpperBound(0)`.

Section 8.9 Sorting an Array with Method `Sort` of Class `Array`

- Sorting data (i.e., arranging the data in some particular order, such as ascending or descending order) is one of the most popular computing applications.
- Class Array provides methods for creating, modifying, sorting and searching arrays.
- `Shared` method `Sort` of class `Array` takes an array as its argument and sorts the elements in the array in ascending order.
- To sort an array in descending order, first call method `Sort` of class array to sort the array, then call method `Reverse` of class `Array` to reverse the order of the elements in the array.

Section 8.10 Searching Arrays

- Often it is necessary to determine whether an array contains a value that matches a certain key value. The process of locating a particular element value in an array is called searching.
- The linear search method works well for small or unsorted arrays. However, it is inefficient for large unsorted arrays. If the array is sorted, the high-speed binary search technique can be used.
- The `Array` class provides method `BinarySearch`, which searches a sorted array for a value using binary search.

Section 8.11 Rectangular Arrays

- One-dimensional arrays contain one row of values.
- Multidimensional arrays require two or more indices to identify particular elements.
- There are two types of two-dimensional arrays—rectangular and jagged.
- Rectangular arrays with two indices often represent tables of values consisting of information arranged in rows and columns. Each row is the same size, and each column is the same size (hence the term "rectangular").

Section 8.13 Variable-Length Parameter Lists

- Methods can be created to receive a variable number of arguments using keyword `ParamArray`.
- All arguments passed to the `ParamArray` array must be of the same type as the array, otherwise a compilation error occurs.

Section 8.14 Jagged Arrays

- Jagged arrays are maintained as arrays of arrays. Unlike rectangular arrays, rows in jagged arrays can be of different lengths.
- In a jagged array, the second dimension is actually an index into the one-dimensional array that represents the current row.
- Arrays of two or more dimensions can be traversed using a nested `For...Next` statement with a separate `For...Next` statement for each dimension.

Section 8.15 Changing the Size of an Array at Execution time: Using the **`ReDim`** *Statement*

- The `ReDim` statement enables you to dynamically change the array size by creating a new array and assigning its reference to the specified variable.
- The `ReDim` statement contains keyword `ReDim`, followed by the name of the array to be resized and the new upper bound in parentheses.
- The `ReDim` statement changes the size of the array and reinitializes the value of the elements to the default value of the type of the array element.
- To save the original data stored in an array, follow the `ReDim` keyword with the optional `Preserve` keyword. If the new array is smaller than the original array, the existing elements that are outside the bounds of the new array are discarded. If the new array is larger than the original array, all the existing elements are preserved in the now larger array, and the extra elements are initialized to the default value of the type of the array element.

Section 8.16 Passing Arrays: **`ByVal`** *vs.* **`ByRef`**

- If an argument passed using keyword `ByVal` is of a reference type, the value being copied is a reference to the original object in memory—any changes you make using that reference will be applied to the original object.
- Visual Basic also allows methods to pass references with keyword `ByRef`.
- When a reference-type object like an array is passed with `ByRef`, the called method gains control over the original reference in the caller, allowing the called method to replace the original reference in the caller with a reference to a different object or `Nothing`. Such behavior can lead to unpredictable effects, which can be disastrous in business-critical and mission-critical applications.
- Visual Basic provides operator `Is` for comparing references to determine whether they are referencing the same object.

• Visual Basic also provides operator `IsNot` for comparing two references. If two references refer to the same object, operator `IsNot` returns `False`; otherwise it returns `True`.

Terminology

allocate an array with `New`
array
array as an object
array bounds
array declaration
array element
array element passed by value
array initialized to zeros
array of arrays
bar chart
binary search
`BinarySearch` method of class `Array`
braces (`{` and `}`)
column
declaration and initialization of array
double-subscripted array
element
exception for invalid array indexing
explicit array bounds
field width
`For Each...Next` statement
`GetUpperBound` method
ignoring array element zero
index
`IndexOutOfRange` exception
indexed array name
initializer list
initializing two-dimensional arrays in declarations
inner `For` statement
inner loop
innermost set of parentheses
`Is` operator
`IsNot` operator
iteration of a `For` loop
iterative binary search
jagged array
key value (in searching)
length of an array
`Length` property
linear search
lvalue ("left value")
m-by-*n* array
multidimensional array
nested `For` statement
`Nothing` keyword
"off-by-one" error
one-dimensional array
outer `For` statement
outer set of parentheses
`ParamArray` keyword
passing an array
passing an array element
position number of an element of an array
`Preserve` keyword
rectangular array
`ReDim` statement
`Reverse` method of class `Array`
search key
searching
size of an array
sorting
`Sort` method of class `Array`
subarray
subscript
`System.Array` class
table
table element
tabular format
two-dimensional array
variable number of arguments
"walk" past end of an array
zero-based counting
zeroth element

Self-Review Exercises

8.1 Fill in the blanks in each of the following statements:
a) Lists and tables of values can be stored in __________.
b) An array is a group of variables containing values that all have the same __________.
c) The number that refers to a particular element of an array is called its __________.
d) The process of placing the elements of an array in order is called __________ the array.
e) Determining whether an array contains a certain value is called __________ the array.
f) Arrays that use two or more indices are referred to as __________ arrays.

g) Keyword __________ in a method definition header indicates that the method receives a variable number of arguments.
h) __________ arrays are maintained as arrays of arrays.
i) All arrays have access to the methods and properties of class __________.
j) When an invalid array reference is made, a(n) __________ exception is thrown.

8.2 State whether each of the following is *true* or *false*. If *false*, explain why.
a) An array can store many different types of values.
b) An array index normally should be of type `Double`.
c) Method `GetUpperBound` returns the highest numbered index in an array.
d) There are two types of two-dimensional arrays—square and jagged.
e) To determine the number of elements in an array, use the `NumberOfElements` property.
f) The linear search works well for unsorted arrays.
g) In an *m*-by-*n* array, the *m* stands for the number of columns and the *n* stands for the number of rows.

Answers to Self-Review Exercises

8.1 a) arrays. b) type. c) index, subscript or position number. d) sorting. e) searching. f) multidimensional. g) `ParamArray`. h) Jagged. i) `System.Array`. j) `IndexOutOfRangeException`.

8.2 a) False. An array can store only values of the same type. b) False. An array index must be a nonnegative integer or integer expression. c) True. d) False. The two different types are called rectangular and jagged. e) False. To determine the number of elements in an array, we can use the `Length` property. f) True. g) False. In an *m*-by-*n* array, the *m* stands for the number of rows and the *n* for the number of columns.

Exercises

8.3 Write statements to accomplish each of the following tasks:
a) Display the value of element 6 of array `numbers`.
b) Using a `For...Next` statement, assign the value `8` to each of the five elements of one-dimensional `Integer` array `values`.
c) Total the 100 elements of floating-point array `results`.
d) Copy 11-element array `source` into the first portion of 34-element array `sourceCopy`.
e) Determine the smallest and largest values contained in 99-element floating-point array `data`.

8.4 Use a one-dimensional array to solve the following problem: A company pays its salespeople on a commission basis. The salespeople receive $200 per week, plus 9% of their gross sales for that week. For example, a salesperson who grosses $5000 in sales in a week receives $200 plus 9% of $5000, or a total of $650. Write a program (using an array of counters) that determines how many of the salespeople earned salaries in each of the following ranges (assume that each salesperson's salary is truncated to an integer amount):
a) $200–299
b) $300–399
c) $400–499
d) $500–599
e) $600–699
f) $700–799
g) $800–899
h) $900–999
i) $1000 and over

8.5 Use a one-dimensional array to solve the following problem: Read in 20 numbers, each of which is between 10 and 100, inclusive. As each number is read, print it only if it is not a duplicate of a number already read. Provide for the "worst case" (in which all 20 numbers are different). Use the smallest possible array to solve this problem.

8.6 Modify the sorting example of Fig. 8.15 so that it lists three columns of data headed "Original values," "Values sorted in ascending order" and "Values sorted in descending order"; your program should display in the last two columns the values sorted in ascending and descending order, respectively.

8.7 *(Telephone-Number Word Generator)* Standard telephone keypads contain the digits zero through nine. The numbers two through nine each have three letters associated with them (Fig. 8.32). Many people find it difficult to memorize phone numbers, so they use the correspondence between digits and letters to develop seven-letter words that correspond to their phone numbers. For example, a person whose telephone number is 686-2377 might use the correspondence indicated in Fig. 8.32 to develop the seven-letter word "NUMBERS." Every seven-letter word corresponds to exactly one seven-digit telephone number. A restaurant wishing to increase its takeout business could surely do so with the number 825-3688 (i.e., "TAKEOUT").

Digit	Letters
2	A B C
3	D E F
4	G H I
5	J K L
6	M N O
7	P R S
8	T U V
9	W X Y

Fig. 8.32 | Telephone keypad digits and letters.

Every seven-letter phone number corresponds to many different seven-letter combinations. Unfortunately, most of these represent unrecognizable juxtapositions of letters. It is possible, however, that the owner of a barbershop would be pleased to know that the shop's telephone number, 424-7288, corresponds to "HAIRCUT." The owner of a liquor store would, no doubt, be delighted to find that the store's number, 233-7226, corresponds to "BEERCAN." A veterinarian with the phone number 738-2273 would be pleased to know that the number corresponds to the letters "PETCARE." An automotive dealership would be pleased to know that the dealership number, 639-2277, corresponds to "NEWCARS."

Write a Windows application (Fig. 8.33) that allows the user to enter a seven-digit number in a `TextBox`, and displays every possible seven-letter word combination corresponding to that number in a multiple line `TextBox` when the user clicks the **Generate Words** button. There are 2,187 (3^7) such combinations. Avoid phone numbers with the digits 0 and 1.

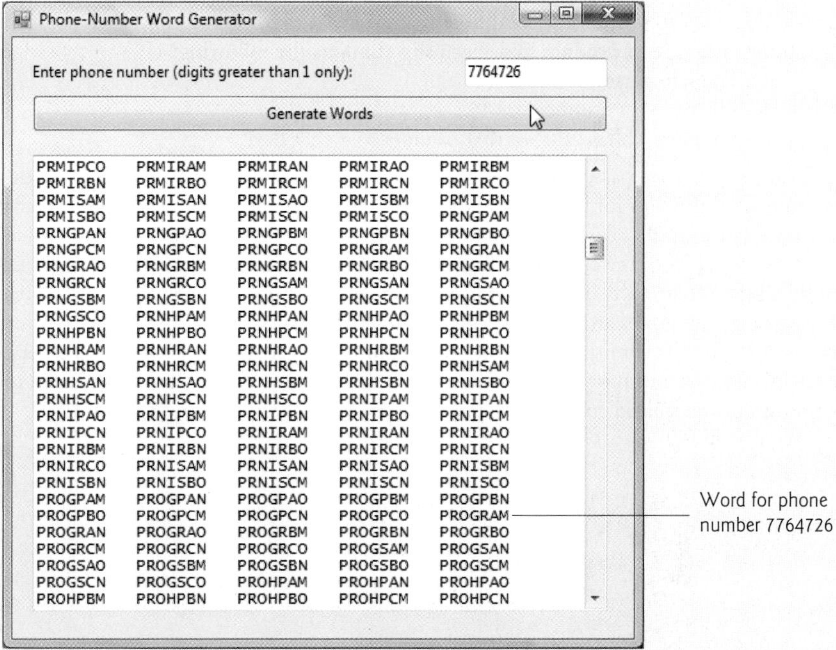

Fig. 8.33 | Windows application to generate the words for a phone number.

8.8 *(Flag Quiz Application)* A geography teacher would like to quiz students on their knowledge of the flags of various countries. The teacher has asked you to write an application that displays a flag and allows students to select the corresponding country by clicking the appropriate buttons. The application should inform the user of whether the answer is correct and display the next flag. The application should display five flags randomly chosen from the flags of Australia, Brazil, China, Italy, Russia, South Africa, Spain and the United States (these images are included with the book's examples). When the application is run, a given flag should be displayed only once.

8.9 *(Airline Reservations System)* A small airline has just purchased a computer for its new automated reservations system. You have been asked to develop the new system. You are to write an application to assign seats on each flight of the airline's only plane (capacity: 10 seats).

Your application should display the following alternatives: `Please type 1 for First Class` and `Please type 2 for Economy`. If the user types `1`, your application should assign a seat in the first-class section (seats 1–5). If the user types `2`, your application should assign a seat in the economy section (seats 6–10). Your application should then display a boarding pass indicating the person's seat number and whether it is in the first-class or economy section of the plane.

Use a one-dimensional array of primitive type `Boolean` to represent the seating chart of the plane. Initialize all the elements of the array to `False` to indicate that all the seats are empty. As each seat is assigned, set the corresponding elements of the array to `True` to indicate that the seat is no longer available.

Your application should never assign a seat that has already been assigned. When the economy section is full, your application should ask the person if it is acceptable to be placed in the first-class section (and vice versa). If yes, make the appropriate seat assignment. If no, display the message `"Next flight leaves in 3 hours."`

8.10 *(Total Sales)* Use a two-dimensional array to solve the following problem: A company has four salespeople (1 to 4) who sell five different products (1 to 5). Once a day, each salesperson passes in a slip for each type of product sold. Each slip contains the following:

a) The salesperson number
b) The product number
c) The total dollar value of that product sold that day

Thus, each salesperson passes in between zero and five sales slips per day. Assume that the information from all of the slips for last month is available. Write an application that will read all this information for last month's sales and summarize the total sales by salesperson and by product. All totals should be stored in the two-dimensional array `sales`. After processing all the information for last month, display the results in tabular format, with each column representing a particular salesperson and each row representing a particular product. Cross-total each row to get the total sales of each product for last month. Cross-total each column to get the total sales by salesperson for last month. Your tabular output should include these cross-totals to the right of the totaled rows and to the bottom of the totaled columns.

9

Introduction to LINQ and Generic Collections

To write it, it took three months; to conceive it three minutes; to collect the data in it—all my life.
—F. Scott Fitzgerald

Science is feasible when the variables are few and can be enumerated; when their combinations are distinct and clear.
—Paul Valéry

You shall listen to all sides and filter them from your self.
—Walt Whitman

The portraitist can select one tiny aspect of everything shown at a moment to incorporate into the final painting.
—Robert Nozick

List, list, O, list!
—William Shakespeare

Be wise to-day; 'tis madness to defer.
—Edward Young

OBJECTIVES

In this chapter you'll learn:

- Basic LINQ concepts.
- How to query an array using LINQ.
- Basic .NET collections concepts.
- How to create and use a generic `List` collection.
- How to write a generic method.
- How to query a generic `List` collection using LINQ.

Outline

9.1 Introduction

The previous chapter introduced arrays—simple data structures used to store data items of specific types. Arrays are commonly used but have limited capabilities. For instance, you must specify the size of an array; if you wish to increase that size at execution time, you must use the `ReDim` statement. Here, we introduce the .NET Framework's collection classes—a set of prepackaged data structures that offer greater capabilities than traditional arrays. The .NET collection classes provide reusable data structures that are reliable, powerful and efficient. These classes have been carefully designed and tested to ensure quality and performance. This chapter focuses on the `List` collection. `List`s are similar to arrays but provide additional functionality, such as dynamic resizing—`List`s automatically increase their size at execution time to accommodate additional elements. We use the `List` collection to implement several examples similar to those used in the previous chapter on arrays.

Large amounts of data are often stored in a database—an organized collection of data. A database management system (DBMS) provides mechanisms for storing, organizing, retrieving and modifying data contained in the database. Today's most popular database systems are relational databases. (We discuss databases in detail in Chapter 20, Databases and LINQ to SQL.) A language called SQL—pronounced "sequel"—is the international standard used almost universally with relational databases to perform queries (i.e., to request information that satisfies given criteria) and to manipulate data. For years, programs that accessed a relational database passed SQL queries, represented as `String`s, to the database management system, then processed the results. This chapter introduces Visual Basic's new LINQ (Language-Integrated Query) capabilities. LINQ allows you to write query expressions (similar to SQL queries) that retrieve information from a wide variety of data sources, not just databases. We use LINQ to Objects in this chapter to query arrays and `List`s, selecting elements that satisfy a set of conditions—this is known as filtering. We'll be using LINQ throughout the book to retrieve information from many data sources. Figure 9.1 shows where and how we use LINQ throughout the book.

Chapter	Used to
Chapter 9, Introduction to LINQ and Generic Collections	Query arrays and `List`s.

Fig. 9.1 | LINQ usage throughout the book. (Part 1 of 2.)

Chapter	Used to
Chapter 17, Strings, Characters and Regular Expressions	Select GUI controls in a Windows Forms application.
Chapter 18, Files and Streams	Search a directory and manipulate text files.
Chapter 19, XML and LINQ to XML	Query an XML document.
Chapter 20, Databases and LINQ to SQL	Retrieve information from a database; insert data into a database.
Chapter 21, ASP.NET and ASP.NET Ajax	Retrieve information from a database to be used in a web-based application.
Chapter 22, Windows Communication Foundation (WCF) Web Services	Query and update a database. Process XML returned by WCF services.
Chapter 23, Silverlight, Rich Internet Applications and Multimedia	Process XML returned by web services to a Silverlight application.
Chapter 24, Data Structures and Generic Collections	Query .NET collections.

Fig. 9.1 | LINQ usage throughout the book. (Part 2 of 2.)

LINQ Providers

The syntax of LINQ is built into the language, but they may be used in many different contexts because of libraries known as providers. A **LINQ provider** is a layer between the LINQ engine and a data source—it consists of a set of classes that implement operations needed by LINQ, such as counting, accessing, comparing and removing elements.

In this book, we discuss LINQ to SQL and LINQ to XML, which allow you to query databases and XML documents using LINQ. These providers, along with LINQ to Objects, mentioned above, are included with Visual Studio and the .NET Framework. There are many more specialized providers, allowing you to interact with a specific website or data format. An extensive list of available providers is located at:

`blogs.msdn.com/charlie/archive/2006/10/05/Links-to-LINQ.aspx`

9.2 Querying an Array Using LINQ

Figure 9.2 demonstrates querying an array of `Integers` using LINQ. Repetition statements that filter arrays focus on the process of getting the results—iterating through the elements and checking whether they satisfy the desired criteria. In contrast, LINQ specifies the conditions that selected elements must satisfy, not the steps necessary to get the results. The query in lines 12–14 specifies that the results should consist of all the `Integers` in the `values` array that are greater than `4`. It does not specify *how* those results are obtained—the Visual Basic compiler generates all the necessary code automatically, which is one of the great strengths of LINQ.

```
' Fig. 9.2: LINQWithSimpleTypeArray.vb
' LINQ to Objects using an Integer array.
Module LINQWithSimpleTypeArray
   Sub Main()
      ' create an integer array
      Dim values As Integer() = {2, 9, 5, 0, 3, 7, 1, 4, 8, 5}

      Display(values, "Original array:") ' display original values

      ' LINQ query that obtains values greater than 4 from the array
      Dim filtered = _
         From value In values _
         Where value > 4 _
         Select value

      ' display filtered results
      Display(filtered, "Array values greater than 4:")

      ' use Order By clause to sort original array in ascending order
      Dim sorted = _
         From value In values _
         Order By value _
         Select value

      Display(sorted, "Original array, sorted:") ' display sorted results

      ' sort the filtered results into descending order
      Dim sortFilteredResults = _
         From value In filtered _
         Order By value Descending _
         Select value

      ' display the sorted results
      Display(sortFilteredResults, _
         "Values greater than 4, descending order (separately):")

      ' filter original array and sort in descending order
      Dim sortAndFilter = _
         From value In values _
         Where value > 4 _
         Order By value Descending _
         Select value

      ' display the filtered and sorted results
      Display(sortAndFilter, _
         "Values greater than 4, descending order (one query):")
   End Sub ' Main

   ' display a sequence of integers with the specified header
   Sub Display(ByVal results As IEnumerable(Of Integer), _
      ByVal header As String)

      Console.Write("{0}", header) ' display header
```

Fig. 9.2 | LINQ to Objects using an `Integer` array. (Part 1 of 2.)

```
54
55          ' display each element, separated by spaces
56          For Each element In results
57             Console.Write(" {0}", element)
58          Next
59
60          Console.WriteLine() ' add end of line
61       End Sub ' Display
62    End Module ' LINQWithSimpleTypeArray
```

```
Original array: 2 9 5 0 3 7 1 4 8 5
Array values greater than 4: 9 5 7 8 5
Original array, sorted: 0 1 2 3 4 5 5 7 8 9
Values greater than 4, descending order (separately): 9 8 7 5 5
Values greater than 4, descending order (one query): 9 8 7 5 5
```

Fig. 9.2 | LINQ to Objects using an `Integer` array. (Part 2 of 2.)

A LINQ query begins with a **`From` clause** (line 12), which specifies a **range variable** (`value`) and the data source to query (`values`). The range variable represents each item in the data source, much like the control variable in a `For Each...Next` statement. Introducing the range variable in the `From` clause at the beginning of the query allows the IDE to provide *IntelliSense* while you write the rest of the query. The IDE knows the type of the range variable, so it can display the methods and properties of the object.

If the condition in the **`Where` clause** (line 13) evaluates to `True`, the element is selected—i.e., it's included in the results. Here, the `Integer`s in the array are included only if they are greater than `4`.

For each item in the data source, the **`Select` clause** (line 14) determines what value appears in the results. In this case, it is the `Integer` that the range variable currently represents. The `Select` clause is usually placed at the end of the query for clarity, though it may be placed after the `From` clause and before other clauses, or omitted entirely. If omitted, the range variable is implicitly selected. Later, you'll see that the `Select` clause can transform the selected items—for example, `Select value * 2` in this example would have multiplied each selected value by `2`.

Line 17 calls the `Display` method to show the query results in the console. Note that the `Display` method (lines 50–61) takes an `IEnumerable(Of Integer)` object as an argument. **`IEnumerable`** is an **interface**. Interfaces define and standardize the ways in which people and systems can interact with one another. For example, the controls on a radio serve as an interface between radio users and the radio's internal components. The controls allow users to perform a limited set of operations (e.g., changing the station, adjusting the volume, and choosing between AM and FM), and different radios may implement the controls in different ways (e.g., using push buttons, dials or voice commands). The interface specifies *what* operations a radio permits users to perform but does not specify *how* the operations are implemented. Similarly, the interface between a driver and a car with a manual transmission includes the steering wheel, the gear shift, the clutch, the gas pedal and the brake pedal. This same interface is found in nearly all manual transmission cars, enabling someone who knows how to drive one particular manual transmission car to drive just about any manual transmission car.

Software objects also communicate via interfaces. A Visual Basic interface describes a set of methods that can be called on an object—to tell the object, for example, to perform some task or return some piece of information. The `IEnumerable` interface describes the functionality of any object that is capable of being iterated over and thus offers methods to access each element. To use an interface, a class must specify that it implements the interface and must define each method in the interface with the signature specified by the interface. Implementing an interface is like signing a contract with the compiler that states, "I will declare all the methods specified by the interface."

Arrays and collections already implement the `IEnumerable` interface—they define the methods described by the interface. You can call any method defined by `IEnumerable` on an array or collection to iterate through its elements. In fact, the `For Each...Next` statement uses `IEnumerable` methods to iterate over each element of an array or collection. AA LINQ query typically returns an object that implements the `IEnumerable` interface (we'll learn about other possibilities in later chapters). Therefore, you can use a `For Each...Next` statement to iterate over the results of any LINQ query. The `For Each...Next` statement in lines 56–58 iterates over the query result, displaying each item in the console.

It would be simple to display the integers greater than 4 using a repetition statement that tests each value before displaying it. However, this intertwines the code that selects elements and the code that prints them. With LINQ, these are kept separate, making the code easier to understand and maintain.

The **`Order By` clause** (line 22) sorts the query results in ascending order. Lines 30 and 41 use the **`Descending`** modifier in the `Order By` clause to sort the results in descending order. An **`Ascending`** modifier also exists but is not normally used, because ascending order is the default. Any value that can be compared with other values of the same type may be used with the `Order By` clause. A value of a simple type (e.g., `Integer`) can always be compared to another value of the same type; we'll say more about comparing values of reference types in Chapter 12, Object-Oriented Programming: Polymorphism.

The queries in lines 29–31 and 39–42 generate the same results, but in different ways. The first query uses LINQ to sort the results of the query from lines 12–14. The second query uses both the `Where` and `Order By` clauses.

Using LINQ to Query an Array of Employee Objects

LINQ is not limited to querying arrays of primitive types such as `Integers`. It can be used with most data types, including `Strings` and classes. It cannot be used when a query does not have a defined meaning—for example, you cannot use `Order By` on objects that are not comparable. Figure 9.3 presents the `Employee` class. Figure 9.4 uses LINQ to query an array of `Employee` objects.

```
' Fig. 9.3: Employee.vb
' Employee class with FirstName, LastName and MonthlySalary properties.
Public Class Employee
   Private firstNameValue As String ' first name of employee
   Private lastNameValue As String ' last name of employee
   Private monthlySalaryValue As Decimal ' monthly salary of employee
```

Fig. 9.3 | `Employee` class with `FirstName`, `LastName` and `MonthlySalary` properties. (Part 1 of 2.)

```
   ' constructor initializes first name, last name and monthly salary
   Public Sub New(ByVal first As String, ByVal last As String, _
      ByVal salary As Decimal)

      FirstName = first
      LastName = last
      MonthlySalary = salary
   End Sub ' New

   ' property that gets and sets the employee's first name
   Public Property FirstName() As String
      Get
         Return firstNameValue
      End Get

      Set(ByVal value As String)
         firstNameValue = value
      End Set
   End Property ' FirstName

   ' property that gets and sets the employee's last name
   Public Property LastName() As String
      Get
         Return lastNameValue
      End Get

      Set(ByVal value As String)
         lastNameValue = value
      End Set
   End Property ' LastName

   ' property that gets and sets the employee's monthly salary
   Public Property MonthlySalary() As Decimal
      Get
         Return monthlySalaryValue
      End Get

      Set(ByVal value As Decimal)
         If value >= 0 Then ' if salary is nonnegative
            monthlySalaryValue = value
         End If
      End Set
   End Property ' MonthlySalary

   ' return a String containing the employee's information
   Public Overrides Function ToString() As String
      Return String.Format("{0,-10} {1,-10} {2,10:C}", _
         FirstName, LastName, MonthlySalary)
   End Function ' ToString
End Class ' Employee
```

Fig. 9.3 | `Employee` class with `FirstName`, `LastName` and `MonthlySalary` properties. (Part 2 of 2.)

```
' Fig. 9.4: LINQWithArrayOfObjects.vb
' LINQ to Objects using an array of Employee objects.
Module LINQWithArrayOfObjects
   Sub Main()
      ' initialize array of employees
      Dim employees As Employee() = { _
         New Employee("Jason", "Red", 5000D), _
         New Employee("Ashley", "Green", 7600D), _
         New Employee("Matthew", "Indigo", 3587.5D), _
         New Employee("James", "Indigo", 4700.77D), _
         New Employee("Luke", "Indigo", 6200D), _
         New Employee("Jason", "Blue", 3200D), _
         New Employee("Wendy", "Brown", 4236.4D)} ' end initializer list

      Display(employees, "Original array") ' display all employees

      ' filter a range of salaries using AndAlso in a LINQ query
      Dim between4K6K = _
         From e In employees _
         Where e.MonthlySalary >= 4000D AndAlso e.MonthlySalary <= 6000D _
         Select e

      ' display employees making between 4000 and 6000 per month
      Display(between4K6K, String.Format( _
         "Employees earning in the range {0:C}-{1:C} per month", _
         4000, 6000))

      ' order the employees by last name, then first name with LINQ
      Dim nameSorted = _
         From e In employees _
         Order By e.LastName, e.FirstName _
         Select e

      Console.WriteLine("First employee when sorted by name:") ' header

      ' attempt to display the first result of the above LINQ query
      If nameSorted.Count() = 0 Then
         Console.WriteLine("not found" & vbNewLine)
      Else
         Console.WriteLine(nameSorted.First().ToString() & vbNewLine)
      End If

      ' use LINQ's Distinct clause to select unique last names
      Dim lastNames = _
         From e In employees _
         Select e.LastName _
         Distinct

      ' display unique last names
      Display(lastNames, "Unique employee last names")

```

Fig. 9.4 | LINQ to Objects using an array of `Employee` objects. (Part 1 of 2.)

```
        ' use LINQ to select first and last names
        Dim names = _
           From e In employees _
           Select e.FirstName, Last = e.LastName

        Display(names, "Names only") ' display full names
     End Sub ' Main

     ' display a sequence of any type, each on a separate line
     Sub Display(Of T)(ByVal results As IEnumerable(Of T), _
        ByVal header As String)

        Console.WriteLine("{0}:", header) ' display header

        ' display each element, separated by spaces
        For Each element As T In results
           Console.WriteLine(element)
        Next

        Console.WriteLine() ' add end of line
     End Sub ' Display
  End Module ' LINQWithArrayOfObjects
```

```
Original array:
Jason      Red        $5,000.00
Ashley     Green      $7,600.00
Matthew    Indigo     $3,587.50
James      Indigo     $4,700.77
Luke       Indigo     $6,200.00
Jason      Blue       $3,200.00
Wendy      Brown      $4,236.40

Employees earning in the range $4,000.00-$6,000.00 per month:
Jason      Red        $5,000.00
James      Indigo     $4,700.77
Wendy      Brown      $4,236.40

First employee when sorted by name:
Jason      Blue       $3,200.00

Unique employee last names:
Red
Green
Indigo
Blue
Brown

Names only:
{ FirstName = Jason, Last = Red }
{ FirstName = Ashley, Last = Green }
{ FirstName = Matthew, Last = Indigo }
{ FirstName = James, Last = Indigo }
{ FirstName = Luke, Last = Indigo }
{ FirstName = Jason, Last = Blue }
{ FirstName = Wendy, Last = Brown }
```

Fig. 9.4 | LINQ to Objects using an array of `Employee` objects. (Part 2 of 2.)

Line 20 of Fig. 9.4 shows a `Where` clause that accesses the properties of the range variable. In this example, the compiler infers that the range variable is of type `Employee` based on its knowledge that `employees` was defined as an array of `Employee` objects (lines 6–13). Any `Boolean` expression can be used in a `Where` clause. Line 20 uses `AndAlso` to combine conditions. Here, only employees that have a salary between $4,000 and $6,000 per month, inclusive, are included in the query result.

Line 31 uses an `Order By` clause to sort the results according to multiple properties—specified in a comma-separated list. In this query, the employees are sorted alphabetically by last name. Each group of `Employees` that have the same last name is then sorted within the group by first name.

Line 37 introduces the query result's **`Count`** method, which returns the number of elements in the result of the query at lines 30–32. The query result's **`First`** method (line 40) returns the first element in the result. You should check that the query result is not empty (line 37) before calling `First`. Note that we have not specified the class that defines methods `First` and `Count`. Your intuition probably tells you they are methods of `IEnumerable`, but they aren't. They're actually extension methods, but can be used as if they are methods of `IEnumerable`. We explain the concept of extension methods in Chapter 10, Classes and Objects: A Deeper Look.

Line 46 uses the `Select` clause in a new way. Instead of simply selecting the range variable, the `LastName` property is selected. This causes the results of the query to consist of only the last names (as `Strings`), instead of complete `Employee` objects. The **`Distinct` clause** (line 47) prevents duplicate values from appearing in the query results. Note that it eliminates duplicate last names—this occurs because the clauses in a LINQ query are applied in the order in which they appear, each using the results of the previous clause in the query.

The last LINQ query in the example (lines 53–55) selects the properties `FirstName` and `LastName`. You can select any number of properties by specifying them in a comma-separated list. The compiler automatically creates a new class having properties `FirstName` and `Last`, and the values are copied from the `Employee` objects. These selected properties can then be accessed when iterating over the results. These compiler-generated classes are called **anonymous types**. Local type inference allows you to use these types without knowing their names. Note that the `LastName` property is assigned to `Last` in the `Select` clause. This specifies a new name for the selected property. In the case of `FirstName`, the name of the property being selected is used as the property's name in the result. When the compiler creates an anonymous type, it automatically generates a `ToString` method that returns a `String` representation of the object. You can see this in the program's output—it consists of the property names and their values, enclosed in braces. Anonymous types are discussed in depth in Chapter 10, Classes and Objects: A Deeper Look.

Using a Generic Method to Display LINQ Query Results

Figure 9.2 used LINQ to select `Integers` from an array, then used method `Display` to output each query's results. Since each query returned an `IEnumerable(Of Integer)`, we used that type as the parameter of method `Display`. Figure 9.4 performs several LINQ queries that return different types—`IEnumerable(Of Employee)`, `IEnumerable(Of String)` and `IEnumerable` of anonymous-type objects. We'd like to output the `String` representations of the elements returned by each query. One way to perform the same operation on multiple types is to define overloaded methods. We could do this for the LINQ queries that return IEnumerable(Of Employee) and IEnumerable(Of String), respectively. Unfortunately, we cannot do this for a query that returns an IEnumerable of anonymous-type objects—there is no type name that we can use to specify the method's parameter type.

If the operations you wish to perform for several types are identical (such as displaying String representations of the elements in query results), overloaded methods can be more compactly and conveniently coded using a generic method. This enables you to create a single method definition that can be called with arguments of many types. The compiler infers the type to process based on the generic method call. So, we can create a generic method that iterates through the results of any query (including an IEnumerable of anonymous-type objects) and outputs each element as a String.

To define a generic method, you must specify a type-parameter list—e.g., the (Of T) in line 61. A type-parameter list—which is placed in parentheses following the method name—begins with the keyword Of and contains one or more type parameters separated by commas. A type parameter (T in this example) is a placeholder for an actual type name. When you call a generic method, the compiler infers from the types of the arguments in the call what each type parameter represents. Type parameters can be used to declare return types, parameter types (e.g., line 61) and local variable types (e.g., line 67) in generic method declarations.

Lines 61–72 define generic method Display. The parameter named results is of type IEnumerable(Of T), indicating that an IEnumerable of any element type can be passed to this method. For example, the call to Display in line 15 passes the employees array as the first element. Since all arrays are also IEnumerables and the employees array contains Employee objects, the compiler infers for this call that the type parameter T should be replaced with the type Employee. In this case, Employee is known as the type argument for the type parameter T. Similarly, for the call in line 50, we pass the results of a query that returns Strings (i.e., an IEnumerable(Of String)). In this case, the compiler infers that the type argument is String. The call in line 57 receives an IEnumerable of an anonymous type. In this case, the compiler infers from the call that the type argument is of the anonymous type that was created in response to the query in lines 54–55.

Notes About Type Parameters and Generic Methods

A type parameter can be declared only once in the type-parameter list but can appear more than once in the method's parameter list and body, and as the method's return type. The type parameter names throughout the method declaration must match those declared in the type-parameter list. For example, line 67 declares element in the For Each statement as type T, which matches the type parameter (T) declared in line 61. Type-parameter names need not be unique among different generic methods.

Common Programming Error 9.1

If you forget to include the type-parameter list when declaring a generic method, the compiler will not recognize the type-parameter names when they're encountered in the method, causing compilation errors.

When compiling a generic method, the compiler also determines whether the operations in the method body can be performed on any type that a type parameter may represent. The only operation performed on the IEnumerable elements in this example is to output their String representations. In .NET, all values and objects have String representations (see Section 10.2), so our Display method works for any type of element. When we discuss generic methods in more detail in Chapter 24, Data Structures and Generic Collections, we'll introduce type constraints, which enable you to restrict the types of values and objects that can be used with a generic method.

9.3 Introduction to Collections

The .NET Framework Class Library provides several classes, called collections, used to store groups of related objects. These classes provide efficient methods that organize, store and retrieve your data without requiring knowledge of how the data is being stored. This reduces application-development time.

You've used arrays to store sequences of objects. Arrays do not automatically change their size at execution time to accommodate additional elements—you must explicitly resize them using a ReDim statement.

The collection class List(Of T) (from namespace System.Collections.Generic) provides a convenient solution to this problem. The T is a placeholder—when declaring a new List, replace it with the type of elements that you want the List to hold. This is similar to specifying the type when declaring an array. For example,

```
Dim list1 As List(Of Integer)
```

declares list1 as a List collection that can store only Integer values, and

```
Dim list2 As List(Of String)
```

declares list2 as a List of Strings. Classes with this kind of placeholder that can be used with any type are called generic classes. Generic classes and additional generic collection classes are discussed in Chapter 24, Data Structures and Generic Collections. Figure 24.8 provides a table of collection classes. Figure 9.5 shows some common methods and properties of class List(Of T).

Method or property	Description
Add	Adds an element to the end of the List.
Capacity	Property that gets or sets the number of elements a List can store.
Clear	Removes all the elements from the List.
Contains	Returns True if the List contains the specified element; otherwise, returns False.
Count	Property that returns the number of elements stored in the List.
IndexOf	Returns the index of the first occurrence of the specified value in the List.
Insert	Inserts an element at the specified index.
Remove	Removes the first occurrence of the specified value.

Fig. 9.5 | Some methods and properties of class List(Of T). (Part 1 of 2.)

Method or property	Description
`RemoveAt`	Removes the element at the specified index.
`RemoveRange`	Removes a specified number of elements starting at a specified index.
`Sort`	Sorts the `List`.
`TrimExcess`	Sets the `Capacity` of the `List` to the number of elements the `List` currently contains (`Count`).

Fig. 9.5 | Some methods and properties of class `List(Of T)`. (Part 2 of 2.)

Figure 9.6 demonstrates dynamically resizing a `List` object. The `Add` and `Insert` methods add elements to the `List` (lines 7–8). The **`Add`** method appends its argument to the end of the `List`. The **`Insert`** method inserts a new element at the specified position. The first argument is an index—as with arrays, collection indices start at zero. The second argument is the value that is to be inserted at the specified index. All elements at the specified index and above are shifted up by one position. This is usually slower than adding an element to the end of the `List`.

```
1  ' Fig. 9.6: ListCollection.vb
2  ' Generic List collection demonstration.
3  Module ListCollection
4     Sub Main()
5        Dim items As New List(Of String) ' create a new List of Strings
6
7        items.Add("red") ' append an item to the List
8        items.Insert(0, "yellow") ' insert the value at index 0
9
10       Console.Write( _
11          "Display list contents with counter-controlled loop:") ' header
12
13       ' display the colors in the list
14       For i = 0 To items.Count - 1
15          Console.Write(" {0}", items(i))
16       Next
17
18       ' display colors using For Each...Next in the Display method
19       Display(items, vbNewLine & _
20          "Display list contents with For Each...Next statement:")
21
22       items.Add("green") ' add "green" to the List
23       items.Add("yellow") ' add "yellow" to the List
24       Display(items, "List with two new elements:") ' display the List
25
26       items.Remove("yellow") ' remove the first "yellow"
27       Display(items, "Remove first instance of yellow:") ' display List
28
```

Fig. 9.6 | Generic `List` collection demonstration. (Part 1 of 2.)

```
29          items.RemoveAt(1) ' remove item at index 1
30          Display(items, "Remove second list element (green):") ' display List
31
32          ' check if a value is in the List
33          Console.WriteLine("""red"" is {0}in the list", _
34             If(items.Contains("red"), String.Empty, "not "))
35
36          ' display number of elements in the List
37          Console.WriteLine(vbNewLine & "Count: {0}", items.Count)
38
39          ' display the capacity of the List
40          Console.WriteLine("Capacity: {0}", items.Capacity)
41       End Sub ' Main
42
43       ' display the List's elements on the console
44       Sub Display(ByVal items As List(Of String), ByVal header As String)
45          Console.Write(header) ' print header
46
47          ' display each element in items
48          For Each item In items
49             Console.Write(" {0}", item)
50          Next
51
52          Console.WriteLine() ' print end of line
53       End Sub ' Display
54    End Module ' ListCollection
```

```
Display list contents with counter-controlled loop: yellow red
Display list contents with For Each...Next statement: yellow red
List with two new elements: yellow red green yellow
Remove first instance of yellow: red green yellow
Remove second list element (green): red yellow
"red" is in the list
Count: 2
Capacity: 4
```

Fig. 9.6 | Generic `List` collection demonstration. (Part 2 of 2.)

Lines 14–16 display the items in the `List`. The **`Count`** property returns the number of elements currently in the `List`. `List`s can be indexed like arrays by placing the index in parentheses after the `List` object's name. The indexed `List` expression is an *lvalue*, and can also be used to modify the element at the index. More elements are then added to the `List`, and it is displayed again (lines 22–24).

The **`Remove`** method is used to remove an element with a specific value (line 26). Note that it removes only the first such element. If the element is not in the `List`, `Remove` does nothing. A similar method, **`RemoveAt`**, removes the element at the specified index (line 29). All elements above that index are shifted down by one—the opposite of the `Insert` method.

Line 34 uses the **`Contains`** method to check if an item is in the `List`. The `Contains` method returns `True` if the element is found in the `List`, and `False` otherwise. Recall that the `If` operator returns its second argument if its first argument is `True`, and its third argument if its first argument is `False`.

Lines 37 and 40 display the List's Count and Capacity. Recall that the Count property (line 37) indicates the number of items in the List. The Capacity property (line 40) indicates how many items the List can hold without growing. List is implemented using an array behind the scenes. When the List grows, it must create a larger internal array and copy each element to the new array. This is a time-consuming operation. It would be inefficient for the List to grow each time an element is added. Instead, the List grows only when an element is added *and* the Count and Capacity properties are equal—there is no space for the new element. The List doubles its Capacity each time it grows. This reduces the number of times the internal array must be recreated.

9.4 Querying a Generic Collection Using LINQ

You can use LINQ to Objects to query Lists just as arrays. In Fig. 9.7, a List of Strings is searched for those that begin with "r", and the Strings are converted to uppercase before being displayed.

Line 15 uses String method StartsWith to select the colors that start with the letter "r". Method StartsWith uses a case sensitive comparison to determine whether a String starts with the String passed to it as an argument. The Where clause determines whether item starts with the character "r". If so, the method returns True, and the element is included in the query results. More powerful String matching can be done using the regular expression capabilities introduced in Chapter 17, Strings, Characters and Regular Expressions. The Select clause (line 17) converts each String included in the result to uppercase using String method ToUpper.

Note that the query is created only once (lines 14–17), yet iterating over the results (lines 20–22 and 30–32) gives two different lists of colors. This demonstrates LINQ's deferred execution—the query is executed only when you iterate over the results, not when the query is defined. This allows you to create a query once and execute it many times. Any changes to the data source are included each time the query executes.

```
1  ' Fig. 9.7: LINQWithListCollection.vb
2  ' LINQ to Objects using a List(Of String).
3  Module LINQWithListCollection
4     Sub Main()
5        ' populate a List of Strings
6        Dim items As New List(Of String)
7        items.Add("aqua") ' add "aqua" to the end of the List
8        items.Add("rust") ' add "rust" to the end of the List
9        items.Add("yellow") ' add "yellow" to the end of the List
10       items.Add("red") ' add "red" to the end of the List
11
12       ' select Strings starting with "r" and convert them to uppercase
13       Dim startsWithR = _
14          From item In items _
15          Where item.StartsWith("r") _
16          Order By item _
17          Select item.ToUpper()
18
```

Fig. 9.7 | LINQ to Objects using a List(Of String). (Part 1 of 2.)

```
         ' display query results
         For Each item In startsWithR
            Console.Write("{0} ", item)
         Next

         Console.WriteLine() ' output end of line

         items.Add("ruby") ' add "ruby" to the end of the List
         items.Add("saffron") ' add "saffron" to the end of the List

         ' print updated query results
         For Each item In startsWithR
            Console.Write("{0} ", item)
         Next

         Console.WriteLine() ' output end of line
      End Sub ' Main
   End Module ' LINQWithListCollection
```

```
RED RUST
RED RUBY RUST
```

Fig. 9.7 | LINQ to Objects using a `List(Of String)`. (Part 2 of 2.)

9.5 Deitel LINQ Resource Center

LINQ is a powerful new programming feature in Visual Basic 2008. This chapter introduced the basic capabilities and syntax. We use more advanced features of LINQ in later chapters. We've also created an extensive LINQ Resource Center that contains many links to additional information, including blogs by Microsoft LINQ team members, sample chapters, tutorials and videos. We encourage you to browse the LINQ Resource Center (`www.deitel.com/LINQ/`) to learn more about this exciting technology.

9.6 Wrap-Up

This chapter introduced LINQ (Language-Integrated Query), a powerful new feature for querying data. We showed how to filter an array or collection using LINQ's `Where` clause, and how to sort the query results using the `Order By` clause. We used the `Select` clause to select specific properties of an object. The `StartsWith` method of class `String` was used to filter `Strings` starting with a specified character or series of characters. We used the `Distinct` clause to remove duplicates from the results.

We introduced the `List(Of T)` generic collection, which provides all the functionality and performance of arrays, along with other useful capabilities such as dynamic resizing. We used the `Add` method to append new items to the end of the `List`. Then we used the `Insert` method to insert new items into specified locations in the `List`. The `Remove` method was used to remove the first occurrence of a specified item, and the `RemoveAt` method was used to remove an item at a specified index. The `Count` property returns the number of items in the `List`, and the `Capacity` property is the size the `List` can grow to without reallocating the internal array. In Chapter 10 we take a deeper look at classes and objects.

Summary

Section 9.1 Introduction

- The .NET collection classes provide reusable data structures that are reliable, powerful and efficient.
- `Lists` automatically increase their size to accommodate additional elements.
- Large amounts of data are often stored in a database—an organized collection of data. Today's most popular database systems are relational databases. SQL is the international standard language used almost universally with relational databases to perform queries (i.e., to request information that satisfies given criteria).
- LINQ allows you to write query expressions (similar to SQL queries) that retrieve information from a wide variety of data sources. We use LINQ to Objects to query arrays and `Lists`, selecting elements that satisfy a set of conditions—this is known as filtering.
- A LINQ provider is a layer between the LINQ engine and a data source—it consists of a set of classes that implement operations needed by LINQ, such as counting, accessing, comparing and removing elements.

Section 9.2 Querying an Array Using LINQ

- Repetition statements focus on the process of iterating through elements and checking whether they satisfy the desired criteria. LINQ specifies the conditions that selected elements must satisfy, not the steps necessary to get the results.
- The Visual Basic compiler generates all the necessary code automatically, which helps explain LINQ's popularity.
- A `From` clause specifies a range variable and the data source to query. The range variable represents each item in the data source, much like the control variable in a `For Each...Next` statement.
- If the condition in the `Where` clause evaluates to `True`, the element is included in the results.
- The `Select` clause determines what value appears in the results. If omitted, the range variable is implicitly selected.
- A Visual Basic interface describes a set of methods that can be called on an object, to tell the object to perform some task or return some piece of information.
- The `IEnumerable` interface describes the functionality of any object that is capable of being iterated over and thus offers methods to access each element in some order.
- A class that `Implements` an interface must define each method in the interface.
- Arrays and collections implement the `IEnumerable` interface.
- A `For Each...Next` statement can iterate over any object that implements the `IEnumerable` interface.
- A LINQ query returns an object that implements the `IEnumerable` interface.
- The `Order By` clause sorts query results in ascending order by default. Results can also be sorted in descending order using the `Descending` modifier.
- LINQ can be used with collections of most data types.
- Any `Boolean` expression can be used in a `Where` clause.
- An `Order By` clause can sort the results according to multiple properties—specified in a comma-separated list.
- The `Count` method returns the number of elements in the query result.
- The `First` method returns the first element in the query result. You should check that the query result is not empty before calling `First`.

- The `Distinct` clause removes duplicate values from query results.
- You can select any number of properties in a `Select` clause by specifying them in a comma-separated list. The compiler automatically creates a new class having these properties—called an anonymous type.
- Generic methods enable you to create a single method definition that can process arguments of many types.
- A generic method's name is followed by a type-parameter list in parentheses that begins with the keyword `Of` and contains one or more type parameters separated by commas.
- A type parameter is a placeholder for an actual type name and can be used to declare the return type, parameter types and local variable types in a generic method declaration.
- Type-parameter names used throughout a generic method declaration must match those declared in the type-parameter list.
- A type parameter can be declared only once in the type-parameter list but can appear more than once in the method's parameter list and body.
- The type parameter is replaced with the type argument specified in the call to a generic method.

Section 9.3 Introduction to Collections

- The .NET collection classes provide efficient methods that organize, store and retrieve data without requiring knowledge of how the data is being stored.
- Class `List(Of T)` is similar to an array but provides richer functionality, such as dynamic resizing.
- The `Add` method appends an element to the end of a `List`.
- The `Insert` method inserts a new element at a specified position in the `List`.
- The `Count` property returns the number of elements currently in a `List`.
- `List`s can be indexed like arrays by placing the index in parentheses after the `List` object's name.
- The `Remove` method is used to remove the first element with a specific value.
- Method `RemoveAt` removes the element at the specified index.
- The `Contains` method returns `True` if the element is found in the `List`, and `False` otherwise.
- The `Capacity` property indicates how many items a `List` can hold without growing. A `List` doubles its `Capacity` each time it grows.

Section 9.4 Querying a Generic Collection Using LINQ

- LINQ to Objects can query `List`s.
- `String` method `StartsWith` determines whether a `String` starts with the `String` passed to it as an argument.
- A LINQ query uses deferred execution—it executes only when you iterate over the results, not when the query is created.

Terminology

`Add` method of class `List(Of T)`
anonymous type
`Ascending` modifier of the `Order By` clause
`Capacity` property of class `List(Of T)`
collections
`Contains` method of class `List(Of T)`
`Count` property of class `List(Of T)`
deferred execution
`Descending` modifier of the `Order By` clause
`Distinct` clause of a LINQ query
dynamic resizing
filtering a collection with LINQ
`From` clause of a LINQ query
generic class

generic method
`IEnumerable` interface
`Insert` method of class `List(Of T)`
interface
LINQ (Language-Integrated Query)
LINQ to Objects
`List(Of T)` collection
`Of` keyword
`Order By` clause of a LINQ query
query expression
query using LINQ
range variable
`Remove` method of class `List(Of T)`
`RemoveAt` method of class `List(Of T)`
`Select` clause of a LINQ query
`StartsWith` method of class `String`
type argument
type parameter
type-parameter list
`Where` clause of a LINQ query

Self-Review Exercises

9.1 Fill in the blanks in each of the following statements:

a) Use the ________ property of the `List` class to find the number of elements in the `List`.
b) The LINQ ________ clause is used for filtering.
c) ________ are classes specifically designed to store groups of values.
d) To add an element to the end of a `List`, use the ________ method.
e) To get only unique results from a LINQ query, use the ________ clause.

9.2 State whether each of the following is *true* or *false*. If *false*, explain why.

a) The `Select` clause in a LINQ query is optional.
b) LINQ queries can be used on both arrays and collections.
c) The `Remove` method of the `List` class removes an element at a specific index.

Answers to Self-Review Exercises

9.1 a) `Count`. b) `Where`. c) Collections. d) `Add`. e) `Distinct`.

9.2 a) True. b) True. c) False. `Remove` removes the first element equal to its argument. `RemoveAt` removes the element at a specific index.

Exercises

9.3 *(Querying an Array of* `Invoice` *Objects)* Use the class `Invoice` provided in the `ex09_03` folder with this chapter's examples to create an array of `Invoice` objects. Use the sample data shown in Fig. 9.8. Class `Invoice` includes four properties—a `PartNumber` (type `Integer`), a `PartDescription` (type `String`), a `Quantity` of the item being purchased (type `Integer`) and a `Price` (type `Decimal`). Write a console application that performs the following queries on the array of `Invoice` objects and displays the results:

a) Use LINQ to sort the `Invoice` objects by `PartDescription`.
b) Use LINQ to sort the `Invoice` objects by `Price`.
c) Use LINQ to select the `PartDescription` and `Quantity` and sort the results by `Quantity`.
d) Use LINQ to select from each `Invoice` the `PartDescription` and the value of the `Invoice` (i.e., `Quantity * Price`). Name the calculated column `InvoiceTotal`. Order the results by `InvoiceTotal`.
e) Using the results of the LINQ query in *Part d*, select the `InvoiceTotals` in the range \$200 to \$500.

9.4 *(Array Sorting Application)* Modify the sorting example of Fig. 8.15 so that it lists three columns of data headed "Original values," "Values sorted in ascending order" and "Values sorted in

Part number	Part description	Quantity	Price
83	Electric sander	7	57.98
24	Power saw	18	99.99
7	Sledge hammer	11	21.50
77	Hammer	76	11.99
39	Lawn mower	3	79.50
68	Screwdriver	106	6.99
56	Jig saw	21	11.00
3	Wrench	34	7.50

Fig. 9.8 | Sample data for Exercise 9.3.

descending order"; your program should display in the last two columns the values sorted in ascending and descending order, respectively. Use LINQ to sort the values. The finished application appears in Fig. 9.9.

9.5 *(Duplicate Word Removal)* Write a console application that inputs a sentence from the user (assume no punctuation), then determines and displays the non-duplicate words in alphabetical order. Treat uppercase and lowercase letters the same. [*Hint:* You can use `String` method `Split` with no arguments, as in `sentence.Split()`, to break a sentence into an array of `String`s containing the individual words. By default, `Split` uses spaces as delimiters. Use `String` method `ToLower` in the `Select` and `Order By` clauses of your LINQ query to obtain the lowercase version of each word.]

9.6 *(Sorting Letters and Removing Duplicates)* Write a console application that inserts 30 random letters into a `List(Of Char)`. Perform the following queries on the `List` and display your results: [*Hint:* Strings can be indexed like arrays to access a character at a specific index.]

a) Use LINQ to sort the `List` in ascending order.
b) Use LINQ to sort the `List` in descending order.
c) Use LINQ to sort the `List` in ascending order with duplicates removed.

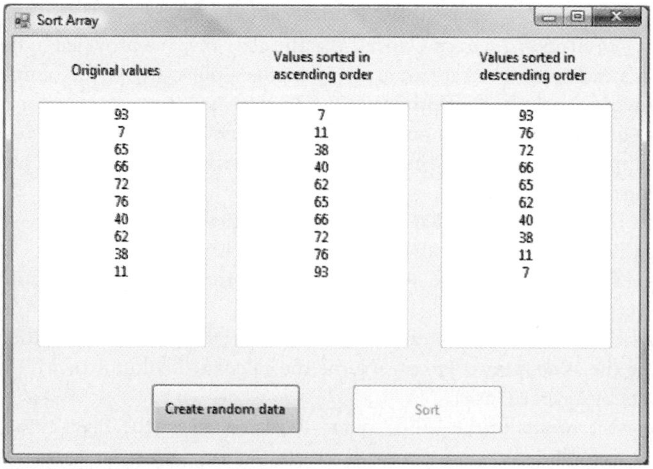

Fig. 9.9 | Completed LINQ array sorting application.

10

Classes and Objects: A Deeper Look

My object all sublime
I shall achieve in time.
—W. S. Gilbert

Is it a world to hide virtues in?
—William Shakespeare

This above all: to thine own self be true.
—William Shakespeare

Don't be "consistent," but be simply true.
—Oliver Wendell Holmes, Jr.

OBJECTIVES

In this chapter you'll learn:

- How class scope affects access to class members.
- To use object initializers to set property values as you create a new object.
- To create overloaded constructors that can initialize objects of a class in a variety of ways.
- How partial classes enable a class to span multiple files.
- How composition enables you to construct classes that are "made out of" other classes.
- To use `Me` to refer to the current object's members.
- How garbage collection helps eliminate "memory leaks."
- How `Shared` class variables help conserve memory.
- To create constant members with `Const` (at compile time) and `ReadOnly` (at runtime).
- To use the **Object Browser** to discover the capabilities of the classes in the .NET Framework Class Library.
- To add functionality to existing classes with extension methods.
- To use delegates and lambda expressions to pass methods to other methods for execution at a later time.
- To create objects of anonymous types.

Outline

10.1 Introduction

Previously, we introduced the basic concepts and terminology of object-oriented programming (OOP) in Visual Basic. This chapter takes a deeper look at classes. We introduce class scope and discuss how it affects where class members can be accessed. We demonstrate that constructors can be overloaded to allow clients to initialize objects of a class in several ways. We discuss how partial classes enable one class to span multiple source-code files. We explain composition—a capability that allows a class to have references to objects of other classes as members. We show how to use the `Me` reference to refer to the current object's members. The chapter presents garbage collection and discusses how it eliminates most "memory leaks." In addition, we discuss `Shared` class variables that are shared among all objects of a class. We then present the differences between constant members created with `Const` and `ReadOnly`. We show how to use the **Object Browser** to discover the capabilities of the classes in the Framework Class Library. We also show how to create a class library for reuse and how to use the classes of the library in an application.

We show how to use extension methods to add functionality to a class without modifying the class's source code. We show you how to use delegates (objects that holds method references) to assign methods to variables and pass methods to other methods. We demonstrate lambda expressions for defining simple, anonymous `Functions` that can also be used with delegates. Finally, you'll learn how to use anonymous types to create simple classes that store data without writing a class definition. Chapters 11–12 introduce inheritance and polymorphism, respectively—two key OOP technologies.

10.2 Time Class Case Study

We begin with a substantial application that uses most of the object-oriented programming concepts presented in Chapters 4–8. We introduce class `Object`, the ultimate "ancestor" of all classes in Visual Basic. Also, we explain method `ToString`, which can be used to obtain a `String` representation of any Visual Basic object.

`Time` Class Declaration

The application consists of classes `Time` (Fig. 10.1) and `TimeTest` (Fig. 10.2). Class `Time` contains the information needed to represent a specific time in two popular formats. Class `TimeTest` represents a GUI for testing class `Time`.

In Fig. 10.1, lines 3–4 begin the `Time` class declaration, indicating that class `Time` inherits from class `Object` of namespace `System`. Programmers use inheritance to quickly create new classes from existing classes (and, as we'll see in Chapter 11, to organize related classes). Keyword `Inherits` (line 4) followed by `Object` indicates that class `Time` inherits class `Object`'s attributes and behaviors. In fact, every class inherits either directly or indirectly from `Object`. If you do not include line 4, the Visual Basic compiler includes it implicitly. You do not need a complete understanding of inheritance to understand the concepts and programs in this chapter. We explore inheritance in detail in Chapter 11.

```
1  ' Fig. 10.1: Time.vb
2  ' Time class declaration maintains the time in 24-hour format.
3  Class Time
4     Inherits Object ' if omitted, Object is inherited implicitly
5
6     ' declare Integer instance variables for the hour, minute and second
7     Private hourValue As Integer ' 0 - 23
8     Private minuteValue As Integer ' 0 - 59
9     Private secondValue As Integer ' 0 - 59
10
11    ' Time constructor initializes instance variables
12    ' when a Time object is created
13    Public Sub New()
14       SetTime(12, 0, 0) ' initialize hour to noon; minute, second to 0
15    End Sub ' New
16
17    ' set a new time value using universal time, check validity of the
18    ' data, set invalid hour to noon, set invalid minute, second to zero
19    Public Sub SetTime(ByVal hh As Integer, _
20       ByVal mm As Integer, ByVal ss As Integer)
21       Hour = hh ' set hourValue using Hour property
22       Minute = mm ' set minuteValue using Minute property
23       Second = ss ' set secondValue using Second property
24    End Sub ' SetTime
25
26    ' property Hour
27    Public Property Hour() As Integer
28       Get ' return hourValue
29          Return hourValue
30       End Get
```

Fig. 10.1 | `Time` class declaration maintains the time in 24-hour format. (Part 1 of 3.)

```

      Set(ByVal value As Integer) ' set hourValue
         If (value >= 0 AndAlso value < 24) Then ' in range 0-23
            hourValue = value ' value is valid
         Else ' value is invalid
            hourValue = 12 ' set to default of noon
         End If
      End Set
   End Property ' Hour

   ' property Minute
   Public Property Minute() As Integer
      Get ' return minuteValue
         Return minuteValue
      End Get

      Set(ByVal value As Integer) ' set minuteValue
         If (value >= 0 AndAlso value < 60) Then ' in range 0-59
            minuteValue = value ' value is valid
         Else ' value is invalid
            minuteValue = 0 ' set to default of 0
         End If
      End Set
   End Property ' Minute

   ' property Second
   Public Property Second() As Integer
      Get ' return secondValue
         Return secondValue
      End Get

      Set(ByVal value As Integer) ' set secondValue
         If (value >= 0 AndAlso value < 60) Then ' in range 0-59
            secondValue = value ' value is valid
         Else ' value is invalid
            secondValue = 0 ' set to default of 0
         End If
      End Set
   End Property ' Second

   ' convert Time to a String in universal-time (24-hour clock) format
   Public Function ToUniversalString() As String
      Return String.Format("{0}:{1:D2}:{2:D2}", Hour, Minute, Second)
   End Function ' ToUniversalString

   ' convert Time to a String in standard-time (12-hour clock) format
   Public Overrides Function ToString() As String
      Dim suffix As String ' AM or PM suffix
      Dim standardHour As Integer ' a standard hour in the range 1-12

      ' determine whether the 12-hour clock suffix should be AM or PM
      If Hour < 12 Then
         suffix = "AM"
```

Fig. 10.1 | Time class declaration maintains the time in 24-hour format. (Part 2 of 3.)

```
84          Else
85             suffix = "PM"
86          End If
87
88          ' convert hour from universal-time format to standard-time format
89          If (Hour = 12 OrElse Hour = 0) Then
90             standardHour = 12
91          Else
92             standardHour = Hour Mod 12 ' 1 through 11, AM or PM
93          End If
94
95          Return String.Format("{0}:{1:D2}:{2:D2} {3}", _
96             standardHour, Minute, Second, suffix)
97       End Function ' ToString
98    End Class ' Time
```

Fig. 10.1 | `Time` class declaration maintains the time in 24-hour format. (Part 3 of 3.)

Lines 3 and 98 delimit with keywords `Class` and `End Class`, respectively, the body of the `Time` class declaration. Any information that we place in this body is contained within the class's scope. Class `Time` declares three `Private Integer` instance variables—`hourValue`, `minuteValue` and `secondValue` (lines 7–9)—that represent the time in universal-time format (24-hour clock format). We prefer to list the instance variables of a class first, so that, when reading the code, you see the name and type of each instance variable before it is used in the class's methods.

It's possible to have `Private` methods and `Public` instance variables. `Private` methods are called utility methods, or helper methods, because they can be called only by other methods of the class to support their operation. Using `Public` instance variables in a class is an uncommon and dangerous programming practice. Providing such access to a class's instance variables is unsafe; other parts of the program could accidentally or maliciously set these members to invalid values, producing potentially disastrous results. Public access to instance variables should be accomplished through properties.

`Time` Class Properties

Class `Time` (Fig. 10.1) declares properties `Hour` (lines 27–39), `Minute` (lines 42–54) and `Second` (lines 57–69) to access instance variables `hourValue`, `minuteValue` and `secondValue`, respectively. Each of these properties contains a `Get` accessor and a `Set` accessor. The `Set` accessors (lines 32–38, 47–53 and 62–68) strictly control the setting of the instance variables to ensure that they contain valid values. An attempt to set any instance variable to an incorrect value causes the instance variable to be set to its default value—12 (noon) for the hour and 0 for the minute and second—leaving the instance variable in a consistent state. Each `Get` accessor (lines 28–30, 43–45 and 58–60) returns the appropriate instance variable's value.

`Time` Class Methods

Class `Time` contains the following `Public` methods—the constructor `New` (lines 13–15), `SetTime` (lines 19–24), `ToUniversalString` (lines 72–74) and `ToString` (lines 77–97). Constructor `New` calls (in line 14) method `SetTime` (discussed shortly) with the `hour` value specified as 12 and the minute and second values specified as `0` to indicate that the default time should be noon. Visual Basic initializes `Integer` variables to 0 by default, so if we did not provide a constructor for class `Time`, instance variables `hourValue`, `minuteValue` and `secondValue` would each be initialized to 0, making the default time midnight. For some classes that would be fine, but we want our `Time` objects to be initialized to noon.

Constructors are implemented as `Sub` procedures, not as `Functions`, because `Sub` procedures cannot return values. Generally, constructors are declared `Public`. `Private` constructors are useful but are beyond the scope of the book. As you'll see, a class can have overloaded constructors with different signatures.

Method `SetTime` (lines 19–24) uses properties `Hour`, `Minute` and `Second` to ensure that instance variables `hourValue`, `minuteValue` and `secondValue` have valid values. For example, the `hourValue` must be greater than or equal to `0` and less than `24`, because universal-time format represents hours as integers from `0` to `23`. Similarly, both the `minuteValue` and `secondValue` must fall between `0` and `59`. Any values outside these ranges are invalid and default to 12 for the `hourValue` or 0 for the `minuteValue` and `secondValue`, ensuring that a `Time` object always contains valid data; that is, the object remains in a consistent state. When a user calls `SetTime` with invalid arguments, the program should indicate that the attempted time setting was invalid. This can be done by "throwing an exception"—we discuss exception handling in Chapter 13.

Method `ToUniversalString` (lines 72–74) takes no arguments and returns a `String` in universal-time format, consisting of the `Hour` property value, two digits for the `Minute` property value and two digits for the `Second` property value. For example, if the time were 1:30:07 PM, method `ToUniversalString` would return the `String "13:30:07"`. Note that format specifier `D2` formats a single-digit integer value with a leading 0.

Method **`ToString`** (lines 77–97) takes no arguments and returns a `String` in standard-time format, consisting of the `Hour`, `Minute` and `Second` property values separated by colons and followed by AM or PM (e.g., `1:27:06 PM`). Lines 82–93 determine the proper formatting for the hour—hours from `0` to `11` print with `AM`, hours from `12` to `23` print with `PM`, hour `0` prints as `12` (midnight), hours `1`–`12` print as is and hours `13`–`23` print as `1`–`11` (`PM`).

Note that method `ToString` contains the keyword **`Overrides`** (line 77) in its declaration. Recall that every class in Visual Basic (such as class `Time`) inherits either directly or indirectly from class `Object`, which is the root of the class hierarchy. Section 11.7 summarizes class `Object`'s seven methods, including method `ToString`, which returns a `String` representation of an object. The default implementation of `ToString` that every class inherits (directly or indirectly) from class `Object` returns the namespace and the class name of the object's class. This implementation is primarily a placeholder that can be overridden by a derived class to specify a more appropriate `String` representation of the data in a derived class object. For class `Time`, we choose to override (i.e., redefine) the `ToString` method to return a `String` which represents the `Time` object in standard-time (i.e., 12-hour clock) format. For most classes, you will need to override the `ToString` method since the default `ToString` method does not display useful or desired information.

After defining the class, we can use it as a type in declarations such as

```
Dim sunset As Time ' reference to object of class Time
```

Using the `Time` Class

Class `TimeTest` (Fig. 10.2) provides a GUI for testing class `Time`. The GUI contains three text boxes in which the user can enter values for the `Time` object's `Hour`, `Minute` and `Second` properties, respectively. Class `TimeTest` creates an object of class `Time` (line 4) and assigns its reference to variable `time`. When the object is instantiated, `New` allocates the memory for the `Time` object, then calls the `Time` constructor (method `New` in lines 13–15 of Fig. 10.1) to initialize the object's instance variables. The constructor invokes `Time` method `SetTime` to initialize the properties, setting the time to noon.

Common Programming Error 10.1

Using a reference type variable (which, as you know, is initialized to the default value `Nothing`) before it refers to an actual object results in a `NullReferenceException` at execution time and causes the program to terminate prematurely. We discuss how to handle exceptions to make programs more robust in Chapter 13, Exception Handling.

```
1  ' Fig. 10.2: TimeTest.vb
2  ' Graphical user interface for testing class Time.
3  Public Class TimeTest
4     Dim time As New Time() ' construct Time with zero arguments
5
6     ' invoked when user clicks the Add 1 to Second button
7     Private Sub addSecondButton_Click(ByVal sender As System.Object, _
8        ByVal e As System.EventArgs) Handles addSecondButton.Click
9        time.Second = (time.Second + 1) Mod 60 ' add 1 to Second
10       setSecondTextBox.Text = Convert.ToString(time.Second)
11
12       ' add one minute if 60 seconds have passed
13       If time.Second = 0 Then
14          time.Minute = (time.Minute + 1) Mod 60 ' add 1 to Minute
15          setMinuteTextBox.Text = Convert.ToString(time.Minute)
16
17          ' add one hour if 60 minutes have passed
18          If time.Minute = 0 Then
19             time.Hour = (time.Hour + 1) Mod 24 ' add 1 to Hour
20             setHourTextBox.Text = Convert.ToString(time.Hour)
21          End If
22       End If
23
24       UpdateDisplay() ' update the text in output1Label and output2Label
25    End Sub ' addSecondButton_Click
26
27    ' handle event when setHourTextBox's text changes
28    Private Sub setHourTextBox_TextChanged( _
29       ByVal sender As System.Object, ByVal e As System.EventArgs) _
30       Handles setHourTextBox.TextChanged
31       time.Hour = Convert.ToInt32(setHourTextBox.Text)
32       UpdateDisplay() ' update the text in output1Label and output2Label
33    End Sub ' setHourTextBox_TextChanged
34
35    ' handle event when setMinuteTextBox's text changes
36    Private Sub setMinuteTextBox_TextChanged( _
37       ByVal sender As System.Object, ByVal e As System.EventArgs) _
38       Handles setMinuteTextBox.TextChanged
39       time.Minute = Convert.ToInt32(setMinuteTextBox.Text)
```

Fig. 10.2 | Graphical user interface for testing class `Time`. (Part 1 of 2.)

```
         UpdateDisplay() ' update the text in output1Label and output2Label
      End Sub ' setMinuteTextBox_TextChanged

      ' handle event when setSecondTextBox's text changes
      Private Sub setSecondTextBox_TextChanged( _
         ByVal sender As System.Object, ByVal e As System.EventArgs) _
         Handles setSecondTextBox.TextChanged
         time.Second = Convert.ToInt32(setSecondTextBox.Text)
         UpdateDisplay() ' update the text in output1Label and output2Label
      End Sub ' setSecondTextBox_Textchanged

      ' update time display
      Private Sub UpdateDisplay()
         setHourTextBox.Text = Convert.ToString(time.Hour)
         setMinuteTextBox.Text = Convert.ToString(time.Minute)
         setSecondTextBox.Text = Convert.ToString(time.Second)
         output1Label.Text = String.Format("Hour: {0}; Minute: {1}; " & _
            "Second: {2}", time.Hour, time.Minute, time.Second)
         output2Label.Text = String.Format("Standard time is: {0}; " & _
            "Universal Time is: {1}", time.ToString(), _
            time.ToUniversalString())
      End Sub ' UpdateDisplay
   End Class ' TimeTest
```

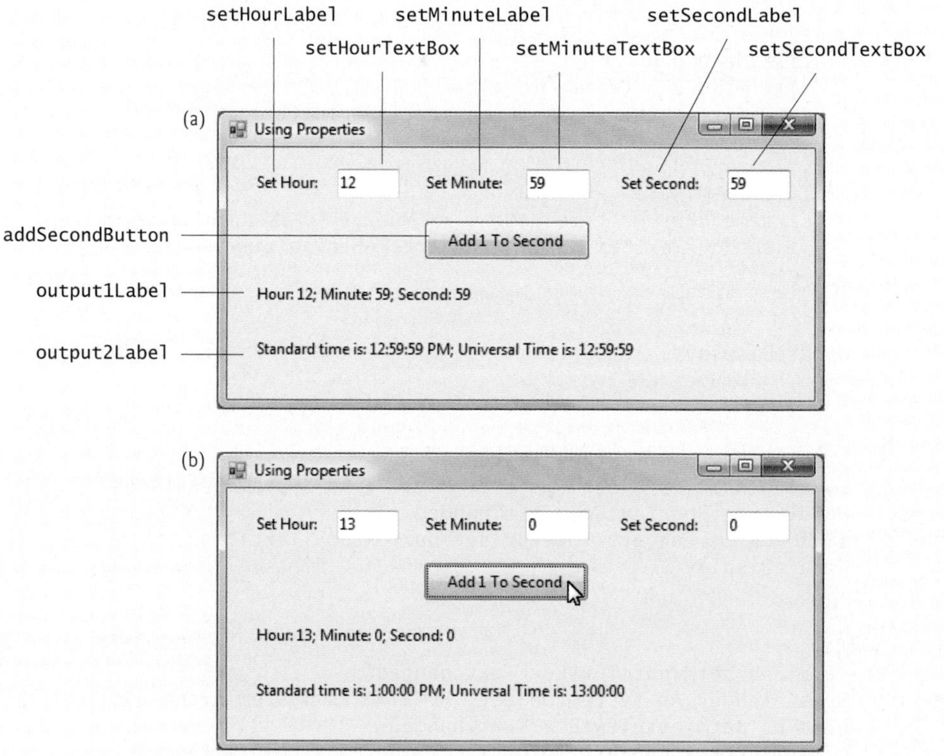

Fig. 10.2 | Graphical user interface for testing class `Time`. (Part 2 of 2.)

Lines 28–49 declare TextChanged event handlers that use the Time object's Hour, Minute and Second properties to alter the corresponding instance variable values. The TextChanged event is raised when the text inside the TextBox is changed in any way. The GUI also contains a button that enables the user to increment the Second property value by 1 without having to use the corresponding text box. Method addSecondButton_Click (lines 7–25) uses properties to determine and set the new time, ensuring that the values for the hour, minute and second are updated properly. For example, 23:59:59 becomes 00:00:00 when the user presses the button. Lines 58–60 display the time in standard-time format (by invoking method ToString of Time) and universal-time format (by invoking method ToUniversalString of Time).

Notes on Importing Namespaces

Note that we are able to use class Time in class TimeTest (Fig. 10.2) even though there is no Imports statement to import class Time. Classes Time and TimeTest are considered to be part of the same namespace by default because we placed them in the same project directory. In fact, every class and module in Visual Basic is part of a namespace. If you do not specify a namespace for a class or module, it is placed in the default namespace, which includes the compiled classes and modules in the current directory—in Visual Studio, this is a project's directory. When a class or module uses another class in the same namespace, an Imports statement is not required. The reason we must import the classes from the .NET Framework is that our classes and modules are in different namespaces from those in the .NET Framework. For console applications, Visual Studio automatically imports namespaces System, System.Data, System.Deployment and System.Xml. For Windows applications, Visual Studio automatically imports namespaces System, System.Deployment, System.Drawing and System.Windows.Forms.

You can see which namespaces have been imported into a project by double clicking the **My Project** folder in the **Solution Explorer** and then selecting **References** in the page that appears (Fig. 10.3). You'll be presented with a list of the application's references to assemblies in the window's **References** area, and a list of the namespaces defined in those references in the **Imported namespaces** area. The namespaces that have been checked are those that are imported for the entire project. Some namespaces that are imported by default are not used in this example. Do not confuse importing namespaces for an entire application with adding references to an application. Adding a reference to an application causes a library (.dll) file to be included into your application. A library file can contain several namespaces. An Imports statement indicates that you'll be using a specific namespace from a library file.

Notes on the **Time** *Class Declaration*

Lines 7–9 of class Time (Fig. 10.1) declare instance variables hourValue, minuteValue and secondValue as Private. The Time constructor initializes the instance variable hourValue to 12 and the instance variables minuteValue and secondValue to 0 (i.e., noon) to ensure that the object is created in a consistent state. The instance variables of a Time object cannot contain invalid values, because they are Private, because the constructor (which calls SetTime) is called when the Time object is created, and because method SetTime uses properties to scrutinize all subsequent attempts by a client to modify the instance variables.

Methods ToUniversalString and ToString take no arguments because, by default, these methods manipulate the instance variables of the particular Time object for which

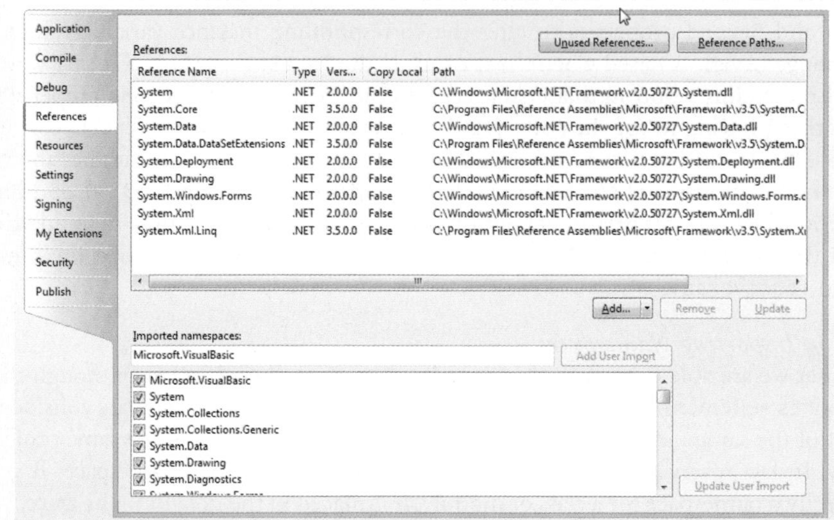

Fig. 10.3 | Imported namespaces in a project.

they are invoked. Any method of a class can access all the instance variables of the class and can call every method of the class. This makes method calls more concise than conventional function calls in procedural programming. It also reduces the likelihood of passing the wrong arguments, the wrong types of arguments or the wrong number of arguments.

Software Engineering Observation 10.1

Using an object-oriented programming approach often simplifies method calls by reducing, or even eliminating, the arguments that must be passed. This benefit of object-oriented programming derives from the encapsulation of instance variables within an object.

One of the reasons why classes simplify programming is that the clients of the class need be concerned only with its `Public` operations. Clients are neither aware of, nor involved in, a class's implementation. Interfaces change less frequently than implementations. When an implementation changes, implementation-dependent code must change accordingly. By hiding the implementation, we eliminate the possibility that the clients of the class will become dependent on the class's implementation details.

You do not always have to create classes from scratch. Rather, you can derive classes by inheritance from other classes that provide capabilities required by the new classes. Classes also can include references to objects of other classes as members—this is called composition. Such software reuse can greatly enhance your productivity. Section 10.8 discusses composition. Chapter 11 discusses inheritance.

10.3 Class Scope

In Section 7.14, we discussed method scope; now we consider class scope. A class's instance variables and methods belong to its scope. Within a class's scope, class members are accessible to all of the class's methods and properties and can be referenced simply by name (without an object reference). Outside a class's scope, class members cannot be referenced directly by name. Those class members that are visible (such as `Public` members) can be accessed through a "handle" (i.e., members can be referenced via names of the form *objectReferenceName*`.`*memberName* or *ClassName*`.`*memberName* for `Shared` members). For example, line 60 of Fig. 10.2 accessess a `Time` object's method with the method call `time.ToUniversalString()`.

If a variable is defined in a method, only that method can access the variable (i.e., the variable is a local variable of that method). Such variables have block scope. If a method defines a local variable that has the same name as an instance variable, the local variable hides the instance variable in that method's scope—this is called shadowing. A shadowed instance variable can be accessed in a method of that class by preceding its name with the keyword `Me` and the dot separator, as in `Me.hourValue`. Section 10.9 discusses keyword `Me`.

10.4 Object Initializers

In Section 6.5, we introduced the `With` statement, which enables you to make multiple references to the same object in a concise manner. Visual Basic 2008 provides a new feature—Object initializers—that uses the `With` keyword to allow you to create an object and initialize its properties in the same statement. This is useful when a class does not provide an appropriate constructor to meet your needs. For example, the `Time` class used here (from Fig. 10.1) provides only a parameterless constructor, so we cannot provide hour, minute and second values in the constructor call. Figure 10.4 creates a new `Time` object (lines 8–9) and uses an object initializer to set its `Hour`, `Minute` and `Second` properties. Notice that `New Time()` is immediately followed by the `With` keyword and an object initializer list—a comma-separated list in curly braces (`{ }`) of properties and their values. The `With` keyword indicates that the new object (`aTime`) is used to access the properties specified in the object-initializer list. Each property name must be preceded by the dot separator (`.`) and can appear only once in the object-initializer list. The object-initializer list cannot be empty and cannot contain `Shared` (Section 10.11), `Const` (Section 10.12) or `ReadOnly` (Section 10.12) properties.

```
1  ' Fig. 10.4: ObjectInitializerTest.vb
2  ' Demonstrate object initializers using class Time.
3  Module ObjectInitializerTest
4     Sub Main()
5        Console.WriteLine("Time object created with object initializer")
6
7        ' create a Time object and initialize its properties
8        Dim aTime As New Time() With _
9           {.Hour = 14, .Minute = 145, .Second = 12}
10
11       ' display the time in both standard and universal format
12       Console.WriteLine("Standard time: {0}" & vbNewLine & _
13          "Universal time: {1}", aTime.ToString(), _
14          aTime.ToUniversalString())
15
16       Console.WriteLine(vbNewLine & _
17          "Time object created with Minute property set")
```

Fig. 10.4 | Demonstrate object initializers using class `Time`. (Part 1 of 2.)

```
18
19         ' create a Time object and initialize its Minute property only
20         Dim anotherTime As New Time() With {.Minute = 45}
21
22         ' display the time in both standard and universal format
23         Console.WriteLine("Standard time: {0}" & vbNewLine & _
24            "Universal time: {1}", anotherTime.ToString(), _
25            anotherTime.ToUniversalString())
26      End Sub ' Main
27   End Module ' ObjectInitializerTest
```

```
Time object created with object initializer
Standard time: 2:00:12 PM
Universal time: 14:00:12

Time object created with Minute property set
Standard time: 12:45:00 PM
Universal time: 12:45:00
```

Fig. 10.4 | Demonstrate object initializers using class `Time`. (Part 2 of 2.)

Lines 8–9 create a `Time` object and initialize it with class `Time`'s parameterless constructor. The object initializer then executes the property initializers in the order in which they appear. Lines 12–14 display the `Time` object in standard and universal time formats. Note that the `Minute` property's value is 0. The value supplied for the `Minute` property in the object initializer (`145`) is invalid. The `Minute` property's `Set` accessor validates the supplied value, setting the `Minute` property to 0.

Line 20 uses an object intializer to create a new `Time` object (`anotherTime`) and set only its `Minute` property. Lines 23–25 display the `Time` object in both standard and universal time formats. Note that the time is set to `12:45:00`. Recall that an object intializer first calls the class's constructor. The `Time` constructor initializes the time to noon (`12:00:00`). The object initializer then sets each specified property to the supplied value. In this case, the `Minute` property is set to `45`. The `Hour` and `Second` properties retain their default values, because no values are specified for them in the object initializer.

10.5 Default and Parameterless Constructors

If a class does not define constructors, the compiler provides a default constructor. This constructor contains no code (i.e., the constructor body is empty) and takes no parameters. You can also provide a constructor—called a parameterless constructor—that contains code (but, again, takes no parameters), as we demonstrated in class `Time` (lines 13–15 of Fig. 10.1), and as we will see again in the next example. If you provide any constructors for a class, the compiler will not provide a default constructor for that class.

Common Programming Error 10.2

If `Public` constructors are provided for a class, but none of them is a parameterless constructor, and an attempt is made to call a constructor with no arguments to initialize an object of the class, a compilation error occurs. A constructor can be called with no arguments only if there are no constructors for the class (in which case the default constructor is called) or if the class includes a parameterless constructor.

10.6 Time Class Case Study: Overloaded Constructors

Like methods, constructors of a class can be overloaded. To do so, provide a separate method declaration with the same name (New) for each version of the method but different numbers, types and/or orders of parameters.

Class Time with Overloaded Constructors

The Time constructor in Fig. 10.1 initialized hourValue to 12 and minuteValue and secondValue to 0 (i.e., noon) with a call to the class's SetTime method. Recall that the declaration in line 4 of Fig. 10.2 supplied no arguments to the Time class constructor. Suppose you would like to create Time objects with any legitimate hour, minute and/or second values. Class Time of Fig. 10.5 includes five overloaded constructors to provide several ways to initialize Time objects. Each constructor calls method SetTime of the Time object, which uses the Set accessors of properties Hour, Minute and Second to ensure that the object begins in a consistent state by setting out-of-range hour, minute and second values to 12, 0 and 0, respectively. The compiler invokes the appropriate constructor by matching the number, types and order of the arguments specified in the constructor call with the number, types and order of the parameters specified in each constructor method declaration.

```
' Fig. 10.5: Time.vb
' Overloaded constructors and Optional arguments.
Class Time
   ' declare Integer instance variables for the hour, minute and second
   Private hourValue As Integer ' 0 - 23
   Private minuteValue As Integer ' 0 - 59
   Private secondValue As Integer ' 0 - 59

   ' constructor initializes hour to 12, minute to 0 and second to 0
   ' to ensure that each Time object starts in a consistent state
   Public Sub New() ' parameterless constructor
      SetTime(12) ' initialize hour to noon; minute and second to 0
   End Sub ' New

   ' Time constructor: hour supplied;
   ' minute and second default to 0
   Public Sub New(ByVal hh As Integer)
      SetTime(hh) ' call SetTime with one argument
   End Sub ' New

   ' Time constructor: hour and minute supplied;
   ' second defaults to 0
   Public Sub New(ByVal hh As Integer, ByVal mm As Integer)
      SetTime(hh, mm) ' call SetTime with two arguments
   End Sub ' New

   ' Time constructor: hour, minute and second supplied
   Public Sub New(ByVal hh As Integer, _
      ByVal mm As Integer, ByVal ss As Integer)
      SetTime(hh, mm, ss) ' call SetTime with three arguments
   End Sub ' New
```

Fig. 10.5 | Overloaded constructors and Optional arguments. (Part 1 of 3.)

```
   ' Time constructor: another Time object supplied
   Public Sub New(ByVal tt As Time)
      SetTime(tt.Hour, tt.Minute, tt.Second)
   End Sub ' New

   ' set a new time value using universal time, check validity of the
   ' data, set invalid hour to 12, set invalid minute/second to zero
   Public Sub SetTime(Optional ByVal hh As Integer = 12, _
      Optional ByVal mm As Integer = 0, Optional ByVal ss As Integer = 0)
      Hour = hh ' set hourValue using the Hour property
      Minute = mm ' set minuteValue using the Minute property
      Second = ss ' set secondValue using the Second property
   End Sub ' SetTime

   ' property Hour
   Public Property Hour() As Integer
      Get ' return hourValue
         Return hourValue
      End Get

      Set(ByVal value As Integer) ' set hourValue
         If (value >= 0 AndAlso value < 24) Then ' in range 0-23
            hourValue = value ' value is valid
         Else ' value is invalid
            hourValue = 12 ' set to default of noon
         End If
      End Set
   End Property ' Hour

   ' property Minute
   Public Property Minute() As Integer
      Get ' return minuteValue
         Return minuteValue
      End Get

      Set(ByVal value As Integer) ' set minuteValue
         If (value >= 0 AndAlso value < 60) Then ' in range 0-59
            minuteValue = value ' value is valid
         Else ' value is invalid
            minuteValue = 0 ' set to default of 0
         End If
      End Set
   End Property ' Minute

   ' property Second
   Public Property Second() As Integer
      Get ' return secondValue
         Return secondValue
      End Get

```

Fig. 10.5 | Overloaded constructors and `Optional` arguments. (Part 2 of 3.)

```
83          Set(ByVal value As Integer) ' set secondValue
84             If (value >= 0 AndAlso value < 60) Then ' in range 0-59
85                secondValue = value ' value is valid
86             Else ' value is invalid
87                secondValue = 0 ' set to default of 0
88             End If
89          End Set
90       End Property ' Second
91
92       ' convert Time to a String in universal-time (24-hour clock) format
93       Public Function ToUniversalString() As String
94          Return String.Format("{0}:{1:D2}:{2:D2}", Hour, Minute, Second)
95       End Function ' ToUniversalString
96
97       ' convert Time to a String in standard-time (12-hour clock) format
98       Public Overrides Function ToString() As String
99          Dim suffix As String ' AM or PM suffix
100         Dim standardHour As Integer ' a standard hour in the range 1-12
101
102         ' determine whether the 12-hour clock suffix should be AM or PM
103         If Hour < 12 Then
104            suffix = "AM"
105         Else
106            suffix = "PM"
107         End If
108
109         ' convert hour from universal-time format to standard-time format
110         If (Hour = 12 OrElse Hour = 0) Then
111            standardHour = 12
112         Else
113            standardHour = Hour Mod 12 ' 1 through 11, AM or PM
114         End If
115
116         Return String.Format("{0}:{1:D2}:{2:D2} {3}", standardHour, _
117            Minute, Second, suffix)
118      End Function ' ToString
119   End Class ' Time
```

Fig. 10.5 | Overloaded constructors and `Optional` arguments. (Part 3 of 3.)

Class `Time`*'s Constructors*

Because most of the code in class `Time` is identical to that in Fig. 10.1, this section concentrates only on the overloaded constructors. Lines 11–13 define the parameterless constructor that calls `SetTime` (line 12), initializing the time to noon. Lines 17–19 define a `Time` constructor with a single `Integer` parameter, representing the hour. Lines 23–25 define a `Time` constructor with two `Integer` parameters, representing the hour and minute. Lines 28–31 define a `Time` constructor with three `Integer` parameters representing the hour, minute and second. Lines 34–36 define a `Time` constructor that receives a reference to another `Time` object. When this last constructor—sometimes called a copy constructor—is called, the values from the `Time` argument are copied to initialize the new object's `hourValue`, `minuteValue` and `secondValue`. Class `Time` declares these values as `Private` (lines

5–7), but the new Time object's constructor obtains these values via the Public properties of its Time parameter by using the expressions tt.Hour, tt.Minute and tt.Second. In fact, line 35 could have accessed the argument Time object's instance variables directly with the expressions tt.hourValue, tt.minuteValue and tt.secondValue.

Software Engineering Observation 10.2

When one object of a class has a reference to another object of the same class, the first object can access all of the second object's data, methods and properties (including those that are Private).

Although the parameter to the constructor in lines 34–36 is passed by value, this does not make a copy of the Time object that is passed as the constructor's argument. Rather, it makes a copy of the reference to the Time object passed as the argument.

Software Engineering Observation 10.3

Visual Basic classes are reference types, so all Visual Basic objects are passed to methods by reference.

Note that each constructor receives a different number and/or different types of parameters. Also, recall that if a method has one or more Optional parameters, the caller has the option of passing a value for each parameter. Method SetTime declares three Optional parameters—hh, mm and ss (lines 40–41). Lines 12 and 18 call method SetTime with one argument, which indicates that the default values for the Optional minuteValue and secondValue parameters should be used. Line 24 calls method SetTime with two arguments, which indicates that the default value for the Optional parameter secondValue is used. Lines 30 and 35 call method SetTime with all three arguments, so that no default values are used.

Common Programming Error 10.3

A constructor can call other class methods that use instance variables not yet initialized. Using instance variables before they have been initialized can lead to logic errors.

Using Class Time's Overloaded Constructors

Figure 10.6 (TimeTest.vb) demonstrates class Time's overloaded constructors. Lines 6–11 create six Time objects that invoke various constructors of the class. Line 6 invokes the parameterless constructor by placing an empty set of parentheses after the class name. Lines 7–11 demonstrate passing arguments to the Time constructors. Line 7 invokes the constructor at lines 17–19 of Fig. 10.5. Line 8 invokes the constructor at lines 23–25 of Fig. 10.5. Lines 9–10 invoke the constructor at lines 28–31 of Fig. 10.5. Line 11 invokes the constructor at lines 34–36 of Fig. 10.5.

Each Time constructor can be written to include a copy of the appropriate statements from method SetTime. This might be slightly more efficient, because it eliminates the extra SetTime call. However, consider what would happen if you changed the representation of the time from three Integer values (requiring 12 bytes of memory) to a single Integer value representing the total number of elapsed seconds since midnight (requiring only 4 bytes of memory). Placing identical code in the Time constructors and method SetTime makes such a change in the class declaration more difficult. If the implementation of SetTime changed, the implementation of all the Time constructors would need to change accordingly. If, on the other hand, the `Time` constructors call method `SetTime` directly, any changes to the implementation of `SetTime` must be made only once, thus reducing the likelihood of a programming error when altering the implementation.

Software Engineering Observation 10.4

If a method of a class provides functionality required by a constructor (or other method) of the class, call that method from the constructor (or other method). This simplifies the maintenance of the code and reduces the likelihood of code errors.

```
' Fig. 10.6: TimeTest.vb
' Overloading constructors.
Module TimeTest
   Sub Main()
      ' use overloaded constructors
      Dim time1 As New Time() ' constructor with zero parameters
      Dim time2 As New Time(2) ' constructor with one parameter
      Dim time3 As New Time(21, 34) ' constructor with two parameters
      Dim time4 As New Time(12, 25, 42) ' three valid arguments
      Dim time5 As New Time(27, 74, 99) ' three invalid arguments
      Dim time6 As New Time(time4) ' copy another Time object

      ' invoke time1 methods
      Console.WriteLine("Constructed with: " & vbNewLine & _
         "time1: all arguments defaulted" & vbNewLine & vbTab & _
         time1.ToUniversalString() & vbNewLine & vbTab & _
         time1.ToString())
      ' invoke time2 methods
      Console.WriteLine( _
         "time2: hour specified; minute and second defaulted" & _
         vbNewLine & vbTab & time2.ToUniversalString() & _
         vbNewLine & vbTab & time2.ToString())
      ' invoke time3 methods
      Console.WriteLine( _
         "time3: hour and minute specified; second defaulted" & _
         vbNewLine & vbTab & time3.ToUniversalString() & _
         vbNewLine & vbTab & time3.ToString())
      ' invoke time4 methods
      Console.WriteLine("time4: hour, minute and second specified" & _
         vbNewLine & vbTab & time4.ToUniversalString() & _
         vbNewLine & vbTab & time4.ToString())
      ' invoke time5 methods
      Console.WriteLine( _
         "time5: invalid hour, minute and second specified" & _
         vbNewLine & vbTab & time5.ToUniversalString() & _
         vbNewLine & vbTab & time5.ToString())
      ' invoke time6 methods
      Console.WriteLine( "time6: Time object copied from time4" & _
         vbNewLine & vbTab & time6.ToUniversalString() & _
         vbNewLine & vbTab & time6.ToString())
   End Sub ' Main
End Module ' TimeTest
```

Fig. 10.6 | Overloading constructors. (Part 1 of 2.)

```
Constructed with:
time1: all arguments defaulted
       12:00:00
       12:00:00 PM
time2: hour specified; minute and second defaulted
       2:00:00
       2:00:00 AM
time3: hour and minute specified; second defaulted
       21:34:00
       9:34:00 PM
time4: hour, minute and second specified
       12:25:42
       12:25:42 PM
time5: invalid hour, minute and second specified
       12:00:00
       12:00:00 PM
time6: Time object copied from time4
       12:25:42
       12:25:42 PM
```

Fig. 10.6 | Overloading constructors. (Part 2 of 2.)

10.7 Partial Classes

Visual Basic allows a class declaration to span multiple source-code files. The separate portions of the class declaration in each file are known as partial classes. We have already created applications that use partial classes—in each GUI application, the code that is auto-generated by the IDE (i.e., the code that declares and creates GUI components in the code-behind file) is marked with the `Partial` modifier and stored in a separate source file. For example, in the GUI application in Fig. 10.2, the lines 2–3 of the auto-generated partial class (stored in `TimeTest.Designer.vb`) are:

```
Partial Class TimeTest
   Inherits System.Windows.Forms.Form
```

which indicates that the code in this file is part of class `TimeTest`. The partial class is stored in a file named `TimeTest.Designer.vb`. To view this file, click the **Show All Files** button on the **Solution Explorer** toolbar and then click the plus sign (+) to the left of the `TimeTest.vb` in the **Solution Explorer** window.

When a class declaration specifies the `Partial` modifier, any class declarations with the same class name in the program will be combined with the partial class declaration to form a single class declaration at compile time. Partial classes must be declared in the same namespace and assembly. If members (e.g., instance variables, methods and properties) in one source file conflict with those in other source files, compilation errors will occur.

Error-Prevention Tip 10.1

When combining all partial classes, at least one class declaration must have a `Partial` *modifier. Otherwise, a compilation error occurs.*

Most of the classes you have seen to this point are small. In real applications, classes can grow to be quite large and might be developed by a team of programmers. Partial classes provide a convenient way to split a large class into small, manageable pieces. With partial classes, several developers can work on the same class at once. Partial classes can also be used to hide auto-generated code in a separate file.

10.8 Composition

A class can have references to objects of other classes as members. This is called composition and is sometimes referred to as a *has-a* relationship. For example, an object of class `AlarmClock` needs to know the current time and the time when it is supposed to sound its alarm, so it's reasonable to include two references to `Time` objects in an `AlarmClock` object.

Software Engineering Observation 10.5

One form of software reuse is composition, in which a class has as members references to objects of other classes.

Our example of composition contains two classes—`Day` (Fig. 10.7) and `Employee` (Fig. 10.8)—and module `CompositionTest` (Fig. 10.9) to demonstrate them. Class `Day` (Fig. 10.7) encapsulates information relating to a specific date. Lines 4–6 declare `Integers` `monthValue`, `dayValue` and `yearValue`. Lines 10–15 declare the constructor, which receives as parameters values for the month, day and year, then assigns these values to the class's properties to ensure that the parameter values are valid.

```
1  ' Fig. 10.7: Day.vb
2  ' Day class encapsulates day, month and year information.
3  Class Day
4     Private monthValue As Integer ' 1-12
5     Private dayValue As Integer ' 1-31 based on month
6     Private yearValue As Integer ' any year (could validate)
7
8     ' constructor confirms proper value for month, then calls
9     ' method CheckDay to confirm proper value for day
10    Public Sub New(ByVal mm As Integer, _
11       ByVal dd As Integer, ByVal yy As Integer)
12
13       Month = mm
14       Year = yy
15       Day = dd
16    End Sub ' New
17
18    ' property Month
19    Public Property Month() As Integer
20       Get
21          Return monthValue
22       End Get
23
24       Set(ByVal mm As Integer)
25          ' ensure month value is valid (in the range 1-12)
26          If (mm > 0 AndAlso mm <= 12) Then
27             monthValue = mm
28          Else
29             monthValue = 1 ' to ensure consistent state
```

Fig. 10.7 | `Day` class encapsulates day, month and year information. (Part 1 of 3.)

```

            ' inform user of error
            Console.WriteLine("Invalid month (" & mm & _
               ") set to 1.")
         End If
      End Set
   End Property ' Month

   ' property Day
   Public Property Day() As Integer
      Get
         Return dayValue
      End Get

      Set(ByVal dd As Integer)
         dayValue = CheckDay(dd) ' validate dd
      End Set
   End Property ' Day

   ' property Year
   Public Property Year() As Integer
      Get
         Return yearValue
      End Get

      Set(ByVal yy As Integer)
         yearValue = yy
      End Set
   End Property ' Year

   ' confirm proper day value based on month and year
   Private Function CheckDay(ByVal testDayValue As Integer) As Integer
      Dim daysPerMonth() As Integer = _
         {0, 31, 28, 31, 30, 31, 30, 31, 31, 30, 31, 30, 31}

      ' validate day
      If (testDayValue > 0 AndAlso _
         testDayValue <= daysPerMonth(Month)) Then
         Return testDayValue
      End If

      ' check for leap year in February
      If (Month = 2 AndAlso testDayValue = 29 AndAlso _
         ((Year Mod 400 = 0) OrElse _
         (Year Mod 4 = 0 AndAlso Year Mod 100 <> 0))) Then
         Return testDayValue
      End If

      ' inform user of error
      Console.WriteLine("Invalid day (" & testDayValue & ") set to 1. ")
      Return 1 ' leave object in consistent state
   End Function ' CheckDay

```

Fig. 10.7 | Day class encapsulates day, month and year information. (Part 2 of 3.)

```
83      ' create string containing month/day/year format
84      Public Overrides Function ToString() As String
85         Return (Month & "/" & Day & "/" & Year)
86      End Function ' ToString
87   End Class ' Day
```

Fig. 10.7 | Day class encapsulates day, month and year information. (Part 3 of 3.)

The `Set` accessor (lines 24–35) of property `Month` ensures that the month value is in the range 1–12. The `Set` accessor (lines 44–46) of property `Day` invokes utility function `CheckDay` to validate the day value. The `Year` property does not perform the validation of the year value. We assume that the `Year` is a valid four-digit year, such as 2008; however, we could have validated the `year` as well.

Function `CheckDay` (lines 61–81) validates whether the `day` is correct based on the current `Month` and `Year`. Lines 66–69 determine whether the day is a valid day for the particular month. If not, lines 72–76 determine whether the `Month` is February, the day is `29` and the `Year` is a leap year. A year is a leap year if it is divisible by 400 (tested at line 73), or if it is divisible by 4 and not divisible by 100 (tested at line 74). If lines 72–76 do not return a correct value for day, line 80 returns `1` to maintain the date in a consistent state.

Using Class `Day` *in Class* `Employee`

Class `Employee` (Fig. 10.8) holds information relating to an employee's birthday and hire date using instance variables `firstName`, `lastName`, `birthDate` and `hireDate` (lines 4–7). Members `birthDate` and `hireDate` are references to `Day` objects, each of which contains instance variables `month`, `day` and `year`. In this example, class `Employee` is *composed of* two references to `Day` objects. The `Employee` constructor (lines 10–23) takes eight arguments (`first`, `last`, `birthMonth`, `birthDay`, `birthYear`, `hireMonth`, `hireDay` and `hireYear`). Line 19 passes arguments `birthMonth`, `birthDay` and `birthYear` to the `Day` constructor to create the `birthDate` object. Similarly, line 22 passes arguments `hireMonth`, `hireDay` and `hireYear` to the `Day` constructor to create the `hireDate` object.

```
1    ' Fig. 10.8: Employee.vb
2    ' Employee class encapsulates employee name, birthday and hire date.
3    Class Employee
4       Private firstName As String
5       Private lastName As String
6       Private birthDate As Day ' member object reference
7       Private hireDate As Day ' member object reference
8
9       ' Employee constructor
10      Public Sub New(ByVal first As String, ByVal last As String, _
11         ByVal birthMonth As Integer, ByVal birthDay As Integer, _
12         ByVal birthYear As Integer, ByVal hireMonth As Integer, _
13         ByVal hireDay As Integer, ByVal hireYear As Integer)
14
15         firstName = first
16         lastName = last
```

Fig. 10.8 | `Employee` class encapsulates employee name, birthday and hire date. (Part 1 of 2.)

```

      ' create Day instance for employee birthday
      birthDate = New Day(birthMonth, birthDay, birthYear)

      ' create Day instance for employee hire date
      hireDate = New Day(hireMonth, hireDay, hireYear)
   End Sub ' New

   ' return employee information as String
   Public Overrides Function ToString() As String
      Return (lastName & ", " & firstName & " Hired: " _
         & hireDate.ToString() & " Birthday: " & birthDate.ToString())
   End Function ' ToString
End Class ' Employee
```

Fig. 10.8 | `Employee` class encapsulates employee name, birthday and hire date. (Part 2 of 2.)

Testing Class `Employee`

Module `CompositionTest` (Fig. 10.9) contains `Main`, which tests the classes in Figs. 10.7–10.8. Lines 5–6 instantiate an `Employee` object (`"Bob Blue"` with birthday `7/24/1949` and hire date `3/12/1988`), and line 7 implicitly calls class `Employee`'s `ToString` method and displays the `Employee` information to the user.

```
1  ' Fig. 10.9: CompositionTest.vb
2  ' Demonstrate an object with member object reference.
3  Module CompositionTest
4     Sub Main()
5        Dim employee As New Employee( _
6           "Bob", "Blue", 7, 24, 1949, 3, 12, 1988)
7        Console.WriteLine(employee)
8     End Sub ' Main
9  End Module ' CompositionTest
```

```
Blue, Bob Hired: 3/12/1988 Birthday: 7/24/1949
```

Fig. 10.9 | Demonstrate an object with member object reference.

10.9 Using Me to Access the Current Object

Every object of a class shares the class's method declarations. We have seen that an object's methods can manipulate the object's data. But how do methods know which object's instance variables to manipulate? Every object has access to itself through a reference called `Me` (a Visual Basic keyword). On every method call, the compiler passes an object's `Me` reference as an implicit argument to each of the object's non-`Shared` methods. The `Me` reference can then be used to access a particular object's members implicitly or explicitly. (Section 10.11 introduces `Shared` class members and explains why the `Me` reference is *not* implicitly passed to `Shared` methods.)

Class `Time` (Fig. 10.10) defines `Private` instance variables `hour`, `minute` and `second` (lines 4–6). The constructor (lines 9–14) receives three `Integer` arguments to initialize a

`Time` object. For this example, we use parameter names (lines 9–10) that are identical to the class's instance-variable names (lines 4–6). When a method has a parameter or local variable with the same name as one of the class's instance variables, the instance variable is shadowed (hidden) in the method's scope. However, the method can use the `Me` reference to refer explicitly to shadowed instance variables. Lines 11–13 of Fig. 10.10 demonstrate this feature.

Method `BuildString` (lines 17–20) returns a `String` created by a statement that uses the `Me` reference first explicitly, then implicitly. Line 18 uses the `Me` reference explicitly to call method `ToUniversalString`, whereas line 19 calls the same method using the `Me` reference implicitly. Note that both lines generate identical outputs.

Error-Prevention Tip 10.2

For a method in which a parameter has the same name as an instance variable, use reference `Me` *to access the instance variable explicitly; otherwise, the method parameter is referenced.*

Error-Prevention Tip 10.3

Avoid parameter names that conflict with instance-variable names to prevent subtle, hard-to-find bugs.

Module `MeTest` (Fig. 10.11) demonstrates the `Me` reference. Line 5 instantiates a `Time` object. Line 6 invokes method `BuildString`, then displays the results to the user.

```
1  ' Fig. 10.10: Time.vb
2  ' Class using the Me reference.
3  Class Time
4     Private hour As Integer
5     Private minute As Integer
6     Private second As Integer
7
8     ' Time constructor
9     Public Sub New(ByVal hour As Integer, _
10       ByVal minute As Integer, ByVal second As Integer)
11       Me.hour = hour ' set instance variable to parameter
12       Me.minute = minute ' set instance variable to parameter
13       Me.second = second ' set instance variable to parameter
14    End Sub ' New
15
16    ' create String using Me explicitly, then implicitly
17    Public Function BuildString() As String
18       Return "Me.ToUniversalString(): " & Me.ToUniversalString() & _
19          vbNewLine & "ToUniversalString(): " & ToUniversalString()
20    End Function ' BuildString
21
22    ' convert to String in universal-time format
23    Public Function ToUniversalString() As String
24       Return String.Format("{0:D2}:{1:D2}:{2:D2}", hour, minute, second)
25    End Function ' ToUniversalString
26 End Class ' Time
```

Fig. 10.10 | Class using the `Me` reference.

```
' Fig. 10.11: MeTest.vb
' Me reference demonstration.
Module MeTest
   Sub Main()
      Dim time As New Time(12, 30, 19)
      Console.WriteLine(time.BuildString())
   End Sub ' Main
End Module ' MeTest
```

```
Me.ToUniversalString(): 12:30:19
ToUniversalString(): 12:30:19
```

Fig. 10.11 | Me reference demonstration.

10.10 Garbage Collection

Every object you create uses various system resources, including the memory that holds the object itself. We need a disciplined way to give resources back to the system when they are no longer needed, so as to avoid "resource leaks." The Common Language Runtime (CLR) performs automatic garbage collection to reclaim the memory occupied by objects that are no longer in use. When there are no more references to an object, the object is marked for garbage collection by the CLR. The memory for such an object can be reclaimed when the runtime executes its garbage collector, which is responsible for retrieving the memory of objects that are no longer used, so that the memory can be used for other objects. Therefore, whereas memory leaks are common in other languages like C and C++ (because memory is not automatically reclaimed in those languages), they are much less likely in Visual Basic (but some can still happen in subtle ways). Resources like memory that are allocated and reclaimed by the CLR are known as managed resources.

Other types of resource leaks can occur. For example, an application may open a file on disk to modify the file's contents. If the application does not close the file, no other application may be allowed to use the file until the application that opened the file finishes. An application that no longer needs a file should close it immediately so that other programs can access the file. Resources like files, network connections and database connections that *you* must manage are known as unmanaged resources (because they are not managed by the CLR). Such resources are typically scarce and should be released as soon as they are no longer needed by a program.

To help prevent resource leaks for unmanaged resources, the garbage collector calls a special method named `Finalize` on each object before it is removed from memory. Recall from Section 10.2 that all classes inherit the methods of class `Object`, one of which is `Finalize`. You will learn more about class `Object` in Chapter 11, Object-Oriented Programming: Inheritance. The `Finalize` method is called by the garbage collector to perform termination housekeeping on an object (such as releasing unmanaged resources used by the object) just before the garbage collector reclaims the object's memory. Method `Finalize` does not take parameters and does not return a value. In Section 10.11, we demonstrate a situation in which method `Finalize` is called by the garbage collector.

Unfortunately, `Finalize` is not ideal for releasing unmanaged resources because the garbage collector is unpredictable—it is not guaranteed to execute at a specified time. In some cases the garbage collector may *never* execute before a program terminates. Thus, it is unclear if, or when, method `Finalize` will be called. Unmanaged resources might not be released for a long time, which would prevent these scarce resources from being used by other programs. For this reason, most programmers should avoid method `Finalize`.

Visual Basic also provides the `Using` statement, which specifies a list of used resources and disposes them at the end of the block, indicated by the `End Using` keywords. This statement ensures the disposal of its resources regardless of how the code in the block is terminated. `Using` statements are discussed in Chapter 13.

In Chapter 12, we discuss interfaces in more detail. As will be explained, an interface describes methods that a class must implement. The Framework Class Library provides interface `IDisposable`, which contains a method named `Dispose` that a client can invoke to immediately release the resources used by an object. When a program creates an object of a class that implements interface `IDisposable`, the client should call that object's `Dispose` method as soon as the client is done using the object. This ensures that the resources used by the object are released promptly so they can be reused. At `msdn.microsoft.com/en-us/events/cc539947.aspx` you can link to a Microsoft Developer Network (MSDN) TV interview describing `IDisposable` in the context of C#. If you study the video carefully, you'll be able to understand the underlying principles.

Software Engineering Observation 10.6

A class that uses unmanaged resources, such as files on disk, should provide a method that clients of the class can call explicitly to release the resources. Many Visual Basic library classes provide `Close` *or* `Dispose` *methods for this purpose. If you write a class using classes that implement* `IDisposable`*, your class should implement* `IDisposable` *as well.*

10.11 Shared Class Members

Each object has its own copy of the instance variables of its class. In certain cases, all objects of a class should share only one copy of a particular variable. Only one copy of a **Shared class variable** exists in memory, no matter how many objects of the class have been instantiated. A `Shared` class variable represents **classwide information**—all class objects share the same variable. The declaration of such a member begins with the keyword `Shared`.

Let us use a video game example to explain the need for `Shared` classwide data. Suppose we have a video game in which `Martians` attack other space creatures. A `Martian` tends to be brave and willing to attack when it is aware that at least four other `Martians` are present. If fewer than five `Martians` are present, a `Martian` becomes cowardly. For this reason, each `Martian` must know the `martianCount`. We could endow class `Martian` with a `martianCount` instance variable. If we were to do this, then every `Martian` would have a separate copy of the instance variable, and every time we create a `Martian`, we would have to update the instance variable `martianCount` in every `Martian`. The redundant copies waste space, and updating those copies is time consuming. Worse yet, while we are updating the individual copies of `martianCount`, there will be periods of time during which some of these copies have not yet been updated, so we could have inconsistent bravery behavior among the `Martians`. Instead, we declare `martianCount` to be `Shared` so that it is classwide data. Each `Martian` can then see the `martianCount` as if it were instance data of that `Martian`, but Visual Basic maintains only one copy of the `Shared martianCount` to save space. We also save time, in that the `Martian` constructor increments only the `Shared martianCount`—there is only one copy, so we do not have to increment separate copies of `martianCount` for each `Martian` object. This also prevents inconsistent bravery behavior among the `Martians`.

`Shared` class members have class scope. A class's `Public Shared` members can be accessed through the class name using the dot separator (e.g., *className*`.`*sharedMemberName*). A class's `Private Shared` class members can be accessed by clients only indirectly through non-`Private` methods of the class. `Shared` class members are available as soon as the class is loaded into memory at execution time; like other variables with class scope, they exist for the duration of program execution, even when no objects of that class exist. To allow clients to access a `Private Shared` class member when no objects of the class exist, you must provide a non-`Private Shared` method or property.

Unlike non-`Shared` methods, a `Shared` method has no `Me` reference, because `Shared` class members exist independently of any class objects and even when there are no objects of that class. So a `Shared` method cannot access non-`Shared` class members.

Common Programming Error 10.4

Using the `Me` reference in a `Shared` method or `Shared` property is a compilation error.

Shared Constructors

When `Shared` variables require more complex initialization than can be accomplished in a `Shared` variable declaration, you can create a **`Shared` constructor** to initialize them. A `Shared` constructor is declared like an instance constructor, but is preceded by the `Shared` modifier and can be used only to initialize `Shared` variables. A `Shared` constructor is implicitly `Public`, must be declared with no parameters, cannot call other constructors of the class and is guaranteed to execute before a program creates any objects of the class or accesses any `Shared` class members. A class can have both a `Shared` constructor and a non-`Shared` parameterless constructor.

Common Programming Error 10.5

Explicitly declaring a `Shared` constructor `Public` is a compilation error, because a `Shared` constructor is `Public` implicitly.

Class `Employee` with `Shared` Variables

Class `Employee` (Fig. 10.12) demonstrates a `Private Shared` class variable and a `Public Shared Property`. The `Shared` class variable `countValue` is initialized to zero by default (line 6). It maintains a count of the number of `Employee` objects that have been instantiated and currently reside in memory, including objects that have already been marked for garbage collection but have not yet been reclaimed by the garbage collector.

When objects of class `Employee` exist, `Shared` member `countValue` can be used in any method of an `Employee` object—in this example, the constructor (lines 9–15) increments `countValue` (line 12) and method `Finalize` (lines 18–23) decrements `countValue` (line 19). (Note that method `Finalize` is declared using keywords `Protected` and `Overrides`—method `Finalize`'s header must contain these keywords, which we discuss in Chapters 11–12.) If no objects of class `Employee` exist, member `countValue` can be referenced through a call to `Property Count` (lines 40–44)—this `Property` is `Shared`, and therefore we do not have to instantiate an `Employee` object to call the `Get` method of the `Property`. Also, by declaring property `Count` as `ReadOnly`, we prevent clients from

```
' Fig. 10.12: Employee.vb
' Employee class objects share a Shared variable and property.
Class Employee
   Private firstNameValue As String ' employee first name
   Private lastNameValue As String ' employee last name
   Private Shared countValue As Integer ' Employee objects in memory

   ' Employee constructor
   Public Sub New(ByVal first As String, ByVal last As String)
      firstNameValue = first
      lastNameValue = last
      countValue += 1 ' increment shared count of employees
      Console.WriteLine("Employee object constructor for " & _
         firstNameValue & " " & lastNameValue)
   End Sub ' New

   ' finalizer method decrements Shared count of employees
   Protected Overrides Sub Finalize()
      countValue -= 1 ' decrement countValue
      Console.WriteLine("Employee object finalizer for " & _
         firstNameValue & " " & lastNameValue & "; count = " & _
         countValue)
   End Sub ' Finalize

   ' return first name
   Public ReadOnly Property FirstName() As String
      Get
         Return firstNameValue
      End Get
   End Property ' FirstName

   ' return last name
   Public ReadOnly Property LastName() As String
      Get
         Return lastNameValue
      End Get
   End Property ' LastName

   ' property Count
   Public Shared ReadOnly Property Count() As Integer
      Get
         Return countValue
      End Get
   End Property ' Count
End Class ' Employee
```

Fig. 10.12 | Employee class objects share a Shared variable and property.

changing the value of countValue directly, thus ensuring that clients can change countValue's value only under the tight control of class Employee's constructors and finalizer.

*Testing **Shared** Variables*

Module SharedTest (Fig. 10.13) demonstrates the Shared members of Fig. 10.12. Lines 5–6 use the ReadOnly Shared Property Count of class Employee to obtain the current

```
1  ' Fig. 10.13: SharedTest.vb
2  ' Shared class member demonstration.
3  Module SharedTest
4     Sub Main()
5        Console.WriteLine("Employees before instantiation: " & _
6           Employee.Count) ' Count is a Shared property
7
8        Dim employee1 As New Employee("Susan", "Baker") ' call constructor
9        Dim employee2 As New Employee("Bob", "Blue") ' call constructor
10
11       ' output number of employees after instantiation
12       ' (use Shared property)
13       Console.WriteLine(vbNewLine & "Employees after instantiation " & _
14          "(via Employee.Count): " & Employee.Count)
15
16       ' display names of first and second employees (using properties)
17       Console.WriteLine(vbNewLine & "Display names of employees " & _
18          "(using properties)" & vbNewLine & "Employee 1: " & _
19          employee1.FirstName & " " & employee1.LastName & vbNewLine & _
20          "Employee 2: " & employee2.FirstName & " " & _
21          employee2.LastName & vbNewLine)
22
23       Console.WriteLine("Marking employees for garbage collection")
24       employee1 = Nothing ' mark employee1 for garbage collection
25       employee2 = Nothing ' mark employee2 for garbage collection
26
27       Console.WriteLine()
28       Console.WriteLine("Explicitly invoking the garbage collector")
29       System.GC.Collect() ' request garbage collection
30    End Sub ' Main
31 End Module ' SharedTest
```

```
Employees before instantiation: 0
Employee object constructor for Susan Baker
Employee object constructor for Bob Blue

Employees after instantiation (via Employee.Count): 2

Display names of employees (using properties)
Employee 1: Susan Baker
Employee 2: Bob Blue

Marking employees for garbage collection

Explicitly invoking the garbage collector
Employee object finalizer for Bob Blue; count = 1
Employee object finalizer for Susan Baker; count = 0
```

Fig. 10.13 | Shared class member demonstration.

value of countValue. No Employee objects exist yet. Since Count is a Shared property, we must access Count using the class name Employee. Lines 8–9 then instantiate two Employee objects, causing countValue to be incremented by 2. Lines 13–14 print the countValue by using ReadOnly Shared Property Count. Lines 17–21 display the names of the employees. Lines 24–25 set these objects' references to Nothing, so that employee1 and employee2 no longer refer to the Employee objects. This "marks" the objects for garbage collection, because there are no more references to these objects in the program.

Common Programming Error 10.6

A compilation error occurs if a Shared method calls an instance (non-Shared) method in the same class by using only the name of the method. Similarly, a compilation error occurs if a Shared method attempts to access an instance variable in the same class by using only the name of the variable.

Normally, the garbage collector is not invoked directly by the user. Either the garbage collector reclaims the memory for objects when it deems garbage collection is appropriate, or the operating system recovers the unneeded memory when the program terminates. Line 29 uses Public Shared method Collect from class GC (namespace System) to request that the garbage collector execute. Before the garbage collector releases the memory occupied by the two Employee objects, it invokes method Finalize for each Employee object, which decrements the countValue value by a total of 2.

The last two lines of the output show that the Employee object for Bob Blue was finalized before the Employee object for Susan Baker. However, the output of this program on your system could differ. The garbage collector is not guaranteed to collect objects in a specific order, nor is it guaranteed to run at all before the program terminates execution.

10.12 Const and ReadOnly Members

Visual Basic allows you to create constants—members whose values cannot change during program execution. To create a constant in a class, declare an identifier as either Const or ReadOnly. An identifier declared as Const must be initialized in its declaration; an identifier declared as ReadOnly can be initialized either in its declaration or in the class constructor. In addition, properties can also be set as read-only. A property with only a Get accessor is called a read-only property and must be declared using keyword ReadOnly; a property with only a Set accessor is called a write-only property and must be declared using keyword WriteOnly. Write-only properties are rarely used.

Const values must be initialized at compile time, whereas ReadOnly values are not initialized until runtime. Neither can be modified once initialized.

Error-Prevention Tip 10.4

If a variable's value should never change, making it a constant prevents it from changing. This helps eliminate errors that might occur if the value of the variable were to change.

Common Programming Error 10.7

Declaring an identifier as Const but failing to initialize it in that declaration is a compilation error.

Common Programming Error 10.8

Assigning a value to a Const member is a compilation error.

Const members must be initialized at compile time; thus, they can be initialized only to constant values, such as integers, string literals, characters and other Const members. Constant members with values that cannot be determined at compile time must be declared ReadOnly. Recall that a ReadOnly member can be assigned a value only once, either when it is declared or within the class's constructor (the Shared constructor for Shared ReadOnly members and a non-Shared constructor for non-Shared ReadOnly members).

Common Programming Error 10.9

Declaring a member as ReadOnly *and attempting to use it before it is initialized is a logic error.*

Common Programming Error 10.10

A Shared ReadOnly *member cannot be initialized in an instance constructor for that class, and a* ReadOnly *member cannot be initialized in a* Shared *constructor for that class. Attempting to define a* ReadOnly *member in an inappropriate constructor is a compilation error.*

Common Programming Error 10.11

Declaring a Const *member as* Shared *is a compilation error, because a* Const *member is* Shared *implicitly.*

Common Programming Error 10.12

Declaring a ReadOnly *member as* Const *is a compilation error, because these two keywords are not allowed to be combined in a variable declaration.*

Class CircleConstants *with* Const *and* ReadOnly *Instance Variables*

Class CircleConstants (Fig. 10.14) demonstrates constants. Line 4 creates constant PI using keyword Const and assigns to PI the Double value 3.14159—an approximation of π. We could have used predefined constant PI of class Math (Math.PI) as the value, but we wanted to demonstrate how you can create your own Const members. The compiler must be able to determine a Const's value to be able to initialize a Const member with that value. The value 3.14159 is acceptable (line 4), but the expression

```
Convert.ToDouble("3.14159")
```

generates a compilation error if used in place of that value. Although this expression uses a constant value (String literal "3.14159") as an argument and produces the same numer-

```
1  ' Fig. 10.14: CircleConstants.vb
2  ' Constants used in class CircleConstants.
3  Class CircleConstants
4     Public Const PI As Double = 3.14159 ' PI is a Const member
5     Public ReadOnly RADIUS As Integer ' RADIUS is uninitialized constant
6
7     ' constructor of class CircleConstants
8     Public Sub New(ByVal radiusValue As Integer)
9        RADIUS = radiusValue ' initialize ReadOnly constant
10    End Sub ' New
11 End Class ' CircleConstants
```

Fig. 10.14 | Constants used in class CircleConstants.

ic value, a compilation error occurs, because the compiler cannot evaluate executable code (such as a method call). This restriction is lifted with ReadOnly members, which are initialized at runtime. Note that line 9 assigns the value of the constructor parameter radiusValue to ReadOnly member RADIUS at runtime. We could also have used a method call, such as Convert.ToInt32, to assign a value to this ReadOnly member.

Using **Const** *and* **ReadOnly**

Module ConstAndReadOnly (Fig. 10.15) demonstrates the Const and ReadOnly values. Line 5 creates a Random object that is used in line 8 to generate a random Integer in the range 1–20 that corresponds to a circle's radius. This enables each program execution to produce different output. The random value is passed to the CircleConstants constructor to initialize a CircleConstants object. Lines 11–13 access the ReadOnly member RADIUS through a reference to object circle, and compute and display the circle's circumference. This calculation employs the Public Const member PI, which we access in line 13 through its class name CircleConstants. Recall that Const members are implicitly Shared; thus we can access a Const member with its class name followed by the dot separator even when no objects of the class are present.

```
1  ' Fig. 10.15: ConstAndReadOnly.vb
2  ' Demonstrates Const and ReadOnly members.
3  Module ConstAndReadOnly
4     Sub Main()
5        Dim random As New Random() ' create Random object
6
7        ' create CircleConstants object with random radius
8        Dim circle As New CircleConstants(random.Next(1, 20))
9
10       ' calculate the circle's circumference
11       Console.WriteLine("Radius = " & circle.RADIUS & vbNewLine & _
12          "Circumference = " & String.Format("{0:F3}", _
13          2 * CircleConstants.PI * circle.RADIUS))
14    End Sub ' Main
15 End Module ' ConstAndReadOnly
```

```
Radius = 9
Circumference = 56.549
```

Fig. 10.15 | Demonstrates Const and ReadOnly members.

10.13 Object Browser

Now we present a powerful feature that Visual Studio provides to facilitate the design of object-oriented applications—the **Object Browser**. The **Object Browser** lists all the libraries that are available to the application, including the Framework Class Library classes and programmer-defined classes. Developers use the **Object Browser** to learn about the functionality provided by specific classes. To open the **Object Browser**, right click any Visual Basic class or method in the code editor and select **Go To Definition** (Figs. 10.16–10.17). Note that if the source code for the selected type (i.e., for a custom class) is available, the source code opens rather than the **Object Browser**.

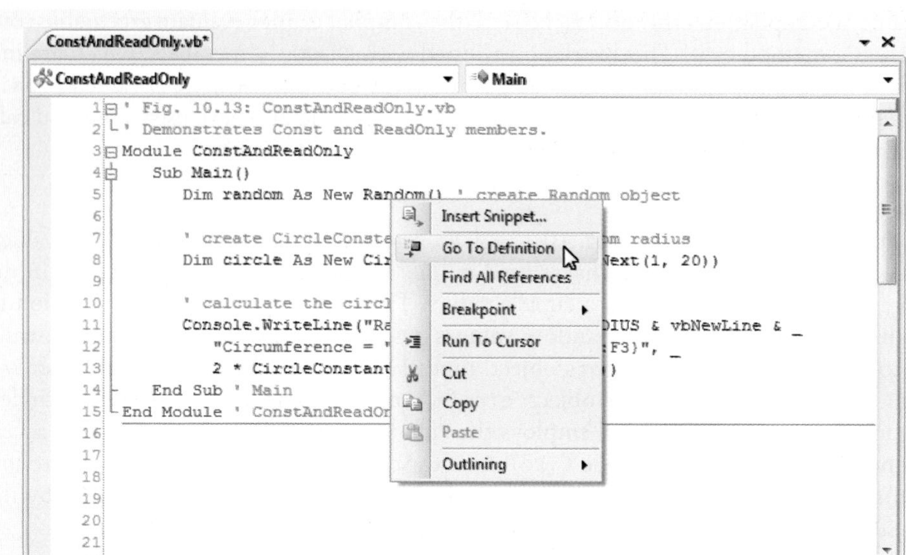

Fig. 10.16 | Invoking the **Object Browser** by right clicking class `Random` and selecting **Go To Definition**.

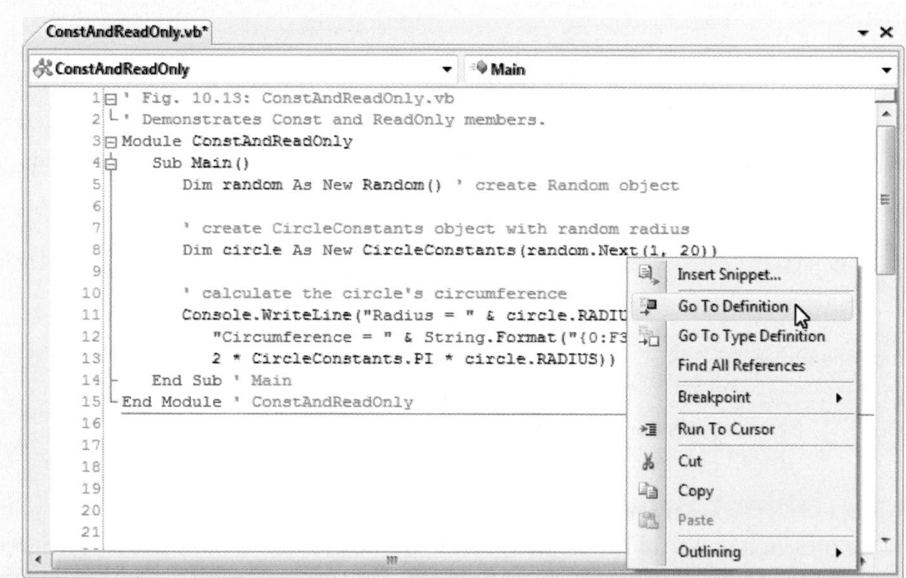

Fig. 10.17 | Invoking the **Object Browser** by right clicking method `Next` and selecting **Go To Definition**.

Figure 10.18 shows the **Object Browser** after the user selects class `Random` in Fig. 10.16. Figure 10.19 shows the **Object Browser** after the user selects method `Next` of class `Random` in Fig. 10.17. The **Object Browser** lists all non-`Private` members provided by class `Random` in the upper-right portion of the window, which offers developers instant access to information regarding the services of the selected class. The menu in Fig. 10.17 also has a **Go To Type Definition** option that allows you to view the selected variable's type definition in the **Object Browser**. This option also works with methods that have a return type. You can also view the details of method `Next` by clicking the method name in the upper-right portion of the windows in Figure 10.18.

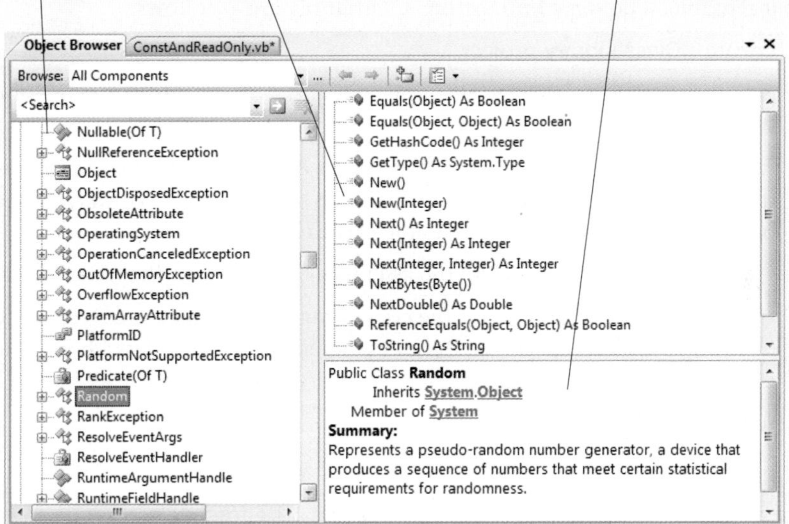

Fig. 10.18 | Object Browser when user selects class `Random` from the code editor.

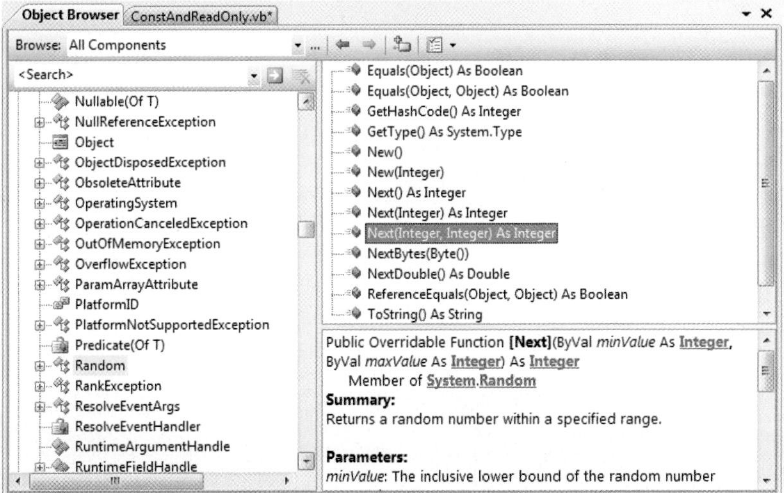

Fig. 10.19 | Object Browser for class `Random`'s `Next` method.

10.14 Time Class Case Study: Creating Class Libraries

We've seen that classes from preexisting libraries, such as .NET's Framework Class Library, can be imported into applications. Each .NET Framework class belongs to a namespace that contains a group of related classes. Class libraries and namespaces facilitate software reuse by enabling applications to add classes from other namespaces. This section demonstrates how to create your own class libraries for reuse.

Making a Class Reusable

Before a class can be imported into multiple applications, it must be placed in an assembly to make it reusable. The steps for creating an assembly are as follows:

1. Create a **Class Library** project.
2. Add the reusable class(es) to the project. [*Note:* You can also create reusable classes from scratch.]
3. Ensure that each reusable class is declared `Public`—only `Public` classes can be imported for use in other projects; non-`Public` classes are typically placed in a library to support the `Public` reusable classes in that library.
4. Compile the project to create the assembly that contains the reusable class(es).
5. In an application that requires the class library's namespace, add a reference to the class library. Then specify an `Imports` statement for the class library and use its class(es) in your application.

Next, we present the five steps in detail.

Step 1: Creating a **Class Library** *Project*

In this example, we'd like to place class `Time` of Fig. 10.1 into a class library to make it a reusable class. To create a class library in Visual Basic 2008 Express, select **File > New Project...** and choose **Class Library** from the list of templates, as shown in Fig. 10.20. Name your project `TimeLibrary`, then click **OK**.

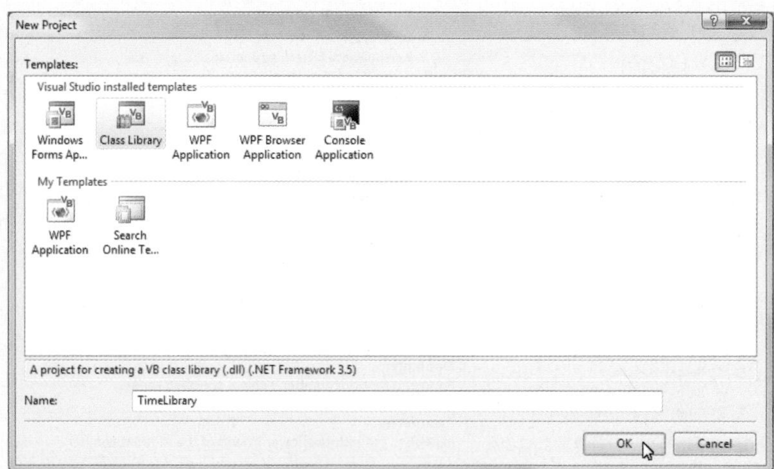

Fig. 10.20 | Creating a **Class Library** Project.

When you create a **Class Library** project, Visual Basic automatically includes the file `Class1.vb` in the project. You can modify the `Public` class in this file to create a reusable class. However, we'll be using the file from the `Time` class in Fig. 10.1, so you can select `Class1.vb` in the **Solution Explorer** and press *Delete* to remove it from the project.

Step 2: Adding Class `Time` to the Project

Next, you must add the file that contains class `Time` to the project. Right click **TimeLibrary** in the **Solution Explorer**. In the menu that appears, select **Add > Existing Item...** to display the **Add Existing Item** dialog box. Locate the `Time.vb` file from Fig. 10.1, select it and click the **Add** button to add the file to this **Class Library** project. [*Note:* We assume that you downloaded the book's examples and placed them on your `C:\` drive. If so, the file is located in the directory `C:\examples\ch10\Fig10_01_02\TimeTest\`.]

Step 3: Making Class `Time Public`

Recall that only `Public` classes can be imported for use in other projects. Thus, you must add the `Public` access modifier to class `Time` to make it reusable. The new version of class `Time` is shown in Fig. 10.21. Notice that line 3 now contains `Public`.

```
1  ' Fig. 10.21: Time.vb
2  ' Creating reusable class Time.
3  Public Class Time
4     Inherits Object ' if not specified, compiler includes it implicitly
5
6     ' declare Integer instance variables for the hour, minute and second
7     Private hourValue As Integer ' 0 - 23
8     Private minuteValue As Integer ' 0 - 59
9     Private secondValue As Integer ' 0 - 59
10
11    ' Time constructor initializes instance variables
12    ' when a Time object is created
13    Public Sub New()
14       SetTime(12, 0, 0) ' initialize hour to noon; minute, second to 0
15    End Sub ' New
16
17    ' set a new time value using universal time, check validity of the
18    ' data, set invalid hour to noon, set invalid minute, second to zero
19    Public Sub SetTime(ByVal hh As Integer, _
20       ByVal mm As Integer, ByVal ss As Integer)
21       Hour = hh ' set hourValue using Hour property
22       Minute = mm ' set minuteValue using Minute property
23       Second = ss ' set secondValue using Second property
24    End Sub ' SetTime
25
26    ' property Hour
27    Public Property Hour() As Integer
28       Get ' return hourValue
29          Return hourValue
30       End Get
31
```

Fig. 10.21 | Creating reusable class `Time`. (Part 1 of 3.)

```
      Set(ByVal value As Integer) ' set hourValue
         If (value >= 0 AndAlso value < 24) Then ' in range 0-23
            hourValue = value ' value is valid
         Else ' value is invalid
            hourValue = 12 ' set to default of noon
         End If
      End Set
   End Property ' Hour

   ' property Minute
   Public Property Minute() As Integer
      Get ' return minuteValue
         Return minuteValue
      End Get

      Set(ByVal value As Integer) ' set minuteValue
         If (value >= 0 AndAlso value < 60) Then ' in range 0-59
            minuteValue = value ' value is valid
         Else ' value is invalid
            minuteValue = 0 ' set to default of 0
         End If
      End Set
   End Property ' Minute

   ' property Second
   Public Property Second() As Integer
      Get ' return secondValue
         Return secondValue
      End Get

      Set(ByVal value As Integer) ' set secondValue
         If (value >= 0 AndAlso value < 60) Then ' in range 0-59
            secondValue = value ' value is valid
         Else ' value is invalid
            secondValue = 0 ' set to default of 0
         End If
      End Set
   End Property ' Second

   ' convert Time to a String in universal-time (24-hour clock) format
   Public Function ToUniversalString() As String
      Return String.Format("{0}:{1:D2}:{2:D2}", Hour, Minute, Second)
   End Function ' ToUniversalString

   ' convert Time to a String in standard-time (12-hour clock) format
   Public Overrides Function ToString() As String
      Dim suffix As String ' AM or PM suffix
      Dim standardHour As Integer ' a standard hour in the range 1-12

      ' determine whether the 12-hour clock suffix should be AM or PM
      If Hour < 12 Then
         suffix = "AM"
```

Fig. 10.21 | Creating reusable class `Time`. (Part 2 of 3.)

```
         Else
            suffix = "PM"
         End If

         ' convert hour from universal-time format to standard-time format
         If (Hour = 12 OrElse Hour = 0) Then
            standardHour = 12
         Else
            standardHour = Hour Mod 12 ' 1 through 11, AM or PM
         End If

         Return String.Format("{0}:{1:D2}:{2:D2} {3}", _
            standardHour, Minute, Second, suffix)
      End Function ' ToString
   End Class ' Time
```

Fig. 10.21 | Creating reusable class `Time`. (Part 3 of 3.)

Step 4: Building the `TimeLibrary`

Save your project and remember where you saved it on your system, so you can locate the `TimeLibrary.dll` file in the next step. To create the assembly containing the reusable class, select **Build > Build TimeLibrary**. When you build a **Class Library** project, the compiler creates a dynamic link library (DLL)—an assembly that you can reference from other applications. This DLL is located in the project's `bin\Release` directory. By default, the file name is the class library's name followed by the `.dll` extension—`TimeLibrary.dll` in this example. The assembly file contains the reusable class `Time`, which can now be imported into other projects. Note that class libraries are not executable, so if you attempt to execute the class library by selecting **Debug > Start**, you'll receive an error message.

Step 5: Create an Application, Add a Reference to the Class Library's Assembly and Import the Library's Namespace

Once the class is compiled and stored in an assembly, it can be imported into a program for reuse. Module `TimeLibraryTest` (Fig. 10.22) uses class `Time` from the assembly `TimeLibrary.dll` to create a `Time` object, set its time and display the time.

```
' Fig. 9.20: TimeLibraryTest.vb
' Module TimeLibraryTest references TimeLibrary.dll.
Imports TimeLibrary ' import namespace TimeLibrary

Module TimeLibraryTest
   Sub Main()
      Dim time As New Time() ' call Time constructor

      Console.WriteLine("The initial universal time is: " & _
         time.ToUniversalString() & vbNewLine & _
         "The initial standard time is: " & time.ToString())

      time.SetTime(13, 27, 6) ' set time with valid settings
```

Fig. 10.22 | Module `TimeLibraryTest` references `TimeLibrary.dll`. (Part 1 of 2.)

```
        Console.WriteLine(vbNewLine & "Universal time after setTime is: " _
           & time.ToUniversalString() & vbNewLine & _
           "Standard time after setTime is: " & time.ToString())

        time.SetTime(99, 99, 99) ' set time with invalid settings
        Console.WriteLine(vbNewLine & _
           "After attempting invalid settings: " & vbNewLine & _
           "Universal time: " & time.ToUniversalString() & _
           vbNewLine & "Standard time: " & time.ToString())
    End Sub ' Main
 End Module ' TimeLibraryTest
```

```
The initial universal time is: 12:00:00
The initial standard time is: 12:00:00 PM

Universal time after setTime is: 13:27:06
Standard time after setTime is: 1:27:06 PM

After attempting invalid settings:
Universal time: 12:00:00
Standard time: 12:00:00 PM
```

Fig. 10.22 | Module `TimeLibraryTest` references `TimeLibrary.dll`. (Part 2 of 2.)

When you create a **Class Library** project, the classes in that library are automatically placed in a namespace that has the same name as the library itself. Thus, class `Time` is located in namespace `TimeLibrary`—part of the assembly `TimeLibrary.dll`. Before you can use the `TimeLibrary` namespace classes in the `TimeLibraryTest` project, you must reference its assembly. Select **Project > Add Reference...**. The **Add Reference** dialog that appears contains a list of class libraries from the .NET Framework. Some class libraries, like the one containing the `System` namespace, are so common that they are added to your application by default. Additional libraries can be selected from this dialog. In the dialog, click the **Browse** tab, then locate and select the `TimeLibrary.dll` file (located in the `bin\Release` directory of the `TimeLibrary` project we created in *Steps 1–4*) as shown in Fig. 10.23. Click **OK** to add the reference to the project.

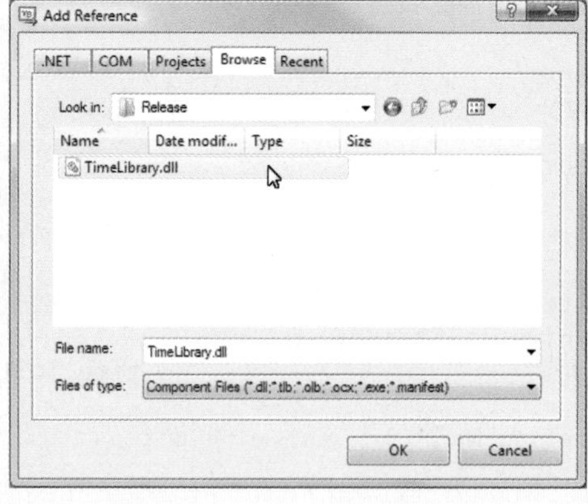

Fig. 10.23 | Adding a Reference.

When developing applications in industry, it's common to have multiple projects in a solution. If some of those projects are class libraries, you can use the **Projects** tab (Fig. 10.23) to locate and add the library references.

After adding the reference, you can use keyword `Imports` followed by the namespace name `TimeLibrary` (line 3) to inform the compiler that you are using classes from this namespace. Module `TimeLibraryTest` and class `Time` are in different namespaces because they are in different projects, so the `Imports` statement at line 3 allows module `TimeLibraryTest` to use class `Time`.

The `Imports` statement at line 3 is not required if you refer to class `Time` with its fully qualified name—`TimeLibrary.Time`—which includes the namespace name and the class name. For example, line 7 could be written as

```
Dim time As New TimeLibrary.Time()
```

You can use this fully qualified name in your programs, or you can import the namespace and use its simple name (the unqualified class name—`Time`). If another namespace also contains a `Time` class, fully qualified class names can be used to distinguish between the two `Time` classes and prevent a name conflict (also called a name collision).

10.15 Time Class Case Study: Extension Methods

In some cases, it is useful to add new functionality to an existing class. However, you cannot modify code for classes in the .NET Framework Class Library or other class libraries that you did not create. In Visual Basic 2008, you can use extension methods to add functionality to an existing class without modifying the class's source code. Many LINQ capabilities are also available as extension methods.

In Section 10.14, you created a `Time` class library. Figure 10.24 uses extension methods and the `TimeLibrary.dll` discussed in Section 10.14 to add functionality to class `Time` without modifying the `Time` class library. The extension method `DisplayTime` (lines 30–34) displays the time in the console window using the `Time` object's `ToString` method. The key new feature of method `DisplayTime` is the attribute `<Extension()>` that precedes the method header (line 30). An attribute specifies additional information about a variable, property, method, class or module. The `<Extension()>` attribute (from the `System.Runtime.CompilerServices` namespace imported in line 4) notifies the compiler that the `DisplayTime` method extends an existing class. The Visual Basic compiler uses this information to inject additional code into the compiled program that enables extension methods to work with existing types. The type of an extension method's first parameter specifies the class that is being extended—extension methods must define at least one parameter. Also, extension methods must be defined in `Modules`, not classes.

```
1  ' Fig. 10.24: TimeLibraryExtension.vb
2  ' Demonstrating extension methods.
3  Imports TimeLibrary ' access the TimeLibrary
4  Imports System.Runtime.CompilerServices ' access Extension attribute
5
6  Module TimeLibraryExtensions
7     Sub Main()
```

Fig. 10.24 | Demonstrating extension methods. (Part 1 of 2.)

```
8         Dim myTime As New Time() ' call Time constructor
9         myTime.SetTime(11, 34, 15) ' set the time to 11:34:15
10
11        ' test the DisplayTime extension method
12        Console.Write("Use the DisplayTime method: ")
13        myTime.DisplayTime()
14
15        ' test the AddHours extension method
16        Console.Write("Add 5 hours to the Time object: ")
17        Dim timeAdded As Time = myTime.AddHours(5) ' add five hours
18        timeAdded.DisplayTime() ' display the new Time object
19
20        ' add hours and display the time in one statement
21        Console.Write("Add 15 hours to the Time object: ")
22        myTime.AddHours(15).DisplayTime() ' add hours and display time
23
24        ' use fully qualified extension-method name to display the time
25        Console.Write("Use fully qualified extension-method name: ")
26        TimeLibraryExtensions.DisplayTime(myTime)
27     End Sub ' Main
28
29     ' display the Time object
30     <Extension()> _
31     Public Sub DisplayTime(ByVal aTime As Time)
32        ' display the time in the console
33        Console.WriteLine(aTime.ToString())
34     End Sub ' DisplayTime
35
36     ' add the specified number of hours to the time
37     ' and return a new Time object
38     <Extension()> _
39     Public Function AddHours(ByVal aTime As Time, _
40        ByVal hours As Integer) As Time
41
42        Dim newTime As New Time() ' create a new Time object
43        newTime.Minute = aTime.Minute ' set the minutes
44        newTime.Second = aTime.Second ' set the seconds
45
46        ' add the specified number of hours to the given time
47        newTime.Hour = (aTime.Hour + hours) Mod 24
48
49        Return newTime ' return the new Time object
50     End Function ' AddHours
51  End Module ' TimeLibraryExtensions
```

```
Use the DisplayTime method: 11:34:15 AM
Add 5 hours to the Time object: 4:34:15 PM
Add 15 hours to the Time object: 2:34:15 AM
Use fully qualified extension-method name: 11:34:15 AM
```

Fig. 10.24 | Demonstrating extension methods. (Part 2 of 2.)

The parameter list for the `DisplayTime` method (line 31) contains a single parameter of type `Time`, indicating that this method extends class `Time`. Line 13 of Fig. 10.24 uses

Time object myTime to call the DisplayTime extension method. Note that line 13 does not provide an argument to the method call. The compiler implicitly passes the object that is used to call the method (myTime in this case) as the extension method's first argument. This allows you to call an extension method as if it were an instance method of the extended class. In fact, *IntelliSense* displays extension methods with the extended class's instance methods (Fig. 10.25). Note the blue down-arrow in the icon to the left of the method name in the *IntelliSense* window—this denotes an extension method. The tool tip shown to the right of the *IntelliSense* window includes the <Extension> attribute to indicate that DisplayTime is an extension method. Also note in the tool tip that the method's signature shows an empty parameter list.

Lines 38–50 of Fig. 10.24 define the AddHours extension method. Again, the method header is preceeded by the <Extension()> attribute (line 38). The first parameter of AddHours is an object of class Time, indicating that the method extends class Time. The second parameter to AddHours is an Integer value specifying the number of hours to add to the time. The AddHours method returns a new Time object with the specified number of hours added. Line 42 creates the new Time object. Lines 43–44 set the new Time's Minute and Second properties using the values of the Time object received as an argument. Line 47 adds the specified number of hours to the value of the original Time object's Hour property, then uses the Mod operator to ensure the values is between 0 and 23. This value is assigned to the new Time object's Hour property. Line 49 returns the new Time object to the caller. Line 17 calls the AddHours extension method to add five hours to the myTime object's hour value. Note that the method call receives one argument—the number of hours to add. Again, the compiler implicitly passes the object that is used to call the method (myTime) as the extension method's first argument. The Time object returned by AddHours is assigned to a local variable (timeAdded) and displayed in the console using the DisplayTime extension method (line 18). Line 22 uses both extension methods (DisplayTime and AddHours) in a single statement to add 15 hours to myTime and display the result in the console. Extension methods, as well as instance methods, allow cascaded method

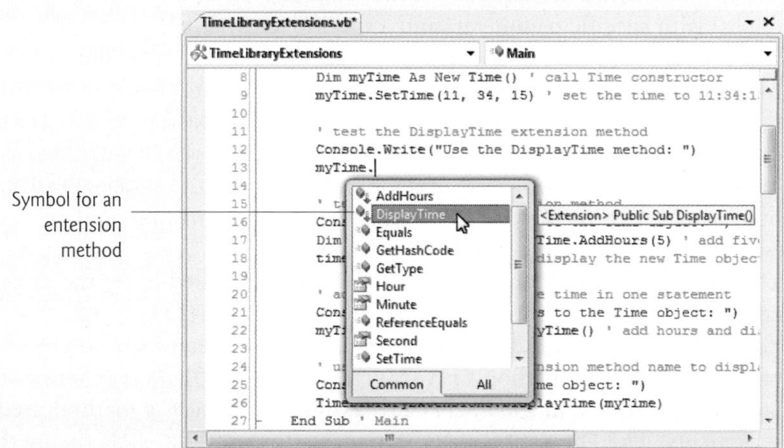

Fig. 10.25 | *IntelliSense* support for extension methods.

calls—that is, invoking multiple methods in the same statement (line 22). The methods are called from left to right. In line 22, the `DisplayTime` method is called on the `Time` object returned by method `AddHours`.

Line 26 calls extension method `DisplayTime` using its fully qualified name—the name of the `Module` in which the extension method is defined (`TimeLibraryExtensions`), followed by the method name (`DisplayTime`) and its argument list. Note in line 26 that the call to `DisplayTime` passes a `Time` object as an argument to the method. When using the fully qualified method name, you must specify an argument for extension method's first parameter. This use of the extension method resembles a call to a `Shared` method.

Extension Method Notes

Be careful when using extension methods to add functionality to pre-existing classes. If the type being extended defines an instance method with the same name as your extension method and a compatible signature, the instance method will shadow the extension method. If a predefined class is later updated to include an instance method that shadows an extension method, the compiler will not report any errors and the extension method would not appear in *IntelliSense*.

10.16 Delegates

A delegate is an object that holds a reference to a method. Delegates allow you to treat methods as data—via delegates, you can assign methods to variables, and pass methods to and from methods. You can also call methods through variables of delegate types. Figure 10.26 uses delegates to customize the functionality of a method that filters an `Integer` array. Lines 37–38 define a delegate type named `NumberPredicate`. A variable of this type can store a reference to any `Function` that takes an `Integer` argument and returns a `Boolean`. A delegate type is declared by preceeding a method header with keyword `Delegate` (placed after any access specifiers, such as `Public` or `Private`). The `Delegate` type declaration includes the method header only—the `Delegate` type simply describes a set of `Functions` (or `Subs`) with specific parameters and a specific return type.

Line 8 declares `evenPredicate` as a variable of type `NumberPredicate` and assigns to it a reference to the `IsEven` method (defined in lines 58–60). Operator `AddressOf` returns a method's reference. Since method `IsEven`'s signature matches the `NumberPredicate` delegate's signature, `IsEven` can be referenced by a variable of type `NumberPredicate`. Variable `evenPredicate` can now be used as an alias for method `IsEven`. A `NumberPredicate` variable can hold a reference to any `Function` that receives an `Integer` and returns a `Boolean`. Lines 11–12 use variable `evenPredicate` to call method `IsEven`, then display the result on the console. The method referenced by the delegate is called using the delegate variable's name in place of the method's name (i.e., `evenPredicate(4)`).

The real power of delegates is the ability to pass a method reference as an argument to another method, as shown by method `FilterArray` (lines 41–55). `FilterArray` takes as arguments an `Integer` array and a `NumberPredicate` that references a method used to filter the array elements. The `For Each...Next` statement (lines 47–52) calls the method referenced by the `NumberPredicate` delegate (line 49) on each element of the array. If the method call returns `True`, the element is included in the result. The `NumberPredicate` is

```
' Fig. 10.26: Delegates.vb
' Using delegates to pass functions as arguments.
Module Delegates
   Sub Main()
      Dim numbers As Integer() = {1, 2, 3, 4, 5, 6, 7, 8, 9, 10}

      ' create an instance of the NumberPredicate delegate type
      Dim evenPredicate As NumberPredicate = AddressOf IsEven

      ' call IsEven using a delegate variable
      Console.WriteLine("Call IsEven using a delegate variable: {0}", _
         evenPredicate(4))

      ' filter the even numbers using method IsEven
      Dim evenNumbers As List(Of Integer) = _
         FilterArray(numbers, evenPredicate)

      ' display the result
      DisplayList("Use IsEven to filter even numbers: ", evenNumbers)

      ' filter the odd numbers using method IsOdd
      Dim oddNumbers As List(Of Integer) = _
         FilterArray(numbers, AddressOf IsOdd)

      ' display the result
      DisplayList("Use IsOdd to filter odd numbers: ", oddNumbers)

      ' filter numbers greater than 5 using method IsOver5
      Dim numbersOver5 As List(Of Integer) = _
         FilterArray(numbers, AddressOf IsOver5)

      ' display the result
      DisplayList("Use IsOver5 to filter numbers over 5: ", numbersOver5)
   End Sub ' Main

   ' Delegate for function that receives an Integer and returns a Boolean
   Public Delegate Function NumberPredicate( _
      ByVal number As Integer) As Boolean

   ' select an array's elements that satisfy the predicate
   Private Function FilterArray(ByVal numbers As Integer(), _
      ByVal predicate As NumberPredicate) As List(Of Integer)

      Dim result As New List(Of Integer) ' hold the selected elements

      ' iterate over each element in the array
      For Each item In numbers
         ' if the element satisfies the predicate
         If predicate(item) Then
            result.Add(item) ' add the element to the result
         End If
      Next

```

Fig. 10.26 | Using delegates to pass functions as arguments. (Part 1 of 2.)

```
54         Return result ' return the result
55      End Function ' FilterArray
56
57      ' determine if an integer is even
58      Private Function IsEven(ByVal number As Integer) As Boolean
59         Return number Mod 2 = 0
60      End Function ' IsEven
61
62      ' determine if an integer is odd
63      Private Function IsOdd(ByVal number As Integer) As Boolean
64         Return number Mod 2 = 1
65      End Function ' IsOdd
66
67      ' determine if a double is greater than 5
68      Private Function IsOver5(ByVal number As Double) As Boolean
69         Return number > 5
70      End Function ' IsOver5
71
72      ' display the elements of a List
73      Private Sub DisplayList(ByVal description As String, _
74         ByVal list As List(Of Integer))
75
76         Console.Write(description) ' display the output's description
77
78         ' iterate over each element in the List
79         For Each item In list
80            Console.Write("{0} ", item) ' print item followed by a space
81         Next
82
83         Console.WriteLine() ' add a new line
84      End Sub ' DisplayList
85   End Module ' Delegates
```

```
Call IsEven using a delegate variable: True
Use IsEven to filter even numbers: 2 4 6 8 10
Use IsOdd to filter odd numbers: 1 3 5 7 9
Use IsOver5 to filter numbers over 5: 6 7 8 9 10
```

Fig. 10.26 | Using delegates to pass functions as arguments. (Part 2 of 2.)

guaranteed to return either `True` or `False`, because any method referenced by a `NumberPredicate` must return a `Boolean`—as specified by the definition of the `NumberPredicate` delegate type. Line 16 passes `FilterArray` the `Integer` array (`numbers`) and the `NumberPredicate` that references the `IsEven` method (`evenPredicate`). `FilterArray` calls the `NumberPredicate` delegate on each array element. `FilterArray` returns a `List(Of Integer)` containing the filtered elements, because we don't know in advance how many elements will be selected. Lines 15–16 assign the `List` returned by `FilterArray` to variable `evenNumbers` and line 19 calls method `DisplayList` to display the results.

Lines 22–23 call method `FilterArray` to select the odd numbers in the array. We use the `AddressOf` operator in `FilterArray`'s second argument to reference method `IsOdd` (defined in lines 63–65), rather than creating a `NumberPredicate` variable. Line 26 displays the results.

Relaxed Delegates

In previous versions of Visual Basic, a method referenced by a delegate was required to match the delegate's signature exactly, just as methods `IsEven` and `IsOdd` exactly match the signature of the `NumberPredicate` delegate type in Fig. 10.26. In Visual Basic 2008, a delegate may reference any method with a compatible signature—meaning the delegate's parameter types can be implicitly converted to the method's parameter types. [*Note:* `Option Strict On` limits what implicit conversions are allowed.] Lines 68–70 of Fig. 10.26 define method `IsOver5`, which takes a `Double` as an argument and returns a `Boolean`. Method `IsOver5` may be referenced by a `NumberPredicate` delegate, because the delegate's parameter type (`Integer`) can be implicitly converted to the method's parameter type (`Double`). Lines 29–30 pass method `IsOver5` to method `FilterArray`. When method `IsOver5` is called, the argument passed to the method is implicitly converted to type `Double` and used in the method's body.

A method with a compatible signature for a delegate must also define a return type that may be implicitly converted to the delegate's return type. For instance, if a delegate defines a return type of `Decimal`, it may reference a method with compatible parameters and a return type of `Integer`, because `Integer` can be implicitly converted to `Decimal`. However, the delegate may not reference a method with compatible parameters and a return type of `Double`, because `Double` cannot be implicitly converted to `Decimal`.

10.17 Lambda Expressions

Lambda expressions (new in Visual Basic 2008)—also known as lambda methods—allow you to define simple, anonymous `Functions`. [*Note:* You cannot use lambda expressions to define a `Sub` procedure.] Figure 10.27 uses lambda expressions to implement the previous example that introduced delegates. A lambda expression (line 9) resembles a `Function` definition. It begins with the keyword `Function` followed by a parameter list. The parameter list is followed by an expression that represents the body of the function defined by the lambda expression. The lambda expression in line 9 uses the `Mod` operator to determine whether the parameter's value is an even `Integer`. The value produced by this expression—`True` if the `Integer` is even, `False` otherwise—is implicitly returned by the lambda expression. Note that we do not specify a return type for the lambda expression—the return type is inferred from the return value. The lambda function in line 9 produces the same results as the `IsEven` method in Fig. 10.26. In fact, the expression used in the body of the `IsEven` method is the same expression used as the body of the lambda expression.

```
1  ' Fig. 10.27: Lambdas.vb
2  ' Using lambda expressions.
3  Module Lambdas
4     Sub Main()
5        Dim numbers As Integer() = {1, 2, 3, 4, 5, 6, 7, 8, 9, 10}
6
7        ' create an instance of the NumberPredicate delegate type
8        Dim evenPredicate As NumberPredicate = _
9           Function(number As Integer) number Mod 2 = 0
10
```

Fig. 10.27 | Using lambda expressions. (Part 1 of 3.)

```
      ' call a lambda expression through a variable
      Console.WriteLine("Use a lambda-expression variable: {0}", _
         evenPredicate(4))

      ' filter the even numbers using a lambda expression
      Dim evenNumbers As List(Of Integer) = _
         FilterArray(numbers, evenPredicate)

      ' display the result
      DisplayList( _
         "Use a lambda expression to filter even numbers: ", evenNumbers)

      ' filter the odd numbers using a lambda expression
      Dim oddNumbers As List(Of Integer) = FilterArray(numbers, _
         Function(number As Integer) number Mod 2 = 1)

      ' display the result
      DisplayList( _
         "Use a lambda expression to filter odd numbers: ", oddNumbers)

      ' filter numbers greater than 5 using a lambda expression
      Dim numbersOver5 As List(Of Integer) = FilterArray(numbers, _
         Function(number As Double) number > 5)

      ' display the result
      DisplayList("Use a lambda expression to filter numbers over 5: ", _
         numbersOver5)
   End Sub ' Main

   ' Delegate for a function that receives an Integer and returns a Boolean
   Public Delegate Function NumberPredicate( _
      ByVal number As Integer) As Boolean

   ' select an array's elements that satisfy the predicate
   Private Function FilterArray(ByVal numbers As Integer(), _
      ByVal predicate As NumberPredicate) As List(Of Integer)

      Dim result As New List(Of Integer) ' hold the selected elements

      ' iterate over each element in the array
      For Each item In numbers
         ' if the element satisfies the predicate
         If predicate(item) Then
            result.Add(item) ' add the element to the result
         End If
      Next

      Return result ' return the result
   End Function ' FilterArray

   ' display the elements of a List
   Private Sub DisplayList(ByVal description As String, _
      ByVal list As List(Of Integer))
```

Fig. 10.27 | Using lambda expressions. (Part 2 of 3.)

```
64
65          Console.Write(description) ' display the output's description
66
67          ' iterate over each element in the List
68          For Each item In list
69             Console.Write("{0} ", item) ' print item followed by a space
70          Next
71
72          Console.WriteLine() ' add a new line
73       End Sub ' DisplayList
74    End Module ' Lambdas
```

```
Use a lambda-expression variable: True
Use a lambda expression to filter even numbers: 2 4 6 8 10
Use a lambda expression to filter odd numbers: 1 3 5 7 9
Use a lambda expression to filter numbers over 5: 6 7 8 9 10
```

Fig. 10.27 | Using lambda expressions. (Part 3 of 3.)

In line 8, the lambda expression is assigned to a variable of type `NumberPredicate` (defined in lines 41–42). Recall that `NumberPredicate` is the delegate type used in the previous example. A delegate can hold a reference to a lambda expression. As with traditional methods, a function defined by a lambda expression must have a signature that is compatible with the delegate type. The `NumberPredicate` delegate can hold a reference to any `Function` procedure that takes an `Integer` as an argument and returns a `Boolean`. The lambda expression in line 9 defines a `Function` that takes an `Integer` as an argument and that returns the `Boolean` result of the expression in its body. So, the signature of the lambda expression matches the signature of the delegate. Lambda expressions are often used as arguments to methods with parameters of delegate types, rather than defining a separate method and using the `AddressOf` operator.

Lines 12–13 display the result of calling the lambda expression defined in line 9. The lambda expression is called via the variable that references it (`evenPredicate`). Lines 16–17 pass `evenPredicate` to method `FilterArray` (lines 45–59), which is identical to Fig. 10.26—it uses the `NumberPredicate` delegate to determine whether an array element should be included in the result. Lines 20–21 display the filtered results.

Lines 24–25 select the odd array elements and store the results. In this case, the lambda expression is passed directly to method `FilterArray` and is implicitly converted to a `NumberPredicate` delegate. The lambda expression in line 25 is equivalent to the `IsOdd` method defined in Fig. 10.26. Lines 28–29 display the filtered results.

Lines 32–33 filter `Integers` greater than `5` from the array and store the results. The lambda expression in line 33 is equivalent to the `IsOver5` method in Fig. 10.26. Note that this lambda expression declares a `Double` parameter. Recall that a method signature is compatible with a delegate signature if the delegate's parameter types can be implicitly converted to the method's parameter types and the method's return type can be implicitly converted to the delegate's return type. The `NumberPredicate`'s parameter type (`Integer`) can be implicitly converted to the lambda expression's parameter type (`Double`). Both `NumberPredicate` and the lambda expression return a `Boolean`. So the lambda expression's signature is compatible with the `NumberPredicate` delegate.

Lambda expressions can help reduce the size of your code and the complexity of working with delegates—the program in Fig. 10.27 performs the same actions as the one in Fig. 10.26 but is 11 lines shorter. Lambda expressions are particularly powerful when combined with the `Where` clause in LINQ queries.

10.18 Anonymous Types

Anonymous types (new in Visual Basic 2008) allow you to create simple classes used to store data without writing a class definition. An anonymous type declaration (line 6 of Fig. 10.28)—also called an anonymous object-creation expression—is similar to an object initializer (discussed in Section 10.4). The declaration begins with the keywords `New` and `With` followed by a member-initializer list. Notice that no class name is specified after the `New` keyword. When line 6 executes, the compiler generates a new class definition based on the anonymous object-creation expression. The new class contains the properties specified in the member-initializer list—`Name` and `Age`. All properties of an anonymous type are `Public`. Each property's type is inferred from value assigned to it. We discuss the `Key` keyword preceeding the `Name` property shortly. Note that no type is specified for the variable `bob` (line 6). The class definition is generated automatically by the compiler, so you don't know the class's type name (hence the term anonymous type). Thus, you must use type inference when working with objects of anonymous types. Line 9 uses the anonymous type's `ToString` method to display the object's information on the console. The compiler defines the `ToString` method when creating the anonymous type's class definition. The method returns a `String` in curly braces containing a comma-separated list of *propertyName* = *value* pairs.

```
1  ' Fig. 10.28: AnonymousTypes.vb
2  ' Using anonymous types.
3  Module AnonymousTypes
4     Sub Main()
5        ' create a "person" object using an anonymous type
6        Dim bob = New With {Key .Name = "Bob Smith", .Age = 37}
7
8        ' display bob's information
9        Console.WriteLine("Bob: " & bob.ToString())
10
11       ' create another "person" object using the same anonymous type
12       Dim steve = New With {Key .Name = "Steve Jones", .Age = 26}
13
14       ' display steve's information
15       Console.WriteLine("Steve: " & steve.ToString())
16
17       ' determine if objects of the same anonymous type are equal
18       Console.WriteLine(vbNewLine & "Bob and Steve are {0}", _
19          If(bob.Equals(steve), "equal", "not equal"))
20
21       ' create a "person" object using an anonymous type
22       Dim bob2 = New With {Key .Name = "Bob Smith", .Age = 37}
23
```

Fig. 10.28 | Using anonymous types. (Part 1 of 2.)

```
24          ' display the bob's information
25          Console.WriteLine(vbNewLine & "Bob2: " & bob2.ToString())
26
27          ' determine whether objects of the same anonymous type are equal
28          Console.WriteLine(vbNewLine & "Bob and Bob2 are {0}" & vbNewLine, _
29             If(bob.Equals(bob2), "equal", "not equal"))
30
31          ' change bob2's age
32          bob2.Age = 45
33
34          ' display the bob2's information
35          Console.WriteLine("Bob2 modified: " & bob2.ToString())
36
37          ' determine whether objects of the same anonymous type are equal
38          Console.WriteLine(vbNewLine & "Bob and Bob2 are {0}", _
39             If(bob.Equals(bob2), "equal", "not equal"))
40       End Sub ' Main
41    End Module ' AnonymousTypes
```

```
Bob: { Name = Bob Smith, Age = 37 }
Steve: { Name = Steve Jones, Age = 26 }

Bob and Steve are not equal

Bob2: { Name = Bob Smith, Age = 37 }

Bob and Bob2 are equal

Bob2 modified: { Name = Bob Smith, Age = 45 }

Bob and Bob2 are equal
```

Fig. 10.28 | Using anonymous types. (Part 2 of 2.)

Line 12 creates another anonymous object and assigns it to variable `steve`. The anonymous object-creation expression uses the same property names (`Name` and `Age`) and types in the member-initializer list as the anonymous type defined in line 6. Two anonymous objects that specify the same property names and types, in the same order, use the same anonymous class definition and are considered to be of the same type.

Lines 18–19 determine if the two anonymous objects, `bob` and `steve`, are equal and display the results. When anonymous objects are compared for equality, only properties marked with the **`Key`** **keyword**—known as **key properties**—are considered. An anonymous type may specify any number of key properties, including none. In this example, `Name` is the only key property, so only the values of `Name` are considered when determining whether `bob` and `steve` are equal. Line 19 uses the anonymous type's `Equals` method, which the compiler generates for any anonymous type that contains at least one key property. The `Equals` method compares the key properties of the anonymous object that calls the method and the anonymous object that it receives as an argument. Since, `bob`'s `Name` property is not equal to `steve`'s `Name` property, the two objects are not equal.

Line 22 creates an object of the same anonymous type as `bob` and `steve` and assigns it to variable `bob2`. This object specifies the same property values as `bob`. Lines 28–29 use the anonymous type's `Equals` method to determine that `bob` and `bob2` are equal—both objects have the same value for the key property Name. Line 32 changes the value of bob2's Age property from 37 to 45, then lines 38–39 test for equality between bob and bob2. The output shows that these objects are still equal, verifying that only key properties are considered when testing the equality of these objects. Note that key properties are ReadOnly—you cannot modify a key property's value once the object is created.

Anonymous Types in LINQ

Anonymous types are frequently used in LINQ queries to select specific properties from the items being queried. Recall the Employee class used in Section 9.2. The class defines three properties—FirstName, LastName and MonthlySalary. The query

```
Dim names = _
   From e In employees _
   Select e.FirstName, Last = e.LastName
```

from lines 54–55 of Fig. 9.4 selects properties FirstName and LastName of each Employee object (e) in an array of Employees (employees). The Select clause creates an anonymous type with properties FirstName and Last to store the selected property values. The syntax used in the Select clause to create the anonymous type is different than what you've seen in this section. The New and With keywords are omitted. Also, the member-initializer list isn't surrounded by curly braces and doesn't specify a name for the FirstName property. As explained in Chapter 9, the compiler implicitly uses the name of the selected property unless you specify otherwise. All properties of an anonymous type created in a LINQ query's Select clause as shown above are key properties. You can use the full anonymous object-creation syntax—as shown to the right of the equal sign in line 6 of Fig. 10.28—in a LINQ query's Select clause to specify which properties should be key properties.

10.19 (Optional) Software Engineering Case Study: Starting to Program the Classes of the ATM System

In the Software Engineering Case Study sections in Chapters 1 and 3–8, we introduced the fundamentals of object orientation and developed an object-oriented design for our ATM system. In Chapters 4–8, we introduced object-oriented programming in Visual Basic. In this chapter, we took a deeper look at the details of programming with classes. We now begin implementing our object-oriented design by converting class diagrams to Visual Basic code. In the final Software Engineering Case Study section (Section 12.8), we modify the code to incorporate the object-oriented concepts of inheritance and polymorphism. We present the full Visual Basic code implementation in Appendix D.

Visibility

We now apply access modifiers to the members of our classes. In Chapter 4, we introduced access modifiers Public and Private. Access modifiers determine the visibility or accessibility of an object's attributes and operations to other objects. Before we can begin implementing our design, we must consider which attributes and methods of our classes should be Public and which should be Private.

In Chapter 4, we observed that attributes normally should be Private and that methods invoked by clients of a class should be Public. Methods that are called only by other methods of the class as "utility functions," however, should be Private. The UML employs visibility markers for modeling the visibility of attributes and operations. Public visibility is indicated by placing a plus sign (+) before an operation or an attribute; a minus sign (–) indicates `Private` visibility. Figure 10.29 shows our updated class diagram with visibility markers included. [*Note:* We do not include any operation parameters in Fig. 10.29. This is perfectly normal. Adding visibility markers does not affect the parameters already modeled in the class diagrams of Figs. 7.26–7.29.]

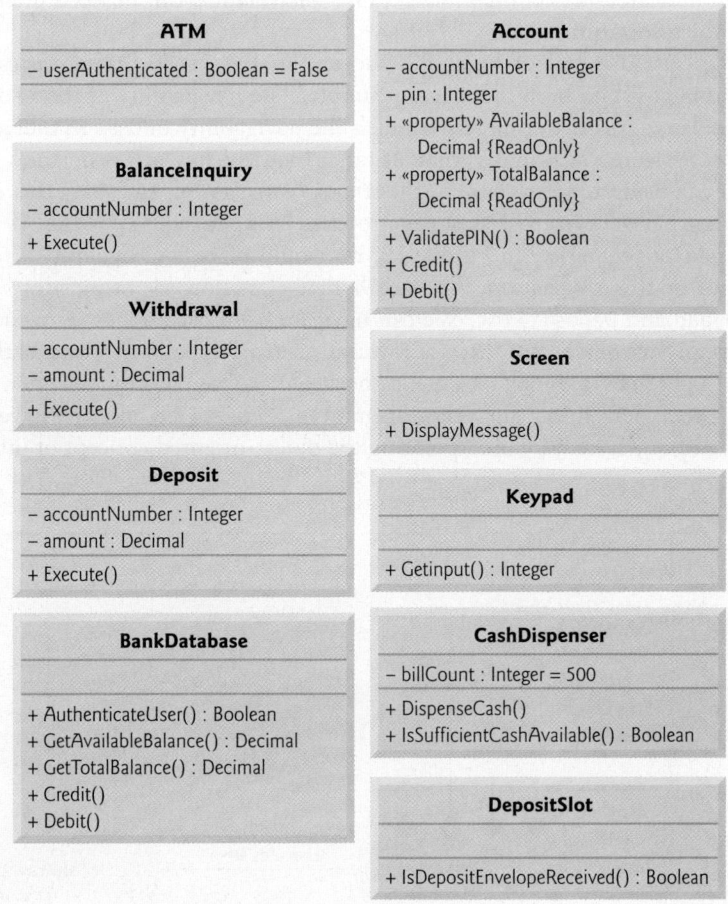

Fig. 10.29 | Class diagram with visibility markers.

Navigability

Before we begin implementing our design in Visual Basic, we introduce an additional UML notation. The class diagram in Fig. 10.30 further refines the relationships among classes in the ATM system by adding navigability arrows to the association lines. Navigability arrows (represented as arrows with stick arrowheads in the class diagram) indicate in which direction an association can be traversed and are based on the collaborations modeled in communication and sequence diagrams (see Section 8.17). When implementing a system designed using the UML, you use navigability arrows to help determine which objects need references to other objects. For example, the navigability arrow pointing from class ATM to class BankDatabase indicates that we can navigate from the former to the latter, thereby enabling the ATM to invoke the BankDatabase's operations. However, since Fig. 10.30 does not contain a navigability arrow pointing from class BankDatabase to class ATM, the BankDatabase cannot access the ATM's operations. Note that associations in a class diagram that have navigability arrows at both ends or do not have navigability arrows at all indicate bidirectional navigability—navigation can proceed in either direction across the association.

Like the class diagram of Fig. 4.22, the one in Fig. 10.30 omits classes BalanceInquiry and Deposit to keep the diagram simple. The navigability of the associations in which these classes participate closely parallels the navigability of class Withdrawal's associations. Recall from Section 4.9 that BalanceInquiry has an association with class Screen. We can navigate from class BalanceInquiry to class Screen along this association, but we cannot navigate from class Screen to class BalanceInquiry. Thus, if we were to model class BalanceInquiry in Fig. 10.30, we would place a navigability arrow at class Screen's end of this association. Also recall that class Deposit associates with classes Screen, Keypad and DepositSlot. We can navigate from class Deposit to each of these classes, but not vice versa. We therefore would place navigability arrows at the Screen, Keypad and DepositSlot ends of these associations. [*Note:* We model these additional classes and associations in our final class diagram in Section 12.8, after we have simplified the structure of our system by incorporating the object-oriented concept of inheritance.]

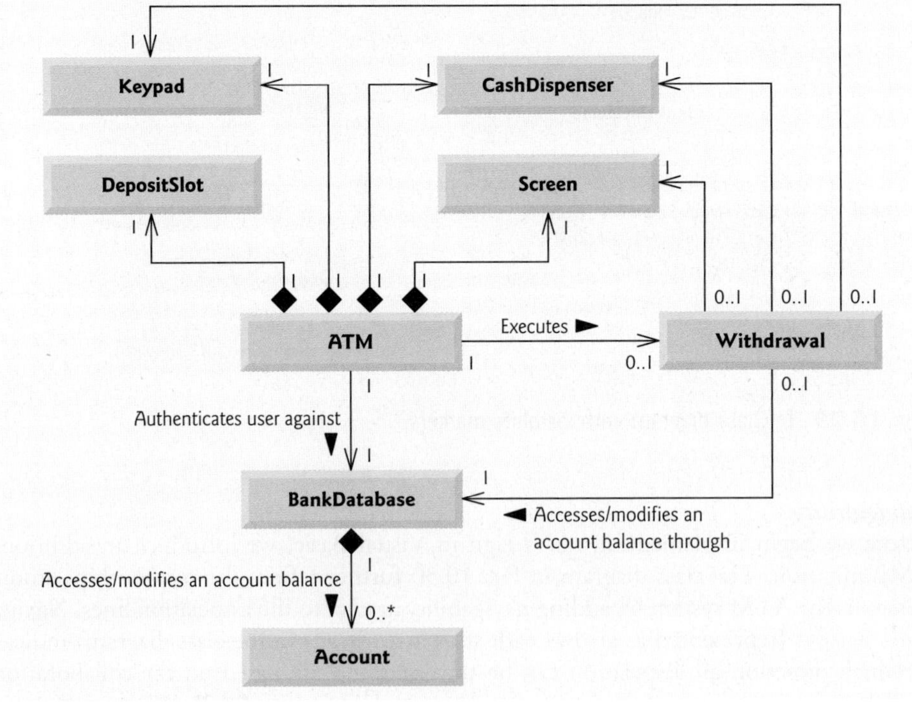

Fig. 10.30 | Class diagram with navigability arrows.

Implementing the ATM System from Its UML Design

We are now ready to begin implementing the ATM system. We first convert the classes in the diagrams of Fig. 10.29 and Fig. 10.30 into Visual Basic code. This code will represent the "skeleton" of the system. In Chapter 12, we modify the code to incorporate the object-oriented concept of inheritance. In Appendix D, we present the complete working Visual Basic code that implements our object-oriented design.

As an example, we begin to develop the code for class `Withdrawal` from our design of class `Withdrawal` in Fig. 10.29. We use this figure to determine the attributes and operations of the class. We use the UML model in Fig. 10.30 to determine the associations among classes. We follow the following four guidelines for each class:

1. Use the name located in the first compartment of a class in a class diagram to declare the class as a `Public` class with an empty parameterless constructor. We include this constructor simply as a placeholder to remind us that most classes will need one or more constructors. In Appendix D, when we complete a working version of this class, we add any necessary arguments and code to the body of the constructor. Class `Withdrawal` initially yields the code in Fig. 10.31. [*Note:* If we find that the class's instance variables require only default initialization, we will remove the empty parameterless constructor because it is unnecessary.]
2. Use the attributes located in the class's second compartment to declare the instance variables. The `Private` attributes `accountNumber` and `amount` of class `Withdrawal` yield the code in Fig. 10.32.

```
' Class Withdrawal represents an ATM withdrawal transaction
Public Class Withdrawal
   ' parameterless constructor
   Public Sub New()
      ' constructor body code
   End Sub ' New
End Class ' Withdrawal
```

Fig. 10.31 | Initial Visual Basic code for class `Withdrawal` based on Figs. 10.29 and 10.30.

```
' Class Withdrawal represents an ATM withdrawal transaction
Public Class Withdrawal
   ' attributes
   Private accountNumber As Integer ' account to withdraw funds from
   Private amount As Decimal ' amount to withdraw from account

   ' parameterless constructor
   Public Sub New()
      ' constructor body code
   End Sub ' New
End Class ' Withdrawal
```

Fig. 10.32 | Visual Basic code incorporating `Private` variables for class `Withdrawal` based on Figs. 10.29 and 10.30.

3. Use the associations described in the class diagram to declare references (or pointers, where appropriate) to other objects. According to Fig. 10.30, `Withdrawal` can access one object of class `Screen`, one object of class `Keypad`, one object of class `CashDispenser` and one object of class `BankDatabase`. Class `Withdrawal` must maintain references to these objects for sending messages to them, so lines 8–11 of Fig. 10.33 declare four references as `Private` instance variables. In the implementation of class `Withdrawal` in Appendix J, a constructor initializes these instance variables with references to the actual objects.
4. Use the operations located in the third compartment of Fig. 10.29 to declare the shells of the methods. If we have not yet specified a return type for an operation, we declare the method with keyword `Sub`. Refer to the class diagrams of Figs. 7.25–7.28 to declare any necessary parameters. Adding the `Public` operation `Execute` (which has an empty parameter list) in class `Withdrawal` yields the code in line 19 of Fig. 10.34. [*Note:* We code the bodies of methods when we implement the complete ATM system in Appendix D.]

```
1  ' Class Withdrawal represents an ATM withdrawal transaction
2  Public Class Withdrawal
3     ' attributes
4     Private accountNumber As Integer ' account to withdraw funds from
5     Private amount As Decimal ' amount to withdraw
6
7     ' references to associated objects
8     Private screenHandle As Screen ' ATM's screen
9     Private keypadHandle As Keypad ' ATM's keypad
10    Private cashDispenserHandle As CashDispenser ' ATM's cash dispenser
11    Private bankDatabaseHandle As BankDatabase ' account info database
12
13    ' parameterless constructor
14    Public Sub New()
15       ' constructor body code
16    End Sub ' New
17 End Class ' Withdrawal
```

Fig. 10.33 | Visual Basic code incorporating `Private` reference handles for the associations of class `Withdrawal` based on Figs. 10.29 and 10.30.

```
1  ' Class Withdrawal represents an ATM withdrawal transaction
2  Public Class Withdrawal
3     ' attributes
4     Private accountNumber As Integer ' account to withdraw funds from
5     Private amount As Decimal ' amount to withdraw
6
7     ' references to associated objects
8     Private screenHandle As Screen ' ATM's screen
```

Fig. 10.34 | Visual Basic code incorporating method `Execute` in class `Withdrawal` based on Figs. 10.29 and 10.30. (Part 1 of 2.)

```
    Private keypadHandle As Keypad ' ATM's keypad
    Private cashDispenserHandle As CashDispenser ' ATM's cash dispenser
    Private bankDatabaseHandle As BankDatabase ' account info database

    ' parameterless constructor
    Public Sub New()
       ' constructor body code
    End Sub ' New

    ' operations
    Public Sub Execute()
       ' Execute method body code
    End Sub ' Execute
 End Class ' Withdrawal
```

Fig. 10.34 | Visual Basic code incorporating method `Execute` in class `Withdrawal` based on Figs. 10.29 and 10.30. (Part 2 of 2.)

Software Engineering Observation 10.7

Many UML modeling tools can convert UML-based designs into Visual Basic code, considerably speeding the implementation process.

This concludes our discussion of the basics of generating class files from UML diagrams. In the final Software Engineering Case Study section (Section 12.8), we demonstrate how to modify the code in Fig. 10.34 to incorporate the object-oriented concepts of inheritance and polymorphism in Chapter 12.

Software Engineering Case Study Self-Review Exercises

10.1 State whether the following statement is *true* or *false*, and if *false*, explain why: If an attribute of a class is marked with a minus sign (-) in a class diagram, the attribute is not directly accessible outside of the class.

10.2 In Fig. 10.30, the association between the `ATM` and the `Screen` indicates that:
a) we can navigate from the `Screen` to the `ATM`
b) we can navigate from the `ATM` to the `Screen`
c) Both a and b; the association is bidirectional
d) None of the above

10.3 Write Visual Basic code to begin implementing the design for class `Account`.

Answers to Software Engineering Case Study Self-Review Exercises

10.1 True. The minus sign (-) indicates `Private` visibility.

10.2 b.

10.3 The design for class `Account` yields the code in Fig. 10.35. Note that we include `Private` instance variables `availableBalance` and `totalBalance` to store the data that properties `AvailableBalance` and `TotalBalance` and methods `Credit` and `Debit` will manipulate. The provided code is simply a "skeleton" of an actual program, and as such it will not compile.

```
' Represents a bank account.
Public Class Account
   Private accountNumber As Integer ' account number
   Private pin As Integer ' PIN for authentication
   Private availableBalance As Decimal ' available withdrawal amount
   Private totalBalance As Decimal ' funds available + pending deposit

   ' parameterless constructor
   Public Sub New()
      ' constructor body code
   End Sub ' New

   ' validates user PIN
   Public Function ValidatePIN() As Boolean
      ' ValidatePIN method body code
   End Function ' ValidatePIN

   ' property AvailableBalance
   Public ReadOnly Property AvailableBalance() As Decimal
      ' AvailableBalance property body code
   End Property ' AvailableBalance

   ' property TotalBalance
   Public ReadOnly Property TotalBalance() As Decimal
      ' TotalBalance property body code
   End Property ' TotalBalance

   ' credits the account
   Public Sub Credit()
      ' Credit method body code
   End Sub ' Credit

   ' debits the account
   Public Sub Debit()
      ' Debit method body code
   End Sub ' Debit
End Class ' Account
```

Fig. 10.35 | Visual Basic code for class `Account` based on Figs. 10.29 and 10.30.

10.20 Wrap-Up

This chapter investigated the object-oriented programming concepts of classes, objects, methods and instance variables in more depth. The `Time` class case study presented a complete class declaration consisting of `Private` data, overloaded constructors for initialization flexibility, properties with `Set` and `Get` accessors for manipulating the class's data, and methods that returned `String` representations of a `Time` object in two different formats.

You learned how to initialize properties of an object as you create it with an object-initializer list. We showed how the `Me` reference is used implicitly in a class's non-`Shared` methods to access the class's instance variables and non-`Shared` methods. We also showed how to use the `Me` reference explicitly to access the class's shadowed instance variables explicitly. You learned about partial classes, which allow the code of a class to span multiple source files.

You learned that a class can have references to objects of other classes as members—a concept known as composition. We discussed how garbage collection reclaims the memory of objects that are no longer needed. You learned how to execute the garbage collector to invoke the method `Finalize` on each object before it is removed from memory. We explained the motivation for `Shared` instance variables in a class, and demonstrated how to declare and use `Shared` variables and methods in your own classes. You learned how to declare and initialize `Const` and `ReadOnly` members. We showed how to use the **Object Browser** to learn the functionality provided by the classes of the Framework Class Library. We also showed how to create a class library for reuse and how to use the classes of the library in an application.

We used extension methods to add functionality to a class without modifying the class's source code. You then learned that a delegate is an object that holds a method reference. We showed you how to use delegates to assign methods to variables and pass methods to other methods. Next we demonstrated lambda expressions for defining simple, anonymous `Function`s that can also be used with delegates. Finally, you learned how to use anonymous types to create simple classes that store data without writing a class definition.

In the next chapter, we continue our discussion of classes by introducing a form of software reuse called inheritance. We will see that classes often share common attributes and behaviors. In such cases, it is possible to define those attributes and behaviors in a common "base" class and "inherit" those capabilities into new class declarations.

Summary

Section 10.1 Introduction

- Composition allows a class to have references to objects of other classes as members.

Section 10.2 `Time` Class Case Study

- Programmers use inheritance to create new classes from existing classes. The `Inherits` keyword followed by class name `Object` indicates that a class inherits existing pieces of class `Object` (of namespace `System`). Every class (except `Object`) inherits from `Object` implicitly if explicit inheritance from `Object` is not indicated.
- Keywords `Class` and `End Class` delimit the body of a class declaration. Any information placed in this body is part of the class's scope.
- Constructors are implemented as `Sub` procedures, not as `Function`s, because constructors cannot return values. Generally, constructors are `Public`.
- If you do not specify a namespace for a class or module, it is placed in the default namespace, which includes the compiled classes and modules in the current directory.
- When a class or module uses another class or module in the same namespace, an `Imports` statement is not required.
- You must import the classes from the .NET Framework because your classes and modules are in different namespaces from those in the .NET Framework.
- Any method of a class can access all the instance variables of the class and can call every method of the class. This reduces the number of arguments needed in a method call, making method calls

more concise than conventional function calls in procedural programming. It also reduces the likelihood of passing the wrong arguments, types of arguments or number of arguments.

- One of the reasons why classes simplify programming is that the clients need be concerned only with the `Public` operations encapsulated in the object. Usually, such operations are designed to be client oriented.
- Clients are neither aware of, nor involved in, a class's implementation. Interfaces change less frequently than implementations. When an implementation changes, implementation-dependent code must change accordingly. By hiding the implementation, we eliminate the possibility that other parts of the program will become dependent on the class implementation details.

Section 10.3 Class Scope

- A class's instance variables and methods belong to that class's scope. Within a class's scope, class members are accessible to all of the class's methods and can be referenced by name.
- Outside a class's scope, class members cannot be referenced directly by name. `Public` class members can be accessed through a "handle," such as a reference to an object of the class (or through the class name if the member is `Shared`).
- If a variable is defined in a method, it is a local variable to that method and can be used only in the method's body. Such variables are said to have block scope.
- If a method defines a local variable that has the same name as an instance variable, the local variable hides the instance variable in the method's scope—this is called shadowing.
- A shadowed instance variable can be accessed in a method of that class by preceding its name with the keyword `Me` and the dot separator.

Section 10.4 Object Initializers

- Object initializers allow you to create an object and initialize its properties in the same statement.
- An object-initializer list is a comma-separated list in curly braces (`{ }`) of properties and their values; it cannot be empty and cannot contain `Shared`, `Const` or `ReadOnly` properties.
- `With` indicates that the new object is used to access properties in the object-initializer list.
- Each property name must be preceded by the dot separator (`.`) and can appear only once in the object-initializer list.
- An object initializer first calls the class's constructor, then sets the value of each property specified in the object-initializer list. The property's `Set` accessor validates the supplied value.

Section 10.5 Default and Parameterless Constructors

- Overloaded constructors provide multiple ways to initialize objects of a class.
- If a class does not define constructors, the compiler provides a default constructor for the class. This constructor contains no code and takes no parameters.
- You can define a parameterless constructor for a class that is similar to a default constructor except that it is defined by you and typically contains statements in its body.
- If you provide any constructors for a class, the compiler will not provide a default constructor.

Section 10.6 `Time` Class Case Study: Overloaded Constructors

- Like methods, constructors of a class can be overloaded.
- The compiler invokes the appropriate overloaded constructor by matching the number, types and order of the arguments specified in the constructor call with the number, types and order of the parameters specified in the various constructor declarations.
- A copy constructor initializes an object by copying values from another object of the same class.

Section 10.7 Partial Classes

- Visual Basic allows a class declaration to span multiple source-code files. The separate portions of the class declaration in each file are known as partial classes. At least one partial class declaration for a given class must be marked with the `Partial` modifier.
- When a class declaration specifies the `Partial` modifier, any class declarations with the same class name in the program are combined at compile time to form a single class declaration.
- Partial classes must be declared in the same namespace and assembly.
- If class members in one partial-class source file conflict with those in other source files for the same class, compilation errors will occur.
- Partial classes provide a convenient way to split a class into small, manageable pieces that enable several developers to work on the same class at once.

Section 10.8 Composition

- A class can have references to objects of other classes as members. Such a capability is called composition and is sometimes referred to as a *has-a* relationship.

Section 10.9 Using `Me` to Access the Current Object

- Every object of a class shares the class's method declarations.
- Every object has access to itself through a reference called `Me`. The compiler passes an object's `Me` reference as an implicit argument to each of the object's non-`Shared` methods. The `Me` reference can then be used to access a particular object's members implicitly or explicitly.
- When a method has a parameter or local variable with the same name as one of the class's instance variables, the instance variable is hidden in that method's scope. However, the method can use the `Me` reference to refer to hidden instance variables explicitly.

Section 10.10 Garbage Collection

- The Common Language Runtime (CLR) performs automatic garbage collection to reclaim the memory occupied by unused objects.
- Managed resources like memory are allocated and reclaimed by the CLR.
- Resources like files, network connections and database connections that you must manage are known as unmanaged resources.
- To help prevent resource leaks for unmanaged resources, the garbage collector calls a special method named `Finalize` on each object before it is removed from memory.
- The `Finalize` method is called by the garbage collector to perform termination housekeeping on an object (such as releasing unmanaged resources used by the object) just before the garbage collector reclaims the object's memory.
- Method `Finalize` is not ideal for releasing unmanaged resources, because the garbage collector is unpredictable—it is not guaranteed to execute at a specified time. In fact, the garbage collector may never execute before a program terminates.
- The .NET Framework Class Library provides interface `IDisposable`, which contains a method named `Dispose` that a client can invoke to immediately release the resources used by an object.

Section 10.11 `Shared` Class Members

- A program contains only one copy of a `Shared` class variable in memory, no matter how many objects of the class have been instantiated. A `Shared` class variable represents classwide information—all class objects share the same piece of data.
- The declaration of a `Shared` member begins with the keyword `Shared`.

- `Shared` class members are accessible in all methods of a class, both `Shared` and non-`Shared`.
- A class's `Public Shared` members can be accessed by clients through the class name using the dot separator.
- A class's `Private Shared` members can be accessed by clients only through non-`Private` methods of the class.
- `Shared` class members are available as soon as the class is loaded into memory at execution time and exist for the duration of program execution, even when no objects of the class exist.
- To allow clients to access a `Private Shared` class member when no objects of the class exist, you must provide a non-`Private Shared` method or property.
- A `Shared` method cannot access non-`Shared` class members. Unlike non-`Shared` methods, a `Shared` method has no `Me` reference, because `Shared` variables and `Shared` methods exist independently of any class objects and even when there are no objects of that class.
- Normally, the garbage collector is not invoked directly by the user. Either the garbage collector reclaims the memory for objects when it deems garbage collection is appropriate, or the operating system recovers the unneeded memory when the program terminates. `Public Shared` method `Collect` from class `GC` of namespace `System` requests that the garbage collector execute.
- When `Shared` variables require more complex initialization than can be accomplished in a `Shared` variable declaration, you can create a `Shared` constructor to initialize those variables.
- A `Shared` constructor is declared like an instance constructor, but is preceded by the `Shared` modifier and can be used only to initialize `Shared` variables.
- A `Shared` constructor is implicitly `Public`, must be declared with no parameters, cannot call other constructors and is guaranteed to execute before a program creates any objects of the class. Explicitly declaring a `Shared` constructor `Public` is a compilation error.

Section 10.12 `Const` *and* `ReadOnly` *Members*

- To create a constant member in a class, declare that member as either `Const` or `ReadOnly`.
- An identifier declared as `Const` must be initialized in its declaration.
- An identifier declared as `ReadOnly` can be initialized either in its declaration or in a constructor.
- `Const` values must be initialized at compile time, but `ReadOnly` values are not initialized until runtime. Once initialized, neither a `Const` nor a `ReadOnly` value can be modified.
- `Const` members must be initialized at compile time, so they can be initialized only to other constant values, such as integers, string literals, characters and other `Const` members.
- Constant members with values that cannot be determined at compile time must be declared with the keyword `ReadOnly`.
- A `Shared` constructor can be used to initialize `Shared ReadOnly` members, and a non-`Shared` (instance) constructor can be used to initialize non-`Shared ReadOnly` members.
- A property with only a `Get` accessor is called a read-only property and must be declared using keyword `ReadOnly`. A property with only a `Set` accessor is called a write-only property and must be declared using keyword `WriteOnly`.

Section 10.13 Object Browser

- The **Object Browser** lists all the namespaces and classes that are available to the application, including the Framework Class Library classes and programmer-defined classes.
- Developers use the **Object Browser** to learn about the functionality provided by specific classes.
- To open the **Object Browser**, right click any Visual Basic class or method in the code editor and select **Go To Definition**.

Section 10.14 `Time` *Class Case Study: Creating Class Libraries*

- Class libraries and namespaces facilitate software reuse by enabling applications to add classes from other namespaces.
- Before a class can be used in multiple applications, it must be declared `Public` and placed in a class library to make it reusable.
- When you compile a class library project, the compiler will create a `.dll` file, known as a dynamic link library—a type of assembly that you can reference from other applications.

Section 10.15 `Time` *Class Case Study: Extension Methods*

- Extension methods add functionality to a class without modifying the class's source code.
- Many LINQ capabilities are also available as extension methods.
- Attributes specify additional information about a variable, property, method, class or module.
- The `<Extension()>` attribute (from the `System.Runtime.CompilerServices` namespace) indicates that the method extends an existing class. The compiler uses this information to add code into the compiled program that enables extension methods to work with existing types.
- The type of an extension method's first parameter specifies the class that is being extended—extension methods must define at least one parameter.
- Extension methods must be defined in `Modules`, not classes.
- The compiler implicitly passes the object that is used to call the method as the extension method's first argument. This allows you to call an extension method as if it were an instance method of the extended class.
- *IntelliSense* displays extension methods with the extended class's instance methods.
- Extension methods, as well as instance methods, allow cascaded method calls—that is, invoking multiple methods in the same statement. The methods are called from left to right.
- An extension method's fully qualified name is the name of the `Module` in which the extension method is defined, followed by the name of the method and its argument list. When using the fully qualified method name, you must specify an argument for first parameter.
- If the type being extended defines an instance method with the same name as your extension method and a compatible signature, the instance method shadows the extension method.

Section 10.16 Delegates

- A delegate is an object that holds a reference to a method.
- Delegates let you assign methods to variables and pass methods to and from methods.
- You can call methods through variables of delegate types.
- A delegate type is declared by preceding a method header with keyword `Delegate`. The `Delegate` type declaration includes the method header only.
- The `AddressOf` operator returns a method's reference.
- A delegate may reference any method with a compatible signature—meaning the delegate's parameter types can be implicitly converted to the method's parameter types and the method's return type can be implicitly converted to the delegate's return type.

Section 10.17 Lambda Expressions

- Lambda expressions allow you to define simple, anonymous `Functions`.
- A lambda expression begins with the keyword `Function` followed by a parameter list. The parameter list is followed by an expression that represents the body of the function.
- The return type is inferred from the return value.

- A delegate can hold a reference to a lambda expression with a compatible signature.
- Often we use lambda expressions as arguments to methods with parameters of delegate types, rather than defining a separate method and using the `AddressOf` operator.
- Lambda expressions are particularly powerful when combined with the LINQ `Where` clause.

Section 10.18 Anonymous Types

- Use anonymous types to create simple classes used to store data without writing a class definition.
- An anonymous type declaration—also called an anonymous object-creation expression—begins with the keywords `New` and `With` followed by a member-initializer list.
- The compiler generates a new class definition based on the anonymous object-creation expression, containing the properties specified in the member-initializer list.
- All properties of an anonymous type are `Public`.
- Each property's type is inferred from the value assigned to it.
- You don't know the auto-generated class's type name (hence the term anonymous type). Thus, you must use type inference when working with objects of anonymous types.
- The compiler defines the `ToString` method when creating the anonymous type's class definition. The method returns a `String` of comma-separated *propertyName* = *value* pairs in curly braces.
- Two anonymous objects that specify the same property names and types, in the same order, use the same anonymous class definition and are considered to be of the same type.
- When anonymous objects are compared for equality, only properties marked with the `Key` keyword—known as key properties—are considered.
- An anonymous type may specify any number of key properties, including none.
- The `Equals` method, generated for any anonymous type that contains at least one key property, compares the key properties of the anonymous object that calls the method and the anonymous object that it receives as an argument.
- Key properties are `ReadOnly`; once the object is created, you cannot modify a key property's value.
- Anonymous types are frequently used with LINQ to select properties from the items being queried.
- The syntax used in a `Select` clause to create an anonymous type omits the `New` and `With` keywords. The member-initializer list isn't surrounded by curly braces and doesn't specify the property names—the compiler uses the name of the selected property unless you specify otherwise.
- All properties of an anonymous type created in a LINQ query's `Select` clause using the shorthand syntax are key properties. You can use the full anonymous object-creation syntax in a LINQ query's select clause to specify which properties should be key properties.

Terminology

`AddressOf` operator
anonymous object-creation expression
anonymous type
assembly
attribute
body of class declaration
cascaded method calls
class library
class scope
"classwide" information
`Collect` method of `System.GC`
compatible signature
composition
`Const` keyword
constructor overloading
copy constructor
default namespace
delegate
`Delegate` keyword
`.dll` file
dynamic link library
`Equals` method of an anonymous type

explicit use of Me reference
<Extension()> attribute
extension method
Finalize method
garbage collection
garbage collector
GC class of namespace System
has-a relationship
helper method
hide an instance variable
implementation-dependent code
implementation hiding
inheritance relationship
initialize Shared class variables
initializer
Key keyword of an anonymous object-creation expression
key property of an anonymous type
lambda expression
lambda method
managed resource
Me reference
memory leak
New keyword of an anonymous object-creation expression
non-Public method
Object Browser
Object class
object initializer
object-initializer list
overloaded constructor
Overrides keyword
parameterless constructor
partial class
Partial modifier
Private Shared member
Public Shared member
read-only property
ReadOnly keyword
reclaim memory
reference to a method
reference to a new object
resource leak
reusable component
service of a class
shadowing a variable
Shared class variable
Shared constructor
Shared keyword
Shared method
software reuse
System.Runtime.CompilerServices namespace
termination housekeeping
ToString method
ToString method of an anonymous type
unmanaged resource
utility method
validity checking
With keyword of an anonymous object-creation expression
With keyword of an object initializer
write-only property
WriteOnly keyword

Self-Review Exercises

10.1 Fill in the blanks in each of the following:

a) A(n) __________ variable represents classwide information.
b) __________ allow a class declaration to span multiple source-code files.
c) The keyword __________ specifies that an object or variable is not modifiable after it is initialized at runtime.
d) A method declared Shared cannot access __________ class members.
e) The class extended by an extension method is specified by the __________ in the extension method's header.
f) Place the __________ at the beginning of a method header to define an extension method.
g) A(n) __________ holds a reference to method which may be used to invoke the method directly or pass the method as an argument to another method.

10.2 State whether each of the following is *true* or *false*. If *false*, explain why.

a) Every class in Visual Basic inherits either directly or indirectly from class Object, which is the root of the class hierarchy.
b) The Me reference of an object is a reference to that object.

c) Setting objects to `Nothing` in a specific order guarantees that those objects are finalized in that order.
d) A `Shared` member of a class can be referenced when no object of that type exists.
e) `ReadOnly` variables must be initialized either in a declaration or in the class constructor.
f) You can modify the properties of an anonymous object created using the shorthand syntax in the `Select` clause of a LINQ query.
g) An object initializer first calls the class's constructor, then assigns the specified property values.
h) Lambda expressions provide a convenient way to write simple `Function` and `Sub` procedures.

10.3 Write a code to accomplish each of the following:
a) Create an anonymous type with properties `FirstName`, `LastName` and `Title`, where equality between objects is determined by the `FirstName` and `LastName` properties.
b) Suppose class `Book` defines properties `Title`, `Author` and `Year`. Use an object initializer to create an object of class `Book` and initialize its properties.
c) Create a lambda method that takes an `Integer` and multiplies it by `2`, then returns the new `Integer` value.

Answers to Self-Review Exercises

10.1 a) `Shared`. b) Partial classes. c) `ReadOnly`. d) non-`Shared`. e) first parameter. f) `<Extension()>` attribute. g) delegate.

10.2 a) True. b) True. c) False. The garbage collector does not guarantee that resources are reclaimed in a specific order or even that they will be reclaimed before the program terminates. d) True. e) True. f) False. All properties of an anonymous type created using the shorthand syntax in the `Select` clause of a LINQ query are key properties, which are declared `ReadOnly`. You must use the full anonymous type syntax to define non-key properties that can be modified. g) True. h) False. Lambda expressions can only be used to define simple `Function` procedures—they must return a value.

10.3 a) `New With {Key .FirstName = "Bob", Key .LastName = "Smith", .Title = "Mr."}`
b)
```
New Book() With {.Title = "Visual Basic 2008 HTP", _
   .Author = "Deitel", .Year = 2009}
```
c) `Function(number As Integer) number * 2`

Exercises

10.4 *(Enhancing Class `Day`)* Modify the `Day` class of Fig. 10.7 to provide validations of the initial values for instance variables `monthValue`, `dayValue` and `yearValue`. For the purposes of this exercise, ensure that the `year` is between 1900 and 2100. Also provide a method `NextDay` to increment the day by 1. The `Day` object should always remain in a consistent state. Write a console application that tests the `NextDay` method and illustrates that it works correctly. Be sure to test the following cases:
a) Incrementing into the next month.
b) Incrementing into the next year.

10.5 *(Savings Account Class)* Create class `SavingsAccount`. Use a `Shared` class variable to store the `annualInterestRate` for all account holders. Each object of the class contains a `Private` instance variable `savingsBalance` indicating the amount the saver currently has on deposit. Provide the `CalculateMonthlyInterest` method to calculate the monthly interest by multiplying the `savingsBalance` by the `annualInterestRate` divided by `12`; this interest should be added to `savingsBalance` and returned to the method caller. Provide a `Shared` method `ModifyInterestRate` that sets the `annualInterestRate` to a new value. Write a console application to test class `SavingsAccount`. Instantiate two `SavingsAccount` objects, `saver1` and `saver2`, with balances of \$2000.00 and \$3000.00, respectively. Set `annualInterestRate` to 4%, then calculate the monthly interest and print the amounts of interest earned and the new balances for each of the savers. Then set the `annualInterestRate` to 5% and calculate the next month's interest and print the amounts of interest earned and the new balances for each of the savers.

10.6 *(Date Format Class)* Create a `DateFormat` class with the following capabilities:

a) Output the date in multiple formats such as

```
MM/DD/YYYY
June 14, 2001
DDD YYYY
```

b) Use overloaded constructors to create `DateFormat` objects initialized with dates of the formats in part a).

10.7 *(Square Class)* Write a class that implements a `Square` shape. Class `Square` should contain a `Side` property for accessing `Private` data. Provide a constructor that takes a `Side` length as a value. Also provide the following methods:

a) `Perimeter` returns `4 × Side`.
b) `Area` returns `Side × Side`.
c) `Diagonal` returns the square root of the expression `(2 × Side²)`.

Test your new `Square` class in a module.

10.8 *(Enhancing Class `Time`)* Write a GUI application that is similar to the output of Fig. 10.2, but with two more buttons—**Add 1 to Minute** and **Add 1 to Hour**. Use extension methods to extend class `Time` of Fig. 10.1 to provide the `Tick` method that increments the time stored in a `Time` object by one second. Also provide method `IncrementMinute` to increment the minute and method `IncrementHour` to increment the hour. The `Time` object should always remain in a consistent state. The `Tick` method, the `IncrementMinute` method and the `IncrementHour` method should be called when you click the **Add 1 to Second** button, the **Add 1 to Minute** button and the **Add 1 to Hour** button, respectively. Be sure to test the following cases:

a) incrementing into the next minute.
b) incrementing into the next hour.
c) incrementing into the next day (i.e., 11:59:59 PM to 12:00:00 AM).

10.9 *(Modifying the Internal Data Representation of a Class)* It would be perfectly reasonable for the `Time` class of Fig. 10.1 to represent the time internally as the number of seconds since midnight rather than the three integer values `hourValue`, `minuteValue` and `secondValue`. Clients could use the same `Public` methods and get the same results. Modify the `Time` class of Fig. 10.1 to implement the `Time` as the number of seconds since midnight and show that no change is visible to the clients of the class.

10.10 *(Account Information Application)* A bank wants you to create a GUI application that will allow bank employees to view the clients' information. The application interface should have four `Labels` and four `TextBoxes`, which are used to display first name, last name, account number and account balance, respectively. The interface should also have two `Buttons`, **Previous** and **Next**, which allow the bank manager to search through each client's information backward and forward, respectively. The application GUI is shown in Fig. 10.36. Create a `Customer` class to represent the client with first name, last name, account number and account balance. When the GUI application is loaded, create an array of `Customer` objects, then display the first client's information to the manager. [*Hint:* Use object initializers in the array's initializer list to create each `Customer` object.] If the current client is the first in the array, the last client in the array is displayed when the manager clicks the **Previous** button. If the current client is the last in the array, the first client in the array is displayed when the manager clicks the **Next** button.

10.11 *(Microwave Oven Application)* An electronics company is considering building microwave ovens. The company has asked you to develop a GUI application that simulates a microwave oven. The oven will contain a keypad that allows the user to specify the microwave cook time and display it for the user. Once a time is entered, the user clicks the **Start** button to begin the cooking process. The microwave's glass window changes color (from gray to yellow) to simulate the oven's light, which remains on while the food cooks, and a timer counts down one second at a time. Once the time expires, the color of the microwave's glass window returns to gray (indicating that the microwave's light is now off) and the microwave displays the text `Done!`. The application GUI is shown in Fig. 10.37. The user can click the **Clear** button at any time to stop the microwave and enter a new time. The user should be able to enter a number of hours no greater than 9, a number of minutes no greater than 59 and a number of seconds no greater than 59; otherwise, the invalid cook time will be set to zero. A beep will be sounded whenever a button is clicked and when the microwave oven has finished a countdown. [*Hint:* Use a `Timer` control to implement the timer countdown. To add a `Timer`, click the `Timer` control in the **Toolbox**, and drag and drop it anywhere on the `Form`. Note that the `Timer` does not actually appear on the `Form`; it appears below the **Designer View** in an area called the component tray. A `Timer` generates a `Tick` event every millisecond (1/1000 of a second). Double click the `Timer` control in the component tray to generate the empty event handler for the `Tick` event. A `Timer` can be started and stopped by setting its `Enabled` property to `True` and `False`, respectively. The statement

```
Beep() ' sound beep
```

causes the computer to make a beep sound.]

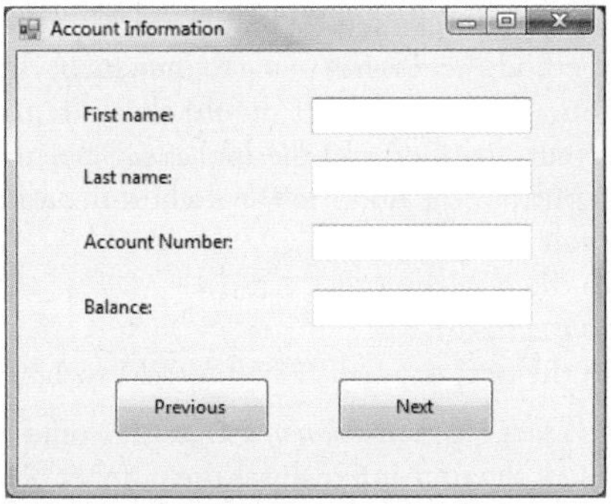

Fig. 10.36 | **Account Information** application GUI.

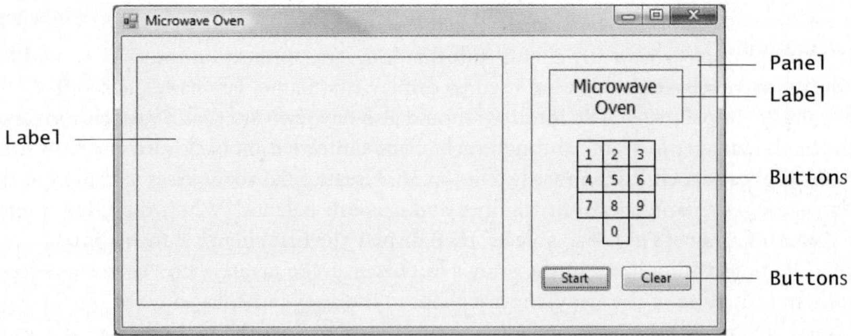

Fig. 10.37 | **Microwave Oven** application GUI.

Object-Oriented Programming: Inheritance

Say not you know another entirely, till you have divided an inheritance with him.

—Johann Kasper Lavater

This method is to define as the number of a class the class of all classes similar to the given class.

—Bertrand Russell

Good as it is to inherit a library, it is better to collect one.

—Augustine Birrell

Save base authority from others' books.

—William Shakespeare

OBJECTIVES

In this chapter you'll learn:

- What inheritance is and how it promotes software reusability.
- The notions of base classes and derived classes.
- To use keyword `Inherits` to create a class that inherits attributes and behaviors from another class.
- To use the access modifier `Protected` in a base class to give derived-class methods access to base class members.
- To access base-class members from a derived class with `MyBase`.
- How constructors are used in inheritance hierarchies.
- To access the current object with `Me` and `MyClass`.
- The methods of class `Object`—the direct or indirect base class of all classes in Visual Basic.

Outline

11.1 Introduction

This chapter continues our discussion of object-oriented programming (OOP) by introducing one of its primary features, inheritance, a form of software reuse in which a new class is created by absorbing an existing class's members and embellishing them with new or modified capabilities. With inheritance, you can save time during program development by reusing proven and debugged high-quality software. This increases the likelihood that a system will be implemented effectively.

When creating a class, rather than declaring completely new members, you can designate that the new class will inherit the members of an existing class. The existing class is called the base class, and the new class is the derived class. (The Java programming language refers to the base class as the superclass and the derived class as the subclass.) A derived class can become the base class for future derived classes.

A derived class normally adds its own instance variables, `Shared` variables, properties and methods. Therefore, a derived class is more specific than its base class and represents a more specialized group of objects. Typically, the derived class exhibits the behaviors of its base class and additional behaviors that are specific to the derived class. [*Note:* A class's instance variables and `Shared` variables are referred to collectively as the class's fields.]

The direct base class is the class from which the derived class explicitly inherits. An indirect base class is inherited from two or more levels up in the class hierarchy. In Visual Basic, the class hierarchy begins with class `Object` (in namespace `System`), which *every* class in Visual Basic directly or indirectly extends (or "inherits from"). Section 11.7 lists the seven methods of class `Object`, which every other class inherits. In the case of single inheritance, a class is derived from one direct base class. Visual Basic, unlike C++, does not support multiple inheritance (which occurs when a class is derived from more than one direct base class). In Chapter 12, Object-Oriented Programming: Polymorphism, we explain how you can use `Interfaces` to realize many of the benefits of multiple inheritance while avoiding the associated problems.

We distinguish between the *is-a* relationship and the *has-a* relationship. *Is-a* represents inheritance. In an *is-a* relationship, an object of a derived class also can be treated as an object of its base class. For example, a car *is a* vehicle. By contrast, the *has-a* relationship represents composition (see Chapter 10). In a *has-a* relationship, an object contains one or more object references as members. For example, a car *has a* steering wheel (and a car object has a reference to a steering-wheel object).

New classes can inherit from classes in class libraries. Organizations develop their own class libraries and can take advantage of others available worldwide. Some day, most new software will probably be constructed from standardized reusable components, just as automobiles and most computer hardware items are constructed today. This will facilitate the development of more powerful, abundant and economical software.

11.2 Base Classes and Derived Classes

Often, an object of one class *is an* object of another class as well. For example, in geometry, a rectangle *is a* quadrilateral (as are squares, parallelograms and trapezoids). Thus, in Visual Basic, class `Rectangle` can be said to inherit from class `Quadrilateral`. In this context, class `Quadrilateral` is a base class and class `Rectangle` is a derived class. A rectangle *is a* specific type of quadrilateral, but it is incorrect to claim that every quadrilateral *is a* rectangle—the quadrilateral could be a parallelogram or some other shape. Figure 11.1 lists several simple examples of base classes and derived classes—note that base classes tend to be "more general" and derived classes tend to be "more specific."

Every derived-class object *is an* object of its base class, and one base class can have many derived classes, so the set of objects represented by a base class is typically larger than the set of objects represented by any of its derived classes. For example, the base class `Vehicle` represents all vehicles, including cars, trucks, boats, bicycles and so on. By contrast, derived class `Car` represents a smaller, more specific subset of vehicles.

Inheritance relationships form treelike hierarchical structures. A base class exists in a hierarchical relationship with its derived classes. When classes participate in inheritance

Base class	Derived classes
`Student`	`GraduateStudent, UndergraduateStudent`
`Shape`	`Circle, Triangle, Rectangle`
`Loan`	`CarLoan, HomeImprovementLoan, MortgageLoan`
`Employee`	`Faculty, Staff`
`BankAccount`	`CheckingAccount, SavingsAccount`

Fig. 11.1 | Inheritance examples.

relationships, they become "affiliated" with other classes. A class becomes either a base class, supplying members to other classes, or a derived class, inheriting its members from other classes. In some cases, a class is both a base class and a derived class.

`CommunityMember` *Inheritance Hierarchy*

Let's develop a sample class hierarchy (Fig. 11.2), also called an inheritance hierarchy. A university community has thousands of members, including employees, students and alumni. Employees are either faculty members or staff members. Faculty members are either administrators (such as deans and department chairpersons) or teachers. The hierarchy could contain many other classes. For example, students can be graduate or undergraduate students. Undergraduate students can be freshmen, sophomores, juniors or seniors.

Each arrow in the inheritance hierarchy represents an *is-a* relationship. As we follow the arrows in this class hierarchy, we can state, for instance, that "an `Employee` *is a* `CommunityMember`" and "a `Teacher` *is a* `Faculty` member." `CommunityMember` is the direct base class of `Employee`, `Student` and `Alumnus`, and is an indirect base class of all the other classes in the diagram. Starting from the bottom of the diagram, you can follow the arrows and apply the *is-a* relationship up to the topmost base class. For example, an `Administrator` *is a* `Faculty` member, *is an* `Employee` and *is a* `CommunityMember`.

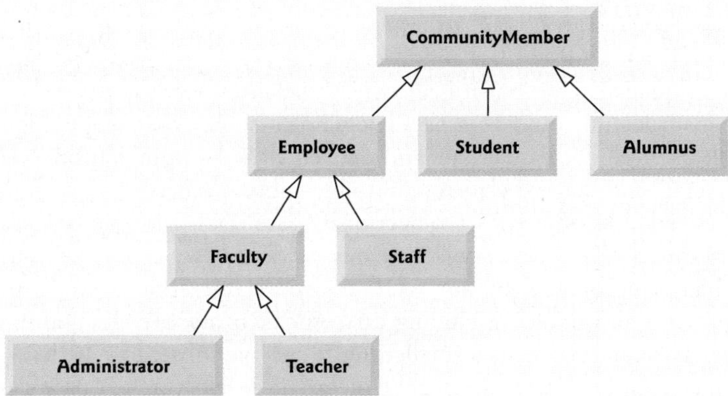

Fig. 11.2 | Inheritance hierarchy for university `CommunityMembers`.

`Shape` *Inheritance Hierarchy*

Now consider the `Shape` inheritance hierarchy in Fig. 11.3. This hierarchy begins with base class `Shape`, which is inherited by derived classes `TwoDimensionalShape` and `ThreeDimensionalShape`—`Shapes` are either `TwoDimensionalShapes` or `ThreeDimensionalShapes`. The third level of the hierarchy contains some more specific types of `TwoDimensionalShapes` and `ThreeDimensionalShapes`. As in Fig. 11.2, we can follow the arrows from the bottom of the diagram to the topmost base class in this class hierarchy to identify several *is-a* relationships. For example, a `Triangle` *is a* `TwoDimensionalShape` and *is a* `Shape`, while a `Sphere` *is a* `ThreeDimensionalShape` and *is a* `Shape`. Note that this hierarchy could contain many other classes. For example, ellipses and trapezoids also are `TwoDimensionalShapes`, and cylinders also are `ThreeDimensionalShapes`.

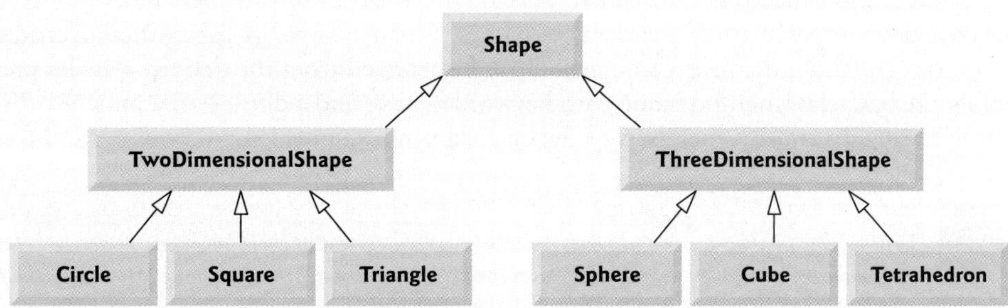

Fig. 11.3 | Inheritance hierarchy for Shapes.

Notes on Inheritance Relationships

Not every class relationship is an inheritance relationship. In Chapter 10, we discussed the *has-a* relationship, in which classes have members that are references to objects of other classes. Such relationships create classes by composition of existing classes. For example, given the classes `Employee`, `BirthDate` and `TelephoneNumber`, it is improper to say that an `Employee` *is a* `BirthDate` or that an `Employee` *is a* `TelephoneNumber`. However, an `Employee` *has a* `BirthDate`, and an `Employee` *has a* `TelephoneNumber`.

It is possible to treat base-class and derived-class objects similarly—their commonalities are expressed in the members of the base class. Objects of all classes that inherit a common base class can be treated as objects of that base class (i.e., such objects have an *is-a* relationship with the base class). However, base-class objects cannot be treated as objects of their derived classes. For example, all cars are vehicles, but not all vehicles are cars (the other vehicles could be trucks, planes or bicycles, for example). Later in this chapter and in Chapter 12, we consider many examples that use the *is-a* relationship.

One problem with inheritance is that a derived class can inherit methods that it does not need or should not have. Even when a base-class method is appropriate for a derived class, the derived class often needs a customized version of the method. In such cases, the derived class can override (redefine) the base-class method with an implementation appropriate for the derived class, as we will see often in the chapter's code examples.

11.3 Protected Members

Chapter 10 discussed access modifiers `Public` and `Private`. A class's `Public` members are accessible wherever the program has a reference to an object of that class or one of its derived classes. A class's `Private` members are accessible only within the class itself. A base class's `Private` members are not inherited by its derived classes. This section introduces the access modifier `Protected`. In Section 11.8, we discuss the access modifier **`Friend`**.

`Protected` access offers an intermediate level of access between `Public` and `Private` access. A base class's `Protected` members can be accessed only by members of that base class and by members of its derived classes.

All `Public` and `Protected` base-class members retain their original access modifier when they become members of the derived class (i.e., `Public` members of the base class become `Public` members of the derived class, and `Protected` members of the base class become `Protected` members of the derived class).

Derived-class methods can refer to `Public` and `Protected` members inherited from the base class simply by using the member names. When a derived-class method overrides a base-class method, the base-class version can be accessed from the derived class by preceding the base-class method name with keyword `MyBase` and a dot (`.`) separator. We discuss accessing overridden members of the base class in Section 11.4.

Software Engineering Observation 11.1

Derived-class methods cannot directly access `Private` members of their base class. A derived class can change the state of `Private` base-class instance variables only through non-`Private` methods provided in the base class and inherited by the derived class.

Software Engineering Observation 11.2

Declaring `Private` instance variables helps programmers test, debug and correctly modify systems. If a derived class could access its base class's `Private` instance variables, classes that inherit from that derived class could access the instance variables as well. This would propagate access to what should be `Private` instance variables, and the benefits of information hiding would be lost.

11.4 Relationship between Base Classes and Derived Classes

In this section, we use a business-oriented inheritance hierarchy containing types of employees in a company's payroll application to discuss the relationship between a base class and a derived class. Commission employees (who will be represented as objects of a base class) are paid a percentage of their sales, while base-salaried commission employees (who will be represented as objects of a derived class) receive a base salary plus a percentage of their sales. We divide our discussion of the relationship between commission employees and base-salaried commission employees into a carefully paced series of five examples:

1. In the first example, we create class `CommissionEmployee`, which contains as `Private` instance variables a first name, last name, social security number, commission rate (percentage) and gross (i.e., total) sales amount.
2. The second example defines class `BasePlusCommissionEmployee`, which contains as `Private` instance variables a first name, last name, social security number, commission rate, gross sales amount *and* a base salary. We create the class by writing every line of code that the class requires—we will soon see that it is much more efficient to create this class simply by inheriting from class `CommissionEmployee`, then adding appropriate attributes and behaviors.
3. The third example defines a new version of class `BasePlusCommissionEmployee` that inherits directly from class `CommissionEmployee` (i.e., a `BasePlusCommissionEmployee` *is a* `CommissionEmployee` who also has a base salary) and attempts to access class `CommissionEmployee`'s `Private` members—this results in compilation errors, because the derived class does not have access to the base class's `Private` data.
4. The fourth example shows that if `CommissionEmployee`'s data is declared as `Protected`, a new version of class `BasePlusCommissionEmployee` that inherits from class `CommissionEmployee` *can* access that data directly. For this purpose, we de-

fine a new version of class CommissionEmployee with Protected data. Both the inherited and noninherited BasePlusCommissionEmployee classes contain identical functionality, but we show how the version of BasePlusCommissionEmployee that inherits from class CommissionEmployee is easier to create and manage.

5. After we discuss the convenience of using protected data, we create the fifth example, which sets the CommissionEmployee data members back to Private to enforce good software engineering. This example demonstrates that derived class BasePlusCommissionEmployee can use base class CommissionEmployee's Public properties and methods to manipulate (in a carefully controlled manner) CommissionEmployee's Private data.

11.4.1 Creating and Using a CommissionEmployee Class

We begin by declaring class CommissionEmployee (Fig. 11.4). Lines 3–4 begin the class declaration and indicate that class CommissionEmployee **Inherits** from class Object (from namespace System). Visual Basic programmers use inheritance to create classes from existing classes. In fact, every class in Visual Basic (except Object) inherits from an existing class. Because class CommissionEmployee is derived from class Object, class CommissionEmployee inherits the methods of class Object—class Object does not have any fields. In fact, every Visual Basic class directly or indirectly inherits Object's methods. If a class does not specify that it inherits another class, the new class implicitly inherits Object. For this reason, programmers typically do not include "Inherits Object" in their code—we do so in this example for demonstration purposes, but then we omit "Inherits Object" in all subsequent examples.

The Public services of class CommissionEmployee include a constructor (lines 13–22), properties FirstName (lines 25–33), LastName (lines 36–44), SocialSecurityNumber (lines 47–55), GrossSales (lines 58–70) and CommissionRate (lines 73–85), and methods CalculateEarnings (lines 88–90) and ToString (lines 93–100). Lines 25–85 declare Public properties for manipulating the class's instance variables firstNameValue, lastNameValue, socialSecurityNumberValue, grossSalesValue and commissionRateValue (declared in lines 6–10). Class CommissionEmployee declares each of its instance variables as Private, so objects of other classes cannot directly access these variables. Properties GrossSales and CommissionRate validate their arguments before assigning the values to instance variables grossSalesValue and commissionRateValue, respectively.

```
1  ' Fig. 11.4: CommmissionEmployee.vb
2  ' CommissionEmployee class represents a commission employee.
3  Public Class CommissionEmployee
4     Inherits Object ' optional
5
6     Private firstNameValue As String ' first name
7     Private lastNameValue As String ' last name
8     Private socialSecurityNumberValue As String ' social security number
9     Private grossSalesValue As Decimal ' gross weekly sales
10    Private commissionRateValue As Double ' commission percentage
```

Fig. 11.4 | CommissionEmployee class represents an employee paid a percentage of gross sales. (Part 1 of 3.)

```
   ' five-argument constructor
   Public Sub New(ByVal first As String, ByVal last As String, _
      ByVal ssn As String, ByVal sales As Decimal, ByVal rate As Double)

      ' implicit call to Object constructor occurs here
      FirstName = first
      LastName = last
      SocialSecurityNumber = ssn
      GrossSales = sales ' validate and store gross sales
      CommissionRate = rate ' validate and store commission rate
   End Sub ' New

   ' property FirstName
   Public Property FirstName() As String
      Get
         Return firstNameValue
      End Get

      Set(ByVal first As String)
         firstNameValue = first ' no validation
      End Set
   End Property ' FirstName

   ' property LastName
   Public Property LastName() As String
      Get
         Return lastNameValue
      End Get

      Set(ByVal last As String)
         lastNameValue = last ' no validation
      End Set
   End Property ' LastName

   ' property SocialSecurityNumber
   Public Property SocialSecurityNumber() As String
      Get
         Return socialSecurityNumberValue
      End Get

      Set(ByVal ssn As String)
         socialSecurityNumberValue = ssn ' no validation
      End Set
   End Property ' SocialSecurityNumber

   ' property GrossSales
   Public Property GrossSales() As Decimal
      Get
         Return grossSalesValue
      End Get
```

Fig. 11.4 | CommissionEmployee class represents an employee paid a percentage of gross sales. (Part 2 of 3.)

```
62
63          Set(ByVal sales As Decimal)
64             If sales < 0D Then ' validate gross sales
65                grossSalesValue = 0D
66             Else
67                grossSalesValue = sales
68             End If
69          End Set
70       End Property ' GrossSales
71
72       ' property CommissionRate
73       Public Property CommissionRate() As Double
74          Get
75             Return commissionRateValue
76          End Get
77
78          Set(ByVal rate As Double)
79             If rate > 0.0 AndAlso rate < 1.0 Then ' validate rate
80                commissionRateValue = rate
81             Else
82                commissionRateValue = 0.0
83             End If
84          End Set
85       End Property ' CommissionRate
86
87       ' calculate earnings
88       Public Function CalculateEarnings() As Decimal
89          Return Convert.ToDecimal(commissionRateValue) * grossSalesValue
90       End Function ' CalculateEarnings
91
92       ' return String representation of CommissionEmployee object
93       Public Overrides Function ToString() As String
94          Return ("commission employee: " & firstNameValue & " " & _
95             lastNameValue & vbNewLine & "social security number: " & _
96             socialSecurityNumberValue & vbNewLine & "gross sales: " & _
97             String.Format("{0:C}", grossSalesValue) & vbNewLine & _
98             "commission rate: " & String.Format("{0:F}", _
99             commissionRateValue))
100      End Function ' ToString
101   End Class ' CommissionEmployee
```

Fig. 11.4 | `CommissionEmployee` class represents an employee paid a percentage of gross sales. (Part 3 of 3.)

Constructors are not inherited, so class `CommissionEmployee` does not inherit class `Object`'s constructor. However, class `CommissionEmployee`'s constructor calls class `Object`'s constructor implicitly. In fact, the first task of any derived-class constructor is to call its direct base class's constructor, either explicitly or implicitly (if no constructor call is specified), to ensure that the instance variables inherited from the base class are initialized properly. The syntax for calling a base-class constructor explicitly is discussed in Section 11.4.3. If the code does not include an explicit call to the base-class constructor, Visual Basic implicitly calls the base class's default or parameterless constructor. The comment in line 16 of Fig. 11.4 indicates where the implicit call to the base class `Object`'s default constructor is made (you do not need to write the code for this call). Object's default constructor does nothing. Note that even if a class does not have constructors, the default constructor that the compiler implicitly declares for the class will call the base class's default or parameterless constructor.

After the implicit call to Object's constructor occurs, lines 17–21 of CommissionEmployee's constructor assign values to the class's instance variables. Note that we do not validate the values of arguments first, last and ssn before assigning them to the corresponding instance variables. We could validate the first and last names—perhaps by ensuring that they are of a reasonable length. Similarly, a social security number could be validated to ensure that it contains nine digits, with or without dashes (e.g., 123-45-6789 or 123456789).

Method CalculateEarnings (lines 88–90) calculates a CommissionEmployee's earnings. Line 89 multiplies the commissionRateValue by the grossSalesValue and returns the result.

Method ToString (lines 93–100) of class CommissionEmployee Overrides (redefines) class Object's ToString method. When invoked, CommissionEmployee's ToString method returns a String containing information about the CommissionEmployee. Without overriding ToString in class CommissionEmployee, the default implementation would return "CommissionEmployeeTest.CommissionEmployee", where CommissionEmployeeTest is the default namespace (which is the same as the project name).

A base-class method must be declared **Overridable** if it is to be overridden in a derived class. Class Object's ToString method is Overridable, so derived class CommissionEmployee can override this method. To view ToString's method header, select **Help > Index...**. Select **.NET Framework** from the **Filtered by:** drop-down menu (if it's not already selected). Finally, enter "Object.ToString method" in the search text box. The page displayed contains a description of method ToString, which includes the following header:

```
Public Overridable Function ToString() As String
```

Common Programming Error 11.1

It is a compilation error to attempt to override a method that is not declared Overridable.

Common Programming Error 11.2

It is a compilation error to override a method with a method that has a different access modifier than the method being overridden.

*Testing Class **CommissionEmployee***

Figure 11.5 tests class CommissionEmployee. Lines 6–7 instantiate a CommissionEmployee object and invoke CommissionEmployee's constructor (lines 13–22 of Fig. 11.4) to initialize it with "Sue" as the first name, "Jones" as the last name, "222-22-2222" as the social security number, 10000 as the gross sales amount and 0.06 as the commission rate. Lines 10–16 access CommissionEmployee's Public properties for output. Lines 18–19 change the values of properties GrossSales and CommissionRate. Lines 22–24 call CommissionEmployee's ToString method to output the string representation of the updated CommissionEmployee. Lines 27–28 display the CommissionEmployee's earnings, calculated by the object's CalculateEarnings method using the updated values of instance variables grossSalesValue and commissionRateValue.

```
' Fig. 11.5: CommissionEmployeeTest.vb
' Testing class CommissionEmployee.
Module CommissionEmployeeTest
   Sub Main()
      ' instantiate CommissionEmployee object
      Dim employee As New CommissionEmployee( _
         "Sue", "Jones", "222-22-2222", 10000D, 0.06)

      ' get commission employee data
      Console.WriteLine("Employee information obtained by properties:" _
         & vbNewLine & "First name is " & employee.FirstName & _
         vbNewLine & "Last name is " & employee.LastName & vbNewLine & _
         "Social Security Number is " & employee.SocialSecurityNumber)
      Console.WriteLine("Gross sales is {0:C}", employee.GrossSales)
      Console.WriteLine("Commission rate is {0:F}", _
         employee.CommissionRate)

      employee.GrossSales = 500D ' set gross sales
      employee.CommissionRate = 0.1 ' set commission rate to 10%

      ' get new employee information
      Console.WriteLine(vbNewLine & _
         "Updated employee information obtained by ToString: " & _
         vbNewLine & employee.ToString() & vbNewLine)

      ' display the employee's earnings
      Console.WriteLine("Employee's earnings: {0:C}", _
         employee.CalculateEarnings())
   End Sub ' Main
End Module ' CommissionEmployeeTest
```

```
Employee information obtained by properties:
First name is Sue
Last name is Jones
Social Security Number is 222-22-2222
Gross sales is $10,000.00
Commission rate is 0.06

Updated employee information obtained by ToString:
commission employee: Sue Jones
social security number: 222-22-2222
gross sales: $500.00
commission rate: 0.10

Employee's earnings: $50.00
```

Fig. 11.5 | CommissionEmployee class test program.

11.4.2 Creating a BasePlusCommissionEmployee Class without Using Inheritance

We now discuss the second part of our introduction to inheritance by declaring and testing a completely new and independent class BasePlusCommissionEmployee (Fig. 11.6), which contains a first name, last name, social security number, gross sales amount, commission rate *and* base salary.

Defining Class **BasePlusCommissionEmployee**

Class `BasePlusCommissionEmployee`'s `Public` services include a `BasePlusCommissionEmployee` constructor (lines 13–24), properties `FirstName` (lines 27–35), `LastName` (lines 38–46), `SocialSecurityNumber` (lines 49–57), `GrossSales` (lines 60–72), `CommissionRate` (lines 75–87) and `BaseSalary` (lines 90–102), and methods `CalculateEarnings` (lines 105–108) and `ToString` (lines 111–119). Lines 27–102 declare `Public` properties for the class's `Private` instance variables `firstNameValue`, `lastNameValue`, `socialSecurityNumberValue`, `grossSalesValue`, `commissionRateValue` and `baseSalaryValue` (declared in lines 5–10). These variables, properties and methods comprise all the necessary features of a base-salaried commission employee. Note the similarity between this class and class `CommissionEmployee` (Fig. 11.4)—in this example, we do not yet exploit that similarity.

```
1  ' Fig. 11.6: BasePlusCommissionEmployee.vb
2  ' BasePlusCommissionEmployee class represents an employee that receives
3  ' a base salary in addition to a commission.
4  Public Class BasePlusCommissionEmployee
5     Private firstNameValue As String ' first name
6     Private lastNameValue As String ' last name
7     Private socialSecurityNumberValue As String ' social security number
8     Private grossSalesValue As Decimal ' gross weekly sales
9     Private commissionRateValue As Double ' commission percentage
10    Private baseSalaryValue As Decimal ' base salary per week
11
12    ' six-argument constructor
13    Public Sub New(ByVal first As String, ByVal last As String, _
14       ByVal ssn As String, ByVal sales As Decimal, _
15       ByVal rate As Double, ByVal salary As Decimal)
16
17       ' implicit call to Object constructor occurs here
18       FirstName = first
19       LastName = last
20       SocialSecurityNumber = ssn
21       GrossSales = sales ' validate and store gross sales
22       CommissionRate = rate ' validate and store commission rate
23       BaseSalary = salary ' validate and store base salary
24    End Sub ' New
25
26    ' property FirstName
27    Public Property FirstName() As String
28       Get
29          Return firstNameValue
30       End Get
31
32       Set(ByVal first As String)
33          firstNameValue = first ' no validation
34       End Set
35    End Property ' FirstName
36
```

Fig. 11.6 | `BasePlusCommissionEmployee` class represents an employee who receives a base salary in addition to a commission. (Part 1 of 3.)

```
   ' property LastName
   Public Property LastName() As String
      Get
         Return lastNameValue
      End Get

      Set(ByVal last As String)
         lastNameValue = last ' no validation
      End Set
   End Property ' LastName

   ' property SocialSecurityNumber
   Public Property SocialSecurityNumber() As String
      Get
         Return socialSecurityNumberValue
      End Get

      Set(ByVal ssn As String)
         socialSecurityNumberValue = ssn ' no validation
      End Set
   End Property ' SocialSecurityNumber

   ' property GrossSales
   Public Property GrossSales() As Decimal
      Get
         Return grossSalesValue
      End Get

      Set(ByVal sales As Decimal)
         If sales < 0D Then ' validate gross sales
            grossSalesValue = 0D
         Else
            grossSalesValue = sales
         End If
      End Set
   End Property ' GrossSales

   ' property CommissionRate
   Public Property CommissionRate() As Double
      Get
         Return commissionRateValue
      End Get

      Set(ByVal rate As Double)
         If rate > 0.0 AndAlso rate < 1.0 Then ' validate rate
            commissionRateValue = rate
         Else
            commissionRateValue = 0.0
         End If
      End Set
   End Property ' CommissionRate
```

Fig. 11.6 | `BasePlusCommissionEmployee` class represents an employee who receives a base salary in addition to a commission. (Part 2 of 3.)

```
88
89       ' property BaseSalary
90       Public Property BaseSalary() As Decimal
91          Get
92             Return baseSalaryValue
93          End Get
94
95          Set(ByVal salary As Decimal)
96             If salary < 0D Then ' validate base salary
97                baseSalaryValue = 0D
98             Else
99                baseSalaryValue = salary
100            End If
101         End Set
102      End Property ' BaseSalary
103
104      ' calculate earnings
105      Public Function CalculateEarnings() As Decimal
106         Return baseSalaryValue + ( _
107            Convert.ToDecimal(commissionRateValue) * grossSalesValue)
108      End Function ' CalculateEarnings
109
110      ' return String representation of BasePlusCommissionEmployee object
111      Public Overrides Function ToString() As String
112         Return ("base-plus-commission employee: " & firstNameValue & " " & _
113            lastNameValue & vbNewLine & "social security number: " & _
114            socialSecurityNumberValue & vbNewLine & "gross sales: " & _
115            String.Format("{0:C}", grossSalesValue) & vbNewLine & _
116            "commission rate: " & String.Format("{0:F}", _
117            commissionRateValue) & vbNewLine & "base salary: " & _
118            String.Format("{0:C}", baseSalaryValue))
119      End Function ' ToString
120   End Class ' BasePlusCommissionEmployee
```

Fig. 11.6 | `BasePlusCommissionEmployee` class represents an employee who receives a base salary in addition to a commission. (Part 3 of 3.)

Note that class `BasePlusCommissionEmployee` does not specify "`Inherits Object`," so the class implicitly inherits `Object`. Also, like class `CommissionEmployee`'s constructor (lines 13–22 of Fig. 11.4), class `BasePlusCommissionEmployee`'s constructor invokes class `Object`'s default constructor implicitly, as noted in the comment in line 17 (Fig. 11.6).

Class `BasePlusCommissionEmployee`'s `CalculateEarnings` method (lines 105–108) computes the earnings of a base-salaried commission employee. Line 106 returns the result of adding the base salary to the product of the commission rate and the gross sales. Class `BasePlusCommissionEmployee` overrides `Object` method `ToString` (lines 111–119) to return a `String` containing the `BasePlusCommissionEmployee`'s information.

Testing Class `BasePlusCommissionEmployee`

Figure 11.7 tests class `BasePlusCommissionEmployee`. Lines 6–7 instantiate a `BasePlusCommissionEmployee` object and pass `"Bob"`, `"Lewis"`, `"333-33-3333"`, `5000`, `0.04` and `300` to the constructor as the first name, last name, social security number, gross sales,

```
1  ' Fig. 11.7: BasePlusCommissionEmployeeTest.vb
2  ' Testing class BasePlusCommissionEmployee.
3  Module BasePlusCommissionEmployeeTest
4     Sub Main()
5        ' instantiate BasePlusCommissionEmployee object
6        Dim employee As New BasePlusCommissionEmployee( _
7           "Bob", "Lewis", "333-33-3333", 5000D, 0.04, 300D)
8
9        ' get base-salaried commission employee data
10       Console.WriteLine("Employee information obtained by properties:" _
11          & vbNewLine & "First name is " & employee.FirstName & _
12          vbNewLine & "Last name is " & employee.LastName & vbNewLine & _
13          "Social Security Number is " & employee.SocialSecurityNumber)
14       Console.WriteLine("Gross sales is {0:C}", employee.GrossSales)
15       Console.WriteLine("Commission rate is {0:F}", _
16          employee.CommissionRate)
17       Console.WriteLine("Base salary is {0:C}", employee.BaseSalary)
18
19       employee.BaseSalary = 1000D ' set base salary
20
21       ' get new employee information
22       Console.WriteLine(vbNewLine & _
23          "Updated employee information obtained by ToString: " & _
24          vbNewLine & employee.ToString() & vbNewLine)
25
26       ' display the employee's earnings
27       Console.WriteLine("Employee's earnings: {0:C}", _
28          employee.CalculateEarnings())
29    End Sub ' Main
30 End Module ' BasePlusCommissionEmployeeTest
```

```
Employee information obtained by properties:
First name is Bob
Last name is Lewis
Social Security Number is 333-33-3333
Gross sales is $5,000.00
Commission rate is 0.04
Base salary is $300.00

Updated employee information obtained by ToString:
base-plus-commission employee: Bob Lewis
social security number: 333-33-3333
gross sales: $5,000.00
commission rate: 0.04
base salary: $1,000.00

Employee's earnings: $1,200.00
```

Fig. 11.7 | `BasePlusCommissionEmployee` test program.

commission rate and base salary, respectively. Lines 10–17 use `BasePlusCommissionEmployee`'s properties to retrieve the values of the object's instance variables for output. Line 19 changes the `BaseSalary` property. Property `BaseSalary`'s `Set` accessor (Fig. 11.6, lines 95–101) ensures that instance variable `baseSalaryValue` is not assigned a negative value, because an employee's base salary cannot be negative. Line 24 of Fig. 11.7 invokes the object's `ToString` method explicitly to get the object's string representation. Lines 27–28 print the `Employee`'s earnings to the console by calling its `CaculateEarnings` method.

*Exploring the Similarities between Class **BasePlusCommissionEmployee** and Class **CommissionEmployee***

Much of the code for class `BasePlusCommissionEmployee` (Fig. 11.6) is similar, if not identical, to the code for class `CommissionEmployee` (Fig. 11.4). For example, both classes contain `Private` instance variables `firstNameValue`, `lastNameValue`, `socialSecurityNumberValue`, `grossSalesValue` and `commissionRateValue`, and properties `FirstName`, `LastName`, `SocialSecurityNumber`, `GrossSales` and `CommissionRate` to manipulate these variables. The `BasePlusCommissionEmployee` constructor is *almost* identical to that of class `CommissionEmployee`, except that `BasePlusCommissionEmployee`'s constructor also sets the `BaseSalary` property. The other additions to class `BasePlusCommissionEmployee` are `Private` instance variable `baseSalaryValue` and property `BaseSalary`. Class `BasePlusCommissionEmployee`'s `ToString` method is nearly identical to that of class `CommissionEmployee` except that `BasePlusCommissionEmployee`'s `ToString` also outputs the value of instance variable `baseSalaryValue`.

To form class `BasePlusCommissionEmployee`, we copied the code from class `CommissionEmployee` and pasted it into class `BasePlusCommissionEmployee`, then modified class `BasePlusCommissionEmployee` to include a base salary and methods that manipulate the base salary. This "copy-and-paste" approach is often error prone and time consuming. Worse yet, it can spread many physical copies of the same code throughout a system, creating a code-maintenance nightmare. Is there a way to "absorb" the instance variables and methods of one class in a way that makes them part of other classes without duplicating code? Indeed there is—using the elegant object-oriented programming technique of inheritance that we demonstrate in the next section.

Software Engineering Observation 11.3

Copying and pasting code from one class to another can spread errors among multiple source-code files. To avoid duplicating code (and possibly errors), use inheritance, rather than the "copy-and-paste" approach, where you want one class to "absorb" the members of another class.

Software Engineering Observation 11.4

With inheritance, the common instance variables and methods of all the classes in the hierarchy are declared in a base class. When changes are required for these common features, software developers need to make the changes only in the base class—derived classes then inherit the changes. Without inheritance, the changes would need to be made to all the source-code files that contain copies of the code in question.

11.4.3 Creating a CommissionEmployee–BasePlusCommissionEmployee Inheritance Hierarchy

Now we declare class `BasePlusCommissionEmployee` (Fig. 11.9), which inherits from class `CommissionEmployee` (Fig. 11.8). Class `CommissionEmployee` is almost identical to Fig. 11.4, except that method `CalculateEarnings` (Fig. 11.8, lines 88–90) is now declared `Overridable` so that a derived class of `CommissionEmployee` can override method `CalculateEarnings` to provide an appropriate earnings calculation. A `BasePlusCommission-`

`Employee` object *is a* `CommissionEmployee` (because inheritance passes on the capabilities of class `CommissionEmployee`), but class `BasePlusCommissionEmployee` also has instance variable `baseSalaryValue` (Fig. 11.9, line 6). Note that Fig. 11.9 does not redeclare the base-class instance variables (lines 6–10 of Fig. 11.8)—these are nevertheless present in the derived class (through inheritance). Even though they are present, they are declared `Private` in the base class, so as we will see in a moment, we will have to make special provision to access this base-class information from the derived class. Keyword `Inherits` in line 4 of the class declaration (Fig. 11.9) indicates inheritance. As a derived class, `BasePlusCommissionEmployee` inherits the `Public` (and `Protected`, if there were any) instance variables and methods of class `CommissionEmployee`. The constructor of class `CommissionEmployee` is not inherited. Thus, the `Public` services of `BasePlusCommissionEmployee` include its constructor (lines 9–16), `Public` methods and properties inherited from class `CommissionEmployee`, property `BaseSalary` (lines 19–31), method `CalculateEarnings` (lines 34–38) and method `ToString` (lines 41–50).

```
1   ' Fig. 11.8: CommmissionEmployee.vb
2   ' CommissionEmployee class represents a commission employee.
3   Public Class CommissionEmployee
4      Inherits Object ' optional
5
6      Private firstNameValue As String ' first name
7      Private lastNameValue As String ' last name
8      Private socialSecurityNumberValue As String ' social security number
9      Private grossSalesValue As Decimal ' gross weekly sales
10     Private commissionRateValue As Double ' commission percentage
11
12     ' five-argument constructor
13     Public Sub New(ByVal first As String, ByVal last As String, _
14        ByVal ssn As String, ByVal sales As Decimal, ByVal rate As Double)
15
16        ' implicit call to Object constructor occurs here
17        FirstName = first
18        LastName = last
19        SocialSecurityNumber = ssn
20        GrossSales = sales ' validate and store gross sales
21        CommissionRate = rate ' validate and store commission rate
22     End Sub ' New
23
24     ' property FirstName
25     Public Property FirstName() As String
26        Get
27           Return firstNameValue
28        End Get
29
30        Set(ByVal first As String)
31           firstNameValue = first ' no validation
32        End Set
33     End Property ' FirstName
34
```

Fig. 11.8 | `CommissionEmployee` class with `Overridable` method `CalculateEarnings`. (Part 1 of 3.)

```
    ' property LastName
    Public Property LastName() As String
       Get
          Return lastNameValue
       End Get

       Set(ByVal last As String)
          lastNameValue = last ' no validation
       End Set
    End Property ' LastName

    ' property SocialSecurityNumber
    Public Property SocialSecurityNumber() As String
       Get
          Return socialSecurityNumberValue
       End Get

       Set(ByVal ssn As String)
          socialSecurityNumberValue = ssn ' no validation
       End Set
    End Property ' SocialSecurityNumber

    ' property GrossSales
    Public Property GrossSales() As Decimal
       Get
          Return grossSalesValue
       End Get

       Set(ByVal sales As Decimal)
          If sales < 0D Then ' validate gross sales
             grossSalesValue = 0D
          Else
             grossSalesValue = sales
          End If
       End Set
    End Property ' GrossSales

    ' property CommissionRate
    Public Property CommissionRate() As Decimal
       Get
          Return commissionRateValue
       End Get

       Set(ByVal rate As Decimal)
          If rate > 0.0 AndAlso rate < 1.0 Then ' validate rate
             commissionRateValue = rate
          Else
             commissionRateValue = 0.0
          End If
       End Set
    End Property ' CommissionRate
```

Fig. 11.8 | `CommissionEmployee` class with `Overridable` method `CalculateEarnings`. (Part 2 of 3.)

```

   ' calculate earnings
   Public Overridable Function CalculateEarnings() As Decimal
      Return Convert.ToDecimal(commissionRateValue) * grossSalesValue
   End Function ' CalculateEarnings

   ' return String representation of CommissionEmployee object
   Public Overrides Function ToString() As String
      Return ("commission employee: " & firstNameValue & " " & _
         lastNameValue & vbNewLine & "social security number: " & _
         socialSecurityNumberValue & vbNewLine & "gross sales: " & _
         String.Format("{0:C}", grossSalesValue) & vbNewLine & _
         "commission rate: " & String.Format("{0:F}", _
         commissionRateValue))
   End Function ' ToString
End Class ' CommissionEmployee
```

Fig. 11.8 | `CommissionEmployee` class with `Overridable` method `CalculateEarnings`. (Part 3 of 3.)

```
' Fig. 11.9: BasePlusCommissionEmployee.vb
' BasePlusCommissionEmployee inherits from class CommissionEmployee.
Public Class BasePlusCommissionEmployee
   Inherits CommissionEmployee

   Private baseSalaryValue As Decimal ' base salary per week

   ' six-argument constructor
   Public Sub New(ByVal first As String, ByVal last As String, _
      ByVal ssn As String, ByVal sales As Decimal, _
      ByVal rate As Double, ByVal salary As Decimal)

      ' use MyBase to invoke CommissionEmployee constructor explicitly
      MyBase.New(first, last, ssn, sales, rate)
      BaseSalary = salary ' validate and store base salary
   End Sub ' New

   ' property BaseSalary
   Public Property BaseSalary() As Decimal
      Get
         Return baseSalaryValue
      End Get

      Set(ByVal salary As Decimal)
         If salary < 0D Then ' validate base salary
            baseSalaryValue = 0D
         Else
            baseSalaryValue = salary
         End If
      End Set
   End Property ' BaseSalary
```

Fig. 11.9 | `Private` base-class members cannot be accessed in a derived class. (Part 1 of 2.)

```
32
33       ' calculate earnings
34       Public Overrides Function CalculateEarnings() As Decimal
35          ' not allowed: attempts to access private base-class members
36          Return baseSalaryValue + ( _
37             Convert.ToDecimal(commissionRateValue) * grossSalesValue)
38       End Function ' CalculateEearnings
39
40       ' return String representation of BasePlusCommissionEmployee object
41       Public Overrides Function ToString() As String
42          ' not allowed: attempts to access private base-class members
43          Return ("base-plus-commission employee: " & firstNameValue & _
44             " " & lastNameValue & vbNewLine & "social security number: " & _
45             socialSecurityNumberValue & vbNewLine & "gross sales: " & _
46             String.Format("{0:C}", grossSalesValue) & vbNewLine & _
47             "commission rate: " & String.Format("{0:F}", _
48             commissionRateValue) & vbNewLine & "base salary: " & _
49             String.Format("{0:C}", baseSalaryValue))
50       End Function ' ToString
51    End Class ' BasePlusCommissionEmployee
```

Error List

8 Errors | 0 Warnings | 0 Messages

	Description	File	Line	Column	Project
1	'Sub Main' was not found in 'BasePlusCommissionEmployee.BasePlusCommissionEmployee'.				BasePlusCommissionEmployee
2	'BasePlusCommissionEmployee.CommissionEmployee.commissionRateValue' is not accessible in this context because it is 'Private'.	BasePlusCommissionEmployee.vb	37	28	BasePlusCommissionEmployee
3	'BasePlusCommissionEmployee.CommissionEmployee.grossSalesValue' is not accessible in this context because it is 'Private'.	BasePlusCommissionEmployee.vb	37	51	BasePlusCommissionEmployee
4	'BasePlusCommissionEmployee.CommissionEmployee.firstNameValue' is not accessible in this context because it is 'Private'.	BasePlusCommissionEmployee.vb	43	51	BasePlusCommissionEmployee
5	'BasePlusCommissionEmployee.CommissionEmployee.lastNameValue' is not accessible in this context because it is 'Private'.	BasePlusCommissionEmployee.vb	44	16	BasePlusCommissionEmployee
6	'BasePlusCommissionEmployee.CommissionEmployee.socialSecurityNumberValue' is not accessible in this context because it is 'Private'.	BasePlusCommissionEmployee.vb	45	10	BasePlusCommissionEmployee
7	'BasePlusCommissionEmployee.CommissionEmployee.grossSalesValue' is not accessible in this context because it is 'Private'.	BasePlusCommissionEmployee.vb	46	33	BasePlusCommissionEmployee
8	'BasePlusCommissionEmployee.CommissionEmployee.commissionRateValue' is not accessible in this context because it is 'Private'.	BasePlusCommissionEmployee.vb	48	10	BasePlusCommissionEmployee

Fig. 11.9 | `Private` base-class members cannot be accessed in a derived class. (Part 2 of 2.)

Each derived-class constructor must implicitly or explicitly call its base-class constructor to ensure that the instance variables inherited from the base class are initialized properly. `BasePlusCommissionEmployee`'s six-argument constructor (lines 9–16 of Fig. 11.9) explicitly calls class `CommissionEmployee`'s five-argument constructor to initialize the baseclass portion of a `BasePlusCommissionEmployee` object (i.e., variables `firstNameValue`, `lastNameValue`, `socialSecurityNumberValue`, `grossSalesValue` and `commissionRateValue`). Line 14 in `BasePlusCommissionEmployee`'s six-argument constructor invokes the `CommissionEmployee`'s five-argument constructor (declared at lines 13–22 of Fig. 11.8) by using the base-class constructor call syntax—keyword **`MyBase`**, followed by the dot (`.`) separator, followed by `New` and a set of parentheses containing the arguments to the base-class constructor. The arguments `first`, `last`, `ssn`, `sales` and `rate` (which were received by the derived-class constructor) are used to initialize base-class members `firstNameValue`, `lastNameValue`, `socialSecurityNumberValue`, `grossSalesValue` and `commissionRateValue`, respectively. If the `BasePlusCommissionEmployee` constructor did not invoke CommissionEmployee's constructor explicitly, Visual Basic would attempt to invoke class CommissionEmployee's parameterless or default constructor—but the class does not have such a constructor, so the compiler would issue an error. The explicit base-class constructor call in line 14 (Fig. 11.9) *must* be the first statement in the derived-class constructor's body. When a base class contains a default or parameterless constructor, you can use MyBase.New() to call that constructor explicitly, but this is unnecessary and is rarely done.

The compiler issues errors for line 37 of Fig. 11.9 because base class CommissionEmployee's instance variables commissionRateValue and grossSalesValue are Private—derived class BasePlusCommissionEmployee's methods are not allowed to access base class CommissionEmployee's Private members. Note that we use red text in Fig. 11.9 (and elsewhere in the book) to indicate erroneous code. The compiler issues additional errors at lines 43–48 of BasePlusCommissionEmployee's ToString method for the same reason. The errors in BasePlusCommissionEmployee could have been prevented by using the properties inherited from class CommissionEmployee. For example, line 37 could have used properties CommissionRate and GrossSales to access CommissionEmployee's Private instance variables commissionRateValue and grossSalesValue, respectively. Lines 43–48 also could have used appropriate properties to retrieve the values of the base class's instance variables.

11.4.4 CommissionEmployee–BasePlusCommissionEmployee Inheritance Hierarchy Using Protected Instance Variables

To enable class BasePlusCommissionEmployee to directly access base-class instance variables firstNameValue, lastNameValue, socialSecurityNumberValue, grossSalesValue and commissionRateValue, we can declare those members as Protected in the base class. As we discussed in Section 11.3, a base class's Protected members *are* inherited by all derived classes of that base class and are directly accessible by derived classes.

Defining Base Class **CommissionEmployee** *with* **Protected** *Data*

Class CommissionEmployee (Fig. 11.10) modifies Fig. 11.8 to declare instance variables firstNameValue, lastNameValue, socialSecurityNumberValue, grossSalesValue and commissionRateValue as Protected (Fig. 11.10, lines 6–10) rather than Private. The rest of the class declaration in Fig. 11.10 is identical to the one in Fig. 11.8.

We could have declared base class CommissionEmployee's instance variables firstNameValue, lastNameValue, socialSecurityNumberValue, grossSalesvalue and commissionRateValue as Public to enable derived class BasePlusCommissionEmployee to access the base-class instance variables. That is dangerous, because it allows unrestricted access to the instance variables, greatly increasing the chance of errors. With Protected base-class instance variables, the derived class gains access to the instance variables, but classes that are not derived classes of this base class cannot access these variables directly.

```
1  ' Fig. 11.10: CommmissionEmployee.vb
2  ' CommissionEmployee class represents a commission employee.
3  Public Class CommissionEmployee
4     Inherits Object ' optional
```

Fig. 11.10 | CommissionEmployee class with Protected instance variables. (Part 1 of 3.)

```

   Protected firstNameValue As String ' first name
   Protected lastNameValue As String ' last name
   Protected socialSecurityNumberValue As String ' social security number
   Protected grossSalesValue As Decimal ' gross weekly sales
   Protected commissionRateValue As Double ' commission percentage

   ' five-argument constructor
   Public Sub New(ByVal first As String, ByVal last As String, _
      ByVal ssn As String, ByVal sales As Decimal, ByVal rate As Double)

      ' implicit call to Object constructor occurs here
      FirstName = first
      LastName = last
      SocialSecurityNumber = ssn
      GrossSales = sales ' validate and store gross sales
      CommissionRate = rate ' validate and store commission rate
   End Sub ' New

   ' property FirstName
   Public Property FirstName() As String
      Get
         Return firstNameValue
      End Get

      Set(ByVal first As String)
         firstNameValue = first ' no validation
      End Set
   End Property ' FirstName

   ' property LastName
   Public Property LastName() As String
      Get
         Return lastNameValue
      End Get

      Set(ByVal last As String)
         lastNameValue = last ' no validation
      End Set
   End Property ' LastName

   ' property SocialSecurityNumber
   Public Property SocialSecurityNumber() As String
      Get
         Return socialSecurityNumberValue
      End Get

      Set(ByVal ssn As String)
         socialSecurityNumberValue = ssn ' no validation
      End Set
   End Property ' SocialSecurityNumber

```

Fig. 11.10 | CommissionEmployee class with Protected instance variables. (Part 2 of 3.)

```
   ' property GrossSales
   Public Property GrossSales() As Decimal
      Get
         Return grossSalesValue
      End Get

      Set(ByVal sales As Decimal)
         If sales < 0D Then ' validate gross sales
            grossSalesValue = 0D
         Else
            grossSalesValue = sales
         End If
      End Set
   End Property ' GrossSales

   ' property CommissionRate
   Public Property CommissionRate() As Double
      Get
         Return commissionRateValue
      End Get

      Set(ByVal rate As Double)
         If rate > 0.0 AndAlso rate < 1.0 Then ' validate rate
            commissionRateValue = rate
         Else
            commissionRateValue = 0.0
         End If
      End Set
   End Property ' CommissionRate

   ' calculate earnings
   Public Overridable Function CalculateEarnings() As Decimal
      Return Convert.ToDecimal(commissionRateValue) * grossSalesValue
   End Function ' CalculateEarnings

   ' return String representation of CommissionEmployee object
   Public Overrides Function ToString() As String
      Return ("commission employee: " & firstNameValue & " " & _
         lastNameValue & vbNewLine & "social security number: " & _
         socialSecurityNumberValue & vbNewLine & "gross sales: " & _
         String.Format("{0:C}", grossSalesValue) & vbNewLine & _
         "commission rate: " & String.Format("{0:F}", _
         commissionRateValue))
   End Function ' ToString
End Class ' CommissionEmployee
```

Fig. 11.10 | `CommissionEmployee` class with `Protected` instance variables. (Part 3 of 3.)

Modifying Derived Class `BasePlusCommissionEmployee`

We now modify class `BasePlusCommissionEmployee` (Fig. 11.9) so that it inherits from the version of class `CommissionEmployee` in Fig. 11.10. Because class `BasePlusCommissionEmployee` inherits from this new version of class `CommissionEmployee`, objects of class `BasePlusCommissionEmployee` (Fig. 11.11) inherit `CommissionEmployee`'s `Protected` instance variables `firstNameValue`, `lastNameValue`, `socialSecurityNumberValue`, `grossSalesValue` and `commissionRateValue`—all these variables are now `Protected` members of `BasePlusCommissionEmployee`. As a result, the compiler does not generate errors when compiling lines 35–36 of method `CalculateEarnings` and lines 41–46 of method `ToString` (so in Fig. 11.11 we have removed the two "not allowed" comments from Fig. 11.9 and we have changed all red text to black). If another class inherits `BasePlusCommissionEmployee`, the new derived class also inherits the `Protected` members.

```
1  ' Fig. 11.11: BasePlusCommissionEmployee.vb
2  ' BasePlusCommissionEmployee inherits from class CommissionEmployee.
3  Public Class BasePlusCommissionEmployee
4     Inherits CommissionEmployee
5
6     Private baseSalaryValue As Decimal ' base salary per week
7
8     ' six-argument constructor
9     Public Sub New(ByVal first As String, ByVal last As String, _
10       ByVal ssn As String, ByVal sales As Decimal, _
11       ByVal rate As Double, ByVal salary As Decimal)
12
13       ' use MyBase reference to CommissionEmployee constructor explicitly
14       MyBase.New(first, last, ssn, sales, rate)
15       BaseSalary = salary ' validate and store base salary
16    End Sub ' New
17
18    ' property BaseSalary
19    Public Property BaseSalary() As Decimal
20       Get
21          Return baseSalaryValue
22       End Get
23
24       Set(ByVal salary As Decimal)
25          If salary < 0D Then ' validate base salary
26             baseSalaryValue = 0D
27          Else
28             baseSalaryValue = salary
29          End If
30       End Set
31    End Property ' BaseSalary
32
33    ' calculate earnings
34    Public Overrides Function CalculateEarnings() As Decimal
35       Return baseSalaryValue + ( _
36          Convert.ToDecimal(commissionRateValue) * grossSalesValue)
37    End Function ' CalculateEarnings
38
39    ' return String representation of BasePlusCommissionEmployee object
40    Public Overrides Function ToString() As String
41       Return ("base-plus-commission employee: " & firstNameValue & _
42          " " & lastNameValue & vbNewLine & "social security number: " & _
```

Fig. 11.11 | `BasePlusCommissionEmployee` inherits `Protected` instance variables from `CommissionEmployee`. (Part 1 of 2.)

```
43             socialSecurityNumberValue & vbNewLine & "gross sales: " & _
44             String.Format("{0:C}", grossSalesValue) & vbNewLine & _
45             "commission rate: " & String.Format("{0:F}", _
46             commissionRateValue) & vbNewLine & "base salary: " & _
47             String.Format("{0:C}", baseSalaryValue))
48       End Function ' ToString
49    End Class ' BasePlusCommissionEmployee
```

Fig. 11.11 | `BasePlusCommissionEmployee` inherits `Protected` instance variables from `CommissionEmployee`. (Part 2 of 2.)

Class `BasePlusCommissionEmployee` does not inherit class `CommissionEmployee`'s constructor. However, class `BasePlusCommissionEmployee`'s six-argument constructor (lines 9–16) calls class `CommissionEmployee`'s five-argument constructor explicitly. `BasePlusCommissionEmployee`'s constructor does this because `CommissionEmployee` does not provide a parameterless constructor that could be invoked implicitly and, more important, because arguments are being passed to the base-class constructor.

Testing the Modified `BasePlusCommissionEmployee` *Class*

Figure 11.12 uses a `BasePlusCommissionEmployee` object to perform the same tasks that Fig. 11.7 performed on an object of the first version of class `BasePlusCommissionEmployee` (Fig. 11.6). Note that the outputs of the two programs are identical. We declared the first class `BasePlusCommissionEmployee` without using inheritance and declared this version of `BasePlusCommissionEmployee` using inheritance—nevertheless, both classes provide the same functionality. Note that the code for class `BasePlusCommissionEmployee` (Fig. 11.11), which is 49 lines, is considerably shorter than the code for the noninherited version of the class (Fig. 11.6), which is 120 lines, because the inherited version absorbs much of its functionality from base class `CommissionEmployee`, whereas the noninherited version absorbs only class `Object`'s functionality.

```
' Fig. 11.12: BasePlusCommissionEmployeeTest.vb
' Testing class BasePlusCommissionEmployee.
Module BasePlusCommissionEmployeeTest
   Sub Main()
      ' instantiate BasePlusCommissionEmployee object
      Dim employee As New BasePlusCommissionEmployee( _
         "Bob", "Lewis", "333-33-3333", 5000D, 0.04, 300D)

      ' get base-salaried commission employee data
      Console.WriteLine("Employee information obtained by properties:" _
         & vbNewLine & "First name is " & employee.FirstName & _
         vbNewLine & "Last name is " & employee.LastName & vbNewLine & _
         "Social Security Number is " & employee.SocialSecurityNumber)
      Console.WriteLine("Gross sales is {0:C}", employee.GrossSales)
      Console.WriteLine("Commission rate is {0:F}", _
         employee.CommissionRate)
      Console.WriteLine("Base salary is {0:C}", employee.BaseSalary)
```

Fig. 11.12 | `Protected` base-class members inherited into derived class `BasePlusCommissionEmployee`. (Part 1 of 2.)

```

      employee.BaseSalary = 1000D ' set base salary

      ' get new employee information
      Console.WriteLine(vbNewLine & _
         "Updated employee information obtained by ToString: " & _
         vbNewLine & employee.ToString() & vbNewLine)

      ' display the employee's earnings
      Console.WriteLine("Employee's earnings: {0:C}", _
         employee.CalculateEarnings())
   End Sub ' Main
End Module ' BasePlusCommissionEmployeeTest
```

```
Employee information obtained by properties:
First name is Bob
Last name is Lewis
Social Security Number is 333-33-3333
Gross sales is $5,000.00
Commission rate is 0.04
Base salary is $300.00

Updated employee information obtained by ToString:
base-plus-commission employee: Bob Lewis
social security number: 333-33-3333
gross sales: $5,000.00
commission rate: 0.04
base salary: $1,000.00

Employee's earnings: $1,200.00
```

Fig. 11.12 | `Protected` base-class members inherited into derived class `BasePlusCommissionEmployee`. (Part 2 of 2.)

Notes on Using **Protected** *Data*

This example declared base-class instance variables as `Protected` so that derived classes could inherit and access them. Inheriting `Protected` instance variables slightly improves performance, because the derived class can directly access the variables without incurring the overhead of calling property `Set` or `Get` accessors. In most cases, it is better to use `Private` instance variables to encourage proper software engineering, and leave code-optimization issues to the compiler. Your code will be easier to maintain, modify and debug.

Using `Protected` instance variables creates several potential problems. First, the derived-class object can set an inherited variable's value directly without using a `Set` accessor. Therefore, a derived-class object can assign an invalid value to the variable, thus leaving the object in an inconsistent state. For example, if we were to declare `CommissionEmployee`'s instance variable `grossSalesValue` as `Protected`, a derived-class object could then assign a negative value to `grossSalesValue`. Another problem with using `Protected` instance variables is that derived-class methods are more likely to be written so that they depend on the base class's data implementation. In practice, derived classes should depend only on the base-class services (i.e., non-`Private` methods and properties) and not on the base-class data implementation. With `Protected` instance variables in the base class, all the derived classes of the base class may need to be modified if the base-class implementation changes. For example, if for some reason we were to change the names of instance variables `firstNameValue` and `lastNameValue` to `first` and `last`, then we would have to do so for all occurrences in which a derived class directly references base-class instance variables `firstNameValue` and `lastNameValue`. In such a case, the software is said to be fragile or brittle, because a small change in the base class can "break" derived-class implementations. We should be able to change the base-class implementation while still providing the same services to the derived classes. Of course, if the base-class services change, we must reimplement our derived classes.

Software Engineering Observation 11.5

Use the `Protected` access modifier on a method when a base class is to provide the method to its derived classes but not to other clients.

11.4.5 CommissionEmployee–BasePlusCommissionEmployee Inheritance Hierarchy Using Private Instance Variables

We now reexamine our hierarchy once more, this time using better software engineering practices. Class `CommissionEmployee` (Fig. 11.13) declares instance variables `firstNameValue`, `lastNameValue`, `socialSecurityNumberValue`, `grossSalesValue` and `commissionRateValue` as `Private` (lines 4–8) and provides `Public` properties `FirstName`, `LastName`, `SocialSecurityNumber`, `GrossSales` and `CommissionRate` for manipulating these values. Note that methods `CalculateEarnings` (lines 86–88) and `ToString` (lines 91–97) obtain the values of the `Private` instance variables via properties. If we decide to change the instance-variable names, the `CalculateEarnings` and `ToString` declarations will not require modification—only the bodies of the `Get` and `Set` accessors that directly manipulate the instance variables will need to change. These changes would occur solely within the base class—no changes to the derived class would be needed. Localizing the effects of changes is good software engineering. Derived class `BasePlusCommissionEmployee` (Fig. 11.14) inherits `CommissionEmployee`'s non-`Private` properties and methods and can access the `Private` base-class members via those properties and methods.

Software Engineering Observation 11.6

Declaring base-class instance variables `Private` (as opposed to `Protected`) enables the base-class implementation of these instance variables to change without affecting derived-class implementations.

Error-Prevention Tip 11.1

When possible, do not include `Protected` instance variables in a base class. Instead, include non-`Private` properties and methods that carefully access `Private` instance variables. This will ensure that objects of the derived classes of this base class maintain consistent states of the base-class instance variables.

```
1  ' Fig. 11.13: CommmissionEmployee.vb
2  ' CommissionEmployee class represents a commission employee.
3  Public Class CommissionEmployee
```

Fig. 11.13 | `CommissionEmployee` class uses properties to manipulate its `Private` instance variables. (Part 1 of 3.)

```
   Private firstNameValue As String ' first name
   Private lastNameValue As String ' last name
   Private socialSecurityNumberValue As String ' social security number
   Private grossSalesValue As Decimal ' gross weekly sales
   Private commissionRateValue As Double ' commission percentage

   ' five-argument constructor
   Public Sub New(ByVal first As String, ByVal last As String, _
      ByVal ssn As String, ByVal sales As Decimal, ByVal rate As Double)

      ' implicit call to Object constructor occurs here
      FirstName = first
      LastName = last
      SocialSecurityNumber = ssn
      GrossSales = sales ' validate and store gross sales
      CommissionRate = rate ' validate and store commission rate
   End Sub ' New

   ' property FirstName
   Public Property FirstName() As String
      Get
         Return firstNameValue
      End Get

      Set(ByVal first As String)
         firstNameValue = first ' no validation
      End Set
   End Property ' FirstName

   ' property LastName
   Public Property LastName() As String
      Get
         Return lastNameValue
      End Get

      Set(ByVal last As String)
         lastNameValue = last ' no validation
      End Set
   End Property ' LastName

   ' property SocialSecurityNumber
   Public Property SocialSecurityNumber() As String
      Get
         Return socialSecurityNumberValue
      End Get

      Set(ByVal ssn As String)
         socialSecurityNumberValue = ssn ' no validation
      End Set
   End Property ' SocialSecurityNumber

```

Fig. 11.13 | CommissionEmployee class uses properties to manipulate its Private instance variables. (Part 2 of 3.)

```
    ' property GrossSales
    Public Property GrossSales() As Decimal
       Get
          Return grossSalesValue
       End Get

       Set(ByVal sales As Decimal)
          If sales < 0D Then ' validate gross sales
             grossSalesValue = 0D
          Else
             grossSalesValue = sales
          End If
       End Set
    End Property ' GrossSales

    ' property CommissionRate
    Public Property CommissionRate() As Double
       Get
          Return commissionRateValue
       End Get

       Set(ByVal rate As Double)
          If rate > 0.0 AndAlso rate < 1.0 Then ' validate rate
             commissionRateValue = rate
          Else
             commissionRateValue = 0.0
          End If
       End Set
    End Property ' CommissionRate

    ' calculate earnings
    Public Overridable Function CalculateEarnings() As Decimal
       Return Convert.ToDecimal(CommissionRate) * GrossSales
    End Function ' CalculateEarnings

    ' return String representation of CommissionEmployee object
    Public Overrides Function ToString() As String
       Return ("commission employee: " & FirstName & " " & _
          LastName & vbNewLine & "social security number: " & _
          SocialSecurityNumber & vbNewLine & "gross sales: " & _
          String.Format("{0:C}", GrossSales) & vbNewLine & _
          "commission rate: " & String.Format("{0:F}", CommissionRate))
    End Function ' ToString
 End Class ' CommissionEmployee
```

Fig. 11.13 | `CommissionEmployee` class uses properties to manipulate its `Private` instance variables. (Part 3 of 3.)

Class `BasePlusCommissionEmployee` (Fig. 11.14) has several changes to its method implementations that distinguish it from class `BasePlusCommissionEmployee` (Fig. 11.11). Methods `CalculateEarnings` (Fig. 11.14, lines 34–36) and `ToString` (lines 39–42) both use property `BaseSalary` to obtain the base salary value, rather than accessing

```
1  ' Fig. 11.14: BasePlusCommissionEmployee.vb
2  ' BasePlusCommissionEmployee inherits from class CommissionEmployee.
3  Public Class BasePlusCommissionEmployee
4     Inherits CommissionEmployee
5
6     Private baseSalaryValue As Decimal ' base salary per week
7
8     ' six-argument constructor
9     Public Sub New(ByVal first As String, ByVal last As String, _
10       ByVal ssn As String, ByVal sales As Decimal, _
11       ByVal rate As Double, ByVal salary As Decimal)
12
13       ' use MyBase reference to CommissionEmployee constructor explicitly
14       MyBase.New(first, last, ssn, sales, rate)
15       BaseSalary = salary ' validate and store base salary
16    End Sub ' New
17
18    ' property BaseSalary
19    Public Property BaseSalary() As Decimal
20       Get
21          Return baseSalaryValue
22       End Get
23
24       Set(ByVal salary As Decimal)
25          If salary < 0D Then ' validate base salary
26             baseSalaryValue = 0D
27          Else
28             baseSalaryValue = salary
29          End If
30       End Set
31    End Property ' BaseSalary
32
33    ' calculate earnings
34    Public Overrides Function CalculateEarnings() As Decimal
35       Return BaseSalary + MyBase.CalculateEarnings()
36    End Function ' CalculateEarnings
37
38    ' return String representation of BasePlusCommissionEmployee object
39    Public Overrides Function ToString() As String
40       Return ("base-plus-" & MyBase.ToString() & vbNewLine & _
41          "base salary: " & String.Format("{0:C}", BaseSalary))
42    End Function ' ToString
43 End Class ' BasePlusCommissionEmployee
```

Fig. 11.14 | `BasePlusCommissionEmployee` class `Inherits` `CommissionEmployee`, which provides only `Private` instance variables.

`baseSalaryValue` directly. If we decide to rename instance variable `baseSalaryValue`, only the bodies of property `BaseSalary` will need to change.

Class `BasePlusCommissionEmployee`'s `CalculateEarnings` method (Fig. 11.14, lines 34–36) overrides class `CommissionEmployee`'s `CalculateEarnings` method (Fig. 11.13, lines 86–88) to calculate the earnings of a base-salaried commission employee. The new version obtains the portion of the employee's earnings based on commission alone by calling `CommissionEmployee`'s `CalculateEarnings` method with the expression `MyBase.CalculateEarnings()` (Fig. 11.14, line 35). `BasePlusCommissionEmployee`'s `CalculateEarnings` method then adds the base salary to this value to calculate the total earnings of the derived-class employee. Note the syntax used to invoke an overridden base-class method from a derived class—place the keyword `MyBase` and a dot (`.`) separator before the base-class method name. By having `BasePlusCommissionEmployee`'s `CalculateEarnings` method invoke `CommissionEmployee`'s `CalculateEarnings` method to calculate part of a `BasePlusCommissionEmployee` object's earnings, we avoid duplicating the code and reduce code-maintenance problems.

Common Programming Error 11.3

When a base-class method is overridden in a derived class, the derived-class version often calls the base-class version to do a portion of the work. Failure to prefix the base-class method name with the keyword `MyBase` and a dot (`.`) separator when referencing the base class's method causes the derived-class method to call itself, usually creating an error called infinite recursion.

Similarly, `BasePlusCommissionEmployee`'s `ToString` method (Fig. 11.14, lines 39–42) overrides class `CommissionEmployee`'s `ToString` method (Fig. 11.13, lines 91–97) to return a string representation that is appropriate for a base-salaried commission employee. The derived class creates part of a `BasePlusCommissionEmployee` object's string representation (i.e., the string `"base-plus-commission employee"` and the values of class `CommissionEmployee`'s `Private` instance variables) by appending `"base-plus-"` in front of the string returned by calling `CommissionEmployee`'s `ToString` method with the expression `MyBase.ToString()` (Fig. 11.14, line 40). `BasePlusCommissionEmployee`'s `ToString` method then outputs the remainder of a `BasePlusCommissionEmployee` object's string representation (i.e., the value of class `BasePlusCommissionEmployee`'s base salary).

Figure 11.15 performs the same manipulations on a `BasePlusCommissionEmployee` object as did Fig. 11.7 and Fig. 11.12. Although each "base-salaried commission employee" class behaves identically, class `BasePlusCommissionEmployee` (Fig. 11.14) is the best engineered. By using inheritance and by calling methods that hide the data and ensure consistency, we have efficiently constructed a well-engineered class.

```
' Fig. 11.15: BasePlusCommissionEmployeeTest.vb
' Testing class BasePlusCommissionEmployee.
Module BasePlusCommissionEmployeeTest
   Sub Main()
      ' instantiate BasePlusCommissionEmployee object
      Dim employee As New BasePlusCommissionEmployee( _
         "Bob", "Lewis", "333-33-3333", 5000D, 0.04, 300D)

      ' get base-salaried commission employee data
      Console.WriteLine("Employee information obtained by properties:" _
         & vbNewLine & "First name is " & employee.FirstName & _
         vbNewLine & "Last name is " & employee.LastName & vbNewLine & _
         "Social Security Number is " & employee.SocialSecurityNumber)
      Console.WriteLine("Gross sales is {0:C}", employee.GrossSales)
```

Fig. 11.15 | Base class `Private` instance variables are accessible to a derived class via the `Public` properties and methods inherited by the derived class. (Part 1 of 2.)

```
        Console.WriteLine("Commission rate is {0:F}", _
           employee.CommissionRate)
        Console.WriteLine("Base salary is {0:C}", employee.BaseSalary)

        employee.BaseSalary = 1000D ' set base salary

        ' get new employee information
        Console.WriteLine(vbNewLine & _
           "Updated employee information obtained by ToString: " & _
           vbNewLine & employee.ToString() & vbNewLine)

        ' display the employee's earnings
        Console.WriteLine("Employee's earnings: {0:C}", _
           employee.CalculateEarnings())
     End Sub ' Main
  End Module ' BasePlusCommissionEmployeeTest
```

```
Employee information obtained by properties:
First name is Bob
Last name is Lewis
Social Security Number is 333-33-3333
Gross sales is $5,000.00
Commission rate is 0.04
Base salary is $300.00

Updated employee information obtained by ToString:
base-plus-commission employee: Bob Lewis
social security number: 333-33-3333
gross sales: $5,000.00
commission rate: 0.04
base salary: $1,000.00

Employee's earnings: $1,200.00
```

Fig. 11.15 | Base class `Private` instance variables are accessible to a derived class via the `Public` properties and methods inherited by the derived class. (Part 2 of 2.)

In this section, you studied five example programs carefully designed to teach key capabilities for good software engineering with inheritance. You learned how to use the keyword `Inherits` to create a derived class using inheritance, how to use `Protected` base-class members to enable a derived class to access inherited base-class instance variables and how to override base-class methods to provide versions that are more appropriate for derived-class objects. Also, you applied software engineering techniques from this chapter and Chapter 10 to create classes that are easy to maintain, modify and debug.

11.5 Constructors in Derived Classes

As we explained in the preceding section, instantiating a derived-class object begins a chain of constructor calls in which the derived-class constructor, before performing its own tasks, invokes its direct base class's constructor either explicitly (via the `MyBase` reference) or implicitly (calling the base class's default or parameterless constructor). Similarly, if the base class is derived from another class (as is every class except `Object`), the base-class constructor invokes the constructor of the next class up the hierarchy, and so on. The last constructor called in the chain is always the constructor for class `Object`. The original derived-class constructor's body finishes executing last. Each base class's constructor manipulates the base-class instance variables that the derived-class object inherits. For example, let's reconsider the `CommissionEmployee`–`BasePlusCommissionEmployee` hierarchy from Figs. 11.13 and 11.14. When a program creates a `BasePlusCommissionEmployee` object, the `BasePlusCommissionEmployee` constructor is called. That constructor, before executing its full body code, immediately calls `CommissionEmployee`'s constructor, which in turn calls `Object`'s constructor. Class `Object`'s constructor has an empty body, so it immediately returns control to the `CommissionEmployee`'s constructor, which then initializes the `Private` instance variables of `CommissionEmployee` that are part of the `BasePlusCommissionEmployee` object. When the `CommissionEmployee`'s constructor completes execution, it returns control to the `BasePlusCommissionEmployee`'s constructor, which initializes the `BasePlusCommissionEmployee` object's `baseSalaryValue`.

Our next example revisits the commission employee hierarchy by redeclaring class `CommissionEmployee` (Fig. 11.16) and class `BasePlusCommissionEmployee` (Fig. 11.17) with each class's constructor printing a message when invoked, enabling us to observe the order in which the constructors in the hierarchy execute.

```
' Fig. 11.16: CommissionEmployee.vb
' CommissionEmployee class represents a commission employee.
Public Class CommissionEmployee
   Private firstNameValue As String ' first name
   Private lastNameValue As String ' last name
   Private socialSecurityNumberValue As String ' social security number
   Private grossSalesValue As Decimal ' gross weekly sales
   Private commissionRateValue As Double ' commission percentage

   ' five-argument constructor
   Public Sub New(ByVal first As String, ByVal last As String, _
      ByVal ssn As String, ByVal sales As Decimal, ByVal rate As Double)

      ' implicit call to Object constructor occurs here
      FirstName = first
      LastName = last
      SocialSecurityNumber = ssn
      GrossSales = sales ' validate and store gross sales
      CommissionRate = rate ' validate and store commission rate
      Console.WriteLine(vbNewLine & _
         "CommissionEmployee constructor:" & vbNewLine & "{0}", Me)
   End Sub ' New

   ' property FirstName
   Public Property FirstName() As String
      Get
         Return firstNameValue
      End Get

```

Fig. 11.16 | `CommissionEmployee`'s constructor outputs text. (Part 1 of 3.)

```
      Set(ByVal first As String)
         firstNameValue = first ' no validation
      End Set
   End Property ' FirstName

   ' property LastName
   Public Property LastName() As String
      Get
         Return lastNameValue
      End Get

      Set(ByVal last As String)
         lastNameValue = last ' no validation
      End Set
   End Property ' LastName

   ' property SocialSecurityNumber
   Public Property SocialSecurityNumber() As String
      Get
         Return socialSecurityNumberValue
      End Get

      Set(ByVal ssn As String)
         socialSecurityNumberValue = ssn ' no validation
      End Set
   End Property ' SocialSecurityNumber

   ' property GrossSales
   Public Property GrossSales() As Decimal
      Get
         Return grossSalesValue
      End Get

      Set(ByVal sales As Decimal)
         If sales < 0D Then ' validate gross sales
            grossSalesValue = 0D
         Else
            grossSalesValue = sales
         End If
      End Set
   End Property ' GrossSales

   ' property CommissionRate
   Public Property CommissionRate() As Double
      Get
         Return commissionRateValue
      End Get

      Set(ByVal rate As Double)
         If rate > 0.0 AndAlso rate < 1.0 Then ' validate rate
            commissionRateValue = rate
```

Fig. 11.16 | CommissionEmployee's constructor outputs text. (Part 2 of 3.)

```
81           Else
82              commissionRateValue = 0.0
83           End If
84        End Set
85     End Property ' CommissionRate
86
87     ' calculate earnings
88     Public Overridable Function CalculateEarnings() As Decimal
89        Return Convert.ToDecimal(CommissionRate) * GrossSales
90     End Function ' CalculateEarnings
91
92     ' return String representation of CommissionEmployee object
93     Public Overrides Function ToString() As String
94        Return ("commission employee: " & FirstName & " " & _
95           LastName & vbNewLine & "social security number: " & _
96           SocialSecurityNumber & vbNewLine & "gross sales: " & _
97           String.Format("{0:C}", GrossSales) & vbNewLine & _
98           "commission rate: " & String.Format("{0:F}", CommissionRate))
99     End Function ' ToString
100 End Class ' CommissionEmployee
```

Fig. 11.16 | `CommissionEmployee`'s constructor outputs text. (Part 3 of 3.)

Class `CommissionEmployee` (Fig. 11.16) contains the same features as the version of the class shown in Fig. 11.13. We have modified the constructor (lines 11–22) to output text upon its invocation (lines 20–21). Note that outputting `Me` with the `{0}` format string (line 21) implicitly invokes the `ToString` method of the `CommissionEmployee` object being constructed to obtain the object's string representation.

Class `BasePlusCommissionEmployee` (Fig. 11.17) is almost identical to Fig. 11.14, except that `BasePlusCommissionEmployee`'s constructor also outputs text when invoked (lines 16–18). Again, we output `Me` using the `{0}` format string (line 18) to implicitly invoke the `ToString` method, this time to obtain the `BasePlusCommissionEmployee` object's string representation.

```
1  ' Fig. 11.17: BasePlusCommissionEmployee.vb
2  ' BasePlusCommissionEmployee inherits from class CommissionEmployee.
3  Public Class BasePlusCommissionEmployee
4     Inherits CommissionEmployee
5
6     Private baseSalaryValue As Decimal ' base salary per week
7
8     ' six-argument constructor
9     Public Sub New(ByVal first As String, ByVal last As String, _
10       ByVal ssn As String, ByVal sales As Decimal, _
11       ByVal rate As Double, ByVal salary As Decimal)
12
13       ' use MyBase reference to CommissionEmployee constructor explicitly
14       MyBase.New(first, last, ssn, sales, rate)
15       BaseSalary = salary ' validate and store base salary
```

Fig. 11.17 | `BasePlusCommissionEmployee`'s constructor outputs text. (Part 1 of 2.)

```
      Console.WriteLine(vbNewLine & _
         "BasePlusCommissionEmployee constructor:" & _
         vbNewLine & "{0}", Me)
   End Sub ' New

   ' property BaseSalary
   Public Property BaseSalary() As Decimal
      Get
         Return baseSalaryValue
      End Get

      Set(ByVal salary As Decimal)
         If salary < 0D Then ' validate base salary
            baseSalaryValue = 0D
         Else
            baseSalaryValue = salary
         End If
      End Set
   End Property ' BaseSalary

   ' calculate earnings
   Public Overrides Function CalculateEarnings() As Decimal
      Return BaseSalary + MyBase.CalculateEarnings()
   End Function ' CalculateEarnings

   ' return String representation of BasePlusCommissionEmployee object
   Public Overrides Function ToString() As String
      Return ("base-plus-" & MyBase.ToString() & vbNewLine & _
         "base salary: " & String.Format("{0:C}", BaseSalary))
   End Function ' ToString
End Class ' BasePlusCommissionEmployee
```

Fig. 11.17 | `BasePlusCommissionEmployee`'s constructor outputs text. (Part 2 of 2.)

Figure 11.18 demonstrates the order in which constructors are called for objects of classes that are part of an inheritance hierarchy. Method `Main` begins by instantiating `CommissionEmployee` object `employee1` (lines 6–7). Next, lines 10–11 instantiate `BasePlusCommissionEmployee` object `employee2`. This invokes the `CommissionEmployee` constructor, which prints output with the values passed from the `BasePlusCommissionEmployee` constructor, then performs the output specified in the `BasePlusCommissionEmployee` constructor.

```
1  ' Fig. 11.18: Constructor.vb
2  ' Display order in which base-class and derived-class constructors
3  ' and finalizers are called.
4  Module Constructor
5     Sub Main()
6        Dim employee1 As New CommissionEmployee( _
7           "Bob", "Lewis", "333-33-3333", 5000D, 0.04)
8        Console.WriteLine()
9
```

Fig. 11.18 | Constructor call order using `Me`. (Part 1 of 2.)

```
      Dim employee2 As New BasePlusCommissionEmployee( _
         "Lisa", "Jones", "555-55-5555", 2000D, 0.06, 800D)
   End Sub ' Main
End Module ' Constructor
```

```
CommissionEmployee constructor:
commission employee: Bob Lewis
social security number: 333-33-3333
gross sales: $5,000.00
commission rate: 0.04

CommissionEmployee constructor:
base-plus-commission employee: Lisa Jones
social security number: 555-55-5555
gross sales: $2,000.00
commission rate: 0.06
base salary: $0.00

BasePlusCommissionEmployee constructor:
base-plus-commission employee: Lisa Jones
social security number: 555-55-5555
gross sales: $2,000.00
commission rate: 0.06
base salary: $800.00
```

Fig. 11.18 | Constructor call order using `Me`. (Part 2 of 2.)

Analyzing the Output

The `CommissionEmployee` constructor and `BasePlusCommissionEmployee` constructor calls each output values for the first name, last name, social security number, gross sales, commission rate *and* base salary of the `BasePlusCommissionEmployee`. When constructing a `BasePlusCommissionEmployee` object, the `Me` reference used in the body of both the `CommissionEmployee` and `BasePlusCommissionEmployee` constructors refers to the `BasePlusCommissionEmployee` object being constructed. When a program invokes method `ToString` on an object, the version of `ToString` that executes is always the version defined in that object's class. This is an example of polymorphism, a key aspect of object-oriented programming that we discuss in detail in Chapter 12. Reference `Me` refers to the current `BasePlusCommissionEmployee` object being constructed, so `BasePlusCommissionEmployee`'s `ToString` method executes even when `ToString` is invoked from the body of class `CommissionEmployee`'s constructor. This would not be the case if the `CommissionEmployee` constructor were called to initialize a new `CommissionEmployee` object. When the `CommissionEmployee` constructor invokes method `ToString` for the `BasePlusCommissionEmployee` being constructed, the program displays `0` for the `BaseSalary` value, because the `BasePlusCommissionEmployee` constructor's body has not yet initialized the `BaseSalary`. The `BasePlusCommissionEmployee` constructor output shows the proper `BaseSalary` value (i.e., `800.00`), because this line is output after the `BaseSalary` is initialized.

Using `MyClass` *in Class* `CommissionEmployee`*'s Constructor*

To force `CommissionEmployee`'s `ToString` method to execute when the `CommissionEmployee`'s constructor is called, we use the `MyClass` reference. Reference **`MyClass`** is similar to `Me`, except that a method call with `MyClass` always invokes the version of the method defined in that particular class—the method called is not affected by the runtime type of the object. For example, if we replace Me in line 21 of Fig. 11.16 with

```
MyClass.ToString()
```

then CommissionEmployee's ToString will be executed (even though the runtime type of the object is BasePlusCommissionEmployee). Thus, the output of the CommissionEmployee's constructor call will not display the base salary value (Fig. 11.19).

Recall that Shared class variables and methods exist independently of a class's objects. They also exist when there are no objects of the class. Hence, the MyClass reference cannot be used in a Shared method, because such a method can be called even when there are no objects of the corresponding class. The Me reference also can't be used in a Shared method.

```
CommissionEmployee constructor:
commission employee: Bob Lewis
social security number: 333-33-3333
gross sales: $5,000.00
commission rate: 0.04

CommissionEmployee constructor:
commission employee: Lisa Jones
social security number: 555-55-5555
gross sales: $2,000.00
commission rate: 0.06

BasePlusCommissionEmployee constructor:
base-plus-commission employee: Lisa Jones
social security number: 555-55-5555
gross sales: $2,000.00
commission rate: 0.06
base salary: $800.00
```

Fig. 11.19 | Constructor call order using MyClass.

11.6 Software Engineering with Inheritance

Novice programmers sometimes have difficulty appreciating the scope of the problems faced by developers who work on large-scale software projects in industry. People experienced with such projects say that effective software reuse improves the software-development process. Object-oriented programming facilitates software reuse, potentially shortening development and maintenance efforts.

This section discusses customizing existing software with inheritance. When a new class inherits from an existing class, the new class inherits the non-Private members of the existing class. We can customize the new class to meet our needs by including additional members and by overriding base-class members. Doing this does not require the derived-class programmer to change the base class's source code. Visual Basic simply requires access to the base class's assembly file so that it can compile and execute any program that uses or inherits the base class. This is attractive to independent software vendors (ISVs), because they develop proprietary classes for sale or license and make them available to users in MSIL format. Users then can derive new classes from these library classes rapidly and without accessing the ISVs' proprietary source code.

Software Engineering Observation 11.7

Even though inheriting from a class does not require access to the class's source code, developers often insist on seeing the source code to see how the class is implemented. They want to ensure that they are extending a solid class that performs well and is implemented securely.

The availability of substantial class libraries helps deliver the maximum benefits of software reuse through inheritance. Application designers build their applications with these libraries, and library designers are compensated when their libraries are included with the applications. The standard Visual Basic class libraries tend to be general purpose. Many special-purpose class libraries exist, and more are being created.

Software Engineering Observation 11.8

At the design stage in an object-oriented system, the designer often finds that certain classes are closely related. The designer should "factor out" common instance variables and methods and place them in a base class. Then the designer should use inheritance to develop derived classes, specializing them with capabilities beyond those inherited from the base class.

Performance Tip 11.1

If derived classes are larger than they need to be (i.e., contain too much functionality), memory and processing resources may be wasted. Extend the base class that contains the functionality that is closest to what you need.

Reading derived-class declarations can be confusing, because inherited members are not declared explicitly in the derived classes, but are nevertheless present in them. A similar problem exists in documenting derived-class members.

11.7 Class `Object`

As we've mentioned, all classes inherit directly or indirectly from class `Object`, so its seven methods are inherited by all other classes. Figure 11.20 summarizes these methods.

Method	Description
`Equals`	Compares two objects for equality; returns `True` if they are equal and `False` otherwise. The method takes any `Object` as an argument. When objects of a class must be compared for equality, the class should override method `Equals` to compare the contents of the two objects. The method's implementation should meet the following requirements: • It should return `False` if the argument is `Nothing`. • It should return `True` if an object is compared to itself, as in `object1.Equals(object1)`. • It should return `True` only if both `object1.Equals(object2)` and `object2.Equals(object1)` would return `True`. • For three objects, if `object1.Equals(object2)` returns `True` and `object2.Equals(object3)` returns `True`, then `object1.Equals(object3)` should also return `True`.

Fig. 11.20 | `Object` methods that are inherited by all classes. (Part 1 of 2.)

Method	Description
`Equals` *(continued)*	• A class that overrides `Equals` must also override `GetHashCode` to ensure that equal objects have identical hashcodes. The default `Equals` implementation determines only whether two references *refer to the same object* in memory.
`Finalize`	This `Protected` method (introduced in Section 10.10) is called by the garbage collector on an object just before the garbage collector reclaims the object's memory. It is not guaranteed that the garbage collector will reclaim an object, so it cannot be guaranteed that the object's `Finalize` method will execute. The method must specify an empty parameter list and must not return a value. The default implementation of this method is a placeholder that does nothing.
`GetHashCode`	A hashtable is a data structure that relates one object, called the key, to another object, called the value. We discuss class `Hashtable` in Chapter 24, Data Structures and Generic Collections. When initially inserting a value into a hashtable, the key's `GetHashCode` method is called. The hashcode value returned is used by the hashtable to determine the location at which to insert the corresponding value. The key's hashcode is also used by the hashtable to locate the key's corresponding value.
`GetType`	Every object in Visual Basic knows its own type at execution time. Method `GetType` (used in Section 12.5) returns an object of class `Type` (namespace `System`) that contains information about the object's type, such as its class name (obtained from `Type` property `FullName`).
`MemberwiseClone`	This `Protected` method, which takes no arguments and returns an `Object` reference, makes a copy of the object on which it is called. The implementation of this method performs a shallow copy—instance-variable values in one object are copied into another object of the same type. For reference types, only the references are copied.
`ReferenceEquals`	This `Shared` method takes two `Object` arguments and returns `True` if two objects are the same instance or if they are `Nothing` references. Otherwise, it returns `False`.
`ToString`	This method (introduced in Section 10.2) returns a `String` representation of an object. The default implementation of this method returns the namespace followed by a dot and the class name of the object's class.

Fig. 11.20 | `Object` methods that are inherited by all classes. (Part 2 of 2.)

We discuss most of `Object`'s methods throughout this book (as indicated in the table). To learn more about these methods from the **Help** menu, select **Help > Index...**, make sure that **.NET Framework** is selected in the **Filtered by:** drop-down list, and enter "`Object` class" in the search text box.

11.8 Friend Members

Another intermediate level of member access is `Friend` access. A class's `Friend` members can be accessed only by code in the same assembly (i.e., the compiled version of a program or class library). Recall that an assembly is a program or a library that consists of one class declaration, declaring a member with `Friend` access has no specific effect. However, if a program uses multiple classes from the same assembly, these classes can access each other's `Friend` members directly through references to objects of the appropriate classes. Unlike `Public` access, any other programs that are declared outside the assembly cannot access these `Friend` members. To access a non-`Shared` `Friend` member within the same assembly, you would first have to create an object of the class that declares the `Friend` member, then invoke the `Friend` member using the dot (`.`) separator. You can access a `Friend` member that is also `Shared` via the name of the class that declares the `Friend` member and a dot (`.`) separator. Note that you can also have `Protected Friend` members that are accessible both from code in the same assembly and by subclasses of the class in which the `Protected Friend` members are declared.

11.9 Wrap-Up

This chapter introduced inheritance—the ability to create a class by absorbing an existing class's members and embellishing them with new capabilities. Through a series of examples using an employee inheritance hierarchy, you learned the notions of base classes and derived classes and used keyword `Inherits` to create derived classes that inherit members from base classes. We introduced the access modifiers `Protected` and `Friend`. Derived-class methods can access `Protected` base-class members. `Friend` members are accessible to classes declared in the same assembly as the class that declares the `Friend` members. You learned how to access base-class members with `MyBase` and how to access the current object with the `Me` and `MyClass` references. You also saw the order in which constructors are called for objects of classes that are part of an inheritance hierarchy. Finally, you learned about the methods of class `Object`—the direct or indirect base class of all classes.

In Chapter 12, Object-Oriented Programming: Polymorphism, we build on our discussion of inheritance by introducing polymorphism—an object-oriented concept that enables us to write programs that handle, in a simple and more general manner, objects of a wide variety of classes related by inheritance. After studying Chapter 12, you will be familiar with classes, objects, encapsulation, inheritance and polymorphism—the most essential aspects of object-oriented programming.

Summary

Section 11.1 Introduction

- Inheritance is a form of software reuse in which a new class is created by absorbing an existing class's members and embellishing them with new or modified capabilities.
- When creating a class, rather than declaring completely new members, you can designate that the new class inherits the members of an existing class. The existing class is called the base class, and the new class is the derived class.
- A derived class is more specific than its base class and normally represents a more specialized group of objects.
- The direct base class is the specific base class from which the derived class inherits.
- An indirect base class is inherited from two or more levels up in the class hierarchy.

- An *is-a* relationship represents inheritance. In an *is-a* relationship, an object of a derived class also can be treated as an object of its base class, but not vice versa.
- A *has-a* relationship represents composition. In a *has-a* relationship, an object contains references to objects of other classes.

Section 11.2 Base Classes and Derived Classes

- A class can be either a base class, supplying members to other classes, or a derived class, inheriting some of its members from other classes.
- A derived class can override (redefine) a base-class method with an appropriate implementation.

Section 11.3 `Protected` Members

- A base class's `Protected` members can be accessed by members of that base class and by members of its derived classes.
- When a derived-class method overrides a base-class method, the base-class method can be accessed from the derived class by preceding the base-class method name with `MyBase` and a dot (`.`).
- Derived-class methods cannot directly access `Private` members of their base class.

Section 11.4.1 Creating and Using a `CommissionEmployee` Class

- Every class directly or indirectly inherits class `Object`'s methods. If a class does not specify that it inherits another class, the new class implicitly inherits `Object`.
- Declaring instance variables as `Private` and providing `Public` properties to manipulate and validate the instance variables help enforce good software engineering.
- A base-class method must be declared `Overridable` if it is to be overridden in a derived class.
- A derived-class method uses keyword `Overrides` to indicate that it overrides (redefines) the corresponding method declared in the base class.

Section 11.4.2 Creating a `BasePlusCommissionEmployee` Class without Using Inheritance

- With inheritance, the common instance variables and methods of all the classes in the hierarchy are declared in a base class.

Section 11.4.3 Creating a `CommissionEmployee`–`BasePlusCommissionEmployee` Inheritance Hierarchy

- Each derived-class constructor must implicitly or explicitly call its base-class constructor to ensure that the instance variables inherited from the base class are initialized properly.
- A derived class can explicitly invoke a constructor of its base class by using the base-class constructor call syntax—keyword `MyBase`, followed by the dot (`.`) separator, followed by `New` and a set of parentheses containing the base-class constructor arguments.

Section 11.4.4 `CommissionEmployee`–`BasePlusCommissionEmployee` Inheritance Hierarchy Using `Protected` Instance Variables

- Declaring `Public` instance variables is poor software engineering, because it allows unrestricted access to the instance variables, greatly increasing the chance of errors.
- With `Protected` instance variables, a derived class gets access to the instance variables, but classes that are not derived classes cannot access these variables directly.
- With `Protected` instance variables, a derived-class object can set an inherited variable directly.
- With `Protected` instance variables in the base class, all the derived classes of the base class may need to be modified if the base-class implementation changes.

Section 11.5 Constructors in Derived Classes

- When a program creates a derived-class object, the derived-class constructor immediately calls the base-class constructor (explicitly via `MyBase`, or implicitly).
- A method call with `MyClass` always invokes the version of the method defined in that particular class—the method called is not affected by the runtime type of the object.
- The `MyClass` reference cannot be used in a `Shared` method, because such a method can be called when no objects exist.

Section 11.6 Software Engineering with Inheritance

- When a new class inherits from an existing class, the new class inherits the non-`Private` members of the existing class.
- Object-oriented programming facilitates software reuse, potentially shortening development and maintenance effort.
- The availability of substantial and useful class libraries helps deliver the maximum benefits of software reuse through inheritance.

*Section 11.7 Class **`Object`***

- Method `Equals` of `Object` compares two objects for equality and returns `True` if they are equal and `False` otherwise.
- The default `Equals` implementation determines whether two references refer to the same object in memory.
- Method `Finalize` of `Object` is called by the garbage collector on an object just before the garbage collector reclaims the object's memory.
- Every object knows its own type. Method `GetType` of `Object` returns an object of class `Type` (namespace `System`) that contains information about the object's type, such as its class name (obtained from `Type` property `FullName`).
- Method `ToString` of `Object` returns a `String` representation of an object. The default implementation of this method returns the namespace and class name of the object's class.
- The default implementation of method `MemberwiseClone` of `Object` performs a so-called shallow copy—instance variable values in one object are copied into another object of the same type.

*Section 11.8 **`Friend`** Members*

- A class's `Friend` members can be accessed only by code in the same assembly.
- To access a non-`Shared` `Friend` member within the same assembly, create an object of the class that declares the `Friend` member, then invoke the `Friend` member using the dot (`.`) separator.
- To access a `Friend` member that is `Shared`, use the name of the class that declares the `Friend` member followed by the dot (`.`) separator.
- You can also have `Protected Friend` members that are accessible both from code in the same assembly and by subclasses of the class in which the `Protected Friend` members are declared.

Terminology

base class
base-class constructor
base-class constructor call syntax
base-class default constructor
base-class parameterless constructor
brittle software
class hierarchy
class library
composition
constructor call order

derived class
derived-class constructor
direct base class
`Equals` method of class `Object`
field of a class
`Finalize` method of `Object`
fragile software
`Friend` access modifier
`FullName` property of `Type`
`GetHashCode` method of class `Object`
`GetType` method of class `Object`
has-a relationship
hierarchical relationship
hierarchy diagram of classes
indirect base class
inheritance
inheritance hierarchy
inherited member
inherited method
`Inherits` keyword
invoke a base-class constructor
invoke a base-class method
is-a relationship
`MemberwiseClone` method of class `Object`
`MyBase` keyword
`MyClass` keyword
object of a base class
object of a derived class
`Overridable` keyword
override a base-class method in a derived class
`Overrides` keyword
`Private` base-class member
`Protected` base-class member
`Protected` keyword
`Public` base-class member
`ReferenceEquals` method of `Object`
reusable component
shallow copy
single inheritance
software reuse
standardized reusable components
subclass
superclass
`ToString` method of class `Object`
`Type` class

Self-Review Exercises

11.1 Fill in the blanks in each of the following statements:

a) ________ is a form of software reusability in which new classes acquire the members of existing classes and enhance those classes with new capabilities.
b) A base class's ________ members can be accessed only in the base-class declaration and in derived-class declarations.
c) In a(n) ________ relationship, an object of a derived class can also be treated as an object of its base class.
d) In a(n) ________ relationship, a class object has references to objects of other classes as members.
e) In single inheritance, a base class exists in a(n) ________ relationship with its derived classes.
f) A base class's ________ members are accessible anywhere that the application has a reference to an object of that base class or to an object of any of its derived classes.
g) When an object of a derived class is instantiated, a base class ________ is called implicitly or explicitly.
h) Derived-class constructors can call base-class constructors via the ________ keyword.

11.2 State whether each of the following is *true* or *false*. If a statement is *false*, explain why.

a) Base-class constructors are not inherited by derived classes.
b) A *has-a* relationship is implemented via inheritance.
c) A `Car` class has *is-a* relationships with the `SteeringWheel` and `Brakes` classes.
d) Inheritance encourages the reuse of proven high-quality software.
e) When a derived class redefines a base-class method by using the same signature and return type, the derived class is said to overload that base-class method.

Answers to Self-Review Exercises

11.1 a) Inheritance. b) `Protected`. c) *is-a* or inheritance. d) *has-a* or composition. e) hierarchical. f) `Public`. g) constructor. h) `MyBase`.

11.2 a) True. b) False. A *has-a* relationship is implemented via composition. An *is-a* relationship is implemented via inheritance. c) False. These are examples of *has-a* relationships. Class `Car` has an *is-a* relationship with class `Vehicle`. d) True. e) False. This is known as overriding, not overloading.

Exercises

11.3 Many applications written with inheritance could be written with composition instead, and vice versa. Rewrite class `BasePlusCommissionEmployee` (Fig. 11.14) of the `CommissionEmployee`–`BasePlusCommissionEmployee` hierarchy to use composition rather than inheritance.

11.4 Discuss the ways in which inheritance promotes software reuse, saves time during application development and helps prevent errors.

11.5 Draw a UML class diagram for an inheritance hierarchy for students at a university similar to the hierarchy shown in Fig. 11.2. Use `Student` as the base class of the hierarchy, then extend `Student` with classes `UndergraduateStudent` and `GraduateStudent`. Continue to extend the hierarchy as deeply (i.e., as many levels) as possible. For example, `Freshman`, `Sophomore`, `Junior` and `Senior` might extend `UndergraduateStudent`, and `DoctoralStudent` and `MastersStudent` might be derived classes of `GraduateStudent`. After drawing the hierarchy, discuss the relationships that exist between the classes. [*Note:* You do not need to write any code for this exercise.]

11.6 The world of shapes is much richer than the shapes included in the inheritance hierarchy of Fig. 11.3. Write down all the shapes you can think of—both two-dimensional and three-dimensional—and form them into a more complete `Shape` hierarchy with as many levels as possible. Your hierarchy should have class `Shape` at the top. Class `TwoDimensionalShape` and class `ThreeDimensionalShape` should extend `Shape`. Add additional derived classes, such as `Quadrilateral` and `Sphere`, at their correct locations in the hierarchy as necessary.

11.7 Some programmers prefer not to use `Protected` access, because they believe it breaks the encapsulation of the base class. Discuss the relative merits of using `Protected` access vs. using `Private` access in base classes.

11.8 Write an inheritance hierarchy for classes `Quadrilateral`, `Trapezoid`, `Parallelogram`, `Rectangle` and `Square`. Use `Quadrilateral` as the base class of the hierarchy. Make the hierarchy as deep (i.e., as many levels) as possible. Specify the instance variables, properties and methods for each class. The `Private` instance variables of `Quadrilateral` should be the *x-y* coordinate pairs for the four endpoints of the `Quadrilateral`. Write an application that instantiates objects of your classes and outputs each object's area (except `Quadrilateral`).

11.9 *(Package Inheritance Hierarchy)* Package-delivery services, such as FedEx®, DHL® and UPS®, offer a number of different shipping options, each with specific costs associated. Create an inheritance hierarchy to represent various types of packages. Use `Package` as the base class of the hierarchy, then include classes `TwoDayPackage` and `OvernightPackage` that derive from `Package`. Base class `Package` should include `Private` instance variables representing the name, address, city, state and ZIP code for the package's sender and recipient, and instance variables that store the weight (in ounces) and cost per ounce to ship the package. `Package`'s constructor should initialize these `Private` instance variables with `Public` properties. Ensure that the weight and cost per ounce contain positive values. `Package` should provide a `Public` method `CalculateCost` that returns a `Decimal` indicating the cost associated with shipping the package. `Package`'s `CalculateCost` method should determine the cost by multiplying the weight by the cost per ounce. Derived class `TwoDayPackage` should inherit the functionality of base class `Package`, but also include an instance variable that represents a flat fee that the shipping company charges for two-day delivery service. `TwoDayPackage`'s constructor should receive a value to initialize this instance variable. `TwoDayPackage` should redefine method `CalculateCost` so that it computes the shipping cost by adding the flat fee to the weight-based cost calculated by base class `Package`'s `CalculateCost` method. Class `OvernightPackage` should inherit directly from class `Package` and contain an instance variable representing an additional fee per ounce charged for overnight-delivery service. `OvernightPackage` should redefine method `CalculateCost` so that it adds the additional fee per ounce to the standard cost per ounce before calculating the shipping cost. Write a test application that creates objects of each type of `Package` and tests method `CalculateCost`.

11.10 *(`Account` Inheritance Hierarchy)* Create an inheritance hierarchy that a bank might use to represent customer bank accounts. All customers at this bank can deposit (i.e., credit) money into their accounts and withdraw (i.e., debit) money from their accounts. More specific types of accounts also exist. Savings accounts, for instance, earn interest on the money they hold. Checking accounts, on the other hand, charge a fee per transaction.

Create base class `Account` and derived classes `SavingsAccount` and `CheckingAccount` that inherit from class `Account`. Base class `Account` should include one `Private` instance variable of type `Decimal` to represent the account balance. The class should provide a constructor that receives an initial balance and uses it to initialize the instance variable with a `Public` property. The property should validate the initial balance to ensure that it is greater than or equal to `0.0`. If not, the balance should be set to `0.0`, and the `set` accessor should display an error message, indicating that the initial balance was invalid. The class should provide two `Public` methods. Method `Credit` should add an amount to the current balance. Method `Debit` should withdraw money from the `Account` and ensure that the debit amount does not exceed the `Account`'s balance. If it does, the balance should be left unchanged, and the method should print the message `"Debit amount exceeded account balance."` The class should also provide a `get` accessor in property `Balance` that returns the current balance.

Derived class `SavingsAccount` should inherit the functionality of an `Account`, but also include a `Decimal` instance variable indicating the interest rate (percentage) assigned to the `Account`. `SavingsAccount`'s constructor should receive the initial balance, as well as an initial value for the interest rate. `SavingsAccount` should provide `Public` method `CalculateInterest` that returns a `Decimal` indicating the amount of interest earned by an account. Method `CalculateInterest` should determine this amount by multiplying the interest rate by the account balance. [*Note:* `SavingsAccount` should inherit methods `Credit` and `Debit` without redefining them.]

Derived class `CheckingAccount` should inherit from base class `Account` and include a `Decimal` instance variable that represents the fee charged per transaction. `CheckingAccount`'s constructor should receive the initial balance, as well as a parameter indicating a fee amount. Class `CheckingAccount` should redefine methods `Credit` and `Debit` so that they subtract the fee from the account balance whenever either transaction is performed successfully. `CheckingAccount`'s versions of these methods should invoke the base-class `Account` version to perform the updates to an account balance. `CheckingAccount`'s `Debit` method should charge a fee only if money is actually withdrawn (i.e., the debit amount does not exceed the account balance). [*Hint:* Define `Account`'s `Debit` method so that it returns a `bool` indicating whether money was withdrawn. Then use the return value to determine whether a fee should be charged.]

After defining the classes in this hierarchy, write an application that creates objects of each class and tests their methods. Add interest to the `SavingsAccount` object by first invoking its `CalculateInterest` method, then passing the returned interest amount to the object's `Credit` method.

12

Object-Oriented Programming: Polymorphism

One Ring to rule them all,
One Ring to find them,
One Ring to bring them all
and in the darkness bind
them.

—J. R. R. Tolkien

General propositions do not decide concrete cases.

—Oliver Wendell Holmes

A philosopher of imposing stature doesn't think in a vacuum. Even his most abstract ideas are, to some extent, conditioned by what is or is not known in the time when he lives.

—Alfred North Whitehead

Why art thou cast down,
O my soul?

—Psalms 42:5

OBJECTIVES

In this chapter you'll learn:

- What polymorphism is.
- To use overridden methods to effect polymorphism.
- To distinguish between abstract and concrete classes.
- To declare abstract methods to create abstract classes.
- How polymorphism makes systems extensible and maintainable.
- To determine an object's type at execution time.
- To declare and implement interfaces.

12.1 Introduction

We now continue our study of object-oriented programming by explaining and demonstrating **polymorphism** with inheritance hierarchies. Polymorphism enables us to "program in the general" rather than "program in the specific." In particular, polymorphism enables us to write programs that process objects that share the same base class in a class hierarchy as simply as if they were all objects of the base class. Yet, as we send method calls in this general way, the specific objects "do the right thing."

Consider the following example of polymorphism. Suppose we create a program that simulates the movement of several types of animals for a biological study. Classes `Fish`, `Frog` and `Bird` represent the three types of animals under investigation. Imagine that each of these classes inherits base class `Animal`, which contains a method `Move` and maintains the animal's current location as *x-y* coordinates. Each derived class implements method `Move`. Our program maintains an array of references to objects of the various `Animal` derived classes. To simulate the animals' movements, the program sends each object the same message—`Move`—once per second. However, each specific type of `Animal` responds to the `Move` message in a unique way—a `Fish` might swim two feet, a `Frog` might jump three feet and a `Bird` might fly ten feet. The program issues the same `Move` message to each animal object generically, but each object knows how to modify its *x-y* coordinates appropriately for its specific type of movement. Relying on each object to know how to "do the right thing" (i.e., what is appropriate for that type of object) in response to the same method call is the key concept of polymorphism. The same message (in this case, `Move`) sent to a variety of objects has "many forms" of results—hence the term polymorphism.

With polymorphism, we can design and implement systems that are easily extensible—new classes can be added with little or no modification to the general portions of the program, as long as the new classes are part of the inheritance hierarchy that the program processes generically. The only parts of a program that must be altered to accommodate new classes are those that require direct knowledge of the new classes that you add to the hierarchy. For example, if we inherit from class `Animal` to create class `Tortoise` (which might respond to a `Move` message by crawling one inch), we need to write only the `Tortoise` class (with a `Move` method) and the part of the simulation that instantiates `Tortoise` objects. The portions of the simulation that process each `Animal` generically can remain the same.

This chapter has several key parts. First, we discuss common examples of polymorphism. We then provide a live-code example demonstrating polymorphic behavior. As you will soon see, you will use base-class references to conveniently manipulate both base-class and derived-class objects polymorphically.

We then present a case study that revisits the employee hierarchy of Section 11.4.5. We develop a simple payroll application that polymorphically calculates the weekly pay of several different types of employees using each employee's `CalculateEarnings` method. Though the earnings of each type of employee are calculated in a specific way, polymorphism allows us to process the employees "in the general." We add two new classes to the hierarchy—`SalariedEmployee` (for people paid a fixed weekly salary) and `HourlyEmployee` (for people paid an hourly salary and "time-and-a-half" for overtime). We declare a common set of functionality for all the classes in the updated hierarchy in a so-called abstract class, `Employee`, from which classes `SalariedEmployee`, `HourlyEmployee` and `CommissionEmployee` inherit directly, and from which class `BasePlusCommissionEmployee` inherits indirectly. As you will see, when we invoke each employee's `CalculateEarnings` method off a base-class `Employee` reference, the correct earnings calculation is performed due to Visual Basic's polymorphic capabilities.

Occasionally, when performing polymorphic processing, we need to program "in the specific." Our `Employee` case study demonstrates that a program can determine an object's type at execution time and act on that object accordingly. The case study uses these capabilities to determine whether a particular employee object *is a* `BasePlusCommissionEmployee`, and, in that specific case, we increase the employee's base salary by 10%.

The chapter continues with an introduction to interfaces. An interface describes a set of methods that can be called on an object but does not provide concrete implementations for the methods. Programmers can declare classes that **implement** (i.e., declare the methods of) one or more interfaces. Each interface method must be declared in all the classes that implement the interface. Once a class implements an interface, all objects of that class have an *is-a* relationship with the interface type, and all objects of the class are guaranteed to provide the functionality described by the interface. This is true of all derived classes of that class as well.

Interfaces are particularly useful for assigning common functionality to possibly unrelated classes. This allows objects of unrelated classes to be processed polymorphically—objects of classes that implement the same interface can respond to the same method calls. To demonstrate creating and using interfaces, we modify our payroll application to create a general accounts payable application that can calculate payments due not only for company employees, but also for invoice amounts to be billed for purchased goods. As you will see, interfaces enable polymorphic capabilities similar to those possible with inheritance.

12.2 Polymorphic Video Game

Suppose we design a video game that manipulates objects of many different types, including objects of classes `Martian`, `Venutian`, `Plutonian`, `SpaceShip` and `LaserBeam`. Imagine that each class inherits from the common base class called `SpaceObject`, which contains method `Draw`. Each derived class implements this method in a manner appropriate to that class. A screen-manager program maintains a collection (e.g., a `SpaceObject` array) of references to objects of the various classes. To refresh the screen, the screen manager periodically sends each object the same message—namely, `Draw`. However, each object responds in a unique way. For example, a `Martian` object might draw itself in red with the appropriate number of antennae. A `SpaceShip` object might draw itself as a bright silver flying saucer. A `LaserBeam` object might draw itself as a bright red beam across the screen. The same message (in this case, `Draw`) sent to a variety of objects has "many forms" of results.

A screen manager might use polymorphism to facilitate adding new classes to a system with minimal modifications to the system's code. Suppose that we want to add `Mercurian` objects to our video game. To do so, we must build a class `Mercurian` that inherits from `SpaceObject` and provides its own `Draw` method implementation. When objects of class `Mercurian` appear in the `SpaceObject` collection, the screen-manager code invokes method `Draw`, exactly as it does for the other objects in the collection, regardless of their types. So the new `Mercurian` class simply "plugs right in" without any modification of the screen-manager code by the programmer. Thus, without modifying the system (other than to build new classes and modify the code that creates new objects), programmers can use polymorphism to include types that were not envisioned when the system was created.

With polymorphism, calls to methods of the same method name, signature and return type can be used to cause different actions to occur, depending on the type of objects on which the method is invoked. This gives you tremendous expressive capability, as you will soon see.

Software Engineering Observation 12.1

Polymorphism promotes extensibility: Software that invokes polymorphic behavior is independent of the object types to which messages are sent. New object types that can respond to existing method calls can be incorporated into a system without requiring modification of the base system. Only client code that instantiates new objects must be modified to accommodate new types.

12.3 Demonstrating Polymorphic Behavior

Section 11.4 created a commission employee class hierarchy, in which class `BasePlusCommissionEmployee` inherited from class `CommissionEmployee`. The examples in that section manipulated `CommissionEmployee` and `BasePlusCommissionEmployee` objects by using references to them to invoke their methods. We aimed base-class references at base-class objects and derived-class references at derived-class objects. These assignments are natural and straightforward—base-class references are intended to refer to base-class objects, and derived-class references are intended to refer to derived-class objects. However, as you will soon see, some "crossover" assignments are possible.

In the next example, we aim a base-class reference at a derived-class object. We then show how invoking a method on a derived-class object via a base class reference invokes the derived-class functionality—*the type of the actual referenced object, not the type of the reference, determines which method is called*. This example demonstrates the key concept that an object of a derived class can be treated as an object of its base class, yet still "do the right thing." This enables various interesting manipulations. A program can create an array of base-class references that refer to objects of many derived-class types. This is allowed because each derived-class object *is an* object of its base class. For instance, we can assign the reference of a `BasePlusCommissionEmployee` object to a base-class `CommissionEmployee` variable because a `BasePlusCommissionEmployee` *is a* `CommissionEmployee`—so we can treat a `BasePlusCommissionEmployee` as a `CommissionEmployee`.

As you will learn later in the chapter, we cannot treat a base-class object as a derived-class object because a base-class object is not an object of any of its derived classes. For example, we cannot assign the reference of a `CommissionEmployee` object to a derived-class `BasePlusCommissionEmployee` variable because a `CommissionEmployee` is not a `BasePlusCommissionEmployee`—a `CommissionEmployee` does not have a `baseSalary` instance variable and does not have property `BaseSalary`. The *is-a* relationship applies only from a derived class to its direct (and indirect) base classes, but not vice versa.

The compiler *does* allow the assignment of a base-class reference to a derived-class variable if we explicitly cast the base-class reference to the derived-class type—a technique we discuss in detail in Section 12.5. Why would we ever want to perform such an assignment? A base-class reference can be used to invoke only the methods declared in the base class—attempting to invoke derived-class-only methods through a base-class reference results in compilation errors. If a program needs to perform a derived-class-specific operation on a derived-class object referenced by a base-class variable, the program must first cast the base class reference to a derived-class reference through a technique known as **downcasting**. This enables the program to invoke derived-class methods that are not in the base class, but only off a derived class reference. We demonstrate downcasting in Section 12.5.

Figure 12.1 shows three ways to use base-class and derived-class variables to store references to base-class and derived-class objects. The first two are straightforward—as in Section 11.4, we assign a base-class reference to a base-class variable, and we assign a derived-class reference to a derived-class variable. Then we demonstrate the relationship between derived classes and base classes (i.e., the *is-a* relationship) by assigning a derived-class reference to a base-class variable. [*Note:* This program uses the `CommissionEmployee` and `BasePlusCommissionEmployee` classes from Figs. 11.13 and 11.14, respectively.]

In Fig. 12.1, lines 10–11 create a `CommissionEmployee` object and assign its reference to a `CommissionEmployee` variable. Lines 14–15 create a `BasePlusCommissionEmployee` object and assign its reference to a `BasePlusCommissionEmployee` variable. These assignments are natural—for example, a `CommissionEmployee` variable's primary purpose is to hold a reference to a `CommissionEmployee` object. Lines 18–20 use reference `commissionEmployee1` to invoke `ToString` explicitly. Because `commissionEmployee1` refers to a `CommissionEmployee` object, base-class `CommissionEmployee`'s version of `ToString` is called, as is evident from the output. Similarly, lines 24–26 use `basePlusCommissionEmployee` to invoke `ToString` explicitly on the `BasePlusCommissionEmployee` object. This invokes derived class `BasePlusCommissionEmployee`'s version of `ToString`, as is also evident from the output.

Lines 29–30 then assign to a base-class `CommissionEmployee` variable `commissionEmployee2` the reference to derived-class object `basePlusCommissionEmployee`, which

```
1  ' Fig. 12.1: PolymorphismTest.vb
2  ' Assigning base-class and derived-class references to base-class and
3  ' derived-class variables.
4  Module PolymorphismTest
5     Sub Main()
6        Dim commissionEmployee1 As CommissionEmployee
7        Dim basePlusCommissionEmployee As BasePlusCommissionEmployee
8
9        ' assign base-class reference to base-class variable
10       commissionEmployee1 = New CommissionEmployee( _
11          "Sue", "Jones", "222-22-2222", 10000D, 0.06)
12
13       ' assign derived-class reference to derived-class variable
14       basePlusCommissionEmployee = New BasePlusCommissionEmployee( _
15          "Bob", "Lewis", "333-33-3333", 5000D, 0.04, 300D)
16
17       ' invoke ToString on base-class object using base-class variable
18       Console.WriteLine("Call CommissionEmployee's ToString with " & _
19          "base-class reference to base-class object: " & vbNewLine & _
20          commissionEmployee1.ToString() & vbNewLine)
21
22       ' invoke ToString on derived-class object using
23       ' derived-class variable
24       Console.WriteLine("Call BasePlusCommissionEmployee's ToString " & _
25          "with derived-class reference to derived-class object: " & _
26          vbNewLine & basePlusCommissionEmployee.ToString() & vbNewLine)
27
28       ' assign derived-class reference to base-class variable
29       Dim commissionEmployee2 As CommissionEmployee = _
30          basePlusCommissionEmployee
31
32       ' invoke ToString on derived-class object using base-class variable
33       Console.WriteLine("Call BasePlusCommissionEmployee's ToString " & _
34          "with base-class reference to derived-class object: " & _
35          vbNewLine & commissionEmployee2.ToString())
36    End Sub ' Main
37 End Module ' PolymorphismTest
```

Fig. 12.1 | Assigning base-class and derived-class references to base-class and derived-class variables. (Part 1 of 2.)

```
Call CommissionEmployee's ToString with base-class reference to base-class
object:
commission employee: Sue Jones
social security number: 222-22-2222
gross sales: $10,000.00
commission rate: 0.06

Call BasePlusCommissionEmployee's ToString with derived-class reference to
derived-class object:
commission employee: Bob Lewis
social security number: 333-33-3333
gross sales: $5,000.00
commission rate: 0.04
base salary: $300.00

Call BasePlusCommissionEmployee's ToString with base-class reference to
derived-class object:
commission employee: Bob Lewis
social security number: 333-33-3333
gross sales: $5,000.00
commission rate: 0.04
base salary: $300.00
```

Fig. 12.1 | Assigning base-class and derived-class references to base-class and derived-class variables. (Part 2 of 2.)

lines 33–35 use to invoke method `ToString`. A base-class variable that contains a reference to a derived-class object and that is used to call a method (which is in both the base class and the derived class) actually calls the derived-class version of the method (polymorphically). Hence, `commissionEmployee2.ToString()` in line 35 actually calls class `BasePlusCommissionEmployee`'s `ToString` method. The compiler allows this "crossover" because an object of a derived class *is an* object of its base class (but not vice versa). When the compiler encounters a method call made through a variable, it determines whether the method can be called by checking the variable's class type. If that class contains the proper method declaration (or inherits one), the compiler allows the call to be compiled. At execution time, the type of the object to which the variable refers determines the actual version of the method to use. This is polymorphic behavior.

12.4 Abstract Classes and Methods

When we think of a class type, we assume that programs will create objects of that type. In some cases, however, it is useful to declare classes for which you never intend to instantiate objects. Such classes are called abstract classes. Because they are used only as base classes in inheritance hierarchies, we refer to them as abstract base classes. These classes cannot be used to instantiate objects, because, as we will soon see, abstract classes are incomplete. We demonstrate abstract classes in Section 12.5.

The purpose of an abstract class is primarily to provide an appropriate base class from which other classes can inherit and thus share a common design. In the `Shape` hierarchy of Fig. 11.3, for example, derived classes inherit the notion of what it means to be a `Shape`—possibly including common properties such as `Location`, `Color` and `Border-`

Thickness, and behaviors such as Draw, Move, Resize and ChangeColor. Classes that can be used to instantiate objects are called concrete classes. Such classes provide implementations of every method they declare (some of the implementations can be inherited). For example, we could derive concrete classes Circle, Square and Triangle from abstract base class TwoDimensionalShape. Similarly, we could derive concrete classes Sphere, Cube and Tetrahedron from abstract base class ThreeDimensionalShape. Abstract base classes are too general to create real objects—they specify only what is common among derived classes. We need to be more specific before we can create objects. For example, if you send the Draw message to abstract class TwoDimensionalShape, it knows that two-dimensional shapes should be *drawable*, but it does not know *what specific shape to draw*, so it cannot implement a real Draw method. Concrete classes provide the specifics that make it reasonable to instantiate objects.

Abstract Classes in Inheritance Hierarchies

Not all inheritance hierarchies contain abstract classes. However, programmers often write client code that uses only abstract base-class types to reduce the client code's dependencies on a range of specific derived-class types. For example, a programmer can write a method with a parameter of an abstract base-class type. When called, such a method can be passed an object of any concrete class that directly or indirectly inherits the base class specified as the parameter's type.

Abstract classes sometimes constitute several levels of the hierarchy. For example, the Shape hierarchy of Fig. 11.3 begins with abstract class Shape. The next level of the hierarchy contains abstract classes TwoDimensionalShape and ThreeDimensionalShape. The next level of the hierarchy declares concrete classes for TwoDimensionalShapes (Circle, Square and Triangle) and ThreeDimensionalShapes (Sphere, Cube and Tetrahedron).

Declaring Abstract Classes and Abstract Methods

You make a class abstract by declaring it with keyword MustInherit. An abstract class normally contains one or more abstract methods. An abstract method is one with keyword MustOverride in its declaration, as in

```
Public MustOverride Sub Draw() ' abstract method
```

Abstract methods do not provide implementations. A class that contains any abstract methods must be declared as an abstract (i.e., MustInherit) class even if it contains some concrete (nonabstract) methods. Each concrete derived class of an abstract base class must provide concrete implementations of all the base class's abstract methods. Constructors and Shared methods cannot be inherited, so they cannot be declared MustOverride.

Software Engineering Observation 12.2

An abstract class declares common attributes and behaviors of the various classes in a class hierarchy. An abstract class typically contains one or more abstract methods that derived classes must override if the derived classes are to be concrete. The instance variables and concrete methods of an abstract class are subject to the normal rules of inheritance.

Common Programming Error 12.1

Attempting to instantiate an object of an abstract class is a compilation error.

Common Programming Error 12.2

Failure to implement a base class's abstract methods in a derived class is a compilation error unless the derived class is also declared `MustInherit` *(i.e., the derived class is also abstract).*

Although we cannot instantiate objects of abstract base classes, soon you will see that we *can* use abstract base classes to declare variables that can hold references to objects of any concrete classes derived from those abstract classes. Programs typically use such variables to manipulate derived-class objects polymorphically.

Using Abstract Classes and Methods to Achieve Polymorphism

Consider another polymorphism application. A drawing program needs to display many shapes, including new shape types that you might add to the system even after writing the drawing program. The drawing program might need to display shapes, such as `Circles`, `Triangles`, `Rectangles` or others, that derive from abstract base class `Shape`. The drawing program uses `Shape` variables to manage the objects that are displayed. To draw any object in this inheritance hierarchy, the drawing program uses a base-class `Shape` variable containing a reference to a derived-class object to invoke the object's `Draw` method. This method is declared `MustOverride` in base class `Shape`, so each concrete derived class *must* implement method `Draw` in a manner specific to that shape. Each object in the `Shape` hierarchy "knows" how to draw itself. The drawing program does not have to worry about the type of each object or whether the drawing program has ever encountered objects of that type.

Polymorphism is particularly effective for implementing so-called layered software systems. Each of the physical devices in an operating system, for example, operates quite differently from the others. Even so, the same commands can be used to read or write data from and to the various devices. For each device, the operating system uses a piece of software called a device driver to control all communication between the system and the device. The write message sent to a device-driver object needs to be interpreted specifically in the context of that driver and how it manipulates devices of that specific type. However, the write call itself really is no different from the write to any other device in the system—place some number of bytes from memory onto that device. An object-oriented operating system might use an abstract base class to provide an "interface" appropriate for all device drivers. Then, through inheritance from that abstract base class, derived classes are formed that all behave similarly. The device-driver methods are declared as abstract methods in the abstract base class. The implementations of these abstract methods are provided in the concrete derived classes that correspond to the specific types of device drivers. New devices are always being developed, often long after the operating system has been released. When you buy a new device, it comes with a device driver provided by the device vendor. The device is immediately operational after you connect it to your computer and install the driver. This is another nice example of how polymorphism makes systems extensible.

It is common in object-oriented programming to declare an iterator class that can traverse all the objects in a collection, such as an array (Chapter 8) or a `List` (Chapter 9). For example, a program can print a `List` of objects by creating an iterator object and using it to obtain the next list element each time the iterator is called. Iterators often are used in polymorphic programming to traverse a collection that contains references to objects from various levels of an inheritance hierarchy. (Chapter 24 presents a thorough treatment of collections and iterators.) A `List` of objects of class `TwoDimensionalShape`, for example, could contain objects from derived classes `Square`, `Circle`, `Triangle` and so on. Calling method `Draw` for each `TwoDimensionalShape` object off a `TwoDimensionalShape` variable would polymorphically draw each object correctly on the screen.

12.5 Case Study: Payroll System Class Hierarchy Using Polymorphism

This section reexamines the `CommissionEmployee`–`BasePlusCommissionEmployee` hierarchy that we explored in Section 11.4. Now we use an abstract method and polymorphism to perform payroll calculations based on the type of employee. We create an enhanced employee hierarchy to solve the following problem:

> *A company pays its employees on a weekly basis. The employees are of four types: Salaried employees are paid a fixed weekly salary regardless of the number of hours worked, hourly employees are paid by the hour and receive overtime pay (1.5 times the regular hourly salary) for all hours worked in excess of 40 hours, commission employees are paid a percentage of their sales, and base-plus-commission employees receive a base salary plus a percentage of their sales. For the current pay period, the company has decided to reward base-plus-commission employees by adding 10% to their base salaries. The company wants to implement a Visual Basic application that performs its payroll calculations polymorphically.*

We use abstract class `Employee` to represent the general concept of an employee. The classes that inherit from `Employee` are `SalariedEmployee`, `CommissionEmployee` and `HourlyEmployee`. Class `BasePlusCommissionEmployee` inherits from `CommissionEmployee`. The UML class diagram in Fig. 12.2 shows our polymorphic employee inheritance hierarchy. Note that abstract class name `Employee` is italicized, as per UML convention; concrete class names are not italicized.

Abstract base class `Employee` declares the "interface" to the hierarchy—that is, the set of methods that a program can invoke on all `Employee` objects. We use the term "interface" here in a general sense to refer to the various ways programs can communicate with objects of any `Employee` derived class. Be careful not to confuse the general notion of an "interface" with the formal notion of a Visual Basic interface, the subject of Section 12.7. Each employee, regardless of the way his or her earnings are calculated, has a first name, a last

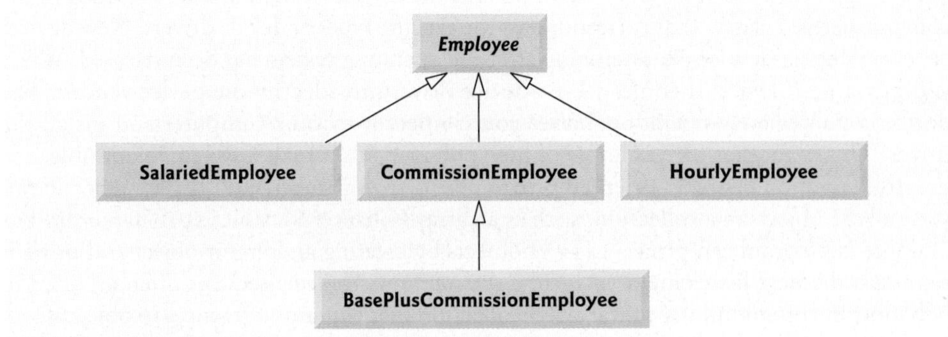

Fig. 12.2 | `Employee` hierarchy UML class diagram.

name and a social security number, so Public properties FirstName, LastName and SocialSecurityNumber appear in abstract base class Employee.

The following sections implement the Employee class hierarchy. The first five sections show the abstract base class Employee and the concrete derived classes SalariedEmployee, CommissionEmployee, HourlyEmployee and the indirectly derived concrete class BasePlusCommissionEmployee. The last section shows a test program that builds objects of these classes and processes the objects polymorphically.

12.5.1 Creating Abstract Base Class Employee

In this example, class Employee provides methods CalculateEarnings and ToString, and properties that manipulate an Employee's instance variables. A CalculateEarnings method certainly applies to all employees, but each earnings calculation depends on the employee's class. So we declare CalculateEarnings as MustOverride in base class Employee because a default implementation does not make sense for that method—there is not enough information to determine what amount CalculateEarnings should return. Each derived class overrides CalculateEarnings with an appropriate implementation. To calculate an employee's earnings, the program assigns to a base class Employee variable a reference to the employee's object, then invokes CalculateEarnings on that variable. We maintain an array of Employee variables, each holding a reference to an Employee object. Of course, there cannot be Employee objects because Employee is an abstract class—thanks to inheritance, however, all objects of all derived classes of Employee may be thought of as Employee objects. The program iterates through the array and calls CalculateEarnings for each Employee object. Visual Basic processes these method calls polymorphically. Including abstract method CalculateEarnings in class Employee forces every directly derived concrete class of Employee to override CalculateEarnings. This enables the class hierarchy designer to demand that each derived concrete class provide an appropriate pay calculation.

Method ToString in class Employee returns a String containing the first name, last name and social security number of the employee. As we will see, each derived class of Employee overrides method ToString to create a string representation of an object of that class that contains the employee's type (e.g., "salaried employee:") followed by the rest of the employee's information.

The diagram in Fig. 12.3 shows the five classes of the hierarchy down the left side and methods CalculateEarnings and ToString across the top. For each class, the diagram shows the desired results of each method. [*Note:* We do not list base class Employee's properties because they are not overridden in any of the derived classes—each of these properties is inherited and used "as is" by each of the derived classes.]

Class Employee (Fig. 12.4) is a MustInherit class, meaning it can be used only as a base class. The class includes a constructor that takes the first name, last name and social security number as arguments (lines 9–14); Get accessors that return the first name, last name and social security number (lines 18–20, 29–31 and 40–42, respectively); Set accessors that set the first name, last name and social security number (lines 22–24, 33–35 and 44–46, respectively); method ToString (lines 50–53), which returns the string representation of an Employee; and abstract (MustOverride) method CalculateEarnings (line 56), which must be implemented by concrete derived classes. Note that the SocialSecurityNumber property does not validate the social security number in this example. In business-critical applications, such validation should be provided.

	CalculateEarnings	ToString
Employee	MustOverride	*FirstName LastName* social security number: *SSN*
Salaried- Employee	*WeeklySalary*	salaried employee: *FirstName LastName* social security number: *SSN* weekly salary: *WeeklySalary*
Hourly- Employee	*If Hours <= 40* *Wage* * *Hours* *If Hours > 40* 40 * *Wage* + ((*Hours* - 40) * *Wage* * 1.5)	hourly employee: *FirstName LastName* social security number: *SSN* hourly wage: *Wage*; hours worked: *Hours*
Commission- Employee	*CommissionRate* * *GrossSales*	commission employee: *FirstName LastName* social security number: *SSN* gross sales: *GrossSales*; commission rate: *CommissionRate*
BasePlus- Commission- Employee	(*CommissionRate* * *GrossSales*) + *BaseSalary*	base-salaried commission employee: *FirstName LastName* social security number: *SSN* gross sales: *GrossSales*; commission rate: *CommissionRate*; base salary: *BaseSalary*

Fig. 12.3 | Polymorphic interface for the `Employee` hierarchy classes.

```
' Fig. 12.4: Employee.vb
' Employee abstract base class.
Public MustInherit Class Employee
   Private firstNameValue As String
   Private lastNameValue As String
   Private socialSecurityNumberValue As String

   ' three-argument constructor
   Public Sub New(ByVal first As String, ByVal last As String, _
      ByVal ssn As String)
      FirstName = first
      LastName = last
      SocialSecurityNumber = ssn
   End Sub ' New

   ' property FirstName
   Public Property FirstName() As String
      Get
         Return firstNameValue
      End Get
```

Fig. 12.4 | `Employee` abstract base class. (Part 1 of 2.)

```

         Set(ByVal first As String)
            firstNameValue = first
         End Set
      End Property ' FirstName

      ' property LastName
      Public Property LastName() As String
         Get
            Return lastNameValue
         End Get

         Set(ByVal last As String)
            lastNameValue = last
         End Set
      End Property ' LastName

      ' property SocialSecurityNumber
      Public Property SocialSecurityNumber() As String
         Get
            Return socialSecurityNumberValue
         End Get

         Set(ByVal ssn As String)
            socialSecurityNumberValue = ssn
         End Set
      End Property ' SocialSecurityNumber

      ' return String representation of Employee object
      Public Overrides Function ToString() As String
         Return (String.Format("{0} {1}", FirstName, LastName) & _
            vbNewLine & "social security number: " & SocialSecurityNumber)
      End Function ' ToString

      ' abstract method overridden by derived class
      Public MustOverride Function CalculateEarnings() As Decimal
   End Class ' Employee
```

Fig. 12.4 | `Employee` abstract base class. (Part 2 of 2.)

Why did we decide to declare `CalculateEarnings` as a `MustOverride` method? It simply does not make sense to provide an implementation of this method in class `Employee`. We cannot calculate the earnings for a general `Employee`—we first must know the specific `Employee` type to determine the appropriate earnings calculation. By declaring this method `MustOverride`, we indicate that each concrete derived class *must* provide an appropriate `CalculateEarnings` implementation and that a program will be able to use base-class `Employee` variables to invoke method `CalculateEarnings` polymorphically for any type of `Employee`.

12.5.2 Creating Concrete Derived Class `SalariedEmployee`

Class `SalariedEmployee` (Fig. 12.5) inherits class `Employee` (line 4) and overrides `CalculateEarnings` (lines 31–33), which makes `SalariedEmployee` a concrete class. The

```
1  ' Fig. 12.5: SalariedEmployee.vb
2  ' SalariedEmployee class inherits Employee
3  Public Class SalariedEmployee
4     Inherits Employee
5
6     Private weeklySalaryValue As Decimal ' employee's weekly salary
7
8     ' four-argument constructor
9     Public Sub New(ByVal first As String, ByVal last As String, _
10       ByVal ssn As String, ByVal salary As Decimal)
11       MyBase.New(first, last, ssn) ' pass to Employee constructor
12       WeeklySalary = salary ' validate and store salary
13    End Sub ' New
14
15    ' property WeeklySalary
16    Public Property WeeklySalary() As Decimal
17       Get
18          Return weeklySalaryValue
19       End Get
20
21       Set(ByVal salary As Decimal)
22          If salary < 0D Then ' validate salary
23             weeklySalaryValue = 0D
24          Else
25             weeklySalaryValue = salary
26          End If
27       End Set
28    End Property ' WeeklySalary
29
30    ' calculate earnings; override abstract method CalculateEarnings
31    Public Overrides Function CalculateEarnings() As Decimal
32       Return WeeklySalary
33    End Function ' CalculateEarnings
34
35    ' return String representation of SalariedEmployee object
36    Public Overrides Function ToString() As String
37       Return ("salaried employee: " & MyBase.ToString() & vbNewLine & _
38          String.Format("weekly salary {0:C}", WeeklySalary))
39    End Function ' ToString
40 End Class ' SalariedEmployee
```

Fig. 12.5 | `SalariedEmployee` class derived from class `Employee`.

class includes a constructor (lines 9–13) that takes a first name, a last name, a social security number and a weekly salary as arguments; a `WeeklySalary` property that has a `Get` accessor (lines 17–19) to return `weeklySalaryValue`'s value and a `Set` accessor (lines 21–27) to assign a new nonnegative value to instance variable `weeklySalaryValue`; a method `CalculateEarnings` (lines 31–33) to calculate a `SalariedEmployee`'s earnings; and a method `ToString` (lines 36–39) that returns a `String` including the employee's type, namely, `"salaried employee: "`, followed by employee-specific information produced by base class `Employee`'s `ToString` method, and the value of `SalariedEmployee`'s `WeeklySalary` property. Class `SalariedEmployee`'s constructor passes the first name, last name and social security number to base class Employee's constructor (line 11). Method CalculateEarnings overrides abstract method CalculateEarnings of Employee with a concrete implementation that returns the SalariedEmployee's weekly salary. If we do not implement CalculateEarnings, class SalariedEmployee must be declared MustInherit—otherwise, a compilation error occurs (and, of course, we want SalariedEmployee to be a concrete class).

SalariedEmployee's ToString method (lines 36–39) overrides Employee method ToString. If class SalariedEmployee did not override ToString, the class would have inherited Employee's ToString method. In that case, SalariedEmployee's ToString method would simply return the employee's full name and social security number, which does not adequately represent a SalariedEmployee. To produce a complete string representation of a SalariedEmployee, the derived class's ToString method returns "salaried employee: " followed by the base-class Employee-specific information (i.e., first name, last name and social security number) obtained by invoking the base class's ToString (line 37)—a nice example of code reuse. The string representation of a SalariedEmployee also contains the employee's weekly salary obtained from the WeeklySalary property.

12.5.3 Creating Concrete Derived Class HourlyEmployee

Class HourlyEmployee (Fig. 12.6) also inherits class Employee (line 4). The class includes a constructor (lines 10–16) that takes as arguments a first name, a last name, a social security number, an hourly wage and the number of hours worked. Lines 24–30 and 39–45

```
1  ' Fig. 12.6: HourlyEmployee.vb
2  ' HourlyEmployee class inherits Employee.
3  Public Class HourlyEmployee
4     Inherits Employee
5
6     Private wageValue As Decimal ' wage per hour
7     Private hoursValue As Decimal ' hours worked for week
8
9     ' five-argument constructor
10    Public Sub New(ByVal first As String, ByVal last As String, _
11       ByVal ssn As String, ByVal hourlyWage As Decimal, _
12       ByVal hoursWorked As Decimal)
13       MyBase.New(first, last, ssn) ' pass to Employee constructor
14       Wage = hourlyWage ' validate and store hourly wage
15       Hours = hoursWorked ' validate and store hours worked
16    End Sub ' New
17
18    ' property Wage
19    Public Property Wage() As Decimal
20       Get
21          Return wageValue
22       End Get
23
24       Set(ByVal hourlyWage As Decimal)
25          If hourlyWage < 0D Then ' validate hourly wage
26             wageValue = 0D
```

Fig. 12.6 | HourlyEmployee class derived from class Employee. (Part 1 of 2.)

```
27             Else
28                wageValue = hourlyWage
29             End If
30          End Set
31       End Property ' Wage
32
33       ' property Hours
34       Public Property Hours() As Decimal
35          Get
36             Return hoursValue
37          End Get
38
39          Set(ByVal hoursWorked As Decimal)
40             If (hoursWorked >= 0.0) AndAlso (hoursWorked <= 168.0) Then
41                hoursValue = hoursWorked ' valid weekly hours
42             Else
43                hoursValue = 0
44             End If
45          End Set
46       End Property ' Hours
47
48       ' calculate earnings; override abstract method CalculateEarnings
49       Public Overrides Function CalculateEarnings() As Decimal
50          If Hours <= 40 Then ' no overtime
51             Return Wage * Hours
52          Else
53             Return 40 * Wage + CDec(Hours - 40) * Wage * 1.5D
54          End If
55       End Function ' CalculateEarnings
56
57       ' return String representation of HourlyEmployee object
58       Public Overrides Function ToString() As String
59          Return ("hourly employee: " & MyBase.ToString() & vbNewLine & _
60             String.Format("hourly wage: {0:C}; hours worked: {1}", _
61             Wage, Hours))
62       End Function ' ToString
63    End Class ' HourlyEmployee
```

Fig. 12.6 | `HourlyEmployee` class derived from class `Employee`. (Part 2 of 2.)

declare `Set` accessors that assign new values to instance variables `wageValue` and `hoursValue`, respectively. The `Set` accessor of property `Wage` (lines 24–30) ensures that `wageValue` is nonnegative, and the `Set` accessor of property `Hours` (lines 39–45) ensures that `hoursValue` is between 0 and 168 (the total number of hours in a week). Properties `Wage` and `Hours` also include `Get` accessors (lines 20–22 and 35–37) to return the values of `wageValue` and `hoursValue`, respectively. Method `CalculateEarnings` (lines 49–55) calculates an `HourlyEmployee`'s earnings. Method `ToString` (lines 58–62) returns the employee's type, namely, `"hourly employee: "`, and employee-specific information, including the full name, the social security number, and the values of properties `Wage` and `Hours`. Note that the `HourlyEmployee` constructor, like the `SalariedEmployee` constructor, passes the first name, last name and social security number to the base-class `Employee` constructor (line 13). In addition, method `ToString` calls base-class method `ToString` (line 59) to obtain the Employee-specific information (i.e., first name, last name and social security number)—this is another nice example of code reuse.

12.5.4 Creating Concrete Derived Class CommissionEmployee

Class CommissionEmployee (Fig. 12.7) inherits class Employee (line 4). The class includes a constructor (lines 10–15) that takes a first name, a last name, a social security number, a sales amount and a commission rate; Get accessors (lines 19–21 and 34–36) that retrieve the values of instance variables grossSalesValue and commissionRateValue, respectively; Set accessors (lines 23–29 and 38–44) that assign new values to these instance variables; method CalculateEarnings (lines 48–50) to calculate a CommissionEmployee's earnings; and method ToString (lines 53–57), which returns the employee's type, namely, "commission employee: " and employee-specific information, including the full name and social security number, and the values of properties GrossSales and CommissionRate. The CommissionEmployee's constructor also passes the first name, last name and social security number to the Employee constructor (line 12) to initialize Employee's Private instance variables. Method ToString calls base-class method ToString (line 54) to obtain the Employee-specific information (i.e., first name, last name and social security number).

```
1  ' Fig. 12.7: CommissionEmployee.vb
2  ' CommissionEmployee class inherits Employee.
3  Public Class CommissionEmployee
4     Inherits Employee
5
6     Private grossSalesValue As Decimal
7     Private commissionRateValue As Double
8
9     ' five-argument constructor
10    Public Sub New(ByVal first As String, ByVal last As String, _
11       ByVal ssn As String, ByVal sales As Decimal, ByVal rate As Double)
12       MyBase.New(first, last, ssn) ' pass to Employee constructor
13       GrossSales = sales ' validate and store gross sales
14       CommissionRate = rate ' validate and store commission rate
15    End Sub ' New
16
17    ' property GrossSales
18    Public Property GrossSales() As Decimal
19       Get
20          Return grossSalesValue
21       End Get
22
23       Set(ByVal sales As Decimal)
24          If sales < 0D Then ' validate gross sales
25             grossSalesValue = 0D
26          Else
27             grossSalesValue = sales
28          End If
29       End Set
30    End Property ' GrossSales
31
```

Fig. 12.7 | CommissionEmployee class derived from Employee. (Part 1 of 2.)

```
   ' property CommissionRate
   Public Property CommissionRate() As Double
      Get
         Return commissionRateValue
      End Get

      Set(ByVal rate As Double)
         If rate > 0.0 AndAlso rate < 1.0 Then ' validate commission rate
            commissionRateValue = rate
         Else
            commissionRateValue = 0.0
         End If
      End Set
   End Property ' CommissionRate

   ' calculate earnings; override abstract method CalculateEarnings
   Public Overrides Function CalculateEarnings() As Decimal
      Return Convert.ToDecimal(CommissionRate) * GrossSales
   End Function ' CalculateEarnings

   ' return String representation of CommissionEmployee object
   Public Overrides Function ToString() As String
      Return ("commission employee: " & MyBase.ToString() & vbNewLine & _
         String.Format("gross sales: {0:C}; commission rate: {1:F}", _
         GrossSales, CommissionRate))
   End Function ' ToString
End Class ' CommissionEmployee
```

Fig. 12.7 | `CommissionEmployee` class derived from `Employee`. (Part 2 of 2.)

12.5.5 Creating Indirect Concrete Derived Class BasePlusCommissionEmployee

Class `BasePlusCommissionEmployee` (Fig. 12.8) inherits class `CommissionEmployee` (line 4) and therefore is an indirect derived class of class `Employee`. Class `BasePlusCommissionEmployee` has a constructor (lines 9–14) that takes as arguments a first name, a last name, a social security number, a sales amount, a commission rate and a base salary. It then passes the first name, last name, social security number, sales amount and commission rate to the `CommissionEmployee` constructor (line 12) to initialize the inherited members. `BasePlusCommissionEmployee` also contains a property `BaseSalary` whose `Set` accessor (lines 22–28) assigns a new value to instance variable `baseSalaryValue`, and whose `Get` accessor (lines 18–20) returns `baseSalaryValue`. Method `CalculateEarnings` (lines 32–34) calculates a `BasePlusCommissionEmployee`'s earnings. Note that line 33 in method `CalculateEarnings` calls base-class `CommissionEmployee`'s `CalculateEarnings` method to calculate the commission-based portion of the employee's earnings. This is another nice example of code reuse. `BasePlusCommissionEmployee`'s `ToString` method (lines 37–40) creates a `String` representation of a `BasePlusCommissionEmployee` that contains `"base-salaried"`, followed by the `String` obtained by invoking base-class `CommissionEmployee`'s `ToString` method (another example of code reuse), then the base salary. The result is a `String` beginning with `"base-salaried commission employee"` followed by the rest of the `BasePlusCommissionEmployee`'s information. Recall that `CommissionEmployee`'s `To-`

```
' Fig. 12.8: BasePlusCommissionEmployee.vb
' BasePlusCommissionEmployee class inherits CommissionEmployee.
Public Class BasePlusCommissionEmployee
   Inherits CommissionEmployee

   Private baseSalaryValue As Decimal ' base salary

   ' six-argument constructor
   Public Sub New(ByVal first As String, ByVal last As String, _
      ByVal ssn As String, ByVal sales As Decimal, _
      ByVal rate As Double, ByVal salary As Decimal)
      MyBase.New(first, last, ssn, sales, rate)
      BaseSalary = salary
   End Sub ' New

   ' property BaseSalary
   Public Property BaseSalary() As Decimal
      Get
         Return baseSalaryValue
      End Get

      Set(ByVal salary As Decimal)
         If salary < 0 Then ' validate salary
            baseSalaryValue = 0
         Else
            baseSalaryValue = salary
         End If
      End Set
   End Property ' BaseSalary

   ' calculate earnings; override method CalculateEarnings
   Public Overrides Function CalculateEarnings() As Decimal
      Return BaseSalary + MyBase.CalculateEarnings()
   End Function ' CalculateEarnings

   ' return String representation of BasePlusCommissionEmployee object
   Public Overrides Function ToString() As String
      Return ("base-salaried " & MyBase.ToString() & _
         String.Format("; base salary: {0:C}", BaseSalary))
   End Function ' ToString
End Class ' BasePlusCommissionEmployee
```

Fig. 12.8 | `BasePlusCommissionEmployee` derived from `CommissionEmployee`.

`String` method obtains the employee's first name, last name and social security number by invoking the `ToString` method of its base class (i.e., `Employee`)—another example of code reuse. Note that `BasePlusCommissionEmployee`'s `ToString` initiates a chain of method calls that spans all three levels of the `Employee` hierarchy.

12.5.6 Demonstrating Polymorphic Processing, Expression TypeOf...Is, TryCast and Downcasting

To test our `Employee` hierarchy, the program in Fig. 12.9 creates an object of each of the four concrete classes `SalariedEmployee`, `HourlyEmployee`, `CommissionEmployee` and

BasePlusCommissionEmployee. The program manipulates these objects, first via variables of each object's own type, then polymorphically, using an array of Employee variables. While processing the objects polymorphically, the program increases the base salary of each BasePlusCommissionEmployee by 10%—this requires that the program determine each object's type at execution time. Finally, the program polymorphically determines and outputs the type of each object in the Employee array. Lines 6–13 create objects of each of the four concrete Employee derived classes. Lines 16–28 output (nonpolymorphically) the string representation and earnings of each of these objects.

Lines 31–32 create and initialize array employees with four Employees. This statement is valid because, through inheritance, a SalariedEmployee *is an* Employee, an HourlyEmployee *is an* Employee, a CommissionEmployee *is an* Employee and a BasePlusCommissionEmployee *is an* Employee. Therefore, we can assign the references of SalariedEmployee, HourlyEmployee, CommissionEmployee and BasePlusCommissionEmployee objects to base-class Employee variables, even though Employee is an abstract class.

```
1  ' Fig. 12.9: PayrollSystemTest.vb
2  ' Employee hierarchy test program.
3  Module PayrollSystemTest
4     Sub Main()
5        ' create derived-class objects
6        Dim salariedEmployee As New SalariedEmployee( _
7           "John", "Smith", "111-11-1111", 800D)
8        Dim hourlyEmployee As New HourlyEmployee( _
9           "Karen", "Price", "222-22-2222", 16.75D, 40)
10       Dim commissionEmployee As New CommissionEmployee( _
11          "Sue", "Jones", "333-33-3333", 10000D, 0.06)
12       Dim basePlusCommissionEmployee As New BasePlusCommissionEmployee( _
13          "Bob", "Lewis", "444-44-4444", 5000D, 0.04, 300D)
14
15       ' display each employee's info nonpolymorphically
16       Console.WriteLine("Employees processed individually:" & vbNewLine)
17       Console.WriteLine(salariedEmployee.ToString() & vbNewLine & _
18          String.Format("earned: {0:C}", _
19          salariedEmployee.CalculateEarnings()) & vbNewLine)
20       Console.WriteLine(hourlyEmployee.ToString() & vbNewLine & _
21          String.Format("earned: {0:C}", _
22          hourlyEmployee.CalculateEarnings()) & vbNewLine)
23       Console.WriteLine(commissionEmployee.ToString() & vbNewLine & _
24          String.Format("earned: {0:C}", _
25          commissionEmployee.CalculateEarnings()) & vbNewLine)
26       Console.WriteLine(basePlusCommissionEmployee.ToString() & _
27          vbNewLine & String.Format("earned: {0:C}", _
28          basePlusCommissionEmployee.CalculateEarnings()) & vbNewLine)
29
30       ' create four-element Employee array
31       Dim employees() As Employee = {salariedEmployee, hourlyEmployee, _
32          commissionEmployee, basePlusCommissionEmployee}
33
34       Console.WriteLine("Employees processed polymorphically:" & _
35          vbNewLine)
```

Fig. 12.9 | Employee class hierarchy test program. (Part 1 of 3.)

```

      ' polymorphically process each element in array employees
      For Each currentEmployee In employees
         Console.WriteLine(currentEmployee.ToString())

         ' determine if currentEmployee is a BasePlusCommissionEmployee
         If (TypeOf currentEmployee Is BasePlusCommissionEmployee) Then

            ' downcast Employee reference to BasePlusCommissionEmployee
            Dim employee As BasePlusCommissionEmployee = _
               TryCast(currentEmployee, BasePlusCommissionEmployee)

            employee.BaseSalary *= 1.1D
            Console.WriteLine(String.Format( _
               "new base salary with 10% increase is: {0:C}", _
               employee.BaseSalary))
         End If

         Console.Write(String.Format("earned {0:C}", _
            currentEmployee.CalculateEarnings()) & vbNewLine & vbNewLine)
      Next

      ' get type name of each object in employees array
      For i As Integer = 0 To employees.Length - 1
         Console.WriteLine(String.Format("Employee {0} is a {1}", _
            i, employees(i).GetType().FullName))
      Next
   End Sub ' Main
End Module ' PayrollSystemTest
```

```
Employees processed individually:

salaried employee: John Smith
social security number: 111-11-1111
weekly salary $800.00
earned: $800.00

hourly employee: Karen Price
social security number: 222-22-2222
hourly wage: $16.75; hours worked: 40
earned: $670.00

commission employee: Sue Jones
social security number: 333-33-3333
gross sales: $10,000.00; commission rate: 0.06
earned: $600.00

base-salaried commission employee: Bob Lewis
social security number: 444-44-4444
gross sales: $5,000.00; commission rate: 0.04; base salary: $300.00
earned: $500.00
```

Fig. 12.9 | Employee class hierarchy test program. (Part 2 of 3.)

```
Employees processed polymorphically:

salaried employee: John Smith
social security number: 111-11-1111
weekly salary $800.00
earned $800.00

hourly employee: Karen Price
social security number: 222-22-2222
hourly wage: $16.75; hours worked: 40
earned $670.00

commission employee: Sue Jones
social security number: 333-33-3333
gross sales: $10,000.00; commission rate: 0.06
earned $600.00

base-salaried commission employee: Bob Lewis
social security number: 444-44-4444
gross sales: $5,000.00; commission rate: 0.04; base salary: $300.00
new base salary with 10% increase is: $330.00
earned $530.00

Employee 0 is a PayrollSystem.SalariedEmployee
Employee 1 is a PayrollSystem.HourlyEmployee
Employee 2 is a PayrollSystem.CommissionEmployee
Employee 3 is a PayrollSystem.BasePlusCommissionEmployee
```

Fig. 12.9 | `Employee` class hierarchy test program. (Part 3 of 3.)

Lines 38–56 iterate through array `employees` and invoke methods `ToString` and `CalculateEarnings` with `Employee` variable `currentEmployee`, which is assigned the reference to a different `Employee` in the array during each iteration. The output illustrates that the appropriate methods for each class are indeed invoked. All calls to method `ToString` and `CalculateEarnings` are resolved at execution time, based on the type of the object to which `currentEmployee` refers. This process is known as **late binding**. For example, line 39 explicitly invokes method `ToString` of the object to which `currentEmployee` refers. As a result of late binding, Visual Basic decides which class's `ToString` method to call at execution time rather than at compile time. Recall that only the methods of class `Employee` can be called via an `Employee` variable (and `Employee`, of course, includes the methods of class `Object`). (Section 11.7 discussed the set of methods that all classes inherit from class `Object`.) A base-class reference can be used to invoke only methods of the base class, even though those method calls polymorphically invoke derived-class method implementations when sent to derived-class objects.

Using Expression `TypeOf...Is` *to Determine Object Type*

We perform special processing on `BasePlusCommissionEmployee` objects—as we encounter these objects, we increase their base salary by 10%. When processing objects polymorphically, we typically do not need to worry about the specifics, but to adjust the base salary, we do have to determine the specific type of `Employee` object at execution time. Line 42 uses a `TypeOf...Is` expression to determine whether a particular `Employee` object's type is

`BasePlusCommissionEmployee`. The condition in line 42 is true if the object referenced by `currentEmployee` *is a* `BasePlusCommissionEmployee`. This would also be true for any object of a `BasePlusCommissionEmployee` derived class (if there are any) because of the *is-a* relationship a derived class has with its base class.

Using `TryCast` *to Downcast from a Base-Class to a Derived-Class Type*

Lines 45–46 use keyword `TryCast` to downcast (i.e., cast from a base-class type to a derived-class type) `currentEmployee` from type `Employee` to type `BasePlusCommissionEmployee`—this cast returns a reference only if the object to which the reference points has an *is-a* relationship with type `BasePlusCommissionEmployee`. The condition at line 42 ensures that this is the case. If the *is-a* relationship does not exist, `TryCast` returns `Nothing`. This cast is required if we are to access derived class `BasePlusCommissionEmployee` property `BaseSalary` on the current `Employee` object—as you will see momentarily, attempting to invoke a derived-class-only method or property directly on a base-class reference is a compilation error. Note that we did not need to use both `TypeOf...Is` and `TryCast`. We used both here so that we could also demonstrate the `TypeOf...Is` expression. We could have simply used `TryCast`, then tested the value of variable `employee` to ensure that it was not `Nothing` before attempting to execute the statements in lines 48–51. Or, we could have used `TypeOf...Is` to first check that there was an *is-a* relationship, then used `DirectCast` to convert the object. Unlike `TryCast`, `DirectCast` does not perform error-checking implicitly. Thus, you must either first check that the *is-a* relationship is valid, or handle the exception that is thrown if the cast fails. We discuss exception handling in Chapter 13.

Common Programming Error 12.3

Assigning a base-class variable to a derived-class variable (without an explicit cast) is a compilation error.

Error-Prevention Tip 12.1

If at execution time the reference of a derived-class object has been assigned to a variable of one of its direct or indirect base classes, it is acceptable to cast the reference stored in that base-class variable back to a reference of the derived-class type. Before performing such a cast, use the `Typeof...Is` *expression to ensure that the object is indeed an object of an appropriate derived-class type. Then use* `DirectCast` *to downcast from the base-class type to the derived-class type. Alternatively, you could use a* `TryCast` *and check that the reference isn't* `Nothing` *afterwards.*

When downcasting an object, `TryCast` returns `Nothing` if at execution time the object being converted does not have an *is-a* relationship with the target type. An object can be cast only to its own type, to one of its base-class types, or to an interface that it implements; otherwise, a compilation error occurs.

If the `Typeof...Is` expression in line 42 is `True`, the body of the `If` statement (lines 45–51) performs the special processing required for the `BasePlusCommissionEmployee` object. Using `BasePlusCommissionEmployee` variable `employee`, lines 48–51 access derived-class-only property `BaseSalary` to retrieve and update the employee's base salary with the 10% raise.

Lines 54–55 invoke method `CalculateEarnings` on `currentEmployee`, which calls the appropriate derived-class object's `CalculateEarnings` method polymorphically. Note that obtaining the earnings of the `SalariedEmployee`, `HourlyEmployee` and `CommissionEmployee` polymorphically in lines 54–55 produces the same result as obtaining these employees' earnings nonpolymorphically in lines 16–25. However, the earnings amount obtained for the `BasePlusCommissionEmployee` in lines 54–55 is higher than that obtained in lines 26–28, due to the 10% increase in its base salary.

Lines 59–62 display each employee's type as a string. Every object in Visual Basic knows its own class and can access this information through method `GetType`, which all classes inherit from class `Object`. Figure 11.20 lists the `Object` methods that are inherited directly or indirectly by all classes. Method `GetType` returns an object of class `Type` (namespace `System`), which contains information about the object's type, including its fully qualified class name. For more information on class `Type`, visit `msdn.microsoft.com/en-us/library/system.type(VS.80).aspx`. Line 61 invokes method `GetType` on the object to get a `Type` object that represents the object's type at execution time. Then line 61 uses the `FullName` property of the object returned by `GetType` to get the class's name fully qualified name (see the last four lines of the program's output).

Notes on Downcasting

We avoid several compilation errors by downcasting an `Employee` variable to a `BasePlusCommissionEmployee` variable in lines 45–46. If we remove the cast expression from line 46 and attempt to assign `Employee` variable `currentEmployee` directly to `BasePlusCommissionEmployee` variable `employee`, we will receive a compilation error (when **Option Strict** is **On**). This error indicates that the attempt to assign the base-class variable `currentEmployee` to derived-class variable `basePlusCommissionEmployee` is not allowed. The compiler prevents this assignment because an `Employee` is not a `BasePlusCommissionEmployee`—the *is-a* relationship applies only between the derived class and its base classes, not vice versa.

Similarly, if lines 48 and 51 were to use base-class variable `currentEmployee`, rather than derived-class variable `employee`, to access derived-class-only property `BaseSalary`, we would receive a compilation error on each of these lines. Attempting to invoke derived-class-only methods and properties on a base-class reference is not allowed. While lines 48 and 51 execute only if the `Typeof...If` expression in line 42 returns `True` to indicate that `currentEmployee` has been assigned a reference to a `BasePlusCommissionEmployee` object, we cannot attempt to invoke derived-class `BasePlusCommissionEmployee` property `BaseSalary` on base-class `Employee` reference `currentEmployee`. The compiler would generate errors in lines 48 and 51, because property `BaseSalary` is not a base-class property and cannot be accessed using a base-class variable. Although the actual method or property that is called depends on the object's type at execution time, a variable can be used to invoke only those methods and properties that are members of that variable's type, which the compiler verifies. Using a base-class `Employee` variable, we can invoke only methods and properties found in class `Employee` (Fig. 12.4)—methods `CalculateEarnings` and `ToString`, and properties `FirstName`, `LastName` and `SocialSecurityNumber`.

12.5.7 Summary of the Allowed Assignments between Base-Class and Derived-Class Variables

Now that you have seen a complete application that processes diverse derived-class objects polymorphically, we summarize what you can and cannot do with base-class and derived-class objects and variables. Although a derived-class object also *is a* base-class object, the two objects are nevertheless different. As discussed previously, derived-class objects can be treated as if they were base-class objects. However, the derived class can have additional derived-class-only members. For this reason, assigning a base-class reference to a derived-class variable is not allowed without a cast—such an assignment would leave the derived-class-only members undefined for the base-class object.

We have discussed four ways to assign base-class and derived-class references to variables of base-class and derived-class types:

1. Assigning a base-class reference to a base-class variable is straightforward.
2. Assigning a derived-class reference to a derived-class variable is straightforward.
3. Assigning a derived-class reference to a base-class variable is safe, because the derived-class object *is an* object of its base class. However, this reference can be used to refer only to base-class members. Referring to a derived-class-only member through the base-class variable is a compilation error.
4. Attempting to assign a base-class reference to a derived-class variable is a compilation error (when **Option Strict** is **On**). To avoid this error, the base-class reference must be cast to a derived-class type explicitly. You can use either a `DirectCast` or a `TryCast` perform a downcast. If you use a `DirectCast` and the object to which the reference refers is not a derived-class object, an exception will occur. (For more on exception handling, see Chapter 13.) If you use a `TryCast`, it returns `Nothing`.

12.6 NotOverridable Methods and NotInheritable Classes

A method that is declared **`NotOverridable`** in a base class cannot be overridden in a derived class. A method that is declared `Overridable` in a base class can be declared `NotOverridable` in a derived class—this prevents overriding the method in classes that inherit from the derived class. All classes derived from the class that contains the `NotOverridable` method use that class's method implementation. Methods that are declared `Private` are implicitly `NotOverridable`.

A class that is declared **`NotInheritable`** cannot be a base class (i.e., a class cannot inherit from a `NotInheritable` class). All methods in a `NotInheritable` class are implicitly `NotOverridable`. A `NotInheritable` class is the opposite of a `MustInherit` class. A `NotInheritable` class is a concrete class that cannot act as a base class, whereas a `MustInherit` class is an abstract class that is intended as a base class. Class `String` is a `NotInheritable` class.

Common Programming Error 12.4

Attempting to inherit a `NotInheritable` class is a compilation error.

12.7 Case Study: Creating and Using Interfaces

Our next example reexamines the payroll system of Section 12.5. Suppose that the company involved wishes to perform several accounting operations in an accounts payable application. In addition to calculating the earnings that must be paid to each employee, the company also wants to calculate the payment due on each of several invoices (i.e., bills for goods and services purchased). Though applied to unrelated things (i.e., employees and invoices), both operations have to do with obtaining some kind of payment amount. For an employee, the payment refers to the employee's earnings. For an invoice, the payment refers to the total cost of the goods and services listed on the invoice. Can we calculate such different things as the payments due for employees and invoices in a single application polymorphically? Does Visual Basic have a capability that forces possibly unrelated classes to implement a set of common methods (e.g., a method that calculates a payment amount)? Visual Basic interfaces offer exactly this capability.

Interfaces define and standardize the ways in which things such as people and systems can interact with one another. For example, the controls on a radio serve as an interface between radio users and a radio's internal components. The controls allow users to perform only a limited set of operations (e.g., changing the station, adjusting the volume, choosing between AM and FM), and different radios may implement the controls in different ways (e.g., using push buttons, dials, voice commands). The interface specifies *what* operations a radio permits users to perform but does not specify *how* the operations are implemented. Similarly, the interface between a driver and a car with a manual transmission includes the steering wheel, the gear shift, and the clutch, gas and brake pedals. This same interface is found in nearly all manual-transmission cars, enabling someone who knows how to drive one particular manual-transmission car to drive just about any manual-transmission car. The components of each individual car may look a bit different, but the components' general purpose is the same—to allow people to drive the car.

Software objects also communicate via interfaces. A Visual Basic interface describes a set of methods that can be called on an object—to tell the object, for example, to perform some task or return some piece of information. An interface is often used in place of a `MustInherit` class when there is no default implementation to inherit—that is, no instance variables and no default method and property implementations. The next example introduces an interface named `IPayable` to describe the functionality of any object that must be capable of being paid and thus must offer a method to determine the proper payment amount due. By convention, the name of an interface is usually prefixed by `I`. An **interface declaration** begins with the keyword `Interface` and can contain abstract methods and properties, but cannot contain instance variables, concrete methods or concrete properties. Unlike classes, interfaces may not specify any implementation details, such as concrete method declarations and instance variables. All members declared in an interface are implicitly `Public`, and may not specify an access modifier.

Common Programming Error 12.5

It is a compilation error to explicitly declare interface methods `Public`*.*

Common Programming Error 12.6

In Visual Basic, an `Interface` *should be declared only as* `Public` *or* `Friend`*; You can declare a* `Private` *or* `Protected` *interface only within another type (i.e., class, interface, etc.).*

To use an interface, a concrete class must specify that it `Implements` the interface and must implement each method in the interface with the signature and return type specified in the interface declaration. A class that does not implement all the methods of the interface is an abstract class and must be declared `MustInherit`. Implementing an interface is like signing a contract with the compiler that states, "I will declare all the methods specified by the interface or I will declare my class `MustInherit`."

Common Programming Error 12.7

Failing to implement any method of an interface in a concrete class that `Implements` the interface results in a syntax error indicating that the class must be declared `MustInherit`.

An interface is typically used when unrelated classes need to share common methods and properties. This allows objects of unrelated classes to be processed polymorphically—objects of classes that implement the same interface have an *is-a* relationship with the interface type and can respond to the same method calls. Programmers can create an interface that describes the desired functionality, then implement this interface in any classes that require that functionality. For example, in the accounts payable application that we develop in the next several subsections, we implement interface `IPayable` in any class that must be able to calculate a payment amount (e.g., `Employee`, `Invoice`).

12.7.1 Developing an `IPayable` Hierarchy

To build an application that can determine payments for employees and invoices alike, we will first create interface `IPayable`. Interface `IPayable` contains a single method called `GetPaymentAmount`, which returns a `Decimal` amount that must be paid for an `IPayable` object. This method is a general-purpose version of the `Employee` hierarchy's `CalculateEarnings` method—method `CalculateEarnings` calculates a payment amount specifically for an `Employee`, while `GetPaymentAmount` can be applied more generally to unrelated objects. After declaring interface `IPayable`, we will introduce class `Invoice`, which implements interface `IPayable`. We then modify class `Employee` so that it, too, implements interface `IPayable`. Finally, we update `Employee` derived class `SalariedEmployee` to "fit" into the `IPayable` hierarchy (i.e., we rename `SalariedEmployee` method `CalculateEarnings` as `GetPaymentAmount`).

Good Programming Practice 12.1

When declaring a method in an interface, choose a method name that describes the method's purpose in a general manner, because the method may be implemented by many unrelated classes.

Classes `Invoice` and `Employee` both represent things for which the company must be able to calculate a payment amount. Both classes implement `IPayable`, so a program can invoke method `GetPaymentAmount` on `Invoice` objects and `Employee` objects alike. As you will soon see, this enables the polymorphic processing of `Invoice`s and `Employee`s required for our accounts payable application.

The UML class diagram in Fig. 12.10 shows the class and interface hierarchy used in our accounts payable application. The hierarchy begins with interface `IPayable`. The UML distinguishes an interface from other classes by placing the word "interface" in guillemets (« ») above the interface name. The UML expresses the relationship between a class and an interface through an association known as a **realization**. A class is said to "realize," or implement, an interface. A class diagram models a realization as a dashed arrow with a hollow arrowhead pointing from the implementing classes to the interface. The diagram in Fig. 12.10 indicates that class `Invoice` realizes (i.e., implements) interface `IPayable`. Class

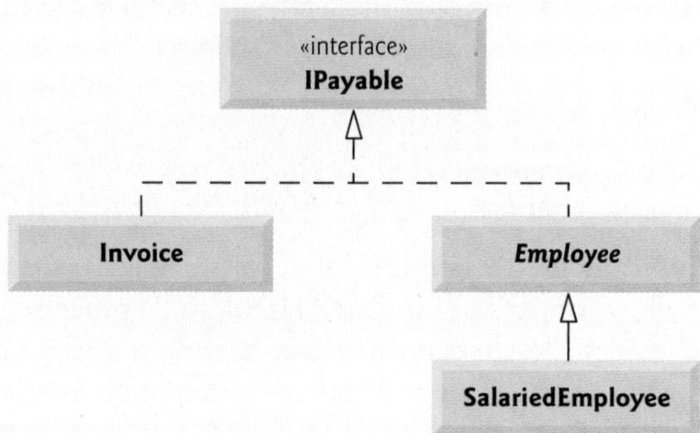

Fig. 12.10 | `IPayable` interface hierarchy UML class diagram.

`Employee` also realizes interface `IPayable`, but it is not required to provide method implementations, because it is an abstract class (note that it appears in italics). Concrete class `SalariedEmployee` inherits from `Employee` and inherits its base class's realization relationship with interface `IPayable`, so `SalariedEmployee` must implement the method(s) of `IPayable`.

12.7.2 Declaring Interface IPayable

The declaration of interface `IPayable` begins in Fig. 12.11 at line 3. Interface `IPayable` contains `Public` method `GetPaymentAmount` (line 4). Note that the method is not explicitly declared `Public`. Interface methods are implicitly `Public`. Interfaces can have any number of methods. Although method `GetPaymentAmount` has no parameters, interface methods can have parameters.

```
1  ' Fig. 12.11: IPayable.vb
2  ' IPayable interface declaration.
3  Public Interface IPayable
4     Function GetPaymentAmount() As Decimal ' calculate payment
5  End Interface ' IPayable
```

Fig. 12.11 | `IPayable` interface declaration.

12.7.3 Creating Class Invoice

We now create class `Invoice` (Fig. 12.12) to represent a simple invoice that contains billing information for only one kind of part. The class declares `Private` instance variables `partNumberValue`, `partDescriptionValue`, `quantityValue` and `pricePerItemValue` (in lines 6–9) that indicate the part number, a description of the part, the quantity of the part ordered and the price per item, respectively. Class `Invoice` also contains a constructor (lines 12–18), and properties `PartNumber` (lines 21–29), `PartDescription`(lines 32–40), `Quantity` (lines 43–55) and `PricePerItem` (lines 58–70) that manipulate the class's instance variables. Note that the `Set` accessors of properties `Quantity` and `PricePerItem` ensure that `quantityValue` and `pricePerItemValue` are assigned only nonnegative values.

Line 4 of Fig. 12.12 indicates that class `Invoice` implements interface `IPayable`. Class `Invoice` also implicitly inherits from `Object`. A derived class cannot inherit from more than one base class, but can inherit from a base class and implement zero or more interfaces. To implement more than one interface, use a comma-separated list of interface names after keyword `Implements` in the class declaration, as in:

```
Public Class ClassName
   Inherits BaseClassName
   Implements IFirstInterface, ISecondInterface, ...
```

```
' Fig. 12.12: Invoice.vb
' Invoice class implements IPayable.
Public Class Invoice
   Implements IPayable

   Private partNumberValue As String
   Private partDescriptionValue As String
   Private quantityValue As Integer
   Private pricePerItemValue As Decimal

   ' four-argument constructor
   Public Sub New(ByVal part As String, ByVal description As String, _
      ByVal count As Integer, ByVal price As Decimal)
      PartNumber = part
      PartDescription = description
      Quantity = count ' validate quantity
      PricePerItem = price ' validate price per item
   End Sub ' New

   ' property PartNumber
   Public Property PartNumber() As String
      Get
         Return partNumberValue
      End Get

      Set(ByVal part As String)
         partNumberValue = part
      End Set
   End Property ' PartNumber

   ' property PartDescription
   Public Property PartDescription() As String
      Get
         Return partDescriptionValue
      End Get

      Set(ByVal description As String)
         partDescriptionValue = description
      End Set
   End Property ' PartDescription

   ' property Quantity
   Public Property Quantity() As Integer
      Get
         Return quantityValue
      End Get
```

Fig. 12.12 | `Invoice` class that implements interface `IPayable`. (Part 1 of 2.)

```
47
48          Set(ByVal count As Integer)
49             If count < 0 Then ' validate quantity
50                quantityValue = 0
51             Else
52                quantityValue = count
53             End If
54          End Set
55       End Property ' Quantity
56
57       ' property PricePerItem
58       Public Property PricePerItem() As Decimal
59          Get
60             Return pricePerItemValue
61          End Get
62
63          Set(ByVal price As Decimal)
64             If price < 0 Then ' validate price
65                pricePerItemValue = 0
66             Else
67                pricePerItemValue = price
68             End If
69          End Set
70       End Property ' PricePerItem
71
72       ' function required to carry out contract with interface IPayable
73       Public Function GetPaymentAmount() As Decimal _
74          Implements IPayable.GetPaymentAmount
75          Return Quantity * PricePerItem ' calculate total cost
76       End Function ' GetPaymentAmount
77
78       ' return String representation of Invoice object
79       Public Overrides Function ToString() As String
80          Return ("invoice:" & vbNewLine & "part number: " & PartNumber & _
81             "(" & PartDescription & ")" & vbNewLine & "quantity: " & _
82             Quantity & vbNewLine & _
83             String.Format("price per item: {0:C}", PricePerItem))
84       End Function ' ToString
85    End Class ' Invoice
```

Fig. 12.12 | `Invoice` class that implements interface `IPayable`. (Part 2 of 2.)

`Inherits` *BaseClassName* is optional if the class implicitly inherits from class `Object`. All objects of a class that implements multiple interfaces have the *is-a* relationship with each implemented interface type.

Class `Invoice` implements the method in interface `IPayable`. Method `GetPaymentAmount` is declared in lines 73–76. Line 74 contains keyword `Implements` followed by `IPayable.GetPaymentAmount` to indicate that the method in lines 73–76 is the implementation of the interface's `GetPaymentAmount` method. Line 75 calculates the total payment required to pay the invoice by multiplying the values of `quantityValue` and `pricePerItemValue` (obtained through the appropriate properties) and returning the result. Implementing method `GetPaymentAmount` in class `Invoice` satisfies the implementation requirement for the method of interface IPayable—concrete class Invoice fulfills the interface contract with the compiler.

Method ToString (lines 79–84) returns the String representation of an Invoice object. Recall that all classes directly or indirectly inherit from class Object. Therefore, class Invoice implicitly inherits Object's ToString method. However, we want to declare a customized ToString method in Invoice that returns a String containing the values of an Invoice's instance variables. Line 79 indicates that Invoice's ToString method overrides the one defined in base class Object.

12.7.4 Modifying Class Employee to Implement Interface IPayable

We now modify class Employee to implement interface IPayable. Figure 12.13 contains the modified Employee class. This class declaration is identical to that of Fig. 12.4 with only three exceptions. First, line 4 of Fig. 12.13 indicates that class Employee now implements interface IPayable. Second, we implement method ToString (lines 52–56), which overrides the version declared in base class Object. Third, since Employee now implements interface IPayable, we rename CalculateEarnings to GetPaymentAmount throughout the Employee hierarchy. As with method CalculateEarnings in the Employee class of Fig. 12.4, however, it does not make sense to implement method GetPaymentAmount in abstract class Employee because we cannot calculate the earnings payment owed to a general Employee—first we must know the specific type of Employee. In Fig. 12.4, we declared method CalculateEarnings as MustOverride for this reason, so class Employee had to be declared MustInherit. This forced each concrete Employee derived class to override CalculateEarnings with an implementation.

```
1  ' Fig. 12.13: Employee.vb
2  ' Employee abstract base class implements IPayable.
3  Public MustInherit Class Employee
4     Implements IPayable
5
6     Private firstNameValue As String
7     Private lastNameValue As String
8     Private socialSecurityNumberValue As String
9
10    ' three-argument constructor
11    Public Sub New(ByVal first As String, ByVal last As String, _
12       ByVal ssn As String)
13       FirstName = first
14       LastName = last
15       SocialSecurityNumber = ssn
16    End Sub ' New
17
18    ' property FirstName
19    Public Property FirstName() As String
20       Get
21          Return firstNameValue
22       End Get
23
```

Fig. 12.13 | Employee class that implements interface IPayable. (Part 1 of 2.)

```
24          Set(ByVal first As String)
25             firstNameValue = first
26          End Set
27       End Property ' FirstName
28
29       ' property LastName
30       Public Property LastName() As String
31          Get
32             Return lastNameValue
33          End Get
34
35          Set(ByVal last As String)
36             lastNameValue = last
37          End Set
38       End Property ' LastName
39
40       ' property SocialSecurityNumber
41       Public Property SocialSecurityNumber() As String
42          Get
43             Return socialSecurityNumberValue
44          End Get
45
46          Set(ByVal ssn As String)
47             socialSecurityNumberValue = ssn
48          End Set
49       End Property ' SocialSecurityNumber
50
51       ' return String representation of Employee object
52       Public Overrides Function ToString() As String
53          Return (String.Format("{0} {1}", FirstName, LastName) & _
54             vbNewLine & "social security number: " & SocialSecurityNumber)
55       End Function ' ToString
56
57       ' Note: We do not implement IPayable function GetPaymentAmount here
58       Public MustOverride Function GetPaymentAmount() As Decimal _
59          Implements IPayable.GetPaymentAmount
60    End Class ' Employee
```

Fig. 12.13 | `Employee` class that implements interface `IPayable`. (Part 2 of 2.)

In Fig. 12.13, we handle this situation similarly. Recall that when a class implements an interface, the class makes a contract with the compiler stating either that the class will implement each of the methods in the interface or that the class will be declared `MustInherit`. If you choose the latter option, you must declare the interface methods as `MustOverride` in the abstract class. Any concrete derived class of the abstract class must implement the interface methods to fulfill the base class's contract with the compiler. If the derived class does not do so, it too must be declared `MustInherit`. As indicated in lines 59–60, class `Employee` of Fig. 12.13 does not implement method `GetPaymentAmount`, so the class is declared `MustInherit` (line 3). Each direct `Employee` derived class inherits the base class's contract to implement method `GetPaymentAmount` and thus must implement this method to become a concrete class from which objects can be instantiated. A class that inherits from one of `Employee`'s concrete derived classes will inherit an implementation of `GetPaymentAmount` and thus will also be a concrete class.

12.7.5 Modifying Class `SalariedEmployee` for Use in the `IPayable` Hierarchy

Figure 12.14 contains a modified version of concrete class `SalariedEmployee` that inherits abstract class `Employee` and fulfills base class `Employee`'s contract to implement interface `IPayable`'s `GetPaymentAmount` method. This `SalariedEmployee` class is identical to that of Fig. 12.5, but this version implements method `GetPaymentAmount` (lines 32–34) instead of method `CalculateEarnings`. These methods contain the same functionality but have different names. Recall that `IPayable`'s `GetPaymentAmount` method has a more general name to be applicable to possibly disparate classes. The remaining `Employee` derived classes (e.g., `HourlyEmployee`, `CommissionEmployee` and `BasePlusCommissionEmployee`) also must be modified to contain `GetPaymentAmount` methods in place of `CalculateEarnings` methods to reflect the fact that `Employee` now implements `IPayable`. We leave these changes as an exercise and use only `SalariedEmployee` in our test program in this section.

```
1  ' Fig. 12.14: SalariedEmployee.vb
2  ' SalariedEmployee class inherits Employee, which implements IPayable.
3  Public Class SalariedEmployee
4     Inherits Employee
5
6     Private weeklySalaryValue As Decimal
7
8     ' four-argument constructor
9     Public Sub New(ByVal first As String, ByVal last As String, _
10       ByVal ssn As String, ByVal salary As Decimal)
11       MyBase.New(first, last, ssn) ' pass to Employee constructor
12       WeeklySalary = salary ' validate and store salary
13    End Sub ' New
14
15    ' property WeeklySalary
16    Public Property WeeklySalary() As Decimal
17       Get
18          Return weeklySalaryValue
19       End Get
20
21       Set(ByVal salary As Decimal)
22          If salary < 0D Then ' validate salary
23             weeklySalaryValue = 0D
24          Else
25             weeklySalaryValue = salary
26          End If
27       End Set
28    End Property ' WeeklySalary
29
30    ' calculate earnings; implements interface IPayable method
31    ' GetPaymentAmount that was MustOverride in base class Employee
```

Fig. 12.14 | `SalariedEmployee` class that implements interface `IPayable` method `GetPaymentAmount`. (Part 1 of 2.)

```
   Public Overrides Function GetPaymentAmount() As Decimal
      Return WeeklySalary
   End Function ' GetPaymentAmount

   ' return String representation of SalariedEmployee object
   Public Overrides Function ToString() As String
      Return ("salaried employee: " & MyBase.ToString() & vbNewLine & _
         String.Format("weekly salary {0:C}", WeeklySalary))
   End Function ' ToString
End Class ' SalariedEmployee
```

Fig. 12.14 | `SalariedEmployee` class that implements interface `IPayable` method `GetPaymentAmount`. (Part 2 of 2.)

When a class implements an interface, the same *is-a* relationship as inheritance applies. For example, class `Employee` implements `IPayable`, so we can say that an `Employee` *is an* `IPayable`. Objects of any classes that inherit from `Employee` are also `IPayable` objects. `SalariedEmployee` objects, for instance, are `IPayable` objects. As with inheritance relationships, an object of a class that implements an interface may be thought of as an object of the interface type. Objects of any derived classes of the class that implements the interface can also be thought of as objects of the interface type. Thus, just as we can assign the reference of a `SalariedEmployee` object to a base-class `Employee` variable, we can assign the reference of a `SalariedEmployee` object to an interface `IPayable` variable. `Invoice` implements `IPayable`, so an `Invoice` object also *is an* `IPayable` object, and we can assign the reference of an `Invoice` object to an `IPayable` variable.

Software Engineering Observation 12.3

Inheritance and interfaces are similar in their implementation of the is-a *relationship. An object of a class that implements an interface may be thought of as an object of that interface type. Objects of any derived classes of a class that implements an interface can also be thought of as objects of the interface type.*

Software Engineering Observation 12.4

The is-a *relationship that exists between derived classes and base classes, and between classes that implement interfaces and the interfaces themselves, holds when passing an object to a method. If a parameter has a base-class type, it can receive either a base-class or derived-class reference as an argument. If a parameter has an interface type, it can receive a reference to an object of any class that implements the interface.*

12.7.6 Using Interface `IPayable` to Process `Invoice`s and `Employee`s Polymorphically

Module `PayableInterfaceTest` (Fig. 12.15) illustrates that interface `IPayable` can be used to process a set of `Invoice`s and `Employee`s polymorphically in a single application, even though these classes represent such different kinds of things.

Line 6 declares `payableObjects` and assigns to it an array of four `IPayable` variables. Lines 9 and 12 assign the references of `Invoice` objects to `payableObjects(0)` and `pay-`

`ableObjects(2)`, respectively. Lines 10–11 and 13–14 assign the references of `SalariedEmployee` objects to `payableObjects(1)` and `payableObjects(3)`, respectively. These assignments are allowed because an `Invoice` *is an* `IPayable`, and a `SalariedEmployee` *is an* `Employee` and an `Employee` *is an* `IPayable`. Lines 20–25 use a `For Each...Next` statement to polymorphically process each `IPayable` object in `payableObjects`, displaying the object as a `String`, along with the payment amount due. Line 22 invokes method `ToString` via an `IPayable` variable to get the `String` representation of each object. Line 24 invokes `IPayable` method `GetPaymentAmount` to obtain the payment amount for each object in `payableObjects`, regardless of the actual type of the object. The output reveals that the method calls in lines 22–24 invoke the appropriate class's implementation of methods `ToString` and `GetPaymentAmount`. For instance, when `currentPayable` refers to an `Invoice` during the first iteration of the `For Each` loop, class `Invoice`'s `ToString` and `GetPaymentAmount` methods execute.

Software Engineering Observation 12.5

Using a base-class reference, you can polymorphically invoke any method specified in the base-class declaration (and in class `Object`). Using an interface reference, you can polymorphically invoke any method specified in the interface declaration (and in class `Object`).

```
 1  ' Fig. 12.15: PayableInterfaceTest.vb
 2  ' Testing interface IPayable.
 3  Module PayableInterfaceTest
 4     Sub Main()
 5        ' create four-element IPayable array
 6        Dim payableObjects() As IPayable = New IPayable(3) {}
 7
 8        ' populate array with objects that implement IPayable
 9        payableObjects(0) = New Invoice("01234", "seat", 2, 375D)
10        payableObjects(1) = New SalariedEmployee( _
11           "John", "Smith", "111-11-1111", 800D)
12        payableObjects(2) = New Invoice("56789", "tire", 4, 79.95D)
13        payableObjects(3) = New SalariedEmployee( _
14           "Lisa", "Barnes", "888-88-8888", 1200D)
15
16        Console.WriteLine( _
17           "Invoices and Employees processed polymorphically:" & vbNewLine)
18
19        ' generically process each element in array payableObjects
20        For Each currentPayable In payableObjects
21           ' output currentPayable and its appropriate payment amount
22           Console.WriteLine(currentPayable.ToString() & vbNewLine & _
23              String.Format("payment due: {0:C}", _
24              currentPayable.GetPaymentAmount()) & vbNewLine)
25        Next
26     End Sub ' Main
27  End Module ' PayableInterfaceTest
```

Fig. 12.15 | `IPayable` interface test program processing `Invoices` and `Employees` polymorphically. (Part 1 of 2.)

```
Invoices and Employees processed polymorphically:

invoice:
part number: 01234(seat)
quantity: 2
price per item: $375.00
payment due: $750.00

salaried employee: John Smith
social security number: 111-11-1111
weekly salary $800.00
payment due: $800.00

invoice:
part number: 56789(tire)
quantity: 4
price per item: $79.95
payment due: $319.80

salaried employee: Lisa Barnes
social security number: 888-88-8888
weekly salary $1,200.00
payment due: $1,200.00
```

Fig. 12.15 | `IPayable` interface test program processing `Invoices` and `Employees` polymorphically. (Part 2 of 2.)

12.7.7 Common Interfaces of the .NET Framework Class Library

In this section, we overview several common interfaces found in the .NET class library. These interfaces are implemented and used in the same manner as the interfaces you create. Figure 12.16 overviews a few of the more popular interfaces of the .NET class library that we use in this book.

Interface	Description
`IComparable`	As you learned in Chapter 3, Visual Basic contains several comparison operators (e.g., <, <=, >, >=, =, <>) that allow you to compare primitive values. However, these operators cannot be used to compare objects. Interface `IComparable` is used to allow objects of a class that implements the interface to be compared to one another. The interface contains one method, `CompareTo`, that compares the object that calls the method to the object passed as an argument to the method. Classes must implement `CompareTo` such that it returns a value indicating whether the object on which it is invoked is less than (negative integer return value), equal to (0 return value) or greater than (positive integer return value) the object passed as an argument, using any criteria specified by the programmer. For example, if class `Employee` implements `IComparable`, its `CompareTo` method could compare `Employee` objects by their earnings amounts. Interface `IComparable` is commonly used for ordering objects in a collection such as an array. We use `IComparable` in Chapter 24, Data Structures and Generic Collections.

Fig. 12.16 | Common interfaces of the .NET Class Library. (Part 1 of 2.)

Interface	Description
`IComponent`	Implemented by any class that represents a component, including Graphical User Interface (GUI) controls (such as buttons or labels). Interface `IComponent` defines the behaviors that components must implement. We discuss `IComponent` and many GUI controls that implement this interface in Chapter 14, Graphical User Interfaces with Windows Forms.
`IEnumerable`	A collection that implements `IEnumerable` (such as `List`) exposes its enumerator for iterating through items. Interface `IEnumerable` contains method `GetEnumerator`, which returns an enumerator for the collection. We discussed this interface in Chapter 9.
`IEnumerator`	Used for iterating through the elements of a collection (such as an array) one element at a time. Interface `IEnumerator` contains method `MoveNext` to move to the next element in a collection, method `Reset` to move to the position before the first element, and property `Current` to return the object at the current location.

Fig. 12.16 | Common interfaces of the .NET Class Library. (Part 2 of 2.)

12.8 (Optional) Software Engineering Case Study: Incorporating Inheritance and Polymorphism into the ATM System

We now revisit our ATM system design to see how it might benefit from inheritance and polymorphism. To apply inheritance, we look for commonality among classes in the system. We create an inheritance hierarchy to model similar classes in an efficient and elegant manner that enables us to process objects of these classes polymorphically. We then modify our class diagram to incorporate the new inheritance relationships. Finally, we demonstrate how to translate the inheritance aspects of our updated design into Visual Basic code.

In Section 4.9, we encountered the problem of representing a financial transaction in the system. Rather than create one class to represent all transaction types, we created three distinct transaction classes—`BalanceInquiry`, `Withdrawal` and `Deposit`—to represent the transactions that the ATM system can perform. The class diagram of Fig. 12.17 shows the attributes and operations of these classes. Note that they have one `Private` attribute (`accountNumber`) and one public operation (`Execute`) in common. Each class requires attribute `accountNumber` to specify the account to which the transaction applies. Each class contains operation `Execute`, which the `ATM` invokes to perform the transaction. Clearly, `BalanceInquiry`, `Withdrawal` and `Deposit` represent *types of* transactions. Figure 12.17 reveals commonality among the transaction classes, so using inheritance to factor out the common features seems appropriate for designing these classes. We place the common functionality in base class `Transaction` and derive classes `BalanceInquiry`, `Withdrawal` and `Deposit` from `Transaction` (Fig. 12.18).

The UML specifies a relationship called a **generalization** to model inheritance. Figure 12.18 is the class diagram that models the inheritance relationship between base class `Transaction` and its three derived classes. The arrows with triangular hollow arrow-

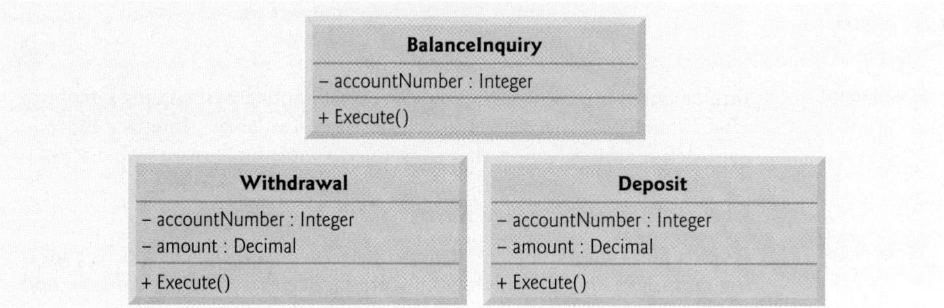

Fig. 12.17 | Attributes and operations of classes `BalanceInquiry`, `Withdrawal` and `Deposit`.

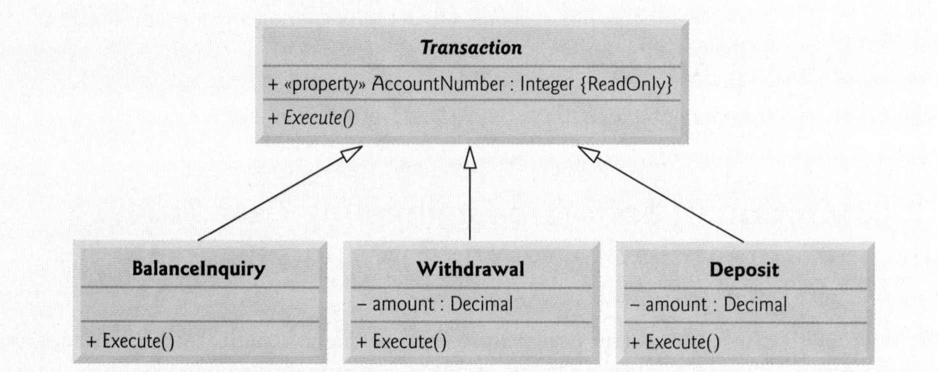

Fig. 12.18 | Class diagram modeling the generalization (i.e., inheritance) relationship between the base class `Transaction` and its derived classes `BalanceInquiry`, `Withdrawal` and `Deposit`.

heads indicate that classes `BalanceInquiry`, `Withdrawal` and `Deposit` are derived from class `Transaction` by inheritance. Class `Transaction` is said to be a generalization of its derived classes. The derived classes are said to be specializations of class `Transaction`.

In Fig. 12.17, you saw that classes `BalanceInquiry`, `Withdrawal` and `Deposit` share `Private Integer` attribute `accountNumber`. We'd like to factor out this common attribute and place it in the base class `Transaction`. However, recall that a base class's `Private` attributes are not accessible in derived classes. The derived classes of `Transaction` require access to attribute `accountNumber` so they can specify which `Account` to process in the `BankDatabase`. As you learned in Chapter 11, a derived class can access only the `Public` and `Protected` members of its base class. However, the derived classes in this case do not need to modify attribute `accountNumber`—they need only to access its value. For this reason, we have chosen to replace `Private` attribute `accountNumber` in our model with the public `ReadOnly` property `AccountNumber`. Since this is a public `ReadOnly` property, it provides a only `Get` accessor to access the account number. Each derived class inherits this property, enabling the derived class to access its account number as needed to execute a transaction. We no longer list accountNumber in the second compartment of each derived class, because the three derived classes inherit property AccountNumber from Transaction.

According to Fig. 12.17, classes BalanceInquiry, Withdrawal and Deposit also share operation Execute, so base class Transaction should contain Public operation Execute. However, it does not make sense to implement Execute in class Transaction, because the functionality that this operation provides depends on the specific type of the actual transaction. We therefore declare Execute as an abstract operation in base class Transaction (i.e., it will become a MustOverride method in the Visual Basic implementation). This makes Transaction an abstract class (i.e., MustInherit class) and forces any class derived from Transaction that must be a concrete class (i.e., BalanceInquiry, Withdrawal and Deposit) to implement the operation Execute to make the derived class concrete. The UML requires that we place abstract class names and abstract operations in italics. Thus, in Fig. 12.18, Transaction and Execute appear in italics for the Transaction class; Execute is not italicized in derived classes BalanceInquiry, Withdrawal and Deposit. Each derived class overrides base-class Transaction's Execute operation with an appropriate concrete implementation. Note that Fig. 12.18 includes operation Execute in the third compartment of classes BalanceInquiry, Withdrawal and Deposit, because each class has a different concrete implementation of the overridden operation.

As you learned in this chapter, a derived class can inherit "interface" and implementation from a base class. Compared to a hierarchy designed for implementation inheritance, one designed for interface inheritance tends to have its functionality lower in the hierarchy—a base class signifies one or more operations that should be defined by each class in the hierarchy, but the individual derived classes provide their own implementations of the operation(s). The inheritance hierarchy designed for the ATM system takes advantage of this type of inheritance, which provides the ATM with an elegant way to execute all transactions "in the general" (i.e., polymorphically). Each class derived from Transaction inherits some implementation details (e.g., property AccountNumber), but the primary benefit of incorporating inheritance into our system is that the derived classes share a common interface (e.g., abstract operation Execute). The ATM can aim a Transaction reference at any transaction, and when the ATM invokes the operation Execute through this reference, the version of Execute specific to that transaction runs automatically. For example, suppose a user chooses to perform a balance inquiry. The ATM aims a Transaction reference at a new object of class BalanceInquiry, which the Visual Basic compiler allows because a BalanceInquiry *is a* Transaction. When the ATM uses this reference to invoke Execute, BalanceInquiry's version of Execute is called.

This polymorphic approach also makes the system easily extensible. Should we wish to create a new transaction type (e.g., funds transfer or bill payment), we would simply create an additional Transaction derived class that overrides the Execute operation with a version appropriate for the new transaction type. We would need to make only minimal changes to the system code to allow users to choose the new transaction type from the main menu and for the ATM to instantiate and execute objects of the new derived class. The ATM could execute transactions of the new type using the current code, because it executes all transactions identically (through polymorphism).

As you learned earlier in the chapter, an abstract class like Transaction is one for which you never intend to (and, in fact, cannot) instantiate objects. An abstract class simply declares common attributes and behaviors for its derived classes in an inheritance hierarchy. Class `Transaction` defines the concept of what it means to be a transaction that has an account number and can be executed. You may wonder why we bother to include abstract operation `Execute` in class `Transaction` if `Execute` lacks a concrete implementation. Conceptually, we include this operation because it is the defining behavior of all transactions—executing. Technically, we must include operation `Execute` in base class `Transaction` so that the `ATM` (or any other class) can invoke each derived class's overridden version of this operation polymorphically via a `Transaction` reference.

Derived classes `BalanceInquiry`, `Withdrawal` and `Deposit` inherit property `AccountNumber` from base class `Transaction`, but classes `Withdrawal` and `Deposit` contain the additional attribute `amount` that distinguishes them from class `BalanceInquiry`. Classes `Withdrawal` and `Deposit` require this additional attribute to store the amount of money that the user wishes to withdraw or deposit. Class `BalanceInquiry` has no need for such an attribute and requires only an account number to execute. Even though two of the three `Transaction` derived classes share the attribute `amount`, we do not place it in base class `Transaction`—we place only features common to *all* the derived classes in the base class, so that derived classes do not inherit unnecessary attributes (and operations).

Figure 12.19 presents an updated class diagram of our model that incorporates inheritance and introduces abstract base class `Transaction`. We model an association between class `ATM` and class `Transaction` to show that the `ATM`, at any given moment, either is exe-

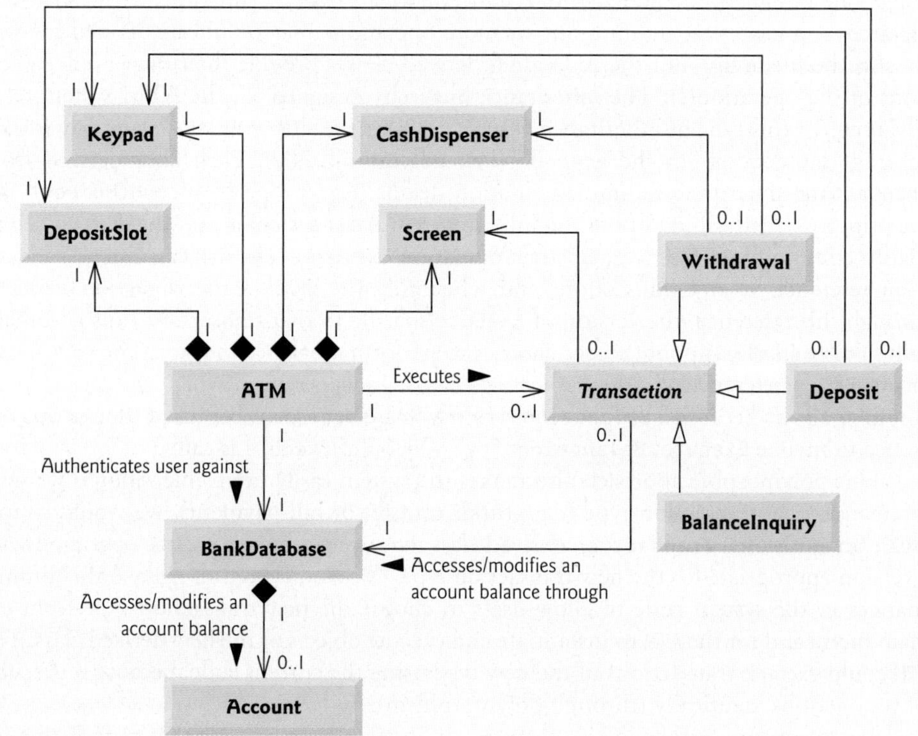

Fig. 12.19 | Class diagram of the ATM system (incorporating inheritance). Note that `MustInherit` class name `Transaction` appears in italics.

cuting a transaction or is not (i.e., zero or one objects of type Transaction exist in the system at a time). Because a Withdrawal is a type of Transaction, we no longer draw an association line directly between class ATM and class Withdrawal—derived class Withdrawal inherits base class Transaction's association with class ATM. Derived classes BalanceInquiry and Deposit also inherit this association, which replaces the previously omitted associations between classes BalanceInquiry and Deposit, and class ATM. Note again the use of triangular hollow arrowheads to indicate the specializations (i.e., derived classes) of class Transaction, as indicated in Fig. 12.18.

We also add an association between class Transaction and the BankDatabase (Fig. 12.19). All Transactions require a reference to the BankDatabase so they can access and modify account information. Each Transaction derived class inherits this reference, so we no longer model the association between class Withdrawal and the BankDatabase. Note that the association between class Transaction and the BankDatabase replaces the previously omitted associations between classes BalanceInquiry and Deposit, and the BankDatabase.

We include an association between class Transaction and the Screen because all Transactions display output to the user via the Screen. Each derived class inherits this association. Therefore, we no longer include the association previously modeled between Withdrawal and the Screen. Class Withdrawal still participates in associations with the CashDispenser and the Keypad, however—these associations apply to derived classes Withdrawal and Deposit, but not to derived class BalanceInquiry, so we do not move these associations to base class Transaction.

Our class diagram incorporating inheritance (Fig. 12.19) also models classes Deposit and BalanceInquiry. We show associations between Deposit and both the DepositSlot and the Keypad. Note that class BalanceInquiry takes part in no associations other than those inherited from class Transaction—a BalanceInquiry interacts only with the BankDatabase and the Screen.

The class diagram of Fig. 10.29 showed attributes, properties and operations with visibility markers. Now we present a modified class diagram in Fig. 12.20 that includes abstract base class Transaction. This abbreviated diagram does not show inheritance relationships (these appear in Fig. 12.19), but instead shows the attributes and operations after we have employed inheritance in our system. Note that abstract class name Transaction and abstract operation name Execute in class Transaction appear in italics. To save space, as we did in Fig. 5.32, we do not include those attributes shown by associations in Fig. 12.19—we do, however, include them in the Visual Basic implementation in Appendix D. We also omit all operation parameters, as we did in Fig. 10.22—incorporating inheritance does not affect the parameters already modeled in Figs. 7.25–7.28.

Software Engineering Observation 12.6

A complete class diagram shows all the associations among classes, and all the attributes and operations for each class. When the number of class attributes, operations and associations is substantial (as in Fig. 12.19 and Fig. 12.20), a good practice that promotes readability is to divide this information between two class diagrams—one focusing on associations and the other on attributes and operations. When examining classes modeled in this fashion, it is crucial to consider both *class diagrams to get a complete picture of the classes. For example, one must refer to Fig. 12.19 to observe the inheritance relationship between* Transaction *and its derived classes; that relationship is omitted from Fig. 12.20.*

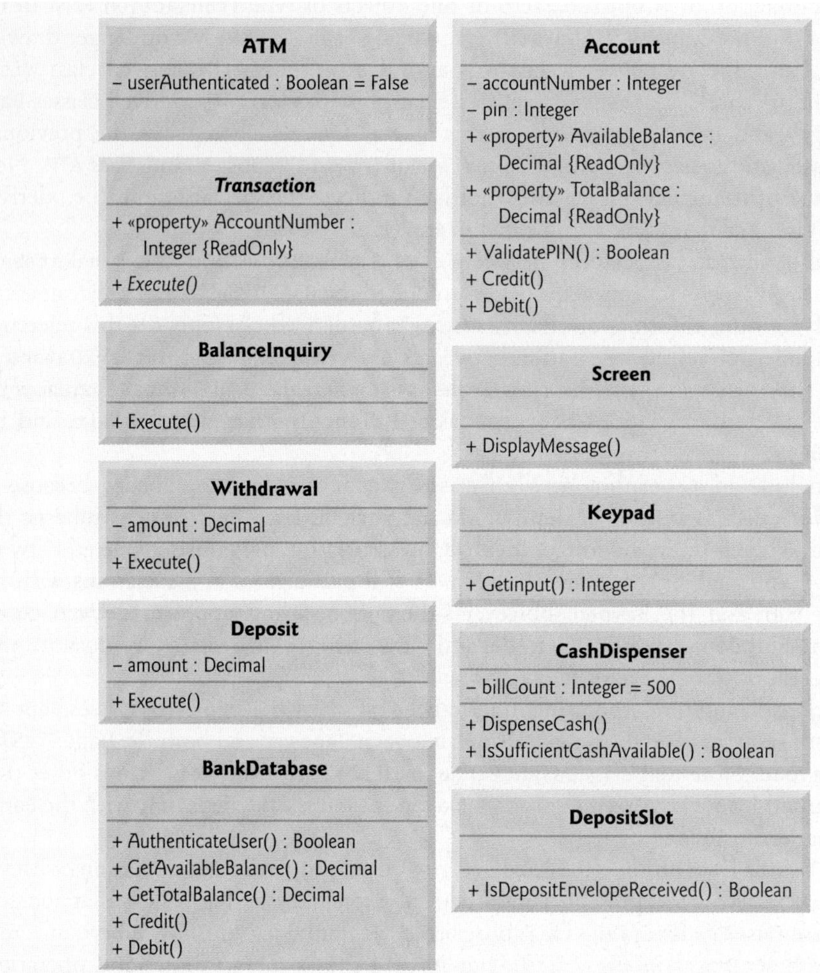

Fig. 12.20 | Class diagram after incorporating inheritance into the system.

Implementing the ATM System Design Incorporating Inheritance

In Section 10.19, we began implementing the ATM system design in Visual Basic. We now incorporate inheritance, using class `Withdrawal` as an example.

1. If a class `A` is a generalization of class `B`, then class `B` is derived from (and is a specialization of) class `A`. For example, abstract base class `Transaction` is a generalization of class `Withdrawal`. Thus, class `Withdrawal` is derived from (and is a specialization of) class `Transaction`. Figure 12.21 contains the shell (i.e., outline with variable, property, and method declarations, but no application logic) of class `Withdrawal`, in which the class definition indicates the inheritance relationship between `Withdrawal` and `Transaction` (line 3).
2. If class `A` is an abstract class and class `B` is derived from class `A`, then class `B` must implement the abstract operations of class `A` if class `B` is to be a concrete class. For

```
' Class Withdrawal represents an ATM withdrawal transaction.
Public Class Withdrawal
   Inherits Transaction

End Class ' Withdrawal
```

Fig. 12.21 | Visual Basic code for shell of class `Withdrawal`.

example, class `Transaction` contains abstract operation `Execute`, so class `Withdrawal` must implement this operation if we want to instantiate a `Withdrawal` object. Figure 12.22 contains the portions of the Visual Basic code for class `Withdrawal` that can be inferred from Fig. 12.19 and Fig. 12.20. Class `Withdrawal` inherits property `AccountNumber` from base class `Transaction`, so `Withdrawal` does not declare this property. Class `Withdrawal` also inherits references to the `Screen` and the `BankDatabase` from class `Transaction`, so we do not include these references in our code. Figure 12.20 specifies attribute `amount` and operation `Execute` for class `Withdrawal`. Line 6 of Fig. 12.22 declares an instance variable for attribute `amount`. Lines 16–18 declare the shell of a method for operation `Execute`. Recall that derived class `Withdrawal` must provide a concrete implementation of the `MustOverride` method `Execute` from base class `Transaction`. The `keypad` and `cashDispenser` references (lines 7–8) are instance variables whose need is apparent from class `Withdrawal`'s associations in Fig. 12.19—in the Visual Basic implementation of this class in Appendix D, a constructor initializes these references to actual objects.

We discuss the polymorphic processing of `Transactions` in Section D.2 of the ATM implementation. Class ATM performs the actual polymorphic call to method `Execute` at line 86 of Fig. D.1.

```
1  ' Class Withdrawal represents an ATM withdrawal transaction.
2  Public Class Withdrawal
3     Inherits Transaction
4
5     ' attributes
6     Private amount As Decimal ' amount to withdraw
7     Private keypad As Keypad ' reference to keypad
8     Private cashDispenser As CashDispenser ' reference to cash dispenser
9
10    ' parameterless constructor
11    Public Sub New()
12       ' constructor body code
13    End Sub ' New
14
15    ' method that overrides Execute
16    Public Overrides Sub Execute()
17       ' Execute method body code
18    End Sub ' Execute
19 End Class ' Withdrawal
```

Fig. 12.22 | Visual Basic code for class `Withdrawal` based on Fig. 12.19 and Fig. 12.20.

ATM Case Study Wrap-Up

This concludes our object-oriented design of the ATM system. A complete Visual Basic implementation of the ATM system in 597 lines of code appears in Appendix D. This working implementation uses all of the key object-oriented programming concepts that we have covered to this point in the book, including classes, objects, encapsulation, visibility, composition, inheritance and polymorphism. The code is abundantly commented and conforms to the coding practices you've learned so far. Mastering this code is a wonderful capstone experience for you after studying the nine Software Engineering Case Study sections in Chapters 1, 3–8, 10 and 12.

Software Engineering Case Study Self-Review Exercises

12.1 The UML uses an arrow with a __________ to indicate a generalization relationship.
a) solid filled arrowhead
b) triangular hollow arrowhead
c) diamond-shaped hollow arrowhead
d) stick arrowhead

12.2 State whether the following statement is *true* or *false*, and if *false*, explain why: The UML requires that we underline abstract class names and abstract operation names.

12.3 Write Visual Basic code to begin implementing the design for class `Transaction` specified in Fig. 12.19 and Fig. 12.20. Be sure to include `Private` references based on class `Transaction`'s associations. Also be sure to include properties with `Public Get` accessors for any of the `Private` instance variables that the derived classes must access to perform their tasks.

Answers to Software Engineering Case Study Self-Review Exercises

12.1 b.

12.2 False. The UML requires that we italicize abstract class names and operation names.

12.3 The design for class `Transaction` yields the code in Fig. 12.23. In the implementation in Appendix D, a constructor initializes `Private` instance variables `screenHandle` and `bankDatabaseHandle` to actual objects, and `ReadOnly` properties `ScreenReference` and `BankDatabaseReference` access these instance variables. These properties allow classes derived from `Transaction` to access the ATM's screen and interact with the bank's database. Note that we use the word "`Reference`" in the names of the `ScreenReference` and `BankDatabaseReference` properties for clarity—we wanted to avoid property names that are the same as the class names `Screen` and `BankDatabase`, which can be confusing.

```
' Abstract base class Transaction represents an ATM transaction.
Public MustInherit Class Transaction
   Private accountNumberValue As Integer ' indicates account involved
   Private screen As Screen ' ATM's screen
   Private bankDatabase As BankDatabase ' account info database

   ' parameterless constructor
   Public Sub New()
      ' constructor body code
   End Sub ' New
```

Fig. 12.23 | Visual Basic code for class `Transaction` based on Fig. 12.19 and Fig. 12.20. (Part 1 of 2.)

```

   ' property AccountNumber
   Public ReadOnly Property AccountNumber() As Integer
      ' AccountNumber property body code
   End Property ' AccountNumber

   ' property Screen
   Public ReadOnly Property ScreenReference() As Screen
      ' ScreenReference property body code
   End Property ' Screen

   ' property BankDatabase
   Public ReadOnly Property BankDatabaseReference() As BankDatabase
      ' BankDatabaseReference property body code
   End Property ' BankDatabase

   ' perform the transaction (overridden by each derived class)
   Public MustOverride Sub Execute()
End Class ' Transaction
```

Fig. 12.23 | Visual Basic code for class `Transaction` based on Fig. 12.19 and Fig. 12.20. (Part 2 of 2.)

12.9 Wrap-Up

In this chapter we discussed polymorphism, which enables you to "program in the general" rather than "program in the specific," and we showed how this makes programs more extensible. We began with an example of how polymorphism would allow a screen manager to display several "space" objects. We then demonstrated how base-class and derived-class references can be assigned to base-class and derived-class variables. We said that assigning base-class references to base-class variables is natural, as is assigning derived-class references to derived-class variables. We then discussed `MustOverride` methods (methods that do not provide an implementation) and `MustInherit` classes (abstract classes that typically have one or more `MustOverride` methods). You learned that abstract classes cannot be used to instantiate objects, whereas concrete classes can. We showed how abstract classes are used in an inheritance hierarchy. You learned that assigning derived-class references to base-class variables is natural, because a derived-class object *is-an* object of its base class. You learned why assigning base-class references to derived-class variables is dangerous and why the compiler disallows such assignments (when **Option Strict** is **On**). We introduced late binding, which enables the proper methods to be called when objects at various levels of an inheritance hierarchy are referenced at execution time via base class variables. You also learned how to determine the type of an object at execution-time by using a `TypeOf...Is` expression; you then can use `TryCast` to downcast from the base-class type to the derived-class type. You learned how interfaces even allow objects of unrelated classes to be processed polymorphically. Objects of classes that implement the same interface have an *is-a* relationship with the interface type. Finally, the chapter discussed how to declare and implement an interface.

You have studied classes, objects, encapsulation, inheritance, interfaces and polymorphism—the most essential aspects of object-oriented programming. In the next chapter, you will learn about exceptions, which are useful for handling errors during a program's execution, thus creating more robust programs.

Summary

Section 12.1 Introduction

- Polymorphism enables us to "program in the general" rather than "program in the specific."
- With polymorphism, we can design and implement systems that are easily extensible—new classes can be added with little or no modification to the general portions of the program, as long as the new classes are part of the inheritance hierarchy that the program processes generically.
- An interface describes a set of methods that can be called on an object, but does not provide concrete implementations for the methods.
- Each interface method must be declared in all the classes that implement the interface.

Section 12.2 Polymorphic Video Game

- With polymorphism, the same method name, signature and return type can be used to cause different actions to occur, depending on the type of object on which the method is invoked.
- Polymorphism enables programmers to deal in generalities and let the execution-time environment handle the specifics.
- Polymorphism promotes extensibility. Software that invokes polymorphic behavior is independent of the object types to which messages are sent.

Section 12.3 Demonstrating Polymorphic Behavior

- Invoking a method on a derived-class object via a base-class reference calls the derived-class version. The referenced object's type, not the reference type, determines which method is called.
- We cannot treat a base-class object as a derived-class object because a base-class object is not an object of any of its derived classes. (Every object of a derived class *is an* object of its base class.)
- Only methods declared in a base class can be invoked through a base-class reference. Attempting to invoke derived-class-only methods through a base-class reference results in compilation errors.
- If a program needs to perform a derived-class-specific operation on a derived-class object referenced by a base-class variable, the program must first cast the base-class reference to a derived-class reference—a technique known as downcasting.

Section 12.4 Abstract Classes and Methods

- Abstract classes are used only as base classes in inheritance hierarchies and cannot be used to instantiate objects.
- Classes that can be used to instantiate objects are called concrete classes. Such classes provide implementations of every method they declare (some of the implementations can be inherited).
- Not all inheritance hierarchies contain abstract classes.
- Abstract classes sometimes constitute several of the top levels of the hierarchy.
- A class is made abstract by declaring it with keyword `MustInherit`. An abstract class normally contains one or more abstract methods.
- An abstract method is one with keyword `MustOverride` in its declaration.
- Abstract methods do not provide implementations. A class that contains abstract methods must be declared `MustInherit` even if it also contains concrete (nonabstract) methods.

- Each concrete derived class of an abstract base class must provide concrete implementations of the base class's abstract (MustOverride) methods.
- Constructors and Shared methods cannot be inherited, so they cannot be declared MustOverride.
- Although objects of an abstract (MustInherit) class cannot be instantiated, a variable of an abstract class can hold a reference to an object of any concrete class derived from that abstract class.
- It is common in object-oriented programming to declare an iterator class that can traverse all the objects in a collection, such as an array or a List. Typically, such traversals process the objects polymorphically.

Section 12.5 Case Study: Payroll System Class Hierarchy Using Polymorphism

- Due to late binding, the specific type of a derived-class (or base-class) object need not be known at compile time for a method call off a base-class variable to be compiled. At execution time, the correct derived-class (or base-class) version of the method is called, based on the type of the reference stored in the base-class variable.
- Expression Typeof...Is checks the type of the object to which the operand to the right of TypeOf refers and determines whether this type has an *is-a* relationship with the type specified as the operand to the right of Is. If the two have an *is-a* relationship, the Typeof...Is expression is True; if not, the Typeof...Is expression is False.
- You can use TryCast to downcast from the base-class type to the derived-class type.
- Every object knows its own class and can access this information through method GetType, which all classes inherit from class Object.
- Method GetType returns an object of class Type (namespace System), which contains information about the object's type that can be accessed using Type's Public methods. Type property FullName, for example, returns the fully qualified name of the class.
- Assigning a derived-class reference to a base-class variable is safe, because the derived-class object *is an* object of its base class.
- Attempting to assign a base-class reference to a derived-class variable is a compilation error (when **Option Strict** is **On**).

*Section 12.6 **NotOverridable** Methods and **NotInheritable** Classes*

- A method that is declared NotOverridable in a base class cannot be overridden in a derived class (so the method must be concrete).
- A method that was declared Overridable in a base class can be declared NotOverridable in a derived class. All classes derived from the class that contains the NotOverridabble method inherit that class's method implementation.
- Methods that are declared Private are implicitly NotOverridable.
- A class that is declared NotInheritable cannot be a base class.
- All methods in a NotInheritable class are implicitly NotOverridable.

Section 12.7 Case Study: Creating and Using Interfaces

- Interfaces specify *what* operations may be performed but not *how* they are implemented.
- A Visual Basic interface describes a set of methods that can be called on an object.
- An interface declaration begins with the keyword Interface and can contain abstract methods and properties, but cannot contain instance variables, concrete methods or concrete properties.
- Interfaces may not specify any implementation details, such as concrete method declarations and instance variables.

- Members declared in an interface are implicitly `Public` and may not specify an access modifier.
- To use an interface, a concrete class must specify that it `Implements` the interface and must define the interface's methods with the signatures and return types specified in the interface declaration.
- A class that does not define all the methods of an interface it `Implements` is an abstract class and must be declared `MustInherit`.
- An interface is often used in place of a `MustInherit` class when there is no default implementation to inherit.
- When a class implements an interface, it establishes an *is-a* relationship with the interface type, as do all of its derived classes. All derived classes implicitly implement the interface.
- To implement more than one interface, provide a comma-separated list of interface names after keyword `Implements` in the class declaration.

Terminology

abstract base class
abstract class
abstract method
base-class reference
concrete class
derived-class reference
downcasting
extensibility
`FullName` property of class `Type`
`GetType` method of class `Object`
`IComparable` interface
`IComponent` interface
`IEnumerator` interface
implement an interface
`Implements` keyword
interface declaration
`Interface` keyword
is-a relationship
iterator class
late binding
`MustInherit` class
`MustOverride` method
`NotInheritable` class
`NotOverridable` method
polymorphism
program in the general
program in the specific
`TryCast` keyword
`Type` class
`TypeOf...Is` expression

Self-Review Exercises

12.1 Fill in the blanks in each of the following statements:

a) If a class contains at least one abstract method, it is a(n) __________ class.
b) Classes from which objects can be instantiated are called __________ classes.
c) __________ involves using a base-class variable to invoke methods on base-class and derived-class objects, enabling you to "program in the general."
d) Methods that are not interface methods and that do not provide implementations must be declared using keyword __________.
e) Classes declared with keyword __________ cannot be base classes.
f) Casting a reference stored in a base-class variable to a derived-class type is called __________.
g) `TryCast` returns __________ if at execution time the object being converted does not have an *is-a* relationship with the target type.

12.2 State whether each of the statements that follows is *true* or *false*. If *false*, explain why.

a) It is possible to treat base-class objects and derived-class objects similarly.
b) All methods in an abstract class must explicitly be declared as `MustOverride` methods.
c) It is a compilation error to invoke a derived-class-only method through a base-class variable.

d) If a base class declares a `MustOverride` method, a derived class must implement that method.
e) An object of a class that implements an interface may be thought of as an object of that interface type.

Answers to Self-Review Exercises

12.1 a) `MustInherit` (i.e., abstract). b) concrete. c) Polymorphism. d) `MustOverride`. e) `NotInheritable`. f) downcasting. g) `Nothing`.

12.2 a) True. b) False. An abstract class can include methods with implementations and `MustOverride` methods. c) True. d) False. Only a concrete derived class must implement the method. Not implementing the method in a derived class causes that class to be abstract (and it must explicitly be declared `MustInherit`). e) True.

Exercises

12.3 How does polymorphism enable you to program "in the general" rather than "in the specific?" Discuss the key advantages of programming "in the general."

12.4 What are abstract methods? Describe the circumstances in which an abstract method would be appropriate.

12.5 How does polymorphism promote extensibility?

12.6 Discuss four ways in which you can assign base-class and derived-class references to variables of base-class and derived-class types.

12.7 Compare and contrast abstract classes and interfaces. When would you use an abstract class? When would you use an interface?

12.8 *(Payroll System Modification)* Modify the payroll system of Figs. 12.4–12.9 to include an additional `Employee` derived class `PieceWorker` that represents an employee whose pay is based on the number of pieces of merchandise produced. Class `PieceWorker` should contain `Private` instance variables `wageValue` (to store the employee's wage per piece) and `piecesValue` (to store the number of pieces produced). Provide a concrete implementation of method `CalculateEarnings` in class `PieceWorker` that calculates the employee's earnings by multiplying the number of pieces produced by the wage per piece. Create an array of `Employee` variables to store references to objects of each concrete class in the new `Employee` hierarchy. For each `Employee`, display its string representation and earnings.

12.9 *(Payroll System Modification)* Modify the payroll system of Figs. 12.4–12.9 to include `Private` instance variable `birthDateValue` and `Public` property `BirthDate` in class `Employee`. Use class `Day` of Fig. 10.5 to represent an employee's birthday. Also declare class `Day` as `Public` and add `ReadOnly` properties for all instance variables. Assume that payroll is processed once per month. Create an array of `Employee` variables to store references to the various employee objects. In a loop, calculate the payroll for each `Employee` (polymorphically), and add a $100.00 bonus to the person's payroll amount if the current month is the month in which the `Employee`'s birthday occurs.

12.10 *(`Shape` Hierarchy)* Implement the `Shape` hierarchy shown in Fig. 11.3. Each `TwoDimensionalShape` should contain method `GetArea` to calculate the area of the two-dimensional shape. Each `ThreeDimensionalShape` should have methods `GetArea` and `GetVolume` to calculate the surface area and volume, respectively, of the three-dimensional shape. You should implement at least two-dimensional shapes (circles and squares) and three-dimensional shapes (spheres and cubes). Use the formulas `4 * Math.PI * Radius * Radius` and `(4 / 3) * Math.PI * Radius * Radius * Radius` to calculate the area and volume of a sphere, respectively, where `Radius` is the radius of the sphere. Create a program that uses an array of `Shape` references to objects of each concrete class in the hierarchy. The program should print a text description of the object to which each array element refers. Also, in the loop that processes all the shapes in the array, determine whether each shape is a `TwoDimensionalShape` or a `ThreeDimensionalShape`. If a shape is a `TwoDimensionalShape`, display its area. If a shape is a `ThreeDimensionalShape`, display its area and volume.

12.11 *(Shape Hierarchy Modification)* Reimplement the program of Exercise 12.10 such that classes `TwoDimensionalShape` and `ThreeDimensionalShape` implement an `IShape` interface rather than inherit `MustInherit` class `Shape`.

12.12 Modify Exercise 11.10 so that class `Account` is abstract. Make property `InterestRate` abstract. For all three derived classes, define this property. If an invalid interest rate is entered (less than 0% or greater than 100%), set a default interest rate. Make the default different for each class.

It is common sense to take a method and try it. If it fails, admit it frankly and try another. But above all, try something.
—Franklin Delano Roosevelt

O! throw away the worser part of it,
And live the purer with the other half.
—William Shakespeare

If they're running and they don't look where they're going I have to come out from somewhere and catch them.
—J. D. Salinger

And oftentimes excusing of a fault
Doth make the fault the worse by the excuse.
—William Shakespeare

O infinite virtue! com'st thou smiling from the world's great snare uncaught?
—William Shakespeare

13 Exception Handling

OBJECTIVES

In this chapter you'll learn:

- What exceptions are and how they are handled.
- When to use exception handling.
- To use `Try` blocks to delimit code in which exceptions might occur.
- To `Throw` exceptions to indicate a problem.
- To use `Catch` blocks to specify exception handlers.
- To use the `Finally` block to release resources.
- The .NET exception class hierarchy.
- `Exception` properties.
- To create user-defined exceptions.

Outline

13.1 Introduction

In this chapter, we introduce exception handling. An exception is an indication of a problem that occurs during a program's execution. The name "exception" refers to a problem that occurs infrequently. If the "rule" is that a statement normally executes correctly, then the occurrence of a problem represents the "exception to the rule." Exception handling enables you to create applications that can resolve (or handle) exceptions. In many cases, handling an exception allows a program to continue executing as if no problems were encountered. However, more severe problems may prevent a program from continuing normal execution, instead requiring the program to notify the user of the problem, then terminate in a controlled manner. The features presented in this chapter help you to write clear, robust and more fault-tolerant programs (i.e., programs that are able to deal with problems that may arise and continue executing). The style and details of Visual Basic exception handling are based in part on the work of Andrew Koenig and Bjarne Stroustrup in the C++ community. "Best practices" for exception handling in Visual Basic 2008 are specified in the Visual Studio documentation.[1]

Error-Prevention Tip 13.1

Exception handling helps improve a program's fault tolerance.

This chapter begins with an overview of exception-handling concepts and demonstrations of basic exception-handling techniques. The chapter also overviews .NET's exception-handling class hierarchy. Programs typically request and release resources (such as files on disk) during program execution. Often these resources are in limited supply or can

1. "Best Practices for Handling Exceptions [Visual Basic]," *.NET Framework Developer's Guide*, Visual Studio .NET Online Help (`msdn.microsoft.com/en-us/library/seyhszts.aspx`).

be used by only one program at a time. We demonstrate a part of the exception-handling mechanism that enables a program to use a resource, then guarantee that the resource will be released for use by other programs, even if an exception occurs. The chapter demonstrates several properties of class `System.Exception` (the base class of all exception classes) and discusses how you can create and use your own exception classes.

13.2 Exception-Handling Overview

Programs frequently test conditions to determine how program execution should proceed. Consider the following pseudocode:

Perform a task

If the preceding task did not execute correctly
    Perform error processing

Perform next task

If the preceding task did not execute correctly
    Perform error processing

...

In this pseudocode, we begin by performing a task; then we test whether that task executed correctly. If not, we perform error processing. Otherwise, we continue with the next task. Although this form of error handling works, intermixing program logic with error-handling logic can make programs difficult to read, modify, maintain and debug—especially in large applications.

Exception handling enables you to remove error-handling code from the "main line" of the program's execution, improving program clarity and enhancing modifiability. You can decide to handle any exceptions you choose—all exceptions, all exceptions of a certain type or all exceptions of a group of related types (i.e., exception types that are related through an inheritance hierarchy). Such flexibility reduces the likelihood that errors will be overlooked, thus making programs more robust.

With programming languages that do not support exception handling, programmers often delay writing error-processing code and sometimes forget to include it. This results in less robust software products. Visual Basic enables you to deal with exception handling easily from the beginning of a project.

13.3 Example: Divide by Zero Without Exception Handling

First we demonstrate what happens when errors arise in a console application that does not use exception handling. Figure 13.1 inputs two integers from the user, then divides the first integer by the second using integer division to obtain an `Integer` result. In this example, we will see that an exception is thrown (i.e., an exception occurs) when a method detects a problem and is unable to handle it.

Running the Application

In most of the examples we have created so far, the application appears to run the same with or without debugging. As we discuss shortly, the example in Fig. 13.1 might cause

```
' Fig. 13.1: DivideByZeroNoExceptionHandling.vb
' Integer division without exception handling.
Module DivideByZeroNoExceptionHandling
   Sub Main()
      ' get numerator and denominator
      Console.Write("Please enter an integer numerator: ")
      Dim numerator As Integer = Convert.ToInt32(Console.ReadLine())
      Console.Write("Please enter an integer denominator: ")
      Dim denominator As Integer = Convert.ToInt32(Console.ReadLine())

      ' divide the two integers, then display the result
      Dim result As Integer = numerator \ denominator
      Console.WriteLine(vbNewLine & _
         "Result: {0:D} \ {1:D} = {2:D}", numerator, denominator, result)
   End Sub ' Main
End Module ' DivideByZeroNoExceptionHandling
```

```
Please enter an integer numerator: 100
Please enter an integer denominator: 7

Result: 100 \ 7 = 14
```

```
Please enter an integer numerator: 100
Please enter an integer denominator: 0

Unhandled Exception: System.DivideByZeroException:
   Attempted to divide by zero.
   at DivideByZeroNoExceptionHandling.Main()
      in C:\examples\ch13\Fig13_01\DivideByZeroNoExceptionHandling\
      DivideByZeroNoExceptionHandling.vb:line 12
```

```
Please enter an integer numerator: 100
Please enter an integer denominator: hello

Unhandled Exception: System.FormatException:
   Input string was not in a correct format.
   at System.Number.StringToNumber(String str, NumberStyles options,
      NumberBuffer& number, NumberFormatInfo info, Boolean parseDecimal)
   at System.Number.ParseInt32(String s, NumberStyles style,
      NumberFormatInfo info)
   at System.Convert.ToInt32(String value)
   at DivideByZeroNoExceptionHandling.Main()
      in C:\examples\ch13\Fig13_01\DivideByZeroNoExceptionHandling\
      DivideByZeroNoExceptionHandling.vb:line 9
```

Fig. 13.1 | Integer division without exception handling.

errors, depending on the user's input. If you run this application using the **Debug > Start Debugging** menu option, the program pauses at the line where an exception occurs, displays the Exception Assistant window and allows you to analyze the current state of the program and debug it. We discuss the Exception Assistant in Section 13.4.3. We discuss debugging in detail in Appendix H.

In this example, we do not wish to debug the application; we simply want to see what happens when errors arise. For this reason, we execute this application from a Command Prompt window. Select **Start > All Programs > Accessories > Command Prompt** to open a Command Prompt window, then use the `cd` command to change to the application's `bin\Debug` directory. If this application resides in the directory `C:\examples\ch13\Fig13_01\DivideByZeroNoExceptionHandling` on your system, you would provide the `cd` command with the argument

```
cd C:\examples\ch13\Fig13_01\DivideByZeroNoExceptionHandling\
   DivideByZeroNoExceptionHandling\bin\Debug
```

in the Command Prompt, then press *Enter* to change to the application's `Debug` directory. To execute the application, type

```
DivideByZeroNoExceptionHandling.exe
```

in the Command Prompt, then press *Enter*. If an error arises during execution, a dialog is displayed indicating that the application has encountered a problem and needs to close. In Windows XP, the dialog also asks whether you'd like to send information about this error to Microsoft. Since we are creating this error for demonstration purposes, you should click **Don't Send**. In Windows Vista, the system tries to find a solution to the problem then asks to choose between closing the program or debugging it. [*Note:* On some systems a **Just-In-Time Debugging** dialog is displayed instead. If this occurs, simply click the **No** button to dismiss the dialog.] At this point, an error message describing the problem is displayed in the Command Prompt. We formatted the error messages in Fig. 13.1 for readability. [*Note:* Selecting **Debug > Start Without Debugging** (or *<Ctrl> F5*) to run the application from Visual Basic 2008 Express executes the application's so-called release version. The error messages produced by this version of the application may differ from those shown in Fig. 13.1 due to optimizations that the compiler performs to create an application's release version.]

Analyzing the Results

The first sample execution in Fig. 13.1 shows a successful division. In the second, the user enters `0` as the denominator. Several lines of information are displayed in response to the invalid input. This information—known as a stack trace—includes the exception name (`System.DivideByZeroException`) in a descriptive message indicating the problem that occurred and the path of execution that led to the exception, method by method. This information helps you debug a program. The first line of the error message specifies that a `DivideByZeroException` has occurred. When division by zero in integer arithmetic occurs, the CLR throws a `DivideByZeroException` (namespace `System`). The text after the name of the exception, "`Attempted to divide by zero`," indicates that this exception occurred as a result of an attempt to divide by zero. Division by zero is not allowed in integer arithmetic. [*Note:* Division by zero with floating-point values is allowed. Such a calculation results in the value infinity, which is represented either by constant `Double.PositiveInfinity` or constant `Double.NegativeInfinity`, depending on whether the numerator is positive or negative. These values are displayed as `Infinity` or `-Infinity`. If both the numerator and denominator are zero, the result of the calculation is the constant `Double.NaN` ("not a number"), which is returned when a calculation's result is undefined.]

Each "at" line in the stack trace indicates a line of code in the method that was executing when the exception occurred. The "at" line contains the namespace, class name and method name in which the exception occurred (DivideByZeroNoExceptionHandling.Main), and sometimes the location and name of the file in which the code resides (C:\examples\ch13\Fig13_01\DivideByZeroNoExceptionHandling\DivideByZeroNoExceptionHandling.vb) and the line number (:line 12) where the exception occurred. In this case, the stack trace indicates that the DivideByZeroException occurred when the program was executing line 12 of method Main. The first "at" line in the stack trace indicates the exception's throw point—the initial point at which the exception occurred (i.e., line 12 in Main). This information makes it easy for you to see where the exception originated and what method calls were made to get to that point in the program.

Now, let's look at a more detailed stack trace. In the third sample execution, the user enters the string "hello" as the denominator. This causes a FormatException, and another stack trace is displayed. Our earlier examples that input numeric values assumed that the user would input an integer value. However, a user could erroneously input a noninteger value. A FormatException (namespace System) occurs, for example, when Convert method ToInt32 receives a string that does not represent a valid integer. Starting from the last "at" line in the stack trace, we see that the exception was detected in line 9 of method Main. The stack trace also shows the other methods that led to the exception being thrown—Convert.ToInt32, Number.ParseInt32 and Number.StringToNumber. To perform its task, Convert.ToInt32 calls method Number.ParseInt32, which in turn calls Number.StringToNumber. The throw point occurs in Number.StringToNumber, as indicated by the first "at" line in the stack trace.

In Fig. 13.1, the program also terminates when exceptions occur and stack traces are displayed. This does not always happen—sometimes a program may continue executing even though an exception has occurred and a stack trace has been printed. In such cases, the application may produce incorrect results. The next section demonstrates how to handle exceptions to enable the program to run to normal completion.

13.4 Example: Handling DivideByZeroExceptions and FormatExceptions

Let us consider a simple example of exception handling. The application in Fig. 13.2 uses exception handling to process any DivideByZeroExceptions and FormatExceptions that might arise. The application displays two TextBoxes in which the user can type integers. When the user presses **Click To Divide**, the program invokes event handler divideButton_Click (lines 6–35), which obtains the user's input, converts the input values to type Integer and divides the first number (numerator) by the second number (denominator). Assuming that the user provides integers as input and does not specify 0 as the denominator, divideButton_Click displays the division result in outputLabel. However, if the user inputs a noninteger value or supplies 0 as the denominator, an exception occurs. This program demonstrates how to catch and handle (i.e., deal with) such exceptions—in this case, displaying an error message and allowing the user to enter another set of values.

Before we discuss the program's details in Sections 13.4.1–13.4.5, let's consider the sample output windows in Fig. 13.2. The window in Fig. 13.2(a) shows a successful calculation, in which the user enters the numerator 100 and the denominator 7. Note that the result (14) is an Integer, because integer division always yields an Integer result. The next two windows, Fig. 13.2(b and c), demonstrate the result of an attempt to divide by zero. In integer arithmetic, the CLR tests for division by zero and, if the denominator is zero, generates a DivideByZeroException. The program detects the exception and displays the error message dialog in Fig. 13.2(c) indicating the attempt to divide by zero. The last two output windows, Fig. 13.2(d) and Fig. 13.2(e), depict the result of inputting a non-Integer value—in this case, the user enters "hello" in the second TextBox, as shown in Fig. 13.2(d). When the user clicks **Click To Divide**, the program attempts to convert the input Strings into Integer values using method Convert.ToInt32 (lines 16 and 18). If an argument passed to Convert.ToInt32 cannot be converted to an Integer value, the method throws a FormatException. The program catches the exception and displays the error message dialog in Fig. 13.2(e) indicating that the user must enter two Integers.

```
1  ' Fig. 13.2: DivideByZeroTest.vb
2  ' FormatException and DivideByZeroException exception handlers.
3  Public Class DivideByZeroTest
4     ' obtain 2 integers from the user
5     ' and divide numerator by denominator
6     Private Sub divideButton_Click(ByVal sender As System.Object, _
7        ByVal e As System.EventArgs) Handles divideButton.Click
8
9        outputLabel.Text = String.Empty ' clear Label outputLabel
10
11       ' retrieve user input and calculate quotient
12       Try
13          ' Convert.ToInt32 generates FormatException
14          ' if argument cannot be converted to an integer
15          Dim numerator As Integer = _
16             Convert.ToInt32(numeratorTextBox.Text)
17          Dim denominator As Integer = _
18             Convert.ToInt32(denominatorTextBox.Text)
19
20          ' division generates DivideByZeroException
21          ' if denominator is 0
22          Dim result As Integer = numerator \ denominator
23
24          ' display result in outputLabel
25          outputLabel.Text = result.ToString()
26       Catch formatExceptionParameter As FormatException
27          MessageBox.Show("You must enter two integers.", _
28             "Invalid Number Format", MessageBoxButtons.OK, _
29             MessageBoxIcon.Error)
30       Catch divideByZeroExceptionParameter As DivideByZeroException
31          MessageBox.Show(divideByZeroExceptionParameter.Message, _
32             "Attempted to Divide by Zero", MessageBoxButtons.OK, _
33             MessageBoxIcon.Error)
34       End Try
35    End Sub ' divideButton_Click
36 End Class ' DivideByZeroTest
```

Fig. 13.2 | FormatException and DivideByZeroException exception handlers. (Part 1 of 2.)

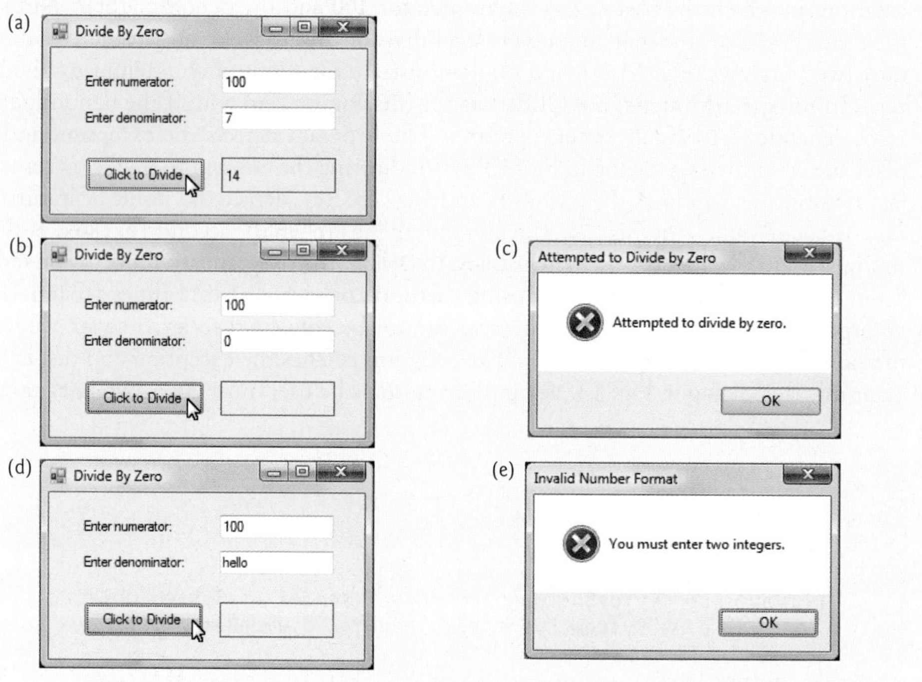

Fig. 13.2 | `FormatException` and `DivideByZeroException` exception handlers. (Part 2 of 2.)

Another way to validate the input is to use the `Int32.TryParse` method, which converts a `String` to an `Integer` value if possible (all of the numeric types have `TryParse` method). The method requires two arguments—one is the `String` to parse and the other is the variable in which the `Integer` value is be stored once the `String` is converted. The method returns a `Boolean` value that is `True` only if the `String` was parsed successfully. If the `String` could not be converted, the value `0` is assigned to the `Integer` argument. This method can be used to validate input in code rather than allowing the code to throw an exception. For errors such as these which are predictable and occur relatively frequently, it is considered a better practice to use in-code validation. We used exceptions in this example strictly for demonstration purposes.

13.4.1 Enclosing Code in a Try Block

Now we consider the user interactions and flow of control that yield the results shown in the sample output windows. The user inputs values into the `TextBoxes` that represent the numerator and denominator, then presses **Click To Divide**. At this point, the program invokes method `divideButton_Click`. Line 9 assigns the empty string to `outputLabel` to clear any prior result in preparation for a new calculation. Lines 12–25 define a `Try` block enclosing the code that might throw exceptions, as well as the code that is skipped when an exception occurs. For example, the program should not display a new result in `outputLabel` (line 25) unless the calculation in line 22 completes successfully.

The two statements that read the `Integers` from the `TextBoxes` (lines 15–18) call method `Convert.ToInt32` to convert `Strings` to `Integer` values. This method throws a

FormatException if it cannot convert its String argument to an Integer. If lines 15–18 convert the values properly (i.e., no exceptions occur), then line 22 divides the numerator by the denominator. If denominator is 0, line 22 causes the CLR to throw a DivideByZeroException. If line 22 does not cause an exception to be thrown, then the result is assigned to variable result and line 25 displays the result of the division.

13.4.2 Catching Exceptions

Exception-handling code appears in a Catch block. In general, when an exception occurs in a Try block, a corresponding Catch block catches the exception and handles it. The Try block in this example is followed by two Catch blocks—one that handles a FormatException (lines 26–29) and one that handles a DivideByZeroException (lines 30–33). A Catch block specifies an exception parameter representing the exception that the Catch block can handle. The Catch block can use the parameter's identifier (which is chosen by the programmer) to interact with a caught exception object. The type of the Catch's parameter is the type of the exception that the Catch block handles. Optionally, you can include a Catch block that does not specify an exception type or an identifier—such a Catch block catches all exception types. At least one Catch block or a Finally block (discussed in Section 13.6) must immediately follow a Try block.

In Fig. 13.2, the first Catch block (lines 26–29) catches FormatExceptions (thrown by method Convert.ToInt32), and the second Catch block (lines 30–33) catches DivideByZeroExceptions (thrown by the CLR). If an exception occurs, the program executes only the first matching Catch block. Both exception handlers in this example display an error-message dialog. After either Catch block terminates, program control continues with the first statement after the last Catch block (the end of the method, in this example). We will soon take a deeper look at how this flow of control works in exception handling.

13.4.3 Uncaught Exceptions

An uncaught exception (or unhandled exception) is an exception for which there is no matching Catch block. You saw the results of uncaught exceptions in the second and third outputs of Fig. 13.1. Recall that when exceptions occur in that example, the application terminates early (after displaying the exception's stack trace). The result of an uncaught exception depends on how you execute the program—Fig. 13.1 demonstrated the results of an uncaught exception when an application is executed in a Command Prompt. If you run the application from Visual Studio with debugging, and the runtime environment detects an uncaught exception, the application pauses and a window called the Exception Assistant appears, indicating where the exception occurred, the type of the exception and links to helpful information on handling the exception. Figure 13.3 shows the Exception Assistant that is displayed if the user attempts to divide by zero in the application of Fig. 13.1.

There is an UnhandledException event that is raised when an exception is passed without being caught by the program. This allows the application to possibly handle the exception before the system handler terminates the program. If enough information about the state of the application is provided, last-minute actions can occur such as saving data for future recovery.

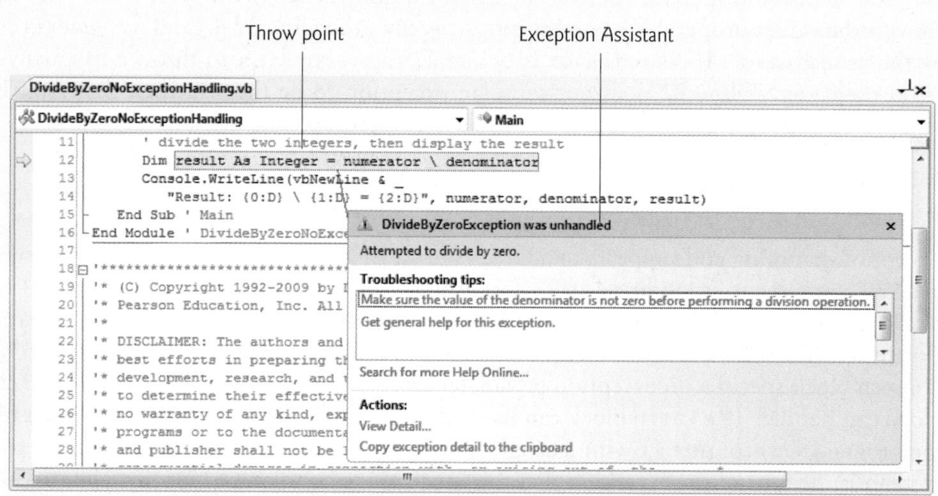

Fig. 13.3 | Exception Assistant.

13.4.4 Termination Model of Exception Handling

When a method called in a program or the CLR detects a problem, the method or the CLR throws an exception. Recall that the point in the program at which an exception occurs is called the throw point—this is an important location for debugging purposes (as we demonstrate in Section 13.7). If an exception occurs in a `Try` block (such as a `FormatException` being thrown as a result of the code in line 17 in Fig. 13.2), the `Try` block terminates immediately, and program control transfers to the first of the following `Catch` blocks in which the exception parameter's type matches the type of the thrown exception. In Fig. 13.2, the first `Catch` block catches `FormatExceptions` (which occur if input of an invalid type is entered); the second `Catch` block catches `DivideByZeroExceptions` (which occur if an attempt is made to divide by zero). After the exception is handled, program control does not return to the throw point because the `Try` block has expired (which also causes any of its local variables to go out of scope). Rather, control resumes after the last `Catch` block. This is known as the termination model of exception handling. [*Note:* Some languages use the resumption model of exception handling, in which, after an exception is handled, control resumes just after the throw point.]

Common Programming Error 13.1

Logic errors can occur if you assume that after an exception is handled, control will return to the first statement after the throw point.

If no exceptions occur in the `Try` block, the program of Fig. 13.2 successfully completes the `Try` block by ignoring the `Catch` blocks in lines 26–29 and 30–33 and passing over line 34. Then the program executes the first statement following the `Try` and `Catch` blocks. In this example, the program reaches the end of event handler `divideButton_Click` (line 35), so the method terminates, and the program awaits the next user interaction.

The Try block and its corresponding Catch and Finally blocks together form a **Try statement**. It is important not to confuse the terms "Try block" and "Try statement"—the term "Try block" refers to the block of code following the keyword Try (but before any Catch or Finally blocks), while the term "Try statement" includes all the code from the opening Try keyword to the closing End Try. This includes the Try block, as well as any associated Catch blocks and Finally block, if there is one.

As with any other block of code, when a Try block terminates, local variables defined in the block go out of scope. If a Try block terminates due to an exception, the CLR searches for the first Catch block that can process the type of exception that occurred. The CLR locates the matching Catch by comparing the type of the thrown exception to each Catch's parameter type. A match occurs if the types are identical or if the thrown exception's type is a derived class of the Catch's parameter type. Once an exception is matched to a Catch block, the code in that block executes and the other Catch blocks in the Try statement are ignored.

13.4.5 Flow of Control When Exceptions Occur

In the sample output of Fig. 13.2(b), the user inputs 0 as the denominator. When the division in line 22 executes, a DivideByZeroException occurs. When the exception occurs, the Try block expires (terminates). Next, the CLR attempts to locate a matching Catch block. In this case, the first Catch block does not match—the exception type in the Catch-handler declaration is not the same as the type of the thrown exception, and FormatException is not a base class of DivideByZeroException. Therefore the program continues to search for a matching Catch block, which it finds in line 30. Line 31 displays the value of property **Message** of class Exception, which contains the error message. Note that our program never "sets" this error-message attribute. This is done by the CLR when it creates the exception object.

In the sample output of Fig. 13.2(d), the user inputs hello as the denominator. When line 15 executes, Convert.ToInt32 cannot convert this String to an Integer, so Convert.ToInt32 throws a FormatException object to indicate that the method was unable to convert the String to an Integer. Once again, the Try block terminates, and the program attempts to locate a matching Catch block. A match occurs with the Catch block in line 26, so the exception handler executes and the program ignores all other exception handlers following the Try block.

Common Programming Error 13.2

Specifying a comma-separated list of parameters in a Catch *block is a syntax error. A* Catch *block can have at most one parameter.*

13.5 .NET Exception Hierarchy

In Visual Basic, the exception-handling mechanism allows only objects of class **Exception** (namespace System) and its derived classes to be thrown and caught. Visual Basic programs may interact with software components written in other .NET languages (such as C++) that do not restrict exception types. Such exceptions are wrapped by the CLR as Exception objects, so they can be caught by a Catch clause of type Exception.

This section overviews several of the .NET Framework's exception classes and focuses exclusively on exceptions that derive from class `Exception`. In addition, we discuss how to determine whether a particular method throws exceptions.

13.5.1 Class SystemException

Class `Exception` of namespace `System` is the base class of the .NET Framework exception-class hierarchy. An important class derived from `Exception` is `SystemException`. The CLR can generate `SystemException`s at any point during program execution. Many of these exceptions can be avoided if applications are coded properly. For example, if a program attempts to access an out-of-range array index, the CLR throws an exception of type `IndexOutOfRangeException` (a derived class of `SystemException`). Similarly, an exception occurs when a program uses an object reference to manipulate an object that does not yet exist (i.e., the reference has the value `Nothing`). Attempting to use a `Nothing` reference causes a `NullReferenceException` (another derived class of `SystemException`). You saw earlier in this chapter that a `DivideByZeroException` occurs in integer division when a program attempts to divide by zero.

Other `SystemException` types thrown by the CLR include `OutOfMemoryException`, `StackOverflowException` and `ExecutionEngineException`. These are thrown when something goes wrong that causes the CLR to become unstable. In some cases, such exceptions cannot even be caught. In general, it is best to simply log such exceptions (possibly by writing information about the problem to a file), then terminate your application.

A benefit of the exception-class hierarchy is that a `Catch` block can catch exceptions of a particular type or—because of the *is-a* relationship of inheritance—can use a base-class type to catch exceptions in a hierarchy of related exception types. For example, Section 13.4.2 discussed the `Catch` block with no parameter, which catches exceptions of all types (including those that are not derived from `Exception`). A `Catch` block that specifies a parameter of type `Exception` can catch all exceptions that derive from `Exception`, because `Exception` is the base class of all exception classes. The advantage of this approach is that the exception handler can access the caught exception's information via the parameter in the `Catch`. We demonstrated accessing the information in an exception in line 31 of Fig. 13.2. We'll say more about accessing exception information in Section 13.7.

Using inheritance with exceptions enables a `Catch` block to catch related exceptions using a concise notation. A set of exception handlers could catch each derived-class exception type individually, but catching the base-class exception type is more concise. However, this technique makes sense only if the handling behavior is the same for a base class and all of its derived classes. Otherwise, catch each derived-class exception individually.

Common Programming Error 13.3

The compiler issues a warning if a `Catch` block that catches a base-class exception is placed before a `Catch` block for any of that class's derived-class types. In this case, the base-class `Catch` block would catch all base-class and derived-class exceptions, so the derived-class exception handler would never execute—a possible logic error.

13.5.2 Determining Which Exceptions a Method Throws

How do we determine that an exception might occur in a program? For methods of the .NET Framework classes, read the detailed descriptions of the methods in the online documentation (accessible through the IDE's **Help** menu). If a method throws an exception, its description contains a section called **Exceptions** that specifies the types of exceptions the method throws and briefly describes possible causes for the exceptions. For example, search for "`Convert.ToInt32` method" in the **Index** of the Visual Studio online documentation (use the **.NET Framework** filter) or find the method in the **Object Browser** described in Chapter 10. Select the document entitled **Convert.ToInt32 Method.** In the document that describes the method, click the link **ToInt32(String).** In the document that appears, the **Exceptions** section (near the bottom of the document) indicates that method `Convert.ToInt32` throws two exception types—`FormatException` and `OverflowException`—and describes the reason why each might occur.

Software Engineering Observation 13.1

If a method throws exceptions, statements that invoke the method directly or indirectly should be placed in `Try` *blocks, and those exceptions should be caught and handled.*

It is more difficult to determine when the CLR throws exceptions. Such information appears in the *Visual Basic Language Specification 9.0* (`go.microsoft.com/fwlink/?LinkId=102846`). This document defines Visual Basic's syntax and specifies cases in which exceptions are thrown. Figure 13.2 demonstrated that the CLR throws a `DivideByZeroException` in integer arithmetic when a program attempts to divide by zero. Section 11.13.6 of the language specification discusses the division operator and when `DivideByZeroException`s occur.

13.6 Finally Block

Programs frequently request and release resources dynamically (i.e., at execution time). For example, a program that reads a file from disk first makes a file-open request (as we'll see in Chapter 18, Files and Streams). If that request succeeds, the program reads the contents of the file. Operating systems typically prevent more than one program from manipulating a file at once. Therefore, when a program finishes processing a file, the program should close the file (i.e., release the resource) so other programs can use it. If the file is not closed, a resource leak occurs. In such a case, the file resource is not available to other programs, possibly because a program using the file has not closed it.

In languages such as C and C++, in which the programmer (not the runtime) is responsible for dynamic memory management, the most common type of resource leak is a memory leak. A memory leak occurs when a program allocates memory (as Visual Basic programmers do via keyword `New`), but does not deallocate the memory when it is no longer needed. Normally, this is not an issue in Visual Basic, because the CLR garbage collects memory that is no longer needed by an executing program (Section 10.10). However, other kinds of resource leaks (such as unclosed files) can occur.

Error-Prevention Tip 13.2

The CLR does not completely eliminate memory leaks. The CLR will not garbage collect an object until the program contains no more references to that object, and even then there may be a delay until the memory is required. Thus, memory leaks can occur if you inadvertently keep references to unwanted objects.

Moving Resource-Release Code to a `Finally` *Block*

Typically, exceptions occur when processing resources that require explicit release. For example, a program that processes a file might receive `IOException`s during the processing. For this reason, file-processing code normally appears in a `Try` block. Regardless of whether a program experiences exceptions while processing a file, the program should close the file when it is no longer needed. Suppose a program places all resource-request and resource-release code in a `Try` block. If no exceptions occur, the `Try` block executes normally and releases the resources after using them. However, if an exception occurs, the `Try` block may expire before the resource-release code can execute. We could duplicate all the resource-release code in each of the `Catch` blocks, but this would make the code more difficult to modify and maintain. We could also place the resource-release code after the `Try` statement; however, if the `Try` block terminated due to a return statement, code following the `Try` statement would never execute.

To address these problems, Visual Basic's exception-handling mechanism provides the optional `Finally` block, which is guaranteed to execute regardless of whether the `Try` block executes successfully or an exception occurs. This makes the `Finally` block an ideal location in which to place resource-release code for resources that are acquired and manipulated in the corresponding `Try` block. If the `Try` block executes successfully, the `Finally` block executes immediately after the `Try` block terminates. If an exception occurs in the `Try` block, the `Finally` block executes immediately after a `Catch` block completes. If the exception is not caught by a `Catch` block associated with the `Try` block, or if a `Catch` block associated with the `Try` block throws an exception itself, the `Finally` block executes before the exception is processed by the next enclosing `Try` block, which could be in the calling method. By placing the resource-release code in a `Finally` block, we ensure that even if the program terminates due to an uncaught exception, the resource will be deallocated. Note that local variables in a `Try` block cannot be accessed in the corresponding `Finally` block. For this reason, variables that must be accessed in both a `Try` block and its corresponding `Finally` block should be declared before the `Try` block.

Error-Prevention Tip 13.3

A `Finally` *block typically contains code to release resources acquired in the corresponding* `Try` *block, which makes the* `Finally` *block an effective mechanism for eliminating resource leaks.*

Performance Tip 13.1

As a rule, resources should be released as soon as they are no longer needed in a program. This makes them available for reuse promptly.

If one or more `Catch` blocks follow a `Try` block, the `Finally` block is optional. However, if no `Catch` blocks follow a `Try` block, a `Finally` block must appear immediately after the `Try` block. If any `Catch` blocks follow a `Try` block, the `Finally` block (if there is one) appears after the last `Catch` block. Only whitespace and comments can separate the blocks in a `Try` statement.

Common Programming Error 13.4

Placing the `Finally` *block before a* `Catch` *block is a syntax error.*

Demonstrating the `Finally` *Block*

The application in Fig. 13.4 demonstrates that the `Finally` block always executes, regardless of whether an exception occurs in the corresponding `Try` block. The program consists of method `Main` (lines 4–36) and four other methods that `Main` invokes to demonstrate `Finally`. These methods are `DoesNotThrowException` (lines 39–50), `ThrowExceptionWithCatch` (lines 53–65), `ThrowExceptionWithoutCatch` (lines 69–81) and `ThrowExceptionCatchRethrow` (lines 83–102).

Line 7 of `Main` invokes method `DoesNotThrowException`. The `Try` block for this method outputs a message (line 42). Because the `Try` block does not throw any exceptions, program control ignores the `Catch` block (lines 43–44) and executes the `Finally` block (lines 45–46), which outputs a message. Program control continues with the first statement after the end of the `Finally` block (line 49), which outputs a message indicating that the end of the method has been reached. Then, program control returns to line 10 of `Main`.

```
1   ' Fig. 13.4: UsingExceptions.vb
2   ' Using Finally blocks demonstrates that Finally always executes.
3   Module UsingExceptions
4      Sub Main()
5         ' Case 1: No exceptions occur in called method
6         Console.WriteLine("Calling DoesNotThrowException")
7         DoesNotThrowException()
8
9         ' Case 2: Exception occurs and is caught in called method
10        Console.WriteLine(vbNewLine & "Calling ThrowExceptionWithCatch")
11        ThrowExceptionWithCatch()
12
13        ' Case 3: Exception occurs, but is not caught in called method
14        ' because there is no Catch block.
15        Console.WriteLine(vbNewLine & "Calling ThrowExceptionWithoutCatch")
16
17        ' call ThrowExceptionWithoutCatch
18        Try
19           ThrowExceptionWithoutCatch()
20        Catch
21           Console.WriteLine("Caught exception from " & _
22              "ThrowExceptionWithoutCatch in Main")
23        End Try
24
25        ' Case 4: Exception occurs and is caught in called method,
26        ' then rethrown to caller.
27        Console.WriteLine(vbNewLine & "Calling ThrowExceptionCatchRethrow")
28
29        ' call ThrowExceptionCatchRethrow
30        Try
31           ThrowExceptionCatchRethrow()
32        Catch
33           Console.WriteLine("Caught exception from " & _
34              "ThrowExceptionCatchRethrow in Main")
35        End Try
36     End Sub ' Main
```

Fig. 13.4 | Using `Finally` blocks demonstrates that `Finally` always executes. (Part 1 of 3.)

```

   ' no exceptions thrown
   Sub DoesNotThrowException()
      ' Try block does not throw any exceptions
      Try
         Console.WriteLine("In DoesNotThrowException")
      Catch
         Console.WriteLine("This catch never executes")
      Finally
         Console.WriteLine("finally executed in DoesNotThrowException")
      End Try

      Console.WriteLine("End of DoesNotThrowException")
   End Sub ' DoesNotThrowException

   ' throws exception and catches it locally
   Sub ThrowExceptionWithCatch()
      ' Try block throws exception
      Try
         Console.WriteLine("In ThrowExceptionWithCatch")
         Throw New Exception("Exception in ThrowExceptionWithCatch")
      Catch exceptionParameter As Exception
         Console.WriteLine("Message: " & exceptionParameter.Message)
      Finally
         Console.WriteLine("finally executed in ThrowExceptionWithCatch")
      End Try

      Console.WriteLine("End of ThrowExceptionWithCatch")
   End Sub ' ThrowExceptionWithCatch

   ' throws exception and does not catch it locally
   Sub ThrowExceptionWithoutCatch()
      ' throw exception, but do not catch it
      Try
         Console.WriteLine("In ThrowExceptionWithoutCatch")
         Throw New Exception("Exception in ThrowExceptionWithoutCatch")
      Finally
         Console.WriteLine("finally executed in " & _
            "ThrowExceptionWithoutCatch")
      End Try

      ' unreachable code; logic error
      Console.WriteLine("End of ThrowExceptionWithoutCatch")
   End Sub ' ThrowExceptionWithoutCatch

   ' throws exception, catches it and rethrows it
   Sub ThrowExceptionCatchRethrow()
      ' Try block throws exception
      Try
         Console.WriteLine("In ThrowExceptionCatchRethrow")
         Throw New Exception("Exception in ThrowExceptionCatchRethrow")
      Catch exceptionParameter As Exception
         Console.WriteLine("Message: " & exceptionParameter.Message)
```

Fig. 13.4 | Using `Finally` blocks demonstrates that `Finally` always executes. (Part 2 of 3.)

```
90
91            ' rethrow exception for further processing
92            Throw
93
94            ' code placed here would be unreachable; logic error
95         Finally
96            Console.WriteLine("finally executed in " & _
97               "ThrowExceptionCatchRethrow")
98         End Try
99
100        ' any code placed here is never reached
101        Console.WriteLine("End of ThrowExceptionCatchRethrow")
102     End Sub ' ThrowExceptionCatchRethrow
103  End Module ' UsingExceptions
```

```
Calling DoesNotThrowException
In DoesNotThrowException
finally executed in DoesNotThrowException
End of DoesNotThrowException

Calling ThrowExceptionWithCatch
In ThrowExceptionWithCatch
Message: Exception in ThrowExceptionWithCatch
finally executed in ThrowExceptionWithCatch
End of ThrowExceptionWithCatch
```

```
Calling ThrowExceptionWithoutCatch
In ThrowExceptionWithoutCatch
finally executed in ThrowExceptionWithoutCatch
Caught exception from ThrowExceptionWithoutCatch in Main

Calling ThrowExceptionCatchRethrow
In ThrowExceptionCatchRethrow
Message: Exception in ThrowExceptionCatchRethrow
finally executed in ThrowExceptionCatchRethrow
Caught exception from ThrowExceptionCatchRethrow in Main
```

Fig. 13.4 | Using `Finally` blocks demonstrates that `Finally` always executes. (Part 3 of 3.)

Throwing Exceptions Using the `Throw` *Statement*

Line 11 of `Main` invokes method `ThrowExceptionWithCatch` (lines 53–65), which begins in its `Try` block (lines 55–57) by outputting a message. Next, the `Try` block creates an `Exception` object and uses a **`Throw` statement** to throw the exception object (line 57). Executing the `Throw` statement indicates that a problem has occurred in the code. So far you have caught exceptions thrown only by called methods. You can throw exceptions by using the `Throw` statement. Just as with exceptions thrown by the Framework Class Library's methods and the CLR, this indicates to client applications that an error has occurred. A `Throw` statement specifies an object to be thrown. The operand of a `Throw` statement can be of type `Exception` or of any type derived from class `Exception`.

Common Programming Error 13.5

It is a compilation error if the argument of a `Throw`*—an exception object—is not of class* `Exception` *or one of its derived classes.*

The `String` passed to the constructor becomes the exception object's error message. When a `Throw` statement in a `Try` block executes, the `Try` block expires immediately, and program control continues with the first matching `Catch` block (lines 58–59) following the `Try` block. In this example, the type thrown (`Exception`) matches the type specified in the `Catch`, so line 59 outputs a message indicating the exception that occurred. Then, the `Finally` block (lines 60–61) executes and outputs a message. At this point, program control continues with the first statement after the end of the `Finally` block (line 64), which outputs a message indicating that the end of the method has been reached. Program control then returns to `Main`. In line 59, note that we use the exception object's `Message` property to retrieve the error message associated with the exception (i.e., the message passed to the `Exception` constructor). Section 13.7 discusses several properties of class `Exception`.

Lines 18–23 of `Main` define a `Try` statement in which `Main` invokes method `ThrowExceptionWithoutCatch` (lines 68–80). The `Try` block enables `Main` to catch any exceptions thrown by `ThrowExceptionWithoutCatch`. The `Try` block in lines 70–72 of `ThrowExceptionWithoutCatch` begins by outputting a message. Next, the `Try` block throws an `Exception` (line 72) and expires immediately.

Normally, program control would continue at the first `Catch` following this `Try` block. However, this `Try` block does not have any `Catch` blocks. Therefore, the exception is not caught in method `ThrowExceptionWithoutCatch`. Program control proceeds to the `Finally` block (lines 73–75), which outputs a message. At this point, program control returns to `Main`—any statements appearing after the `Finally` block (e.g., line 79) do not execute. In this example, such statements could cause logic errors, because the exception thrown in line 72 is not caught. In `Main`, the `Catch` block in lines 20–22 catches the exception and displays a message indicating that the exception was caught in `Main`.

Rethrowing Exceptions

Lines 30–35 of `Main` define a `Try` statement in which `Main` invokes method `ThrowExceptionCatchRethrow` (lines 83–102). The `Try` statement enables `Main` to catch any exceptions thrown by `ThrowExceptionCatchRethrow`. The `Try` statement in lines 85–98 of `ThrowExceptionCatchRethrow` begins by outputting a message. Next, the `Try` block throws an `Exception` (line 87). The `Try` block expires immediately, and program control continues at the first `Catch` (lines 88–92) following the `Try` block. In this example, the type thrown (`Exception`) matches the type specified in the `Catch`, so line 89 outputs the exception's message, which in this case indicates where the exception was thrown. Line 92 uses the `Throw` statement to rethrow the exception. This indicates that the `Catch` block performed partial processing of the exception and now is throwing the exception again (in this case, back to method `Main`) for further processing. In general, it is considered better practice to throw a new exception and pass the original one to the new exception's constructor. This maintains all of the stack trace information for the original exception. Rethrowing an exception loses the original exception's stack trace information.

You can also rethrow an exception with a version of the `Throw` statement which takes an operand that is the reference to the exception that was caught. It's important to note, however, that this form of `Throw` statement resets the throw point, so the original throw point's stack trace information is lost. Section 13.7 demonstrates using a `Throw` statement with an operand from a `Catch` block. In that section, you will see that after an exception is caught, you can create and throw a different type of exception object from the `Catch` block and you can include the original exception as part of the new exception object. Class library designers often do this to customize the exception types thrown from methods in their class libraries or to provide additional debugging information.

The exception handling in method `ThrowExceptionCatchRethrow` does not complete, because the method rethrows the exception with the `Throw` statement in line 92. This causes method `ThrowExceptionCatchRethrow` to terminate and return control to `Main`. Once again, the `Finally` block (lines 95–97) executes and outputs a message before control returns to `Main`. When control returns to `Main`, the `Catch` block in lines 32–34 catches the exception and displays a message indicating that the exception was caught. Then the program terminates.

Returning After a `Finally` *Block*

Note that the next statement to execute after a `Finally` block terminates depends on the exception-handling state. If the `Try` block successfully completes, or if a `Catch` block catches and handles an exception, the program continues its execution with the next statement after the `Finally` block. However, if an exception is not caught, or if a `Catch` block rethrows an exception, program control continues in the next enclosing `Try` block, which could be in the calling method or in one of its callers. It also is possible to nest a `Try` statement in a `Try` block; in such a case, the outer `Try` statement's `Catch` blocks would process any exceptions that were not caught in the inner `Try` statement. If a `Try` block executes and has a corresponding `Finally` block, the `Finally` block executes even if the `Try` block terminates due to a `Return` statement—the `Return` occurs after executing the `Finally` block.

Common Programming Error 13.6

Throwing an exception from a `Finally` block can be dangerous. If an uncaught exception is awaiting processing when the `Finally` block executes, and the `Finally` block throws a new exception that is not caught in the `Finally` block, the first exception is lost, and the new exception is passed to the next enclosing `Try` block.

Error-Prevention Tip 13.4

When placing code that can throw an exception in a `Finally` block, always enclose the code in a `Try` statement that catches the appropriate exception types. This prevents the loss of any uncaught and rethrown exceptions that occur before the `Finally` block executes.

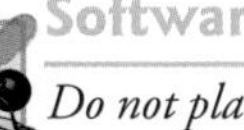

Software Engineering Observation 13.2

Do not place `Try` blocks around every statement that might throw an exception, because this can make programs difficult to read. It is better to place one `Try` block around a significant portion of code, and follow this `Try` block with `Catch` blocks that handle each of the possible exceptions. Then follow the `Catch` blocks with a single `Finally` block. Separate `Try` blocks should be used when it is important to distinguish between multiple statements that can throw the same exception type.

The `Using` *Statement*

Recall from earlier in this section that resource-release code should be placed in a `Finally` block to ensure that a resource is released, regardless of whether exceptions occurred when the resource was used in the corresponding `Try` block. An alternative notation—the `Using` statement—simplifies writing code in which you obtain a resource, use the resource in a `Try` block and release the resource in a corresponding `Finally` block. For example, a file-processing application (Chapter 18) could process a file with a `Using` statement to ensure that the file is closed properly when it is no longer needed. The resource must be an object that implements the `IDisposable` interface and therefore has a `Dispose` method. The general form of a `Using` statement is

```
Using exampleObject As New ExampleObject()
   exampleObject.SomeMethod()
End Using
```

where `ExampleObject` is a class that implements the `IDisposable` interface. This code creates an object of type `ExampleObject` and uses it in a statement, then calls its `Dispose` method to release any resources used by the object. The `Using` statement implicitly places the code in its body in a `Try` block with a corresponding `Finally` block that calls the object's `Dispose` method. For instance, the preceding `Using` statement is equivalent to the following code

```
Dim exampleObject As New ExampleObject()

Try
   exampleObject.SomeMethod()
Finally
   If Not (exampleObject Is Nothing) Then
      exampleObject.Dispose()
   End If
End Try
```

Note that the `If` statement ensures that `exampleObject` still references an object; otherwise, a `NullReferenceException` might occur. You can read more about the `Using` statement in Section 10.13 of the *Visual Basic Language Specification*.

13.7 Exception Properties

As we discussed in Section 13.5, exception types derive from class `Exception`, which has several properties. These frequently are used in error messages indicating a caught exception. Two important properties are `Message` and `StackTrace`.

Property `Message` stores the error message associated with an `Exception` object. This message can be a default message associated with the exception type or a customized message passed to an `Exception` object's constructor when the `Exception` object is thrown.

Property `StackTrace` contains a (normally lengthy) `String` that represents the method-call stack. Recall that the runtime environment at all times keeps a list of open method calls that have been made but have not yet returned. The `StackTrace` represents the series of methods that have not finished processing at the time the exception occurs.

Error-Prevention Tip 13.5

A stack trace shows the complete method-call stack at the time an exception occurred. This enables you to view the series of method calls that led to the exception. Information in the stack trace includes the names of the methods on the call stack at the time of the exception, the names

of the classes in which the methods are defined and the names of the namespaces in which the classes are defined. The IDE creates program database (PDB) files to maintain the debugging information for your projects. If the PDB file that contains the debugging information for the method is accessible to the IDE, the stack trace also includes line numbers; the first line number indicates the throw point, and subsequent line numbers indicate the locations from which the methods in the stack trace were called.

Property InnerException

Another property used frequently by class-library programmers is `InnerException`. Typically, class-library programmers "wrap" exception objects caught in their code so they then can throw new exception types that are specific to their libraries. For example, a programmer implementing an accounting system might have some account-number processing code in which account numbers are input as `Strings` but represented as `Integers` in the code. Recall that a program can convert `Strings` to `Integer` values with `Convert.ToInt32`, which throws a `FormatException` when it encounters an invalid number format. When an invalid account number format occurs, the accounting-system programmer might wish to employ a different error message than the default message supplied by `FormatException` or might wish to indicate a new exception type, such as `InvalidAccountNumberFormatException`. In such cases, the programmer would provide code to catch the `FormatException`, then create an appropriate type of `Exception` object in the `Catch` block and pass the original exception as one of the constructor arguments. The original exception object becomes the `InnerException` of the new exception object. When an `InvalidAccountNumberFormatException` occurs in code that uses the accounting-system library, the `Catch` block that catches the exception can obtain a reference to the original exception via property `InnerException`. Thus the exception indicates both that the user specified an invalid account number and that the problem was an invalid number format. If the `InnerException` property is `Nothing`, this indicates that the exception was not caused by another exception.

Other Exception *Properties*

Class `Exception` provides other properties, including `HelpLink`, `Source` and `TargetSite`. Property `HelpLink` specifies the location of the help file that describes the problem that occurred. This property is `Nothing` if no such file exists. Property `Source` specifies the name of the application or object that caused the exception. Property `TargetSite` specifies the method where the exception originated.

Demonstrating Exception *Properties and Stack Unwinding*

Our next example (Fig. 13.5) demonstrates properties `Message`, `StackTrace` and `InnerException`, and method `ToString`, of class `Exception`. In addition, the example introduces stack unwinding—when an exception is thrown but not caught in a particular scope, the method-call stack is "unwound," and an attempt is made to catch the exception in the next outer `Try` block. We keep track of the methods on the call stack as we discuss property `StackTrace` and the stack-unwinding mechanism. To see the proper stack trace, you should execute this program using steps similar to those presented in Section 13.3.

Program execution begins with `Main`, which becomes the first method on the method-call stack. Line 8 of the `Try` block in `Main` invokes `Method1` (declared in lines 28–30), which becomes the second method on the stack. If `Method1` throws an exception, the `Catch` block in lines 9–23 handles the exception and outputs information about the exception that occurred. Line 29 of `Method1` invokes `Method2` (lines 33–35), which becomes the third method on the stack. Then line 34 of `Method2` invokes `Method3` (lines 38–47), which becomes the fourth method on the stack.

```
1  ' Fig. 13.5: Properties.vb
2  ' Exception properties and stack unwinding.
3  Module Properties
4     Sub Main()
5        ' call Method1; any Exception generated is caught
6        ' in the catch block that follows
7        Try
8           Method1()
9        Catch exceptionParameter As Exception
10          ' output the string representation of the Exception, then output
11          ' properties InnerException, Message and StackTrace
12          Console.WriteLine("exceptionParameter.ToString: " & _
13             vbNewLine & "{0}" & vbNewLine, _
14             exceptionParameter.ToString())
15          Console.WriteLine("exceptionParameter.Message: " & _
16             vbNewLine & "{0}" & vbNewLine, _
17             exceptionParameter.Message)
18          Console.WriteLine("exceptionParameter.StackTrace: " & _
19             vbNewLine & "{0}" & vbNewLine, _
20             exceptionParameter.StackTrace)
21          Console.WriteLine("exceptionParameter.InnerException: " & _
22             vbNewLine & "{0}" & vbNewLine, _
23             exceptionParameter.InnerException.ToString())
24       End Try
25    End Sub ' Main
26
27    ' calls Method2
28    Sub Method1()
29       Method2()
30    End Sub ' Method1
31
32    ' calls Method3
33    Sub Method2()
34       Method3()
35    End Sub ' Method2
36
37    ' throws an Exception containing an InnerException
38    Sub Method3()
39       ' attempt to convert string to integer
40       Try
41          Convert.ToInt32("Not an integer")
42       Catch formatExceptionParameter As FormatException
43          ' wrap FormatException in new Exception
44          Throw New Exception("Exception occurred in Method3", _
45             formatExceptionParameter)
46       End Try
47    End Sub ' Method3
48 End Module ' Properties
```

Fig. 13.5 | `Exception` properties and stack unwinding. (Part 1 of 2.)

```
exceptionParameter.ToString:
System.Exception: Exception occurred in Method3 --->
   System.FormatException: Input string was not in a correct format.
   at System.Number.StringToNumber(String str, NumberStyles options,
      NumberBuffer& number, NumberFormatInfo info, Boolean parseDecimal)
   at System.Number.ParseInt32(String s, NumberStyles style,
      NumberFormatInfo info)
   at System.Convert.ToInt32(String value)
   at Properties.Method3() in C:\examples\ch13\Fig13_05\Properties\
      Properties\Properties.vb:line 42
   --- End of inner exception stack trace ---
   at Properties.Method3() in C:\examples\ch13\Fig13_05\Properties\
      Properties\Properties.vb:line 45
   at Properties.Method2() in C:\examples\ch13\Fig13_05\Properties\
      Properties\Properties.vb:line 35
   at Properties.Method1() in C:\examples\ch13\Fig13_05\Properties\
      Properties\Properties.vb:line 30
   at Properties.Main() in C:\examples\ch13\Fig13_05\Properties\
      Properties\Properties.vb:line 9

exceptionParameter.Message:
Exception occurred in Method3

exceptionParameter.StackTrace:
   at Properties.Method3() in C:\examples\ch13\Fig13_05\Properties\
      Properties\Properties.vb:line 45
   at Properties.Method2() in C:\examples\ch13\Fig13_05\Properties\
      Properties\Properties.vb:line 35
   at Properties.Method1() in C:\examples\ch13\Fig13_05\Properties\
      Properties\Properties.vb:line 30
   at Properties.Main() in C:\examples\ch13\Fig13_05\Properties\
      Properties\Properties.vb:line 9

exceptionParameter.InnerException:
System.FormatException: Input string was not in a correct format.
   at System.Number.StringToNumber(String str, NumberStyles options,
      NumberBuffer& number, NumberFormatInfo info, Boolean parseDecimal)
   at System.Number.ParseInt32(String s, NumberStyles style,
      NumberFormatInfo info)
   at System.Convert.ToInt32(String value)
   at Properties.Method3() in C:\examples\ch13\Fig13_05\Properties\
      Properties\Properties.vb:line 42
```

Fig. 13.5 | `Exception` properties and stack unwinding. (Part 2 of 2.)

At this point, the method-call stack (from top to bottom) for the program is:

```
Method3
Method2
Method1
Main
```

The method called most recently (`Method3`) appears at the top of the stack; the first method called (`Main`) appears at the bottom. The `Try` statement (lines 40–46) in `Method3` invokes `Convert.ToInt32` (line 41), which attempts to convert a `String` to an `Integer`. At this point, `Convert.ToInt32` becomes the fifth and final method on the call stack.

Throwing an **Exception** *with an* **InnerException**

Because the argument to Convert.ToInt32 is not in Integer format, line 41 throws a FormatException that is caught in line 42 of Method3. When the exception occurs, the call to Convert.ToInt32 terminates, so the method is removed (or unwound) from the method-call stack. The Catch block in Method3 then creates and throws an Exception object. The first argument to the Exception constructor is the custom error message for our example, "Exception occurred in Method3". The second argument is the InnerException—the FormatException that was caught. The StackTrace for this new exception object reflects the point at which the exception was thrown (line 44). Now Method3 terminates, because the exception thrown in the Catch block is not caught in the method body. Thus, control returns to the statement that invoked Method3 in the prior method in the call stack (Method2). This removes, or unwinds, Method3 from the method-call stack.

When control returns to line 34 in Method2, the CLR determines that line 34 is not in a Try block. Therefore the exception cannot be caught in Method2, and Method2 terminates. This unwinds Method2 from the call stack and returns control to line 29 in Method1.

Here again, line 29 is not in a Try block, so Method1 cannot catch the exception. The method terminates and is unwound from the call stack, returning control to line 8 in Main, which *is* located in a Try block. The Try block in Main expires and the Catch block (lines 9–23) catches the exception. The Catch block uses method ToString and properties Message, StackTrace and InnerException to create the output. Note that stack unwinding continues until a Catch block catches the exception or the program terminates.

Displaying Information About the **Exception**

The first block of output (which we reformatted for readability) in Fig. 13.5 contains the exception's String representation, which is returned from method ToString. The String begins with the name of the exception class followed by the Message property value. The next four items present the stack trace of the InnerException object. The remainder of the block of output shows the StackTrace for the exception thrown in Method3. Note that the StackTrace represents the state of the method-call stack at the throw point of the exception, rather than at the point where the exception eventually is caught. Each StackTrace line that begins with "at" represents a method on the call stack. These lines indicate the method in which the exception occurred, the file in which the method resides and the line number of the throw point in the file. Note that the inner-exception information includes the inner-exception stack trace.

Error-Prevention Tip 13.6

When catching and rethrowing an exception, provide additional debugging information in the rethrown exception. To do so, create an Exception *object containing more specific debugging information, then pass the original caught exception to the new exception object's constructor to initialize the* InnerException *property.*

The next block of output (two lines) simply displays the Message property's value (Exception occurred in Method3) of the exception thrown in Method3.

The third block of output displays the StackTrace property of the exception thrown in Method3. Note that this StackTrace property contains the stack trace starting from line 44 in Method3, because that is the point at which the Exception object was created and thrown. The stack trace always begins with the exception's throw point.

Finally, the last block of output displays the `String` representation of the `InnerException` property, which includes the namespace and class name of the exception object, as well as its `Message` and `StackTrace` properties.

13.8 User-Defined Exception Classes

In many cases, you can use existing exception classes from the .NET Framework Class Library to indicate exceptions that occur in your programs. However, in some cases, you might wish to create new exception classes specific to the problems that occur in your programs. User-defined exception classes should derive directly or indirectly from class `Exception` of namespace `System`. When you create code that throws exceptions, they should be well documented so that other developers who use your code will know how to handle them.

Good Programming Practice 13.1

Associating each type of malfunction with an appropriately named exception class improves program clarity.

Software Engineering Observation 13.3

Before creating a user-defined exception class, investigate the existing exceptions in the .NET Framework Class Library to determine whether an appropriate exception type already exists.

Figures 13.6 and 13.7 demonstrate a user-defined exception class. Class `NegativeNumberException` (Fig. 13.6) is a user-defined exception class representing exceptions that occur when a program performs an illegal operation on a negative number, such as

```
' Fig. 13.6: NegativeNumberException.vb
' Exception derived class thrown when a program performs an illegal
' operation on a negative number.
Public Class NegativeNumberException
   Inherits Exception
   ' default constructor
   Public Sub New()
      MyBase.New("Illegal operation for a negative number")
   End Sub ' New

   ' constructor for customizing error message
   Public Sub New(ByVal messageValue As String)
      MyBase.New(messageValue)
   End Sub ' New

   ' constructor for customizing the exception's error
   ' message and specifying the InnerException object
   Public Sub New(ByVal messageValue As String, ByVal inner As Exception)
      MyBase.New(messageValue, inner)
   End Sub ' New
End Class ' NegativeNumberException
```

Fig. 13.6 | `Exception` derived class thrown when a program performs an illegal operation on a negative number.

attempting to calculate its square root. Note that this class was created only for demonstration purposes. In real-world applications, it would be better to anticipate and handle this frequent error in your code with argument validation rather than with exceptions.

According to Microsoft's "Best Practices for Handling Exceptions [Visual Basic]," user-defined exceptions should typically extend class `Exception`, have a class name that ends with "Exception" and define three constructors: a parameterless constructor; a constructor that receives a `String` argument (the error message); and a constructor that receives a `String` argument and an `Exception` argument (the error message and the inner exception object). Defining these three constructors makes your exception class more flexible, allowing other programmers to easily use and extend it.

`NegativeNumberException`s most frequently occur during arithmetic operations, so it seems logical to derive class `NegativeNumberException` from class `ArithmeticException`. However, class `ArithmeticException` derives from class `SystemException`—the category of exceptions thrown by the CLR. Per Microsoft's best practices for exception handling, user-defined exception classes should inherit from `Exception` rather than `SystemException`. In this case, we could have used the built in `ArgumentException` class which is recommended in the best practices for invalid argument values. We create our own exception type here for demonstration purposes.

Class `SquareRootTest` (Fig. 13.7) demonstrates our user-defined exception class. The application enables the user to input a numeric value, then invokes method `SquareRoot` (lines 6–14) to calculate the square root of that value. To perform this calculation, `SquareRoot` invokes class `Math`'s `Sqrt` method, which receives a `Double` value as its argument. Normally, if the argument is negative, method `Sqrt` returns `NaN`. In this program, we would like to prevent the user from calculating the square root of a negative number. If the numeric value that the user enters is negative, the `SquareRoot` method throws a `NegativeNumberException` (lines 9–10). Otherwise, `SquareRoot` invokes class `Math`'s method `Sqrt` to compute the square root (line 12).

```
1  ' Fig. 13.7: SquareRootTest.vb
2  ' SquareRootForm throws an exception if a negative number is entered.
3  Public Class SquareRootForm
4     ' computes square root of parameter; throws
5     ' NegativeNumberException if parameter is negative
6     Public Function SquareRoot(ByVal value As Double) As Double
7        ' if negative operand, throw NegativeNumberException
8        If value < 0.0 Then
9           Throw New NegativeNumberException( _
10             "Square root of negative number not permitted")
11       Else
12          Return Math.Sqrt(value) ' compute square root
13       End If
14    End Function ' SquareRoot
15
16    ' obtain user input, convert to double, calculate square root
17    Private Sub squareRootButton_Click(ByVal sender As System.Object, _
18       ByVal e As System.EventArgs) Handles squareRootButton.Click
```

Fig. 13.7 | `SquareRootForm` throws an exception if a negative number is entered. (Part 1 of 2.)

```
19
20          outputLabel.Text = String.Empty ' clear outputLabel
21
22          ' catch any NegativeNumberException thrown
23          Try
24             Dim result As Double = _
25                SquareRoot(Convert.ToDouble(inputTextBox.Text))
26
27             outputLabel.Text = result.ToString()
28          Catch formatExceptionParameter As FormatException
29             MessageBox.Show(formatExceptionParameter.Message, _
30                "Invalid Number Format", MessageBoxButtons.OK, _
31                MessageBoxIcon.Error)
32          Catch negativeNumberExceptionParameter As NegativeNumberException
33             MessageBox.Show(negativeNumberExceptionParameter.Message, _
34                "Invalid Operation", MessageBoxButtons.OK, _
35                MessageBoxIcon.Error)
36          End Try
37       End Sub ' squareRootButton_Click
38    End Class ' SquareRootTest
```

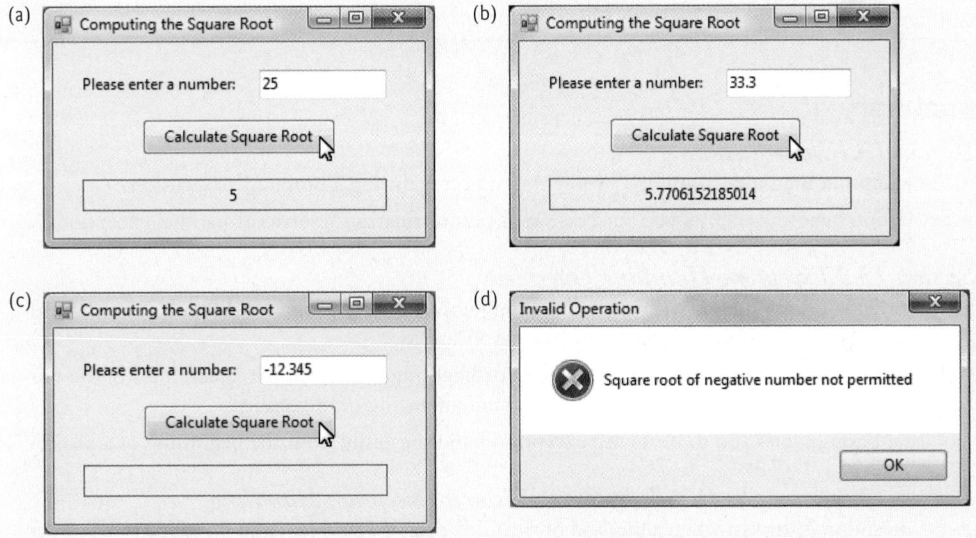

(a) Computing the Square Root
Please enter a number: 25
Calculate Square Root
5

(b) Computing the Square Root
Please enter a number: 33.3
Calculate Square Root
5.7706152185014

(c) Computing the Square Root
Please enter a number: -12.345
Calculate Square Root

(d) Invalid Operation
Square root of negative number not permitted
OK

Fig. 13.7 | `SquareRootForm` throws an exception if a negative number is entered. (Part 2 of 2.)

When the user inputs a value and clicks the **Calculate Square Root** button, the program invokes event handler `squareRootButton_Click` (lines 17–37). The `Try` statement (lines 23–36) attempts to invoke `SquareRoot` using the value input by the user. If the user input is not a valid number, a `FormatException` occurs, and the `Catch` block in lines 28–31 processes the exception. If the user inputs a negative number, method `SquareRoot` throws a `NegativeNumberException` (lines 9–10); the `Catch` block in lines 32–35 catches and handles this type of exception.

13.9 Wrap-Up

In this chapter, you learned how to use exception handling to deal with errors in an application. We showed how exception handling enables you to remove error-handling code from the "main line" of the program's execution. You saw exception handling in the context of a divide-by-zero example. You learned how to use `Try` blocks to enclose code that may throw an exception, and how to use `Catch` blocks to deal with exceptions that may arise. We discussed the termination model of exception handling, in which, after an exception is handled, program control does not return to the throw point. We also discussed several important classes of the .NET `Exception` hierarchy, including `Exception` (from which user-defined exception classes are derived) and `SystemException`. You learned how to use the `Finally` block to release resources whether or not an exception occurs, and how to throw and rethrow exceptions with the `Throw` statement. We also discussed how the `Using` statement can be used to automate the process of releasing a resource. You then learned how to obtain information about an exception using `Exception` properties `Message`, `StackTrace` and `InnerException`, and method `ToString`. You learned how to create your own exception classes. In the next two chapters, we present an in-depth treatment of graphical user interfaces. In these chapters and throughout the rest of the book, we use exception handling to make our examples more robust.

Summary

Section 13.1 Introduction

- An exception is an indication of a problem that occurs during a program's execution.
- Exception handling enables you to create applications that can resolve (or handle) exceptions.

Section 13.2 Exception-Handling Overview

- Intermixing program logic with error-handling logic can make programs difficult to read, modify, maintain and debug—especially in large applications.
- Exception handling enables you to remove error-handling code from the "main line" of the program's execution, improving program clarity and enhancing modifiability.
- Visual Basic enables you to deal with exception handling easily from the beginning of a project.

Section 13.3 Example: Divide by Zero Without Exception Handling

- An exception is thrown when a method or the CLR detects a problem and is unable to handle it.
- A stack trace includes the name of the exception in a descriptive message that indicates the problem that occurred and the complete method-call stack at the time the exception occurred.
- Division by zero is not allowed in integer arithmetic.
- Division by zero with floating-point values results in the value infinity, which is represented by either constant `Double.PositiveInfinity` or constant `Double.NegativeInfinity`, depending on whether the numerator is positive or negative. If both the numerator and denominator are zero, the result of the calculation is the constant `Double.NaN`, which stands for "not a number."
- When division by zero occurs in integer arithmetic, a `DivideByZeroException` is thrown.
- A `FormatException` occurs when `Convert` method `ToInt32` receives a string that does not represent a valid integer.

Section 13.4 Example: Handling `DivideByZeroException`s and `FormatException`s

- A `Try` block encloses the code that might throw exceptions, as well as the code that should not execute if an exception occurs.
- A `Catch` block can specify an identifier of the exception type that the `Catch` block can handle.
- At least one `Catch` block and/or a `Finally` block must immediately follow the `Try` block.
- An uncaught exception is an exception that occurs for which there is no matching `Catch` block.
- When a method called in a program detects an exception, or when the CLR detects a problem, the method or the CLR throws an exception.
- The point in the program at which an exception occurs is called the throw point.
- If an exception occurs in a `Try` block, the `Try` block terminates immediately, and program control transfers to the first of the following `Catch` blocks in which the exception parameter's type matches the type of the thrown exception.
- After the exception is handled, program control does not return to the throw point because the `Try` block has expired (which also causes any of its local variables to be lost). Instead control resumes after the last `Catch` block. This is known as the termination model of exception handling.
- The `Try` block and its corresponding `Catch` and `Finally` blocks together form a `Try` statement.
- The CLR locates the matching `Catch` by comparing the thrown exception's type to each `Catch`'s exception-parameter type. A match occurs if the types are identical or if the thrown exception's type is a derived class of the exception-parameter type.
- Once an exception is matched to a `Catch` block, that `Catch` block executes and the other `Catch` blocks are ignored.

Section 13.5 .NET `Exception` Hierarchy

- The Visual Basic exception-handling mechanism allows objects only of class `Exception` and its derived classes to be thrown and caught.
- Class `Exception` of namespace `System` is the base class of the .NET Framework Class Library exception class hierarchy.
- The CLR generates `SystemException`s, which can occur at any point during the execution of the program. Many of these exceptions can be avoided if applications are coded properly.
- A benefit of using the exception class hierarchy is that a `Catch` block can catch exceptions of a particular type or—because of the *is-a* relationship of inheritance—can use a base-class type to catch exceptions in a hierarchy of related exception types.
- A `Catch` block that specifies an exception parameter of type `Exception` can catch all exceptions that derive from `Exception`, because `Exception` is the base class of all exception classes.
- Using inheritance with exceptions enables an exception handler to catch related exceptions using a concise notation.

Section 13.6 `Finally` Block

- The most common type of resource leak is a memory leak.
- A memory leak occurs when a program allocates memory but does not deallocate it when it is no longer needed. Normally, this is not an issue in Visual Basic, because the CLR garbage collects memory that is no longer needed by an executing program.
- Visual Basic's exception-handling mechanism provides the `Finally` block, which is guaranteed to execute if program control enters the corresponding `Try` block.

- The `Finally` block executes regardless of whether the corresponding `Try` block executes successfully or an exception occurs. This makes the `Finally` block an ideal location in which to place resource-release code for resources acquired and manipulated in the corresponding `Try` block.
- If the `Try` block executes successfully, the `Finally` block executes immediately after the `Try` block terminates. If an exception occurs in the `Try` block, the `Finally` block executes immediately after a `Catch` block completes.
- If the exception is not caught by a `Catch` block associated with the `Try` block, or if a `Catch` block associated with the `Try` block throws an exception, the `Finally` block executes before the exception is processed by the next enclosing `Try` block (if there is one).
- The `Throw` statement can be used to rethrow an exception, indicating that a `Catch` block performed partial processing of the exception and now is throwing the exception again for further processing.
- If a `Try` block executes and has a corresponding `Finally` block, the `Finally` block always executes—even if the `Try` block terminates due to a `Return` statement. The `Return` occurs after the execution of the `Finally` block.
- The `Using` statement simplifies writing code in which you obtain a resource, use the resource in a `Try` block and release the resource in a corresponding `Finally` block.

Section 13.7 `Exception` Properties

- Property `Message` of class `Exception` stores the error message associated with an `Exception` object.
- Property `StackTrace` of class `Exception` contains a `String` that represents the method-call stack.
- Another `Exception` property used frequently by class-library programmers is `InnerException`. Typically, you use this property to "wrap" exception objects caught in your code so that you then can throw new exception types specific to your libraries.
- When an exception is thrown but not caught in a particular scope, the method-call stack is "unwound," and an attempt is made to catch the exception in the next outer `Try` block—this is known as stack unwinding.

Section 13.8 User-Defined Exception Classes

- User-defined exception classes should derive directly or indirectly from class `Exception` of namespace `System`.
- User-defined exceptions should typically extend `Exception`, have a class name that ends with "Exception" and define a parameterless constructor, a constructor that receives a `String` argument (the error message), and a constructor that receives a `String` argument and an `Exception` argument (the error message and the inner exception object).

Terminology

catch an exception
`Catch` block
divide by zero
`DivideByZeroException` class
error-processing code
exception
Exception Assistant
`Exception` class
exception handler
exception handling
`ExecutionEngineException` class
fault-tolerant program
`Finally` block
`FormatException` class
handle an exception
`HelpLink` property of class `Exception`
inheritance with exceptions
`IndexOutOfRangeException` class
`InnerException` property of class `Exception`
memory leak
`Message` property of class `Exception`
method-call stack

NaN constant of structure Double
NegativeInfinity constant of structure Double
NullReferenceException class
OutOfMemoryException class
out-of-range array index
PositiveInfinity constant of structure Double
program database (PDB) file
resource leak
resumption model of exception handling
rethrow an exception
robust program
Source property of class Exception
stack trace
stack unwinding
StackTrace property of class Exception
SystemException class
TargetSite property of class Exception
termination model of exception handling
throw an exception
throw point
Throw statement
Try block
Try statement
TryParse method of structure Int32
uncaught exception
unhandled exception
unwind a method from call stack
user-defined exception class
Using statement

Self-Review Exercises

13.1 Fill in the blanks in each of the following statements:

a) A method is said to ________ an exception when it detects that a problem has occurred.
b) When present, the ________ block associated with a Try block always executes.
c) Exception classes are derived from class ________ of namespace System.
d) The statement that throws an exception is called the ________ of the exception.
e) Visual Basic uses the ________ model of exception handling as opposed to the ________ model of exception handling.
f) An uncaught exception in a method causes the method to ________ from the method-call stack.
g) Method Convert.ToInt32 throws a(n) ________ exception if its argument is not a valid integer value.

13.2 State whether each of the following is *true* or *false*. If *false*, explain why.

a) Exceptions always are handled in the method that initially detects the exception.
b) User-defined exception classes should extend class SystemException.
c) Accessing an out-of-bounds array index causes the CLR to throw an exception.
d) A Finally block is optional after a Try block that does not have any corresponding Catch blocks.
e) A Finally block that appears in a method is guaranteed to execute.
f) It is possible to return to the throw point of an exception (in that same method) using keyword Return.
g) Exceptions can be rethrown.
h) Property Message of class Exception returns a String indicating the method from which the exception was thrown.

Answers to Self-Review Exercises

13.1 a) throw. b) Finally. c) Exception. d) throw point. e) termination, resumption. f) unwind. g) FormatException.

13.2 a) False. Exceptions can be handled by other methods on the method-call stack. b) False. User-defined exception classes should typically extend class Exception. c) True. d) False. A Try block that does not have any Catch blocks requires a Finally block. e) False. The Finally block executes only if program control enters the corresponding Try block. f) False. Return causes control to return to the caller. g) True. h) False. Property `Message` of class `Exception` returns a `String` representing the error message.

Exercises

13.3 Use inheritance to create an exception base class and various exception-derived classes. Write a program to demonstrate that the `Catch` specifying the base class catches derived-class exceptions.

13.4 Write a program that demonstrates how various exceptions are caught with

```
Catch exceptionParameter As Exception
```

13.5 To demonstrate the importance of the order of exception handlers, write two programs, one with correct ordering of `Catch` blocks (i.e., place the base-class exception handler after all derived-class exception handlers) and another with improper ordering (i.e., place the base-class exception handler before the derived-class exception handlers). What happens when you attempt to compile the second program?

13.6 Exceptions can be used to indicate problems that occur when an object is being constructed. Write a program that shows a constructor passing information about constructor failure to an exception handler. The exception thrown also should contain the arguments sent to the constructor.

13.7 Write a program that demonstrates rethrowing an exception.

13.8 Write a program demonstrating that a method with its own `Try` block does not have to catch every possible exception that occurs within the `Try` block—some exceptions can slip through to, and be handled in, other scopes.

13.9 Write a program that `Throws` an exception from a deeply nested method. The `Catch` block should follow the `Try` block that encloses the call chain. The exception caught should be one you defined yourself. In catching the exception, display its message and stack trace.

13.10 Create a GUI application that inputs miles driven and gallons used, and calculates miles per gallon. The example should use exception handling to process the `FormatExceptions` that occur when converting the strings in the `TextBoxes` to `Doubles`. If invalid data is entered, a `MessageBox` should be displayed informing the user.

13.11 Create a **Vending Machine** application (Fig. 13.8) that displays images for four snacks and corresponding `Labels` that indicate numbers for each snack (the snacks should be numbered 0–3). Use a `String` array that contains the names of each snack. The GUI should contain a `TextBox` in which the user specifies the number of the desired snack. When the **Dispense Snack** `Button` is clicked, the name of the selected snack (retrieved from the array) should be displayed. If the user enters a snack value not in the range 0–3, an `IndexOutOfRangeException` will occur. Use exception handling so that whenever an `IndexOutOfRangeException` occurs, a `MessageBox` is displayed indicating the proper range of values. Also handle any possible `FormatExceptions` that may occur. The images used in this application can be found in the examples folder for this chapter, in the `images` directory.

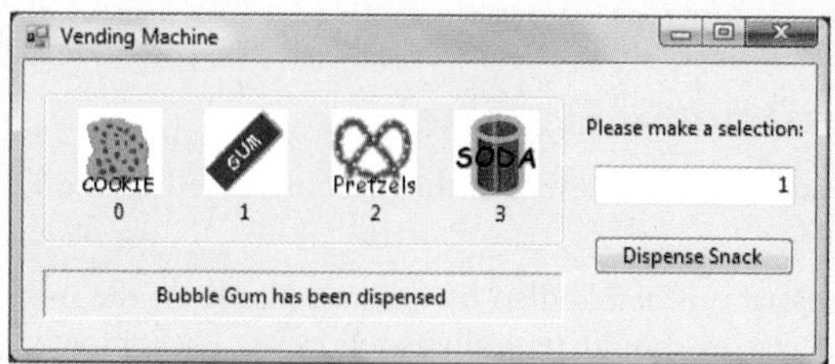

Fig. 13.8 | **Vending Machine** application.

14 Graphical User Interfaces with Windows Forms

. . . The user should feel in control of the computer; not the other way around. This is achieved in applications that embody three qualities: responsiveness, permissiveness, and consistency.

—Apple Computer, Inc.

All the better to see you with, my dear.

—The Big Bad Wolf to Little Red Riding Hood

. . . the wisest prophets make sure of the event first.

—Horace Walpole

OBJECTIVES

In this chapter you will learn:

- Design principles of graphical user interfaces (GUIs).
- How to create graphical user interfaces.
- How to process events that are generated by user interactions with GUI controls, including general mouse and keyboard events.
- How to create and manipulate `Button`, `Label`, `RadioButton`, `CheckBox`, `TextBox`, `GroupBox`, `Panel`, `PictureBox`, `ToolTip`, `NumericUpDown`, `MonthCalendar`, `LinkLabel`, `ListBox`, `CheckedListBox`, `ComboBox`, `TreeView`, and `ListView` controls.
- To create menus, tabbed windows and multiple document interface (MDI) programs.
- How to create custom controls.

14.1 Introduction

A graphical user interface (GUI) allows a user to interact visually with a program. A GUI (pronounced "GOO-ee") gives a program a distinctive look-and-feel.

Look-and-Feel Observation 14.1

Consistent user interfaces enable a user to learn new applications faster because the applications have the same look-and-feel.

As an example of a GUI, consider Fig. 14.1, which shows a Visual Basic 2008 Express Edition window containing various GUI controls. Near the top of the window, there is a

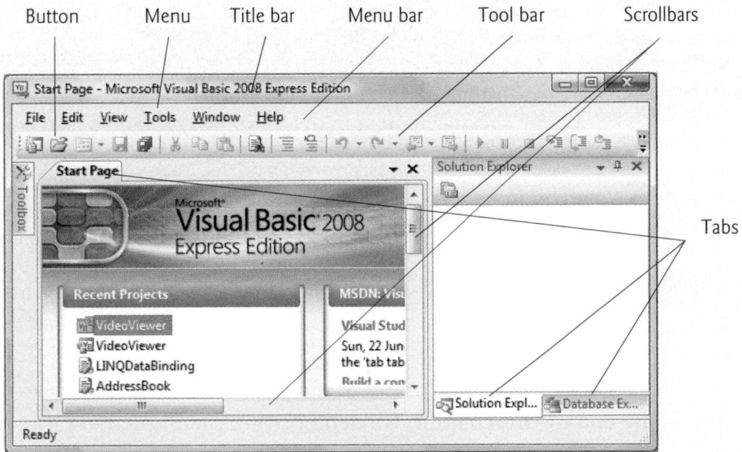

Fig. 14.1 | GUI controls in an Internet Explorer window.

menu bar containing the menus **File**, **Edit**, **View**, **Tools**, **Window**, and **Help**. Below the menu bar is a tool bar of buttons, each with a defined task in Visual Basic 2008 Express Edition, such as creating a new project, opening an existing project, or finding a word in the text. Scrollbars are located at the right side and bottom of the **Start Page** section. Usually, scrollbars appear when an object contains more information than can be displayed in its viewable area. Scrollbars enable a user to view different portions of an object's contents, in this case the **Start Page**. In the bottom right corner are two tabs, which present information in a tabbed view and allows users to switch between them. These controls form a user-friendly interface through which you have been interacting with the Visual Basic 2008 Express Edition IDE.

GUIs are built from GUI controls (which are sometimes called components or widgets—short for window gadgets). GUI controls are objects that can display information on the screen or enable users to interact with an application via the mouse, keyboard or some other form of input (such as voice commands). Several common GUI controls are listed in Fig. 14.2. In the sections that follow, we discuss each of these in detail. We also explore the features and properties of additional GUI controls.

Control	Description
`Label`	Displays images or uneditable text.
`TextBox`	Enables the user to enter data via the keyboard. Also can be used to display editable or uneditable text.
`Button`	Triggers an event when clicked with the mouse.
`CheckBox`	Specifies an option that can be selected (checked) or unselected (not checked).

Fig. 14.2 | Some basic GUI controls. (Part 1 of 2.)

Control	Description
`ComboBox`	Provides a drop-down list of items from which the user can make a selection either by clicking an item in the list or by typing in a box.
`ListBox`	Provides a list of items from which the user can make a selection by clicking an item in the list. Multiple elements can be selected.
`Panel`	A container in which controls can be placed and organized.
`NumericUpDown`	Enables the user to select from a range of numeric input values.

Fig. 14.2 | Some basic GUI controls. (Part 2 of 2.)

Towards the end of this chapter, we demonstrate the implementation of tab controls and multiple document interface (MDI) windows. These components enable you to create real-world programs with sophisticated GUIs. In addition, we introduce visual inheritance and how to maintain a consistent look-and-feel throughout an application.

Visual Studio provides a large set of GUI components, many of which are discussed in this chapter. Visual Studio also enables you to design custom controls and add them to the **ToolBox**, as we demonstrate in the last example of this chapter. The techniques presented in this chapter form the groundwork for creating more substantial GUIs and custom controls.

14.2 Windows Forms

Windows Forms are used to create the GUIs for programs. A `Form` is a graphical element that appears on your computer's desktop; it can be a dialog, a window or an MDI window (multiple document interface window)—discussed in Section 14.23. A component is an instance of a class that implements the `IComponent` interface, which defines the behaviors that components must implement, such as how the component is loaded. A control, such as a `Button` or `Label`, has a graphical representation at runtime. Some components lack graphical representations (e.g., class `Timer` of namespace `System.Windows.Forms`—see Section 14.25). Such components are not visible at execution time.

Figure 14.3 displays the Windows Forms controls and components from the Visual Basic **Toolbox**. The controls and components are organized into categories by functionality. Selecting the category **All Windows Forms** at the top of the **Toolbox** allows you to view all the controls and components from the other tabs in one list (as shown in Fig. 14.3). In this chapter, we discuss many of these controls and components. To add a control or component to a `Form`, select that control or component from the **Toolbox** and drag it onto the `Form`. To deselect a control or component, select the **Pointer** item in the **Toolbox** (the icon at the top of the list).

When there are several windows on the screen, the active window is the front-most and has a highlighted title bar—typically darker than the other windows on the screen. A window becomes the active window when the user clicks somewhere inside it. The active window is said to "have the focus." For example, in Visual Studio the active window is the **Toolbox** when you are selecting an item from it, or the **Properties** window when you are editing a control's properties.

Fig. 14.3 | Components and controls for Windows Forms.

A `Form` is a **container** for controls and components. When you drag a control or component from the **Toolbox** onto the `Form`, Visual Studio generates code that instantiates the object and sets its basic properties to default values. This code is updated when the control or component's properties are modified in the IDE. If a control or component is removed from the `Form`, the generated code for that control is deleted. The generated code is placed by the IDE in a separate file using partial classes (introduced in Section 10.7). Although we could write this code ourselves, it is much easier to create and modify controls and components using the **Toolbox** and **Properties** windows and allow Visual Studio to handle the details. We introduced visual programming concepts in Chapter 2. In this chapter and the next, we use visual programming to build more substantial GUIs.

Each control or component we present in this chapter is located in namespace `System.Windows.Forms`. To create a Windows application, you generally create a Windows `Form`, set its properties, add controls to the `Form`, set their properties and implement event handlers (methods) that respond to events generated by the controls. Figure 14.4 lists common `Form` properties, methods and events.

When you create controls and event handlers, Visual Studio generates much of the GUI-related code. In visual programming, the IDE maintains GUI-related code and you write the bodies of the event handlers to indicate what actions the program should take when particular events occur.

Form properties, methods and an event	Description
Common Properties	
AcceptButton	Button that is clicked when *Enter* is pressed.
AutoScroll	Boolean value that allows or disallows scrollbars when needed.
CancelButton	Button that is clicked when the *Escape* key is pressed.
FormBorderStyle	Border style for the Form (e.g., none, single, three-dimensional).
Font	Font of text displayed on the Form, and the default font for controls added to the Form.
Text	Text in the Form's title bar.
Common Methods	
Close	Closes a Form and releases all resources, such as the memory used for the Form's controls and components. A closed Form cannot be reopened.
Hide	Hides a Form, but does not destroy the Form or release its resources.
Show	Displays a hidden Form.
Common Event	
Load	Occurs before a Form is displayed to the user. The handler for this event is displayed in the Visual Studio editor when you double click the Form in the Visual Studio designer.

Fig. 14.4 | Common Form properties, methods and an event.

14.3 Event Handling

Normally, a user interacts with an application's GUI to indicate the tasks that the application should perform. For example, when you write an e-mail in an e-mail application, clicking the **Send** button tells the application to send the e-mail to the specified e-mail addresses. GUIs are event driven. When the user interacts with a GUI component, the interaction—known as an event—drives the program to perform a task. Common events (user interactions) that might cause an application to perform a task include clicking a Button, typing in a TextBox, selecting an item from a menu, closing a window and moving the mouse. All GUI controls have events associated with them. Objects of other types can also have associated events. A method that performs a task in response to an event is called an event handler, and the overall process of responding to events is known as event handling. Event-handling methods don't return values, so they are implemented as Sub procedures.

14.3.1 A Simple Event-Driven GUI

The `Form` in the application of Fig. 14.5 contains a `Button` that a user can click to display a `MessageBox`. You have already created several GUI examples that execute an event handler in response to clicking a `Button`. In this example, we discuss Visual Studio's auto-generated code in more depth.

Using the techniques presented earlier in the book, create a `Form` containing a `Button`. First, create a new Windows application and add a `Button` to the `Form`. In the **Properties** window for the `Button`, set the `(Name)` property to `clickMeButton` and the `Text` property to `Click Me`. You'll notice that each variable name we create for a control ends with the type of the control. For example, the variable name `clickMeButton` ends with `Button`. This is a widely used naming practice in the Visual Basic community. Another common convention is to prefix every name with a three letter abbreviation of the control type. For example, the **Click Me** button's name would be `btnClickMe`.

When the user clicks the `Button` in this example, we want the application to respond by displaying a `MessageBox`. To do this, you must create an event handler for the `Button`'s `Click` event. You can create this event handler by double clicking the `Button` on the `Form`, which declares the following empty event handler in the program code:

```
Private Sub clickMeButton_Click(ByVal sender As System.Object, _
   ByVal e As System.EventArgs) Handles clickMeButton.Click

End Sub
```

By convention, Visual Basic names the event-handler method as *objectName_eventName* (e.g., `clickMeButton_Click`). The `clickMeButton_Click` event handler executes when the user clicks the `clickMeButton` control.

Each event handler receives two parameters. The first—an `Object` reference named `sender`—is a reference to the object that generated the event. The second is a reference to an event arguments object (typically named `e`) of type `System.EventArgs` (or one of its derived classes). This object contains information about the event that occurred. `System.EventArgs` is the base class of all classes that represent event information.

Software Engineering Observation 14.1

Event handlers do not return values—they are designed to execute code based on an action and return control to the main program.

```
' Fig. 14.5: SimpleEventExampleForm.vb
' Using Visual Studio to create event handlers.
Public Class SimpleEventExampleForm
   ' event handler for clickMeButton's Click event
   Private Sub clickMeButton_Click(ByVal sender As System.Object, _
      ByVal e As System.EventArgs) Handles clickMeButton.Click

      MessageBox.Show("Button was clicked.")
   End Sub ' clickMeButton_Click
End Class ' SimpleEventExampleForm
```

Fig. 14.5 | Simple event-handling example using visual programming. (Part 1 of 2.)

Fig. 14.5 | Simple event-handling example using visual programming. (Part 2 of 2.)

Good Programming Practice 14.1

Use the event-handler naming convention controlName_eventName *so that your method names will be meaningful. Such names tell users what event a method handles for what control. This convention is not required, but it makes your code easier to read, understand, modify and maintain.*

To display a `MessageBox` in response to the event, insert the statement

```
MessageBox.Show("Button was clicked.")
```

in the event handler's body. The resulting event handler appears in lines 5–9 of Fig. 14.5. When you execute the application and click the `Button`, a `MessageBox` appears displaying the text `"Button was clicked"`.

14.3.2 Another Look at the Visual Studio Generated Code

Visual Studio generates the code that creates and initializes the GUI you build in the GUI design window. This auto-generated code is placed in the `Designer.vb` file of the `Form` (`SimpleEventExampleForm.Designer.vb` in this example). You can open this file by expanding the node for the file you are currently working in (`SimpleEventExampleForm.vb`) and double clicking the file name that ends with `Designer.vb`. (You might need to click the **Show All Files** button first.) Figures 14.6 and 14.7 show this file's contents.

SimpleEventExamp...Form.Designer.vb

SimpleEventExampleForm | (Declarations)

```
<Global.Microsoft.VisualBasic.CompilerServices.DesignerGenerated()> _
Partial Class SimpleEventExampleForm
   Inherits System.Windows.Forms.Form

   'Form overrides dispose to clean up the component list.
   <System.Diagnostics.DebuggerNonUserCode()> _
   Protected Overrides Sub Dispose(ByVal disposing As Boolean)
      Try
         If disposing AndAlso components IsNot Nothing Then
            components.Dispose()
         End If
      Finally
         MyBase.Dispose(disposing)
      End Try
   End Sub

```

Fig. 14.6 | First half of the Visual Studio generated code file.

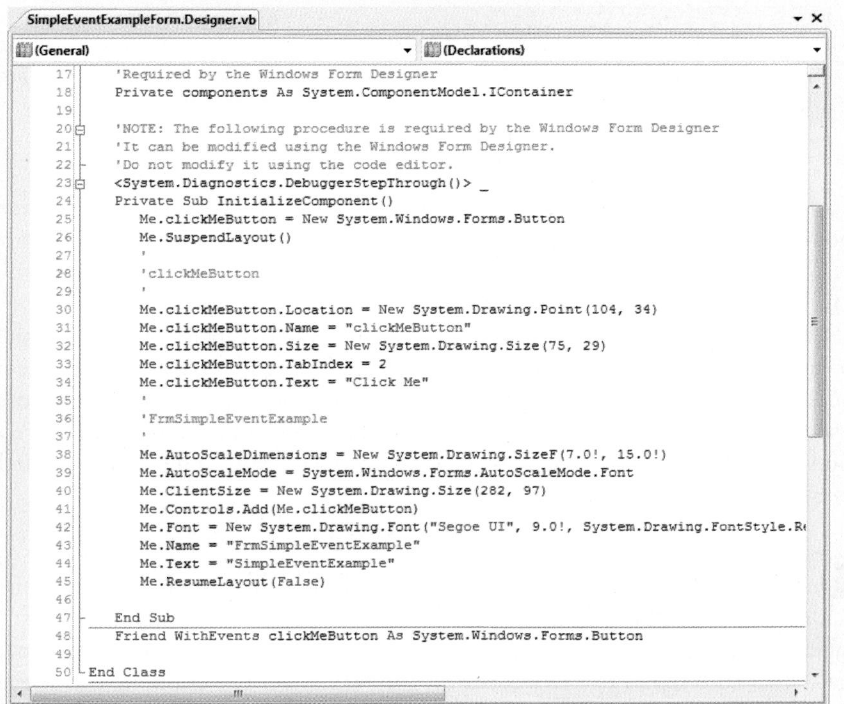

Fig. 14.7 | Second half of the Visual Studio generated code file.

Now that you have studied classes and objects in detail, this code will be easier to understand. Since this code is created and maintained by Visual Studio, you generally don't need to look at it. In fact, you do not need to understand most of the code shown here to build GUI applications. However, we now take a closer look to help you understand how GUI applications work.

The auto-generated code that defines the GUI is actually part of the `Form`'s class—in this case, `SimpleEventExampleForm`. Line 2 of Fig. 14.6 uses the `Partial` modifier, which allows this class to be split among multiple files. Line 48 declares as an instance variable of class `SimpleEventExampleForm` the `Button` control `clickMeButton` that we created in **Design** mode. By default, all variable declarations for controls created through Visual Basic's design window have a `Friend` access modifier. The code also includes the `Dispose` method for releasing resources (lines 7–15) and method `InitializeComponent` (lines 24–48), which contains the code that creates the `Button`, then sets some of the `Button`'s and the `Form`'s properties. The property values correspond to the values set in the **Properties** window for each control. Note that Visual Studio adds comments to the code that it generates, as in lines 27–29.

When the application begins executing, its `Form` is created, and the `Form's InitializeComponent` method is called automatically to establish such properties as the `Form`'s title and size, and the location, size and text for each control. Visual Studio also uses the code in this method to create the GUI you see in design view. Changing the code in `InitializeComponent` may prevent Visual Studio from displaying the GUI properly.

Error-Prevention Tip 14.1

The code generated by building a GUI in **Design** *mode is not meant to be modified directly, and doing so can make an application function incorrectly. You should modify control properties through the* **Properties** *window.*

14.3.3 Delegates and the Event-Handling Mechanism

The control that generates an event is known as the event sender. An event-handling method—known as the event receiver—responds to a particular event that a control generates. When the event occurs, the event sender calls its event receiver to perform a task (i.e., to "handle the event").

The .NET event-handling mechanism allows you to choose your own names for event-handling methods. However, each event-handling method must declare the proper parameters to receive information about the event it handles. Since you can choose your own method names, an event sender such as a `Button` cannot know in advance which method will respond to its events. So we need a mechanism to indicate which method is the event receiver for an event.

Delegates

Event handlers are connected to a control's events via delegates. Recall from Section 10.16 that a delegate object holds a reference to a method. The method's signature must match the signature specified by the delegate type's declaration. GUI controls have predefined delegates that correspond to every event they can generate. For example, the delegate for a `Button`'s `Click` event is of type `EventHandler` (namespace `System`). If you look at this type in the online help documentation, you will see that it is declared as follows:

```
Public Delegate Sub EventHandler(sender As Object, e As EventArgs)
```

where `Object` and `EventArgs` are classes from the `System` namespace. This uses the `Delegate` keyword to declare a delegate type named `EventHandler`, which can hold a reference to a method that does not return a value and receives two parameters—one of type `Object` (the event sender) and one of type `EventArgs`. If you compare the delegate declaration with `clickMeButton_Click`'s header (Fig. 14.5, lines 5–6), you will see that this event handler indeed meets the requirements of the `EventHandler` delegate. Note that the preceding declaration actually creates an entire class for you. The details of this special class's declaration are handled by the compiler.

Indicating the Method That a Delegate Should Call

An event sender uses a delegate object like a method call. Since each event handler must have the same signature as the control's delegate for a particular event, the event sender can simply "call" the appropriate delegate when an event occurs. For example, a `Button` calls its `Click` delegate in response to a click. The delegate's job is to invoke the appropriate event-handler method. To enable the `clickMeButton_Click` method to be called when the user clicks the `Button`, Visual Basic inserts the clause

`Handles` *controlName*`.`*eventName*

following the event handler's parameter list. For example, `Handles clickMeButton.Click` in line 6 of Fig. 14.5 indicates that `clickMeButton_Click` will be called when the user clicks the `clickMeButton` control (i.e., when the button's `Click` event occurs). The **`Handles` clause**, which is added by Visual Studio when you double click the `Button` control in **Design** mode, causes Visual Basic to "register" your event handler as the method to call in response to the event. You can also manually add and remove event handlers at runtime by using the `AddHandler` and `RemoveHandler` statements (see `msdn2.microsoft.com/en-us/library/6yyk8z93.aspx`).

14.3.4 Other Ways to Create Event Handlers

In all the GUI applications you have created so far, you double clicked a control on the `Form` to create an event handler for that control. This technique creates an event handler for a control's **default event**—the event most frequently used with that control. Typically, controls can generate many different types of events, and each type can have its own event handler. For instance, you have already created `Click` event handlers for `Buttons` by double clicking a `Button` in design view (`Click` is the default event for a `Button`). However your application can also provide an event handler for a `Button`'s `MouseHover` event, which occurs when the mouse pointer remains positioned over the `Button`. We now discuss how to create an event handler for an event that is not a control's default event.

Creating Event Handlers in the **Code** *Editor*

Visual Basic 2008 Express Edition allows you to create event handlers while editing your form's code. If you select a control from the **Class Name** combobox in the top left while in the **Code** editor, the **Method Name** combobox is populated with all the events for that control (Fig. 14.8). When you select an event, your text cursor will move to its location in the code. If the event handler does not already exist, it will be created.

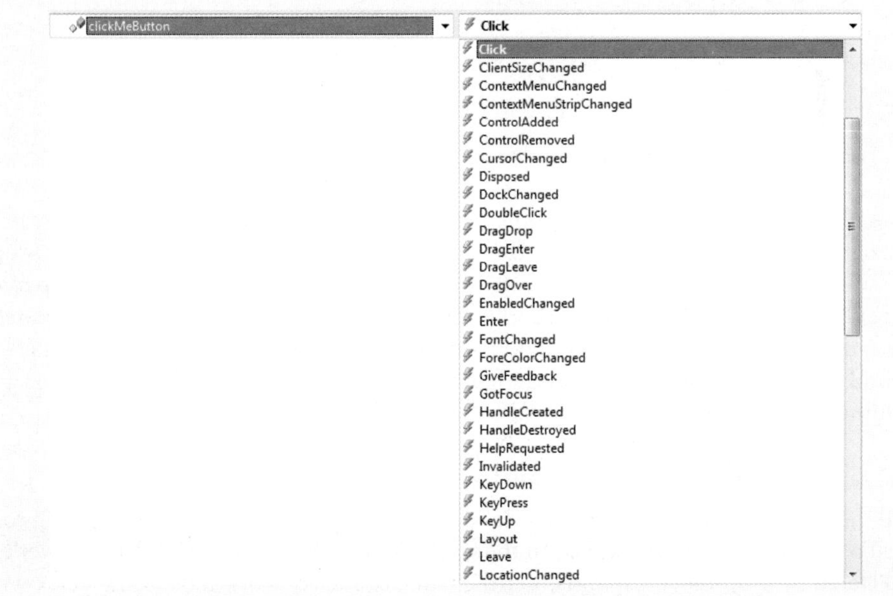

Fig. 14.8 | Creating an event handler in the **Code** editor.

Using the Properties *Window to Create Event Handlers*

You can create also additional event handlers through the **Properties** window. If you select a control on the `Form`, then click the **Events** icon (the lightning bolt icon in Fig. 14.9) in the **Properties** window, all the events for that control are listed in the window. You can double click an event's name to display the event handler in the editor. If the event handler does not already exist, it will be created. You can also select an event, then use the drop-down list to its right to choose an existing method that will be used as the event handler for that event. The methods that appear in this drop-down list are the class's methods that have the proper signature to be an event handler for the selected event. You can return to viewing the properties of a control by selecting the **Properties** icon (Fig. 14.9).

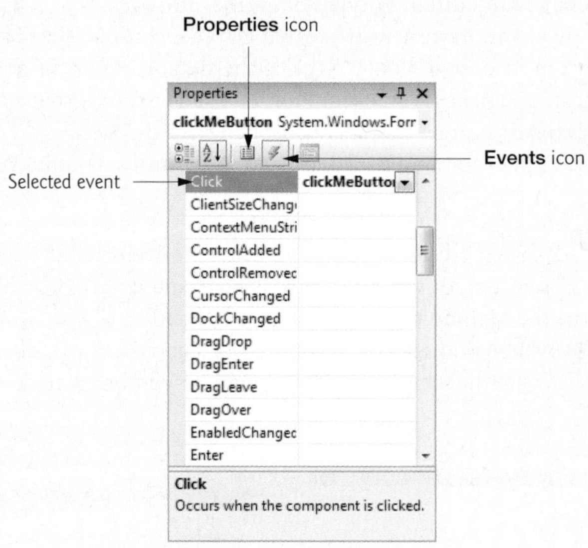

Fig. 14.9 | Viewing events for a `Button` control in the **Properties** window.

A single method can handle events from many controls. For example, to create a `Click` event handler that can handle the events of three `Button`s, select them in **Design** view, then double click the event you want to handle in the **Events** tab of the **Properties** window. If you create a new event handler this way, you should rename it appropriately. You can also select each control individually and use the **Events** tab to select an existing method as the event handler. The event handler's `Handles` clause specifies a comma-separated list of all the events that will invoke the event handler.

14.3.5 Locating Event Information

Read the Visual Studio documentation to learn about the different events raised by a control. To do this, select **Help > Index**. In the window that appears, select **.NET Framework** in the **Filtered by** drop-down list and enter the name of the control's class in the **Index** window. To ensure that you are selecting the proper class, enter the fully qualified class name (e.g., `System.Windows.Forms.Button`). Once you select a control's class in the documentation, basic information about the class is displayed. To display a list of all the class's members (Fig. 14.10), click the **Members** link. This list includes the events that the class can generate. In Fig. 14.10, we scrolled to class `Button`'s events. Click the name of an event to view its description and examples of its use (Fig. 14.11). Note that the `Click` event is listed as a member of class `Control`, because class `Button`'s `Click` event is inherited from class `Control`.

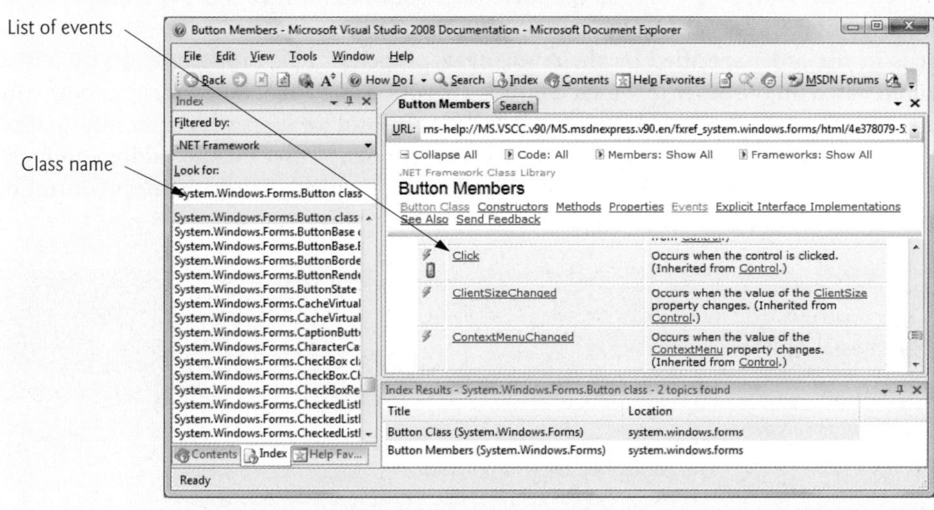

Fig. 14.10 | List of `Button` events.

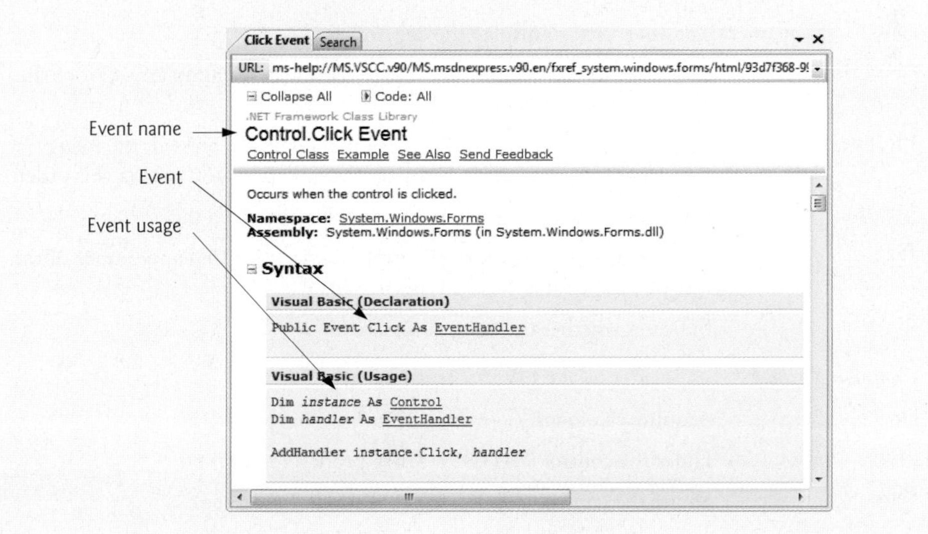

Fig. 14.11 | `Click` event details.

14.4 Control Properties and Layout

This section overviews properties that are common to many controls. Controls derive from class `Control` (namespace `System.Windows.Forms`). Figure 14.12 lists some of class `Control`'s properties and methods. The properties shown here can be set for many controls. For example, the `Text` property specifies the text that appears on a control. The location of this text varies depending on the control. In a Windows Form, the text appears in the title bar, but the text of a `Button` appears on its face.

The `Focus` method transfers the focus to a control and makes it the active control. When you press the *Tab* key in an executing Windows application, controls receive the focus in the order specified by their `TabIndex` property. This property is set by Visual Studio based on the order in which controls are added to a `Form`, but you can modify this property to change the tabbing order. `TabIndex` is helpful for users who enter information in many controls, such as a set of `TextBox`es that represent a user's name, address and telephone number. The user can enter information, then quickly select the next control by pressing the *Tab* key.

Class `Control` properties and methods	Description
Common Properties	
`BackColor`	The control's background color.
`BackgroundImage`	The control's background image.
`Enabled`	Specifies whether the user can interact with the control. A disabled control typically appears "grayed out."
`Focused`	Indicates whether the control has the focus.
`Font`	The `Font` used to display the control's text.
`ForeColor`	The control's foreground color. This usually determines the color of the text in the `Text` property.
`TabIndex`	The tab order of the control. When the *Tab* key is pressed, the focus transfers between controls based on the tab order. You can set this order.
`TabStop`	If `True`, then a user can give focus to this control via the *Tab* key.
`Text`	The text associated with the control. The location and appearance of the text vary depending on the type of control.
`Visible`	Indicates whether the control is visible.
Common Methods	
`Focus`	Acquires the focus.
`Hide`	Hides the control (sets the `Visible` property to `False`).
`Show`	Shows the control (sets the `Visible` property to `True`).

Fig. 14.12 | Class `Control` properties and methods.

The Enabled property indicates whether the user can interact with a control to generate an event. If a control is disabled, it is often because an option is unavailable to the user at that time. For example, text editor applications often disable the "paste" command until the user copies some text. In most cases, a disabled control's text appears in gray (rather than in black). You can also hide a control from the user without disabling the control by setting the Visible property to False or by calling method Hide. In each case, the control still exists but is not visible on the Form.

You can use anchoring and docking to specify the layout of controls inside a container (such as a Form). Anchoring causes controls to remain at a fixed distance from the sides of the container even when the container is resized. Anchoring enhances the user experience. For example, if the user expects a control to appear in a certain corner of the application, anchoring ensures that the control will always be in that corner—even if the user resizes the Form. Docking attaches a control to a container such that the control stretches across an entire side or fill an entire area. For example, a button docked to the top of a container stretches across the entire top of that container regardless of the container's width.

When parent containers are resized, anchored controls are moved (and possibly resized) so that the distance from the sides to which they are anchored does not vary. By default, most controls are anchored to the top-left corner of the Form. To see the effects of anchoring a control, create a simple Windows application that contains two Buttons. Anchor one control to the right and bottom sides by setting the **Anchor** property as shown in Fig. 14.13. Leave the other control unanchored. Execute the application and enlarge the Form. Note that the Button anchored to the bottom-right corner is always the same distance from the Form's bottom-right corner (Fig. 14.14), but that the other control stays its original distance from the top-left corner of the Form.

Sometimes, it is desirable for a control to span an entire side of the Form, even when the Form is resized. For example, a control such as a status bar typically should remain at the bottom of the Form. Docking allows a control to span an entire side (left, right, top or bottom) of its parent container or to fill the entire container. When the parent control is resized, the docked control resizes as well. In Fig. 14.15, a Button is docked at the top of the Form (spanning the top portion). When the Form is resized, the Button is resized to the Form's new width. Forms have a Padding property that specifies the distance between the

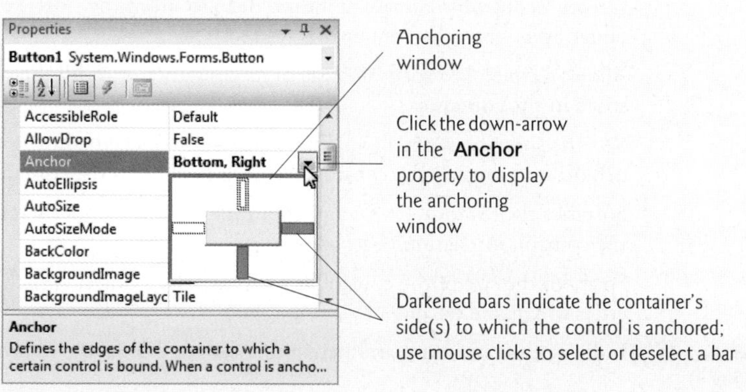

Fig. 14.13 | Manipulating the **Anchor** property of a control.

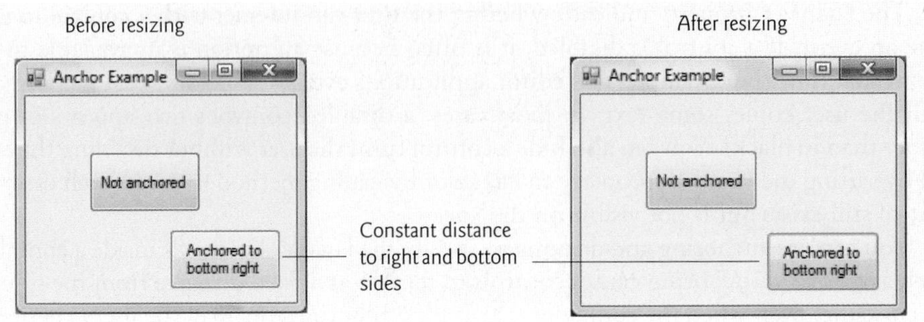

Fig. 14.14 | Anchoring demonstration.

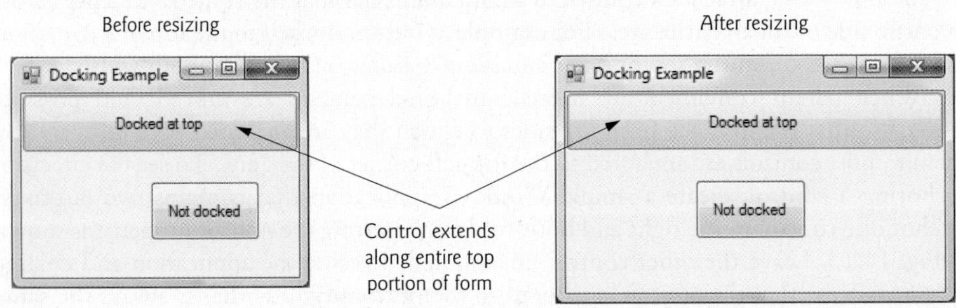

Fig. 14.15 | Docking a `Button` to the top of a `Form`.

docked controls and the `Form` edges. This property specifies four values (one for each side), and each value is set to `0` by default. Some common control-layout properties are summarized in Fig. 14.16.

`Control` layout properties	Description
`Anchor`	Causes a control to remain at a fixed distance from the side(s) of the container even when the container is resized.
`Dock`	Allows a control to span one side of its container or to fill the remaining space in the container.
`Padding`	Sets the space between a container's edges and docked controls. The default is `0`, causing the control to appear flush with the container's sides.
`Location`	Specifies the location (as a set of coordinates) of the upper-left corner of the control, in relation to its container.
`Size`	Specifies the size of the control in pixels as a `Size` object, which has properties `Width` and `Height`.
`MinimumSize`, `MaximumSize`	Indicate the minimum and maximum sizes of a `Control`, respectively.

Fig. 14.16 | `Control` layout properties.

The Anchor and Dock properties of a Control are set with respect to the Control's parent container, which could be a Form or another parent container (such as a Panel; discussed in Section 14.6). The minimum and maximum Form (or other Control) sizes can be set via properties MinimumSize and MaximumSize, respectively. Both are of type Size, which has properties Width and Height to specify the size of the Form. Properties MinimumSize and MaximumSize allow you to design the GUI layout for a given size range. The user cannot make a Form smaller than the size specified by property MinimumSize and cannot make a Form larger than the size specified by property MaximumSize. To set a Form to a fixed size (where the Form cannot be resized by the user), set its minimum and maximum sizes to the same values or set its FormBorderStyle property to FixedSingle.

Look-and-Feel Observation 14.2

For resizable Forms, ensure that the GUI layout appears consistent across various Form sizes.

Using Visual Studio To Edit a GUI's Layout

Visual Studio provides tools that help you with GUI layout. You may have noticed when dragging a control across a Form, that blue lines (known as snap lines) appear to help you position the control with respect to other controls (Fig. 14.17) and the Form's edges. This new feature of Visual Studio 2008 makes the control you are dragging appear to "snap into place" alongside other controls. Visual Studio also provides the **Format** menu, which contains several options for modifying your GUI's layout. The **Format** menu does not appear in the IDE unless you select a control (or set of controls) in design view. When you select multiple controls, you can use the **Format** menu's **Align** submenu to align the controls. The **Format** menu also enables you to modify the amount of space between controls or to center a control on the Form.

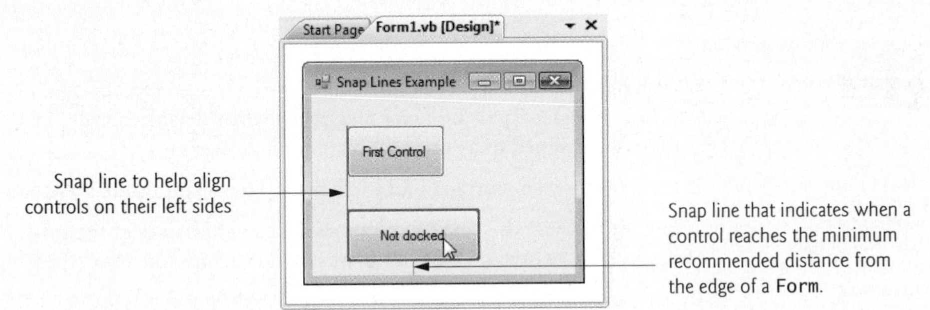

Fig. 14.17 | Snap lines in Visual Studio 2008.

14.5 Labels, TextBoxes and Buttons

Labels provide text information (as well as optional images) and are defined with class Label (a derived class of Control). A Label displays text that the user cannot directly modify. A Label's text can be changed programmatically by modifying the Label's Text property. Figure 14.18 lists common Label properties.

A TextBox is an area in which text can be displayed by a program or the user can type text via the keyboard. A password TextBox is a TextBox that hides the information entered

Common Label properties	Description
Font	The font of the text on the Label.
Text	The text on the Label.
TextAlign	The alignment of the Label's text on the control—horizontally (left, center or right) and vertically (top, middle or bottom).

Fig. 14.18 | Common Label properties.

by the user. As the user types characters, the password TextBox masks the user input by displaying a character you specify (usually *). If you set property **UseSystemPasswordChar** to True, the TextBox becomes a password TextBox. Users often encounter both types of TextBoxes when logging into a computer or website—the username TextBox allows users to input their usernames; the password TextBox allows users to enter their passwords. Figure 14.19 lists the common properties and a common event of TextBoxes.

A button is a control that the user clicks to trigger a specific action or to select an option in a program. As you will see, a program can use various button types, such as **checkboxes** and **radio buttons**. All the button classes derive from **ButtonBase** (namespace System.Windows.Forms), which defines common button features. In this section, we discuss class Button, which typically enables a user to issue a command to an application. Figure 14.20 lists common properties and a common event of class Button.

TextBox properties and an event	Description
Common Properties	
AcceptsReturn	If True in a multiline TextBox, pressing *Enter* in the TextBox creates a new line. If False, pressing *Enter* presses the Form's default Button (i.e., the Button assigned to a Form's AcceptButton property).
Multiline	If True, the TextBox can span multiple lines. The default value is False.
UseSystem-PasswordChar	When set to True, the TextBox becomes a password box, and the system-specified password character masks each character the user types.
ReadOnly	If True, the TextBox has a gray background, and its text cannot be edited. The default value is False.
ScrollBars	For multiline textboxes, this property indicates which scrollbars appear (None, Horizontal, Vertical or Both).
Text	The TextBox's text content.
Common Event	
TextChanged	Generated when the text changes in a TextBox. Double clicking the TextBox in **Design** mode creates an empty event handler for this event.

Fig. 14.19 | TextBox properties and an event.

Button properties and an event	Description
Common Properties	
`Text`	Specifies the text displayed on the `Button` face.
`FlatStyle`	Modifies a `Button`'s appearance—attribute `Flat` (displays the `Button` without a three-dimensional appearance), `Popup` (displays the `Button` flat until the user moves the mouse pointer over the `Button`), `Standard` (three-dimensional) and `System` (the `Button`'s appearance is controlled by the operating system). The default value is `Standard`.
Common Event	
`Click`	Generated when the user clicks the `Button`. When you double click a `Button` in design view, an empty event handler for this event is created.

Fig. 14.20 | `Button` properties and an event.

Look-and-Feel Observation 14.3

Although `Labels`, `TextBoxes` and other controls can respond to mouse clicks, `Buttons` are more natural for this purpose.

Figure 14.21 uses a `TextBox`, a `Button` and a `Label`. When the user clicks the **Show Me** `Button`, this application retrieves the text that the user typed in the password `TextBox` and displays it in a `Label`. Normally, we would not display this text—the purpose of password `TextBoxes` is to hide the text being entered by the user. When the user clicks the **Show Me** `Button`, this application retrieves the text that the user typed in the password `TextBox` and displays it in another `TextBox`.

First, create the GUI by dragging the controls (a `TextBox`, a `Button` and a `Label`) onto the `Form`. Once the controls are positioned, change their names in the **Properties** window from the default values—`textBox1`, `button1` and `label1`—to the more descriptive names `displayPasswordLabel`, `displayPasswordButton` and `inputPasswordTextBox`. The `(Name)` property in the **Properties** window enables us to change the variable name for a

```
' Fig. 14.21: LabelTextBoxButtonTestForm.vb
' Using a TextBox, Label and Button to display
' the hidden text in a password TextBox.
Public Class LabelTextBoxButtonTestForm
   ' event handler for btnDisplayPassword's Click event
   Private Sub displayPasswordButton_Click( _
      ByVal sender As System.Object, ByVal e As System.EventArgs) _
      Handles displayPasswordButton.Click
      ' display the text that the user typed
      displayPasswordLabel.Text = inputPasswordTextBox.Text
   End Sub ' displayPasswordButton_Click
End Class ' LabelTextBoxButtonTestForm
```

Fig. 14.21 | Program to display hidden text in a password box. (Part 1 of 2.)

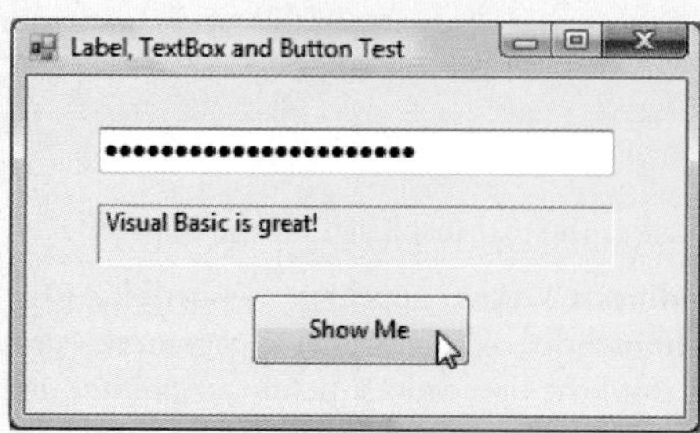

Fig. 14.21 | Program to display hidden text in a password box. (Part 2 of 2.)

control. Visual Studio creates the necessary code and places it in method `InitializeComponent` of the partial class in the file `LabelTextBoxButtonTestForm.Designer.vb`.

We then set `displayPasswordButton`'s `Text` property to "`Show Me`" and clear the `Text` of `displayPasswordLabel` and `inputPasswordTextBox` so that they are blank when the program begins executing. The `BorderStyle` property of `displayPasswordLabel` is set to `Fixed3D`, giving our `Label` a three-dimensional appearance. The `BorderStyle` property of all `TextBoxes` is set to `Fixed3D` by default. The password character for `inputPasswordTextBox` is set by assigning the asterisk character (*) to the `PasswordChar` property. This property accepts only one character.

We create an event handler for `displayPasswordButton` by double clicking this control in **Design** mode. We add line 10 to the event handler's body. When the user clicks the **Show Me** `Button` in the executing application, line 10 obtains the text entered by the user in `inputPasswordTextBox` and displays the text in `displayPasswordLabel`.

14.6 GroupBoxes and Panels

`GroupBoxes` and `Panels` arrange controls on a GUI. `GroupBoxes` and `Panels` are typically used to group several controls of similar functionality or several controls that are related in a GUI. All of the controls in a `GroupBox` or `Panel` move together when the `GroupBox` or `Panel` is moved.

The primary difference between these two controls is that `GroupBoxes` can display a caption (i.e., text) and do not include scrollbars, whereas `Panels` can include scrollbars and do not include a caption. `GroupBoxes` have thin borders by default; `Panels` can be set so that they also have borders by changing their `BorderStyle` property. Figures 14.22 and 14.23 list the common properties of `GroupBoxes` and `Panels`, respectively.

GroupBox properties	Description
`Controls`	The set of controls that the `GroupBox` contains.
`Text`	Specifies the caption text displayed at the top of the `GroupBox`.

Fig. 14.22 | `GroupBox` properties.

Panel properties	Description
AutoScroll	Indicates whether scrollbars appear when the Panel is too small to display all of its controls. The default value is False.
BorderStyle	Sets the border of the Panel. The default value is None; other options are Fixed3D and FixedSingle.
Controls	The set of controls that the Panel contains.

Fig. 14.23 | Panel properties.

Look-and-Feel Observation 14.4

Panels and GroupBoxes can contain other Panels and GroupBoxes for more complex layouts.

Look-and-Feel Observation 14.5

You can organize a GUI by anchoring and docking controls inside a GroupBox or Panel. The GroupBox or Panel can then be anchored or docked inside a Form. This divides controls into functional "groups" that can be arranged easily.

To create a GroupBox, drag its icon from the **Toolbox** onto the Form. Then drag new controls from the **Toolbox** into the GroupBox. These controls are added to the GroupBox's Controls property and become part of the GroupBox. The GroupBox's Text property specifies the caption.

To create a Panel, drag its icon from the **Toolbox** onto the Form. You can then add controls directly to the Panel by dragging them from the **Toolbox** onto the Panel. To enable the scrollbars, set the Panel's AutoScroll property to True. If the Panel is resized and cannot display all of its controls, scrollbars appear (Fig. 14.24). The scrollbars can be used to view all the controls in the Panel—both at design time and at execution time. In Fig. 14.24, we set the Panel's BorderStyle property to FixedSingle so that you can see the Panel in the Form.

The program in Fig. 14.25 uses a GroupBox and a Panel to arrange Buttons. When these Buttons are clicked, their event handlers change the text on a Label.

The GroupBox (named mainGroupBox) has two Buttons—hiButton (which displays the text **Hi**) and byeButton (which displays the text **Bye**). The Panel (named mainPanel) also has two Buttons, leftButton (which displays the text **Far Left**) and rightButton (which displays the text **Far Right**). The mainPanel has its AutoScroll property set to True, allowing scrollbars to appear when the contents of the Panel require more space than the Panel's visible area. The Label (named messageLabel) is initially blank. To add controls to mainGroupBox or mainPanel, Visual Studio calls method Add of each container's Controls property. This code is placed in the partial class located in the file GroupBoxPanelExampleForm.Designer.vb.

The event handlers for the four Buttons are located in lines 4–26. We added a line in each event handler (lines 7, 13, 19 and 25) to change the text of messageLabel to indicate which Button the user pressed.

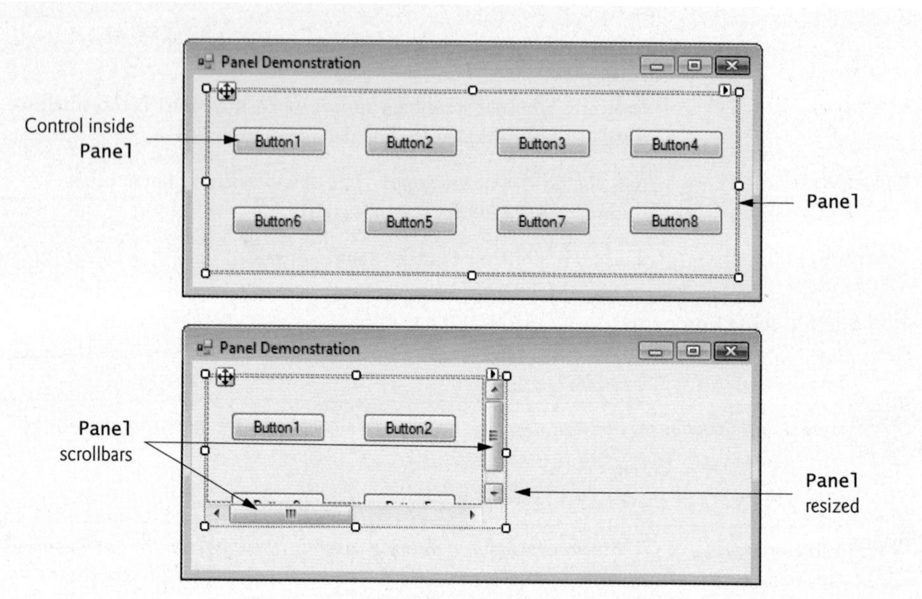

Fig. 14.24 | Creating a `Panel` with scrollbars.

```
' Fig. 14.25: GroupboxPanelExampleForm.vb
' Using GroupBoxes and Panels to hold Buttons.
Public Class GroupBoxPanelExampleForm
   ' event handler for hiButton's Click event
   Private Sub hiButton_Click(ByVal sender As System.Object, _
      ByVal e As System.EventArgs) Handles hiButton.Click
      messageLabel.Text = "Hi pressed" ' change text in Label
   End Sub ' hiButton_Click

   ' event handler for byeButton's Click event
   Private Sub byeButton_Click(ByVal sender As System.Object, _
      ByVal e As System.EventArgs) Handles byeButton.Click
      messageLabel.Text = "Bye pressed" ' change text in Label
   End Sub ' byeButton_Click

   ' event handler for leftButton's Click event
   Private Sub leftButton_Click(ByVal sender As System.Object, _
      ByVal e As System.EventArgs) Handles leftButton.Click
      messageLabel.Text = "Far left pressed" ' change text in Label
   End Sub ' leftButton_Click

   ' event handler for rightButton's Click event
   Private Sub rightButton_Click(ByVal sender As System.Object, _
      ByVal e As System.EventArgs) Handles rightButton.Click
      messageLabel.Text = "Far right pressed" ' change text in Label
   End Sub ' rightButton_Click
End Class ' GroupBoxPanelExampleForm
```

Fig. 14.25 | Using `GroupBoxes` and `Panels` to arrange `Buttons`. (Part 1 of 2.)

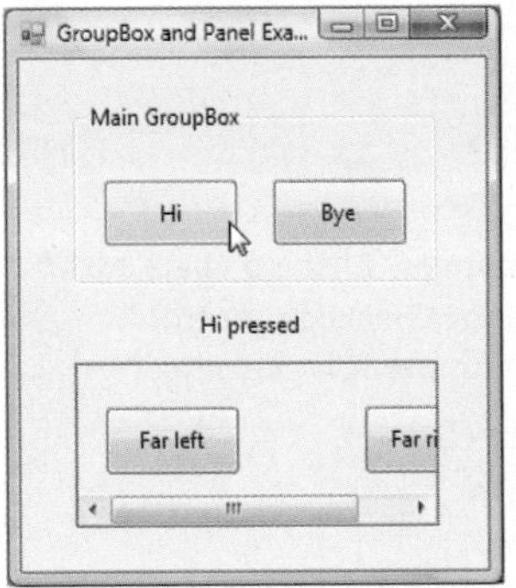

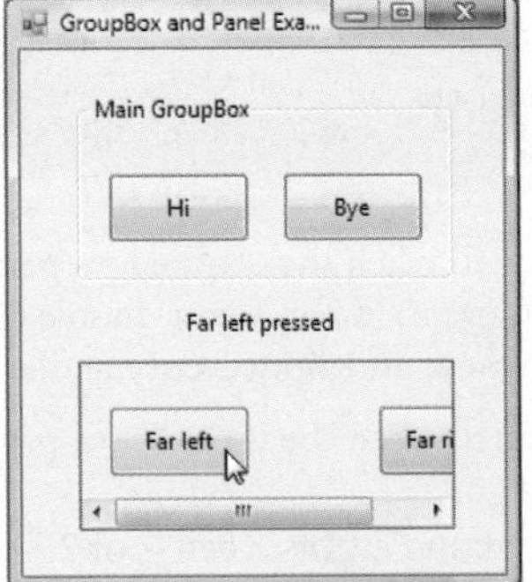

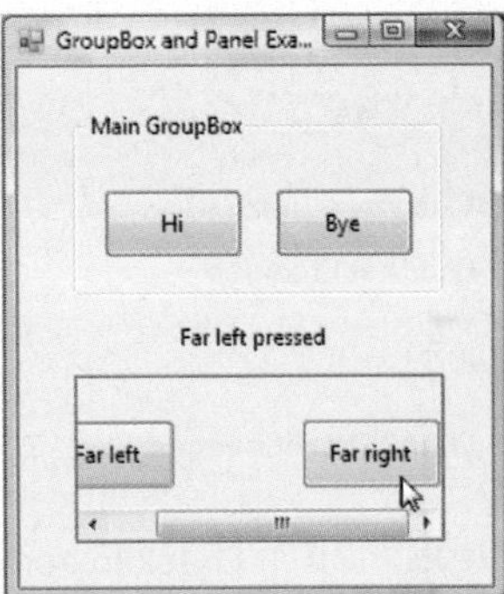

Fig. 14.25 | Using `GroupBox`es and `Panel`s to arrange `Button`s. (Part 2 of 2.)

14.7 CheckBoxes and RadioButtons

Visual Basic has two types of **state buttons** that can be in the on/off or true/false states—**CheckBoxes** and **RadioButtons**. Like class `Button`, classes `CheckBox` and `RadioButton` are derived from class `ButtonBase`.

CheckBoxes

A `CheckBox` is a small square that either is blank or contains a check mark. When the user clicks a `CheckBox` to select it, a check mark appears in the box. If the user clicks the `CheckBox` again to deselect it, the check mark is removed. Any number of `CheckBox`es can be selected at a time. A list of common `CheckBox` properties and events appears in Fig. 14.26.

The program in Fig. 14.27 allows the user to select `CheckBox`es to change a `Label`'s font style. The event handlers for the `CheckBox`es apply bold or italic. If both `CheckBox`es are selected, the font style is set to bold and italic. Initially, neither `CheckBox` is checked.

CheckBox properties and events	Description
Common Properties	
`Checked`	Indicates whether the `CheckBox` is checked (contains a check mark) or unchecked (blank). This property returns a `Boolean` value.
`CheckState`	Indicates whether the `CheckBox` is checked or unchecked with a value from the `CheckState` enumeration (`Checked`, `Unchecked` or `Indeterminate`). `Indeterminate` is used when it is unclear whether the state should be `Checked` or `Unchecked`. For example, in Microsoft Word, when you select a paragraph that contains several character formats, then go to **Format > Font**, some of the `CheckBox`es appear in the `Indeterminate` state. When `CheckState` is set to `Indeterminate`, the `CheckBox` is usually shaded.
`Text`	Specifies the text displayed to the right of the `CheckBox`.

Fig. 14.26 | `CheckBox` properties and events. (Part 1 of 2.)

CheckBox properties and events	Description
Common Events	
CheckedChanged	Generated when the Checked property changes. This is a CheckBox's default event. When a user double clicks the CheckBox control in design view, an empty event handler for this event is generated.
CheckStateChanged	Generated when the CheckState property changes.

Fig. 14.26 | CheckBox properties and events. (Part 2 of 2.)

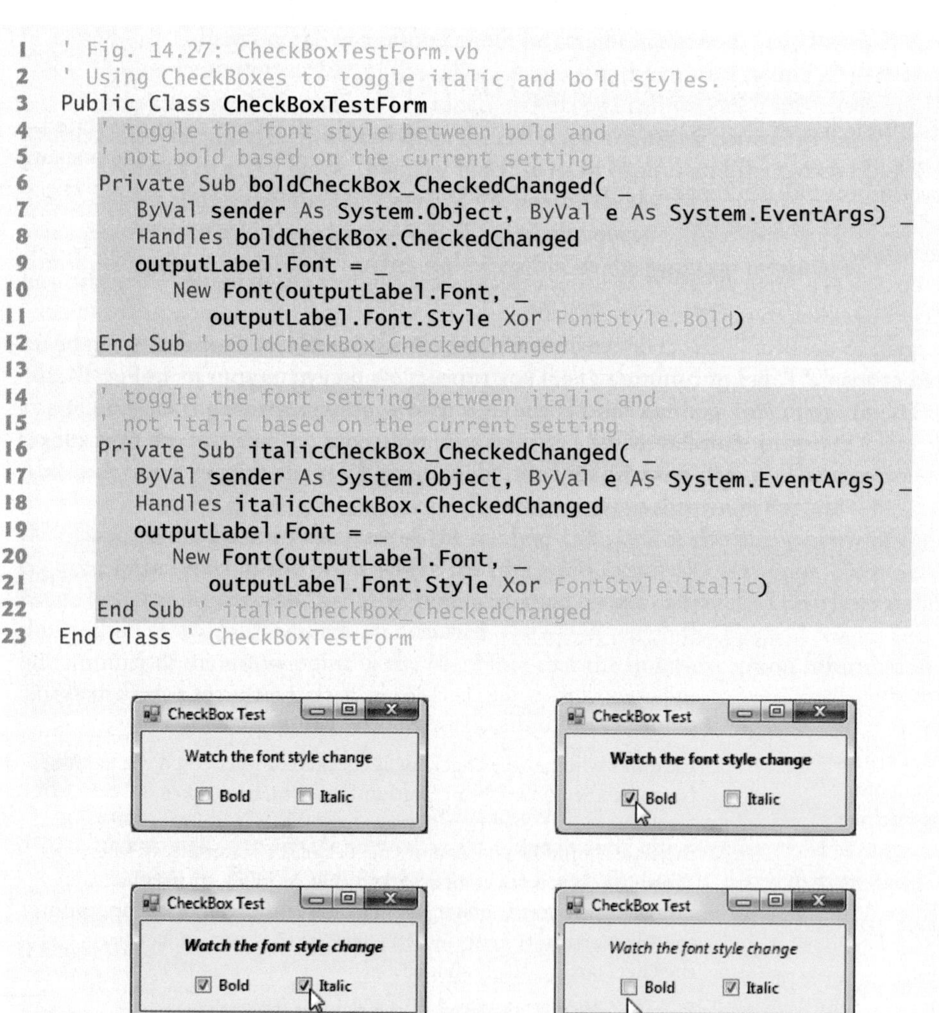

```
' Fig. 14.27: CheckBoxTestForm.vb
' Using CheckBoxes to toggle italic and bold styles.
Public Class CheckBoxTestForm
   ' toggle the font style between bold and
   ' not bold based on the current setting
   Private Sub boldCheckBox_CheckedChanged( _
      ByVal sender As System.Object, ByVal e As System.EventArgs) _
      Handles boldCheckBox.CheckedChanged
      outputLabel.Font = _
         New Font(outputLabel.Font, _
            outputLabel.Font.Style Xor FontStyle.Bold)
   End Sub ' boldCheckBox_CheckedChanged

   ' toggle the font setting between italic and
   ' not italic based on the current setting
   Private Sub italicCheckBox_CheckedChanged( _
      ByVal sender As System.Object, ByVal e As System.EventArgs) _
      Handles italicCheckBox.CheckedChanged
      outputLabel.Font = _
         New Font(outputLabel.Font, _
            outputLabel.Font.Style Xor FontStyle.Italic)
   End Sub ' italicCheckBox_CheckedChanged
End Class ' CheckBoxTestForm
```


Fig. 14.27 | Using CheckBoxes to change font styles.

The boldCheckBox has its Text property set to Bold. The italicCheckBox has its Text property set to Italic. The Text property of outputLabel is set to Watch the font style change. After creating the controls, we define their event handlers. Double clicking the CheckBoxes at design time creates empty CheckedChanged event handlers.

To change the font style on a Label, set its Font property to a new Font object (lines 9–11 and 19–21). The Font constructor used here takes the current font and new style as arguments. The first argument—outputLabel.Font—uses outputLabel's original font and size. The style is specified with a member of the FontStyle enumeration, which contains Regular, Bold, Italic, Strikeout and Underline. (Strikeout displays text with a line through it.) A Font object's Style property is read-only, so it can be set only when the Font object is created.

Styles can be combined via bitwise operators—operators that perform manipulations on bits of information. All data is represented in the computer as combinations of 0s and 1s. Each 0 or 1 represents a bit. FontStyle has a System.FlagAttribute, meaning that the FontStyle bit values are selected in a way that allows us to combine different FontStyle elements to create compound styles, using bitwise operators. These styles are not mutually exclusive, so we can combine different styles and remove them without affecting the combination of previous FontStyle elements. We can combine these various font styles using either the Or operator or the Xor operator. When the Or operator is applied to two bits, if at least one bit of the two has the value 1, then the result is 1. Combining styles using the Or operator works as follows. Assume that FontStyle.Bold is represented by bits 01 and that FontStyle.Italic is represented by bits 10. When we use the Or operator to combine the styles, we obtain the bits 11.

```
01   =   Bold
10   =   Italic
--
11   =   Bold and Italic
```

The Or operator helps create style combinations. However, what happens if we want to undo a style combination, as we did in Fig. 14.27?

The Xor operator enables us to combine styles and to undo existing style settings. When Xor is applied to two bits, if both bits have the same value, then the result is 0. If both bits are different, then the result is 1.

Combining styles using Xor works as follows. Assume, again, that FontStyle.Bold is represented by bits 01 and that FontStyle.Italic is represented by bits 10. When we use Xor on both styles, we obtain the bits 11.

```
01   =   Bold
10   =   Italic
--
11   =   Bold and Italic
```

Now suppose that we would like to remove the FontStyle.Bold style from the previous combination of FontStyle.Bold and FontStyle.Italic. The easiest way to do so is to reapply the Xor operator to the compound style and FontStyle.Bold.

```
11   =   Bold and Italic
01   =   Bold
--
10   =   Italic
```

This is a simple example. The advantages of using bitwise operators to combine FontStyle values become more evident when we consider that there are five different FontStyle values (Bold, Italic, Regular, Strikeout and Underline), resulting in 16 different FontStyle combinations. Using bitwise operators to combine font styles greatly reduces the amount of code required to check all possible font combinations.

In Fig. 14.27, we need to set the FontStyle so that the text appears in bold if it was not bold originally, and vice versa. Note that line 11 uses the Xor operator to do this. If outputLabel.Font.Style is bold, then the resulting style is not bold. If the text is originally italic, the resulting style is bold and italic rather than just bold. The same applies for FontStyle.Italic in line 21.

If we did not use bitwise operators to compound FontStyle elements, we would have to test for the current style and change it accordingly. For example, in event handler boldCheckBox_CheckChanged, we could test for the regular style and make it bold, test for the bold style and make it regular, test for the italic style and make it bold italic, and test for the italic bold style and make it italic. This is cumbersome because for every new style we add, we double the number of combinations. Adding a CheckBox for underline would require testing eight additional styles. Adding a CheckBox for strikeout would require testing 16 additional styles.

RadioButtons

Radio buttons (defined with class RadioButton) are similar to CheckBoxes in that they also have two states—selected and not selected (also called deselected). However, RadioButtons normally appear as a group, in which only one RadioButton can be selected at a time. Selecting one RadioButton in the group forces all the others to be deselected. Therefore, RadioButtons are used to represent a set of mutually exclusive options (i.e., a set in which multiple options cannot be selected at the same time).

Look-and-Feel Observation 14.6

Use RadioButtons when the user should choose only one option in a group.

Look-and-Feel Observation 14.7

Use CheckBoxes when the user should be able to choose multiple options (or no options at all) in a group.

All RadioButtons added to a container are part of the same group. To divide them into several groups, the RadioButtons must be added to separate GroupBoxes or Panels. Class RadioButton's common properties and a common event are listed in Fig. 14.28.

RadioButton properties and an event	Description
Common Properties	
Checked	Indicates whether the RadioButton is checked.
Text	Specifies the RadioButton's text.

Fig. 14.28 | RadioButton properties and an event. (Part 1 of 2.)

RadioButton properties and an event	Description
Common Event	
CheckedChanged	Generated every time the RadioButton is checked or unchecked. When you double click a RadioButton control in design view, an empty event handler for this event is generated.

Fig. 14.28 | RadioButton properties and an event. (Part 2 of 2.)

Software Engineering Observation 14.2

Forms, GroupBoxes and Panels act as logical groups for RadioButtons. The RadioButtons within each group are mutually exclusive to each other, but not to those in different logical groups.

The program in Fig. 14.29 uses RadioButtons to enable users to select options for a MessageBox. After selecting the desired attributes, the user presses the **Display** Button to display the MessageBox. A Label in the lower-left corner shows the result of the MessageBox (i.e., which Button the user clicked—**Yes**, **No**, **Cancel**, etc.).

```
' Fig. 14.29: RadioButtonsTestForm.vb
' Using RadioButtons to set message window options.
Public Class RadioButtonsTestForm
   ' create variables that store the user's choice of options
   Private iconType As MessageBoxIcon
   Private buttonType As MessageBoxButtons

   ' set button type to OK
   Private Sub okRadioButton_CheckedChanged( _
      ByVal sender As System.Object, ByVal e As System.EventArgs) _
      Handles okRadioButton.CheckedChanged
      buttonType = MessageBoxButtons.OK
   End Sub ' okRadioButton_CheckedChanged

   ' set button type to OKCancel
   Private Sub okCancelRadioButton_CheckedChanged( _
      ByVal sender As System.Object, ByVal e As System.EventArgs) _
      Handles okCancelRadioButton.CheckedChanged
      buttonType = MessageBoxButtons.OKCancel
   End Sub ' okCancelRadioButton_CheckedChanged

   ' set button type to AbortRetryIgnore
   Private Sub abortRetryIgnoreRadioButton_CheckedChanged( _
      ByVal sender As System.Object, ByVal e As System.EventArgs) _
      Handles abortRetryIgnoreRadioButton.CheckedChanged
      buttonType = MessageBoxButtons.AbortRetryIgnore
   End Sub ' abortRetryIgnoreRadioButton_CheckedChanged

```

Fig. 14.29 | Using RadioButtons to set message-window options. (Part 1 of 4.)

```
   ' set button type to YesNoCancel
   Private Sub yesNoCancelRadioButton_CheckedChanged( _
      ByVal sender As System.Object, ByVal e As System.EventArgs) _
      Handles yesNoCancelRadioButton.CheckedChanged
      buttonType = MessageBoxButtons.YesNoCancel
   End Sub ' yesNoCancelRadioButton_CheckedChanged

   ' set button type to YesNo
   Private Sub yesNoRadioButton_CheckedChanged( _
      ByVal sender As System.Object, ByVal e As System.EventArgs) _
      Handles yesNoRadioButton.CheckedChanged
      buttonType = MessageBoxButtons.YesNo
   End Sub ' yesNoRadioButton_CheckedChanged

   ' set button type to RetryCancel
   Private Sub retryCancelRadioButton_CheckedChanged( _
      ByVal sender As System.Object, ByVal e As System.EventArgs) _
      Handles retryCancelRadioButton.CheckedChanged
      buttonType = MessageBoxButtons.RetryCancel
   End Sub ' retryCancelRadioButton_CheckedChanged

   ' set icon type to Asterisk
   Private Sub asteriskRadioButton_CheckedChanged( _
      ByVal sender As System.Object, ByVal e As System.EventArgs) _
      Handles asteriskRadioButton.CheckedChanged
      iconType = MessageBoxIcon.Asterisk
   End Sub ' asteriskRadioButton_CheckedChanged

   ' set icon type to Error
   Private Sub errorRadioButton_CheckedChanged( _
      ByVal sender As System.Object, ByVal e As System.EventArgs) _
      Handles errorRadioButton.CheckedChanged
      iconType = MessageBoxIcon.Error
   End Sub ' errorRadioButton_CheckedChanged

   ' set icon type to Exclamation
   Private Sub exclamationRadioButton_CheckedChanged( _
      ByVal sender As System.Object, ByVal e As System.EventArgs) _
      Handles exclamationRadioButton.CheckedChanged
      iconType = MessageBoxIcon.Exclamation
   End Sub ' exclamationRadioButton_CheckedChanged

   ' set icon type to Hand
   Private Sub handRadioButton_CheckedChanged( _
      ByVal sender As System.Object, ByVal e As System.EventArgs) _
      Handles handRadioButton.CheckedChanged
      iconType = MessageBoxIcon.Hand
   End Sub ' handRadioButton_CheckedChanged

   ' set icon type to Information
   Private Sub informationRadioButton_CheckedChanged( _
      ByVal sender As System.Object, ByVal e As System.EventArgs) _
      Handles informationRadioButton.CheckedChanged
```

Fig. 14.29 | Using `RadioButtons` to set message-window options. (Part 2 of 4.)

```
         iconType = MessageBoxIcon.Information
      End Sub ' informationRadioButton_CheckedChanged

      ' set icon type to Question
      Private Sub questionRadioButton_CheckedChanged( _
         ByVal sender As System.Object, ByVal e As System.EventArgs) _
         Handles questionRadioButton.CheckedChanged
         iconType = MessageBoxIcon.Question
      End Sub ' questionRadioButton_CheckedChanged

      ' set icon type to Stop
      Private Sub stopRadioButton_CheckedChanged( _
         ByVal sender As System.Object, ByVal e As System.EventArgs) _
         Handles stopRadioButton.CheckedChanged
         iconType = MessageBoxIcon.Stop
      End Sub ' stopRadioButton_CheckedChanged

      ' set icon type to Warning
      Private Sub warningRadioButton_CheckedChanged( _
         ByVal sender As System.Object, ByVal e As System.EventArgs) _
         Handles warningRadioButton.CheckedChanged
         iconType = MessageBoxIcon.Warning
      End Sub ' warningRadioButton_CheckedChanged

      ' display MessageBox and Button user pressed
      Private Sub displayButton_Click(ByVal sender As System.Object, _
         ByVal e As System.EventArgs) Handles displayButton.Click
         ' display MessageBox and store
         ' the value of the Button that was pressed
         Dim result As DialogResult = MessageBox.Show( _
            "This is your custom MessageBox.", _
            "Custom MessageBox", buttonType, iconType, 0, 0)

         ' check to see which Button was pressed in the MessageBox
         ' change text displayed accordingly
         Select Case result
            Case DialogResult.OK
               displayLabel.Text = "OK was pressed"
            Case DialogResult.Cancel
               displayLabel.Text = "Cancel was pressed"
            Case DialogResult.Abort
               displayLabel.Text = "Abort was pressed"
            Case DialogResult.Retry
               displayLabel.Text = "Retry was pressed"
            Case DialogResult.Ignore
               displayLabel.Text = "Ignore was pressed"
            Case DialogResult.Yes
               displayLabel.Text = "Yes was pressed"
            Case DialogResult.No
               displayLabel.Text = "No was pressed"
         End Select
      End Sub ' displayButton_Click
   End Class ' RadioButtonsTestForm
```

Fig. 14.29 | Using RadioButtons to set message-window options. (Part 3 of 4.)

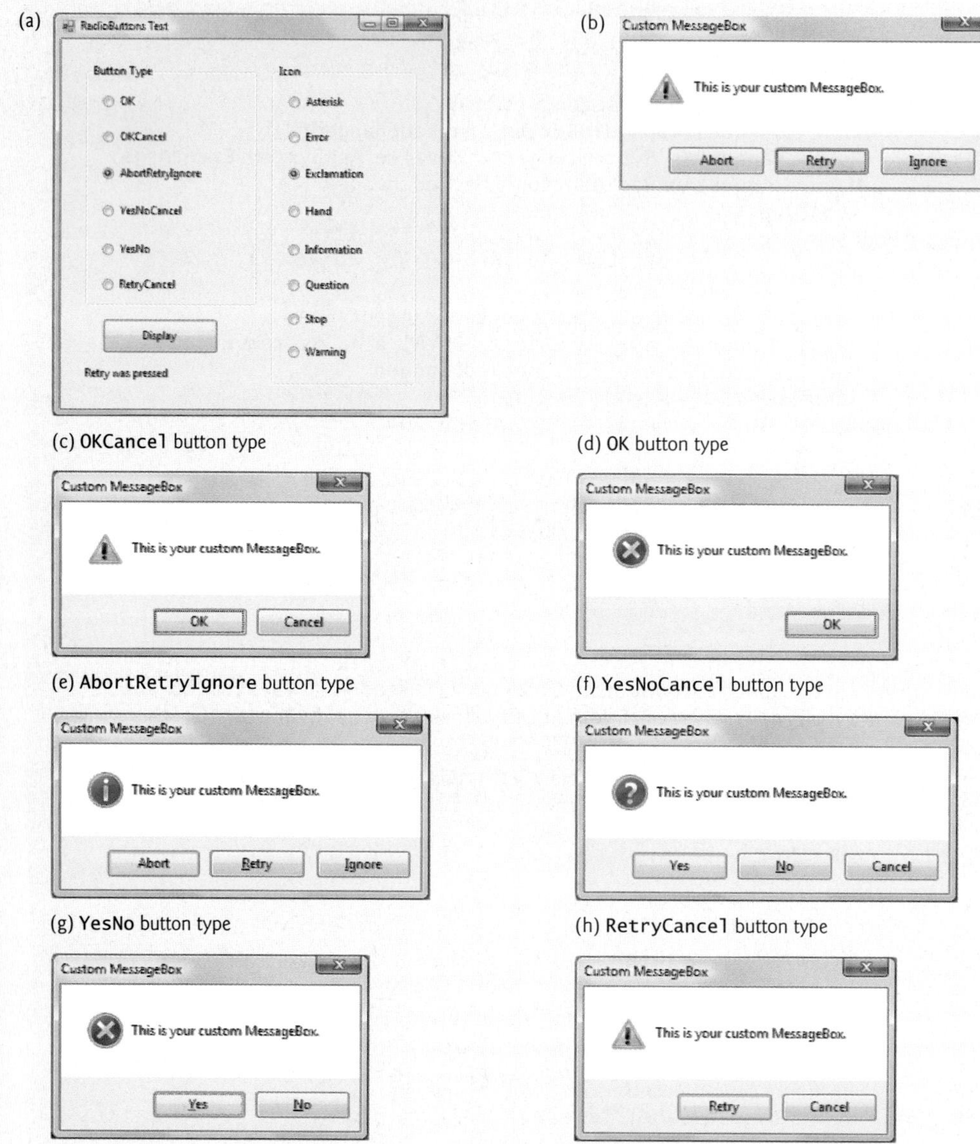

Fig. 14.29 | Using `RadioButtons` to set message-window options. (Part 4 of 4.)

To store the user's choices, we create and initialize variables `iconType` and `buttonType` (lines 5–6). `iconType` is of type `MessageBoxIcon`, and can have values `Asterisk`, `Error`, `Exclamation`, `Hand`, `Information`, `None`, `Question`, `Stop` and `Warning`. The sample output shows only the `Error`, `Exclamation`, `Information` and `Question` icons.

Object `buttonType` is of type `MessageBoxButtons`, and can have values `AbortRetryIgnore`, `OK`, `OKCancel`, `RetryCancel`, `YesNo` and `YesNoCancel`. The name indicates the options that are presented to the user in the `MessageBox`. The sample output windows show `MessageBoxes` for all of the `MessageBoxButtons` enumeration values.

We created two GroupBoxes, one for each set of enumeration values. The GroupBox captions are **Button Type** and **Icon**. The GroupBoxes contain RadioButtons for the corresponding enumeration options, and the RadioButtons' Text properties are set appropriately. Because the RadioButtons are grouped, only one RadioButton can be selected from each GroupBox. There is also a Button (displayButton) labeled **Display.** When a user clicks this Button, a customized MessageBox is displayed. A Label (displayLabel) displays which Button the user pressed in the MessageBox.

The event handler for each RadioButton handles the CheckedChanged event for that RadioButton. When a RadioButton contained in the **Button Type** GroupBox is checked, the checked RadioButton's corresponding event handler sets buttonType to the appropriate value. Lines 8–48 contain the event handling for these RadioButtons. Similarly, when the user checks the RadioButtons belonging to the **Icon** GroupBox, the event handlers associated with these events (lines 50–104) set iconType to its corresponding value.

The displayButton_Click event handler (lines 106–133) creates a MessageBox (lines 111–113) with options specified by the values of iconType and buttonType. When the user clicks one of the MessageBox's buttons, the result of the message box is returned to the application. This result is a value from the DialogResult enumeration that contains Abort, Cancel, Ignore, No, None, OK, Retry or Yes. The Select Case statement in lines 117–132 tests for the result and sets displayLabel.Text appropriately.

14.8 PictureBoxes

A PictureBox displays an image. The image can be one of several formats, such as bitmap, GIF (Graphics Interchange Format) and JPEG. A PictureBox's Image property specifies the image that is displayed, and the SizeMode property indicates how the image is displayed (Normal, StretchImage, Autosize, CenterImage or Zoom). Figure 14.30 describes common PictureBox properties and a common event.

PictureBox properties and an event	Description
Common Properties	
Image	Sets the image to display in the PictureBox.
SizeMode	Enumeration that controls image sizing and positioning. Values are Normal (default), StretchImage, AutoSize and CenterImage. Normal places the image in the top-left corner of the PictureBox; CenterImage puts the image in the middle. Both options truncate the image if it is too large. StretchImage resizes the image to fit in the PictureBox. AutoSize resizes the PictureBox to fit the image.
Common Event	
Click	Occurs when the user clicks the control. Double clicking this control design mode generates an empty event handler for this event.

Fig. 14.30 | PictureBox properties and an event.

Figure 14.31 uses a `PictureBox` named `picImage` to display one of three bitmap images—`image0`, `image1` or `image2`. These images are located in the project's `Resources` subdirectory. Whenever a user clicks the **Next Image** `Button`, the image changes to the next image in sequence. When the last image is displayed and the user clicks the **Next Image** `Button`, the first image is displayed again. Event handler `nextButton_Click` (lines 10–19) uses `Integer` variable `imageNum` to store the number of the image we want to display. We then retrieve the corresponding image as a resource (lines 15–17). Finally, we set the `Image` property of `imagePictureBox` to the `Image` resource (lines 19–20).

```
1  ' Fig. 14.31: PictureBoxTestForm.vb
2  ' Using a PictureBox to display images.
3  Imports System.IO
4
5  Public Class PictureBoxTestForm
6     ' determines which image is displayed
7     Private imageNum As Integer = -1
8
9     ' change image whenever Next Button is clicked
10    Private Sub nextButton_Click(ByVal sender As System.Object, _
11       ByVal e As System.EventArgs) Handles nextButton.Click
12
13       imageNum = (imageNum + 1) Mod 3 ' imageNum cycles from 0 to 2
14
15       ' retrieve specific image from resources
16       Dim pictureResource = My.Resources.ResourceManager.GetObject( _
17          String.Format("image{0}", imageNum))
18
19       ' convert pictureResource to image type and load into PictureBox
20       imagePictureBox.Image = CType(pictureResource, Image)
21    End Sub ' nextButton_Click
22 End Class ' PictureBoxTestForm
```

(a)

(b)

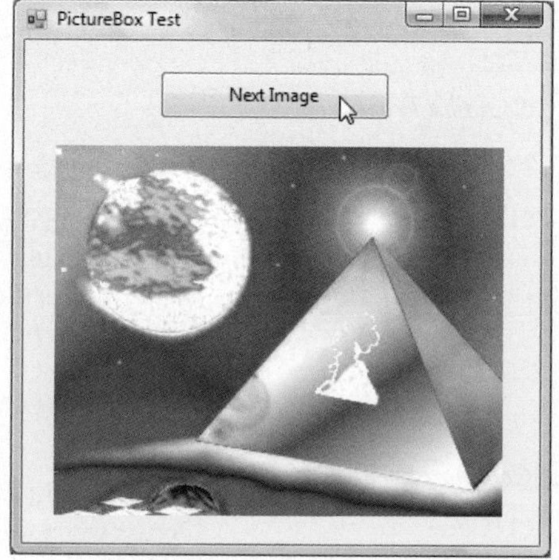

Fig. 14.31 | Using a `PictureBox` to display images. (Part 1 of 2.)

(c)

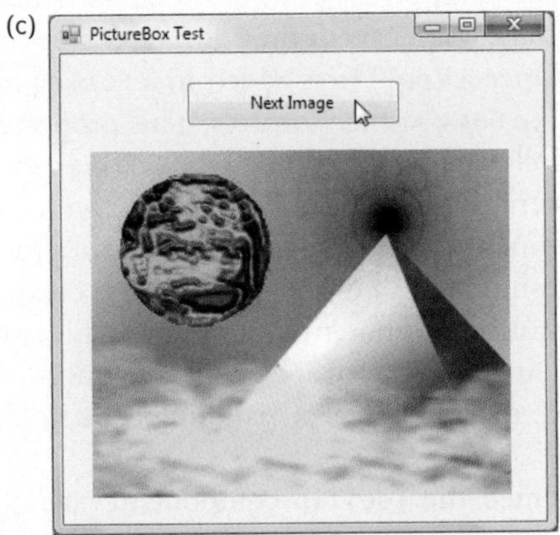

Fig. 14.31 | Using a `PictureBox` to display images. (Part 2 of 2.)

14.9 ToolTips

In Chapter 2, we discussed tool tips—the helpful text that appears when the mouse hovers over a GUI control. The tool tips displayed in Visual Studio serve as useful reminders of each toolbar icon's functionality. Many programs use tool tips to remind users of each control's purpose. For example, Microsoft Word has tool tips that help users determine the purpose of the application's icons. This section demonstrates how to use the `ToolTip` component to add tool tips to your applications. Figure 14.32 describes common properties, a common event, and a common method of class `ToolTip`.

`ToolTip` properties an event, and a method	Description
Common Properties	
`AutoPopDelay`	The amount of time (in milliseconds) that the tool tip appears while the mouse is over a control.
`InitialDelay`	The amount of time (in milliseconds) that a mouse must hover over a control before a tool tip appears.
`ReshowDelay`	The amount of time (in milliseconds) between which two different tool tips appear (when the mouse is moved from one control to another).
Common Event	
`Draw`	Raised when the tool tip is displayed. This event allows programmers to modify the appearance of the tool tip.
Common Method	
`Show`	Sets the tool tip's text and displays it.

Fig. 14.32 | `ToolTip` properties, an event and a method.

When you add a `ToolTip` component from the **Toolbox** (which can only be found in the **All Windows Forms** section), it appears in the component tray—the gray region below the `Form` in **Design** mode. Once a `ToolTip` is added to a `Form`, a new property appears in the **Properties** window for the `Form`'s other controls. This property appears in the **Properties** window as **ToolTip on**, followed by the name of the `ToolTip` component. For instance, if our `Form`'s `ToolTip` were named `helpfulToolTip`, you would set a control's **ToolTip on helpfulToolTip** property value to specify the control's tool tip text. Figure 14.33 demonstrates the `ToolTip` component. For this example, we create a GUI containing two `Label`s so that we can demonstrate a different tool tip for each `Label`. To make the sample outputs clearer, we set the `BorderStyle` property of each `Label` to `FixedSingle`, which displays a solid border. Since there is no event-handling code in this example, the class in Fig. 14.33 is empty.

In this example, we named the `ToolTip` component `labelsToolTip`. Figure 14.34 shows the `ToolTip` in the component tray. We set the tool tip text for the first `Label` to "`First Label`" and the tool tip text for the second `Label` to "`Second Label`." Figure 14.35 demonstrates setting the tool tip text for the first `Label`.

```
' Fig. 14.33: ToolTipDemonstrationForm.vb
' Demonstrating the ToolTip component.
Public Class ToolTipDemonstrationForm
   ' no event handlers needed for this example
End Class ' ToolTipDemonstrationForm
```

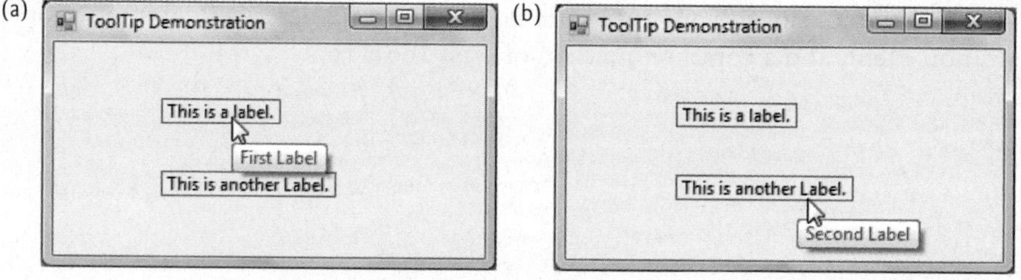

Fig. 14.33 | Demonstrating the `ToolTip` component.

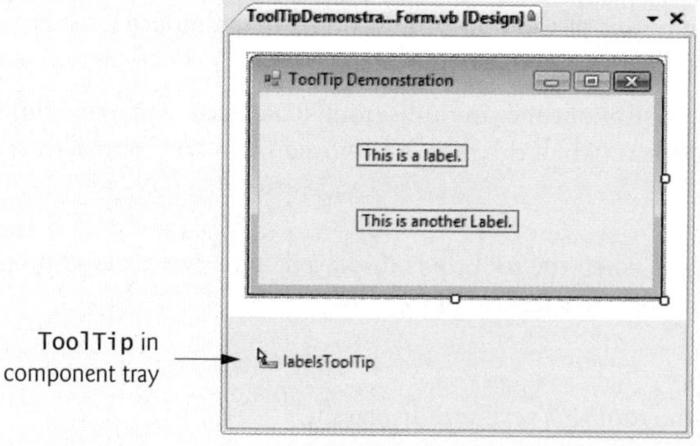

Fig. 14.34 | `ToolTip` component in the component tray.

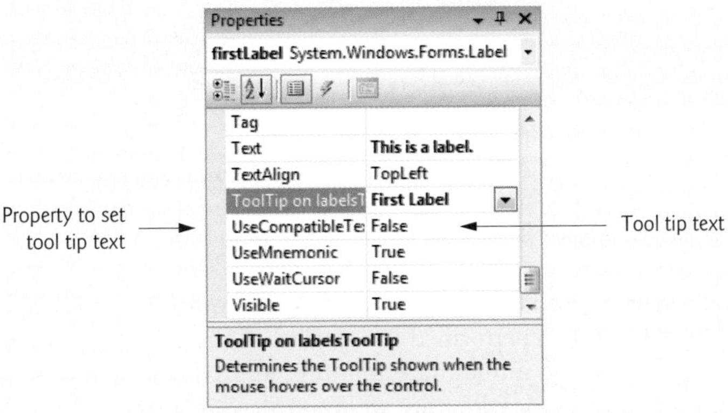

Fig. 14.35 | Setting a control's tool tip text.

14.10 NumericUpDown Control

At times, we will want to restrict a user's input choices to a specific range of numeric values. This is the purpose of the **NumericUpDown control**. This control appears as a `TextBox`, with two small `Buttons` on the right side—one with an up arrow and one with a down arrow. By default, a user can type numeric values into this control as if it were a `TextBox` or click the up and down arrows to increase or decrease the value in the control, respectively. The largest and smallest values in the range are specified with the **`Maximum`** and **`Minimum`** properties, respectively (both of type `Decimal`). The **`Increment`** property (also of type `Decimal`) specifies by how much the current number in the control changes when the user clicks the control's up and down arrows. The **`DecimalPlaces`** property specifies the number of decimal places to the control should display. Figure 14.36 describes common properties and a common event of class `NumericUpDown`.

`NumericUpDown` properties and an event	Description
Common Properties	
`DecimalPlaces`	Sets the number of decimal places to display.
`Increment`	Specifies by how much the current number in the control changes when the user clicks the control's up and down arrows.
`Maximum`	Largest value in the control's range.
`Minimum`	Smallest value in the control's range.
`UpDownAlign`	Modifies the control's up and down `Button` alignment to either the left or the right of the control.
`Value`	The numeric value currently displayed in the control.

Fig. 14.36 | `NumericUpDown` properties and an event. (Part 1 of 2.)

NumericUpDown properties and an event	Description
Common Event	
ValueChanged	This event is raised when the value in the control is changed. It is the default event for the NumericUpDown control.

Fig. 14.36 | NumericUpDown properties and an event. (Part 2 of 2.)

Figure 14.37 demonstrates using a NumericUpDown control for a GUI that calculates interest rate. The calculations performed are similar to those in Fig. 6.8. TextBoxes are used to input the principal and interest rate amounts, and a NumericUpDown control is used to input the number of years for which we want to calculate interest.

For the NumericUpDown control named yearUpDown, we set the Minimum property to 1 and the Maximum property to 10. We left the Increment property's default value (1). These settings specify that users can enter a number of years in the range 1 to 10 in increments of 1. If we had set the Increment to 0.5, we could also input values such as 1.5 or 2.5.

```
' Fig. 14.37: NumericUpDownTestForm.vb
' Demonstrating the NumericUpDown control.
Public Class NumericUpDownTestForm

   Private Sub calculateButton_Click(ByVal sender As System.Object, _
      ByVal e As System.EventArgs) Handles calculateButton.Click
      ' declare variables to store user input
      Dim principal As Decimal ' store principal
      Dim rate As Double ' store interest rate
      Dim year As Integer ' store number of years
      Dim amount As Decimal ' store amount

      ' retrieve user input
      principal = Convert.ToDecimal(principalTextBox.Text)
      rate = Convert.ToDouble(interestTextBox.Text)
      year = Convert.ToInt32(yearUpDown.Value)

      ' set output header
      displayTextBox.Text = "Year" & vbTab & "Amount on Deposit" & _
         vbNewLine

      ' calculate amount after each year and append to output
      For yearCounter As Integer = 1 To year
         amount = principal * Convert.ToDecimal( _
            Math.Pow(1 + rate / 100.0, yearCounter))
         displayTextBox.Text &= (yearCounter & vbTab & _
            String.Format("{0:C}", amount) & vbNewLine)
      Next
   End Sub ' calculateButton_Click
End Class ' NumericUpDownTestForm
```

Fig. 14.37 | Demonstrating the NumericUpDown control. (Part 1 of 2.)

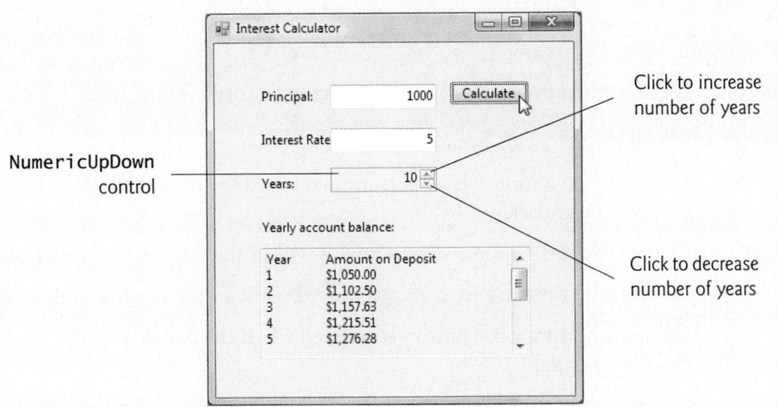

Fig. 14.37 | Demonstrating the `NumericUpDown` control. (Part 2 of 2.)

Note that if you don't modify the `DecimalPlaces` property (`0` by default), `1.5` and `2.5` would display as `2` and `3`, respectively. We set the `NumericUpDown`'s `ReadOnly` property to `True` to indicate that the user cannot type a number into the control to make a selection. Thus, the user must click the up and down arrows (or use the arrow keys on the keyboard) to modify the value in the control. By default, the `ReadOnly` property is set to `False`. The output for this application is displayed in a multiline read-only `TextBox` with a vertical scrollbar so that the user can scroll through the entire output.

14.11 Mouse-Event Handling

This section explains how to handle mouse events, such as clicks, presses and moves, which are generated when the user interacts with a control via the mouse. Mouse events can be handled for any control that derives from class `System.Windows.Forms.Control`. For most mouse events, information about the event is passed to the event-handling method through an object of class `MouseEventArgs`, and the delegate used to create the mouse-event handlers is `MouseEventHandler`. Each mouse-event-handling method for these events requires an `Object` and a `MouseEventArgs` object as arguments.

Class `MouseEventArgs` contains information related to the mouse event, such as the mouse pointer's *x*- and *y*-coordinates, the mouse button pressed (`Right`, `Left` or `Middle`) and the number of times the mouse was clicked. Note that the *x*- and *y*-coordinates of the `MouseEventArgs` object are relative to the control that generated the event—that is point *(0,0)* represents the upper-left corner of the control where the mouse event occurred. Several common mouse events are described in Fig. 14.38.

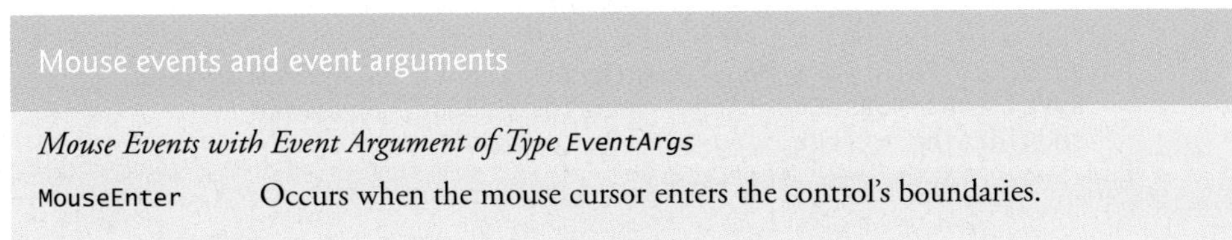

Mouse events and event arguments	
Mouse Events with Event Argument of Type `EventArgs`	
`MouseEnter`	Occurs when the mouse cursor enters the control's boundaries.

Fig. 14.38 | Mouse events and event arguments. (Part 1 of 2.)

Mouse events and event arguments	
`MouseLeave`	Occurs when the mouse cursor leaves the control's boundaries.
Mouse Events with Event Argument of Type `MouseEventArgs`	
`MouseDown`	Occurs when a mouse button is pressed while the mouse cursor is within a control's boundaries.
`MouseHover`	Occurs when the mouse cursor hovers within the control's boundaries.
`MouseMove`	Occurs when the mouse cursor is moved while in the control's boundaries.
`MouseUp`	Occurs when a mouse button is released when the cursor is within the control's boundaries.
Class `MouseEventArgs` *Properties*	
`Button`	Specifies which mouse button was pressed (`Left`, `Right`, `Middle` or `none`).
`Clicks`	The number of times the mouse button was clicked.
`X`	The *x*-coordinate within the control where the event occurred.
`Y`	The *y*-coordinate within the control where the event occurred.

Fig. 14.38 | Mouse events and event arguments. (Part 2 of 2.)

Figure 14.39 uses mouse events to draw on a `Form`. Whenever the user drags the mouse (i.e., moves the mouse while a mouse button is pressed), small circles appear on the `Form` at the position where each mouse event occurs during the drag operation.

Line 4 declares variable `shouldPaint`, which determines whether to draw on the `Form`. We want to draw only while the mouse button is pressed (i.e., held down). Thus, when the user clicks or holds down a mouse button, the system generates a `MouseDown` event, and the event handler `PainterForm_MouseDown` (lines 6–10) sets `shouldPaint` to `True`. When the user releases the mouse button, the system generates a `MouseUp` event, `shouldPaint` is set to `False` in the `PainterForm_MouseUp` event handler (lines 12–16) and the program stops drawing. Unlike `MouseMove` events, which occur continuously as the user moves the mouse, the system generates a `MouseDown` event only when a mouse button is first pressed and generates a `MouseUp` event only when a mouse button is released.

```
1   ' Fig. 14.39: PaintForm.vb
2   ' Using the mouse to draw on a Form.
3   Public Class PaintForm
4      Private shouldPaint As Boolean = False ' determines whether to paint
5
6      ' should paint when mouse button is pressed down
7      Private Sub PaintForm_MouseDown(ByVal sender As System.Object, _
8         ByVal e As MouseEventArgs) Handles MyBase.MouseDown
9         shouldPaint = True
10     End Sub ' PaintForm_MouseDown
11
```

Fig. 14.39 | Using the mouse to draw on a `Form`. (Part 1 of 2.)

```
12        ' stop painting when mouse button is released
13        Private Sub PaintForm_MouseUp(ByVal sender As System.Object, _
14           ByVal e As MouseEventArgs) Handles MyBase.MouseUp
15           shouldPaint = False
16        End Sub ' PaintForm_MouseUp
17
18        ' draw circle whenever mouse moves with its button held down
19        Private Sub Paint_MouseMove(ByVal sender As System.Object, _
20           ByVal e As MouseEventArgs) Handles MyBase.MouseMove
21           ' check if mouse button is being pressed
22           If (shouldPaint) Then
23              ' draw a circle where the mouse pointer is present
24              Dim g As Graphics = CreateGraphics()
25              g.FillEllipse( _
26                 New SolidBrush(Color.BlueViolet), e.X, e.Y, 4, 4)
27              g.Dispose()
28           End If
29        End Sub ' Paint_MouseMove
30     End Class ' PaintForm
```

Fig. 14.39 | Using the mouse to draw on a Form. (Part 2 of 2.)

Whenever the mouse moves over a control, the `MouseMove` event for that control occurs. Inside the `PainterForm_MouseMove` event handler (lines 18–29), the program draws only if `shouldPaint` is `True` (i.e., a mouse button is pressed). Line 24 calls inherited `Form` method `CreateGraphics` to create a **`Graphics`** object that allows the program to draw on the `Form`. Class `Graphics` provides methods that draw various shapes. For example, lines 25–26 use method **`FillEllipse`** to draw a circle. The first parameter to method `FillEllipse` in this case is an object of class **`SolidBrush`**, which specifies the solid color that will fill the shape. The color is provided as an argument to class `SolidBrush`'s constructor. Type **`Color`** contains many predefined color constants—we selected `Color.BlueViolet`. `FillEllipse` draws an oval in a bounding rectangle that is specified by the *x*- and *y*-coordinates of its upper-left corner, its width and its height—the final four arguments to the method. The *x*- and *y*-coordinates represent the location of the mouse event and can be taken from the mouse-event arguments (`e.X` and `e.Y`). To draw a circle, we set the width and height of the bounding rectangle so that they are equal—in this example, both are 4 pixels. Line 27 invokes the `Graphics` object's `Dispose` method to return the `Graphics` object's resources back to the system. `Graphics`, `SolidBrush` and

Color are all part of the System.Drawing namespace. Rather than manually disposing of the Graphics object, lines 24–27 could be have been replaced with a Using statement (Section 13.6) as follows:

```
Using g As Graphics = CreateGraphics()
   g.FillEllipse(New SolidBrush(Color.BlueViolet), e.X, e.Y, 4, 4)
End Using
```

14.12 Keyboard-Event Handling

Key events occur when keyboard keys are pressed and released. Such events can be handled for any control that inherits from System.Windows.Forms.Control. There are three key events—KeyPress, KeyUp and KeyDown. The KeyPress event occurs when the user presses a key that represents an ASCII character. The specific key can be determined with property KeyChar of the event handler's KeyPressEventArgs argument. ASCII is a 128-character set of alphanumeric symbols, a full listing of which can be found in Appendix F.

The KeyPress event does not indicate whether modifier keys (e.g., *Shift*, *Alt* and *Ctrl*) were pressed when a key event occurred. If this information is important, the KeyUp or KeyDown events can be used. The KeyEventArgs argument for each of these events contains information about modifier keys. Often, modifier keys are used in conjunction with the mouse to select or highlight information. Figure 14.40 lists important key-event information. Several properties return values from the Keys enumeration, which provides constants that specify the various keys on a keyboard. Like the FontStyle enumeration (Section 14.7), the Keys enumeration has the System.FlagAttribute, so the enumeration's constants can be combined to indicate multiple keys pressed at the same time.

Keyboard events and event arguments	
Key Events with Event Arguments of Type KeyEventArgs	
KeyDown	Generated when a key is initially pressed.
KeyUp	Generated when a key is released.
Key Event with Event Argument of Type KeyPressEventArgs	
KeyPress	Generated when a key is pressed.
Class KeyPressEventArgs *Properties*	
KeyChar	Returns the ASCII character for the key pressed.
Handled	Indicates whether the KeyPress event was handled.
Class KeyEventArgs *Properties*	
Alt	Indicates whether the *Alt* key was pressed.
Control	Indicates whether the *Ctrl* key was pressed.
Shift	Indicates whether the *Shift* key was pressed.
Handled	Indicates whether the event was handled.

Fig. 14.40 | Keyboard events and event arguments. (Part 1 of 2.)

Keyboard events and event arguments	
`KeyCode`	Returns the key code for the key as a value from the `Keys` enumeration. This does not include modifier-key information. It is used to test for a specific key.
`KeyData`	Returns the key code for a key combined with modifier information as a `Keys` value. This property contains all the information about the pressed key.
`KeyValue`	Returns the key code as an `int`, rather than as a value from the `Keys` enumeration. This property is used to obtain a numeric representation of the pressed key. The `int` value is known as a Windows virtual key code.
`Modifiers`	Returns a `Keys` value indicating any pressed modifier keys (*Alt*, *Ctrl* and *Shift*). This property is used to determine modifier-key information only.

Fig. 14.40 | Keyboard events and event arguments. (Part 2 of 2.)

Figure 14.41 demonstrates the use of the key-event handlers to display a key pressed by a user. The program is a `Form` with two `Label`s that displays the pressed key on one `Label` and modifier-key information on the other.

```
' Fig. 14.41: KeyDemoForm.vb
' Displaying information about the key the user pressed.
Public Class KeyDemoForm

   ' display the character pressed using KeyChar
   Private Sub KeyDemoForm_KeyPress(ByVal sender As System.Object, _
      ByVal e As KeyPressEventArgs) Handles MyBase.KeyPress

      charLabel.Text = "Key pressed: " & e.KeyChar
   End Sub ' KeyDemoForm_KeyPress

   ' display modifier keys, key code, key data and key value
   Private Sub KeyDemoForm_KeyDown(ByVal sender As System.Object, _
      ByVal e As KeyEventArgs) Handles MyBase.KeyDown

      If e.Alt Then ' key is Alt
         keyInfoLabel.Text = "Alt: Yes" & vbNewLine
      Else ' key is not Alt
         keyInfoLabel.Text = "Alt: No" & vbNewLine
      End If

      If e.Shift Then ' key is Shift
         keyInfoLabel.Text &= "Shift: Yes" & vbNewLine
      Else ' key is not Shift
         keyInfoLabel.Text &= "Shift: No" & vbNewLine
      End If

      If e.Control Then ' key is Control
         keyInfoLabel.Text &= "Control: Yes" & vbNewLine
```

Fig. 14.41 | Demonstrating keyboard events. (Part 1 of 2.)

```
30         Else ' key is not Control
31            keyInfoLabel.Text &= "Control: No" & vbNewLine
32         End If
33
34         ' diplay key code, key data and key value
35         keyInfoLabel.Text &= "KeyCode: " & e.KeyCode.ToString() & _
36         vbNewLine & "KeyData: " & e.KeyData.ToString() & vbNewLine & _
37            "KeyValue: " & e.KeyValue.ToString()
38      End Sub ' KeyDemoForm_KeyDown
39
40      ' clear Labels when keys are released
41      Private Sub KeyDemoForm_KeyUp(ByVal sender As System.Object, _
42         ByVal e As KeyEventArgs) Handles MyBase.KeyUp
43
44         charLabel.Text = String.Empty
45         keyInfoLabel.Text = String.Empty
46      End Sub ' KeyDemoForm_KeyUp
47   End Class ' KeyDemoForm
```

Fig. 14.41 | Demonstrating keyboard events. (Part 2 of 2.)

Initially, the two `Labels` (`charLabel` and `keyInfoLabel`) contain `"Just Press"` and `"A Key..."`, respectively. When the user presses a key, `charLabel` displays the key's character value, and `keyInfoLabel` displays related information. Because the `KeyDown` and `KeyPress` events convey different information, the `Form` (`KeyDemoForm`) handles both.

The `KeyPress` event handler (lines 5–10) accesses the `KeyChar` property of the `KeyPressEventArgs` object. This returns the pressed key as a `Char`, which we then display in `charLabel` (line 9). If the pressed key is not an ASCII character, then the `KeyPress` event will not occur, and `charLabel` will not display any text. ASCII is a common encoding format for letters, numbers, punctuation marks and other characters. It does not support keys such as the function keys (such as *F1*) or the modifier keys (*Alt*, *Ctrl* and *Shift*).

The `KeyDown` event handler (lines 12–38) displays information from its `KeyEventArgs` object. The event handler tests for the *Alt*, *Shift* and *Ctrl* keys by using the `Alt`, `Shift` and `Control` properties, each of which returns a `Boolean` value—`True` if the corresponding key is pressed and `False` if otherwise. The event handler then displays the `KeyCode`, `KeyData` and `KeyValue` properties.

The `KeyCode` property returns a `Keys` enumeration value (line 35). The `KeyCode` property returns the pressed key, but does not provide any information about modifier keys. Thus, both a capital "A" and a lowercase "a" are represented as the *A* key.

The `KeyData` property (line 36) also returns a `Keys` enumeration value, but this property includes data about modifier keys. Thus, if "A" is input, the `KeyData` shows that both the *A* key and the *Shift* key were pressed. Lastly, `KeyValue` (line 37) returns the key code of the pressed key as an `Integer`. This `Integer` is the key code, which provides an `Integer` value for a wide range of keys and for mouse buttons. The key code is useful when one is testing for non-ASCII keys (such as *F12*).

The `KeyUp` event handler (lines 40–46) clears both `Label`s when the key is released. As we can see from the output, non-ASCII keys are not displayed in `charLabel`, because the `KeyPress` event is not generated. For example, `charLabel` does not display any text when you press the *F12* or *Insert* keys, as shown in Fig. 14.41(b) and (c). However, the `KeyDown` event is still generated, and `keyInfoLabel` displays information about the key that is pressed. The `Keys` enumeration can be used to test for specific keys by comparing the key pressed to a specific `KeyCode`.

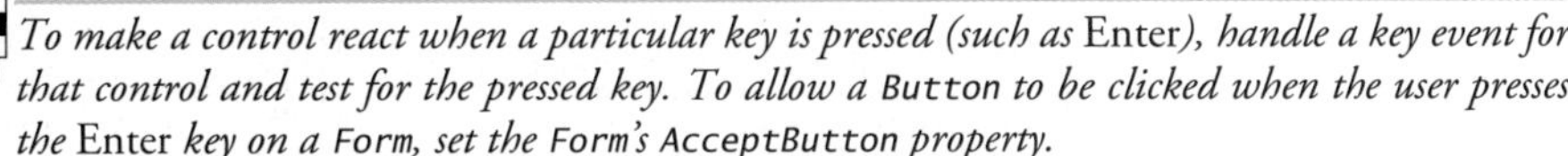

Software Engineering Observation 14.3

To make a control react when a particular key is pressed (such as Enter*), handle a key event for that control and test for the pressed key. To allow a `Button` to be clicked when the user presses the* Enter *key on a `Form`, set the `Form`'s `AcceptButton` property.*

14.13 Menus

Menus provide groups of related commands. Although commands vary between applications, some—such as **Open** and **Save**—are common to many applications. Menus organize commands without "cluttering" the application's user interface.

In Fig. 14.42, an expanded menu from Visual Basic 2008 Express lists various commands (called menu items), plus submenus (menus within a menu). Menu items are typically displayed down and indented to the right of the top-level menu, but they can be displayed to the left if there is not enough space to the right. The menu that contains a menu item is called the menu item's parent menu. A menu item that contains a submenu is considered to be the parent of the submenu.

All menu items can have *Alt* key shortcuts (also called access shortcuts or hotkeys), which are accessed by pressing *Alt* and the underlined letter (for example, *Alt V* typically expands the **View** menu in Visual Basic 2008 Express). Menus that are not top-level menus can have shortcut keys as well (combinations of *Ctrl*, *Shift*, *Alt*, *F1*, *F2*, letter keys, etc.). Some menu items display check marks, usually indicating that multiple options on the menu can be selected at once.

To create a menu, open the **Toolbox** and drag a `MenuStrip` control onto the `Form`. This creates a menu bar across the top of the `Form` (below the title bar) and places a `MenuStrip` icon in the component tray. To select the `MenuStrip`, click this icon. You can now use **Design** mode to create and edit menus for your application. Menus, like other controls, have properties and events, which can be accessed through the **Properties** window.

To add menu items to the menu, click the **Type Here** `TextBox` (Fig. 14.43) and type the menu item's name. This action adds an entry to the menu of type `ToolStripMenuItem`. After you press the *Enter* key, the menu item name is added to the menu. Additional **Type Here** `TextBox`es appear, allowing you to add items underneath or to the right of the original menu item (Fig. 14.44).

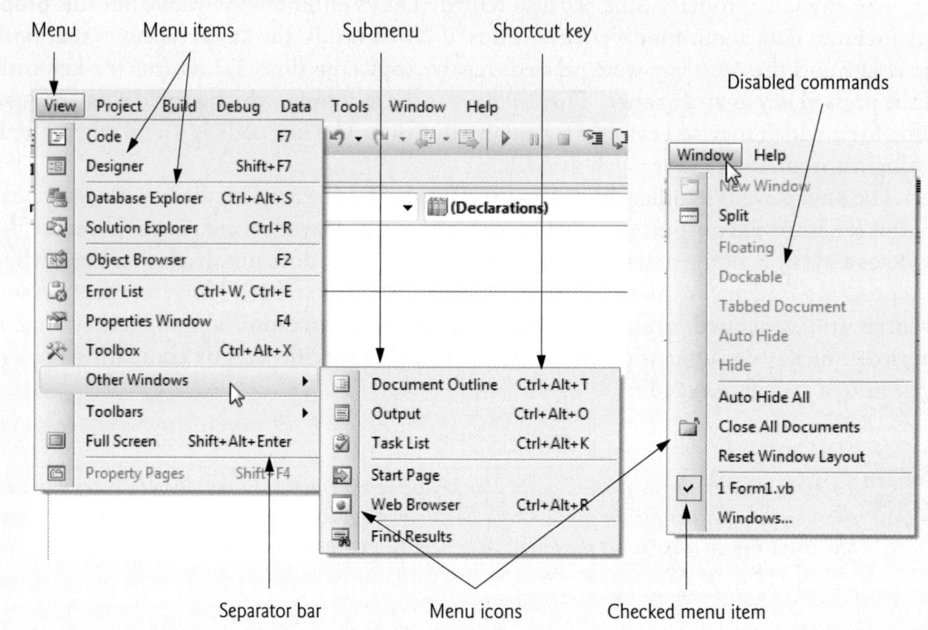

Fig. 14.42 | Menus, submenus, menu items and menu icons.

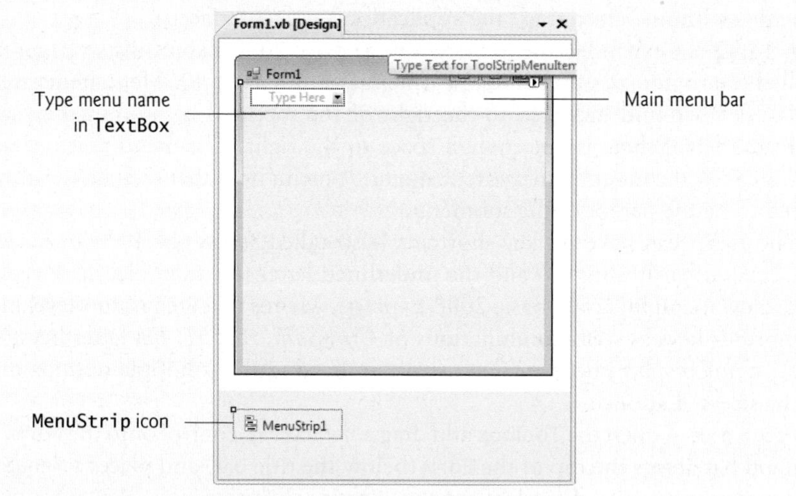

Fig. 14.43 | Editing menus in Visual Studio.

To create an access shortcut (or keyboard shortcut), type an ampersand (&) before the character to be underlined. For example, to create the **File** menu item with the letter **F** underlined, type `&File`. To display an ampersand, type &&. To add other shortcut keys (like those shown in Fig. 14.42) for menu items, set the `ShortcutKeys` property of the appropriate `ToolStripMenuItems`. To do this, select the down arrow to the right of this

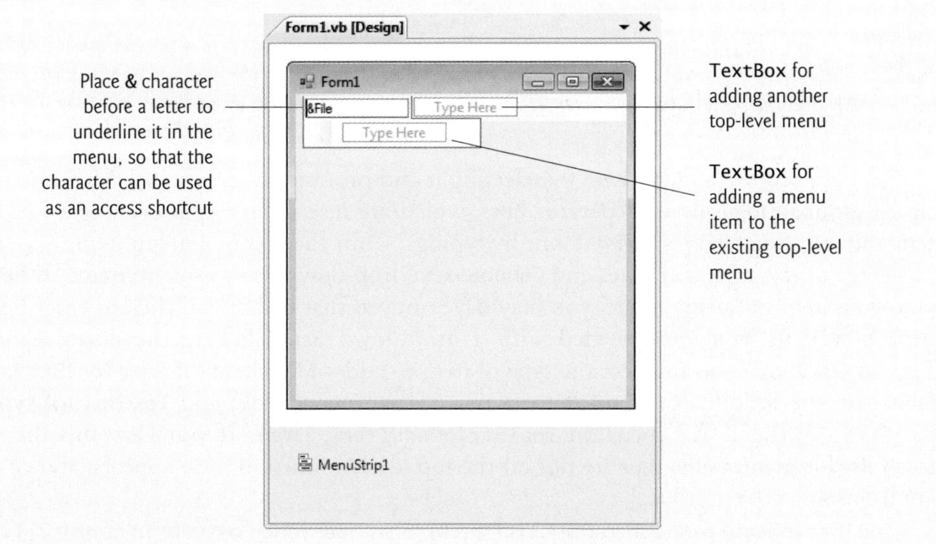

Fig. 14.44 | Adding `ToolStripMenuItems` to a `MenuStrip`.

property in the **Properties** window. In the window that appears (Fig. 14.45), use the `CheckBoxes` and drop-down list to select the shortcut keys. When you are finished, click elsewhere on the screen. You can hide the shortcut keys by setting property `ShowShortcutKeys` to `False`, and you can modify how the control keys are displayed in the menu item by modifying property `ShortcutKeyDisplayString`.

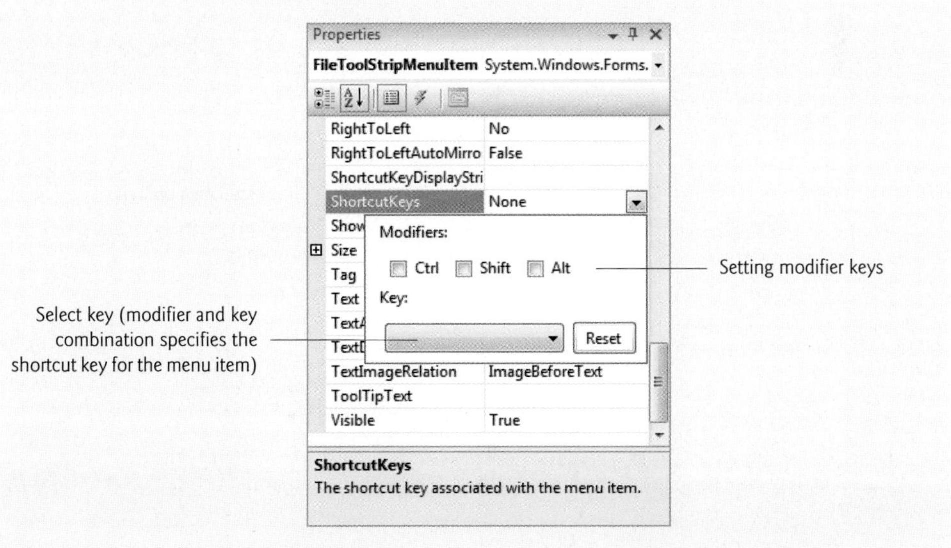

Fig. 14.45 | Setting a menu item's shortcut keys.

Look-and-Feel Observation 14.8

Buttons can have access shortcuts. Place the & symbol immediately before the desired character in the Button's text. To press the button by using its access key in the running application, press Alt *and the underlined character. If the underlines are not visible at runtime, press the* Alt *key to display the underlines.*

You can remove a menu item by selecting it and pressing the *Delete* key. Menu items can be grouped logically by separator bars, which are inserted by right clicking a menu item and selecting **Insert > Separator** or by typing "-" for the text of a menu item.

You can also add TextBoxes and ComboBoxes (drop-down lists) as menu items. When adding an item in **Design** mode, you may have noticed that before you click to enter text for a new item, you are provided with a drop-down list. Clicking the down arrow (Fig. 14.46) allows you to select the type of item to add—**MenuItem** (of type ToolStripMenuItem, the default), **ComboBox** (of type ToolStripComboBox) and **TextBox** (of type ToolStripTextBox). We focus on ToolStripMenuItems. [*Note:* If you view this drop-down list for menu items that are not on the top level, a fourth option appears, allowing you to insert a separator bar.]

ToolStripMenuItems generate a Click event when selected. To create an empty Click event handler, double click the menu item in **Design** mode. Common actions in response to these events include displaying dialogs and setting application properties. Common properties of MenuStrip and ToolStripMenuItem and a common event of a ToolStripMenuItem are summarized in Fig. 14.47.

Look-and-Feel Observation 14.9

It is a convention to place an ellipsis (...) after the name of a menu item that, when selected, displays a dialog (e.g. **Save As...***). A menu item that causes an immediate action without prompting the user for more information (e.g.,* **Save***) should not have an ellipsis following its name.*

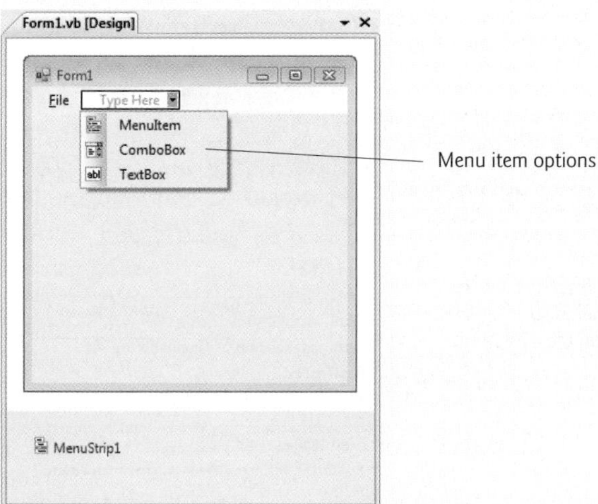

Fig. 14.46 | Menu item options.

MenuStrip and ToolStripMenuItem properties and an event	Description
MenuStrip Properties	
MenuItems	Contains the top-level menu items for this MenuStrip.
HasChildren	Indicates whether MenuStrip has any child controls (menu items).
RightToLeft	Causes text to display from right to left. This is useful for languages that are read from right to left.
ToolStripMenuItem Properties	
Checked	Indicates whether a menu item is checked. The default value is False, meaning that the menu item is unchecked.
CheckOnClick	Indicates that a menu item should appear checked or unchecked as the item is clicked.
MenuItems	Lists the submenu items for a particular menu item.
ShortcutKey-DisplayString	Specifies text that should appear beside a menu item for a shortcut key. If left blank, the key names are displayed.
ShortcutKeys	Specifies the shortcut key for the menu item.
ShowShortcutKeys	Indicates whether a shortcut key is shown beside the menu item text. The default is True, which displays the shortcut key.
Text	Specifies the menu item's text. To create an *Alt* access shortcut, precede a character with & (e.g., &File to specify a menu named **File** with the letter **F** underlined).
Common ToolStripMenuItem Event	
Click	Generated when an item is clicked or a shortcut key is used to select a menu item.

Fig. 14.47 | MenuStrip and ToolStripMenuItem properties and an event.

Class MenuTestForm (Fig. 14.48) creates a simple menu on a Form. The Form has a top-level **File** menu with menu items **About** (which displays a MessageBox) and **Exit** (which terminates the program). The program also includes a **Format** menu, which contains menu items that change the format of the text on a Label. The **Format** menu has submenus **Color** and **Font**, which change the color and font of the text on a Label.

To create this GUI, begin by dragging the MenuStrip from the **ToolBox** onto the Form. Then use **Design** mode to create the menu structure shown in the sample outputs. The **File** menu (fileToolStripMenuItem) has menu items **About** (aboutToolStripMenuItem) and **Exit** (exitToolStripMenuItem); the **Format** menu (formatToolStripMenuItem) has two submenus. The first submenu, **Color** (colorToolStripMenuItem), contains menu items **Black** (blackToolStripMenuItem), **Blue** (blueToolStripMenuItem), **Red** (redToolStripMenuItem) and **Green** (greenToolStripMenuItem). The second submenu, **Font** (fontToolStripMenuItem), contains menu items **Times New Roman** (timesToolStripMenuItem), **Courier New** (courierToolStripMenuItem), **Comic Sans MS** (comicToolStripMenuItem), a separator bar (dashToolStripMenuItem), **Bold** (boldToolStripMenuItem) and **Italic** (italicToolStripMenuItem).

```
' Fig. 14.48: MenuTestForm.vb
' Using Menus to change font colors and styles.
Public Class MenuTestForm

   ' display MessageBox when About menu item is selected
   Private Sub aboutToolStripMenuItem_Click( _
      ByVal sender As System.Object, ByVal e As System.EventArgs) _
      Handles aboutToolStripMenuItem.Click

      MessageBox.Show("This is an example" & vbNewLine & _
         "of using menus.", "About", MessageBoxButtons.OK, _
         MessageBoxIcon.Information)
   End Sub ' aboutToolStripMenuItem_Click

   ' exit program when Exit menu item is selected
   Private Sub exitToolStripMenuItem_Click( _
      ByVal sender As System.Object, ByVal e As System.EventArgs) _
      Handles exitToolStripMenuItem.Click

      Application.Exit()
   End Sub ' exitToolStripMenuItem_Click

   ' reset checkmarks for Color menu items
   Private Sub ClearColor()
      ' clear all checkmarks
      blackToolStripMenuItem.Checked = False
      blueToolStripMenuItem.Checked = False
      redToolStripMenuItem.Checked = False
      greenToolStripMenuItem.Checked = False
   End Sub ' ClearColor

   ' update Menu state and color display black
   Private Sub blackToolStripMenuItem_Click( _
      ByVal sender As System.Object, ByVal e As System.EventArgs) _
      Handles blackToolStripMenuItem.Click

      ClearColor() ' reset checkmarks for Color menu items
      displayLabel.ForeColor = Color.Black ' set Color to Black
      blackToolStripMenuItem.Checked = True
   End Sub ' blackToolStripMenuItem_Click

   ' update Menu state and color display blue
   Private Sub blueToolStripMenuItem_Click( _
      ByVal sender As System.Object, ByVal e As System.EventArgs) _
      Handles blueToolStripMenuItem.Click

      ClearColor() ' reset checkmarks for Color menu items
      displayLabel.ForeColor = Color.Blue ' set Color to Blue
      blueToolStripMenuItem.Checked = True
   End Sub ' blueToolStripMenuItem_Click
```

Fig. 14.48 | Menus for changing text font and color. (Part 1 of 4.)

```
   ' update Menu state and color display red
   Private Sub redToolStripMenuItem_Click( _
      ByVal sender As System.Object, ByVal e As System.EventArgs) _
      Handles redToolStripMenuItem.Click

      ClearColor() ' reset checkmarks for Color menu items
      displayLabel.ForeColor = Color.Red ' set Color to Red
      redToolStripMenuItem.Checked = True
   End Sub ' redToolStripMenuItem_Click

   ' update Menu state and color display green
   Private Sub greenToolStripMenuItem_Click( _
      ByVal sender As System.Object, ByVal e As System.EventArgs) _
      Handles greenToolStripMenuItem.Click

      ClearColor() ' reset checkmarks for Color menu items
      displayLabel.ForeColor = Color.Green ' set Color to Green
      greenToolStripMenuItem.Checked = True
   End Sub ' greenToolStripMenuItem_Click

   ' reset checkmarks for Font menu items
   Private Sub ClearFont()
      timesToolStripMenuItem.Checked = False
      courierToolStripMenuItem.Checked = False
      comicToolStripMenuItem.Checked = False
   End Sub ' ClearFont

   ' update Menu state and set Font to Times New Roman
   Private Sub timesToolStripMenuItem_Click( _
      ByVal sender As System.Object, ByVal e As System.EventArgs) _
      Handles timesToolStripMenuItem.Click

      ClearFont() ' reset checkmarks for Font menu items
      timesToolStripMenuItem.Checked = True

      ' set Times New Roman font
      displayLabel.Font = _
         New Font("Times New Roman", 14, displayLabel.Font.Style)
   End Sub ' timesToolStripMenuItem_Click

   ' update Menu state and set Font to Courier New
   Private Sub courierToolStripMenuItem_Click( _
      ByVal sender As System.Object, ByVal e As System.EventArgs) _
      Handles courierToolStripMenuItem.Click

      ClearFont() ' reset checkmarks for Font menu items
      courierToolStripMenuItem.Checked = True

      ' set Courier font
      displayLabel.Font = _
         New Font("Courier New", 14, displayLabel.Font.Style)
   End Sub ' courierToolStripMenuItem_Click
```

Fig. 14.48 | Menus for changing text font and color. (Part 2 of 4.)

```

   ' update Menu state and set Font to Comic Sans MS
   Private Sub comicToolStripMenuItem_Click( _
      ByVal sender As System.Object, ByVal e As System.EventArgs) _
      Handles comicToolStripMenuItem.Click

      ClearFont() ' reset checkmarks for Font menu items
      comicToolStripMenuItem.Checked = True

      ' set Comic Sans MS font
      displayLabel.Font = _
         New Font("Comic Sans MS", 14, displayLabel.Font.Style)
   End Sub ' comicToolStripMenuItem_Click

   ' toggle checkmark and toggle bold style
   Private Sub boldToolStripMenuItem_Click( _
      ByVal sender As System.Object, ByVal e As System.EventArgs) _
      Handles boldToolStripMenuItem.Click
      ' toggle menu item checkmark
      boldToolStripMenuItem.Checked = Not boldToolStripMenuItem.Checked

      ' use Xor to toggle bold, keep all other styles
      displayLabel.Font = New Font(displayLabel.Font.FontFamily, 14, _
         displayLabel.Font.Style Xor FontStyle.Bold)
   End Sub ' boldToolStripMenuItem_Click

   ' toggle checkmark and toggle italic style
   Private Sub italicToolStripMenuItem_Click( _
      ByVal sender As System.Object, ByVal e As System.EventArgs) _
      Handles italicToolStripMenuItem.Click
      ' toggle menu item checkmark
      italicToolStripMenuItem.Checked = _
         Not italicToolStripMenuItem.Checked

      ' use Xor to toggle italic, keep all other styles
      displayLabel.Font = New Font(displayLabel.Font.FontFamily, 14, _
         displayLabel.Font.Style Xor FontStyle.Italic)
   End Sub ' italicToolStripMenuItem_Click
End Class ' MenuTestForm
```

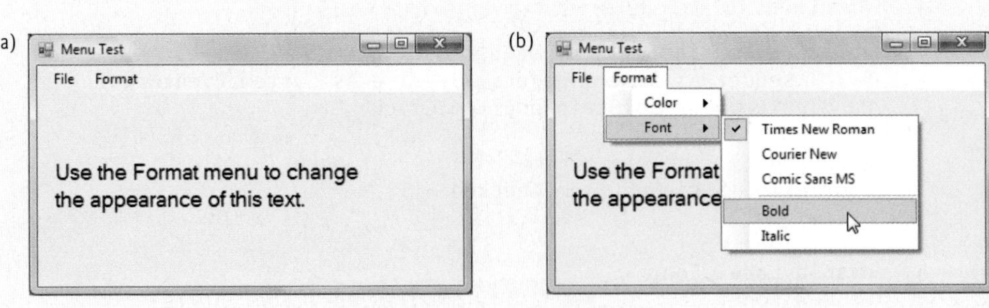

Fig. 14.48 | Menus for changing text font and color. (Part 3 of 4.)

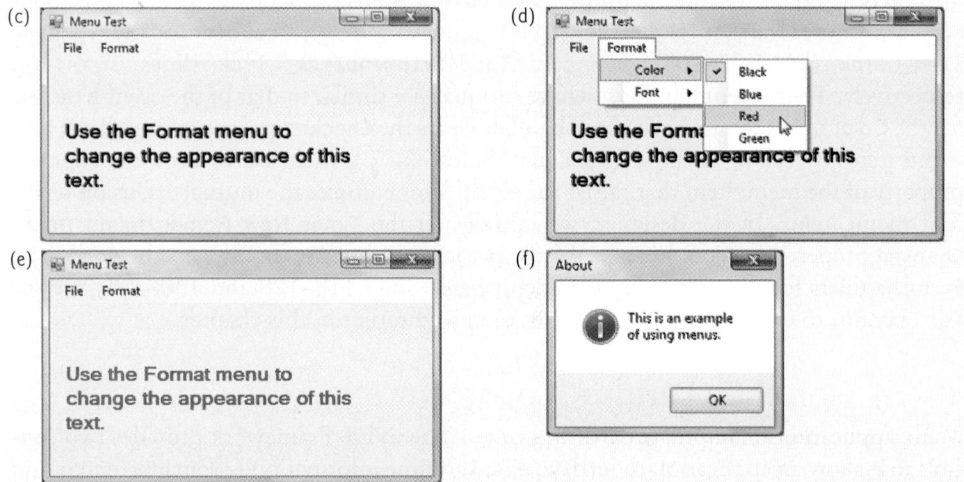

Fig. 14.48 | Menus for changing text font and color. (Part 4 of 4.)

The **About** menu item in the **File** menu displays a `MessageBox` when clicked (lines 5–13). The **Exit** menu item closes the application through `Shared` method `Exit` of class `Application` (line 20). Class `Application`'s `Shared` methods control program execution. Method `Exit` causes our application to terminate.

We made the items in the **Color** submenu (**Black**, **Blue**, **Red** and **Green**) mutually exclusive—the user can select only one at a time (we explain how we did this shortly). To indicate that a menu item is selected, we will set each **Color** menu item's `Checked` property to `True`. This causes a check to appear to the left of a menu item.

Each **Color** menu item has its own `Click` event handler. The event handler for color **Black** is `blackToolStripMenuItem_Click` (lines 32–40). Similarly, the event handlers for colors **Blue**, **Red** and **Green** are `blueToolStripMenuItem_Click` (lines 42–50), `redToolStripMenuItem_Click` (lines 52–60) and `greenToolStripMenuItem_Click` (lines 62–70), respectively. The **Color** menu items must be mutually exclusive, so each event handler calls method `ClearColor` (lines 23–30) before setting its corresponding `Checked` property to `True`. Method `ClearColor` sets the `Checked` property of each color `MenuItem` to `False`, effectively preventing more than one menu item from being selected at a time. In the designer, we initially set the **Black** menu item's `Checked` property to `True`, because at the start of the program, the text on the `Form` is black.

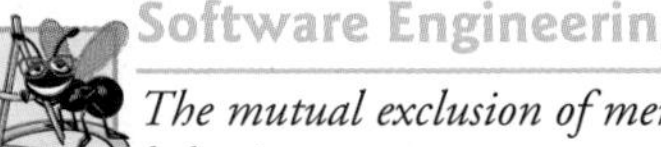

Software Engineering Observation 14.4

The mutual exclusion of menu items is not enforced by the `MenuStrip`*. You must program this behavior.*

The **Font** menu contains three menu items for fonts (**Times New Roman**, **Courier New** and **Comic Sans MS**) and two menu items for font styles (**Bold** and **Italic**). We added a separator bar between the font and font-style menu items to indicate that these are separate options. A `Font` object can specify multiple styles at once (e.g., a font can be both bold and italic). We set the font menu items to display checks. As with the **Color** menu, we must enforce mutual exclusion of these items in our event handlers.

Event handlers for font menu items **Times New Roman**, **Courier New** and **Comic Sans MS** are `timesToolStripMenuItem_Click` (lines 79–90), `courierToolStripMenuItem_Click` (lines 92–103) and `comicToolStripMenuItem_Click` (lines 105–116), respectively. These event handlers behave in a manner similar to that of the event handlers for the **Color** menu items. Each event handler clears the `Checked` properties for all the font menu items by calling method `ClearFont` (lines 72–77), then sets to `True` the `Checked` property of the menu item that raised the event. This enforces the mutual exclusion of the font menu items. In the designer, we initially set the **Times New Roman** menu item's `Checked` property to `True`, because this is the original font for the text on the `Form`. The event handlers for the **Bold** and **Italic** menu items (lines 118–128 and 130–141) use the `Xor` operator to combine font styles as we discussed earlier in this chapter.

14.14 MonthCalendar Control

Many applications manipulate dates and times. The .NET Framework provides two controls that allow an application to retrieve date and time information—`MonthCalendar` and `DateTimePicker` (Section 14.15).

The `MonthCalendar` control (Fig. 14.49) displays a monthly calendar on the `Form`. The user can select a date from the currently displayed month or can use the provided links to navigate to another month. When a date is selected, it is highlighted. Multiple dates can be selected by clicking dates on the calendar while holding down the *Shift* key. The default event for this control is `DateChanged`, which is generated when a new date is selected. Properties are provided that allow you to modify the appearance of the calendar, how many dates can be selected at once, and the minimum and maximum dates that may be selected. `MonthCalendar` properties and a common event are summarized in Fig. 14.50.

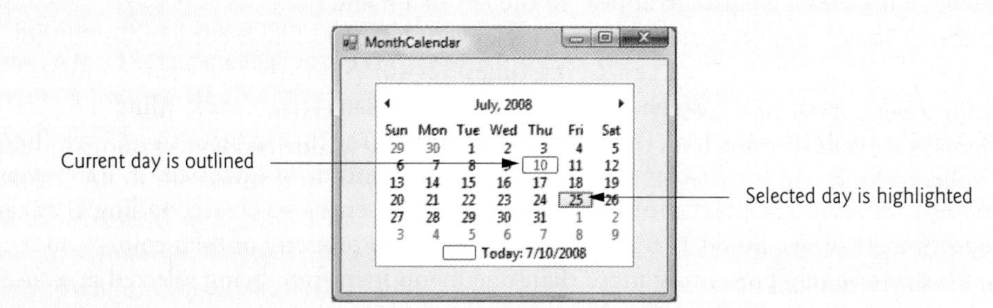

Fig. 14.49 | `MonthCalendar` control.

`MonthCalendar` properties and an event	Description
`MonthCalendar` Properties	
`FirstDayOfWeek`	Sets which day of the week is the first displayed for each week.
`MaxDate`	The last date that can be selected.

Fig. 14.50 | `MonthCalendar` properties and an event. (Part 1 of 2.)

MonthCalendar properties and an event	Description
MaxSelectionCount	The maximum number of dates that can be selected at once.
MinDate	The first date that can be selected.
MonthlyBoldedDates	An array of dates that will displayed in bold in the calendar.
SelectionEnd	The last of the dates selected by the user.
SelectionRange	The dates selected by the user.
SelectionStart	The first of the dates selected by the user.
Common MonthCalendar *Event*	
DateChanged	Generated when a date is selected in the calendar.

Fig. 14.50 | MonthCalendar properties and an event. (Part 2 of 2.)

14.15 DateTimePicker Control

The **DateTimePicker** control (see output of Fig. 14.52) is similar to the MonthCalendar control, but displays the calendar when the user clicks the down arrow. The DateTimePicker can be used to retrieve date and time information from the user. A DateTimePicker's **Value** property stores a DateTime, which always contains both date and time information. You can retrieve the date information alone by using **Date** property, and you can retrieve only the time information by using the **TimeOfDay** property. By default, this control stores the current date and time.

The DateTimePicker is also more customizable than a MonthCalendar control—more properties are provided to edit the look-and-feel of the drop-down calendar. Property **Format** specifies the user's selection options using the **DateTimePickerFormat** enumeration. The values in this enumeration are **Long** (displays the date in long format, as in **Thursday, July 10 2008**), **Short** (displays the date in short format, as in **7/10/2008**), **Time** (displays a time value, as in **5:31:02 PM**) and **Custom** (indicates that a custom format will be used). If value Custom is used, the display in the DateTimePicker is specified using property **CustomFormat**. The default event for this control is **ValueChanged**, which occurs when the selected value (whether a date or a time) is changed. DateTimePicker properties and a common event are summarized in Fig. 14.51.

DateTimePicker properties and an event	Description
DateTimePicker *Properties*	
CalendarForeColor	Sets the text color for the calendar.
CalendarMonthBackground	Sets the calendar's background color.

Fig. 14.51 | DateTimePicker properties and an event. (Part 1 of 2.)

DateTimePicker properties and an event	Description
`CustomFormat`	Sets the custom format string for the user's options.
`Date`	Sets the date.
`Format`	Sets the format of the date and/or time used for the user's options.
`MaxDate`	The maximum date and time that can be selected.
`MinDate`	The minimum date and time that can be selected.
`ShowCheckBox`	Indicates whether a `CheckBox` should be displayed to the left of the selected date and time.
`ShowUpDown`	Used to indicate that the control should have up and down `Buttons`. This is helpful for instances when the `DateTimePicker` is used to select a time—the `Buttons` can be used to increase or decrease hour, minute and second values.
`TimeOfDay`	Sets the time.
`Value`	The data selected by the user.
Common `DateTimePicker` *Event*	
`ValueChanged`	Generated when the `Value` property changes, including when the user selects a new date or time.

Fig. 14.51 | `DateTimePicker` properties and an event. (Part 2 of 2.)

Figure 14.52 demonstrates using the `DateTimePicker` control to select an item's drop-off date. Many companies use such functionality. For instance, several online DVD-rental companies specify the day a movie is sent out, and the estimated time that the movie will arrive at your home. In this application, the user selects a drop-off day, and then an estimated arrival date is displayed. The date is always two days after drop off, three days if a Sunday is reached (mail is not delivered on Sunday).

```
' Fig. 14.52: DateTimePickerForm.vb
' Using a DateTimePicker to select a drop off date.
Public Class DateTimePickerTest
   ' set DateTimePicker's MinDate and MaxDate properties
   Private Sub DateTimePickerTest_Load(ByVal sender As System.Object, _
      ByVal e As System.EventArgs) Handles MyBase.Load
      ' user cannot select days before today
      dropOffDateTimePicker.MinDate = DateTime.Today

      ' user can select days up to one year from now
      dropOffDateTimePicker.MaxDate = DateTime.Today.AddYears(1)
   End Sub ' DateTimePickerTest_Load

```

Fig. 14.52 | Demonstrating `DateTimePicker`. (Part 1 of 2.)

```
14     ' display delivery date
15     Private Sub dropOffDateTimePicker_ValueChanged( _
16        ByVal sender As System.Object, ByVal e As System.EventArgs) _
17        Handles dropOffDateTimePicker.ValueChanged
18
19        Dim dropOffDate As DateTime = dropOffDateTimePicker.Value
20
21        ' add an extra day when items are dropped off Friday-Sunday
22        If dropOffDate.DayOfWeek = DayOfWeek.Friday Or _
23           dropOffDate.DayOfWeek = DayOfWeek.Saturday Or _
24           dropOffDate.DayOfWeek = DayOfWeek.Sunday Then
25           ' estimate three days for delivery
26           outputLabel.Text = dropOffDate.AddDays(3).ToLongDateString()
27        Else ' otherwise estimate only two days for delivery
28           outputLabel.Text = dropOffDate.AddDays(2).ToLongDateString()
29        End If
30     End Sub ' dateTimePickerDropOff_ValueChanged
31  End Class ' DateTimePickerTest
```

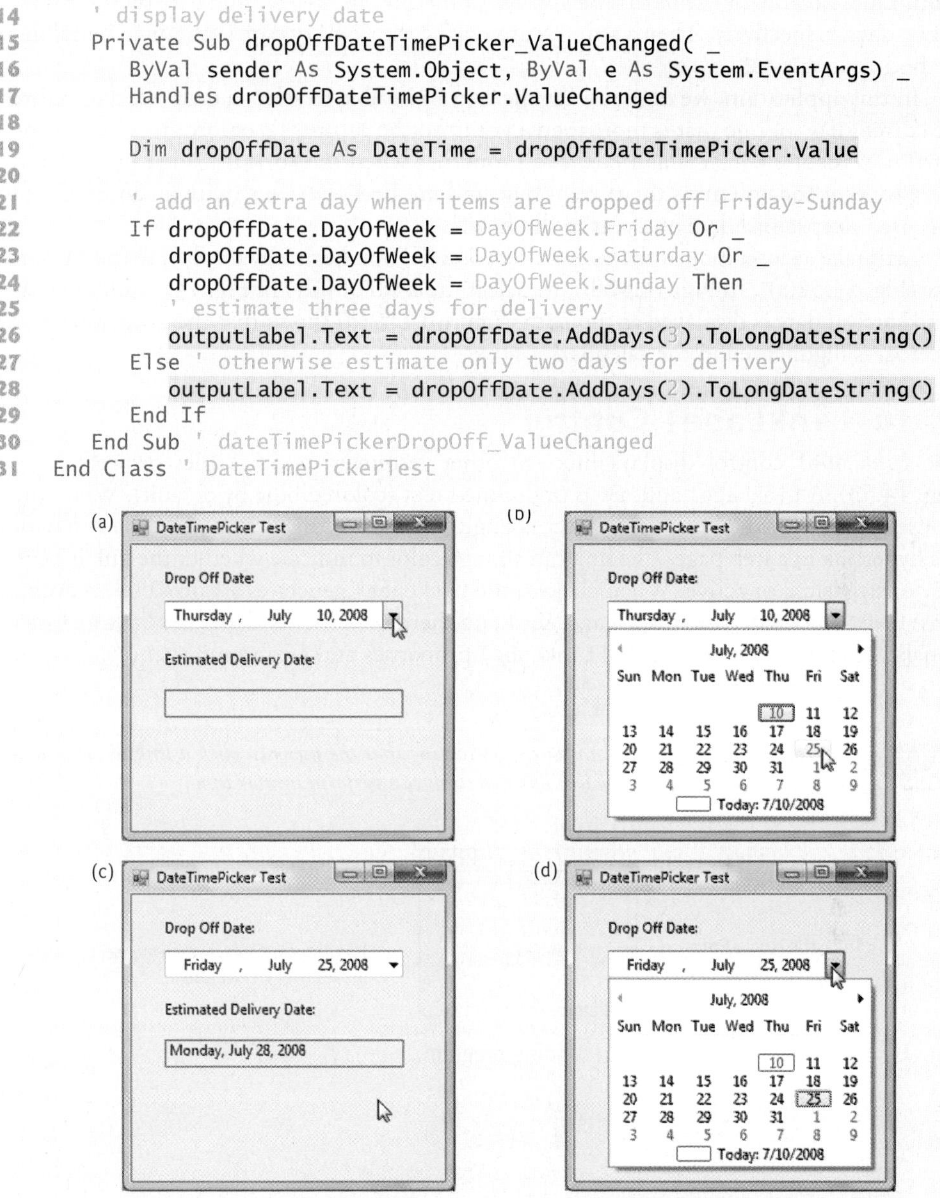

Fig. 14.52 | Demonstrating `DateTimePicker`. (Part 2 of 2.)

The `DateTimePicker` (`dropOffDateTimePicker`) has its `Format` property set to `Long`, so the user can select a date and not a time in this application. When the user selects a date, the `ValueChanged` event occurs. The event handler for this event (lines 15–30) first retrieves the selected date from the `DateTimePicker`'s **`Value`** property (line 19). Lines 22–24 use the `DateTime` structure's **`DayOfWeek`** property to determine the day of the week on which the selected date falls. The day values are represented using the **`DayOfWeek`** enumeration. Lines 26 and 28 use DateTime's AddDays method to increase the date by three days or two days, respectively. Then a string representing the delivery date is obtained by calling method ToLongDateString.

In this application, we do not want the user to be able to select a drop-off day before the current day, or one that is more than a year into the future. To enforce this, we set the DateTimePicker's MinDate and MaxDate properties when the Form is loaded (lines 8 and 11). Property Today returns the current day, and method AddYears (with an argument of 1) is used to specify a date one year in the future.

Let's take a closer look at the output. This application begins by displaying the current date (Fig. 14.52(a)). In Fig. 14.52(b), we select the 25th of July. In Fig. 14.52(c), the estimated arrival date is displayed as the 28th. Figure 14.52(d) shows that the 25th, after it is selected, is highlighted in the calendar.

14.16 LinkLabel Control

The LinkLabel control displays links to other resources, such as files or web pages (Fig. 14.53). A LinkLabel appears as underlined text (colored blue by default). When the mouse moves over the link, the pointer changes to a hand; this is similar to the behavior of a hyperlink in a web page. The link can change color to indicate whether the link is new, previously visited or active. When clicked, the LinkLabel generates a LinkClicked event. Class LinkLabel is derived from class Label and therefore inherits all of class Label's functionality. Figure 14.54 lists several LinkLabel properties and a common event.

Look-and-Feel Observation 14.10

A LinkLabel is the preferred control for indicating that the user can click a link to jump to a resource such as a web page, though other controls can perform similar tasks.

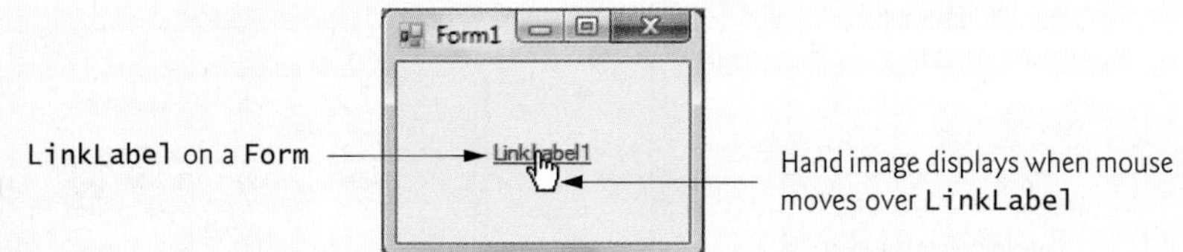

Fig. 14.53 | LinkLabel control in running program.

LinkLabel properties and an event	Description
Common Properties	
ActiveLinkColor	Specifies the color of the link when clicked.
LinkArea	Specifies which portion of text in the LinkLabel is part of the link.
LinkBehavior	Specifies the link's behavior, such as how the link appears when the mouse is placed over it.

Fig. 14.54 | LinkLabel properties and an event. (Part 1 of 2.)

LinkLabel properties and an event	Description
LinkColor	Specifies the original color of all links before they have been visited. The default color is set by the system, but is usually blue.
LinkVisited	If True, the link appears as though it has been visited (its color is changed to that specified by property VisitedLinkColor). The default value is False.
Text	Specifies the control's text.
UseMnemonic	If True, the & character can be used in the Text property to create a shortcut (similar to the *Alt* shortcut in menus).
VisitedLinkColor	Specifies the color of visited links. The default color is set by the system, but is usually purple.
Common Event (event argument type is LinkLabelLinkClickedEventArgs)	
LinkClicked	Generated when the link is clicked.

Fig. 14.54 | LinkLabel properties and an event. (Part 2 of 2.)

Class LinkLabelTestForm (Fig. 14.55) uses three LinkLabels to link to the C: drive, the Deitel web site (www.deitel.com) and the Notepad application, respectively. The Text properties of the LinkLabel's cDriveLinkLabel, deitelLinkLabel and notepadLinkLabel describe each link's purpose.

```
' Fig. 14.55: LinkLabelTestForm.vb
' Using LinkLabels to create hyperlinks.

Public Class LinkLabelTestForm
   ' browse C:\ drive
   Private Sub cDriveLinkLabel_LinkClicked(ByVal sender As _
      System.Object, ByVal e As LinkLabelLinkClickedEventArgs) _
      Handles cDriveLinkLabel.LinkClicked

      cDriveLinkLabel.LinkVisited = True ' change LinkColor after click
      Process.Start("C:\")
   End Sub ' cDriveLinkLabel_LinkClicked

   ' browse www.deitel.com in Internet Explorer
   Private Sub deitelLinkLabel_LinkClicked(ByVal sender As _
      System.Object, ByVal e As LinkLabelLinkClickedEventArgs) _
      Handles deitelLinkLabel.LinkClicked

      deitelLinkLabel.LinkVisited = True ' change LinkColor after click
      Process.Start("http://www.deitel.com")
   End Sub ' deitelLinkLabel_LinkClicked

```

Fig. 14.55 | LinkLabels used to link to a drive, a web page and an application. (Part 1 of 2.)

```
    ' run the Notepad application
    Private Sub notepadLinkLabel_LinkClicked(ByVal sender As _
       System.Object, ByVal e As LinkLabelLinkClickedEventArgs) _
       Handles notepadLinkLabel.LinkClicked

       notepadLinkLabel.LinkVisited = True ' change LinkColor after click
       Process.Start("notepad")
    End Sub ' notepadLinkLabel_LinkClicked
 End Class ' LinkLabelTestForm
```

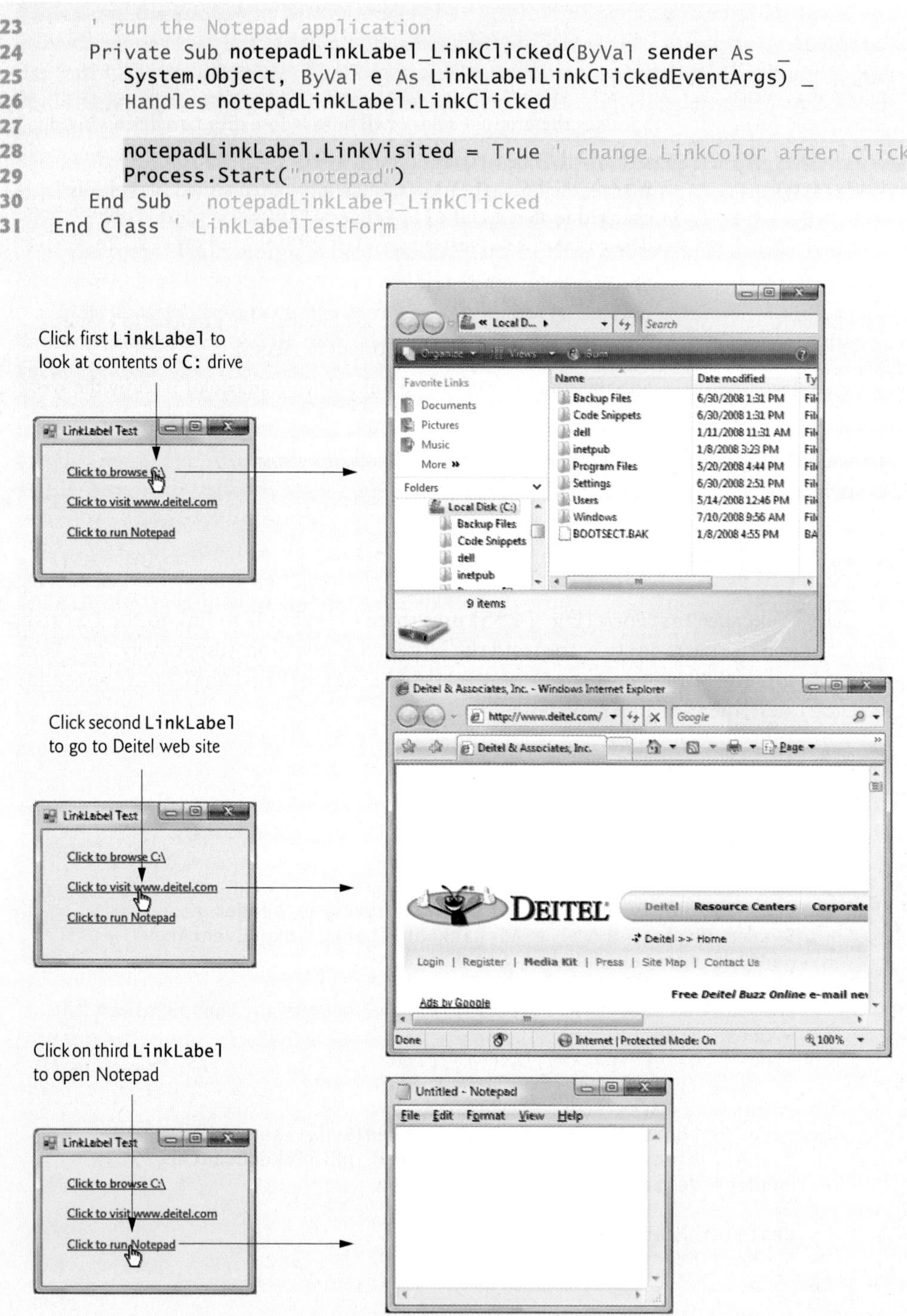

Fig. 14.55 | `LinkLabel`s used to link to a drive, a web page and an application. (Part 2 of 2.)

The event handlers for the LinkLabels call method Start of class Process (namespace System.Diagnostics), which allows you to execute other programs from an application. Method Start can take one argument, the file to open (a String), or two arguments, the application to run and its command-line arguments (two Strings). Method Start's arguments can be in the same form as if they were provided for input to the Windows **Run** command (**Start > Run...**). For applications that are known to Windows (such as Notepad), full path names are not required, and the .exe extension often can be omitted. To open a file that has a file type that Windows recognizes, simply use the file's full path name. The Windows operating system must be able to use the application associated with the given file's extension to open the file.

The event handler for cDriveLinkLabel's LinkClicked event browses the C: drive (lines 6–12). Line 10 sets the LinkVisited property to True, which changes the link's color from blue to purple (the LinkVisited colors can be configured through the **Properties** window in Visual Studio). The event handler then passes "C:\" to method Start (line 11), which opens a **Windows Explorer** window.

The event handler for deitelLinkLabel's LinkClicked event (lines 15–21) opens the web page www.deitel.com in the user's default Internet browser. We achieve this by passing the web page address as a String (line 20), which opens the web page. Line 19 sets the LinkVisited property to True.

The event handler for notepadLinkLabel's LinkClicked event (lines 24–30) opens the Notepad application. Line 28 sets the LinkVisited property to True so that the link appears as a visited link. Line 29 passes the argument "notepad" to method Start, which runs notepad.exe. Note that in line 29, the .exe extension is not required—Windows automatically recognizes the argument given to method Start as an executable file.

14.17 ListBox Control

The ListBox control allows the user to view and select from multiple items in a list. The CheckedListBox control (Section 14.18) extends a ListBox by including CheckBoxes next to each item in the list. This allows users to place checks on multiple items at once, as is possible with CheckBox controls. (Users also can select multiple items from a ListBox by setting the ListBox's SelectionMode property, which is discussed shortly.) Figure 14.56 displays a ListBox and a CheckedListBox. In both controls, scrollbars appear if the number of items exceeds the ListBox's viewable area.

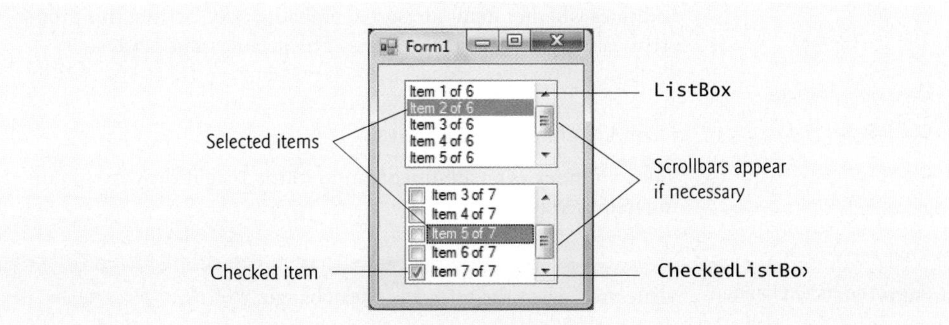

Fig. 14.56 | ListBox and CheckedListBox on a Form.

Figure 14.57 lists common `ListBox` properties and methods, and a common event. The `SelectionMode` property determines the number of items that can be selected. This property has the possible values `None`, `One`, `MultiSimple` and `MultiExtended` (from the `SelectionMode` enumeration)—the differences among these settings are explained in Fig. 14.57. The `SelectedIndexChanged` event occurs when the user selects a new item.

Both the `ListBox` and `CheckedListBox` have properties `Items`, `SelectedItem` and `SelectedIndex`. Property `Items` returns all the list items as an `ObjectCollection`. Many .NET GUI components (e.g., `ListBox`es) use collections to expose lists of internal objects (e.g., items contained within a `ListBox`). Property `SelectedItem` returns the `ListBox`'s currently selected item. If the user can select multiple items, use collection `SelectedItems` to obtain all the selected items as a collection. Property `SelectedIndex` returns the index

`ListBox` properties, methods and an event	Description
Common Properties	
`Items`	The collection of items in the `ListBox`.
`MultiColumn`	Indicates whether the `ListBox` can break a list into multiple columns, which eliminates vertical scrollbars from the display.
`SelectedIndex`	Returns the index of the selected item, or `-1` if no items have been selected. If the user selects multiple items, this property returns only one of the selected indices. For this reason, if multiple items are selected, you should use property `SelectedIndices`.
`SelectedIndices`	Returns a collection containing the indices of all selected items.
`SelectedItem`	Returns a reference to the selected item. If multiple items are selected, it returns the item with the lowest index number.
`SelectedItems`	Returns a collection of the selected item(s).
`SelectionMode`	Determines the number of items that can be selected and the means through which multiple items can be selected. Values `None`, `One`, `MultiSimple` (multiple selection allowed) or `MultiExtended` (multiple selection allowed using a combination of arrow keys or mouse clicks and *Shift* and *Ctrl* keys).
`Sorted`	Indicates whether items are sorted alphabetically. Setting this property's value to `True` sorts the items. The default value is `False`.
Common Methods	
`ClearSelected`	Deselects all items in the `ListBox`.
`GetSelected`	Takes an index as an argument, and returns `True` if the corresponding item is selected.
Common Event	
`SelectedIndexChanged`	Generated when the selected index changes.

Fig. 14.57 | `ListBox` properties, methods and an event.

of the selected item—if there could be more than one, use property `SelectedIndices`. If no items are selected, property `SelectedIndex` returns `-1`. Method `GetSelected` takes an index and returns `True` if the corresponding item is selected.

To add items to a `ListBox` or to a `CheckedListBox`, we must add objects to its `Items` collection. This can be accomplished by calling method `Add` to add a `String` to the `ListBox`'s or `CheckedListBox`'s `Items` collection. For example, we could write

myListBox`.Items.Add(` *myListItem* `)`

to add `String` *myListItem* to `ListBox` *myListBox*. To add multiple objects, you can either call method `Add` multiple times or call method `AddRange` to add an array of objects. Classes `ListBox` and `CheckedListBox` each call the submitted object's `ToString` method to determine the `Label` for the corresponding object's entry in the list. This allows you to add non-`String` objects to a `ListBox` or a `CheckedListBox` that later can be returned through properties `SelectedItem` and `SelectedItems`.

Alternatively, you can add items to `ListBoxes` and `CheckedListBoxes` visually by examining the `Items` property in the **Properties** window. Clicking the ellipsis button opens the **String Collection Editor**, which contains a text area for adding items; each item appears on a separate line (Fig. 14.58). Visual Studio then writes code to add these `Strings` to the `Items` collection inside method `InitializeComponent` in the `Form`'s `Designer.vb` file.

Figure 14.59 uses class `ListBoxTestForm` to add, remove and clear items from `ListBox displayListBox`. Class `ListBoxTestForm` uses `TextBox inputTextBox` to allow the user to enter new items. When the user clicks the **Add** `Button`, the new item appears in `displayListBox`. Similarly, if the user selects an item and clicks **Remove**, the item is deleted. When clicked, **Clear** deletes all entries in `displayListBox`. The user terminates the application by clicking **Exit**.

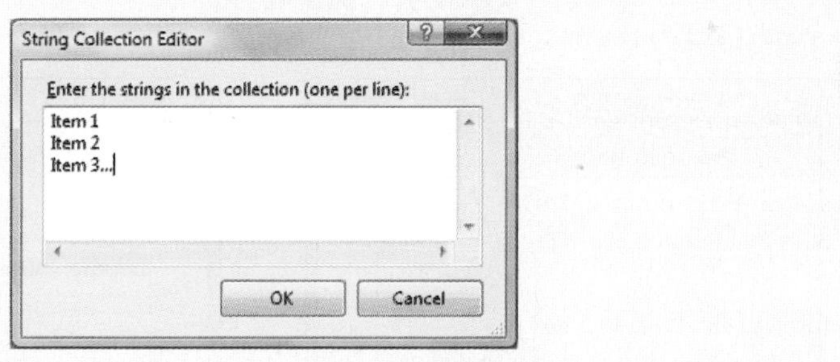

Fig. 14.58 | **String Collection Editor**.

```
' Fig. 14.59: ListBoxTestForm.vb
' Program to add, remove and clear ListBox items
Public Class ListBoxTestForm
   ' add to displayListBox the item the user enters in inputTextBox,
   ' then clear inputTextBox
   Private Sub addButton_Click(ByVal sender As System.Object, _
      ByVal e As System.EventArgs) Handles addButton.Click
```

Fig. 14.59 | Program that adds, removes and clears `ListBox` items. (Part 1 of 3.)

```

         displayListBox.Items.Add(inputTextBox.Text)
         inputTextBox.Clear()
      End Sub ' addButton_Click

      ' remove an item from displayListBox if one is selected
      Private Sub removeButton_Click(ByVal sender As System.Object, _
         ByVal e As System.EventArgs) Handles removeButton.Click

         ' if an item is selected, remove that item
         If displayListBox.SelectedIndex <> -1 Then
            displayListBox.Items.RemoveAt(displayListBox.SelectedIndex)
         End If
      End Sub ' removeButton_Click

      ' clear all the items in displayListBox
      Private Sub clearButton_Click(ByVal sender As System.Object, _
         ByVal e As System.EventArgs) Handles clearButton.Click

         displayListBox.Items.Clear()
      End Sub ' clearButton_Click

      ' terminate the application
      Private Sub exitButton_Click(ByVal sender As System.Object, _
         ByVal e As System.EventArgs) Handles exitButton.Click

         Application.Exit()
      End Sub ' exitButton_Click
   End Class ' ListBoxTestForm
```

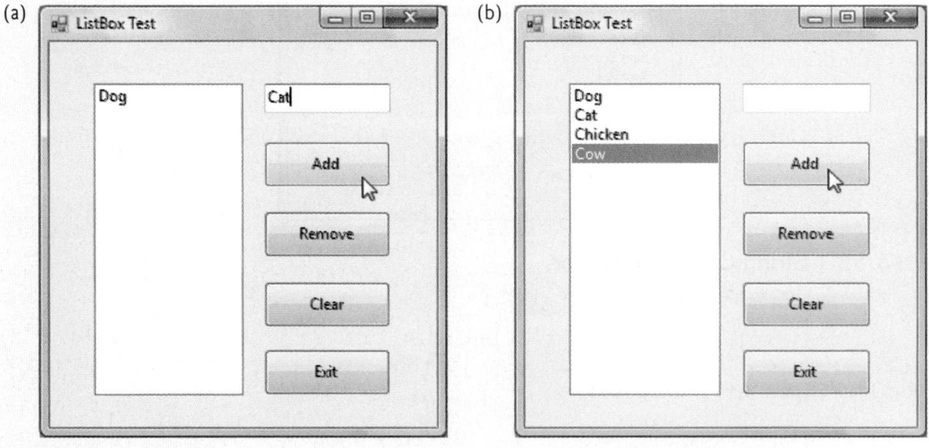

Fig. 14.59 | Program that adds, removes and clears `ListBox` items. (Part 2 of 3.)

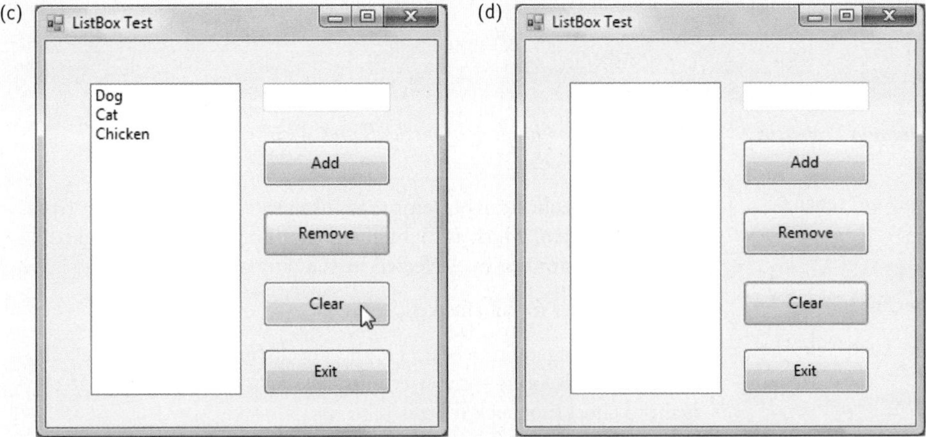

Fig. 14.59 | Program that adds, removes and clears `ListBox` items. (Part 3 of 3.)

The `addButton_Click` event handler (lines 6–11) calls method **Add** of the `ListBox`'s `Items` collection. This method takes an `Object` as the item to add to `displayListBox`. In this case, the `Object` used is the text entered by the user—`inputTextBox.Text` (line 9). After the item is added, `inputTextBox.Text` is cleared (line 10).

The `removeButton_Click` event handler (lines 14–21) uses method **RemoveAt** to remove an item from the `ListBox`. Lines 17–20 first use property `SelectedIndex` to determine which index is selected. If `SelectedIndex` is not `-1` (i.e., an item is selected) line 19 removes the item that corresponds to the selected index.

The `clearButton_Click` event handler (lines 24–28) calls method **Clear** of the `Items` collection (line 27) to remove all the entries in `displayListBox`. Finally, event handler `exitButton_Click` (lines 31–35) terminates the application by calling method `Application.Exit` (line 34).

14.18 CheckedListBox Control

The `CheckedListBox` control derives from class `ListBox` and includes a `CheckBox` next to each item. As in `ListBoxes`, items can be added via methods `Add` and `AddRange` or through the **String Collection Editor**. `CheckedListBoxes` imply that multiple items can be selected, and the only possible values for the `SelectionMode` property are `None` and `One`. `One` allows multiple selection, because `CheckBoxes` imply that there are no logical restrictions on the items—the user can select as many items as required. Thus, the only choice is whether to give the user multiple selection or no selection at all. This keeps the `CheckedListBox`'s behavior consistent with that of `CheckBoxes`. Figure 14.60 lists some common properties, a common method and a common event of class `CheckedListBox`.

Common Programming Error 14.1

*The IDE displays an error message if you attempt to set the `SelectionMode` property to `MultiSimple` or `MultiExtended` in the **Properties** window of a `CheckedListBox`. If this value is set programmatically, a runtime error occurs.*

CheckedListBox properties, methods and an event	Description
Common Properties	*(All the `ListBox` properties, methods and events are inherited by `CheckedListBox`.)*
`CheckedItems`	Contains the collection of items that are checked. This is distinct from the selected item, which is highlighted (but not necessarily checked). There can be at most one selected item at any given time.
`CheckedIndices`	Returns indices for all checked items.
`CheckOnClick`	If `True`, clicking an item selects it and checks/unchecks it. By default this property is `False`—the user must select an item, then click it again to check/uncheck it.
`SelectionMode`	Determines how many items can be checked. The only possible values are `One` (allows multiple checks to be placed) or `None` (does not allow any checks to be placed).
Common Method	
`GetItemChecked`	Takes an index and returns `True` if the corresponding item is checked.
Common Event (Event arguments `ItemCheckEventArgs`)	
`ItemCheck`	Generated when an item is checked or unchecked.
`ItemCheckEventArgs` Properties	
`CurrentValue`	Indicates whether the current item is checked or unchecked. Possible values are `Checked`, `Unchecked` and `Indeterminate`.
`Index`	Returns the zero-based index of the item that changed.
`NewValue`	Specifies the new state of the item.

Fig. 14.60 | `CheckedListBox` properties, a method and an event.

Event **`ItemCheck`** occurs when a user checks or unchecks a `CheckedListBox` item. Event argument properties `CurrentValue` and `NewValue` return `CheckState` values for the current and new state of the item, respectively. A comparison of these values allows you to determine whether the `CheckedListBox` item was checked or unchecked. The `CheckedListBox` control inherits the `SelectedItems` and `SelectedIndices` properties from class `ListBox`. It also includes properties `CheckedItems` and `CheckedIndices`, which return information about the checked items and indices.

In Fig. 14.61, class `checkedListBoxTestForm` uses a `CheckedListBox` and a `ListBox` to display a user's book selections. The `CheckedListBox` allows the user to select multiple titles. In the **String Collection Editor**, we added items for some Deitel books—C, C++, Internet & WWW, Java, VB 2008, Visual C# 2008, and Visual C++ 2008 (the acronym HTP stands for "How to Program"). The `ListBox` (named `displayListBox`) displays the user's selections.

```
1  ' Fig. 14.61: CheckedListBoxTestForm.vb
2  ' Using the checked ListBox to add items to a display ListBox
3  Public Class CheckedListBoxTestForm
4     ' add an item to or remove an item from lstDisplay
5     Private Sub itemCheckedListBox_ItemCheck( _
6        ByVal sender As System.Object, ByVal e As ItemCheckEventArgs) _
7        Handles itemCheckedListBox.ItemCheck
8
9        ' obtain selected item
10       Dim item As String = itemCheckedListBox.SelectedItem.ToString()
11
12       ' if the selected item is checked add it to displayListBox;
13       ' otherwise, remove it from displayListBox
14       If e.NewValue = CheckState.Checked Then
15          displayListBox.Items.Add(item)
16       Else
17          displayListBox.Items.Remove(item)
18       End If
19    End Sub ' itemCheckedListBox_ItemCheck
20 End Class ' CheckedListBoxTestForm
```

(a) (b) (c) (d)

Fig. 14.61 | CheckedListBox and ListBox used in a program to display a user selection.

When the user checks or unchecks an item in `itemCheckedListBox`, an `ItemCheck` event occurs and event handler `itemCheckedListBox_ItemCheck` (lines 5–19) executes. An `If...Else` statement (lines 14–18) determines whether the user checked or unchecked an item in the `CheckedListBox`. Line 14 uses the `ItemCheckEventArgs` property `NewValue` to determine whether the item is being checked (`CheckState.Checked`). If the user checks an item, line 15 adds the checked entry to `displayListBox`. If the user unchecks an item, line 17 removes the corresponding item from `displayListBox`. This event handler was created by selecting the `CheckedListBox` in **Design** mode, viewing the control's events in the **Properties** window and double clicking the `ItemCheck` event.

14.19 ComboBox Control

The ComboBox control combines `TextBox` features with a drop-down list—a GUI component that contains a list from which a value can be selected. A `ComboBox` usually appears as a TextBox with a down arrow to its right. By default, the user can enter text into the TextBox or click the down arrow to display a list of predefined items. If a user chooses an element from this list, that element is displayed in the TextBox. If the list contains more elements than can be displayed in the drop-down list, a scrollbar appears. The maximum number of items that a drop-down list can display at one time is set by property MaxDropDownItems. Figure 14.62 shows a sample ComboBox in three different states.

As with the ListBox control, you can add objects to collection Items programmatically, using methods Add and AddRange, or visually, with the **String Collection Editor.** Figure 14.63 lists common properties and a common event of class ComboBox.

Look-and-Feel Observation 14.11

Use a ComboBox to save space on a GUI. It has the disadvantage, however, that unlike with a ListBox, the user cannot see available items without expanding the drop-down list.

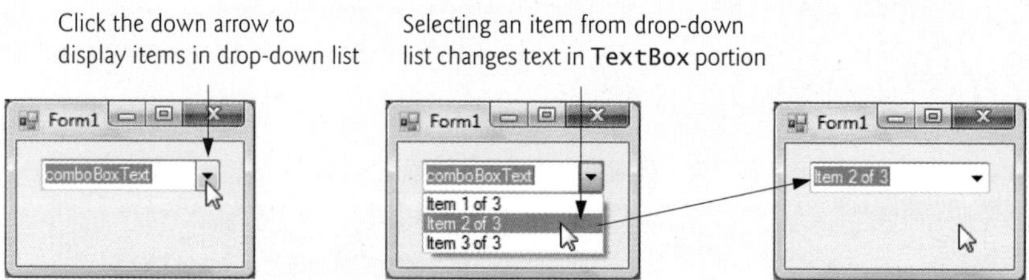

Fig. 14.62 | ComboBox demonstration.

ComboBox properties and an event	Description
Common Properties	
DropDownStyle	Determines the ComboBox type. Value Simple means that the text portion is editable, and the list portion is always visible. Value DropDown (the default) means that the text portion is editable, but the user must click an arrow button to see the list portion. Value DropDownList means that the text portion is not editable, and the user must click the arrow button to see the list portion.
Items	The collection of items in the ComboBox control.
MaxDropDownItems	Specifies the maximum number of items (between 1 and 100) that the drop-down list can display. If the number of items exceeds the maximum number of items to display, a scrollbar appears.
SelectedIndex	Returns the index of the selected item, or -1 if there is no selected item.
SelectedItem	Returns a reference to the selected item.
Sorted	Indicates whether items are sorted alphabetically. Setting this property's value to True sorts the items. The default is False.

Fig. 14.63 | ComboBox properties and an event. (Part 1 of 2.)

ComboBox properties and an event	Description
Common Event	
`SelectedIndexChanged`	Generated when the selected index changes (such as when a different item is selected). This is the default event when control is double clicked in the designer.

Fig. 14.63 | `ComboBox` properties and an event. (Part 2 of 2.)

Property **`DropDownStyle`** determines the type of `ComboBox` and is represented as a value of the **`ComboBoxStyle`** enumeration, which contains values `Simple`, `DropDown` and `DropDownList`. Option **`Simple`** does not display a drop-down arrow. Instead, a scrollbar appears next to the control, allowing the user to select a choice from the list. The user also can type in a selection. Style **`DropDown`** (the default) displays a drop-down list when the down arrow is clicked (or the down-arrow key is pressed). The user can type a new item in the `ComboBox`. The last style is **`DropDownList`**, which displays a drop-down list but does not allow the user to type in the `ComboBox`.

The `ComboBox` control has properties **`Items`** (a collection), **`SelectedItem`** and **`SelectedIndex`**, which are similar to the corresponding properties in `ListBox`. There can be at most one selected item in a `ComboBox`. If no items are selected, then `SelectedIndex` is `-1`. When the selected item changes, a **`SelectedIndexChanged`** event occurs.

Class `ComboBoxTestForm` (Fig. 14.64) allows users to select a shape to draw—circle, ellipse, square or pie (in both filled and unfilled versions)—by using a `ComboBox`. The `ComboBox` in this example is uneditable, so the user cannot type in the `ComboBox`.

Look-and-Feel Observation 14.12

Make lists (such as `ComboBox`es) editable only if the program is designed to accept user-submitted elements. Otherwise, the user might try to enter a custom item that is improper for the purposes of your application.

```
' Fig. 14.64: ComboBoxTest.vb
' Using ComboBox to select a shape to draw.
Public Class ComboBoxTest
   ' get index of selected shape, then draw the shape
   Private Sub imageComboBox_SelectedIndexChanged( _
      ByVal sender As System.Object, ByVal e As System.EventArgs) _
      Handles imageComboBox.SelectedIndexChanged
      ' create graphics object, Pen and SolidBrush
      Dim myGraphics As Graphics = MyBase.CreateGraphics()

      ' create Pen using color DarkRed
      Dim myPen As Pen = New Pen(Color.DarkRed)

      ' create SolidBrush using color DarkRed
      Dim mySolidBrush As SolidBrush = New SolidBrush(Color.DarkRed)
```

Fig. 14.64 | `ComboBox` used to draw a selected shape. (Part 1 of 2.)

```

         ' clear drawing area setting it to color white
         myGraphics.Clear(Color.White)

         ' find index, draw proper shape
         Select Case imageComboBox.SelectedIndex
            Case 0 ' case Circle is selected
               myGraphics.DrawEllipse(myPen, 50, 50, 150, 150)
            Case 1 ' case Rectangle is selected
               myGraphics.DrawRectangle(myPen, 50, 50, 150, 150)
            Case 2 ' case Ellipse is selected
               myGraphics.DrawEllipse(myPen, 50, 85, 150, 115)
            Case 3 ' case Pie is selected
               myGraphics.DrawPie(myPen, 50, 50, 150, 150, 0, 45)
            Case 4 ' case Filled Circle is selected
               myGraphics.FillEllipse(mySolidBrush, 50, 50, 150, 150)
            Case 5 ' case Filled Rectangle is selected
               myGraphics.FillRectangle(mySolidBrush, 50, 50, 150, 150)
            Case 6 ' case Filled Ellipse is selected
               myGraphics.FillEllipse(mySolidBrush, 50, 85, 150, 115)
            Case 7 ' case Filled Pie is selected
               myGraphics.FillPie(mySolidBrush, 50, 50, 150, 150, 0, 45)
         End Select

         myGraphics.Dispose() ' release the Graphics object
      End Sub ' imageComboBox_SelectedIndexChanged
   End Class ' ComboBoxTest
```

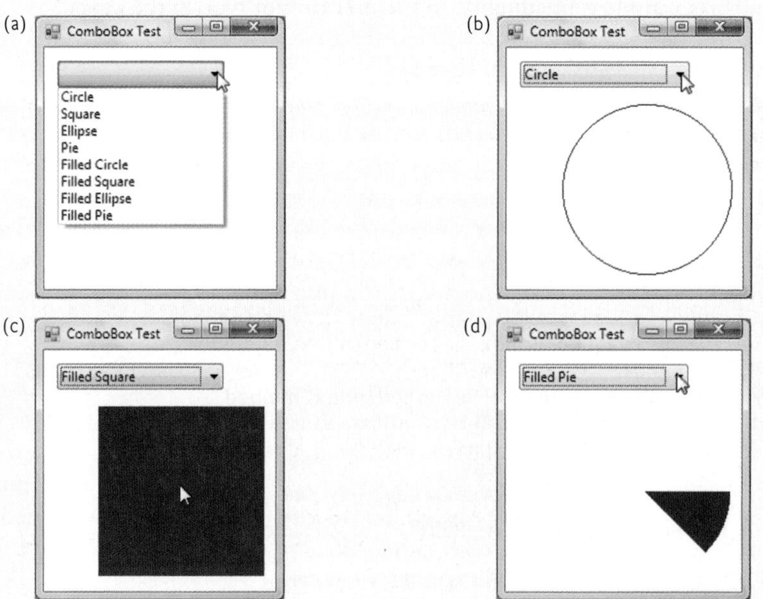

Fig. 14.64 | ComboBox used to draw a selected shape. (Part 2 of 2.)

After creating ComboBox imageComboBox, make it uneditable by setting its DropDownStyle to DropDownList in the **Properties** window. Next, add items Circle, Square, Ellipse, Pie, Filled Circle, Filled Square, Filled Ellipse and Filled Pie to the Items collection using the **String Collection Editor**. Whenever the user selects an item from cboImage, a SelectedIndexChanged event occurs and event handler cboImage_SelectedIndexChanged (lines 4–41) executes. Lines 8–15 create a Graphics object, a Pen and a SolidBrush, which are used to draw on the Form. The Graphics object (line 9) allows a pen or brush to draw on a component using one of several Graphics methods. The Pen object (line 12) is used by methods DrawEllipse, DrawRectangle and DrawPie (lines 23, 25, 27 and 29) to draw the outlines of their corresponding shapes. The SolidBrush object (line 15) is used by methods FillEllipse, FillRectangle and FillPie (lines 31, 33, 35 and 37) to fill their corresponding solid shapes. Line 18 colors the entire Form White, using Graphics method Clear.

The application draws a shape based on the selected item's index. The Select Case statement (lines 20–38) uses cboImage.SelectedIndex to determine which item the user selected. Graphics method DrawEllipse (line 23) takes a Pen, the *x*- and *y*-coordinates of the center and the width and height of the ellipse to draw. The origin of the coordinate system is in the upper-left corner of the Form; the *x*-coordinate increases to the right, and the *y*-coordinate increases toward the bottom of the Form. A circle is a special case of an ellipse with equal width and height. Line 23 draws a circle. Line 27 draws an ellipse that has different values for width and height.

Class Graphics method DrawRectangle (line 25) takes a Pen, the *x*- and *y*-coordinates of the upper-left corner and the width and height of the rectangle to draw. Method DrawPie (line 29) draws a pie as a portion of an ellipse. The ellipse is bounded by a rectangle. Method DrawPie takes a Pen, the *x*- and *y*-coordinates of the upper-left corner of the rectangle, its width and height, the start angle (in degrees) and the sweep angle (in degrees) of the pie. Angles increase clockwise. The FillEllipse (lines 31 and 35), FillRectangle (line 33) and FillPie (line 37) methods are similar to their unfilled counterparts, except that they take a SolidBrush instead of a Pen. Some of the drawn shapes are illustrated in the screen shots of Fig. 14.64.

14.20 TreeView Control

The TreeView control displays nodes hierarchically in a tree. Traditionally, nodes are objects that contain values and can refer to other nodes. A parent node contains child nodes, and the child nodes can be parents to other nodes. Two child nodes that have the same parent node are considered sibling nodes. A tree is a collection of nodes, usually organized in a hierarchical manner. The first parent node of a tree is the root node (a TreeView can have multiple roots). For example, the file system of a computer can be represented as a tree. The top-level directory (perhaps C:\) would be the root, each subfolder of C:\ would be a child node and each child folder could have its own children. TreeView controls are useful for displaying hierarchal information, such as the file structure that we just mentioned. We cover nodes and trees in greater detail in Chapter 24, Data Structures and Generic Collections. Figure 14.65 displays a sample TreeView control on a Form.

A parent node can be expanded or collapsed by clicking the plus box or minus box to its left. This box does not appear next to a node without children.

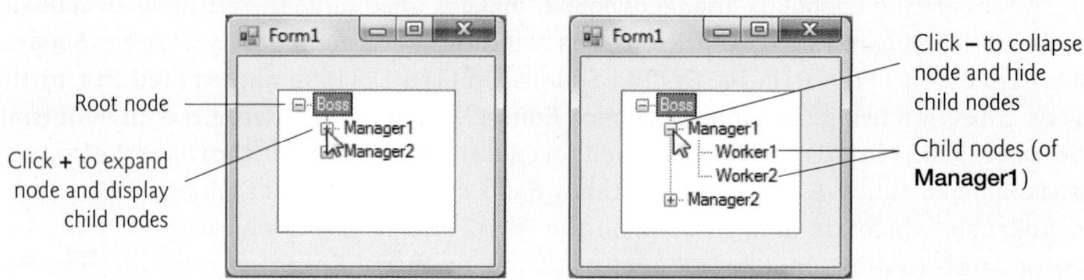

Fig. 14.65 | `TreeView` displaying a sample tree.

The nodes in a `TreeView` are instances of class **`TreeNode`**. Each `TreeNode` has a **`Nodes` collection** (type **`TreeNodeCollection`**), which contains a list of other `TreeNode`s—known as its children. The `Parent` property returns a reference to the parent node (or `Nothing` if the node is a root node). Figure 14.66 and Fig. 14.67 list the common properties of `TreeView`s and `TreeNode`s, common `TreeNode` methods and a common `TreeView` event.

`TreeView` properties and an event	Description
Common Properties	
`CheckBoxes`	Indicates whether `CheckBox`es appear next to nodes. A value of `True` displays `CheckBox`es. The default value is `False`.
`ImageList`	Specifies an `ImageList` object containing the node icons. An **`ImageList`** object is a collection that contains `Image` objects.
`Nodes`	Collection of `TreeNode`s with methods `Add` (adds a `TreeNode` object), `Clear` (deletes the entire collection) and `Remove` (deletes a specific node). Removing a parent node deletes all of its children.
`SelectedNode`	The selected node.
Common Event (Event arguments `TreeViewEventArgs`)	
`AfterSelect`	Generated after selected node changes.

Fig. 14.66 | `TreeView` properties and an event.

`TreeNode` properties and a methods	Description
Common Properties	
`Checked`	Indicates whether the `TreeNode` is checked (`CheckBoxes` property must be set to `True` in the parent `TreeView`).
`FirstNode`	Specifies the first node in the `Nodes` collection (i.e., the first child in the tree).

Fig. 14.67 | `TreeNode` properties and methods. (Part 1 of 2.)

TreeNode properties and a methods	Description
`FullPath`	Indicates the path of the node, starting at the root of the tree.
`ImageIndex`	Specifies the index of the image shown when the node is deselected.
`LastNode`	Specifies the `Nodes` collection's last node (i.e., the last child in the tree).
`NextNode`	Next sibling node.
`Nodes`	Collection of the current node's child `TreeNodes` (i.e., the current node's children). The `Nodes` collection has methods `Add` (adds a `TreeNode`), `Clear` (deletes the entire collection) and `Remove` (deletes a specific node). Removing a parent node deletes all of its children.
`Parent`	Parent node of the current node.
`PrevNode`	Previous sibling node.
`SelectedImageIndex`	Specifies the index of the image to use when the node is selected.
`Text`	Specifies the `TreeNode`'s text.
Common Methods	
`Collapse`	Collapses a node.
`Expand`	Expands a node.
`ExpandAll`	Expands all the children of a node.
`GetNodeCount`	Returns the number of child nodes.

Fig. 14.67 | `TreeNode` properties and methods. (Part 2 of 2.)

To add nodes to the `TreeView` visually, click the ellipsis next to the `Nodes` property in the **Properties** window. This opens the **TreeNode Editor** (Fig. 14.68), which displays an empty tree representing the `TreeView`. There are `Buttons` to create a root, and to add or delete a node. To the right are the properties of current node. Here you can rename the node and specify the text it should display.

To add nodes programmatically, first create a root node. Create a new `TreeNode` object and pass it a `String` to display. Then call method `Add` to add this new `TreeNode` to the `TreeView`'s `Nodes` collection. Thus, to add a root node to `TreeView` *myTreeView*, write

```
myTreeView.Nodes.Add(rootLabel)
```

where *myTreeView* is the `TreeView` to which we are adding nodes, and *rootLabel* is the text to display in *myTreeView*. To add children to a root node, add new `TreeNodes` to its `Nodes` collection. We select the appropriate root node from the `TreeView` by writing

```
myTreeView.Nodes(myIndex)
```

where *myIndex* is the root node's index in *myTreeView*'s `Nodes` collection. We add nodes to child nodes through the same process by which we added root nodes to *myTreeView*. To add a child to the root node at index *myIndex*, write

```
myTreeView.Nodes(myIndex).Nodes.Add(childNodeText)
```

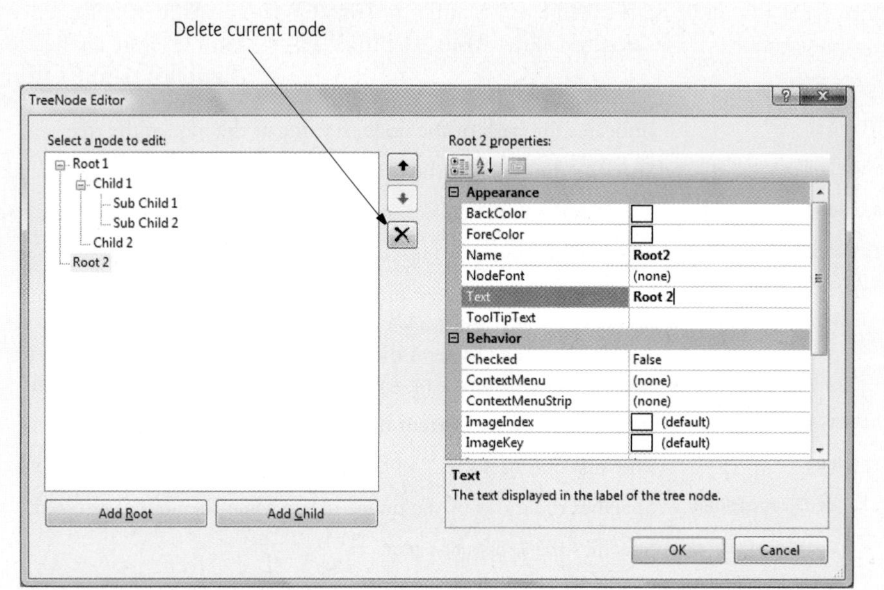

Fig. 14.68 | TreeNode Editor.

Class `TreeViewDirectoryStructureForm` (Fig. 14.69) uses a `TreeView` to display the contents of a directory chosen by the user. A `TextBox` and a `Button` are used to specify the directory. First, enter the full path of the directory you want to display. Then click the `Button` to set the specified directory as the root node in the `TreeView`. Each subdirectory of this directory becomes a child node. This layout is similar to the one used in **Windows Explorer**. Folders can be expanded or collapsed by clicking the plus or minus boxes that appear to their left.

When the user clicks the `enterButton`, all the nodes in `directoryTreeView` are cleared (line 10). Then the path entered in `inputTextBox` is used to create the root node. Line 16 adds the directory to `directoryTreeView` as the root node, and line 19 calls method `PopulateTreeView` (lines 28–61), which receives as arguments a directory (as a `String`) and a parent node (as a `TreeNode`). Method `PopulateTreeView` then creates child nodes corresponding to the subdirectories of the directory it receives as an argument.

```
 1  ' Fig. 14.69: TreeViewDirectoryStructureForm.vb
 2  ' Using TreeView to display directory structure.
 3  Imports System.IO
 4
 5  Public Class TreeViewDirectoryStructureForm
 6     ' clear directoryTreeView, then call PopulateTreeView
 7     Private Sub enterButton_Click(ByVal sender As System.Object, _
 8        ByVal e As System.EventArgs) Handles enterButton.Click
 9
10        directoryTreeView.Nodes.Clear() ' clear all nodes
```

Fig. 14.69 | `TreeView` used to display directories. (Part 1 of 3.)

```
      ' if the directory specified by the user exists, fill in the
      ' TreeView; otherwise, display an error message
      If (Directory.Exists(inputTextBox.Text)) Then
         ' add full path name to directoryTreeView
         directoryTreeView.Nodes.Add(inputTextBox.Text)

         ' insert subfolders
         PopulateTreeView(inputTextBox.Text, directoryTreeView.Nodes(0))
      Else ' display error MessageBox if directory not found
         MessageBox.Show(inputTextBox.Text & " could not be found.", _
            "Directory Not Found", MessageBoxButtons.OK, _
            MessageBoxIcon.Error)
      End If
   End Sub ' enterButton_Click

   ' populate current node with subdirectories
   Private Sub PopulateTreeView( _
      ByVal directoryValue As String, ByVal parentNode As TreeNode)
      ' array stores all subdirectories in the directory
      Dim directoryArray As String() = _
         Directory.GetDirectories(directoryValue)

      ' populate current node with subdirectories
      Try
         ' check to see if any subdirectories are present
         If directoryArray.Length <> 0 Then
            ' for every subdirectory, create new TreeNode,
            ' add as a child of current node and recursively
            ' populate child nodes with subdirectories
            For Each directory In directoryArray
               ' obtain last part of path name from the full path name
               ' by calling the GetFileNameWithoutExtension method of the
               ' Path class
               Dim directoryName As String = _
                  Path.GetFileNameWithoutExtension(directory)

               ' create TreeNode for current directory
               Dim myNode As TreeNode = New TreeNode(directoryName)

               ' add current directory node to parent node
               parentNode.Nodes.Add(myNode)

               ' recursively populate every subdirectory
               PopulateTreeView(directory, myNode)
            Next
         End If
      Catch e As UnauthorizedAccessException
         parentNode.Nodes.Add("Access denied")
      End Try
   End Sub ' PopulateTreeView
End Class ' TreeViewDirectoryStructureForm
```

Fig. 14.69 | TreeView used to display directories. (Part 2 of 3.)

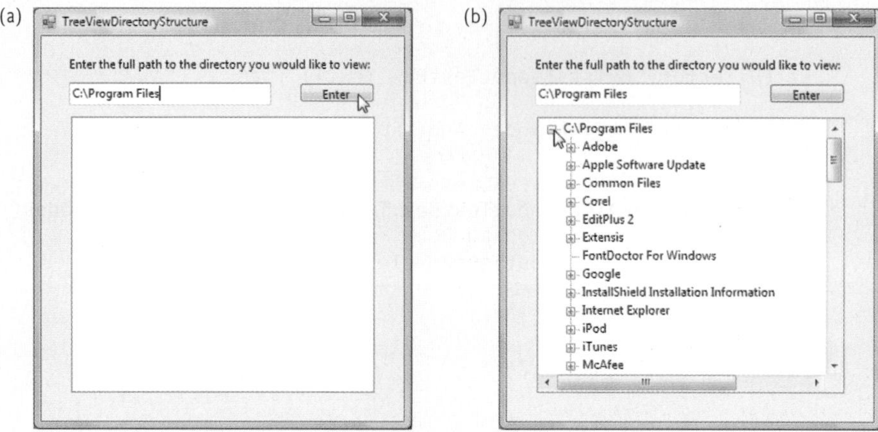

Fig. 14.69 | `TreeView` used to display directories. (Part 3 of 3.)

`PopulateTreeView` (lines 28–61) obtains a list of subdirectories, using method `GetDirectories` of class `Directory` (namespace `System.IO`) in lines 30–32. Method `GetDirectories` receives the current directory (as a `String`) and returns an array of `Strings` representing its subdirectories. If a directory is not accessible for security reasons, an `UnauthorizedAccessException` is thrown. Lines 58–60 catch this exception and add a node containing "`Access Denied`."

If there are accessible subdirectories, lines 45–46 use the `GetFileNameWithoutExtension` method of class `Path` to increase readability by shortening the full path name to just the directory name. Next, each `String` in the `directoryArray` is used to create a new child node (line 49). We use method `Add` (line 52) to add each child node to the parent. `PopulateTreeView` calls itself recursively on each subdirectory (line 55), which eventually populates the `TreeView` with the entire directory structure. Note that our recursive algorithm may cause a delay when the program loads directories with many subdirectories. However, once the folder names are added to the appropriate `Nodes` collection, they can be expanded and collapsed without delay. In the next section, we present an alternative algorithm to solve this problem.

14.21 ListView Control

The `ListView` control is similar to a `ListBox` in that both display lists from which the user can select one or more items (an example of a `ListView` can be found in Fig. 14.72). The important differences between the two classes are that a `ListView` can display icons next to the list items (controlled by its `ImageList` property) and display the details of items in columns. Property `MultiSelect` (a `Boolean`) determines whether multiple items can be selected. `CheckBoxes` can be included by setting property `CheckBoxes` (a `Boolean`) to `True`, making the `ListView` similar in appearance to a `CheckedListBox`. The `View` property specifies the layout of the `ListBox`. Property `Activation` determines the method by which the user selects a list item. Figure 14.70 presents some of the `ListView` class's common properties and its `ItemActivate` event.

ListView properties and an event	Description
Common Properties	
Activation	Determines how the user activates an item. This property takes a value in the ItemActivation enumeration. Possible values are OneClick (single-click activation), TwoClick (double-click activation, item changes color when selected) and Standard (double-click activation, item does not change color).
CheckBoxes	Indicates whether items appear with CheckBoxes. True displays CheckBoxes. The default is False.
LargeImageList	Specifies the ImageList containing large icons for display.
Items	Returns the collection of ListViewItems in the control.
MultiSelect	Determines whether multiple selection is allowed. The default is True, which enables multiple selection.
SelectedItems	Gets the collection of selected items.
SmallImageList	Specifies the ImageList containing small icons for display.
View	Determines appearance of ListViewItems. Possible values are LargeIcon (large icon displayed, items can be in multiple columns), SmallIcon (small icon displayed, items can be in multiple columns), List (small icons displayed, items appear in a single column), Details (like List, but multiple columns of information can be displayed per item) and Tile (large icons displayed, information provided to right of icon, valid only in Windows XP or later).
Common Event	
ItemActivate	Generated when an item in the ListView is activated. Does not contain the specifics of the item activated.

Fig. 14.70 | ListView properties and an event.

ListView allows you to define the images used as icons for ListView items. To display images, an ImageList component is required. Create one by dragging it to a Form from the **ToolBox**. Then select the **Images** property in the **Properties** window to display the **Image Collection Editor** (Fig. 14.71). Here you can browse for images that you wish to add to the ImageList, which contains an array of Images. Once the images have been defined, set property SmallImageList of the ListView to the new ImageList object. Property **SmallImageList** specifies the image list for the small icons. Property **LargeImageList** sets the ImageList for large icons. The items in a ListView are each of type **ListViewItem**. Icons for the ListView items are selected by setting the item's **ImageIndex** property to the appropriate index.

Class ListViewTestForm (Fig. 14.72) displays files and folders in a ListView, along with small icons representing each file or folder. If a file or folder is inaccessible because of permission settings, a MessageBox appears. The program scans the contents of the directory as it browses, rather than indexing the entire drive at once.

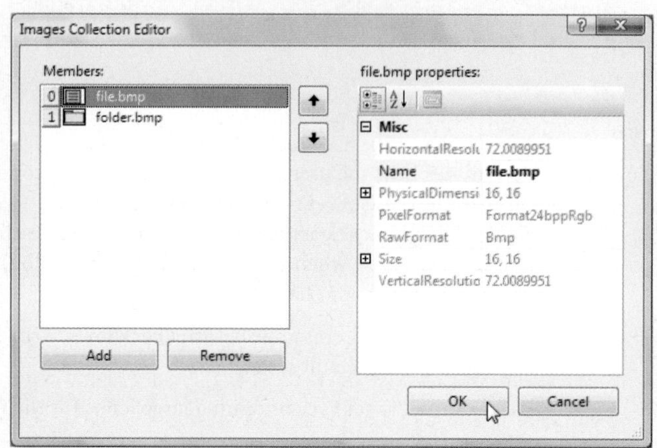

Fig. 14.71 | **Image Collection Editor** window for an `ImageList` component.

```
' Fig. 14.72: ListViewTestForm.vb
' Displaying directories and their contents in ListView.
Imports System.IO

Public Class ListViewTestForm
   ' store current directory
   Private currentDirectory As String = Directory.GetCurrentDirectory()

   ' display files/subdirectories of current directory
   ' (i.e., the one from which the application is executed)
   Private Sub ListViewTest_Load(ByVal sender As Object, _
      ByVal e As System.EventArgs) Handles Me.Load

      ' set Image list
      ' retrieve specific image from resources
      Dim folderImageResource = My.Resources.ResourceManager.GetObject( _
         "folder")
      Dim fileImageResource = My.Resources.ResourceManager.GetObject( _
         "file")

      ' convert picture resources to Images and load into PictureBoxes
      fileFolderImageList.Images.Add(CType(folderImageResource, Image))
      fileFolderImageList.Images.Add(CType(fileImageResource, Image))

      ' load current directory into browserListView
      LoadFilesInDirectory(currentDirectory)
      displayLabel.Text = currentDirectory
   End Sub ' ListViewTest_Load

   ' browse directory user clicked or go up one level
   Private Sub browserListView_Click(ByVal sender As System.Object, _
      ByVal e As System.EventArgs) Handles browserListView.Click
```

Fig. 14.72 | `ListView` displaying files and folders. (Part 1 of 4.)

```
         ' ensure an item is selected
         If browserListView.SelectedItems.Count <> 0 Then
            ' if first item selected, go up one level
            If browserListView.Items(0).Selected Then
               ' create DirectoryInfo object for directory
               Dim directoryObject As DirectoryInfo = _
                  New DirectoryInfo(currentDirectory)

               ' if directory has parent, load it
               If directoryObject.Parent IsNot Nothing Then
                  LoadFilesInDirectory(directoryObject.Parent.FullName)
                  displayLabel.Text = currentDirectory
               End If
            Else ' selected directory or file
               ' directory or file chosen
               Dim chosen As String = browserListView.SelectedItems(0).Text

               ' if item selected is directory, load selected directory
               If Directory.Exists( _
                  Path.Combine(currentDirectory, chosen)) Then

                  LoadFilesInDirectory( _
                     Path.Combine(currentDirectory, chosen)

                  ' update displayLabel
                  displayLabel.Text = currentDirectory
               End If
            End If
         End If
      End Sub ' browserListView_Click

      ' display files/subdirectories of current directory
      Private Sub LoadFilesInDirectory( _
         ByVal currentDirectoryValue As String)
         ' load directory information and display
         Try
            ' clear ListView and set first item
            browserListView.Items.Clear()
            browserListView.Items.Add("Go Up One Level")

            ' update current directory
            currentDirectory = currentDirectoryValue
            Dim newCurrentDirectory As DirectoryInfo = _
               New DirectoryInfo(currentDirectory)

            ' put files and directories into arrays
            Dim directoryArray As DirectoryInfo() = _
               newCurrentDirectory.GetDirectories()
            Dim fileArray As FileInfo() = newCurrentDirectory.GetFiles()

```

Fig. 14.72 | ListView displaying files and folders. (Part 2 of 4.)

```
            ' add directory names to ListView
            For Each dir In directoryArray
               ' add directory to ListView
               Dim newDirectoryItem As ListViewItem = _
                  browserListView.Items.Add(dir.Name)

               newDirectoryItem.ImageIndex = 0 ' set directory image
            Next

            ' add file names to ListView
            For Each file In fileArray
               ' add file to ListView
               Dim newFileItem As ListViewItem = _
                  browserListView.Items.Add(file.Name)

               newFileItem.ImageIndex = 1 ' set file image
            Next
         Catch e As UnauthorizedAccessException
            MessageBox.Show("Warning: Some files may not be " & _
               "visible due to permission settings", _
               "Attention", 0, MessageBoxIcon.Warning)
         End Try
      End Sub ' LoadFilesInDirectory
   End Class ' ListViewTestForm
```

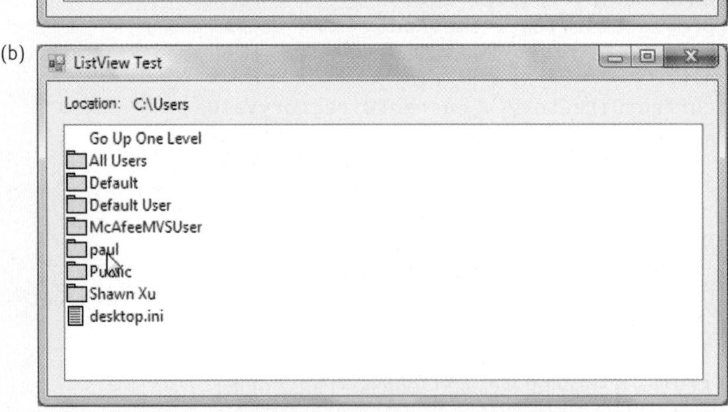

Fig. 14.72 | `ListView` displaying files and folders. (Part 3 of 4.)

(c) 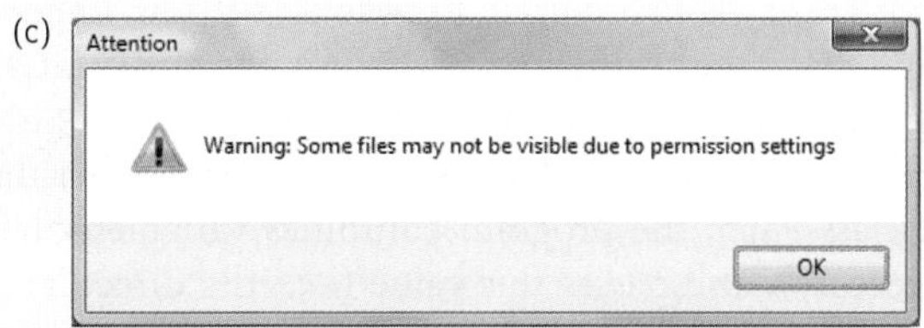

Fig. 14.72 | `ListView` displaying files and folders. (Part 4 of 4.)

To display icons beside list items, create an `ImageList` for the `ListView` `browserListView`. First, drag and drop an `ImageList` on the `Form` and open the **Image Collection Editor**. Select our two simple bitmap images, provided in the `bin\Debug` and `bin\Release` folders of this example—one for a folder (array index `0`) and the other for a file (array index `1`). Then set the object `browserListView` property `SmallImageList` to the new `ImageList` in the **Properties** window.

Method `LoadFilesInDirectory` (lines 65–105) populates `browserListView` with the directory passed to it (`currentDirectoryValue`). It clears `browserListView` and adds the element `"Go Up One Level"`. When the user clicks this element, the program attempts to move up one level (we see how shortly). The method then creates a `DirectoryInfo` object initialized with the `String currentDirectory` (lines 75–76). If you do not have permission to browse the directory, an exception is thrown (and caught in line 100). Method `LoadFilesInDirectory` works differently from method `PopulateTreeView` in the previous program (Fig. 14.69). Rather than loading the names of all the folders on the hard drive, method `LoadFilesInDirectory` loads only the names of folders in the current directory. In this example, we also load the names of the files in the current directory.

Class **`DirectoryInfo`** (namespace `System.IO`) makes it easy to browse or manipulate the directory structure. Method **`GetDirectories`** (line 80) returns an array of `DirectoryInfo` objects containing the subdirectories of the current directory. Similarly, method **`GetFiles`** (line 81) returns an array of class **`FileInfo`** objects containing the files in the current directory. Property **`Name`** (of both class `DirectoryInfo` and class `FileInfo`) contains only the directory or file name, such as `Users` instead of `C:\Users`. To access the full name and location, use property **`FullName`**.

Lines 84–90 and lines 93–99 iterate through the subdirectories and files of the current directory and add them to `browserListView`. Lines 89 and 98 set the `ImageIndex` properties of the newly created items. If an item is a directory, we set its icon to a directory icon (index `0`); if an item is a file, we set its icon to a file icon (index `1`).

Method `browserListView_Click` (lines 31–62) responds when the user clicks control `browserListView`. Line 34 checks whether anything is selected. If a selection has been made, line 36 determines whether the user chose the first item in `browserListView`. The first item in `browserListView` is always **Go Up One Level**; if it is selected, the program attempts to go up a level. Lines 37–39 create a `DirectoryInfo` object for the current directory. Line 42 tests property `Parent` to ensure that the user is not at the root of the directory tree. Property **`Parent`** indicates the parent directory as a `DirectoryInfo` object; if no parent directory exists, `Parent` returns the value `Nothing`. If a parent directory does exist, then line 43 passes the full name of the parent directory to method `LoadFilesInDirectory`, and line 44 displays the new current directory's name.

If the user did not select the first item in browserListView, lines 48–59 allow the user to continue navigating through the directory structure. Line 48 creates String chosen and assigns it the text of the selected item (the first item in collection SelectedItems). Lines 51–52 determine whether the user selected a valid directory (rather than a file). Using the Combine method of class Path, the program combines variables currentDirectory and chosen (the new directory), and passes this value (i.e., the directory's full name) to class Directory's method Exists. Note the that Combine method automaticallys adds a backslash (\), if necessary, between the two pieces. Method Exists returns True if its String parameter is a directory. In this case, the program passes the directory's name to method LoadFilesInDirectory. Finally, displayLabel is updated to display the new directory (line 58).

This program loads quickly, because it displays the names of only the current directory's contents. This means that a small delay may occur each time you choose another directory. However, changes that occur in the directory structure while this program executes will appear when you reload a directory. The previous program (Fig. 14.69) may have a large initial delay as it loads an entire directory structure, but the program displays directory contents with no delay once the directory structure is loaded. Also, that program does not dynamically show directory structure changes—you would need to execute the program again. Trade-offs of this kind are typical in the software world.

Software Engineering Observation 14.5

When designing applications that run for long periods of time, you might choose a large initial delay to improve performance throughout the rest of the program. However, in applications that run for only short periods, developers often prefer fast initial loading times and small delays after each action.

14.22 TabControl Control

The TabControl control creates tabbed windows, such as the ones we have seen in Visual Studio (Fig. 14.73). Tabs allow you to organize more complex GUIs. TabControls contain TabPage objects, similar to Panels and GroupBoxes, on which you can place controls. Figure 14.74 depicts a sample TabControl.

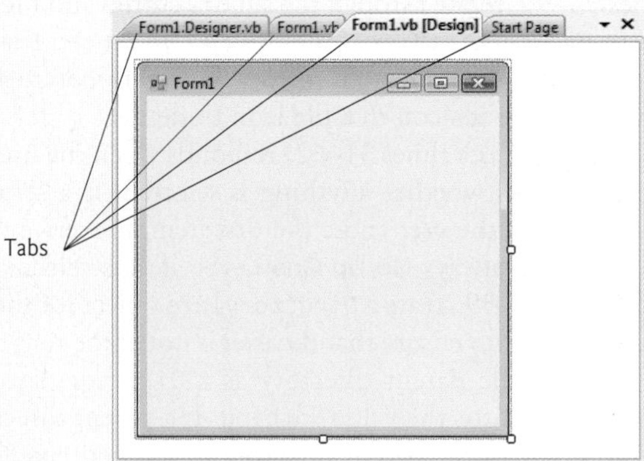

Fig. 14.73 | Tabbed windows in Visual Studio.

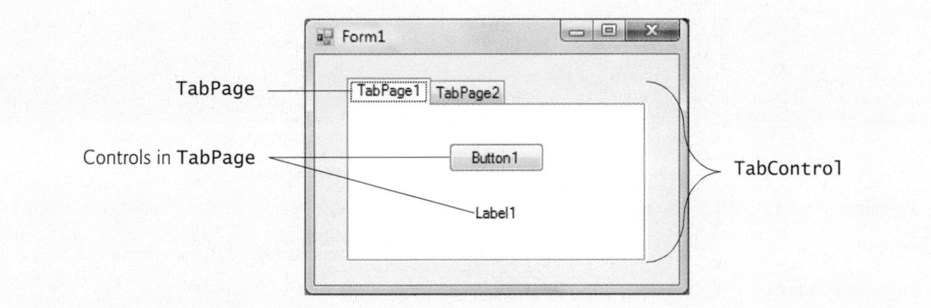

Fig. 14.74 | TabControl with TabPages example.

You can add TabControls visually by dragging and dropping them onto a Form in **Design** mode. To add TabPages in **Design** mode, right click the TabControl and select **Add Tab** (Fig. 14.75). Alternatively, click the TabPages property in the **Properties** window, and add tabs in the dialog that appears. To change a tab label, set the Text property of the TabPage. Note that clicking the tabs selects the TabControl—to select the TabPage, click the control area underneath the tabs. You can add controls to the TabPage by dragging and dropping items from the **ToolBox**. To view different TabPages (in **Design** mode or when the program is running), simply click the appropriate tab. When a TabPage is clicked at execution time, it generates a Click event. To create the event handler for this event, double click the body of a TabPage in **Design** mode. Common properties and a common event of TabControls are described in Fig. 14.76.

You can add controls to a TabPage object and add TabPages to a TabControl object programmatically, with statements like

```
myTabPage.Controls.Add(myControl)
myTabControl.TabPages.Add(myTabPage)
```

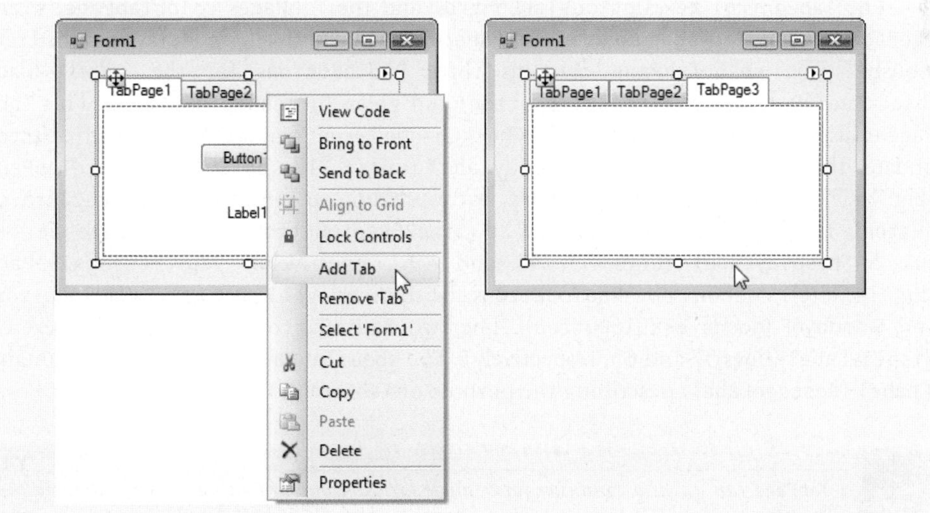

Fig. 14.75 | TabPages added to a TabControl.

TabControl properties and an event	Description
Common Properties	
ImageList	Specifies images to be displayed on tabs.
ItemSize	Specifies the tab size.
Multiline	Indicates whether multiple rows of tabs can be displayed.
SelectedIndex	Index of the selected TabPage.
SelectedTab	The selected TabPage.
TabCount	Returns the number of tab pages.
TabPages	Collection of TabPages within the TabControl.
Common Event	
SelectedIndexChanged	Generated when SelectedIndex changes (i.e., another TabPage is selected).

Fig. 14.76 | TabControl properties and an event.

These statements call method Add of the Controls collection and method Add of the TabPages colection. The first statement adds a control to TabPage *myTabPage*, and the second statement adds *myTabPage* to TabControl *myTabControl.* Alternatively, you can use method AddRange to add an array of controls or TabPages to a TabPage or TabControl, respectively.

Class UsingTabsForm (Fig. 14.77) uses a TabControl to display various options related to the text on a label (**Color, Size** and **Message**). The last TabPage displays an **About** message, which describes how TabControls are used.

The TabControl textOptionsTabControl and the TabPages colorTabPage, sizeTabPage, messageTabPage and aboutTabPage are created in the designer (as described previously). The colorTabPage contains three RadioButtons for the colors—black (blackRadioButton), red (redRadioButton) and green (greenRadioButton). This TabPage is displayed in Fig. 14.77(a). The CheckChanged event handler for each RadioButton updates the color of the text in displayLabel (lines 9, 17 and 25). The sizeTabPage (Fig. 14.77(b)) has three RadioButtons, corresponding to font sizes 12 (size12RadioButton), 16 (size16RadioButton) and 20 (size20RadioButton), which change the font size of displayLabel (lines 33, 41 and 49, respectively). The messageTabPage (Fig. 14.77(c)) contains two RadioButtons for the messages **Hello!** (helloRadioButton) and **Goodbye!** (goodbyeRadioButton). The two RadioButtons determine the text on displayLabel (lines 57 and 65, respectively). The aboutTabPage (Fig. 14.77(d)) contains a Label (messageLabel) describing the purpose of TabControls.

Software Engineering Observation 14.6

A TabPage can act as a container for a single logical group of RadioButtons, enforcing their mutual exclusivity. To place multiple RadioButton groups inside a single TabPage, group the RadioButtons within Panels or GroupBoxes and attach these containers to the TabPage.

```
' Fig. 14.77: UsingTabsForm.vb
' Using TabControl to display various font settings.
Public Class UsingTabsForm
   ' event handler for Black RadioButton
   Private Sub blackRadioButton_CheckedChanged( _
      ByVal sender As System.Object, ByVal e As System.EventArgs) _
      Handles blackRadioButton.CheckedChanged

      displayLabel.ForeColor = Color.Black ' change font color to black
   End Sub ' blackRadioButton_CheckedChanged

   ' event handler for Red RadioButton
   Private Sub redRadioButton_CheckedChanged( _
      ByVal sender As System.Object, ByVal e As System.EventArgs) _
      Handles redRadioButton.CheckedChanged

      displayLabel.ForeColor = Color.Red ' change font color to red
   End Sub ' redRadioButton_CheckedChanged

   ' event handler for Green RadioButton
   Private Sub greenRadioButton_CheckedChanged( _
      ByVal sender As System.Object, ByVal e As System.EventArgs) _
      Handles greenRadioButton.CheckedChanged

      displayLabel.ForeColor = Color.Green ' change font color to green
   End Sub ' greenRadioButton_CheckedChanged

   ' event handler for 12 point RadioButton
   Private Sub size12RadioButton_CheckedChanged( _
      ByVal sender As System.Object, ByVal e As System.EventArgs) _
      Handles size12RadioButton.CheckedChanged
      ' change font size to 12
      displayLabel.Font = New Font(displayLabel.Font.Name, 12)
   End Sub ' size12RadioButton_CheckedChanged

   ' event handler for 16 point RadioButton
   Private Sub size16RadioButton_CheckedChanged( _
      ByVal sender As System.Object, ByVal e As System.EventArgs) _
      Handles size16RadioButton.CheckedChanged
      ' change font size to 16
      displayLabel.Font = New Font(displayLabel.Font.Name, 16)
   End Sub ' size16RadioButton_CheckedChanged

   ' event handler for 20 point RadioButton
   Private Sub size20RadioButton_CheckedChanged( _
      ByVal sender As System.Object, ByVal e As System.EventArgs) _
      Handles size20RadioButton.CheckedChanged
      ' change font size to 20
      displayLabel.Font = New Font(displayLabel.Font.Name, 20)
   End Sub ' size20RadioButton_CheckedChanged

```

Fig. 14.77 | TabControl used to display various font settings. (Part 1 of 2.)

```
    ' event handler for Hello! RadioButton
    Private Sub helloRadioButton_CheckedChanged( _
       ByVal sender As System.Object, ByVal e As System.EventArgs) _
       Handles helloRadioButton.CheckedChanged

       displayLabel.Text = "Hello!" ' change text to Hello!
    End Sub ' helloRadioButton_CheckedChanged

    ' event handler for Goodbye! RadioButton
    Private Sub goodbyeRadioButton_CheckedChanged( _
       ByVal sender As System.Object, ByVal e As System.EventArgs) _
       Handles goodbyeRadioButton.CheckedChanged

       displayLabel.Text = "Goodbye!" ' change text to Goodbye!
    End Sub ' goodbyeRadioButton_CheckedChanged
End Class ' UsingTabsForm
```

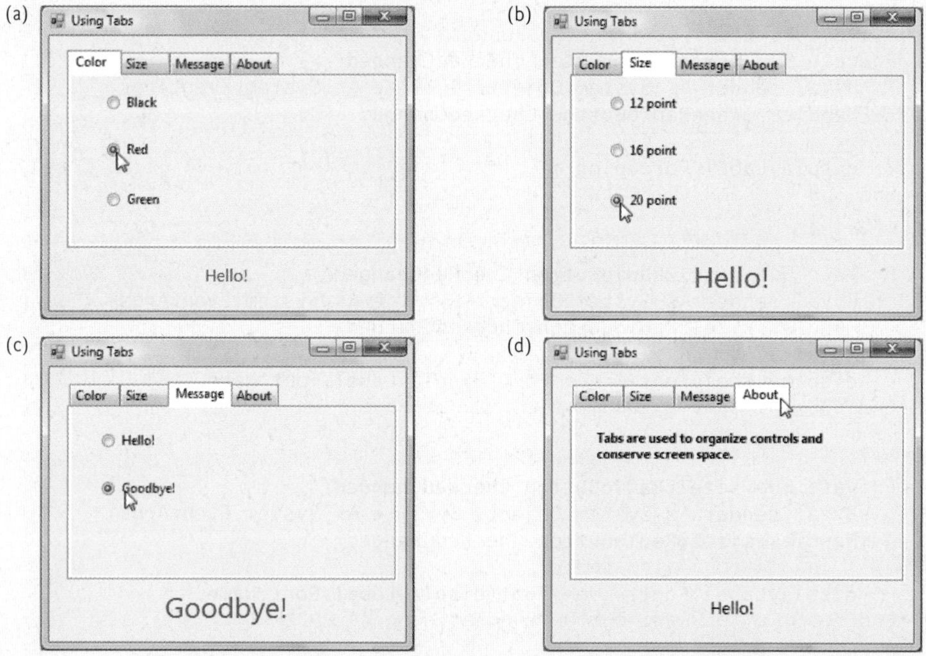

Fig. 14.77 | `TabControl` used to display various font settings. (Part 2 of 2.)

14.23 Multiple Document Interface (MDI) Windows

In previous chapters, we have built only single document interface (SDI) applications. Such programs (including Microsoft's Notepad and Paint) can support only one open window or document at a time. SDI applications usually have limited abilities—Paint and Notepad, for example, have limited image- and text-editing features. To edit multiple documents, the user must execute another instance of the SDI application.

Most recent applications have multiple document interfaces (MDIs), which allow users to edit multiple documents at once—for example, graphics applications like Corel PaintShop Pro and Adobe Photoshop allow you to edit multiple images at once. MDI programs also tend to be more complex—PaintShop Pro and Photoshop have a greater number of image-editing features than does Paint.

The main application window of an MDI program is called the parent window, and each window inside the application is referred to as a child window. Although an MDI application can have many child windows, there is only one parent window. Furthermore, a maximum of one child window can be active at once. Child windows cannot be parents themselves and cannot be moved outside their parent. In all other ways (closing, minimizing, resizing, etc.), a child window behaves like any other window. A child window's functionality can be different from the functionality of other child windows of the parent. For example, one child window might allow the user to edit images, another might allow the user to edit text and a third might display network traffic graphically, but all could belong to the same MDI parent. Figure 14.78 depicts a sample MDI application.

To create an MDI `Form`, create a new `Form` and set its `IsMdiContainer` property to `True`. The `Form` changes appearance, as in Fig. 14.79.

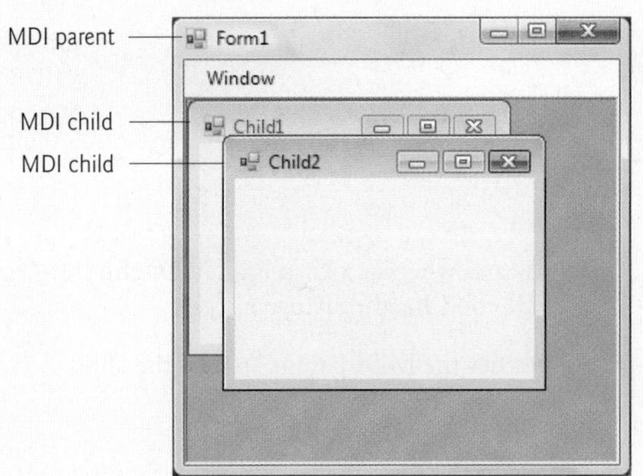

Fig. 14.78 | MDI parent window and MDI child windows.

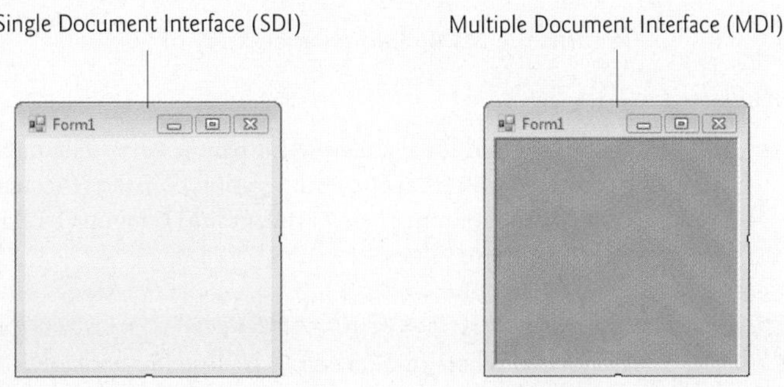

Fig. 14.79 | SDI and MDI forms.

Next, create a child Form class to be added to the Form. To do this, right click the project in the **Solution Explorer**, select **Add > Windows Form...** and name the file. Edit the Form as you like. To add the child Form to the parent, we must create a new child Form object, set its MdiParent property to the parent Form and call the child Form's Show method. In general, to add a child Form to a parent, you would write

```
Dim childForm As New ChildFormClass()
childForm.MdiParent = parentForm
childForm.Show()
```

In most cases, the parent Form creates the child, so the *parentForm* reference is Me. The code to create a child usually resides in an event handler, which creates a new window in response to a user action. Menu selections (such as **File > New > Window**) are commonly used to create new child windows.

Class Form property MdiChildren returns an array of child Form references. This is useful if the parent window wants to check the status of all its children (for example, ensuring that all are saved before the parent closes). Property ActiveMdiChild returns a reference to the active child window; it returns Nothing if there are no active child windows. Other features of MDI windows are described in Fig. 14.80.

MDI Form properties, a method and an event	Description
Common MDI Child Properties	
IsMdiChild	Indicates whether a Form is an MDI child. If True, the Form is an MDI child (read-only property).
MdiParent	Specifies the MDI parent Form of the child.
Common MDI Parent Properties	
ActiveMdiChild	Returns the Form that is the currently active MDI child (returns Nothing if no children are active).
IsMdiContainer	Indicates whether a Form can be an MDI parent. If True, the Form can be an MDI parent. The default value is False.
MdiChildren	Returns the MDI children as an array of Forms.
Common Method	
LayoutMdi	Arranges child forms in an MDI parent Form. The method takes as a parameter an MdiLayout enumeration constant (ArrangeIcons, Cascade, TileHorizontal or TileVertical). Figure 14.83 depicts the effects of these values.
Common Event	
MdiChildActivate	Generated when an MDI child is closed or activated.

Fig. 14.80 | MDI Form properties, a method and an event.

Child windows can be minimized, maximized and closed independent of the parent window. Figure 14.81 shows two images—one containing two minimized child windows and a second containing a maximized child window. When the parent is minimized or closed, the child windows are minimized or closed as well. Note that the title bar in Fig. 14.81(b) is **Form1 - [Child2]**. When a child window is maximized, its title bar text is inserted into the parent window's title bar. When a child window is minimized or maximized, its title bar displays a restore icon, which can be used to return the child window to its previous size (i.e., its size before it was minimized or maximized).

Visual Basic provides a property that helps track which child windows are open in an MDI container. Property `MdiWindowListItem` of class `MenuStrip` specifies which menu, if any, displays a list of open child windows. When a new child window is opened, an entry is added to the list (as in the first screen of Figure 14.82). If nine or more child windows are open, the list includes the option **More Windows...**, which allows the user to select a window from a list in a dialog.

Good Programming Practice 14.2

When creating MDI applications, include a menu that displays a list of the open child windows. This helps the user select a child window quickly, rather than having to search for it in the parent window.

MDI containers allow you to organize child windows by calling method `LayoutMdi` of the parent `Form`. Method `LayoutMdi` receives as its argument one of the `MdiLayout` enumeration constants—`ArrangeIcons`, `Cascade`, `TileHorizontal` and `TileVertical`. Tiled windows completely fill the parent and do not overlap; such windows can be arranged horizontally (value `TileHorizontal`) or vertically (value `TileVertical`). Cascaded windows (value `Cascade`) overlap—each is the same size and displays a visible title bar, if possible. Value `ArrangeIcons` arranges the icons for any minimized child windows. If minimized windows are scattered around the parent window, value `ArrangeIcons` orders them neatly at the bottom-left corner of the parent window. Figure 14.83 illustrates the values of the `MdiLayout` enumeration.

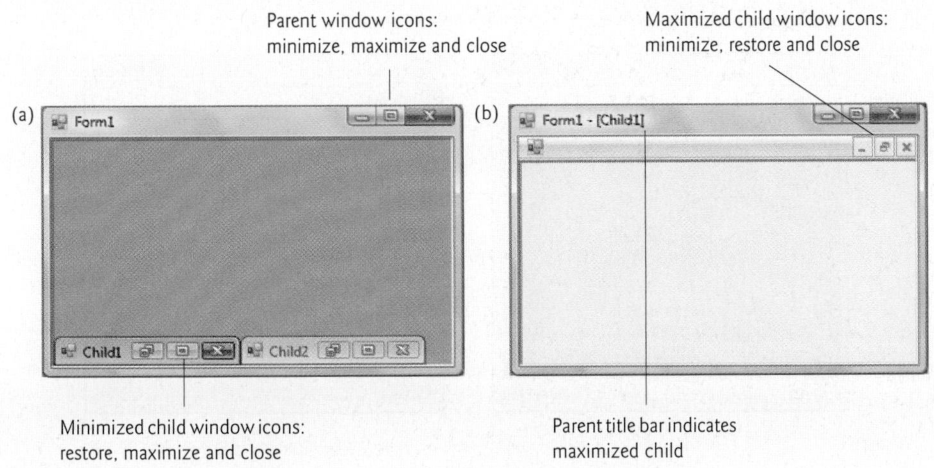

Fig. 14.81 | Minimized and maximized child windows.

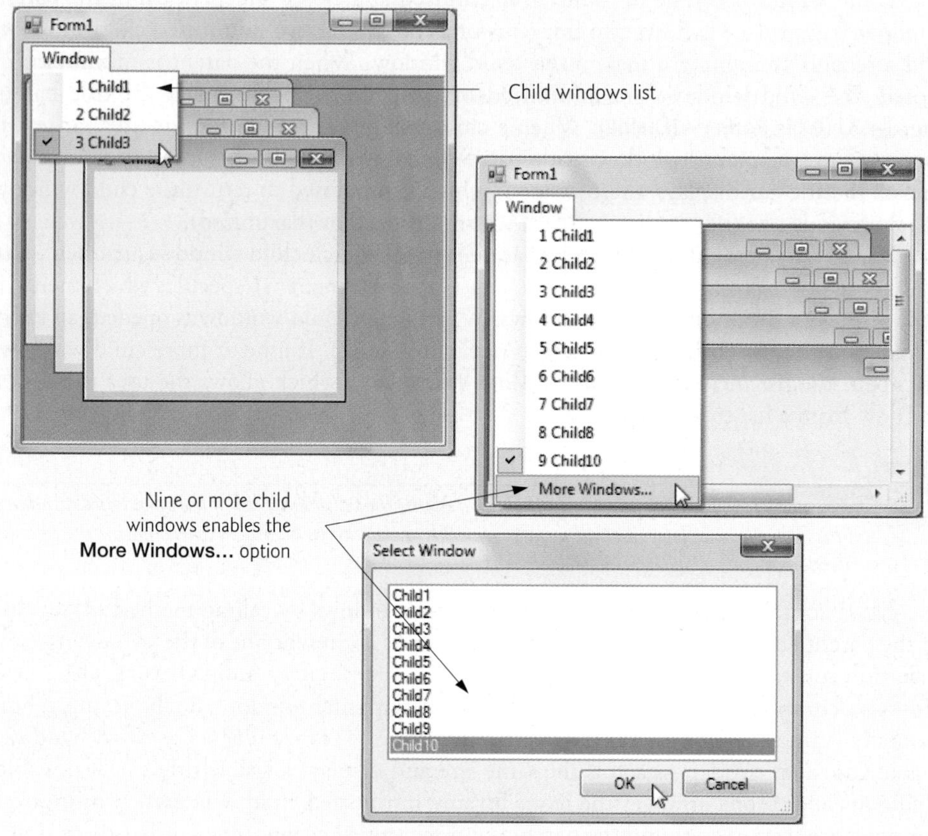

Fig. 14.82 | `MenuStrip` property `MdiWindowListItem` example.

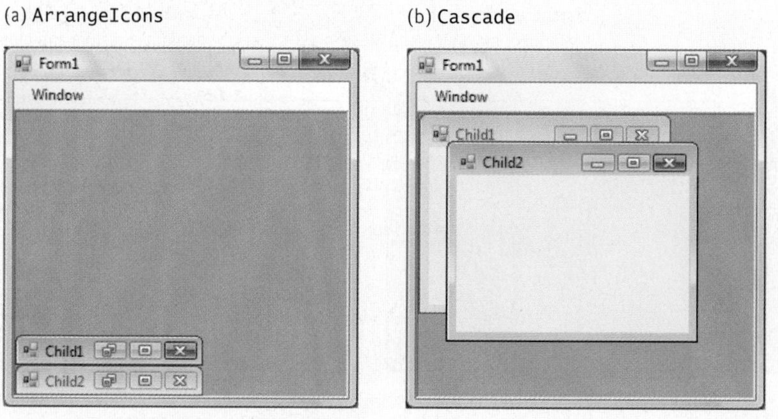

Fig. 14.83 | `MdiLayout` enumeration values. (Part 1 of 2.)

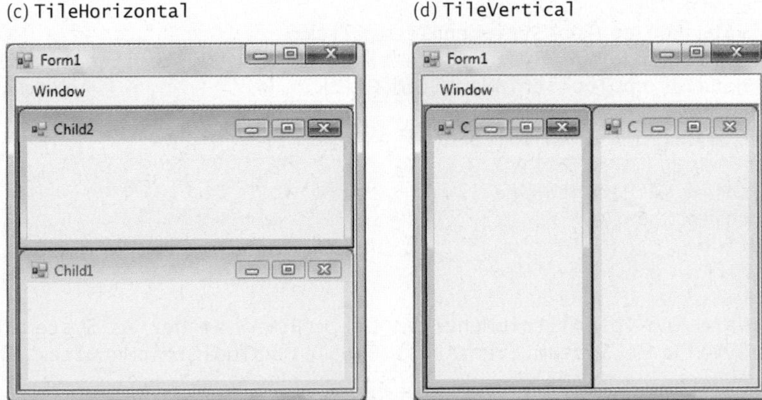

Fig. 14.83 | `MdiLayout` enumeration values. (Part 2 of 2.)

Class `UsingMDIForm` (Fig. 14.84) demonstrates MDI windows. Class `UsingMDIForm` uses three instances of child `ChildForm` (Fig. 14.85), each containing a `PictureBox` that displays an image. The parent MDI `Form` contains menus that enable users to create and arrange child `Forms`.

UsingMDIForm

Figure 14.84 presents class `UsingMDIForm`—the application's MDI parent `Form`. This `Form`, which is created first, contains two top-level menus. The first of these menus, **File** (`fileToolStripMenuItem`), contains both an **Exit** item (`exitToolStripMenuItem`) and a **New** submenu (`newToolStripMenuItem`) consisting of items for each child window. The second menu, **Window** (`windowToolStripMenuItem`), provides options for laying out the MDI children, plus a list of the active MDI children.

In the **Properties** window, we set the `Form`'s `IsMdiContainer` property to `True`, making the `Form` an MDI parent. In addition, we set the `MenuStrip`'s `MdiWindowListItem` property to `windowToolStripMenuItem` so that the **Window** menu can list the open MDI child windows.

```
' Fig. 14.84: UsingMDI.vb
' MDI parent and child windows.
Public Class UsingMDIForm
   ' create Visual C# image window
   Private Sub csToolStripMenuItem_Click(ByVal sender As System.Object, _
      ByVal e As System.EventArgs) Handles csToolStripMenuItem.Click
      ' create new child
      Dim child As New ChildForm("Visual C# 2008 How to Program", _
         "vcs2008htp")
      child.MdiParent = Me ' set parent
      child.Show() ' display child
   End Sub ' csToolStripMenuItem_Click

```

Fig. 14.84 | MDI parent-window class. (Part 1 of 3.)

```
   ' create Visual C++ image window
   Private Sub cppToolStripMenuItem_Click( _
      ByVal sender As System.Object, ByVal e As System.EventArgs) _
      Handles cppToolStripMenuItem.Click
      ' create new child
      Dim child As New ChildForm("Visual C++ 2008 How to Program", _
         "vcpp2008htp")
      child.MdiParent = Me ' set parent
      child.Show() ' display child
   End Sub ' cppToolStripMenuItem_Click

   ' create Visual Basic window
   Private Sub vbToolStripMenuItem_Click(ByVal sender As System.Object, _
      ByVal e As System.EventArgs) Handles vbToolStripMenuItem.Click
      ' create new child
      Dim child As New ChildForm("Visual Basic 2008 How to Program", _
         "vb2008htp")
      child.MdiParent = Me ' set parent
      child.Show() ' display child
   End Sub ' vbToolStripMenuItem_Click

   ' exit application
   Private Sub exitToolStripMenuItem_Click( _
      ByVal sender As System.Object, ByVal e As System.EventArgs) _
      Handles exitToolStripMenuItem.Click

      Application.Exit()
   End Sub ' exitToolStripMenuItem_Click

   ' set Cascade layout
   Private Sub cascadeToolStripMenuItem_Click( _
      ByVal sender As System.Object, ByVal e As System.EventArgs) _
      Handles cascadeToolStripMenuItem.Click

      Me.LayoutMdi(MdiLayout.Cascade)
   End Sub ' cascadeToolStripMenuItem_Click

   ' set TileHorizontal layout
   Private Sub tileHorizontalToolStripMenuItem_Click( _
      ByVal sender As System.Object, ByVal e As System.EventArgs) _
      Handles tileHorizontalToolStripMenuItem.Click

      Me.LayoutMdi(MdiLayout.TileHorizontal)
   End Sub ' tileHorizontalToolStripMenuItem_Click

   ' set TileVertical layout
   Private Sub tileVerticalToolStripMenuItem_Click( _
      ByVal sender As System.Object, ByVal e As System.EventArgs) _
      Handles tileVerticalToolStripMenuItem.Click

      Me.LayoutMdi(MdiLayout.TileVertical)
   End Sub ' tileVerticalToolStripMenuItem_Click
End Class ' UsingMDIForm
```

Fig. 14.84 | MDI parent-window class. (Part 2 of 3.)

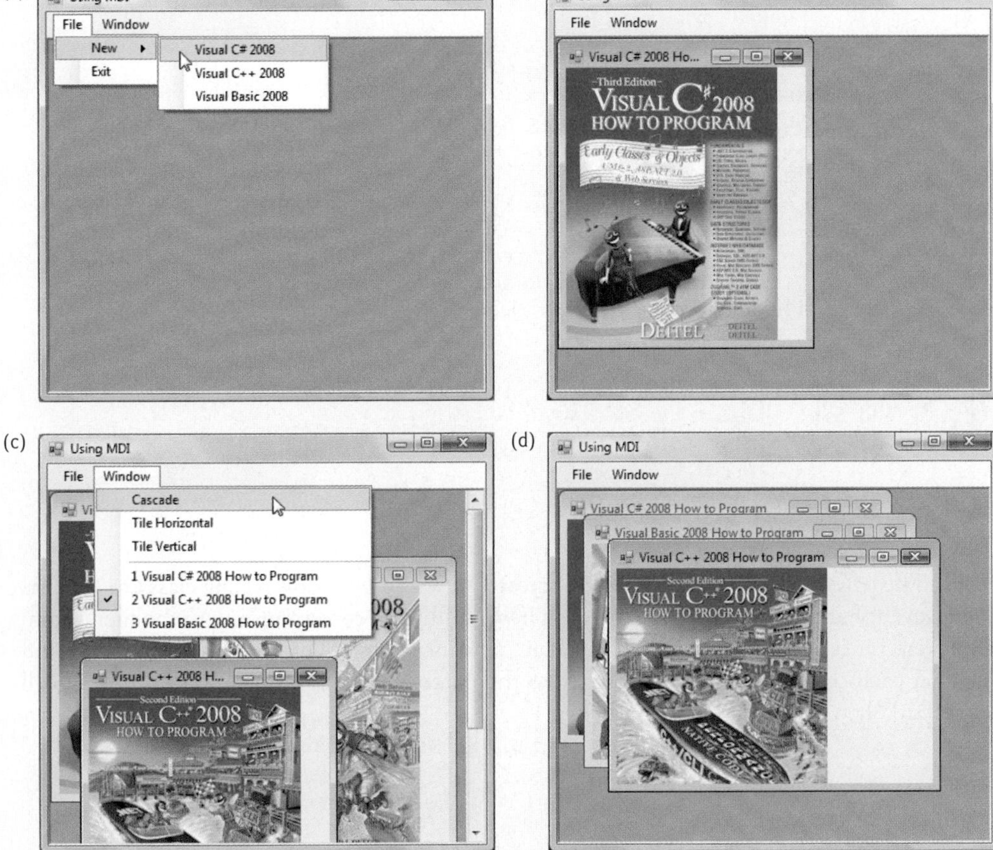

Fig. 14.84 | MDI parent-window class. (Part 3 of 3.)

The **Cascade** menu item's (`cascadeToolStripMenuItem`) event handler (lines 43–49) cascades the child windows by calling the parent `Form`'s `LayoutMdi` method with the argument `MdiLayout.Cascade` (line 48). The **Tile Horizontal** menu item's (`tileHorizontalToolStripMenuItem`) event handler (lines 51–57) arranges the child windows horizontally by calling the parent `Form`'s `LayoutMdi` method with the argument `MdiLayout.TileHorizontal` (line 56). Finally, the **Tile Vertical** menu item's (`tileVerticalToolStripMenuItem`) event handler (lines 59–65) arranges the child windows vertically by calling the parent `Form`'s `LayoutMdi` method with the argument `MdiLayout.TileVertical` (line 64).

`ChildForm`

At this point, the application is still incomplete—we must define the MDI child class. To do this, right click the project in the **Solution Explorer** and select **Add > Windows Form....** Then name the new class in the dialog as `ChildForm` (Fig. 14.85). Next, add a `PictureBox` (`displayPictureBox`) to `ChildForm`. In the constructor, line 9 sets the title bar text. In lines 11–16, we retrieve the appropriate image file (`fileName`) as a resource, convert it to an `Image`, and set `displayPicture`'s `Image` property.

```
' Fig. 14.85: ChildForm.vb
' Child window of MDI parent.
Imports System.IO

Public Class ChildForm
   Public Sub New(ByVal title As String, ByVal fileName As String)
      ' ensure that Designer generated code executes
      InitializeComponent()
      Text = title ' set title text

      ' retrieve specific image from resources
      Dim pictureResource = My.Resources.ResourceManager.GetObject( _
         fileName)

      ' convert pictureResource to image type and load into PictureBox
      displayPictureBox.Image = CType(pictureResource, Image)
   End Sub ' New
End Class ' ChildForm
```

Fig. 14.85 | MDI child `FrmChild`.

The parent MDI `Form` (Fig. 14.84) creates new child windows using class `ChildForm`. The event handlers in lines 5–33 create a new child `Form` corresponding to the menu item clicked. Lines 8–9, 19–20 and 29–30 create new instances of `ChildForm`. Lines 10, 21 and 31 set each child's `MdiParent` property to the parent `Form` (`Me`). Lines 11, 22 and 32 call method `Show` to display each child `Form`.

14.24 Visual Inheritance

Chapter 11 discussed how to create classes by inheriting from other classes. We have also used inheritance to create `Form`s that display a GUI, by deriving our new `Form` classes from class `System.Windows.Forms.Form` (the code that indicates the inheritance relationship appears in the `Form`'s `Designer.vb` file). This is an example of visual inheritance. The derived `Form` class contains the functionality of its `Form` base class, including any base-class properties, methods, variables and controls. The derived class also inherits all visual aspects—such as size, component layout, spacing between GUI components, colors and fonts—from its base class.

Visual inheritance enables you to achieve visual consistency across your applications by giving them a common look-and-feel. This also reduces the learning curve as your users move between applications. For example, you could define a base `Form` that contains a product's logo, a specific background color, a predefined menu bar and other elements. You then could use the base `Form` throughout an application for uniformity and branding.

Class `VisualInheritanceForm` (Fig. 14.86) derives from `Form`. The output depicts the workings of the `Form`. The GUI contains two `Label`s with the text **Bugs, Bugs, Bugs** and **Copyright 2006, by Deitel & Associates, Inc.**, as well as one `Button` displaying the text **Learn More**. When a user presses the **Learn More** `Button`, the event handler `learnMoreButton_Click` (lines 4–12) displays a `MessageBox` that provides some informative text.

```
' Fig. 14.86: VisualInheritanceForm.vb
' Base Form for use with visual inheritance.
Public Class VisualInheritanceForm
   ' display MessageBox when Button is clicked
   Private Sub learnMoreButton_Click(ByVal sender As System.Object, _
      ByVal e As System.EventArgs) Handles learnMoreButton.Click

      MessageBox.Show( _
         "Bugs, Bugs, Bugs is a product of Deitel & Associates, Inc.", _
         "Learn More", MessageBoxButtons.OK, _
         MessageBoxIcon.Information)
   End Sub ' learnMoreButton_Click
End Class ' VisualInheritanceForm
```

Fig. 14.86 | Class `FrmVisualInheritance`, which inherits from class `Form`, contains a `Button` (**Learn More**).

To allow other `Forms` to inherit from `VisualInheritanceForm`, we must package it as a class library in a `.dll` file. To do so, right click the project name in the **Solution Explorer** and select **Properties**, then choose the **Application** tab. In the **Application type** drop-down list, change **Windows Application** to **Class Library**. Building the project produces the `.dll`. The name of the solution that contains `VisualInheritanceForm` becomes parts of the class's fully qualified name—in this case, `VisualInheritance.FrmVisualInheritance`. [*Note:* A class library cannot be executed as a standalone application. The screenshots in Fig. 14.86 were taken before changing the project to be a class library.]

To visually inherit from `VisualInheritanceForm`, first create a new Windows application. In this application, add a reference to the `.dll` you just created (located in the `bin/Release` folder of the solution containing Fig. 14.86). Then open the `Designer.vb` file for the new application's `Form` and modify the line

```
Inherits System.Windows.Forms.Form
```

to indicate that the application's `Form` should inherit from class `VisualInheritanceForm` instead. The `Inherits` line in the `Designer.vb` file should now appear as follows:

```
Inherits VisualInheritance.VisualInheritanceForm
```

Note that you must either specify `VisualInheritanceForm`'s fully qualified name or use an `Imports` declaration to indicate that the new application uses classes from the namespace `VisualInheritance`. In **Design** view, the new application's `Form` now displays the inherited controls of the base class `VisualInheritanceForm` (as shown in Fig. 14.87). You can now add more components to the `Form`.

Class `VisualInheritanceTestForm` (Fig. 14.88) derives from `VisualInheritanceForm` (Fig. 14.86). The GUI contains the components inherited from `VisualInheritanceForm` and a `Button` with the text **About this Program**. When the user presses this `Button`, the event handler `aboutButton_Click` (lines 5–12) displays another `MessageBox` providing different informative text.

Figure 14.88 demonstrates that the components, their layouts and the functionality of base-class `VisualInheritanceForm` (Fig. 14.86) are inherited by `VisualInheritanceTestForm`. If a user clicks the button **Learn More**, the base class event handler `learnMoreButton_Click` displays a `MessageBox`. `VisualInheritanceForm` uses a `Private` access modifier to declare its controls (in its `Designer.vb` file), so derived class `VisualInheritanceTestForm` cannot modify the inherited controls.

Fig. 14.87 | `Form` demonstrating visual inheritance.

```
 1  ' Fig. 14.88: VisualInheritanceTestForm.vb
 2  ' Derived Form using visual inheritance.
 3  Public Class VisualInheritanceTestForm
 4     ' display MessageBox when Button is clicked
 5     Private Sub aboutButton_Click(ByVal sender As System.Object, _
 6        ByVal e As System.EventArgs) Handles aboutButton.Click
 7
 8        MessageBox.Show( _
 9           "This program was created by Deitel & Associates", _
10            "About this Program", MessageBoxButtons.OK, _
11           MessageBoxIcon.Information)
12     End Sub ' aboutButton_Click
13  End Class ' VisualInheritanceTestForm
```

Fig. 14.88 | Class `VisualInheritanceTestForm`, which inherits from class `VisualInheritanceForm`, contains an additional `Button`. (Part 1 of 2.)

Fig. 14.88 | Class `VisualInheritanceTestForm`, which inherits from class `VisualInheritanceForm`, contains an additional `Button`. (Part 2 of 2.)

14.25 User-Defined Controls

The .NET Framework allows you to create custom controls. These custom controls appear in the user's **Toolbox** and can be added to `Forms`, `Panels` or `GroupBoxes` in the same way that we add `Buttons`, `Labels` and other predefined controls. The simplest way to create a custom control is to derive a class from an existing control, such as a `Label`. This is useful if you want to add functionality to an existing control rather than re-implement the existing control to include the desired functionality. For example, you can create a new type of `Label` that behaves like a normal `Label` but has a different appearance. You accomplish this by inheriting from class `Label` and overriding method `OnPaint`.

All controls contain method `OnPaint`, which the system calls when a component must be redrawn (such as when the component is resized). Method `OnPaint` is passed a `PaintEventArgs` object, which contains graphics information—property `Graphics` is the graphics object used to draw, and property `ClipRectangle` defines the rectangular boundary of the control. Whenever the system raises the `Paint` event, polymorphism enables the system to call the new control's `OnPaint`. The base class's `OnPaint` method is not called, so you must call it explicitly from the derived class's `OnPaint` implementation before performing any customized painting operation. In most cases, you want to do this to ensure that the original painting code executes in addition to the code you define in the custom control's class, so that the control will be displayed correctly.

To create a new control that is composed of existing controls, use class `UserControl`. Controls added to a custom control are called constituent controls. For example, you could create a `UserControl` composed of a `Button`, a `Label` and a `TextBox`, each associated with some functionality (for example, the `Button` might set the `Label`'s text to the text contained in the `TextBox`). The `UserControl` acts as a container for the controls added to it. The `UserControl` contains constituent controls but does not determine how these constituent controls are displayed. Method `OnPaint` of the `UserControl` cannot be overridden. To control the appearance of each constituent control, you must handle each control's `Paint` event. The `Paint` event handler is passed a `PaintEventArgs` object, which can be used to draw graphics (lines, rectangles, etc.) on the constituent controls.

Using another technique, you can create a brand new control by inheriting from class `Control`. This class does not define any specific behavior; that task is left to you. Instead, class `Control` handles the items associated with all controls, such as events and sizing handles. Method `OnPaint` should contain a call to the base class's `OnPaint` method. Inside the overridden `OnPaint` method, you can add code that draws custom graphics when drawing the control. This technique allows for the greatest flexibility, but also requires the most planning. All three approaches are summarized in Fig. 14.89.

We create a "clock" control in Fig. 14.90. This is a `UserControl` composed of a `Label` and a `Timer`—whenever the `Timer` raises an event (once per second in this example), the `Timer`'s event handler updates the `Label` to reflect the current time.

`Timers` (`System.Windows.Forms` namespace) are invisible components that reside on a `Form`, generating **`Tick`** events at set intervals. The interval is set by the `Timer`'s **`Interval`** property, which defines the number of milliseconds (thousandths of a second) between events. By default, timers are disabled and do not generate events.

Custom control techniques and `PaintEventArgs` properties	Description
Custom Control Techniques	
Inherit from Windows Forms control	You can do this to add functionality to a pre-existing control. If you override method `OnPaint`, call the base class's `OnPaint` method. Note that you only can add to the original control's appearance, not redesign it.
Create a `UserControl`	You can create a `UserControl` composed of multiple pre-existing controls (e.g., to combine their functionality). Note that you cannot override the `OnPaint` methods of custom controls. Instead, you must place drawing code in a `Paint` event handler. Again, note that you only can add to the original control's appearance, not redesign it
Inherit from class `Control`	Define a brand-new control. Override method `OnPaint`, then call base class method `OnPaint` and include methods to draw the control. With this method you can customize control appearance and functionality.
`PaintEventArgs` Properties	
`Graphics`	The graphics object of the control. It is used to draw on the control.
`ClipRectangle`	Specifies the rectangle indicating the boundary of the control.

Fig. 14.89 | Custom control techniques and `PaintEventArgs` properties.

```
1  ' Fig. 14.90: ClockUserControl.vb
2  ' User-defined control with a timer and a Label.
3  Public Class ClockUserControl
4     ' update label for each clock tick
5     Private Sub clockTimer_Tick(ByVal sender As System.Object, _
6        ByVal e As System.EventArgs) Handles clockTimer.Tick
7        ' get current time (Now), convert to String
8        displayLabel.Text = DateTime.Now.ToLongTimeString()
9     End Sub ' clockTimer_Tick
10 End Class ' ClockUserControl
```

Fig. 14.90 | `UserControl`-defined clock.

This application contains a user control (`ClockUserControl`) and a `Form` that displays the user control. We begin by creating a Windows application. Next, we create a `UserControl` class for the project by selecting **Project > Add User Control....** This displays a dialog from which we can select the type of control to add—**User Control** is already selected. We then name the file (and the class) `ClockUserControl`. Our empty `ClockUserControl` is displayed as a gray rectangle.

You can treat this control like a Windows Form, meaning that you can add controls using the **ToolBox** and set properties using the **Properties** window. However, rather than creating an application's `Form`, you are simply creating a new control composed of other controls. Add a `Label` (`displayLabel`) and a `Timer` (`clockTimer`) to the `UserControl`. Set the `Timer`'s `Interval` property to 1000 milliseconds. To generate events, `clockTimer` must be enabled by setting property `Enabled` to `True` in the **Properties** window. Finally, create an event handler for `clockTimer`'s `Tick` event, which updates `displayLabel`'s text with each tick (lines 4–9).

Line 8 sets `displayLabel`'s text to the current time. Structure **`DateTime`** (namespace `System`) contains property **`Now`**, which is the current time. Method **`ToLongTimeString`** converts `Now` to a `String` containing the current hour, minute and second followed by AM or PM. Once you build the project containing the custom user control, the control is automatically added to the IDE's **Toolbox**. You may need to switch to the application's `Form` in the **Designer** before the custom user control appears in the **Toolbox**.

To use the custom control, simply drag it onto the `Form` and run the Windows application. We gave the `ClockUserControl` object a white background to make it stand out in the `Form`. Figure 14.90 shows the output of `UserControlTestForm`, which contains our `ClockUserControl`. There are no event handlers in `UserControlTestForm`, so we show only the code for `ClockUserControl`.

Sharing Custom Controls with Other Developers

Visual Studio allows you to share custom controls with other developers. To create a `UserControl` that can be exported to other solutions, do the following:

1. Create a new **Class Library** project.
2. Delete the file `Class1.vb` that is initially provided with the project.
3. Right click the project in the **Solution Explorer** and select **Add > User Control....** In the dialog that appears, name the user control file and click **Add**.
4. In the project, create your custom control by adding controls and functionality to the `UserControl` (e.g., Fig. 14.91).
5. Build the project. Visual Studio creates a `.dll` file for the `UserControl` in the solution's `bin/Release` directory. The file is not executable; class libraries are used to define classes that are reused in other executable applications.
6. Create a new Windows application.
7. In the new Windows application, right click the **Toolbox** and select **Choose Items....** In the **Choose Toolbox Items** dialog that appears, click **Browse...** and locate the `.dll` file for the class library you created in *Steps 1–5*. The item will then appear in the **Choose Toolbox Items** dialog (Fig. 14.92). If it is not already checked, check this item. Click **OK** to add the item to the **Toolbox**. This control can now be added to the `Form` as if it were any other control (Fig. 14.93).

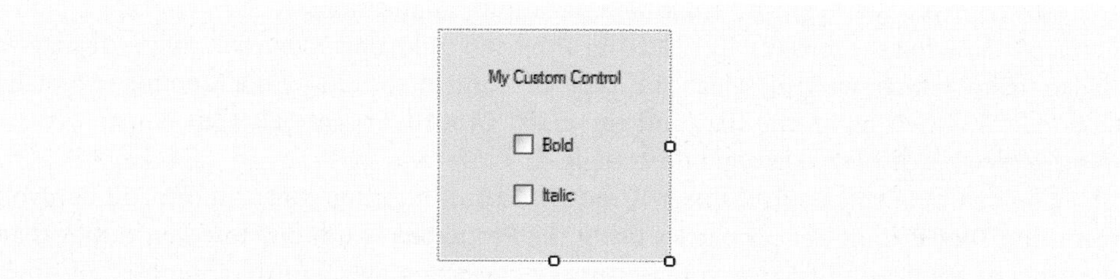

Fig. 14.91 | Custom-control creation.

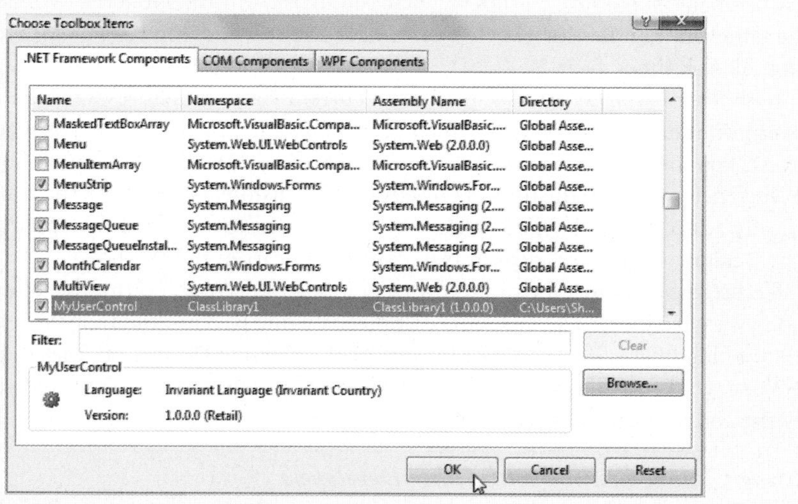

Fig. 14.92 | Custom control added to the **ToolBox**.

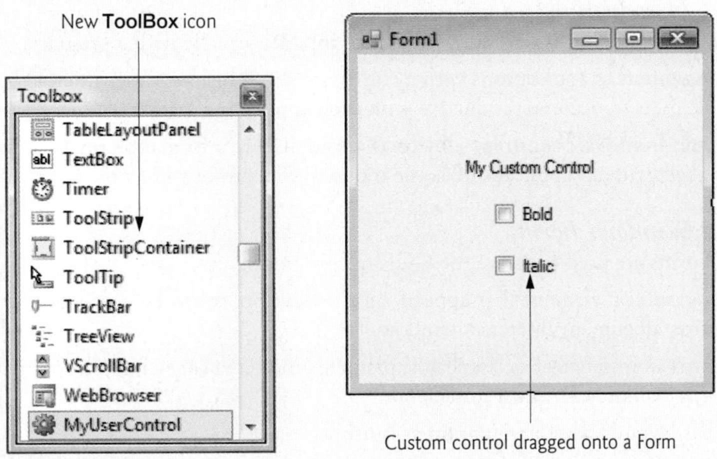

Fig. 14.93 | Custom control added to a `Form`.

14.26 Wrap-Up

This chapter introduced many Windows Forms GUI controls. We discussed event handling in detail, and showed how to create event handlers. We also discussed how delegates are used to connect event handlers to the events of specific controls. You learned how to use a control's properties and Visual Studio to specify the layout of your GUI.

We then introduced numerous controls, beginning with `Label`s, `Button`s and `TextBox`es. You learned how to use `GroupBox`es and `Panel`s to organize other controls. We demonstrated `CheckBox`es and `RadioButton`s, which are state buttons that allow users to select among several options. We displayed images in `PictureBox` controls, displayed helpful text on a GUI with `ToolTip` components and specified a range of input values for users with a `NumericUpDown` control. We then demonstrated how to handle mouse and keyboard events.

We then explained how to create menus that provide users easy access to an application's functionality. You learned the `DateTimePicker` and `MonthCalendar` controls, which allow users to input date and time values. We used `LinkLabel`s to link the user to an application or a web page. You used several controls that provide lists of data to the user—`ListBox`es, `CheckedListBox`es and `ListView`s. We used the `ComboBox` control to create drop-down lists, and the `TreeView` control to display data in hierarchical form. We then introduced complex GUIs that use tabbed windows and multiple document interfaces. The chapter concluded with demonstrations of visual inheritance and creating custom controls.

The next chapter shows how to create a different type of GUI using a new technology called Windows Presentation Foundation (WPF). Although you'll apply many of the concepts that you've learned in this chapter, you'll also find that creating a WPF GUI is significantly different from creating a Windows Forms GUI.

Summary

Section 14.1 Introduction

- A graphical user interface (GUI) allows a user to interact visually with a program.
- By providing different applications with a consistent set of intuitive user-interface components, GUIs enable users to become productive with each application faster.
- GUIs are built from GUI controls—objects that can display information on the screen or enable users to interact with an application via the mouse, keyboard or some other form of input.

Section 14.2 Windows Forms

- Windows Forms are used to create the GUIs for programs.
- A `Form` is a graphical element that appears on the desktop; it can be a dialog, a window or an MDI (multiple document interface) window.
- A `component` is an instance of a class that implements the `IComponent` interface, which defines the behaviors that components must implement.
- A control has a graphical representation at runtime.
- Some components lack graphical representations (e.g., class `Timer` of namespace `System.Windows.Forms`). Such components are not visible at runtime.
- When there are several windows on the screen, the active window is the frontmost and has a highlighted title bar—typically darker than the other windows on the screen. A window becomes the active window when the user clicks somewhere inside it.
- The active window is said to "have the focus."
- A `Form` is a container for controls and components.

Section 14.3 Event Handling

- A user interacts with an application's GUI to indicate the tasks that the application can perform on the user's behalf.
- GUIs are event driven.
- When the user interacts with a control, the interaction—known as an event—drives the program to perform a task. Common events include clicking a `Button`, typing in a `TextBox`, selecting an item from a menu, closing a window and moving the mouse.
- A method that performs a task in response to an event is called an event handler, and the overall process of responding to events is known as event handling.

Section 14.3.1 A Simple Event-Driven GUI

- By convention, event-handler methods are named as *objectName_eventName*.
- An event handler executes only when the user performs the specific event.
- Each event handler receives two parameters when it is called. The first—an `Object` reference named `sender`—is a reference to the object that generated the event. The second is a reference to an event arguments object of type `EventArgs` (or one of its derived classes), which is typically named `e`. This object contains additional information about the event that occurred.
- `EventArgs` is the base class of all classes that represent event information.

Section 14.3.2 Another Look at the Visual Studio Generated Code

- Visual Studio generates the code that creates and initializes the GUI you build in the GUI design window. This auto-generated code is placed in the `Designer.vb` file of the `Form`.

- The auto-generated code that defines the GUI is part of the `Form`'s class. The use of the `Partial` modifier in the class declaration allows the class to be split among multiple files.
- The `Designer.vb` file contains the declarations of the controls you create in **Design** mode. By default, all variable declarations for controls created through Visual Basic's design window have a `Friend` access modifier.
- The `Designer.vb` file includes the `Dispose` method for releasing resources and method `InitializeComponent`, which sets the properties of the `Form` and its controls.
- Visual Studio uses the code in `InitializeComponent` to create the GUI you see in design view. Changing the code in this method may prevent Visual Studio from displaying the GUI properly.

Section 14.3.3 Delegates and the Event-Handling Mechanism

- The control that generates an event is known as the event sender.
- An event-handling method—known as the event receiver—responds to a particular event that a control generates.
- When an event occurs, the event sender calls its event receiver to perform a task.
- The .NET event-handling mechanism allows you to choose your own names for event-handling methods. However, each event-handling method must declare the proper parameters to receive information about the event it handles.
- Event handlers are connected to a control's events via special objects called delegates.
- A delegate object holds a reference to a method. The method's signature must match the signature specified by the delegate type's declaration.
- GUI controls have predefined delegates that correspond to every event they can generate.
- An event uses a delegate object like a method call.
- Since each event handler is declared as a delegate, the event sender can simply call the appropriate delegate when an event occurs. The delegate's job is to invoke the appropriate method.

Section 14.3.4 Other Ways to Create Event Handlers

- Double clicking a control on the `Form` creates an event handler for a control's default event.
- Typically, controls can generate many different events, and each can have its own event handler.
- If you select a control from the **Class Name** combobox in the top left while in the **Code** editor, the **Method Name** combobox is populated with all the events for that control. When you select an event, your text cursor will move to its location in the code. If the event handler does not already exist, it will be created.
- You can create additional event handlers through the **Properties** window.
- If you select a control on the `Form`, then click the **Events** icon (the lightning bolt icon) in the **Properties** window, all the events for that control are listed in the window. You can double click an event's name to display the event handler in the editor, if the event handler already exists, or to create the corresponding event handler.
- You can select an event, then use the drop-down list to its right to choose an existing method that will be used as the event handler for that event. The methods that appear in this drop-down list are the class's methods that have the proper signature to be an event handler for the selected event.

Section 14.3.5 Locating Event Information

- Read the Visual Studio documentation to learn about the different events raised by a control.
- To do this, select **Help > Index**. In the window that appears, select **.NET Framework** in the **Filtered by:** drop-down list and enter the name of the control's class in the **Index** window. To ensure that you are selecting the proper class, enter the fully qualified class name.

- Once you select a control's class in the documentation, a list of all the class's members are displayed. This list includes the events the class can generate.
- Click the name of an event to view its description and examples of its use.

Section 14.4 Control Properties and Layout

- Controls derive from class `Control` (of namespace `System.Windows.Forms`).
- The `Focus` method transfers the focus to a control and makes it the active control.
- The `Enabled` property indicates whether the user can interact with a control to generate an event.
- A programmer can hide a control from the user without disabling the control by setting the `Visible` property to `False` or by calling method `Hide`.
- Anchoring causes controls to remain at a fixed distance from the sides of the container even when the container is resized.
- Docking attaches a control to a container such that the control stretches across an entire side.
- `Forms` have a `Padding` property that specifies the distance between the docked controls and the `Form` edges.
- The `Anchor` and `Dock` properties of a `Control` are set with respect to the `Control`'s parent container, which could be a `Form` or other parent container (such as a `Panel`).
- The minimum and maximum `Form` (or other `Control`) sizes can be set via properties `MinimumSize` and `MaximumSize`, respectively.
- When dragging a control across a `Form`, blue lines (known as snap lines) appear to help you position the control with respect to other controls and the `Form`'s edges.
- Visual Studio also provides the **Format** menu, which contains several options for modifying your GUI's layout.

Section 14.5 `Labels`, `TextBoxes` and `Buttons`

- Labels provide text information (as well as optional images) that the user cannot directly modify.
- A textbox (class `TextBox`) is an area in which text can be displayed by a program or the user can type text via the keyboard.
- A password `TextBox` is a `TextBox` that hides the information entered by the user. As the user types characters, the password `TextBox` masks the user input by displaying a character you specify (usually *). If you set the `PasswordChar` property, the `TextBox` becomes a password `TextBox`.
- The user clicks a button to trigger a specific action in a program or to select an option.
- All the button classes derive from class `ButtonBase` (namespace `System.Windows.Forms`), which defines common button features.

Section 14.6 `GroupBoxes` and `Panels`

- `GroupBoxes` and `Panels` arrange controls on a GUI.
- `GroupBoxes` and `Panels` are typically used to group several controls of similar functionality or several controls that are related in a GUI.
- `GroupBoxes` can display a caption (i.e., text) and do not include scrollbars, whereas `Panels` can include scrollbars and do not include a caption.
- `GroupBoxes` have thin borders by default; `Panels` can be set so that they also have borders, by changing their `BorderStyle` property.
- The controls of a `GroupBox` or `Panel` are added to the container's `Controls` property.
- To enable a `Panel`'s scrollbars, set the `Panel`'s `AutoScroll` property to `True`. If the `Panel` is resized and cannot display all of its controls, scrollbars appear.

Section 14.7 CheckBoxes and RadioButtons

- CheckBoxes and RadioButtons can be in the on/off or true/false states.
- Classes CheckBox and RadioButton are derived from class ButtonBase.
- A CheckBox is a small square that either is blank or contains a check mark. When a CheckBox is selected, a check mark appears in the box. Any number of CheckBoxes can be selected at a time.
- Styles can be combined via bitwise operators, such as the Or operator or the Xor operator.
- RadioButtons (defined with class RadioButton) are similar to CheckBoxes in that they also have two states—selected and not selected (also called deselected).
- RadioButtons normally appear as a group, in which only one RadioButton can be selected at a time. The selection of one RadioButton in the group forces all the others to be deselected. Therefore, RadioButtons are used to represent a set of mutually exclusive options.
- All RadioButtons added to a container become part of the same group.

Section 14.8 PictureBoxes

- A PictureBox displays the image specified by the Image property.
- The SizeMode property indicates how the image is displayed (Normal, StretchImage, Autosize or CenterImage).

Section 14.9 ToolTips

- Tool tips help you become familiar with the IDE's features and serve as useful reminders of each toolbar icon's functionality. This property appears in the **Properties** window as **ToolTip on** followed by the name of the ToolTip component.
- Once a ToolTip is added to a Form, a new property appears in the **Properties** window for the other controls on the Form.
- The ToolTip component can be used to add tool tips to your application.
- The component tray is the gray region below the Form in **Design** mode.

Section 14.10 NumericUpDown Control

- The NumericUpDown control restricts a user's input choices to a specific range of numeric values.
- The NumericUpDown control appears as a TextBox, with two small Buttons on the right side, one with an up arrow and one with a down arrow. By default, a user can type numeric values into this control as if it were a TextBox or click the up and down arrows to increase or decrease the value in the control, respectively.
- The largest and smallest values in the range are specified with the Maximum and Minimum properties, respectively (both are of type Decimal).
- The Increment property (of type Decimal) specifies by how much the current number in the control changes when the user clicks the control's up and down arrows.
- Setting a NumericUpDown control's ReadOnly property to True specifies that the user can only use the up and down arrows to modify the value in the NumericUpDown control.

Section 14.11 Mouse-Event Handling

- Mouse events, such as clicks, presses and moves, are generated when the mouse interacts with any control that derives from class System.Windows.Forms.Control.
- Class MouseEventArgs contains information related to the mouse event, such as the *x*- and *y*-coordinates of the mouse pointer, the mouse button pressed (Right, Left or Middle) and the number of times the mouse was clicked.

- Whenever the user clicks or holds down a mouse button, the system generates a MouseDown event.
- When the user releases the mouse button (to complete a "click" operation), the system generates a single MouseUp event.
- Moving the mouse over a control causes a MouseMove event for that control.

Section 14.12 Keyboard-Event Handling

- Key events KeyPress, KeyUp and KeyDown occur when various keys on the keyboard are pressed and released.
- The KeyPress event occurs when the user presses a key that represents an ASCII character. The specific key can be determined with property KeyChar of the event handler's KeyPressEventArgs argument.
- The KeyPress event does not indicate whether modifier keys (e.g., *Shift*, *Alt* and *Ctrl*) were pressed when a key event occurred. If this information is important, the KeyUp or KeyDown events can be used.
- The KeyEventArgs argument for each Key event contains information about modifier keys. Several properties return values from the Keys enumeration, which provides constants that specify the various keys on a keyboard.
- The KeyCode property returns the pressed key, but does not provide any information about modifier keys.
- The KeyData property returns a Keys enumeration value, including data about modifier keys.

Section 14.13 Menus

- Menus provide groups of related commands and organize them without "cluttering" the GUI.
- An expanded menu lists various menu items and submenus (menus within a menu).
- A menu that contains a menu item is called the menu item's parent menu. A menu item that contains a submenu is considered to be the parent of the submenu.
- All menu items can have *Alt* key shortcuts (also called access shortcuts or hotkeys), which are accessed by pressing *Alt* and the underlined letter.
- Menus that are not top-level menus can have shortcut keys as well (combinations of *Ctrl*, *Shift*, *Alt*, *F1*, *F2*, letter keys, etc.).
- Some menu items display check marks, indicating that multiple options on the menu can be selected at once.
- The MenuStrip control is used to create menus in a GUI.
- Top-level menus and their menu items are represented using ToolStripMenuItems.
- To create an access shortcut, type an ampersand (&) before the character to be underlined.
- To add other shortcut keys, set the ShortcutKeys property of the ToolStripMenuItem.
- You can hide the shortcut keys by setting property ShowShortcutKeys to False, and you can modify how the control keys are displayed in the menu item by modifying property ShortcutKeyDisplayString.
- A menu item's Checked property is used to display a check to the left of the menu item.

Section 14.14 **MonthCalendar** *Control*

- The MonthCalendar control displays a monthly calendar.
- The user can select a date from the currently displayed month or use the links to navigate to another month.
- A MonthCalendar's DateChanged event occurs when a new date is selected.

Section 14.15 `DateTimePicker` Control

- The `DateTimePicker` control can be used to retrieve date and/or time information from the user.
- `DateTimePicker` property `Format` specifies the user's selection options by using constants from the `DateTimePickerFormat` enumeration.
- The `DateTimePicker`'s `ValueChanged` event occurs when the selected value changes.

Section 14.16 `LinkLabel` Control

- The `LinkLabel` control displays links to other resources, such as files or web pages.
- A `LinkLabel` appears as underlined text (colored blue by default). When the mouse moves over the link, the pointer changes to a hand; this is similar to a hyperlink in a web page.
- The link can change color to indicate whether the link is new, previously visited or active.
- When clicked, the `LinkLabel` generates a `LinkClicked` event.

Section 14.17 `ListBox` Control

- The `ListBox` control allows the user to view and select items in a list.
- `ListBox` property `SelectionMode` determines the number of items that can be selected. This property has the possible values `None`, `One`, `MultiSimple` and `MultiExtended` (from the `SelectionMode` enumeration).
- The `SelectedIndexChanged` event of class `ListBox` occurs when the user selects a new item.
- Property `Items` returns all the list items as a collection.
- Property `SelectedItem` returns the currently selected item.
- To add items to a `ListBox`, add objects to its `Items` collection. Call method `Add` to add a `String` to the `ListBox`'s `Items` collection.
- You can add items to `ListBox`es and `CheckedListBox`es visually by examining the `Items` property in the **Properties** window.

Section 14.18 `CheckedListBox` Control

- The `CheckedListBox` control extends a `ListBox` by including `CheckBox`es next to each item.
- Items can be added to a `CheckedListBox` control via methods `Add` and `AddRange` or through the **String Collection Editor**.
- `CheckedListBox`es imply that multiple items can be selected.
- An `ItemCheck` event occurs whenever a user checks or unchecks a `CheckedListBox` item.

Section 14.19 `ComboBox` Control

- The `ComboBox` control combines `TextBox` features with a drop-down list.
- `MaxDropDownItems` specifies the maximum number of items that a drop-down list can display.
- As with the `ListBox` control, you can add objects to collection `Items` programmatically, using methods `Add` and `AddRange`, or visually, with the **String Collection Editor**.
- Property `DropDownStyle` determines the type of `ComboBox` and is represented as a value of the `ComboBoxStyle` enumeration, which contains values `Simple`, `DropDown` and `DropDownList`.
- There can be at most one selected item in a `ComboBox` (if none are selected, then the property `SelectedIndex` contains `-1`).
- When the selected item changes in a `ComboBox`, a `SelectedIndexChanged` event occurs.

Section 14.20 `TreeView` Control

- The `TreeView` control displays nodes hierarchically in a tree.

- Traditionally, nodes are objects that contain values and can refer to other nodes.
- A parent node contains child nodes, and the child nodes can be parents to other nodes.
- Two child nodes that have the same parent node are considered sibling nodes.
- A tree is a collection of nodes, usually organized in a hierarchical manner. The first parent node of a tree is the root node.
- `TreeView` controls are useful for displaying hierarchical information.
- In a `TreeView`, a parent node can be expanded or collapsed by clicking the plus box or minus box to its left. Nodes without children do not have these boxes.
- The nodes displayed in a `TreeView` are instances of class `TreeNode`.
- Each `TreeNode` has a `Nodes` collection (of type `TreeNodeCollection`), which contains a list of the node's children.
- To add nodes to a `TreeView` visually, click the ellipsis next to the `Nodes` property in the **Properties** window, then use the **TreeNode Editor**, which displays an empty tree representing the `TreeView`.
- To add nodes programmatically, create a root `TreeNode` object and pass it a `String` to display. Then call method `Add` to add this new `TreeNode` to the `TreeView`'s `Nodes` collection.

Section 14.21 `ListView` Control

- The `ListView` control is similar to a `ListBox` in that both display lists from which the user can select one or more items. The important difference between the two classes is that a `ListView` can display icons next to list items.
- Property `MultiSelect` (a `Boolean`) determines whether multiple items can be selected.
- To display images in a `ListView`, an `ImageList` component is required.
- Property `SmallImageList` of class `ListView` sets the `ImageList` for the small icons.
- Property `LargeImageList` of class `ListView` sets the `ImageList` for large icons.
- The items in a `ListView` are each of type `ListViewItem`.

Section 14.22 `TabControl` Control

- A `TabControl` creates tabbed windows. This allows you to organize more complex GUIs.
- `TabPage` objects are containers for other controls.
- Only one `TabPage` is displayed at a time.
- You can add `TabControls` visually by dragging and dropping them on a `Form` in **Design** mode. You can also right click the `TabControl` in **Design** mode and select **Add Tab**, or click the `TabPages` property in the **Properties** window and add tabs in the dialog that appears.
- Each `TabPage` raises a `Click` event when its tab is clicked.

Section 14.23 Multiple Document Interface (MDI) Windows

- Multiple document interface (MDI) programs enable users to edit multiple documents at once.
- The application window of an MDI program is called the parent window, and each window inside the application is referred to as a child window.
- Child windows cannot be parents themselves and cannot be moved outside their parent.
- To create an MDI `Form`, create a new `Form` and set its `IsMdiContainer` property to `True`.
- To add a child `Form` to the parent, create a new child `Form` object, set its `MdiParent` property to the parent `Form` and call the child `Form`'s `Show` method.
- Child windows can be minimized, maximized and closed independent of each other and of the parent window.

- Property MdiWindowListItem of class MenuStrip specifies which menu, if any, displays a list of open child windows.
- MDI containers allow you to organize the placement of child windows. The child windows in an MDI application can be arranged by calling method LayoutMdi of the parent Form.

Section 14.24 Visual Inheritance

- Visual inheritance allows you to create a new Form by inheriting from an existing Form. The derived Form class contains the functionality of its base class.
- Visual inheritance enables you to achieve visual consistency across applications by reusing code.
- A Form can inherit from another Form as long as that Form (or its assembly) is included in the project.

Section 14.25 User-Defined Controls

- The .NET Framework allows you to create custom controls.
- Custom controls appear in the user's **Toolbox** and can be added to Forms, Panels or GroupBoxes in the same way that Buttons, Labels and other predefined controls are added.
- The simplest way to create a custom control is to derive a class from an existing control, such as a Label. This is useful if you want to add functionality to an existing control rather than reimplement the existing control to include the desired functionality.
- To create a new control composed of existing controls, use class UserControl.
- Controls added to a custom control are called constituent controls.
- You can create a brand-new control by inheriting from class Control.
- Timers are invisible components that reside on a Form, generating Tick events at set intervals. The interval is set by the Timer's Interval property, which defines the number of milliseconds (thousandths of a second) between events.
- A Timer's Enabled property must be set to True before the Timer will generate events.

Terminology

Activation property of class ListView
active control
active window
ActiveMdiChild property of class Form
Add method of class ObjectCollection
AddDays method of structure DateTime
AddYears method of structure DateTime
anchor a control
ArrangeIcons value of enumeration MdiLayout
bitwise operator
Button properties and events
Button property of class MouseEventArgs
ButtonBase class
Cascade value of enumeration MdiLayout
cascaded window
checkbox
CheckBox class
CheckBoxes property of class ListView
Checked property of class CheckBox
Checked property of class RadioButton
Checked property of class ToolStripMenuItem
CheckedChanged event of class CheckBox
CheckedChanged event of class RadioButton
CheckedListBox class
CheckState property of class CheckBox
CheckStateChanged event of class CheckBox
child node
child window
Clear method of class Graphics
Clear method of class ObjectCollection
Click event of class ToolStripMenuItem
ClipRectangle property of class PaintEventArgs
Color structure
ComboBox class
ComboBoxStyle enumeration
component
component tray
constituent controls
container

menu access shortcut
menu item
MenuStrip class
MinDate property of class DateTimePicker
Minimum property of class NumericUpDown
MinimumSize property of class Control
modifier key
MonthCalendar class
mouse click
mouse event
mouse move
mouse press
MouseDown event of class Control
MouseEventArgs class
MouseEventHandler delegate
MouseMove event of class Control
MouseUp event of class Control
MultiExtended value of enumeration SelectionMode
multiple document interface (MDI)
MultiSelect property of class ListView
MultiSimple value of enumeration SelectionMode
mutual exclusion
Name property of class DirectoryInfo
Name property of class FileInfo
node
Nodes collection
None value of enumeration SelectionMode
"not-selected" state
Now property of structure DateTime
NumericUpDown class
ObjectCollection class
One value of enumeration SelectionMode
OnPaint method of class Control
Padding property of class Control
PaintEventArgs class
Panel class
parent menu
parent node
Parent property of class DirectoryInfo
parent window
password TextBox
PasswordChar property of class TextBox
Process class
radio button
radio button group
RadioButton class
ReadOnly property of class NumericUpDown
RemoveAt method of class ObjectCollection
root node
selected state
SelectedIndex property of class ComboBox
SelectedIndex property of class ListBox
SelectedIndexChanged event of class ComboBox
SelectedIndexChanged event of class ListBox
SelectedIndices property of class ListBox
SelectedItem property of class ComboBox
SelectedItem property of class ListBox
SelectedItems property of class ListBox
SelectionMode enumeration
SelectionMode property of class ListBox
separator bar
Short value of enumeration DateTimePickerFormat
ShortcutKeyDisplayString property of class ToolStripMenuItem
ShortcutKeys property of class ToolStripMenuItem
ShowShortcutKeys property of class ToolStripMenuItem
sibling node
Simple value of enumeration ComboBoxStyle
Single document interface (SDI)
Size property of class Control
Size structure
SmallImageList property of class ListView
snap line
SolidBrush class
Start method of class Process
state button
Style property of class Font
submenu
System.Diagnostics namespace
TabControl class
TabIndex property of class Control
TabPage class
TabPages property
TabPages property of class TabControl
TabStop property of class Control
Text property
Text property of class TabPage
Tick event of class Timer
tiled window
TileHorizontal value of enumeration MdiLayout
TileVertical value of enumeration MdiLayout
Time value of enumeration DateTimePickerFormat

`TimeOfDay` property of class `DateTimePicker`
`Timer` class
`ToLongDateString` method of structure `DateTime`
`ToLongTimeString` method of structure `DateTime`
`ToolStripMenuItem` class
`ToolTip` class
tree
`TreeNode` class
`TreeNodeCollection` type
`TreeView` class
`TreeViewEventArgs` class
`UpDownAlign` property of class `NumericUpDown`
`UserControl` class
`Value` property of class `DateTimePicker`
`Value` property of class `NumericUpDown`
`ValueChanged` event of class `DateTimePicker`
`View` property of class `ListView`
`Visible` property of class `Control`
visual inheritance
widget
`Width` property of structure `Size`
window gadget
Windows Form

Self-Review Exercises

14.1 State whether each of the following is *true* or *false*. If *false*, explain why.

a) The `KeyData` property includes data about modifier keys.
b) Windows Forms commonly are used to create GUIs.
c) A `Form` is a container.
d) All `Forms`, components and controls are classes.
e) `CheckBoxes` are used to represent a set of mutually exclusive options.
f) A `Label` displays text that a user running an application can edit.
g) `Button` presses generate events.
h) All mouse events use the same event arguments class.
i) The `NumericUpDown` control is used to specify a range of input values.
j) A control's tool tip text is set with the `ToolTip` property of class `Control`.
k) Menus organize groups of related classes.
l) Menu items can display `ComboBoxes`, checkmarks and access shortcuts.
m) The `ListBox` control allows only single selection (like a `RadioButton`).
n) A `ComboBox` control typically has a drop-down list.
o) Deleting a parent node in a `TreeView` control deletes its child nodes.
p) The user can select only one item in a `ListView` control.
q) A `TabPage` can act as a container for `RadioButtons`.
r) An MDI child window can have MDI children.
s) MDI child windows can be moved outside the boundaries of their parent window.
t) There are two basic ways to create a customized control.

14.2 Fill in the blanks in each of the following statements:

a) The active control is said to have the __________.
b) The `Form` acts as a(n) __________ for the controls that are added.
c) GUIs are __________ driven.
d) Every method that handles the same event must have the same __________.
e) A(n) __________ `TextBox` masks user input with a character used repeatedly.
f) Class __________ and class __________ help arrange controls on a GUI and provide logical groups for radio buttons.
g) Typical mouse events include __________, __________ and __________.
h) __________ events are generated when a key on the keyboard is pressed or released.
i) The modifier keys are __________, __________ and __________.
j) Method _______ of class `Process` can open files and web pages, similar to the **Run...** command in Windows.

k) If more elements appear in a `ComboBox` than can fit, a(n) ________ appears.
l) The top-level node in a `TreeView` is the ________ node.
m) A(n) ________ and a(n) ________ can display icons contained in an `ImageList` control.
n) The ________ property of class `MenuStrip` allows a menu to display a list of active child windows.
o) Class ________ allows you to combine several controls into a single custom control.
p) The ________ saves space by layering `TabPages` on top of each other.
q) The ________ window layout option makes all MDI windows the same size and layers them so that every title bar is visible (if possible).
r) ________ are typically used to display hyperlinks to other resources, files or web pages.

Answers To Self-Review Exercises

14.1 a) True. b) True. c) True. d) True. e) False. `RadioButtons` are used to represent a set of mutually exclusive options. f) False. A `Label`'s text cannot be edited by the user. g) True. h) False. Some mouse events use `EventArgs`, others use `MouseEventArgs`. i) True. j) False. A control's tool tip text is set using a `ToolTip` component that must be added to the application. k) False. Menus organize groups of related commands. l) True. m) False. The `ListBox` control allows single or multiple selection. n) True. o) True. p) False. The user can select one or more items. q) True. r) False. Only an MDI parent window can have MDI children. An MDI parent window cannot be an MDI child. s) False. MDI child windows cannot be moved outside their parent window. t) False. There are three ways—derive from an existing control, derive a new control from class `UserControl` (to create a control that contains other controls) or derive a new control from class `Control` (to create a control from scratch).

14.2 a) focus. b) container. c) event. d) signature. e) password. f) `GroupBox`, `Panel`. g) mouse clicks, mouse presses, mouse moves. h) `Key`. i) *Shift*, *Ctrl*, *Alt*. j) `Start`. k) scrollbar. l) root. m) `ListView`, `TreeView`. n) `MdiWindowListItem`. o) `UserControl`. p) `TabControl`. q) `Cascade`. r) `LinkLabels`.

Exercises

14.3 Extend the program in Fig. 14.27 to include a `CheckBox` for every font-style option. [*Hint:* Use `Xor` rather than test for every bit explicitly.]

14.4 Create the GUI in Fig. 14.94 (you do not have to provide functionality).

14.5 Create the GUI in Fig. 14.95 (you do not have to provide functionality).

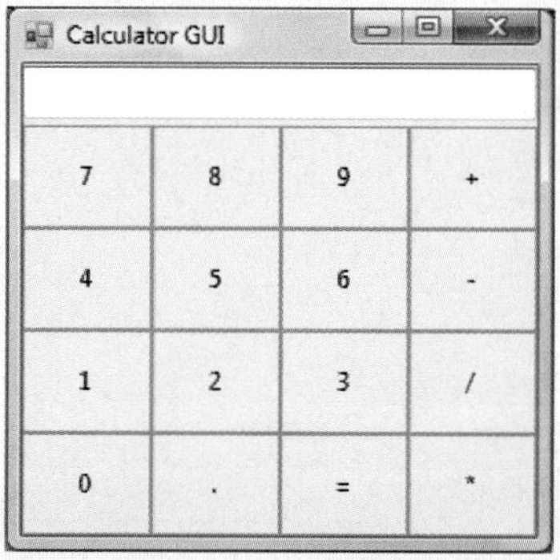

Fig. 14.94 | Calculator GUI.

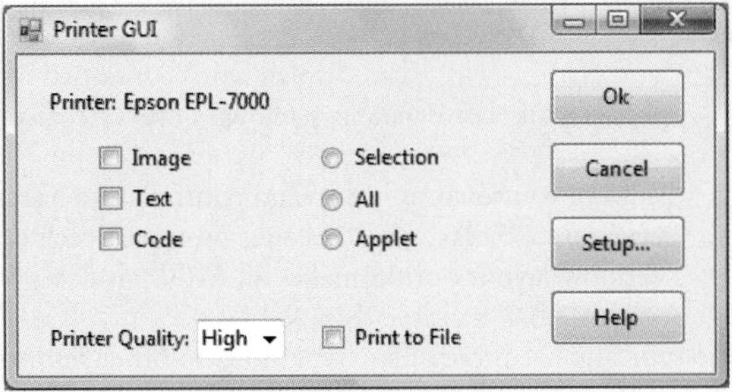

Fig. 14.95 | Printer GUI.

14.6 Write a temperature-conversion program that converts from Fahrenheit to Celsius. The Fahrenheit temperature should be entered from the keyboard (via a `TextBox`). A `Label` should be used to display the converted temperature. Use the following formula for the conversion:

$$Celsius = (5 / 9) \times (Fahrenheit - 32)$$

14.7 Extend the program of Fig. 14.39 to include options for changing the size and color of the lines drawn. Create a GUI similar to Fig. 14.96. The user should be able to draw on the application's `Panel`. To retrieve a `Graphics` object for drawing, call method *panelName*`.CreateGraphics()`, substituting in the name of your `Panel`. Remember to call the `Graphics` object's `Dispose` method when the object is no longer needed.

14.8 Write a program that plays "guess the number" as follows: Your program chooses the number to be guessed by selecting an `Integer` at random in the range 1–1000. The program then displays the following text in a label:

```
I have a number between 1 and 1000--can you guess my number?
Please enter your first guess.
```

A `TextBox` should be used to input the guess. As each guess is input, the background color should change to red or blue. Red indicates that the user is getting "warmer," blue that the user is getting "colder." A `Label` should display either "`Too High`" or "`Too Low`," to help the user zero in on the cor-

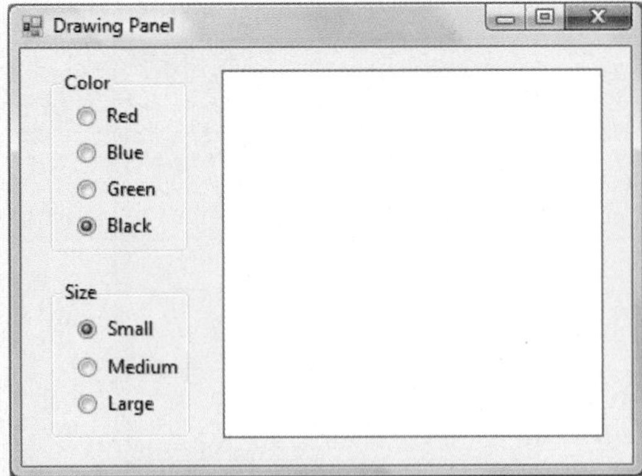

Fig. 14.96 | Drawing Panel GUI.

rect answer. When the user guesses the correct answer, display "Correct!" in a message box, change the Form's background color to green and disable the TextBox. Recall that a TextBox (like other controls) can be disabled by setting the control's Enabled property to False. Provide a Button that allows the user to play the game again. When the Button is clicked, generate a new random number, change the background to the default color and enable the TextBox.

14.9 Write a program that displays the names of 15 states in a ComboBox. When an item is selected from the ComboBox, remove it.

14.10 Modify your solution to Exercise 14.3 to add a ListBox. When the user selects an item from the ComboBox, remove the item from the ComboBox and add it to the ListBox. Your program should check to ensure that the ComboBox contains at least one item. If it does not, display a message, using a message box, then terminate program execution when the user dismisses the message box.

14.11 Write a program that allows the user to enter Strings in a TextBox. Add each String the user inputs to a ListBox. As each String is added to the ListBox, ensure that the Strings are in sorted order. [*Note:* Use property Sorted.]

14.12 Create a file browser (similar to Windows Explorer) based on the programs in Fig. 14.55, Fig. 14.69 and Fig. 14.72. The file browser should have a TreeView that allows the user to browse directories. There should also be a ListView that displays the contents (all subdirectories and files) of the directory being browsed. Double clicking a file in the ListView should open it, and double clicking a directory in either the ListView or the TreeView should browse it. If a file or directory cannot be accessed because of its permission settings, notify the user.

14.13 Create an MDI text editor. Each child window should contain a multiline RichTextBox. The MDI parent should have a **Format** menu with submenus to control the size, font and color of the text in the active child window. Each submenu should have at least three options. In addition, the parent should have a **File** menu with menu items **New** (create a new child), **Close** (close the active child) and **Exit** (exit the application). The parent should have a **Window** menu to display a list of the open child windows and their layout options.

14.14 Create a UserControl called LoginPasswordUserControl. The LoginPasswordUserControl contains a Label (loginLabel) that displays String "Login:", a TextBox (loginTextBox) where the user inputs a login name, a Label (passwordLabel) that displays the String "Password:" and finally, a TextBox (passwordTextBox) where a user inputs a password (do not forget to set property PasswordChar to "*" in the TextBox's **Properties** window). LoginPasswordUserControl must provide Public read-only properties Login and Password that allow an application to retrieve the user input from a login TextBox and a password TextBox. Use the new control in an application that displays the values input by the user in LoginPasswordUserControl.

14.15 A restaurant wants an application that calculates a table's bill. The application should display all the menu items from Fig. 14.97 in four ComboBoxes. Each ComboBox should contain a category of food offered by the restaurant (Beverage, Appetizer, Main Course and Dessert). The user can choose from one of these ComboBoxes to add an item to a table's bill. As each item is selected in the ComboBoxes, add the price of the item to the bill. The user can click the Clear Button to restore the Subtotal:, Tax: and Total: fields to $0.00.

14.16 Create an application that contains three TabPages. On the first TabPage, place a CheckedListBox with six items. On the second TabPage, place six TextBoxes. On the last TabPage, place six LinkLabels. The user's selections on the first TabPage should specify which of the six LinkLabels will be displayed. To hide or display a LinkLabel's value, use its Visible property. Use the second TabPage to modify the web page that is opened by the LinkLabels. [*Note:* To change the LinkLabels' Visible properties, you will need to change the currently displayed TabPage to the last one. To do this, use the TabPage's SelectedTab property.]

Name	Category	Price
Soda	Beverage	$1.95
Tea	Beverage	$1.50
Coffee	Beverage	$1.25
Mineral Water	Beverage	$2.95
Juice	Beverage	$2.50
Milk	Beverage	$1.50
Buffalo Wings	Appetizer	$5.95
Buffalo Fingers	Appetizer	$6.95
Potato Skins	Appetizer	$8.95
Nachos	Appetizer	$8.95
Mushroom Caps	Appetizer	$10.95
Shrimp Cocktail	Appetizer	$12.95
Chips and Salsa	Appetizer	$6.95
Seafood Alfredo	Main Course	$15.95
Chicken Alfredo	Main Course	$13.95
Chicken Picatta	Main Course	$13.95
Turkey Club	Main Course	$11.95
Lobster Pie	Main Course	$19.95
Prime Rib	Main Course	$20.95
Shrimp Scampi	Main Course	$18.95
Turkey Dinner	Main Course	$13.95
Stuffed Chicken	Main Course	$14.95
Apple Pie	Dessert	$5.95
Sundae	Dessert	$3.95
Carrot Cake	Dessert	$5.95
Mud Pie	Dessert	$4.95
Apple Crisp	Dessert	$5.95

Fig. 14.97 | Food items and prices.

14.17 Create an MDI application with child windows that each have a `Panel` for drawing. Add menus to the MDI application that allow the user to modify the size and color of the paint brush. When running this application, be aware that the `Panel` will be cleared if one of the windows overlaps another.

15

GUI with Windows Presentation Foundation

My function is to present old masterpieces in modern frames.
—Rudolf Bing

Instead of being a static one-time event, bonding is a process, a dynamic and continuous one.
—Julius Segal

. . . they do not declare but only hint.
—Friedrich Nietzsche

Science is the knowledge of consequences, and dependence of one fact upon another.
—Thomas Hobbes

Here form is content, content is form.
—Samuel Beckett

OBJECTIVES

In this chapter you'll learn:

- What Windows Presentation Foundation (WPF) is.
- Differences between WPF and Windows Forms.
- To mark up data using XML.
- How XML namespaces help provide unique XML element and attribute names.
- To define a WPF GUI with Extensible Application Markup Language (XAML).
- To handle WPF user-interface events.
- To use WPF's commands feature to handle common application tasks such as cut, copy and paste.
- To customize the look-and-feel of WPF GUIs using styles and control templates.
- To use data binding to display data in WPF controls.

Outline

15.1 Introduction

In Chapter 14, you built GUIs using Windows `Forms`. In this chapter, you'll build GUIs using **Windows Presentation Foundation (WPF)**—Microsoft's new framework for GUI, graphics, animation and multimedia. In Chapter 16, WPF Graphics and Multimedia, you'll learn how to incorporate 2D graphics, 3D graphics, animation, audio and video in WPF applications. In Chapter 23, Silverlight, Rich Internet Applications and Multimedia, we'll demonstrate how to use Silverlight (a subset of WPF and a new platform for web applications) to create Internet applications.

We begin with an introduction to WPF. Next, we discuss an important tool for creating WPF applications called **XAML** (pronounced "zammel")—**Extensible Application Markup Language**. XAML is a descriptive markup language that can be used to define and arrange GUI controls without any Visual Basic code. Its syntax is **XML** (**Extensible Markup Language**), a widely supported standard for describing data that is commonly used to exchange that data between applications over the Internet. We present an introduction to XML in Sections 15.3–15.5. Section 15.6 demonstrates how to define a WPF GUI with XAML. Sections 15.7–15.10 demonstrate the basics of creating a WPF GUI—layout, controls and events. You'll also learn new capabilities that are available in WPF controls and event handling.

WPF allows you to easily customize the look-and-feel of a GUI beyond what is possible in Windows `Forms`. Sections 15.11–15.14 demonstrate several techniques for manipulating the appearance of your GUIs. WPF also allows you to create data-driven GUIs that interact with many types of data. We demonstrate how to do this in Section 15.15.

15.2 Windows Presentation Foundation (WPF)

Previously, you often had to use multiple technologies to build client applications. If a Windows Forms application required video and audio capabilities, you needed to incorporate an additional technology such as Windows Media Player. Likewise, if your application required 3D graphics capabilities, you had to incorporate a separate technology such as Direct3D. WPF provides a single platform capable of handling both of these requirements, and more. It enables you to use one technology to build applications containing GUI, images, animation, 2D or 3D graphics, audio and video capabilities. In this chapter and Chapters 16 and 23, we demonstrate each of these capabilities.

WPF can interoperate with existing technologies. For example, you can include WPF controls in Windows Forms applications to incorporate multimedia content (such as audio or video) without converting the entire application to WPF, which could be a costly and time-consuming process. You can also use Windows Forms controls in WPF applications.

WPF's ability to use the acceleration capabilities of your computer's graphics hardware increases your applications' performance. In addition, WPF generates vector-based graphics and is resolution independent. Vector-based graphics are defined, not by a grid of pixels as raster-based graphics are, but rather by mathematical models. An advantage of vector-based graphics is that when you change the resolution, there is no loss of quality. Hence, the graphics become portable to a great variety of devices. Moreover, your applications won't appear smaller on higher-resolution screens. Instead, they'll remain the same size and display sharper. Chapter 16, WPF Graphics and Multimedia, presents more information about vector-based graphics and resolution independence.

Building a GUI with WPF is similar to building a GUI with Windows Forms—you drag-and-drop predefined controls from the **Toolbox** onto the design area. Many WPF controls correspond directly to those in Windows Forms. Just as in a Windows Forms application, the functionality is event driven. Many of the Windows Forms events you're familiar with are also in WPF. A WPF `Button`, for example, is similar to a Windows Forms `Button`, and both raise `Click` events.

There are several important differences between the two technologies. The WPF layout scheme is different. WPF properties and events have more capabilities. Most notably, WPF allows designers to define the appearance and content of a GUI without any Visual Basic code by defining it in XAML, a descriptive markup language (i.e., a text-based notation for describing something).

Introduction to XAML

In Windows Forms, when you use the designer to create a GUI, the IDE generates code statements that create and configure the controls. In WPF, it generates XAML markup (i.e., a text-based notation for describing data). Because markup is designed to be readable by both humans and computers, you can also manually write XAML markup to define GUI controls. When you compile your WPF application, a XAML compiler generates code to create and configure controls based on your XAML markup. This technique of defining *what* the GUI should contain without specifying *how* to generate it is an example of declarative programming.

XAML allows designers and programmers to work together more efficiently. Without writing any code, a graphic designer can edit the look-and-feel of an application using a design tool, such as Microsoft's Expression Blend—a XAML graphic design program. A programmer can import the XAML markup into Visual Studio and focus on coding the logic that gives an application its functionality. Even if you are working alone, however, this separation of front-end appearance from back-end logic improves your program's organization and makes it easier to maintain. XAML is an essential component of WPF programming.

Because XAML implemented with XML, it is important that you understand the basics of XML before we continue our discussion of XAML and WPF GUIs.

15.3 XML Basics

The Extensible Markup Language was developed in 1996 by the World Wide Web Consortium's (W3C's) XML Working Group. XML is a widely supported standard for describing data that is commonly used to exchange that data between applications over the Internet. It permits document authors to create markup for virtually any type of information. This enables them to create entirely new markup languages for describing any type of data, such as mathematical formulas, software-configuration instructions, chemical molecular structures, music, news, recipes and financial reports. XML describes data in a way that both human beings and computers can understand.

Figure 15.1 is a simple XML document that describes information for a baseball player. We focus on lines 5–11 to introduce basic XML syntax. You will learn about the other elements of this document in Section 15.4.

XML documents contain text that represents content (i.e., data), such as `John` (line 6), and elements that specify the document's structure, such as `firstName` (line 6). XML documents delimit elements with start tags and end tags. A start tag consists of the element name in angle brackets (e.g., `<player>` and `<firstName>` in lines 5 and 6, respectively). An end tag consists of the element name preceded by a forward slash (/) in angle brackets (e.g., `</firstName>` and `</player>` in lines 6 and 11, respectively). An element's start and end tags enclose text that represents a piece of data (e.g., the `firstName` of the `player`—`John`—in line 6, which is enclosed by the `<firstName>` start tag and and `</firstName>` end tag) or other elements (e.g., the `firstName`, `lastName`, and `battingAverage` elements in the `player` element. Every XML document must have exactly one root element that contains all the other elements. In Fig. 15.1, `player` (lines 5–11) is the root element.

Some XML-based markup languages include XHTML (Extensible HyperText Markup Language—HTML's replacement for marking up web content), MathML (for

```
1  <?xml version = "1.0"?>
2  <!-- Fig. 15.1: player.xml -->
3  <!-- Baseball player structured with XML -->
4
5  <player>
6     <firstName>John</firstName>
7
8     <lastName>Doe</lastName>
9
10    <battingAverage>0.375</battingAverage>
11 </player>
```

Fig. 15.1 | XML that describes a baseball player's information.

mathematics), VoiceXML™ (for speech), CML (Chemical Markup Language—for chemistry) and XBRL (Extensible Business Reporting Language—for financial data exchange). ODF (Open Document Format—developed by Sun Microsystems) and OOXML (Office Open XML—developed by Microsoft as a replacement for the old proprietary Microsoft Office formats) are two competing standards for electronic office documents such as spreadsheets, presentations, and word processing documents. These markup languages are called XML vocabularies and provide a means for describing particular types of data in standardized, structured ways.

Massive amounts of data are currently stored on the Internet in a variety of formats (e.g., databases, web pages, text files). Based on current trends, it is likely that much of this data, especially that which is passed between systems, will soon take the form of XML. Organizations see XML as the future of data encoding. Information-technology groups are planning ways to integrate XML into their systems. Industry groups are developing custom XML vocabularies for most major industries that will allow computer-based business applications to communicate in common languages. For example, web services, which we discuss in Chapter 22, allow web-based applications to exchange data seamlessly through standard protocols based on XML. Also, web services are described by an XML vocabulary called WSDL (Web Services Description Language).

The next generation of the Internet and World Wide Web is being built on a foundation of XML, which enables the development of more sophisticated web-based applications. XML allows you to assign meaning to what would otherwise be random pieces of data. As a result, programs can "understand" the data they manipulate. For example, a web browser might view a street address listed on a simple HTML web page as a string of characters without any real meaning. In an XML document, however, this data can be clearly identified (i.e., marked up) as an address. A program that uses the document can recognize this data as an address and provide links to a map of that location, driving directions from that location or other location-specific information. Likewise, an application can recognize names of people, dates, ISBN numbers and any other type of XML-encoded data. Based on this data, the application can present users with other related information, providing a richer, more meaningful user experience.

Viewing and Modifying XML Documents

XML documents are portable. Viewing or modifying an XML document—a text file, usually with the `.xml` file-name extension—does not require special software, although many software tools exist, and new ones are frequently released that make it more convenient to develop XML-based applications. Most text editors can open XML documents for viewing and editing. Visual Basic Express includes an XML editor that provides *IntelliSense* for tag and attribute names. The editor also checks that the document is well formed and is valid if a schema (discussed shortly) is present. Also, most web browsers can display an XML document in a formatted manner that shows its structure. We demonstrate this using Internet Explorer in Section 15.4. One important characteristic of XML is that it is both human readable and machine readable.

Processing XML Documents

Processing an XML document requires software called an XML parser (or XML processor). A parser makes the document's data available to applications. While reading the contents of an XML document, a parser checks that the document follows the syntax rules specified by the W3C's XML Recommendation (www.w3.org/XML). XML syntax requires a single root element, a start tag and end tag for each element, and properly nested tags (i.e., the end tag for a nested element must appear before the end tag of the enclosing element). Furthermore, XML is case sensitive, so the proper capitalization must be used in elements. A document that conforms to this syntax is a well-formed XML document, and is syntactically correct. We present fundamental XML syntax in Section 15.4. If an XML parser can process an XML document successfully, that XML document is well formed. Parsers can provide access to XML-encoded data in well-formed documents only—if a document is not well-formed, the parser will report an error to the user or calling application.

Often, XML parsers are built into software such as Visual Studio or available for download over the Internet. Popular parsers include Microsoft XML Core Services (MSXML), the .NET Framework's `XmlReader` class, the Apache Software Foundation's Xerces (available from `xerces.apache.org`) and the open-source Expat XML Parser (available from `expat.sourceforge.net`).

Validating XML Documents

An XML document can optionally reference a Document Type Definition (DTD) or a W3C XML Schema (referred to simply as a "schema" for the rest of this book) that defines the XML document's proper structure. When an XML document references a DTD or a schema, some parsers (called validating parsers) can use the DTD/schema to check that it has the appropriate structure. If the XML document conforms to the DTD/schema (i.e., the document has the appropriate structure), the XML document is valid. For example, if in Fig. 15.1 we were referencing a DTD that specifies that a `player` element must have `firstName`, `lastName` and `battingAverage` elements, then omitting the `lastName` element (line 8) would cause the XML document `player.xml` to be invalid. The XML document would still be well formed, however, because it follows proper XML syntax (i.e., it has one root element, and each element has a start and an end tag). By definition, a valid XML document is well formed. Parsers that cannot check for document conformity against DTDs/schemas are nonvalidating parsers—they determine only whether an XML document is well formed.

For more information about validation, DTDs and schemas, as well as the key differences between these two types of structural specifications, see Chapter 19. For now, note that schemas are XML documents themselves, whereas DTDs are not. As you will learn in Chapter 19, this difference presents several advantages in using schemas over DTDs.

Software Engineering Observation 15.1

DTDs and schemas are essential for business-to-business (B2B) transactions and mission-critical systems. Validating XML documents ensures that disparate systems can manipulate data structured in standardized ways and prevents errors caused by missing or malformed data.

Formatting and Manipulating XML Documents

XML documents contain only data, not formatting instructions, so applications that process XML documents must decide how to manipulate or display each document's data. For example, a PDA (personal digital assistant) may render an XML document differently than a wireless phone or a desktop computer. You can use Extensible Stylesheet Language (XSL) to specify rendering instructions for different platforms. We discuss XSL in Chapter 19.

XML-processing programs can also search, sort and manipulate XML data using technologies such as XSL. Some other XML-related technologies are XPath (XML Path Language—a language for accessing parts of an XML document), XSL-FO (XSL Formatting Objects—an XML vocabulary used to describe document formatting) and XSLT (XSL Transformations—a language for transforming XML documents into other documents). We present XSLT and XPath in Chapter 19. We'll also present new Visual Basic 2008 features that greatly simplify working with XML in your code. With these new features, XSLT and similar technologies are not needed while coding in Visual Basic, but they remain relevant on platforms where Visual Basic and .NET are not available.

15.4 Structuring Data

In Fig. 15.2, we present an XML document that marks up a simple article using XML. The line numbers shown are for reference only and are not part of the XML document.

This document begins with an **XML declaration** (line 1), which identifies the document as an XML document. The **version attribute** specifies the XML version to which the document conforms. The current XML standard is version 1.0. Though the W3C released a version 1.1 specification in February 2004, this newer version is not yet widely supported. The W3C may continue to release new versions as XML evolves to meet the requirements of different fields.

Some XML documents also specify an **encoding attribute** in the XML declaration. An encoding specifies how characters are stored in memory and on disk—historically, the way an uppercase "A" was stored on one computer architecture was different than the way it was stored on a different computer architecture. Appendix G describes Unicode, which specifies encodings that can describe characters in any written language. An introduction to different encodings in XML can be found at the website msdn.microsoft.com/en-us/library/aa468560.aspx.

```
1  <?xml version = "1.0"?>
2  <!-- Fig. 15.2: article.xml -->
3  <!-- Article structured with XML -->
4
5  <article>
6     <title>Simple XML</title>
7
8     <date>July 24, 2008</date>
9
10    <author>
11       <firstName>John</firstName>
12       <lastName>Doe</lastName>
13    </author>
14
15    <summary>XML is pretty easy.</summary>
16
17    <content>
18       In this chapter, we present a wide variety of examples that use XML.
19    </content>
20 </article>
```

Fig. 15.2 | XML used to mark up an article.

Portability Tip 15.1

Documents should include the XML declaration to identify the version of XML used. A document that lacks an XML declaration might be assumed erroneously to conform to the latest version of XML—in which case, errors could result.

Common Programming Error 15.1

Placing whitespace characters before the XML declaration is an error.

XML comments (lines 2–3), which begin with <!-- and end with -->, can be placed almost anywhere in an XML document. XML comments can span to multiple lines—an end marker on each line is not needed; the end marker can appear on a subsequent line, as long as there is exactly one end marker (-->) for each begin marker (<!--). Comments are used in XML for documentation purposes. Line 4 is a blank line. As in a Visual Basic program, blank lines, whitespaces and indentation are used in XML to improve readability. Later you will see that the blank lines are normally ignored by XML parsers.

Common Programming Error 15.2

In an XML document, each start tag must have a matching end tag; omitting either tag is an error. Soon, you will learn how such errors are detected.

Common Programming Error 15.3

XML is case sensitive. Using different cases for the start-tag and end-tag names for the same element is a syntax error.

In Fig. 15.2, `article` (lines 5–20) is the root element. The lines that precede the root element (lines 1–4) are the XML prolog. In an XML prolog, the XML declaration must appear before the comments and any other markup.

The elements we used in the example do not come from any specific markup language. Instead, we chose the element names and markup structure that best describe our particular data. You can invent whatever elements make sense for the particular data you are dealing with. For example, element `title` (line 6) contains text that describes the article's title (e.g., `Simple XML`). Similarly, `date` (line 8), `author` (lines 10–13), `firstName` (line 11), `lastName` (line 12), `summary` (line 15) and `content` (lines 17–19) contain text that describes the date, author, the author's first name, the author's last name, a summary and the content of the document, respectively. XML element and attribute names can be of any length and may contain letters, digits, underscores, hyphens and periods. However, they must begin with either a letter or an underscore, and they should not begin with "`xml`" in any combination of uppercase and lowercase letters (e.g., `XML`, `Xml`, `xMl`), as this is reserved for use in the XML standards.

Common Programming Error 15.4

Using a whitespace character in an XML element name is an error.

Good Programming Practice 15.1

XML element names should be meaningful to humans and should not use abbreviations.

XML elements are nested to form hierarchies—with the root element at the top of the hierarchy. This allows document authors to create parent/child relationships between data. For example, elements `title`, `date`, `author`, `summary` and `content` are nested within `article`. Elements `firstName` and `lastName` are nested within `author`.

Common Programming Error 15.5

Nesting XML tags improperly is a syntax error—it causes an XML document to not be well-formed. For example, `<x><y>hello</x></y>` *is an error, because the* `</y>` *tag must precede the* `</x>` *tag.*

Any element that contains other elements (e.g., `article` or `author`) is a container element. Container elements also are called parent elements. Elements nested inside a container element are child elements (or children) of that container element.

Viewing an XML Document in Internet Explorer

The XML document in Fig. 15.2 is simply a text file named `article.xml`. This document does not contain formatting information for the article. The reason is that XML is a technology for describing the structure of data. Formatting and displaying data from an XML document are application-specific issues. For example, when the user loads `article.xml` in Internet Explorer (IE), MSXML (Microsoft XML Core Services) parses and displays the document's data. Internet Explorer uses a built-in style sheet to format the data. Note that the resulting format of the data (Fig. 15.3) is similar to the format of the listing in Fig. 15.2. In Chapter 19, we show how to create style sheets to transform your XML data into various formats suitable for display.

Note the minus sign (-) and plus sign (+) in the screenshots of Fig. 15.3. Although these symbols are not part of the XML document, Internet Explorer places them next to every container element. A minus sign indicates that Internet Explorer is displaying the container element's child elements. Clicking the minus sign next to an element collapses that element (i.e., causes Internet Explorer to hide the container element's children and

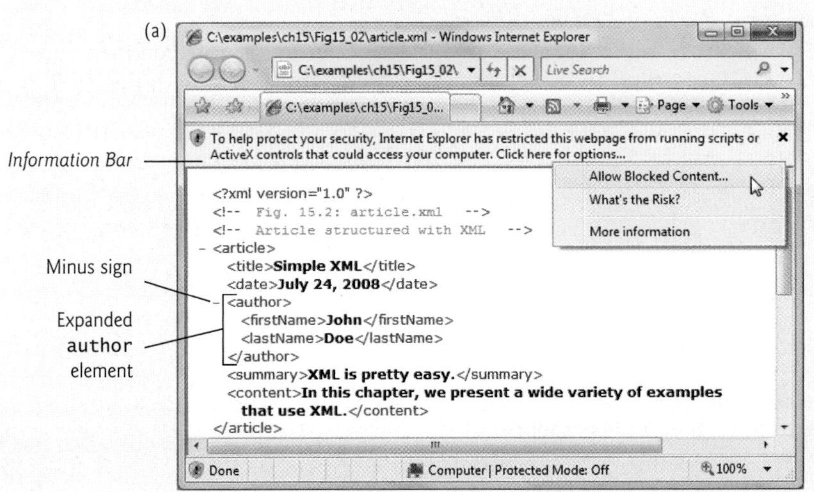

Fig. 15.3 | `article.xml` displayed by Internet Explorer. (Part 1 of 2.)

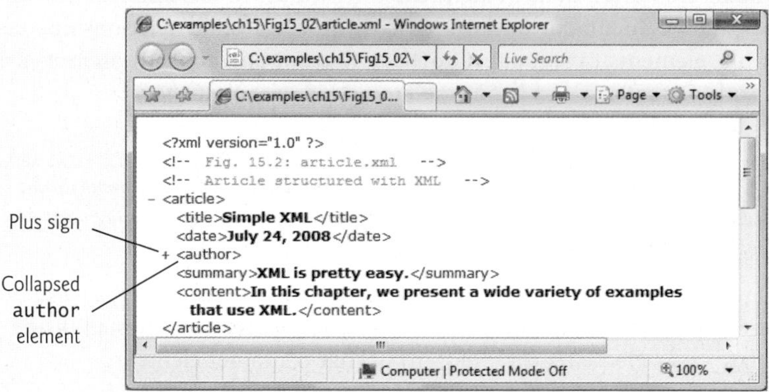

Fig. 15.3 | `article.xml` displayed by Internet Explorer. (Part 2 of 2.)

replace the minus sign with a plus sign). Conversely, clicking the plus sign next to an element expands that element (i.e., causes Internet Explorer to display the container element's children and replace the plus sign with a minus sign). This behavior is similar to viewing the directory structure using Windows Explorer. In fact, a directory structure often is modeled as a series of tree structures, in which the **root** of a tree represents a drive letter (e.g., `C:`), and **nodes** in the tree represent directories. Parsers often store XML data as tree structures to facilitate efficient manipulation.

[*Note:* In Windows XP Service Pack 2 and Windows Vista, by default Internet Explorer displays all the XML elements in expanded view, and clicking the minus sign (Fig. 15.3(a)) does not do anything. So, by default, Windows will not be able to collapse the element. To enable this functionality, right click the *Information Bar* just below the **Address** field and select **Allow Blocked Content....** Then click **Yes** in the popup window that appears.]

XML Markup for a Business Letter

Now that we have seen a simple XML document, let's examine a more complex one that marks up a business letter (Fig. 15.4). Again, we begin the document with the XML declaration (line 1) that states the XML version to which the document conforms.

```
1  <?xml version = "1.0"?>
2  <!-- Fig. 15.4: letter.xml -->
3  <!-- Business letter marked up as XML -->
4
5  <!DOCTYPE letter SYSTEM "letter.dtd">
6
7  <letter>
8     <contact type = "sender">
9        <name>Jane Doe</name>
10       <address1>Box 12345</address1>
11       <address2>15 Any Ave.</address2>
12       <city>Othertown</city>
```

Fig. 15.4 | Business letter marked up as XML. (Part 1 of 2.)

```
13          <state>Otherstate</state>
14          <zip>67890</zip>
15          <phone>555-4321</phone>
16          <flag gender = "F" />
17       </contact>
18
19       <contact type = "receiver">
20          <name>John Doe</name>
21          <address1>123 Main St.</address1>
22          <address2></address2>
23          <city>Anytown</city>
24          <state>Anystate</state>
25          <zip>12345</zip>
26          <phone>555-1234</phone>
27          <flag gender = "M" />
28       </contact>
29
30       <salutation>Dear Sir:</salutation>
31
32       <paragraph>It is our privilege to inform you about our new database
33          managed with XML. This new system allows you to reduce the
34          load on your inventory list server by having the client machine
35          perform the work of sorting and filtering the data.
36       </paragraph>
37
38       <paragraph>Please visit our website for availability
39          and pricing.
40       </paragraph>
41
42       <closing>Sincerely,</closing>
43       <signature>Ms. Jane Doe</signature>
44    </letter>
```

Fig. 15.4 | Business letter marked up as XML. (Part 2 of 2.)

Line 5 specifies that this XML document references a DTD. Recall from Section 15.3 that DTDs define the structure of the data for an XML document. For example, a DTD specifies the elements and parent/child relationships between elements permitted in an XML document.

Error-Prevention Tip 15.1

An XML document is not required to reference a DTD, but validating XML parsers can use a DTD to ensure that the document has the proper structure.

Portability Tip 15.2

Validating an XML document helps guarantee that independent developers will exchange data in a standardized form that conforms to the DTD.

The DTD reference (line 5) contains three items: the name of the root element that the DTD specifies (`letter`); the keyword **`SYSTEM`** (which denotes an **external DTD**—a DTD declared in a separate file, as opposed to a DTD declared locally in the same file);

and the DTD's name and location (i.e., `letter.dtd` in the same directory as the XML document). DTD document file names typically end with the `.dtd` extension. We discuss DTDs and `letter.dtd` in detail in Chapter 19.

Root element `letter` (lines 7–44 of Fig. 15.4) contains the child elements `contact`, `contact`, `salutation`, `paragraph`, `paragraph`, `closing` and `signature`. Besides being placed between tags, data also can be placed in attributes—name/value pairs that appear within the angle brackets of start tags. Elements can have any number of attributes (separated by spaces) in their start tags, provided all the attribute names are unique. The first `contact` element (lines 8–17) has an attribute named `type` with attribute value `"sender"`, which indicates that this `contact` element identifies the letter's sender. The second `contact` element (lines 19–28) has attribute `type` with value `"receiver"`, which indicates that this `contact` element identifies the letter's recipient. Like element names, attribute names are case sensitive, can be of any length, may contain letters, digits, underscores, hyphens and periods, and must begin with either a letter or an underscore character. A `contact` element stores various items of information about a contact, such as the contact's name (represented by element `name`), address (represented by elements `address1`, `address2`, `city`, `state` and `zip`), phone number (represented by element `phone`) and gender (represented by attribute `gender` of element `flag`). Element `salutation` (line 30) marks up the letter's salutation. Lines 32–40 mark up the letter's body using two `paragraph` elements. Elements `closing` (line 42) and `signature` (line 43) mark up the closing sentence and the author's "signature," respectively.

Common Programming Error 15.6

Failure to enclose attribute values in double ("") or single ('') quotes is a syntax error.

Line 16 introduces the empty element `flag`. An empty element contains no content. However, an it may sometimes contain data in the form of attributes. Empty element `flag` contains an attribute that indicates the gender of the contact (represented by the parent `contact` element). Document authors can close an empty element either by placing a slash immediately preceding the right angle bracket, as shown in line 16, or by explicitly writing an end tag, as in line 22

```
<address2></address2>
```

Line 22 can also be written as:

```
<address2/>
```

Note that the `address2` element in line 22 is empty, because there is no second part to this contact's address. However, we must include this element to conform to the structural rules specified in the XML document's DTD—`letter.dtd` (which we present in Chapter 19). This DTD specifies that each `contact` element must have an `address2` child element (even if it is empty). In Chapter 19, you will learn how DTDs indicate that certain elements are required while others are optional.

15.5 XML Namespaces

XML allows document authors to create custom elements. This extensibility can result in naming collisions—elements with identical names that represent different things—when combining content from multiple sources. For example, we may use the element book to mark up data about a Deitel publication. A stamp collector may use the element book to mark up data about a book of stamps. Using both of these elements in the same document could create a naming collision, making it difficult to determine which kind of data each element contains.

An XML namespace is a collection of element and attribute names. Like Visual Basic namespaces, XML namespaces provide a means for document authors to unambiguously refer to elements that have the same name (i.e., prevent collisions). For example,

```
<subject>Math</subject>
```

and

```
<subject>Cardiology</subject>
```

use element subject to mark up data. In the first case, the subject is something one studies in school, whereas in the second case, the subject is a field of medicine. Namespaces can differentiate these two subject elements. For example,

```
<school:subject>Math</school:subject>
```

and

```
<medical:subject>Cardiology</medical:subject>
```

Both school and medical are namespace prefixes. A document author places a namespace prefix and colon (:) before an element name to specify the namespace to which that element belongs. Document authors can create their own namespace prefixes using virtually any name except the reserved namespace prefixes xml and xmlns. In the subsections that follow, we demonstrate how document authors ensure that namespaces are unique.

Common Programming Error 15.7

Attempting to create a namespace prefix named xml *in any mixture of uppercase and lowercase letters is a syntax error—the* xml *namespace prefix is reserved for internal use by XML itself.*

Differentiating Elements with Namespaces

Figure 15.5 demonstrates namespaces. In this document, namespaces differentiate two distinct elements—the file element related to a text file and the file document related to an image file.

```
<?xml version = "1.0"?>
<!-- Fig. 15.5: namespace.xml -->
<!-- Demonstrating namespaces -->

<text:directory
   xmlns:text = "urn:deitel:textInfo"
   xmlns:image = "urn:deitel:imageInfo">

   <text:file filename = "book.xml">
      <text:description>A book list</text:description>
   </text:file>
```

Fig. 15.5 | XML namespaces demonstration. (Part 1 of 2.)

```
12
13    <image:file filename = "funny.jpg">
14       <image:description>A funny picture</image:description>
15       <image:size width = "200" height = "100" />
16    </image:file>
17 </text:directory>
```

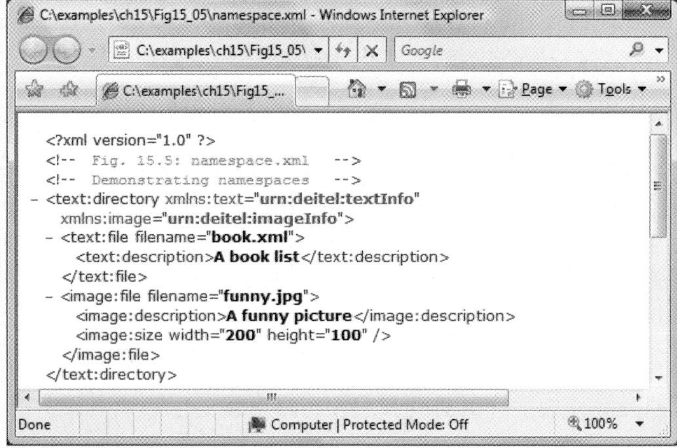

Fig. 15.5 | XML namespaces demonstration. (Part 2 of 2.)

Lines 6–7 use the XML-namespace reserved attribute `xmlns` to create two namespace prefixes—`text` and `image`. Creating a namespace prefix is similar to using an `Imports` statement in Visual Basic—it allows you to access XML elements from a given namespace. Each namespace prefix is bound to a series of characters called a Uniform Resource Identifier (URI) that uniquely identifies the namespace. Document authors create their own namespace prefixes and URIs. A URI is a way to identify a resource, typically on the Internet. Two popular types of URI are Uniform Resource Name (URN) and Uniform Resource Locator (URL).

To ensure that namespaces are unique, document authors must provide unique URIs. In this example, we use the text `urn:deitel:textInfo` and `urn:deitel:imageInfo` as URIs. These URIs employ the URN scheme frequently used to identify namespaces. Under this naming scheme, a URI begins with `"urn:"`, followed by a unique series of additional names separated by colons. Note that these URIs are not guaranteed to be unique—the idea is simply that creating a long URI in this way makes it unlikely that two authors will use the same namespace.

Another common practice is to use URLs, which specify the location of a file or a resource on the Internet. For example, `http://www.deitel.com` is the URL that identifies the home page of the Deitel & Associates website. Using URLs guarantees that the namespaces are unique, because the domain names (e.g., `www.deitel.com`) are guaranteed to be unique. For example, lines 5–7 could be rewritten as

```
<text:directory
   xmlns:text = "http://www.deitel.com/xmlns-text"
   xmlns:image = "http://www.deitel.com/xmlns-image">
```

where URLs related to the Deitel & Associates, Inc. domain name serve as URIs to identify the `text` and `image` namespaces. The parser does not visit these URLs, nor do these URLs need to refer to actual web pages. Each simply represents a unique series of characters used to differentiate URI names. In fact, any string can represent a namespace. For example, our `image` namespace URI could be `hgjfkdlsa4556`, in which case our prefix assignment would be

```
xmlns:image = "hgjfkdlsa4556"
```

Lines 9–11 use the `text` namespace prefix for elements `file` and `description`. Note that the end tags must also specify the namespace prefix `text`. Lines 13–16 apply namespace prefix `image` to the elements `file`, `description` and `size`. Note that attributes do not require namespace prefixes (although they can have them), because each attribute is already part of an element that specifies the namespace prefix. For example, attribute `filename` (line 9) is already uniquely identified by being in the context of the `filename` start tag, which is prefixed with `text`.

Specifying a Default Namespace

To eliminate the need to place namespace prefixes in each element, document authors may specify a default namespace for an element and its children. Figure 15.6 demonstrates using a default namespace (`urn:deitel:textInfo`) for element `directory`.

Line 5 defines a default namespace using attribute `xmlns` with a URI as its value. Once we define this default namespace, child elements which do not specify a prefix belong to the default namespace. Thus, element `file` (lines 8–10) is in the default namespace `urn:deitel:textInfo`. Compare this to lines 9–11 of Fig. 15.5, where we had to prefix the `file` and `description` element names with the namespace prefix `text`.

Common Programming Error 15.8

The default namespace can be overridden at any point in the document with another `xmlns` *attribute. All direct and indirect children of the element with the* `xmlns` *attribute use the new default namespace.*

```
1  <?xml version = "1.0"?>
2  <!-- Fig. 15.6: defaultnamespace.xml -->
3  <!-- Using default namespaces -->
4
5  <directory xmlns = "urn:deitel:textInfo"
6     xmlns:image = "urn:deitel:imageInfo">
7
8     <file filename = "book.xml">
9        <description>A book list</description>
10    </file>
11
12    <image:file filename = "funny.jpg">
13       <image:description>A funny picture</image:description>
14       <image:size width = "200" height = "100" />
15    </image:file>
16 </directory>
```

Fig. 15.6 | Default namespace demonstration. (Part 1 of 2.)

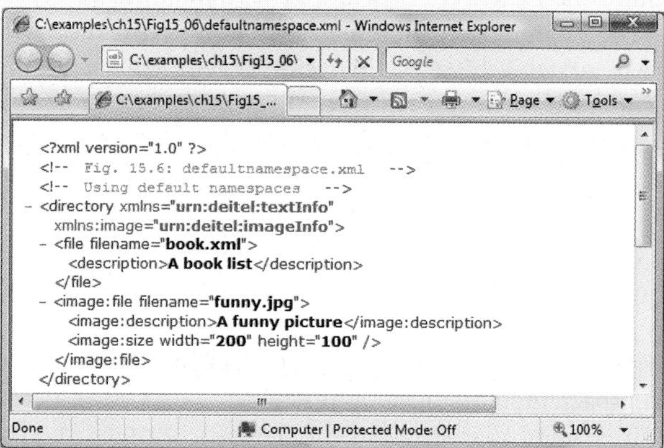

Fig. 15.6 | Default namespace demonstration. (Part 2 of 2.)

The default namespace applies to the `directory` element and all elements that are not qualified with a namespace prefix. However, we can use a namespace prefix to specify a different namespace for particular elements. For example, the `file` element in lines 12–15 includes the `image` namespace prefix, indicating that this element is in the `urn:deitel:imageInfo` namespace, not the default namespace.

Namespaces in XML Vocabularies

XML-based languages, such as XML Schema, Extensible Stylesheet Language (XSL) and BizTalk (`www.microsoft.com/biztalk`), often use namespaces to identify their elements. Each of these vocabularies defines special-purpose elements that are grouped in namespaces. These namespaces help prevent naming collisions between predefined elements and user-defined elements.

15.6 Declarative GUI Programming Using XAML

A XAML document defines the appearance of a WPF application. Figure 15.7 is a simple XAML document that defines a window that displays `Welcome to WPF!`

Since XAML documents are XML documents, a XAML document consists of many nested elements, delimited by start tags and end tags. As with any other XML document, each XAML document must contain a single root element. Just as in XML, data is placed as nested content or in attributes.

```
<!-- Fig. 15.7: XAMLIntroduction.xaml -->
<!-- A simple XAML document. -->

<!-- the Window control is the root element of the GUI -->
<Window x:Class="XAMLIntroduction"
   xmlns="http://schemas.microsoft.com/winfx/2006/xaml/presentation"
   xmlns:x="http://schemas.microsoft.com/winfx/2006/xaml"
   Title="A Simple Window" Height="150" Width="250">
```

Fig. 15.7 | A simple XAML document. (Part 1 of 2.)

```
 9
10       <!-- a layout container -->
11       <Grid Background="Gold">
12
13          <!-- a Label control -->
14          <Label HorizontalAlignment="Center" VerticalAlignment="Center">
15             Welcome to WPF!
16          </Label>
17       </Grid>
18    </Window>
```

Fig. 15.7 | A simple XAML document. (Part 2 of 2.)

Two standard namespaces must be defined in every XAML document so that the XAML compiler can interpret your markup—the **presentation XAML namespace**, which defines WPF-specific elements and attributes, and the **standard XAML namespace**, which defines elements and attributes that are standard to all types of XAML documents. Usually, the presentation XAML namespace (`http://schemas.microsoft.com/winfx/2006/xaml/presentation`) is defined as the default namespace (line 6), and the standard XAML namespace (`http://schemas.microsoft.com/winfx/2006/xaml`) is mapped to the key `x` (line 7). These are both automatically included in the `Window` element's start tag when you create a WPF application in Visual Studio.

WPF **controls** are represented by elements in XAML markup. The root element of the XAML document in Fig. 15.7 is a **`Window`** control (lines 5–18), which defines the application's window—this corresponds to the `Form` control in Windows `Forms`.

The `Window` start tag (line 5) also defines another important attribute, **`x:Class`**, which specifies the class name of the associated code-behind class that provides the GUI's functionality (line 5). The `x:` signifies that the `Class` attribute is located in the standard XAML namespace. A XAML document must have an associated code-behind file to handle events.

Using attributes, you can define a control's properties in XAML. For example, the `Window`'s `Title`, `Width` and `Height` properties are set in line 8. A `Window`'s `Title` specifies the text that is displayed in the `Window`'s title bar. The `Width` and `Height` properties apply to a control of any type and specify the control's width and height, respectively, using machine-independent pixels.

`Window` is a **content control** (a control derived from class **`ContentControl`**), meaning it can have exactly one child element or text content. You'll almost always set a **layout container** (a control derived from the **`Panel`** class) as the child element so that you can host multiple controls in a `Window`. A layout container such as a `Grid` (lines 11–17) can have many child elements, allowing it to contain many controls. In Section 15.8, you'll use content controls and layout containers to arrange a GUI.

Like `Window`, a `Label`—corresponding to the `Label` control in Windows `Forms`—is also a `ContentControl`. It is generally used to display a small amount of information.

15.7 Creating a WPF Application in Visual Basic Express

To create a new WPF application, open the **New Project** dialog (Fig. 15.8) and select **WPF Application** from the list of template types. The IDE for a WPF application looks nearly identical to that of a Windows `Forms` application. You'll recognize the familiar **Toolbox**, **Design** view, **Solution Explorer** and **Properties** window.

There are differences, however. One is the new **XAML view** (Fig. 15.9) that appears when you open a XAML document. This view is linked to the **Design** view and the **Properties** window. When you edit content in the **Design** view, the **XAML** view automatically updates, and vice versa. Likewise, when you edit properties in the **Properties** window, the **XAML** view automatically updates, and vice versa.

When you create a WPF application, four files are generated and can be viewed in the **Solution Explorer**. `Application.xaml` defines the `Application` object and its settings. The most noteworthy setting is the `StartupUri` attribute, which defines the XAML document that executes first when the `Application` loads (`Window1.xaml` by default). `Application.xaml.vb` is its code-behind class and handles application-level events. `Window1.xaml`

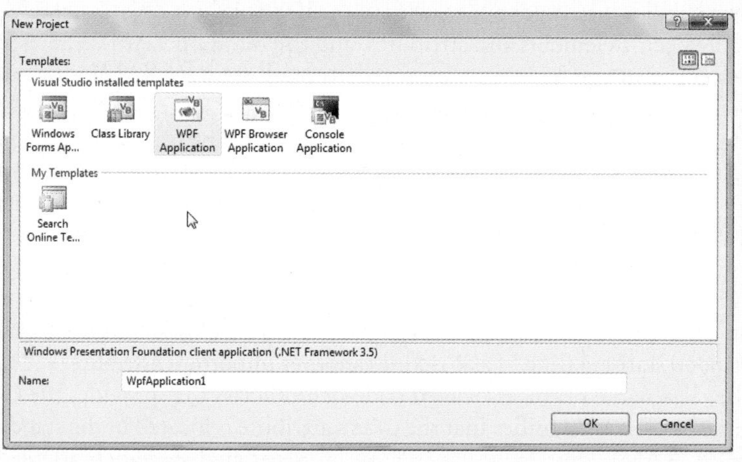

Fig. 15.8 | **New Project** dialog.

Design | XAML

```
<Window x:Class="Window1"
    xmlns="http://schemas.microsoft.com/winfx/2006/xaml/presentation"
    xmlns:x="http://schemas.microsoft.com/winfx/2006/xaml"
    Title="Window1" Height="300" Width="300">
    <Grid>

    </Grid>
</Window>
```

Fig. 15.9 | **XAML** view.

defines the application window, and `Window1.xaml.vb` is its code-behind class, which handles the window's events. The file name of the code-behind class is always the file name of the associated XAML document appended by the `.vb` file-name extension.

[*Note:* At the time of this writing (pre Visual Studio 2008 Service Pack 1), if you have `Option Strict` turned `On`, you'll get an implicit conversion error when you compile your WPF application. To fix it, double click the error message. This displays the file `MyWpfExtension.vb` in **Code** view. Next, click the **Error Correction Options** icon (![]) and apply the suggested correction (Fig. 15.10).]

Error-Prevention Tip 15.2

Before you begin designing and coding your WPF application, make sure that the `StartupUri` *attribute of* `Application.xaml` *points to the correct XAML document. You can do this either by editing the XAML markup or by changing the property in the* **Application** *tab of the* **My Project** *properties view. In addition, ensure that every XAML document references the correct class name (not file name) of its associated code-behind class.*

We use three-space indents in our code. To ensure that your code appears the same as the book's examples, change the tab spacing for XAML documents to three spaces (the default is four). Select **Tools > Options** and ensure that the **Show all settings** checkbox is checked. In **Text Editor > XAML > Tabs** change both the **Tab size** and **Indent size** properties to `3` (Fig. 15.11). In addition, you should configure the **XAML** editor to display line numbers by checking the **Line numbers** checkbox in **Text Editor > XAML > General**. You are now ready to create your first WPF application.

Creating a WPF application in Visual Basic Express is similar to creating a Windows `Forms` application. Just as you did in the last chapter to create a Windows `Forms` application, you can drag-and-drop controls onto the **Design** view of your WPF GUI. A control's

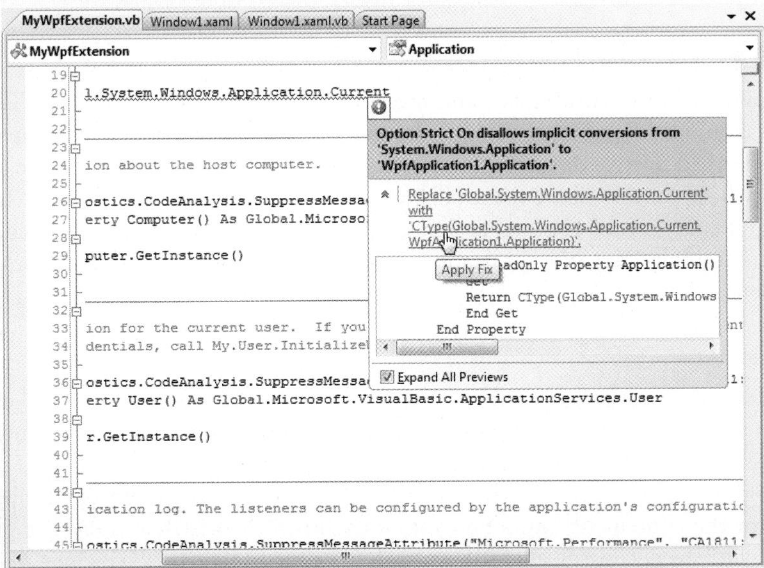

Fig. 15.10 | Casting the application type to comply with `Option Strict`.

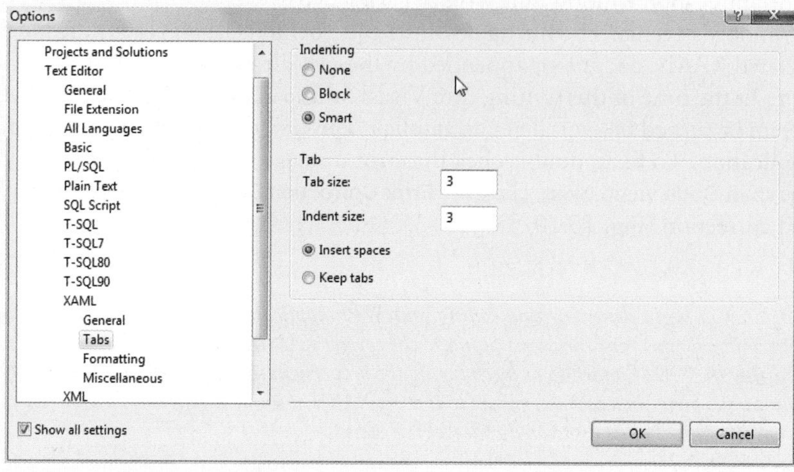

Fig. 15.11 | Changing the tab spacing.

properties can be edited in the **Properties** window. Event handlers can be created using the **Class Name** and **Method Name** menus at the top of the **Code** editor. However, at the time of this writing, there is no way to create event handlers from the **Properties** window in a WPF application—this feature is part of Visual Studio 2008 Service Pack 1.

Because XAML is easy to understand and edit, it is often less difficult to manually edit your GUI's XAML markup than to do everything through the IDE. In some cases, you must manually write XAML markup in order to take full advantage of the features that are offered in WPF. Nevertheless, the visual programming tools in Visual Studio are often handy, and we'll point out the situations in which they might be useful as they occur.

15.8 Laying Out Controls

In Windows `Forms`, a control's size and location are specified explicitly. In WPF, a control's size should be specified as a range of possible values rather than fixed values, and its location specified relative to those of other controls. This type of layout scheme, in which you specify how controls share the available space, is called **flow-based layout**. Its advantage is that it enables your GUIs, if designed properly, to be aesthetically pleasing, no matter how a user might resize the application. Likewise, it enables your GUIs to be resolution independent.

15.8.1 General Layout Principles

Layout refers to the size and positioning of controls. The WPF layout scheme addresses both of these in a flow-based fashion and can be summarized by two fundamental principles.

Unless necessary, a control's size should not be defined explicitly. Doing so often creates a design that looks pleasing when it first loads, but deteriorates when the application is resized or the content updates. Thus, in addition to the `Width` and `Height` properties associated with every control, all WPF controls have the **`MinWidth`**, **`MinHeight`**, **`MaxHeight`** and **`MaxHeight`** properties. If the `Width` and `Height` properties are both `Auto` (which is the default), you can use these minimum and maximum properties to specify a range of acceptable sizes for a control. Its size will automatically adjust as the size of its container changes.

A control's position should not be defined in absolute terms. Instead, it should be specified based on its position relative to the layout container in which it is included and the other controls in the same container. All controls have three properties for doing this—**Margin**, **HorizontalAlignment** and **VerticalAlignment**. Margin specifies how much space to put around a control's edges. The parameters of Margin are a comma-separated list of four integers, representing the left, top, right and bottom margins. Additionally, you can pass it two integers, which it interprets as the left–right and top–bottom margins. If you pass it just one integer, it uses the same margin on all four sides.

HorizontalAlignment and VerticalAlignment specify how to align a control within its layout container. Valid options of HorizontalAlignment are Left, Center, Right and Stretch. Valid options of VerticalAlignment are Top, Center, Bottom and Stretch. Stretch means that the object will occupy as much space as possible.

A control can have other layout properties specific to the layout container in which it is contained. We'll discuss these as we examine the specific layout containers. WPF provides many controls for laying out a GUI. Figure 15.12 lists some of the common controls used for layout.

Control	Description
Layout containers (derived from Panel*)*	
Grid	Layout is defined by a grid of rows and columns, depending on the RowDefinitions and ColumnDefinitions properties. Elements are placed into cells.
Canvas	Layout is coordinate based. Element positions are defined explicitly by their distance from the top and left edges of the Canvas.
StackPanel	Elements are arranged in a single row or column, depending on the Orientation property.
DockPanel	Elements are positioned based on which edge they are docked to. If the LastChildFill property is True, the last element gets the remaining space in the middle.
WrapPanel	A wrapping StackPanel. Elements are arranged sequentially in rows or columns (depending on the Orientation), each row or column wrapping to start a new one when it reaches the WrapPanel's right or bottom edge, respectively.
Content controls (derived from ContentControl*)*	
Border	Adds a background or a border to the child element.
GroupBox	Surrounds the child element with a titled box.
Window	The application window. Also the root element.
Expander	Puts the child element in a titled area that collapses to display just the header and expands to display the header and the content.

Fig. 15.12 | Common controls used for layout.

15.8.2 Layout in Action

Figure 15.13 shows the XAML document and the GUI display of a painter application. Note the use of `Margin`, `HorizontalAlignment` and `VerticalAlignment` throughout the markup. This example introduces several WPF controls that are commonly used for layout, as well as a few other basic ones.

Note that the controls in this application look similar to Windows `Forms` controls. WPF **`RadioButtons`** function as mutually exclusive options, just like their Windows `Forms` counterparts. However, a WPF `RadioButton` does not have a `Text` property. Instead, it is a `ContentControl`, meaning it can have exactly one child or text content. This makes the control more versatile, enabling it to be labeled by an image or other item. In this example, each `RadioButton` is labeled by plain text (e.g., lines 28–30). A WPF **`Button`** behaves like a Windows `Forms` `Button` but is a `ContentControl`. As such, a WPF `Button` can display any single element as its content, not just text. Lines 61–69 define the two buttons seen in the `Painter` application. You can drag and drop controls onto the WPF designer and create their event handlers, just as you do in the Windows `Forms` designer.

```
1   <!-- Fig. 15.13: Painter.xaml -->
2   <!-- XAML of a painter application. -->
3   <Window x:Class="PainterWindow"
4       xmlns="http://schemas.microsoft.com/winfx/2006/xaml/presentation"
5       xmlns:x="http://schemas.microsoft.com/winfx/2006/xaml"
6       Title="Painter" Height="340" Width="350" Background="Beige">
7
8       <Grid> <!-- creates a Grid -->
9          <Grid.ColumnDefinitions> <!-- specifies the columns -->
10            <ColumnDefinition Width="Auto" /> <!-- defines a column -->
11            <ColumnDefinition Width="*" />
12         </Grid.ColumnDefinitions>
13
14         <!-- creates a Canvas -->
15         <Canvas Grid.Column="1" Margin="0" Name="paintCanvas"
16            Background="White" />
17
18         <StackPanel Margin="3"> <!-- creates a StackPanel-->
19
20            <!-- creates a GroupBox for color options -->
21            <GroupBox Grid.ColumnSpan="1" Header="Color" Margin="3"
22               Name="colorGroupBox" HorizontalAlignment="Stretch"
23               VerticalAlignment="Top">
24               <StackPanel Name="colorStackPanel" Margin="3"
25                  HorizontalAlignment="Left" VerticalAlignment="Top">
26
27                  <!-- creates RadioButtons for selecting color -->
28                  <RadioButton Name="redRadioButton" Margin="3">
29                     Red
30                  </RadioButton>
31                  <RadioButton Name="blueRadioButton" Margin="3">
32                     Blue
33                  </RadioButton>
```

Fig. 15.13 | XAML of a painter application. (Part 1 of 2.)

```
               <RadioButton Name="greenRadioButton" Margin="3">
                  Green
               </RadioButton>
               <RadioButton Name="blackRadioButton" Margin="3"
                  IsChecked="True">
                  Black
               </RadioButton>
            </StackPanel>
         </GroupBox>

         <!-- creates GroupBox for size options -->
         <GroupBox Header="Size" Name="sizeGroupBox" Margin="3">
            <StackPanel Name="StackPanel1" Margin="3">
               <RadioButton Name="smallRadioButton" Margin="3">
                  Small
               </RadioButton>
               <RadioButton Name="mediumRadioButton" Margin="3"
                  IsChecked="True">
                  Medium
               </RadioButton>
               <RadioButton Name="largeRadioButton" Margin="3">
                  Large
               </RadioButton>
            </StackPanel>
         </GroupBox>

         <!-- creates a Button-->
         <Button Height="23" Name="undoButton" Width="75"
            Margin="3,10,3,3">
            Undo
         </Button>

         <Button Height="23" Name="clearButton" Width="75"
            Margin="3">
            Clear
         </Button>
      </StackPanel>
   </Grid>
</Window>
```

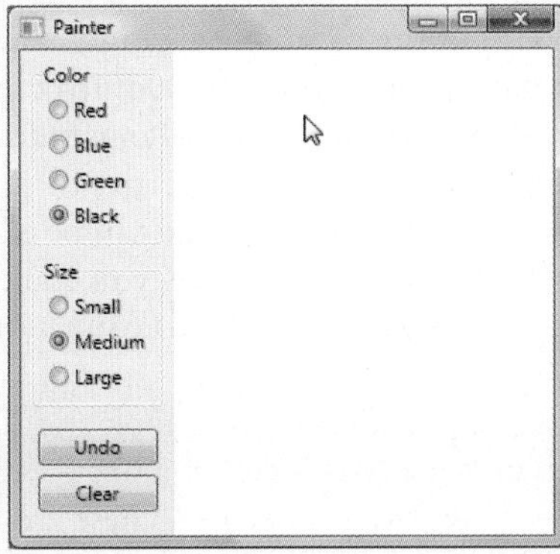

Fig. 15.13 | XAML of a painter application. (Part 2 of 2.)

GroupBox Control

A WPF GroupBox arranges controls and displays just as a Windows Forms GroupBox would, but using one is slightly different. The Header property replaces the Windows Forms version's Text property. In addition, a GroupBox is a ContentControl, so to place multiple controls in it, you must place them in a layout container (e.g., lines 21–42).

StackPanel Control

In the Painter application, we organized each GroupBox's RadioButtons by placing them in StackPanels (e.g., lines 24–41). A StackPanel is the simplest of layout containers. It arranges its content in either vertically or horizontally, depending on the Orientation property's setting. The default Orientation is Vertical, which is used by every StackPanel in the Painter example.

Grid Control

The Painter Window's contents are contained within a Grid—a flexible, all-purpose layout container. A Grid organizes controls into a user-defined number of rows and columns (one row and one column by default). You can define a Grid's rows and columns by setting its Grid.RowDefinitions and Grid.ColumnDefinitions properties, whose values are a collection of RowDefinition and ColumnDefinition objects, respectively. Because these properties do not take String values, they cannot be specified as attributes in the Grid tag. Another syntax is used instead. A class's property can be defined in XAML as a nested element with the name *ClassName.PropertyName*. For example, the Grid.ColumnDefinitions element in lines 9–12 sets the Grid's ColumnDefinitions property and defines two columns, which separate the options from the painting area, as shown in Fig. 15.13.

You can specify the Width of a ColumnDefinition and the Height of a RowDefinition with an explicit size, a relative size (using *) or Auto. Auto makes the row or column only as big as it needs to be to fit its contents. The setting * specifies the size of a row or column with respect to the Grid's other rows and columns. For example, a column with a Height of 2* would be twice the size of a column that is 1* (or just *). A Grid first allocates its space to the rows and columns whose sizes are defined explicitly or determined automatically. The remaining space is divided among the other rows and columns. By default, all Widths and Heights are set to *, so every cell in the grid is of equal size. In the Painter application, the first column is just wide enough to fit the controls, and the rest of the space is allotted to the painting area (lines 10–11). If you resize the Painter window, you'll notice that only the width of the paintable area increases or decreases.

If you click the ellipsis button next to the RowDefinitions or ColumnDefinitions property in the **Properties** window, the **Collection Editor** window will appear. This tool can be used to add, remove, reorder, and edit the properties of rows and columns in a Grid. In fact, any property that takes a collection as a value can be edited in a version of the **Collection Editor** specific to that collection. For example, you could edit the Items property of a ComboBox (i.e., drop-down list) in such a way. The ColumnDefinitions **Collection Editor** is shown in Fig. 15.14.

The control properties we've introduced so far look and function just like their Windows Forms counterparts. To indicate which cell of a Grid a control belongs in, however, you use the Grid.Row and Grid.Column properties. These are known as attached properties—they are defined by a different control than that to which they are applied. In this case, Row and Column are defined by the Grid itself but applied to the controls contained

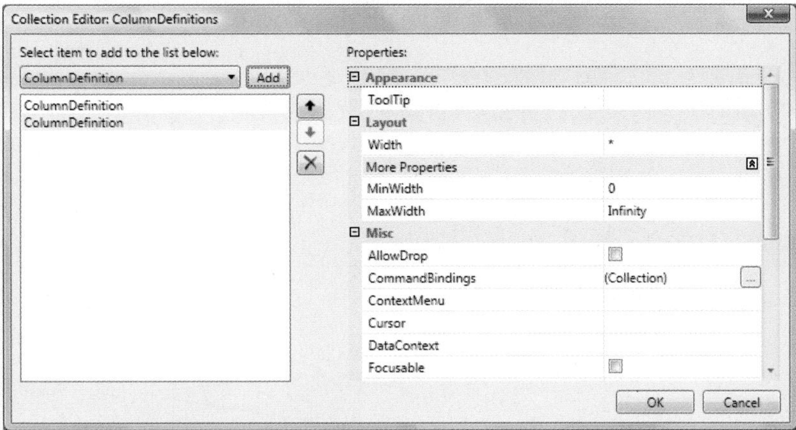

Fig. 15.14 | Using the **Collection Editor**.

in the `Grid` (e.g., line 15). To specify the number of rows or columns that a control spans, you can use the **`Grid.RowSpan`** or **`Grid.ColumnSpan`** attached properties, respectively (e.g., line 21). By default, a control spans the entire `Grid`, unless the `Grid.Row` or `Grid.Column` property is set, in which case the control spans only the specified row or column by default.

`Canvas` Control

The painting area of the `Painter` application is a **`Canvas`** (lines 15–16), another layout container. A `Canvas` allows users to position controls by defining explicit coordinates. Controls in a `Canvas` have the attached properties, **`Canvas.Left`** and **`Canvas.Top`**, which specify the control's coordinate position based on its distance from the `Canvas`'s left and top borders, respectively. If two controls overlap, the one with the greater **`Canvas.ZIndex`** displays in the foreground. If this property is not defined for the controls, then the last control added to the canvas displays in the foreground.

Layout in **Design** *Mode*

As you are creating your GUI in **Design** mode, you'll notice many helpful layout features. For example, as you resize a control, its width and height are displayed. In addition, red snaplines appear as necessary to help you align the edges of elements. These lines will also appear when you move controls around the design area.

When you select a control, margin lines that extend from the control to the edges of its container appear, as shown in Fig. 15.15. If a line extends to the edge of the container, then the distance between the control and that edge is fixed. If it displays as a little circular stub, then the distance between the control and that edge is dynamic and changes as its surroundings change. You can toggle between the two by clicking on the margin line.

Furthermore, the **Design** view also helps you use a `Grid`. As shown in Fig. 15.15, when you select a control in a `Grid`, the `Grid`'s rulers appear to the left and on top of it. The widths and heights of each column and row, respectively, appear on the rulers. Gridlines that outline the `Grid`'s rows and columns also appear, helping you align and position the `Grid`'s elements. You can also create more rows and columns by clicking where you want to separate them on the ruler.

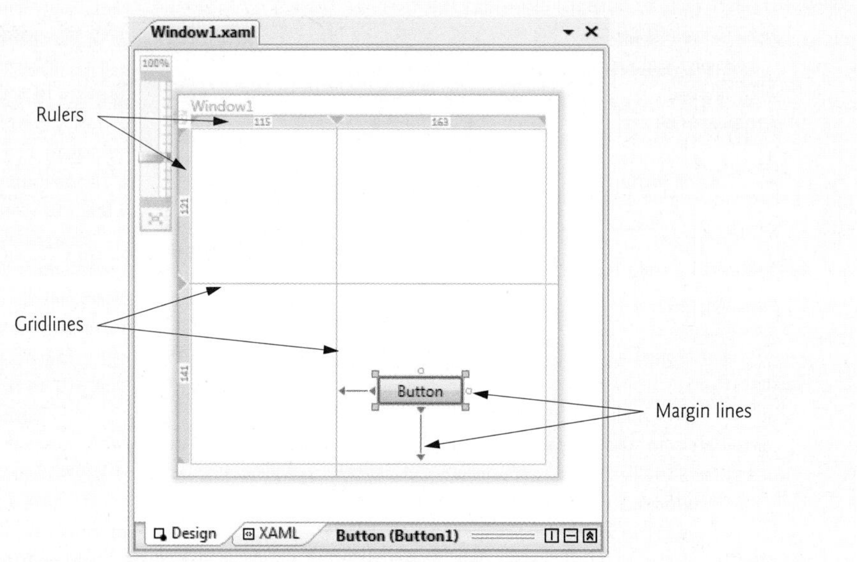

Fig. 15.15 | Margin lines and gridlines in **Design** view.

15.9 Event Handling

Basic event handling in WPF is almost identical to Windows `Forms` event handling, but there is a fundamental difference, which we'll explain later in this section. We'll use the `Painter` example to introduce WPF event handling. Figure 15.16 provides the code-behind class for the `Painter` `Window`.

The `Painter` application "draws" by placing colored circles on the `Canvas` at the mouse pointer's position as you drag the mouse. The `PaintCircle` method (lines 16–29 in Fig. 15.16) creates the circle by defining an `Ellipse` object (lines 19–23), and positions it using the **`Canvas.SetLeft`** and **`Canvas.SetTop`** methods (lines 25–26), which change the circle's `Canvas.Left` and `Canvas.Top` attached properties, respectively.

```
1  ' Fig. 15.16: Painter.xaml.vb
2  ' Code-behind class for Painter.
3  Class PainterWindow
4     Private diameter As Integer = 8 ' set diameter of circle
5     Private brushColor As Brush = Brushes.Black ' set the color to draw in
6     Private shouldErase As Boolean = False ' specify whether to erase
7     Private shouldPaint As Boolean = False ' specify whether to paint
8
9     Private Enum Sizes ' size constants for diameter of the circle
10       SMALL = 4
11       MEDIUM = 8
12       LARGE = 10
13    End Enum
14
```

Fig. 15.16 | Code-behind class for `Painter`. (Part 1 of 4.)

```
   ' paints a circle on the Canvas
   Private Sub PaintCircle(ByVal circleColor As Brush, _
      ByVal position As Point)

      Dim newEllipse As Ellipse = New Ellipse() ' create an Ellipse

      newEllipse.Fill = circleColor ' set Ellipse's color
      newEllipse.Width = diameter ' set its horizontal diameter
      newEllipse.Height = diameter ' set its vertical diameter

      Canvas.SetTop(newEllipse, position.Y) ' set its distance from top
      Canvas.SetLeft(newEllipse, position.X) ' set its distance from left

      paintCanvas.Children.Add(newEllipse) ' add it to the Canvas
   End Sub ' PaintCircle

   ' handles paintCanvas's MouseLeftButtonDown event
   Private Sub paintCanvas_MouseLeftButtonDown(ByVal sender As Object, _
      ByVal e As MouseButtonEventArgs) _
      Handles paintCanvas.MouseLeftButtonDown

      shouldPaint = True ' OK to draw on the Canvas
   End Sub ' paintCanvas_MouseLeftButtonDown

   ' handles paintCanvas's MouseLeftButtonUp event
   Private Sub paintCanvas_MouseLeftButtonUp(ByVal sender As Object, _
      ByVal e As MouseButtonEventArgs) _
      Handles paintCanvas.MouseLeftButtonUp

      shouldPaint = False ' do not draw on the Canvas
   End Sub ' paintCanvas_MouseLeftButtonUp

   ' handles paintCanvas's MouseMove event
   Private Sub paintCanvas_MouseMove(ByVal sender As Object, _
      ByVal e As MouseEventArgs) _
      Handles paintCanvas.MouseMove

      If shouldPaint = True Then
         ' draw a circle in the selected color at current mouse position
         Dim mousePosition As Point = e.GetPosition(paintCanvas)
         PaintCircle(brushColor, mousePosition)
      ElseIf shouldErase = True Then
         ' erase by drawing circles of the Canvas's background color
         Dim mousePosition As Point = e.GetPosition(paintCanvas)
         PaintCircle(paintCanvas.Background, mousePosition)
      End If
   End Sub ' paintCanvas_MouseMove

   ' handles paintCanvas's MouseRightButtonDown event
   Private Sub paintCanvas_MouseRightButtonDown(ByVal sender As Object, _
      ByVal e As MouseButtonEventArgs) _
      Handles paintCanvas.MouseRightButtonDown

```

Fig. 15.16 | Code-behind class for `Painter`. (Part 2 of 4.)

```
      shouldErase = True ' OK to erase the Canvas
   End Sub ' paintCanvas_MouseRightButtonDown

   ' handles paintCanvas's MouseRightButtonUp event
   Private Sub paintCanvas_MouseRightButtonUp(ByVal sender As Object, _
      ByVal e As MouseButtonEventArgs) _
      Handles paintCanvas.MouseRightButtonUp

      shouldErase = False ' do not erase the Canvas
   End Sub ' paintCanvas_MouseRightButtonUp

   ' handles Red RadioButton's Checked event
   Private Sub redRadioButton_Checked(ByVal sender As Object, _
      ByVal e As RoutedEventArgs) Handles redRadioButton.Checked

      brushColor = Brushes.Red
   End Sub ' redRadioButton_Checked

   ' handles Blue RadioButton's Checked event
   Private Sub blueRadioButton_Checked(ByVal sender As Object, _
      ByVal e As RoutedEventArgs) Handles blueRadioButton.Checked

      brushColor = Brushes.Blue
   End Sub ' blueRadioButton_Checked

   ' handles Green RadioButton's Checked event
   Private Sub greenRadioButton_Checked(ByVal sender As Object, _
      ByVal e As RoutedEventArgs) Handles greenRadioButton.Checked

      brushColor = Brushes.Green
   End Sub ' greenRadioButton_Checked

   ' handles Black RadioButton's Checked event
   Private Sub blackRadioButton_Checked(ByVal sender As Object, _
      ByVal e As RoutedEventArgs) Handles blackRadioButton.Checked

      brushColor = Brushes.Black
   End Sub ' blackRadioButton_Checked

   ' handles Small RadioButton's Checked event
   Private Sub smallRadioButton_Checked(ByVal sender As Object, _
      ByVal e As RoutedEventArgs) Handles smallRadioButton.Checked

      diameter = Sizes.SMALL
   End Sub ' smallRadioButton_Checked

   ' handles Medium RadioButton's Checked event
   Private Sub mediumRadioButton_Checked(ByVal sender As Object, _
      ByVal e As RoutedEventArgs) Handles mediumRadioButton.Checked

      diameter = Sizes.MEDIUM
   End Sub ' mediumRadioButton_Checked

```

Fig. 15.16 | Code-behind class for `Painter`. (Part 3 of 4.)

```
121    ' handles Large RadioButton's Checked event
122    Private Sub largeRadioButton_Checked(ByVal sender As Object, _
123       ByVal e As RoutedEventArgs) Handles largeRadioButton.Checked
124
125       diameter = Sizes.LARGE
126    End Sub ' largeRadioButton_Checked
127
128    ' handles Undo Button's Click event
129    Private Sub undoButton_Click(ByVal sender As Object, _
130       ByVal e As RoutedEventArgs) Handles undoButton.Click
131
132       ' if there are any shapes on the canvas
133       If paintCanvas.Children.Count > 0 Then
134          ' remove the last one that was added
135          paintCanvas.Children.RemoveAt(paintCanvas.Children.Count - 1)
136       End If
137    End Sub ' undoButton_Click
138
139    ' handles Clear Button's Click event
140    Private Sub clearButton_Click(ByVal sender As Object, _
141       ByVal e As RoutedEventArgs) Handles clearButton.Click
142
143       paintCanvas.Children.Clear() ' clear the canvas
144    End Sub ' clearButton_Click
145 End Class ' PainterWindow
```

Fig. 15.16 | Code-behind class for `Painter`. (Part 4 of 4.)

The **`Children`** property stores a list (of type **`UIElementCollection`**) of a layout container's child elements. This allows you to edit the layout container's child elements with Visual Basic code as you would any other implementation of the `IEnumerable` interface. For example, you can add an element to the container by calling the **`Add`** method of the `Children` list (e.g., line 28). The **Undo** and **Clear** buttons work by invoking the **`RemoveAt`** and **`Clear`** methods of the `Children` list (lines 135 and 143), respectively.

Just as with a Windows Forms RadioButton, a WPF RadioButton has a Checked event. Lines 80–126 handle the Checked event for each of the RadioButtons in this example, which change the color and the size of the circles painted on the Canvas. The Button control's Click event also functions the same in WPF as it did in Windows Forms. Lines 129–144 handle the **Undo** and **Clear** Buttons. The event-handler declarations look almost identical to how they would look in a Windows Forms application, except that the event-arguments object (e) is a RoutedEventArgs object instead of an EventArgs object. We'll explain why later in this section.

Mouse and Keyboard Events

WPF has built-in support for keyboard and mouse events that is nearly identical to the support in Windows Forms. Painter uses the MouseMove event of the paintable Canvas to paint and erase (lines 48–61). A control's MouseMove event is triggered whenever the mouse moves while within the boundaries of the control. Information for the event is passed to the event handler using MouseEventArgs, which contains mouse-specific information. The GetPosition method of MouseEventArgs, for example, returns the current position of the mouse relative to the control that triggered the event (e.g., lines 54 and 58). MouseMove works exactly the same as it does in Windows Forms. [*Note:* Much of the funcionality in our sample Painter application is already provided by the WPF InkCanvas control. We chose not to use this control so we could demonstrate various other WPF features.]

WPF has additional mouse events. Painter also uses the MouseLeftButtonDown and MouseLeftButtonUp events to toggle painting on and off (lines 32–45), and the MouseRightButtonDown and MouseRightButtonUp events to toggle erasing on and off (lines 64–77). All of these events pass information to the event handler using the MouseButtonEventArgs object, which has properties specific to a mouse button (e.g., ButtonState or ClickCount) in addition to mouse-specific ones. These events are new to WPF and are more specific versions of MouseUp and MouseDown (which are still available in WPF). A summary of commonly used mouse and keyboard events is provided in Fig. 15.17.

Common mouse and keyboard events	
Mouse Events with an Event Argument of Type MouseEventArgs	
MouseMove	Raised when the mouse cursor is moved while within the control's boundaries.
Mouse Events with an Event Argument of Type MouseButtonEventArgs	
MouseLeftButtonDown	Raised when the left mouse button is pressed.
MouseLeftButtonUp	Raised when the left mouse button is released.
MouseRightButtonDown	Raised when the right mouse button is pressed.
MouseRightButtonUp	Raised when the right mouse button is released.
Mouse Events with an Event Argument of Type MouseWheelEventArgs	
MouseWheel	Raised when the mouse wheel is rotated.

Fig. 15.17 | Common mouse and keyboard events. (Part 1 of 2.)

Common mouse and keyboard events	
Keyboard Events with an Event Argument of Type `KeyEventArgs`	
`KeyDown`	Raised when a key is pressed.
`KeyUp`	Raised when a key is released.

Fig. 15.17 | Common mouse and keyboard events. (Part 2 of 2.)

Routed Events

WPF events have a significant distinction from their Windows `Forms` counterparts—they can travel either up (from child to parent) or down (from parent to child) the containment hierarchy—the hierarchy of nested elements defined within a control. This is called event routing, and all WPF events are routed events.

This explains why the event-arguments object that is passed to the event handler of a `Button`'s `Click` event or a `RadioButton`'s `Check` event is of the type `RoutedEventArgs`. In fact, all event-argument objects in WPF are of type `RoutedEventArgs` or one of its subclasses. As an event travels up or down the hierarchy, it may be useful to stop it before it reaches the end. When the `Handled` property of the `RoutedEventArgs` parameter is set to `True`, event handlers ignore the event. It may also be useful to know the source where the event was first triggered. The `Source` property stores this information.

Figures 15.18 and 15.19 show the XAML and code-behind for a program that demonstrates event routing. The program contains two `GroupBox`es, each with a `Label` inside (lines 15–29 in Fig. 15.18). One group handles a left-mouse-button press with `MouseLeftButtonUp`, and the other with `PreviewMouseLeftButtonUp`. As the event travels up or down the containment hierarchy, a log of where the event has traveled is displayed in a `TextBox` (line 31). The WPF `TextBox` functions just like its Windows `Forms` counterpart.

```
1  <!-- Fig. 15.18: RoutedEvents.xaml -->
2  <!-- Routed-events example (XAML). -->
3  <Window x:Class="RoutedEvents"
4     xmlns="http://schemas.microsoft.com/winfx/2006/xaml/presentation"
5     xmlns:x="http://schemas.microsoft.com/winfx/2006/xaml"
6     Title="Routed Events" Height="300" Width="300"
7     Name="routedEventsWindow">
8     <Grid>
9        <Grid.RowDefinitions>
10          <RowDefinition Height="Auto" />
11          <RowDefinition Height="Auto" />
12          <RowDefinition Height="*" />
13       </Grid.RowDefinitions>
14
15       <GroupBox Name="tunnelingGroupBox" Grid.Row="0" Header="Tunneling"
16          Margin="5" >
17          <Label Margin="5" Name="tunnelingLabel"
18             HorizontalAlignment="Center">
19             Click Here
```

Fig. 15.18 | Routed-events example (XAML). (Part 1 of 2.)

```
         </Label>
      </GroupBox>

      <GroupBox Name="bubblingGroupBox" Grid.Row="1" Header="Bubbling"
         Margin="5">
         <Label Margin="5" Name="bubblingLabel"
            HorizontalAlignment="Center">
            Click Here
         </Label>
      </GroupBox>

      <TextBox Name="logTextBox" Grid.Row="2" Margin="5" />
   </Grid>
</Window>
```

Fig. 15.18 | Routed-events example (XAML). (Part 2 of 2.)

```
' Fig. 15.19: RoutedEvents.xaml.vb
' Routed-events example (code-behind).
Class RoutedEvents
   Private bubblingEventStep As Integer = 1 ' step counter for Bubbling
   Private tunnelingLogText As String = "" ' temporary log for Tunneling
   Private tunnelingEventStep As Integer = 1 ' step counter for Tunneling

   ' MouseUp is a bubbling event
   Private Sub Bubbling(ByVal sender As Object, _
      ByVal e As MouseButtonEventArgs) _
      Handles bubblingLabel.MouseLeftButtonUp, _
      bubblingGroupBox.MouseLeftButtonUp

      ' execution goes from child to parent, starting at the source
      If e.Source.Equals(sender) Then
         logTextBox.Clear() ' clear logTextBox
         bubblingEventStep = 1 ' reset counter
         logTextBox.Text = "This is a bubbling event:" & vbNewLine
      End If

      ' append step number and sender
      logTextBox.Text = logTextBox.Text & "(" & bubblingEventStep & _
         "):" & CType(sender, Control).Name & vbNewLine
      bubblingEventStep += 1 ' increment counter
   End Sub ' Bubbling

   ' PreviewMouseUp is a tunneling event
   Private Sub Tunneling(ByVal sender As Object, _
      ByVal e As MouseButtonEventArgs) _
      Handles tunnelingLabel.PreviewMouseLeftButtonUp, _
      tunnelingGroupBox.PreviewMouseLeftButtonUp

      ' append step number and sender
      tunnelingLogText = tunnelingLogText & "(" & tunnelingEventStep & _
         "): " & CType(sender, Control).Name & vbNewLine
```

Fig. 15.19 | Routed-events example (code-behind). (Part 1 of 2.)

```
36         tunnelingEventStep += 1 ' increment counter
37
38         ' execution goes from parent to child, ending with the source
39         If e.Source.Equals(sender) Then
40            tunnelingLogText = "This is a tunneling event:" & vbNewLine & _
41               tunnelingLogText
42            logTextBox.Text = tunnelingLogText ' set logTextBox text
43            tunnelingLogText = "" ' clear temporary log
44            tunnelingEventStep = 1 ' reset counter
45         End If
46      End Sub ' Tunneling
47   End Class ' RoutedEvents
```

Fig. 15.19 | Routed-events example (code-behind). (Part 2 of 2.)

There are three types of routed events—direct events, bubbling events and tunneling events. Direct events are like ordinary Windows `Forms` events—they do not travel up or down the containment hierarchy. Bubbling events start at the `Source` and travel up the hierarchy ending at the `Window` or until you set `Handled` to `True`. Tunneling events start at the top and travel down the hierarchy until they reach the `Source` or `Handled` is `True`. To help you distinguish tunneling events from bubbling events, WPF prefixes the names of tunneling events with `Preview`. For example, `PreviewMouseLeftButtonDown` is the tunneling version of `MouseLeftButtonDown`, which is a bubbling event.

If you click the **Click Here** `Label` in the **Tunneling** `GroupBox`, the click is handled first by the `GroupBox`, then by the contained `Label`. The event handler that responds to the click handles the `PreviewMouseLeftButtonUp` event—a tunneling event. Note that the `Tunneling` method handles the events of both the `GroupBox` and the `Label` (lines 30–31 in Fig. 15.19). An event handler can handle events for many controls, specified in the `Handles` clause by a comma-separated list. If you click the other `Label`, the click is handled first by the `Label`, then by the containing `GroupBox`. The event that is handled in this case is `MouseLeftButtonUp`—the bubbling event (lines 11–12).

15.10 Commands and Common Application Tasks

In Windows `Forms`, event handling is the only way to respond to user actions. WPF provides an alternate technique called a command—an action or a task that may be triggered by many different user interactions. In Visual Studio, for example, you can cut, copy and paste code. You can execute these tasks through the **Edit** menu, a toolbar or keyboard shortcuts. To program this functionality in WPF, you can define a single command for each task. In Windows Forms, you must code and maintain the handling of an event for each menu item, one for each toolbar item and one to handle the key presses.

Commands also enable you to synchronize a task's availability to the state of its corresponding controls. For example, users should be able to copy something only if they have content selected. When you define the copy command, you can specify this as a requirement. As a result, if the user has no content selected, then the menu item, toolbar item and keyboard shortcut for copying are all automatically disabled.

Commands are implementations of the **ICommand** interface. Every ICommand has a Name and a collection of **InputGestures** (i.e., keyboard shortcuts) associated with it. When a command is executed, the **Execute** method is called. However, the command's execution logic (i.e., how it should execute) is not defined in its Execute method. You must specify this logic when implementing the command. An ICommand's **CanExecute** method works in the same way. The logic that specifies when a command is enabled and disabled is not determined by the CanExecute method and must instead be specified at implementation. Class RoutedCommand is the standard implementation of ICommand. RoutedUICommand is an extension of RoutedCommand with a Text property, which specifies the default text to display on a GUI element that triggers the command.

WPF provides a command library of built-in commands. These commands have their standard keyboard shortcuts already associated with them. For example, Copy is a built-in command and has *Ctrl-C* associated with it. Figure 15.20 provides a list of some common built-in commands, listed by the class in which they are defined. Like any command, none of these commands contains any built-in application logic.

Figures 15.21 and 15.22 are the XAML markup and Visual Basic code for a simple text-editor application that allows users to format text into bold and italics, and also to cut, copy and paste text. The example uses the **RichTextBox** control (line 52), which allows users to enter, edit and format text. We use this application to demonstrate several built-in commands from the command library.

A command is executed when it is triggered by a command source. For example, the Close command is triggered by a MenuItem (line 23 in Fig. 15.21). The Cut command has two sources, a MenuItem and a ToolBar Button (lines 26 and 39, respectively). A command can have many sources.

Common built-in commands from the WPF command library			
ApplicationCommands properties			
New	Open	Save	Close
Cut	Copy	Paste	
EditingCommands properties			
ToggleBold	ToggleItalic	ToggleUnderline	
MediaCommands properties			
Play	Stop	Rewind	FastForward
IncreaseVolume	DecreaseVolume	NextTrack	PreviousTrack

Fig. 15.20 | Common built-in commands from the WPF command library.

To make use of a command, you must create a command binding—a link between a command and the methods containing its application logic. You can declare a command binding by creating a `CommandBinding` object in XAML and setting its `Command` property to the name of the associated command (line 10). A command binding raises the `Executed` and `PreviewExecuted` events (bubbling and tunneling versions of the same event) when its associated command is executed. You program the command's functionality into an event handler for one of these events. In line 10, we set the `Executed` attribute to a method name, telling the program that the specified method (`closeCommand_Executed`) handles the command binding's `Executed` event. The syntax used here for defining an event handler in XAML can be applied to controls as well. For example, you can define a `Button`'s `Click` handler by setting the `Click` attribute of the `Button` element, as in `<Button Click="`*EventHandlerName*`">`.

```
1  <!-- Fig. 15.21: TextEditor.xaml -->
2  <!-- Creating menus and toolbars, and using commands (XAML). -->
3  <Window x:Class="TextEditor"
4     xmlns="http://schemas.microsoft.com/winfx/2006/xaml/presentation"
5     xmlns:x="http://schemas.microsoft.com/winfx/2006/xaml"
6     Title="Text Editor" Height="300" Width="300">
7
8     <Window.CommandBindings> <!-- define command bindings -->
9        <!-- bind the Close command to handler -->
10       <CommandBinding Command="Close" Executed="closeCommand_Executed" />
11    </Window.CommandBindings>
12
13    <Grid> <!-- define the GUI -->
14       <Grid.RowDefinitions>
15          <RowDefinition Height="Auto" />
16          <RowDefinition Height="Auto" />
17          <RowDefinition Height="*" />
18       </Grid.RowDefinitions>
19
20       <Menu Grid.Row="0"> <!-- create the menu -->
21          <!-- map each menu item to corresponding command -->
22          <MenuItem Header="File">
23             <MenuItem Header="Exit" Command="Close" />
24          </MenuItem>
25          <MenuItem Header="Edit">
26             <MenuItem Header="Cut" Command="Cut" />
27             <MenuItem Header="Copy" Command="Copy" />
28             <MenuItem Header="Paste" Command="Paste" />
29             <Separator /> <!-- separates groups of menu items -->
30             <MenuItem Header="Bold" Command="ToggleBold"
31                FontWeight="Bold" />
32             <MenuItem Header="Italic" Command="ToggleItalic"
33                FontStyle="Italic" />
34          </MenuItem>
35       </Menu>
36
```

Fig. 15.21 | Creating menus and toolbars, and using commands (XAML). (Part 1 of 2.)

```
37        <ToolBar Grid.Row="1"> <!-- create the toolbar -->
38           <!-- map each toolbar item to corresponding command -->
39           <Button Command="Cut">Cut</Button>
40           <Button Command="Copy">Copy</Button>
41           <Button Command="Paste">Paste</Button>
42           <Separator /> <!-- separates groups of toolbar items -->
43           <Button FontWeight="Bold" Command="ToggleBold">
44              Bold
45           </Button>
46           <Button FontStyle="Italic" Command="ToggleItalic">
47              Italic
48           </Button>
49        </ToolBar>
50
51        <!-- display editable, formattable text -->
52        <RichTextBox Grid.Row="2" Margin="5" />
53     </Grid>
54  </Window>
```

Fig. 15.21 | Creating menus and toolbars, and using commands (XAML). (Part 2 of 2.)

In this example, we demonstrate the use of a command binding by implementing the `Close` command. When it executes, it shuts down the application. The method that executes this task is `Application.Current.Shutdown`, as shown in line 9 of Fig. 15.22. Note that the method that handles the `Close` command binding's `Executed` event does not have a `Handles` clause (lines 6–10). If you have already defined an event's handler in XAML (line 10 of Fig. 15.21), there is no need to specify it again in the `Handles` clause of the event handler's method definition.

You can also use a command binding to specify the application logic for determining when a command should be enabled or disabled. You can do so by handling either the `CanExecute` or `PreviewCanExecute` (bubbling and tunneling versions of the same events) events in the same way that you handle the `Executed` or `PreviewExecuted` events. Because we do not define such a handler for the `Close` command in its command binding, it is always enabled. Command bindings should be defined within the `Window.CommandBindings` element (e.g., lines 8–11).

```
1   ' Fig. 15.22: TextEditor.xaml.vb
2   ' Code-behind class for a simple text editor.
3   Class TextEditor
4
5      ' exit the application
6      Private Sub closeCommand_Executed(ByVal sender As Object, _
7         ByVal e As RoutedEventArgs)
8
9         Application.Current.Shutdown() ' shut down application
10     End Sub ' closeCommand_Executed
11  End Class ' TextEditor
```

Fig. 15.22 | Code-behind class for a simple text editor. (Part 1 of 2.)

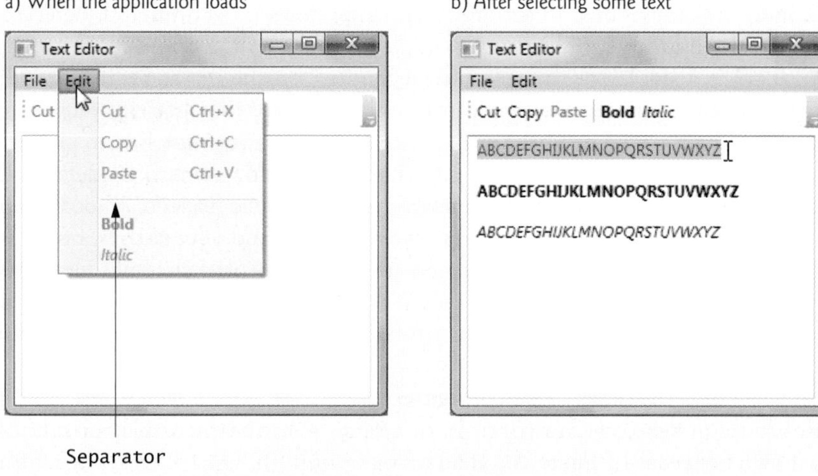

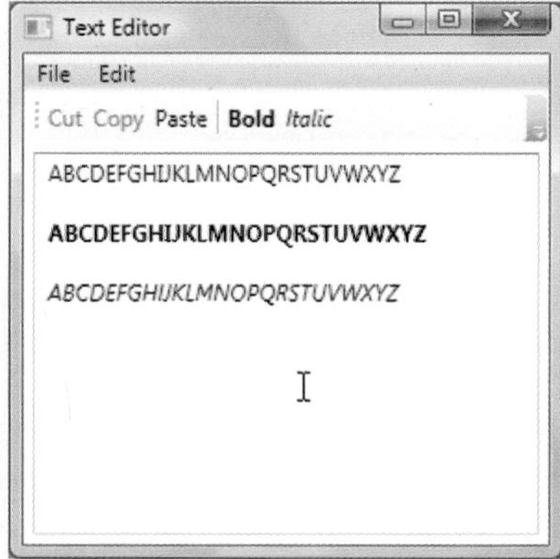

Fig. 15.22 | Code-behind class for a simple text editor. (Part 2 of 2.)

The only time a command binding is not necessary is when a control has built-in functionality for dealing with a command. A `Button` or `MenuItem` linked to the `Cut`, `Copy`, or `Paste` commands is an example (e.g., lines 26–28 and lines 39–41). As Fig. 15.22(a) shows, all three commands are disabled when the application loads. If you select some text, the `Cut` and `Copy` commands are enabled, as shown in Fig. 15.22(b). Once you have copied some text, the `Paste` command is enabled, as evidenced by Fig. 15.22(c). Note that we did not have to define any associated command bindings or event handlers to implement these commands. The `ToggleBold` and `ToggleItalic` commands are also implemented without any command bindings.

Menus and Toolbars

The text editor uses menus and toolbars. The **`Menu`** control creates a menu containing **`MenuItem`**s. `MenuItem`s can be top-level menus such as **File** or **Edit** (lines 24 and 27 in Fig. 15.21), submenus, or items in a menu, which function like `Button`s (e.g., lines 28–

30). If a MenuItem has nested MenuItems, then it's a top-level menu or a submenu. Otherwise, it's an item that executes an action via either an event or a command. MenuItems are content controls and thus can display any single GUI element as content.

A ToolBar is a single row or column (depending on the Orientation property) of options. A ToolBar's Orientation is a read-only property that gets its value from the parent ToolBarTray, which can host multiple ToolBars. If a ToolBar has no parent ToolBarTray, as is the case in this example, its Orientation is Horizontal by default. Unlike elements in a Menu, a ToolBar's child elements are not of a specific type. A ToolBar usually contains Buttons, CheckBoxes, ComboBoxes, RadioButtons and Separators, but any WPF control can be used. ToolBars overwrite the look-and-feel of their child elements with their own specifications, so that the controls look seamless together. You can override the default specifications to create your own look-and-feel. Lines 37–49 define the text editor's ToolBar.

Both Menus and ToolBars can incorporate Separators (e.g., lines 29 and 42) that differentiate groups of MenuItems or controls. In a Menu, a Separator displays as a horizontal bar—as shown between the **Paste** and **Bold** menu options in Fig. 15.22(a). In a horizontal ToolBar, it displays as a short vertical bar—as shown in Fig. 15.22(b). You can use Separators in any type of control that can contain multiple child elements, such as a StackPanel.

15.11 WPF GUI Customization

One advantage of WPF over Windows Forms is the ability to customize controls. WPF provides several techniques to customize the look and behavior of controls. The simplest takes full advantage of a control's properties. The value of a control's Background property, for example, is a brush (i.e, Brush object). This allows you to create a gradient or an image and use it as the background rather than a solid color. For more information about brushes, see Section 16.5. In addition, many controls that allowed only text content in Windows Forms are ContentControls in WPF, which can host any type of content—including other controls. The caption of a WPF Button, for example, could be an image or even a video.

In Section 15.12, we demonstrate how to use styles in WPF to achieve a uniform look-and-feel. In Windows Forms, if you want to make all your Buttons look the same, you have to manually set properties for every Button, or copy and paste. To achieve the same result in WPF, you can define the properties once as a style and apply the style to each Button. This is similar to the CSS/XHTML implementation of styles. XHTML specifies the content and structure of a website, and CSS defines styles that specify the presentation of elements in a website. For more information on CSS and XHTML, see Chapter 21, ASP.NET and ASP.NET AJAX, or visit our XHTML and CSS Resource Centers at www.deitel.com/xhtml/ and www.deitel.com/css21/, respectively.

Styles are limited to modifying a control's look-and-feel through its properties. In Section 15.14, we introduce control templates, which offer you the freedom to define a control's appearance by modifying its visual structure. With a custom control template, you can completely strip a control of all its visual settings and rebuild it to look exactly the way you like, while maintaining its existing functionality. A Button with a custom control template might look structurally different from a default Button, but it still functions the same as any other Button.

If you want to change only the appearance of an element, a style or control template should suffice. However, you can also create entirely new custom controls that have their own functionality, properties, methods and events. We demonstrate how to create a custom control in Section 23.4.3.

15.12 Using Styles to Change the Appearance of Controls

Once defined, a WPF style is a collection of property-value and event-handler definitions that can be reused. Style prevent you from writing repetitive code or markup. For example, if you want to change the look-and-feel of the standard `Button` throughout a section of your application, you can define a style and apply it to all the `Buttons` in that section. Without styles, you have to set the properties for each individual `Button`. Furthermore, if you later decided that you wanted to tweak the appearance of these `Buttons`, you would have to modify your markup or code several times. By using a style, you would need to make the change only once in the style and it would automatically be applied to any control which used that style.

Styles are WPF resources. A resource is an object that is defined for an entire section of your application and can be reused multiple times. A resource can be as simple as a property or as complex as a control template. Every WPF control can hold a collection of resources that can be accessed by any element down the containment hierarchy. In a way, this is similar in approach to the concept of variable scope that you learned about in Chapter 7. For example, if you define a style as a resource of a `Window`, then the contents of the `Window` can apply that style. If you define a style as a resource of a layout container, then only the elements of the layout container can apply that style. You can also define application-level resources for an `Application` object in the `Application.xaml` file. These resources can be accessed in any file in the application.

Figure 15.23 provides the XAML markup and Fig. 15.24 provides the Visual Basic code for a color-chooser application. This example demonstrates the use of styles and introduces the `Slider` user input control.

```
<!-- Fig. 15.23: ColorChooser.xaml -->
<!-- Color-chooser application showing the use of styles (XAML). -->
<Window x:Class="ColorChooser"
   xmlns="http://schemas.microsoft.com/winfx/2006/xaml/presentation"
   xmlns:x="http://schemas.microsoft.com/winfx/2006/xaml"
   Title="Color Chooser" Height="150" Width="450">

   <Window.Resources> <!-- define Window's resources -->
      <Style x:Key="SliderStyle"> <!-- define style for Sliders -->

         <!-- set properties for Sliders -->
         <Setter Property="Slider.Width" Value="256" />
         <Setter Property="Slider.Minimum" Value="0" />
         <Setter Property="Slider.Maximum" Value="255" />
         <Setter Property="Slider.IsSnapToTickEnabled" Value="True" />
         <Setter Property="Slider.VerticalAlignment" Value="Center" />
```

Fig. 15.23 | Color-chooser application showing the use of styles (XAML). (Part 1 of 2.)

```
         <Setter Property="Slider.HorizontalAlignment" Value="Center" />
         <Setter Property="Slider.Value" Value="0" />
         <Setter Property="Slider.AutoToolTipPlacement"
            Value="TopLeft" />

         <!-- set event handler for ValueChanged event -->
         <EventSetter Event="Slider.ValueChanged"
            Handler="slider_ValueChanged" />
      </Style>
   </Window.Resources>

   <Grid Margin="5"> <!-- define GUI -->
      <Grid.RowDefinitions>
         <RowDefinition />
         <RowDefinition />
         <RowDefinition />
         <RowDefinition />
      </Grid.RowDefinitions>
      <Grid.ColumnDefinitions>
         <ColumnDefinition Width="Auto" />
         <ColumnDefinition Width="Auto" />
         <ColumnDefinition />
      </Grid.ColumnDefinitions>

      <!-- define Labels for Sliders -->
      <Label Grid.Row="0" Grid.Column="0" HorizontalAlignment="Right"
         VerticalAlignment="Center">Red:</Label>
      <Label Grid.Row="1" Grid.Column="0" HorizontalAlignment="Right"
         VerticalAlignment="Center">Green:</Label>
      <Label Grid.Row="2" Grid.Column="0" HorizontalAlignment="Right"
         VerticalAlignment="Center">Blue:</Label>
      <Label Grid.Row="3" Grid.Column="0" HorizontalAlignment="Right"
         VerticalAlignment="Center">Alpha:</Label>

      <Label Name="colorLabel" Grid.RowSpan="4" Grid.Column="2"
         Margin="10" /> <!-- define Label that displays the color -->

      <!-- define Sliders and apply style to them -->
      <Slider Name="redSlider" Grid.Row="0" Grid.Column="1"
         Style="{StaticResource SliderStyle}" />
      <Slider Name="greenSlider" Grid.Row="1" Grid.Column="1"
         Style="{StaticResource SliderStyle}" />
      <Slider Name="blueSlider" Grid.Row="2" Grid.Column="1"
         Style="{StaticResource SliderStyle}" />
      <Slider Name="alphaSlider" Grid.Row="3" Grid.Column="1"
         Style="{StaticResource SliderStyle}" Value="255" />
   </Grid>
</Window>
```

Fig. 15.23 | Color-chooser application showing the use of styles (XAML). (Part 2 of 2.)

The color-chooser application uses the RGBA system of color selection. Every color is represented by its red, green and blue color values, each ranging from 0 to 255, where 0 denotes no color and 255 full color. For example, a color with a red value of 0 would

```
1  ' Fig. 15.24: ColorChooser.xaml.vb
2  ' Color-chooser application showing the use of styles (code-behind).
3  Class ColorChooser
4     ' handles the ValueChanged event for the Sliders
5     Private Sub slider_ValueChanged(ByVal sender As Object, _
6        ByVal e As RoutedPropertyChangedEventArgs(Of Double))
7
8        ' generate new color
9        Dim backgroundColor As New SolidColorBrush()
10       backgroundColor.Color = Color.FromArgb(CByte(alphaSlider.Value), _
11          CByte(redSlider.Value), CByte(greenSlider.Value), _
12          CByte(blueSlider.Value))
13
14       ' set colorLabel's background to new color
15       colorLabel.Background = backgroundColor
16    End Sub ' slider_ValueChanged
17 End Class ' ColorChooser
```

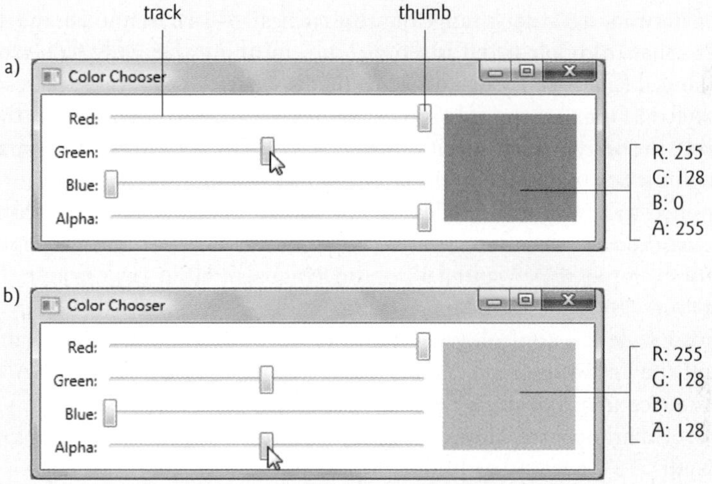

Fig. 15.24 | Color-chooser application showing the use of styles (code-behind).

contain no red component. The alpha value (A)—which also ranges from 0 to 255—represents a color's opacity, with 0 being completely transparent and 255 completely opaque. For example, the two colors in Fig. 15.24 have the same base color, but the color displayed in Fig. 15.24(b) is semitransparent.

The color-chooser GUI is composed of four **`Slider`** controls that change the RGBA values of a color displayed by a `Label`. A `Slider`, as shown in Fig. 15.24(a), is a numeric user input control that allows users to drag a "thumb" along a track to select the value. Whenever the user moves a `Slider`, the application generates a new color, and the `Label` displays the new color as its background. The new color is generated by using class `Color`'s `FromArgb` method, which returns a color based on the four RGBA byte values you pass it (lines 10–12). The color is then applied as the background of the `Label` using a `SolidColorBrush`. For more information about brushes, please see Chapter 16.

Styles can be defined as a resource of any control. In the color-chooser application, we defined the style as a resource of the entire Window. We also could have defined it as a resource of the Grid. To define resources for a control, you set a control's Resources property. Thus, to define a resource for a Window, as we did in this example, you would use Window.Resources (lines 8–26 in Fig. 15.23). To define a resource for a Grid, you would use Grid.Resources.

Style objects can be defined in XAML using the Style element. The x:Key attribute (i.e., attribute Key from the standard XAML namespace) must be set in every style (or other resource) so that it can be referenced later by other controls (line 9). The children of a Style element set properties and define event handlers. A Setter sets a property to a specific value (e.g., line 12, which sets the styled Slider's Width property to 256). An EventSetter specifies the method that responds to an event (e.g., lines 23–24, which specifies that method slider_ValueChanged handles the Slider's ValueChanged event).

The Style in the color-chooser example (SliderStyle) primarily uses Setters. It lays out the color Sliders by specifying their Width, HorizontalAlignment and VerticalAlignment properties (lines 12, 16 and 17). It also sets the Minimum and Maximum properties, which determine a Slider's range of values (lines 13–14). In line 18, the default Value is set to 0. IsSnapToTickEnabled is set to True, meaning that only values that fall on a "tick" are allowed (line 15). By default, each tick is separated by a value of 1, so this setting makes the styled Slider accept only integer values. Lastly, the style also sets the AutoToolTipPlacement property, which specifies where a Slider's tooltip should appear, if at all.

Although the Style defined in the color-chooser example is clearly meant for Sliders, it can be applied to any control. Styles are not control specific. You can make all controls of one type use the same default style by setting the style's TargetType attribute to the control type. For example, if we wanted all of the Window's Sliders to use a Style, we would add TargetType="Slider" to the its start tag.

To apply a style to a control, you create a resource binding between a control's Style property and the Style resource. You can create a resource binding in XAML by specifying the resource in a markup extension—an expression enclosed in curly braces ({}). The form of a markup extension calling a resource is {*ResourceType ResourceKey*} (e.g., {StaticResource SliderStyle} in line 56).

There are two types of resources. Static resources are applied at initialization time only. Dynamic resources are applied every time the resource is modified by the application. To use a style as a static resource, use StaticResource as the type in the markup extension. To use a style as a dynamic resource, use DynamicResource as the type. Because styles don't normally change during runtime, they are usually used as static resources. However, using one as a dynamic resource is sometimes necessary, such as when you wish to enable users to customize a style at runtime.

In the color-chooser application, we apply SliderStyle as a static resource to each of the four Sliders (lines 56, 58, 60 and 62). Note that once you apply a style to a control, the **Design** view and **Properties** window update to display the control's new appearance settings. If you then modify the control through the **Properties** window, the control itself is updated, not the style. We changed the alpha value Slider's Value to 255.

Dependency Properties

Most WPF properties, though they might look and behave exactly like ordinary ones, are in fact dependency properties. They are coded differently than ordinary properties and are more advanced. They have built-in support for change notification—that is, an application knows and can be made to respond when a property has been modified. In addition, they support inheritance down the control-containment hierarchy. For example, when you specify `FontSize` in a `Window`, every control in the `Window` inherits it as the default `FontSize`. You can also specify a control's property in one of its child elements. This is how attached properties work.

A control's properties may be set at many different levels in WPF, so instead of holding a fixed value, a dependency property's value is determined during execution by a value-determination system. If a property is defined at several levels at once, then the current value is the one defined at the level with the highest precedence. A style, for example, overwrites the default appearance of a control, because it takes higher precedence. A summary of the levels, in order from highest to lowest precedence, is shown in Fig. 15.25.

As shown in Fig. 15.26, the `Slider` that adjusts the alpha value in the color-chooser example starts with a value of 255, whereas the R, G and B `Sliders`' values start at 0. The `Value` property is defined by a `Setter` in the style to be `0` (line 20 in Fig. 15.23). This is why the R, G and B values are 0. The `Value` property of the alpha `Slider` is locally defined to be `255` (line 62). Because a local declaration takes precedence over a style setter, the alpha `Slider`'s value starts at 255 when the application loads.

Levels of value-determination system	
Animation	The value is defined by an active animation. For more information about animation, see Chapter 16.
Local declaration	The value is defined as an attribute in XAML or set in code. This is how ordinary properties are set.
Trigger	The value is defined by an active trigger. For more information about triggers, see Section 15.14.
Style	The value is defined by a setter in a style.
Inherited value	The value is inherited from a definition in a containing element.
Default value	The value is not explicitly defined.

Fig. 15.25 | Levels of property-value determination from highest to lowest precedence.

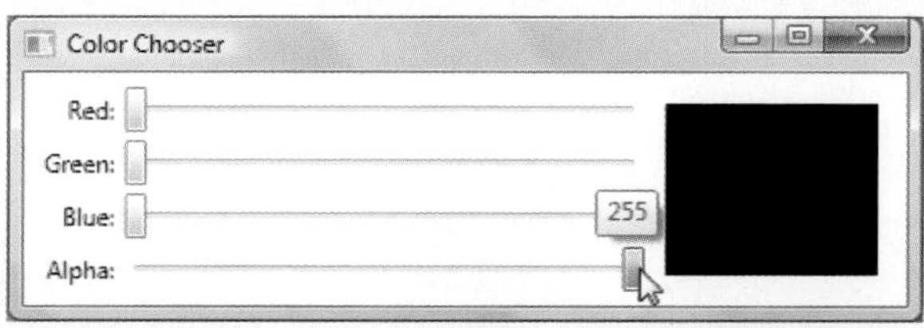

Fig. 15.26 | GUI of the color-chooser application at initialization.

15.13 Customizing Windows

For over a decade, the standard design of an application window has remained practically the same—a framed rectangular box with a header in the top left and a set of buttons in the top right for minimizing, maximizing and closing the window. Cutting-edge applications, however, have begun to use custom windows that diverge from this standard to create a more interesting look.

WPF lets you do this more easily. To create a custom window, set the **WindowStyle** property to `None`. This removes the standard frame around your `Window`. To make your `Window` irregularly shaped, you set the **AllowsTransparency** property to `True` and the `Background` property to `Transparent`. If you then add controls, only the space within the boundaries of those controls behaves as part of the window. This works because a user cannot interact with any part of a `Window` that is transparent. You still define your `Window` as a rectangle with a width and a height, but when a user clicks in a transparent part of the `Window`, it behaves as if the user clicked outside the `Window`'s boundaries—that is, the window does not respond to the click.

Figure 15.27 is the XAML markup that defines a GUI for a circular digital clock. Note that the `Window`'s `WindowStyle` is set to `None` and `AllowsTransparency` is set to `True` (line 7). In this example, we set the background to be an image using an `ImageBrush` (lines 9–11). The background image is a circle with a drop shadow surrounded by transparency. Thus, the `Window` appears circular.

```
1  <!-- Fig. 15.27: BasicClock.xaml -->
2  <!-- Creating custom windows and using timers (XAML). -->
3  <Window x:Class="Clock"
4     xmlns="http://schemas.microsoft.com/winfx/2006/xaml/presentation"
5     xmlns:x="http://schemas.microsoft.com/winfx/2006/xaml"
6     Title="Clock" Name="clockWindow" Height="118" Width="118"
7     WindowStyle="None" AllowsTransparency="True">
8
9     <Window.Background> <!-- Set background image -->
10       <ImageBrush ImageSource="images/circle.png" />
11    </Window.Background>
12
13    <Grid>
14       <TextBox Name="timeTextBox" Grid.Row="1" Margin="0,42,0,0"
15          Background="Transparent" TextAlignment="Center"
16          FontWeight="Bold" Foreground="White" FontSize="16"
17          BorderThickness="0" Cursor="Arrow" Focusable="False" />
18    </Grid>
19 </Window>
```

Fig. 15.27 | Creating custom windows and using timers (XAML).

The time is displayed in the center of the window in a `TextBox` (lines 14–17). Its `Background` is set to `Transparent` so that the text displays directly on the circular background (line 15). We configured the text to be size 16, bold, and white by setting the `FontSize`, `FontWeight`, and `Foreground` properties. The `Cursor` property is set to `Arrow`, so that the mouse cursor doesn't change when it moves over the time (line 17). Setting `Focusable` to `False` disables the user's ability to select the text (line 17).

When you create a custom window, there is no built-in functionality for doing the simple tasks that normal windows do. For example, there is no way for the user to move, resize, minimize, maximize, or close a window unless you write the code to enable these features. You can move the clock around, because we implemented this functionality in the `Window`'s code-behind class (Fig. 15.28). Whenever the left mouse button is held down on the clock (handled by the `MouseLeftButtonDown` event), the `Window` is dragged around using the **`DragMove`** method (e.g., lines 17–22). Because we did not define how to close or minimize the `Window`, there is no way of doing so (the only way to shut down the clock is to press *Alt-F4*—this is a feature built into Windows).

```
1  ' Fig. 15.28: Clock.xaml.vb
2  ' Creating custom windows and using timers (code-behind).
3  Class Clock
4
5     ' create a timer to control clock
6     Private WithEvents timer As New Windows.Threading.DispatcherTimer()
7
8     ' enable timer when window is loaded
9     Private Sub clockWindow_Loaded(ByVal sender As Object, _
10       ByVal e As RoutedEventArgs) Handles clockWindow.Loaded
11
12       timer.Interval = New TimeSpan(0, 0, 1) ' tick every second
13       timer.IsEnabled = True ' enable timer
14    End Sub ' clockWindow_Loaded
15
16    ' drag Window when the left mouse button is held down
17    Private Sub clockWindow_MouseLeftButtonDown(ByVal sender As Object, _
18       ByVal e As MouseButtonEventArgs) _
19       Handles clockWindow.MouseLeftButtonDown
20
21       Me.DragMove() ' moves the window
22    End Sub ' clockWindow_MouseLeftButtonDown
23
24    ' update the time every time the timer ticks
25    Private Sub timer_Tick(ByVal sender As Object, _
26       ByVal e As System.EventArgs) Handles timer.Tick
27
28       Dim currentTime As Date = Date.Now ' get the current time
29
30       ' display the time as hh:mm:ss
31       timeTextBox.Text = currentTime.ToLongTimeString()
32    End Sub ' timer_Tick
33 End Class ' Clock
```

Fig. 15.28 | Creating custom windows and using timers (code-behind).

The clock works by getting the current time every second and displaying it in the TextBox. To do this, the clock uses a DispatcherTimer object (of the Windows.Threading namespace), which raises the Tick event repeatedly at a prespecified time interval. Visual Basic will not listen for a variable's events, however, unless you specify when you declare the variable that it will raise an event. To do this, add the WithEvents keyword after specifying the scope. Thus, the DispatcherTimer variable must be declared WithEvents (line 6 in Fig. 15.28). After it is declared, you must specify the interval between Ticks by setting the Interval property, which takes a TimeSpan as its value. The TimeSpan class has several different constructors, one of which takes three integers as its parameters, which specify the duration of time by the number of hours, minutes, and seconds. In line 12, we create a one-second TimeSpan and set it as the DispatcherTimer's Interval. A DispatcherTimer is disabled by default. Until you enable it by setting the IsEnabled property to True (line 13), it will not Tick. In this example, the Tick event handler gets the current time and displays it in the TextBox.

You may recall that the Timer component provided the same capabilities in Windows Forms. A similar object that you can drag-and-drop onto your GUI doesn't exist in WPF. Instead, you must create a DispatcherTimer object, as illustrated in this example.

15.14 Defining a Control's Appearance with Control Templates

We now update the clock example to include buttons for minimizing and closing the application. We also introduce control templates—a powerful tool for customizing the look-and-feel of your GUIs. As previously mentioned, a custom control template can redefine the appearance of any control without changing its functionality. In Windows Forms, if you want to create a round button, you have to create a new control and simulate the functionality of a Button. With control templates, you can simply redefine the visual elements that compose the Button control and still use the preexisting functionality.

All WPF controls are lookless—that is, a control's properties, methods and events are coded into the control's class, but its appearance is not. Instead, the appearance of a control is determined by a control template, which is a hierarchy of visual elements. Every control has a built-in default control template. All of the GUIs discussed so far have used these default templates.

The hierarchy of visual elements defined by a control template can be represented as a tree, called a control's visual tree. Figure 15.29(b) shows the visual tree of a default Button (Fig. 15.30). This is a more detailed version of the same Button's logical tree, which is shown in Fig. 15.29(a). A logical tree depicts how a control is a defined, whereas a visual tree depicts how a control is graphically rendered.

A control's logical tree always mirrors its definition in XAML. For example, you'll notice that the Button's logical tree, which comprises only the Button and its String caption, exactly represents the hierarchy outlined by its XAML definition, which is

```
<Button>
   Click Me
</Button>
```

To actually render the Button, WPF displays a ContentPresenter with a Border around it. These elements are included in the Button's visual tree. A ContentPresenter is

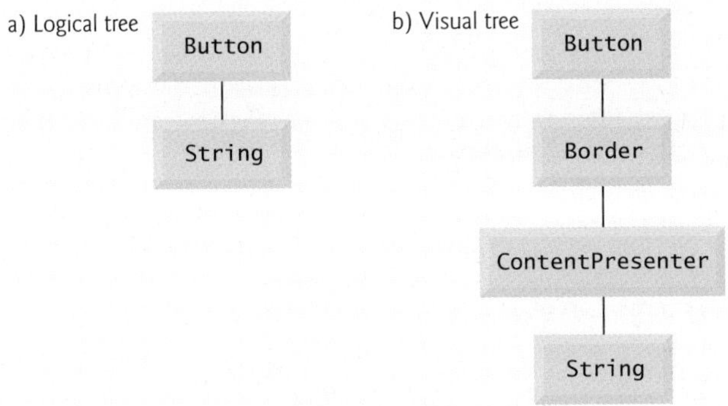

Fig. 15.29 | The logical and visual trees for a default `Button`.

Click Me

Fig. 15.30 | The default `Button`.

an object used to display a single element of content on the screen. It is often used in a template to specify where to display content.

In the updated clock example, we create a custom control template (named `ButtonTemplate`) for rendering `Buttons` and apply it to the two `Buttons` in the application. The XAML markup is shown in Fig. 15.31. Like a style, a control template is usually defined as a resource, and applied by binding a control's `Template` property to the control template using a resource binding (e.g., lines 45 and 49). After you apply a control template to a control, the **Design** view will update to display the new appearance of the control. Note that the **Properties** window remains unchanged, since a control template does not modify a control's properties.

```
1  <!-- Fig. 15.31: Clock.xaml -->
2  <!-- Using control templates (XAML). -->
3  <Window x:Class="Clock"
4     xmlns="http://schemas.microsoft.com/winfx/2006/xaml/presentation"
5     xmlns:x="http://schemas.microsoft.com/winfx/2006/xaml"
6     Title="Clock" Name="clockWindow" Height="118" Width="118"
7     WindowStyle="None" AllowsTransparency="True">
8
9     <Window.Resources>
10       <!-- control template for Buttons -->
11       <ControlTemplate x:Key="ButtonTemplate" TargetType="Button">
12          <Border Name="Border" BorderThickness="2" CornerRadius="2"
13             BorderBrush="RoyalBlue">
14
15             <!-- Template binding to Button.Content -->
16             <ContentPresenter Margin="0" Width="8"
17                Content="{TemplateBinding Content}" />
18          </Border>
```

Fig. 15.31 | Using control templates (XAML). (Part 1 of 2.)

```

            <ControlTemplate.Triggers>
               <!-- if mouse is over the button -->
               <Trigger Property="IsMouseOver" Value="True">
                  <Setter TargetName="Border" Property="Background"
                     Value="LightBlue" /> <!-- make the background blue -->
               </Trigger>
            </ControlTemplate.Triggers>
         </ControlTemplate>
   </Window.Resources>

   <Window.Background> <!-- Set background image -->
      <ImageBrush ImageSource="images/circle.png" />
   </Window.Background>

   <Grid>
      <Grid.RowDefinitions>
         <RowDefinition Height="Auto" />
         <RowDefinition />
      </Grid.RowDefinitions>

      <StackPanel Grid.Row="0" Orientation="Horizontal"
         HorizontalAlignment="Right">

         <!-- these buttons use the control template -->
         <Button Name="minimizeButton" Margin="0" Focusable="False"
            IsTabStop="False" Template="{StaticResource ButtonTemplate}">
            <Image Source="images/minimize.png" Margin="0" />
         </Button>
         <Button Name="closeButton" Margin="1,0,0,0" Focusable="False"
            IsTabStop="False" Template="{StaticResource ButtonTemplate}">
            <Image Source="images/close.png" Margin="0"/>
         </Button>
      </StackPanel>

      <TextBox Name="timeTextBox" Grid.Row="1" Margin="0,30,0,0"
         Background="Transparent" TextAlignment="Center"
         FontWeight="Bold" Foreground="White" FontSize="16"
         BorderThickness="0" Cursor="Arrow" Focusable="False" />
   </Grid>
</Window>
```

Fig. 15.31 | Using control templates (XAML). (Part 2 of 2.)

To define a control template in XAML, you create a `ControlTemplate` element. Just as with a style, you must specify the control template's `x:Key` attribute so you can reference it later (e.g., line 11). You must also set the `TargetType` attribute to the type of control for which the template is designed (e.g., line 11). Inside the `ControlTemplate` element, you can build the control using any WPF visual element (e.g., lines 12–18). In this example, we replace the default `Border` and `ContentPresenter` with our own custom ones.

Sometimes, when defining a control template, it may be beneficial to use the value of one of the templated control's properties. For example, if you want several controls of different sizes to use the same control template, you may need to use the values of their `Wi` and `Height` properties in the template. WPF allows you to do this with a template binding, which can be created in XAML with the markup extension, `{TemplateBinding` *PropertyName*`}`. To bind a property of an element in a control template to one of the properties of the templated control (i.e., the control that the template is applied to), you need to set the appropriate markup extension as the value of that property. In `ButtonTemplate`, we bind the `Content` property of a `ContentPresenter` to the `Content` property of the templated `Button` (line 17). Note that the nested element of a `ContentControl` is the value of its `Content` property. Thus, the images defined in lines 45 and 49 are the `Content` of the `Buttons` and are displayed by the `ContentPresenters` in their respective control templates. You can also create template bindings to a control's events.

Often you'll use a combination of control templates, styles and local declarations to define the appearance of your application. Recall that a control template defines the default appearance of a control and thus has a lower precedence than a style in dependency property-value determination.

Triggers

The control template for `Buttons` used in the updated clock example defines a trigger, which changes a control's appearance when that control enters a certain state. For example, when your mouse is over the clock's minimize or close `Buttons`, the `Button` is highlighted with a light blue background, as shown in Fig. 15.31(b). This simple change in appearance is caused by a trigger that fires whenever the `IsMouseOver` property becomes `True`.

A trigger must be defined in the `Style.Triggers` or `ControlTemplate.Triggers` element of a style or a control template, respectively (e.g., lines 20–26). You can create a trigger by defining a `Trigger` object. The `Property` and `Value` attributes define the state when a trigger is active. `Setters` nested in the `Trigger` element are carried out when the trigger is fired. When the trigger no longer applies, the changes are removed. A `Setter`'s `TargetName` property specifies the name of the element that the `Setter` applies to (e.g., line 23).

Lines 22–25 define the `IsMouseOver` trigger for the minimize and close `Buttons`. When the mouse is over the `Button`, `IsMouseOver` becomes `True`, and the trigger becomes active. The trigger's `Setter` makes the background of the `Border` in the control template temporarily light blue. When the mouse exits the boundaries of the `Button`, `IsMouseOver` becomes `False`. Thus, the `Border`'s background returns to its default setting, which in this case is transparent.

Functionality

Figure 15.32 shows the code-behind class for the clock application. Although the custom control template makes the `Buttons` in this application look different, it doesn't change how they behave. Lines 1–32 remain unchanged from the code in first clock example

(Fig. 15.28). The functionality for the close and minimize `Buttons` is implemented in the same way as any other button—by handling the `Click` event (lines 42–46 and 35–39 of Fig. 15.32, respectively). To minimize the window, we set the **`WindowState`** of the `Window` to **`Windows.WindowState.Minimized`** (line 45).

```
1  ' Fig. 15.32: Clock.xaml.vb
2  ' Using control templates (code-behind).
3  Class Clock
4
5     ' create a timer to control clock
6     Private WithEvents timer As New Windows.Threading.DispatcherTimer()
7
8     ' enable timer when window is loaded
9     Private Sub clockWindow_Loaded(ByVal sender As Object, _
10       ByVal e As RoutedEventArgs) Handles clockWindow.Loaded
11
12       timer.Interval = New TimeSpan(0, 0, 1) ' tick every second
13       timer.IsEnabled = True ' enable timer
14    End Sub ' clockWindow_Loaded
15
16    ' drag Window when the left mouse button is held down
17    Private Sub clockWindow_MouseLeftButtonDown(ByVal sender As Object, _
18       ByVal e As MouseButtonEventArgs) _
19       Handles clockWindow.MouseLeftButtonDown
20
21       Me.DragMove()
22    End Sub ' clockWindow_MouseLeftButtonDown
23
24    ' update the time every time the timer ticks
25    Private Sub timer_Tick(ByVal sender As Object, _
26       ByVal e As System.EventArgs) Handles timer.Tick
27
28       Dim currentTime As Date = Date.Now ' get the current time
29
30       ' display the time as hh:mm:ss
31       timeTextBox.Text = currentTime.ToLongTimeString()
32    End Sub ' timer_Tick
33
34    ' close the application
35    Private Sub closeButton_Click(ByVal sender As Object, _
36       ByVal e As RoutedEventArgs) Handles closeButton.Click
37
38       Application.Current.Shutdown() ' shut down application
39    End Sub
40
41    ' minimize the application
42    Private Sub minimizeButton_Click(ByVal sender As Object, _
43       ByVal e As RoutedEventArgs) Handles minimizeButton.Click
44
45       Me.WindowState = Windows.WindowState.Minimized ' minimize window
46    End Sub ' minimizeButton_Click
47 End Class
```

Fig. 15.32 | Using control templates (code-behind).

15.15 Data-Driven GUIs with Data Binding

Often, an application needs to edit and display data. WPF provides a comprehensive model for allowing GUIs to interact with data.

Bindings

A data binding is a pointer to data, represented by a `Binding` object. WPF allows you to create a binding to a broad range of data types. At the simplest level, you could create a binding to a single property. Often, however, it is useful to create a binding to a data object—an object of a class with properties that describe the data. You can also create a binding to objects like arrays, collections and data in an XML document. The versatility of the WPF data model even allows you to bind to data represented by LINQ statements.

Like other binding types, a data binding can be created declaratively in XAML markup with a markup extension. To declare a data binding, you must specify the data's source. If it's another element in the XAML markup, use property `ElementName`. Otherwise, use `Source`. Then, if you are binding to a specific data point of the source, such as a property of a control, you must specify the `Path` to that piece of information. Use a comma to separate the binding's property declarations. For example, to create a binding to a control's property, you would use `{Binding ElementName=`*ControlName*`, Path=`*PropertyName*`}`.

Figure 15.33 presents the XAML markup of a book-cover viewer that lets the user select from a list of books, and displays the cover of the currently selected book. The list of books is presented in a `ListView` control (lines 14–24), which displays a set of data as items in a selectable list. Its current selection can be retrieved from the `SelectedItem` property. A large image of the currently selected book's cover is displayed in an `Image` control (lines 27–28), which automatically updates when the user makes a new selection. Each book is represented by a `Book` object, which stores four properties:

1. `ThumbImage` (`String`)—the full path to the small cover image of the book.
2. `LargeImage` (`String`)—the full path to the large cover image of the book.
3. `Title` (`String`)—the title of the book.
4. `ISBN` (`String`)—the 10-digit ISBN of the book.

```
1  <!-- Fig. 15.33: BookViewer.xaml -->
2  <!-- Using data binding (XAML). -->
3  <Window x:Class="BookViewer"
4     xmlns="http://schemas.microsoft.com/winfx/2006/xaml/presentation"
5     xmlns:x="http://schemas.microsoft.com/winfx/2006/xaml"
6     Title="Book Viewer" Height="400" Width="600">
7
8     <Grid> <!-- define GUI -->
9        <Grid.ColumnDefinitions>
10          <ColumnDefinition Width="Auto" />
11          <ColumnDefinition />
12       </Grid.ColumnDefinitions>
13
```

Fig. 15.33 | Using data binding (XAML). (Part 1 of 2.)

```
14          <!-- use ListView and GridView to display data -->
15          <ListView Grid.Column="0" Name="booksListView" MaxWidth="250">
16             <ListView.View>
17                <GridView>
18                   <GridViewColumn Header="Title" Width="100"
19                      DisplayMemberBinding="{Binding Path=Title}" />
20                   <GridViewColumn Header="ISBN" Width="80"
21                      DisplayMemberBinding="{Binding Path=ISBN}" />
22                </GridView>
23             </ListView.View>
24          </ListView>
25
26          <!-- bind to selected item's full-size image -->
27          <Image Grid.Column="1" Source="{Binding ElementName=booksListView,
28             Path=SelectedItem.LargeImage}" Margin="5" />
29       </Grid>
30    </Window>
```

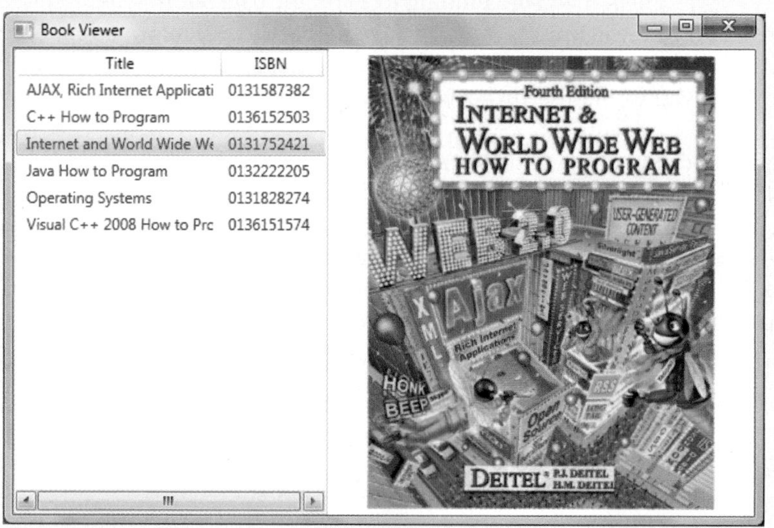

Fig. 15.33 | Using data binding (XAML). (Part 2 of 2.)

Class `Book` also contains a constructor that initializes a `Book` and sets each of its properties. The full source code of the `Book` class is not presented here but is included in the directory containing this chapter's examples.

To synchronize the book cover that is being displayed with the currently selected book, we bind the `Image`'s `Source` property to the file location of the currently selected book's large cover image (lines 27–28). The `Binding`'s `ElementName` property is the name of the selector control, `booksListView`. The `Path` property is `SelectedItem.LargeImage`. This indicates that the binding should be linked to the `LargeImage` property of the `Book` object that is currently `booksListView`'s `SelectedItem`.

Some controls have built-in support for data binding, and a separate `Binding` object doesn't need to be created. A `ListView`, for example, has a built-in **`ItemsSource`** property that specifies the data source from which the items of the list are determined. There is no need to create a binding—instead, you can just set the `ItemsSource` property as you would any other property. When you set `ItemsSource` to a collection of data, the objects in the collection automatically become the items in the list. Figure 15.34 presents the code-behind class for the book-cover viewer. When the `Window` loads, a list of six `Book` objects is initialized (lines 11–25) and set as the `ItemsSource` of of the `booksListView`, meaning that each item displayed in the selector is one of the `Books`.

```
1  ' Fig. 15.34: BookViewer.xaml.vb
2  ' Using data binding (code-behind).
3  Class BookViewer
4     Public books As New List(Of Book)
5
6     ' add books to list when loaded
7     Private Sub bookViewerWindow_Loaded(ByVal sender As Object, _
8        ByVal e As System.EventArgs) Handles MyBase.Loaded
9
10       ' add Book objects to the List
11       books.Add(New Book("AJAX, Rich Internet Applications, and Web " & _
12          "Development for Programmers", "0131587382", _
13          "images/small/ajax.jpg", "images/large/ajax.jpg"))
14       books.Add(New Book("C++ How to Program", "0136152503", _
15          "images/small/cppHTP6e.jpg", "images/large/cppHTP6e.jpg"))
16       books.Add(New Book("Internet and World Wide Web How to Program", _
17          "0131752421", "images/small/iw3htp4.jpg", _
18          "images/large/iw3htp4.jpg"))
19       books.Add(New Book("Java How to Program", "0132222205", _
20          "images/small/jhtp7.jpg", "images/large/jhtp7.jpg"))
21       books.Add(New Book("Operating Systems", "0131828274", _
22          "images/small/os3e.jpg", "images/large/os3e.jpg"))
23       books.Add(New Book("Visual C++ 2008 How to Program", _
24          "0136151574", "images/small/vcpp2008htp2e.jpg", _
25          "images/large/vcpp2008htp2e.jpg"))
26
27       booksListView.ItemsSource = books ' bind data to the display list
28    End Sub ' bookViewerWindow_Loaded
29 End Class ' BookViewer
```

Fig. 15.34 | Using data binding (code-behind).

Data Templates

For a `ListView` to display objects in a useful manner, you must specify how. For example, if you don't specify how to display each `Book`, the `ListView` simply displays the result of the item's `ToString` method, as shown in Fig. 15.35.

BookViewer.Book
BookViewer.Book
BookViewer.Book
BookViewer.Book
BookViewer.Book
BookViewer.Book

Fig. 15.35 | `ListView` display with no data template.

There are many ways to format the display of a ListView. One such method is to display each item as a row in a tabular grid, as shown in Fig. 15.33. This can be achieved by setting a **GridView** as the View property of a ListView (lines 16–23). A GridView consists of many **GridViewColumns**, each representing a property. In this example, we define two columns, one for **Title** and one for **ISBN** (lines 18–19 and 20–21, respectively). A GridViewColumn's Header property specifies what to display as its header. The values displayed in each column are determined by its **DisplayMemberBinding** property. We set the **Title** column's DisplayMemberBinding to a Binding object that points to the Title property (line 19), and the **ISBN** column's to one that points to the ISBN property (line 21). Note that neither of the Bindings has a specified ElementName or Source. Because the ListView has already specified the data source (line 27 of Fig. 15.34), the two data bindings inherit this source, and we do not need specify it again.

A much more powerful technique for formatting a ListView is to specify a template for displaying each item in the list. This template defines how to display bound data and is called a **data template**. Figure 15.36 is the XAML markup that describes modified version of the book-cover viewer GUI. Each book, instead of being displayed as a row in a table, is represented by a small thumbnail of its cover image with its title and ISBN. Lines 11–32 define the data template (i.e., **DataTemplate** object) that specifies how to display a Book object. Note the similarity between the structure of a data template and that of a control template. If you define a data template as a resource, you apply it by using a resource binding, just as you would a style or control template. To apply a data template to items in a ListView, use the **ItemTemplate** property (e.g., line 41).

A data template uses data bindings to specify how to display data. Once again, we can omit the data binding's ElementName and Source properties, because its source has already been specified by the ListView (line 27 of Fig. 15.34). The same principle can be applied in other scenarios as well. If you bind an element's DataContext property to a data source, then its child elements can access data within that source without your having to specify it again. In other words, if a binding already has a context (i.e, a DataContext has already been defined by a parent), it automatically inherits the data source. For example, if you bind a data source to the DataContext property of a Grid, then any data binding created in the Grid uses that source by default. You can, however, override this source by explicitly defining a new one when you define a binding.

```
1  <!-- Fig. 15.36: BookViewer.xaml -->
2  <!-- Using data templates (XAML). -->
3  <Window x:Class="BookViewer"
4     xmlns="http://schemas.microsoft.com/winfx/2006/xaml/presentation"
5     xmlns:x="http://schemas.microsoft.com/winfx/2006/xaml"
6     Title="Book Viewer" Height="400" Width="600" Name="bookViewerWindow">
7
8     <Window.Resources> <!-- Define Window's resources -->
9
10       <!-- define data template -->
11       <DataTemplate x:Key="BookTemplate">
12          <Grid MaxWidth="250" Margin="3">
13             <Grid.ColumnDefinitions>
14                <ColumnDefinition Width="Auto" />
```

Fig. 15.36 | Using data templates (XAML). (Part 1 of 3.)

```
               <ColumnDefinition />
            </Grid.ColumnDefinitions>

            <!-- bind image source -->
            <Image Grid.Column="0" Source="{Binding Path=ThumbImage}"
               Width="50" />

            <StackPanel Grid.Column="1">
               <!-- bind Title and ISBN -->
               <TextBlock Margin="3,0" Text="{Binding Path=Title}"
                  FontWeight="Bold" TextWrapping="Wrap" />
               <StackPanel Margin="3,0" Orientation="Horizontal">
                  <TextBlock Text="ISBN: " />
                  <TextBlock Text="{Binding Path=ISBN}" />
               </StackPanel>
            </StackPanel>
         </Grid>
      </DataTemplate>
   </Window.Resources>

   <Grid> <!-- define GUI -->
      <Grid.ColumnDefinitions>
         <ColumnDefinition Width="Auto" />
         <ColumnDefinition />
      </Grid.ColumnDefinitions>

      <!-- use ListView and template to display data -->
      <ListView Grid.Column="0" Name="booksListView"
         ItemTemplate="{StaticResource BookTemplate}" />

      <!-- bind to selected item's full-size image -->
      <Image Grid.Column="1" Source="{Binding ElementName=booksListView,
         Path=SelectedItem.LargeImage}" Margin="5" />
   </Grid>
</Window>
```

a)

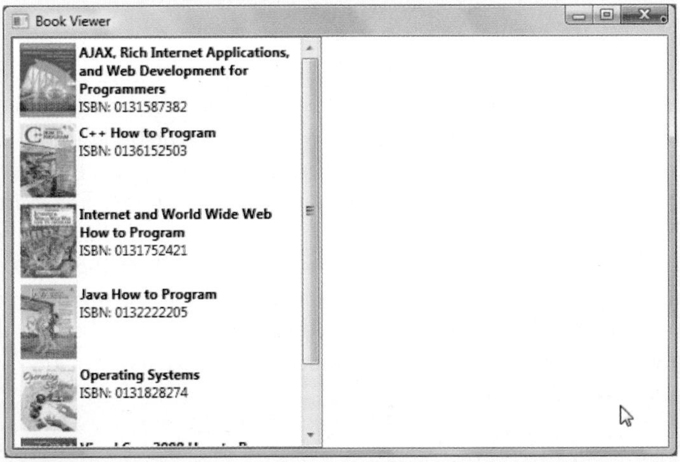

Book Viewer

AJAX, Rich Internet Applications, and Web Development for Programmers
ISBN: 0131587382

C++ How to Program
ISBN: 0136152503

Internet and World Wide Web How to Program
ISBN: 0131752421

Java How to Program
ISBN: 0132222205

Operating Systems
ISBN: 0131828274

Fig. 15.36 | Using data templates (XAML). (Part 2 of 3.)

b)

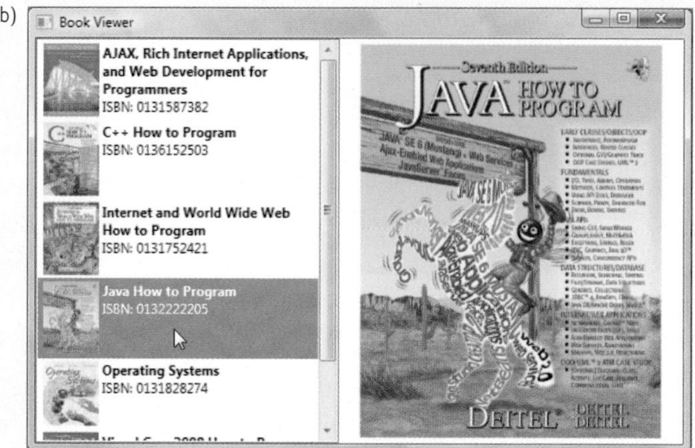

Fig. 15.36 | Using data templates (XAML). (Part 3 of 3.)

In the `Book` data template, lines 19–20 of Fig. 15.36 define an `Image` whose `Source` is bound to the `Book`'s `ThumbImage` property, which stores the relative file path to the thumbnail cover image. The `Book`'s `Title` and `ISBN` are displayed to the right of the book using `TextBlocks`—lightweight controls for displaying text. The `TextBlock` in lines 24–25 displays the `Book`'s `Title` because the `Text` property is bound to it. Because some of the books' titles are long, we set the `TextWrapping` property to `Wrap` (line 25) so that, if the title is too long, it will wrap to multiple lines. We also set the `FontWeight` property to `Bold`. Lines 26–29 displays two additional `TextBlocks`, one that displays `ISBN:`, and another that is bound to the `Book`'s `ISBN` property.

Figure 15.36(a) shows the book-viewer application when it first loads. Each item in the `ListView` is represented by a thumbnail of its cover image, its title and its ISBN, as specified in the data template. As illustrated by Fig. 15.36(b), when you select an item in the `ListView`, the large cover image on the right automatically updates, because it is bound to the `SelectedItem` property of the list.

Data Views

A data view (of class type `CollectionView`) is a wrapper around a collection of data that can provide us with multiple "views" of the same data based on how we filter, sort and group the data. A default view is automatically created in the background every time a data binding is created. To retrieve the data view, use the `CollectionViewSource.GetDefaultView` method and pass it the source of your data binding. For example, to retrieve the default view of `bookListView` in the book-viewer application, you would use `CollectionViewSource.GetDefaultView(bookListView.ItemsSource)`.

You can then modify the view to create the exact view of the data that you want to display. The methods of filtering, sorting and grouping data are beyond the scope of this book. For more information, see `msdn.microsoft.com/en-us/library/ms752347.aspx#what_are_collection_views`.

Asynchronous Data Binding

Sometimes you may wish to create asynchronous data bindings that don't hold up your application while data is being transmitted. To do this, you set the `IsAsync` property of a data binding to `True` (it is `False` by default). Often, however, it is not the transmission but the instantiation of data that is the most expensive operation. An asynchronous data binding does not provide a solution for instantiating data asynchronously.

To do so, you must use a data provider, a class that can create or retrieve data. There are two types of data providers, `XmlDataProvider` (for XML) and `ObjectDataProvider` (for data objects). Both can be declared as a resource in XAML markup. If you set a data provider's `IsAsynchronous` property to `True`, the provider will run in the background. Creating and using data providers is beyond the scope of this book. For more information, see `msdn.microsoft.com/en-us/library/aa480224.aspx`.

15.16 Wrap-Up

In this chapter, we discussed some basic XML terminology and introduced the concepts of markup, XML vocabularies and XML parsers (validating and nonvalidating). We then demonstrated how to describe and structure data in XML, illustrating these points with examples marking up an article and a business letter. Next, we discussed XML namespaces and namespace prefixes. You learned that each namespace has a unique name that provides a means for document authors to unambiguously refer to elements with the same name (i.e., prevent naming collisions) from different namespaces. We presented examples of defining two namespaces in the same document, as well as setting the default namespace for a document.

Many of today's commercial applications provide GUIs that are easy to use and manipulate. The demand for sophisticated and user-friendly GUIs makes GUI design an essential programming skill. In Chapter 14, we showed you how to create GUIs with Windows `Forms`. In this chapter, we demonstrated how to create GUIs with WPF. You learned how to design a WPF GUI with XAML markup and how to give it functionality in a Visual Basic code-behind class. We presented WPF's new flow-based layout scheme, in which a control's size and position are both defined relatively. You learned not only to handle events just as you did in a Windows `Forms` application, but also to implement WPF commands when you want multiple user interactions to execute the same task. We demonstrated the flexibility WPF offers for customizing the look-and-feel of your GUIs. You learned how to use styles, control templates and triggers to define a control's appearance. The chapter concluded with a demonstration of how to create data-driven GUIs with data bindings and data templates.

But WPF is not merely a GUI-building platform. Chapter 16, , explores some of the many other capabilities of WPF, showing you how to incorporate 2D and 3D graphics, animation and multimedia into your WPF applications. Chapter 23, , demonstrates how to create Internet applications using a subset of WPF's features that are available in the Silverlight runtime, which executes as a plug-in for several popular browsers and platforms.

15.17 Web Resources

There is a tremendous amount of material on the web to help you learn more about WPF. Check out our Windows Presentation Foundation Resource Center

```
www.deitel.com/wpf/
```

for the latest WPF articles, books, sample chapters, tutorials, webcasts, blogs and more.

Summary

Section 15.2 Windows Presentation Foundation (WPF)

- Windows Presentation Foundation (WPF) is a single platform capable of integrating GUI components, images, animation, 2D graphics, 3D graphics, audio and video capabilities.
- WPF generates vector-based graphics and is resolution independent.
- Just as in Windows `Forms`, you use predefined controls to create GUI elements in WPF.
- Just as in Windows `Forms`, the functionality of a WPF GUI is event driven.
- In WPF, you can write XAML markup to define the layout and appearance of a GUI.
- Declarative programming is defining *what* something is without specifying *how* to generate it. Writing XAML markup to define GUI controls is an example of declarative programming.
- XAML separates front-end appearance from back-end logic, allowing designers and programmers to work together more efficiently.

Section 15.3 XML Basics

- XML documents should be readable by both humans and machines.
- XML permits document authors to create custom markup for any type of information. This enables document authors to create entirely new markup languages that describe specific types of data, including mathematical formulas, chemical molecular structures, music and recipes.
- An XML parser is responsible for identifying components of XML documents (typically files with the `.xml` extension) and then storing those components in a data structure for manipulation.
- An XML document can optionally reference a Document Type Definition (DTD) or W3C XML Schema that defines the XML document's structure.
- An XML document that conforms to a DTD/schema (i.e., has the appropriate structure) is valid.
- If an XML parser (validating or nonvalidating) can process an XML document successfully, that XML document is well formed.

Section 15.4 Structuring Data

- An XML document begins with an optional XML declaration. The `version` attribute specifies the version of XML syntax used in the document. The `encoding` attribute specifies what character encoding is used in the document.
- XML comments begin with <!-- and end with -->.
- An XML document contains text that represents its content (i.e., data) and elements that specify its structure. XML documents delimit an element with start and end tags.
- The root element of an XML document encompasses all its other elements.
- XML element names can be of any length and can contain letters, digits, underscores, hyphens and periods. However, they must begin with either a letter or an underscore, and they should not begin with "`xml`" in any combination of uppercase and lowercase letters, as this is reserved for use in the XML standards.
- When a user loads an XML document in Internet Explorer, MSXML parses the document, and Internet Explorer uses a style sheet to format the data for display.
- Internet Explorer displays minus (–) or plus (+) signs next to all container elements. A minus sign indicates that all child elements are being displayed. When clicked, a minus sign becomes a plus sign (which collapses the container element and hides all the children), and vice versa.
- Data can be placed between tags or in attributes (name/value pairs that appear within the angle brackets of start tags). Elements can have any number of attributes, but attribute names within a single element must be unique.

Section 15.5 XML Namespaces

- XML allows document authors to create their own markup, and as a result, naming collisions (i.e., two different elements that have the same name) can occur. XML namespaces provide a means for document authors to prevent collisions.
- Each namespace prefix is bound to a uniform resource identifier (URI) that uniquely identifies the namespace. A URI is a series of characters that differentiate names. Document authors create their own namespace prefixes. Any name can be used as a namespace prefix, but the namespace prefix `xml` is reserved for use in XML standards.
- To eliminate the need to place a namespace prefix in each element, authors can specify a default namespace for an element and its children. We declare a default namespace using keyword `xmlns` with a URI (Uniform Resource Identifier) as its value.
- Document authors commonly use URLs (Uniform Resource Locators) for URIs, because domain names (e.g., `deitel.com`) in URLs must be unique.

Section 15.6 Declarative GUI Programming Using XAML

- WPF controls are represented by elements in XAML markup.
- Every XAML document must have a single root element.
- The presentation XAML namespace and the standard XAML namespace must be defined with the `Window` control in every XAML document so that the XAML compiler can interpret your markup.
- A XAML document must have an associated code-behind class in order to handle events. The `x:Class` attribute of `Window` specifies the class name of the code-behind class.
- A `Window` is a content control that can have exactly one child element or text. To place multiple controls in a `Window`, you must set a layout container as the `Window`'s child element.
- WPF `Label`s are content controls that typically display a small amount of data.

Section 15.7 Creating a WPF Application in Visual Basic Express

- To create a new WPF application in Visual Basic Express, open the **New Project** dialog and select **WPF Application** from the list of template types.
- When you select a XAML document from the **Solution Explorer**, a **XAML view** that allows you to edit XAML markup appears in your IDE.
- Every WPF project has an `Application.xaml` document that defines the `Application` object and its settings and an `Application.xaml.vb` code-behind class that handles application-level events.
- The `StartupUri` attribute in `Application.xaml` specifies the XAML document that executes first.
- The file name of a code-behind file is the file name of the XAML document followed by `.vb`.

Section 15.8.1 General Layout Principles

- WPF layout is flow based and defined relatively.
- A control's size should be defined as a range of acceptable sizes using the `MinHeight`, `MinWidth`, `MaxHeight` and `MaxWidth` properties.
- A control's position should be defined based on its position relative to the layout container in which it is included and the other controls in the same container.
- A control's `Margin` specifies how much space to put around the edges of a control.
- A control's `HorizontalAlignment` and `VerticalAlignment` specify how to align a control within its layout container.

Section 15.8.2 Layout in Action

- WPF `RadioButtons` represent mutually exclusive options.
- WPF `Buttons` are objects that respond to mouse clicks.
- A WPF `GroupBox` surrounds its child element with a titled box.
- A `StackPanel` is a layout container that arranges its content vertically or horizontally.
- A `Grid` is a flexible, all-purpose layout container that organizes controls into a user-defined grid of rows and columns.
- The `RowDefinitions` and `ColumnDefinitions` properties of `Grid` define its rows and columns. They take collections of `RowDefinition` and `ColumnDefinition` objects, respectively. You can specify the `Width` of a `ColumnDefinition` and the `Height` of a `RowDefinition` to be an explicit size, a relative size (using *) or `Auto`.
- You can use the **Collection Editor** to edit properties that take collection values, such as `RowDefinitions` or `ColumnDefinitions`.
- The `Grid.Row` and `Grid.Column` properties specify a control's location in the `Grid`.
- To specify the number of rows or columns of a `Grid` that a contained control spans, use the `Grid.RowSpan` or `Grid.ColumnSpan` attached properties, respectively.
- Attached properties are defined by a parent control and used by its children.
- A `Canvas` is a layout container that allows users to position controls in absolute terms.
- The `Canvas.Left` and `Canvas.Top` properties specify a control's coordinate position based on its distance from the left and top borders, respectively, of the `Canvas` in which it is contained. If two controls overlap, the one with the greater `Canvas.ZIndex` displays in front.
- When editing a GUI in **Design** mode, snaplines, margin lines, and gridlines help you lay out your GUI.

Section 15.9 Event Handling

- WPF event handling is similar to Windows `Forms` event handling.
- All layout containers have a `Children` property that stores all of a layout container's children. You can manipulate the content of a layout container as you would any other `IEnumerable`.
- A WPF `RadioButton` raises the `Checked` event every time it becomes checked.
- A WPF `Button` raises the `Click` event every time it is clicked.
- Just as in Windows `Forms`, WPF has built-in support for keyboard and mouse events.
- Class `MouseEventArgs` contains mouse-specific information.
- Class `MouseButtonEventArgs` contains information specific to a mouse button.
- The `MouseLeftButtonDown` and `MouseRightButtonDown` events are raised when the user presses the left and right mouse buttons, respectively.
- The `MouseLeftButtonUp` and `MouseRightButtonUp` events are raised when the user releases the left and right mouse buttons, respectively.
- WPF events can travel either up or down the containment hierarchy of controls. This is called event routing, and all WPF events are routed events.
- `RoutedEventArgs` contains information specific to routed events. If its `Handled` property is `True`, then event handlers ignore the event. The `Source` property specifies where the event occurred.
- WPF `TextBoxes` display editable unformatted text.
- There are three types of routed events. Direct events do not travel up or down the containment hierarchy. Bubbling events start at the `Source` and travel up the hierarchy, ending at the `Window`

or until you set Handled to True. Tunneling events start at the top and travel down the hierarchy until they reach the Source or Handled is True.

- A tunneling event has the same name as the corresponding bubbling event prefixed by Preview.
- An event handler can handle multiple events, specified in the Handles clause by a comma-separated list.

Section 15.10 Commands and Common Application Tasks

- A WPF command is an action or a task that may be triggered by many different user interactions.
- Commands enable you to synchronize the availability of a task to the state of its corresponding controls and keyboard shortcuts.
- Commands are implementation of the ICommand interface. Every ICommand has a Name and a collection of InputGestures (keyboard shortcuts) associated with it.
- When an ICommand executes, its Execute method is called. The command's execution logic is not defined in its Execute method.
- An ICommand's CanExecute method is called to determine when the command should be enabled. The application logic is not defined in this method.
- WPF provides a command library of built-in commands. These commands have their standard keyboard shortcuts already associated with them.
- A command executes when it is triggered by a command source.
- To use a command, you must specify a method that handles either the Executed and PreviewExecuted event in a command binding. You can declare a command binding by creating a CommandBinding object in XAML, setting the Command attribute to the command, and setting the value of either the Executed or PreviewExecuted attribute to the event-handler name.
- You can declare an event handler for any event in XAML by setting the event's attribute to be the name of the event-handler method.
- Application.Current.Shutdown shuts down an application.
- Command bindings should be defined within the Window.CommandBindings element.
- Some controls have built-in functionality for using certain commands. In these cases, a command binding is not necessary.
- A RichTextBox allows users to enter, edit and format text.
- A Menu creates a menu containing MenuItems. If a MenuItem contains additional nested MenuItems, then it's a top-level menu or a submenu. Otherwise, it's a menu option, and it executes an action via either an event or a command.
- A ToolBar is a single row or column of controls. ToolBars overwrite the look-and-feel of their child elements with their own specifications so that the controls look seamless together. You can place multiple ToolBars inside a ToolBarTray.
- A Separator creates a divider to separate content into groups. You can use Separators in any control that can contain multiple child elements.

Section 15.11 WPF GUI Customization

- You can change the appearance of a WPF control just by adjusting its properties.
- You can define the appearance of many controls at once by creating and applying a style.
- With a customized control template, you can completely redefine the appearance of a control without changing its functionality.
- You can create a custom control with its own functionality, properties, methods and events.

Section 15.12 Using Styles to Change the Appearance of Controls

- Styles can define property values and event handlers.
- A resource is an object that is defined for an entire section of your application and can be reused multiple times. Every WPF control can hold a collection of resources that can be accessed by its children. To define resources for a control, you use a control's `Resources` property.
- A `Slider` is a numeric user input control that allows users to drag a "thumb" along a track to select the value.
- Style objects are easily defined in XAML using the `Style` element.
- A `Setter` sets a property to a certain value.
- An `EventSetter` specifies the method that responds to an event.
- You can make all controls of one type automatically use the same default style by setting the style's `TargetType` attribute to the control type.
- You can create a resource binding in XAML by calling the resource in a markup extension. The form of a markup extension calling a resource is {*ResourceType ResourceKey*}.
- There are two types of resources. Static resources are applied at initialization time only. Dynamic resources are applied every time the resource is modified by the application.
- Most WPF properties are dependency properties. A dependency property's value is determined during execution by a value-determination system. If a property is defined at several levels, then the current value is the one defined at the level with the highest precedence.

Section 15.13 Customizing `Windows`

- To create a custom window, set the `WindowStyle` property to `None`. This removes the standard frame around your `Window`.
- To make an irregularly shaped `Window`, set the `AllowsTransparency` property to `True` and the `Background` property to `Transparent`.
- A `Window` can be dragged around the screen with the `DragMove` method.
- A `DispatcherTimer` object is designed to raise the `Tick` event once every prespecified time interval. To use it, you must specify the `Interval` between `Ticks` and set `IsEnabled` to `True`.
- To define a variable that will raise events, you must use the `WithEvents` keyword.
- WPF does not have any components like those in Windows `Forms`.

Section 15.14 Defining a Control's Appearance with Control Templates

- All WPF controls are lookless. A control's properties, methods and events are coded into the control's class, but its appearance is not.
- A control's appearance is determined by a control template.
- A control's logical tree depicts how it is a defined, and a control's visual tree depicts how it is graphically rendered. A control template defines a control's visual tree.
- A control template is usually defined as a resource and applied by binding a control's `Template` property to the control template using a resource binding.
- To define a control template in XAML, you create a `ControlTemplate` element. You must set the `TargetType` attribute to the type of control for which the template is designed. Inside the `ControlTemplate` element, you have the freedom to build the control using any WPF visual element.
- You can use a control's property within the definition of its control template by using a template binding, which can be created in XAML with the markup extension, `{TemplateBinding` *PropertyName*`}`.

- A trigger changes the appearance of a control when that control enters a certain state.
- A trigger must be contained within a style or a control template. You can create a trigger with a `Trigger` object. `Setters` nested in the `Trigger` element are carried out when the trigger is fired. When the trigger no longer applies, the changes are removed.
- To minimize a window, set the `WindowState` property to `Windows.WindowState.Minimized`.

Section 15.15 Data-Driven GUIs with Data Binding

- A data binding is a pointer to some type of data, represented by a `Binding` object.
- A data binding can be created declaratively in XAML markup using a markup extension. You must specify the data source by setting either the `Source` or `ElementName` property. To obtain a specific data point, you must specify the `Path` relative to the data source.
- A `ListView` displays data in a selectable list format.
- A `ListView` has a built-in `ItemsSource` property that specifies the data source from which the items of the list are determined.
- A `GridView` displays each item of a `ListView` as a row in a grid.
- A `GridViewColumn` represents a column of a `GridView`. The `DisplayMemberBinding` property specifies the data field that is displayed.
- A `DataTemplate` object that defines how to display data can be created and used as a resource.
- To apply a data template to a `ListView`, bind the `ItemsTemplate` property to the template.
- If you bind an element's `DataContext` to a data object, then its child elements can access specific data points within that object without respecifying it as the source.
- A data view (of class type `CollectionView`) is a wrapper around a collection of data that can provide us with multiple "views" of the same data based on how we filter, sort and group the data.
- A data provider is a class that can create or retrieve data. There are two types of data providers, `XmlDataProvider` (for XML) and `ObjectDataProvider` (for data objects). If you set a data provider's `IsAsynchronous` property to `True`, the provider will run in the background.

Terminology

Sections 15.3–15.5

angle brackets (<>)
attribute of XML element
child element
container element
default namespace
Document Type Definition (DTD)
`.dtd` file-name extension
element
empty element
`encoding` attribute of an XML declaration
end tag
Expat XML parser
Extensible Stylesheet Language (XSL)
external DTD
forward-slash character (/)
markup
Microsoft XML Core Services (MSXML)
namespace in an XML document
namespace prefix
naming collision
nested element
node
nonvalidating XML parser
parent element
root element
schema
start tag
style sheet
`SYSTEM` keyword in XML
Uniform Resource Identifier (URI)
Uniform Resource Locator (URL)
Uniform Resource Name (URN)
valid XML document
validating XML parser
`version` attribute of an XML declaration
W3C XML Schema

well-formed XML document
World Wide Web Consortium (W3C)
Xerces XML parser
XML (Extensible Markup Language)
XML declaration
.xml file-name extensions
XML parser
XML prolog
XML vocabulary
xmlns attribute in an XML document
XmlReader class

Section 15.2 and Sections 15.6–15.15

Add method of UIElementCollection class
AllowsTransparency property of Window control
Application.Current.Shutdown method
Application.xaml
Application.xaml.vb
attached properties
Binding class
bubbling events
Button control
CanExecute event of CommandBinding class
Canvas control
Checked event of RadioButton control
Children property of Panel control
Clear method of UIElementCollection class
Click event of Button control
CollectionView class
Column attached property of Grid control
ColumnDefinition class
ColumnDefinitions property of Grid control
ColumnSpan attached property of Grid control
command
command binding
CommandBinding class
CommandBindings property of Window control
content control
Content property of ContentPresenter class
ContentControl control
ContentPresenter class
control template
ControlTemplate class
data binding
data template
DataContext property of WPF controls
DataTemplate class
declarative programming
dependency property
DispatcherTimer class
DisplayMemberBinding property of GridView class
DragMove method of Window control
dynamic resource
ElementName property of Binding class
Event property of EventSetter class
EventSetter class
Execute method of ICommand class
Executed event of CommandBinding class
Expression Blend
flow-based layout
GetDefaultView method of CollectionViewSource class
GetPosition method of MouseEventArgs class
Grid control
GridView class
GridViewColumn class
GroupBox control
Handled property of RoutedEventArgs class
Handler property of EventSetter class
Header property of GroupBox control
HorizontalAlignment property of controls
ICommand interface
Image control
InputGestures property of ICommand class
Interval property of DispatcherTimer class
IsEnabled property of DispatcherTimer class
IsMouseOver property of WPF controls
IsSnapToTickEnabled property of a Slider
ItemsSource property of ListView
ItemTemplate property of ListView control
Label control
layout container
Left attached property of Canvas control
ListView control
logical tree
lookless control
Margin property of a control
markup extension
MaxHeight property of a control
MaxWidth property of a control
Menu control
MenuItem control
MinHeight property of a control
Minimized constant of Windows.WindowState class
MinWidth property of WPF controls
MouseButtonEventArgs class

- MouseEventArgs class
- MouseLeftButtonDown event
- MouseLeftButtonUp event
- MouseMove event
- MouseRightButtonDown event
- MouseRightButtonUp event
- ObjectDataProvider class
- Orientation property of StackPanel control
- Panel control
- Path property of Binding class
- PreviewCanExecute event of CommandBinding class
- PreviewExecuted event of CommandBinding class
- PreviewMouseLeftButtonDown event
- PreviewMouseLeftButtonUp event
- Property property of Setter class
- Property property of Trigger class
- RadioButton control
- raster-based graphics
- resolution independence
- resource
- resource binding
- Resources property of a control
- RichTextBox control
- routed events
- RoutedEventArgs class
- Row attached property of Grid control
- RowDefinition class
- RowDefinitions property of Grid control
- RowSpan attached property of Grid control
- SelectedItem property of ListView control
- Separator control
- SetLeft method of Canvas control
- Setter class
- SetTop method of Canvas control
- Shutdown method of Application.Current
- Slider control
- Source property of Binding class
- Source property of RoutedEventArgs class
- StackPanel control
- StartupUri property of Application.xaml
- static resource
- style
- Style class
- TargetType property of ControlTemplate class
- TargetType property of Style class
- template binding
- Template property of a control
- TextBox control
- Tick event of DispatcherTimer class
- TimeSpan class
- ToolBar control
- ToolBarTray control
- Top attached property of Canvas control
- Trigger class
- Triggers property of ControlTemplate class
- Triggers property of Style class
- tunneling events
- UIElementCollection class
- Value property of Setter class
- Value property of Trigger class
- vector-based graphics
- version attribute in an XML declaration
- VerticalAlignment property of a control
- visual tree
- Window control
- Windows Presentation Foundation
- Windows.WindowState.Minimized constant
- WindowState property of Window control
- WindowStyle property of Window control
- WithEvents
- WPF (Windows Presentation Foundation)
- x:Class attribute
- XAML (Extensible Application Markup Language)
- XAML view
- XmlDataProvider class
- ZIndex attached property of Canvas control

Self-Review Exercises

Sections 15.3–15.5

15.1 Which of the following are valid XML element names? (Select all that apply.)

a) `yearBorn`
b) `year.Born`
c) `year Born`
d) `year-Born1`
e) `2_year_born`
f) `_year_born_`

15.2 State whether each of the following is *true* or *false*. If *false*, explain why.

a) XML is a technology for creating markup languages called XML vocabularies.
b) XML markup is delimited by forward and backward slashes (/ and \).
c) All XML start tags must have corresponding end tags.
d) Parsers check an XML document's syntax.
e) XML does not support namespaces.
f) When creating XML elements, document authors must use the set of standard XML tags provided by the W3C.
g) The pound character (#), dollar sign ($), ampersand (&) and angle brackets (< and >) are examples of XML reserved characters.

15.3 In Fig. 15.2, we subdivided the `author` element into more detailed pieces. How might you subdivide the `date` element? Use the date May 5, 2005, as an example.

Section 15.2 and Sections 15.6–15.15

15.4 State whether each of the following is *true* or *false*. If *false*, explain why.

a) WPF has GUI, animation, 2D graphics, 3D graphics and multimedia capabilities
b) All of a WPF application's Visual Basic code can be replaced by XAML markup.
c) You lay out a WPF GUI in the same way you lay out a `Windows Forms` GUI.
d) Events in WPF are the same as they are in `Windows Forms`.
e) A WPF command can be executed through many user interactions.
f) If a WPF resource is defined for a `Window`, then it can be used by any of the `Window`'s child elements.
g) A WPF style must be defined for a specific control type.
h) A WPF control template must be defined for a specific control type.
i) A WPF control's logical and visual trees are the same.
j) Data bindings in WPF can be specified in XAML by markup extensions.

15.5 Fill in the blanks in each of the following statements:.

a) XAML documents consists of a hierarchy of __________.
b) A `Window` is a(n) __________, meaning it can have exactly one child element or text.
c) Properties such as `Grid.Row` or `Canvas.Left` are examples of __________ properties.
d) `MouseLeftButtonDown` is a bubbling event. The name of its corresponding tunneling event is __________.
e) When a WPF command is executed, it raises the __________ and __________ events.
f) A menu usually has only __________ and __________ as children.
g) __________ resources are applied at initialization only, whereas __________ resources are reapplied every time the resource is modified.
h) A WPF control template defines a control's __________ tree.
i) To declare a variable that may raise an event, you must add the __________ keyword to its declaration.
j) To format the display of items in a `ListView`, you would use a(n) __________.

Answers to Self-Review Exercises

Sections 15.3–15.5

15.1 a, b, d, f. [Choice c is incorrect because it contains a space. Choice e is incorrect because the first character is a digit.]

15.2 a) True. b) False. In an XML document, markup text is delimited by tags enclosed in angle brackets (< and >) with a forward slash just after the < in the end tag. c) True. d) True. e) False. XML does support namespaces. f) False. When creating tags, document authors can use any valid name but should avoid ones that begin with the reserved word `xml` (also `XML`, `Xml`, and so on). g) False. XML reserved characters include the ampersand (&), the left-angle bracket (<) and the right-angle bracket (>), but not `#` and `$`.

15.3
```
<date>
    <month>May</month>
    <day>5</day>
    <year>2005</year>
</date>.
```

Section 15.2 and Sections 15.6–15.15

15.4 a) True. b) False. XAML is designed to be used alongside Visual Basic, not to replace it. c) False. The layout in WPF is primarily flow based, whereas layout in `Windows Forms` is primarily coordinate based. d) False. Events in WPF are routed events. e) True. f) True. g) False. A style may be applied to any type of control. h) True. i) False. A control's visual tree represents how a control is rendered, whereas a logical tree represents how it is defined. j) True.

15.5 a) elements. b) content control. c) attached. d) `PreviewMouseLeftButtonDown`. e) `Executed`, `PreviewExecuted`. f) `MenuItems`, `Separators`. g) Static, dynamic. h) visual. i) `WithEvents`. j) data template.

Exercises

Sections 15.3–15.5

15.6 *(Nutrition Information XML Document)* Create an XML document that marks up the nutrition facts for a package of Grandma White's cookies. A package of cookies has a serving size of 28 grams and the following nutritional value per serving: 140 calories, 60 fat calories, 8 grams of fat, 2 grams of saturated fat, 5 milligrams of cholesterol, 110 milligrams of sodium, 15 grams of total carbohydrates, 2 grams of fiber, 15 grams of sugars and 1 gram of protein. Name this document `nutrition.xml`. Load the XML document into Internet Explorer. [*Hint:* Your markup should contain individual elements describing the product name, serving size, calories, sodium, cholesterol, proteins, and so on. Mark up each nutrition fact/ingredient listed above.]

Section 15.2 and Sections 15.6–15.15

15.7 Create the GUI in Fig. 15.37 (you do not have to provide functionality) using WPF. Do not use a `Canvas`. Do not use explicit sizing or positioning.

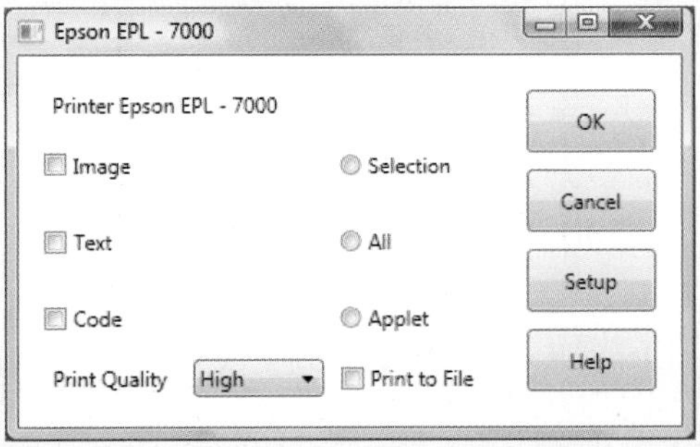

Fig. 15.37 | Printer GUI.

15.8 Incorporate an RGBA color chooser into the `Painter` example to look like Fig. 15.38. Let the user select the brush color using the color chooser instead of the group of `RadioButtons`. You should use a style to make all the sliders look the same.

Fig. 15.38 | Painter with color-chooser GUI.

15.9 Create a cash-register application modeled after the one presented in Fig. 15.39. It should allow users to enter a series of prices, then obtain the total. The **Delete** button should clear the current entry, and the **Clear** button should reset the application.

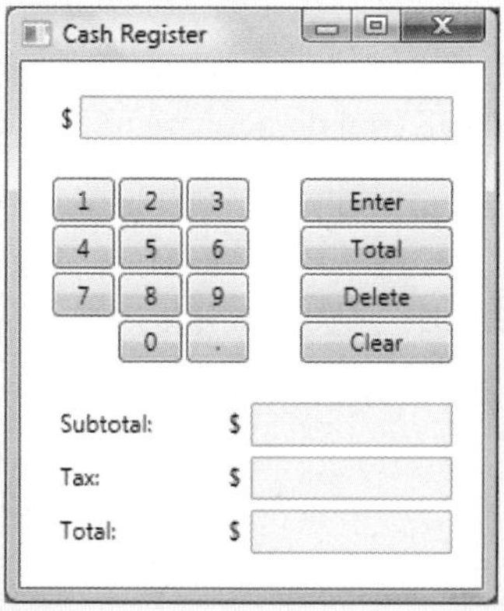

Fig. 15.39 | Cash-register GUI.

15.10 Create an application that quizzes users on their knowledge of national flags. The application should display a series of flags in random order (with no repeats). As each flag is displayed, the user should be able to select the flag's country from a drop-down list and submit his answer

(Fig. 15.40). The application should keep a running tally of how the user has performed. The flag images are available in the `exerciseImages` folder.

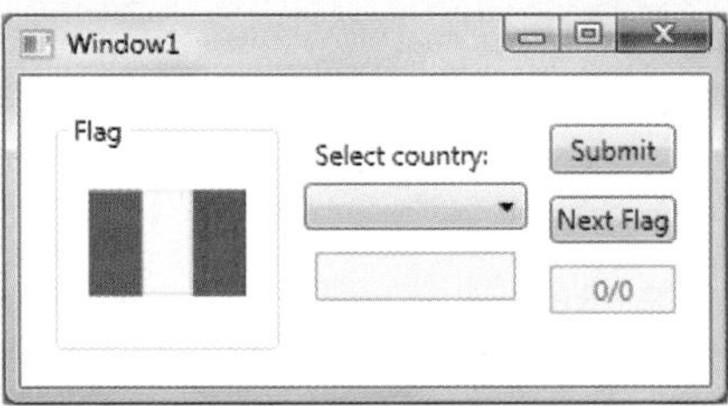

Fig. 15.40 | Flag-quiz GUI.

Because the flag `Image` needs to change from country to country, its `Source` property needs to be set in Visual Basic code. In XAML, you can set a `String` file path to be an `Image`'s `Source`, but the `Source` property actually takes an `ImageSource` object as its value. When your XAML document is compiled, the `String` file path is converted. To set an `Image`'s `Source` in Visual Basic, you must specify an `ImageSource` object. To create an `ImageSource` object from a `String` file path, you can write

```
Dim converter As New ImageSourceConverter
Dim source As ImageSource = _
   CType(converter.ConvertFromString(Path), ImageSource)
```

where *Path* is the `String` file path,

15.11 Using WPF, create a GUI that represents a simple microwave, as shown in Fig. 15.41 (you do not have to provide functionality). To create the **Start**, **Clear** and numerical `Buttons`, you'll need to make use of control templates. To apply a control template automatically for a control type, you can create a style (with a `TargetType`) that sets the `Template` property.

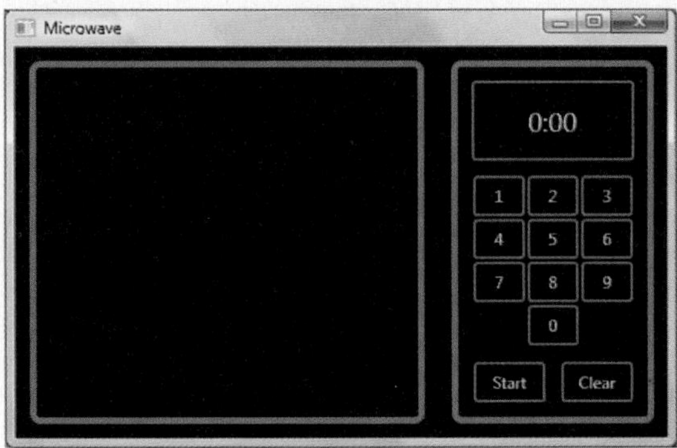

Fig. 15.41 | Microwave GUI.

15.12 WPF allows two-way data bindings. In a normal data binding, if the data source is updated, the binding's target will update, but not vice versa. In a two-way binding, if the value is changed in either the binding's source or its target, the other will be automatically updated. To create a two-way binding, set the `Mode` property to `TwoWay` at the `Binding`'s declaration. Create a phone-book application modeled after the one shown in Fig. 15.42. When the user selects a contact from the contacts list, its information should display in an editable `GridView`. As the information is modified, the contacts list should display each change.

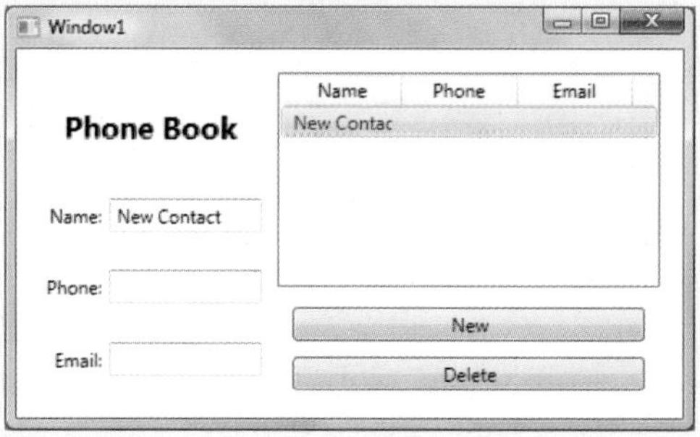

Fig. 15.42 | Phone-book GUI.

15.13 You can create data bindings to LINQ statements. Modify the example given by Fig. 9.4 to display a list of all employees' earnings and a list of employees earning between $4000 and $6000 per month (Fig. 15.43). Allow users to set a different salary range and update the filtered list of employees. Use a data template to display each employee in this format—*LastName, FirstName: $PerMonth Salary.*

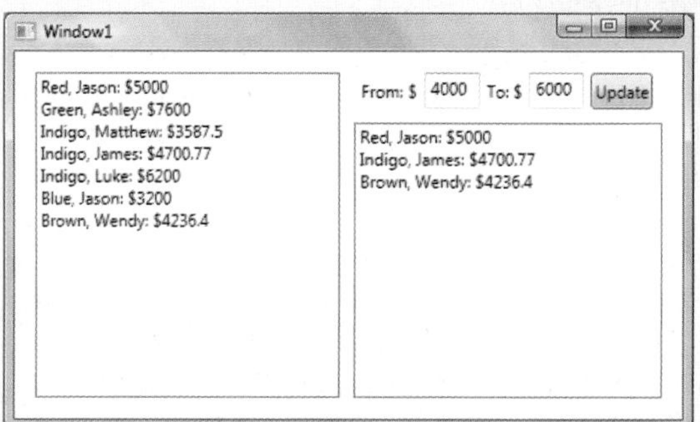

Fig. 15.43 | Lists-of-employees GUI.

16

WPF Graphics and Multimedia

Nowadays people's visual imagination is so much more sophisticated, so much more developed, particularly in young people, that now you can make an image which just slightly suggests something, they can make of it what they will.

—Robert Doisneau

In shape, it is perfectly elliptical. In texture, it is smooth and lustrous. In color, it ranges from pale alabaster to warm terra cotta.

—Sydney J Harris, "Tribute to an Egg"

There are painters who transform the sun into a yellow spot, but there are others who, thanks to their art and intelligence, transform a yellow spot into the sun.

—Pablo Picasso

OBJECTIVES

In this chapter you'll learn:

- To manipulate fonts.
- To draw basic shapes like `Line`s, `Rectangle`s, `Ellipse`s and `Polygon`s.
- To use brushes to customize the `Fill` or `Background` of an object.
- To use transforms to reposition or reorient GUI elements.
- To completely customize the look of a control while maintaining its functionality.
- To animate the properties of a GUI element.
- To transform and animate 3-D objects.

Outline

16.1 Introduction

This chapter overviews WPF's graphics and multimedia capabilities, including two-dimensional and three-dimensional shapes, fonts, transformations, animations, audio and video. WPF integrates drawing and animation features that were previously available only in special libraries (such as Microsoft Windows GDI+). The graphics system in WPF is designed to use your computer's graphics hardware to reduce the load on the CPU.

WPF graphics use resolution-independent units of measurement, making applications more uniform and portable across devices. The size properties of graphic elements in WPF are measured in machine-independent pixels, where one pixel typically represents 1/96 of an inch—however, this depends on the computer's DPI (dots per inch) setting. The graphics engine determines the correct pixel count so that all users see elements of the same size on all devices.

Graphic elements are rendered on screen using a vector-based system in which calculations determine how to size and scale each element, allowing graphic elements to be preserved across any rendering size. This produces smoother graphics than the so called raster-based systems, in which the precise pixels are specified for each graphical element. Raster-based graphics tend to degrade in appearance as they are scaled larger. Vector-based graphics appear smooth at any scale. Graphic elements other than images and video are drawn using WPF's vector-based system.

The basic 2-D shapes are `Lines`, `Rectangles` and `Ellipses`. WPF also has controls that can be used to create custom shapes or curves. Brushes can be used to fill an element with solid colors, complex patterns, gradients, images or videos, allowing for unique and interesting visual experiences. WPF's robust animation and transform capabilities allow you to further customize GUIs. Transforms reposition and reorient graphic elements.

WPF also includes 3-D modeling and rendering capabilities. In addition, 2-D manipulations can be applied to 3-D objects as well. You can find more information on WPF in our WPF Resource Center at `www.deitel.com/wpf/`.

16.2 Controlling Fonts

This section introduces how to control fonts by modifying the font properties of a `TextBlock` control in the XAML code. Figure 16.1 shows how to use `TextBlocks` and how to change the properties to control the appearance of the displayed text.

```
1  <!-- Fig. 16.1: UsingFonts.xaml -->
2  <!-- Formatting fonts in XAML code. -->
3  <Window x:Class="UsingFonts"
4     xmlns="http://schemas.microsoft.com/winfx/2006/xaml/presentation"
5     xmlns:x="http://schemas.microsoft.com/winfx/2006/xaml"
6     Title="UsingFonts" Height="120" Width="400">
7
8     <StackPanel>
9        <!-- make a font bold using the FontWeight -->
10       <TextBlock FontFamily="Arial" FontSize="12" FontWeight="Bold">
11          Arial 12 point bold.</TextBlock>
12
13       <!-- if no font size is specified, default is 12 -->
14       <TextBlock FontFamily="Times New Roman">
15          Times New Roman 12 point plain.</TextBlock>
16
17       <!-- specifying a different font size and using FontStyle -->
18       <TextBlock FontFamily="Courier New" FontSize="16"
19          FontStyle="Italic" FontWeight="Bold">
20          Courier New 16 point bold and italic.
21       </TextBlock>
22
23       <!-- using Overline and Baseline TextDecorations -->
24       <TextBlock>
25          <TextBlock.TextDecorations>
26             <TextDecoration Location="OverLine" />
27             <TextDecoration Location="Baseline" />
28          </TextBlock.TextDecorations>
29          Default font with overline and baseline.
30       </TextBlock>
31
32       <!-- using Strikethrough and Underline TextDecorations -->
33       <TextBlock>
34          <TextBlock.TextDecorations>
35             <TextDecoration Location="Strikethrough" />
36             <TextDecoration Location="Underline" />
37          </TextBlock.TextDecorations>
38          Default font with strikethrough and underline.
39       </TextBlock>
40    </StackPanel>
41 </Window>
```

UsingFonts
Arial 12 point bold.
Times New Roman 12 point plain.
Courier New 16 point bold and italic.
Default font with overline and baseline.
Default font with strikethrough and underline.

Fig. 16.1 | Formatting fonts in XAML code.

The text that you want to display in the `TextBlock` is placed between the `TextBlock` tags. The **`FontFamily`** property defines the font of the displayed text. This property can be set to any font. Lines 10, 14 and 18 define the separate `TextBlock` fonts to be Arial, Times

New Roman and Courier New, respectively. If the font is not specified or is not available, the default font, Segoe UI for Windows Vista, is used (lines 24 and 33).

The **FontSize** property defines the text size measured in points. When no `FontSize` is specified, the property is set to the default value of 12. The font sizes are defined in lines 10 and 18. Notice in lines 14, 24 and 33 that the `FontSize` is not defined, assigning the default value of 12 to each corresponding block of text.

`TextBlock`s have various properties that can further modify the font. Lines 10 and 19 set the **FontWeight** property to `Bold` to make the font thicker. This property can be set either to a numeric value (1–999) or to a predefined descriptive value—such as `Light` or `UltraBold`—to define the thickness of the text. You can use the **FontStyle** property to make the text either `Italic` or `Oblique`—which is simply a more emphasized italic. Line 19 sets the `FontStyle` property to `Italic`.

You can also define **TextDecorations** for a `TextBlock` to draw a horizontal line through the text. **Overline** and **Baseline**—shown in the fourth `TextBlock` of Fig. 16.1—create lines above the text and at the base of the text, respectively (lines 26–27). **Strikethrough** and **Underline**—shown in the fifth `TextBlock`—create lines through the middle of the text and under the text, respectively (lines 35–36). The `Underline` option leaves a small amount of space between the text and the line, unlike the `Baseline`. The **Location** property of the **TextDecoration** class defines which decoration you want to apply.

16.3 Basic Shapes

WPF has several built-in shapes. The `BasicShapes` example (Fig. 16.2) shows you how to display `Line`s, `Rectangle`s and `Ellipse`s.

```
<!-- Fig. 16.2: BasicShapes.xaml -->
<!-- Drawing basic shapes in XAML. -->
<Window x:Class="BasicShapes"
    xmlns="http://schemas.microsoft.com/winfx/2006/xaml/presentation"
    xmlns:x="http://schemas.microsoft.com/winfx/2006/xaml"
    Title="BasicShapes" Height="200" Width="500">
  <Canvas>
     <!-- Rectangle with fill but no stroke -->
     <Rectangle Canvas.Left="90" Canvas.Top="30" Width="150" Height="90"
        Fill="Blue" />

     <!-- Lines defined by starting points and ending points-->
     <Line X1="90" Y1="30" X2="110" Y2="40" Stroke="Black" />
     <Line X1="90" Y1="120" X2="110" Y2="130" Stroke="Black" />
     <Line X1="240" Y1="30" X2="260" Y2="40" Stroke="Black" />
     <Line X1="240" Y1="120" X2="260" Y2="130" Stroke="Black" />

     <!-- Rectangle with stroke but no fill -->
     <Rectangle Canvas.Left="110" Canvas.Top="40" Width="150"
        Height="90" Stroke="Black" />

     <!-- Ellipse with fill and no stroke -->
     <Ellipse Canvas.Left="280" Canvas.Top="75" Width="100" Height="50"
        Fill="Red" />
```

Fig. 16.2 | Drawing basic shapes in XAML. (Part 1 of 2.)

```
25          <Line X1="380" Y1="55" X2="380" Y2="100" Stroke="Black" />
26          <Line X1="280" Y1="55" X2="280" Y2="100" Stroke="Black" />
27
28          <!-- Ellipse with stroke and no fill -->
29          <Ellipse Canvas.Left="280" Canvas.Top="30" Width="100" Height="50"
30             Stroke="Black" />
31       </Canvas>
32    </Window>
```

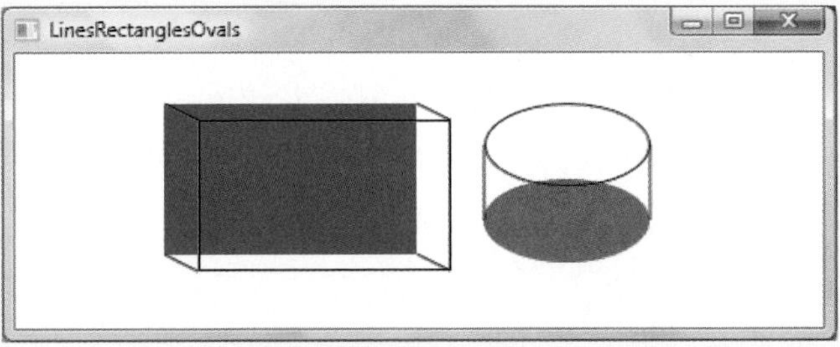

Fig. 16.2 | Drawing basic shapes in XAML. (Part 2 of 2.)

The first shape drawn uses the **Rectangle** object to create a filled rectangle in the window. Notice that the layout control is a Canvas allowing us to use coordinates to position the shapes. To specify the upper-left corner of the Rectangle at lines 9–10, we set the Canvas.Left and Canvas.Top properties to 90 and 30, respectively. We then set the Width and Height properties to 150 and 90, respectively, to specify the size. To define the Rectangle's color, we use the **Fill** property (line 10). You can assign any Color or Brush to this property. Rectangles also have a **Stroke** property, which defines the color of the outline of the shape (line 20). If either the Fill or the Stroke is not specified, that property will be rendered transparently. For this reason, the blue Rectangle in the window has no outline, while the second Rectangle drawn has only an outline (with a transparent center). Shape objects have a **StrokeThickness** property which defines the thickness of the outline. The default value for StrokeThickness is 1 pixel.

A **Line** is defined by its two endpoints—X1, Y1 and X2, Y2. Lines have a Stroke property that defines the color of the line. In this example, the lines are all set to have black Strokes (lines 13–16).

To draw a circle or ellipse, you can use the **Ellipse** control. The placement and size of an Ellipse is defined like a Rectangle—with the Canvas.Left and Canvas.Top properties for the upper-left corner, and the Width and Height properties for the size (line 23). Together, the Canvas.Left, Canvas.Top, Width and Height of an Ellipse define a "bounding rectangle" in which the Ellipse touches the center of each side of the rectangle. To draw a circle, provide the same value for the Width and Height properties. As with Rectangles, having an unspecified Fill property for an Ellipse makes the shape transparent (lines 29–30).

16.4 Polygons and Polylines

There are two shape controls for drawing multisided shapes—**Polyline** and **Polygon**. Polyline draws a series of connected lines defined by a set of points, while Polygon does the same but connects the start and end points to make a closed figure. The application `DrawPolygons` (Fig. 16.3) allows you to click anywhere on the `Canvas` to define points for one of three shapes. You select which shape you want to display by selecting one of the `RadioButton`s in the second column. The difference between the **Filled Polygon** and the **Polygon** options is that the former has a `Fill` property specified while the latter does not.

```
<!-- Fig. 16.3: DrawPolygons.xaml -->
<!-- Defining Polylines and Polygons in XAML. -->
<Window x:Class="DrawPolygons"
    xmlns="http://schemas.microsoft.com/winfx/2006/xaml/presentation"
    xmlns:x="http://schemas.microsoft.com/winfx/2006/xaml"
    Title="DrawPolygons" Height="400" Width="450" Name="mainWindow">
    <Grid>
      <Grid.ColumnDefinitions>
         <ColumnDefinition />
         <ColumnDefinition Width="Auto" />
      </Grid.ColumnDefinitions>

      <!-- Canvas contains two polygons and a polyline -->
      <!-- Only the shape selected by the radio button is visible -->
      <Canvas Name="drawCanvas" Grid.Column="0" Background="White">
         <Polyline Name="polyLine" Stroke="Black"
            Visibility="Collapsed" />
         <Polygon Name="polygon" Stroke="Black" Visibility="Collapsed" />
         <Polygon Name="filledPolygon" Fill="DarkBlue"
            Visibility="Collapsed" /> <!-- Filled -->
      </Canvas>

      <!-- StackPanel containing the RadioButton options -->
      <StackPanel Grid.Column="1" Orientation="Vertical"
         Background="WhiteSmoke">
         <GroupBox Header="Select Type" Margin="10">
            <StackPanel>
               <RadioButton Name="lineRadio" Margin="5">Polyline
                  </RadioButton> <!-- Polyline option -->

               <!-- unfilled Polygon option -->
               <RadioButton Name="polygonRadio" Margin="5">Polygon
                  </RadioButton>

               <!-- filled Polygon option -->
               <RadioButton Name="filledPolygonRadio" Margin="5">
                  Filled Polygon</RadioButton>
            </StackPanel>
         </GroupBox>

         <!-- Button clears the shape from the canvas -->
         <Button Name="clearButton" Margin="5">Clear</Button>
      </StackPanel>
   </Grid>
</Window>
```

Fig. 16.3 | Defining Polylines and Polygons in XAML. (Part 1 of 2.)

a) Application with the Polyline option selected.

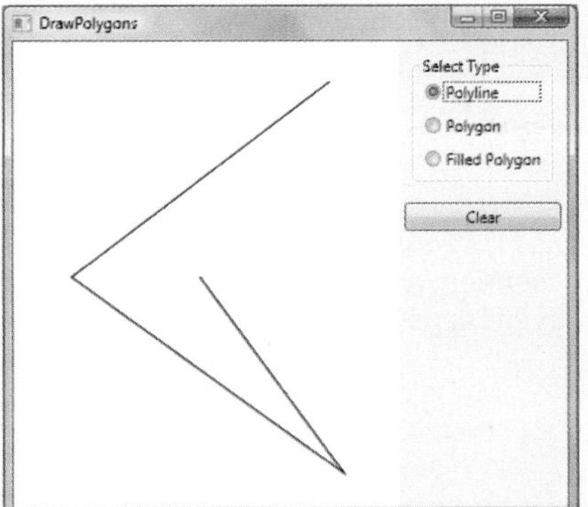

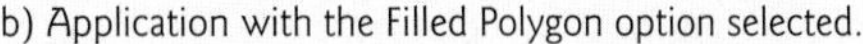
b) Application with the Filled Polygon option selected.

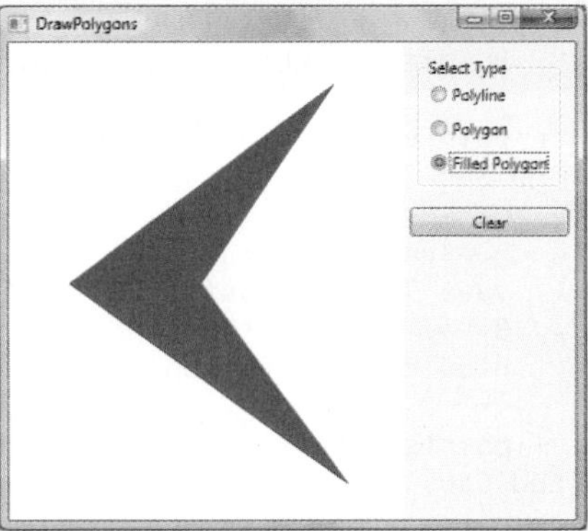

Fig. 16.3 | Defining Polylines and Polygons in XAML. (Part 2 of 2.)

The code defines a two-column GUI (lines 9–10). The first column contains a `Canvas` (lines 15–21) that the user interacts with to create the points of the selected shape. Embedded in the `Canvas` are a `Polyline` (lines 16–17) and two `Polygons`—one with a `Fill` (lines 19–20) and one without (line 18). The **`Visibility`** of a control can be set to **`Visible`**, **`Collapsed`** or **`Hidden`**. This property is initially set to `Collapsed` for all three shapes (lines 17, 18 and 20), because we'll display only the shape that corresponds to the selected `RadioButton`. The difference between `Hidden` and `Collapsed` is that a `Hidden` object occupies space in the GUI but is not visible, while a `Collapsed` object has a `Width` and `Height` of 0. As you can see, `Polyline` and `Polygon` objects have `Fill` and `Stroke` properties like the simple shapes we discussed earlier.

The `RadioButtons` (lines 28–37) allow you to select which shape appears in the `Canvas`. There is also a `Button` (line 42) that clears the shape's points to allow you start over. The code-behind file for this application is shown in Fig. 16.4.

```
' Fig. 16.4: DrawPolygons.xaml.vb
' Drawing Polylines and Polygons.
Class DrawPolygons
   ' stores the collection of points for the multisided shapes
   Private points As New PointCollection()

   ' when the window loads, assign the PointCollection to shape points
   Private Sub mainWindow_Loaded(ByVal sender As System.Object, _
      ByVal e As System.Windows.RoutedEventArgs) _
      Handles mainWindow.Loaded

      polyLine.Points = points ' assign Polyline points
      polygon.Points = points ' assign Polygon points
      filledPolygon.Points = points ' assign filled Polygon points
   End Sub ' mainWindow_Loaded

```

Fig. 16.4 | Drawing `Polylines` and `Polygons`. (Part 1 of 2.)

```
17       ' adds a new point when the user clicks on the canvas
18       Private Sub drawCanvas_MouseDown(ByVal sender As Object, _
19          ByVal e As System.Windows.Input.MouseButtonEventArgs) _
20          Handles drawCanvas.MouseDown
21
22          points.Add(e.GetPosition(drawCanvas)) ' add point to collection
23       End Sub ' drawCanvas_MouseDown
24
25       ' when the clear Button is clicked
26       Private Sub clearButton_Click(ByVal sender As Object, _
27          ByVal e As System.Windows.RoutedEventArgs) _
28          Handles clearButton.Click
29
30          points.Clear() ' clear the points from the collection
31       End Sub ' clearButton_Click
32
33       ' when the user selects the Polyline
34       Private Sub lineRadio_Checked(ByVal sender As Object, _
35          ByVal e As System.Windows.RoutedEventArgs) _
36          Handles lineRadio.Checked
37
38          ' Polyline is visible, the other two are not
39          polyLine.Visibility = Windows.Visibility.Visible
40          polygon.Visibility = Windows.Visibility.Collapsed
41          filledPolygon.Visibility = Windows.Visibility.Collapsed
42       End Sub ' lineRadio_Checked
43
44       ' when the user selects the Polygon
45       Private Sub polygonRadio_Checked(ByVal sender As Object, _
46          ByVal e As System.Windows.RoutedEventArgs) _
47          Handles polygonRadio.Checked
48
49          ' Polygon is visible, the other two are not
50          polyLine.Visibility = Windows.Visibility.Collapsed
51          polygon.Visibility = Windows.Visibility.Visible
52          filledPolygon.Visibility = Windows.Visibility.Collapsed
53       End Sub ' polygonRadio_Checked
54
55       ' when the user selects the filled Polygon
56       Private Sub filledPolygonRadio_Checked(ByVal sender As Object, _
57          ByVal e As System.Windows.RoutedEventArgs) _
58          Handles filledPolygonRadio.Checked
59
60          ' filled Polygon is visible, the other two are not
61          polyLine.Visibility = Windows.Visibility.Collapsed
62          polygon.Visibility = Windows.Visibility.Collapsed
63          filledPolygon.Visibility = Windows.Visibility.Visible
64       End Sub ' filledPolygonRadio_Checked
65    End Class ' DrawPolygons
```

Fig. 16.4 | Drawing `Polylines` and `Polygons`. (Part 2 of 2.)

To allow the user to specify a variable number of points, line 5 declares a **`PointCollection`**, which is a collection that stores `Point` objects. This keeps track of each mouse-click location. The collection's Add method adds new points to the end of the collection. When the window is loaded, we set the Points property (lines 12–14) of each shape to reference the PointCollection instance variable created in line 5.

We created a MouseDown event handler to capture mouse clicks on the Canvas (lines 18–23). When the user clicks the mouse on the Canvas, the mouse coordinates are recorded (line 22) and the points collection is updated. Since the Points property of each of the three shapes has a reference to our PointCollection object, the shapes are automatically updated with the new Point. The Polyline and Polygon shapes connect the Points based on the ordering in the collection.

Each RadioButton's Checked event handler sets the corresponding shape's Visibility property to Visible and sets the other two to Collapsed to display the correct shape in the Canvas. For example, the lineRadio_Checked event handler (lines 34–42) makes polyLine Visible (line 39) and makes polygon and filledPolygon Collapsed (lines 40–41). The other two RadioButton event handlers are defined similarly in lines 45–53 and lines 56–64.

The clearButton_Click event handler erases the stored collection of Points (line 30). The Clear method of PointCollection, points, erases its elements.

16.5 Brushes

Brushes change an element's graphic properties, such as the Fill, Stroke or Background. A SolidColorBrush fills the element with the specified color. To customize elements further, you can use ImageBrushes, VisualBrushes and gradient brushes. Run the UsingBrushes application (Fig. 16.5) to see Brushes applied to TextBlocks and Ellipses.

ImageBrush

An ImageBrush paints an image into the property it is assigned to (such as a Background). For instance, the TextBlock with the text "Image" and the Ellipse next to it are both filled with the same flower picture. To fill the text, we can assign the ImageBrush to the Foreground property of the TextBlock. The Foreground property specifies the fill for the text itself while the Background property specifies the fill for the area surrounding the text. Notice in lines 32–35 we apply the ImageBrush with its ImageSource set to the file we want to display (the image file must be included in the project). We can also assign the brush to the Fill of the Ellipse (lines 41–43) to display the image inside the shape.

```
1  <!-- Fig. 16.5: UsingBrushes.xaml -->
2  <!-- Applying brushes to various XAML elements. -->
3  <Window x:Class="UsingBrushes"
4     xmlns="http://schemas.microsoft.com/winfx/2006/xaml/presentation"
5     xmlns:x="http://schemas.microsoft.com/winfx/2006/xaml"
6     Title="UsingBrushes" Height="450" Width="700">
7     <Grid>
8        <Grid.RowDefinitions>
9           <RowDefinition />
10          <RowDefinition />
11          <RowDefinition />
12       </Grid.RowDefinitions>
```

Fig. 16.5 | Applying brushes to various XAML elements. (Part 1 of 3.)

```

      <Grid.ColumnDefinitions>
         <ColumnDefinition />
         <ColumnDefinition />
      </Grid.ColumnDefinitions>

      <!-- TextBlock with a SolidColorBrush -->
      <TextBlock FontSize="100" FontWeight="999">
         <TextBlock.Foreground>
            <SolidColorBrush Color="#5F2CAE" />
         </TextBlock.Foreground>
         Color
      </TextBlock>

      <!-- Ellipse with a SolidColorBrush (just a Fill) -->
      <Ellipse Grid.Column="1" Height="100" Width="300" Fill="#5F2CAE" />

      <!-- TextBlock with an ImageBrush -->
      <TextBlock Grid.Row="1" FontSize="100" FontWeight="999">
         <TextBlock.Foreground>
            <!-- Flower image as an ImageBrush -->
            <ImageBrush ImageSource="flowers.jpg" />
         </TextBlock.Foreground>
         Image
      </TextBlock>

      <!-- Ellipse with an ImageBrush -->
      <Ellipse Grid.Row="1" Grid.Column="1" Height="100" Width="300">
         <Ellipse.Fill>
            <ImageBrush ImageSource="flowers.jpg" />
         </Ellipse.Fill>
      </Ellipse>

      <!-- TextBlock with a MediaElement as a VisualBrush -->
      <TextBlock Grid.Row="2" FontSize="100" FontWeight="999">
         <TextBlock.Foreground>
            <!-- VisualBrush with an embedded MediaElement-->
            <VisualBrush>
               <VisualBrush.Visual>
                  <MediaElement Source="nasa.wmv" />
               </VisualBrush.Visual>
            </VisualBrush>
         </TextBlock.Foreground>
         Video
      </TextBlock>

      <!-- Ellipse with a MediaElement as a VisualBrush -->
      <Ellipse Grid.Row="2" Grid.Column="1" Height="100" Width="300">
         <Ellipse.Fill>
            <VisualBrush>
               <VisualBrush.Visual>
                  <MediaElement Source="nasa.wmv" />
               </VisualBrush.Visual>
```

Fig. 16.5 | Applying brushes to various XAML elements. (Part 2 of 3.)

```
                </VisualBrush>
            </Ellipse.Fill>
        </Ellipse>
    </Grid>
</Window>
```

Fig. 16.5 | Applying brushes to various XAML elements. (Part 3 of 3.)

VisualBrush and MediaElement

This example displays a video in a TextBlock's Foreground and an Ellipse's Fill. To use audio or video in a WPF application, you use the MediaElement control. Before using a video file in your application, add it to your Visual Studio project by first selecting the **Add Existing Item...** option in the **Project** menu. In the file dialog that appears, find and select the video you want to use. Note that in the drop-down menu next to the **File Name** TextBox, you must change the selection to **All Files (*.*)** to be able to find your file. Once you have selected your file, click **Add**. Select the newly added video in the **Solution Explorer**. Then, in the **Properties** window, change the **Copy to Output Directory** property to **Copy if newer**. This tells the project to copy your video to the project's output directory where it can directly reference the file. You can now set the Source property of your MediaElement to the video. In the UsingBrushes application, we use nasa.wmv (line 52 and 64).

We use the VisualBrush element to display a video in the desired controls. Lines 50–54 define the Brush with a MediaElement assigned to its Visual property. In this property you can completely customize the look of the brush. By assigning the video to this property, we can apply the brush to the Foreground of the TextBlock (lines 48–55) and the Fill of the Ellipse (lines 61–67) to play the video inside the controls. Notice that the Fill of the third Row's elements is different in each screen capture in Fig. 16.5. This is because the video is playing inside the two elements.

Gradients

A gradient is a gradual transition through two or more colors. Gradients can be applied as the background or fill for various elements. There are two types of gradients in WPF—LinearGradientBrush and RadialGradientBrush. The LinearGradientBrush transitions through colors along a straight path. The RadialGradientBrush transitions through colors radially outward from a specified point. Linear gradients are discussed in the UsingGradients example, which displays a gradient across the window. This was created by applying a LinearGradientBrush to a Rectangle's Fill. The gradient starts white and transitions linearly to black from left to right. You can set the RGBA values of the start and end colors to change the look of the gradient. Note that the values entered in the TextBoxes must be in the range of 0–255 for the application to run properly. If you set either color's Alpha value to less than 255, you'll see the text "Transparency test" in the background, showing that the Rectangle is semitransparent. The XAML code for this application is shown in Fig. 16.6.

The GUI for this application contains a single Rectangle with a LinearGradientBrush applied to its Fill (lines 19–29). We define the StartPoint and EndPoint of the gradient in line 21. You must assign logical points to these properties, meaning the *x*- and *y*-coordinates take values between 0 and 1, inclusive. Logical points are used to reference

```
1  <!-- Fig. 16.6: UsingGradients.xaml -->
2  <!-- Defining gradients in XAML. -->
3  <Window x:Class="UsingGradients"
4     xmlns="http://schemas.microsoft.com/winfx/2006/xaml/presentation"
5     xmlns:x="http://schemas.microsoft.com/winfx/2006/xaml"
6     Title="UsingGradients" Height="200" Width="450">
```

Fig. 16.6 | Defining gradients in XAML. (Part 1 of 3.)

```
   <Grid>
      <Grid.RowDefinitions>
         <RowDefinition />
         <RowDefinition Height="Auto" />
         <RowDefinition Height="Auto" />
         <RowDefinition Height="Auto" />
      </Grid.RowDefinitions>

      <!-- TextBlock in the background to show transparency -->
      <TextBlock FontSize="30" HorizontalAlignment="Center"
         VerticalAlignment="Center">Transparency test</TextBlock>

      <Rectangle> <!-- sample rectangle with gradient fill -->
         <Rectangle.Fill> <!-- a gradient -->
            <LinearGradientBrush  StartPoint="0,0" EndPoint="1,0">
               <!-- gradient stop can define a color at any offset -->
               <GradientStop x:Name="startGradient" Offset="0.0"
                  Color="White" />
               <GradientStop x:Name="stopGradient" Offset="1.0"
                  Color="Black" />
            </LinearGradientBrush>
         </Rectangle.Fill>
      </Rectangle>

      <!-- shows which TextBox corresponds with which RGBA value-->
      <StackPanel Grid.Row="1" Orientation="Horizontal">
         <TextBlock Width="75" Margin="5">Alpha:</TextBlock>
         <TextBlock Width="75" Margin="5">Red:</TextBlock>
         <TextBlock Width="75" Margin="5">Green:</TextBlock>
         <TextBlock Width="75" Margin="5">Blue:</TextBlock>
      </StackPanel>

      <!-- GUI to select the color of the first GradientStop -->
      <StackPanel Grid.Row="2" Orientation="Horizontal">
         <TextBox Name="fromAlpha" Width="75" Margin="5">255</TextBox>
         <TextBox Name="fromRed" Width="75" Margin="5">255</TextBox>
         <TextBox Name="fromGreen" Width="75" Margin="5">255</TextBox>
         <TextBox Name="fromBlue" Width="75" Margin="5">255</TextBox>
         <Button Name="fromButton" Width="75" Margin="5">Start Color
            </Button>
      </StackPanel>

      <!-- GUI to select the color of second GradientStop -->
      <StackPanel Grid.Row="3" Orientation="Horizontal">
         <TextBox Name="toAlpha" Width="75" Margin="5">255</TextBox>
         <TextBox Name="toRed" Width="75" Margin="5">0</TextBox>
         <TextBox Name="toGreen" Width="75" Margin="5">0</TextBox>
         <TextBox Name="toBlue" Width="75" Margin="5">0</TextBox>
         <Button Name="toButton" Width="75" Margin="5">End Color
            </Button>
      </StackPanel>
   </Grid>
</Window>
```

Fig. 16.6 | Defining gradients in XAML. (Part 2 of 3.)

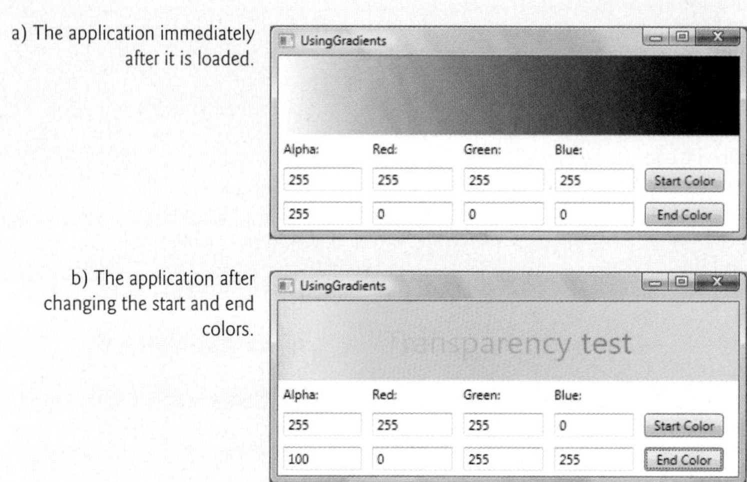

Fig. 16.6 | Defining gradients in XAML. (Part 3 of 3.)

locations in the control independent of the actual size. The point (0,0) represents the top-left corner while the point (1,1) represents the bottom-right corner. The gradient will transition linearly from the start to the end—for `RadialGradientBrush`, the `StartPoint` represents the center of the gradient.

A gradient is defined using `GradientStop` controls. A **`GradientStop`** defines a single color along the gradient. You can define as many stops as you want by embedding them in the brush element. A `GradientStop` is defined by its `Offset` and `Color` properties. The **`Color`** property defines the color you want the gradient to transition to—lines 24 and 26 indicate that the gradient transitions through white and black. The **`Offset`** property defines where along the linear transition you want the color to appear. You can assign any `Double` value between 0 and 1, inclusive, which represent the start and end of the gradient. In the example we use 0.0 and 1.0 offsets (lines 23 and 25), indicating that these colors appear at the start and end of the gradient (which were defined in line 21), respectively. The code in Fig. 16.7 allows the user to set the `Colors` of the two stops.

When `fromButton` is clicked, we use the `Text` properties of the corresponding `TextBoxes` to obtain the RGBA values and create a new color. We then assign it to the `Color` property of `startGradient` (lines 10–12). When the `toButton` is clicked, we do the same for `stopGradient`'s `Color` (lines 20–22).

```
1  ' Fig. 16.7: UsingGradients.xaml.vb
2  ' Customizing gradients.
3  Class UsingGradients
4     ' change the starting color of the gradient when the user clicks
5     Private Sub fromButton_Click(ByVal sender As System.Object, _
6        ByVal e As System.Windows.RoutedEventArgs) _
7        Handles fromButton.Click
8
```

Fig. 16.7 | Customizing gradients. (Part 1 of 2.)

```
        ' change the color to use the ARGB values specified by user
        startGradient.Color = Color.FromArgb( _
           Convert.ToByte(fromAlpha.Text), Convert.ToByte(fromRed.Text), _
           Convert.ToByte(fromGreen.Text), Convert.ToByte(fromBlue.Text))
     End Sub ' fromButton_Click

     ' change the ending color of the gradient when the user clicks
     Private Sub toButton_Click(ByVal sender As System.Object, _
        ByVal e As System.Windows.RoutedEventArgs) Handles toButton.Click

        ' change the color to use the ARGB values specified by user
        stopGradient.Color = Color.FromArgb( _
           Convert.ToByte(toAlpha.Text), Convert.ToByte(toRed.Text), _
           Convert.ToByte(toGreen.Text), Convert.ToByte(toBlue.Text))
     End Sub ' toButton_Click
  End Class ' UsingGradients
```

Fig. 16.7 | Customizing gradients. (Part 2 of 2.)

16.6 Transforms

A transform can be applied to any UI element to reposition or reorient the graphic. There are four types of transforms—`TranslateTransform`, `RotateTransform`, `SkewTransform` and `ScaleTransform`. A `TranslateTransform` moves an object to a new location. A `RotateTransform` rotates the object around a point and by a specified `RotationAngle`. A `SkewTransform` skews (or shears) the object. A `ScaleTransform` scales the object's *x*- and *y*-coordinate points by different specified amounts. See Section 16.7 for an example using a `RotateTransform` and a `ScaleTransform`.

In the following `DrawStars` example, we draw a star using the `Polygon` control and use `RotateTransforms` to create a circle of randomly colored stars. Figure 16.8 shows the XAML code and a screen capture of the example. Lines 10–11 define a `Polygon` in the shape of a star. The `Points` property of the `Polygon` in this example is defined here in a new syntax. Each `Point` in the collection is defined with a comma separating the *x*- and *y*-coordinates. A single space separates each `Point`. Note that we defined ten `Points` in the collection. The code-behind file is shown in Fig. 16.9.

```
1  <!-- Fig. 16.8: DrawStars.xaml -->
2  <!-- Defining a Polygon representing a star in XAML. -->
3  <Window x:Class="DrawStars"
4     xmlns="http://schemas.microsoft.com/winfx/2006/xaml/presentation"
5     xmlns:x="http://schemas.microsoft.com/winfx/2006/xaml"
6     Title="DrawStars" Height="330" Width="330" Name="DrawStars">
7     <Canvas Name="mainCanvas"> <!-- Main canvas of the application -->
8
9        <!-- Polygon with points that make up a star -->
10       <Polygon Name="star" Fill="Green" Points="205,150 217,186 259,186
11          223,204 233,246 205,222 177,246 187,204 151,186 193,186" />
12    </Canvas>
13 </Window>
```

Fig. 16.8 | Defining a `Polygon` representing a star in XAML. (Part 1 of 2.)

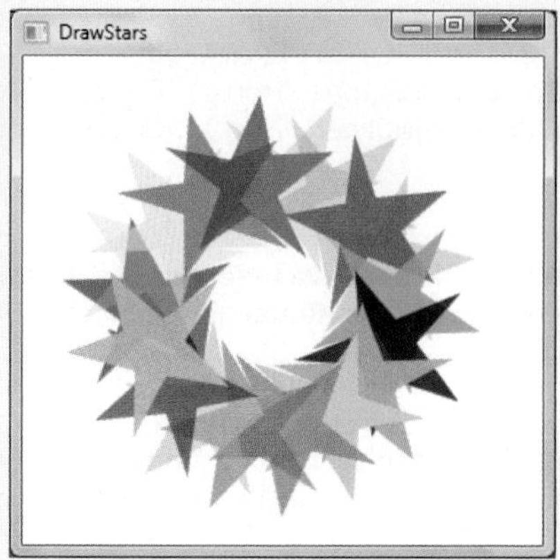

Fig. 16.8 | Defining a `Polygon` representing a star in XAML. (Part 2 of 2.)

```
1  ' Fig. 16.9: DrawStars.xaml.vb
2  ' Applying transforms to a Polygon.
3  Class DrawStars
4     ' duplicate the polygon several times and rotate each
5     Private Sub DrawStars_Loaded(ByVal sender As System.Object, _
6        ByVal e As System.Windows.RoutedEventArgs) Handles MyBase.Loaded
7
8        Dim random As New Random() ' used to get random values for colors
9
10       ' create 18 more stars
11       For count = 1 To 18
12          Dim newStar = New Polygon() ' create a new polygon object
13          newStar.Points = star.Points ' copy the points collection
14
15          Dim colorValues(3) As Byte ' create a four-element Byte array
16          random.NextBytes(colorValues) ' creates four random values
17          newStar.Fill = New SolidColorBrush(Color.FromArgb( _
18             colorValues(0), colorValues(1), colorValues(2), _
19             colorValues(3))) ' creates a random-color brush
20
21          ' apply a rotation to the shape
22          Dim rotate = New RotateTransform(count * 20, 150, 150)
23          newStar.RenderTransform = rotate
24          mainCanvas.Children.Add(newStar) ' add the polygon to the window
25       Next ' count
26    End Sub ' DrawStars_Loaded
27 End Class ' DrawStars
```

Fig. 16.9 | Applying transforms to a `Polygon`.

In the code-behind, we replicate `star` 18 times and apply a different `RotateTransform` to each to get the circle of `Polygons` shown in the screen capture of Fig. 16.8. Each iteration of the loop duplicates `star` by creating a new `Polygon` with the same set of points (lines 12–13). To generate the random colors for each star, we use the `Random` class's **`NextBytes`** method, which assigns a random value in the range 0–255 to each element in its

Byte array argument. Lines 15–16 define a four-element Byte array and supply the array to the NextBytes method. We then create a new Brush with a color that uses the four randomly generated values as its RGBA values (lines 17–19).

To apply a rotation to the new Polygon, we set the **RenderTransform** property to a new RotateTransform object (lines 22–23). Each iteration of the For...Next statement assigns a new rotation-angle value by using the control variable multiplied by 20 as the RotationAngle argument. The first argument in the RotateTransform's constructor is the angle by which to rotate the object. The next two arguments are the *x*- and *y*-coordinates of the point of rotation. The center of the circle of stars is the point (150,150) because all 18 stars were rotated about that point. Each new shape is added as a new Child element to mainCanvas (line 24) so it can be rendered on screen.

16.7 WPF Customization: A Television GUI

In Chapter 15, we introduced several techniques for customizing the appearance of WPF controls. We revisit them in this section, now that we have a basic understanding of how to create and manipulate 2-D graphics in WPF. You'll learn to apply combinations of shapes, brushes and transforms to define every aspect of a control's appearance and to create graphically sophisticated GUIs.

This case study presents a WPF application that models a television. The GUI depicts a 3-D-looking environment featuring a TV that can be turned on and off. When it is on, the user can play, pause and stop the TV's video. When the video plays, a semitransparent reflection plays simultaneously on what appears to be a flat surface in front of the screen (Fig. 16.10).

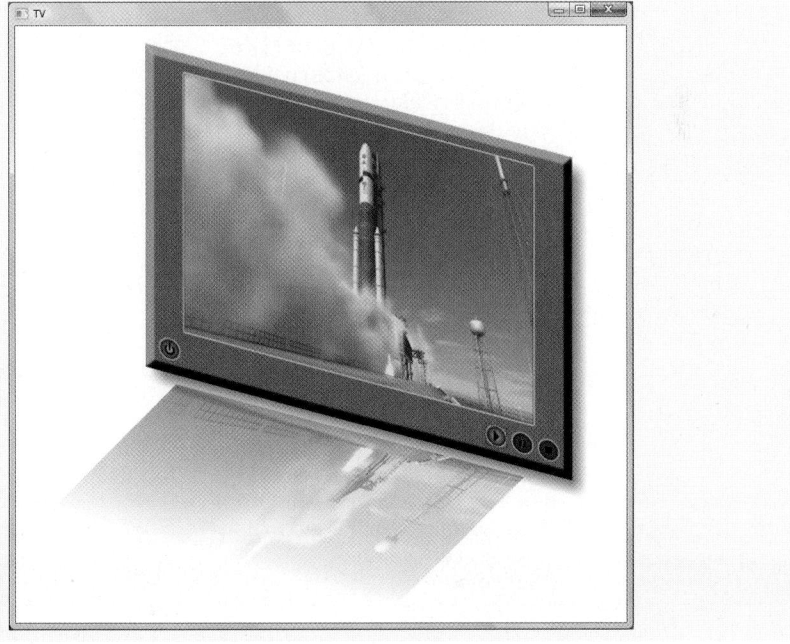

Fig. 16.10 | GUI representing a television.

The TV GUI may appear overwhelmingly complex, but it's actually just a basic WPF GUI built using controls with modified appearances. This example demonstrates the use of WPF bitmap effects to apply simple visual effects to some of the GUI elements. In addition, it introduces opacity masks, which can be used to hide parts of an element. Other than these two new concepts, the TV application is created using only the WPF elements and concepts that you've already learned. Figure 16.11 presents the XAML markup and a screen capture of the application when it first loads. The video used in this case study is a public-domain NASA video entitled *Animation: To the Moon* and can be downloaded from the NASA website (`www.nasa.gov/multimedia/hd/index.html`).

```
<!-- Fig. 16.11: TV.xaml -->
<!-- TV GUI showing the versatility of WPF customization. -->
<Window x:Class="TV"
   xmlns="http://schemas.microsoft.com/winfx/2006/xaml/presentation"
   xmlns:x="http://schemas.microsoft.com/winfx/2006/xaml"
   Title="TV" Height="720" Width="720">
   <Window.Resources>
      <!-- define template for play, pause and stop buttons -->
      <ControlTemplate x:Key="RadioButtonTemplate"
         TargetType="RadioButton">
         <Grid>
            <!-- create a circular border -->
            <Ellipse Width="25" Height="25" Fill="Silver" />

            <!-- create an "illuminated" background -->
            <Ellipse Name="backgroundEllipse" Width="22" Height="22">
               <Ellipse.Fill> <!-- enabled and unchecked state -->
                  <RadialGradientBrush> <!-- red "light" -->
                     <GradientStop Offset="0" Color="Red" />
                     <GradientStop Offset="1.25" Color="Black" />
                  </RadialGradientBrush>
               </Ellipse.Fill>
            </Ellipse>

            <!-- display button image -->
            <ContentPresenter Content="{TemplateBinding Content}" />
         </Grid>

         <!-- change appearance when state changes -->
         <ControlTemplate.Triggers>
            <!-- disabled state -->
            <Trigger Property="RadioButton.IsEnabled" Value="False">
               <Setter TargetName="backgroundEllipse" Property="Fill">
                  <Setter.Value>
                     <RadialGradientBrush> <!-- dim "light" -->
                        <GradientStop Offset="0" Color="LightGray" />
                        <GradientStop Offset="1.25" Color="Black" />
                     </RadialGradientBrush>
                  </Setter.Value>
               </Setter>
            </Trigger>
```

Fig. 16.11 | TV GUI showing the versatility of WPF customization (XAML). (Part 1 of 5.)

```

            <!-- checked state -->
            <Trigger Property="RadioButton.IsChecked" Value="True">
               <Setter TargetName="backgroundEllipse" Property="Fill">
                  <Setter.Value>
                     <RadialGradientBrush> <!-- green "light" -->
                        <GradientStop Offset="0" Color="LimeGreen" />
                        <GradientStop Offset="1.25" Color="Black" />
                     </RadialGradientBrush>
                  </Setter.Value>
               </Setter>
            </Trigger>
         </ControlTemplate.Triggers>
      </ControlTemplate>
   </Window.Resources>

   <!-- define the GUI -->
   <Canvas>
      <!-- define the "TV" -->
      <Border Canvas.Left="150" Height="370" Width="490"
         Canvas.Top="20" Background="DimGray">
         <Grid>
            <Grid.RowDefinitions>
               <RowDefinition />
               <RowDefinition Height="Auto" />
            </Grid.RowDefinitions>

            <!-- define the screen -->
            <Border Margin="0,20,0,10" Background="Black"
               HorizontalAlignment="Center" VerticalAlignment="Center"
               BorderThickness="2" BorderBrush="Silver" CornerRadius="2">
               <MediaElement Height="300" Width="400"
                  Name="videoMediaElement" Source="Video/future_nasa.wmv"
                  LoadedBehavior="Manual" Stretch="Fill" />
            </Border>

            <!-- define the play, pause, and stop buttons -->
            <StackPanel Grid.Row="1" HorizontalAlignment="Right"
               Orientation="Horizontal">
               <RadioButton Name="playRadioButton" IsEnabled="False"
                  HorizontalAlignment="Right" Margin="0,0,5,15"
                  Template="{StaticResource RadioButtonTemplate}">
                  <Image Height="20" Width="20"
                     Source="Images/play.png" Stretch="Uniform" />
               </RadioButton>
               <RadioButton Name="pauseRadioButton" IsEnabled="False"
                  HorizontalAlignment="Right" Margin="0,0,5,15"
                  Template="{StaticResource RadioButtonTemplate}">
                  <Image Height="20" Width="20"
                     Source="Images/pause.png" Stretch="Uniform" />
               </RadioButton>
               <RadioButton Name="stopRadioButton" IsEnabled="False"
                  HorizontalAlignment="Right" Margin="0,0,15,15"
```

Fig. 16.11 | TV GUI showing the versatility of WPF customization (XAML). (Part 2 of 5.)

```
               Template="{StaticResource RadioButtonTemplate}">
               <Image Height="20" Width="20"
                  Source="Images/stop.png" Stretch="Uniform" />
            </RadioButton>
         </StackPanel>

         <!-- define the power button -->
         <CheckBox Name="powerCheckBox" Grid.Row="1" Width="25"
            Height="25" HorizontalAlignment="Left"
            Margin="15,0,0,15">
            <CheckBox.Template> <!-- set the template -->
               <ControlTemplate TargetType="CheckBox">
                  <Grid>
                     <!-- create a circular border -->
                     <Ellipse Width="25" Height="25"
                        Fill="Silver" />

                     <!-- create an "illuminated" background -->
                     <Ellipse Name="backgroundEllipse" Width="22"
                        Height="22">
                        <Ellipse.Fill> <!-- unchecked state -->
                           <RadialGradientBrush> <!-- dim "light" -->
                              <GradientStop Offset="0"
                                 Color="LightGray" />
                              <GradientStop Offset="1.25"
                                 Color="Black" />
                           </RadialGradientBrush>
                        </Ellipse.Fill>
                     </Ellipse>

                     <!-- display power-button image-->
                     <Image Source="Images/power.png" Width="20"
                        Height="20" />
                  </Grid>

                  <!-- change appearance when state changes -->
                  <ControlTemplate.Triggers>
                     <!-- checked state -->
                     <Trigger Property="CheckBox.IsChecked"
                        Value="True">
                        <Setter TargetName="backgroundEllipse"
                           Property="Fill">
                           <Setter.Value> <!-- green "light" -->
                              <RadialGradientBrush>
                                 <GradientStop Offset="0"
                                    Color="LimeGreen" />
                                 <GradientStop Offset="1.25"
                                    Color="Black" />
                              </RadialGradientBrush>
                           </Setter.Value>
                        </Setter>
                     </Trigger>
                  </ControlTemplate.Triggers>
```

Fig. 16.11 | TV GUI showing the versatility of WPF customization (XAML). (Part 3 of 5.)

```
                  </ControlTemplate>
               </CheckBox.Template>
            </CheckBox>
         </Grid>

         <!-- skew "TV" to give a 3-D appearance -->
         <Border.RenderTransform>
            <SkewTransform AngleY="15" />
         </Border.RenderTransform>

         <!-- apply bitmap effects to "TV" -->
         <Border.BitmapEffect>
            <BitmapEffectGroup>
               <!-- make "TV" panel look "raised" -->
               <BevelBitmapEffect BevelWidth="10" />
               <DropShadowBitmapEffect Color="Gray" ShadowDepth="15"
                  Softness="1" /> <!-- create a drop shadow -->
            </BitmapEffectGroup>
         </Border.BitmapEffect>
      </Border>

      <!-- define reflection -->
      <Border Canvas.Left="185" Canvas.Top="410" Height="300"
         Width="400">
         <Rectangle Name="reflectionRectangle">
            <Rectangle.Fill>
               <!-- create a reflection of the video -->
               <VisualBrush
                  Visual="{Binding ElementName=videoMediaElement}">
                  <VisualBrush.RelativeTransform>
                     <ScaleTransform ScaleY="-1" CenterY="0.5" />
                  </VisualBrush.RelativeTransform>
               </VisualBrush>
            </Rectangle.Fill>

            <!-- make reflection more transparent the further it gets
               from the screen -->
            <Rectangle.OpacityMask>
               <LinearGradientBrush StartPoint="0,0" EndPoint="0,1">
                  <GradientStop Color="Black" Offset="-0.25" />
                  <GradientStop Color="Transparent" Offset="0.5" />
               </LinearGradientBrush>
            </Rectangle.OpacityMask>
         </Rectangle>

         <!-- skew reflection to look 3-D -->
         <Border.RenderTransform>
            <SkewTransform AngleY="15" AngleX="-45" />
         </Border.RenderTransform>
      </Border>
   </Canvas>
</Window>
```

Fig. 16.11 | TV GUI showing the versatility of WPF customization (XAML). (Part 4 of 5.)

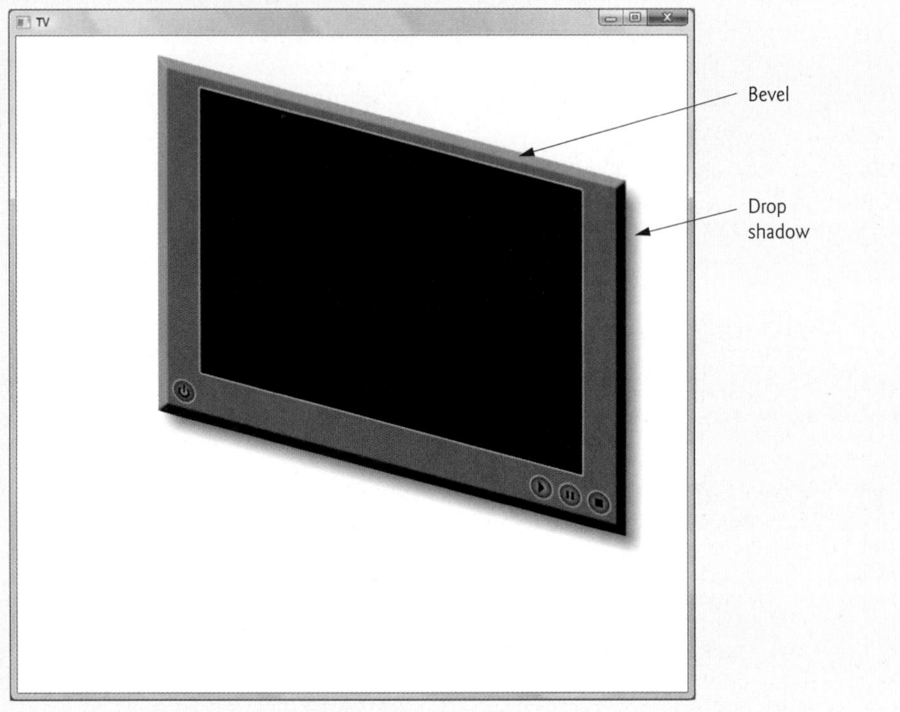

Fig. 16.11 | TV GUI showing the versatility of WPF customization (XAML). (Part 5 of 5.)

WPF Bitmap Effects

There are five bitmap effects that can be applied to any WPF graphic element. Figure 16.12 summarizes the effects of each. The TV GUI uses two of these effects—the `BevelBitmapEffect` and the `DropShadowBitmapEffect`. As shown in Fig. 16.11, the `BevelBitmapEffect` appears to raise an element's edges to give it a three-dimensional look. The `DropShadowBitmapEffect` gives an element a shadow as if a light were shining at it.

WPF bitmap effects	
`BevelBitmapEffect`	"Raises" the edges of an element.
`BlurBitmapEffect`	Blurs an element.
`DropShadowBitmapEffect`	Gives an element a shadow.
`EmbossBitmapEffect`	Uses changes in color to make an element appear raised out of the screen or lowered into the screen.
`OuterGlowBitmapEffect`	Surrounds an element with a small amount of color to make it look like it's glowing.

Fig. 16.12 | Summary of WPF bitmap effects.

You can apply a single bitmap effect to any element by setting its **`BitmapEffect`** property. To apply more than one effect, you must define the effects in a **`BitmapEffectGroup`**, then set it as the `BitmapEffect` property's value (lines 159–166). Each bitmap effect has its own set of unique properties. The **`BevelWidth`** property of a `BevelBitmapEffect` sets the size of its raised edge (line 162). A `DropShadowBitmapEffect`'s **`ShadowDepth`** property sets the distance from the element to the shadow (line 163). The `DropShadowBitmapEffect`'s **`Softness`** property defines how sharp the outline of the shadow is. This property takes values between 0 (sharp) and 1 (blurry), inclusive.

Performance Tip 16.1

Bitmap effects should be used sparingly in your applications. Bitmap effects are not hardware accelerated so they require a large amount of processing power and can degrade the machine's performance.

Creating Buttons on the TV

The representations of TV buttons in this example are not `Button` controls. The play, pause, and stop buttons are `RadioButtons`, and the power button is a `CheckBox`. Lines 9–55 and 106–148 define the `ControlTemplates` used to render the `RadioButtons` and `CheckBox`, respectively. The two templates are defined similarly, so we discuss only the `RadioButton` template in detail.

In the background of each button are two circles, defined by `Ellipse` objects. The larger `Ellipse` acts as a border (line 13). The smaller `Ellipse` is colored by a `RadialGradientBrush`. The gradient is a light color in the center and becomes black as it extends farther out. This makes it appear to be a source of light (lines 16–23). The content of the `RadioButton` is then applied on top of the two `Ellipses` (line 26).

The images used in this example are transparent outlines of the play, pause, and stop symbols on a black background. When the button os applied over the `RadialGradientBrush`, it appears to be illuminated. In its default state (enabled and unchecked), each playback button glows red. This represents the TV being on, with the playback option not active. When the application first loads, the TV is off, so the playback buttons are disabled. In this state, the background gradient is gray. When a playback option is active (i.e. `RadioButton` is checked), it glows green. The latter two deviations in appearance when the control changes states are defined by triggers (lines 30–54).

The power button, represented by a `CheckBox`, behaves similarly. When the TV is off (i.e. `CheckBox` is unchecked), the control is gray. When the user presses the power button and turns the TV on (i.e. `CheckBox` becomes checked), the control turns green. The power button is never disabled.

Creating the TV Interface

The TV panel is represented by a beveled `Border` with a gray background (lines 61–167). Recall that a `Border` is a `ContentControl` and can host only one direct child element. Thus, all of the `Border`'s elements are contained in a `Grid` layout container. Nested within the TV panel is another `Border` with a black background containing a `MediaElement` control (lines 70–76). This portrays the TV's screen. The power button is placed in the bottom-left corner, and the playback buttons are bound in a `StackPanel` in the bottom-right corner (lines 79–150).

Creating the Reflection of the TV Screen

Lines 170–197 define the GUI's video reflection using a `Rectangle` element nested in a `Border`. The `Rectangle`'s `Fill` is a `VisualBrush` that is bound to the `MediaElement` (lines 173–181). To invert the video, we define a `ScaleTransform` and specify it as the `RelativeTransform` property, which is common to all brushes (lines 177–179). You can invert an element by setting the `ScaleX` or `ScaleY`—the amounts by which to scale the respective coordinates—property of a `ScaleTransform` to a negative number. In this example, we set `ScaleY` to `-1` and `CenterY` to `0.5`, inverting the `VisualBrush` vertically centered around the midpoint. The `CenterX` and `CenterY` properties specify the point from which the image expands or contracts. When you scale an image, most of the points move as a result of the altered size. The center point is the only point that stays at its original location when `ScaleX` and `ScaleY` are set to values other than 1.

To achieve the semitransparent look, we applied an opacity mask to the `Rectangle` by setting the `OpacityMask` property (lines 185–190). The mask uses a `LinearGradientBrush` that changes from black near the top to transparent near the bottom. When the gradient is applied as an opacity mask, the gradient translates to a range from completely opaque, where it is black, to completely transparent. In this example, we set the `Offset` of the black `GradientStop` to `-0.25`, so that even the opaque edge of the mask is slightly transparent. We also set the `Offset` of the transparent `GradientStop` to `0.5`, indicating that only the top half of the `Rectangle` (or bottom half of the movie) should display.

Skewing the GUI Components to Create a 3-D Look

When you draw a three-dimensional object on a two-dimensional plane, you are creating a 2-D projection of that 3-D environment. For example, to represent a simple box, you draw three adjoining parallelograms. Each face of the box is actually a flat, skewed rectangle rather than a 2-D view of a 3-D object. You can apply the same concept to create simple 3-D-looking GUIs without using a 3-D engine.

In this case study, we applied a `SkewTransform` to the TV representation, skewing it vertically by 15 degrees clockwise from the *x*-axis (lines 154–156). The reflection is then skewed vertically by 15 degrees clockwise from the *x*-axis and horizontally by 45 degrees clockwise from the *y*-axis (lines 194–196). Thus the GUI becomes a 2-D orthographic projection of a 3-D space with the axes 105, 120, and 135 degrees from each other, as shown in Fig. 16.13. Unlike a perspective projection, an orthographic projection does not show depth. Thus, the TV GUI does not present a realistic 3-D view, but rather a graphical representation. In Section 16.9, we present a 3-D object in perspective.

Examining the Code-Behind Class

Figure 16.14 presents the code-behind class that provides the functionality for the TV application. When the user turns on the TV (i.e. checks the `powerCheckBox`), the reflection is made visible and the playback options are enabled (lines 6–16). When the user turns off the TV, the `MediaElement`'s `Close` method is called to close the media. In addition, the reflection is made invisible and the playback options are disabled (lines 19–34).

Whenever one of the `RadioButtons` that represent each playback option is checked, the `MediaElement` executes the corresponding task (lines 37–55). The methods that execute these tasks are built into the `MediaElement` control. Playback can be modified programmatically only if the `LoadedBehavior` is `Manual` (line 75 in Fig. 16.11).

Fig. 16.13 | The effect of skewing the TV application's GUI components.

```
' Fig. 16.14: TV.xaml.vb
' TV GUI showing the versatility of WPF customization (code-behind)
Class TV

   ' turns "on" the TV
   Private Sub powerCheckBox_Checked(ByVal sender As Object, _
      ByVal e As RoutedEventArgs) Handles powerCheckBox.Checked

      ' render the reflection visible
      reflectionRectangle.Visibility = Windows.Visibility.Visible

      ' enable play, pause, and stop buttons
      playRadioButton.IsEnabled = True
      pauseRadioButton.IsEnabled = True
      stopRadioButton.IsEnabled = True
   End Sub ' powerCheckBox_Checked

   ' turns "off" the TV
   Private Sub powerCheckBox_Unchecked(ByVal sender As Object, _
      ByVal e As RoutedEventArgs) Handles powerCheckBox.Unchecked

      videoMediaElement.Close() ' shut down the screen

      ' hide the reflection
      reflectionRectangle.Visibility = Windows.Visibility.Hidden

```

Fig. 16.14 | TV GUI showing the versatility of WPF customization (code-behind). (Part 1 of 2.)

```
         ' disable the play, pause, and stop buttons
         playRadioButton.IsChecked = False
         pauseRadioButton.IsChecked = False
         stopRadioButton.IsChecked = False
         playRadioButton.IsEnabled = False
         pauseRadioButton.IsEnabled = False
         stopRadioButton.IsEnabled = False
      End Sub ' powerCheckBox_Unchecked

      ' plays the video
      Private Sub playRadioButton_Checked(ByVal sender As Object, _
         ByVal e As RoutedEventArgs) Handles playRadioButton.Checked

         videoMediaElement.Play()
      End Sub ' playRadioButton_Checked

      ' pauses the video
      Private Sub pauseRadioButton_Checked(ByVal sender As Object, _
         ByVal e As RoutedEventArgs) Handles pauseRadioButton.Checked

         videoMediaElement.Pause()
      End Sub ' pauseRadioButton_Checked

      ' stops the video
      Private Sub stopRadioButton_Checked(ByVal sender As Object, _
         ByVal e As RoutedEventArgs) Handles stopRadioButton.Checked

         videoMediaElement.Stop()
      End Sub ' stopRadioButton_Checked
   End Class ' VideoViewer
```

Fig. 16.14 | TV GUI showing the versatility of WPF customization (code-behind). (Part 2 of 2.)

16.8 Animations

An animation in WPF applications simply means a transition of a property from one value to another in a specified amount of time. Most graphic properties of a control can be animated. The `UsingAnimations` example (Fig. 16.15) shows a video's size being animated. A `MediaElement` along with two input `TextBoxes`—one for `Width` and one for `Height`—and an animate `Button` are created in the GUI. When you click the animate `Button`, the video's `Width` and `Height` properties animate to the values typed in the corresponding `TextBoxes` by the user.

As you can see, the animations create a smooth transition from the original `Height` and `Width` to the new values. Lines 31–43 define a **`Storyboard`** element embedded in the `Button`'s click event `Trigger`. A `Storyboard` contains embedded animation elements. When the `Storyboard` begins executing (line 30), all embedded animations execute. A `Storyboard` has two important properties—**`TargetName`** and **`TargetProperty`**. The `TargetName` (line 31) specifies which control to animate. The `TargetProperty` specifies which property of the animated control to change. In this case, the `Height` (line 34) and `Width` (line 40) are the `TargetProperties`, because we're changing the size of the video. Both the `TargetName` and `TargetProperty` can be defined in the `Storyboard` or in the animation element itself.

To animate a property, you can use one of several animation classes available in WPF. We use the `DoubleAnimation` for the size properties—`PointAnimations` and `ColorAnimations` are two other commonly used animation classes. A **`DoubleAnimation`** animates properties of type `Double`. The `Width` and `Height` animations are defined in lines 33–36 and 39–42, respectively. Lines 35–36 define the **`To`** property of the `Width` animation, which specifies the value of the `Width` at the end of the animation. We use data binding to set this to the value in the `widthValue` `TextBox`. The animation also has a **`Duration`** property that specifies how long the animation takes. Notice in line 33 that we set the `Duration` of the `Width` animation to 0:0:2, meaning the animation takes 0 hours, 0 minutes and 2 seconds. You can specify fractions of a second by using a decimal point. Hour and minute values must be integers. Animations also have a **`From`** property which defines a constant starting value of the animated property.

```
1  <!-- Fig. 16.15: UsingAnimations.xaml -->
2  <!-- Animating graphic elements with Storyboards. -->
3  <Window x:Class="UsingAnimations"
4     xmlns="http://schemas.microsoft.com/winfx/2006/xaml/presentation"
5     xmlns:x="http://schemas.microsoft.com/winfx/2006/xaml"
6     Title="UsingAnimations" Height="400" Width="500">
7     <Grid>
8        <Grid.ColumnDefinitions>
9           <ColumnDefinition />
10          <ColumnDefinition Width="Auto" />
11       </Grid.ColumnDefinitions>
12
13       <MediaElement Name="video" Height="100" Width="100" Stretch="Fill"
14          Source="newfractal.wmv" /> <!-- Animated video -->
15
16       <StackPanel Grid.Column="1">
17          <!-- TextBox will contain the new Width for the video -->
18          <TextBlock Margin="5,0,0,0">Width:</TextBlock>
19          <TextBox Name="widthValue" Width="75" Margin="5">100</TextBox>
20
21          <!-- TextBox will contain the new Height for the video -->
22          <TextBlock Margin="5,0,0,0">Height:</TextBlock>
23          <TextBox Name="heightValue" Width="75" Margin="5">100</TextBox>
24
25          <!-- When clicked, rectangle animates to the input values -->
26          <Button Width="75" Margin="5">Animate
27             <Button.Triggers> <!-- Use trigger to call animation -->
28                <!-- When button is clicked -->
29                <EventTrigger RoutedEvent="Button.Click">
30                   <BeginStoryboard> <!-- Begin animation -->
31                      <Storyboard Storyboard.TargetName="video">
32                         <!-- Animates the Width -->
33                         <DoubleAnimation Duration="0:0:2"
34                            Storyboard.TargetProperty="Width"
35                            To="{Binding ElementName=widthValue,
36                            Path=Text}" />
37
```

Fig. 16.15 | Animating the width and height of a video. (Part 1 of 3.)

```
                        <!-- Animates the Height -->
                        <DoubleAnimation Duration="0:0:2"
                           Storyboard.TargetProperty="Height"
                           To="{Binding ElementName=heightValue,
                           Path=Text}" />
                     </Storyboard>
                  </BeginStoryboard>
               </EventTrigger>
            </Button.Triggers>
         </Button>
      </StackPanel>
   </Grid>
</Window>
```

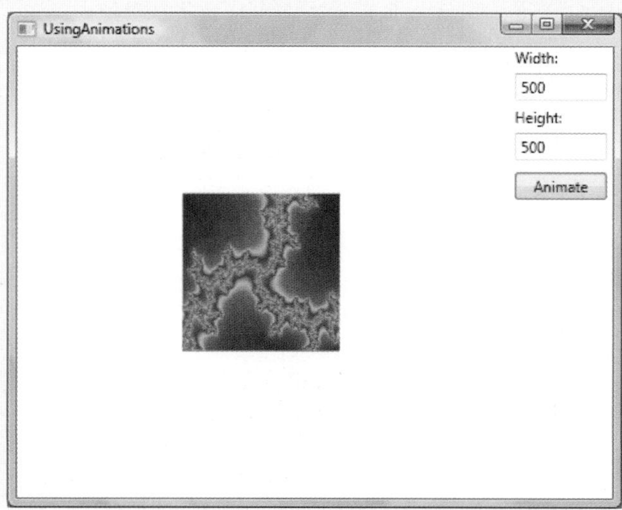

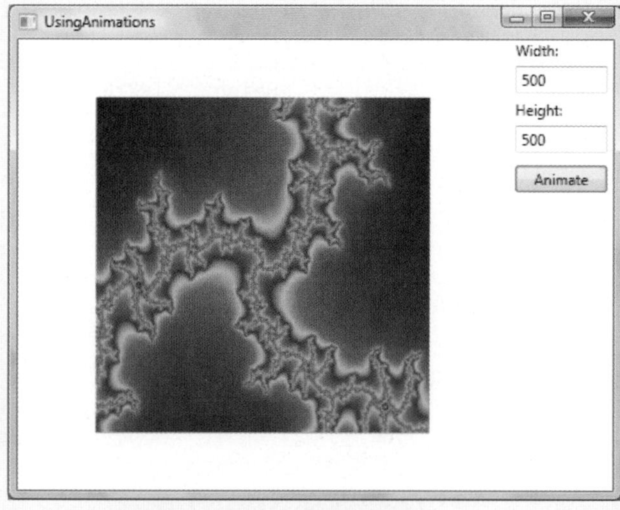

Fig. 16.15 | Animating the width and height of a video. (Part 2 of 3.)

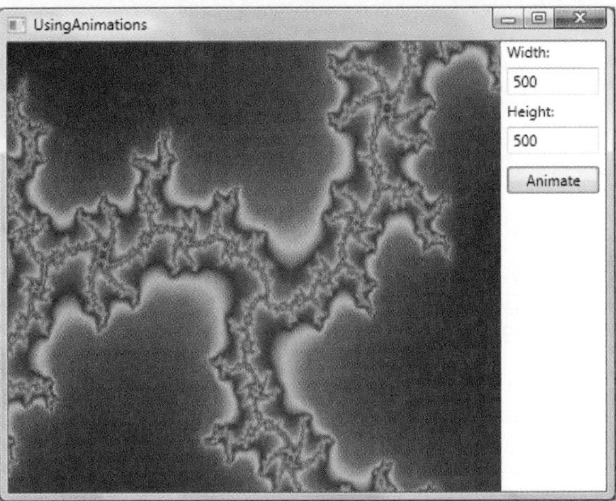

Fig. 16.15 | Animating the width and height of a video. (Part 3 of 3.)

Since we're animating the video's `Width` and `Height` properties separately, it is not always displayed at its original width and height. In line 13, we define the `MediaElement`'s `Stretch` property. This is a property for graphic elements and determines how the media stretches to fit the size of its enclosure. This property can be set to `None`, `Uniform`, `UniformToFill` or `Fill`. `None` allows the media to stay at its native size regardless of the container's size. `Uniform` resizes the media to its largest possible size while maintaining its native aspect ratio. A video's aspect ratio is the proportion between its width and height. Keeping this ratio at its original value ensures that the video does not look "stretched." `UniformToFill` resizes the media to completely fill the container while still keeping its aspect ratio—as a result, it could be cropped. When an image or video is cropped, the pieces of the edges are cut off from the media in order to fit the shape of the container. `Fill` forces the media to be resized to the size of the container (aspect ratio is not preserved). In the example, we use `Fill` to show the changing size of the container.

16.9 (Optional) 3-D Objects and Transforms

WPF has substantial three-dimensional graphics capabilities. Once a 3-D shape is created, it can be manipulated using 3-D transforms and animations. This section requires an understanding of 3-D analytical geometry. Readers without a strong background in these geometric concepts can still enjoy this section. We overview several advanced WPF 3-D capabilities.

The next example creates a rotating pyramid. The user can change the axis of rotation to see all sides of the object. The XAML code for this application is shown in Fig. 16.16.

```
<!-- Fig. 16.16: Application3D.xaml -->
<!-- Animating a 3-D object. -->
<Window x:Class="Application3D"
```

Fig. 16.16 | Animating a 3-D object. (Part 1 of 3.)

```
   xmlns="http://schemas.microsoft.com/winfx/2006/xaml/presentation"
   xmlns:x="http://schemas.microsoft.com/winfx/2006/xaml"
   Title="Application3D" Height="300" Width="300">
  <Grid>
     <Grid.RowDefinitions>
        <RowDefinition />
        <RowDefinition Height="Auto" />
     </Grid.RowDefinitions>

     <Grid.Triggers>
        <!-- when the window has loaded, begin the animation -->
        <EventTrigger RoutedEvent="Grid.Loaded">
           <BeginStoryboard>
              <Storyboard Storyboard.TargetName="rotation"
                 RepeatBehavior="Forever">

                 <!-- rotate the object 360 degrees -->
                 <DoubleAnimation Storyboard.TargetProperty="Angle"
                    To="360" Duration="0:0:3" />
              </Storyboard>
           </BeginStoryboard>
        </EventTrigger>
     </Grid.Triggers>

     <!-- viewport window for viewing the 3D object -->
     <Viewport3D>
        <Viewport3D.Camera>
           <!-- camera represents what user sees -->
           <PerspectiveCamera x:Name="camera" Position="6,0,1"
              LookDirection="-1,0,0" UpDirection="0,0,1" />
        </Viewport3D.Camera>

        <!-- defines the 3-D content in the viewport -->
        <ModelVisual3D>
           <ModelVisual3D.Content>
              <Model3DGroup>

                 <!-- two light sources to illuminate the objects-->
                 <DirectionalLight Color="White" Direction="-1,0,0" />
                 <DirectionalLight Color="White" Direction="0,0,-1" />

                 <GeometryModel3D>
                    <!-- rotate the geometry about the z-axis -->
                    <GeometryModel3D.Transform>
                       <RotateTransform3D>
                          <RotateTransform3D.Rotation>
                             <AxisAngleRotation3D x:Name="rotation"
                                Angle="0" Axis="0,0,1" />
                          </RotateTransform3D.Rotation>
                       </RotateTransform3D>
                    </GeometryModel3D.Transform>

```

Fig. 16.16 | Animating a 3-D object. (Part 2 of 3.)

```
56                         <!-- defines the pyramid -->
57                         <GeometryModel3D.Geometry>
58                            <MeshGeometry3D Positions="1,1,0 1,-1,0 -1,1,0
59                               -1,-1,0 0,0,2" TriangleIndices="0,4,1 2,4,0
60                               3,4,2 3,1,4 2,0,1 3,2,1"
61                               TextureCoordinates="0,0 1,0 0,1 1,1 0,0" />
62                         </GeometryModel3D.Geometry>
63
64                         <!-- defines the surface of the object -->
65                         <GeometryModel3D.Material>
66                            <DiffuseMaterial>
67                               <DiffuseMaterial.Brush>
68                                  <ImageBrush ImageSource="cover.png" />
69                               </DiffuseMaterial.Brush>
70                            </DiffuseMaterial>
71                         </GeometryModel3D.Material>
72                      </GeometryModel3D>
73                   </Model3DGroup>
74                </ModelVisual3D.Content>
75             </ModelVisual3D>
76          </Viewport3D>
77
78          <!-- RadioButtons to change the axis of rotation -->
79          <GroupBox Grid.Row="1" Header="Axis of rotation">
80             <StackPanel Orientation="Horizontal"
81                HorizontalAlignment="Center">
82                <RadioButton Name="xRadio" Margin="5">x-axis</RadioButton>
83                <RadioButton Name="yRadio" Margin="5">y-axis</RadioButton>
84                <RadioButton Name="zRadio" Margin="5">z-axis</RadioButton>
85             </StackPanel>
86          </GroupBox>
87       </Grid>
88    </Window>
```

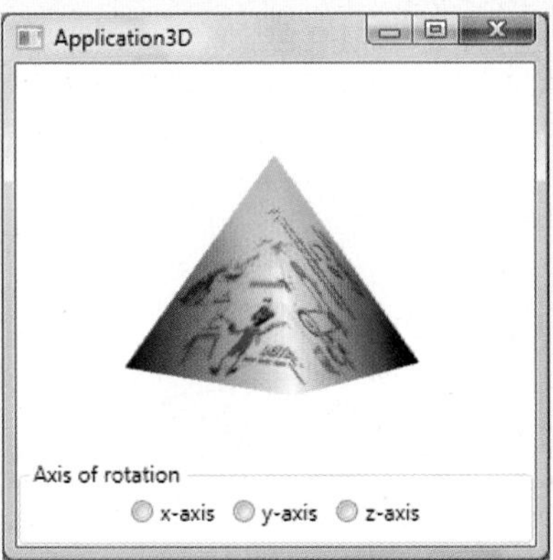

Fig. 16.16 | Animating a 3-D object. (Part 3 of 3.)

The first step in creating a 3-D object is to create a `Viewport3D` control (lines 29–76). The viewport represents the 2-D view the user sees when the application executes. This control defines a rendering surface for the content and contains content that represents the 3-D objects to render.

Create a `ModelVisual3D` object (lines 37–75) to define a 3-D object in a `Viewport3D` control. `ModelVisual3D`'s `Content` property contains the shapes you wish to define in your space. To add multiple objects to the `Content`, embed them in a `Model3DGroup` element.

Creating the 3-D Object

3-D objects in WPF are modeled as sets of triangles, because you need a minimum of three points to make a flat surface. Every surface must be created or approximated as a collection of triangles. For this reason, shapes with flat surfaces (like cubes) are relatively simple to create, while curved surfaces (like spheres) are extremely complex. To make more complicated 3-D elements, you can use 3-D application development tools such as Electric Rain's ZAM 3D (`erain.com/products/zam3d/DefaultPDC.asp`), which generates the XAML markup.

Use the `GeometryModel3D` element to define a shape (lines 45–72). This control creates and textures your 3-D model. First we discuss this control's `Geometry` property (lines 57–62). Use the `MeshGeometry3D` control (lines 58–61) to specify the exact shape of the object you want to create in the `Geometry` property. To create the object, you need two collections—one is a set of points to represent the vertices, and the other uses those vertices to specify the triangles that define the shape. These collections are assigned to the `Positions` and `TriangleIndices` properties of `MeshGeometry3D`, respectively. The points that we assigned to the `Positions` attribute (lines 58–59) are shown in a 3-D space in Fig. 16.17. The view in the figure does not directly correspond to the view of the pyramid shown in the application. In the application, if you change the camera's `Position` to `"5,5,5"`, `LookDirection` to `"-1,-1,-1"` and `UpDirection` to `"0,1,0"`, you'll see the pyramid in the same orientation as in Fig. 16.17.

The points are labeled in the order they are defined in the `Positions` collection. For instance, the text `0. (1,1,0)` in the diagram refers to the first defined point, which has an index of 0 in the collection. Points in 3-D are defined with the notation "(*x*-coordinate, *y*-coordinate, *z*-coordinate)." With these points, we can define the triangles that we use to model the 3-D shape. The `TriangleIndices` property specifies the three corners of each individual triangle in the collection. Note that the first element in the collection defined

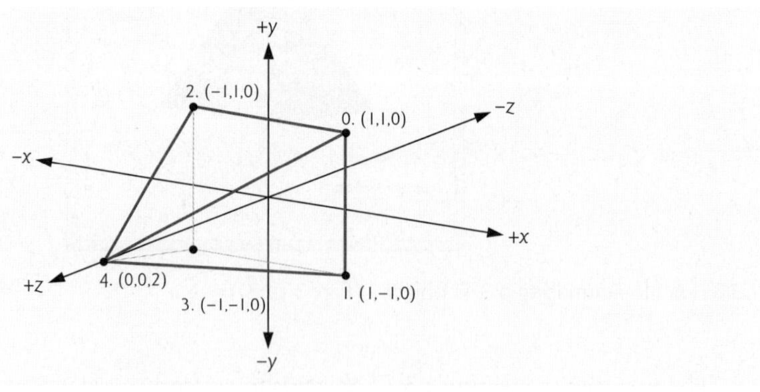

Fig. 16.17 | 3-D points making up a pyramid with a square base.

in line 59 is (0,4,1). This indicates that we want to create a triangle with corners at points 0, 4 and 1 defined in the Positions collection. You can see this triangle in Fig. 16.17 (the frontmost triangle in the picture). We can define all the sides of the pyramid by defining the rest of the triangles. Note also that while the pyramid has five flat surfaces, there are six triangles defined, because we need two triangles to create the pyramid's square base.

The order in which you define the corners of the triangle dictates which side of the triangle is considered the "front" versus the "back." Suppose you want to create a flat square in your viewport. This can be done using two triangles, as shown in Fig. 16.18. If you want the surface facing toward you to be the "front," you must define the corners in counterclockwise order. So, to define the lower-left triangle, you need to define the triangle as "0,1,3". The upper-right triangle needs to be "1,2,3". By default, the "front" of the triangle is drawn with your defined Material (described in the next section) while the "back" is made transparent. Therefore, the order in which you define the triangle's vertices is significant.

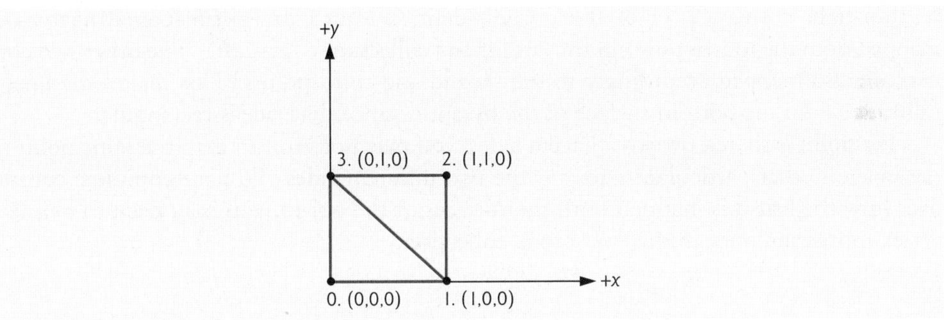

Fig. 16.18 | Defining two triangles to create a square in 3-D space.

Using a Brush on the Surface of a 3-D Object

By defining the Material property of the GeometryModel3D, we can specify what type of brush to use when painting each surface of the 3-D object. There are several different controls you can use to set the Material property. Each control gives a different "look" to the surface. Figure 16.19 describes the available controls.

3-D material controls	
DiffuseMaterial	Creates a "flat" surface that reflects light evenly in all directions.
SpecularMaterial	Creates a glossy-looking material. It creates a surface similar to that of metal or glass.
EmissiveMaterial	Creates a glowing surface that generates its own light (this light does not act as a light source for other objects).
MaterialGroup	Allows you to combine multiple materials, which are layered in the order they are added to the group.

Fig. 16.19 | 3-D material controls.

In the example, we use the DiffuseMaterial control. We can assign the brushes described in Section 16.5 to the material's Brush property to define how to paint the 3-D object's surface. We use an ImageBrush with cover.png as its source (line 68) to draw an image on the pyramid.

Notice in line 61 of Fig. 16.16 that we define the TextureCoordinates of the 3-D object. This property takes a PointCollection and determines how the Material is mapped onto the object's surfaces. If this property is not defined, the brush may not render correctly on the surface. The TextureCoordinates property defines which point on the image is mapped onto which vertex—an intersection of two or more edges—of the object. Notice we assigned the String "0,0 1,0 0,1 1,1 0,0" to the TextureCoordinates property. This String is translated into a PointCollection containing Points (0,0), (1,0), (0,1), (1,1) and (0,0). These points are logical points—as described in Section 16.5—on the image. The five points defined here correspond directly to the five points defined in the Positions collection. The image's top-left corner (0,0)—defined first in TextureCoordinates—is mapped onto the first point in the Positions collection (1,1,0). The bottom-right corner (1,1) of the image—defined fourth in TextureCoordinates—is mapped onto the fourth point in the Positions collection (-1,-1,0). The other two corners are also mapped accordingly to the second and third points. This makes the image fully appear on the bottom surface of the pyramid, since that face is rectangular.

If a point is shared by two adjacent sides, you may not want to map the same point of the image to that particular vertex for the two different sides. To have complete control over how the brush is mapped onto the surfaces of the object, you may need to define a vertex more than once in the Positions collection.

Defining a Camera and a Light Source

The Camera property of Viewport3D (lines 30–34) defines a virtual camera for viewing the defined 3-D space. In this example, we use a PerspectiveCamera to define what the user sees. We must set the camera's Position, LookDirection and UpDirection (lines 32–33). The Position property requires a Point3D object which defines a 3-D point, while the LookDirection and UpDirection require Vector3D objects which define vectors in 3-D space. 3-D vectors are defined by an *x*-, a *y*- and a *z*-component (defined in that order in the XAML markup). For instance, the vector applied to the UpDirection is written as "0,0,1" (line 33) and represents a vector with an *x*- and *y*-component of 0, and a *z*-component of 1. This vector points in the positive direction of the *z*-axis.

The Position defines the location of the camera in the 3-D space. The LookDirection defines the direction in which the camera is pointed. The UpDirection defines the orientation of the camera by specifying the upward direction in the viewport. Note that if the UpDirection in this example were set to "0,0,-1" then the pyramid would appear "upside-down" in the viewport.

Unlike 2-D objects, a 3-D object needs a virtual light source so the camera can actually "see" the 3-D scene. In the Model3DGroup, which groups all of the ModelVisual3D's objects, we define two DirectionalLight objects (lines 42–43) to illuminate the pyramid. This control creates uniform rays of light pointing in the direction specified by the Direction property. This property receives a vector that points in the direction of the light. You can also define the Color property to change the light's color.

Animating the 3-D Object

As with 2-D animations, there is a set of 3-D animations that can be applied to 3-D objects. Lines 47–54 define the `Transform` property of the `GeometryModel3D` element that models a pyramid. We use the `RotateTransform3D` control to implement a rotation of the pyramid. We then use the `AxisAngleRotation3D` to strictly define the transform's rotation (lines 50–51). The `Angle` and `Axis` properties can be modified to customize the transform. The `Angle` is initially set to 0 (i.e., not rotated) and the `Axis` of rotation to the *z*-axis, represented by the vector defined as `"0,0,1"` (line 51).

To animate the rotation, we created a `Storyboard` that modifies the `Angle` property of the `AxisAngleRotation3D` (lines 17–23). Notice we set the `RepeatBehavior` of the `Storyboard` to `Forever` (line 18), indicating that the animation repeats continuously while the window is open. This `Storyboard` is set to begin when the page loads (line 15).

The application contains `RadioButton`s at the bottom of the window that change the axis of rotation. The code-behind for this functionality appears in Fig. 16.20.

With each `RadioButton`'s `Checked` event, we change the `Axis` of rotation to the appropriate `Vector3D`. We also change the `Position` of the `PerspectiveCamera` to give a better view of the rotating object. For instance, when `xButton` is clicked, we change the axis of rotation to the *x*-axis (line 10) and the camera's position to give a better view (line 11).

```
1  ' Fig. 16.20: Application3D.xaml.vb
2  ' Changing the axis of rotation for a 3-D animation.
3  Imports System.Windows.Media.Media3D
4
5  Class Application3D
6     ' when user selects xRadio, set axis of rotation
7     Private Sub xRadio_Checked(ByVal sender As System.Object, _
8        ByVal e As System.Windows.RoutedEventArgs) Handles xRadio.Checked
9
10       rotation.Axis = New Vector3D(1, 0, 0) ' set rotation axis
11       camera.Position = New Point3D(6, 0, 0) ' set camera position
12    End Sub ' xRadio_Checked
13
14    ' when user selects yRadio, set axis of rotation
15    Private Sub yRadio_Checked(ByVal sender As System.Object, _
16       ByVal e As System.Windows.RoutedEventArgs) Handles yRadio.Checked
17
18       rotation.Axis = New Vector3D(0, 1, 0) ' set rotation axis
19       camera.Position = New Point3D(6, 0, 0) ' set camera position
20    End Sub ' yRadio_Checked
21
22    ' when user selects zRadio, set axis of rotation
23    Private Sub zRadio_Checked(ByVal sender As System.Object, _
24       ByVal e As System.Windows.RoutedEventArgs) Handles zRadio.Checked
25
26       rotation.Axis = New Vector3D(0, 0, 1) ' set rotation axis
27       camera.Position = New Point3D(6, 0, 1) ' set camera position
28    End Sub ' zRadio_Checked
29 End Class ' Application3D
```

Fig. 16.20 | Changing the axis of rotation for a 3-D animation.

16.10 Wrap-Up

In this chapter you learned how to manipulate graphic elements in your WPF application. We introduced how to control fonts using the properties of `TextBlocks`. You learned to change the `TextBlock`'s `FontFamily`, `FontSize`, `FontWeight` and `FontStyle` in XAML. We also demonstrated the `TextDecorations` `Underline`, `Overline`, `Baseline` and `Strikethrough`.

Next, you learned how to create basic shapes such as `Lines`, `Rectangles` and `Ellipses`. You set the `Fill` and `Stroke` of these shapes. We then discussed an application that created a `Polyline` and two `Polygons`. These controls allow you to create multisided objects using a set of `Points` in a `PointCollection`.

You learned that there are several types of brushes for customizing an object's `Fill`. We demonstrated the `SolidColorBrush`, the `ImageBrush`, the `VisualBrush` and the `LinearGradientBrush`. Though the `VisualBrush` was used only with a `MediaElement`, this brush has a wide range of capabilities.

We explained how to apply transforms to an object to reposition or reorient any graphic element. You used transforms such as the `TranslateTransform`, the `RotateTransform`, the `SkewTransform` and the `ScaleTransform` to manipulate various controls.

The television GUI application used `ControlTemplates` and `BitmapEffects` to create a completely customized 3-D-looking television set. You saw how to use `ControlTemplates` to customize the look of `RadioButtons` and `CheckBoxes`. The application also included an opacity mask, which can be used on any shape to define the opaque or transparent regions of the control. Opacity masks are particularly useful with images and video where you cannot change the `Fill` to directly control transparency.

We showed how animations can be applied to transition properties from one value to another. Common 2-D animation types include `DoubleAnimations`, `PointAnimations` and `ColorAnimations`.

Finally, you learned how to create a 3-D space using a `Viewport3D` control. You saw how to model 3-D objects as sets of triangles using the `MeshGeometry3D` control. The `ImageBrush`, which was previously applied to a 2-D object, was used to display a book-cover image on the surface of the 3-D pyramid using `GeometryModel3D`'s mapping techniques. We discussed how to include lighting and camera objects in your `Viewport3D` to modify the view shown in the application. We showed how similar transforms and animations are in 2-D and 3-D. In Chapter 17, we introduce `String` and character processing.

Summary

Section 16.1 Introduction

- WPF integrates drawing and animation features that were previously available only in special libraries (such as Microsoft Windows GDI+).
- WPF graphics use resolution-independent units of measurement.
- A machine-independent pixel measures 1/96 of an inch.
- WPF graphics use a vector-based system in which calculations determine how to size and scale each element.

Section 16.2 Controlling Fonts

- A `TextBlock` is a control that displays and modifies text.

- The FontFamily property of TextBlock defines the font of the displayed text.
- The FontSize property of TextBlock defines the text size measured in points.
- The FontWeight property of TextBlock defines the thickness of the text and can be assigned to either a numeric value or a predefined descriptive value.
- The FontStyle property of TextBlock can be used to make the text Italic or Oblique.
- You can also define the TextDecorations property of a TextBlock to give the text any of four TextDecorations: Underline, Baseline, Strikethrough and Overline.

Section 16.3 Basic Shapes

- Shape controls have Height and Width properties as well as Fill, Stroke and StrokeThickness properties to define the appearance of the shape.
- The Line, Rectangle and Ellipse are three basic shapes available in WPF.
- A Line is defined by its two endpoints.
- The Rectangle and the Ellipse are defined by Width and Height properties.
- If a Stroke or Fill of a shape is not specified, that property will be rendered transparently.

Section 16.4 Polygons and Polylines

- Polyline draws a series of connected lines defined by a set of points.
- Polygon draws a series of connected lines defined by a set of points and connects the first and last points to create a closed figure.
- The Polyline and Polygon shapes connect the points based on the ordering in the collection.
- The Visibility of a graphic control can be set to Visible, Collapsed or Hidden.
- The difference between Hidden and Collapsed is that a Hidden object occupies space in the GUI but is not visible, while a Collapsed object has a Width and Height of 0.
- A PointCollection is a collection that stores Point objects.
- PointCollection's Add method adds another point to the end of the collection.
- PointCollection's Clear method empties the collection.

Section 16.5 Brushes

- Brushes can be used to change the graphic properties of an element, such as the Fill, Stroke or Background.
- An ImageBrush paints an image into the property it is assigned to (such as a Background).
- A VisualBrush can display a fully customized graphic into the property it is assigned to.
- To use audio and video in a WPF application, you use the MediaElement control.
- LinearGradientBrush transitions linearly through the colors specified by GradientStops.
- RadialGradientBrush transitions through the specified colors radially outward from a specified point.
- Logical points are used to reference locations in the control independent of the actual size. The point (0,0) represents the top-left corner and the point (1,1) represents the bottom-right corner.
- A GradientStop defines a single color along the gradient.
- The Offset property of a GradientStop defines where the color appears along the transition.

Section 16.6 Transforms

- A TranslateTransform moves the object based on given *x*- and *y*-offset values.
- A RotateTransform rotates the object around a Point and by a specified RotationAngle.

- A `SkewTransform` skews (or shears) the object, meaning it rotates the *x*- or *y*-axis based on specified `AngleX` and `AngleY` values.
- A `ScaleTransform` scales the image's *x*- and *y*-coordinate points by different specified amounts.
- The `Random` class's `NextBytes` method assigns a random value in the range 0–255 to each element in its `Byte` array argument.
- The `RenderTransform` property of a GUI element contains embedded transforms that are applied to the control.

Section 16.7 WPF Customization: A Television GUI

- WPF bitmap effects can be used to apply simple visual effects to GUI elements. They can be applied by setting an element's `BitmapEffect` property
- A `BevelBitmapEffect` appears to raise an element's edges to give it a three-dimensional look. A `DropShadowBitmapEffect` gives an element a shadow as if a light were shining at it.
- To apply more than one effect to an element, define the effects as a `BitmapEffectGroup`.
- By setting the `ScaleX` or `ScaleY` property of a `ScaleTransform` to a negative number, you can invert an element horizontally or vertically, respectively.
- An opacity mask translates a partially transparent brush into a mapping of opacity values and applies it to an object. You can define an opacity mask by specifying a brush as the `OpacityMask` property.
- A `SkewTransform` creates an oblique distortion of an element.
- An orthographic projection depicts a 3-D space graphically, and does not account for depth. A perspective projection presents a realistic representation of a 3-D space.
- The `MediaElement` control has built-in playback methods. These methods can be called only if the `LoadedBehavior` property of the `MediaElement` is set to `Manual`.

Section 16.8 Animations

- A `Storyboard` contains embedded animation elements. When the `Storyboard` begins executing, all embedded animations execute.
- The `TargetProperty` of a `Storyboard` specifies which property of the control you want to change.
- A `DoubleAnimation` animates properties of type `Double`. `PointAnimations` and `ColorAnimations` are two other commonly used animation controls.
- The `Stretch` property of images and videos determines how the media stretches to fit the size of its enclosure. This property can be set to `None`, `Uniform`, `UniformToFill` or `Fill`.
- `None` value for the `Stretch` property allows the media to stay at its native size regardless of the container's size.
- `Uniform` value for the `Stretch` property resizes the media to its largest possible size while still being confined inside the container with its native aspect ratio.
- `UniformToFill` value for the `Stretch` property resizes the media to completely fill the container while still keeping its aspect ratio—as a result, it could be cropped.
- `Fill` value for the `Stretch` property forces the media to be resized to the size of the container (aspect ratio is not preserved).

Section 16.9 (Optional) 3-D Objects and Transforms

- WPF has substantial three-dimensional graphics capabilities which require an understanding of 3-D analytical geometry.
- The `Viewport3D` represents the 2-D view of the 3-D space the user sees.

- Create a ModelVisual3D object to define a 3-D object in a Viewport3D control.
- 3-D objects in WPF are modeled as sets of triangles.
- Use the GeometryModel3D element to define a shape.
- Use the MeshGeometry3D control to specify the exact shape of the object you want to create in the Geometry property of GeometryModel3D. The Positions and TriangleIndices properties of MeshGeometry3D are used to define the triangles modeling the shape.
- Corners of the triangles in the TriangleIndices property of MeshGeometry3D must be defined in counterclockwise order to be viewed.
- Specify a brush in a GeometryModel3D's Material property to paint the surface of the 3-D object.
- The TextureCoordinates property of MeshGeometry3D determines how a Material is mapped onto the 3-D object's surface. You may need to define a vertex more than once in the Positions collection to get proper mapping.
- The Camera property of Viewport3D defines a virtual camera for viewing the defined 3-D space.
- A 3-D object needs a virtual light source so the camera can actually "see" the 3-D scene.
- A DirectionalLight control creates uniform rays of light pointing in a specified direction.
- Use the AxisAngleRotation3D to strictly define the RotateTransform3D's rotation.
- The RepeatBehavior of a Storyboard or animation indicates whether it repeats when the animation is complete.

Terminology

Add method of class PointCollection
Angle property of AxisAngleRotation3D control
aspect ratio
Axis property of AxisAngleRotation3D control
AxisAngleRotation3D control
Background property of TextBlock control
BevelBitmapEffect control
BevelWidth property of BevelBitmapEffect control
bitmap effects
BitmapEffect property of a WPF UI element
BitmapEffectGroup control
BlurBitmapEffect control
Brush property of DiffuseMaterial control
Camera property of Viewport3D control
CenterX property of ScaleTransform control
CenterY property of ScaleTransform control
Clear method of class PointCollection
Collapsed state
Color property of DirectionalLight control
Color property of GradientStop control
ColorAnimation control
Content property of ModelVisual3D control
cropping
DiffuseMaterial control
Direction property of DirectionalLight control
DirectionalLight control
DoubleAnimation control
DropShadowBitmapEffect control
Duration property of DoubleAnimation control
Ellipse control
EmbossBitmapEffect control
EndPoint property of LinearGradientBrush control
Fill property of a shape control
Fill value for Stretch property of a multimedia element
FontFamily property of TextBlock control
FontSize property of TextBlock control
FontStyle property of TextBlock control
FontWeight property of TextBlock control
Foreground property of TextBlock control
From property of DoubleAnimation control
Geometry property of GeometryModel3D control
GeometryModel3D control
gradient
GradientStop control
Hidden state
ImageBrush control
ImageSource property of ImageBrush control
Line control
LinearGradientBrush control
Location property of TextDecoration control

logical point
LookDirection property of PerspectiveCamera control
machine-independent pixel
Material property of GeometryModel3D control
MediaElement control
MeshGeometry3D control
Model3DGroup control
ModelVisual3D control
NextBytes method of class Random
None value for Stretch property of a multimedia element
Offset property of GradientStop control
OpacityMask property of Rectangle control
orthographic projection
OuterGlowBitmapEffect control
perspective projection
PerspectiveCamera control
Point3D control
PointAnimation control
PointCollection class
Points property of Polyline control
Polygon control
Polyline control
Position property of PerspectiveCamera
Positions property of MeshGeometry3D control
RadialGradientBrush control
raster-based graphics
Rectangle control
RenderTransform property of a WPF UI element
RepeatBehavior property of Storyboard control
RepeatBehavior.Forever
RotateTransform control
RotateTransform3D control
Rotation property of RotateTransform3D
ScaleTransform control
ScaleX property of ScaleTransform control
ScaleY property of ScaleTransform control
ShadowDepth property of DropShadowBitmapEffect control
SkewTransform control
Softness property of a DropShadowBitmapEffect control
Source property of MediaElement control
StartPoint property of LinearGradientBrush control
Storyboard control
Stretch property of a multimedia element
Stroke property of a shape controls
StrokeThickness property of a shape controls
TargetName property of Storyboard control
TargetProperty property of Storyboard control
TextBlock control
TextDecoration control
TextDecorations property of TextBlock control
TextureCoordinates property of MeshGeometry3D control
To property of DoubleAnimation control
TranslateTransform control
TriangleIndices property of MeshGeometry3D control
Uniform value for Stretch property of a multimedia element
UniformToFill value for Stretch property of a multimedia element
UpDirection property of PerspectiveCamera control
vector-based graphics
Vector3D control
Viewport3D control
Visible state
Visibility property of a WPF UI element
Visual property of VisualBrush control
VisualBrush control

Self-Review Exercises

16.1 State whether each of the following is *true* or *false*. If *false*, explain why.

a) The unit of measurement for the FontSize property is machine independent.
b) A Line is defined by its length and its direction.
c) If an object's Fill is not defined, it uses the default White color.
d) A Polyline and Polygon are the same, except that the Polygon connects the first point in the PointCollection with the last point.
e) A Collapsed element is still created in the window, but it is transparent.
f) A MediaElement is used for audio or video playback.
g) A LinearGradientBrush always defines a gradient that transitions through colors from left to right.
h) A transform can be applied to a WPF UI element to reposition or reorient the graphic.

i) An element's `BitmapEffect` property takes a collection of bitmap effects as its value.
j) A `Storyboard` is the main control for implementing animations into the application.
k) A 3-D object can be manipulated much as a 2-D object would be manipulated.

16.2 Fill in the blanks in each of the following statements:
a) A(n) ________ control can be used to display text in the window.
b) A(n) ________ control can apply `Underlines`, `Overlines`, `Baselines` or `Strikethroughs` to a piece of text.
c) The ________ property of the `DoubleAnimation` defines the final value taken by the animated property.
d) The four types of transforms are ________, ________, `TranslateTransform` and `RotateTransform`.
e) The ________ property of a `GradientStop` defines where along the transition the corresponding color appears.
f) The ________ property of a `Storyboard` defines what property you want to animate.
g) A `Polygon` connects the set of points defined in a(n) ________ object.
h) The `Position` of a `PerspectiveCamera` is defined with a(n) ________ object while the `Direction` is defined with a(n) ________ object.
i) The three basic available shape controls are `Line`, ________ and ________.
j) A(n) ________ creates an opacity mapping from a brush and applies it to an element.
k) ________ points are used to define the `StartPoint` and `EndPoint` of a gradient to reference locations independently of the control's size.

Answers to Self-Review Exercises

16.1 a) True. b) False. A `Line` is defined by a start point and an end point. c) False—When no `Fill` is defined, the object is transparent. d) True. e) False. A `Collapsed` object has a `Width` and `Height` of 0. f) True. g) False. You can define start and end points for the gradient to change the direction of the transitions. h) True. i) False. It takes a single bitmap effect or a `BitmapEffectGroup`. j) True. k) True.

16.2 a) `TextBlock`. b) `TextDecoration`. c) `To`. d) `SkewTransform`, `ScaleTransform`. e) `Offset`. f) `TargetProperty`. g) `PointCollection`. h) `Point3D`, `Vector3D`. i) `Rectangle`, `Ellipse`. j) opacity mask. k) Logical.

Exercises

16.3 *(Enhanced `UsingGradients` application)* Modify the `UsingGradients` example in Section 16.5 to allow the user to switch between having a `RadialGradient` or a `LinearGradient` in the `Rectangle`. Users can still modify either gradient with the RGBA values as before. Place the `RadioButtons` at the bottom of the window. When the user switches between types of gradients, the colors should be kept consistent. In other words, if there is currently a `LinearGradient` on screen with a purple start color and a black stop color, the `RadialGradient` should have those start and stop colors as well when switched to. The GUI should appear as shown in Fig. 16.21.

16.4 *(Enhanced `DrawStars` application)* Modify the `DrawStars` example in Section 16.6 so that all the stars animate in a circular motion. Do this by animating the `Angle` property of the `Rotation` applied to each `Polygon`. The GUI should look as shown in Fig. 16.22, which is how it looked in the example in the chapter. Notice that the stars have changed positions between the two screen captures. [*Hint:* Controls have a `BeginAnimation` method which can be used to apply an animation without predefining it in a `Storyboard` element.]

16.5 *(Optional: Modified `Application3D` application)* Modify the `Application3D` example from Section 16.9 to create a 3-D die that can be animated along each axis. An image of all six faces of a

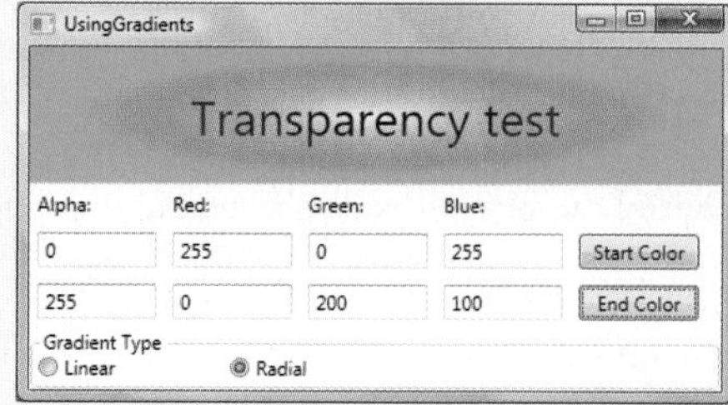

Fig. 16.21 | `UsingGradients` example after `RadioButton` enhancement.

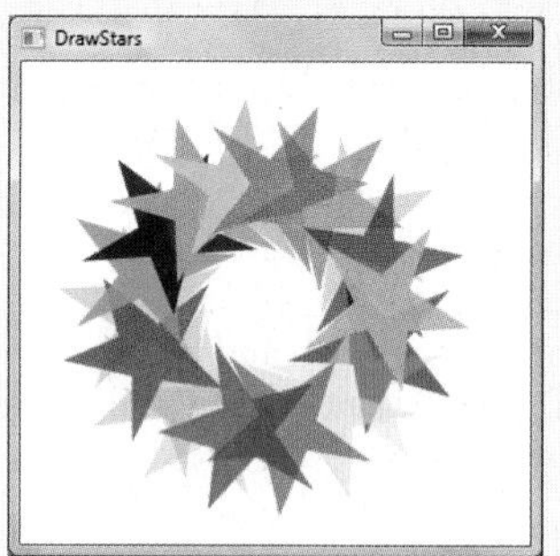

Fig. 16.22 | Animated `Polygons` rotating along the same circle.

die is in `C:\Chapter 16\Exercises\`. You have to map the correct part of the image onto the sides of a cube. The application should look like the screen capture in Fig. 16.23.

16.6 *(`Image` reflector application)* Create an application that has the same GUI as shown in Fig. 16.24(a). The cover images are included in your `C:\Chapter 16\Exercises\` folder. When the mouse hovers over any one of the covers, that cover and its reflection should animate to a larger size. Figure 16.24(b) shows one of the enlarged covers with a mouse over it.

16.7 *(Snake `PolyLine` application)* Create an application that creates a `Polyline` object that acts like a snake following your cursor around the window. The application, once the `Polyline` is created, should appear as shown in Fig. 16.25. You need to create an `Ellipse` for the head and a `Polyline` for the body of the snake. The head should always be at the location of the mouse cursor, while the `Polyline` continuously follows the head (make sure the length of the snake does not increase forever).

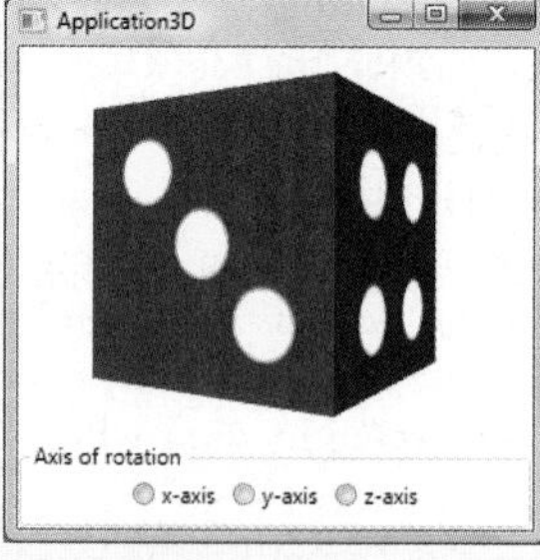

Fig. 16.23 | Creating a rotating 3-D die.

Fig. 16.24 | Cover images and their reflections. Each cover expands when the mouse hovers over it.

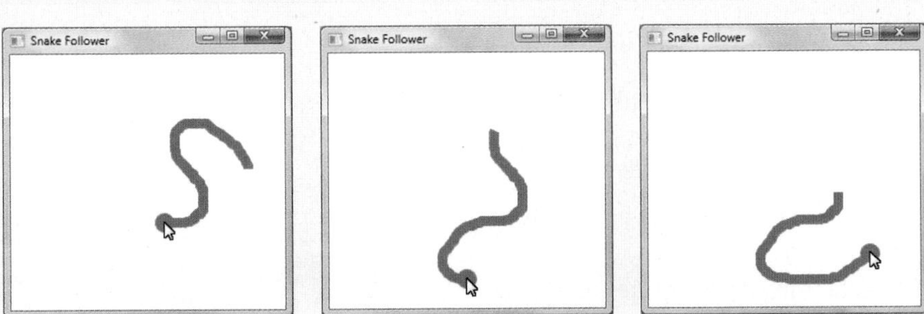

Fig. 16.25 | Snake follows the mouse cursor inside the window.

17

Strings, Characters and Regular Expressions

The chief defect of Henry King
Was chewing little bits of string.
—Hilaire Belloc

Vigorous writing is concise. A sentence should contain no unnecessary words, a paragraph no unnecessary sentences.
—William Strunk, Jr.

I have made this letter longer than usual, because I lack the time to make it short.
—Blaise Pascal

The difference between the almost-right word and the right word is really a large matter—it's the difference between the lightning bug and the lightning.
—Mark Twain

Mum's the word.
—Miguel de Cervantes

OBJECTIVES

In this chapter you'll learn:

- To create and manipulate immutable character String objects of class `String`.
- To create and manipulate mutable character String objects of class `StringBuilder`.
- To manipulate character objects of structure `Char`.
- What regular expressions are and when they are useful.
- To use regular expressions in conjunction with classes `Regex` and `Match`.
- To iterate through matches to a regular expression.
- To use character classes to match any character from a set of characters.
- To use quantifiers to match a pattern multiple times.
- To search for complex patterns in text using regular expressions.
- To validate data using regular expressions.
- To modify `String`s using regular expressions and class `Regex`.

Outline

17.1 Introduction

This chapter introduces the .NET Framework Class Library's string- and character-processing capabilities, and demonstrates how to use regular expressions to search for patterns in text. The techniques we present can be employed in text editors, word processors, page-layout software, computerized typesetting systems and other kinds of text-processing software. Previous chapters presented some basic string-processing capabilities. In this chapter, we discuss in detail the text-processing capabilities of class `String` and type `Char` from the `System` namespace and class `StringBuilder` from the `System.Text` namespace.

We begin with an overview of the fundamentals of characters and strings in which we discuss character literals and string literals. We then provide examples of class `String`'s many constructors and methods. The examples demonstrate how to determine the length of strings, copy strings, access individual characters in strings, search strings, obtain substrings from larger strings, compare strings, concatenate strings, replace characters in strings and convert strings to uppercase or lowercase letters.

Next we introduce class `StringBuilder`, which is used to build strings dynamically. We demonstrate `StringBuilder` capabilities for determining and specifying the size of a `StringBuilder` object, as well as appending, inserting, removing and replacing characters in a `StringBuilder` object. We then introduce the character-testing methods of the `Char` structure that enable a program to determine whether a character is a digit, a letter, a lowercase letter, an uppercase letter, a punctuation mark or a symbol other than a punctuation mark. Such methods are useful for validating individual characters in user input. In addition, type `Char` provides methods for converting a character to uppercase or lowercase.

The chapter concludes with a discussion of regular expressions. We discuss classes `Regex` and `Match` from the `System.Text.RegularExpressions` namespace as well as the symbols that are used to form regular expressions. We then demonstrate how to find patterns in a string, match entire strings to patterns, replace characters in a string that match a pattern and split strings at delimiters specified as a pattern.

17.2 Fundamentals of Characters and Strings

Characters are the fundamental building blocks of Visual Basic source code. Every program is composed of characters that, when grouped together meaningfully, create a sequence that the compiler interprets as instructions describing how to accomplish a task. In addition to normal characters, a program also can contain character literals, also called character constants. A character literal is a character that is represented internally as an integer value, called a *character code*. For example, the integer value `97` corresponds to the character literal `"a"c`, and the integer value `122` corresponds to the character literal `"z"c`. The letter `c` following the closing double quote is Visual Basic's syntax for a character literal. Character literals are established according to the Unicode character set, an international character set that contains many more symbols and letters than the ASCII character set (listed in Appendix F). To learn more about Unicode, see Appendix G.

A string is a series of characters treated as a single unit. These characters can be uppercase letters, lowercase letters, digits and various special characters: `+`, `-`, `*`, `/`, `$` and others. A string is an object of class `String` in the `System` namespace. We write string literals, also called string constants, as sequences of characters in double quotation marks, as follows:

```
"John Q. Doe"
"9999 Main Street"
"Waltham, Massachusetts"
"(201) 555-1212"
```

A declaration can assign a `String` literal to a `String` variable. The declaration

```
Dim color As String = "blue"
```

initializes `String` variable `color` to refer to the `String` literal object `"blue"`.

Performance Tip 17.1

If there are multiple occurrences of the same `String` literal in an application, a single copy of the `String` literal object will be referenced from each location in the program that uses that `String` literal. It is possible to share the object in this manner because `String` literal objects are implicitly constant. Such sharing conserves memory.

Common Programming Error 17.1

Assigning `Nothing` to a `String` variable can lead to logic errors if you attempt to compare `Nothing` to an empty `String` (`String.Empty` or `""`). The keyword `Nothing` is a null reference, not an empty `String` (which is a `String` that is of length 0 and contains no characters).

17.3 String Constructors

Figure 17.1 demonstrates three constructors of class `String`. Lines 6-7 allocate the `Char` array `characterArray`, which contains nine characters. Lines 10–14 declare and initialize the `String` variables `originalString`, `string1`, `string2`, `string3` and `string4`. Line 10 initializes `originalString` with the `String` literal `"Welcome to VB programming!"`. Line 11 initializes `string1` to refer to the same `String` literal as `originalString`.

Line 12 initializes `string2` with a new `String`, using the `String` constructor that takes a character array as an argument. The new `String` contains a copy of the characters in array `characterArray`.

Software Engineering Observation 17.1

In most cases, it is not necessary to make a copy of an existing `String`. All `String`s are immutable—their character contents cannot be changed after they are created. Also, if there are one or more references to a `String` (or any object, for that matter), the object cannot be reclaimed by the garbage collector. When a new value is assigned to a `String` variable, the variable simply refers to a different `String` object in memory.

Line 13 initializes `string3` with a new `String`, using the `String` constructor that takes a `Char` array and two `Integer` arguments. The second argument specifies the starting

```
1  ' Fig. 17.1: StringConstructor.vb
2  ' Demonstrating string class constructors.
3
4  Module StringConstructor
5     Sub Main()
6        Dim characterArray() As Char = _
7           {"b"c, "i"c, "r"c, "t"c, "h"c, " "c, "d"c, "a"c, "y"c}
8
9        ' string initialization
10       Dim originalString As String = "Welcome to VB programming!"
11       Dim string1 As String = originalString
12       Dim string2 As New String(characterArray)
13       Dim string3 As New String(characterArray, 6, 3)
14       Dim string4 As New String("C"c, 5)
15
16       Console.WriteLine("string1 = " & Chr(34) & string1 & Chr(34) & _
17          vbNewLine & "string2 = " & Chr(34) & string2 & Chr(34) & _
18          vbNewLine & "string3 = " & Chr(34) & string3 & Chr(34) & _
19          vbNewLine & "string4 = " & Chr(34) & string4 & Chr(34) & _
20          vbNewLine)
21    End Sub ' Main
22 End Module ' StringConstructor
```

```
string1 = "Welcome to VB programming!"
string2 = "birth day"
string3 = "day"
string4 = "CCCCC"
```

Fig. 17.1 | `String` constructors.

index position from which characters in the array are to be copied. The third argument specifies the number of characters (the count) to be copied from the specified starting position in the array. The new String contains a copy of the specified characters in the array. If the starting index or count causes the program to access an element outside the character array's bounds, an ArgumentOutOfRangeException is thrown.

Line 14 initializes string4 with a new String, using the String constructor that takes as arguments a character and an Integer specifying the number of times to repeat that character in the String. Lines 16–20 output the contents of variables string1, string2, string3 and string4. Note the use of the Visual Basic Chr function with the argument 34, which represents the double-quote (") character in the Unicode character set. This inserts the double-quote character in the String being output. Recall that the double-quote character is a delimiter for a String literal. To insert a double-quote character in a String literal, place two double-quote characters where you want the double-quote character to appear. For example, the statement

```
Console.WriteLine("The word ""four"" contains 4 characters")
```

outputs

```
The word "four" contains 4 characters
```

17.4 String Indexer, Length Property and CopyTo Method

Figure 17.2 uses the String indexer (a property that provides array-like access to the String's contents) to access individual characters in a String, and demonstrates String property Length, which returns the length of the String. The program also uses String method CopyTo to copy a specified number of characters from a String into a Char array. This application determines the length of a String, reverses the order of the characters in the String and copies a series of characters from the String to a character array.

```
' Fig. 17.2: StringMethods.vb
' Using the indexer, property Length and method CopyTo
' of class string.

Module StringMethods
   Sub Main()
      Dim string1 As String = "hello there"
      Dim characterArray() As Char = New Char(5) {}

      ' output string1
      Console.WriteLine("string1: " & Chr(34) & string1 & Chr(34))

      ' test Length property
      Console.WriteLine("Length of string1: " & string1.Length)

      ' loop through characters in string1 and display reversed
      Console.Write("The string reversed is: ")
```

Fig. 17.2 | String indexer, Length property and CopyTo method. (Part 1 of 2.)

```
18
19          For i = string1.Length - 1 To 0 Step -1
20             Console.Write(string1(i))
21          Next i
22
23          ' copy characters from string1 into characterArray
24          string1.CopyTo(0, characterArray, 0, 5)
25          Console.Write(vbNewLine & "The character array is: ")
26
27          For i = 0 To characterArray.Length - 1
28             Console.Write(characterArray(i))
29          Next i
30
31          Console.WriteLine(vbNewLine)
32       End Sub ' Main
33    End Module ' StringMethods
```

```
string1: "hello there"
Length of string1: 11
The string reversed is: ereht olleh
The character array is: hello
```

Fig. 17.2 | `String` indexer, `Length` property and `CopyTo` method. (Part 2 of 2.)

Line 14 uses `String` property `Length` to determine the number of characters in `string1`. Like arrays, `String`s always know their own size.

Lines 19–21 output the characters of `string1` in reverse order using the `String` indexer, which treats a `String` as an array of `Char`s and returns the character at a specific index in the `String`. The indexer receives an integer argument as the index and returns the character at that index. As with arrays, the first element of a `String` is considered to be at position 0.

Common Programming Error 17.2

Attempting to access a character that is outside the bounds of a `String` (i.e., an index less than 0 or an index greater than or equal to the `String`'s length) results in an `IndexOutOfRangeException`.

Line 24 uses `String` method `CopyTo` to copy the characters of a `String` (`string1`) into a character array (`characterArray`). `CopyTo`'s first argument is the index from which the method begins copying characters in the `String`. The second argument is the character array into which the characters are copied. The third argument is the index specifying the starting location at which the method begins placing the copied characters into the character array. The last argument is the number of characters that the method will copy from the `String`. Lines 27–29 output the `Char` array contents one character at a time.

17.5 Comparing Strings

The next two examples demonstrate the various methods for comparing `String`s. To understand how one `String` can be "greater than" or "less than" another `String`, consider the process of alphabetizing a series of last names. The reader would, no doubt, place

"Jones" before "Smith", because the first letter of "Jones" comes before the first letter of "Smith" in the alphabet. The alphabet is more than just a set of 26 letters—it is an ordered list of characters in which each letter occurs in a specific position. For example, Z is more than just a letter of the alphabet; Z is specifically the 26th letter of the alphabet.

Computers can order characters alphabetically because the characters are represented internally as Unicode numeric codes. When comparing two Strings, the string comparison methods simply compare the numeric codes of the characters in the Strings.

Comparing Strings with = and **String** *Methods* **Equals** *and* **CompareTo**

Class String provides several ways to compare Strings. Figure 17.3 demonstrates method Equals, method CompareTo and the equality operator (=).

```
' Fig. 17.3: StringCompare.vb
' Comparing strings

Module StringCompare
   Sub Main()
      Dim string1 As String = "hello"
      Dim string2 As String = "good bye"
      Dim string3 As String = "Happy Birthday"
      Dim string4 As String = "happy birthday"

      ' output values of four strings
      Console.WriteLine("string1 = " & Chr(34) & string1 & Chr(34) & _
         vbNewLine & "string2 = " & Chr(34) & string2 & Chr(34) & _
         vbNewLine & "string3 = " & Chr(34) & string3 & Chr(34) & _
         vbNewLine & "string4 = " & Chr(34) & string4 & Chr(34) & _
         vbNewLine)

      ' test for equality using Equals method
      If string1.Equals("hello") Then
         Console.WriteLine("string1 equals " & Chr(34) & "hello" & _
            Chr(34))
      Else
         Console.WriteLine("string1 does not equal " & Chr(34) & _
            "hello" & Chr(34))
      End If

      ' test for equality with =
      If string1 = "hello" Then
         Console.WriteLine("string1 equals " & Chr(34) & "hello" & _
            Chr(34))
      Else
         Console.WriteLine("string1 does not equal " & Chr(34) & _
            "hello" & Chr(34))
      End If

      ' test for equality comparing case
      If String.Equals(string3, string4) Then ' Shared method
         Console.WriteLine("string3 equals string4")
```

Fig. 17.3 | String test to determine equality. (Part 1 of 2.)

```
39         Else
40            Console.WriteLine("string3 does not equal string4")
41         End If
42
43         ' test CompareTo
44         Console.WriteLine(vbNewLine & _
45            "string1.CompareTo( string2 ) is " & _
46            string1.CompareTo(string2) & vbNewLine & _
47            "string2.CompareTo( string1 ) is " & _
48            string2.CompareTo(string1) & vbNewLine & _
49            "string1.CompareTo( string1 ) is " & _
50            string1.CompareTo(string1) & vbNewLine & _
51            "string3.CompareTo( string4 ) is " & _
52            string3.CompareTo(string4) & vbNewLine & _
53            "string4.CompareTo( string3 ) is " & _
54            string4.CompareTo(string3) & vbNewLine)
55      End Sub ' Main
56   End Module ' StringCompare
```

```
string1 = "hello"
string2 = "good bye"
string3 = "Happy Birthday"
string4 = "happy birthday"

string1 equals "hello"
string1 equals "hello"
string3 does not equal string4

string1.CompareTo( string2 ) is 1
string2.CompareTo( string1 ) is -1
string1.CompareTo( string1 ) is 0
string3.CompareTo( string4 ) is 1
string4.CompareTo( string3 ) is -1
```

Fig. 17.3 | `String` test to determine equality. (Part 2 of 2.)

The condition in the `If` statement (line 19) uses `String` method `Equals` to compare `string1` and the `String` literal `"hello"` to determine whether they are equal. Method `Equals` (inherited by `String` from class `Object`) tests any two objects for equality (i.e., whether the objects have the same contents). The method returns `True` if the objects are equal and `False` otherwise. In this instance, the preceding condition returns `True` because `string1` references the `String` literal object `"hello"`. Method `Equals` uses a lexicographical comparison—the integer Unicode values that represent each character in each `String` are compared. Comparing `"hello"` with `"HELLO"` would return `False`, because the numeric representations of lowercase letters are different from those of corresponding uppercase letters.

The condition in the second `If` statement (line 28) uses the equality operator (=) to compare `string1` with the `String` literal `"hello"` for equality. In Visual Basic, the equality operator also uses a lexicographical comparison to compare two `Strings`. Thus, the condition in the `If` statement evaluates to `True` because the values of `string1` and `"hello"` are equal.

Line 37 compares `string3` and `string4` for equality to illustrate that comparisons are indeed case sensitive. `Shared` method `Equals` is used to compare the values of two `Strings`. `"Happy Birthday"` does not equal `"happy birthday"`, so the condition of the `If` statement fails, and the message `"string3 does not equal string4"` is output (line 40).

Lines 44–54 use `String` method `CompareTo` to compare `Strings`. Method `CompareTo` returns `0` if the `Strings` are equal, `-1` if the `String` that invokes `CompareTo` is less than the `String` passed as an argument and `1` if the `String` that invokes `CompareTo` is greater than the `String` passed as an argument. Method `CompareTo` uses a lexicographical comparison.

Note that `CompareTo` considers `string3` to be larger than `string4`. The only difference between these two `Strings` is that `string3` contains two uppercase letters in positions where `string4` contains lowercase letters. `string3` is greater than `string4` because the integer Unicode values representing uppercase letters are greater than the values representing lowercase letters.

Using `String` *Methods* `StartsWith` *and* `EndsWith`

The application in Fig. 17.4 shows how to test whether a `String` begins or ends with a given `String`. Method `StartsWith` determines whether a `String` starts with the `String` passed to it as an argument. Method `EndsWith` determines whether a `String` ends with the `String` passed to it as an argument. Module `StringStartEnd`'s `Main` method defines an

```
' Fig. 17.4: StringStartEnd.vb
' Demonstrating StartsWith and EndsWith methods.

Module StringStartEnd
   Sub Main()
      Dim strings As String() = _
         {"started", "starting", "ended", "ending"}

      ' test every string to see if it starts with "st"
      For Each element In strings
         If element.StartsWith("st") Then
            Console.WriteLine(Chr(34) & element & Chr(34) & _
               " starts with " & Chr(34) & "st" & Chr(34))
         End If
      Next

      Console.WriteLine()

      ' test every string to see if it ends with "ed"
      For Each element In strings
         If element.EndsWith("ed") Then
            Console.WriteLine(Chr(34) & element & Chr(34) & _
               " ends with " & Chr(34) & "ed" & Chr(34))
         End If
      Next

      Console.WriteLine()
   End Sub ' Main
End Module ' StringStartEnd
```

Fig. 17.4 | `StartsWith` and `EndsWith` methods. (Part 1 of 2.)

```
"started" starts with "st"
"starting" starts with "st"

"started" ends with "ed"
"ended" ends with "ed"
```

Fig. 17.4 | StartsWith and EndsWith methods. (Part 2 of 2.)

array of Strings (called strings), which contains "started", "starting", "ended" and "ending". The remainder of method Main tests the elements of the array to determine whether they start or end with a particular set of characters.

Line 11 uses method StartsWith, which takes a String argument. The condition in the If statement determines whether the String starts with the characters "st". If so, the method returns True, and lines 12–13 output a message.

Line 21 uses method EndsWith, which also takes a String argument. The condition in the If statement determines whether the String ends with the characters "ed". If so, the method returns True, and lines 22–23 output a message.

17.6 Locating Characters and Substrings in Strings

Many applications search for a character or set of characters in a String. For example, a programmer creating a word processor would want to provide capabilities for searching documents. Figure 17.5 demonstrates some versions of String methods IndexOf, IndexOfAny, LastIndexOf and LastIndexOfAny, which search for a specified character or substring in a String.

```
' Fig. 17.5: StringIndexMethods.vb
' Using string searching methods.

Module StringIndexMethods
   Sub Main()
      Dim letters As String = "abcdefghijklmabcdefghijklm"
      Dim searchLetters As Char() = {"c"c, "a"c, "$"c}

      ' test IndexOf to find a character in a string
      Console.WriteLine("First 'c' is located at index " & _
         letters.IndexOf("c"c))
      Console.WriteLine("First 'a' starting at 1 is located at index " _
         & letters.IndexOf("a"c, 1))
      Console.WriteLine("First '$' in the 5 positions starting at 3 " & _
         "is located at index " & letters.IndexOf("$"c, 3, 5))

      ' test LastIndexOf to find a character in a string
      Console.WriteLine(vbNewLine & "Last 'c' is located at index " & _
         letters.LastIndexOf("c"c))
      Console.WriteLine("Last 'a' up to position 25 is located at " & _
         "index " & letters.LastIndexOf("a"c, 25))
      Console.WriteLine("Last '$' in the 5 positions starting at 15 " & _
         "is located at index " & letters.LastIndexOf("$"c, 15, 5))
```

Fig. 17.5 | Searching for characters and substrings in Strings. (Part 1 of 3.)

```

        ' test IndexOf to find a substring in a string
        Console.WriteLine(vbNewLine & "First " & Chr(34)& "def" & _
           Chr(34) & " is located at index " & letters.IndexOf("def"))
        Console.WriteLine("First " & Chr(34) & "def" & Chr(34) & _
           " starting at 7 is located at " & "index " & _
           letters.IndexOf("def", 7))
        Console.WriteLine("First " & Chr(34) & "hello" & Chr(34) & _
           " in the 15 positions starting at 5 is located at index " & _
           letters.IndexOf("hello", 5, 15))

        ' test LastIndexOf to find a substring in a string
        Console.WriteLine(vbNewLine & "Last " & Chr(34) & "def" & _
           Chr(34) & " is located at index " & letters.LastIndexOf("def"))
        Console.WriteLine("Last " & Chr(34) & "def" & Chr(34) & _
           " up to position 25 is located at index " & _
           letters.LastIndexOf("def", 25))
        Console.WriteLine("Last " & Chr(34) & "hello" & Chr(34) & _
           " in the 15 positions ending at 20 is located at index " & _
           letters.LastIndexOf("hello", 20, 15))

        ' test IndexOfAny to find first occurrence of character in array
        Console.WriteLine(vbNewLine & "First 'c', 'a' or '$' is " & _
           "located at index " & letters.IndexOfAny(searchLetters))
        Console.WriteLine("First 'c', 'a' or '$' starting at 7 is " & _
           "located at index " & letters.IndexOfAny(searchLetters, 7))
        Console.WriteLine("First 'c', 'a' or '$' in the 5 positions " & _
           "starting at 7 is located at index " & _
           letters.IndexOfAny(searchLetters, 7, 5))

        ' test LastIndexOfAny to find last occurrence of character
        ' in array
        Console.WriteLine(vbNewLine & "Last 'c', 'a' or '$' is " & _
           "located at index " & letters.LastIndexOfAny(searchLetters))
        Console.WriteLine("Last 'c', 'a' or '$' up to position 1 is " & _
           "located at index " & letters.LastIndexOfAny(searchLetters, 1))
        Console.WriteLine("Last 'c', 'a' or '$' in the 5 positions " & _
           "ending at 25 is located at index " & _
           letters.LastIndexOfAny(searchLetters, 25, 5))
     End Sub ' Main
  End Module ' StringIndexMethods
```

```
First 'c' is located at index 2
First 'a' starting at 1 is located at index 13
First '$' in the 5 positions starting at 3 is located at index -1

Last 'c' is located at index 15
Last 'a' up to position 25 is located at index 13
Last '$' in the 5 positions starting at 15 is located at index -1

First "def" is located at index 3
First "def" starting at 7 is located at index 16
First "hello" in the 15 positions starting at 5 is located at index -1
```

Fig. 17.5 | Searching for characters and substrings in `Strings`. (Part 2 of 3.)

```
Last "def" is located at index 16
Last "def" up to position 25 is located at index 16
Last "hello" in the 15 positions ending at 20 is located at index -1

First 'c', 'a' or '$' is located at index 0
First 'c', 'a' or '$' starting at 7 is located at index 13
First 'c', 'a' or '$' in the 5 positions starting at 7 is located at index -1

Last 'c', 'a' or '$' is located at index 15
Last 'c', 'a' or '$' up to position 1 is located at index 0
Last 'c', 'a' or '$' in the 5 positions ending at 25 is located at index -1
```

Fig. 17.5 | Searching for characters and substrings in `Strings`. (Part 3 of 3.)

This example searches the `String letters` which is initialized with `"abcdefghijklmabcdefghijklm"` (line 6). Lines 11, 13 and 15 use method `IndexOf` to locate the first occurrence of a character in a `String`. If it finds a character, `IndexOf` returns the index of the specified character in the `String`; otherwise, `IndexOf` returns `-1`. Line 13 uses a version of method `IndexOf` that takes two arguments—the character to search for and the starting index in the `String` at which the search should begin. The method does not examine any characters before the starting index (in this case, `1`). Line 15 uses another version of method `IndexOf` that takes three arguments—the character to search for, the index at which to start searching and the number of characters to search.

Lines 19, 21 and 23 use method `LastIndexOf` to find the last occurrence of a character in a `String`. `LastIndexOf` searches from the end of the `String` toward the beginning. If `LastIndexOf` finds the character, it returns the index of the character in the `String`; otherwise, it returns `-1`. There are three versions of `LastIndexOf`. Line 19 uses the version of method `LastIndexOf` that takes as an argument the character for which to search. Line 21 uses the version of method `LastIndexOf` that takes two arguments—the character for which to search and the highest index from which to begin searching backward for the character. The expression in line 23 uses a third version of method `LastIndexOf` that takes three arguments—the character for which to search, the starting index from which to start searching backward and the number of characters (the portion of the `String`) to search.

Lines 26–43 use versions of `IndexOf` and `LastIndexOf` that take a `String` instead of a character as the first argument. These versions of the methods perform identically to the ones described above except that they search for sequences of characters (or substrings) that are specified by their `String` arguments.

Lines 46–62 use methods `IndexOfAny` and `LastIndexOfAny`, which take an array of characters as the first argument. These versions of the methods also perform identically to those described above except that they return the index of the first occurrence of any of the characters in the character-array argument. Class `String` also provides method `Contains`, which takes a `String` as an argument and returns a `Boolean` indicating whether the `String` argument was found in the `String`.

Common Programming Error 17.3

In the overloaded methods `LastIndexOf` and `LastIndexOfAny` that take three parameters, the second argument must be greater than or equal to the third argument; otherwise, an `ArgumentOutOfRangeException` occurs. This might seem counterintuitive, but remember that the search moves from the end of the string toward the beginning.

17.7 Extracting Substrings from Strings

Class `String` provides two `Substring` methods, which are used to create a new `String` by copying part of an existing `String`. Each method returns a new `String`. Figure 17.6 demonstrates both methods.

Line 11 uses the `Substring` method that takes one `Integer` argument. The argument specifies the starting index, from which the method copies characters in the original `String`. The substring returned contains a copy of the characters from the starting index to the end of the `String`. If the index specified in the argument is outside the bounds of the `String`, an `ArgumentOutOfRangeException` occurs.

The second version of method `Substring` (line 15) takes two `Integer` arguments. The arguments specify the starting index from which to copy characters and the length of the substring to copy. The substring returned contains a copy of the specified characters from the original `String`. If the starting index plus the length is greater than the number of characters in the `String`, an `ArgumentOutOfRangeException` occurs.

```
1  ' Fig. 17.6: Substring.vb
2  ' Demonstrating the String Substring method.
3
4  Module Substring
5     Sub Main()
6        Dim letters As String = "abcdefghijklmabcdefghijklm"
7        Dim output As String = String.Empty
8
9        ' invoke Substring method and pass it one parameter
10       Console.WriteLine("Substring from index 20 to end is " & _
11          Chr(34) & letters.Substring(20) & Chr(34))
12
13       ' invoke Substring method and pass it two parameters
14       Console.WriteLine("Substring from index 0 of length 6 is " & _
15          Chr(34) & letters.Substring(0, 6) & Chr(34))
16    End Sub ' Main
17 End Module ' SubString
```

```
Substring from index 20 to end is "hijklm"
Substring from index 0 of length 6 is "abcdef"
```

Fig. 17.6 | Substrings generated from `Strings`.

17.8 Concatenating Strings

Like the `&` operator, the `String` class's `Shared` method `Concat` (Fig. 17.7) can be used to concatenate two `Strings`. The method returns a new `String` containing the combined characters from both original `Strings`. Line 13 appends the characters from `string2` to the end of a copy of `string1`, using method `Concat`. The original `Strings` are not modified. Overloaded versions of the `Concat` method allow you to concatenate any number of `Strings` by passing an array of `Strings` as the argument—each `String` in the array is merged into one `String`. You can also use method `Concat` to concatenate the `String` representation of any number of `Objects`. A complete list of overloads can be found at `msdn.microsoft.com/en-us/library/system.string.concat.aspx`.

```
' Fig. 17.7: StringConcatenation.vb
' Demonstrating string class Concat method.

Module StringConcatenation
   Sub Main()
      Dim string1 As String = "Happy "
      Dim string2 As String = "Birthday"

      Console.WriteLine("string1 = " & Chr(34) & string1 & Chr(34) & _
         vbNewLine & "string2 = " & Chr(34) & string2 & Chr(34))
      Console.WriteLine(vbNewLine & _
         "Result of String.Concat( string1, string2 ) = " & _
         String.Concat(string1, string2))
      Console.WriteLine("string1 after concatenation = " & string1)
   End Sub ' Main
End Module ' StringConcatenation
```

```
string1 = "Happy "
string2 = "Birthday"

Result of String.Concat( string1, string2 ) = Happy Birthday
string1 after concatenation = Happy
```

Fig. 17.7 | Concat Shared method.

17.9 Miscellaneous String Methods

Class String provides several methods that return modified copies of Strings. Figure 17.8 demonstrates String methods Replace, ToLower, ToUpper and Trim. None of these methods modifies the original String.

Line 18 uses String method Replace to return a new String, replacing every occurrence in string1 of character 'e' with character 'E'. Method Replace takes two arguments—a Char for which to search and another Char with which to replace all matching occurrences of the first argument. This method is also overloaded to receive two String parameters. If there are no occurrences of the first argument in the String, the method returns the original String.

```
1  ' Fig. 17.8: StringMethods2.vb
2  ' Demonstrating String methods Replace, ToLower, ToUpper, Trim,
3  ' and ToString.
4
5  Module StringMethods2
6     Sub Main()
7        Dim string1 As String = "cheers!"
8        Dim string2 As String = "GOOD BYE "
9        Dim string3 As String = "   spaces   "
10
11       Console.WriteLine("string1 = " & Chr(34) & string1 & Chr(34) & _
12          vbNewLine & "string2 = " & Chr(34) & string2 & Chr(34) & _
13          vbNewLine & "string3 = " & Chr(34) & string3 & Chr(34))
14
```

Fig. 17.8 | String methods Replace, ToLower, ToUpper and Trim. (Part 1 of 2.)

```
15         ' call method Replace
16         Console.WriteLine(vbNewLine & "Replacing " & Chr(34) & "e" & _
17            Chr(34) & " with " & Chr(34) & "E" & Chr(34) & _
18            " in string1: " & Chr(34) & string1.Replace("e"c, "E"c) & _
19            Chr(34))
20
21         ' call ToLower and ToUpper
22         Console.WriteLine(vbNewLine & "string1.ToUpper() = " & Chr(34) & _
23            string1.ToUpper() & Chr(34) & vbNewLine & _
24            "string2.ToLower() = " & Chr(34) & string2.ToLower() & Chr(34))
25
26         ' call Trim method
27         Console.WriteLine(vbNewLine & "string3 after trim = " & Chr(34) & _
28            string3.Trim() & Chr(34))
29
30         Console.WriteLine(vbNewLine & "string1 = " & Chr(34) & string1 & _
31            Chr(34))
32      End Sub ' Main
33   End Module ' StringMethods2
```

```
string1 = "cheers!"
string2 = "GOOD BYE "
string3 = "   spaces   "

Replacing "e" with "E" in string1: "chEErs!"

string1.ToUpper() = "CHEERS!"
string2.ToLower() = "good bye "

string3 after trim = "spaces"

string1 = "cheers!"
```

Fig. 17.8 | `String` methods `Replace`, `ToLower`, `ToUpper` and `Trim`. (Part 2 of 2.)

`String` method `ToUpper` returns a new `String` (line 23) that replaces any lowercase letters in `string1` with their uppercase equivalent. If there are no characters to convert, the method returns the original `String`. Line 24 uses `String` method `ToLower` to return a new `String` in which any uppercase letters in `string2` are replaced by their lowercase equivalents. As with `ToUpper`, if there are no characters to convert to lowercase, method `ToLower` returns the original `String`. Lines 30–31 demonstrate that `string1` did not change.

Line 28 uses `String` method `Trim` to remove all whitespace characters that appear at the beginning and end of a `String`. The method returns a new `String` that contains the original `String`, but omits leading or trailing whitespace characters. This is particularly useful when working with user input. Another version of method `Trim` takes a character array and returns a `String` that does not contain the characters in the array argument at the start or end of the `String`. `String` methods `TrimStart` and `TrimEnd` can be used to remove whitespace characters (or the characters contained in a character array argument) from the beginning or end of a `String`, respectively.

17.10 Class StringBuilder

The String class provides many capabilities for processing Strings. However, a String's contents can never change. Operations that seem to concatenate Strings are in fact creating new Strings (e.g., the &= operator creates a new String and assigns it to the String variable on the left side of the operator).

The next several sections discuss the features of class StringBuilder (namespace System.Text), used to create and manipulate dynamic string information—that is, mutable strings. Every StringBuilder can store the number of characters specified by its capacity. Exceeding the capacity of a StringBuilder makes the capacity expand to accommodate the additional characters. As we will see, members of class StringBuilder, such as methods Append and AppendFormat, can be used for concatenation like the operators &, and &= for class String.

Performance Tip 17.2

Objects of class String are constant strings, whereas object of class StringBuilder are mutable sequences of characters. The CLR can perform certain optimizations with Strings (such as referring to one String with many variables) because it knows the Strings will not change.

Performance Tip 17.3

When you have a choice between using a String or a StringBuilder to represent a sequence of characters, always use a String if the contents of the object will not change. When appropriate, using Strings instead of StringBuilder objects improves performance.

Class StringBuilder provides six overloaded constructors. Class StringBuilderConstructor (Fig. 17.9) demonstrates three of them. Line 7 employs the parameterless StringBuilder constructor to create a StringBuilder that contains no characters and has a default initial capacity of 16 characters. Line 8 uses the StringBuilder constructor that takes an Integer argument to create a StringBuilder that contains no characters and has

```
1  ' Fig. 17.9: StringBuilderConstructor.vb
2  ' Demonstrating StringBuilder class constructors.
3  Imports System.Text
4
5  Module StringBuilderConstructor
6     Sub Main()
7        Dim buffer1 As New StringBuilder()
8        Dim buffer2 As New StringBuilder(10)
9        Dim buffer3 As New StringBuilder("hello")
10
11       Console.WriteLine("buffer1 = " & Chr(34) & buffer1.ToString() & _
12          Chr(34))
13       Console.WriteLine("buffer2 = " & Chr(34) & buffer2.ToString() & _
14          Chr(34))
15       Console.WriteLine("buffer3 = " & Chr(34) & buffer3.ToString() & _
16          Chr(34))
17    End Sub ' Main
18 End Module ' StringBuilderConstructor
```

Fig. 17.9 | StringBuilder class constructors. (Part 1 of 2.)

```
buffer1 = ""
buffer2 = ""
buffer3 = "hello"
```

Fig. 17.9 | `StringBuilder` class constructors. (Part 2 of 2.)

the initial capacity specified in the `Integer` argument (i.e., `10`). Line 9 uses the `StringBuilder` constructor that takes a `String` argument to create a `StringBuilder` containing the characters of the `String` argument. The initial capacity is the smallest power of two greater than or equal to the number of characters in the argument `String`, with a minimum of 16. The `String` passed to the constructor in line 9 is five characters long. The smallest power of two greater than or equal to five is eight (two to the power of three). However, the minimum initial capacity is 16, so the initial capacity of `buffer3` (line 9) is 16. Lines 11–16 use `StringBuilder` method `ToString` to obtain `String` representations of the `StringBuilders`' contents.

17.11 Length and Capacity Properties, EnsureCapacity Method and Indexer of Class StringBuilder

Class `StringBuilder` provides the `Length` and `Capacity` properties to return the number of characters currently in a `StringBuilder` and the number of characters that a `StringBuilder` can store without allocating more memory, respectively. These properties also can increase or decrease the length or the capacity of the `StringBuilder`.

Method `EnsureCapacity` allows you to reduce the number of times a `StringBuilder`'s capacity must be increased. Method `EnsureCapacity` increases the `StringBuilder` instance's capacity to accommodate *at least* the number of elements specified as the argument. Figure 17.10 demonstrates these methods and properties.

```
' Fig. 17.10: StringBuilderFeatures.vb
' Demonstrating some features of class StringBuilder.
Imports System.Text

Module StringBuilderFeatures
   Sub Main()
      Dim buffer As New StringBuilder("Hello, how are you?")

      ' use Length and Capacity properties
      Console.WriteLine("buffer = " & buffer.ToString() & vbNewLine & _
         "Length = " & buffer.Length & vbNewLine & "Capacity = " & _
         buffer.Capacity)

      buffer.EnsureCapacity(75) ' ensure a capacity of at least 75
      Console.WriteLine(vbNewLine & "New capacity = " & buffer.Capacity)

```

Fig. 17.10 | `StringBuilder` size manipulation. (Part 1 of 2.)

```
17        ' truncate StringBuilder by setting Length property
18        buffer.Length = 10
19        Console.Write(vbNewLine & "New length = " & _
20           buffer.Length & vbNewLine & "buffer = ")
21
22        ' use StringBuilder indexer
23        For i = 0 To buffer.Length - 1
24           Console.Write(buffer(i))
25        Next i
26
27        Console.WriteLine()
28     End Sub ' Main
29  End Module ' StringBuilderFeatures
```

```
buffer = Hello, how are you?
Length = 19
Capacity = 32

New capacity = 75

New length = 10
buffer = Hello, how
```

Fig. 17.10 | `StringBuilder` size manipulation. (Part 2 of 2.)

The program contains one `StringBuilder`, called `buffer`. Line 7 uses the `StringBuilder` constructor that takes a `String` argument to instantiate a `StringBuilder` and initialize its value to `"Hello, how are you?"`. Lines 10–12 output the content, length and capacity of the `StringBuilder`. In the output window, note that the capacity of the `StringBuilder` is initially `32`. Remember, the `StringBuilder` constructor that takes a `String` argument creates a `StringBuilder` object with an initial capacity that is the smallest power of two greater than or equal to the number of characters in the `String` passed as an argument. The default initial capacity is `16`, which is two to the power of four. The `String` is too large for the default capacity, so the `StringBuilder` constructor determines the smallest power of two that is greater than or equal to the number of characters in the `String` (`19`). Two to the power of five is `32`, which is greater than `19`, so the initial capacity is set to `32`.

Line 14 expands the capacity of the `StringBuilder` to a minimum of 75 characters. The current capacity (`32`) multiplied by two is less than 75, so method `EnsureCapacity` increases the capacity to `75`. If new characters are added to a `StringBuilder` so that its length exceeds its capacity, the capacity grows to accommodate the additional characters in the same manner as if method `EnsureCapacity` had been called.

Line 18 uses property `Length` to set the length of the `StringBuilder` to `10`. If the specified length is less than the current number of characters in the `StringBuilder`, the contents of the `StringBuilder` are truncated to the specified length. If the specified length is greater than the number of characters currently in the `StringBuilder`, null characters (characters with the numeric representation `0`) are appended to the `StringBuilder` until the total number of characters in the `StringBuilder` is equal to the specified length. Lines 23–25 use the `StringBuilder` indexer to output the characters in the `StringBuilder` one character at a time.

17.12 Append and AppendFormat Methods of Class StringBuilder

Class StringBuilder provides 19 overloaded Append methods for appending values of various types to the end of a StringBuilder's contents. This method has versions for each primitive type and for character arrays, Strings and Objects. Recall that ToString produces a String representation of any Object, so any Object's string representation can be appended to a StringBuilder. Each method takes an argument, converts it to a String and appends it to the StringBuilder. Figure 17.11 demonstrates several Append methods.

```
' Fig. 17.11: StringBuilderAppend.vb
' Demonstrating StringBuilder Append methods.
Imports System.Text

Module StringBuilderAppend
   Sub Main()
      Dim objectValue As Object = "hello"
      Dim stringValue As String = "good bye"
      Dim characterArray As Char() = {"a"c, "b"c, "c"c, "d"c, "e"c, "f"c}
      Dim booleanValue As Boolean = True
      Dim characterValue As Char = "Z"c
      Dim integerValue As Integer = 7
      Dim longValue As Long = 1000000
      Dim floatValue As Single = 2.5F ' F indicates that 2.5 is a float
      Dim doubleValue As Double = 33.333
      Dim buffer As New StringBuilder()

      ' use method Append to append values to buffer
      buffer.Append(objectValue)
      buffer.Append("  ")
      buffer.Append(stringValue)
      buffer.Append("  ")
      buffer.Append(characterArray)
      buffer.Append("  ")
      buffer.Append(characterArray, 0, 3)
      buffer.Append("  ")
      buffer.Append(booleanValue)
      buffer.Append("  ")
      buffer.Append(characterValue)
      buffer.Append("  ")
      buffer.Append(integerValue)
      buffer.Append("  ")
      buffer.Append(longValue)
      buffer.Append("  ")
      buffer.Append(floatValue)
      buffer.Append("  ")
      buffer.Append(doubleValue)

      Console.WriteLine("buffer = " & buffer.ToString() & vbNewLine)
   End Sub ' Main
End Module ' StringBuilderAppend
```

Fig. 17.11 | Append methods of StringBuilder. (Part 1 of 2.)

```
buffer = hello  good bye  abcdef  abc  True  Z  7  1000000  2.5  33.333
```

Fig. 17.11 | Append methods of `StringBuilder`. (Part 2 of 2.)

Lines 19–37 use 10 different overloaded `Append` methods to append the `String` representations of the variables created in lines 7–16 to the end of the `StringBuilder`. `Append` behaves similarly to the `&` operator, which is used to concatenate `String`s.

Class `StringBuilder` also provides method `AppendFormat`, which converts a `String` to a specified format, then appends it to the `StringBuilder`. The example in Fig. 17.12 demonstrates this method.

```
' Fig. 17.12: StringBuilderAppendFormat.vb
' Demonstrating method AppendFormat.
Imports System.Text

Module StringBuilderAppendFormat
   Sub Main()
      Dim buffer As New StringBuilder()

      ' formatted string
      Dim string1 As String = "This {0} costs: {1:C}." & vbNewLine

      ' string1 argument array
      Dim objectArray(2) As Object

      objectArray(0) = "car"
      objectArray(1) = 1234.56

      ' append to buffer formatted string with argument
      buffer.AppendFormat(string1, objectArray)

      ' formatted string
      Dim string2 As String = "Number:{0:d3}." & vbNewLine & _
         "Number right aligned with spaces:{0, 4}." & vbNewLine & _
         "Number left aligned with spaces:{0, -4}."

      ' append to buffer formatted string with argument
      buffer.AppendFormat(string2, 5)

      ' display formatted strings
      Console.WriteLine(buffer.ToString())
   End Sub ' Main
End Module ' StringBuilderAppendFormat
```

```
This car costs: $1,234.56.
Number:005.
Number right aligned with spaces:   5.
Number left aligned with spaces:5   .
```

Fig. 17.12 | `StringBuilder`'s `AppendFormat` method.

Line 10 creates and initializes a `String` that contains formatting information. The information enclosed within the braces specifies how to format a specific piece of information. Formats have the form `{X[,Y][:FormatString]}`, where `X` is the number of the argument to be formatted, counting from zero. `Y` is an optional argument, which can be positive or negative, indicating how many characters should be in the formatted `String`. If the resulting `String` has fewer characters than the number `Y`, the `String` will be padded with spaces to make up for the difference. A positive integer aligns the `String` to the right; a negative integer aligns it to the left. The optional `FormatString` applies a particular format to the argument—currency, decimal or scientific, among others. In this case, `{0}` means that the first argument's `String` representation will be included in the formatted `String`. `{1:C}` specifies that the second argument will be formatted as a currency value.

Line 19 shows a version of `AppendFormat` that takes two parameters—a `String` specifying the format and an array of objects to serve as the arguments to the format `String`. The argument referred to by `{0}` is in the object array at index `0`.

Lines 22–24 create and initialize another `String` used for formatting. The first format `{0:D3}`, specifies that the first argument will be formatted as a three-digit decimal, meaning any number that has fewer than three digits will have leading zeros, so the total number of formatted digits will be 3. The next format, `{0, 4}`, specifies that the formatted `String` should have four characters and should be right aligned. The third format, `{0, -4}`, specifies that the `String` should be aligned to the left. For more formatting options, please refer to the online help documentation.

Line 27 uses a version of `AppendFormat` that takes two parameters—a `String` containing a format and an object to which the format is applied. In this case, the object is the number `5`. The output of Fig. 17.12 displays the result of applying these versions of `AppendFormat` with their respective arguments.

17.13 Insert, Remove and Replace Methods of Class StringBuilder

Class `StringBuilder` provides 18 overloaded `Insert` methods to allow values of various types to be inserted at any position in a `StringBuilder`. There are versions of `Insert` for each of the primitive types and for character arrays, `Strings` and `Objects`. Each version takes its second argument, converts it to a `String` and inserts the `String` into the `StringBuilder` at the index specified by the first argument. The index must be greater than or equal to `0` and less than the length of the `StringBuilder`; otherwise, an `ArgumentOutOfRangeException` occurs.

Class `StringBuilder` also provides method `Remove` for deleting characters in a `StringBuilder`. Method `Remove` takes two arguments—the index at which to begin deletion and the number of characters to delete. The sum of the starting subscript and the number of characters to be deleted must always be less than the `StringBuilder`'s length; otherwise, an `ArgumentOutOfRangeException` occurs. Figure 17.13 demonstrates the `Insert` and `Remove` methods. Lines 20–37 use nine different overloaded `Insert` methods to insert the `String` representations of the variables created in lines 7–17 at index 0 in the `StringBuilder`.

```
' Fig. 17.13: StringBuilderInsertRemove.vb
' Insert and Remove methods of class StringBuilder.
Imports System.Text

Module StringBuilderInsertRemove
   Sub Main()
      Dim objectValue As Object = "hello"
      Dim stringValue As String = "good bye"
      Dim characterArray As Char() = _
         {"a"c, "b"c, "c"c, "d"c, "e"c, "f"c}
      Dim booleanValue As Boolean = True
      Dim characterValue As Char = "K"c
      Dim integerValue As Integer = 7
      Dim longValue As Long = 10000000
      Dim floatValue As Single = 2.5F ' F indicates that 2.5 is a float
      Dim doubleValue As Double = 33.333
      Dim buffer As New StringBuilder()

      ' insert values into buffer
      buffer.Insert(0, objectValue)
      buffer.Insert(0, "  ")
      buffer.Insert(0, stringValue)
      buffer.Insert(0, "  ")
      buffer.Insert(0, characterArray)
      buffer.Insert(0, "  ")
      buffer.Insert(0, booleanValue)
      buffer.Insert(0, "  ")
      buffer.Insert(0, characterValue)
      buffer.Insert(0, "  ")
      buffer.Insert(0, integerValue)
      buffer.Insert(0, "  ")
      buffer.Insert(0, longValue)
      buffer.Insert(0, "  ")
      buffer.Insert(0, floatValue)
      buffer.Insert(0, "  ")
      buffer.Insert(0, doubleValue)
      buffer.Insert(0, "  ")

      Console.WriteLine("buffer after inserts: " & vbNewLine & _
         buffer.ToString() & vbNewLine)

      buffer.Remove(10, 1) ' delete 2 in 2.5
      buffer.Remove(4, 4) ' delete .333 in 33.333

      Console.WriteLine("buffer after Removes:" & vbNewLine & _
         buffer.ToString())
   End Sub ' Main
End Module ' StringBuilderInsertRemove
```

```
buffer after inserts:
  33.333  2.5  10000000  7  K  True  abcdef  good bye  hello

buffer after Removes:
  33  .5  10000000  7  K  True  abcdef  good bye  hello
```

Fig. 17.13 | StringBuilder text insertion and removal.

Another useful `StringBuilder` method is `Replace`, which searches for a specified `String` or character and substitutes another `String` or character in its place. Figure 17.14 demonstrates `Replace`.

Line 13 uses method `Replace` to replace all instances of the `String` `"Jane"` with the `String` `"Greg"` in `builder1`. An overloaded version of this method takes two characters as parameters and replaces each occurrence of the first character with the second character. Line 14 uses an overload of `Replace` that takes four parameters—two characters and two `Integers`. The method replaces all instances of the first character with the second character, beginning at the index specified by the first `Integer` and continuing for a count specified by the second `Integer`. In this case, `Replace` looks at only five characters, starting with the character at index `0`. As the output illustrates, this version of `Replace` replaces `g` with `G` in the word `"good"`, but not in `"greg"`—the `g`s in `"greg"` are not in the range indicated by the `Integer` arguments (i.e., between indexes `0` and `4`). An overloaded version takes two `Strings` and two `Integers`, replacing all instances of the first `String` with the second `String`, beginning at the index specified by the first `Integer` and continuing for a count specified by the second `Integer`.

```
1  ' Fig. 17.14: StringBuilderReplace.vb
2  ' Demonstrating method Replace.
3  Imports System.Text
4
5  Module StringBuilderReplace
6     Sub Main()
7        Dim builder1 As New StringBuilder("Happy Birthday Jane")
8        Dim builder2 As New StringBuilder("good bye greg")
9
10       Console.WriteLine("Before replacements:" & vbNewLine & _
11          builder1.ToString() & vbNewLine & builder2.ToString())
12
13       builder1.Replace("Jane", "Greg")
14       builder2.Replace("g"c, "G"c, 0, 5)
15
16       Console.WriteLine(vbNewLine & "After replacements:" & vbNewLine & _
17          builder1.ToString() & vbNewLine & builder2.ToString())
18    End Sub ' Main
19 End Module ' StringBuilderReplace
```

```
Before replacements:
Happy Birthday Jane
good bye greg

After replacements:
Happy Birthday Greg
Good bye greg
```

Fig. 17.14 | `StringBuilder` text replacement.

17.14 Char Methods

Visual Basic provides a construct called a structure that is similar to a class. Although structures and classes are comparable in many ways, structures represent value types. Like classes, structures include methods and properties. Both use the same access modifiers (such as `Public`, `Protected` and `Private`) and access members via the member-access operator (`.`). Structures are created using the keyword **`Structure`**.

Many of the primitive types that we have used in this book are actually aliases for different structures. For instance, an `Integer` is defined by structure `System.Int32`, a `Long` by `System.Int64` and so on. These structures derive from class **`ValueType`**, which in turn derives from class `Object`. In this section, we present structure **`Char`**, which is the structure for characters.

Most `Char` methods are `Shared`, take at least one character argument and perform either a test or a manipulation on the character. We present several of these methods in the next example. Figure 17.15 demonstrates `Shared` methods that test characters to determine whether they are of a specific character type and `Shared` methods that perform case conversions on characters.

This Windows Forms application contains a prompt, a `TextBox` in which the user can input a character, a button that the user can press after entering a character and a second `TextBox` that displays the output of our analysis. When the user clicks the **Analyze Character** button, event handler `analyzeButton_Click` (lines 7–28) converts the entered data from a `String` to a `Char`, using method `Convert.ToChar` (line 12).

```
 1  ' Fig. 17.15: SharedCharMethodsForm.vb
 2  ' Demonstrates Shared character testing methods
 3  ' from Char structure
 4
 5  Public Class SharedCharMethodsForm
 6     ' handle analyzeButton_Click
 7     Private Sub analyzeButton_Click(ByVal sender As System.Object, _
 8        ByVal e As System.EventArgs) Handles analyzeButton.Click
 9
10        If inputTextBox.Text.Length = 1 Then
11           ' convert String entered to type Char
12           Dim character As Char = Convert.ToChar(inputTextBox.Text)
13           Dim output As String
14
15           output = "is digit: " & Char.IsDigit(character) & vbNewLine
16           output &= "is letter: " & Char.IsLetter(character) & vbNewLine
17           output &= "is letter or digit: " & _
18              Char.IsLetterOrDigit(character) & vbNewLine
19           output &= "is lowercase: " & Char.IsLower(character) & vbNewLine
20           output &= "is uppercase: " & Char.IsUpper(character) & vbNewLine
21           output &= "to uppercase: " & Char.ToUpper(character) & vbNewLine
22           output &= "to lower: " & Char.ToLower(character) & vbNewLine
23           output &= "is punctuation: " & _
24              Char.IsPunctuation(character) & vbNewLine
25           output &= "is symbol: " & Char.IsSymbol(character)
26           outputTextBox.Text = output
27        End If
28     End Sub ' analyzeButton_Click
29  End Class ' SharedCharMethodsForm
```

Fig. 17.15 | `Char`'s `Shared` character-testing and case-conversion methods. (Part 1 of 2.)

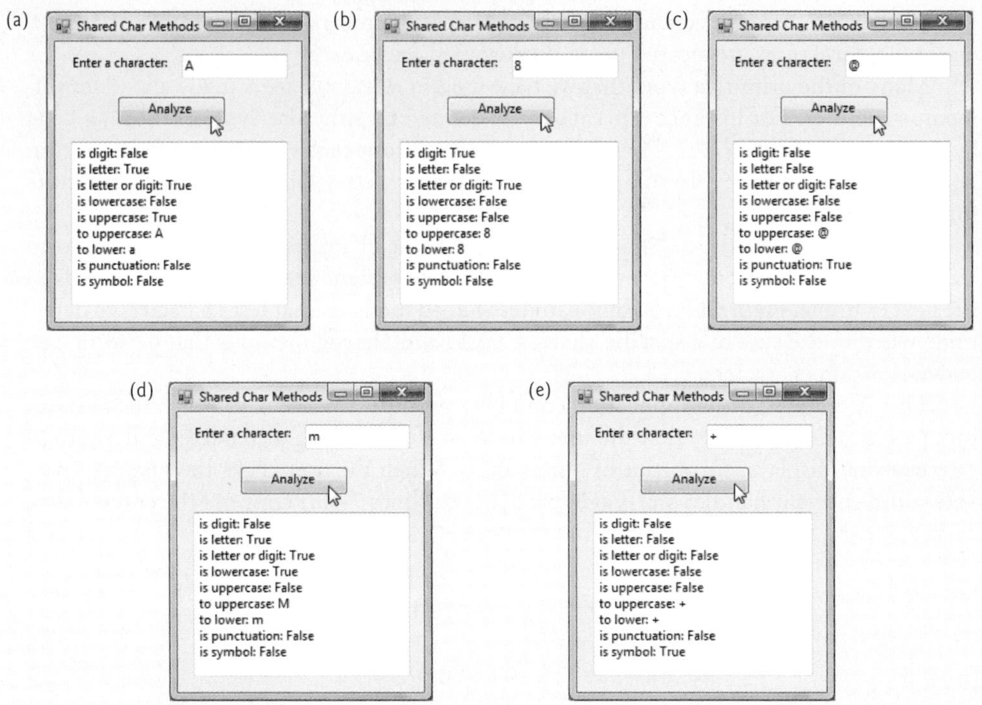

Fig. 17.15 | `Char`'s `Shared` character-testing and case-conversion methods. (Part 2 of 2.)

Line 15 uses `Char` method `IsDigit` to determine whether `character` is a digit. If so, the method returns `True`; otherwise, it returns `False`. Line 16 uses `Char` method `IsLetter` to determine whether `character` is a letter. Line 18 uses `Char` method `IsLetterOrDigit` to determine whether `character` is a letter or a digit.

Line 19 uses `Char` method `IsLower` to determine whether `character` is a lowercase letter. Line 20 uses `Char` method `IsUpper` to determine whether `character` is an uppercase letter. Line 21 uses `Char` method `ToUpper` to convert `character` to its uppercase equivalent. The method returns the converted character if the character has an uppercase equivalent; otherwise, the method returns its original argument. Line 22 uses `Char` method `ToLower` to convert `character` to its lowercase equivalent. The method returns the converted character if the character has a lowercase equivalent; otherwise, the method returns its original argument.

Line 24 uses `Char` method `IsPunctuation` to determine whether `character` is a punctuation mark, such as `"!"`, `":"` or `")"`. Line 25 uses `Char` method `IsSymbol` to determine whether `character` is a symbol, such as `"+"`, `"="` or `"^"`.

Structure `Char` also contains other methods not shown in this example. Many of the `Shared` methods are similar—for instance, `IsWhiteSpace` determines whether a character is a whitespace character (e.g., newline, tab or space). `Char` also contains several `Public` instance methods; many of these, such as methods `ToString` and `Equals`, are methods that we have seen before in other classes. This group includes method `CompareTo`, which is used to compare two character values.

17.15 Card Shuffling and Dealing Simulation

In this section, we use random-number generation to develop a program that simulates card shuffling and dealing. These techniques can form the basis of programs that implement specific card games. We include several exercises at the end of this chapter that require card shuffling and dealing capabilities.

Class `Card` (Fig. 17.16) contains two `String` instance variables—`face` and `suit`—that store references to the face value and suit name of a specific card. The constructor for the class receives two `Strings` that it uses to initialize `face` and `suit`. Method `ToString` (lines 12–14) creates a `String` consisting of the `face` of the card and the `suit` of the card to identify the card when it is dealt.

The `DeckForm` application (Fig. 17.17) creates a deck of 52 `Card` objects. Users can deal each card by clicking the **Deal Card** button. Each dealt card is displayed in a `Label`. Users can also shuffle the deck at any time by clicking the **Shuffle Cards** button.

```
1  ' Fig. 17.16: Card.vb
2  ' Stores suit and face information on each card.
3  Public Class Card
4     Private face As String
5     Private suit As String
6
7     Public Sub New(ByVal faceValue As String, ByVal suitValue As String)
8        face = faceValue
9        suit = suitValue
10    End Sub ' New
11
12    Public Overrides Function ToString() As String
13       Return face & " of " & suit
14    End Function ' ToString
15 End Class ' Card
```

Fig. 17.16 | `Card` class.

```
' Fig. 17.17: DeckForm.vb
' Simulating card shuffling and dealing.
Public Class DeckForm
   Private deck(51) As Card ' deck of 52 cards
   Private currentCard As Integer ' count which card was just dealt

   ' handles form at load time
   Private Sub DeckForm_Load(ByVal sender As System.Object, _
      ByVal e As System.EventArgs) Handles MyBase.Load

      Dim faces As String() = _
         {"Ace", "Deuce", "Three", "Four", "Five", "Six", "Seven", _
         "Eight", "Nine", "Ten", "Jack", "Queen", "King"}
      Dim suits As String() = {"Hearts", "Diamonds", "Clubs", "Spades"}

      currentCard = -1 ' no cards have been dealt
```

Fig. 17.17 | Card shuffling and dealing simulation. (Part 1 of 3.)

```

      ' initialize deck
      For i = 0 To deck.Length - 1
         deck(i) = New Card(faces(i Mod 13), suits(i \ 13))
      Next
   End Sub ' DeckForm_Load

   ' deal a card
   Private Sub dealButton_Click(ByVal sender As System.Object, _
      ByVal e As System.EventArgs) Handles dealButton.Click

      Dim dealt As Card = DealCard()

      ' if dealt card is Nothing, then no cards left
      ' player must shuffle cards
      If Not (dealt Is Nothing) Then
         displayLabel.Text = dealt.ToString()
         statusLabel.Text = "Card #: " & currentCard
      Else
         displayLabel.Text = "NO MORE CARDS TO DEAL"
         statusLabel.Text = "Shuffle cards to continue"
      End If
   End Sub ' dealButton_Click

   ' shuffle cards
   Private Sub Shuffle()
      Dim randomNumber As New Random()
      Dim temporaryValue As Card

      currentCard = -1

      ' swap each card with randomly selected card (0-51)
      For i = 0 To deck.Length - 1
         Dim j = randomNumber.Next(52)

         ' swap cards
         temporaryValue = deck(i)
         deck(i) = deck(j)
         deck(j) = temporaryValue
      Next

      dealButton.Enabled = True ' shuffled deck can now deal cards
   End Sub ' Shuffle

   ' deal a card if the deck is not empty
   Private Function DealCard() As Card
      ' if there is a card to deal, then deal it;
      ' otherwise, signal that cards need to be shuffled by
      ' disabling dealButton and returning Nothing
      If currentCard + 1 < deck.Length Then
         currentCard += 1 ' increment count
         Return deck(currentCard) ' return new card
```

Fig. 17.17 | Card shuffling and dealing simulation. (Part 2 of 3.)

```
69         Else
70            dealButton.Enabled = False ' empty deck cannot deal cards
71            Return Nothing ' do not return a card
72         End If
73      End Function ' DealCard
74
75      ' handles shuffleButton Click
76      Private Sub shuffleButton_Click(ByVal sender As System.Object, _
77         ByVal e As System.EventArgs) Handles shuffleButton.Click
78
79         displayLabel.Text = "SHUFFLING..."
80         Shuffle()
81         displayLabel.Text = "DECK IS SHUFFLED"
82      End Sub ' shuffleButton_Click
83   End Class ' DeckForm
```

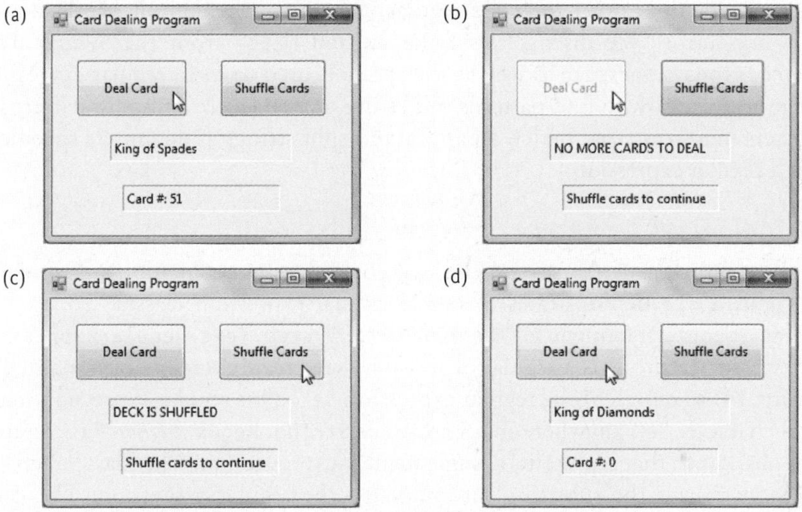

Fig. 17.17 | Card shuffling and dealing simulation. (Part 3 of 3.)

Method `DeckForm_Load` (lines 8–22 of Fig. 17.17) uses a loop (lines 19–21) to fill the `deck` array with `Card`s. Each `Card` is instantiated and initialized with two `Strings`—one from the `faces` array (`Strings` `"Ace"` through `"King"`) and one from the `suits` array (`"Hearts"`, `"Diamonds"`, `"Clubs"` or `"Spades"`). The calculation `i Mod 13` always results in a value from `0` to `12` (the 13 subscripts of the `faces` array), and the calculation `i \ 13` always results in an `Integer` value from `0` to `3` (the four subscripts in the `suits` array). The initialized `deck` array contains the cards with faces Ace through King for each suit.

When the user clicks the **Deal Card** button, event handler `dealButton_Click` (lines 25–39) invokes method `DealCard` (defined in lines 62–73) to get the next card in the `deck` array. If the `deck` is not empty, the method returns a `Card` object reference; otherwise, it returns `Nothing`. If the reference is not `Nothing`, lines 33–34 display the `Card` in `displayLabel` and display the card number in `statusLabel`. If `DealCard` returns `Nothing`, the `String` `"NO MORE CARDS TO DEAL"` is displayed in `displayLabel`, and the `String` `"Shuffle cards to continue"` is displayed in `statusLabel`.

When the user clicks the **Shuffle Cards** button, event handler `shuffleButton_Click` (lines 76–82) invokes method `Shuffle` (defined in lines 42–59) to shuffle the cards. The method loops through all 52 cards (array subscripts `0–51`). For each card, the method randomly picks a number between `0` and `51`. Then the current `Card` object and the randomly selected `Card` object are swapped in the array. To shuffle the cards, method `Shuffle` makes a total of only 52 swaps during a single pass of the entire array. When the shuffling is complete, `displayLabel` displays the `String` `"DECK IS SHUFFLED"`.

17.16 Introduction to Regular Expression Processing

This section introduces regular expressions—specially formatted strings that are used to find patterns in text. They can be used to ensure that data is in a particular format. For example, a U.S. zip code must consist of five digits, or five digits followed by a dash followed by four more digits. Compilers use regular expressions to validate program syntax. If the program code does not match the regular expression, the compiler indicates that there is a syntax error. We discuss classes `Regex` and `Match` from the `System.Text.RegularExpressions` namespace as well as the symbols used to form regular expressions. We then demonstrate how to find patterns in a string, match entire strings to patterns, replace characters in a string that match a pattern and split strings at delimiters specified as a pattern in a regular expression.

17.16.1 Simple Regular Expressions and Class Regex

The .NET Framework provides several classes to help developers manipulate regular expressions. Figure 17.18 demonstrates the basic regular-expression classes. To use these classes, add an `Imports` statement for the namespace `System.Text.RegularExpressions` (line 3). Class **`Regex`** represents a regular expression. We create a `Regex` object named `expression` (line 14) to represent the regular expression `"e"`. This regular expression matches the literal character `"e"` anywhere in an arbitrary `String`. `Regex` *method* **`Match`** returns an object of *class* **`Match`** that represents a single regular-expression match. Class `Match`'s `ToString` method returns the substring that matched the regular expression. The call to method `Match` (line 15) matches the leftmost occurrence of the character `"e"` in `testString`. `Regex` also provides method `Matches` (line 19), which finds all matches of the regular expression in an arbitrary `String` and returns a `MatchCollection` object containing all the `Matches`. A `MatchCollection` is a collection, similar to an `array`, and can be used with a `for each` statement to iterate through the collection's elements. We introduced collections in Chapter 9 and we discuss collections in more detail in Chapter 24, Data Structures and Generic Collections. We use a `For Each` statement (lines 19–21) to print all the matches to `expression` in `testString`. The elements in the `MatchCollection` are `Match` objects, so the `For Each` statement infers variable `myMatch` to be of type `Match`. For each `Match`, line 20 outputs the text that matched the regular expression.

```
1  ' Fig. 17.18: BasicRegex.vb
2  ' Demonstrate basic regular expressions.
3  Imports System.Text.RegularExpressions ' regular-expression classes
4
```

Fig. 17.18 | Demonstrating basic regular expressions. (Part 1 of 2.)

```
5  Module BasicRegex
6     Sub Main()
7        Dim testString As String = _
8           "regular expressions are sometimes called regex or regexp"
9        Console.WriteLine("The test string is:" & vbNewLine & _
10          "   """ & testString & """")
11       Console.Write("Match 'e' in the test string: ")
12
13       ' match 'e' in the test string
14       Dim expression As New Regex("e")
15       Console.WriteLine(expression.Match(testString))
16       Console.Write("Match every 'e' in the test string: ")
17
18       ' match 'e' multiple times in the test string
19       For Each myMatch In expression.Matches(testString)
20          Console.Write("{0} ", myMatch)
21       Next
22
23       Console.Write(vbNewLine & "Match ""regex"" in the test string: ")
24
25       ' match 'regex' in the test string
26       For Each myMatch In Regex.Matches(testString, "regex")
27          Console.Write("{0} ", myMatch)
28       Next
29
30       Console.Write(vbNewLine & _
31          "Match ""regex"" or ""regexp"" using an optional 'p': ")
32
33       ' use the ? quantifier to include an optional 'p'
34       For Each myMatch In Regex.Matches(testString, "regexp?")
35          Console.Write("{0} ", myMatch)
36       Next
37
38       ' use alternation to match either 'cat' or 'hat'
39       expression = New Regex("(c|h)at")
40       Console.WriteLine(vbNewLine & _
41          """hat cat"" matches {0}, but ""cat hat"" matches {1}", _
42          expression.Match("hat cat"), expression.Match("cat hat"))
43    End Sub ' Main
44 End Module ' BasicRegex
```

```
The test string is:
  "regular expressions are sometimes called regex or regexp"
Match 'e' in the test string: e
Match every 'e' in the test string: e e e e e e e e e e e
Match "regex" in the test string: regex regex
Match "regex" or "regexp" using an optional 'p': regex regexp
"hat cat" matches hat, but "cat hat" matches cat
```

Fig. 17.18 | Demonstrating basic regular expressions. (Part 2 of 2.)

Regular expressions can also be used to match a sequence of literal characters anywhere in a `String`. Lines 26–28 print all the occurrences of the character sequence `"regex"` in `testString`. Here we use the `Regex Shared` method `Matches`. Class `Regex` provides Shared versions of both methods Match and Matches. The Shared versions take a regular expression as an argument in addition to the String to be searched. This is useful when you want to use a regular expression only once. The call to method Matches (line 26) returns two matches to the regular expression "regex". Notice that "regexp" in the test String matches the regular expression "regex", but the "p" is excluded. We use the regular expression "regexp?" (line 34) to match occurrences of both "regex" and "regexp". The question mark (?) is a metacharacter—a character with special meaning in a regular expression. More specifically, the question mark is a quantifier—a metacharacter that describes how many times a part of the pattern may occur in a match. The ? quantifier matches zero or one occurrence of the pattern to its left. In line 34, we apply the ? quantifier to the character "p". This means that a match to the regular expression contains the sequence of characters "regex" and may be followed by a "p". Notice that the For Each statement (lines 34–36) prints both "regex" and "regexp".

Metacharacters allow you to create more complex patterns. The "|" (alternation) metacharacter matches the expression to its left or to its right. We use alternation in the regular expression "(c|h)at" (line 39) to match either "cat" or "hat". Parentheses are used to group parts of a regular expression, much as you group parts of a mathematical expression. The "|" causes the pattern to match a sequence of characters starting with either "c" or "h", followed by "at". Note that the "|" character attempts to match the entire expression to its left or to its right. If we didn't use the parentheses around "c|h", the regular expression would match either the single character "c" or the sequence of characters "hat". Line 42 uses the regular expression (line 39) to search the Strings "hat cat" and "cat hat". Notice in the output that the first match in "hat cat" is "hat", while the first match in "cat hat" is "cat". Alternation chooses the leftmost match in the String for either of the alternating expressions—the order of the expressions in the alternation doesn't matter.

Regular-Expression Character Classes and Quantifiers

The table in Fig. 17.19 lists some character classes that can be used with regular expressions. A character class represents a group of characters that might appear in a String. For example, a word character (\w) is any alphanumeric character (a-z, A-Z and 0-9) or underscore. A whitespace character (\s) is a space, a tab, a carriage return, a newline or a form feed. A digit (\d) is any numeric character.

Figure 17.20 uses character classes in regular expressions. For this example, we use method DisplayMatches (lines 51–59) to display all matches to a regular expression. Method DisplayMatches takes two Strings representing the String to search and the regular expression to match. The method uses a For Each statement to print each Match in the MatchCollection object returned by the Shared method Matches of class Regex.

Character class	Matches	Character class	Matches
\d	any digit	\D	any nondigit
\w	any word character	\W	any nonword character
\s	any whitespace	\S	any nonwhitespace

Fig. 17.19 | Character classes.

The first regular expression (line 12) matches digits in the `testString`. We use the digit character class (`\d`) to match any digit (0-9). The output shows that the regular expression matches `1`, `2`, and `3` in the `testString`. You can also match anything that *isn't* a member of a particular character class using an uppercase letter instead of a lowercase letter. For example, the regular expression `"\D"` (line 16) matches any character that isn't a digit. Notice in the output that this includes punctuation and whitespace. Negating a character class matches *everything* that *isn't* a member of the character class.

```
1  ' Fig. 17.20: CharacterClasses.vb
2  ' Demonstrate using character classes and quantifiers.
3  Imports System.Text.RegularExpressions ' regular-expression classes
4
5  Module CharacterClasses
6     Sub Main()
7        Dim testString As String = "abc, DEF, 123"
8        Console.WriteLine("The test string is: ""{0}""", testString)
9
10       ' find the digits is the test string
11       Console.WriteLine("Match any digit")
12       DisplayMatches(testString, "\d")
13
14       ' find anything that isn't a digit
15       Console.WriteLine(vbNewLine & "Match any nondigit")
16       DisplayMatches(testString, "\D")
17
18       ' find the word characters in the test string
19       Console.WriteLine(vbNewLine & "Match any word character")
20       DisplayMatches(testString, "\w")
21
22       ' find sequences of word characters
23       Console.WriteLine(vbNewLine & _
24          "Match a group of at least one word character")
25       DisplayMatches(testString, "\w+")
26
27       ' use a lazy quantifier
28       Console.WriteLine(vbNewLine & _
29          "Match a group of at least one word character (lazy)")
30       DisplayMatches(testString, "\w+?")
31
32       ' match characters from 'a' to 'f'
33       Console.WriteLine(vbNewLine & "Match anything from 'a' - 'f'")
34       DisplayMatches(testString, "[a-f]")
35
36       ' match anything that isn't in the range 'a' to 'f'
37       Console.WriteLine(vbNewLine & "Match anything not from 'a' - 'f'")
38       DisplayMatches(testString, "[^a-f]")
39
40       ' match any sequence of letters in any case
41       Console.WriteLine( _
42          vbNewLine & "Match a group of at least one letter")
43       DisplayMatches(testString, "[a-zA-Z]+")
```

Fig. 17.20 | Demonstrating using character classes and quantifiers. (Part 1 of 2.)

```
44
45          ' use the . (dot) metacharacter to match any character
46          Console.WriteLine(vbNewLine & "Match a group of any characters")
47          DisplayMatches(testString, ".*")
48       End Sub ' Main
49
50       ' display the matches to a regular expression
51       Private Sub DisplayMatches( _
52          ByVal input As String, ByVal expression As String)
53
54          For Each regexMatch In Regex.Matches(input, expression)
55             Console.Write("{0} ", regexMatch)
56          Next
57
58          Console.WriteLine() ' move to the next line
59       End Sub ' DisplayMatches
60    End Module ' CharacterClasses
```

```
The test string is: "abc, DEF, 123"
Match any digit
1 2 3

Match any nondigit
a b c ,   D E F ,

Match any word character
a b c D E F 1 2 3

Match a group of at least one word character
abc DEF 123

Match a group of at least one word character (lazy)
a b c D E F 1 2 3

Match anything from 'a' - 'f'
a b c

Match anything not from 'a' - 'f'
,   D E F ,   1 2 3

Match a group of at least one letter
abc DEF

Match a group of any characters
abc, DEF, 123
```

Fig. 17.20 | Demonstrating using character classes and quantifiers. (Part 2 of 2.)

The next regular expression (line 20) uses the character class `\w` to match any word character in the `testString`. Notice that each match consists of a single character. It would be useful to match a sequence of word characters rather than a single character. The regular expression in line 25 uses the + quantifier to match a sequence of word characters. The **+ quantifier** matches one or more occurrences of the pattern to its left. There are three matches for this expression, each three characters long. Quantifiers are **greedy**—they match the *longest* occurrence of the pattern as possible. You can follow a quantifier with a question mark (?) to make it **lazy**—it matches the *shortest* occurrence of the pattern as possible. The regular expression "\w+?" (line 30) uses a lazy + quantifier to match the shortest sequence of word characters possible. This produces nine matches of length one instead of three matches of length three. Figure 17.21 lists other quantifiers that you can place after a pattern in a regular expression, and the purpose of each quantifier.

Regular expressions are not limited to the character classes in Fig. 17.19. You can create your own character class by listing the members of the character class between square brackets, `[` and `]`. [*Note:* Metacharacters in square brackets are treated as literal characters.] You can include a range of characters using the `"-"` character. The regular expression in line 34 of Fig. 17.20 creates a character class to match any lowercase letter from `a` to `f`. These custom character classes match a single character that is a member of the class. The output shows three matches, `a`, `b` and `c`. Notice that `D`, `E` and `F` don't match the character class `[a-f]` because they are uppercase. You can negate a custom character class by placing a `"^"` character after the opening square bracket. The regular expression in line 38 matches any character that *isn't* in the range `a-f`. As with the predefined character classes, negating a custom character class matches *everything* that isn't a member, including punctuation and whitespace. You can use quantifiers with custom character classes. The regular expression in line 43 uses a character class with two ranges of characters, `a-z` and `A-Z`, and the `+` quantifier to match a sequence of lowercase or uppercase letters. You can also use the `"."` (dot) character to match any character other than a newline. The regular expression `".*"` (line 47) matches any sequence of characters. The `*` quantifier matches zero or more occurrences of the pattern to its left. Unlike the `+` quantifier, the `*` quantifier can be used to match an empty string.

Quantifier	Matches
`*`	Matches zero or more occurrences of the preceding pattern.
`+`	Matches one or more occurrences of the preceding pattern.
`?`	Matches zero or one occurrences of the preceding pattern.
`.`	Matches any single character.
`{n}`	Matches exactly `n` occurrences of the preceding pattern.
`{n,}`	Matches at least `n` occurrences of the preceding pattern.
`{n,m}`	Matches between `n` and `m` (inclusive) occurrences of the preceding pattern.

Fig. 17.21 | Quantifiers used in regular expressions.

17.16.2 Complex Regular Expressions

The program of Fig. 17.22 tries to match birthdays to a regular expression. For demonstration purposes, the expression matches only birthdays that do not occur in April and that belong to people whose names begin with `"J"`. We can do this by combining the basic regular-expression techniques we've already discussed.

Line 8 creates a `Regex` object and passes a regular-expression pattern `String` to its constructor. The first character in the regular expression, `"J"`, is a literal character. Any `String` matching this regular expression must start with `"J"`. The next part of the regular expression (`".*"`) matches any number of unspecified characters except newlines. The pattern `"J.*"` matches a person's name that starts with J and any characters that may come after that.

```
1  ' Fig. 17.22: RegexMatches.vb
2  ' A more complex regular expression.
3  Imports System.Text.RegularExpressions ' regular-expression classes
4
5  Module RegexMatches
6     Sub Main()
7        ' create a regular expression
8        Dim expression As New Regex("J.*\d[\d-[4]]-\d\d-\d\d")
9
10       Dim testString As String = _
11          "Jane's Birthday is 05-12-75" & vbNewLine & _
12          "Dave's Birthday is 11-04-68" & vbNewLine & _
13          "John's Birthday is 04-28-73" & vbNewLine & _
14          "Joe's Birthday is 12-17-77"
15
16       ' print out all matches to the regular expression
17       For Each regexMatch In expression.Matches(testString)
18          Console.WriteLine(regexMatch)
19       Next
20    End Sub ' Main
21 End Module ' RegexMatches
```

```
Jane's Birthday is 05-12-75
Joe's Birthday is 12-17-77
```

Fig. 17.22 | A more complex regular expression.

Next we match the person's birthday. We use the `\d` character class to match the first digit of the month. Since the birthday must not occur in April, the second digit in the month can't be `4`. We could use the character class `"[0-35-9]"` to match any digit other than `4`. However, .NET regular expressions allow you to subtract members from a character class, called **character-class subtraction**. In line 8, we use the pattern `"[\d-[4]]"` to match any digit other than `4`. When the `"-"` character in a character class is followed by a character class instead of a literal character, the `"-"` is interpreted as subtraction instead of a range of characters. The members of the character class following the `"-"` are removed from the character class preceding the `"-"`. When using character-class subtraction, the class being subtracted (`[4]`) must be the last item in the enclosing square brackets (`[\d-[4]]`). This notation allows you to write shorter, easier-to-read regular expressions.

Although the `"-"` character indicates a range or character-class subtraction when it is enclosed in square brackets, instances of the `"-"` character outside a character class are treated as literal characters. Thus, the regular expression in line 8 searches for a `String` that starts with the letter `"J"`, followed by any number of characters, followed by a two-digit number (of which the second digit cannot be `4`), followed by a dash, another two-digit number, a dash and another two-digit number.

Lines 17–19 use a `For Each` statement to iterate through the `MatchCollection` object returned by method `Matches`, which received `testString` as an argument. For each `Match`, line 18 outputs the text that matched the regular expression. The output in Fig. 17.22 displays the two matches that were found in `testString`. Notice that both matches conform to the pattern specified by the regular expression.

17.16.3 Validating User Input with Regular Expressions

The application in Fig. 17.23 presents a more involved example that uses regular expressions to validate name, address and telephone-number information input by a user.

When a user clicks **OK**, the program uses a LINQ query to select any empty `TextBoxes` (lines 12–17) from the `Controls` collections. The first `Where` clause (line 13) uses the `TypeOf...Is` operator to determine whether the control is a `TextBox`. The `Let` clause (line 14) creates and initializes a variable in a LINQ query for use later in the query. Here, we use the `Let` clause to define variable `box` as a `TextBox`, which contains the control converted to a `TextBox`. This allows us to use the control in the LINQ query as a `TextBox`, enabling access to its properties (such as `Text`). You may include a second `Where` clause after the `Let` clause. The second `Where` clause determines whether the `TextBox`'s `Text`

```
1  ' Fig. 17.23: Validate.vb
2  ' Validate user information using regular expressions.
3  Imports System.Text.RegularExpressions ' regular expression classes
4
5  Public Class ValidateForm
6     ' handles OK Button's Click event
7     Private Sub okButton_Click(ByVal sender As System.Object, _
8        ByVal e As System.EventArgs) Handles okButton.Click
9
10       ' find blank TextBoxes and order by TabIndex
11       Dim emptyBoxes = _
12          From control In Controls _
13          Where TypeOf control Is TextBox _
14          Let box As TextBox = CType(control, TextBox) _
15          Where String.IsNullOrEmpty(box.Text) _
16          Order By box.TabIndex _
17          Select box
18
19       If emptyBoxes.Count() > 0 Then
20          ' display popup box
21          MessageBox.Show("Please fill in all fields", _
22             "Missing Information", MessageBoxButtons.OK, _
23             MessageBoxIcon.Error)
24
25          emptyBoxes.First().Focus() ' set focus to first empty TextBox
26       Else
27          ' check for invalid input
28          Select Case False
29             ' last-name format is invalid
30             Case ValidateInput(lastNameTextBox.Text, _
31                "^[A-Z][a-zA-Z]*$", "Invalid last name")
32
33                lastNameTextBox.Focus() ' focus on invalid TextBox
34                ' first-name format is invalid
35             Case ValidateInput(firstNameTextBox.Text, _
36                "^[A-Z][a-zA-Z]*$", "Invalid first name")
37
38                firstNameTextBox.Focus() ' focus on invalid TextBox
```

Fig. 17.23 | Validating user information using regular expressions. (Part 1 of 4.)

```
               ' address format is invalid
               Case ValidateInput(addressTextBox.Text, _
                  "^[0-9]+\s+([a-zA-Z]+|[a-zA-Z]+\s[a-zA-Z]+)$", _
                  "Invalid address")

                  addressTextBox.Focus() ' focus on invalid TextBox
                  ' city format is invalid
               Case ValidateInput(cityTextBox.Text, _
                  "^([a-zA-Z]+|[a-zA-Z]+\s[a-zA-Z]+)$", "Invalid city")

                  cityTextBox.Focus() ' focus on invalid TextBox
                  ' state format is invalid
               Case ValidateInput(stateTextBox.Text, _
                  "^([a-zA-Z]+|[a-zA-Z]+\s[a-zA-Z]+)$", "Invalid state")

                  stateTextBox.Focus() ' focus on invalid TextBox
                  ' zip code format is invalid
               Case ValidateInput(zipCodeTextBox.Text, _
                  "^\d{5}$", "Invalid zip code")

                  zipCodeTextBox.Focus() ' focus on invalid TextBox
                  ' phone-number format is invalid
               Case ValidateInput(phoneTextBox.Text, _
                  "^[1-9]\d{2}-[1-9]\d{2}-\d{4}$", "Invalid phone number")

                  phoneTextBox.Focus() ' focus on invalid TextBox
               Case Else
                  ' information is valid, signal user and exit application
                  Me.Hide() ' hide main window while MessageBox displays
                  MessageBox.Show("Thank You!", "Information Correct", _
                     MessageBoxButtons.OK, MessageBoxIcon.Information)
                  Application.Exit() ' exit the application
            End Select
         End If
      End Sub ' okButton_Click

      ' use regular expressions to validate user input
      Public Function ValidateInput(ByVal input As String, _
         ByVal expression As String, ByVal message As String) As Boolean

         ' store whether the input is valid
         Dim valid As Boolean = Regex.Match(input, expression).Success

         ' if the input doesn't match the regular expression
         If Not valid Then
            ' signal user input was invalid
            MessageBox.Show(message, "Invalid Input", _
               MessageBoxButtons.OK, MessageBoxIcon.Error)
         End If

         Return valid ' return whether the input is valid
      End Function ' ValidateInput
   End Class ' ValidateForm
```

Fig. 17.23 | Validating user information using regular expressions. (Part 2 of 4.)

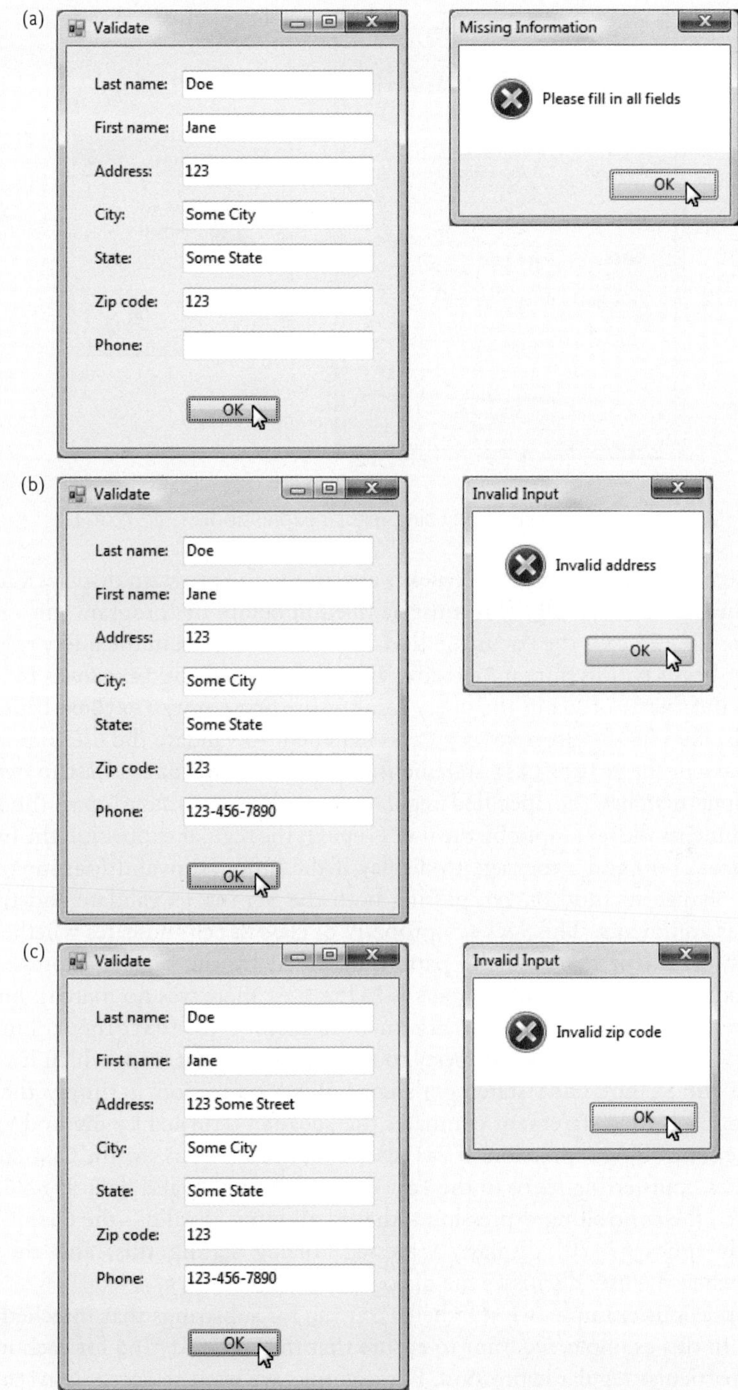

Fig. 17.23 | Validating user information using regular expressions. (Part 3 of 4.)

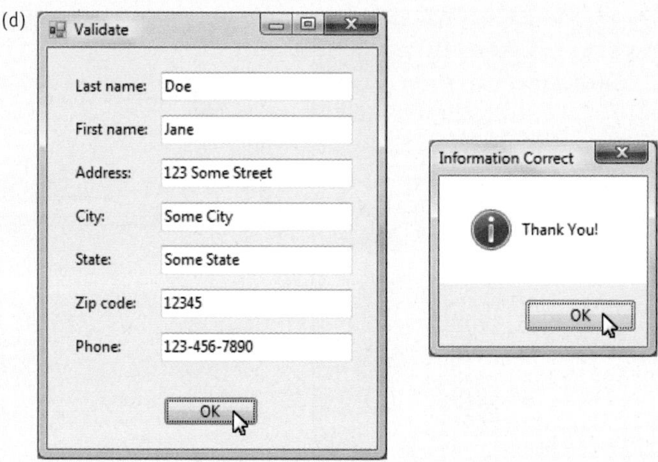

Fig. 17.23 | Validating user information using regular expressions. (Part 4 of 4.)

property is empty. If one or more `TextBox`es are empty, the program displays a message to the user (lines 21–23) that all fields must be filled in before the program can validate the information. Line 25 calls the `Focus` method of the first `TextBox` in the query result so that the user can begin typing in that `TextBox`. The query sorted the `TextBox`es by `TabIndex` (line 16) so the first `TextBox` in the query result is the first empty `TextBox`. If there are no empty fields, lines 28–64 use a `Select Case` statement to validate the user input.

Each `Case` in the `Select Case` statement calls method `ValidateInput` to determine if the user input matches the specified regular expression. `ValidateInput` (lines 76–90) takes as arguments the text input by the user (`input`), the regular expression the input must match (`expression`) and a message to display if the input is invalid (`message`). Line 80 calls `Regex Shared` method `Match`, passing both the `String` to validate and the regular expression as arguments. The **`Success`** property of class `Match` indicates whether method `Match`'s first argument matched the pattern specified by the regular expression in the second argument. If the value of `Success` is `False` (i.e., there was no match), lines 85–86 display the error message passed as an argument to method `ValidateInput`. Line 89 then returns the value of the `Success` property to the `Case` statement from which it was called. Notice that the `Select Case` statement's controlling expression is simply the `Boolean` value `False`. Each `Case` statement compares the `Boolean` returned by method `ValidateInput` to the controlling expression. If `ValidateInput` returns `False`, the `Case` statement's body executes, transferring focus to the `TextBox` containing invalid data. If no `Case` statement's match the controlling expression—that is, all input is valid—the `Case Else` statement's body (lines 67–70) displays a message dialog stating this, and the program terminates when the user dismisses the dialog.

In the previous example, we searched a `String` for substrings that matched a regular expression. In this example, we want to ensure that the entire `String` for each input conforms to a particular regular expression. For example, we want to accept `"Smith"` as a last name, but not `"9@Smith#"`. In a regular expression that begins with a `"^"` character and ends with a `"$"` character, the characters `"^"` and `"$"` represent the beginning and end of a `String`, respectively. These characters force a regular expression to return a match only if the entire `String` being processed matches the regular expression.

The regular expression in line 31 uses a character class to match an uppercase first letter followed by letters of any case—`a-z` matches any lowercase letter, and `A-Z` matches any uppercase letter. The * quantifier signifies that the second range of characters may occur zero or more times in the `String`. Thus, this expression matches any `String` consisting of one uppercase letter, followed by zero or more additional letters.

The `\s` character class matches a single whitespace character (lines 41, 47 and 52). In the expression `"\d{5}"`, used for the `zipCode` `String` (line 57), `{5}` is a quantifier (see Fig. 17.21). The pattern to the left of `{n}` must occur exactly `n` times. Thus `"\d{5}"` matches any five digits. Recall that the character `"|"` (lines 41, 47 and 52) matches the expression to its left *or* the expression to its right. In line 41, we use the character `"|"` to indicate that the address can contain a word of one or more characters *or* a word of one or more characters followed by a space and another word of one or more characters. Note the use of parentheses to group parts of the regular expression. This ensures that `"|"` is applied to the correct parts of the pattern.

The **Last Name:** and **First Name:** `TextBox`es each accept `String`s that begin with an uppercase letter (lines 31 and 36). The regular expression for the **Address:** `TextBox` (line 41) matches a number of at least one digit, followed by a space and then either one or more letters or else one or more letters followed by a space and another series of one or more letters. Therefore, `"10 Broadway"` and `"10 Main Street"` are both valid addresses. As currently formed, the regular expression in line 41 doesn't match an address that does not start with a number, or that has more than two words. The regular expressions for the **City:** (line 47) and **State:** (line 52) `TextBox`es match any word of at least one character or, alternatively, any two words of at least one character if the words are separated by a single space. This means both `Waltham` and `West Newton` would match. Again, these regular expressions would not accept names that have more than two words. The regular expression for the **Zip code:** `TextBox` (line 57) ensures that the zip code is a five-digit number. The regular expression for the **Phone:** `TextBox` (line 62) indicates that the phone number must be of the form `xxx-yyy-yyyy`, where the `x`s represent the area code and the `y`s the number. The first `x` and the first `y` cannot be zero, as specified by the range `[1-9]` in each case.

17.16.4 Regex Methods Replace and Split

Sometimes it is useful to replace parts of one `String` with another or to split a `String` according to a regular expression. For this purpose, class `Regex` provides `Shared` and instance versions of methods `Replace` and `Split`, which are demonstrated in Fig. 17.24.

```
' Fig. 17.24: RegexSubstitution.vb
' Using Regex methods Replace and Split.
Imports System.Text.RegularExpressions ' regular expression classes

Module RegexSubstitution
   Sub Main()
      Dim testString1 As String = _
         "This sentence ends in 5 stars *****"
```

Fig. 17.24 | Using `Regex` method `Replace`. (Part 1 of 2.)

```
      Dim testString2 As String = "1, 2, 3, 4, 5, 6, 7, 8"
      Dim testRegex1 As New Regex("\d")
      Dim output As String = String.Empty

      Console.WriteLine("First test string: " & testString1)

      ' replace every '*' with a '^' and display the result
      testString1 = Regex.Replace(testString1, "\*", "^")
      Console.WriteLine("^ substituted for *: " & testString1)

      ' replace the word "starts" with "carets" and display the result
      testString1 = Regex.Replace(testString1, "stars", "carets")
      Console.WriteLine("""carets"" substituted for ""stars"": " & _
         testString1)

      ' replace every word with "word" and display the result
      Console.WriteLine("Every word replaced by ""word"": " & _
         Regex.Replace(testString1, "\w+", "word"))

      Console.WriteLine(vbNewLine & "Second test string: " & testString2)

      ' replace the first three digits with the word "digit"
      Console.WriteLine("Replace first 3 digits by ""digit"": " & _
         testRegex1.Replace(testString2, "digit", 3))

      Console.Write("string split at commas [")

      ' split the string into individual strings, each containing a digit
      Dim result As String() = Regex.Split(testString2, ",\s")

      ' add each digit to the output string
      For Each resultString In result
         output &= """" & resultString & """, "
      Next

      ' Delete ", " at the end of output string
      Console.WriteLine(output.Substring(0, output.Length - 2) & "]")
   End Sub ' Main
End Module ' RegexSubstitution
```

```
First test string: This sentence ends in 5 stars *****
^ substituted for *: This sentence ends in 5 stars ^^^^^
"carets" substituted for "stars": This sentence ends in 5 carets ^^^^^
Every word replaced by "word": word word word word word word ^^^^^

Second test string: 1, 2, 3, 4, 5, 6, 7, 8
Replace first 3 digits by "digit": digit, digit, digit, 4, 5, 6, 7, 8
string split at commas ["1", "2", "3", "4", "5", "6", "7", "8"]
```

Fig. 17.24 | Using Regex method Replace. (Part 2 of 2.)

Regex method **Replace** replaces text in a String with new text wherever the original String matches a regular expression. We use two versions of this method in Fig. 17.24.

The first version (line 16) is a Shared method and takes three parameters—the String to modify, the String containing the regular expression to match and the replacement String. Here, Replace replaces every instance of "*" in testString1 with "^". Notice that the regular expression ("*") precedes character * with a backslash (\). Normally, * is a quantifier indicating that a regular expression should match any number of occurrences of a preceding pattern. However, in line 16, we want to find all occurrences of the literal character *; to do this, we must escape character * with character \. By escaping a special regular-expression character, we tell the regular-expression matching engine to find the actual character * rather than use it as a quantifier.

The second version of method Replace (line 32) is an instance method that uses the regular expression passed to the constructor for testRegex1 (line 10) to perform the replacement operation. Line 10 instantiates testRegex1 with argument "\d". The call to instance method Replace in line 32 takes three arguments—a String to modify, a String containing the replacement text and an Integer specifying the number of replacements to make. In this case, line 32 replaces the first three instances of a digit ("\d") in testString2 with the text "digit".

Method Split divides a String into several substrings. The original String is broken at delimiters that match a specified regular expression. Method Split returns an array containing the substrings. In line 37, we use Shared method Split to separate a String of comma-separated Integers. The first argument is the String to split; the second argument is the regular expression that represents the delimiter. The regular expression ",\s" separates the substrings at each comma. By matching a whitespace character (\s in the regular expression), we eliminate the extra spaces from the resulting substrings.

17.17 Wrap-Up

This chapter presented the .NET Framework Class Library's string- and character-processing capabilities. We overviewed the fundamentals of characters and strings. You saw how to determine the length of strings, copy strings, access the individual characters in strings, search strings, obtain substrings from larger strings, compare strings, concatenate strings, replace characters in strings and convert strings to uppercase or lowercase letters.

We showed how to use class StringBuilder to build sequences of characters dynamically. You learned how to determine and specify the size of a StringBuilder object, and how to append, insert, remove and replace characters in a StringBuilder object. We then introduced the character-testing methods of type Char that enable a program to determine whether a character is a digit, a letter, a lowercase letter, an uppercase letter, a punctuation mark or a symbol other than a punctuation mark, and the methods for converting a character to uppercase or lowercase.

Finally, we discussed classes Regex, Match and MatchCollection from namespace System.Text.RegularExpressions and the symbols that are used to form regular expressions. You learned how to find patterns in a string and match entire strings to patterns with Regex methods Match and Matches, how to replace characters in a string with Regex method Replace and how to split strings at delimiters with Regex method Split. In the next chapter, you will learn how to read data from and write data to files.

Summary

Section 17.2 Fundamentals of Characters and Strings

- Characters are the fundamental building blocks of Visual Basic source code. Every program is composed of characters that, when grouped together meaningfully, create a sequence that the compiler interprets as instructions describing how to accomplish a task.
- A character literal is a character represented internally as an integer value, called a character code. For example, the integer value `97` corresponds to the character literal `"a"c`. The letter `c` following the closing double quote is Visual Basic's syntax for a character literal.
- Character literals are established according to the Unicode character set.
- A string is a series of characters treated as a single unit. These characters can be uppercase letters, lowercase letters, digits and various special characters: `+`, `-`, `*`, `/`, `$` and others.
- A string is an object of class `String` in the `System` namespace. We write string literals, also called string constants, as sequences of characters in double quotation marks.
- A declaration can assign a `String` literal to a `String` variable.

Section 17.3 `String` Constructors

- Class `String` provides three constructors for initializing `String`s.

Section 17.4 `String` Indexer, `Length` Property and `CopyTo` Method

- The `String` indexer provides access to individual characters in a `String`.
- `String` property `Length` returns the length of the `String`.
- `String` method `CopyTo` copies a specified number of characters from a `String` into a `Char` array. `CopyTo`'s first argument is the index from which the method begins copying characters in the `String`. The second argument is the character array into which the characters are copied. The third argument is the index specifying the starting location at which the method begins placing the copied characters into the character array. The last argument is the number of characters that the method will copy from the `String`.
- The `String` indexer receives an integer argument as the index and returns the character at that index. As with arrays, the first element of a `String` is considered to be at position 0.

Section 17.5 Comparing `String`s

- Computers can order characters alphabetically, because the characters are represented internally as Unicode numeric codes. When comparing two `String`s, the string-comparison methods simply compare the numeric codes of the characters in the `String`s.
- `String` method `Equals` compares two `String`s to determine whether they are equal, and returns `True` if the objects are equal and `False` otherwise. Method `Equals` uses a lexicographical comparison—the integer Unicode values that represent each character in each `String` are compared.
- The equality operator (`=`) can be used to compare two `String`s for equality. This operator also uses a lexicographical comparison to compare two `String`s.
- `String` method `CompareTo` returns `0` if two `String`s are equal, `-1` if the `String` that invokes `CompareTo` is less than the method's argument and `1` if the `String` that invokes `CompareTo` is greater than the method's argument. Method `CompareTo` uses a lexicographical comparison.
- `String` method `StartsWith` determines whether a `String` starts with the `String` passed to it as an argument.
- `String` method `EndsWith` determines whether a `String` ends with the `String` passed to it as an argument.

Section 17.6 Locating Characters and Substrings in `Strings`

- `String` method `IndexOf` locates the first occurrence of a character in a `String`. If it finds the character, `IndexOf` returns the character's index in the `String`; otherwise, `IndexOf` returns `-1`.
- `String` method `LastIndexOf` locates the last occurrence of a character in a `String`. Method `LastIndexOf` searches from the end of the `String` toward the beginning. If it finds the character, `LastIndexOf` returns the character's index in the `String`; otherwise, `LastIndexOf` returns `-1`.
- There are also versions of `IndexOf` and `LastIndexOf` that take `Strings` rather than characters as their first argument.
- `String` methods `IndexOfAny` and `LastIndexOfAny` each take an array of characters as the first argument. These methods return the index of the first occurrence of any of the characters in the character-array argument.

Section 17.7 Extracting Substrings from `Strings`

- Class `String` provides two `Substring` methods that are used to create a new `String` by copying part of an existing `String`. Each method returns a new `String`.
- One `Substring` method takes one `Integer` argument that specifies the starting index from which the method copies characters in the original `String`.
- The second version of method `Substring` takes two `Integer` arguments. The arguments specify the starting index from which to copy characters and the length of the substring to copy.

Section 17.8 Concatenating `Strings`

- Like the `&` operator, the `String` class's `Shared` method `Concat` can be used to concatenate two `Strings`. The method returns a new `String` containing the combined characters from both original `Strings`. The original `Strings` are not modified.

Section 17.9 Miscellaneous `String` *Methods*

- Class `String` provides several methods that return modified copies of `Strings`. None of these methods modifies the original `String`.
- `String` method `Replace` takes two arguments—a `Char` for which to search and another `Char` with which to replace all matching occurrences of the first argument. This method is also overloaded to receive two `String` parameters. If there are no occurrences of the first argument in the `String`, the method returns the original `String`.
- `String` method `ToUpper` returns a new `String` that replaces any lowercase letters in a `String` with their uppercase equivalent. If there are no characters to convert to uppercase, the method returns the original `String`.
- `String` method `ToLower` returns a new `String` in which any uppercase letters in a `String` are replaced by their lowercase equivalents. As with `ToUpper`, if there are no characters to convert to lowercase, method `ToLower` returns the original `String`.
- `String` method `Trim` removes all whitespace characters that appear at the beginning and end of a `String`. The method returns a new `String` that contains the original `String`, but omits leading or trailing whitespace characters.

Section 17.10 Class `StringBuilder`

- A `String`'s contents can never change. Operations that seem to concatenate `Strings` are in fact creating new `Strings`.
- Class `StringBuilder` (namespace `System.Text`) is used to create and manipulate dynamic string information.

- A `StringBuilder` can store the number of characters specified by its capacity. Exceeding the capacity of a `StringBuilder` makes the capacity expand to accommodate the additional characters.
- Class `StringBuilder` provides six overloaded constructors.

Section 17.11 `Length` *and* `Capacity` *Properties,* `EnsureCapacity` *Method and Indexer of Class* `StringBuilder`

- Class `StringBuilder` provides the `Length` and `Capacity` properties to return the number of characters currently in a `StringBuilder` and the number of characters that a `StringBuilder` can store without allocating more memory, respectively. These properties also can increase or decrease the length or the capacity of the `StringBuilder`.
- Method `EnsureCapacity` increases the `StringBuilder` instance's capacity to accommodate at least the number of elements specified as the argument.
- The `StringBuilder` constructor that takes a `String` argument creates a `StringBuilder` object with an initial capacity that is the smallest power of two greater than or equal to the number of characters in the `String` passed as an argument.

Section 17.12 `Append` *and* `AppendFormat` *Methods of Class* `StringBuilder`

- Class `StringBuilder` provides 19 overloaded `Append` methods for appending values of various types to the end of a `StringBuilder`'s contents. There are versions of this method for each of the primitive types and for character arrays, `Strings` and `Objects`.
- `StringBuilder` method `AppendFormat` converts a `String` to a specified format, then appends it to the `StringBuilder`.

Section 17.13 `Insert`*,* `Remove` *and* `Replace` *Methods of Class* `StringBuilder`

- Class `StringBuilder` provides 18 overloaded `Insert` methods to allow values of various types to be inserted at any position in a `StringBuilder`. There are versions of `Insert` for each of the primitive types and for character arrays, `Strings` and `Objects`. Each version takes its second argument, converts it to a `String` and inserts the `String` into the `StringBuilder` at the index specified by the first argument. The index must be greater than or equal to `0` and less than the length of the `StringBuilder`; otherwise, an `ArgumentOutOfRangeException` occurs.
- `StringBuilder` method `Remove` deletes characters in a `StringBuilder`. Method `Remove` takes two arguments—the index at which to begin deletion and the number of characters to delete. The sum of the starting subscript and the number of characters to be deleted must always be less than the `StringBuilder`'s length; otherwise, an `ArgumentOutOfRangeException` occurs.
- `StringBuilder` method `Replace` searches for a specified `String` or character and substitutes another `String` or character in its place.

Section 17.14 `Char` *Methods*

- Visual Basic provides a type called a structure that is similar to a class. Although structures and classes are comparable in many ways, structures represent value types.
- Like classes, structures include methods and properties. Both use the same access modifiers (such as `Public`, `Protected` and `Private`) and access members via the member-access operator (`.`).
- Structures are created using the keyword `Structure`.
- The primitive types are actually aliases for different structures. For instance, an `Integer` is defined by structure `System.Int32`, a `Long` by `System.Int64` and so on.
- Structures derive from class `ValueType`, which in turn derives from class `Object`.
- Most `Char` methods are `Shared`, take at least one character argument and perform either a test or a manipulation on the character.

- Method Convert.ToChar converts a String to a Char.
- Char method IsDigit determines whether a character is a digit.
- Char method IsLetter determines whether a character is a letter.
- Char method IsLetterOrDigit determines whether a character is a letter or a digit.
- Char method IsLower determines whether a character is a lowercase letter.
- Char method IsUpper determines whether a character is an uppercase letter.
- Char method ToUpper converts a character to its uppercase equivalent. The method returns the converted character if the character has an uppercase equivalent; otherwise, the method returns its original argument.
- Char method ToLower converts a character to its lowercase equivalent. The method returns the converted character if the character has a lowercase equivalent; otherwise, the method returns its original argument.
- Char method IsPunctuation determines whether a character is a punctuation mark.
- Char method IsSymbol determines whether a character is a symbol.
- Char method IsWhiteSpace determines whether a character is a whitespace character.

Section 17.16.1 Simple Regular Expressions and Class **Regex**

- The .NET Framework provides several classes to help developers manipulate regular expressions. To use these classes, add an Imports statement for the System.Text.RegularExpressions namespace.
- Class Regex represents a regular expression.
- Regex method Match returns an object of *class* Match that represents a single regular-expression match. Method Match matches the leftmost occurrence of the pattern.
- Class Regex method Matches finds all matches of the regular expression in an arbitrary String and returns an object of the class MatchCollection containing all the matches. The elements in the MatchCollection are Match objects.
- Class Regex provides Shared versions of both methods Match and Matches. The Shared versions take a regular expression as an argument in addition to the String to be searched. This is useful when you want to use a regular expression only once.
- A quantifier is a metacharacter that describes how many times a part of the pattern may occur.
- The ? quantifier matches zero or one occurrences of the pattern to its left.
- The "|" (alternation) metacharacter matches the expression to its left or to its right. Alternation chooses the leftmost match in the string for either of the alternating expressions—the order of the expressions in the alternation doesn't matter.
- Parentheses, (and), are used to group parts of the regular expression, much as you group parts of a mathematical expression.
- A character class represents a group of characters that might appear in a String.
- A word character is any alphanumeric character (a-z, A-Z and 0-9) or underscore.
- A whitespace character is a space, a tab, a carriage return, a newline or a form feed.
- A digit is any numeric character.
- You can match anything that isn't a member of a particular predefined character class using an uppercase letter instead of a lowercase letter. Negating a character class matches everything that isn't a member of the character class.
- The + quantifier matches one or more occurrences of the pattern to its left.

- Quantifiers are greedy—they match the *longest* possible occurrence of the pattern. A quantifier followed by a question mark (?) is lazy—it matches the *shortest* possible occurrence as possible.
- You can create your own character class by listing the members of the character class between square brackets, [and]. You can include a range of characters using the "-" character. You can negate a custom character class by placing a "^" character at the beginning.
- The "." (dot) character matches any character other than a newline (\n).
- The * quantifier matches zero or more occurrences of the pattern to its left. The * quantifier can be used to match an empty String.

Section 17.16.2 Complex Regular Expressions

- When the "-" character in a character class is followed by a character class instead of a literal character, the "-" represents character-class subtraction. The members of the character class following the "-" are removed from the character class preceding the "-". When using character-class subtraction, the class being subtracted must be the last item in the enclosing square brackets.
- Instances of the "-" character outside square brackets are treated as literal characters.

Section 17.16.3 Validating User Input with Regular Expressions

- The Success property of class Match is a Boolean indicating whether the String matched a regular expression.
- In a regular expression that begins with a "^" character and ends with a "$" character, "^" and "$" represent the beginning and end of a String, respectively. These force a regular expression to return a match only if the entire String being processed matches the regular expression.
- The {n} quantifier matches the pattern to its left exactly n times.

Section 17.16.4 **Regex** *Methods* **Replace** *and* **Split**

- Regex method Replace replaces text in a String with new text wherever the original String matches a regular expression. By default, Replace replaces every instance of the pattern found in the String.
- By escaping a special regular-expression character, we tell the regular-expression matching engine to find the actual character rather than use its special meaning.
- Regex method Split divides a String into several substrings. The original String is broken at delimiters that match a specified regular expression. Method Split returns an array containing the substrings.

Terminology

\d (regular expressions)
\w (regular expressions)
\s (regular expressions)
\D (regular expressions)
\W (regular expressions)
\S (regular expressions)
$ (regular expressions)
^ (regular expressions)
+ quantifier
* quantifier
{n} quantifier
|, alternation
& operator
&= concatenation operator
alphabetizing
Append method of class StringBuilder
AppendFormat method of class StringBuilder
ArgumentOutOfRangeException
Capacity property of StringBuilder
Char array
Char structure
character
character class, in regular expressions
character-class subtraction

character constant
character literal
CompareTo method of class String
CompareTo method of structure Char
Concat method of class String
CopyTo method of class String
Enabled property of class Control
EndsWith method of class String
EnsureCapacity method of class StringBuilder
Equals method of class String
Equals method of structure Char
format string
greedy quantifier
immutable String
IndexOf method of class String
IndexOfAny method of class String
Insert method of class StringBuilder
IsDigit method of structure Char
IsLetter method of structure Char
IsLetterOrDigit method of structure Char
IsLower method of structure Char
IsPunctuation method of structure Char
IsSymbol method of structure Char
IsUpper method of structure Char
IsWhiteSpace method of structure Char
LastIndexOf method of class String
LastIndexOfAny method of class String
lazy quantifier
Length property of class String
Length property of class StringBuilder
Let clause of a LINQ query
lexicographical comparison
literal character
Match class
Match method of class Regex
MatchCollection class
Matches method of class Regex
metacharacter
pattern
quantifier in a regular expression
Regex class for regular expressions
regular expression
Remove method of class StringBuilder
Replace method of class Regex
Replace method of class String
Replace method of class StringBuilder
special characters
Split method of class Regex
StartsWith method of class String
String class
string literal
StringBuilder class
Structure keyword
Substring method of class String
Success property of class Match
System.Text namespace
System.Text.RegularExpressions namespace
ToLower method of class String
ToLower method of structure Char
ToString method of StringBuilder
ToUpper method of class String
ToUpper method of structure Char
trailing whitespace characters
Trim method of class String
Unicode character set
ValueType class
whitespace character
word character

Self-Review Exercises

17.1 State whether each of the following is *true* or *false*. If *false*, explain why.

a) When Strings are compared with =, the result is True if the Strings contain the same values.
b) A String can be modified after it is created.
c) StringBuilder method EnsureCapacity sets the StringBuilder instance's length to the argument's value.
d) Method Equals and the equality operator work the same for Strings.
e) Method Trim removes all whitespace at the beginning and the end of a String.
f) A regular expression matches a String to a pattern.
g) It is always better to use Strings rather than StringBuilders, because Strings containing the same value will reference the same object in memory.
h) String method ToUpper capitalizes just the first letter of the String.
i) The expression \d in a regular expression denotes a letter.

17.2 Fill in the blanks in each of the following statements:

a) Operators ______ and ______ can be used to concatenate Strings.
b) Method Equals of class String uses a(n) ______ comparison of Strings.
c) Class Regex is located in namespace ______.
d) StringBuilder method ______ first formats the specified String, then appends it to the end of the StringBuilder's contents.
e) If the arguments to a Substring method call are out of range, an exception of type ______ occurs.
f) Regex method ______ changes all occurrences of a pattern in a String to a specified String.
g) A C in a format string means to output the number as ______.
h) Regular-expression quantifier ______ matches zero or more occurrences of an expression.
i) Regular-expression operator ______ inside square brackets will not match any of the characters in that set of brackets.

17.3 Write statements to accomplish each of the following tasks:

a) Create a regular expression to match either a five-letter word or five-digit number.
b) Create a regular expression to match a phone number in the form of (123) 456-7890.

Answers to Self-Review Exercises

17.1 a) True. b) False. Strings are immutable; they cannot be modified after they are created. However, many methods return new Strings containing modified copies of existing Strings. c) False. EnsureCapacity sets the instance's capacity to at least the value of its argument. d) True. e) True. f) True. g) False. StringBuilder should be used when a program needs to modify a sequence of characters repeatedly. h) False. String method ToUpper capitalizes all letters in the String. i) False. The expression \d in a regular expression denotes a digit.

17.2 a) &, &=. b) lexicographical. c) System.Text.RegularExpressions. d) AppendFormat e) ArgumentOutOfRangeException. f) Replace. g) currency. h) *. i) ^.

17.3 a) `Dim regex As New Regex("\w{5}|\d{5}")`
b) `Dim regex As New Regex("\([1-9]\d{2}\)\s[1-9]\d{2}-\d{4}")`

Exercises

17.4 Modify the program in Fig. 17.17 so that the card-dealing method deals a five-card poker hand. Then write the following additional methods:

a) Determine whether the hand contains a pair.
b) Determine whether the hand contains two pairs.
c) Determine whether the hand contains three of a kind (e.g., three jacks).
d) Determine whether the hand contains four of a kind (e.g., four aces).
e) Determine whether the hand contains a flush (i.e., all five cards of the same suit).
f) Determine whether the hand contains a straight (i.e., five cards of consecutive face values).
g) Determine whether the hand contains a full house (i.e., two cards of one face value and three cards of another face value).

17.5 Write an application that uses String method CompareTo to compare two Strings input by the user. Output whether the first String is less than, equal to or greater than the second.

17.6 Write an application that uses random-number generation to create sentences. Use four arrays of Strings, called article, noun, verb and preposition. Create a sentence by selecting a word at random from each array in the following order: `article`, `noun`, `verb`, `preposition`, `article`, `noun`. As each word is picked, concatenate it to the previous words in the sentence. The words should be separated by spaces. When the sentence is output, it should start with a capital letter and end with a period. The program should generate 10 sentences and output them to a text area.

The arrays should be filled as follows: The `article` array should contain the articles `"the"`, `"a"`, `"one"`, `"some"` and `"any"`; the `noun` array should contain the nouns `"boy"`, `"girl"`, `"dog"`, `"town"` and `"car"`; the `verb` array should contain the past-tense verbs `"drove"`, `"jumped"`, `"ran"`, `"walked"` and `"skipped"`; and the `preposition` array should contain the prepositions `"to"`, `"from"`, `"over"`, `"under"` and `"on"`.

After the preceding program is written, modify the program to produce a short story consisting of several of these sentences. (How about the possibility of a random term-paper writer!)

17.7 *(Pig Latin)* Write a program that encodes English-language phrases into pig Latin. Pig Latin is a form of coded language often used for amusement. Many variations exist in the methods used to form pig Latin phrases. For simplicity, use the following algorithm:

To translate each English word into a pig Latin word, place the first letter of the English word at the end of the word and add the letters "`ay`." Thus, the word "`jump`" becomes "`umpjay`," the word "`the`" becomes "`hetay`" and the word "`computer`" becomes "`omputercay`." Blanks between words remain blanks. Assume the following: The English phrase consists of words separated by blanks, there are no punctuation marks and all words have two or more letters. Have the user input a sentence. Use techniques discussed in this chapter to divide the sentence into separate words. Function `GetPigLatin` should translate a single word into pig Latin.

17.8 Write a program that reads a five-letter word from the user and produces all possible three-letter words that can be derived from the letters of the five-letter word. For example, the three-letter words produced from the word "bathe" include the commonly used words "ate," "bat," "bet," "tab," "hat," "the" and "tea."

17.9 Write a program that uses regular expressions to convert the first letter of all words to uppercase. Have it do this for an arbitrary string input by the user.

17.10 Use a regular expression to count the number of digits, characters and whitespace characters in a string. [*Hint:* `Regex` function `Matches` returns an `IEnumerable`, which has a `Count` property.]

17.11 Write a regular expression that will search a string and match a valid number. A number can have any number of digits, but it can have only digits and a decimal point. The decimal point is optional, but if it appears in the number, there must be only one, and it must have digits on its left and its right. There should be whitespace or a beginning- or end-of-line character on either side of a valid number. Negative numbers are preceded by a minus sign.

17.12 Write a program that asks the user to enter a sentence and uses a regular expression to check whether the sentence contains more than one space between words. If so, the program should remove the extra spaces. For example, `"Hello    World"` should be `"Hello World"`.

18

Files and Streams

Consciousness … does not appear to itself chopped up in bits. … A "river" or a "stream" are the metaphors by which it is most naturally described.

—William James

I read part of it all the way through.

—Samuel Goldwyn

I can only assume that a "Do Not File" document is filed in a "Do Not File" file.

—Senator Frank Church, Senate Intelligence Subcommittee Hearing, 1975

OBJECTIVES

In this chapter you'll learn:

- To create, read, write and update files.
- The .NET framework streams class hierarchy.
- To use classes `File` and `Directory` to obtain information about files and directories on your computer.
- To become familiar with sequential-access file processing.
- To use classes `FileStream`, `StreamReader` and `StreamWriter` to read text from and write text to files.
- To use classes `FileStream` and `BinaryFormatter` to read objects from and write objects to files.

Outline

18.1 Introduction

Variables and arrays offer only temporary storage of data—the data is lost when a local variable "goes out of scope" or when the program terminates. By contrast, files (and databases, which we cover in Chapter 20, Databases and LINQ to SQL) are used for long-term retention of large amounts of data, even after the program that created the data terminates. Data maintained in files is often called persistent data. Computers store files on secondary storage devices, such as magnetic disks, optical disks and magnetic tapes. In this chapter, we explain how to create, update and process data files.

We begin with an overview of the data hierarchy from bits to files. Next, we overview some of the .NET Framework Class Library's file-processing classes. We then present two examples that show how you can determine information about the files and directories on your computer. The remainder of the chapter shows how to write to and read from text files that are human readable and binary files that store entire objects in binary format.

18.2 Data Hierarchy

Ultimately, all data items that computers process are reduced to combinations of `0`s and `1`s. This occurs because it is simple and economical to build electronic devices that can assume two stable states—one state represents `0` and the other represents `1`. It is remarkable that the impressive functions performed by computers involve only the most fundamental manipulations of `0`s and `1`s!

The smallest data item that computers support is called a bit (short for "binary digit"—a digit that can assume one of two values). Each data item, or bit, can assume either the value `0` or the value `1`. Computer circuitry performs various simple bit manipulations, such as examining the value of a bit, setting the value of a bit and reversing a bit (from `1` to `0` or from `0` to `1`).

Programming with data in the low-level form of bits is cumbersome. It is preferable to program with data in forms such as decimal digits (i.e., `0`, `1`, `2`, `3`, `4`, `5`, `6`, `7`, `8` and `9`), letters (i.e., the uppercase letters `A`–`Z` and the lowercase letters `a`–`z`) and special symbols (i.e., `$`, `@`, `%`, `&`, `*`, `(`, `)`, `-`, `+`, `"`, `:`, `?`, `/` and many others). Digits, letters and special symbols are referred to as characters. The set of all characters used to write programs and represent data items on a particular computer is called that computer's character set. Because computers can process only 0s and 1s, every character in a computer's character set is represented as a pattern of 0s and 1s. Bytes are composed of eight bits. Visual Basic uses the Unicode character set (www.unicode.org), in which each character is composed of two bytes. Programmers create programs and data items with characters; computers manipulate and process these characters as patterns of bits.

Just as characters are composed of bits, fields are composed of characters. A field is a group of characters that conveys meaning. For example, a field consisting of uppercase and lowercase letters can represent a person's name.

Data items processed by computers form a data hierarchy (Fig. 18.1), in which data items become larger and more complex in structure as we progress up the hierarchy from bits to characters to fields to larger data aggregates.

Typically, a record (which can be represented as a `Class`) is composed of several related fields. In a payroll system, for example, a record for a particular employee might include the following fields:

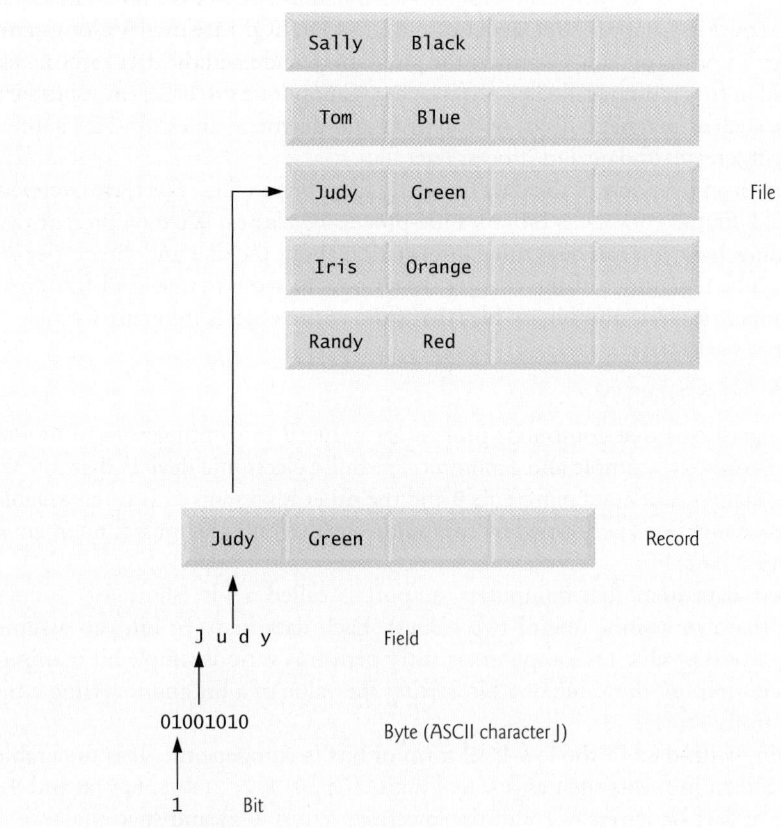

Fig. 18.1 | Data hierarchy.

1. Employee identification number
2. Name
3. Address
4. Hourly pay rate
5. Number of exemptions claimed
6. Year-to-date earnings
7. Amount of taxes withheld

In the preceding example, each field is associated with the same employee. A data file is a group of related records.[1] A company's payroll file normally contains one record for each employee. A payroll file for a small company might contain only 22 records, whereas one for a large company might contain 100,000 records. Companies typically have many files, some containing millions, billions or even trillions of characters of information.

To facilitate the retrieval of specific records from a file, at least one field in each record is chosen as a record key, which identifies a record as belonging to a particular person or entity and distinguishes that record from all others. For example, in a payroll record, the employee identification number normally would be the record key.

There are many ways to organize records in a file. A common organization is called a sequential file, in which records typically are stored in order by a record-key field. In a payroll file, records usually are placed in order by employee identification number. The first employee record in the file contains the lowest employee identification number, and subsequent records contain increasingly higher ones.

Most businesses use many different files to store data. For example, a company might have payroll files, accounts-receivable files (listing money due from clients), accounts-payable files (listing money due to suppliers), inventory files (listing facts about all the items handled by the business) and many other files. Related files often are stored in a database. A collection of programs designed to create and manage databases is called a database management system (DBMS). We discuss databases in Chapter 20.

18.3 Files and Streams

Visual Basic views a file as a sequential stream of bytes (Fig. 18.2). Depending on the operating system, each file ends either with an end-of-file marker or at a specific byte number that is recorded in a system-maintained administrative data structure. For example, the Windows operating system keeps track of the number of bytes in a file. When you open a

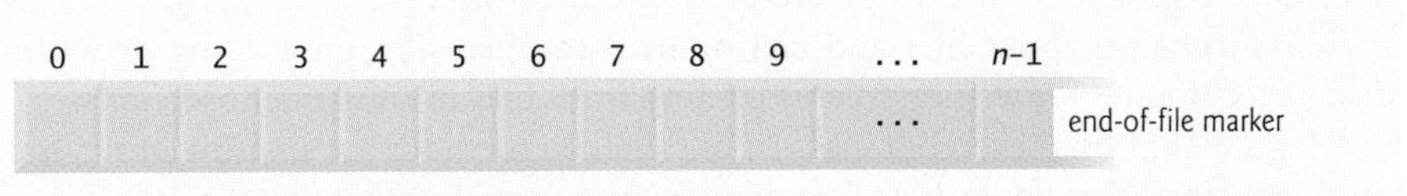

Fig. 18.2 | Visual Basic's view of an n-byte file.

1. Generally, a file can contain arbitrary data in arbitrary formats. In some operating systems, a file is viewed as nothing more than a collection of bytes, and any organization of the bytes in a file (such as organizing the data into records) is a view created by the application programmer.

file from a Visual Basic program, an object is created and a stream is associated with the object. When a program executes, the runtime environment creates three stream objects that are accessible via properties Console.Out, Console.In and Console.Error, respectively. These objects facilitate communication between a program and a particular file or device. Console.In refers to the standard input-stream object, which enables a program to input data from the keyboard. Console.Out refers to the standard output-stream object, which enables a program to output data to the screen. Console.Error refers to the standard error-stream object, which enables a program to output error messages to the screen. We have been using Console.Out and Console.In in our console applications—Console methods Write and WriteLine use Console.Out to perform output, and Console methods Read and ReadLine use Console.In to perform input.

There are many file-processing classes in the .NET framework. The System.IO namespace includes stream classes such as StreamReader (for text input), StreamWriter (for text output) and FileStream (for both input from and output to a file). These stream classes inherit from the MustInherit classes TextReader, TextWriter and Stream, respectively. Actually, properties Console.In and Console.Out are of type TextReader and TextWriter, respectively. The system creates objects of TextReader and TextWriter classes to initialize Console properties Console.In and Console.Out.

MustInherit class Stream provides functionality for representing streams that are made of bytes. Classes FileStream, MemoryStream and BufferedStream (all in namespace System.IO) inherit from class Stream. Class FileStream can be used to write data to and read data from files. Class MemoryStream enables the transfer of data directly to and from memory—this is much faster than reading from and writing to external devices. Class BufferedStream uses buffering to transfer data to or from a stream. Buffering is an I/O performance-enhancement technique, in which each output operation is directed to a region in memory, called a buffer, that is large enough to hold the data from many output operations. Then actual transfer to the output device is performed more efficiently in one large physical output operation each time the buffer fills. The output operations directed to the output buffer in memory are often called logical output operations. Buffering can also be used to speed input operations by initially reading more data than is required into a buffer, so that subsequent reads get data from memory rather than an external device. In this chapter, we use key stream classes to implement file-processing programs that create and manipulate sequential-access files.

18.4 Classes File and Directory

Information is stored in files, which are organized in directories. Classes File and Directory enable programs to manipulate files and directories on disk. Class File can determine information about files and can be used to open files for reading or writing. We discuss techniques for writing to and reading from files in subsequent sections.

Figure 18.3 lists several of class File's Shared methods for manipulating and determining information about files. We demonstrate several of these methods in Fig. 18.5.

Class Directory provides capabilities for manipulating directories. Figure 18.4 lists some of class Directory's Shared methods for directory manipulation. Figure 18.5 demonstrates several of these methods, as well. The DirectoryInfo object returned by method CreateDirectory contains information about a directory. Much of the information contained in class DirectoryInfo also can be accessed via the methods of class Directory.

File class Shared methods and descriptions	
AppendText	Returns a StreamWriter that appends text to an existing file or creates a file if one does not exist.
Copy	Copies a file to a new file.
Create	Creates a file and returns its associated FileStream.
CreateText	Creates a text file and returns its associated StreamWriter.
Delete	Deletes the specified file.
Exists	Returns True if the specified file exists and False otherwise.
GetCreationTime	Returns a DateTime object representing when the file was created.
GetLastAccessTime	Returns a DateTime object representing when the file was last accessed.
GetLastWriteTime	Returns a DateTime object representing when the file was last modified.
Move	Moves the specified file to a specified location.
Open	Returns a FileStream associated with the specified file and equipped with the specified read/write permissions.
OpenRead	Returns a read-only FileStream associated with the specified file.
OpenText	Returns a StreamReader associated with the specified file.
OpenWrite	Returns a read/write FileStream associated with the specified file.

Fig. 18.3 | File class Shared methods (partial list).

Directory class Shared methods and descriptions	
CreateDirectory	Creates a directory and returns its associated DirectoryInfo object.
Delete	Deletes the specified directory.
Exists	Returns True if the specified directory exists and False otherwise.
GetDirectories	Returns a String array containing the names of the subdirectories in the specified directory.
GetFiles	Returns a String array containing the names of the files in the specified directory.
GetCreationTime	Returns a DateTime object representing when the directory was created.
GetLastAccessTime	Returns a DateTime object representing when the directory was last accessed.
GetLastWriteTime	Returns a DateTime object representing when items were last written to the directory.
Move	Moves the specified directory to a specified location.

Fig. 18.4 | Directory class Shared methods (partial list).

Demonstrating Classes `File` and `Directory`

Class `FileTestForm` (Fig. 18.5) uses `File` and `Directory` methods to access file and directory information. This `Form` contains the control `inputTextBox`, in which the user enters a file or directory name. For each key that the user presses while typing in the `TextBox`, the program calls event handler `inputTextBox_KeyDown` (lines 8–56). If the user presses the *Enter* key (line 11), this method displays either the file's or the directory's contents, depending on the text the user input. (If the user does not press the *Enter* key, this method returns without displaying any content.) Line 18 uses `File` method `Exists` to determine whether the user-specified text is the name of an existing file. If so, line 20 invokes `Private` method `GetInformation` (lines 59–78), which calls `File` methods `GetCreationTime` (line 67), `GetLastWriteTime` (line 71) and `GetLastAccessTime` (line 75) to access file information. When method `GetInformation` returns, line 25 instantiates a `StreamReader` for reading text from the file. The `StreamReader` constructor takes as an argument a `String` containing the name of the file to open. Line 26 calls `StreamReader` method `ReadToEnd` to read the file's entire contents as a `String`, then appends the `String` to `outputTextBox`. Lines 27 calls `StreamReader` method `Close` to close the file stream and line 28 calls `StreamReader` method `Dispose` to release the file resources back to the system.

If line 18 determines that the user-specified text is not a file, line 34 determines whether it is a directory, using `Directory` method `Exists`. If the user specified an existing directory, line 38 invokes method `GetInformation` to access the directory information. Line 41 calls `Directory` method `GetDirectories` to obtain a `String` array containing the names of subdirectories in the specified directory. Lines 47–49 display each element in the `String` array. If line 34 determines that the user-specified text is not a directory name, lines 52–53 notify the user (via a `MessageBox`) that the name the user entered does not exist as a file or directory.

```
1  ' Fig 18.5: FileTestForm.vb
2  ' Testing classes File and Directory.
3  Imports System.IO
4
5  ' displays contents of files and directories
6  Public Class FileTestForm
7     ' invoked when user presses key
8     Private Sub inputTextBox_KeyDown(ByVal sender As System.Object, _
9        ByVal e As KeyEventArgs) Handles inputTextBox.KeyDown
10       ' determine whether user pressed Enter key
11       If e.KeyCode = Keys.Enter Then
12          Dim fileName As String ' name of file or directory
13
14          ' get user-specified file or directory
15          fileName = inputTextBox.Text
16
17          ' determine whether fileName is a file
18          If File.Exists(fileName) Then
19             ' get file's creation date, modification date, etc.
20             outputTextBox.Text = GetInformation(fileName)
21
```

Fig. 18.5 | Testing classes `File` and `Directory`. (Part 1 of 3.)

```
            ' display file contents through StreamReader
            Try
               ' obtain reader and file contents
               Dim stream As New StreamReader(fileName)
               outputTextBox.Text &= stream.ReadToEnd()
               stream.Close() ' close file
               stream.Dispose() ' release file resources back to system
            Catch ex As IOException
               MessageBox.Show("Error reading from file", "File Error", _
                  MessageBoxButtons.OK, MessageBoxIcon.Error)
            End Try
         ' determine whether fileName is a directory
         ElseIf Directory.Exists(fileName) Then
            Dim directoryList() As String ' array for directories

            ' get directory's creation date, modification date, etc.
            outputTextBox.Text = GetInformation(fileName)

            ' obtain directory list of specified directory
            directoryList = Directory.GetDirectories(fileName)

            outputTextBox.Text &= vbNewLine & vbNewLine & _
               "Directory contents:" & vbNewLine

            ' output directoryList contents
            For Each directoryName In directoryList
               outputTextBox.Text &= directoryName & vbNewLine
            Next
         Else
            ' notify user that neither file nor directory exists
            MessageBox.Show(inputTextBox.Text & " does not exist", _
               "File Error", MessageBoxButtons.OK, MessageBoxIcon.Error)
         End If
      End If
   End Sub ' inputTextBox_KeyDown

   ' get information on file or directory
   Private Function GetInformation(ByVal fileName As String) As String
      Dim information As String

      ' output that file or directory exists
      information = fileName & " exists" & vbNewLine & vbNewLine

      ' output when file or directory was created
      information &= "Created: " & _
         File.GetCreationTime(fileName) & vbNewLine

      ' output when file or directory was last modified
      information &= "Last modified: " & _
         File.GetLastWriteTime(fileName) & vbNewLine

```

Fig. 18.5 | Testing classes File and Directory. (Part 2 of 3.)

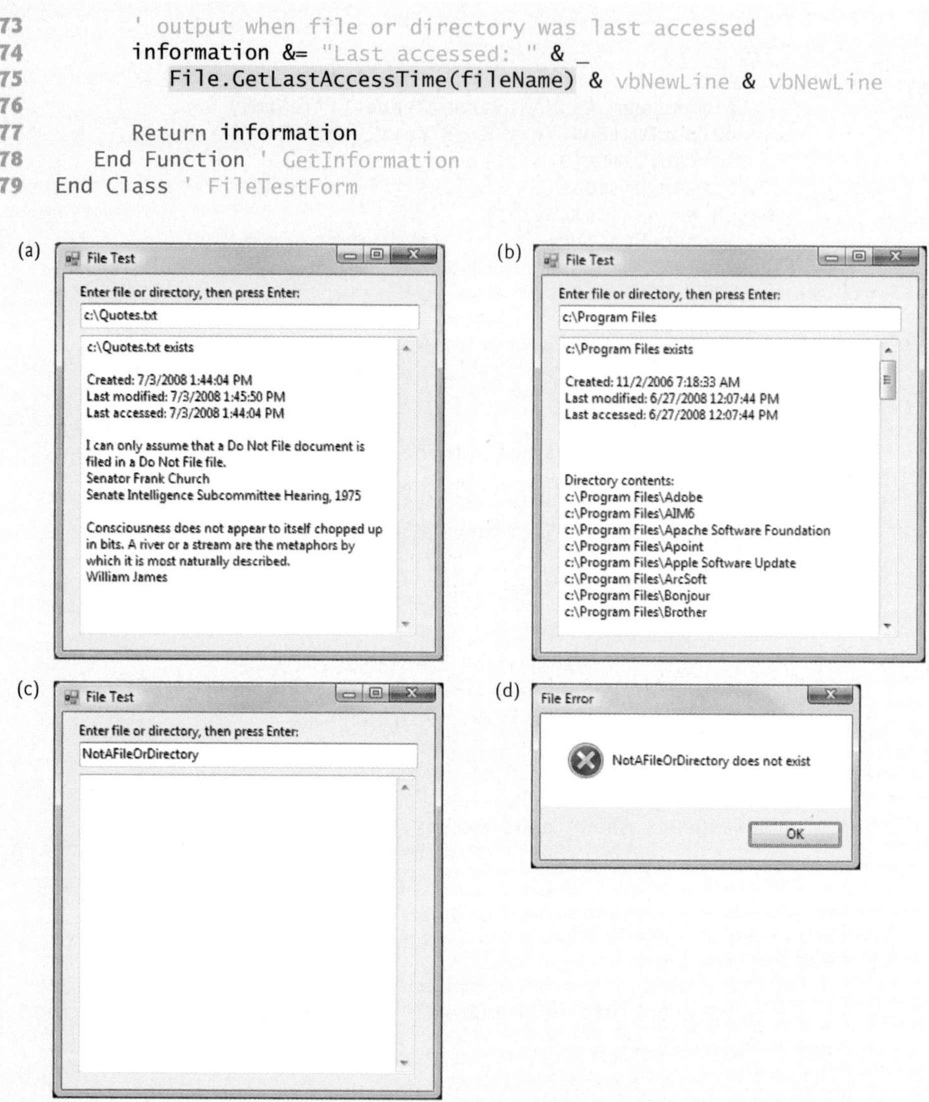

```
            ' output when file or directory was last accessed
            information &= "Last accessed: " & _
               File.GetLastAccessTime(fileName) & vbNewLine & vbNewLine

            Return information
         End Function ' GetInformation
      End Class ' FileTestForm
```


Fig. 18.5 | Testing classes `File` and `Directory`. (Part 3 of 3.)

Finding Directories with LINQ

We now consider another example that uses the .NET framework's file- and directory-manipulation capabilities. Class `LINQToFileDirectoryForm` (Fig. 18.6) uses classes `File` and `Directory`, and LINQ, to report the number of files of each file type that exist in the specified directory path. The program also serves as a "clean-up" utility—when a file that has the `.bak` file-name extension (i.e., a backup file) is encountered, the program displays a `MessageBox` asking the user whether that file should be removed, then responds appropriately to the user's input. This example also uses LINQ to Objects to help summarize the files and types in the specified directory and to help delete the backup files.

```
' Fig 18.6: LINQToFileDirectoryForm.vb
' Using LINQ to determine file types.
Imports System.IO

Public Class SearchDirectoryForm
   Private currentDirectory As String ' directory to search
   Private directoryList() As String ' subdirectories
   Private fileArray() As String ' file names

   ' store extensions found and number found
   Dim found As New Dictionary(Of String, Integer)

   ' handles the Search Directory Button's Click event
   Private Sub searchButton_Click(ByVal sender As System.Object, _
      ByVal e As System.EventArgs) Handles searchButton.Click

      ' check if user specified path exists
      If pathTextBox.Text <> String.Empty AndAlso _
         Not (Directory.Exists(pathTextBox.Text)) Then

         ' show error if user does not specify valid directory
         MessageBox.Show("Invalid Directory", "Error", _
            MessageBoxButtons.OK, MessageBoxIcon.Error)
      Else
         ' use current directory if no directory is specified
         If pathTextBox.Text = String.Empty Then
            currentDirectory = Directory.GetCurrentDirectory()
         Else
            currentDirectory = pathTextBox.Text ' use specified directory
         End If

         directoryTextBox.Text = currentDirectory ' display the directory

         ' clear text boxes
         pathTextBox.Clear()
         resultsTextBox.Clear()

         SearchDirectory(currentDirectory) ' search directory

         ' allow user to delete .bak files
         CleanDirectory(currentDirectory)

         ' summarize and print results
         For Each current In found.Keys
            resultsTextBox.Text &= "* Found " & found(current) & _
               " " & current & " files." & vbNewLine
         Next current

         found.Clear() ' clear output for new search
      End If
   End Sub ' searchButton_Click

```

Fig. 18.6 | Using LINQ to determine file types. (Part 1 of 3.)

```
   ' search directory using LINQ
   Private Sub SearchDirectory(ByVal folder As String)
      ' files contained in the directory
      Dim files As String() = Directory.GetFiles(folder)

      ' subdirectories in the directory
      Dim directories As String() = Directory.GetDirectories(folder)

      ' find all file extensions in this directory
      Dim extensions = _
         From file In files _
         Select Path.GetExtension(file) Distinct

      ' count the number of files using each extension
      For Each extension In extensions
         Dim temporaryExtension = extension

         ' count the number of files with the extension
         Dim extensionCount = _
            (From file In files _
            Where Path.GetExtension(file) = temporaryExtension _
            Select file).Count

         ' if the Dictionary already contains a key for the extension
         If found.ContainsKey(extension) Then
            found(extension) += extensionCount ' update the count
         Else
            found.Add(extension, extensionCount) ' add the new count
         End If
      Next

      ' recursive call to search subdirectories
      For Each subdirectory In directories
         SearchDirectory(subdirectory)
      Next
   End Sub ' SearchDirectory

   ' allow user to delete backup files (.bak)
   Private Sub CleanDirectory(ByVal folder As String)
      ' files contained in the directory
      Dim files As String() = Directory.GetFiles(folder)

      ' subdirectories in the directory
      Dim directories As String() = Directory.GetDirectories(folder)

      ' select all the backup files in this directory
      Dim backupFiles = _
         From file In files _
         Where Path.GetExtension(file) = ".bak" _
         Select file

```

Fig. 18.6 | Using LINQ to determine file types. (Part 2 of 3.)

```
104          ' iterate over all the backup files (.bak)
105          For Each backup In backupFiles
106             ' prompt user to delete (.bak) file
107             Dim result As DialogResult = MessageBox.Show( _
108                "Found backup file " & Path.GetFileName(backup) _
109                & ". Delete?", "Delete Backup", MessageBoxButtons.YesNo, _
110                MessageBoxIcon.Question)
111
112             ' delete file if user clicked 'yes'
113             If result = Windows.Forms.DialogResult.Yes Then
114                File.Delete(backup)
115                found(".bak") -= 1
116
117                ' if there are no backup files, delete key from Dictionary
118                If found(".bak") = 0 Then
119                   found.Remove(".bak")
120                End If
121             End If
122          Next
123
124          ' recursive call to clean subdirectories
125          For Each subdirectory In directories
126             CleanDirectory(subdirectory)
127          Next
128       End Sub ' CleanDirectory
129    End Class ' LINQToFileDirectoryForm
```

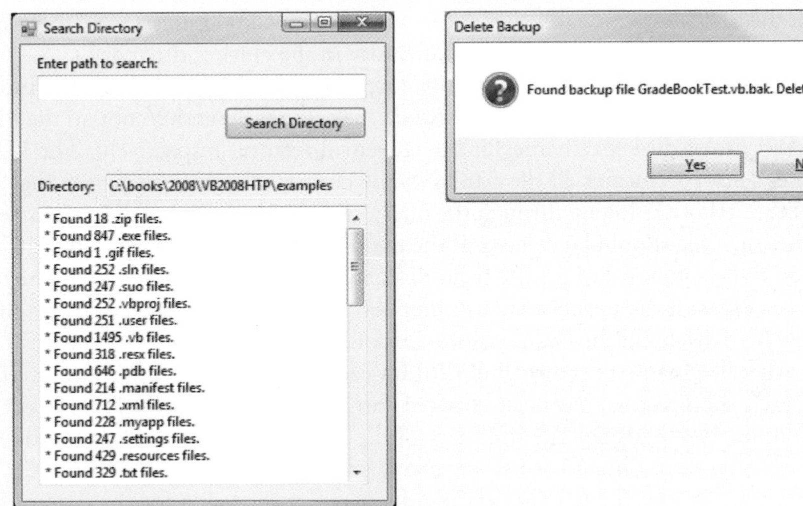

Fig. 18.6 | Using LINQ to determine file types. (Part 3 of 3.)

When the user clicks the **Search Directory** button, the program invokes method `searchButton_Click` (lines 14–51), which searches recursively through the directory path specified by the user. If the user inputs text in the `TextBox`, line 19 calls `Directory` method `Exists` to determine whether that text is a valid directory. If not, lines 22–23 notify the user of the error.

Lines 26–30 get the current directory (if the user did not specify a path) or the specified directory. Line 38 passes the directory name to recursive method `SearchDirectory` (lines 54–88). Line 56 calls `Directory` method **`GetFiles`** to get a `String` array containing file names in the specified directory. Line 59 calls `Directory` method `GetDirectories` to get a `String` array containing the subdirectory names in the specified directory.

Lines 62–64 use LINQ to get the `Distinct` file-name extensions in the `files` array. **`Path`** method **`GetExtension`** obtains the extension for the specified file name. For each file-name extension returned by the LINQ query, lines 67–82 determine the number of occurrences of that extension in the `files` array. The LINQ query at lines 72–74 compares each file-name extension in the `files` array with the current extension being processed (line 73). All matches are included in the result. We then use LINQ method `Count` to determine the total number of files that matched the current extension.

Class `SearchDirectoryForm` uses a `Dictionary` (declared in line 11) to store each file-name extension and the corresponding number of file names with that extension. A **`Dictionary`** (namespace `System.Collections.Generic`) is a collection of key/value pairs, in which each key has a corresponding value. Class `Dictionary` is a generic class like class `List` (presented in Section 9.3). Line 11 indicates that the `Dictionary found` contains pairs of `Strings` and `Integers`, which represent the file-name extensions and the number of files with those extensions, respectively. Line 77 uses `Dictionary` method **`ContainsKey`** to determine whether the specified file-name extension has been placed in the `Dictionary` previously. If this method returns `True`, line 78 adds the `extensionCount` determined in lines 71–74 to the current total for that extension that is stored in the `Dictionary`. Otherwise, line 80 uses `Dictionary` method **`Add`** to insert a new key/value pair into the `Dictionary` for the new file-name extension and its `extensionCount`. Lines 85–87 recursively call `SearchDirectory` (line 86) for each subdirectory in the current directory.

When method `SearchDirectory` returns, line 41 calls `CleanDirectory` (defined at lines 91–128) to search for all files with extension `.bak`. Lines 93 and 96 obtain the list of file names and list of directory names in the current directory, respectively. The LINQ query in lines 100–102 locates all file names in the current directory that have the `.bak` extension. Lines 105–122 iterate through the query's results and prompt the user to determine whether each file should be deleted. If the user clicks **Yes** in the dialog, line 114 uses `File` method **`Delete`** to remove the file from disk, and line 115 subtracts 1 from the total number of `.bak` files. If the number of `.bak` files remaining is `0`, line 119 uses `Dictionary` method **`Remove`** to delete the key/value pair for `.bak` files from the `Dictionary`. Lines 125–127 recursively call `CleanDirectory` (line 126) for each subdirectory in the current directory. After each subdirectory has been checked for `.bak` files, method `CleanDirectory` returns, and lines 44–47 display the summary of file-name extensions and the number of files with each extension. Line 44 uses `Dictionary` property **`Keys`** to get all the keys in the `Dictionary`. Line 46 uses the `Dictionary`'s indexer to get the value for the current key. Finally, line 49 uses `Dictionary` method **`Clear`** to delete the contents of the `Dictionary`.

18.5 Creating a Sequential-Access Text File

Visual Basic imposes no structure on files. Thus, the concept of a "record" does not exist in Visual Basic files. This means that you must structure files to meet the requirements of your applications. In the next few examples, we use text and special characters to organize our own concept of a "record."

Class **BankUIForm**

The next several examples demonstrate file processing in a bank-account maintenance application. These programs have similar user interfaces, so we used the Visual Studio `Form` designer to create reusable base class `BankUIForm` (Fig. 18.7), which encapsulates the common GUI components (see the screen capture in Fig. 18.7). Class `BankUIForm` contains four `Label`s and four `TextBox`es. Method `ClearTextBoxes` (lines 18–27) clears the `TextBox`es' contents. Method `SetTextBoxValues` (lines 30–45) sets the text in the `TextBox`es. Method `GetTextBoxValues` (lines 48–58) gets the values from the `TextBox`es.

```
1  ' Fig. 18.7: BankUIForm.vb
2  ' Base class for GUIs in our file-processing applications.
3  Imports System.Windows.Forms
4
5  Public Class BankUIForm
6     ' number of TextBoxes on Form
7     Protected TextBoxCount As Integer = 4
8
9     ' enumeration constants specify TextBox indices
10    Public Enum TextBoxIndices
11       ACCOUNT
12       FIRST
13       LAST
14       BALANCE
15    End Enum ' TextBoxIndices
16
17    ' clear all TextBoxes
18    Public Sub ClearTextBoxes()
19       ' iterate through every Control on form
20       For Each guiControl In Controls
21          ' determine whether Control is TextBox
22          If TypeOf guiControl Is TextBox Then
23             ' clear Text property (set to empty string)
24             CType(guiControl, TextBox).Text = String.Empty
25          End If
26       Next
27    End Sub ' ClearTextBoxes
28
29    ' set text box values to string array values
30    Public Sub SetTextBoxValues(ByVal values() As String)
31       ' determine whether string array has correct length
32       If values.Length <> TextBoxCount Then
33          ' throw exception if not correct length
34          Throw New ArgumentException( _
35             "There must be " & (TextBoxCount) & _
36             " strings in the array")
37       ' set array values if array has correct length
38       Else
39          ' set array values to text box values
40          accountTextBox.Text = values(TextBoxIndices.ACCOUNT)
41          firstNameTextBox.Text = values(TextBoxIndices.FIRST)
42          lastNameTextBox.Text = values(TextBoxIndices.LAST)
```

Fig. 18.7 | Base class for GUIs in our file-processing applications. (Part 1 of 2.)

```
            balanceTextBox.Text = values(TextBoxIndices.BALANCE)
         End If
      End Sub ' SetTextBoxValues

      ' return text box values as string array
      Public Function GetTextBoxValues() As String()
         Dim values(TextBoxCount) As String

         ' copy text box fields to string array
         values(TextBoxIndices.ACCOUNT) = accountTextBox.Text
         values(TextBoxIndices.FIRST) = firstNameTextBox.Text
         values(TextBoxIndices.LAST) = lastNameTextBox.Text
         values(TextBoxIndices.BALANCE) = balanceTextBox.Text

         Return values
      End Function ' GetTextBoxValues
   End Class ' BankUIForm
```

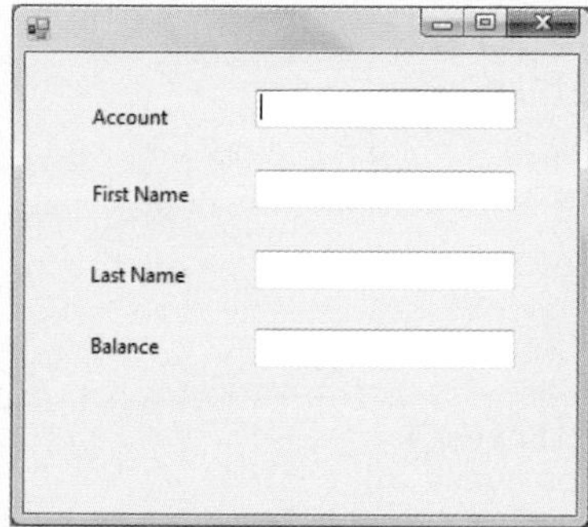

Fig. 18.7 | Base class for GUIs in our file-processing applications. (Part 2 of 2.)

To reuse class `BankUIForm`, you must compile the GUI into a DLL (we called it `BankLibrary`) as described in Section 14.24. We provide the `BankLibrary` with the examples for this chapter. When you copy these examples to your system, you might need to delete the reference to `BankLibrary` and add it again, since the library most likely will reside in a different location on your system.

Class `Record`

Figure 18.8 contains class `Record`, which Figs. 18.9, 18,11 and 18.12 use to maintain the data in each record that is written to or read from a file. This class also belongs to the `BankLibrary` DLL, so it is located in the same project as class `BankUIForm`.

Class `Record` contains `Private` instance variables `accountValue`, `firstNameValue`, `lastNameValue` and `balanceValue` (lines 4–7), which collectively represent all the information for a record. The parameterless constructor (lines 10–12) sets these members by calling the four-argument constructor with `0` for the account number, empty strings for the first and last names and `0D` for the balance. The four-argument constructor (lines 15–23) sets these members to the arguments. Class `Record` also provides properties `Account` (lines 26–33), `FirstName` (lines 36–43), `LastName` (lines 46–53) and `Balance` (lines 56–63) to access each record's account number, first name, last name and balance, respectively.

```
' Fig. 18.8: Record.vb
' Class that represents a data record.
Public Class Record
   Private accountValue As Integer
   Private firstNameValue As String
   Private lastNameValue As String
   Private balanceValue As Decimal

   ' parameterless constructor sets members to default values
   Public Sub New()
      MyClass.New(0, String.Empty, String.Empty, 0D)
   End Sub ' New

   ' overloaded constructor sets members to parameter values
   Public Sub New(ByVal newAccount As Integer, _
      ByVal newFirstName As String, ByVal newLastName As String, _
      ByVal newBalance As Decimal)

      Account = newAccount
      FirstName = newFirstName
      LastName = newLastName
      Balance = newBalance
   End Sub ' New

   ' property that gets and sets Account
   Public Property Account() As Integer
      Get
         Return accountValue
      End Get
      Set(ByVal value As Integer)
         accountValue = value
      End Set
   End Property ' Account

   ' property that gets and sets FirstName
   Public Property FirstName() As String
      Get
         Return firstNameValue
      End Get
      Set(ByVal value As String)
         firstNameValue = value
      End Set
   End Property ' FirstName

   ' property that gets and sets LastName
   Public Property LastName() As String
      Get
         Return lastNameValue
      End Get
      Set(ByVal value As String)
         lastNameValue = value
      End Set
   End Property ' LastName
```

Fig. 18.8 | Class that represents a data record. (Part 1 of 2.)

```

   ' property that gets and sets Balance
   Public Property Balance() As Decimal
      Get
         Return balanceValue
      End Get
      Set(ByVal value As Decimal)
         balanceValue = value
      End Set
   End Property ' Balance
End Class ' Record
```

Fig. 18.8 | Class that represents a data record. (Part 2 of 2.)

Using a Character Stream to Create an Output File

Class `CreateFileForm` (Fig. 18.9) uses instances of class `Record` to create a sequential-access file that might be used in an accounts-receivable system—a program that organizes data regarding money owed by a company's credit clients. For each client, the program obtains an account number and the client's first name, last name and balance (i.e., the amount of money that the client owes to the company for previously received goods and services). The data obtained for each client constitutes a record for that client. In this application, the account number is used as the record key—files are created and maintained in account-number order. This program assumes that the user enters records in account-number order. However, a comprehensive accounts-receivable system would provide a sorting capability so that the user could enter the records in any order.

```
' Fig. 18.9: CreateFileForm.vb
' Creating and writing to a sequential-access file.
Imports System.IO
Imports BankLibrary ' imports classes from Figs. 18.7 and 18.8

Public Class CreateFileForm
   Private fileWriter As StreamWriter ' writes data to text file
   Private output As FileStream ' maintains connection to file

   ' event handler for Save Button
   Private Sub saveButton_Click(ByVal sender As System.Object, _
      ByVal e As System.EventArgs) Handles saveButton.Click

      Dim result As DialogResult ' stores result of Save dialog
      Dim fileName As String ' name of file to save data

      ' display dialog so user can choose name of file to save
      Using fileChooser As New SaveFileDialog()
         result = fileChooser.ShowDialog()
         fileName = fileChooser.FileName ' get specified file name
      End Using ' automatic call to fileChooser.Dispose() occurs here

```

Fig. 18.9 | Creating and writing to a sequential-access file. (Part 1 of 5.)

```
         ' if user did not click Cancel
         If result <> Windows.Forms.DialogResult.Cancel Then
            ' save file via FileStream if user specified file
            Try
               ' open file with write access
               output = New FileStream( _
                  fileName, FileMode.OpenOrCreate, FileAccess.Write)

               ' sets file to where data is written
               fileWriter = New StreamWriter(output)

               ' disable Save button and enable Enter button
               saveButton.Enabled = False
               enterButton.Enabled = True
            ' handle exception if there is a problem opening the file
            Catch ex As IOException
               ' notify user if file does not exist
               MessageBox.Show("Error Opening File", "Error", _
                  MessageBoxButtons.OK, MessageBoxIcon.Error)
            End Try
         End If
      End Sub ' saveButton_Click

      ' event handler for Enter Button
      Private Sub enterButton_Click(ByVal sender As System.Object, _
         ByVal e As System.EventArgs) Handles enterButton.Click
         ' store TextBox values string array
         Dim values As String() = GetTextBoxValues()

         ' Record containing TextBox values to serialize
         Dim record As New Record()

         ' determine whether TextBox account field is empty
         If values(TextBoxIndices.ACCOUNT) <> String.Empty Then
            ' store TextBox values in Record and serialize Record
            Try
               ' get account number value from TextBox
               Dim accountNumber As Integer = _
                  Convert.toInt32(values(TextBoxIndices.ACCOUNT))

               ' determine whether accountNumber is valid
               If accountNumber > 0 Then
                  ' store TextBox fields in Record
                  record.Account = accountNumber
                  record.FirstName = values(TextBoxIndices.FIRST)
                  record.LastName = values(TextBoxIndices.LAST)
                  record.Balance = _
                     Convert.toDecimal(values(TextBoxIndices.BALANCE))

                  ' write Record to file, fields separated by commas
                  fileWriter.WriteLine( _
                     record.Account & "," & record.FirstName & "," & _
                     record.LastName & "," & record.Balance)
```

Fig. 18.9 | Creating and writing to a sequential-access file. (Part 2 of 5.)

```
            Else
               ' notify user if invalid account number
               MessageBox.Show("Invalid Account Number", "Error", _
                  MessageBoxButtons.OK, MessageBoxIcon.Error)
            End If
         ' notify user if error occurs in serialization
         Catch ex As IOException
            MessageBox.Show("Error Writing to File", "Error", _
               MessageBoxButtons.OK, MessageBoxIcon.Error)
         Catch ex As FormatException
            MessageBox.Show("Invalid Format", "Error", _
               MessageBoxButtons.OK, MessageBoxIcon.Error)
         End Try
      End If

      ClearTextBoxes() ' clear TextBox values
      accountTextBox.Select() ' give focus to accountTextBox
   End Sub ' enterButton_Click

   ' event handler for Exit Button
   Private Sub exitButton_Click(ByVal sender As System.Object, _
      ByVal e As System.EventArgs) Handles exitButton.Click
      ' determine whether file exists
      If output IsNot Nothing Then
         Try
            fileWriter.Close() ' close StreamWriter
         ' notify user of error closing file
         Catch ex As IOException
            MessageBox.Show("Cannot close file", "Error", _
               MessageBoxButtons.OK, MessageBoxIcon.Error)
         End Try
      End If

      Application.Exit()
   End Sub ' exitButton_Click
End Class ' CreateFileForm
```

(a)

BankUIForm graphical user interface

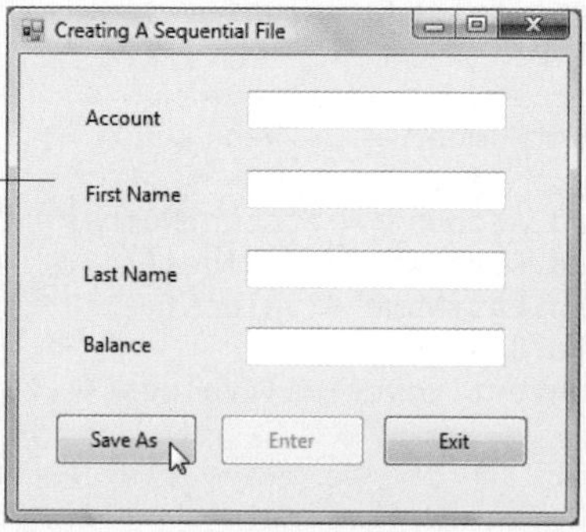

Creating A Sequential File

Account

First Name

Last Name

Balance

Save As Enter Exit

Fig. 18.9 | Creating and writing to a sequential-access file. (Part 3 of 5.)

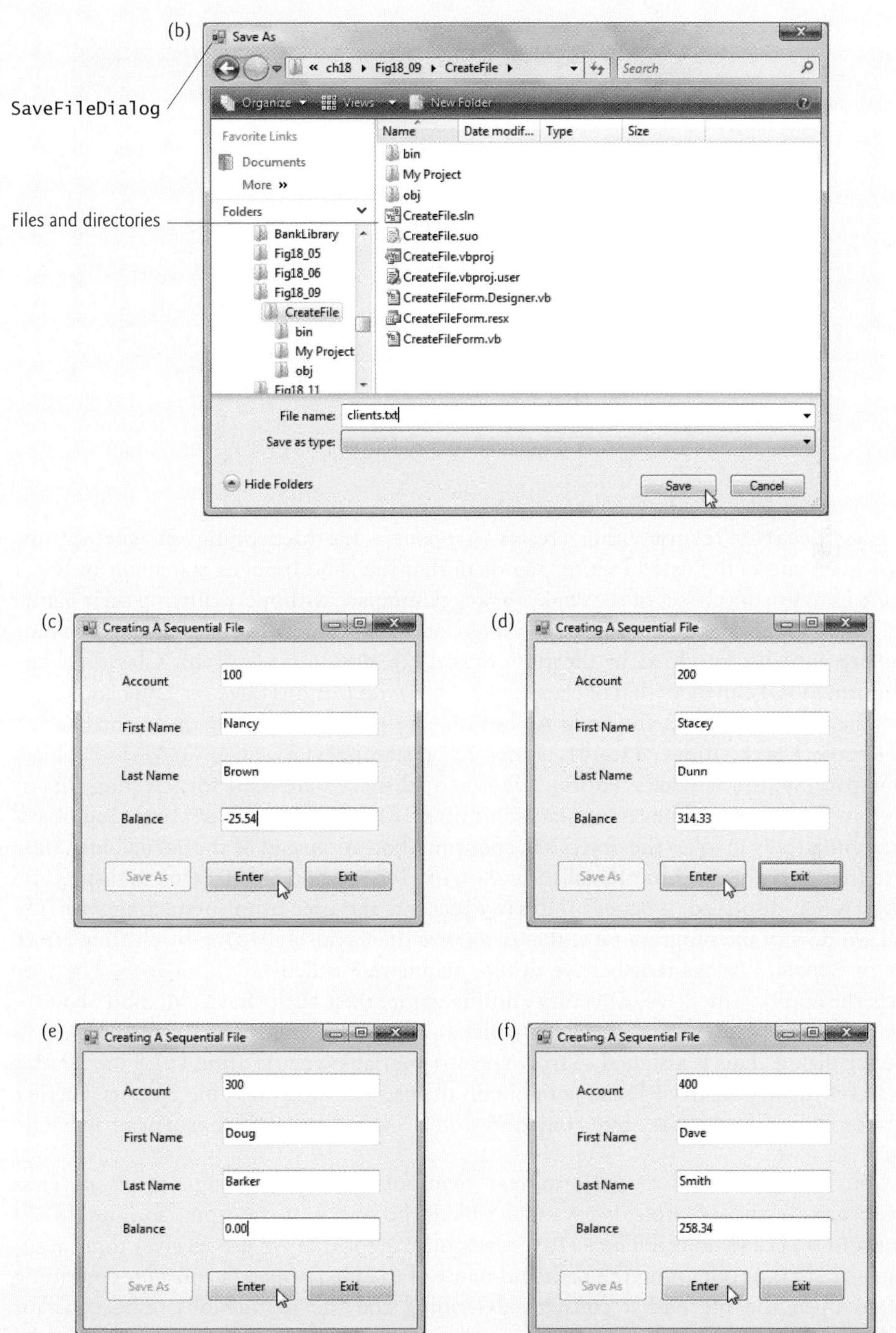

Fig. 18.9 | Creating and writing to a sequential-access file. (Part 4 of 5.)

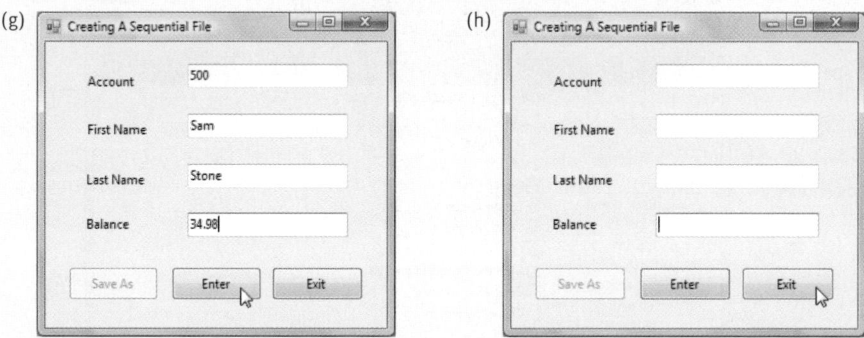

Fig. 18.9 | Creating and writing to a sequential-access file. (Part 5 of 5.)

Class `CreateFileForm` either creates or opens a file (depending on whether one exists), then allows the user to write records to that file. The `Imports` statement in line 4 enables us to use the classes of the `BankLibrary` namespace without qualifying their names with "`BankLibrary`"; this namespace contains class `BankUIForm`, from which class `CreateFileForm` inherits (specified in the file `CreateFileForm.Designer.vb`). Class `CreateFileForm`'s GUI enhances that of class `BankUIForm` with buttons **Save As**, **Enter** and **Exit**.

When the user clicks the **Save As** button, the program invokes the event handler `saveButton_Click` (lines 11–44). Line 18 instantiates a `SaveFileDialog` object (namespace `System.Windows.Forms`). Objects of this class are used for selecting files as shown in Fig. 18.9(b). The `Using` statement (line 18) creates the `SaveFileDialog` object and automatically invokes the object's `Dispose` method at the end of the `Using` block (line 21) to free up resources. Line 19 calls `SaveFileDialog` method `ShowDialog` to display the dialog. When displayed, a `SaveFileDialog` prevents the user from interacting with any other window in the program until the user closes the `SaveFileDialog` by clicking either **Save** or **Cancel**. Dialogs that behave in this manner are called modal dialogs. The user selects the appropriate drive, directory and file name, then clicks **Save**. Method `ShowDialog` returns a `DialogResult` specifying which button (**Save** or **Cancel**) the user clicked to close the dialog. This is assigned to `DialogResult` variable `result` (line 19). Line 20 uses `SaveFileDialog` property `FileName` to obtain the user-selected file. Line 24 tests whether the user clicked **Cancel** by comparing this value to `Windows.Forms.DialogResult.Cancel`.

You can open files to perform text manipulation by creating objects of class `FileStream`. In this example, we want the file to be opened for output, so lines 28–29 create a `FileStream` object. The `FileStream` constructor that we use receives three arguments—a `String` containing the path and name of the file to open, a constant describing how to open the file and a constant describing the file permissions. The constant `FileMode.OpenOrCreate` (line 29) indicates that the `FileStream` object should open the file if the file exists and create the file if it does not exist. There are other `FileMode` constants describing how to open files; we introduce these constants as we use them in examples. The constant `FileAccess.Write` (from the `FileAccess` enumeration) indicates that the program can perform only write operations with the `FileStream` object. There are two other constants for the third constructor parameter—`FileAccess.Read` for read-only access and `FileAccess.ReadWrite` for both read and write access. The `StreamWriter` object (line 32) is constructed with a `FileStream` argument that specifies the file to which the `StreamWriter` will output text. Class `StreamWriter` belongs to the `System.IO` namespace. Line 38 catches an `IOException` if there is a problem opening the file or creating the `StreamWriter`. If so, the program displays an error message (lines 40–41). If no exception occurs, the file is open for writing.

Common Programming Error 18.1

Failure to open a file before attempting to reference it in a program is a logic error.

After typing information in each `TextBox`, the user clicks the **Enter** button, which calls event handler `enterButton_Click` (lines 47–93) to save the data from the `TextBoxes` into the user-specified file. If the user entered a valid account number (i.e., an integer greater than zero), lines 66–70 store the `TextBox` values in an object of type `Record` (created in line 53). If the user entered invalid data in one of the `TextBoxes` (such as nonnumeric characters in the **Balance** field), the program throws a `FormatException`. The `Catch` block in lines 85–87 handles such exceptions by notifying the user (via a `MessageBox`) of the improper format.

If the user entered valid data, lines 73–75 write the record to the file by invoking method `WriteLine` of the `StreamWriter` object that was created at line 32. Method `WriteLine` writes a sequence of characters to a file. We separate each field with a comma in this example, and we place each record on its own line in the file.

When the user clicks the **Exit** button, event handler `exitButton_Click` (lines 96–110) exits the application. Line 101 closes the `StreamWriter` and the underlying `FileStream`, then line 109 terminates the program. Note that the call to method `Close` is located in a `Try` block. Method `Close` throws an `IOException` if the file or stream cannot be closed properly. In this case, it is important to notify the user that the information in the file or stream might be corrupted.

Performance Tip 18.1

Close each file explicitly when the program no longer needs to reference the file. This can reduce resource usage in programs that continue executing long after they finish using a specific file. The practice of explicitly closing files also improves program clarity.

Performance Tip 18.2

Releasing resources explicitly when they are no longer needed makes them immediately available for reuse by other programs, thus improving resource utilization.

In the sample execution for the program in Fig. 18.9, we entered information for the five accounts shown in Fig. 18.10. The program does not depict how the data records are rendered in the file. To verify that the file has been created successfully, we create a program in the next section to read and display the file. Since this is a text file, you can open it in any text editor to see its contents.

Account	First Name	Last Name	Balance
100	Nancy	Brown	-25.54
200	Stacey	Dunn	314.33
300	Doug	Barker	0.00
400	Dave	Smith	258.34
500	Sam	Stone	34.98

Fig. 18.10 | Sample data for the program in Fig. 18.9.

18.6 Reading Data from a Sequential-Access Text File

The preceding section demonstrated how to create a file for use in sequential-access applications. In this section, we discuss how to read (or retrieve) data sequentially from a file. Class `ReadSequentialAccessFileForm` (Fig. 18.11) reads records from the file created in Fig. 18.9, then displays the contents of each record. Much of the code in this example is similar to that in Fig. 18.9, so we discuss only the unique aspects of the application.

When the user clicks the **Open File** button, the program calls event handler `openButton_Click` (lines 11–36). Line 18 creates an `OpenFileDialog`, and line 19 calls its `ShowDialog` method to display the **Open** dialog shown in Fig. 18.11(b). The behavior and GUI for the **Save** and **Open** dialog types are identical, except that **Save** is replaced by **Open**. If the user inputs a valid file name, line 28 creates a `FileStream` object and assigns it to reference `input`. We pass constant `FileMode.Open` as the second argument to the

```
1  ' Fig. 18.11: ReadSequentialAccessFileForm.vb
2  ' Reading a sequential-access file.
3  Imports System.IO
4  Imports BankLibrary ' imports classes from Figs. 18.7 and 18.8
5
6  Public Class ReadSequentialAccessFileForm
7     Private input As FileStream ' maintains connection to a file
8     Private fileReader As StreamReader ' reads data from a text file
9
10    ' invoked when user clicks the Open button
11    Private Sub openButton_Click(ByVal sender As System.Object, _
12       ByVal e As System.EventArgs) Handles openButton.Click
13
14       Dim result As DialogResult ' stores result of Open dialog
15       Dim fileName As String ' name of file to open
16
17       ' create dialog box enabling user to open file
18       Using fileChooser As New OpenFileDialog()
19          result = fileChooser.ShowDialog()
20          fileName = fileChooser.FileName ' get specified file name
21       End Using
22
```

Fig. 18.11 | Reading sequential-access files. (Part 1 of 4.)

```
      ' if user did not click Cancel
      If result <> DialogResult.Cancel Then
         ClearTextBoxes()

         ' create FileStream to obtain read access to file
         input = New FileStream(fileName, FileMode.Open, FileAccess.Read)

         ' set file from where data is read
         fileReader = New StreamReader(input)

         openButton.Enabled = False ' disable Open File button
         nextButton.Enabled = True ' enable Next Record button
      End If
   End Sub ' openButton_Click

   ' invoked when user clicks Next button
   Private Sub nextButton_Click(ByVal sender As System.Object, _
      ByVal e As System.EventArgs) Handles nextButton.Click

      Try
         ' get next record available in file
         Dim inputRecord As String = fileReader.ReadLine()

         If inputRecord IsNot Nothing Then
            ' store individual pieces of data
            Dim inputFields() As String = inputRecord.Split(","c)

            Dim record As New Record(Convert.ToInt32( _
               inputFields(0)), inputFields(1), inputFields(2), _
               Convert.ToDecimal(inputFields(3)))

            ' copy string array values to TextBox values
            SetTextBoxValues(inputFields)
         Else
            fileReader.Close() ' close StreamReader
            openButton.Enabled = True ' enable Open File button
            nextButton.Enabled = False ' disable Next Record button
            ClearTextBoxes()

            ' notify user if no Records in file
            MessageBox.Show("No more records in file", String.Empty, _
               MessageBoxButtons.OK, MessageBoxIcon.Information)
         End If
      Catch ex As IOException
         MessageBox.Show("Error Reading from File", "Error", _
            MessageBoxButtons.OK, MessageBoxIcon.Error)
      Catch ex As FormatException
         MessageBox.Show("Invalid Format", "Error", _
            MessageBoxButtons.OK, MessageBoxIcon.Error)
      End Try
   End Sub ' nextButton_Click
End Class ' ReadSequentialAccessFileForm
```

Fig. 18.11 | Reading sequential-access files. (Part 2 of 4.)

(a)

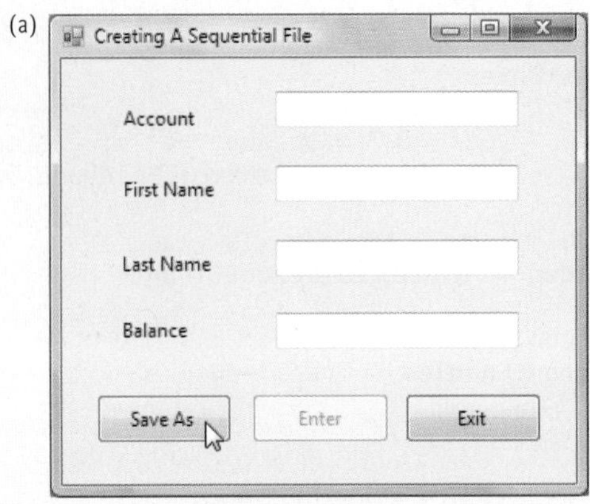

(b)

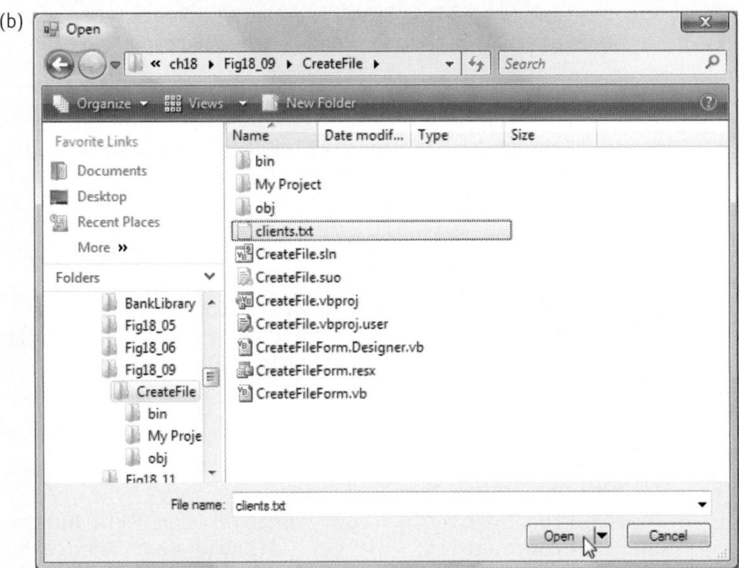

(c)

(d)

Fig. 18.11 | Reading sequential-access files. (Part 3 of 4.)

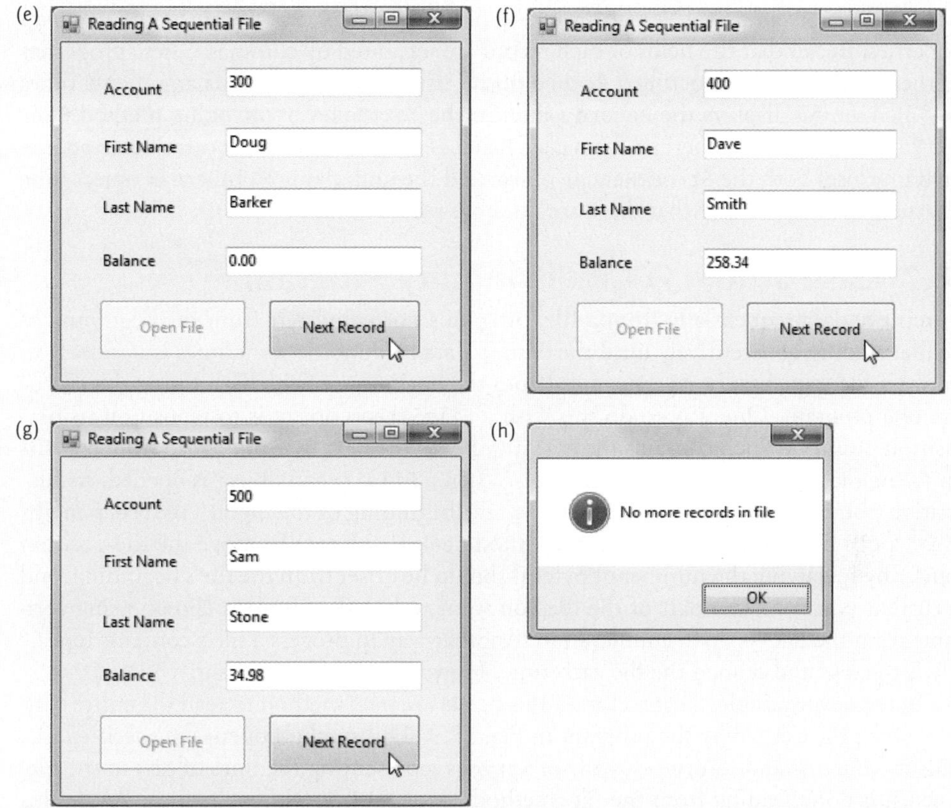

Fig. 18.11 | Reading sequential-access files. (Part 4 of 4.)

`FileStream` constructor to indicate that the `FileStream` should open the file if it exists and throw a `FileNotFoundException` if the file does not exist. In the last example (Fig. 18.9), we wrote text to the file using a `FileStream` object with write-only access. In this example (Fig. 18.11), we specify read-only access to the file by passing constant `File-Access.Read` as the third argument to the `FileStream` constructor (line 28). This `FileStream` object is used to create a `StreamReader` object in line 31. The `FileStream` object specifies the file from which the `StreamReader` object will read text.

Error-Prevention Tip 18.1

Open a file with the `FileAccess.Read` file-open mode if the contents of the file should not be modified. This prevents unintentional modification of the contents.

When the user clicks **Next Record**, the program calls event handler `nextButton_Click` (lines 39–73) to read the next record from the user-specified file. (The user must click **Next Record** after opening the file to view the first record.) Line 44 calls `StreamReader` method `ReadLine` to read the next record. If an error occurs while reading the file, an `IOException` is thrown (caught at line 66), and the user is notified (line 67–68). Otherwise, line 46 determines whether `StreamReader` method `ReadLine` returned `Nothing` (i.e., there is no more text in the file). If not, line 48 uses method `Split` of class `String` to separate the stream of characters that was read from the file into strings that represent the `Record`'s properties. Recall that the fields of each record are separated by commas. These properties are then stored by constructing a `Record` object using the properties as arguments (lines 50–52). Line 55 displays the `Record` values in the `TextBoxes` by invoking method `SetTextBoxes`, which was inherited from class `BankUIForm`. If `ReadLine` returns `Nothing`, the program closes both the `StreamReader` object and the underlying `FileStream` object (line 57), then notifies the user that there are no more records (lines 70–71).

18.7 Case Study: A Credit-Inquiry Program

To retrieve data sequentially from a file, programs normally start from the beginning of the file, reading consecutively until the desired data is found. It sometimes is necessary to process a file sequentially several times (from the beginning of the file) during the execution of a program. One way to do this with a `FileStream` object is to reposition its file-position pointer (which contains the byte number of the next byte to be read from or written to the file) to the beginning of the file. When a `FileStream` object is opened, its file-position pointer is set to byte position `0` (i.e., the beginning of the file). `FileStream` method `Seek` can be used for this purpose. Method `Seek` allows you to move the file-position pointer by specifying the number of bytes it should be offset from the file's beginning, end or current position. The part of the file you want to be offset from is chosen using constants from the `SeekOrigin` enumeration. Another way to process a file's contents repeatedly is to close and reopen the file each time. However, this is inefficient.

In the next example, we use class `File`'s `ReadAllLines` method to read the entire contents of the file created by the program in Fig. 18.9. This method opens the specified file, reads its contents and returns an array of `Strings` representing the lines of text in the file. When it is done reading from the file, method `ReadAllLines` closes the file. We use this technique so that we can process the files contents using LINQ to Objects.

Class `CreditInquiryForm` (Fig. 18.12) enables a credit manager to search for and display account information for customers with credit balances (i.e., customers to whom the company owes money), zero balances (i.e., customers who do not owe the company money) and debit balances (i.e., customers who owe the company money for previously received goods and services). We use a `RichTextBox` in the program to display the account information. `RichTextBoxes` provide more functionality than regular `TextBoxes`—for example, `RichTextBoxes` offer method `Find` for searching individual strings and method `LoadFile` for displaying file contents. Classes `RichTextBox` and `TextBox` both inherit from `MustInherit` class `System.Windows.Forms.TextBoxBase`. We chose a `RichTextBox` in this example because it displays multiple lines of text by default, whereas a regular `TextBox` displays only one. Alternatively, we could have specified that a `TextBox` object display multiple lines of text by setting its `Multiline` property to `True`.

```
' Fig. 18.12: CreditInquiryForm.vb
' Read a file sequentially and display contents based on
' account type specified by user (credit, debit or zero balances).
```

Fig. 18.12 | Read a file sequentially and display contents based on account type specified by user (credit, debit or zero balances). (Part 1 of 5.)

```
Imports System.IO
Imports BankLibrary

Public Class CreditInquiryForm
   ' name of file that stores credit, debit and zero balances
   Private fileName As String

   ' invoked when user clicks Open File button
   Private Sub openButton_Click(ByVal sender As System.Object, _
      ByVal e As System.EventArgs) Handles openButton.Click

      Dim result As DialogResult ' stores result of Open dialog

      ' create dialog box enabling user to open file
      Using fileChooser As New OpenFileDialog()
         result = fileChooser.ShowDialog()
         fileName = fileChooser.FileName ' get name from user
      End Using

      ' if user did not click Cancel
      If result <> Windows.Forms.DialogResult.Cancel Then
         ' enable all GUI buttons, except for Open File button
         openButton.Enabled = False
         creditButton.Enabled = True
         debitButton.Enabled = True
         zeroButton.Enabled = True
      End If
   End Sub ' openButton_Click

   ' invoked when user clicks credit balances,
   ' debit balances or zero balances button
   Private Sub getBalances_Click( _
      ByVal sender As System.Object, ByVal e As System.EventArgs) _
      Handles creditButton.Click, zeroButton.Click, debitButton.Click

      ' delegate variable used to check a balance against
      ' a certain condition
      Dim balanceChooser As Func(Of Decimal, Boolean)

      ' convert sender explicitly to object of type button
      Dim senderButton As Button = CType(sender, Button)

      ' determine the condition the account balances must satisfy
      Select Case senderButton.Text
         Case "Credit Balances" ' positive balances
            balanceChooser = _
               Function(balance As Decimal) balance > 0D
         Case "Debit Balances" ' negative balances
            balanceChooser = _
               Function(balance As Decimal) balance < 0D
```

Fig. 18.12 | Read a file sequentially and display contents based on account type specified by user (credit, debit or zero balances). (Part 2 of 5.)

```
         Case Else ' zero balances
            balanceChooser = _
               Function(balance As Decimal) balance = 0D
      End Select

      ' read and display file information
      Try
         displayRichTextBox.AppendText("The accounts are:" & vbNewLine)

         ' select records that match account type
         Dim balanceQuery = _
            From line In File.ReadAllLines(fileName) _
            Let creditInfo As String() = line.Split(","c) _
            Where balanceChooser(Convert.ToDecimal(creditInfo(3))) _
            Select New Record With _
            { _
               .Account = Convert.ToInt32(creditInfo(0)), _
               .FirstName = creditInfo(1), _
               .LastName = creditInfo(2), _
               .Balance = Convert.ToDecimal(creditInfo(3)) _
            } ' end LINQ query that selects Record objects

         Dim output As String = String.Empty ' hold output String

         ' display each selected Record
         For Each creditRecord In balanceQuery
            output &= _
               creditRecord.Account & vbTab & _
               creditRecord.FirstName & vbTab & _
               creditRecord.LastName & vbTab

            output &= _
               String.Format("{0:C}", creditRecord.Balance) & vbNewLine
         Next

         displayRichTextBox.AppendText(output) ' copy output to screen

      ' handle exception when file cannot be read
      Catch ex As IOException
         MessageBox.Show("Cannot Read File", "Error", _
            MessageBoxButtons.OK, MessageBoxIcon.Error)
      End Try
   End Sub ' getBalances_Click

   ' invoked when user clicks Done button
   Private Sub doneButton_Click(ByVal sender As System.Object, _
      ByVal e As System.EventArgs) Handles doneButton.Click

      Application.Exit()
   End Sub ' doneButton_Click
End Class ' CreditInquiryForm
```

Fig. 18.12 | Read a file sequentially and display contents based on account type specified by user (credit, debit or zero balances). (Part 3 of 5.)

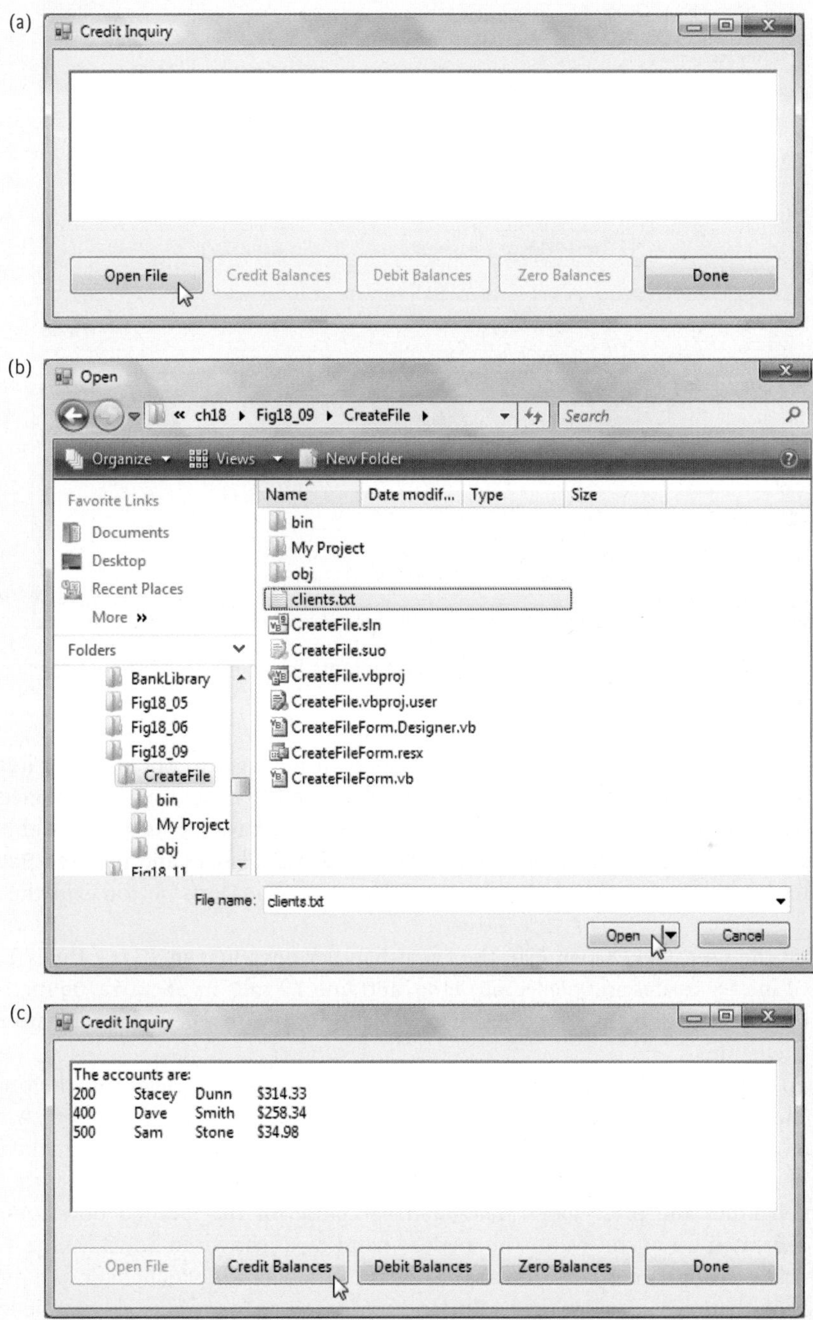

Fig. 18.12 | Read a file sequentially and display contents based on account type specified by user (credit, debit or zero balances). (Part 4 of 5.)

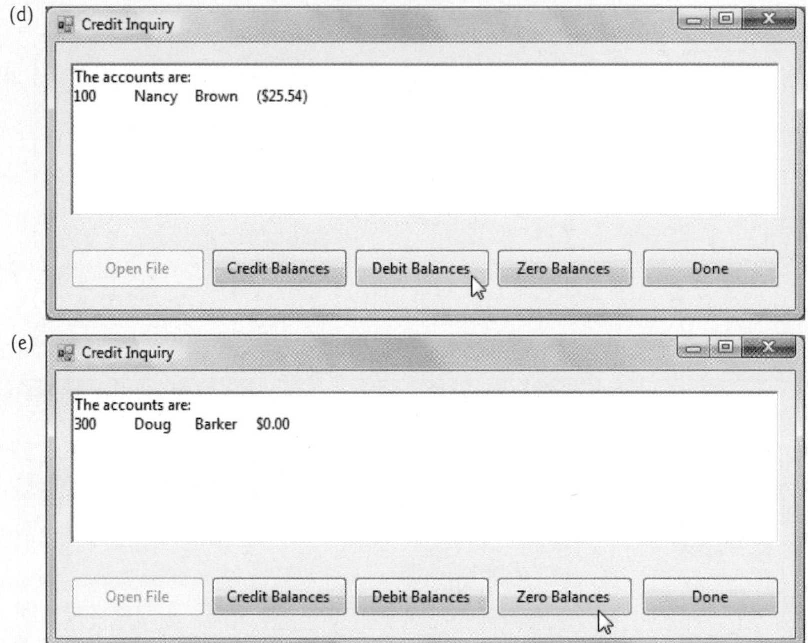

Fig. 18.12 | Read a file sequentially and display contents based on account type specified by user (credit, debit or zero balances). (Part 5 of 5.)

The program displays buttons that enable a credit manager to obtain credit information. The **Open File** button enables the user to select the file containing the balance data. The **Credit Balances** button displays a list of accounts that have credit balances, the **Debit Balances** button displays a list of accounts that have debit balances and the **Zero Balances** button displays a list of accounts that have zero balances. The **Done** button exits the application.

When the user clicks **Open File**, the event handler `openButton_Click` (lines 12–31) executes. Line 18 creates an `OpenFileDialog`, and line 19 calls its `ShowDialog` method to display the **Open** dialog, in which the user selects the file to open. Line 20 stores the selected file name.

When the user clicks **Credit Balances**, **Debit Balances** or **Zero Balances**, the program invokes method `getBalances_Click` (lines 35–96). To create a single method that handles the events for multiple `Buttons`, select all the `Buttons` at once then select the `Click` event in the events tab of the **Properties** window. Next, type the name you wish to use for the event handler and press *Enter*. The `Handles` clause for the method now contains a comma-separated list of the events the method handles, as shown in line 37. Line 41 uses the `Func` class (from namespace `System`) to declare variable `balanceChooser` as a delegate to a function that receives a `Decimal` value and returns a `Boolean` value. The value for this variable is set in lines 47–57. This variable is used in the LINQ query in lines 65–74 to determine which accounts are selected. Line 44 uses the `CType` function to convert the `sender` parameter's type to type `Button`. The `sender` parameter represents the control that generated the event. This conversion allows the event handler to use the properties and methods of the Button the user pressed. Line 47 obtains the Button object's text, which the program uses to determine which type of accounts to display.

Depending on the Button that was pressed, lines 47–57 create lambda expressions (Section 10.17) that determine the appropriate balances to select. For credit balances, lines 48–50 assign balanceChooser a lambda expression that returns True if a balance is greater than 0. For debit balances, lines 51–53 assign balanceChooser a lambda expression that returns True if a balance is less than 0. For zero balances, lines 54–56 assign balanceChooser a lambda expression that returns True if a balance is equal to 0. The AppendText method of the RichTextBox class is used to append text to the current text in displayRichTextBox (lines 61 and 89).

The LINQ query in lines 65–74 begins by getting all the lines from the file (line 65). Line 66 creates a variable (creditInfo) to store the data for one record in the file (split into an array of Strings). The Where clause (line 67) invokes the balanceChooser delegate to determine whether the current account should be selected. The last element of the creditInfo array contains a String representation of the account's balance, which we convert to a Decimal value before passing it to the delegate. If the delegate returns True, the LINQ query selects a new Record object containing that account's data. Lines 79–87 process the LINQ query's results and build a String to display in the RichTextBox. Notice in Fig. 18.12(d) that the currency output format displays negative values in parentheses.

18.8 Serialization

Section 18.5 demonstrated how to write the individual fields of a Record object to a text file, and Section 18.6 demonstrated how to read those fields from a file and place their values in a Record object in memory. In the examples, Record was used to aggregate the information for one record. When the instance variables for a Record were output to a disk file, certain information was lost, such as the type of each value. For instance, if the value "3" is read from a file, there is no way to tell whether the value came from an Integer, a String or a Decimal. We have only data, not type information, on disk. If the program that is going to read this data "knows" what object type the data corresponds to, then the data can be read directly into objects of that type. For example, in Fig. 18.11 we know that we are inputting an Integer (the account number), followed by two Strings (the first and last names) and a Decimal (the balance). We also know that these values are separated by commas, with only one record on each line. Thus we are able to parse the strings and convert the account number to an Integer and the balance to a Decimal. Sometimes it would be easier to read or write entire objects. .NET provides such a mechanism, called object serialization. A serialized object is an object represented as a sequence of bytes that includes the object's data, as well as information about the object's type and the types of data stored in the object. After a serialized object has been written to a file, it can be read from the file and deserialized—that is, the type information and bytes that represent the object and its data can be used to recreate the object in memory.

Class BinaryFormatter (namespace System.Runtime.Serialization.Formatters.Binary) enables entire objects to be written to or read from a stream. BinaryFormatter method Serialize writes an object's representation to a file. BinaryFormatter method Deserialize reads this representation from a file and reconstructs the original object. Both methods throw a SerializationException if an error occurs during serialization or deserialization. Both methods require a Stream object (e.g., the FileStream) as a parameter so that the BinaryFormatter can access the correct stream.

Sections 18.9–18.10 create and manipulate sequential-access files using object serialization. Object serialization is performed with byte-based streams, so the sequential files created and manipulated will be binary files. Binary files are not human readable. For this reason, we write a separate application that reads and displays serialized objects.

18.9 Creating a Sequential-Access File Using Object Serialization

We begin by creating and writing serialized objects to a sequential-access file. In this section, we reuse much of the code from Section 18.5, so we focus only on the new features.

Defining the **RecordSerializable** *Class*

Let us begin by modifying our Record class (Fig. 18.8) so that objects of this class can be serialized. Class RecordSerializable (Fig. 18.13) is marked with the **<Serializable()>** attribute (line 3), which indicates to the CLR that objects of class RecordSerializable can be serialized. The classes for objects that we wish to write to or read from a stream must include this attribute in their declarations or must implement interface **ISerializable** (from namespace System.Runtime.Serialization). The remainder of class RecordSerializable is identical to class Record (Fig. 18.8).

In a class that is marked with the <Serializable()> attribute or that implements interface ISerializable, you must ensure that every instance variable of the class is also serializable. All simple-type variables and Strings are serializable. For variables of reference types, you must check the class declaration (and possibly its base classes) to ensure that the type is serializable. By default, array objects are serializable. However, if the array contains references to other objects, those objects may or may not be serializable.

```
1  ' Fig. 18.13: RecordSerializable.vb
2  ' Serializable class that represents a data record.
3  <Serializable()> _
4  Public Class RecordSerializable
5     Private accountValue As Integer
6     Private firstNameValue As String
7     Private lastNameValue As String
8     Private balanceValue As Decimal
9
10    ' default constructor sets members to default values
11    Public Sub New()
12       MyClass.New(0, String.Empty, String.Empty, 0D)
13    End Sub ' New
14
15    ' overloaded constructor sets members to parameter values
16    Public Sub New(ByVal newAccount As Integer, _
17       ByVal newFirstName As String, ByVal newLastName As String, _
18       ByVal newBalance As Decimal)
```

Fig. 18.13 | Serializable class that represents a data record. (Part 1 of 2.)

```

      Account = newAccount
      FirstName = newFirstName
      LastName = newLastName
      Balance = newBalance
   End Sub ' New

   ' property Account
   Public Property Account() As Integer
      Get
         Return accountValue
      End Get
      Set(ByVal value As Integer)
         accountValue = value
      End Set
   End Property ' Account

   ' property FirstName
   Public Property FirstName() As String
      Get
         Return firstNameValue
      End Get
      Set(ByVal value As String)
         firstNameValue = value
      End Set
   End Property ' FirstName

   ' property LastName
   Public Property LastName() As String
      Get
         Return lastNameValue
      End Get
      Set(ByVal value As String)
         lastNameValue = value
      End Set
   End Property ' LastName

   ' property Balance
   Public Property Balance() As Decimal
      Get
         Return balanceValue
      End Get
      Set(ByVal value As Decimal)
         balanceValue = value
      End Set
   End Property ' Balance
End Class ' RecordSerializable
```

Fig. 18.13 | Serializable class that represents a data record. (Part 2 of 2.)

Using a Serialization Stream to Create an Output File

Now let's create a sequential-access file with serialization (Fig. 18.14). Line 10 creates a `BinaryFormatter` for writing serialized objects. Lines 31–32 open the `FileStream` to which this program writes the serialized objects. The `String` argument `fileName` that is passed to the `FileStream`'s constructor represents the name and path of the file to be opened. This specifies the file to which the serialized objects will be written.

Common Programming Error 18.2

It is a logic error to open an existing file for output when the user wishes to preserve the file—the original file's contents will be lost.

This program assumes that data is input correctly and in the proper record-number order. Event handler `enterButton_Click` (lines 47–93) performs the write operation. Line 53 creates a `RecordSerializable` object, which is assigned values in lines 66–72. Line 75 calls method `Serialize` to write the `RecordSerializable` object to the output file. Method `Serialize` receives as its first argument the `FileStream` object into which the `BinaryFormatter` writes its second argument. Note that only one statement is required to write the entire object.

In the sample execution for the program in Fig. 18.14, we entered information for five accounts—the same information shown in Fig. 18.10. The program does not show how the data records actually appear in the file. Remember that we are now using binary files, which are not human readable. To verify that the file was created successfully, the next section presents a program to read the file's contents and deserialize the objects.

```
1  ' Fig 18.14: CreateFileForm.vb
2  ' Creating a sequential-access file using serialization.
3  Imports System.IO
4  Imports System.Runtime.Serialization.Formatters.Binary
5  Imports System.Runtime.Serialization
6  Imports BankLibrary
7
8  Public Class CreateFileForm
9     ' object for serializing Records in binary format
10    Private formatter As New BinaryFormatter()
11    Private output As FileStream ' stream for writing to a file
12
13    ' handler for saveButton_Click
14    Private Sub saveButton_Click(ByVal sender As System.Object, _
15       ByVal e As System.EventArgs) Handles saveButton.Click
16
17       Dim result As DialogResult ' stores result of Save dialog
18       Dim fileName As String ' name of file to save data
19
20       ' create dialog box enabling user to save file
21       Using fileChooser As New SaveFileDialog()
22          result = fileChooser.ShowDialog()
23          fileName = fileChooser.FileName ' get specified file name
24       End Using
25
26       ' if user did not click cancel
27       If result <> Windows.Forms.DialogResult.Cancel Then
```

Fig. 18.14 | Creating a sequential-access file using serialization. (Part 1 of 5.)

```
            ' save file via FileStream if user specified valid file
            Try
               ' open file with write access
               output = New FileStream( _
                  fileName, FileMode.OpenOrCreate, FileAccess.Write)

               ' disable Save button and enable Enter button
               saveButton.Enabled = False
               enterButton.Enabled = True
            ' handle exception if there is a problem opening the file
            Catch ex As IOException
               ' notify user if file does not exist
               MessageBox.Show("Error opening file", "Error", _
                  MessageBoxButtons.OK, MessageBoxIcon.Error)
            End Try
         End If
      End Sub ' saveButton_Click

      ' handler for enterButton_Click
      Private Sub enterButton_Click(ByVal sender As System.Object, _
         ByVal e As System.EventArgs) Handles enterButton.Click
         ' store TextBox values string array
         Dim values As String() = GetTextBoxValues()

         ' Record containing TextBox values to serialize
         Dim record As New RecordSerializable()

         ' determine whether TextBox account field is empty
         If values(TextBoxIndices.ACCOUNT) <> String.Empty Then
            ' store TextBox values in Record and serialize Record
            Try
               ' get account number value from TextBox
               Dim accountNumber As Integer = _
                  Convert.ToInt32(values(TextBoxIndices.ACCOUNT))

               ' determine whether accountNumber is valid
               If accountNumber > 0 Then
                  ' store TextBox fields in Record
                  record.Account = accountNumber
                  record.FirstName = _
                     values(TextBoxIndices.FIRST)
                  record.LastName = _
                     values(TextBoxIndices.LAST)
                  record.Balance = _
                     Convert.ToDecimal(values(TextBoxIndices.BALANCE))

                  ' write Record to FileStream ( serialize object )
                  formatter.Serialize(output, record)
               Else
                  ' notify user if invalid account number
                  MessageBox.Show("Invalid Account Number", "Error", _
                     MessageBoxButtons.OK, MessageBoxIcon.Error)
               End If
```

Fig. 18.14 | Creating a sequential-access file using serialization. (Part 2 of 5.)

```
         ' notify user if error occurs in serialization
         Catch ex As SerializationException
            MessageBox.Show("Error Writing to File", "Error", _
               MessageBoxButtons.OK, MessageBoxIcon.Error)
         ' notify user if error occurs regarding parameter format
         Catch ex As FormatException
            MessageBox.Show("Invalid Format", "Error", _
               MessageBoxButtons.OK, MessageBoxIcon.Error)
         End Try
      End If

      ClearTextBoxes() ' clear TextBox values
   End Sub ' enterButton_Click

   ' handler for exitButton_Click
   Private Sub exitButton_Click(ByVal sender As System.Object, _
      ByVal e As System.EventArgs) Handles exitButton.Click
      ' determine whether file exists
      If output IsNot Nothing Then
         ' close file
         Try
            output.Close()
         ' notify user of error closing file
         Catch ex As IOException
            MessageBox.Show("Cannot close file", "Error", _
               MessageBoxButtons.OK, MessageBoxIcon.Error)
         End Try
      End If

      Application.Exit()
   End Sub ' enterButton_Click
End Class ' CreateFileForm
```

(a)

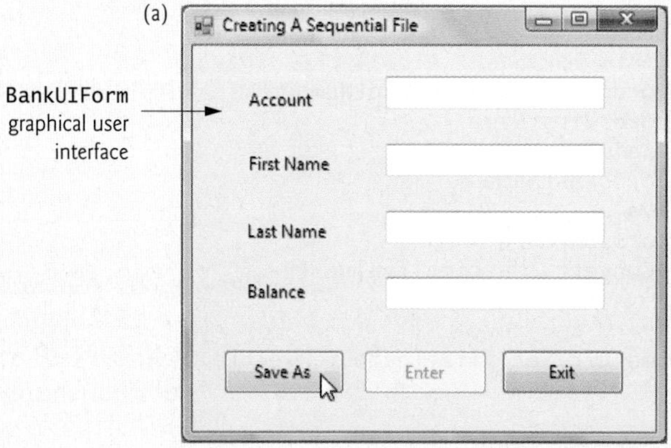

BankUIForm graphical user interface

Creating A Sequential File

Account

First Name

Last Name

Balance

Save As Enter Exit

Fig. 18.14 | Creating a sequential-access file using serialization. (Part 3 of 5.)

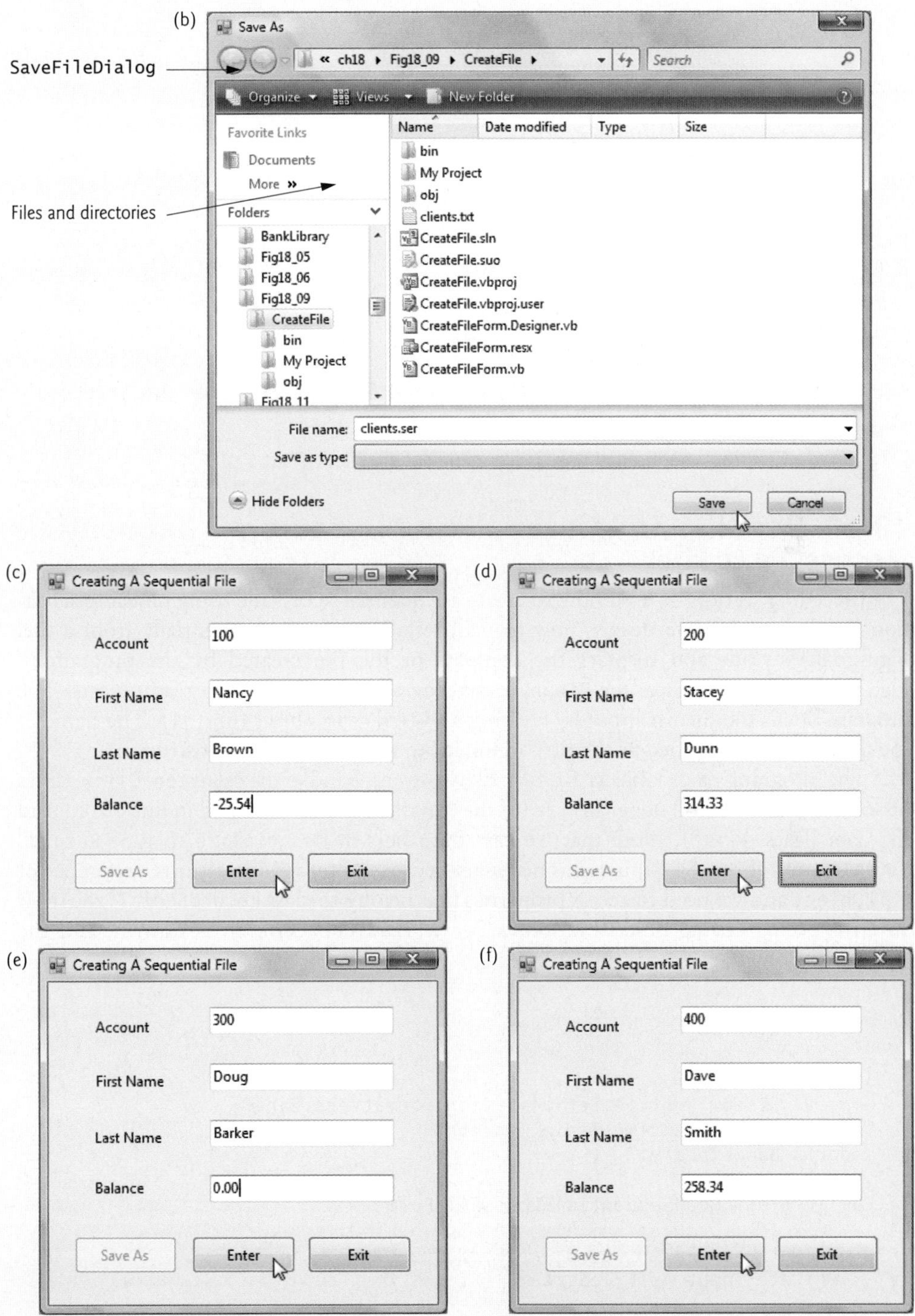

Fig. 18.14 | Creating a sequential-access file using serialization. (Part 4 of 5.)

(g)

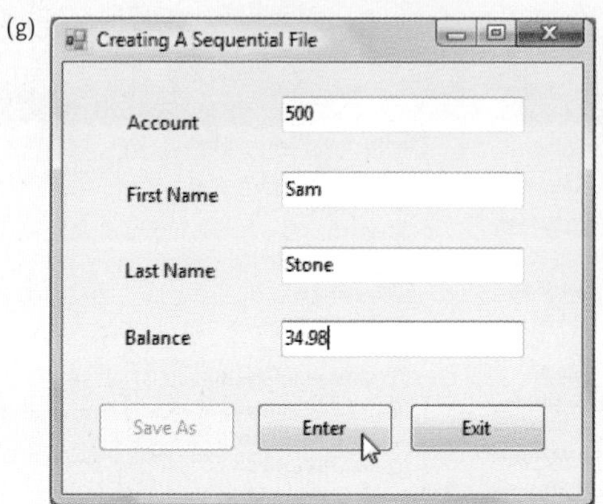

Fig. 18.14 | Creating a sequential-access file using serialization. (Part 5 of 5.)

18.10 Reading and Deserializing Data from a Sequential-Access Text File

The preceding section showed how to create a sequential-access file using object serialization. In this section, we discuss how to read serialized objects sequentially from a file. Figure 18.15 reads and displays the contents of the file created by the program in Fig. 18.14. Line 10 creates the `BinaryFormatter` that will be used to read objects. The program opens the file for input by creating a `FileStream` object (line 31). The name of the file to open is specified as the first argument to the `FileStream` constructor.

The program reads objects from a file in event handler `nextButton_Click` (lines 39–66). We use method `Deserialize` (of the `BinaryFormatter` created in line 10) to read the data (lines 44–45). Note that we cast the result of `Deserialize` to type `RecordSerializable` (line 45)—this cast is necessary because `Deserialize` returns a reference of type `Object` and we need to access properties that belong to class `RecordSerializable`. If an error occurs during deserialization, a `SerializationException` is thrown, and the `FileStream` object is closed (line 56).

```
1   ' Fig. 18.15: ReadSequentialAccessFileForm.vb
2   ' Reading a sequential-access file using deserialization.
3   Imports System.IO
4   Imports System.Runtime.Serialization.Formatters.Binary
5   Imports System.Runtime.Serialization
6   Imports BankLibrary
7
8   Public Class ReadSequentialAccessFileForm
9      ' object for deserializing Record in binary format
10     Private reader As New BinaryFormatter()
11     Private input As FileStream ' stream for reading from a file
12
```

Fig. 18.15 | Reading a sequential-access file using deserialization. (Part 1 of 4.)

```
   ' invoked when user clicks Open button
   Private Sub openButton_Click(ByVal sender As System.Object, _
      ByVal e As System.EventArgs) Handles openButton.Click

      Dim result As DialogResult ' stores result of Open dialog
      Dim fileName As String ' name of file to open

      ' create dialog box enabling user to open file
      Using fileChooser As New OpenFileDialog()
         result = fileChooser.ShowDialog()
         fileName = fileChooser.FileName ' get specified file name
      End Using

      ' if user did not click Cancel
      If result <> Windows.Forms.DialogResult.Cancel Then
         ClearTextBoxes()

         ' create FileStream to obtain read access to file
         input = New FileStream(fileName, FileMode.Open, FileAccess.Read)

         openButton.Enabled = False ' disable Open File button
         nextButton.Enabled = True ' enable Next Record button
      End If
   End Sub ' openButton_Click

   ' invoked when user clicks Next button
   Private Sub nextButton_Click(ByVal sender As System.Object, _
      ByVal e As System.EventArgs) Handles nextButton.Click
      ' deserialize Record and store data in TextBoxes
      Try
         ' get next RecordSerializable available in file
         Dim record As RecordSerializable = _
            CType(reader.Deserialize(input), RecordSerializable)

         ' store Record values in temporary string array
         Dim values() As String = { _
            record.Account.ToString(), record.FirstName.ToString(), _
            record.LastName.ToString(), record.Balance.ToString()}

         ' copy string array values to TextBox values
         SetTextBoxValues(values)
      ' handle exception when there are no Records in file
      Catch ex As SerializationException
         input.Close() ' close FileStream if no Records in file
         openButton.Enabled = True ' enable Open File button
         nextButton.Enabled = False ' disable Next Record button

         ClearTextBoxes()

         ' notify user if no Records in file
         MessageBox.Show("No more records in file", String.Empty, _
            MessageBoxButtons.OK, MessageBoxIcon.Information)
      End Try
```

Fig. 18.15 | Reading a sequential-access file using deserialization. (Part 2 of 4.)

```
    End Sub ' nextButton_Click
End Class ' ReadSequentialAccessFileForm
```

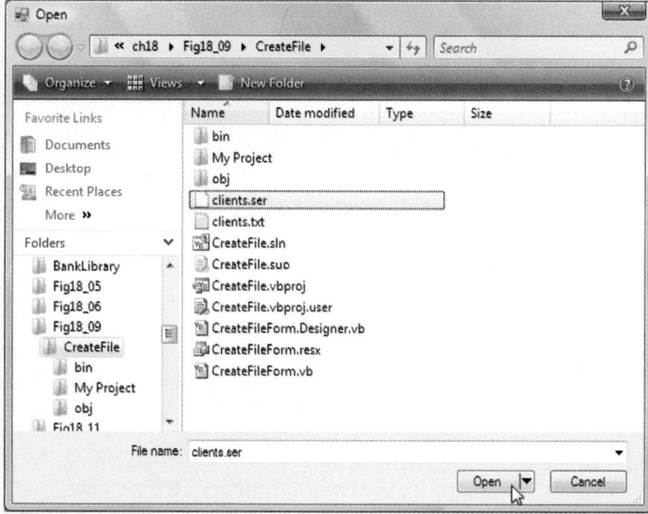

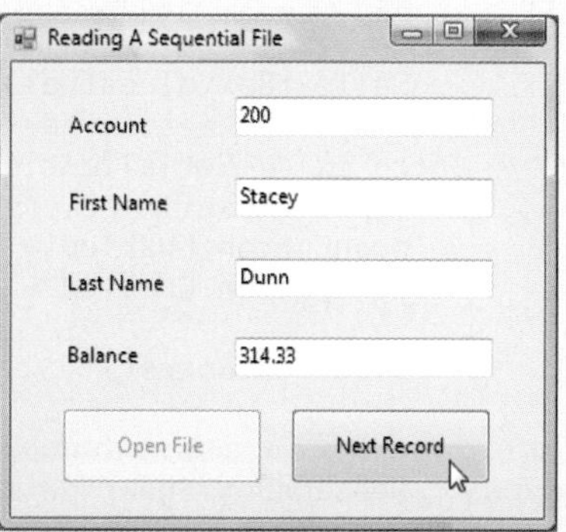

Fig. 18.15 | Reading a sequential-access file using deserialization. (Part 3 of 4.)

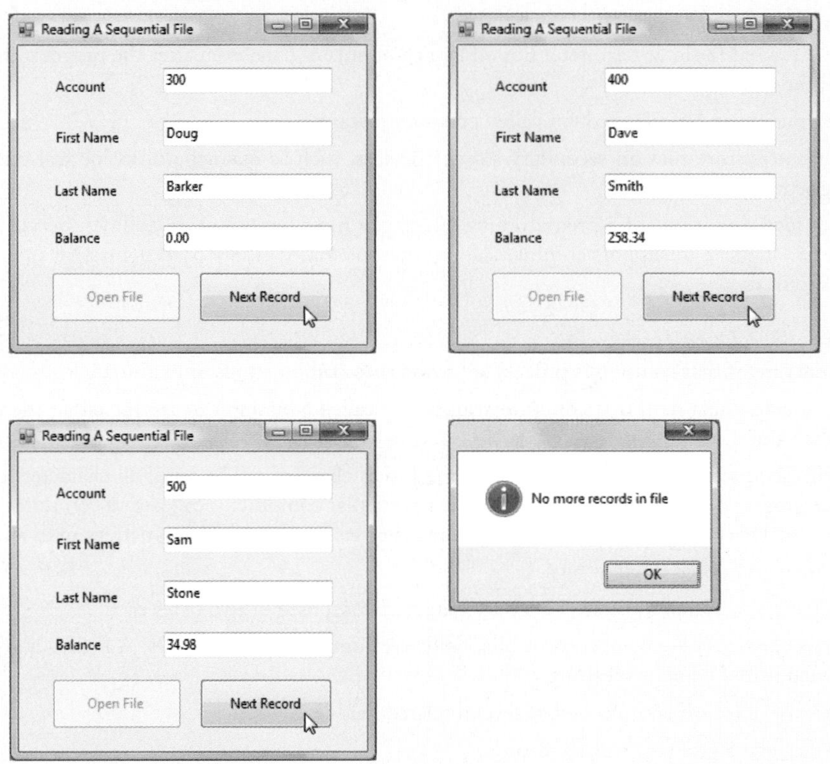

Fig. 18.15 | Reading a sequential-access file using deserialization. (Part 4 of 4.)

18.11 Wrap-Up

In this chapter, you learned how to use file processing to manipulate persistent data. You learned that data is stored in computers as `0`s and `1`s, and that combinations of these values are used to form bytes, fields, records and eventually files. We overviewed the differences between character-based and byte-based streams, as well as several file-processing classes from the `System.IO` namespace. You used class `File` to manipulate files and class `Directory` to manipulate directories. Next, you learned how to use sequential-access file processing to manipulate records in text files. We then discussed the differences between text-file processing and object serialization, and used serialization to store entire objects in and retrieve entire objects from files.

In Chapter 19, XML and LINQ to XML, we present Extensible Markup Language (XML)—a widely supported technology for describing data. Using XML, we can describe any type of data, such as mathematical formulas, music and financial reports. We demonstrate how to describe data with XML and how to write programs that can process XML-encoded data. XML is having an important influence on the development of web applications, which we discuss in detail in Chapters 21 and 22.

Summary

Section 18.1 Introduction

- Files are used for long-term retention of large amounts of data, even after the program that created the data terminates.
- Data maintained in files is often called persistent data.
- Computers store files on secondary storage devices, such as magnetic disks, optical disks and magnetic tapes.
- File processing is one of a programming language's most important capabilities, because it enables a language to support commercial applications that typically process massive amounts of persistent data.

Section 18.2 Data Hierarchy

- All data items that computers process are reduced to combinations of `0`s and `1`s.
- The smallest data item that computers support is called a bit and can assume either the value `0` or the value `1`.
- Digits, letters and special symbols are referred to as characters. The set of all characters used to write programs and represent data items on a particular computer is called that computer's character set. Every character in a computer's character set is represented as a pattern of `0`s and `1`s.
- A byte is composed of eight bits.
- Characters in Visual Basic are Unicode characters composed of two bytes each.
- Just as characters are composed of bits, fields are composed of characters. A field is a group of characters that conveys meaning.
- Typically, a record is composed of several related fields.
- A data file is a group of related records.
- At least one field in each record is chosen as a record key, which uniquely identifies a record as belonging to a particular person or entity and distinguishes that record from all others.
- The most common type of file organization is a sequential file, in which records typically are stored in order by record-key field.
- A group of related files is called a database. A collection of programs designed to create and manage databases is called a database management system (DBMS).

Section 18.3 Files and Streams

- Visual Basic views each file as a sequential stream of bytes.
- Each file ends either with an end-of-file marker or at a specific byte number that is recorded in a system-maintained administrative data structure.
- Files are opened by creating an object that has a stream associated with it.
- Streams provide communication channels between files and programs.
- The `System.IO` namespace includes definitions for stream classes, such as `StreamReader` (for text input from a file), `StreamWriter` (for text output to a file) and `FileStream` (for both input from and output to a file).
- Class `Stream` provides functionality for representing streams as bytes. This class is a `MustInherit` class, so objects of this class cannot be instantiated.
- Classes `FileStream`, `MemoryStream` and `BufferedStream` (all from namespace `System.IO`) inherit from class `Stream`.

- Class `FileStream` can be used to read data to and write data from sequential-access files.
- Class `MemoryStream` enables the transfer of data directly to and from memory—this is much faster than other types of data transfer (e.g., to and from disk).
- Class `BufferedStream` uses buffering to transfer data to or from a stream. Buffering is an I/O performance-enhancement technique, in which each output operation is directed to a region in memory, called a buffer, that is large enough to hold the data from many output operations. Then actual transfer to the output device is performed in one large physical output operation each time the buffer fills. The output operations directed to the output buffer in memory are often called logical output operations. Buffering can also be used to speed input operations.

Section 18.4 Classes `File` and `Directory`

- Information on computers is stored in files, which are organized in directories. Classes `File` and `Directory` enable programs to manipulate files and directories on disk.
- Class `File` provides `Shared` methods determining information about files and can be used to open files for reading or writing.
- Class `Directory` provides `Shared` methods for manipulating directories.
- The `DirectoryInfo` object returned by `Directory` method `CreateDirectory` contains information about a directory. Much of the information contained in class `DirectoryInfo` also can be accessed via the methods of class `Directory`.
- `File` method `Exists` determines whether a `String` is the name of an existing file.
- A `StreamReader` can be used to read text from a file. The `StreamReader` constructor takes as an argument a `String` containing the name of the file to open. `StreamReader` method `ReadToEnd` reads the entire contents of a file.
- `Directory` method `Exists` determines whether a `String` is the name of an existing directory.
- `Directory` method `GetDirectories` obtains a `String` array containing the names of subdirectories in the specified directory.
- A `Dictionary` (namespace `System.Collections.Generic`) is a collection of key/value pairs, in which each key has a corresponding value. Class `Dictionary` is a generic class like class `List`.

Section 18.5 Creating a Sequential-Access Text File

- Visual Basic imposes no structure on files, so it does not recognize concepts like "record." This means that you must structure files to meet the requirements of your applications.
- A `SaveFileDialog` is a modal dialog.
- The three-argument `FileStream` constructor receives a `String` containing the name of the file to open, a constant describing how to open the file and a constant describing the file permissions.
- A `StreamWriter` object can be constructed with a `FileStream` argument that specifies the file to which `StreamWriter` outputs text.
- Class `StreamWriter` belongs to the `System.IO` namespace.

Section 18.6 Reading Data from a Sequential-Access Text File

- Data is stored in files so that it can be retrieved for processing when it is needed.
- To retrieve data sequentially from a file, programs normally start from the beginning of the file, reading data consecutively until the desired data is found. It sometimes is necessary to process a file sequentially several times during the execution of a program.
- An `OpenFileDialog` allows a user to select files to open. Method `ShowDialog` displays the dialog.

Section 18.7 Case Study: A Credit-Inquiry Program

- FileStream method Seek allows you to reset the file-position pointer by specifying the number of bytes it should be offset from the file's beginning, end or current position. The part of the file you want to be offset from is chosen using constants from the SeekOrigin enumeration.

Section 18.8 Serialization

- A serialized object is represented as a sequence of bytes that includes the object's data, as well as information about the object's type and the types of data stored in the object.
- After a serialized object has been written to a file, it can be read from the file and deserialized (recreated in memory).
- Class BinaryFormatter (namespace System.Runtime.Serialization.Formatters.Binary) enables entire serializable objects to be read from or written to a stream.
- BinaryFormatter methods Serialize and Deserialize write objects to and read objects from streams, respectively.
- Both method Serialize and method Deserialize require a Stream object (e.g., the FileStream) as a parameter so that the BinaryFormatter can access the correct file.

Section 18.9 Creating a Sequential-Access File Using Object Serialization

- Classes that are marked with the Serializable attribute indicate to the CLR that objects of the class can be serialized. Objects that we wish to write to or read from a stream must include this attribute in their class definitions or implement the ISerializable interface.
- In a serializable class, you must ensure that every instance variable of the class is also serializable. By default, all simple-type variables are serializable. For reference-type variables, you must check the declaration of the class (and possibly its superclasses) to ensure that the type is serializable.

Section 18.10 Reading and Deserializing Data from a Sequential-Access Text File

- Method Deserialize (of class BinaryFormatter) reads a serialized object from a stream and reforms the object in memory.
- Method Deserialize returns a reference of type Object which must be cast to the appropriate type to manipulate the object.
- If an error occurs during deserialization, a SerializationException is thrown.

Terminology

Add method of class Dictionary
AppendText method of class RichTextBox
binary digit (bit)
BinaryFormatter class
bit
bit manipulation
buffer
BufferedStream class
buffering
character
character set
Clear method of class Dictionary
close a file
Close method of class FileStream
Close method of class StreamWriter
Console class
ContainsKey method of class Dictionary
Copy method of class File
Create method of class File
CreateDirectory method of class Directory
CreateText method of class File
data hierarchy
database
database management system (DBMS)
decimal digit
Delete method of class Directory
Delete method of class File
Deserialize method of class BinaryFormatter
deserialized object
DialogResult enumeration

`Dictionary` class
`Directory` class
`DirectoryInfo` class
end-of-file marker
`Error` property of class `Console`
`Exists` method of class `Directory`
field
file
`File` class
file-position pointer
file-processing programs
`FileAccess` enumeration
`FileName` property of class `SaveFileDialog`
`FileStream` class
fixed-length records
`Func` class
`GetCreationTime` method of class `Directory`
`GetCreationTime` method of class `File`
`GetDirectories` method of class `Directory`
`GetExtension` method of class `Path`
`GetFiles` method of class `Directory`
`GetLastAccessTime` method of class `Directory`
`GetLastAccessTime` method of class `File`
`GetLastWriteTime` method of class `Directory`
`GetLastWriteTime` method of class `File`
`In` property of class `Console`
`IOException` class
`ISerializable` interface
`Keys` property of class `Dictionary`
logical output operation
`MemoryStream` class
modal dialog
`Move` method of class `Directory`
`Move` method of class `File`
object serialization
`Open` method of class `File`
`OpenFileDialog` class
`OpenRead` method of class `File`
`OpenText` method of class `File`
`OpenWrite` method of class `File`
`Out` property of class `Console`
`Path` class
pattern of `0`s and `1`s
persistent data
physical output operation
`Read` method of class `Console`
`ReadAllLines` method of class `File`
`ReadLine` method of class `Console`
`ReadLine` method of class `StreamReader`
record
record key
`Remove` method of class `Dictionary`
`RichTextBox` control
`SaveFileDialog` class
secondary storage device
`Seek` method of class `FileStream`
`SeekOrigin` enumeration
sequential file
`Serializable` attribute
`SerializationException` class
`Serialize` method of class `BinaryFormatter`
serialized object
`OpenFileDialog`
`ShowDialog` method of class `OpenFileDialog`
`ShowDialog` method of class `SaveFileDialog`
standard error-stream object
standard input-stream object
standard output-stream object
`Stream` class
stream of bytes
`StreamReader` class
`StreamWriter` class
`System.IO` namespace
`System.Runtime.Serialization.Formatters.Binary` namespace
`TextReader` class
`TextWriter` class
`Write` method of class `Console`
`WriteLine` method of class `Console`
`WriteLine` method of class `StreamWriter`

Self-Review Exercises

18.1 State whether each of the following is *true* or *false*. If *false*, explain why.

a) Creating instances of classes `File` and `Directory` is not possible.
b) Typically, a sequential file stores records in order by the record-key field.
c) Class `StreamReader` inherits from class `Stream`.
d) Any class can be serialized to a file.
e) Method `Seek` of class `FileStream` always seeks relative to the beginning of a file.
f) Classes `StreamReader` and `StreamWriter` are used with sequential-access files.
g) You cannot instantiate objects of type `Stream`.

18.2 Fill in the blanks in each of the following statements:

a) Ultimately, all data items processed by a computer are reduced to combinations of __________ and __________.
b) The smallest data item a computer can process is called a(n) __________.
c) A(n) __________ is a group of related records.
d) Digits, letters and special symbols are collectively referred to as __________.
e) A group of related files is called a(n) __________.
f) The `StreamReader` method __________ reads a line of text from a file.
g) The `StreamWriter` method __________ writes a line of text to a file.
h) Method `Serialize` of class `BinaryFormatter` takes a(n) __________ and a(n) __________ as arguments.
i) The __________ namespace contains most of the .NET framework's file-processing classes.
j) The __________ namespace contains the `BinaryFormatter` class.

Answers to Self-Review Exercises

18.1 a) True. b) True. c) False. Class `StreamReader` inherits from class `TextReader`. d) False. Only classes with the `Serializable` attribute or implement the `ISerializable` interface can be serialized. e) False. It seeks relative to the `SeekOrigin` enumeration member that is passed as one of the arguments. f.) True. g) True.

18.2 a) `0s`, `1s`. b) bit. c) file. d) characters. e) database. f) `ReadLine`. g) `WriteLine`. h) `Stream`, `object`. i) `System.IO`. j) `System.Runtime.Serialization.Formatters.Binary`.

Exercises

18.3 Create a program that stores student grades in a text file. The file should contain the first name, last name, ID number, class taken and grade of every student. Output the fields separated by tab characters. Open the resulting text file in a text editor to confirm that the data was output properly.

18.4 Modify the preceding program to use objects of a class that can be serialized to and deserialized from a file.

18.5 Create a program that combines the ideas of Fig. 18.9 and Fig. 18.11 to allow a user to write records to and read records from a file. Add an extra field of type `Boolean` to the record to indicate whether the account has overdraft protection.

18.6 *(Telephone-Number Word Generator)* Standard telephone keypads contain the digits 0 through 9. The numbers 2 through 9 each have three letters associated with them (Fig. 18.16). Many people find it difficult to memorize phone numbers, so they use the correspondence between digits and letters to develop seven-letter words that correspond to their phone numbers. For example, a person whose telephone number is 686-2377 might use the correspondence indicated in Fig. 18.16 to develop the seven-letter word "NUMBERS." Every seven-letter word corresponds to exactly one seven-digit telephone number. A restaurant wishing to increase its takeout business could surely do so with the number 825-3688 (i.e., "TAKEOUT").

Every seven-letter phone number corresponds to many different seven-letter words. Unfortunately, most of these words represent unrecognizable juxtapositions of letters. It is possible, however, that the owner of a barbershop would be pleased to know that the shop's telephone number, 424-7288, corresponds to "HAIRCUT." A veterinarian with the phone number 738-2273 would be pleased to know that the number corresponds to the letters "PETCARE." An automotive dealership would be pleased to know that its phone number, 639-2277, corresponds to "NEWCARS."

Digit	Letter	Digit	Letter
2	A B C	6	M N O
3	D E F	7	P R S
4	G H I	8	T U V
5	J K L	9	W X Y

Fig. 18.16 | Letters that correspond to the digits on a telephone keypad.

Write a GUI-based application (Fig. 18.17) that, given a seven-digit number, uses a `StreamWriter` object to write to a file every possible seven-letter word combination corresponding to that number. There are 2,187 (3^7) such combinations. Avoid phone numbers with the digits 0 and 1.

Fig. 18.17 | Sample GUI for telephone-number word-generation application.

18.7 *(Student Poll)* Figure 8.5 contains an array of survey responses that is hard-coded into the program. Suppose we wish to process survey results that are stored in a file. First, create a Windows `Form` that prompts the user for survey responses and outputs each response to a file. Use `StreamWriter` to create a file called `numbers.txt`. Each integer should be written using method `Write`. Then add a `TextBox` that will output the frequency of survey responses. Modify the code in Fig. 8.5 to read the survey responses from `numbers.txt`. The responses should be read from the file by using a `StreamReader`. Class `String`'s `Split` method should be used to split the input string into separate responses, then each response should be converted to an integer. The program should continue to read responses until it reaches the end of file. The results should be output to the `TextBox`.

19

XML and LINQ to XML

Knowing trees, I understand the meaning of patience. Knowing grass, I can appreciate persistence.
—Hal Borland

Like everything metaphysical, the harmony between thought and reality is to be found in the grammar of the language.
—Ludwig Wittgenstein

I played with an idea, and grew willful; tossed it into the air; transformed it; let it escape and recaptured it; made it iridescent with fancy, and winged it with paradox.
—Oscar Wilde

OBJECTIVES

In this chapter you'll learn:

- To create DTDs and schemas for specifying and validating the structure of an XML document.
- To create and use simple XSL style sheets to render XML document data.
- To retrieve and modify XML data programmatically using .NET Framework classes.
- To use XML axis properties to access data in XML documents.
- To use XML literals and embedded expressions to create XML documents and work with them directly in Visual Basic code.
- To use LINQ to XML to extract and manipulate data from XML documents.
- To transform XML documents into XHTML using class `XslCompiledTransform`.

Outline

19.1 Introduction

In Chapter 15, we began our introduction to XML to help explain the syntax of XAML (eXtensible Application Markup Language). You learned the syntax of XML, how to use XML namespaces and were introduced to the concept of DTDs and schemas. In this chapter, you learn how to create your own DTDs (Section 19.2) and schemas (Section 19.3) to validate your XML documents.

The .NET Framework uses XML extensively. Many of the configuration files that Visual Studio creates—such as those that represent project settings—use XML format. XML is also used heavily in serialization, as you'll see in Chapter 22, Windows Communication Foundation (WCF) Web Services. You've already used XAML—an XML vocabulary used for creating user interfaces—in Chapters 15–16. XAML is also used in Chapter 23, Silverlight, Rich Internet Applications and Multimedia.

Sections 19.4–19.8 demonstrate techniques for working with XML documents in Visual Basic applications. Visual Basic 2008 introduces many new language features for working with XML. LINQ to XML provides a convenient way to manipulate data in XML documents using the same LINQ syntax you used on arrays and collections in Chapter 9. You'll learn XML axis properties, which provide direct access to XML elements, collections of XML elements and XML data. Finally, we'll discuss XML literals, which allow you to create and work with XML directly in your code with standard XML syntax.

19.2 Document Type Definitions (DTDs)

Document Type Definitions (DTDs) are one of two techniques you can use to specify XML document structure. Section 19.3 presents W3C XML Schema documents, which provide an improved method of specifying XML document structure.

Software Engineering Observation 19.1

XML documents can have many different structures, and for this reason an application cannot be certain whether a particular document it receives is complete, ordered properly, and not missing data. DTDs and schemas (Section 19.3) solve this problem by providing an extensible way to describe XML document structure. Applications should use DTDs or schemas to confirm whether XML documents are valid.

Software Engineering Observation 19.2

Many organizations and individuals are creating DTDs and schemas for a broad range of applications. These collections—called repositories—are available free for download from the web (e.g., `www.xml.org`, `www.oasis-open.org`).

Creating a Document Type Definition

Figure 15.4 presented a simple business letter marked up with XML. Recall that line 5 of `letter.xml` references a DTD—`letter.dtd` (Fig. 19.1). This DTD specifies the business letter's element types and attributes, and their relationships to one another.

A DTD describes the structure of an XML document and enables an XML parser to verify whether an XML document is valid (i.e., whether its elements contain the proper attributes and appear in the proper sequence). DTDs allow users to check document structure and to exchange data in a standardized format. A DTD expresses the set of rules for document structure using an EBNF (Extended Backus-Naur Form) grammar. [*Note:* EBNF grammars are commonly used to define programming languages. For more information on EBNF grammars, please see `en.wikipedia.org/wiki/EBNF` or `www.garshol.priv.no/download/text/bnf.html`.]

Common Programming Error 19.1

For documents validated with DTDs, any document that uses elements, attributes or relationships not explicitly defined by a DTD is an invalid document.

```
<!-- Fig. 19.1: letter.dtd       -->
<!-- DTD document for letter.xml -->

<!ELEMENT letter ( contact+, salutation, paragraph+,
   closing, signature )>

<!ELEMENT contact ( name, address1, address2, city, state,
   zip, phone, flag )>
<!ATTLIST contact type CDATA #IMPLIED>

<!ELEMENT name ( #PCDATA )>
<!ELEMENT address1 ( #PCDATA )>
<!ELEMENT address2 ( #PCDATA )>
<!ELEMENT city ( #PCDATA )>
<!ELEMENT state ( #PCDATA )>
<!ELEMENT zip ( #PCDATA )>
<!ELEMENT phone ( #PCDATA )>
<!ELEMENT flag EMPTY>
<!ATTLIST flag gender (M | F) "M">

<!ELEMENT salutation ( #PCDATA )>
<!ELEMENT closing ( #PCDATA )>
<!ELEMENT paragraph ( #PCDATA )>
<!ELEMENT signature ( #PCDATA )>
```

Fig. 19.1 | Document Type Definition (DTD) for a business letter.

Defining Elements in a DTD

The `ELEMENT` element type declaration in lines 4–5 defines the rules for element `letter`. In this case, `letter` contains one or more `contact` elements, one `salutation` element, one or more `paragraph` elements, one `closing` element and one `signature` element, in that sequence. The plus sign (+) occurrence indicator specifies that the DTD allows one or more occurrences of an element. Other occurrence indicators include the asterisk (*), which indicates an optional element that can occur zero or more times, and the question mark (?), which indicates an optional element that can occur at most once (i.e., zero or one occurrence). If an element does not have an occurrence indicator, the DTD allows exactly one occurrence.

The `contact` element type declaration (lines 7–8) specifies that a `contact` element contains child elements `name`, `address1`, `address2`, `city`, `state`, `zip`, `phone` and `flag`—in that order. The DTD requires exactly one occurrence of each of these elements.

Defining Attributes in a DTD

Line 9 uses the `ATTLIST` attribute-list declaration to define an attribute named `type` for the `contact` element. Keyword `#IMPLIED` specifies that the `type` attribute of the `contact` element is optional—a missing `type` attribute will not invalidate the document. Other keywords that can be used in place of `#IMPLIED` in an `ATTLIST` declaration include `#REQUIRED` and `#FIXED`. Keyword `#REQUIRED` specifies that the attribute must be present in the element, and keyword `#FIXED` specifies that the attribute (if present) must have the given fixed value. For example,

```
<!ATTLIST address zip CDATA #FIXED "01757">
```

indicates that attribute `zip` (if present in element `address`) must have the value `01757` for the document to be valid. If the attribute is not present, then the parser, by default, uses the fixed value that the `ATTLIST` declaration specifies. You can supply a default value instead of one of these keywords. Doing so makes the attribute optional, but the default value will be used if the attribute's value is not specified.

Character Data vs. Parsed Character Data

Keyword `CDATA` (line 9) specifies that attribute `type` contains character data (i.e., a string). A parser will pass such data to an application without modification.

Software Engineering Observation 19.3

DTD syntax cannot describe an element's (or attribute's) type. For example, a DTD cannot specify that a particular element or attribute can contain only integer data.

Keyword `#PCDATA` (line 11) specifies that an element (e.g., `name`) may contain parsed character data (i.e., data that is processed by an XML parser). Elements with parsed character data cannot contain markup characters, such as less than (<), greater than (>) or ampersand (&). The document author should replace any markup character in a `#PCDATA` element with the character's corresponding character entity reference. For example, the character entity reference `<` should be used in place of the less-than symbol (<), and the character entity reference `>` should be used in place of the greater-than symbol (>). A document author who wishes to use a literal ampersand should use the entity reference `&` instead—parsed character data can contain ampersands (&) only for inserting entities. The final two entities defined by XML are `'` and `"`, representing the single (`'`) and double (`"`) quote characters, respectively.

Common Programming Error 19.2

Using markup characters (e.g., <, > and &) in parsed character data is an error. Use character entity references (e.g., `<`, `>` and `&` instead).

Defining Empty Elements in a DTD

Line 18 defines an empty element named `flag`. Keyword `EMPTY` specifies that the element does not contain any data between its start and end tags. Empty elements commonly describe data via attributes. For example, `flag`'s data appears in its `gender` attribute (line 19). Line 19 specifies that the `gender` attribute's value must be one of the enumerated values (`M` or `F`) enclosed in parentheses and delimited by a vertical bar (`|`) meaning "or." Note that line 19 also indicates that `gender` has a default value of `M`.

Well-Formed Documents vs. Valid Documents

Recall that a well-formed document is syntactically correct (i.e., each start tag has a corresponding end tag, the document contains only one root element, etc.), and a valid document contains the proper elements with the proper attributes in the proper sequence. An XML document cannot be valid unless it is well formed.

Visual Studio 2008 can validate XML documents against both DTDs and schemas. You do not have to create a project to use this facility—simply open the XML file in Visual Studio as in Fig. 19.2. If the DTD or schema referenced in the XML document can be retrieved, Visual Studio will automatically validate the XML. If the XML file does not validate, Visual Studio will display a warning just as it does with errors in your Visual Basic code (Fig. 19.2). Visit `www.w3.org/XML/Schema` for a list of additional validation tools.

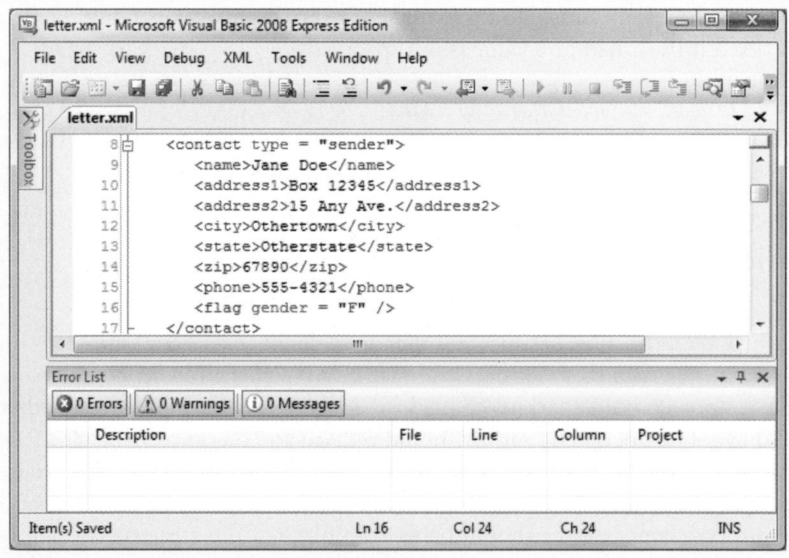

Fig. 19.2 | An XML file open in Visual Basic 2008 Express Edition. (Part 1 of 2.)

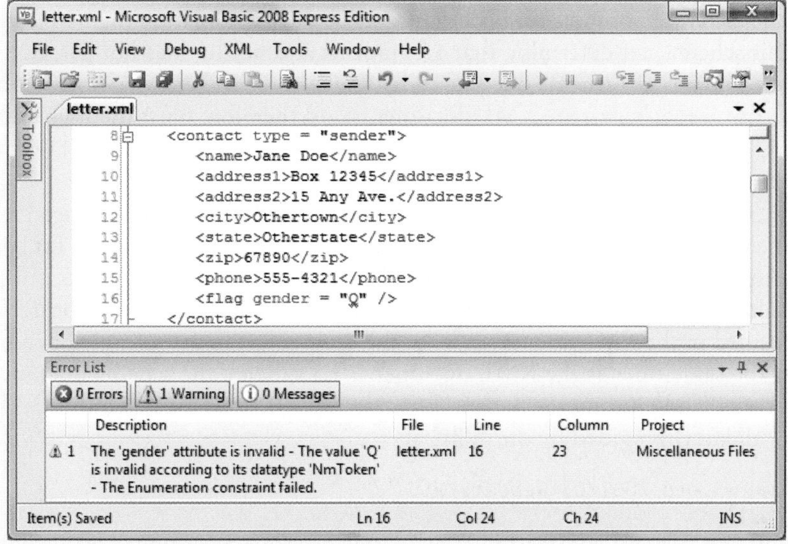

Fig. 19.2 | An XML file open in Visual Basic 2008 Express Edition. (Part 2 of 2.)

19.3 W3C XML Schema Documents

In this section, we introduce schemas for specifying XML document structure and validating XML documents. Many developers in the XML community believe that DTDs are not flexible enough to meet today's programming needs. For example, DTDs lack a way of indicating what specific type of data (e.g., numeric, text) an element can contain and DTDs are not themselves XML documents, making it difficult to manipulate them programmatically. These and other limitations have led to the development of schemas.

Unlike DTDs, schemas do not use EBNF grammar. Instead, schemas use XML syntax and are actually XML documents that programs can manipulate. Like DTDs, schemas are used by validating parsers to validate documents.

In this section, we focus on the W3C's XML Schema vocabulary. For the latest information on XML Schema, visit `www.w3.org/XML/Schema`. For tutorials on XML Schema concepts beyond what we present here, visit `www.w3schools.com/schema/default.asp`.

A DTD describes an XML document's structure, not the content of its elements. For example,

```
<quantity>5</quantity>
```

contains character data. If the document that contains element `quantity` references a DTD, an XML parser can validate the document to confirm that this element indeed does contain `PCDATA` content. However, the parser cannot validate that the content is numeric; DTDs do not provide this capability. So, unfortunately, the parser also considers

```
<quantity>hello</quantity>
```

to be valid. An application that uses the XML document containing this markup should test that the data in element `quantity` is numeric and take appropriate action if it is not.

XML Schema enables schema authors to specify that element `quantity`'s data must be numeric or, even more specifically, an integer. A parser validating the XML document against this schema can determine that `5` conforms and `hello` does not. An XML document that conforms to a schema document is schema valid, and one that does not conform is schema invalid. Schemas are XML documents and therefore must themselves be valid.

Validating Against an XML Schema Document

Figure 19.3 shows a schema-valid XML document named `book.xml`, and Fig. 19.4 shows the pertinent XML Schema document (`book.xsd`) that defines the structure for `book.xml`. By convention, schemas use the `.xsd` extension. Recall that Visual Studio can perform schema validation if it can locate the schema document. Visual Studio can locate a schema if it is specified in the XML document, is in the same solution or is simply open in Visual Studio at the same time as the XML document. To validate the schema document itself (i.e., `book.xsd`) and produce the output shown in Fig. 19.4, we used an online XSV (XML Schema Validator) provided by the W3C at

```
www.w3.org/2001/03/webdata/xsv
```

These tools are free and enforce the W3C's specifications regarding XML Schemas and schema validation.

Figure 19.3 contains markup describing several Deitel books. The `books` element (line 5) has the namespace prefix `deitel`, indicating that the `books` element is a part of the

```
1  <?xml version = "1.0"?>
2  <!-- Fig. 19.3: book.xml -->
3  <!-- Book list marked up as XML -->
4
5  <deitel:books xmlns:deitel = "http://www.deitel.com/booklist">
6     <book>
7        <title>Visual Basic 2008 How to Program</title>
8     </book>
9
10    <book>
11       <title>Visual C# 2008 How to Program, 3/e</title>
12    </book>
13
14    <book>
15       <title>Java How to Program, 7/e</title>
16    </book>
17
18    <book>
19       <title>C++ How to Program, 6/e</title>
20    </book>
21
22    <book>
23       <title>Internet and World Wide Web How to Program, 4/e</title>
24    </book>
25 </deitel:books>
```

Fig. 19.3 | Schema-valid XML document describing a list of books.

```
1  <?xml version = "1.0"?>
2  <!-- Fig. 19.4: book.xsd                   -->
3  <!-- Simple W3C XML Schema document -->
4
5  <schema xmlns = "http://www.w3.org/2001/XMLSchema"
6     xmlns:deitel = "http://www.deitel.com/booklist"
7     targetNamespace = "http://www.deitel.com/booklist">
8
9     <element name = "books" type = "deitel:BooksType"/>
10
11    <complexType name = "BooksType">
12       <sequence>
13          <element name = "book" type = "deitel:SingleBookType"
14             minOccurs = "1" maxOccurs = "unbounded"/>
15       </sequence>
16    </complexType>
17
18    <complexType name = "SingleBookType">
19       <sequence>
20          <element name = "title" type = "string"/>
21       </sequence>
22    </complexType>
23 </schema>
```

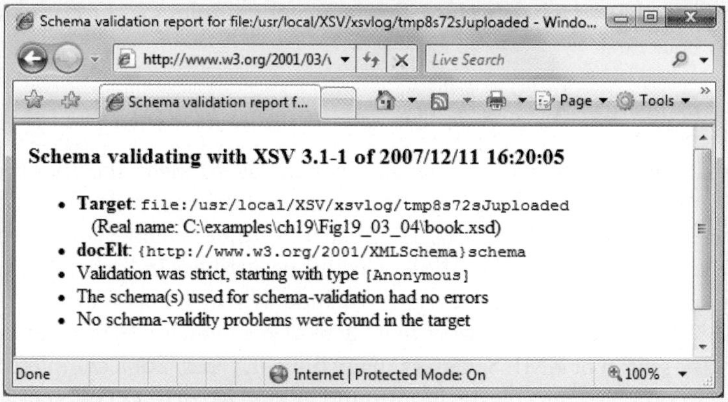

Schema validation report for file:/usr/local/XSV/xsvlog/tmp8s72sJuploaded - Windo...

http://www.w3.org/2001/03/\ Live Search

Schema validation report f... Page Tools

Schema validating with XSV 3.1-1 of 2007/12/11 16:20:05

- **Target**: `file:/usr/local/XSV/xsvlog/tmp8s72sJuploaded` (Real name: C:\examples\ch19\Fig19_03_04\book.xsd)
- **docElt**: `{http://www.w3.org/2001/XMLSchema}schema`
- Validation was strict, starting with type `[Anonymous]`
- The schema(s) used for schema-validation had no errors
- No schema-validity problems were found in the target

Done Internet | Protected Mode: On 100%

Fig. 19.4 | XML Schema document for `book.xml`.

`http://www.deitel.com/booklist` namespace. Note that we declare the namespace prefix `deitel` in line 5.

Creating an XML Schema Document

Figure 19.4 presents the XML Schema document that specifies the structure of `book.xml` (Fig. 19.3). This document defines an XML-based language (i.e., a vocabulary) for writing XML documents about collections of books. The schema defines the elements, attributes and parent-child relationships that such a document can (or must) include. The schema also specifies the type of data that these elements and attributes may contain.

Root element `schema` (Fig. 19.4, lines 5–23) contains elements that define the structure of an XML document such as `book.xml`. Line 5 specifies as the default namespace the standard W3C XML Schema namespace URI—`http://www.w3.org/2001/XMLSchema`. This namespace contains predefined elements (e.g., root element `schema`) that comprise the XML Schema vocabulary—the language used to write an XML Schema document.

Portability Tip 19.1

W3C XML Schema authors specify URI `http://www.w3.org/2001/XMLSchema` when referring to the XML Schema namespace. This namespace contains predefined elements that comprise the XML Schema vocabulary. Specifying this URI ensures that validation tools correctly identify XML Schema elements and do not confuse them with those defined by document authors.

Line 6 binds the URI `http://www.deitel.com/booklist` to namespace prefix `deitel`. As we discuss momentarily, the schema uses this namespace to differentiate names created by us from names that are part of the XML Schema namespace. Line 7 also specifies `http://www.deitel.com/booklist` as the `targetNamespace` of the schema. This attribute identifies the namespace of the XML vocabulary that this schema defines. Note that the `targetNamespace` of `book.xsd` is the same as the namespace referenced in line 5 of `book.xml` (Fig. 19.3). This is what "connects" the XML document with the schema that defines its structure. When an XML schema validator examines `book.xml` and `book.xsd`, it will recognize that `book.xml` uses elements and attributes from the `http://www.deitel.com/booklist` namespace. The validator also will recognize that this namespace is the namespace defined in `book.xsd` (i.e., the schema's `targetNamespace`). Thus the validator knows where to look for the structural rules for the elements and attributes used in `book.xml`.

Defining an Element in XML Schema

In XML Schema, the `element` tag (line 9) defines an element to be included in an XML document that conforms to the schema. In other words, `element` specifies the actual *elements* that can be used to mark up data. Line 9 defines the `books` element, which we use as the root element in `book.xml` (Fig. 19.3). Attributes `name` and `type` specify the `element`'s name and type, respectively. An element's `type` attribute indicates the data type that the element may contain. Possible types include XML Schema–defined types (e.g., `string`, `double`) and user-defined types (e.g., `BooksType`, which is defined in lines 11–16). Figure 19.5 lists several of XML Schema's many built-in types. For a complete list of built-in types, see Section 3 of the specification found at `www.w3.org/TR/xmlschema-2`.

In this example, `books` is defined as an element of type `deitel:BooksType` (line 9). `BooksType` is a user-defined type (lines 11–16) in the `http://www.deitel.com/booklist` namespace and therefore must have the namespace prefix `deitel`. It is not an existing XML Schema type.

Two categories of type exist in XML Schema—simple types and complex types. Simple and complex types differ only in that simple types cannot contain attributes or child elements and complex types can.

A user-defined type that contains attributes or child elements must be defined as a complex type. Lines 11–16 use element `complexType` to define `BooksType` as a complex type that has a child element named `book`. The `sequence` element (lines 12–15) allows you to specify the sequential order in which child elements must appear. The `element` (lines 13–14) nested within the `complexType` element indicates that a `BooksType` element (e.g., `books`) can contain child elements named `book` of type `deitel:SingleBookType` (defined in lines 18–22). Attribute `minOccurs` (line 14), with value `1`, specifies that elements of type `BooksType` must contain a minimum of one `book` element. Attribute `maxOccurs` (line 14), with value `unbounded`, specifies that elements of type `BooksType` may have any number of `book` child elements. Both of these attributes have default values of `1`.

Lines 18–22 define the complex type `SingleBookType`. An element of this type contains a child element named `title`. Line 20 defines element `title` to be of simple type `string`. Recall that elements of a simple type cannot contain attributes or child elements. The `schema` end tag (`</schema>`, line 23) declares the end of the XML Schema document.

A Closer Look at Types in XML Schema

Every element in XML Schema has a type. Types include the built-in types provided by XML Schema (Fig. 19.5) or user-defined types (e.g., `SingleBookType` in Fig. 19.4).

Type	Description	Ranges or Structures	Examples
`string`	A character string.		`"hello"`
`boolean`	True or false.	`true`, `false`	`true`
`decimal`	A decimal numeral.	`i * (10`^{n}`)`, where `i` is an integer and `n` is an integer that is less than or equal to zero.	`5, -12, -45.78`
`float`	A floating-point number.	`m * (2`^{e}`)`, where `m` is an integer whose absolute value is less than 2^{24} and `e` is an integer in the range `-149` to `104`. Plus three additional numbers: positive infinity (`INF`), negative infinity (`-INF`) and not-a-number (`NaN`).	`0, 12, -109.375, NaN`
`double`	A floating-point number.	`m * (2`^{e}`)`, where `m` is an integer whose absolute value is less than 2^{53} and `e` is an integer in the range `-1075` to `970`. Plus three additional numbers: positive infinity, negative infinity and not-a-number (`NaN`).	`0, 12, -109.375, NaN`
`long`	A whole number.	`-9223372036854775808` to `9223372036854775807`, inclusive.	`1234567890, -1234567890`
`int`	A whole number.	`-2147483648` to `2147483647`, inclusive.	`1234567890, -1234567890`
`short`	A whole number.	`-32768` to `32767`, inclusive.	`12, -345`
`date`	A date consisting of a year, month and day.	`yyyy-mm` with an optional `dd` and an optional time zone, where `yyyy` is four digits long and `mm` and `dd` are two digits long. The time zone is specified as `+hh:mm` or `-hh:mm`, giving an offset in hours and minutes.	`2008-07-25+01:00`

Fig. 19.5 | Some XML Schema types. (Part 1 of 2.)

Type	Description	Ranges or Structures	Examples
`time`	A time consisting of hours, minutes and seconds.	`hh:mm:ss` with an optional time zone, where `hh`, `mm` and `ss` are two digits long.	`16:30:25-05:00`

Fig. 19.5 | Some XML Schema types. (Part 2 of 2.)

Every simple type defines a **restriction** on an XML Schema-defined type or a restriction on a user-defined type. Restrictions limit the possible values that an element can hold.

Complex types are divided into two groups—those with **simple content** and those with **complex content**. Both can contain attributes, but only complex content can contain child elements. Complex types with simple content must extend or restrict some other existing type. Complex types with complex content do not have this limitation. We demonstrate complex types with each kind of content in the next example.

The schema document in Fig. 19.6 creates both simple types and complex types. The XML document in Fig. 19.7 (`laptop.xml`) follows the structure defined in Fig. 19.6 to describe parts of a laptop computer. A document such as `laptop.xml` that conforms to a schema is known as an **XML instance document**—the document is an instance (i.e., example) of the schema.

```
<?xml version = "1.0"?>
<!-- Fig. 19.6: computer.xsd -->
<!-- W3C XML Schema document -->

<schema xmlns = "http://www.w3.org/2001/XMLSchema"
   xmlns:computer = "http://www.deitel.com/computer"
   targetNamespace = "http://www.deitel.com/computer">

   <simpleType name = "gigahertz">
      <restriction base = "decimal">
         <minInclusive value = "2.1"/>
      </restriction>
   </simpleType>

   <complexType name = "CPU">
      <simpleContent>
         <extension base = "string">
            <attribute name = "model" type = "string"/>
         </extension>
      </simpleContent>
   </complexType>

   <complexType name = "portable">
      <all>
         <element name = "processor" type = "computer:CPU"/>
         <element name = "monitor" type = "int"/>
         <element name = "CPUSpeed" type = "computer:gigahertz"/>
```

Fig. 19.6 | XML Schema document defining simple and complex types. (Part 1 of 2.)

```
28             <element name = "RAM" type = "int"/>
29          </all>
30          <attribute name = "manufacturer" type = "string"/>
31       </complexType>
32
33       <element name = "laptop" type = "computer:portable"/>
34    </schema>
```

Fig. 19.6 | XML Schema document defining simple and complex types. (Part 2 of 2.)

```
<?xml version = "1.0"?>
<!-- Fig. 19.7: laptop.xml                  -->
<!-- Laptop components marked up as XML -->

<computer:laptop xmlns:computer = "http://www.deitel.com/computer"
   manufacturer = "IBM">

   <processor model = "Centrino">Intel</processor>
   <monitor>17</monitor>
   <CPUSpeed>2.4</CPUSpeed>
   <RAM>256</RAM>
</computer:laptop>
```

Fig. 19.7 | XML document using the `laptop` element defined in `computer.xsd`.

Line 5 declares the default namespace as the standard XML Schema namespace—any elements without a prefix are assumed to be in the XML Schema namespace. Line 6 binds the namespace prefix `computer` to the namespace `http://www.deitel.com/computer`. Line 7 identifies this namespace as the `targetNamespace`—the namespace being defined by the current XML Schema document.

To design the XML elements for describing laptop computers, we first create a simple type in lines 9–13 using the **`simpleType`** element. We name this `simpleType` `gigahertz` because it will be used to describe the clock speed of the processor in gigahertz. Simple types are restrictions of a type typically called a **base type**. For this `simpleType`, line 10 declares the base type as `decimal`, and we restrict the value to be at least `2.1` by using the **`minInclusive`** element in line 11.

Next, we declare a `complexType` named `CPU` that has **`simpleContent`** (lines 16–20). Remember that a complex type with simple content can have attributes but not child elements. Also recall that complex types with simple content must extend or restrict some XML Schema type or user-defined type. The **`extension`** element with attribute **`base`** (line 17) sets the base type to `string`. In this `complexType`, we extend the base type `string` with an attribute. The **`attribute`** element (line 18) gives the `complexType` an attribute of type `string` named `model`. Thus an element of type `CPU` must contain `string` text (because the base type is `string`) and may contain a `model` attribute that is also of type `string`.

Lastly we define type `portable`, which is a `complexType` with complex content (lines 23–31). Such types are allowed to have child elements and attributes. The element **`all`** (lines 24–29) encloses elements that must each be included once in the corresponding XML instance document. These elements can be included in any order. This complex type holds four elements—processor, monitor, CPUSpeed and RAM. They are given types CPU, int, gigahertz and int, respectively. When using types CPU and gigahertz, we must include the namespace prefix computer, because these user-defined types are part of the computer namespace (http://www.deitel.com/computer)—the namespace defined in the current document (line 7). Also, portable contains an attribute defined in line 30. The attribute element indicates that elements of type portable contain an attribute of type string named manufacturer.

Line 33 declares the actual element that uses the three types defined in the schema. The element is called laptop and is of type portable. We must use the namespace prefix computer in front of portable.

We have now created an element named laptop that contains child elements processor, monitor, CPUSpeed and RAM, and an attribute manufacturer. Figure 19.7 uses the laptop element defined in the computer.xsd schema. We used Visual Studio's schema validator to ensure that this XML instance document adheres to the schema's structural rules.

Line 5 declares namespace prefix computer. The laptop element requires this prefix because it is part of the http://www.deitel.com/computer namespace. Line 6 sets the laptop's manufacturer attribute, and lines 8–11 use the elements defined in the schema to describe the laptop's characteristics.

Automatically Creating Schemas using Visual Studio

Visual Studio includes a tool that allows you to create a schema from an existing XML document, using the document as a template. With an XML document open, select **XML > Create Schema** to use this feature. A new schema file opens that conforms to the standards of the XML document. You can now save it and add it to the project.

Good Programming Practice 19.1

The schema generated by Visual Studio is a good starting point, but you should refine the restrictions and types it specifies so they are appropriate for your XML documents.

19.4 Extensible Stylesheet Language and XSL Transformations

Extensible Stylesheet Language (XSL) documents specify how programs are to render XML document data. XSL is a group of three technologies—XSL-FO (XSL Formatting Objects), XPath (XML Path Language) and XSLT (XSL Transformations). XSL-FO is a vocabulary for specifying formatting, and XPath is a string-based language of expressions used by XML and many of its related technologies for effectively and efficiently locating structures and data (such as specific elements and attributes) in XML documents.

The third portion of XSL—XSL Transformations (XSLT)—is a technology for transforming XML documents into other documents—i.e., transforming the structure of the XML document data to another structure. XSLT provides elements that define rules for transforming one XML document to produce a different XML document. This is useful when you want to use data in multiple applications or on multiple platforms, each of which may be designed to work with documents written in a particular vocabulary. For example, XSLT allows you to convert a simple XML document to an XHTML (Extensible HyperText Markup Language) document that presents the XML document's data (or a subset of the data) formatted for display in a web browser. (See Fig. 19.8 for a sample "before" and "after" view of such a transformation.) XHTML is the W3C technical recommendation that replaces HTML for marking up web content. For more information on XHTML, visit `www.deitel.com/xhtml/`.

Transforming an XML document using XSLT involves two tree structures—the source tree (i.e., the XML document to be transformed) and the result tree (i.e., the XML document to be created). XPath is used to locate parts of the source tree document that match templates defined in an XSL style sheet. When a match occurs (i.e., a node matches a template), the matching template executes and adds its result to the result tree. When there are no more matches, XSLT has transformed the source tree into the result tree. The XSLT does not analyze every node of the source tree; it selectively navigates the source tree using XSLT's `select` and `match` attributes. For XSLT to function, the source tree must be properly structured. Schemas, DTDs and validating parsers can validate document structure before using XPath and XSLTs.

A Simple XSL Example

Figure 19.8 lists an XML document that describes various sports. The output shows the result of the transformation (specified in the XSLT template of Fig. 19.9) rendered by Internet Explorer 7. Right click with the page open in Internet Explorer and select **View Source** to view the generated XHTML.

To perform transformations, an XSLT processor is required. Popular XSLT processors include Microsoft's MSXML, the Apache Software Foundation's Xalan (`xalan.apache.org`) and the `XslCompiledTransform` class from the .NET Framework that we use in Section 19.8. The XML document shown in Fig. 19.8 is transformed into an XHTML document by MSXML when the document is loaded in Internet Explorer. MSXML is both an XML parser and an XSLT processor.

```
<?xml version = "1.0"?>
<?xml-stylesheet type = "text/xsl" href = "sports.xsl"?>

<!-- Fig. 19.8: sports.xml -->
<!-- Sports Database -->

<sports>
   <game id = "783">
      <name>Cricket</name>

      <paragraph>
         More popular among commonwealth nations.
      </paragraph>
   </game>

   <game id = "239">
      <name>Baseball</name>

      <paragraph>
         More popular in America.
      </paragraph>
   </game>
```

Fig. 19.8 | XML document that describes various sports. (Part 1 of 2.)

```

   <game id = "418">
      <name>Soccer (Futbol)</name>

      <paragraph>
         Most popular sport in the world.
      </paragraph>
   </game>
</sports>
```

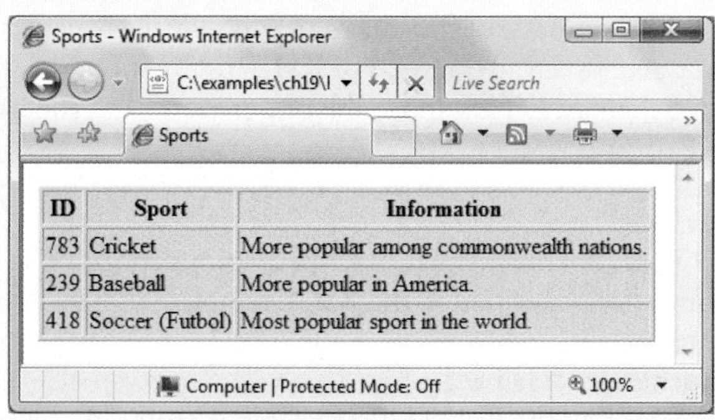

Fig. 19.8 | XML document that describes various sports. (Part 2 of 2.)

```
<?xml version = "1.0"?>
<!-- Fig. 19.9: sports.xsl -->
<!-- A simple XSLT transformation -->

<!-- reference XSL style sheet URI -->
<xsl:stylesheet version = "1.0"
   xmlns:xsl = "http://www.w3.org/1999/XSL/Transform">

   <xsl:output method = "xml" omit-xml-declaration = "no"
      doctype-system =
         "http://www.w3c.org/TR/xhtml1/DTD/xhtml1-strict.dtd"
      doctype-public = "-//W3C//DTD XHTML 1.0 Strict//EN"/>

   <xsl:template match = "/"> <!-- match root element -->

   <html xmlns = "http://www.w3.org/1999/xhtml">
      <head>
         <title>Sports</title>
      </head>

      <body>
         <table border = "1" bgcolor = "wheat">
            <thead>
               <tr>
                  <th>ID</th>
                  <th>Sport</th>
```

Fig. 19.9 | XSLT that creates elements and attributes in an XHTML document. (Part 1 of 2.)

```
27                 <th>Information</th>
28             </tr>
29         </thead>
30
31         <!-- insert each name and paragraph element value -->
32         <!-- into a table row. -->
33         <xsl:for-each select = "/sports/game">
34             <tr>
35                 <td><xsl:value-of select = "@id"/></td>
36                 <td><xsl:value-of select = "name"/></td>
37                 <td><xsl:value-of select = "paragraph"/></td>
38             </tr>
39         </xsl:for-each>
40     </table>
41     </body>
42 </html>
43
44 </xsl:template>
45 </xsl:stylesheet>
```

Fig. 19.9 | XSLT that creates elements and attributes in an XHTML document. (Part 2 of 2.)

Line 2 (Fig. 19.8) is a **processing instruction** (**PI**) that references the XSL style sheet `sports.xsl` (Fig. 19.9). A processing instruction is embedded in an XML document and provides application-specific information to whichever XML processor the application uses. In this particular case, the processing instruction specifies the location of an XSLT document with which to transform the XML document. The characters `<?` and `?>` (line 2, Fig. 19.8) delimit a processing instruction, which consists of a **PI target** (e.g., `xml-stylesheet`) and a **PI value** (e.g., `type = "text/xsl" href = "sports.xsl"`). The PI value's `type` attribute specifies that `sports.xsl` is a `text/xsl` file (i.e., a text file containing XSL content). The `href` attribute specifies the name and location of the style sheet to apply—in this case, `sports.xsl` in the current directory.

Software Engineering Observation 19.4

XSL enables document authors to separate data presentation (specified in XSL documents) from data description (specified in XML documents).

Figure 19.9 shows the XSL document for transforming the structured data of the XML document of Fig. 19.8 into an XHTML document for presentation. By convention, XSL documents have the filename extension **`.xsl`**.

Lines 6–7 begin the XSL style sheet with the **`stylesheet`** start tag. Attribute **`version`** specifies the XSLT version to which this document conforms. Line 7 binds namespace prefix **`xsl`** to the W3C's XSLT URI (i.e., `http://www.w3.org/1999/XSL/Transform`).

Lines 9–12 use element **`xsl:output`** to write an XHTML document type declaration (`DOCTYPE`) to the result tree (i.e., the XML document to be created). The `DOCTYPE` identifies XHTML as the type of the resulting document. Attribute `method` is assigned `"xml"`, which indicates that XML is being output to the result tree. (Recall that XHTML is a type of XML.) Attribute **`omit-xml-declaration`** specifies whether the transformation should write the XML declaration to the result tree. In this case, we do not want to omit the XML declaration, so we assign to this attribute the value "no". Attributes doctype-system and doctype-public write the DOCTYPE DTD information to the result tree.

XSLT uses templates (i.e., xsl:template elements) to describe how to transform particular nodes from the source tree to the result tree. A template is applied to nodes that are specified in the match attribute. Line 14 uses the match attribute to select the document root (i.e., the conceptual part of the document that contains the root element and everything below it) of the XML source document (i.e., sports.xml). The XPath character / (a forward slash) is used as a separator between element names. Recall that XPath is a string-based language used to locate parts of an XML document easily. In XPath, a leading forward slash specifies that we are using absolute addressing (i.e., we are starting from the root and defining paths down the source tree). In the XML document of Fig. 19.8, the child nodes of the document root are the two processing instruction nodes (lines 1–2), the two comment nodes (lines 4–5) and the sports element node (lines 7–31). The template in Fig. 19.9, line 14, matches a node (i.e., the document root), so the contents of the template are now added to the result tree.

The XSLT processor writes the XHTML in lines 16–29 (Fig. 19.9) to the result tree exactly as it appears in the XSL document. Now the result tree consists of the DOCTYPE definition and the XHTML code from lines 16–29. Lines 33–39 use element xsl:for-each to iterate through the source XML document, searching for game elements. The xsl:for-each element is similar to Visual Basic's For Each statement. Attribute select is an XPath expression that specifies the nodes (called the node set) on which the xsl:for-each operates. Again, the first forward slash means that we are using absolute addressing. The forward slash between sports and game indicates that game is a child node of sports. Thus, the xsl:for-each finds game nodes that are children of the sports node. The XML document sports.xml contains only one sports node, which is also the document root element. After finding the elements that match the selection criteria, the xsl:for-each processes each element with the code in lines 34–38 (these lines produce one row in an XHTML table each time they execute) and places the result of lines 34–38 in the result tree.

Line 35 uses element value-of to retrieve attribute id's value and place it in a td element in the result tree. The XPath symbol @ specifies that id is an attribute node of the game context node (i.e., the current node being processed). Lines 36–37 place the name and paragraph element values in td elements and insert them in the result tree. When an XPath expression has no beginning forward slash, the expression uses relative addressing. Omitting the beginning forward slash tells the xsl:value-of select statements to search for name and paragraph elements that are children of the context node, not the root node. Due to the last XPath expression selection, the current context node is game, which indeed has an id attribute, a name child element and a paragraph child element.

Using XSLT to Sort and Format Data

Figure 19.10 presents an XML document (sorting.xml) that marks up information about a book. Note that several elements of the markup describing the book appear out of order (e.g., the element describing Chapter 3 appears before the element describing Chapter 2). We arranged them this way purposely to demonstrate that the XSL style sheet referenced in line 5 (sorting.xsl) can sort the XML file's data for presentation purposes.

Figure 19.11 presents an XSL document (sorting.xsl) for transforming sorting.xml (Fig. 19.10) to XHTML. Recall that an XSL document navigates a source

```
<?xml version = "1.0"?>
<!-- Fig. 19.10: sorting.xml -->
<!-- XML document containing book information -->

<?xml-stylesheet type = "text/xsl" href = "sorting.xsl"?>

<book isbn = "999-99999-9-X">
   <title>Deitel&apos;s XML Primer</title>

   <author>
      <firstName>Jane</firstName>
      <lastName>Blue</lastName>
   </author>

   <chapters>
      <frontMatter>
         <preface pages = "2" />
         <contents pages = "5" />
         <illustrations pages = "4" />
      </frontMatter>

      <chapter number = "3" pages = "44">Advanced XML</chapter>
      <chapter number = "2" pages = "35">Intermediate XML</chapter>
      <appendix number = "B" pages = "26">Parsers and Tools</appendix>
      <appendix number = "A" pages = "7">Entities</appendix>
      <chapter number = "1" pages = "28">XML Fundamentals</chapter>
   </chapters>

   <media type = "CD" />
</book>
```

Fig. 19.10 | XML document containing book information.

tree and builds a result tree. In this example, the source tree is XML, and the output tree is XHTML. Line 14 of Fig. 19.11 matches the root element of the document in Fig. 19.10. Line 15 outputs an `html` start tag to the result tree. The `<xsl:apply-templates/>` element (line 16) specifies that the XSLT processor is to apply the `xsl:templates` defined in this XSL document to the current node's (i.e., the document root's) children. The content from the applied templates is output in the `html` element that ends at line 17. Lines 21–86 specify a template that matches element `book`. The template indicates how to format the information contained in `book` elements of `sorting.xml` (Fig. 19.10) as XHTML.

```
1  <?xml version = "1.0"?>
2  <!-- Fig. 19.11: sorting.xsl -->
3  <!-- Transformation of book information into XHTML -->
4
5  <xsl:stylesheet version = "1.0"
6     xmlns:xsl = "http://www.w3.org/1999/XSL/Transform">
7
```

Fig. 19.11 | XSL document that transforms `sorting.xml` into XHTML. (Part 1 of 3.)

```
    <!-- write XML declaration and DOCTYPE DTD information -->
    <xsl:output method = "xml" omit-xml-declaration = "no"
       doctype-system = "http://www.w3.org/TR/xhtml11/DTD/xhtml11.dtd"
       doctype-public = "-//W3C//DTD XHTML 1.1//EN"/>

    <!-- match document root -->
    <xsl:template match = "/">
       <html xmlns = "http://www.w3.org/1999/xhtml">
          <xsl:apply-templates/>
       </html>
    </xsl:template>

    <!-- match book -->
    <xsl:template match = "book">
       <head>
          <title>ISBN <xsl:value-of select = "@isbn"/> -
             <xsl:value-of select = "title"/></title>
       </head>

       <body>
          <h1 style = "color: blue"><xsl:value-of select = "title"/></h1>
          <h2 style = "color: blue">by
             <xsl:value-of select = "author/firstName"/>
             <xsl:text> </xsl:text>
             <xsl:value-of select = "author/lastName"/>
          </h2>

          <table style = "border-style: groove; background-color: wheat">

             <xsl:for-each select = "chapters/frontMatter/*">
                <tr>
                   <td style = "text-align: right">
                      <xsl:value-of select = "name()"/>
                   </td>

                   <td>
                      ( <xsl:value-of select = "@pages"/> pages )
                   </td>
                </tr>
             </xsl:for-each>

             <xsl:for-each select = "chapters/chapter">
                <xsl:sort select = "@number" data-type = "number"
                     order = "ascending"/>
                <tr>
                   <td style = "text-align: right">
                      Chapter <xsl:value-of select = "@number"/>
                   </td>

                   <td>
                      <xsl:value-of select = "text()"/>
                      ( <xsl:value-of select = "@pages"/> pages )
                   </td>
```

Fig. 19.11 | XSL document that transforms `sorting.xml` into XHTML. (Part 2 of 3.)

```
               </tr>
            </xsl:for-each>

            <xsl:for-each select = "chapters/appendix">
               <xsl:sort select = "@number" data-type = "text"
                  order = "ascending"/>
               <tr>
                  <td style = "text-align: right">
                     Appendix <xsl:value-of select = "@number"/>
                  </td>

                  <td>
                     <xsl:value-of select = "text()"/>
                     ( <xsl:value-of select = "@pages"/> pages )
                  </td>
               </tr>
            </xsl:for-each>
         </table>

         <br /><p style = "color: blue">Pages:
            <xsl:variable name = "pagecount"
               select = "sum(chapters//*/@pages)"/>
            <xsl:value-of select = "$pagecount"/>
         <br />Media Type: <xsl:value-of select = "media/@type"/></p>
      </body>
   </xsl:template>
</xsl:stylesheet>
```

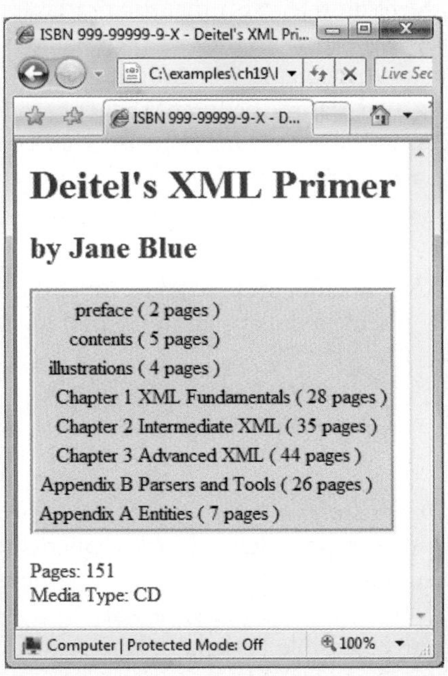

Fig. 19.11 | XSL document that transforms `sorting.xml` into XHTML. (Part 3 of 3.)

Lines 23–24 create the title for the XHTML document. We use the book's ISBN (from attribute isbn) and the contents of element title to create the string that appears in the browser window's title bar (**ISBN 999-99999-9-X - Deitel's XML Primer**).

Line 28 creates a header element that contains the book's title. Lines 29–33 create a header element that contains the book's author. Because the context node (i.e., the current node being processed) is book, the XPath expression author/lastName selects the author's last name, and the expression author/firstName selects the author's first name. The xsl:text element (line 31) is used to insert literal text. Because XML (and therefore XSLT) ignores whitespace, the author's name would appear as **JaneBlue** without inserting the explicit space.

Line 37 selects each element (indicated by an asterisk) that is a child of element frontMatter. Line 40 calls node-set function name to retrieve the current node's element name (e.g., preface). The current node is the context node specified in the xsl:for-each (line 37). Line 44 retrieves the value of the pages attribute of the current node.

Line 49 selects each chapter element. Lines 50–51 use element xsl:sort to sort chapters by number in ascending order. Attribute select selects the value of attribute number in context node chapter. Attribute data-type, with value "number", specifies a numeric sort, and attribute order, with value "ascending", specifies ascending order. Attribute data-type also accepts the value "text" (line 65), and attribute order also accepts the value "descending". Line 58 uses node-set function text to obtain the text between the chapter start and end tags (i.e., the name of the chapter). Line 59 retrieves the value of the pages attribute of the current node. Lines 64–77 perform similar tasks for each appendix.

Lines 81–82 use an XSL variable to store the value of the book's total page count and output the page count to the result tree. Note that such variables cannot be modified after they are initialized. Attribute name specifies the variable's name (i.e., pagecount), and attribute select assigns a value to the variable. Function sum (line 82) totals the values for all page attribute values. The two slashes between chapters and * indicate a recursive descent—the XSLT processor will search for elements that contain an attribute named pages in all descendant nodes of chapters. The XPath expression

```
//*
```

selects all the nodes in an XML document. Line 83 retrieves the value of the newly created XSL variable pagecount by placing a dollar sign in front of its name.

Performance Tip 19.1

Selecting all nodes in a document when it is not necessary slows XSLT processing.

Summary of XSL Style Sheet Elements

This section's examples used several predefined XSL elements to perform various operations. Figure 19.12 lists commonly used XSL elements. For more information on these elements and XSL in general, see www.w3.org/Style/XSL.

This section introduced Extensible Stylesheet Language (XSL) and showed how to create XSL transformations to convert XML documents from one format to another. We showed how to transform XML documents to XHTML documents for display in a web

Element	Description
`<xsl:apply-templates>`	Applies the templates of the XSL document to the children of the current node.
`<xsl:apply-templates match = "`*expression*`">`	Applies the templates of the XSL document to the children of the nodes matching *expression*. The value of the attribute match (i.e., *expression*) must be an XPath expression that specifies elements.
`<xsl:template>`	Contains rules to apply when a specified node is matched.
`<xsl:value-of select = "`*expression*`">`	Selects the value of an XML element and adds it to the output tree of the transformation. The required `select` attribute contains an XPath expression.
`<xsl:for-each select = "`*expression*`">`	Applies a template to every node selected by the XPath specified by the `select` attribute.
`<xsl:sort select = "`*expression*`">`	Used as a child element of an `<xsl:apply-templates>` or `<xsl:for-each>` element. Sorts the nodes selected by the `<xsl:apply-template>` or `<xsl:for-each>` element so that the nodes are processed in sorted order.
`<xsl:output>`	Has various attributes to define the format (e.g., XML, XHTML), version (e.g., 1.0, 2.0), document type and MIME type of the output document. MIME types are discussed in Section 21.2. This tag is a top-level element—it can be used only as a child element of an `xsl:stylesheet`.
`<xsl:copy>`	Adds the current node to the output tree.

Fig. 19.12 | XSL style sheet elements.

browser. In most business applications, XML documents are transferred between business partners and are transformed to other XML vocabularies programmatically. In Section 19.8, we demonstrate how to perform XSL transformations using the `XslCompiledTransform` class provided by the .NET Framework.

19.5 LINQ to XML: Document Object Model (DOM)

Although an XML document is a text file, retrieving data from the document using traditional sequential file processing techniques is not practical, especially for adding and removing elements dynamically.

On successfully parsing a document, some XML parsers store document data as trees in memory. Figure 19.13 illustrates the tree structure for the document `article.xml` discussed in Fig. 15.2. This hierarchical tree structure is called a Document Object Model (DOM) tree, and an XML parser that creates such a tree is known as a DOM parser. DOM gets its name from the conversion of an XML document's tree structure into a tree of objects that are then manipulated using an object-oriented programming language such

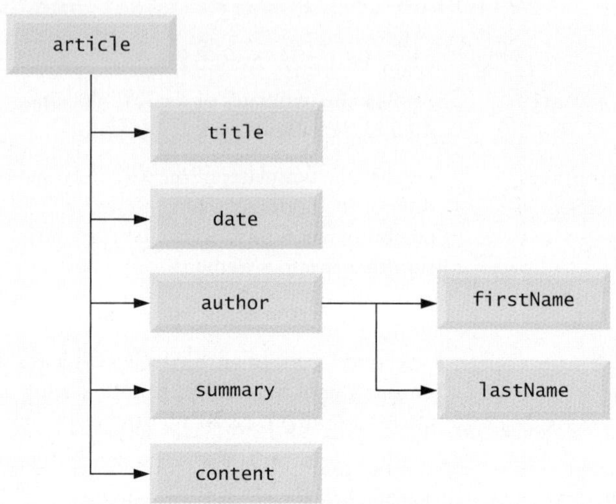

Fig. 19.13 | Tree structure for the document `article.xml`.

as Visual Basic. Each element name (e.g., `article`, `date`, `firstName`) is represented by a node. A node that contains other nodes (called child nodes or children) is called a parent node (e.g., `author`). A parent node can have many children, but a child node can have only one parent node. Nodes that are peers (e.g., `firstName` and `lastName`) are called sibling nodes. A node's descendant nodes include its children, its children's children and so on. A node's ancestor nodes include its parent, its parent's parent and so on.

The DOM tree has a single root node, which contains all the other nodes in the document. For example, the root node of the DOM tree that represents `article.xml` (Fig. 15.2) contains a node for the XML declaration (line 1), two nodes for the comments (lines 2–3) and a node for the XML document's root element `article` (line 5).

Classes for creating, reading and manipulating XML documents are located in the `System.Xml` namespace, which also contains additional namespaces that provide other XML-related operations.

Reading an XML Document with an `XDocument`

Namespace `System.Xml.Linq` contains the classes used to manipulate a DOM in the .NET framework—though LINQ query expressions are not required to use them, the technologies used are collectively referred to as LINQ to XML. Previous versions of the .NET Framework used a different DOM implementation in the `System.Xml` namespace. These classes (such as `XmlDocument`) were made obsolete by LINQ to XML. The `XElement` class represents a DOM element node—a full XML document is represented by a tree of `XElement` objects. The `XDocument` class represents an entire XML document. Unlike `XElements`, `XDocuments` cannot be nested. Figure 19.14 uses these classes to load the `article.xml` document presented in Fig. 15.2 and display its data in a `TextBox`. The program displays a formatted version of its input XML file. If `article.xml` were poorly formatted, such as being all on one line, this application would allow you to convert it into a form that is much easier to understand.

```
' Fig. 19.14: XDocumentTestForm.vb
' Reading an XML document and displaying it in a TextBox.
Imports System.Xml.Linq ' import namespace for XDocument and XElement

Public Class XDocumentTestForm
   ' read XML document and display its content
   Private Sub XDocumentTestForm_Load(ByVal sender As System.Object, _
      ByVal e As System.EventArgs) Handles MyBase.Load

      ' load the XML file into an XDocument
      Dim xmlFile = XDocument.Load("article.xml")
      Dim indent As Integer = 0 ' no indentation for root element
      PrintElement(xmlFile.Root, indent) ' print elements recursively
   End Sub ' XDocumentTestForm_Load

   ' print an element (and its children, if any) in the TextBox
   Private Sub PrintElement(ByVal element As XElement, _
      ByVal indentLevel As Integer)

      Dim name = element.Name.LocalName ' element name without namespace

      ' display the element's name within its tag
      IndentOutput(indentLevel) ' add correct amount of indentation
      outputTextBox.AppendText("<" & name & ">" & vbNewLine)

      ' check for child elements and print value if none contained
      If element.HasElements Then
         ' print all child elements
         For Each child In element.Elements()
            ' print the contained element at the next indentation level
            PrintElement(child, indentLevel + 1)
         Next
      Else
         ' increase the indentation amount for text elements
         IndentOutput(indentLevel + 1)

         ' display the text inside this element
         outputTextBox.AppendText(element.Value.Trim() & vbNewLine)
      End If

      ' display end tag
      IndentOutput(indentLevel)
      outputTextBox.AppendText("</" & name & ">" & vbNewLine)
   End Sub ' PrintElement

   ' add the specified amount of indentation to the current line
   Private Sub IndentOutput(ByVal number As Integer)
      For i = 1 To number
         outputTextBox.AppendText("   ")
      Next
   End Sub ' IndentOutput
End Class ' XDocumentTestForm
```

Fig. 19.14 | Reading an XML document and displaying it in a `TextBox`. (Part 1 of 2.)

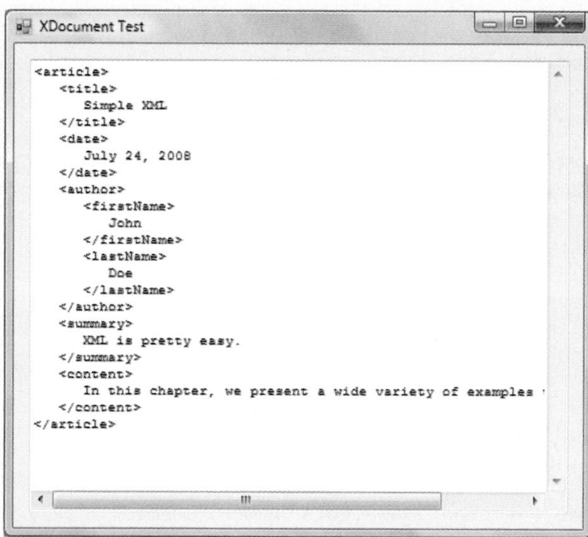

Fig. 19.14 | Reading an XML document and displaying it in a `TextBox`. (Part 2 of 2.)

To create an `XDocument` from an existing XML document, we use its `Shared` `Load` method, giving the location of the document as an argument (line 11). The returned `XDocument` contains a tree representation of the loaded XML file, which is used to navigate the file's contents. The `XDocument`'s `Root` property (line 13) returns an `XElement` representing the root element of the XML file.

Method `PrintElement` (lines 17–44) displays an `XElement` in `outputTextBox`. Because nested elements should be at different indentation levels, `PrintElement` takes an `Integer` specifying the amount of indentation to use in addition to the `XElement` it is displaying. The `indentLevel` parameter is passed to the `IndentOutput` method (lines 47–51) to add the correct amount of spacing before the begin (line 24) and end (line 43) tags are displayed.

As you've seen in previous sections, tag and attribute names often have a namespace prefix. Because the full names consist of two parts (the prefix and name), tag and attribute names are not simply stored as `Strings`, but as objects of class `XName`. The `Name` property of an `XElement` (line 20) returns an `XName` object containing the tag name and namespace—we are not interested in the namespace, so we retrieve the unqualified name using the `XName`'s `LocalName` property.

`XElements` with and without children are treated differently in the program—this test is performed using the `XElement`'s `HasElements` property (line 27). For `XElements` with children, the children are iterated through using the `Elements` method and printed recursively by calling `PrintElement` (line 31). For `XElements` that do not have children, the text they contain is displayed using the `Value` property. If used on an element with children, the `Value` property returns all of the text contained within its descendants, with the tags removed. For simplicity, elements with attributes and those with both elements and text as children are not handled. The indentation is increased by one in both cases to allow for proper formatting.

19.6 LINQ to XML: XML Axis Properties

As you saw in the previous section, `XElement` objects provide several methods for quickly traversing the DOM tree they represent. XML axis properties are a new feature in Visual Basic 2008 that provide a convenient syntax for navigating an `XElement` DOM tree. They provide functionality similar to XPath , but with axis properties the IDE can provide *IntelliSense* and refactoring tools just as it can with Visual Basic code.

XML axis properties can be used in concert with normal method calls on `XElement` objects. Figure 19.15 uses XML axis properties to provide functionality similar to the XPath strings introduced in Section 19.4. It displays the structure of an XML document in a `TreeView` control and allows the user to navigate within the DOM tree. The file used as a data source (`sports.xml`) is shown in Fig. 19.8.

The interface for this example allows the user to select which elements to display, and navigate through the DOM tree in the lower `TreeView`. Initially, the `TextBox` is blank, and the `TreeView` is initialized to show the `sports` element—the root of the tree. The `ComboBox` at the top of the `Form` contains XPath expressions. These are not used directly—instead, the example uses XML axis properties and a LINQ query to retrieve the same results. As in the previous example, the `XDocument`'s `Load` method (line 15) is used to load the contents of the XML file into memory. The `sports` element is accessed by passing the XPath string `"/sports"` to `XPathSelectElement`, an extension method from namespace `System.Xml.XPath` (imported at line 4) that allows you to use an XPath expression to navigate `XDocument` and `XElement` objects. Line 19 creates a `TreeNode` for the `XElement` with the correct text, which is then inserted into the `TreeView` (lines 20–21). The `TreeRefresh` method (lines 132–136), refreshes the `treePath` control so that the user interface updates correctly.

The `SelectedIndexChanged` event handler of `locateComboBox` (lines 25–53) uses XML axis properties to fill the `TextBox` with the elements corresponding to the path the user selected. There are three kinds of axis properties. A child axis (line 32) refers to elements that are direct children of the current element and have the specified name. Note the similarity to XPath expressions, except the `/` separator is replaced by the dot (`.`) operator typically used for accessing methods or properties and the tag names are enclosed in angle brackets. Child axes also function like XPath—they return a collection of `XElement` objects—an `IEnumerable(Of XElement)`—instead of a single object.

```
1  ' Fig. 19.15: PathNavigatorForm.vb
2  ' Document navigation using XNode and axis properties.
3  Imports System.Xml ' for XmlNodeType Enumeration
4  Imports System.Xml.XPath ' for XPathSelectElement extension method
5
6  Public Class PathNavigatorForm
7     Private current As XNode ' currently selected element
8     Private document As XDocument ' the document to navigate
9     Private tree As TreeNode ' TreeNode used by TreeView control
10
11    ' initialize variables and TreeView control
12    Private Sub PathNavigatorForm_Load(ByVal sender As System.Object, _
13       ByVal e As System.EventArgs) Handles MyBase.Load
14
```

Fig. 19.15 | Document navigation using `XNode` and axis properties. (Part 1 of 6.)

```
      document = XDocument.Load("sports.xml") ' load sports.xml

      ' create first element representation using an XPath Expression
      current = document.XPathSelectElement("/sports")
      tree = New TreeNode(NodeText(current)) ' create root TreeNode
      treePath.Nodes.Add(tree) ' add TreeNode to TreeView
      TreeRefresh() ' reset the tree display
   End Sub ' PathNavigatorForm_Load

   ' print the elements of the selected path
   Private Sub locateComboBox_SelectedIndexChanged( _
      ByVal sender As System.Object, ByVal e As System.EventArgs) _
      Handles locateComboBox.SelectedIndexChanged

      ' retrieve the set of elements to output
      Select Case locateComboBox.SelectedIndex
         Case 0 ' print all sports elements
            PrintElements(document.<sports>)
         Case 1 ' print all game elements
            ' could also be document.<sports>.<game>
            PrintElements(document...<game>)
         Case 2 ' print all name elements
            ' could also be document.<sports>.<game>.<name>
            PrintElements(document...<name>)
         Case 3 ' print all paragraph elements
            ' could also be document.<sports>.<game>.<paragraph>
            PrintElements(document...<paragraph>)
         Case 4 ' print game elements with a name element of "Cricket"
            ' use LINQ to XML to retrieve the correct node
            Dim cricket = _
               From game In document...<game> _
               Where game.<name>.Value = "Cricket" _
               Select game
            PrintElements(cricket)
         Case 5 ' print all id attributes of game
            ' could also be document.<sports>.<game>
            PrintIDs(document...<game>)
      End Select
   End Sub ' locateComboBox_SelectedIndexChanged

   ' traverse to first child
   Private Sub firstChildButton_Click(ByVal sender As System.Object, _
      ByVal e As System.EventArgs) Handles firstChildButton.Click

      ' if current is an element and has children, move to first child
      If current.NodeType = XmlNodeType.Element AndAlso _
         CType(current, XElement).Nodes().Any() Then

         current = CType(current, XElement).Nodes().First() ' first child

         ' create new TreeNode for this node with correct label
         Dim newNode As New TreeNode(NodeText(current))
         tree.Nodes.Add(newNode) ' add node to TreeNode Nodes list
```

Fig. 19.15 | Document navigation using XNode and axis properties. (Part 2 of 6.)

```
         tree = newNode ' move current selection to newNode '
         TreeRefresh() ' reset the tree display
      Else ' current is not an element or is an element with no children
         MessageBox.Show("Current node has no children.", "Warning", _
            MessageBoxButtons.OK, MessageBoxIcon.Information)
      End If
   End Sub ' firstChildButton_Click

   ' traverse to node's parent
   Private Sub parentButton_Click(ByVal sender As System.Object, _
      ByVal e As System.EventArgs) Handles parentButton.Click

      ' if current node is not the root, move to parent
      If current.Parent IsNot Nothing Then
         current = current.Parent ' get parent node
         tree = tree.Parent ' get parent in tree structure
         tree.Nodes.Clear() ' remove all children
         TreeRefresh() ' reset the tree display
      Else ' element has no parent (root element)
         MessageBox.Show("Current node has no parent.", "Warning", _
            MessageBoxButtons.OK, MessageBoxIcon.Information)
      End If
   End Sub ' parentButton_Click

   ' traverse to previous node
   Private Sub previousButton_Click(ByVal sender As System.Object, _
      ByVal e As System.EventArgs) Handles previousButton.Click

      ' if current node is not first, move to previous node
      If current.PreviousNode IsNot Nothing AndAlso _
         current.Parent IsNot Nothing Then

         current = current.PreviousNode ' move to previous node
         Dim treeParent = tree.Parent ' get parent node
         treeParent.Nodes.Remove(tree) ' delete current node
         tree = treeParent.LastNode ' set current position for display
         TreeRefresh() ' reset the tree display
      Else ' current element is last among its siblings
         MessageBox.Show("Current node is first sibling.", "Warning", _
            MessageBoxButtons.OK, MessageBoxIcon.Information)
      End If
   End Sub ' previousButton_Click

   ' traverse to next node
   Private Sub nextButton_Click(ByVal sender As System.Object, _
      ByVal e As System.EventArgs) Handles nextButton.Click

      ' if current node is not last, move to next node
      If current.NextNode IsNot Nothing AndAlso _
         current.Parent IsNot Nothing Then

         current = current.NextNode ' move to next node
         Dim treeParent = tree.Parent ' get parent node
```

Fig. 19.15 | Document navigation using XNode and axis properties. (Part 3 of 6.)

```
            Dim newNode As New TreeNode(NodeText(current)) ' create new node
            treeParent.Nodes.Add(newNode) ' add to parent node
            tree = newNode ' set current position for display
            TreeRefresh() ' reset the tree display
         Else ' current node is last among its siblings
            MessageBox.Show("Current node is last sibling.", "Warning", _
               MessageBoxButtons.OK, MessageBoxIcon.Information)
         End If
      End Sub ' nextButton_Click

      ' update TreeView control
      Private Sub TreeRefresh()
         treePath.ExpandAll() ' expand tree node in TreeView
         treePath.Refresh() ' force TreeView update
         treePath.SelectedNode = tree ' highlight current node
      End Sub ' TreeRefresh

      ' print values in the given collection
      Private Sub PrintElements(ByVal elements As IEnumerable(Of XElement))
         locateTextBox.Clear() ' clear the text area

         ' display text inside all elements
         For Each element In elements
            locateTextBox.AppendText(element.Value.Trim() & vbNewLine)
         Next
      End Sub ' PrintElements

      ' print the ID numbers of all games in elements
      Private Sub PrintIDs(ByVal elements As IEnumerable(Of XElement))
         locateTextBox.Clear() ' clear the text area

         ' display "id" attribute of all elements
         For Each element In elements
            locateTextBox.AppendText(element.@id.Trim() & vbNewLine)
         Next
      End Sub ' PrintIDs

      ' returns text used to represent an element in the tree
      Private Function NodeText(ByVal element As XNode) As String
         ' if node is an element then use its name
         If element.NodeType = XmlNodeType.Element Then
            ' represent node by tag name
            Return CType(element, XElement).Name.LocalName
         ElseIf element.NodeType = XmlNodeType.Text Then ' if node is XText
            ' represent node by text stored in Value property
            Return CType(element, XText).Value.Trim()
         Else
            ' all nodes in this example are elements or text;
            ' return a reasonable default value for other nodes
            Return element.NodeType.ToString()
         End If
      End Function ' NodeText
   End Class ' PathNavigatorForm
```

Fig. 19.15 | Document navigation using XNode and axis properties. (Part 4 of 6.)

a) **Path Navigator** form upon loading.

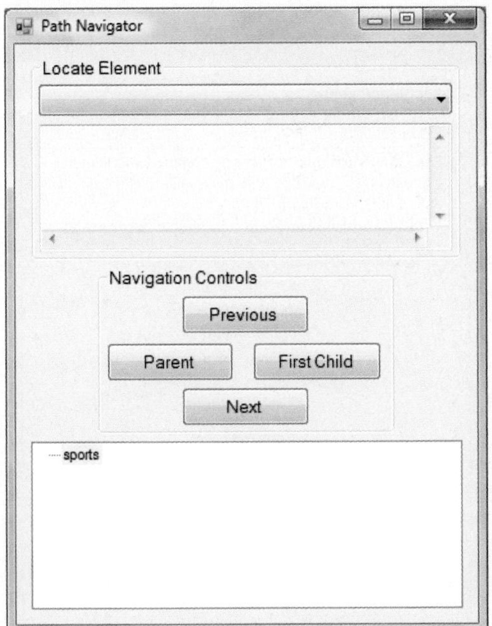

b) The **//name** path is selected.

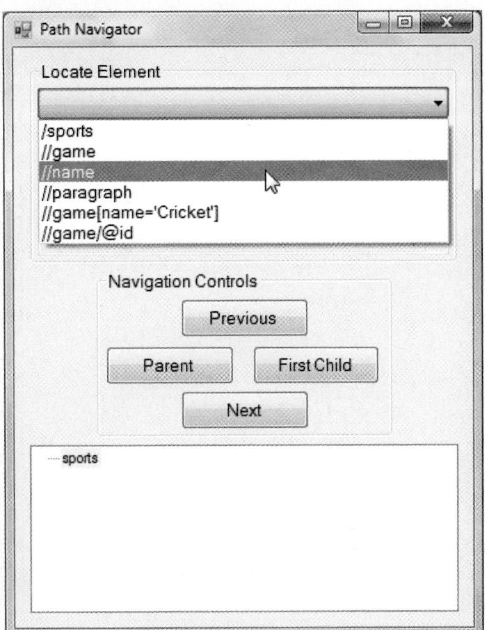

c) The **//name** path displays all **name** elements in the document.

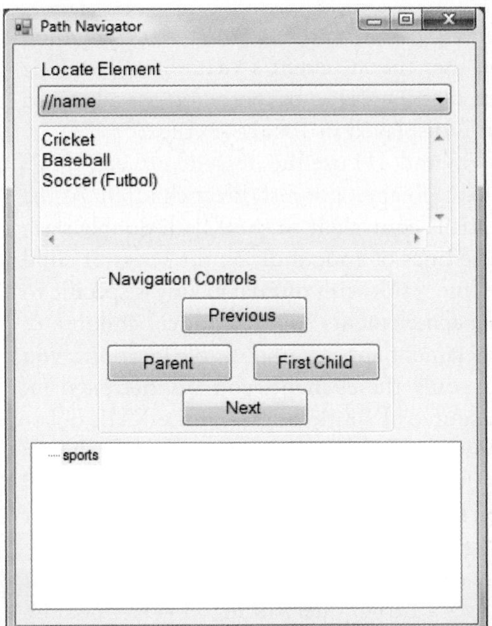

d) The **//game[name='Cricket']** path displays **game** elements with a **name** element containing "Cricket."

Fig. 19.15 | Document navigation using `XNode` and axis properties. (Part 5 of 6.)

e) The **First Child** button expands the tree to show the first element in that group.

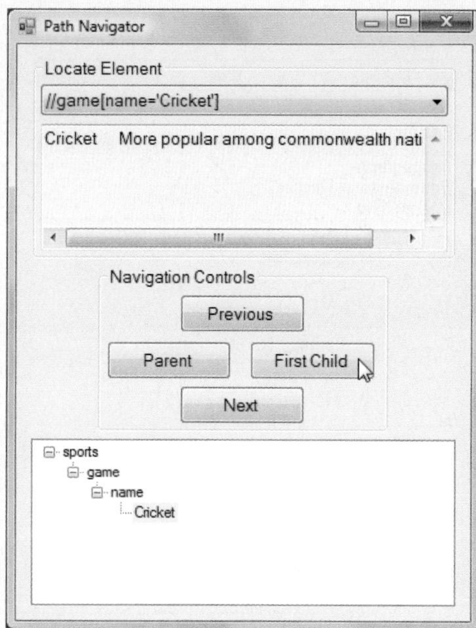

f) The **Next** button lets you view siblings of the current element

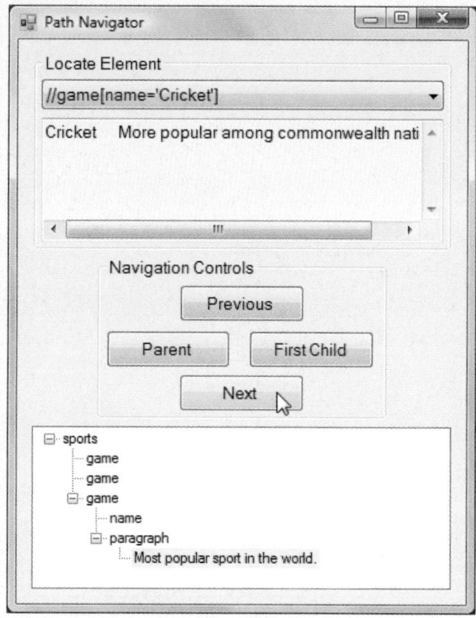

Fig. 19.15 | Document navigation using `XNode` and axis properties. (Part 6 of 6.)

The results of this axis property expression are passed to the `PrintElements` method (lines 139–146). The `PrintElements` method uses the `XElement`'s `Value` property (line 144) introduced in the previous example. Note that the `Value` property returns all text in the current node and its descendants. The text is displayed in `locateTextBox`.

The next three `Case` statements (lines 35, 38 and 41) use the descendant axis (`...`), which retrieves all descendants with the specified tag name, not just direct children. As the text in the `ComboBox` indicates, a descendant axis is equivalent to the XPath double slash (//) operator. The comments above these three lines of code indicate the series of child axes that could have been used to achieve the same result with our data. This is specific to `sports.xml`—for example, all `name` and `paragraph` elements appear as direct children of `game` elements. In a document where a specific element appears in multiple locations, you may need to use child axes explicitly to return only the elements you are interested in. Using descendant axes in these cases can be a source of subtle bugs— if the XML document's structure changes, your code could silently accept input that the program should not treat as valid. Descendant axes are best used for tags that can appear at any nesting level within the document, such as formatting tags in HTML, which can occur in many distinct parts of the text.

The fifth `Case` statement retrieves only the `game` elements containing a `name` element containing the text `"Cricket"`. To do this, it uses a LINQ query (lines 45–47)—because axis properties return an `IEnumerable`, they can be used as the subject of a LINQ query. The `Where` clause (line 46) uses a child axis property to retrieve all `name` elements that are children of the game element the range variable represents. It calls the Value property directly on the result of the axis property—this is an extension property that returns the Value of the first XElement in the collection, or Nothing if the collection is empty.

The PrintIDs method (lines 149–156) displays the id attributes of the XElement objects passed to it—specifically, the game elements in the document (line 51). To do this, it uses an attribute axis, which returns a String with the contents of the specified attribute name. If the attribute does not exist, the axis returns Nothing. An attribute axis can also be used to add or modify attributes by using the axis as an *lvalue*.

There are strings that are valid XML attribute and tag names that are not valid Visual Basic identifiers. For example, XML allows the use of the hyphen (-) as part of an identifier—in Visual Basic, this is the subtraction operator. To use an attribute named like this inside attribute axes, enclose the name of the attribute in angle brackets. The expression at line 154 of the example could have been written as element.@<id>.Trim().

The Click event handlers for the Buttons in the example are used to update the data displayed in the TreeView. These functions introduce two new classes from the System.Xml.Linq namespace—XText and XNode. The XText class holds plain text nodes. An XNode represents any node in the DOM—XText and XElement both inherit from it, so it provides a common base class that can be used to keep track of our current location as we step through the DOM tree.

The firstChildButton_Click event handler (lines 56–74) uses the NodeType property of the XNode class to determine if the current node is an XElement or not. The NodeType property returns a value of the XmlNodeType enumeration from the System.Xml namespace (imported at line 3) indicating what type of node that object is. If current is an element and not some other type of node such as a text field (line 60), we verify that it has children (line 61) before moving current to its first child (line 63). These operations use the Nodes method of class XElement, which returns an IEnumerable(Of XNode) containing all children of the given XElement. The Any extension method is equivalent to checking that Count is nonzero—it returns True if there is at least one element, and False if there are none. The event handler then inserts a TreeNode into the TreeView to display the child element that current now references (lines 66–69).

Line 66 uses the NodeText method (lines 159–172) to determine what text to display in the TreeNode. It also uses the NodeType property and the XmlNodeType enumeration to determine the type of the XNode. For elements, NodeText returns the tag name (line 163). For text nodes, it uses XText's Value property to return the contained text (line 166). Other node types are not used in this example, but a default case returning the name of the node type is included for completeness (line 170).

The event handlers for the other Buttons are structured similarly—each moves current and updates the TreeView accordingly. The parentButton_Click method (lines 77–90) ensures that the current node has a parent—that is, it is not the root of the XDocument—before it tries to move current (line 81). It uses the Parent property of XNode, which returns the parent of the given XNode or Nothing if the parent does not exist.

The event handlers for the **Previous** (lines 93–109) and **Next** (lines 112–129) Buttons use the PreviousNode (lines 97 and 100) and NextNode (lines 116 and 119) properties of XNode, respectively. As their names imply, they return the previous or next sibling node in the tree. If there is no previous or next node, the properties return Nothing. We also check the Parent property because the comments at the top and bottom of the file are also counted as sibling nodes. We are not interested in them, so we verify that there is a parent node before moving to the next or previous node.

19.7 LINQ to XML: XML Literals and Embedded Expressions

Visual Basic 2008 introduces a new feature known as **XML literals**, which allow you to write XML documents and elements directly in your code. XML literals are compiled into an `XElement` object, allowing you to use the techniques we've already shown to further manipulate the data. Without XML literals, you would have to manually call the `XElement` constructors—multiple nested constructor calls are not nearly as clear as plain XML.

In addition to XML literals, Visual Basic 2008 introduces **embedded expressions**, which allow you to write Visual Basic code inside XML literals. Using embedded expressions, you can insert values obtained in your code when you create the `XElement` from the XML literal instead of having to insert them later after creating the static components.

Figure 19.16 uses these new features to update an XML document to a new format and combine the data in it with data from a document already in the new format. Figures 19.17 and 19.18 contain the XML files in the old and new formats, respectively. Figure 19.19 displays the file output by the program.

```
' Fig. 19.16: XMLCombine.vb
' Transforming an XML document and splicing its contents with another.
Imports <xmlns:old="http://www.deitel.com/employeesold">
Imports <xmlns="http://www.deitel.com/employeesnew">

Module XMLCombine
   Sub Main()
      ' do processing in a Try block to catch errors
      Try
         ' attempt to load files
         Dim newDocument = XDocument.Load("employeesNew.xml")
         Dim oldDocument = XDocument.Load("employeesOld.xml")

         ' convert from old to new format
         oldDocument = Transform(oldDocument)

         ' combine documents and write to output file
         SaveFinalDocument(newDocument, oldDocument)

         ' tell user we succeeded
         Console.WriteLine("Documents successfully combined.")
      Catch ' catch everything
         ' inform the user that there was a problem combining
         Console.WriteLine("Files could not be combined.")
         Console.WriteLine("This was probably caused by an I/O error.")
      End Try
   End Sub ' Main

```

Fig. 19.16 | Transforming an XML document and splicing its contents with another. (Part 1 of 2.)

```
    ' convert the given XDocument in the old format to the new format
    Private Function Transform(ByVal document As XDocument) As XDocument
       ' use a LINQ query, embedded in an XML literal, to fill the new
       ' XML root with the correct data; the values within each employee
       ' listing become attributes in the new document
       Dim newDocumentRoot = _
          <employeelist>
             <%= From employee In document.Root.Elements() _
                Select _
                <employee name=
                   <%= employee.<old:firstname>.Value & _
                      " " & employee.<old:lastname>.Value %>
                   salary=<%= employee.<old:salary>.Value %>/> _
             %>
          </employeelist>

       Return New XDocument(newDocumentRoot) ' return transformed document
    End Function ' Transform

    ' take two validated XDocuments and combine
    ' them into one, then save to output.xml
    Private Sub SaveFinalDocument(ByVal document1 As XDocument, _
       ByVal document2 As XDocument)

       ' create root element, and fill with the elements
       ' contained in the roots of both documents
       Dim root = _
          <employeelist>
             <%= document1.Root.Elements() %>
             <%= document2.Root.Elements() %>
          </employeelist>

       Dim finalDocument As New XDocument(root) ' create new document
       finalDocument.Save("output.xml") ' save document to file
    End Sub ' SaveFinalDocument
End Module ' XMLCombine
```

Fig. 19.16 | Transforming an XML document and splicing its contents with another. (Part 2 of 2.)

```
<?xml version="1.0"?>
<!-- Fig. 19.17: employeesOld.xml -->
<!-- Sample old-format input for the XMLCombine application. -->
<employees xmlns="http://www.deitel.com/employeesold">
   <employeelisting>
      <firstname>Christopher</firstname>
      <lastname>Green</lastname>
      <salary>1460</salary>
   </employeelisting>
   <employeelisting>
      <firstname>Michael</firstname>
      <lastname>Red</lastname>
```

Fig. 19.17 | Sample old-format input for the `XMLCombine` application. (Part 1 of 2.)

```
        <salary>1420</salary>
    </employeelisting>
</employees>
```

Fig. 19.17 | Sample old-format input for the `XMLCombine` application. (Part 2 of 2.)

```
<?xml version="1.0"?>
<!-- Fig. 19.18: employeesNew.xml -->
<!-- Sample new-format input for the XMLCombine application. -->
<employeelist xmlns="http://www.deitel.com/employeesnew">
   <employee name="Jenn Brown" salary="2300"/>
   <employee name="Percy Indigo" salary="1415"/>
</employeelist>
```

Fig. 19.18 | Sample new-format input for the `XMLCombine` application.

```
<?xml version="1.0" encoding="utf-8"?>
<employeelist xmlns="http://www.deitel.com/employeesnew">
  <employee name="Jenn Brown" salary="2300" />
  <employee name="Percy Indigo" salary="1415" />
  <employee name="Christopher Green" salary="1460" />
  <employee name="Michael Red" salary="1420" />
</employeelist>
```

Fig. 19.19 | XML file generated by `XMLCombine`(Fig. 19.16).

Lines 3 and 4 of Fig. 19.16 use `Imports` statements with XML namespaces instead of .NET namespaces. The namespace prefix `old` is used for the data in the old format, and the default namespace is used for data in the new format. Note that the syntax is the same as that used for specifying a namespace in an XML document, except there is no tag name. This allows us to use namespaces in XML literals and axis properties the same way they are used in normal XML documents.

The `Transform` method (Fig. 19.16, lines 30–46) converts an XML document from the old format to the new format. It uses an XML literal (lines 35–43) to create a new root node for the document, then creates a new `XDocument` and returns it (line 45). Note that there is no special syntax for starting or ending an XML literal—the XML is written into the Visual Basic source file exactly as it would be in a plain XML file, with no Visual Basic line continuations. Literals are implemented in this way because it allows you to copy and paste XML directly into the IDE, which then automatically formats the XML. As mentioned above, the type of an XML literal is the `XElement` class. The created object contains the entire structure of the XML literal, with all attributes, text elements, and nested tags.

Embedded expressions are delimited by <%= and %> (e.g., lines 36–42)—a Visual Basic expression between them is executed and its value is inserted into the XML. Embedded expressions must contain only a single expression. Multiple statements are not allowed, but can be emulated by calling a function containing the desired statements. Since the expressions retrieve data, LINQ is commonly used in this situation.

The LINQ query (lines 36–41) selects an XML literal that creates a new `employee` element for the given employee. This XML literal contains additional embedded expressions (lines 39–40, 41) that set the `name` and `salary` attributes. When setting attribute values, the embedded expression is not enclosed in quotes as it is for a literal value—in fact, it is a syntax error to include them. These embedded expressions use namespace prefixes in their child axes. This is needed because the elements with the old format use the namepace `http://www.deitel.com/employeesold`, which is given the prefix `old` at line 3 instead of being put in the default namespace like it is in the `employeesOld.xml` file.

As you learned in Chapter 9, LINQ queries return an object of type `IEnumerable(Of T)`. In this case, because an XML literal is used in the `Select` clause, the type is `IEnumerable(Of XElement)`. When an embedded expression returns this type, the `XElements` in the collection are added as children into the enclosing `XElement`. Here, the `employee` elements are included as children of the `employeelist` element.

While not shown in this example, embedded expressions can also be used to specify tag and attribute names. Names and values are treated differently when the value returned by the embedded expression is `Nothing`. Tag names cannot be `Nothing`. Attribute names are allowed to be `Nothing` only if their corresponding value is also `Nothing`—causing the attribute to be ignored and not appear in the generated `XElement` object.

The `SaveFinalDocument` method (lines 50–63) uses an XML literal to create a root element for the new merged document. The two embedded expressions use the `Elements` method to retrieve the elements contained in the root elements of the two documents. As above, the returned `IEnumerable(Of XElement)` has all of its elements added as children of the `employeelist` element. A namespace prefix is not needed when creating the new root because the `http://www.deitel.com/employeesnew` namespace was defined as the default namespace (line 4).

Using XML Literals and Embedded Expressions to Convert XML to XHTML

Figure 19.20 uses XML literals and embedded expressions to transform an XML document into XHTML. You've already seen how to create XHTML using an XSL stylesheet in Fig. 19.11—this example also uses the `sorting.xml` file presented in Fig. 19.10. While useful, XSL is a special-purpose language—its functionality is limited to transforming XML. If you understand how to perform the same operation in a general-purpose language such as Visual Basic, you can combine it with other language features to do operations that XSL cannot.

```
' Fig. 19.20: LINQTransformer.vb
' Transforming an XML document to XHTML using XML literals.
Public Class LINQTransformer
   ' open the file dialog for the file to be converted
   Private Sub browseButton_Click(ByVal sender As System.Object, _
      ByVal e As System.EventArgs) Handles browseButton.Click

      ' make sure the user clicks OK
      If xmlOpenDialog.ShowDialog() = Windows.Forms.DialogResult.OK Then
         ' user clicked OK
         fileTextBox.Text = xmlOpenDialog.FileName
      End If
   End Sub ' browseButton_Click

```

Fig. 19.20 | Transforming an XML document to XHTML using XML literals. (Part 1 of 4.)

```
   ' convert the specified file to XHTML
   Private Sub convertButton_Click(ByVal sender As System.Object, _
      ByVal e As System.EventArgs) Handles convertButton.Click

      Dim document As XElement = Nothing

      ' attempt to load the XML document
      Try
         document = XElement.Load(fileTextBox.Text)
      Catch ex As Exception
         MessageBox.Show("Error: File could not be read.", _
            "Error", MessageBoxButtons.OK, MessageBoxIcon.Error)
         Return ' loading failed, give up
      End Try

      Dim totalPages As Integer = 0 ' store total pages in document

      ' determine the number of total pages in the document;
      ' the Descendants method is used because the frontmatter
      ' elements are one level down from the other chapters
      For Each section In document.<chapters>.Descendants()
         totalPages += Convert.ToInt32(section.@pages)
      Next

      ' define the XHTML document
      Dim xhtmlPage As XElement = _
         <html>
            <head>
               <title>
                  ISBN <%= document.@isbn & "-" & _
                           document.<title>.Value %>
               </title>
            </head>

            <body>
               <h1 style="color: blue">
                  <%= document.<title>.Value %></h1>
               <h2 style="color: blue">
                  by <%= document.<author>.<firstName>.Value & " " & _
                        document.<author>.<lastName>.Value %>
               </h2>

               <table style="border-style: groove;
                  background-color: wheat">
                  <!-- use a LINQ query to create table rows for -->
                  <!-- each <frontMatter> element in the document; -->
                  <!-- this row contains a column for name and a -->
                  <!-- column for pages -->
                  <%= From element In _
                     document.<chapters>.<frontMatter>.Elements() _
                     Select _
                     <tr>
                        <td style="text-align: right">
```

Fig. 19.20 | Transforming an XML document to XHTML using XML literals. (Part 2 of 4.)

```
                           <%= element.Name.LocalName %>
                        </td>

                        <td>
                           <!-- retrieve the pages attribute -->
                           <!-- from the element -->
                           ( <%= element.@pages & " pages" %> )
                        </td>
                     </tr> %>

                  <!-- the Order By clause sorts the chapters -->
                  <!-- by their @number attribute -->
                  <%= From chapter In document.<chapters>.<chapter> _
                     Order By Convert.ToInt32(chapter.@number) _
                     Select _
                     <tr>
                        <td style="text-align: right">
                           Chapter <%= chapter.@number %>
                        </td>

                        <td>
                           <%= chapter.Value & " ( " _
                              & chapter.@pages & " pages )" %>
                        </td>
                     </tr> %>
                  <%= From appendix In document.<chapters>.<appendix> _
                     Order By appendix.@number _
                     Select _
                     <tr>
                        <td style="text-align: right">
                           Appendix <%= appendix.@number %>
                        </td>

                        <td>
                           <%= appendix.Value & " ( " _
                              & appendix.@pages & " pages )" %>
                        </td>
                     </tr> %>
               </table>

               <br/><p style="color: blue">Pages:
                     <%= totalPages %>
                  <br/>Media Type: <%= document.<media>.@type %></p>
            </body>
         </html>

      xhtmlPage.Save("final.html") ' save the XHTML document

      ' open XHTML page in web browser
      System.Diagnostics.Process.Start("IExplore", _
         Application.StartupPath & "\final.html")
   End Sub ' convertButton_Click
End Class ' LinqTransformer
```

Fig. 19.20 | Transforming an XML document to XHTML using XML literals. (Part 3 of 4.)

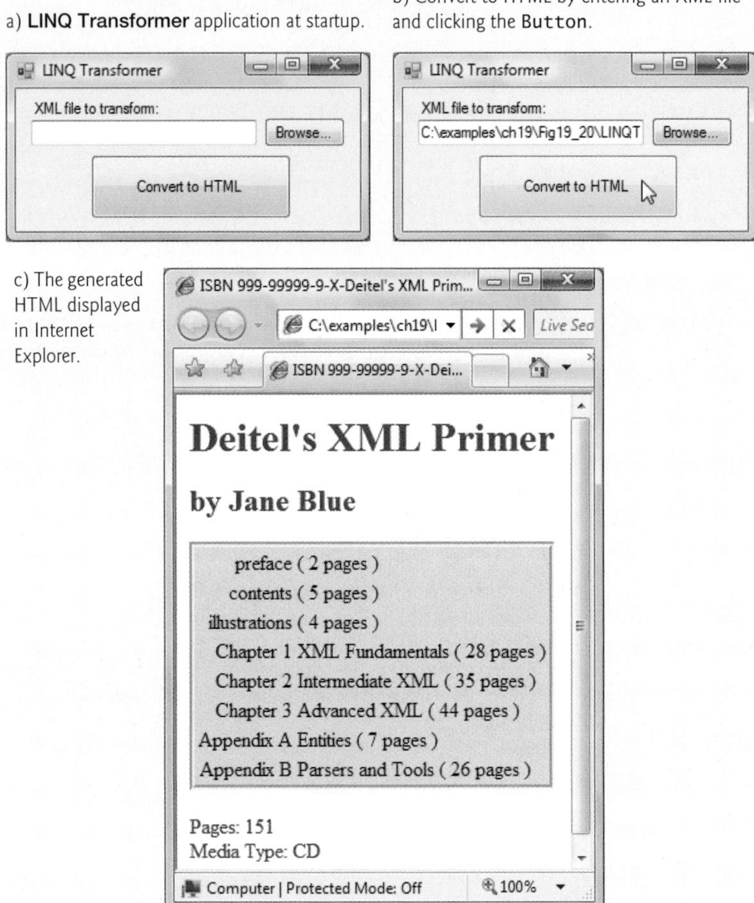

Fig. 19.20 | Transforming an XML document to XHTML using XML literals. (Part 4 of 4.)

Lines 5–13 allow the user to enter a filename or browse for one. When the user clicks the **Convert to HTML** button the event handler at lines 16–119 begins generating the XHTML from the given XML file.

Lines 35–37 calculate the total number of pages in the front matter, sections and appendices of the document described in the loaded XML file. These lines use a `For Each...Next` statement and XML axis properties to add the number of pages in each item, yielding the total number of pages. The **`Descendants` method** of the `XElement` class (line 35) returns all elements that are descendants of the given element. We cannot use an axis property here because axis properties do not support wildcards like XPath.

The three LINQ queries in this example (lines 63–76, 80–92, 93–105) all use XML literals in their `Select` clauses. These XML literals contain embedded expressions to transform the data. There is no limit on the nesting depth of XML literals and embedded expressions, though high levels of nesting can negatively affect the readability and maintainability of your code.

Embedded expressions are also used to write the footer after the table. Line 109 displays the total number of pages that was calculated earlier. The media type is also retrieved from the XML input and displayed (line 110).

Line 111 uses an attribute axis on the result of a child axis. This behaves like the `Value` property—when called on a collection, this is applied to the collection's first element.

After the XHTML is generated and written to disk, the program launches Internet Explorer to view the generated XHTML (lines 117–118) as shown in Fig. 19.20(c). It must pass the file's full path to Internet Explorer, so it uses the `Application.StartupPath` property to retrieve the full path to the current directory, then appends the name of the file in which the XHTML document was saved.

19.8 XSLT with Class XslCompiledTransform

Recall from Section 19.4 that XSL elements define rules for transforming one type of XML document to another type of XML document. We showed how to transform XML documents into XHTML documents and displayed the results in Internet Explorer. The XSLT processor included in Internet Explorer performed the transformations. We now perform a similar task in a Visual Basic program.

Performing an XSL Transformation in Visual Basic Using the .NET Framework

Figure 19.21 applies the style sheet `sports.xsl` (Fig. 19.9) to the XML document `sports.xml` (Fig. 19.8) programmatically. The result of the transformation is written to an XHTML file on disk and displayed in a text box. Figure 19.21(c) shows the resulting XHTML document (`sports.html`) when you view it in Internet Explorer.

Line 3 imports the **`System.Xml.Xsl`** namespace, which contains class **`XslCompiledTransform`** for applying XSL style sheets to XML documents. Line 7 creates `XslCompiledTransform` object `transformer`, which serves as an XSLT processor to transform XML data from one format to another.

```
1   ' Fig. 19.21: TransformTestForm.vb
2   ' Applying an XSLT style sheet to an XML Document.
3   Imports System.Xml.Xsl ' contains class XslCompiledTransform
4
5   Public Class TransformTestForm
6      ' applies the transformation
7      Private transformer As New XslCompiledTransform()
8
9      ' initialize variables
10     Private Sub TransformTestForm_Load(ByVal sender As System.Object, _
11        ByVal e As System.EventArgs) Handles MyBase.Load
12
13        transformer.Load("sports.xsl") ' load and compile the style sheet
14     End Sub ' TransformTestForm_Load
15
16     ' transform XML data on Transform XML Button Click event
17     Private Sub transformButton_Click(ByVal sender As System.Object, _
18        ByVal e As System.EventArgs) Handles transformButton.Click
19
```

Fig. 19.21 | Applying an XSLT style sheet to an XML document. (Part 1 of 2.)

```
20          ' perform the transformation and store the result in new file
21          transformer.Transform("sports.xml", "sports.html")
22
23          ' read and display the XHTML document's text in a TextBox
24          consoleTextBox.Text = System.IO.File.ReadAllText("sports.html")
25       End Sub ' transformButton_Click
26    End Class ' TransformTestForm
```

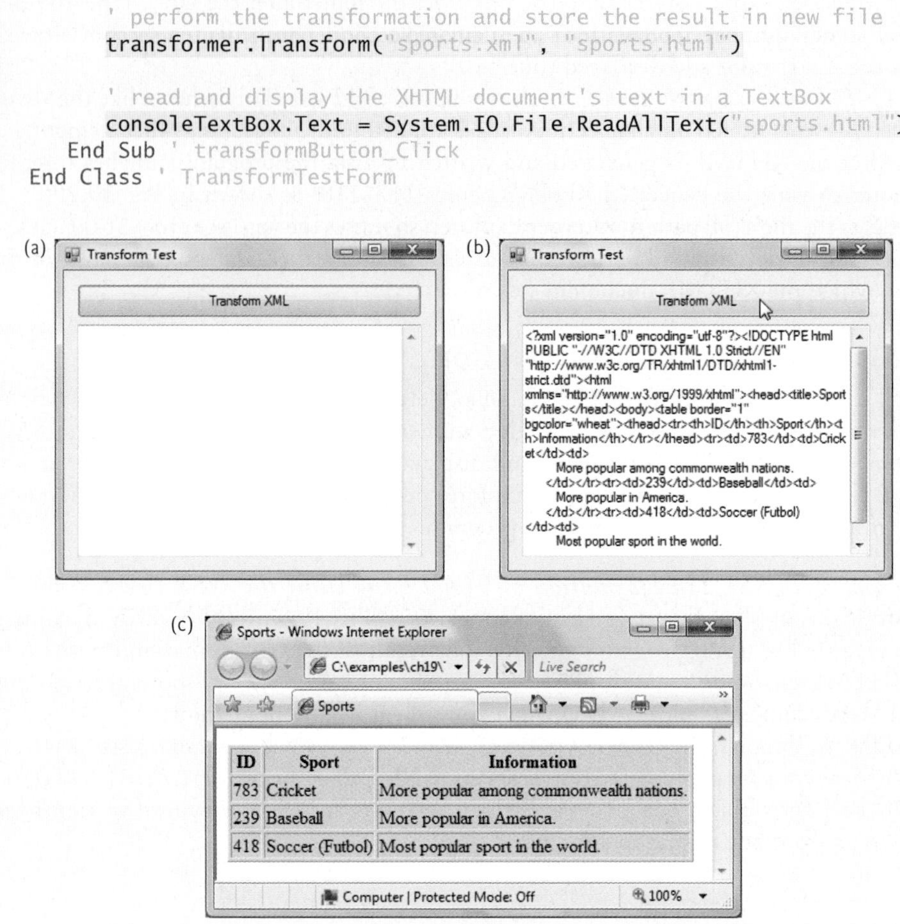

Fig. 19.21 | Applying an XSLT style sheet to an XML document. (Part 2 of 2.)

In event handler `TransformTestForm_Load` (lines 10–14), line 13 calls the `XslCompiledTransform` object's **`Load`** method, which loads and parses the style sheet that this application uses. This method takes an argument specifying the name and location of the style sheet—`sports.xsl` (Fig. 19.9) located in the current directory.

Event handler `transformButton_Click` (lines 17–25) calls method **`Transform`** of class `XslCompiledTransform` to apply the style sheet (`sports.xsl`) to `sports.xml` (line 21). This method takes two `String` arguments—the first specifies the XML file to which the style sheet should be applied, and the second specifies the file in which the result of the transformation should be stored on disk. Thus the `Transform` method call in line 21 transforms `sports.xml` to XHTML and writes the result to disk as the file `sports.html`. Figure 19.21(c) shows the new XHTML document rendered in Internet Explorer. Note that the output is identical to that of Fig. 19.8—in the current example, though, the XHTML is stored on disk rather than generated dynamically by MSXML.

After applying the transformation, the program displays the content of the new file `sports.html` in `consoleTextBox`, as shown in Fig. 19.21(b). Line 24 obtains the text of the file by passing its name to method `ReadAllText` of the `System.IO.File` class provided by the .NET framework to simplify file-processing tasks on the local system.

19.9 Wrap-Up

In this chapter, we continued our XML introduction that began in Chapter 15 by demonstrating several technologies related to XML. We discussed how to create DTDs and schemas for specifying and validating the structure of an XML document. We showed how to use various tools to confirm whether XML documents are valid (i.e., conform to a DTD or schema).

You learned how to create and use XSL documents to specify rules for converting XML documents between formats. Specifically, you learned how to format and sort XML data and output it as XHTML for display in a web browser.

The final sections of the chapter presented more advanced uses of XML in Visual Basic applications. We demonstrated how to retrieve and display data from an XML document using various .NET classes. We illustrated how a Document Object Model (DOM) tree represents each element of an XML document as a node in the tree. The chapter also demonstrated loading data from an XML document using the `Load` method of the `XDocument` class. We demonstrated the new features for working with XML in Visual Basic 2008—XML axis properties, XML literals, and embedded expressions. Finally, we showed how to use the `XslCompiledTransform` class to perform XSL transformations.

In Chapter 20, we begin our discussion of databases, which organize data in such a way that the data can be selected and updated quickly. We introduce Structured Query Language (SQL) for writing simple database queries. We then introduce LINQ to SQL, which allows you to write LINQ queries that are automatically converted into SQL queries. These SQL queries are then used to query the database.

19.10 Web Resources

`www.deitel.com/XML/`

The Deitel XML Resource Center focuses on the vast amount of free XML content available online, plus some for-sale items. Start your search here for tools, downloads, tutorials, podcasts, wikis, documentation, conferences, FAQs, books, e-books, sample chapters, articles, newsgroups, forums, downloads from CNET's download.com, jobs and contract opportunities, and more that will help you develop XML applications.

Summary

Section 19.1 Introduction

- XML is a widely supported standard for describing data that is commonly used to exchange that data between applications over the Internet.
- The .NET Framework uses XML extensively. Many of the internal files that Visual Studio creates, such as those that represent project settings, are formatted as XML.
- XML is used heavily in serialization.

- XAML (from WPF) is an XML vocabulary used for creating user interfaces.
- LINQ to XML provides a convenient way to extract data from XML documents using the same LINQ syntax used on arrays and collections.
- XML literals allow you to write XML documents in your Visual Basic code.

Section 19.2 Document Type Definitions (DTDs)

- DTDs and schemas specify documents' element types and attributes, and their relationships to one another.
- DTDs and schemas enable an XML parser to verify whether an XML document is valid (i.e., its elements contain the proper attributes and appear in the proper sequence).
- A DTD expresses the set of rules for document structure using an EBNF (Extended Backus-Naur Form) grammar.
- In a DTD, an `ELEMENT` element type declaration defines the rules for an element. An `ATTLIST` attribute-list declaration defines attributes for a particular element.

Section 19.3 W3C XML Schema Documents

- Unlike DTDs, schemas do not use EBNF grammar. Instead, they use XML syntax and are themselves XML documents that programs can manipulate.
- Unlike DTDs, XML Schema documents can specify what type of data (e.g., numeric, text) an element can contain.
- An XML document that conforms to a schema document is schema valid.
- Two categories of types exist in XML Schema: simple types and complex types. Simple types cannot contain attributes or child elements; complex types can.
- Every simple type defines a restriction on an XML Schema–defined schema type or on a user-defined type.
- Complex types can have either simple content or complex content. Both simple content and complex content can contain attributes, but only complex content can contain child elements.
- Whereas complex types with simple content must extend or restrict some other existing type, complex types with complex content do not have this limitation.

Section 19.4 Extensible Stylesheet Language and XSL Transformations

- XSL can convert XML into any text-based document. XSL documents have the extension `.xsl`.
- XPath is a string-based language of expressions used by XML and many of its related technologies for effectively and efficiently locating structures and data (such as specific elements and attributes) in XML documents.
- XPath is used to locate parts of the source tree document that match templates defined in an XSL style sheet. When a match occurs (i.e., a node matches a template), the matching template executes and adds its result to the result tree. When there are no more matches, XSLT has transformed the source tree into the result tree.
- XSLT selectively navigates the source tree using the `select` and `match` attributes.
- For XSLT to function, the source tree must be properly structured. Schemas, DTDs and validating parsers can validate document structure before using XPath and XSLT.
- XSL style sheets can be connected directly to an XML document by adding an `xml-stylesheet` processing instruction to the XML document.
- Two tree structures are involved in transforming an XML document using XSLT—the source tree (the document being transformed) and the result tree (the result of the transformation).

- The XPath character / (a forward slash) always selects the document root. In XPath, a leading forward slash specifies that we are using absolute addressing.
- An XPath expression with no beginning forward slash uses relative addressing.
- XSL element value-of retrieves an attribute's or element's value. The @ symbol specifies an attribute node.
- XSL node-set function name retrieves the current node's element name.
- XSL node-set function text retrieves the text between an element's start and end tags.
- The XPath expression //* selects all the nodes in an XML document.

Section 19.5 LINQ to XML: Document Object Model (DOM)

- On successfully parsing a document, some XML parsers store document data as tree structures in memory. This hierarchical tree structure is called a Document Object Model (DOM) tree, and an XML parser that creates this type of structure is known as a DOM parser.
- The DOM represents each element as a node. A parent node contains other nodes. A child node can have only one parent node. Nodes that are peers are called sibling nodes.
- A node's descendant nodes include its children, its children's children and so on. A node's ancestor nodes include its parent, its parent's parent and so on.
- The DOM tree has a single root node, which contains all the other nodes in the document.
- Namespace System.Xml and its contained namespaces contain the classes for creating, reading and manipulating XML documents.
- Namespace System.Xml.Linq contains the classes used to manipulate a LINQ to XML DOM in the .NET framework.
- The XElement class represents a node in the DOM—a full XML document is represented by a tree of XElement objects.
- The XDocument class represents an entire XML document.
- To create an XDocument from an existing XML file, we use its Shared Load method, giving the location of the file as an argument.
- An XDocument's Root property returns an XElement representing the root element of the XML.
- Tag and attribute names are stored as objects of class XName. The Name property of an XElement returns an XName object. The unqualified name is accessed using the XName's LocalName property.
- The text in an XElement can be accessed using property Value. If used on an element with children, Value returns all of the text contained within its descendants, with the tags removed.

Section 19.6 LINQ to XML: XML Axis Properties

- XML axis properties are a new syntax for navigating XElements along specified axes.
- XML axis properties can be used in concert with normal method calls on XElement objects.
- XML axis properties, when combined with LINQ queries, can retrieve the same results as XPath expressions.
- XPathSelectElement is an extension method from namespace System.Xml.XPath that allows you to use an XPath expression to navigate XDocument and XElement objects.
- A child axis refers to elements that are direct children of the current element and have the specified name. Note the similarity to XPath expressions, except the / separator is replaced by the dot (.) operator typically used for accessing methods or properties and the tag names are enclosed in angle brackets. Child axes return an IEnumerable(Of XElement), not a single object.

- A descendant axis retrieves all descendants with the specified tag name, not just direct children. A descendant axis is equivalent to the XPath double slash (//) operator.
- Because axis properties return an `IEnumerable`, they can be used as the subject of a LINQ query.
- When the `Value` property is applied to the result of an axis property, the `Value` property returns the value of the first `XElement` in the collection returned by the axis property, or `Nothing` if the collection is empty.
- An attribute axis returns a `String` with the contents of the specified attribute name. If the attribute does not exist, the axis returns `Nothing`. An attribute axis can also be used to add or modify attributes by using the axis as an *lvalue*.
- Some valid XML attribute and tag names are not valid Visual Basic identifiers. To use an attribute named like this inside attribute axes, enclose the name of the attribute in angle brackets.
- The `XText` class holds plain text nodes.
- An `XNode` represents any node in the DOM. `XText` and `XElement` both inherit from it.
- An `XNode`'s `NodeType` property returns an `XmlNodeType` constant indicating the node's type.
- `XElement`'s `Nodes` method returns an `IEnumerable(Of XNode)` of the `XElement`'s children.
- The `Any` extension method of `IEnumerable` is equivalent to checking that `Count` is nonzero—it returns `True` if there is at least one element, and `False` if there are none.
- The `Value` property of class `XText` returns the contained text.
- `XNode`'s `Parent` property returns the parent of the given `XNode` or `Nothing` for the root node.
- The `PreviousNode` and `NextNode` properties of class `XNode` return the previous or next sibling node in the tree, respectively. If there is no previous or next node, the properties return `Nothing`.

Section 19.7 LINQ to XML: XML Literals and Embedded Expressions

- XML literals allow you to write XML documents and elements directly in your code.
- XML literals are compiled into an `XElement` object. Using XML literals prevents you from having to manually call the `XElement` constructors.
- Embedded expressions allow you to write Visual Basic code inside XML literals. The results of the Visual Basic code are placed in the XML literal.
- XML namespaces can be used in an `Imports` statement, allowing you to use namespaces in XML literals and axis properties the same way they are used in XML documents.
- An XML literal is written in the Visual Basic exactly as it would be in a plain XML file.
- Embedded expressions are delimited by <%= and %>.
- Embedded expressions can also be used to specify tag and attribute names.
- When setting attribute values, the embedded expression is not enclosed in quotes as it is for a literal value—in fact, it is a syntax error to include them.
- Embedded expressions must contain only a single expression. Multiple statements are not allowed, but can be emulated by calling a function containing the desired statements. Since the expressions retrieve data, LINQ is commonly used in this situation.
- When an embedded expression returns an `IEnumerable(Of XElement)`, the `XElements` in the collection are added as children into the enclosing `XElement`.
- The `Descendants` method of class `XElement` returns all elements that are descendants of the given element.
- There is no limit on the nesting depth of XML literals and embedded expressions.
- When an attribute axis is used on the result of a child axis, it is applied to the first element.

Section 19.8 XSLT with Class `XslCompiledTransform`

- The `System.Xml.Xsl` namespace contains class `XslCompiledTransform` for applying XSLT style sheets to XML documents.
- `XslCompiledTransform` method `Load` loads and compiles a style sheet.
- `XslCompiledTransform` method `Transform` applies the compiled style sheet to a specified XML document. This method takes two `string` arguments: the name of the XML file to which the style sheet should be applied and the name of the file to store the transformation result.

Terminology

Sections 19.1–19.3

`all` element
asterisk (*) occurrence indicator
`ATTLIST` attribute-list declaration
`base` attribute of element `extension`
`base` attribute of element `restriction`
base type
`CDATA` keyword
character data
character entity reference
complex content in XML Schema
complex type
`complexType` element
Document Type Definition (DTD)
`element` element (XML Schema)
`ELEMENT` element type declaration
`EMPTY` keyword
Extensible HyperText Markup Language (XHTML)
`extension` element
`#FIXED` keyword
`#IMPLIED` keyword
LINQ to XML
`maxOccurs` attribute of `element` element
`minInclusive` element
`minOccurs` attribute of `element` element
`name` attribute of `element` element
occurrence indicator
parsed character data
parser
`#PCDATA` keyword
plus sign (+) occurrence indicator
prolog of an XML document
question mark (?) occurrence indicator
`#REQUIRED` keyword
restriction on built-in schema type
schema
`schema` element
schema-invalid XML document
schema repository
schema-valid XML document
simple content in XML Schema
simple type
`simpleContent` XML Schema element
`simpleType` XML Schema element
`targetNamespace` attribute of `schema` element
`type` attribute of `element` element
`unbounded` value of attribute `maxOccurs`
W3C XML Schema
World Wide Web Consortium (W3C)
XML instance document
XML Schema
XML Validator
`.xsd` filename extension

Sections 19.4–19.8

/ forward slash character (XPath)
@ XPath attribute symbol
<? and ?> XML delimiters
absolute addressing
ancestor node
`Any` extension method of interface `IEnumerable`
attribute (`@attribute`) axis
automatic schema generation
child (`.<element>`) axis
child node
context node
`data-type` attribute of `xsl:sort` element
descendant (`...<element>`) axis
descendant node
`Descendants` method of class `XElement`
Document Object Model (DOM)
document root
DOM parser

- Elements method of class XElement
- embedded expression (<%= and %>)
- ExpandAll method of class TreeView
- HasElements property of class XElement
- Load method of class XDocument
- Load method of class XslCompiledTransform
- LocalName property of class XName
- LINQ to XML
- match attribute of xsl:template element
- name node-set function
- Name property of class XElement
- NextNode property of class XNode
- node-set function
- node set of an xsl:for-each element
- Nodes method of class XElement
- NodeType property of class XNode
- order attribute of xsl:sort element
- parent node
- Parent property of class TreeNode
- Parent property of class XNode
- PI target
- PI value
- PreviousNode property of class XNode
- processing instruction (PI)
- recursive descent
- Refresh method of class TreeView
- relative addressing
- result tree (XSLT)
- root node
- Root property of class XDocument
- select attribute of xsl:for-each element
- sibling node
- source tree (XSLT)
- stylesheet start tag
- sum function (XSL)
- System.Xml namespace
- System.Xml.Linq namespace
- System.Xml.XPath namespace
- System.Xml.Xsl namespace
- text node-set function
- TreeNode class
- TreeView control
- transformations using LINQ
- Transform method of class XslCompiledTransform
- type attribute in a processing instruction
- Value property of class XElement
- Value property of class XText
- version attribute of xsl:stylesheet element
- Xalan XSLT processor
- XDocument class
- XElement class
- XML axis property
- XML literal
- XML Path Language (XPath)
- XmlNodeType enumeration
- XName class
- XNode class
- XPathSelectElement extension method of class XDocument
- XslCompiledTransform class
- .xsl filename extension
- XSL Formatting Objects (XSL-FO)
- XSL style sheet
- XSL template
- XSL Transformations (XSLT)
- XSL variable
- xsl:for-each element
- xsl:output element
- xsl:sort element
- xsl:stylesheet element
- xsl:template element
- xsl:text element
- xsl:value-of element
- XText class

Self-Review Exercises

Sections 19.1–19.3

19.1 Fill in the blanks for each of the following:

a) ________ embed application-specific information into an XML document.
b) ________ is Microsoft's XML parser used in Internet Explorer.
c) XSL element ________ writes a DOCTYPE to the result tree.
d) XML Schema documents have root element ________.
e) XSL element ________ is the root element in an XSL document.
f) XSL element ________ selects specific XML elements using repetition.

19.2 State whether each of the following is *true* or *false*. If *false*, explain why.

a) XML Schemas are better than DTDs, because DTDs lack a way of indicating what specific type of data (e.g., numeric, text) an element can contain and DTDs are not themselves XML documents.
b) DTDs are written using an XML vocabulary.
c) Schema is a technology for locating information in an XML document.

Sections 19.7–19.10

19.3 Write a processing instruction that includes style sheet `wap.xsl` for use in Internet Explorer.

19.4 Give a brief description of the child, descendant and attribute XML axis properties.

19.5 Write an XPath expression that locates `contact` nodes in `letter.xml` (Fig. 15.4).

19.6 Describe how an XML literal with LINQ can be used similarly to an XSL stylesheet.

Answers to Self-Review Exercises

Sections 19.1–19.3

19.1 a) Processing instructions. b) MSXML. c) `xsl:output`. d) `schema`. e) `xsl:stylesheet`. f) `xsl:for-each`.

19.2 a) True. b) False. DTDs use an EBNF grammar, which is not an XML vocabulary. c) False. XPath is a technology for locating information in an XML document. XML Schema provides a means for type checking XML documents and verifying their validity.

Sections 19.7–19.10

19.3 `<?xml-stylesheet type = "text/xsl" href = "wap.xsl"?>`

19.4 The child axis property is denoted by `.<element>` and represents elements contained directly within the current element. The descendant axis property is denoted by `...<element>` and represents all elements, contained directly or indirectly within the current element. The attribute axis is denoted by `@attribute` and provides access to the attributes of an element.

19.5 `/letter/contact`.

19.6 In place of `xsl:` namespace items, you may use Visual Basic code through embedded expressions.

Exercises

Sections 19.1–19.3

19.7 *(Nutrition Information XML Schema)* Write an XML Schema document (`nutrition.xsd`) specifying the structure of the XML document created in Exercise 15.6.

Sections 19.4–19.8

19.8 *(Nutrition Information XHTML Conversion)* Using the file you created in Exercise 15.6, write a program that uses XML literals and LINQ to create an XHTML table of each nutritional value. Save the resulting XHTML document.

19.9 *(Sorting XSLT Modification)* Modify Fig. 19.11 (`sorting.xsl`) to sort by the number of pages rather than by chapter number. Save the modified document as `sorting_byPage.xsl`.

19.10 *(Filtering LINQ Transformations)* Modify Fig. 19.20 (`LINQTransformer.vb`) so that any backmatter with two or fewer pages are not included in the resulting document. Add a `WebBrowser` control to the form so that the resulting XHTML page is displayed in your program. Open the XHTML file in this control once it has been generated by passing the file's location to the `WebBrowser`'s `Navigate` method. [*Hint:* Use `Application.StartupPath` as in Fig. 19.20 to get the file's location.]

19.11 *(`XMLCombine` Format Checking)* Create a GUI application based on the `XMLCombine` application in Fig. 19.16. Instead of hard-coding the filenames, create two sets of radio buttons that allow the user to choose the two input files (Fig. 19.22). Each set should let the user choose between the `employeesOld.xml` and `employeesNew.xml` from Section 19.7, and the `employeesExtra.xml` included in the `Exercises` folder with this chapter's examples. If either file is in the old format, convert it to the new format, then merge the entries in the two files. Do not worry about duplicate entries. Use the file's structure, not the selected radio button, to determine if it is in the old or new format.

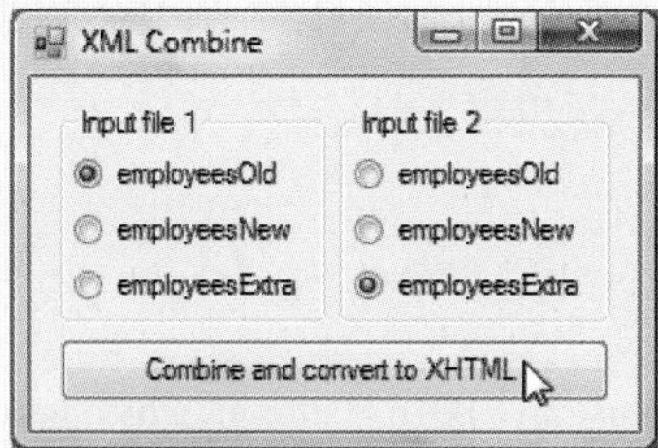

Fig. 19.22 | **XML Combine** GUI application.

19.12 *(Nutrition XHTML Modification)* Modify your program from Exercise 19.8 to also read file `nutrition2.xml` (included in the `Exercises` folder), and combine its elements with those of `nutrition.xml`. Then, sort all of the elements by their local name before outputting them as XHTML. Use the product title of the first document when writing the final document's title.

20

Databases and LINQ to SQL

It is a capital mistake to theorize before one has data.
—Arthur Conan Doyle

Now go, write it before them in a table, and note it in a book, that it may be for the time to come for ever and ever.
—Isaiah 30:8

Get your facts first, and then you can distort them as much as you please.
—Mark Twain

I like two kinds of men: domestic and foreign.
—Mae West

OBJECTIVES

In this chapter you will learn:

- The relational database model.
- To write basic database queries in SQL.
- To use LINQ to SQL to retrieve and manipulate data from a database.
- To add data sources to projects.
- To use the Object Relational Designer to create LINQ to SQL classes.
- To use the IDE's drag-and-drop capabilities to display database tables in applications.
- To use data binding to move data seamlessly between GUI controls and databases.
- To create Master/Detail views.

Outline

20.1 Introduction

A database is an organized collection of data. Many strategies exist for organizing data to facilitate easy access and manipulation. A database management system (DBMS) provides mechanisms for storing, organizing, retrieving and modifying data for many users. Database management systems allow access to and storage of data independently of its internal representation.

Today's most popular DBMSs manage relational databases, which organize data simply as tables with rows and columns. A language called Structured Query Language (SQL)—pronounced "sequel," or as its individual letters—is the international standard language used almost universally with relational databases to perform queries (i.e., to request information that satisfies given criteria) and to manipulate data in a database. In this book, we pronounce SQL as "sequel."

Some popular proprietary database management systems are Microsoft SQL Server, Oracle, Sybase and IBM DB2. PostgreSQL and MySQL are open-source DBMSs that can be downloaded and used freely by anyone. You may also be familiar with Microsoft Access—a relational database system that is part of Microsoft Office. In this chapter, we use Microsoft SQL Server 2005 Express—included on the DVD that came with this book. It can also be downloaded separately from Microsoft (www.microsoft.com/express/sql). As of this writing, SQL Server 2008 Express was still in development.

When it becomes available, we'll post information on using it with this book at the book's website—`www.deitel.com/books/vb2008htp/`.

Chapter 9 introduced LINQ to Objects, which allows you to manipulate data stored in arrays and collections using a syntax similar to SQL. LINQ to SQL allows you to manipulate relational data stored in a SQL Server database. LINQ to SQL provides the expressiveness of SQL with the additional benefits of the Visual Basic compiler's type checking and the IDE's *IntelliSense*.

This chapter introduces general concepts of relational databases and SQL, then explores LINQ to SQL and the IDE's tools for working with databases. In the next two chapters, you'll see other practical database and LINQ to SQL applications. Chapter 21, ASP.NET and ASP.NET Ajax, presents a web-based bookstore case study that retrieves user and book information from a database. Chapter 22, Windows Communication Foundation (WCF) Web Services, uses a database to store airline reservation data for a web service (i.e., a class that allows its methods to be called by methods on other machines via common data formats and protocols).

20.2 Relational Databases

A relational database is a logical representation of data that allows the data to be accessed independently of its physical structure. A relational database organizes data in tables. Figure 20.1 illustrates a sample `Employees` table that might be used in a personnel system. The table stores the attributes of employees. Tables are composed of rows and columns in which values are stored. This table consists of six rows and five columns. The `ID` column of each row is the table's primary key—a column (or group of columns) requiring a unique value that cannot be duplicated in other rows. This guarantees that a primary key value can be used to uniquely identify a row. A primary key composed of two or more columns is known as a composite key. Good examples of primary-key columns in other applications are an employee ID number in a payroll system and a part number in an inventory system—values in each of these columns are guaranteed to be unique. The rows in Fig. 20.1 are displayed in order by primary key. In this case, the rows are listed in increasing (ascending) order, but they could also be listed in decreasing (descending) order or in no particular order at all. As we will demonstrate in an upcoming example, programs can specify ordering criteria when requesting data from a database.

Table `Employees`

ID	Name	Department	Salary	Location
23603	Jones	413	1100	New Jersey
24568	Kerwin	413	2000	New Jersey
34589	Larson	642	1800	Los Angeles
35761	Myers	611	1400	Orlando
47132	Neumann	413	9000	New Jersey
78321	Stephens	611	8500	Orlando

Row (34589 row); Primary key (ID column); Column (Department column)

Fig. 20.1 | `Employees` table sample data.

Each column represents a different data attribute. Rows are normally unique (by primary key) within a table, but some column values may be duplicated between rows. For example, three different rows in the Employees table's Department column contain the number 413, indicating that these employees work in the same department.

Different database users are often interested in different data and different relationships among the data. Most users require only subsets of the rows and columns. To obtain these subsets, programs use SQL to define queries that select subsets of the data from a table. For example, a program might select data from the Employees table to create a query result that shows where each department is located, in increasing order by Department number (Fig. 20.2). SQL queries are discussed in Section 20.4.

```
Department    Location

413           New Jersey
611           Orlando
642           Los Angeles
```

Fig. 20.2 | Distinct Department and Location data from the Employees table.

20.3 Relational Database Overview: Books Database

We now overview relational databases in the context of a simple Books database. The database stores information about some recent Deitel publications. First, we overview the Books database's tables. A database's tables, their fields and the relationships between them are collectively known as a database schema. After overviewing the database, we introduce database concepts, such as how to use SQL to retrieve information from the Books database and to manipulate the data. We provide the database file—Books.mdf—with the examples for this chapter (downloadable from www.deitel.com/books/vb2008htp/). SQL Server database files typically end with the .mdf ("master data file") file-name extension. Sections 20.6–20.9 explain how to use this file in an application.

Authors Table of the Books Database

The database consists of three tables: Authors, AuthorISBN and Titles. The Authors table (described in Fig. 20.3) consists of three columns that maintain each author's unique ID number, first name and last name, respectively. Figure 20.4 contains the data from the Authors table. We list the rows in order by the table's primary key—AuthorID. You will learn how to sort data by other criteria (e.g., in alphabetical order by last name) using SQL's ORDER BY clause in Section 20.4.3.

Column	Description
AuthorID	Author's ID number in the database. In the Books database, this integer column is defined as an identity column, also known as an autoincremented column—for each row inserted in the table, the AuthorID value is increased by 1 automatically to ensure that each row has a unique AuthorID. This is the primary key.

Fig. 20.3 | Authors table of the Books database. (Part 1 of 2.)

Column	Description
FirstName	Author's first name (a string).
LastName	Author's last name (a string).

Fig. 20.3 | Authors table of the Books database. (Part 2 of 2.)

AuthorID	FirstName	LastName
1	Harvey	Deitel
2	Paul	Deitel
3	Greg	Ayer
4	Dan	Quirk

Fig. 20.4 | Data from the Authors table of the Books database.

Titles Table of the Books Database

The Titles table (described in Fig. 20.5) consists of four columns that maintain information about each book in the database, including the ISBN, title, edition number and copyright year. Figure 20.6 contains the data from the Titles table.

Column	Description
ISBN	ISBN of the book (a string). The table's primary key. ISBN is an abbreviation for "International Standard Book Number"—a numbering scheme that publishers worldwide use to give every book a unique identification number.
Title	Title of the book (a string).
EditionNumber	Edition number of the book (an integer).
Copyright	Copyright year of the book (a string).

Fig. 20.5 | Titles table of the Books database.

ISBN	Title	Edition-Number	Copy-right
0131752421	Internet & World Wide Web How to Program	4	2008
0132222205	Java How to Program	7	2007
0132404168	C How to Program	5	2007

Fig. 20.6 | Data from the Titles table of the Books database. (Part 1 of 2.)

ISBN	Title	Edition-Number	Copy-right
0136053033	Simply Visual Basic 2008	3	2009
013605305X	Visual Basic 2008 How to Program	4	2009
013605322X	Visual C# 2008 How to Program	3	2009
0136151574	Visual C++ 2008 How to Program	2	2008
0136152503	C++ How to Program	6	2008

Fig. 20.6 | Data from the `Titles` table of the `Books` database. (Part 2 of 2.)

`AuthorISBN` Table of the `Books` Database

The `AuthorISBN` table (described in Fig. 20.7) consists of two columns that maintain ISBNs for each book and their corresponding authors' ID numbers. This table associates authors with their books. The `AuthorID` column is a **foreign key**—a column in this table that matches the primary-key column in another table (i.e., `AuthorID` in the `Authors` table). The `ISBN` column is also a foreign key—it matches the primary-key column (i.e., `ISBN`) in the `Titles` table. Together the `AuthorID` and `ISBN` columns in this table form a composite primary key. Every row in this table uniquely matches one author to one book's ISBN. Figure 20.8 contains the data from the `AuthorISBN` table of the `Books` database.

Column	Description
`AuthorID`	The author's ID number, a foreign key to the `Authors` table.
`ISBN`	The ISBN for a book, a foreign key to the `Titles` table.

Fig. 20.7 | `AuthorISBN` table of the `Books` database.

AuthorID	ISBN	AuthorID	ISBN
1	0131752421	2	0132222205
1	0132222205	2	0132404168
1	0132404168	2	0136053033
1	0136053033	2	013605305X
1	013605305X	2	013605322X
1	013605322X	2	0136151574
1	0136151574	2	0136152503
1	0136152503	3	0136053033
2	0131752421	4	0136151574

Fig. 20.8 | Data from the `AuthorISBN` table of `Books`.

Foreign Keys

Foreign keys can be specified when creating a table. A foreign key helps maintain the *Rule of Referential Integrity*—every foreign-key value must appear as another table's primary-key value. This enables the DBMS to determine whether the `AuthorID` value for a particular row of the `AuthorISBN` table is valid. Foreign keys also allow related data in multiple tables to be selected from those tables—this is known as joining the data. (You will learn how to join data using SQL's `INNER JOIN` operator in Section 20.4.4.) There is a one-to-many relationship between a primary key and a corresponding foreign key (e.g., one author can write many books). This means that a foreign key can appear many times in its own table but only once (as the primary key) in another table. For example, the `ISBN` `0131450913` can appear in several rows of `AuthorISBN` (because this book has several authors) but only once in `Titles`, where `ISBN` is the primary key.

Entity-Relationship Diagram for the **Books** *Database*

Figure 20.9 is an entity-relationship (ER) diagram for the `Books` database. This diagram shows the tables in the database and the relationships among them. The first compartment in each box contains the table's name. The names in italic font are primary keys (e.g., *`AuthorID`* in the `Authors` table). A table's primary key uniquely identifies each row in the table. Every row must have a value in the primary-key column, and the value of the key must be unique in the table. This is known as the *Rule of Entity Integrity*. Note that the names `AuthorID` and `ISBN` in the `AuthorISBN` table are both italic—together these form a composite primary key for the `AuthorISBN` table.

Common Programming Error 20.1

Not providing a value for every column in a primary key breaks the Rule of Entity Integrity *and causes the DBMS to report an error.*

Common Programming Error 20.2

Providing the same value for the primary key in multiple rows breaks the Rule of Entity Integrity *and causes the DBMS to report an error.*

The lines connecting the tables in Fig. 20.9 represent the relationships among the tables. Consider the line between the `Authors` and `AuthorISBN` tables. On the `Authors` end of the line, there is a `1`, and on the `AuthorISBN` end, an infinity symbol (∞). This indicates a one-to-many relationship—for each author in the `Authors` table, there can be an arbitrary number of ISBNs for books written by that author in the `AuthorISBN` table (i.e., an author can write any number of books). Note that the relationship line links the `AuthorID`

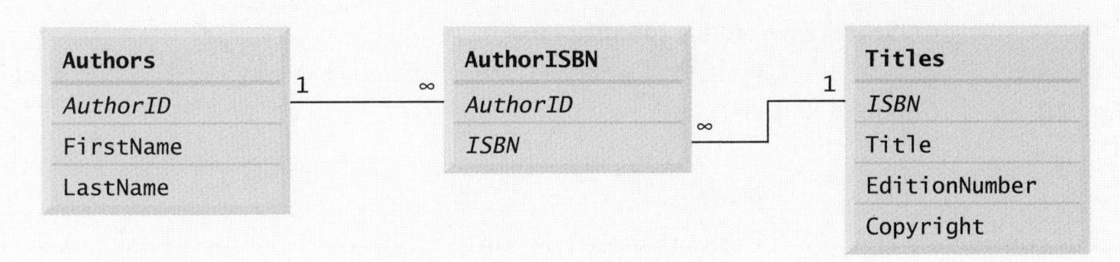

Fig. 20.9 | Entity-relationship diagram for the `Books` database.

column in the Authors table (where AuthorID is the primary key) to the AuthorID column in the AuthorISBN table (where AuthorID is a foreign key)—the line between the tables links the primary key to the matching foreign key.

Common Programming Error 20.3

Providing a foreign-key value that does not appear as a primary-key value in another table breaks the Rule of Referential Integrity *and causes the DBMS to report an error.*

The line between the Titles and AuthorISBN tables illustrates a one-to-many relationship—a book can be written by many authors. Note that the line between the tables links the primary key ISBN in table Titles to the corresponding foreign key in table AuthorISBN. The relationships in Fig. 20.9 illustrate that the sole purpose of the AuthorISBN table is to provide a many-to-many relationship between the Authors and Titles tables—an author can write many books, and a book can have many authors.

20.4 SQL

We now overview SQL in the context of the Books database. Though LINQ to SQL and the Visual Basic IDE hide the SQL used to manipulate databases, it is nevertheless important to understand SQL basics. Knowing the types of operations you can perform will help you develop more advanced database-intensive applications.

Figure 20.10 lists some common SQL keywords used to form complete SQL statements—we discuss these keywords in the next several subsections. Other SQL keywords exist, but they are beyond the scope of this text.

SQL keyword	Description
SELECT	Retrieves data from one or more tables.
FROM	Specifies the tables involved in a query. Required in every query.
WHERE	Specifies optional criteria for selection that determine the rows to be retrieved, deleted or updated.
ORDER BY	Specifies optional criteria for ordering rows (e.g., ascending, descending).
INNER JOIN	Specifies optional operator for merging rows from multiple tables.
INSERT	Inserts rows in a specified table.
UPDATE	Updates rows in a specified table.
DELETE	Deletes rows from a specified table.

Fig. 20.10 | Common SQL keywords.

20.4.1 Basic SELECT Query

Let us consider several SQL queries that retrieve information from database Books. A SQL query "selects" rows and columns from one or more tables in a database. Such selections are performed by queries with the SELECT keyword. The basic form of a SELECT query is

```
SELECT * FROM tableName
```

in which the asterisk (*) indicates that all the columns from the *tableName* table should be retrieved. For example, to retrieve all the data in the `Authors` table, use

```
SELECT * FROM Authors
```

Note that the rows of the `Authors` table are not guaranteed to be returned in any particular order. You will learn how to specify criteria for sorting rows in Section 20.4.3.

Most programs do not require all the data in a table—in fact, selecting all the data from a large table is discouraged. To retrieve only specific columns from a table, replace the asterisk (*) with a comma-separated list of the column names. For example, to retrieve only the columns `AuthorID` and `LastName` for all the rows in the `Authors` table, use the query

```
SELECT AuthorID, LastName FROM Authors
```

This query returns only the data listed in Fig. 20.11.

AuthorID	LastName
1	Deitel
2	Deitel
3	Ayer
4	Quirk

Fig. 20.11 | `AuthorID` and `LastName` data from the `Authors` table.

20.4.2 WHERE Clause

When users search a database for rows that satisfy certain **selection criteria** (formally called **predicates**), only rows that satisfy the selection criteria are selected. SQL uses the optional **`WHERE` clause** in a query to specify the selection criteria for the query. The basic form of a query with selection criteria is

```
SELECT columnName1, columnName2, ... FROM tableName WHERE criteria
```

For example, to select the `Title`, `EditionNumber` and `Copyright` columns from table `Titles` for which the `Copyright` date is more recent than `2007`, use the query

```
SELECT Title, EditionNumber, Copyright
FROM Titles
WHERE Copyright > '2007'
```

Note that string literals in SQL are delimited by single quotes instead of double quotes as in Visual Basic. In SQL, double quotes are used around table and column names that would otherwise be invalid—names containing SQL keywords, spaces, or other punctuation characters. Figure 20.12 shows the result of the preceding query.

Title	EditionNumber	Copyright
Internet & World Wide Web How to Program	4	2008
Simply Visual Basic 2008	3	2009
Visual Basic 2008 How to Program	4	2009
Visual C# 2008 How to Program	3	2009
Visual C++ 2008 How to Program	2	2008
C++ How to Program	6	2008

Fig. 20.12 | Titles with copyright dates after 2007 from table `Titles`.

The `WHERE` clause criteria can contain the comparison operators <, >, <=, >=, = (equality), <> (inequality) and `LIKE`, as well as the logical operators `AND`, `OR` and `NOT` (discussed in Section 20.4.6). Operator **`LIKE`** is used for **pattern matching** with wildcard characters **percent** (%) and **underscore** (_). Pattern matching allows SQL to search for strings that match a given pattern.

A pattern that contains a percent character (%) searches for strings that have zero or more characters at the percent character's position in the pattern. For example, the following query locates the rows of all the authors whose last names start with the letter `D`:

```
SELECT AuthorID, FirstName, LastName
FROM Authors
WHERE LastName LIKE 'D%'
```

The preceding query selects the two rows shown in Fig. 20.13, because two of the four authors in our database have a last name starting with the letter `D` (followed by zero or more characters). The `%` in the `WHERE` clause's `LIKE` pattern indicates that any number of characters can appear after the letter `D` in the `LastName` column. Note that the pattern string is surrounded by single-quote characters.

An underscore (_) in the pattern string indicates a single wildcard character at that position in the pattern. For example, the following query locates the rows of all the authors whose last names start with any character (specified by _), followed by the letter `y`, followed by any number of additional characters (specified by `%`):

```
SELECT AuthorID, FirstName, LastName
FROM Authors
WHERE LastName LIKE '_y%'
```

The preceding query produces the row shown in Fig. 20.14, because only one author in our database has a last name that contains the letter `y` as its second letter.

AuthorID	FirstName	LastName
1	Harvey	Deitel
2	Paul	Deitel

Fig. 20.13 | Authors from the `Authors` table whose last names start with `D`.

AuthorID	FirstName	LastName
3	Greg	Ayer

Fig. 20.14 | The only author from the `Authors` table whose last name contains `y` as the second letter.

20.4.3 ORDER BY Clause

The rows in the result of a query can be sorted into ascending or descending order by using the optional **ORDER BY clause**. The basic form of a query with an `ORDER BY` clause is

SELECT *columnName1*, *columnName2*, … FROM *tableName* ORDER BY *column* ASC
SELECT *columnName1*, *columnName2*, … FROM *tableName* ORDER BY *column* DESC

where **ASC** specifies ascending order (lowest to highest), **DESC** specifies descending order (highest to lowest) and *column* specifies the column on which the sort is based. For example, to obtain the list of authors in ascending order by last name (Fig. 20.15), use the query

```
SELECT AuthorID, FirstName, LastName
FROM Authors
ORDER BY LastName ASC
```

The default sorting order is ascending, so `ASC` is optional in the preceding query. To obtain the same list of authors in descending order by last name (Fig. 20.16), use

```
SELECT AuthorID, FirstName, LastName
FROM Authors
ORDER BY LastName DESC
```

AuthorID	FirstName	LastName
3	Greg	Ayer
1	Harvey	Deitel
2	Paul	Deitel
4	Dan	Quirk

Fig. 20.15 | Authors from table `Authors` in ascending order by `LastName`.

AuthorID	FirstName	LastName
4	Dan	Quirk
1	Harvey	Deitel
2	Paul	Deitel
3	Greg	Ayer

Fig. 20.16 | Authors from table `Authors` in descending order by `LastName`.

Multiple columns can be used for sorting with an ORDER BY clause of the form

```
ORDER BY column1 sortingOrder, column2 sortingOrder, ...
```

where *sortingOrder* is either ASC or DESC. Note that the *sortingOrder* does not have to be identical for each column. For example, the query

```
SELECT Title, EditionNumber, Copyright
FROM Titles
ORDER BY Copyright DESC, Title ASC
```

returns the rows of the Titles table sorted first in descending order by copyright date, then in ascending order by title (Fig. 20.17). This means that rows with higher Copyright values are returned before rows with lower Copyright values, and any rows that have the same Copyright values are sorted in ascending order by title.

The WHERE and ORDER BY clauses can be combined. If used, ORDER BY must be the last clause in the query. For example, the query

```
SELECT ISBN, Title, EditionNumber, Copyright
FROM Titles
WHERE Title LIKE '%How to Program'
ORDER BY Title ASC
```

returns the ISBN, Title, EditionNumber and Copyright of each book in the Titles table that has a Title ending with "How to Program" and sorts them in ascending order by Title. The query results are shown in Fig. 20.18.

Title	EditionNumber	Copyright
Simply Visual Basic 2008	3	2009
Visual Basic 2008 How to Program	4	2009
Visual C# 2008 How to Program	3	2009
C++ How to Program	6	2008
Internet & World Wide Web How to Program	4	2008
Visual C++ 2008 How to Program	2	2008
C How to Program	5	2007
Java How to Program	7	2007

Fig. 20.17 | Data from Titles in descending order by Copyright and ascending order by Title.

ISBN	Title	EditionNumber	Copyright
0132404168	C How to Program	5	2007
0136152503	C++ How to Program	6	2008
0131752421	Internet & World Wide Web How to Program	4	2008

Fig. 20.18 | Books from table Titles whose titles end with How to Program in ascending order by Title. (Part 1 of 2.)

ISBN	Title	EditionNumber	Copyright
0132222205	Java How to Program	7	2007
013605305X	Visual Basic 2008 How to Program	4	2009
013605322X	Visual C# 2008 How to Program	3	2009
0136151574	Visual C++ 2008 How to Program	2	2008

Fig. 20.18 | Books from table `Titles` whose titles end with `How to Program` in ascending order by `Title`. (Part 2 of 2.)

20.4.4 Retrieving Data from Multiple Tables: INNER JOIN

Database designers typically **normalize** databases—i.e., split related data into separate tables to ensure that a database does not store redundant data. For example, the `Books` database has tables `Authors` and `Titles`. We use an `AuthorISBN` table to store "links" between authors and titles. If we did not separate this information into individual tables, we would need to include author information with each entry in the `Titles` table. This would result in the database storing duplicate author information for authors who have written more than one book.

Often, it is desirable to merge data from multiple tables into a single result. This is referred to as joining the tables, and is specified by an **`INNER JOIN` operator** in the query. An `INNER JOIN` merges rows from two tables by testing for matching values in a column that is common to the tables (though the column names can differ among the tables). The basic form of an `INNER JOIN` is:

```
SELECT columnName1, columnName2, ...
FROM table1 INNER JOIN table2
   ON table1.columnName = table2.columnName
```

The **`ON` clause** of the `INNER JOIN` specifies the columns from each table that are compared to determine which rows are merged. For example, the following query produces a list of authors accompanied by the ISBNs for books written by each author:

```
SELECT FirstName, LastName, ISBN
FROM Authors INNER JOIN AuthorISBN
   ON Authors.AuthorID = AuthorISBN.AuthorID
ORDER BY LastName, FirstName
```

The query combines the `FirstName` and `LastName` columns from table `Authors` and the `ISBN` column from table `AuthorISBN`, sorting the results in ascending order by `LastName` and `FirstName`. Note the use of the syntax *tableName*`.`*columnName* in the `ON` clause. This syntax (called a **qualified name**) specifies the columns from each table that should be compared to join the tables. The "*tableName*`.`" syntax is required if the columns have the same name in both tables. The same syntax can be used in any query to distinguish columns that have the same name in different tables.

Common Programming Error 20.4

In a SQL query, failure to qualify names for columns that have the same name in two or more tables is an error.

As always, the query can contain an ORDER BY clause. Figure 20.19 depicts the results of the preceding query, ordered by LastName and FirstName.

FirstName	LastName	ISBN
Greg	Ayer	0136053033
Harvey	Deitel	0131752421
Harvey	Deitel	0132222205
Harvey	Deitel	0132404168
Harvey	Deitel	0136053033
Harvey	Deitel	013605305X
Harvey	Deitel	013605322X
Harvey	Deitel	0136151574
Harvey	Deitel	0136152503
Paul	Deitel	0131752421
Paul	Deitel	0132222205
Paul	Deitel	0132404168
Paul	Deitel	0136053033
Paul	Deitel	013605305X
Paul	Deitel	013605322X
Paul	Deitel	0136151574
Paul	Deitel	0136152503
Dan	Quirk	0136151574

Fig. 20.19 | Authors and ISBNs for their books in ascending order by LastName and FirstName.

20.4.5 INSERT Statement

The **INSERT statement** inserts a row into a table. The basic form of this statement is

```
INSERT INTO tableName ( columnName1, columnName2, ..., columnNameN )
VALUES ( value1, value2, ..., valueN )
```

where *tableName* is the table in which to insert the row. The *tableName* is followed by a comma-separated list of column names in parentheses. The list of column names is followed by the SQL keyword **VALUES** and a comma-separated list of values in parentheses. The values specified here must match up with the columns specified after the table name in both order and type (e.g., if *columnName1* is supposed to be the FirstName column, then *value1* should be a string in single quotes representing the first name). Although the list is not required if the INSERT operation specifies a value for every table column in the correct order, you should always explicitly list the columns when inserting rows—if the order of the columns in the table changes, using only VALUES may cause an error. The INSERT statement

```
INSERT INTO Authors ( FirstName, LastName )
VALUES ( 'Sue', 'Smith' )
```

inserts a row into the `Authors` table. The statement indicates that the values `'Sue'` and `'Smith'` are provided for the `FirstName` and `LastName` columns, respectively.

Some database tables allow `NULL` columns—that is, columns without values. `NULL` is used similarly to `Nothing` in Visual Basic. All of the columns in the `Books` database are required, so they must be given values in an `INSERT` statement.

We do not specify an `AuthorID` in this example because `AuthorID` is an identity column in the `Authors` table (see Fig. 20.3). For every row added to this table, SQL Server assigns a unique `AuthorID` value that is the next value in an autoincremented sequence (i.e., 1, 2, 3 and so on). In this case, Sue Smith would be assigned `AuthorID` number `5`. Figure 20.20 shows the `Authors` table after the `INSERT` operation.

Common Programming Error 20.5

It is an error to specify a value for an identity column in an `INSERT` statement.

Common Programming Error 20.6

SQL uses the single-quote (`'`) character to delimit strings. To specify a string containing a single quote (e.g., O'Malley) in a SQL statement, there must be two single quotes in the position where the single-quote character appears in the string (e.g., `'O''Malley'`). The first of the two single-quote characters acts as an escape character for the second. Not escaping single-quote characters in a string that is part of a SQL statement is a syntax error.

AuthorID	FirstName	LastName
1	Harvey	Deitel
2	Paul	Deitel
3	Greg	Ayer
4	Dan	Quirk
5	Sue	Smith

Fig. 20.20 | Table `Authors` after an `INSERT` operation.

20.4.6 UPDATE Statement

An **`UPDATE` statement** modifies data in a table. The basic form of the `UPDATE` statement is

```
UPDATE tableName
SET columnName1 = value1, columnName2 = value2, ..., columnNameN = valueN
WHERE criteria
```

where *tableName* is the table to update. The *tableName* is followed by keyword **`SET`** and a comma-separated list of column name/value pairs in the format *columnName = value*. The optional `WHERE` clause provides criteria that determine which rows to update. Though not required, the `WHERE` clause is typically used, unless a change is to be made to every row. The `UPDATE` statement

```
UPDATE Authors
SET LastName = 'Jones'
WHERE LastName = 'Smith' AND FirstName = 'Sue'
```

updates a row in the `Authors` table. Keyword **AND** is a logical operator that, like the Visual Basic `AndAlso` operator, returns true *if and only if* both of its operands are true. Thus, the preceding statement assigns to `LastName` the value `Jones` for the row in which `LastName` is equal to `Smith` *and* `FirstName` is equal to `Sue`. [*Note:* If there are multiple rows with the first name "Sue" and the last name "Smith," this statement modifies all such rows to have the last name "Jones."] Figure 20.21 shows the `Authors` table after the `UPDATE` operation has taken place. SQL also provides other logical operators, such as **OR** and **NOT**, which behave like their Visual Basic counterparts.

AuthorID	FirstName	LastName
1	Harvey	Deitel
2	Paul	Deitel
3	Greg	Ayer
4	Dan	Quirk
5	Sue	Jones

Fig. 20.21 | Table `Authors` after an `UPDATE` operation.

20.4.7 DELETE Statement

A **DELETE statement** removes rows from a table. The basic form of a `DELETE` statement is

```
DELETE FROM tableName WHERE criteria
```

where *tableName* is the table from which to delete. The optional `WHERE` clause specifies the criteria used to determine which rows to delete. If the `WHERE` clause is omitted, the `DELETE` applies to all rows of the table. The `DELETE` statement

```
DELETE FROM Authors
WHERE LastName = 'Jones' AND FirstName = 'Sue'
```

deletes the row for Sue Jones in the `Authors` table. `DELETE` statements can delete multiple rows if the rows all meet the criteria in the `WHERE` clause. Figure 20.22 shows the `Authors` table after the `DELETE` operation has taken place.

AuthorID	FirstName	LastName
1	Harvey	Deitel
2	Paul	Deitel
3	Greg	Ayer
4	Dan	Quirk

Fig. 20.22 | Table `Authors` after a `DELETE` operation.

SQL Wrap-Up

This concludes our SQL introduction. We demonstrated several commonly used SQL keywords, formed SQL queries that retrieved data from databases and formed other SQL statements that manipulated data in a database. Next, we introduce LINQ to SQL, which allows Visual Basic applications to interact with databases. As you will see, LINQ to SQL translates LINQ queries like the ones you wrote in Chapter 9 into SQL statements like those presented here.

20.5 LINQ to SQL

LINQ to SQL provides an API for accessing data in SQL Server databases using the same LINQ syntax used to query arrays and collections. For many applications, the LINQ to SQL API can entirely replace the ADO.NET API from previous versions of the .NET framework, though ADO.NET is still used internally by LINQ to SQL.

You interact with LINQ to SQL via classes that are automatically generated by the IDE's LINQ to SQL Designer based on the database schema. The IDE creates a class for each table, with a property for each column in the table. Objects of these classes hold the data from individual rows in the database's tables. Foreign-key relationships are taken into account in both directions. For each foreign key, a property is created that returns the row object that the foreign key references. Every object also contains a property that returns a collection of the rows that reference it. Once generated, these classes are normal Visual Basic classes with full *IntelliSense* support in the IDE.

A cache is a temporary store created for fast access to data that would otherwise be costly to retrieve or regenerate. LINQ to SQL caches all row objects that it creates, making interacting with the database more efficient in two significant ways. First, it does not have to recreate row objects each time data is retrieved from the database—it can simply reuse the ones it already has in memory. Second, having these row objects in memory allows you to manipulate them as much as necessary, then submit the changes you make all at once. This can reduce round trips to the database—a slow operation compared to manipulating objects that are already in memory. The cache needs a way to uniquely identify individual rows to determine if a cached row is the same as a new row. For this reason, LINQ to SQL requires every table to have a primary key.

LINQ to SQL works through the `IQueryable` interface, which inherits from the `IEnumerable` interface introduced in Chapter 9. With LINQ to Objects, LINQ iterates through the entire collection and applies the query operators one at a time—each operator uses the results of applying the previous operator. In contrast, LINQ queries on an `IQueryable` object are processed together—LINQ to SQL converts the entire query into a single SQL statement to execute against the database. If each query operator were handled separately, multiple round trips to the database would be needed, and the database management system would not be able to use its intimate knowledge of its data structures to optimize the query. When the results are returned from the database, they are loaded into the corresponding LINQ to SQL classes for convenient access in your code.

All LINQ to SQL queries occur via a `DataContext` class, which controls the flow of data between the program and the database. A specific `DataContext` class, which inherits from the class `System.Data.Linq.DataContext`, is created when the classes representing each row of the table are generated. When instantiated, the `DataContext` has properties for each table in the database—these can be used as subjects of a LINQ query. When cached objects have been changed, these changes are saved back to the database using the `DataContext`'s `SubmitChanges` method.

20.6 LINQ to SQL: Extracting Information from a Database

In this section, we demonstrate how to connect to a database, query it and display the result of the query. There is little code in this section—the IDE provides visual programming tools and wizards that simplify accessing data in your projects. These tools establish database connections and create the data-binding objects necessary to view and manipulate the data through Windows `Forms` GUI controls.

The next example performs a simple query on the `Books` database from Section 20.3. The program retrieves the entire `Authors` table and uses data binding to display its data in a `DataGridView`—a control from namespace `System.Windows.Forms` that can display a data source in a GUI. First, we connect to the `Books` database and create the LINQ to SQL classes required to use it. Then, we add the `Authors` table as a data source. Finally, we drag the `Authors` table data source onto the **Design** view to create a GUI for displaying the table's data.

20.6.1 Creating LINQ to SQL Classes

This section presents the steps required to create LINQ to SQL classes for a database. Though we create a **Windows Forms Application** here, *Steps 2–4* apply to any type of application that manipulates a database via LINQ to SQL.

Step 1: Creating the Project

Create a new **Windows Forms Application** named `DisplayTable`. Change the name of the source file to `DisplayTableForm.vb`. The IDE updates the `Form`'s class name to match the source file. Set the `Form`'s **Text** property to `Display Table`.

Step 2: Adding a Database to the Project

To interact with a database, you must first add it to the project. Select **Tools > Connect to Database...**. If the **Choose Data Source** dialog appears, select **Microsoft SQL Server Database File** from the **Data source:** `ListBox`. If you check the **Always use this selection** `CheckBox`, Visual Basic will use this type of database file by default when you add databases to your projects in the future. Click **Continue** to open the **Add Connection** dialog. Notice that the **Data source:** `TextBox` reflects your selection in the **Choose Data Source** dialog. You can click the **Change...** `Button` to select a different type of database. Next, click **Browse...** and locate the `Books.mdf` file in the `Databases` directory included with this chapter's examples. You can click **Test Connection** to verify that the IDE can connect to the database through SQL Server Express. Click **OK** to create the connection.

Error-Prevention Tip 20.1

SQL Server Express allows only one application at a time to access a database file. Ensure that no other program is using the database file before you attempt to add it to the project.

Step 3: Generating the LINQ to SQL classes

After the database has been added, you must create the classes based on the database schema. To do this, right click the project name in the **Solution Explorer** and select **Add > New Item...** to display the **Add New Item** dialog. Select **LINQ to SQL classes**, name the new item `Books.dbml` and click the **Add** button. After a few moments, the **Object Relational**

Designer window appears. You can also double click the `Books.dbml` file in the **Solution Explorer** to open the **Object Relational Designer**.

The **Database Explorer** window, which lets you navigate the structure of databases, should have appeared on the left side of the IDE when you added the database to the project. If not, open it by selecting **View > Database Explorer**. Expand the `Books.mdf` database node, then expand the **Tables** node. Drag the `Authors`, `Titles` and `AuthorISBN` tables onto the **Object Relational Designer**. The IDE prompts whether you want to copy the database to the project directory. Select **Yes**. Then save the `Books.dbml` file. At this point, the IDE generates the LINQ to SQL classes—the next steps will not work if you do not save the `.dbml` file.

Error-Prevention Tip 20.2

Be sure to save the file in the **Object Relational Designer** *before trying to use the LINQ to SQL classes in code. The IDE does not generate the classes until you save the file.*

20.6.2 Creating Data Bindings

While they are not a part of LINQ to SQL, the automatic data bindings that the IDE provides greatly simplify the creation of applications to view and modify the data stored in the database's tables. You must write a small amount of code to bridge the gap between the autogenerated data-binding classes and the autogenerated LINQ to SQL classes.

Step 1: Adding a Data Source

To use the LINQ to SQL classes in our bindings, we must first add them as a data source. Select **Data > Add New Data Source...** to display the **Data Source Configuration Wizard**. Since the LINQ to SQL classes can be used to create objects representing the tables in the database, we'll use an object data source. In the dialog, select **Object** and click **Next >**. Expand the tree view in the next screen and select **DisplayTable > DisplayTable > Author**. The first **DisplayTable** is the project's name, the second is the `DisplayTable` namespace where the automatically generated classes are located, and the last is the `Author` class—an object of this class will be used as the data source. Click **Next >** then **Finish**. The `Authors` table in the database is now a data source that can be used by the bindings.

Step 2: Create GUI Elements

Open the **Data Sources** window by selecting **Data > Show Data Sources**. The `Author` class that you added in the previous step should appear. The columns of the `Authors` table should appear below it, as well as an `AuthorISBNs` entry showing the relationship between the two tables.

Open the `DisplayTableForm` in **Design** view. Click the **Author** node in the **Data Sources** window—it should change to a drop-down list. Open the drop-down and ensure that the `DataGridView` option is selected—this is the GUI control that will be used to display and interact with the data.

Drag the **Author** node from the **Data Sources** window to the `DisplayTableForm`. The IDE creates a `DataGridView` with the correct column names and a `BindingNavigator`. The **`BindingNavigator`** contains `Buttons` for moving between entries, adding entries, deleting entries and saving changes to the database. The IDE also generates a **`BindingSource`**, which handles the transfer of data between the data source and the data-bound controls on the Form. Nonvisual components such as the BindingSource and the nonvisual aspects of the BindingNavigator appear in the component tray—the gray region below the Form in **Design** view (Fig. 20.23). We use the default names for automatically generated components throughout this chapter to show exactly what the IDE creates.

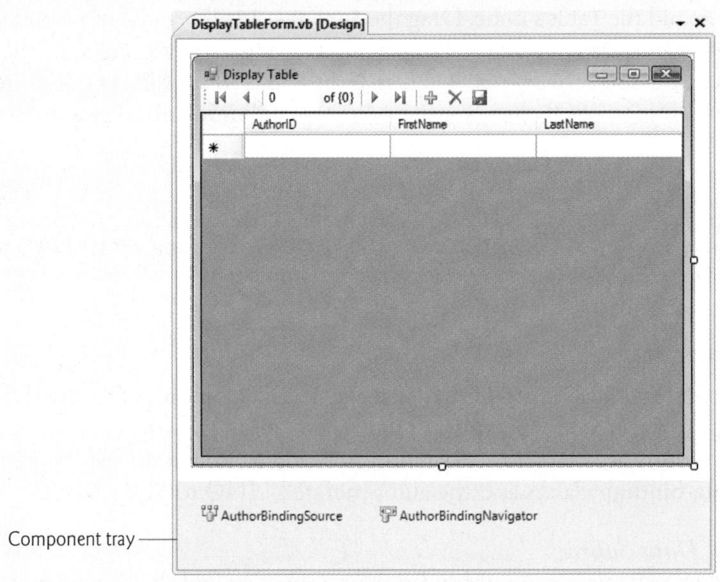

Fig. 20.23 | Component tray holds nonvisual components in **Design** view.

Step 3: Connect the **BooksDataContext** *to the* **AuthorBindingSource**

Now that we've created the back-end LINQ to SQL classes and the front-end DataGridView and BindingNavigator, we must connect them with a small amount of code. The DataGridView is already connected to the BindingSource by the IDE, so we simply need to connect BooksDataContext you declared in the previous section and the AuthorBindingSource you created above. Figure 20.24 shows the small amount of code needed to move data back and forth between the database and GUI.

As mentioned in the previous section, we must use a DataContext object to interact with the database. The BooksDataContext class is automatically generated by the IDE to allow access to the Books database. Line 4 defines an object of this class named database.

```
1  ' Fig. 20.24: DisplayTableForm.vb
2  ' Displaying data from a database table in a DataGridView.
3  Public Class DisplayTableForm
4     Private database As New BooksDataContext() ' LINQ to SQL data context
5
6     ' load data from database into DataGridView
7     Private Sub DisplayTableForm_Load(ByVal sender As System.Object, _
8        ByVal e As System.EventArgs) Handles MyBase.Load
9
```

Fig. 20.24 | Displaying data from a database table in a DataGridView. (Part 1 of 2.)

```
10         ' use LINQ to order the data for display
11         AuthorBindingSource.DataSource = _
12            From author In database.Authors _
13            Order By author.AuthorID _
14            Select author
15      End Sub ' DisplayTableForm_Load
16
17      ' Click event handler for the Save Button in the
18      ' BindingNavigator saves the changes made to the data
19      Private Sub AuthorBindingNavigatorSaveItem_Click( _
20         ByVal sender As System.Object, ByVal e As System.EventArgs) _
21         Handles AuthorBindingNavigatorSaveItem.Click
22
23         Validate() ' validate input fields
24         AuthorBindingSource.EndEdit() ' indicate edits are complete
25         database.SubmitChanges() ' write changes to database file
26      End Sub ' AuthorBindingNavigatorSaveItem_Click
27   End Class ' DisplayTableForm
```

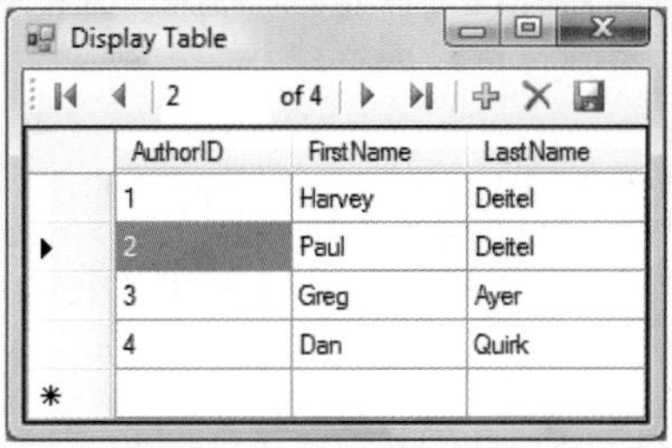

Display Table

2 of 4

	AuthorID	FirstName	LastName
	1	Harvey	Deitel
▶	2	Paul	Deitel
	3	Greg	Ayer
	4	Dan	Quirk
*			

Fig. 20.24 | Displaying data from a database table in a `DataGridView`. (Part 2 of 2.)

Create the `Form`'s `Load` handler by double clicking the title bar in **Design** view. We allow data to move between the `DataContext` and the `BindingSource` by creating a LINQ query that extracts data from the `DataContext`'s `Authors` property (lines 12–14), which corresponds to the `Authors` table in the database. The `BindingSource`'s **`DataSource` property** is set to the results of this query (line 11). The `BindingSource` uses its `DataSource` to extract data from the database and to populate the `DataGridView`.

Step 4: Saving Modifications Back to the Database

We would also like to save data back to the database if the user modifies it. By default, the `BindingNavigator`'s save `Button` (💾) is disabled. Enable it via the save `Button`'s right-click menu or the **Properties** window. Then, double click the save `Button` to create its event handler.

Saving the data entered into the `DataGridView` back to the database is a three-step process (lines 23–25). First, all controls on the form are validated (line 23)—if any of the controls have validation event handlers, those execute to determine whether the controls' contents are valid. Second, line 24 calls **`EndEdit`** on the `BindingSource`, which forces it to save any pending changes to its `DataSource`. Finally, with the data saved back to the LINQ to SQL classes, we call `SubmitChanges` on the `BooksDataContext` to store the changes in the database. For efficiency reasons, LINQ to SQL sends only data that has changed.

Step 5: Configuring the Database File to Persist Changes
By default, the original database file is copied to the project's `bin` directory—the location of the program's executable—each time you execute the program. To persist changes between program executions, select the database in the **Solution Explorer** and set the **Copy to Output Directory** property in the **Properties** window to **Copy if newer**.

Testing the Application
Run the application to verify that it works. The `DataGridView` should be filled with the author data as shown in the screenshot. You can add and remove rows, and save your changes back to the database. Note that empty (`NULL`) values are not allowed in the database, so attempting to save the data with some of the fields empty will cause an error.

20.7 More Complex LINQ Queries and Data Binding

Now that you've seen how to display an entire database table in a `DataGridView`, we demonstrate how to execute more advanced queries against the database and display the results. Perform the following steps to build the example application, which executes custom queries against the `Titles` table of the `Books` database.

Step 1: Creating the Project
First, create a new **Windows Forms Application** named `DisplayQueryResult`. Rename the source file to `DisplayQueryResultForm.vb`. The IDE will rename the `Form` class to `DisplayQueryResultForm`. Set the `Form`'s **Text** property to `Display Query Result`.

Step 2: Creating the LINQ to SQL Classes
Follow the steps in Section 20.6.1 to add the `Books` database to the project and generate the LINQ to SQL classes.

Step 3: Creating a **`DataGridView`** *to Display the* **`Titles`** *Table*
Follow *Steps 1* and *2* in Section 20.6.2 to create the data source and the `DataGridView`. In this example, select the `Title` class (rather than the `Author` class) as the data source, and drag the **Title** node from the **Data Sources** window onto the form.

Step 4: Adding a **`ComboBox`** *to the* **`Form`**
Leave the `Form`'s **Design** view open and add a `ComboBox` named `queriesComboBox` below the `DataGridView` on the `Form`. From this control users select options representing the queries to execute. Open the **String Collection Editor** by selecting **Edit Items** from the right-click or smart tag menu of `queriesComboBox`. You can open the **smart tag menu** by clicking the small arrowhead that appears in the upper-right corner of the control in **Design** view. The Visual Basic IDE displays smart tag menus for many GUI controls to facilitate common tasks. Add the following three items to `queriesComboBox`—one for each of the queries we'll create:

1. `All titles`
2. `Titles with 2008 copyright`
3. `Titles ending with "How to Program"`

Step 5: Programming an Event Handler for the **ComboBox**

Next you must write code that executes the appropriate query each time the user chooses a different item from `queriesComboBox`. Double click `queriesComboBox` in **Design** view to generate a `queriesComboBox_SelectedIndexChanged` event handler (lines 33–63) in the `DisplayQueryResultForm.vb` file (Fig. 20.25). In the event handler, add a `Select Case` statement (lines 38–60) to change the `TitleBindingSource`'s `DataSource` property to a LINQ query that returns the correct set of data. The data bindings created by the IDE update the `TitlesDataGridView` each time we change the `DataSource`. The **`MoveFirst` method** of the `BindingSource` (line 62) is used to move the focus to the first element each time a query executes.

```
1  ' Fig. 20.25: DisplayQueryResultForm.vb
2  ' Displaying the result of a user-selected query in a DataGridView.
3  Public Class DisplayQueryResultForm
4     Private database As New BooksDataContext() ' LINQ to SQL data context
5
6     ' load data from database into DataGridView
7     Private Sub DisplayQueryResultForm_Load( _
8        ByVal sender As System.Object, ByVal e As System.EventArgs) _
9        Handles MyBase.Load
10
11       database.Log = Console.Out ' write SQL to standard output stream
12
13       ' set the ComboBox to show the default query that
14       ' selects all books from the Titles table
15       queriesComboBox.SelectedIndex = 0
16    End Sub ' DisplayQueryResultForm_Load
17
18    ' Click event handler for the Save Button in the
19    ' BindingNavigator saves the changes made to the data
20    Private Sub TitleBindingNavigatorSaveItem_Click( _
21       ByVal sender As System.Object, ByVal e As System.EventArgs) _
22       Handles TitleBindingNavigatorSaveItem.Click
23
24       Validate() ' validate input fields
25       TitleBindingSource.EndEdit() ' indicate edits are complete
26       database.SubmitChanges() ' write changes to database file
27
28       ' when saving, return to "all titles" query
29       queriesComboBox.SelectedIndex = 0
30    End Sub ' TitleBindingNavigatorSaveItem_Click
31
32    ' loads data into TitleBindingSource based on user-selected query
33    Private Sub queriesComboBox_SelectedIndexChanged( _
34       ByVal sender As System.Object, ByVal e As System.EventArgs) _
35       Handles queriesComboBox.SelectedIndexChanged
36
37       ' set the data displayed according to what is selected
38       Select Case queriesComboBox.SelectedIndex
39          Case 0 ' all titles
40             ' use LINQ to order the books by title
```

Fig. 20.25 | Displaying the result of a user-selected query in a `DataGridView`. (Part 1 of 2.)

```
41                TitleBindingSource.DataSource = _
42                   From title In database.Titles _
43                   Order By title.Title _
44                   Select title
45             Case 1 ' titles with 2008 copyright
46                ' use LINQ to get titles with 2008 copyright and sort them
47                TitleBindingSource.DataSource = _
48                   From title In database.Titles _
49                   Where title.Copyright = "2008" _
50                   Order By title.Title _
51                   Select title
52             Case 2 ' titles ending with "How to Program"
53                ' use LINQ to get titles ending with
54                ' "How to Program" and sort them
55                TitleBindingSource.DataSource = _
56                   From title In database.Titles _
57                   Where title.Title.EndsWith("How to Program") _
58                   Order By title.Title _
59                   Select title
60          End Select
61
62          TitleBindingSource.MoveFirst() ' move to first entry
63       End Sub ' queriesComboBox_SelectedIndexChanged
64    End Class ' DisplayQueryResultForm
```

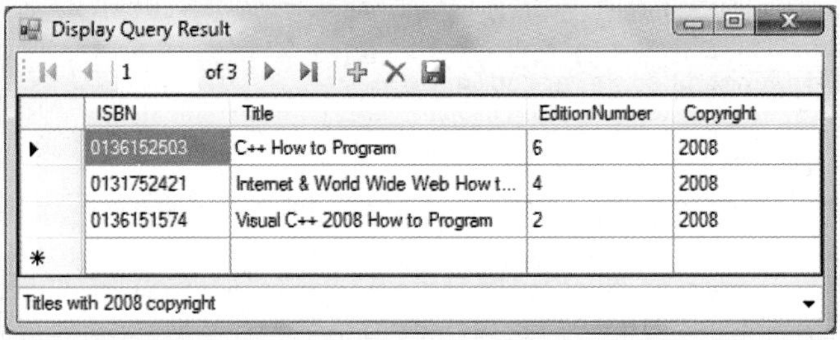

Display Query Result

1 of 3

	ISBN	Title	EditionNumber	Copyright
▶	0136152503	C++ How to Program	6	2008
	0131752421	Internet & World Wide Web How t...	4	2008
	0136151574	Visual C++ 2008 How to Program	2	2008
*				

Titles with 2008 copyright

Fig. 20.25 | Displaying the result of a user-selected query in a `DataGridView`. (Part 2 of 2.)

Step 6: Customizing the **Form***'s* **Load** *Event Handler*

Create the `Form`'s `Load` event handler by double clicking the title bar in **Design** view. Add a line setting the `SelectedIndex` of the `queriesComboBox` to `0` (line 15). This causes the program to show all titles when it executes.

Step 7: Saving Changes

Follow the instructions in the previous example to add a handler for the `BindingNavigator`'s save `Button` (lines 20–30). Note that, except for changes to the names, the three lines are identical. The last statement (line 29) makes the `DataGridView` reset to the `All titles` query. Also, set the database's **Copy to Output Directory** property to **Copy if newer**, as was done in the preceding example.

Testing the Application

You may now run the application. As in the previous example, you can add and remove rows to and from the table, and save your changes to the database. Additionally, selecting one of the queries from the `ComboBox` will filter the results so that only some of the rows are displayed.

The `BooksDataContext`*'s* `Log` *Property*

Line 11 sets the database `BooksDataContext`'s **Log** property. When you set this property, the `DataContext` object logs all queries it runs on the database to the specified stream—in this case, `Console.Out`. Recall from Chapter 18 that `Console.Out` is the standard output stream object. In a GUI application, "standard output" is sent to the IDE's **Output** window, shown in Fig. 20.26. The **Output** window can be opened while the program is running by selecting **View > Other Windows > Output** in the IDE. [*Note:* The output log is displayed only when running in debug mode.]

The SQL syntax in Fig. 20.26 is slightly different from the syntax we presented earlier in this chapter. Microsoft SQL Server uses a SQL variant known as Transact-SQL. The square brackets are used to quote table and column names—required if the table names contain spaces. The SQL generated by LINQ to SQL quotes all table and column names even if it is not required.

The identifier `t0` used throughout the SQL in Fig. 20.26 is an alias for the table named `dbo.Titles`. This alias is defined in the `FROM` clause using SQL's `AS` keyword. The alias simply provides a shorter name for the table. The identifier `dbo` stands for "database owner." This represents the database user that is allowed to perform all operations on a SQL Server database. The lines starting with `--` are comments in the `Log` output.

The `@p0` seen in the third line of the second query is a placeholder for a parameter to the SQL statement. The first comment line for the second SQL statement shows the value of the parameter at the end of the line in square brackets (i.e., `[%How to Program]`).

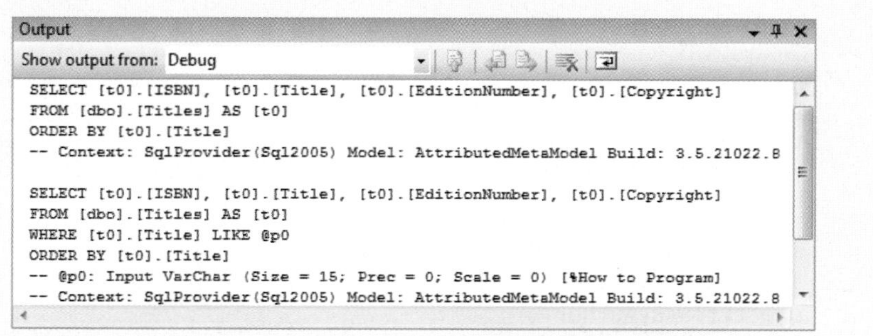

Fig. 20.26 | **Output** window after starting the **Display Query Result** application and selecting the `Titles ending with "How to Program"` query.

20.8 Retrieving Data from Multiple Tables with LINQ

In the two previous examples, we used data bindings to display data extracted using LINQ to SQL. In this section, we concentrate on LINQ to SQL features that simplify querying and combining data from multiple tables. You've already seen the SQL `INNER JOIN` operator in Section 20.4.4—LINQ to SQL provides similar capabilities and allows more complex operations as well. Figure 20.27 uses LINQ to SQL to combine and organize data from multiple tables.

```
' Fig. 20.27: JoiningWithLINQ.vb
' Using LINQ to perform a join and aggregate data across tables.
Module JoiningWithLINQ
   Sub Main()
      Dim database As New BooksDataContext() ' create database connection

      ' get authors and ISBNs of each book they co-authored
      Dim authorsAndISBNs = _
         From author In database.Authors _
         Join book In database.AuthorISBNs _
            On author.AuthorID Equals book.AuthorID _
         Order By author.LastName, author.FirstName _
         Select author.FirstName, author.LastName, book.ISBN

      Console.WriteLine("Authors and ISBNs:") ' display header

      ' display authors and ISBNs in tabular format
      For Each element In authorsAndISBNs
         Console.WriteLine(vbTab & "{0,-10} {1,-10} {2,-10}", _
            element.FirstName, element.LastName, element.ISBN)
      Next

      ' get authors and titles of each book they co-authored
      Dim authorsAndTitles = _
         From title In database.Titles _
         From book In title.AuthorISBNs _
         Let author = book.Author _
         Order By author.LastName, author.FirstName, title.Title _
         Select author.FirstName, author.LastName, title.Title

      Console.WriteLine(vbNewLine & "Authors and titles:") ' header

      ' display authors and titles in tabular format
      For Each element In authorsAndTitles
         Console.WriteLine(vbTab & "{0,-10} {1,-10} {2}", _
            element.FirstName, element.LastName, element.Title)
      Next

      ' get authors and titles of each book
      ' they co-authored; group by author
      Dim titlesByAuthor = _
         From author In database.Authors _
         Order By author.LastName, author.FirstName _
         Select Name = author.FirstName & " " & author.LastName, _
            Titles = _
               From book In author.AuthorISBNs _
               Order By book.Title.Title _
               Select book.Title.Title

      Console.WriteLine(vbNewLine & "Titles grouped by author:") ' header

      ' display titles written by each author, grouped by author
      For Each author In titlesByAuthor
```

Fig. 20.27 | Using LINQ to perform a join and aggregate data across tables. (Part 1 of 3.)

```
         Console.WriteLine(vbTab & author.Name & ":") ' display author

         ' display titles written by that author
         For Each title In author.Titles
            Console.WriteLine(vbTab & vbTab & title)
         Next title
      Next author
   End Sub ' Main
End Module ' JoiningWithLINQ
```

```
Authors and ISBNs:
        Greg        Ayer        0136053033
        Harvey      Deitel      0131752421
        Harvey      Deitel      0132222205
        Harvey      Deitel      0132404168
        Harvey      Deitel      0136053033
        Harvey      Deitel      013605305X
        Harvey      Deitel      013605322X
        Harvey      Deitel      0136151574
        Harvey      Deitel      0136152503
        Paul        Deitel      0131752421
        Paul        Deitel      0132222205
        Paul        Deitel      0132404168
        Paul        Deitel      0136053033
        Paul        Deitel      013605305X
        Paul        Deitel      013605322X
        Paul        Deitel      0136151574
        Paul        Deitel      0136152503
        Dan         Quirk       0136151574
Authors and titles:
        Greg        Ayer        Simply Visual Basic 2008
        Harvey      Deitel      C How to Program
        Harvey      Deitel      C++ How to Program
        Harvey      Deitel      Internet & World Wide Web How to Program
        Harvey      Deitel      Java How to Program
        Harvey      Deitel      Simply Visual Basic 2008
        Harvey      Deitel      Visual Basic 2008 How to Program
        Harvey      Deitel      Visual C# 2008 How to Program
        Harvey      Deitel      Visual C++ 2008 How to Program
        Paul        Deitel      C How to Program
        Paul        Deitel      C++ How to Program
        Paul        Deitel      Internet & World Wide Web How to Program
        Paul        Deitel      Java How to Program
        Paul        Deitel      Simply Visual Basic 2008
        Paul        Deitel      Visual Basic 2008 How to Program
        Paul        Deitel      Visual C# 2008 How to Program
        Paul        Deitel      Visual C++ 2008 How to Program
        Dan         Quirk       Visual C++ 2008 How to Program

Titles grouped by author:
        Greg Ayer:
                Simply Visual Basic 2008
        Harvey Deitel:
                C How to Program
```

Fig. 20.27 | Using LINQ to perform a join and aggregate data across tables. (Part 2 of 3.)

```
            C++ How to Program
            Internet & World Wide Web How to Program
            Java How to Program
            Simply Visual Basic 2008
            Visual Basic 2008 How to Program
            Visual C# 2008 How to Program
            Visual C++ 2008 How to Program
    Paul Deitel:
            C How to Program
            C++ How to Program
            Internet & World Wide Web How to Program
            Java How to Program
            Simply Visual Basic 2008
            Visual Basic 2008 How to Program
            Visual C# 2008 How to Program
            Visual C++ 2008 How to Program
    Dan Quirk:
            Visual C++ 2008 How to Program
```

Fig. 20.27 | Using LINQ to perform a join and aggregate data across tables. (Part 3 of 3.)

The code combines data from the three tables in the Books database and displays the relationships between the book titles and authors in three different ways. It uses LINQ to SQL classes that have been created using the same steps as the first two examples. As in previous examples, the BooksDataContext object (declared in line 5) is needed to be able to query the database.

The first query in the example (lines 9–13) returns results identical to those in Fig. 20.19. It uses LINQ's Join query operator, which functions like SQL's INNER JOIN operator—the generated SQL is nearly identical to the SQL given earlier in Section 20.4.4. The LINQ syntax is similar to the corresponding SQL. The key differences are the Select clause's placement and the use of a range variable to access columns rather than the column names by themselves—i.e., LINQ uses author.FirstName while SQL uses FirstName.

The second query (lines 25–29) gives similar output, but it does not use the Join query operator. Operations that would require a join in SQL often do not need one in LINQ to SQL, because it automatically creates properties based on foreign-key relationships. These properties enable you to easily access related rows in other tables. Line 26 uses the generated AuthorISBNs property of the Title class to query only the rows in the AuthorISBN table that link to that row of the Titles table. LINQ also allows functionality similar to a join by using multiple From clauses (lines 25–26). Like nested repetition statements, these cause multiple range variables to be in scope—other clauses can access both range variables to combine data from multiple tables (lines 28–29).

The second query also introduces the Let query operator (line 27). The Let clause lets you declare a new variable, usually to create a shorter name for an expression. The variable can be accessed in later statements just like a range variable, but it does not represent a specific range of values. The author variable created in the Let clause refers to book.Author, demonstrating the automatically generated link between the AuthorISBN and Authors tables based on the foreign-key relationship between them.

Lines 42–48 contain the final query in the example. Instead of returning a flat result set, with data laid out in relational-style rows and columns, the results from this query are hierarchical. Each element in the results contains the name of an `Author` and a list of `Titles` that the author wrote. The LINQ query does this by using a nested query in the `Select` clause. The outer query iterates over the authors in the database. The inner query takes a specific author and retrieves all titles that the author worked on. This list of titles is placed into the `Titles` property that is selected along with the `Name` property that contains the author's full name. These results are then displayed using nested `For Each...Next` statements (lines 53–60).

Relational databases cannot return this kind of hierarchical result set, so unlike the previous two examples, it would be impossible to write a query like this in SQL. Before LINQ, one would have had to retrieve the results in a flat table like the other two queries, then transform them into the desired format. LINQ does this work for you, allowing you to concentrate on the format you want the data to be in, instead of the way it is stored.

Notice the duplicate `Title` identifier in `book.Title.Title` used in the inner `Order By` and `Select` clauses (lines 47–48). This is due to the database having a `Title` column in the `Titles` table, and is another example of following foreign-key relationships. The range variable `book` iterates over the rows of the `AuthorISBN` table that the current `author` helped write. The `Title` property contains the row in the `Titles` table that `book` refers to, and the second `Title` returns the `Title` column of that row—the title of the book.

20.9 Creating a Master/Detail View Application

The previous examples demonstrated using LINQ to SQL to combine data from different tables and displaying data from a database in a GUI. It is often necessary to combine the two, as the example in this section does. Figure 20.28 demonstrates a master/detail view—one part of the interface (the master) allows you to select an entry, and another part (the details) displays detailed information about that entry. In this example, you select either a book title or an author, and the details displayed are the co-authors of the book or the titles the author has written, respectively.

In the previous examples, the IDE automatically generated the `BindingSource`, `BindingNavigator` and GUI elements when you dragged a data source onto the `Form`. While this works for simple applications, those with more complex operations involve writing more substantial amounts of code. Before explaining the code, we list the steps required to create the interface the code manipulates.

```
' Fig. 20.28: MasterDetailForm.vb
' Using a DataGridView to display details based on a selection.
Public Class MasterDetailForm
   Private database As New BooksDataContext() ' connection to database

   ' this class helps us display each author's first
   ' and last name in the authors drop-down list
   Private Class AuthorBinding
      Private authorValue As Author ' contained Author object
      Private nameValue As String ' author's full name

```

Fig. 20.28 | Using a `DataGridView` to display details based on a selection. (Part 1 of 4.)

```
      ' property to get and set the contained Author object
      Public Property Author() As Author
         Get
            Return authorValue
         End Get
         Set(ByVal value As Author)
            authorValue = value
         End Set
      End Property ' Author

      ' property to get and set the Author's full name
      Public Property Name() As String
         Get
            Return nameValue
         End Get
         Set(ByVal value As String)
            nameValue = value
         End Set
      End Property ' Name
   End Class ' AuthorBinding

   ' initialize data sources when the Form is loaded
   Private Sub MasterDetailForm_Load(ByVal sender As System.Object, _
      ByVal e As System.EventArgs) Handles MyBase.Load

      authorComboBox.DisplayMember = "Name" ' display AuthorBinding.Name

      ' set the authorComboBox's DataSource to the list of authors
      authorComboBox.DataSource = _
         From author In database.Authors _
         Order By author.LastName, author.FirstName _
         Select New AuthorBinding With _
         { _
            .Author = author, _
            .Name = author.FirstName & " " & author.LastName _
         }

      titleComboBox.DisplayMember = "Title" ' display Title.Title

      ' set the titleComboBox's DataSource to the list of titles
      titleComboBox.DataSource = _
         From title In database.Titles _
         Order By title.Title _
         Select title

      booksDataGridView.DataSource = Nothing ' initially, display no data
   End Sub ' MasterDetailForm_Load

   ' display titles that were co-authored by the selected author
   Private Sub authorComboBox_SelectedIndexChanged( _
      ByVal sender As System.Object, ByVal e As System.EventArgs) _
      Handles authorComboBox.SelectedIndexChanged
```

Fig. 20.28 | Using a `DataGridView` to display details based on a selection. (Part 2 of 4.)

```

      ' get the selected Author object from the ComboBox
      Dim currentAuthor = _
         CType(authorComboBox.SelectedItem, AuthorBinding).Author

      ' set the titleBindingSource's DataSource to the
      ' list of titles written by the selected author
      titleBindingSource.DataSource = _
         From book In currentAuthor.AuthorISBNs _
         Select book.Title

      ' display the titles in the DataGridView
      booksDataGridView.DataSource = titleBindingSource
   End Sub ' authorComboBox_SelectedIndexChanged

   ' display the authors of the selected title
   Private Sub titleComboBox_SelectedIndexChanged( _
      ByVal sender As System.Object, ByVal e As System.EventArgs) _
      Handles titleComboBox.SelectedIndexChanged

      ' get the selected Title object from the ComboBox
      Dim currentTitle = CType(titleComboBox.SelectedItem, Title)

      ' set the authorBindingSource's DataSource to the
      ' list of authors for the selected title
      authorBindingSource.DataSource = _
         From book In currentTitle.AuthorISBNs _
         Select book.Author

      ' display the authors in the DataGridView
      booksDataGridView.DataSource = authorBindingSource
   End Sub ' titleComboBox_SelectedIndexChanged
End Class ' MasterDetailForm
```

a) **Master/Detail** application when it begins execution

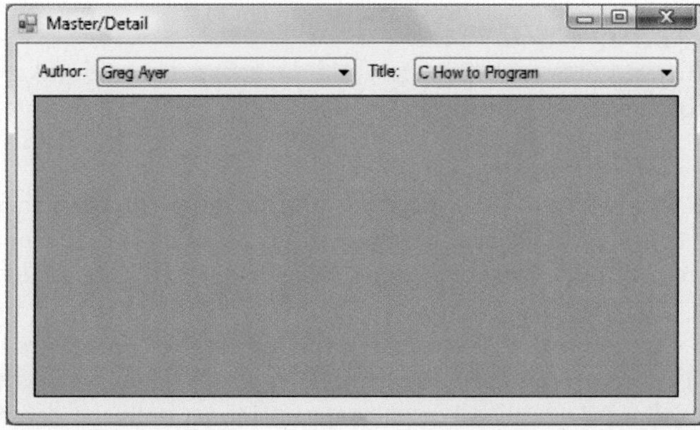

Fig. 20.28 | Using a `DataGridView` to display details based on a selection. (Part 3 of 4.)

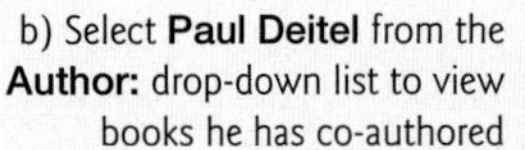
b) Select **Paul Deitel** from the **Author:** drop-down list to view books he has co-authored

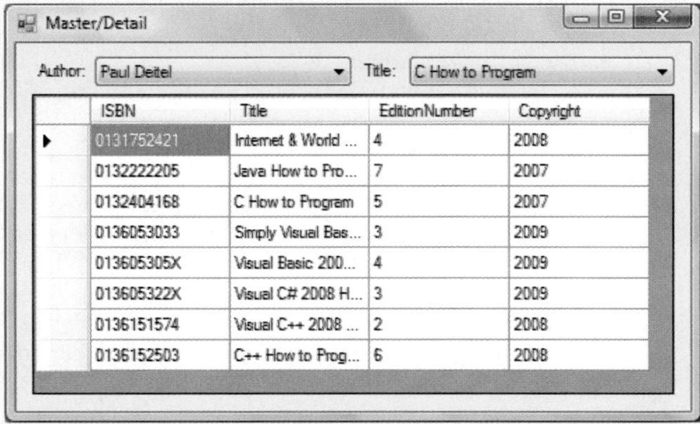

c) Select **Simply Visual Basic 2008** from the **Title:** drop-down to view the authors who wrote that book

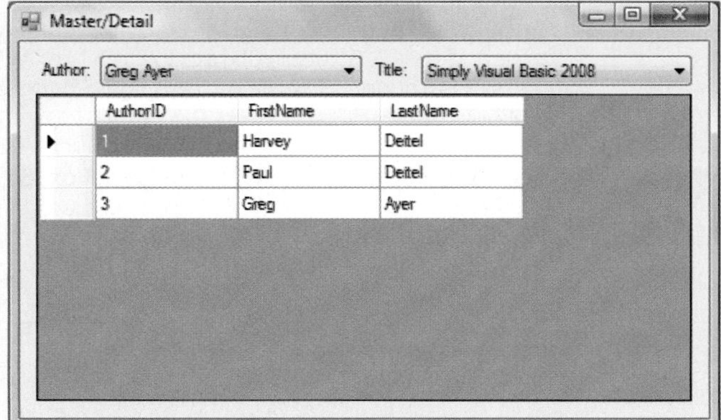

Fig. 20.28 | Using a `DataGridView` to display details based on a selection. (Part 4 of 4.)

Step 1: Creating the Project

Create a new **Windows Forms Application** called `MasterDetail`. Name the source file and class as indicated in Fig. 20.28, and set the `Form`'s `Text` property to **Master/Detail**.

Step 2: Creating LINQ to SQL Classes

Follow the instructions in Section 20.6.1 to add the `Books` database and create the LINQ to SQL classes to interact with the database.

Step 3: Creating GUI Elements

Add two `Label`s and two `ComboBox`es to the top of the `Form`. Position them as shown in Fig. 20.29. The `Label` and `ComboBox` on the left should be named `authorLabel` and `authorComboBox`, respectively. The `Label` and `ComboBox` on the right should be named `titleLabel` and `titleComboBox`. Set the `Text` property of the `Label`s as indicated in the screenshot. Also change the `DropDownStyle` properties of the `ComboBox`es from `DropDown` to `DropDownList`—this prevents the user from being able to type in the control.

Create a `DataGridView` called `booksDataGridView` to hold the details that are displayed. Unlike previous examples, do not automatically create it by dragging a data source from the **Data Sources** window, because this example sets the data source programmatically. Instead, manually add it from the **Toolbox**. Resize the `DataGridView` so that it fills

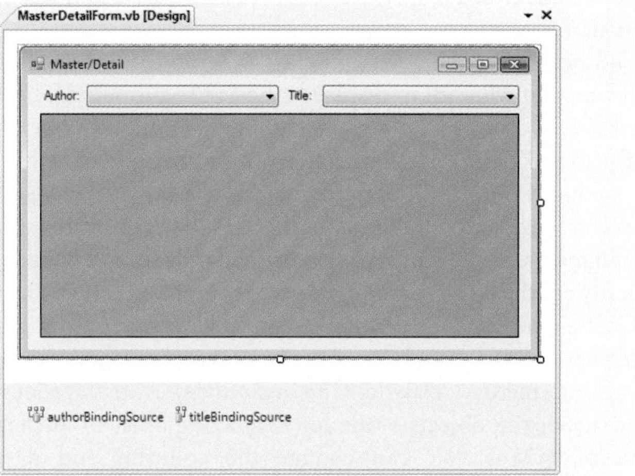

Fig. 20.29 | Finished design of **MasterDetail** application.

the remainder of the `Form`. Because this control is only for viewing data, set its `ReadOnly` property to `True` using the **Properties** window.

Finally, we need to add two `BindingSources` from the **Data** section of the **Toolbox**, one for information from the `Titles` table and one for information from the `Authors` table. Name these `titleBindingSource` and `authorBindingSource`. As in the previous examples, they do not appear as visible components on the `Form`, but appear in the component tray. These `BindingSources` are used as data sources for the `DataGridView`—the data source switches between them, depending on whether we want to view a list of `Titles` or a list of `Authors`. With the GUI creation complete, we can now write the code to provide the functionality we require.

The **Master/Detail** *Application*

When the code has been written, the **Master/Detail** application allows the user to select an author or book title from one of two drop-down lists, and view the details of the titles that author worked on or the authors of that book, respectively.

Class `MasterDetailForm` contains the nested class `AuthorBinding` (lines 8–31). Class definitions may be nested inside other classes. `AuthorBinding` is marked `Private` because it should be accessed only from irs containing class. We created the `AuthorBinding` class to allow us to associate a full `Author` object—the `Author` class is automatically generated by LINQ to SQL—with each row in the drop-down list, but have it display the author's full name. Recall that the author's name is stored as two separate fields in the database, so the `Author` class does not have single property that retrieves the full name. The `Name` property of the `AuthorBinding` class stores the author's full name, and the `Author` property stores the `Author` object that contains the author's information from the database.

The `ComboBox`'s `DisplayMember` property is set to the `String` `"Name"` (line 37), which tells the `ComboBox` to use the `Name` property of `AuthorBinding` to determine what text to display for each `AuthorBinding` object. Lines 40–47 create an `AuthorBinding` object for each author and assign it to the `authorComboBox`'s `DataSource` property. This makes `authorComboBox` create one entry per author. Recall from Section 10.4 that object initializers using the `With` keyword (e.g., lines 43–47) can be used to initialize an object without calling a constructor.

There is no need to create a custom class to wrap the `Title` class, because it already has a property for what we want to display—the `Title` property. The text in the `ComboBox` is set to be retrieved from the `Title` property (line 49). Lines 52–55 create and assign the `DataSource` for `titleComboBox`—a sorted list of `Title` objects.

Initially, we don't want to display any data in the `DataGridView`. However, when the `ComboBoxes` are created and initialized with their `DataSources`, their `SelectedIndex-Changed` event handlers are called, setting a `DataSource` for the `DataGridView`. To prevent this, we explicitly set the `DataSource` property to `Nothing` (line 57).

Simple GUI elements like `ComboBoxes` can work directly from a data source—in this case, the result of a LINQ to SQL query. However, the `DataGridView` is more complex and requires an intermediary class (a `BindingSource`) as its `DataSource`. Earlier, we created two `BindingSource` objects—one for displaying a list of `Authors`, and one for displaying a list of `Titles`. We can change the columns and data displayed in the `DataGridView` merely by changing its `DataSource` between the two `BindingSource` objects. The `DataGridView` automatically determines the column names it needs to display from the `BindingSource`.

The `authorComboBox_SelectedIndexChanged` event handler performs three distinct operations. First, it retrieves the selected `Author` (lines 66–67). The `ComboBox`'s `Selected-Item` property returns an `Object`, so the `SelectedItem` property's value must be cast to the `AuthorBinding` class we used as the data source. The event handler then accesses the `AuthorBinding`'s `Author` property to retrieve the wrapped `Author` object. Second, the event handler uses LINQ to retrieve the `Title` objects representing books the `Author` worked on (lines 72–73)—the mechanism for this was explained in the preceding example. The results of the LINQ query are assigned to the `DataSource` property of `titleBindingSource` (line 71)—note that the `authorComboBox` sets the `titleBinding-Source` because we want to display `Title` objects associated with that `Author`. Finally, the `DataGridView`'s `DataSource` is assigned to `titleBindingSource` to make the correct information display in the GUI (line 76).

The event handler for `titleComboBox` is structured identically to the `authorComboBox` one. The primary difference is that the author and title names are switched. Also, the first step is slightly simpler, because the `Title` class did not need to be wrapped to display correctly in the `ComboBox`.

20.10 Programming with LINQ to SQL: Address-Book Case Study

Our next example implements a simple address-book application that enables users to insert rows into, locate rows from and update the database `AddressBook.mdf`, which is included in the directory with this chapter's examples.

The `AddressBook` application (Fig. 20.30) provides a GUI through which users can query the database with LINQ. However, rather than displaying a database table in a `DataGridView`, this example presents data from a table one row at a time, using several `TextBoxes` that display the values of each of the row's columns. A `BindingNavigator` allows you to control which row of the table is in view at any given time. The `Binding-Navigator` also allows you to add rows, delete rows, and save changes to the data. We discuss the application's functionality and the code that implements it momentarily. First we show the steps to create this application.

```
' Fig. 20.30: AddressBookForm.vb
' Manipulating an address book.
Public Class AddressBookForm
   ' LINQ to SQL data context
   Private database As New AddressBookDataContext()

   ' fill our AddressBindingSource with all rows, ordered by name
   Private Sub BindDefault()
      ' use LINQ to create a data source from the database
      AddressBindingSource.DataSource = _
         From address In database.Addresses _
         Order By address.LastName, address.FirstName _
         Select address

      AddressBindingSource.MoveFirst() ' go to the first result
      findTextBox.Clear() ' clear the Find TextBox
   End Sub ' BindDefault

   ' when the form loads, fill it with data from the database
   Private Sub AddressBookForm_Load(ByVal sender As System.Object, _
      ByVal e As System.EventArgs) Handles MyBase.Load

      BindDefault() ' fill binding with data from database
   End Sub ' AddressBookForm_Load

   ' Click event handler for the Save Button in the
   ' BindingNavigator saves the changes made to the data
   Private Sub AddressBindingNavigatorSaveItem_Click( _
      ByVal sender As System.Object, ByVal e As System.EventArgs) _
      Handles AddressBindingNavigatorSaveItem.Click

      Validate() ' validate input fields
      AddressBindingSource.EndEdit() ' indicate edits are complete
      database.SubmitChanges() ' write changes to database file

      BindDefault() ' change back to initial unfiltered data on save
   End Sub ' AddressBindingNavigatorSaveItem_Click

   ' load data for the rows with the specified
   ' last name into the AddressBindingSource
   Private Sub findButton_Click(ByVal sender As System.Object, _
      ByVal e As System.EventArgs) Handles findButton.Click

      ' use LINQ to create a data source that contains
      ' only people with the specified last name
      AddressBindingSource.DataSource = _
         From address In database.Addresses _
         Where address.LastName = findTextBox.Text _
         Order By address.LastName, address.FirstName _
         Select address
```

Fig. 20.30 | Manipulating an address book. (Part 1 of 2.)

```

        AddressBindingSource.MoveFirst() ' go to first result
    End Sub ' findButton_Click

    ' reload AddressBindingSource with all rows
    Private Sub browseAllButton_Click(ByVal sender As System.Object, _
        ByVal e As System.EventArgs) Handles browseAllButton.Click

        BindDefault() ' change back to initial unfiltered data
    End Sub ' browseAllButton_Click
End Class ' AddressBookForm
```

Fig. 20.30 | Manipulating an address book. (Part 2 of 2.)

Step 1: Creating the Project

Create a new **Windows Forms Application** named `AddressBook`. Rename the `Form` `AddressBookForm` and its source file `AddressBookForm.vb`, then set the `Form`'s **Text** property to `AddressBook`.

Step 2: Create LINQ to SQL Classes and Data Source

Follow the instructions in Section 20.6.1 to add a database to the project and generate the LINQ to SQL classes. For this example, add the `AddressBook` database and name the file `AddressBook.dbml` instead of `Books.dbml`. You must also add the `Addresses` table as a data source, as was done with the `Authors` table in *Step 1* of Section 20.6.2.

Step 3: Indicating that the IDE Should Create a Set of `Label`*s and* `TextBox`*es to Display Each Row of Data*

In the earlier sections, you dragged a node from the **Data Sources** window to the `Form` to create a `DataGridView` bound to the data-source member represented by that node. The IDE allows you to specify the type of control(s) that it creates when you drag and drop a data-source member onto a `Form`. In **Design** view, click the `Addresses` node in the **Data Sources** window. Note that this becomes a drop-down list when you select it. Click the down arrow to view the items in the list. The item to the left of **DataGridView** is initially highlighted in blue, because the default control to be bound to a table is a `DataGridView` (as you saw in the earlier examples). Select the **Details** option in the drop-down list to indicate that the IDE should create a set of `Label`/`TextBox` pairs for each column-name/column-value pair when you drag and drop the `Addresses` table onto the `Form`. The drop-down list contains suggestions for controls to display the table's data, but you can also choose the **Customize...** option to select other controls that can be bound to a table's data.

Step 4: Dragging the `Addresses` *Data-Source Node to the* `Form`

Drag the `Addresses` node from the **Data Sources** window to the `Form`. This automatically creates a `BindingNavigator` and the `Label`s and `TextBox`es corresponding to the columns of the database table. The fields may be placed out of order, with the `Email` at the top. Reorder the components, using **Design** view, so they are in the proper order shown in Fig. 20.30.

Step 5: Making the `AddressID` `TextBox` `ReadOnly`

The `AddressID` column of the `Addresses` table is an autoincremented identity column, so users should not be allowed to edit the values in this column. Select the `TextBox` for the `AddressID` and set its `ReadOnly` property to `True` using the **Properties** window. Note that you may need to click in an empty part of the `Form` to deselect the other `Label`s and `TextBox`es before selecting the `AddressID` `TextBox`.

Step 6: Connecting the `BindingSource` *to the* `DataContext`

As in previous examples, we must connect the `AddressBindingSource` that controls the GUI with the `AddressBookDataContext` that controls the connection to the database. This is done using the `BindDefault` method (lines 8–17), which sets the `AddressBindingSource`'s `DataSource` property to the result of a LINQ query on the `Addresses` table. The need for a separate function becomes apparent later, when we have two places that need to set the `DataSource` to the result of that query.

The `BindDefault` method must be called from the `Form`'s `Load` event handler for the data to be displayed when the application starts (line 23). As before, you create the `Load` event handler by double clicking the `Form`'s title bar.

We must also create an event handler to save the changes to the database when the `BindingNavigator`'s save `Button` is clicked (lines 28–37). Note that, besides the names of the variables, the three-statement save logic remains the same. We also call `BindDefault` after saving to re-sort the data and move back to the first element. Recall from Section 20.6 that to allow changes to the database to save between runs of the application, you must select the database in the **Solution Explorer**, then change its **Copy to Output Directory** property to **Copy if newer** in the **Properties** window.

The `AddressBook` database is configured to require values for the first name, last name, phone number or e-mail. We have not checked for errors to simplify the code, but an exception (of type `System.Data.SqlClient.SqlException`) will be thrown if you attempt to save when any of the fields are empty.

Step 7: Running the Application

Run the application and experiment with the controls in the `BindingNavigator` at the top of the window. Like the previous examples, this example fills a `BindingSource` object (specifically an `AddressBindingSource` object) with all the rows of a database table (i.e., `Addresses`). However, only a single row of the database appears at any given time. The CD- or DVD-like buttons of the `BindingNavigator` allow you to change the currently displayed row (i.e., change the values in each of the `TextBox`es). The `Button`s to add a row, delete a row and save changes also perform their designated tasks. Adding a row clears the

TextBoxes and sets the TextBox to the right of **Address ID** to zero. After entering several address-book entries, click the **Save** Button to record the new rows to the database—the **Address ID** field is be automatically changed from zero to a unique number by the database. When you close and restart the application, you should be able to use the BindingNavigator controls to browse your entries.

Step 8: Adding Controls to Allow Users to Specify a Last Name to Locate
While the BindingNavigator allows you to browse the address book, it would be more convenient to be able to find a specific entry by last name. To add this functionality to the application, we must create controls to allow the user to enter a last name, then event handlers to actually perform the search.

Go to **Design** view and add to the Form a Label named findLabel, a TextBox named findTextBox, and a Button named findButton. Place these controls in a GroupBox named findGroupBox, then set its Text property to **Find an entry by last name.** Set the Text properties of the Label and Button as shown in Fig. 20.30.

Step 9: Programming an Event Handler that Locates the User-Specified Last Name
Double click findButton to create a Click event handler for this Button. In the event handler, use LINQ to select only people with the last name entered in findTextBox and sort them by last name then first name (lines 47–50). Start the application to test the new functionality. When you enter a last name and click **Find**, the BindingNavigator allows the user to browse only the rows containing the specified last name. This is because the data source bound to the Form's controls (the result of the LINQ query) has changed and now contains only a limited number of rows. The database in this example is initially empty, so you'll need to add several records before testing the find capability.

Step 10: Allowing the User to Return to Browsing All Rows of the Database
To allow users to return to browsing all the rows after searching for specific rows, add a Button named browseAllButton below the findGroupBox. Set the Text property of browseAllButton to **Browse All Entries.** Double click browseAllButton to create a Click event handler. Have the event handler call BindDefault (line 59) to restore the data source to the full list of people. Also modify BindDefault so that it clears findTextBox (line 16).

Data Binding in the **AddressBook** *Application*
Dragging and dropping the Addresses node from the **Data Sources** window onto the AddressBookForm caused the IDE to generate several components in the component tray. These serve the same purposes as those generated for the earlier examples that use the Books database. In this example, AddressBindingSource uses LINQ to manipulate the AddressBookDataContext's Addresses table. The AddressBindingNavigator is bound to the AddressBindingSource object, enabling the user to manipulate the Addresses table through the GUI.

In each of the earlier examples using a DataGridView to display all the rows of a database table, the DataGridView's DataSource property was set to the corresponding BindingSource object. In this example, you selected **Details** from the drop-down list for the Addresses table in the **Data Sources** window, so the values from a single row of the table appear on the Form in a set of TextBoxes. In this example, the IDE binds each TextBox to a specific column of the Addresses table in the AddressBookDataContext. To do this, the

IDE sets the TextBox's DataBindings.Text property. You can view this property by clicking the plus sign next to **(DataBindings)** in the **Properties** window. Clicking the drop-down list for this property (as in Fig. 20.31) allows you to choose a BindingSource object and a property (i.e., column) within the associated data source to bind to the TextBox.

Consider the TextBox that displays the FirstName value—named FirstNameTextBox by the IDE. This control's DataBindings.Text property is set to the FirstName property of the AddressBindingSource (which refers to the Addresses table in the database). Thus, FirstNameTextBox always displays the value of the FirstName column in the currently selected row of the Addresses table. Each IDE-created TextBox on the Form is configured in a similar manner. Browsing the address book with the AddressBindingNavigator changes the current position in AddressBindingSource, and thus changes the values displayed in each TextBox. Regardless of changes to the contents of the Addresses table in the database, the TextBoxes remain bound to the same properties of the table and always display the appropriate data. The TextBoxes do not display any values if the AddressesBindingSource is empty.

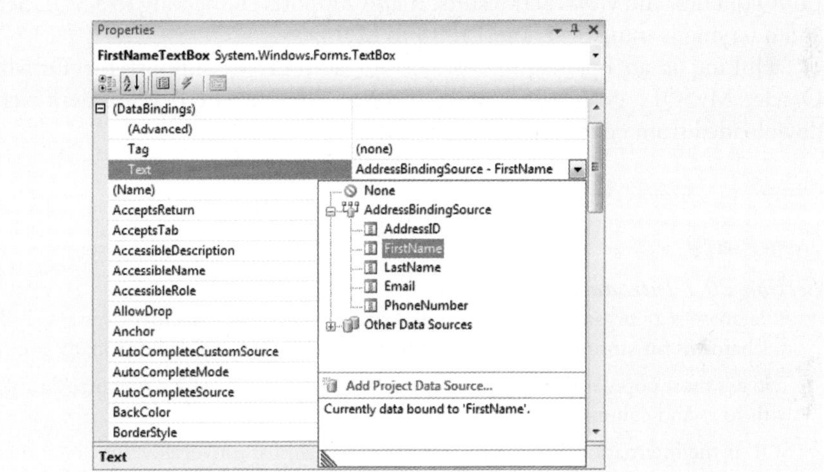

Fig. 20.31 | Data bindings for FirstNameTextBox in the **AddressBook** application.

20.11 Wrap-Up

This chapter introduced relational databases, SQL, LINQ to SQL and the IDE's visual programming tools for working with databases. You examined the contents of a simple Books database and learned about the relationships among the tables in the database. You then learned basic SQL statements to retrieve data from, add new data to, delete data from and update data in a database.

We discussed the LINQ to SQL classes automatically generated by the IDE, such as the DataContext that controls interactions with the database. We also explained that LINQ to SQL transforms the LINQ queries you write into SQL, which is then sent to the database software.

Next, the chapter focused on using the IDE's tools and wizards to access and manipulate data sources like databases in GUI applications. You learned how to generate LINQ to SQL classes and how to use the IDE's drag-and-drop capabilities to display database tables in applications. We discussed the IDE's wizards that help you create fully functional applications requiring just a few lines of code.

In the next chapter, we demonstrate how to build web applications using Microsoft's ASP.NET technology. We also introduce the concept of a three-tier application, which is divided into three pieces that can reside on the same computer or be distributed among separate computers across a network such as the Internet. One of these tiers—the information tier—typically stores data in an DBMS like SQL Server.

20.12 Tools and Web Resources

Deitel has created an extensive LINQ Resource Center at `www.deitel.com/LINQ` that contains many links to additional information, including blogs by Microsoft LINQ team members, sample chapters, tutorials and videos.

A useful tool for learning LINQ is LINQPad (`www.linqpad.net`), which defines itself as a *code snippet IDE*. It allows you to execute any Visual Basic or C# expression, including LINQ queries, and view their results. It also supports connecting to a SQL Server database and querying it using SQL and LINQ to SQL.

DbLinq is an open-source project to add LINQ support for DBMSs including Oracle, MySQL, PostgreSQL and SQLite. The current development version can be downloaded from `code2code.net/DB_Linq/`.

Summary

Section 20.1 Introduction

- A database is an organized collection of data. A database management system (DBMS) provides mechanisms for storing, organizing, retrieving and modifying data for many users.
- Today's most popular DBMSs manage relational databases, which organize data simply as tables with rows and columns.
- SQL is the international standard language used almost universally with relational databases to perform queries and manipulate data.
- LINQ to SQL allows you to run LINQ queries directly on relational data. LINQ to SQL provides all the expressiveness of SQL, with the added benefit of the Visual Basic compiler providing type checking and the IDE providing *IntelliSense*.

Section 20.2 Relational Databases

- A relational database stores data in tables. Tables are composed of rows and columns in which values are stored.
- A primary key provides a unique value that cannot be duplicated in other rows of the same table. The primary key uniquely identifies each row.
- Each row of a table represents a record.
- Each column of a table represents a different attribute.
- The primary key can be composed of more than one column.

Section 20.3 Relational Database Overview: **Books** *Database*

- A foreign key is a column (or columns) in a table that matches the primary key in another table.

- The foreign key helps maintain the *Rule of Referential Integrity*: Every foreign-key value must appear as another table's primary-key value. Foreign keys enable information from multiple tables to be joined together. There is a one-to-many relationship between a primary key and its corresponding foreign key.
- Every column in a primary key must have a value, and the value of the primary key must be unique. This is known as the *Rule of Entity Integrity*.
- A one-to-many relationship between tables indicates that a row in one table can have many related rows in a separate table.

Section 20.4 SQL

- SQL provides a rich set of language constructs that enable you to define complex queries to retrieve data from a database.

Section 20.4.1 Basic **SELECT** *Query*

- The basic form of a `SELECT` query is

  ```
  SELECT * FROM tableName
  ```

  where the asterisk (*) indicates that all columns from *tableName* should be selected and *tableName* specifies the table in the database from which rows will be retrieved.
- To retrieve specific columns from a table, replace the asterisk (*) with a comma-separated list of column names. Specifying columns explicitly guarantees that they are always returned in the specified order, even if the actual order in the table(s) is different.

Section 20.4.2 **WHERE** *Clause*

- The optional `WHERE` clause in a query specifies the selection criteria for the query. The basic form of a query with selection criteria is

  ```
  SELECT columnName1, columnName2, … FROM tableName WHERE criteria
  ```

- The `WHERE` clause can contain operators <, >, <=, >=, =, <> and `LIKE`. Operator `LIKE` is used for string pattern matching with wildcard characters percent (`%`) and underscore (_).
- A percent character (`%`) in a pattern indicates that a string matching the pattern can have zero or more characters at the percent character's location in the pattern.
- An underscore (_) in the pattern string indicates a single character at that position in the pattern.

Section 20.4.3 **ORDER BY** *Clause*

- The result of a query can be sorted in ascending or descending order using the optional `ORDER BY` clause. The simplest form of an `ORDER BY` clause is

  ```
  SELECT columnName1, columnName2, … FROM tableName ORDER BY column ASC
  SELECT columnName1, columnName2, … FROM tableName ORDER BY column DESC
  ```

  where `ASC` specifies ascending order, `DESC` specifies descending order and *column* specifies the column on which the sort is based. The default sorting order is ascending, so `ASC` is optional.
- Multiple columns can be used for ordering purposes with an `ORDER BY` clause of the form

  ```
  ORDER BY column1sortingOrder, column2 sortingOrder, …
  ```

- The `WHERE` and `ORDER BY` clauses can be combined in one query. If used, `ORDER BY` must be the last clause in the query.

Section 20.4.4 Retrieving Data from Multiple Tables: **INNER JOIN**

- An INNER JOIN merges rows from two tables by testing for matching values in a column that is common to the tables (though the column names can differ). The basic form for the INNER JOIN operator is:

```
SELECT columnName1, columnName2, ...
FROM table1 INNER JOIN table2
   ON table1.columnName = table2.columnName
```

  The ON clause specifies the columns from each table that are compared to determine which rows are joined.
- If a SQL statement uses columns with the same name from multiple tables, the column names must be fully qualified by prefixing them with their table names and a dot (.).

Section 20.4.5 **INSERT** *Statement*

- An INSERT statement inserts a new row into a table. The basic form of this statement is

```
INSERT INTO tableName ( columnName1, columnName2, ..., columnNameN )
VALUES ( value1, value2, ..., valueN )
```

  where *tableName* is the table in which to insert the row. The *tableName* is followed by a comma-separated list of column names in parentheses. The list of column names is followed by the SQL keyword VALUES and a comma-separated list of values in parentheses.
- SQL uses single quotes (') as the delimiter for strings. To specify a string containing a single quote in SQL, the single quote must be escaped with another single quote.

Section 20.4.6 **UPDATE** *Statement*

- An UPDATE statement modifies data in a table. The basic form of an UPDATE statement is

```
UPDATE tableName
SET columnName1 = value1, columnName2 = value2, ..., columnNameN = valueN
WHERE criteria
```

  where *tableName* is the table in which to update data. The *tableName* is followed by keyword SET and a comma-separated list of column name/value pairs in the format *columnName* = *value*. The optional WHERE clause *criteria* determines which rows to update. If the WHERE clause is omitted, the UPDATE applies to all rows of the table.

Section 20.4.7 **DELETE** *Statement*

- A DELETE statement removes rows from a table. The simplest form for a DELETE statement is

```
DELETE FROM tableName WHERE criteria
```

  where *tableName* is the table from which to delete a row (or rows). The optional WHERE *criteria* determines which rows to delete—if it is omitted, the DELETE applies to all rows of the table.

Section 20.5 LINQ to SQL

- LINQ to SQL provides an API for accessing SQL Server databases using the same LINQ syntax used to query Visual Basic objects.
- You interact with LINQ to SQL via classes that are automatically generated by the IDE based on the database schema.
- A cache is a temporary store created for fast access to data that would otherwise be costly to retrieve or generate. LINQ to SQL uses a cache to make its interactions with the database more efficient.
- LINQ to SQL requires every table to have a primary key.

- All LINQ to SQL queries occur via a `DataContext` class, which controls the flow of data between the program and the database.
- When cached objects have been changed, these changes are saved back to the database using the `DataContext`'s `SubmitChanges` method.

Section 20.6 LINQ to SQL: Extracting Information from a Database

- The IDE provides visual programming tools and wizards that simplify accessing data in your projects. These tools establish database connections and create the data-binding objects necessary to view and manipulate the data through GUI controls.
- A `DataGridView` is a control from namespace `System.Windows.Forms` that can display a data source in a GUI.

Section 20.6.1 Creating LINQ to SQL Classes

- To interact with a database, you must first add it to the project using the **Add Connection** dialog.
- After a database has been added, drag tables from the **Database Explorer** window onto the **Object Relational Designer** to create the LINQ to SQL classes.

Section 20.6.2 Creating Data Bindings

- To use the LINQ to SQL classes in bindings, they must first be added as a data source. Use the **Data Source Configuration Wizard** to create **Object** bindings—select the class representing rows of the table you want in the binding.
- Dragging the table's node in the **Data Sources** window to the `Form` creates a `DataGridView` with the correct columns. It also creates a `BindingNavigator` and a `BindingSource`.
- A `BindingNavigator` contains `Buttons` that allow you to move between entries, as well as `Buttons` to add and delete entries and save the changes to the database.
- A `BindingSource` handles the transfer of data between the data source and the data-bound controls on the `Form`.
- Nonvisual components that the IDE generates appear in the component tray—the gray region below the `Form` in **Design** view.
- A `BindingSource`'s `DataSource` property can be set to the results of a LINQ query.
- Saving the data entered into the `DataGridView` back to the database is a three-step process. First, all controls on the form are validated. Second, the `BindingSource` saves any pending changes to its `DataSource`. Finally, the `DataContext` sends all the changes back to the database.
- To have changes persist between runs of the program, select the database in the **Solution Explorer** and set the **Copy to Output Directory** property in the **Properties** window to **Copy if newer**.

Section 20.7 More Complex LINQ Queries and Data Binding

- The data bindings created by the IDE update the `DataGridView` each time we change the `BindingSource`'s `DataSource` property.
- If its `Log` property is set, a `DataContext` object logs all queries it runs on the database to the given stream, typically standard output. In a GUI application, "standard output" is the **Output** window, which can be opened while the program is running by selecting **View > Other Windows > Output** in the IDE.

Section 20.8 Retrieving Data from Multiple Tables with LINQ

- LINQ's `Join` query operator functions like SQL's `INNER JOIN` operator. The syntax is also similar, with the only real differences being the placement of the `Select` clause and the accessing of properties on the range variables instead of using single identifiers.

- Operations that would require a join in SQL often do not need one in LINQ to SQL, because it automatically creates properties based on foreign-key relationships, enabling you to easily access related rows from other tables.
- LINQ also allows functionality similar to a join by using multiple `From` clauses. Like nested repetition statements, these cause multiple range variables to be in scope—other clauses can access both range variables to combine data from multiple tables.
- The `Let` clause in a LINQ query lets you declare a new variable, usually to create a shorter name for an expression. The variable can be accessed in later statements just like a range variable, but it does not represent a specific range of values.
- LINQ can return hierarchical results, but relational databases using SQL cannot. Before LINQ, one would have to retrieve the results in a flat table, then transform them into the desired format. LINQ does this work for you, allowing you to concentrate on the format you want the data to be in, instead of the way it is stored.

Section 20.9 Creating a Master/Detail View Application

- In a master/detail view, one part of the interface (the master) allows you to select an entry, and another part (the details) displays detailed information about that entry.
- The IDE can automatically generate a `BindingSource`, `BindingNavigator` and GUI elements when you drag a data source onto a `Form`. While this works for simple applications, those with more complex operations involve writing more substantial amounts of code and manually adding the controls from the **Toolbox**.
- Class definitions may be nested inside other classes.
- When using data bindings, it is sometimes necessary to create a simple wrapper class if the original class does not have a property that returns the text to be displayed.
- The `ComboBox`'s `DisplayMember` property tells the `ComboBox` to use a specific property of the class contained in its `DataSource` property to determine what text to display for each object.
- Simple GUI elements like `ComboBox`es can work directly from a data source. A `DataGridView` is more complex and requires an intermediary class (a `BindingSource`) as its `DataSource`. You can change the columns and data displayed in a `DataGridView` merely by changing its `DataSource`. The `DataGridView` automatically determines the column names it needs to display from the `BindingSource`.

Section 20.10 Programming with LINQ to SQL: Address-Book Case Study

- The IDE allows you to specify the type of control(s) that it creates when you drag and drop a data-source member onto a `Form`. You've already seen **DataGridView**—the **Details** option indicates that the IDE should create a set of `Label`/`TextBox` pairs for each column-name/column-value pair in the data source.
- The CD- or DVD-like buttons of the `BindingNavigator` allow you to change the currently displayed row (i.e., change the values in each of the `TextBox`es). The `Button`s to add a row, delete a row and save changes also perform their designated tasks.
- When using the **Details** binding, the IDE binds each `TextBox` to a specific column of the data source. To do this, the IDE sets the `TextBox`'s `DataBindings.Text` property.

Terminology

`%` SQL wildcard character
`_` SQL wildcard character
Add Connection dialog
`AND` SQL operator
`ASC` (ascending order)
autoincremented database column

BindingNavigator class
BindingSource class
BindingSource property of class BindingNavigator
cache of data in local memory
Choose Data Source dialog
column in a relational database
component tray
composite key
data binding
data source
Data Source Configuration Wizard
Data Sources window
database
Database Explorer window
database management system (DBMS)
database schema
DataBindings.Text property of class TextBox
DataContext class
DataGridView class
DataSource property of class BindingSource
DataSource property of class ComboBox
DataSource property of class DataGridView
DELETE SQL statement
DESC (descending order)
DisplayMember property of class ComboBox
EndEdit method of class BindingSource
entity-relationship (ER) diagram
foreign key in a database table
identity column in a database table
INNER JOIN SQL operator
INSERT SQL statement
IQueryable interface
Join clause of a LINQ query
joining database tables
Let clause of a LINQ query
LIKE SQL clause
LINQ to SQL
Log property of a DataContext
master/detail view
Microsoft SQL Server 2005 Express
MoveFirst method of class BindingSource
normalizing a database
NOT SQL operator
Object Relational Designer window
ON SQL clause in an INNER JOIN SQL operation
one-to-many relationship
OR SQL operator
ORDER BY SQL clause
pattern matching
predicate in a SQL WHERE clause
primary key in a database table
qualified name of a database table
query of a database
relational database
row in a relational database
Rule of Entity Integrity
Rule of Referential Integrity
SELECT SQL query
selection criteria in a WHERE SQL clause
SET SQL clause
smart tag menu
SQL (Structured Query Language)
SQL keyword
SQL statement
SubmitChanges method of class DataContext
table in a relational database
UPDATE SQL statement
VALUES SQL clause
WHERE SQL clause

Self-Review Exercises

20.1 Fill in the blanks in each of the following statements:

a) The international standard database query language is __________.
b) A table in a relational database consists of __________ and __________ in which values are stored.
c) The __________ uniquely identifies each row in a relational database table.
d) A relational database can be manipulated in Visual Basic via a(n) __________ object, which contains properties for accessing each table in the database.
e) The __________ control (presented in this chapter) displays data in rows and columns that correspond to the rows and columns of the underlying data source.
f) The optional __________ clause in a SQL SELECT query specifies selection criteria for the query.
g) The optional __________ clause in a SQL SELECT query specifies the order in which rows are sorted in a query.

h) Merging data from multiple relational database tables is called ________ the data.
i) A(n) ________ is a column (or group of columns) in a relational database table that matches the primary-key column in another table.
j) A(n) ________ object serves as an intermediary between a data source and its corresponding data-bound GUI control.
k) LINQ to SQL stores all row objects it creates in a ________ for efficiency of reads and writes to and from the database.
l) The ________ property of a control specifies where it gets the data it displays.
m) The ________ clause declares a new temporary variable within a LINQ query.

20.2 State whether each of the following is *true* or *false*. If *false*, explain why.
a) Only the SQL `UPDATE` statement can change the data in a database.
b) Providing the same value for a foreign key in multiple rows breaks the *Rule of Entity Integrity*.
c) Providing a foreign-key value that does not appear as a primary-key value in another table breaks the *Rule of Referential Integrity*.
d) The result of a query can be sorted in ascending or descending order.
e) SQL `SELECT` queries can merge data from multiple relational database tables.
f) A SQL `DELETE` statement deletes only one row in a relational database table.
g) A `BindingNavigator` object can extract data from a database.
h) LINQ to SQL automatically saves changes made back to the database.

Answers to Self-Review Exercises

20.1 a) SQL. b) rows, columns. c) primary key. d) `DataContext`. e) `DataGridView`. f) `WHERE`. g) `ORDER BY`. h) joining. i) foreign key. j) `BindingSource`. k) cache. l) `DataSource`. m) `Let`.

20.2 a) False. The SQL `INSERT` and `DELETE` statements also change the database. b) False. Multiple rows can have the same value for a foreign key. Providing the same value for the primary key in multiple rows breaks the *Rule of Entity Integrity*—doing so prevents each row from being identified uniquely. c) True. d) True. e) True. f) False. A SQL `DELETE` statement deletes all rows satisfying the selection criteria in its `WHERE` clause, or all the rows if no `WHERE` clause is specified. g) False. A `BindingNavigator` allows users to browse and manipulate data displayed by another GUI control. A `DataContext` can extract data from a database. h) False. You must call the `SubmitChanges` method of the `DataContext` to save the changes made back to the database.

Exercises

20.3 *(**DisplayTable** Application Modification)* Modify the **DisplayTable** application in Section 20.6 to contain a `TextBox` and a `Button` that allow the user to search for specific authors by last name. Include a `Label` to identify the `TextBox`. Using the techniques presented in Section 20.10, create a LINQ query that changes the `DataSource` property of `AuthorBindingSource` to contain only the specified authors.

20.4 *(**DisplayQueryResult** Application Modification)* Modify the **DisplayQueryResult** application in Section 20.7 to contain a `TextBox` and a `Button` that allow the user to perform a search of the book titles in the `Titles` table of the `Books` database. Use a `Label` to identify the `TextBox`. When the user clicks the `Button`, the application should execute and display the result of a query that selects all the rows in which the search term entered by the user in the `TextBox` appears anywhere in the `Title` column. For example, if the user enters the search term "Visual," the `DataGridView` should display the rows for *Simply Visual Basic 2008*, *Visual Basic 2008 How to Program*, *Visual C# 2008 How to Program* and *Visual C++ 2008 How to Program*. If the user enters "Simply," the `DataGridView` should display only the row for *Simply Visual Basic 2008*. [*Hint:* Use the `Contains` method of the `String` class.]

20.5 *(`Baseball` Database Application)* Build an application that executes a query against the `Players` table of the `Baseball` database included in the `databases` folder with this chapter's examples. Display the table in a `DataGridView`, and add a `TextBox` and `Button` to allow the user to search for a specific player by last name. Use a `Label` to identify the `TextBox`. Clicking the `Button` should execute the appropriate query.

20.6 *(`Baseball` Database Application Modification)* Modify Exercise 20.5 to allow the user to locate players with batting averages in a specific range. Add a `TextBox` `minimumTextBox` for the minimum batting average (`0.000` by default) and a `TextBox` `maximumTextBox` for the maximum batting average (`1.000` by default). Use a `Label` to identify each `TextBox`. Add a `Button` for executing a query that selects rows from the `Players` table in which the `BattingAverage` column is greater than or equal to the specified minimum value and less than or equal to the specified maximum value. [*Hint:* Use method `Convert.ToDecimal` to convert the values in the `TextBoxes` to `Decimal` values before using them in the LINQ to SQL query.]

20.7 *(`AdventureWorks` Command-Line Application)* In this exercise, use Microsoft's sample `AdventureWorks` database. There are several versions available, depending on what version of SQL Server you're using and your operating system. We used the `LT` version of the database—a smaller version with fewer tables and less data than the full version. The files for SQL Server 2005 can be downloaded from

```
www.codeplex.com/MSFTDBProdSamples/Release/ProjectReleases.aspx?ReleaseId=4004
```

The files for SQL Server 2008 can be downloaded from

```
www.codeplex.com/MSFTDBProdSamples/Release/
ProjectReleases.aspx?ReleaseId=14274
```

Most people will need the SQL Server 2005 version of the database (`AdventureWorksLT.msi`). When SQL Server 2008 becomes available, we'll post additional instructions at

```
www.deitel.com/books/vb2008htp/
```

showing how to obtain and use the SQL Server 2008 version of the database.

Use the `AdventureWorks` database in a command-line application that runs multiple queries on the database and displays the results. First, it should list customers and their addresses. As this is a large list, limit the number of results to ten. Second, if a category has subcategories, the output should show the category with its subcategories indented below it. The queries described here require the `AdventureWorks` tables `Address`, `Customer`, `CustomerAddress` and `ProductCategory`. [*Hint:* Use LINQ's `Take` clause at the end of the query to return a limited number of results. The `Take` clause consists of the `Take` operator, then an `Integer` specifying how many rows to take.]

20.8 *(`AdventureWorks` Master/Detail view)* Use the Microsoft `AdventureWorks` database from Exercise 20.7 to create a master/detail view. One master list should be customers, and the other should be products—these should show the details of products the customers purchased, and customers who purchased those products, respectively. Note that there are many customers in the database who did not order any products, and many products that no one ordered. Restrict the drop-down lists so that only customers that have submitted at least one order and products that have been included in at least one order are displayed. The queries in this exercise require the `Customer`, `Product`, `SalesOrderHeader` and `SalesOrderDetail` tables.

21

ASP.NET and ASP.NET AJAX

If any man will draw up his case, and put his name at the foot of the first page, I will give him an immediate reply. Where he compels me to turn over the sheet, he must wait my leisure.

—Lord Sandwich

Rule One: Our client is always right
Rule Two: If you think our client is wrong, see Rule One.

—Anonymous

A fair question should be followed by a deed in silence.

—Dante Alighieri

… the challenges are for the designers of these applications: to forget what we think we know about the limitations of the Web, and begin to imagine a wider, richer range of possibilities. It's going to be fun.

—Jesse James Garrett

OBJECTIVES

In this chapter you'll learn:

- Web application development using Active Server Pages .NET (ASP.NET).
- To create Web Forms.
- To create ASP.NET applications consisting of multiple Web Forms.
- To maintain state information about a user with session tracking and cookies.
- To use the **Web Site Administration Tool** to modify web-application configuration settings.
- To control user access to web applications using forms authentication and ASP.NET login controls.
- To use databases in ASP.NET applications.
- To design a master page and content pages to create a uniform look-and-feel for a website.
- To use ASP.NET AJAX to improve the user interactivity of your web applications.

21.1 Introduction

In previous chapters, we used Windows `Forms` and WPF to develop Windows applications. In this chapter, we introduce web-application development with Microsoft's Active Server Pages .NET (ASP.NET) 3.5 technology. Web-based applications create web content for web-browser clients. This web content includes Extensible HyperText Markup Language (XHTML), client-side scripting, images and binary data. If you are not familiar with XHTML, check out our XHTML resource center at `www.deitel.com/xhtml/` for links to online tutorials and other resources.

We present several examples that demonstrate web-application development using Web Forms, web controls (also called ASP.NET server controls) and Visual Basic programming. Web Form files have the file-name extension `.aspx` and contain the web page's GUI. You customize Web Forms by adding web controls including labels, textboxes, images, buttons and other GUI components. The Web Form file represents the web page that is sent to the client browser. From this point onward, we refer to Web Form files as ASPX files.

An ASPX file created in Visual Studio typically has a corresponding class written in a .NET language, such as Visual Basic. This class contains event handlers, initialization code, utility methods and other supporting code. The file that contains this class is called the code-behind file and provides the ASPX file's programmatic implementation.

To develop the code and GUIs in this chapter, we used Microsoft Visual Web Developer 2008 Express—an IDE designed for developing ASP.NET web applications. Visual Web Developer and Visual Basic 2008 Express share many common features and visual programming tools that simplify building complex applications, such as those that access a database (presented in Sections 21.7–21.8). The full version of Visual Studio 2008 includes the functionality of Visual Web Developer, so the instructions we present for Visual Web Developer apply also to Visual Studio 2008. Note that you must install either Visual Web Developer 2008 Express (available from `msdn.microsoft.com/vstudio/express/vwd/default.aspx`) or a complete version of Visual Studio 2008 to implement the programs in this chapter and Chapter 22, Windows Communication Foundation (WCF) Web Services.

21.2 Simple HTTP Transactions

In this section, we discuss what occurs behind the scenes when a user requests a web page in a browser. The HTTP protocol allows clients and servers to interact and exchange information in a uniform and reliable manner.

In its simplest form, a web page is nothing more than an XHTML document that describes to a web browser how to display and format the document's information. XHTML documents normally contain hyperlinks that link to different pages or to other parts of the same page. When the user clicks a hyperlink, the requested web page loads into the user's web browser. Similarly, the user can type the address of a page into the browser's address field.

URIs

HTTP uses URIs (Uniform Resource Identifiers) to identify data on the Internet. URIs that specify document locations are called URLs (Uniform Resource Locators). Common URLs refer to files, directories or objects that perform complex tasks, such as database lookups and Internet searches. If you know the URL of a publicly available resource or file anywhere on the web, you can access it through HTTP.

Parts of a URL

A URL contains information that directs a browser to the resource that the user wishes to access. Computers that run web-server software make such resources available. Let's examine the components of the URL

```
http://www.deitel.com/books/downloads.html
```

The `http://` indicates that the resource is to be obtained using the HTTP protocol. The middle portion, `www.deitel.com`, is the server's fully qualified hostname—the name of the server on which the resource resides. This computer usually is referred to as the host, because it houses and maintains resources. The hostname `www.deitel.com` is translated into an IP address—a unique numerical value that identifies the server much as a telephone number uniquely defines a particular phone line. More information on IP addresses is available at `en.wikipedia.org/wiki/IP_address`. This translation is performed by a domain-name system (DNS) server—a computer that maintains a database of hostnames and their corresponding IP addresses—and the process is called a DNS lookup.

The remainder of the URL (i.e., `/books/downloads.html`) specifies both the name of the requested resource (the XHTML document `downloads.html`) and its path, or location (`/books`), on the web server. The path could specify the location of an actual directory on the web server's file system. For security reasons, however, the path normally specifies the location of a virtual directory. The server translates the virtual directory into a real location on the server (or on another computer on the server's network), thus hiding the true location of the resource. Some resources are created dynamically using other information stored on the server computer, such as a database. The hostname in the URL for such a resource specifies the correct server; the path and resource information identify the resource with which to interact to respond to the client's request.

Making a Request and Receiving a Response

When given a URL, a web browser performs a simple HTTP transaction to retrieve and display the web page found at that address. Figure 21.1 illustrates the transaction, showing the interaction between the web browser (the client side) and the web-server application (the server side).

In Fig. 21.1, the web browser sends an HTTP request to the server. The request (in its simplest form) is

```
GET /books/downloads.html HTTP/1.1
```

The word `GET` is an HTTP method indicating that the client wishes to obtain a resource from the server. The remainder of the request provides the path name of the resource (e.g., an XHTML document) and the protocol's name and version number (`HTTP/1.1`). The client's request also contains some required and optional headers.

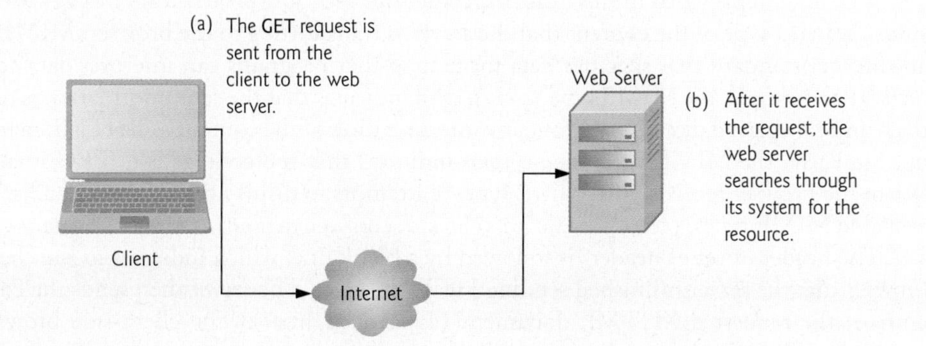

Fig. 21.1 | Client interacting with web server. *Step 1:* The `GET` request.

Any server that understands HTTP (version 1.1) can translate this request and respond appropriately. Figure 21.2 depicts the server responding to a request. The server first responds by sending a line of text that indicates the HTTP version, followed by a numeric code and a phrase describing the status of the transaction. For example,

```
HTTP/1.1 200 OK
```

indicates success, whereas

```
HTTP/1.1 404 Not found
```

informs the client that the web server could not locate the requested resource. A complete list of numeric codes indicating the status of an HTTP transaction can be found at `www.w3.org/Protocols/rfc2616/rfc2616-sec10.html`.

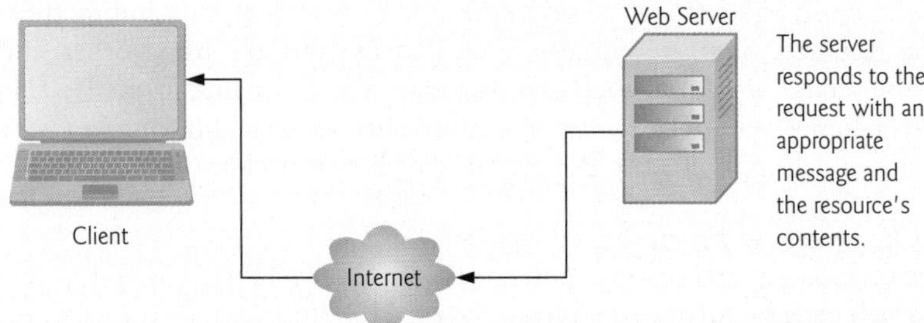

Fig. 21.2 | Client interacting with web server. *Step 2:* The HTTP response.

HTTP Headers

The server then sends one or more HTTP headers, which provide additional information about the data that will be sent. In this case, the server is sending an XHTML text document, so one HTTP header for this example would read:

```
Content-type: text/html
```

The information provided in this header specifies the Multipurpose Internet Mail Extensions (MIME) type of the content that the server is transmitting to the browser. MIME is an Internet standard that specifies data formats so that programs can interpret data correctly. For example, the MIME type `text/plain` indicates that the sent information is text that can be displayed directly, without any interpretation of the content as XHTML markup. Similarly, the MIME type `image/jpeg` indicates that the content is a JPEG image. When the browser receives this MIME type, it attempts to display the image. For a list of available MIME types, please see `www.w3schools.com/media/media_mimeeref.asp`.

The header or set of headers is followed by a blank line, which indicates to the client browser that the server is finished sending HTTP headers. The server then sends the contents of the requested XHTML document (`downloads.html`). The client-side browser parses the XHTML markup it receives and renders (or displays) the results. The server normally keeps the connection open to process other requests from the client.

HTTP `get` *and* `post` *Requests*

The two most common HTTP request types (also known as request methods) are `get` and `post`. A `get` request typically gets (or retrieves) information from a server. Common uses of `get` requests are to retrieve an XHTML document or an image, or to fetch search results based on a user-submitted search term. A `post` request typically posts (or sends) data to a server. Common uses of `post` requests are to send form data or documents to a server.

An HTTP request often posts data to a server-side form handler that processes the data. For example, when a user performs a search or participates in a web-based survey, the web server receives the information specified in the XHTML form as part of the request. `Get` requests and `post` requests can both be used to send form data to a web server, yet each request type sends the information differently.

A `get` request sends information to the server in the URL, e.g., `www.google.com/search?q=deitel`. In this case, `search` is the name of Google's server-side form handler, `q` is the `name` of a variable in Google's search form and `deitel` is the search term. A `?` separates the query string from the rest of the URL in a request. A *name*/*value* pair is passed to the server with the *name* and the *value* separated by an equals sign (`=`). If more than one *name*/*value* pair is submitted, each pair is separated by an ampersand (`&`). The server uses data passed in a query string to retrieve an appropriate resource from the server. The server then sends a response to the client. A `get` request may be initiated by submitting an XHTML form whose `method` attribute is set to `"get"`, or by typing the URL (possibly containing a query string) directly into the browser's address bar.

A `post` request sends form data as part of the HTTP message, not as part of the URL. A `get` request typically limits the query string (i.e., everything to the right of the `?`) to a specific number of characters (2083 in Internet Explorer; more in other browsers), so it is often necessary to send large pieces of information using the `post` method. The `post` method is also sometimes preferred because it hides the submitted data from the user by embedding it in an HTTP message. If a form submits hidden input values along with user-submitted data, the `post` method might generate a URL like `www.searchengine.com/search`. The form data still reaches the server for processing, but the user does not see the exact information sent.

Software Engineering Observation 21.1

The data sent in a `post` *request is not part of the URL, and the user can't see the data by default. However, there are tools available that expose this data, so you should not assume that the data is secure just because a* `post` *request is used.*

Client-Side Caching

Browsers often cache (save on disk) web pages for quick reloading. If there are no changes between the version stored in the cache and the current version on the web, this speeds up your browsing experience. An HTTP response can indicate the length of time for which the content remains "fresh." If this amount of time has not been reached, the browser can avoid another request to the server. Otherwise, the browser requests the document from the server. Thus, the browser minimizes the amount of data that must be downloaded for you to view a web page. Browsers typically do not cache the server's response to a `post` request, because the next `post` might not return the same result. For example, in a survey, many users could visit the same web page and answer a question. The survey results could then be displayed for the user. Each new answer changes the overall results of the survey.

When you use a web-based search engine, the browser normally supplies the information you specify in an XHTML form to the search engine with a `get` request. The search engine performs the search, then returns the results to you as a web page. Such pages are sometimes cached by the browser in case you perform the same search again.

21.3 Multitier Application Architecture

Web-based applications are **multitier applications** (sometimes referred to as ***n*-tier applications**). Multitier applications divide functionality into separate **tiers** (i.e., logical groupings of functionality). Although tiers can be located on the same computer, the tiers of web-based applications typically reside on separate computers. Figure 21.3 presents the basic structure of a three-tier web-based application.

The **information tier** (also called the **data tier** or the **bottom tier**) maintains data pertaining to the application. This tier typically stores data in a relational database management system (RDBMS). We discussed RDBMSs in Chapter 20. For example, a retail store might have a database for storing product information, such as descriptions, prices and quantities in stock. The same database also might contain customer information, such as user names, billing addresses and credit card numbers. This tier can contain multiple databases, which together comprise the data needed for our application.

The **middle tier** implements **business logic**, **controller logic** and **presentation logic** to control interactions between the application's clients and the application's data. The middle tier acts as an intermediary between data in the information tier and the application's clients. The middle-tier controller logic processes client requests (such as requests to view a product catalog) and retrieves data from the database. The middle-tier presentation logic then processes data from the information tier and presents the content to the client. Web applications typically present data to clients as XHTML documents.

Business logic in the middle tier enforces **business rules** and ensures that data is reliable before the server application updates the database or presents the data to users. Business rules dictate how clients can and cannot access application data, and how applications process data. For example, a business rule in the middle tier of a retail store's web-based application might ensure that all product quantities remain positive. A client request to set a negative quantity in the bottom tier's product information database would be rejected by the middle tier's business logic.

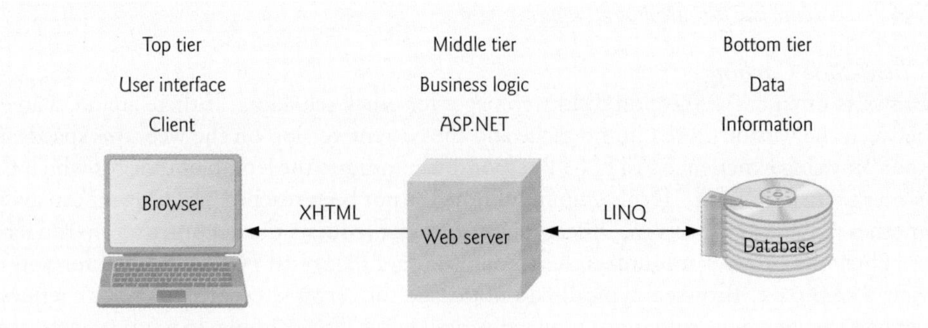

Fig. 21.3 | Three-tier architecture.

The client tier, or top tier, is the application's user interface, which gathers input and displays output. Users interact directly with the application through the user interface (typically viewed in a web browser), keyboard and mouse. In response to user actions (e.g., clicking a hyperlink), the client tier interacts with the middle tier to make requests and to retrieve data from the information tier. The client tier then displays the data retrieved from the middle tier to the user. The client tier never directly interacts with the information tier.

21.4 Creating and Running a Simple Web-Form Example

Our first example displays the web server's time of day in a browser window. When run, this program displays the text `Current time on the Web server:`, followed by the web server's time. As mentioned previously, the program consists of two related files—an ASPX file (Fig. 21.4) and a Visual Basic code-behind file (Fig. 21.5). We first display the markup and code, then we carefully guide you through the step-by-step process of creating this program. [*Note:* The markup in Fig. 21.4 and other ASPX file listings in this chapter is the same as the markup that appears in Visual Web Developer, but we have reformatted the markup for presentation purposes to make the code more readable.]

Visual Web Developer generates all the markup shown in Fig. 21.4 when you set the web page's title, type text in the Web Form, drag a `Label` onto the Web Form and set the properties of the page's text and the `Label`. We discuss these steps in Section 21.4.6.

```
<%-- Fig. 21.4: WebTime.aspx --%>
<%-- A page that displays the current time in a Label. --%>
<%@ Page Language="VB" AutoEventWireup="false" CodeFile="WebTime.aspx.vb"
   Inherits="WebTime" EnableSessionState="False" %>

<!DOCTYPE html PUBLIC "-//W3C//DTD XHTML 1.0 Transitional//EN"
   "http://www.w3.org/TR/xhtml1/DTD/xhtml1-transitional.dtd">

<html xmlns="http://www.w3.org/1999/xhtml" >
<head runat="server">
   <title>A Simple Web Form Example</title>
</head>
<body>
   <form id="form1" runat="server">
   <div>
      <h2>
      Current time on the web server:</h2>
      <p>
         <asp:Label ID="timeLabel" runat="server" BackColor="Black"
            EnableViewState="False" Font-Size="XX-Large"
            ForeColor="Yellow"></asp:Label>
      </p>
   </div>
   </form>
</body>
</html>
```

Fig. 21.4 | ASPX file that displays the web server's time.

21.4.1 Examining an ASPX File

The ASPX file contains other information in addition to XHTML. Lines 1–2 are ASP.NET comments that indicate the figure number, the file name and the purpose of the file. ASP.NET comments begin with `<%--` and terminate with `--%>`, and can span multiple lines. We added these comments to the file. Lines 3–4 use a `Page` directive (in an ASPX file a directive is delimited by `<%@` and `%>`) to specify information needed by ASP.NET to process this file. The `Language` attribute of the `Page` directive specifies the language of the code-behind file as Visual Basic (`"VB"`); the code-behind file (i.e., the `CodeFile`) is `WebTime.aspx.vb`. A code-behind file name usually consists of the full ASPX file name (e.g., `WebTime.aspx`) followed by the `.vb` extension.

The `AutoEventWireup` attribute (line 3) determines how Web Form event handling is recognized. When `AutoEventWireup` is set to `true`, ASP.NET automatically treats a method of name `Page_`*EventName* as an event handler for the associated event of the `Page` without you having to explicitly define it as such in the method's `Handles` clause. For example, ASP.NET will call methods `Page_Init` and `Page_Load` in the code-behind file to handle the `Page`'s `Init` and `Load` events, respectively. (We discuss these events later in the chapter.) When `AutoEventWireup` is set to `false`, ASP.NET looks for the `Handles` clause when one of the `Page`'s events are raised, as per the traditional event handling model in Windows `Forms`.

The `Inherits` attribute (line 4) specifies the page's class name—in this case, `WebTime`. We say more about `Inherits` momentarily. [*Note:* We explicitly set the `EnableSessionState` attribute (line 4) to `False`. We explain the significance of this attribute later in the chapter. The IDE sometimes generates attribute values (e.g., `true` and `false`) and control names (as you will see later in the chapter) that do not adhere to our standard code capitalization conventions (i.e., `True` and `False`). Like Visual Basic, ASP.NET markup is not case sensitive, so using a different case is not problematic. To remain consistent with the code generated by the IDE, we do not modify these values in our code listings or in our accompanying discussions.]

For this first ASPX file, we provide a brief discussion of the XHTML markup. We do not discuss most of the XHTML in subsequent ASPX files. Lines 6–7 contain the document type declaration, which specifies the document element name (`HTML`) and the `PUBLIC` Uniform Resource Identifier (URI) for the DTD that defines the XHTML vocabulary.

Lines 9–10 contain the `<html>` and `<head>` start tags, respectively. XHTML documents have the root element `html` and markup information about the document in the `head` element. Also note that the `html` element specifies the XML namespace of the document using the `xmlns` attribute (see Section 15.5).

Notice the `runat` attribute in line 10, which is set to `"server"`. This attribute indicates that when a client requests this ASPX file, ASP.NET processes the `head` element and its nested elements on the server and generates the corresponding XHTML, which is then sent to the client. In this case, the XHTML sent to the client will be identical to the markup in the ASPX file. However, as you will see, ASP.NET can generate complex XHTML markup from simple elements in an ASPX file.

Line 11 sets the title of this web page. We demonstrate how to set the title through a property in the IDE shortly. Line 13 contains the `<body>` start tag, which begins the body of the XHTML document; the body contains the main content that the browser displays. The `form` that contains our XHTML text and controls is defined in lines 14–24. Again, the runat attribute in the form element indicates that this element executes on the server, which generates equivalent XHTML and sends it to the client. Lines 15–23 contain a div element that groups the elements of the form in a block of markup.

Lines 16–17 are an XHTML h2 heading element that contains text indicating the web page's purpose. As we demonstrate shortly, the IDE generates this element in response to typing text directly in the Web Form and selecting the text as a second-level heading.

Lines 18–22 contain a p element to mark up a paragraph of content in the browser. Lines 19–21 mark up a label web control. The properties that we set in the **Properties** window, such as Font-Size and BackColor (i.e., background color), are attributes here. The ID attribute (line 19) assigns a name to the control so that it can be manipulated programmatically in the code-behind file. We set the control's EnableViewState attribute (line 20) to False. We explain the significance of this attribute later in the chapter.

The asp: tag prefix in the declaration of the Label tag (line 19) indicates that the label is an ASP.NET web control, not an XHTML element. Each web control maps to a corresponding XHTML element (or group of elements)—when processing a web control on the server, ASP.NET generates XHTML markup that will be sent to the client to represent that control in a web browser.

Portability Tip 21.1

The same web control can map to different XHTML elements, depending on the client browser and the web control's property settings.

In this example, the asp:Label control maps to the XHTML span element (i.e., ASP.NET creates a span element to represent this control in the client's web browser). A span element contains text that is displayed in a web page. This particular element is used because span elements allow formatting styles to be applied to text. Several of the property values that were applied to our label are represented as part of the style attribute of the span element. You will soon see what the generated span element's markup looks like.

The web control in this example contains the runat="server" attribute/value pair (line 19), because this control must be processed on the server so that the server can translate the control into XHTML that can be rendered in the client browser. If this attribute/value pair is not present, the asp:Label element is written as text to the client (i.e., the control is not converted into a span element and does not render properly).

21.4.2 Examining a Code-Behind File

Figure 21.5 presents the code-behind file. Recall that the ASPX file in Fig. 21.4 references this file in line 3. Line 3 of Fig. 21.5 begins the declaration of class WebTime. Recall from Section 10.7 that a class declaration can span multiple source-code files and that the separate portions of the class declaration in each file are known as partial classes. The Partial modifier in line 3 indicates that the code-behind file is a partial class. We discuss the remainder of this class shortly.

Line 4 indicates that WebTime inherits from class Page in namespace System.Web.UI. This namespace contains classes and controls that assist in building web-based applications. Class Page provides event handlers and objects necessary for creating web-based applications. In addition to class Page (from which all web applications directly or indirectly inherit), System.Web.UI also includes class Control—the base class that provides common functionality for all web controls.

```
1  ' Fig. 21.5: WebTime.aspx.vb
2  ' Code-behind file for a page that displays the current time.
3  Partial Class WebTime
4     Inherits System.Web.UI.Page
5
6     ' initializes the contents of the page
7     Protected Sub Page_Init(ByVal sender As Object, _
8        ByVal e As System.EventArgs) Handles Me.Init
9        ' display the server's current time in timeLabel
10       timeLabel.Text = DateTime.Now.ToString("hh:mm:ss")
11    End Sub ' Page_Init
12 End Class ' WebTime
```

Fig. 21.5 | Code-behind file for a page that displays the web server's time.

Lines 7–11 define method `Page_Init`, which handles the page's `Init` event. This event indicates that the page is ready to be initialized. The only initialization required for this page is setting `timeLabel`'s `Text` property to the time on the server (i.e., the computer on which this code executes). The statement in line 10 retrieves the current time and formats it as *hh*:*mm*:*ss*. For example, 9 AM is formatted as 09:00:00, and 2:30 PM is formatted as 02:30:00. Notice that the code-behind file can access `timeLabel` (the `ID` of the `Label` in the ASPX file) programmatically, even though the file does not contain a declaration for a variable named `timeLabel`. You will learn why momentarily.

21.4.3 Relationship Between an ASPX File and a Code-Behind File

How are the ASPX and code-behind files used to create the web page that is sent to the client? First, recall that class `WebTime` is the base class specified in line 4 of the ASPX file (Fig. 21.4). This class (partially declared in the code-behind file) inherits from `Page`, which defines general web page functionality. Partial class `WebTime` inherits this functionality and defines some of its own (i.e., displaying the current time). The code in the code-behind file displays the time, whereas the code in the ASPX file defines the GUI.

When a client requests an ASPX file, ASP.NET creates two partial classes behind the scenes. The code-behind file contains one partial class named `WebTime`, and ASP.NET generates another partial class containing the remainder of class `WebTime`, based on the markup in the ASPX file. For example, `WebTime.aspx` contains a `Label` web control with `ID timeLabel`, so the generated partial class would contain a declaration for a variable named `timeLabel` of type `System.Web.UI.WebControls.Label`. Class `Label` represents a web control defined in namespace `System.Web.UI.WebControls`, which contains various web controls for designing a page's user interface. Web controls in this namespace derive from class WebControl. When compiled, the partial class that declares timeLabel combines with the code-behind file's partial class declaration to form the complete WebTime class. This explains why line 10 in Fig. 21.5 can access timeLabel, which is created in lines 19–21 of WebTime.aspx (Fig. 21.4)—method Page_Init and control timeLabel are actually members of the same class, but defined in separate partial classes.

The partial class generated by ASP.NET is based on the ASPX file that defines the page's visual representation. This partial class is combined with the one in Fig. 21.5, which defines the page's logic. The first time the page is requested, this class is compiled and an instance is created. This instance represents the page and creates the XHTML that is sent to the client. The assembly for the compiled partial classes is placed in a subdirectory of

```
C:\WINDOWS\Microsoft.NET\Framework\v2.0.50727\
   Temporary ASP.NET Files\WebTime
```

on Windows XP. On Windows Vista, the assembly is placed in

```
C:\Users\User\AppData\Local\Temp\Temporary ASP.NET Files\webtime
```

Once an instance of the web page has been created, multiple clients can use it to access the page—no recompilation is necessary. The project will be recompiled only when you modify the application; changes are detected by the runtime environment, and the application is recompiled to reflect the altered content.

21.4.4 How the Code in an ASP.NET Web Page Executes

Let's look briefly at how the code for our web page executes. When an instance of the page is created, the PreInit event occurs first, invoking method Page_PreInit. Method Page_PreInit can be used to set a page's theme and look-and-feel (and perform other tasks that are beyond this chapter's scope). The Init event occurs next, invoking method Page_Init. Method Page_Init is used to initialize objects and other aspects of the page. After Page_Init executes, the Load event occurs, and the Page_Load event handler executes. Although not present in this example, the PreInit and Load events are inherited from class Page. You will see examples of the Page_Load event handler later in the chapter. After the Load event handler finishes executing, the page processes events that are generated by the page's controls, such as user interactions with the GUI. When the Web Form object is ready for garbage collection, an Unload event occurs, which calls the Page_Unload event handler. This event, too, is inherited from class Page. Page_Unload typically contains code that releases resources used by the page. Other events occur as well, but are typically used only by ASP.NET controls to render themselves. You can learn more about a Page's event lifecycle at msdn2.microsoft.com/en-US/library/ms178472.aspx.

21.4.5 Examining the XHTML Generated by an ASP.NET Application

Figure 21.6 shows the XHTML generated by ASP.NET when a client browser requests WebTime.aspx (Fig. 21.4). To view this code, select **View > Source** in Internet Explorer. We added the comments in lines 1–2 and reformatted the XHTML for readability.

The markup in this page is similar to the ASPX file. Lines 7–9 define a document header comparable to that in Fig. 21.4. Lines 10–25 define the document's body. Line 11

```
1  <!-- Fig. 21.6: WebTime.html -->
2  <!-- The XHTML generated when WebTime.aspx is loaded. -->
3  <!DOCTYPE html PUBLIC "-//W3C//DTD XHTML 1.1//EN"
4     "http://www.w3.org/TR/xhtml11/DTD/xhtml11.dtd">
5
6  <html xmlns="http://www.w3.org/1999/xhtml" >
7  <head>
8     <title>A Simple Web Form Example</title>
9  </head>
10 <body>
11    <form name="form1" method="post" action="WebTime.aspx" id="form1">
12       <div>
13          <input type="hidden" name="__VIEWSTATE" id="__VIEWSTATE" value=
14             "/wEPDwUJODExMDE5NzY5ZGSzVbs789nqEeoNueQCnCJQEUgykw==" />
15       </div>
16
17       <div>
18          <h2>Current time on the web server:</h2>
19          <p>
20             <span id="timeLabel" style="color:Yellow;
21                background-color:Black;font-size:XX-Large;">03:11:49</span>
22          </p>
23       </div>
24    </form>
25 </body>
26 </html>
```

Fig. 21.6 | XHTML response when the browser requests `WebTime.aspx`.

begins the form, a mechanism for collecting user information and sending it to the web server. In this particular program, the user does not submit data to the web server for processing; however, processing user data is a crucial part of many applications that is facilitated by forms. We demonstrate how to submit form data to the server in later examples.

XHTML forms can contain visual and nonvisual components. Visual components include buttons and other GUI components with which users interact. Nonvisual components, called **hidden inputs**, store data, such as e-mail addresses, that the document author specifies. A hidden input is defined in lines 13–14. We discuss the precise meaning of this hidden input later in the chapter. Attribute **`method`** of the `form` element (line 11) specifies the method by which the web browser submits the form to the server. The **`action`** attribute identifies the name and location of the resource that will be requested when this form is submitted—in this case, `WebTime.aspx`. Recall that the ASPX file's `form` element contained the `runat="server"` attribute/value pair (line 14 of Fig. 21.4). When the `form` is processed on the server, the `runat` attribute is removed. The `method` and `action` attributes are added, and the resulting XHTML `form` is sent to the client browser.

In the ASPX file, the form's `Label` (i.e., `timeLabel`) is a web control. Here, we are viewing the XHTML created by our application, so the `form` contains a `span` element (lines 20–21 of Fig. 21.6) to represent the text in the label. In this particular case, ASP.NET maps the **`Label`** web control to an XHTML `span` element. The formatting options that were specified as properties of `timeLabel`, such as the font size and color of the text in the `Label`, are now specified in the `style` attribute of the `span` element.

Notice that only those elements in the ASPX file marked with the `runat="server"` attribute/value pair are modified or replaced when the file is processed by the server. The literal XHTML elements, such as the `h2` in line 18 of Fig. 21.6, are sent to the browser as they appear in the ASPX file (lines 16–17 of Fig. 21.4).

21.4.6 Building an ASP.NET Web Application

Now that we've presented the ASPX file, the code-behind file and the resulting web page sent to the web browser, we show the steps we used to create this application in Visual Web Developer.

Step 1: Creating the Web Site Project

Select **File > New Web Site...** to display the **New Web Site** dialog (Fig. 21.7). In this dialog, select **ASP.NET Web Site** in the **Templates** pane. Below this pane, are two fields in which you can specify the location and language of the web application you are creating. If it is not already selected, select **File System** from the drop-down list closest to **Location.** This indicates that the web application should be built on your local file system. You will be able to test the application using Visual Web Developer's internal ASP.NET Development Server, but you will not be able to access the application remotely over the Internet. Later, you can publish your application to a web server as an IIS application that uses HTTP. You should create your project in a directory named `WebTime`.

The **Language** drop-down list in the **New Web Site** dialog allows you to specify the language (i.e., Visual Basic or Visual C#) in which you will write the code-behind file(s) for the web application. Change the setting to Visual Basic. Click **OK** to create the web-application project. In addition to the directory in which your web-application files will be created, this action also creates a `WebTime` directory in your `My Documents` (Windows XP) or `Documents` (Windows Vista) folder under `Visual Studio 2008\Projects`. This folder contains the project's solution files (e.g., `WebTime.sln`). We do not provide solution files with the examples in this chapter. To open a website, select **File > Open Web Site**, select the root folder where it resides, and click **Open**.

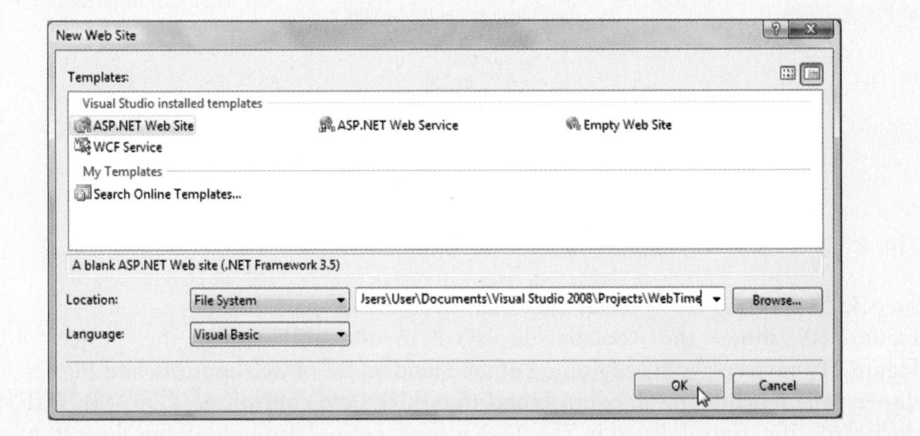

Fig. 21.7 | Creating an **ASP.NET Web Site** in Visual Web Developer.

Step 2: Examining the Solution Explorer *of the Newly Created Project*

The next several figures describe the new project's content, beginning with the **Solution Explorer** shown in Fig. 21.8. Like Visual Basic 2008 Express, Visual Web Developer creates several files when you create a new project. It creates an ASPX file (i.e., Web Form) named `Default.aspx` for each new **ASP.NET Web Site** project. This file is open by default in the Web Forms Designer in **Source** mode when the project first loads (we discuss this momentarily). As mentioned previously, a code-behind file is included as part of the project. Visual Web Developer creates a code-behind file named `Default.aspx.vb`. To open the ASPX file's code-behind file, right click the ASPX file and select **View Code** or click the **View Code** button ( ) at the top of the **Solution Explorer**. Alternatively, you can expand the node for the ASPX file to reveal the node for the code-behind file (see Fig. 21.8). You can also choose to list all the files in the project individually (instead of nested) by clicking the **Nest Related Files** button—this option is turned on by default, so clicking the button toggles the option off.

The **Properties** and **Refresh** buttons in Visual Web Developer's **Solution Explorer** behave like those in Visual Basic 2008 Express. Visual Web Developer's **Solution Explorer** also contains the buttons **View Designer**, **Copy Web Site** and **ASP.NET Configuration**. The **View Designer** button allows you to open the Web Form in **Design** mode, which we discuss shortly. The **Copy Web Site** button opens a dialog that allows you to move the files in this project to another location, such as a remote web server. This is useful if you are developing the application on your local computer but want to make it available to the public from a different location. Finally, the **ASP.NET Configuration** button takes you to a web page called the **Web Site Administration Tool**, where you can manipulate various settings and security options for your application. We discuss this tool in greater detail in Section 21.8.

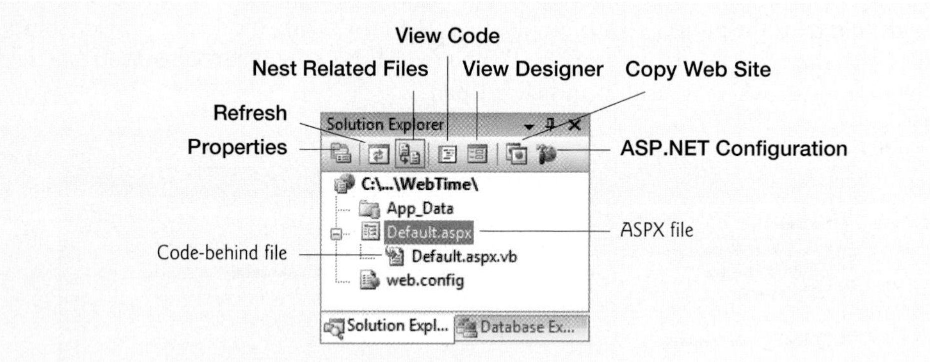

Fig. 21.8 | **Solution Explorer** window for project `WebTime`.

Step 3: Examining the Toolbox *in Visual Web Developer*

Figure 21.9 shows the **Toolbox** displayed in the IDE when the project loads. Figure 21.9(a) displays the beginning of the **Standard** list of web controls, and Fig. 21.9(b) displays the remaining web controls and the list of **Data** controls used in ASP.NET. We discuss specific controls listed in Fig. 21.9 as they are used throughout the chapter. Notice that some controls in the **Toolbox** are similar to the Windows controls presented earlier in the book.

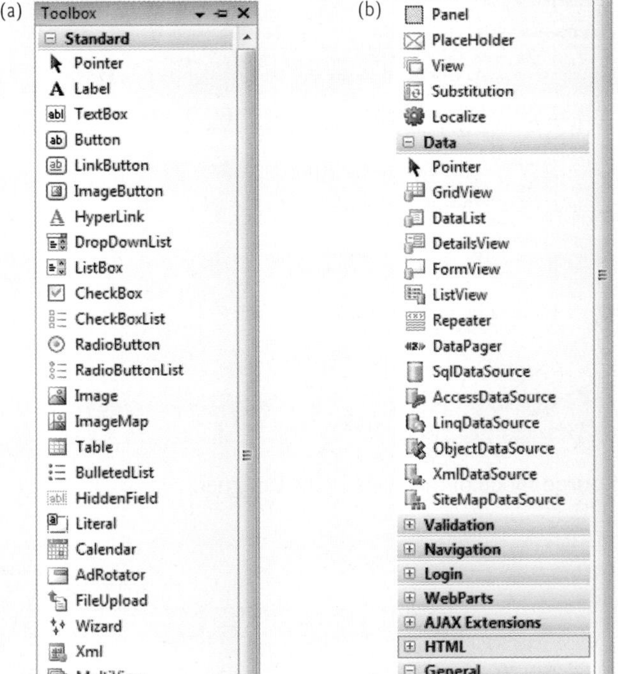

Fig. 21.9 | **Toolbox** in Visual Web Developer.

Step 4: Examining the Web Forms Designer

Figure 21.10 shows the Web Forms Designer in **Source** mode, which appears in the center of the IDE. When the project loads for the first time, the Web Forms Designer displays the autogenerated ASPX file (i.e., `Default.aspx`) in **Source** mode, which allows you to view and edit the markup that comprises the web page. The markup listed in Fig. 21.10 was created by the IDE and serves as a template that we will modify shortly. Clicking the **Design** button in the lower-left corner of the Web Forms Designer switches to **Design** mode (Fig. 21.11), which allows you to drag and drop controls from the **Toolbox** on the Web Form. You can also type at the current cursor location to add text to the web page. We demonstrate this shortly. In response to such actions, the IDE generates the appropriate markup in the ASPX file. Notice that **Design** mode indicates the XHTML element where the cursor is currently located. Clicking the **Source** button returns the Web Forms Designer to **Source** mode, where you can see the generated markup. You can also view both the markup and the web page at the same time by using **Split** mode, as shown in Fig. 21.12.

Step 5: Examining the Code-Behind File in the IDE

The next figure (Fig. 21.13) displays `Default.aspx.vb`—the code-behind file generated by Visual Web Developer for `Default.aspx`. Right click the ASPX file in the **Solution Explorer** and select **View Code** to open the code-behind file. When it is first created, this file contains nothing more than a partial class declaration. We will add the `Page_Init` event handler to this code momentarily.

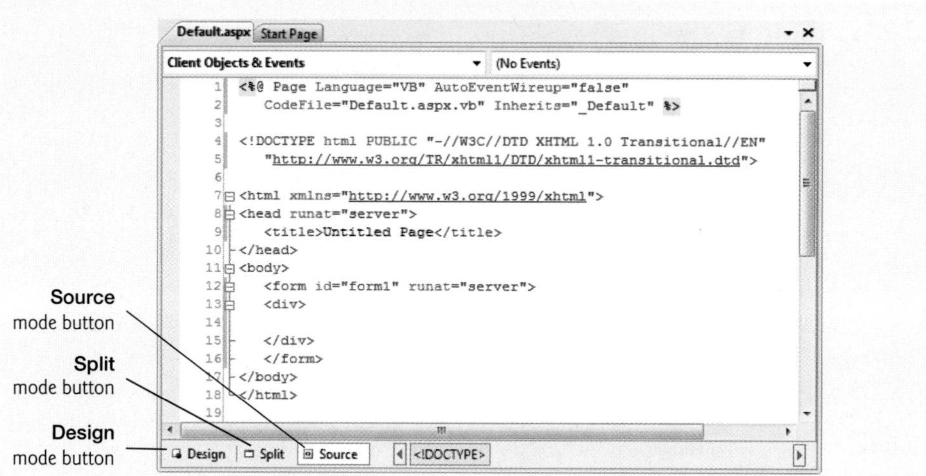

Fig. 21.10 | **Source** mode of the Web Forms Designer.

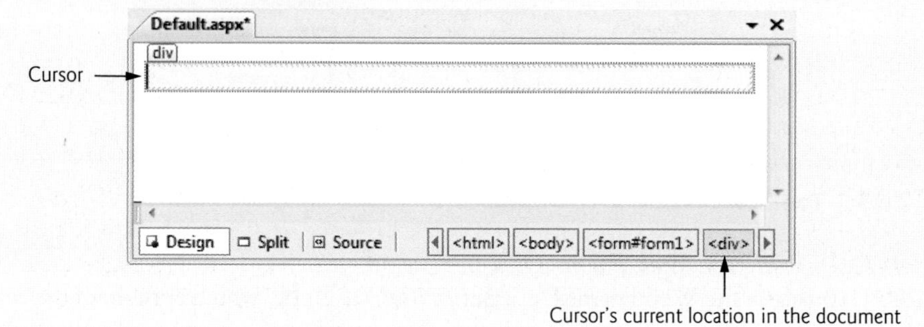

Fig. 21.11 | **Design** mode of the Web Forms Designer.

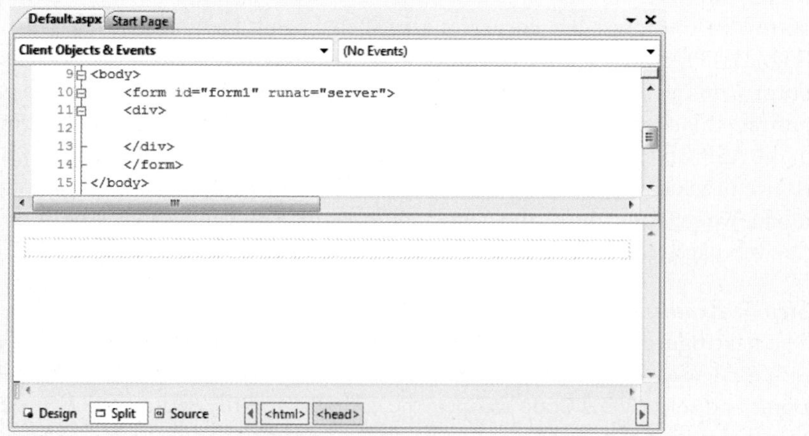

Fig. 21.12 | **Split** mode of the Web Forms Designer.

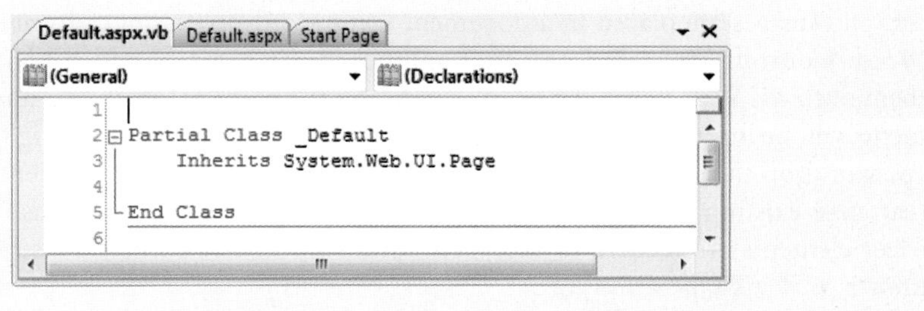

Fig. 21.13 | Code-behind file for `Default.aspx` generated by Visual Web Developer.

Step 6: Renaming the ASPX File

Now that you've seen the contents of the default ASPX and code-behind files, let's rename these files. Right click the ASPX file in the **Solution Explorer** and select **Rename**. Enter the new file name `WebTime.aspx` and press *Enter*. This updates the name of both the ASPX file and the code-behind file. The IDE also updates the `Page` directive's `CodeFile` attribute in `WebTime.aspx`.

Step 7: Renaming the Class in the Code-Behind File and Updating the ASPX File

Although renaming the ASPX file causes the name of the code-behind file to change, this action does not affect the name of the partial class declared in the code-behind file. Open the code-behind file and change the class name from `_Default` (line 2 in Fig. 21.13) to `WebTime`, so the partial class declaration appears as in line 3 of Fig. 21.5. Recall that this class is also referenced by the `Page` directive in the ASPX file. Using the Web Forms Designer's **Source** mode, modify the `Inherits` attribute of the `Page` directive in `WebTime.aspx`, so it appears as in line 4 of Fig. 21.4. The value of the `Inherits` attribute and the class name in the code-behind file must be identical; otherwise, you'll get errors when you build the web application.

Step 8: Changing the Title of the Page

Before designing the content of the Web Form, we change its title from the default `Untitled Page` (line 9 of Fig. 21.10) to `A Simple Web Form Example`. To do so, open the ASPX file in **Source** mode and modify the text in the `title` element—i.e., the text between the tags `<title>` and `</title>`). Alternatively, you can open the ASPX file in **Design** mode and modify the Web Form's `Title` property in the **Properties** window. To view the Web Form's properties, select `DOCUMENT` from the drop-down list in the **Properties** window; `DOCUMENT` represents the Web Form in the **Properties** window.

Step 9: Designing the Page

Designing a Web Form is as simple as designing a Windows Form. To add controls to the page, drag-and-drop them from the **Toolbox** onto the Web Form in **Design** mode. Like the Web Form itself, each control is an object that has properties, methods and events. You can set these properties and events visually using the **Properties** window or programmatically in the code-behind file. However, unlike working with a Windows Form, you can type text directly on a Web Form at the cursor location or insert XHTML elements using menu commands.

Controls and other elements are placed sequentially on a Web Form, much as how text and images are placed in a document using word-processing software like Microsoft Word. Controls are placed one after another in the order in which you drag-and-drop them onto the Web Form. The cursor indicates the point at which text and XHTML elements will be inserted. If you want to position a control between existing text or controls, you can drop the control at a specific position within the existing elements. You can also rearrange existing controls using drag-and-drop actions. The positions of controls and other elements are relative to the Web Form's upper-left corner. This type of layout is known as relative positioning.

An alternate type of layout is known as absolute positioning, in which controls are located exactly where they are dropped on the Web Form. You can enable absolute positioning in **Design** mode by selecting **Tools > Options...**., to display the **Options** dialog. If it isn't checked already, check the **Show all settings** checkbox. Next, open the **HTML Designer > CSS Styling** node and ensure that the checkbox labeled **Change positioning to absolute for controls added using Toolbox, paste or drag and drop** is selected.

Portability Tip 21.2

Absolute positioning is discouraged, because pages designed in this manner may not render correctly on computers with different screen resolutions and font sizes. This could cause absolutely positioned elements to overlap each other or display off-screen, requiring the client to scroll to see the full page content.

In this example, we use one piece of text and one `Label`. To add the text to the Web Form, click the blank Web Form in **Design** mode and type `Current time on the Web server:`. Visual Web Developer is a WYSIWYG (What You See Is What You Get) editor—whenever you make a change to a Web Form in **Design** mode, the IDE creates the markup (visible in **Source** mode) necessary to achieve the desired visual effects seen in **Design** mode. After adding the text to the Web Form, switch to **Source** mode. You should see that the IDE added this text to the `div` element that appears in the ASPX file by default. Back in **Design** mode, highlight the text you added. From the **Block Format** drop-down list (see Fig. 21.14), choose **Heading 2** to format this text as a heading that will appear bold in a font slightly larger than the default. This action encloses the text in an `h2` element. Finally, click to the right of the text and press the *Enter* key to start a new paragraph. This action generates a `p` (paragraph) element in the ASPX file's markup. The IDE should now look like Fig. 21.14.

You can place a `Label` on a Web Form either by dragging-and-dropping or by double clicking the **Toolbox**'s **Label** control. Ensure that the cursor is in the new paragraph, then add a `Label` that will be used to display the time. Using the **Properties** window, set the `(ID)` property of the `Label` to `timeLabel` and delete `timeLabel`'s text in its `Text` property, because this text will be set programmatically in the code-behind file. When a `Label` does not contain text, its name is displayed in square brackets in the Web Forms Designer (Fig. 21.15) as a placeholder for design and layout purposes. This text is not displayed at execution time. We set `timeLabel`'s `BackColor`, `ForeColor` and `Font-Size` properties to `Black`, `Yellow` and `XX-Large`, respectively. To change the `Label`'s font properties, select the `Label`, expand the `Font` node in the **Properties** window and change each relevant property. As the `Label`'s properties are set, Visual Web Developer updates the ASPX file's contents. Figure 21.15 shows the IDE after setting these properties.

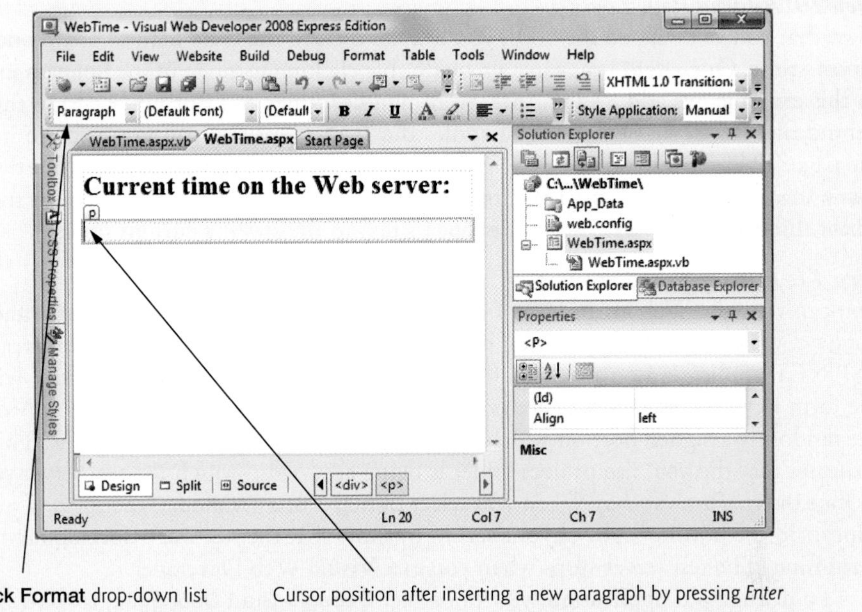

Fig. 21.14 | `WebTime.aspx` after inserting text and a new paragraph.

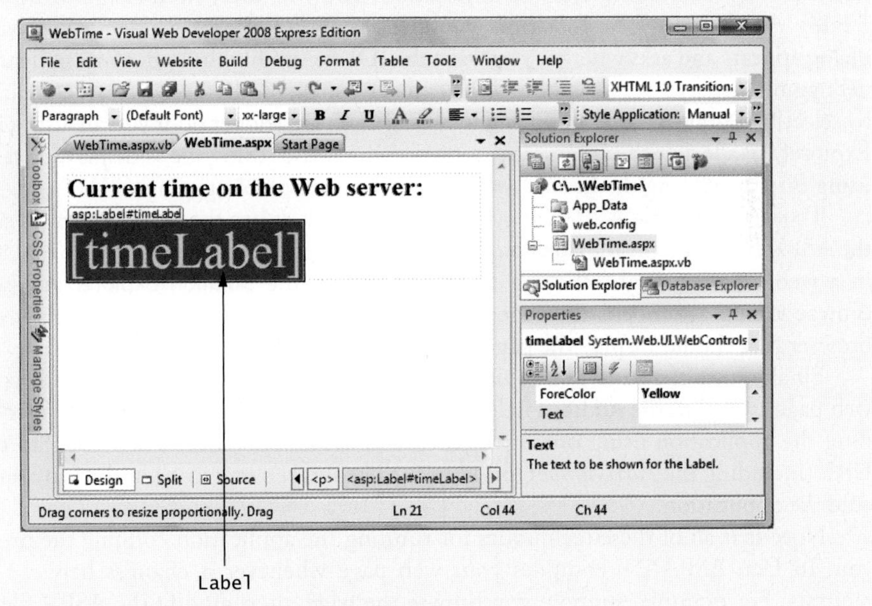

Fig. 21.15 | `WebTime.aspx` after adding a `Label` and setting its properties.

Next, set the `Label`'s `EnableViewState` property to `False`. Finally, select `DOCUMENT` from the drop-down list in the **Properties** window and set the Web Form's `EnableSessionState` property to `False`. We discuss both of these properties later in the chapter.

Step 10: Adding Page Logic

Now that you've designed the GUI, you'll write code in the code-behind file to obtain the server's time. Open `WebTime.aspx.vb` by double clicking its node in the **Solution Explorer**. In this example, we add a `Page_Init` event handler (lines 7–11 of Fig. 21.5) to the code-behind file. Recall that `Page_Init` handles the `Init` event and contains code to initialize the page. This event handler can be generated by selecting `(Page Events)` from the **Class Name** drop-down menu and `Init` from the **Method Name** drop-down menu in the **Code** editor. Line 10 of Fig. 21.5 sets `timeLabel`'s text to the server's current time.

Step 11: Running the Program

You can view the Web Form several ways. First, you can select **Debug > Start Without Debugging**, which runs the application by opening it in a browser window. If you created the ASP.NET application on the local file system, the URL shown in the browser will have the form `http://localhost:`*PortNumber*`/WebTime/WebTime.aspx`, where *PortNumber* is the randomly assigned port on which the ASP.NET Development Server runs. This URL indicates that the `WebTime` project folder is being accessed through the test server running at `localhost:`*PortNumber*. When you select **Debug > Start Without Debugging**, a tray icon appears in the bottom-right of your screen to show that the **ASP.NET Development Server** is running. The test server stops when you exit Visual Web Developer.

To debug your application, you can select **Debug > Start Debugging** to view the web page in a web browser with debugging enabled. You cannot debug a web application unless debugging is explicitly enabled by the **`Web.config`** file—a file that stores configuration settings for an ASP.NET web application. You will rarely need to manually create or modify `Web.config`. The first time you select **Debug > Start Debugging** in a project, a dialog appears and asks whether you want the IDE to modify the `Web.config` file to enable debugging. After you click **OK**, the IDE enters **Running** mode. You can exit **Running** mode by selecting **Debug > Stop Debugging** in Visual Web Developer or, if you are using Internet Explorer, by closing the browser window in which the ASPX file is displayed. If you are using Firefox, closing the browser window will not stop debuggging.

To view a specific ASPX file, you can right click either the Web Forms Designer or the ASPX file name (in the **Solution Explorer**) and select **View In Browser** to load the page in a web browser. Right clicking the ASPX file in the **Solution Explorer** and selecting **Browse With...** also opens the page in a browser, but first allows you to specify the web browser that should display the page and its screen resolution.

Finally, you can run your application by opening a browser window and typing the web page's URL in the **Address** field. First start the **ASP.NET Development Server** by running the application using one of the methods described above. Then you can type the URL (including the *PortNumber* found in the test server's tray icon) in the browser to execute the application.

Note that all of these techniques for running the application compile the project for you. In fact, ASP.NET compiles your web page whenever it changes between HTTP requests. For example, suppose you browse the page, then modify the ASPX file or add code to the code-behind file. When you reload the page, ASP.NET recompiles the page on the server before returning the HTTP response to the browser. This important behavior of ASP.NET 3.5 ensures that clients always see the latest version of the page. You can manually compile a web page or an entire website by selecting **Build Page** or **Build Site**, respectively, from the **Build** menu in Visual Web Developer.

Windows Firewall Settings

If you are using a local IIS web server to test web applications (rather than the built-in test server in Visual Web Developer) and would like to test your web applications over a network, you may need to change your Windows Firewall settings. For security reasons, Windows Firewall does not allow remote access to a web server on your local computer by default. To change this, open the Windows Firewall utility in the Windows Control Panel. Click the **Advanced** tab and select your network connection from the **Network Connection Settings** list, then click **Settings....** On the **Services** tab of the **Advanced Settings** dialog, ensure that **Web Server (HTTP)** is checked.

21.5 Web Controls

This section introduces some of the web controls located in the **Standard** section of the **Toolbox** (Fig. 21.9). Figure 21.16 summarizes some of the web controls used in the chapter examples.

Web control	Description
`Label`	Displays text that the user cannot edit.
`TextBox`	Gathers user input and displays text.
`Button`	Triggers an event when clicked.
`HyperLink`	Displays a hyperlink.
`DropDownList`	Displays a drop-down list of choices from which a user can select an item.
`RadioButtonList`	Groups radio buttons.
`Image`	Displays images (e.g., GIF and JPG).

Fig. 21.16 | Commonly used web controls.

21.5.1 Text and Graphics Controls

Figure 21.17 depicts a simple form for gathering user input. This example uses all the controls listed in Fig. 21.16, except `Label`, which you used in Section 21.4. The code in Fig. 21.17 was generated by Visual Web Developer in response to dragging controls onto the page in **Design** mode. To begin, create an **ASP.NET Web Site** named `WebControls`. [*Note:* This example does not contain any functionality—i.e., no action occurs when the user clicks **Register**. We ask you to provide the functionality as an exercise. In subsequent examples, we demonstrate how to add functionality to many of these web controls.]

Before discussing the web controls used in this ASPX file, we explain the XHTML that creates the layout seen in Fig. 21.17. The page contains an `h3` heading element (line 28), followed by a series of additional XHTML blocks. We place most of the web controls inside `p` elements (i.e., paragraphs), but we use an XHTML `table` element (lines 37–67) to organize the `Image` and `TextBox` controls in the user-information section of the page. In the preceding section, we described how to add heading elements and paragraphs visually without manipulating any XHTML in the ASPX file directly. Visual Web Developer allows you to add a table in a similar manner.

```
<%-- Fig. 21.17: WebControls.aspx --%>
<%-- Registration form that demonstrates web controls. --%>
<%@ Page Language="VB" AutoEventWireup="false"
   CodeFile="WebControls.aspx.vb" Inherits="WebControls" %>

<!DOCTYPE html PUBLIC "-//W3C//DTD XHTML 1.0 Transitional//EN"
   "http://www.w3.org/TR/xhtml1/DTD/xhtml1-transitional.dtd">

<html xmlns="http://www.w3.org/1999/xhtml">
<head runat="server">
     <title>Web Controls Demonstration</title>
     <style type="text/css">
        .style1
        {
           width: 230px;
           height: 21px;
        }
        .style2
        {
           width: 231px;
           height: 21px;
        }
     </style>
</head>
<body>
   <form id="form1" runat="server">
   <div>
      <h3>This is a sample registration form.</h3>
      <p>
         <em>Please fill in all fields and click Register.</em></p>
      <p>
         <asp:Image ID="userInformationImage" runat="server"
            EnableViewState="False" ImageUrl="~/Images/user.png" />  
         <span style="color: teal">
            Please fill out the fields below.</span>
      </p>
      <table id="TABLE1">
         <tr>
            <td valign="top" class="style1">
               <asp:Image ID="firstNameImage" runat="server"
                  EnableViewState="False" ImageUrl="~/Images/fname.png" />
               <asp:TextBox ID="firstNameTextBox" runat="server"
                  EnableViewState="False"></asp:TextBox>
            </td>
            <td valign="top" class="style1">
               <asp:Image ID="lastNameImage" runat="server"
                  EnableViewState="False" ImageUrl="~/Images/lname.png" />
               <asp:TextBox ID="lastNameTextBox" runat="server"
                  EnableViewState="False"></asp:TextBox>
            </td>
         </tr>
         <tr>
            <td style="width: 230px" valign="top">
```

Fig. 21.17 | Web Form that demonstrates web controls. (Part 1 of 3.)

```
               <asp:Image ID="emailImage" runat="server"
                  EnableViewState="False" ImageUrl="~/Images/email.png" />
               <asp:TextBox ID="emailTextBox" runat="server"
                  EnableViewState="False"></asp:TextBox>
            </td>
            <td style="width: 231px" valign="top">
               <asp:Image ID="phoneImage" runat="server"
                  EnableViewState="False" ImageUrl="~/Images/phone.png" />
               <asp:TextBox ID="phoneTextBox" runat="server"
                  EnableViewState="False"></asp:TextBox>
               Must be in the form (555) 555-5555.
            </td>
         </tr>
      </table>
      <p>
         <asp:Image ID="publicationsImage" runat="server"
            EnableViewState="False"
            ImageUrl="~/Images/publications.png" />  
         <span style="color: teal">
            Which book would you like information about?</span>
      </p>
      <p>
         <asp:DropDownList ID="booksDropDownList" runat="server"
            EnableViewState="False">
            <asp:ListItem>Visual Basic 2008 How to Program</asp:ListItem>
            <asp:ListItem>Visual C# 2008 How to Program</asp:ListItem>
            <asp:ListItem>Java How to Program 6e</asp:ListItem>
            <asp:ListItem>C++ How to Program 5e</asp:ListItem>
            <asp:ListItem>C How to Program 5e</asp:ListItem>
            <asp:ListItem>Internet and World Wide Web How to Program 4e
               </asp:ListItem>
         </asp:DropDownList>
      </p>
      <p>
         <asp:HyperLink ID="booksHyperLink" runat="server"
            EnableViewState="False" NavigateUrl="http://www.deitel.com"
            Target="_blank">
            Click here to view more information about our books
         </asp:HyperLink>
      </p>
      <p>
         <asp:Image ID="osImage" runat="server" EnableViewState="False"
            ImageUrl="~/Images/os.png" />  
         <span style="color: teal">
            Which operating system are you using?</span>
      </p>
      <p>
         <asp:RadioButtonList ID="operatingSystemRadioButtonList"
            runat="server" EnableViewState="False">
            <asp:ListItem>Windows Vista</asp:ListItem>
            <asp:ListItem>Windows XP</asp:ListItem>
            <asp:ListItem>Mac OS X</asp:ListItem>
            <asp:ListItem>Linux</asp:ListItem>
```

Fig. 21.17 | Web Form that demonstrates web controls. (Part 2 of 3.)

```
                <asp:ListItem>Other</asp:ListItem>
            </asp:RadioButtonList>
        </p>
        <p>
            <asp:Button ID="registerButton" runat="server"
                EnableViewState="False" Text="Register" />
        </p>
    </div>
    </form>
</body>
</html>
```

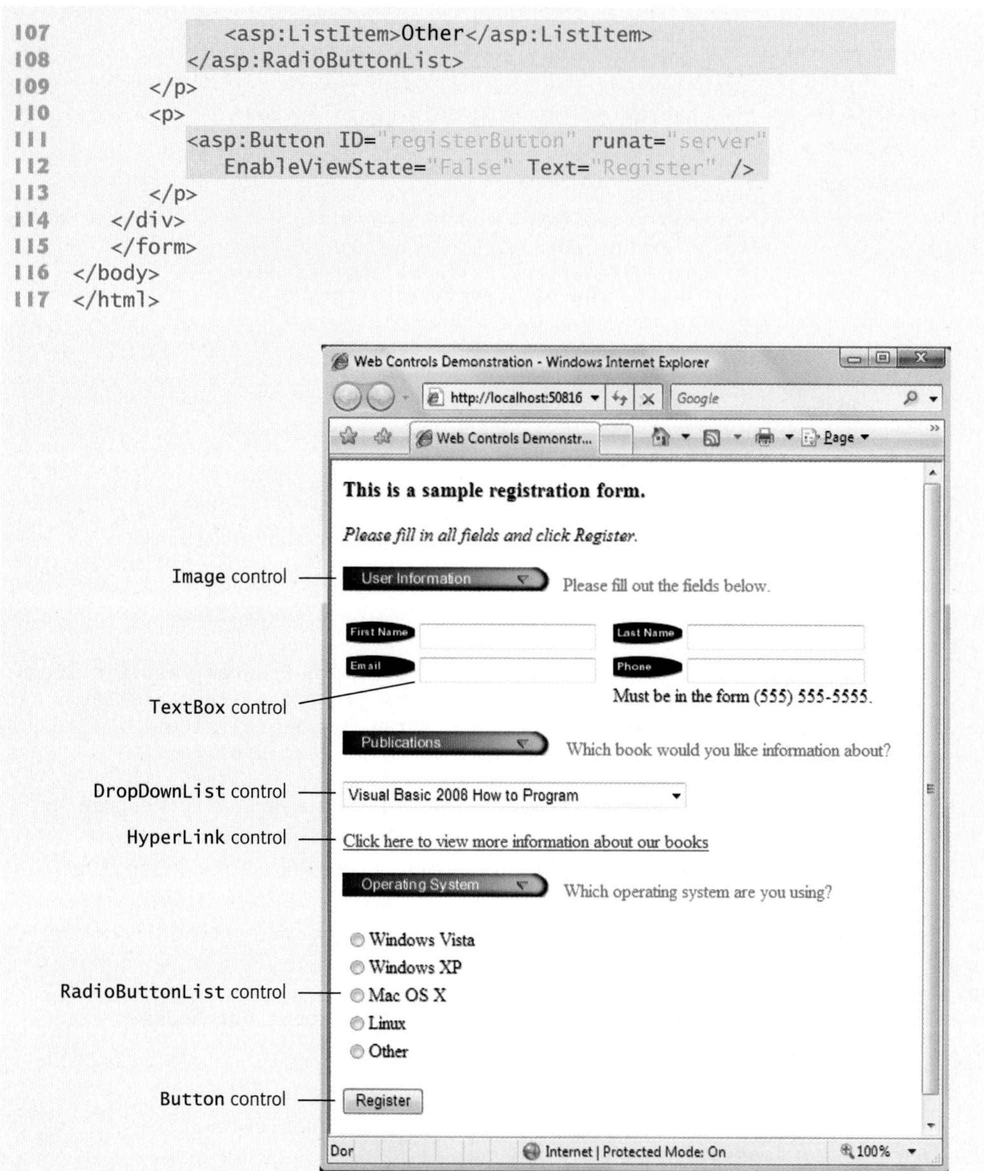

Fig. 21.17 | Web Form that demonstrates web controls. (Part 3 of 3.)

Adding an XHTML Table to a Web Form

To create a table with two rows and two columns in **Design** mode, select the **Insert Table** command from the **Table** menu to display the **Insert Table** dialog (Fig. 21.18). In the **Size** group box, change the values of **Rows** and **Columns** to 2. Click **OK** to close the **Insert Table** dialog and create the table. By default, the contents of a table cell are aligned vertically in the middle of the cell. We changed the vertical alignment of all cells in the table (i.e., `td` elements by setting the `valign` property to `top` in the **Properties** window. This causes the content of each table cell to align with the top of the cell. Once a table is created, controls and text can be added to particular cells to create a neatly organized layout. Alternatively, you can drag and drop a `Table` (in the **HTML** tab) onto the form and edit it in **Design mode** and the **Properties** window.

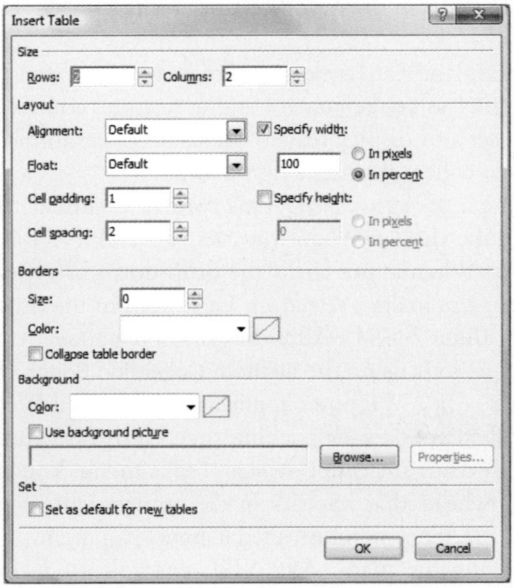

Fig. 21.18 | **Insert Table** dialog.

Setting the Color of Text on a Web Form

Notice that some of the instructions to the user on the form appear in a teal color. To set the color of a specific piece of text, highlight the text and select **Format > Font...**. In the **Font** dialog that appears, you can choose a color from the ones provided in the drop-down menu or click **More Colors...**. This displays the **More Colors** dialog, which offers a greater selection of colors and allows you to specify a custom color by clicking the **Colors...** button. Note that the IDE places the colored text in an XHTML `span` element (e.g., lines 34–35) and applies the color using CSS styling. We explain CSS styling of Web content at the end of this section.

Examining Web Controls on a Sample Registration Form

Lines 32–33 of Fig. 21.17 define an `Image` control, which inserts an image into a web page. The images used in this example are located in the chapter's examples directory. You can download the examples from `www.deitel.com/books/vb2008htp`. Before an image can be displayed on a web page using an `Image` web control, the image must first be added to the project. We added an `Images` folder to this project by right clicking the location of the project in the **Solution Explorer**, selecting **New Folder** and entering the folder name `Images`. We then added each of the images used in the example to this folder by right clicking the folder, selecting **Add Existing Item...** and browsing for the files to add. You can also drag a folder full of images onto the project's location in the **Solution Explorer** to add the folder and all the images to the project.

The **ImageUrl** property (line 33) specifies the location of the image to display in the Image control. To select an image, click the ellipsis next to the ImageUrl property in the **Properties** window and use the **Select Image** dialog to browse for the desired image in the project's Images folder. When the IDE fills in the ImageUrl property based on your selection, it includes a tilde and forward slash (~/) at the beginning of the ImageUrl—this indicates that the Images folder is in the root directory of the project. This syntax can be used only in server controls.

Lines 37–67 contain the table element created by the steps discussed previously. Each td element contains an Image control and a **TextBox** control, which allows you to obtain text from the user and display text to the user. For example, lines 42–43 define a TextBox control used to collect the user's first name.

Lines 76–85 define a **DropDownList**. This control is similar to the Windows Forms ComboBox control. Unlike the ComboBox however, an ASP.NET DropDownList doesn't allow users to type text. When a user clicks the drop-down list, it expands and displays a list from which the user can make a selection. Each item in the drop-down list is defined by a **ListItem** element (lines 78–84). After dragging a DropDownList control onto a Web Form, you can add items to it using the **ListItem Collection Editor**. This process is similar to customizing a ListBox in a Windows application. In Visual Web Developer, you can access the **ListItem Collection Editor** by clicking the ellipsis next to the Items property of the DropDownList, or by using the **DropDownList Tasks** menu. You can open this menu by clicking the small arrowhead that appears in the upper-right corner of the control in **Design** mode (Fig. 21.19). This menu is called a **smart-tag menu**. Visual Web Developer displays smart-tag menus for many ASP.NET controls to facilitate common tasks. Clicking **Edit Items...** in the **DropDownList Tasks** menu opens the **ListItem Collection Editor**, which allows you to add ListItem elements to the DropDownList.

The **HyperLink** control (lines 88–92 of Fig. 21.17) adds a hyperlink to a web page. The **NavigateUrl** property (line 89) of this control specifies the resource (i.e., http://www.deitel.com) that is requested when a user clicks the hyperlink. Setting the **Target** property to _blank specifies that the requested web page should open in a new browser window. By default, HyperLink controls cause pages to open in the same browser window.

Lines 101–108 define a **RadioButtonList** control, which provides a series of radio buttons from which the user can select only one. Like options in a DropDownList, individual radio buttons are defined by ListItem elements. Note that, like the **DropDownList Tasks** smart-tag menu, the **RadioButtonList Tasks** smart-tag menu also provides an **Edit Items...** link to open the **ListItem Collection Editor.**

The final web control in Fig. 21.17 is a **Button** (lines 111–112). A Button web control represents a button that triggers an action when clicked. This control typically maps to an XHTML input element with attribute type set to "button". As stated earlier, clicking the **Register** button in this example does not do anything.

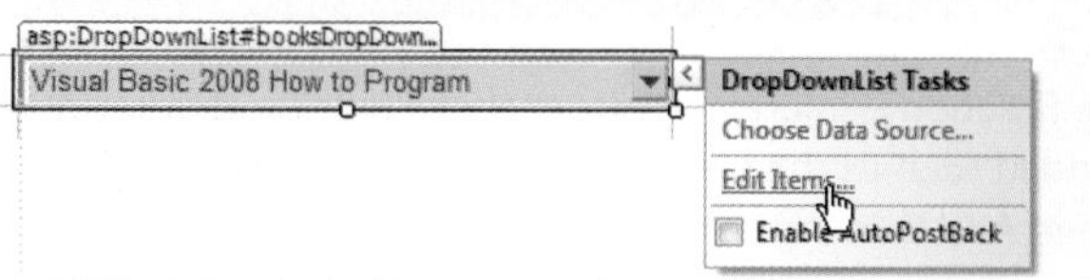

Fig. 21.19 | **DropDownList Tasks** smart-tag menu.

CSS Inline Styles and Embedded Style Sheets

When you style an XHTML element through the **Design** view, **Properties** window, or a wizard, Visual Web Developer often generates CSS (Cascading Style Sheets™) code to specify the presentation of the element. In the `head` element of your `.aspx` file, the `style` element defines embedded style sheets (lines 12–23). The `style` element's `type` attribute specifes the MIME type of its content. The body of the style sheet declares CSS rules (styles), each of which is composed of a CSS selector and a series of property specifications separated by semicolons and (`;`) and enclosed in curly braces (`{}`). Each specification is composed of a property followed by a colon and a value (lines 15, 16, 20, and 21). When you use one of the visual programming tools to define an XHTML element's appearance, Visual Web Developer sometimes creates a style class, which can be used as a selector by prefixing it with a period (lines 13 and 18). The style class can then be applied to any element in the document by setting the XHTML attribute `class` (lines 39 and 45).

Another way to apply styles is to use inline styles, which are composed of a series of property specifications separated by semicolons. Inline styles declare an individual element's format using the XHTML attribute `style`. These are interchangeable with embedded style sheets, and Visual Web Developer generates a mixture of both. You can also write your own CSS code in **Source** mode. For more information on CSS, please visit our CSS Resource Center at `www.deitel.com/CSS21/`.

21.5.2 AdRotator Control

Web pages often contain product or service advertisements, which usually consist of images. Although website authors want to include as many sponsors as possible, web pages can display only a limited number of advertisements. To address this problem, ASP.NET provides the `AdRotator` web control for displaying advertisements. Using advertisement data located in an XML file, an `AdRotator` randomly selects an image to display and generates a hyperlink to the web page associated with that image. Browsers that do not support images display alternate text that is specified in the XML document. If a user clicks the image or substituted text, the browser loads the web page associated with that image.

Demonstrating the `AdRotator` *Web Control*

Figure 21.20 demonstrates the `AdRotator` web control. In this example, the "advertisements" that we rotate are the flags of 10 countries. When a user clicks the displayed flag image, the browser is redirected to a web page containing information about the country that the flag represents. If a user refreshes the browser or requests the page again, one of the eleven flags is again chosen at random and displayed.

```
<%-- Fig. 21.20: FlagRotator.aspx --%>
<%-- A Web Form that displays flags using an AdRotator control. --%>
<%@ Page Language="VB" AutoEventWireup="false"
   CodeFile="FlagRotator.aspx.vb" Inherits="FlagRotator" %>

<!DOCTYPE html PUBLIC "-//W3C//DTD XHTML 1.0 Transitional//EN"
   "http://www.w3.org/TR/xhtml1/DTD/xhtml1-transitional.dtd">

```

Fig. 21.20 | Web Form that demonstrates the `AdRotator` web control. (Part 1 of 2.)

```
 9  <html xmlns="http://www.w3.org/1999/xhtml" >
10  <head runat="server">
11      <title>Flag Rotator</title>
12  </head>
13  <body background="Images/background.png">
14      <form id="form1" runat="server">
15      <div>
16          <h3>AdRotator Example</h3>
17          <p>
18              <asp:AdRotator ID="countryRotator" runat="server"
19                 DataSourceID="adXmlDataSource" />
20              <asp:XmlDataSource ID="adXmlDataSource" runat="server"
21                 DataFile="~/App_Data/AdRotatorInformation.xml">
22              </asp:XmlDataSource>
23          </p>
24      </div>
25      </form>
26  </body>
27  </html>
```

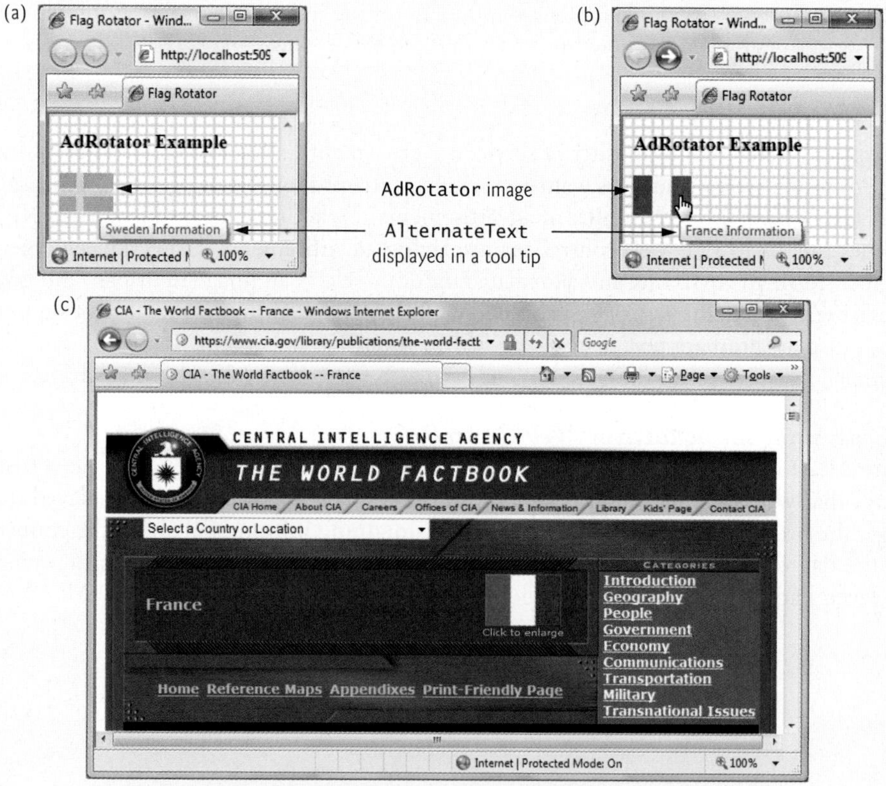

(a) (b)

AdRotator image

AlternateText displayed in a tool tip

(c)

Fig. 21.20 | Web Form that demonstrates the `AdRotator` web control. (Part 2 of 2.)

The ASPX file in Fig. 21.20 is similar to that in Fig. 21.4. However, instead of XHTML text and a `Label`, this page contains XHTML text (the `h3` element in line 16) and an `AdRotator` control named `countryRotator` (lines 18–19). This page also contains an `XmlDataSource` control (lines 20–22), which supplies the data to the `AdRotator` control. The `background` attribute of the page's `body` element (line 13) is set to the image `background.png`, located in the project's `Images` folder. To specify this file, click the ellipsis provided next to the `Background` property of `DOCUMENT` in the **Properties** window and use the resulting dialog to select `background.png` from the `Images` folder. The images and XML file used in this example are both located in the chapter's examples directory.

You do not need to add any code to the code-behind file, because the `AdRotator` control "does all the work." The output depicts two different requests. Figure 21.20(a) shows the first time the page is requested, when the Swedish flag is displayed. In the second request, as shown in Fig. 21.20(b), the French flag is displayed. Figure 21.20(c) depicts the web page that loads when you click the French flag.

Connecting Data to an **`AdRotator`** *Control*

An `AdRotator` control accesses an XML file to determine what advertisement (i.e., flag) image, hyperlink URL and alternate text to display and include in the page. To connect the `AdRotator` control to the XML file, we create an `XmlDataSource` control—one of several ASP.NET data controls (found in the **Data** section of the **Toolbox**) that encapsulate data sources and make such data available for web controls. An `XmlDataSource` references an XML file containing data that will be used in an ASP.NET application. Later in the chapter, you'll learn more about data-bound web controls, as well as the `LinqDataSource` control, which retrieves data from a LINQ data context.

To build this example, we first add the XML file `AdRotatorInformation.xml` to the project. Each project created in Visual Web Developer contains an `App_Data` folder, which is intended to store all the data used by the project. Right click this folder in the **Solution Explorer** and select **Add Existing Item...**, then browse for `AdRotatorInformation.xml` in this chapter's examples folder. We provide this file in the chapter's examples directory in the subdirectory named `exampleXMLFiles`.

After adding the XML file to the project, drag an `AdRotator` control from the **Toolbox** to the Web Form. The **AdRotator Tasks** smart-tag menu opens automatically. From this menu, select **<New Data Source...>** from the **Choose Data Source** drop-down list to start the **Data Source Configuration Wizard**. Select **XML File** as the data-source type. This causes the wizard to create an `XmlDataSource` with the `ID` specified in the bottom half of the wizard dialog. We set the `ID` of the control to `adXmlDataSource`. Click **OK** in the **Data Source Configuration Wizard** dialog. The **Configure Data Source - adXmlDataSource** dialog appears next. In this dialog's **Data File** section, click **Browse...** and, in the **Select XML File** dialog, locate and select the XML file you added to the `App_Data` folder. Click **OK** to exit this dialog, then click **OK** to exit the **Configure Data Source - adXmlDataSource** dialog. After completing these steps, the `AdRotator` is configured to use the XML file to determine which advertisements to display.

Examining an XML File Containing Advertisement Information

XML document `AdRotatorInformation.xml`—or any XML document used with an `AdRotator` control—must contain one **`Advertisements`** root element. Within that element can be as many **`Ad`** elements as you need. Each `Ad` element is similar to the following:

```
<Ad>
   <ImageUrl>Images/france.png</ImageUrl>
   <NavigateUrl>https://www.cia.gov/library/publications/
      the-world-factbook/geos/fr.html</NavigateUrl>
   <AlternateText>France Information</AlternateText>
   <Impressions>1</Impressions>
</Ad>
```

and provides information about an advertisement. Element `ImageUrl` specifies the path (location) of the advertisement's image, and element `NavigateUrl` specifies the URL for the web page that loads when a user clicks the advertisement. Note that we reformatted this `NavigateUrl` element above for presentation purposes. The actual XML file cannot contain any whitespace before or after the URL in the `NavigateUrl` element, or the whitespace will be considered part of the URL, and the page will not load properly.

The `AlternateText` element nested in each `Ad` element contains text that displays in place of the image when the browser cannot locate or render the image for some reason (i.e., the file is missing, or the browser is not capable of displaying it), or to assist the visually impaired. The `AlternateText` element's text is also a tool tip that Internet Explorer displays when a user places the mouse pointer over the image (Fig. 21.20). The `Impressions` element specifies how often a particular image appears, relative to the other images. An advertisement that has a higher `Impressions` value displays more frequently than an advertisement with a lower value. In our example, the advertisements display with equal probability, because the value of each `Impressions` element is set to `1`.

The advertisement XML file can also include other elements. For more information, please see, `msdn.microsoft.com/en-us/library/system.web.ui.webcontrols.adrotator.advertisementfile.aspx`.

21.5.3 Validation Controls

This section introduces a different type of web control, called a **validation control** (or **validator**), which determines whether the data in another web control is in the proper format. For example, validators could determine whether a user has provided information in a required field or whether a zip-code field contains exactly five digits. Validators provide a mechanism for validating user input on the client. When the XHTML for our page is created, the validator is converted into **JavaScript** that performs the validation. JavaScript is a scripting language that enhances the functionality and appearance of web pages and is typically executed on the client. However, some clients do not support scripting or disable scripting, and so validation must be performed on the server. ASP.NET validation controls can function on the client, on the server or both.

Validating Input in a Web Form

The example in this section prompts the user to enter a name, e-mail address and phone number. A website could use a form like this to collect contact information from site visitors. After the user enters any data, but before the data is sent to the web server, validators ensure that the user entered a value in each field and that the e-mail address and phone-number values are in an acceptable format. In this example, (555) 123-4567, 555-123-4567 and 123-4567 are all considered valid phone numbers. Once the data is submitted, the web server responds by displaying an appropriate message and an XHTML table repeating the submitted information. Note that a real business application would typically store the submitted data in a database or in a file on the server. We simply send the data back to the form to demonstrate that the server received the data.

Figure 21.21 presents the ASPX file. Like the Web Form in Fig. 21.17, this Web Form uses a `table` to organize the page's contents. Lines 24–25, 36–37 and 58–59 define `TextBoxes` for retrieving the user's name, e-mail address and phone number, respectively, and line 78 defines a **Submit** button. Lines 80–82 create a `Label` named `outputLabel` that displays the response from the server when the user successfully submits the form. Notice that `outputLabel`'s `Visible` property is initially set to `False` (line 81), so the `Label` does not appear in the client's browser when the page loads for the first time.

Using `RequiredFieldValidator` Controls

In this example, we use three `RequiredFieldValidator` controls (found in the **Validation** section of the **Toolbox**) to ensure that the name, e-mail address and phone number `TextBoxes` are not empty when the form is submitted. A `RequiredFieldValidator` makes an input control a required field. If such a field is empty, validation fails. For example, lines

```
1  <%-- Fig. 21.21: Validation.aspx --%>
2  <%-- Form that demonstrates using validators to validate user input. --%>
3  <%@ Page Language="VB" AutoEventWireup="false"
4     CodeFile="Validation.aspx.vb" Inherits="Validation" %>
5
6  <!DOCTYPE html PUBLIC "-//W3C//DTD XHTML 1.0 Transitional//EN"
7     "http://www.w3.org/TR/xhtml1/DTD/xhtml1-transitional.dtd">
8
9  <html xmlns="http://www.w3.org/1999/xhtml" >
10 <head runat="server">
11     <title>Demonstrating Validation Controls</title>
12 </head>
13 <body>
14    <form id="form1" runat="server">
15    <div>
16       Please fill out the following form.<br /><em>All fields are
17       required and must contain valid information.</em><br />
18       <br />
19       <table>
20          <tr>
21             <td style="width: 100px" valign="top">
22                Name:</td>
23             <td style="width: 450px" valign="top">
24                <asp:TextBox ID="nameTextBox" runat="server">
25                </asp:TextBox><br />
26                <asp:RequiredFieldValidator
27                   ID="nameInputValidator" runat="server"
28                   ControlToValidate="nameTextBox" Display="Dynamic"
29                   ErrorMessage="Please enter your name.">
30                </asp:RequiredFieldValidator>
31             </td>
32          </tr>
33          <tr>
34             <td style="width: 100px" valign="top">E-mail address:</td>
```

Fig. 21.21 | Validators used in a Web Form that retrieves user contact information. (Part 1 of 4.)

```
            <td style="width: 450px" valign="top">
               <asp:TextBox ID="emailTextBox" runat="server">
               </asp:TextBox>
                e.g., user@domain.com<br />
               <asp:RequiredFieldValidator
                  ID="emailInputValidator" runat="server"
                  ControlToValidate="emailTextBox" Display="Dynamic"
                  ErrorMessage="Please enter your e-mail address.">
               </asp:RequiredFieldValidator>
               <asp:RegularExpressionValidator
                  ID="emailFormatValidator" runat="server"
                  ControlToValidate="emailTextBox" Display="Dynamic"
                  ErrorMessage=
                     "Please enter an e-mail address in a valid format."
                  ValidationExpression=
                     "\w+([-+.']\w+)*@\w+([-.]\w+)*\.\w+([-.]\w+)*">
               </asp:RegularExpressionValidator>
            </td>
         </tr>
         <tr>
            <td style="width: 100px; height: 21px" valign="top">
               Phone number:</td>
            <td style="width: 450px; height: 21px" valign="top">
               <asp:TextBox ID="phoneTextBox" runat="server">
               </asp:TextBox>
                e.g., (555) 555-1234<br />
               <asp:RequiredFieldValidator
                  ID="phoneInputValidator" runat="server"
                  ControlToValidate="phoneTextBox" Display="Dynamic"
                  ErrorMessage="Please enter your phone number.">
               </asp:RequiredFieldValidator>
               <asp:RegularExpressionValidator
                  ID="phoneFormatValidator" runat="server"
                  ControlToValidate="phoneTextBox" Display="Dynamic"
                  ErrorMessage=
                     "Please enter a phone number in a valid format."
                  ValidationExpression=
                     "((\(\d{3}\) ?)|(\d{3}-))?\d{3}-\d{4}">
               </asp:RegularExpressionValidator>
            </td>
         </tr>
      </table>
      <br />
      <asp:Button ID="submitButton" runat="server" Text="Submit" /><br />
      <br />
      <asp:Label ID="outputLabel" runat="server"
         Text="Thank you for your submission." Visible="False">
      </asp:Label>
   </div>
   </form>
</body>
</html>
```

Fig. 21.21 | Validators used in a Web Form that retrieves user contact information. (Part 2 of 4.)

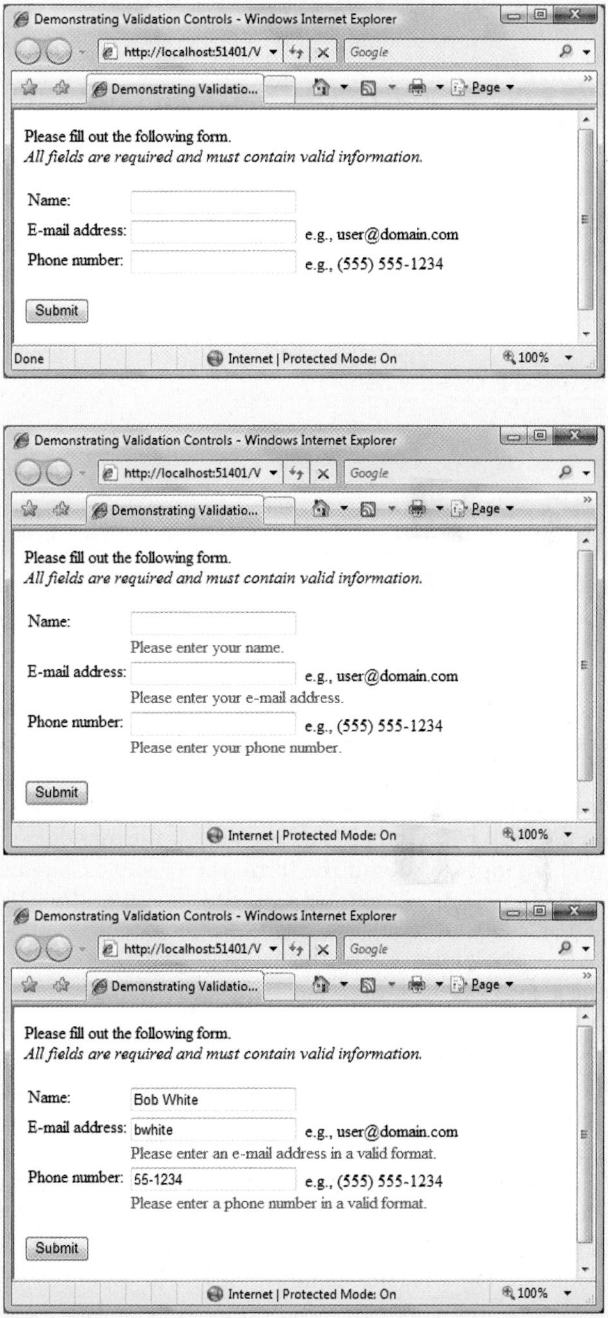

(a)

(b)

(c)

Fig. 21.21 | Validators used in a Web Form that retrieves user contact information. (Part 3 of 4.)

(d)

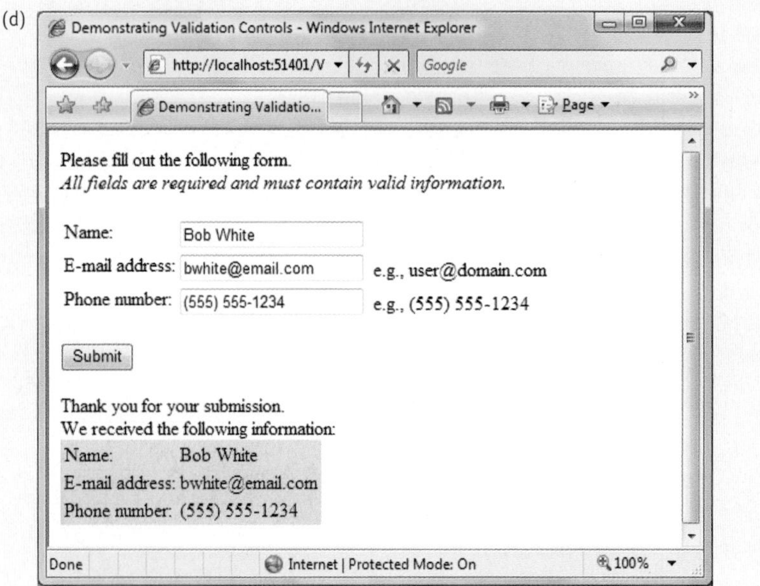

Fig. 21.21 | Validators used in a Web Form that retrieves user contact information. (Part 4 of 4.)

26–30 define `RequiredFieldValidator nameInputValidator`, which makes sure that `nameTextBox` is not empty. Line 28 associates `nameTextBox` with `nameInputValidator` by setting the validator's **`ControlToValidate`** property to `nameTextBox`. This indicates that `nameInputValidator` verifies the `nameTextBox`'s contents. We set the value of this property (and the validator's other properties) by selecting the validator in **Design** mode and using the **Properties** window to specify property values. Property **`ErrorMessage`**'s text (line 29) is displayed on the Web Form if the validation fails. If the user does not input any data in `nameTextBox` and attempts to submit the form, the `ErrorMessage` text is displayed in red. Because we set the validator's **`Display`** property to `Dynamic` (line 28), the validator is displayed on the Web Form only when validation fails. Space is allocated dynamically when validation fails, causing the controls below the validator to shift downward to accommodate the `ErrorMessage`, as seen in Fig. 21.21(a)–(b).

Using `RegularExpressionValidator` *Controls*

This example also uses **`RegularExpressionValidator`** controls to match the e-mail address and phone number entered by the user against regular expressions. (Regular expressions were introduced in Chapter 17.) These controls determine whether the e-mail address and phone number were each entered in a valid format. For example, lines 44–51 create a `RegularExpressionValidator` named `emailFormatValidator`. Line 46 sets property `ControlToValidate` to `emailTextBox` to indicate that `emailFormatValidator` verifies the `emailTextBox`'s contents. Fig. 21.21(c) demonstrates their responses when there is an error.

A `RegularExpressionValidator`'s **`ValidationExpression`** property specifies the regular expression that validates the `ControlToValidate`'s contents. Clicking the ellipsis next to property `ValidationExpression` in the **Properties** window displays the **Regular Expres-**

sion Editor dialog, which contains a list of **Standard expressions** for phone numbers, zip codes and other formatted information. You can also write your own custom expression. For the `emailFormatValidator`, we selected the standard expression **Internet e-mail address**, which uses the validation expression

```
\w+([-+.']\w+)*@\w+([-.]\w+)*\.\w+([-.]\w+)*
```

This regular expression indicates that an e-mail address is valid if the part of the address before the `@` symbol contains one or more word characters (i.e., alphanumeric characters or underscores), followed by zero or more strings comprised of a hyphen, plus sign, period or apostrophe and additional word characters. After the `@` symbol, a valid e-mail address must contain one or more groups of word characters potentially separated by hyphens or periods, followed by a required period and another group of one or more word characters potentially separated by hyphens or periods. For example, `bob.white@email.com`, `bob-white@my-email.com` and `bob's-personal.email@white.email.com` are all valid e-mail addresses. If the user enters text in the `emailTextBox` that does not have the correct format and either clicks in a different text box or attempts to submit the form, the `ErrorMessage` text is displayed in red.

We also use `RegularExpressionValidator phoneFormatValidator` (lines 66–73) to ensure that the `phoneTextBox` contains a valid phone number before the form is submitted. In the **Regular Expression Editor** dialog, we select **U.S. phone number**, which assigns

```
((\(\d{3}\) ?)|(\d{3}-))?\d{3}-\d{4}
```

to the `ValidationExpression` property. This expression indicates that a phone number can contain a three-digit area code either in parentheses and followed by an optional space or without parentheses and followed by required hyphen. After an optional area code, a phone number must contain three digits, a hyphen and another four digits. For example, `(555) 123-4567`, `555-123-4567` and `123-4567` are all valid phone numbers.

If all five validators are successful (i.e., each `TextBox` is filled in, and the e-mail address and phone number provided are valid), clicking the **Submit** button sends the form's data to the server. As shown in Fig. 21.21(d), the server then responds by displaying the submitted data in the `outputLabel` (lines 80–82).

Examining the Code-Behind File for a Web Form That Receives User Input

Figure 21.22 depicts the code-behind file for the ASPX file in Fig. 21.21. Notice that this code-behind file does not contain any implementation related to the validators. We say more about this soon.

```
' Fig. 21.22: Validation.aspx.vb
' Code-behind file for the form demonstrating validation controls.
Partial Class Validation
   Inherits System.Web.UI.Page

   ' Page_Load event handler executes when the page is loaded
   Protected Sub Page_Load(ByVal sender As Object, _
      ByVal e As System.EventArgs) Handles Me.Load
```

Fig. 21.22 | Code-behind file for a Web Form that obtains a user's contact information. (Part 1 of 2.)

```
9            ' if this is not the first time the page is loading
10           ' (i.e., the user has already submitted form data)
11           If IsPostBack Then
12              Validate() ' validate the form
13
14              If IsValid Then
15                 ' retrieve the values submitted by the user
16                 Dim name As String = nameTextBox.Text
17                 Dim email As String = emailTextBox.Text
18                 Dim phone As String = phoneTextBox.Text
19
20                 ' create a table indicating the submitted values
21                 outputLabel.Text &= _
22                    "<br />We received the following information:" & _
23                    "<table style=""background-color: yellow"">" & _
24                    "<tr><td>Name: </td><td>" & name & "</td></tr>" & _
25                    "<tr><td>E-mail address: </td>" & _
26                    "<td>" & email & "</td></tr>" & _
27                    "<tr><td>Phone number: </td>" & _
28                    "<td>" & phone & "</td></tr>" & _
29                    "<table>"
30                 outputLabel.Visible = True ' display the output message
31              End If
32           End If
33        End Sub ' Page_Load
34     End Class ' Validation
```

Fig. 21.22 | Code-behind file for a Web Form that obtains a user's contact information. (Part 2 of 2.)

Web programmers using ASP.NET often design their web pages so that the current page reloads when the user submits the form; this enables the program to receive input, process it as necessary and display the results in the same page when it is loaded the second time. These pages usually contain a form that, when submitted, sends the values of all the controls to the server and causes the current page to be requested again. This event is known as a postback. Line 11 uses the `IsPostBack` property of class `Page` to determine whether the page is being loaded due to a postback. The first time that the web page is requested, `IsPostBack` is `False`, and the page displays only the form for user input. When the postback occurs (from the user clicking **Submit**), `IsPostBack` is `True`.

Server-side Web Form validation must be implemented programmatically. Line 12 calls the current `Page`'s `Validate` method to validate the information in the request. This validates the information as specified by the validation controls in the Web Form. Line 14 uses the `IsValid` property of class `Page` to check whether the validation succeeded. If this property is set to `True` (i.e., validation succeeded and the Web Form is valid), then we display the Web Form's information. Otherwise, the web page loads without any changes, except any validator that failed now displays its `ErrorMessage`.

Lines 16–18 retrieve the values of `nameTextBox`, `emailTextBox` and `phoneTextBox`. When data is posted to the web server, the XHTML form's data becomes accessible to the web application through the properties of the various web controls. Lines 21–29 append to `outputLabel`'s `Text` a line break, an additional message and an XHTML table containing the submitted data so the user knows that the server received the data correctly. In a real business application, the data would be stored in a database or file at this point in the application. Line 30 sets the `outputLabel`'s `Visible` property to `True`, so the user can see the thank-you message and submitted data.

Examining the Client-Side XHTML for a Web Form with Validation

If a validation control's `EnableClientScript` property is `True` (which it is by default), then the validator performs client-side validation as the user edits the Web Form. If you wish, you can view the XHTML and JavaScript sent to the client browser when `Validation.aspx` loads after the postback by selecting **View > Source** in Internet Explorer or **View > Page Source** in Firefox (other browsers have similar capabilities). As you look through the code, you'll see several `<script></script>` elements which define the client-side JavaScript code that performs the validation. You do not need to be able to create or even understand JavaScript—the functionality defined for the controls in our application is converted to working JavaScript by ASP.NET.

The `EnableViewState` attribute determines whether a web control's current state is remembered each time a postback occurs. Previously, we explicitly set this attribute to `False`. The default value, `True`, indicates that the control's state at the last postback is retained. A `hidden` input in the XHTML generated for the page contains this information. This element is always named `__VIEWSTATE` and stores the controls' data as an encoded string. This data allows the server to determine whether anything about the control, such as its value, has changed since the last postback. For example, to determine whether a `TextBox`'s `TextChanged` event should be raised on a postback, the server compares the control's current text to that specified by the `__VIEWSTATE`. If there's a difference, then the text has changed and the `TextChanged` event is raised.

Performance Tip 21.1

Setting `EnableViewState` to `False` reduces the amount of data passed to the web server with each request.

21.6 Session Tracking

Originally, critics accused the Internet and e-business of failing to provide the customized service typically experienced in "brick-and-mortar" stores. To address this problem, e-businesses began to establish mechanisms by which they could personalize users' browsing experiences, tailoring content to individual users while enabling them to bypass irrelevant information. Businesses achieve this level of service by tracking each customer's movement through the Internet and combining the collected data with information provided by the consumer, including billing information, personal preferences, interests and hobbies.

Personalization

Personalization makes it possible for e-businesses to communicate effectively with their customers and also improves users' ability to locate desired products and services. Companies that provide content of particular interest to users can establish relationships with customers and build on those relationships over time. Furthermore, by targeting consumers with personal offers, recommendations, advertisements, promotions and services, e-businesses create customer loyalty. Websites can use sophisticated technology to allow visitors to customize home pages to suit their individual needs and preferences. Similarly, online shopping sites often store personal information for customers, tailoring notifications and special offers to their interests. Such services encourage customers to visit sites more frequently and make purchases more regularly.

Privacy
A trade-off exists, however, between personalized e-business service and protection of privacy. Some consumers embrace the idea of tailored content, but others fear the possible adverse consequences if the info they provide to e-businesses is released or collected by tracking technologies. Consumers and privacy advocates ask: What if the e-business to which we give personal data sells or gives that information to another organization without our knowledge? What if we do not want our actions on the Internet—a supposedly anonymous medium—to be tracked and recorded by unknown parties? What if unauthorized parties gain access to sensitive private data, such as credit-card numbers or medical history? All of these are questions that must be debated and addressed by programmers, consumers, e-businesses and lawmakers alike.

Recognizing Clients
To provide personalized services to consumers, e-businesses must be able to recognize clients when they request information from a site. As we have discussed, the request/response system on which the web operates is facilitated by HTTP. Unfortunately, HTTP is a stateless protocol—it does not support persistent connections that would enable web servers to maintain state information regarding particular clients. This means that web servers cannot determine whether a request comes from a particular client or whether the same or different clients generate a series of requests. To circumvent this problem, sites can provide mechanisms by which they identify individual clients. A session represents a unique client on a website. If the client leaves a site and then returns later, the client will still be recognized as the same user. When the user closes the browser, the session ends. To help the server distinguish among clients, each client must identify itself to the server. Tracking individual clients, known as session tracking, can be achieved in a number of ways. One popular technique uses cookies (Section 21.6.1); another uses ASP.NET's `HttpSessionState` object (Section 21.6.2). Additional session-tracking techniques include the use of `input` `form` elements of type "`hidden`" and URL rewriting. Using "`hidden`" form elements, a Web Form can write session-tracking data into a `form` in the web page that it returns to the client in response to a prior request. When the user submits the form in the new web page, all the form data, including the "`hidden`" fields, is sent to the form handler on the web server. When a website performs URL rewriting, the Web Form embeds session-tracking information directly in the URLs of hyperlinks that the user clicks to send subsequent requests to the web server.

Note that in the `WebTime` example, we set the Web Form's `EnableSessionState` property to `False`. We could have also used this setting for each of the previous examples, since we didn't need to use session tracking in any of them. However, because we wish to use session tracking in the following examples, we *must* keep this property's default setting—`True`.

21.6.1 Cookies

Cookies provide web developers with a tool for personalizing web pages. A cookie is a piece of data stored in a small text file on the user's computer. A cookie maintains information about the client during and between browser sessions. The first time a user visits the website, the user's computer might receive a cookie; this cookie is then reactivated each time the user revisits that site. The collected information is intended to be an anonymous record containing data that is used to personalize the user's future visits to the site. For example, cookies in a shopping application might store unique identifiers for users. When a user adds items to an online shopping cart or performs another task resulting in a request to the web server, the server receives a cookie containing the user's unique identifier. The server then uses the unique identifier to locate the shopping cart and perform any necessary processing.

In addition to identifying users, cookies also can indicate users' shopping preferences. When a Web Form receives a request from a client, the Web Form can examine the cookie(s) it sent to the client during previous communications, identify the users's preferences and immediately display products of interest to the client.

Every HTTP-based interaction between a client and a server includes a header containing information either about the request (when the communication is from the client to the server) or about the response (when the communication is from the server to the client). When a Web Form receives a request, the header includes information such as the request type (e.g., `get`) and any cookies that have been sent previously from the server to be stored on the client machine. When the server formulates its response, the header information contains any cookies the server wants to store on the client computer and other information, such as the MIME type of the response.

The **expiration date** of a cookie determines how long the cookie remains on the client's computer. If you do not set an expiration date for a cookie, the web browser maintains the cookie for the duration of the browsing session. Otherwise, the web browser maintains the cookie until the expiration date occurs. When the browser requests a resource from a web server, cookies previously sent to the client by that web server are returned to the web server as part of the request formulated by the browser. Cookies are deleted when they **expire**.

Portability Tip 21.3

Users may disable cookies in their web browsers help ensure their privacy. Such users will experience difficulty using web applications that depend on cookies to maintain state information.

Using Cookies to Provide Book Recommendations

The next web application demonstrates the use of cookies. The example contains two pages. In the first page (Figs. 21.23–21.24), users select a favorite programming language from a group of radio buttons and submit the XHTML form to the web server for processing. The web server responds by creating a cookie that stores a record of the chosen language, as well as the ISBN number for a book on that topic. The server then returns an XHTML document to the browser, allowing the user either to select another favorite programming language or to view the second page in our application (Figs. 21.25 and 21.26), which lists recommended books pertaining to the programming language that the user selected previously. When the user clicks the hyperlink, the cookies previously stored on the client are read and used to form the list of book recommendations.

The ASPX file in Fig. 21.23 contains five radio buttons (lines 20–26) with the values **Visual Basic 2008**, **Visual C# 2008**, **C**, **C++**, and **Java**. Recall that you can set the values of radio buttons via the **ListItem Collection Editor**, which you open either by clicking the `RadioButtonList`'s `Items` property in the **Properties** window or by clicking the **Edit**

Items... link in the **RadioButtonList Tasks** smart tag menu. The user selects a programming language by clicking one of the radio buttons. When the user clicks **Submit**, we'll create a cookie containing the selected language. Then we'll add this cookie to the HTTP response header, so the cookie will be stored on the user's computer. Each time the user chooses a language and clicks **Submit**, a cookie is written to the client. Each time the client requests information from our web application, the cookies are sent back to the server.

```
<%-- Fig. 21.23: Options.aspx --%>
<%-- Allows client to select programming languages and access --%>
<%-- book recommendations. --%>
<%@ Page Language="VB" AutoEventWireup="false"
   CodeFile="Options.aspx.vb" Inherits="Options" %>

<!DOCTYPE html PUBLIC "-//W3C//DTD XHTML 1.0 Transitional//EN"
   "http://www.w3.org/TR/xhtml1/DTD/xhtml1-transitional.dtd">

<html xmlns="http://www.w3.org/1999/xhtml" >
<head runat="server">
    <title>Cookies</title>
</head>
<body>
   <form id="form1" runat="server">
   <div>
      <asp:Label ID="promptLabel" runat="server" Font-Bold="True"
         Font-Size="Large" Text="Select a programming language:">
      </asp:Label>
      <asp:RadioButtonList ID="languageList" runat="server">
         <asp:ListItem>Visual Basic 2008</asp:ListItem>
         <asp:ListItem>Visual C# 2008</asp:ListItem>
         <asp:ListItem>C</asp:ListItem>
         <asp:ListItem>C++</asp:ListItem>
         <asp:ListItem>Java</asp:ListItem>
      </asp:RadioButtonList>
      <asp:Button ID="submitButton" runat="server" Text="Submit" />
      <asp:Label ID="responseLabel" runat="server" Font-Bold="True"
         Font-Size="Large" Text="Welcome to cookies!" Visible="False">
      </asp:Label><br />
      <br />
      <asp:HyperLink ID="languageLink" runat="server"
         NavigateUrl="~/Options.aspx" Visible="False">
         Click here to choose another language
      </asp:HyperLink><br />
      <br />
      <asp:HyperLink ID="recommendationsLink" runat="server"
         NavigateUrl="~/Recommendations.aspx" Visible="False">
         Click here to get book recommendations
      </asp:HyperLink>
   </div>
   </form>
</body>
</html>
```

Fig. 21.23 | ASPX file that presents a list of programming languages. (Part 1 of 2.)

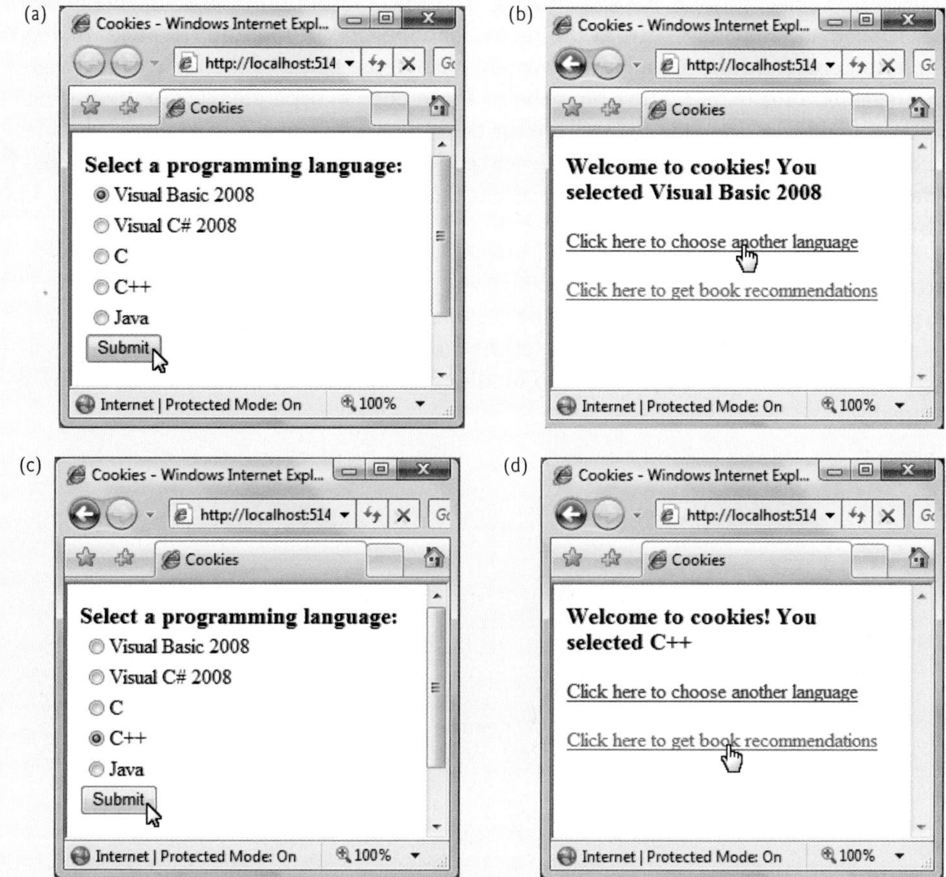

Fig. 21.23 | ASPX file that presents a list of programming languages. (Part 2 of 2.)

When the postback occurs, certain controls are hidden and others are displayed. The `Label`, `RadioButtonList` and `Button` used to select a language are hidden. Toward the bottom of the page, a `Label` and two `HyperLinks` are displayed. One link requests this page (lines 32–35), and the other requests `Recommendations.aspx` (lines 37–40). Clicking the first hyperlink (the one that requests the current page) does not cause a postback to occur. The file `Options.aspx` is specified in the `NavigateUrl` property of the hyperlink. When the hyperlink is clicked, a new request for this page occurs. Recall that earlier in the chapter, we set `NavigateUrl` to a remote website (`http://www.deitel.com`). To set this property to a page within the same ASP.NET application, click the ellipsis button next to the `NavigateUrl` property in the **Properties** window to open the **Select URL** dialog. Use this dialog to select a page within your project as the destination for the `HyperLink`.

Adding and Linking to a New Web Form

Setting the `NavigateUrl` property to a page in the current application requires that the destination page exist already. Thus, to set the `NavigateUrl` property of the second link (the one that requests the page with book recommendations) to `Recommendations.aspx`, you must first create this file by right clicking the project location in the **Solution Explorer** and selecting **Add New Item...** from the menu that appears. In the **Add New Item** dialog, select **Web Form** from the **Templates** pane and change the name of the file to `Recommendations.aspx`. Finally, check the box labeled **Place code in separate file** to indicate that the IDE should create a code-behind file for this ASPX file. Click **Add** to create the file. (We discuss the contents of this ASPX file and code-behind file shortly.) Once the `Recommendations.aspx` file exists, you can select it as the `NavigateUrl` value for a `HyperLink` in the **Select URL** dialog.

Writing Cookies in a Code-Behind File

Figure 21.24 presents the code-behind file for `Options.aspx` (Fig. 21.23). This file contains the code that writes a cookie to the client machine when the user selects a programming language. The code-behind file also modifies the appearance of the page in response to a postback.

```
' Fig. 21.24: Options.aspx.vb
' Processes user's selection of a programming language
' by displaying links and writing a cookie to the user's machine.
Partial Class Options
   Inherits System.Web.UI.Page
   ' stores values to represent books as cookies
   Private books As New Dictionary(Of String, String)

   ' initializes the Dictionary of values to be stored as cookies
   Protected Sub Page_Init(ByVal sender As Object, _
      ByVal e As System.EventArgs) Handles Me.Init
      books.Add("Visual Basic 2008", "0-13-605305-X")
      books.Add("Visual C# 2008", "0-13-605322-X")
      books.Add("C", "0-13-240416-8")
      books.Add("C++", "0-13-615250-3")
      books.Add("Java", "0-13-222220-5")
   End Sub ' Page_Init

   ' if postback, hide form and display links to make additional
   ' selections or view recommendations
   Protected Sub Page_Load(ByVal sender As Object, _
      ByVal e As System.EventArgs) Handles Me.Load

      If IsPostBack Then
         ' user has submitted information, so display message
         ' and appropriate hyperlinks
         responseLabel.Visible = True
         languageLink.Visible = True
         recommendationsLink.Visible = True

         ' hide other controls used to make language selection
         promptLabel.Visible = False
         languageList.Visible = False
         submitButton.Visible = False

```

Fig. 21.24 | Code-behind file that writes a cookie to the client. (Part 1 of 2.)

```
36             ' if the user made a selection, display it in responseLabel
37             If languageList.SelectedItem IsNot Nothing Then
38                responseLabel.Text &= " You selected " & _
39                   languageList.SelectedItem.Text
40             Else
41                responseLabel.Text &= " You did not select a language."
42             End If
43          End If
44       End Sub ' Page_Load
45 
46       ' write a cookie to record the user's selection
47       Protected Sub submitButton_Click(ByVal sender As Object, _
48          ByVal e As System.EventArgs) Handles submitButton.Click
49          ' if the user made a selection
50          If languageList.SelectedItem IsNot Nothing Then
51             Dim language As String = languageList.SelectedItem.Text
52 
53             ' get ISBN number of book for the given language
54             Dim ISBN As String = books(language)
55 
56             ' create cookie using language-ISBN name-value pair
57             Dim cookie As New HttpCookie(language, ISBN)
58 
59             ' add cookie to response to place it on the user's machine
60             Response.Cookies.Add(cookie)
61          End If
62       End Sub ' submitButton_Click
63    End Class ' Options
```

Fig. 21.24 | Code-behind file that writes a cookie to the client. (Part 2 of 2.)

Line 7 creates variable `books` as a **`Dictionary`**—a data structure that stores **key/value pairs**. A program uses the key to store and retrieve the associated value in the `Dictionary`. In this example, the keys are `String`s containing the programming languages' names, and the values are `String`s containing the ISBN numbers for the recommended books. Class `Dictionary` provides method **`Add`**, which takes as arguments a key and a value. A value that is added via method `Add` is placed in the `Dictionary` at a location determined by the key. The value for a specific `Dictionary` entry can be determined by indexing the `Dictionary` with that value's key. The expression

DictionaryName(*keyName*)

returns the value in the key/value pair in which *keyName* is the key. For example, the expression `books(language)` in line 54 returns the value that corresponds to the key contained in `language`. Class `Dictionary` is discussed in detail in Section 24.2.2.

Clicking the **Submit** button creates a cookie if a language is selected and causes a postback to occur. In the `submitButton_Click` event handler (lines 47–62), a new cookie object (of type **`HttpCookie`**) is created to store the `language` and its corresponding `ISBN` number (line 57). This cookie is then `Add`ed to the **`Cookies`** collection sent as part of the HTTP response header (line 60). The postback causes the condition in the `If` statement of `Page_Load` (line 24) to evaluate to `True`, and lines 27–42 execute. Lines 27–29 reveal the initially hidden controls `responseLabel`, `languageLink` and `recommendationsLink`.

Lines 32–34 hide the controls used to obtain the user's language selection. Line 37 determines whether the user selected a language. If so, that language is displayed in `responseLabel` (lines 38–39). Otherwise, text indicating that a language was not selected is displayed in `responseLabel` (line 41).

Displaying Book Recommendations Based on Cookie Values

After the postback of `Options.aspx`, the user may request a book recommendation. The book-recommendation hyperlink forwards the user to `Recommendations.aspx` (Fig. 21.25) to display the recommendations based on the user's language selections.

`Recommendations.aspx` contains a `Label` (lines 16–18), a `ListBox` (lines 20–21) and a `HyperLink` (lines 23–26). The `Label` displays the text **Recommendations** if the user selects one or more languages; otherwise, it displays **No Recommendations.** The `ListBox` displays the recommendations specified by the code-behind file (Fig. 21.26). The `HyperLink` allows the user to return to `Options.aspx` to select additional languages.

Code-Behind File That Creates Book Recommendations From Cookies

In Fig. 21.26, method `Page_Init` (lines 7–28) retrieves the cookies from the client, using the `Request` object's `Cookies` property (line 10). This returns a collection of type `HttpCookieCollection`, containing cookies that were previously written to the client. Cookies

```
1  <%-- Fig. 21.25: Recommendations.aspx --%>
2  <%-- Displays book recommendations using cookies. --%>
3  <%@ Page Language="VB" AutoEventWireup="false"
4     CodeFile="Recommendations.aspx.vb" Inherits="Recommendations" %>
5
6  <!DOCTYPE html PUBLIC "-//W3C//DTD XHTML 1.0 Transitional//EN"
7     "http://www.w3.org/TR/xhtml1/DTD/xhtml1-transitional.dtd">
8
9  <html xmlns="http://www.w3.org/1999/xhtml" >
10 <head runat="server">
11     <title>Book Recommendations</title>
12 </head>
13 <body>
14     <form id="form1" runat="server">
15     <div>
16         <asp:Label ID="recommendationsLabel" runat="server"
17            Font-Bold="True" Font-Size="X-Large" Text="Recommendations">
18         </asp:Label><br />
19         <br />
20         <asp:ListBox ID="booksListBox" runat="server" Height="125px"
21            Width="450px"></asp:ListBox><br />
22         <br />
23         <asp:HyperLink ID="languageLink" runat="server"
24            NavigateUrl="~/Options.aspx">
25            Click here to choose another language
26         </asp:HyperLink> </div>
27     </form>
28 </body>
29 </html>
```

Fig. 21.25 | ASPX file that displays book recommendations based on cookies. (Part 1 of 2.)

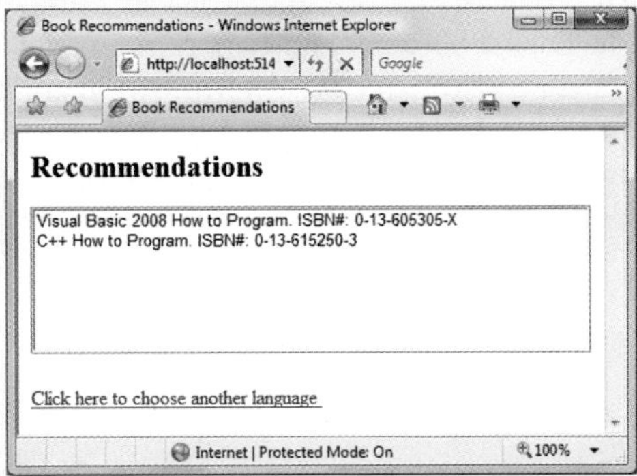

Fig. 21.25 | ASPX file that displays book recommendations based on cookies. (Part 2 of 2.)

```
' Fig. 21.26: Recommendations.aspx.vb
' Creates book recommendations based on cookies.
Partial Class Recommendations
   Inherits System.Web.UI.Page

   ' read cookies and populate ListBox with any book recommendations
   Protected Sub Page_Init(ByVal sender As Object, _
      ByVal e As System.EventArgs) Handles Me.Init
      ' retrieve client's cookies
      Dim cookies As HttpCookieCollection = Request.Cookies

      ' if there are cookies, list the appropriate books and ISBN numbers
      If cookies.Count <> 0 Then
         For i As Integer = 0 To cookies.Count - 1
            booksListBox.Items.Add(cookies(i).Name & _
               " How to Program. ISBN#: " & cookies(i).Value)
         Next
      Else
         ' if there are no cookies, then no language was chosen, so
         ' display appropriate message and clear and hide booksListBox
         recommendationsLabel.Text = "No Recommendations"
         booksListBox.Items.Clear()
         booksListBox.Visible = False

         ' modify languageLink because no language was selected
         languageLink.Text = "Click here to choose a language"
      End If
   End Sub ' Page_Init
End Class ' Recommendations
```

Fig. 21.26 | Reading cookies from a client to determine book recommendations.

can be read by an application only if they were created in the domain in which the application is running—a web server can never access cookies created outside its domain. For example, a cookie created by the `deitel.com` web server cannot be read by a web server in any other domain. [*Note:* Depending on the settings in `web.config` and whether other pages store cookies, other cookie values may be displayed by this web application.]

Line 13 determines whether at least one cookie exists. Lines 14–17 add the information in the cookie(s) to the booksListBox. The loop retrieves the name and value of each cookie using i, the loop's control variable, to determine the current value in the cookie collection. The Name and Value properties of class HttpCookie, which contain the language and corresponding ISBN, respectively, are concatenated with " How to Program. ISBN# " and added to the ListBox. Lines 21–26 execute if no language was selected. We summarize some commonly used HttpCookie properties in Fig. 21.27.

Properties	Description
Domain	Returns a String containing the cookie's domain (i.e., the domain of the web server running the application that wrote the cookie). This determines which web servers can receive the cookie. By default, cookies are sent to the web server that originally sent the cookie. Changing the Domain property causes the cookie to be returned to a web server other than the one that originally wrote it.
Expires	Returns a DateTime object indicating when the browser can delete the cookie. You can delete a cookie by setting this property to be a DateTime in the past.
Name	Returns a String containing the cookie's name.
Path	Returns a String containing the path to a directory on the server (i.e., the Domain) to which the cookie applies. Cookies can be "targeted" to specific directories on the web server. By default, a cookie is returned only to applications operating in the same directory as the application that sent the cookie or a subdirectory of that directory. Changing the Path property causes the cookie to be returned to a directory other than the one from which it was originally written.
Secure	Returns a Boolean value indicating whether the cookie should be transmitted through a secure protocol. The value True causes a secure protocol to be used.
Value	Returns a String containing the cookie's value.

Fig. 21.27 | HttpCookie properties.

21.6.2 Session Tracking with HttpSessionState

Session-tracking capabilities are provided by the .NET class HttpSessionState. To demonstrate basic session-tracking techniques, we modified the example of Figs. 21.23–21.26 to use HttpSessionState objects. Figures 21.28–21.29 present the ASPX file and code-behind file for Options.aspx. Figures 21.31–21.32 present the ASPX file and code-behind file for Recommendations.aspx. Options.aspx is similar to the version presented in Fig. 21.23, but Fig. 21.28 contains two additional Labels (lines 32–33 and lines 35–36), which we discuss shortly.

Every Web Form includes an HttpSessionState object, which is accessible through property Session of class Page. Throughout this section, we use property Session to manipulate our page's HttpSessionState object. When the web page is requested, an HttpSessionState object is created and assigned to the Page's Session property. As a result, we often refer to property Session as the Session object.

```
<%-- Fig. 21.28: Options.aspx --%>
<%-- Allows client to select programming languages and access --%>
<%-- book recommendations. --%>
<%@ Page Language="VB" AutoEventWireup="false"
   CodeFile="Options.aspx.vb" Inherits="Options" %>

<!DOCTYPE html PUBLIC "-//W3C//DTD XHTML 1.0 Transitional//EN"
   "http://www.w3.org/TR/xhtml1/DTD/xhtml1-transitional.dtd">

<html xmlns="http://www.w3.org/1999/xhtml" >
<head id="Head1" runat="server">
    <title>Sessions</title>
</head>
<body>
   <form id="form1" runat="server">
   <div>
      <asp:Label ID="promptLabel" runat="server" Font-Bold="True"
         Font-Size="Large" Text="Select a programming language:">
      </asp:Label>
      <asp:RadioButtonList ID="languageList" runat="server">
         <asp:ListItem>Visual Basic 2008</asp:ListItem>
         <asp:ListItem>Visual C# 2008</asp:ListItem>
         <asp:ListItem>C</asp:ListItem>
         <asp:ListItem>C++</asp:ListItem>
         <asp:ListItem>Java</asp:ListItem>
      </asp:RadioButtonList>
      <asp:Button ID="submitButton" runat="server" Text="Submit" />
      <asp:Label ID="responseLabel" runat="server" Font-Bold="True"
         Font-Size="Large" Text="Welcome to sessions!" Visible="False">
      </asp:Label><br />
      <br />
      <asp:Label ID="idLabel" runat="server" Visible="False">
      </asp:Label><br />
      <br />
      <asp:Label ID="timeoutLabel" runat="server" Visible="False">
      </asp:Label><br />
      <br />
      <asp:HyperLink ID="languageLink" runat="server"
         NavigateUrl="~/Options.aspx" Visible="False">
         Click here to choose another language
      </asp:HyperLink><br />
      <br />
      <asp:HyperLink ID="recommendationsLink" runat="server"
         NavigateUrl="~/Recommendations.aspx" Visible="False">
         Click here to get book recommendations
      </asp:HyperLink>
   </div>
   </form>
</body>
</html>
```

Fig. 21.28 | ASPX file that presents a list of programming languages. (Part 1 of 2.)

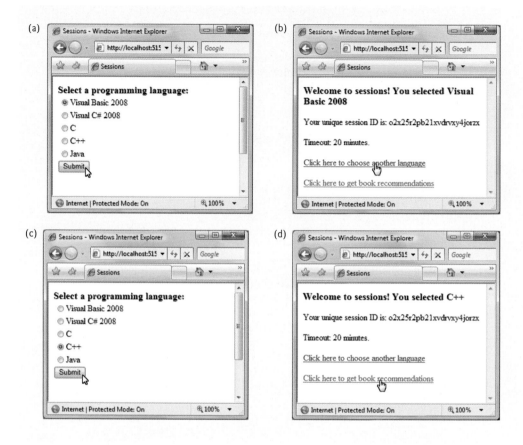

(a)

(b)

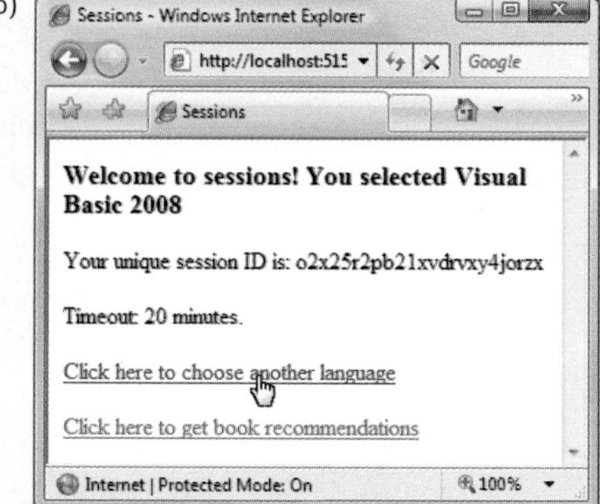

(c)

(d)

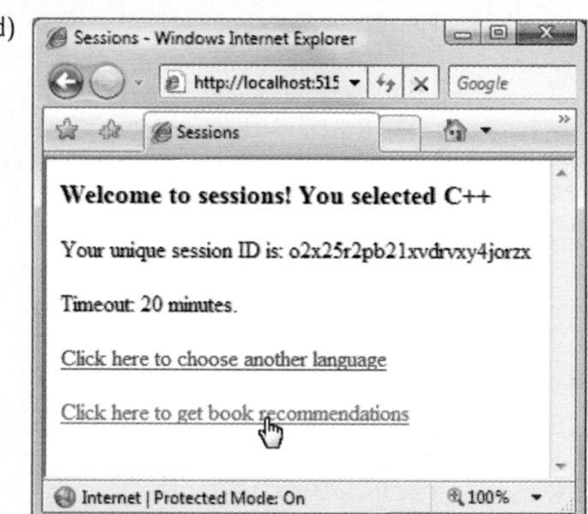

Fig. 21.28 | ASPX file that presents a list of programming languages. (Part 2 of 2.)

Adding Session Items

When the user presses **Submit** on the Web Form, `submitButton_Click` is invoked in the code-behind file (Fig. 21.29). Method `submitButton_Click` responds by adding a key/value pair to our `Session` object, specifying the language chosen and the ISBN number for a book on that language. These key/value pairs are often referred to as session items. Next, a postback occurs. Each time the user clicks **Submit**, `submitButton_Click` adds a new session item to the `HttpSessionState` object. Because much of this example is identical to the last example, we concentrate on the new features.

```
' Fig. 21.29: Options.aspx.vb
' Processes user's selection of a programming language
' by displaying links and writing information in a Session object.
Partial Class Options
   Inherits System.Web.UI.Page
```

Fig. 21.29 | Creates a session item for each programming language selected by the user on the ASPX page. (Part 1 of 3.)

```
   ' stores values to represent books
   Private books As New Dictionary(Of String, String)

   ' initializes the Dictionary of values to be stored in a Session
   Protected Sub Page_Init(ByVal sender As Object, _
      ByVal e As System.EventArgs) Handles Me.Init
      books.Add("Visual Basic 2008", "0-13-605305-X")
      books.Add("Visual C# 2008", "0-13-605322-X")
      books.Add("C", "0-13-240416-8")
      books.Add("C++", "0-13-615250-3")
      books.Add("Java", "0-13-222220-5")
   End Sub ' Page_Init

   ' if postback, hide form and display links to make additional
   ' selections or view recommendations
   Protected Sub Page_Load(ByVal sender As Object, _
      ByVal e As System.EventArgs) Handles Me.Load

      If IsPostBack Then
         ' user has submitted information, so display message
         ' and appropriate hyperlinks
         responseLabel.Visible = True
         idLabel.Visible = True
         timeoutLabel.Visible = True
         languageLink.Visible = True
         recommendationsLink.Visible = True

         ' hide other controls used to make language selection
         promptLabel.Visible = False
         languageList.Visible = False
         submitButton.Visible = False

         ' if the user made a selection, display it in responseLabel
         If languageList.SelectedItem IsNot Nothing Then
            responseLabel.Text &= " You selected " & _
               languageList.SelectedItem.Text
         Else
            responseLabel.Text &= " You did not select a language."
         End If

         ' display session ID
         idLabel.Text = "Your unique session ID is: " & Session.SessionID

         ' display the timeout
         timeoutLabel.Text = "Timeout: " & Session.Timeout & " minutes."
      End If
   End Sub ' Page_Load

   ' record the user's selection in the Session
   Protected Sub submitButton_Click(ByVal sender As Object, _
      ByVal e As System.EventArgs) Handles submitButton.Click
```

Fig. 21.29 | Creates a session item for each programming language selected by the user on the ASPX page. (Part 2 of 3.)

```
57          ' if the user made a selection
58          If languageList.SelectedItem IsNot Nothing Then
59             Dim language As String = languageList.SelectedItem.Text
60
61             ' get ISBN number of book for the given language
62             Dim ISBN As String = books(language)
63
64             Session.Add(language, ISBN) ' add name/value pair to Session
65          End If
66       End Sub ' submitButton_Click
67    End Class ' Options
```

Fig. 21.29 | Creates a session item for each programming language selected by the user on the ASPX page. (Part 3 of 3.)

Software Engineering Observation 21.2

A Web Form should not use instance variables to maintain client state information, because each new request or postback is handled by a new instance of the page. Instead, maintain client state information in `HttpSessionState` *objects, because such objects are specific to each client.*

Like a cookie, an `HttpSessionState` object can store name/value pairs. These session items are placed in an `HttpSessionState` object by calling method **`Add`**. Line 64 calls `Add` to place the language and its corresponding recommended book's ISBN number in the `HttpSessionState` object. If the application calls method `Add` to add an attribute that has the same name as an attribute previously stored in a session, the object associated with that attribute is replaced. Another common syntax for placing a session item in the `HttpSessionState` object is `Session(`*Name*`) = `*Value*. For example, we could have replaced line 64 with `Session(language) = ISBN`.

Software Engineering Observation 21.3

A benefit of using `HttpSessionState` *objects (rather than cookies) is that* `HttpSessionState` *objects can store any type of object (not just* `Strings`*) as attribute values. This provides you with increased flexibility in determining the type of state information to maintain for clients.*

The application handles the postback event (lines 24–51) in method `Page_Load`. Here, we retrieve information about the current client's session from the `Session` object's properties and display this information in the web page. The ASP.NET application contains information about the `HttpSessionState` object for the current client. Property **`SessionID`** (line 47) contains the **unique session ID**—a sequence of random letters and numbers. The first time a client connects to the web server, a unique session ID is created for that client and a temporary cookie is written to the client so the server can identify the client on subsequent requests. When the client makes additional requests, the client's session ID from that temporary cookie is compared with the session IDs stored in the web server's memory to retrieve the client's `HttpSessionState` object. Property **`Timeout`** (line 50) specifies the maximum amount of time that an `HttpSessionState` object can be inactive before it is discarded. Figure 21.30 lists some common `HttpSessionState` properties. For more information on the `HttpSessionState` class, please visit: `msdn.microsoft.com/en-us/library/h6bb9cz9.aspx`.

Properties	Description
`Count`	Specifies the number of key/value pairs in the `Session` object.
`IsNewSession`	Indicates whether this is a new session (i.e., whether the session was created during loading of this page).
`IsReadOnly`	Indicates whether the `Session` object is read-only.
`Keys`	Returns a collection containing the `Session` object's keys.
`SessionID`	Returns the session's unique ID.
`Timeout`	Specifies the maximum number of minutes during which a session can be inactive (i.e., no requests are made) before the session expires. By default, this property is set to 20 minutes.

Fig. 21.30 | `HttpSessionState` properties.

Displaying Recommendations Based on Session Values

As in the cookies example, this application provides a link to `Recommendations.aspx` (Fig. 21.31), which displays a list of book recommendations based on the user's language selections. Lines 20–21 define a `ListBox` web control that is used to present the recommendations to the user.

```
1  <%-- Fig. 21.31: Recommendations.aspx --%>
2  <%-- Displays book recommendations using a Session object. --%>
3  <%@ Page Language="VB" AutoEventWireup="false"
4     CodeFile="Recommendations.aspx.vb" Inherits="Recommendations" %>
5
6  <!DOCTYPE html PUBLIC "-//W3C//DTD XHTML 1.0 Transitional//EN"
7     "http://www.w3.org/TR/xhtml1/DTD/xhtml1-transitional.dtd">
8
9  <html xmlns="http://www.w3.org/1999/xhtml" >
10 <head id="Head1" runat="server">
11     <title>Book Recommendations</title>
12 </head>
13 <body>
14     <form id="form1" runat="server">
15     <div>
16        <asp:Label ID="recommendationsLabel" runat="server"
17           Font-Bold="True" Font-Size="X-Large" Text="Recommendations">
18        </asp:Label><br />
19        <br />
20        <asp:ListBox ID="booksListBox" runat="server" Height="125px"
21           Width="450px"></asp:ListBox><br />
22        <br />
23        <asp:HyperLink ID="languageLink" runat="server"
24           NavigateUrl="~/Options.aspx">
25           Click here to choose another language
26        </asp:HyperLink> </div>
```

Fig. 21.31 | Session-based book recommendations displayed in a `ListBox`. (Part 1 of 2.)

```
        </form>
    </body>
    </html>
```

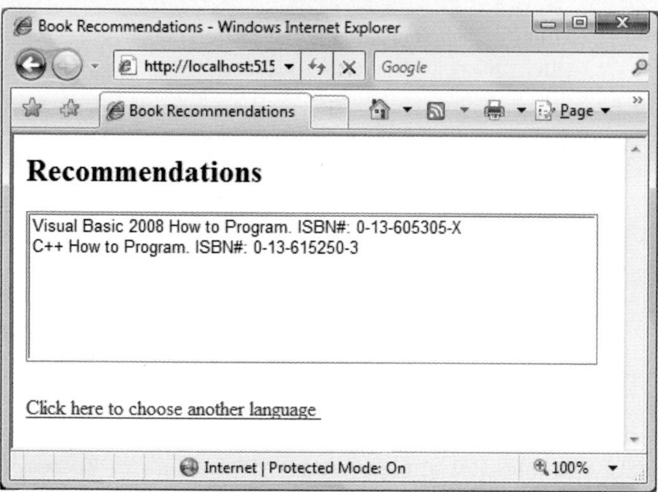

Fig. 21.31 | Session-based book recommendations displayed in a `ListBox`. (Part 2 of 2.)

Code-Behind File That Creates Book Recommendations from a Session

Figure 21.32 presents the code-behind file for `Recommendations.aspx`. Event handler `Page_Init` (lines 7–30) retrieves the session information. If a user has not selected a language on `Options.aspx`, our `Session` object's **`Count`** property will be `0`. This property provides the number of session items contained in a `Session` object. If `Session` object's `Count` property is `0` (i.e., no language was selected), then we display the text **No Recommendations** and update the `Text` of the `HyperLink` back to `Options.aspx`.

If the user has chosen a language, the loop in lines 11–19 iterates through our `Session` object's session items, temporarily storing each key name (line 13). The value in a key/value pair is retrieved from the `Session` object by indexing the `Session` object with the key name, using the same process by which we retrieved a value from our `Dictionary` in the preceding section.

Line 13 accesses the **`Keys`** property of class `HttpSessionState`, which returns a collection containing all the keys in the session. Line 13 indexes this collection to retrieve the current key. Lines 16–18 concatenate `keyName`'s value to the `String " How to Program. ISBN#: "` and the value from the `Session` object for which `keyName` is the key. This `String` is the recommendation that appears in the `ListBox`.

```
1   ' Fig. 21.32: Recommendations.aspx.vb
2   ' Creates book recommendations based on a Session object.
3   Partial Class Recommendations
4      Inherits System.Web.UI.Page
5
```

Fig. 21.32 | Session data used to provide book recommendations to the user. (Part 1 of 2.)

```
   ' read Session items and populate ListBox with any book recommendations
   Protected Sub Page_Init(ByVal sender As Object, _
      ByVal e As System.EventArgs) Handles Me.Init
      ' determine whether Session contains any information
      If Session.Count <> 0 Then
         For i As Integer = 0 To Session.Count - 1
            ' get current key name from Session object
            Dim keyName As String = Session.Keys(i)

            ' use keyName to display one of Session's name/value pairs
            booksListBox.Items.Add(keyName & _
               " How to Program. ISBN#: " & _
               Session(keyName).ToString())
         Next
      Else
         ' if there are no session items, no language was chosen, so
         ' display appropriate message and clear and hide booksListBox
         recommendationsLabel.Text = "No Recommendations"
         booksListBox.Items.Clear()
         booksListBox.Visible = False

         ' modify languageLink because no language was selected
         languageLink.Text = "Click here to choose a language"
      End If
   End Sub ' Page_Init
End Class ' Recommendations
```

Fig. 21.32 | Session data used to provide book recommendations to the user. (Part 2 of 2.)

21.7 Case Study: Connecting to a Database in ASP.NET

Many websites allow users to provide feedback about the website in a guestbook. Typically, users click a link on the website's home page to request the guestbook page. This page usually consists of an XHTML form that contains fields for the user's name, e-mail address, message/feedback and so on. Data submitted on the guestbook form is then stored in a database located on the web server's machine.

In this section, we create a guestbook Web Form application. This example's GUI is slightly more complex than that of earlier examples. It contains a `GridView` ASP.NET data control, as shown in Fig. 21.33, which displays all the entries in the guestbook in tabular format. We explain how to create and configure this data control shortly. Note that the `GridView` displays **abc** in **Design** mode to indicate string data that will be retrieved from a data source at runtime.

The XHTML form presented to the user consists of a name field, an e-mail address field and a message field. The form also contains a **Submit** button to send the data to the server and a **Clear** button to reset each of the fields on the form. The application stores the guestbook information in a SQL Server database called `Guestbook.mdf` located on the web server. (We provide this database in the examples directory for this chapter. You can download the examples from `www.deitel.com/books/vb2008htp`.) Below the XHTML form, the `GridView` displays the data (i.e., guestbook entries) in the database's `Messages` table.

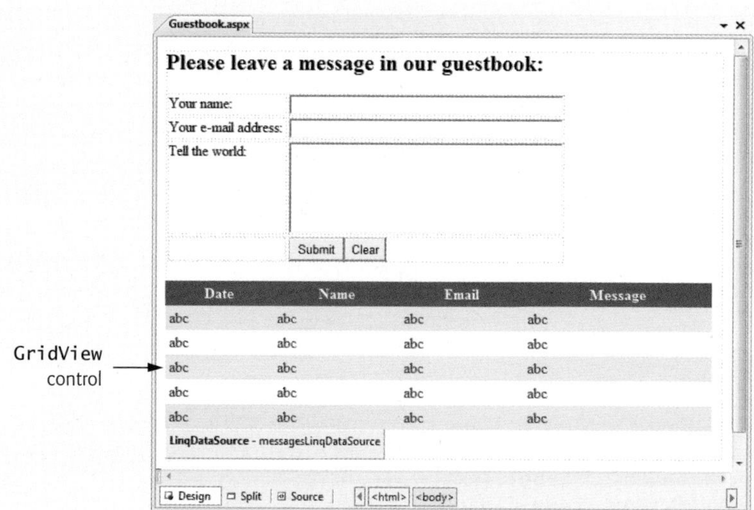

Fig. 21.33 | Guestbook application GUI in **Design** mode.

21.7.1 Building a Web Form That Displays Data from a Database

We now explain how to build this GUI and set up the data binding between the `GridView` control and the database. Many of these steps are similar to those performed in Chapter 20 to access and interact with a database in a Windows application. We present the ASPX file generated from the GUI later in this section, and we discuss the related code-behind file in the next subsection. To build the guestbook application, perform the following steps:

Step 1: Creating the Project

Create an **ASP.NET Web Site** named `Guestbook` and name the ASPX file `Guestbook.aspx`. Rename the class in the code-behind file `Guestbook`, and update the `Page` directive in the ASPX file accordingly.

Step 2: Creating the Form for User Input

In **Design** mode for the ASPX file, add the text `Please leave a message in our guestbook:` formatted as an `h2` header. Insert an XHTML table with two columns and four rows, configured so that the text in each cell aligns with the top of the cell. Place the appropriate text (see Fig. 21.33) in the top three cells in the table's left column. Then place `TextBox`es named `nameTextBox`, `emailTextBox` and `messageTextBox` in the top three table cells in the right column. Set `messageTextBox` to be a multiline `TextBox`. Finally, add `Button`s named `submitButton` and `clearButton` to the bottom-right table cell. Set the buttons' `Text` properties to `Submit` and `Clear`, respectively. We discuss the buttons' event handlers when we present the code-behind file.

Step 3: Adding a `GridView` Control to the Web Form

Add a `GridView` named `messagesGridView` that will display the guestbook entries. This control appears in the **Data** section of the **Toolbox**. The colors for the `GridView` are specified through the **Auto Format...** link in the **GridView Tasks** smart-tag menu that opens when you place the `GridView` on the page. Clicking this link causes an **AutoFormat** dialog to open with several choices. In this example, we chose **Simple**. We show how to set the GridView's data source (i.e., where it gets the data to display in its rows and columns) shortly.

Step 4: Adding a Database to an ASP.NET Web Application

To use a SQL Server 2005 Express database file in an ASP.NET web application, you must first add the file to the project's App_Data folder. Right click this folder in the **Solution Explorer** and select **Add Existing Item....** Locate the Guestbook.mdf file in the databases subdirectory of the chapter's examples directory, then click **Add**.

To create LINQ to SQL classes so that you can interact with the database using LINQ, right click the project in the **Solution Explorer** and select **Add New Item....** In the **Add New Item** dialog, select **LINQ to SQL Classes**, enter GuestbookDB.dbml as the **Name**, and click **OK**. A dialog appears asking if you would like to put your new LINQ to SQL classes in the App_Code folder; click **Yes**. If the **Object Relational Designer** does not open automatically, double click GuestbookDB.dbml in the **Solution Explorer**. Next, drag the Guestbook database's Messages table from the **Database Explorer** onto the **Object Relational Designer**. Finally, save your project by selecting **File > Save All**.

Step 5: Binding the GridView to the Messages Table of the Guestbook Database

Now that the Guestbook.mdf database is part of the project and we have created LINQ to SQL classes for interacting with it, we can configure the GridView to display the database's data. Open the **GridView Tasks** smart-tag menu, then select **<New data source...>** from the **Choose Data Source** drop-down list. In the **Data Source Configuration Wizard** that appears, select LINQ. In this example, we use a LinqDataSource control that allows the application to interact with the Guestbook.mdf database through LINQ. Set the ID of the data source to messagesLinqDataSource and click **OK** to begin the **Configure Data Source** wizard. In the **Choose a Context Object** screen, select GuestbookDBDataContext from the drop-down list (Fig. 21.34), then click **Next >**.

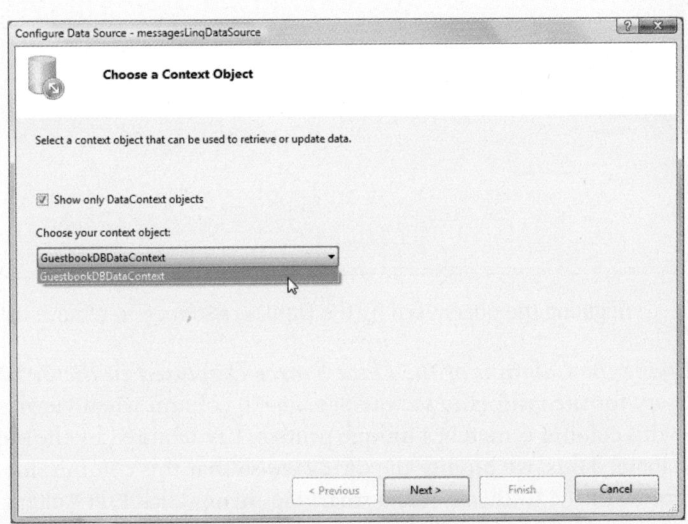

Fig. 21.34 | **Configure Data Source** dialog in Visual Web Developer.

The **Configure Data Source** dialog (Fig. 21.35) allows you to specify which data the `LinqDataSource` should retrieve from the data context. Your choices on this page design a `SELECT` LINQ query. The **Table** drop-down list identifies a table in the data context. The `GuestbookDB` data context contains one table named `Messages`, which is selected by default. If you haven't saved your project since creating your LINQ to SQL classes (*Step 4*), the list of tables will not appear. Next, in the **Select** pane, select the checkbox marked with an asterisk (*) to indicate that you want to retrieve all the columns in the `Messages` table. Click the **Advanced...** button, then check the box next to **Enable the LinqDataSource to perform automatic inserts.** This configures the `LinqDataSource` control to allow us to insert new data into the database. We discuss inserting new guestbook entries based on users' form submissions shortly. Click **Finish** to complete the wizard.

A control named `messagesLinqDataSource` now appears on the Web Form directly below the `GridView` (Fig. 21.36). This control is represented in **Design** mode as a gray box containing its type and name. It will *not* appear on the web page—the gray box simply provides a way to manipulate the control visually through **Design** mode. Also notice that the `GridView` now has column headers that correspond to the columns in the `Messages` table and that the rows each contain either a number (which signifies an autoincremented column) or **abc** (which indicates string data). The actual data from the `Guestbook.mdf` database file will appear in these rows when you view the ASPX file in a web browser.

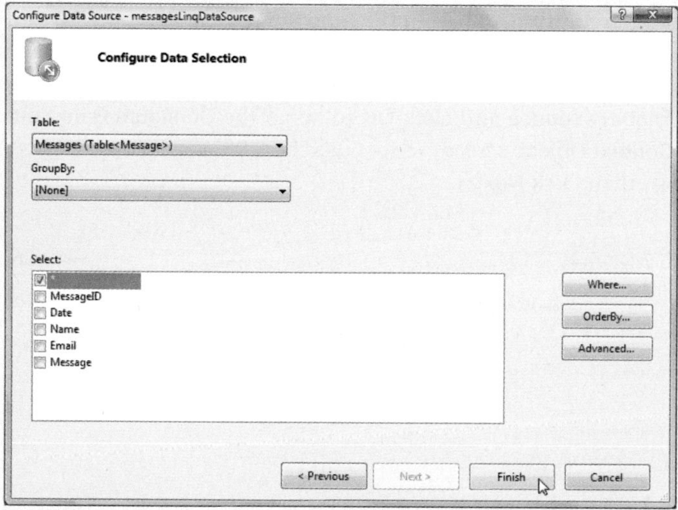

Fig. 21.35 | Configuring the query used by the `LinqDataSource` to retrieve data.

Step 6: Modifying the Columns of the Data Source Displayed in the `GridView`

It is not necessary for site visitors to see the `MessageID` column when viewing past guestbook entries—this column is merely a unique primary key required by the `Messages` table within the database. Thus, we modify the `GridView` so that this column does not display on the Web Form. In the **GridView Tasks** smart tag menu, click **Edit Columns.** In the resulting **Fields** dialog (Fig. 21.37), select **MessageID** in the **Selected fields** pane, then click the **X**. This removes the `MessageID` column from the `GridView`. Click **OK** to return to the main IDE window. The `GridView` should now appear as in Fig. 21.33.

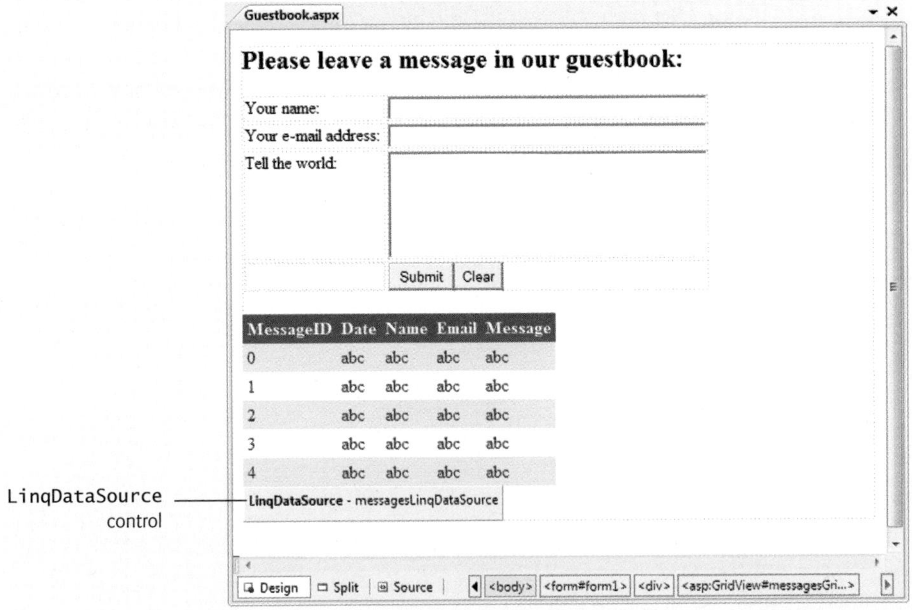

LinqDataSource control

Fig. 21.36 | **Design** mode displaying `LinqDataSource` control for a `GridView`.

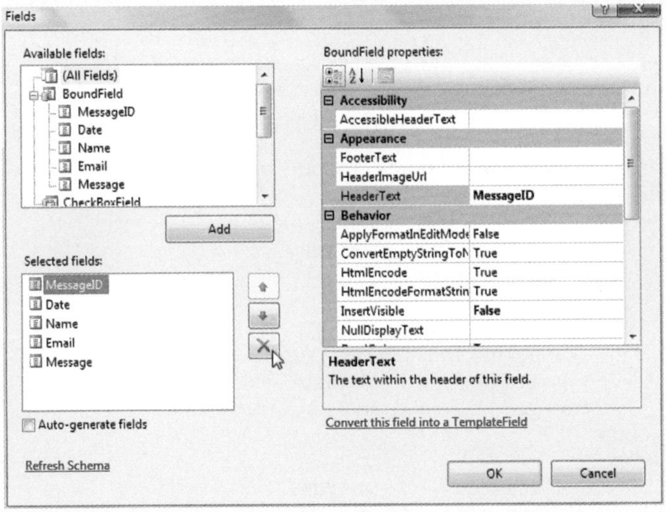

Fig. 21.37 | Removing the `MessageID` column from the `GridView`.

ASPX File for a Web Form That Interacts with a Database

The ASPX file generated by the guestbook GUI (and `messagesLinqDataSource` control) is shown in Fig. 21.38. This file contains a large amount of generated markup. We discuss only those parts that are new or noteworthy for the current example. Lines 29–68 contain the XHTML and ASP.NET elements that comprise the form that gathers user input. The

GridView control appears in lines 70–95. The <asp:GridView> start tag (lines 70–73) contains properties that set various aspects of the GridView's appearance and behavior, such as whether grid lines should be displayed between rows and columns. The **DataSourceID** property identifies the data source that is used to fill the GridView with data at runtime.

```
1  <%-- Fig. 21.38: Guestbook.aspx --%>
2  <%-- Guestbook Web application with a form for users to submit --%>
3  <%-- guestbook entries and a GridView to view existing entries. --%>
4  <%@ Page Language="VB" AutoEventWireup="false"
5     CodeFile="Guestbook.aspx.vb" Inherits="Guestbook" %>
6
7  <!DOCTYPE html PUBLIC "-//W3C//DTD XHTML 1.0 Transitional//EN"
8     "http://www.w3.org/TR/xhtml1/DTD/xhtml1-transitional.dtd">
9
10 <html xmlns="http://www.w3.org/1999/xhtml" >
11 <head runat="server">
12    <title>Guestbook</title>
13    <style type="text/css">
14       .style1
15       {
16          width: 100%
17       }
18       .style2
19       {
20          width: 130px
21       }
22    </style>
23 </head>
24 <body>
25    <form id="form1" runat="server">
26    <div>
27       <h2>
28          Please leave a message in our guestbook:</h2>
29       <table class="style1">
30          <tr>
31             <td class="style2" valign="top">
32                Your name:<br />
33             </td>
34             <td valign="top">
35                <asp:TextBox ID="nameTextBox" runat="server"
36                   Width="300px"></asp:TextBox>
37             </td>
38          </tr>
39          <tr>
40             <td class="style2" valign="top">
41                Your e-mail address:<br />
42             </td>
43             <td valign="top">
44                <asp:TextBox ID="emailTextBox" runat="server"
45                   Width="300px"></asp:TextBox>
46             </td>
47          </tr>
```

Fig. 21.38 | ASPX file for the guestbook application. (Part 1 of 3.)

```
            <tr>
               <td class="style2" valign="top">
                  Tell the world:<br />
               </td>
               <td valign="top">
                  <asp:TextBox ID="messageTextBox" runat="server" Rows="8"
                     Height="100px" Width="300px" TextMode="MultiLine">
                  </asp:TextBox>
               </td>
            </tr>
            <tr>
               <td class="style2" valign="top">
               </td>
               <td valign="top">
                  <asp:Button ID="submitButton" runat="server"
                     Text="Submit" />
                  <asp:Button ID="clearButton" runat="server"
                     Text="Clear" />
               </td>
            </tr>
         </table>
         <br />
         <asp:GridView ID="messagesGridView" runat="server"
            AutoGenerateColumns="False" CellPadding="4"
            DataKeyNames="MessageID" DataSourceID="messagesLinqDataSource"
            ForeColor="#333333" GridLines="None" Width="600px">
            <FooterStyle BackColor="#1C5E55" Font-Bold="True"
               ForeColor="White" />
            <Columns>
               <asp:BoundField DataField="Date" HeaderText="Date"
                  SortExpression="Date" />
               <asp:BoundField DataField="Name" HeaderText="Name"
                  SortExpression="Name" />
               <asp:BoundField DataField="Email" HeaderText="Email"
                  SortExpression="Email" />
               <asp:BoundField DataField="Message" HeaderText="Message"
                  SortExpression="Message" />
            </Columns>
            <RowStyle BackColor="#E3EAEB" />
            <EditRowStyle BackColor="#7C6F57" />
            <SelectedRowStyle BackColor="#C5BBAF" Font-Bold="True"
               ForeColor="#333333" />
            <PagerStyle BackColor="#666666" ForeColor="White"
               HorizontalAlign="Center" />
            <HeaderStyle BackColor="#1C5E55" Font-Bold="True"
               ForeColor="White" />
            <AlternatingRowStyle BackColor="White" />
         </asp:GridView>
         <asp:LinqDataSource ID="messagesLinqDataSource" runat="server"
            ContextTypeName="GuestbookDBDataContext" EnableInsert="True"
            TableName="Messages">
         </asp:LinqDataSource>
      </div>
```

Fig. 21.38 | ASPX file for the guestbook application. (Part 2 of 3.)

```
    </form>
</body>
</html>
```

(a)

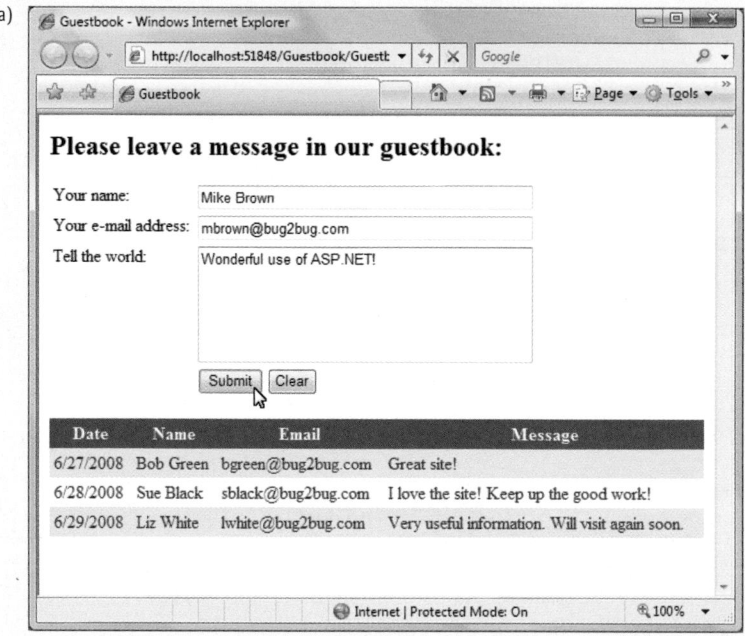

(b)

Fig. 21.38 | ASPX file for the guestbook application. (Part 3 of 3.)

Lines 76–85 define the `Columns` that appear in the `GridView`. Each column is represented as a `BoundField`, because the values in the columns are bound to values retrieved from the data source (i.e., the `Messages` table of the `Guestbook` database). The `DataField` property of each `BoundField` identifies the column in the data source to which the column in the `GridView` is bound. The `HeaderText` property indicates the text that appears as the column header. By default, this is the name of the column in the data source, but you can change this property as desired. The `SortExpression` property specifies the expression used to sort the `GridView`'s elements when the user chooses to sort by the column. Because the `GridView` cannot be sorted in this example, we could have omitted this auto-generated code. Lines 86–94 contain nested elements that define the styles used to format the `GridView`'s rows. The IDE configured these styles based on your selection of the **Simple** style in the **Auto Format** dialog for the `GridView`.

The `messagesLinqDataSource` is defined in lines 96–99 in Fig. 21.38. The `ContextTypeName` property (line 97) indicates the data context that the `LinqDataSource` interacts with. Recall that we specified this value earlier in this section using the **Configure Data Source** wizard. As determined by our actions in the same wizard, the `TableName` property in line 98 specifies the table from which to retrieve data. The `EnableInsert` property in line 97 is set to `True`, allowing the data source to insert records into the data context.

21.7.2 Modifying the Code-Behind File for the Guestbook Application

After building the Web Form and configuring the data controls used in this example, double click the **Submit** and **Clear** buttons in **Design** view to create their corresponding `Click` event handlers in the code-behind file (Fig. 21.39). The IDE generates empty event handlers, so we must add the appropriate code to make these buttons work properly. The event handler for `clearButton` (lines 36–41) clears each `TextBox` by setting its `Text` property to an empty string. This resets the form for a new guestbook submission.

```
1  ' Fig. 21.39: Guestbook.aspx.vb
2  ' Code-behind file that defines event handlers for the guestbook.
3  Partial Class Guestbook
4     Inherits System.Web.UI.Page
5
6     ' Submit Button adds a new guestbook entry to the database,
7     ' clears the form and displays the updated list of guestbook entries
8     Protected Sub submitButton_Click(ByVal sender As Object, _
9        ByVal e As System.EventArgs) Handles submitButton.Click
10
11       ' create dictionary of parameters for inserting
12       Dim insertParameters As New ListDictionary()
13
14       ' add current date and the user's name, e-mail address and message
15       ' to dictionary of insert parameters
16       insertParameters.Add("Date", Date.Now.ToShortDateString())
17       insertParameters.Add("Name", nameTextBox.Text)
18       insertParameters.Add("Email", emailTextBox.Text)
19       insertParameters.Add("Message", messageTextBox.Text)
20
```

Fig. 21.39 | Code-behind file for the guestbook application. (Part 1 of 2.)

```
21          ' execute an INSERT LINQ statement to add a new entry to the
22          ' Messages table in the Guestbook data context that contains the
23          ' current date and the user's name, e-mail address and message
24          messagesLinqDataSource.Insert(InsertParameters)
25
26          ' clear the TextBoxes
27          nameTextBox.Text = String.Empty
28          emailTextBox.Text = String.Empty
29          messageTextBox.Text = String.Empty
30
31          ' update the GridView with the new database table contents
32          messagesGridView.DataBind()
33       End Sub ' submitButton_Click
34
35       ' Clear Button clears the Web Form's TextBoxes
36       Protected Sub clearButton_Click(ByVal sender As Object, _
37          ByVal e As System.EventArgs) Handles clearButton.Click
38          nameTextBox.Text = String.Empty
39          emailTextBox.Text = String.Empty
40          messageTextBox.Text = String.Empty
41       End Sub ' clearButton_Click
42    End Class ' Guestbook
```

Fig. 21.39 | Code-behind file for the guestbook application. (Part 2 of 2.)

Lines 8–33 contain `submitButton`'s event-handling code, which adds the user's information to the `Guestbook` database's `Messages` table. To use the values of the `TextBox`es on the Web Form as the parameter values inserted into the database, we must create a `ListDictionary`—a list of key/value pairs—of insert parameters. Line 12 creates a `ListDictionary` object. Lines 16–19 populate the `ListDictionary` with a key/value pair to represent each of the four insert parameters—the current date and the user's name, e-mail address, and message. Invoking the `LinqDataSource` method `Insert` (line 24) executes the `INSERT` LINQ command against the data context and adds a row to the `Messages` table. We pass the `ListDictionary` object as an argument for the `Insert` method to specify the insert parameters. After the data is inserted into the database, lines 27–29 clear the `TextBox`es, and line 32 invokes `messagesGridView`'s `DataBind` method to refresh the data that the `GridView` displays. This causes `messagesLinqDataSource` (the `GridView`'s source) to execute its `SELECT` command to obtain the `Messages` table's newly updated data.

21.8 Case Study: Secure Books Database Application

This case study presents a web application in which a user logs into a secure website to view a list of publications by a selected author. The application consists of several ASPX files. Section 21.8.1 presents the application and explains the purpose of each of its web pages. Section 21.8.2 provides step-by-step instructions to guide you through building the application and presents the markup in the ASPX files.

21.8.1 Examining the Completed Secure Books Database Application

This example uses a technique known as forms authentication to protect a page so that only users known to the website can access it. Such users are known as the site's members.

Authentication is a crucial tool for sites that allow only members to enter the site or a portion of the site. In this application, website visitors must log in before they are allowed to view the publications in the `Books` database. The first page that a user would typically request is `Login.aspx` (Fig. 21.40). You will soon learn to create this page using a `Login` control, one of several ASP.NET login controls that help create secure applications using authentication. These controls are found in the **Login** section of the **Toolbox**.

The `Login.aspx` page allows a site visitor to enter an existing user name and password to log into the website. A first-time visitor must click the link below the **Log In** button to create a new user before logging in. Doing so redirects the visitor to `CreateNewUser.aspx` (Fig. 21.41), which contains a `CreateUserWizard` control that presents the visitor with a user registration form. We discuss the `CreateUserWizard` control in detail in Section 21.8.2. In Fig. 21.41, we use the password `pa$$word` for testing purposes—as you

Fig. 21.40 | `Login.aspx` page of the secure books database application.

Fig. 21.41 | `CreateNewUser.aspx` page of the secure books database application.

will learn, the `CreateUserWizard` requires that the password contain special characters for security purposes. Clicking **Create User** establishes a new user account. After creating the account, the user is automatically logged in and shown a success message (Fig. 21.42).

Clicking the **Continue** button on the confirmation page sends the user to `Books.aspx` (Fig. 21.43), which provides a drop-down list of authors and a table containing the ISBNs, titles, edition numbers and copyright years of books in the database. By default, all the books by Harvey Deitel are displayed. Links appear at the bottom of the table that allow you to access additional pages of data. When the user chooses an author, a postback occurs, and the page is updated to display information about books written by the selected author (Fig. 21.44).

Fig. 21.42 | Message displayed to indicate that a user account was created successfully.

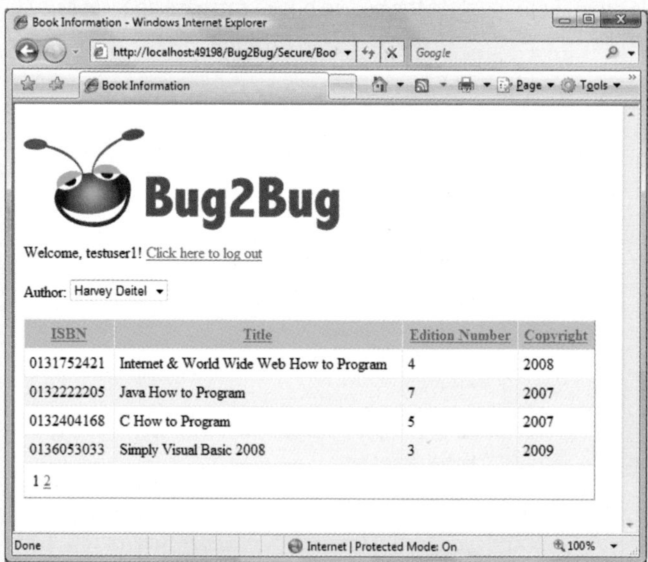

Fig. 21.43 | `Books.aspx` displaying books by Harvey Deitel (by default).

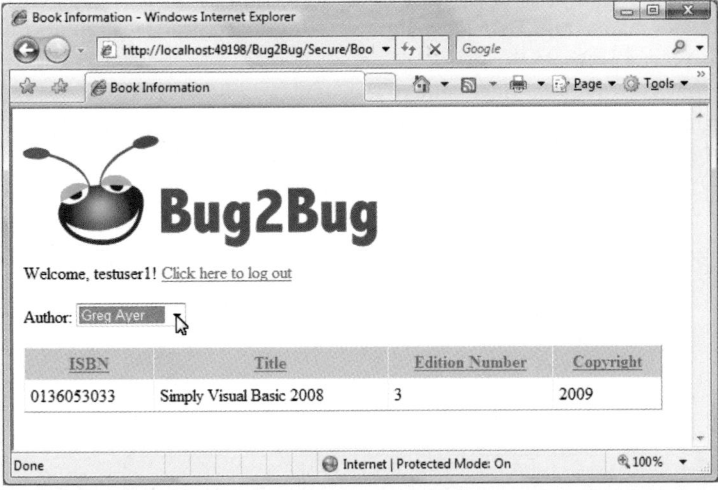

Fig. 21.44 | `Books.aspx` displaying books by Greg Ayer.

Note that once the user creates an account and is logged in, `Books.aspx` displays a welcome message customized for the particular logged-in user. As you will soon see, a `LoginName` control provides this functionality. After you add this control to the page, ASP.NET handles the details of determining the user name.

Clicking the **Click here to log out** link logs the user out, then sends the user back to `Login.aspx` (Fig. 21.45). This link is created by a `LoginStatus` control, which handles the log-out details. After logging out, the user would need to log in through `Login.aspx` to view the book listing again. The `Login` control on this page receives the username and password entered by a visitor. ASP.NET compares these values with usernames and passwords stored in a database on the server. If there is a match, the visitor is authenticated (i.e., the user's identity is confirmed). We explain the authentication process in detail in

Fig. 21.45 | Logging in using the `Login` control.

Section 21.8.2. When an existing user is successfully authenticated, `Login.aspx` redirects the user to `Books.aspx` (Fig. 21.43). If the user's login attempt fails, an appropriate error message is displayed (Fig. 21.46).

Notice that `Login.aspx`, `CreateNewUser.aspx` and `Books.aspx` share the same page header containing the logo image from the fictional company Bug2Bug. Instead of placing this image at the top of each page, we use a master page to achieve this. As we demonstrate shortly, a master page defines common GUI elements that are inherited by each page in a set of content pages. Just as Visual Basic classes can inherit instance variables and methods from existing classes, content pages inherit elements from master pages—this is known as visual inheritance.

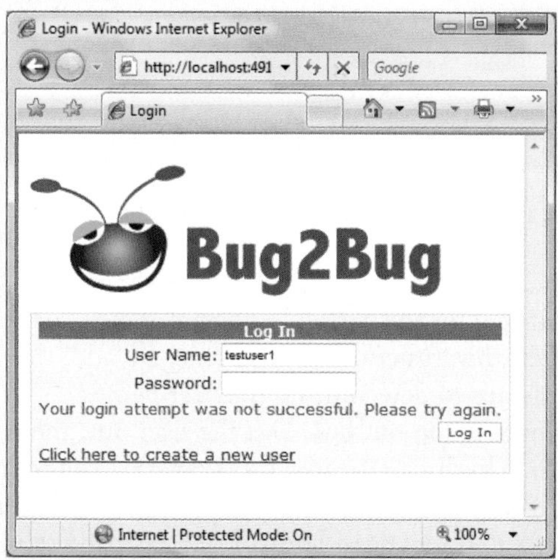

Fig. 21.46 | Error message displayed for an unsuccessful login attempt using the `Login` control.

21.8.2 Creating the Secure Books Database Application

Now that you are familiar with how this application behaves, you'll learn how to create it from scratch. Thanks to the rich set of login and data controls provided by ASP.NET, you will have to write almost no Visual Basic code to create this application. Most of the functionality is specified through properties of controls, many of which are set through wizards and other visual programming tools. ASP.NET hides the details of authenticating users against a database of user names and passwords, displaying appropriate success or error messages and redirecting the user to the correct page based on the authentication results. We now discuss the steps you must perform to create the secure books database application.

Step 1: Creating the Website

Create a new **ASP.NET Web Site** at `http://localhost/Bug2Bug` as described previously. We will explicitly create each of the ASPX files that we need in this application, so delete the IDE-generated `Default.aspx` file (and its corresponding code-behind file) by selecting `Default.aspx` in the **Solution Explorer** and pressing the *Delete* key. Click **OK** in the confirmation dialog to delete these files.

Step 2: Setting Up the Website's Folders

Before building any of the pages in the website, we create folders to organize its contents. First, create an `Images` folder by right clicking the location of the website in the **Solution Explorer** and selecting **New Folder**, then add the `bug2bug.png` file to it. This image can be found in the examples directory for this chapter. Next, add the `Books.mdf` database file (located in the `exampleDatabases` subdirectory examples directory) to the project's `App_Data` folder. We show how to retrieve data from this database later in the section.

Step 3: Configuring the Application's Security Settings

In this application, we want to ensure that only authenticated users are allowed to access `Books.aspx` (created in *Step 9* and *Step 10*) to view the information in the database. Previously, we created all of our ASPX pages in the web application's root directory (e.g., `http://localhost/`*ProjectName*). By default, any website visitor (regardless of whether the visitor is authenticated) can view pages in the root directory. ASP.NET allows you to restrict access to particular folders of a website. We do not want to restrict access to the root of the website, however, because all users must be able to view `Login.aspx` and `CreateNewUser.aspx` to log in and create user accounts, respectively. Thus, if we want to restrict access to `Books.aspx`, it must reside in a directory other than the root directory. Create a folder named `Secure`. Later in the section, we will create `Books.aspx` in this folder. First, let's enable forms authentication in our application and configure the `Secure` folder to restrict access to authenticated users only.

Select **Website > ASP.NET Configuration** to open the **Web Site Administration Tool** in a web browser (Fig. 21.47). This tool allows you to configure various options that determine how your application behaves. Click either the **Security** link or the **Security** tab to open a web page in which you can set security options (Fig. 21.48), such as the type of authentication the application should use. In the **Users** column, click **Select authentication type**. On the resulting page (Fig. 21.49), select the radio button next to **From the internet** to indicate that users will log in via a form on the website in which they can enter a username and password (i.e., the application will use forms authentication). The default set-

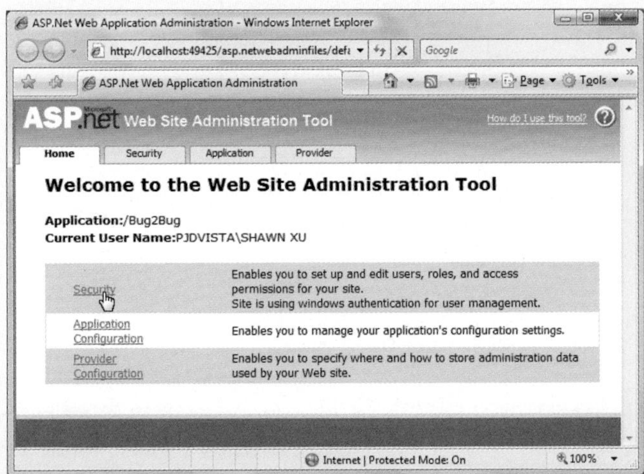

Fig. 21.47 | **Web Site Administration Tool** for configuring a web application.

ting—**From a local network**—relies on users' Windows usernames and passwords for authentication purposes. Click the **Done** button to save this change.

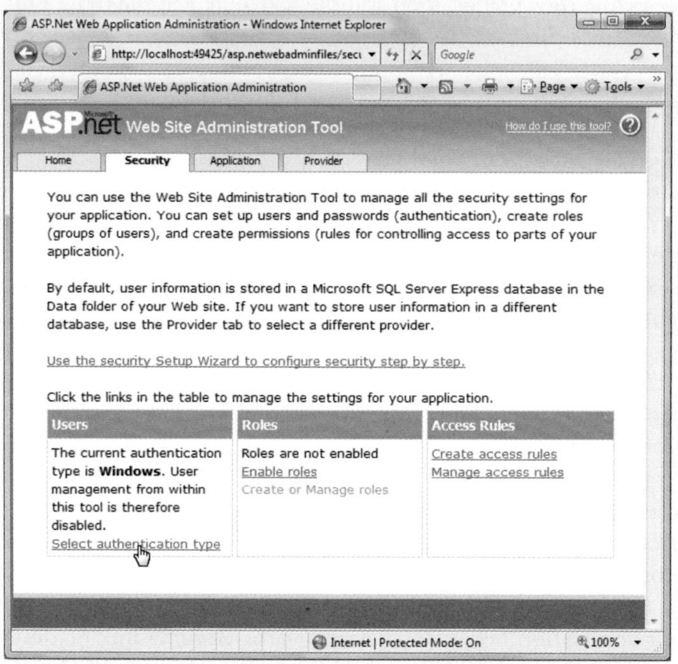

Fig. 21.48 | **Security** page of the **Web Site Administration Tool**.

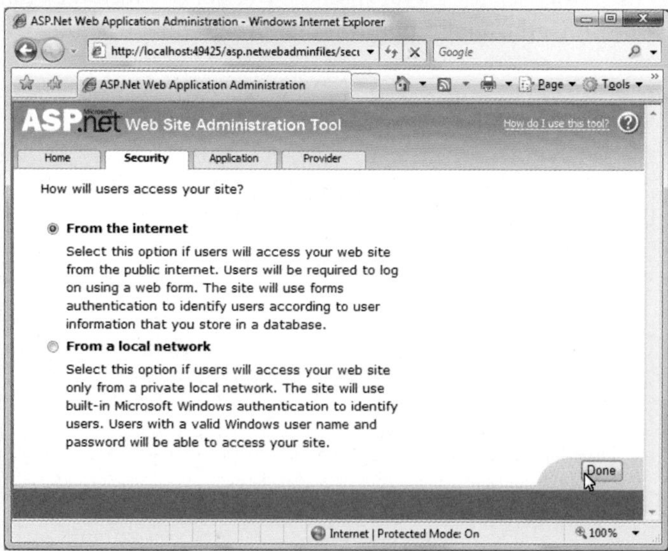

Fig. 21.49 | Choosing the type of authentication used by an ASP.NET Web application.

Now that forms authentication is enabled, the **Users** column on the main page of the **Web Site Administration Tool** (Fig. 21.50) provides links to create and manage users. As you saw in Section 21.8.1, our application provides the `CreateNewUser.aspx` page in which users can create their own accounts. Thus, while it is possible to create users through the **Web Site Administration Tool**, we do not do so here.

Even though no users exist at the moment, we configure the `Secure` folder to grant access only to authenticated users (i.e., deny access to all unauthenticated users). Click the **Create access rules** link in the **Access Rules** column of the **Web Site Administration Tool** (Fig. 21.50) to view the **Add New Access Rule** page (Fig. 21.51). This page is used to create an access rule—a rule that grants or denies access to a particular web-application directory for a specific user or group of users. Click the `Secure` directory in the left column of the page to identify the directory to which our access rule applies. In the middle column, select the radio button marked **Anonymous users** to specify that the rule applies to users who have not been authenticated. Finally, select **Deny** in the right column, labeled **Permission**, then click **OK**. This rule indicates that anonymous users (i.e., users who have not identified themselves by logging in) should be denied access to any pages in the `Secure` directory (e.g., `Books.aspx`). By default, anonymous users who attempt to load a page in the `Secure` directory are redirected to the `Login.aspx` page so that they can identify themselves. Note that, because we did not set up any access rules for the `Bug2Bug` root directory, anonymous users may still access pages there (e.g., `Login.aspx`, `CreateNewUser.aspx`). We create these pages momentarily.

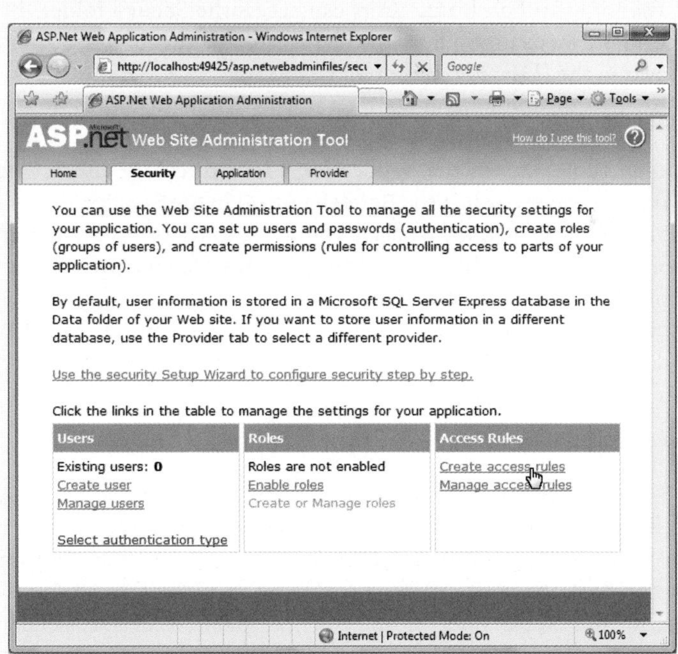

Fig. 21.50 | Main page of the **Web Site Administration Tool** after enabling forms authentication.

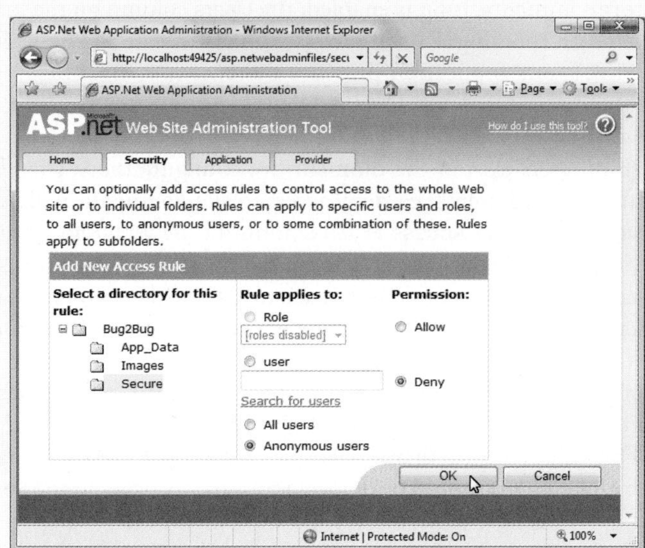

Fig. 21.51 | **Add New Access Rule** page used to configure directory access.

Step 4: Examining the Autogenerated `Web.config` *Files*

We have now configured the application to use forms authentication and created an access rule to ensure that only authenticated users can access the `Secure` folder. Before creating the website's content, we examine how the changes made through the **Web Site Administration Tool** appear in the IDE. Recall that `Web.config` is an XML file used for application configuration, such as enabling debugging or storing database connection strings. Visual Web Developer generates two `Web.config` files in response to our actions using the **Web Site Administration Tool**—one in the application's root directory and one in the `Secure` folder. [*Note:* You may need to click the **Refresh** button in the **Solution Explorer** to see these files.] In an ASP.NET application, a page's configuration settings are determined by the current directory's `Web.config` file. The settings in this file take precedence over the settings in the root directory's `Web.config` file.

After setting the authentication type for the web application, the IDE generates a `Web.config` file at `http://localhost:`*PortNumber*`/Bug2Bug/Web.config`, which contains an `authentication` element

```
<authentication mode="Forms" />
```

This element appears in the root directory's `Web.config` file, so the setting applies to the entire website. The value `"Forms"` of the `mode` attribute specifies that we want to use forms authentication. Had we left the authentication type set to **From a local network** in the **Web Site Administration Tool**, the `mode` attribute would be set to `"Windows"`.

After creating the access rule for the `Secure` folder, the IDE generates a second `Web.config` file in that folder. This file contains an `authorization` element that indicates who is, and who is not, authorized to access this folder over the web. In this application, we want to allow only authenticated users to access the contents of the `Secure` folder, so the authorization element appears as

```
<authorization>
   <deny users="?" />
</authorization>
```

Rather than grant permission to each individual authenticated user, we deny access to those who are not authenticated (i.e., those who have not logged in). The `deny` element inside the `authorization` element specifies the users to whom we wish to deny access. When the `users` attribute's value is set to `"?"`, all anonymous (i.e., unauthenticated) users are denied access to the folder. Thus, an unauthenticated user will not be able to load `http://localhost:`*PortNumber*`/Bug2Bug/Secure/Books.aspx`. Instead, such a user will be redirected to the `Login.aspx` page—when a user is denied access to a part of a site, ASP.NET by default sends the user to a page named `Login.aspx` in the application's root directory.

Step 5: Creating a Master Page

Now that you have established the application's security settings, you can create the application's web pages. We begin with the master page, which defines the elements we want to appear on each page. A master page is like a base class in a visual inheritance hierarchy, and content pages are like derived classes. The master page contains placeholders for custom content created in each content page. The content pages visually inherit the master page's content, then add content in place of the master page's placeholders.

For example, you might want to include a navigation bar (i.e., a series of buttons for navigating a website) on every page of a site. If the site encompasses a large number of pages, adding markup to create the navigation bar for each page can be time consuming. Moreover, if you subsequently modify the navigation bar, every page on the site that uses it must be updated. By creating a master page, you can specify the navigation-bar markup in one file and have it appear on all the content pages, with only a few lines of markup. If the navigation bar changes, only the master page changes—any content pages that use it are updated the next time the page is requested.

In this example, we want the Bug2Bug logo to appear as a header at the top of every page, so we will place an `Image` control in the master page. Each subsequent page we create will be a content page based on this master page and thus will include the header. To create a master page, right click the location of the website in the **Solution Explorer** and select **Add New Item....** In the **Add New Item** dialog, select **Master Page** from the template list and specify `Bug2Bug.master` as the filename. Master pages have the file-name extension `.master` and, like Web Forms, can optionally use a code-behind file to define additional functionality. In this example, we do not need to specify any code for the master page, so leave the box labeled **Place code in a separate file** unchecked. Click **Add** to create the page.

The IDE opens the master page in **Source** mode (Fig. 21.52) when the file is first created. [*Note:* We added a line break in the `DOCTYPE` element for presentation purposes.] The markup for a master page is almost identical to that of a Web Form. One difference is that a master page contains a `Master` directive (line 1 in Fig. 21.52), which specifies that this file defines a master page using the indicated `Language` for any code. Because we chose not to use a code-behind file, the master page also contains a `script` element (lines 6–8). Code that would usually be placed in a code-behind file can be placed in a `script` element. However, we could have omitted the `script` element from this page, because we do not need to write any additional code. After deleting this block of markup, set the `title` of the page to `Bug2Bug`. Finally, notice that the master page contains two `ContentPlaceHolder` controls

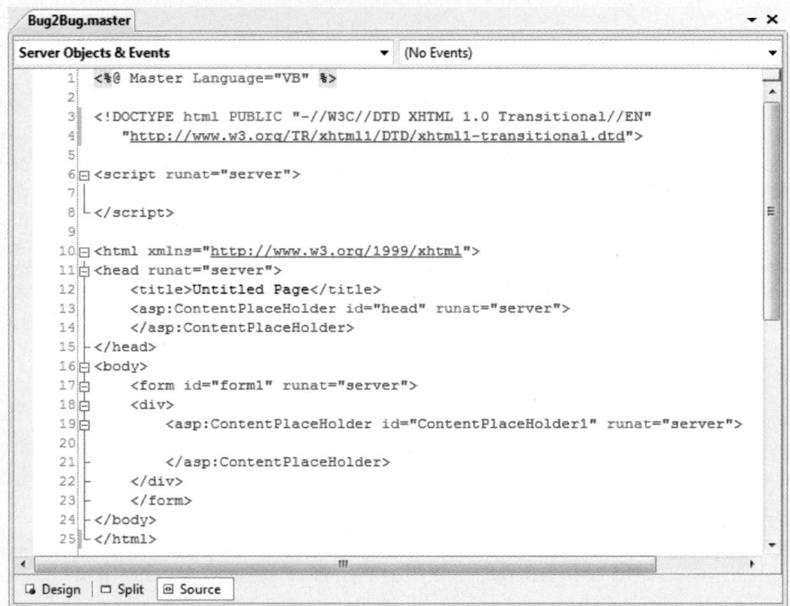

Fig. 21.52 | Master page in **Source** mode.

(lines 13–14 and 19–21 of Fig. 21.52). These serve as a placeholders for content that will be defined by a content page. You will see how to define content to replace `ContentPlaceHolders` shortly.

At this point, you can edit the master page in **Design** mode (Fig. 21.53) as if it were an ASPX file. Notice that the `ContentPlaceHolder` control appears as a rectangle with a purple outline indicating the control's type and `ID`. Using the **Properties** window, change the `ID` of this control to `bodyContent`.

To create a header in the master page that will appear at the top of each content page, we insert a table into the master page. Place the cursor to the left of `ContentPlaceHolder` and select **Table > Insert Table**. In the **Insert Table** dialog, set **Rows** to `2` and **Columns** to `1`. In the **Layout** section, specify a **Cell padding** of `0` and a **Cell spacing** of `0`. Set both the width and height of the table to `100` percent. Make sure that the **Size** value in the **Borders** section is `0`. Click **OK** to create a table that fills the page and contains two rows.

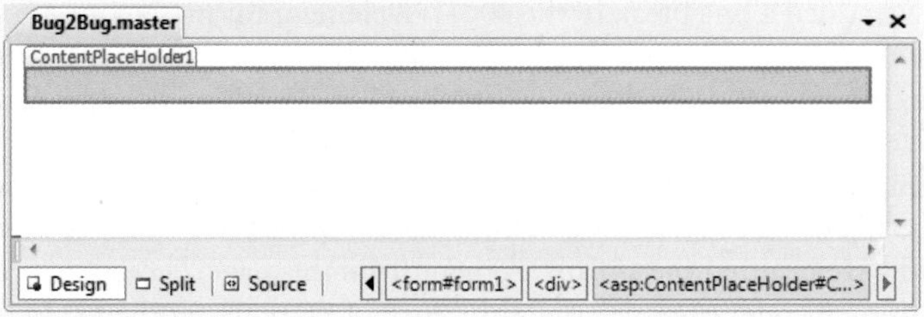

Fig. 21.53 | Master page in **Design** mode.

Drag-and-drop the `ContentPlaceHolder` into the bottom table cell. Change the `valign` property of this cell to `top`, so the `ContentPlaceHolder` vertically aligns with the top of the cell. Next, set the `Height` of the top table cell to `130`. Add to this cell an `Image` control named `headerImage` with its `ImageUrl` property set to the `bug2bug.png` file in the project's `Images` folder. (You can also simply drag the image from the **Solution Explorer** into the top cell.) Figure 21.54 shows the markup and **Design** view of the completed master page. As you will see in *Step 6*, a content page based on this master page displays the logo image defined here, as well as the content designed for that specific page (in place of the `ContentPlaceHolder`).

```
<%-- Fig. 21.54: Bug2Bug.Master --%>
<%-- Master page that defines commmon features of all pages in the --%>
<%-- secure books database application. --%>
<%@ Master Language="VB" %>

<!DOCTYPE html PUBLIC "-//W3C//DTD XHTML 1.0 Transitional//EN"
   "http://www.w3.org/TR/xhtml1/DTD/xhtml1-transitional.dtd">

<script runat="server">

</script>

<html xmlns="http://www.w3.org/1999/xhtml">
<head runat="server">
   <title>Bug2Bug</title>
   <asp:ContentPlaceHolder id="head" runat="server">
   </asp:ContentPlaceHolder>
   <style type="text/css">
    .style1
    {
       width: 100%;
       height: 100%;
    }
   </style>
</head>
<body>
   <form id="form1" runat="server">
   <div>
      <table cellpadding="0" cellspacing="0" class="style1">
         <tr>
            <td height="130">
               <asp:Image ID="headerImage" runat="server"
               ImageUrl="~/Images/bug2bug.png" />
            </td>
         </tr>
         <tr>
            <td valign="top">
               <asp:ContentPlaceHolder id="bodyContent" runat="server">
               </asp:ContentPlaceHolder>
            </td>
```

Fig. 21.54 | `Bug2Bug.master` page that defines a logo image header for all pages in the secure books database application. (Part 1 of 2.)

```
            </tr>
        </table>
    </div>
    </form>
</body>
</html>
```

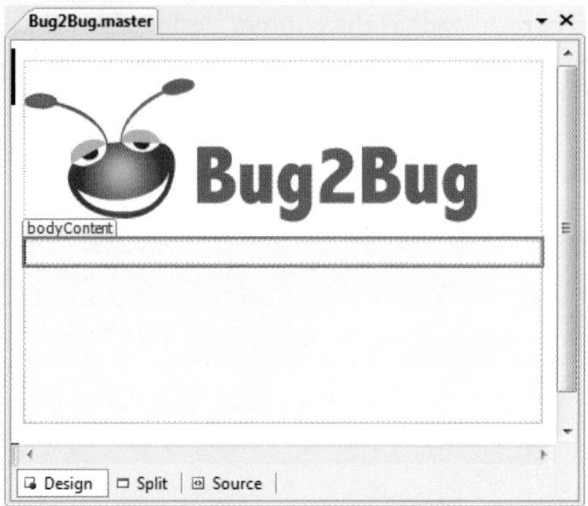

Fig. 21.54 | `Bug2Bug.master` page that defines a logo image header for all pages in the secure books database application. (Part 2 of 2.)

Step 6: Creating a Content Page

We now create a content page based on `Bug2Bug.master`. We begin by building `CreateNewUser.aspx`. To create this file, right click the master page in the **Solution Explorer** and select **Add Content Page**. This action causes a `Default.aspx` file, configured to use the master page, to be added to the project. Rename this file `CreateNewUser.aspx`, then open it in **Source** mode (Fig. 21.55). Note that this file contains a `Page` directive with a `Language` property, a `MasterPageFile` property and a `Title` property. The `Page` directive indicates the `MasterPageFile` that is used as a starting point for this new page's design. In this case, the `MasterPageFile` property is set to `"~/Bug2Bug.master"` to indicate that the current file is based on the master page we just created. The `Title` property specifies the title that will be displayed in the web browser's title bar when the content page is loaded. This value, which we set to `Create a New User`, replaces the value (i.e., `Bug2Bug`) set in the `title` element of the master page.

Because `CreateNewUser.aspx`'s `Page` directive specifies `Bug2Bug.master` as the page's `MasterPageFile`, the content page implicitly contains the contents of the master page, such as the `DOCTYPE`, `html` and `body` elements. The content page file does not duplicate the XHTML elements found in the master page. Instead, the content page contains `Content` controls (e.g. lines 7–8 and 9–11 in Fig. 21.55), in which we will place page-specific content that will replace the master page's `ContentPlaceHolders` when the content page is requested. The `ContentPlaceHolderID` property of the `Content` control identifies the `ContentPlaceHolder` in the master page that the control should replace—in this case, `head` and `bodyContent` (lines 7 and 9, respectively).

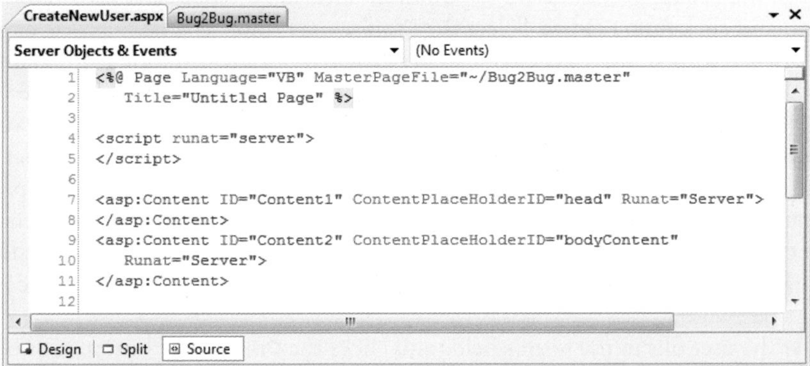

Fig. 21.55 | Content page `CreateNewUser.aspx` in **Source** mode.

The relationship between a content page and its master page is more evident in **Design** mode (Fig. 21.56). The gray-shaded region contains the contents of the master page `Bug2Bug.master` as they will appear in `CreateNewUser.aspx` when rendered in a web browser. The contents are grayed out in the IDE to indicate that they are uneditable, but they will display normally when you run the web application. The only editable part of this page is the `bodyContent` `Content` control, which appears in place of the master page's `ContentPlaceHolder`. The `head` `Content` control is for adding elements to the page's head element, and can only be edited in **Source** mode.

Fig. 21.56 | Content page `CreateNewUser.aspx` in **Design** mode.

Step 7: Adding a `CreateUserWizard` *Control to a Content Page*

Recall from Section 21.8.1 that `CreateNewUser.aspx` is the page in our website that allows first-time visitors to create user accounts. To provide this functionality, we use a `CreateUserWizard` control. Place the cursor inside the `Content` control in **Design** mode and double click `CreateUserWizard` in the **Login** section of the **Toolbox** to add it to the page at the current cursor position. You can also drag-and-drop the control onto the page.

To change the `CreateUserWizard`'s appearance, open the **CreateUserWizard Tasks** smart-tag menu and click **Auto Format**. Select the **Professional** color scheme.

As discussed previously, a `CreateUserWizard` provides a registration form that site visitors can use to create a user account. ASP.NET creates a SQL Server database (named `ASPNETDB.MDF` and located in the `App_Data` folder) to store the user names, passwords and other account information of the application's users. ASP.NET also enforces a default set of requirements for filling out the form. Each field on the form is required, the password must contain at least seven characters (including at least one nonalphanumeric character) and the two passwords entered must match. The form also asks for a security question and answer that can be used to identify a user in case the user needs to reset or recover the account's password.

After the user fills in the form's fields and clicks the **Create User** button to submit the account information, ASP.NET verifies that all the form's requirements were fulfilled and attempts to create the user account. If an error occurs (e.g., the username already exists), the `CreateUserWizard` displays a message below the form. If the account is created successfully, the form is replaced by a confirmation message and a button that allows the user to continue. You can view this confirmation message in **Design** mode by selecting **Complete** from the **Step** drop-down list in the **CreateUserWizard Tasks** smart-tag menu.

When a user account is created, ASP.NET automatically logs the user into the site (we say more about the login process shortly). At this point, the user is authenticated and allowed to access the `Secure` folder. After we create `Books.aspx` later in this section, we set the `CreateUserWizard`'s `ContinueDestinationPageUrl` property to `~/Secure/Books.aspx` to indicate that the user should be redirected to `Books.aspx` after clicking the **Continue** button on the confirmation page.

Figure 21.57 presents the completed `CreateNewUser.aspx` file (reformatted for readability). Inside the `Content` control, the `CreateUserWizard` control is defined by the markup in lines 13–40. The start tag (lines 13–16) contains several properties that specify formatting styles for the control, as well as the `ContinueDestinationPageUrl` property, which you will set later in the chapter. Lines 36–39 specify the wizard's two steps—`CreateUserWizardStep` and `CompleteWizardStep`—in a `WizardSteps` element. `CreateUserWizardStep` and `CompleteWizardStep` are classes that encapsulate the details of creating a user and issuing a confirmation message. Finally, lines 17–35 contain elements that define additional styles used to format specific parts of the control.

```
1  <%-- Fig. 21.57: CreateNewUser.aspx --%>
2  <%-- Content page using a CreateUserWizard control to register users. --%>
3  <%@ Page Language="VB" MasterPageFile="~/Bug2Bug.master"
4     Title="Create a New User" %>
5
6  <script runat="server">
7  </script>
8
9  <asp:Content ID="Content1" ContentPlaceHolderID="head" Runat="Server">
10 </asp:Content>
11 <asp:Content ID="Content2" ContentPlaceHolderID="bodyContent"
12    Runat="Server">
```

Fig. 21.57 | `CreateNewUser.aspx` page that provides a user registration form. (Part 1 of 3.)

```
   <asp:CreateUserWizard ID="CreateUserWizard1" runat="server"
      BackColor="#F7F6F3" BorderColor="#E6E2D8" BorderStyle="Solid"
      BorderWidth="1px" Font-Names="Verdana" Font-Size="0.8em"
      ContinueDestinationPageUrl="~/Secure/Books.aspx">
      <SideBarStyle BackColor="#5D7B9D" BorderWidth="0px"
         Font-Size="0.9em" VerticalAlign="Top" />
      <SideBarButtonStyle BorderWidth="0px" Font-Names="Verdana"
         ForeColor="White" />
      <ContinueButtonStyle BackColor="#FFFBFF" BorderColor="#CCCCCC"
         BorderStyle="Solid" BorderWidth="1px" Font-Names="Verdana"
         ForeColor="#284775" />
      <NavigationButtonStyle BackColor="#FFFBFF" BorderColor="#CCCCCC"
         BorderStyle="Solid" BorderWidth="1px" Font-Names="Verdana"
         ForeColor="#284775" />
      <HeaderStyle BackColor="#5D7B9D" BorderStyle="Solid"
         Font-Bold="True" Font-Size="0.9em" ForeColor="White"
         HorizontalAlign="Center" />
      <CreateUserButtonStyle BackColor="#FFFBFF" BorderColor="#CCCCCC"
         BorderStyle="Solid" BorderWidth="1px" Font-Names="Verdana"
         ForeColor="#284775" />
      <TitleTextStyle BackColor="#5D7B9D" Font-Bold="True"
         ForeColor="White" />
      <StepStyle BorderWidth="0px" />
      <WizardSteps>
         <asp:CreateUserWizardStep runat="server" />
         <asp:CompleteWizardStep runat="server" />
      </WizardSteps>
   </asp:CreateUserWizard>
</asp:Content>
```

(a)

(b)

Fig. 21.57 | `CreateNewUser.aspx` page that provides a user registration form. (Part 2 of 3.)

(c)

Fig. 21.57 | `CreateNewUser.aspx` page that provides a user registration form. (Part 3 of 3.)

The sample outputs in Fig. 21.57(a) and Fig. 21.57(b) demonstrate successfully creating a user account with `CreateNewUser.aspx`. We use the password `pa$$word` for testing purposes. This password satisfies the minimum length and special character requirement imposed by ASP.NET, but in a real application, you should use a password that is more difficult for someone to guess. Figure 21.57(c) illustrates the error message that appears when you attempt to create a second user account with the same username—ASP.NET requires that each username be unique.

Step 8: Creating a Login Page

Recall from Section 21.8.1 that `Login.aspx` is the page in our website that allows returning visitors to log into their user accounts. To create this functionality, add another content page named `Login.aspx` and set its title to `Login`. In **Design** mode, drag a `Login` control (located in the **Login** section of the **Toolbox**) to the page's `Content` control. Open the **Auto Format** dialog from the **Login Tasks** smart-tag menu and set the control's color scheme to **Professional**.

Next, configure the `Login` control to display a link to the page for creating new users. Set the `Login` control's `CreateUserUrl` property to `CreateNewUser.aspx` by clicking the ellipsis button to the right of this property in the **Properties** window and selecting the `CreateNewUser.aspx` file in the resulting dialog. Then set the `CreateUserText` property to `Click here to create a new user`. These property values cause a link to appear in the `Login` control.

Finally, change the value of the `Login` control's `DisplayRememberMe` property to `False`. By default, the control displays a checkbox and the text `Remember me next time`.

This can be used to allow a user to remain authenticated beyond a single browser session on the user's current computer. However, we want to require that users log in each time they visit the site, so we disable this option.

The `Login` control encapsulates the details of logging a user into a web application (i.e., authenticating a user). When a user enters a username and password, then clicks the **Log In** button, ASP.NET determines whether the information provided matches that of an account in the membership database (i.e., `ASPNETDB.MDF` created by ASP.NET). If they match, the user is authenticated (i.e., the user's identity is confirmed), and the browser is redirected to the page specified by the `Login` control's `DestinationPageUrl` property. We set this property to the `Books.aspx` page after creating it in the next section. If the user's identity cannot be confirmed (i.e., the user is not authenticated), the `Login` control displays an error message (see Fig. 21.58), and the user can attempt to log in again.

Figure 21.58 presents the completed `Login.aspx` page. Note that, as in `CreateNewUser.aspx`, the `Page` directive indicates that this content page inherits content from `Bug2Bug.master`. In the `Content` control that replaces the master page's `ContentPlaceHolder` with `ID bodyContent`, lines 12–25 create a `Login` control. Note the `CreateUserText` and `CreateUserUrl` properties (lines 14–15) that we set using the **Properties** window. Line 17 in the start tag for the `Login` control contains the `DestinationPageUrl` (you will set this property in the next step). The elements in lines 18–24 define various formatting styles applied to parts of the control. Note that all of the functionality related to actually logging the user in or displaying error messages is completely hidden from you.

```
1  <%-- Figure 21.58: Login.aspx --%>
2  <%-- Content page using a Login control that authenticates users. --%>
3  <%@ Page Language="VB" MasterPageFile="~/Bug2Bug.master" Title="Login" %>
4
5  <script runat="server">
6  </script>
7
8  <asp:Content ID="Content1" ContentPlaceHolderID="head" Runat="Server">
9  </asp:Content>
10 <asp:Content ID="Content2" ContentPlaceHolderID="bodyContent"
11    Runat="Server">
12    <asp:Login ID="Login1" runat="server" BackColor="#F7F6F3"
13       BorderColor="#E6E2D8" BorderPadding="4" BorderStyle="Solid"
14       BorderWidth="1px" CreateUserText="Click here to create a new user"
15       CreateUserUrl="~/CreateNewUser.aspx" DisplayRememberMe="False"
16       Font-Names="Verdana" Font-Size="0.8em" ForeColor="#333333"
17       DestinationPageUrl="~/Secure/Books.aspx">
18       <TextBoxStyle Font-Size="0.8em" />
19       <LoginButtonStyle BackColor="#FFFBFF" BorderColor="#CCCCCC"
20          BorderStyle="Solid" BorderWidth="1px" Font-Names="Verdana"
21          Font-Size="0.8em" ForeColor="#284775" />
22       <InstructionTextStyle Font-Italic="True" ForeColor="Black" />
23       <TitleTextStyle BackColor="#5D7B9D" Font-Bold="True"
24          Font-Size="0.9em" ForeColor="White" />
25    </asp:Login>
26 </asp:Content>
```

Fig. 21.58 | `Login.aspx` content page using a Login control. (Part 1 of 2.)

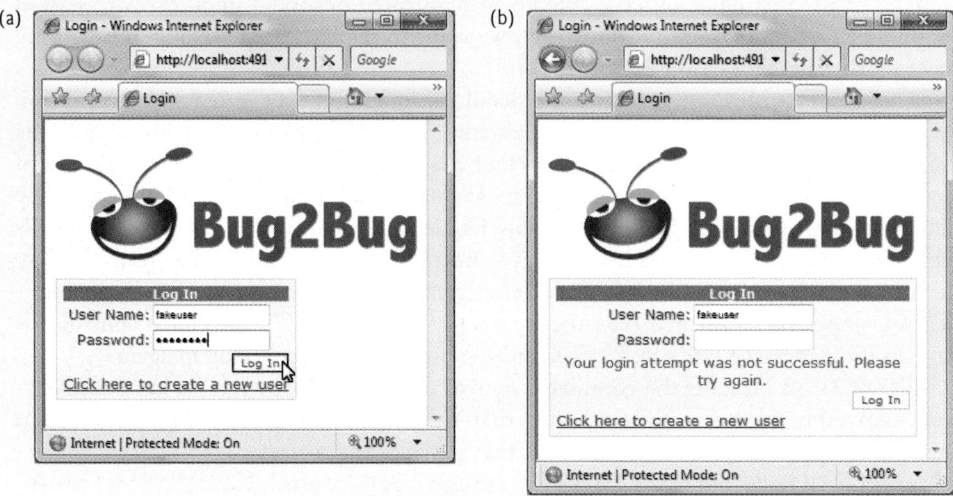

Fig. 21.58 | `Login.aspx` content page using a Login control. (Part 2 of 2.)

When a user enters the username and password of an existing user account, ASP.NET authenticates the user and writes to the client an encrypted cookie containing information about the authenticated user. Encrypted data is data translated into a code that only the sender and receiver can understand—thereby keeping it private. The encrypted cookie contains a `String` user name and a `Boolean` value that specifies whether this cookie should persist (i.e., remain on the client's computer) beyond the current session. Our application authenticates the user only for the current session.

Step 9: Creating a Content Page That Only Authenticated Users Can Access

A user who has been authenticated will be redirected to `Books.aspx`. We now create the `Books.aspx` file in the `Secure` folder—the folder for which we set an access rule denying access to anonymous users. If an unauthenticated user requests this file, the user will be redirected to `Login.aspx`. From there, the user can either log in or create a new account, both of which will authenticate the user, thus allowing the user to return to `Books.aspx`.

To create `Books.aspx`, right click the `Secure` folder in the **Solution Explorer** and select **Add New Item...**. In the resulting dialog, select **Web Form** and specify the file name `Books.aspx`. You'll need to write event handlers for this form, so check the box **Place code in separate file.** Also check the box **Select master page** to indicate that this Web Form should be created as a content page that references a master page, then click **Add**. In the **Select a Master Page** dialog, select `Bug2Bug.master` and click **OK**. The IDE creates the file and opens it in **Source** mode. Change the `Title` property of the `Page` directive to `Book Information`.

Step 10: Customizing the Secure Page

To customize the `Books.aspx` page for a particular user, we add a welcome message containing a `LoginName` control, which displays the current authenticated username. Open `Books.aspx` in **Design** mode. In the `Content` control, type `Welcome` followed by a comma and a space. Then drag a `LoginName` control from the **Toolbox** onto the page. When this page executes on the server, the text `[UserName]` that appears in this control in **Design** mode will be replaced by the current username. In **Source** mode, type an exclamation point (`!`) directly after the `LoginName` control (with no spaces in between). [*Note:* If you add the exclamation point in **Design** mode, the IDE may insert extra spaces or a line break between this character and the preceding control. Entering the `!` in **Source** mode ensures that it appears adjacent to the user's name.]

Next, add a `LoginStatus` control, which will allow the user to log out of the website when finished viewing the listing of books in the database. A `LoginStatus` control renders on a web page in one of two ways—by default, if the user is not authenticated, the control displays a hyperlink with the text `Login`; if the user is authenticated, the control displays a hyperlink with the text `Logout`. Each link performs the stated action. Add a `LoginStatus` control to the page by dragging it from the **Toolbox** onto the page. In this example, any user who reaches this page must already be authenticated, so the control will always render as a `Logout` link. The **LoginStatus Tasks** smart-tag menu allows you switch between the control's **Views**. Select the **Logged In** view to see the `Logout` link. To change the actual text of this link, modify the control's `LogoutText` property to `Click here to log out`. Next, set the `LogoutAction` property to `RedirectToLoginPage`.

*Step 11: Connecting the **`CreateUserWizard`** and **`Login`** Controls to the Secure Page*

Now that we have created `Books.aspx`, we can specify that this is the page to which the `CreateUserWizard` and `Login` controls redirect users after they are authenticated. Open `CreateNewUser.aspx` in **Design** mode and set the `CreateUserWizard` control's `ContinueDestinationPageUrl` property to `Books.aspx`. Next, open `Login.aspx` and select `Books.aspx` as the `DestinationPageUrl` of the `Login` control.

At this point, you can run the web application by selecting **Debug > Start Without Debugging**. First, create a user account on `CreateNewUser.aspx`, then notice how the `LoginName` and `LoginStatus` controls appear on `Books.aspx`. Next, log out of the site and log back in using `Login.aspx`.

*Step 12: Generating LINQ to SQL Classes Based on the **`Books.mdf`** Database*

Now let's add the content (i.e., book information) to the secure page `Books.aspx`. This page will provide a `DropDownList` containing authors' names and a `GridView` displaying information about books written by the author selected in the `DropDownList`. A user will select an author from the `DropDownList` to cause the `GridView` to display information about only the books written by the selected author.

To work with the `Books` database through LINQ, we use the same approach as the preceding case study in which we accessed the `Guestbook` database. First you need to generate the LINQ to SQL classes based on the `Books` database, which is provided in the `databases` subfolder of this chapter's examples folder. Name the classes `BooksDB.dbml` When you drag the tables of the `Books` database onto the **Object Relation Designer** of `BooksDB.dbml`, you'll find that associations (represented by arrows) between the two tables are automatically generated (Fig. 21.59).

To obtain data from this data context, you'll use two `LinqDataSource` controls. In both cases however, the `LinqDataSource` control's built-in data selection functionality won't be versatile enough, so the implementation will be slightly different than in the preceding case study. In *Steps 13* and *14*, you'll learn to use a custom `SELECT` LINQ statement as the query of a `LinqDataSource`.

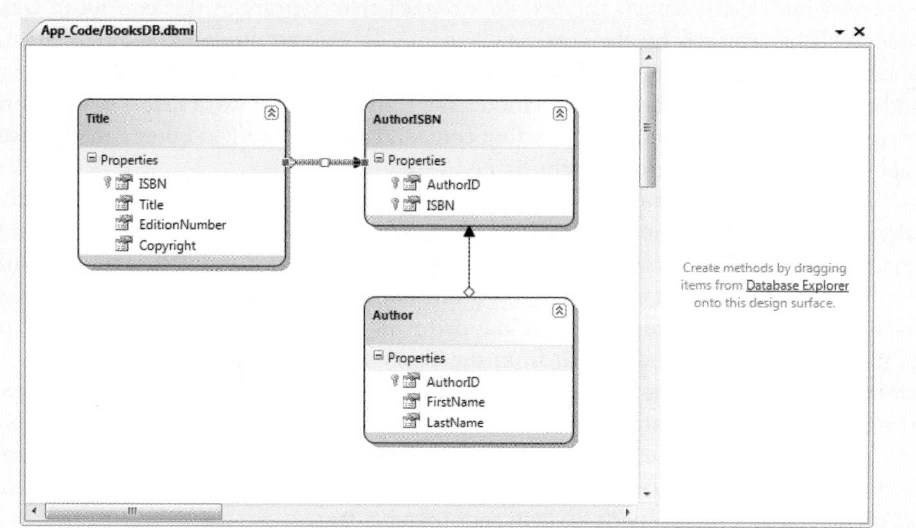

Fig. 21.59 | Object Relation Designer of `Books` database.

Step 13: Adding a `DropDownList` *Containing Authors' First and Last Names*

Now that we have created a `BooksDBDataContext` (one of the generated LINQ to SQL classes), we add controls to `Books.aspx` that will display the data on the web page. We first add the `DropDownList` from which users can select an author. Open `Books.aspx` in **Design** mode, then add the text `Author:` and a `DropDownList` control named `authorsDropDownList` in the page's `Content` control, below the existing content. The `DropDownList` initially displays the text `[Unbound]`. We now bind the list to a data source, so the list displays the author information in the `Authors` table of the `Books` database.

Because the **Configure Data Source** wizard only allows us to create `LinqDataSources` with simple `SELECT` LINQ statements, we cannot use it here. Instead, add a `LinqDataSource` object below the `DropDownList` named `authorsLinqDataSource`. In the **DropDownList Tasks** smart-tag menu, click **Choose Data Source...** to start the **Data Source Configuration Wizard** (Fig. 21.60). Select `authorsLinqDataSource` from the **Select a data source** drop-down list in the first screen of the wizard. Set `Name` as the data field to display and `AuthorID` as the data field to use as the value. [*Note:* Because `authorsLinqDataSource` has no defined `SELECT` query, you must manually type these values in; they will not appear in the drop-down list.] Thus, when `authorsDropDownList` is rendered in a web browser, the list items will display the names of the authors, but the underlying values associated with each item will be the `AuthorID`s of the authors. Click **OK** to bind the `DropDownList` to the specified data.

In the Visual Basic code-behind file (`Books.aspx.vb`), create an instance of `BooksDBDataContext` as a class variable. In the **Design** view of `Books.aspx`, double click `authorsLinqDataSource`. Double-clicking a `LinqDataSource` control creates an event handler for its **`Selecting`** event. This event is raised every time the `LinqDataSource` selects data from its data context, and can be used to implement custom `SELECT` queries against the data context. To do so, define the **`Result`** property of the event handler's arguments object to be the custom LINQ query. The results of the query become the data source's

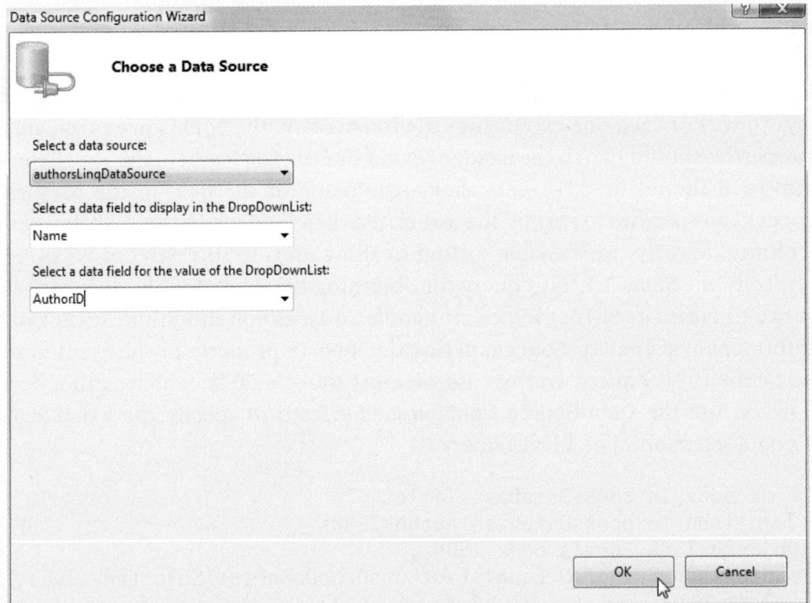

Fig. 21.60 | Choosing a data source for a `DropDownList`.

data. In this case, we must create a custom anonymous type in the `SELECT` clause with properties `Name` and `AuthorID` that contain the author's full name and ID. The LINQ query is

```
From author In booksDatabase.Authors _
Select Name = author.FirstName & " " & author.LastName, _
   author.AuthorID
```

The limitations of the **Configure Data Source** wizard prevent us from using a custom field such as `Name` (a combination of first name and last name, separated by a space) that isn't one of the data table's columns.

The last step in configuring the `DropDownList` on `Books.aspx` is to set the control's `AutoPostBack` property to `True`. This property indicates that a postback occurs each time the user selects an item in the `DropDownList`. As you will see shortly, this causes the page's `GridView` (created in the next step) to display new data.

Step 14: Creating a `GridView` to Display the Selected Author's Books

We now add a `GridView` to `Books.aspx` for displaying the book information by the author selected in the `authorsDropDownList`. Add a `GridView` named `titlesGridView` below the other controls in the page's `Content` control.

To bind the `GridView` to data from the `Books` database, create a `LinqDataSource` named `titlesLinqDataSource` beneath the `GridView`. Select `titlesLinqDataSource` from the **Choose Data Source** drop-down list in the **GridView Tasks** smart-tag menu. Because `titlesLinqDataSource` has no defined `SELECT` query, the `GridView` will not automatically be configured.

To configure the columns of the `GridView` to display the appropriate data, select **Edit Columns...** from the **GridView Tasks** smart-tag menu to initiate the **Fields** dialog (Fig. 21.61). Uncheck the **Auto-generate fields** box to indicate that you'll manually define the fields to display. Create `BoundFields` with `HeaderTexts` `ISBN`, `Title`, `Edition Number`, and `Copyright`. For each one except for `Edition Number`, the `SortExpression` and `DataField` properties should match the `HeaderText`. For `Edition Number`, the `SortExpression` and `DataField` should be `EditionNumber`—the name of the field in the database. The `SortExpression` specifies to sort by the associated data field when the user chooses to sort by the column. Shortly, we'll enable sorting to allow users to sort this `GridView`.

To specify the `SELECT` LINQ query for obtaining the data, double click `titlesLinqDataSource` to create its `Selecting` event handler. Just as you did in the `Selecting` event handler for `authorsLinqDataSource`, define the `Result` property of the event-arguments object to be the LINQ query. In this case we must to use a `JOIN`, which cannot be accomplished if you use the **Data Source Configuration Wizard** to specify the `LinqDataSource` control's data selection. The LINQ query is

```
From book In booksDatabase.Titles _
Join isbn In booksDatabase.AuthorISBNs _
On isbn.ISBN Equals book.ISBN _
Where isbn.AuthorID.Equals(authorsDropDownList.SelectedValue) _
Select book
```

The `GridView` needs to update every time the user makes a new author selection. To implement this, double click the `DropDownList` to create an event handler for its `SelectedIndexChanged` event. Make the `GridView` update by invoking its `DataBind` method. Figure 21.62 shows the code for the completed code-behind file. Line 8 defines the data

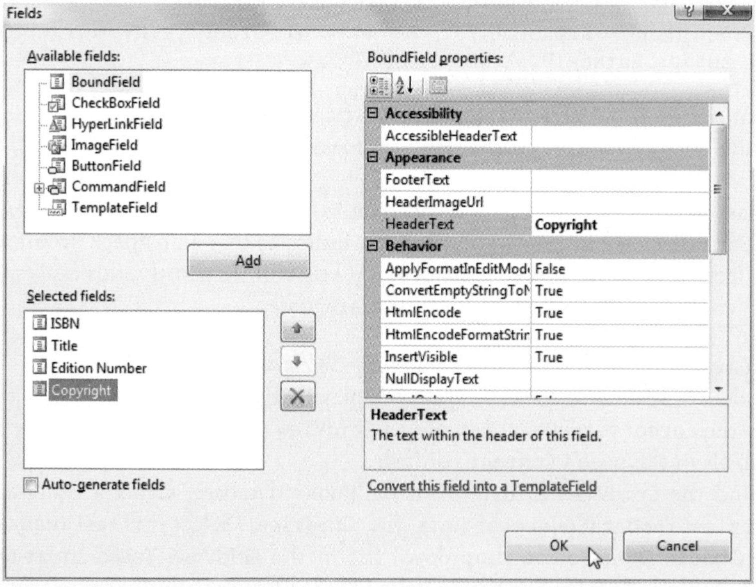

Fig. 21.61 | Creating `GridView` fields in the **Fields** dialog.

```
1  ' Fig. 21.62: Books.aspx.vb
2  ' Code-behind file that defines event handlers for the secure books
3  ' database application.
4  Partial Class Books
5     Inherits System.Web.UI.Page
6
7     ' data context queried by data sources
8     Private booksDatabase As New BooksDBDataContext()
9
10    ' runs a query and uses the result as authorsLinqDataSource's data
11    Protected Sub authorsLinqDataSource_Selecting( _
12       ByVal sender As Object, ByVal e As LinqDataSourceSelectEventArgs) _
13       Handles authorsLinqDataSource.Selecting
14
15       ' SELECT LINQ query returning all authors
16       e.Result = From author In booksDatabase.Authors _
17          Select Name = author.FirstName & " " & author.LastName, _
18             author.AuthorID
19    End Sub ' authorsLinqDataSource_Selecting
20
21    ' runs a query and uses the result as titlesLinqDataSource's data
22    Protected Sub titlesLinqDataSource_Selecting(ByVal sender As Object, _
23       ByVal e As LinqDataSourceSelectEventArgs) _
24       Handles titlesLinqDataSource.Selecting
25
26       ' SELECT LINQ query returning all books by the selected author
27       e.Result = From book In booksDatabase.Titles _
28          Join isbn In booksDatabase.AuthorISBNs _
29          On isbn.ISBN Equals book.ISBN _
30          Where isbn.AuthorID.Equals(authorsDropDownList.SelectedValue) _
31          Select book
32    End Sub ' titlesLinqDataSource_Selecting
33
34    ' updates the books whenever the user makes a new author selection
35    Protected Sub authorsDropDownList_SelectedIndexChanged( _
36       ByVal sender As Object, ByVal e As System.EventArgs) _
37       Handles authorsDropDownList.SelectedIndexChanged
38
39       titlesGridView.DataBind() ' update the GridView
40    End Sub ' authorsDropDownList_SelectedIndexChanged
41 End Class ' Books
```

Fig. 21.62 | Code-behind file that defines event handlers for the secure books database application.

context object that is used as the source of both data sources. Lines 11–19 and 22–32 define the two data source's `Selecting` events. Lastly, `authorsDropDownList`'s `SelectedIndexChanged` event handler is defined in lines 35–40.

Now that the `GridView` is tied to a data source, we modify several of the control's properties to adjust its appearance and behavior. Set the `GridView`'s `CellPadding` property to 5, set the `BackColor` of the `AlternatingRowStyle` to `LightYellow`, and set the `BackColor` of the `HeaderStyle` to `LightGreen`. Change the `Width` of the control to `600px` to accommodate long data values.

Next, in the **GridView Tasks** smart-tag menu, check **Enable Sorting** to make the column headings in the `GridView` to hyperlinks that allow users to sort the data in the `GridView` using the sort expressions specified by each column. For example, clicking the `Titles` heading in the web browser will cause the displayed data to appear sorted in alphabetical order. Clicking this heading a second time will cause the data to be sorted in reverse alphabetical order. ASP.NET hides the details required to achieve this functionality.

Finally, in the **GridView Tasks** smart-tag menu, check **Enable Paging**. This causes the `GridView` to split across multiple pages. The user can click the numbered links at the bottom of the `GridView` control to display a different page of data. `GridView`'s `PageSize` property determines the number of entries per page. Set the `PageSize` property to `4` using the **Properties** window so that the `GridView` displays only four books per page. This technique for displaying data makes the site more readable and enables pages to load more quickly (because less data is displayed at one time). Note that, as with sorting data in a `GridView`, you do not need to add any code to achieve paging functionality. Figure 21.63 displays the completed `Books.aspx` file in **Design** mode.

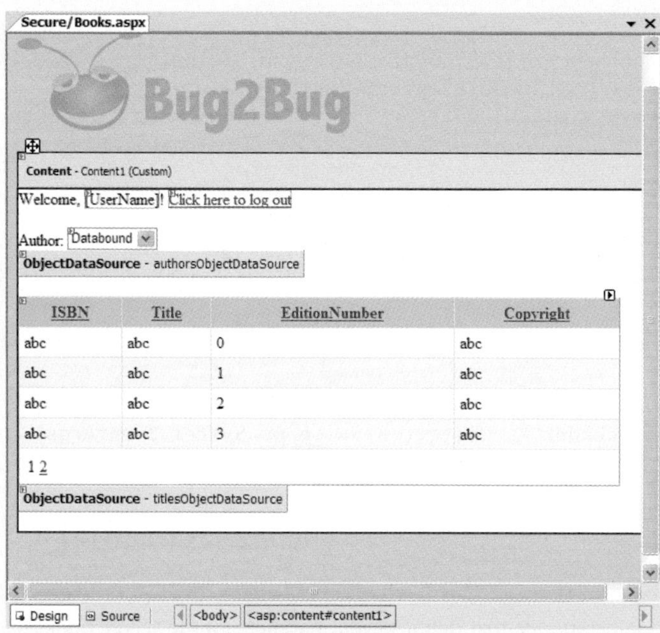

Fig. 21.63 | Completed `Books.aspx` in **Design** mode.

Step 17: Examining the Markup in `Books.aspx`

Figure 21.64 presents the markup in `Books.aspx` (reformatted for readability). Aside from the exclamation point in line 12, which we added manually in **Source** mode, all the remaining markup was generated by the IDE in response to the actions we performed in **Design** mode. The `Content` control (lines 9–46) defines page-specific content that will replace the `ContentPlaceHolder` named `bodyContent`. Recall that this control is located in the master page specified in line 3. Line 12 creates the `LoginName` control, which displays the authenticated user's name when the page is requested and viewed in a browser. Lines 13–15 create the `LoginStatus` control. Recall that this control is configured to redirect the user to the login page after logging out (i.e., clicking the hyperlink with the `LogoutText`).

Lines 19–22 define the `DropDownList` that displays the names of the authors in the `Books` database. Line 21 contains the control's `AutoPostBack` property, which indicates that changing the selected item in the list causes a postback to occur. The `DataSourceID` property in line 20 specifies that the `DropDownList`'s items are created based on the data obtained through the `authorsLinqDataSource` (defined in lines 23–24).

```
1  <%-- Fig. 21.64: Books.aspx --%>
2  <%-- Displays information from the Books database. --%>
3  <%@ Page Language="VB" MasterPageFile="~/Bug2Bug.master"
4     AutoEventWireup="false" CodeFile="Books.aspx.vb" Inherits="Books"
5     title="Book Information" %>
6
7  <asp:Content ID="Content1" ContentPlaceHolderID="head" Runat="Server">
8  </asp:Content>
9  <asp:Content ID="Content2" ContentPlaceHolderID="bodyContent"
10    Runat="Server">
11    Welcome,
12    <asp:LoginName ID="LoginName1" runat="server" />!
13    <asp:LoginStatus ID="LoginStatus1" runat="server"
14       LogoutText="Click here to log out"
15       LogoutAction="RedirectToLoginPage" />
16    <br />
17    <br />
18    Author:
19    <asp:DropDownList ID="authorsDropDownList" runat="server"
20       DataSourceID="authorsLinqDataSource" DataTextField="Name"
21       DataValueField="AuthorID" AutoPostBack="True">
22    </asp:DropDownList>
23    <asp:LinqDataSource ID="authorsLinqDataSource" runat="server">
24    </asp:LinqDataSource>
25    <br />
26    <br />
27    <asp:GridView ID="titlesGridView" runat="server" AllowPaging="True"
28       AllowSorting="True" CellPadding="5" Width="600px"
29       DataSourceID="titlesLinqDataSource" PageSize="4"
30       AutoGenerateColumns="False">
31       <Columns>
32          <asp:BoundField DataField="ISBN" HeaderText="ISBN"
33             SortExpression="ISBN" />
34          <asp:BoundField DataField="Title" HeaderText="Title"
35             SortExpression="Title" />
36          <asp:BoundField DataField="EditionNumber"
37             HeaderText="Edition Number" SortExpression="EditionNumber" />
38          <asp:BoundField DataField="Copyright" HeaderText="Copyright"
39             SortExpression="Copyright" />
40       </Columns>
```

Fig. 21.64 | Displays information from the Books database. (Part 1 of 3.)

```
            <HeaderStyle BackColor="LightGreen" />
            <AlternatingRowStyle BackColor="LightYellow" />
        </asp:GridView>
        <asp:LinqDataSource ID="titlesLinqDataSource" runat="server">
        </asp:LinqDataSource>
    </asp:Content>
```

(a)

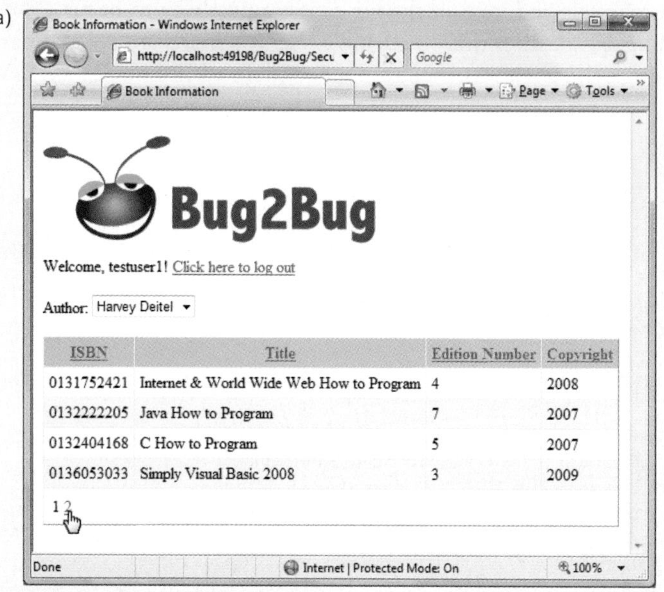

(b)

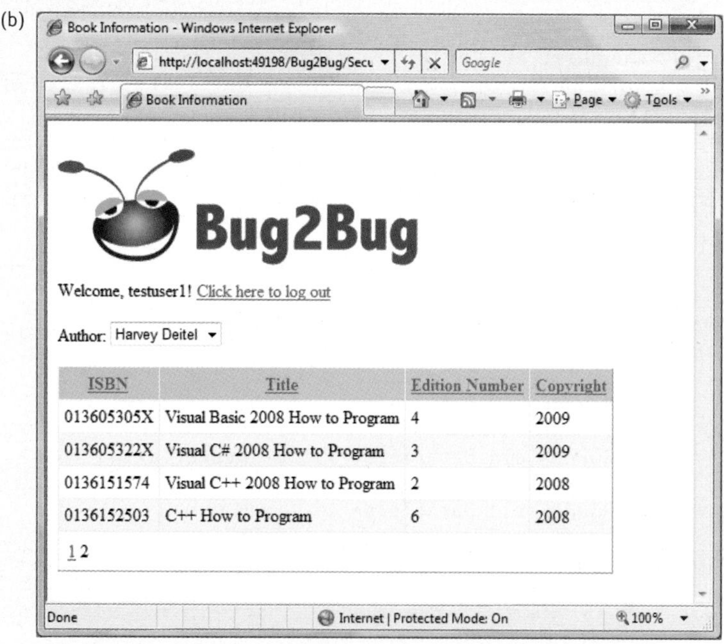

Fig. 21.64 | Displays information from the Books database. (Part 2 of 3.)

(c)

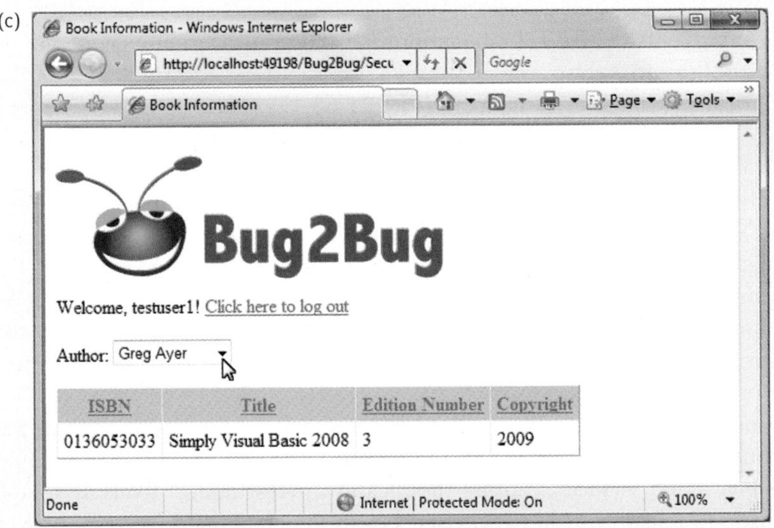

Fig. 21.64 | Displays information from the Books database. (Part 3 of 3.)

Lines 27–43 create the `GridView` that displays information about the books written by the selected author. The start tag (lines 27–30) indicates that paging (with a page size of `4`) and sorting are enabled in the `GridView`. Property `AutoGenerateColumns` indicates whether the columns in the `GridView` are generated automatically at runtime based on the fields in the data source. This property is set to `False`, reflecting our choice in the **Fields** dialog. The IDE-generated `Columns` element (lines 31–40) specifies the columns for the `GridView` using `BoundFields`. Lines 44–45 define the `LinqDataSource` used to fill the `GridView` with data. Recall that we configured the selections of both the `LinqDataSource` controls programatically, so there are almost no properties defined in the markup.

Figure 21.64(a) depicts the default appearance of `Books.aspx` in a web browser. By default, the author with `AuthorID 1` (i.e., Harvey Deitel) is selected, and his books are displayed when the page first loads. Note that the `GridView` displays paging links below the data, because the number of rows of data in `titlesLinqDataSource` is greater than the page size. Figure 21.64(b) shows the `GridView` after clicking the `2` link to view the second page of data. Figure 21.64(c) presents `Books.aspx` after the user selects a different author from the `authorsDropDownList`. The data fits on one page, so the `GridView` does not display paging links.

21.9 ASP.NET AJAX

In this section, you learn the difference between a traditional web application and an Ajax (Asynchronous JavaScript and XML) web application. You also learn how to use ASP.NET AJAX to quickly and easily improve the user experience for your web applications. To demonstrate ASP.NET AJAX capabilities, you enhance the validation example by displaying the submitted form information without reloading the entire page. The only modifications to this web application appear in `Validation.aspx` file. You use Ajax-enabled controls to add this feature.

21.9.1 Traditional Web Applications

Figure 21.65 presents the typical interactions between the client and the server in a traditional web application, such as one that uses a user registration form. The user first fills in the form's fields, then submits the form (Fig. 21.65, *Step 1*). The browser generates a request to the server, which receives the request and processes it (*Step 2*). The server generates and sends a response containing the exact page that the browser renders (*Step 3*), which causes the browser to load the new page (*Step 4*) and temporarily makes the browser window blank. Note that the client *waits* for the server to respond and *reloads the entire page* with the data from the response (*Step 4*). While such a synchronous request is being processed on the server, the user cannot interact with the web page. Frequent long periods of waiting, due perhaps to Internet congestion, have led some users to refer to the World Wide Web as the "World Wide Wait." If the user interacts with and submits another form, the process begins again (*Steps 5–8*).

This model was designed for a web of hypertext documents—what some people call the "brochure web." As the web evolved into a full-scale applications platform, the model shown in Fig. 21.65 yielded "choppy" application performance. Every full-page refresh required users to reload the full page. Users began to demand a more responsive model.

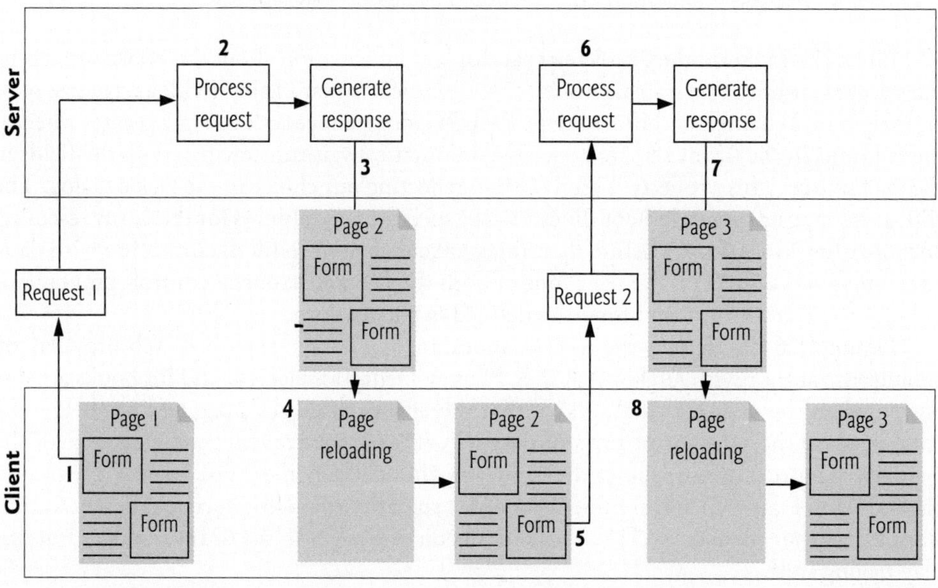

Fig. 21.65 | Class web application reloading the page for every user interaction.

21.9.2 Ajax Web Applications

Ajax web applications add a layer between the client and the server to manage communication between the two (Fig. 21.66). When the user interacts with the page, the client requests information from the server (*Step 1*). The request is intercepted by the ASP.NET AJAX controls and sent to the server as an asynchronous request (*Step 2*)—the user can continue interacting with the application in the client browser while the server processes the request. Other user interactions could result in additional requests to the server (*Steps 3* and *4*). Once the server responds to the original request (*Step 5*), the ASP.NET AJAX control that issued the request calls a client-side function to process the data returned by the server. This function—known as a callback function—uses partial-page updates (*Step 6*) to display the data in the existing web page *without reloading the entire page*. At the same time, the server may be responding to the second request (*Step 7*) and the client browser may be starting another partial-page update (*Step 8*). The callback function updates only a designated part of the page. Such partial-page updates help make web applications more responsive, making them feel more like desktop applications. The web application does not load a new page while the user interacts with it. In the following section, you use ASP.NET AJAX controls to enhance the `Validation.aspx` page.

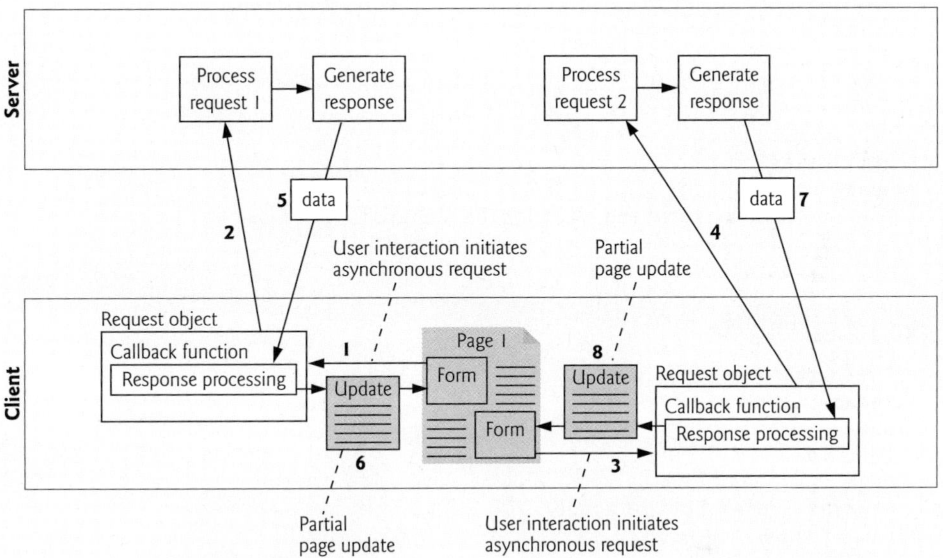

Fig. 21.66 | Ajax-enabled web application interacting with the server asynchronously.

21.9.3 Examining an ASP.NET AJAX Application

ASP.NET AJAX is built into .NET 3.5, and the Ajax Extensions package that implements basic Ajax functionality comes pre-installed in Visual Web Developer 2008. You'll notice that there is a tab of basic **AJAX Extensions** controls in the **Toolbox**. Microsoft also provides the ASP.NET AJAX Control Toolkit, which contains rich, Ajax-enabled GUI controls. You can download the latest version of the Ajax Control Toolkit from `www.asp.net/ajax/ajaxcontroltoolkit`. Be sure to download the .NET Framework 3.5 version. The toolkit does not come with an installer, so you must extract the contents of the toolkit's ZIP file to your hard drive.

To make using the ASP.NET AJAX Control Toolkit more convenient, you'll want to add its controls to the **Toolbox** in Visual Web Developer (or in Visual Studio) so you can drag and drop controls onto your Web Forms. To do so, right click the **Toolbox** and choose **Add Tab**. Type `Ajax Toolkit` in the new tab. Then right click the tab and select **Choose Items**. Navigate to the folder in which you extracted the Ajax Control Toolkit and select `AjaxControlToolkit.dll` from the `SampleWebSite\Bin` folder. A list of available Ajax controls will appear under the **Ajax Toolkit** tab when you are in **Design** mode.

To demonstrate ASP.NET AJAX capabilities we'll enhance the `Validation` application from Fig. 21.21. The only modifications to this application will appear in its `.aspx` file. We'll use Ajax-enabled controls to add Ajax features to this application. Figure 21.67 is a modified `Validation.aspx` file that enhances the application by using the `ToolkitScriptManager`, `TabContainer`, `UpdatePanel` and `ValidatorCalloutExtender` controls.

```
<%-- Fig. 21.67: Validation.aspx --%>
<%-- Validation application enchanced by ASP.NET AJAX. --%>
<%@ Page Language="VB" AutoEventWireup="false"
   CodeFile="Validation.aspx.vb" Inherits="Validation" %>
<%@ Register Assembly="AjaxControlToolkit" Namespace="AjaxControlToolkit"
   TagPrefix="ajax" %>

<!DOCTYPE html PUBLIC "-//W3C//DTD XHTML 1.0 Transitional//EN"
   "http://www.w3.org/TR/xhtml1/DTD/xhtml1-transitional.dtd">

<html xmlns="http://www.w3.org/1999/xhtml">
<head runat="server">
    <title>Demonstrating Validation Controls</title>
    <style type="text/css">
       .style1
       {
          width: 100%;
       }
    </style>
</head>
<body>
<form id="form1" runat="server">
<div>
   <ajax:ToolkitScriptManager ID="ToolkitScriptManager1"
      runat="server">
   </ajax:ToolkitScriptManager>
   Please fill out the following form.<br /><em>All fields are required
   and must contain valid information</em><br /><br />
   <ajax:TabContainer ID="TabContainer1" runat="server"
      ActiveTabIndex="0" Width="450px">
      <ajax:TabPanel runat="server" HeaderText="Name" ID="TabPanel1">
         <ContentTemplate>
         <table class="style1">
            <tr>
               <td align="right">First Name:</td>
               <td>
                  <asp:TextBox ID="firstNameTextBox" runat="server">
                  </asp:TextBox>
                  <asp:RequiredFieldValidator
                     ID="firstNameInputValidator" runat="server"
                     ControlToValidate="firstNameTextBox" Display="None"
                     ErrorMessage="Please enter your first name.">
                  </asp:RequiredFieldValidator>
```

Fig. 21.67 | Validation application enhanced by ASP.NET AJAX. (Part 1 of 4.)

```
                  <ajax:ValidatorCalloutExtender
                     ID="firstNameInputCallout" runat="server"
                     Enabled="True"
                     TargetControlID="firstNameInputValidator">
                  </ajax:ValidatorCalloutExtender>
               </td>
            </tr>
            <tr>
               <td align="right">Last Name:</td>
               <td>
                  <asp:TextBox ID="lastNameTextBox" runat="server">
                  </asp:TextBox>
                  <asp:RequiredFieldValidator ID="lastNameInputValidator"
                     runat="server" ControlToValidate="lastNameTextBox"
                     Display="None"
                     ErrorMessage="Please enter your last name.">
                  </asp:RequiredFieldValidator>
                  <ajax:ValidatorCalloutExtender
                     ID="lastNameInputCallout" runat="server"
                     Enabled="True"
                     TargetControlID="lastNameInputValidator">
                  </ajax:ValidatorCalloutExtender>
               </td>
            </tr>
         </table>
         </ContentTemplate>
      </ajax:TabPanel>
      <ajax:TabPanel ID="TabPanel2" runat="server" HeaderText="Contact">
         <ContentTemplate>
         <table class="style1">
            <tr>
               <td align="right">E-mail address:</td>
               <td>
                  <asp:TextBox ID="emailTextBox" runat="server">
                  </asp:TextBox>
                  e.g., user@domain.com
                  <asp:RequiredFieldValidator ID="emailInputValidator"
                     runat="server" ControlToValidate="emailTextBox"
                     Display="None"
                     ErrorMessage="Please enter your e-mail address.">
                  </asp:RequiredFieldValidator>
                  <ajax:ValidatorCalloutExtender ID="emailInputCallout"
                     runat="server" Enabled="True"
                     TargetControlID="emailInputValidator">
                  </ajax:ValidatorCalloutExtender>
                  <asp:RegularExpressionValidator
                     ID="emailFormatValidator" runat="server"
                     ControlToValidate="emailTextBox" Display="None"
                     ErrorMessage="Please enter a valid e-mail address."
                     ValidationExpression=
                        "\w+([-+.']\w+)*@\w+([-.]\w+)*\.\w+([-.]\w+)*">
                  </asp:RegularExpressionValidator>
```

Fig. 21.67 | Validation application enhanced by ASP.NET AJAX. (Part 2 of 4.)

```
               <ajax:ValidatorCalloutExtender ID="emailFormatCallout"
                  runat="server" Enabled="True"
                  TargetControlID="emailFormatValidator">
               </ajax:ValidatorCalloutExtender>
            </td>
         </tr>
         <tr>
            <td align="right">Phone number:</td>
            <td>
               <asp:TextBox ID="phoneTextBox" runat="server">
               </asp:TextBox>
               e.g., (555) 555-1234
               <asp:RequiredFieldValidator ID="phoneInputValidator"
                  runat="server" ControlToValidate="phoneTextBox"
                  Display="None"
                  ErrorMessage="Please enter your phone number.">
               </asp:RequiredFieldValidator>
               <ajax:ValidatorCalloutExtender ID="phoneInputCallout"
                  runat="server" Enabled="True"
                  TargetControlID="phoneInputValidator">
               </ajax:ValidatorCalloutExtender>
               <asp:RegularExpressionValidator
                  ID="phoneFormatValidator" runat="server"
                  ControlToValidate="phoneTextBox" Display="None"
                  ErrorMessage="Please enter a valid phone number."
                  ValidationExpression=
                     "((\(\d{3}\) ?)|(\d{3}-))?\d{3}-\d{4}">
               </asp:RegularExpressionValidator>
               <ajax:ValidatorCalloutExtender ID="phoneFormatCallout"
                  runat="server" Enabled="True"
                  TargetControlID="phoneFormatValidator">
               </ajax:ValidatorCalloutExtender>
            </td>
         </tr>
      </table>
      </ContentTemplate>
   </ajax:TabPanel>
</ajax:TabContainer>
<br />
<asp:Button ID="submitButton" runat="server" Text="Submit" />
<br /><br />
<asp:UpdatePanel ID="outputUpdatePanel" runat="server">
   <ContentTemplate>
      <asp:Label ID="outputLabel" Visible="false" runat="server"
         Text="Thank you for your submission.">
      </asp:Label>
   </ContentTemplate>
   <Triggers>
      <asp:AsyncPostBackTrigger ControlID="submitButton"
         EventName="Click">
      </asp:AsyncPostBackTrigger>
   </Triggers>
</asp:UpdatePanel>
```

Fig. 21.67 | Validation application enhanced by ASP.NET AJAX. (Part 3 of 4.)

```
</div>
</form>
</body>
</html>
```

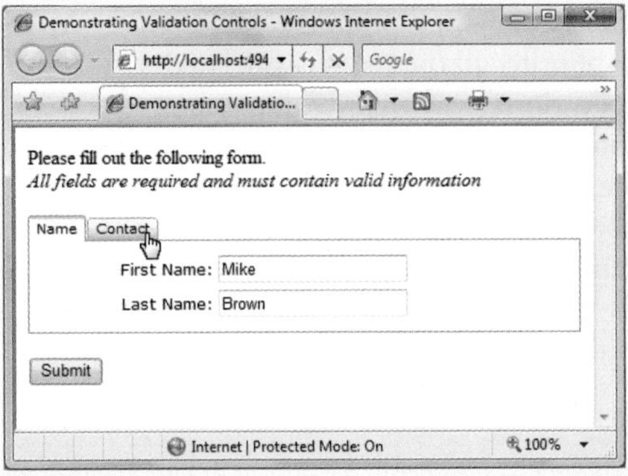

a) The user enters his first and last name and proceeds to the Contact tab.

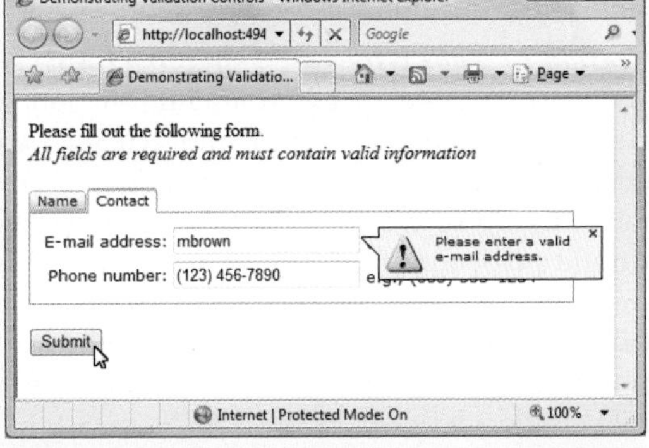

b) The user enters an e-mail address in an incorrect format and presses *Tab* to move to the next input field. A callout appears informing the user to enter an e-mail address in a valid format.

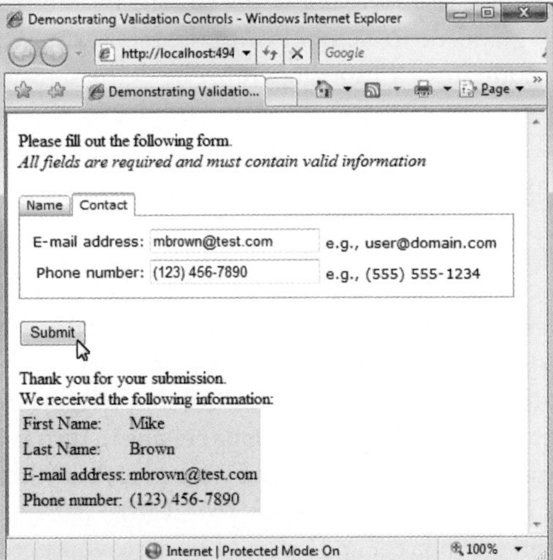

c) After the user fills out the form properly and clicks the **Submit** button, the submitted data is displayed at the bottom of the page with a partial page update.

Fig. 21.67 | Validation application enhanced by ASP.NET AJAX. (Part 4 of 4.)

ScriptManager Control

The key control in every ASP.NET AJAX-enabled application is the ScriptManager, which manages the client-side scripts that enable asynchronous Ajax functionality. There can be only one ScriptManager per page. To incorporate controls from the Ajax Control Toolkit you should use the ToolkitScriptManager that comes with the toolkit controls, rather than the ScriptManager from the ASP.NET AJAX Extensions. The ToolkitScriptManager bundles all the scripts associated with ASP. NET Ajax Toolkit controls to optimize the application's performance. Drag the ToolkitScriptManager from the **Ajax Toolkit** tab in the toolbox to the top of the page—a script manager must appear before any controls that use the scripts it manages. This generates lines 5–6 and lines 24–26. Lines 5–6 associate the AjaxControlToolkit assembly with a tag prefix, allowing us to put Ajax Control Toolkit elements on the page. To improve readability, we have changed the prefix from cc1, which is what's assigned by default, to ajax. Lines 24–26 load the ToolkitScriptManager on the page.

Common Programming Error 21.1

Putting more than one instance of the ScriptManager control on a Web Form causes the application to throw an InvalidOperationException when the page is initialized.

Grouping Information in Tabs Using the TabContainer Control

The TabContainer control enables you to group information into tabs that are displayed only if they are selected. The information in an unselected tab won't be displayed, and thus won't be sent to the client. To create multiple tabs, drag the TabContainer control from the **Ajax Toolkit** tab in the **Toolbox** to your form. This creates a container for hosting tabs (lines 29–133). To add a tab, open the **TabContainer Tasks** smart-tag menu and select **Add Tab Panel**. This adds a TabPanel object—representing a tab—to the TabContainer. Change the TabPanel's HeaderText property to specify the tab's header. In this example, we created two tabs to separate the form's name information from its contact information (lines 31–70 and 71–132).

In **Design** view, you can navigate between tabs by holding *Ctrl* and clicking the tab header. You can drag-and-drop elements into the tab as you would anywhere else. In actuality, however, the content of a TabPanel must be defined inside its ContentTemplate element (e.g., line 32–69 and 72–131). In this example, we created a layout table in each tab and moved the old input controls into the tabs. The name input field has been separated into first and last name.

Partial-Page Updates Using the UpdatePanel Control

The UpdatePanel control eliminates full-page refreshes by isolating a section of a page for a partial-page update. To implement a partial-page update, drag the UpdatePanel control from the **AJAX Extensions** tab in the **Toolbox** to your form. Then, drag into the UpdatePanel the control to update and the control that triggers the update. For this example, drag the outputLabel element into the UpdatePanel. Just as in a TabPanel, the components that are managed by the UpdatePanel are placed in the ContentTemplate element (lines 138–142) of the UpdatePanel (lines 137–148).

To specify when an UpdatePanel should update, you need to define an UpdatePanel trigger. Click the ellipsis button next to the control's Triggers property in the **Properties** window. In the **UpdatePanelTrigger Collection** dialog that appears (Fig. 21.68), click **Add** to add an AsyncPostBackTrigger. Set the ControlID property to submitButton and the EventName property to Click. Now, when the user clicks the **Submit** button, the UpdatePanel intercepts the request and makes an asynchronous request to the server instead. Then the response is inserted in the outputLabel element, and the UpdatePanel reloads the label to display the new text without refreshing the entire page.

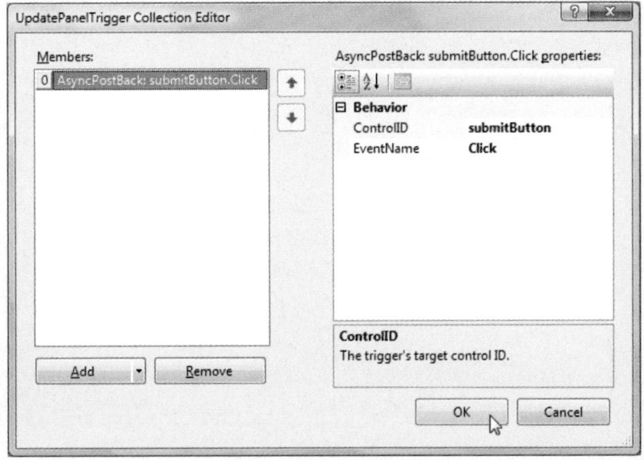

Fig. 21.68 | Creating a trigger for an UpdatePanel.

Adding Ajax Functionality to ASP.NET Validation Controls Using Ajax Extenders

Several controls in the Ajax Control Toolkit are extenders—components that enhance regular ASP.NET controls. Lines 44–48, 61–65, 85–88, 96–99, 113–116, and 124–127 in Fig. 21.67 define ValidatorCalloutExtender controls that display error messages in small yellow callouts next to the input fields. To create a ValidatorCalloutExtender, you can either drag-and-drop it into the form, just as you do with any other control, or you can select the **Add Extender** option in a validator's smart-tag menu. In the **Extender Wizard** dialog that displays (Fig. 21.69), choose ValidatorCalloutExtender from the list of available extenders, specify its ID, and click **OK**.

Line 47 of Fig. 21.67 sets the first ValidatorCalloutExtender's targetControlID property, which indicates the validator control from which the extender should obtain the error message to display. This is automatically determined if you created the extender through the **Extender Wizard**. The ValidatorCalloutExtenders display error messages with a nicer look-and-feel, so we no longer need the validator controls to display these messages on their own. For this reason, line 41 sets the Display property of the first validator to None. The remaining control extenders and validator controls are configured similarly.

Additional ASP.NET Information

The Ajax Control Toolkit contains many other extenders and independent controls. You can check them out using the sample website included with the toolkit. The live version of the sample website can be found at www.asp.net/ajax/ajaxcontroltoolkit/samples/. For more information on ASP.NET AJAX, check out our ASP.NET AJAX Resource Center at www.deitel.com/aspdotnetajax.

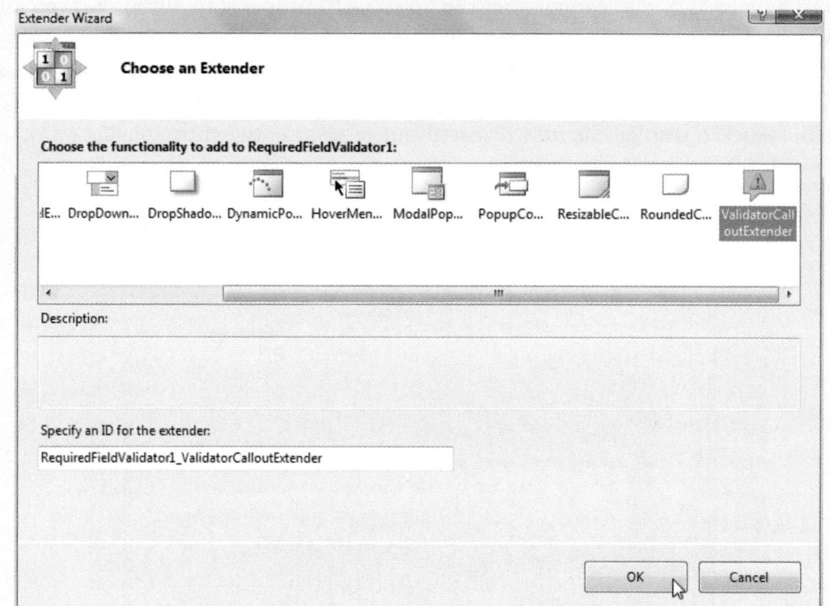

Fig. 21.69 | Creating a control extender using the **Extender Wizard**.

21.10 New ASP.NET 3.5 Data Controls

ASP.NET 3.5 introduces two new server-side data controls, the `ListView` and the `DataPager`. The `ListView` is highly customizable control for displaying data. Its implementation is similar to that of a WPF `ListView`. You can define an assortment of templates such as `ItemsTemplate`, `SelectedItemTemplate`, `ItemSeparatorTemplate`, and `GroupTemplate` to customize how to display data. For more information about the ASP.NET `ListView` control please see `msdn.microsoft.com/en-us/library/bb398790.aspx`.

The `DataPager` control works alongside a data control, such as `GridView` or `ListView`, and customizes how it pages through data. With a data pager, you can customize the combination of page-navigation buttons (such as next, previous, or page numbers) that are displayed. For more information about the ASP.NET `DataPager` control, please see `msdn.microsoft.com/en-us/library/system.web.ui.webcontrols.datapager.aspx`.

21.11 Wrap-Up

In this chapter, we introduced web-application development using ASP.NET and Visual Web Developer 2008 Express. We began by discussing the simple HTTP transactions that take place when you request and receive a web page through a web browser. You then learned about the three tiers (i.e., the client or top tier, the business logic or middle tier and the information or bottom tier) that comprise most web applications.

Next, we explained the role of ASPX files (i.e., Web Form files) and code-behind files, and the relationship between them. We discussed how ASP.NET compiles and executes web applications so that they can be displayed as XHTML in a web browser. You also learned how to build an ASP.NET web application using Visual Web Developer.

The chapter demonstrated several common ASP.NET web controls used for displaying text and images on a Web Form. You learned how to use an AdRotator control to display randomly selected images. We also discussed validation controls, which allow you to ensure that user input on a web page satisfies certain requirements.

We discussed the benefits of maintaining a user's state information across multiple pages of a website. We then demonstrated how you can include such functionality in a web application using either cookies or session tracking with HttpSessionState objects.

We presented two case studies on building ASP.NET applications that interact with databases. First, we showed how to build a guestbook application that allows users to submit comments about a website. You learned how to save the user input in a SQL Server database and how to display past submissions on the web page.

The second case study presented a secure web application that requires users to log in before accessing information from the Books database (discussed in Chapter 20). You used the **Web Site Administration Tool** to configure the application to use forms authentication and prevent anonymous users from accessing the book information. This case study explained how to use the Login, CreateUserWizard, LoginName and LoginStatus controls to simplify user authentication. You also learned to create a uniform look-and-feel for a website using a master page and several content pages.

Finally, you learned the difference between a traditional web application and an Ajax web application. We introduced ASP.NET AJAX and Microsoft's Ajax Control Toolkit. You learned how to build an Ajax-enabled web application by using a ScriptManager and the Ajax-enabled controls of the Ajax Extensions package and the Ajax Control Toolkit.

In the next chapter, we introduce web services, which allow methods on one machine to call methods on other machines via common data formats and protocols, such as XML and HTTP. You will learn how web services promote software reusability and interoperability across multiple computers on a network such as the Internet.

21.12 Web Resources

We provide links to many online resources for ASP.NET and ASP.NET AJAX in our Resource Centers:

```
www.deitel.com/aspdotnet3.5/
www.deitel.com/aspdotnetajax/
```

Start your searches here for tutorials, articles, books, blogs, sample code, forums, training courses, videos, webcasts and more. For related technologies, see our complete list of Resource Centers at www.deitel.com/ResourceCenters.html.

Summary

Section 21.1 Introduction

- Microsoft's ASP.NET technology is used for web-application development.
- Web-based applications create web content for web-browser clients. This web content includes XHTML, client-side scripting, images and binary data.

- A Web Form file represents a web page that is sent to the client browser. Web Form files have the file-name extension `.aspx` and contain a web page's GUI. You customize Web Forms by adding web controls.
- Every ASPX file created in Visual Studio has a corresponding class written in a .NET language. The file that contains this class is called the code-behind file and provides the ASPX file's programmatic implementation.

Section 21.2 Simple HTTP Transactions

- The HTTP protocol allows clients and servers to interact and exchange information in a uniform and reliable manner.
- HTTP uses URIs (Uniform Resource Identifiers) to identify data on the Internet.
- URIs that specify document locations are called URLs. Common URLs refer to files, directories or objects that perform complex tasks, such as database lookups and Internet searches.
- A URL contains information that directs a browser to the resource that the user wishes to access.
- `http://` indicates that the resource is to be obtained using the HTTP protocol.
- A hostname is translated into an IP address—a unique numerical value which identifies the server much as a telephone number uniquely defines a particular phone line. This translation is performed by a domain-name system (DNS) server—a computer that maintains a database of hostnames and their corresponding IP addresses—and the process is called a DNS lookup.
- The part of a URL after the hostname specifies both the name of the requested resource and its path, or location, on the web server.
- For security reasons, a resource's path normally specifies the location of a virtual directory. The server translates the virtual directory into a real location on the server (or on another computer on the server's network), thus hiding the true location of the resource.
- Some resources are created dynamically and do not reside anywhere on a server.
- When given a URL, a web browser performs a simple HTTP transaction to retrieve and display the web page found at that address.
- HTTP method `get` indicates that the client wishes to obtain a resource from the server. The remainder of a request provides the resource's path name and the protocol's name and version.
- Any server that understands HTTP can receive a `get` request and respond appropriately.
- HTTP status code `200` indicates success. Status code `404` informs the client that the web server could not locate the requested resource. A complete list of numeric codes indicating the status of an HTTP transaction can be found at `www.w3.org/Protocols/rfc2616/rfc2616-sec10.html`.
- In a response, the server sends one or more HTTP headers, which provide additional information about the data that will be sent.
- Multipurpose Internet Mail Extensions (MIME) is an Internet standard that specifies data formats so that programs can interpret data correctly. The MIME type `text/plain` indicates that the sent information is text that can be displayed directly, without any interpretation of the content as XHTML markup. The MIME type `image/jpeg` indicates that the content is a JPEG image. When the browser receives this MIME type, it attempts to display the image.
- The header or set of headers is followed by a blank line, which indicates to the client browser that the server is finished sending HTTP headers.
- The two most common HTTP request types (also known as request methods) are `get` and `post`.
- A `get` request typically gets (or retrieves) information from a server. Common uses of `get` requests are to retrieve an XHTML document or an image, or to fetch search results based on a user-submitted search term.

- A `post` request typically sends data to a server. Common uses of `post` requests are to send authentication information or data from a form that gathers user input.
- An HTTP request often posts data to a server-side form handler that processes the data.
- A `get` request sends information to the server as part of the URL in a query string. A `?` separates the query string from the rest of the URL in a `get` request. A *name*/*value* pair is passed to the server with the *name* and the *value* separated by an equals sign (`=`). If more than one *name*/*value* pair is submitted, each pair is separated by an ampersand (`&`).
- A `get` request may be initiated by submitting a form whose `method` attribute is set to `"get"`, or by typing the URL (possibly containing a query string) directly into the browser's address bar.
- A `post` request is specified in an XHTML form by the `method "post"`. The `post` method sends form data as an HTTP message, not as part of the URL.
- Large pieces of information must be sent using the `post` method.
- Browsers often cache web pages so they can quickly reload them. If there are no changes between the version stored in the cache and the current version on the web, this helps speed up your browsing experience.

Section 21.3 Multitier Application Architecture

- Web applications are multitier applications (sometimes referred to as *n*-tier applications). Multitier applications divide functionality into separate tiers (i.e., logical groupings of functionality).
- The information tier, or bottom tier, maintains data pertaining to the application.
- The middle tier implements business logic, controller logic and presentation logic to control interactions between the application's clients and the application's data.
- The client (or top) tier is the application's user interface (typically viewed in a web browser).

Section 21.4 Creating and Running a Simple Web-Form Example

- An ASP.NET Web Form typically consists of an ASPX file and a Visual Basic code-behind file.
- Visual Web Developer generates markup when you change a Web Form's properties and when you add text or controls to a Web Form.

Section 21.4.1 Examining an ASPX File

- ASP.NET comments begin with `<%--` and terminate with `--%>`.
- A `Page` directive (delimited by `<%@` and `%>`) specifies information needed by ASP.NET to process an ASPX file. The `CodeFile` attribute of the `Page` directive indicates the name of the corresponding code-behind file. The `Language` attribute specifies the .NET language used in this file.
- When a control's `runat` attribute is set to `"server"`, the control is processed by ASP.NET on the server, generating an XHTML equivalent.
- The `asp:` tag prefix in a control declaration indicates that a control is an ASP.NET web control.
- Each web control maps to a corresponding XHTML element (or group of elements)—when processing a web control on the server, ASP.NET generates XHTML markup that will be sent to the client to represent that control in a web browser.

Section 21.4.2 Examining a Code-Behind File

- The code-behind file is a partial class.
- Namespace `System.Web.UI` contains classes for the creation of web applications and controls.
- Class `Page` defines a standard web page, providing event handlers and objects necessary for creating web-based applications. All web applications directly or indirectly inherit from class `Page`.

- Class `Control` is the base class that provides common functionality for all web controls.
- Method `Page_Init` handles the `Init` event, which indicates that a page is ready to be initialized.

Section 21.4.3 Relationship Between an ASPX File and a Code-Behind File

- When a client requests an ASPX file, ASP.NET combines two partial classes—the one defined in the code-behind file and the one that ASP.NET generates based on the markup in the ASPX file that defines the page's GUI.
- ASP.NET compiles the combined partial classes and creates an instance that represents the page. This instance creates the XHTML that is sent to the client.
- Namespace `System.Web.UI.WebControls` contains web controls (derived from class `WebControl`) for designing a page's user interface.

Section 21.4.4 How the Code in an ASP.NET Web Page Executes

- When an instance of a page is created, the `PreInit` event occurs first, invoking method `Page_PreInit`. The `Init` event occurs next, invoking method `Page_Init`. Then the `Load` event occurs, invoking method `Page_Load`.
- After `Page_Load` finishes executing, the page processes any events raised by the page's controls.
- When a Web Form object is ready for garbage collection, an `Unload` event occurs. Event handler `Page_Unload` is inherited from class `Page` and contains any code that releases resources.

Section 21.4.5 Examining the XHTML Generated by an ASP.NET Application

- A form is a mechanism for collecting user information and sending it to the web server.
- XHTML forms can contain visual and nonvisual components.
- Nonvisual components in an XHTML form, called hidden inputs, can store any data that the document author specifies.

Section 21.4.6 Building an ASP.NET Web Application

- `DOCUMENT` is the name used to represent a Web Form in the **Properties** window.
- The Web Forms Designer's **Source** mode allows you to view the markup that represents the user interface of a page. The **Design** mode allows you to view the page as it will look and modify it by dragging-and-dropping controls from the **Toolbox** onto the Web Form. The **Split** mode allows you to view both at the same time.
- Controls and other elements are placed sequentially on a Web Form. The positions of controls and other elements are relative to the Web Form's upper-left corner.
- An alternate type of layout is known as absolute positioning, in which controls are located exactly where they are dropped on the Web Form.
- Visual Web Developer is a WYSIWYG editor.
- `Web.config` is a file that stores configuration settings for an ASP.NET web application.

Section 21.5 Web Controls

- The **Standard** section of the **Toolbox** in Visual Web Developer contains several web controls.

Section 21.5.1 Text and Graphics Controls

- The **Insert Table** command from the **Table** menu in **Design** mode allows you to add an XHTML table to a Web Form.
- An `Image` control inserts an image into a web page. The `ImageUrl` property specifies the file location of the image to display.

- A `TextBox` control allows the you to obtain text from the user and display text to the user.
- A `DropDownList` control provides a list of options to the user. Each item in the drop-down list is defined by a `ListItem` element.
- Visual Web Developer displays smart-tag menus for many ASP.NET controls to facilitate performing common tasks. A smart-tag menu is opened by clicking the small arrowhead that appears in the upper-right corner of the control in **Design** mode.
- A `HyperLink` control adds a hyperlink to a web page. The `NavigateUrl` property of this control specifies the resource that is requested when a user clicks the hyperlink.
- A `RadioButtonList` control provides a series of radio buttons for the user.

Section 21.5.2 `AdRotator` Control

- ASP.NET provides the `AdRotator` web control for displaying advertisements (or any other images). Using data from an XML file, the `AdRotator` control randomly selects an image to display and generates a hyperlink to the web page associated with that image.
- An `XmlDataSource` references an XML file containing data that will be used in an ASP.NET application. The **AdRotator Tasks** smart-tag menu allows you to create a new `XmlDataSource` that retrieves advertisement data from an XML file.
- The advertisement file used for an `AdRotator` control contains `Ad` elements, each of which provides information about a different advertisement.
- Element `ImageUrl` in an advertisement file specifies the path (location) of the advertisement's image, and element `NavigateUrl` specifies the URL that loads when a user clicks the advertisement.
- The `AlternateText` element contains text that displays as a tooltip or in place of the image when the browser cannot locate or render the image for some reason, or to assist the visually impaired.
- Element `Impressions` specifies how often an image appears, relative to the other images.

Section 21.5.3 Validation Controls

- A validation control (or validator) determines whether the data in another web control is in the proper format. Validators provide a mechanism for validating user input on the client.
- When the XHTML for a page is created, a validator is converted into JavaScript. JavaScript is a scripting language that enhances the functionality and appearance of web pages.
- The `Visible` property of a control indicates whether the control appears in the client's browser.
- A `RequiredFieldValidator` ensures that a control receives user input before a form is submitted.
- A validator's `ControlToValidate` property indicates which control will be validated.
- A validator's `ErrorMessage` property contains text to be displayed if the validation fails.
- A `RegularExpressionValidator` matches a web control's content against a regular expression. The regular expression that validates the input is assigned to property `ValidationExpression`.
- Web programmers using ASP.NET often design their web pages so that the current page reloads when the user submits the form. This event is known as a postback.
- A `Page`'s `IsPostBack` property determines whether the page is being loaded due to a postback.
- The `Validate` method of class `Page` validates a Web Form based on the validators in the `Page`.
- The `IsValid` property of class `Page` stores whether a Web Form is valid.
- The `EnableClientScript` property of a validator specifies whether to generate JavaScript for performing client-side validation.
- The `EnableViewState` attribute determines whether a web control's previous state should be stored as hidden data in the web page.

Section 21.6 Session Tracking

- Personalization makes it possible for e-businesses to communicate effectively with their customers and also improves users' ability to locate desired products and services.
- To provide personalized services to consumers, e-businesses must be able to recognize clients when they request information from a site.
- The request/response system on which the web operates is facilitated by HTTP. Unfortunately, HTTP is a stateless protocol—it does not support persistent connections that would enable web servers to maintain state information regarding particular clients.
- A session represents a unique client on a website. If the client leaves a site and then returns later, the client will still be recognized as the same user. To help the server distinguish among clients, each client must identify itself to the server.
- Tracking individual clients is known as session tracking.

Section 21.6.1 Cookies

- A cookie is a piece of data stored in a small text file on the user's computer. A cookie maintains information about the client during and between browser sessions.
- A cookie object is of type `HttpCookie`. Properties `Name` and `Value` of class `HttpCookie` can be used to retrieve the key and value in a key/value pair (both strings) in a cookie.
- Cookies are sent and received as a collection of type `HttpCookieCollection`. An application on a server can write cookies to a client using the `Response` object's `Cookies` property. Cookies can be accessed programmatically using the `Request` object's `Cookies` property. Cookies can be read by an application only if they were created in the domain in which the application is running.
- When a Web Form receives a request, the header includes information such as the request type and any cookies that have been sent previously from the server to be stored on the client machine.
- When the server formulates its response, the header information includes any cookies the server wants to store on the client computer.
- The expiration date of a cookie determines how long the cookie remains on the client's computer. If you do not set an expiration date for a cookie, the web browser maintains the cookie for the duration of the browsing session.
- Certain web applications will not work if the client has cookies disabled.

Section 21.6.2 Session Tracking with `HttpSessionState`

- Session-tracking capabilities are provided by .NET class `HttpSessionState`. Every Web Form includes an `HttpSessionState` object, which is accessible through property `Session` of class `Page`.
- When the web page is requested, an `HttpSessionState` object is created and assigned to the `Page`'s `Session` property. Also, a unique session ID is created for that client and a temporary cookie is written to the client so the server can identify the client on subsequent requests.
- The `Page`'s `Session` property is often referred to as the `Session` object.
- The `Session` object's key/value pairs are often referred to as session items.
- Session items are placed into an `HttpSessionState` object by calling method `Add`.
- `HttpSessionState` objects can store any type of object (not just `Strings`) as attribute values. This provides increased flexibility in maintaining client state information.
- Property `SessionID` contains the unique session ID. The first time a client connects to the web server, a unique session ID is created for that client. When the client makes additional requests, the client's session ID is compared with the session IDs stored in the web server's memory to retrieve the `HttpSessionState` object for that client.

- Property `Timeout` specifies the maximum amount of time that an `HttpSessionState` object can be inactive before it is discarded.
- Property `Count` provides the number of session items contained in a `Session` object.
- Indexing the `Session` object with a key name retrieves the corresponding value.
- Property `Keys` of class `HttpSessionState` returns a collection containing all the session's keys.

Section 21.7 Case Study: Connecting to a Database in ASP.NET

- A `GridView` ASP.NET data control displays data on a Web Form in a tabular format.

Section 21.7.1 Building a Web Form That Displays Data from a Database

- A `GridView`'s colors can be set using the **Auto Format...** link in the **GridView Tasks** smart tag menu.
- A SQL Server 2005 Express database used by an ASP.NET website should be located in the project's `App_Data` folder.
- A `LinqDataSource` control allows a web application to interact with any LINQ data context. Thus, to use it with a database, you'll need to generate LINQ to SQL files.
- Each column in a `GridView` is represented as a `BoundField`.
- `LinqDataSource` property `ContextTypeName` indicates the data context that the `LinqDataSource` interacts with. Property `TableName` indicates the specific table in the data context.

Section 21.7.2 Modifying the Code-Behind File for the Guestbook Application

- If you allow a `LinqDataSource` to perform automatic inserts, you can invoke its `Insert` method to insert an entry into the data context.
- `LinqDataSource` method `Insert` executes the control's `INSERT` command against the database. It takes a `Dictionary` of parameters as its argument.
- `GridView` method `DataBind` refreshes the information displayed in the `GridView`.

Section 21.8.1 Examining the Completed Secure Books Database Application

- Forms authentication is a technique that protects a page so that only users known to the website can access it. Such users are known as the site's members.
- ASP.NET login controls help create secure applications using authentication. These controls are found in the **Login** section of the **Toolbox**.
- When a user's identity is confirmed, the user is said to have been authenticated.
- A master page defines common GUI elements that are inherited by each page in a set of content pages.

Section 21.8.2 Creating the Secure Books Database Application

- ASP.NET hides the details of authenticating users, displaying appropriate success or error messages and redirecting the user to the correct page based on the authentication results.
- The **Web Site Administration Tool** allows you to configure an application's security settings, add site users and create access rules that determine who is allowed to access the site.
- By default, anonymous users who attempt to load a page in a directory to which they are denied access are redirected to a page named `Login.aspx` so that they can identify themselves.
- An ASPX page's configuration settings are determined by the current directory's `Web.config` file. The settings in this file take precedence over the settings in the root directory's `Web.config` file.
- A master page contains placeholders for custom content created in a content page, which visually inherits the master page's content, then adds content in place of the placeholders.

- Master pages have the file-name extension `.master` and, like Web Forms, can optionally use a code-behind file to define additional functionality.
- A `Master` directive in an ASPX file specifies that the file defines a master page.
- A `ContentPlaceHolder` control serves as a placeholder for page-specific content defined by a content page using a `Content` control. The `Content` control will appear in place of the master page's `ContentPlaceHolder` when the content page is requested.
- A `CreateUserWizard` control provides a registration form that site visitors can use to create a user account. ASP.NET handles the details of creating a SQL Server database to store the usernames, passwords and other account information of the application's users.
- A `Login` control encapsulates the details of authenticating a user. If the user is authenticated, the browser is redirected to the page specified by the `Login` control's `DestinationPageUrl` property. If the user is not authenticated, the `Login` control displays an error message.
- ASP.NET writes to the client an encrypted cookie containing data about an authenticated user.
- Encrypted data is data translated into a code that only the sender and receiver can understand.
- A `LoginName` control displays the current authenticated username on a Web Form.
- A `LoginStatus` control renders on a web page in one of two ways—by default, if the user is not authenticated, the control displays a hyperlink with the text `Login`; if the user is authenticated, the control displays a hyperlink with the text `Logout`. The `LogoutText` determines the text of the link in the **Logged In** view.
- Instead of using the `ContextTypeName` and `TableName` properties, you can specify data selection for a `LinqDataSource` with a custom `SELECT` LINQ statement by handling the data source's `Selecting` event. Setting the `Result` property of `Selecting` event handler's event-arguments object sets the data of the data source.
- A `DropDownList`'s `AutoPostBack` property indicates whether a postback occurs each time the user selects an item.
- When you **Enable Sorting** for a `GridView`, the column headings in the `GridView` turn into hyperlinks that allow users to sort the data it displays.
- When you **Enable Paging** for a `GridView`, the `GridView` divides its data among multiple pages. The user can click the numbered links at the bottom of the `GridView` control to display a different page of data. `GridView`'s `PageSize` property determines the number of entries per page.

Section 21.9 ASP.NET AJAX

- A traditional web application must make synchronous requests and must wait for a response, whereas an AJAX (Asynchronous JavaScript and XML) web applications can make asynchronous requests and do not need to wait for a response.

Section 21.9.3 Examining an ASP.NET AJAX Application

- ASP.NET AJAX is an extension of ASP.NET that provides a fast and simple way to create Ajax-enabled applications.
- The ASP.NET AJAX Control Toolkit contains rich controls that implement Ajax functionality.
- The key part of every ASP.NET AJAX-enabled application is the `ScriptManager` control, which manages the client-side scripts that enable asynchronous functionality.
- The `ToolkitScriptManager` bundles all the scripts associated with ASP.NET AJAX Toolkit controls to optimize the application's performance.
- The `TabContainer` control separates information into tabs, represented by `TabPanel` objects. The information in a tab is sent to the client and displayed only if it is selected.

- The `UpdatePanel` control eliminates full-page refreshes by isolating a section of a page for a partial-page update.
- The `AsyncPostBackTrigger` specifies a control and an event that triggers a partial-page refresh.
- A `TabPanel`'s or `UpdatePanel`'s components must be placed in a `ContentTemplate` element.
- Several controls in the Ajax Control Toolkit are extenders—components that enhance regular ASP.NET controllers.

Terminology

<%-- --%> ASP.NET comment delimiters
<%@ %> ASP.NET directive delimiters
absolute positioning
access rule in ASP.NET
action attribute of XHTML element `form`
`Ad` XML element in an `AdRotator` advertisement file
`Add` method of class `Dictionary`
`Add` method of class `HttpSessionState`
`AdRotator` ASP.NET web control
`Advertisements` XML element in an `AdRotator` advertisement file
Ajax (Asynchronous JavaScript and XML)
Ajax Extensions package
Ajax web application
`AlternateText` element in an `AdRotator` advertisement file
anonymous user
`asp:` tag prefix
ASP.NET 3.5
ASP.NET AJAX
ASP.NET AJAX Control Toolkit
ASP.NET comment
ASP.NET expression
ASP.NET login control
ASP.NET server control
ASP.NET Web Site in Visual Web Developer
ASPX file
`.aspx` file-name extension
asynchronous request
`AsyncPostBackTrigger` class
authenticating a user
`authentication` element in `Web.config`
`authorization` element in `Web.config`
`AutoEventWireup` attribute of ASP.NET page
`AutoPostBack` property of a `DropDownList`
bottom tier
`BoundField` ASP.NET element
Build Page command in Visual Web Developer
Build Site command in Visual Web Developer
business logic
business rule
`Button` ASP.NET web control
callback function
`class` XHTML attribute
client tier
code-behind file
`CodeFile` attribute in a `Page` directive
`Content` ASP.NET control
content page in ASP.NET
`ContentPlaceHolder` ASP.NET control
`ContextTypeName` property of `LinqDataSource` control
`Control` class
controller logic
`ControlToValidate` property of a validation control
cookie
`Cookies` collection of the `Response` object
`Cookies` property of class `Request`
`Count` property of class `HttpSessionState`
`CreateUserWizard` ASP.NET login control
CSS (Cascading Style Sheets™)
CSS rule
CSS selector
data tier
`DataSourceID` property of a `GridView`
`deny` element in `Web.config`
Design mode in Visual Web Developer
`Dictionary` class
directive in ASP.NET
`Display` property of a validation control
DNS (domain-name system) server
DNS lookup
`DOCUMENT` property of a Web Form
domain-name system (DNS) server
`DropDownList` ASP.NET web control
embedded style sheet
Enable Paging setting for a `GridView`
Enable Sorting setting for a `GridView`
`EnableClientScript` property of a validation control

EnableSessionState property of a Web Form
EnableViewState property of a web control
encrypted data
ErrorMessage property of a validation control
expiration date of a cookie
extender
forms authentication
GET HTTP request
GridView ASP.NET data control
guestbook on a website
hidden input in an XHTML form
host
hostname
HTTP (Hypertext Transfer Protocol)
HTTP header
HTTP method
HttpCookie class
HttpCookieCollection class
HttpSessionState class
hyperlink
HyperLink ASP.NET web control
hypertext
ID attribute of an ASP.NET web control
IIS (Internet Information Services)
Image ASP.NET web control
ImageUrl element in an AdRotator advertisement file
ImageUrl property of an Image web control
Impressions element in an AdRotator advertisement file
information tier
Inherits attribute of an ASP.NET page
Init event of an ASP.NET web page
inline style
IP address
IsPostBack property of class Page
IsValid property of class Page
JavaScript
key/value pair
Keys property of HttpSessionState class
Label ASP.NET web control
Language attribute in a Page directive
ListDictionary class
ListItem ASP.NET class
Load event of an ASP.NET web page
localhost
Login ASP.NET control
LoginName ASP.NET login control
LoginStatus ASP.NET login control
Master directive
.master file-name extension
master page in ASP.NET
MasterPageFile property of a Page directive
method attribute of XHTML element form
middle tier
MIME (Multipurpose Internet Mail Extensions)
mode attribute of element authentication in Web.config
multitier application
n-tier application
Name property of class HttpCookie
NavigateUrl element in an AdRotator advertisement file
NavigateUrl property of a HyperLink control
navigation bar on a website
Page class
Page directive in ASP.NET
Page_Init event handler
Page_Load event handler
Page_PreInit event handler
Page_Unload event handler
PageSize property of a GridView
partial-page update
personalization
postback event of an ASP.NET page
PreInit event of an ASP.NET web page
presentation logic
RadioButtonList ASP.NET web control
RegularExpressionValidator ASP.NET validation control
relative positioning
rendering XHTML in a web browser
Request object in ASP.NET
RequiredFieldValidator ASP.NET validation control
Result property of LinqDataSourceSelect-EventArgs class
runat ASP.NET attribute
script element in ASP.NET
ScriptManager control
Selecting event of LinqDataSource
server
server control
session item
Session property of class Page
session tracking
SessionID property of class HttpSessionState
smart-tag menu in Visual Web Developer
Source mode in Visual Web Developer

span XHTML element
style class
style XHTML attribute
style XHTML element
synchronous request
System.Web.UI namespace
System.Web.UI.WebControls namespace
TabContainer control
TableName property of LinqDataSource control
TabPanel class
Target property of a HyperLink control
TextBox ASP.NET web control
tier in a multitier application
Timeout property of class HttpSessionState
Title property of a Page directive
Title property of a Web Form
title XHTML element
ToolkitScriptManager control
top tier
trigger of UpdatePanel control
unique session ID of an ASP.NET client
Unload event of an ASP.NET page
UpdatePanel control
Validate method of class Page
validation control
ValidationExpression property of a RegularExpressionValidator control
validator
ValidatorCalloutExtender control
Value property of class HttpCookie
View In Browser command in Visual Web Developer
__VIEWSTATE hidden input
virtual directory
Visible property of an ASP.NET web control
visual inheritance
web-application development
web control
Web Form
web server
Web Site Administration Tool
Web.config ASP.NET configuration file
WebControl class
WYSIWYG (What You See Is What You Get) editor
XHTML markup
XHTML tag
XmlDataSource ASP.NET data control

Self-Review Exercises

21.1 State whether each of the following is *true* or *false*. If *false*, explain why.

a) Web Form file names end in .aspx.
b) App.config is a file that stores configuration settings for an ASP.NET web application.
c) A maximum of one validation control can be placed on a Web Form.
d) If no expiration date is set for a cookie, that cookie will be destroyed at the end of the browser session.
e) A LoginStatus control displays the current authenticated username on a Web Form.
f) ASP.NET directives are delimited by <%@ and %>.
g) An AdRotator control always displays all ads with equal frequency.
h) Each web control maps to exactly one corresponding XHTML element.
i) A LinqDataSource control allows a web application to interact with a database.
j) The Ajax-enabled TabContainer control sends only the information displayed in the selected tab to the client.

21.2 Fill in the blanks in each of the following statements:

a) Web applications contain three basic tiers: ________, ________, and ________.
b) The ________ web control is similar to the ComboBox Windows control.
c) A control which ensures that the data in another control is in the correct format is called a(n) ________.
d) A(n) ________ occurs when a page requests itself.
e) Every ASP.NET page inherits from class ________.
f) When a page loads, the ________ event occurs first, followed by the ________ event.
g) The ________ file contains the functionality for an ASP.NET page.

h) A(n) ________ control provides a registration form that site visitors can use to create a user account.
i) A(n) ________ defines common GUI elements that are inherited by each page in a set of ________.
j) In a multitier application, the ________ tier controls interactions between the application's clients and the application's data.
k) The main difference between a traditional web application and an Ajax web application is that the latter supports ________ requests.

Answers to Self-Review Exercises

21.1 a) True. b) False. `Web.config` is the file that stores configuration settings for an ASP.NET web application. c) False. An unlimited number of validation controls can be placed on a Web Form. d) True. e) False. A `LoginName` control displays the current authenticated username on a Web Form. A `LoginStatus` control displays a link to either log in or log out, depending on whether the user is currently authenticated. f) True. g) False. The frequency with which the `AdRotator` displays ads is specified in the `AdvertisementFile`. h) False. A web control can map to a group of XHTML elements—ASP.NET can generate complex XHTML markup from simple elements in an ASPX file. i) True. j) True.

21.2 a) bottom (information), middle (business logic), top (client). b) `DropDownList`. c) validator. d) postback. e) `Page`. f) `PreInit`, `Init`. g) code-behind. h) `CreateUserWizard`. i) master page, content pages. j) middle. k) asynchronous.

Exercises

21.3 *(`WebTime` Modification)* Modify the `WebTime` example to contain drop-down lists that allow the user to modify such `Label` properties as `BackColor`, `ForeColor` and `Font-Size`. Configure these drop-down lists so that a postback occurs whenever the user makes a selection. When the page reloads, it should reflect the specified changes to the properties of the `Label` displaying the time.

21.4 *(Page Hit Counter)* Create an ASP.NET page that uses a persistent cookie (i.e., a cookie with a distant expiration date) to keep track of how many times the client computer has visited the page. Set the `HttpCookie` object's `Expires` property to `DateTime.Now.AddMonths(1)` to cause the cookie to remain on the client's computer for one month. Display the number of page hits (i.e., the cookie's value) every time the page loads.

21.5 *(Guestbook Application Modification)* Add validation to the guestbook application in Section 21.7. Use validation controls to ensure that the user provides a name, a valid e-mail address and a message.

21.6 *(Guestbook Application Modification)* Add Ajax functionality to the `Guestbook` application in Exercise 21.5. Use control extenders to display error callouts when one of the user input fields is invalid. Use a `UpdatePanel` so only the `GridView` updates when the user submits the form. Because only the `UpdatePanel` will be updated, you cannot clear the user input fields in the submit button's `Click` event, so you can remove this functionality.

22

Windows Communication Foundation (WCF) Web Services

A client is to me a mere unit, a factor in a problem.
—Sir Arthur Conan Doyle

...if the simplest things of nature have a message that you understand, rejoice, for your soul is alive.
—Eleonora Duse

Protocol is everything.
—Francoise Giuliani

They also serve who only stand and wait.
—John Milton

OBJECTIVES

In this chapter you'll learn:

- What a WCF service is.
- How to create WCF web services.
- How XML, JSON, XML-Based Simple Object Access Protocol (SOAP) and Representational State Transfer Architecture (REST) enable WCF web services.
- The elements that comprise WCF web services, such as service references, service endpoints, service contracts and service bindings.
- How to create a client that consumes a WCF web service.
- How to use WCF web services with Windows applications and web applications.
- How to use session tracking in WCF web services to maintain state information for the client.
- How to pass user-defined types to a WCF web service.

Outline

22.1 Introduction

This chapter introduces Windows Communication Foundation (WCF) services. WCF is a set of technologies for building distributed systems in which system components communicate with one another over networks. In earlier versions of .NET, the various types of communication used different technologies and programming models. WCF uses a common framework for all communication between systems, so you need to learn only one programming model to use WCF.

This chapter focuses on WCF web services, which promote software reusability in distributed systems that typically execute across the Internet. A web service is a class that allows its methods to be called by methods on other machines via common data formats and protocols, such as XML (see Chapter 19), JSON (Section 22.5) and HTTP. In .NET, the over-the-network method calls are commonly implemented through Simple Object Access Protocol (SOAP) or the Representational State Transfer (REST) architecture. SOAP is an XML-based protocol describing how to mark up requests and responses so that they can be sent via protocols such as HTTP. SOAP uses a standardized XML-based format to enclose data in a message that can be sent between a client and a server. REST is a network architecture that uses the web's traditional request/response mechanisms such as `GET` and `POST` requests. REST-based systems do not require data to be wrapped in a special message format.

We build the WCF web services presented in this chapter in Visual Web Developer 2008 Express, and we create client applications that invoke these services using both Visual Basic 2008 Express and Visual Web Developer 2008 Express. Full versions of Visual Studio 2008 include the functionality of both Express editions.

Requests to and responses from web services created with Visual Web Developer are typically transmitted via SOAP or REST, so any client capable of generating and processing SOAP or REST messages can interact with a web service, regardless of the language in which the web service is written. We say more about SOAP and REST in Section 22.3 and Section 22.4, respectively.

22.2 WCF Services Basics

Microsoft's Windows Communication Foundation (WCF) was created as a single platform to encompass many existing communication technologies. WCF increases productivity, because you learn only one straightforward programming model. Each WCF service has three key components—addresses, bindings and contracts (usually called the ABCs of a WCF service):

- An address represents the service's location (also known as its endpoint), which includes the protocol (e.g., HTTP) and network address (e.g., `www.deitel.com`) used to access the service.
- A binding specifies how a client communicates with the service (e.g., SOAP, REST, and so on). Bindings can also specify other options, such as security constraints.
- A contract is an interface representing the service's methods and their return types. The service's contract allows clients to interact with the service.

The machine on which the web service resides is referred to as a web service host. The client application that accesses the web service sends a method call over a network to the web service host, which processes the call and returns a response over the network to the application. This kind of distributed computing benefits systems in various ways. For example, an application without direct access to data on another system might be able to retrieve this data via a web service. Similarly, an application lacking the processing power necessary to perform specific computations could use a web service to take advantage of another system's superior resources.

22.3 Simple Object Access Protocol (SOAP)

The Simple Object Access Protocol (SOAP) is a platform-independent protocol that uses XML to make remote procedure calls, typically over HTTP. Each request and response is packaged in a SOAP message—an XML message containing the information that a web service requires to process the message. SOAP messages are written in XML so that they are computer readable, human readable and platform independent. Most firewalls—security barriers that restrict communication among networks—allow HTTP traffic to pass through, so that clients can browse the Internet by sending requests to and receiving responses from web servers. Thus, SOAP-based services can send and receive SOAP messages over HTTP connections with few limitations.

SOAP supports an extensive set of types. The wire format used to transmit requests and responses must support all types passed between the applications. SOAP types include the primitive types (e.g., `Integer`), as well as `DateTime`, `XmlNode` and others. SOAP can also transmit arrays of these types. In Section 22.11, you'll see that you can also transmit user-defined types in SOAP messages.

When a program invokes a method of a SOAP web service, the request and all relevant information are packaged in a SOAP message enclosed in a SOAP envelope and sent to the server on which the web service resides. When the web service receives this SOAP message, it parses the XML representing the message, then processes the message's contents. The message specifies the method that the client wishes to execute and the arguments the client passed to that method. Next, the web service calls the method with the specified arguments (if any) and sends the response back to the client in another SOAP message. The client parses the response to retrieve the method's result. In Section 22.6, you'll build and consume a basic SOAP web service.

22.4 Representational State Transfer (REST)

Representational State Transfer (REST) refers to an architectural style for implementing web services. Such web services are often called RESTful web services. Though REST itself is not a standard, RESTful web services are implemented using web standards. Each operation in a RESTful web service is identified by a unique URL. Thus, when the server receives a request, it immediately knows what operation to perform. Such web services can be used in a program or directly from a web browser. The results of a particular operation may be cached locally by the browser when the service is invoked with a `GET` request. This can make subsequent requests for the same operation faster by loading the result directly from the browser's cache. Amazon's web services (`aws.amazon.com`) are RESTful, as are many others.

RESTful web services are alternatives to those implemented with SOAP. Unlike SOAP-based web services, the request and response of REST services are not wrapped in envelopes. REST is also not limited to returning data in XML format. It can use a variety of formats, such as XML, JSON, HTML, plain text and media files. In Sections 22.7–22.8, you'll build and consume basic RESTful web services.

22.5 JavaScript Object Notation (JSON)

JavaScript Object Notation (JSON) is an alternative to XML for representing data. JSON is a text-based data-interchange format used to represent objects in JavaScript as collections of name/value pairs represented as `Strings`. It is commonly used in Ajax applications. JSON is a simple format that makes objects easy to read, create and parse, and allows programs to transmit data efficiently across the Internet because it is much less verbose than XML. Each JSON object is represented as a list of property names and values contained in curly braces, in the following format:

```
{ propertyName1 : value1, propertyName2 : value2 }
```

Arrays are represented in JSON with square brackets in the following format:

```
[ value1, value2, value3 ]
```

Each value in an array can be a string, a number, a JSON object, `true`, `false` or `null`. To appreciate the simplicity of JSON data, examine this representation of an array of address-book entries

```
[ { first: 'Cheryl', last: 'Black' },
  { first: 'James', last: 'Blue' },
  { first: 'Mike', last: 'Brown' },
  { first: 'Meg', last: 'Gold' } ]
```

Many programming languages now support the JSON data format.

22.6 Publishing and Consuming SOAP-Based WCF Web Services

This section presents our first example of publishing (enabling for client access) and consuming (using) a web service. We begin with a SOAP-based web service.

22.6.1 Creating a WCF Web Service

To build a SOAP-based WCF web service in Visual Web Developer, you first create a project of type **WCF Service**. SOAP is the default protocol for WCF web services, so no special configuration is required to create them. Visual Web Developer then generates files for the WCF service code, an SVC file (`Service.svc`, which provides access to the service), and a `Web.config` file (which specifies the service's binding and behavior).

Visual Web Developer also generates code files for the WCF service class and any other code that is part of the WCF service implementation. In the service class, you define the methods that your WCF web service makes available to client applications.

22.6.2 Code for the `WelcomeSOAPXMLService`

Figures 22.1 and 22.2 present the code-behind files for the `WelcomeSOAPXMLService` WCF web service that you build in Section 22.6.3. When creating services in Visual Web Developer, you work almost exclusively in the code-behind files. The service provides a method that takes a name (represented as a `String`) as an argument and appends it to the welcome message that is returned to the client. We use a parameter in the method definition to demonstrate that a client can send data to a web service.

Figure 22.1 is the service's interface, which describes the service's contract—the set of methods and properties the client uses to access the service. The `ServiceContract` attribute (line 4) exposes a class that implements this interface as a WCF web service. The `OperationContract` attribute (line 7) exposes the `Welcome` method to clients for remote calls. Optional parameters can be assigned to these contracts to change the data format and method behavior, as we'll show in later examples.

```
' Fig. 22.1: IWelcomeSOAPXMLService.vb
' WCF web service interface that returns a welcome message through SOAP
' protocol and XML format.
<ServiceContract()> _
Public Interface IWelcomeSOAPXMLService
   ' returns a welcome message
   <OperationContract()> _
   Function Welcome(ByVal yourName As String) As String
End Interface ' IWelcomeSOAPXMLService
```

Fig. 22.1 | WCF web service interface that returns a welcome message through SOAP protocol and XML format.

Figure 22.2 defines the class that implements the interface declared as the `ServiceContract`. Lines 8–13 define the method `Welcome`, which returns a `String` welcoming you to WCF web services. Next, we build the web service from scratch.

```
1  ' Fig. 22.2: WelcomeSOAPXMLService.vb
2  ' WCF web service that returns a welcome message through SOAP protocol and
3  ' XML format.
4  Public Class WelcomeSOAPXMLService
5     Implements IWelcomeSOAPXMLService
6
7     ' returns a welcome message
8     Public Function Welcome(ByVal yourName As String) _
9        As String Implements IWelcomeSOAPXMLService.Welcome
10
11       Return "Welcome to WCF Web Services with SOAP and XML, " _
12          & yourName & "!"
13    End Function ' Welcome
14 End Class ' WelcomeSOAPXMLService
```

Fig. 22.2 | WCF web service that returns a welcome message through the SOAP protocol and XML format.

22.6.3 Building a SOAP WCF Web Service

In the following steps, you create a **WCF Service** project for the `WelcomeSOAPXMLService` and test it using the built-in ASP.NET Development Server that comes with Visual Web Developer Express and Visual Studio.

Step 1: Creating the Project

To create a project of type **WCF Service**, select **File > New Web Site...** to display the **New Web Site** dialog (Fig. 22.3). Click **WCF Service** in the **Templates** pane. Select **File System** from the **Location** drop-down list to indicate that the files should be placed on your local hard disk. By default, Visual Web Developer places files on the local machine in a directory named `WCFService1`. Rename this folder to `WelcomeSOAPXMLService`. We modified the default path as well. Select **Visual Basic** from the **Language** drop-down list to indicate that you'll use Visual Basic as the language in the code-behind files. Click **OK** to create the project.

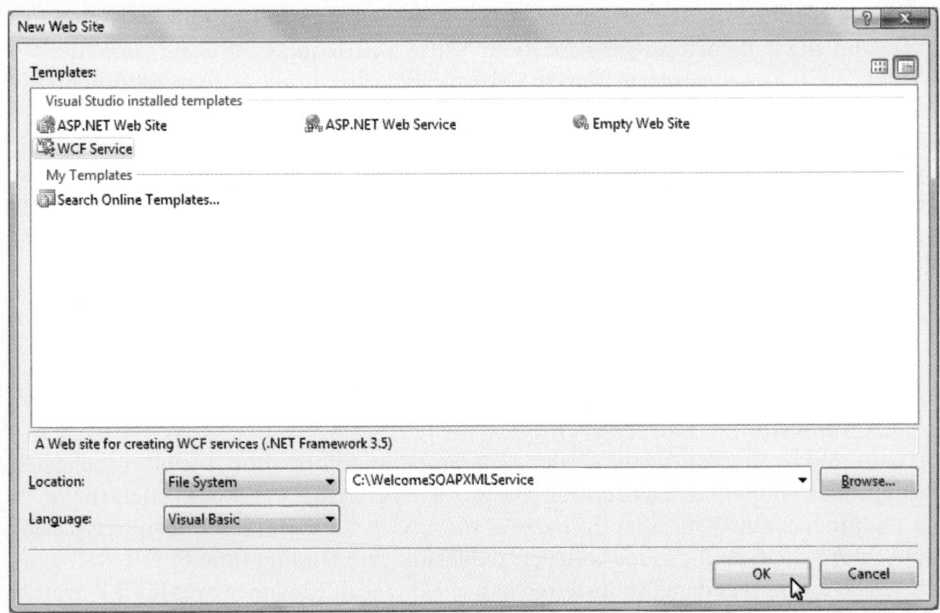

Fig. 22.3 | Creating a **WCF Service** in Visual Web Developer.

Step 2: Examining the Newly Created Project

After you create the project, the code-behind file `Service.vb`, which contains code for a simple web service, is displayed by default. If the code-behind file is not open, open it by double clicking the file in the **App_Code** directory listed in the **Solution Explorer**. By default, a new code-behind file implements an interface named `IService` that is marked with the `ServiceContract` and `OperationContract` attributes. In addition, the `IService.vb` file defines a class named `CompositeType` with a `DataContract` attribute (discussed in Section 22.8). The interface contains two sample service methods named `GetData` and `GetDataUsingContract`. The `Service.vb` contains the code that defines these methods.

Step 3: Modifying and Renaming the Code-Behind File

To create the `WelcomeSOAPXMLService` service developed in this section, modify `IService.vb` and `Service.vb` by replacing the sample code provided by Visual Web Developer with the code from the `IWelcomeSOAPXMLService` and `WelcomeSOAPXMLService` files (Figs. 22.1 and 22.2, respectively). Then rename the files to `IWelcomeSOAPXMLService.vb` and `WelcomeSOAPXMLService.vb` by right clicking each file in the Solution Explorer and choosing **Rename**.

Step 4: Examining the SVC File

The `Service.svc` file, when accessed through a web browser, provides information about the web service. However, if you open the SVC file on disk, note that it contains only

```
<%@ ServiceHost Language="VB" Debug="true" Service="Service"
   CodeBehind="~/App_Code/Service.vb" %>
```

to indicate the programming language in which the web service's code-behind file is written, the `Debug` attribute (enables a page to be compiled for debugging), the name of the service and the code-behind file's location. When you request the SVC page in a web browser, WCF uses this information to dynamically generate the WSDL document.

Step 5: Modifying the SVC File

If you change the code-behind file name or the class name that defines the web service, you must modify the SVC file accordingly. Thus, after defining class `WelcomeSOAPXMLService` in the code-behind file `WelcomeSOAPXMLService.vb`, modify the SVC file as follows:

```
<%@ ServiceHost Language="VB" Debug="true"
   Service="WelcomeSOAPXMLService"
   CodeBehind="~/App_Code/WelcomeSOAPXMLService.vb" %>
```

Step 6: Examining the `Web.config` File

The `Web.config` file specifies the service's configuration information, including behaviors, bindings and endpoints. Figure 22.4 shows the `System.ServiceModel` element of the `Web.config` file. Line 3 specifies the name of the service. Lines 6–11 define the service endpoint, where client applications connect. By default, the binding (line 6) is `wsHttpBinding`, which means that data is transferred in a secure, reliable manner over HTTP protocol using XML as the data format. This is the default binding for SOAP-based services. The `contract` specifies the name of the interface class. In later examples, we'll discuss the `behaviors` element (line 16–23).

```
1  <system.serviceModel>
2     <services>
3        <service name="Service"
4           behaviorConfiguration="ServiceBehavior">
5           <!-- Service Endpoints -->
6           <endpoint address="" binding="wsHttpBinding"
7              contract="IService">
8              <identity>
9                 <dns value="localhost"/>
10             </identity>
11          </endpoint>
12          <endpoint address="mex" binding="mexHttpBinding"
13             contract="IMetadataExchange"/>
14       </service>
15    </services>
16    <behaviors>
17       <serviceBehaviors>
18          <behavior name="ServiceBehavior">
19             <serviceMetadata httpGetEnabled="true"/>
20             <serviceDebug includeExceptionDetailInFaults="false"/>
21          </behavior>
22       </serviceBehaviors>
23    </behaviors>
24 </system.serviceModel>
```

Fig. 22.4 | Default `Web.config` file's service model configuration for WCF service.

Step 7: Modifying the Web.config File

After changing the `ServiceContract`'s code-behind file name, the web-service class name or interface name, you must change the `Web.config` file to reference the appropriate names. In Fig. 22.5, we change the service name from `Service` to `WelcomeSOAPXMLService` (line 3) and the contract from `IService` to `IWelcomeSOAPXMLService` (line 7).

```
1  <system.serviceModel>
2     <services>
3        <service name="WelcomeSOAPXMLService"
4           behaviorConfiguration="ServiceBehavior">
5           <!-- Service Endpoints -->
6           <endpoint address="" binding="wsHttpBinding"
7              contract="IWelcomeSOAPXMLService">
8              <identity>
9                 <dns value="localhost"/>
10             </identity>
11          </endpoint>
12          <endpoint address="mex" binding="mexHttpBinding"
13             contract="IMetadataExchange"/>
14       </service>
15    </services>
16    <behaviors>
17       <serviceBehaviors>
18          <behavior name="ServiceBehavior">
19             <serviceMetadata httpGetEnabled="true"/>
20             <serviceDebug includeExceptionDetailInFaults="false"/>
21          </behavior>
22       </serviceBehaviors>
23    </behaviors>
24 </system.serviceModel>
```

Fig. 22.5 | `Web.config` file's service model configuration for `WelcomeSOAPXMLService` web service.

22.6.4 Deploying the `WelcomeSOAPXMLService`

You can choose **Build Web Site** from the **Build** menu to ensure that the web service compiles without errors. You can also test the web service directly from Visual Web Developer by selecting **Start Debugging** from the **Debug** menu. The first time you do this, the **Debugging Not Enabled** dialog appears. Click **OK** if you want to enable debugging. Next, a browser window opens and displays information about the service. This information is generated dynamically when the SVC file is requested. Figure 22.6 shows a web browser displaying the `Service.svc` file for the `WelcomeSOAPXMLService` WCF web service. [*Note:* To view the `Service.svc` file, you must set the `.svc` file as the project's start page by right clicking it in **Solution Explorer** and selecting **Set As Start Page**.]

Once the service is running, you can also access the SVC page from your browser by typing a URL of the following form in a web browser:

`http://localhost:`*portNumber*`/`*virtualPath*`/Service.svc`

(See the actual URL in Fig. 22.6.) By default, the ASP.NET Development Server assigns a random port number to each website it hosts. You can change this behavior by going to

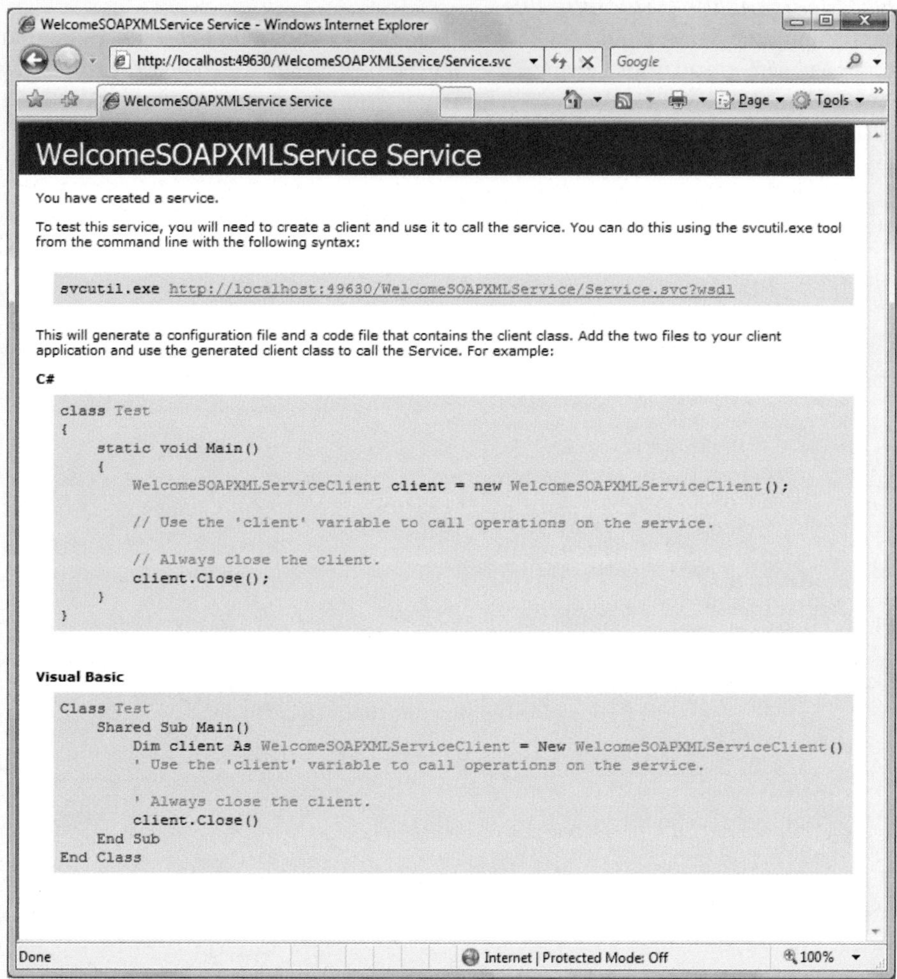

Fig. 22.6 | SVC file rendered in a web browser.

the **Solution Explorer** and clicking on the project name to view the **Properties** window (Fig. 22.7). Set the **Use dynamic ports** property to **False** and set the **Port number** property to the port number that you want to use, which can be any unused TCP port. Generally, you don't do this for web services that will be deployed to a real web server. You can also change the service's virtual path, perhaps to make the path shorter or more readable.

Web Services Description Language

To consume a web service, a client must determine the service's functionality and how to use it. For this purpose, web services normally contain a service description. This is an XML document that conforms to the Web Service Description Language (WSDL)—an XML vocabulary that defines the methods a web service makes available and how clients interact with them. The WSDL document also specifies lower-level information that clients might need, such as the required formats for requests and responses.

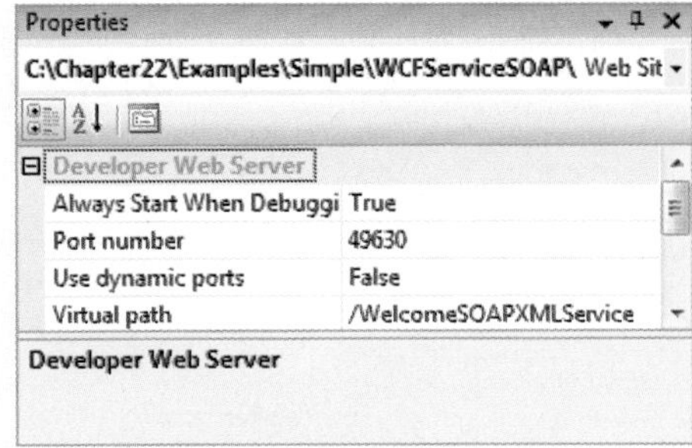

Fig. 22.7 | WCF web service **Properties** window.

WSDL documents help applications determine how to interact with the web services described in the documents. When viewed in a web browser, an SVC file presents a link to the service's WSDL document and information on using the utility `svcutil.exe` to generate test console applications. The `svcutil.exe` tool is included with Visual Studio 2008 and Visual Web Developer. We do not use `svcutil.exe` to test our services, opting instead to build our own test applications. When a client requests the SVC file's URL followed by `?wsdl`, the server autogenerates the WSDL that describes the web service and returns the WSDL document. Copy the SVC URL (which ends with `.svc`) from the browser's address `ComboBox` in Fig. 22.6, as you'll need it in the next section to build the client application. Also, leave the web service running so the client can interact with it.

22.6.5 Creating a Client to Consume the `WelcomeSOAPXMLService`

Now that you've defined and deployed the web service, let's consume it from a client application. A .NET web-service client can be any type of .NET application, such as a Windows application, a console application or a web application. You can enable a client application to consume a web service by adding a service reference to the client. Figure 22.8 diagrams the parts of a client for a SOAP-based web service after a service reference has been added. [*Note*: This section discusses Visual Basic 2008 Express, but the discussion also applies to Visual Web Developer 2008 Express.]

An application that consumes a SOAP-based web service actually consists of two parts—a proxy class representing the web service and a client application that accesses the web service via a proxy object (i.e., an instance of the proxy class). A proxy class handles all the "plumbing" required for service method calls (i.e., the networking details and the formation of SOAP messages). Whenever the client application calls a web service's method, the application actually calls a corresponding method in the proxy class. This method has the same name and parameters as the web service's method that is being called, but formats the call to be sent as a request in a SOAP message. The web service receives this request as a SOAP message, executes the method call and sends back the result as another SOAP message. When the client application receives the SOAP message containing the response, the proxy class deserializes it and returns the results as the return value of the web-service method that was called. Figure 22.9 depicts the interactions among the client code, proxy class and web service. The proxy class is not shown in the project unless you click the **Show All Files** button in the **Solution Explorer**.

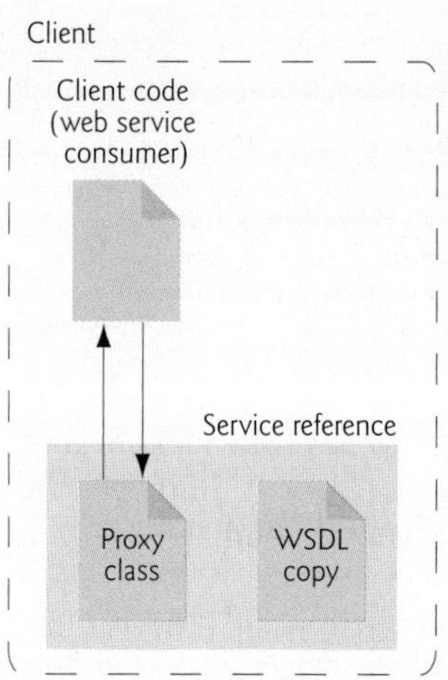

Fig. 22.8 | .NET WCF web service client after a web-service reference has been added.

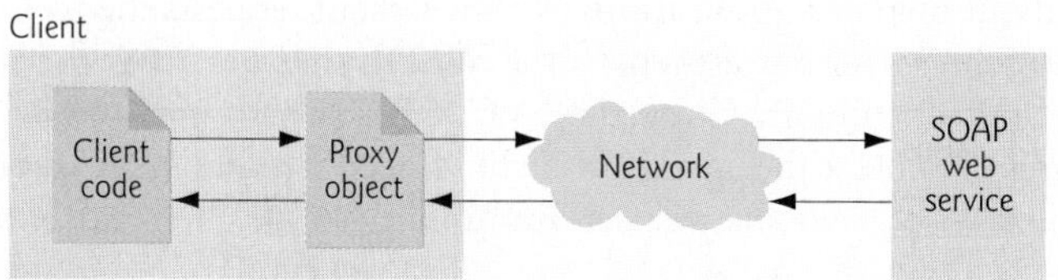

Fig. 22.9 | Interaction between a web-service client and a SOAP web service.

Many aspects of web-service creation and consumption—such as generating WSDL files and proxy classes—are handled by Visual Web Developer, Visual Basic 2008 and WCF. Although developers are relieved of the tedious process of creating these files, they can still modify the files if necessary. This is required only when developing advanced web services—none of our examples require modifications to these files.

We now create a client and generate a proxy class that allows the client to access the `WelcomeSOAPXMLService` web service. First create a Windows application named `WelcomeSOAPXMLClient` in Visual Basic 2008, then perform the following steps.

Step 1: Opening the Add Service Reference *Dialog*

Right click the project name in the **Solution Explorer** and select **Add Service Reference...** to display the **Add Service Reference** dialog.

Step 2: Specifying the Web Service's Location

In the dialog, enter the URL of `WelcomeSOAPXMLService`'s `.svc` file (i.e., the URL you copied from Fig. 22.6) in the **Address** field. When you specify the service you want to consume, the IDE accesses the web service's WSDL information and copies it into a WSDL file that is stored in the client project's `Service References` folder. This file is visible when you view all of your project's files in the **Solution Explorer**. [*Note:* A copy of the WSDL file provides the client application with local access to the web service's description. To ensure that the WSDL file is up to date, Visual Basic 2008 provides an **Update Service Reference** option (available by right clicking the service reference in the **Solution Explorer**), which updates the files in the `Service References` folder.]

Many companies that provide web services simply distribute the exact URLs at which their web services can be accessed. The **Add Service Reference** dialog also allows you to search for services on your local machine or on the Internet.

Step 3: Renaming the Service Reference's Namespace

In the **Add Service Reference** dialog, rename the service reference's namespace by changing the **Namespace** field to `ServiceReference`.

Step 4: Adding the Service Reference

Click the **Ok** button to add the service reference.

Step 5: Viewing the Service Reference in the **Solution Explorer**

The **Solution Explorer** should now contain a **Service References** folder with a node showing the namespace you specified in *Step 3*.

22.6.6 Consuming the `WelcomeSOAPXMLService`

The application in Fig. 22.10 uses the `WelcomeSOAPXMLService` service to send a welcome message. You are already familiar with Visual Basic applications that use `Labels`, `TextBoxes` and `Buttons`, so we focus our discussions on the web-services concepts in this chapter's applications.

Line 5 defines a new `ServiceReference.WelcomeSOAPXMLServiceClient` proxy object named `client`. The event handler uses this object to call methods of the `Welcome-`

```
1  ' Fig. 22.10: WelcomeSOAPXMLForm.vb
2  ' Client that consumes WelcomeSOAPXMLService.
3  Public Class WelcomeSOAPXMLForm
4     ' reference to web service
5     Private client As New ServiceReference.WelcomeSOAPXMLServiceClient()
6
7     ' creates welcome message from text input and web service
8     Private Sub submitButton_Click(ByVal sender As System.Object, _
9        ByVal e As System.EventArgs) Handles submitButton.Click
10
11       MessageBox.Show(client.Welcome(textBox.Text))
12    End Sub ' submitButton_Click
13 End Class ' WelcomeSOAPXMLForm
```

a) User inputs name.

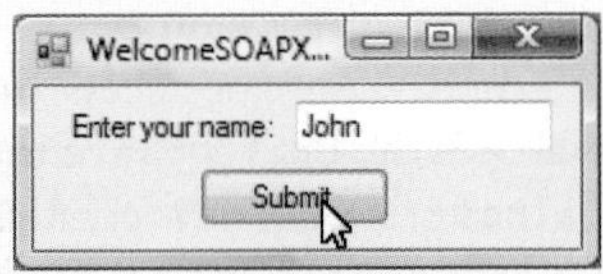

Fig. 22.10 | Client that consumes `WelcomeSOAPXMLService`. (Part 1 of 2.)

b) Message sent from **WelcomeSOAPXMLService**.

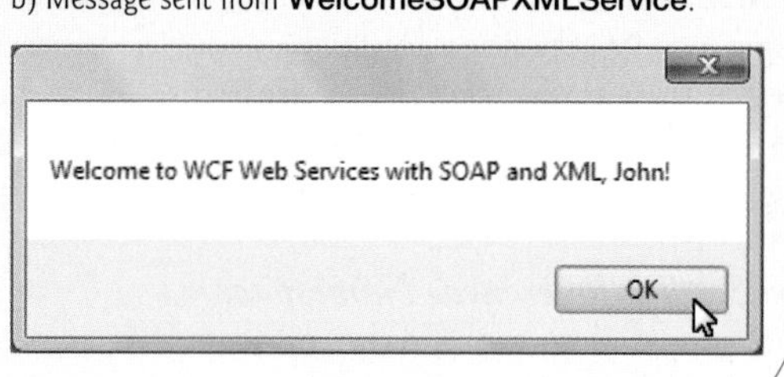

Fig. 22.10 | Client that consumes `WelcomeSOAPXMLService`. (Part 2 of 2.)

`SOAPXMLService` web service. Line 11 invokes the `WelcomeSOAPXMLService` web service's `Welcome` method. Note that the call is made via the local proxy object `client`, which then communicates with the web service on the client's behalf. If you downloaded the example from `www.deitel.com/books/vb2008htp/`, you may need to regenerate the proxy by removing the service reference, then adding it again, because ASP.NET Development Server may use a different port number on your computer. To do so, right click `ServiceReference` in the **Service References** folder in the **Solution Explorer** and select option **Delete**. Then follow the instructions in Section 22.6.5 to add the service reference to the project.

When the application runs, enter your name and click the **Submit** button. The application invokes the `Welcome` service method to perform the appropriate task and return the result, then displays the result in a `MessageBox`.

22.7 Publishing and Consuming REST-Based XML Web Services

In the previous section, we used a proxy object to pass data to and from a WCF web service using the SOAP protocol. In this section, we access a WCF web service using the REST architecture. We modify the `IWelcomeSOAPXMLService` example to return data in plain XML format. You can create a **WCF Service** project as you did in Section 22.6 to begin.

22.7.1 Creating a REST-Based XML WCF Web Service

Step 1: Adding the **WebGet** *Attribute*

`IWelcomeRESTXMLService` interface (Fig. 22.11) is a modified version of the `IWelcomeSOAPXMLService` interface. The `Welcome` method's `WebGet` attribute (line 10) maps a method to a unique URL that can be accessed via an HTTP `GET` operation programmatically or in a web browser. To use the `WebGet` attribute, we import the `System.ServiceModel.Web` namespace (line 4). `WebGet`'s `UriTemplate` property (line 10) specifies the URI format that is used to invoke the method. You can access the `Welcome` method in a web browser by appending text that matches the `UriTemplate` definition to the end of the service's location, as in `http://localhost:50000/WelcomeRESTXMLService/Service.svc/welcome/Bruce`. `WelcomeRESTXMLService` (Fig. 22.12) is the class that implements the `IWelcomeRESTXMLService` interface; it is similar to the `WelcomeSOAPXMLService` class (Fig. 22.2).

```
' Fig. 22.11: IWelcomeRESTXMLService.vb
' WCF web-service interface. A class that implements this interface
' returns a welcome message through REST architecture and XML data format.
Imports System.ServiceModel.Web

<ServiceContract()> _
Public Interface IWelcomeRESTXMLService
   ' returns a welcome message
   <OperationContract()> _
   <WebGet(UriTemplate:="welcome/{yourName}")> _
   Function Welcome(ByVal yourName As String) As String
End Interface ' IWelcomeRESTXMLService
```

Fig. 22.11 | WCF web-service interface. A class that implements this interface returns a welcome message through REST architecture and XML data format.

```
' Fig. 22.12: WelcomeRESTXMLService.vb
' WCF web service that returns a welcome message using REST architecture
' and XML data format.
Public Class WelcomeRESTXMLService
   Implements IWelcomeRESTXMLService

   ' returns a welcome message
   Public Function Welcome(ByVal yourName As String) _
      As String Implements IWelcomeRESTXMLService.Welcome

      Return "Welcome to WCF Web Services with REST and XML, " _
         & yourName & "!"
   End Function ' Welcome
End Class ' WelcomeRESTXMLService
```

Fig. 22.12 | WCF web service that returns a welcome message using REST architecture and XML data format.

Step 2: Modifying the `Web.config` File

Figure 22.13 shows part of the default `Web.config` file modified to use REST architecture. First, the service binding in the `endpoint` element must be changed from `wsHttpBinding` to **`webHttpBinding`** (line 6) to respond to REST-based HTTP requests rather than SOAP-based messages. You must also add a new **`behaviorConfiguration`** (we called it `RESTBehavior`) at line 8 of the endpoint to define the endpoint's behavior. This behavior is configured in the `endpointBehaviors` section at lines 25–27. Line 25 specifies the name of the behavior being configured, and line 26 uses the **`webHttp`** element to specify that clients communicate with this service using the standard HTTP request/response mechanism.

```
1 <system.serviceModel>
2    <services>
3       <service name="WelcomeRESTXMLService"
4          behaviorConfiguration="ServiceBehavior">
```

Fig. 22.13 | `WelcomeRESTXMLService Web.config` file. (Part 1 of 2.)

```
            <!-- Service Endpoints -->
            <endpoint address="" binding="webHttpBinding"
               contract="IWelcomeRESTXMLService"
               behaviorConfiguration="RESTBehavior">
               <identity>
                  <dns value="localhost"/>
               </identity>
            </endpoint>
            <endpoint address="mex" binding="mexHttpBinding"
               contract="IMetadataExchange"/>
         </service>
      </services>
      <behaviors>
         <serviceBehaviors>
            <behavior name="ServiceBehavior">
               <serviceMetadata httpGetEnabled="true"/>
               <serviceDebug includeExceptionDetailInFaults="false"/>
            </behavior>
         </serviceBehaviors>
         <endpointBehaviors>
            <behavior name="RESTBehavior">
               <webHttp />
            </behavior>
         </endpointBehaviors>
      </behaviors>
   </system.serviceModel>
```

Fig. 22.13 | `WelcomeRESTXMLService` `Web.config` file. (Part 2 of 2.)

Figure 22.14 tests the `WelcomeRESTXMLService`'s `Welcome` method in a web browser. The URL specifies the location of the `Service.svc` file and uses the URI template to invoke method `Welcome` with the argument `Bruce`. The browser displays the XML data response from `WelcomeRESTXMLService`. Next, you'll learn how to consume this service.

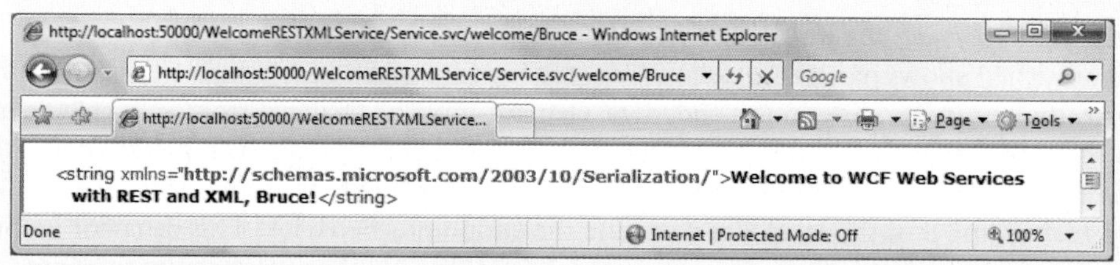

Fig. 22.14 | Response from `WelcomeRESTXMLService` in XML data format.

22.7.2 Consuming a REST-Based XML WCF Web Service

`WelcomeRESTXMLForm` (Fig. 22.15) uses the **`WebClient`** class to invoke the web service and receive its response. In line 5, we import the XML message's namespace (seen in Fig. 22.14), which is required to parse the service's XML response. The keyword `WithEvents` in line 9 indicates that the `WebClient` object has events associated with it and enables you to use the variable's name in an event handler's `Handles` clause.

```
' Fig. 22.15: WelcomeRESTXMLForm.vb
' Client that consumes the WelcomeRESTXMLService.
Imports System.Net
Imports System.Xml.Linq
Imports <xmlns="http://schemas.microsoft.com/2003/10/Serialization/">

Public Class WelcomeRESTXMLForm
   ' object to invoke the WelcomeRESTXMLService
   Private WithEvents service As New WebClient()

   ' get user input and pass it to the web service
   Private Sub submitButton_Click(ByVal sender As System.Object, _
      ByVal e As System.EventArgs) Handles submitButton.Click

      ' send request to WelcomeRESTXMLService
      service.DownloadStringAsync(New Uri( _
         "http://localhost:50000/WelcomeRESTXMLService/Service.svc/" _
         & "welcome/" & textBox.Text))
   End Sub ' submitButton_Click

   ' process web-service response
   Private Sub service_DownloadStringCompleted(ByVal sender As Object, _
      ByVal e As System.Net.DownloadStringCompletedEventArgs) _
      Handles service.DownloadStringCompleted

      ' check if any errors occurred in retrieving service data
      If e.Error Is Nothing Then
         ' parse the returned XML string (e.Result)
         Dim xmlResponse = XDocument.Parse(e.Result)

         ' use XML axis property to access the <string> element's value
         MessageBox.Show(xmlResponse.<string>.Value)
      End If
   End Sub ' service_DownloadStringCompleted
End Class ' WelcomeRESTXMLForm
```

a) User inputs name.

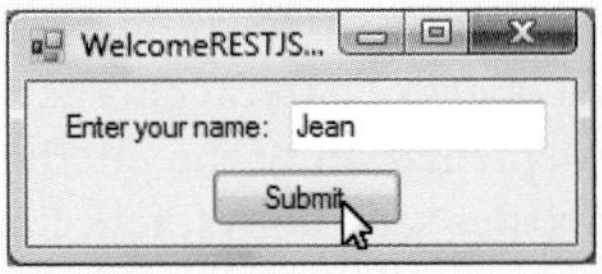

WelcomeRESTJS...
Enter your name: Jean
Submit

b) Message sent from **WelcomeRESTXMLService**.

Welcome to WCF Web Services with REST and XML, Jane!
OK

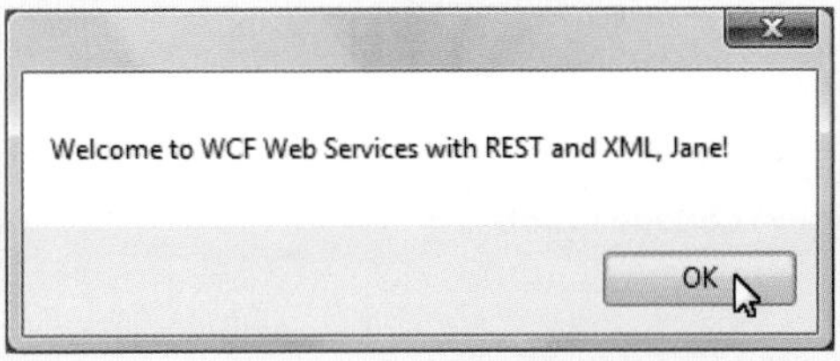

Fig. 22.15 | Client that consumes the `WelcomeRESTXMLService`.

In this example, we process the `WebClient`'s `DownloadStringCompleted` event, which occurs when the client receives the completed response from the web service. Line 16 calls the `service` object's `DownloadStringAsync` method to invoke the web service asynchronously. (There is also a synchronous `DownloadString` method that does not return until it receives the response.) The method's argument (i.e., the URL to invoke the web service) must be specified as an object of class `Uri`. Class `Uri`'s constructor receives a `String` representing a uniform resource identifier. [*Note:* The URL's port number must match the one issued to the web service by the ASP.NET Development Server.] When the call to the web service completes, the `WebClient` object raises the `DownloadStringCompleted` event. Its event handler has a parameter `e` of type `DownloadStringCompletedEventArgs` which contains the information returned by the web service. We can use this variable's properties to get the returned XML document (`e.Result`) and any errors that may have occurred during the process (`e.Error`). We then parse the XML response using `XDocument` method `Parse` (line 29) and display our welcome `String` in a `MessageBox` (line 32).

22.8 Publishing and Consuming REST-Based JSON Web Services

We now build a RESTful web service that returns data in JSON format.

22.8.1 Creating a REST-Based JSON WCF Web Service

By default, a web-service method with the `WebGet` attribute returns data in XML format. In Fig. 22.16, we modify the `WelcomeRESTXMLService` to return data in JSON format by setting `WebGet`'s `ResponseFormat` property to `WebMessageFormat.Json` (line 10). (`WebMessageFormat.XML` is the default value.) For JSON serialization to work properly, the objects being converted to JSON must have `Public` properties. This enables the JSON serialization to create name/value pairs representing each `Public` property and its corresponding value. The previous examples return `String` objects containing the responses. Even though `String`s are objects, `String`s do not have any `Public` properties that represent their contents. So, lines 17–30 define a `TextMessage` class that encapsulates a `String` value and defines a `Public` property `Message` to access that value. The `DataContract` attribute (line 16) exposes the `TextMessage` class to the client access. Similarly, the `DataMember` attribute exposes a property of this class to the client. This property will appear in the JSON object as a name/value pair. Only `DataMember`s of a `DataContract` are serialized.

Figure 22.17 shows the implementation of the interface of Fig. 22.16. The `Welcome` method (lines 8–15) returns a `TextMessage` object, reflecting the changes we made to the interface class. This object is automatically serialized in JSON format (as a result of line 10 in Fig. 22.16) and sent to the client.

```
1  ' Fig. 22.16: IWelcomeRESTJSONService.vb
2  ' WCF web-service interface that returns a welcome message through REST
3  ' architecture and JSON format.
4  Imports System.ServiceModel.Web
5
```

Fig. 22.16 | WCF web-service interface that returns a welcome message through REST architecture and JSON format. (Part 1 of 2.)

```
<ServiceContract()> _
Public Interface IWelcomeRESTJSONService
   ' returns a welcome message
   <OperationContract()> _
   <WebGet(ResponseFormat:=WebMessageFormat.Json, _
      UriTemplate:="welcome/{yourName}")> _
   Function Welcome(ByVal yourName As String) As TextMessage
End Interface ' IWelcomeRESTJSONService

' class to encapsulate a String to send in JSON format
<DataContract()> _
Public Class TextMessage
   Public messageValue As String

   ' property message
   <DataMember()> _
   Public Property Message() As String
      Get
         Return messageValue
      End Get
      Set(ByVal value As String)
         messageValue = value
      End Set
   End Property ' Message
End Class ' TextMessage
```

Fig. 22.16 | WCF web-service interface that returns a welcome message through REST architecture and JSON format. (Part 2 of 2.)

```
' Fig. 22.17: WelcomeRESTJSONService.vb
' WCF web service that returns a welcome message through REST architecture
' and JSON format.
Public Class WelcomeRESTJSONService
   Implements IWelcomeRESTJSONService

   ' returns a welcome message
   Public Function Welcome(ByVal yourName As String) _
      As TextMessage Implements IWelcomeRESTJSONService.Welcome
      ' add welcome message to field of TextMessage object
      Dim welcomeString As New TextMessage
      welcomeString.Message = "Welcome to WCF Web Services with REST " _
         & "and JSON, " & yourName & "!"
      Return welcomeString
   End Function ' Welcome
End Class ' WelcomeRESTJSONService
```

Fig. 22.17 | WCF web service that returns a welcome message through REST architecture and JSON format.

We can once again test the web service using a web browser, by accessing the `Service.svc` file (`http://localhost:50000/WelcomeRESTJSONService/Service.svc`) and appending the URI template (`welcome/`*yourName*) to the address. The response prompts you to download a file called *yourName*, which is a text file. If you save it to disk, the file will have the `.json` extension. This contains the JSON formatted data. By opening the file in a text editor such as Notepad (Fig. 22.18), you can see the service response as a JSON object. Notice that the property named `Message` has the welcome message as its value.

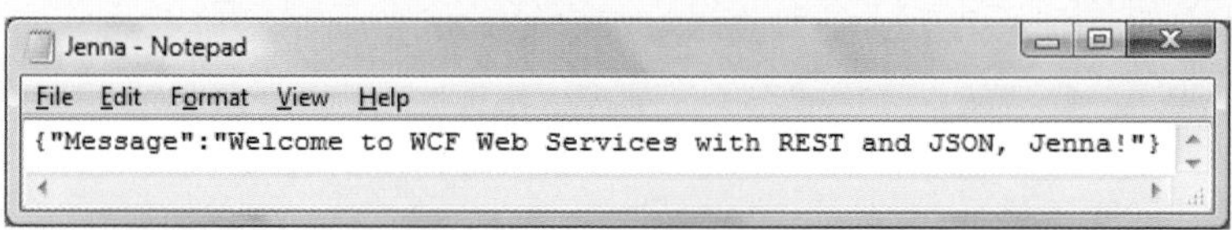

Fig. 22.18 | Response from `WelcomeRESTJSONService` in JSON data format.

22.8.2 Consuming a REST-Based JSON WCF Web Service

We mentioned earlier that all types passed to and from web services can be supported by REST. Custom types that are sent to or from a REST web service are converted to XML or JSON data format. This process is referred to as XML serialization or JSON serialization, respectively. In Fig. 22.19, we consume the `WelcomeRESTJSONService` service using an object of the `System.Runtime.Serialization.Json` library's `DataContractJsonSerializer` class (lines 30–31). To use the `System.Runtime.Serialization.Json` library and `DataContractJsonSerializer` class, you must include a reference to the `System.ServiceModel.Web` and `System.Runtime.Serialization` assemblies in the project. To do so, right click the project name, select **Add Reference** and add the `System.ServiceModel.Web` and `System.Runtime.Serialization` assemblies. The `TextMessage` class (lines 43–45) maps the JSON response's fields for the `DataContractJsonSerializer` to deserialize. We add the `Serializable` attribute (line 42) to the `TextMessage` class to recognize it as a valid serializable object we can convert to and from JSON format. Also, this class on the client must have `Public` data or properties that match the `Public` data or properties in the corresponding class from the web service. Since we want to convert the JSON response into a `TextMessage` object, we set the `DataContractJsonSerializer`'s type parameter to `TextMessage` (line 31). In line 33, we use the `System.Text` namespace's `Encoding.Unicode.GetBytes` method to convert the JSON response to a Unicode encoded byte array, and encapsulate the byte array in a `MemoryStream` object so we can read data from the array using stream semantics. The bytes in the `MemoryStream` object are read by the `DataContractJsonSerializer` and deserialized into a `TextMessage` object (line 32).

```
1  ' Fig. 22.19: WelcomeRESTJSONForm.vb
2  ' Client that consumes WelcomeRESTJSONService.
3  Imports System.IO
4  Imports System.Net
5  Imports System.Runtime.Serialization.Json
6  Imports System.Text
7
8  Public Class WelcomeRESTJSONForm
9     ' object to invoke the WelcomeRESTJSONService
10    Private WithEvents service As New WebClient()
```

Fig. 22.19 | Client that consumes `WelcomeRESTJSONService`. (Part 1 of 2.)

```

    ' creates welcome message from text input and web service
    Private Sub submitButton_Click(ByVal sender As System.Object, _
       ByVal e As System.EventArgs) Handles submitButton.Click

       ' send request to WelcomeRESTJSONService
       service.DownloadStringAsync(New Uri( _
          "http://localhost:50000/WelcomeRESTJSONService/Service.svc/" _
          & "welcome/" & textBox.Text))
    End Sub ' submitButton

    ' process web-service response
    Private Sub service_DownloadStringCompleted(ByVal sender As Object, _
       ByVal e As System.Net.DownloadStringCompletedEventArgs) _
       Handles service.DownloadStringCompleted

       ' check if any errors occurred in retrieving service data
       If e.Error Is Nothing Then
          ' deserialize response into a TextMessage object
          Dim JSONSerializer _
             As New DataContractJsonSerializer(GetType(TextMessage))
          Dim welcomeString = JSONSerializer.ReadObject( _
             New MemoryStream(Encoding.Unicode.GetBytes(e.Result)))

          ' display Message text
          MessageBox.Show(CType(welcomeString, TextMessage).Message)
       End If
    End Sub ' service_DownloadStringCompleted
 End Class ' WelcomeRESTJSONForm

 ' TextMessage class representing a JSON object
 <Serializable()> _
 Public Class TextMessage
    Public Message As String
 End Class ' TextMessage
```

a) User inputs name.

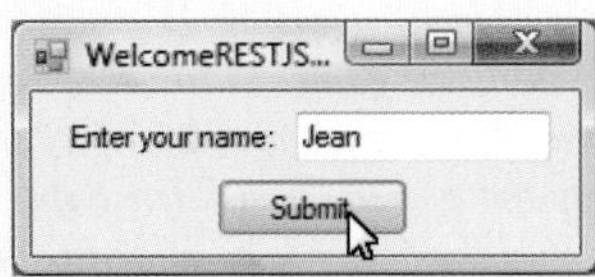

b) Message sent from `WelcomeRESTJSONService`.

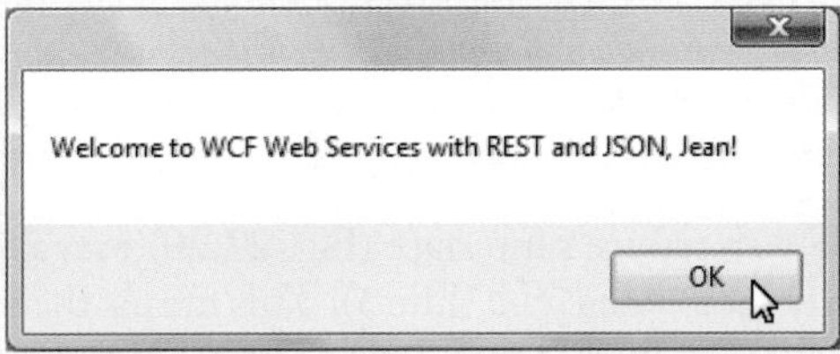

Fig. 22.19 | Client that consumes `WelcomeRESTJSONService`. (Part 2 of 2.)

22.9 Blackjack Web Service: Using Session Tracking in a SOAP-Based WCF Web Service

In Chapter 21, we described the advantages of maintaining information about users to personalize their experiences. In particular, we discussed session tracking using cookies and `HttpSessionState` objects. Next, we incorporate session tracking into a SOAP-based WCF web service.

Suppose a client application needs to call several methods from the same web service, possibly several times each. In such a case, it can be beneficial for the web service to maintain state information for the client. Session tracking eliminates the need for information about the client to be passed between the client and the web service multiple times. For example, a web service providing access to local restaurant reviews would benefit from storing the client user's street address. Once the user's address is stored in a session variable, web service methods can return personalized, localized results without requiring that the address be passed in each method call. This not only improves performance but also requires less effort on your part—less information is passed in each method call.

22.9.1 Creating a Blackjack Web Service

Web services store session information to provide more intuitive functionality. Our next example is a SOAP-based web service that assists programmers in developing a blackjack card game. The web service provides methods to deal a card and to evaluate a hand of cards. After presenting the web service, we use it to serve as the dealer for a game of blackjack. The blackjack web service creates a session variable to maintain a unique deck of cards for each client application. Several clients can use the service at the same time, but method calls made by a specific client use only the deck stored in that client's session. Our example uses a simple subset of casino blackjack rules:

> *Two cards each are dealt to the dealer and the player. The player's cards are dealt face up. Only the dealer's first card is dealt face up. Each card has a value. A card numbered 2 through 10 is worth its face value. Jacks, queens and kings each count as 10. Aces can count as 1 or 11—whichever value is more beneficial to the player (as we'll soon see). If the sum of the player's two initial cards is 21 (i.e., the player was dealt a card valued at 10 and an ace, which counts as 11 in this situation), the player has "blackjack" and immediately wins the game. Otherwise, the player can begin taking additional cards one at a time. These cards are dealt face up, and the player decides when to stop taking cards. If the player "busts" (i.e., the sum of the player's cards exceeds 21), the game is over, and the player loses. When the player is satisfied with the current set of cards, the player "stays" (i.e., stops taking cards), and the dealer's hidden card is revealed. If the dealer's total is 16 or less, the dealer must take another card; otherwise, the dealer must stay. The dealer must continue to take cards until the sum of the dealer's cards is greater than or equal to 17. If the dealer exceeds 21, the player wins. Otherwise, the hand with the higher point total wins. If the dealer and the player have the same point total, the game is a "push" (i.e., a tie), and no one wins.*

The blackjack WCF web service's interface (Fig. 22.20) uses a `ServiceContract` with the `SessionMode` property set to `Required` (line 3). This means the service requires sessions to execute correctly. By default, the `SessionMode` property is set to `Allowed`. It can also be set to `NotAllowed` to disable sessions.

```
' Fig. 22.20: IBlackjackService.vb
' Blackjack game WCF web-service interface.
<ServiceContract(SessionMode:=SessionMode.Required)> _
Public Interface IBlackjackService
   ' deals a card that has not been dealt
   <OperationContract()> _
   Function DealCard() As String

   ' creates and shuffles the deck
   <OperationContract()> _
   Sub Shuffle()

   ' calculates value of a hand
   <OperationContract()> _
   Function GetHandValue(ByVal dealt As String) As Integer
End Interface ' IBlackjackService
```

Fig. 22.20 | Blackjack game WCF web-service interface.

The web-service class (Fig. 22.21) provides methods to deal a card, shuffle the deck and determine the point value of a hand. For this example, we want a separate object of the `BlackjackService` class to handle each client session, so we can maintain a unique deck for each client. To do this, we must specify this behavior in the `ServiceBehavior` attribute (line 5). Setting the `ServiceBehavior`'s `InstanceContextMode` property to `PerSession` creates a new instance of the class for each session. The `InstanceContextMode` property can also be set to `PerCall` or `Single`. `PerCall` uses a new object of the web-service class to handle every method call to the service. `Single` uses the same object of the web-ervice class to handle all calls to the service.

We represent each card as a `String` consisting of a digit (i.e., `1`–`13`) representing the card's face (e.g., ace through king), followed by a space and a digit (i.e., `0`–`3`) representing the card's suit (e.g., clubs, diamonds, hearts or spades). For example, the jack of hearts is represented as `"11 2"`, and the two of clubs as `"2 0"`. After deploying the web service, we create a Windows `Forms` application that uses the `BlackjackService`'s methods to implement a blackjack game.

```
1  ' Fig. 22.21: BlackjackService.vb
2  ' Blackjack game WCF web service.
3  Imports System.Collections.Generic
4
5  <ServiceBehavior(InstanceContextMode:=InstanceContextMode.PerSession)> _
6  Public Class BlackjackService
7     Implements IBlackjackService
8     ' create persistent session deck-of-cards object
9     Dim deck As New List(Of String)
10
11    ' deals card that has not yet been dealt
12    Public Function DealCard() As String _
13       Implements IBlackjackService.DealCard
```

Fig. 22.21 | Blackjack game WCF web service. (Part 1 of 3.)

```

      Dim card As String = Convert.ToString(deck(0)) ' get first card
      deck.RemoveAt(0) ' remove card from deck
      Return card
   End Function ' DealCard

   ' creates and shuffles a deck of cards
   Public Sub Shuffle() Implements IBlackjackService.Shuffle
      Dim randomObject As New Random() ' generates random numbers

      deck.Clear() ' clears deck for new game

      ' generate all possible cards
      For face = 1 To 13 ' loop through face values
         For suit As Integer = 0 To 3 ' loop through suits
            deck.Add(face & " " & suit) ' add card (string) to deck
         Next suit
      Next face

      ' shuffles deck by swapping each card with another card randomly
      For i = 0 To deck.Count - 1
         ' get random index
         Dim newIndex = randomObject.Next(deck.Count - 1)
         Dim temporary = deck(i) ' save current card in temporary variable
         deck(i) = deck(newIndex) ' copy randomly selected card
         deck(newIndex) = temporary ' copy current card back into deck
      Next
   End Sub ' Shuffle

   ' computes value of hand
   Public Function GetHandValue(ByVal dealt As String) As Integer _
      Implements IBlackjackService.GetHandValue
      ' split string containing all cards
      Dim tab As Char = Convert.ToChar(vbTab)
      Dim cards As String() = dealt.Split(tab) ' get array of cards
      Dim total As Integer = 0 ' total value of cards in hand
      Dim face As Integer ' face of the current card
      Dim aceCount As Integer = 0 ' number of aces in hand

      ' loop through the cards in the hand
      For Each card In cards
         ' get face of card
         face = Convert.ToInt32(card.Substring(0, card.IndexOf(" ")))

         Select Case face
            Case 1 ' if ace, increment aceCount
               aceCount += 1
            Case 11 To 13 ' if jack, queen or king add 10
               total += 10
            Case Else ' otherwise, add value of face
               total += face
         End Select
      Next
```

Fig. 22.21 | Blackjack game WCF web service. (Part 2 of 3.)

```
67
68          ' if there are any aces, calculate optimum total
69          If aceCount > 0 Then
70             ' if it is possible to count one ace as 11, and the rest
71             ' as 1 each, do so; otherwise, count all aces as 1 each
72             If (total + 11 + aceCount - 1 <= 21) Then
73                total += 11 + aceCount - 1
74             Else
75                total += aceCount
76             End If
77          End If
78
79          Return total
80       End Function ' GetHandValue
81    End Class ' BlackjackService
```

Fig. 22.21 | Blackjack game WCF web service. (Part 3 of 3.)

Method `DealCard` (lines 12–18) removes a card from the deck and sends it to the client. Without using session tracking, the deck of cards would need to be passed back and forth with each method call. Using session state makes the method easy to call (it requires no arguments) and avoids the overhead of sending the deck over the network multiple times.

Method `DealCard` (lines 12–18) manipulates the current user's deck (the `List` of `Strings` defined at line 9). From the user's deck, `DealCard` obtains the current top card (line 15), removes the top card from the deck (line 16) and returns the card's value as a `String` (line 17).

Method `Shuffle` (lines 21–41) fills the `List` object representing a deck of cards and shuffles it. Lines 27–31 generate `Strings` in the form "*face suit*" to represent each card in a deck. Lines 34–40 shuffle the deck by swapping each card with another randomly selected card in the deck.

Method `GetHandValue` (lines 44–80) determines the total value of cards in a hand by trying to attain the highest score possible without going over 21. Recall that an ace can be counted as either 1 or 11, and all face cards count as 10.

As you'll see in Fig. 22.22, the client application maintains a hand of cards as a `String` in which each card is separated by a tab character. Line 48 of Fig. 22.21 tokenizes the hand of cards (represented by `dealt`) into individual cards by calling `String` method `Split` and passing to it the tab character. `Split` uses the delimiter characters to separate tokens in the `String`. Lines 54–66 count the value of each card. Line 56 retrieves the first integer—the face—and uses that value in the `Select Case` statement (lines 58–65). If the card is an ace, the method increments variable `aceCount` (line 60). We discuss how this variable is used shortly. If the card is an 11, 12 or 13 (jack, queen or king), the method adds 10 to the total value of the hand (line 62). If the card is anything else, the method increases the total by that value (line 64).

Because an ace can represent 1 or 11, additional logic is required to process aces. Lines 69–77 process the aces after all the other cards. If a hand contains several aces, only one ace can be counted as 11 (if two aces each are counted as 11, the hand would have a losing value of at least 22). The condition in line 72 determines whether counting one ace as 11 and the rest as 1 results in a total that does not exceed 21. If this is possible, line 73 adjusts the total accordingly. Otherwise, line 75 adjusts the total, counting each ace as 1.

Method `GetHandValue` maximizes the value of the current cards without exceeding 21. Imagine, for example, that the dealer has a 7 and receives an ace. The new total could be either 8 or 18. However, `GetHandValue` always maximizes the value of the cards without going over 21, so the new total is 18.

22.9.2 Consuming the Blackjack Web Service

Now we use our blackjack web service in a Windows application (Fig. 22.22). This application uses an instance of `BlackjackServiceClient` (declared in line 7 and created in line 30) to represent the dealer. The web service keeps track of the player's and the dealer's cards (i.e., all the cards that have been dealt). As in Section 22.6.5, you must add a service reference to your project so it can access the web service. The code and images for this example are provided with the chapter's examples, which can be downloaded from our website `www.deitel.com/books/vb2008htp`.

```
1  ' Fig. 22.22: BlackjackForm.vb
2  ' Blackjack game that uses the BlackjackService web service.
3  Imports System.Net
4
5  Public Class BlackjackForm
6     ' reference to web service
7     Private dealer As ServiceReference.BlackJackServiceClient
8
9     ' string representing the dealer's cards
10    Private dealersCards As String
11
12    ' string representing the player's cards
13    Private playersCards As String
14    Private cardBoxes As List(Of PictureBox) ' list of card images
15    Private currentPlayerCard As Integer ' player's current card number
16    Private currentDealerCard As Integer ' dealer's current card number
17
18    ' enum representing the possible game outcomes
19    Public Enum GameStatus
20       PUSH ' game ends in a tie
21       LOSE ' player loses
22       WIN ' player wins
23       BLACKJACK ' player has blackjack
24    End Enum ' GameStatus
25
26    ' sets up the game
27    Private Sub BlackjackForm_Load(ByVal sender As Object, _
28       ByVal e As System.EventArgs) Handles Me.Load
29       ' instantiate object allowing communication with web service
30       dealer = New ServiceReference.BlackJackServiceClient()
31
32       cardBoxes = New List(Of PictureBox)
```

Fig. 22.22 | Blackjack game that uses the `BlackjackService` web service. (Part 1 of 8.)

```

      ' put PictureBoxes into cardBoxes List
      cardBoxes.Add(pictureBox1)
      cardBoxes.Add(pictureBox2)
      cardBoxes.Add(pictureBox3)
      cardBoxes.Add(pictureBox4)
      cardBoxes.Add(pictureBox5)
      cardBoxes.Add(pictureBox6)
      cardBoxes.Add(pictureBox7)
      cardBoxes.Add(pictureBox8)
      cardBoxes.Add(pictureBox9)
      cardBoxes.Add(pictureBox10)
      cardBoxes.Add(pictureBox11)
      cardBoxes.Add(pictureBox12)
      cardBoxes.Add(pictureBox13)
      cardBoxes.Add(pictureBox14)
      cardBoxes.Add(pictureBox15)
      cardBoxes.Add(pictureBox16)
      cardBoxes.Add(pictureBox17)
      cardBoxes.Add(pictureBox18)
      cardBoxes.Add(pictureBox19)
      cardBoxes.Add(pictureBox20)
      cardBoxes.Add(pictureBox21)
      cardBoxes.Add(pictureBox22)
   End Sub ' BlackjackForm_Load

   ' deals cards to dealer while dealer's total is less than 17,
   ' then computes value of each hand and determines winner
   Private Sub DealerPlay()
      ' reveal dealer's second card
      Dim tab As Char = Convert.ToChar(vbTab)
      Dim cards As String() = dealersCards.Split(tab)
      DisplayCard(1, cards(1))

      Dim nextCard As String

      ' while value of dealer's hand is below 17,
      ' dealer must take cards
      While dealer.GetHandValue(dealersCards) < 17
         nextCard = dealer.DealCard() ' deal new card
         dealersCards &= vbTab & nextCard

         ' update GUI to show new card
         MessageBox.Show("Dealer takes a card")
         DisplayCard(currentDealerCard, nextCard)
         currentDealerCard += 1
      End While

      Dim dealerTotal As Integer = dealer.GetHandValue(dealersCards)
      Dim playerTotal As Integer = dealer.GetHandValue(playersCards)

```

Fig. 22.22 | Blackjack game that uses the `BlackjackService` web service. (Part 2 of 8.)

```
         ' if dealer busted, player wins
         If dealerTotal > 21 Then
            GameOver(GameStatus.WIN)
         Else
            ' if dealer and player have not exceeded 21,
            ' higher score wins; equal scores is a push.
            If dealerTotal > playerTotal Then ' player loses game
               GameOver(GameStatus.LOSE)
            ElseIf playerTotal > dealerTotal Then ' player wins game
               GameOver(GameStatus.WIN)
            Else ' player and dealer tie
               GameOver(GameStatus.PUSH)
            End If
         End If
      End Sub ' DealerPlay

      ' displays card represented by cardValue in specified PictureBox
      Public Sub DisplayCard( _
         ByVal card As Integer, ByVal cardValue As String)
         ' retrieve appropriate PictureBox
         Dim displayBox As PictureBox = cardBoxes(card)

         ' if string representing card is empty,
         ' set displayBox to display back of card
         If String.IsNullOrEmpty(cardValue) Then
            displayBox.Image = _
               Image.FromFile("blackjack_images/cardback.png")
            Return
         End If

         ' retrieve face value of card from cardValue
         Dim face As String = _
            cardValue.Substring(0, cardValue.IndexOf(" "))

         ' retrieve the suit of the card from cardValue
         Dim suit As String = _
            cardValue.Substring(cardValue.IndexOf(" ") + 1)

         Dim suitLetter As Char ' suit letter used to form image file name

         ' determine the suit letter of the card
         Select Case Convert.ToInt32(suit)
            Case 0 ' clubs
               suitLetter = "c"c
            Case 1 ' diamonds
               suitLetter = "d"c
            Case 2 ' hearts
               suitLetter = "h"c
            Case Else ' spades
               suitLetter = "s"c
         End Select

```

Fig. 22.22 | Blackjack game that uses the `BlackjackService` web service. (Part 3 of 8.)

```
      ' set displayBox to display appropriate image
      displayBox.Image = Image.FromFile( _
      "blackjack_images/" & face & suitLetter & ".png")
   End Sub ' DisplayCard

   ' displays all player cards and shows
   ' appropriate game status message
   Public Sub GameOver(ByVal winner As GameStatus)
      ' display appropriate status image
      If winner = GameStatus.PUSH Then ' push
         statusPictureBox.Image = _
            Image.FromFile("blackjack_images/tie.png")
      ElseIf winner = GameStatus.LOSE Then ' player loses
         statusPictureBox.Image = _
            Image.FromFile("blackjack_images/lose.png")
      ElseIf winner = GameStatus.BLACKJACK Then
         ' player has blackjack
         statusPictureBox.Image = _
            Image.FromFile("blackjack_images/blackjack.png")
      Else ' player wins
         statusPictureBox.Image = _
            Image.FromFile("blackjack_images/win.png")
      End If

      ' display final totals for dealer and player
      dealerTotalLabel.Text = _
         "Dealer: " & dealer.GetHandValue(dealersCards)
      playerTotalLabel.Text = _
         "Player: " & dealer.GetHandValue(playersCards)

      ' reset controls for new game
      stayButton.Enabled = False
      hitButton.Enabled = False
      dealButton.Enabled = True
   End Sub ' GameOver

   ' deal two cards each to dealer and player
   Private Sub dealButton_Click(ByVal sender As System.Object, _
      ByVal e As System.EventArgs) Handles dealButton.Click
      Dim card As String ' stores a card temporarily until added to a hand

      ' clear card images
      For Each cardImage As PictureBox In cardBoxes
         cardImage.Image = Nothing
      Next

      statusPictureBox.Image = Nothing ' clear status image
      dealerTotalLabel.Text = String.Empty ' clear final total for dealer
      playerTotalLabel.Text = String.Empty ' clear final total for player

      ' create a new, shuffled deck on the web service host
      dealer.Shuffle()
```

Fig. 22.22 | Blackjack game that uses the `BlackjackService` web service. (Part 4 of 8.)

```

      ' deal two cards to player
      playersCards = dealer.DealCard() ' deal a card to player's hand

      ' update GUI to display new card
      DisplayCard(11, playersCards)
      card = dealer.DealCard() ' deal a second card
      DisplayCard(12, card) ' update GUI to display new card
      playersCards &= vbTab & card ' add second card to player's hand

      ' deal two cards to dealer, only display face of first card
      dealersCards = dealer.DealCard() ' deal a card to dealer's hand
      DisplayCard(0, dealersCards) ' update GUI to display new card
      card = dealer.DealCard() ' deal a second card
      DisplayCard(1, String.Empty) ' update GUI to show face-down card
      dealersCards &= vbTab & card ' add second card to dealer's hand

      stayButton.Enabled = True ' allow player to stay
      hitButton.Enabled = True ' allow player to hit
      dealButton.Enabled = False ' disable Deal Button

      ' determine the value of the two hands
      Dim dealerTotal As Integer = dealer.GetHandValue(dealersCards)
      Dim playerTotal As Integer = dealer.GetHandValue(playersCards)

      ' if hands equal 21, it is a push
      If dealerTotal = playerTotal And dealerTotal = 21 Then
         GameOver(GameStatus.PUSH)
      ElseIf dealerTotal = 21 Then ' if dealer has 21, dealer wins
         GameOver(GameStatus.LOSE)
      ElseIf playerTotal = 21 Then ' player has blackjack
         GameOver(GameStatus.BLACKJACK)
      End If

      currentDealerCard = 2 ' next dealer card has index 2 in cardBoxes
      currentPlayerCard = 13 ' next player card has index 13 in cardBoxes
   End Sub ' dealButton_Click

   ' deal another card to player
   Private Sub hitButton_Click(ByVal sender As System.Object, _
      ByVal e As System.EventArgs) Handles hitButton.Click
      ' get player another card
      Dim card As String = dealer.DealCard() ' deal new card
      playersCards &= vbTab & card ' add new card to player's hand

      ' update GUI to show new card
      DisplayCard(currentPlayerCard, card)
      currentPlayerCard += 1

      ' determine the value of the player's hand
      Dim total As Integer = dealer.GetHandValue(playersCards)

```

Fig. 22.22 | Blackjack game that uses the `BlackjackService` web service. (Part 5 of 8.)

```
         ' if player exceeds 21, house wins
         If total > 21 Then
            GameOver(GameStatus.LOSE)
         End If

         ' if player has 21,
         ' they cannot take more cards, and dealer plays
         If total = 21 Then
            hitButton.Enabled = False
            DealerPlay()
         End If
      End Sub ' hitButton_Click

      ' play the dealer's hand after the play chooses to stay
      Private Sub stayButton_Click(ByVal sender As System.Object, _
         ByVal e As System.EventArgs) Handles stayButton.Click
         stayButton.Enabled = False ' disable Stay Button
         hitButton.Enabled = False ' disable Hit Button
         dealButton.Enabled = True ' re-enable Deal Button
         DealerPlay() ' player chose to stay, so play the dealer's hand
      End Sub ' stayButton_Click
   End Class ' BlackjackForm
```

a) Initial cards dealt to the player and the dealer when the user presses the **Deal** button.

Fig. 22.22 | Blackjack game that uses the `BlackjackService` web service. (Part 6 of 8.)

b) Cards after the player presses the **Hit** button once, then the **Stay** button. In this case, the player wins the game with a higher total than the dealer.

c) Cards after the player presses the **Hit** button once, then the **Stay** button. In this case, the player busts (exceeds 21) and the dealer wins the game.

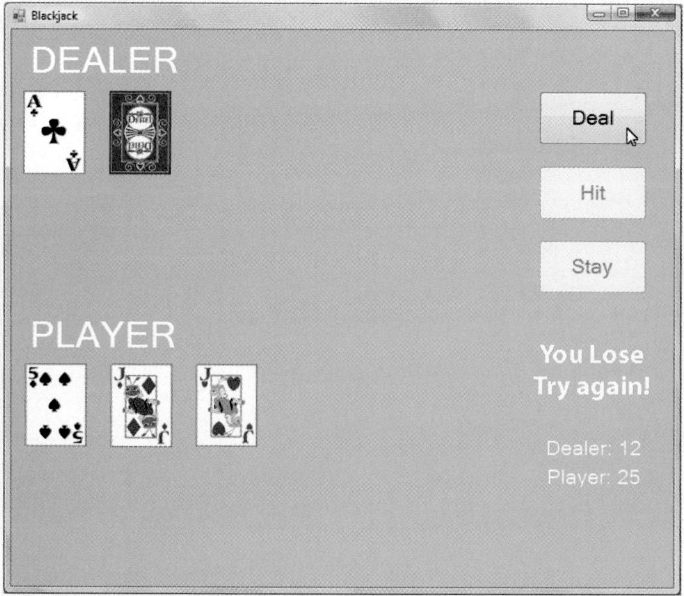

Fig. 22.22 | Blackjack game that uses the `BlackjackService` web service. (Part 7 of 8.)

d) Cards after the player presses the **Deal** button. In this case, the player wins with Blackjack because the first two cards are an ace and a card with a value of 10 (a jack in this case).

e) Cards after the player presses the **Stay** button. In this case, the player and dealer push—they have the same card total.

Fig. 22.22 | Blackjack game that uses the `BlackjackService` web service. (Part 8 of 8.)

Each player has 11 PictureBoxes—the maximum number of cards that can be dealt without exceeding 21 (i.e., four aces, four twos and three threes). These PictureBoxes are placed in a List (lines 35–56), so we can index the List during the game to determine which PictureBox should display a particular card image.

Method GameOver (lines 143–170) shows an appropriate message in the status PictureBox and displays the final point totals of both the dealer and the player. These values are obtained by calling the web service's GetHandValue method in lines 162 and 164. Method GameOver receives as an argument a member of the GameStatus enumeration (defined in lines 19–24). The enumeration represents whether the player tied, lost or won the game; its four members are PUSH, LOSE, WIN and BLACKJACK.

When the player clicks the **Deal** button, the event handler (lines 173–224) clears the PictureBoxes and the Labels displaying the final point totals. Line 187 shuffles the deck by calling the web service's Shuffle method, then the player and dealer receive two cards each (returned by calls to the web service's DealCard method in lines 190, 194, 199 and 201). Lines 210–211 evaluate both the dealer's and player's hands by calling the web service's GetHandValue method. If the player and the dealer both obtain scores of 21, the program calls method GameOver, passing GameStatus.PUSH. If only the player has 21 after the first two cards are dealt, the program passes GameStatus.BLACKJACK to method GameOver. If only the dealer has 21, the program passes GameStatus.LOSE to method GameOver.

If dealButton_Click does not call GameOver, the player can take more cards by clicking the **Hit** button. The event handler for this button is in lines 227–251. Each time a player clicks **Hit**, the program deals the player one more card (line 230), displaying it in the GUI. Line 238 evaluates the player's hand. If the player exceeds 21, the game is over, and the player loses. If the player has exactly 21, the player cannot take any more cards, and method DealerPlay (lines 61–98) is called, causing the dealer to keep taking cards until the dealer's hand has a value of 17 or more (lines 71–79). If the dealer exceeds 21, the player wins (line 86); otherwise, the values of the hands are compared, and GameOver is called with the appropriate argument (lines 90–96).

Clicking the **Stay** button indicates that a player does not want to be dealt another card. The event handler for this button (lines 254–260) disables the **Hit** and **Stay** buttons, then calls method DealerPlay.

Method DisplayCard (lines 101–139) updates the GUI to display a newly dealt card. The method takes as arguments an integer representing the index of the PictureBox in the List that must have its image set, and a String representing the card. An empty String indicates that we wish to display the card face down. If method DisplayCard receives a String that's not empty, the program extracts the face and suit from the String and uses this information to find the correct image. The Select Case statement (lines 125–134) converts the number representing the suit to an Integer and assigns the appropriate character literal to suitLetter (c for clubs, d for diamonds, h for hearts and s for spades). The character in suitLetter is used to complete the image's file name (lines 137–138).

22.10 Airline Reservation Web Service: Database Access and Invoking a Service from ASP.NET

Our prior examples accessed web services from Windows Forms applications. You can just as easily use web services in ASP.NET web applications. In fact, because web-based businesses are becoming increasingly prevalent, it is common for web applications to consume web services. Figures 22.23 and 22.24 present the interface and class, respectively, for an airline reservation service that receives information regarding the type of seat a customer wishes to reserve, checks a database to see if such a seat is available and, if so, makes a reservation. Later in this section, we present an ASP.NET web application that allows a customer to specify a reservation request, then uses the airline reservation web service to attempt to execute the request. The code and database used in this example are provided with the chapter's examples, which can be downloaded from `www.deitel.com/books/vb2008htp`.

```
' Fig. 22.23: IReservationService.vb
' Airline reservation WCF web-service interface.
<ServiceContract()> _
Public Interface IReservationService
   ' reserves a seat
   <OperationContract()> _
   Function Reserve(ByVal seatType As String, _
      ByVal classType As String) As Boolean
End Interface ' IReservationService
```

Fig. 22.23 | Airline reservation WCF web-service interface.

```
' Fig. 22.24: ReservationService.vb
' Airline reservation WCF web service.
Public Class ReservationService
   Implements IReservationService

   ' create ticketsDB object to access Tickets database
   Private ticketsDB As New TicketsDataContext()

   ' checks database to determine whether matching seat is available
   Public Function Reserve(ByVal seatType As String, _
      ByVal classType As String) As Boolean _
      Implements IReservationService.Reserve

      ' LINQ query to find seats matching the parameters
      Dim result = _
         From seat In ticketsDB.Seats _
         Where (seat.Taken = 0) And (seat.SeatType = seatType) _
            And (seat.SeatClass = classType)

      ' if the number of seats returned is nonzero,
      ' obtain the first matching seat number and mark it as taken
      If result.Count() <> 0 Then
         ' get first available seat
         Dim firstAvailableSeat As Seat = result.First()
         firstAvailableSeat.Taken = 1 ' mark the seat as taken
         ticketsDB.SubmitChanges() ' update
         Return True ' seat was reserved
      End If
```

Fig. 22.24 | Airline reservation WCF web service. (Part 1 of 2.)

```
29
30       Return False ' no seat was reserved
31    End Function ' Reserve
32 End Class ' ReservationService
```

Fig. 22.24 | Airline reservation WCF web service. (Part 2 of 2.)

In Chapter 20, you learned how to use LINQ to SQL to extract data from a database. We added the `Tickets.mdf` database and corresponding LINQ to SQL classes to create a `DataContext` object (line 7) for our ticket reservation system. `Tickets.mdf` database contains the `Seats` table with four columns—the seat number (1–10), the seat type (`Window`, `Middle` or `Aisle`), the class type (`Economy` or `First`) and a column containing either `1` (true) or `0` (false) to indicate whether the seat is taken.

This web service has a single method—`Reserve` (lines 10–31)—which searches a seat database (`Tickets.mdf`) to locate a seat matching a user's request. If it finds an appropriate seat, `Reserve` updates the database, makes the reservation and returns `True`; otherwise, no reservation is made, and the method returns `False`. Note that the statements in lines 15–18 and lines 22–28, which query and update the database, use LINQ to SQL.

`Reserve` receives two parameters—a `String` representing the seat type (i.e., `Window`, `Middle` or `Aisle`) and a `String` representing the class type (i.e., `Economy` or `First`). Our database contains four columns—the seat number (i.e., `1`–`10`), the seat type (i.e., `Window`, `Middle` or `Aisle`), the class type (i.e., `Economy` or `First`) and a column containing either `1` (true) or `0` (false) to indicate whether the seat is taken. Lines 16–18 retrieve the seat numbers of any available seats matching the requested seat and class type with the results of a query. In line 22, if the number of results in the query is not zero, there was at least one seat that matched the user's request. In this case, the web service reserves the first matching seat. We obtain the seat in line 24 by accessing the query's first result. Line 25 marks the seat as taken and line 26 submits the changes to the database. Method `Reserve` returns `True` (line 27) to indicate that the reservation was successful. If there are no matching seats, `Reserve` returns `False` (line 30) to indicate that no seats matched the user's request.

Creating a Web Form to Interact with the Airline Reservation Web Service

Figure 22.25 presents the code for an ASP.NET page through which users can select seat types. This page allows users to reserve a seat on the basis of its class (`Economy` or `First`) and location (`Aisle`, `Middle` or `Window`) in a row of seats. The page then uses the airline reservation web service to carry out user requests. If the database request is not successful, the user is instructed to modify the request and try again. When you create this ASP.NET application, remember to add a service reference to the `ReservationService`.

```
<%-- Fig. 22.25: ReservationClient.aspx                    --%>
<%-- Web Form that allows users to reserve seats on a plane. --%>
<%@ Page Language="VB" AutoEventWireup="false"
   CodeFile="ReservationClient.aspx.vb" Inherits="ReservationClient" %>

<!DOCTYPE html PUBLIC "-//W3C//DTD XHTML 1.0 Transitional//EN"
   "http://www.w3.org/TR/xhtml11/DTD/xhtml11-transitional.dtd">
```

Fig. 22.25 | ASPX file that takes reservation information. (Part 1 of 2.)

```
8
9  <html xmlns="http://www.w3.org/1999/xhtml" >
10 <head runat="server">
11    <title>Ticket Reservation</title>
12 </head>
13 <body>
14    <form id="form1" runat="server">
15    <div>
16       <asp:Label ID="instructionsLabel" runat="server"
17          Text="Please select the seat type and class to reserve:">
18       </asp:Label>
19       <br /><br />
20       <%-- seat options --%>
21       <asp:DropDownList ID="seatList" runat="server"
22          Height="22px" Width="100px">
23          <asp:ListItem>Aisle</asp:ListItem>
24          <asp:ListItem>Middle</asp:ListItem>
25          <asp:ListItem>Window</asp:ListItem>
26       </asp:DropDownList>
27           
28       <%-- class options --%>
29       <asp:DropDownList ID="classList" runat="server" Width="100px">
30          <asp:ListItem>Economy</asp:ListItem>
31          <asp:ListItem>First</asp:ListItem>
32       </asp:DropDownList>
33           
34       <%-- submits selections to server --%>
35       <asp:Button ID="reserveButton" runat="server" Text="Reserve"
36          Width="102px" />
37       <br /><br />
38       <asp:Label ID="errorLabel" runat="server" ForeColor="#C00000"
39          Height="19px" Width="343px"></asp:Label>
40    </div>
41    </form>
42 </body>
43 </html>
```

Fig. 22.25 | ASPX file that takes reservation information. (Part 2 of 2.)

This page defines two `DropDownList` objects and a `Button`. One `DropDownList` (lines 21–26) displays all the seat types from which users can select. The second (lines 29–32) provides choices for the class type. Users click the `Button` named `reserveButton` (lines 35–36) to submit requests after making selections from the `DropDownLists`. The page also defines an initially blank `Label` named `errorLabel` (lines 38–39), which displays an appropriate message if no seat matching the user's selection is available. Line 9 of the code-behind file (Fig. 22.26) attaches an event handler to `reserveButton`.

Line 6 of Fig. 22.26 creates a `ReservationServiceClient` proxy object. When the user clicks **Reserve** (Fig. 22.27), the `reserveButton_Click` event handler (lines 8–29 of Fig. 22.26) executes, and the page reloads. The event handler calls the web service's `Reserve` method and passes to it the selected seat and class type as arguments (lines 12–13). If `Reserve` returns `True`, the application hides the GUI controls and displays a

```
1  ' Fig. 22.26: ReservationClient.aspx.vb
2  ' ReservationClient code-behind file.
3  Partial Class ReservationClient
4     Inherits System.Web.UI.Page
5     ' object of proxy type used to connect to Reservation service
6     Private ticketAgent As New ServiceReference.ReservationServiceClient()
7
8     Protected Sub reserveButton_Click(ByVal sender As Object, _
9        ByVal e As System.EventArgs) Handles reserveButton.Click
10
11       ' if the ticket is reserved
12       If ticketAgent.Reserve(seatList.SelectedItem.Text, _
13          classList.SelectedItem.Text.ToString()) Then
14
15          ' hide other controls
16          instructionsLabel.Visible = False
17          seatList.Visible = False
18          classList.Visible = False
19          reserveButton.Visible = False
20          errorLabel.Visible = False
21
22          ' display message indicating success
23          Response.Write("Your reservation has been made. Thank you.")
24       Else ' service method returned false, so signal failure
25          ' display message in the initially blank errorLabel
26          errorLabel.Text = "This type of seat is not available. " & _
27             "Please modify your request and try again."
28       End If
29    End Sub ' reserveButton_Click
30 End Class ' ReservationClient
```

Fig. 22.26 | `ReservationClient` code-behind file.

message thanking the user for making a reservation (line 23); otherwise, the application notifies the user that the type of seat requested is not available and instructs the user to try again (lines 26–27). You can use the techniques presented in Chapter 21 to build this ASP.NET Web Form. Figure 22.27 shows several user interactions with this web application.

a) Selecting a seat.

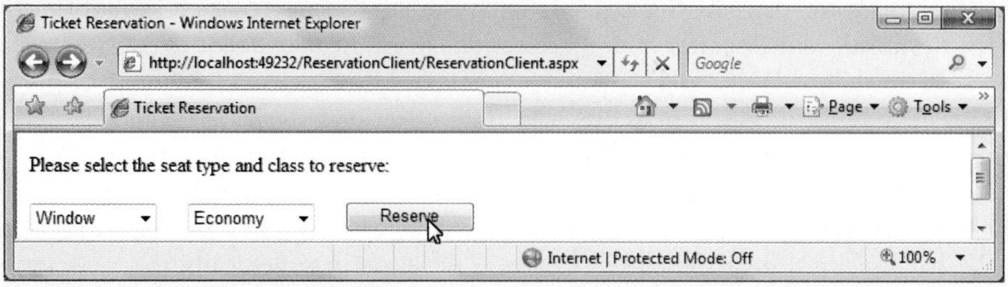

Ticket Reservation - Windows Internet Explorer

http://localhost:49232/ReservationClient/ReservationClient.aspx

Please select the seat type and class to reserve:

Window | Economy | Reserve

Fig. 22.27 | Ticket reservation web-application sample execution. (Part 1 of 2.)

b) Seat is reserved successfully.

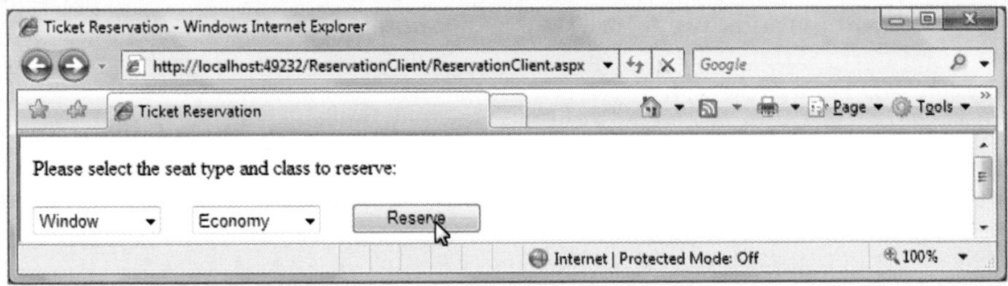

c) Attempting to reserve another seat.

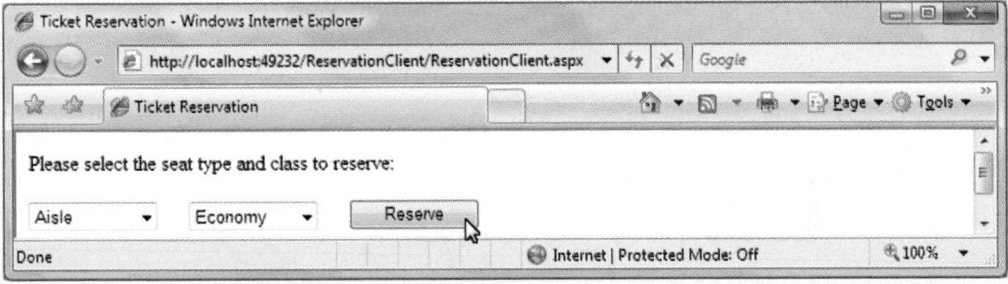

d) No seats match the requested type and class.

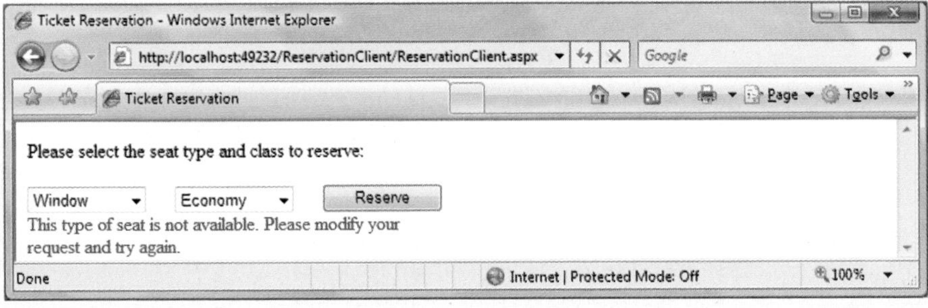

Fig. 22.27 | Ticket reservation web-application sample execution. (Part 2 of 2.)

22.11 Equation Generator: Returning User-Defined Types

With the exception of the `WelcomeRESTJSONService` (Fig. 22.17), the web services we've demonstrated all received and returned primitive-type instances. It is also possible to process instances of complete user-defined types in a web service. These types can be passed to or returned from web-service methods.

This section presents an `EquationGenerator` web service that generates random arithmetic equations of type `Equation`. The client is a math-tutoring application that inputs information about the mathematical question that the user wishes to attempt (addition, subtraction or multiplication) and the skill level of the user (1 specifies equations using numbers from 1 to 10, 2 specifies equations involving numbers from 10 to 100, and 3 specifies equations containing numbers from 100 to 1000). The web service then generates an equation consisting of random numbers in the proper range. The client application receives the `Equation` and displays the sample question to the user.

Defining Class **`Equation`**

We define class `Equation` in Fig. 22.28. Lines 16–33 define a constructor that takes three arguments—two `Integers` representing the left and right operands and a `String` that represents the arithmetic operation to perform. The constructor sets the `leftOperand`, `rightOperand` and `operationType` instance variables, then calculates the appropriate result. The parameterless constructor (lines 11–13) calls the three-argument constructor (lines 16–33) and passes default values.

```
1  ' Fig. 22.28: Equation.vb
2  ' Class Equation that contains information about an equation.
3  <DataContract()> _
4  Public Class Equation
5     Private leftOperand As Integer ' number to the left of the operator
6     Private rightOperand As Integer ' number to the right of the operator
7     Private resultValue As Integer ' result of the operation
8     Private operationType As String ' type of the operation
9
10    ' required default constructor
11    Public Sub New()
12       MyClass.New(0, 0, "add")
13    End Sub ' parameterless New
14
15    ' three-argument constructor for class Equation
16    Public Sub New(ByVal leftValue As Integer, _
17       ByVal rightValue As Integer, ByVal type As String)
18
19       Left = leftValue
20       Right = rightValue
21
22       Select Case type ' perform appropriate operation
23          Case "add" ' addition
24             Result = leftOperand + rightOperand
25             operationType = "+"
26          Case "subtract" ' subtraction
27             Result = leftOperand - rightOperand
28             operationType = "-"
29          Case "multiply" ' multiplication
30             Result = leftOperand * rightOperand
31             operationType = "*"
32       End Select
33    End Sub ' three-parameter New
34
35    ' return string representation of the Equation object
36    Public Overrides Function ToString() As String
37       Return leftOperand.ToString() & " " & operationType & " " & _
38          rightOperand.ToString() & " = " & resultValue.ToString()
39    End Function ' ToString
```

Fig. 22.28 | Class `Equation` that contains information about an equation. (Part 1 of 3.)

```
      ' property that returns a string representing left-hand side
      <DataMember()> _
      Public Property LeftHandSide() As String
         Get
            Return leftOperand.ToString() & " " & operationType & " " & _
               rightOperand.ToString()
         End Get

         Set(ByVal value As String) ' required set accessor
            ' empty body
         End Set
      End Property ' LeftHandSide

      ' property that returns a string representing right-hand side
      <DataMember()> _
      Public Property RightHandSide() As String
         Get
            Return resultValue.ToString()
         End Get

         Set(ByVal value As String) ' required set accessor
            ' empty body
         End Set
      End Property ' RightHandSide

      ' property to access the left operand
      <DataMember()> _
      Public Property Left() As Integer
         Get
            Return leftOperand
         End Get

         Set(ByVal value As Integer)
            leftOperand = value
         End Set
      End Property ' Left

      ' property to access the right operand
      <DataMember()> _
      Public Property Right() As Integer
         Get
            Return rightOperand
         End Get

         Set(ByVal value As Integer)
            rightOperand = value
         End Set
      End Property ' Right

      ' property to access the result of applying
      ' an operation to the left and right operands
```

Fig. 22.28 | Class `Equation` that contains information about an equation. (Part 2 of 3.)

```
92        <DataMember()> _
93        Public Property Result() As Integer
94           Get
95              Return resultValue
96           End Get
97
98           Set(ByVal value As Integer)
99              resultValue = value
100          End Set
101       End Property ' Result
102
103       ' property to access the operation
104       <DataMember()> _
105       Public Property Operation() As String
106          Get
107             Return operationType
108          End Get
109
110          Set(ByVal value As String)
111             operationType = value
112          End Set
113       End Property ' Operation
114    End Class ' Equation
```

Fig. 22.28 | Class `Equation` that contains information about an equation. (Part 3 of 3.)

Class `Equation` defines properties `LeftHandSide` (lines 43–52), `RightHandSide` (lines 56–64), `Left` (lines 68–76), `Right` (lines 80–88), `Result` (lines 93–101) and `Operation` (lines 105–113). The web service client does not need to modify the values of properties `LeftHandSide` and `RightHandSide`. However, recall that a property can be serialized only if it has both a `Get` and a `Set` accessor—this is true even if the `Set` accessor has an empty body. Each of the properties is preceded by the `DataMember` attribute to indicate that it should be serialized. `LeftHandSide` (lines 43–52) returns a `String` representing everything to the left of the equals (=) sign in the equation, and `RightHandSide` (lines 56–64) returns a `String` representing everything to the right of the equals (=) sign. `Left` (lines 68–76) returns the `Integer` to the left of the operator (known as the left operand), and `Right` (lines 80–88) returns the `Integer` to the right of the operator (known as the right operand). `Result` (lines 93–101) returns the solution to the equation, and `Operation` (lines 105–113) returns the operator in the equation. The client in this case study does not use the `RightHandSide` property, but we included it in case future clients choose to use it. Method `ToString` (lines 36–39) returns a `String` representation of the equation.

22.11.1 Creating the REST-Based XML EquationGenerator Web Service

Figures 22.29 and 22.30 present the interface and class for the `EquationGeneratorService` web service, which creates random, customized `Equation`s. This web service contains only method `GenerateEquation` (lines 7–27 of Fig. 22.30), which takes two parameters—a `String` representing the mathematical operation (`"add"`, `"subtract"` or `"multiply"`) and a `String` representing the difficulty level. When line 26 of Fig. 22.30 returns the `Equation`, it is serialized as XML by default and sent to the client. We'll do this with JSON as well in Section 22.11.3. Recall from Section 22.7.1 that you must modify the `Web.config` file to enable REST support as well.

```
' Fig. 22.29: IEquationGeneratorService.vb
' WCF REST service interface to create random equations based on a
' specified operation and difficulty level.
Imports System.ServiceModel.Web

<ServiceContract()> _
Public Interface IEquationGeneratorService
   ' method to generate a math equation
   <OperationContract()> _
   <WebGet(UriTemplate:="equation/{operation}/{level}")> _
   Function GenerateEquation(ByVal operation As String, _
      ByVal level As String) As Equation
End Interface ' IEquationGeneratorService
```

Fig. 22.29 | WCF REST service interface to create random equations based on a specified operation and difficulty level.

```
' Fig. 22.30: EquationGeneratorService.vb
' WCF REST service to create random equations based on a
' specified operation and difficulty level.
Public Class EquationGeneratorService
   Implements IEquationGeneratorService
   ' method to generate a math equation
   Public Function GenerateEquation(ByVal operation As String, _
      ByVal level As String) As Equation _
      Implements IEquationGeneratorService.GenerateEquation

      ' convert level from String to Integer
      Dim digits = Convert.ToInt32(level)

      ' calculate maximum and minimum number to be used
      Dim maximum As Integer = Convert.ToInt32(Math.Pow(10, digits))
      Dim minimum As Integer = Convert.ToInt32(Math.Pow(10, digits - 1))

      Dim randomObject As New Random() ' used to generate random numbers

      ' create Equation consisting of two random
      ' numbers in the range minimum to maximum
      Dim newEquation As New Equation( _
         randomObject.Next(minimum, maximum), _
         randomObject.Next(minimum, maximum), operation)

      Return newEquation
   End Function ' GenerateEquation
End Class ' EquationGeneratorService
```

Fig. 22.30 | WCF REST service to create random equations based on a specified operation and difficulty level.

22.11.2 Consuming the REST-Based XML EquationGenerator Web Service

The `MathTutor` application (Fig. 22.31) calls the `EquationGenerator` web service's `GenerateEquation` method to create an `Equation` object. The tutor then displays the left-hand side of the `Equation` and waits for user input.

```
' Fig. 22.31: MathTutorForm.vb
' Math tutor using EquationGeneratorServiceXML to create equations.
Imports System.Net
Imports System.Xml.Linq
Imports <xmlns="http://schemas.datacontract.org/2004/07/">

Public Class MathTutorForm
   Private operation As String = "add" ' the default operation
   Private level As Integer = 1 ' the default difficulty level
   Private leftHandSide As String ' the left side of the equation
   Private result As Integer ' the answer

   Private WithEvents service As New WebClient() ' used to invoke service

   ' generates a new equation when user clicks button
   Private Sub generateButton_Click(ByVal sender As System.Object, _
      ByVal e As System.EventArgs) Handles generateButton.Click

      ' send request to EquationGeneratorServiceXML
      service.DownloadStringAsync(New Uri( _
         "http://localhost:49593/EquationGeneratorServiceXML/" _
         & "Service.svc/equation/" & operation & "/" & level))
   End Sub ' generateButton_Click

   ' process web-service response
   Private Sub service_DownloadStringCompleted(ByVal sender As Object, _
      ByVal e As System.Net.DownloadStringCompletedEventArgs) _
      Handles service.DownloadStringCompleted

      ' check if any errors occurred in retrieving service data
      If e.Error Is Nothing Then
         ' parse response and get LeftHandSide and Result values
         Dim xmlResponse = XDocument.Parse(e.Result)
         leftHandSide = xmlResponse.<Equation>.<LeftHandSide>.Value
         result = Convert.ToInt32(xmlResponse.<Equation>.<Result>.Value)

         questionLabel.Text = leftHandSide ' display left side of equation
         okButton.Enabled = True ' enable okButton
         answerTextBox.Enabled = True ' enable answerTextBox
      End If
   End Sub ' service_DownloadStringCompleted

   ' check user's answer
   Private Sub okButton_Click(ByVal sender As System.Object, _
      ByVal e As System.EventArgs) Handles okButton.Click
```

Fig. 22.31 | Math tutor using `EquationGeneratorServiceXML` to create equations. (Part 1 of 3.)

```

      If Not String.IsNullOrEmpty(answerTextBox.Text) Then
         ' get user's answer
         Dim userAnswer As Integer = Convert.ToInt32(answerTextBox.Text)

         ' determine whether user's answer is correct
         If result = userAnswer Then
            questionLabel.Text = String.Empty ' clear question
            answerTextBox.Clear() ' clear answer
            okButton.Enabled = False ' disable OK button
            MessageBox.Show("Correct! Good job!")
         Else
            MessageBox.Show("Incorrect. Try again.")
         End If
      End If
   End Sub ' okButton_Click

   ' set the operation to addition
   Private Sub additionRadioButton_CheckedChanged( _
      ByVal sender As System.Object, ByVal e As System.EventArgs) _
      Handles additionRadioButton.CheckedChanged
      operation = "add"
   End Sub ' additionRadioButton_CheckedChanged

   ' set the operation to subtraction
   Private Sub subtractionRadioButton_CheckedChanged( _
      ByVal sender As System.Object, ByVal e As System.EventArgs) _
      Handles subtractionRadioButton.CheckedChanged
      operation = "subtract"
   End Sub ' subtractionRadioButton_CheckedChanged

   ' set the operation to multiplication
   Private Sub multiplicationRadioButton_CheckedChanged( _
      ByVal sender As System.Object, ByVal e As System.EventArgs) _
      Handles multiplicationRadioButton.CheckedChanged
      operation = "multiply"
   End Sub ' multiplicationRadioButton_CheckedChanged

   ' set difficulty level to 1
   Private Sub levelOneRadioButton_CheckedChanged( _
      ByVal sender As System.Object, ByVal e As System.EventArgs) _
      Handles levelOneRadioButton.CheckedChanged
      level = 1
   End Sub ' levelOneRadioButton_CheckedChanged

   ' set difficulty level to 2
   Private Sub levelTwoRadioButton_CheckedChanged( _
      ByVal sender As System.Object, ByVal e As System.EventArgs) _
      Handles levelTwoRadioButton.CheckedChanged
      level = 2
   End Sub ' levelTwoRadioButton_CheckedChanged

```

Fig. 22.31 | Math tutor using `EquationGeneratorServiceXML` to create equations. (Part 2 of 3.)

```
98         ' set difficulty level to 3
99         Private Sub levelThreeRadioButton_CheckedChanged( _
100           ByVal sender As System.Object, ByVal e As System.EventArgs) _
101           Handles levelThreeRadioButton.CheckedChanged
102           level = 3
103        End Sub ' levelThreeRadioButton_CheckedChanged
104     End Class ' MathTutorForm
```

a) Generating a level 1 addition equation.

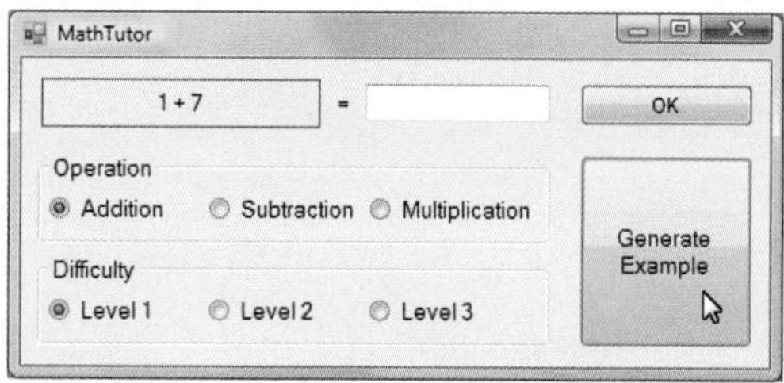

b) Answering the question incorrectly.

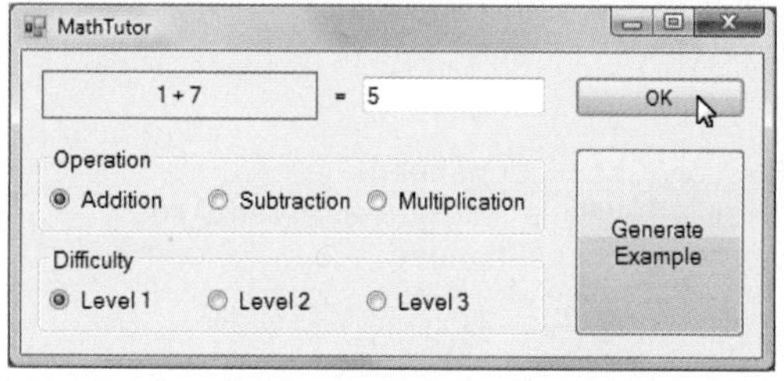

c) Answering the question correctly.

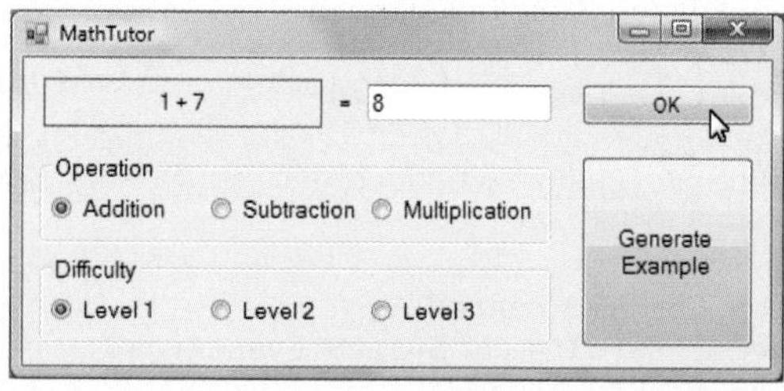

Fig. 22.31 | Math tutor using `EquationGeneratorServiceXML` to create equations. (Part 3 of 3.)

The default setting for the difficulty level is `1`, but the user can change this by choosing a level from the `RadioButton`s in the `GroupBox` labeled **Difficulty**. Clicking any of the levels invokes the corresponding `RadioButton`'s `CheckedChanged` event handler (lines 85–103), which sets integer `level` to the level selected by the user. Although the default setting for the question type is **Addition**, the user also can change this by selecting one of the `RadioButton`s in the `GroupBox` labeled **Operation**. Doing so invokes the corresponding operation's event handlers in lines 64–82, which assigns to `String operation` the symbol corresponding to the user's selection. Each event handler also updates the `Text` property of the **Generate** button to match the newly selected operation.

Line 13 defines the `WebClient` that is used to invoke the web service. Event handler `generateButton_Click` (lines 16–23) invokes `EquationGeneratorService` method `GenerateEquation` (line 20–22) asynchronously using the web service's `UriTemplate` specified at line 10 in Fig. 22.29. When the response arrives, the `DownloadStringCompleted` event handler (lines 26–41) parses the XML response (line 33), uses XML Axis properties to obtain the left side of the equation (line 34) and stores the result (line 35). Then, the handler displays the left-hand side of the equation in `questionLabel` (line 37) and enables `okButton` so that the user can enter an answer. When the user clicks **OK**, `okButton_Click` (lines 44–61) checks whether the user provided the correct answer.

22.11.3 Creating the REST-Based JSON WCF EquationGenerator Web Service

You can set the web service to return JSON data instead of XML. Figure 22.32 is a modified `IEquationGeneratorService` interface for a service that returns an `Equation` in JSON format. The `ResponseFormat` property (line 10) is added to the `WebGet` attribute and set to `WebMessageFormat.Json`. We don't show the implementation of this interface here, because it is identical to that of Fig. 22.30. This shows how flexible WCF can be.

```
1  ' Fig. 22.32: IEquationGeneratorService.vb
2  ' WCF REST service interface to create random equations based on a
3  ' specified operation and difficulty level.
4  Imports System.ServiceModel.Web
5
6  <ServiceContract()> _
7  Public Interface IEquationGeneratorService
8     ' method to generate a math equation
9     <OperationContract()> _
10    <WebGet(ResponseFormat:=WebMessageFormat.Json, _
11       UriTemplate:="equation/{operation}/{level}")> _
12    Function GenerateEquation(ByVal operation As String, _
13       ByVal level As String) As Equation
14 End Interface ' IEquationGeneratorService
```

Fig. 22.32 | WCF REST service interface to create random equations based on a specified operation and difficulty level.

22.11.4 Consuming the REST-Based JSON WCF EquationGenerator Web Service

A modified `MathTutor` application (Fig. 22.33) accesses the URI of the `EquationGenerator` web service to get the JSON object (lines 19–21). We define a JSON representation of an `Equation` object for the serializer in Fig. 22.34. The JSON object is deserialized using a `DataContractJsonSerializer` (lines 32–35) and converted into an `Equation` object. We use the `LeftHandSide` field of the deserialized object (line 38) to display the left side of the equation and the `Result` field (line 51–52) to obtain the answer.

```
' Fig. 22.33: MathTutorForm.vb
' Math tutor using EquationGeneratorServiceJSON to create equations.
Imports System.Net
Imports System.IO
Imports System.Text
Imports System.Runtime.Serialization.Json

Public Class MathTutorForm
   Private operation As String = "add" ' the default operation
   Private level As Integer = 1 ' the default difficulty level
   Private currentEquation As Equation ' represents the Equation
   Private WithEvents service As New WebClient() ' used to invoke service

   ' generates a new equation when user clicks button
   Private Sub generateButton_Click(ByVal sender As System.Object, _
      ByVal e As System.EventArgs) Handles generateButton.Click

      ' send request to EquationGeneratorServiceJSON
      service.DownloadStringAsync(New Uri( _
         "http://localhost:49672/EquationGeneratorServiceJSON/" _
         & "Service.svc/equation/" & operation & "/" & level))
   End Sub ' generateButton_Click

   ' process web-service response
   Private Sub service_DownloadStringCompleted(ByVal sender As Object, _
      ByVal e As System.Net.DownloadStringCompletedEventArgs) _
      Handles service.DownloadStringCompleted

      ' check if any errors occurred in retrieving service data
      If e.Error Is Nothing Then
         ' deserialize response into an equation object
         Dim JSONSerializer As New _
            DataContractJsonSerializer(GetType(Equation))
         currentEquation = CType(JSONSerializer.ReadObject(New _
            MemoryStream(Encoding.Unicode.GetBytes(e.Result))), Equation)

         ' display left side of equation
         questionLabel.Text = currentEquation.LeftHandSide
         okButton.Enabled = True ' enable okButton
         answerTextBox.Enabled = True ' enable answerTextBox
      End If
   End Sub ' service_DownloadStringCompleted

   ' check user's answer
   Private Sub okButton_Click(ByVal sender As System.Object, _
      ByVal e As System.EventArgs) Handles okButton.Click

      ' check if answer field is filled
      If Not String.IsNullOrEmpty(answerTextBox.Text) Then
         ' determine whether user's answer is correct
         If currentEquation.Result = _
            Convert.ToInt32(answerTextBox.Text) Then
```

Fig. 22.33 | Math tutor using EquationGeneratorServiceJSON to create equations. (Part 1 of 3.)

```

            questionLabel.Text = String.Empty ' clear question
            answerTextBox.Clear() ' clear answer
            okButton.Enabled = False ' disable OK button
            MessageBox.Show("Correct! Good job!")
         Else
            MessageBox.Show("Incorrect. Try again.")
         End If
      End If
   End Sub ' okButton_Click

   ' set the operation to addition
   Private Sub additionRadioButton_CheckedChanged( _
      ByVal sender As System.Object, ByVal e As System.EventArgs) _
      Handles additionRadioButton.CheckedChanged
      operation = "add"
   End Sub ' additionRadioButton_CheckedChanged

   ' set the operation to subtraction
   Private Sub subtractionRadioButton_CheckedChanged( _
      ByVal sender As System.Object, ByVal e As System.EventArgs) _
      Handles subtractionRadioButton.CheckedChanged
      operation = "subtract"
   End Sub ' subtractionRadioButton_CheckedChanged

   ' set the operation to multiplication
   Private Sub multiplicationRadioButton_CheckedChanged( _
      ByVal sender As System.Object, ByVal e As System.EventArgs) _
      Handles multiplicationRadioButton.CheckedChanged
      operation = "multiply"
   End Sub ' multiplicationRadioButton_CheckedChanged

   ' set difficulty level to 1
   Private Sub levelOneRadioButton_CheckedChanged( _
      ByVal sender As System.Object, ByVal e As System.EventArgs) _
      Handles levelOneRadioButton.CheckedChanged
      level = 1
   End Sub ' levelOneRadioButton_CheckedChanged

   ' set difficulty level to 2
   Private Sub levelTwoRadioButton_CheckedChanged( _
      ByVal sender As System.Object, ByVal e As System.EventArgs) _
      Handles levelTwoRadioButton.CheckedChanged
      level = 2
   End Sub ' levelTwoRadioButton_CheckedChanged

   ' set difficulty level to 3
   Private Sub levelThreeRadioButton_CheckedChanged( _
      ByVal sender As System.Object, ByVal e As System.EventArgs) _
      Handles levelThreeRadioButton.CheckedChanged
      level = 3
   End Sub ' levelThreeRadioButton_CheckedChanged
```

Fig. 22.33 | Math tutor using EquationGeneratorServiceJSON to create equations. (Part 2 of 3.)

```
End Class ' MathTutorForm
```

a) Generating a level 2 multiplication equation.

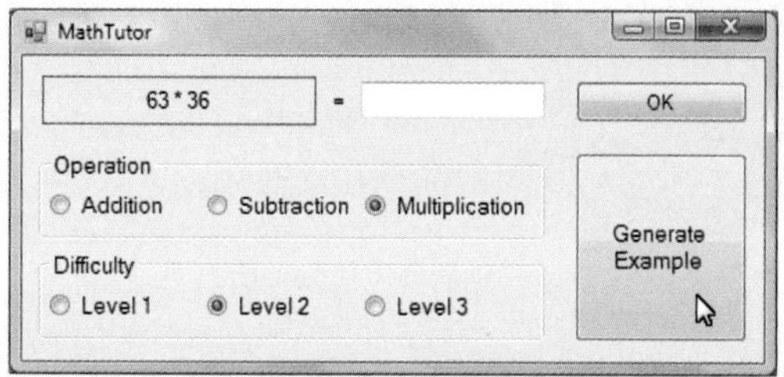

b) Answering the question incorrectly.

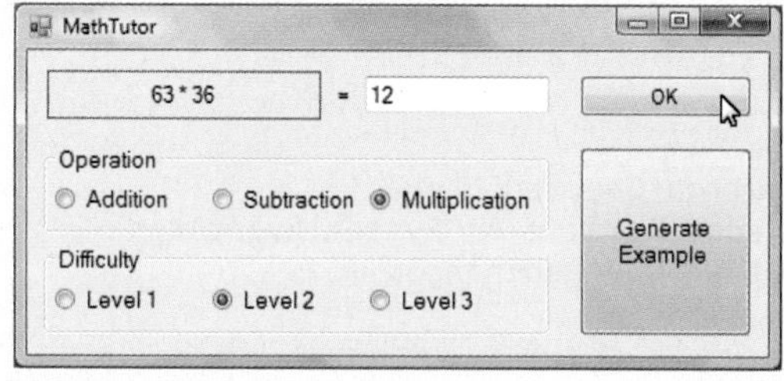

c) Answering the question correctly.

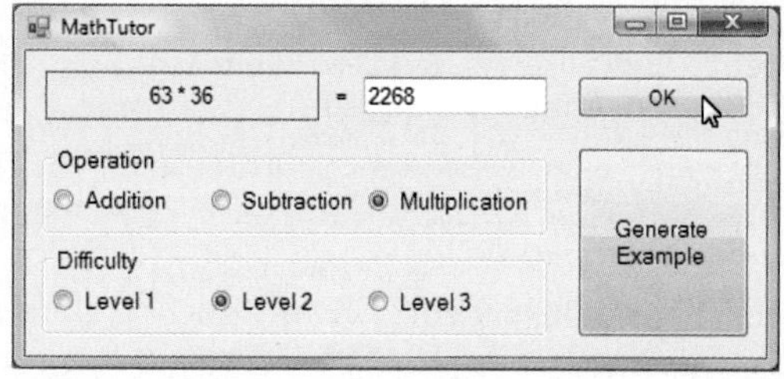

Fig. 22.33 | Math tutor using `EquationGeneratorServiceJSON` to create equations. (Part 3 of 3.)

```
' Fig. 22.34: Equation.vb
' Equation class representing a JSON object.
<Serializable()> _
Public Class Equation
   Public Left As Integer
   Public LeftHandSide As String
   Public Operation As String
   Public Result As Integer
   Public Right As Integer
   Public RightHandSide As String
End Class ' Equation
```

Fig. 22.34 | `Equation` class representing a JSON object.

22.12 Wrap-Up

This chapter introduced WCF web services—a set of technologies for building distributed systems in which system components communicate with one another over networks. You learned that a web service is a class that allows client software to call the web service's methods remotely via common data formats and protocols, such as XML, JSON, HTTP, SOAP and REST. We also discussed several benefits of distributed computing with web services.

We discussed how Visual Basic 2008 Express, Visual Web Developer 2008 Express, and WCF facilitate publishing and consuming web services. You learned how to define web services and methods using both SOAP protocol and REST architecture, and how to return data in both XML and JSON formats. You consumed SOAP-based web services using proxy classes to call the web service's methods. You also consumed REST-based web services using class `WebClient`. We built both Windows applications and ASP.NET web applications as web-service clients. After explaining the mechanics of web services through our `Welcome` examples, we demonstrated more sophisticated web services that use session tracking, database access and user-defined types.

22.13 Deitel Web Services Resource Centers

To learn more about web services, check out our web services Resource Centers at:

```
www.deitel.com/WebServices/
www.deitel.com/RESTWebServices/
```

You'll find articles, samples chapters and tutorials that discuss XML, web-services specifications, SOAP, WSDL, UDDI, .NET web services, consuming XML web services, and web-services architecture. You'll learn how to build your own Yahoo! maps mashup and applications that work with the Yahoo! Music Engine. You'll find information about Amazon's web services including the Amazon E-Commerce Service (ECS), Amazon historical pricing, Amazon Mechanical Turk, Amazon S3 (Simple Storage Service) and the Scalable Simple Queue Service (SQS). You'll learn how to use web services from several other companies including eBay, Google and Microsoft. You'll find REST web services best practices and guidelines. You'll also learn how to use REST web services with other technologies including SOAP, Rails, Windows Communication Foundation (`WCF`) and more. You can view the complete list of Deitel Resource Centers at `www.deitel.com/ResourceCenters.html`.

Summary

Section 22.1 Introduction

- WCF is a set of technologies for building distributed systems in which system components communicate with one another over networks. WCF uses a common framework for all communication between systems, so you need to learn only one programming model to use WCF.
- WCF web services promote software reusability in distributed systems that typically execute across the Internet.
- Simple Object Access Protocol (SOAP) is an XML-based protocol describing how to mark up requests and responses so that they can be sent via protocols such as HTTP. SOAP uses a standardized XML-based format to enclose data in a message.

- Representational State Transfer (REST) is a network architecture that uses the web's traditional request/response mechanisms such as `GET` and `POST` requests. REST-based systems do not require data to be wrapped in a special message format.

Section 22.2 WCF Services Basics

- WCF service has three key components—addresses, bindings and contracts.
- An address represents the service's location or endpoint, which includes the protocol and network address used to access the service.
- A binding specifies how a client communicates with the service, such as through SOAP protocol or REST architecture. Bindings can also specify other options, such as security constraints.
- A contract is an interface representing the service's methods and their return types. The service's contract allows clients to interact with the service.
- The machine on which the web service resides is referred to as a web service host.

Section 22.3 Simple Object Access Protocol (SOAP)

- The Simple Object Access Protocol (SOAP) is a platform-independent protocol that uses XML to make remote procedure calls, typically over HTTP.
- Each request and response is packaged in a SOAP message—an XML message containing the information that a web service requires to process the message.
- SOAP messages are written in XML so that they are computer readable, human readable and platform independent.
- SOAP supports an extensive set of types—the primitive types, as well as `DateTime`, `XmlNode` and others. SOAP can also transmit arrays of these types.
- When a program invokes a method of a SOAP web service, the request and all relevant information are packaged in a SOAP message enclosed in a SOAP envelope and sent to the server on which the web service resides.
- When a web service receives a SOAP message, it parses the XML representing the message, then processes the message's contents. The message specifies the method that the client wishes to execute and the arguments the client passed to that method.
- After a web service parses a SOAP message, it calls the appropriate method with the specified arguments (if any), and sends the response back to the client in another SOAP message. The client parses the response to retrieve the method's result.

Section 22.4 Representational State Transfer (REST)

- Representational State Transfer (REST) refers to an architectural style for implementing web services. Such web services are often called RESTful web services. Though REST itself is not a standard, RESTful web services are implemented using web standards.
- Each operation in a RESTful web service is identified by a unique URL.
- REST can return data in formats such as XML, JSON, HTML, plain text and media files.

Section 22.5 JavaScript Object Notation (JSON)

- JavaScript Object Notation (JSON) is an alternative to XML for representing data.
- JSON is a text-based data-interchange format used to represent objects in JavaScript as collections of name/value pairs represented as `Strings`.
- JSON is a simple format that makes objects easy to read, create and parse, and allows programs to transmit data efficiently across the Internet because it is much less verbose than XML.
- Each value in a JSON array can be a string, a number, a JSON object, `true`, `false` or `null`.

Section 22.6 Publishing and Consuming SOAP-Based WCF Web Services

- Enabling a web service for client usage is also known as publishing the web service.
- Using a web service is also known as consuming the web service.

Section 22.6.1 Creating a WCF Web Service

- To create a SOAP-based WCF web service in Visual Web Developer, you first create a project of type **WCF Service**. SOAP is the default protocol for WCF web services, so no special configuration is required to create SOAP-based services.
- Visual Web Developer automatically generates files for a **WCF Service** project, including an SVC file, which provides access to the service, and a `Web.config` file, which specifies the service's binding and behavior, and code files for the WCF service class and any other code that is part of the WCF service implementation. In the service class, you define the methods that your WCF web service makes available to client applications.

Section 22.6.2 Code for the `WelcomeSOAPXMLService`

- The service interface describes the service's contract—the set of methods and properties the client uses to access the service.
- The `ServiceContract` attribute exposes a class that implements the service interface as a WCF web service.
- The `OperationContract` attribute exposes a method for remote calls.

Section 22.6.3 Building a SOAP WCF Web Service

- By default, a new code-behind file implements an interface named `IService` that is marked with the `ServiceContract` and `OperationContract` attributes. In addition, the `IService.vb` file defines a class named `CompositeType` with a `DataContract` attribute. The interface contains two sample service methods named `GetData` and `GetDataUsingContract`. The `Service.vb` file contains the code that defines these methods.
- The `Service.svc` file, when accessed through a web browser, provides access to information about the web service.
- When you display the SVC file in the **Solution Explorer**, you see the programming language in which the web service's code-behind file is written, the `Debug` attribute, the name of the service and the code-behind file's location.
- If you change the code-behind file name or the class name that defines the web service, you must modify the SVC file accordingly.
- The `Web.config` file specifies a service's configuration information, including behaviors, bindings and endpoints. The default binding for SOAP is `wsHttpBinding`—data is transferred in a secure, reliable manner over HTTP protocol using XML as the data format. The `contract` setting specifies the name of the interface class.
- If you change the code-behind file name, the web service class name or interface name for the `ServiceContract`, you must change the corresponding values in the `Web.config` file accordingly.

Section 22.6.4 Deploying the `WelcomeSOAPXMLService`

- You can choose **Build Web Site** from the **Build** menu to ensure that the web service compiles without errors. You can also test the web service directly from Visual Web Developer by selecting **Start Without Debugging** from the **Debug** menu. This opens a browser window that contains the SVC page. Once the service is running, you can also access the SVC page from your browser by typing the URL in a web browser.

- By default, the ASP.NET Development Server assigns a random port number to each website it hosts. You can change this behavior by going to the **Solution Explorer** and clicking on the project name to view the **Properties** window. Set the **Use dynamic ports** property to **False** and specify the port number you want to use, which can be any unused TCP port. You can also change the service's virtual path, perhaps to make the path shorter or more readable.
- Web services normally contain a service description that conforms to the Web Service Description Language (WSDL)—an XML vocabulary that defines the methods a web service makes available and how clients interact with them. WSDL documents help applications determine how to interact with the web services described in the documents.
- When viewed in a web browser, an SVC file presents a link to the service's WSDL file and information on using the utility `svcutil.exe` to generate test console applications.
- When a client requests the WSDL URL, the server autogenerates the WSDL that describes the web service and returns the WSDL document.
- Many aspects of web-service creation and consumption—such as generating WSDL files and proxy classes—are handled by Visual Web Developer, Visual Basic 2008 and WCF.

Section 22.6.5 Creating a Client to Consume the `WelcomeSOAPXMLService`

- An application that consumes a SOAP-based web service consists of a proxy class representing the web service and a client application that accesses the web service via a proxy object. The proxy object passes arguments from the client application to the web service as part of the web-service method call. When the method completes its task, the proxy object receives the result and parses it for the client application.
- A proxy object communicates with the web service on the client's behalf. The proxy object is part of the client application, making web-service calls appear to interact with local objects.
- To add a proxy class, right click the project name in the **Solution Explorer** and select **Add Service Reference...** to display the **Add Service Reference** dialog. In the dialog, enter the URL of the service's `.svc` file in the **Address** field. The tools will automatically use that URL to request the web service's WSDL document. You can rename the service reference's namespace by changing the **Namespace** field. Click the **OK** button to add the service reference.
- A proxy object handles the networking details and the formation of SOAP messages. Whenever the client application calls a web method, the application actually calls a corresponding method in the proxy class. This method has the same name and parameters as the web method that is being called, but formats the call to be sent as a request in a SOAP message. The web service receives this request as a SOAP message, executes the method call and sends back the result as another SOAP message. When the client application receives the SOAP message containing the response, the proxy class deserializes it and returns the results as the return value of the web method that was called.

Section 22.7.1 Creating a REST-Based XML WCF Web Service

- `WebGet` maps a method to a unique URL that can be accessed via an HTTP `GET` operation.
- `WebGet`'s `UriTemplate` property specifies the URI format that is used to invoke a method.
- The service binding in the `endpoint` element must be changed from `wsHttpBinding` to `webHttpBinding` to respond to REST HTTP requests instead of SOAP-based messages. A new `behaviorConfiguration` with a `webHttp` property must be added to the endpoint to support the HTTP `GET` and `POST` request methods of `webHttpBinding`.
- You can test a REST-based service method using a web browser by going to the `Service.svc` file's network address and appending to the address the URI template with the appropriate arguments.

Section 22.7.2 Consuming a REST-Based XML WCF Web Service

- The `WebClient` class invokes a web service and receives its response.
- `WebClient`'s `DownloadStringAsync` method invokes a web service asynchronously. The `DownloadStringCompleted` event occurs when the `WebClient` receives the completed response from the web service.
- If a service is invoked asynchronously, the application can continue executing and the user can continue interacting with it while waiting for a response from the web service. `DownloadStringCompletedEventArgs` contains the information returned by the web service. We can use this variable's properties to get the returned XML document and any errors that may have occurred during the process.

Section 22.8.1 Creating a REST-Based JSON WCF Web Service

- By default, a web-service method with the `WebGet` attribute returns data in XML format. To return data in JSON format, set `WebGet`'s `ResponseFormat` property to `WebMessageFormat.Json`.
- Objects being converted to JSON must have `Public` properties. This enables the JSON serialization to create name/value pairs that represent each `Public` property and its corresponding value.
- The `DataContract` attribute exposes a class to the client access.
- The `DataMember` attribute exposes a property of this class to the client.
- When we test the web service using a web browser, the response prompts you to download a text file containing the JSON formatted data. You can see the service response as a JSON object by opening the file in a text editor such as Notepad.

Section 22.8.2 Consuming a REST-Based JSON WCF Web Service

- XML serialization converts a custom type into XML data format.
- JSON serialization converts a custom type into JSON data format.
- The `System.Runtime.Serialization.Json` library's `DataContractJsonSerializer` class serializes custom types as JSON objects. To use the `System.Runtime.Serialization.Json` library, you must include a reference to the `System.ServiceModel.Web` assembly in the project.
- Attribute `Serializable` indicates that a class can be used in serialization.
- A `MemoryStream` object is used to encapsulate the JSON object so we can read data from the byte array using stream semantics. The `MemoryStream` object is read by the `DataContractJsonSerializer` and then converted into a custom type.

Section 22.9 Blackjack Web Service: Using Session Tracking in a SOAP-Based WCF Web Service

- Using session tracking eliminates the need for information about the client to be passed between the client and the web service multiple times.

Section 22.9.1 Creating a Blackjack Web Service

- Web services store session information to provide more intuitive functionality.
- A service's interface uses a `ServiceContract` with the `SessionMode` property set to `Required` to indicate that the service needs a session to run. The `SessionMode` property is `Allowed` by default and can also be set to `NotAllowed` to disable sessions.
- Setting the `ServiceBehavior`'s `InstanceContextMode` property to `PerSession` creates a new instance of the class for each session. The `InstanceContextMode` property can also be set to `PerCall` or `Single`. `PerCall` uses a new object of the web-service class to handle every method call to the service. `Single` uses the same object of the web-service class to handle all calls to the service.

Section 22.10 Airline Reservation Web Service: Database Access and Invoking a Service from ASP.NET

- You can add a database and corresponding LINQ to SQL classes to create a `DataContext` object to support database operations of your web service.

Section 22.11 Equation Generator: Returning User-Defined Types

- Instances of user-defined types can be passed to or returned from web-service methods.

Terminology

adding a service reference
address for WCF web service
`behaviorConfiguration` property
binding for WCF web service
consume a WCF web service
contract for WCF web service
`DataContract` attribute
`DataContractJsonSerializer` class
`DataMember` attribute
`DownloadStringAsync` method
`DownloadStringCompleted` event
`DownloadStringCompletedEventArgs` class
endpoint of a WCF web service
`Error` property of class `DownloadStringCompletedEventArgs`
firewall
`InstanceContextMode` property of a `ServiceBehavior` attribute
JavaScript Object Notation (JSON)
JSON serialization
`OperationContract` attribute
proxy class for a web service
publish a web service
Representational State Transfer (REST)
`ResponseFormat` property
RESTful web services
`Result` property of class `DownloadStringCompletedEventArgs`
`Serializable` attribute
`ServiceBehavior` attribute
`ServiceContract` attribute
service description for a web service
service references
`SessionMode` property of a `ServiceContract` attribute
session tracking in web services
`.svc` file-name extension
SVC file
`svcutil.exe` utility
Simple Object Access Protocol (SOAP)
SOAP envelope
SOAP message
`System.Net` namespace
`System.Web` namespace
`UriTemplate` property
user-defined types in web services
WCF Service class
WCF Service project
web service
Web Service Description Language (WSDL)
web service host
web service method
`Web.config` file
`WebClient` class
`WebGet` attribute
`webHttp` property
`webHttpBinding` setting
Windows Communication Foundation (WCF)
wire format
`wsHttpBinding` setting
XML serialization

Self-Review Exercises

22.1 State whether each of the following is *true* or *false*. If *false*, explain why.

a) The purpose of a web service is to create objects of a class located on a web service host. This class then can be instantiated and used on the local machine.
b) You must explicitly create the proxy class after you add a service reference for a SOAP-based service to a client application.
c) A client application can invoke only those methods of a web service that are tagged with the `OperationContract` attribute.

d) To enable session tracking in a web-service method, no action is required other than setting the `SessionMode` property to `SessionMode.Required` in the `ServiceContract` attribute.
e) Operations in a REST web service are defined by their own unique URLs.
f) A SOAP-based web service can return data in JSON format.
g) For a client application to deserialize a JSON object, the client must define a `Serializable` class with public instance variables or properties that match those serialized by the web service.

22.2 Fill in the blanks for each of the following statements:
a) A key difference between SOAP and REST is that SOAP messages have data wrapped in a(n) ________.
b) A WCF web service exposes its methods to clients by adding the ________ and ________ attributes to the service interface.
c) Web-service requests are typically transported over the Internet via the protocol.
d) To return data in JSON format from a REST-based web service, the ________ property of the `WebGet` attribute is set to ________.
e) ________ transforms an object into a format that can be sent between a web service and a client.
f) To parse a HTTP response in XML data format, the client application must import the response's ________.

Answers to Self-Review Exercises

22.1 a) False. Web services are used to execute methods on web service hosts. The web service receives the arguments it needs to execute a particular method, executes the method and returns the result to the caller. b) False. The proxy class is created by Visual Basic or Visual Web Developer when you add a Service Reference to your project. The proxy class itself is hidden from you. c) True. d) True. e) True. f)) False. A SOAP web service implicitly returns data in XML format. h) True.

22.2 a) envelope. b) `ServiceContract`, `OperationContract`. c) HTTP. d) `ResponseFormat`, `WebMessageFormat.Json`. e) Serialization. f) namespace.

Exercises

22.3 *(Phone-Book Web Service)* Create a REST-based web service that stores phone-book entries in a database (`PhoneBook.mdf`, which is provided in the examples directory for this chapter) and a client application that consumes this service. Give the client user the capability to enter a new contact (service method `AddEntry`) and to find contacts by last name (service method `GetEntries`). Pass only primitive types as arguments to the web service. Add a `DataContext` to the web-service project to enable the web service to interact with the database. The `GetEntries` method should return an array of `Strings` that contains the matching phone-book entries. Each `String` in the array should consist of the last name, first name and phone number for one phone-book entry separated by commas. Build an ASP.NET client (Fig. 22.35) to interact with this web service. To use an asynchronous web request from an ASP.NET client, you must set the `Async` property to true by adding `Async="true"` to the `.aspx` page directive. Since the `AddEntry` method accepts a request and does not return a response to the client, you can use `WebClient's` `OpenRead` method to access the service method. You can use the `ToArray` method on the LINQ query to return an array containing LINQ query results.

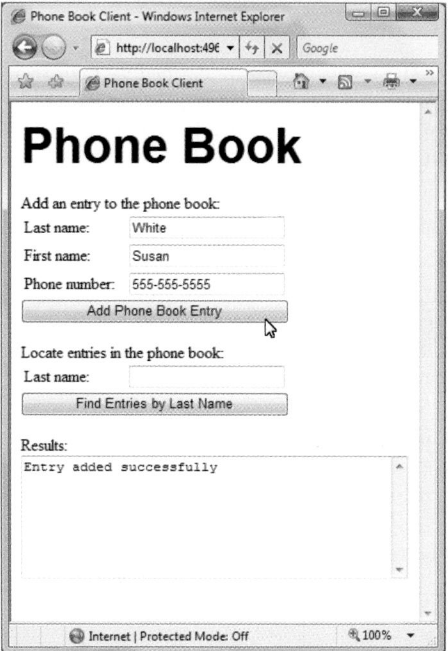

Fig. 22.35 | Template web form for phone book client.

22.4 *(Phone-Book Web Service Modification)* Modify Exercise 22.3 so that it uses a class named `PhoneBookEntry` to represent a row in the database. The web service should return objects of type `PhoneBookEntry` in XML format for the `GetEntries` service method, and the client application should use XML document parsing to interpret the `PhoneBookEntry` object.

22.5 *(Phone-Book Web Service with JSON)* Modify Exercise 22.4 so that the `PhoneBookEntry` class is passed to and from the web service as a JSON object. Use serialization to convert the JSON object into an object of type `PhoneBookEntry`.

22.6 *(Blackjack Modification)* Modify the blackjack web-service example in Section 22.9 to include class `Card`. Change service method `DealCard` so that it returns an object of type `Card` and modify method `GetHandValue` to receive an array of `Card`s. Also modify the client application to keep track of what cards have been dealt by using `Card` objects. Your `Card` class should include properties for the face and suit of the card. [*Note:* When you create the `Card` class, be sure to add the `DataContract` attribute to the class and the `DataMember` attribute to the properties. Also, in a SOAP-based service, you don't need to define your own `Card` class on the client as well. The `Card` class will be exposed to the client through the service reference that you add to the client. If the service reference is named `ServiceReference`, you'll access the card type as `ServiceReference.Card`.]

22.7 *(Airline Reservation Web-Service Modification)* Modify the airline reservation web service in Section 22.10 so that it contains two separate methods—one that allows users to view all available seats, and another that allows users to reserve a particular seat that is currently available. Use an object of type `Ticket` to pass information to and from the web service. The web service must be able to handle cases in which two users view available seats, one reserves a seat and the second user tries to reserve the same seat, not knowing that it is now taken. The names of the methods that execute should be `Reserve` and `GetAllAvailableSeats`.

23

Silverlight, Rich Internet Applications and Multimedia

Had I the heavens' embroidered cloths, Enwrought with gold and silver light.
—William Butler Yeats

This world is but a canvas to our imaginations.
—Henry David Thoreau

Something deeply hidden had to be behind things.
—Albert Einstein

Individuality of expression is the beginning and end of all art.
—Johann Wolfgang von Goethe

It is my intention to present—through the medium of photography—intuitive observations of the natural world which may have meaning to the spectators.
—Ansel Adams

OBJECTIVES

In this chapter you'll learn:

- What Silverlight is and how it relates to Windows Presentation Foundation.
- To use Silverlight controls to create Rich Internet Applications.
- To create custom Silverlight controls.
- To use animation for enhanced GUIs.
- To display and manipulate images.
- To use Silverlight with Flickr's web services to build an online photo-searching application.
- To create Silverlight deep zoom applications.
- To include audio and video in Silverlight applications.

Outline

23.1 Introduction

Silverlight™ is Microsoft's platform for building Rich Internet Applications (RIAs)—web applications comparable in responsiveness and rich user interactivity to desktop applications. Silverlight is a robust, cross-platform, cross-browser subset of the .NET platform that competes with RIA technologies such as Adobe Flash and Flex and Sun's JavaFX, and complements Microsoft's ASP.NET and ASP.NET AJAX (which we discussed in Chapter 21). Since Silverlight is a subset of WPF, developers familiar with programming WPF applications are able to adapt quickly to creating Silverlight applications.

Multimedia may be the largest revolution in the history of the computer industry. Those who entered the field decades ago used computers primarily to perform arithmetic calculations at high speed. As the field evolved, we began to see computers data-manipulation capabilities as perhaps far more important. The "sizzle" of Silverlight is multimedia—the use of images, graphics, animation, sound and video to make applications "come alive." Silverlight includes strong multimedia support, including state-of-the-art high-definition video streaming. Microsoft also provides a service called Silverlight Streaming (`streaming.live.com`) for distributing multimedia-intensive Silverlight applications.

Multimedia programming offers many new challenges. The field is already enormous and growing rapidly. Most new computers sold today are "multimedia ready," with CD-RW and DVD drives, audio boards and special video capabilities. Today's desktop and laptop computers are so powerful that they can store and play DVD-quality sound and video, and we anticipate further advances in the programmable multimedia capabilities available through programming languages. One thing we've learned is to plan for the "impossible"—in the computer and communications fields, the "impossible" has repeatedly become reality.

Among users who want graphics, many now want three-dimensional, high-resolution graphics. True three-dimensional imaging may become available within the next decade.

Imagine having high-resolution "theater-in-the-round"—three-dimensional television. Sporting and entertainment events will appear to take place in your living room! And, you'll be able to zoom in as if you had the best seats in the house! Medical students worldwide will use web applications to see operations being performed thousands of miles away, as if they were occurring in the same room. People will be able to learn how to drive with extremely realistic driving simulators in their homes before they get behind the wheel. The possibilities are exciting and endless.

Multimedia demands extraordinary computing power. Until recently, affordable computers with that kind of power were not available. Today's ultrapowerful processors make effective multimedia possible and economical. The computer and communications industries will be primary beneficiaries of the multimedia revolution. Users will be willing to pay for the faster processors, larger memories and wider communications bandwidths that support demanding multimedia applications, just as they're willing to pay more for high-definition television today. Ironically, users may not have to pay more, because the fierce competition in these industries continues to drive prices down.

We need tools that make creating multimedia applications easy. Most programming languages do not incorporate such capabilities. WPF and Silverlight, through the .NET 3.5 class libraries, provide extensive multimedia facilities that enable you to start developing powerful multimedia applications immediately. Among these facilities is **deep zoom**, which allows the user to view high-resolution images over the web as if the images were stored on the local computer. Users can interactively "explore" a high-resolution image by zooming in and out and panning—while maintaining the original image's quality. Silverlight supports deep zoom images up to one billion by one billion pixels in size!

To find the latest Silverlight information and additional Silverlight web resources, visit our Silverlight 2 Resource Center at `www.deitel.com/silverlight20/`. There you'll find Silverlight demos, articles, tutorials, downloads, sample code, training courses, forums, FAQs, books, eBooks, sample chapters and more. We've also included overviews of several Silverlight demo sites in Section 23.9. All Silverlight code examples and exercises in this chapter were implemented using Silverlight 2 Beta 2. As new versions of Silverlight are released, updates for the examples and exercises will be posted at `www.deitel.com/books/vb2008htp/`.

23.2 Platform Overview

Silverlight runs as a browser plug-in for Internet Explorer, Firefox and Safari on recent versions of Microsoft Windows and Mac OS X. The system requirements for the runtime can be found at `microsoft.com/silverlight/resources/install.aspx?v=2.0#sysreq`. Silverlight is also available on Linux systems via the Mono Project's Moonlight (`mono-project.com/Moonlight`).

Like WPF applications, Silverlight applications consist of user interfaces described in XAML and code-behind files containing application logic. The XAML used in Silverlight is a subset of that used in WPF.

The subset of the .NET Framework available in Silverlight 2 includes APIs for collections, input/output, generics, multithreading, globalization, XML and LINQ. It also includes APIs for interacting with JavaScript and the elements in a web page, and APIs for local storage data to help you create more robust web-based applications.

Silverlight 2 is an implementation of the .NET Platform, so you can create Silverlight applications in .NET languages such as Visual Basic, Visual C#, IronRuby and IronPython. (IronRuby and IronPython require the Silverlight Dynamic Languages SDK from www.codeplex.com/sdlsdk/.) This makes it easy for .NET programmers to create applications that run in a web browser. Silverlight 2 also provides a substantial performance improvement over Silverlight 1.0, which used JavaScript that was interpreted on the client. Silverlight 2's .NET code is compiled and the compiled code executes on the client in the Silverlight plug-in.

Silverlight 2's graphics and GUI capabilities are a subset of the Windows Presentation Foundation (WPF) framework. Some capabilities supported in Silverlight include GUI controls, layout management, graphics, animation and multimedia. There are also styles and template-based "skinning" capabilities to manage the look-and-feel of a Silverlight user interface. Like WPF, Silverlight provides a powerful data-binding model that makes it easy to display data from objects, collections, databases, XML and even other GUI controls. Silverlight 2 also provides rich networking support, enabling you to write browser-based applications that invoke web services and use other networking technologies.

23.3 Silverlight Runtime and Tools Installation

Silverlight runs in web browsers as a plug-in. To view websites programmed in Silverlight, you need the Silverlight 2 Runtime plug-in from www.microsoft.com/silverlight/resources/installationFiles.aspx?v=2.0. After installing the plug-in, go to Microsoft's Silverlight Gallery website at silverlight.net/themes/silverlight/community/gallerydetail.aspx?cat=6 to try some sample applications. See Section 23.9 for more Silverlight demo and resource websites.

At the time of this writing, Silverlight 2 development is not yet supported in Microsoft's Visual Studio Express editions. When the final version of Service Pack 1 is released for the Express Editions, it will include Silverlight compatibility, but until then you'll need a complete version of Visual Studio 2008 to build a Silverlight application. In addition, the Visual Web Developer feature must be installed. Trial versions are available from msdn.microsoft.com/en-us/vstudio/products/aa700831.aspx. You'll also need the Silverlight Tools Beta 2 for Visual Studio 2008 from go.microsoft.com/fwlink/?LinkId=120319. Download and execute the file silverlight_chainer.exe, then follow the on-screen instructions to install the tools for developing Silverlight 2 applications in Visual Studio 2008. Watch www.deitel.com/books/VB2008HTP/ for updates.

If you don't have access to a complete version of Visual Studio 2008, Microsoft also provides the Silverlight 2 SDK Beta 2. You can get the SDK by going to www.microsoft.com/downloads/ and searching for "Silverlight 2 SDK". The SDK provides documentation, sample code and tools to help you build applications for Silverlight 2 Beta 2. We do not cover the SDK in this book.

23.4 Building a Silverlight WeatherViewer Application

Silverlight is a subset of WPF, so the two share many capabilities. Since Silverlight produces Internet applications instead of desktop applications, the setup of a Silverlight project is different from that of WPF.

A basic Silverlight application has two XAML files—Page.xaml and App.xaml. Page.xaml defines the application's GUI, and its code-behind file Page.xaml.vb declares the GUI event handlers and other methods required by the application. `App.xaml` declares your application's shared resources that can be applied to various GUI elements. The code-behind file `App.xaml.vb` defines application-level event handlers, such as an event handler for unhandled exceptions. Content in these files can be used by all the application's pages. Since our example applications contain only a single page, we do not use `App.xaml` and `App.xaml.vb` in this chapter.

Differences Between WPF and Silverlight

To create a new Silverlight project, select **File > New Project...** in Visual Studio 2008. In the **Project types** window under **Visual Basic**, select the **Silverlight** option. Then in the **Templates** window, select **Silverlight Application**. When you've entered the information, click **OK**. An **Add Silverlight Application** dialog appears, asking how you would like to host your application. Select the **Add a new Web to the solution for hosting the control** option. In the **Project Type** drop-down menu, select **Web Site**. Keep the default **Name** and click **OK**.

The `Page.xaml` file displayed in the XAML tab of Visual Studio (Fig. 23.1) is similar to the default XAML for a WPF application. In a WPF application, the root XAML element is a `Window`. In Silverlight, the root element is a `UserControl`. The default `UserControl` has a class name specified with the `x:Class` attribute (line 1), specifies the namespaces (lines 2–3) to provide access to the Silverlight controls throughout the XAML,

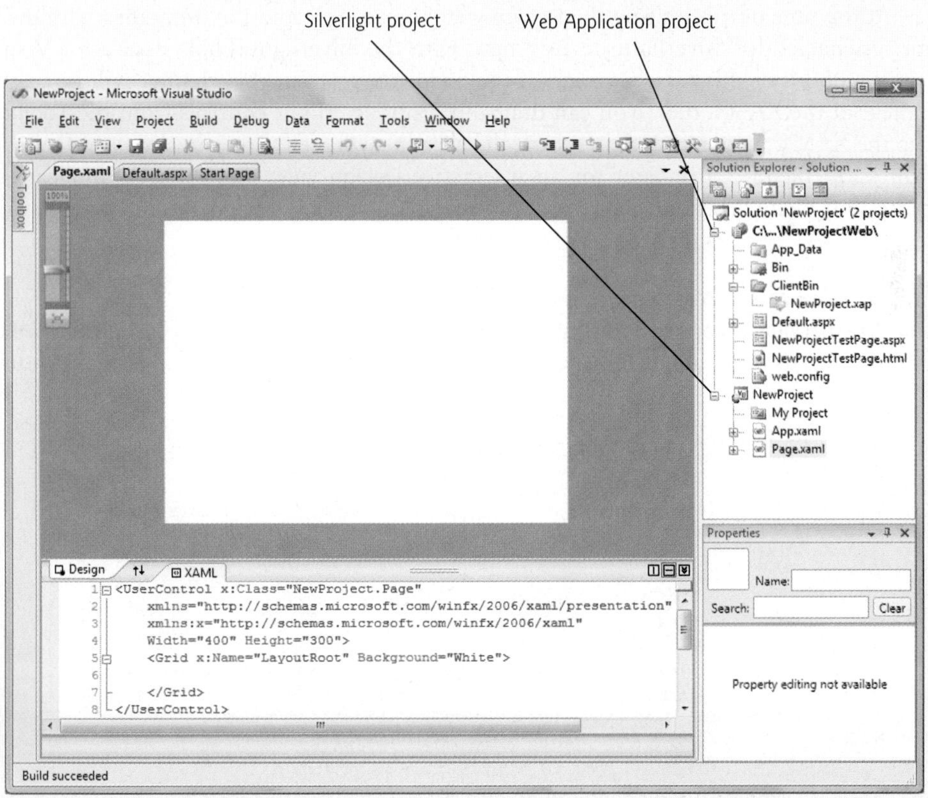

Fig. 23.1 | New Silverlight application in Visual Studio.

and has a `Width` and `Height` of 400 and 300 pixels, respectively. These numbers are system-independent pixel measurements, where each pixel represents 1/96th of an inch. Lines 5–7 are the default `Grid` layout container. Unlike a WPF application, the `x:Name` (the name used in code that manipulates the control) and `Background` attributes are set by default in a Silverlight application.

A compiled Silverlight application is packaged by the IDE as a `.xap` file containing the application and its supporting resources (such as images or other files used by the application). The web page that hosts the Silverlight application references the Silverlight plug-in and the application's `.xap` file. The Silverlight plug-in then executes the application. The test web application that was created for you contains the file `NewProjectTestPage.aspx`, which loads and executes the Silverlight application.

A Silverlight application must be hosted in a web page. The **Web Application Project** is used to test the Silverlight application in a web browser. Building the solution automatically copies the compiled application into the **Web Application Project**. You can then test it using the built-in web server in Visual Studio. After the application is built in the IDE, this part of the application contains the `.xap` file that was described in the preceding paragraph.

Note that the first time you start debugging a Silverlight application, a **Debugging Not Enabled** dialog appears. It states that debugging is not enabled in the **Web.config** file. If you would like to run your project in debug mode, you can select the **Modify the Web.Config file to enable debugging** option.

At the time of this writing the **Design** view is read-only and the **Properties** window is not yet enabled for Silverlight development with the Silverlight Tools Beta 2 for Visual Studio 2008. For this reason, much of the code you write in this chapter will be in the context of the XAML files. You can drag and drop Silverlight controls from the **Toolbox** into the XAML view, rather than typing the elements yourself. You can also use Microsoft Expression Blend 2.5 or later for an interactive **Design** view of your web application. Expression Blend is beyond the scope of this chapter. Trial and preview versions are available from `www.microsoft.com/expression/`.

Introduction to the WeatherViewer *Application*

Our **WeatherViewer** application (Fig. 23.2) allows the user to input a zip code and invokes a web service to get weather information for that location. The application receives weath-

a)
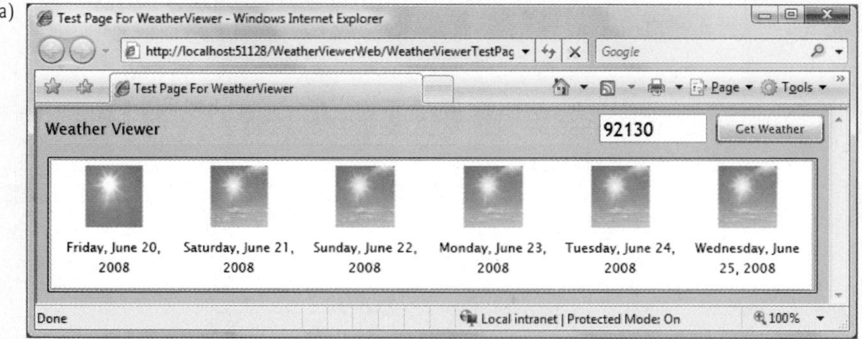

Fig. 23.2 | **WeatherViewer** application displays a six-day weather forecast. The program can also display detailed information for a selected day. (Part 1 of 2.)

b)

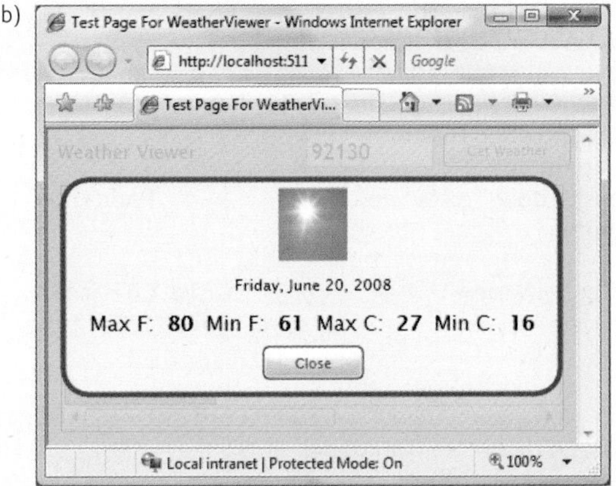

Fig. 23.2 | **WeatherViewer** application displays a six-day weather forecast. The program can also display detailed information for a selected day. (Part 2 of 2.)

er data from `www.webservicex.net`—a site offering several web services that return XML. This application uses LINQ to XML to process the weather data that is returned by the web service. The application also includes a custom control that displays more specific weather information for a single day of the week. Figure 23.2 shows a preview of the application after the user enters a zip code and clicks a specific day to see its weather details. You can test the example online at `www.deitel.com/books/vb2008htp/`.

23.4.1 GUI Layout

The main layout controls of WPF described in Chapter 15—`Grid`, `StackPanel` and `Canvas`—are also available in Silverlight. The XAML for the layout of the **WeatherViewer** application is shown in Fig. 23.3. This application uses nested `Grid` controls to lay out its elements.

```
<!-- Fig. 23.3: Page.xaml -->
<!-- WeatherViewer displays day-by-day weather data (XAML). -->
<UserControl xmlns:Weather="clr-namespace:WeatherViewer"
   x:Class="WeatherViewer.Page"
   xmlns="http://schemas.microsoft.com/winfx/2006/xaml/presentation"
   xmlns:x="http://schemas.microsoft.com/winfx/2006/xaml">
   <Grid x:Name="LayoutRoot" Background="LightSkyBlue">
      <Grid.RowDefinitions>
         <RowDefinition Height="35" />
         <RowDefinition />
      </Grid.RowDefinitions>

      <Grid> <!-- Grid contains border, textbox, and search button -->
         <Grid.ColumnDefinitions>
            <ColumnDefinition Width="*" />
            <ColumnDefinition Width="110" />
```

Fig. 23.3 | **WeatherViewer** displays day-by-day weather data (XAML). (Part 1 of 3.)

```
            <ColumnDefinition Width="110" />
         </Grid.ColumnDefinitions>

      <!-- Border containing the title "Weather Viewer" -->
         <Border Grid.Column="0" CornerRadius="10"
            Background="LightGray" Margin="2">
            <TextBlock Text="Weather Viewer" Padding="6" />
         </Border>

         <TextBox x:Name="inputTextBox" Grid.Column="1" FontSize="18"
            Margin="4" /> <!-- zip code goes into this text box -->

         <!-- Click to invoke web service -->
         <Button x:Name="submitButton" Content="Get Weather"
            Grid.Column="2" Margin="4" />
      </Grid>

      <!-- Contains weather images for several upcoming days -->
      <ListBox x:Name="forecastList" Grid.Row="1" Margin="10">
         <ListBox.ItemsPanel>
            <ItemsPanelTemplate>

               <!-- Arrange items horizontally -->
               <StackPanel Orientation="Horizontal" />
            </ItemsPanelTemplate>
         </ListBox.ItemsPanel>

         <ListBox.ItemTemplate>
            <DataTemplate>

               <!-- Represents item for a single day -->
               <StackPanel Width="120" Orientation="Vertical"
                  HorizontalAlignment="Center">

                  <!-- Displays image for a single day -->
                  <Image Source="{Binding WeatherImage}"
                     Margin="5" Width="55" Height="58" />

                  <!-- Displays the day of the week -->
                  <TextBlock Text="{Binding DayOfWeek}"
                     TextAlignment="Center" FontSize="12"
                     Margin="5" TextWrapping="Wrap" />
               </StackPanel>
            </DataTemplate>
         </ListBox.ItemTemplate>
      </ListBox>

      <!-- Custom control for displaying detailed information -->
      <Weather:WeatherDetailsView x:Name="completeDetails"
         Visibility="Collapsed" Grid.RowSpan="2" />
   </Grid>
</UserControl>
```

Fig. 23.3 | **WeatherViewer** displays day-by-day weather data (XAML). (Part 2 of 3.)

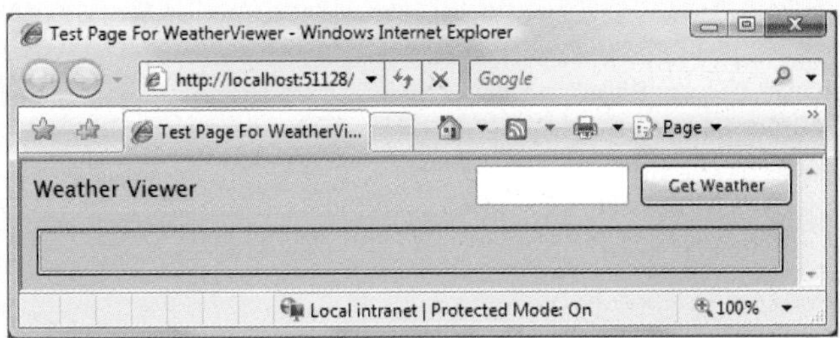

Fig. 23.3 | **WeatherViewer** displays day-by-day weather data (XAML). (Part 3 of 3.)

Lines 8–11 contain the `RowDefinitions` of the main `Grid`. Lines 14–18 contain the `ColumnDefinitions` of a nested `Grid` element which displays the top row of the page containing the light gray title `Border`, the search `TextBox` and the search `Button`, as shown in the screen capture in Fig. 23.3.

Line 23 defines the `Border`'s **`Padding`** property, which specifies the distance between the inside edge of the border and the outside edge of any embedded elements. Lines 35–62 define the `ListBox` used on the main page to display each day's weather image. Line 40 defines the `StackPanel` that is used as a template by the `ListBox`'s `ItemsPanel`, allowing the `ListBox`'s items to display horizontally. Lines 48–59 define a `StackPanel` for each individual item, displaying the weather `Image` and the `TextBlock` containing the day of the week in a vertical orientation. Lines 52 and 56 bind data from the web service's XML response to the two elements that display weather information.

Lines 65–66 create a `WeatherDetailsView` custom control element. The code for the custom control appears later in the chapter. This control's `Visibility` property is initially set to `Collapsed`, so it is not visible when the page loads. The `Visibility` of a control defines whether it is rendered on the screen. We also set the `Grid.RowSpan` property to 2. By taking up two rows, the GUI is blocked when the custom control is displayed, so the user can no longer interact with the main page until the control is closed. Notice that `WeatherDetailsView` is in the namespace `Weather`. This namespace (defined in line 3 of the XAML file) allows you to use the custom control in the application. The custom control must be referenced through the namespace since it is not a pre-defined control. If we did not define the namespace, there would be no way to reference `WeatherDetailsView`.

23.4.2 Obtaining and Displaying Weather Forecast Data

The **WeatherViewer** example uses Silverlight's web services, LINQ to XML and data-binding capabilities. The application's code-behind file appears in Fig. 23.4.

```
' Fig. 23.4: Page.xaml.vb
' WeatherViewer displays day-by-day weather data (code-behind).
Imports System.Net ' to access the Uri class
Imports System.Xml.Linq ' to access LINQ to XML features

' import the namespace for the XML returned by webservicex.net's
' web service; required to access the data properly
```

Fig. 23.4 | **WeatherViewer** displays day-by-day weather data (code-behind). (Part 1 of 3.)

```
Imports <xmlns="http://www.webservicex.net">

Partial Public Class Page
   Inherits UserControl

   ' object to invoke weather forecast web service
   Dim WithEvents weatherService As New WebClient()

   ' constructor
   Public Sub New()
      InitializeComponent()
   End Sub ' New

   ' process submitButton's Click event
   Private Sub submitButton_Click(ByVal sender As System.Object, _
      ByVal e As System.Windows.RoutedEventArgs) _
      Handles submitButton.Click

      Dim zipcode As String = inputTextBox.Text ' get zipcode
      Me.Cursor = System.Windows.Input.Cursors.Wait ' wait cursor

      ' webserviceX.net's WeatherForecast web service URL
      Dim forecastURL As String = _
         "http://www.webservicex.net/WeatherForecast.asmx/" & _
         "GetWeatherByZipCode?ZipCode=" & zipcode

      ' asynchronously invoke the web service
      weatherService.DownloadStringAsync(New Uri(forecastURL))
   End Sub ' submitButton_Click

   ' event handler to process weather forecast
   Private Sub weatherService_DownloadStringCompleted( _
      ByVal sender As Object, _
      ByVal e As DownloadStringCompletedEventArgs) _
      Handles weatherService.DownloadStringCompleted

      If e.Error Is Nothing AndAlso e.Result.Contains("Day") Then
         DisplayWeatherForecast(e.Result)
      End If

      Me.Cursor = System.Windows.Input.Cursors.Arrow ' arrow cursor
   End Sub ' weatherService_DownloadStringCompleted

   ' display weather forecast
   Private Sub DisplayWeatherForecast(ByVal xmlData As String)
      ' parse the XML data for use with LINQ
      Dim weatherXML As XDocument = XDocument.Parse(xmlData)

      ' convert XML into WeatherData objects using XML literals
      Dim weatherInformation = _
         From item In weatherXML...<WeatherData> _
         Where Not item.IsEmpty _
         Select New WeatherData With _
```

Fig. 23.4 | **WeatherViewer** displays day-by-day weather data (code-behind). (Part 2 of 3.)

```
61        { _
62          .DayOfWeek = item.<Day>.Value, _
63          .WeatherImage = item.<WeatherImage>.Value, _
64          .MaxTemperatureF = Convert.ToInt32( _
65            item.<MaxTemperatureF>.Value), _
66          .MinTemperatureF = Convert.ToInt32( _
67            item.<MinTemperatureF>.Value), _
68          .MaxTemperatureC = Convert.ToInt32( _
69            item.<MaxTemperatureC>.Value), _
70          .MinTemperatureC = Convert.ToInt32( _
71            item.<MinTemperatureC>.Value) _
72        } ' end LINQ to XML that creates WeatherData objects
73
74      ' bind forecastList.ItemSource to the weatherInformation
75      forecastList.ItemsSource = weatherInformation
76    End Sub ' DisplayWeatherForecast
77
78    ' Show details of the selected day
79    Private Sub forecastList_SelectionChanged( _
80      ByVal sender As Object, ByVal e As _
81      System.Windows.Controls.SelectionChangedEventArgs) _
82      Handles forecastList.SelectionChanged
83
84      If forecastList.SelectedItem IsNot Nothing Then
85        ' specify the WeatherData object containing the details
86        completeDetails.DataContext = forecastList.SelectedItem
87
88        ' show the complete weather details
89        completeDetails.Visibility = Windows.Visibility.Visible
90      End If
91    End Sub ' forecastList_SelectionChanged
92
93    ' clear the Grid when the text in inputTextBox changes
94    Private Sub inputTextBox_TextChanged(ByVal sender As Object, _
95      ByVal e As System.Windows.Controls.TextChangedEventArgs) _
96      Handles inputTextBox.TextChanged
97
98      forecastList.ItemsSource = Nothing ' clear the ListBox
99    End Sub ' inputTextBox_TextChanged
100 End Class ' Page
```

Fig. 23.4 | **WeatherViewer** displays day-by-day weather data (code-behind). (Part 3 of 3.)

The code for the main page of the **WeatherViewer** invokes the web service and binds all the necessary data to the proper elements of the page. Notice that we import the `System.Xml.Linq` namespace (line 4), which enables the LINQ to XML that is used in the example. You must also add a reference to this assembly. To do so, right click the **WeatherViewer** project in the **Solution Explorer** and select **Add Reference…**. In the dialog that appears, locate the assembly `System.Xml.Linq` in the **.NET** tab and click **OK**. Line 8 imports the namespace for the XML returned by the web service. Note that this is the default XML namespace. You can also specify a namespace name and qualify each XML element with that name. For example, if line 8 were written as:

```
Imports <xmlns:weather="http://www.webservicex.net">
```

then each XML element we referenced in the code would be qualified with "`weather:`", as in `<weather:MaxTemperatureF>`.

Error-Prevention Tip 23.1

When invoking a web service that returns XML, ensure that the namespace you specify in your code precisely matches the namespace specified in the returned XML. Otherwise, the elements in the returned XML will not be recognized in your code.

This application also uses the class `WeatherData` (line 60) that includes all the necessary weather information for a single day of the week. We created this class for you. It contains six weather information properties—`DayOfWeek`, `WeatherImage`, `MaxTemperatureF`, `MinTemperatureF`, `MaxTemperatureC` and `MinTemperatureC`. To add the code for this class to the project, right click the **WeatherViewer** project in the **Solution Explorer** and select **Add > Existing Item….** Find the file `WeatherData.vb` in this chapter's examples folder and click **OK**. We use this class to bind the necessary information to the `ListBox` and the custom control in our application. Note that if this were a WPF application, we could use an anonymous class here instead of our `WeatherData` class. However, in Silverlight applications, you cannot bind to anonymous types, which is why we needed to create the new class.

Using the `WebClient` Class to Invoke a Web Service

The application's method for handling the `submitButton` click grabs the zip code entered by the user in the `TextBox` (line 26), formats the web service URL with the zip code (lines 30–32) and asynchronously invokes the web service (line 35). We use the `WebClient` class to use the web service and retrieve the desired information. The keyword `WithEvents` on line 14 indicates that the `WebClient` object has events associated with it and enables you to include the `WebClient` variable in a `Handles` clause of an event handler.

Line 35 calls the `weatherService` object's `DownloadStringAsync` method to invoke the web service. The web service's location must be specified as an object of class `Uri`. Class `Uri`'s constructor receives a `String` representing a uniform resource identifier, such as `"http://www.deitel.com"`. In this example, the web service is invoked asynchronously. When the web service returns its result, the `WebClient` object raises the `DownloadString-Completed` event. Its event handler (lines 39–49) has a parameter `e` of type `Download-StringCompletedEventArgs` which contains information returned by the web service. We can use this variable's properties to get the returned XML (`e.Result`) and any errors that may have occurred during the process (`e.Error`).

Using LINQ to XML to Process the Weather Data

Once the `WebClient` has received the response, the application checks for an error and ensures that the result contains the desired information (line 44). If the user enters an incorrect zip code, the service responds without error and sends back XML that does not contain a weather forecast. If the XML contains the string `"Day"`, then the response includes weather forecast data. A sample of the web service's XML response appears in Fig. 23.5. The web service returns XML data that describes the high and low temperatures for the corresponding city over a period of several days. The data for each day also contains a link to an image that represents the weather for that day. If there is no error, the application calls the `DisplayWeatherForecast` method (defined in lines 52–76).

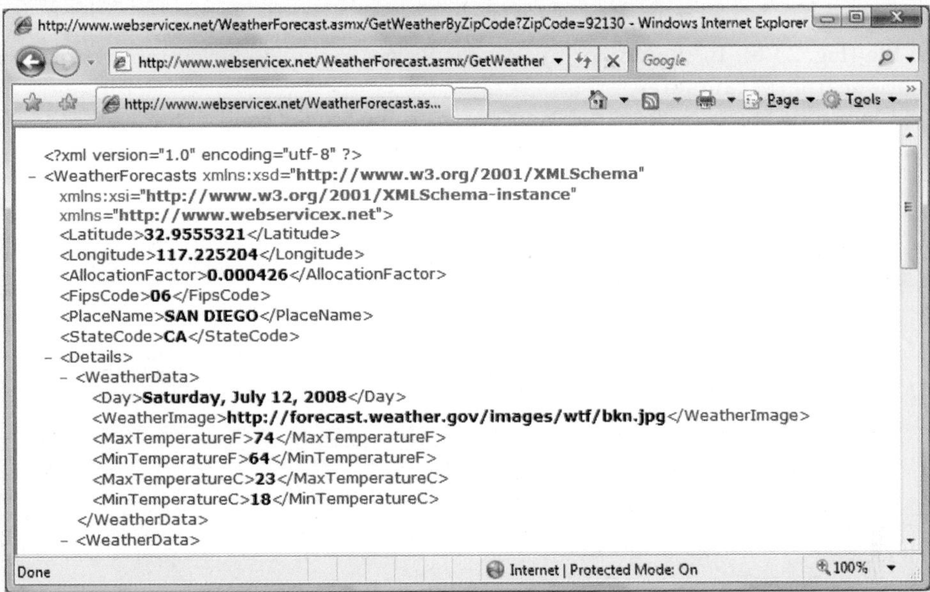

Fig. 23.5 | Sample web service XML response.

We use class `XDocument`'s **Parse** method (line 54) to convert a `String`—containing the contents of the XML response—to an `XDocument` to use in the LINQ to XML query (lines 57–72). The query gathers the weather information and sets the corresponding values for a `WeatherData` object. The LINQ query gathers more information from the XML than is initially displayed on the main page of the application. This is because the selected object is also passed to the custom control where more detailed information about the weather is displayed.

Using Data Binding to Display the Weather Data

We first bind the results of the `weatherInformation` LINQ query (an `IEnumerable(Of WeatherData)`) to the `ListBox` (line 75). This displays the summary of the six-day weather forecast. When the user selects a particular day, we bind the `WeatherData` object for the selected day to the custom control, which displays the details for that day. The `ListBox`'s `SelectionChanged` event handler (lines 79–91) sets the `DataContext` of our custom control (line 86) to the `WeatherData` object for the selected day. The method also changes the custom control's `Visibility` to `Visible`, so the user can see the weather details.

23.4.3 Custom Controls

There are many ways to customize controls in Silverlight, including WPF's `Styles` and `ControlTemplates`. As with WPF, if deeper customization is desired, you can create **custom controls** by using the `UserControl` element as a template. The **WeatherViewer** example creates a custom control that displays detailed weather information for a particular day of the week. The control has a simple GUI and is displayed when you change your selection in the `ListBox` on the main page.

To add a new `UserControl` to the project, right click the project in the **Solution Explorer** and select **Add > New Item...**. Select the **Silverlight User Control** template and name the file (Fig. 23.6). In the case of the **WeatherViewer** example, our custom control was named `WeatherDetailsView`.

Once added to the project, the `UserControl` can be coded similar to any other Silverlight application. The XAML code for the GUI appears in Fig. 23.7.

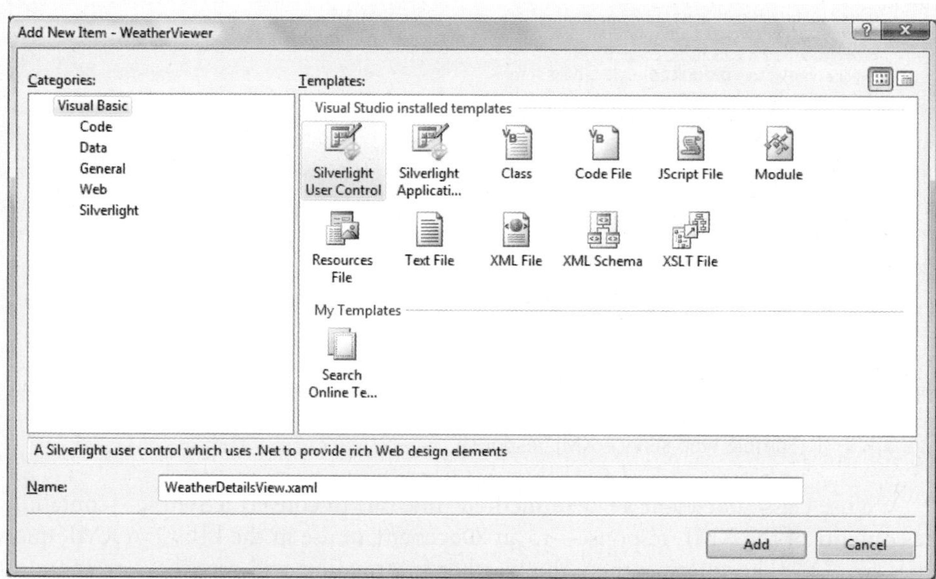

Fig. 23.6 | Adding a new `UserControl` to a Silverlight application.

```
<!-- Fig. 23.7: WeatherDetailsView.xaml -->
<!-- WeatherViewer's WeatherDetailsView custom control (XAML). -->
<UserControl x:Class="WeatherViewer.WeatherDetailsView"
   xmlns="http://schemas.microsoft.com/winfx/2006/xaml/presentation"
   xmlns:x="http://schemas.microsoft.com/winfx/2006/xaml">
   <Grid>
      <!-- Background semitransparent rectangle -->
      <Rectangle HorizontalAlignment="Stretch" Fill="Aquamarine"
         VerticalAlignment="Stretch" Opacity="0.8" />

      <!-- Border containing all the elements of the control -->
      <Border CornerRadius="20" Background="AliceBlue"
         BorderBrush="Blue" BorderThickness="4"
         Width="400" Height="175">

         <!-- StackPanel contains all the displayed weather info -->
         <StackPanel>
            <Image Source="{Binding WeatherImage}" Margin="5" Width="55"
               Height="58" /> <!-- The day's weather image -->
```

Fig. 23.7 | **WeatherViewer**'s `WeatherDetailsView` custom control (XAML). (Part 1 of 2.)

```
20                <TextBlock Text="{Binding DayOfWeek}" Margin="5"
21                   TextAlignment="Center" FontSize="12"
22                   TextWrapping="Wrap" /> <!-- Day of the week -->
23
24                <!-- Displays the temperature info in C and F -->
25                <StackPanel HorizontalAlignment="Center"
26                   Orientation="Horizontal">
27                   <TextBlock Text="Max F:" Margin="5" FontSize="16" />
28                   <TextBlock Text="{Binding MaxTemperatureF}"
29                      Margin="5" FontSize="16" FontWeight="Bold" />
30                   <TextBlock Text="Min F:" Margin="5" FontSize="16" />
31                   <TextBlock Text="{Binding MinTemperatureF}"
32                      Margin="5" FontSize="16" FontWeight="Bold" />
33                   <TextBlock Text="Max C:" Margin="5" FontSize="16" />
34                   <TextBlock Text="{Binding MaxTemperatureC}"
35                      Margin="5" FontSize="16" FontWeight="Bold" />
36                   <TextBlock Text="Min C:" Margin="5" FontSize="16" />
37                   <TextBlock Text="{Binding MinTemperatureC}"
38                      Margin="5" FontSize="16" FontWeight="Bold" />
39                </StackPanel>
40
41                <!-- Closes the control to go back to the main page -->
42                <Button x:Name="closeButton" Content="Close" Width="80" />
43             </StackPanel>
44          </Border>
45       </Grid>
46    </UserControl>
```

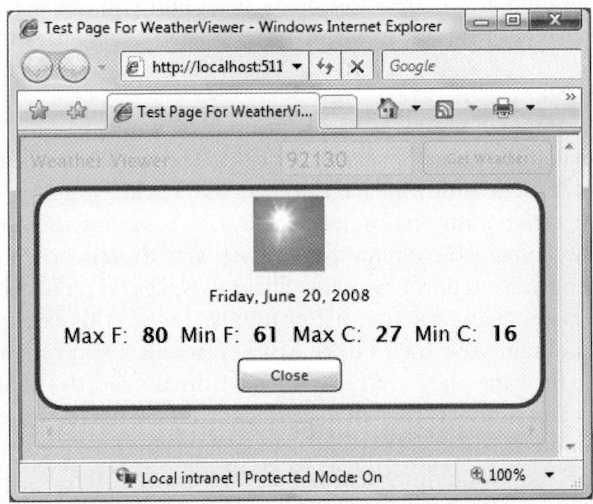

Fig. 23.7 | WeatherViewer's `WeatherDetailsView` custom control (XAML). (Part 2 of 2.)

This control contains two `StackPanel`s embedded in a `Grid`. Since the aquamarine `Rectangle` (lines 8–9) in the background has an `Opacity` of 0.8, you can see that the control is treated as another element "on top of" the main page. Figure 23.8 shows the code-behind file for this control. The Button's Click event handler collapses the control, so the user can continue interacting with the main page of the application.

```
' Fig. 23.8: WeatherDetailsView.xaml.vb
' WeatherViewer's WeatherDetailsView custom control (code-behind).
Partial Public Class WeatherDetailsView
   Inherits UserControl

   Public Sub New()
      InitializeComponent()
   End Sub ' New

   ' close the details view
   Private Sub closeButton_Click(ByVal sender As Object, _
      ByVal e As System.Windows.RoutedEventArgs) _
      Handles closeButton.Click

      Me.Visibility = Windows.Visibility.Collapsed
   End Sub ' closeButton_Click
End Class ' WeatherDetailsView
```

Fig. 23.8 | **WeatherViewer**'s WeatherDetailsView custom control (code-behind).

23.5 Animations and the FlickrViewer

Animations in Silverlight are defined in Storyboards, which are created as Resources of a layout control and contain one or more animation elements. When a Storyboard's Begin method is called, its animations are applied. In Silverlight you can use WPF's three animation types—DoubleAnimations, PointAnimations, and ColorAnimations.

FlickrViewer Example

Our **FlickrViewer** example (a sample screen capture is shown in Fig. 23.9) uses a web service provided by the public photo-sharing site Flickr. The application allows you to search by tag for photos that users worldwide have uploaded to Flickr. Tagging—or labeling content—is part of the collaborative nature of Web 2.0. A tag is any user-generated word or phrase that helps organize web content. Tagging items with self-chosen words or phrases creates a strong identification of the content. Flickr uses tags on uploaded files to improve its photo-search service, giving the user better results. To run this example on your computer, you need to obtain your own Flickr API key at www.flickr.com/services/api/keys/ and add it to the Page.xaml.vb file (which we discuss shortly). This key is a unique string of characters and numbers that enables Flickr to track usage of their APIs. You can test the example online at www.deitel.com/books/vb2008htp/.

The application shows you thumbnails of the first twenty (or fewer) public results and allows you to click a thumbnail to view its full-sized image. As you change your selection, the application animates out the previously selected image and animates in the new selection. The Border shrinks until the current Image is no longer visible, then expands to display the new selected Image.

As shown in Fig. 23.9, you can type one or more tags (e.g., "deitel flowers") into the application's TextBox. When you click the **Search** Button, the application invokes the

Flickr web service, which responds with an XML document containing links to the photos that match the tags. The application parses the XML and displays thumbnails of these photos. The application's XAML is shown in Fig. 23.10.

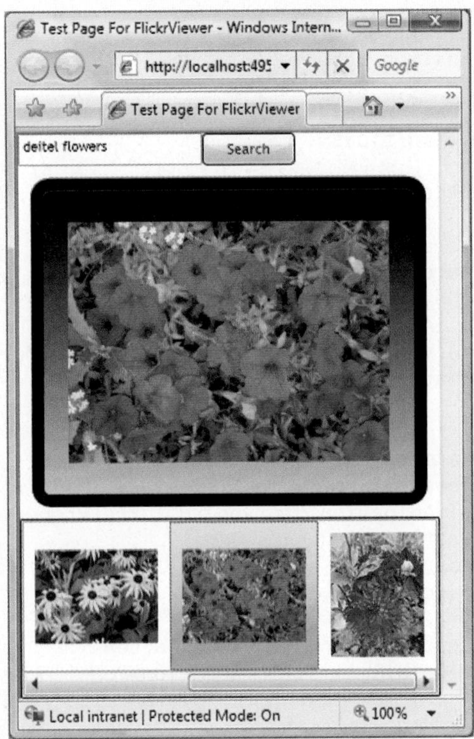

Fig. 23.9 | **FlickrViewer** allows users to search photos by tag.

Lines 13–28 define the `Grid`'s `Resources`, which contain two `Storyboard` elements to animate the large image in and out. The `animateIn Storyboard` (lines 16–20) contains a `DoubleAnimation` that animates the `Height` property of the `largeCoverImage`'s `Border`. Though this animation is a `From/To/By` animation, the `To` property is not set. We set this value in the Visual Basic code to allow the border to fill the available space in the window regardless of the browser window size. The `animateOut Storyboard` (lines 23–27) shrinks the `Border` until the image inside is no longer visible.

The rest of the layout is similar to that of the **WeatherViewer**. Lines 7–11 define the main `Grid`'s three rows. The first row contains a `StackPanel` with an embedded search `TextBox` and a `Button` (lines 31–34). The second row contains the `Border` with an embedded `Image` (lines 37–49) to display the large version of the selected thumbnail. The third row contains the `ListBox` (lines 52–65), which displays the thumbnails of the photos returned from Flickr. This `ListBox` is organized and coded in the same way as in the **WeatherViewer**, except that the `DataTemplate` contains only one `Image`—one of the photos returned by the web service.

```
<!-- Fig. 23.10: Page.xaml -->
<!-- FlickrViewer allows users to search for tagged photos (XAML). -->
<UserControl x:Class="FlickrViewer.Page"
   xmlns="http://schemas.microsoft.com/winfx/2006/xaml/presentation"
   xmlns:x="http://schemas.microsoft.com/winfx/2006/xaml">
   <Grid x:Name="LayoutRoot">
      <Grid.RowDefinitions> <!-- Defines the rows of the main grid -->
         <RowDefinition Height="Auto" />
         <RowDefinition x:Name="imageRow" />
         <RowDefinition Height="Auto" />
      </Grid.RowDefinitions>

      <Grid.Resources> <!-- Contains the page's animations -->

         <!-- Enlarges the Border to display a new image -->
         <Storyboard x:Name="animateIn"
            Storyboard.TargetName="largeCoverImage">
            <DoubleAnimation x:Name="animate"
               Storyboard.TargetProperty="Height" Duration="0:0:0.45" />
         </Storyboard>

         <!-- Collapses the Border in preparation for a new image -->
         <Storyboard x:Name="animateOut"
            Storyboard.TargetName="largeCoverImage">
            <DoubleAnimation Storyboard.TargetProperty="Height" To="60"
               Duration="0:0:0.25" />
         </Storyboard>
      </Grid.Resources>

      <!-- Contains the search box and button for user interaction -->
      <StackPanel Grid.Row="0" Orientation="Horizontal">
         <TextBox x:Name="searchBox" Width="150" />
         <Button x:Name="searchButton" Content="Search" Width="75" />
      </StackPanel>

      <!-- Border that contains the large main image -->
      <Border Grid.Row="1" x:Name="largeCoverImage" Height="60"
         BorderBrush="Black" BorderThickness="10" CornerRadius="10"
         Padding="20" Margin="10" HorizontalAlignment="Center">
         <Border.Background>
            <LinearGradientBrush StartPoint="0,0" EndPoint="0,1">
               <GradientStop Offset="0" Color="Black" />
               <GradientStop Offset="1" Color="LightGray" />
            </LinearGradientBrush>
         </Border.Background>

         <!-- Displays the image that the user selected -->
         <Image Source="{Binding}" Stretch="Uniform" />
      </Border>

      <!-- Listbox displays thumbnails of the search results -->
      <ListBox x:Name="thumbsListBox" Grid.Row="2"
         HorizontalAlignment="Center">
```

Fig. 23.10 | **FlickrViewer** allows users to search for tagged photos (XAML). (Part 1 of 2.)

```
            <ListBox.ItemsPanel>
               <ItemsPanelTemplate>
                  <StackPanel Orientation="Horizontal"/>
               </ItemsPanelTemplate>
            </ListBox.ItemsPanel>

            <ListBox.ItemTemplate>
               <DataTemplate>
                  <Image Source="{Binding}" Margin="10" />
               </DataTemplate>
            </ListBox.ItemTemplate>
         </ListBox>
      </Grid>
   </UserControl>
```

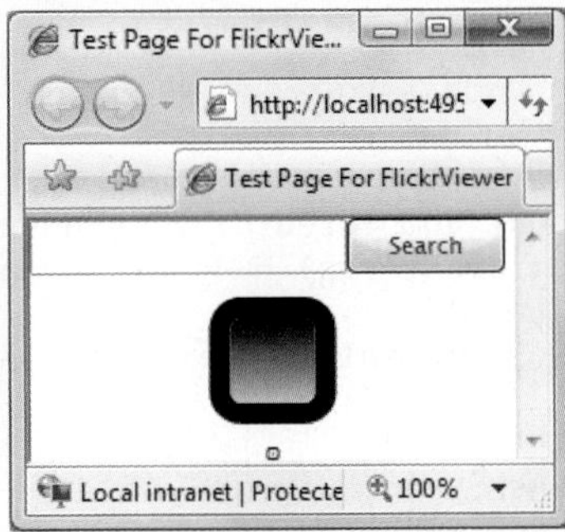

Fig. 23.10 | **FlickrViewer** allows users to search for tagged photos (XAML). (Part 2 of 2.)

The screen capture in Fig. 23.10 shows the empty layout of the **FlickrViewer** before a search query has been made. The Visual Basic code for the application can be seen in Fig. 23.11. This example uses web services and LINQ to XML.

```
' Fig. 23.11: Page.xaml.vb
' FlickrViewer allows users to search for tagged photos (code-behind).
Imports System.Xml.Linq ' Allows us to use LINQ to XML

Partial Public Class Page
   Inherits UserControl

   Const key As String = "Your API Key goes here as String" ' API key

   ' Object used to invoke Flickr web service
   Private WithEvents flickr As New WebClient()

   ' Constructor
   Public Sub New()
      InitializeComponent()
   End Sub ' New
```

Fig. 23.11 | **FlickrViewer** allows users to search for tagged photos (code-behind). (Part 1 of 3.)

```

   ' Changes the large image displayed when the selection is changed
   Private Sub thumbsListBox_SelectionChanged(ByVal sender As Object, _
      ByVal e As System.Windows.Controls.SelectionChangedEventArgs) _
      Handles thumbsListBox.SelectionChanged

      ' Set the height back to a value so that it can be animated
      largeCoverImage.Height = largeCoverImage.ActualHeight

      animateOut.Begin() ' begin shrinking animation
   End Sub ' thumbsListBox_SelectionChanged

   ' This makes sure that the border will resize with the window
   Private Sub animateIn_Completed(ByVal sender As Object, _
      ByVal e As System.EventArgs) Handles animateIn.Completed

      largeCoverImage.Height = Double.NaN ' image height = Auto
   End Sub ' animateIn_Completed

   ' Once the box has animated to no longer show the image
   Private Sub animateOut_Completed(ByVal sender As Object, _
      ByVal e As System.EventArgs) Handles animateOut.Completed

      If thumbsListBox.SelectedItem IsNot Nothing Then

         ' Grab the URL of the selected item, but grab full image
         Dim photoURL As String = _
            thumbsListBox.SelectedItem.ToString.Replace("_t.jpg", ".jpg")

         ' Specify the URL of the large image shown
         largeCoverImage.DataContext = photoURL

         ' Set the animation to stop at height available in the window
         animate.To = imageRow.ActualHeight - 20
         animateIn.Begin() ' begin expanding animation
      End If
   End Sub ' animateOut_Completed

   ' Begin the search when the user clicks the search button
   Private Sub searchButton_Click(ByVal sender As Object, _
      ByVal e As System.Windows.RoutedEventArgs) _
      Handles searchButton.Click

      ' Flickr's web service URL for searches
      Dim flickrURL As String = _
         "http://api.flickr.com/services/rest/" & _
         "?method=flickr.photos.search&api_key=" & key & "&tags=" & _
         searchBox.Text.Replace(" ", ",") & _
         "&tag_mode=all&per_page=20&privacy_filter=1"

      ' Invokes the web service
      flickr.DownloadStringAsync(New Uri(flickrURL))

```

Fig. 23.11 | **FlickrViewer** allows users to search for tagged photos (code-behind). (Part 2 of 3.)

```
70        searchButton.Content = "Loading..." ' Disable the search button
71        searchButton.IsEnabled = False
72     End Sub ' searchButton_Click
73
74     ' Once we have received the XML file from Flickr
75     Private Sub flickr_DownloadStringCompleted(ByVal sender As Object, _
76        ByVal e As System.Net.DownloadStringCompletedEventArgs) _
77        Handles flickr.DownloadStringCompleted
78
79        searchButton.Content = "Search" ' Re-enable the search button
80        searchButton.IsEnabled = True
81
82        If e.Error Is Nothing Then ' If no error occurs
83
84           ' We will parse the data with LINQ
85           Dim flickrXML As XDocument = XDocument.Parse(e.Result)
86
87           ' Gather information on all public photos
88           Dim flickrPhotos = _
89              From photo In flickrXML...<photo> _
90              Select New With _
91              { _
92                 .id = photo.@id, _
93                 .secret = photo.@secret, _
94                 .server = photo.@server, _
95                 .farm = photo.@farm _
96              }
97
98           ' Format the information received into the proper URL
99           Dim thumbURLs = _
100             From photo In flickrPhotos _
101             Select "http://farm" & photo.farm & ".static.flickr.com/" _
102                & photo.server & "/" & photo.id & "_" & photo.secret & _
103                "_t.jpg"
104
105          ' Set thumbsListBox's item source to the URLs we received
106          thumbsListBox.ItemsSource = thumbURLs
107       End If
108    End Sub ' flickr_DownloadStringCompleted
109 End Class ' Page
```

Fig. 23.11 | **FlickrViewer** allows users to search for tagged photos (code-behind). (Part 3 of 3.)

Line 8 defines a constant `String` for the API key that is required to use the Flickr API. To run this application insert your Flickr API key here.

Recall that the `To` property of the `DoubleAnimation` in the `animateIn` `Storyboard` is set programatically. Line 50 sets the `To` property to the `Height` of the page's second row (minus 20 to account for the `Border`'s `Margin`), animating the `Height` to the largest possible value while keeping the `Border` completely visible on the page.

For animations to function properly, the properties being animated must contain numeric values—relative values `"*"` and `"Auto"` do not work. So before `animateOut` begins, we assign the value `largeImageCover.ActualHeight` to the `Border`'s `Height` (line 24). When the `Border` is not being animated, we want it to take up as much space as possible on screen while still being resizable based on the changing size of the browser window. Line 33 resets the `Border`'s `Height` back to `Double.NaN`, which allows the border to be resized with the window.

Notice that when you click a new picture that you have not previously viewed, the `Border`'s `Height` increases without displaying a new picture inside. This is because the animation begins before the application can download the entire image. The picture is not displayed until its download is complete. If you click the thumbnail of an image you've viewed previously, it displays properly, because the image has already been downloaded to your system and cached by the browser. Viewing the image again causes it to be loaded from the browser's cache rather than over the web.

Lines 88–96 of Fig. 23.11 use a LINQ statement and an anonymous class to gather the necessary information from the attributes of the `photo` elements in the XML returned by the web service. A sample of the XML response is shown in Fig. 23.12. The four values collected in the anonymous type are required to form the URL to the online photos. The thumbnail URLs are created (lines 99–103) in the second LINQ statement, which builds a URL in its `Select` clause. The "`_t`" before the "`.jpg`" in each URL indicates that we want the thumbnail of the photo rather than the full-sized file. These URLs are passed to the `ItemsSource` of `thumbsListBox`, which displays all the thumbnails at the bottom of the page. To load the large `Image`, use the URL of the thumbnail and remove the "`_t`" from the link (lines 43–44), then change the source of the `Image` element in the `Border` (line 47). Notice that the data binding in lines 48 and 62 of Fig. 23.10 use the simple `"{Binding}"` syntax. We can use this syntax since we bind a single `String` to the object rather than a class with separate properties.

```
<?xml version="1.0" encoding="utf-8" ?>
<rsp stat="ok">
   <photos page="1" pages="1" perpage="20" total="5">
      <photo id="2608518732" owner="8832668@N04" secret="76dab8eb42"
         server="3185" farm="4" title="Red Flowers 1" ispublic="1"
         isfriend="0" isfamily="0" />
      <photo id="2608518654" owner="8832668@N04" secret="57d35c8f64"
         server="3293" farm="4" title="Lavender Flowers" ispublic="1"
         isfriend="0" isfamily="0" />
      <photo id="2608518890" owner="8832668@N04" secret="98fcb5fb42"
         server="3121" farm="4" title="Yellow Flowers" ispublic="1"
         isfriend="0" isfamily="0" />
      <photo id="2608518370" owner="8832668@N04" secret="0099e12778"
         server="3076" farm="4" title="Fuscia Flowers" ispublic="1"
         isfriend="0" isfamily="0" />
      <photo id="2607687273" owner="8832668@N04" secret="4b630e31ba"
         server="3283" farm="4" title="Red Flowers 2" ispublic="1"
         isfriend="0" isfamily="0" />
   </photos>
</rsp>
```

Fig. 23.12 | Sample XML response from the Flickr APIs.

23.6 Images and Deep Zoom

One feature in Silverlight that is not in WPF is the `MultiScaleImage`. In most desktop applications, you'll have no trouble viewing and zooming in on a high-resolution image. Doing this over the Internet is problematic, however, because transferring large images usually takes significant time, which prevents web-based applications from having the feel of desktop applications.

This problem is addressed by Silverlight's deep zoom capabilities, which use `MultiScaleImages` to allow you to zoom far into an image in a web browser while maintaining quality. One of the best demonstrations of this technology is the Hard Rock Cafe's memorabilia page (`memo.hardrock.com`), which uses Silverlight's deep zoom capabilities to display a large collage of rock and roll memorabilia. You can zoom in on any individual item to see its high-resolution image. The photographs were taken at such high resolution that you can actually see fingerprints on the surfaces of some of the guitars!

Deep zoom works by sending only the necessary image data for the part of the image you are viewing to your machine. To split an image or collage of images into the Silverlight-ready format used by `MultiScaleImages`, you use the Deep Zoom Composer (available from `silverlight.net/GetStarted/`). The original images are split into smaller pieces to support various zoom levels. This enables the server to send smaller chunks of the picture rather than the entire file. If you zoom in close to an image, the server sends only the small section that you are viewing at its highest available resolution (which depends on the resolution of the original image). If you zoom out, the server sends only a lower-resolution version of the image. In either case, the server sends just enough data to give the user a rich image-viewing experience.

A `MultiScaleImage`'s `Source` is an XML document—created by Deep Zoom Composer. The `MultiScaleImage` uses the data in the XML to display an image or collage of images. A `MultiScaleSubImage` of a `MultiScaleImage` contains information on a single image in a collage.

The DeepZoomCoverCollage *Example*

Our **DeepZoomCoverCollage** application contains a high-resolution collage of 12 of our book covers. You can test the example online at `www.deitel.com/books/vb2008htp/`. You can zoom in and out and pan the image with simple keystroke and mouse-click combinations. Figure 23.13 shows screen captures of the application. Figure 23.13(a) shows the application when it's first loaded with all 12 cover images displayed. Eight large images and three tiny images are clearly visible. One cover is hidden within one of these eleven covers. Test-run the program to see if you can find it. Figure 23.13(b) shows the application after we've zoomed in closely on the leftmost small cover image. As you can see in the second screen capture, the small cover image still comes up clearly, because it was originally created in the Deep Zoom Composer with a high-resolution image. Figure 23.13(c) shows the application with an even deeper zoom on a different cover. Rather than being pixelated, the image displays the details of the original picture.

23.6.1 Getting Started With Deep Zoom Composer

To create the collection of files that is used by `MultiScaleImage`, you need to import the image or set of images into Deep Zoom Composer. When you first open the program, create a new project through the **File** menu, and specify the project's **Name** and **Location**. We named the project **CoverCollage** and saved it to the **Location** `C:\examples\ch23\DeepZoomProject`. Figure 23.14 shows the **New Project** dialog.

a)

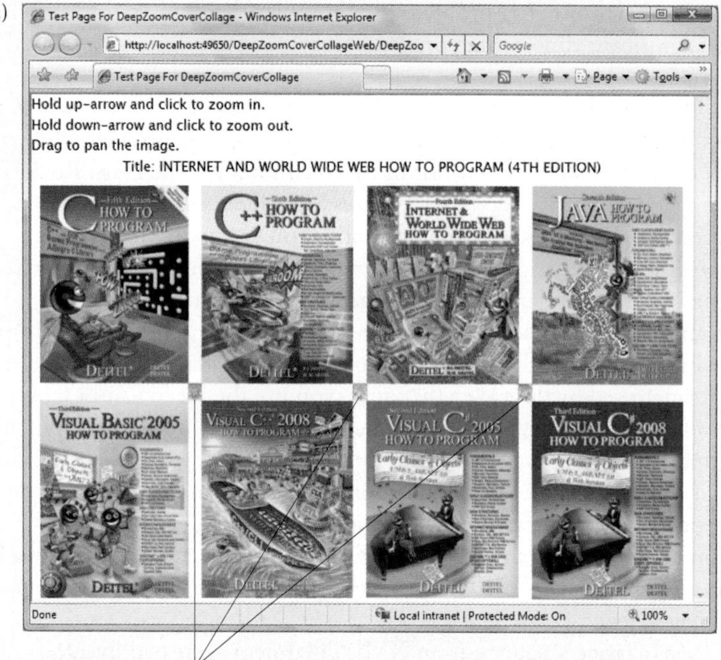

Small images nested among larger images in the collage

b)

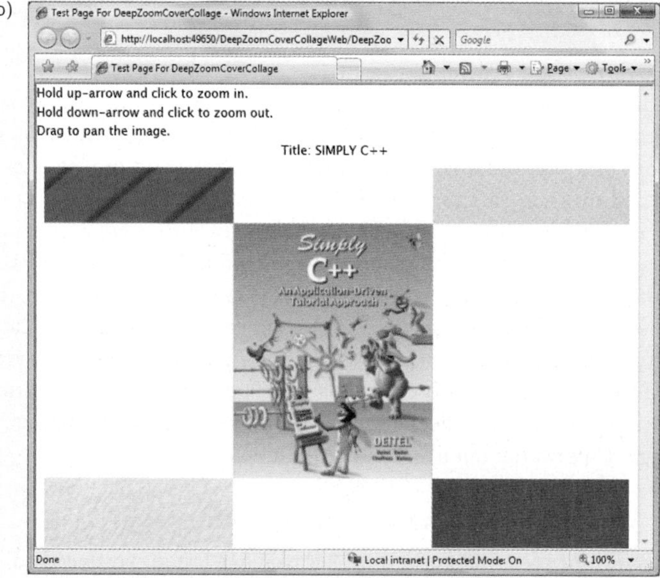

Fig. 23.13 | Main page of the **DeepZoomCoverCollage**. (Part 1 of 2.)

c)

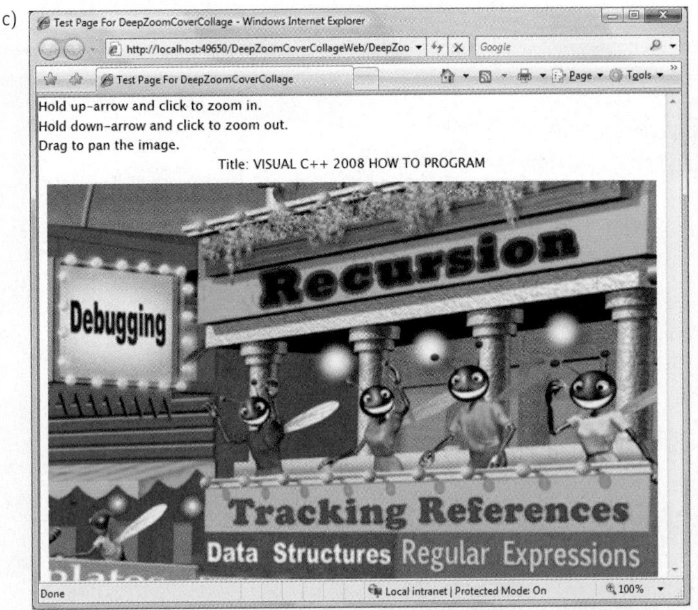

Fig. 23.13 | Main page of the **DeepZoomCoverCollage**. (Part 2 of 2.)

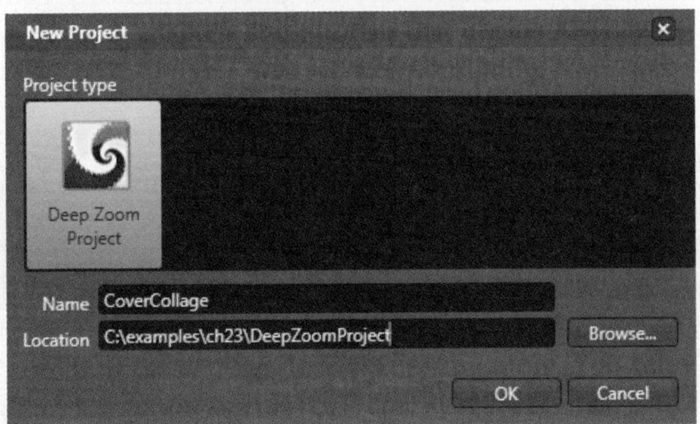

Fig. 23.14 | Deep Zoom Composer's **New Project** dialog.

The **Import** tab in Deep Zoom Composer is displayed by default. It enables you to add the image(s) that you want in the collage. Click the **Add Image...** button to add your images. (We provided our book-cover images with this chapter's examples in the `CoverImages` folder.) Once you've added your images, you'll see their thumbnails on the right side of the window. A larger version of the selected image appears in the middle of the window. Figure 23.15 shows the window with the **Import** tab open after the book-cover images have been imported to the project.

For our **CoverCollage** example, we use high-resolution `.jpg` images. Deep Zoom Composer also supports `.tif`, `.bmp` and `.png` formats. After importing the images, you can go to the **Compose** tab to organize them on your collage.

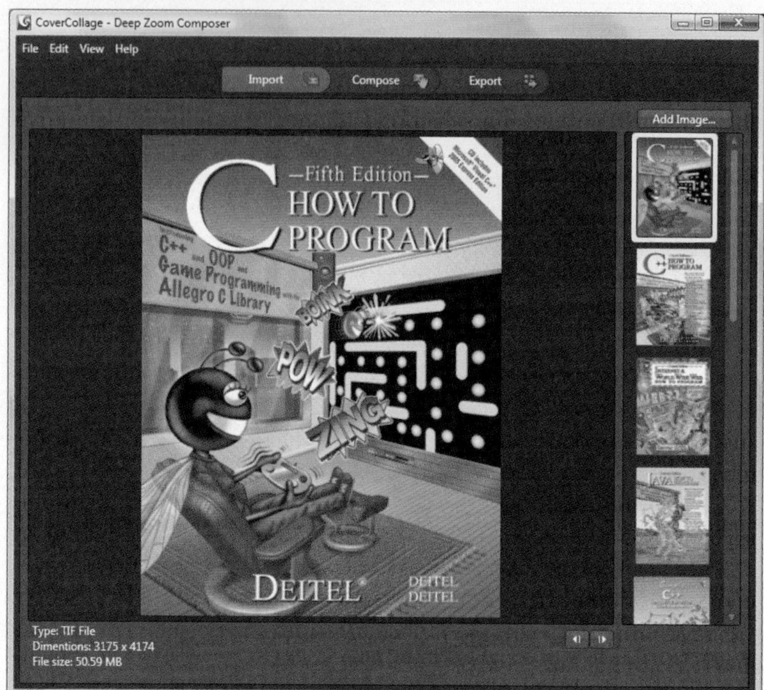

Fig. 23.15 | Deep Zoom Composer showing the imported image files.

a)

Fig. 23.16 | Deep Zoom Composer showing the editable composition.

b)

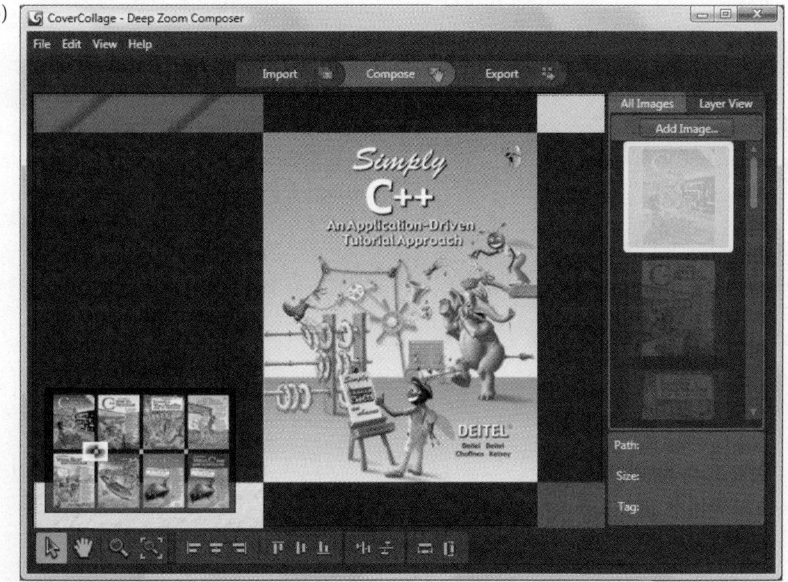

Fig. 23.16 | Deep Zoom Composer showing the editable composition.

Drag the thumbnail of each desired image onto the main canvas of the window. When you drag a file into the collage, its thumbnail is grayed out in the side bar and you cannot add it to the collage again. Figure 23.16 shows what the composer looks like, once you bring files into the project.

When images are in the composition, you can move the images to the canvas and resize them to be as large or small as you want. Deep Zoom Composer has features such as snapping and alignment tools that help you lay out the images. The yellow pins throughout the collage in Fig. 23.16(a) indicate that there are small images at those locations. You can zoom in on the composition by scrolling the mouse wheel to see the smaller image. Figure 23.16(b) shows the smaller cover that one of the yellow pins indicates. A small screen in the bottom-left corner shows the entire collage and a white rectangle indicating the view displayed in the window.

The panel on the right showing all the images also has a **Layer View** option, which indicates the layer ordering of all the composition's images. This view is used to control the order of overlapping images. The layers can be rearranged to allow you to place certain images on top of others.

Once you have a completed collage, go to the **Export** tab to export the files to be used by a `MultiScaleImage` in your application. Figure 23.17 shows the contents of the window when the **Export** tab is open.

You'll need to name the project. For this example, name the project **CoverCollage-Collection** and keep the default **Export Location**. The files are exported to a new folder inside the directory that you created earlier for the Deep Zoom Composer project. By default, Deep Zoom Composer selects the **Export as Collection** option using a PNG file format. By exporting as a collection instead of a composition, subimage information is included in the output XML files. Change the file format to **JPEG** and keep the **Quality** at

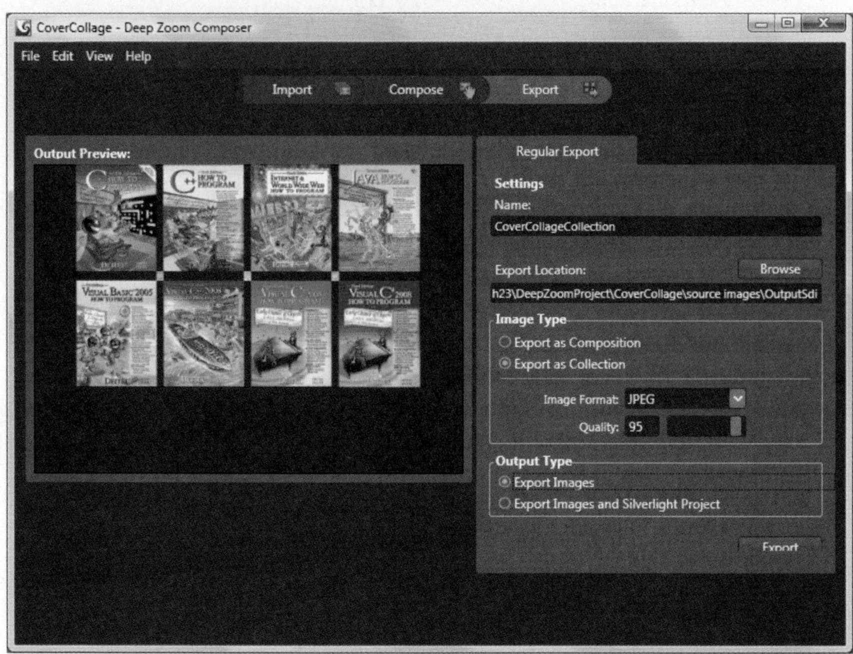

Fig. 23.17 | Deep Zoom Composer's exporting capabilities.

95—lower values result in smaller file sizes and lower-quality images. Also by default, the composer selects the **Export Images and Silverlight Project** output type. Select the **Export Images** option, since we are using the export in our own Silverlight project. Once the project is done exporting, you'll be ready to import these files into a Silverlight project and use them to create a deep zoom application.

23.6.2 Creating a Silverlight Deep Zoom Application

Deep zoom images are created in Silverlight Projects by using the `MultiScaleImage` element, which takes an XML file as its source. A `MultiScaleImage` can be treated in the XAML code similar to a simple `Image` element. Earlier in the chapter we showed you screen captures of the **DeepZoomCoverCollage** example. Figure 23.18 is the XAML code that produces the layout of this application.

```
<!-- Fig. 23.18: Page.xaml -->
<!-- DeepZoomCoverCollage employs Silverlight's deep zoom (XAML). -->
<UserControl x:Class="DeepZoomCoverCollage.Page"
   xmlns="http://schemas.microsoft.com/winfx/2006/xaml/presentation"
   xmlns:x="http://schemas.microsoft.com/winfx/2006/xaml">
   <Grid x:Name="LayoutRoot">

      <!-- instructions on how to interact with the page -->
```

Fig. 23.18 | **DeepZoomCoverCollage** employs Silverlight's deep zoom (XAML). (Part 1 of 2.)

```
        <StackPanel Orientation="Vertical">
           <TextBlock Text="Hold up-arrow and click to zoom in." />
           <TextBlock Text="Hold down-arrow and click to zoom out." />
           <TextBlock Text="Drag to pan the image." />

           <TextBlock x:Name="titleTextBlock" Text="Title:"
              HorizontalAlignment="Center" /> <!-- book title -->

           <!-- deep zoom collage that was created in Composer -->
           <MultiScaleImage x:Name="Image" Margin="10"
              Source="/CoverCollageCollection/dzc_output.xml" />
        </StackPanel>
     </Grid>
  </UserControl>
```

Fig. 23.18 | **DeepZoomCoverCollage** employs Silverlight's deep zoom (XAML). (Part 2 of 2.)

The main page contains only a `StackPanel` with embedded `TextBlocks` that display instructions, a `TextBlock` to display the selected book's title and the `MultiScaleImage` to display the collage we created in the previous section. To use the collage, you must add the entire **CoverCollageCollection** folder to your Silverlight project. If you kept the default Deep Zoom Composer export location, this folder can be found in the `CoverCollage` project's folder under the subfolder `\source images\OutputSdi\`. Copy the `CoverCollageCollection` folder into the `ClientBin` folder of the web application (`C:\examples\ch23\Examples\DeepZoomCoverCollage\DeepZoomCoverCollageWeb\ClientBin\`) in Windows Explorer. Right click **Client Bin** under the **DeepZoomCoverCollageWeb** project in the **Solution Explorer** in Visual Studio and click **Refresh Folder**. If the `CoverCollageCollection` folder was copied correctly, you should see a **CoverCollageCollection** folder (Fig. 23.19). You can now refer to this collection in your application.

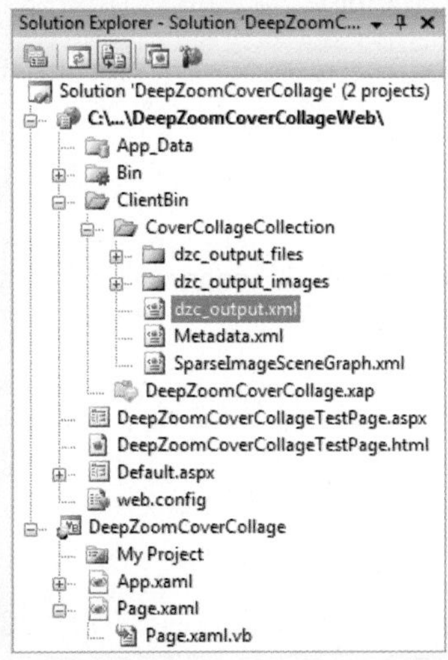

Fig. 23.19 | **Solution Explorer** after the deep zoom files have been added to the project.

Once the necessary files are in the project, they can be used by the `MultiScaleImage` element that displays the deep zoom image. Line 19 of Fig. 23.18 defines the source of the `MultiScaleImage` to `"/CoverCollageCollection/dzc_output.xml"`. The source address in this case is relative to the **Client Bin**, meaning that the application searches for the given path in the **Client Bin** folder of the project. Now that the `MultiScaleImage` is ready, we can program the application's event handlers for zooming and panning the image, and for displaying a book's title when its cover is clicked (Fig. 23.20).

```
' Fig. 23.20: Page.xaml.vb
' DeepZoomCoverCollage employs Silverlight's deep zoom (code-behind).
Imports System.Xml.Linq

Partial Public Class Page
   Inherits UserControl

   Const ZOOMFACTOR As Double = 2.0 ' factor by which to zoom in or out

   Private zoomIn As Boolean = False ' true if up button is pressed
   Private zoomOut As Boolean = False ' true if down button is pressed
   Private mouseDown As Boolean = False ' true if mouse button is down
   Private currentPosition As Point ' position of image when clicked
   Private dragOffset As Point ' mouse offset used for panning

   ' constructor
   Public Sub New()
      InitializeComponent()
   End Sub ' New

   ' when a key is pressed, set the correct variables to true
   Private Sub Page_KeyDown(ByVal sender As Object, _
      ByVal e As System.Windows.Input.KeyEventArgs) Handles Me.KeyDown

      If e.Key = Key.Up Then ' button pressed is UP
         zoomIn = True ' prepare to zoom in
      ElseIf e.Key = Key.Down Then ' button pressed is DOWN
         zoomOut = True ' prepare to zoom out
      End If
   End Sub ' Page_KeyDown

   ' when a key is released, set the correct variables to false
   Private Sub Page_KeyUp(ByVal sender As Object, _
      ByVal e As System.Windows.Input.KeyEventArgs) Handles Me.KeyUp

      If e.Key = Key.Up Then ' button released is UP
         zoomIn = False ' don't zoom in
      ElseIf e.Key = Key.Down Then ' button released is DOWN
         zoomOut = False ' don't zoom out
      End If
   End Sub ' Page_KeyUp

```

Fig. 23.20 | **DeepZoomCoverCollage** employs Silverlight's deep zoom (code-behind). (Part 1 of 3.)

```
   ' when the mouse leaves the area of the image we don't want to pan
   Private Sub Image_MouseLeave(ByVal sender As Object, _
      ByVal e As System.Windows.Input.MouseEventArgs) _
      Handles Image.MouseLeave

      mouseDown = False ' If mouse leaves area, no more panning
   End Sub ' Image_MouseLeave

   ' handle events when user clicks the mouse
   Private Sub Image_MouseLeftButtonDown(ByVal sender As Object, _
      ByVal e As System.Windows.Input.MouseButtonEventArgs) _
      Handles Image.MouseLeftButtonDown

      mouseDown = True ' mouse button is down
      currentPosition = Image.ViewportOrigin ' current position of image
      dragOffset = e.GetPosition(Image) ' current of mouse position

      ' logical position (between 0 and 1) of mouse
      Dim click As Point = Image.ElementToLogicalPoint(dragOffset)

      If zoomIn Then ' zoom in when UP key is pressed
         Image.ZoomAboutLogicalPoint(ZOOMFACTOR, click.X, click.Y)
      ElseIf zoomOut Then ' zoom out when DOWN key is pressed
         Image.ZoomAboutLogicalPoint(1 / ZOOMFACTOR, click.X, click.Y)
      End If

      ' determine which book cover was pressed to display the title
      Dim index As Integer = subImageIndex(click)

      ' XDocument that contains info on all subimages in the collage
      Dim xmlDocument As XDocument = _
         XDocument.Load("SparseImageSceneGraph.xml")

      ' LINQ to XML to find the title based on index of clicked image
      Dim bookTitle = _
         From info In xmlDocument...<SceneNode> _
         Where Convert.ToInt32(info.<ZOrder>.Value) = index + 1 _
         Select info.<FileName>.Value

      If bookTitle.Any Then ' if any cover was actually clicked
         Dim title As String = bookTitle.Single ' gets book title

         ' only want title of book, not the rest of the file name
         title = title.Substring(title.LastIndexOf("\") + 1)

         ' make slight changes from file names to make the title correct
         title = title.Replace("pp", "++")
         title = title.Replace("sharp", "#")

         ' display the title on the page
         titleTextBlock.Text = "Title: " & title.Replace(".jpg", _
            String.Empty).ToUpper
```

Fig. 23.20 | **DeepZoomCoverCollage** employs Silverlight's deep zoom (code-behind). (Part 2 of 3.)

```
      Else ' User clicked on blank space
         titleTextBlock.Text = "Title:"
      End If
   End Sub ' Image_MouseLeftButtonDown

   ' if the mouse button is released, we don't want to pan any more
   Private Sub Image_MouseLeftButtonUp(ByVal sender As Object, _
      ByVal e As System.Windows.Input.MouseButtonEventArgs) _
      Handles Image.MouseLeftButtonUp

      mouseDown = False ' no more panning
   End Sub ' Image_MouseLeftButtonUp

   ' handle when the mouse moves: panning
   Private Sub Image_MouseMove(ByVal sender As Object, _
      ByVal e As System.Windows.Input.MouseEventArgs) _
      Handles Image.MouseMove

      ' if no zoom occurs, we want to pan
      If mouseDown AndAlso zoomIn = False AndAlso zoomOut = False Then
         Dim click As New Point() ' records point to move to
         click.X = currentPosition.X - Image.ViewportWidth * _
            (e.GetPosition(Image).X - dragOffset.X) / Image.ActualWidth
         click.Y = currentPosition.Y - Image.ViewportWidth * _
            (e.GetPosition(Image).Y - dragOffset.Y) / Image.ActualWidth
         Image.ViewportOrigin = click ' shifts the image
      End If
   End Sub ' Image_MouseMove

   ' used to find out which image was clicked (if anything was clicked)
   Private Function subImageIndex(ByVal click As Point) As Integer

      ' go through images backward so images on top are processed first
      For i = Image.SubImages.Count - 1 To 0 Step -1
         Dim subImage = Image.SubImages(i) ' select a single subimage

         ' create a rect around the area of the cover. used to check if
         ' the point clicked is within the area taken up by the cover
         Dim scale As Double = 1 / subImage.ViewportWidth
         Dim area As New Rect(-subImage.ViewportOrigin.X * scale, _
            -subImage.ViewportOrigin.Y * scale, scale, _
            scale / subImage.AspectRatio)

         If area.Contains(click) Then
            Return i ' returns the index of the clicked cover
         End If
      Next ' i

      Return -1 ' if no cover was clicked
   End Function ' subImageIndex
End Class ' Page
```

Fig. 23.20 | **DeepZoomCoverCollage** employs Silverlight's deep zoom (code-behind). (Part 3 of 3.)

Line 3 imports the LINQ to XML namespace. We use a LINQ query to find the title of the cover image the user selects. We have several instance variables that help us determine which operation is to occur when you click the mouse.

Zooming a `MultiScaleImage`

To zoom in or out with a `MultiScaleImage`, we call its `ZoomAboutLogicalPoint` method (lines 64 and 66), which takes a zoom factor, an *x*-coordinate and a *y*-coordinate as parameters. A zoom factor of 1 keeps the image at its current size. Values less than 1 zoom out and values greater than 1 zoom in. The method zooms toward or away from the coordinates passed to the method. The coordinates need to be absolute points divided by the entire collage's `Width`. To convert the absolute coordinates raised by a mouse event to these coordinates, we use `MultiScaleImage`'s `ElementToLogicalPoint` method (line 61), which takes the `Point`'s absolute coordinates as parameters.

Panning a `MultiScaleImage`

The viewport of a `MultiScaleImage` represents the portion of the image that is rendered on screen. To pan, change the `ViewportOrigin` property of the `MultiScaleImage` (line 120). By keeping track of the offset between where the user initially clicked (line 58) and where the user has dragged the mouse, we can calculate where we need to move the origin (lines 116–119) to shift the image. Figures 23.21–23.22 demonstrate what values are returned by various `MultiScaleImage` properties. Assume the "container" of Fig. 23.21 is the viewport while the "image" is the entire collage.

To determine the new *x*-coordinate of the `ViewportOrigin`, we first find the difference between the *x*-coordinates of the current mouse position (`e.GetPosition(Image).X`) and the mouse position where the user initially clicked (`dragOffset.X`), which we'll refer to as the mouse offset. To convert this value to one we can use for the `ViewportOrigin`, we need to divide it by the width of the collage. The `MultiScaleImage`'s `ViewportWidth` returns the ratio of the viewport's width and the collage's width. A `MultiScaleImage`'s `ActualWidth` property returns the width of the piece of the collage rendered on-screen (viewport's width). Multiplying the mouse offset by the `ViewportWidth` and dividing by the `ActualWidth` returns the ratio of the mouse offset and the collage's width. We then subtract this value

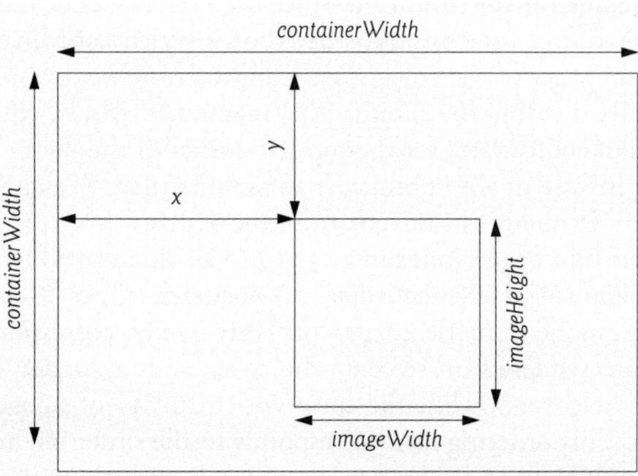

Fig. 23.21 | Various values used to by `MultiScaleImage`'s properties.

Property	Value
ViewportOrigin	$\left(\frac{-x}{imageWidth}, \frac{-y}{imageWidth}\right)$
ViewportWidth	$\frac{containerWidth}{imageWidth}$
AspectRatio	$\frac{imageWidth}{imageHeight}$
ActualWidth	$containerWidth$

Fig. 23.22 | Ratios returned by MultiScaleImage's properties.

from the ViewportOrigin's original *x*-coordinate to obtain the new value. A similar calculation is performed for the *y*-coordinate (keep in mind we still use ActualWidth in this calculation since ViewportOrigin's coordinates are given in terms of the width).

Determining the Title of the Clicked Cover

To determine a clicked image's book title requires the SparseImageSceneGraph.xml file created by Deep Zoom Composer. In the **Solution Explorer**, find this XML file in the collection folder we imported and drag the file to your Silverlight deep zoom project so that you can use it in a LINQ query later in the application. The file contains information on where each subimage is located in the collage.

To determine which cover the user clicked, we create a **Rect** object (lines 134–136) for each subimage that represents the on-screen area that the image occupies. A Rect defines a rectangular area on the page. If the Point returned by the mouse-click event is inside the Rect, the user clicked the cover in that Rect. We can use Rect method **Contains** to determine whether the click was inside the rectangle. If a cover was clicked, method subImageIndex returns the index of the subimage. Otherwise the method returns -1.

A MultiScaleSubImage's properties return the same ratios as a MultiScaleImage's properties (Figs. 23.21–23.22), except that the "container" represents the entire collage while the "image" represents the subimage. Since the ElementToLogicalPoint method of a MultiScaleImage control returns points based on a scaled coordinate system with the origin at the top-left corner of the collage, we want to create Rect objects using the same coordinate system. By dividing the subimage's ViewportOrigin by the subimage's ViewportWidth, we obtain coordinates for the top-left corner of the Rect. To find the Rect's Width, we take the inverse of the subimage's ViewportWidth. We can then use the subimage's AspectRatio to obtain the Height from the Width.

Next, we use the subimage's index in a LINQ to XML query to locate the subimage's information in the SparseImageSceneGraph.xml document (lines 78–80). Each subimage in the collage has a unique numeric ZOrder property, which corresponds to the order in which the images are rendered on screen—the cover with a ZOrder of 1 is drawn first (behind the rest of the covers), while the cover with a ZOrder of 12 is drawn last (on top of all other covers). This ordering also corresponds to the order of the subimages in the collection Image.SubImages and therefore corresponds with the index that we found in the subImageIndex method. To determine which cover was clicked, we can compare the returned index with the ZOrder of each subimage in the collection using our LINQ to XML query. We add 1 to the returned index (line 79), because the indices in a collection start at 0 while the ZOrder properties of the subimages start at 1. We then obtain the title from the subimage's original file name and display the title above the deep zoom image (lines 83–94). If none of the covers were clicked, then no title is displayed (line 96).

23.7 Audio and Video

Silverlight uses the MediaElement control to embed audio or video files into your application. The source for MediaElements can be either a file stored with the Silverlight application or a source on the Internet. MediaElement supports playback in the following encoded formats (more information is available at msdn.microsoft.com/en-us/library/cc189080(vs.95).aspx):

- Video: WMV1, WMV2, WMV3, WMVA, WMVC1
- Audio: WMA7, WMA8, WMA9, MP3

Silverlight also supports high-definition video. While Silverlight is compatible with only Windows media files, Microsoft's Expression Encoder can be used to convert files into a supported format. Other encoders that can convert to Windows media format will work as well, including the free online media encoder at media-convert.com/

MediaElements can be in one of the following states—Buffering, Closed, Paused, Error, Opening, Playing or Stopped. A MediaElement's state is determined by its **CurrentState** property. When in the Buffering state, the MediaElement is loading the media in preparation for playback. When in the Closed state, the MediaElement contains no media and displays a transparent frame.

Our **VideoSelector** application (Fig. 23.23) shows some of Silverlight's media-playing capabilities. This application obtains its video sources from a user-created XML file and displays small previews of those videos on the left side of the screen. When you click a preview, the application loads that video in the application's main area. The application plays the audio only for the video in the main area. You can test the example online at www.deitel.com/books/vb2008htp/.

```
<!-- Fig. 23.23: Page.xaml -->
<!-- VideoSelector lets users watch several videos at once (XAML). -->
<UserControl x:Class="VideoSelector.Page"
   xmlns="http://schemas.microsoft.com/winfx/2006/xaml/presentation"
   xmlns:x="http://schemas.microsoft.com/winfx/2006/xaml">
   <Grid x:Name="LayoutRoot">
      <Grid.ColumnDefinitions> <!-- Defines the page's two columns -->
         <ColumnDefinition Width="Auto" />
         <ColumnDefinition />
      </Grid.ColumnDefinitions>

      <Grid.Resources> <!-- Contains the page's animations -->

         <!-- Fades the main screen in, displaying the new video -->
         <Storyboard x:Name="fadeIn" Storyboard.TargetName="screen">
```

Fig. 23.23 | **VideoSelector** lets users watch several videos at once (XAML). (Part 1 of 2.)

```
            <DoubleAnimation Storyboard.TargetProperty="Opacity"
               From="0" To="1" Duration="0:0:0.5" />
         </Storyboard>

         <!-- Fades the main screen out when a new video is selected -->
         <Storyboard x:Name="fadeOut" Storyboard.TargetName="screen">
            <DoubleAnimation Storyboard.TargetProperty="Opacity"
               From="1" To="0" Duration="0:0:0.5" />
         </Storyboard>
      </Grid.Resources>

      <!-- ListBox containing all available videos -->
      <ListBox x:Name="previewListBox">
         <ListBox.ItemsPanel>
            <ItemsPanelTemplate>
               <StackPanel Orientation="Vertical" />
            </ItemsPanelTemplate>
         </ListBox.ItemsPanel>
      </ListBox>

      <!-- Rectangle object with a video brush showing the main video -->
      <Rectangle x:Name="screen" Grid.Column="1">
         <Rectangle.Fill>
            <VideoBrush x:Name="brush" Stretch="Uniform" />
         </Rectangle.Fill>
      </Rectangle>
   </Grid>
</UserControl>
```

Fig. 23.23 | **VideoSelector** lets users watch several videos at once (XAML). (Part 2 of 2.)

The videos for this example were downloaded from the Wikimedia Commons website (`commons.wikimedia.org`) and are in the public domain. This site contains many images and sound and video files that you can use in your programs—not all items are in the public domain. The videos in the screen capture in Fig. 23.23 were obtained under the science videos section at

`commons.wikimedia.org/wiki/Category:Science_videos`

The files were `.ogg` files that we converted to `.wmv` files using the online video converter at `media-convert.com/`.

The application displays one preview video on the side of the page for each source defined in a user-created XML file (discussed shortly). The GUI contains a `Grid` with two `Columns`. The first `Column` contains a `ListBox` that allows you to scroll through previews of the videos (lines 28–34). The second `Column` contains a `Rectangle` element with a `VideoBrush` for its `Fill` (lines 37–41). A **`VideoBrush`** displays a video as a graphics object's `Fill`—similar to an `ImageBrush`. The `SetSource` method of `VideoBrush` takes a `MediaElement` as a parameter and sets the video to be played in the brush.

The `Grid` element contains two `Storyboard Resources`, which contain the main video's fade-in and fade-out animations (lines 12–25). These animations are `DoubleAnimations` that target the `Opacity` property of the `Rectangle` that displays the video. To make the `Rectangle` display the selected video, we'll change the `VideoBrush`'s source to the video the user clicks.

When the page loads, the application performs several initialization tasks. It first loads a new `MediaElement` for each source that is included in the `sources.xml` file (Fig. 23.24). We query this XML file using LINQ to XML. To specify your own list of videos, you must edit our `sources.xml` file, or create a new one and add it to the project. To do this, open a new XML file by right clicking the application project—in this case **VideoSelector**—in the **Solution Explorer** and go to **Add > New Item...**. Select **Visual Basic** in the **Categories** section of the window, then select **XML File** in the **Templates** section. Change the file's **Name** to **sources.xml** and click **Add**. Open the file to begin editing it. The sample file in Fig. 23.24 shows the format required to list the sources of the desired videos.

The XML document defines a `videos` element that may contain any number of `video` elements. Each `video` element contains a `url` element whose value is the source URL for

```
<?xml version="1.0" encoding="utf-8" ?>

<!-- Fig. 23.24: sources.xml -->
<!-- VideoSelector's list of video sources. -->
<videos>
   <video> <!-- each video child contains a url source property -->
      <url>/newfractal.wmv</url> <!-- source for first video -->
   </video>
   <video>
      <url>/fractal.wmv</url> <!-- source for second video -->
   </video>
   <video>
      <url>/bailey.wmv</url> <!-- source for third video -->
   </video>
</videos>
```

Fig. 23.24 | **VideoSelector's** list of video sources.

the corresponding `MediaElement`. Simply replace the value in the `url` tag(s) with the path to your video(s). These videos also need to be included in your **Web Project**'s **Client Bin** if you want to play them from the same location as the Silverlight application. If your source URLs link to online videos, then you don't need to add anything else to your project. To add these files, right click the **Client Bin** folder in the **Web Project** associated with your Silverlight application (**VideoSelectorWeb**) in the **Solution Explorer** and select **Add Existing Item...**. Locate the videos you want to add and click **Add**. Now that we've added the necessary files to the project, we can continue with the code-behind file shown in Fig. 23.25.

```
' Fig. 23.25: Page.xaml.vb
' VideoSelector lets users watch several videos (code-behind).
Imports System.Xml.Linq

Partial Public Class Page
   Inherits UserControl

   Dim currentVideo As New MediaElement() ' currently playing video

   ' constructor
   Public Sub New()
      InitializeComponent()
   End Sub ' New

   ' read the sources of the videos that should be displayed from XML
   Private Sub Page_Loaded(ByVal sender As Object, _
      ByVal e As System.Windows.RoutedEventArgs) Handles Me.Loaded

      ' sources.xml contains the URL for all the videos
      Dim sources As XDocument = XDocument.Load("sources.xml")

      ' LINQ to XML to create new MediaElements with the listed sources
      Dim videos = From video In sources...<video> _
         Where Not video.<url>.Value = String.Empty _
         Select New MediaElement With _
         { _
            .Source = New Uri(video.<url>.Value, UriKind.Relative), _
            .Width = 150, _
            .Margin = New Thickness(10), _
            .IsMuted = True _
         }

      ' send all videos to the ListBox
      previewListBox.ItemsSource = videos
   End Sub ' Page_Loaded

   ' once animation completes, change the main video
   Private Sub fadeOut_Completed(ByVal sender As Object, _
      ByVal e As System.EventArgs) Handles fadeOut.Completed

      ' if there is a selection
      If previewListBox.SelectedItem IsNot Nothing Then
```

Fig. 23.25 | **VideoSelector** lets users watch several videos (code-behind). (Part 1 of 2.)

```
43
44             ' grab the new video to be played
45             Dim newVideo = CType(previewListBox.SelectedItem, MediaElement)
46
47             ' if new video has finished playing, restart it
48             If newVideo.CurrentState = MediaElementState.Paused Then
49                newVideo.Stop()
50                newVideo.Play()
51             End If
52
53             currentVideo.IsMuted = True ' mute the old video
54             newVideo.IsMuted = False ' play audio for main video
55
56             currentVideo = newVideo ' set the currently playing video
57             brush.SetSource(newVideo) ' set source of video brush
58          End If
59
60          fadeIn.Begin() ' begin fade in animation
61       End Sub ' fadeOut_Completed
62
63       ' when the user makes a new selection
64       Private Sub previewListBox_SelectionChanged(ByVal sender As Object, _
65          ByVal e As System.Windows.Controls.SelectionChangedEventArgs) _
66          Handles previewListBox.SelectionChanged
67
68          fadeOut.Begin() ' begin fade out animation
69       End Sub ' previewListBox_SelectionChanged
70    End Class ' Page
```

Fig. 23.25 | **VideoSelector** lets users watch several videos (code-behind). (Part 2 of 2.)

The **VideoSelector** uses LINQ to XML to determine which videos to display in the side bar. Line 20 defines the `XDocument` that loads `sources.xml`. Lines 23–31 contain a LINQ query that gets each `video` element from the XML file. For each `video` element that has a non-empty `url` element, the query creates a new `MediaElement` with that `url` as its relative `Source`. If your video is in the same location as the application or any subdirectory of that location, you may use a relative `Source` value. Otherwise, you need to use an absolute `Source`, which specifies the full path of the video. We set each element's `Width`, `Margin` and `IsMuted` properties to specify how the videos appear and perform when the application loads. Setting a `MediaElement`'s `IsMuted` property to `True` (line 30) mutes its audio—the default value is `False`—so that we do not hear the audio from all videos at once. We then feed the videos to the `ItemsSource` (line 34) of the `ListBox` to display the preview videos.

The application uses `previewListBox`'s `SelectionChanged` event handler to determine which video the user wants to view in the main area. When this event occurs, we begin the fade-out animation (line 68). After the fade-out animation completes, the application determines which video was clicked by grabbing `previewListBox`'s `SelectedItem` object and stores it in a `MediaElement` variable (line 45).

When a video has finished playing, it is placed in the `Paused` state. Lines 48–51 ensure that the selected video is restarted if it is in this state. We then mute the audio of the old video and enable the audio of the selected video (lines 53 and 54 respectively). Next, we set the source for the `VideoBrush` of the `Rectangle`'s `Fill` to the selected video (line 57). Finally, we begin the fade-in animation to show the new video in the main area (line 60).

23.8 Isolated Storage

Just as web applications can store data on a client's computer via cookies, Silverlight allows applications to store data on client computers. This feature, called isolated storage, is used to save user-specific data associated with one or more Silverlight applications from a single domain. These files can store any kind of data that the application needs, such as the user's preferences for the application. The current limit for isolated data storage on a client machine is 1 MB; however, the application can request a higher quota, and Silverlight will automatically prompt the user to approve the request. The quota is for all applications from one domain, not each individual application. The isolated storage is shared among all Silverlight applications from a given domain.

Applications use isolated storage to store data in a virtual file system. The file system is considered virtual because it is not stored at a specific location on the client computer. Rather, storage files—called stores—contain the information on the physical location of the data. The same isolated storage is used by all browsers on the client's computer. For example, if a client accesses a Silverlight application from Internet Explorer, then accesses the same application from Firefox, the application running in Firefox has access to any data stored in the isolated storage when the application was running in Internet Explorer (and vice versa). This system is particularly useful in offering cross-browser operability of Silverlight applications, since the user's browser has no effect on the site's ability to retrieve the data. More information on isolated storage can be found at

`msdn.microsoft.com/en-us/library/bdts8hk0(VS.95).aspx`

23.9 Silverlight Demos and Web Resources

A great way to get into the "Silverlight world" is to visit the growing number of demo sites and general resource sites on the web.

`www.deitel.com/ResourceCenters/Microsoft/Silverlight20/tabid/2985/Default.aspx`
Start your search here for Silverlight 2.0 resources, including sample applications, articles, blogs, videos, tutorials, downloads, training courses, forums, FAQs, books, eBooks, sample chapters and more.

`www.silverlight.net/Showcase/`
A gallery of hundreds of Silverlight applications and demos. Includes Developer Express (a layout-management tool for creating advanced web applications powered by Silverlight), Silverlight Virtual Earth Draw Tools, The Bragosphere, Silverlight.net (mouse-gesture recognition), Media Player, ABC Shop Online, Movie Trailers, Buddy Knavery (adventure game), Suboost (for adding tags and subtitles to videos), Fragmenti (puzzle game), AllMusic Streaming, Shidonni (virtual world for children), Dortik Solitaire Games, AgLite Effects (animation library), EyeRollerWEB (this widget displays a face whose eyes follow mouse moves around a web page), Silverlight Weather Widget and Knight's Tour Classic Chess Puzzle.

`silverlight.net/community/gallerydetail.aspx?cat=6&sort=1`
Dozens of Silverlight 2 samples, including Disco Floor (smooth animation), Color Picker Control, Binary Clock, Shiver Mario, DeepView Lite (to share your DeepZoom data), Spider Solitaire Game, Silverlight Klotski (sliding block puzzle), MinoPlayer, SilverLander: A Silverlight 2 Game, Silverlight Controls demo (DropDownList, TreeView, Popup Dialogs and more), Image Snipper, LINQ

Food Finder, Syndication-RSS/Atom Feed Reader, Silverlight Control Demo Sample (24 Silverlight 2 controls), Silverlight Airline Sample, Silverlight Surface, Clock VB.NET and Clock C#, Bumble Beegger (2D Silverlight action game), Digital Clock, and Tetrislight.

`www.vectorform.com/silverlight/`
Vectorform Labs Silverlight Examples. Samples include Tile Navigation (allows user to select different videos using an animated GUI), Video Player (Microsoft Surface), and Breakout.

`blogs.msdn.com/tims/archive/2007/07/07/from-a-to-z-50-silverlight-applications.aspx`
Tim Sneath of Microsoft put together a list of 50 sample Silverlight applications from numerous websites, including 2D Physics Simulation, Grand Piano, Silverlight Mind Map, 3D Teapot Demo, Infragistics Controls Demo, Silverlight Pad, Amazon Search Visualization, JavaScript/.NET Chess, Silverlight Playground, AOL Social Mail Gadget, Laugh-o-Sphere, Silverlight Rocks, Binary Clock, LiveStation, SilverNibbles, Popfly, Telerik RadControls 3D Cube, Disco Dance Floor, Windows Journal-to-Silverlight Converter, Windows Vista Simulator, XamlWebPad, Gradient Animations, and Silverlight Chess Game Replay (playback of a few full games of chess).

`memorabilia.hardrock.com/`
Silverlight demo: Hard Rock Memorabilia. This site allows users to view all of the memorabilia items on display in the Hard Rock Cafes worldwide (clicking on an item will zoom it in).

`www.youtube.com/results?search_query=silverlight+2&search_type=&aq=f`
59 Silverlight 2 videos and demos on YouTube. The videos are anywhere from one to ten minutes long. Includes Silverlight 2 Control Unit Tests (demonstration from MIX conference), Deep Zoom, iTunes as Silverlight media Display (a Silverlight application that mimics iTunes), the Silverlight announcement by Bill Gates, Silverlight Talking, the Silverlight video for the MIX08 conference and more.

`sessions.visitmix.com/?selectedSearch=CT01`
Video: "Building Rich Internet Applications Using Microsoft Silverlight," with Mike Harsh and Joe Stegman at MIX08. The video, roughly 80 minutes long, discusses and demos Silverlight. Topics include an overview of Silverlight, getting started with Silverlight, building an application, networking, XML, controls, data binding, control templating, custom controls, custom layouts, OpenFile Dialog, HTML integration, Deep Zoom and more.

23.10 Wrap-Up

In this chapter, you learned how to use Silverlight (a cross-platform, cross-browser subset of .NET) to build Rich Internet Applications (RIAs) in Visual Studio 2008. We began by introducing the **WeatherViewer** application to portray some of the key features of a new Silverlight application. Since Silverlight is a subset of WPF, the two have similar programming environments with slight minor variations. The GUI of any Silverlight page is created by a XAML file in the project. All event handlers and other methods are created in the code-behind files.

With the **WeatherViewer** example, we showed that you can use web services, LINQ to XML and data binding to create a web application with desktoplike capabilities. We also showed you how to create a custom control by using a `UserControl` as a template. Unlike `Styles` and `ControlTemplates`, custom controls allow you to manipulate the control's functionality rather than just the visual aspects. The GUI and code-behind of a custom control are created as if it were a new page in the application.

We showed you our **FlickrViewer** example, which, similar to the **WeatherViewer**, shows how to use web services to enhance the capabilities of your application—specifically in this example with the `Image` control. This application combines a web service—provided by Flickr—and animations to create a photo-searching website.

You learned about Silverlight's deep zoom capabilities. You saw how to use Deep Zoom Composer and Silverlight to create your own deep zoom application. We showed how to implement zooming, panning, and subimage recognition in the code-behind file of your application using `MultiScaleImage` and `MultiScaleSubImage`.

Silverlight supports audio and video playback using the `MediaElement` control. This control supports embedding Windows media format files into the application. We introduced our **VideoSelector** application to show how to program `MediaElements` in your application. The example also showed the `VideoBrush` control being applied to the `Fill` of a `Rectangle` (applicable to any graphics object) to display the video within the graphic.

We introduced the concept of isolated storage, which allows the application to store user-specific data on the client machine or on the server. These files are stored in a virtual file system and can be used to save state information. In the next chapter, we discuss data structures concepts, generics and generic collections.

Summary

Section 23.1 Introduction

- Silverlight™ is Microsoft's platform for Rich Internet Applications (RIAs) and is a subset of the .NET platform.
- RIAs are web applications that offer responsiveness and rich GUI features comparable to those of desktop applications.
- Silverlight competes with Adobe Flash and Flex and Sun's JavaFX, and complements Microsoft's ASP.NET and ASP.NET AJAX.
- Silverlight runs as a web-browser plug-in.

Section 23.2 Platform Overview

- Silverlight applications consist of XAML files describing the GUI and a code-behind files defining the program logic.
- The subset of .NET available in Silverlight 2 includes APIs for collections, input/output, generics, multithreading, globalization, XML and LINQ. It also includes APIs for interacting with JavaScript and the elements in a web page.
- Silverlight 2 applications can be created in .NET languages such as Visual Basic, Visual C#, IronRuby and IronPython.

Section 23.3 Silverlight Runtime and Tools Installation

- Silverlight 2, at the time of this writing, is not supported in Microsoft's Visual Studio Express editions. Visual Studio 2008 is required to make Silverlight applications.
- The Silverlight 2 SDK can be used to create Silverlight applications if you don't have access to a complete version of Visual Studio.

Section 23.4 Building a Silverlight **WeatherViewer** *Application*

- Silverlight is a subset of WPF, so the two share many capabilities.
- A default Silverlight project contains `Page.xaml`, `Page.xaml.vb`, `App.xaml` and `App.xaml.vb`. The latter two contain code that is shared across all of the application's pages.

- `UserControl` is Silverlight's primary control, similar to the `Window` control in WPF.
- `UserControl` has a class name specified with the `x:Class` attribute.
- A compiled Silverlight application is packaged as a `.xap` file containing the application and its supporting resources.

Section 23.4.1 GUI Layout

- The main layout controls in Silverlight are `Grids`, `StackPanels` and `Canvases`.
- The `ItemsPanel` of a `ListBox` defines how the collection of items is displayed.
- The `ItemTemplate` of a `ListBox` contains a `DataTemplate` which defines the layout of a particular item in the collection.

Section 23.4.2 Obtaining and Displaying Weather Forecast Data

- The `WebClient` class can be used to invoke a web service.
- The `WithEvents` keyword lets you handle events for the associated object.
- The `DownloadStringAsync` method of `WebClient` invokes the web service and takes a `Uri` object containing the web-service address as a parameter.
- The `DownloadStringCompleted` event of `WebClient` is raised when the result of the web-service call has finished downloading.
- The `DownloadStringCompletedEventArgs` parameter of the `DownloadStringCompleted` event handler contains the returned information and any errors that occurred.
- `XDocument`'s `Parse` method converts a `String` to an `XDocument`.
- You can bind data to a `ListBox`'s `ItemsSource` to change the set of items the `ListBox` displays.
- A control has a `Visibility` property that determines whether the control is visible on the page.

Section 23.4.3 Custom Controls

- `Styles` and `ControlTemplates` can be used to customize the visual aspects of a control.
- Custom controls can be created by using a `UserControl` as a template.
- Custom controls can be programmed similarly to a separate Silverlight application.

Section 23.5 Animations and the FlickrViewer

- Silverlight has three types of animations—`DoubleAnimations`, `PointAnimations`, and `ColorAnimations`.
- Properties with relative values such as `"*"` and `"Auto"` do not animate.
- A `Storyboard` contains one or more animations that can be invoked by the `Begin` method.
- A `Storyboard` is created as a `Resource` element of a layout control.
- A tag is any user-generated word or phrase that helps organize web content.

Section 23.6 Images and Deep Zoom

- Silverlight's deep zoom allows you to view high-resolution images in a browser at different zoom levels while maintaining quality.
- Deep zoom works by sending only the necessary image information to the client machine.
- Silverlight's `MultiScaleImage` element is used to display deep zoom images. It takes an XML file as its source.
- A `MultiScaleSubImage` contains information on a single image in the deep zoom collage.

Section 23.6.1 Getting Started With Deep Zoom Composer

- Deep Zoom Composer splits a collage into separate images for different zoom levels.
- The **Import** tab allows you to add images on your computer to the collection.
- The **Compose** tab allows you to create the collage using the imported images. There are snapping and alignment tools to help you lay out the images.
- The **Export** tab allows you to export the collection to the format required by `MultiScaleImage`.
- When exporting, the split images of the collage can be in the original image format or compressed as `.jpg` or `.png`.
- The **Quality** value of `.jpg` files determines the balance between file size and image resolution.

Section 23.6.2 Creating a Silverlight Deep Zoom Application

- Exported deep zoom collages need to be included in the **ClientBin** folder of the web project that executes your Silverlight application.
- The `ZoomAboutLogicalPoint` method zooms into or out of a `MultiScaleImage`.
- The viewport of the `MultiScaleImage` represents the part of the image that is currently visible. The `ViewportOrigin` property can be changed to pan the image.
- A deep zoom collage's `SparseImageSceneGraph.xml` file contains information on the location of each subimage.
- The `ZOrder` property defines the order in which the subimages are rendered. This value is unique to each subimage.
- The `Rect` class represents a rectangular area on the page. The class's `Contains` method can be used to determine whether the user clicked within the specified area.

Section 23.7 Audio and Video

- Silverlight uses the `MediaElement` control to embed audio or video files into the application.
- A `MediaElement` supports windows media audio, MP3 or video sources.
- Microsoft's Expression Encoder can convert videos into a supported windows media format.
- A `VideoBrush` can be applied to the `Fill` property of a graphics element. This imposes the video onto the background of that graphics element.
- The `IsMuted` property of a `MediaElement` specifies whether the media's audio is audible.
- `MediaElements` can be in the `Buffering`, `Closed`, `Error`, `Opening`, `Playing`, `Paused` or `Stopped` states.

Section 23.8 Isolated Storage

- Silverlight allows applications to store data on client computers via isolated storage
- Isolated storage saves user-specific data associated with one or more Silverlight applications from a single domain.
- The current limit for isolated data storage on a client machine is 1 MB; however, the application can request a higher quota. The quota is for all applications from one domain.
- Applications use isolated storage to store data in a virtual file system.
- The same isolated storage is used by all browsers on the client's computer.

Terminology

`App.xaml`
`App.xaml.vb`
`Begin` method of `Storyboard`
`Border` control
`Button` control
Compose tab of Deep Zoom Composer

`Contains` method of `Rect`
cross-browser capabilities of Silverlight
`CurrentState` property of `MediaElement`
custom control
Deep Zoom
Deep Zoom Composer
`DoubleAnimation`
`ElementToLogicalPoint` method of `MultiScaleImage`
Export tab of Deep Zoom Composer
Import tab of Deep Zoom Composer
`IsMuted` property of `MediaElement`
isolated storage
`ListBox` control
Microsoft Expression Blend 2.5
Microsoft Expression Encoder
`MultiScaleImage`
`MultiScaleSubImage`
`Padding` property of a control
`Page.xaml`
`Page.xaml.vb`
`Paused` state of `MediaElement`
`Playing` state of `MediaElement`
`Rect` structure
Rich Internet Applications (RIAs)
Silverlight
Silverlight 2 Runtime
Silverlight 2 SDK
Silverlight Application project template
`Stopped` state of `MediaElement`
tagging
`UserControl`
`VideoBrush` control
`ViewportOrigin` property of `MultiScaleImage`
`ViewportWidth` property of `MultiScaleImage`
virtual file system
`Visibility` attribute of a control
Web Application Project
`WithEvents` keyword
`.xap` file
`x:Name` attribute of a Silverlight control
`XDocument` class
`XDocument.Parse` method
Zoom and pan capabilities of deep zoom.
`ZoomAboutLogicalPoint` method of `MultiScaleImage`

Self-Review Exercises

23.1 Say whether the statement is *true* or *false*. If it is *false*, explain why.

a) Silverlight employs all of the same functionality as WPF but in the form of an Internet application.
b) Silverlight competes with RIA technologies such as Adobe Flash and Flex and Sun's JavaFX, and complements Microsoft's ASP.NET and ASP.NET AJAX.
c) The `.xap` file contains the application and its supporting resources and is packaged by the IDE.
d) Silverlight's template control is `Window`.
e) Users can create custom controls by using the Silverlight `Style` and `ControlTemplate` controls.
f) When you call `WebClient`'s `DownloadStringAsync` method, the user can still interact with the application while the string is downloading.
g) A deep zoom image is just a high-resolution image.

23.2 Fill in the blanks with the appropriate answer.

a) The three basic animation controls are ________, ________, and ________.
b) An object of class ________ can be used to invoke a web service.
c) The `XDocument` method ________ converts a `String` containing XML into an object that can be used with LINQ to XML.
d) Namespace ________ is required to use LINQ to XML in your application.
e) The ________ keyword, used when creating an object, indicates that the object has events and enables you to write code that can respond to those events.
f) When a `MediaElement` has finished playing, it is in the ________ state.
g) The three layout controls for Silverlight are ________, ________ and ________.
h) The ________ of a `MultiScaleImage` represents the area of the deep zoom image that the user is currently viewing.

Answers to Self-Review Exercises

23.1 a) False—Silverlight is a subset of WPF, therefore it does not contain all of the same functionality as a WPF application. b) True c) True d) False—Unlike WPF applications, the template control for Silverlight applications is the `UserControl`. e) False—While `Styles` and `ControlTemplates` can be used to customize existing controls, `UserControl` is the template used to create custom controls. f) True g) False—A deep zoom image is really a collection of images. Deep Zoom Composer separates your original collage into these images, which are sent over the Internet to the client machine.

23.2 a) `DoubleAnimation`, `PointAnimation`, `ColorAnimation`. b) `WebClient`. c) `Parse`. d) `System.Xml.Linq`. e) `WithEvents`. f) `Paused`. g) `Grid`, `StackPanel`, `Canvas`. h) viewport.

Exercises

23.3 *(Enhanced* **Weather Viewer** *Application)* Modify the **Weather Viewer** application (Section 23.4) to display the name of the city and state for the zip code input by the user. These are specified by elements named `PlaceName` and `StateCode` in the XML returned by the web service. The new GUI should appear as shown in Fig. 23.26. You can test the updated **Weather Viewer** application at `www.deitel.com/books/vb2008htp/`. To update the application's layout, you'll need to:

a) Add a new `RowDefinition` in the main `Grid` to accommodate the additional information.
b) Change the `ListBox`'s `Grid.Row` attribute so that it appears in the bottom row of the main `Grid`.
c) Insert a horizontal `StackPanel` before the `ListBox`. This `StackPanel` should contain four `TextBlocks`—two to label the city and state, and two to display the values for the city and state.
d) Add the `CityState` class (provided in the exercises folder with this chapter's examples) to your project. This class consists of `String` properties `City` and `State`.
e) Use LINQ to XML to create a `CityState` object containing the values of the elements named `PlaceName` and `StateCode` in XML returned by the web service.
f) Set the `DataContext` of the `StackPanel` in *Step c* to the `CityState` object from *Step e*.
g) Use binding markup extensions to bind the city and state information to the appropriate `TextBlocks` you created in *Step c*.

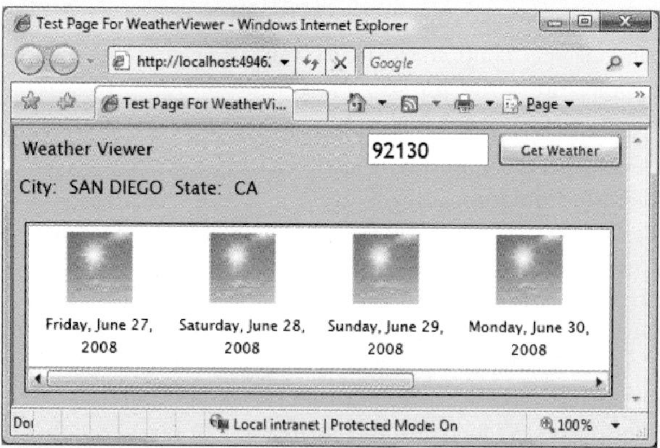

Fig. 23.26 | Displaying the city and state information in the **Weather Viewer**.

23.4 *(Length/Distance Converter)* The website `www.webservicex.net` provides several useful web services, including a length/distance converter. Use this web service and the techniques you learned in this chapter to create a Silverlight length/distance converter. The GUI for this application should appear as shown in Fig. 23.27. You can test the application at `www.deitel.com/books/vb2008htp/`.

You can invoke the web service with a URL of the form:

```
http://www.webservicex.net/length.asmx/ChangeLengthUnit?LengthValue= 100&from-
LengthUnit=Inches&toLengthUnit=Centimeters
```

If you try the preceding URL in your web browser, you'll see that 100 inches converts to 254 centimeters. The XML returned by the web service appears as follows:

```
<?xml version="1.0" encoding="utf-8" ?>
<double xmlns="http://www.webserviceX.NET/">254</double>
```

The element `double` contains the result. The web-service method `ChangeLengthUnit` requires three parameters named `LengthValue`, `fromLengthUnit` and `toLengthUnit`, each of type `String`. The complete list of values you can supply for the `fromLengthUnit` and `toLengthUnit` parameters can be found by looking at the bottom of the following web page in the section labeled **WSDL Schema:**

```
http://www.webservicex.net/WCF/ServiceDetails.aspx?SID=71
```

The user should be able to enter a number in a `TextBox`, then select the two units of measurement from `ListBoxes` and click a `Button` to invoke the web service. You can bind each `ListBox`'s `ItemsSource` property to an array of `Strings` containing the complete list of measurement names.

23.5 *(Enhanced* **VideoSelector** *Application)* Modify the **VideoSelector** application (Section 23.7) to include a **Play/Pause** and a **Stop** button. When the **Play/Pause** button is clicked, its text should change from **Play** to **Pause** or from **Pause** to **Play**, respectively. Place the buttons below the currently selected video. These buttons should allow the user to play, pause or stop the current video. The GUI should appear as shown in Fig. 23.28. You can test the application at `www.deitel.com/books/vb2008htp/`.

23.6 Combine capabilities of the **FlickrViewer** application (Section 23.5) and the **DeepZoomCoverCollage** application (Section 23.6.2) to create a Deitel Book-Cover Viewer with the following features. The `ListBox` should display thumbnails of the book-cover images (provided in the exercises folder with this chapter's examples). When the user selects a book-cover thumbnail from the `List-`

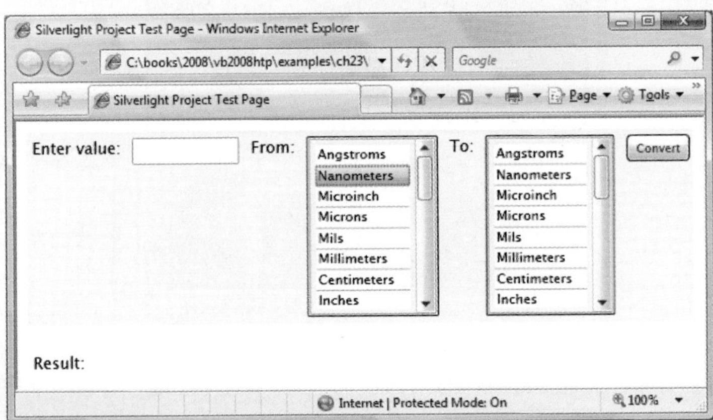

Fig. 23.27 | **LengthDistanceConverter** exercise sample GUI.

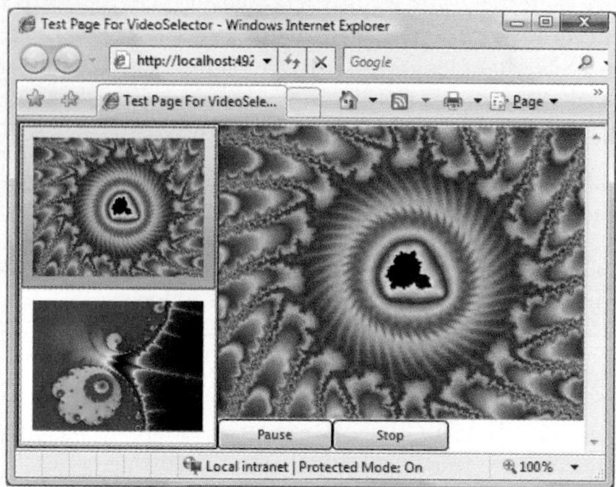

Fig. 23.28 | **VideoSelector** with **Play/Pause** and **Stop** buttons.

`Box`, the application should display a deep zoom image of that cover. Use the code from the **DeepZoomCoverCollage** application to implement the zooming and panning. You will need to change the code to use keys other than the up-arrow and down-arrow, because those buttons change the selection in the `ListBox`. We suggest the *I* key for zooming in and the *O* key for zooming out. The GUI should appear as shown in Fig. 23.29. You can test the application at `www.deitel.com/books/vb2008htp/`.

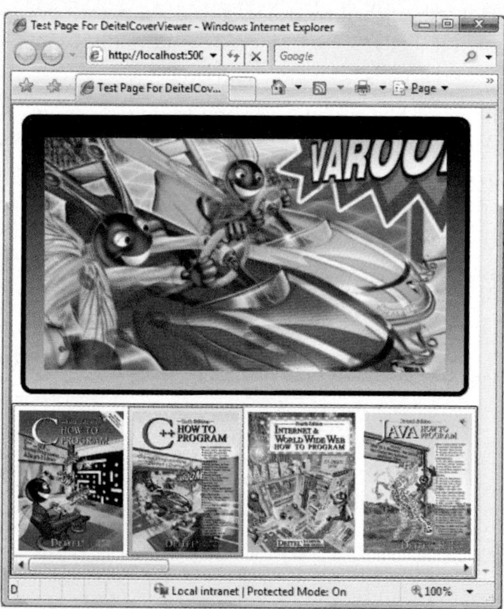

Fig. 23.29 | **DeitelCoverViewer** displays deep zoom images of Deitel covers.

24

Data Structures and Generic Collections

There is always room at the top.
—Daniel Webster

I think that I shall never see
A poem lovely as a tree.
—Joyce Kilmer

The shapes a bright container can contain!
—Theodore Roethke

I think this is the most extraordinary collection of talent, of human knowledge, that has ever been gathered together at the White House—with the possible exception of when Thomas Jefferson dined alone.
—John F. Kennedy

…our special individuality, as distinguished from our generic humanity.
—Oliver Wendell Holmes, Sr.

Every man of genius sees the world at a different angle from his fellows.
—Havelock Ellis

Born under one law, to another bound.
—Lord Brooke

OBJECTIVES

In this chapter you'll learn:

- Dynamic data structures, such as linked lists, queues, stacks and binary trees.
- Applications of linked data structures.
- The generic collections that are provided by the .NET Framework.
- To use generic collection classes `LinkedList`, `Dictionary` and `SortedDictionary`.
- To create generic methods that perform identical tasks on arguments of different types.
- To create a generic `Stack` class that can be used to store objects of any class or interface type.
- To understand the `New` constraint of a type parameter.
- To apply multiple constraints to a type parameter.

Outline

24.1 Introduction to Data Structures

In Chapter 8, we studied data structures that normally have fixed sizes, such as one- and two-dimensional arrays—these can grow and shrink at execution time, but only if they are explicitly resized by the programmer via the **ReDim** statement. In Chapter 9, we introduced the `List(Of T)` generic collection, which had arraylike behavior but could grow and shrink dynamically based on the application's needs. In this chapter, we continue our discussion of dynamic data structures. First we discuss some general theory, introducing four of the most widely used types of data structures. Linked lists are collections of data items "lined up in a row"—in some sense like arrays, but users can make insertions and deletions anywhere in a linked list without having to displace existing elements. Stacks are important in compilers and operating systems; insertions and deletions are made at only one end—the **top** of the stack. Queues represent waiting lines; insertions are made only at the back (also referred to as the **tail**) of a queue, and deletions are made only from the front (also referred to as the **head**) of a queue. Binary trees facilitate high-speed searching and sorting of data, efficient elimination of duplicate data items, representation of file-system directories and compilation of expressions. All these data structures have many other interesting applications as well.

We introduce the notion of linked data structures and show how these can be used to implement lists, stacks, queues and trees. We discuss the .NET framework's predefined generic collection classes that implement various common data structures. We then take a deeper look at generics, which allow you to declare your own data structures that can be easily adapted to contain data of any type. Programmers used to have to "roll their own" data structures—and to do that they needed to be aware of the intimate details of how popular data structures are implemented. .NET's generic collection classes are prebuilt data structures that provide the functionality of many popular data structures—you can use these classes effectively without having to be familiar with how they are implemented. This is the essence of simplicity. We begin with a discussion of linked data structures.

24.1.1 Linked Lists

A linked list is a linear collection (i.e., a sequence) of objects called nodes. Each node contains a link—a reference member that refers to another node—thus the term "linked" list (Fig. 24.1). A program accesses a linked list via a reference to the first node of the list. Each subsequent node is accessed via the link-reference member stored in the previous node. By convention, the link reference in the last node of a list is set to `Nothing` to mark the end of the list. Data is stored in a linked list dynamically—that is, each node is created as necessary. You can declare a node's class to store data of any type, including references to objects of other classes. Stacks and queues are also linear data structures—in fact, they are constrained versions of linked lists. Trees are nonlinear data structures.

Lists of data can be stored in arrays, but linked lists provide several advantages. A linked list is appropriate when the number of data elements to be represented in the data structure is unpredictable. Unlike a linked list, the size of a conventional Visual Basic array is fixed at creation time and can be changed only by explicitly using the `ReDim` statement. Conventional arrays can become full if the programmer does not explicitly allocate sufficient space, but linked lists become full only when the system has insufficient memory to satisfy additional dynamic memory allocation requests.

Performance Tip 24.1

An array can be declared to contain more elements than the number of items expected, possibly wasting memory. Linked lists provide better memory utilization in these situations, because they can grow and shrink at execution time.

Performance Tip 24.2

After locating the insertion point for a new item in a sorted linked list (which can be time consuming), inserting an element in the list is fast—only two references have to be modified. All existing nodes remain at their current locations in memory.

Programmers can maintain linked lists in sorted order simply by inserting each new element at the proper point in the list. Existing list elements do not need to be moved.

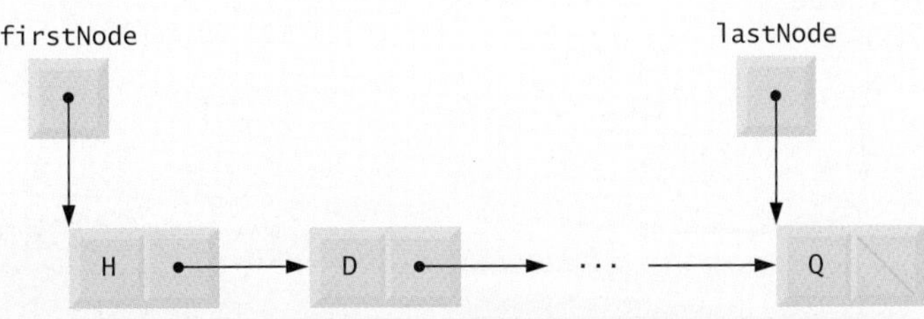

Fig. 24.1 | Linked-list graphical representation showing nodes connected by references.

Performance Tip 24.3

The elements of an array are stored contiguously in memory to allow immediate access to any array element—the address of any element can be calculated directly from its index. Linked lists do not afford such immediate access to their elements—an element can be accessed only by traversing the list from the front.

Performance Tip 24.4

Insertion and deletion in a sorted array can be time consuming—all the elements following the inserted or deleted element must be shifted appropriately.

Normally, linked-list nodes are not stored contiguously in memory. Rather, the nodes are said to be logically contiguous. Figure 24.1 illustrates a linked list with several nodes. [*Note:* the box containing the backslash represents a `Nothing` reference.]

Performance Tip 24.5

Using linked data structures and dynamic memory allocation (instead of arrays) for data structures that grow and shrink can save memory. Keep in mind, however, that reference links occupy space, and dynamic memory allocation incurs the overhead of method calls.

Linear and Circular Singly Linked and Doubly Linked Lists

The kind of linked list we've been discussing is a singly linked list—it begins with a reference to the first node, and each node contains a reference to the next node "in sequence." This list terminates with a node whose reference member has the value `Nothing`. A singly linked list may be traversed in only one direction.

A circular, singly linked list (Fig. 24.2) begins with a reference to the first node, and each node contains a reference to the next node. The "last node" does not contain a `Nothing` reference. Instead the reference in the last node points back to the first node, thus closing the "circle."

A doubly linked list (Fig. 24.3) allows traversals both forward and backward. Such a list is often implemented with two "start references"—one that refers to the first element of the list to allow front-to-back traversals of the list, and one that refers to the last element to allow back-to-front traversals. Each node has both a forward reference to the next node in the list and a backward reference to the previous node in the list. If your list contains an alphabetized telephone directory, for example, a search for someone whose name begins with a letter near the front of the alphabet might begin from the front of the list. A search for someone whose name begins with a letter near the end of the alphabet might begin from the back of the list.

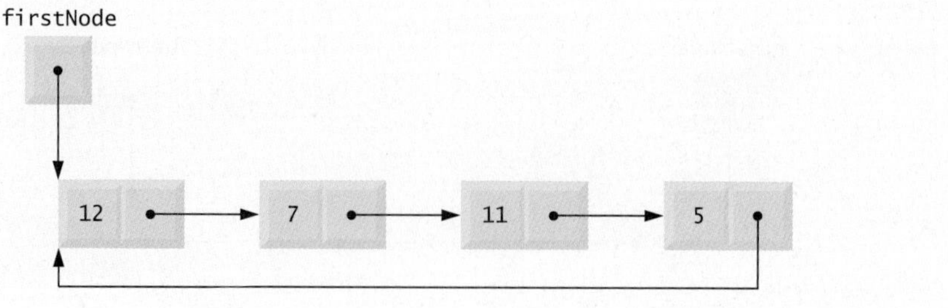

Fig. 24.2 | Circular, singly linked list.

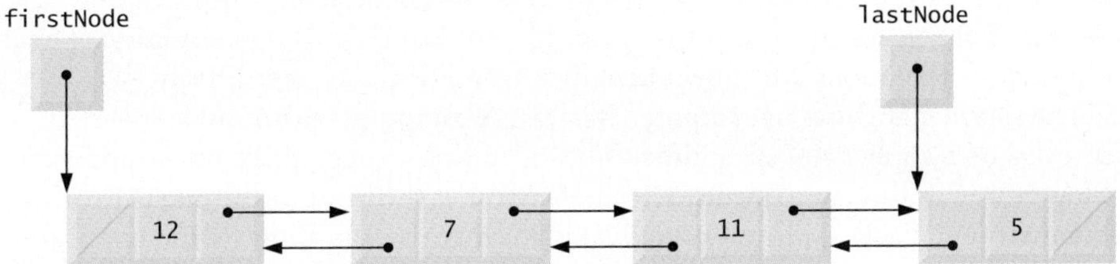

Fig. 24.3 | Doubly linked list.

In a circular, doubly linked list (Fig. 24.4), the forward reference of the last node refers to the first node, and the backward reference of the first node refers to the last node, thus closing the "circle."

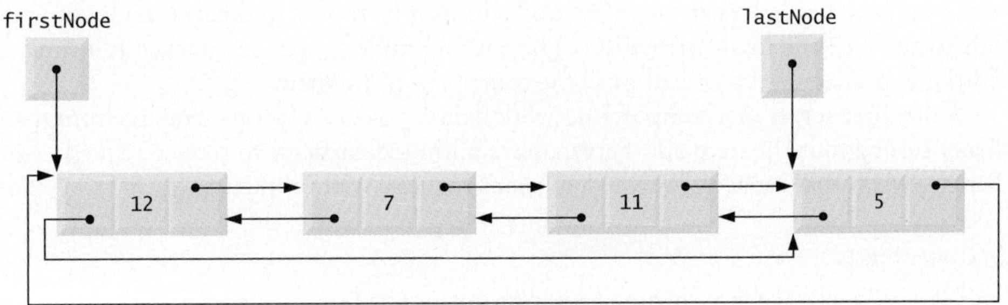

Fig. 24.4 | Circular, doubly linked list.

24.1.2 Stacks

A stack is a constrained version of a list—a stack adds new nodes and releases nodes only at the top. For this reason, a stack is referred to as a last-in, first-out (LIFO) data structure. The primary operations to manipulate a stack are push and pop. Operation push adds a new node to the top of the stack. Operation pop removes a node from the top of the stack and returns the data item from the popped node.

Stacks have many interesting applications. For example, when a program calls a method, the called method must know how to return to its caller, so the return address is pushed onto the method call stack by the system. If a series of method calls occurs, the successive return values are pushed onto the stack in last-in, first-out order, so that each method can return to its caller. Stacks support recursive method calls in the same manner that they do conventional nonrecursive method calls.

The `System.Collections.Generics` namespace contains class `Stack(Of T)` for implementing and manipulating stacks that can grow and shrink during program execution. We discuss our own generic class `Stack (Of T)` in Section 24.3.5.

24.1.3 Queues

Another commonly used data structure is the queue. A queue is similar to a checkout line in a supermarket—the cashier services the person at the beginning of the line first. Other customers, if they are polite, enter the line only at the end and wait for service. Queue nodes are removed only from the head (or front) of the queue and are inserted only at the tail (or end). For this reason, a queue is a first-in, first-out (FIFO) data structure. The insert and remove operations are known as enqueue and dequeue, respectively.

Queues have many uses in computer systems. A computer with a single processor can service only one application at a time. The operating system places each application requiring processor time in a queue. The application at the front of the queue is the next to receive service. Each application gradually advances to the front as the applications before it receive service.

Queues also support print spooling. For example, a single printer might be shared by all the users in a network. Many users can send print jobs to the printer, even when the printer is busy. An operating-system component, called a spooler, places these print jobs in a queue until the printer becomes available. As each print job completes, the spooler sends the next print job to the printer.

Information packets in computer networks, such as the Internet, also wait in queues. Each time a packet arrives at a network node, it must be routed to the next node along the path to the packet's final destination. The routing node routes one packet at a time, so additional packets are enqueued until the router can route them.

A database server in a computer network handles database-access requests from many clients throughout the network. Servers have a limited capacity to service requests from clients—when that capacity is exceeded, client requests wait in queues.

24.1.4 Trees

Linked lists, stacks and queues are linear data structures (i.e., sequences). A tree is a nonlinear, two-dimensional data structure. Tree nodes contain two or more links.

Basic Terminology

We now discuss binary trees (Fig. 24.5)—trees whose nodes all contain two links (none, one or both of which may be `Nothing`). The root node is the first node in a tree. Each link in the root node refers to a child. The left child is the first node in the left subtree, and the right child is the first node in the right subtree. The children of a specific node are

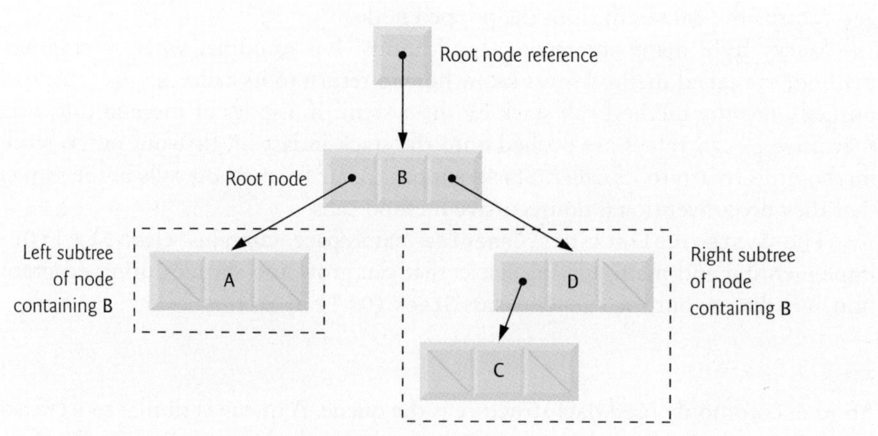

Fig. 24.5 | Binary-tree graphical representation.

called siblings. A node with no children is called a leaf node. Computer scientists normally draw trees from the root node down—exactly the opposite of the way trees naturally grow.

Binary Search Trees

A binary search tree (containing no duplicate node values) has the characteristic that the values in any left subtree are less than the value in the subtree's parent node, and the values in any right subtree are greater than the value in the subtree's parent node. Figure 24.6 illustrates a binary search tree with nine integer values. Note that the shape of the binary search tree that corresponds to a set of data can depend on the order in which the values are inserted into the tree.

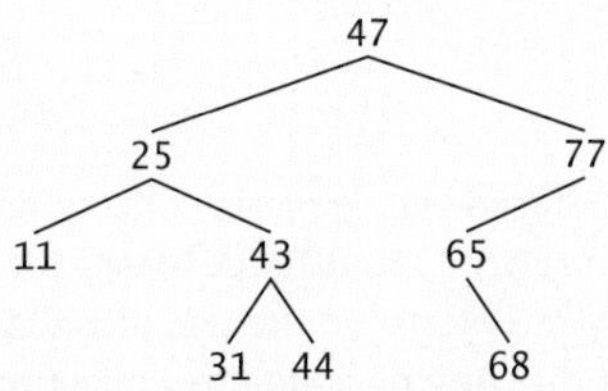

Fig. 24.6 | Binary search tree containing nine values.

Duplicate Elimination

The binary search tree facilitates duplicate elimination. While building a tree, the insertion operation recognizes attempts to insert a duplicate value, because a duplicate follows the same "go left" or "go right" decisions on each comparison as the original value did. Thus the insertion operation eventually compares the duplicate with a node containing the same value. At this point, the insertion operation simply discards the duplicate value.

24.2 Generic Collections Overview

Previously, programmers painstakingly created each element of each data structure dynamically with `New` and modified the data structures by directly manipulating their elements and references to their elements. Next, we consider the prepackaged data-structures classes provided by the .NET Framework. These classes are known as collection classes—they store collections of data. Each instance of one of these classes is a collection of items. Some examples of collections are the cards you hold in a card game, the songs stored in your computer, the real-estate records in your local registry of deeds (which map book numbers and page numbers to property owners), and the players on your favorite sports team.

Collection classes enable you to store sets of items by using existing data structures without concern for how they are implemented. This is a nice example of code reuse. You can code faster and expect excellent performance, maximizing execution speed and minimizing memory consumption. We discuss the collection interfaces that list the capabilities of each collection type and the implementation classes.

The .NET Framework provides three collections namespaces. The `System.Collections` namespace contains collections that store references to `Object`s. The **`System.Collections.Generic`** namespace contains generic classes that store collections of specified types. The **`System.Collections.Specialized`** namespace contains several collections that support specific types, such as Strings and bits. The collections in these namespaces provide standardized components that are written for broad reuse—you do not need to write your own collection classes.

Generic Collection Interfaces

All the generic collection classes in the .NET Framework implement some combination of the collection interfaces. These interfaces declare the operations to be performed on various types of generic collections. Figure 24.7 lists some of the generic interfaces of namespace System.Collections.Generic. Implementations of these interfaces are provided within the framework. You may also create your own custom implementations.

Interface	Description
ICollection(Of T)	The interface in the generic collections hierarchy from which interfaces IList(Of T) and IDictionary(Of T) inherit. Contains a Count property to determine the size of a generic collection and a CopyTo method for copying a generic collection's contents into a traditional array.
IList(Of T)	An ordered generic collection that can be manipulated like an array. Provides an indexer for accessing elements by position. Also has methods for modifying and searching a generic collection, including Add, Remove, Contains and IndexOf.
IDictionary(Of K, V))	A generic collection of values, indexed by arbitrary "keys." Provides an indexer for accessing elements by key and methods for modifying the collection (e.g., Add, Remove). Property Keys returns a collection of the keys in the Dictionary, and property Values returns a collection of the values in the Dictionary.
IEnumerable(Of T)	An object that supports iteration over a collection of elements (typically in a For Each statement). ICollection(Of T) implements IEnumerable(Of T), so all collection classes implement IEnumerable(Of T) directly or indirectly. Any class that implements IEnumerable(Of T) can be used as the data source in a LINQ query.

Fig. 24.7 | Some common collection interfaces.

Generic Collections

The System.Collections.Generic namespace contains generic classes that allow us to create collections of specific types. Figure 24.8 summarizes many of these generic collection classes. These collections allow you to specify the exact type to store. You then receive the benefits of compile-time type checking—the compiler ensures that you are using appropriate types with your generic collection and, if not, issues compile-time error messages. Also, once you specify the type stored in a generic collection, any item you retrieve from the generic collection will have the correct type. In the following subsections, we demonstrate three generic collection classes—LinkedList, Dictionary and SortedDictionary.

Class	Implements	Description
`System.Collections.Generic` namespace:		
`List(Of T)`	`IList(Of T)`	A generic array-based list. See Section 9.3.
`LinkedList(Of T)`	`ICollection(Of T)`	A generic doubly linked list. See Section 24.2.1.
`Stack(Of T)`	`ICollection(Of T)`	A generic last-in, first-out (LIFO) collection.
`Queue(Of T)`	`ICollection(Of T)`	A generic first-in, first-out (FIFO) collection.
`Dictionary(Of K, V)`	`IDictionary(Of K, V)`	A generic, unordered collection of key/value pairs that can be accessed by key. See Section 24.2.2.
`SortedDictionary (Of K, V)`	`IDictionary(Of K, V)`	A generic `Dictionary` that sorts data by the keys in a binary tree. See Section 24.2.3.
`SortedList(Of K, V)`	`IDictionary(Of K, V)`	A generic `Dictionary` that sorts data by keys in an array of key/value pairs. Values can be accessed either by key or by index.

[*Note: All collection classes directly or indirectly implement generic interfaces* `ICollection(Of T)` *and* `IEnumerable(Of T)`*).*]

Fig. 24.8 | Some generic collection classes of the .NET Framework.

Nongeneric Collections

The older collections from namespace `System.Collection` store and manipulate `Object` references. Any `Object` can be placed in such a collection. In fact, one collection could store objects of many different types, which typically is not necessary. One inconvenient aspect of storing `Object` references occurs when you access the elements in the collection. An application normally needs to process specific types of objects, so the `Object` references obtained from a collection typically need to be downcast to an appropriate type so you can invoke methods of that type.

Collections that store `Object` references can also store values of Visual Basic's primitive types. Each primitive type (see Appendix B, Primitive Types) has a corresponding `Structure` in namespace `System` that declares the primitive type. These `Structures` are called `Boolean`, `Byte`, `SByte`, `Char`, `Decimal`, `Double`, `Single`, `Int16`, `UInt16`, `Int32`, `UInt32`, `Int64` and `UInt64`. Types declared with keyword `Structure` are implicitly value types. Primitive types are actually aliases for their corresponding `Structures`, so a variable of a primitive type can be declared using the primitive type's keyword or the `Structure` name—e.g., `Integer` and `Int32` are interchangeable.

Boxing

All primitive-type `Structures` inherit from class `ValueType` (namespace `System`), which inherits from class `Object`. Thus, any primitive-type value can be assigned to an `Object` variable or stored in a collection of `Objects`. Assigning a primitive-type variable is referred to as boxing. With boxing, a primitive-type value is copied into an object so that the primitive-type value can be manipulated as an `Object`. Boxing can be performed either explicitly or implicitly, as shown in the following statements:

```
Dim i As Integer = 5 ' create an Integer value
Dim object1 As Object = _
   CType(i, Object) ' explicitly box the Integer value
Dim object2 As Object = i ' implicitly box the Integer value
```

After executing the preceding code, both `object1` and `object2` refer to two different objects that contain a copy of the value in `Integer` variable `i`.

Unboxing can be used to explicitly convert an `Object` reference to a primitive value, as shown in the following statement:

```
' explicitly unbox the Integer value
Dim int1 As Integer = CType(object1, Integer)
```

Explicitly attempting to unbox an `Object` reference that does not refer to the correct primitive value type causes an `InvalidCastException`. Boxing and unboxing can cause performance issues and should be avoided when unnecessary.

24.2.1 Generic Collection Class `LinkedList`

This chapter began our discussion of data structures with the concept of a linked list. We now discuss the .NET Framework's generic `LinkedList` class. This class is a doubly linked list—we can navigate it both backward and forward with nodes of generic class `LinkedListNode`. Each node contains property `Value` and read-only properties `Previous` and `Next`. The `Value` property's type matches `LinkedList`'s single type parameter, because it contains the data stored in the node. The `Previous` property gets a reference to the preceding node in the linked list (or `Nothing` if the node is the first in the list). Similarly, the `Next` property gets a reference to the subsequent reference in the linked list (or `Nothing` if the node is the last in the list). We demonstrate a few linked-list manipulations in Fig. 24.9.

```
' Fig. 24.9: LinkedListTest.vb
' Using LinkedLists.
Module LinkedListTest
   Private colors As String() = _
      {"black", "yellow", "green", "blue", "violet", "silver"}
   Private colors2 As String() = _
      {"gold", "white", "brown", "blue", "gray"}

   ' set up and manipulate LinkedList objects
   Sub Main()
      Dim list1 As New LinkedList(Of String)()

      ' add elements to first LinkedList
      For Each color In colors
         list1.AddLast(color)
      Next

```

Fig. 24.9 | Using `LinkedList`s. (Part 1 of 3.)

```
      ' add elements to second LinkedList via constructor
      Dim list2 As New LinkedList(Of String)(colors2)

      Concatenate(list1, list2) ' concatenate list2 onto list1
      PrintList(list1) ' print list1 elements

      Console.WriteLine(vbNewLine & _
         "Converting strings in list1 to uppercase" & vbNewLine)
      ToUppercaseStrings(list1) ' convert to uppercase string
      PrintList(list1) ' print list1 elements

      Console.WriteLine(vbNewLine & _
         "Deleting strings between BLACK and BROWN" & vbNewLine)
      RemoveItemsBetween(list1, "BLACK", "BROWN")

      PrintList(list1) ' print list1 elements
      Console.WriteLine()
      PrintReversedList(list1) ' print list in reverse order
   End Sub ' Main

   ' output list contents
   Private Sub PrintList(Of T)(ByVal list As LinkedList(Of T))
      Console.WriteLine("Linked list: ")

      For Each value In list
         Console.Write("{0} ", value)
      Next

      Console.WriteLine()
   End Sub ' PrintList

   ' concatenate the second list on the end of the first list
   Private Sub Concatenate(Of T)(ByVal list1 As LinkedList(Of T), _
      ByVal list2 As LinkedList(Of T))
      ' concatenate lists by copying element values
      ' in order from the second list to the first list
      For Each value In list2
         list1.AddLast(value) ' add new node
      Next
   End Sub ' Concatenate

   ' locate string objects and convert to uppercase
   Private Sub ToUppercaseStrings(ByVal list As LinkedList(Of String))
      ' iterate over the list by using the nodes
      Dim currentNode As LinkedListNode(Of String) = list.First

      While currentNode IsNot Nothing
         currentNode.Value = _
            currentNode.Value.ToUpper() ' convert to uppercase
         currentNode = currentNode.Next ' get next node
      End While
   End Sub ' ToUppercaseStrings

```

Fig. 24.9 | Using `LinkedList`s. (Part 2 of 3.)

```
71        ' delete list items between two given items
72        Private Sub RemoveItemsBetween(Of T)(ByVal list As LinkedList(Of T), _
73           ByVal startItem As T, ByVal endItem As T)
74           ' get the nodes corresponding to the start and end item
75           Dim currentNode As LinkedListNode(Of T) = list.Find(startItem)
76           Dim endNode As LinkedListNode(Of T) = list.Find(endItem)
77
78           ' remove items after the start item
79           ' until we find the last item or the end of the LinkedList
80           While currentNode.Next IsNot Nothing And _
81              Not currentNode.Next.Equals(endNode)
82              ' remove next node
83              list.Remove(currentNode.Next)
84           End While
85        End Sub ' RemoveItemsBetween
86
87        ' print reversed list
88        Private Sub PrintReversedList(Of T)(ByVal list As LinkedList(Of T))
89           Console.WriteLine("Reversed List:")
90
91           ' iterate over the list by using the nodes
92           Dim currentNode As LinkedListNode(Of T) = list.Last
93
94           While currentNode IsNot Nothing
95              Console.Write("{0} ", currentNode.Value)
96              currentNode = currentNode.Previous ' get previous node
97           End While
98
99           Console.WriteLine()
100       End Sub ' PrintReversedList
101    End Module ' LinkedListTest
```

```
Linked list:
black yellow green blue violet silver gold white brown blue gray

Converting strings in list1 to uppercase

Linked list:
BLACK YELLOW GREEN BLUE VIOLET SILVER GOLD WHITE BROWN BLUE GRAY

Deleting strings between BLACK and BROWN

Linked list:
BLACK BROWN BLUE GRAY

Reversed List:
GRAY BLUE BROWN BLACK
```

Fig. 24.9 | Using `LinkedLists`. (Part 3 of 3.)

Lines 11–19 create `LinkedLists` `list1` and `list2` of `Strings` and fill them with the contents of arrays `colors` and `colors2`, respectively. This example uses the type argument `String` for class `LinkedList`'s type parameter (lines 11 and 19). We demonstrate two ways to fill the lists. Lines 14–16 use the `For Each` statement and method **`AddLast`** to fill `list1`. The `AddLast` method creates a new `LinkedListNode` and appends it to the end of the list.

There is also an `AddFirst` method that inserts a node at the beginning of the list. Line 19 invokes the `LinkedList` constructor that takes a parameter of type `IEnumerable(Of String)`. All arrays implicitly inherit from the generic interfaces `IList` and `IEnumerable` with the type of the array as the type argument, so the `String` array `colors2` implements `IEnumerable(Of String)`. The type parameter of this generic `IEnumerable` matches the type parameter of the generic `LinkedList` object. This constructor call (line 19) copies the contents of the array `colors2` to `list2`.

`Concatenate` *method*

Line 21 calls generic method `Concatenate` (lines 50–57) to append all elements of `list2` to the end of `list1`. Line 22 calls method `PrintList` (lines 39–47) to output `list1`'s contents. Line 26 calls method `ToUppercaseStrings` (lines 60–69) to convert each `String` element to uppercase, then line 27 calls `PrintList` again to display the modified `String`s. Line 31 calls method `RemoveItemsBetween` (lines 72–85) to remove the elements between `"BLACK"` and `"BROWN"`, but not including either. Line 33 outputs the list again, then line 35 invokes method `PrintReversedList` (lines 88–100) to print the list in reverse order.

Generic method `Concatenate` (lines 50–57) iterates over `list2` with a `For Each` statement and calls method `AddLast` to append each value to the end of `list1`. The loop iterates through the elements of the `LinkedList` to obtain the value in each node. The loop creates a new node in `list1` for each node in `list2`. One `LinkedListNode` cannot be a member of more than one `LinkedList`. Any attempt to add a node from one `LinkedList` to another generates an `InvalidOperationException`. If you want the same data to belong to more than one `LinkedList`, you must make a copy of the node for each list. Generic method `PrintList` (lines 39–47) also uses a `For Each` statement to iterate over the values in a `LinkedList` and output them.

`ToUppercaseStrings` *method*

Method `ToUppercaseStrings` (lines 60–69) takes a linked list of `String`s and converts each `String` to uppercase. This method replaces the `String`s stored in the list, so we cannot use a `For Each` statement as in the preceding two methods. Recall that `For Each` cannot be used to modify the elements in a collection. In this case, we cannot replace a `String` in the collection with an uppercase `String`. Instead, we obtain the first `LinkedListNode` via the `First` property (line 62), then loop through the list (lines 64–68). Each iteration of the loop obtains and updates the contents of `currentNode` via property `Value`, using `String` method `ToUpper` to create an uppercase version of the `String`. At the end of each iteration, we move the current node to the next node in the list by assigning to `currentNode` the node obtained by its own `Next` property (line 67). The `Next` property of the last node of the list returns `Nothing`, so when the loop iterates past the end of the list, the loop exits.

Note that we did not declare `ToUppercaseStrings` as a generic method, because it uses the `String`-specific methods of the values in the nodes. Methods `PrintList` (lines 39–47) and `Concatenate` (lines 50–57) do not need to use any `String`-specific methods, so they can be declared with generic type parameters to promote maximal code reuse.

`RemoveItemsBetween` *method*

Generic method `RemoveItemsBetween` (lines 72–85) removes a range of items between two nodes. Lines 75–76 obtain the two "boundary" nodes of the range by using method `Find`. This method performs a linear search and returns the first node that contains a value equal to the passed argument. Method `Find` returns `Nothing` if the value is not found. We store the node preceding the range in local variable `currentNode` and the node following the range in `endNode`.

The loop in lines 80–84 removes all the elements between `currentNode` and `endNode`. On each iteration of the loop, we remove the node following `currentNode` by invoking method `Remove` (line 83). Method `Remove` takes a `LinkedListNode`, deletes that node from the `LinkedList` and fixes the references of the surrounding nodes. During the `Remove` call, `currentNode`'s `Next` property is assigned the node *following* the removed node, and that node's `Previous` property is assigned `currentNode`. The loop continues until there are no nodes left between `currentNode` and `endNode`, or until `currentNode` is the last node in the list. (There is also an overloaded version of method `Remove` that performs a linear search for the specified value and removes the first node in the list that contains it.)

`PrintReversedList` method

Method `PrintReversedList` (lines 88–100) prints the list backward by navigating the nodes manually. Line 92 obtains the last element of the list via the `Last` property and stores it in `currentNode`. The loop in lines 94–97 iterates through the list backward by moving the `currentNode` reference to the previous node at the end of each iteration, then exits when it moves past the beginning of the list. Note how similar this code is to lines 64–68, which iterated through the list from the beginning to the end.

24.2.2 Generic Collection Class `Dictionary`

When an application creates objects, it needs to manage them efficiently. This includes storing and retrieving objects. Storing and retrieving information with arrays is efficient if some aspect of your data directly matches the key value and if the keys are unique and tightly packed. If you have 100 employees with nine-digit social security numbers and you want to store and retrieve employee data by using the social security number as a key, it would nominally require an array with 999,999,999 elements, because there are 999,999,999 unique nine-digit numbers. If you had an array that large, you could get very high performance storing and retrieving employee records by simply using the social security number as the array index, but it would be a massive waste of memory. Many applications have this problem—either the keys are of the wrong type (i.e., not nonnegative integers), or they are of the right type but are sparsely spread over a large range.

Hashing and Collisions

What is needed is a high-speed scheme for converting keys such as social security numbers and inventory part numbers to unique array indices. Then, when an application needs to store something, the scheme could convert the application key rapidly to an index, and the record of information could be stored at that location in the array. Retrieval occurs the same way—once the application has a key for which it wants to retrieve the data record, the application simply applies the conversion to the key, which produces the array subscript where the data resides in the array and retrieves the data.

The scheme we describe here is the basis of a technique called hashing, in which we store data in a data structure called a dictionary (often called a hash table). Why the name? Because, when we convert a key into an array subscript, we literally scramble the bits, making a "hash" of the number. The number actually has no real significance beyond its usefulness in storing and retrieving this particular data record.

A glitch in the scheme occurs when collisions occur (i.e., two different keys "hash into" the same cell, or element, in the array). Since we cannot store two different data records in the same space, we need to find an alternative home for all records beyond the first that hash to a particular array subscript. One scheme for doing this is to "hash again" (i.e., to reapply the hashing transformation to the key to provide a next candidate cell in the array). The hashing process is designed to distribute keys throughout the `Dictionary`—it is assumed that an available cell will be found with just a few hashes.

Another scheme uses one hash to locate the first candidate cell. If the cell is occupied, successive cells are searched linearly until an available cell is found. Retrieval works the same way—the key is hashed once, and the resulting cell is checked to determine whether it contains the desired data. If it does, the search is complete. If it does not, successive cells are searched linearly until the desired data is found.

The most popular solution to dictionary collisions is to have each cell of the table be a hash "bucket"—typically, a linked list of all the key/value pairs that hash to that cell. This is the solution that the generic `Dictionary` class implements.

The load factor affects the performance of hashing schemes. The load factor is the ratio of the number of objects stored in the dictionary to the total number of cells of the hash table. As this ratio gets higher, the chance of collisions increases.

Performance Tip 24.6

The load factor in a dictionary is a classic example of a space/time trade-off: By increasing the load factor, we get better memory utilization, but owing to increased hashing collisions the application runs slower. By decreasing the load factor, we get better application speed because of reduced hashing collisions, but we get poorer memory utilization because a larger portion of the dictionary remains empty.

Class `Dictionary`

The .NET Framework provides class `Dictionary` to enable you to easily employ hashing in applications. A hash function performs a calculation that determines where to place data in the dictionary. The hash function is applied to the key in a key/value pair of objects. Class `Dictionary` can accept any `Object` as a key. For this reason, class `Object` defines method `GetHashCode`, which all classes inherit. Most classes that are candidates to be used as keys in a dictionary override this method to provide one that performs efficient hash-code calculations for a specific type. For example, a `String` has a hash-code calculation that is based on the contents of the `String`. Figure 24.10 uses a `Dictionary` to count the number of occurrences of each word in a `String`.

```
' Fig. 24.10: DictionaryTest.vb
' Application counts the number of occurrences of each word in a String
' and stores them in a dictionary.
Module DictionaryTest
   Sub Main()
      ' create dictionary based on user input
      Dim table As Dictionary(Of String, Integer) = CollectWords()

```

Fig. 24.10 | Application counts the number of occurrences of each word in a `String` and stores this information in a dictionary. (Part 1 of 3.)

```
      ' display dictionary content
      DisplayDictionary(table)
   End Sub ' Main

   ' create dictionary from user input
   Private Function CollectWords() As Dictionary(Of String, Integer)
      ' create a new dictionary
      Dim table As New Dictionary(Of String, Integer)

      Console.WriteLine("Enter a string: ") ' prompt for user input
      Dim input As String = Console.ReadLine() ' get input

      ' split input text into tokens (words)
      Dim words As String() = input.Split()

      ' processing input words
      For Each word In words
         Dim wordKey As String = word.ToLower() ' get word in lowercase

         ' if the dictionary contains the word
         If table.ContainsKey(wordKey) Then
            table(wordKey) = table(wordKey) + 1
         Else
            ' add new word with a count of 1 to dictionary
            table.Add(wordKey, 1)
         End If
      Next

      Return table
   End Function ' CollectWords

   ' display dictionary content
   Private Sub DisplayDictionary( _
      ByVal table As Dictionary(Of String, Integer))
      Console.WriteLine(vbNewLine & "Dictionary contains:" & _
         vbNewLine & "{0,-12}{1,-12}", "Key:", "Value:")

      ' generate output for each key in dictionary by
      ' iterating through the Keys property with a For Each statement
      For Each key In table.Keys
         Console.WriteLine("{0,-12}{1,-12}", key, table(key))
      Next

      Console.WriteLine(vbNewLine & "size: {0}", table.Count)
   End Sub ' DisplayDictionary
End Module ' DictionaryTest
```

```
Enter a string:
As idle as a painted ship upon a painted ocean
```

Fig. 24.10 | Application counts the number of occurrences of each word in a `String` and stores this information in a dictionary. (Part 2 of 3.)

```
Dictionary contains:
Key:        Value:
as          2
idle        1
a           2
painted     2
ship        1
upon        1
ocean       1

size: 7
```

Fig. 24.10 | Application counts the number of occurrences of each word in a `String` and stores this information in a dictionary. (Part 3 of 3.)

Class `DictionaryTest` declares three methods. Method `CollectWords` (lines 14–38) inputs a `String` and returns a `Dictionary` in which each value stores the number of times that word appears in the `String` and the word is used as the key. Method `DisplayDictionary` (lines 41–53) displays in column format the `Dictionary` passed to it. The `Main` method (lines 5–11) invokes `CollectWords` (line 7), then passes the `Dictionary` returned by `CollectWords` to `DisplayDictionary` (line 10).

Method `CollectWords` (lines 14–38) initializes local variable `table` with a new `Dictionary` (line 16). Lines 18–19 prompt the user and input a `String`. We use `String` method `Split` in line 22 to divide the `String` into words. This creates an array of "words," which we then store in local variable `words`.

The `For Each` statement in lines 25–35 iterates through the elements of array `words`. Each word is converted to lowercase with `String` method `ToLower`, then stored in variable `wordKey` (line 26). Line 29 calls `Dictionary` method **`ContainsKey`** to determine whether the word is in the dictionary (and thus has occurred previously in the `String`). If the `Dictionary` does not contain an entry for the word, line 33 uses `Dictionary` method `Add` to create a new entry in the dictionary, with the lowercase word as the key and an object containing `1` as the value.

Common Programming Error 24.1

Using the `Add` method to add a key that already exists in the dictionary causes an `ArgumentException`.

If the word is already a key in the dictionary, line 30 uses the `Dictionary`'s indexer to obtain and set the key's associated value (the word count) in the dictionary. We then increment the value by 1 and use the indexer to store the key's associated value.

Invoking the `Get` accessor of a `Dictionary` indexer with a key that does not exist in the dictionary throws a `KeyNotFoundException`. Using the `Set` accessor with a key that does not exist in the dictionary creates a new entry, as if you had used the `Add` method.

Line 37 returns the dictionary to the `Main` method, which then passes it to method `DisplayDictionary` (lines 41–53), which displays all the entries. This method uses read-only property **`Keys`** (line 48) to get an `ICollection` that contains all the keys. Because `ICollection` extends `IEnumerable`, we can use this collection in the `For Each` statement in lines 48–50 to iterate over the keys of the dictionary. This loop accesses and outputs each key and its value in a field width of `-12`. The negative field width indicates that the output should be left justified. Note that a dictionary is not sorted, so the key/value pairs are not displayed in any particular order. Line 52 uses `Dictionary` property **`Count`** to get the number of key/value pairs in the `Dictionary`.

Lines 48–50 could also have used the `For Each` statement with the `Dictionary` object itself, rather than the `Keys` property. If you use a `For Each` statement with a `Dictionary` object, the iteration variable will be of type **`KeyValuePair`**, which has properties `Key` and `Value` for retrieving the key and value of the current element. If you do not need the key, class `Dictionary` also provides a read-only **`Values`** property that gets an `ICollection` of all the values stored in the `Dictionary`.

24.2.3 Generic Collection Class SortedDictionary

A **dictionary** is the general term for a collection of key/value pairs. A hash table is one way to implement a dictionary. The .NET Framework provides several implementations of dictionaries. Each implements a version of the `IDictionary` interface (Fig. 24.7). The application in Fig. 24.11 is a modification of Fig. 24.10 that uses the generic class **`SortedDictionary`**. Generic class `SortedDictionary` stores its key/value pairs in a binary search tree. We discussed binary trees in Section 24.1.4. As the class name suggests, the entries in `SortedDictionary` are sorted in the tree by key. When the key implements generic interface `IComparable`, the `SortedDictionary` uses the results of `IComparable` method `CompareTo` to sort the keys. Notice in the output of Fig. 24.11 that the keys are in alphabetical order. Note that, despite these implementation details, we use the same `Public` methods, properties and indexers with classes `Dictionary` and `SortedDictionary` in the same ways. Fig. 24.11 looks remarkably similar to Fig. 24.10. That is the beauty of object-oriented programming.

```
' Fig. 24.11: SortedDictionaryTest.vb
' Application counts the number of occurrences of each word in a String
' and stores them in a generic sorted dictionary.
Module SortedDictionaryTest
   Sub Main()
      ' create sorted dictionary based on user input
      Dim dictionary As SortedDictionary(Of String, Integer) = _
         CollectWords()

      ' display sorted dictionary content
      DisplayDictionary(dictionary)
   End Sub ' Main

   ' create sorted dictionary from user input
   Private Function CollectWords() As SortedDictionary( _
      Of String, Integer)
      ' create a new sorted dictionary
      Dim dictionary As New SortedDictionary(Of String, Integer)()
```

Fig. 24.11 | Application counts the number of occurrences of each word in a `String` and stores them in a generic sorted dictionary. (Part 1 of 2.)

```

      Console.WriteLine("Enter a string: ") ' prompt for user input
      Dim input As String = Console.ReadLine() ' get input

      ' split input text into tokens
      Dim words As String() = input.Split()

      ' processing input words
      For Each word In words
         Dim wordKey As String = word.ToLower() ' get word in lowercase

         ' if the dictionary contains the word
         If dictionary.ContainsKey(wordKey) Then
            dictionary(wordKey) += 1
         Else
            ' add new word with a count of 1 to the dictionary
            dictionary.Add(wordKey, 1)
         End If
      Next

      Return dictionary
   End Function ' CollectWords

   ' display dictionary content
   Private Sub DisplayDictionary(Of K, V)( _
      ByVal dictionary As SortedDictionary(Of K, V))

      Console.WriteLine(vbNewLine & "Sorted dictionary contains:" _
         & vbNewLine & "{0,-12}{1,-12}", "Key:", "Value:")

      ' generate output for each key in the sorted dictionary
      ' by iterating through the Keys property with a For Each statement
      For Each key In dictionary.Keys
         Console.WriteLine("{0,-12}{1,-12}", key, dictionary(key))
      Next

      Console.WriteLine(vbNewLine & "size: {0}", dictionary.Count)
   End Sub ' DisplayDictionary
End Module ' SortedDictionaryTest
```

```
Enter a string:
we few, we happy few, we band of brothers

Sorted dictionary contains:
Key:        Value:
band        1
brothers    1
few,        2
happy       1
of          1
we          3

size: 6
```

Fig. 24.11 | Application counts the number of occurrences of each word in a `String` and stores them in a generic sorted dictionary. (Part 2 of 2.)

The generic class `SortedDictionary` takes two type arguments—the first specifies the type of key (i.e., `String`), and the second specifies the type of value (i.e., `Integer`). Method `DisplayDictionary` (lines 43–56) takes type parameters `K` and `V`. These parameters are used in line 44 to indicate that `DisplayDictionary` takes a `SortedDictionary` with keys of type `K` and values of type `V`. This use of generics is a marvelous example of code reuse. If we decided to change the application to count the number of times each character appeared in a `String`, method `DisplayDictionary` could receive an argument of type `SortedDictionary(Of Char, Integer)` without modification. This is precisely what you will do in Exercise 24.12.

Common Programming Error 24.2

Invoking the `Get` accessor of a `SortedDictionary` indexer with a key that does not exist in the collection causes a `KeyNotFoundException`.

24.3 Generic Classes and Methods

.NET's nongeneric collections store and manipulate `Object` references. You could store any `Object` in these data structures. One inconvenient aspect of storing `Object` references occurs when retrieving them from a collection. An application normally needs to process specific types of objects. As a result, the `Object` references obtained from a collection typically need to be downcast to an appropriate type to allow the application to process the objects correctly. In addition, data of value types (e.g., `Integer` and `Double`) must be boxed to be manipulated with `Object` references, which increases the overhead of processing such data. Also, processing all data as type `Object` limits the Visual Basic compiler's ability to perform type checking.

Though we can easily create data structures that manipulate any type of data as `Object`s, it would be nice if we could detect type mismatches at compile time—this is known as compile-time type safety. For example, if a `Stack` should store only `Integer` values, attempting to push a `String` onto that `Stack` should cause a compile-time error. Similarly, a `Sort` method should be able to compare elements that are all guaranteed to have the same type. If we created type-specific versions of class `Stack` and method `Sort`, the Visual Basic compiler would certainly be able to ensure compile-time type safety. However, this would require that we create many copies of the same basic code.

Generics provide the means to create the general models mentioned above. Generic methods enable you to specify a set of related methods with a single method declaration. Generic classes enable you to specify a set of related classes with a single class declaration. Similarly, generic interfaces enable you to specify a set of related interfaces with a single interface declaration. Generics provide compile-time type safety. [*Note:* You can also implement generic `Structure`s and `Delegate`s. For more information, see the Visual Basic Language Specification 9.0, available at `go.microsoft.com/fwlink/?LinkId=102846`.]

We can write a generic method for sorting an array of objects, then invoke the generic method separately with an `Integer` array, a `Double` array, a `String` array and so on, to sort each type of array. The compiler performs type checking to ensure that the array passed to the sorting method contains only elements of the same type. We can write a single generic `Stack` class that manipulates a stack of objects, then instantiate `Stack` objects for a stack of `Integer`s, a stack of `Double`s, a stack of `String`s and so on. The compiler performs type checking to ensure that the `Stack` stores only elements of the same type.

24.3.1 Motivation for Generic Methods

Overloaded methods are often used to perform similar operations on different types of data. To motivate the concept of generic methods, let's begin with an example (Fig. 24.12) that contains three overloaded `PrintArray` methods (lines 19–25, 28–34 and 37–43). These methods display the elements of an `Integer` array, a `Double` array and a `Char` array, respectively. In Section 24.3.2, we reimplement this program more concisely and elegantly, using a single generic method.

```
1  ' Fig. 24.12: OverloadedMethods.vb
2  ' Using overloaded methods to print arrays of different types.
3  Module OverloadedMethods
4     Sub Main()
5        ' create arrays of Integer, Double and Char types
6        Dim integerArray As Integer() = {1, 2, 3, 4, 5, 6}
7        Dim doubleArray As Double() = {1.1, 2.2, 3.3, 4.4, 5.5, 6.6, 7.7}
8        Dim charArray As Char() = {"H"c, "E"c, "L"c, "L"c, "O"c}
9
10       Console.WriteLine("Array integerArray contains:")
11       PrintArray(integerArray) ' pass an Integer array argument
12       Console.WriteLine("Array doubleArray contains:")
13       PrintArray(doubleArray) ' pass a Double array argument
14       Console.WriteLine("Array charArray contains:")
15       PrintArray(charArray) ' pass a Char array
16    End Sub ' Main
17
18    ' output Integer array
19    Sub PrintArray(ByVal inputArray() As Integer)
20       For Each element In inputArray
21          Console.Write(element.ToString() & " ")
22       Next
23
24       Console.WriteLine(vbNewLine)
25    End Sub ' PrintArray
26
27    ' output Double array
28    Sub PrintArray(ByVal inputArray() As Double)
29       For Each element In inputArray
30          Console.Write(element.ToString() & " ")
31       Next
32
33       Console.WriteLine(vbNewLine)
34    End Sub ' PrintArray
```

Fig. 24.12 | Displaying arrays of different types using overloaded methods. (Part 1 of 2.)

```
35
36      ' output Char array
37      Sub PrintArray(ByVal inputArray() As Char)
38         For Each element In inputArray
39            Console.Write(element.ToString() & " ")
40         Next
41
42         Console.WriteLine(vbNewLine)
43      End Sub ' PrintArray
44   End Module ' OverloadedMethods
```

```
Array integerArray contains:
1 2 3 4 5 6

Array doubleArray contains:
1.1 2.2 3.3 4.4 5.5 6.6 7.7

Array charArray contains:
H E L L O
```

Fig. 24.12 | Displaying arrays of different types using overloaded methods. (Part 2 of 2.)

The program begins by declaring and initializing three arrays—six-element `Integer` array `integerArray` (line 6), seven-element `Double` array `doubleArray` (line 7) and five-element `Char` array `charArray` (line 8). Then lines 10–15 output the arrays.

When the compiler encounters a method call, it attempts to locate a method declaration that has the same method name and parameters that match the argument types in the method call. In this example, each `PrintArray` call exactly matches one of the `PrintArray` method declarations. For example, line 11 calls `PrintArray` with `integerArray` as its argument. At compile time, the compiler determines argument `integerArray`'s type (i.e., `Integer()`), attempts to locate a method named `PrintArray` that specifies a single `Integer()` parameter (which it finds in lines 19–25) and sets up a call to that method. Similarly, when the compiler encounters the `PrintArray` call in line 13, it determines argument `doubleArray`'s type (i.e., `Double()`), then attempts to locate a method named `PrintArray` that specifies a single `Double()` parameter (which it finds in lines 28–34) and sets up a call to that method. Finally, when the compiler encounters the `PrintArray` call in line 15, it determines argument `charArray`'s type (i.e., `Char()`), then attempts to locate a method named `PrintArray` that specifies a single `Char()` parameter (which it finds in lines 37–43) and sets up a call to that method.

Study each `PrintArray` method. Note that the array element type (`Integer`, `Double` or `Char`) appears in two locations in each method—the method header (lines 19, 28 and 37) and the `For Each` statement header (lines 20, 29 and 38). If we replace the element type in each method with a generic name—we chose `T` to represent the element type—then all three methods would look like the one in Fig. 24.13. It appears that if we can replace the array element type in each of the three methods with a single "generic type parameter," then we should be able to declare one `PrintArray` method that can display the elements of *any* array. The method in Fig. 24.13 will not compile because its syntax is not correct—we declare a generic `PrintArray` method with the proper syntax in Fig. 24.14.

```
Public Sub PrintArray(ByVal inputArray() As T)
   For Each element In inputArray
      Console.Write(element.ToString() & " ")
   Next

   Console.WriteLine(vbNewLine)
End Sub ' PrintArray
```

Fig. 24.13 | `PrintArray` method in which actual type names are replaced by convention with the generic name `T` (for "type").

24.3.2 Generic-Method Implementation

The overloaded methods of Fig. 24.12 can be more compactly and conveniently coded using a single generic method. You can write a single generic-method declaration that can be called at different times with arguments of different types. Based on the types of the arguments passed to the generic method, the compiler handles each method call appropriately.

Figure 24.14 reimplements the application of Fig. 24.12 using a single generic `PrintArray` method (lines 19–25). Note that the `PrintArray` method calls in lines 11, 13 and 15 are identical to those in Fig. 24.12, the outputs of the two applications are identical and the code in Fig. 24.14 is 18 lines shorter than the code in Fig. 24.12. As illustrated in Fig. 24.14, generics enable us to create and test our code once, then reuse the code for many different types of data. This demonstrates the expressive power of generics.

```
1  ' Fig. 24.14: GenericMethod.vb
2  ' Using overloaded methods to print arrays of different types.
3  Module GenericMethod
4     Sub Main()
5        ' create arrays of Integer, Double and Char types
6        Dim integerArray As Integer() = {1, 2, 3, 4, 5, 6}
7        Dim doubleArray As Double() = {1.1, 2.2, 3.3, 4.4, 5.5, 6.6, 7.7}
8        Dim charArray As Char() = {"H"c, "E"c, "L"c, "L"c, "O"c}
9
10       Console.WriteLine("Array integerArray contains:")
11       PrintArray(integerArray) ' pass an Integer array argument
12       Console.WriteLine("Array doubleArray contains:")
13       PrintArray(doubleArray) ' pass a Double array argument
14       Console.WriteLine("Array charArray contains:")
15       PrintArray(charArray) ' pass a Char array argument
16    End Sub ' Main
17
18    ' outputs array of any type
19    Public Sub PrintArray(Of T)(ByVal inputArray() As T)
20       For Each element In inputArray
21          Console.Write(element.ToString() & " ")
22       Next
23
24       Console.WriteLine(vbNewLine)
25    End Sub ' PrintArray
26 End Module ' GenericMethod
```

Fig. 24.14 | Printing array elements using generic method `PrintArray`. (Part 1 of 2.)

```
Array integerArray contains:
1 2 3 4 5 6

Array doubleArray contains:
1.1 2.2 3.3 4.4 5.5 6.6 7.7

Array charArray contains:
H E L L O
```

Fig. 24.14 | Printing array elements using generic method `PrintArray`. (Part 2 of 2.)

Line 19 begins method `PrintArray`'s declaration. All generic-method declarations have a type-parameter list delimited by parentheses—`(Of T)` in this example—that follows the method's name. Each type-parameter list begins with the keyword `Of` and contains one or more type parameters separated by commas. A type parameter is an identifier that is used in place of actual type names. The type parameters can be used to declare the return type, the parameter types and the local variable types in a generic-method declaration; the type parameters act as placeholders for the types of the arguments passed to the generic method. A generic method's body is declared like that of any other method. Note that the type-parameter names throughout the method declaration must match those declared in the type-parameter list. Also, a type parameter can be declared only once in the type-parameter list but can appear more than once in the method's parameter list. Type-parameter names need not be unique among different generic methods.

Common Programming Error 24.3

If you forget to include the type-parameter list when declaring a generic method, the compiler will not recognize the type-parameter names when they are encountered in the method. This results in compilation errors.

`PrintArray`'s type-parameter list (line 19) declares type parameter `T` as the placeholder for the array-element type that `PrintArray` will output. Note that `T` appears in the method's parameter list as the array-element type (line 19). The `For Each` statement header (line 20) also uses `T` as the `element` type. These are the same two locations where the overloaded `PrintArray` methods of Fig. 24.12 specified `Integer`, `Double` or `Char` as the array-element type. The remainder of `PrintArray` is identical to the version in Fig. 24.12.

Good Programming Practice 24.1

According to `msdn.microsoft.com/en-us/library/aa479858.aspx`, it is recommended that type parameters be specified as individual capital letters. Typically, a type parameter that represents the type of an element in an array (or other collection) is named `T` for "type" or `E` for "element."

As in Fig. 24.12, the program in Fig. 24.14 begins by declaring and initializing six-element `Integer` array `integerArray` (line 6), seven-element `Double` array `doubleArray` (line 7) and five-element `Char` array `charArray` (line 8). Then each array is output by calling `PrintArray` (lines 11, 13 and 15)—once with argument `integerArray`, once with argument `doubleArray` and once with argument `charArray`.

When the compiler encounters a method call, such as line 11, it analyzes the set of methods (both nongeneric and generic) that might match the method call, looking for a method that matches the call exactly. If there are no exact matches, the compiler picks the best match. If there are no matching methods, or if there is more than one best match, the compiler generates an error. The complete details of method-call resolution can be found in Section 11.8.1 of the *Visual Basic Language Specification 9.0*, available at `http://go.microsoft.com/fwlink/?LinkId=102846`.

For line 11, the compiler determines that an exact match occurs if the type parameter `T` in lines 19 and 20 of method `PrintArray`'s declaration is replaced with the type of the elements in the method call's argument `integerArray` (i.e., `Integer`). Then the compiler sets up a call to `PrintArray` with `Integer` as the type argument for the type parameter `T`. This is known as the type-inferencing process. The same process is repeated for the calls to method `PrintArray` in lines 13 and 15.

Common Programming Error 24.4

If the compiler cannot find a single nongeneric or generic method declaration that is a best match for a method call, or if there are multiple best matches, a compilation error occurs.

You can also use explicit type arguments to indicate the exact type that should be used to call a generic function. For example, line 11 could be written as

```
PrintArray(Of Integer)(integerArray) ' call Integer version
```

In the preceding method call, the first set of parentheses contains the explicit type argument `Integer` that should be used to replace type parameter `T` in lines 19 and 20 of method `PrintArray`'s declaration.

The compiler also determines whether the operations performed on the method's type parameters can be applied to elements of the type stored in the array argument. The only operation performed on the array elements in this example is to output the `String` representation of the elements. Line 21 calls `ToString` on the current array element being processed. Since all objects have a `ToString` method, the compiler is satisfied that line 21 performs a valid operation for any array element.

By declaring `PrintArray` as a generic method in Fig. 24.14, we eliminated the need for the overloaded methods of Fig. 24.12, saving 18 lines of code and creating a reusable method that can output the string representations of the elements of *any* array, not just arrays of `Integer`, `Double` or `Char` elements.

24.3.3 Type Constraints

In this section, we present a generic `Maximum` method that determines and returns the largest of its three arguments (all of the same type). The generic method in this example uses the type parameter to declare both the method's return type and its parameters. Normally, when comparing values to determine which one is greater, you would use the > operator. However, this operator is not overloaded for use with every type that is built into the .NET Framework Class Library or that might be defined by extending those types. Generic code is restricted to performing operations that are guaranteed to work for every possible type. Thus, an expression like `variable1 < variable2` is not allowed unless the compiler can ensure that the operator < is provided for every type that will ever be used in the generic code. Similarly, you cannot call a method on a generic-type variable unless the compiler can ensure that all types that will ever be used in the generic code support that method.

`IComparable(Of T)` Interface

It is possible to compare two objects of the same type if that type implements the generic interface `IComparable(Of T)` from namespace `System`. A benefit of implementing this interface is that `IComparable(Of T)` objects can be used with the sorting and searching methods of classes in the `System.Collections.Generic` namespace. The structures in the .NET framework that correspond to the primitive types (such as `Int32` for primitive type `Integer`) all implement this interface. Types that implement `IComparable(Of T)` must declare a `CompareTo` method for comparing objects. For example, if we have two `Integers`, `integer1` and `integer2`, they can be compared with the expression:

```
integer1.CompareTo(integer2)
```

Method `CompareTo` must return `0` if the objects are equal, a negative integer if `integer1` is less than `integer2` or a positive integer if `integer1` is greater than `integer2`. It is the responsibility of the programmer who declares a type that implements `IComparable(Of T)` to declare method `CompareTo` such that it compares the contents of two objects of that type and returns the appropriate result.

Specifying Type Constraints

Even though `IComparable` objects can be compared, they cannot be used with generic code by default, because not all types implement interface `IComparable(Of T)`. We can, however, restrict the types that can be used with a generic method or class to ensure that they meet certain requirements. This feature—known as a type constraint—limits the type arguments that can be supplied to a particular type parameter. Figure 24.15 declares method `Maximum` with a type constraint (line 16) that requires each of the method's arguments to be of type `IComparable(Of T)`. This restriction is important, because not all objects can be compared. However, all `IComparable(Of T)` objects are guaranteed to have a `CompareTo` method that can be used in method `Maximum` to determine the largest of its three arguments.

```
1  ' Fig. 24.15: MaximumTest.vb
2  ' Generic method Maximum with a type constraint on its type parameter.
3  Module MaximumTest
4     Sub Main()
5        Console.WriteLine("Maximum of {0}, {1} and {2} is {3}" & _
6           vbNewLine, 3, 4, 5, Maximum(3, 4, 5))
7        Console.WriteLine("Maximum of {0}, {1} and {2} is {3}" & _
8           vbNewLine, 6.6, 8.8, 7.7, Maximum(6.6, 8.8, 7.7))
9        Console.WriteLine("Maximum of {0}, {1} and {2} is {3}" & _
10          vbNewLine, "pear", "apple", "orange", _
11          Maximum("pear", "apple", "orange"))
12    End Sub ' Main
13
14    ' generic function determines the
15    ' largest of the IComparable objects
16    Public Function Maximum(Of T As IComparable(Of T)) _
17       (ByVal x As T, ByVal y As T, ByVal z As T) As T
```

Fig. 24.15 | Generic method `Maximum` with a type constraint on its type parameter. (Part 1 of 2.)

```
18          Dim max As T = x ' assume x is initially the largest
19
20          ' compare y with max
21          If y.CompareTo(max) > 0 Then
22             max = y ' y is the largest so far
23          End If
24
25          ' compare z with max
26          If z.CompareTo(max) > 0 Then
27             max = z ' z is the largest
28          End If
29
30          Return max ' return largest object
31       End Function ' Maximum
32    End Module ' MaximumTest
```

```
Maximum of 3, 4 and 5 is 5

Maximum of 6.6, 8.8 and 7.7 is 8.8

Maximum of pear, apple and orange is pear
```

Fig. 24.15 | Generic method `Maximum` with a type constraint on its type parameter. (Part 2 of 2.)

Generic method `Maximum` uses type parameter `T` as the return type of the method (line 17), as the type of method parameters `x`, `y` and `z` (line 17), and as the type of local variable `max` (line 18). Generic method `Maximum` specifies the type constraint for type parameter `T` in its type-parameter list in line 16. In this case, the type-parameter list `(Of T As IComparable(Of T))` indicates that this method requires the type arguments to implement interface `IComparable(Of T)`. If no type constraint is specified, the default type constraint is `Object`.

Visual Basic provides several kinds of type constraints. A class constraint indicates that the type argument must be an object of a specific base class or one of its subclasses. An interface constraint indicates that the type argument's class must implement a specific interface. The type constraint in line 16 is an example of an interface constraint, because `IComparable(Of T)` is an interface. You can specify that the type argument must be a reference type or a value type by using the reference-type constraint (`Class`) or the value-type constraint (`Structure`), respectively. Finally, you can specify a `New` constraint to indicate that the generic code can use operator `New` to create new objects of the type represented by the type parameter. If a type parameter is specified with a `New` constraint, the type argument's class must be a concrete class. Also, the class must provide a `Public` parameterless or default constructor to ensure that objects of the class can be created without passing constructor arguments; otherwise, a compilation error occurs.

It is possible to apply multiple constraints to a type parameter. To do so, simply provide a comma-separated list of constraints enclosed in curly braces (`{}`) in the type-parameter list (e.g., `F(Of T As {Class, New})`). If you have a class constraint, reference-type constraint or value-type constraint, it must be listed first—only one of these types of constraints can be used for each type parameter. Interface constraints (if any) are listed next. The `New` constraint is listed last (if there is one).

Analyzing the Code

Method Maximum assumes that its first argument (x) is the largest and assigns it to local variable max (line 18). Next, lines 21–23 determine whether y is greater than max. The condition invokes y's CompareTo method to compare y to max. If y is greater than max, then y is assigned to variable max (line 22). Similarly, lines 26–28 determine whether z is greater than max. If so, line 27 assigns z to max. Then line 30 returns max to the caller.

In Main (lines 4–12), line 6 calls Maximum with the integers 3, 4 and 5. Generic method Maximum is a match for this call, but its arguments must implement interface IComparable(Of T) to ensure that they can be compared. Type Integer is a synonym for Structure Int32, which implements interface IComparable(Of Integer). Thus, Integers (and other primitive types) are valid arguments to method Maximum.

Line 8 passes three Double arguments to Maximum. Again, this is allowed because primitive type Double is a synonym for the .NET framework's Double Structure, which implements IComparable(Of Double). Line 11 passes Maximum three Strings, which are also IComparable(Of String) objects. Note that we intentionally placed the largest value in a different position in each method call (lines 6, 8 and 11) to show that the generic method always finds the maximum value, regardless of its position in the argument list and regardless of the inferred type argument.

24.3.4 Overloading Generic Methods

Generic methods can be overloaded. A class can provide two or more generic methods with the same name but different method parameters. For example, we could provide a second version of generic method PrintArray (Fig. 24.14) with the additional parameters lowIndex and highIndex that specify the portion of the array to output (see Exercise 24.21). A generic method can also be overloaded by another generic method with the same method name and a different number of type parameters, or by a generic method with different numbers of type parameters and method parameters.

A generic method can be overloaded by nongeneric methods that have the same method name and number of parameters. When the compiler encounters a method call, it searches for the method declaration that most precisely matches the method name and the argument types specified in the call. For example, generic method PrintArray of Fig. 24.14 could be overloaded with a version specific to Strings that outputs the Strings in neat, tabular format (see Exercise 24.22). If the compiler cannot match a method call to either a nongeneric method or a generic method, or if there is ambiguity due to multiple possible matches, the compiler generates an error. Generic methods can also be overloaded by nongeneric methods that have the same method name but a different number of method parameters.

24.3.5 Creating a Generic Stack Class

Recall that a generic class enables you to describe a class's capabilities in a type-independent manner. You can then instantiate type-specific objects of the generic class. This capability is an opportunity for software reusability. In addition, the compiler ensures the type safety of your code, and the runtime system replaces type parameters with actual arguments to enable your client code to interact with the generic class.

We now build a generic Stack class declaration (Fig. 24.16). The Framework Class Library provides a generic Stack class. We implement our own here for demonstration purposes only. You should use the Stack class provided by .NET in your applications.

In a generic class declaration, the class name is followed by a type-parameter list (line 3). Type parameter `T` represents the element type the `Stack` will manipulate. As with generic methods, the type-parameter list of a generic class can have one or more type parameters separated by commas. (You will create a generic class with two type parameters in Exercise 24.24.) Type parameter `T` is used throughout the `Stack` class declaration (Fig. 24.16) to represent the element type. Class `Stack` declares variable `elements` as an array of type `T` (line 5). This array (created at line 15 or 17) will store the `Stack`'s elements. [*Note:* This example implements a `Stack` as an array. As you have seen earlier in the chapter, `Stack`s also are commonly implemented as linked lists.]

```
1  ' Fig. 24.16: Stack.vb
2  ' Generic class Stack
3  Public Class Stack(Of T)
4     Private top As Integer ' location of the top element
5     Private elements() As T ' array that stores Stack elements
6
7     ' parameterless constructor creates a Stack of the default size
8     Public Sub New()
9        MyClass.New(10) ' default stack size 10 elements
10    End Sub ' New
11
12    ' constructor creates a Stack of the specified number of elements
13    Public Sub New(ByVal stackSize As Integer)
14       If stackSize > 0 Then ' validate stackSize
15          elements = New T(stackSize - 1) {} ' create stackSize elements
16       Else
17          elements = New T(9) {} ' create 10 elements
18       End If
19
20       top = -1 ' Stack initially empty
21    End Sub ' New
22
23    ' push element onto the Stack; if successful, return true
24    ' otherwise, throw FullStackException
25    Public Sub Push(ByVal pushValue As T)
26       If top = elements.Length - 1 Then ' Stack is full
27          Throw New FullStackException(String.Format( _
28             "Stack is full, cannot push {0}", pushValue))
29       End If
30
31       top += 1 ' increment top
32       elements(top) = pushValue ' place pushValue on Stack
33    End Sub ' Push
34
35    ' return the top element if not empty
36    ' else throw EmptyStackException
37    Public Function Pop() As T
38       If top = -1 Then ' Stack is empty
39          Throw New EmptyStackException("Stack is empty, cannot pop")
40       End If
```

Fig. 24.16 | Generic class `Stack` declaration. (Part 1 of 2.)

```
41
42          top -= 1 ' decrement top
43          Return elements(top + 1) ' return top value
44       End Function ' Pop
45    End Class ' Stack
```

Fig. 24.16 | Generic class `Stack` declaration. (Part 2 of 2.)

Class `Stack` has two constructors. The parameterless constructor (lines 8–10) passes the default stack size (`10`) to the one-argument constructor (line 9) by invoking the constructor in lines 13–21. The one-argument constructor (lines 13–21) validates the `stackSize` argument and creates an array of the specified `stackSize` if it is greater than `0` or an array of 10 elements otherwise.

Method `Push` (lines 25–33) first determines whether an attempt is being made to push an element onto a full `Stack`. If so, lines 27–28 throw a `FullStackException` (declared in Fig. 24.17). If the `Stack` is not full, line 31 increments the `top` counter to indicate the new top position, and line 32 places the argument in that location of array `elements`.

Method `Pop` (lines 37–44) first determines whether an attempt is being made to pop an element from an empty `Stack`. If so, line 39 throws an `EmptyStackException` (declared in Fig. 24.18). Otherwise, line 42 decrements the `top` counter to indicate the new top position, and line 43 returns the original top element of the `Stack`.

Classes `FullStackException` (Fig. 24.17) and `EmptyStackException` (Fig. 24.18) each provide a parameterless constructor and a one-argument constructor. The parameterless constructor sets the default error message, and the one-argument constructor sets a custom error message.

```
' Fig. 24.17: FullStackException.vb
' Indicates a stack is full.
Public Class FullStackException
   Inherits Exception

   ' parameterless constructor
   Public Sub New()
      MyBase.New("Stack is full")
   End Sub ' New

   ' one-parameter constructor
   Public Sub New(ByVal exception As String)
      MyBase.New(exception)
   End Sub ' New

   ' two-parameter constructor
   Public Sub New(ByVal message As String, _
      ByVal innerException As Exception)

      MyBase.New(exception, innerException)
   End Sub ' New
End Class ' FullStackException
```

Fig. 24.17 | `FullStackException` class declaration.

```
' Fig. 24.18: EmptyStackException.vb
' Indicates a stack is empty
Public Class EmptyStackException
   Inherits Exception

   ' parameterless constructor
   Public Sub New()
      MyBase.New("Stack is empty")
   End Sub ' New

   ' one-parameter constructor
   Public Sub New(ByVal exception As String)
      MyBase.New(exception)
   End Sub ' New

   ' two-parameter constructor
   Public Sub New(ByVal message As String, _
      ByVal innerException As Exception)

      MyBase.New(exception, innerException)
   End Sub ' New
End Class ' EmptyStackException
```

Fig. 24.18 | `EmptyStackException` class declaration.

As with generic methods, when a generic class is compiled, the compiler performs type checking on the class's type parameters to ensure that they can be used with the code in the generic class. The constraints determine the operations that can be performed on the type parameters. The runtime system replaces the type parameters with the actual types. For class `Stack` (Fig. 24.16), no type constraint is specified, so the default type constraint, `Object`, is used. The scope of a generic class's type parameter is the entire class.

Now let's consider an application (Fig. 24.19) that uses the `Stack` generic class. Lines 8–9 declare variables of type `Stack(Of Double)` (pronounced "`Stack` of `Double`") and `Stack(Of Integer)` (pronounced "`Stack` of `Integer`"). The types `Double` and `Integer` are the type arguments. The compiler replaces the type parameters in the generic class with the type arguments so that the compiler can perform type checking. Method `Main` instantiates objects `doubleStack` of size `5` (line 12) and `integerStack` of size `10` (line 13), then calls methods `TestPushDouble` (lines 22–38), `TestPopDouble` (lines 41–58), `TestPushInteger` (lines 61–77) and `TestPopInteger` (lines 80–97) to manipulate the two `Stacks` in this example.

```
1  ' Fig. 24.19: StackTest.vb
2  ' Generic class Stack test program.
3  Module StackTest
4     ' create arrays of doubles and integers
5     Dim doubleElements() As Double = {1.1, 2.2, 3.3, 4.4, 5.5, 6.6}
6     Dim integerElements() As Integer = {1, 2, 3, 4, 5, 6, 7, 8, 9, 10, 11}
7
```

Fig. 24.19 | Generic class `Stack` test program. (Part 1 of 4.)

```
    Dim doubleStack As Stack(Of Double) ' stack stores double objects
    Dim integerStack As Stack(Of Integer) ' stack stores integer objects

    Sub Main()
       doubleStack = New Stack(Of Double)(5) ' Stack of doubles
       integerStack = New Stack(Of Integer)(10) ' Stack of integers

       TestPushDouble() ' push doubles onto doubleStack
       TestPopDouble() ' pop doubles from doubleStack
       TestPushInteger() ' push integers onto integerStack
       TestPopInteger() ' pop integers from integerStack
    End Sub ' Main

    ' test Push method with doubleStack
    Sub TestPushDouble()
       ' push elements onto stack
       Try
          Console.WriteLine(vbNewLine & _
             "Pushing elements onto doubleStack")

          ' push elements onto stack
          For Each element As Double In doubleElements
             Console.Write("{0:F1} ", element)
             doubleStack.Push(element) ' push onto doubleStack
          Next element
       Catch exception As FullStackException
          Console.Error.WriteLine()
          Console.Error.WriteLine("Message: " & exception.Message)
          Console.Error.WriteLine(exception.StackTrace)
       End Try
    End Sub ' TestPushDouble

    ' test Pop method with doubleStack
    Sub TestPopDouble()
       ' pop elements from stack
       Try
          Console.WriteLine(vbNewLine & _
             "Popping elements from doubleStack")
          Dim popValue As Double ' store element removed from stack

          ' remove all elements from stack
          While True
             popValue = doubleStack.Pop() ' pop from doubleStack
             Console.Write("{0:F1} ", popValue)
          End While
       Catch exception As EmptyStackException
          Console.Error.WriteLine()
          Console.Error.WriteLine("Message: " & exception.Message)
          Console.Error.WriteLine(exception.StackTrace)
       End Try
    End Sub ' TestPopDouble

```

Fig. 24.19 | Generic class `Stack` test program. (Part 2 of 4.)

```
   ' test Push method with integerStack
   Sub TestPushInteger()
      ' push elements onto stack
      Try
         Console.WriteLine(vbNewLine & _
            "Pushing elements onto integerStack")

         ' push elements onto stack
         For Each element As Integer In integerElements
            Console.Write("{0} ", element)
            integerStack.Push(element) ' push onto integerStack
         Next element
      Catch exception As FullStackException
         Console.Error.WriteLine()
         Console.Error.WriteLine("Message: " & exception.Message)
         Console.Error.WriteLine(exception.StackTrace)
      End Try
   End Sub ' TestPushInteger

   ' test Pop method with integerStack
   Sub TestPopInteger()
      ' pop elements from stack
      Try
         Console.WriteLine(vbNewLine & _
            "Popping elements from integerStack")
         Dim popValue As Integer ' store element removed from stack

         ' remove all elements from stack
         While True
            popValue = integerStack.Pop() ' pop from integerStack
            Console.Write("{0} ", popValue)
         End While
      Catch exception As EmptyStackException
         Console.Error.WriteLine()
         Console.Error.WriteLine("Message: " & exception.Message)
         Console.Error.WriteLine(exception.StackTrace)
      End Try
   End Sub ' TestPopInteger
End Module ' StackTest
```

```
Pushing elements onto doubleStack
1.1 2.2 3.3 4.4 5.5 6.6
Message: Stack is full, cannot push 6.6
   at Stack.Stack`1.Push(T pushValue) in
      C:\examples\ch24\Fig24_16-19\Stack\Stack.vb:line 27
   at Stack.StackTest.TestPushDouble() in
      C:\examples\ch24\Fig24_16-19\Stack\StackTest.vb:line 31

Popping elements from doubleStack
5.5 4.4 3.3 2.2 1.1
Message: Stack is empty, cannot pop
```

Fig. 24.19 | Generic class Stack test program. (Part 3 of 4.)

```
   at Stack.Stack`1.Pop() in
      C:\examples\ch24\Fig24_16-19\Stack\Stack.vb:line 39
   at Stack.StackTest.TestPopDouble() in
      C:\examples\ch24\Fig24_16-19\Stack\StackTest.vb:line 50

Pushing elements onto integerStack
1 2 3 4 5 6 7 8 9 10 11
Message: Stack is full, cannot push 11
   at Stack.Stack`1.Push(T pushValue) in
      C:\examples\ch24\Fig24_16-19\Stack\Stack.vb:line 27
   at Stack.StackTest.TestPushInteger() in
      C:\examples\ch24\Fig24_16-19\Stack\StackTest.vb:line 70

Popping elements from integerStack
10 9 8 7 6 5 4 3 2 1
Message: Stack is empty, cannot pop
   at Stack.Stack`1.Pop() in
      C:\examples\ch24\Fig24_16-19\Stack\Stack.vb:line 39
   at Stack.StackTest.TestPopInteger() in
      C:\examples\ch24\Fig24_16-19\Stack\StackTest.vb:line 89
```

Fig. 24.19 | Generic class `Stack` test program. (Part 4 of 4.)

Method `TestPushDouble` (lines 22–38) invokes method `Push` to place the `Double` values `1.1`, `2.2`, `3.3`, `4.4` and `5.5` stored in array `doubleElements` onto `doubleStack`. The loop in lines 29–32 terminates when the test program attempts to `Push` a sixth value onto `doubleStack` (which is full, because `doubleStack` can store only five elements). In this case, the method throws a `FullStackException` (Fig. 24.17) to indicate that the `Stack` is full. Lines 33–36 catch this exception, and print the message and stack-trace information (see the output of Fig. 24.19). The stack trace indicates the exception that occurred and shows that `Stack` method `Push` generated the exception in line 27 of the file `Stack.vb` (Fig. 24.16). The trace also shows that method `Push` was called by `StackTest` method `TestPushDouble` in line 31 of `StackTest.vb`. This information enables you to determine the methods that were on the method-call stack at the time that the exception occurred. The program catches the exception, so the Visual Basic runtime environment considers the exception to have been handled, and the program can continue executing.

Method `TestPopDouble` (lines 41–58) invokes `Stack` method `Pop` in an infinite loop to remove all the values from the stack. Note in the output that the values are popped in last-in, first-out (LIFO) order—this, of course, is the defining characteristic of stacks. The loop in lines 49–52 continues until the stack is empty. An `EmptyStackException` occurs when an attempt is made to pop from the empty stack. This causes the program to proceed to the `Catch` block (lines 53–56) and handle the exception, so that the program can continue executing. When the test program attempts to `Pop` a sixth value, the `doubleStack` is empty, so method `Pop` throws an `EmptyStackException`.

Method `TestPushInteger` (lines 61–77) invokes `Stack` method `Push` to place values onto `integerStack` until it is full. Method `TestPopInteger` (lines 80–97) invokes `Stack` method `Pop` to remove values from `integerStack` until it is empty. Once again, note that the values pop off in last-in, first-out (LIFO) order.

Creating Generic Methods to Test Class `Stack(Of T)`

The code is almost identical in methods `TestPushDouble` and `TestPushInteger` for pushing values onto a `Stack(Of Double)` or a `Stack(Of Integer)`, respectively. Similarly the code is almost identical in methods `TestPopDouble` and `TestPopInteger` for popping values from a `Stack(Of Double)` or a `Stack(Of Integer)`, respectively. This presents another opportunity to use generic methods. Figure 24.20 declares generic method `TestPush` (lines 25–41) to perform the same tasks as `TestPushDouble` and `TestPushInteger` in Fig. 24.19—that is, `Push` values onto a `Stack(Of T)`. Similarly, generic method `TestPop` (lines 43–60) performs the same tasks as `TestPopDouble` and `TestPopInteger` in Fig. 24.19—that is, `Pop` values off a `Stack(Of T)`. Except for the slight differences in the stack traces, the output of Fig. 24.20 matches the output of Fig. 24.19.

```
1  ' Fig. 24.20: StackTest.vb
2  ' Stack generic class test program.
3  Module StackTest
4     ' create arrays of doubles and integers
5     Dim doubleElements() As Double = {1.1, 2.2, 3.3, 4.4, 5.5, 6.6}
6     Dim integerElements() As Integer = {1, 2, 3, 4, 5, 6, 7, 8, 9, 10, 11}
7
8     Dim doubleStack As Stack(Of Double) ' stack stores double objects
9     Dim integerStack As Stack(Of Integer) ' stack stores integer objects
10
11    Sub Main()
12       doubleStack = New Stack(Of Double)(5) ' Stack of doubles
13       integerStack = New Stack(Of Integer)(10) ' Stack of integers
14
15       ' push doubles onto doubleStack
16       TestPush("doubleStack", doubleStack, doubleElements)
17       ' pop doubles from doubleStack
18       TestPop("doubleStack", doubleStack)
19       ' push integers onto integerStack
20       TestPush("integerStack", integerStack, integerElements)
21       ' pop integers from integerStack
22       TestPop("integerStack", integerStack)
23    End Sub ' Main
24
25    Sub TestPush(Of T)(ByVal name As String, ByVal stack As Stack(Of T), _
26       ByVal elements() As T)
27       ' push elements onto stack
28       Try
29          Console.WriteLine(vbNewLine & "Pushing elements onto " & name)
30
31          ' push elements onto stack
32          For Each element As T In elements
33             Console.Write("{0} ", element)
34             stack.Push(element) ' push onto stack
35          Next element
36       Catch exception As FullStackException
37          Console.Error.WriteLine()
38          Console.Error.WriteLine("Message: " & exception.Message)
```

Fig. 24.20 | Passing a generic type `Stack` to a generic method. (Part 1 of 2.)

```
            Console.Error.WriteLine(exception.StackTrace)
        End Try
    End Sub ' TestPush

    Sub TestPop(Of T)(ByVal name As String, ByVal stack As Stack(Of T))
        ' pop elements off stack
        Try
            Console.WriteLine(vbNewLine & "Popping elements from " & name)

            Dim popValue As T ' store element removed from stack

            ' remove all elements from stack
            While True
                popValue = stack.Pop() ' pop from stack
                Console.Write("{0} ", popValue)
            End While
        Catch exception As EmptyStackException
            Console.Error.WriteLine()
            Console.Error.WriteLine("Message: " & exception.Message)
            Console.Error.WriteLine(exception.StackTrace)
        End Try
    End Sub ' TestPop
End Module ' StackTest
```

```
Pushing elements onto doubleStack
1.1 2.2 3.3 4.4 5.5 6.6
Message: Stack is full, cannot push 6.6
   at Stack.Stack`1.Push(T pushValue) in
      C:\examples\ch24\Fig24_20\Stack\Stack.vb:line 27
   at Stack.StackTest.TestPush[T](String name, Stack`1 stack, T[] elements)
      in C:\examples\ch24\Fig24_20\Stack\StackTest.vb:line 34

Popping elements from doubleStack
5.5 4.4 3.3 2.2 1.1
Message: Stack is empty, cannot pop
   at Stack.Stack`1.Pop()
      in C:\examples\ch24\Fig24_20\Stack\Stack.vb:line 39
   at Stack.StackTest.TestPop[T](String name, Stack`1 stack)
      in C:\examples\ch24\Fig24_20\Stack\StackTest.vb:line 52

Pushing elements onto integerStack
1 2 3 4 5 6 7 8 9 10 11
Message: Stack is full, cannot push 11
   at Stack.Stack`1.Push(T pushValue)
      in C:\examples\ch24\Fig24_20\Stack\Stack.vb:line 27
   at Stack.StackTest.TestPush[T](String name, Stack`1 stack, T[] elements)
      in C:\examples\ch24\Fig24_20\Stack\StackTest.vb:line 34

Popping elements from integerStack
10 9 8 7 6 5 4 3 2 1
Message: Stack is empty, cannot pop
   at Stack.Stack`1.Pop()
      in C:\examples\ch24\Fig24_20\Stack\Stack.vb:line 39
   at Stack.StackTest.TestPop[T](String name, Stack`1 stack)
      in C:\examples\ch24\Fig24_20\Stack\StackTest.vb:line 52
```

Fig. 24.20 | Passing a generic type `Stack` to a generic method. (Part 2 of 2.)

Method `Main` (lines 11–23) creates the `Stack(Of Double)` and `Stack(Of Integer)` objects (lines 12–13). Lines 16–22 invoke generic methods `TestPush` and `TestPop` to test the `Stack` objects.

Generic method `TestPush` (lines 25–41) uses type parameter `T` (specified in line 25) to represent the type stored in the `Stack`. The generic method takes three arguments—a `String` that represents the name of the `Stack` object for output purposes, an object of type `Stack(Of T)` and an array of type `T` that contains the elements that will be `Push`ed onto `Stack(Of T)`. Note that the compiler enforces consistency between the type of the `Stack` and the elements that will be pushed onto the `Stack` when `Push` is invoked, which is the type argument of the generic method call. Generic method `TestPop` (lines 43–60) takes two arguments—a `String` that represents the name of the `Stack` object for output purposes and an object of type `Stack(Of T)`.

Stack(Of T)

The .NET Framework provides a generic `Stack(Of T)` class as part of the `System.Collections.Generic` namespace. Figure 24.21 describes the most common methods of the `Stack(Of T)` class. For more information about the generic `Stack` class visit `msdn.microsoft.com/en-us/library/3278tedw.aspx`.

Method	Description
`Push`	Adds a new node to the top of the `Stack`.
`Pop`	Removes a node from the top of the `Stack` and returns the data item from the popped node.
`Peek`	Returns the data item from the top node without removing the node from the `Stack`.

Fig. 24.21 | `Stack(Of T)` methods.

24.4 Wrap-Up

In this chapter, you studied the four most common types of data structures. You learned that linked lists are collections of data items that are "linked together in a chain" and that a program can perform insertions and deletions anywhere in a linked list. We discussed the stack and queue data structures. Stacks allow insertions and deletions only at the top—so stacks are last-in, first-out (LIFO) data structures. Queues represent waiting lines—insertions are made at the tail and deletions are made from the head—so queues are first-in, first-out (FIFO) data structures. We also presented the binary tree data structure and several of its key applications, including duplicate elimination.

We introduced the .NET Framework generic collection classes and interfaces. You learned that the `System.Collections.Generic` namespace contains many generic collection classes. We presented the generic classes `Dictionary`, `SortedDictionary` and `LinkedList`. In doing so, we discussed data structures in greater depth. We discussed dynamically expanding collections, hashing schemes, and two implementations of a dictionary. We demonstrated the `For Each` statement with several collections.

We introduced generics and discussed how generics ensure compile-time type safety by checking for type mismatches at compile time. You learned that the compiler will allow generic code to compile only if all the operations performed on the type parameters in the generic code are supported for all the types that could be used with the generic code. You also learned how to declare generic methods and classes using type parameters. We demonstrated how to use a type constraint to specify the requirements for a type parameter—a key component of compile-time type safety. We discussed several kinds of type constraints, including reference-type constraints, value type constraints, class constraints, interface constraints and `New` constraints. You learned that a `New` constraint indicates that the type argument's class must be concrete and must provide a `Public` parameterless or default constructor so that objects of that type can be created with `New`. We also discussed how to implement multiple type constraints for a type parameter. Finally, we showed how generics improve code reuse.

Summary

Section 24.1 Introduction to Data Structures

- Dynamic data structures can grow and shrink at execution time.

Section 24.1.1 Linked Lists

- A linked list is a linear collection (i.e., a sequence) of objects called nodes, connected by reference links.
- A node can contain instance variables of any type, including references to objects of other classes.
- A linked list is accessed via a reference to the first node of the list. Each subsequent node is accessed via the link-reference member stored in the previous node.
- By convention, the last node's link reference is set to `Nothing` to mark the end of the list.

Section 24.1.2 Stacks

- A stack is a constrained version of a linked list—new nodes can be added to and removed from a stack only at the top. A stack is referred to as a last-in, first-out (LIFO) data structure.
- The primary stack operations are push and pop. Operation push adds a new node to the top of the stack. Operation pop removes a node from the top of the stack and returns the data object from the popped node.
- Stacks have many interesting applications, including method call-return handling.

Section 24.1.3 Queues

- Queues represent waiting lines. Insertions occur at the back (also referred to as the tail) of a queue, and deletions occur from the front (also referred to as the head) of a queue.
- A queue is similar to a checkout line in a supermarket: The first person in line is served first; other customers enter the line at the end and wait to be served.
- Queue nodes are removed only from the head of the queue and are inserted only at the tail of the queue. For this reason, a queue is referred to as a first-in, first-out (FIFO) data structure.
- The insert and remove operations for a queue are known as enqueue and dequeue.

Section 24.1.4 Trees

- Tree nodes contain two or more links.

- A binary tree is a tree whose nodes all contain two links. The root node is the first node in a tree.
- Each link in the root node refers to a child. The left child is the root node of the left subtree, and the right child is the root node of the right subtree.
- The children of a node are called siblings. A node with no children is called a leaf node.
- A binary search tree (with no duplicate node values) has the characteristic that the values in any left subtree are less than the value in the subtree's parent node, and the values in any right subtree are greater than the value in the subtree's parent node.
- A binary search tree facilitates duplicate elimination. As the tree is created, attempts to insert a duplicate value are recognized because a duplicate follows the same "go left" or "go right" decision on each comparison as the original value did. Thus, the duplicate eventually is compared with a node containing the same value, and can then be discarded.

Section 24.2 Generic Collections Overview

- The prepackaged data-structure classes provided by the .NET Framework are known as collection classes—they store collections of data.
- With collection classes, instead of creating data structures to store these sets of items, you simply use existing data structures, without concern for how they are implemented.
- The .NET Framework collections provide high-performance, high-quality implementations of common data structures and enable effective software reuse.
- The `System.Collections.Generic` namespace contains classes that take advantage of .NET's generics capabilities.
- All primitive-type names are aliases for corresponding `Structures` in namespace `System`. Each primitive type `Structure` has methods that manipulate the corresponding primitive-type values.
- `Structures` that represent primitive types inherit from class `ValueType` in namespace `System`.
- A boxing conversion creates an object that contains a copy of a primitive-type value.
- An unboxing conversion retrieves a primitive-type value from an object.

Section 24.2.1 Generic Collection Class `LinkedList`

- The `LinkedList` class implements a doubly linked list.
- Each node contains property `Value` and read-only properties `Previous` and `Next`.
- One `LinkedListNode` cannot be a member of more than one `LinkedList`. Any attempt to add a node from one `LinkedList` to another generates an `InvalidOperationException`.
- The `LinkedList` constructor that takes a parameter of type `IEnumerable(Of T)` copies the contents of the `IEnumberable` into the list.
- Method `AddLast` creates a new `LinkedListNode` and appends it to the end of the list. Method `AddFirst` inserts a node at the beginning of the list.
- Method `Find` performs a linear search on the list, and returns the first node that contains a value equal to the passed argument.
- Method `Remove` deletes a node from a `LinkedList`.

Section 24.2.2 Generic Collection Class `Dictionary`

- Many applications need a high-speed scheme for converting keys to unique array indices. One such scheme is called hashing, in which we store data in a data structure called a dictionary (or hash table). The .NET Framework provides class `Dictionary` to enable you to employ hashing.
- Class `Dictionary` can accept any `Object` as a key.

- Invoking the Get accessor of a Dictionary indexer with a key that does not exist in the collection causes a KeyNotFoundException.
- Method ContainsKey determines whether a key is in the dictionary.
- Dictionary method Add creates a new entry in the hash table, with the first argument as the key and the second argument as the value.
- A Dictionary's indexer obtains or sets the key's associated value in the dictionary.
- Dictionary property Keys returns an ICollection that contains all the keys.
- If you use a For Each statement with a Dictionary, the iteration variable is of type KeyValuePair, which has properties Key and Value for retrieving the key and value of the current element.

Section 24.2.3 Generic Collection Class ***SortedDictionary***

- A dictionary is the general term for a collection of key/value pairs. A hash table is one way to implement a dictionary.
- Generic class SortedDictionary stores its key/value pairs in a binary search tree.
- Generic class SortedDictionary takes two type arguments—the first specifies the type of key, and the second specifies the type of value.

Section 24.3 Generic Classes and Methods

- Generic methods enable you to specify a set of related methods with a single method declaration.
- Generic classes enable you to specify a set of related classes with a single class declaration.
- Generic interfaces enable you to specify a set of related interfaces with a single interface declaration.
- Generics provide compile-time type safety.

Section 24.3.1 Motivation for Generic Methods

- Overloaded methods are often used to perform similar operations on different types of data.
- When the compiler encounters a method call, it attempts to locate a method declaration that has the same method name and parameters that match the argument types in the method call.

Section 24.3.2 Generic-Method Implementation

- If the same operations are performed by several overloaded methods, the overloaded methods can be more compactly and conveniently coded using a generic method.
- You can write a single generic method declaration that can be called at different times with arguments of different types. Based on the types of the arguments passed to the generic method, the compiler handles each method call appropriately.
- All generic methods have a type-parameter list delimited by parentheses that follows the method's name. Each type-parameter list contains one or more type parameters, separated by commas.
- A type parameter is used in place of actual type names. The type parameters can be used to declare the return type, parameter types and local variable types in a generic-method declaration; the type parameters act as placeholders for the types of the arguments passed to the method.
- A generic method's body is declared like that of any other method. The type-parameter names throughout the method declaration must match those declared in the type-parameter list.
- A type parameter can be declared only once in the type-parameter list but can appear more than once in the method's parameter list. Type-parameter names need not be unique among different generic methods.
- When the compiler encounters a method call, it analyzes the set of methods (both nongeneric and generic) that might match the method call, looking for a method that matches the call ex-

actly. If there are no exact matches, the compiler picks the best match. If there are no matching methods, or if there is more than one best match, the compiler generates an error.

- You can use explicit type arguments to indicate the exact type that should be used to call a generic method.

Section 24.3.3 Type Constraints

- Generic code is restricted to performing operations that are guaranteed to work for every possible type. Thus, an expression like `variable1 < variable2` is not allowed unless the compiler can ensure that the operator `<` is provided for every type that will ever be used in the generic code. Similarly, you cannot call a method on a variable of a generic type unless the compiler can ensure that all types that will ever be used for the variable support that method.
- It is possible to compare two objects of the same type if that type implements the generic interface `IComparable(Of T)` (of namespace `System`), which declares method `CompareTo`.
- `IComparable(Of T)` objects can be used with the sorting and searching methods of classes in the `System.Collections.Generic` namespace.
- The structures in the .NET framework that correspond to the primitive types all implement interface `IComparable(Of T)`.
- If you declare a type that implements `IComparable(Of T)`, you must define the method `CompareTo` such that it compares the contents of two objects of that type and returns the appropriate result.
- You can restrict the types that can be used with a generic method or class to ensure that they meet certain requirements. This feature—known as a type constraint—restricts the type of the argument supplied to a particular type parameter. For example, the type-parameter list `(Of T As IComparable(Of T))` indicates that the type arguments must implement interface `IComparable(Of T)`. If no type constraint is specified, the default type constraint is `Object`.
- A class constraint indicates that the type argument must be an object of a specific base class or one of its subclasses.
- An interface constraint indicates that the type argument's class must implement that interface.
- You can specify that the type argument must be a reference type or a value type by using the reference-type constraint (`Class`) or the value type constraint (`Structure`), respectively.
- You can specify a `New` constraint to indicate that the generic code can use operator `New` to create new objects of the type represented by the type parameter. If a type parameter is specified with a `New` constraint, the type argument's class must be concrete and must provide a `Public` parameterless or default constructor to ensure that objects of the class can be created without passing constructor arguments; otherwise, a compilation error occurs.
- It is possible to apply multiple constraints to a type parameter by providing a comma-separated list of constraints enclosed in curly braces (`{}`) in the type-parameter list.
- If you have a class constraint, reference-type constraint or value-type constraint, it must be listed first—only one of these types of constraints can be used for each type parameter. Interface constraints (if any) are listed next. The `New` constraint is listed last (if there is one).

Section 24.3.4 Overloading Generic Methods

- A generic method may be overloaded. A class can provide two or more generic methods with the same name but different method parameters.
- A generic method can also be overloaded by another generic method with the same method name and a different number of type parameters, or by a generic method with different numbers of type parameters and method parameters.

- A generic method can be overloaded by nongeneric methods that have the same method name and number of parameters. When the compiler encounters a method call, it searches for the method that most precisely matches the method name and argument types specified in the call.
- Generic methods can also be overloaded by nongeneric methods that have the same method name but a different number of method parameters.

Section 24.3.5 Creating a Generic Stack Class

- A generic class declaration is similar to a nongeneric class declaration, except that the class name is followed by a type-parameter list and possibly constraints on its type parameters.
- As with generic methods, the type-parameter list of a generic class can have one or more type parameters separated by commas.
- When a generic class is compiled, the compiler performs type checking on the class's type parameters to ensure that they can be used with the code in the generic class. The constraints determine the operations that can be performed on the type parameters.

Terminology

`Add` method of class `Dictionary(Of T)`
`AddLast` method of class `LinkedList(Of T)`
`ArgumentException`
binary search tree
binary tree
capacity of a collection
child node
circular, doubly linked list
circular, singly linked list
class constraint
collection
collection class
collision of keys in a `Dictionary`
`CompareTo` method of interface `IComparable(Of T)`
compile-time type safety
`ContainsKey` method of class `Dictionary(Of T)`
`CopyTo` method of interface `ICollection(Of T)`
`Count` property of interface `ICollection(Of T)`
data structures
default type constraint (`Object`) of a type parameter
dequeue operation of a queue
dictionary
`Dictionary(Of T)` class
doubly linked list
duplicate elimination
dynamic data structures
dynamic memory allocation
enqueue operation of a queue
explicit type argument
`Find` method of class `LinkedList(Of T)`
`First` property of class `LinkedList(Of T)`
first-in, first-out (FIFO) data structure
generic class
generic collection class
generic interface
generic method
generics
`GetHashCode` method of class `Object`
head of a queue
hash function
hash table
hashing keys in a `Dictionary`
`ICollection(Of T)` interface
`IComparable(Of T)` interface
`IDictionary(Of T)` interface
`IEnumerator(Of T)` interface
`IList(Of T)` interface
interface constraint
`InvalidOperationException`
`KeyNotFoundException`
`Keys` property of interface `IDictionary(Of T)`
`KeyValuePair` structure
last-in, first-out (LIFO) data structure
leaf node
left child node
left subtree
linear data structure
link in a node of a data structure
linked list
`Last` property of class `LinkedList(Of T)`
`LinkedList(Of T)` generic class
`LinkedListNode(Of T)` generic class
load factor
multiple constraints

New constraint
Next property of class LinkedListNode(Of T)
node of a data structure
Of keyword
overloading generic methods
parent node in a data structure
pop stack operation
Previous property of class LinkedListNode(Of T)
print spooling
push stack operation
queue
reference-type constraint (Class)
Remove method of class LinkedList(Of T)
right child node
right subtree
root node
scope of a type parameter
searching
sequences
sibling node
singly linked list
SortedDictionary(Of T) generic class
sorting
space/time trade-off
spooler
stack
Stack(Of T)
System.Collections namespace
System.Collections.Generic namespace
tail of a queue
top of a stack
tree
type argument
type checking
type constraint
type inference
type parameter
type-parameter list
Value property of class LinkedListNode(Of T)
value-type constraint (Structure)
Values property of interface IDictionary(Of T)

Self-Review Exercises

24.1 State whether each of the following is *true* or *false*. If *false*, explain why.

a) In a queue, the first item to be added is the last item to be removed.
b) Trees can have no more than two child nodes per node.
c) A tree node with no children is called a leaf node.
d) Linked-list nodes are stored contiguously in memory.
e) The primary operations of the stack data structure are enqueue and dequeue.
f) Lists, stacks and queues are linear data structures.

24.2 Fill in the blanks in each of the following statements:

a) Operator __________ allocates memory dynamically; this operator returns a reference to the allocated memory.
b) A(n) __________ is a constrained version of a linked list in which nodes can be inserted and deleted only from the start of the list; this data structure returns node values in last-in, first-out order.
c) A queue is a(n) __________ data structure, because the first nodes inserted are the first nodes removed.
d) A(n) __________ is a constrained version of a linked list in which nodes can be inserted only at the end of the list and deleted only from the start of the list.
e) A(n) __________ is a nonlinear, two-dimensional data structure that contains nodes with two or more links.
f) The nodes of a(n) __________ tree contain two link members.

24.3 State whether each of the following is *true* or *false*. If *false*, explain why.

a) A Dictionary stores key/value pairs.
b) A Dictionary can contain duplicate keys.
c) A LinkedList can contain duplicate values.
d) With hashing, as the load factor increases, the chance of collisions decreases.
e) Property First gets the first node in a LinkedList.

24.4 State whether each of the following is *true* or *false*. If *false*, explain why.
a) A generic method cannot have the same method name as a nongeneric method.
b) All generic-method declarations have a type-parameter list that immediately precedes the method name.
c) A generic method can be overloaded by another generic method with the same method name but a different number of type parameters.
d) A type parameter can be declared only once in the type-parameter list but can appear more than once in the method's parameter list.
e) Type-parameter names among different generic methods must be unique.
f) The scope of a generic class's type parameter is the entire class.
g) A type parameter can have at most one interface constraint, but multiple class constraints.
h) Class `Stack(Of T)` is in the `System.Collections.Generics` namespace.

24.5 Fill in the blanks in each of the following:
a) ________ enable you to specify, with a single method declaration, a set of related methods; ________ enable you to specify, with a single class declaration, a set of related classes.
b) A type-parameter list is delimited by ________.
c) The ________ of a generic method can be used to specify the types of the arguments to the method, to specify the return type of the method and to declare variables within the method.
d) The statement "`Dim objectStack As New Stack(Of Integer)()`" indicates that `objectStack` stores ________.
e) In a generic-class declaration, the class name is followed by a(n) ________.
f) The ________ constraint requires that the type argument must have a `Public` parameterless constructor.

Answers to Self-Review Exercises

24.1 a) False. A queue is a first-in, first-out data structure—the first item added is the first item removed. b) False. In general, trees may have as many child nodes per node as necessary. Only binary trees are restricted to no more than two child nodes per node. c) True. d) False. Linked-list nodes are logically contiguous, but they need not be stored physically contiguously. e) False. They are the primary operations of a queue. The primary operations of a stack are push and pop. f) True.

24.2 a) `New`. b) stack. c) first-in, first-out (FIFO). d) queue. e) tree. f) binary.

24.3 a) True. b) False. A `Dictionary` cannot contain duplicate keys. c) True. d) False. With hashing, as the load factor increases, there are fewer available slots relative to the total number of slots, so the chance of selecting an occupied slot (a collision) with a hashing operation increases. e) True.

24.4 a) False. A generic method can be overloaded by nongeneric methods with the same or a different number of arguments. b) False. All generic-method declarations have a type-parameter list that immediately follows the method's name. c) True. d) True. e) False. Type-parameter names among different generic methods need not be unique. f) True. g) False. A type parameter can have at most one class constraint, but multiple interface constraints. h) True.

24.5 a) Generic methods, Generic classes. b) parentheses. c) type parameters. d) `Integers`. e) type-parameter list. f) `New`.

Exercises

24.6 Write a program that merges two ordered-list objects of integers into a single ordered-list object of integers. Method `Merge` of class `ListMerge` should receive references to each of the list objects to be merged and should return a reference to the merged-list object.

24.7 Write a program that inputs a line of text and uses a stack object to print the line reversed.

24.8 Write a program that uses a stack to determine whether a string is a palindrome (i.e., the string is spelled identically backward and forward). The program should ignore capitalization, spaces and punctuation.

24.9 Define each of the following terms:

a) `ICollection(Of T)`
b) `IList(Of T)`
c) load factor
d) collision
e) space/time trade-off in hashing
f) `Dictionary(Of T)`

24.10 Explain briefly the operation of each of the following methods and properties of class `Dictionary`:

a) `Add`
b) `Keys`
c) `Values`
d) `ContainsKey`

24.11 Write an application that reads in a series of first names and stores them in a `LinkedList`. Do not store duplicate names. Allow the user to search for a first name.

24.12 Modify the application in Fig. 24.11 to count the number of occurrences of each letter rather than of each word. For example, the string `"HELLO THERE"` contains two `H`s, three `E`s, two `L`s, one `O`, one `T` and one `R`. Display the results.

24.13 Use a `SortedDictionary` to create a reusable class for choosing from some of the predefined colors in class `Color` (in the `System.Drawing` namespace). The names of the colors should be used as keys, and the predefined `Color` objects should be used as values. Place this class in a class library that can be referenced from any Visual Basic application. Use your new class in a Windows application that allows the user to select a color and then changes the background color of the `Form`.

24.14 Write an application that determines and prints the number of duplicate words in a sentence. Treat uppercase and lowercase letters the same. Ignore punctuation.

24.15 Write an application that creates a `LinkedList` object of 10 characters, then creates a second list object containing a copy of the first list, but in reverse order.

24.16 Explain the use of the following notation in a Visual Basic program:

```
Public Class List(Of T)
```

24.17 How can generic methods be overloaded?

24.18 The compiler performs a matching process to determine which method to call when a method is invoked. Under what circumstances does an attempt to make a match result in a compile-time error?

24.19 Explain why a Visual Basic program might use the statement

```
Dim workerlist As New List(Of Employee)()
```

24.20 Write a generic method, `Search`, that implements the linear search algorithm. Method `Search` should compare the search key with each element in the array until the search key is found or the end of the array is reached. If the search key is found, return its location in the array; otherwise, return `-1`. Write a test application that inputs and searches an `Integer` array and a `Double` array. Provide buttons that the user can click to randomly generate `Integer` and `Double` values.

Display the generated values in a TextBox, so that the user knows what values they can search for. [*Hint:* The type parameter for method Search should be constrained with IComparable(Of T) so that you can use method CompareTo to compare the search key to the elements in the array.]

24.21 Overload generic method PrintArray of Fig. 24.14 so that it takes two additional Integer arguments: lowIndex and highIndex. A call to this method prints only the designated portion of the array. Validate lowIndex and highIndex. If either is out of range, or if highIndex is less than or equal to lowIndex, the overloaded PrintArray method should throw an InvalidIndexException; otherwise, PrintArray should return the number of elements printed. Then modify Main to exercise both versions of PrintArray on arrays integerArray, doubleArray and charArray. Test all capabilities of both versions of PrintArray.

24.22 Overload generic method PrintArray of Fig. 24.14 with a nongeneric version that prints an array of strings in neat, tabular format, as shown in the sample output that follows:

```
Array stringArray contains:
one      two      three    four
five     six      seven    eight
```

24.23 Write a simple generic version of method IsEqualTo that compares its two arguments with the Equals method, and returns True if they are equal and False otherwise. Use this generic method in a program that calls IsEqualTo with a variety of primitive types, such as Double or Integer. What result do you get when you attempt to run this program?

24.24 Write a generic class Pair which has two type parameters, F and S, representing the types of the first and second element of the pair, respectively. Add properties (with Get and Set accessors) for the first and second elements of the pair. [*Hint:* The class header should be Public Class Pair(Of F, S).]

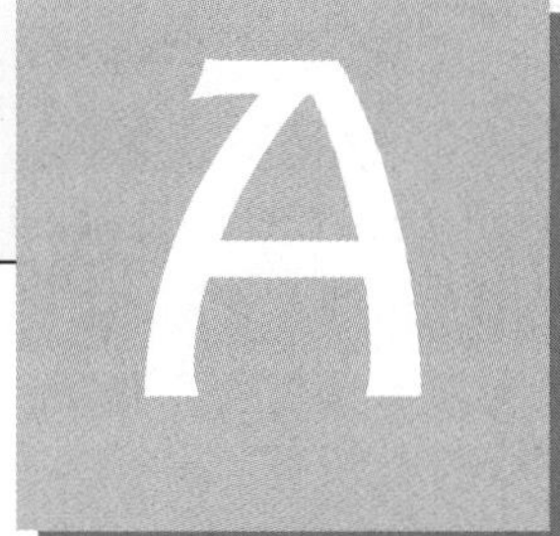

Operator Precedence Chart

Operators are shown in decreasing order of precedence from top to bottom, with each level of precedence separated by a horizontal line. Visual Basic operators associate from left to right.

Operator	Type
`TypeOf`	type comparison
`^`	exponentiation
`+` `-`	unary plus unary minus
`*` `/`	multiplication division
`\`	integer division
`Mod`	modulus
`+` `-`	addition subtraction
`&`	concatenation
`<<` `>>`	bitwise left shift bitwise right shift

Fig. A.1 | Operator precedence chart. (Part 1 of 2.)

Operator	Type
`=`	relational is equal to
`<>`	relational is not equal to
`<`	relational less than
`<=`	relational less than or equal to
`>`	relational greater than
`>=`	relational greater than or equal to
`Like`	pattern matching
`Is`	reference comparison
`IsNot`	reference comparison
`Not`	logical negation
`And`	logical AND without short-circuit evaluation
`AndAlso`	logical AND with short-circuit evaluation
`Or`	logical inclusive OR without short-circuit evaluation
`OrElse`	logical inclusive OR with short-circuit evaluation
`Xor`	logical exclusive OR

Fig. A.1 | Operator precedence chart. (Part 2 of 2.)

B

Primitive Types

Type	Size in bytes	Value range
`SByte`	1	–128 to 127, inclusive
`Byte`	1	0 to 255, inclusive
`Boolean`	2	`True` or `False`
`Char`	2	0 to 65,535, inclusive (representing the Unicode character set)
`Short`	2	–32,768 to 32,767, inclusive
`UShort`	2	0 to 65,535, inclusive
`Integer`	4	–2,147,483,648 to 2,147,483,647, inclusive
`UInteger`	4	0 to 4,294,967,295, inclusive
`Single`	4	negative range: –3.4028235E+38 to –1.401298E-45 positive range: 1.401298E–45 to 3.4028235E+38
`Long`	8	–9,223,372,036,854,775,808 to 9,223,372,036,854,775,807, inclusive
`ULong`	8	0 to 18,446,744,073,709,551,615, inclusive
`Double`	8	negative range: –1.79769313486231570E+308 to –4.94065645841246544E–324 positive range: 4.94065645841246544E–324 to 1.79769313486231570E+308
`Date`	8	0:00:00 on 1 January 0001 to 23:59:59 on 31 December 9999

Fig. B.1 | Primitive types. (Part 1 of 2.)

Type	Size in bytes	Value range
`Decimal`	16	Range with no decimal point: ±79,228,162,514,264,337,593,543,950,335 Range with 28 places to the right of the decimal point: ±7.9228162514264337593543950335 The smallest nonzero number is ±0.0000000000000000000000000001 (±1E–28)
`String`	Depends on platform	Up to approximately 2 billion Unicode characters

Fig. B.1 | Primitive types. (Part 2 of 2.)

Additional Primitive Type Information

This appendix is based on information from Section 7.3 of *The Microsoft Visual Basic Language Specification* (available at `msdn2.microsoft.com/en-us/library/ms234437.aspx`).

C Number Systems

Here are only numbers ratified.

—William Shakespeare

Nature has some sort of arithmetic-geometrical coordinate system, because nature has all kinds of models. What we experience of nature is in models, and all of nature's models are so beautiful.

It struck me that nature's system must be a real beauty, because in chemistry we find that the associations are always in beautiful whole numbers—there are no fractions.

—Richard Buckminster Fuller

OBJECTIVES

In this appendix you will learn:

- To understand basic number-systems concepts, such as base, positional value and symbol value.
- To understand how to work with numbers represented in the binary, octal and hexadecimal number systems.
- To abbreviate binary numbers as octal numbers or hexadecimal numbers.
- To convert octal numbers and hexadecimal numbers to binary numbers.
- To convert back and forth between decimal numbers and their binary, octal and hexadecimal equivalents.
- To understand binary arithmetic and how negative binary numbers are represented using two's-complement notation.

Outline

C.1 Introduction

In this appendix, we introduce the key number systems that programmers use, especially when they are working on software projects that require close interaction with machine-level hardware. Projects like this include operating systems, computer networking software, compilers, database systems and applications requiring high performance.

When we write an integer such as 227 or –63 in a program, the number is assumed to be in the decimal (base-10) number system. The digits in the decimal number system are 0, 1, 2, 3, 4, 5, 6, 7, 8 and 9. The lowest digit is 0 and the highest is 9—one less than the base of 10. Internally, computers use the binary (base-2) number system. The binary number system has only two digits, namely 0 and 1. Its lowest digit is 0 and its highest is 1—one less than the base of 2.

As you will see, binary numbers tend to be much longer than their decimal equivalents. Programmers who work in assembly languages and in high-level languages that enable programmers to reach down to the machine level find it cumbersome to work with binary numbers. So, two other number systems—the octal number system (base 8) and the hexadecimal number system (base 16)—are popular primarily because they make it convenient to abbreviate binary numbers.

In the octal number system, the digits range from 0 to 7. Because both the binary and the octal number systems have fewer digits than the decimal number system, their digits are the same as the corresponding digits in decimal.

The hexadecimal number system poses a problem because it requires 16 digits—a lowest digit of 0 and a highest digit with a value equivalent to decimal 15 (one less than the base of 16). By convention, the letters A through F represent the hexadecimal digits corresponding to decimal values 10 through 15. Thus, in hexadecimal, you can have numbers like 876 consisting solely of decimal-like digits, numbers like 8A55F consisting of digits and letters and numbers like FFE consisting solely of letters. Occasionally, a hexadecimal number spells a common word such as FACE or FEED—this can appear strange to programmers accustomed to working with numbers. The digits of the binary, octal, decimal and hexadecimal number systems are summarized in Figs. C.1 and C.2.

Each of these number systems uses positional notation—each position in which a digit is written has a different positional value. For example, in the decimal number 937 (the 9, the 3 and the 7 are referred to as symbol values), we say that the 7 is written in the ones position, the 3 is written in the tens position and the 9 is written in the hundreds position. Note that each of these positions is a power of the base (base 10) and that these powers begin at 0 and increase by 1 as we move left in the number (Fig. C.3).

Binary digit	Octal digit	Decimal digit	Hexadecimal digit
0	0	0	0
1	1	1	1
	2	2	2
	3	3	3
	4	4	4
	5	5	5
	6	6	6
	7	7	7
		8	8
		9	9
			A (decimal value of 10)
			B (decimal value of 11)
			C (decimal value of 12)
			D (decimal value of 13)
			E (decimal value of 14)
			F (decimal value of 15)

Fig. C.1 | Digits of the binary, octal, decimal and hexadecimal number systems.

Attribute	Binary	Octal	Decimal	Hexadecimal
Base	2	8	10	16
Lowest digit	0	0	0	0
Highest digit	1	7	9	F

Fig. C.2 | Comparing the binary, octal, decimal and hexadecimal number systems.

Positional values in the decimal number system			
Decimal digit	9	3	7
Position name	Hundreds	Tens	Ones
Positional value	100	10	1
Positional value as a power of the base (10)	10^2	10^1	10^0

Fig. C.3 | Positional values in the decimal number system.

For longer decimal numbers, the next positions to the left would be the thousands position (10 to the 3rd power), the ten-thousands position (10 to the 4th power), the hundred-thousands position (10 to the 5th power), the millions position (10 to the 6th power), the ten-millions position (10 to the 7th power) and so on.

In the binary number 101, the rightmost 1 is written in the ones position, the 0 is written in the twos position and the leftmost 1 is written in the fours position. Each position is a power of the base (base 2), and these powers begin at 0 and increase by 1 as we move left in the number (Fig. C.4). So, $101 = 1 * 2^2 + 0 * 2^1 + 1 * 2^0 = 4 + 0 + 1 = 5$.

For longer binary numbers, the next positions to the left would be the eights position (2 to the 3rd power), the sixteens position (2 to the 4th power), the thirty-twos position (2 to the 5th power), the sixty-fours position (2 to the 6th power) and so on.

In the octal number 425, we say that the 5 is written in the ones position, the 2 is written in the eights position and the 4 is written in the sixty-fours position. Note that each of these positions is a power of the base (base 8) and that these powers begin at 0 and increase by 1 as we move left in the number (Fig. C.5).

For longer octal numbers, the next positions to the left would be the five-hundred-and-twelves position (8 to the 3rd power), the four-thousand-and-ninety-sixes position (8 to the 4th power), the thirty-two-thousand-seven-hundred-and-sixty-eights position (8 to the 5th power) and so on.

In the hexadecimal number 3DA, we say that the A is written in the ones position, the D is written in the sixteens position and the 3 is written in the two-hundred-and-fifty-sixes position. Note that each of these positions is a power of the base (base 16) and that these powers begin at 0 and increase by 1 as we move left in the number (Fig. C.6).

For longer hexadecimal numbers, the next positions to the left would be the four-thousand-and-ninety-sixes position (16 to the 3rd power), the sixty-five-thousand-five-hundred-and-thirty-sixes position (16 to the 4th power) and so on.

Positional values in the binary number system			
Binary digit	1	0	1
Position name	Fours	Twos	Ones
Positional value	4	2	1
Positional value as a power of the base (2)	2^2	2^1	2^0

Fig. C.4 | Positional values in the binary number system.

Positional values in the octal number system			
Decimal digit	4	2	5
Position name	Sixty-fours	Eights	Ones
Positional value	64	8	1
Positional value as a power of the base (8)	8^2	8^1	8^0

Fig. C.5 | Positional values in the octal number system.

Positional values in the hexadecimal number system			
Decimal digit	3	D	A
Position name	Two-hundred-and-fifty-sixes	Sixteens	Ones
Positional value	256	16	1
Positional value as a power of the base (16)	16^2	16^1	16^0

Fig. C.6 | Positional values in the hexadecimal number system.

C.2 Abbreviating Binary Numbers as Octal and Hexadecimal Numbers

The main use for octal and hexadecimal numbers in computing is for abbreviating lengthy binary representations. Figure C.7 highlights the fact that lengthy binary numbers can be expressed concisely in number systems with higher bases than the binary number system.

Decimal number	Binary representation	Octal representation	Hexadecimal representation
0	0	0	0
1	1	1	1
2	10	2	2
3	11	3	3
4	100	4	4
5	101	5	5
6	110	6	6
7	111	7	7
8	1000	10	8
9	1001	11	9
10	1010	12	A
11	1011	13	B
12	1100	14	C
13	1101	15	D
14	1110	16	E
15	1111	17	F
16	10000	20	10

Fig. C.7 | Decimal, binary, octal and hexadecimal equivalents.

A particularly important relationship that both the octal and the hexadecimal number system have to the binary system is that the bases of octal and hexadecimal (8 and 16, respectively) are powers of the base of the binary number system (base 2). Consider the following 12-digit binary number and its octal and hexadecimal equivalents. See if you can determine how this relationship makes it convenient to abbreviate binary numbers in octal or hexadecimal. The answer follows the numbers.

Binary number	Octal equivalent	Hexadecimal equivalent
100011010001	4321	8D1

To see how the binary number converts easily to octal, simply break the 12-digit binary number into groups of three consecutive bits each and write those groups over the corresponding digits of the octal number as follows:

```
100     011     010     001
4       3       2       1
```

Note that the octal digit you have written under each group of three bits corresponds precisely to the octal equivalent of that 3-digit binary number, as shown in Fig. C.7.

The same kind of relationship can be observed in converting from binary to hexadecimal. Break the 12-digit binary number into groups of four consecutive bits each and write those groups over the corresponding digits of the hexadecimal number, as follows:

```
1000    1101    0001
8       D       1
```

Notice that the hexadecimal digit you wrote under each group of four bits corresponds precisely to the hexadecimal equivalent of that 4-digit binary number as shown in Fig. C.7.

C.3 Converting Octal and Hexadecimal Numbers to Binary Numbers

In the previous section, you learned how to convert binary numbers to their octal and hexadecimal equivalents by forming groups of binary digits and simply rewriting them as their equivalent octal digit values or hexadecimal digit values. This process may be used in reverse to produce the binary equivalent of a given octal or hexadecimal number.

For example, the octal number 653 is converted to binary simply by writing the 6 as its 3-digit binary equivalent 110, the 5 as its 3-digit binary equivalent 101 and the 3 as its 3-digit binary equivalent 011 to form the 9-digit binary number 110101011.

The hexadecimal number FAD5 is converted to binary simply by writing the F as its 4-digit binary equivalent 1111, the A as its 4-digit binary equivalent 1010, the D as its 4-digit binary equivalent 1101 and the 5 as its 4-digit binary equivalent 0101 to form the 16-digit binary number 1111101011010101.

C.4 Converting from Binary, Octal or Hexadecimal to Decimal

We are accustomed to working in decimal, and therefore it is often convenient to convert a binary, octal, or hexadecimal number to decimal to get a sense of what the number is "really" worth. Our diagrams in Section C.1 express the positional values in decimal. To convert a number to decimal from another base, multiply the decimal equivalent of each digit by its positional value and sum these products. For example, the binary number 110101 is converted to decimal 53, as shown in Fig. C.8.

To convert octal 7614 to decimal 3980, we use the same technique, this time using appropriate octal positional values, as shown in Fig. C.9.

To convert hexadecimal AD3B to decimal 44347, we use the same technique, this time using appropriate hexadecimal positional values, as shown in Fig. C.10.

C.5 Converting from Decimal to Binary, Octal or Hexadecimal

The conversions in Section C.4 follow naturally from the positional notation conventions. Converting from decimal to binary, octal, or hexadecimal also follows these conventions.

Converting a binary number to decimal						
Positional values:	32	16	8	4	2	1
Symbol values:	1	1	0	1	0	1
Products:	1*32=32	1*16=16	0*8=0	1*4=4	0*2=0	1*1=1
Sum:	= 32 + 16 + 0 + 4 + 0s + 1 = 53					

Fig. C.8 | Converting a binary number to decimal.

Converting an octal number to decimal				
Positional values:	512	64	8	1
Symbol values:	7	6	1	4
Products	7*512=3584	6*64=384	1*8=8	4*1=4
Sum:	= 3584 + 384 + 8 + 4 = 3980			

Fig. C.9 | Converting an octal number to decimal.

Converting a hexadecimal number to decimal				
Positional values:	4096	256	16	1
Symbol values:	A	D	3	B
Products	A*4096=40960	D*256=3328	3*16=48	B*1=11
Sum:	= 40960 + 3328 + 48 + 11 = 44347			

Fig. C.10 | Converting a hexadecimal number to decimal.

Suppose we wish to convert decimal 57 to binary. We write the positional values of the columns right to left until we reach a column whose positional value is greater than the decimal number. We don't need that column, so we discard it. Thus, we first write:

Positional values:	64	32	16	8	4	2	1

Then we discard the column with positional value 64, leaving:

Positional values:	32	16	8	4	2	1

Next we work from the leftmost column to the right. We divide 32 into 57 and observe that there is one 32 in 57 with a remainder of 25, so we write 1 in the 32 column. We divide 16 into 25 and observe that there is one 16 in 25 with a remainder of 9 and write 1 in the 16 column. We divide 8 into 9 and observe that there is one 8 in 9 with a remainder of 1. The next two columns each produce quotients of 0 when their positional values are divided into 1, so we write 0s in the 4 and 2 columns. Finally, 1 into 1 is 1, so we write 1 in the 1 column. This yields:

Positional values:	32	16	8	4	2	1
Symbol values:	1	1	1	0	0	1

and thus decimal 57 is equivalent to binary 111001.

To convert decimal 103 to octal, we write the positional values of the columns until we reach a column whose positional value is greater than the decimal number. We do not need that column, so we discard it. Thus, we first write:

Positional values:	512	64	8	1

Then we discard the column with positional value 512, yielding:

Positional values:	64	8	1

Next we work from the leftmost column to the right. We divide 64 into 103 and observe that there is one 64 in 103 with a remainder of 39, so we write 1 in the 64 column. We divide 8 into 39 and observe that there are four 8s in 39 with a remainder of 7, so we write 4 in the 8 column. Finally, we divide 1 into 7 and observe that there are seven 1s in 7 with no remainder, so we write 7 in the 1 column. This yields:

Positional values:	64	8	1
Symbol values:	1	4	7

and thus decimal 103 is equivalent to octal 147.

To convert decimal 375 to hexadecimal, we write the positional values of the columns until we reach a column whose positional value is greater than the decimal number. We do not need that column, so we discard it. Thus, we first write:

Positional values:	4096	256	16	1

Then we discard the column with positional value 4096, yielding:

Positional values:	256	16	1

Next we work from the leftmost column to the right. We divide 256 into 375 and observe that there is one 256 in 375 with a remainder of 119, so we write 1 in the 256 column. We divide 16 into 119 and observe that there are seven 16s in 119 with a remainder of 7, so we write 7 in the 16 column. Finally, we divide 1 into 7 and observe that there are seven 1s in 7 with no remainder, so we write 7 in the 1 column. This yields:

```
Positional values: 256    16    1
Symbol values:     1      7     7
```

and thus decimal 375 is equivalent to hexadecimal 177.

C.6 Negative Binary Numbers: Two's-Complement Notation

The discussion so far in this appendix has focused on positive numbers. In this section, we explain how computers represent negative numbers using *two's-complement notation*. First we explain how the two's complement of a binary number is formed, then we show why it represents the negative value of the given binary number.

Consider a machine with 32-bit integers. Suppose

```
Dim value As Integer = 13
```

The 32-bit representation of `value` is

```
00000000 00000000 00000000 00001101
```

To form the negative of `value` we first form its *one's complement* by combining `value` with `&H7FFFFFFF` using Visual Basic's `Xor` operator, as in:

```
onesComplement = value Xor &H7FFFFFFF
```

Internally, `onesComplement` is now `value` with each of its bits reversed—ones become zeros and zeros become ones, as follows:

```
value:
00000000 00000000 00000000 00001101

onesComplement
11111111 11111111 11111111 11110010
```

To form the two's complement of `value`, we simply add 1 to `value`'s one's complement, which produces

```
Two's complement of value:
11111111 11111111 11111111 11110011
```

Now if this is in fact equal to –13, we should be able to add it to binary 13 and obtain a result of 0. Let us try this:

```
 00000000 00000000 00000000 00001101
+11111111 11111111 11111111 11110011
------------------------------------
 00000000 00000000 00000000 00000000
```

The carry bit coming out of the leftmost column is discarded and we indeed get 0 as a result. If we add the one's complement of a number to the number, the result will be all 1s. The key to getting a result of all zeros is that the two's complement is one more than the one's complement. The addition of 1 causes each column to add to 0 with a carry of 1. The carry keeps moving leftward until it is discarded from the leftmost bit, and thus the resulting number is all zeros.

Computers actually perform a subtraction, such as

```
x = a - value;
```

by adding the two's complement of `value` to a, as follows:

```
x = a + (onesComplement + 1);
```

Suppose a is 27 and `value` is 13, as before. If the two's complement of `value` is actually the negative of `value`, then adding the two's complement of value to a should produce the result 14. Let us try this:

```
a (i.e., 27)                  00000000 00000000 00000000 00011011
+(onesComplement + 1)        +11111111 11111111 11111111 11110011
                              -----------------------------------
                              00000000 00000000 00000000 00001110
```

which is indeed equal to 14.

Summary

- An integer such as 19 or 227 or –63 in a program is assumed to be in the decimal (base-10) number system. The digits in the decimal number system are 0, 1, 2, 3, 4, 5, 6, 7, 8 and 9. The lowest digit is 0 and the highest digit is 9—one less than the base of 10.
- Internally, computers use the binary (base-2) number system. The binary number system has only two digits, namely 0 and 1. Its lowest digit is 0 and its highest digit is 1—one less than the base of 2.
- The octal number system (base 8) and the hexadecimal number system (base 16) are popular primarily because they make it convenient to abbreviate binary numbers.
- The digits of the octal number system range from 0 to 7.
- The hexadecimal number system poses a problem because it requires 16 digits—a lowest digit of 0 and a highest digit with a value equivalent to decimal 15 (one less than the base of 16). By convention, we use the letters A through F to represent the hexadecimal digits corresponding to decimal values 10 through 15.
- Each number system uses positional notation—each position in which a digit is written has a different positional value.
- A particularly important relationship of both the octal number system and the hexadecimal number system to the binary system is that the bases of octal and hexadecimal (8 and 16 respectively) are powers of the base of the binary number system (base 2).
- To convert an octal to a binary number, replace each octal digit with its three-digit binary equivalent.
- To convert a hexadecimal number to a binary number, simply replace each hexadecimal digit with its four-digit binary equivalent.
- Because we are accustomed to working in decimal, it is convenient to convert a binary, octal or hexadecimal number to decimal to get a sense of the number's "real" worth.
- To convert a number to decimal from another base, multiply the decimal equivalent of each digit by its positional value and sum the products.
- Computers represent negative numbers using two's-complement notation.
- To form the negative of a value in binary, first form its one's complement by combining the value with `&H7FFFFFFF` using Visual Basic's `Xor` operator. This reverses the bits of the value. To form the two's complement of a value, simply add one to the value's one's complement.

Terminology

base
base-2 number system
base-8 number system
base-10 number system
base-16 number system
binary number system
conversions
decimal number system
digit
hexadecimal number system
negative value
octal number system
one's-complement notation
positional notation
positional value
symbol value
two's-complement notation

Self-Review Exercises

C.1 Fill in the blanks in each of the following statements:

a) The bases of the decimal, binary, octal and hexadecimal number systems are ________, ________, ________ and ________, respectively.

b) The positional value of the rightmost digit of any number in either binary, octal, decimal or hexadecimal is always ________.

c) The positional value of the digit to the left of the rightmost digit of any number in binary, octal, decimal or hexadecimal is always equal to ________.

C.2 State whether each of the following is *true* or *false*. If *false*, explain why.

a) A popular reason for using the decimal number system is that it forms a convenient notation for abbreviating binary numbers simply by substituting one decimal digit per group of four binary bits.

b) The highest digit in any base is one more than the base.

c) The lowest digit in any base is one less than the base.

C.3 In general, the decimal, octal and hexadecimal representations of a given binary number contain (more/fewer) digits than the binary number contains.

C.4 The (octal / hexadecimal / decimal) representation of a large binary value is the most concise (of the given alternatives).

C.5 Fill in the missing values in this chart of positional values for the rightmost four positions in each of the indicated number systems:

decimal	1000	100	10	1
hexadecimal	...	256	...	...
binary	...	...	...	...
octal	512	...	8	...

C.6 Convert binary 110101011000 to octal and to hexadecimal.

C.7 Convert hexadecimal FACE to binary.

C.8 Convert octal 7316 to binary.

C.9 Convert hexadecimal 4FEC to octal. [*Hint:* First convert 4FEC to binary, then convert that binary number to octal.]

C.10 Convert binary 1101110 to decimal.

C.11 Convert octal 317 to decimal.

C.12 Convert hexadecimal EFD4 to decimal.

C.13 Convert decimal 177 to binary, to octal and to hexadecimal.

C.14 Show the binary representation of decimal 417. Then show the one's complement of 417 and the two's complement of 417.

C.15 What is the result when a number and its two's complement are added to each other?

Answers to Self-Review Exercises

C.1 a) 10, 2, 8, 16. b) 1 (the base raised to the zero power). c) The base of the number system.

C.2 a) False. Hexadecimal does this. b) False. The highest digit in any base is one less than the base. c) False. The lowest digit in any base is zero.

C.3 Fewer.

C.4 Hexadecimal.

C.5 Fill in the missing values in this chart of positional values for the rightmost four positions in each of the indicated number systems:

decimal	1000	100	10	1
hexadecimal	4096	256	16	1
binary	8	4	2	1
octal	512	64	8	1

C.6 Octal 6530; Hexadecimal D58.

C.7 Binary 1111 1010 1100 1110.

C.8 Binary 111 011 001 110.

C.9 Binary 0 100 111 111 101 100; Octal 47754.

C.10 Decimal 2 + 4 + 8 + 32 + 64 = 110.

C.11 Decimal 7 + 1 * 8 + 3 * 64 = 7 + 8 + 192 = 207.

C.12 Decimal 4 + 13 * 16 + 15 * 256 + 14 * 4096 = 61396.

C.13 Decimal 177
to binary:

```
256 128 64 32 16 8 4 2 1
128 64 32 16 8 4 2 1
(1*128)+(0*64)+(1*32)+(1*16)+(0*8)+(0*4)+(0*2)+(1*1)
10110001
```

to octal:

```
512 64 8 1
64 8 1
(2*64)+(6*8)+(1*1)
261
```

to hexadecimal:

```
256 16 1
16 1
(11*16)+(1*1)
(B*16)+(1*1)
B1
```

C.14 Binary:

```
512 256 128 64 32 16 8 4 2 1
256 128 64 32 16 8 4 2 1
(1*256)+(1*128)+(0*64)+(1*32)+(0*16)+(0*8)+(0*4)+(0*2)+(1*1)
110100001
```

One's complement: 001011110
Two's complement: 001011111
Check: Original binary number + its two's complement

```
110100001
001011111
---------
000000000
```

C.15 Zero.

Exercises

C.16 Some people argue that many of our calculations would be easier in the base-12 number system because 12 is divisible by so many more numbers than 10 (for base 10). What is the lowest digit in base 12? What would be the highest symbol for the digit in base 12? What are the positional values of the rightmost four positions of any number in the base-12 number system?

C.17 Complete the following chart of positional values for the rightmost four positions in each of the indicated number systems:

decimal	1000	100	10	1
base 6	...	...	6	...
base 13	...	169	...	...
base 3	27	...	...	...

C.18 Convert binary 100101111010 to octal and to hexadecimal.

C.19 Convert hexadecimal 3A7D to binary.

C.20 Convert hexadecimal 765F to octal. (*Hint:* First convert 765F to binary, then convert that binary number to octal.)

C.21 Convert binary 1011110 to decimal.

C.22 Convert octal 426 to decimal.

C.23 Convert hexadecimal FFFF to decimal.

C.24 Convert decimal 299 to binary, to octal and to hexadecimal.

C.25 Show the binary representation of decimal 779. Then show the one's complement of 779 and the two's complement of 779.

C.26 Show the two's complement of integer value –1 on a machine with 32-bit integers.

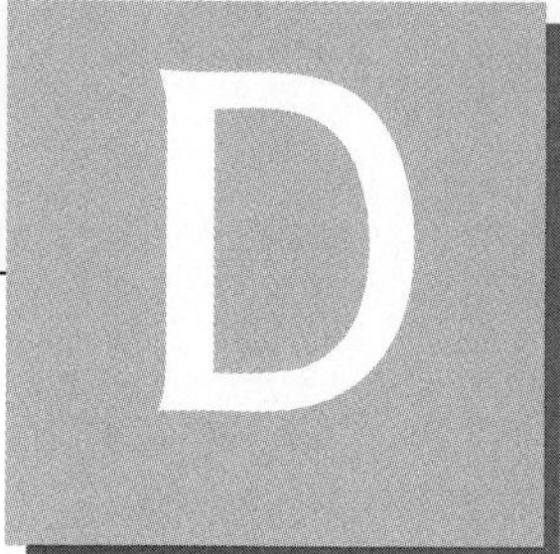

ATM Case Study Code

D.1 ATM Case Study Implementation

This appendix contains the complete working implementation of the ATM system that we designed in the nine Software Engineering Case Study sections in Chapters 1, 3–8, 10 and 12. The implementation comprises 597 lines of Visual Basic code. We consider the 11 classes in the order in which we identified them in Section 4.9 (with the exception of `Transaction`, which was introduced in Chapter 12 as the base class of classes `BalanceInquiry`, `Withdrawal` and `Deposit`):

- `ATM`
- `Screen`
- `Keypad`
- `CashDispenser`
- `DepositSlot`
- `Account`
- `BankDatabase`
- `Transaction`
- `BalanceInquiry`
- `Withdrawal`
- `Deposit`

We apply the guidelines discussed in Section 10.19 and Section 12.8 to code these classes based on how we modeled them in the UML class diagrams of Fig. 12.19 and Fig. 12.20. To develop the bodies of class methods, we refer to the activity diagrams presented in Section 6.11 and the communication and sequence diagrams presented in Section 7.20. Note that our ATM design does not specify all the program logic and may not specify all the attributes and operations required to complete the ATM implementation. This is a normal part of the object-oriented design process. As we implement the system, we complete the program logic and add attributes and behaviors as necessary to construct the ATM system specified by the requirements document in Section 3.10.

We conclude the discussion by presenting a Visual Basic application (`ATMCaseStudy` in Section D.13) that creates an object of class `ATM` and starts it by calling its `run` method. Recall that we are developing a first version of the ATM system that runs on a personal computer and uses the keyboard and monitor to approximate the ATM's keypad and screen. Also, we simulate the actions of the ATM's cash dispenser and deposit slot. We attempt to implement the system, however, so that real hardware versions of these devices could be integrated without significant code changes.

D.2 Class ATM

Class `ATM` (Fig. D.1) represents the ATM as a whole. Lines 4–10 implement the class's attributes. We determine all but one of these attributes from the UML class diagrams of Fig. 12.19 and Fig. 12.20. Line 4 declares the `Boolean` attribute `userAuthenticated` from Fig. 12.21. Line 5 declares an attribute not found in our UML design—an `Integer` attribute `currentAccountNumber` that keeps track of the account number of the current authenticated user. We will soon see how the class uses this attribute. Lines 6–10 declare reference-type attributes corresponding to the `ATM` class's associations modeled in the class diagram of Fig. 12.19. These attributes allow the ATM to access its parts (i.e., its `Screen`, `Keypad`, `CashDispenser` and `DepositSlot`) and interact with the bank's account-information database (i.e., a `BankDatabase` object).

```
1  ' ATM.vb
2  ' Represents an automated teller machine.
3  Public Class ATM
4     Private userAuthenticated As Boolean ' whether user is authenticated
5     Private currentAccountNumber As Integer ' user's account number
6     Private screenHandle As Screen ' ATM's screen
7     Private keypadHandle As Keypad ' ATM's keypad
8     Private cashDispenserHandle As CashDispenser ' ATM's cash dispenser
9     Private depositSlotHandle As DepositSlot ' ATM's deposit slot
10    Private bankDatabaseHandle As BankDatabase ' account database
11
12    ' enumeration constants represent main-menu options
13    Private Enum MenuOption
14       BALANCE_INQUIRY = 1
15       WITHDRAWAL
16       DEPOSIT
17       EXIT_ATM
18    End Enum ' MenuOption
19
20    ' parameterless constructor initializes instance variables
21    Public Sub New()
22       userAuthenticated = False ' user is not authenticated to start
23       currentAccountNumber = 0 ' no current account number to start
24       screenHandle = New Screen() ' create screen
```

Fig. D.1 | Class `ATM` represents the ATM. (Part 1 of 3.)

```
      keypadHandle = New Keypad() ' create keypad
      cashDispenserHandle = New CashDispenser() ' create cash dispenser
      depositSlotHandle = New DepositSlot() ' create deposit slot
      bankDatabaseHandle = New BankDatabase() ' create database
   End Sub ' New

   ' start ATM
   Public Sub Run()
      ' welcome and authenticate users; perform transactions
      While (True) ' infinite loop
         ' loop while user is not yet authenticated
         While (Not userAuthenticated)
            screenHandle.DisplayMessageLine(vbCrLf & "Welcome!")
            AuthenticateUser() ' authenticate user
         End While

         PerformTransactions() ' for authenticated user
         userAuthenticated = False ' reset before next ATM session
         currentAccountNumber = 0 ' reset before next ATM session
         screenHandle.DisplayMessageLine(vbCrLf & "Thank you! Goodbye!")
      End While
   End Sub ' Run

   ' attempt to authenticate user against database
   Private Sub AuthenticateUser()
      screenHandle.DisplayMessage(vbCrLf & _
         "Please enter your account number: ")
      Dim accountNumber As Integer = keypadHandle.GetInput()
      screenHandle.DisplayMessage(vbCrLf & "Enter your PIN: ") ' prompt
      Dim pin As Integer = keypadHandle.GetInput() ' get PIN

      ' set userAuthenticated to Boolean value returned by database
      userAuthenticated = _
         bankDatabaseHandle.AuthenticateUser(accountNumber, pin)

      ' check whether authentication succeeded
      If userAuthenticated Then
         currentAccountNumber = accountNumber ' save user's account #
      Else
         screenHandle.DisplayMessageLine( _
            "Invalid account number or PIN. Please try again.")
      End If
   End Sub ' AuthenticateUser

   ' display the main menu and perform transactions
   Private Sub PerformTransactions()
      Dim currentTransaction As Transaction ' transaction being processed
      Dim userExited As Boolean = False ' user has not chosen to exit

      ' loop while user has not chosen exit option
      While (Not userExited)
         ' show main menu and get user selection
         Dim mainMenuSelection As Integer = DisplayMainMenu()
```

Fig. D.1 | Class ATM represents the ATM. (Part 2 of 3.)

```

         ' decide how to proceed based on user's menu selection
         Select Case (mainMenuSelection)
            ' user chooses to perform one of three transaction types
            Case MenuOption.BALANCE_INQUIRY, MenuOption.WITHDRAWAL, _
               MenuOption.DEPOSIT
               ' initialize as new object of chosen type
               currentTransaction = CreateTransaction(mainMenuSelection)
               currentTransaction.Execute() ' execute transaction
            Case MenuOption.EXIT_ATM ' user chose to terminate session
               screenHandle.DisplayMessageLine( _
                  vbCrLf & "Exiting the system...")
               userExited = True ' this ATM session should end
            Case Else ' user did not enter an integer from 1-4
               screenHandle.DisplayMessageLine(vbCrLf & _
                  "You did not enter a valid selection. Try again.")
         End Select
      End While
   End Sub ' PerformTransactions

   ' display the main menu and return an input selection
   Private Function DisplayMainMenu() As Integer
      screenHandle.DisplayMessageLine(vbCrLf & "Main menu:")
      screenHandle.DisplayMessageLine("1 - View my balance")
      screenHandle.DisplayMessageLine("2 - Withdraw cash")
      screenHandle.DisplayMessageLine("3 - Deposit funds")
      screenHandle.DisplayMessageLine("4 - Exit" & vbCrLf)
      screenHandle.DisplayMessage("Enter a choice: ")
      Return keypadHandle.GetInput() ' return user's selection
   End Function ' DisplayMainMenu

   ' return object of specified Transaction derived class
   Private Function CreateTransaction(ByVal type As Integer) _
      As Transaction
      Dim temp As Transaction = Nothing ' temporary Transaction object

      ' determine which type of Transaction to create
      Select Case (type)
         ' create new BalanceInquiry transaction
         Case MenuOption.BALANCE_INQUIRY
            temp = New BalanceInquiry( _
               currentAccountNumber, screenHandle, bankDatabaseHandle)
         Case MenuOption.WITHDRAWAL ' create new Withdrawal transaction
            temp = New Withdrawal(currentAccountNumber, screenHandle, _
               bankDatabaseHandle, keypadHandle, cashDispenserHandle)
         Case MenuOption.DEPOSIT ' create new Deposit transaction
            temp = New Deposit(currentAccountNumber, screenHandle, _
               bankDatabaseHandle, keypadHandle, depositSlotHandle)
      End Select

      Return temp
   End Function ' CreateTransaction
End Class ' ATM
```

Fig. D.1 | Class ATM represents the ATM. (Part 3 of 3.)

Lines 13–18 declare an enumeration that corresponds to the four options in the ATM's main menu (i.e., balance inquiry, withdrawal, deposit and exit). Lines 21–29 declare class ATM's constructor, which initializes the class's attributes. When an ATM object is first created, no user is authenticated, so line 22 initializes userAuthenticated to False. Line 23 initializes currentAccountNumber to 0, because there is no current user yet. Lines 24–27 instantiate new objects to represent the parts of the ATM. Recall that class ATM has composition relationships with classes Screen, Keypad, CashDispenser and DepositSlot, so class ATM is responsible for their creation. Line 28 creates a new BankDatabase. As you will soon see, the BankDatabase creates two Account objects that can be used to test the ATM. [*Note:* If this were a real ATM system, the ATM class would receive a reference to an existing database object created by the bank. However, in this implementation we are only simulating the bank's database, so class ATM creates the BankDatabase object with which it interacts.]

Implementing the Operation

The class diagram of Fig. 12.20 does not list any operations for class ATM. We now implement one operation (i.e., Public method) in class ATM that allows an external client of the class (i.e., module ATMCaseStudy; Section D.13) to tell the ATM to run. ATM method Run (lines 32–46) uses an infinite loop (lines 34–45) to repeatedly welcome a user, attempt to authenticate the user and, if authentication succeeds, allow the user to perform transactions. After an authenticated user performs the desired transactions and chooses to exit, the ATM resets itself, displays a goodbye message to the user and restarts the process. We use an infinite loop here to simulate the fact that an ATM appears to run continuously until the bank turns it off (an action beyond the user's control). An ATM user has the option to exit the system, but does not have the ability to turn off the ATM completely.

Inside method Run's infinite loop, lines 36–39 cause the ATM to repeatedly welcome and attempt to authenticate the user as long as the user has not been authenticated (i.e., the condition Not userAuthenticated is True). Line 37 invokes method DisplayMessageLine of the ATM's screen to display a welcome message. Like Screen method DisplayMessage designed in the case study, method DisplayMessageLine (declared in lines 10–12 of Fig. D.2) displays a message to the user, but this method also outputs a newline after displaying the message. We add this method during implementation to give class Screen's clients more control over the placement of displayed messages. Line 38 invokes class ATM's Private utility method AuthenticateUser (declared in lines 49–67) to attempt to authenticate the user.

Authenticating the User

We refer to the requirements document to determine the steps necessary to authenticate the user before allowing transactions to occur. Lines 50–51 of method AuthenticateUser invoke method DisplayMessage of the ATM's screen to prompt the user to enter an account number. Line 52 invokes method GetInput of the ATM's keypad to obtain the user's input, then stores the integer value entered by the user in local variable accountNumber. Method AuthenticateUser next prompts the user to enter a PIN (line 53), and stores the PIN input by the user in local variable pin (line 54). Next, lines 57–58 attempt to authenticate the user by passing the accountNumber and pin entered by the user to the bank database's AuthenticateUser method. Class ATM sets its userAuthenticated attribute to the Boolean value returned by this method—userAuthenticated becomes True if authentication succeeds (i.e., accountNumber and pin match those of an existing Account in the bank database) and remains `False` otherwise. If `userAuthenticated` is `True`, line 62 saves the account number entered by the user (i.e., `accountNumber`) in the ATM attribute `currentAccountNumber`. The other methods of class `ATM` use this variable whenever an ATM session requires access to the user's account number. If `userAuthenticated` is `False`, lines 64–65 use the `screenHandle`'s `DisplayMessageLine` method to indicate that an invalid account number and/or PIN was entered, so the user must try again. Note that we set `currentAccountNumber` only after authenticating the user's account number and the associated PIN—if the database could not authenticate the user, `currentAccountNumber` remains `0`.

After method `Run` attempts to authenticate the user (line 38), if `userAuthenticated` is still `False` (line 36), the `While` loop body (lines 37–38) executes again. If `userAuthenticated` is now `True`, the loop terminates and control continues with line 41, which calls class `ATM`'s `Private` utility method `PerformTransactions`.

Performing Transactions

Method `PerformTransactions` (lines 70–96) carries out an ATM session for an authenticated user. Line 71 declares local variable `Transaction` to which we assign a `BalanceInquiry`, `Withdrawal` or `Deposit` object representing the ATM transaction currently being processed. Note that we use a `Transaction` variable here to allow us to take advantage of polymorphism. Also note that we name this variable after the role name included in the class diagram of Fig. 4.19—`currentTransaction`. Line 72 declares another local variable—a `Boolean` called `userExited` that keeps track of whether the user has chosen to exit. This variable controls a `While` loop (lines 75–95) that allows the user to execute an unlimited number of transactions before choosing to exit. Within this loop, line 77 displays the main menu and obtains the user's menu selection by calling `ATM` utility method `DisplayMainMenu` (declared in lines 99–107). This method displays the main menu by invoking methods of the `ATM`'s screen and returns a menu selection obtained from the user through the `ATM`'s keypad. Line 77 stores the user's selection returned by `DisplayMainMenu` in local variable `mainMenuSelection`.

After obtaining a main-menu selection, method `PerformTransactions` uses a `Select Case` statement (lines 80–94) to respond to the selection appropriately. If `mainMenuSelection` is equal to any of the three integer constants representing transaction types (i.e., if the user chose to perform a transaction), line 85 calls utility method `CreateTransaction` (declared in lines 110–129) to return a newly instantiated object of the type that corresponds to the selected transaction. Variable `currentTransaction` is assigned the reference returned by method `CreateTransaction`, then line 86 invokes method `Execute` of this transaction to execute it. We will discuss `Transaction` method `Execute` and the three `Transaction` derived classes shortly. Note that we assign to the `Transaction` variable `currentTransaction` an object of one of the three `Transaction` derived classes so that we can execute transactions polymorphically. For example, if the user chooses to perform a balance inquiry, `mainMenuSelection` equals `MenuOption.BALANCE_INQUIRY`, and `CreateTransaction` returns a `BalanceInquiry` object (line 85). Thus, `currentTransaction` refers to a `BalanceInquiry` and invoking `currentTransaction.Execute()` (line 86) results in `BalanceInquiry`'s version of `Execute` being called.

Creating Transactions

Method `CreateTransaction` (lines 110–129) uses a `Select Case` statement (lines 115–126) to instantiate a new `Transaction` derived class object of the type indicated by the parameter type. Recall that method PerformTransactions passes mainMenuSelection to method CreateTransaction only when mainMenuSelection contains a value corresponding to one of the three transaction types. So parameter type (line 110) receives one of the values MenuOption.BALANCE_INQUIRY, MenuOption.WITHDRAWAL or MenuOption.DEPOSIT. Each Case in the Select Case statement instantiates a new object by calling the appropriate Transaction derived class constructor. Note that each constructor has a unique parameter list, based on the specific data required to initialize the derived class object. A BalanceInquiry (lines 118–119) requires only the account number of the current user and the ATM's screenHandle and bankDatabaseHandle. In addition to these parameters, a Withdrawal (lines 121–122) requires the ATM's keypadHandle and cashDispenserHandle, and a Deposit (lines 124–125) requires the ATM's keypadHandle and depositSlotHandle. We discuss the transaction classes in more detail in Sections D.9–D.12.

After a transaction is executed (line 86 in method PerformTransactions), userExited remains False and the While loop in lines 75–95 repeats, returning the user to the main menu. However, if a user does not perform a transaction and instead selects the main menu option to exit, line 90 sets userExited to True, causing the condition in line 75 of the While loop (Not userExited) to become False. This While is the final statement of method PerformTransactions, so control returns to line 42 of the calling method Run. If the user enters an invalid main-menu selection (i.e., not an integer in the range 1–4), lines 92–93 display an appropriate error message, userExited (as set in line 72) remains False and the user returns to the main menu to try again.

When method PerformTransactions returns control to method Run, the user has chosen to exit the system, so lines 42–43 reset the ATM's attributes userAuthenticated and currentAccountNumber to False and 0, respectively, to prepare for the next ATM user. Line 44 displays a goodbye message to the current user before the ATM welcomes the next user.

D.3 Class Screen

Class Screen (Fig. D.2) represents the screen of the ATM and encapsulates all aspects of displaying output to the user. Class Screen simulates a real ATM's screen with the computer monitor and outputs text messages using standard console output methods Console.Write and Console.WriteLine. In the design portion of this case study, we endowed class Screen with one operation—DisplayMessage. For greater flexibility in displaying messages to the Screen, we now declare three Screen methods—DisplayMessage, DisplayMessageLine and DisplayDollarAmount.

```
' Screen.vb
' Represents the screen of the ATM
Public Class Screen
   ' displays a message without a terminating carriage return
   Public Sub DisplayMessage(ByVal message As String)
      Console.Write(message)
   End Sub ' DisplayMessage

```

Fig. D.2 | Class Screen represents the screen of the ATM. (Part 1 of 2.)

```
9    ' display a message with a terminating carriage return
10   Public Sub DisplayMessageLine(ByVal message As String)
11      Console.WriteLine(message)
12   End Sub ' DisplayMessageLine
13
14   ' display a dollar amount
15   Public Sub DisplayDollarAmount(ByVal amount As Decimal)
16      Console.Write("{0:C}", amount)
17   End Sub ' DisplayDollarAmount
18 End Class ' Screen
```

Fig. D.2 | Class `Screen` represents the screen of the ATM. (Part 2 of 2.)

Method `DisplayMessage` (lines 5–7) takes a `String` as an argument and prints it to the screen using `Console.Write`. The cursor stays on the same line, making this method appropriate for displaying prompts to the user. Method `DisplayMessageLine` (lines 10–12) does the same using `Console.WriteLine`, which outputs a newline to move the cursor to the next line. Finally, method `DisplayDollarAmount` (lines 15–17) outputs a properly formatted dollar amount (e.g., `$1,234.56`). Line 16 uses method `Console.Write` to output a `Decimal` value formatted as currency with two decimal places and commas to increase the readability of large dollar amounts.

D.4 Class Keypad

Class `Keypad` (Fig. D.3) represents the keypad of the ATM and is responsible for receiving all user input. Recall that we are simulating this hardware, so we use the computer's keyboard to approximate the keypad. We use method `Console.ReadLine` to obtain keyboard input from the user. A computer keyboard contains many keys not found on the ATM's keypad. We assume that the user presses only the keys on the computer keyboard that also appear on the keypad—the keys numbered 0–9 and the *Enter* key.

Method `GetInput` (lines 5–7) invokes `Convert` method `ToInt32` to convert the input returned by `Console.ReadLine` (line 6) to an `Integer` value. [*Note:* Method `ToInt32` can throw a `FormatException` if the user enters noninteger input. Because the real ATM's keypad permits only integer input, we simply assume that no exceptions will occur. See Chapter 13, Exception Handling, for information on catching and processing exceptions.] Recall that `ReadLine` obtains all the input used by the ATM. Class `Keypad`'s `GetInput` method simply returns the integer input by the user. If a client of class `Keypad` requires

```
1 ' Keypad.vb
2 ' Represents the keypad of the ATM.
3 Public Class Keypad
4    ' return an integer value entered by user
5    Public Function GetInput() As Integer
6       Return Convert.ToInt32(Console.ReadLine())
7    End Function ' GetInput
8 End Class ' Keypad
```

Fig. D.3 | Class `Keypad` represents the ATM's keypad.

input that satisfies some particular criteria (i.e., a number corresponding to a valid menu option), the client must perform the appropriate error checking.

D.5 Class CashDispenser

Class `CashDispenser` (Fig. D.4) represents the cash dispenser of the ATM. Line 5 declares constant `INITIAL_COUNT`, which indicates the initial count of bills in the cash dispenser when the ATM starts (i.e., `500`). Line 6 implements attribute `billCount` (modeled in Fig. 12.20), which keeps track of the number of bills remaining in the `CashDispenser` at any time. The constructor (lines 9–11) sets `billCount` to the initial count. [*Note:* We assume that the process of adding more bills to the `CashDispenser` and updating the `billCount` occurs outside the ATM system.] Class `CashDispenser` has two `Public` methods—`DispenseCash` (lines 14–18) and `IsSufficientCashAvailable` (lines 21–31). The class trusts that a client (i.e., `Withdrawal`) calls method `DispenseCash` only after establishing that sufficient cash is available by calling method `IsSufficientCashAvailable`. Thus, `DispenseCash` simply simulates dispensing the requested amount without checking whether sufficient cash is available.

```
1  ' CashDispenser.vb
2  ' Represents the cash dispenser of the ATM
3  Public Class CashDispenser
4     ' the default initial number of bills in the cash dispenser
5     Private Const INITIAL_COUNT As Integer = 500
6     Private billCount As Integer ' number of $20 bills remaining
7
8     ' parameterless constructor initializes billCount to INITIAL_COUNT
9     Public Sub New()
10       billCount = INITIAL_COUNT ' set billCount to INITIAL_COUNT
11    End Sub ' New
12
13    ' simulates dispensing of specified amount of cash
14    Public Sub DispenseCash(ByVal amount As Decimal)
15       ' number of $20 bills required
16       Dim billsRequired As Integer = (Convert.ToInt32(amount) \ 20)
17       billCount -= billsRequired
18    End Sub ' DispenseCash
19
20    ' indicates whether cash dispenser can dispense desired amount
21    Public Function IsSufficientCashAvailable(ByVal amount As Decimal) _
22       As Boolean
23       ' number of $20 bills required
24       Dim billsRequired As Integer = (Convert.ToInt32(amount) \ 20)
25
26       If (billCount >= billsRequired) Then
27          Return True ' enough bills available
28       Else
29          Return False ' not enough bills available
30       End If
31    End Function ' IsSufficientCashAvailable
32 End Class ' CashDispenser
```

Fig. D.4 | Class `CashDispenser` represents the ATM's cash dispenser.

Method `IsSufficientCashAvailable` (lines 21–31) has a parameter `amount` that specifies the amount of cash in question. Line 24 calculates the number of $20 bills required to dispense the specified `amount`. The ATM allows the user to choose only withdrawal amounts that are multiples of $20, so we convert `amount` to an integer value and divide it by `20` to obtain the number of `billsRequired`. Lines 26–30 return `True` if the `CashDispenser`'s `billCount` is greater than or equal to `billsRequired` (i.e., enough bills are available) and `False` otherwise (i.e., not enough bills). For example, if a user wishes to withdraw $80 (i.e., `billsRequired` is `4`), but only three bills remain (i.e., `billCount` is `3`), the method returns `False`.

Method `DispenseCash` (lines 14–18) simulates cash dispensing. If our system were hooked up to a real hardware cash dispenser, this method would interact with the hardware device to physically dispense cash. Our simulated version of the method simply decreases the `billCount` of bills remaining by the number required to dispense the specified `amount` (line 17). Note that it is the responsibility of the client of the class (i.e., `Withdrawal`) to inform the user that cash has been dispensed—`CashDispenser` does not interact directly with `Screen`.

D.6 Class DepositSlot

Class `DepositSlot` (Fig. D.5) represents the deposit slot of the ATM. Like the version of class `CashDispenser` presented here, this version of class `DepositSlot` merely simulates the functionality of a real hardware deposit slot. `DepositSlot` has no attributes and only one method—`IsDepositEnvelopeReceived` (lines 6–8)—that indicates whether a deposit envelope was received.

Recall from the requirements document that the ATM allows the user up to two minutes to insert an envelope. The current version of method `IsDepositEnvelopeReceived` simply returns `True` immediately (line 7), because this is only a software simulation, and we assume that the user inserts an envelope within the required time frame. If an actual hardware deposit slot were connected to our system, method `IsDepositEnvelopeReceived` would be implemented to wait for a maximum of two minutes to receive a signal from the hardware deposit slot indicating that the user has indeed inserted a deposit envelope. If `IsDepositEnvelopeReceived` were to receive such a signal within two minutes, the method would return `True`. If two minutes were to elapse and the method still had not received a signal, then the method would return `False`.

```
1  ' DepositSlot.vb
2  ' Represents the deposit slot of the ATM
3  Public Class DepositSlot
4     ' indicates whether envelope was received (always returns true,
5     ' because this is only a software simulation of a real deposit slot)
6     Public Function IsDepositEnvelopeReceived() As Boolean
7        Return True ' deposit envelope was received
8     End Function ' IsDepositEnvelopeReceived
9  End Class ' DepositSlot
```

Fig. D.5 | Class `DepositSlot` represents the ATM's deposit slot.

D.7 Class Account

Class Account (Fig. D.6) represents a bank account. Each Account has four attributes (modeled in Fig. 12.20)—accountNumber, pin, availableBalance and totalBalance. Lines 4–7 implement these attributes as Private instance variables. Note that when we provide a property to access an instance variable, we create the instance-variable name by appending Value to the end of the attribute name that was listed in the model. We provide a property with the same name as the attribute name (but starting with a capital letter) to access the instance variable. For example, property AccountNumber corresponds to the accountNumber attribute modeled in Fig. 12.20. Since clients of this class do not need to modify the accountNumberValue instance variable, AccountNumber is a ReadOnly property (i.e., it provides only a Get accessory).

```
1  ' Account.vb
2  ' Represents a bank account.
3  Public Class Account
4     Private accountNumberValue As Integer ' account number
5     Private pin As Integer ' PIN for authentication
6     Private availableBalanceValue As Decimal ' available withdrawal amount
7     Private totalBalanceValue As Decimal ' funds available+pending deposit
8
9     ' constructor initializes attributes
10    Public Sub New(ByVal theAccountNumber As Integer, _
11       ByVal thePIN As Integer, ByVal theAvailableBalance As Decimal, _
12       ByVal theTotalBalance As Decimal)
13       accountNumberValue = theAccountNumber
14       pin = thePIN
15       availableBalanceValue = theAvailableBalance
16       totalBalanceValue = theTotalBalance
17    End Sub ' New
18
19    ' property AccountNumber
20    Public ReadOnly Property AccountNumber() As Integer
21       Get
22          Return accountNumberValue
23       End Get
24    End Property ' AccountNumber
25
26    ' property AvailableBalance
27    Public ReadOnly Property AvailableBalance() As Decimal
28       Get
29          Return availableBalanceValue
30       End Get
31    End Property ' AvailableBalance
32
33    ' property TotalBalance
34    Public ReadOnly Property TotalBalance() As Decimal
35       Get
36          Return totalBalanceValue
37       End Get
38    End Property ' TotalBalance
```

Fig. D.6 | Class Account represents a bank account. (Part 1 of 2.)

```
39
40     ' determines whether a user-specified PIN matches PIN in Account
41     Public Function ValidatePIN(ByVal userPIN As Integer) As Boolean
42        If userPIN = pin Then
43           Return True
44        Else
45           Return False
46        End If
47     End Function ' ValidatePIN
48
49     ' credits the account (funds have not yet cleared)
50     Public Sub Credit(ByVal amount As Decimal)
51        totalBalanceValue += amount ' add to total balance
52     End Sub ' Credit
53
54     ' debits the account
55     Public Sub Debit(ByVal amount As Decimal)
56        availableBalanceValue -= amount ' subtract from available balance
57        totalBalanceValue -= amount ' subtract from total balance
58     End Sub ' Debit
59  End Class ' Account
```

Fig. D.6 | Class `Account` represents a bank account. (Part 2 of 2.)

Class `Account` has a constructor (lines 10–17) that takes an account number, the PIN established for the account, the initial available balance and the initial total balance as arguments. Lines 13–16 assign these values to the class's attributes (i.e., instance variables). Note that `Account` objects would normally be created externally to the ATM system. However, in this simulation, the `Account` objects are created in the `BankDatabase` class (Fig. D.7).

`Public ReadOnly` Properties of Class `Account`

`ReadOnly` property `AccountNumber` (lines 20–24) provides access to an `Account`'s `accountNumberValue`. We include this property in our implementation so that a client of the class (e.g., `BankDatabase`) can identify a particular `Account`. For example, `BankDatabase` contains many `Account` objects, and it can access this property on each of its `Account` objects to locate the one with a specific account number.

`ReadOnly` properties `AvailableBalance` (lines 27–31) and `TotalBalance` (lines 34–38) allow clients to retrieve the values of `Private Decimal` instance variables `availableBalanceValue` and `totalBalanceValue`, respectively. Property `AvailableBalance` represents the amount of funds available for withdrawal. Property `TotalBalance` represents the amount of funds available, plus the amount of deposited funds still pending confirmation (of cash in deposit envelopes) or clearance (of checks in deposit envelopes).

`Public` Methods of Class `Account`

Method `ValidatePIN` (lines 41–47) determines whether a user-specified PIN (i.e., parameter `userPIN`) matches the PIN associated with the account (i.e., attribute `pin`). Recall that we modeled this method's parameter `userPIN` in the UML class diagram of Fig. 7.26. If the two PINs match, the method returns `True` (line 43); otherwise, it returns `False` (line 45).

Method Credit (lines 50–52) adds an amount of money (i.e., parameter amount) to an Account as part of a deposit transaction. Note that this method adds the amount only to instance variable totalBalanceValue (line 45). The money credited to an account during a deposit does not become available immediately, so we modify only the total balance. We assume that the bank updates the available balance appropriately at a later time when the amount of cash in the deposit envelope has been verified and when the checks in the deposit envelope have cleared. Our implementation of class Account includes only methods required for carrying out ATM transactions. Therefore, we omit the methods that some other bank system would invoke to add to instance variable availableBalanceValue (to confirm a deposit) or subtract from attribute totalBalanceValue (to reject a deposit).

Method Debit (lines 55–58) subtracts an amount of money (i.e., parameter amount) from an Account as part of a withdrawal transaction. This method subtracts the amount from both instance variable availableBalanceValue (line 56) and instance variable totalBalanceValue (line 57), because a withdrawal affects both measures of an account balance.

D.8 Class BankDatabase

Class BankDatabase (Fig. D.7) models the bank's database with which the ATM interacts to access and modify a user's account information. We determine one reference-type attribute for class BankDatabase based on its composition relationship with class Account. Recall from Fig. 12.19 that a BankDatabase is composed of zero or more objects of class Account. Line 4 implements attribute accounts—an array that will store Account objects—to implement this composition relationship. Class BankDatabase has a parameterless constructor (lines 7–13) that initializes accounts with new Account objects. We create two new Account objects with test data and place them in the array (lines 11–12). Note that the Account constructor has four parameters—the account number, the PIN assigned to the account, the initial available balance and the initial total balance.

Recall that class BankDatabase serves as an intermediary between class ATM and the actual Account objects that contain users' account information. Thus, methods of class BankDatabase invoke the corresponding methods and properties of the Account object belonging to the current ATM user.

Private Utility Method GetAccount

We include Private utility method GetAccount (lines 16–25) to allow the BankDatabase to obtain a reference to a particular Account within the accounts ArrayList. To locate the user's Account, the BankDatabase compares the value returned by property AccountNumber for each element of accounts to a specified account number until it finds a match. Lines 18–22 traverse the accounts ArrayList. If currentAccount's account number equals the value of parameter accountNumber, the method returns currentAccount. If no account has the given account number, then line 24 returns Nothing.

Public Methods

Method AuthenticateUser (lines 29–40) proves or disproves the identity of an ATM user. This method takes a user-specified account number and a user-specified PIN as arguments and indicates whether they match the account number and PIN of an Account in

```
' BankDatabase.vb
' Represents the bank account-information database
Public Class BankDatabase
   Private accounts As Account() ' array of the bank's Accounts

   ' parameterless BankDatabase constructor initializes accounts
   Public Sub New()
      ' create two Account objects for testing and
      ' place them in the accounts array
      accounts = New Account(0 To 1) {} ' create accounts array
      accounts(0) = New Account(12345, 54321, 1000, 1200)
      accounts(1) = New Account(98765, 56789, 200, 200)
   End Sub ' New

   ' retrieve Account object containing specified account number
   Private Function GetAccount(ByVal accountNumber As Integer) As Account
      ' loop through accounts searching for matching account number
      For Each currentAccount As Account In accounts
         If currentAccount.AccountNumber = accountNumber Then
            Return currentAccount
         End If
      Next

      Return Nothing
   End Function ' GetAccount

   ' determine whether user-specified account number and PIN match
   ' those of an account in the database
   Public Function AuthenticateUser(ByVal userAccountNumber As Integer, _
      ByVal userPIN As Integer) As Boolean
      ' attempt to retrieve the account with the account number
      Dim userAccount As Account = GetAccount(userAccountNumber)

      ' if account exists, return result of Account function ValidatePIN
      If (userAccount IsNot Nothing) Then
         Return userAccount.ValidatePIN(userPIN)
      Else
         Return False ' account number not found, so return false
      End If
   End Function ' AuthenticateUser

   ' return available balance of Account with specified account number
   Public Function GetAvailableBalance( _
      ByVal userAccountNumber As Integer) As Decimal
      Dim userAccount As Account = GetAccount(userAccountNumber)
      Return userAccount.AvailableBalance
   End Function ' GetAvailableBalance

   ' return total balance of Account with specified account number
   Public Function GetTotalBalance( _
      ByVal userAccountNumber As Integer) As Decimal
      Dim userAccount As Account = GetAccount(userAccountNumber)
```

Fig. D.7 | Class BankDatabase represents the bank's account-information database. (Part 1 of 2.)

```
53          Return userAccount.TotalBalance
54       End Function ' GetTotalBalance
55
56       ' credit the Account with specified account number
57       Public Sub Credit(ByVal userAccountNumber As Integer, _
58          ByVal amount As Decimal)
59          Dim userAccount As Account = GetAccount(userAccountNumber)
60          userAccount.Credit(amount)
61       End Sub ' Credit
62
63       ' debit the Account with specified account number
64       Public Sub Debit(ByVal userAccountNumber As Integer, _
65          ByVal amount As Decimal)
66          Dim userAccount As Account = GetAccount(userAccountNumber)
67          userAccount.Debit(amount)
68       End Sub ' Debit
69    End Class ' BankDatabase
```

Fig. D.7 | Class `BankDatabase` represents the bank's account-information database. (Part 2 of 2.)

the database. Line 32 calls method `GetAccount`, which returns either an `Account` with `userAccountNumber` as its account number or `Nothing` to indicate that `userAccountNumber` is invalid. If `GetAccount` returns an `Account` object, line 36 returns the `Boolean` value returned by that object's `ValidatePIN` method. Note that `BankDatabase`'s `AuthenticateUser` method does not perform the PIN comparison itself—rather, it forwards `userPIN` to the `Account` object's `ValidatePIN` method to do so. The value returned by `Account` method `ValidatePIN` (line 36) indicates whether the user-specified PIN matches the PIN of the user's `Account`, so method `AuthenticateUser` simply returns this value (line 36) to the client of the class (i.e., `ATM`).

`BankDatabase` trusts the `ATM` to invoke method `AuthenticateUser` and receive a return value of `True` before allowing the user to perform transactions. `BankDatabase` also trusts that each `Transaction` object created by the `ATM` contains the valid account number of the current authenticated user and that this is the account number passed to the remaining `BankDatabase` methods as argument `userAccountNumber`. Methods `GetAvailableBalance` (lines 43–47), `GetTotalBalance` (lines 50–54), `Credit` (lines 57–61) and `Debit` (lines 64–68) therefore simply retrieve the user's `Account` object with utility method `GetAccount`, then invoke the appropriate `Account` method on that object. We know that the calls to `GetAccount` within these methods will never return `Nothing`, because `userAccountNumber` must refer to an existing `Account`. Note that `GetAvailableBalance` and `GetTotalBalance` return the values returned by the corresponding `Account` properties. Also note that methods `Credit` and `Debit` simply redirect parameter `amount` to the `Account` methods they invoke.

D.9 Class Transaction

Class `Transaction` (Fig. D.8) is an abstract base class that represents the notion of an ATM transaction. It contains the common features of derived classes `BalanceInquiry`, `Withdrawal` and `Deposit`. This class expands upon the "skeleton" code first developed in Section 12.8. Line 3 declares this class to be `MustInherit` (the Visual Basic equivalent of

```
1   ' Transaction.vb
2   ' MustInherit base class Transaction represents an ATM transaction.
3   Public MustInherit Class Transaction
4      Private accountNumberValue As Integer ' indicates account involved
5      Private screenHandle As Screen ' ATM's screen
6      Private bankDatabaseHandle As BankDatabase ' account info database
7
8      ' constructor invoked by derived classes using MyBase.New
9      Public Sub New(ByVal userAccount As Integer, _
10        ByVal userScreen As Screen, ByVal database As BankDatabase)
11        accountNumberValue = userAccount
12        screenHandle = userScreen
13        bankDatabaseHandle = database
14     End Sub ' New
15
16     ' property AccountNumber
17     Public ReadOnly Property AccountNumber() As Integer
18        Get
19           Return accountNumberValue
20        End Get
21     End Property ' AccountNumber
22
23     ' property ScreenReference
24     Public ReadOnly Property ScreenReference() As Screen
25        Get
26           Return screenHandle
27        End Get
28     End Property ' ScreenReference
29
30     ' property BankDatabaseReference
31     Public ReadOnly Property BankDatabaseReference() As BankDatabase
32        Get
33           Return bankDatabaseHandle
34        End Get
35     End Property ' BankDatabaseReference
36
37     ' perform the transaction (overridden by each derived class)
38     Public MustOverride Sub Execute()
39  End Class ' Transaction
```

Fig. D.8 | `MustInherit` base class `Transaction` represents an ATM transaction.

an abstract class). Lines 4–6 declare the class's `Private` instance variables. Recall from the class diagram of Fig. 12.20 that class `Transaction` contains an property `AccountNumber` that indicates the account involved in the `Transaction`. Line 4 implements the instance variable `accountNumberValue` to maintain the `AccountNumber` property's data. We derive attributes `screen` (implemented as instance variable `screenHandle` in line 7) and `bankDatabase` (implemented as instance variable `bankDatabaseHandle` in line 8) from class `Transaction`'s associations modeled in Fig. 12.19. All transactions require access to the ATM's screen and the bank's database.

Class `Transaction` has a constructor (lines 9–14) that takes the current user's account number and references to the ATM's screen and the bank's database as arguments. Because

Transaction is a MustInherit class (line 3), this constructor will never be called directly to instantiate Transaction objects. Instead, it will be invoked by the constructors of the Transaction derived classes via MyBase.New.

Class Transaction has three Public ReadOnly properties—AccountNumber (lines 17–21), ScreenReference (lines 24–28) and BankDatabaseReference (lines 31–35). Derived classes of Transaction inherit these properties and use them to gain access to class Transaction's Private instance variables. Note that we use the word "Reference" in the names of the ScreenReference and BankDatabaseReference properties for clarity—we wanted to avoid property names that are the same as the class names Screen and BankDatabase, which can be confusing.

Class Transaction also declares a MustOverride method Execute (line 38). It does not make sense to provide an implementation for this method in class Transaction, because a generic transaction cannot be executed. Thus, we declare this method to be MustOverride, forcing each Transaction derived class to provide its own concrete implementation that executes the particular type of transaction.

D.10 Class BalanceInquiry

Class BalanceInquiry (Fig. D.9) inherits from Transaction (line 4) and represents an ATM balance-inquiry transaction. BalanceInquiry does not have any attributes of its own, but it inherits Transaction attributes accountNumber, screen and bankDatabase, which are accessible through Transaction's Public ReadOnly properties. The BalanceInquiry constructor (lines 7–10) takes arguments corresponding to these attributes and simply forwards them to Transaction's constructor using MyBase.New (line 9).

```
1  ' BalanceInquiry.vb
2  ' Represents a balance-inquiry ATM transaction
3  Public Class BalanceInquiry
4     Inherits Transaction
5
6     ' BalanceInquiry constructor initializes base-class variables
7     Public Sub New(ByVal userAccountNumber As Integer, _
8        ByVal atmScreen As Screen, ByVal atmBankDatabase As BankDatabase)
9        MyBase.New(userAccountNumber, atmScreen, atmBankDatabase)
10    End Sub ' New
11
12    ' performs transaction; overrides Transaction's MustOverride method
13    Public Overrides Sub Execute()
14       ' get the available balance for the current user's Account
15       Dim availableBalance As Decimal = _
16          BankDatabaseReference.GetAvailableBalance(AccountNumber)
17
18       ' get the total balance for the current user's Account
19       Dim totalBalance As Decimal = _
20          BankDatabaseReference.GetTotalBalance(AccountNumber)
21
22       ' display the balance information on the screen
23       ScreenReference.DisplayMessageLine(vbCrLf & "Balance Information:")
```

Fig. D.9 | Class BalanceInquiry represents a balance-inquiry ATM transaction. (Part 1 of 2.)

```
24         ScreenReference.DisplayMessage(" - Available balance: ")
25         ScreenReference.DisplayDollarAmount(availableBalance)
26         ScreenReference.DisplayMessage(vbCrLf & " - Total balance: ")
27         ScreenReference.DisplayDollarAmount(totalBalance)
28         ScreenReference.DisplayMessageLine("")
29      End Sub ' Execute
30   End Class ' BalanceInquiry
```

Fig. D.9 | Class `BalanceInquiry` represents a balance-inquiry ATM transaction. (Part 2 of 2.)

Class `BalanceInquiry` overrides `Transaction`'s `MustOverride` method `Execute` to provide a concrete implementation (lines 13–29) that performs the steps involved in a balance inquiry. Lines 15–16 obtain the specified `Account`'s available balance by invoking the inherited property `BankDatabaseReference`'s `GetAvailableBalance` method. Note that line 16 uses the inherited property `AccountNumber` to get the account number of the current user. Lines 19–24 retrieve the specified `Account`'s total balance. Lines 23–28 display the balance information on the ATM's screen using the inherited property `ScreenReference`. Recall that `DisplayDollarAmount` takes a `Decimal` argument and outputs it to the screen formatted as a dollar amount. For example, if a user's available balance is `1000.5`, line 25 outputs `$1,000.50`. Note that line 28 inserts a blank line of output to separate the balance information from subsequent output (i.e., the main menu repeated by class `ATM` after executing the `BalanceInquiry`).

D.11 Class `Withdrawal`

Class `Withdrawal` (Fig. D.10) extends `Transaction` and represents an ATM withdrawal transaction. This class expands upon the "skeleton" code for this class developed in Fig. 12.22. Recall from the class diagram of Fig. 12.19 that class `Withdrawal` has one attribute, `amount`, which line 6 implements as a `Decimal` instance variable. Figure 12.19 models associations between class `Withdrawal` and classes `Keypad` and `CashDispenser`, for which lines 7–8 implement reference attributes `keypadHandle` and `dispenserHandle`, respectively. Line 11 declares a constant corresponding to the cancel menu option. We will soon discuss how the class uses this constant.

Class `Withdrawal`'s constructor (lines 14–23) has five parameters. It uses `MyBase.New` to pass parameters `userAccountNumber`, `atmScreen` and `atmBankDatabase` to base class `Transaction`'s constructor to set the attributes that `Withdrawal` inherits from `Transaction`. The constructor also takes references `atmKeypad` and `atmCashDispenser` as parameters and assigns them to variables `keypadHandle` and `dispenserHandle`.

Overriding `MustOverride` *Method* `Execute`

Class `Withdrawal` overrides `Transaction`'s `MustOverride` method `Execute` with a concrete implementation (lines 26–74) that performs the steps involved in a withdrawal. Line 27 declares and initializes a local `Boolean` variable `cashDispensed`. This variable indicates whether cash has been dispensed (i.e., whether the transaction has completed successfully) and is initially `False`. Line 30 declares and initializes to `False` a `Boolean` variable `transactionCanceled` to indicate that the transaction has not yet been canceled by the user.

```
' Withdrawal.vb
' Class Withdrawal represents an ATM withdrawal transaction.
Public Class Withdrawal
   Inherits Transaction

   Private amount As Decimal ' amount to withdraw
   Private keypadHandle As Keypad ' reference to Keypad
   Private dispenserHandle As CashDispenser ' reference to cash dispenser

   ' constant that corresponds to menu option to cancel
   Private Const CANCELED As Integer = 6

   ' Withdrawal constructor
   Public Sub New(ByVal userAccountNumber As Integer, _
      ByVal atmScreen As Screen, ByVal atmBankDatabase As BankDatabase, _
      ByVal atmKeypad As Keypad, ByVal atmCashDispenser As CashDispenser)
      ' initialize base-class variables
      MyBase.New(userAccountNumber, atmScreen, atmBankDatabase)

      ' initialize references to keypad and cash dispenser
      keypadHandle = atmKeypad
      dispenserHandle = atmCashDispenser
   End Sub ' New

   ' perform transaction
   Public Overrides Sub Execute()
      Dim cashDispensed As Boolean = False ' cash was not dispensed yet

      ' transaction was not canceled yet
      Dim transactionCanceled As Boolean = False

      ' loop until cash is dispensed or the user cancels
      Do
         ' obtain the chosen withdrawal amount from the user
         Dim selection As Integer = DisplayMenuOfAmounts()

         ' check whether user chose a withdrawal amount or canceled
         If (selection <> CANCELED) Then
            amount = selection ' set amount to the selected dollar amount

            ' get available balance of account involved
            Dim availableBalance As Decimal = _
               BankDatabaseReference.GetAvailableBalance(AccountNumber)

            ' check whether the user has enough money in the account
            If (amount <= availableBalance) Then
               ' check whether the cash dispenser has enough money
               If (dispenserHandle.IsSufficientCashAvailable(amount)) Then
                  ' update the account involved to reflect withdrawal
                  BankDatabaseReference.Debit(AccountNumber, amount)

                  dispenserHandle.DispenseCash(amount) ' dispense cash
                  cashDispensed = True ' cash was dispensed
```

Fig. D.10 | Class `Withdrawal` represents an ATM withdrawal transaction. (Part 1 of 3.)

```

                  ' instruct user to take cash
                  ScreenReference.DisplayMessageLine(vbCrLf & _
                     "Please take your cash from the cash dispenser.")
               Else ' cash dispenser does not have enough cash
                  ScreenReference.DisplayMessageLine(vbCrLf & _
                     "Insufficient cash available in the ATM." & _
                     vbCrLf & vbCrLf & "Please choose a smaller amount.")
               End If
            Else ' not enough money available in user's account
               ScreenReference.DisplayMessageLine(vbCrLf & _
                  "Insufficient cash available in your account." & _
                  vbCrLf & vbCrLf & "Please choose a smaller amount.")
            End If
         Else
            ScreenReference.DisplayMessageLine( _
               vbCrLf & "Canceling transaction...")
            transactionCanceled = True ' user canceled the transaction
         End If
      Loop While ((Not cashDispensed) And (Not transactionCanceled))
   End Sub ' Execute

   ' display a menu of withdrawal amounts and the option to cancel;
   ' return the chosen amount or 0 if the user chooses to cancel
   Private Function DisplayMenuOfAmounts() As Integer
      Dim userChoice As Integer = 0 ' variable to store return value

      ' array of amounts to correspond to menu numbers
      Dim amounts As Integer() = New Integer() { _
         0, 20, 40, 60, 100, 200}

      ' loop while no valid choice has been made
      While (userChoice = 0)
         ' display the menu
         ScreenReference.DisplayMessageLine( _
            vbCrLf & "Withdrawal options:")
         ScreenReference.DisplayMessageLine("1 - $20")
         ScreenReference.DisplayMessageLine("2 - $40")
         ScreenReference.DisplayMessageLine("3 - $60")
         ScreenReference.DisplayMessageLine("4 - $100")
         ScreenReference.DisplayMessageLine("5 - $200")
         ScreenReference.DisplayMessageLine("6 - Cancel transaction")
         ScreenReference.DisplayMessage( _
            vbCrLf & "Choose a withdrawal option (1-6): ")

         ' get user input through keypad
         Dim input As Integer = keypadHandle.GetInput()

         ' determine how to proceed based on the input value
         Select Case (input)
            ' if the user chose a withdrawal amount (i.e., option
            ' 1, 2, 3, 4, or 5), return the corresponding amount
            ' from the amounts array
```

Fig. D.10 | Class `Withdrawal` represents an ATM withdrawal transaction. (Part 2 of 3.)

```
107             Case 1 To 5
108                userChoice = amounts(input) ' save user's choice
109             Case CANCELED ' the user chose to cancel
110                userChoice = CANCELED ' save user's choice
111             Case Else
112                ScreenReference.DisplayMessageLine( _
113                   vbCrLf & "Invalid selection. Try again.")
114          End Select
115       End While
116
117       Return userChoice
118    End Function ' DisplayMenuOfAmounts
119 End Class ' Withdrawal
```

Fig. D.10 | Class `Withdrawal` represents an ATM withdrawal transaction. (Part 3 of 3.)

Lines 33–73 contain a `Do...Loop While` statement that executes its body until cash is dispensed (i.e., until `cashDispensed` becomes `True`) or until the user chooses to cancel (i.e., until `transactionCanceled` becomes `True`). We use this loop to continuously return the user to the start of the transaction if an error occurs (i.e., the requested withdrawal amount is greater than the user's available balance or greater than the amount of cash in the cash dispenser). Line 35 displays a menu of withdrawal amounts and obtains a user selection by calling `Private` utility method `DisplayMenuOfAmounts` (declared in lines 78–118). This method displays the menu of amounts and returns either an `Integer` withdrawal amount or an `Integer` constant `CANCELED` to indicate that the user has chosen to cancel the transaction.

Displaying Options With `Private` *Utility Method* `DisplayMenuOfAmounts`

Method `DisplayMenuOfAmounts` (lines 81–121) first declares local variable `userChoice` (initially `0`) to store the value that the method will return (line 82). Lines 82–83 declare an integer array of withdrawal amounts that correspond to the amounts displayed in the withdrawal menu. We ignore the first element in the array (index `0`) because the menu has no option 0. The `While` statement at lines 86–115 repeats until `userChoice` takes on a value other than `0`. We will see shortly that this occurs when the user makes a valid selection from the menu. Lines 88–97 display the withdrawal menu on the screen and prompt the user to enter a choice. Line 100 obtains integer `input` through the keypad. The `Select Case` statement at lines 103–114 determines how to proceed based on the user's input. If the user selects a number between `1` and `5`, line 108 sets `userChoice` to the value of the element in the `amounts` array at index `input`. For example, if the user enters `3` to withdraw $60, line 108 sets `userChoice` to the value of `amounts(3)` (i.e., `60`). Variable `userChoice` no longer equals `0`, so the `While` at lines 86–115 terminates and line 117 returns `userChoice`. If the user selects the cancel menu option, line 110 executes, setting `userChoice` to `CANCELED` and causing the method to return this value. If the user does not enter a valid menu selection, lines 112–113 display an error message and the user is returned to the withdrawal menu.

The `If` statement at line 38 in method `Execute` determines whether the user has selected a withdrawal amount or chosen to cancel. If the user cancels, lines 69–70 display an appropriate message to the user before returning control to the calling method (i.e., `ATM` method PerformTransactions). If the user has chosen a withdrawal amount, lines 39 assigns local variable selection to instance variable amount. Lines 42–43 retrieve the available balance of the current user's Account and store it in a local Decimal variable availableBalance. Next, the If statement at line 46 determines whether the selected amount is less than or equal to the user's available balance. If it is not, lines 64–66 display an error message. Control then continues to the end of the Do...Loop While, and the loop repeats, because both cashDispensed and transactionCanceled are still False. If the user's balance is high enough, the If statement at line 48 determines whether the cash dispenser has enough money to satisfy the withdrawal request by invoking the cash dispenser's IsSufficientCashAvailable method. If this method returns False, lines 59–61 display an error message and the Do...Loop While repeats. If sufficient cash is available, then the requirements for the withdrawal are satisfied, and line 50 debits the user's account in the database by amount. Lines 52–53 then instruct the cash dispenser to dispense the cash to the user and set cashDispensed to True. Finally, lines 56–57 display a message to the user to take the dispensed cash. Because cashDispensed is now True, control continues after the Do...Loop While. No additional statements appear below the loop, so the method returns control to class ATM.

D.12 Class Deposit

Class Deposit (Fig. D.11) inherits from Transaction and represents an ATM deposit transaction. Recall from the class diagram of Fig. 12.20 that class Deposit has one attribute, amount, which line 6 implements as a Decimal instance variable. Lines 7–8 create reference attributes keypadHandle and depositSlotHandle that implement the associations between class Deposit and classes Keypad and DepositSlot modeled in Fig. 12.19. Line 11 declares a constant CANCELED that corresponds to the value a user enters to cancel. We will soon discuss how the class uses this constant.

```
1  ' Deposit.vb
2  ' Represents a deposit ATM transaction.
3  Public Class Deposit
4     Inherits Transaction
5
6     Private amount As Decimal ' amount to deposit
7     Private keypadHandle As Keypad ' reference to Keypad
8     Private depositSlotHandle As DepositSlot ' reference to deposit slot
9
10    ' constant representing cancel option
11    Private Const CANCELED As Integer = 0
12
13    ' Deposit constructor initializes class's instance variables
14    Public Sub New(ByVal userAccountNumber As Integer, _
15       ByVal atmScreen As Screen, ByVal atmBankDatabase As BankDatabase, _
16       ByVal atmKeypad As Keypad, ByVal atmDepositSlot As DepositSlot)
17       ' initialize base class variables
18       MyBase.New(userAccountNumber, atmScreen, atmBankDatabase)
19
```

Fig. D.11 | Class Deposit represents an ATM deposit transaction. (Part 1 of 3.)

```
      ' initialize references to keypad and deposit slot
      keypadHandle = atmKeypad
      depositSlotHandle = atmDepositSlot
   End Sub ' New

   ' perform transaction; overrides Transaction's MustOverride method
   Public Overrides Sub Execute()
      amount = PromptForDepositAmount() ' get deposit amount from user

      ' check whether user entered a deposit amount or canceled
      If (amount <> CANCELED) Then
         ' request deposit envelope containing specified amount
         ScreenReference.DisplayMessage(vbCrLf & _
            "Please insert a deposit envelope containing ")
         ScreenReference.DisplayDollarAmount(amount)
         ScreenReference.DisplayMessageLine(" in the deposit slot.")

         ' retrieve deposit envelope
         Dim envelopeReceived As Boolean = _
            depositSlotHandle.IsDepositEnvelopeReceived()

         ' check whether deposit envelope was received
         If envelopeReceived Then
            ScreenReference.DisplayMessageLine(vbCrLf & _
               "Your envelope has been received." & vbCrLf & _
               "The money just deposited will not be available " & _
               "until we" & vbCrLf & "verify the amount of any " & _
               "enclosed cash, and any enclosed checks clear.")

            ' credit account to reflect the deposit
            BankDatabaseReference.Credit(AccountNumber, amount)
         Else
            ScreenReference.DisplayMessageLine(vbCrLf & _
               "You did not insert an envelope, so the ATM has " & _
               "canceled your transaction.")
         End If
      Else
         ScreenReference.DisplayMessageLine( _
            vbCrLf & "Canceling transaction...")
      End If
   End Sub ' Execute

   ' prompt user to enter a deposit amount to credit
   Private Function PromptForDepositAmount() As Decimal
      ' display the prompt and receive input
      ScreenReference.DisplayMessage(vbCrLf & _
         "Please input a deposit amount in CENTS (or 0 to cancel): ")
      Dim input As Integer = Convert.ToInt32(keypadHandle.GetInput())

      ' check whether the user canceled or entered a valid amount
      If (input = CANCELED) Then
         Return CANCELED
```

Fig. D.11 | Class `Deposit` represents an ATM deposit transaction. (Part 2 of 3.)

```
72          Else
73             Return Convert.ToDecimal(input / 100)
74          End If
75       End Function ' PromptForDepositAmount
76    End Class ' Deposit
```

Fig. D.11 | Class `Deposit` represents an ATM deposit transaction. (Part 3 of 3.)

Like class `Withdrawal`, class `Deposit` contains a constructor (lines 14–23) that passes three parameters to base class `Transaction`'s constructor using `MyBase.New`. The constructor also has parameters `atmKeypad` and `atmDepositSlot`, which it assigns to corresponding reference attributes (lines 21–22).

Overriding `MustOverride` *Method* `Execute`

Method `Execute` (lines 26–60) overrides `MustOverride` method `Execute` in base class `Transaction` with a concrete implementation that performs the steps required in a deposit transaction. Line 27 prompts the user to enter a deposit amount by invoking `Private` utility method `PromptForDepositAmount` (declared in lines 63–75) and sets attribute `amount` to the value returned. Method `PromptForDepositAmount` asks the user to enter a deposit amount as an integer number of cents (because the ATM's keypad does not contain a decimal point; this is consistent with many real ATMs) and returns the `Decimal` value representing the dollar amount to be deposited.

Getting Deposit Amount With `Private` *Utility Method* `PromptForDepositAmount`

Lines 65–66 in method `PromptForDepositAmount` display a message on the screen asking the user to input a deposit amount as a number of cents or "0" to cancel the transaction. Line 67 receives the user's input from the keypad. The `If` statement at lines 70–74 determines whether the user has entered a real deposit amount or chosen to cancel. If the user chooses to cancel, line 71 returns the constant `CANCELED`. Otherwise, line 73 returns the deposit amount after converting from the number of cents to a dollar amount by dividing `input` by `100`, then converting the result to a `Decimal`. For example, if the user enters `125` as the number of cents, line 73 returns `125` divided by `100`, or `1.25`—125 cents is $1.25.

Lines 30–59 in method `Execute` determine whether the user chose to cancel the transaction rather than enter a deposit amount. If the user cancels, lines 57–58 display an appropriate message and the method returns. If the user enters a deposit amount, lines 32–35 instruct the user to insert a deposit envelope with the correct amount. Recall that `Screen` method `DisplayDollarAmount` outputs a `Decimal` value formatted as a dollar amount.

Lines 38–39 sets a local `Boolean` variable to the value returned by the deposit slot's `IsDepositEnvelopeReceived` method, indicating whether a deposit envelope has been received. Recall that we coded method `IsDepositEnvelopeReceived` (lines 6–8 of Fig. D.5) to always return `True`, because we are simulating the functionality of the deposit slot and assume that the user always inserts an envelope. However, we code method `Execute` of class `Deposit` to test for the possibility that the user does not insert an envelope—good software engineering demands that programs account for all possible return values. Thus, class `Deposit` is prepared for future versions of `IsDepositEnvelopeReceived` that could return `False`. Lines 43–50 execute if the deposit slot receives an envelope. Lines 43–47 display an appropriate message to the user. Line 50 credits the user's account in the database with the deposit amount. Lines 52–54 execute if the deposit slot does not receive a deposit envelope. In this case, we display a message to the user stating that the ATM has canceled the transaction. The method then returns without modifying the user's account.

D.13 Module ATMCaseStudy

Module `ATMCaseStudy` (Fig. D.12) simply allows us to start, or "turn on," the ATM and test the implementation of our ATM system model. Module `ATMCaseStudy`'s `Main` method (lines 4–7) does nothing more than instantiate a new `ATM` object named `theATM` (line 5) and invoke its `Run` method (line 6) to start the ATM.

D.14 Wrap-Up

Now that we have presented the complete ATM implementation, you can see that many issues arose during implementation for which we did not provide detailed UML diagrams. This is not uncommon in an object-oriented design-and-implementation experience. For example, many attributes listed in the class diagrams were implemented as Visual Basic properties so that clients of the classes could gain controlled access to the underlying `Private` instance variables. We did not make these properties during our design process, because there was nothing in the requirements document or our design process to indicate that certain attributes would eventually need to be accessed outside of their classes.

We also encountered various issues with simulating hardware. A real-world ATM is a hardware device that does not have a complete computer keyboard. One problem with using a computer keyboard to simulate the keypad is that the user can enter nondigits as input. We did not spend much time dealing with such issues, because this problem is not possible in a real ATM, which has only a numeric keypad. However, having to think about issues like this is a good thing. Quite typically, software designs for complete systems involve simulating hardware devices like the cash dispenser and keypad. Although some aspects of our ATM may seem contrived, in real-world systems hardware design and implementation often occurs in parallel with software design and implementation. In such cases, the software cannot be implemented in final form because the hardware is not yet ready. So, software developers must simulate the hardware as we have done in this case study with the keypad, cash dispenser and deposit slot.

Congratulations on completing the entire software engineering ATM case study! We hope you found this experience to be valuable and that it reinforced many of the concepts that you learned in Chapters 1–12. We would sincerely appreciate your comments, criticisms and suggestions. You can reach us at `deitel@deitel.com`. We will respond promptly.

```
1  ' ATMCaseStudy.vb
2  ' Module for testing the ATM case study.
3  Module ATMCaseStudy
4     Sub Main()
5        Dim theATM As New ATM()
6        theATM.Run()
7     End Sub ' Main
8  End Module ' ATMCaseStudy
```

Fig. D.12 | `ATMCaseStudy.vb` starts the ATM.

E

UML 2: Additional Diagram Types

E.1 Introduction

If you have read the optional Software Engineering Case Study sections in Chapters 3–8, 10 and 12, you should now have a comfortable grasp of the UML diagram types that we use to model our ATM system. The case study is intended for use in first- or second-semester courses, so we limit our discussion to a concise subset of the UML. The UML 2 provides 13 diagram types. The end of Section 3.10 summarizes the six diagram types that we use in the case study. This appendix lists and briefly defines the seven remaining diagram types.

E.2 Additional Diagram Types

The following are the seven diagram types that we have chosen not to use in our Software Engineering Case Study.

- Object diagrams model a "snapshot" of the system by modeling a system's objects and their relationships at a specific point in time. Each object represents an instance of a class from a class diagram, and several objects may be created from one class. For our ATM system, an object diagram could show several distinct `Account` objects side by side, illustrating that they are all part of the bank's account database.
- Component diagrams model the artifacts and components—resources (which include source files)—that make up the system.
- Deployment diagrams model the system's runtime requirements (such as the computer or computers on which the system will reside), memory requirements, or other devices the system requires during execution.
- Package diagrams model the hierarchical structure of packages (which are groups of classes) in the system at compile time and the relationships that exist between the packages.

- Composite structure diagrams model the internal structure of a complex object at runtime. New in UML 2, they allow system designers to hierarchically decompose a complex object into smaller parts. Composite structure diagrams are beyond the scope of our case study. They are more appropriate for larger industrial applications, which exhibit complex groupings of objects at execution time.
- Interaction overview diagrams, new in UML 2, provide a summary of control flow in the system by combining elements of several types of behavioral diagrams (e.g., activity diagrams, sequence diagrams).
- Timing diagrams, also new in UML 2, model the timing constraints imposed on stage changes and interactions between objects in a system.

To learn more about these diagrams and advanced UML topics, please visit `www.uml.org` and the web resources listed at the end of Section 3.10.

F

ASCII Character Set

ASCII character set

	0	1	2	3	4	5	6	7	8	9
0	nul	soh	stx	etx	eot	enq	ack	bel	bs	ht
1	lf	vt	ff	cr	so	si	dle	dc1	dc2	dc3
2	dc4	nak	syn	etb	can	em	sub	esc	fs	gs
3	rs	us	sp	!	"	#	$	%	&	'
4	(	)	*	+	,	-	.	/	0	1
5	2	3	4	5	6	7	8	9	:	;
6	<	=	>	?	@	A	B	C	D	E
7	F	G	H	I	J	K	L	M	N	O
8	P	Q	R	S	T	U	V	W	X	Y
9	Z	[	\	]	^	_	`	a	b	c
10	d	e	f	g	h	i	j	k	l	m
11	n	o	p	q	r	s	t	u	v	w
12	x	y	z	{	|	}	~	del		

Fig. F.1 | ASCII character set.

The digits at the left of the table are the left digits of the decimal equivalent (0–127) of the character code, and the digits at the top of the table are the right digits of the character code. For example, the character code for "F" is 70, and the character code for "&" is 38.

Most users of this book are interested in the ASCII character set used to represent English characters on many computers. The ASCII character set is a subset of the Unicode character set used by Visual Basic to represent characters from most of the world's languages. For more information on the Unicode character set, see Appendix G.

G

Unicode®

OBJECTIVES

In this appendix you'll learn:

- The mission of the Unicode Consortium.
- The design basis of Unicode.
- The three Unicode encoding forms: UTF-8, UTF-16 and UTF-32.
- Characters and glyphs.
- The advantages and disadvantages of using Unicode.
- About the Unicode Consortium's website.

G.1 Introduction

The use of inconsistent character **encodings** (i.e., numeric values associated with characters) in the developing of global software products causes serious problems, because computers process information as numbers. For instance, the character "a" is converted to a numeric value so that a computer can manipulate that piece of data. Many countries and corporations have developed their own encoding systems that are incompatible with the encoding systems of other countries and corporations. For example, the Microsoft Windows operating system assigns the value 0xC0 to the character "A with a grave accent"; the Apple Macintosh operating system assigns that same value to an upside-down question mark. This results in the misrepresentation and possible corruption of data when it is not processed as intended.

In the absence of a widely implemented universal character-encoding standard, global software developers had to **localize** their products extensively before distribution. Localization includes the language translation and cultural adaptation of content. The process of localization usually includes significant modifications to the source code (such as the conversion of numeric values and the underlying assumptions made by programmers), which results in increased costs and delays releasing the software. For example, some English-speaking programmers might design global software products assuming that a single character can be represented by one byte. However, when those products are localized for Asian markets, the programmer's assumptions are no longer valid; thus, the majority, if not the entirety, of the code needs to be rewritten. Localization is necessary with each release of a version. By the time a software product is localized for a particular market, a newer version, which needs to be localized as well, may be ready for distribution. As a result, it is cumbersome and costly to produce and distribute global software products in a market where there is no universal character-encoding standard.

In response to this situation, the **Unicode Standard**, an encoding standard that facilitates the production and distribution of software, was created. The Unicode Standard outlines a specification to produce consistent encoding of the world's characters and symbols. Software products that handle text encoded in the Unicode Standard need to be localized, but the localization process is simpler and more efficient, because the numeric values need not be converted and the assumptions made by programmers about the character encoding are universal. The Unicode Standard is maintained by a nonprofit organization called the **Unicode Consortium**, whose members include Apple, IBM, Microsoft, Oracle, Sun Microsystems, Sybase and many others.

When the Consortium envisioned and developed the Unicode Standard, they wanted an encoding system that was universal, efficient, uniform and unambiguous. A universal encoding system encompasses all commonly used characters. An efficient encoding system allows text files to be parsed easily. A uniform encoding system assigns fixed values to all characters. An unambiguous encoding system represents a given character in a consistent manner. These four terms are referred to as the Unicode Standard design basis.

G.2 Unicode Transformation Formats

Although Unicode incorporates the limited ASCII character set (i.e., a collection of characters), it encompasses a more comprehensive character set. In ASCII each character is represented by a byte containing 0s and 1s. One byte is capable of storing the binary numbers from 0 to 255. Each character is assigned a number between 0 and 255; thus, ASCII-based systems can support only 256 characters, a tiny fraction of world's characters. Unicode extends the ASCII character set by encoding the vast majority of the world's characters. The Unicode Standard encodes all of those characters in a uniform numerical space from 0 to 10FFFF hexadecimal. An implementation will express these numbers in one of several transformation formats, choosing the one that best fits the particular application at hand.

Three such formats are in use, called UTF-8, UTF-16 and UTF-32, depending on the size of the units—in bits—being used. UTF-8, a variable-width encoding form, requires one to four bytes to express each Unicode character. UTF-8 data consists of 8-bit bytes (sequences of one, two, three or four bytes depending on the character being encoded) and is well suited for ASCII-based systems, where there is a predominance of one-byte characters (ASCII represents characters as one byte). Currently, UTF-8 is widely implemented in UNIX systems and in databases.

The variable-width UTF-16 encoding form expresses Unicode characters in units of 16 bits (i.e., as two adjacent bytes, or a short integer in many machines). Most characters of Unicode are expressed in a single 16-bit unit. However, characters with values above FFFF hexadecimal are expressed with an ordered pair of 16-bit units called surrogates. Surrogates are 16-bit integers in the range D800 through DFFF, which are used solely for the purpose of "escaping" into higher-numbered characters. Approximately one million characters can be expressed in this manner. Although a surrogate pair requires 32 bits to represent characters, it is space efficient to use these 16-bit units. Surrogates are rare characters in current implementations. Many string-handling implementations are written in terms of UTF-16. [*Note:* Details and sample code for UTF-16 handling are available on the Unicode Consortium website at `www.unicode.org`.]

Implementations that require significant use of rare characters or entire scripts encoded above FFFF hexadecimal should use UTF-32, a 32-bit, fixed-width encoding form that usually requires twice as much memory as UTF-16 encoded characters. The major advantage of the fixed-width UTF-32 encoding form is that it expresses all characters uniformly, so it is easy to handle in arrays.

There are few guidelines that state when to use a particular encoding form. The best encoding form to use depends on computer systems and business protocols, not on the data itself. Typically, the UTF-8 encoding form should be used where computer systems and business protocols require data to be handled in 8-bit units, particularly in legacy systems being upgraded, because it often simplifies changes to existing programs. For this reason, UTF-8 has become the encoding form of choice on the Internet. Likewise, UTF-

16 is the encoding form of choice on Microsoft Windows applications. UTF-32 is likely to become more widely used in the future, as more characters are encoded with values above FFFF hexadecimal. Also, UTF-32 requires less sophisticated handling than UTF-16 in the presence of surrogate pairs. Figure G.1 shows the different ways in which the three encoding forms handle character encoding.

Character	UTF-8	UTF-16	UTF-32
Latin Capital Letter A	0x41	0x0041	0x00000041
Greek Capital Letter Alpha	0xCD 0x91	0x0391	0x00000391
CJK Unified Ideograph-4e95	0xE4 0xBA 0x95	0x4E95	0x00004E95
Old Italic Letter A	0xF0 0x80 0x83 0x80	0xDC00 0xDF00	0x00010300

Fig. G.1 | Correlation between the three encoding forms.

G.3 Characters and Glyphs

The Unicode Standard consists of characters, written components (i.e., alphabetic letters, numerals, punctuation marks, accent marks, and so on) that can be represented by numeric values. Examples of characters include: U+0041 LATIN CAPITAL LETTER A. In the first character representation, U+*yyyy* is a code value, in which U+ refers to Unicode code values, as opposed to other hexadecimal values. The *yyyy* represents a four-digit hexadecimal number of an encoded character. Code values are bit combinations that represent encoded characters. Characters are represented with glyphs, various shapes, fonts and sizes for displaying characters. There are no code values for glyphs in the Unicode Standard. Examples of glyphs are shown in Fig. G.2.

The Unicode Standard encompasses the alphabets, ideographs, syllabaries, punctuation marks, diacritics, mathematical operators and so on that comprise the written languages and scripts of the world. A diacritic is a special mark added to a character to distinguish it from another letter or to indicate an accent (e.g., in Spanish, the tilde "~" above the character "n"). Currently, Unicode provides code values for 94,140 character representations, with more than 880,000 code values reserved for future expansion.

Fig. G.2 | Various glyphs of the character A.

G.4 Advantages/Disadvantages of Unicode

The Unicode Standard has several significant advantages that promote its use. One is its impact on the performance of the international economy. Unicode standardizes the characters for the world's writing systems to a uniform model that promotes transferring and sharing data. Programs developed using such a schema maintain their accuracy, because each character has a single definition (i.e., *a* is always U+0061, *%* is always U+0025). This enables corporations to manage the high demands of international markets by processing different writing systems at the same time. Also, all characters can be managed in an identical manner, thus avoiding any confusion caused by different character-code architectures. Moreover, managing data in a consistent manner eliminates data corruption, because data can be sorted, searched and manipulated via a consistent process.

Another advantage of the Unicode Standard is portability (i.e., the ability to execute software on disparate computers or with disparate operating systems). Most operating systems, databases, programming languages and web browsers currently support, or are planning to support, Unicode. Additionally, Unicode includes more characters than any other character set in common use (although it does not yet include all of the world's characters).

A disadvantage of the Unicode Standard is the amount of memory required by UTF-16 and UTF-32. ASCII character sets are 8 bits in length, so they require less storage than the default 16-bit Unicode character set. However, the double-byte character set (DBCS) and the multibyte character set (MBCS) that encode Asian characters (ideographs) require two to four bytes, respectively. In such instances, the UTF-16 or the UTF-32 encoding forms may be used with little hindrance to memory and performance.

G.5 Unicode Consortium's Website

If you would like to learn more about the Unicode Standard, visit `www.unicode.org`. This site provides a wealth of information about the Unicode Standard. Currently, the home page is organized into various sections: New to Unicode, General Information, The Consortium, The Unicode Standard, Work in Progress and For Members.

The New to Unicode? section consists of four subsections: **What is Unicode?**, **How to Use this Site**, **FAQ** and **Glossary of Unicode Terms**. The first subsection (recommended reading for anyone new to Unicode) provides a technical introduction to Unicode by describing design principles, character interpretations and assignments, text processing and Unicode conformance. Also, this subsection gives related links that provide the reader with additional information about Unicode. The **How to Use this Site** subsection contains information about using and navigating the site as well hyperlinks to additional resources.

The General Information section contains eight subsections: **Where is my Character?**, **Display Problems?**, **Case Studies**, **Useful Resources**, **Last Resort Font**, **Unicode Enabled Products**, **Mail Lists**, and **Subset of the Unicode website in French**. The main areas covered in this section include a link to the Unicode code charts (a complete listing of code values) assembled by the Unicode Consortium as well as a detailed outline on how to locate an encoded character in the code chart. Also, the section contains advice on how to configure different operating systems and web browsers so that the Unicode characters can be viewed properly. Moreover, from this section, the user can navigate to other sites that provide information on various topics, such as fonts, linguistics and such other standards as the Armenian Standards Page and the Chinese GB 18030 Encoding Standard.

The Consortium section consists of seven subsections: **Who we are**, **Our Members**, **How to Join**, **Conferences**, **Press Info**, **Policies & Positions** and **Contact Us**. This section provides a list of the current Unicode Consortium members as well as information on how to become a member. Privileges for each member type—*full*, *associate*, *specialist* and *individual*—and the fees assessed to each member are listed here.

The For Members Only section consists of two subsections that are available only to consortium members: **Member Resources** and **Working Documents**.

The Unicode Standard section consists of eight subsections: **Start Here**, **Latest Version**, **Archive of Earlier Versions**, **Referencing the Standard**, **Code Charts**, **Unicode Character Database**, **Unihan Database** and **Ideographic Variation Database**. This section describes the updates applied to the latest version of the Unicode Standard and categorizes all defined encoding. The user can learn how the latest version has been modified to encompass more features and capabilities. For instance, one enhancement of Version 3.1 is that it contains additional encoded characters.

The Key Specifications and Technical Publications sections provide all the Unicode technical documentation.

The Work in Progress section consists of the subsections **Calendar of Meetings**, **Proposals for Public Review**, **Unicode Technical Committee**, **UTC Meeting Minutes**, **Proposed Characters (Pipeline)**, **Submitting Proposals**, **CLDR Technical Committee** and **UDHR in Unicode**. This section presents the user with a catalog of the recent characters included into the Unicode Standard scheme as well as those characters being considered for inclusion. If users determine that a character has been overlooked, then they can submit a written proposal for its inclusion. The **Submitting Proposals** subsection contains strict guidelines that must be adhered to when submitting written proposals. In addition, this section provides information about upcoming and past technical committee meetings.

G.6 Using Unicode

Visual Studio uses Unicode UTF-16 encoding to represent all characters. Figure G.3 uses Visual Basic to display the text "Welcome to Unicode!" in eight different languages: English, French, German, Japanese, Portuguese, Russian, Spanish and Traditional Chinese.

```
' Fig. G.3: UnicodeDemonstration.vb
' Using Unicode encoding.
Public Class unicodeForm
   Private Sub UnicodeDemonstration_Load(ByVal sender As System.Object, _
      ByVal e As System.EventArgs) Handles MyBase.Load
      'English
      englishLabel.Text = ChrW(&H57) & ChrW(&H65) & ChrW(&H6C) & _
         ChrW(&H63) & ChrW(&H6F) & ChrW(&H6D) & ChrW(&H65) & _
         ChrW(&H20) & ChrW(&H74) & ChrW(&H6F) & ChrW(&H20) & _
         "Unicode" & ChrW(&H21)

      ' French
      frenchLabel.Text = ChrW(&H42) & ChrW(&H69) & ChrW(&H65) & _
         ChrW(&H6E) & ChrW(&H76) & ChrW(&H65) & ChrW(&H6E) & _
         ChrW(&H75) & ChrW(&H65) & ChrW(&H20) & ChrW(&H61) & _
         ChrW(&H75) & ChrW(&H20) & "Unicode" & ChrW(&H21)

      ' German
      germanLabel.Text = ChrW(&H57) & ChrW(&H69) & ChrW(&H6C) & _
         ChrW(&H6B) & ChrW(&H6F) & ChrW(&H6D) & ChrW(&H6D) & _
         ChrW(&H65) & ChrW(&H6E) & ChrW(&H20) & ChrW(&H7A) & _
         ChrW(&H75) & ChrW(&H20) & "Unicode" & ChrW(&H21)

```

Fig. G.3 | Windows application demonstrating Unicode encoding. (Part 1 of 2.)

```
24          ' Japanese
25          japaneseLabel.Text = "Unicode " & ChrW(&H3078) & _
26             ChrW(&H3087) & ChrW(&H3045) & ChrW(&H3053) & _
27             ChrW(&H305D) & ChrW(&H21)
28
29          ' Portuguese
30          portugueseLabel.Text = ChrW(&H53) & ChrW(&HE9) & ChrW(&H6A) & _
31             ChrW(&H61) & ChrW(&H20) & ChrW(&H42) & _
32             ChrW(&H65) & ChrW(&H6D) & ChrW(&H76) & _
33             ChrW(&H69) & ChrW(&H6E) & ChrW(&H64) & _
34             ChrW(&H6F) & ChrW(&H20) & "Unicode" & ChrW(&H21)
35
36          ' Russian
37          russianLabel.Text = ChrW(&H414) & ChrW(&H43E) & ChrW(&H431) & _
38             ChrW(&H440) & ChrW(&H43E) & ChrW(&H20) & _
39             ChrW(&H43F) & ChrW(&H43E) & ChrW(&H436) & _
40             ChrW(&H430) & ChrW(&H43B) & ChrW(&H43E) & _
41             ChrW(&H432) & ChrW(&H430) & ChrW(&H442) & _
42             ChrW(&H44A) & ChrW(&H20) & ChrW(&H432) & _
43             ChrW(&H20) & "Unicode" & ChrW(&H21)
44
45          ' Spanish
46          spanishLabel.Text = ChrW(&H42) & ChrW(&H69) & ChrW(&H65) & _
47             ChrW(&H6E) & ChrW(&H76) & ChrW(&H65) & _
48             ChrW(&H6E) & ChrW(&H69) & ChrW(&H64) & _
49             ChrW(&H61) & ChrW(&H20) & ChrW(&H61) & _
50             ChrW(&H20) & "Unicode" & ChrW(&H21)
51
52          ' Traditional Chinese
53          chineseLabel.Text = ChrW(&H6B22) & ChrW(&H8FCE) & _
54             ChrW(&H4F7F) & ChrW(&H7528) & ChrW(&H20) & _
55             "Unicode" & ChrW(&H21)
56       End Sub ' UnicodeDemonstration_Load
57    End Class ' UnicodeDemonstration
```

Unicode Demonstration

Welcome to Unicode! | Séja Bemvindo Unicode!
Bienvenue au Unicode! | Добро пожаловатъ в Unicode!
Wilkommen zu Unicode! | Bienvenida a Unicode!
Unicode へょうこそ! | 欢迎使用 Unicode!

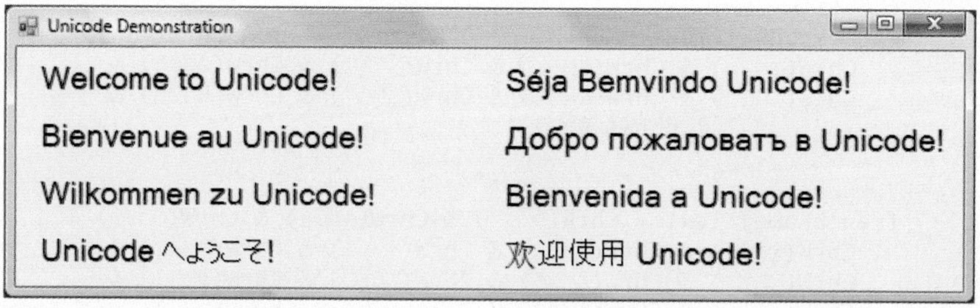

Fig. G.3 | Windows application demonstrating Unicode encoding. (Part 2 of 2.)

The first welcome message (lines 7–10) contains the hexadecimal codes for the English text. The **Code Charts** page on the Unicode Consortium website contains a document that lists the code values for the **Basic Latin** block (or category), which includes the English alphabet. The hexadecimal codes in lines 7–8 equate to "Welcome." When using Unicode characters in Visual Basic, the format `&Hyyyy` is used, where *yyyy* represents the hexadecimal Unicode encoding. For example, the letter "W" (in "Welcome") is denoted by &H57. [*Note:* The actual code for the letter "W" is &H0057, but Visual Studio removes the two zeros.] Line 9 contains the hexadecimal for the *space* character (&H20). The hexadecimal value for the word "to" is on lines 9, and the word "Unicode" is on line 10. "Unicode" is not encoded because it is a registered trademark and has no equivalent translation in most languages. Line 10 also contains the &H21 notation for the exclamation mark (!).

The remaining welcome messages (lines 13–55) contain the hexadecimal codes for the other seven languages. The code values used for the French, German, Portuguese and Spanish text are located in the **Basic Latin** block, the code values used for the Traditional Chinese text are located in the **CJK Unified Ideographs** block, the code values used for the Russian text are located in the **Cyrillic** block and the code values used for the Japanese text are located in the **Hiragana** block.

[*Note:* To render the Asian characters in a Windows application, you would need to install the proper language files on your computer. To do this, open the **Regional Options** dialog from the **Control Panel** (**Start > Control Panel > Clock, Language, and Region**). Under the **Keyboard and Languages** tab, click the **Change Keyboards...** button. At the bottom of the **General** tab is a list of languages. Click **Add...** then search the tree view for the **Japanese** and the **Traditional Chinese** checkboxes and press **OK**. Follow the directions of the install wizard to install the languages. For additional assistance, visit www.unicode.org/help/display_problems.html.]

G.7 Character Ranges

The Unicode Standard assigns code values, which range from 0000 (**Basic Latin**) to E007F (**Tags**), to the written characters of the world. Currently, there are code values for 94,140 characters. To simplify the search for a character and its associated code value, the Unicode Standard generally groups code values by script and function (i.e., Latin characters are grouped in a block, mathematical operators are grouped in another block, and so on). As a rule, a script is a single writing system that is used for multiple languages (e.g., the Latin script is used for English, French, Spanish, and so on). The **Code Charts** page on the Unicode Consortium website lists all the defined blocks and their respective code values. Figure G.4 lists some blocks (scripts) from the website and their range of code values.

Script	Range of code values
Arabic	U+0600–U+06FF
Basic Latin	U+0000–U+007F
Bengali (India)	U+0980–U+09FF
Cherokee (Native America)	U+13A0–U+13FF
CJK Unified Ideographs (East Asia)	U+4E00–U+9FAF
Cyrillic (Russia and Eastern Europe)	U+0400–U+04FF
Ethiopic	U+1200–U+137F

Fig. G.4 | Some character ranges. (Part 1 of 2.)

Script	Range of code values
Greek	U+0370–U+03FF
Hangul Jamo (Korea)	U+1100–U+11FF
Hebrew	U+0590–U+05FF
Hiragana (Japan)	U+3040–U+309F
Khmer (Cambodia)	U+1780–U+17FF
Lao (Laos)	U+0E80–U+0EFF
Mongolian	U+1800–U+18AF
Myanmar	U+1000–U+109F
Ogham (Ireland)	U+1680–U+169F
Runic (Germany and Scandinavia)	U+16A0–U+16FF
Sinhala (Sri Lanka)	U+0D80–U+0DFF
Telugu (India)	U+0C00–U+0C7F
Thai	U+0E00–U+0E7F

Fig. G.4 | Some character ranges. (Part 2 of 2.)

Summary

- Before Unicode, software developers were plagued by the use of inconsistent character encoding (i.e., numeric values for characters). Most countries and organizations had their own encoding systems, which were incompatible. A good example is the individual encoding systems on the Windows and Macintosh platforms.
- Computers process data by converting characters to numeric values. For instance, the character "a" is converted to a numeric value so that a computer can manipulate that piece of data.
- Without Unicode, localization of global software requires significant modifications to the source code, which results in increased cost and delays in releasing the product.
- Localization is necessary with each release of a version. By the time a software product is localized for a particular market, a newer version, which needs to be localized as well, is ready for distribution. As a result, it is cumbersome and costly to produce and distribute global software products in a market where there is no universal character-encoding standard.
- The Unicode Consortium developed the Unicode Standard in response to the serious problems created by multiple character encodings and the use of those encodings.
- The Unicode Standard facilitates the production and distribution of localized software. It outlines a specification for the consistent encoding of the world's characters and symbols.

- Software products that handle text encoded in the Unicode Standard need to be localized, but the localization process is simpler and more efficient because the numeric values need not be converted.
- The Unicode Standard is designed to be universal, efficient, uniform and unambiguous.
- A universal encoding system encompasses all commonly used characters; an efficient encoding system parses text files easily; a uniform encoding system assigns fixed values to all characters; and an unambiguous encoding system represents the same character for any given value.
- Unicode extends the limited ASCII character set to include all the major characters of the world.
- Unicode makes use of three Unicode Transformation Formats (UTF): UTF-8, UTF-16 and UTF-32, each of which may be appropriate for use in different contexts.
- UTF-8 data consists of 8-bit bytes (sequences of one, two, three or four bytes depending on the character being encoded) and is well suited for ASCII-based systems, where there is a predominance of one-byte characters (ASCII represents characters as one byte).
- UTF-8 is a variable-width encoding form that is more compact for text involving mostly Latin characters and ASCII punctuation.
- UTF-16 is the default encoding form of the Unicode Standard. It is a variable-width encoding form that uses 16-bit code units instead of bytes. Most characters are represented by a single unit, but some characters require surrogate pairs.
- Surrogates are 16-bit integers in the range D800 through DFFF, which are used solely for the purpose of "escaping" into higher-numbered characters.
- Without surrogate pairs, the UTF-16 encoding form can encompass only 65,000 characters, but with the surrogate pairs, this is expanded to include over a million characters.
- UTF-32 is a 32-bit encoding form. The major advantage of the fixed-width encoding form is that it uniformly expresses all characters, so that they are easy to handle in arrays and so forth.
- The Unicode Standard consists of characters. A character is any written component that can be represented by a numeric value.
- Characters are represented with glyphs (various shapes, fonts and sizes for displaying characters).
- Code values are bit combinations that represent encoded characters. The Unicode notation for a code value is U+*yyyy*, in which U+ refers to the Unicode code values, as opposed to other hexadecimal values. The *yyyy* represents a four-digit hexadecimal number.
- Currently, the Unicode Standard provides code values for 94,140 character representations.
- An advantage of the Unicode Standard is its impact on the overall performance of the international economy. Applications that conform to an encoding standard can be processed easily by computers anywhere.
- Another advantage of the Unicode Standard is its portability. Applications written in Unicode can be easily transferred to different operating systems, databases, web browsers and so on. Most companies currently support, or are planning to support, Unicode.
- To obtain more information about the Unicode Standard and the Unicode Consortium, visit `www.unicode.org`. It contains a link to the code charts, which contain the 16-bit code values for the currently encoded characters.
- The Unicode Standard has become the default encoding system for XML and any language derived from XML, such as XHTML.
- The Visual Basic IDE uses Unicode UTF-16 encoding to represent all characters.
- In the marking up of Visual Basic documents, the entity reference &H*yyyy* is used, where *yyyy* represents the hexadecimal code value.

Terminology

&Hyyyy notation
ASCII
block
character
character set
code value
diacritic
double-byte character set (DBCS)
efficient (Unicode design basis)
encode
entity reference
glyph
hexadecimal notation
localization
multibyte character set (MBCS)
portability
script
surrogate
symbol
unambiguous (Unicode design basis)
Unicode Consortium
Unicode design basis
Unicode Standard
Unicode Transformation Format (UTF)
uniform (Unicode design basis)
universal (Unicode design basis)
UTF-8
UTF-16
UTF-32

Self-Review Exercises

G.1 Fill in the blanks in each of the following.

a) Global software developers had to _________ their products to a specific market before distribution.

b) The Unicode Standard is a(n) _________ standard that facilitates the uniform production and distribution of software products.

c) The four design bases that constitute the Unicode Standard are: _________, _________, _________ and _________.

d) A(n) _________ is the smallest written component that can be represented with a numeric value.

e) Software that can execute on different operating systems is said to be _________.

f) Of the three encoding forms, _________ is currently supported by Internet Explorer 5.5 and Netscape Communicator 6.

G.2 State whether each of the following is *true* or *false*. If *false*, explain why.

a) The Unicode Standard encompasses all the world's characters.

b) A Unicode code value is represented as U+*yyyy*, where *yyyy* represents a number in binary notation.

c) A diacritic is a character with a special mark that emphasizes an accent.

d) Unicode is portable.

e) When designing Visual Basic programs, the entity reference is denoted by #U+*yyyy*.

Answers to Self-Review exercises

G.1 a) localize. b) encoding. c) universal, efficient, uniform, unambiguous. d) character. e) portable. f) UTF-8.

G.2 a) False. It encompasses the majority of the world's characters. b) False. The *yyyy* represents a hexadecimal number. c) False. A diacritic is a special mark added to a character to distinguish it from another letter or to indicate an accent. d) True. e) False. The entity reference is denoted by &H*yyyy*.

Exercises

G.3 Navigate to the Unicode Consortium website (`www.unicode.org`) and write the hexadecimal code values for the following characters. In which block are they located?

a) Latin letter 'Z.'
b) Latin letter 'n' with the 'tilde (~).'
c) Greek letter 'delta.'
d) Mathematical operator 'less than or equal to.'
e) Punctuation symbol 'open quote (").'

G.4 Describe the Unicode Standard design basis.

G.5 Define the following terms:

a) code value.
b) surrogates.
c) Unicode Standard.
d) UTF-8.
e) UTF-16.
f) UTF-32.

G.6 Describe a scenario where it is optimal to store your data in UTF-16 format.

G.7 Using the Unicode Standard code values, create a program that prints your first and last name. If you know other writing systems, print your first and last name in those as well. Use a `Label` to display your name.

G.8 Write an ASP.NET program that prints "Welcome to Unicode!" in English, French, German, Japanese, Portuguese, Russian, Spanish and Traditional Chinese. Use the code values provided in Fig. G.3. In ASP.NET, a code value is represented the same way as in a Windows application (&H*yyyy*, where *yyyy* is a four-digit hexadecimal number).

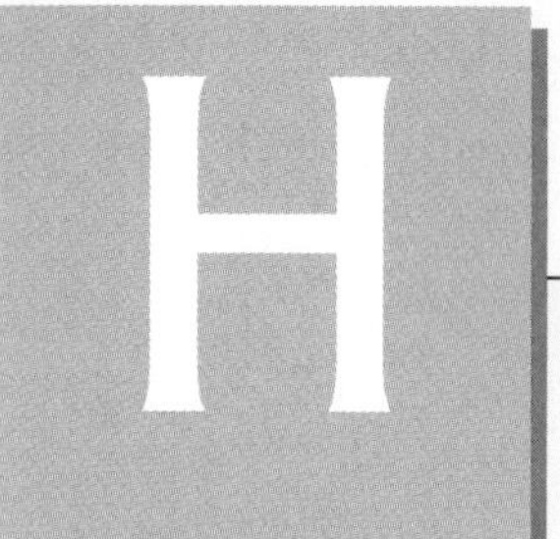

Using the Visual Basic 2008 Debugger

We are built to make mistakes, coded for error.
—Lewis Thomas

What we anticipate seldom occurs; what we least expect generally happens.
—Benjamin Disraeli

It is one thing to show a man that he is in error, and another to put him in possession of truth.
—John Locke

He can run but he can't hide.
—Joe Louis

And so shall I catch the fly.
—William Shakespeare

OBJECTIVES

In this appendix you will learn:

- To use the debugger to locate and correct logic errors in a program.
- To use breakpoints to pause program execution and allow you to examine the values of variables.
- To set, disable and remove breakpoints.
- To use the **Continue** command to continue execution from a breakpoint.
- To use the **Locals** window to view and modify variable values.
- To use the **Watch** window to evaluate expressions.
- To use the **Step Into**, **Step Out** and **Step Over** commands to execute a program line by line.
- To use the debugging features Edit and Continue and Just My Code™ debugging.

Outline

H.1 Introduction

In this appendix, you'll learn about tools and techniques that can be used to address compilation errors and logic errors. In Chapter 3, you were introduced to syntax errors—violations of Visual Basic's language rules. Syntax errors are a type of compilation error—an error that prevents code from compiling. Logic errors, also called bugs, do not prevent a program from compiling successfully, but can cause a running program to produce erroneous results or terminate prematurely. Most compiler vendors, like Microsoft, package their IDEs with a tool called a debugger. Debuggers allow you to monitor the execution of your programs to locate and remove logic errors. A program must successfully compile before it can be used in the debugger. The debugger allows you to suspend program execution, examine and set variable values and much more. In this appendix, we introduce the Visual Basic 2008 IDE and debugger features for fixing errors in your programs.

H.2 Resolving Compilation Errors

As you know, compilation errors appear before the program runs, and can be found by the IDE as you write your code. Some common compilation errors can be quickly removed using a Visual Basic feature called *Smart Compile Auto Correction*. Sometimes, a compilation error displays the rectangular symbol (▭) under what the compiler recognizes as the cause of the compilation error. If you hover the mouse over this symbol, you'll see the **Error Correction Options** icon. You can click the icon to open the **Error Correction Options** Window. This window, which you'll see shortly, displays suggestions for correcting the problem and a preview of what the code will look like once a fix has been made.

Line 7 in Fig. H.1, contains a compilation error. The problem is a missing parenthesis in the `Console.Write()` function call. Visual Basic automatically detects such errors and in some cases allows you to use automatic correction. Figure H.2 shows the ▭ symbol that represents an error that can be autocorrected. By hovering the mouse over this symbol, you see the **Error Correction Options** exclamation point (Fig. H.3). When you click the down

```
' Fig. H.1: Login.vb
' Login application used to demonstrate compiler errors.
Module Login
   Sub Main()
      ' obtain username from user
      Console.WriteLine("Please enter your username and password.")
      Console.Write("Username: "
      Dim user = Console.ReadLine()

      Console.Write("Password: ") ' obtain password from user
      Dim password = Console.ReadLine()

      ' check whether given username and password are valid
      If user = "admin" AndAlso password = "opensesame" Then
         ' username and password are correct
         Console.WriteLine("Access granted.")
      Else
         ' username and password are incorrect
         Console.WriteLine("Access denied.")
      End If
   End Sub ' Main
End Module ' Login
```

Fig. H.1 | **Login** program.

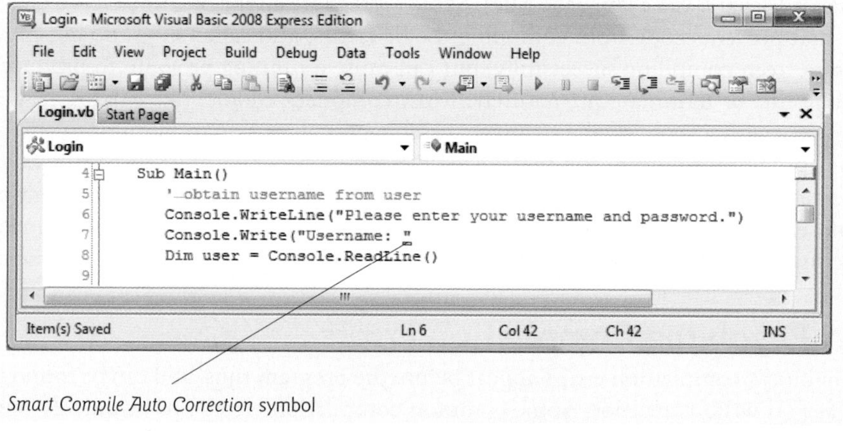

Fig. H.2 | Compilation error.

arrow, the **Error Correction Options** window appears (Fig. H.4), showing the error message "**')' expected**" and suggesting the code fix "**Insert the missing ')'.**" In the text area below the error suggestion, you can see a preview of the code if this fix were to be applied. Clicking the link "**Insert the missing ')'**" fixes the code and the **Error Correction Options** window closes.

Getting Help with Errors

When you receive a compilation error, you can typically right click the error in the **Error List** (Fig. H.5) and select **Show Error Help** to learn more about the error and how to fix it

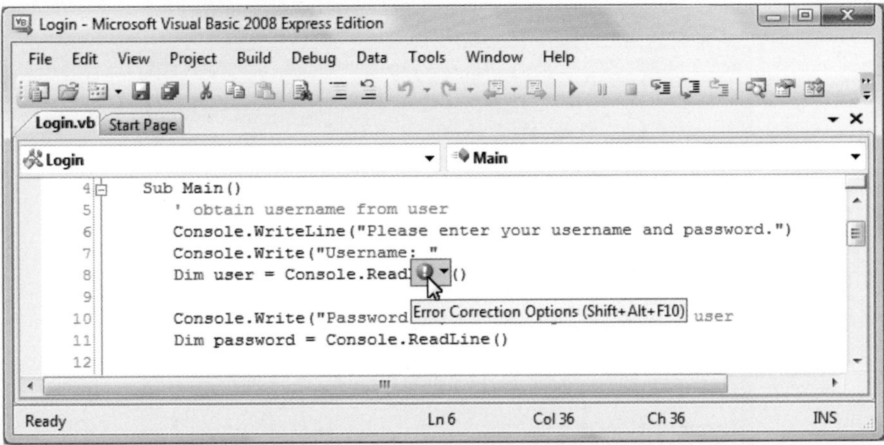

Fig. H.3 | **Error Correction Options** icon shown when hovering over the error.

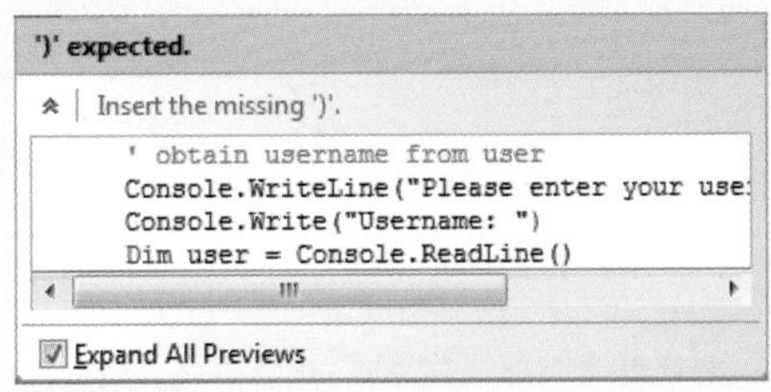

Fig. H.4 | **Error Correction Options** window

(if the **Error List** is not visible, you can show it by selecting **View > Error List**). This opens the MSDN (Microsoft Developer Network) page for the appropriate compiler error in the **Microsoft Visual Studio 2008 Documentation** window (Fig. H.6). This website includes the problem's description as well as one or more recommended methods of fixing it.

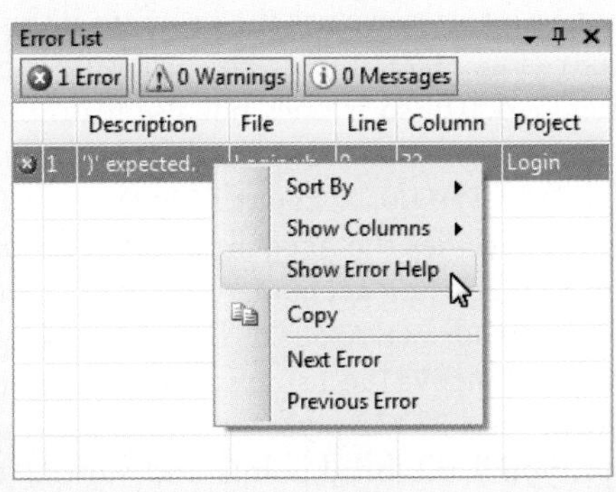

Fig. H.5 | **Show Error Help** option in **Error List**.

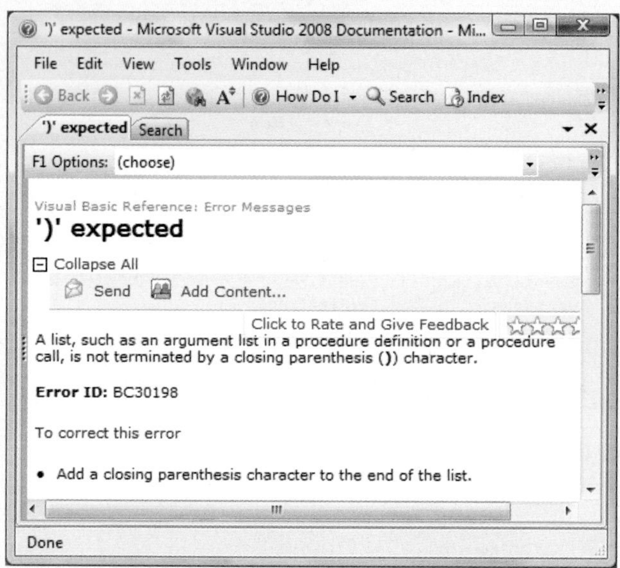

Fig. H.6 | MSDN page for the **')' expected** error

H.3 Breakpoints and the Continue Command

While compilation errors can be found automatically by the compiler, it can be much more difficult to determine the cause of logic errors. To help with this, we investigate the concept of breakpoints. Breakpoints are special markers that can be set at any executable line of code. They cannot be placed on comments or whitespace. When a running program reaches a breakpoint, execution pauses, allowing you to examine the values of variables to help determine whether logic errors exist. For example, you can examine the value of a variable that stores a calculation's result to determine whether the calculation was performed correctly. You can also examine the value of an expression.

To illustrate the debugger features, we use the program in Figs. H.7–H.8 that creates and manipulates an `Account` (Fig. H.7) object. This example is based on an exercise you created in Chapter 4 (Exercise 4.10), so it does not use features that are presented after Chapter 4. Execution begins in `Main` (lines 4–33 of Fig. H.8). Line 5 creates an `Account` object with an initial balance of $50.00. `Account`'s constructor (lines 8–14 of Fig. H.7) accepts one argument, which specifies the `Account`'s initial `balance`. Line 8 of Fig. H.8 outputs the initial account balance using `Account` property `Balance`. Lines 11–12 prompt the user for and input the `withdrawalAmount`. Lines 14–16 subtract the withdrawal amount from the `Account`'s `balanceValue` using its `Debit` method. Lines 19–20 display the new `balanceValue`. Next, lines 23–32 perform similar steps to credit the account.

In the following steps, you'll use breakpoints and various debugger commands to examine the variable `withdrawalAmount`'s value (declared in Fig. H.8) while the program executes.

```
' Fig. H.7: Account.vb
' Account class with a constructor to initialize a customer's balance.
Public Class Account
   ' instance variable that stores the balance
   Private balanceValue As Integer

   ' constructor
   Public Sub New(ByVal initialBalance As Integer)
      ' if initialBalance is not greater than 0,
      ' balance is still initialized to 0 by default
      If initialBalance > 0 Then
         Balance = initialBalance
      End If
   End Sub ' New

   ' credit (increases) the account by amount
   Public Sub Credit(ByVal amount As Integer)
      Balance = Balance + amount ' add amount to balance
   End Sub ' Credit

   ' debit (decreases) the account by amount
   Public Sub Debit(ByVal amount As Integer)
      If amount > Balance Then
         Console.WriteLine("Debit amount exceeded account balance.")
      End If

      If amount <= Balance Then
         Balance = Balance - amount ' subtract amount to balance
      End If
   End Sub ' Debit

   ' property makes balanceValue available to clients;
   ' no validation required
   Public Property Balance() As Integer
      Get ' returns the account balance
         Return balanceValue
      End Get

      Set(ByVal value As Integer) ' sets the balance value
         balanceValue = value
      End Set
   End Property ' Balance
End Class ' Account
```

Fig. H.7 | Account class with a constructor to initialize property Balance.

```
' Fig. H.8: AccountTest.vb
' Create and manipulate an Account object.
Module AccountTest
   Sub Main() ' begins execution
      Dim account1 As New Account(50) ' create Account object
```

Fig. H.8 | Creating and manipulating an Account object. (Part 1 of 2.)

```
6
7            ' display initial balance of each object
8            Console.WriteLine("account1 balance: " & account1.Balance)
9
10           ' obtain withdrawal input from Command Prompt
11           Console.Write("Enter withdrawal amount for account1: ")
12           Dim withdrawalAmount As Integer = Console.ReadLine()
13
14           Console.WriteLine(vbCrLf & "Subtracting " & withdrawalAmount & _
15              " from account1 balance")
16           account1.Debit(withdrawalAmount) ' subtract amount from account1
17
18           ' display balance
19           Console.WriteLine("account1 balance: " & account1.Balance)
20           Console.WriteLine()
21
22           ' obtain credit input from Command Prompt
23           Console.Write("Enter credit amount for account1: ")
24           Dim creditAmount As Integer = Console.ReadLine()
25
26           Console.WriteLine(vbCrLf & "Adding " & creditAmount & _
27              " to account1 balance")
28           account1.Credit(creditAmount) ' add amount to account1
29
30           ' display balance
31           Console.WriteLine("account1 balance: " & account1.Balance)
32           Console.WriteLine()
33        End Sub ' Main
34     End Module ' AccountTest
```

```
account1 balance: 50

Enter withdrawal amount for account1: 25

Subtracting 25 from account1 balance
account1 balance: 25

Enter credit amount for account1: 33

Adding 33 to account1 balance
account1 balance: 58
```

Fig. H.8 | Creating and manipulating an `Account` object. (Part 2 of 2.)

1. ***Inserting breakpoints in Visual Basic.*** First, ensure that `AccountTest.vb` is open in the IDE's code editor. To insert a breakpoint, left click inside the margin indicator bar (the gray margin at the left of the code window in Fig. H.9) next to the line of code at which you wish to break, or right click that line of code and select **Breakpoint > Insert Breakpoint**. Additionally, you can also press *F9* when your cursor is on the line. You may set as many breakpoints as you like. Set breakpoints at lines 11, 16 and 33 of your code. A solid circle appears in the margin indicator bar where you clicked and the entire code statement is highlighted, indicating that breakpoints have been set (Fig. H.9). When the program runs, the

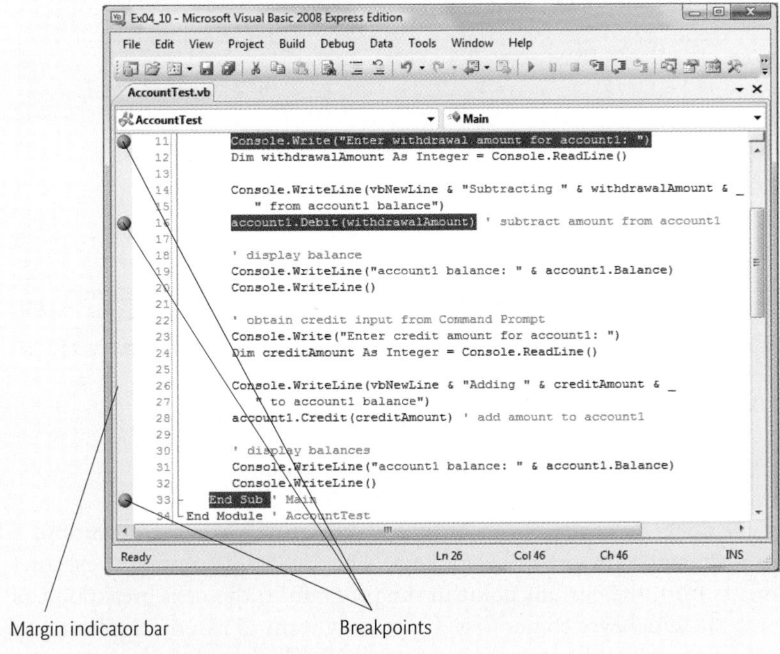

Fig. H.9 | Setting breakpoints.

debugger suspends execution at any line that contains a breakpoint. The program then enters break mode. Breakpoints can be set before running a program, both in break mode and during execution. To show a list of all break points in a project, select **Debug > Windows > Breakpoints**. This features is only available in the full version of Visual Studio 2008.

2. ***Beginning the debugging process.*** After setting breakpoints in the code editor, select **Build > Build Account** to compile the program, then select **Debug > Start Debugging** (or press the *F5* key) to begin the debugging process. While debugging a console application, the **Command Prompt** window appears (Fig. H.10), allowing program interaction (input and output).
3. ***Examining program execution.*** Program execution pauses at the first breakpoint (line 11), and the IDE becomes the active window (Fig. H.11). The yellow arrow to the left of line 11, also called the *Instruction Pointer*, indicates that this line contains the next statement to execute. The IDE also highlights the line as well.

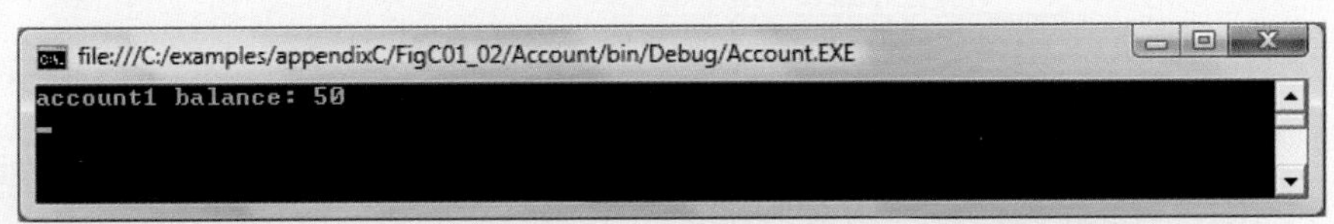

Fig. H.10 | **Account** program running.

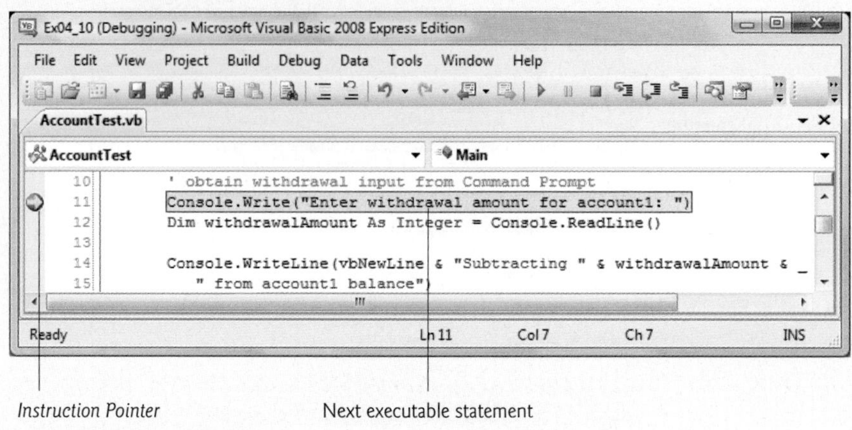

Fig. H.11 | Program execution suspended at the first breakpoint.

4. ***Using the* Continue *command to resume execution.*** To resume execution, select **Debug > Continue** (or press the *F5* key). The Continue command executes the statements from the current point in the program to the next breakpoint or the end of `Main`, whichever comes first. If you only want to run the application until a specific line, you can place your cursor on that line, and then use the **Run To Cursor** command to execute the program until that line. Here, we use the **Continue** command and the program continues executing and pauses for input at line 12. Enter `25` in the **Command Prompt** window as the withdrawal amount. When you press *Enter*, the program executes until it stops at the next breakpoint (line 16). Notice that when you place the mouse pointer over the variable name `withdrawalAmount`, its value is displayed in a *Quick Info* box (Fig. H.12). As you'll see, this can help you spot logic errors in your programs.
5. ***Continuing program execution.*** Use the **Debug > Continue** command to execute line 16. The program then asks you to input a credit (deposit) amount. Enter `33`, then press *Enter*. The program displays the result of its calculation (Fig. H.13).

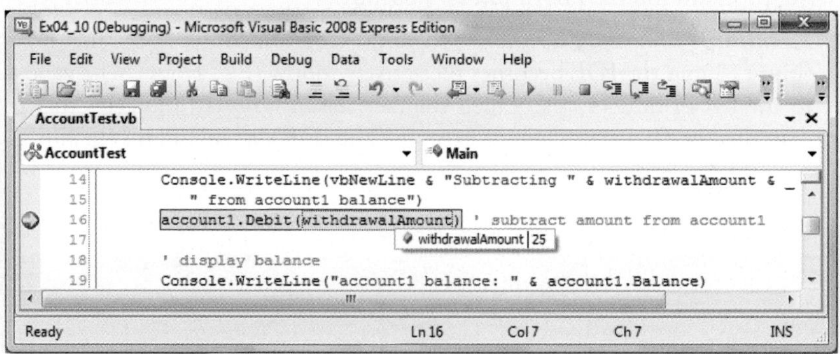

Fig. H.12 | *Quick Info* box displays value of variable `depositAmount`.

```
file:///C:/examples/appendixC/FigC01_02/Account/bin/Debug/Account.EXE
account1 balance: 50
Enter withdrawal amount for account1: 25

Subtracting 25 from account1 balance
account1 balance: 25

Enter credit amount for account1: 33

Adding 33 to account1 balance
account1 balance: 58
```

Fig. H.13 | Sample execution of `Account.EXE` in debug mode.

6. ***Disabling a breakpoint.*** To disable a breakpoint, right click a line of code in which the breakpoint has been set and select **Breakpoint > Disable Breakpoint.** The disabled breakpoint is indicated by a hollow circle (Fig. H.14)—the breakpoint can be re-enabled by right clicking the line marked by the hollow circle and selecting **Breakpoint > Enable Breakpoint.**
7. ***Removing a breakpoint.*** To remove a breakpoint that you no longer need, right click the line of code on which the breakpoint has been set and select **Breakpoint > Delete Breakpoint.** You also can remove a breakpoint by clicking the circle in the margin indicator bar or pressing *F9* when the cursor is on the line.
8. ***Finishing program execution.*** Select **Debug > Continue** to execute the program to completion. Then delete all the breakpoints.

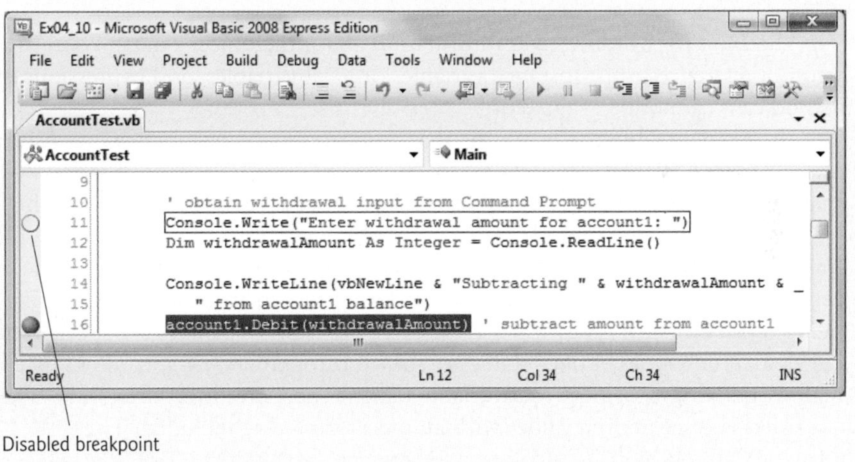

Fig. H.14 | Disabled breakpoint.

H.4 *DataTips* and Visualizers

You already know how to use the *Quick Info* window to view a variable's value. However, often you may want to check the status of an `Object`. For example, you may want to check the `Text` value of a `TextBox` control. When you hover the mouse over a reference-type variable, the *DataTip* window appears (Fig. H.15). When you hover over the + sign in the

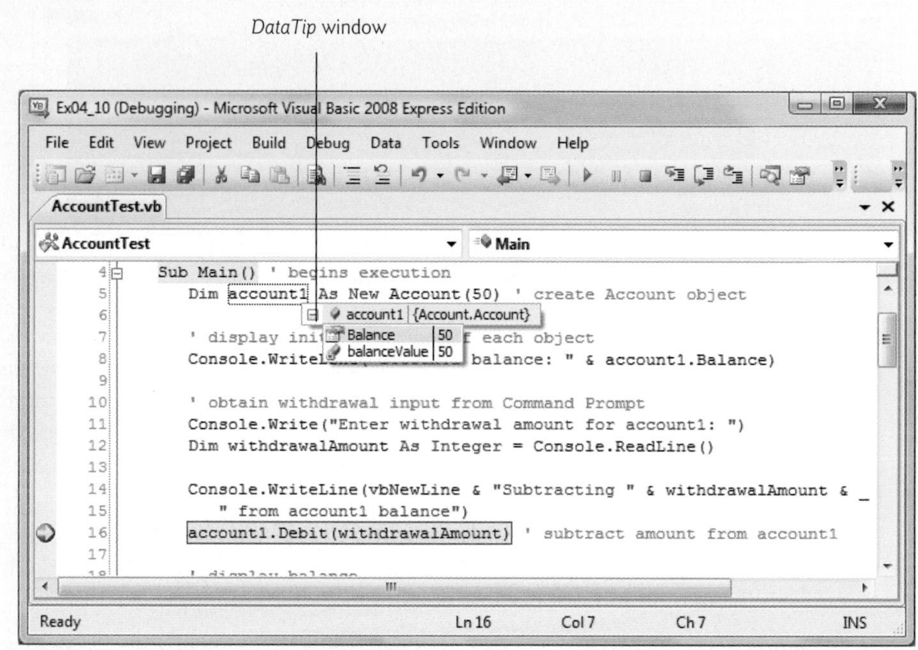

Fig. H.15 | A *DataTip* displayed for the `account1` variable.

DataTip, the *DataTip* window gives information about the object's data. There are some limitations—references must instance variables or local variables, and expressions involving method calls cannot be evaluated.

For the `Account` object, this means that you can see the `balanceValue` inside it (as well as the `Balance` property used to access it). Just like the *Quick Info* window, you can also change the value of a property or variable inside it by clicking on one of the values listed, then typing the new value.

DataTips do not intuitively display information for all variables. For example, a variable representing an XML document cannot be viewed in its natural form using most debugging tools. For such types, visualizers can be useful. Visualizers are specialized windows to view certain types of data. They are shown through *DataTip* windows by clicking the small magnifying glass next to a variable name. There are three visualizers. The **Text Visualizer** lets you see `String` values with all their formatting included. The **XML Visualizer** formats XML objects into a color-coded format. Finally, the **HTML Visualizer** parses HTML code (in `String` or XML form) into a web page, which is displayed in the small window.

H.5 The Locals and Watch Windows

In the preceding section, you learned how to use the *Quick Info* and *DataTip* features to examine the variable's value. In this section, you'll learn how to use the **Locals** window to view all variables that are in use while your program is running. You'll also use the **Watch** window to examine the values of expressions.

1. ***Inserting breakpoints.*** Set a breakpoint at line 16 (Fig. H.16) in the source code by left clicking in the margin indicator bar to the left of line 16. Use the same technique to set breakpoints at lines 19 and 20 as well.
2. ***Starting debugging.*** Select **Debug > Start Debugging.** Type 25 at the **Enter withdrawal amount for account1:** prompt (Fig. H.17) and press *Enter* so that the program reads the value you just entered. The program executes until the breakpoint at line 16.
3. ***Suspending program execution.*** When the program reaches line 16, Visual Basic suspends program execution and switches the program into break mode (Fig. H.18). At this point, the statement in line 12 (Fig. H.8) has input the `withdrawalAmount` that you entered (25), the statement in lines 14–15 has output that the program is subtracting that amount from the `account1` balance and the statement in line 16 is the next statement that executes.
4. ***Examining data.*** Once the program has entered break mode, you can explore the values of your local variables using the debugger's **Locals** window. To view the **Locals** window, select **Debug > Windows > Locals.** Click the plus box to the left of `account1` in the **Locals** window's **Name** column (Fig. H.19). This allows you to view each of `account1`'s instance variable values individually, including the value for `balanceValue` (50). Note that the **Locals** window displays a class' properties as data, which is why you see both the `Balance` property and the `balanceValue` instance variable in the **Locals** window. In addition, the current value of local variable `withdrawalAmount` (25) is also displayed.

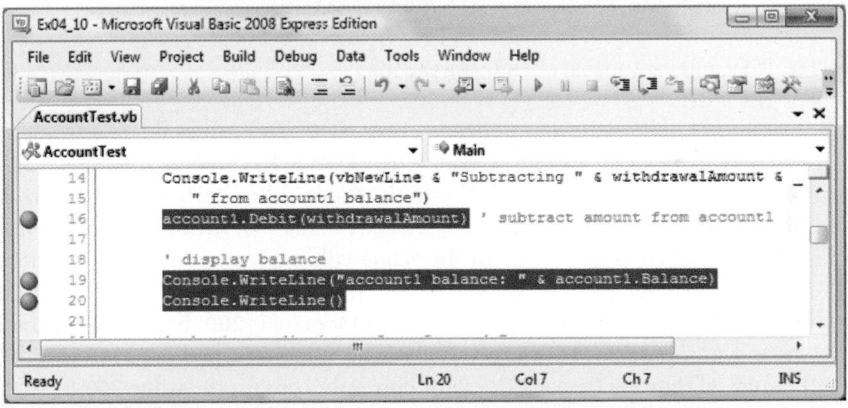

Fig. H.16 | Setting breakpoints at lines 16, 19 and 20.

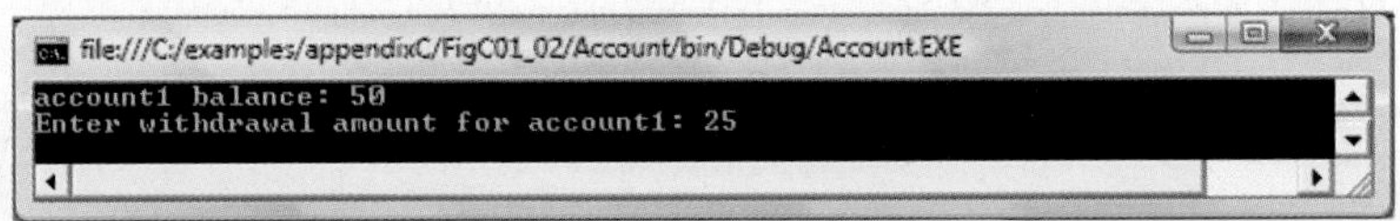

Fig. H.17 | Entering the deposit amount before the breakpoint is reached.

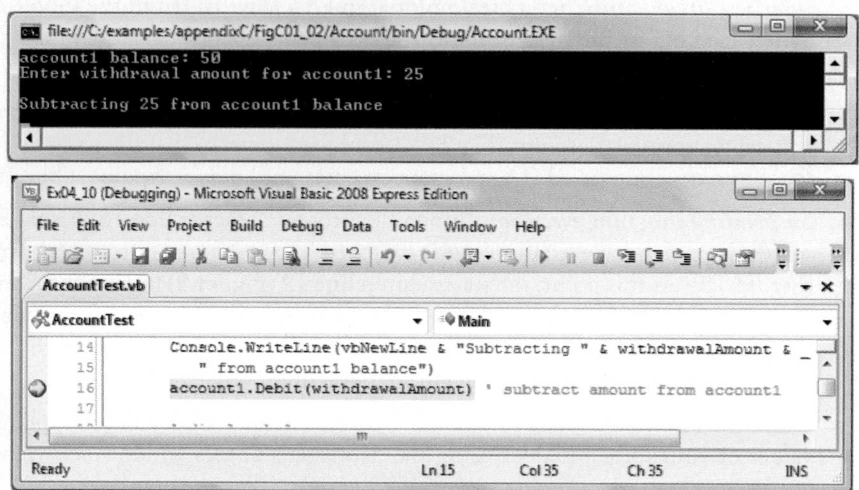

Fig. H.18 | Program execution pauses when debugger reaches the breakpoint at line 16.

Locals

Name	Value	Type
account1	{Account.Account}	Account.Account
Balance	50	Integer
balanceValue	50	Integer
creditAmount	0	Integer
withdrawalAmount	25	Integer

Fig. H.19 | Examining variable `withdrawalAmount`.

5. ***Evaluating arithmetic and*** `Boolean` ***expressions.*** You can evaluate arithmetic and `Boolean` expressions using the **Watch** window. Select **Debug > Windows > Watch** to display the window (Fig. H.20). In the **Name** column's first row (which should be blank initially), type `(withdrawalAmount + 10) * 5`, then press *Enter*. The value `175` is displayed (Fig. H.20). In the **Name** column's next row in the **Watch** window, type `withdrawalAmount = 200`, then press *Enter*. This expression determines whether the value contained in `withdrawalAmount` is `200`. Expressions containing the `=` symbol are `Boolean` expressions. The value returned is `False` (Fig. H.20), because `withdrawalAmount` does not currently contain the value `200`.

6. ***Resuming execution.*** Select **Debug > Continue** to resume execution. Line 16 executes, subtracting the account with the withdrawal amount, and the program

Watch

Name	Value	Type
(withdrawalAmount + 10) * 5	175	Integer
withdrawalAmount = 200	False	Boolean

Evaluating an arithmetic expression

Evaluating a `Boolean` expression

Fig. H.20 | Examining the values of expressions.

enters break mode again at line 19. Select **Debug > Windows > Locals.** The updated `balanceValue` instance variable and `Balance` property value are now displayed (Fig. H.21). The values in red indicate the values that have just been modified.

7. ***Modifying values.*** Based on the value input by the user (`25`), the account balance output by the program should be `25`. However, you can use the **Locals** window to change variable values during program execution. This can be valuable for experimenting with different values and for locating logic errors in programs. In the **Locals** window, click the **Value** field in the `balanceValue` row to select the value `25`. Type `37`, then press *Enter*. The debugger changes the value of `balanceValue` (and the `Balance` property as well), then displays its new value in red (Fig. H.22). Now select **Debug > Continue** to execute lines 19–20. Notice that the new value of `balanceValue` is displayed in the **Command Prompt** window.
8. ***Stopping the debugging session.*** Select **Debug > Stop Debugging.** Delete all breakpoints, which can be done by pressing *Ctrl-Shift-F9*.

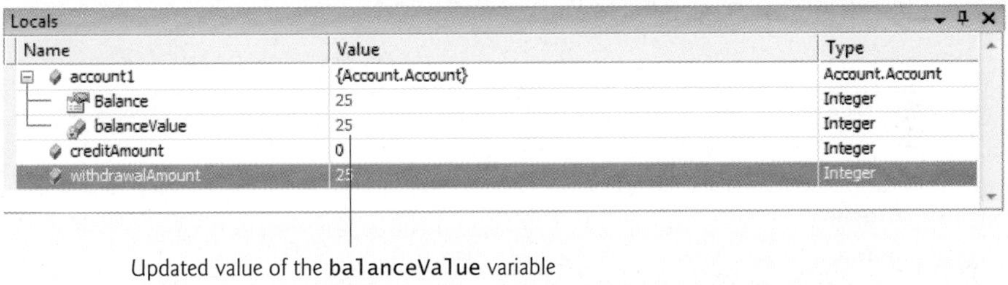

Updated value of the `balanceValue` variable

Fig. H.21 | Displaying the value of local variables.

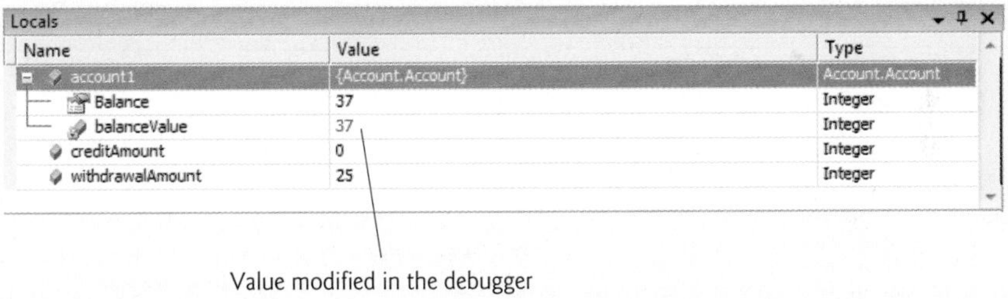

Value modified in the debugger

Fig. H.22 | Modifying the value of a variable.

H.6 Controlling Execution Using the Step Into, Step Over, Step Out and Continue Commands

Sometimes you need to execute a program line by line to find and fix logic errors. Stepping through a portion of your program this way can help you verify that a method's code executes correctly. The commands you learn in this section allow you to execute a method line by line, execute all of a method's statements or execute only a method's remaining statements (if you have already executed some statements in the method).

1. ***Setting a breakpoint.*** Set a breakpoint at line 16 by left clicking in the margin indicator bar (Fig. H.23).
2. ***Starting the debugger.*** Select **Debug > Start Debugging.** Enter the value `25` at the **Enter withdrawal amount for account1:** prompt. Program execution halts when the program reaches the breakpoint at line 16.
3. ***Using the* Step Into *command.*** The **Step Into** command executes the next statement in the program (the yellow highlighted line of Fig. H.24) and immediately halts. If the statement to execute is a method call, control transfers to the called method. The **Step Into** command allows you to follow execution into a method and confirm its execution by individually executing each statement inside the method. Select **Debug > Step Into** (or press *F8*) to enter the `Debit` method (Fig. H.25).
4. ***Using the* Step Over *command.*** Select **Debug > Step Over** to enter the `Debit` method's body and transfer control to line 23 (Fig. H.26). The **Step Over** command behaves like the **Step Into** command when the next statement to execute does not contain a method call or access a property. You'll see how the **Step Over** command differs from the **Step Into** command in *Step 10.*

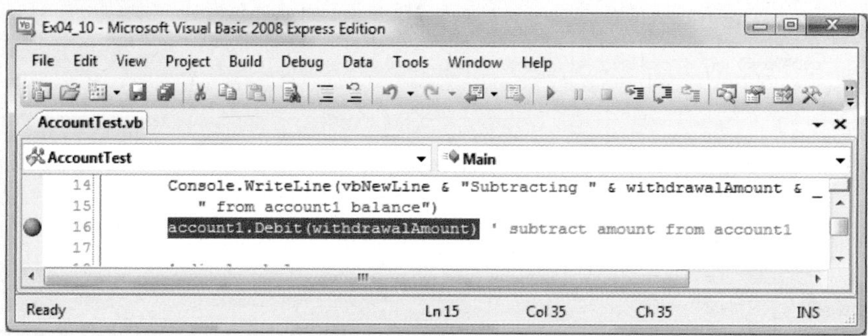

Fig. H.23 | Setting a breakpoint in the program.

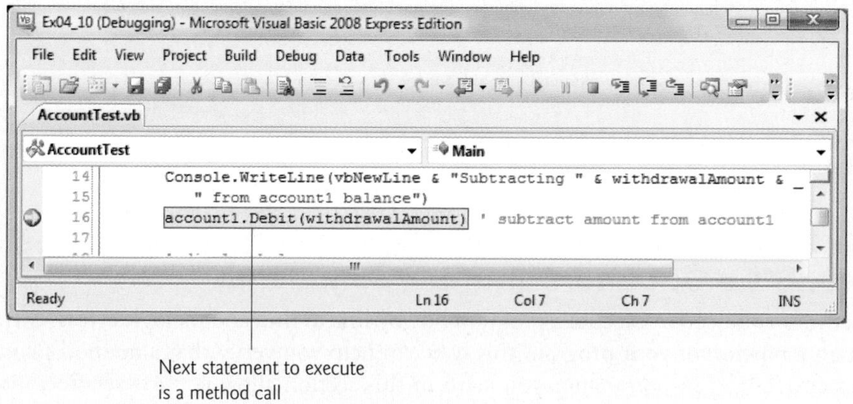

Fig. H.24 | **Step Into** command enters the `Debit` method.

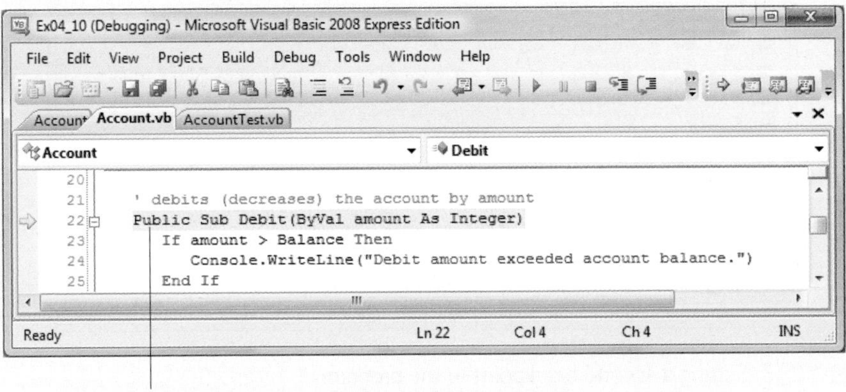

Fig. H.25 | Stepping into the `Debit` method.

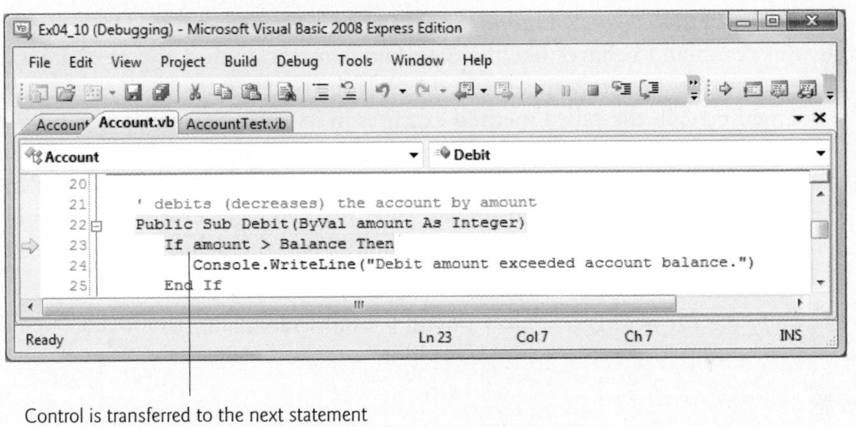

Fig. H.26 | Stepping over a statement in the `Debit` method.

5. ***Using the* Step Out *command.*** Select **Debug > Step Out** or press *Shift-F11* to execute the remaining statements in the method and return control to the calling method. Often, in lengthy methods, you may want to look at a few key lines of code, then continue debugging the caller's code. The **Step Out** command executes the remainder of a method and returns to the caller.
6. ***Setting a breakpoint.*** Set a breakpoint (Fig. H.27) at line 20 of Fig. H.8. This breakpoint is used in the next step.
7. ***Using the* Continue *command.*** Select **Debug > Continue** to execute until the next breakpoint is reached at line 20. This feature saves time when you do not want to step line by line through many lines of code to reach the next breakpoint.
8. ***Stopping the debugger.*** Select **Debug > Stop Debugging** to end the debugging session.

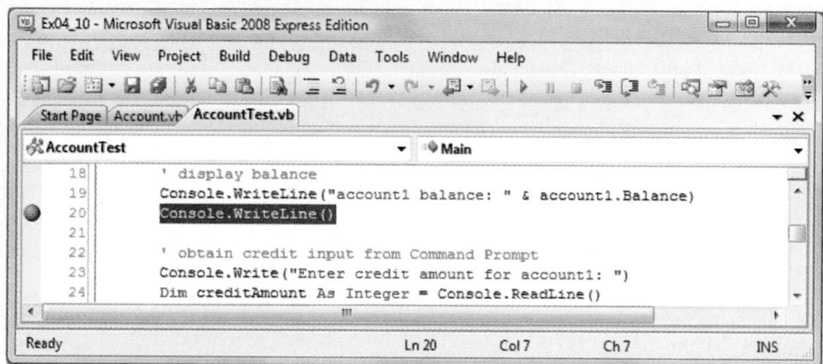

Fig. H.27 | Setting a second breakpoint in the program.

9. ***Starting the debugger.*** Before we can demonstrate the next debugger feature, you must restart the debugger. Start it, as you did in *Step 2*, and enter the same value (`25`). The debugger pauses execution at line 16.
10. ***Using the* Step Over *command.*** Select **Debug > Step Over** (Fig. H.28). Recall that this command behaves like the **Step Into** command when the next statement to execute does not contain a method call. If the next statement to execute contains a method call, the called method executes in its entirety (without pausing execution at any statement inside the method—unless there is a breakpoint in the method), and the arrow advances to the next executable line (after the method call) in the current method. In this case, the debugger executes line 16 in `Main` (Fig. H.8), which calls the `Debit` method. Then the debugger pauses execution at line 19, the next executable statement.
11. ***Stopping the debugger.*** Select **Debug > Stop Debugging**. Remove all remaining breakpoints.

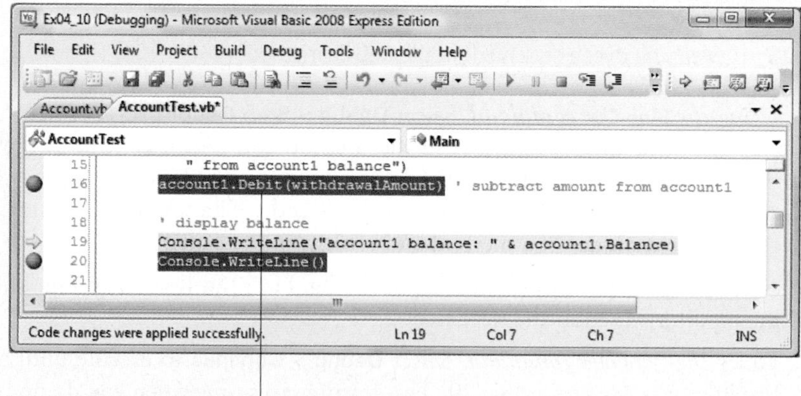

Fig. H.28 | Using the debugger's **Step Over** command.

H.7 Other Debugging Features

Visual Basic 2008 provides many other debugging features that simplify the testing and debugging process. We discuss some of these features in this section.

H.7.1 Edit and Continue

The **Edit and Continue** feature allows you to make modifications or changes to your code in debug mode, then continue executing the program without having to recompile your code.

1. ***Setting a breakpoint.*** Set a breakpoint at line 11 in your example (Fig. H.29).
2. ***Starting the debugger.*** Select **Debug > Start Debugging**. When execution begins, the `account1` balance is displayed. The debugger enters break mode when it reaches the breakpoint at line 11.
3. ***Changing the input prompt text.*** Suppose you wish to modify the input prompt text to provide the user with a range of values for variable `withdrawalAmount`. Rather than stopping the debugging process, add the text `"(from 1 to 49):"` to the end of `"Enter withdrawal amount for account1"` at line 11 in the code view window. Select **Debug > Continue**. The application prompts you for input using the updated text (Fig. H.30).

In this example, we wanted to make a change in the text for our input prompt before line 11 executes. However, if you want to make a change to a line that has already executed, you must select a prior statement in your code from which to continue execution.

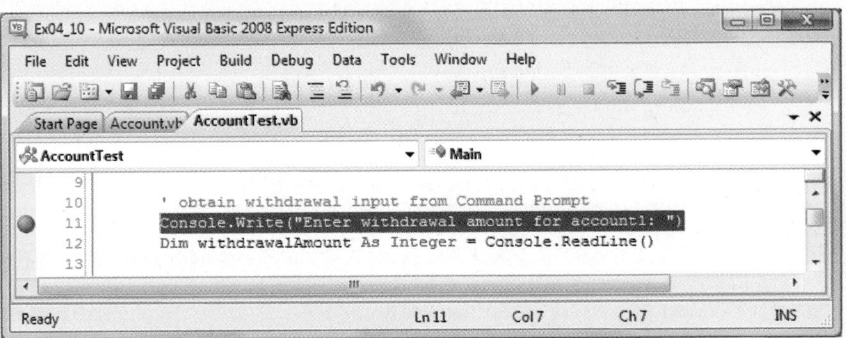

Fig. H.29 | Setting a breakpoint at line 11.

```
file:///C:/examples/appendixC/FigC01_02/Account/bin/Debug/Account.EXE
account1 balance: 50
Enter withdrawal amount for account1 (from 1 to 49): _
```

Fig. H.30 | Application prompt displaying the updated text.

1. ***Setting a breakpoint.*** Delete the breakpoint at line 11 and set a new breakpoint at line 14 (Fig. H.31).
2. ***Starting the debugger.*** Delete the `"(from 1 to 49)"` text you just added in the previous steps. Select **Debug > Start Debugging.** When execution begins, the prompt **Enter withdrawal amount for account1:** appears. Enter the value `22` at the prompt (Fig. H.32). The debugger enters break mode at line 14 (Fig. H.32).
3. ***Changing the input prompt text.*** Let's say that you once again wish to modify the input prompt text to provide the user with a range of values for variable `withdrawalAmount`. Add the text `"(from 1 to 49):"` to the end of `"Enter withdrawal amount for account1"` in line 11 inside the code view window.
4. ***Setting the next statement.*** For the program to update the input prompt text correctly, you must set the execution point to a previous line of code. Right click in line 11 and select **Set Next Statement** from the menu that appears (Fig. H.33). Alternatively, you can also drag the yellow arrow that is displayed in th left margin.

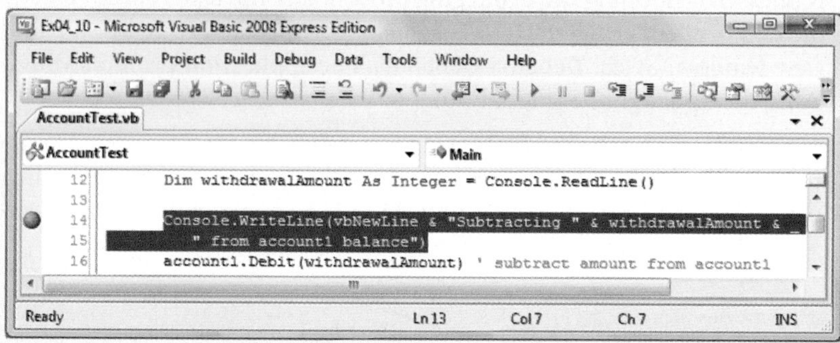

Fig. H.31 | Setting a breakpoint at line 14.

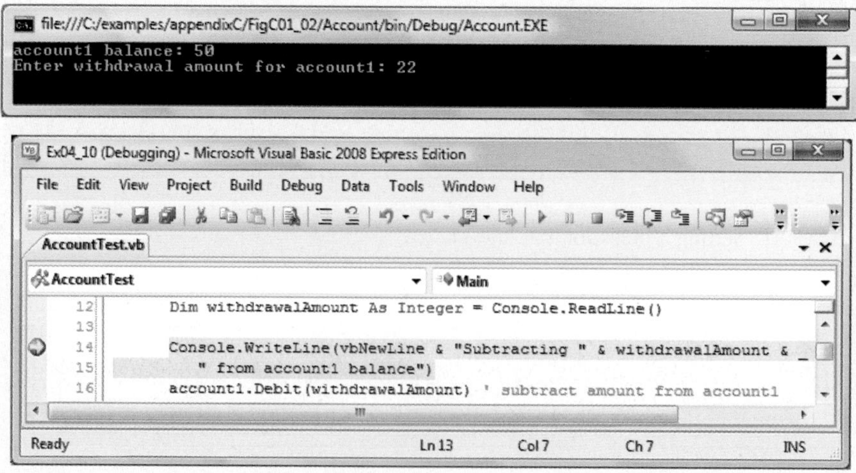

Fig. H.32 | Stopping execution at the breakpoint in line 14.

5. Select **Debug > Continue.** The application prompts you again for input using the updated text (Fig. H.34).
6. ***Stopping the debugger.*** Select **Debug > Stop Debugging.**

Certain types of changes are not allowed with the **Edit and Continue** feature, once the program begins execution. These include changing class names, adding or removing method parameters, adding `public` fields to a class and adding or removing methods. If a particular change that you make to your program is not allowed during the debugging process, Visual Basic displays a dialog box as shown in Fig. H.35.

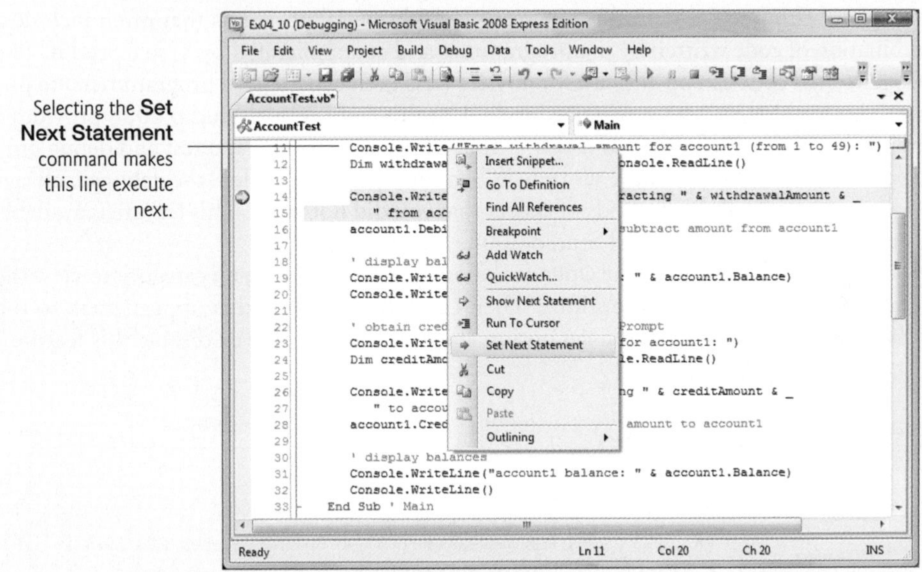

Fig. H.33 | Setting the next statement to execute.

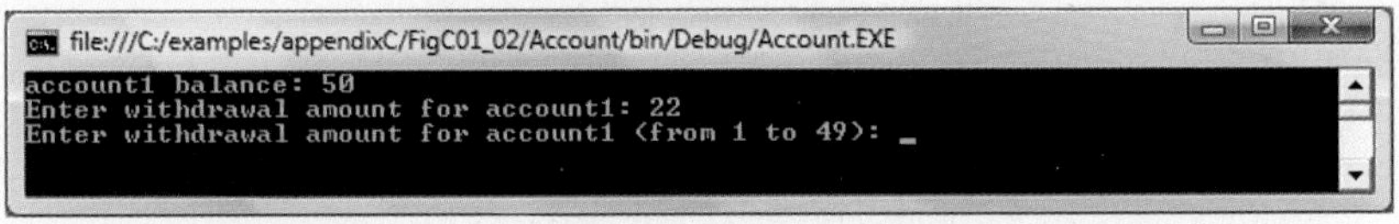

file:///C:/examples/appendixC/FigC01_02/Account/bin/Debug/Account.EXE

```
account1 balance: 50
Enter withdrawal amount for account1: 22
Enter withdrawal amount for account1 (from 1 to 49): _
```

Fig. H.34 | Program execution continues with updated prompt text.

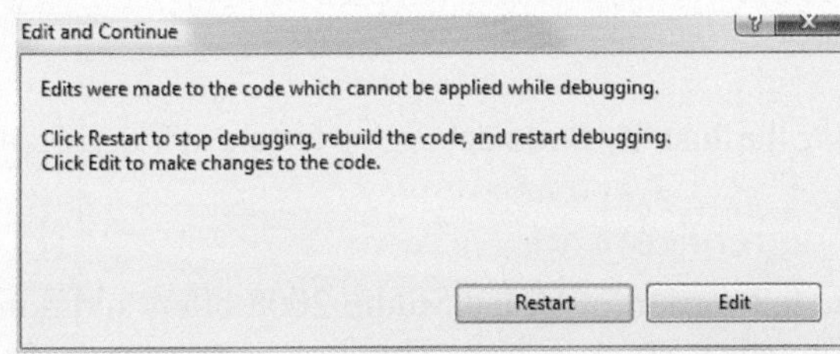

Fig. H.35 | Dialog box stating that program edits are not allowed during program execution.

H.7.2 Exception Assistant

Another debugging feature is the **Exception Assistant**. You can run a program by selecting either **Debug > Start Debugging** or **Debug > Start Without Debugging**. If you select the option **Debug > Start Debugging** and the runtime environment detects uncaught exceptions, the application pauses, and a window called the **Exception Assistant** appears, indicating where the exception occurred, the exception type and links to helpful information on handling the exception. We discuss the **Exception Assistant** in detail in Section 13.4.3.

H.7.3 Just My Code™ Debugging

Throughout this book, we produce increasingly substantial programs that often include a combination of code written by the programmer and code generated by Visual Studio. The IDE-generated code can be difficult for novices (and even experienced programmers) to understand—fortunately, you rarely need to look at this code. Visual Studio 2008 provides a debugging feature called **Just My Code**™ that allows programmers to test and debug only the portion of the code they have written. When this option is enabled, the debugger always steps over method calls to methods of classes that you did not write. This feature is available **only** in the full version of Visual Studio 2008.

To enable this option, in the **Options** dialog, select the **Debugging** category to view the available debugging tools and options. Then click the checkbox that appears next to the **Enable Just My Code (Managed only)** option (Fig. H.36) to enable or disable this feature.

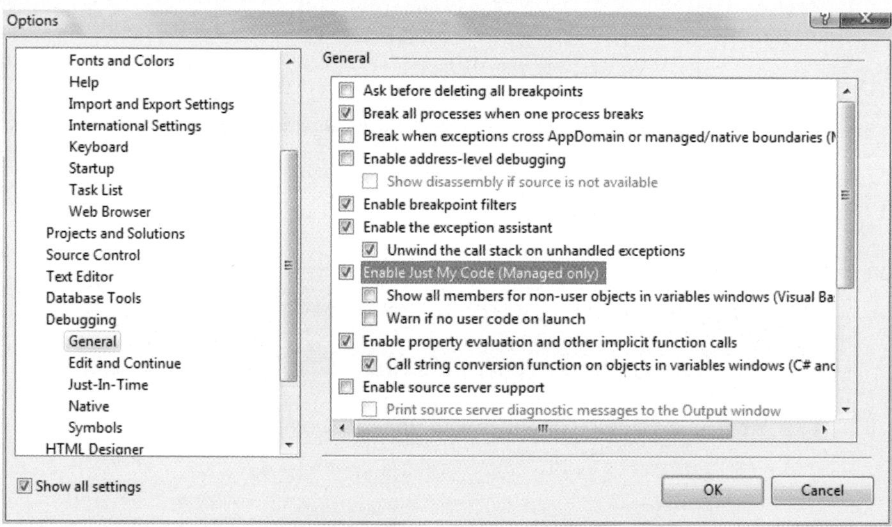

Fig. H.36 | Enabling the **Just My Code** debugging feature in Visual Studio.

H.7.4 Other Debugger Features

The debugger for the full version of Visual Studio 2008 offers additional features, such as tracepoints and more, which you can learn about at `msdn.microsoft.com/vstudio/express/vb/features/debug/default.aspx`.

H.8 Wrap-Up

In this appendix, you learned what compilation errors are and how to use *Smart Compile Auto Correction* to fix them. You can get further help with compiler errors using the **Show Error Help** option. You learned how to enable the debugger and set breakpoints so that you can examine your code and results while a program executes. This capability enables you to locate and fix logic errors in your programs. You also learned how to continue execution after a program suspends execution at a breakpoint and how to disable and remove breakpoints.

We used *DataTips* to find additional information on nonprimitive variables, and **Visualizers** to view certain data types in a detailed view. We showed how to use the debugger's **Watch** and **Locals** windows to evaluate arithmetic and `Boolean` expressions. We also demonstrated how to modify a variable's value during program execution so that you can see how changes in values affect your results.

You learned how to use the debugger's **Step Into** command to debug methods called during your program's execution. You saw how the **Step Over** command can be used to execute a method call without stopping the called method. You used the **Step Out** command to continue execution until the current method's end. You also learned that the **Continue** command continues execution until another breakpoint is found or the program terminates.

Finally, we discussed the Visual Studio 2008 debugger's additional features, including **Edit and Continue**, the **Exception Assistant** and **Just My Code™** debugging.

Summary

Section H.1 Introduction

- Most compiler vendors, like Microsoft, provide software called a debugger, which allows you to monitor the execution of your programs to locate and remove logic errors.
- The debugger allows you to suspend program execution, examine and set variables and much more.

Section H.2 Resolving Compilation Errors

- Compilation errors appear as you write your program.
- Some common compilation errors can be quickly removed using a Visual Basic feature called *Smart Compile Auto Correction.*
- If you hover the mouse over the compilation error symbol, you see the **Error Correction Options** icon. Click the icon to open the **Error Correction Options** Window, which displays suggested corrections and a preview of what the code will look like, once the fix is applied.
- When you receive a compilation error, you can typically right click the error in the **Error List** and select **Show Error Help** to learn more about the error and how to fix it. This opens the MSDN (Microsoft Developer Network) page for the appropriate compiler error, which includes the problem's description as well as one or more recommended methods of fixing it.

Section H.3 Breakpoints and the **Continue** *Command*

- Breakpoints are markers that can be set at any executable line of code. When program execution reaches a breakpoint, execution pauses, allowing you to examine the values of variables to help you locate and correct logic errors.
- To insert a breakpoint, left click the margin indicator bar next to the line of code at which you wish to break, or right click that line of code and select **Breakpoint > Insert Breakpoint.**

- A program is said to be in break mode when the debugger pauses the program's execution. Breakpoints can be set before running a program, in break mode or while a program is running.
- The **Continue** command will execute any statements between the next executable statement and the next breakpoint or the end of `Main`, whichever comes first.
- The **Run To Cursor** command will execute any statements between the next executable statement and the line where your cursor currently is.
- The value that the variable stores is displayed in a *Quick Info* box. In a sense, you are peeking inside the computer at the value of one of your variables.
- To disable a breakpoint, right click a line of code in which the breakpoint has been set and select **Breakpoint > Disable Breakpoint.**
- To remove a breakpoint that you no longer need, right click the line of code on which the breakpoint has been set and select **Breakpoint > Delete Breakpoint**. You also can remove a breakpoint by clicking the solid circle in the margin indicator bar.

Section H.4 DataTips and Visualizers

- When you hover the mouse over a reference-type variable, the *DataTip* window appears. When you click the + sign, the *DataTip* window gives information about the object's data.
- The *DataTip* window has some limitations—references must be instance variables or local variables, and expressions involving method calls cannot be evaluated.
- Just as with the *Quick Info* window, you can also change the value of a property or variable inside an object by clicking one of the values listed, then typing the new value.
- **Visualizers** are specialized windows to view certain types of data. They are shown through *DataTip* windows by clicking the small magnifying glass next to a variable name.
- The **Text Visualizer** lets you see `String` values with all their formatting included.
- The **XML Visualizer** formats XML objects into a color-coded format.
- The **HTML Visualizer** parses HTML code (in `String` or XML form) into a web page, which is displayed in a small window.

Section H.5 The **Locals** *and* **Watch** *Windows*

- The **Locals** window enables you to assign new values to variables while your program is running.
- The **Watch** window allows you to examine the value of arithmetic and Boolean expressions.

Section H.6 Controlling Execution Using the **Step Into, Step Over, Step Out** *and* **Continue** *Commands*

- You can step through a portion of your program line by line to find and fix logic errors and verify that a method's code executes correctly.
- The **Step Into** command executes the next statement in the program and immediately halts. If the statement to be executed as a result of the **Step Into** command is a method call, control is transferred to the called method. The **Step Into** command allows you to enter a method and confirm its execution by individually executing each statement in the method.
- The **Step Over** command behaves like the **Step Into** command when the next statement to execute does not contain a method call or access a property. If it does contain a method call or access a property, the application executes the statement and advances to the next line.
- The **Step Out** command is used for situations where you do not want to continue stepping through the entire method line by line.

Section H.7 Other Debugging Features

- The **Edit and Continue** feature allows you to make modifications or changes to your code as the debugger is running.
- If you want to make a change to a particular line that has been executed, you must select a prior statement in your code from which to continue execution. The **Set Next Statement** will allow you to do this
- Certain types of change are not allowed with the Edit and Continue feature, once the program begins execution. These include changing the name of a class, adding or removing method parameters, adding public fields to a class and adding or removing methods.
- The Exception Assistant indicates where the exception occurred, the type of the exception and links to helpful information on handling the exception.
- The Just My Code™ feature allows programmers to test and debug only the portion of code which they have written.

Terminology

break mode
breakpoint
bug
compilation error
Continue command
DataTip
debugger
disable a breakpoint
Edit and Continue
Error Correction Options
Error Help
Exception Assistant
HTML Visualizer
insert a breakpoint
Instruction Pointer
Just My Code™ debugging
Locals window
logic error
margin indicator bar
Quick Info box
Run To Cursor command
Smart Compile Auto Correction
solid breakpoint circle
Step Into command
Step Out command
Step Over command
suspend program execution
Text Visualizer
Visualizer
Visual Basic debugger
Watch window
XML Visualizer

Self-Review Exercises

H.1 Fill in the blanks in each of the following statements:

a) When the debugger suspends program execution at a breakpoint, the program is said to be in __________ mode.
b) The __________ feature in Visual Basic .NET allows you to "peek into the computer" and look at the value of a variable.
c) You can examine the value of an expression by using the debugger's __________ window.
d) The __________ command behaves like the **Step Into** command when the next statement to execute does not contain a method call or access a property.

H.2 State whether each of the following is *true* or *false*. If *false*, explain why.

a) When program execution suspends at a breakpoint, the next statement to be executed is the statement after the breakpoint.
b) When a variable's value is changed, the value changes to yellow in the **Locals** windows.
c) During debugging, the **Step Out** command executes the remaining statements in the current method and returns program control to the place where the method was called.

Answers to Self-Review Exercises

H.1 a) break. b) *Quick Info* box. c) **Watch**. d) **Step Over**.

H.2 a) False. When program execution suspends at a breakpoint, the next statement to be executed is the statement at the breakpoint. b) False. A variable's value turns red when it is changed. c) True.

Index

Symbols

A

B

J

K

M

N

O

S

T

X

Y

Z

The DEITEL® Suite of Products...

HOW TO PROGRAM BOOKS

C++ How to Program Sixth Edition

BOOK / CD-ROM

©2008, 1504 pp., paper (0-13-615250-3)

The complete authoritative DEITEL® *LIVE-CODE* introduction to programming with C++! The Sixth Edition takes an easy-to-follow, carefully developed early classes and objects approach to programming in C++. The text includes comprehensive coverage of the fundamentals of object-oriented programming in C++. It includes an optional automated teller machine (ATM) case study that teaches the fundamentals of software engineering and object-oriented design with the UML 2.0 in Chapters 1-7, 9 and 13. Additional integrated case studies appear throughout the text, including the `Time` class (Chapter 9), the `Employee` class (Chapters 12 and 13) and the `GradeBook` class (Chapters 3-7). This new edition includes a chapter on C++ game programming with the OGRE and OpenAL libraries, and a chapter on the Boost C++ Libraries, Technical Report 1 (TR1) and the forthcoming C++0X standard.

Small C++ How to Program Fifth Edition

BOOK / CD-ROM

©2005, 848 pp., paper (0-13-185758-4)

Based on chapters 1-13 (except the optional OOD/UML case study) and appendices of *C++ How to Program, Fifth Edition, Small C++* features comprehensive coverage of the fundamentals of object-oriented programming in C++. Key topics include applications, variables, memory concepts, data types, control statements, functions, arrays, pointers and strings, inheritance and polymorphism.

Now available for both *C++ How to Program, 6/e,* and *Small C++ How to Program, 5/e:* C++ Web-based *Cyber Classroom* included with the purchase of a new textbook. The *Cyber Classroom* includes a complete e-book, audio walk-throughs of the code examples, a Lab Manual and selected student solutions. See the *Cyber Classroom* section of this advertorial for more information.

Java™ How to Program Seventh Edition

BOOK / CD-ROM

©2007, 1500 pp., paper (0-13-222220-5)

The complete authoritative DEITEL® *LIVE-CODE* introduction to programming with Java™ Standard Edition 6! *Java How to Program, Seventh Edition* is up-to-date with Java™ SE 6 and includes comprehensive coverage of object-oriented programming in Java, classes, objects, inheritance, polymorphism and interfaces; and an optional automated teller machine (ATM) case study that teaches the fundamentals of software engineering and object oriented design with the UML 2.0 in Chapters 1-8 and 10. Additional integrated case studies appear throughout the text, including GUI and graphics (Chapters 3-12), the `Time` class (Chapter 8), the `Employee` class (Chapters 9 and 10) and the `GradeBook` class (Chapters 3-8). New topics covered include Java Desktop Integration Components, Ajax Web application development with JavaServer Faces, web services and more.

Small Java™ How to Program Sixth Edition

BOOK / CD-ROM

©2005, 624 pp., paper (0-13-148660-8)

Based on chapters 1-10 of *Java™ How to Program, Sixth Edition, Small Java* is for use with J2SE™ 5.0, features an early classes and objects approach and comprehensive coverage of the fundamentals of object-oriented programming in Java. Key topics include applications, variables, data types, control statements, methods, arrays, object-based programming, inheritance and polymorphism.

Now available for both *Java How to Program, 7/e,* and *Small Java How to Program, 6/e:* Java Web-based *Cyber Classroom* included with the purchase of a new textbook. The *Cyber Classroom* includes a complete e-book, audio walk-throughs of the code examples, a Lab Manual and selected student solutions. See the *Cyber Classroom* section of this advertorial for more information.

Sign up now for the FREE ***DEITEL® Buzz Online*** newsletter at:
`www.deitel.com/newsletter/subscribe.html`
Question? Write to the authors at `deitel@deitel.com`

Visual Basic® 2008 How to Program

BOOK / DVD

©2009, 1568 pp., paper (0-13-605305-X)

The complete authoritative DEITEL® *LIVE-CODE* introduction to Visual Basic programming. *Visual Basic® 2008 How to Program* is up-to-date with Microsoft's Visual Basic 2008. The text includes comprehensive coverage of the fundamentals of object-oriented programming in Visual Basic including an optional automated teller machine (ATM) case study that teaches the fundamentals of software engineering and object-oriented design with the UML 2.0 in Chapters 1,3–9 and 11. Additional integrated case studies appear throughout the text, including the `Time` class (Chapter 9), the `Employee` class (Chapters 10 and 11) and the `Gradebook` class (Chapters 4–9). This book also includes discussions of more advanced topics such as XML, database processing and web application development. New Visual Basic 2008 topics covered include LINQ, WPF, WCF Web Services, ASP.NET 3.5, ASP.NET Ajax and Silverlight.

Visual C#® 2008 How to Program, Third Edition

BOOK / DVD

©2009, 1648 pp., paper (0-13-605322-X)

The complete authoritative DEITEL® *LIVE-CODE* introduction to C# programming. *Visual C#® 2008 How to Program, Third Edition,* is up-to-date with Microsoft's Visual C# 2008. The text includes comprehensive coverage of the fundamentals of object-oriented programming in C#, including an optional automated teller machine (ATM) case study that teaches the fundamentals of software engineering and object-oriented design with the UML 2.0 in Chapters 1, 3–9 and 11. Additional integrated case studies appear throughout the text, including the `Time` class (Chapter 9), the `Employee` class (Chapters 10 and 11) and the `Gradebook` class (Chapters 4–9). This book also includes discussions of more advanced topics such as XML, database processing and web application development. New Visual C#2008 topics covered include LINQ, WPF, WCF Web Services, ASP.NET 3.5, ASP.NET Ajax and Silverlight.

Visual C++® 2008 How to Program, Second Edition

BOOK / CD-ROM

©2008, 1552 pp., paper (0-13-615157-4)

This Second Edition is based on our C++-standard-compliant textbook, *C++ How to Program, Sixth Edition*, and is intended for courses that offer a Microsoft-specific C++ programming focus using Visual C++ 2008. Microsoft has determined that most Visual C++ developers primarily use native C++. As a result, the book now focuses on native C++ and presents examples of .NET managed code programming with C++/CLI, where appropriate. The book presents an easy-to-follow, carefully developed, comprehensive coverage of object-oriented programming. The optional automated teller machine (ATM) case study teaches the fundamentals of software engineering and object-oriented design with the UML 2.0. Additional integrated case studies appear throughout the text. This edition includes new coverage of .NET generics, collections and regular expressions.

C How to Program, Fifth Edition

BOOK / CD-ROM

©2007, 1184 pp., paper (0-13-240416-8)

C How to Program, Fifth Edition—the world's best-selling C textbook—is designed for introductory through intermediate courses and programming languages survey courses. This comprehensive text is aimed at readers with little or no programming experience through intermediate audiences. Highly practical in approach, it introduces fundamental notions of structured programming and software engineering and gets up to speed quickly. The Fifth Edition features new chapters on the C99 standard and an introduction to game programming with the Allegro C Library.

Internet & World Wide Web How to Program Fourth Edition

BOOK / CD-ROM

©2008, 1424 pp., paper (0-13-175242-1)

This book introduces students with little or no programming experience to the exciting world of Web-based applications. It has been substantially reworked to reflect today's Web 2.0 rich Internet application-development methodologies. The book teaches the skills and tools for creating dynamic Web applications. Topics include introductory programming principles, markup languages (XHTML/ XML), scripting languages (JavaScript, PHP and Ruby/Ruby on Rails), Ajax, web services, web servers (IIS/Apache), relational databases (MySQL/SQL Server 2008 Express/Apache Derby/ Java DB), ASP .NET 2.0 and JavaServer™ Faces (JSF). You'll build Ajax-enabled rich Internet applications (RIAs)—using Ajax frameworks, Adobe® Flex™ and Microsoft® Silverlight—with the look-and-feel of desktop applications. The Dive Into® Web 2.0 chapter exposes readers to many other topics associated with Web 2.0 applications and businesses. After mastering the material in this book, students will be well prepared to build real-world, industrial-strength, Web-based applications.

Python How to Program

BOOK / CD-ROM

©2002, 1376pp., paper (0-13-092361-3)

This exciting textbook provides a comprehensive introduction to Python—a powerful object-oriented programming language with clear syntax and the ability to bring together various technologies quickly and easily. The book covers introductory programming techniques and more advanced topics such as graphical user interfaces, databases, networking, security, process management, multithreading, XHTML, CSS, PSP and multimedia. Readers will learn principles that are applicable to both systems development and Web programming.

"As always, I am impressed with the Deitel organization and its books. I love teaching from them not only because the content is so sound, but also because of the competent and timely expertise and support provided." — Robert A. Long, Indiana University

"In my courses, I've read several Deitel books. I really enjoy reading and learning from them because they're written in a fashion that's very easy to follow. It's almost like someone is speaking to you, and you don't get lost in a lot of unnecessarily complicated paragraphs. There are sections that have some humor and the real world examples they use help you understand why some things that are good in theory don't work as well in practice. I think Paul and Harvey Deitel have done an amazing job researching the latest technologies and then presenting them in a very understandable way. Whenever I take a new class and find out that we are to use a Deitel book, I'm very happy about that because they're my favorite. I know I can rely upon the book to explain the subject clearly."

— Christine Spencer, Graduate of MIT

XML How to Program

BOOK / CD-ROM

©2001, 1112 pp., paper (0-13-028417-3)

This book is a comprehensive guide to programming in XML. It teaches how to use XML to create customized tags and includes chapters that address markup languages for science and technology, multimedia, commerce and many other fields. Concise introductions to Java, JavaServer Pages, VBScript, Active Server Pages and Perl/CGI provide readers with the essentials of these programming languages and server-side development technologies to enable them to work effectively with XML. The book also covers topics such as XSL, DOM™, SAX, a real-world e-commerce case study and a complete chapter on Web accessibility that addresses Voice XML. Other topics covered include XHTML, CSS, DTD, schema, parsers, XPath, XLink, namespaces, XBase, XInclude, XPointer, XSLT, XSL Formatting Objects, JavaServer Pages, XForms, topic maps, X3D, MathML, OpenMath, CML, BML, CDF, RDF, SVG, Cocoon, WML, XBRL and BizTalk™ and SOAP™ Web resources.

Perl How to Program

©2001, 1057 pp., paper (0-13-028418-1)

This comprehensive guide to Perl programming emphasizes the use of the Common Gateway Interface (CGI) with Perl to create powerful, dynamic multi-tier Web-based client/server applications. The book begins with a clear and careful introduction to programming concepts at a level suitable for beginners, and proceeds through advanced topics such as references and complex data structures. Key Perl topics such as regular expressions and string manipulation are covered in detail. The authors address important and topical issues such as object-oriented programming, the Perl database interface (DBI), graphics and security. Also included is a treatment of XML, a bonus chapter introducing the Python programming language, supplemental material on career resources and a complete chapter on Web accessibility.

For ordering information,
visit us on the Web at www.prenhall.com.

INTERNATIONAL ORDERING INFORMATION

CANADA:
Pearson Education Canada
26 Prince Andrew Place
PO Box 580
Don Mills, Ontario M3C 2T8 Canada
Tel.: 416-925-2249; Fax: 416-925-0068
e-mail: phcinfo.pubcanada@pearsoned.com

EUROPE, MIDDLE EAST, AND AFRICA:
Pearson Education
Edinburgh Gate
Harlow, Essex CM20 2JE UK
Tel: 01279 623928; Fax: 01279 414130
e-mail: enq.orders@pearsoned-ema.com

BENELUX REGION:
Pearson Education
Concertgebouwplein 25
1071 LM Amsterdam
The Netherlands
Tel: 31 20 5755 800; Fax: 31 20 664 5334
e-mail: amsterdam@pearsoned-ema.com

ASIA:
Pearson Education Asia Pte. Ltd.
23/25 First Lok Yang Road
Jurong, 629733 Singapore
Tel: 65 476 4688; Fax: 65 378 0370

JAPAN:
Pearson Education Japan
Ogikubo TM Bldg. 6F. 5-26-13 Ogikubo
Suginami-ku, Tokyo 167-0051 Japan
Tel: 81 3 3365 9001; Fax: 81 3 3365 9009

INDIA:
Pearson Education
Indian Branch
482 FIE, Patparganj
Delhi – 110092 India
Tel: 91 11 2059850 & 2059851
Fax: 91 11 2059852

AUSTRALIA:
Pearson Education Australia
Unit 4, Level 2, 14 Aquatic Drive
Frenchs Forest, NSW 2086, Australia
Tel: 61 2 9454 2200; Fax: 61 2 9453 0089
e-mail: marketing@pearsoned.com.au

NEW ZEALAND/FIJI:
Pearson Education
46 Hillside Road
Auckland 10, New Zealand
Tel: 649 444 4968; Fax: 649 444 4957
E-mail: sales@pearsoned.co.nz

SOUTH AFRICA:
Maskew Miller Longman
Central Park Block H
16th Street Midrand 1685
South Africa
Tel: 27 21 686 6356; Fax: 27 21 686 4590

LATIN AMERICA:
Pearson Education Latin America
Attn: Tina Sheldon
1 Lake Street
Upper Saddle River, NJ 07458

The SIMPLY SERIES!

The Deitels' *Simply Series* takes an engaging new approach to teaching programming languages from the ground up. The pedagogy of this series combines the DEITEL® signature *LIVE-CODE Approach* with an *APPLICATION-DRIVEN Tutorial Approach* to teach programming with outstanding pedagogical features that help students learn. They have merged the notion of a lab manual with that of a conventional textbook, creating a book in which readers build and execute complete applications from start to finish, while learning the fundamental concepts of programming!

Simply Visual Basic® 2008 An APPLICATION-DRIVEN Tutorial Approach, Third Edition

©2009, 848 pp., paper (0-13-605303-3)

Simply Visual Basic® 2008 An APPLICATION-DRIVEN Tutorial Approach, 3/e, guides readers through building real-world applications that incorporate Visual Basic 2008 programming fundamentals. Learn GUI design, controls, methods, functions, data types, control statements, procedures, arrays, object-oriented programming, exception-handling, collections, strings and characters, sequential files and more in this comprehensive introduction to Visual Basic 2008. Higher-end topics include LINQ, ASP .NET 3.5, ASP.NET AJAX, Visual Web Developer 2008 Express, database programming, multimedia and graphics, Silverlight and Web applications development.

Simply C# An APPLICATION-DRIVEN Tutorial Approach

©2004, 992 pp., paper (0-13-142641-9)

Simply C# An APPLICATION-DRIVEN Tutorial Approach guides readers through building real-world applications that incorporate C# programming fundamentals. Learn GUI design, controls, methods, functions, data types, control statements, procedures, arrays, object-oriented programming, strings and characters, sequential files and more in this comprehensive introduction to C#. We also include higher-end topics such as database programming, multimedia and graphics and Web applications development.

Simply Java™ Programming An APPLICATION-DRIVEN Tutorial Approach

©2004, 1300 pp., paper (0-13-142648-6)

Simply Java™ Programming An APPLICATION-DRIVEN Tutorial Approach guides readers through building real-world applications that incorporate Java programming fundamentals. Learn GUI design, components, methods, event-handling, types, control statements, arrays, object-oriented programming, exception-handling, strings and characters, sequential files and more in this comprehensive introduction to Java. We also include higher-end topics such as database programming, multimedia, graphics and Web applications development.

Simply C++ An APPLICATION-DRIVEN Tutorial Approach

©2005, 704 pp., paper (0-13-142660-5)

Simply C++ An APPLICATION-DRIVEN Tutorial Approach guides readers through building real-world applications that incorporate C++ programming fundamentals. Learn methods, functions, data types, control statements, procedures, arrays, object-oriented programming, strings and characters, pointers, references, templates, operator overloading and more in this comprehensive introduction to C++.

THE BUZZ ABOUT THE DEITEL® SUITE OF PRODUCTS!

Deitel & Associates garners worldwide praise for its best-selling *How to Program Series* and *Simply Series* of books and its signature *LIVE-CODE Approach.* See for yourself what our readers have to say:

"Richly detailed programming examples and explanation of the concepts. An enjoyable read—many 'light bulb' moments throughout. I'm a big fan of the gradually developed GradeBook case study! Building the ATM application chapter-by-chapter really shows the amount of work in programming a major application. Excellent bank account [file processing] examples. The Silverlight Weather Viewer application is great."
—James Keysor, Florida Institute of Technology

"Covers the state-of-the-art technologies in Visual Basic 2008. I can't wait to see what amazing things your readers do once they are armed with this new found knowledge."
—Chris Lovett, Software Architect, Microsoft

"An excellent 'objects first' coverage of C++ that remains accessible to beginners. The example-driven presentation is enriched by the optional UML case study that contextualizes the material in an ongoing software engineering project."—Gavin Osborne, Saskatchewan Institute of Applied Science and Technology

"Ogre is a free world-class rendering engine that has been used in several commercial games. The Ogre chapter is a great introduction, providing well documented and easy to understand examples that will have you creating your own simple computer games in no time!"
—Casey Borders (Creator of OgreAL), Sensis Corp.

"I am continually impressed with the Deitels' ability to clearly explain concepts and ideas, which allows the student to gain a well-rounded understanding of the language and software development."
— Karen Arlien, Bismarck State College

"Great early introduction to classes and objects. The combination of live-code examples and detailed figures provides a unique visualization of C++ concepts."
— Earl LaBatt, University of New Hampshire

"Probably the most complete coverage of learning through examples in published material today. This material is such high quality—it is unbelievable. The ATM is super."
— Anne Horton,
AT&T Bell Laboratories

"*Java How to Program, 6/e* is an excellent book to learn how to program in Java. The book does an excellent job describing the new features included in the JDK 5.0, including generics and formatted output. The book is easy to read with numerous, simple-to-follow code examples."
— Doug Kohlert, Sun Microsystems

"This book is a must have for any C# student because of its thorough explanations, its carefully developed and commented examples, and its numerous and interesting exercises. The idea of introducing a bit of UML in each chapter through a case study is great and should be in every book! It's the book I'll recommend to my students!"
—José Antonio González Seco, Andalucia's Parliament

"I'm glad to see the early treatment of objects done so well. The UML material is well explained and will help students better understand OOP. A comprehensive introduction to XML, and one of the clearest tutorials on Web services I've read, with great examples. An excellent chapter on generics. Explains data structures with a clarity that is hard to come by."
—Gavin Osborne, Saskatchewan Institute of Applied Science and Technology

"The writing style is comprehensive, systematic and clear. Nothing is either skipped or glossed over. Of particular note is the authors' attention to good software engineering concepts, and the wide selection of code examples provides excellent reinforcement for the practical application of developing Java skills."— Dean Mellas, Computer and Information Sciences, Cerritos College

"Good job! Introduces OOP without burying the reader in complexity. I think the level of conceptual detail is perfect. This will be a great help the next time I teach 101."
— Walt Bunch, Chapman University

"The new edition... is by far the best student-oriented textbook on programming in the C language—the Deitels have set the standard-again! A thorough, careful, student-oriented treatment of not just the langauge, but more importantly, the ideas, concepts, and techniques of programming! The addition of 'live code' is also a big plus—encouraging active participation by the student. A great text!" —Richard Albright, Goldey-Beacom College

"A fun way of learning VB. Tips and hands-on guidance give readers an amazing running start in software development."—April Reagan, Microsoft Corp.

"The use of graphics and common application topics will capture student interest. The step-by-step approach enables students to work independently. The integrated debugging is superior to the pedagogical approach taken by competing textbooks. [The ASP.NET 3.5 case study with ASP.NET AJAX] would be an excellent starting example for my classes on ASP.NET programming."
—Douglas Bock Southern Illinois University

"I've already decided to adopt! Showing the student what an application will do, then building it, engages the student and provides superior motivation. A great teaching vehicle!"
—Peter van de Goes, Rose State College Business and IT Division

www.deitel.com www.prenhall.com/deitel
Check out our Resource Centers at www.deitel.com/resourcecenters.html
Question? Write to the authors at deitel@deitel.com

MULTIMEDIA CYBER CLASSROOMS

Premium content available with *Java™ How to Program, Seventh Edition* and *C++ How to Program, Sixth Edition!*

Java How to Program, 7/e, and *C++ How to Program, 6/e,* are now available with 12-month access to the web-based *Multimedia Cyber Classroom* for students who purchase new copies of these books! The *Cyber Classroom* is an interactive, multimedia, tutorial version of DEITEL textbooks. *Cyber Classrooms* are a great value, giving students additional hands-on experience and study aids.

NOW AVAILABLE for *Java How to Program, 7/e* and *C++ How to Program, 6/e* (with purchase of a new book)

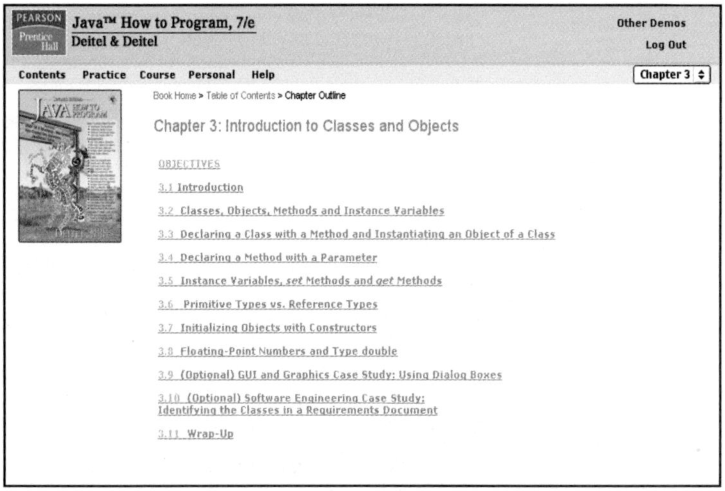

DEITEL® Multimedia Cyber Classrooms *feature an e-book with the complete text of their corresponding* How to Program *titles.*

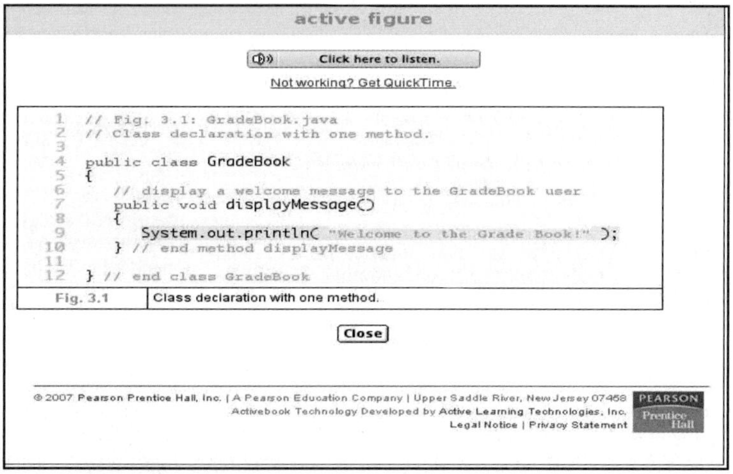

Unique audio "walkthroughs" of code examples reinforce key concepts.

Sign up now for the FREE ***DEITEL® Buzz Online*** newsletter at:
www.deitel.com/newsletter/subscribe.html
Question? Write to the authors at deitel@deitel.com

MULTIMEDIA CYBER CLASSROOMS

DEITEL® *Multimedia Cyber Classrooms* include:

- The full text, illustrations and program listings of its corresponding *How to Program* book.
- Hours of detailed, expert audio descriptions of hundreds of lines of code that help to reinforce important concepts.
- An abundance of self-assessment material, including practice exams, hundreds of programming exercises and self-review questions and answers.

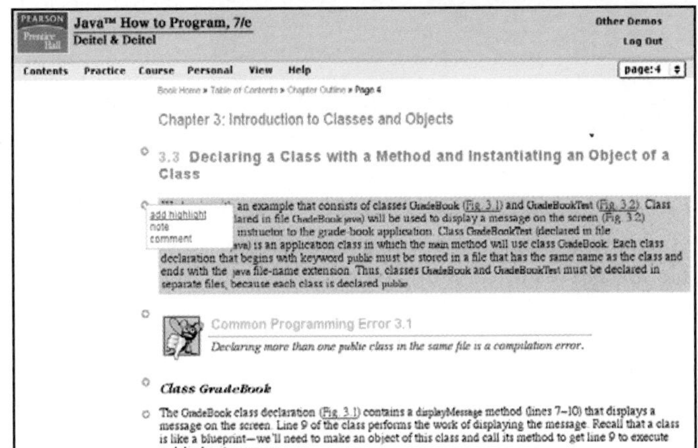

DEITEL® Multimedia Cyber Classrooms *offer a host of interactive features, such as highlighting of key sections of the text...*

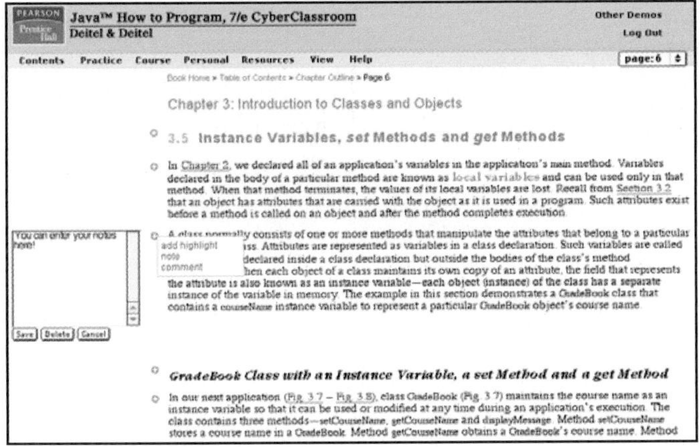

...and the ability to write notes in the margin of a given page for future reference.

- Intuitive browser-based interface designed to be easy and accessible.
- A Lab Manual featuring lab exercises as well as pre- and post-lab activities.
- Student Solutions to approximately one-half of the exercises in the textbook.

Students receive 12-month access to a protected web site via access code cards packaged with these new textbooks. (Simply tear the strip on the inside of the Cyber Classroom package to reveal access code.)

For more information, please visit:
www.prenhall.com/deitel/cyberclassroom

www.deitel.com www.prenhall.com/deitel
Check out our Resource Centers at www.deitel.com/resourcecenters.html
Question? Write to the authors at deitel@deitel.com

DEITEL® BUZZ ONLINE NEWSLETTER

Each issue of our free, e-mail newsletter, the *DEITEL® BUZZ ONLINE*, is now sent to about 50,000 opt-in subscribers. This weekly newsletter provides updates on our publishing program, our instructor-led professional training courses, timely industry topics and the continuing stream of innovations and new Web 2.0 business ventures emerging from Deitel.

The DEITEL® Buzz Online includes:

- Resource centers on programming, software development, Web 2.0 and more.
- Updates on all Deitel publications of interest to students, instructors and professionals.
- Free tutorials and guest articles (part of the Deitel Free Content Initiative).
- Information on our instructor-led professional training courses taught worldwide.
- Detailed ordering information, additional book resources, code downloads and more.
- Available in both HTML or plain-text format.
- Previous issues are archived at: `www.deitel.com/newsletter/backissues.html`.
- Check out the complete list of Resource Centers at `www.deitel.com/ResourceCenters.html`.

Your Information Resource for Building Web 2.0 Businesses

Cutting-Edge Textbooks, E-Learning and Media Solutions Published by Pearson/Prentice Hall!
Cutting-Edge Programming Languages Training Delivered at Organizations Worldwide!

Welcome to the June 20th, 2008 issue of the *Deitel Buzz Online Newsletter*! In this issue we introduce our new Firefox 3 Resource Center. You can also visit our complete Resource Center list.

In upcoming newsletters we'll preview our new books *Simply Visual Basic 2008, 3/e* (now available), *Visual Basic 2008 How to Program* and *Visual C# 2008 How to Program, 3/e* (coming this summer).

New! Firefox 3 Resource Center

To sponsor Deitel Resource Centers or to commission custom Resource Centers, contact Abbey Deitel.

Welcome to the Firefox 3 Resource Center. Firefox 3—the latest version of Mozilla's popular web browser—features improved performance, one-click bookmarking, instant web site ID, a password manager and more. Firefox 3 was officially launched on June 17, 2008. Within 24 hours of the launch, over 8 million copies were downloaded. Start your search here to find Firefox 3 downloads, tutorials, sample chapters, books, training courses, FAQs, newsgroups, and more. In the Firefox 3 Resource Center, you'll find links to:

- Mozilla's list of the top new Firefox 3 features.
- The 15-minute video tutorial, "Firefox Ultimate Tutorial: Faster, Uncluttered and More Efficient," that demonstrates several new features of Firefox 3.
- Firefox 3 Tips and Tricks.
- The article, "A Field Guide to Firefox 3: What's New and Improved," by Debra Lyn Richardson.
- The article, "Hands on with Firefox 3," by Rob Griffiths.
- Mozilla's Firefox 3 wiki.
- The article, "A First Look at Firefox 3.0," by Ryan Paul.
- The free Firefox 3 download with the Google toolbar.
- Firefox 3 Build Documentation and release notes.
- The "Places" wiki from Mozilla that discusses the new system for storing bookmarks, history and web page information.
- Firefox 3 add-ons including alerts, updates, bookmarks, feeds, blogging, photos and music, videos and more.
- The article, "On Firefox 3 and Microformats with Michael Kaply," by Percy Cabello.
- The Extend Firefox 3 Developer Contest. Prize categories include best new add-on, best updated add-on, and best music add-on.
- The article, "JavaScript Updates in Firefox 3.0a3," by John Resig.
- The article, "Firefox 3 Beta Offers Numerous Features for Developers," by Tony Patton.
- The free, self-paced training course, "Mozilla Firefox," from GCFLearnFree.org.
- The tutorial, "Using Firefox."
- The "Firefox Bookmarks Tutorial."
- The 370 Firefox videos (including several Firefox 3 videos) available on Metacafe that discuss extensions, Firefox tweaks, passwords, bookmarks, hidden pages and more.
- Firefox 3 blogs, books, sample chapters, documentation, tutorials, FAQs, newsgroups, videos and downloads.
- And more...

Now Available! *Simply Visual Basic 2008 An Application Driven Tutorial Approach, 3/e*

Now Available! *Visual C++ 2008 How to Program*

Now Available! *Internet and World Wide Web How to Program, 4/e*

35% Discount at Informit.com! *AJAX, Rich Internet Applications, and Web Development for Programmers*

35% Discount at Informit.com! *Java Fundamentals I and II (LiveLessons Video Training)*

Check it Out! The Free 81-Page *Dive Into Web 2.0* e-Book

Last Week's Newsletter

Complete Resource Center List

Instructor Resources Information for Instructors Teaching from our Books

Corporate Training On-Site Programming-Languages Training

Recent Publications *AJAX, Rich Internet Applications, and Web Development for Programmers (Deitel Developer Series professional book based on Internet and World Wide Web How to Program, 4/e)*

Simply Visual Basic 2008, 2/e

Visual C++ 2008 How to Program, 2/e

Internet and World Wide Web How to Program, 4/e

C++ How to Program, 6/e

C How to Program, 5/e

C# for Programmers, 2/e (Deitel Developer Series professional book based on *Visual C# 2005 How to Program*)

Java How to Program, 7/e

Simply C++

Simply C#

Turn the page to find out more about Deitel & Associates!

To sign up for the *DEITEL® BUZZ ONLINE* newsletter, visit `www.deitel.com/newsletter/subscribe.html`.

DIVE INTO® SERIES CORPORATE TRAINING DELIVERED WORLDWIDE

Deitel & Associates, Inc. provides intensive, lecture-and-laboratory courses to organizations worldwide. The programming courses use our signature *Live-Code Approach*, presenting complete working programs.

Deitel & Associates, Inc. has trained over one million students and professionals worldwide through Dive Into® Series corporate training courses, public seminars, university teaching, *How to Program Series* textbooks, *Deitel® Developer Series* books, *Simply Series* textbooks, *Cyber Classroom Series and Live Lessons* multimedia video packages, *Complete Training Course Series* textbook and multimedia packages, broadcast-satellite courses and Web-based training.

Educational Consulting

Deitel & Associates, Inc. offers complete educational consulting services for corporate training programs and professional schools including:

- Curriculum design and development
- Preparation of Instructor Guides
- Customized courses and course materials
- Design and implementation of professional training certificate programs
- Instructor certification
- Train-the-trainers programs
- Delivery of software-related corporate training programs

Visit our Web site for more information on our Dive Into® Series corporate training curriculum and to purchase our training products and services.

www.deitel.com/training

Would you like to review upcoming publications?

If you are a professor or senior industry professional interested in being a reviewer of our forthcoming publications, please contact us by email at deitel@deitel.com. Insert "Content Reviewer" in the subject heading.

Are you interested in a career in computer education, publishing and training?

We offer a limited number of **full-time** positions available for college graduates in computer science, information systems, information technology, management information systems, advertising and marketing. Please check our Web site for the latest job postings or contact us by email at deitel@deitel.com. Insert "Full-time Job" in the subject heading.

Are you a College student looking for an internship or co-op?

We have a limited number of competitive summer positions and 15-20-hr./week school-year opportunities for computer science, IT/IS, MIS and marketing majors. Students work at our headquarters west of Boston. We also offer full-time co-ops for students taking a semester off from school. This is an excellent opportunity for students looking to gain industry experience and earn money to pay for school. Please contact us by email at deitel@deitel.com. Insert "Internship" in the subject heading.

Would you like to explore contract training opportunities with us?

Deitel & Associates, Inc. is looking for contract instructors to teach software-related topics at our clients' sites in the United States and worldwide. Applicants should be experienced professional trainers or college professors. For more information, please visit www.deitel.com and send your resume to Abbey Deitel at deitel@deitel.com.

Are you a training company in need of quality course materials?

Corporate training companies worldwide use our *How to Program Series* textbooks, *Complete Training Course Series* book and multimedia packages, *Simply Series* textbooks and our *Deitel® Developer Series* books in their classes. We have extensive ancillary instructor materials for many of our products. For more details, please visit www.deitel.com or contact us by email at deitel@deitel.com.

PROGRAMMING LANGUAGE TEXTBOOK AUTHORS

Check out our Dive Into® Series Corporate On-site Seminars...

Java™

- Java for Nonprogrammers
- Java for Programmers
- Advanced Java™

Internet & World Wide Web Programming

- Client-Side Internet & Web Programming
- Server-Side Internet & Web Programming

C/C++

- C and C++ Programming: Part 1 (for Nonprogrammers)
- C and C++ Programming: Part 2 (for Non-C Programmers)
- C++ and Object-Oriented Programming
- Advanced C++ and Object-Oriented Programming

XML

- XML Programming for programmers with Java, Web or other programming experience

.NET Programming

- Visual C# 2008 Programming
- Visual Basic® 2008 Programming
- Visual C++® 2008 Programming
- Visual C# 2005 Programming
- Visual Basic® 2005 Programming

Other Topics

- Object-Oriented Analysis and Design with the UML
- SQL Server

For Detailed Course Descriptions, Visit Our Web Site: **www.deitel.com**

Through our worldwide network of trainers, we would be happy to attempt to arrange corporate on-site courses for you in virtually any software-related field.

For Additional Information about Our Dive Into® Series Corporate On-Site Courses, contact:

Abbey Deitel, President
Email: deitel@deitel.com
Phone: (978) 823-0130

Our training clients include:

3Com
Argonne National Laboratories
Art Technology
Avid Technology
Bank of America
BEA Systems
BlueCross BlueShield
Boeing
Bristol-Myers Squibb
Cap Gemini
Cisco
Concord Communications
Dell
Dunn & Bradstreet
Eastman Kodak
EMC
Federal Reserve Bank of Chicago
Fidelity
GE
General Dynamics Electric Boat Corporation
Gillette
GTE
Hitachi
IBM
Invensys
iRobot
JPL Laboratories
Lockheed Martin
Lucent
MapInfo Corporation
MCI
Motorola
NASA's Kennedy Space Center
NASDAQ
NOAA
Nortel Networks
One Wave
Open Market
Oracle
Pacific Capital Bank Corporation
PalmSource
Philips Medical Systems
Pragmatics
Primavera
Progress Software
Puma
Rogue Wave Software
Schlumberger
Sun Microsystems
Symmetrix
Teleflora
Thompson Technology
Tivoli Systems
TJX Companies
Toys "R" Us
U.S. Army at Ft. Leavenworth
Visa International
Washington Post Newsweek Interactive
Westinghouse Nuclear Services
White Sands Missile Range
and more!

LOOK HERE
for the latest buzz on
DEITEL PRODUCTS
from Prentice Hall.